NJ   Eckhardt,
974.903 Charles.
Eck   Our brothers
     gone before

Clark Public Library
303 Westfield Ave.
Clark, NJ 07066
(732)388-5999

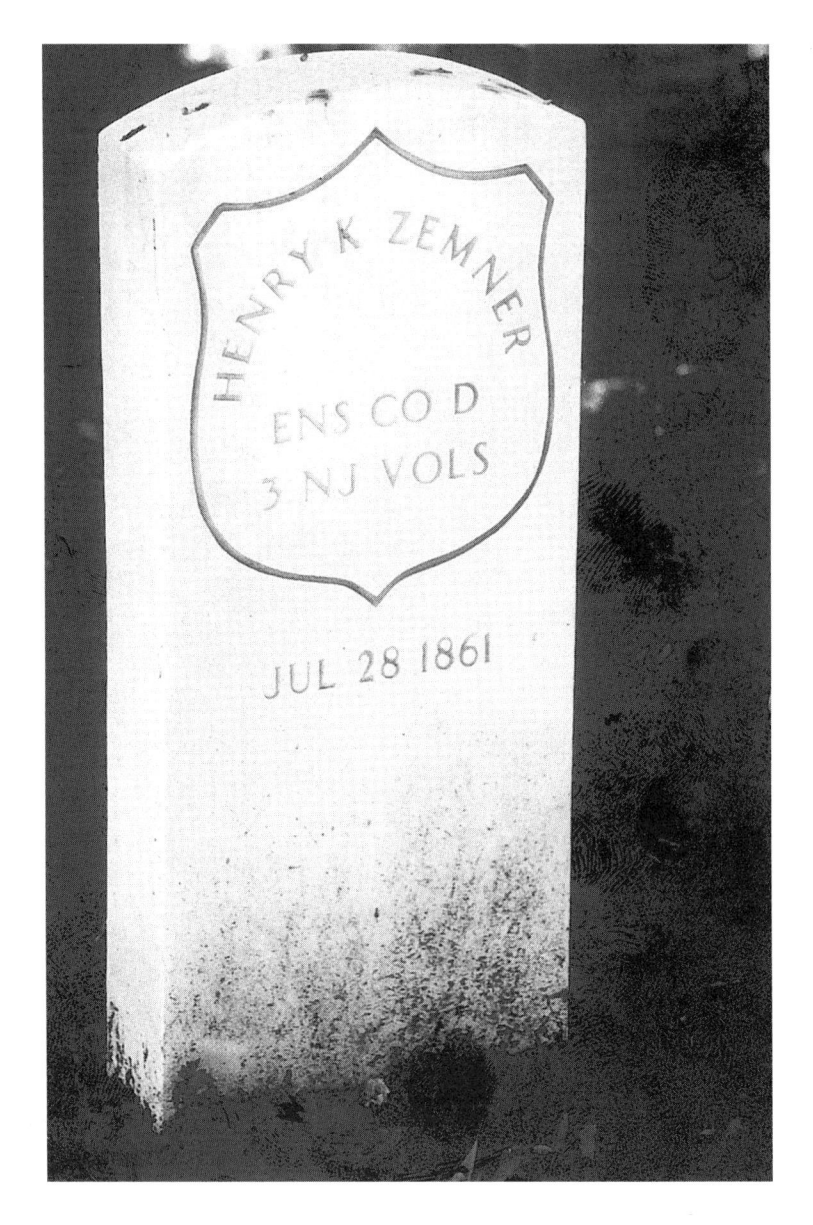

Grave of Henry K. Zemner (Zehner). The first New Jersey officer to die in Civil War service. Died of Debility at Washington, D.C. Buried in Mercer Cemetery, Trenton. (Photo courtesy of Chuck Eckhardt)

Our Brothers

Gone Before

Volume I

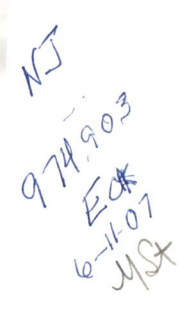

DEDICATIONS

To my wife Diane, daughters Diana and Jennifer, sons Robert Jr. and Joseph, without whose support, encouragement and intellectual discourse I would be lost. — Bob MacAvoy

In memory of the Boys of 1861 to 1865 and all the veterans who have answered their final roll call. — Charles Eckhardt

Copyright © 2006 by Charles Eckhardt and Robert MacAvoy

All rights reserved. Permission to reproduce in any form must be secured from the copyright holders and the publisher.

First Edition.

Please direct all correspondence and book orders to:

Longstreet House
P.O. Box 730
Hightstown, NJ 08520

ISBN number 0-944413-70-6

Printed in the United States of America

CONTENTS OF VOLUME I

List of Illustrations	iii
Our Brothers Gone Before	v
Foreword	vii
Preface	ix
Whatever Happened to Andrew Hopper Ackerman's Body?	xv
Acknowledgments	xix
Military Abbreviations	xxii
State Abbreviations	xxiii
List of Burials	1

NOTE:
Each entry consists of the soldier's name, unit, date of death, and cemetery. A full list of cemeteries, with their locations, is located on pages 1609-1668 at the end of Volume II. The cemeteries are listed there by county and town. A list of corrections and deletions to the burial roster can be found at the end of Volume II.

LIST OF ILLUSTRATIONS

Grave of Henry Zemner	front.
Grave of Ellis Hamilton	iv
Andrew H. Ackerman	xiv
James MacAvoy	xviii
Grave of James Theodore Calhoun	xxiv

Grave of Ellis Hamilton.
Enlisted as 2nd Lt., Company E, 15th NJ Infantry at the age of 16 years. Mortally wounded in 1864 at the age of 18 while serving as Captain of Company F, 15th NJ. Buried in Mercer Cemetery, Trenton. (Photo courtesy of Chuck Eckhardt)

OUR BROTHERS GONE BEFORE

Supreme Court Justice Oliver Wendell Holmes, Jr. – thrice-wounded soldier of the Union – on one occasion regretted, "We do not save our traditions in this country. The regiments whose battle-flags were not large enough to hold the names of the battles they had fought, vanished with the surrender of Lee, though their memories inherited would have made heroes for a century." Holmes thought it "a noble and pious thing to do whatever we may by written word and moulded bronze and sculpted stone to keep our memories, our reverence and our love alive, and to hand them on to new generations all too ready to forget."

Like so many veterans of the Civil War, Holmes bore the scars of that terrible conflict upon his body as its legacy was seared upon his soul. Those men could never forget. It is testimony to the power of that epic and defining era of American history, that more than 130 years later the lives and events of 1861-65 still touch a responsive chord in the American psyche. Though the veterans are long departed, their memories remain.

The Centennial of the War inspired a resurgence of interest that has continued unabated; indeed, if anything, it has grown over the past three decades. Despite the vast indifference of many to our nation's past, it seems that those memories have indeed been inherited by no small number of devotees, kept alive in a copious outpouring of books and documentaries – as well as the occasional film – discussed and debated in dozens of Civil War roundtables, and reenacted by "living history" enthusiasts who don the woolen uniforms and carry the muskets and accoutrements of Yanks and Rebs.

Hundreds of thousands of visitors annually travel to the battlefields – some as tourists, merely – others in something approaching a pilgrimage. They seek, as that soulful warrior Joshua Lawrence Chamberlain put it, "to see where and by whom great things were suffered and done for them." The humble farm lanes, rail fences, stone walls, wheatfields – immortalized in the blood of fallen heroes – are touchstones that hearken to that stirring, tragic time when so many died for ideals they valued above life itself. And for all the cynicism, apathy and selfish negation of our own time, those things and those places stand for that which is eternal.

In the last decade the loss of Hallowed Ground to the cancer-like sprawl of suburbanization has sparked a battlefield preservation movement that despite many defeats has managed to achieve some notable victories. Refusing to accept the rape of our heritage as the inevitable byproduct of what passes for "progress," zealous volunteers have organized and battled on behalf of those who selflessly gave their all, on those fields, so long ago. The battle is never over, so long as greed and ignorance persist, but these preservation efforts testify to the veneration that beats on in the hearts of those who refuse to forget.

Yet despite the enduring fascination with the events, the battle sites and the people of the American Civil War, there is another aspect of that evocative legacy so far largely ignored by scholars, students, buffs and preservationists. That is the location, enumeration and maintenance of the last resting places of the combatants, North and South.

Most of the 620,000 soldiers who fell in action or succumbed to wounds or disease were initially buried on the field, or close by the hospitals where they died. In time many were reinterred in National Cemeteries, while others were brought home, by their grieving loved ones, and laid to rest in family plots. Down through the decades the surviving veterans would gather on Memorial Days to decorate the graves of fallen comrades, until, in time, they too joined the silent army "On Fame's Eternal Camping Ground."

Sadly, the passage of time has not been kind to the monuments that often remain the last tangible legacy of those vanished veterans of the Civil War. Hundreds of small family graveyards have been obliterated – plowed under and paved over by the concrete and steel of office buildings, shopping malls and housing developments. And vandalism and neglect have in many cases taken a shocking toll of once beautiful, park-like city cemeteries – all but abandoned amidst the crime, decay and hopelessness that surrounds them. Even where memorial stones survive, the effects of acid rain has often made it difficult, if not impossible, to decipher the inscriptions. Weathered, broken, or missing altogether – the loss of those tombstones in a very real sense obliterates an important connection between us and those we seek to honor, venerate, remember.

It comes as both an encouragement and an inspiration to find that a cadre of dedicated researchers have undertaken the challenging task of chronicling the burial places of New Jersey's Civil War veterans. Not alone the patriotic volunteers who served in the ranks of New Jersey's 52 organized units – though that would have been daunting enough – but all veterans of that war whose mortal remains found final rest within the boundaries of the state.

This worthy, heartfelt undertaking is one that will hopefully serve to inspire others – in states throughout this nation – to attempt a similar enumeration of civil War graves. For if we do not do so, in our time, with our devotion, it may well be too late. This is an effort we cannot afford to defer to future generations. This is our duty, our gesture of love and remembrance, to "Our Brothers Gone Before."

Brian C. Pohanka
Alexandria, Virginia

FOREWORD

Our Brothers Gone Before is the result of the most comprehensive and detailed New Jersey historical and genealogical research project ever conducted. Chuck Eckhardt and Bob MacAvoy engaged in a more than twelve year intellectual and physical odyssey through long forgotten records in archives, libraries and historical societies and down highways, city streets and back country dirt roads to cemeteries often abandoned to urban decay or overgrown by deer tick infested thickets. In the hands of lesser men than Eckhardt and MacAvoy, the goal-- producing as complete a burial list as possible of the state's Civil War soldiers, veterans and civilian contributors to the war effort, including nurses -- may well have gone unaccomplished.

Eckhardt and MacAvoy's book details, for the first time ever, a comprehensive statewide record of Civil War related interments in New Jersey. It is much more than just a list, however, and includes additional information on the lives and service of its subjects whenever possible. One such fascinating historical tidbit is the fact that Union navy veteran Anton Basting, who was buried in Holy Name Cemetery in Jersey City in 1915, was the last surviving crewman of the famous iron clad *Monitor*. At the time of his death in 1946, African American veteran George Ashby, who served in the 45th United States Colored Infantry and is interred in Allentown, was the state's last living Civil War veteran.

Some interesting anomalies broaden the scope of the study even further. The vast majority of New Jersey Union soldiers who died of disease or were killed or mortally wounded during the war were buried not far from where they died, often in National Cemeteries such as Gettysburg, and most New Jersey soldier burials are veterans who died in the postwar period. There were exceptions, however. Captain Edward A. Acton of the 5th New Jersey Infantry, killed in action at Second Bull Run in 1862, was disinterred, brought home and reburied at the Old Friends Cemetery in Salem. The body of Captain Ellis Hamilton of the 15th New Jersey Infantry, who died of his wounds in a Washington hospital in 1864, was shipped home to be buried in Trenton's Mercer cemetery. Hamilton, who as a sixteen year old lieutenant became the youngest New Jersey commissioned officer, lies a long stone's throw from much honored veteran Sergeant John Beech, a Medal of Honor winner.

Not only New Jerseyans make the list. A number of Union soldiers from other states who died at local army hospitals from disease or wounds received on Southern battlefields were buried in New Jersey, most at the Beverly National Cemetery. Likewise, a number of Confederates, including Private Adolphus C. Alexander of Company H, 7th North Carolina Infantry, found their final resting-place in the state. Alexander was wounded on July 3, 1863 at Gettysburg, captured by Union forces and incarcerated as a prisoner of war at Fort Delaware. He died of typhoid fever on September 7,1863 and, along with a number of other Rebels, is buried at Finn's Point National Cemetery in Pennsville. Other Confederates moved from the impoverished South to New Jersey after the war, lived out their lives in the state and were buried here.

Military historians writing the story of a particular New Jersey regiment will, of course, find the information in *Our Brothers Gone Before* of utmost importance in closing a tale begun in the early 1860s. The book will also prove a valuable resource for scholars studying the demographics of Civil War units and the communities they were recruited from and came home to. Veteran burials are revelatory of the number of veterans who remained in a community and state following the war, and the lack of such a record indicates a pattern of out-migration, which may be socially significant. Similarly, a study of veterans from other states who moved to New Jersey following the war and lived out their lives here might also prove instructive. There is much raw material to mull over for historians of the Grand Army of the Republic, the first broad based American veterans' association, as well.

For many years William S. Stryker's *Stryker's Record of Officers and Men of New Jersey in the Civil War, 1861-1865*, a comprehensive, indexed listing of New Jerseyans' Civil War service originally published in 1876, has been a basic and invaluable source for genealogists. *Our Brothers Gone Before* will join Stryker's work as an essential volume on the genealogical bookshelf. Both works will complement each other in verifying both service and its aftermath and placing old family Civil War stories in their proper context.

Despite the vast amount of work involved in creating this landmark publication, MacAvoy and Eckhardt will frankly tell you that by its very nature, it is a work in progress, and always will be. There will always be one more gravesite discovered back down some Pine Barrens sand lane or urban back lot. The authors are still looking, and they welcome input from the public.

Eckhardt and MacAvoy have already, however, given us a wonderful snapshot in time. We will not lose the information they so painstakingly gathered, and so a significant part of New Jersey's Civil War heritage will no longer slowly slip away through acid rain gravestone erosion and feckless trashing of written records. For this we in the state's historical and genealogical community owe them our eternal thanks.

Joseph G. Bilby
Wall Township, NJ

PREFACE

Little did my partner or I realize that a meeting one brisk Saturday morning in the autumn of 1989 would launch us on a 15-plus year odyssey and ultimately result in the volume you hold in your hands. But this tome and its companions are indeed the result of that meeting and what came after: a several thousand-mile journey across the width and breadth of New Jersey to document the memory of all those soldiers who served in the U.S. Civil War and fought for the North or South and their way of life. We hope that our effort will preserve their legacy and memory from the ravages of time, in a way that not even etchings on a granite tombstone – as we learned from firsthand experience – can resist. Let this record stand hereafter as our testament to those brave soldiers.

I first met Chuck Eckhardt after reading about him in an article in one of our local newspapers, the Home News Tribune. Chuck had been visiting area cemeteries documenting the graves and taking photographs of the tombstones of Civil War veterans. Having always had a passion for the Civil War, I had some knowledge of local war history. So, I contacted Chuck and offered to help him with his research.

We met on a Saturday morning in Rahway Cemetery, where I had worked for three years as a lad in high school. As we wandered around the grounds, Chuck told me his story. He had been introduced to the Civil War by his grandfather, a veteran of WWI who had known Civil War veterans. Through reading about the war and a 1963 visit to Gettysburg, his interest grew. At a living history event in Woodbridge in 1987, a historical discussion had turned to the burial places of members of Company H of the 5th NJ Infantry. Company H was recruited primarily in the Union/Middlesex County region and many of its members are interred there. A historian of this regiment gave Chuck a tour of several local cemeteries, and pointed out the graves of the Company H soldiers whom he had documented. Excited, Chuck decided to undertake a more serious documentation of all Civil War soldiers buried locally, with a special interest in those who died during the war and those who were awarded the Medal of Honor.

As we discovered, Chuck's interests in the Civil War and New Jersey local history coincided with mine in many ways. My own great-grandfather James MacAvoy had fought for the Union as a member of the 1st New Jersey Cavalry, after lying about his age as a 15-year old in order to enlist. I'm sure as a "Bound Boy" to a store keeper in New Brunswick, the idea of fighting for the North must have involved grand visions of excitement and adventure, certainly something better than the life of an indentured servant in a canal store. Knowledge of my great-grandfather, as well as several visits to Gettysburg and inspiration from tales of Pickett's Charge and Joshua Chamberlain's heroics on Little Round Top, gave me an abiding passion for the Civil War.

As we wandered through the rows of graves in Rahway Cemetery (some of which I may have actually dug during my high school job there) I asked Chuck, "Why document just those who were buried locally? Why not document all who were buried in all New Jersey cemeteries?"

This innocent question was the official beginning of our project. We started out with a Union County map in hand and a tank full of gas in the "War Wagon", my 1979 Chevrolet van that has seen better days. Eventually, we purchased as many different New Jersey County maps as we could find, and started the outward expansion from Union County to encompass the rest of the state. In the New Jersey Historical Society files in Newark, we discovered and copied a previously attempted Civil War burial survey. Although it was incomplete, it proved to be extremely helpful because it contained the names of many cemeteries that are not found on road maps. The maps, the survey, and a complete photocopied set of US Geological Survey maps from Rutgers University, were our navigation charts as we visited the approximately 1400-1500 cemeteries scattered across our nation's 3rd state. We've tried to find every single human being who served the North or South and were buried in New Jersey - white men, black men, foreigners, women, and children. Despite the twelve plus years of work after our fateful meeting, we realize this is a project that will never be "finished" because this type of research can never be an exact science. We are sure there must be literally thousands of veterans resting in peace (or perhaps not) who may never be found.

We documented any individual with a military gravestone or any sort of veteran's marker that indicated a Civil War veteran was buried there. We realized quickly, after several trips to the local graveyards, that we were going to have many problems with our methodology. It is not easy to right a tombstone toppled by vandals that is lying face down and weighs hundreds of pounds. Many of the marble headstones in the more populated and polluted areas of New Jersey had not held up well to acid rain and were quickly deteriorating. Many were completely illegible, and many more would be in a few years. We were only able to read many of these stones by rubbing them lightly with railroad crayon that highlights the lettering, making them somewhat legible. Obscure, out of the way, and abandoned cemeteries required a different approach because they are usually not well maintained. Jungle fatigues, machetes, and bug spray became the tools of our trade as we searched for soldiers' graves in these places. Simply put, there are cemeteries in New Jersey that are maintained like country clubs, cemeteries that have become garbage dumps riddled with graffiti and trash, and everything in between. In addition to the physical difficulties, once we were able to decipher the information, we found that many of the government-issue tombstones contained erroneous data, such as misspellings, incorrect ranks, wrong regiment numbers, wrong State service, etc.

Right information or wrong, we used micro-cassettes to record the information from the tombstones. Then we transcribed our data and entered it into our computer files. The next step was to verify the individual soldiers' service, and note whether a soldier was killed in action, died of wounds, died of disease, was wounded in action, served in more than one regiment or branch of service, or achieved some notable accomplishment worthy of additional comment. Since 80% of the soldiers we found served in New Jersey regiments, we had to locate a copy of the New Jersey Adjutant Generals' report for the Civil War. Luckily, the local library in Rahway (since razed due to flooding!) had a set of these volumes, and I spent many a lunch hour and Saturday poring over these records. Eventually, we purchased our own copies for New Jersey, and for many of the Union states that published records of their soldiers. This was a very expensive proposition, but an expense we felt was necessary to be as complete as possible.

The final piece of the puzzle was to obtain all paper or microfilm veterans' burial records we could find to assist us in locating unmarked graves, reading illegible gravestones, and other information we were missing. This led us to many different sources. The primary source was the Veterans' Interment Officer in each county. Tombstone application microfilm was obtained from the National Archives. Additional county burial microfilm came from the Latter Day Saints in Utah. In the 1930's, during the Great Depression, the Works Project Administration created the Veterans Graves Registration Division of the WPA. These people traveled from cemetery to cemetery documenting all veterans' graves, both physically and by examining each cemetery's records. On the whole, they did an excellent job, and the result of each survey was turned over to the appropriate County Clerk's office. In the one or two counties where these records existed, they had been placed in private hands, and were accessible to us. We believe the rest of the counties threw them out, had them stored away where no one can find them, or don't even know they exist.

Some partial veterans' burial files resided in the various county archives. Historical societies and associations possessed some Grand Army of the Republic Posts' records. Alexander Library at Rutgers University in New Brunswick had some veterans' records, tombstone inscription files, and cemetery interment books. Last but not least, were the records in possession of those individuals willing to share information with us. Naturally, there were many other sources that we used to a lesser extent - books, periodicals, regimental histories, and GAR encampment pamphlets. The internet proved to be a great place to find information, but, as anywhere else, the information must be scoured carefully for errors and the verification of sources.

Of course, not every aspect of this endeavor ran smoothly. Four counties – Atlantic, Bergen, Cumberland, and Passaic – did not have any paper records that could be found and remain lost, stolen, misplaced, trashed, or in unknown private hands. We thought that each county would have maintained these records in a similar fashion, but nothing is further from the truth. Each county is supposed to have a Veterans' Interment Officer who is responsible for maintaining the burial records, handling the veteran gravestone applications, etc., but this is also not true. In the counties where these Veterans' Interment Officers exist, we received the utmost cooperation from them, but this was also a mixed bag. Unfortunately, some of the Interment Officers had turned their older burial records (prior to WWI) over to the County Clerk or to a historical society. We believe they did this for preservation purposes and should be commended for the attempt, but we have often wondered about the legality of doing this with public records.

The County Clerks who possess the records were also very cooperative, but, in one county the clerk threw them in the trash and they were lost forever. The historical societies that have burial records are, for the most part, very helpful, but not always easily accessible. Many queries directed to various New Jersey veterans' organizations, New Jersey State agencies, the Federal Government, and many cemeteries went unanswered. If it were not for the interest taken by individual members of these various groups and organizations who discovered our project, and went out of their way to contribute on their own, we would not have completed this volume.

As our project became more well known as a result of several newspaper articles, we received offers from individuals willing to volunteer their time to assist us in researching records we did not have access to. Armed with this additional assistance, we were able to tie up many loose ends and verify 95% of the veterans we have documented.

As with any work of this magnitude, errors are sure to crop up, regardless of the amount of time spent proof reading the documentation. We have made a concerted effort to be as accurate as possible. Many of the records and sources we used in our research leave a lot to be desired and contained inaccuracies that we corrected as we progressed. Because the educational level in the latter half of the 19th century was not nearly as high as it is today, spelling and handwriting generally suffered. Trying to interpret and comprehend handwritten documents proved difficult at times, and in some cases we used prevailing historical information from other sources to make a final determination of the intent of the writer. We tried to keep speculation to an extreme minimum, and when forced to do so, we erred on the side of inclusion. This is why there are many names listed with no military information or incomplete data. We cannot prove or disprove that these men served, so we felt we had to include them based upon that fact.

The names of many cemeteries in New Jersey have changed over the course of time. Many churches have changed affiliations, both religiously, and ethnically. Some have changed their physical locations and left behind their cemeteries. Others have relocated their cemeteries to newer incorporated cemeteries. Farm cemeteries have generally suffered the same fate as old churchyards; some still exist, some have been relocated, and others destroyed. We decided early on in the project to use the name of the church, farm, or farm family where the cemetery was located at the time we surveyed it. If no name was evident, we used the county records or historical society information to find the commonly used name of the cemetery located there. In a very few cases we were forced to use the street name as the cemetery name. City cemeteries and public burial grounds have generally maintained their identification over the years of their existence and presented less of a problem.

Cemetery locations presented only a minor problem. We decided to use place names and actual physical locations of the cemeteries as opposed to the Post Office address used by the cemetery administrators. While this may cause some confusion since an address might be in one town or county, but the physical location of the cemetery is in a different town or county, we felt that for historical accuracy it should be done this way. Hopefully, because there are so few cemeteries in this category, it will not cause any future confusion.

In a few rare cases, during our surveying trips across the state, there were some small cemeteries we could not locate even though the maps we were using at the time clearly showed that one existed at that location. We noted such cemeteries in our files as "not found". Subsequent to the completion of our physical survey, new information has come to light indicating that some of these cemeteries do indeed exist and our maps were incorrect. Since correct locations were provided by the individual or group bringing such information to our attention, and because we had previously obtained documentation listing the known Civil War veterans buried in these "lost" cemeteries, we felt it was unnecessary to return to the field. We decided in these rare cases to search for information from various official sources for additional verification. If we could not support the existence of these cemeteries with additional research, they were not included.

Despite the years that have passed since we left on our journey from Rahway Cemetery to here, these volumes do not mean that we have arrived at our destination – merely that we have reached a way station. We will continue to maintain and revise our files, and we encourage readers to contact us with information that will ensure any future editions will be as accurate as possible. The publishing of this work represents a "snapshot" of our journey to memorialize our brave forebears – a journey that we hope will continue and inspire others to join and assist.

Robert F. MacAvoy

Andrew H. Ackerman.
Captain, Company C, 11th N.J. Infantry. Killed in action at
Gettysburg, Pa., July 2, 1863. (John W. Kuhl Collection)

Whatever Happened to Andrew Hopper Ackerman's body?
Robert F. MacAvoy

Many years ago there was a television crime drama titled "The Naked City". The stories revolved around everyday police detective activity in New York City. The show's tag line was, "There are eight million stories in the Naked City... this has been one of them."

To paraphrase their tag line, "There are poignant stories of the American Civil War and its aftermath... the following is just one of many."

July 2nd, 1863 was the last day in the life of Andrew Hopper Ackerman, Captain of Company C, Eleventh New Jersey Infantry. However, his death caused by a Rebel bullet and an eventual hero's funeral in his hometown of Paterson, New Jersey is not the end of this tale, just the beginning. You see, Captain Ackerman's body is missing and resting in an unknown and probably unmarked location.

My involvement with Andrew Hopper Ackerman began Fourteen years ago when my partner Chuck Eckhardt and I began in earnest a project he had started before we met, the documentation of the graves of Union Civil War veterans who were buried in New Jersey cemeteries. We modified his original idea and decided to include all men, women, and children who served in any capacity for the Union or the Confederacy. Our proximity to the Gettysburg battlefield, and our interest in the epic struggle that took place there, led us to pay particular attention during our research to the casualties from that conflict.

Andrew Hopper Ackerman was born in 1835 to Jacob and Marretje Hopper Ackerman and was raised in the Passaic County city of Paterson. Just over a year after his first wife, Sophia Jane Alyea, passed away, he married his second wife, Margaret L. Willis, on October 14, 1858. This marriage produced two sons, Nelson and Albert, born in 1859 and 1860, respectively. At the outbreak of the war he volunteered his services as a Private in Company I of the Second New Jersey Infantry. On July 21, 1862 he was discharged from the Second for promotion, and on August 18, 1862 he was commissioned a 1st Lieutenant in Company A of the Eleventh New Jersey Infantry. He was promoted Captain of Company C on March 6, 1863, and went on to fight with distinction at Fredericksburg and Chancellorsville. As one soldier, a member of his regiment, said after the battle of Chancellorsville, "Captain Ackerman was struck in the leg by a piece of shell, but gallantly remained with his regiment until it was withdrawn from the field". On June 11, 1863 the Eleventh began its march northward with General Daniel Sickles Third Army Corps to the field where Andrew Hopper Ackerman would lose his life.

On that fateful day of July 2nd, 1863, the Eleventh New Jersey Infantry would suffer the loss or incapacitation of many of its officers in the fight on the low ground north and east of the Peach Orchard and near

Emmitsburg Road. Colonel McAllister, Captain Lloyd, Lieutenants Schoonover, Provost, Fausett, Good, and Axtell wounded. Major Kearny mortally wounded. Captains Ackerman, Logan, and Martin killed. Including the 18 enlisted men killed, the 6 mortally wounded, and the 115 wounded, the regiment suffered a 62% loss.

Ackerman's family brought his body back to Paterson, NJ for burial. The July 17, 1863 edition of the Paterson Daily Guardian noted: "The splendid glass hearse was drawn by four gray horses led by four of Uncle Abraham's free American citizens of African descent. A large concourse of the returned NJ Volunteers and other citizens followed the noble and patriotic Captain to his final resting place". This should have been the somber end of the journey for Captain Ackerman, at peace beneath his native soil.

After finding the graves of most of the officers of the Eleventh NJ Infantry in New Jersey cemeteries, including Gettysburg casualties Captains Logan and Martin, we began to wonder about the eventual fate of Captain Ackerman's body. The New Jersey State Archives revealed nothing pertaining to his burial, and neither did the Hugh Irish GAR Post burial records in the New Jersey Historical Society. We checked the military tombstone application microfilm from the National Archives in Washington, DC, and found no application for a military marker for his grave. With the knowledge that his family reclaimed his body from Gettysburg, we went in search of some of his personal information. Conversations with several Ackerman family researchers proved only partially successful, since they had no knowledge of his final resting place. However, we did obtain information on his parents, wives, and children. We found that his widow, Margaret applied for a widow's pension on July 28, 1863. She remarried a gentleman by the name of Noyes G. Palmer on December 9 1872 and, on July 17, 1873 she was granted a pension as guardian of her two minor children fathered by Captain Ackerman.

At this point we turned to Roger D. Hunt, co-author of *Brigadier Generals in Blue* and one of this country's finest Civil War researchers. We asked him to search the multitude of files in the National Archives for any information that could be found on Ackerman and his final resting-place. Despite his success doing research for our project for many years, Roger was unable to find any documentation in reference to Captain Ackerman's interment. However, he did unearth enough new information for us to determine that Ackerman is not buried in Cypress Hills Cemetery in Brooklyn, NY with his second wife and her family.

In 1994 and again in 1999, William Gordon of the Newark *Star Ledger* newspaper wrote articles on our project in which our Ackerman conundrum was mentioned. This provided several leads, all of which reached a dead end. Having scoured the Internet by placing queries on several web sites, we picked up small amounts of information including a copy of the article on Ackerman's funeral, which mentioned the Second

Dutch Reformed Church Cemetery. Our research found that at the time of Ackerman's death, there were two Dutch Reformed Churches in Paterson and each had its own cemetery. This led to another roadblock. Both cemeteries were condemned at different times, and the bodies removed either by the families, the churches, or the City of Paterson. The Second Dutch Reformed Church Cemetery on Ryle Avenue had begun removing some of its dead in 1888 to the First Dutch Reformed Church Cemetery at Sandy Hill. The Sandy Hill area was actually a conglomeration of seven small burial grounds, each of a different religious denomination. From 1911 through 1914, after all the Sandy Hill cemeteries were condemned, the remaining bodies were removed. Of course, many families had started removing their loved ones earlier when several new cemeteries were incorporated in the Paterson area: Cedar Lawn in Paterson in 1865. Holy Sepulchre in 1867 and Laurel Grove in 1881, both located in Totowa. Most of the later reinterments were in these newer cemeteries, and were fairly well documented. Ackerman's name does not appear anywhere on the existing removal records.

In 1958 the Second Dutch Reformed Church relocated to Wyckoff, NJ and became the Wyckoff Reformed Church. Correspondence with Reverend Bruce J. Hoffman revealed that the old church records were turned over to the archives at the New Jersey Theological Seminary located on the campus of Rutgers University in New Brunswick, NJ. Mr. Russell L. Gasero, the archivist at the Seminary, wrote that the records for the old church are very sketchy and found no reference to the removals from the cemetery or to Andrew Hopper Ackerman. A recent posting on the website of the Passaic County Historical Society Genealogy Club contains the list of lot owners for the old Sandy Hill cemeteries, but none of the names listed seemed to provide any additional clues.

This is where our search for Captain Ackerman stands at the moment, with no prospects for the eventual discovery of his grave in the near future. With our project nearing completion, we have accumulated the names of 40,000+ Civil War soldiers and nurses buried under New Jersey soil. We had hoped to add Andrew Hopper Ackerman to our growing list of the graves of men and women who sacrificed a part or all of their lives fighting for their beliefs. Perhaps in the final analysis he was never meant to be found, but only to be included with the thousands of other Civil War soldiers lying buried in unknown or unmarked New Jersey graves that we cannot locate.

Marbaker's *History of the Eleventh New Jersey Infantry* contains a biographical sketch of Captain Ackerman, a portion of which reads, "and to be taken thus early in his military career deprived the regiment of the services of one of its most valuable and promising officers". We will continue our search for Ackerman, and hopefully, by finding him someday, ensure that he will not remain one of the lost and forgotten heroes who gave their lives for the cause in which they believed. We owe them all at least that much.

James MacAvoy (aka James Avoy)
Enlisted at the age of 16 in 3rd New York Cavalry, 1861.
Transferred to 1st New Jersey Cavalry, 1862. Captured by
Stonewall Jackson's troops at Manassas Junction during the
2nd Bull Run campaign. Discharged 1865. (CDV courtesy of
Bob MacAvoy)

ACKNOWLEDGMENTS

A work of this magnitude could not be accomplished without the contributions of many individuals. Above and beyond the normal acknowledgments, there are four gentlemen who deserve special praise and recognition. Civil War researcher and collector, Kurt D. Kabelac of Ithaca, New York, volunteered in the summer of 1994 to research the Adjutant General's records for the New York state's soldiers we were documenting. Because of our States geographical proximity to each other, we kept him quite busy researching the many thousands of New York veterans buried in New Jersey cemeteries. Howard D. Lanza of Garfield, New Jersey, an author, historian, and Civil War buff who in early 1994 was in the process of compiling information for his book on the history of Cedar Lawn Cemetery in Paterson, New Jersey, offered to provide us access to his accumulated research data. He also volunteered to undertake research for us in the historical societies and libraries of northern New Jersey. In the Fall of 2000, George C. Burgey of East Windsor, New Jersey answered one of our many Internet queries for information on Civil War soldiers' burials in New Jersey and graciously volunteered to research the microfilmed death certificates in the New Jersey State Archives in Trenton. He has spent countless hours there successfully searching for the many "mystery" soldiers we had discovered on paper records, but for whom we could not find final resting places. Finally, and most importantly, we were assisted by author and Civil War historian Roger D. Hunt of Rockville, Maryland who contacted us in the spring of 1996 and volunteered to undertake research on our behalf in the massive Civil War files of the National Archives in Washington, DC. Not surprisingly, we took him up on his immeasurably generous offer and relied upon him most heavily. He answered literally thousands of requests with a dedication to accuracy and completeness that is rare in this day and age. If there is a finer Civil War researcher alive today we have yet to find him, and without his help we would most certainly not be where we stand at this moment.

We also thank these dedicated individuals: Samuel Asbell of Cherry Hill, NJ; Jan Bachman of Bloomfield, NJ; Peter Bartus the Union County Supervisor of Veterans Interment; Ron Becker at Rutgers University; Joe Bilby of Wall, NJ; Kristen Blauvelt of Los Angeles, CA; Robert Boone the Salem County Supervisor of Veterans Interment; J. Delbert Brandt of Vineland, NJ; Lois Broomell of Seaville, NJ; Christian Christiansen of Cranbury, NJ; Vincent F. Byrnes of Willingboro, NJ; James K. Campbell of Cold Spring, NJ; Richard Caramanga of Bloomfield, NJ; Patrick and Linda Carry of Waukegan, IL; Steven M. Cassese of Newark, NJ; Valerie N. Caulfield of Auburn, NJ; Kemper Chambers of Morristown, NJ; Somers Coursen of Cape May, NJ; Tom

Crossen of East Windsor, NJ; Lonnie and Janet Cryan of Oxford, NJ; Nick DeRose of Dover, NJ; Melinda Deuchar of Imlaystown, NJ; Donna DiFiore at Harleigh Cemetery in Camden, NJ; Cathy DiPietro of Franklin, NJ; Kathleen S. Dodds at the Walsh Library, Seton Hall University, South Orange, NJ; Ted Dombroski of Hazleton, PA; Gary Drake of Colonia, NJ; Terry and Donna Ellis of Ocala, FL; Lou Evans of the United States Navy; Evergreen Cemetery, Hillside, NJ; Robert J. Fahrenholz at Hillside Cemetery in Scotch Plains, NJ; Flower Hill Cemetery, North Bergen, NJ; Miss Janet Foisset of Buffalo, NY; John Fosa of Forked River, NJ; Stuart Foulks of Florence, NJ; Glenn and Jill Geisheimer of Iselin, NJ; Neil Genzlinger at the New York Times; Marcia Glamp of Greensburg, PA; William Gordon at the Newark Star Ledger; Fred Greenbaum the Monmouth County Supervisor of Veterans Interment; Larry Greene at the Hunterdon County Hall of Records; Bob Griffin of Englewood, NJ; Grove Church, North Bergen, NJ; Anne Haines of East Brunswick, NJ; Katherine Hawkins of Summit, NY; Jeff Heckelmann of Keyport, NJ; Bob Heistand of Hanover, PA; Robert Helm of New Brunswick, NJ; Ed Henkler of Lansdale, PA; J. Nolan Higgins of Freehold, NJ; Hoboken Cemetery, North Bergen, NJ; Edith Hoelle at the Gloucester County Historical Society; Edward Huelbig the Hudson County Supervisor of Veterans Interment;

Also: Evelyn Huey of East Hanover, NJ; Bob Illig of the Newark Police Museum; Lance W. Ingmire of Pittsford, NY; Jack Kelley of Vineland, NJ; Sue Kerekgyarto of Chicago, IL; Mary Ann Kiernan at the Monmouth County Archives; Trevor Kirkpatrick of Toms River, NJ; Joe Klett at the New Jersey State Archives; Jeanne Kolva of Highland Park, NJ; Susan Kornutick of Jersey City, NJ; Ivan Kossak of Lincoln Park, NJ; Kearney Kulthau Jr. of New Brunswick, NJ; Joan Lanphear at the Burlington County Historical Society; Richard J. Lesser of Mt. Pleasant, SC; Mary Lish of Nutley, NJ; Bob Longcore of Hamburg, NJ; Thomas Love the Superintendent of Holy Sepulchre Cemetery in Orange, NJ; Walter Lovett of Egg Harbor, NJ; Jeff Maddalena of Vineland, NJ; James Madden of Wood-Ridge, NJ; Ms. Paula Lynch Manzella at the Burlington County Library in Westampton, NJ; Mr. Masterton of South Amboy, NJ; Fred McElhenny of Woodbridge, NJ; Ed McGuinn of Port Reading, NJ; Richard Kingdon Meyers of Princeton, NJ; Susanne D. Miller of Matawan, NJ; Patricia Mirabella of Bayonne, NJ; Dave Mitros of Basking Ridge, NJ; Carol Reading Morris of Virginia Beach, VA; Betty Mumm of Metuchen, NJ; Tom Murphy at the Middlesex County Archives; Iris H. Naylor of Stockton, NJ; Scott Newkirk of Mickleton, NJ; Karl Niederer at the New Jersey State Archives; R.E. Niederer the Superintendent of Riverview Cemetery in Trenton, NJ; Edward O'Donnell of Rahway, NJ; Judy Olsen of Pemberton, NJ; Jane W. Ott of Belvidere, NJ; George Paulton the Ocean County Supervisor of Veterans Interment; Brian Pohanka of Alexandria, VA; Michael D. Pongracz the Superintendent of Fairmount Cemetery in Newark, NJ; Randy B. Rauscher of Colts Neck,

NJ; Gill Riddle of Easton, PA; Jacqueline H. Ross-Foulkrod of Hazlet, NJ; George Rummell of Brick, NJ; Gary D. Saretzky at the Monmouth County Archives; John Andrew Sass of Bloomfield, NJ; Tony Scacifero of Scotch Plains, NJ; Paul W. Schopp at the Camden County Historical Society; Irving Scolnick the Morris County Supervisor of Veterans Interment;

Also: Wayne Sherrer of Phillipsburg, NJ; Andrew Shick at the Passaic County Historical Society; William Skinner of Mullica Hill, NJ; Ed Skipworth at Rutgers University; Tom Slack of New Brunswick, NJ; Diane and Jamie Smyczynski of Livingston, NJ; Ed Smyk of Paterson, NJ; Debra Spayd of Stockton, NJ; Dr. Charles Speierl and his class at the Raritan Valley Community College in North Branch, NJ; James A. Stewart at the Delaware State Museum; Walter Studdiford of Bridgewater, NJ; Bill Styple of Kearny, NJ; the staff at the Sussex County Hall of Records in Newton, NJ; Herbert Tinning of Millburn, NJ; Kathleen Tortoriello, Somerville, MA; Raymond C. Trepkau of Lake Hiawatha, NJ; Holly VanCamp of Trenton, NJ; Robert Viering of Iselin, NJ; Jean Volz of Nutley, NJ; Lloyd E. Washington of Maplewood, NJ; Charles Webster IV of Trenton, NJ; Weehawken Cemetery, North Bergen, NJ; George J. Weinmann, Brooklyn, NY; Agnes Wolf of West Orange, NJ; Stanley Yard of Three Bridges, NJ; the Office Staff of Alpine Cemetery in Perth Amboy, NJ; the Research Department of Dowdell Library in South Amboy, NJ; the staff at the Warren County Clerks office in Belvidere, NJ; Oliver Tilden Camp 26, SUVCW in New York City; James A. Garfield Camp 4, SUVCW in Trenton, NJ.

There are many other people not listed who contributed a name, a date, a location, or other bits of information we used to track down many of the soldiers noted in these volumes. To these unnamed individuals we also owe our gratitude.

Military Abbreviations

AAG	Assistant Adjutant General
Actg	Acting
ADC	Aide de Camp
Adj	Adjutant
AIG	Assistant Inspector General
aka	also known as (Alias)
Art	Artillery
Asst	Assistant
Brig	Brigade
Brig Gen	Brigadier General
Bttn	Battalion
Btty	Battery
Bvt	Brevet
Capt	Captain
Cav	Cavalry
CHA	Colored Heavy Artillery
Cl	Class
Co	Company
Col	Colonel
Com	Commissary
Corp	Corporal
CSA	Confederate States Army
CT	Colored Troops
Div	Division
Eng	Engineer (or Engineers)
GAR	Grand Army of the Republic
Hosp	Hospital
IG	Inspector General
Ind	Independent
Inf	Infantry
Lt	Lieutenant
Lt Col	Lieutenant Colonel
Maj	Major
Maj Gen	Major General
Musc	Musician
Pvt	Private
QM	Quartermaster
Res	Reserve (or Reserves)
RQM	Regimental Quartermaster
Sgt	Sergeant
Surg	Surgeon
Unatt	Unattached
Unass	Unassigned
U.S.	United States
U.S.M.A.	United States Military Academy
USS	United States Ship
Vet	Veteran
Vol	Volunteer (or Volunteers)
VRC	Veteran Reserve Corps
*	next to surname indicates service in multiple regiments, ships or branches

State Abbreviations

AL	Alabama
AR	Arkansas
CA	California
CO	Colorado
CT	Connecticut
DE	Delaware
DC	District of Columbia
FL	Florida
GA	Georgia
IL	Illinois
IN	Indiana
IA	Iowa
KS	Kansas
KY	Kentucky
LA	Louisiana
ME	Maine
MD	Maryland
MA	Massachusetts
MI	Michigan
MN	Minnesota
MS	Mississippi
MO	Missouri
NE	Nebraska
NH	New Hampshire
NJ	New Jersey
NM	New Mexico
NY	New York
NC	North Carolina
OH	Ohio
OR	Oregon
PA	Pennsylvania
RI	Rhode Island
SC	South Carolina
TN	Tennessee
TX	Texas
VT	Vermont
VA	Virginia
WV	West Virginia
WI	Wisconsin

Grave of James Theodore Calhoun, Surgeon, 74th N.Y. Infantry; Medical Director, 2nd Division, 3rd Corps; Surgeon in Chief, Ward U.S. Army Hospital, Newark, N.J. Died July 19, 1866 of Cholera at Hart Island Depot, N.Y. Buried in Hazelwood Cemetery, Rahway. (Photo courtesy of Chuck Eckhardt)

New Jersey Civil War Burials

AAB, GEORGE L. Pvt, B, 20th NY Inf, [Wounded 9-17-1862 at Antietam, MD.] 1-20-1895. Fairmount Cemetery, Newark, Essex County.

AARON, SIMON Sgt, A, 41st U.S. CT, 11-26-1880. Rahway Cemetery, Rahway, Union County.

AARONSON, BENJAMIN Corp, I, 23rd NJ Inf, 2-24-1915. Oddfellows Cemetery, Burlington, Burlington County.

AARONSON, NAPOLEON B. Capt, F, 4th NJ Inf, 2-1-1902. Evergreen Cemetery, Camden, Camden County.

ABBOT, MICHAEL Pvt, B, 5th PA Cav, DoD Unknown. Riverside Cemetery, Riverside, Burlington County.

ABBOT, THOMAS Pvt, K, 13th NJ Inf, 6-6-1898. Laurel Grove Cemetery, Totowa, Passaic County.

ABBOTT, ABDEN Pvt, D, 12th NJ Inf, 1- -1869. Chickory Chapel Baptist Church Cemetery, Elk, Gloucester County.

ABBOTT, ANDREW 1927. Presbyterian Church Cemetery, Mays Landing, Atlantic County.

ABBOTT, BENJAMIN Corp, H, 6th NJ Inf, 1905. Old Rock Church Cemetery, West Amwell, Hunterdon County.

ABBOTT, BENJAMIN TREEN 1911. Union Cemetery, Clarkstown, Atlantic County.

ABBOTT, CHARLES A. Pvt, A, 3rd NJ Cav, 1-16-1889. Mount Hope Presbyterian Cemetery, Lambertville, Hunterdon County.

ABBOTT, CHARLES CONRAD Pvt, A, PA Emerg NJ Militia, 7-27-1919. Riverview Cemetery, Trenton, Mercer County.

ABBOTT, CHARLES S. Pvt, I, 18th VA Inf (CSA), [Captured 7-3-1863 at Gettysburg, PA. Died of typhoid.] 9-22-1863. Finn's Point National Cemetery, Pennsville, Salem County.

ABBOTT, CHARLES V. Pvt, A, 3rd NJ Inf, 10-17-1908. Methodist Church Cemetery, Hurffville, Gloucester County.

ABBOTT*, EDWARD P. 1st Lt, B, 1st NH Cav, [Wounded on Wilsons raid at Nottoway CH, VA.] 6-26-1901. United Methodist Church Cemetery, Vernon, Sussex County.

ABBOTT, GEORGE A. Pvt, F, 57th NY Inf, 7-14-1920. Cedar Lawn Cemetery, Paterson, Passaic County.

ABBOTT, GEORGE H. Pvt, C, 2nd DC Inf, 6-11-1907. Cedar Lawn Cemetery, Paterson, Passaic County.

ABBOTT, GEORGE W. Pvt, C, 21st NJ Inf, 3-4-1880. Rosedale Cemetery, Orange, Essex County.

ABBOTT, JAMES Pvt, A, 79th NY Inf, [Wounded 7-21-1861 at 1st Bull Run, VA.] 1-30-1902. Arlington Cemetery, Kearny, Hudson County.

ABBOTT, JAMES MILES Pvt, A, 46th GA Inf (CSA), [Captured 11-27-1863 at Ringgold, GA. Died of lung inflammation.] 6-11-1864. Finn's Point National Cemetery, Pennsville, Salem County.

ABBOTT, JESSE 12-10-1898. Evergreen Cemetery, New Brunswick, Middlesex County.

ABBOTT, JOHN Pvt, B, 10th NJ Inf, 6-10-1899. Methodist-Episcopal Church Cemetery, Aura, Gloucester County.

ABBOTT, JOHN G. Sgt, D, 48th NY Inf, [Died at Fort Schuyler, NY of wounds received 7-18-1863 at Fort Wagner, SC.] 1863. Union Cemetery, Clarkstown, Atlantic County.

ABBOTT, JOHN J. Sgt, F, 95th NY Inf, [Wounded 8-21-1864 at Weldon Railroad, VA.] 1-27-1915. Glendale Cemetery, Bloomfield, Essex County.

ABBOTT, JOSEPH Pvt, A, 213th PA Inf, DoD Unknown. Overlook Cemetery, Bridgeton, Cumberland County.

ABBOTT, JOSEPH (JR.) Capt, E, 7th NJ Inf, [Killed in action at 2nd Bull Run, VA.] 8-29-1862. Riverview Cemetery, Trenton, Mercer County.

Our Brothers Gone Before

ABBOTT, MORGAN H. Sgt, A, 7th NJ Inf, 10-10-1910. Methodist-Episcopal Church Cemetery, Aura, Gloucester County.

ABBOTT, RICHARD J. Pvt, E, 10th NJ Inf, [Accidently killed.] 7-12-1862. Batsto/Pleasant Mills Methodist Church Cemetery, Pleasant Mills, Atlantic County.

ABBOTT, ROBERT Pvt, K, 4th NJ Inf, 9-30-1901. Oak Hill Cemetery, Vineland, Cumberland County.

ABBOTT, THOMAS Pvt, D, 36th PA Inf, [Wounded 9-14-1862 at South Mountain, MD.] 1-16-1894. St. Mary's Cemetery, Hamilton, Mercer County.

ABBOTT, WILLIAM T. Chaplain, 23rd NJ Inf 6-9-1925. Glenwood Cemetery, West Long Branch, Monmouth County.

ABBOTT*, WILLIAM W. Capt, E, 38th NJ Inf, 3-26-1878. Mount Hope Presbyterian Cemetery, Lambertville, Hunterdon County.

ABBOTT, ZEPHANIAH S. Pvt, I, 38th NJ Inf, 1932. Baptist Cemetery, Hopewell Boro, Mercer County.

ABDILL, DECATUR Pvt, Unassigned, 2nd PA Heavy Art, 6-8-1922. Oddfellows Cemetery, Burlington, Burlington County.

ABDILL, JOHN S. Pvt, F, 51st PA Militia, 1-14-1888. Methodist-Episcopal Cemetery, Burlington, Burlington County.

ABDILL, SYLVESTER WATSON Pvt, Btty D, 2nd PA Heavy Art, 5-2-1908. Baptist Cemetery, Burlington, Burlington County.

ABEEL*, GUSTAVUS N. Bvt Col, 34th NJ Inf 9-4-1887. Mount Pleasant Cemetery, Newark, Essex County.

ABEEL, JACOB H. Pvt, Btty K, 10th NY Heavy Art, [Died at Beverly, NJ.] 12-7-1864. Beverly National Cemetery, Edgewater Park, Burlington County.

ABEL, JOHANN (see: Aberle, John) Union Cemetery, Frenchtown, Hunterdon County.

ABEL, THEODORE Pvt, F, 97th PA Inf, [Wounded 6-10-1862 at James Island, SC.] 1908. Soldier's Home Cemetery, Vineland, Cumberland County.

ABEL, WILLIAM Pvt, I, 14th NJ Inf, [Died at Newark, NJ. of wounds received 7-9-1864 at Monocacy, MD.] 9-5-1864. Methodist Cemetery, Pennington, Mercer County.

ABELE, MATTHIAS Pvt, C, 46th NY Inf, [Died of disease at Petersburg, VA.] 10-27-1864. Beverly National Cemetery, Edgewater Park, Burlington County.

ABELL, WILLIAM DoD Unknown. Evergreen Cemetery, Morristown, Morris County.

ABER, CALEB Pvt, F, 12th NJ Inf, 10-30-1926. Pequest Union Cemetery, Great Meadows, Warren County.

ABER, CHARLES H. Pvt, E, 11th NJ Inf, 7-12-1895. Walnut Grove Cemetery, Mount Freedom, Morris County.

ABER, EDWARD C. 8-13-1878. Mount Pleasant Cemetery, Newark, Essex County.

ABER, JACOB Y. Pvt, B, 33rd NJ Inf, 12-17-1908. Baptist Cemetery, Mount Freedom, Morris County.

ABERGER, WILLIAM (see: Alberger, William) Holy Sepulchre Cemetery, East Orange, Essex County.

ABERLE*, JACOB Pvt, B, 178th NY Inf, 5-15-1898. Fairmount Cemetery, Newark, Essex County.

ABERLE, JOHN (aka: Abel, Johann) Pvt, 29th NY Ind Btty 9-7-1902. Union Cemetery, Frenchtown, Hunterdon County.

ABERS, PETER K. Wagoner, B, 27th NJ Inf, 8-10-1908. Walnut Grove Cemetery, Mount Freedom, Morris County.

ABLE, JAMES S. Pvt, D, 13th AL Inf (CSA), 10-1-1863. Finn's Point National Cemetery, Pennsville, Salem County.

ABLE, JOSEPH Pvt, K, 2nd NJ Cav, 1-26-1917. Monument Cemetery, Edgewater Park, Burlington County.

ABLE, REUBEN 10-6-1922. St. Bernard's Cemetery, Bridgewater, Somerset County.

New Jersey Civil War Burials

ABLE, THOMAS Pvt, C, 31st NJ Inf, 8-31-1892. Union Cemetery, Frenchtown, Hunterdon County.

ABOS, GEORGE Pvt, E, 33rd NJ Inf, 8-16-1870. Fairmount Cemetery, Newark, Essex County.

ABRAHAMS, CORNELIUS (aka: Abrams,Cornelius) Pvt, G, 1st NJ Cav, 5-15-1862. Tennent Church Cemetery, Tennent, Monmouth County.

ABRAHAMS, CORNELIUS S. 2nd Lt, B, 1st NJ Inf, 6-18-1915. Riverview Cemetery, Trenton, Mercer County.

ABRAHAMS, JOHN P. 2-19-1869. Mount Pleasant Cemetery, Newark, Essex County.

ABRAHAMS, JOSEPH (see: Abrams, Joseph S.) 1st Baptist Cemetery, Cape May Court House, Cape May County.

ABRAHAMS, PETER M. Pvt, K, 2nd IL Cav, [Cenotaph.] 11-4-1861. Brainerd Cemetery, Cranbury, Middlesex County.

ABRAMS, ADAM Pvt, I, 25th NJ Inf, DoD Unknown. Asbury Methodist-Episcopal Church Cemetery, Swainton, Cape May County.

ABRAMS, CHARLES Pvt, F, 25th NJ Inf, 3-5-1901. Calvary Baptist Church Cemetery, Ocean View, Cape May County.

ABRAMS, CORNELIUS (see: Abrahams, Cornelius) Tennent Church Cemetery, Tennent, Monmouth County.

ABRAMS, ENOCH T. Pvt, K, 38th NJ Inf, [Wounded in action.] 2-11-1915. Calvary Baptist Church Cemetery, Ocean View, Cape May County.

ABRAMS, JACOB 2-4-1903. United Presbyterian Church Cemetery, Perrineville, Monmouth County.

ABRAMS, JOSEPH S. (aka: Abrahams, Joseph) Corp, B, 10th NJ Inf, [Wounded 10-19-1864 at Cedar Creek, VA.] 6-5-1925. 1st Baptist Cemetery, Cape May Court House, Cape May County.

ABRAMS*, SKIDMORE Pvt, K, 38th NJ Inf, 10-17-1871. Asbury Methodist-Episcopal Church Cemetery, Swainton, Cape May County.

ABRAMS*, WILLIAM H. Pvt, B, 127th NY Inf, 6-7-1899. Rahway Cemetery, Rahway, Union County.

ABRION, F. DoD Unknown. Old Camden Cemetery, Camden, Camden County.

ABRON, JAMES S. 4-30-1884. Lake Park Cemetery, Swedesboro, Gloucester County.

ABSLEY, ALEXANDER Pvt, I, 39th NJ Inf, 6-3-1906. Holy Sepulchre Cemetery, East Orange, Essex County.

ACCOO, CHARLES Pvt, F, 25th U.S. CT, 5-19-1910. Mount Peace Cemetery, Lawnside, Camden County.

ACCOO, NAPPY Pvt, F, 22nd U.S. CT, 11-30-1903. Mount Zion AME Cemetery, Swedesboro, Gloucester County.

ACKELEY, CHARLES (aka: Ackley, Chauncey) Com Sgt, F, 11th PA Cav, 1914. Presbyterian Church Cemetery, Pleasant Grove, Morris County.

ACKEN, CROWELL Pvt, I, 28th NJ Inf, 3-21-1866. Alpine Cemetery, Perth Amboy, Middlesex County.

ACKEN, SAMUEL Master, U.S. Navy, [Wounded in action.] 12-13-1892. Elmwood Cemetery, New Brunswick, Middlesex County.

ACKER, FRANCIS Pvt, B, 9th NJ Inf, 2-9-1906. St. Peter's Cemetery, New Brunswick, Middlesex County.

ACKER, GEORGE W. (aka: Akers, George) Pvt, G, 30th NJ Inf, 2-20-1882. Methodist Church Cemetery, Liberty, Warren County.

ACKER*, JAMES Pvt, Btty M, 15th NY Heavy Art, 2-19-1916. Laurel Grove Cemetery, Totowa, Passaic County.

ACKER, JOHN Pvt, B, 22nd NJ Inf, [Wounded in action.] 11-24-1910. Zion Lutheran Church Cemetery, Saddle River, Bergen County.

ACKER, PHILIP Pvt, B, 9th NJ Inf, [Wounded in action at Newbern, NC.] 7-24-1904. Van Liew Cemetery, North Brunswick, Middlesex County.

Our Brothers Gone Before

ACKERMAN, AARON E. Sgt, H, 13th NJ Inf, 6-14-1914. Maple Grove Cemetery, Hackensack, Bergen County.
ACKERMAN, ABRAHAM Sgt, K, 153rd PA Inf, 3-7-1899. Fairview Cemetery, Columbia, Warren County.
ACKERMAN, ABRAHAM A. 1908. Reformed Church Cemetery, Wyckoff, Bergen County.
ACKERMAN, ABRAHAM J. Pvt, H, 22nd NJ Inf, 5-26-1865. Valleau Cemetery, Ridgewood, Bergen County.
ACKERMAN, ABRAM RUTAN Pvt, D, 22nd NJ Inf, 3-6-1900. Valleau Cemetery, Ridgewood, Bergen County.
ACKERMAN, ABRAM W. Sgt, K, 13th NJ Inf, 7- -1902. Laurel Grove Cemetery, Totowa, Passaic County.
ACKERMAN, ALBERT D. 1925. Valleau Cemetery, Ridgewood, Bergen County.
ACKERMAN, ALEXANDER F. 2-23-1910. Old 1st Reformed Church Cemetery, Hackensack, Bergen County.
ACKERMAN, BENJAMIN F. Pvt, 6th NY Ind Btty 5-13-1910. Evergreen Cemetery, Hillside, Union County.
ACKERMAN*, CHARLES D. Corp, F, 174th NY Inf, 2-10-1911. Evergreen Cemetery, Morristown, Morris County.
ACKERMAN, CORNELIUS D. Corp, B, 22nd NJ Inf, 1881. Valleau Cemetery, Ridgewood, Bergen County.
ACKERMAN, CORNELIUS D. DoD Unknown. 1st Reformed Church Cemetery, Pompton Plains, Morris County.
ACKERMAN, DAVID 1934. Maple Grove Cemetery, Hackensack, Bergen County.
ACKERMAN, DAVID D. Wagoner, K, 25th NJ Inf, 9-30-1905. Cedar Lawn Cemetery, Paterson, Passaic County.
ACKERMAN, DAVID R. 2-4-1865. Willow Grove Cemetery, New Brunswick, Middlesex County.
ACKERMAN, EDWIN Pvt, I, 22nd NJ Inf, 8-3-1901. Woodside Cemetery, Dumont, Bergen County.
ACKERMAN, FREDERICK WILLIAM Musc, D, 6th NY Inf, 4-15-1906. Flower Hill Cemetery, North Bergen, Hudson County.
ACKERMAN, GARRET A. Pvt, D, 22nd NJ Inf, 1-4-1914. Old Stone Reformed Church Cemetery, Upper Saddle River, Bergen County.
ACKERMAN, GARRETT 5-26-1925. Zion Lutheran Church Cemetery, Saddle River, Bergen County.
ACKERMAN, GARRETT A.N. 4-21-1883. Valleau Cemetery, Ridgewood, Bergen County.
ACKERMAN, GEORGE W. Pvt, D, 22nd NJ Inf, 11-26-1912. Valleau Cemetery, Ridgewood, Bergen County.
ACKERMAN, GEORGE W. Pvt, C, 30th NJ Inf, 3-28-1904. Old 1st Methodist Church Cemetery, West Long Branch, Monmouth County.
ACKERMAN, HENRY 2nd Lt, C, 3rd NJ Cav, 9-7-1906. Fairmount Cemetery, Newark, Essex County.
ACKERMAN, HENRY A. Pvt, C, 26th NJ Inf, 1923. Franklin Reformed Church Cemetery, Nutley, Essex County.
ACKERMAN, JAMES H. Pvt, I, 70th NY Inf, 3-30-1919. Cedar Lawn Cemetery, Paterson, Passaic County.
ACKERMAN, JAMES P. Pvt, D, 22nd NJ Inf, 3-23-1879. Old Hook Cemetery, Westwood, Bergen County.
ACKERMAN, JAMES W. Pvt, D, 22nd NJ Inf, 8-21-1893. Valleau Cemetery, Ridgewood, Bergen County.
ACKERMAN, JOHN Corp, C, 22nd NJ Inf, DoD Unknown. Old South Church Cemetery, Bergenfield, Bergen County.

New Jersey Civil War Burials

ACKERMAN, JOHN Pvt, H, 26th NJ Inf, 7-16-1905. Rosedale Cemetery, Orange, Essex County.

ACKERMAN, JOHN Pvt, F, 26th NJ Inf, 11-29-1884. Mount Olivet Cemetery, Bloomfield, Essex County.

ACKERMAN, JOHN 3-29-1921. Evergreen Cemetery, Morristown, Morris County.

ACKERMAN, JOHN A. Pvt, H, 25th NJ Inf, 1-6-1897. Valleau Cemetery, Ridgewood, Bergen County.

ACKERMAN, JOHN A. 11-15-1879. Ponds Church Cemetery, Oakland, Bergen County.

ACKERMAN, JOHN J. Pvt, D, 3rd NJ Cav, 4-6-1918. Valleau Cemetery, Ridgewood, Bergen County.

ACKERMAN, JOHN J. Pvt, C, 2nd NJ Cav, 2-10-1918. Newton Cemetery, Newton, Sussex County.

ACKERMAN, JOSEPH Corp, A, 11th NJ Inf, 1-16-1893. Laurel Grove Cemetery, Totowa, Passaic County.

ACKERMAN, PETER J. Pvt, C, 22nd NJ Inf, 3-3-1909. Old 1st Reformed Church Cemetery, Hackensack, Bergen County.

ACKERMAN*, PETER J. Pvt, C, 87th NY Inf, [Wounded 6-30-1862 at Fair Oaks, VA.] DoD Unknown. Laurel Grove Cemetery, Totowa, Passaic County.

ACKERMAN*, PHILLIP Pvt, E, 7th NJ Inf, 12-8-1910. Evergreen Cemetery, Hillside, Union County.

ACKERMAN, RICHARD Pvt, K, 5th NY Inf, [Died of wounds received 8-30-1862 at 2nd Bull Run, VA.] 12-19-1862. Willow Grove Cemetery, New Brunswick, Middlesex County.

ACKERMAN*, THEODORE F. Pvt, 26th NY Ind Btty 10-9-1878. Willow Grove Cemetery, New Brunswick, Middlesex County.

ACKERMAN, THEODORE F. Pvt, Btty B, 1st NJ Light Art, 5-14-1920. 1st Reformed Church Cemetery, Pompton Plains, Morris County.

ACKERMAN, THOMAS 1-20-1905. 1st Presbyterian Union Cemetery, Ramsey, Bergen County.

ACKERMAN, THOMAS Corp, G, 7th NJ Inf, 1-16-1875. Cedar Lawn Cemetery, Paterson, Passaic County.

ACKERMAN, WILLIAM Sgt, K, 79th NY Inf, 2-8-1917. Oak Hill Cemetery, Vineland, Cumberland County.

ACKERMAN, WILLIAM Pvt, I, 22nd NJ Inf, 6-7-1880. Pascack Reformed Cemetery, Park Ridge, Bergen County.

ACKERMAN, WILLIAM H. Pvt, A, 22nd NJ Inf, 11-6-1913. Hackensack Cemetery, Hackensack, Bergen County.

ACKERMANN, JOHN Pvt, Btty E, 1st NJ Light Art, 6-17-1874. Palisade Cemetery, North Bergen, Hudson County.

ACKERSON, CHARLES Pvt, K, 1st NJ Cav, 11-10-1937. Headley Cemetery, Milton, Morris County.

ACKERSON, EMANUEL 1st Lt, G, 15th NJ Inf, 7-10-1887. Fairmount Cemetery, Newark, Essex County.

ACKERSON, JOHN C. Pvt, D, 22nd NJ Inf, 4-11-1893. Old Hook Cemetery, Westwood, Bergen County.

ACKERSON, STEPHEN Pvt, Btty B, 2nd NY Heavy Art, 6-24-1911. Arlington Cemetery, Kearny, Hudson County.

ACKERSON*, WILLIAM T. Capt, F, 51st NY Inf, [Wounded 9-17-1862 at Antietam, MD.] 11-29-1923. Manalapan Cemetery, Manalapan, Monmouth County.

ACKERT, JOHN (see: Eckert, John) Holy Sepulchre Cemetery, Totowa, Passaic County.

ACKLEY, CHAUNCEY (see: Ackeley, Charles) Presbyterian Church Cemetery, Pleasant Grove, Morris County.

ACKLEY, DEWITT C. Sgt, 14th OH Art 12-1-1908. Atlantic View Cemetery, Manasquan, Monmouth County.

Our Brothers Gone Before

ACKLEY*, ELIJAH N. Pvt, G, 14th NJ Inf, 10-5-1907. Fairview Cemetery, Fairview, Monmouth County.
ACKLEY, ERASTUS J. Corp, C, 67th NY Inf, [Died of disease at Georgetown, DC.] 11-11-1861. Evergreen Cemetery, Morristown, Morris County.
ACKLEY, GEORGE F. Coal Heaver, U.S. Navy, USS Magnolia, 6-27-1915. Rahway Cemetery, Rahway, Union County.
ACKLEY, HEZEKIAH Pvt, C, 104th PA Inf, 1896. Lake Park Cemetery, Swedesboro, Gloucester County.
ACKLEY, JESSE C. 12-19-1902. Mount Pleasant Cemetery, Millville, Cumberland County.
ACKLEY, JOHN BOLTON Asst Surg, U.S. Navy, 9-11-1874. St. Mary's Episcopal Church Cemetery, Burlington, Burlington County.
ACKLEY, JOSEPH Pvt, D, 26th NJ Inf, DoD Unknown. Evergreen Cemetery, Morristown, Morris County.
ACKLEY, MAURICE (see: Salkize, Moritz) Oheb Sholem Cemetery, Hillside, Union County.
ACKLEY, WILLIAM Pvt, G, 24th NJ Inf, 11-26-1897. Methodist-Episcopal Cemetery, Olivet, Salem County.
ACKLEY, WILLIAM S. Pvt, F, 24th NJ Inf, 7-29-1920. Arlington Cemetery, Kearny, Hudson County.
ACKMAN, JOSEPH Sgt, E, 58th NY Inf, DoD Unknown. Weehawken Cemetery, North Bergen, Hudson County.
ACQUAVELLA, FRANCESCO 1914. Holy Sepulchre Cemetery, East Orange, Essex County.
ACTON, BENJAMIN Maj, U.S. Volunteers, [Disbursing Officer and Quartermaster at Camp Stockton. Woodbury, NJ.] 12-18-1877. Old Friends Cemetery, Salem, Salem County.
ACTON, EDWARD A. Capt, K, 5th NJ Inf, [Killed in action at 2nd Bull Run, VA.] 8-29-1862. Old Friends Cemetery, Salem, Salem County.
ACTON, FRANKLIN M. Capt, F, 12th NJ Inf, 8-15-1895. Old Friends Cemetery, Salem, Salem County.
ADAIR, GEORGE (see: Ader, George) Fairmount Cemetery, Fairmount, Hunterdon County.
ADAIR, GEORGE W. Pvt, I, 1st NJ Cav, 10-20-1918. Arlington Cemetery, Kearny, Hudson County.
ADAIR, JAMES 3-3-1896. New Somerville Cemetery, Somerville, Somerset County.
ADAM, JOHN Pvt, I, 82nd NY Inf, 7-2-1915. Van Liew Cemetery, North Brunswick, Middlesex County.
ADAMS, __ Pvt, I, 14th TN Inf (CSA), 9-8-1863. Finn's Point National Cemetery, Pennsville, Salem County.
ADAMS*, ABRAHAM L. Corp, C, 3rd NJ Inf, 4-4-1928. Harleigh Cemetery, Camden, Camden County.
ADAMS, AMAZIAH Pvt, Btty M, 1st NY Light Art, 5-8-1911. Pequest Union Cemetery, Great Meadows, Warren County.
ADAMS, ANDREW Landsman, U.S. Navy, USS Sonoma, 11-23-1896. Methodist-Episcopal Cemetery, Olivet, Salem County.
ADAMS, B. DoD Unknown. Jersey City Cemetery, Jersey City, Hudson County.
ADAMS*, CASPER K. Pvt, H, 57th NY Inf, 11-5-1909. Oddfellows Cemetery, Burlington, Burlington County.
ADAMS, CHARLES Pvt, A, 23rd NJ Inf, 2-22-1904. Fairmount Cemetery, Newark, Essex County.
ADAMS*, CHARLES W. Pvt, F, 57th NY Inf, 3- -1923. Monument Cemetery, Edgewater Park, Burlington County.

New Jersey Civil War Burials

ADAMS, CHARLES W. Sgt, B, 14th NJ Inf, 7-3-1875. Riverview Cemetery, Trenton, Mercer County.

ADAMS, CLEMENT J. Pvt, B, 25th NJ Inf, 5-29-1922. Atlantic City Cemetery, Pleasantville, Atlantic County.

ADAMS, DAVID Pvt, I, 34th NJ Inf, 2-9-1895. Evergreen Cemetery, Camden, Camden County.

ADAMS, DAVID (see: Snell, David Adams) Mount Hebron Cemetery, Montclair, Essex County.

ADAMS, DAVID W. Pvt, G, 4th NJ Inf, 3-25-1866. Miller's Cemetery, New Gretna, Burlington County.

ADAMS, EDGAR Pvt, B, 14th NJ Inf, 5-24-1906. Riverview Cemetery, Trenton, Mercer County.

ADAMS, EDWARD Pvt, F, 33rd NJ Inf, DoD Unknown. Christ Church Cemetery, Belleville, Essex County.

ADAMS, EDWARD G. Pvt, G, 2nd DC Inf, 12-30-1898. Fairmount Cemetery, Newark, Essex County.

ADAMS, EDWARD P. Corp, F, 1st NJ Cav, 7-7-1866. Columbus Cemetery, Columbus, Burlington County.

ADAMS, EDWIN Pvt, K, 2nd CT Inf, 1914. Oak Grove Cemetery, Hammonton, Atlantic County.

ADAMS, ELMER Corp, K, 23rd NJ Inf, 1922. St. Paul's Methodist Church Cemetery, Port Republic, Atlantic County.

ADAMS, FRANCIS Pvt, F, 2nd NJ Militia, 5-5-1908. Arlington Cemetery, Kearny, Hudson County.

ADAMS, FRANCIS (see: Adams, Frank) Arlington Cemetery, Kearny, Hudson County.

ADAMS, FRANK (aka: Adams, Francis) Pvt, Btty I, 1st NY Light Art, DoD Unknown. Arlington Cemetery, Kearny, Hudson County.

ADAMS, FRANKLIN Pvt, G, 23rd NJ Inf, 3-13-1915. Oddfellows Cemetery, Burlington, Burlington County.

ADAMS*, FRANKLIN Pvt, B, 199th PA Inf, 2-10-1912. Cedar Grove Cemetery, Gloucester City, Camden County.

ADAMS, GEORGE 1-17-1865. Wallen's Cemetery, Blackwood, Camden County.

ADAMS*, GEORGE Corp, C, 79th NY Inf, 1-29-1891. Laurel Grove Cemetery, Totowa, Passaic County.

ADAMS, GEORGE Pvt, E, 1st NJ Inf, [Killed in action at Wilderness, VA.] 5-6-1864. Baptist Cemetery, Burlington, Burlington County.

ADAMS, GEORGE B. Pvt, I, 7th NJ Inf, 8-26-1920. Clinton Cemetery, Irvington, Essex County.

ADAMS, GEORGE H. Pvt, A, 38th NJ Inf, 12-26-1901. Maplewood Cemetery, Freehold, Monmouth County.

ADAMS, GEORGE W. Landsman, U.S. Navy, USS North Carolina, DoD Unknown. Hedding Methodist-Episcopal Church Cemetery, Bellmawr, Camden County.

ADAMS, GEORGE W. Pvt, C, 3rd NJ Inf, 1-4-1896. Flower Hill Cemetery, North Bergen, Hudson County.

ADAMS, GEORGE W. 7-17-1872. Riverview Cemetery, Trenton, Mercer County.

ADAMS, GIDEON H. Corp, B, 25th NJ Inf, 1905. Mount Pleasant Methodist Cemetery, Pleasantville, Atlantic County.

ADAMS, GIDEON L. Pvt, B, 1st NJ Cav, [Died of consumption at Bargaintown, NJ.] 3-11-1865. Zion Methodist Church Cemetery, Bargaintown, Atlantic County.

ADAMS, HENRY 6-10-1903. St. Paul's Methodist Church Cemetery, Port Republic, Atlantic County.

ADAMS, HENRY Seaman, U.S. Navy, USS Honduras, DoD Unknown. White Ridge Cemetery, Eatontown, Monmouth County.

ADAMS, HENRY C. DoD Unknown. Hackensack Cemetery, Hackensack, Bergen County.

Our Brothers Gone Before

ADAMS, HUGH WHITE Maj, 7th KY Inf 8-6-1916. Evergreen Cemetery, Hillside, Union County.

ADAMS, JACOB Pvt, G, 3rd NJ Cav, 1934. Mount Pleasant Cemetery, Millville, Cumberland County.

ADAMS, JAMES Pvt, Btty D, 5th NY Heavy Art, DoD Unknown. Grove Church Cemetery, North Bergen, Hudson County.

ADAMS, JAMES Pvt, B, 15th GA Inf (CSA), [Captured 7-3-1863 at Gettysburg, PA. Died of typhoid.] 9-24-1863. Finn's Point National Cemetery, Pennsville, Salem County.

ADAMS, JAMES Pvt, H, 27th NJ Inf, DoD Unknown. Branchville Cemetery, Branchville, Sussex County.

ADAMS, JAMES C. Corp, C, 5th PA Cav, 3-18-1899. Atlantic City Cemetery, Pleasantville, Atlantic County.

ADAMS, JAMES D. Pvt, D, 1st (Turney's) TN Inf (CSA), 7-29-1863. Finn's Point National Cemetery, Pennsville, Salem County.

ADAMS, JAMES H. Pvt, K, 23rd NJ Inf, [Wounded in action.] 4-15-1884. United Methodist Church Cemetery, Absecon, Atlantic County.

ADAMS, JAMES H. Pvt, B, 5th MA Colored Cav, 5-1-1921. Mount Peace Cemetery, Lawnside, Camden County.

ADAMS, JAMES M. Pvt, B, 23rd NJ Inf, 12-31-1915. Evergreen Cemetery, Camden, Camden County.

ADAMS, JAMES M. Pvt, B, 2nd NJ Inf, 1911. Elwood Rural Cemetery, Elwood, Atlantic County.

ADAMS, JAMES R. Pvt, D, 15th NJ Inf, 8-17-1898. Salem Cemetery, Pleasantville, Atlantic County.

ADAMS, JAMES SYLVESTER 1st Lt, I, 30th NJ Inf, 1-18-1916. Presbyterian Church Cemetery, Mendham, Morris County.

ADAMS, JEREMIAH ELIGH Pvt, D, 13th NY State Militia, 6-22-1915. Evergreen Cemetery, Hillside, Union County.

ADAMS, JESSE Pvt, A, 2nd DC Inf, 8-24-1884. Monument Cemetery, Edgewater Park, Burlington County.

ADAMS, JESSE DoD Unknown. Quaker Cemetery, Quaker Church, Warren County.

ADAMS, JESSE S. Pvt, F, 24th NJ Inf, 1-21-1917. Oddfellows Cemetery, Burlington, Burlington County.

ADAMS, JOHN Pvt, G, 3rd NJ Cav, 7-5-1919. Oddfellows Cemetery, Burlington, Burlington County.

ADAMS, JOHN Pvt, G, 54th PA Inf, 2-2-1900. Phillipsburg Cemetery, Phillipsburg, Warren County.

ADAMS, JOHN Pvt, E, 2nd NJ Inf, 2-10-1888. Woodland Cemetery, Newark, Essex County.

ADAMS, JOHN B. 7-26-1865. Beemerville Cemetery, Beemerville, Sussex County.

ADAMS, JOHN D. Pvt, F, 1st NJ Cav, 12-17-1896. Riverview Cemetery, Trenton, Mercer County.

ADAMS, JOHN H. Pvt, B, 25th NJ Inf, 1-14-1919. Atlantic City Cemetery, Pleasantville, Atlantic County.

ADAMS, JOHN H. Pvt, G, 23rd NJ Inf, 12-5-1919. Coopertown Meeting House Cemetery, Edgewater Park, Burlington County.

ADAMS, JOHN H. Pvt, C, 77th NY Inf, 4-15-1907. Fairmount Cemetery, Newark, Essex County.

ADAMS, JOHN H. (SR.) Pvt, F, 1st NJ Cav, 1909. Columbus Cemetery, Columbus, Burlington County.

ADAMS, JOHN L. Corp, B, 23rd NJ Inf, [Died of diarrhea at White Oak Church, VA.] 3-13-1863. Bordentown/Old St. Mary's Catholic Cemetery, Bordentown, Burlington County.

New Jersey Civil War Burials

ADAMS, JOHN Q. Sgt, B, 5th NJ Inf, 7-18-1884. Speer Cemetery, Jersey City, Hudson County.
ADAMS*, JOHN R. Pvt, L, 3rd MA Cav, 9-15-1884. Fairmount Cemetery, Newark, Essex County.
ADAMS, JOHN S. 8-21-1869. Evergreen Cemetery, Camden, Camden County.
ADAMS*, JOHN S. Pvt, F, 6th NJ Inf, 3-6-1902. Chestnut Grove Cemetery, Elmer, Salem County.
ADAMS, JOHN W. Pvt, A, 6th U.S. Cav, 7-2-1902. Presbyterian Church Cemetery, Mays Landing, Atlantic County.
ADAMS, JOHN W. Pvt, C, 2nd NJ Militia, 4- -1927. Monument Cemetery, Edgewater Park, Burlington County.
ADAMS, JOHN W. Pvt, 8th Btty, WI Light Art, 1904. Cedar Ridge Cemetery, Blairstown, Warren County.
ADAMS, JOHN WESLEY Pvt, I, 24th NJ Inf, 7-18-1919. Siloam Cemetery, Vineland, Cumberland County.
ADAMS, JOSEPH Pvt, G, 4th NJ Inf, 11-29-1902. St. Paul's Methodist Church Cemetery, Port Republic, Atlantic County.
ADAMS, JOSEPH W. Pvt, F, 23rd NJ Inf, 7-25-1910. Baptist Cemetery, Medford, Burlington County.
ADAMS, JOSHUA P. Corp, I, 23rd NJ Inf, 2-8-1876. Baptist Cemetery, Burlington, Burlington County.
ADAMS, L. 1922. Jericho/Oddfellows Cemetery, Deptford, Gloucester County.
ADAMS, LAMAR Pvt, K, 35th NJ Inf, 4-20-1907. Riverview Cemetery, Trenton, Mercer County.
ADAMS*, NAPOLEON BONAPARTE QM Sgt, I, 1st NJ Cav, 12-3-1887. Monument Cemetery, Edgewater Park, Burlington County.
ADAMS, NAPOLEON BONAPARTE 3-31-1907. Mount Pleasant Cemetery, Newark, Essex County.
ADAMS, OLIVER E. Pvt, 3rd Btty, VT Light Art, [Died of disease.] 10-18-1864. Beverly National Cemetery, Edgewater Park, Burlington County.
ADAMS, OREGON Pvt, K, 12th AL Inf (CSA), 6- -1865. Finn's Point National Cemetery, Pennsville, Salem County.
ADAMS, PITMAN Pvt, E, 10th NJ Inf, [Died of wounds received 6-1-1864 at Cold Harbor, VA.] 9-18-1864. St. Paul's Methodist Church Cemetery, Port Republic, Atlantic County.
ADAMS, RICHARD S. Pvt, G, 23rd NJ Inf, 5-1-1905. Coopertown Meeting House Cemetery, Edgewater Park, Burlington County.
ADAMS, ROBERT Pvt, E, 34th NJ Inf, 1915. Mount Pleasant Cemetery, Newark, Essex County.
ADAMS, ROBERT K. Com Sgt, M, 1st NJ Cav, 4-30-1878. Methodist Church Cemetery, Sparta, Sussex County.
ADAMS, SAMUEL F. Fireman, U.S. Navy, USS Vandalia, DoD Unknown. Christ Church Cemetery, Belleville, Essex County.
ADAMS, SAMUEL R. Pvt, H, 57th NY Inf, [Wounded 9-17-1862 at Antietam, MD.] 11-25-1895. Oddfellows Cemetery, Burlington, Burlington County.
ADAMS, SAMUEL S. Pvt, H, 4th PA Cav, 1-17-1868. Trinity Bible Church Cemetery, Glassboro, Gloucester County.
ADAMS, SYLVESTER J. Pvt, K, 150th NY Inf, 4-19-1912. Savage Cemetery, Denville, Morris County.
ADAMS, THEODORE Pvt, I, 119th PA Inf, 4-2-1926. Bordentown/Old St. Mary's Catholic Cemetery, Bordentown, Burlington County.
ADAMS*, THEODORE Pvt, E, 8th NJ Inf, 12-3-1917. Evergreen Cemetery, Camden, Camden County.

Our Brothers Gone Before

ADAMS, THEOPHILUS H. Pvt, H, 41st VA Inf (CSA), 1919. Methodist-Episcopal Cemetery, Lower Bank, Burlington County.

ADAMS, THOMAS Pvt, C, 12th NJ Inf, 4-12-1901. Baptist Cemetery, Pemberton, Burlington County.

ADAMS*, THOMAS Sgt, G, 86th NY Inf, 3-3-1915. Bayview-New York Bay Cemetery, Jersey City, Hudson County.

ADAMS, THOMAS 1-8-1901. Mount Pleasant Cemetery, Newark, Essex County.

ADAMS, THOMAS C. Pvt, E, 10th NJ Inf, 3-22-1916. Mount Pleasant Methodist Cemetery, Pleasantville, Atlantic County.

ADAMS*, WESLEY Pvt, C, 28th NJ Inf, 1-19-1904. Bayview-New York Bay Cemetery, Jersey City, Hudson County.

ADAMS, WILLIAM Pvt, A, 3rd NJ Inf, [Died at Philadelphia, PA.] 8-17-1862. Fairmount Cemetery, Newark, Essex County.

ADAMS, WILLIAM Corp, K, 2nd NJ Inf, 4-11-1897. Fairmount Cemetery, Newark, Essex County.

ADAMS, WILLIAM Seaman, U.S. Navy, USS Santiago de Cuba, 10-5-1909. Cedar Lawn Cemetery, Paterson, Passaic County.

ADAMS, WILLIAM D. 2-22-1913. Maple Grove Cemetery, Hackensack, Bergen County.

ADAMS*, WILLIAM DEXTER 1st Lt, H, 79th U.S. CT, 4-3-1917. Rosedale Cemetery, Orange, Essex County.

ADAMS, WILLIAM F. Pvt, B, 7th NJ Inf, 5-17-1864. Mount Pleasant Cemetery, Newark, Essex County.

ADAMS*, WILLIAM H. Pvt, F, 8th NJ Inf, 12-23-1918. Fairmount Cemetery, Newark, Essex County.

ADAMS, WILLIAM H. Pvt, F, 12th NJ Inf, 8-6-1920. Coopertown Meeting House Cemetery, Edgewater Park, Burlington County.

ADAMS, WILLIAM H. Pvt, I, 79th NY Inf, 2-26-1926. Laurel Grove Cemetery, Totowa, Passaic County.

ADAMS, WILLIAM L. Pvt, E, 10th NJ Inf, 12-1-1894. Fairmount Cemetery, Newark, Essex County.

ADAMS, WILLIAM P. Pvt, F, 43rd NC Inf (CSA), [Wounded 7-3-1863 and captured 7-4-1863 at Gettysburg, PA. Died of disease.] 1-3-1864. Finn's Point National Cemetery, Pennsville, Salem County.

ADAMS*, WILSON Pvt, I, 2nd NJ Inf, 2-15-1917. Greenwood Cemetery, Pleasantville, Atlantic County.

ADAMSON, GEORGE 7-21-1909. Eglington Cemetery, Clarksboro, Gloucester County.

ADARE, CHARLES H. Pvt, K, 23rd NJ Inf, 10-27-1882. Miller's Cemetery, New Gretna, Burlington County.

ADDIS, WILLIAM Pvt, 6th NY Ind Btty 10-24-1921. Hillside Cemetery, Scotch Plains, Union County.

ADDISON, DAVID (see: Swinn, David A.) Bloomfield Cemetery, Bloomfield, Essex County.

ADDISON, GEORGE Pvt, A, 3rd NJ Cav, 8-26-1908. Fairview Cemetery, Westfield, Union County.

ADELBERG*, OSCAR Pvt, Btty C, 13th NY Heavy Art, 5-10-1913. Evergreen Cemetery, Hillside, Union County.

ADELMAN, PHILLIP Pvt, L, 1st NY Cav, 1-13-1872. Palisade Cemetery, North Bergen, Hudson County.

ADER, GEORGE (aka: Adair, George) Pvt, K, 1st NJ Inf, 11-21-1919. Fairmount Cemetery, Fairmount, Hunterdon County.

ADER, JACOB (aka: Aider, Jacob) Pvt, A, 2nd NJ Cav, 1918. Fairmount Cemetery, Fairmount, Hunterdon County.

ADER, JACOB W. Pvt, A, 43rd U.S. CT, 8-15-1903. Fairmount Cemetery, Newark, Essex County.

New Jersey Civil War Burials

ADKINS, A.J. Pvt, Alexander's Btty, 2nd VA Light Art (CSA), 11-21-1863. Finn's Point National Cemetery, Pennsville, Salem County.

ADKINS, B.F.T. Pvt, E, 16th VA Cav (CSA), 9-11-1864. Finn's Point National Cemetery, Pennsville, Salem County.

ADKINS, HENRY A. Pvt, E, 57th VA Inf (CSA), [Captured 7-3-1863 at Gettysburg, PA. Died of diarrhea.] 8-7-1863. Finn's Point National Cemetery, Pennsville, Salem County.

ADKINS, JOHN W. Pvt, A, 2nd MS Inf (CSA), [Wounded 6-27-1862 at Gaines' Mill, VA. Wounded and captured 7-3-1863 at Gettysburg, PA. Died of disease.] 11-12-1863. Finn's Point National Cemetery, Pennsville, Salem County.

ADKINS, WILSON J. Pvt, B, 18th VA Inf (CSA), [Wounded 9-14-1862 at South Mountain, MD. Wounded and captured 7-3-1863 at Gettysburg, PA.] 10-15-1863. Finn's Point National Cemetery, Pennsville, Salem County.

ADLER, FRANCIS A. 2nd Lt, L, 9th NJ Inf, 12-28-1906. Fairmount Cemetery, Newark, Essex County.

ADOLPH*, CARL Pvt, B, 3rd NY Inf, 5-9-1890. Fairmount Cemetery, Newark, Essex County.

AERTZ, JOSEPH A. Pvt, K, 107th PA Inf, 3-26-1904. Pascack Reformed Church Cemetery, Park Ridge, Bergen County.

AFFLEBACK, JACOB W. Corp, E, 91st PA Inf, [Wounded 12-13-1862 at Fredericksburg, VA.] 5-20-1909. Baptist Church Cemetery, Slabtown, Salem County.

AGANS*, ISAAC S. (aka: Agens, Isaac S.) Pvt, B, 11th NJ Inf, 1919. Reformed Church Cemetery, Three Bridges, Hunterdon County.

AGANS, PETER K. Pvt, A, 31st NJ Inf, 8-3-1873. Reformed Church Cemetery, Readington, Hunterdon County.

AGAR, ISAAC H. 2nd Lt, B, 34th NJ Inf, 1886. Baptist/St. Andrew's Cemetery, Mount Holly, Burlington County.

AGAR*, JOHN J. (aka: Ager, John) Landsman, U.S. Navy, USS North Carolina, 2-13-1932. Rosedale Cemetery, Orange, Essex County.

AGEE, J.M. Pvt, E, 61st (Pitts') TN Mtd Inf (CSA), 9-17-1863. Finn's Point National Cemetery, Pennsville, Salem County.

AGEN, THOMAS DoD Unknown. Old St. Mary's Cemetery, Gloucester City, Camden County.

AGENS, CONDIT J. 1913. Mount Pleasant Cemetery, Newark, Essex County.

AGENS, ISAAC S. (see: Agans, Isaac S.) Reformed Church Cemetery, Three Bridges, Hunterdon County.

AGENS, JAMES H. Wagoner, G, 9th NJ Inf, 12-14-1903. Rosedale Cemetery, Orange, Essex County.

AGER, JOHN (see: Agar, John J.) Rosedale Cemetery, Orange, Essex County.

AGGINGS, WILLIAM H. (aka: Agins, William) Corp, H, 28th NJ Inf, 5-8-1897. Baptist Church Cemetery, Mullica Hill, Gloucester County.

AGIN, BAXTER Pvt, I, 14th NJ Inf, 1925. Old Rock Church Cemetery, West Amwell, Hunterdon County.

AGIN*, JAMES Pvt, H, 6th NJ Inf, 9-7-1896. Union Cemetery, Ringoes, Hunterdon County.

AGIN, WILLIAM H. Pvt, A, 15th NJ Inf, 2-2-1908. Riverview Cemetery, Trenton, Mercer County.

AGINS, JACOB Pvt, F, 38th NJ Inf, 1903. Princeton Cemetery, Princeton, Mercer County.

AGINS, WILLIAM (see: Aggings, William H.) Baptist Church Cemetery, Mullica Hill, Gloucester County.

AGNEW, ROBERT E. Pvt, D, 28th NJ Inf, 4-19-1875. Pitman Methodist-Episcopal Cemetery, New Brunswick, Middlesex County.

AGNEW, THOMAS R. 1st Lt, G, 7th NJ Inf, 2-20-1912. Hoboken Cemetery, North Bergen, Hudson County.

Our Brothers Gone Before

AGNEW, W.G. 6-5-1880. Mount Holly Cemetery, Mount Holly, Burlington County.
AHEARN, CORNELIUS Sgt, E, 88th NY Inf, 2-3-1902. Madonna Cemetery, Leonia, Bergen County.
AHLSTED, OSWALD (aka: Alsted, Andreas) Pvt, I, 1st NY Inf, 11-15-1912. Fairmount Cemetery, Newark, Essex County.
AHN*, JESSE Pvt, E, 3rd PA Prov Cav, [Wounded 6-15-1864 at St. Marys Church, VA.] 2-14-1904. Fairmount Cemetery, Newark, Essex County.
AHRENS, ALEXANDER J. Pvt, K, 11th NY Inf, 8-5-1897. Grove Church Cemetery, North Bergen, Hudson County.
AHRENS, LOUIS Pvt, C, 72nd NY Inf, [Wounded 7-2-1863 at Gettysburg, PA.] 4-10-1926. Flower Hill Cemetery, North Bergen, Hudson County.
AIDER, JACOB (see: Ader, Jacob) Fairmount Cemetery, Fairmount, Hunterdon County.
AIKEN, CHARLES (see: Aitken, Charles R.) Riverview Cemetery, Trenton, Mercer County.
AIKINS, GEORGE L. Sgt, I, 4th NJ Inf, 3-3-1892. Oddfellows Cemetery, Burlington, Burlington County.
AINSWORTH, WILLIAM Pvt, D, 8th NJ Inf, 10-31-1900. Fairmount Cemetery, Newark, Essex County.
AINSWORTH, WILLIAM (aka: Speakman, William H.) Sgt, Btty G, 5th NY Heavy Art, 11-5-1913. Weehawken Cemetery, North Bergen, Hudson County.
AIRGOTT, THOMAS (aka: Ehrgott, Francis) Pvt, A, 33rd NJ Inf, 1- -1913. Laurel Grove Cemetery, Totowa, Passaic County.
AIRY, JOHN Pvt, A, 4th U.S. Cav, 10-19-1912. Arlington Cemetery, Kearny, Hudson County.
AITKEN, ALEXANDER Pvt, K, 10th NJ Inf, 7-14-1899. Greenmount Cemetery, Hammonton, Atlantic County.
AITKEN*, CHARLES R. (aka: Aiken, Charles) Pvt, F, 197th PA Inf, 11-24-1890. Riverview Cemetery, Trenton, Mercer County.
AITKEN, THOMAS (see: Atkins, Thomas W.G.) Arlington Cemetery, Kearny, Hudson County.
AITKEN, THOMAS B. 1st Sgt, B, 14th NJ Inf, 7-29-1904. Riverview Cemetery, Trenton, Mercer County.
AITKEN, THOMAS W.G. Pvt, I, 22nd NJ Inf, 6-22-1906. Arlington Cemetery, Kearny, Hudson County.
AKENS, WILLIAM DoD Unknown. Cedar Grove Cemetery, Gloucester City, Camden County.
AKER, CARRINGTON R. Sgt, A, 38th NY Inf, [Wounded 12-13-1862 at Fredericksburg, VA.] 3-25-1892. Old 1st Methodist Church Cemetery, West Long Branch, Monmouth County.
AKERS, ABNER Pvt, I, 14th NJ Inf, DoD Unknown. Mount Pleasant Cemetery, Newark, Essex County.
AKERS, CHARLES D. Corp, G, 30th NJ Inf, 5-26-1914. Mount Hope Presbyterian Cemetery, Lambertville, Hunterdon County.
AKERS, CHARLES R. Pvt, I, 3rd NJ Militia, 9-1-1861. Bloomfield Cemetery, Bloomfield, Essex County.
AKERS, DAVID Pvt, M, 5th NY Cav, 3-5-1913. Ramapo Reformed Church Cemetery, Mahwah, Bergen County.
AKERS, FARLEY F. Pvt, H, 6th NJ Inf, 8-30-1879. 2nd Presbyterian Church Cemetery, Mount Airy, Hunterdon County.
AKERS, FERDINAND H. Pvt, H, 6th NJ Inf, 5-6-1902. Holcomb-Riverview Cemetery, Lambertville, Hunterdon County.
AKERS, GEORGE (see: Acker, George W.) Methodist Church Cemetery, Liberty, Warren County.

New Jersey Civil War Burials

AKERS, GEORGE W. Pvt, G, 30th NJ Inf, 1920. Reformed Church Cemetery, Clover Hill, Somerset County.

AKERS, GERSHOM L. Sgt, G, 30th NJ Inf, 1911. Mount Hope Presbyterian Cemetery, Lambertville, Hunterdon County.

AKERS, JOHN A. Pvt, F, 22nd NJ Inf, 9-26-1900. Highland Cemetery, Hopewell Boro, Mercer County.

AKERS, JOSEPH Pvt, K, 1st PA Inf, 7-6-1935. Mount Hope Presbyterian Cemetery, Lambertville, Hunterdon County.

AKERS, JOSEPH H. Pvt, G, 30th NJ Inf, 10-5-1890. Holcomb-Riverview Cemetery, Lambertville, Hunterdon County.

AKERS, SAMUEL N. Pvt, E, 36th VA Inf (CSA), [Captured 3-2-1865 at Waynesboro, VA. Died of pneumonia.] 4-2-1865. Finn's Point National Cemetery, Pennsville, Salem County.

AKIN, ANDREW J. Pvt, G, 35th GA Inf (CSA), [Captured 5-12-1864 at Spotsylvania CH, VA. Died of smallpox.] 7-29-1864. Finn's Point National Cemetery, Pennsville, Salem County.

AKIN, JAMES Pvt, C, 1st NY Inf, 3-24-1913. Cedar Lawn Cemetery, Paterson, Passaic County.

AKIN, JOHN Pvt, F, 79th NY Inf, 8-21-1895. Cedar Lawn Cemetery, Paterson, Passaic County.

AKINS, JOHN Corp, C, 1st NJ Cav, 12-7-1900. Baptist Cemetery, Pemberton, Burlington County.

AKINS, THOMAS E. Pvt, I, 23rd NJ Inf, 8-17-1902. Baptist/St. Andrew's Cemetery, Mount Holly, Burlington County.

ALBEE, WILLIAM Pvt, K, 110th NY Inf, 10-22-1915. Grove Church Cemetery, North Bergen, Hudson County.

ALBEE, WILLIAM H. 2-19-1919. Bayview-New York Bay Cemetery, Jersey City, Hudson County.

ALBEN*, FRANCIS Landsman, U.S. Navy, USS Ironsides, 1-8-1884. Presbyterian Church Cemetery, Bridgeton, Cumberland County.

ALBERGER, WILLIAM (aka: Aberger, William) Pvt, K, 41st NY Inf, 2-2-1929. Holy Sepulchre Cemetery, East Orange, Essex County.

ALBERS, JOSEPH Pvt, G, 60th NY Inf, 8-29-1862. Fairmount Cemetery, Newark, Essex County.

ALBERSON, SMITH Pvt, B, 25th NJ Inf, [Died of measles at Fairfax Seminary, VA.] 11-11-1862. Asbury United Methodist Church Cemetery, English Creek, Atlantic County.

ALBERT, CHARLES 3-29-1903. St. John's Evangelical Church Cemetery, Orange, Essex County.

ALBERT, HENRY Pvt, F, 29th NJ Inf, 1-4-1886. Holy Sepulchre Cemetery, East Orange, Essex County.

ALBERT, JOHN E. Boy, U.S. Navy, USS Gennessee, 4-26-1897. Fairmount Cemetery, Newark, Essex County.

ALBERT, MICHAEL Pvt, U.S. Marine Corps, 8-8-1909. Fairmount Cemetery, Newark, Essex County.

ALBERT, MICHAEL Pvt, I, 30th NJ Inf, 5-12-1936. Trinity United Church Cemetery, Coontown, Somerset County.

ALBERT, SAMUEL Pvt, G, 153rd PA Inf, 6-12-1902. Methodist-Episcopal Cemetery, Columbia, Warren County.

ALBERT*, WILLIAM Pvt, G, 7th NJ Inf, [Wounded 5-6-1864 at Wilderness, VA.] DoD Unknown. Pine Brook Cemetery, Pine Brook, Morris County.

ALBERTS, ROBERT H. Corp, C, 9th NY Inf, 1-28-1915. Grove Church Cemetery, North Bergen, Hudson County.

Our Brothers Gone Before

ALBERTSON, BENJAMIN 2nd Lt, F, 104th PA Inf, 10-3-1911. Riverview Cemetery, Trenton, Mercer County.

ALBERTSON, DERICK 1st Sgt, I, 31st NJ Inf, [Died of typhoid at Belle Plain, VA.] 4-14-1863. Presbyterian Church Cemetery, Harmony, Warren County.

ALBERTSON, EDWARD H. Pvt, H, 31st NJ Inf, 1931. Union Cemetery, Hope, Warren County.

ALBERTSON, JETHRO V. 1st Lt, B, 25th NJ Inf, 1-6-1911. Salem Cemetery, Pleasantville, Atlantic County.

ALBERTSON, LEVI C. Coal Heaver, U.S. Navy, USS Kansas, 1-3-1913. Atlantic City Cemetery, Pleasantville, Atlantic County.

ALBERTSON, WILLIAM M. 5-8-1876. Berlin Cemetery, Berlin, Camden County.

ALBERTY, A.P.J. Pvt, H, 22nd NC Inf (CSA), [Wounded and captured 7-3-1863 at Gettysburg, PA.] 10-11-1863. Finn's Point National Cemetery, Pennsville, Salem County.

ALBIN, SAMUEL Musc, 3rd NJ Inf Band DoD Unknown. 1st United Methodist Church Cemetery, Bridgeton, Cumberland County.

ALBRECHT, BERNHARDT Pvt, G, 13th OH Inf, 9-15-1888. Atlantic City Cemetery, Pleasantville, Atlantic County.

ALBRECHT, CHRISTOPHER Pvt, D, 2nd NJ Inf, [Wounded in action.] 8-11-1900. Fairmount Cemetery, Newark, Essex County.

ALBUTH, GEORGE H. Pvt, C, 2nd DC Inf, DoD Unknown. Cedar Lawn Cemetery, Paterson, Passaic County.

ALCHIN, GEORGE L. Pvt, Btty G, 2nd PA Heavy Art, 7-22-1889. Evergreen Cemetery, Camden, Camden County.

ALCORN, ROBERT Musc, I, 9th NJ Inf, 4-14-1908. Shinn GAR Post Cemetery, Port Norris, Cumberland County.

ALCOTT, CHARLES W. Pvt, Btty M, 2nd PA Heavy Art, 9-17-1881. Baptist Cemetery, Burlington, Burlington County.

ALCOTT, THOMAS J. QM Sgt, 23rd NJ Inf 6-28-1915. Mount Holly Cemetery, Mount Holly, Burlington County.

ALCOTT, WILLIAM H. Pvt, I, 23rd NJ Inf, 8-31-1927. Colestown Cemetery, Cherry Hill, Camden County.

ALDENDORF, LOUIS Pvt, H, 5th NY State Militia, 7-31-1906. Fairmount Cemetery, Newark, Essex County.

ALDERMAN, RUFUS S. 1st Lt,RQM, 161st NY Inf 5-23-1904. Fairmount Cemetery, Newark, Essex County.

ALDERSON, W.H. 2nd Lt, F, 6th (Wheeler's) TN Cav (CSA), 3-30-1865. Finn's Point National Cemetery, Pennsville, Salem County.

ALDRICH, AARON Com Sgt, K, 5th NY Cav, DoD Unknown. Oak Hill Cemetery, Vineland, Cumberland County.

ALDRIDGE, A.J. Pvt, C, 1st (Butler's) KY Cav (CSA), [Captured 6-7-1863 at Liberty, TN.] 12-26-1863. Finn's Point National Cemetery, Pennsville, Salem County.

ALDRIDGE*, RICHARD Pvt, B, 21st NJ Inf, 8-30-1875. Old Bergen Church Cemetery, Jersey City, Hudson County.

ALE, ELIJAH K. 2nd Lt, I, 12th NJ Inf, 1898. Presbyterian Cemetery, Salem, Salem County.

ALE, JAMES Pvt, A, 24th NJ Inf, 2-24-1912. United Methodist Church Cemetery, Hainesneck, Salem County.

ALECK, FRANK 5-31-1887. Flower Hill Cemetery, North Bergen, Hudson County.

ALEO, PHILIP DoD Unknown. New Catholic Cemetery, Newton, Sussex County.

ALEXANDER, ADOLPHUS C. Pvt, K, 7th NC Inf (CSA), [Wounded 7-3-1863 and captured 7-4/5-1863 at Gettysburg, PA. Died of typhoid.] 9-7-1863. Finn's Point National Cemetery, Pennsville, Salem County.

New Jersey Civil War Burials

ALEXANDER, ARCHIBALD Pvt, A, 63rd IL Inf, 4-8-1882. Princeton Cemetery, Princeton, Mercer County.
ALEXANDER, HOWARD Seaman, U.S. Navy, 10-30-1901. Mount Pleasant Cemetery, Newark, Essex County.
ALEXANDER, JAMES Pvt, H, 25th NJ Inf, 9- -1865. Cedar Lawn Cemetery, Paterson, Passaic County.
ALEXANDER, JAMES Pvt, I, 26th AL Inf (CSA), [Captured at Gettysburg, PA.] 10-12-1863. Finn's Point National Cemetery, Pennsville, Salem County.
ALEXANDER, JAMES J. Pvt, I, 34th NJ Inf, 9-27-1916. Mount Pleasant Cemetery, Newark, Essex County.
ALEXANDER, JOHN Pvt, B, 52nd PA Militia, 12-29-1865. St. Mary's Episcopal Church Cemetery, Burlington, Burlington County.
ALEXANDER, JOSEPH Pvt, E, 10th NJ Inf, 4-10-1872. Presbyterian Church Cemetery, Mays Landing, Atlantic County.
ALEXANDER, JOSEPH Pvt, F, 52nd PA Militia, 11-7-1906. St. John's Episcopal Church Cemetery, Chews Landing, Camden County.
ALEXANDER, SAMUEL 1st Corp, K, 20th GA Inf (CSA), [Captured 7-2-1863 at Gettysburg, PA. Died of lung inflammation.] 1-6-1864. Finn's Point National Cemetery, Pennsville, Salem County.
ALEXANDER, WILLIAM C. Pvt, G, 15th AL Inf (CSA), [Captured at Gettysburg, PA.] 2-8-1864. Finn's Point National Cemetery, Pennsville, Salem County.
ALEXANDER, WILLIAM H. Pvt, K, 2nd NJ Inf, [Wounded in action.] 12-29-1895. Fairmount Cemetery, Newark, Essex County.
ALEXANDER, WILLIAM R. Pvt, B, 39th NJ Inf, 1-13-1898. Fairmount Cemetery, Newark, Essex County.
ALFORD, DANIEL W. Pvt, A, 17th VT Inf, 4-24-1923. St. Bernard's Cemetery, Bridgewater, Somerset County.
ALFORD, THOMAS R. Pvt, B, 3rd LA Inf (CSA), [Wounded in action. Captured 5-20-1863 at Milldale Hospital, MS.] 8-6-1863. Finn's Point National Cemetery, Pennsville, Salem County.
ALGER, WILLIAM B. (aka: Algore, William) Pvt, K, 10th NJ Inf, 5-13-1910. Greenwood Cemetery, Tuckerton, Ocean County.
ALGIER, LEWIS Pvt, F, 8th NJ Inf, 8-28-1894. Fairmount Cemetery, Newark, Essex County.
ALGOR, BLOOMFIELD Pvt, K, 10th NJ Inf, [Died of diarrhea at Newark, NJ.] 8-23-1864. Greenwood Cemetery, Tuckerton, Ocean County.
ALGOR, THOMAS Pvt, K, 29th NJ Inf, 5-9-1917. Atlantic View Cemetery, Manasquan, Monmouth County.
ALGORE, WILLIAM (see: Alger, William B.) Greenwood Cemetery, Tuckerton, Ocean County.
ALKIRE, ANDREW J. Pvt, E, 72nd PA Inf, 11-7-1876. Presbyterian Church Cemetery, Bridgeton, Cumberland County.
ALKIRE, CHARLES M. Pvt, F, 24th NJ Inf, 8-20-1913. Presbyterian Church Cemetery, Bridgeton, Cumberland County.
ALKIRE, ISAAC Pvt, K, 10th NJ Inf, 5-28-1900. Presbyterian Church Cemetery, Bridgeton, Cumberland County.
ALLAIRE*, GEORGE M. 3rd Cl Boy, U.S. Navy, USS Huntsville, 1-23-1910. Bayview-New York Bay Cemetery, Jersey City, Hudson County.
ALLAN, J.S. 12-30-1870. Rahway Cemetery, Rahway, Union County.
ALLAN, WILLIAM Corp, F, 12th NY National Guard, 6-15-1918. Macphelah Cemetery, North Bergen, Hudson County.
ALLANSON*, WILLIAM H. (aka: Allison, William) Pvt, C, 3rd NJ Inf, 7-1-1867. St. Mary's Episcopal Church Cemetery, Burlington, Burlington County.

Our Brothers Gone Before

ALLBRIGHT, WILLIAM 1914. Hope Christian Church Cemetery, Marlton, Burlington County.
ALLCOTT, JOHN H. Maj, 133rd NY Inf 8-1-1883. Bayview-New York Bay Cemetery, Jersey City, Hudson County.
ALLDER, PETER (see: Harmour, Peter Allder) Princeton Cemetery, Princeton, Mercer County.
ALLDRIDGE, HIRAM Sgt, B, 19th AL Inf (CSA), 6-13-1864. Finn's Point National Cemetery, Pennsville, Salem County.
ALLEAUME, ARMAND D. Capt, E, 38th U.S. CT, 3-5-1891. Bayview-New York Bay Cemetery, Jersey City, Hudson County.
ALLEGAR, EZRA M. Pvt, B, 38th NJ Inf, 1907. Locust Grove Cemetery, Quakertown, Hunterdon County.
ALLEGAR, GEORGE R. Pvt, E, 30th NJ Inf, 1904. Methodist-Episcopal Cemetery, Whitehouse, Hunterdon County.
ALLEGAR, GEORGE W. Pvt, A, 31st NJ Inf, DoD Unknown. Methodist-Episcopal Cemetery, Whitehouse, Hunterdon County.
ALLEGAR*, JOHN L. (aka: Allegear, John) Pvt, E, 3rd NJ Cav, 3-29-1906. Voorhees Burying Ground Cemetery, Rowlands Mills, Hunterdon County.
ALLEGAR, PETER S. Pvt, G, 3rd NJ Inf, 1913. Rural Hill Cemetery, Whitehouse, Hunterdon County.
ALLEGEAR, JOHN (see: Allegar, John L.) Voorhees Burying Ground Cemetery, Rowlands Mills, Hunterdon County.
ALLEGER, ELIN WESLEY Pvt, I, 31st NJ Inf, 3- -1900. Mansfield/Washington Cemetery, Washington, Warren County.
ALLEGER, HIRAM W. Corp, I, 31st NJ Inf, 1924. Mansfield/Washington Cemetery, Washington, Warren County.
ALLEN, AARON W. Pvt, B, 23rd NJ Inf, 11-29-1896. Bordentown/Old St. Mary's Catholic Cemetery, Bordentown, Burlington County.
ALLEN*, ABRAHAM K. Pvt, H, 7th NJ Inf, 3-4-1905. Green Cemetery, Woodbury, Gloucester County.
ALLEN, ALEXANDER Pvt, I, 70th NY Inf, 3-10-1878. Holy Sepulchre Cemetery, Totowa, Passaic County.
ALLEN, ALFRED E. 1874. Mount Pleasant Cemetery, Newark, Essex County.
ALLEN, ARCHIBALD W. 1877. Baptist Cemetery, Burlington, Burlington County.
ALLEN, ARTHUR Pvt, K, 8th U.S. CT, 4-18-1924. Mount Salem Church Cemetery, Fenwick, Salem County.
ALLEN, AUGUSTUS Pvt, E, PA Emerg NJ Militia, DoD Unknown. Evergreen Cemetery, Morristown, Morris County.
ALLEN, BENJAMIN F. Pvt, G, 28th NJ Inf, 9-5-1905. Methodist Episcopal/Methodist Protestant Cemetery, Bridgeport, Gloucester County.
ALLEN, CARLOS (aka: Allen, Charles) Pvt, G, 18th MI Inf, DoD Unknown. United Methodist Church Cemetery, Vernon, Sussex County.
ALLEN, CASPAR (see: Allen, Casper) Pearson/Colonial Memorial Park Cemetery, Whitehorse, Mercer County.
ALLEN*, CASPER (aka: Allen, Caspar) Pvt, K, 35th NJ Inf, 3-14-1931. Pearson/Colonial Memorial Park Cemetery, Whitehorse, Mercer County.
ALLEN, CHARLES (see: Allen, Carlos) United Methodist Church Cemetery, Vernon, Sussex County.
ALLEN, CHARLES G. Pvt, B, 95th PA Inf, 8-20-1908. Brotherhood Cemetery, Hainesport, Burlington County.
ALLEN, CHARLES H. Corp, B, 95th PA Inf, DoD Unknown. Methodist-Episcopal Church Cemetery, Medford, Burlington County.
ALLEN, CHARLES N. Pvt, F, 29th NJ Inf, 6-29-1925. United Methodist Church Cemetery, Little Silver, Monmouth County.

New Jersey Civil War Burials

ALLEN, CHARLES R. Wagoner, B, 37th IA Inf, 1895. Cedar Hill Cemetery, Florence, Burlington County.
ALLEN, CHRISTOPHER C. Pvt, A, 26th NJ Inf, 8-14-1917. Evergreen Cemetery, Hillside, Union County.
ALLEN, DANIEL Corp, A, 37th NJ Inf, 1898. Evergreen Cemetery, Lumberton, Burlington County.
ALLEN*, DANIEL Pvt, Btty B, 7th NY Heavy Art, 2-9-1887. Rosedale Cemetery, Orange, Essex County.
ALLEN, DANIEL P. 1-8-1903. Oddfellows Cemetery, Burlington, Burlington County.
ALLEN, DAVID H. Corp, A, 39th NJ Inf, 7-9-1915. Union Cemetery, Mount Olive, Morris County.
ALLEN*, DAVID H. Pvt, Btty B, 1st NJ Light Art, 3-16-1894. Clinton Cemetery, Irvington, Essex County.
ALLEN*, DAVID S. Capt, K, 39th NJ Inf, [Wounded at Petersburg, VA.] 12-31-1914. Chestnut Cemetery, Dover, Morris County.
ALLEN*, DEWITT C. Corp, E, 13th NJ Inf, 3-29-1903. South Orange Cemetery, South Orange, Essex County.
ALLEN, E. Pvt, E, 7th VA Cav (CSA), 7-31-1864. Finn's Point National Cemetery, Pennsville, Salem County.
ALLEN, E. LIVINGSTON Sgt, K, 13th NJ Inf, 1920. Valleau Cemetery, Ridgewood, Bergen County.
ALLEN, EDWARD I. 1-18-1919. Mount Hope Presbyterian Cemetery, Lambertville, Hunterdon County.
ALLEN, EDWARD K. Pvt, D, 1st NJ Cav, 10-22-1909. Bethel Cemetery, Pennsauken, Camden County.
ALLEN, EDWARD N. Corp, G, 7th NJ Inf, 6-6-1899. Baptist Cemetery, Vincentown, Burlington County.
ALLEN, EDWIN F. Pvt, A, 9th MD Inf, 12-3-1914. Evergreen Cemetery, Camden, Camden County.
ALLEN, ERAMUS D. Pvt, I, 102nd NY Inf, 5-7-1924. Fairmount Cemetery, Newark, Essex County.
ALLEN, ERASTUS D. Pvt, E, PA Emerg NJ Militia, DoD Unknown. Evergreen Cemetery, Morristown, Morris County.
ALLEN, ERASTUS H. Pvt, H, 30th NJ Inf, 4-16-1908. Fairmount Cemetery, Newark, Essex County.
ALLEN, FREDERICK Pvt, B, 2nd U.S. CT, 9-25-1913. Brookside Cemetery, Englewood, Bergen County.
ALLEN, GEORGE A. Capt, H, 3rd NJ Militia, 12-26-1879. Presbyterian Church Cemetery, Flemington, Hunterdon County.
ALLEN, GEORGE C. 11-19-1888. Eglington Cemetery, Clarksboro, Gloucester County.
ALLEN, GEORGE W. __, __, __ U.S. Sharpshooters, 11-20-1881. Presbyterian Church Cemetery, Mount Freedom, Morris County.
ALLEN, GEORGE W. Pvt, A, U.S. Inf, [Permanent Party, General Service. Wounded in action.] 1-25-1886. Evergreen Cemetery, Hillside, Union County.
ALLEN, GERSHOM C. Pvt, A, 39th NJ Inf, 4-19-1906. New Somerville Cemetery, Somerville, Somerset County.
ALLEN, HENRY A. Pvt, E, 35th GA Inf (CSA), [Captured 5-6-1864 at Wilderness, VA. Died of diarrhea.] 1-19-1865. Finn's Point National Cemetery, Pennsville, Salem County.
ALLEN, ISAAC N. Musc, E, 15th NJ Inf, DoD Unknown. 1st United Methodist Church Cemetery, Bridgeton, Cumberland County.
ALLEN, J.B. Pvt, B, 51st VA Inf (CSA), [Captured 3-2-1865 at Waynesboro, VA.] 5-6-1865. Finn's Point National Cemetery, Pennsville, Salem County.

Our Brothers Gone Before

ALLEN, JAMES Corp, B, 4th NJ Inf, 9-19-1878. Riverview Cemetery, Trenton, Mercer County.
ALLEN, JAMES Pvt, G, 33rd NJ Inf, 12-23-1875. Greenwood Cemetery, Boonton, Morris County.
ALLEN, JAMES Pvt, C, 11th NJ Inf, [Wounded 5-3-1863 at Chancellorsville, VA.] 9-29-1867. Holy Sepulchre Cemetery, East Orange, Essex County.
ALLEN, JESSE F. Pvt, A, 3rd Bttn MO Cav (CSA), 7-5-1863. Finn's Point National Cemetery, Pennsville, Salem County.
ALLEN, JOHN 1st Lt, I, 2nd NJ Inf, 10-30-1905. Cedar Lawn Cemetery, Paterson, Passaic County.
ALLEN*, JOHN Pvt, F, 40th NJ Inf, 11-21-1874. Baptist Cemetery, Burlington, Burlington County.
ALLEN, JOHN B. Pvt, K, 35th NJ Inf, 5-6-1908. Riverview Cemetery, Trenton, Mercer County.
ALLEN*, JOHN C. Pvt, G, 1st NJ Cav, DoD Unknown. Mount Pleasant Cemetery, Newark, Essex County.
ALLEN, JOHN C. 11-17-1937. Atlantic City Cemetery, Pleasantville, Atlantic County.
ALLEN, JOHN FREDERICK Landsman, U.S. Navy, USS Tuscarora, 1-2-1890. Bordentown/Old St. Mary's Catholic Cemetery, Bordentown, Burlington County.
ALLEN*, JOHN H. Pvt, B, 15th NJ Inf, 10-16-1922. Greenwood Cemetery, Hamilton, Mercer County.
ALLEN, JOHN J. Pvt, K, 68th PA Inf, 10-22-1913. Soldier's Home Cemetery, Vineland, Cumberland County.
ALLEN, JOHN L. Pvt, C, 27th NJ Inf, DoD Unknown. German Valley Rural Cemetery, Naughright, Morris County.
ALLEN*, JOHN L. Pvt, G, 102nd NY Inf, 8-3-1922. Locust Hill Cemetery, Dover, Morris County.
ALLEN, JOHN S. DoD Unknown. Greenmount Cemetery, Hammonton, Atlantic County.
ALLEN, JOHN T. Musc, I, 30th NJ Inf, 9-24-1914. Arlington Cemetery, Kearny, Hudson County.
ALLEN, JONATHAN Pvt, I, 32nd U.S. CT, 3-22-1923. Bordentown/Old St. Mary's Catholic Cemetery, Bordentown, Burlington County.
ALLEN, JOSEPH C. Pvt, H, 2nd NJ Cav, 3-5-1873. Union Cemetery, Washington, Morris County.
ALLEN*, JOSEPH I. Hosp Steward, 5th PA Cav 8-30-1894. Cedar Grove Cemetery, Gloucester City, Camden County.
ALLEN, JOSEPH WARNER Col, 9th NJ Inf [Drowned off Hatteras Inlet, NC.] 1-15-1862. Christ Episcopal Church Cemetery, Bordentown, Burlington County.
ALLEN, JOSIAH Pvt, K, 23rd NC Inf (CSA), [Captured 7-2-1863 at Gettysburg, PA. Died of typhoid.] 8-26-1863. Finn's Point National Cemetery, Pennsville, Salem County.
ALLEN, KINSEY C. Pvt, A, 1st NJ Cav, 5-18-1878. Evergreen Cemetery, Camden, Camden County.
ALLEN, LEONARD A.D. Pvt, H, 12th NJ Inf, 1915. Friends Cemetery, Woodstown, Salem County.
ALLEN, LEVI Pvt, A, 22nd U.S. CT, [Died at Salem, NJ.] 1-29-1864. Spencer African Methodist Church Cemetery, Woodstown, Salem County.
ALLEN, MATTHEW DoD Unknown. Friends Cemetery, Mullica Hill, Gloucester County.
ALLEN, MERRITT Pvt, C, 53rd NY Inf, 3-15-1902. Bayview-New York Bay Cemetery, Jersey City, Hudson County.
ALLEN, PETER R. Pvt, D, 43rd U.S. CT, 2-23-1924. Lodi Cemetery, Lodi, Bergen County.
ALLEN, RICHARD Pvt, E, 11th U.S. Inf, 10-26-1897. Methodist Cemetery, Bridgeboro, Burlington County.

New Jersey Civil War Burials

ALLEN, RICHARD Pvt, I, 110th PA Inf, 7-22-1904. Mount Holly Cemetery, Mount Holly, Burlington County.

ALLEN, RICHARD Pvt, C, 35th NJ Inf, 1-14-1908. Mount Pleasant Cemetery, Newark, Essex County.

ALLEN, SAMUEL Pvt, I, 192nd NY Inf, 12-26-1915. Weehawken Cemetery, North Bergen, Hudson County.

ALLEN*, SAMUEL Pvt, H, 2nd NJ Cav, 7-2-1919. Union Cemetery, Mount Olive, Morris County.

ALLEN, SAMUEL A. 2nd Lt, I, 30th NJ Inf, DoD Unknown. Evergreen/Bishop Jaynes Cemetery, Basking Ridge, Somerset County.

ALLEN, SAMUEL C. Pvt, Btty B, 2nd U.S. Art, 5-19-1907. Zion Methodist Church Cemetery, Porchtown, Gloucester County.

ALLEN, SAMUEL S. Pvt, Btty A, 1st NJ Light Art, 1-21-1930. Greenwood Cemetery, Boonton, Morris County.

ALLEN, SCOTT Pvt, G, 2nd NJ Cav, DoD Unknown. Union Cemetery, Frenchtown, Hunterdon County.

ALLEN, SILAS A. Pvt, B, 1st NJ Inf, DoD Unknown. New Germantown Cemetery, Oldwick, Hunterdon County.

ALLEN, STEPHEN W. 1st Lt, F, 10th NJ Inf, 3-1-1899. Cedar Lawn Cemetery, Paterson, Passaic County.

ALLEN, THEODORE Pvt, D, 24th NJ Inf, 12-1-1900. Eglington Cemetery, Clarksboro, Gloucester County.

ALLEN, THEODORE Pvt, D, 1st NJ Inf, [Wounded 6-27-1862 at Gaines' Farm, VA.] 3-10-1875. Old & New Lutheran Cemetery, Lebanon, Hunterdon County.

ALLEN, THERON A. Pvt, K, 7th NJ Inf, [Died of fever at Jersey City, NJ.] 6-7-1862. Hillside Cemetery, Madison, Morris County.

ALLEN, THOMAS Pvt, K, 158th NY Inf, 9-15-1870. St. Peter's Cemetery, Jersey City, Hudson County.

ALLEN, THOMAS Pvt, E, 23rd NJ Inf, 3-29-1907. Mount Holly Cemetery, Mount Holly, Burlington County.

ALLEN, THOMAS E. Wagoner, D, 10th NJ Inf, 1911. 7th Day Baptist Church Cemetery, Shiloh, Cumberland County.

ALLEN*, THOMAS W. Pvt, C, 11th NJ Inf, [Died of diarrhea at Annapolis, MD.] 12-4-1864. Baptist Church Cemetery, Hamilton Square, Mercer County.

ALLEN, WADE 2nd Lt, D, 3rd SC Inf (CSA), [Captured 12-4-1863 at Knoxville, TN. Died of lung inflammation.] 5-6-1864. Finn's Point National Cemetery, Pennsville, Salem County.

ALLEN, WASHINGTON IRVING Capt, E, 31st MA Inf, [Wounded 6-14-1863 at Port Hudson, LA.] 1918. Newton Cemetery, Newton, Sussex County.

ALLEN, WILLIAM D 2nd Lt, I, 60th (Crawford's) TN Mtd Inf (CSA), [Captured 5-17-1863 at Big Black River Bridge, MS.] 9-25-1863. Finn's Point National Cemetery, Pennsville, Salem County.

ALLEN*, WILLIAM D. Pvt, Btty E, 1st NJ Light Art, 12-21-1916. Presbyterian Cemetery, Springfield, Union County.

ALLEN, WILLIAM F. Pvt, A, 3rd NJ Inf, 7-11-1902. Trinity Bible Church Cemetery, Glassboro, Gloucester County.

ALLEN*, WILLIAM H. Pvt, I, 12th NJ Inf, 8-13-1908. Presbyterian Church Cemetery, Bridgeton, Cumberland County.

ALLEN, WILLIAM H. Pvt, C, 3rd NJ Inf, 12-30-1923. Soldier's Home Cemetery, Vineland, Cumberland County.

ALLEN, WILLIAM H. 1903. Mount Pleasant Cemetery, Newark, Essex County.

ALLEN*, WILLIAM H. 1867. Hainesburg Cemetery, Hainesburg, Warren County.

ALLEN, WILLIAM L. Pvt, K, 35th NJ Inf, 11-5-1909. Mercer Cemetery, Trenton, Mercer County.

Our Brothers Gone Before

ALLEN, WILLIAM L. Pvt, G, 40th NJ Inf, 5-11-1883. Chestnut Cemetery, Dover, Morris County.
ALLEN*, WILLIAM OGDEN Pvt, A, 39th NJ Inf, 9-22-1931. Fairmount Cemetery, Newark, Essex County.
ALLEN, WILLIAM S. Sgt, K, 23rd NJ Inf, 1902. Greenwood Cemetery, Tuckerton, Ocean County.
ALLEN, WILLIAM W. Pvt, E, 5th NJ Inf, 3-17-1913. Coopertown Meeting House Cemetery, Edgewater Park, Burlington County.
ALLENBACK, CHARLES Pvt, A, 12th NJ Inf, 12-20-1888. Union Cemetery, Gloucester City, Camden County.
ALLER, HENRY T. Pvt, B, 22nd NJ Inf, 11-12-1884. Reformed Church Cemetery, Wyckoff, Bergen County.
ALLER, JOHN M. Pvt, I, 8th NJ Inf, 2-22-1863. Methodist Church Cemetery, Allerton, Hunterdon County.
ALLES, JOHN J. Pvt, C, 96th PA Inf, 1-19-1895. Baptist Church Cemetery, Cherryville, Hunterdon County.
ALLEWAY, COLLINS L. (aka: Alloways, Collins) Pvt, C, 34th NJ Inf, 5-25-1915. Evergreen Cemetery, Camden, Camden County.
ALLEY*, WILLIAM W. Pvt, D, 12th NJ Inf, 10-22-1894. 1st Methodist Church Cemetery, Williamstown, Gloucester County.
ALLGEYER*, PHILIP Pvt, E, 39th NJ Inf, 2-27-1887. Holy Sepulchre Cemetery, East Orange, Essex County.
ALLGOR, BENJAMIN S. Pvt, K, 29th NJ Inf, 12-14-1882. Methodist-Episcopal Cemetery, Glendola, Monmouth County.
ALLGOR, ISRAEL J. Landsman, U.S. Navy, USS Vandalia, 1922. Methodist-Episcopal Cemetery, Glendola, Monmouth County.
ALLGOR, ZACHARIAH Pvt, K, 29th NJ Inf, 3-10-1896. Methodist-Episcopal Cemetery, Glendola, Monmouth County.
ALLIBONE, JOSEPH Pvt, B, 6th NJ Inf, 2-7-1914. Riverview Cemetery, Trenton, Mercer County.
ALLICE, ROBERT (aka: Mount, Barney) Pvt, D, 119th PA Inf, [Wounded in action.] 2-10-1919. Brotherhood Cemetery, Hainesport, Burlington County.
ALLING, WILLIAM R. 7-17-1905. Mount Pleasant Cemetery, Newark, Essex County.
ALLINGTON, DAVID (see: Arlington, David G.) Bloomfield Cemetery, Bloomfield, Essex County.
ALLINGTON, JOHN (see: Arlington, John) Fairmount Cemetery, Newark, Essex County.
ALLINGTON, PETER (aka: Arlington, Peter) Pvt, C, 13th NJ Inf, [Died of wounds received at Antietam, MD.] 6-11-1863. Laurel Grove Cemetery, Totowa, Passaic County.
ALLINGTON, THOMAS R. Pvt, F, 124th NY Inf, 12-29-1902. Fairmount Cemetery, Newark, Essex County.
ALLINSON, JOSEPH Pvt, D, 1st NJ Inf, [Died at Washington, DC of wounds received at 2nd Bull Run, VA.] 10-2-1862. Methodist-Episcopal Cemetery, Burlington, Burlington County.
ALLINSON, WILLIAM H. Pvt, A, 23rd NJ Inf, 2-6-1916. Oddfellows Cemetery, Burlington, Burlington County.
ALLIS, JEREMIAH PRATT 1st Lt, F, 114th NY Inf, [Wounded 10-19-1864 at Cedar Creek, VA.] 12-31-1903. Hillside Cemetery, Scotch Plains, Union County.
ALLISON, BENJAMIN Pvt, K, 22nd NC Inf (CSA), [Captured 7-3-1863 at Gettysburg, PA. Died of smallpox.] 11-9-1863. Finn's Point National Cemetery, Pennsville, Salem County.
ALLISON, CHARLES E. Pvt, D, 40th NJ Inf, 12-20-1913. Baptist/St. Andrew's Cemetery, Mount Holly, Burlington County.

New Jersey Civil War Burials

ALLISON*, DAVID Pvt, G, 2nd NJ Inf, 6-1-1912. Fairmount Cemetery, Newark, Essex County.

ALLISON, EDGAR 5-6-1904. Mount Pleasant Cemetery, Newark, Essex County.

ALLISON, GARRETT Pvt, G, 9th NY Inf, [Wounded in action 4-19-1862.] 6-20-1867. Edgewater Cemetery, Edgewater, Bergen County.

ALLISON, GARRETT E. Pvt, H, 17th NY Inf, 12-29-1899. Edgewater Cemetery, Edgewater, Bergen County.

ALLISON, HENRY Pvt, H, 3rd NJ Cav, 3-18-1924. Cedar Run/Greenwood Cemetery, Manahawkin, Ocean County.

ALLISON, J.F. Pvt, A, 2nd (Ashby's) TN Cav (CSA), 7-11-1864. Finn's Point National Cemetery, Pennsville, Salem County.

ALLISON, JACOB Pvt, F, 1st NJ Cav, 4-23-1902. Evergreen Cemetery, Lakewood, Ocean County.

ALLISON*, JAMES Pvt, H, 4th U.S. Hancock Corps, 5-8-1895. Monument Cemetery, Edgewater Park, Burlington County.

ALLISON, JOHN Pvt, F, 1st NJ Cav, 1-25-1876. Whitesville Cemetery, Whitesville, Ocean County.

ALLISON*, JOHN W. Corp, H, 22nd NJ Inf, 6-6-1902. Old Hook Cemetery, Westwood, Bergen County.

ALLISON, JOSEPH Corp, B, 11th NJ Inf, 4-18-1927. Arlington Cemetery, Kearny, Hudson County.

ALLISON, THOMAS STUBBS Bvt Lt Col, U.S. Army, [Additional Paymaster.] 2-14-1871. Riverview Cemetery, Trenton, Mercer County.

ALLISON, WILLIAM Sgt, C, 5th PA Cav, 7-24-1890. Beverly National Cemetery, Edgewater Park, Burlington County.

ALLISON, WILLIAM (see: Allanson, William H.) St. Mary's Episcopal Church Cemetery, Burlington, Burlington County.

ALLKIRE, HENRY J. Pvt, H, 8th CA Inf, 1929. Soldier's Home Cemetery, Vineland, Cumberland County.

ALLMAN, CHARLES H. Seaman, U.S. Navy, 2-28-1895. Arlington Cemetery, Kearny, Hudson County.

ALLMAN, MITCHELL G. Corp, A, 8th FL Inf (CSA), [Captured 7-2-1863 at Gettysburg, PA. Died of smallpox.] 11-22-1863. Finn's Point National Cemetery, Pennsville, Salem County.

ALLMOND, JOHN Pvt, B, 3rd MI Cav, 8-2-1904. Cedar Lawn Cemetery, Paterson, Passaic County.

ALLOWAY, ANDREW JACKSON Pvt, D, 19th PA Cav, 9-23-1893. Methodist-Episcopal Cemetery, Vincentown, Burlington County.

ALLOWAY, ELIAS Corp, H, McKeage's Bttn PA Militia, 7-20-1888. Mount Holly Cemetery, Mount Holly, Burlington County.

ALLOWAY, JOSEPH Corp, F, 23rd NJ Inf, 10-24-1896. Methodist-Episcopal Cemetery, Vincentown, Burlington County.

ALLOWAYS, COLLINS (see: Alleway, Collins L.) Evergreen Cemetery, Camden, Camden County.

ALLSHOUSE, JACOB A. Musc, C, 31st NJ Inf, 5-19-1910. St. James Cemetery, Greenwich, Warren County.

ALLSTROM, JOHN V. Maj, 3rd NJ Cav 8-3-1906. Glenwood Cemetery, West Long Branch, Monmouth County.

ALLWARD*, WILLIAM H. Pvt, G, 8th NJ Inf, [Died of wounds received while on picket duty at Petersburg, VA.] 11-8-1864. Alpine Cemetery, Perth Amboy, Middlesex County.

ALLYN, STEPHEN D. Pvt, A, 2nd NJ Militia, 9-7-1901. Grove Church Cemetery, North Bergen, Hudson County.

Our Brothers Gone Before

ALMAND, W.F. Pvt, H, 19th (Dockery's) AR Inf (CSA), [Captured 5-16-1863 at Champion's Hill, MS.] 6-18-1864. Finn's Point National Cemetery, Pennsville, Salem County.
ALPAUGH*, DAVID B. Pvt, E, 11th NJ Inf, [Wounded 5-6-1864 at Wilderness, VA.] 1-30-1896. Reformed Church Cemetery, Lebanon, Hunterdon County.
ALPAUGH, DAVID B. 5-28-1892. Methodist Church Cemetery, Norton, Hunterdon County.
ALPAUGH, GEORGE W. 12-8-1906. Methodist Church Cemetery, Asbury, Warren County.
ALPAUGH, PETER A. Pvt, Btty B, 1st NJ Light Art, 3-18-1893. Methodist-Episcopal Cemetery, Whitehouse, Hunterdon County.
ALPAUGH, WILLIAM E. Pvt, E, 31st NJ Inf, 1-29-1906. Hillside Cemetery, Scotch Plains, Union County.
ALPHONSE*, EDWIN C. Pvt, F, 83rd NY Inf, 10-16-1900. Fairmount Cemetery, Newark, Essex County.
ALRUTH, HENRY Corp, E, 33rd NJ Inf, 11-9-1890. Fairmount Cemetery, Newark, Essex County.
ALSTED, ANDREAS (see: Ahlsted, Oswald) Fairmount Cemetery, Newark, Essex County.
ALSTON, ANTHONY Pvt, E, 24th U.S. CT, 3-13-1895. Johnson Cemetery, Camden, Camden County.
ALSTON, DAVID Pvt, C, 3rd NJ Inf, 2-3-1907. Greenwood Cemetery, Hamilton, Mercer County.
ALSTON, ISAAC J. Sgt, H, 1st MA Inf, [Wounded 8-29-1862 at 2nd Bull Run, VA.] 5-30-1926. Baptist Cemetery, Pemberton, Burlington County.
ALSTON, JAMES W. Pvt, H, 2nd DC Inf, 9-30-1885. Fairmount Cemetery, Newark, Essex County.
ALSTON, SAUL Pvt, B, ___ U.S. CT, DoD Unknown. Mount Peace Cemetery, Lawnside, Camden County.
ALSTON, THEODORE W. 2nd Lt, F, 2nd NJ Inf, 4-2-1922. Fairmount Cemetery, Newark, Essex County.
ALSTON, WILLIAM W. Pvt, H, 1st NJ Cav, 9-1-1896. Van Liew Cemetery, North Brunswick, Middlesex County.
ALT*, CHARLES Musc, A, 15th MO Inf, 3-25-1897. Fairmount Cemetery, Newark, Essex County.
ALTEMUS, ALEXANDER Sgt, E, 31st NJ Inf, 9-21-1890. Bethlehem Presbyterian Church Cemetery, Grandin, Hunterdon County.
ALTEMUS, CHARLES HYLER Pvt, E, 31st NJ Inf, [Died of typhoid at Washington, DC.] 11-13-1862. Bethlehem Presbyterian Church Cemetery, Grandin, Hunterdon County.
ALTEMUS, HERMAN Pvt, E, 31st NJ Inf, 1904. Bethlehem Presbyterian Church Cemetery, Grandin, Hunterdon County.
ALTMAN, GERHARDT (see: Ultman, Gerhardt) St. Mary's Cemetery, Plainfield, Union County.
ALTOP, LOUIS 2nd Lt, K, 19th VA Inf (CSA), 5-7-1865. Finn's Point National Cemetery, Pennsville, Salem County.
ALVATER, GEORGE 1924. Prospect Hill Cemetery, Flemington, Hunterdon County.
ALVERSON, WILLIAM W. (aka: Alverson, Willis) Pvt, E, 51st AL Cav (CSA), 10-4-1863. Finn's Point National Cemetery, Pennsville, Salem County.
ALVERSON, WILLIS (see: Alverson, William W.) Finn's Point National Cemetery, Pennsville, Salem County.
ALVORD, HENRY Pvt, H, 15th NJ Inf, 4-26-1900. New Somerville Cemetery, Somerville, Somerset County.

New Jersey Civil War Burials

ALWARD, ELISHA 1-19-1900. Methodist-Episcopal Church Cemetery, Sergeantsville, Hunterdon County.

AMBACK, JOSEPH (see: Ausback, Joseph) Tabernacle Baptist Church Cemetery, Erma, Cape May County.

AMBERG, WILLIAM (aka: Ambery, William) Pvt, Btty E, 1st NJ Light Art, 10-3-1909. Holy Sepulchre Cemetery, East Orange, Essex County.

AMBERY, WILLIAM (see: Amberg, William) Holy Sepulchre Cemetery, East Orange, Essex County.

AMBRECHT, ALOYSIUS Pvt, G, 102nd NY Inf, DoD Unknown. Holy Sepulchre Cemetery, East Orange, Essex County.

AMBROS, GEORGE (see: Armbruster, George) Fairmount Cemetery, Newark, Essex County.

AMBROSE, ANTHONY (aka: Andone, Ambrose) Pvt, G, 35th NJ Inf, [Wounded in action.] 1-16-1892. Holy Sepulchre Cemetery, East Orange, Essex County.

AMBROSE, BENJAMIN Pvt, Btty K, 2nd PA Heavy Art, 2-25-1907. St. Peter's Cemetery, New Brunswick, Middlesex County.

AMBROSE, GRAGOR (see: Armbruster, Gregory) Holy Sepulchre Cemetery, East Orange, Essex County.

AMBROSE*, JOSEPH Pvt, B, 6th U.S. Vet Vol Inf, 1-14-1911. Holy Sepulchre Cemetery, East Orange, Essex County.

AMBROSE, KISER (see: Kiser, Ambrose) Arlington Cemetery, Kearny, Hudson County.

AMEND, JOHN E. Pvt, C, 3rd NJ Cav, [Killed in action at Kearneysville, VA.] 8-26-1864. Presbyterian Church Cemetery, Basking Ridge, Somerset County.

AMER, JAMES C. Seaman, U.S. Navy, 6-10-1903. All Saints Episcopal Church Cemetery, Navesink, Monmouth County.

AMERMAN, ABRAHAM 5-27-1888. Reformed Church Cemetery, South Branch, Somerset County.

AMERMAN, DANIEL H. Pvt, E, 30th NJ Inf, 6-3-1925. New Somerville Cemetery, Somerville, Somerset County.

AMERMAN, JOHN B. Corp, Btty D, 1st NJ Light Art, DoD Unknown. New Vernon Cemetery, New Vernon, Morris County.

AMERMAN, LOUIS D. Pvt, B, 71st NY Inf, 4-14-1896. Bayview-New York Bay Cemetery, Jersey City, Hudson County.

AMERMAN, PETER (aka: Ammerman, Philip M.) Sgt, A, 18th KY Inf, 12-3-1908. Woodland Cemetery, Newark, Essex County.

AMERMAN, WILLIAM H. Pvt, E, 30th NJ Inf, 1902. Reformed Church Cemetery, South Branch, Somerset County.

AMERMAN, WILLIAM H. 3-7-1896. Methodist Cemetery, Bernardsville, Somerset County.

AMERMAN, WILLIAM P. Pvt, E, 9th NJ Inf, 1-22-1921. Hackensack Cemetery, Hackensack, Bergen County.

AMERMAN, WOODHULL F. Pvt, G, 3rd NJ Inf, 6-12-1876. Union Cemetery, Washington, Morris County.

AMERY, JOHN Pvt, I, 12th NY State Militia, 5-14-1897. Cedar Lawn Cemetery, Paterson, Passaic County.

AMES, AMAZIAH (see: Ames, Erasmus) Presbyterian Church Cemetery, Sparta, Sussex County.

AMES, ERASMUS (aka: Ames, Amaziah) Pvt, E, 22nd CT Inf, 4-25-1899. Presbyterian Church Cemetery, Sparta, Sussex County.

AMES, HORACE L. Drum Major, 2nd NJ Inf 5-20-1875. Phillipsburg Cemetery, Phillipsburg, Warren County.

AMES, NATHAN M. Capt, H, 7th NH Inf, 9-5-1872. Siloam Cemetery, Vineland, Cumberland County.

Our Brothers Gone Before

AMICK, JOHN Pvt, H, 16th NC Inf (CSA), [Captured 7-3-1863 at Gettysburg, PA.] 7-25-1863. Finn's Point National Cemetery, Pennsville, Salem County.
AMMERMAN, PETER Pvt, I, 27th NJ Inf, DoD Unknown. Fairmount Cemetery, Fairmount, Hunterdon County.
AMMERMAN, PHILIP M. (see: Amerman, Peter) Woodland Cemetery, Newark, Essex County.
AMOLAL, LEWIS GOLDING 1871. St. Peter's Cemetery, Perth Amboy, Middlesex County.
AMOS, CHARLES Colored Cook, C, 3rd NJ Cav, 11-5-1922. Jordan Lawn Cemetery, Pennsauken, Camden County.
AMOS, HENRY Pvt, B, 41st U.S. CT, 10-2-1887. Jordan Lawn Cemetery, Pennsauken, Camden County.
AMRHEIN, ANDREW (aka: Amrine, Andrew) Pvt, A, 1st NJ Militia, 11-21-1923. Fairmount Cemetery, Newark, Essex County.
AMRINE, ANDREW (see: Amrhein, Andrew) Fairmount Cemetery, Newark, Essex County.
AMSBY, F. MARION Pvt, A, 17th NY Inf, DoD Unknown. Arlington Cemetery, Kearny, Hudson County.
AMSDEN, HENRY Pvt, H, 66th NY Inf, 10-13-1865. Bayview-New York Bay Cemetery, Jersey City, Hudson County.
AMSDEN*, WILLIAM Sgt, K, 11th NJ Inf, 11-23-1898. Bayview-New York Bay Cemetery, Jersey City, Hudson County.
AMTMAN*, JACOB Sgt, E, 7th NJ Inf, 10-8-1903. Holy Sepulchre Cemetery, East Orange, Essex County.
AMWAKE, WILLIAM F.H. Sgt, C, 122nd PA Inf, 4-22-1916. Evergreen Cemetery, Camden, Camden County.
ANABLE, SAMUEL LOW Maj, 7th NY Heavy Art [Wounded 6-16-1864 at Petersburg, VA.] 7-29-1913. Elmwood Cemetery, New Brunswick, Middlesex County.
ANDE, CHARLES E. (aka: Aude, Charles) Pvt, H, 34th PA Inf, 1-19-1905. Alpine Cemetery, Perth Amboy, Middlesex County.
ANDEM, JAMES L. 1st Lt, E, 74th U.S. CT, 3-28-1932. Rosedale Cemetery, Orange, Essex County.
ANDERS, CARL R. Pvt, Btty E, 3rd PA Heavy Art, 4-18-1893. New Camden Cemetery, Camden, Camden County.
ANDERSON, AARON H. Pvt, K, 38th NJ Inf, 2-1-1883. United Presbyterian Church Cemetery, Perrineville, Monmouth County.
ANDERSON, ABIJAH 1st Sgt, F, 73rd IL Inf, 1893. Riverview Cemetery, Trenton, Mercer County.
ANDERSON, ABRAHAM Pvt, D, 3rd U.S. CT, 1-8-1906. St. Matthew's Methodist-Episcopal Cemetery, Morrisville, Camden County.
ANDERSON, ABRAHAM (see: Anderson, Abram J.) Dayton Cemetery, Dayton, Middlesex County.
ANDERSON, ABRAM J. (aka: Anderson, Abraham) Pvt, K, 111th NY Inf, 1910. Dayton Cemetery, Dayton, Middlesex County.
ANDERSON*, ALEXANDER Pvt, F, 110th PA Inf, 7-9-1899. Harleigh Cemetery, Camden, Camden County.
ANDERSON, ALEXANDER Pvt, B, 24th NJ Inf, 1899. Laurel Grove Cemetery, Totowa, Passaic County.
ANDERSON, ALEXANDER 1st Lt, E, 12th TN Cav (CSA), 4-8-1864. Finn's Point National Cemetery, Pennsville, Salem County.
ANDERSON, ALFRED C. Pvt, A, 10th NJ Inf, 8-12-1904. Baptist Church Cemetery, Haddonfield, Camden County.
ANDERSON, BENJAMIN Pvt, G, 6th NJ Inf, 9-2-1872. Old Camden Cemetery, Camden, Camden County.

New Jersey Civil War Burials

ANDERSON, BENJAMIN 12-29-1893. Newell Cemetery, Stanton Station, Hunterdon County.

ANDERSON, BENJAMIN P. Pvt, Btty K, 2nd PA Heavy Art, 1-5-1913. Elmwood Cemetery, New Brunswick, Middlesex County.

ANDERSON, BURZILAR B. 2-15-1915. Trinity United Methodist Church Cemetery, Bayville, Ocean County.

ANDERSON, CHARLES Pvt, A, 43rd U.S. CT, 8-10-1910. Oddfellows Cemetery, Burlington, Burlington County.

ANDERSON, CHARLES 4-3-1864. Evergreen Cemetery, Camden, Camden County.

ANDERSON*, CHARLES Pvt, B, 13th NY Cav, 9-10-1910. Flower Hill Cemetery, North Bergen, Hudson County.

ANDERSON, CHARLES A. 2nd Lt, A, 4th NY Inf, DoD Unknown. Arlington Cemetery, Kearny, Hudson County.

ANDERSON, CHARLES A. Pvt, L, 1st NJ Cav, 11-13-1916. United Presbyterian Church Cemetery, Perrineville, Monmouth County.

ANDERSON, CHARLES E. Pvt, C, 19th LA Inf (CSA), [Captured 9-20-1863 at Chattanooga, TN.] 5-7-1865. Finn's Point National Cemetery, Pennsville, Salem County.

ANDERSON*, CHRISTIAN Pvt, D, 6th NJ Inf, 1-14-1898. Methodist-Episcopal Cemetery, Mullica Hill, Gloucester County.

ANDERSON, CHRISTIAN 2-10-1906. Alpine Cemetery, Perth Amboy, Middlesex County.

ANDERSON, CORNELIUS C. Pvt, H, 13th NJ Inf, 5-17-1928. Weehawken Cemetery, North Bergen, Hudson County.

ANDERSON, CYRENUS V. Pvt, H, 6th NJ Inf, 10-7-1891. Mount Hope Presbyterian Cemetery, Lambertville, Hunterdon County.

ANDERSON, DANIEL A. Corp, A, 25th U.S. CT, DoD Unknown. Jordan Lawn Cemetery, Pennsauken, Camden County.

ANDERSON, DANIEL H. Pvt, H, 31st NJ Inf, 1877. Presbyterian Church Cemetery, Hampton, Hunterdon County.

ANDERSON, DAVID Pvt, E, 1st NJ Inf, 8-6-1877. Mount Pleasant Cemetery, Newark, Essex County.

ANDERSON, DAVID S. 3-20-1878. Mercer Cemetery, Trenton, Mercer County.

ANDERSON, DAVID W. QM Sgt, A, 3rd NJ Cav, 12-14-1866. 2nd Presbyterian Church Cemetery, Mount Airy, Hunterdon County.

ANDERSON, EDWARD Pvt, Btty B, 1st NJ Light Art, [Died of diarrhea at Beverly, NJ.] 2-17-1865. Beverly National Cemetery, Edgewater Park, Burlington County.

ANDERSON, EDWARD J. Seaman, U.S. Navy, USS Princeton, 2-7-1905. Mount Pleasant Cemetery, Newark, Essex County.

ANDERSON, EDWARD L. Pvt, C, 15th PA Cav, 2-14-1904. Fairmount Cemetery, Newark, Essex County.

ANDERSON, EDWARD M. 1st Lt, K, 4th NJ Inf, 8-19-1918. Riverview Cemetery, Trenton, Mercer County.

ANDERSON, EDWARD S. Corp, H, 1st NJ Cav, [Killed in action at Hawe's Shop, VA.] 5-28-1864. Brainerd Cemetery, Cranbury, Middlesex County.

ANDERSON, ELI D. Pvt, E, 37th VA Inf (CSA), [Captured 5-12-1864 at Spotsylvania CH, VA. Died of pneumonia.] 12-9-1864. Finn's Point National Cemetery, Pennsville, Salem County.

ANDERSON, ELIAS J. Pvt, I, 8th NJ Inf, 1903. Methodist Church Cemetery, Pleasant Grove, Ocean County.

ANDERSON, EVI DAYTON Corp, I, 15th NJ Inf, [Died of chronic diarrhea at Culpepper CH, VA.] 9-29-1863. Presbyterian Church Cemetery, Newton, Sussex County.

ANDERSON, EZRA S. 4-13-1876. Baptist Church Cemetery, Alloway, Salem County.

Our Brothers Gone Before

ANDERSON, FINDLATUR CARMAN (see: Anderson, Findlatus Cameron) Hillside Cemetery, Scotch Plains, Union County.

ANDERSON, FINDLATUS CAMERON (aka: Anderson, Findlatur Carman) Pvt, C, 4th MI Inf, 9-29-1923. Hillside Cemetery, Scotch Plains, Union County.

ANDERSON*, GARRETT (aka: Trout, Garrett) Pvt, D, 1st NJ Inf, 5-23-1929. Oddfellows Cemetery, Burlington, Burlington County.

ANDERSON, GARRETT T. Pvt, H, 1st NJ Cav, [Died of disease at Camp Custis, VA.] 3-28-1862. Brainerd Cemetery, Cranbury, Middlesex County.

ANDERSON, GEORGE (aka: Calkins, A.) Pvt, B, 28th MI Inf, 11-8-1915. New Camden Cemetery, Camden, Camden County.

ANDERSON, GEORGE Pvt, F, 7th NJ Inf, 3-31-1899. Presbyterian Church Cemetery, Mendham, Morris County.

ANDERSON*, GEORGE B. Sgt, H, 10th NJ Inf, 12-21-1901. Evergreen Cemetery, Camden, Camden County.

ANDERSON, GEORGE B. Landsman, U.S. Navy, 1913. Bayview-New York Bay Cemetery, Jersey City, Hudson County.

ANDERSON, GEORGE E. Pvt, H, 21st NJ Inf, 9-8-1908. Presbyterian Church Cemetery, Ewing, Mercer County.

ANDERSON, GEORGE F. Pvt, K, 35th NJ Inf, 1-3-1895. Baptist Cemetery, Wertsville, Hunterdon County.

ANDERSON, GEORGE H. Pvt, K, 34th NJ Inf, 9-10-1906. Mount Pleasant Cemetery, Newark, Essex County.

ANDERSON, GEORGE P. 1st Lt, F, 114th PA Inf, DoD Unknown. Newtonville Cemetery, Newtonville, Atlantic County.

ANDERSON, GEORGE V. Landsman, U.S. Navy, USS Yorktown, 12-26-1903. Bayview-New York Bay Cemetery, Jersey City, Hudson County.

ANDERSON*, GEORGE W. Pvt, I, 162nd NY Inf, 9-27-1913. Grove Church Cemetery, North Bergen, Hudson County.

ANDERSON, H.B. Pvt, B, 12th NC Inf (CSA), [Captured 10-1-1862 at Frederick City, MD.] 10-8-1862. Finn's Point National Cemetery, Pennsville, Salem County.

ANDERSON, HENRY A. Pvt, H, 14th NJ Inf, [Cenotaph. Drowned at Frederick City, MD.] 7-3-1863. Brainerd Cemetery, Cranbury, Middlesex County.

ANDERSON, HENRY G. Fireman, U.S. Navy, USS Minnesota, 10-29-1935. Old & New Lutheran Cemetery, Lebanon, Hunterdon County.

ANDERSON, HENRY (JR.) Pvt, D, 14th NJ Inf, 8-16-1902. Mount Pleasant Cemetery, Newark, Essex County.

ANDERSON, J. Pvt, A, 1st VA Light Art (CSA), 9-19-1863. Finn's Point National Cemetery, Pennsville, Salem County.

ANDERSON, JACOB B. Corp, I, 11th PA Cav, 12-4-1900. Belvidere/Catholic Cemetery, Belvidere, Warren County.

ANDERSON, JAMES QM Sgt, A, 47th NY Inf, 2-3-1903. Hackensack Cemetery, Hackensack, Bergen County.

ANDERSON, JAMES Musc, G, 1st NJ Cav, DoD Unknown. Harleigh Cemetery, Camden, Camden County.

ANDERSON, JAMES Pvt, M, 2nd NJ Cav, 1912. Presbyterian Church Cemetery, Clinton, Hunterdon County.

ANDERSON, JAMES 11-13-1882. Evergreen Cemetery, Morristown, Morris County.

ANDERSON, JAMES Pvt, Btty L, 12th U.S. CHA, 3-13-1909. Greenwood Cemetery, Hamilton, Mercer County.

ANDERSON, JAMES H. Corp, E, 25th U.S. CT, 1914. Mount Pisgah Cemetery, Elsinboro, Salem County.

New Jersey Civil War Burials

ANDERSON, JAMES HARVEY 3-15-1911. Mount Pleasant Cemetery, Newark, Essex County.

ANDERSON, JAMES M. Corp, H, 5th PA Cav, 8-26-1915. Arlington Cemetery, Kearny, Hudson County.

ANDERSON, JAMES T. Pvt, F, 56th GA Inf (CSA), [Captured 5-17-1863 at Baker's Creek, MS.] 7-8-1863. Finn's Point National Cemetery, Pennsville, Salem County.

ANDERSON, JAMES TRESHAM Pvt, A, 25th U.S. CT, 2-11-1897. Fairmount Cemetery, Newark, Essex County.

ANDERSON, JOHN Pvt, D, 23rd PA Inf, 6-15-1899. New Camden Cemetery, Camden, Camden County.

ANDERSON, JOHN Seaman, U.S. Navy, USS Satelette, 1-24-1899. Johnson Cemetery, Camden, Camden County.

ANDERSON, JOHN Pvt, C, 25th NJ Inf, 8-2-1911. Laurel Grove Cemetery, Totowa, Passaic County.

ANDERSON, JOHN Pvt, K, 13th NJ Inf, [Wounded 9-17-1862 at Antietam, MD.] 11-11-1913. Cedar Lawn Cemetery, Paterson, Passaic County.

ANDERSON, JOHN Pvt, K, 24th NJ Inf, DoD Unknown. Moose Cemetery, Perkintown, Salem County.

ANDERSON, JOHN Pvt, H, 11th NJ Inf, DoD Unknown. Evergreen Cemetery, Morristown, Morris County.

ANDERSON, JOHN (see: Perry, Albert Gilkerson) Hillside Cemetery, Scotch Plains, Union County.

ANDERSON, JOHN A. Corp, C, 8th WV Inf, 4-7-1892. 1st United Methodist Church Cemetery, Bridgeton, Cumberland County.

ANDERSON, JOHN B. Pvt, B, 7th NJ Inf, 3-19-1873. Evergreen Cemetery, Hillside, Union County.

ANDERSON, JOHN C. Maj, 1st U.S. Colored Cav 1911. Brookside Cemetery, Englewood, Bergen County.

ANDERSON, JOHN C. Pvt, D, 63rd NY Inf, 9-5-1917. St. Peter's Cemetery, New Brunswick, Middlesex County.

ANDERSON*, JOHN H. Pvt, L, 1st NJ Cav, 6-9-1884. United Presbyterian Church Cemetery, Perrineville, Monmouth County.

ANDERSON, JOHN I. Pvt, A, 57th NY Inf, 4-13-1875. Cedar Lawn Cemetery, Paterson, Passaic County.

ANDERSON, JOHN J. Pvt, A, 19th U.S. Inf, [Wounded in action.] 2-22-1899. Presbyterian Church Cemetery, Rockaway, Morris County.

ANDERSON*, JOHN L.T. Principal Musc, 4th NJ Inf 6- -1871. Mercer Cemetery, Trenton, Mercer County.

ANDERSON*, JOHN N. 2nd Lt, F, 38th NJ Inf, 4-3-1909. Riverview Cemetery, Trenton, Mercer County.

ANDERSON, JOHN N. 4-2-1909. Mercer Cemetery, Trenton, Mercer County.

ANDERSON, JOHN P. Pvt, E, 2nd NJ Cav, 3-5-1905. Windsor Burial Grounds Cemetery, East Windsor, Mercer County.

ANDERSON*, JOHN R. Seaman, U.S. Navy, USS Potomac, 9-26-1929. Mount Hebron Cemetery, Montclair, Essex County.

ANDERSON, JOHN W. Pvt, K, 22nd NJ Inf, [Died of typhoid at White Oak Church, VA.] 6-9-1863. Woodland Cemetery, Englewood Cliffs, Bergen County.

ANDERSON, JOSEPH Pvt, C, 10th NJ Inf, 7-23-1924. Baptist Cemetery, Medford, Burlington County.

ANDERSON, LEWIS Pvt, I, 16th VA Cav (CSA), 4-9-1865. Finn's Point National Cemetery, Pennsville, Salem County.

ANDERSON*, LEWIS Pvt, Btty F, 11th U.S. CHA, 3-21-1915. Rahway Cemetery, Rahway, Union County.

Our Brothers Gone Before

ANDERSON, MANLY S. (aka: Anderson, S.M.) Pvt, K, 15th AL Inf (CSA), [Captured at Gettysburg.] 4-6-1864. Finn's Point National Cemetery, Pennsville, Salem County.

ANDERSON, MATTHIAS ROSS Wagoner, F, 11th NJ Inf, 12-11-1866. Dayton Cemetery, Dayton, Middlesex County.

ANDERSON, MOSES Pvt, F, 22nd NJ Inf, 1892. Methodist Church Cemetery, Pleasant Grove, Ocean County.

ANDERSON, NELSON 1903. Methodist Church Cemetery, Mount Bethel, Warren County.

ANDERSON, PATRICK Pvt, Btty B, 1st NJ Light Art, 4-4-1909. Holy Sepulchre Cemetery, East Orange, Essex County.

ANDERSON, PETER F. Sgt, D, 48th NY Inf, 3-13-1897. Mercer Cemetery, Trenton, Mercer County.

ANDERSON*, REUBEN Pvt, K, 2nd U.S. Cav, 10-21-1931. Riverview Cemetery, Trenton, Mercer County.

ANDERSON, RISDEN Pvt, F, 127th U.S. CT, DoD Unknown. Atlantic City Cemetery, Pleasantville, Atlantic County.

ANDERSON, ROBERT Pvt, F, 33rd NJ Inf, 11-6-1868. Fairmount Cemetery, Newark, Essex County.

ANDERSON*, ROBERT 2nd Lt, I, 51st NY Inf, [Wounded 9-17-1862 at Antietam, MD.] 10-7-1877. Palisade Cemetery, North Bergen, Hudson County.

ANDERSON, ROBERT DoD Unknown. Riverview Cemetery, Trenton, Mercer County.

ANDERSON, ROBERT S. Corp, C, 5th NY Cav, 8-25-1891. Evergreen/Bishop Jaynes Cemetery, Basking Ridge, Somerset County.

ANDERSON, S.M. (see: Anderson, Manly S.) Finn's Point National Cemetery, Pennsville, Salem County.

ANDERSON, SAMUEL Pvt, G, 1st NJ Cav, 3-17-1907. Laurel Grove Cemetery, Totowa, Passaic County.

ANDERSON, STEPHEN Pvt, Btty D, 1st NJ Light Art, 2-22-1904. Fairmount Cemetery, Newark, Essex County.

ANDERSON*, STEWART M. Pvt, E, 14th NJ Inf, [Wounded 5-5-1862 at Williamsburg, VA.] 2-21-1911. Rahway Cemetery, Rahway, Union County.

ANDERSON, SYLVESTER H. Pvt, I, 38th NJ Inf, 9-20-1902. Presbyterian Church Cemetery, Hamilton Square, Mercer County.

ANDERSON*, THADDEUS Pvt, I, 116th NY Inf, 11-30-1899. Fairmount Cemetery, Newark, Essex County.

ANDERSON, THEODORE Pvt, E, 2nd NJ Cav, [Cenotaph. Died of dysentery while prisoner at Andersonville, GA.] 8-28-1864. Cedar Hill Cemetery, Hightstown, Mercer County.

ANDERSON, THOMAS Pvt, B, 9th NJ Inf, 5-19-1885. Presbyterian Cemetery, North Plainfield, Somerset County.

ANDERSON, THOMAS Capt, D, 27th NJ Inf, 11-11-1917. Presbyterian Church Cemetery, Newton, Sussex County.

ANDERSON, THOMAS B. 1886. Baptist/Evergreen Methodist Cemetery, Plainfield, Union County.

ANDERSON, W.F. Pvt, C, 8th VA Cav (CSA), 4-8-1865. Finn's Point National Cemetery, Pennsville, Salem County.

ANDERSON, WILLIAM Pvt, E, 23rd NJ Inf, 10-20-1903. Baptist Cemetery, Pemberton, Burlington County.

ANDERSON, WILLIAM A. Pvt, D, 14th NJ Inf, 1-10-1878. United Presbyterian Church Cemetery, Perrineville, Monmouth County.

ANDERSON, WILLIAM C. 11-26-1888. Mercer Cemetery, Trenton, Mercer County.

ANDERSON*, WILLIAM D. Sgt, C, 11th PA Cav, 1913. Cedar Grove Cemetery, Gloucester City, Camden County.

New Jersey Civil War Burials

ANDERSON, WILLIAM H. Pvt, G, 25th U.S. CT, DoD Unknown. Arlington Cemetery, Kearny, Hudson County.

ANDERSON, WILLIAM H. Corp, E, 1st NJ Cav, 8-6-1909. Riverview Cemetery, Trenton, Mercer County.

ANDERSON, WILLIAM H. Pvt, Btty G, 10th U.S. CHA, 2-14-1910. Mount Prospect Cemetery, Neptune, Monmouth County.

ANDERSON, WILLIAM H. Pvt, E, 10th NJ Inf, 1-16-1897. Masonic Cemetery, Barnegat, Ocean County.

ANDERSON*, WILLIAM P. Pvt, B, 11th NJ Inf, 1-3-1905. Methodist Church Cemetery, Mount Bethel, Warren County.

ANDERSON, WILLIAM R. Pvt, E, 1st NJ Inf, 3-30-1916. New Camden Cemetery, Camden, Camden County.

ANDERSON, WILLIAM R. 2-10-1894. Mount Hebron Cemetery, Montclair, Essex County.

ANDERSON, WILLIAM W. Pvt, G, 4th NJ Inf, DoD Unknown. 2nd Presbyterian Church Cemetery, Mount Airy, Hunterdon County.

ANDERSON, WILLIAM W. Pvt, M, 3rd NJ Cav, 3-9-1922. Presbyterian Church Cemetery, Ewing, Mercer County.

ANDERSON, WILLIAM W. 2-23-1890. Mansfield/Washington Cemetery, Washington, Warren County.

ANDIS, SIMON P. Sgt, K, 64th VA Inf (CSA), [Captured 9-9-1863 at Cumberland Gap, TN. Died of dysentery.] 5-17-1865. Finn's Point National Cemetery, Pennsville, Salem County.

ANDOG, WILLIAM Pvt, G, 1st NJ Cav, DoD Unknown. Elmwood Cemetery, New Brunswick, Middlesex County.

ANDONE, AMBROSE (see: Ambrose, Anthony) Holy Sepulchre Cemetery, East Orange, Essex County.

ANDRES, JOHN C. 7-20-1884. Van Liew Cemetery, North Brunswick, Middlesex County.

ANDRESS, THEODORE H. Sgt, G, 31st NJ Inf, [Died of fever at Falmouth, VA.] 6-3-1863. Presbyterian Church Cemetery, Marksboro, Warren County.

ANDRESS, THEOPHILUS H. Medical Cadet, U.S. Army, 8-26-1913. Newton Cemetery, Newton, Sussex County.

ANDREW, ALEXANDER S. Pvt, H, 39th NJ Inf, 2-11-1925. Bloomfield Cemetery, Bloomfield, Essex County.

ANDREW, ISAAC W. Corp, G, 1st MD Inf (ES), 3-24-1903. New Camden Cemetery, Camden, Camden County.

ANDREW, THOMAS Pvt, F, 26th NJ Inf, 7-11-1871. Bloomfield Cemetery, Bloomfield, Essex County.

ANDREWS, ABRAM Pvt, I, 8th U.S. CT, [Wounded in action.] 1-21-1909. Mansfield/Washington Cemetery, Washington, Warren County.

ANDREWS, ALFRED W. Pvt, C, 23rd NJ Inf, DoD Unknown. Methodist-Episcopal Church Cemetery, Medford, Burlington County.

ANDREWS, BENJAMIN B. Pvt, A, 25th U.S. CT, 5-4-1892. Mansfield/Washington Cemetery, Washington, Warren County.

ANDREWS, CHARLES B. Pvt, A, 1st MD Inf, DoD Unknown. Finn's Point National Cemetery, Pennsville, Salem County.

ANDREWS, CHAUNCEY Pvt, I, 2nd NJ Inf, 4-9-1868. Cedar Lawn Cemetery, Paterson, Passaic County.

ANDREWS, DANIEL Pvt, B, 25th NJ Inf, 5- -1922. Mount Pleasant Methodist Cemetery, Pleasantville, Atlantic County.

ANDREWS, EDWARD Fireman, U.S. Navy, USS Princeton, DoD Unknown. Old Camden Cemetery, Camden, Camden County.

Our Brothers Gone Before

ANDREWS, EDWARD Pvt, B, 24th U.S. CT, 8-16-1901. Fairmount Cemetery, Newark, Essex County.

ANDREWS, GEORGE B. Pvt, E, 25th U.S. CT, 6-29-1903. Mansfield/Washington Cemetery, Washington, Warren County.

ANDREWS*, GEORGE E. Pvt, E, 7th CT Inf, [Wounded 10-13-1864 at Richmond, VA.] 2-22-1913. Van Liew Cemetery, North Brunswick, Middlesex County.

ANDREWS, GEORGE S. Musc, G, 35th NJ Inf, 3-28-1927. Fairmount Cemetery, Newark, Essex County.

ANDREWS, GEORGE W. Pvt, E, 50th AL Inf (CSA), 5-6-1864. Finn's Point National Cemetery, Pennsville, Salem County.

ANDREWS*, GIBSON C. Pvt, K, 3rd PA Cav, 1906. Shinn GAR Post Cemetery, Port Norris, Cumberland County.

ANDREWS, HENRY E. Pvt, B, 95th PA Inf, 1918. Greenmount Cemetery, Hammonton, Atlantic County.

ANDREWS, ISAAC Pvt, E, 10th NJ Inf, 2-19-1914. Mount Pleasant Methodist Cemetery, Pleasantville, Atlantic County.

ANDREWS, ISAAC B. Wagoner, D, 30th NJ Inf, 2-19-1913. Phillipsburg Cemetery, Phillipsburg, Warren County.

ANDREWS*, ISAAC M. Pvt, H, 2nd NJ Inf, 1919. Mansfield/Washington Cemetery, Washington, Warren County.

ANDREWS, JAMES C. Pvt, D, 17th NY Inf, 4-25-1887. All Saints Episcopal Church Cemetery, Navesink, Monmouth County.

ANDREWS, JESSE Pvt, D, 2nd NJ Cav, DoD Unknown. Mount Pleasant Cemetery, Millville, Cumberland County.

ANDREWS, JOHN Pvt, D, 29th CT Inf, 9-2-1884. Presbyterian Cemetery, Woodbury, Gloucester County.

ANDREWS*, JOHN C. Pvt, H, 15th NJ Inf, DoD Unknown. St. Peter's Cemetery, New Brunswick, Middlesex County.

ANDREWS*, JOHN C. Pvt, Btty D, 2nd U.S. Art, 11-18-1905. Mansfield/Washington Cemetery, Washington, Warren County.

ANDREWS, JOSEPH 1-14-1893. Old South Church Cemetery, Bergenfield, Bergen County.

ANDREWS, JOSEPH B. Pvt, B, 95th PA Inf, 8-30-1909. Oddfellows-Friends Cemetery, Medford, Burlington County.

ANDREWS, JUDSON B. Pvt, I, 13th AL Inf (CSA), 10-16-1863. Finn's Point National Cemetery, Pennsville, Salem County.

ANDREWS, LEWIS A. Pvt, K, 5th PA Cav, 12-26-1908. Shinn GAR Post Cemetery, Port Norris, Cumberland County.

ANDREWS, PHILIP 11-15-1919. Bloomfield Cemetery, Bloomfield, Essex County.

ANDREWS, ROBERT Pvt, B, 1st MD Inf (ES), 1923. Soldier's Home Cemetery, Vineland, Cumberland County.

ANDREWS, ROBERT Pvt, G, 71st NY State Militia, 4-8-1902. Macphelah Cemetery, North Bergen, Hudson County.

ANDREWS, SAMUEL F. Pvt, B, 8th PA Cav, 9-1-1916. Cedar Grove Cemetery, Gloucester City, Camden County.

ANDREWS, THOMAS Pvt, B, 95th PA Inf, 10-30-1908. Baptist Cemetery, Pemberton, Burlington County.

ANDREWS, THOMAS F. Pvt, G, 3rd (Howard's) Confederate States Cav (CSA), 7-21-1864. Finn's Point National Cemetery, Pennsville, Salem County.

ANDREWS, THOMAS H. Pvt, G, 28th NJ Inf, [Wounded in action.] 6-20-1907. Green Cemetery, Woodbury, Gloucester County.

ANDREWS, THOMAS S. Corp, K, 23rd NJ Inf, [Wounded in action.] 4-20-1900. Greenwood Cemetery, Tuckerton, Ocean County.

New Jersey Civil War Burials

ANDREWS, WILLIAM W. Pvt, I, 8th U.S. CT, [Wounded 2-20-1864 at Olustee, FL.] 2-23-1890. Mansfield/Washington Cemetery, Washington, Warren County.

ANG, GODFREY (aka: Godfrey, August) Pvt, D, 7th NJ Inf, 8-18-1887. Atlantic City Cemetery, Pleasantville, Atlantic County.

ANGEL*, ASHBEL WELCH Lt Col, 38th NJ Inf [Cenotaph.] 7-5-1884. Mount Hope Presbyterian Cemetery, Lambertville, Hunterdon County.

ANGEL, CHARLES AUGUSTUS Capt, A, 35th NJ Inf, [Cenotaph. Killed in action at Ruffs Mill, GA.] 7-4-1864. Mount Hope Presbyterian Cemetery, Lambertville, Hunterdon County.

ANGELHART, SEBASTIAN Pvt, C, 2nd NJ Inf, 8-6-1880. Holy Sepulchre Cemetery, East Orange, Essex County.

ANGELO, CHARLES P. (aka: Anglo, Charles) Pvt, C, 9th NJ Inf, 8-25-1898. Trinity Bible Church Cemetery, Glassboro, Gloucester County.

ANGELO, RICHARD E. (aka: Angelow, Richard) Ordinary Seaman, U.S. Navy, USS North Carolina, 1922. 1st Methodist Church Cemetery, Williamstown, Gloucester County.

ANGELOW, RICHARD (see: Angelo, Richard E.) 1st Methodist Church Cemetery, Williamstown, Gloucester County.

ANGEN, ANTHONY Pvt, D, 33rd NJ Inf, 1-24-1919. Cedar Lawn Cemetery, Paterson, Passaic County.

ANGERBAUER, JOSEPH Sgt, I, 89th NY National Guard, 3-2-1913. Hillside Cemetery, Scotch Plains, Union County.

ANGEVINE, AMORY (see: Angevine, Emery P.) Fairview Cemetery, Westfield, Union County.

ANGEVINE, EMERY P. (aka: Angevine, Amory) Pvt, B, 84th NY National Guard, 3-30-1930. Fairview Cemetery, Westfield, Union County.

ANGLE, JACOB J. Pvt, G, 31st NJ Inf, 3-13-1876. Ramseyburg Cemetery, Ramseyburg, Warren County.

ANGLE, JEREMIAH (see: Angle, Samuel D.) Methodist Cemetery, Newfoundland, Morris County.

ANGLE, SAMUEL D. (aka: Angle, Jeremiah) Pvt, K, 80th NY Inf, 11-5-1910. Methodist Cemetery, Newfoundland, Morris County.

ANGLE, WILLIAM N. Capt, B, 35th NY Inf, 1890. Eglington Cemetery, Clarksboro, Gloucester County.

ANGLEMAN, HENRY W. Pvt, K, 7th NJ Inf, 1920. Baptist/Evergreen Methodist Cemetery, Plainfield, Union County.

ANGLER, GEORGE R. Pvt, B, 12th MA Inf, 11-26-1878. Evergreen Cemetery, Camden, Camden County.

ANGLIN, SAMUEL H. Pvt, D, 38th VA Inf (CSA), [Wounded 7-3-1863 and captured 7-4-1863 at Gettysburg, PA.] 10-8-1863. Finn's Point National Cemetery, Pennsville, Salem County.

ANGLO, CHARLES (see: Angelo, Charles P.) Trinity Bible Church Cemetery, Glassboro, Gloucester County.

ANGLUM, JOHN Pvt, H, 10th U.S. Inf, 1-4-1910. St. Mary's Cemetery, Boonton, Morris County.

ANGUS, JAMES C. Pvt, G, 12th NY State Militia, 5-29-1930. Hoboken Cemetery, North Bergen, Hudson County.

ANIN, HENRY Pvt, A, 41st U.S. CT, 6-9-1890. Fairmount Cemetery, Newark, Essex County.

ANKER, JOHN Corp, D, 104th PA Inf, 7-3-1898. Bethel Cemetery, Pennsauken, Camden County.

ANNAN, GEORGE 5-27-1887. Methodist Cemetery, Bridgeboro, Burlington County.

ANSBRO, PATRICK (aka: Ensbro, Patrick) Pvt, B, 29th NJ Inf, 6-12-1893. St. Joseph's Cemetery, Keyport, Monmouth County.

Our Brothers Gone Before

ANSEL, JOHN (aka: Ensel, John) Pvt, B, 48th NY Inf, 3-7-1908. Oak Hill Cemetery, Vineland, Cumberland County.
ANSHUTZ, VALENTINE Pvt, E, 39th NJ Inf, 3-26-1874. Woodland Cemetery, Newark, Essex County.
ANSON, CHARLES H. Pvt, B, 4th NJ Inf, 1913. Riverview Cemetery, Trenton, Mercer County.
ANSON, JOSEPH J. Pvt, B, 1st NJ Inf, 2-10-1903. Walnut Grove Cemetery, Mount Freedom, Morris County.
ANTES, WILLIAM Pvt, Btty C, 1st U.S. Art, 1-24-1910. Prospect Hill Cemetery, Flemington, Hunterdon County.
ANTHONY, CYRUS (see: Anthony, George W.) Oddfellows Cemetery, Burlington, Burlington County.
ANTHONY, GEORGE Pvt, A, 31st NJ Inf, 1909. New Germantown Cemetery, Oldwick, Hunterdon County.
ANTHONY, GEORGE W. (aka: Anthony, Cyrus) Pvt, I, 110th PA Inf, 3-17-1937. Oddfellows Cemetery, Burlington, Burlington County.
ANTHONY, JOHN D. 1st Corp, D, 44th GA Inf (CSA), [Captured 5-10-1864 at Spotsylvania CH, VA. Died of disease.] 9-10-1864. Finn's Point National Cemetery, Pennsville, Salem County.
ANTHONY, JOHN H. Pvt, F, 3rd U.S. CT, 10-14-1902. Trinity AME Church Cemetery, Wrightsville, Burlington County.
ANTHONY, JOSEPH Pvt, G, 37th NJ Inf, 3-31-1929. Cedar Lawn Cemetery, Paterson, Passaic County.
ANTHONY, MARK 2nd Lt, D, 23rd PA Inf, 2-20-1915. East Ridgelawn Cemetery, Clifton, Passaic County.
ANTHONY, NATHANIEL R. Pvt, H, 21st NJ Inf, 1932. Greenwood Cemetery, Hamilton, Mercer County.
ANTHONY, WILLIAM SHEPPARD (aka: Sheppard, William) Corp, B, 6th NJ Inf, 8-8-1918. Riverview Cemetery, Trenton, Mercer County.
ANTREY, ELIAS Pvt, E, 197th PA Inf, 8-14-1920. Greenwood Cemetery, Hamilton, Mercer County.
ANTRIM, WATSON Pvt, 6th NY Ind Btty 9-25-1902. Methodist Church Cemetery, Pemberton, Burlington County.
APELT, AUGUST C. 1923. Laurel Grove Cemetery, Totowa, Passaic County.
APGAR, ABRAHAM Pvt, M, 2nd NJ Cav, 4-25-1907. Evergreen Cemetery, Hillside, Union County.
APGAR, AUSTIN C. 3-4-1908. Greenwood Cemetery, Hamilton, Mercer County.
APGAR, BENJAMIN A. Pvt, A, 2nd NJ Cav, 1915. Fairmount Cemetery, Fairmount, Hunterdon County.
APGAR, DANIEL P. Pvt, C, 27th NJ Inf, DoD Unknown. Fairmount Cemetery, Fairmount, Hunterdon County.
APGAR, EBENEZER ALBERT Pvt, K, 1st NJ Inf, 2-20-1892. Fairmount Cemetery, Fairmount, Hunterdon County.
APGAR, FREDERICK H. Pvt, K, 31st NJ Inf, 5-21-1908. Arlington Cemetery, Kearny, Hudson County.
APGAR, GEORGE Pvt, E, 11th NJ Inf, 2-1-1869. Presbyterian Church Cemetery, Califon, Hunterdon County.
APGAR, GEORGE N. 12-18-1891. Reformed Church Cemetery, Lebanon, Hunterdon County.
APGAR, ISAAC H. 12-13-1906. Presbyterian Cemetery, Cokesbury, Hunterdon County.
APGAR, JACOB D. Pvt, A, 15th NJ Inf, [Cenotaph. Killed in action at Spotsylvania CH, VA.] 5-12-1864. Presbyterian Church Cemetery, Califon, Hunterdon County.
APGAR*, JACOB WANDLING Pvt, Btty E, 1st NJ Light Art, 2-7-1890. Phillipsburg Cemetery, Phillipsburg, Warren County.

APGAR, JOHN (see: Flomerfelt, David N.) Fairmount Cemetery, Fairmount, Hunterdon County.
APGAR, JOHN R. Pvt, A, 31st NJ Inf, 2-9-1922. Reformed Church Cemetery, Lebanon, Hunterdon County.
APGAR, MATTHIAS H. Pvt, Btty B, 1st NJ Light Art, DoD Unknown. Fairmount Cemetery, Fairmount, Hunterdon County.
APGAR, MORRIS Pvt, A, 2nd NJ Cav, 4-9-1906. Fairmount Cemetery, Fairmount, Hunterdon County.
APGAR, PETER N. 1-10-1898. Presbyterian Church Cemetery, Califon, Hunterdon County.
APGAR, SEARING P. (aka: Apgar, Surren) Pvt, B, 134th NY Inf, 9-22-1876. Presbyterian Cemetery, Cokesbury, Hunterdon County.
APGAR, SURREN (see: Apgar, Searing P.) Presbyterian Cemetery, Cokesbury, Hunterdon County.
APP, GEORGE WASHINGTON Corp, I, 183rd PA Inf, 10-2-1922. Beverly National Cemetery, Edgewater Park, Burlington County.
APPEL, CHRISTIAN (SR.) Pvt, H, 28th NJ Inf, 1879. Trinity Bible Church Cemetery, Glassboro, Gloucester County.
APPLE, NATHAN B. Pvt, A, 69th PA Inf, [Died at Beverly, NJ.] 10-14-1864. Beverly National Cemetery, Edgewater Park, Burlington County.
APPLEBE, HERBERT (see: Appleby, Herbert) Chestnut Hill Cemetery, East Brunswick, Middlesex County.
APPLEBEE, CEPHAS Artificer, Btty M, 1st VT Heavy Art, 8-30-1910. Siloam Cemetery, Vineland, Cumberland County.
APPLEBY, GEORGE J. Pvt, F, 14th NJ Inf, 1901. Methodist Church Cemetery, Groveville, Mercer County.
APPLEBY*, HERBERT (aka: Applbe, Herbert) Pvt, E, 84th NY National Guard, 3-4-1921. Chestnut Hill Cemetery, East Brunswick, Middlesex County.
APPLEBY, J. RANDOLPH 1st Lt, A, 28th NJ Inf, 7-22-1884. Washington Monumental Cemetery, South River, Middlesex County.
APPLEBY*, WILLIAM M. Yeoman, U.S. Navy, USS Nantucket, 10-10-1910. Chestnut Hill Cemetery, East Brunswick, Middlesex County.
APPLEGATE, ALLEN E. Pvt, D, 23rd NJ Inf, 7-20-1923. Springfield-Upper Springfield-Friends Cemetery, Springfield, Burlington County.
APPLEGATE, ASHER Pvt, D, 14th NJ Inf, [Wounded in action.] 1-4-1886. Adelphia Cemetery, Adelphia, Monmouth County.
APPLEGATE, BARTON 1st Lt, F, 14th NJ Inf, 6-5-1904. Riverside Cemetery, Toms River, Ocean County.
APPLEGATE, BURRIS Pvt, K, 2nd NJ Cav, DoD Unknown. Overlook Cemetery, Bridgeton, Cumberland County.
APPLEGATE, BURRIS J. DoD Unknown. Cedar Grove Methodist Church Cemetery, Toms River, Ocean County.
APPLEGATE, CHARLES Pvt, L, 2nd NJ Cav, 7-14-1885. Baptist Church Cemetery, Jacobstown, Burlington County.
APPLEGATE, CHARLES 10-11-1911. Tennent Church Cemetery, Tennent, Monmouth County.
APPLEGATE, CHARLES E. Corp, F, 29th NJ Inf, 1930. Fairview Cemetery, Fairview, Monmouth County.
APPLEGATE, CHARLES L. 8-13-1907. Riverside Cemetery, Toms River, Ocean County.
APPLEGATE, CHARLES S. Pvt, F, 14th NJ Inf, 4-3-1919. Riverside Cemetery, Toms River, Ocean County.
APPLEGATE, DANIEL Pvt, E, 29th NJ Inf, 5-28-1931. Adelphia Cemetery, Adelphia, Monmouth County.

Our Brothers Gone Before

APPLEGATE, DISBROW Pvt, C, 29th NJ Inf, 1-19-1907. Fernwood Cemetery, Jamesburg, Middlesex County.

APPLEGATE, EDWIN Pvt, D, 9th NJ Inf, DoD Unknown. Methodist-Episcopal Cemetery, Old Bridge, Middlesex County.

APPLEGATE, EDWIN FORREST Col, 29th NJ Inf 1-23-1885. Maplewood Cemetery, Freehold, Monmouth County.

APPLEGATE*, EDWIN R. Pvt, E, 9th NJ Inf, 12-25-1910. Cedar Grove Methodist Church Cemetery, Toms River, Ocean County.

APPLEGATE, ELI Pvt, I, 2nd NJ Cav, 3-15-1900. Brainerd Cemetery, Cranbury, Middlesex County.

APPLEGATE*, ELIAS Pvt, H, 35th NJ Inf, 8-7-1865. Evergreen Cemetery, Hillside, Union County.

APPLEGATE, ENOCH Pvt, I, 38th NJ Inf, 5-15-1909. Presbyterian Church Cemetery, Hamilton Square, Mercer County.

APPLEGATE, GEORGE DoD Unknown. Christ Church Cemetery, Morgan, Middlesex County.

APPLEGATE, GEORGE Veterinary Surg, 1st NJ Cav 3-15-1914. Van Liew Cemetery, North Brunswick, Middlesex County.

APPLEGATE, GEORGE B. Pvt, I, 38th NJ Inf, 5-30-1891. Riverview Cemetery, Trenton, Mercer County.

APPLEGATE, GEORGE H. Corp, G, 11th NJ Inf, [Died of typhoid at Potomac Creek, VA.] 5-21-1863. Baptist Church Cemetery, Jacobstown, Burlington County.

APPLEGATE, ISAIAH Pvt, L, 1st NJ Cav, 8-2-1867. Brainerd Cemetery, Cranbury, Middlesex County.

APPLEGATE, JACOB (see: Applegit, Jacob) Presbyterian/Methodist-Episcopal Cemetery, Succasunna, Morris County.

APPLEGATE, JACOB S. Pvt, B, 28th NJ Inf, 3-30-1930. Fernwood Cemetery, Jamesburg, Middlesex County.

APPLEGATE, JACOB S. DoD Unknown. Van Liew Cemetery, North Brunswick, Middlesex County.

APPLEGATE, JACOB T. Pvt, D, 48th NY Inf, 11-6-1907. Evergreen Cemetery, Farmingdale, Monmouth County.

APPLEGATE, JAMES H. Pvt, A, 38th NJ Inf, 11-2-1900. Evergreen Cemetery, Farmingdale, Monmouth County.

APPLEGATE, JAMES H. 6-15-1904. Old Baptist Cemetery, Freehold, Monmouth County.

APPLEGATE, JAMES M. Pvt, A, 38th NJ Inf, [Died of consumption at Fort Powhattan, VA.] 11-17-1864. Brainerd Cemetery, Cranbury, Middlesex County.

APPLEGATE, JAMES R. Pvt, F, 1st NJ Cav, [Died of diarrhea at Philadelphia, PA.] 4-19-1863. Osbornville Protestant Church Cemetery, Breton Woods, Ocean County.

APPLEGATE, JOHN (aka: Appleget, John) Pvt, A, 9th NJ Inf, [Wounded 6-30-1864.] 5-11-1913. Brainerd Cemetery, Cranbury, Middlesex County.

APPLEGATE, JOHN A. Pvt, I, 38th NJ Inf, 12-20-1902. Fairmount Cemetery, Newark, Essex County.

APPLEGATE, JOHN H. Pvt, I, 14th NJ Inf, 1-11-1890. Elmwood Cemetery, New Brunswick, Middlesex County.

APPLEGATE, JOHN L. Sgt, D, 29th NJ Inf, 4-14-1885. Fairview Cemetery, Fairview, Monmouth County.

APPLEGATE, JOHN S. Pvt, H, 31st NJ Inf, 2-27-1907. Union Cemetery, Washington, Morris County.

APPLEGATE, JOHN W. Wagoner, A, 6th NJ Inf, 4-13-1888. Cedar Grove Methodist Church Cemetery, Toms River, Ocean County.

New Jersey Civil War Burials

APPLEGATE, JOSEPH Pvt, E, 23rd NJ Inf, 11-21-1890. New Camden Cemetery, Camden, Camden County.
APPLEGATE, JOSEPH H. Pvt, G, 11th NJ Inf, 4-18-1910. Baptist Church Cemetery, Jacobstown, Burlington County.
APPLEGATE, JOSEPH H.C. Pvt, F, 24th NJ Inf, DoD Unknown. Overlook Cemetery, Bridgeton, Cumberland County.
APPLEGATE, LLOYD Pvt, E, 2nd NJ Cav, 5-31-1917. Emleys Hill United Methodist Church Cemetery, Upper Freehold, Monmouth County.
APPLEGATE*, MOSES Pvt, G, 11th NJ Inf, 12-23-1919. Methodist Cemetery, Allentown, Monmouth County.
APPLEGATE, NOAH Pvt, K, 28th NJ Inf, 4-20-1873. Christ Church Cemetery, Morgan, Middlesex County.
APPLEGATE, OSCAR Corp, D, 28th NJ Inf, 1-8-1865. Riverview Cemetery, Trenton, Mercer County.
APPLEGATE, PETER (see: Lampey, Peter) Baptist Church Cemetery, Penns Neck, Mercer County.
APPLEGATE*, PETER C. Pvt, F, 14th NJ Inf, 12-17-1918. Cedar Grove Methodist Church Cemetery, Toms River, Ocean County.
APPLEGATE, RALPH Sgt, C, 29th NJ Inf, 4-19-1900. Methodist-Protestant Cemetery, Union Valley, Middlesex County.
APPLEGATE, SAMUEL Pvt, I, 23rd NJ Inf, 6-20-1888. Coopertown Meeting House Cemetery, Edgewater Park, Burlington County.
APPLEGATE, SAMUEL Pvt, A, 6th NJ Inf, [Wounded 8-29-1862 at 2nd Bull Run, VA.] 3-17-1907. Brainerd Cemetery, Cranbury, Middlesex County.
APPLEGATE, SMITH Corp, A, 6th NJ Inf, [Wounded 7-3-1863 at Gettysburg, PA.] 4-10-1915. Baptist Cemetery, Burlington, Burlington County.
APPLEGATE, THOMAS Pvt, E, 35th NJ Inf, 7-15-1876. Presbyterian Church Cemetery, Pleasant Grove, Morris County.
APPLEGATE, THOMAS F. Pvt, H, 14th NJ Inf, [Killed in action at Cedar Creek, VA.] 10-19-1864. Cedar Grove Methodist Church Cemetery, Toms River, Ocean County.
APPLEGATE, WILLIAM Pvt, G, 4th NJ Inf, [Died of fever at Absecon, NJ.] 1-10-1863. United Methodist Church Cemetery, Absecon, Atlantic County.
APPLEGATE, WILLIAM Pvt, A, 28th NJ Inf, 3-16-1906. Fairmount Cemetery, Newark, Essex County.
APPLEGATE, WILLIAM B. Pvt, K, 34th NJ Inf, 4-22-1878. Methodist-Episcopal Cemetery, Vincentown, Burlington County.
APPLEGATE, WILLIAM C. Wagoner, E, 28th NJ Inf, 3-15-1917. Lakewood-Hope Cemetery, Lakewood, Ocean County.
APPLEGATE, WILLIAM G. Pvt, F, 22nd NJ Inf, 1875. Riverview Cemetery, Trenton, Mercer County.
APPLEGATE, WILLIAM H. Pvt, D, 23rd NJ Inf, 12-5-1923. Woodlane Graveyard Cemetery, Westampton, Burlington County.
APPLEGATE, WILLIAM H. 3-18-1908. Greenwood Cemetery, Hamilton, Mercer County.
APPLEGATE*, WILLIAM J. Pvt, F, 7th NJ Inf, 4-13-1921. Riverside Cemetery, Toms River, Ocean County.
APPLEGATE, WILLIAM L. Pvt, F, 14th NJ Inf, 8-23-1898. Tennent Church Cemetery, Tennent, Monmouth County.
APPLEGATE, WILLIAM P. 1st Sgt, C, 29th NJ Inf, 4-9-1896. Brainerd Cemetery, Cranbury, Middlesex County.
APPLEGET*, ADRIAN S. 2nd Lt, C, 2nd NJ Cav, 8-6-1927. Brainerd Cemetery, Cranbury, Middlesex County.

Our Brothers Gone Before

APPLEGET, ARUNAH D. 2nd Lt, A, 9th NJ Inf, 1-23-1918. Brainerd Cemetery, Cranbury, Middlesex County.

APPLEGET, JOHN (see: Applegate, John) Brainerd Cemetery, Cranbury, Middlesex County.

APPLEGET, THEODORE F. 1st Sgt, E, 21st NJ Inf, 5-8-1910. Riverview Cemetery, Trenton, Mercer County.

APPLEGET, THOMAS BAIRD Maj, 9th NJ Inf 2-23-1904. Cedar Hill Cemetery, Hightstown, Mercer County.

APPLEGIT, JACOB (aka: Applegate, Jacob) Pvt, C, 27th NJ Inf, 3-30-1897. Presbyterian/Methodist-Episcopal Cemetery, Succasunna, Morris County.

APPLETON, GEORGE W. Capt, H, 45th PA Militia, 12-11-1886. Baptist Church Cemetery, Haddonfield, Camden County.

APPLETON*, PETER WILSON Pvt, G, 34th NJ Inf, 8-25-1869. St. Mary's Episcopal Church Cemetery, Burlington, Burlington County.

APPO, WILLIAM Corp, I, 30th NY Inf, [Killed in action at 2nd Bull Run, VA.] 8-30-1862. St. Mary's Episcopal Church Cemetery, Burlington, Burlington County.

APTHORP*, WILLIAM LEE Lt Col, 34th U.S. CT 1-24-1879. St. Stephen's Cemetery, Millburn, Essex County.

ARBOGAST, JOHN (see: August, John W.) Riverview Cemetery, Trenton, Mercer County.

ARBUGUST, JOHN Pvt, Btty I, 2nd PA Heavy Art, 8-3-1904. Riverside Cemetery, Riverside, Burlington County.

ARBUTHNOT*, CHARLES Pvt, H, 2nd NJ Inf, DoD Unknown. Mount Pleasant Cemetery, Newark, Essex County.

ARBUTHNOT, FREDERICK Pvt, K, 11th NJ Inf, 2-13-1881. Mount Pleasant Cemetery, Newark, Essex County.

ARBUTHNOT, WILLIAM J. Sgt, G, 8th NJ Inf, 4-25-1878. Mount Pleasant Cemetery, Newark, Essex County.

ARCHER, A.W. 3rd Lt, E, 1st (Symon's) GA Res Inf (CSA), 3-26-1865. Finn's Point National Cemetery, Pennsville, Salem County.

ARCHER, BENJAMIN 3-24-1872. New Episcopal Church Cemetery, Swedesboro, Gloucester County.

ARCHER, CHARLES H. Pvt, F, 14th NJ Inf, 7-14-1896. Zion Baptist Church Cemetery, New Egypt, Ocean County.

ARCHER, CHARLES R. Pvt, F, 4th NJ Inf, 2-7-1903. New Camden Cemetery, Camden, Camden County.

ARCHER, EDWARD Pvt, A, 10th NJ Inf, 1884. Zion Baptist Church Cemetery, New Egypt, Ocean County.

ARCHER, EDWARD R. Landsman, U.S. Navy, USS Nereus, 12-6-1900. Baptist Church Cemetery, Slabtown, Salem County.

ARCHER, ELWOOD Pvt, E, 33rd NJ Inf, 1931. Good Luck Cemetery, Murray Grove, Ocean County.

ARCHER, GEORGE W. Corp, D, 4th NJ Inf, 7-31-1926. Jacobstown Masonic Cemetery, Jacobstown, Burlington County.

ARCHER, HARRY H. Corp, G, 10th NJ Inf, 11-21-1898. Bordentown/Old St. Mary's Catholic Cemetery, Bordentown, Burlington County.

ARCHER, HENRY H. Corp, G, 10th NJ Inf, 1898. Oddfellows Cemetery, Burlington, Burlington County.

ARCHER, ISAAC Pvt, K, 4th NJ Militia, 2-2-1911. Oddfellows Cemetery, Pemberton, Burlington County.

ARCHER, JASPER N. Sgt, D, 4th NJ Inf, 9-8-1880. Zion Baptist Church Cemetery, New Egypt, Ocean County.

ARCHER, JOHN W. Pvt, B, 1st NJ Inf, 8-6-1933. Mount Holly Cemetery, Mount Holly, Burlington County.

New Jersey Civil War Burials

ARCHER, LEVI Pvt, E, 9th VA Inf (CSA), [Captured 7-3-1863 at Gettysburg, PA.] 10-13-1863. Finn's Point National Cemetery, Pennsville, Salem County.

ARCHER, SAMUEL L. 1915. Zion Baptist Church Cemetery, New Egypt, Ocean County.

ARCHER, SAVILLIAN W.L. Pvt, A, MD Emerg NJ Militia, 12-4-1886. Mount Holly Cemetery, Mount Holly, Burlington County.

ARCHER, THOMAS Capt, M, 1st NY Eng, 2-23-1876. Hazelwood Cemetery, Rahway, Union County.

ARCHIMANN, CHARLES A. Sgt, B, 22nd __ Inf, 11-11-1932. Fairmount Cemetery, Newark, Essex County.

ARCHINAL, WILLIAM J. Corp, I, 30th OH Inf, [Awarded the Medal of Honor.] 5-10-1919. Riverview Cemetery, Trenton, Mercer County.

ARCULARIUS, CHARLES T. Corp, H, 26th NJ Inf, 12-10-1919. Rosedale Cemetery, Orange, Essex County.

ARCULARIUS, GEORGE H. Wagoner, E, 8th NJ Inf, 9-11-1888. Woodland Cemetery, Newark, Essex County.

ARD, JOHN J. Pvt, G, 15th SC Inf (CSA), [Captured 7-2-1863 at Gettysburg, PA. Died of smallpox.] 11-28-1863. Finn's Point National Cemetery, Pennsville, Salem County.

ARDELL, RICHARD F. Pvt, A, 21st AR Inf (CSA), 9-26-1863. Finn's Point National Cemetery, Pennsville, Salem County.

ARESON, GEORGE W. Sgt, Btty K, 6th NY Heavy Art, 1-27-1914. Laurel Grove Cemetery, Totowa, Passaic County.

ARESON, SAMUEL Pvt, D, 9th NY Inf, 4-16-1928. Rosedale Cemetery, Orange, Essex County.

ARESON, WILLIAM H. (aka: Mountjoy, William) 1st Sgt, Btty E, 3rd NY Light Art, 9-25-1888. Rosedale Cemetery, Orange, Essex County.

AREY, JOHN H. Capt, G, 13th NJ Inf, 1910. Cedar Hill Cemetery, Hightstown, Mercer County.

ARING, AUGUSTUS F. Fireman, U.S. Navy, USS Nantucket, 1911. Evergreen Cemetery, Farmingdale, Monmouth County.

ARLINGTON*, DAVID G. (aka: Allington, David) Sgt, I, 13th NJ Inf, 9-6-1917. Bloomfield Cemetery, Bloomfield, Essex County.

ARLINGTON, JOHN (aka: Allington, John) Pvt, E, 37th NJ Inf, 10-18-1912. Fairmount Cemetery, Newark, Essex County.

ARLINGTON, PETER (see: Allington, Peter) Laurel Grove Cemetery, Totowa, Passaic County.

ARLITZ, WILLIAM Pvt, C, 41st NY Inf, 12-13-1900. Greenmount Cemetery, Hammonton, Atlantic County.

ARLOW, ROBERT K. Pvt, A, 9th NJ Inf, 1913. Elmwood Cemetery, New Brunswick, Middlesex County.

ARMBRUSTER, GEORGE (aka: Ambros, George) Pvt, G, 26th NJ Inf, 5-11-1920. Fairmount Cemetery, Newark, Essex County.

ARMBRUSTER, GREGORY (aka: Ambrose, Gragor) Pvt, F, 39th NJ Inf, 7-28-1917. Holy Sepulchre Cemetery, East Orange, Essex County.

ARMENT*, MOSES E. Pvt, K, 102nd NY National Guard, 7-17-1910. Maple Grove Cemetery, Hackensack, Bergen County.

ARMINGTON, GEORGE H. Pvt, U.S. Volunteers, [Signal Corps.] 11-5-1917. Evergreen Cemetery, Camden, Camden County.

ARMINGTON*, PHILIP M. 1st Lt, E, 12th NJ Inf, 11-18-1882. Old Camden Cemetery, Camden, Camden County.

ARMITAGE, SHEWBART B. Pvt, F, 17th PA Inf, 2-10-1901. Evergreen Cemetery, Camden, Camden County.

ARMOUR, ALOUS 1917. Atlantic City Cemetery, Pleasantville, Atlantic County.

ARMSTEAD, NATHAN H. Pvt, E, 41st U.S. CT, 1-15-1897. Atlantic City Cemetery, Pleasantville, Atlantic County.
ARMSTRONG*, ABRAHAM Pvt, C, 34th NJ Inf, 2-7-1916. Mount Holly Cemetery, Mount Holly, Burlington County.
ARMSTRONG, ALEXANDER Seaman, U.S. Navy, USS Potapsco, 1-7-1915. Phillipsburg Cemetery, Phillipsburg, Warren County.
ARMSTRONG*, ALFRED M. Pvt, C, 15th NJ Inf, 11-12-1892. Evergreen Cemetery, Morristown, Morris County.
ARMSTRONG, AUSTIN E. Sgt, H, 9th NJ Inf, [Killed in action at Roanoke Island, NC.] 2-8-1862. Presbyterian Church Cemetery, Yellow Frame, Warren County.
ARMSTRONG, CHARLES A. Pvt, I, 91st PA Inf, 11-9-1934. Harleigh Cemetery, Camden, Camden County.
ARMSTRONG, CHARLES B. Pvt, G, 22nd U.S. CT, 1-14-1904. Riverview Cemetery, Trenton, Mercer County.
ARMSTRONG, CHRISTIAN Pvt, C, 104th OH Inf, DoD Unknown. Methodist-Episcopal Cemetery, Glassboro, Gloucester County.
ARMSTRONG*, FRANKLIN Pvt, C, 11th NJ Inf, [Wounded in action.] 1927. Baptist/St. Andrew's Cemetery, Mount Holly, Burlington County.
ARMSTRONG, ISAAC DoD Unknown. Colestown Cemetery, Cherry Hill, Camden County.
ARMSTRONG, JACOB J. Pvt, D, 14th NJ Inf, [Died of wounds received at Petersburg, VA.] 12-20-1864. Old Baptist Cemetery, Freehold, Monmouth County.
ARMSTRONG*, JAMES F. Commander, U.S. Navy, USS San Jacinto, [Cenotaph.] 4-19-1873. Presbyterian Cemetery, Woodbury, Gloucester County.
ARMSTRONG, JOHN Pvt, A, 7th NJ Inf, [Died on furlough at Glassboro, NJ.] 4-3-1865. Methodist-Episcopal Cemetery, Glassboro, Gloucester County.
ARMSTRONG, JOHN JAMES Principal Musc, 25th U.S. CT 2-23-1918. Oddfellows Cemetery, Burlington, Burlington County.
ARMSTRONG, JOHN S. 6-26-1912. Baptist Cemetery, Salem, Salem County.
ARMSTRONG, JOSEPH T. Pvt, C, 23rd U.S. CT, 1-30-1917. Butler Cemetery, Camden, Camden County.
ARMSTRONG, LOUIS B. Pvt, D, 22nd U.S. CT, 5-11-1903. Timbuctoo Cemetery, Timbuctoo, Burlington County.
ARMSTRONG, ROBERT Pvt, F, 34th NJ Inf, 1866. Tennent Church Cemetery, Tennent, Monmouth County.
ARMSTRONG, ROBERT H. 3rd Sgt, H, 22nd GA Inf (CSA), [Captured 7-2-1862 at Gettysburg, PA.] 10-30-1863. Finn's Point National Cemetery, Pennsville, Salem County.
ARMSTRONG, SAMUEL STROUD 1930. Riverview Cemetery, Trenton, Mercer County.
ARMSTRONG, THOMAS G. 1902. Glenwood Cemetery, West Long Branch, Monmouth County.
ARMSTRONG, THOMAS J. Sgt, I, 93rd NY Inf, 1896. Holy Name Cemetery, Jersey City, Hudson County.
ARMSTRONG, THOMAS SWAIN 12-14-1929. Hillside Cemetery, Scotch Plains, Union County.
ARMSTRONG*, URIAH Musc, D, 176th NY Inf, 5-12-1920. Laurel Grove Cemetery, Totowa, Passaic County.
ARMSTRONG, WILLIAM Pvt, F, 25th NJ Inf, 8-21-1915. Methodist Church Cemetery, Goshen, Cape May County.
ARMSTRONG, WILLIAM Pvt, K, 4th NJ Inf, 11-26-1876. Methodist-Episcopal Cemetery, Pennsville, Salem County.
ARMSTRONG, WILLIAM Pvt, D, 9th NJ Inf, 1-26-1880. Evergreen Cemetery, Hillside, Union County.

New Jersey Civil War Burials

ARMSTRONG, WILLIAM C. Pvt, D, 1st NJ Cav, 1-30-1896. Riverview Cemetery, Trenton, Mercer County.
ARMSTRONG, WILLIAM H. QM Sgt, 2nd NY Cav 10-11-1923. Arlington Cemetery, Kearny, Hudson County.
ARMSTRONG, WILLIAM H.L. Sgt, C, 1st DE Inf, 6-7-1912. Berlin Cemetery, Berlin, Camden County.
ARMSTRONG, WILLIAM J. Pvt, G, 5th NJ Inf, 11-26-1864. Mount Pleasant Cemetery, Newark, Essex County.
ARNET, JAMES Pvt, C, 27th NJ Inf, 5-28-1886. Methodist Church Cemetery, Flanders, Morris County.
ARNETT, CHARLES W. 2nd Lt, C, 5th NJ Inf, [Died of wounds.] 11-11-1862. Mount Hope Presbyterian Cemetery, Lambertville, Hunterdon County.
ARNETT, CORNELIUS Pvt, H, 118th U.S. CT, 1-11-1886. Mount Hope Presbyterian Cemetery, Lambertville, Hunterdon County.
ARNETT, JOHN G. Corp, K, 4th NJ Inf, 1925. Presbyterian Church Cemetery, Bridgeton, Cumberland County.
ARNETT*, WILLIAM Pvt, K, 4th NJ Inf, 6-7-1926. Soldier's Home Cemetery, Vineland, Cumberland County.
ARNOLD, CHARLES A. Pvt, G, 40th NY Inf, 11-22-1880. Hoboken Cemetery, North Bergen, Hudson County.
ARNOLD*, EDMUND Pvt, D, 33rd NJ Inf, 3-31-1890. St. Vincent Martyr Cemetery, Madison, Morris County.
ARNOLD, ELWOOD (aka: Decker, Elwood) Seaman, U.S. Navy, USS Mercedita, 11-4-1878. Whitelawn Cemetery, Point Pleasant, Ocean County.
ARNOLD, FRANCIS W. 1st Lt,RQM, 93rd OH Inf 8-22-1866. Constable Hook Cemetery, Bayonne, Hudson County.
ARNOLD, JAMES (aka: Dalton, James) Pvt, H, 33rd NJ Inf, 6-18-1914. Arlington Cemetery, Kearny, Hudson County.
ARNOLD, JAMES A. (aka: Hinhold, James) Pvt, B, 12th NJ Inf, 8-28-1893. Mount Pleasant Cemetery, Newark, Essex County.
ARNOLD, JOHN Pvt, E, 3rd NJ Cav, 3-21-1879. Mount Pleasant Cemetery, Newark, Essex County.
ARNOLD, MICHAEL Pvt, A, 33rd NJ Inf, 7-5-1920. Cedar Lawn Cemetery, Paterson, Passaic County.
ARNOLD, MOSES Pvt, Btty D, 3rd U.S. Art, 7-15-1900. Jersey City Cemetery, Jersey City, Hudson County.
ARNOLD, W.H. Pvt, Fry's Btty, VA Light Art (CSA), 8-6-1864. Finn's Point National Cemetery, Pennsville, Salem County.
ARNOLD*, WILLIAM Pvt, F, 7th NJ Inf, 7-24-1895. Evergreen Cemetery, Camden, Camden County.
AROSE, ABRAHAM Pvt, K, 28th NJ Inf, [Died of typhoid at Falmouth, VA.] 3-14-1863. Rose Hill Cemetery, Matawan, Monmouth County.
AROSE, ABRAHAM (see: Rose, Abraham) Rose Hill Cemetery, Matawan, Monmouth County.
AROSE*, DANIEL Pvt, I, 14th NJ Inf, 11-23-1899. Rose Hill Cemetery, Matawan, Monmouth County.
AROSE, ELISHA Pvt, K, 28th NJ Inf, 1889. Rose Hill Cemetery, Matawan, Monmouth County.
AROSE, WILLIAM CARMAN Pvt, K, 28th NJ Inf, [Wounded in action.] 11-11-1921. Rose Hill Cemetery, Matawan, Monmouth County.
ARRISON, JOSEPH Pvt, C, 3rd NJ Militia, 11-29-1906. Mercer Cemetery, Trenton, Mercer County.
ARRISON, THOMAS B. Corp, K, 104th PA Inf, [Wounded in action.] 2-18-1914. Evergreen Cemetery, Camden, Camden County.

Our Brothers Gone Before

ARROWSMITH, EDWIN Coal Heaver, U.S. Navy, USS New Ironsides, [Died at Salisbury, NC.] 1-2-1865. Rose Hill Cemetery, Matawan, Monmouth County.
ARROWSMITH*, GEORGE W. Lt Col, 157th NY Inf [Killed in action at Gettysburg, PA.] 7-1-1863. Fairview Cemetery, Fairview, Monmouth County.
ARROWSMITH, STEPHEN V. 1-17-1910. Fairview Cemetery, Fairview, Monmouth County.
ARROWSMITH, THOMAS A. Bvt Capt, E, 8th PA Cav, 2-11-1893. Fairview Cemetery, Fairview, Monmouth County.
ARTERBURN, ISAAC Pvt, U.S. Marine Corps, 2-22-1870. Methodist Cemetery, Haddonfield, Camden County.
ARTHER, F.M. Corp, H, 9th (Malone's) AL Cav (CSA), 8-17-1863. Finn's Point National Cemetery, Pennsville, Salem County.
ARTHUR, ELKANAH Pvt, B, 14th VA Inf (CSA), [Captured 7-3-1863 at Gettysburg, PA. Died of smallpox.] 12-13-1863. Finn's Point National Cemetery, Pennsville, Salem County.
ARTHUR, ISAIAH DoD Unknown. Mount Peace Cemetery, Lawnside, Camden County.
ARTHUR, JAMES H. 3-11-1922. Mount Peace Cemetery, Lawnside, Camden County.
ARTHUR, JOHN ANDREW Pvt, Btty A, 3rd PA Heavy Art, 1914. Baptist Cemetery, Burlington, Burlington County.
ARTHUR, MICHAEL Pvt, H, 2nd DC Inf, 10-19-1884. Fairmount Cemetery, Newark, Essex County.
ARTLOLAUF, PHILIP (see: Orthlouf, Philip) Evergreen Cemetery, Hillside, Union County.
ARUNDALE, MERRICK Pvt, C, 1st NJ Cav, [Killed in action at Deep Bottom, VA.] 8-14-1864. Mercer Cemetery, Trenton, Mercer County.
ARVINE, JAMES C. Pvt, H, 8th NJ Inf, 9-1-1878. Ramseyburg Cemetery, Ramseyburg, Warren County.
ASAY, AMBROSE E. Pvt, A, 23rd NJ Inf, 2-5-1926. Oddfellows Cemetery, Burlington, Burlington County.
ASAY*, GEORGE W. Pvt, E, 8th NJ Inf, 4-17-1895. Oddfellows Cemetery, Burlington, Burlington County.
ASAY, HENRY M. Pvt, A, 38th NJ Inf, 4-29-1905. Whitelawn Cemetery, Point Pleasant, Ocean County.
ASAY*, JACOB Pvt, E, 12th NJ Inf, 7-13-1911. Berlin Cemetery, Berlin, Camden County.
ASAY, JAMES JOHN Pvt, C, 29th NJ Inf, 3-8-1863. Old Baptist Cemetery, Freehold, Monmouth County.
ASAY, RIDGWAY S. Sgt, F, 1st NJ Cav, 2-23-1934. Mount Holly Cemetery, Mount Holly, Burlington County.
ASAY, WILLIAM Musc, B, 97th PA Inf, 4-19-1911. Baptist Church Cemetery, Blackwood, Camden County.
ASAY, WILLIAM H. Corp, D, 23rd NJ Inf, [Wounded 5-4-1863 at Banks Ford, VA.] 6-13-1931. United Methodist Church Cemetery, Jacobstown, Burlington County.
ASBELL, SYLVESTER Pvt, D, 5th NJ Inf, [Wounded in action at Chancellorsville, VA.] 4-1-1901. Laurel Grove Cemetery, Totowa, Passaic County.
ASBURY, LEMUEL (aka: Asbury, Samuel) Pvt, H, 19th U.S. CT, 1915. Riverview Cemetery, Trenton, Mercer County.
ASBURY, SAMUEL (see: Asbury, Lemuel) Riverview Cemetery, Trenton, Mercer County.
ASCHENBACH, FREDERICK L.H. Pvt, F, 13th NY Cav, 7-28-1912. Maplewood Cemetery, Freehold, Monmouth County.
ASH, CALEB Pvt, E, 5th MA Cav, 5-7-1921. Cedar Hill Cemetery, Hightstown, Mercer County.
ASH*, GEORGE W. Pvt, K, 9th NJ Inf, 6-1-1914. Arlington Cemetery, Kearny, Hudson County.

New Jersey Civil War Burials

ASH, JOSEPH VAIL Pvt, K, 1st NJ Militia, 8-7-1934. Clinton Cemetery, Irvington, Essex County.
ASH, SYLVESTER Pvt, B, 11th MD Inf, 5-3-1908. Evergreen Cemetery, Camden, Camden County.
ASH, SYLVESTER H. Pvt, I, 6th PA Cav, 4-11-1926. Wesley United Methodist Church Cemetery, Petersburg, Cape May County.
ASH, WILLIAM Pvt, G, 2nd NJ Cav, 1924. Siloam Cemetery, Vineland, Cumberland County.
ASHBACH, RUDOLPH (see: Assbach, Rudolph) Weehawken Cemetery, North Bergen, Hudson County.
ASHBACK, GEORGE H. Seaman, U.S. Navy, USS Portsmouth, 3-2-1914. Woodland Cemetery, Newark, Essex County.
ASHBROOK, ___?___ DoD Unknown. Baptist Church Cemetery, Haddonfield, Camden County.
ASHBROOK, JOSEPH J. Pvt, F, 12th NJ Inf, DoD Unknown. Methodist-Episcopal Cemetery, Mullica Hill, Gloucester County.
ASHBY, GEORGE 1st Sgt, H, 45th U.S. CT, [Last living Civil War Veteran from New Jersey.] 4-26-1946. Hamilton Cemetery, Allentown, Monmouth County.
ASHBY, GEORGE (see: Ashley, George) Greenwood Cemetery, Hamilton, Mercer County.
ASHBY, JAMES Pvt, B, 7th WV Inf, [Died of disease.] 10-19-1864. Beverly National Cemetery, Edgewater Park, Burlington County.
ASHCROFT, C.D. 1899. Presbyterian Cemetery, Salem, Salem County.
ASHCROFT*, JAMES Sgt, G, 38th NJ Inf, DoD Unknown. Union Cemetery, Frenchtown, Hunterdon County.
ASHCROFT, WILLIAM Pvt, G, 15th NJ Inf, [Wounded in action at Spotsylvania CH, VA.] 11-6-1922. Union Cemetery, Frenchtown, Hunterdon County.
ASHFIELD, JAMES Pvt, A, 70th NY Inf, 12-4-1907. Laurel Grove Cemetery, Totowa, Passaic County.
ASHLEY, GEORGE (aka: Ashby, George) 1st Sgt, H, 45th U.S. CT, 1-18-1915. Greenwood Cemetery, Hamilton, Mercer County.
ASHLEY, LEONARD H. 1st Lt, K, 23rd NJ Inf, 1911. St. Paul's Methodist Church Cemetery, Port Republic, Atlantic County.
ASHLEY, WILLIAM Pvt, K, 9th NJ Inf, 12-8-1872. Mount Pleasant Cemetery, Newark, Essex County.
ASHLEY, WILLIAM Pvt, K, 9th NJ Inf, 1-5-1870. Bloomfield Cemetery, Bloomfield, Essex County.
ASHMAN*, MATTHEW Pvt, G, 38th NJ Inf, 10-8-1888. Greenwood Cemetery, Hamilton, Mercer County.
ASHMORE, HENRY Corp, I, 14th NJ Inf, 6-12-1901. Riverview Cemetery, Trenton, Mercer County.
ASHMORE, HENRY J. 3-2-1878. Mercer Cemetery, Trenton, Mercer County.
ASHMORE, JABEZ Pvt, I, 14th NJ Inf, 10-1-1895. Riverview Cemetery, Trenton, Mercer County.
ASHMORE, JOHN Pvt, E, 5th NJ Inf, 1-3-1911. Riverview Cemetery, Trenton, Mercer County.
ASHTON, ENOCH W. Pvt, A, 3rd NJ Inf, DoD Unknown. Methodist Cemetery, Mantua, Gloucester County.
ASHTON, HENRY Corp, B, 3rd PA Cav, 10-26-1876. Calvary Baptist Church Cemetery, Ocean View, Cape May County.
ASHTON, JOHN S. 1-18-1881. Lodi Cemetery, Lodi, Bergen County.
ASHTON, JOHN SHERRINGTON Sgt, G, 23rd NJ Inf, 11-20-1864. Monument Cemetery, Edgewater Park, Burlington County.

Our Brothers Gone Before

ASHTON, THOMAS W. Corp, B, 82nd PA Inf, [Wounded in action.] 7-8-1911. Arlington Cemetery, Kearny, Hudson County.
ASHTON, WILLIAM W. Pvt, C, 40th NJ Inf, 10-14-1918. Mount Hope Presbyterian Cemetery, Lambertville, Hunterdon County.
ASHWORTH, JOHN 7-7-1913. Glendale Cemetery, Bloomfield, Essex County.
ASHWORTH, JOHN Sgt, C, 4th NJ Inf, 1-22-1898. Riverview Cemetery, Trenton, Mercer County.
ASHWORTH, THOMAS Pvt, K, 43rd GA Inf (CSA), [Died of disease.] 7-9-1863. Finn's Point National Cemetery, Pennsville, Salem County.
ASHWORTH, THOMAS Corp, C, 4th NJ Inf, [Killed in action at Gaines' Farm, VA.] 6-27-1862. Riverview Cemetery, Trenton, Mercer County.
ASPDEN, NICHOLAS (aka: Aspen, Nicholas) 1st Lt, K, 33rd NJ Inf, 1-18-1882. Fairmount Cemetery, Newark, Essex County.
ASPEN, NICHOLAS (see: Aspden, Nicholas) Fairmount Cemetery, Newark, Essex County.
ASPER*, JOSEPH E. Pvt, E, 5th OH Inf, 5-2-1919. East Ridgelawn Cemetery, Clifton, Passaic County.
ASPINAL, H.C. DoD Unknown. Pompton Reformed Church Cemetery, Pompton Lakes, Passaic County.
ASPINWALL, SUMNER D. Pvt, G, 2nd NJ Inf, 9-4-1912. Evergreen Cemetery, Hillside, Union County.
ASSBACH*, RUDOLPH (aka: Ashbach, Rudolph) Sgt, B, 58th NY Inf, [Wounded 6-8-1862 at Cross Keys, VA, 5-3-1863 at Chancellorsville, VA, and 7-1-1863 at Gettysburg, PA.] 1-8-1892. Weehawken Cemetery, North Bergen, Hudson County.
ASSMAN, ALBERT Pvt, C, 30th NJ Inf, 12-25-1902. Rahway Cemetery, Rahway, Union County.
ASTFALK, JOHN E. Eng, U.S. Navy, USS Miami, 9-17-1917. Arlington Cemetery, Kearny, Hudson County.
ASTLE, DAVID Corp, A, 31st NJ Inf, 3-22-1926. Chestnut Grove Cemetery, Elmer, Salem County.
ASTLEY*, ERNEST A. 1st Cl Seaman, U.S. Navy, 12-19-1925. Fairmount Cemetery, Newark, Essex County.
ASTLEY, WILLIAM Pvt, Btty B, 1st NJ Light Art, 6-23-1916. Fairmount Cemetery, Newark, Essex County.
ASTLEY, WILLIAM ANDREW Pvt, K, 1st NJ Militia, 7-18-1913. Fairmount Cemetery, Newark, Essex County.
ASTLEY, WILLIAM C. Artificer, F, 1st NY Eng, 5-5-1911. Fairmount Cemetery, Newark, Essex County.
ATCHINSON, ROBERT O. Pvt, A, 13th NJ Inf, 2-15-1906. Evergreen Cemetery, Hillside, Union County.
ATCHINSON, WALTER (aka: Atchison, Walter) Pvt, G, 95th NY Inf, DoD Unknown. Cedar Lawn Cemetery, Paterson, Passaic County.
ATCHISON, JAMES Corp, I, 2nd NJ Inf, 1899. Bayview-New York Bay Cemetery, Jersey City, Hudson County.
ATCHISON, WALTER (see: Atchinson, Walter) Cedar Lawn Cemetery, Paterson, Passaic County.
ATCHISON*, WILLIAM J. (JR.) Pvt, I, 2nd NJ Inf, [Wounded 8-26-1862 at 2nd Bull Run, VA.] 9-2-1914. Cedar Lawn Cemetery, Paterson, Passaic County.
ATHERTON, C.D. 7-11-1863. Laurel Grove Cemetery, Totowa, Passaic County.
ATKINS, ABRAM Pvt, D, 13th NJ Inf, 4- -1920. Locust Hill Cemetery, Dover, Morris County.
ATKINS*, ALFRED Capt, B, 98th NY Inf, [Wounded in action 6-27-1862 at Gaines' Mill, VA.] 10-18-1919. Evergreen Cemetery, Hillside, Union County.

New Jersey Civil War Burials

ATKINS, GEORGE Pvt, B, 38th NY Inf, 7-31-1903. Maple Grove Cemetery, Hackensack, Bergen County.

ATKINS, NICHOLAS Pvt, Unassigned, 33rd NJ Inf, 5-24-1904. Locust Hill Cemetery, Dover, Morris County.

ATKINS, THOMAS W.G. (aka: Aitken, Thomas) Pvt, I, 22nd NJ Inf, 6-22-1906. Arlington Cemetery, Kearny, Hudson County.

ATKINS, WILLIAM M. Pvt, K, 2nd DC Inf, 10-25-1915. Greenwood Cemetery, Boonton, Morris County.

ATKINSON*, ABRAHAM Pvt, I, 37th NJ Inf, 10-24-1907. Baptist/St. Andrew's Cemetery, Mount Holly, Burlington County.

ATKINSON, ALONZO Pvt, E, 2nd OH Inf, DoD Unknown. Friends Cemetery, Mullica Hill, Gloucester County.

ATKINSON, ANDREW H. Pvt, H, 10th NJ Inf, 3-3-1871. Bethesda Methodist-Episcopal Church Cemetery, Swedesboro, Gloucester County.

ATKINSON, BENJAMIN A. Pvt, D, 8th (Wade's) Confederate States Cav (CSA), 3-20-1864. Finn's Point National Cemetery, Pennsville, Salem County.

ATKINSON, BENJAMIN S. Pvt, B, 12th NJ Inf, 8-3-1875. Fairmount Cemetery, Newark, Essex County.

ATKINSON, CHARLES H. Corp, H, 12th NJ Inf, 9-29-1916. 1st Baptist Church Cemetery, Woodstown, Salem County.

ATKINSON, CHARLES P. Pvt, Btty F, 3rd PA Heavy Art, 10-26-1907. Methodist-Episcopal Cemetery, Olivet, Salem County.

ATKINSON, DAVID H. Pvt, H, 12th NJ Inf, [Wounded in action.] 11-23-1892. Cedar Green Cemetery, Clayton, Gloucester County.

ATKINSON, HOWARD D. DoD Unknown. Presbyterian Church Cemetery, Bridgeton, Cumberland County.

ATKINSON, J. Pvt, F, 8th NJ Inf, 6-4-1902. Rahway Cemetery, Rahway, Union County.

ATKINSON, JAMES C 1926. Brotherhood Cemetery, Hainesport, Burlington County.

ATKINSON*, JOHN Pvt, E, 198th PA Inf, 1-20-1897. Greenmount Cemetery, Hammonton, Atlantic County.

ATKINSON, JOHN C. Pvt, D, 24th NJ Inf, 4-22-1926. Chickory Chapel Baptist Church Cemetery, Elk, Gloucester County.

ATKINSON, JOSEPH A. Captains Clerk, U.S. Navy, USS Hendrick Hudson, 12-17-1924. Fairmount Cemetery, Newark, Essex County.

ATKINSON*, JOSEPH W. Pvt, H, 1st NJ Inf, 4-21-1888. Mount Holly Cemetery, Mount Holly, Burlington County.

ATKINSON, LEVI H. Pvt, I, 24th NJ Inf, 5-7-1895. Cedar Green Cemetery, Clayton, Gloucester County.

ATKINSON, PHINEAS Corp, G, 4th NJ Inf, 3-4-1921. Evergreen Cemetery, Camden, Camden County.

ATKINSON, ROBERT Pvt, D, 8th NJ Inf, 12-21-1883. Dutch Reformed Church Cemetery, Spotswood, Middlesex County.

ATKINSON*, ROBERT G. Pvt, G, 4th IA Inf, 7-11-1910. Free Burying Ground Cemetery, Alloway, Salem County.

ATKINSON, S.S. Pvt, H, 5th SC Inf (CSA), [Captured 5-12-1864 at Spotsylvania CH, VA. Died of lung inflammation.] 3-19-1865. Finn's Point National Cemetery, Pennsville, Salem County.

ATKINSON, SPAFFORD W. Pvt, H, 186th PA Inf, 3-6-1921. Beverly National Cemetery, Edgewater Park, Burlington County.

ATKINSON, STACY Pvt, I, 23rd NJ Inf, 3-18-1873. Baptist/St. Andrew's Cemetery, Mount Holly, Burlington County.

ATKINSON, STACY L. Pvt, D, 23rd NJ Inf, 12-26-1882. Bordentown/Old St. Mary's Catholic Cemetery, Bordentown, Burlington County.

Our Brothers Gone Before

ATKINSON, THOMAS A. Corp, E, 150th PA Inf, 9-7-1885. Zion Methodist Church Cemetery, Porchtown, Gloucester County.

ATKINSON, THOMAS B. DoD Unknown. Old Camden Cemetery, Camden, Camden County.

ATKINSON, WILLIAM H. Pvt, F, 3rd NJ Militia, 10-9-1927. Evergreen Cemetery, Farmingdale, Monmouth County.

ATKINSON*, WILLIAM L. Sgt, I, 29th NJ Inf, 6-11-1912. Rose Hill Cemetery, Matawan, Monmouth County.

ATNO, JOHN Pvt, K, 27th NJ Inf, 9-18-1912. Stanhope-Union Cemetery, Netcong, Morris County.

ATTENBOROUGH, SAMUEL Pvt, A, 25th NJ Inf, 10-7-1895. Fairmount Cemetery, Newark, Essex County.

ATTERSON, JOSEPH (see: Attison, Joseph W.) Riverside Cemetery, Toms River, Ocean County.

ATTISON, JOSEPH W. (aka: Atterson, Joseph) Pvt, D, 9th NJ Inf, [Died of wounds received at Roanoke Island, NC.] 5-1-1862. Riverside Cemetery, Toms River, Ocean County.

ATWATER, ELIAS Pvt, D, 29th NJ Inf, 4-18-1892. Bay View Cemetery, Leonardo, Monmouth County.

ATWOOD, JOHN HENRY Pvt, Ind Btty, Landis' PA Light Art, 2-23-1901. Phillipsburg Cemetery, Phillipsburg, Warren County.

AUBERTIN*, JOHN N. (aka: Oberton, John) Pvt, Btty E, 1st NJ Light Art, 3-23-1923. Woodland Cemetery, Newark, Essex County.

AUCH, JACOB (aka: Ouh, Jacob) Pvt, 13th NY Ind Btty 12-2-1908. Berry Lawn Cemetery, Carlstadt, Bergen County.

AUCH, JOHN (aka: Ouh, John) Pvt, 13th NY Ind Btty 7-4-1915. East Ridgelawn Cemetery, Clifton, Passaic County.

AUDE, CHARLES (see: Ande, Charles E.) Alpine Cemetery, Perth Amboy, Middlesex County.

AUER, AUGUSTUS F. Pvt, I, 39th NJ Inf, 2-22-1897. Fairmount Cemetery, Newark, Essex County.

AUER, HENRY Pvt, K, 34th NJ Inf, 4-17-1877. Evergreen Cemetery, Hillside, Union County.

AUGHEY, JOHN H. Chaplain, 6th IL Cav 7-30-1911. Newton Cemetery, Newton, Sussex County.

AUGUST, JOHN W. (aka: Arbogast, John) Pvt, A, 158th PA Inf, 12-11-1918. Riverview Cemetery, Trenton, Mercer County.

AUGUSTIN, BERNHARD Pvt, C, 54th NY Inf, 4-18-1893. Fairmount Cemetery, Newark, Essex County.

AULEB, HERMAN Pvt, E, 2nd U.S. Inf, 2-28-1918. Fairmount Cemetery, Newark, Essex County.

AULTER, GEORGE M. Pvt, F, 25th OH Inf, [Wounded in action at Camp Allegheny, WV.] 10-20-1878. Fairmount Cemetery, Newark, Essex County.

AUMACK, GEORGE Pvt, H, 38th NJ Inf, 1924. Methodist-Episcopal Cemetery, Lake, Gloucester County.

AUMACK, PETER J. Pvt, F, 29th NJ Inf, 1-14-1890. United Methodist Church Cemetery, Little Silver, Monmouth County.

AUMACK, RICHARD (JR.) Pvt, H, 38th NJ Inf, 1923. Union Cemetery, Clarkstown, Atlantic County.

AUMACK, SIDNEY Pvt, A, 29th NJ Inf, [Died of typhoid at Belle Plain, VA.] 4-8-1863. Old 1st Methodist Church Cemetery, West Long Branch, Monmouth County.

AUMACK, THOMAS BAILEY Pvt, C, 87th NY Inf, [Wounded 9-17-1862 at Antietam, MD. Died of diarrhea at Hazlet, NJ.] 10-13-1862. Aumack Family Cemetery, Hazlet, Monmouth County.

New Jersey Civil War Burials

AUMACK, WILLIAM 1st Lt, A, 29th NJ Inf, 4-16-1908. Greenlawn Cemetery, West Long Branch, Monmouth County.

AUMAN, LUCIEN Pvt, I, 53rd PA Inf, 10-4-1901. Fairview Cemetery, Wantage, Sussex County.

AUMICK, JOHN L. Pvt, II, 9th NJ Inf, 8-23-1889. Branchville Cemetery, Branchville, Sussex County.

AUMOCK, JOHN H. Pvt, I, 29th NJ Inf, 3-9-1905. Evergreen Cemetery, Farmingdale, Monmouth County.

AUSBACK, JOSEPH (aka: Amback, Joseph) Corp, F, 99th PA Inf, [Wounded 12-13-1862 at Fredericksburg, VA. and 4-6-1865 at Saylers Creek, VA.] 3-4-1882. Tabernacle Baptist Church Cemetery, Erma, Cape May County.

AUSBURN, ALBERT A. Sgt, D, 11th PA Inf, 12-3-1902. Evergreen Cemetery, Camden, Camden County.

AUSTEN, J.R. 5-25-1932. Eglington Cemetery, Clarksboro, Gloucester County.

AUSTERMUHL, CONRAD F. 11-29-1911. Evergreen Cemetery, Camden, Camden County.

AUSTIN, AMBROSE L. Sgt, L, 25th NY Cav, 1905. Valleau Cemetery, Ridgewood, Bergen County.

AUSTIN, BENJAMIN A. Corp, D, 4th NJ Inf, 6-28-1916. Coopertown Meeting House Cemetery, Edgewater Park, Burlington County.

AUSTIN, BESSEN J. 5-29-1905. United Methodist Church Cemetery, Little Silver, Monmouth County.

AUSTIN, CORNELIUS 1884. Atlantic City Cemetery, Pleasantville, Atlantic County.

AUSTIN*, EDWARD B. Pvt, C, 82nd NY Inf, 5-5-1922. Hillside Cemetery, Scotch Plains, Union County.

AUSTIN, JOHN H. Pvt, G, 4th NJ Inf, 12-28-1897. Greenwood Cemetery, Tuckerton, Ocean County.

AUSTIN, MATTHEW S. 2nd Lt, G, 5th NJ Inf, 1-13-1904. Mercer Cemetery, Trenton, Mercer County.

AUSTIN, SEVER Pvt, L, 2nd MN Inf, 10-9-1864. Beverly National Cemetery, Edgewater Park, Burlington County.

AUSTIN, WILLARD Capt, G, 7th CT Inf, [Wounded in action.] 2-21-1914. Vincent Methodist-Episcopal Cemetery, Nutley, Essex County.

AUSTIN, WILLIAM A. Corp, G, 23rd NJ Inf, 7-6-1913. Coopertown Meeting House Cemetery, Edgewater Park, Burlington County.

AUTEN, CORNELIUS W. Pvt, E, 30th NJ Inf, 1-6-1905. New Somerville Cemetery, Somerville, Somerset County.

AUTON, ALBERT (see: Orton, Albert) New Somerville Cemetery, Somerville, Somerset County.

AVERBECK, FERDINAND M. Pvt, K, 186th OH Inf, 3-26-1934. Baptist Church Cemetery, Cherryville, Hunterdon County.

AVERELL, SAMUEL F. Sgt, A, 7th MN Inf, 12-10-1917. Soldier's Home Cemetery, Vineland, Cumberland County.

AVERY, DAVID H. Landsman, U.S. Navy, USS Rhode Island, 4-14-1882. Methodist-Episcopal Cemetery, Burlington, Burlington County.

AVERY*, GEORGE B. Pvt, Btty D, 1st NJ Light Art, 12-10-1920. Hazelwood Cemetery, Rahway, Union County.

AVERY, JAMES Pvt, C, 7th NJ Inf, [Wounded in action.] 5-15-1891. Prospect Hill Cemetery, Caldwell, Essex County.

AVERY, JOHN W. 3-21-1863. Cedar Hill Cemetery, Hightstown, Mercer County.

AVERY, RICHARD H. Pvt, I, 2nd NJ Inf, 10-17-1900. Rahway Cemetery, Rahway, Union County.

AVERY, THOMAS Pvt, Btty D, 1st NJ Light Art, 5-7-1872. Hazelwood Cemetery, Rahway, Union County.

45

Our Brothers Gone Before

AVIS, HENRY M. Sgt, F, 12th NJ Inf, 5-20-1923. Eglington Cemetery, Clarksboro, Gloucester County.
AVIS, JEDEDIAH Pvt, ___, 109th PA Inf, 4-16-1862. Bethesda Methodist-Episcopal Church Cemetery, Swedesboro, Gloucester County.
AVIS, JOSEPH R. Landsman, U.S. Navy, USS Mondola, 11-13-1903. Lake Park Cemetery, Swedesboro, Gloucester County.
AVIS*, WILLIAM Pvt, F, 12th NJ Inf, 1926. Chestnut Grove Cemetery, Elmer, Salem County.
AVISON, JEREMIAH (see: Everson, Jeremiah) Hackensack Cemetery, Hackensack, Bergen County.
AVOY, JAMES (see: MacAvoy, James) Evergreen Cemetery, New Brunswick, Middlesex County.
AXTELL, CHARLES F. Corp, E, NJ National Guard, 12-12-1913. Evergreen Cemetery, Morristown, Morris County.
AXTELL, CYRUS L. Pvt, A, 26th NJ Inf, 5-8-1915. Evergreen Cemetery, Hillside, Union County.
AXTELL, EZRA S. Pvt, A, 26th NJ Inf, 2-2-1918. Fairmount Cemetery, Newark, Essex County.
AYARES, ENOS Pvt, A, 24th NJ Inf, 7-29-1913. Baptist Church Cemetery, Canton, Salem County.
AYARES, WILLIAM W. 8-29-1894. Baptist Church Cemetery, Canton, Salem County.
AYARS, DANIEL S. Pvt, A, 12th NJ Inf, 1-8-1899. 1st United Methodist Church Cemetery, Bridgeton, Cumberland County.
AYARS, EDGAR (aka: Ayars, Edward) Pvt, H, 24th NJ Inf, 5-27-1883. 1st United Methodist Church Cemetery, Bridgeton, Cumberland County.
AYARS, EDWARD (see: Ayars, Edgar) 1st United Methodist Church Cemetery, Bridgeton, Cumberland County.
AYARS, EPHRIAM R. Musc, H, 24th NJ Inf, 1919. Overlook Cemetery, Bridgeton, Cumberland County.
AYARS, JEREMIAH Corp, K, 1st DE Inf, [Wounded in action at Gettysburg, PA. and 5-5-1864 at Wilderness, VA.] 8-14-1867. Baptist Church Cemetery, Bridgeton, Cumberland County.
AYARS, JESSE B. DoD Unknown. 7th Day Baptist Church Cemetery, Shiloh, Cumberland County.
AYARS, JOHN C. 7-20-1893. St. Paul's United Methodist Church Cemetery, Paulsboro, Gloucester County.
AYARS, JOHN D. Corp, D, 10th NJ Inf, 7-13-1901. 7th Day Baptist Church Cemetery, Shiloh, Cumberland County.
AYARS*, JOSEPH A. Pvt, I, 12th NJ Inf, 12-15-1913. Baptist Church Cemetery, Canton, Salem County.
AYARS, RICHARD R. Pvt, H, 24th NJ Inf, 11-9-1916. Soldier's Home Cemetery, Vineland, Cumberland County.
AYARS, SAMUEL L. Pvt, H, 24th NJ Inf, 8-30-1887. 1st United Methodist Church Cemetery, Bridgeton, Cumberland County.
AYARS, THEOPHILUS P. Pvt, D, 10th NJ Inf, 1-31-1898. 7th Day Baptist Church Cemetery, Shiloh, Cumberland County.
AYDLOTTE, PETER (aka: Idley, Peter) Pvt, D, 30th U.S. CT, 7-20-1898. Atlantic City Cemetery, Pleasantville, Atlantic County.
AYERS, BENJAMIN S. Corp, F, 24th NJ Inf, DoD Unknown. Overlook Cemetery, Bridgeton, Cumberland County.
AYERS, CHARLES Corp, B, 23rd NJ Inf, 2-7-1896. Bordentown/Old St. Mary's Catholic Cemetery, Bordentown, Burlington County.
AYERS*, CLARK H. Pvt, E, 8th NJ Inf, DoD Unknown. Alpine Cemetery, Perth Amboy, Middlesex County.

New Jersey Civil War Burials

AYERS, DANIEL S. Pvt, A, 12th NJ Inf, 6-20-1893. Presbyterian Church Cemetery, Great Meadows, Warren County.
AYERS*, DAVID H. Capt, E, 7th NJ Inf, 7-31-1882. Fairmount Cemetery, Newark, Essex County.
AYERS, ELLIS F. (JR.) Pvt, F, 84th PA Inf, [Wounded 5-3-1863 at Chancellorsville, VA.] 10-27-1911. Presbyterian Church Cemetery, Metuchen, Middlesex County.
AYERS, ELLIS F. (SR.) 12-23-1890. Presbyterian Church Cemetery, Metuchen, Middlesex County.
AYERS, EVI B. (aka: Ayers, Levi) Pvt, H, 3rd NJ Cav, 1930. Clove Cemetery, Wantage, Sussex County.
AYERS, HENRY B. Pvt, A, 24th NJ Inf, 9-30-1915. Arlington Cemetery, Kearny, Hudson County.
AYERS, HENRY F. Pvt, K, 2nd NJ Cav, 1-2-1900. Presbyterian Church Cemetery, Metuchen, Middlesex County.
AYERS, ISAIAH Pvt, K, 29th NJ Inf, 4-4-1914. Evergreen Cemetery, Farmingdale, Monmouth County.
AYERS, JAMES Pvt, B, 23rd NJ Inf, 5-26-1899. Bordentown/Old St. Mary's Catholic Cemetery, Bordentown, Burlington County.
AYERS, JAMES E. Pvt, H, 31st NJ Inf, 1-21-1910. Union Cemetery, Washington, Morris County.
AYERS, JOHN W. Pvt, F, 2nd NJ Cav, 5-9-1909. Evergreen Cemetery, Camden, Camden County.
AYERS, LEVI (see: Ayers, Evi B.) Clove Cemetery, Wantage, Sussex County.
AYERS, LEVI ELWOOD 1st Lt, F, 6th NJ Inf, [Wounded 7-2-1863 at Gettysburg, PA.] 11-8-1900. Methodist Cemetery, Crosswicks, Burlington County.
AYERS, LEWIS 2nd Lt, B, 23rd NJ Inf, 2-9-1912. Bordentown/Old St. Mary's Catholic Cemetery, Bordentown, Burlington County.
AYERS, LOUIS H. Pvt, H, 30th NJ Inf, DoD Unknown. Presbyterian Cemetery, North Plainfield, Somerset County.
AYERS*, OLIVER C. Landsman, U.S. Navy, USS North Carolina, 10-18-1913. Fairview Cemetery, Fairview, Monmouth County.
AYERS, STEWART 1910. Union Cemetery, Washington, Morris County.
AYERS, THOMAS Seaman, U.S. Navy, USS Shawmut, 11-16-1926. Evergreen Cemetery, Camden, Camden County.
AYERS, W.T.F. 7-4-1896. New Somerville Cemetery, Somerville, Somerset County.
AYERS, WALTER B. Wagoner, F, 4th NJ Inf, 3-12-1893. Evergreen Cemetery, Camden, Camden County.
AYERS, WESLEY R. Sgt, I, 28th NJ Inf, 3-20-1916. St. Stephen's Cemetery, Millburn, Essex County.
AYERS, WILLIAM Pvt, A, 14th NJ Inf, 12-25-1884. Evergreen Cemetery, Farmingdale, Monmouth County.
AYERS, WILLIAM B. Pvt, C, 14th NJ Inf, 2-21-1908. Hillside Cemetery, Scotch Plains, Union County.
AYRES, DANIEL S. Pvt, A, 12th NJ Inf, DoD Unknown. Cedar Hill Cemetery, Hightstown, Mercer County.
AYRES, DAVID Seaman, U.S. Navy, USS Rhode Island, 8-15-1867. Presbyterian Church Cemetery, Basking Ridge, Somerset County.
AYRES, EZRA F. Pvt, Btty C, 1st U.S. Art, [Died at 10th Army Corps hospital of wounds received at Petersburg, VA.] 9-12-1864. Presbyterian Church Cemetery, New Providence, Union County.
AYRES, GEORGE W. Pvt, B, 124th PA Inf, 7-31-1917. United Methodist Church Cemetery, Alloway, Salem County.
AYRES, ISAAC Pvt, I, 8th NJ Inf, 7-6-1887. Lodi Cemetery, Lodi, Bergen County.

Our Brothers Gone Before

AYRES, JAMES B. Capt, B, 14th NY Cav, 1-25-1864. Presbyterian Church Cemetery, Woodbridge, Middlesex County.

AYRES, JAMES M. Capt, F, 22nd NJ Inf, 1919. Maplewood Cemetery, Freehold, Monmouth County.

AYRES, JOEL W. (JR.) Sgt, H, 104th NY Inf, 5-1-1917. United Methodist Church Cemetery, Little Silver, Monmouth County.

AYRES, JOHN H. Sgt, C, 37th NJ Inf, 11-22-1914. Bordentown/Old St. Mary's Catholic Cemetery, Bordentown, Burlington County.

AYRES, MARCELLUS Pvt, K, 35th NJ Inf, 9-21-1893. Riverview Cemetery, Trenton, Mercer County.

AYRES, NATHAN 5-16-1867. Evergreen Cemetery, Camden, Camden County.

AYRES, RICHMOND Corp, H, 23rd NJ Inf, DoD Unknown. Riverview Cemetery, Trenton, Mercer County.

AYRES, SAMUEL Pvt, H, 24th NJ Inf, 1-1-1896. Presbyterian Church Cemetery, Metuchen, Middlesex County.

AYRES, WILLIAM J. Wagoner, H, 30th NJ Inf, 12-18-1865. Baptist/Evergreen Methodist Cemetery, Plainfield, Union County.

AYRES*, WILLIAM S. Sgt, K, 12th NJ Inf, 1902. 7th Day Baptist Church Cemetery, Shiloh, Cumberland County.

BAADE, CHARLES Musc, 12th MO Inf 2-10-1885. Fairmount Cemetery, Newark, Essex County.

BABBITT, DAYTON L. Corp, E, PA Emerg NJ Militia, 11-3-1902. Evergreen Cemetery, Morristown, Morris County.

BABBITT, HAMPTON M. Pvt, H, 2nd NJ Inf, 1-9-1889. Evergreen Cemetery, Morristown, Morris County.

BABBITT, LEMUEL G. Corp, E, PA Emerg NJ Militia, 1-4-1878. Rosedale Cemetery, Orange, Essex County.

BABBITT, STEPHEN I. Pvt, B, 15th NJ Inf, 3-10-1883. Fairmount Cemetery, Newark, Essex County.

BABBITT, SYDNEY Pvt, G, 40th NJ Inf, 5-15-1889. Presbyterian Church Cemetery, Rockaway, Morris County.

BABCOCK, ANTHONY M. Pvt, E, 25th NJ Inf, 4-13-1892. Laurel Grove Cemetery, Totowa, Passaic County.

BABCOCK, BARTHOLOMEW Pvt, K, 15th NJ Inf, 12-10-1901. Holland Cemetery, Holland, Morris County.

BABCOCK, CHARLES Seaman, U.S. Navy, USS Galatea, 11-30-1891. Preakness Reformed Church Cemetery, Wayne, Passaic County.

BABCOCK, ELIHU L. (aka: Babcock, Elisha L.) Pvt, Btty A, 1st CT Heavy Art, 1882. Cedar Green Cemetery, Clayton, Gloucester County.

BABCOCK, ELISHA L. (see: Babcock, Elihu L.) Cedar Green Cemetery, Clayton, Gloucester County.

BABCOCK, FREDERICK Pvt, I, 2nd NJ Inf, DoD Unknown. Laurel Grove Cemetery, Totowa, Passaic County.

BABCOCK, GEORGE E. (aka: Lee, Edward) Sgt, D, 69th NY Inf, 5-11-1910. Laurel Grove Cemetery, Totowa, Passaic County.

BABCOCK, GEORGE W. Pvt, H, 22nd NJ Inf, 3-8-1884. Stanhope-Union Cemetery, Netcong, Morris County.

BABCOCK, GEORGE W. 1904. Midvale Cemetery, Midvale, Passaic County.

BABCOCK, ISAAC J. Pvt, B, 41st NY Inf, 1-9-1900. Fairmount Cemetery, Newark, Essex County.

BABCOCK, JACOB 3-11-1912. Methodist Church Cemetery, Liberty, Warren County.

BABCOCK, JAMES Pvt, G, 1st U.S. Hancock Corps, DoD Unknown. Evergreen Cemetery, Morristown, Morris County.

New Jersey Civil War Burials

BABCOCK*, JOHN G. Pvt, D, 2nd U.S. Cav, 5-26-1900. Deckertown-Union Cemetery, Papakating, Sussex County.

BABCOCK, JOSEPH W. 3-20-1909. Asbury United Methodist Church Cemetery, English Creek, Atlantic County.

BABCOCK, LEVI M. Pvt, E, 35th NJ Inf, [Cenotaph. Died of disease at Andersonville Prison, GA.] 8-18-1864. Methodist Church Cemetery, Liberty, Warren County.

BABCOCK, LUCIEN (see: Babcock, Lucius F.) Oak Hill Cemetery, Vineland, Cumberland County.

BABCOCK*, LUCIUS F. (aka: Babcock, Lucien) Corp, F, 10th MA Inf, [Also served in the U.S. Secret Service.] 4-27-1910. Oak Hill Cemetery, Vineland, Cumberland County.

BABCOCK, MATTHEW Pvt, B, 124th NY Inf, [Wounded 5-30-1864 at Totopotomoy Creek, VA.] 2-23-1881. Hardyston Cemetery, North Church, Sussex County.

BABCOCK*, MATTHIAS Pvt, G, 1st NJ Cav, 3-7-1922. New Presbyterian Cemetery, Hanover, Morris County.

BABCOCK, MINARD E. Pvt, E, 25th NJ Inf, 5-27-1884. Cuff Cemetery, Newfoundland, Morris County.

BABCOCK*, PAUL (JR.) Capt, U.S. Army, [Signal Corps, Army of the Cumberland.] 10-6-1903. Mount Hebron Cemetery, Montclair, Essex County.

BABCOCK, PETER P. Blacksmith, K, 1st NJ Cav, [Wounded in action.] 1-30-1918. Hardyston Cemetery, North Church, Sussex County.

BABCOCK, ROBERT M. Pvt, F, 33rd NJ Inf, DoD Unknown. Holy Sepulchre Cemetery, Totowa, Passaic County.

BABCOCK, WILLIAM Pvt, C, 124th NY Inf, 1-2-1902. Hardyston Cemetery, North Church, Sussex County.

BABCOCK, WILLIAM (see: Barcock, William O.) Presbyterian Church Cemetery, Sparta, Sussex County.

BABCOCK, WILLIAM C.V. Pvt, K, 2nd DC Inf, 3-13-1920. Evergreen Cemetery, Morristown, Morris County.

BABCOOK, WILLIAM DoD Unknown. Deckertown-Union Cemetery, Papakating, Sussex County.

BABER, JAMES R. Pvt, G, 3rd AL Cav (CSA), 10-12-1863. Finn's Point National Cemetery, Pennsville, Salem County.

BABEUF, RICHARD P. Pvt, A, 17th NY Vet Inf, 12-19-1917. Bayview-New York Bay Cemetery, Jersey City, Hudson County.

BABINGTON, FRANCIS ASBURY 6-22-1896. Bayview-New York Bay Cemetery, Jersey City, Hudson County.

BABRICK, ADAM Pvt, K, 26th NJ Inf, 9-21-1905. Fairmount Cemetery, Newark, Essex County.

BABSER, FREDERICK Pvt, I, 9th NJ Inf, 7-13-1875. Palisade Cemetery, North Bergen, Hudson County.

BABSON, BERRY Pvt, K, 20th NC Inf (CSA), [Wounded 7-1-1862 at Malvern Hill, VA. Captured 7-1-1863 at Gettysburg, PA.] 10-3-1863. Finn's Point National Cemetery, Pennsville, Salem County.

BACHELDER, S. KENNARD Pvt, D, 24th NJ Inf, 1-26-1889. Evergreen Cemetery, Camden, Camden County.

BACHELLER, JOHN COLLINS (aka: Batchelor, John) Pvt, G, 26th NJ Inf, 2-6-1928. Mount Pleasant Cemetery, Newark, Essex County.

BACHMAN, EDWARD A. Corp, A, 194th NY Inf, 1915. Oddfellows Cemetery, Burlington, Burlington County.

BACHMAN, JOHN Pvt, Btty E, 1st NJ Light Art, 12-31-1925. Mount Pleasant Cemetery, Newark, Essex County.

Our Brothers Gone Before

BACHOLAR, ZENO Pvt, I, 60th VA Inf (CSA), [Captured 3-2-1865 at Waynesboro, VA. Died of fever.] 6-20-1865. Finn's Point National Cemetery, Pennsville, Salem County.
BACHTOLD, JACOB (see: Bechtold, Jacob) Woodland Cemetery, Newark, Essex County.
BACHUS, CHARLES Pvt, H, 31st AL Inf (CSA), 6-15-1863. Finn's Point National Cemetery, Pennsville, Salem County.
BACIGALUPO, ALBERT (aka: Tecorney, Giuseppe) Pvt, D, 7th CT Inf, [Wounded 6-7-1864 at Bermuda Hundred, VA.] 5-16-1899. Holy Name Cemetery, Jersey City, Hudson County.
BACKER, DAVID A. 10-2-1919. Pompton Reformed Church Cemetery, Pompton Lakes, Passaic County.
BACKER, WILLIAM DoD Unknown. Evergreen Cemetery, Morristown, Morris County.
BACKSTER, JOHN C. 9-4-1895. Glenwood Cemetery, Glenwood, Sussex County.
BACKSTER II, JOHN HENRY Pvt, F, 27th NJ Inf, [Died of disease at Windmill Point, VA.] 1-27-1863. Glenwood Cemetery, Glenwood, Sussex County.
BACON, ANTHONY (see: Bickon, Anthony) Mercer Cemetery, Trenton, Mercer County.
BACON, CHARLES H. Pvt, F, 3rd NJ Inf, [Killed in action at Crampton's Pass, MD.] 9-14-1862. Presbyterian Church Cemetery, Bridgeton, Cumberland County.
BACON, CHARLES P. Pvt, G, 24th NJ Inf, 9-26-1924. Shinn GAR Post Cemetery, Port Norris, Cumberland County.
BACON, EDWIN F. (aka: Warren, Edwin F.) Sgt, K, 7th NH Inf, [Wounded 2-20-1864 at Olustee, FL. and 10-7-1864 at New Market Road, VA.] 4-5-1895. Evergreen Cemetery, Camden, Camden County.
BACON, GEORGE DoD Unknown. Old 1st Methodist Church Cemetery, West Long Branch, Monmouth County.
BACON, GEORGE GLAGDEN Pvt, D, 7th NJ Inf, 9-15-1876. Rosedale Cemetery, Orange, Essex County.
BACON, HENRY H. Pvt, B, 73rd PA Inf, DoD Unknown. Overlook Cemetery, Bridgeton, Cumberland County.
BACON, JOHN HENRY Pvt, U.S. Marine Corps, USS Lancaster, 8-25-1916. Soldier's Home Cemetery, Vineland, Cumberland County.
BACON, JOHN J. 2-13-1900. Evergreen Cemetery, Camden, Camden County.
BACON, LOTT Pvt, G, 24th NJ Inf, [Died of jaundice at Washington, DC.] 1-2-1863. 7th Day Baptist Church Cemetery, Shiloh, Cumberland County.
BACON, SMITH Corp, K, 10th NJ Inf, 9-28-1915. Overlook Cemetery, Bridgeton, Cumberland County.
BACORN, ABRAM Pvt, E, 39th NJ Inf, 11-6-1872. Fairmount Cemetery, Newark, Essex County.
BACORN*, WILLIAM (JR.) Pvt, Unassigned, 33rd NJ Inf, 12-25-1908. Fairmount Cemetery, Newark, Essex County.
BADDEN, JOHN Pvt, F, 24th NJ Inf, 12-1-1896. Union Bethel Cemetery, Erma, Cape May County.
BADENHAUSEN, EDMUND 10-5-1902. Hoboken Cemetery, North Bergen, Hudson County.
BADENHAUSER, H. Seaman, U.S. Navy, 5-5-1880. Rahway Cemetery, Rahway, Union County.
BADER, ALBERT Pvt, C, 10th CT Inf, 9-27-1909. Fairmount Cemetery, Newark, Essex County.
BADER, ANDREAS (see: Bader, Andrew) Fairmount Cemetery, Newark, Essex County.
BADER, ANDREW (aka: Bader, Andreas) Pvt, Btty K, 15th NY Heavy Art, 9-5-1911. Fairmount Cemetery, Newark, Essex County.
BADER, MAGNUS 1st Lt, C, 39th NY Inf, 8-31-1907. Hoboken Cemetery, North Bergen, Hudson County.

New Jersey Civil War Burials

BADGER, JOSEPH M. Pvt, I, 29th MA Inf, [Died of disease.] 6-3-1862. Methodist-Episcopal Cemetery, Mullica Hill, Gloucester County.
BADGLEY*, AMOS Pvt, I, 3rd NJ Inf, 5-14-1888. Methodist Church Cemetery, Springfield, Union County.
BADGLEY, EUGENE D. Wagoner, B, 30th NJ Inf, 1924. Presbyterian Church Cemetery, New Providence, Union County.
BADGLEY, NOAH Pvt, C, 30th NJ Inf, 4-18-1891. Fairmount Cemetery, Newark, Essex County.
BAECHNER, GEORGE M. 1904. Presbyterian Cemetery, Janvier, Gloucester County.
BAEHR, GEORGE Sgt, E, 20th NY Inf, 5-8-1879. Hoboken Cemetery, North Bergen, Hudson County.
BAER, FREDERICK Pvt, E, 29th NJ Inf, 8-15-1895. Old Brick Reformed Church Cemetery, Marlboro, Monmouth County.
BAEZNER, PHILIP (aka: Basenor, Philip) Pvt, I, 38th NJ Inf, 3-19-1906. Riverview Cemetery, Trenton, Mercer County.
BAGEAT, CAMILLE (see: Baquet, Camille) St. Mary's Episcopal Church Cemetery, Burlington, Burlington County.
BAGGETT, THOMAS C. Pvt, K, 38th AL Inf (CSA), 7-17-1863. Finn's Point National Cemetery, Pennsville, Salem County.
BAGGITT*, WILLIAM Pvt, K, 12th NJ Inf, 9-23-1901. St. Rose of Lima Cemetery, Freehold, Monmouth County.
BAGLEY*, GEORGE W. Pvt, D, 84th NY Inf, 9-19-1919. Evergreen Cemetery, Morristown, Morris County.
BAGLEY*, JOSIAH Pvt, I, 32nd NY Inf, 2-9-1893. English Neighborhood Reformed Church Cemetery, Ridgefield, Bergen County.
BAGLIN, JAMES Pvt, D, 139th NY Inf, 7-4-1918. St. Mary's Cemetery, Plainfield, Union County.
BAGNALL, JAMES Pvt, K, 25th NJ Inf, 2-10-1907. Jersey City Cemetery, Jersey City, Hudson County.
BAGNELL, ROBERT F. Sgt, E, 38th MA Inf, [Wounded 10-19-1864 at Cedar Creek, VA.] 6-26-1906. Oak Hill Cemetery, Vineland, Cumberland County.
BAGWELL, EUGENE (see: Boswell, Eugene) Soldier's Home Cemetery, Vineland, Cumberland County.
BAGWELL, GEORGE W.J. Pvt, F, 3rd U.S. CT, 2-1-1901. White Ridge Cemetery, Eatontown, Monmouth County.
BAGWELL, JOHN Pvt, E, 21st GA Inf (CSA), [Captured 5-10-1864 at Spotsylvania CH, VA. Died of lung inflammation.] 6-22-1864. Finn's Point National Cemetery, Pennsville, Salem County.
BAHNMULLER, CHARLES (see: Bomm, Charles H.) Fairmount Cemetery, Newark, Essex County.
BAHR, HERMAN DoD Unknown. Evergreen Cemetery, Morristown, Morris County.
BAIER, GEORGE GOTTLIEB Pvt, H, 27th PA Inf, 8-10-1904. Willow Grove Cemetery, New Brunswick, Middlesex County.
BAIERLE, PHILIP Pvt, F, 75th PA Inf, 1-21-1885. Fairmount Cemetery, Newark, Essex County.
BAILEY, ALEXANDER Pvt, A, 43rd U.S. CT, 10-6-1897. Presbyterian Cemetery, Woodbury, Gloucester County.
BAILEY, ALEXANDER (see: Baillie, Alexander F.) Baptist/St. Andrew's Cemetery, Mount Holly, Burlington County.
BAILEY, ALVIN M. Pvt, A, 147th PA Inf, 1884. Greenmount Cemetery, Hammonton, Atlantic County.
BAILEY, AUGUSTUS F. Pvt, B, 29th NJ Inf, 12-15-1889. Cedarwood Cemetery, Hazlet, Monmouth County.

Our Brothers Gone Before

BAILEY, CHARLES A. Pvt, D, 33rd NJ Inf, 12-18-1907. Bloomfield Cemetery, Bloomfield, Essex County.
BAILEY, CHARLES HOWELL 2nd Lt, Btty E, 14th NY Heavy Art, 1907. Bloomfield Cemetery, Bloomfield, Essex County.
BAILEY, COLUMBUS C. Pvt, B, 8th NJ Inf, 1-12-1927. Evergreen Cemetery, Hillside, Union County.
BAILEY*, CORNELIUS B. Corp, H, 1st NJ Cav, 10-9-1902. Elmwood Cemetery, New Brunswick, Middlesex County.
BAILEY*, DANIEL Capt, B, 123rd U.S. CT, 12-8-1923. Glenwood Cemetery, Glenwood, Sussex County.
BAILEY, DAVID S. Corp, F, 9th NJ Inf, 8-20-1902. Methodist Cemetery, Pennington, Mercer County.
BAILEY, EDWARD P. Pvt, B, 29th NJ Inf, 5-4-1873. Cedarwood Cemetery, Hazlet, Monmouth County.
BAILEY, ELIJAH Pvt, B, 29th NJ Inf, 2-3-1873. Cedarwood Cemetery, Hazlet, Monmouth County.
BAILEY, GARDINER (aka: Figotts, Gardiner) Sgt, B, 38th NY Inf, 2-18-1892. St. Peter's Cemetery, Perth Amboy, Middlesex County.
BAILEY, GEORGE W. Sgt, E, 24th NJ Inf, 1916. Eglington Cemetery, Clarksboro, Gloucester County.
BAILEY, HENRY 1st Sgt, F, 13th NY Militia, DoD Unknown. Arlington Cemetery, Kearny, Hudson County.
BAILEY, HENRY Pvt, F, 14th U.S. Inf, 10-18-1912. Arlington Cemetery, Kearny, Hudson County.
BAILEY, ISAAC P. Pvt, F, 9th NJ Inf, 1-24-1904. New Somerville Cemetery, Somerville, Somerset County.
BAILEY, JAMES Pvt, A, 7th NJ Inf, 4-19-1890. Methodist Church Cemetery, Haleyville, Cumberland County.
BAILEY, JAMES Pvt, E, 56th NY Inf, 6-6-1892. Laurel Grove Cemetery, Totowa, Passaic County.
BAILEY, JAMES Pvt, B, 4th (Russell's) AL Cav (CSA), 10-16-1863. Finn's Point National Cemetery, Pennsville, Salem County.
BAILEY*, JAMES W. Pvt, H, 60th GA Inf (CSA), [Wounded and captured 7-3-1863 at Gettysburg, PA. Died of typhoid.] 9-14-1863. Finn's Point National Cemetery, Pennsville, Salem County.
BAILEY, JEREMIAH S. Pvt, K, 22nd NJ Inf, 1921. Greengrove Cemetery, Keyport, Monmouth County.
BAILEY, JOHN Corp, I, 23rd NJ Inf, 1-7-1915. Mount Holly Cemetery, Mount Holly, Burlington County.
BAILEY, JOHN H. Pvt, K, 33rd NC Inf (CSA), [Captured 7-3-1863 at Gettysburg, PA. Died of diarrhea.] 11-17-1863. Finn's Point National Cemetery, Pennsville, Salem County.
BAILEY, JOHN H. Pvt, A, 3rd U.S. CT, 5-10-1894. Johnson Cemetery, Camden, Camden County.
BAILEY, JOSEPH B. Pvt, E, 24th NJ Inf, 5-1-1902. Evergreen Cemetery, Camden, Camden County.
BAILEY, LEVI Pvt, C, 38th NJ Inf, 12-6-1910. Shinn GAR Post Cemetery, Port Norris, Cumberland County.
BAILEY, LOGAN Corp, B, 29th NJ Inf, 3-6-1902. Cedarwood Cemetery, Hazlet, Monmouth County.
BAILEY, MATTHEW A. 1st Lt, I, 188th NY Inf, 1-1-1890. Edgewater Cemetery, Edgewater, Bergen County.
BAILEY, P.E. DoD Unknown. Riverside Cemetery, Toms River, Ocean County.

New Jersey Civil War Burials

BAILEY, RICHARD Pvt, D, 8th NJ Inf, DoD Unknown. Cedarwood Cemetery, Hazlet, Monmouth County.

BAILEY, SAMUEL C. Bvt Lt Col, 14th NJ Inf 2-28-1918. Riverside Cemetery, Toms River, Ocean County.

BAILEY, STEPHEN G. Pvt, G, 4th NJ Inf, 10-13-1882. Cedarwood Cemetery, Hazlet, Monmouth County.

BAILEY, SYLVESTER Pvt, E, 26th NJ Inf, 1-27-1915. Clinton Cemetery, Irvington, Essex County.

BAILEY, THOMAS Pvt, K, 10th NJ Inf, DoD Unknown. 1st United Methodist Church Cemetery, Bridgeton, Cumberland County.

BAILEY, THOMAS Pvt, A, 33rd NJ Inf, 2-14-1873. Holy Sepulchre Cemetery, East Orange, Essex County.

BAILEY, W. (see: Baley, William Henry) Methodist Church Cemetery, Stockholm, Sussex County.

BAILEY, WILLIAM 3-26-1865. Eglington Cemetery, Clarksboro, Gloucester County.

BAILEY, WILLIAM Pvt, D, 7th NJ Inf, 10-14-1892. Laurel Grove Cemetery, Totowa, Passaic County.

BAILEY, WILLIAM (see: Baily, William P.) Hillside Cemetery, Scotch Plains, Union County.

BAILEY, WILLIAM B. Pvt, C, 15th NJ Inf, 1928. Stanhope-Union Cemetery, Netcong, Morris County.

BAILEY, WILLIAM COOK Pvt, B, 29th NJ Inf, 7-26-1917. Cedarwood Cemetery, Hazlet, Monmouth County.

BAILEY, WILLIAM H. Pvt, A, 7th U.S. Hancock Corps, 12-31-1890. Eastview Cemetery, Salem, Salem County.

BAILEY, WILLIAM HENRY 2nd Lt, H, 22nd VA Inf (CSA), [Captured 9-19-1864 at Winchester, VA. Died of diarrhea. Wounded in action 1863.] 5-2-1865. Finn's Point National Cemetery, Pennsville, Salem County.

BAILIS, WILLIAM (aka: Baylis, Willis) Pvt, B, 29th CT Inf, 1897. White Ridge Cemetery, Eatontown, Monmouth County.

BAILLIE, ALEXANDER F. (aka: Bailey, Alexander) Pvt, A, 43rd U.S. CT, 1893. Baptist/St. Andrew's Cemetery, Mount Holly, Burlington County.

BAILY, WILLIAM P. (aka: Bailey, William) Lt Col, 2nd DE Inf [Wounded 12-13-1862 at Fredericksburg, VA.] 2-1-1873. Hillside Cemetery, Scotch Plains, Union County.

BAIN, JOHN Pvt, U.S. Marine Corps, 3-4-1905. Bayview-New York Bay Cemetery, Jersey City, Hudson County.

BAIN, PETER (see: Baines, Peter) Laurel Grove Cemetery, Totowa, Passaic County.

BAINES, PETER (aka: Bain, Peter) Pvt, A, 35th NJ Inf, 3-4-1890. Laurel Grove Cemetery, Totowa, Passaic County.

BAINTON, JOHN S. (SR.) Corp, F, 29th NJ Inf, 3-27-1914. Fairview Cemetery, Fairview, Monmouth County.

BAIR, JOHN H. Pvt, C, 186th PA Inf, 12-15-1920. Holcomb-Riverview Cemetery, Lambertville, Hunterdon County.

BAIRD*, ABRAHAM D. Sgt, E, 2nd NJ Inf, 8-8-1898. Flagtown Dutch Reformed Cemetery, Frankfort, Somerset County.

BAIRD, ARCHIBALD Pvt, H, 160th OH Inf, DoD Unknown. Evergreen/Bishop Jaynes Cemetery, Basking Ridge, Somerset County.

BAIRD, BARNEY M. (see: Baird, Luther M.) Evergreen Cemetery, Morristown, Morris County.

BAIRD, CHARLES H. Pvt, F, 127th U.S. CT, 1-21-1876. Princeton Cemetery, Princeton, Mercer County.

BAIRD, CHARLES W.V. Pvt, E, 22nd WI Inf, [Wounded in action at Resaca, GA.] 3-14-1906. Mount Prospect Cemetery, Neptune, Monmouth County.

Our Brothers Gone Before

BAIRD, DAVID Pvt, I, 27th NJ Inf, 1903. Manalapan Cemetery, Manalapan, Monmouth County.
BAIRD, DAVID SAMUEL Pvt, D, 28th NJ Inf, 10-6-1930. Elmwood Cemetery, New Brunswick, Middlesex County.
BAIRD, ISAAC Pvt, G, 1st NJ Inf, [Died of diarrhea at Six Mile Run, NJ.] 6-29-1862. Ten Mile Run Cemetery, Ten Mile Run, Somerset County.
BAIRD, JAMES Seaman, U.S. Navy, 12-26-1929. Elmwood Cemetery, New Brunswick, Middlesex County.
BAIRD, JAMES H. Sgt, B, 3rd NJ Cav, 1921. Old Brick Reformed Church Cemetery, Marlboro, Monmouth County.
BAIRD, JAMES O. 10-15-1886. Evergreen/Bishop Jaynes Cemetery, Basking Ridge, Somerset County.
BAIRD, JOHN Pvt, A, 9th NJ Inf, 2-20-1903. Fairmount Cemetery, Newark, Essex County.
BAIRD, JOHN 12-13-1925. Elmwood Cemetery, New Brunswick, Middlesex County.
BAIRD*, LUTHER M. (aka: Baird, Barney M.) Pvt, Btty H, 10th NY Heavy Art, 9-16-1904. Evergreen Cemetery, Morristown, Morris County.
BAIRD, SAMUEL (see: Bard, Samuel F.) Presbyterian Church Cemetery, Bridgeton, Cumberland County.
BAIRD, SYLVESTER (see: Byard, Sylvester) Laurel Grove Cemetery, Totowa, Passaic County.
BAIRD, WILLIAM G. Sgt, F, 13th AL Inf (CSA), [Captured 7-1-1863 at Gettysburg, PA.] 3-16-1864. Finn's Point National Cemetery, Pennsville, Salem County.
BAISDEN, JAMES (see: Basden, James) Finn's Point National Cemetery, Pennsville, Salem County.
BAISDER, Z. Pvt, D, 34th VA Cav (CSA), 8-7-1864. Finn's Point National Cemetery, Pennsville, Salem County.
BAISLER, WILLIAM H. Pvt, Btty D, 1st NJ Light Art, 1-3-1898. Elmwood Cemetery, New Brunswick, Middlesex County.
BAITON, RICHARD Pvt, B, 6th NJ Inf, [Died of typhoid at Bottom Bridge, VA.] 7-2-1862. Riverview Cemetery, Trenton, Mercer County.
BAIZICKS, GEORGE (see: Beesicks, George H.) Fairmount Cemetery, Newark, Essex County.
BAKELEY, STEWARD D. Pvt, F, 4th NJ Inf, DoD Unknown. New Camden Cemetery, Camden, Camden County.
BAKELY, GEORGE H. Pvt, H, 7th NJ Inf, 8-25-1907. Baptist Cemetery, Medford, Burlington County.
BAKELY, JESSE S. Pvt, C, 9th NJ Inf, 7-30-1903. Greenmount Cemetery, Hammonton, Atlantic County.
BAKELY*, MILES G. Corp, F, 4th NJ Inf, 5-29-1886. Cedar Grove Cemetery, Gloucester City, Camden County.
BAKER, AARON Pvt, G, 38th NJ Inf, 9-15-1874. Methodist Church Cemetery, Springfield, Union County.
BAKER, ABRAM P. Pvt, F, 1st MN Inf, 1909. Evergreen Cemetery, Hillside, Union County.
BAKER, BASSETT W. Pvt, E, 23rd NJ Inf, 6-19-1881. Baptist Cemetery, Burlington, Burlington County.
BAKER, CHARLES Pvt, D, 37th NJ Inf, 10-18-1885. Bayview-New York Bay Cemetery, Jersey City, Hudson County.
BAKER, CHARLES (aka: Boker, Charles) Pvt, I, 11th NJ Inf, [Wounded 6-16-1864 at Petersburg, VA.] 1-27-1892. Atlantic View Cemetery, Manasquan, Monmouth County.
BAKER, CHARLES Pvt, A, 1st NJ Inf, 12-11-1889. Mount Hope Presbyterian Cemetery, Lambertville, Hunterdon County.

New Jersey Civil War Burials

BAKER, CHARLES C. Sgt, I, 118th PA Inf, 2-15-1918. Arlington Cemetery, Kearny, Hudson County.
BAKER, CHARLES J. Pvt, K, 80th NY Inf, 4-23-1923. Arlington Cemetery, Kearny, Hudson County.
BAKER, CHARLES W. DoD Unknown. 1st Methodist-Episcopal Cemetery, New Brunswick, Middlesex County.
BAKER, CHAUNCEY Pvt, B, 89th NY Inf, 5-24-1908. Flower Hill Cemetery, North Bergen, Hudson County.
BAKER, CHRISTOPHER COLUMBUS Sgt, A, 47th NY Inf, [Wounded in action at Drury's Bluff, VA.] 11-23-1921. Hillside Cemetery, Fairfield, Essex County.
BAKER, CORNELIUS DoD Unknown. Reformed Church Cemetery, Wyckoff, Bergen County.
BAKER, CORNELIUS Pvt, D, 1st NJ Cav, [Died of spotted fever at Trenton, NJ.] 3-22-1864. Riverview Cemetery, Trenton, Mercer County.
BAKER, DAVID (see: Baker, William H.) Arlington Cemetery, Kearny, Hudson County.
BAKER, EDMUND (aka: Baker, Edward) Pvt, B, 99th NY Inf, [Wounded 5-1-1863 at South Quay Bridge, VA.] DoD Unknown. Hazelwood Cemetery, Rahway, Union County.
BAKER, EDWARD (see: Baker, Edmund) Hazelwood Cemetery, Rahway, Union County.
BAKER, EDWARD T. Pvt, G, 21st NJ Inf, 10-30-1882. Episcopal Cemetery, Waterford, Camden County.
BAKER, ELIJAH Pvt, A, 40th MS Inf (CSA), 6-30-1863. Finn's Point National Cemetery, Pennsville, Salem County.
BAKER, GEORGE Pvt, A, 1st NC Cav (CSA), [Captured at Jefferson, PA. Died of typhoid] 9-5-1863. Finn's Point National Cemetery, Pennsville, Salem County.
BAKER, GEORGE Pvt, I, 40th NJ Inf, 7-10-1875. Greenwood Cemetery, Boonton, Morris County.
BAKER, HENRY G. Musc, I, 13th NJ Inf, 3-6-1939. Fairmount Cemetery, Newark, Essex County.
BAKER*, HENRY MICHAEL Col, 88th NY Inf 11-8-1872. St. Peter's Cemetery, Jersey City, Hudson County.
BAKER, HENRY R. Pvt, B, 10th NJ Inf, 12-17-1908. Mount Pleasant Cemetery, Newark, Essex County.
BAKER, HERMAN J. Corp, B, 29th IL Inf, 12-8-1910. Evergreen Cemetery, Camden, Camden County.
BAKER, ISAAC COLLINS Pvt, B, 34th NJ Inf, 9-17-1906. Methodist Cemetery, Haddonfield, Camden County.
BAKER, JACOB W. Pvt, B, 31st NJ Inf, 1920. Mansfield/Washington Cemetery, Washington, Warren County.
BAKER, JEHU Pvt, K, 23rd NC Inf (CSA), [Wounded 5-3-1863 at Chancellorsville, VA. Captured 7-3-1863 at Gettysburg, PA.] 10-10-1863. Finn's Point National Cemetery, Pennsville, Salem County.
BAKER, JOHN Sgt, D, 3rd NJ Cav, 4-7-1919. Lodi Cemetery, Lodi, Bergen County.
BAKER, JOHN DoD Unknown. Old Camden Cemetery, Camden, Camden County.
BAKER, JOHN Pvt, E, 23rd OH Inf, 9-2-1917. Presbyterian Church Cemetery, Cold Spring, Cape May County.
BAKER, JOHN A. 2nd Cl Fireman, U.S. Navy, USS Princeton, 1922. Cedar Grove Cemetery, Gloucester City, Camden County.
BAKER*, JOHN C. Corp, H, 5th NY Vet Inf, 4-21-1874. Evergreen Cemetery, Hillside, Union County.
BAKER, JOHN C. Pvt, L, 1st NJ Cav, 12-26-1894. Mount Pleasant Cemetery, Newark, Essex County.
BAKER, JOHN F. Pvt, C, 24th NJ Inf, 5-22-1867. Baptist Cemetery, Salem, Salem County.

Our Brothers Gone Before

BAKER, JOHN H. Pvt, D, 12th NJ Inf, 11-30-1891. Evergreen Cemetery, Camden, Camden County.
BAKER, JOHN L. Pvt, G, 42nd VA Inf (CSA), [Captured 7-3-1863 at Gettysburg, PA. Died of smallpox.] 11-13-1863. Finn's Point National Cemetery, Pennsville, Salem County.
BAKER, JOHN THOMAS 5-16-1907. Hillside Cemetery, Scotch Plains, Union County.
BAKER, LEWIS F. Pvt, E, 34th NJ Inf, 2-25-1905. Riverview Cemetery, Trenton, Mercer County.
BAKER, LEWIS FREDERICK Asst Surg, 67th NY Inf 9-5-1864. Van Liew Cemetery, North Brunswick, Middlesex County.
BAKER, MILTON Pvt, F, 30th NJ Inf, 11-23-1907. Riverview Cemetery, Trenton, Mercer County.
BAKER, NICHOLAS Pvt, G, 5th NJ Inf, 9-7-1894. Rosedale Cemetery, Orange, Essex County.
BAKER, NICHOLAS Pvt, D, 28th NJ Inf, DoD Unknown. 1st Methodist-Episcopal Cemetery, New Brunswick, Middlesex County.
BAKER, PHILIP PONTIUS Pvt, D, 3rd NJ Cav, 8-14-1920. 1st Baptist Cemetery, Cape May Court House, Cape May County.
BAKER, R.M. Corp, C, 5th AR Inf (CSA), 7-31-1864. Finn's Point National Cemetery, Pennsville, Salem County.
BAKER, RALPH PRIESTLY 1st Lt, C, 1st NJ Inf, 10-18-1906. Evergreen Cemetery, Hillside, Union County.
BAKER, SAMUEL E. Pvt, C, 28th NJ Inf, [Died of typhoid at Newark, NJ.] 3-23-1863. Hazelwood Cemetery, Rahway, Union County.
BAKER, SAMUEL W. Seaman, U.S. Navy, 2-2-1920. Evergreen Cemetery, Hillside, Union County.
BAKER, W.A. Pvt, G, 46th AL Inf (CSA), 7-1-1863. Finn's Point National Cemetery, Pennsville, Salem County.
BAKER, WILLIAM A. 1911. Methodist Church Cemetery, Haleyville, Cumberland County.
BAKER*, WILLIAM A. (JR.) Pvt, F, 5th NJ Inf, 4-21-1885. Old Friends Cemetery, Salem, Salem County.
BAKER, WILLIAM H. (aka: Baker, David) Pvt, C, 17th NY Inf, 5-15-1912. Arlington Cemetery, Kearny, Hudson County.
BAKLEY, CHARLES Pvt, F, 4th NJ Inf, [Wounded in action.] 1919. Chew's United Methodist Church Cemetery, Glendora, Camden County.
BAKLEY, GAMALIEN D. Pvt, C, 12th NJ Inf, 8-6-1926. Fairmount Cemetery, Newark, Essex County.
BAKLEY, HENRY H. (aka: Beakley, Henry) Pvt, D, 25th NJ Inf, 11-4-1912. Methodist Church Cemetery, Hurffville, Gloucester County.
BAKLEY, JOHN Pvt, Btty B, 5th U.S. Art, 5-20-1872. Methodist Cemetery, Haddonfield, Camden County.
BAKLEY*, JOSEPH G. Pvt, F, 4th NJ Inf, [Died at Wilmington, DE.] 12-1-1863. Chew's United Methodist Church Cemetery, Glendora, Camden County.
BALBACH, ARTHUR Maj, 8th Bttn DC Inf 7-11-1868. Rosedale Cemetery, Orange, Essex County.
BALDIN, GEORGE (see: Boldin, George W.) AME Cemetery, Pennington, Mercer County.
BALDRIDGE, JOHN E. Corp, G, 50th NY Eng, 1913. New Somerville Cemetery, Somerville, Somerset County.
BALDWIN, ALEXANDER Wagoner, K, 2nd NJ Inf, 6-17-1914. Fairmount Cemetery, Newark, Essex County.
BALDWIN, ALFRED Corp, F, 28th NJ Inf, 3-13-1902. Fairmount Cemetery, Newark, Essex County.

New Jersey Civil War Burials

BALDWIN, ALFRED C. Pvt, A, 2nd MD Inf (ES), 1-14-1918. Brotherhood Cemetery, Hainesport, Burlington County.
BALDWIN, ALFRED M. Pvt, D, 26th NJ Inf, 4-24-1885. Fairmount Cemetery, Newark, Essex County.
BALDWIN, AMZI W. Sgt, E, 13th NJ Inf, 4-18-1929. Bloomfield Cemetery, Bloomfield, Essex County.
BALDWIN, BENJAMIN F. 5-25-1912. Bloomfield Cemetery, Bloomfield, Essex County.
BALDWIN, CHARLES S. Pvt, C, 39th NJ Inf, 2-22-1916. Prospect Hill Cemetery, Caldwell, Essex County.
BALDWIN, CHARLES WILLIAM (JR.) Pvt, G, 5th NY Inf, [Killed in action at 2nd Bull Run, VA.] 8-30-1862. Rosedale Cemetery, Orange, Essex County.
BALDWIN, CLOUD Sgt, F, 5th PA Cav, 1-10-1890. Methodist Cemetery, Haddonfield, Camden County.
BALDWIN, DANIEL W. Musc, D, 26th NJ Inf, 5-15-1910. Prospect Hill Cemetery, Caldwell, Essex County.
BALDWIN, DANIEL W. Pvt, E, 52nd NC Inf (CSA), [Captured 7-5-1863 at Gettysburg, PA. Died of disease.] 11-25-1863. Finn's Point National Cemetery, Pennsville, Salem County.
BALDWIN, DAVID (see: Kane, David) Fairmount Cemetery, Newark, Essex County.
BALDWIN, EDWARD 1st Sgt, 13th NY Ind Btty 4-19-1914. Hazelwood Cemetery, Rahway, Union County.
BALDWIN, EDWARD S. Capt, K, 27th NJ Inf, 2-1-1878. Bloomfield Cemetery, Bloomfield, Essex County.
BALDWIN, EZRA T. Pvt, C, 15th NJ Inf, 7-28-1899. Presbyterian Church Cemetery, Mendham, Morris County.
BALDWIN*, FREDERICK A. Pvt, K, 2nd NJ Inf, [Wounded 9-14-1862 at Crampton's Pass, MD.] 5-22-1891. Fairmount Cemetery, Newark, Essex County.
BALDWIN, GEORGE Corp, D, 26th NJ Inf, 3-20-1906. Prospect Hill Cemetery, Caldwell, Essex County.
BALDWIN, GEORGE E. Pvt, B, 84th NY Inf, [Died of wounds received 5-8-1864 at Piney Church, VA.] 6-12-1864. Bloomfield Cemetery, Bloomfield, Essex County.
BALDWIN*, GIBSON Pvt, A, 13th NJ Inf, 3-21-1864. Prospect Hill Cemetery, Caldwell, Essex County.
BALDWIN, GILSEN Pvt, E, 15th NJ Inf, 9-23-1888. Evergreen/Bishop Jaynes Cemetery, Basking Ridge, Somerset County.
BALDWIN, HARVEY Pvt, D, 26th NJ Inf, [Died of typhoid at Washington, DC.] 1-7-1863. Prospect Hill Cemetery, Caldwell, Essex County.
BALDWIN, HENRY D. Pvt, F, 8th NJ Inf, 6-2-1896. Presbyterian Cemetery, North Plainfield, Somerset County.
BALDWIN, HENRY MOORE 2nd Lt, Btty E, 5th U.S. Art, [Died at Winchester, VA. of wounds received 10-19-1864 at Cedar Creek, VA.] 11-8-1864. Bloomfield Cemetery, Bloomfield, Essex County.
BALDWIN, HORACE E. Sgt, E, 26th NJ Inf, [Wounded in action.] 10-24-1900. Evergreen Cemetery, Hillside, Union County.
BALDWIN, IRA Pvt, D, 26th NJ Inf, [Died of diarrhea at Newark, NJ.] 3-12-1863. Prospect Hill Cemetery, Caldwell, Essex County.
BALDWIN, JAMES S. 2nd Lt, C, 1st NY Eng, 2-17-1919. Arlington Cemetery, Kearny, Hudson County.
BALDWIN, JOHN Pvt, I, 14th NJ Inf, 5-28-1866. Mount Pleasant Cemetery, Newark, Essex County.
BALDWIN, JOHN 3-4-1891. Rosedale Cemetery, Orange, Essex County.
BALDWIN*, JOHN GABLE Pvt, G, 15th NY Cav, 8-15-1904. Laurel Grove Cemetery, Totowa, Passaic County.
BALDWIN, JOHN H. 10-11-1906. Mount Pleasant Cemetery, Newark, Essex County.

Our Brothers Gone Before

BALDWIN, JOHN HENRY 4-3-1894. Mount Pleasant Cemetery, Newark, Essex County.

BALDWIN, JOHN M. Com Sgt, 27th NJ Inf 2-9-1902. Evergreen Cemetery, Hillside, Union County.

BALDWIN, JOHN W. Pvt, Btty F, 5th NY Heavy Art, 12-13-1872. Clinton Cemetery, Irvington, Essex County.

BALDWIN, JONATHAN Pvt, Btty H, 5th U.S. Art, 7-11-1909. Evergreen Cemetery, Hillside, Union County.

BALDWIN, JOSEPH Seaman, U.S. Navy, 10-21-1890. Mount Pleasant Cemetery, Newark, Essex County.

BALDWIN, JOSEPH A. Pvt, F, 26th NJ Inf, 1912. Bloomfield Cemetery, Bloomfield, Essex County.

BALDWIN, JOSEPH C. 2nd Lt, G, 26th IL Inf, 5-2-1888. Union Cemetery, Washington, Morris County.

BALDWIN, JOSEPH CONDIT 2nd Lt, E, 11th NJ Inf, [Killed in action at Spotsylvania CH, VA.] 5-15-1864. Reformed Church Cemetery, Fairfield, Essex County.

BALDWIN, JOSEPH S. Pvt, A, 13th NJ Inf, 8-31-1881. Bloomfield Cemetery, Bloomfield, Essex County.

BALDWIN, JOSEPH S. Pvt, G, 13th NJ Inf, [Died of wounds received 5-3-1863 at Chancellorsville, VA.] 7-27-1863. Fairmount Cemetery, Newark, Essex County.

BALDWIN, JUSTIN H. Pvt, K, 26th NJ Inf, 4-9-1876. Rosedale Cemetery, Orange, Essex County.

BALDWIN, LEWIS B. Sgt, K, 2nd NJ Inf, DoD Unknown. Rosedale Cemetery, Orange, Essex County.

BALDWIN, LEWIS M. Pvt, G, 26th NJ Inf, 1-26-1902. 1st Presbyterian Church Cemetery, Orange, Essex County.

BALDWIN, MARCUS E. Musc, G, 26th NJ Inf, 7-5-1925. Fairmount Cemetery, Newark, Essex County.

BALDWIN, MARCUS F. Pvt, D, 26th NJ Inf, 2-19-1889. Prospect Hill Cemetery, Caldwell, Essex County.

BALDWIN, MILTON Contract Surgeon, U.S. Volunteers, 2-29-1892. Fairmount Cemetery, Newark, Essex County.

BALDWIN, MOSES Pvt, A, 3rd NJ Cav, 1-28-1883. Reformed Church Cemetery, Montville, Morris County.

BALDWIN, MOSES G. 6-17-1885. Mount Pleasant Cemetery, Newark, Essex County.

BALDWIN, NOAH O. Pvt, K, 39th NJ Inf, [Killed in action at Petersburg, VA.] 4-2-1865. Whitehall Cemetery, Towaco, Morris County.

BALDWIN, OSCAR A. 2-8-1908. Mount Pleasant Cemetery, Newark, Essex County.

BALDWIN, ROBERT Musc, M, 2nd NJ Cav, 6-11-1897. Mount Pleasant Cemetery, Newark, Essex County.

BALDWIN, ROBERT J. QM Sgt, B, 26th NJ Inf, 10-22-1906. Mount Pleasant Cemetery, Newark, Essex County.

BALDWIN*, SAMUEL H. Capt, F, 13th NJ Inf, 9-1-1893. Mount Pleasant Cemetery, Newark, Essex County.

BALDWIN, SAMUEL SEARS 1-5-1885. Bloomfield Cemetery, Bloomfield, Essex County.

BALDWIN, STEPHEN Y. Pvt, G, 27th NJ Inf, 11-17-1866. Whitehall Cemetery, Towaco, Morris County.

BALDWIN, THEODORE W. Pvt, H, 26th NJ Inf, 3-10-1923. Arlington Cemetery, Kearny, Hudson County.

BALDWIN, THOMAS J. QM Sgt, 8th NJ Inf 7-19-1884. Cedar Lawn Cemetery, Paterson, Passaic County.

BALDWIN, WILLIAM Pvt, C, 40th NJ Inf, DoD Unknown. Lady of Lourdes/Holy Sepulchre Cemetery, Hamilton, Mercer County.

New Jersey Civil War Burials

BALDWIN, WILLIAM BOLLES 4-10-1919. Mount Pleasant Cemetery, Newark, Essex County.

BALDWIN*, WILLIAM H. Coal Heaver, U.S. Navy, USS Princeton, 3-7-1911. Fairmount Cemetery, Newark, Essex County.

BALDWIN*, WILLIAM H. Pvt, 6th NY Ind Btty 10-10-1911. Princeton Cemetery, Princeton, Mercer County.

BALDWIN, WILLIAM H. 7-10-1925. Rosedale Cemetery, Orange, Essex County.

BALDWIN, WILLIAM J. 1877. Mount Pleasant Cemetery, Newark, Essex County.

BALDWIN, WILLIAM JAMES Pvt, 14th OH Ind Btty 2-21-1922. Bloomfield Cemetery, Bloomfield, Essex County.

BALDWIN, WILLIAM M. Corp, F, 26th NJ Inf, 12-21-1905. Bloomfield Cemetery, Bloomfield, Essex County.

BALDWIN, WILLIAM R. Corp, F, 28th NJ Inf, 10-10-1917. Hazelwood Cemetery, Rahway, Union County.

BALDWIN, WILLIAM R. Pvt, H, 26th NJ Inf, 2-16-1886. Prospect Hill Cemetery, Caldwell, Essex County.

BALDWIN, WILLIAM S. Pvt, I, 26th NJ Inf, 1-23-1882. Mount Pleasant Cemetery, Newark, Essex County.

BALEY, GEORGE (see: Daley, George) Mount Peace Cemetery, Lawnside, Camden County.

BALEY, WILLIAM HENRY (aka: Bailey, W.) Sgt, A, 2nd U.S. Cav, [Cenotaph. Died at Alexandria, VA. of wounds received at Aldie, VA.] 6-30-1863. Methodist Church Cemetery, Stockholm, Sussex County.

BALKENBERG, LEWIS (aka: Bergenbach, Lewis) Pvt, B, 31st NJ Inf, 3-26-1911. St. Rose of Lima Cemetery, Oxford, Warren County.

BALL, ABRAM Sgt, C, 7th NJ Inf, 7-21-1926. St. Teresa's Cemetery, Summit, Union County.

BALL, ABRAM S. Pvt, C, 13th NJ Inf, 6-13-1887. Fairmount Cemetery, Newark, Essex County.

BALL*, AMON G. Pvt, F, 15th NJ Inf, DoD Unknown. Stanhope-Union Cemetery, Netcong, Morris County.

BALL, CHARLES WESLEY 8-13-1915. Mount Pleasant Cemetery, Newark, Essex County.

BALL, DANIEL O. Pvt, Btty A, 4th U.S. Art, 9-8-1913. Riverview Cemetery, Trenton, Mercer County.

BALL, DAVID W. Pvt, E, 13th NJ Inf, 3-7-1913. South Orange Cemetery, South Orange, Essex County.

BALL, ELIAS HONUS Pvt, Walpoles Ind SC Cav (CSA) 1872. St. Mary's Episcopal Church Cemetery, Burlington, Burlington County.

BALL, GEORGE Pvt, M, 1st NJ Cav, 4-26-1886. Mosier Cemetery, Highland Lakes, Sussex County.

BALL, GEORGE B. Pvt, G, 40th PA Militia, 5-5-1892. Fairmount Cemetery, Newark, Essex County.

BALL, GEORGE DAYTON Pvt, D, 26th NJ Inf, 1872. Prospect Hill Cemetery, Caldwell, Essex County.

BALL*, GEORGE MURRAY Pvt, C, 39th NJ Inf, 10-18-1875. Evergreen Cemetery, Hillside, Union County.

BALL, HENRY J. Pvt, A, 9th NJ Inf, 10-24-1890. Holy Sepulchre Cemetery, East Orange, Essex County.

BALL, HENRY M. Corp, B, 7th NJ Inf, [Died of consumption at Falmouth, VA.] 2-15-1863. Presbyterian Church Cemetery, Hanover, Morris County.

BALL, ISAAC Pvt, K, 26th NJ Inf, 8-21-1903. Fairmount Cemetery, Newark, Essex County.

Our Brothers Gone Before

BALL, JARVIS Pvt, I, 1st NJ Cav, 4-20-1895. Fairmount Cemetery, Newark, Essex County.

BALL, JARVIS W. Pvt, G, 47th NY Inf, 4-21-1895. Fairmount Cemetery, Newark, Essex County.

BALL, JOHN DoD Unknown. South Orange Cemetery, South Orange, Essex County.

BALL, JOHN BALDWIN Pvt, I, 8th NJ Inf, 8-7-1917. Rosedale Cemetery, Orange, Essex County.

BALL, JOHN H. Pvt, A, 13th NJ Inf, 1-4-1895. Mount Pleasant Cemetery, Newark, Essex County.

BALL, JOHN H. Pvt, A, 26th NJ Inf, DoD Unknown. St. Peter's Cemetery, Jersey City, Hudson County.

BALL, L. 1914. Oak Hill Cemetery, Vineland, Cumberland County.

BALL, LORENZO F. Pvt, A, 26th NJ Inf, 10-2-1871. Clinton Cemetery, Irvington, Essex County.

BALL, PETER A. Pvt, H, 39th NJ Inf, 1-3-1907. Arlington Cemetery, Kearny, Hudson County.

BALL, ROBERT R. Pvt, H, 1st NY Cav, 1907. Rosedale Cemetery, Orange, Essex County.

BALL, SAMUEL M. Sgt, C, 1st NY Eng, 12-13-1898. Hillside Cemetery, Scotch Plains, Union County.

BALL, THOMAS F. Pvt, A, 26th NJ Inf, 9-8-1913. Mount Pleasant Cemetery, Newark, Essex County.

BALL, WILLIAM Pvt, D, 11th NJ Inf, 3-24-1896. Fairmount Cemetery, Newark, Essex County.

BALL, WILLIAM C. Corp, G, 26th NJ Inf, DoD Unknown. Hollywood Cemetery, Union, Union County.

BALL, WILLIAM M. Sgt, D, Cocke's AR Inf (CSA), [Captured 7-4-1863 at Helena, AR. Died of scurvy.] 8-7-1864. Finn's Point National Cemetery, Pennsville, Salem County.

BALL, WILLIAM M. Pvt, I, 2nd MS Inf (CSA), [Captured 7-1-1863 at Gettysburg, PA. Died of lung inflammation.] 2-27-1865. Finn's Point National Cemetery, Pennsville, Salem County.

BALL, WILLIAM T. Pvt, Btty F, 1st CT Heavy Art, 7-18-1896. Fairmount Cemetery, Newark, Essex County.

BALLARD, HENRY FENTON Pvt, E, 28th VA Inf (CSA), 11-30-1906. Rosedale Cemetery, Orange, Essex County.

BALLENGER, EDWARD (see: Ballinger, Edward) Methodist Cemetery, Mantua, Gloucester County.

BALLENGER, JACOB (see: Ballinger, Jacob) Methodist Cemetery, Mantua, Gloucester County.

BALLENTINE*, GEORGE F. Pvt, I, 33rd NJ Inf, 1877. Presbyterian Church Cemetery, Mendham, Morris County.

BALLENTINE, JOSEPH B. Corp, K, 7th U.S. Inf, 7-31-1896. Fairmount Cemetery, Newark, Essex County.

BALLENTINE, SAMUEL R. Pvt, B, 15th U.S. Inf, 8-8-1915. Presbyterian Church Cemetery, Mendham, Morris County.

BALLIET*, WILLIAM Pvt, Btty C, 5th U.S. Art, 10-16-1913. Union Cemetery, Milford, Hunterdon County.

BALLINGER*, CLEMENT E. Pvt, F, 34th NJ Inf, 12-6-1905. Baptist Church Cemetery, Alloway, Salem County.

BALLINGER, EDWARD (aka: Ballenger, Edward) Pvt, G, 28th NJ Inf, 6-3-1881. Methodist Cemetery, Mantua, Gloucester County.

BALLINGER, JACOB (aka: Ballenger, Jacob) Pvt, G, 28th NJ Inf, 2-12-1923. Methodist Cemetery, Mantua, Gloucester County.

New Jersey Civil War Burials

BALLOU, FRANCIS Pvt, D, 28th NJ Inf, 5-7-1882. Elmwood Cemetery, New Brunswick, Middlesex County.
BALLS, G.N. (see: Boals, C.M.) Finn's Point National Cemetery, Pennsville, Salem County.
BALM, JOHN Pvt, D, 215th PA Inf, 10-31-1900. Baptist/St. Andrew's Cemetery, Mount Holly, Burlington County.
BALMER, EDWARD Pvt, D, 3rd NJ Cav, DoD Unknown. Jersey City Cemetery, Jersey City, Hudson County.
BALZAU, CHARLES 1890. Harleigh Cemetery, Camden, Camden County.
BAMBER*, HENRY Corp, G, 94th NY Inf, DoD Unknown. Egg Harbor Cemetery, Egg Harbor, Atlantic County.
BAMFORD, EDWARD H. Pvt, D, 38th NJ Inf, 11-30-1900. Riverview Cemetery, Trenton, Mercer County.
BAMFORD, GEORGE H. Pvt, K, 38th NJ Inf, 9-18-1912. Greenwood Cemetery, Hamilton, Mercer County.
BAMFORD*, JAMES Corp, A, 5th NJ Inf, DoD Unknown. Mercer Cemetery, Trenton, Mercer County.
BAMFORD, JOHN QM, 3rd NJ Cav 3-2-1890. Evergreen Cemetery, Camden, Camden County.
BAMFORD, THOMAS W. Pvt, I, 70th NY Inf, 1918. Hancock Cemetery, Florham Park, Morris County.
BAMFORTH, WILLIAM Pvt, E, 23rd NJ Inf, 4-6-1909. Columbus Cemetery, Columbus, Burlington County.
BAMLE, GEORGE (see: Burlie, George) Fairmount Cemetery, Newark, Essex County.
BAMPER, THEODORE Corp, Btty B, 7th NY Heavy Art, 9-2-1923. Arlington Cemetery, Kearny, Hudson County.
BANCHERT, AUGUSTE (see: Bauschert, Auguste) Rosedale Cemetery, Orange, Essex County.
BANCROFT, ISAAC DoD Unknown. St. Stephen's Episcopal Church Cemetery, Beverly, Burlington County.
BANCROFT, JOHN MILTON 1st Lt, B, 4th MI Inf, 7-27-1918. Glendale Cemetery, Bloomfield, Essex County.
BANCROFT, WILLIAM C. 1907. Colestown Cemetery, Cherry Hill, Camden County.
BANDER, CHARLES F. Sgt, E, 2nd NJ Inf, 3-21-1885. Fairmount Cemetery, Newark, Essex County.
BANE, WILLIAM H. Pvt, I, 36th VA Inf (CSA), 6-23-1865. Finn's Point National Cemetery, Pennsville, Salem County.
BANER, GEORGE Pvt, G, 25th NJ Inf, 4-9-1904. Baptist Church Cemetery, Palermo, Cape May County.
BANER, JAMES E. Pvt, F, 9th NJ Inf, 9-30-1919. Eastview Cemetery, Salem, Salem County.
BANFIELD, JOHN Sgt, Btty B, 2nd NY Heavy Art, [Wounded 6-17-1864 at Petersburg, VA.] 3-23-1903. Fairmount Cemetery, Newark, Essex County.
BANGHART, JOHN S. Pvt, I, 31st NJ Inf, 4-15-1916. Methodist Church Cemetery, Buttzville, Warren County.
BANHAM, SAMUEL P. Corp, H, 84th NY Inf, 4-21-1884. Jersey City Cemetery, Jersey City, Hudson County.
BANISTER, COLUMBUS Pvt, E, 21st GA Inf (CSA), [Captured 5-10-1864 at Spotsylvania CH, VA.] 11-4-1864. Finn's Point National Cemetery, Pennsville, Salem County.
BANISTER, N. Pvt, B, 3rd Bttn KY Mounted Rifles (CSA), 11-2-1863. Finn's Point National Cemetery, Pennsville, Salem County.
BANKER, JOHN W. Pvt, H, 13th NJ Inf, 4-2-1884. Fairmount Cemetery, Newark, Essex County.

Our Brothers Gone Before

BANKER, ROBERT D. Pvt, G, 7th NJ Inf, 3-13-1887. Cedar Lawn Cemetery, Paterson, Passaic County.
BANKHEAD, W.C. 11-8-1872. St. Peter's Cemetery, Jersey City, Hudson County.
BANKS, ALEXANDER 1st Sgt, B, 1st U.S. CT, 6-23-1910. Masonic Cemetery, Springside, Burlington County.
BANKS, CHARLES Corp, Btty B, 1st NJ Light Art, 12-6-1911. Elmwood Cemetery, New Brunswick, Middlesex County.
BANKS, CHARLES Pvt, A, 24th NJ Inf, 10-17-1906. Baptist Church Cemetery, Slabtown, Salem County.
BANKS, CHARLES H. Sgt, E, 25th U.S. CT, 8-26-1927. Fairmount Cemetery, Newark, Essex County.
BANKS, CHARLES S. Pvt, A, 15th NJ Inf, DoD Unknown. Overlook Cemetery, Bridgeton, Cumberland County.
BANKS, GEORGE F. Pvt, H, 1st CA Inf, 5-31-1916. Fairmount Cemetery, Newark, Essex County.
BANKS, HENRY WARD Capt, A, 47th NY National Guard, 2-5-1905. Brookside Cemetery, Englewood, Bergen County.
BANKS, ISAIAH Seaman, U.S. Navy, 2-3-1911. Woodlane Graveyard Cemetery, Westampton, Burlington County.
BANKS, JAMES N. Pvt, B, 118th PA Inf, 5-16-1914. Presbyterian Church Cemetery, Bridgeton, Cumberland County.
BANKS, JOHN C. Landsman, U.S. Navy, USS Princeton, 2-13-1914. Riverview Cemetery, Trenton, Mercer County.
BANKS, JOSEPH Pvt, F, 5th NJ Inf, [Wounded in action.] 1-14-1916. Methodist Church Cemetery, Sharptown, Salem County.
BANKS, MOSES R. Pvt, A, 24th NJ Inf, 4-8-1908. Baptist Church Cemetery, Slabtown, Salem County.
BANKS, WILLIAM (aka: Brown, William) Sgt, G, 25th NY Cav, 3-21-1910. Holy Sepulchre Cemetery, East Orange, Essex County.
BANKSON, LEVI W. Pvt, E, 25th U.S. CT, 3-16-1909. Mount Zion Methodist Church Cemetery, Lawnside, Camden County.
BANNEN, CHARLES W. Pvt, G, 2nd NJ Inf, 5-13-1907. Fairmount Cemetery, Newark, Essex County.
BANNER, JAMES Pvt, D, 22nd NJ Inf, 11-20-1921. Boonton Cemetery, Boonton, Morris County.
BANNER, JOHN C. Pvt, D, 1st NJ Inf, 1930. Presbyterian Cemetery, Asbury, Warren County.
BANNER, JOHN W. Pvt, D, 57th NC Inf (CSA), [Captured 7-14-1863 at Hagerstown, MD. Died of pneumonia.] 8-10-1863. Finn's Point National Cemetery, Pennsville, Salem County.
BANNER, ROBERT Sgt, G, 4th NY Cav, 1-4-1896. Valleau Cemetery, Ridgewood, Bergen County.
BANNIGAN, AUGUSTUS Artificer, C, 1st NY Eng, 2-28-1922. Cedar Lawn Cemetery, Paterson, Passaic County.
BANNISTER, DEWITT Pvt, C, 39th NJ Inf, 9-2-1903. Rosedale Cemetery, Orange, Essex County.
BANNISTER*, WILLIAM H. Sgt, A, 6th NY Cav, 8-1-1905. Arlington Cemetery, Kearny, Hudson County.
BANNISTER, WILLIAM H. Sgt, C, 39th NJ Inf, 7-15-1873. Fairmount Cemetery, Newark, Essex County.
BANNON*, OWEN Pvt, F, 7th NJ Inf, 8-2-1886. St. John's Cemetery, Hamilton, Mercer County.
BANNON, WILLIAM Pvt, I, 33rd NJ Inf, 1-23-1883. Holy Sepulchre Cemetery, East Orange, Essex County.

New Jersey Civil War Burials

BANTA, AARON V. Pvt, D, 22nd NJ Inf, 8-11-1925. Valleau Cemetery, Ridgewood, Bergen County.
BANTA, ABRAHAM P. Pvt, D, 22nd NJ Inf, 2-2-1902. Old Hook Cemetery, Westwood, Bergen County.
BANTA, DANIEL 1st Lt, I, 66th NY Inf, [Wounded 7-2-1863 at Gettysburg, PA.] 11-22-1884. Hackensack Cemetery, Hackensack, Bergen County.
BANTA, ELLEN (WILLIAMS) Nurse, 1-23-1932. Valleau Cemetery, Ridgewood, Bergen County.
BANTA, HENRY H. Corp, A, 22nd NJ Inf, 7-16-1899. Fairmount Cemetery, Newark, Essex County.
BANTA, JOHN H. Pvt, I, 22nd NJ Inf, 5-14-1883. Old Hook Cemetery, Westwood, Bergen County.
BANTA, MATHIAS 1895. Maple Grove Cemetery, Hackensack, Bergen County.
BANTA, PETER Pvt, L, 25th NY Cav, 11-22-1917. Maple Grove Cemetery, Hackensack, Bergen County.
BANTA, THOMAS T. Pvt, B, 22nd NJ Inf, 8-9-1911. Ramapo Reformed Church Cemetery, Mahwah, Bergen County.
BANTA, WEST DoD Unknown. Old South Church Cemetery, Bergenfield, Bergen County.
BANTA, WILLIAM Pvt, C, 5th NY Inf, 1911. Ramapo Reformed Church Cemetery, Mahwah, Bergen County.
BANTA, WILLIAM B. Pvt, D, 33rd NJ Inf, DoD Unknown. Reformed Church Cemetery, Wyckoff, Bergen County.
BANTA, WILLIAM B. 12-22-1902. Mount Pleasant Cemetery, Newark, Essex County.
BANZHAF, THEODORE Sgt, E, 2nd NJ Inf, 1-14-1875. Fairmount Cemetery, Newark, Essex County.
BAPTIST, JAMES S. Pvt, I, 1st NJ Inf, [Wounded 6-27-1862 at Gaines' Farm, VA.] DoD Unknown. Grove Church Cemetery, North Bergen, Hudson County.
BAPTISTE, EDWARD Sgt, F, 1st U.S. Colored Cav, 1883. Fairmount Cemetery, Newark, Essex County.
BAQUET*, CAMILLE (aka: Bageat, Camille) 2nd Lt, A, 1st NJ Inf, 3-27-1880. St. Mary's Episcopal Church Cemetery, Burlington, Burlington County.
BAQUET, FRANCISCO H.M.A. Pvt, K, 4th NJ Militia, 7-8-1862. St. Mary's Episcopal Church Cemetery, Burlington, Burlington County.
BARBARIN, THOMAS 2-28-1877. St. Peter's Cemetery, Perth Amboy, Middlesex County.
BARBARY, JOHN M. Pvt, H, 37th VA Inf (CSA), [Wounded 5-8-1862 at McDowell, VA. Captured 5-12-1864 at Spotsylvania CH, VA.] 12-26-1864. Finn's Point National Cemetery, Pennsville, Salem County.
BARBER, ALFRED Pvt, D, 41st U.S. CT, 12-21-1929. Greenwood Cemetery, Lakewood, Ocean County.
BARBER, CHARLES S. 11-13-1862. Riverview Cemetery, Penns Grove, Salem County.
BARBER*, CHARLES W. Pvt, C, 9th NJ Inf, 12-30-1891. Riverview Cemetery, Trenton, Mercer County.
BARBER, DANIEL A. Corp, B, 10th NJ Inf, 5-5-1910. Soldier's Home Cemetery, Vineland, Cumberland County.
BARBER, DAVID R. Sgt, B, 14th NJ Inf, 3-30-1917. Riverview Cemetery, Trenton, Mercer County.
BARBER*, DAVID W. Pvt, K, 20th OH Inf, 1-13-1892. Siloam Cemetery, Vineland, Cumberland County.
BARBER, EDWARD G. Pvt, A, 3rd NJ Inf, 11-4-1886. Trinity Bible Church Cemetery, Glassboro, Gloucester County.
BARBER, ELI M. 1st Sgt, D, 10th CT Inf, [Wounded in action.] 5-12-1893. Presbyterian Cemetery, Springfield, Union County.

Our Brothers Gone Before

BARBER, ISAAC Pvt, C, 32nd IL Inf, 2-16-1917. Fairmount Cemetery, Newark, Essex County.
BARBER, JAMES Pvt, K, 8th NJ Inf, 4-3-1874. Fairmount Cemetery, Newark, Essex County.
BARBER, JEREMIAH P. Corp, B, 10th NJ Inf, 6-27-1902. Presbyterian Church Cemetery, Bridgeton, Cumberland County.
BARBER*, JOHN WELLING Pvt, B, 14th NJ Inf, 5-3-1910. Riverview Cemetery, Trenton, Mercer County.
BARBER, JONATHAN Pvt, B, 10th NJ Inf, 1-13-1891. United Methodist Church Cemetery, Port Elizabeth, Cumberland County.
BARBER, JULIUS F. Pvt, C, 51st GA Inf (CSA), [Died of brain congestion.] 8-12-1863. Finn's Point National Cemetery, Pennsville, Salem County.
BARBER, LUKE DoD Unknown. Anabaptist Cemetery, Franklin Boro, Sussex County.
BARBER, NATHANIEL A. Corp, G, 11th NJ Inf, 5-10-1910. Mount Holly Cemetery, Mount Holly, Burlington County.
BARBER, NICHOLAS P. Pvt, A, 12th NJ Inf, 6-14-1884. Pierce Cemetery, Almonessen, Gloucester County.
BARBER, PETER M. Corp, K, 28th NJ Inf, 3-16-1905. Rose Hill Cemetery, Matawan, Monmouth County.
BARBER, PHINEAS (see: VanSyckel, Phineas Barber) Princeton Cemetery, Princeton, Mercer County.
BARBER, R.A. Pvt, K, 14th AL Inf (CSA), 2-13-1865. Finn's Point National Cemetery, Pennsville, Salem County.
BARBER, RANSOM R. Pvt, C, 5th NC Inf (CSA), [Captured 7-1-1863 at Gettysburg, PA. Died of typhoid.] 10-31-1863. Finn's Point National Cemetery, Pennsville, Salem County.
BARBER, RENSLAER Pvt, E, 107th PA Inf, 11-21-1901. Union Cemetery, Gloucester City, Camden County.
BARBER, WILLIAM H. Corp, G, 23rd CT Inf, 7-23-1898. Barber's Burying Ground Cemetery, Dilts Corner, Hunterdon County.
BARBER, WILLIAM TAYLOR Corp, A, 15th NJ Inf, 4-19-1910. Prospect Hill Cemetery, Flemington, Hunterdon County.
BARBER, WILLIAM W. Pvt, E, 7th NJ Inf, 5-16-1884. Mercer Cemetery, Trenton, Mercer County.
BARBREE*, JOHN S. Pvt, I, 31st GA Inf (CSA), [Captured 7-3-1863 at Gettysburg, PA.] 9-19-1863. Finn's Point National Cemetery, Pennsville, Salem County.
BARCALOW, CULVER 6-1-1886. New Somerville Cemetery, Somerville, Somerset County.
BARCALOW, JOHN L. Sgt, A, 28th NJ Inf, 1909. Tennent Church Cemetery, Tennent, Monmouth County.
BARCALOW, JOHN S. Corp, K, 30th NJ Inf, DoD Unknown. Cedar Grove Cemetery, Middlebush, Somerset County.
BARCALOW, WILLIAM H. Pvt, K, 30th NJ Inf, 1875. Cedar Hill Cemetery, East Millstone, Somerset County.
BARCKLEY, ROBERT Fireman, U.S. Navy, 1884. Oddfellows Cemetery, Burlington, Burlington County.
BARCLAY, ALEXANDER (JR.) Asst Surg, 30th NJ Inf 6-18-1865. New Germantown Cemetery, Oldwick, Hunterdon County.
BARCLAY, JAMES 1st Lt, F, 24th NY Inf, 7-3-1896. Bayview-New York Bay Cemetery, Jersey City, Hudson County.
BARCLAY, JAMES C. Pvt, D, 149th PA Inf, [Wounded 2-7-1865 at Dabneys Mills, VA.] DoD Unknown. New Somerville Cemetery, Somerville, Somerset County.
BARCLAY, JOHN M. (JR.) Pvt, B, 1st NJ Inf, 9-24-1869. Mercer Cemetery, Trenton, Mercer County.

New Jersey Civil War Burials

BARCLAY, JOHN W. Pvt, D, 9th NJ Inf, 2-14-1906. Evergreen Cemetery, Camden, Camden County.

BARCLAY, MARK WILKS COLLET 2nd Lt, G, 121st PA Inf, [Killed in action at Fredericksburg, VA.] 12-13-1862. St. Mary's Episcopal Church Cemetery, Burlington, Burlington County.

BARCLAY, ROBERT J. Sgt, D, 3rd NJ Cav, 2-3-1893. Old Camden Cemetery, Camden, Camden County.

BARCLAY, THOMAS Pvt, K, 12th NY State Militia, 11-26-1883. Bayview-New York Bay Cemetery, Jersey City, Hudson County.

BARCLAY, THOMAS Pvt, Btty L, 4th U.S. Art, DoD Unknown. Arlington Cemetery, Kearny, Hudson County.

BARCO, JOSEPH P. 1st Lt, G, 9th FL Inf (CSA), [Captured 2-10-1864 at Baldwin, FL. Died of typhoid.] 7-29-1864. Finn's Point National Cemetery, Pennsville, Salem County.

BARCOCK, WILLIAM O. (aka: Babcock, William) Pvt, Btty I, 4th NY Heavy Art, 7-27-1911. Presbyterian Church Cemetery, Sparta, Sussex County.

BARD, SAMUEL F. (aka: Baird, Samuel) Pvt, B, 24th NJ Inf, 11-1-1931. Presbyterian Church Cemetery, Bridgeton, Cumberland County.

BARDELL, CONRAD (aka: Bordel, Conrad) Pvt, H, 96th PA Inf, [Died at Newark, NJ.] 10-8-1862. Fairmount Cemetery, Newark, Essex County.

BARDEN, WILLIAM R. Pvt, M, 1st NY Mounted Rifles, 1-17-1911. Clinton Cemetery, Irvington, Essex County.

BARDER, EDWARD 12-27-1861. 1st Methodist Church Cemetery, Williamstown, Gloucester County.

BARE, JOHN (see: Barry, John J.) Soldier's Home Cemetery, Vineland, Cumberland County.

BAREFOOT, J.B. Pvt, I, 55th NC Inf (CSA), [Wounded and captured 7-1-1863 at Gettysburg, PA.] 10-9-1863. Finn's Point National Cemetery, Pennsville, Salem County.

BAREFOOT, JOHN M. Pvt, A, 24th MS Inf (CSA), 10-24-1863. Finn's Point National Cemetery, Pennsville, Salem County.

BAREFORD, SAMUEL A. Ordinary Seaman, U.S. Navy, USS Princeton, 1911. Colestown Cemetery, Cherry Hill, Camden County.

BAREFORD, THOMAS B. Sgt, A, 10th NJ Inf, 5-24-1897. Harleigh Cemetery, Camden, Camden County.

BAREMORE, ENOS Pvt, G, 10th NJ Inf, 12-31-1906. Cedar Hill Cemetery, Hightstown, Mercer County.

BAREMORE, JAMES Pvt, G, 11th NJ Inf, 1914. Cedar Hill Cemetery, Hightstown, Mercer County.

BARFIELD, ALBERT (aka: Pound, Albert) Pvt, C, 24th U.S. CT, 1915. Whitelawn Cemetery, Point Pleasant, Ocean County.

BARFIELD, ROGERS Pvt, K, 25th GA Inf (CSA), [Captured 4-11-1862 at Fort Pulaski, GA. Died of pneumonia.] 7-15-1862. Finn's Point National Cemetery, Pennsville, Salem County.

BARGER, CHARLES D. Pvt, F, 183rd PA Inf, 3-27-1922. Evergreen Cemetery, Camden, Camden County.

BARICKLOW, NELSON Corp, A, 9th NJ Inf, 5-6-1894. Fairmount Cemetery, Newark, Essex County.

BARKALOW, CORNELIUS M. Corp, E, 29th NJ Inf, 6-2-1898. Maplewood Cemetery, Freehold, Monmouth County.

BARKALOW, CORNELIUS S. Bvt Maj, 14th NJ Inf 2-12-1866. Adelphia Cemetery, Adelphia, Monmouth County.

BARKALOW, GARRETT W. Pvt, E, 29th NJ Inf, 3-28-1907. Adelphia Cemetery, Adelphia, Monmouth County.

Our Brothers Gone Before

BARKALOW, MATHIAS A. Pvt, E, 29th NJ Inf, 2-28-1901. Adelphia Cemetery, Adelphia, Monmouth County.
BARKALOW, RICHARD 1907. Clinton Cemetery, Irvington, Essex County.
BARKALOW, WILLIAM H. 1862. Tennent Church Cemetery, Tennent, Monmouth County.
BARKER, B. Pvt, G, 12th (Green's) TN Cav (CSA), 7-21-1863. Finn's Point National Cemetery, Pennsville, Salem County.
BARKER, DAVID SANFORD 5-19-1901. Mount Hebron Cemetery, Montclair, Essex County.
BARKER, FRANK E. Pvt, G, 150th NY Inf, 8-22-1931. Grove Church Cemetery, North Bergen, Hudson County.
BARKER*, GEORGE V. Corp, H, 56th MA Inf, 5-20-1918. Arlington Cemetery, Kearny, Hudson County.
BARKER, J.W. Pvt, A, 5th KY Cav (CSA), 7-5-1864. Finn's Point National Cemetery, Pennsville, Salem County.
BARKER, JACOB 1899. Reformed Church Cemetery, Pluckemin, Somerset County.
BARKER, JOHN H. Pvt, E, 18th VA Inf (CSA), [Captured 7-3-1863 at Gettysburg, PA. Died of diarrhea.] 10-19-1863. Finn's Point National Cemetery, Pennsville, Salem County.
BARKER, JOHN T. Pvt, F, 6th AL Inf (CSA), [Captured at Gettysburg, PA.] 9-29-1863. Finn's Point National Cemetery, Pennsville, Salem County.
BARKER, JOSEPH (see: Carnall, Herbert) Greenwood Cemetery, Hamilton, Mercer County.
BARKER, RICHARD Pvt, E, 2nd NJ Cav, 9-15-1865. Cedar Hill Cemetery, Hightstown, Mercer County.
BARKER, SAMUEL E. Pvt, G, 12th NJ Inf, 2-21-1875. Lake Park Cemetery, Swedesboro, Gloucester County.
BARKER, SMITH W. Pvt, G, 2nd DC Inf, 3-12-1882. Mount Pleasant Cemetery, Newark, Essex County.
BARKER, THOMAS M. Pvt, G, 5th NJ Inf, 4-10-1891. Baptist Church Cemetery, Port Murray, Warren County.
BARKER, WILLIAM R. Pvt, B, 15th NJ Inf, 7-2-1901. Newton Cemetery, Newton, Sussex County.
BARKER, WILLIAM R. 12-31-1903. Presbyterian Church Cemetery, Newton, Sussex County.
BARKLEY, IRWIN (see: Irwin, Barclay F.) Berlin Cemetery, Berlin, Camden County.
BARKLEY, JOHN O'CONNOR Surg, U.S. Navy, 12-7-1865. St. Mary's Episcopal Church Cemetery, Burlington, Burlington County.
BARKLEY, JONATHAN 3-22-1903. Holcomb-Riverview Cemetery, Lambertville, Hunterdon County.
BARKMAN, JOHN C. Corp, B, 8th NJ Inf, 1939. German Valley Rural Cemetery, Naughright, Morris County.
BARKMAN, WILLIAM P. 6-28-1934. Peapack Reformed Church Cemetery, Gladstone, Somerset County.
BARKSDALE, ALBERT A. Sgt, D, 11th PA Inf, 12-3-1902. Evergreen Cemetery, Camden, Camden County.
BARLETT, JOSEPH (aka: Barnett, Joseph) Pvt, E, 5th NJ Inf, 5-18-1897. Fairmount Cemetery, Newark, Essex County.
BARLIS, WILLIAM (aka: Baylis, William) Pvt, B, 29th CT Inf, 3-13-1926. Fairmount Cemetery, Newark, Essex County.
BARLOW, ABRAHAM Pvt, A, 3rd PA Cav, DoD Unknown. East Ridgelawn Cemetery, Clifton, Passaic County.
BARLOW, ARABELLA WHARTON (GRIFFITH) Nurse, 7-27-1864. Old Somerville Cemetery, Somerville, Somerset County.

New Jersey Civil War Burials

BARLOW, JOHN S. Lt Col, 37th NJ Inf [Died of pulmonary consumption at City Point, VA.] 9-12-1864. Fairmount Cemetery, Newark, Essex County.

BARLOW*, THOMAS Pvt, C, 111th PA Inf, [Wounded in action 6-16-1864.] 6-1-1917. Siloam Cemetery, Vineland, Cumberland County.

BARLOW*, WILLIAM Pvt, L, 1st NY Eng, 2-3-1878. Weehawken Cemetery, North Bergen, Hudson County.

BARNABY*, LEVI Pvt, F, 8th NJ Inf, [Wounded 10-27-1864 at Boydton Plank Road, VA.] 3-3-1897. Green Cemetery, Woodbury, Gloucester County.

BARNARD, ALFRED T. Pvt, G, 2nd NJ Inf, [Wounded 9-14-1862 at Crampton's Pass, MD.] 5-4-1904. Fairmount Cemetery, Newark, Essex County.

BARNARD, CHARLES H. Pvt, D, 214th PA Inf, 10-24-1921. Cedar Grove Cemetery, Gloucester City, Camden County.

BARNARD, CHARLES S. 8-17-1916. Evergreen Cemetery, Camden, Camden County.

BARNARD, EDWARD DoD Unknown. Johnson Cemetery, Camden, Camden County.

BARNARD, EDWIN 1911. Vincent Methodist-Episcopal Cemetery, Nutley, Essex County.

BARNARD, GEORGE F. (see: Foerster, Bernhard) Grove Church Cemetery, North Bergen, Hudson County.

BARNARD, HENRY H. Corp, Btty E, 1st OH Light Art, 4-27-1880. St. Stephen's Cemetery, Millburn, Essex County.

BARNARD, JOSEPH P. Pvt, C, 37th NJ Inf, 10-19-1914. Mercer Cemetery, Trenton, Mercer County.

BARNARD, LEVI 1st Lt, G, 2nd NJ Cav, 12-19-1915. Mount Pleasant Cemetery, Newark, Essex County.

BARNARD, WILLIAM C. 2nd Lt, G, 3rd NJ Inf, [Killed in action at Williamsburg, VA. Aide-de-Camp to General Philip Kearny.] 5-5-1862. Evergreen Cemetery, Camden, Camden County.

BARNARD, WILLIAM H. Pvt, B, 23rd NJ Inf, 1-8-1900. Flower Hill Cemetery, North Bergen, Hudson County.

BARNER, JAMES (see: Barnes, James) Cedar Lawn Cemetery, Paterson, Passaic County.

BARNES, ALBERT 2nd Lt, H, 7th NJ Inf, 10-21-1865. Bethesda Methodist-Episcopal Church Cemetery, Swedesboro, Gloucester County.

BARNES, ALBERT H. 9-26-1891. Mount Pleasant Cemetery, Newark, Essex County.

BARNES*, ALEXANDER Pvt, C, 13th NJ Inf, 1-11-1882. Cedar Lawn Cemetery, Paterson, Passaic County.

BARNES, ALFRED Pvt, A, 20th U.S. CT, 4-17-1906. Bayview-New York Bay Cemetery, Jersey City, Hudson County.

BARNES, BENJAMIN H. Pvt, G, 11th NJ Inf, 1894. New Camden Cemetery, Camden, Camden County.

BARNES, CHARLES Corp, I, 43rd U.S. CT, 1-29-1897. Johnson Cemetery, Camden, Camden County.

BARNES, CHARLES W. Pvt, I, 95th NY Inf, 1-7-1909. Laurel Grove Cemetery, Totowa, Passaic County.

BARNES, E.J. Pvt, B, 23rd AL Inf (CSA), 8-6-1864. Finn's Point National Cemetery, Pennsville, Salem County.

BARNES, EDWARD H. Pvt, C, 4th WI Cav, [Died of disease at Baton Rouge, LA.] 5-8-1864. Newton Cemetery, Newton, Sussex County.

BARNES, EDWARD S. 1st Lt, D, 30th NJ Inf, [Died of fever at Aquia Creek, VA.] 12-29-1862. Baptist Church Cemetery, Port Murray, Warren County.

BARNES*, GEORGE Pvt, D, 2nd NJ Inf, 5-14-1885. Cedar Lawn Cemetery, Paterson, Passaic County.

BARNES, GEORGE DoD Unknown. Cedar Lawn Cemetery, Paterson, Passaic County.

BARNES*, GEORGE W. Pvt, Btty F, Hampton's Ind PA Art, DoD Unknown. Presbyterian Church Cemetery, Cold Spring, Cape May County.

Our Brothers Gone Before

BARNES, GEORGE W. Pvt, F, 4th NY Inf, 2-3-1902. Jersey City Cemetery, Jersey City, Hudson County.
BARNES*, GIDEON A. Pvt, C, 147th PA Inf, 1919. Presbyterian Cemetery, North Plainfield, Somerset County.
BARNES, H.J. Pvt, K, 2nd AR Inf (CSA), 2-12-1865. Finn's Point National Cemetery, Pennsville, Salem County.
BARNES, HENRY (aka: Barns, Henry) Pvt, A, 21st NJ Inf, 4-16-1906. Bayview-New York Bay Cemetery, Jersey City, Hudson County.
BARNES, HENRY S. Sgt, B, 4th MI Inf, [Wounded in action at Hatchers Run, VA.] 9-24-1919. Rahway Cemetery, Rahway, Union County.
BARNES*, HORACE E. Pvt, E, 120th NY Inf, 3-2-1903. Eglington Cemetery, Clarksboro, Gloucester County.
BARNES, J. MORGAN QM Sgt, 12th NJ Inf DoD Unknown. Bethesda Methodist-Episcopal Church Cemetery, Swedesboro, Gloucester County.
BARNES, JACOB H. Pvt, C, 5th NC Inf (CSA), [Wounded and captured 7-1-1863 at Gettysburg, PA. Died of rubella.] 8-25-1863. Finn's Point National Cemetery, Pennsville, Salem County.
BARNES, JAMES (aka: Barner, James) Pvt, F, 72nd NY Inf, [Wounded 7-1-1862 at Malvern Hill, VA.] 2-5-1907. Cedar Lawn Cemetery, Paterson, Passaic County.
BARNES, JOHN EDWARD Pvt, U.S. Marine Corps, 10-14-1938. Fairview Cemetery, Fairview, Bergen County.
BARNES, JOHN J. Pvt, D, 82nd PA Inf, [Wounded 6-1-1864 at Cold Harbor, VA.] 1930. Oddfellows Cemetery, Burlington, Burlington County.
BARNES*, JONATHAN Pvt, E, 8th NJ Inf, 8-11-1908. Riverside Cemetery, Riverside, Burlington County.
BARNES, JOSHUA Pvt, Unassigned, 71st NY State Militia, DoD Unknown. Arlington Cemetery, Kearny, Hudson County.
BARNES, PETER H. Pvt, D, 1st NJ Inf, 7-12-1895. Fairmount Cemetery, Newark, Essex County.
BARNES, RICHARD Corp, H, 12th NJ Inf, 1899. Methodist Church Cemetery, Aldine, Salem County.
BARNES, SAMUEL Pvt, H, 38th NJ Inf, 8-28-1893. Asbury Methodist-Episcopal Church Cemetery, Swainton, Cape May County.
BARNES, SAMUEL Pvt, G, 25th NJ Inf, 8-27-1892. Methodist Cemetery, Weymouth, Atlantic County.
BARNES, SAMUEL F. Pvt, D, 38th NJ Inf, DoD Unknown. Overlook Cemetery, Bridgeton, Cumberland County.
BARNES, SAMUEL G. Sgt, Btty E, 5th NY Heavy Art, 1-18-1933. Fairmount Cemetery, Newark, Essex County.
BARNES, STEPHEN Artificer, K, 1st NY Eng, 12-13-1926. Laurel Grove Cemetery, Totowa, Passaic County.
BARNES, THOMAS (see: Barron, Thomas) Finn's Point National Cemetery, Pennsville, Salem County.
BARNES, WHITFIELD E. Pvt, I, 21st PA Cav, DoD Unknown. Ramseyburg Cemetery, Ramseyburg, Warren County.
BARNES, WILLIAM 11-23-1872. Evergreen Cemetery, Camden, Camden County.
BARNES, WILLIAM Pvt, B, 12th NJ Inf, DoD Unknown. Methodist Cemetery, Weymouth, Atlantic County.
BARNES, WILLIAM M. Pvt, H, 24th NJ Inf, 3-23-1897. Cedar Green Cemetery, Clayton, Gloucester County.
BARNES, WILLIAM R. Corp, F, 2nd FL Inf (CSA), [Wounded 6-26-1862 at Ellison's Mills, VA. Captured 7-5-1863 at Gettysburg, PA. Died of smallpox.] 12-9-1863. Finn's Point National Cemetery, Pennsville, Salem County.

New Jersey Civil War Burials

BARNETT, C.A. Pvt, E, 1st (Butler's) KY Cav (CSA), 12-25-1864. Finn's Point National Cemetery, Pennsville, Salem County.
BARNETT, FURMAN Pvt, F, 25th NJ Inf, 12-16-1922. Presbyterian Church Cemetery, Cold Spring, Cape May County.
BARNETT, GEORGE Pvt, D, 11th NJ Inf, 12-15-1865. Presbyterian Church Cemetery, Caldwell, Essex County.
BARNETT, GEORGE S. Pvt, K, 24th NJ Inf, 10-21-1899. Church of Christ Cemetery, Fairton, Cumberland County.
BARNETT, JAMES W. Pvt, E, 27th AL Inf (CSA), 6-13-1863. Finn's Point National Cemetery, Pennsville, Salem County.
BARNETT, JOHN S. Sgt, F, 3rd NJ Cav, 9-2-1897. Phillipsburg Cemetery, Phillipsburg, Warren County.
BARNETT, JOSEPH Pvt, E, 5th NJ Inf, 5-18-1897. Fairmount Cemetery, Newark, Essex County.
BARNETT, JOSEPH (see: Barlett, Joseph) Fairmount Cemetery, Newark, Essex County.
BARNETT, MORRIS Pvt, F, 116th NY Inf, [Wounded 9-19-1864 at Winchester, VA.] 10-14-1913. Mount Nebo Cemetery, Totowa, Passaic County.
BARNETT, THOMAS Pvt, K, 10th NJ Inf, DoD Unknown. Presbyterian Church Cemetery, Bridgeton, Cumberland County.
BARNETT, WILLIAM (see: Morton, William B. (Sr.)) Harleigh Cemetery, Camden, Camden County.
BARNETT, WILLIAM (see: Burnett, William H.) Tranquility Cemetery, Tranquility, Sussex County.
BARNETT, WILLIAM H. Pvt, B, 15th NJ Inf, [Cenotaph. Died of wounds received 6-2-1864 at Cold Harbor, VA.] 7-15-1864. Presbyterian Church Cemetery, Bridgeton, Cumberland County.
BARNEY, MARTIN M. Pvt, Btty K, 2nd PA Heavy Art, 3-20-1931. Evergreen Cemetery, Camden, Camden County.
BARNEY, WILLIAM D. Pvt, D, 4th GA Inf (CSA), 9-14-1864. Finn's Point National Cemetery, Pennsville, Salem County.
BARNHART, HENRY Pvt, H, 61st NY Inf, 4-29-1921. Greenwood Cemetery, Hamilton, Mercer County.
BARNHART, WILLIAM H. Musc, E, 1st NJ Cav, 3-7-1904. New Camden Cemetery, Camden, Camden County.
BARNHART, WILLIAM M. Corp, D, 34th NC Inf (CSA), [Captured 7-3-1863 at Gettysburg, PA. Died of diarrhea.] 9-1-1863. Finn's Point National Cemetery, Pennsville, Salem County.
BARNS, HENRY (see: Barnes, Henry) Bayview-New York Bay Cemetery, Jersey City, Hudson County.
BARR, CHARLES Pvt, I, 22nd NJ Inf, 8-3-1923. Brookside Cemetery, Englewood, Bergen County.
BARR, JOHN Landsman, U.S. Navy, USS Sabine, DoD Unknown. Mount Carmel Cemetery, West Moorestown, Burlington County.
BARR, THOMAS S. Pvt, H, 13th MS Inf (CSA), 12-28-1863. Finn's Point National Cemetery, Pennsville, Salem County.
BARR, WILLIAM M. Pvt, B, 192nd PA Inf, 4-5-1922. Holy Sepulchre Cemetery, Totowa, Passaic County.
BARR, WILLIAM T. Pvt, B, 5th FL Inf (CSA), [Captured 6-7-1862 at Fair Oaks, VA. Died of disease.] 10-24-1862. Finn's Point National Cemetery, Pennsville, Salem County.
BARRACKS, SAMUEL Pvt, E, 10th CT Inf, 4-1-1892. United Presbyterian Church Cemetery, Perrineville, Monmouth County.
BARRACLIFF, BENJAMIN F. Pvt, H, 3rd NJ Cav, DoD Unknown. Presbyterian Church Cemetery, Bridgeton, Cumberland County.

Our Brothers Gone Before

BARRACLIFF, THOMAS M. Pvt, G, 24th NJ Inf, DoD Unknown. Presbyterian Church Cemetery, Upper Deerfield, Cumberland County.
BARRASS*, EDWARD Pvt, B, 38th NJ Inf, 8-27-1905. Union Cemetery, Clinton, Hunterdon County.
BARRASS, EDWARD J. Landsman, U.S. Navy, USS Princeton, 8-26-1913. New Somerville Cemetery, Somerville, Somerset County.
BARRASS, THOMAS Pvt, E, 31st NJ Inf, 4-3-1900. Presbyterian Church Cemetery, Hampton, Hunterdon County.
BARRATT, GEORGE Pvt, C, 206th PA Inf, 1932. Colestown Cemetery, Cherry Hill, Camden County.
BARRETT, EDWARD Sgt, B, 33rd NJ Inf, 2-7-1890. Fairmount Cemetery, Newark, Essex County.
BARRETT, EDWARD Fireman, U.S. Navy, USS Reliance, 5-27-1903. St. John's Evangelical Church Cemetery, Orange, Essex County.
BARRETT, GEORGE P. 3-4-1904. Fairview Cemetery, Westfield, Union County.
BARRETT*, JAMES F. Pvt, H, 2nd NJ Inf, 3-21-1910. Holy Sepulchre Cemetery, East Orange, Essex County.
BARRETT, JOHN Pvt, E, 71st NY Inf, 10-3-1863. St. John's Evangelical Church Cemetery, Orange, Essex County.
BARRETT, JOHN J. Pvt, A, 190th NY Inf, 4-4-1937. St. Peter's Church Cemetery, Belleville, Essex County.
BARRETT, JOHN L. Pvt, D, 3rd AR Inf (CSA), [Captured 7-2-1863 at Gettysburg, PA. Died of measles.] 8-23-1863. Finn's Point National Cemetery, Pennsville, Salem County.
BARRETT, REUBEN F. Pvt, F, 3rd NJ Inf, 1885. 7th Day Baptist Church Cemetery, Shiloh, Cumberland County.
BARRETT, THOMAS Musc, 3rd NJ Inf Band 11- -1933. Immaculate Conception Cemetery, Montclair, Essex County.
BARRETT, THOMAS TOWNSEND (see: Townsend, Thomas Barrett) Hillside Cemetery, Scotch Plains, Union County.
BARRETT, WILLIAM H. Pvt, B, 21st NJ Inf, 4-6-1889. Fairmount Cemetery, Newark, Essex County.
BARRICKS, WILLIAM Pvt, K, 5th NJ Inf, 12-4-1867. Westminster Cemetery, Cranbury, Middlesex County.
BARRIES, PETER H. 7-12-1895. Fairmount Cemetery, Newark, Essex County.
BARRIGAN, JAMES Pvt, H, 9th NJ Inf, DoD Unknown. Holy Sepulchre Cemetery, East Orange, Essex County.
BARRINGER, AMASA (see: Barringer, Charles Amasa) Evergreen Cemetery, Hillside, Union County.
BARRINGER*, CHARLES AMASA (aka: Barringer, Amasa) Principal Musc, 22nd U.S. VRC 6-18-1898. Evergreen Cemetery, Hillside, Union County.
BARRON, ALFRED GIBSON Pvt, A, 3rd NJ Cav, 8-15-1891. Mount Hope Presbyterian Cemetery, Lambertville, Hunterdon County.
BARRON*, DALLAS Pvt, G, 18th PA Cav, 9-18-1885. Mount Hope Presbyterian Cemetery, Lambertville, Hunterdon County.
BARRON, JOHN CONNER Asst Surg, 69th NY State Militia 2-6-1908. Presbyterian Church Cemetery, Woodbridge, Middlesex County.
BARRON*, ROBERT Pvt, A, 21st U.S. VRC, 8-6-1894. Fairmount Cemetery, Newark, Essex County.
BARRON, THOMAS (aka: Barnes, Thomas) Pvt, F, 60th (Crawford's) TN Mtd Inf (CSA) [Captured 5-17-1863 at Big Black River Bridge, MS.] 8-1-1863. Finn's Point National Cemetery, Pennsville, Salem County.
BARRON, THOMAS J. Seaman, U.S. Navy, USS Ossipee, 4-23-1900. Mount Hope Presbyterian Cemetery, Lambertville, Hunterdon County.

New Jersey Civil War Burials

BARROWCLOUGH, CHARLES Pvt, B, 37th NJ Inf, 1-19-1929. Cedar Lawn Cemetery, Paterson, Passaic County.
BARROWS, HORATIO N. (aka: Burroughs, Horatio) Pvt, E, 21st MA Inf, [Wounded 9-17-1862 at Antietam, MD.] 3-1-1919. Evergreen Cemetery, Hillside, Union County.
BARROWS*, WALTER A. Capt, C, 115th U.S. CT, 3-9-1926. Presbyterian Church Cemetery, Cold Spring, Cape May County.
BARRY, EDWARD Pvt, F, 29th NJ Inf, 12-8-1906. Bordentown/Old St. Mary's Catholic Cemetery, Bordentown, Burlington County.
BARRY, EDWARD (see: Berry, Edward) Holy Sepulchre Cemetery, Totowa, Passaic County.
BARRY, JAMES (aka: Barry, Joseph) Pvt, E, 5th CT Inf, 6-30-1891. Holy Name Cemetery, Jersey City, Hudson County.
BARRY, JAMES W. Seaman, U.S. Navy, USS Baron de Kalb, 4-28-1907. Soldier's Home Cemetery, Vineland, Cumberland County.
BARRY, JOHN J. (aka: Bare, John) Corp, C, 127th U.S. CT, 1-23-1916. Soldier's Home Cemetery, Vineland, Cumberland County.
BARRY, JOHN M. Pvt, K, 70th NY Inf, 7-28-1902. Holy Sepulchre Cemetery, East Orange, Essex County.
BARRY, JOSEPH (see: Barry, James) Holy Name Cemetery, Jersey City, Hudson County.
BARRY, LYMAN FRANK Pvt, I, 71st NY National Guard, 11-9-1922. Arlington Cemetery, Kearny, Hudson County.
BARRY, MARTIN (see: Barry, William) Baptist Cemetery, Pemberton, Burlington County.
BARRY*, MICHAEL Seaman, U.S. Navy, USS Monocacy, 2-11-1922. Holy Sepulchre Cemetery, East Orange, Essex County.
BARRY, MICHAEL Corp, D, 7th NJ Inf, [Wounded in action.] 4-10-1891. Bordentown/Old St. Mary's Catholic Cemetery, Bordentown, Burlington County.
BARRY, NAPOLEON Seaman, U.S. Navy, 1-29-1905. Arlington Cemetery, Kearny, Hudson County.
BARRY, PATRICK Pvt, Btty A, 1st NJ Light Art, 3-10-1936. Holy Name Cemetery, Jersey City, Hudson County.
BARRY*, WILLIAM (aka: Barry, Martin) Pvt, A, 76th NY Inf, 12-24-1893. Baptist Cemetery, Pemberton, Burlington County.
BARRY, WILLIAM (see: Berry, William A.) Woodland Cemetery, Newark, Essex County.
BARSOTTI, EMILIO Seaman, U.S. Navy, 4-10-1916. Bayview-New York Bay Cemetery, Jersey City, Hudson County.
BART, MATTHEW S. (aka: Hart, Matthew) 4-15-1891. Fairmount Cemetery, Newark, Essex County.
BARTELS, FREDERICK Seaman, U.S. Navy, USS Princeton, 9-30-1918. Harleigh Cemetery, Camden, Camden County.
BARTH, FREDERICK Pvt, A, 2nd NJ Cav, 8-25-1904. Woodland Cemetery, Newark, Essex County.
BARTH, JACOB 3-13-1895. Flower Hill Cemetery, North Bergen, Hudson County.
BARTH, THEODORE Pvt, B, 5th PA Cav, 9-15-1902. Evergreen Cemetery, Camden, Camden County.
BARTHOLF, DAVID G. Sgt, Btty H, 5th NY Heavy Art, 1-29-1897. Mount Pleasant Cemetery, Newark, Essex County.
BARTHOLF, PETER Pvt, B, 22nd NJ Inf, 9-28-1889. Bayview-New York Bay Cemetery, Jersey City, Hudson County.
BARTHOLOMEW, HENRY Pvt, C, 30th NJ Inf, 4-26-1883. Rahway Cemetery, Rahway, Union County.
BARTHOLOMEW*, LUZERNE 1st Lt, G, 38th NJ Inf, 5-27-1910. Van Liew Cemetery, North Brunswick, Middlesex County.

Our Brothers Gone Before

BARTHOLOMEW, MARSHALL MILES Pvt, Ind, OH Inf, 1-7-1933. Rosedale Cemetery, Orange, Essex County.
BARTHOULOT, SEVERIN A. 1st Sgt, D, 18th PA Inf, 3-11-1902. Oak Hill Cemetery, Vineland, Cumberland County.
BARTHURST, BENJAMIN (see: Bathurst, Benjamin M.) Finn's Point National Cemetery, Pennsville, Salem County.
BARTLEMAN, FREDOLIN Pvt, A, 104th PA Inf, [Wounded in action.] 5-3-1902. Prospect Hill Cemetery, Flemington, Hunterdon County.
BARTLES, ANDREW Pvt, E, 31st NJ Inf, 1889. Prospect Hill Cemetery, Flemington, Hunterdon County.
BARTLES, JOHN H. Pvt, 8th NY Ind Btty 9-24-1914. Locust Hill Cemetery, Dover, Morris County.
BARTLESON, SAMUEL V. Pvt, G, 104th PA Inf, 8-29-1929. Bay View Cemetery, Leonardo, Monmouth County.
BARTLETT*, ALONZO F. Pvt, A, 31st MA Inf, 12-29-1892. Christ Church Cemetery, Morgan, Middlesex County.
BARTLETT, CHARLES Pvt, G, 3rd NJ Cav, DoD Unknown. Mount Pleasant Cemetery, Millville, Cumberland County.
BARTLETT, CHARLES B. 2-6-1934. Cedar Lawn Cemetery, Paterson, Passaic County.
BARTLETT, E.H. Pvt, E, 8th AL Inf (CSA), 8-20-1863. Finn's Point National Cemetery, Pennsville, Salem County.
BARTLETT*, EDWARD Pvt, H, 57th NY Inf, 12-28-1910. St. Mary's Episcopal Church Cemetery, Burlington, Burlington County.
BARTLETT, JOSEPH R. 4-11-1876. Presbyterian Church Cemetery, Mays Landing, Atlantic County.
BARTLETT, THOMAS H. Pvt, H, 57th NY Inf, 2-19-1900. Oddfellows Cemetery, Burlington, Burlington County.
BARTLETT, WILLIAM Pvt, E, 10th NJ Inf, 3-15-1898. Mount Pleasant Cemetery, Millville, Cumberland County.
BARTLETT, WILLIAM J. Pvt, A, 21st U.S. VRC, 4-17-1897. Evergreen Cemetery, Camden, Camden County.
BARTLEY*, JAMES E. Pvt, A, 48th NY Inf, [Wounded 7-18-1863 at Fort Wagner, SC.] 10-3-1915. Greengrove Cemetery, Keyport, Monmouth County.
BARTLEY, JOHN W. Pvt, H, 6th NJ Inf, [Died of typhoid at Budds Ferry, MD.] 2-23-1862. 2nd Baptist Church Cemetery, Harbourtown, Mercer County.
BARTMAN, HORATIO N. (aka: Bateman, Horatio) Pvt, E, 71st PA Inf, 9-10-1921. Mount Holly Cemetery, Mount Holly, Burlington County.
BARTO*, GILES G. Pvt, H, 3rd WI Cav, DoD Unknown. Union Cemetery, Clarkstown, Atlantic County.
BARTOLETTE, JOHN C. Musc, 4th NJ Inf Band [Died at U.S. Army Hospital Brooklyn, NY.] 7-23-1862. Old Somerville Cemetery, Somerville, Somerset County.
BARTON, ALEXANDER A. Sgt, D, 58th PA Inf, 7-16-1892. Evergreen Cemetery, Camden, Camden County.
BARTON, AUGUSTUS Pvt, F, 28th NJ Inf, 3-24-1920. Trinity Episcopal Church Cemetery, Woodbridge, Middlesex County.
BARTON, CHARLES G. Sgt, Btty L, 6th PA Heavy Art, 7-11-1889. Fairmount Cemetery, Newark, Essex County.
BARTON*, EDWARD W. Pvt, F, 1st PA Prov Cav, 8-4-1889. Greenwood Cemetery, Hamilton, Mercer County.
BARTON, EMANUEL Pvt, C, 15th NJ Inf, [Wounded in action.] 7-29-1915. Savage Cemetery, Denville, Morris County.
BARTON, FRANK DoD Unknown. Cedar Green Cemetery, Clayton, Gloucester County.
BARTON, GEORGE H. Clerk, CSA Navy, CSS Artic, 1910. Greengrove Cemetery, Keyport, Monmouth County.

New Jersey Civil War Burials

BARTON, HIRAM E.W. Pvt, A, 118th PA Inf, 2-21-1900. Oak Hill Cemetery, Vineland, Cumberland County.

BARTON, JAMES Pvt, D, 22nd NJ Inf, 2-10-1916. Zion Lutheran Church Cemetery, Saddle River, Bergen County.

BARTON, JAMES 1-14-1865. Methodist-Episcopal Church Cemetery, Blackwood, Camden County.

BARTON, JAMES 12-31-1922. Cedar Lawn Cemetery, Paterson, Passaic County.

BARTON, JAMES Pvt, D, 17th U.S. Inf, 10-1-1877. Woodland Cemetery, Newark, Essex County.

BARTON, JOHN Pvt, B, 13th NJ Inf, [Wounded in action.] 7-20-1905. Arlington Cemetery, Kearny, Hudson County.

BARTON, JOHN HENRY Corp, I, 54th NY Inf, 11-23-1887. Siloam Cemetery, Vineland, Cumberland County.

BARTON, JOSEPH DoD Unknown. Cedar Grove Cemetery, Gloucester City, Camden County.

BARTON, JOSEPH M. Pvt, C, 10th NJ Inf, 10-9-1914. Arlington Cemetery, Pennsauken, Camden County.

BARTON*, LUKE L. Pvt, D, 2nd NJ Inf, 6-21-1906. Savage Cemetery, Denville, Morris County.

BARTON, PAUL R. Pvt, D, 26th NJ Inf, 4-18-1885. Savage Cemetery, Denville, Morris County.

BARTON, RICHARD P. Pvt, I, 28th NJ Inf, 1884. St. Peter's Cemetery, Perth Amboy, Middlesex County.

BARTON, ROBERT E. Pvt, A, 1st NJ Inf, 3-7-1899. Holy Sepulchre Cemetery, East Orange, Essex County.

BARTON, SAMUEL C. Sgt, I, 58th PA Inf, 3-30-1918. Presbyterian Church Cemetery, Cold Spring, Cape May County.

BARTON, THOMAS Pvt, B, 14th NJ Inf, 6-11-1915. Riverview Cemetery, Trenton, Mercer County.

BARTON, THOMAS S. Pvt, G, 38th NY Inf, 9-15-1906. Beverly National Cemetery, Edgewater Park, Burlington County.

BARTON, WESLEY D. Pvt, D, 25th NJ Inf, 10-23-1895. Methodist Church Cemetery, Sicklerville, Camden County.

BARTON, WILLIAM Pvt, C, 33rd VA Inf (CSA), [Captured 5-12-1864 at Spotsylvania CH, VA. Died of dysentery.] 8-10-1864. Finn's Point National Cemetery, Pennsville, Salem County.

BARTON*, WILLIAM Pvt, E, 140th NY Inf, 7-5-1899. Holy Name Cemetery, Jersey City, Hudson County.

BARTON, WILLIAM Pvt, D, 28th NJ Inf, 9-27-1876. Evergreen Cemetery, New Brunswick, Middlesex County.

BARTON, WILLIAM 9-27-1876. Pitman Methodist-Episcopal Cemetery, New Brunswick, Middlesex County.

BARTON, WILLIAM BRAINERD Bvt Brig Gen, U.S. Volunteers, [Colonel, 48th New York Infantry. Wounded 6-1-1864 at Cold Harbor, VA.] 6-13-1891. Presbyterian Church Cemetery, Woodbridge, Middlesex County.

BARTON, WILLIAM H. Pvt, D, 12th NJ Inf, 2-5-1902. Methodist-Episcopal Church Cemetery, South Dennis, Cape May County.

BARTON, WILLIAM H. Pvt, K, 2nd NJ Inf, 12-22-1922. Bloomfield Cemetery, Bloomfield, Essex County.

BARTON, WILLIAM H. Actg Gunner, U.S. Navy, USS Vindicator, [Mississippi Squadron.] 3-27-1904. Savage Cemetery, Denville, Morris County.

BARTON, WILLIAM H. (JR.) Seaman, U.S. Navy, 6-12-1918. Cedar Lawn Cemetery, Paterson, Passaic County.

BARTOW, GEORGE W. 1907. Greengrove Cemetery, Keyport, Monmouth County.

Our Brothers Gone Before

BARTOW, HENRY Pvt, C, 39th NJ Inf, 12-20-1885. Fairmount Cemetery, Newark, Essex County.
BARTRAM, ELI S. Corp, G, 28th CT Inf, 1-9-1937. Rosedale Cemetery, Orange, Essex County.
BARTRAM*, JAMES Pvt, C, 90th NY Inf, 5-4-1929. Fairmount Cemetery, Newark, Essex County.
BARTRAM, OSCAR F. Pvt, I, 8th CT Inf, 1901. Soldier's Home Cemetery, Vineland, Cumberland County.
BARTRON, WILLIAM H. Pvt, G, 38th NJ Inf, 7-23-1893. New Somerville Cemetery, Somerville, Somerset County.
BARULT*, JOHN (aka: Barrell, John) Pvt, Btty K, 1st ME Heavy Art, [Wounded 6-22-1864 at Weldon Railroad, VA.] 8-30-1917. Arlington Cemetery, Kearny, Hudson County.
BARWICK, JOHN Pvt, A, 5th MD Inf, 4-30-1924. New Camden Cemetery, Camden, Camden County.
BARWIS, EDMUND 5-15-1893. Mercer Cemetery, Trenton, Mercer County.
BARWIS, HOWARD S. Pvt, G, 119th PA Inf, 5-15-1911. Greenwood Cemetery, Hamilton, Mercer County.
BARWIS, SAMUEL Pvt, Btty G, 2nd PA Heavy Art, [Wounded 9-29-1864 at Chapin's Farm, VA.] 7-11-1900. Cedar Grove Cemetery, Gloucester City, Camden County.
BARY, JAMES L. (aka: Berry, James) Pvt, G, 31st NJ Inf, 1-19-1901. Presbyterian Church Cemetery, Great Meadows, Warren County.
BASCOME, DANIEL B. Surg, 12-5-1887. Hillside Cemetery, Scotch Plains, Union County.
BASDEN, JAMES (aka: Baisden, James) Pvt, I, 1st NC Cav (CSA), [Captured 7-3-1863 at Gettysburg, PA.] 10-18-1863. Finn's Point National Cemetery, Pennsville, Salem County.
BASENOR, PHILIP (see: Baezner, Philip) Riverview Cemetery, Trenton, Mercer County.
BASH, GEORGE P. Pvt, A, 28th NJ Inf, 12-15-1892. St. Peter's Episcopal Church Cemetery, Spotswood, Middlesex County.
BASHFORD, RICHARD Pvt, I, 39th NJ Inf, DoD Unknown. Alpine Cemetery, Perth Amboy, Middlesex County.
BASHFORD, SAMUEL Pvt, I, 28th NJ Inf, [Wounded in action.] 7-24-1900. Fairmount Cemetery, Newark, Essex County.
BASMIGHT, AMOS Pvt, F, 11th (Bethel) NC Inf (CSA), 10-6-1863. Finn's Point National Cemetery, Pennsville, Salem County.
BASS, JACOB (see: Boss, Jacob) Evergreen Cemetery, Morristown, Morris County.
BASSENGER, WILLIAM P. Pvt, G, 186th NY Inf, 1894. Brown Cemetery, Butler, Morris County.
BASSETT, C. EDWIN Corp, A, 24th NJ Inf, 12-5-1896. Old Friends Cemetery, Salem, Salem County.
BASSETT, DARIUS Sgt, Btty F, 1st MI Light Art, 3-20-1919. Friends Cemetery, Cropwell, Burlington County.
BASSETT, FREDERICK B. Pvt, F, 7th NY State Militia, 11-4-1922. Evergreen Cemetery, Hillside, Union County.
BASSETT, HOWARD Capt, A, 24th NJ Inf, 1894. Friends Cemetery, Woodstown, Salem County.
BASSETT, ISAAC G. Pvt, K, 110th PA Inf, 1-9-1927. Arlington Cemetery, Pennsauken, Camden County.
BASSETT, JOSEPH (JR.) Pvt, D, 12th NJ Inf, 12-24-1892. Eastview Cemetery, Salem, Salem County.
BASSETT, STACY H. Pvt, K, 8th PA Cav, 8-9-1892. Evergreen Cemetery, Camden, Camden County.

BASSETT, WILLIAM Pvt, B, 95th PA Inf, DoD Unknown. Baptist Cemetery, Burlington, Burlington County.
BASSETT, WILLIAM Pvt, E, 4th NJ Inf, 10-10-1918. Berlin Cemetery, Berlin, Camden County.
BASSETT, WILLIAM H. (SR.) Pvt, E, 4th NJ Inf, 1877. Harleigh Cemetery, Camden, Camden County.
BASSINGER, ROBERT Pvt, D, 70th NY Inf, [Wounded 7-2-1863 at Gettysburg, PA.] 12-21-1905. Fairmount Cemetery, Newark, Essex County.
BASTAN, JEROME A. (aka: Bastine, Jerome) Pvt, G, 61st PA Inf, 9-4-1892. Bayview-New York Bay Cemetery, Jersey City, Hudson County.
BASTEDO, ABNER Pvt, L, 27th NJ Inf, 9-25-1890. Zeek Cemetery, Marcella, Morris County.
BASTEDO, GIDEON Pvt, L, 27th NJ Inf, [Drowned while crossing the Cumberland River, KY.] 5-6-1863. Union Cemetery, Marcella, Morris County.
BASTEDO, JOSEPH H. Pvt, 3rd NY Ind Btty 1911. Vail Presbyterian Cemetery, Parsippany, Morris County.
BASTEDO, THOMAS Pvt, I, 29th NJ Inf, 1-7-1907. Maplewood Cemetery, Freehold, Monmouth County.
BASTGEN, MATTHIAS WILLIAM Pvt, I, 7th NJ Inf, 8-5-1921. Weehawken Cemetery, North Bergen, Hudson County.
BASTIAN, JEREMIAH A. (aka: Bastine, Jerome) Pvt, G, 61st PA Inf, DoD Unknown. Hoboken Cemetery, North Bergen, Hudson County.
BASTINE, JEROME (see: Bastan, Jerome A.) Bayview-New York Bay Cemetery, Jersey City, Hudson County.
BASTINE, JEROME (see: Bastian, Jeremiah A.) Hoboken Cemetery, North Bergen, Hudson County.
BASTING, ANTON Seaman, U.S. Navy, USS Monitor, [Last survivor of the ironclad USS Monitor.] 1915. Holy Name Cemetery, Jersey City, Hudson County.
BATAILLE, EDWARD Pvt, C, 2nd NJ Inf, 2-12-1920. Rosedale Cemetery, Orange, Essex County.
BATCHELOR, CHARLES F. Corp, I, 39th NJ Inf, 1-15-1900. Fairmount Cemetery, Newark, Essex County.
BATCHELOR*, JAMES M. Pvt, H, 2nd NJ Inf, 12-30-1903. Fairmount Cemetery, Newark, Essex County.
BATCHELOR, JOHN (see: Bacheller, John Collins) Mount Pleasant Cemetery, Newark, Essex County.
BATCHELOR, WILLIAM C. Pvt, G, 47th NC Inf (CSA), [Captured 7-3-1863 at Gettysburg, PA. Died of scurvy.] 10-17-1863. Finn's Point National Cemetery, Pennsville, Salem County.
BATEMAN, A. JUDSON Pvt, F, 24th NJ Inf, 12-17-1894. Old Stone Church Cemetery, Fairton, Cumberland County.
BATEMAN, ALBERT B. Sgt, H, 7th NJ Inf, 8-8-1878. Presbyterian Church Cemetery, Bridgeton, Cumberland County.
BATEMAN, DARIUS Pvt, I, 25th NJ Inf, 8-30-1900. 1st Baptist Cemetery, Cape May Court House, Cape May County.
BATEMAN, DAVID EUGENE Pvt, D, 25th NJ Inf, 3-27-1923. Old Stone Church Cemetery, Fairton, Cumberland County.
BATEMAN, EPHRIAM F. Corp, D, 25th NJ Inf, [Died of typhoid at Washington, DC.] 2-19-1863. Presbyterian Church Cemetery, Cedarville, Cumberland County.
BATEMAN, FRANK Seaman, U.S. Navy, 1-19-1924. Presbyterian Church Cemetery, Blackwood, Camden County.
BATEMAN, HORATIO (see: Bartman, Horatio N.) Mount Holly Cemetery, Mount Holly, Burlington County.

Our Brothers Gone Before

BATEMAN, JAMES S. Sgt, A, 51st NY Inf, 3-26-1890. Mount Prospect Cemetery, Neptune, Monmouth County.
BATEMAN, JOHN Pvt, K, 13th NC Inf (CSA), [Captured 7-1-1863 at Gettysburg, PA. Died of fever.] 9-27-1863. Finn's Point National Cemetery, Pennsville, Salem County.
BATEMAN, JOSEPH 2nd Lt, D, 25th NJ Inf, 2-25-1917. Old Stone Church Cemetery, Fairton, Cumberland County.
BATEMAN, ROBERT M. Asst Surg, 25th NJ Inf 6-4-1878. Presbyterian Church Cemetery, Cedarville, Cumberland County.
BATEMAN, TIMOTHY Sgt, K, 12th NJ Inf, 12-10-1926. Methodist-Episcopal Cemetery, Port Norris, Cumberland County.
BATES, BENJAMIN Corp, I, 14th NJ Inf, [Cenotaph. Died of typhoid at Monocacy, MD.] 11-3-1862. Bates Mills Cemetery, Waterford Works, Camden County.
BATES*, BENJAMIN Pvt, H, 15th NJ Inf, 1-15-1866. Methodist Church Cemetery, Asbury, Warren County.
BATES, BENJAMIN FRANKLIN Pvt, G, 23rd NJ Inf, 9-29-1932. Methodist Church Cemetery, New Albany, Burlington County.
BATES, CHARLES J. Pvt, D, 11th NJ Inf, 10-24-1883. Riverview Cemetery, Trenton, Mercer County.
BATES*, DANIEL SPENCER (aka: Spencer, Bates D.) Corp, G, 15th PA Cav, [Died of typhoid fever at Wilkin's Crossroads, TN.] 1-29-1863. Oddfellows-Friends Cemetery, Medford, Burlington County.
BATES, EDWARD G. Pvt, G, 21st NJ Inf, 5-12-1870. Zeek Cemetery, Marcella, Morris County.
BATES, ENOS W. Pvt, E, 24th NJ Inf, 1925. Eglington Cemetery, Clarksboro, Gloucester County.
BATES*, FRANKLIN Corp, C, 12th NJ Inf, 3-10-1916. Baptist Church Cemetery, Haddonfield, Camden County.
BATES, GEORGE (see: Battest, George) Union Bethel Cemetery, Erma, Cape May County.
BATES, GEORGE E. 3-3-1906. Methodist Cemetery, Haddonfield, Camden County.
BATES*, HARVEY M. Pvt, Btty D, 2nd MA Heavy Art, 4-17-1918. Brotherhood Cemetery, Hainesport, Burlington County.
BATES, HENRY A. Pvt, K, 23rd NJ Inf, 11-13-1913. St. Paul's Methodist Church Cemetery, Port Republic, Atlantic County.
BATES, HENRY C. 7-4-1912. Evergreen Cemetery, Camden, Camden County.
BATES, JAMES Corp, Btty D, 4th U.S. Art, 12-11-1928. Fairmount Cemetery, Newark, Essex County.
BATES, JOHN Pvt, H, 28th NJ Inf, 9-25-1916. Chestnut Grove Cemetery, Elmer, Salem County.
BATES, JOSEPH D. Sgt, D, 24th NJ Inf, 1889. Wenonah Cemetery, Mantua, Gloucester County.
BATES, JOSIAH 1902. Berlin Cemetery, Berlin, Camden County.
BATES, LEVI E. Corp, U.S. Marine Corps, 2-25-1864. Baptist Church Cemetery, Haddonfield, Camden County.
BATES, MILES Pvt, I, 24th NJ Inf, 7-30-1888. Methodist Cemetery, Haddonfield, Camden County.
BATES, ROBERT W. Pvt, A, 2nd NJ Cav, 1918. Tabernacle Baptist Church Cemetery, Erma, Cape May County.
BATES, SAMUEL A. Pvt, I, 24th NJ Inf, 10-23-1894. Methodist Cemetery, Haddonfield, Camden County.
BATES, SAMUEL M. Pvt, Btty I, 2nd PA Heavy Art, 2-17-1921. Evergreen Cemetery, Camden, Camden County.

New Jersey Civil War Burials

BATES, THOMAS Pvt, C, 24th NJ Inf, [Died of typhoid at Georgetown, DC.] 12-7-1862. Methodist-Episcopal Church Cemetery, Aura, Gloucester County.

BATES, THOMAS (JR.) DoD Unknown. Old Camden Cemetery, Camden, Camden County.

BATES, THOMAS (SR.) Pvt, D, 6th NJ Inf, [Wounded 5-5-1862 at Williamsburg, VA.] 3-24-1880. Old Camden Cemetery, Camden, Camden County.

BATES, WESLEY Pvt, I, 6th NJ Inf, 7-16-1913. Asbury Methodist-Episcopal Church Cemetery, Swainton, Cape May County.

BATES*, WILLIAM Pvt, F, 8th NJ Inf, 6-5-1893. Bates Mills Cemetery, Waterford Works, Camden County.

BATES, WILLIAM D. 2-19-1888. Baptist Church Cemetery, Haddonfield, Camden County.

BATES, WILLIAM H. Sgt Maj, 199th PA Inf 12-18-1890. Eastview Cemetery, Salem, Salem County.

BATH, WILLIAM D. Corp, B, 4th DE Inf, 3-7-1869. Baptist Church Cemetery, Mullica Hill, Gloucester County.

BATHE, ALBERT 3-8-1890. Bethel Cemetery, Pennsauken, Camden County.

BATHURST, BENJAMIN M. (aka: Barthurst, Benjamin) Pvt, F, 157th PA Inf, DoD Unknown. Finn's Point National Cemetery, Pennsville, Salem County.

BATICH*, ANTONIO (aka: Langlois, Antonio) Pvt, E, 15th CT Inf, 1-13-1895. Holy Sepulchre Cemetery, Totowa, Passaic County.

BATSON, GEORGE D. Pvt, C, 2nd NJ Inf, 10-27-1941. Stanhope-Union Cemetery, Netcong, Morris County.

BATT, MOSES Pvt, K, 5th VA Inf (CSA), [Wounded 5-3-1863 at Chancellorsville, VA. Captured 10-15-1864.] 4-29-1864. Finn's Point National Cemetery, Pennsville, Salem County.

BATTAIS, LOUIS Capt, C, 55th NY Inf, 8-5-1897. Flower Hill Cemetery, North Bergen, Hudson County.

BATTEN, FRANCIS P. Sgt, F, 6th PA Cav, 1916. Cedar Green Cemetery, Clayton, Gloucester County.

BATTEN, GEORGE 1-9-1893. New Episcopal Church Cemetery, Swedesboro, Gloucester County.

BATTEN, GEORGE W. 1-28-1918. Eglington Cemetery, Clarksboro, Gloucester County.

BATTEN, ISAAC S. Pvt, B, 5th U.S. Inf, 8-10-1900. Methodist-Episcopal Cemetery, Blackwood, Camden County.

BATTEN, JOHN B. Corp, D, 38th NJ Inf, 7-1-1877. Bethesda Methodist-Episcopal Church Cemetery, Swedesboro, Gloucester County.

BATTEN, MOSES H. 1911. Methodist-Episcopal Church Cemetery, Blackwood, Camden County.

BATTEN, WEST Corp, D, 37th NJ Inf, 3-23-1917. New Camden Cemetery, Camden, Camden County.

BATTERSHALL, WILLIAM H. Pvt, G, 13th NJ Inf, 11-21-1885. Fairmount Cemetery, Newark, Essex County.

BATTERSON*, WILLIAM B. Pvt, K, 11th NJ Inf, 9-6-1895. Fairmount Cemetery, Newark, Essex County.

BATTEST, GEORGE (aka: Bates, George) Pvt, K, 22nd U.S. CT, 8-12-1897. Union Bethel Cemetery, Erma, Cape May County.

BATTISH, JOHN (see: Jacques, John) Cedar Lawn Cemetery, Paterson, Passaic County.

BATTS*, ELIJAH D. Pvt, K, 38th NJ Inf, 3-12-1904. Methodist Church Cemetery, Goshen, Cape May County.

BATTS, WILLIAM H.M. Corp, I, 25th NJ Inf, 7-6-1877. Methodist Church Cemetery, Goshen, Cape May County.

BAUER, ADAM (aka: Bowers, Adam) Pvt, K, 192nd PA Inf, DoD Unknown. Riverside Cemetery, Riverside, Burlington County.

Our Brothers Gone Before

BAUER, CHRISTIAN Pvt, Btty A, 1st NJ Light Art, 1907. Clinton Cemetery, Irvington, Essex County.

BAUER, JACOB (aka: Bowers, Jacob) Pvt, D, 1st NY Mounted Rifles, 7-11-1884. Weehawken Cemetery, North Bergen, Hudson County.

BAUER, JOHN Pvt, A, 8th Bttn DC Inf, 9-10-1895. Fairmount Cemetery, Newark, Essex County.

BAUER, JOHN Pvt, F, 39th NJ Inf, 1-27-1901. Fairmount Cemetery, Newark, Essex County.

BAUER, JOHN (aka: Bower, John) Pvt, E, 5th NJ Inf, 2-21-1921. Woodland Cemetery, Newark, Essex County.

BAUER, JOHN A. 1st Lt, H, 4th NY Cav, 4-22-1925. Palisade Cemetery, North Bergen, Hudson County.

BAUER, JOHN FREDERICK Capt, I, 41st NY Inf, 3-22-1896. Fairmount Cemetery, Newark, Essex County.

BAUER, MICHAEL Pvt, B, 1st NJ Cav, 4-28-1901. Fairmount Cemetery, Newark, Essex County.

BAUER*, MORRIS (SR.) Sgt, D, 28th NJ Inf, 4-11-1898. Willow Grove Cemetery, New Brunswick, Middlesex County.

BAUERMANN, JULIUS Pvt, D, 8th NY Inf, [Wounded 7-21-1861 at 1st Bull Run, VA.] 4-4-1904. Evergreen Cemetery, Hillside, Union County.

BAUGH, HARMAN 1911. Baptist/St. Andrew's Cemetery, Mount Holly, Burlington County.

BAUGHAN, WILLIAM Pvt, H, 132nd NY Inf, 2-20-1903. Bayview-New York Bay Cemetery, Jersey City, Hudson County.

BAUGHN, JOHN ROBERT Pvt, C, 2nd NJ Militia, 8-4-1906. Bayview-New York Bay Cemetery, Jersey City, Hudson County.

BAUGHN, T.C. Pvt, C, Jones' Bttn VA Inf (CSA), 5-22-1864. Finn's Point National Cemetery, Pennsville, Salem County.

BAULIG, GEORGE (aka: Boaler, George) Pvt, Btty G, 3rd PA Heavy Art, 4-12-1912. Egg Harbor Cemetery, Egg Harbor, Atlantic County.

BAULSER, JOSEPH A. 10-18-1894. Arlington Cemetery, Kearny, Hudson County.

BAUM, CONRAD Pvt, Btty A, 1st NJ Light Art, 1-1-1902. Grove Church Cemetery, North Bergen, Hudson County.

BAUM, JOSEPH P. Musc, F, 20th PA Cav, 10-3-1900. Riverview Cemetery, Trenton, Mercer County.

BAUM*, TIMOTHY Landsman, U.S. Navy, USS Wyalusing, 1914. Locust Hill Cemetery, Dover, Morris County.

BAUMAN, CONRAD Pvt, C, 9th NJ Inf, 7-7-1899. Fairmount Cemetery, Newark, Essex County.

BAUMAN, EDWARD E. Pvt, A, 9th NJ Inf, 11-19-1890. Fairmount Cemetery, Newark, Essex County.

BAUMAN, HENRY Pvt, G, 9th NJ Inf, 1-24-1919. Evergreen Cemetery, Hillside, Union County.

BAUMAN, JOHN Pvt, F, 39th NJ Inf, 10-14-1908. Hillside Cemetery, Scotch Plains, Union County.

BAUMAN, MATTHEW Pvt, E, 2nd NJ Inf, 6-23-1875. Fairmount Cemetery, Newark, Essex County.

BAUMGARTNER, FREDOLIN Pvt, G, 35th NJ Inf, 11-15-1867. Holy Sepulchre Cemetery, East Orange, Essex County.

BAUMGARTNER, JOHN Pvt, F, 39th NJ Inf, 10-9-1877. Palisade Cemetery, North Bergen, Hudson County.

BAUS, PETER L. Pvt, B, 23rd NJ Inf, 10-15-1922. Methodist Church Cemetery, Groveville, Mercer County.

New Jersey Civil War Burials

BAUSCHERT, AUGUSTE (aka: Banchert, Auguste) Pvt, Btty A, 1st NJ Light Art, 8-19-1887. Rosedale Cemetery, Orange, Essex County.

BAUSEL, JOSEPH Pvt, C, 62nd VA Inf (CSA), [Captured 7-5-1863 at Gettysburg, PA.] 8-21-1863. Finn's Point National Cemetery, Pennsville, Salem County.

BAXENDALE, ROBERT V. Pvt, G, 73rd PA Inf, 2-2-1916. Calvary Baptist Church Cemetery, Ocean View, Cape May County.

BAXTER, EDWARD (see: Baxter, Israel P.) Evergreen Cemetery, Hillside, Union County.

BAXTER, FRANKLIN A. Pvt, F, 8th NY State Militia, DoD Unknown. Valleau Cemetery, Ridgewood, Bergen County.

BAXTER, GEORGE (SR.) Pvt, G, 4th NJ Militia, 1884. Evergreen Cemetery, Camden, Camden County.

BAXTER, ISRAEL P. (aka: Baxter, Edward) Pvt, I, 36th NY Inf, 7-27-1904. Evergreen Cemetery, Hillside, Union County.

BAXTER, JAMES N. Pvt, D, 150th NY Inf, 3-6-1890. Rosedale Cemetery, Orange, Essex County.

BAXTER, JOHN Pvt, A, 70th NY Inf, 3-13-1895. Cedar Lawn Cemetery, Paterson, Passaic County.

BAXTER, JOSEPH Pvt, C, 34th NJ Inf, 4-12-1905. Oddfellows Cemetery, Pemberton, Burlington County.

BAXTER, RICHARD 11-27-1911. United Methodist Church Cemetery, Waterloo, Sussex County.

BAXTER, WILLIAM Pvt, I, 158th NY Inf, 5-19-1877. Cedar Lawn Cemetery, Paterson, Passaic County.

BAY, BERTEL (aka: Baye, Thomas B.) Pvt, B, 2nd AL Cav (CSA), [Wounded in action.] 3-14-1903. Bayview-New York Bay Cemetery, Jersey City, Hudson County.

BAY, WILLIAM H. Landsman, U.S. Navy, USS Princeton, DoD Unknown. Holy Sepulchre Cemetery, East Orange, Essex County.

BAYARD, GEORGE DASHIELL Brig Gen, U.S. Army, [Died of wounds received 12-13-1862 at Fredericksburg, VA.] 12-14-1862. Princeton Cemetery, Princeton, Mercer County.

BAYE, THOMAS B. (see: Bay, Bertel) Bayview-New York Bay Cemetery, Jersey City, Hudson County.

BAYER, WILLIAM Pvt, A, 54th NY Inf, 3-19-1880. Hoboken Cemetery, North Bergen, Hudson County.

BAYGEANTS, K.W. (aka: Beipgents, K.) Pvt, E, 6th AL Inf (CSA), [Captured at Gettysburg, PA.] 9-20-1863. Finn's Point National Cemetery, Pennsville, Salem County.

BAYLES, CHARLES Pvt, Btty A, 2nd PA Heavy Art, 5-17-1877. St. Mary's Episcopal Church Cemetery, Burlington, Burlington County.

BAYLES*, GEORGE F. Pvt, K, 7th NJ Inf, 6-24-1921. Evergreen Cemetery, Morristown, Morris County.

BAYLES, JOHN R. Pvt, B, 15th NJ Inf, 2- -1868. Presbyterian Church Cemetery, Sparta, Sussex County.

BAYLES, STEPHEN Pvt, K, 15th NJ Inf, 1-11-1908. Methodist Church Cemetery, Sparta, Sussex County.

BAYLES*, THEODORE P. Corp, K, 7th NJ Inf, 7-4-1902. Evergreen Cemetery, Morristown, Morris County.

BAYLES*, WILLIAM N. Pvt, I, 15th NJ Inf, 4-13-1900. Presbyterian Church Cemetery, Sparta, Sussex County.

BAYLEY, HORACE DoD Unknown. Elmwood Cemetery, New Brunswick, Middlesex County.

BAYLIE, ROBERT N. Pvt, E, 109th PA Inf, 2-26-1903. New Camden Cemetery, Camden, Camden County.

Our Brothers Gone Before

BAYLIS, ELIAS Pvt, M, 9th NJ Inf, 10-21-1862. Pitman Methodist-Episcopal Cemetery, New Brunswick, Middlesex County.
BAYLIS, WILLIAM (see: Barlis, William) Fairmount Cemetery, Newark, Essex County.
BAYLIS, WILLIS (see: Bailis, William) White Ridge Cemetery, Eatontown, Monmouth County.
BAYLOR, JAMES R. Pvt, F, 50th NY Eng, 1-13-1895. Sergeant's Hill Cemetery, Sand Brook, Hunterdon County.
BAYLOR, NELSON J. Pvt, D, 1st NJ Inf, 12-8-1911. Holcomb-Riverview Cemetery, Lambertville, Hunterdon County.
BAYNE, WILLIAM Pvt, I, 2nd NJ Cav, 3-4-1906. Evergreen Cemetery, Camden, Camden County.
BAYOR, MATTHEW (see: Byer, Matthew) Fairmount Cemetery, Newark, Essex County.
BAYS*, WILLIAM 2nd Lt, F, 149th IL Inf, 4-6-1899. Bayview-New York Bay Cemetery, Jersey City, Hudson County.
BAZIN, CHARLES H. Landsman, U.S. Navy, USS Santiago de Cuba, 6-23-1901. Mount Pleasant Cemetery, Millville, Cumberland County.
BAZIRE, CHARLES I. Pvt, A, 26th NJ Inf, 1904. Clinton Cemetery, Irvington, Essex County.
BAZZLE, HENRY Musc, H, 23rd NJ Inf, 4-3-1890. Bordentown/Old St. Mary's Catholic Cemetery, Bordentown, Burlington County.
BEA, JACOB DoD Unknown. Holy Sepulchre Cemetery, East Orange, Essex County.
BEACH, ALBERT B. 1st Lt, E, 9th NJ Inf, DoD Unknown. Newton Cemetery, Newton, Sussex County.
BEACH, ALEXANDER (JR.) 1st Lt, Adj, 11th NJ Inf 4-9-1902. Mount Pleasant Cemetery, Newark, Essex County.
BEACH, AMZI A. Corp, I, 27th NJ Inf, 12-13-1876. Evergreen Cemetery, Morristown, Morris County.
BEACH, CHARLES D. Pvt, I, 15th NJ Inf, 7-19-1883. Newton Cemetery, Newton, Sussex County.
BEACH, GEORGE A. Pvt, F, 114th NY Inf, [Wounded 6-14-1863 at Port Hudson, LA.] 6-22-1926. Arlington Cemetery, Kearny, Hudson County.
BEACH, GEORGE P. Pvt, I, 10th NJ Inf, 6-23-1895. Riverview Cemetery, Trenton, Mercer County.
BEACH, HARVEY Pvt, I, 24th NJ Inf, 7-17-1904. Oak Grove Cemetery, Hammonton, Atlantic County.
BEACH, HENRY O. Capt, D, 1st NJ Militia, 1912. New Presbyterian Cemetery, Hanover, Morris County.
BEACH, HENRY O. Pvt, H, 26th NJ Inf, 1876. Walnut Grove Cemetery, Mount Freedom, Morris County.
BEACH, HENRY O. 4-29-1888. Mount Pleasant Cemetery, Newark, Essex County.
BEACH, ISAAC P. Pvt, K, 24th NJ Inf, 7-27-1872. Methodist-Episcopal Church Cemetery, Penns Grove, Salem County.
BEACH, JOHN Corp, A, 11th NJ Inf, 8-26-1884. Newton Cemetery, Newton, Sussex County.
BEACH, JOHN HENRY Pvt, H, 135th IN Inf, [Died of disease at Bridgeport, AL.] 6-30-1864. Presbyterian Church Cemetery, Rockaway, Morris County.
BEACH, JOHN POINTON Sgt, B, 4th NJ Inf, [Awarded the Medal of Honor.] 11-27-1926. Mercer Cemetery, Trenton, Mercer County.
BEACH, JONAS Pvt, E, 11th NJ Inf, 1908. Presbyterian Church Cemetery, Rockaway, Morris County.
BEACH, JOSEPH Pvt, B, 4th NJ Inf, 5-11-1881. Mercer Cemetery, Trenton, Mercer County.
BEACH, JOSEPH G. Pvt, F, 3rd U.S. Inf, 2-29-1908. Mount Pleasant Cemetery, Newark, Essex County.

New Jersey Civil War Burials

BEACH, JOSHUA Pvt, E, 11th NJ Inf, [Cenotaph. Died of scurvy while prisoner at Andersonville, GA.] 8-1-1864. Presbyterian Church Cemetery, Rockaway, Morris County.

BEACH, MOSES Pvt, B, 27th NJ Inf, DoD Unknown. Presbyterian Church Cemetery, Rockaway, Morris County.

BEACH, ROBERT J. Capt, F, 26th NJ Inf, 2-28-1903. Bloomfield Cemetery, Bloomfield, Essex County.

BEACH, ROBERT N. Corp, C, 7th NJ Inf, 6-21-1924. New Presbyterian Cemetery, Hanover, Morris County.

BEACHER, HENRY Pvt, F, 11th NJ Inf, 11-30-1910. Rosedale Cemetery, Orange, Essex County.

BEADLE, GEORGE Pvt, C, 26th NJ Inf, 2-24-1917. Arlington Cemetery, Kearny, Hudson County.

BEAHAN, BARTLEY Pvt, B, 35th NJ Inf, 8-31-1906. Lady of Lourdes/Holy Sepulchre Cemetery, Hamilton, Mercer County.

BEAHEN*, MICHAEL Capt, A, 8th NJ Inf, [Wounded in action at Boydton Plank Road, VA.] 8-11-1872. Fairmount Cemetery, Newark, Essex County.

BEAKES, SAMUEL Pvt, C, 4th NJ Inf, 7-15-1865. Presbyterian Church Cemetery, Pennington, Mercer County.

BEAKLEY, HENRY (see: Bakley, Henry H.) Methodist Church Cemetery, Hurffville, Gloucester County.

BEAKLEY, ISAAC H. (aka: Bradley, Isaac) Pvt, B, 24th NJ Inf, 4-26-1917. Mount Pleasant Cemetery, Millville, Cumberland County.

BEAL, ALBERT J. 8-18-1919. Hillside Cemetery, Scotch Plains, Union County.

BEALE*, EDWARD E. Pvt, C, 95th PA Inf, 1934. Methodist Cemetery, Mantua, Gloucester County.

BEALE, JOHN 1st Sgt, C, 1st NY Marine Art, 12-27-1900. Rosedale Cemetery, Linden, Union County.

BEAM, ADAM (aka: Keeth, Adam) Pvt, D, 26th NJ Inf, 2-20-1907. Prospect Hill Cemetery, Caldwell, Essex County.

BEAM, ANDREW Pvt, H, 31st NJ Inf, 1917. Baptist Church Cemetery, Port Murray, Warren County.

BEAM, DAVID Pvt, C, 27th NJ Inf, 7-28-1921. Little Valley Cemetery, Middle Valley, Morris County.

BEAM, DAVID A. 1884. Mount Pleasant Cemetery, Newark, Essex County.

BEAM, GEORGE Corp, D, 26th NJ Inf, DoD Unknown. Prospect Hill Cemetery, Caldwell, Essex County.

BEAM, GEORGE T. Pvt, E, 39th NJ Inf, 6-25-1892. Fairmount Cemetery, Newark, Essex County.

BEAM, JOHN E. Capt, Btty B, 1st NJ Light Art, [Killed in action at Malvern Hill, VA.] 7-1-1862. Mount Pleasant Cemetery, Newark, Essex County.

BEAM, JOHN P. Pvt, F, 15th NJ Inf, 4-8-1901. Presbyterian Church Cemetery, Rockaway, Morris County.

BEAM, JOSEPH Pvt, Btty A, 1st NJ Light Art, DoD Unknown. Palisade Cemetery, North Bergen, Hudson County.

BEAM*, NELSON Pvt, C, 138th NY Inf, 7-12-1911. Macphelah Cemetery, North Bergen, Hudson County.

BEAM, PHILIP Pvt, C, 27th NJ Inf, DoD Unknown. Presbyterian Church Cemetery, Fairmount, Hunterdon County.

BEAM, THEODORE Pvt, Btty A, 1st NJ Light Art, 1-3-1921. Presbyterian Church Cemetery, Rockaway, Morris County.

BEAM, THEODORE Pvt, B, 27th NJ Inf, 1899. Little Valley Cemetery, Middle Valley, Morris County.

Our Brothers Gone Before

BEAM*, WILLIAM H. Pvt, F, 7th NJ Inf, 12-28-1909. Arlington Cemetery, Kearny, Hudson County.
BEAM, WILLIAM H. Pvt, Btty D, 1st NJ Light Art, 1-24-1886. Evergreen Cemetery, Morristown, Morris County.
BEAM, WILLIAM L. Pvt, A, 7th NJ Inf, 4-17-1889. Methodist Church Cemetery, Buttzville, Warren County.
BEAMISH, ALLEN (see: Beemis, Allen H.) Harleigh Cemetery, Camden, Camden County.
BEAN, GEORGE J. Pvt, D, 5th NH Inf, [Died at Newark, NJ.] 9-9-1862. Fairmount Cemetery, Newark, Essex County.
BEAN, IRA Pvt, G, 16th VT Inf, 1-16-1920. Soldier's Home Cemetery, Vineland, Cumberland County.
BEAN, JAMES Corp, F, 114th U.S. CT, 3-31-1880. Evergreen Cemetery, Hillside, Union County.
BEAN, JOHN (see: Beine, John) St. Nicholas Cemetery, Lodi, Bergen County.
BEAN, T.D. Pvt, B, Nelson's Bttn VA Light Art (CSA), 5-28-1865. Finn's Point National Cemetery, Pennsville, Salem County.
BEAN, WILEY JACKSON Pvt, E, 13th AL Inf (CSA), [Captured 7-1-1863 at Gettysburg, PA. Died of scurvy.] 1-13-1864. Finn's Point National Cemetery, Pennsville, Salem County.
BEAR, JOHN W. 1-12-1881. Evergreen Cemetery, Camden, Camden County.
BEAR, SEBASTIAN Pvt, H, 5th PA Cav, 8-16-1899. Fairmount Cemetery, Newark, Essex County.
BEAR, WILLIAM R. (see: Beare, William R.) Mount Holly Cemetery, Mount Holly, Burlington County.
BEARD, AARON Pvt, K, 25th U.S. CT, 1-30-1876. Princeton Cemetery, Princeton, Mercer County.
BEARD, JOHN A. Pvt, A, 7th NC Inf (CSA), [Captured 7-3-1863 at Gettysburg, PA. Died of fever.] 8-18-1863. Finn's Point National Cemetery, Pennsville, Salem County.
BEARD, JOHN H. (SR.) Sgt, A, 2nd PA Cav, 12-15-1920. Arlington Cemetery, Pennsauken, Camden County.
BEARD, JOHN W. Pvt, C, 5th VA Inf (CSA), [Captured 5-5-1864 at Wilderness, VA.] 3-7-1865. Finn's Point National Cemetery, Pennsville, Salem County.
BEARDSLEE*, SAMUEL R. 1st Lt, B, 13th NJ Inf, [Wounded 5-15-1864 at Resaca, GA.] 11-23-1867. Presbyterian Church Cemetery, Sparta, Sussex County.
BEARDSLEY, GEORGE A. Maj, 13th NJ Inf 12-17-1898. Mount Pleasant Cemetery, Newark, Essex County.
BEARDSLEY, HENRY B. Corp, B, 2nd WI Inf, 11-15-1892. Oak Hill Cemetery, Vineland, Cumberland County.
BEARDSLEY, JAMES Pvt, I, 2nd NJ Inf, 12-12-1910. Cedar Lawn Cemetery, Paterson, Passaic County.
BEARE, WILLIAM R. (aka: Bear, William R.) Pvt, A, 1st PA Cav, [Wounded 6-21-1864 at White House, VA.] DoD Unknown. Mount Holly Cemetery, Mount Holly, Burlington County.
BEARMAN, JOHN C. Pvt, A, 1st DE Cav, 4-4-1897. Harleigh Cemetery, Camden, Camden County.
BEARMORE, HIRAM Wagoner, G, 11th NJ Inf, 1-30-1881. Cedar Hill Cemetery, Hightstown, Mercer County.
BEASLEY, J.C. Pvt, B, 15th AL Inf (CSA), [Captured at Gettysburg, PA.] 3-5-1864. Finn's Point National Cemetery, Pennsville, Salem County.
BEATLE, VALENTINE (see: Bettel, Valentine) Woodland Cemetery, Newark, Essex County.
BEATTIE, ESTILLE Pvt, K, 39th NJ Inf, 2-13-1888. Laurel Grove Cemetery, Totowa, Passaic County.

New Jersey Civil War Burials

BEATTY, ALEXANDER (aka: Bums, Alexander) Pvt, F, 19th U.S. Inf, 1-8-1887. Pearson/Colonial Memorial Park Cemetery, Whitehorse, Mercer County.

BEATTY, DANIEL Corp, I, 1st MN Inf, 2-13-1923. Bayview-New York Bay Cemetery, Jersey City, Hudson County.

BEATTY, GEORGE W. Pvt, D, 9th NJ Inf, 10-27-1924. Baptist Church Cemetery, Jacobstown, Burlington County.

BEATTY, JOHN Pvt, H, 7th NJ Inf, 3-23-1880. St. John's Cemetery, Hamilton, Mercer County.

BEATTY, JOHN Pvt, A, 6th NJ Inf, 1-14-1909. Riverside Cemetery, Toms River, Ocean County.

BEATTY, JOHN JAMES Pvt, G, 2nd NJ Cav, 3-22-1911. Evergreen Cemetery, Hillside, Union County.

BEATTY, JOSEPH S. Com Sgt, 57th IL Inf 8-25-1922. Arlington Cemetery, Kearny, Hudson County.

BEATTY, MATTHEW Pvt, F, 164th NY Inf, 8-25-1888. Evergreen Cemetery, Hillside, Union County.

BEATTY, SAMUEL 1-27-1878. Zion United Methodist Church Cemetery, Clarksboro, Gloucester County.

BEATTY*, SAMUEL H. Pvt, H, 8th CA Inf, 3-16-1897. Evergreen Cemetery, Camden, Camden County.

BEATTY, STEPHEN Corp, G, 9th NJ Inf, 2-16-1869. Evergreen Cemetery, Hillside, Union County.

BEATTY, THOMAS C. Pvt, Btty A, 13th NY Heavy Art, 5-28-1885. Fairmount Cemetery, Newark, Essex County.

BEATTY, WHITFIELD H. Wagoner, D, 130th OH Inf, 11-21-1907. Presbyterian Church Cemetery, Sparta, Sussex County.

BEATTY, WILLIAM Pvt, I, 11th NJ Inf, 11-10-1891. Cedar Lawn Cemetery, Paterson, Passaic County.

BEATTY, WILLIAM H. Corp, D, 124th PA Inf, 11-4-1890. Fairmount Cemetery, Newark, Essex County.

BEATTY, WILLIAM H.H. Corp, Btty F, 5th NY Heavy Art, 2-7-1921. Alpine Cemetery, Perth Amboy, Middlesex County.

BEATTY, WILLIAM H. (SR.) Fireman, U.S. Navy, 6-12-1908. Monument Cemetery, Edgewater Park, Burlington County.

BEAUMONT, HORATION NELSON Sgt, F, 11th PA Militia, 6-26-1911. Holcomb-Riverview Cemetery, Lambertville, Hunterdon County.

BEAVENS, JOHN DoD Unknown. Riverside Cemetery, Toms River, Ocean County.

BEAVER, JOSEPH CHATTLE Pvt, A, 31st NJ Inf, 2-10-1865. Methodist Church Cemetery, Fairmount, Hunterdon County.

BEAVER, MONROE Sgt, E, 5th NC Inf (CSA), [Wounded 5-5-1862 at Williamsburg, VA. Captured 7-4-1863 at Gettysburg, PA. Died of smallpox.] 4-17-1865. Finn's Point National Cemetery, Pennsville, Salem County.

BEAVERS, GEORGE Corp, A, 31st NJ Inf, [Died of typhoid at Fitzhugh House, VA.] 5-28-1863. Methodist Church Cemetery, Fairmount, Hunterdon County.

BEAVERS, GEORGE S. Corp, A, 15th NJ Inf, 10-31-1922. Presbyterian Church Cemetery, Mendham, Morris County.

BEAZLY, RICHARD R. Sgt, Btty K, 1st U.S. Art, 1904. Berlin Cemetery, Berlin, Camden County.

BECHLER, JOSEPH Corp, B, 3rd NJ Inf, 10-31-1914. Rahway Cemetery, Rahway, Union County.

BECHLER, VALENTINE Pvt, E, 8th NJ Inf, 1-6-1870. Holy Sepulchre Cemetery, East Orange, Essex County.

BECHMANN*, ADOLPH Pvt, Btty A, 1st NJ Light Art, 11-2-1899. Fair Lawn Cemetery, Fair Lawn, Bergen County.

Our Brothers Gone Before

BECHT, JOHANN Pvt, H, 9th NJ Inf, 10-2-1879. Woodland Cemetery, Newark, Essex County.

BECHT, OTTO Pvt, Btty C, 1st NJ Light Art, 12-22-1882. Woodland Cemetery, Newark, Essex County.

BECHTEL, CHARLES R. Pvt, E, 6th NJ Inf, [Killed in action at Williamsburg, VA.] 5-5-1862. Bordentown/Old St. Mary's Catholic Cemetery, Bordentown, Burlington County.

BECHTEL, FREDERICK Pvt, G, 23rd NJ Inf, 12-4-1919. Harleigh Cemetery, Camden, Camden County.

BECHTEL, ROBERT Corp, C, 50th PA Inf, 1-19-1898. Bayview-New York Bay Cemetery, Jersey City, Hudson County.

BECHTEL*, WILLIAM Pvt, E, 10th NJ Inf, 8- -1921. Monument Cemetery, Edgewater Park, Burlington County.

BECHTEL*, WILLIAM H. 1st Lt, C, 4th NJ Inf, 9-17-1923. Harleigh Cemetery, Camden, Camden County.

BECHTER, PETER Pvt, D, 8th NY Inf, 1-26-1906. Soldier's Home Cemetery, Vineland, Cumberland County.

BECHTOLD, JACOB (aka: Bachtold, Jacob) Pvt, C, 8th NJ Inf, 2-8-1887. Woodland Cemetery, Newark, Essex County.

BECHTOLD*, JOHN Corp, F, 39th NJ Inf, [Wounded 8-27-1862 at 2nd Bull Run, VA.] 2-20-1909. Fairmount Cemetery, Newark, Essex County.

BECHTOLD, MICHAEL Pvt, F, 39th NJ Inf, 3-4-1900. East Ridgelawn Cemetery, Clifton, Passaic County.

BECHTOLDT, GEORGE Pvt, E, 5th NY State Militia, 7-28-1913. Palisade Cemetery, North Bergen, Hudson County.

BECK, ALEXANDER (aka: Beck, Andrew) Pvt, C, 97th PA Inf, 4-15-1902. Harleigh Cemetery, Camden, Camden County.

BECK, ANDREW (see: Beck, Alexander) Harleigh Cemetery, Camden, Camden County.

BECK*, CHARLES Pvt, 30th NY Ind Btty 7-27-1899. Fairmount Cemetery, Newark, Essex County.

BECK, CHARLES E. 1st Lt, C, 15th PA Cav, 2-25-1916. Bethel Cemetery, Pennsauken, Camden County.

BECK, EDMUND Pvt, E, 37th NJ Inf, 3-21-1898. Fairmount Cemetery, Newark, Essex County.

BECK, FREDERICK (JR.) Maj, 108th OH Inf 2-19-1907. Flower Hill Cemetery, North Bergen, Hudson County.

BECK, GEORGE J. [Wounded in action.] 4-21-1888. Greengrove Cemetery, Keyport, Monmouth County.

BECK*, HEINRICH C. Corp, A, 96th NY Inf, 4-24-1922. Bloomfield Cemetery, Bloomfield, Essex County.

BECK, JACOB 11-6-1907. Palisade Cemetery, North Bergen, Hudson County.

BECK, JACOB Pvt, H, 12th NJ Inf, 9-14-1908. St. Mary's Cemetery, Clark, Union County.

BECK, JACOB J. DoD Unknown. Hainesburg Cemetery, Hainesburg, Warren County.

BECK, JOHN Pvt, H, 12th NJ Inf, 1888. Hainesburg Cemetery, Hainesburg, Warren County.

BECK, JOSEPH A. DoD Unknown. Evergreen Cemetery, Camden, Camden County.

BECK, JOSEPH F. Pvt, H, 2nd NY Mounted Rifles, 8-24-1893. Fairmount Cemetery, Newark, Essex County.

BECK, LEWIS F. 12-7-1911. Fairmount Cemetery, Newark, Essex County.

BECK, PETER Pvt, F, 37th NY State Militia, 1-21-1888. Flower Hill Cemetery, North Bergen, Hudson County.

BECK, PHILIP Sgt, G, 75th PA Inf, 7-21-1913. Greenwood Cemetery, Hamilton, Mercer County.

New Jersey Civil War Burials

BECK, RUDOLF FREDERICK Pvt, I, 96th NY Inf, 7-14-1885. Grove Church Cemetery, North Bergen, Hudson County.

BECK, SARAH (BINNEY) Nurse, U.S. Volunteers, 1904. Bloomfield Cemetery, Bloomfield, Essex County.

BECK*, THOMAS R. 2nd Lt, G, 7th NJ Inf, 1-4-1884. Laurel Grove Cemetery, Totowa, Passaic County.

BECK, WILLIAM Sgt, E, 55th NY Inf, DoD Unknown. Berry Lawn Cemetery, Carlstadt, Bergen County.

BECKER, ADOLPH Lt Col, 46th NY Inf 2-8-1902. Fairmount Cemetery, Newark, Essex County.

BECKER, CHARLES Pvt, E, 3rd NJ Cav, DoD Unknown. Harleigh Cemetery, Camden, Camden County.

BECKER*, CHARLES Capt, G, 119th NY Inf, [Wounded in action.] 12-6-1899. Prospect Hill Cemetery, Caldwell, Essex County.

BECKER, CHARLES (see: Kohlbecker, Cornelius) St. Mary's Cemetery, East Orange, Essex County.

BECKER, FREDERICK G. Pvt, H, 30th NJ Inf, 1-27-1902. Evergreen Cemetery, Hillside, Union County.

BECKER, HENRY Corp, G, 162nd NY Inf, [Wounded 4-8-1864 at Sabine Cross Roads, LA.] 2-20-1915. Atco Cemetery, Atco, Camden County.

BECKER, JOSEPH Corp, C, 8th MO Inf, 6-5-1908. Rosedale Cemetery, Linden, Union County.

BECKER, JULIUS L.F. Pvt, D, 165th OH Inf, 11-27-1886. Old Camden Cemetery, Camden, Camden County.

BECKER, WILLIAM 3rd Cl Musc, 1st NJ Brigade Band 7-8-1900. Evergreen Cemetery, Morristown, Morris County.

BECKETT, ANDREW Pvt, A, 127th U.S. CT, 7-5-1904. Mount Peace Cemetery, Lawnside, Camden County.

BECKETT, CHARLES H. Corp, D, 25th U.S. CT, 12-27-1895. Johnson Cemetery, Camden, Camden County.

BECKETT, GEORGE W. Pvt, C, 24th NJ Inf, DoD Unknown. Berlin Cemetery, Berlin, Camden County.

BECKETT*, HIRAM D. Pvt, A, 9th NJ Inf, 1919. Cedar Green Cemetery, Clayton, Gloucester County.

BECKETT, ISAAC Pvt, K, 8th U.S. CT, 6-13-1889. Zion AME Church Cemetery, Marshalltown, Salem County.

BECKETT, J.D. Pvt, D, 27th VA Inf (CSA), [Died of disease.] 7-16-1864. Finn's Point National Cemetery, Pennsville, Salem County.

BECKETT*, JAMES P. Pvt, H, 12th NJ Inf, 5-8-1918. Methodist Church Cemetery, Union Grove, Salem County.

BECKETT, JOHN S. Pvt, I, 24th NJ Inf, 2-14-1900. Mount Pleasant Cemetery, Millville, Cumberland County.

BECKETT, JOHN W. Seaman, U.S. Navy, USS Princeton, 7-3-1896. Johnson Cemetery, Camden, Camden County.

BECKETT, JOSIAH Landsman, U.S. Navy, USS John Adams, 5-21-1905. Evergreen Cemetery, Camden, Camden County.

BECKETT, SAMUEL T. Pvt, H, 7th NJ Inf, 1-27-1867. Bethesda Methodist-Episcopal Church Cemetery, Swedesboro, Gloucester County.

BECKHARDT, HENRY Pvt, Btty A, 1st NJ Light Art, 12-9-1893. Palisade Cemetery, North Bergen, Hudson County.

BECKING, JULIUS Musc, D, 18th NY Inf, 2-3-1902. Siloam Cemetery, Vineland, Cumberland County.

BECKMAN, ADOLPH Pvt, Btty A, 1st NJ Light Art, 11-4-1899. Fairmount Cemetery, Newark, Essex County.

Our Brothers Gone Before

BECKMAN, JOHN W. Seaman, U.S. Navy, 1-16-1896. Flower Hill Cemetery, North Bergen, Hudson County.

BECKWITH, THOMAS (see: Beckworth, Thomas) Methodist Church Cemetery, Eldora, Cape May County.

BECKWORTH, THOMAS (aka: Beckwith, Thomas) Pvt, F, 25th NJ Inf, [Died of measles at Washington, DC.] 11-7-1862. Methodist Church Cemetery, Eldora, Cape May County.

BEDELL, BRICE 4-27-1892. Branchville Cemetery, Branchville, Sussex County.

BEDELL, DANIEL Pvt, C, 14th NJ Inf, 11-6-1878. Evergreen Cemetery, Hillside, Union County.

BEDELL, JAMES OLIVER 2nd Lt, E, 14th NJ Inf, 1905. Cedarwood Cemetery, Hazlet, Monmouth County.

BEDELL, LEWIS A. Pvt, I, 27th NJ Inf, 1928. United Methodist Church Cemetery, New Providence, Union County.

BEDELL, MELANCTHON Pvt, D, 8th NJ Inf, [Died of wounds received 5-3-1863 at Chancellorsville, VA.] 6-9-1863. Mount Pleasant Cemetery, Newark, Essex County.

BEDELL, STEPHEN A. Artificer, K, 1st NY Eng, 5-2-1889. Fairview Cemetery, Fairview, Monmouth County.

BEDELL, WILLIAM E. Pvt, I, 27th NJ Inf, 5-19-1912. Presbyterian Cemetery, New Vernon, Morris County.

BEDFORD, HENRY Pvt, E, 13th NJ Inf, [Cenotaph. Killed in action at Atlanta, GA.] 7-27-1864. Northfield Baptist Cemetery, Livingston, Essex County.

BEDFORD*, RANDOLPH Pvt, C, 2nd NJ Inf, 5-18-1902. Fairmount Cemetery, Newark, Essex County.

BEDLE, HOLMES Pvt, D, 38th NJ Inf, DoD Unknown. Rose Hill Cemetery, Matawan, Monmouth County.

BEDLE, SEPTIMUS STEPHENS Corp, B, 29th NJ Inf, 12-23-1934. Greengrove Cemetery, Keyport, Monmouth County.

BEDLE, THOMAS Landsman, U.S. Navy, USS North Carolina, 1920. Greengrove Cemetery, Keyport, Monmouth County.

BEDLE, WILLIAM (JR.) Sgt, B, 29th NJ Inf, 1919. Greengrove Cemetery, Keyport, Monmouth County.

BEDMAN, CHARLES Pvt, F, 28th NJ Inf, 4-21-1898. Trinity Episcopal Church Cemetery, Woodbridge, Middlesex County.

BEDMAN, LEWIS WASHINTON 1-11-1882. Trinity Episcopal Church Cemetery, Woodbridge, Middlesex County.

BEE, JACOB L. Pvt, F, 105th PA Inf, 12-21-1904. New Camden Cemetery, Camden, Camden County.

BEEBE*, BENJAMIN H. Pvt, I, 7th CT Inf, 1-12-1901. Presbyterian Church Cemetery, Bridgeton, Cumberland County.

BEEBE, DAVID 7-14-1875. Bates Mills Cemetery, Waterford Works, Camden County.

BEEBE*, EBENEZER Pvt, F, 8th NJ Inf, 1926. Bates Mills Cemetery, Waterford Works, Camden County.

BEEBE*, HENRY C. Pvt, H, 3rd NJ Cav, DoD Unknown. Chestnut Hill Cemetery, East Brunswick, Middlesex County.

BEEBE*, JOSIAH Pvt, F, 8th NJ Inf, 8-2-1906. Bates Mills Cemetery, Waterford Works, Camden County.

BEEBE, LEWIS Pvt, I, 10th NJ Inf, [Died of cholera at Philadelphia, PA.] 8-1-1863. United Methodist Church Cemetery, Winslow, Camden County.

BEEBE, OLIVER Pvt, G, 1st PA Inf, 7-10-1889. Presbyterian Church Cemetery, Mays Landing, Atlantic County.

BEEBE, WILLIAM H. Pvt, G, 3rd NJ Cav, DoD Unknown. Cedar Green Cemetery, Clayton, Gloucester County.

New Jersey Civil War Burials

BEECROFT, CHARLES H. Corp, D, 1st NJ Cav, 7-9-1914. Riverview Cemetery, Trenton, Mercer County.

BEECROFT, JOSEPH 6-26-1890. Riverview Cemetery, Trenton, Mercer County.

BEEGLE*, JACOB (aka: Clark, George) Pvt, G, 1st ME Cav, 2-2-1923. Mount Hope Presbyterian Cemetery, Lambertville, Hunterdon County.

BEEKMAN, ABRAHAM J. 1st Lt, F, 35th NJ Inf, 4-4-1892. Laurel Hill Cemetery, Elwood, Atlantic County.

BEEKMAN, DANIEL D. 10-21-1916. New Somerville Cemetery, Somerville, Somerset County.

BEEKMAN, GARRETT V. Capt, I, 1st NJ Cav, 12-14-1884. Rocky Hill Cemetery, Rocky Hill, Somerset County.

BEEKMAN, GEORGE C. Pvt, C, 127th U.S. CT, 10-11-1865. Princeton Cemetery, Princeton, Mercer County.

BEEKMAN, JOSHUA Pvt, E, 15th NJ Inf, 1-28-1864. Methodist Church Cemetery, Mount Horeb, Somerset County.

BEEKMAN, SAMUEL J. 2nd Lt, F, 35th NJ Inf, [Died of disease at Memphis, TN.] 3-21-1864. New Somerville Cemetery, Somerville, Somerset County.

BEEL, ERNEST (see: Biehl, Ernest) Woodland Cemetery, Newark, Essex County.

BEELHER, CHARLES (see: Buehler, Charles) Fairmount Cemetery, Newark, Essex County.

BEEMAN, JOHN M. Pvt, K, 1st NJ Inf, 6-17-1872. Hoboken Cemetery, North Bergen, Hudson County.

BEEMER, ALBERT H. Pvt, I, 7th NJ Inf, 1925. Branchville Cemetery, Branchville, Sussex County.

BEEMER, EZRA Corp, H, 27th NJ Inf, DoD Unknown. Old Clove Church Cemetery, Wantage, Sussex County.

BEEMER, FRANKLIN Pvt, H, 27th NJ Inf, DoD Unknown. Old Clove Church Cemetery, Wantage, Sussex County.

BEEMER, HARRISON Corp, M, 1st NJ Cav, 1913. Beemerville Cemetery, Beemerville, Sussex County.

BEEMER, SOLOMON Pvt, Btty D, 1st NJ Light Art, [Died of diarrhea at Fort Monroe, VA.] 3-25-1865. Brink Cemetery, Colesville, Sussex County.

BEEMER, WILLIAM S. (aka: Beemer, William T.) Corp, A, 87th NY Inf, [Died of mumps at Yorktown, VA.] 4-16-1862. Old Beemer Church Cemetery, Roys, Sussex County.

BEEMER, WILLIAM T. (see: Beemer, William S.) Old Beemer Church Cemetery, Roys, Sussex County.

BEEMIS, ALLEN H. (aka: Beamish, Allen) Pvt, E, 82nd PA Inf, 5-1-1926. Harleigh Cemetery, Camden, Camden County.

BEER, FRANK Pvt, F, 75th PA Inf, 1-27-1896. St. Paul's Lutheran Church Cemetery, Hainesport, Burlington County.

BEERS, CHARLES M. Pvt, F, 3rd NJ Cav, 3-8-1890. Phillipsburg Cemetery, Phillipsburg, Warren County.

BEERS, CHARLES Y. Pvt, K, 7th NJ Inf, [Died of wounds received 7-2-1863 at Gettysburg, PA.] 7-6-1863. Evergreen Cemetery, Morristown, Morris County.

BEERS*, GEORGE Corp, D, 156th NY Inf, 4-23-1888. Locust Hill Cemetery, Dover, Morris County.

BEERS, JABEZ Pvt, E, 7th NJ Inf, [Killed in action at Petersburg, VA.] 6-16-1864. Evergreen Cemetery, Morristown, Morris County.

BEERS*, JACOB H. Com Sgt, D, 83rd NY Inf, 11-11-1909. Riverview Cemetery, Trenton, Mercer County.

BEERS, JOHN Pvt, H, 16th PA Inf, 11-15-1868. Phillipsburg Cemetery, Phillipsburg, Warren County.

Our Brothers Gone Before

BEERS, SAMUEL Pvt, G, 29th NJ Inf, [Died of typhoid at Washington, DC.] 1-29-1863. Holmdel Cemetery, Holmdel, Monmouth County.
BEERS, THEODORE Pvt, C, 37th NJ Inf, 12-10-1915. Mansfield/Washington Cemetery, Washington, Warren County.
BEERS, WILLIAM H. Corp, C, 15th NJ Inf, [Wounded 5-3-1863 at Salem Heights, VA.] 10-12-1896. St. Vincent Martyr Cemetery, Madison, Morris County.
BEERS, WILLIAM W. 8-21-1907. Evergreen Cemetery, Morristown, Morris County.
BEESE, HENRY Pvt, Castellano's Btty, LA Light Art (CSA), 4-26-1874. Fairmount Cemetery, Newark, Essex County.
BEESICKS, GEORGE H. (aka: Baizicks, George) Pvt, C, 22nd U.S. CT, [Died at Newark, NJ.] 8-15-1864. Fairmount Cemetery, Newark, Essex County.
BEET, THOMAS C. 6-28-1933. Fairview Cemetery, Fairview, Monmouth County.
BEETHAM, JOHN W. 1929. New Presbyterian Cemetery, Bound Brook, Somerset County.
BEETLE, JOHN BARTON Pvt, E, 99th PA Inf, [Died at Philadelphia, PA.] 8-19-1862. Hedding Methodist-Episcopal Church Cemetery, Bellmawr, Camden County.
BEGBIE, EUGENE Corp, A, 13th NJ Inf, 7-19-1924. Fairmount Cemetery, Newark, Essex County.
BEGBIE, GEORGE L. 1st Lt, F, 33rd NJ Inf, 4-7-1910. Fairmount Cemetery, Newark, Essex County.
BEGGS, JAMES Pvt, I, 2nd NJ Inf, 7-19-1889. Cedar Lawn Cemetery, Paterson, Passaic County.
BEGGS, JOSEPH Pvt, D, 28th NJ Inf, 10-18-1891. St. Peter's Cemetery, New Brunswick, Middlesex County.
BEGGS, WILLIAM C. Pvt, E, 11th NY Cav, [Died at Washington, DC. of an accidental gun shot wound to the head.] 8-17-1863. Cedar Lawn Cemetery, Paterson, Passaic County.
BEHAN, JOHN R. Pvt, U.S. Army, [Quartermasters Department.] 8-9-1902. St. Teresa's Cemetery, Summit, Union County.
BEHM, HENRY Pvt, D, 7th NJ Inf, 3-11-1904. Egg Harbor Cemetery, Egg Harbor, Atlantic County.
BEHM, HENRY J. DoD Unknown. St. Mary's Cemetery, East Orange, Essex County.
BEHNE, FREDERICK Pvt, Unassigned, 68th OH Inf, DoD Unknown. Hackensack Cemetery, Hackensack, Bergen County.
BEHNNE, HUGO Sgt, I, 12th NY Inf, DoD Unknown. Bayview-New York Bay Cemetery, Jersey City, Hudson County.
BEHRENS*, WILLIAM H. 1st Lt, F, 39th NJ Inf, 11-27-1908. Rosedale Cemetery, Orange, Essex County.
BEHRINGER*, MICHAEL Musc, 103rd NY Inf Band 3-29-1899. Osage Cemetery, East Brunswick, Middlesex County.
BEHRINGER, PHILIP Pvt, D, 2nd NJ Inf, 8-1-1891. Fairmount Cemetery, Newark, Essex County.
BEHRMANN, HENRY G. Pvt, E, 61st NY Inf, 8-13-1900. Cedar Lawn Cemetery, Paterson, Passaic County.
BEIDELMAN, EDWIN M. Pvt, I, 38th NJ Inf, 7-12-1883. Union Cemetery, Frenchtown, Hunterdon County.
BEIDEMAN, JOHN Pvt, G, 4th NJ Militia, 3-20-1910. Evergreen Cemetery, Camden, Camden County.
BEIDERMAN, HENRY 7-4-1930. Valleau Cemetery, Ridgewood, Bergen County.
BEIERLE, LEWIS (see: Beuerle, Louis) New Camden Cemetery, Camden, Camden County.
BEINE, JOHN (aka: Bean, John) Pvt, B, 169th NY Inf, 2-22-1896. St. Nicholas Cemetery, Lodi, Bergen County.

New Jersey Civil War Burials

BEINEMANN*, ALBERT Pvt, F, 162nd NY Inf, 5-21-1903. Flower Hill Cemetery, North Bergen, Hudson County.
BEING, J.P. (see: Bing, Joshua P.) Finn's Point National Cemetery, Pennsville, Salem County.
BEIPGENTS, K. (see: Baygeants, K.W.) Finn's Point National Cemetery, Pennsville, Salem County.
BEIRNE, CHARLES (aka: Burns, Charles) Pvt, B, 48th NY Inf, DoD Unknown. Holy Sepulchre Cemetery, Totowa, Passaic County.
BELCHER, AMHERST W. 1st Sgt, Btty M, 15th NY Heavy Art, 1-1-1919. Oddfellows Cemetery, Burlington, Burlington County.
BELCHER, CHARLES 1904. Clinton Cemetery, Irvington, Essex County.
BELCHER, JACOB Pvt, F, 27th NJ Inf, 6-22-1901. Glenwood Cemetery, Glenwood, Sussex County.
BELCHER*, SYLVESTER Pvt, D, 112th NY Inf, 9-1-1907. Glenwood Cemetery, Glenwood, Sussex County.
BELDEN, HENRY A. Pvt, K, 70th NY Inf, 3-21-1890. Fairmount Cemetery, Newark, Essex County.
BELDEN, OLIVER S. Asst Surg, 5th NJ Inf 10-25-1904. Presbyterian Cemetery, Salem, Salem County.
BELDIN, GEORGE A. 2nd Lt, H, 40th NJ Inf, 7-25-1873. St. Mary's Episcopal Church Cemetery, Burlington, Burlington County.
BELDING, AUGUSTUS 1-1-1902. Canfield Cemetery, Cedar Grove, Essex County.
BELEW, GEORGE T. Pvt, Charlottesville Btty, VA Light Art (CSA), [Captured 5-12-1864 at Spotsylvania CH, VA. Died of disease.] 3-18-1865. Finn's Point National Cemetery, Pennsville, Salem County.
BELFIELD*, WILLIAM Corp, F, 7th NJ Inf, DoD Unknown. Bayview-New York Bay Cemetery, Jersey City, Hudson County.
BELGER, JAMES Fireman, U.S. Navy, 1-8-1890. Holy Name Cemetery, Jersey City, Hudson County.
BELK, JOHN W. Pvt, H, 2nd (Ashby's) TN Cav (CSA), 3-16-1864. Finn's Point National Cemetery, Pennsville, Salem County.
BELL, ALEXANDER B. Pvt, C, 5th VA Inf (CSA), [Wounded 6-9-1862 at Port Republic, VA. Captured 7-5-1863 at Gettysburg, PA. Died of diptheria.] 9-22-1863. Finn's Point National Cemetery, Pennsville, Salem County.
BELL*, ALVAH T. Pvt, H, 3rd VT Inf, 11-12-1888. Fairmount Cemetery, Newark, Essex County.
BELL, BENJAMIN Pvt, A, 24th NJ Inf, 11-28-1901. Old Friends Cemetery, Salem, Salem County.
BELL, BENJAMIN D. Pvt, F, 43rd NC Inf (CSA), [Wounded 7-1-1863 at Gettysburg, PA. Captured 7-5-1863 at South Mountain, MD.] 10-8-1863. Finn's Point National Cemetery, Pennsville, Salem County.
BELL, CHARLES Pvt, B, 1st NJ Inf, 6-1-1864. Baptist Church Cemetery, Jacobstown, Burlington County.
BELL, CHARLES H. Commodore, U.S. Navy, 2-19-1875. Elmwood Cemetery, New Brunswick, Middlesex County.
BELL, CHARLES S. Pvt, G, __ U.S. __, 5-9-1864. Rahway Cemetery, Rahway, Union County.
BELL, DAVID A. Pvt, G, 2nd NJ Inf, 12-19-1893. Rosedale Cemetery, Orange, Essex County.
BELL, EDWARD M. (SR.) Pvt, B, 105th OH Inf, DoD Unknown. Branchville Cemetery, Branchville, Sussex County.
BELL, FRANCIS (see: Bell, Franklin) 1st Baptist Cemetery, New Brunswick, Middlesex County.

Our Brothers Gone Before

BELL, FRANKLIN (aka: Bell, Francis) Pvt, K, 45th U.S. CT, 1872. 1st Baptist Cemetery, New Brunswick, Middlesex County.
BELL, GEORGE 2-22-1896. Methodist Cemetery, Bridgeboro, Burlington County.
BELL, GEORGE Pvt, I, 4th NJ Inf, [Died of typhoid at New York, NY.] 5-29-1862. Baptist Church Cemetery, Jacobstown, Burlington County.
BELL, HENRY Pvt, M, 2nd NJ Cav, 7-15-1895. Bayview-New York Bay Cemetery, Jersey City, Hudson County.
BELL, HENRY FRAZIER Pvt, Btty A, Stark's Bttn Confederate Light Art (CSA), 7-30-1896. Overlook Cemetery, Bridgeton, Cumberland County.
BELL, HENRY T. Pvt, B, 23rd VA Inf (CSA), [Wounded 5-2-1863 at Chancellorsville, VA. Captured 5-12-1864 at Spotsylvania CH, VA. Died of lung inflammation.] 3-26-1865. Finn's Point National Cemetery, Pennsville, Salem County.
BELL, ISAIAH Pvt, A, 24th NJ Inf, 7-14-1914. 1st Baptist Church Cemetery, Woodstown, Salem County.
BELL, JACOB J. Pvt, A, 22nd NJ Inf, 5-2-1900. Woodside Cemetery, Dumont, Bergen County.
BELL, JAMES Pvt, C, 3rd NJ Cav, 10-25-1920. Weller Cemetery, Willow Grove, Warren County.
BELL, JAMES Sgt, D, 150th NY Inf, [Wounded 5-25-1864 at Dallas, GA. and 3-16-1865 at Averysboro, NC.] 5-7-1892. Evergreen Cemetery, Hillside, Union County.
BELL, JAMES Pvt, A, 5th NJ Inf, 6-8-1892. Greenwood Cemetery, Hamilton, Mercer County.
BELL, JAMES (see: Bell, John) Montana Cemetery, Montana, Warren County.
BELL, JAMES E. 12-8-1870. Monument Cemetery, Edgewater Park, Burlington County.
BELL, JAMES EDWARD Cadet, U.S.M.A., 9-11-1873. Riverview Cemetery, Trenton, Mercer County.
BELL, JOB K. Pvt, G, 23rd NJ Inf, 1- -1923. Methodist Church Cemetery, New Albany, Burlington County.
BELL, JOHN Pvt, E, 37th NJ Inf, 2-11-1917. Fairmount Cemetery, Newark, Essex County.
BELL, JOHN Pvt, A, 59th NY Inf, [Wounded 9-17-1862 at Antietam, MD.] 10-8-1927. Washington Monumental Cemetery, South River, Middlesex County.
BELL, JOHN (aka: Bell, James) Pvt, D, 81st PA Inf, 5-23-1904. Montana Cemetery, Montana, Warren County.
BELL, JOHN C. Pvt, E, 51st GA Inf (CSA), [Captured 7-3-1863 at Gettysburg, PA. Died of measles.] 12-17-1863. Finn's Point National Cemetery, Pennsville, Salem County.
BELL, JOHN HANN Bvt Brig Gen, U.S. Volunteers, [Lt. Colonel, 12th Veteran Reserve Corps.] 4-20-1875. Rosedale Cemetery, Orange, Essex County.
BELL, JOHN WILLIAM Seaman, U.S. Navy, 12-23-1866. Union Cemetery, Washington, Morris County.
BELL, JOSEPH G. Pvt, C, PA Emerg NJ Militia, 1918. Greenwood Cemetery, Hamilton, Mercer County.
BELL, MAURICE Pvt, I, 26th NJ Inf, 3-16-1892. Holy Sepulchre Cemetery, East Orange, Essex County.
BELL, MILLER G. Corp, E, 3rd NJ Cav, 4-3-1881. Fountain Grove Cemetery, Glen Gardner, Hunterdon County.
BELL, OLIN Pvt, B, 15th AL Inf (CSA), [Captured at Gettysburg, PA.] 2-7-1864. Finn's Point National Cemetery, Pennsville, Salem County.
BELL, PETER Pvt, E, 30th NJ Inf, 4-19-1911. Prospect Hill Cemetery, Flemington, Hunterdon County.
BELL, SAMUEL C. 1st Sgt, 15th (Northwest) AR Inf (CSA) [Captured 5-16-1863 at Big Black River Bridge, MS.] 9-21-1863. Finn's Point National Cemetery, Pennsville, Salem County.
BELL, TALMADGE L. Sgt, H, 31st NJ Inf, 8-1-1906. Union Cemetery, Washington, Morris County.

New Jersey Civil War Burials

BELL, THOMAS Seaman, U.S. Navy, USS Vermont, 8-10-1912. Greenwood Cemetery, Pleasantville, Atlantic County.

BELL, THOMAS F. Pvt, C, 4th NJ Inf, 3-31-1906. Bordentown/Old St. Mary's Catholic Cemetery, Bordentown, Burlington County.

BELL, THOMAS G. Boatswain, U.S. Navy, 8-9-1883. Evergreen Cemetery, Camden, Camden County.

BELL, THOMAS G. Seaman, U.S. Navy, 3-5-1907. Berry Lawn Cemetery, Carlstadt, Bergen County.

BELL, W.J. Pvt, D, 2nd FL Inf (CSA), [Captured 7-4-1863 at Gettysburg, PA. Died of smallpox.] 10-24-1863. Finn's Point National Cemetery, Pennsville, Salem County.

BELL, WILLIAM Pvt, U.S. Marine Corps, 6-16-1906. Monument Cemetery, Edgewater Park, Burlington County.

BELL, WILLIAM Pvt, A, 2nd NJ Militia, 12-4-1906. Bayview-New York Bay Cemetery, Jersey City, Hudson County.

BELL, WILLIAM C. Pvt, D, 3rd NJ Inf, [Died at Fredericksburg, VA. of wounds received 5-3-1863 at Salem Heights, VA.] 5-18-1863. Layton Cemetery, Layton, Sussex County.

BELL*, WILLIAM G. Pvt, C, 165th NY Inf, 8-31-1907. Laurel Grove Cemetery, Totowa, Passaic County.

BELL, WILLIAM H. Pvt, B, 38th NJ Inf, 8-14-1927. Greenwood Cemetery, Hamilton, Mercer County.

BELLANGEE, JAMES B. Surg, U.S. Army, [Died of yellow fever at Morehead City, NC.] 10-6-1864. North Crosswicks Cemetery, North Crosswicks, Mercer County.

BELLARD, ALFRED Pvt, E, 5th NJ Inf, 9-19-1891. Fairmount Cemetery, Newark, Essex County.

BELLAS, BENJAMIN Pvt, I, 143rd PA Inf, DoD Unknown. Elmwood Cemetery, New Brunswick, Middlesex County.

BELLERJEAU*, SAMUEL OAKLEY Pvt, D, 4th NJ Inf, 10-17-1901. Mercer Cemetery, Trenton, Mercer County.

BELLIS, ANDREW J. Pvt, D, 31st NJ Inf, 7-29-1911. Prospect Hill Cemetery, Flemington, Hunterdon County.

BELLIS*, GABRIEL H. Pvt, C, 59th NY Inf, 4-7-1908. Baptist/Evergreen Methodist Cemetery, Plainfield, Union County.

BELLIS, GODFREY Wagoner, F, 31st NJ Inf, 5-4-1906. Christian Cemetery, Milford, Hunterdon County.

BELLIS*, JAMES O. Sgt, G, 7th NJ Inf, 12-8-1912. Mount Hope Presbyterian Cemetery, Lambertville, Hunterdon County.

BELLIS, JOHN (see: Billes, John W.) Cedar Hill Cemetery, East Millstone, Somerset County.

BELLIS, PETER S. Corp, A, 30th NJ Inf, 12-12-1919. Old Somerville Cemetery, Somerville, Somerset County.

BELLIS, PETER S. 3-30-1886. Hainesburg Cemetery, Hainesburg, Warren County.

BELLIS, STEWART Pvt, D, 31st NJ Inf, 9-19-1922. Prospect Hill Cemetery, Flemington, Hunterdon County.

BELLIS, THEODORE B. Pvt, A, 15th NJ Inf, 12-21-1911. Prospect Hill Cemetery, Flemington, Hunterdon County.

BELLIS, WILLIAM DUKE Pvt, F, 30th NJ Inf, 12-24-1893. Amwell Ridge Cemetery, Larisons Corner, Hunterdon County.

BELLIS, WILLIAM R. Pvt, H, 3rd NJ Militia, 8-12-1928. Arlington Cemetery, Kearny, Hudson County.

BELLMAN, DANIEL Pvt, H, 88th PA Inf, 9-28-1922. Arlington Cemetery, Kearny, Hudson County.

Our Brothers Gone Before

BELT, GEORGE Pvt, K, 5th NJ Inf, 1928. Bayview-New York Bay Cemetery, Jersey City, Hudson County.

BELVILLE*, ROBERT C. 1st Lt, A, PA Emerg NJ Militia, 8-16-1875. Mercer Cemetery, Trenton, Mercer County.

BELVILLE, SAMUEL S. 7-10-1886. Eglington Cemetery, Clarksboro, Gloucester County.

BEMLER, GEORGE A. Corp, I, 31st NJ Inf, 1-5-1900. Methodist Church Cemetery, Buttzville, Warren County.

BEMSPACH, MICHAEL Pvt, B, 9th NJ Inf, DoD Unknown. Bayview-New York Bay Cemetery, Jersey City, Hudson County.

BENDALOW*, DANIEL P. Pvt, G, 8th NJ Inf, 4-24-1874. Green Cemetery, Woodbury, Gloucester County.

BENDELO, MICHAEL Pvt, I, 21st PA Inf, 3-19-1905. Pascack Reformed Cemetery, Park Ridge, Bergen County.

BENDER, AUGUST Pvt, H, 8th NJ Inf, 9-18-1929. Old Gloucester Burial Grounds Cemetery, Clarksboro, Gloucester County.

BENDER, CHARLES A. 9-15-1899. Evergreen Cemetery, Camden, Camden County.

BENDER, CHARLES F. Sgt, I, 34th NJ Inf, 5-30-1921. Bloomfield Cemetery, Bloomfield, Essex County.

BENDER, CHARLES F. Pvt, E, Stewart's PA Inf, 5-28-1921. Bloomfield Cemetery, Bloomfield, Essex County.

BENDER, JACOB Pvt, A, 8th NJ Inf, 4-8-1889. Fairmount Cemetery, Newark, Essex County.

BENDER, JACOB Pvt, F, 12th NJ Inf, 10-15-1914. Eglington Cemetery, Clarksboro, Gloucester County.

BENDER, JOHN 8-16-1880. Old Camden Cemetery, Camden, Camden County.

BENDER, JOHN Pvt, G, 37th NJ Inf, 2-26-1881. Fairmount Cemetery, Newark, Essex County.

BENDER, LEWIS Corp, G, 4th NJ Inf, [Wounded in action.] 8-29-1919. Maplewood Cemetery, Freehold, Monmouth County.

BENDER, ROBERT S. Pvt, B, 32nd PA Inf, 7-10-1912. Harleigh Cemetery, Camden, Camden County.

BENDY, JOB Pvt, E, 29th NJ Inf, 2-12-1902. Fairview Cemetery, Fairview, Monmouth County.

BENDY, WESLEY L. Pvt, H, 21st NJ Inf, 5-17-1901. Riverview Cemetery, Trenton, Mercer County.

BENDY, WILLIAM H. Corp, A, 9th NJ Inf, 3-8-1897. Riverview Cemetery, Trenton, Mercer County.

BENEDICT, CYRUS D. Pvt, K, 2nd NJ Inf, 2-27-1915. Rosedale Cemetery, Orange, Essex County.

BENEDICT, EDWARD E. Pvt, G, 2nd NJ Inf, 4-5-1903. Fairmount Cemetery, Newark, Essex County.

BENEDICT, EDWIN S. Landsman, U.S. Navy, USS Newbern, 2-23-1906. St. Stephen's Cemetery, Millburn, Essex County.

BENEDICT, OSCAR B. Pvt, F, 13th NJ Inf, [Died of diarrhea at Maryland Heights, MD.] 10-20-1862. Mount Pleasant Cemetery, Newark, Essex County.

BENGLESS, JOHN D. Chaplain, 2nd RI Inf 1887. Oddfellows Cemetery, Burlington, Burlington County.

BENJAMIN, CHARLES A. Sgt Maj, A, 7th LA Inf (CSA), [Wounded in action.] 1-7-1911. Fairmount Cemetery, Newark, Essex County.

BENJAMIN, DANIEL Pvt, K, 2nd DC Inf, 12-10-1921. Greenwood Cemetery, Boonton, Morris County.

BENJAMIN, HARRY S. Pvt, Btty E, 1st U.S. Art, 10-27-1912. Locust Hill Cemetery, Dover, Morris County.

New Jersey Civil War Burials

BENJAMIN, THOMAS Pvt, H, 26th U.S. CT, 10-21-1909. Methodist Church Cemetery, Asbury, Warren County.

BENJAMIN, WILLIAM B. Pvt, I, 26th PA Inf, DoD Unknown. Evergreen Cemetery, Camden, Camden County.

BENJAMIN, WILLIAM S. Pvt, G, 1st NY Marine Art, 7-14-1879. Bayview-New York Bay Cemetery, Jersey City, Hudson County.

BENKER, HENRY Pvt, F, 115th NY Inf, [Wounded 2-20-1864 at Olustee, FL.] 12-16-1894. Weehawken Cemetery, North Bergen, Hudson County.

BENKERT, LEONARD 1st Sgt, K, 21st PA Inf, 8-23-1865. Evergreen Cemetery, Camden, Camden County.

BENNARD, EDWARD (aka: Brainard, Edward) Pvt, C, 22nd U.S. CT, 8-13-1884. Johnson Cemetery, Camden, Camden County.

BENNER, GEORGE Pvt, E, 2nd NJ Inf, 4-20-1869. Fairmount Cemetery, Newark, Essex County.

BENNER, JOSEPH Pvt, K, 19th PA Militia, DoD Unknown. Phillipsburg Cemetery, Phillipsburg, Warren County.

BENNETT, A.M. 1931. Greengrove Cemetery, Keyport, Monmouth County.

BENNETT, ABRAM DoD Unknown. 1st Reformed Church Cemetery, New Brunswick, Middlesex County.

BENNETT, ADOLPHUS Actg Ensign, U.S. Navy, 6-15-1876. Cedar Green Cemetery, Clayton, Gloucester County.

BENNETT, AMOS Pvt, I, 38th NJ Inf, 12-29-1921. Greenwood Cemetery, Hamilton, Mercer County.

BENNETT, BENJAMIN Pvt, C, 25th U.S. CT, 8-4-1914. Riverview Cemetery, Trenton, Mercer County.

BENNETT*, BENJAMIN F. Pvt, E, 5th NY Vet Inf, 4-20-1931. Hoboken Cemetery, North Bergen, Hudson County.

BENNETT, CALEB Pvt, E, 28th NJ Inf, 8-16-1874. Methodist Church Cemetery, Harmony, Ocean County.

BENNETT, CHARLES 1-17-1905. Baptist/St. Andrew's Cemetery, Mount Holly, Burlington County.

BENNETT, CHARLES Pvt, E, 7th U.S. CT, 1886. Old Methodist Cemetery, New Egypt, Ocean County.

BENNETT, CHARLES 1st Sgt, C, 34th NJ Inf, 1870. Methodist-Episcopal Cemetery, Vincentown, Burlington County.

BENNETT*, CHARLES K. Pvt, H, 40th NJ Inf, 2-22-1927. Riverview Cemetery, Trenton, Mercer County.

BENNETT, CHARLES L. Corp, K, 104th PA Inf, 7-31-1891. Evergreen Cemetery, Camden, Camden County.

BENNETT, CHARLES L. 1881. Old 1st Methodist Church Cemetery, West Long Branch, Monmouth County.

BENNETT, CYRENUS G. 2nd Lt, B, 3rd __ __, 1912. Glenwood Cemetery, West Long Branch, Monmouth County.

BENNETT, EDEN BOICE Pvt, H, 9th NJ Inf, 10-18-1917. Hillside Cemetery, Scotch Plains, Union County.

BENNETT, EDWARD Pvt, E, 71st NY Inf, 8-31-1886. St. John's Evangelical Church Cemetery, Orange, Essex County.

BENNETT, EDWIN 10-8-1894. Bayview-New York Bay Cemetery, Jersey City, Hudson County.

BENNETT*, ELDRIDGE Pvt, B, 2nd NJ Cav, 6-1-1916. Greenwood Cemetery, Hamilton, Mercer County.

BENNETT, GEORGE Pvt, D, 23rd NJ Inf, 5-22-1902. Riverview Cemetery, Trenton, Mercer County.

Our Brothers Gone Before

BENNETT*, GEORGE ACKERLY 1st Lt, C, 4th NJ Inf, 11-23-1924. Mercer Cemetery, Trenton, Mercer County.

BENNETT, GEORGE W. Pvt, 6th NY Ind Btty [Died of disease at DeCamp General Hospital.] 7-9-1862. Hazelwood Cemetery, Rahway, Union County.

BENNETT, HARRISON Pvt, A, 29th NJ Inf, 1923. Cedar Grove Cemetery, Middlebush, Somerset County.

BENNETT, HENRY Pvt, D, 1st NJ Militia, 3-23-1917. Arlington Cemetery, Kearny, Hudson County.

BENNETT, HENRY (aka: Bennett, John) Pvt, D, 29th NJ Inf, 1-6-1926. Fairview Cemetery, Fairview, Monmouth County.

BENNETT, HENRY B. Pvt, A, 29th NJ Inf, 11-17-1886. Old 1st Methodist Church Cemetery, West Long Branch, Monmouth County.

BENNETT, HENRY J. Pvt, A, PA Emerg NJ Militia, 7-23-1901. Mercer Cemetery, Trenton, Mercer County.

BENNETT, HENRY R. Pvt, Btty E, 1st NJ Light Art, 11-17-1891. United Methodist Church Cemetery, Winslow, Camden County.

BENNETT, HOLMES C. Pvt, A, 14th NJ Inf, [Wounded in action.] 7-18-1899. Methodist Cemetery, Hamilton, Monmouth County.

BENNETT*, HUGH M. Pvt, K, 14th NJ Inf, 1-3-1872. 1st Methodist-Episcopal Cemetery, New Brunswick, Middlesex County.

BENNETT, ISAAC SCUDDER Pvt, A, 28th NJ Inf, 2-7-1931. Brainerd Cemetery, Cranbury, Middlesex County.

BENNETT, J. MILTON Pvt, A, 29th NJ Inf, 3-30-1930. Glenwood Cemetery, West Long Branch, Monmouth County.

BENNETT*, JAMES Pvt, D, 5th NJ Inf, 2-10-1917. Holy Sepulchre Cemetery, East Orange, Essex County.

BENNETT, JAMES W. Pvt, K, 8th AL Inf (CSA), 9-20-1863. Finn's Point National Cemetery, Pennsville, Salem County.

BENNETT, JERVIS H. Pvt, B, 14th NJ Inf, 5-7-1908. Riverview Cemetery, Trenton, Mercer County.

BENNETT, JESSE L. Sgt, D, 9th NJ Inf, [Cenotaph. Died while prisoner at Andersonville, GA.] 2-25-1865. Masonic Cemetery, Barnegat, Ocean County.

BENNETT, JOHN 1st Lt, B, 9th NJ Inf, 11-29-1904. Arlington Cemetery, Kearny, Hudson County.

BENNETT, JOHN Pvt, B, 22nd VA Inf (CSA), [Wounded and captured 11-6-1863 at Droop Mountain, WV. Died of measles.] 4-15-1864. Finn's Point National Cemetery, Pennsville, Salem County.

BENNETT, JOHN (see: Bennett, Henry) Fairview Cemetery, Fairview, Monmouth County.

BENNETT, JOHN A. Corp, F, 31st PA Militia, 8-14-1898. Evergreen Cemetery, Camden, Camden County.

BENNETT, JOHN B.W. Pvt, B, 30th NJ Inf, 2-11-1907. Evergreen Cemetery, Hillside, Union County.

BENNETT, JOHN G. QM Sgt, 38th NJ Inf 9-6-1884. Mercer Cemetery, Trenton, Mercer County.

BENNETT, JOHN G. 8-16-1893. United Methodist Church Cemetery, Little Silver, Monmouth County.

BENNETT, JOHN H. Pvt, B, 35th NJ Inf, 11-24-1892. Evergreen Cemetery, Hillside, Union County.

BENNETT, JOHN J. Pvt, Btty A, 1st NJ Light Art, 1-2-1889. St. John's Evangelical Church Cemetery, Orange, Essex County.

BENNETT, JOHN J. Corp, A, 150th NY Inf, 5-23-1897. Fairmount Cemetery, Newark, Essex County.

New Jersey Civil War Burials

BENNETT*, JOHN J. Pvt, I, 146th NY Inf, [Wounded 8-18-1864 at Weldon Railroad, VA.] 2-6-1891. Evergreen Cemetery, Hillside, Union County.

BENNETT, JOHN M. Corp, I, 33rd NJ Inf, 8-22-1874. Fairmount Cemetery, Newark, Essex County.

BENNETT*, JOHN P. Pvt, I, 12th NJ Inf, 9-26-1921. Arlington Cemetery, Kearny, Hudson County.

BENNETT, JOHN RANDOLPH Pvt, A, 22nd NJ Inf, 6-20-1908. Evergreen Cemetery, Hillside, Union County.

BENNETT, JOHN RODGER Corp, K, 10th NJ Inf, 12-29-1925. Greenwood Cemetery, Tuckerton, Ocean County.

BENNETT, JOHN S. Pvt, F, 14th NJ Inf, 3-5-1915. Arlington Cemetery, Kearny, Hudson County.

BENNETT, JOHN W. Actg Ensign, U.S. Navy, 9-10-1912. Masonic Cemetery, Barnegat, Ocean County.

BENNETT, JOHN Y. Pvt, M, 2nd NJ Cav, 3-1-1896. Presbyterian Church Cemetery, Clinton, Hunterdon County.

BENNETT, JOHNSON H. Musc, K, 31st NJ Inf, 12-31-1903. Presbyterian Church Cemetery, Califon, Hunterdon County.

BENNETT, JONATHAN W. Pvt, A, 29th NJ Inf, 8-27-1907. Greenlawn Cemetery, West Long Branch, Monmouth County.

BENNETT, JOSEPH 4-21-1904. United Methodist Church Cemetery, Little Silver, Monmouth County.

BENNETT*, JOSEPH Fireman, U.S. Navy, USS North Carolina, 11-30-1864. Old Oakhurst Cemetery, West Long Branch, Monmouth County.

BENNETT, JOSEPH L. Pvt, D, 14th NJ Inf, 9-5-1909. Arlington Cemetery, Kearny, Hudson County.

BENNETT, JOSEPH L. 11-30-1867. Greenlawn Cemetery, West Long Branch, Monmouth County.

BENNETT, JOSEPH R. 1912. Locust Grove Cemetery, Quakertown, Hunterdon County.

BENNETT, JOSEPH R. Pvt, 6th NY Ind Btty 5-21-1900. Rahway Cemetery, Rahway, Union County.

BENNETT, JOSHUA Pvt, K, 10th NJ Inf, 7-5-1864. Methodist Cemetery, Tuckerton, Ocean County.

BENNETT, MARTIN Pvt, B, 28th NJ Inf, 6-4-1909. Van Liew Cemetery, North Brunswick, Middlesex County.

BENNETT, MARTIN V. Pvt, E, 26th NJ Inf, 5-12-1914. Clinton Cemetery, Irvington, Essex County.

BENNETT, NATHANIEL B. Pvt, D, PA Emerg NJ Militia, 1885. Tennent Church Cemetery, Tennent, Monmouth County.

BENNETT, NATHANIEL HAYES Pvt, K, 34th NJ Inf, 8-27-1904. Methodist-Episcopal Cemetery, Vincentown, Burlington County.

BENNETT, NELSON Capt, K, 31st NJ Inf, 8-18-1891. Presbyterian Church Cemetery, Clinton, Hunterdon County.

BENNETT, P. FRANK 12-28-1907. Oddfellows Cemetery, Burlington, Burlington County.

BENNETT, RENWICK Pvt, G, 29th NJ Inf, 11-18-1917. Mount Prospect Cemetery, Neptune, Monmouth County.

BENNETT, ROBERT M. Pvt, D, 25th NJ Inf, 4-23-1909. Mount Pleasant Cemetery, Millville, Cumberland County.

BENNETT, RUFUS E. Corp, D, 25th NJ Inf, 5-21-1902. Overlook Cemetery, Bridgeton, Cumberland County.

BENNETT, SAMUEL F. Pvt, G, 3rd NJ Cav, 1908. Mount Pleasant Cemetery, Millville, Cumberland County.

Our Brothers Gone Before

BENNETT, SEDGWICK R. Sgt, A, 27th NJ Inf, 8-12-1910. Chestnut Cemetery, Dover, Morris County.
BENNETT*, SETH Pvt, D, 2nd U.S. Cav, 12-22-1907. Methodist Church Cemetery, Juliustown, Burlington County.
BENNETT, SOLOMON Pvt, E, 10th MS Cav (CSA), 3-5-1865. Finn's Point National Cemetery, Pennsville, Salem County.
BENNETT, STEPHEN DECATUR (JR.) Pvt, A, 7th NJ Inf, [Died of wounds received 5-5-1862 at Williamsburg, VA.] 5-28-1862. Presbyterian Church Cemetery, Cold Spring, Cape May County.
BENNETT, THOMAS Pvt, K, 10th NJ Inf, 12-15-1901. 7th Day Baptist Church Cemetery, Shiloh, Cumberland County.
BENNETT, THOMAS F. Sgt, E, 1st NY Eng, 7-19-1892. Old 1st Methodist Church Cemetery, West Long Branch, Monmouth County.
BENNETT, WILLIAM Corp, F, 1st NJ Militia, 3-19-1900. Fairmount Cemetery, Newark, Essex County.
BENNETT, WILLIAM A. (aka: Bothner, William) Pvt, A, 132nd NY Inf, 1-15-1881. Princeton Cemetery, Princeton, Mercer County.
BENNETT, WILLIAM G. Pvt, A, 68th PA Inf, 3-26-1918. Cedar Green Cemetery, Clayton, Gloucester County.
BENNETT, WILLIAM H. 1st Sgt, E, 28th NJ Inf, DoD Unknown. Methodist Church Cemetery, Harmony, Ocean County.
BENNETT, WILLIAM H. Corp, B, 14th NJ Inf, 1-1-1893. Methodist Church Cemetery, Groveville, Mercer County.
BENNETT, WILLIAM H. Corp, K, 12th NJ Inf, 1-22-1910. Presbyterian Church Cemetery, Bridgeton, Cumberland County.
BENNETT, WILLIAM (JR.) Pvt, H, 53rd NC Inf (CSA), 1-4-1864. Finn's Point National Cemetery, Pennsville, Salem County.
BENNETT, WILLIAM O. Corp, G, 53rd NY Inf, DoD Unknown. Old Brick Reformed Church Cemetery, Marlboro, Monmouth County.
BENNETT, WILLIAM W. Pvt, I, 95th PA Inf, 5-6-1905. Harleigh Cemetery, Camden, Camden County.
BENNETT, WINCHESTER T. Corp, D, 1st NJ Inf, [Killed in action at Gaines' Farm, VA.] 6-27-1862. Brainerd Cemetery, Cranbury, Middlesex County.
BENNEY, CHARLES E. (aka: Bluner, Charles) Pvt, G, 20th PA Cav, 8-29-1914. Oddfellows Cemetery, Burlington, Burlington County.
BENSINGER, BYRON (see: Bininger, Byron) Arlington Cemetery, Kearny, Hudson County.
BENSON, CHARLES Artificer, K, 15th NY Eng, DoD Unknown. Old Bergen Church Cemetery, Jersey City, Hudson County.
BENSON, CHARLES J.B. Corp, A, 34th NJ Inf, 7-2-1904. Old Methodist-Episcopal Cemetery, Fresh Ponds, Middlesex County.
BENSON, CORNELIUS H. Landsman, U.S. Navy, USS Vermont, 3-15-1905. Arlington Cemetery, Kearny, Hudson County.
BENSON, ELIJAH H. Pvt, L, 1st NJ Cav, 3-15-1875. United Presbyterian Church Cemetery, Perrineville, Monmouth County.
BENSON*, GARRETT B. Corp, G, 2nd NJ Inf, 1-15-1912. Cedar Lawn Cemetery, Paterson, Passaic County.
BENSON, HENRY Capt, Btty A, 2nd U.S. Art, [Died of wounds received 8-5-1862 at Malvern Hill, VA.] 8-11-1862. Reformed Church Cemetery, Belleville, Essex County.
BENSON, JAMES Pvt, E, 12th NY Inf, 5-4-1925. Rosedale Cemetery, Orange, Essex County.
BENSON, JEREMIAH (see: Burns, Jeremiah) St. James Cemetery, Woodbridge, Middlesex County.

New Jersey Civil War Burials

BENSON, JOHN Pvt, C, 21st NJ Inf, DoD Unknown. Old Bergen Church Cemetery, Jersey City, Hudson County.
BENSON, JOSEPH F. 8-30-1889. New Somerville Cemetery, Somerville, Somerset County.
BENSON, JOSIAH Pvt, B, 45th U.S. CT, 12-8-1892. Mount Pisgah Cemetery, Elsinboro, Salem County.
BENSON, MARTIN V.B. Pvt, F, 91st NY Inf, 2-17-1922. Baptist/Evergreen Methodist Cemetery, Plainfield, Union County.
BENSON, MONMOUTH H. Pvt, K, 27th NJ Inf, 12-22-1887. Pleasant Hill Cemetery, Pleasant Hill, Morris County.
BENSON, ROBERT Pvt, B, 24th U.S. CT, 1-10-1899. Mount Zion Methodist Church Cemetery, Lawnside, Camden County.
BENSON, WILLIAM Pvt, B, 24th U.S. CT, 3-3-1916. Mount Zion Methodist Church Cemetery, Lawnside, Camden County.
BENSON, WILLIAM Pvt, H, 29th NJ Inf, 5-5-1892. Old Methodist Cemetery, Toms River, Ocean County.
BENSON, WILLIAM H. 4-25-1913. Laurel Grove Cemetery, Totowa, Passaic County.
BENT, FITZ EDWARD Capt, B, 60th MA Militia, 3-8-1917. Rosedale Cemetery, Orange, Essex County.
BENTELL, EDWARD (see: Beutell, Ernest Emanuel) Methodist Cemetery, Hamilton, Monmouth County.
BENTLEY, JAMES Pvt, F, 17th NY Inf, 8-9-1890. Fairmount Cemetery, Newark, Essex County.
BENTLEY, JAMES Pvt, C, 28th CT Inf, 8-31-1884. Cedar Lawn Cemetery, Paterson, Passaic County.
BENTLEY*, JAMES V. Hosp Steward, 24th NY Inf 8-10-1890. Fairmount Cemetery, Newark, Essex County.
BENTLEY, JAMES V. 2nd Lt, H, 15th NJ Inf, 10-5-1881. Evergreen Cemetery, Morristown, Morris County.
BENTLEY, PETER 4-30-1888. Old Bergen Church Cemetery, Jersey City, Hudson County.
BENTNER, EDWARD CHARLES Pvt, F, 3rd NJ Cav, [Wounded in action.] 7-2-1901. Fairmount Cemetery, Newark, Essex County.
BENTON*, JOHN Pvt, Btty G, 11th U.S. CHA, 12-22-1897. Mount Zion AME Cemetery, Swedesboro, Gloucester County.
BENTON, WEBSTER (see: Burton, Webster) Laurel Grove Cemetery, Totowa, Passaic County.
BENWARD, HENRY K. Pvt, G, 30th NJ Inf, 1-25-1903. Presbyterian Cemetery, West Stewartsville, Warren County.
BENWARD*, JAMES L. Pvt, 6th NY Ind Btty 2- -1914. Rosemont Cemetery, Rosemont, Hunterdon County.
BENWARD, MOSES (see: Benwood, Moses) Presbyterian Cemetery, Asbury, Warren County.
BENWOOD, MOSES (aka: Benward, Moses) Wagoner, H, 8th NJ Inf, 5-7-1903. Presbyterian Cemetery, Asbury, Warren County.
BENYAURD, EUGENE C. Pvt, H, 20th PA Militia, 1924. Trinity Episcopal Church Cemetery, Moorestown, Burlington County.
BENZ, FREDERICK J. Pvt, K, 114th U.S. CT, DoD Unknown. Evergreen Cemetery, Hillside, Union County.
BENZ, JOSEPH Corp, F, 39th NJ Inf, 4-8-1876. Woodland Cemetery, Newark, Essex County.
BEPLER, ADOLPH (aka: Beppler, Adolph) Pvt, I, 8th NY Inf, 1-19-1919. Evergreen Cemetery, Morristown, Morris County.

Our Brothers Gone Before

BEPPLER, ADOLPH (see: Bepler, Adolph) Evergreen Cemetery, Morristown, Morris County.
BERCAW, HENRY Pvt, I, 35th NJ Inf, 1-18-1905. Phillipsburg Cemetery, Phillipsburg, Warren County.
BERDAN, ALBERT Pvt, I, 2nd NJ Inf, 5-28-1889. Cedar Lawn Cemetery, Paterson, Passaic County.
BERDAN, JACOB H. Pvt, K, 13th NJ Inf, 1-7-1920. Cedar Lawn Cemetery, Paterson, Passaic County.
BERDAN, JOHN D. Pvt, K, 13th NJ Inf, DoD Unknown. Laurel Grove Cemetery, Totowa, Passaic County.
BERDAN, RALPH CONOVER (aka: Berdan, Rulif) Corp, A, 190th NY Inf, 6-22-1897. Valleau Cemetery, Ridgewood, Bergen County.
BERDAN, RICHARD J. QM, 9th NJ Inf 1-30-1911. Cedar Lawn Cemetery, Paterson, Passaic County.
BERDAN, RULIF (see: Berdan, Ralph Conover) Valleau Cemetery, Ridgewood, Bergen County.
BERDINE, WILLIAM QM, 28th NJ Inf 12-26-1865. Three Mile Run Cemetery, New Brunswick, Middlesex County.
BERDUN, HENRY (see: Berdux, Henry) Phillipsburg Cemetery, Phillipsburg, Warren County.
BERDUX, HENRY (aka: Berdun, Henry) Pvt, F, 162nd NY Inf, [Wounded 4-9-1864 at Pleasant Hill, LA.] 12-27-1906. Phillipsburg Cemetery, Phillipsburg, Warren County.
BEREN, THOMAS Pvt, F, 12th NJ Inf, DoD Unknown. Lake Park Cemetery, Swedesboro, Gloucester County.
BERESFORD, CHARLES H. Pvt, F, 37th NJ Inf, 10-21-1918. Cedar Lawn Cemetery, Paterson, Passaic County.
BERESFORD, WILLIAM J. Pvt, I, 13th NJ Inf, [Cenotaph. Died of fever at Chattanooga, TN.] 11-30-1864. Cedar Lawn Cemetery, Paterson, Passaic County.
BERG, CHARLES A. Pvt, F, 33rd NJ Inf, 8-21-1925. Arlington Cemetery, Kearny, Hudson County.
BERG, FREDERICK Pvt, H, 26th NJ Inf, 2-20-1908. Rosedale Cemetery, Orange, Essex County.
BERG, JOSEPH FREDERICK (JR.) Asst Surgeon, 28th NJ Inf 11-2-1923. Baptist/Evergreen Methodist Cemetery, Plainfield, Union County.
BERGEN, ADAM MILLER (aka: Miller, Adam) Pvt, D, 28th NJ Inf, 3-1-1910. Elmwood Cemetery, New Brunswick, Middlesex County.
BERGEN, ADRIAN W. Corp, D, 28th NJ Inf, 3-1-1914. Evergreen Cemetery, New Brunswick, Middlesex County.
BERGEN, ALFRED W. Pvt, F, 8th NJ Inf, 4-4-1880. Mount Pleasant Cemetery, Newark, Essex County.
BERGEN, CORNELIUS P. 1st Lt, I, 22nd U.S. CT, 12-6-1870. Old Somerville Cemetery, Somerville, Somerset County.
BERGEN, EDWARD Corp, H, 2nd DC Inf, 11-17-1902. Holy Sepulchre Cemetery, East Orange, Essex County.
BERGEN, EDWARD (see: Berger, Edward) Woodland Cemetery, Newark, Essex County.
BERGEN, GEORGE D. Pvt, B, 28th NJ Inf, [Wounded in action.] 1931. Princeton Cemetery, Princeton, Mercer County.
BERGEN, GEORGE H. Pvt, D, 10th NJ Inf, 1-23-1911. Presbyterian Church Cemetery, Hampton, Hunterdon County.
BERGEN, GEORGE H. DoD Unknown. Washington Monumental Cemetery, South River, Middlesex County.
BERGEN, IRA S. Pvt, H, 127th U.S. CT, 6-22-1930. Princeton Cemetery, Princeton, Mercer County.

New Jersey Civil War Burials

BERGEN, JAMES Pvt, C, 5th NJ Inf, DoD Unknown. St. Peter's Cemetery, New Brunswick, Middlesex County.

BERGEN, JOHN Pvt, F, 2nd NJ Inf, [Wounded 9-14-1862 at Crampton's Pass, MD.] 11-31-1901. Fairmount Cemetery, Newark, Essex County.

BERGEN, JOHN H. Pvt, D, 28th NJ Inf, 9-27-1926. Elmwood Cemetery, New Brunswick, Middlesex County.

BERGEN, JOHN V.D. 4-30-1911. Harlingen Cemetery, Belle Mead, Somerset County.

BERGEN, LEWIS Corp, H, 127th U.S. CT, 6-9-1893. Fairmount Cemetery, Newark, Essex County.

BERGEN, MARTIN Musc, G, 5th NJ Inf, 9-17-1917. Holy Cross Cemetery, North Arlington, Bergen County.

BERGEN, PETER D. Pvt, D, 5th NJ Inf, 1864. Presbyterian Church Cemetery, Dutch Neck, Mercer County.

BERGEN, THOMAS 10-11-1928. Evergreen Cemetery, Hillside, Union County.

BERGEN, WILLIAM Capt, G, 2nd NJ Inf, [Died of wounds received 5-3-1863 at Salem Heights, VA.] 5-4-1863. St. John's Evangelical Church Cemetery, Orange, Essex County.

BERGENBACH, LEWIS (see: Balkenberg, Lewis) St. Rose of Lima Cemetery, Oxford, Warren County.

BERGER, CHARLES B. 1914. New Somerville Cemetery, Somerville, Somerset County.

BERGER, EDWARD (aka: Bergen, Edward) Pvt, Btty L, 3rd U.S. Art, 1-24-1913. Woodland Cemetery, Newark, Essex County.

BERGER, FREDERICK 11-2-1903. Trinity Bible Church Cemetery, Glassboro, Gloucester County.

BERGER, HIRAM (aka: Burger, Hiram) Pvt, E, 176th PA Inf, 5-4-1907. Lutheran Cemetery, East Stewartsville, Warren County.

BERGER, LOUIS Pvt, G, 39th NJ Inf, 3-15-1919. Fairmount Cemetery, Newark, Essex County.

BERGER, LOUIS DoD Unknown. Berry Lawn Cemetery, Carlstadt, Bergen County.

BERGERON, NEMORIN Pvt, B, 7th LA Inf (CSA), [Captured 5-30-1862 at Front Royal, VA.] 7-16-1862. Finn's Point National Cemetery, Pennsville, Salem County.

BERGFELS*, JOHN G. Pvt, B, 1st NJ Cav, [Killed in action at Todds Tavern, VA.] 5-5-1864. Evergreen Cemetery, Hillside, Union County.

BERGNER, AUGUSTUS M. Seaman, U.S. Navy, USS Hetzell, 1-22-1890. Rosedale Cemetery, Orange, Essex County.

BERGQUIST, JOHN P.F. (see: Borgquist, John P.F.) Holy Name Cemetery, Jersey City, Hudson County.

BERGSTRESSER, ISRAEL (see: Burgstresser, Israel) Riverview Cemetery, Trenton, Mercer County.

BERGYSER, CHRISTIAN (aka: Berkheyser, Christian) Pvt, C, 79th PA Inf, 1-20-1889. Methodist Church Cemetery, Groveville, Mercer County.

BERKEHEISER, WILLIAM (see: Berkeyheiser, William) Methodist Church Cemetery, Groveville, Mercer County.

BERKEYHEISER*, WILLIAM (aka: Berkeheiser, William) Pvt, 38th, 2nd Bttn U.S. VRC, 3-27-1923. Methodist Church Cemetery, Groveville, Mercer County.

BERKHEYSER, CHRISTIAN (see: Bergyser, Christian) Methodist Church Cemetery, Groveville, Mercer County.

BERKLE, GEORGE Pvt, Btty B, 1st NJ Light Art, 4-12-1871. Fairmount Cemetery, Newark, Essex County.

BERLEW, CAROLINE Nurse, 9-8-1897. Christ Church Cemetery, Morgan, Middlesex County.

BERLEW, JOHN C. (aka: Burlew, John C.) Pvt, D, 13th NJ Inf, DoD Unknown. Greengrove Cemetery, Keyport, Monmouth County.

Our Brothers Gone Before

BERLEW, SYLVESTER B. Pvt, E, 14th NJ Inf, 2-6-1910. Greengrove Cemetery, Keyport, Monmouth County.

BERLIN, RICHARD 4-14-1890. Bayview-New York Bay Cemetery, Jersey City, Hudson County.

BERMAN, AUGUST (see: Buermann, August) Fairmount Cemetery, Newark, Essex County.

BERMINGHAM, ANDREW 1st Lt, A, 69th NY Inf, [Died of wounds received 12-13-1862 at Fredericksburg, VA.] 12-17-1862. St. Mary's Cemetery, Wharton, Morris County.

BERMINGHAM, WILLIAM (aka: Birmingham, William) Pvt, A, 69th NY Inf, 5-17-1915. St. Mary's Cemetery, Wharton, Morris County.

BERNARD, ALFRED T. Pvt, G, 2nd NJ Inf, 5-7-1904. Fairmount Cemetery, Newark, Essex County.

BERNARD, ALFRED T. Pvt, G, 2nd NJ Inf, DoD Unknown. Old Camden Cemetery, Camden, Camden County.

BERNARD, CHARLES E. Pvt, G, 2nd MI Inf, 5-31-1887. Maplewood Cemetery, Freehold, Monmouth County.

BERNARD, W.H. Pvt, G, 1st Bttn (Stirman's) AR Cav (CSA), [Died of smallpox.] 10-8-1863. Finn's Point National Cemetery, Pennsville, Salem County.

BERNARDO, CARLOS J. (aka: Donnelly, John M.) Pvt, K, 2nd MO Cav, 5-21-1917. Grove Church Cemetery, North Bergen, Hudson County.

BERNATSKI, JOHN Seaman, U.S. Navy, 1924. Holy Sepulchre Cemetery, East Orange, Essex County.

BERNER, FRANZ (see: Borner, Franz) St. John's Evangelical Church Cemetery, Orange, Essex County.

BERNER, HENRY Pvt, E, 26th NJ Inf, 11-8-1891. Mount Hebron Cemetery, Montclair, Essex County.

BERNER, MARTIN J. Pvt, C, 67th OH Inf, 12-16-1887. Egg Harbor Cemetery, Egg Harbor, Atlantic County.

BERNHAMMER, GEORGE F. (aka: Bonheimer, George) Pvt, Btty A, 1st NJ Light Art, 6- -1887. Grove Church Cemetery, North Bergen, Hudson County.

BERNHAMMER, HENRY (see: Bernheimer, Henry) Grove Church Cemetery, North Bergen, Hudson County.

BERNHARD, JOHN Musc, 20th NY Inf Band 11-21-1862. Rahway Cemetery, Rahway, Union County.

BERNHEIMER, HENRY (aka: Bernhammer, Henry) 2nd Cl Fireman, U.S. Navy, USS North Carolina, 12-23-1905. Grove Church Cemetery, North Bergen, Hudson County.

BERRIAN, JOHN G. Sgt, C, 2nd NJ Militia, 3-2-1895. Arlington Cemetery, Kearny, Hudson County.

BERRIE, JOHN (see: Biers, John E.) Arlington Cemetery, Pennsauken, Camden County.

BERRIEN, JOHN M. Capt, U.S. Navy, 11-21-1883. Princeton Cemetery, Princeton, Mercer County.

BERRIEN, JOHN W. Sgt, C, 2nd NJ Militia, DoD Unknown. Princeton Cemetery, Princeton, Mercer County.

BERRIEN, LAWRENCE R. Pvt, A, 5th NY Vet Inf, 6-18-1933. Riverside Cemetery, Toms River, Ocean County.

BERRIEN, WILLIAM Pvt, H, 21st NJ Inf, 2-28-1910. Brainerd Cemetery, Cranbury, Middlesex County.

BERRIGAN, JAMES Pvt, H, 9th NJ Inf, 1-15-1889. Holy Sepulchre Cemetery, East Orange, Essex County.

BERRIGAN, WILLIAM Pvt, M, 1st NJ Cav, 2-27-1893. Old Catholic Cemetery, Franklin Boro, Sussex County.

BERRY, ABRAHAM H. Ensign, U.S. Navy, USS Hatteras, DoD Unknown. Hackensack Cemetery, Hackensack, Bergen County.

BERRY, ALEXANDER H. Pvt, K, 9th NJ Inf, 10-20-1908. Phillipsburg Cemetery, Phillipsburg, Warren County.

BERRY, ALFRED J. Pvt, A, 41st U.S. CT, 5-26-1897. Pinebrook Cemetery, Macedonia, Monmouth County.

BERRY, ANDREW W. Pvt, D, 24th NJ Inf, 12-15-1889. Cedar Green Cemetery, Clayton, Gloucester County.

BERRY, AUGUSTUS R. Pvt, H, 10th VA Inf (CSA), [Captured 5-12-1864 at Spotsylvania CH, VA. Died of diarrhea.] 5-10-1865. Finn's Point National Cemetery, Pennsville, Salem County.

BERRY, CHARLES Pvt, A, 3rd NJ Cav, 7-19-1904. Holy Sepulchre Cemetery, East Orange, Essex County.

BERRY*, CHARLES Steward, U.S. Navy, USS Brooklyn, DoD Unknown. Baptist Church Cemetery, Scotch Plains, Union County.

BERRY, CHESTER D. Pvt, I, 20th MI Inf, [Survived the Sultana disaster of April 27th, 1865.] 11-22-1926. Glendale Cemetery, Bloomfield, Essex County.

BERRY, CHRISTOPHER Corp, D, 25th U.S. CT, DoD Unknown. Johnson Cemetery, Camden, Camden County.

BERRY, DANIEL P. Seaman, U.S. Navy, 4-16-1869. Mount Pleasant Cemetery, Newark, Essex County.

BERRY, EDWARD 1887. Pinebrook Cemetery, Macedonia, Monmouth County.

BERRY*, EDWARD (aka: Barry, Edward) Corp, Btty F, 5th NY Heavy Art, 10-9-1886. Holy Sepulchre Cemetery, Totowa, Passaic County.

BERRY, EDWARD L. 2-21-1919. Cedar Lawn Cemetery, Paterson, Passaic County.

BERRY, EDWARD P. Capt, E, 5th NJ Inf, [Died of wounds received at Gettysburg, PA.] 7-6-1863. Chestnut Cemetery, Dover, Morris County.

BERRY, GEORGE Pvt, A, 25th U.S. CT, 12-4-1896. Fairmount Cemetery, Newark, Essex County.

BERRY, GREENE (see: Greenwood, Berry) Bethel AME Cemetery, Cookstown, Burlington County.

BERRY, HENRY H. Pvt, F, 15th NJ Inf, 1916. Pleasant Hill Cemetery, Pleasant Hill, Morris County.

BERRY, HULDAH 4-25-1892. Stillwater Cemetery, Stillwater, Sussex County.

BERRY, JAMES Seaman, U.S. Navy, 10-29-1893. Methodist Church Cemetery, Allerton, Hunterdon County.

BERRY, JAMES (see: Bary, James L.) Presbyterian Church Cemetery, Great Meadows, Warren County.

BERRY, JAMES H. Pvt, C, 8th NJ Inf, 4-3-1898. 1st Reformed Church Cemetery, Pompton Plains, Morris County.

BERRY, JAMES L. Pvt, G, 31st NJ Inf, DoD Unknown. Pequest Union Cemetery, Great Meadows, Warren County.

BERRY, JEREMIAH Pvt, D, 205th PA Inf, 7-4-1886. Evergreen Cemetery, Camden, Camden County.

BERRY, JOHN Corp, A, 127th U.S. CT, 1-1-1909. Mount Peace Cemetery, Lawnside, Camden County.

BERRY, JOHN Pvt, D, 37th Bttn VA Res Inf (CSA), 5-28-1865. Finn's Point National Cemetery, Pennsville, Salem County.

BERRY*, JOHN G. Pvt, G, 14th PA Cav, 1923. Community Church Cemetery, Leeds Point, Atlantic County.

BERRY, JOHN J. Pvt, E, 25th NJ Inf, 11-21-1919. Holy Sepulchre Cemetery, Totowa, Passaic County.

BERRY, JOHN J. Pvt, I, 12th NJ Inf, 10-29-1917. Deckertown-Union Cemetery, Papakating, Sussex County.

Our Brothers Gone Before

BERRY, JOSEPH Wagoner, E, 5th NY Inf, 8-7-1868. Greenwood Cemetery, Tuckerton, Ocean County.

BERRY, JOSEPH H. Pvt, E, 11th NJ Inf, 5-16-1923. Evergreen Cemetery, Morristown, Morris County.

BERRY, MATTHEW DoD Unknown. Deckertown-Union Cemetery, Papakating, Sussex County.

BERRY, MOSES A. Pvt, K, 7th NJ Inf, [Died of pneumonia at Lower Potomac, VA.] 1-29-1862. Methodist Cemetery, Hurdtown, Morris County.

BERRY, R.W. Pvt, H, 23rd NC Inf (CSA), [Captured 7-1-1863 at Gettysburg, PA. Died of measles.] 9-14-1863. Finn's Point National Cemetery, Pennsville, Salem County.

BERRY, ROBERT WARD Capt, A, 22nd NJ Inf, 2-28-1878. Hackensack Cemetery, Hackensack, Bergen County.

BERRY, SAMUEL J. Pvt, H, 7th NY State Militia, 1922. Evergreen Cemetery, Hillside, Union County.

BERRY*, THEODORE Ordinary Seaman, U.S. Navy, USS Maumee, DoD Unknown. Pleasantdale Cemetery, West Orange, Essex County.

BERRY, THEODORE Pvt, M, 2nd NJ Cav, DoD Unknown. Presbyterian Church Cemetery, Andover, Sussex County.

BERRY*, THOMAS Pvt, Btty I, 11th U.S. CHA, 10-8-1911. Laurel Grove Cemetery, Totowa, Passaic County.

BERRY, TIMOTHY HALSEY Pvt, D, 1st NJ Inf, [Wounded in action.] 7-2-1915. Presbyterian Church Cemetery, Hampton, Hunterdon County.

BERRY, TITUS (JR.) 2nd Lt, E, 11th NJ Inf, 4-25-1911. Chestnut Cemetery, Dover, Morris County.

BERRY, WILLIAM 1872. Bordentown/Old St. Mary's Catholic Cemetery, Bordentown, Burlington County.

BERRY, WILLIAM Pvt, H, 8th NJ Inf, 12-23-1910. Presbyterian Cemetery, Asbury, Warren County.

BERRY, WILLIAM A. (aka: Barry, William) Pvt, K, 70th NY Inf, [Wounded at Gettysburg, PA.] 8-30-1873. Woodland Cemetery, Newark, Essex County.

BERRY, WILLIAM C. 1st Lt, H, 5th NJ Inf, [Killed in action at Williamsburg, VA.] 5-5-1862. Alpine Cemetery, Perth Amboy, Middlesex County.

BERRY*, WILLIAM H. Musc, K, 12th NJ Inf, 11-13-1899. Methodist Church Cemetery, Haleyville, Cumberland County.

BERRY, WILLIAM W. Pvt, E, 39th NJ Inf, DoD Unknown. Holy Sepulchre Cemetery, East Orange, Essex County.

BERRYMAN*, JOHN Pvt, D, 6th NJ Inf, 1-27-1905. Cedar Grove Cemetery, Gloucester City, Camden County.

BERRYMAN, JOHN M. Pvt, I, 192nd PA Inf, 10-18-1898. Evergreen Cemetery, Camden, Camden County.

BERRYMAN, ROBERT Musc, H, 4th NJ Militia, DoD Unknown. Cedar Grove Cemetery, Gloucester City, Camden County.

BERSTLER, GEORGE W. Pvt, E, 2nd NJ Cav, 1924. Presbyterian Cemetery, Springfield, Union County.

BERT, WILLIAM 7-5-1871. Presbyterian Cemetery, North Plainfield, Somerset County.

BERTELE, ENGLEBERT Pvt, C, 4th NJ Inf, 8-14-1889. St. Francis Cemetery, Trenton, Mercer County.

BERTHOLF, GEORGE W. Pvt, D, 39th NJ Inf, 9-21-1889. Fairmount Cemetery, Newark, Essex County.

BERTHOLF, JOHN H. Pvt, F, 11th NY Inf, 10-12-1905. Cedar Lawn Cemetery, Paterson, Passaic County.

BERTHOLF, JOHN J. 1st Lt, Adj, 79th U.S. CT 5-6-1895. Maple Grove Cemetery, Hackensack, Bergen County.

New Jersey Civil War Burials

BERTHOLF, JOSEPH H. Pvt, L, 1st NJ Cav, 4-16-1915. Laurel Grove Cemetery, Totowa, Passaic County.
BERTHOLF, PETER A. 2nd Lt, G, 1st NJ Cav, [Died of heart disease at Washington, DC.] 2-9-1862. Greenlawn Cemetery, West Long Branch, Monmouth County.
BERTINSHAW, JOSHUA Pvt, C, 33rd NJ Inf, 9-29-1868. Fairmount Cemetery, Newark, Essex County.
BERTRAM, CASPER Pvt, F, 15th NJ Inf, [Wounded in action.] 3-7-1873. Holy Sepulchre Cemetery, East Orange, Essex County.
BERTRAM, CORNELIUS Corp, E, 39th NJ Inf, 1-7-1903. Holy Sepulchre Cemetery, East Orange, Essex County.
BERTRAM, KARL 7-1-1910. Bayview-New York Bay Cemetery, Jersey City, Hudson County.
BERTRAM, RICHARD S. (aka: Burtrone, Richard) Sgt, D, 11th NJ Inf, 3-5-1893. Fairmount Cemetery, Newark, Essex County.
BERTRAND, ALBERT Pvt, H, 9th NJ Inf, 3-7-1897. Fairmount Cemetery, Newark, Essex County.
BERTSCH, DAVID Pvt, D, 2nd NJ Inf, 8-11-1888. Fairmount Cemetery, Newark, Essex County.
BERTSCH, JACOB Pvt, U.S. Army, [General Service.] 3-5-1862. Finn's Point National Cemetery, Pennsville, Salem County.
BERZELL, JOHN DoD Unknown. Old St. Mary's Cemetery, Gloucester City, Camden County.
BESCHER, ANDREW Pvt, Btty A, 1st NJ Light Art, 1-12-1911. Fairmount Cemetery, Newark, Essex County.
BESCHEVER, JOHN H. Pvt, I, 31st NJ Inf, 3-25-1922. Union Brick Cemetery, Blairstown, Warren County.
BESSER, WILLIAM P. Fireman, U.S. Navy, USS Arkansas, 6-30-1865. Evergreen Cemetery, Camden, Camden County.
BESSIMIER, JOHN 5-7-1894. Trinity Episcopal Church Cemetery, Woodbridge, Middlesex County.
BESSINGER, CARL F. 10-22-1880. Speer Cemetery, Jersey City, Hudson County.
BEST, WILLIAM B. Pvt, A, 8th (Wade's) Confederate States Cav (CSA), 9-30-1863. Finn's Point National Cemetery, Pennsville, Salem County.
BESWICK, BENJAMIN J. Pvt, G, 23rd NJ Inf, 11-9-1888. Monument Cemetery, Edgewater Park, Burlington County.
BETCES, JOHN (aka: Betz, John) Pvt, E, 26th NJ Inf, 5-9-1882. Woodland Cemetery, Newark, Essex County.
BETHMANN, FREDERICK H. Pvt, F, 7th NY Inf, 9-15-1893. Grove Church Cemetery, North Bergen, Hudson County.
BETTEL, VALENTINE (aka: Beatle, Valentine) Pvt, F, 1st NJ Militia, 1-3-1923. Woodland Cemetery, Newark, Essex County.
BETTINGER, JACOB Pvt, H, 9th NJ Inf, 8-24-1870. Fairmount Cemetery, Newark, Essex County.
BETTINGER, JOHN Pvt, H, 9th NJ Inf, 3-13-1894. Fairmount Cemetery, Newark, Essex County.
BETTS, JOHN BROOKS Pvt, Ind Btty, Woodward's PA Light Art, 8-29-1931. Harleigh Cemetery, Camden, Camden County.
BETZ, ALBERT Pvt, G, 7th U.S. Inf, 6-6-1916. New Camden Cemetery, Camden, Camden County.
BETZ, GEORGE V. Pvt, F, 8th NJ Inf, 12-24-1910. Arlington Cemetery, Kearny, Hudson County.
BETZ, JOHN Pvt, I, 20th NY Inf, 7-18-1919. Jersey City Cemetery, Jersey City, Hudson County.
BETZ, JOHN (see: Betces, John) Woodland Cemetery, Newark, Essex County.

Our Brothers Gone Before

BETZEL, HENRY Pvt, E, 2nd NJ Inf, 4-3-1890. Woodland Cemetery, Newark, Essex County.
BETZELL, JACOB (see: Betzler, Jacob) Fairmount Cemetery, Newark, Essex County.
BETZLER, JACOB (aka: Betzell, Jacob) Pvt, Btty E, 1st NJ Light Art, 11-27-1919. Fairmount Cemetery, Newark, Essex County.
BEUERLE*, LOUIS (aka: Beierle, Lewis) Pvt, C, 27th PA Inf, 2-5-1905. New Camden Cemetery, Camden, Camden County.
BEUETELL, JULIUS (see: Beutel, Julius) Evergreen Cemetery, Hillside, Union County.
BEURET*, CONSTANTINE (aka: Burritt, Constantine) Pvt, G, 8th NJ Inf, [Wounded in action.] 3-9-1894. Holy Sepulchre Cemetery, East Orange, Essex County.
BEUTEL, JULIUS (aka: Beuetell, Julius) Pvt, C, 30th NJ Inf, 2-11-1913. Evergreen Cemetery, Hillside, Union County.
BEUTELL, ERNEST EMANUEL (aka: Bentell, Edward) Pvt, E, 1st NY Inf, 12-25-1930. Methodist Cemetery, Hamilton, Monmouth County.
BEUTINGER, CHRISTOF QM Sgt, 11th U.S. Inf 7-11-1916. Prospect Hill Cemetery, Caldwell, Essex County.
BEVANS, BENJAMIN R. 12-1-1885. Hainesville Cemetery, Hainesville, Sussex County.
BEVEL, B.G. (aka: Bevils, B.G.) Pvt, H, 3rd (Clack's) TN Inf (CSA), 8-14-1863. Finn's Point National Cemetery, Pennsville, Salem County.
BEVERIDGE, THOMAS Sgt, I, 26th NY Inf, 10-17-1907. Cedar Lawn Cemetery, Paterson, Passaic County.
BEVERLY, WILLIAM H. Pvt, B, 29th U.S. CT, 4-12-1936. New Somerville Cemetery, Somerville, Somerset County.
BEVERS, JOSEPH A. HENRY Artificer, F, 50th NY Eng, [Wounded 6-5-1863 at Franklins Crossing, VA.] 10-7-1892. Weehawken Cemetery, North Bergen, Hudson County.
BEVILS, B.G. (see: Bevel, B.G.) Finn's Point National Cemetery, Pennsville, Salem County.
BEYEA, HARVEY Capt, H, 25th NJ Inf, 1-6-1911. Laurel Grove Cemetery, Totowa, Passaic County.
BEYER, CHARLES (see: Franks, Charles Beyer) Fairmount Cemetery, Newark, Essex County.
BEYER, HERMAN C. Hosp Steward, U.S. Army, 2-9-1903. Woodland Cemetery, Newark, Essex County.
BIBB, JOHN HENRY (JR.) Pvt, Charlottesville Btty, VA Light Art (CSA), [Wounded and captured 5-12-1864 at Spotsylvania CH, VA. Died of wounds.] 12-21-1864. Finn's Point National Cemetery, Pennsville, Salem County.
BIBBY*, ISAAC (aka: Bilbey, Isaac) Pvt, B, 37th NJ Inf, 6-28-1909. Cedar Lawn Cemetery, Paterson, Passaic County.
BICE, CHARLES J. Pvt, A, 35th NJ Inf, 1922. Holcomb-Riverview Cemetery, Lambertville, Hunterdon County.
BICE, JOHN (SR.) Pvt, A, 3rd NJ Cav, 2-13-1916. Riverview Cemetery, Trenton, Mercer County.
BICKEL, FRANCIS (see: Hall, Francis B.) Bayview-New York Bay Cemetery, Jersey City, Hudson County.
BICKEL, JACOB Pvt, B, 9th NJ Inf, 8-16-1877. Bloomfield Cemetery, Bloomfield, Essex County.
BICKETT, WILLIAM Pvt, D, 107th U.S. CT, 1910. White Ridge Cemetery, Eatontown, Monmouth County.
BICKFORD, NATHANIEL G. Pvt, D, 17th ME Inf, [Wounded 7-2-1863 at Gettysburg, PA.] 1-22-1922. Brotherhood Cemetery, Hainesport, Burlington County.
BICKHARD, CONRAD (aka: Brickhardt, Conrad) Pvt, D, 6th NJ Inf, 10-15-1874. Grove Church Cemetery, North Bergen, Hudson County.

New Jersey Civil War Burials

BICKHARDT*, HENRY Pvt, Btty C, 1st NJ Light Art, 12-9-1893. Flower Hill Cemetery, North Bergen, Hudson County.

BICKLEY, HORACE P. Sgt, K, 10th NJ Inf, 8-8-1910. United Methodist Church Cemetery, Leesburg, Cumberland County.

BICKLEY, JOHN H. Pvt, F, 10th PA Inf, 7-4-1921. Locust Hill Cemetery, Dover, Morris County.

BICKNER, GEORGE H.L. Seaman, U.S. Navy, USS Midnight, 2-1-1874. Oak Grove Cemetery, Hammonton, Atlantic County.

BICKON, ANTHONY (aka: Bacon, Anthony) Pvt, D, 4th NJ Inf, [Died of diarrhea at Camp Seminary, VA.] 10-7-1861. Mercer Cemetery, Trenton, Mercer County.

BIDDLE, AARON H. Pvt, K, 24th NJ Inf, [Wounded in action.] 5-16-1894. Atlantic City Cemetery, Pleasantville, Atlantic County.

BIDDLE, ABEL Pvt, F, 4th NJ Inf, 10-1-1909. St. Rose of Lima Cemetery, Millburn, Essex County.

BIDDLE, ALFRED Pvt, E, 6th NJ Inf, [Died at Fort Monroe, VA. of wounds received 5-5-1862 at Williamsburg, VA.] 5-22-1862. Methodist Church Cemetery, Groveville, Mercer County.

BIDDLE, CHARLES Pvt, D, 25th NJ Inf, 9-26-1900. Old Stone Church Cemetery, Fairton, Cumberland County.

BIDDLE, GEORGE K. Landsman, U.S. Navy, USS Sarah Bruen, 9-6-1896. Methodist-Episcopal Church Cemetery, Penns Grove, Salem County.

BIDDLE*, JACOB Pvt, I, 12th NJ Inf, [Died at Washington, DC.] 9-2-1863. Methodist-Episcopal Church Cemetery, Penns Grove, Salem County.

BIDDLE, JEREMIAH S. Pvt, I, 1st DE Inf, 2-26-1914. Arlington Cemetery, Pennsauken, Camden County.

BIDDLE, JOHN Pvt, K, 24th NJ Inf, 1-25-1907. Methodist-Episcopal Church Cemetery, Penns Grove, Salem County.

BIDDLE, JOHN WESLEY Coal Heaver, U.S. Navy, USS Pequot, 4-1-1891. Prospect Hill Cemetery, Flemington, Hunterdon County.

BIDDLE, JONATHAN S. Sgt, K, 1st DE Inf, [Wounded 9-17-1862 at Antietam, MD.] 3-24-1905. Presbyterian Church Cemetery, Bridgeton, Cumberland County.

BIDDLE, PHILIP (see: Bittle, Philip) Mount Pleasant Cemetery, Newark, Essex County.

BIDDLE, URIAH B. Pvt, I, 1st DE Inf, 11-15-1913. Evergreen Cemetery, Camden, Camden County.

BIDWELL, CHARLES KNOWLES 8-21-1921. Bloomsbury Cemetery, Kennedy Mills, Warren County.

BIDWELL, EDWIN C. Surg, 31st MA Inf 11-14-1905. Oak Hill Cemetery, Vineland, Cumberland County.

BIDWELL, JAMES (see: Boswell, James) Fairmount Cemetery, Newark, Essex County.

BIEHL, ERNEST (aka: Beel, Ernest) Pvt, D, 9th NJ Inf, 10-3-1880. Woodland Cemetery, Newark, Essex County.

BIERKELBAUGH, JACOB (aka: Deighlebohr, Joseph) Pvt, D, 7th NJ Inf, 8- -1866. Methodist Cemetery, Malaga, Gloucester County.

BIERMAN*, WILLIAM Pvt, G, 9th NJ Inf, 12-10-1881. Lady of Lourdes/Holy Sepulchre Cemetery, Hamilton, Mercer County.

BIERS, JOHN E. (aka: Berrie, John) Pvt, H, 4th NY Cav, 9-30-1913. Arlington Cemetery, Pennsauken, Camden County.

BIERWIRTH*, HENRY Pvt, I, 16th NY Cav, 11-12-1901. Hazelwood Cemetery, Rahway, Union County.

BIERWITH*, FRANCIS J. Capt, G, 69th PA Inf, [Cenotaph. Killed in action at Antietam, MD.] 9-17-1862. Egg Harbor Cemetery, Egg Harbor, Atlantic County.

BIGALOW, JONATHAN Pvt, C, 69th NY Inf, 3-15-1922. Methodist Cemetery, Newfoundland, Morris County.

Our Brothers Gone Before

BIGELOW*, CHARLES D. Pvt, Btty H, 4th MA Heavy Art, DoD Unknown. Locust Hill Cemetery, Dover, Morris County.

BIGELOW, JOHN G. Pvt, F, 8th NY State Militia, 6-27-1907. Mercer Cemetery, Trenton, Mercer County.

BIGGER, ROBERT M. Pvt, Btty G, Young's Ind PA Art, [Died at Fort Delaware.] 10-10-1864. Finn's Point National Cemetery, Pennsville, Salem County.

BIGGERS, ALISON H. Pvt, E, 4th NC Cav (CSA), [Captured 7-4-1863 at South Mountain, MD. Died of apoplexy.] 1-29-1865. Finn's Point National Cemetery, Pennsville, Salem County.

BIGGS*, DAVID Pvt, C, 86th OH Inf, 1-6-1914. Reformed Church Cemetery, Readington, Hunterdon County.

BIGGS, GEORGE P. Pvt, G, 3rd NJ Cav, 4-20-1923. Mount Pleasant Cemetery, Millville, Cumberland County.

BIGGS, HERMAN Bvt Brig Gen, U.S. Volunteers, [Colonel, Chief Quartermaster, Philadelphia, PA Depot.] 10-11-1887. Greenmount Cemetery, Hammonton, Atlantic County.

BIGGS, JOHN C. Sgt, D, 26th NJ Inf, 1-5-1886. Prospect Hill Cemetery, Caldwell, Essex County.

BIGGS, JOSEPH F. Pvt, C, 38th NJ Inf, 1-19-1921. 1st United Methodist Church Cemetery, Bridgeton, Cumberland County.

BIGGS, LEWIS Pvt, I, 8th PA Cav, 1-24-1909. Union Cemetery, Gloucester City, Camden County.

BIGGS, MOSES Pvt, C, 22nd U.S. CT, 5-30-1901. Fairmount Cemetery, Newark, Essex County.

BIGGS, NICHOLAS O. Pvt, A, 30th NJ Inf, 2-26-1913. Baptist Church Cemetery, Flemington, Hunterdon County.

BIGGS, WILLIAM H. Pvt, D, 26th NJ Inf, 9-3-1877. Prospect Hill Cemetery, Caldwell, Essex County.

BIGGS, WILLIAM H. DoD Unknown. 1st United Methodist Church Cemetery, Bridgeton, Cumberland County.

BIGHAM, JAMES A. Pvt, (CSA) 1-2-1892. Maplewood Cemetery, Freehold, Monmouth County.

BIGHARDT, CHARLES (aka: Richardt, Charles) Pvt, K, 26th NJ Inf, 1876. Fairmount Cemetery, Newark, Essex County.

BIGLE, JOHN Pvt, G, 25th MI Inf, DoD Unknown. Stillwater Cemetery, Stillwater, Sussex County.

BIGLER, J. (see: Peagler, Thomas H.) Finn's Point National Cemetery, Pennsville, Salem County.

BIGNELL, DAVID E. Pvt, D, 3rd DE Inf, [Wounded in action.] 11-15-1902. Bordentown/Old St. Mary's Catholic Cemetery, Bordentown, Burlington County.

BIGNELL, JOHN R. Corp, I, 27th PA Inf, 1916. Cedar Green Cemetery, Clayton, Gloucester County.

BIGOT, JOHN (see: Bogert, John) Redeemer Cemetery, Mahwah, Bergen County.

BIJOTAT, GEORGE Pvt, H, 131st NY Inf, 2-7-1916. Hollywood Cemetery, Union, Union County.

BILBEE, GEORGE W. Pvt, D, 104th PA Inf, 12-17-1891. Riverview Cemetery, Trenton, Mercer County.

BILBEY, HENRY (see: Bilby, Henry D.) Methodist Church Cemetery, Mount Bethel, Warren County.

BILBEY, ISAAC (see: Bibby, Isaac) Cedar Lawn Cemetery, Paterson, Passaic County.

BILBY, HENRY D. (aka: Bilbey, Henry) Pvt, H, 31st NJ Inf, 12-24-1911. Methodist Church Cemetery, Mount Bethel, Warren County.

BILBY, NICHOLAS S. Pvt, H, 31st NJ Inf, 6-16-1865. Union Cemetery, Washington, Morris County.

New Jersey Civil War Burials

BILDERBACK, JOHN Corp, C, 24th NJ Inf, 5-21-1866. Baptist Church Cemetery, Alloway, Salem County.

BILDERBACK, SMITH 2nd Lt, F, 34th NJ Inf, 11-8-1905. Eastview Cemetery, Salem, Salem County.

BILDERBACK, WILLIAM H. Musc, 5th NJ Inf Band 2-24-1884. Methodist-Episcopal Church Cemetery, Penns Grove, Salem County.

BILES, AUGUSTINE S. Pvt, F, 33rd PA Militia, 10-28-1891. Methodist Church Cemetery, Hurffville, Gloucester County.

BILL, HENRY WEIR 12-6-1885. Presbyterian Church Cemetery, Metuchen, Middlesex County.

BILLANEY, HARRISON Sgt, F, 15th NY Eng, DoD Unknown. Presbyterian Church Cemetery, Woodbridge, Middlesex County.

BILLES, JOHN W. (aka: Bellis, John) 2nd Lt, I, 1st NJ Cav, [Killed in action at Hawe's Shop, VA.] 5-28-1864. Cedar Hill Cemetery, East Millstone, Somerset County.

BILLIG, LAFAYETTE Sgt, G, 95th PA Inf, 12-26-1911. Arlington Cemetery, Pennsauken, Camden County.

BILLINGS, CHARLES M. Hosp Steward, U.S. Volunteers, 8-25-1885. Evergreen Cemetery, Camden, Camden County.

BILLINGS, LEWIS Pvt, A, 57th PA Inf, 8-15-1895. Hainesburg Cemetery, Hainesburg, Warren County.

BILLINGS, PETER H. Musc, H, 29th CT Inf, 12-5-1902. Gethsemane Cemetery, Little Ferry, Bergen County.

BILLINGS, STEPHEN B. 2-15-1891. Old 1st Methodist Church Cemetery, West Long Branch, Monmouth County.

BILLINGS*, THOMAS Pvt, G, 1st DE Inf, 1-7-1919. Overlook Cemetery, Bridgeton, Cumberland County.

BILLINGTON, SAMUEL H. Pvt, C, 47th PA Inf, [Wounded 10-22-1862 at Pocotaligo, SC.] 3-28-1893. Evergreen Cemetery, Camden, Camden County.

BILLS, ABRAHAM L. Pvt, H, 97th PA Inf, 10-21-1877. Greenlawn Cemetery, West Long Branch, Monmouth County.

BILLS, THOMAS Pvt, D, 39th NJ Inf, 1-10-1868. Riverside Cemetery, Toms River, Ocean County.

BILLS, WILLIAM H. Pvt, D, 14th NJ Inf, [Killed in action at Cold Harbor, VA.] 6-1-1864. Evergreen Cemetery, Farmingdale, Monmouth County.

BILYEA, JEREMIAH L. Pvt, H, 30th NJ Inf, DoD Unknown. Baptist/Evergreen Methodist Cemetery, Plainfield, Union County.

BILYOU, JEREMIAH L. 3-8-1895. Methodist Church Cemetery, Mount Horeb, Somerset County.

BIMBLE, ANDREW Pvt, F, 39th NJ Inf, 5-21-1906. Holy Sepulchre Cemetery, East Orange, Essex County.

BIMSON, ROBERT (aka: Brinson, Robert) Pvt, C, 25th NJ Inf, [Wounded in action at Fredericksburg, VA.] 2-24-1918. Cedar Lawn Cemetery, Paterson, Passaic County.

BINDE, AUGUSTUS W.F. 3-27-1936. Dayton Cemetery, Dayton, Middlesex County.

BINDER, GUSTAV Pvt, C, 9th NJ Inf, 6-21-1896. Fairmount Cemetery, Newark, Essex County.

BINES, FREDERICK W. Corp, F, 13th NJ Inf, [Died of diptheria at Sharpsburg, MD.] 12-4-1862. Fairmount Cemetery, Newark, Essex County.

BING, JOSHUA P. (aka: Being, J.P.) Pvt, D, 36th (Broyle's) GA Inf (CSA), [Captured 5-16-1863 at Baker's Creek, MS.] 7-24-1863. Finn's Point National Cemetery, Pennsville, Salem County.

BINGHAM, EDWARD B. QM Sgt, 21st NJ Inf 8-21-1899. Rosedale Cemetery, Orange, Essex County.

Our Brothers Gone Before

BINGHAM, ERNEST K. Pvt, 20th NY Ind Btty 3-28-1922. Holy Sepulchre Cemetery, East Orange, Essex County.

BINGHAM, FRANCIS E. Pvt, Unassigned, 161st NY Inf, 3-29-1911. Rosedale Cemetery, Orange, Essex County.

BINGHAM, GEORGE A. 2nd Lt, I, 28th NY Inf, 5-16-1897. Harleigh Cemetery, Camden, Camden County.

BINGHAM, THOMAS Pvt, A, 1st NY Cav, 12-21-1895. St. Nicholas Cemetery, Lodi, Bergen County.

BINGHAM, WELLS A. (see: Bingham, William A.) Bloomfield Cemetery, Bloomfield, Essex County.

BINGHAM, WILLIAM A. (aka: Bingham, Wells A.) Corp, H, 16th CT Inf, 1921. Bloomfield Cemetery, Bloomfield, Essex County.

BINGLER, EUGENE G. Pvt, B, 3rd U.S. Cav, 3-31-1919. Fairmount Cemetery, Newark, Essex County.

BININGER, BYRON (aka: Bensinger, Byron) Pvt, A, 47th PA Inf, 12-26-1903. Arlington Cemetery, Kearny, Hudson County.

BINLEY, HENRY Pvt, B, 197th PA Inf, 2-23-1901. Atlantic City Cemetery, Pleasantville, Atlantic County.

BINN, WILLIAM Pvt, H, 6th U.S. CT, 1892. Old Methodist Cemetery, New Egypt, Ocean County.

BINTCLIFF, JOSEPH Pvt, I, 37th NJ Inf, 1-11-1905. Beverly National Cemetery, Edgewater Park, Burlington County.

BIONEN, JAMES CANNON Pvt, C, 65th OH Inf, 1925. Fairmount Cemetery, Newark, Essex County.

BIRCH, BENJAMIN O. Pvt, I, 5th NJ Inf, 4-22-1902. Fairmount Cemetery, Newark, Essex County.

BIRCH, JOHN S. Pvt, C, 24th NJ Inf, 1926. Methodist Church Cemetery, Newport, Cumberland County.

BIRCH, LEWIS Pvt, I, 3rd NJ Inf, [Wounded in action.] 1-22-1922. Friendship United Methodist Church Cemetery, Landisville, Atlantic County.

BIRCH*, PETER Ordinary Seaman, U.S. Navy, USS Sassacus, 11-12-1894. Holy Sepulchre Cemetery, East Orange, Essex County.

BIRCH, THEODORE F. Pvt, E, 213th PA Inf, 8-14-1915. Mount Pleasant Cemetery, Millville, Cumberland County.

BIRCH, W.J. Pvt, F, 6th VA Cav (CSA), 7-20-1864. Finn's Point National Cemetery, Pennsville, Salem County.

BIRCK, JOHN A. (aka: Burk, John) Pvt, K, 11th NJ Inf, 9-24-1908. Flower Hill Cemetery, North Bergen, Hudson County.

BIRD, AZEL M. Pvt, K, 23rd NJ Inf, 6-29-1868. United Methodist Church Cemetery, Smithville, Atlantic County.

BIRD, BRITTON H. 1903. Sandy Ridge Cemetery, Sandy Ridge, Hunterdon County.

BIRD, CHETWOOD 1st Sgt, B, 30th NJ Inf, 2-23-1893. Riverview Cemetery, Trenton, Mercer County.

BIRD, EDWARD Pvt, K, 10th NJ Inf, 4-9-1900. Greenwood Cemetery, Tuckerton, Ocean County.

BIRD, GEORGE R. Pvt, D, 1st NJ Cav, 2-10-1908. Methodist Cemetery, Crosswicks, Burlington County.

BIRD, GEORGE SAMUEL 12-11-1943. Colestown Cemetery, Cherry Hill, Camden County.

BIRD, ISAAC (aka: Burd, Isaac) Pvt, G, 6th NY Heavy Art, 2-5-1900. Baptist Church Cemetery, Mount Bethel, Somerset County.

BIRD, JAMES Capt, H, 6th NJ Inf, 1-20-1899. Mount Hope Presbyterian Cemetery, Lambertville, Hunterdon County.

New Jersey Civil War Burials

BIRD, JAMES (JR.) Pvt, K, 23rd NJ Inf, [Died of typhoid at White Oak Church, VA.] 1-19-1863. Greenwood Cemetery, Tuckerton, Ocean County.
BIRD, JAMES R. 1-16-1879. Mount Pleasant Cemetery, Newark, Essex County.
BIRD, JAMES W. Pvt, B, 26th NJ Inf, 4-13-1922. Fairmount Cemetery, Newark, Essex County.
BIRD, JESSE Pvt, K, 10th NJ Inf, 3-2-1907. Greenwood Cemetery, Tuckerton, Ocean County.
BIRD, JOHN Pvt, F, 3rd NJ Cav, 11-3-1909. Fairmount Cemetery, Newark, Essex County.
BIRD, JOHN Wagoner, E, 12th NJ Inf, 9-3-1899. Bayview-New York Bay Cemetery, Jersey City, Hudson County.
BIRD, JOHN 6-3-1873. Mansfield/Washington Cemetery, Washington, Warren County.
BIRD, JOHN J. Maj, 14th PA Cav 3-19-1886. Greenwood Cemetery, Hamilton, Mercer County.
BIRD, JOHN S. Pvt, H, 2nd NJ Cav, 1917. Union Cemetery, Washington, Morris County.
BIRD, JOHN Y. 1st Sgt, I, 30th NJ Inf, 3-13-1882. Presbyterian Church Cemetery, Liberty Corners, Somerset County.
BIRD, LAWRENCE Pvt, K, 10th NJ Inf, 6-15-1938. Greenwood Cemetery, Tuckerton, Ocean County.
BIRD, LAWRENCE A. Pvt, G, 23rd NJ Inf, 8-23-1888. Methodist Cemetery, Bridgeboro, Burlington County.
BIRD, LEONARD (see: Burd, Leonard G.) Prospect Hill Cemetery, Flemington, Hunterdon County.
BIRD, LEONARD G. Sgt, D, 31st NJ Inf, 5-15-1884. Methodist Cemetery, Bernardsville, Somerset County.
BIRD, MICHAEL E. Pvt, K, 10th NJ Inf, 1906. Friends United Methodist-Episcopal Church Cemetery, Linwood, Atlantic County.
BIRD, PETER (JR.) Pvt, C, 27th NJ Inf, 4-28-1892. Phillipsburg Cemetery, Phillipsburg, Warren County.
BIRD*, PHILIP ACKOR Pvt, H, 115th IL Inf, 11-3-1919. Hillside Cemetery, Scotch Plains, Union County.
BIRD, SAMUEL Pvt, K, 10th NJ Inf, 3-27-1902. Greenwood Cemetery, Tuckerton, Ocean County.
BIRD, THOMAS Pvt, G, 4th NJ Inf, 3-12-1904. Mount Pleasant Cemetery, Millville, Cumberland County.
BIRD, THOMAS (see: Burd, Thomas) Fairmount Cemetery, Fairmount, Hunterdon County.
BIRD*, THOMAS J. Pvt, I, 16th PA Cav, 10-11-1909. Bayview-New York Bay Cemetery, Jersey City, Hudson County.
BIRD, THOMAS S. Pvt, H, 31st NJ Inf, 8-13-1922. Union Cemetery, Washington, Morris County.
BIRD, W. HENRY Pvt, H, 23rd NJ Inf, 4-15-1927. Riverside Cemetery, Toms River, Ocean County.
BIRD, WESLEY Corp, D, 36th IN Inf, DoD Unknown. Hardyston Cemetery, North Church, Sussex County.
BIRD, WILLIAM A. Pvt, G, 38th NJ Inf, 10-23-1874. Methodist Cemetery, Bridgeboro, Burlington County.
BIRD, WILLIAM D. DoD Unknown. Holy Sepulchre Cemetery, Totowa, Passaic County.
BIRD, WILLIAM H. Landsman, U.S. Navy, 4-27-1887. Presbyterian Church Cemetery, Woodbridge, Middlesex County.
BIRD, WILLIAM TINSMAN Pvt, E, 31st NJ Inf, 1894. Bethlehem Presbyterian Church Cemetery, Grandin, Hunterdon County.
BIRDSALL, GEORGE E. Seaman, U.S. Navy, USS Lafayette, 1927. Atlantic View Cemetery, Manasquan, Monmouth County.

Our Brothers Gone Before

BIRDSALL, JAMES H. Seaman, U.S. Navy, USS Princeton, 12-21-1902. Holy Name Cemetery, Jersey City, Hudson County.

BIRDSALL, JOHN G. Pvt, Btty F, 6th NY Heavy Art, 7-3-1927. Evergreen Cemetery, Hillside, Union County.

BIRDSELL, BARNET (see: Burdsell, Barnet) 7th Day Baptist Church Cemetery, Shiloh, Cumberland County.

BIRGEN, MICHAEL Pvt, U.S. Marine Corps, USS Circassian, 3-25-1883. St. James Cemetery, Woodbridge, Middlesex County.

BIRKENSTOCK*, A.E. Sgt, C, 103rd NY Inf, DoD Unknown. Grove Church Cemetery, North Bergen, Hudson County.

BIRKLEY, H.C. Pvt, C, White's VA Cav (CSA), 7-14-1864. Finn's Point National Cemetery, Pennsville, Salem County.

BIRKMIRE*, WILLIAM H. Pvt, I, 33rd PA Inf, 1901. Monument Cemetery, Edgewater Park, Burlington County.

BIRLEY, MILTON 1st Sgt, A, 22nd NJ Inf, 9-14-1887. Hackensack Cemetery, Hackensack, Bergen County.

BIRMELY*, JOHN JACOB Seaman, U.S. Navy, USS Scotia, 2-6-1908. Bayview-New York Bay Cemetery, Jersey City, Hudson County.

BIRMINGHAM, ISRAEL Pvt, B, 95th PA Inf, DoD Unknown. Baptist Cemetery, Medford, Burlington County.

BIRMINGHAM, WILLIAM (see: Bermingham, William) St. Mary's Cemetery, Wharton, Morris County.

BIRNEY, DAVID (aka: Burney, David) Pvt, Btty E, 2nd PA Heavy Art, 1-10-1904. German Valley Rural Cemetery, Naughright, Morris County.

BIRNIE, WILLIAM Pvt, Parker's SC Light Art (CSA) [Marion Artillery. Charleston Marine Artillery.] DoD Unknown. Evergreen Cemetery, Hillside, Union County.

BIRRELL, DAVID A. (aka: Burrill, David) Pvt, G, 8th NJ Inf, [Killed in action at Williamsburg, VA.] 5-5-1862. Fairmount Cemetery, Newark, Essex County.

BIRRELL, WILLIAM (aka: Dease, William) Pvt, F, 8th NJ Inf, [Died of apoplexy at Manassas Junction, VA.] 11-18-1862. Fairmount Cemetery, Newark, Essex County.

BIRTWISTLE, GEORGE Pvt, A, 12th U.S. Inf, 1865. Vincent Methodist-Episcopal Cemetery, Nutley, Essex County.

BISCHOF, FREDERICK 1st Lt, D, 2nd NJ Militia, 4-3-1893. Bayview-New York Bay Cemetery, Jersey City, Hudson County.

BISCHOFF, JOHN Pvt, Btty C, 15th NY Heavy Art, 10-20-1880. Egg Harbor Cemetery, Egg Harbor, Atlantic County.

BISCHOFF*, WILLIAM QM Sgt, 30th NY Ind Btty 12-21-1888. South Orange Cemetery, South Orange, Essex County.

BISHOFF, WILLIAM (aka: Bishop, William) Sgt, 6th NY Ind Btty 2-15-1880. Rahway Cemetery, Rahway, Union County.

BISHOP, BRAZILLA Pvt, H, 29th NJ Inf, 1885. Evergreen Cemetery, Lakewood, Ocean County.

BISHOP*, CHARLES Wagoner, C, 34th NJ Inf, 2-20-1919. Columbus Cemetery, Columbus, Burlington County.

BISHOP, CHARLES Pvt, C, 33rd NJ Inf, 1925. Midvale Cemetery, Midvale, Passaic County.

BISHOP, CHARLES B. 9-13-1914. Mount Pleasant Cemetery, Newark, Essex County.

BISHOP, EDWARD Pvt, K, 23rd PA Inf, 3-24-1869. Cedar Lawn Cemetery, Paterson, Passaic County.

BISHOP, EDWIN Capt, H, 2nd NJ Inf, 11-6-1902. Boonton Cemetery, Boonton, Morris County.

BISHOP*, EDWIN S. Pvt, B, 1st NJ Cav, 5-1-1888. Riverview Cemetery, Trenton, Mercer County.

New Jersey Civil War Burials

BISHOP, FRANK V. (aka: Bishop, T.W.) Pvt, K, 4th LA Inf (CSA), 3-21-1869. Cedar Lawn Cemetery, Paterson, Passaic County.

BISHOP, FRANKLIN S. Pvt, K, 15th NJ Inf, [Killed in action at Salem Heights, VA.] 5-3-1863. Beemerville Cemetery, Beemerville, Sussex County.

BISHOP, GEORGE Pvt, E, 3rd U.S. CT, 12-4-1924. Mount Peace Cemetery, Lawnside, Camden County.

BISHOP, GEORGE A. Pvt, K, 83rd PA Inf, 2-15-1863. Fairmount Cemetery, Newark, Essex County.

BISHOP, GEORGE D. Pvt, K, 15th NJ Inf, [Cenotaph. Died of debility at Danville, VA.] 1-30-1865. Beemerville Cemetery, Beemerville, Sussex County.

BISHOP, GEORGE S. Pvt, H, 23rd NJ Inf, 11-13-1912. Trinity Episcopal Church Cemetery, Delran, Burlington County.

BISHOP, GEORGE SAYES 3-12-1914. Rosedale Cemetery, Orange, Essex County.

BISHOP, GEORGE W. Pvt, E, 37th NJ Inf, 5-28-1928. Fairmount Cemetery, Newark, Essex County.

BISHOP, HOWARD Pvt, F, 71st NY State Militia, 9-11-1866. 1st Methodist-Episcopal Cemetery, New Brunswick, Middlesex County.

BISHOP, ISAAC H. Corp, G, 23rd NJ Inf, 10-20-1907. Coopertown Meeting House Cemetery, Edgewater Park, Burlington County.

BISHOP, JAMES Musc, M, 1st NJ Cav, DoD Unknown. Riverview Cemetery, Trenton, Mercer County.

BISHOP, JAMES (see: McCline, James) Reformed Church Cemetery, Readington, Hunterdon County.

BISHOP, JAMES T. 4-4-1888. Willow Grove Cemetery, New Brunswick, Middlesex County.

BISHOP, JOHN Pvt, E, 29th NJ Inf, 12-11-1887. Maplewood Cemetery, Freehold, Monmouth County.

BISHOP*, JOHN Pvt, F, 93rd NY Inf, 4-7-1898. Hardyston Cemetery, North Church, Sussex County.

BISHOP, JOHN S. Pvt, L, 3rd KY Mtd Inf (CSA), [Captured 5-16-1863 at Baker's Creek, MS.] 9-8-1863. Finn's Point National Cemetery, Pennsville, Salem County.

BISHOP, JOSEPH Pvt, H, 29th NJ Inf, DoD Unknown. New 1st Methodist Meeting House Cemetery, Manahawkin, Ocean County.

BISHOP, MICHAEL S. Pvt, H, 29th NJ Inf, 8-14-1910. Cedar Run/Greenwood Cemetery, Manahawkin, Ocean County.

BISHOP, MILES Corp, K, 25th U.S. CT, 12-9-1906. Mount Peace Cemetery, Lawnside, Camden County.

BISHOP, PRESTON (JR.) Seaman, U.S. Navy, 9-11-1886. Monument Cemetery, Edgewater Park, Burlington County.

BISHOP, ROBERT M. Pvt, I, 31st NJ Inf, 11-13-1888. Belvidere/Catholic Cemetery, Belvidere, Warren County.

BISHOP, T.W. (see: Bishop, Frank V.) Cedar Lawn Cemetery, Paterson, Passaic County.

BISHOP, WALTER H. Pvt, D, 26th NJ Inf, 5-31-1889. Methodist Church Cemetery, Roseland, Essex County.

BISHOP, WARREN S. Pvt, B, 26th NJ Inf, 1-6-1882. St. Mark's Cemetery, Orange, Essex County.

BISHOP, WILLIAM Pvt, K, 39th NJ Inf, 1925. Midvale Cemetery, Midvale, Passaic County.

BISHOP, WILLIAM (see: Bishoff, William) Rahway Cemetery, Rahway, Union County.

BISHOP, WILLIAM H. Pvt, B, 2nd NY Cav, 3-3-1870. Vaughn Cemetery, Ackerson, Sussex County.

BISHOP, WILLIAM S. Surg, U.S. Navy, 12-28-1868. Evergreen Cemetery, Camden, Camden County.

Our Brothers Gone Before

BISPHAM, JOHN E. Pvt, Ind, PA Art, 3-24-1919. Baptist/St. Andrew's Cemetery, Mount Holly, Burlington County.
BISSERT, MICHAEL (see: Burkhardt, Michael J.) Old Camden Cemetery, Camden, Camden County.
BISSET*, JOHN J. 2nd Asst Eng, U.S. Navy, USS Nyack, 1915. Washington Monumental Cemetery, South River, Middlesex County.
BISSETT*, FREDERICK W. 2nd Asst Eng, U.S. Navy, USS Colorado, 11-30-1906. Washington Monumental Cemetery, South River, Middlesex County.
BISSEY, CHARLES P. Sgt, K, 104th PA Inf, 11-3-1915. Union Cemetery, Frenchtown, Hunterdon County.
BISSEY, JOHN W. Pvt, E, 104th PA Inf, 11-21-1912. Bloomsbury Cemetery, Kennedy Mills, Warren County.
BISSMAN, JOHN Pvt, F, 52nd NY Inf, 6-19-1900. Bayview-New York Bay Cemetery, Jersey City, Hudson County.
BITTERS, BENJAMIN H. Pvt, D, 10th NJ Inf, [Died of typhoid at Washington, DC.] 6-1-1862. Presbyterian Church Cemetery, Bridgeton, Cumberland County.
BITTLE, CHARLES P. Pvt, K, 6th U.S. Cav, 12-31-1906. Fairmount Cemetery, Newark, Essex County.
BITTLE, DANIEL M. 8-30-1900. Berlin Cemetery, Berlin, Camden County.
BITTLE, GEORGE W. Pvt, B, 95th PA Inf, 9-2-1922. Berlin Cemetery, Berlin, Camden County.
BITTLE, PHILIP (aka: Biddle, Philip) Pvt, A, 2nd DC Inf, 7-8-1916. Mount Pleasant Cemetery, Newark, Essex County.
BITTLE, SOCRATES T. Pvt, B, 95th PA Inf, 2-9-1934. Berlin Cemetery, Berlin, Camden County.
BIVINS, BENJAMIN FRANKLIN Pvt, D, 10th NJ Inf, [Died of chronic debility at Washington, DC.] 9-8-1862. 7th Day Baptist Church Cemetery, Shiloh, Cumberland County.
BIVINS, THOMAS J. Corp, D, 10th NJ Inf, [Died of typhoid at Hampton, VA.] 7-1-1863. 7th Day Baptist Church Cemetery, Shiloh, Cumberland County.
BLACK, ALBERT Pvt, A, 3rd NJ Cav, [Cenotaph. Died at Washington, DC. of wounds received in action.] 8-28-1864. Mount Hope Presbyterian Cemetery, Lambertville, Hunterdon County.
BLACK, BENJAMIN F. Corp, F, 3rd (Howard's) Confederate States Cav (CSA), 11-27-1863. Finn's Point National Cemetery, Pennsville, Salem County.
BLACK, CRAWFORD QM, U.S. Navy, USS Princeton, DoD Unknown. Atlantic City Cemetery, Pleasantville, Atlantic County.
BLACK, DOZIER C. Pvt, E, 3rd (Howard's) Confederate States Cav (CSA), 12-1-1863. Finn's Point National Cemetery, Pennsville, Salem County.
BLACK, EDWARD H. Pvt, K, 10th NY Inf, 11-18-1895. Rose Hill Cemetery, Matawan, Monmouth County.
BLACK, EDWARD H. (SR.) Pvt, D, 38th NJ Inf, 12-18-1904. Lake Park Cemetery, Swedesboro, Gloucester County.
BLACK*, HENRY Pvt, G, 8th NJ Inf, 6-8-1908. Cedar Grove Cemetery, Gloucester City, Camden County.
BLACK, J.R. ___, B, ___ NY Cav, DoD Unknown. Old Bergen Church Cemetery, Jersey City, Hudson County.
BLACK, JAMES Pvt, G, 6th U.S. CT, 6-3-1928. Fairmount Cemetery, Newark, Essex County.
BLACK, JAMES C. Pvt, F, 10th NJ Inf, 7-22-1916. Riverview Cemetery, Trenton, Mercer County.
BLACK, JOHN Pvt, C, 2nd NJ Cav, 4-7-1904. Pompton Reformed Church Cemetery, Pompton Lakes, Passaic County.
BLACK, JOHN DoD Unknown. Riverview Cemetery, Trenton, Mercer County.

New Jersey Civil War Burials

BLACK, LEWIS Pvt, I, 7th NJ Inf, 2-28-1897. Branchville Cemetery, Branchville, Sussex County.

BLACK, SAMUEL Pvt, A, 3rd U.S. CT, 3-27-1917. Oddfellows Cemetery, Pemberton, Burlington County.

BLACK, SAMUEL Pvt, E, 28th NJ Inf, 4-16-1914. Presbyterian Cemetery, Holmanville, Ocean County.

BLACK, SAMUEL PERRYMAN Pvt, K, 13th AL Inf (CSA), 9-10-1863. Finn's Point National Cemetery, Pennsville, Salem County.

BLACK, THOMAS 8-5-1881. English Neighborhood Reformed Church Cemetery, Ridgefield, Bergen County.

BLACK, THOMAS Pvt, H, 10th NJ Inf, 4-28-1930. Cedar Grove Cemetery, Gloucester City, Camden County.

BLACK, WILLIAM Pvt, B, 34th PA Inf, 11-24-1903. Stanhope-Union Cemetery, Netcong, Morris County.

BLACK, WILLIAM Pvt, H, 15th NJ Inf, [Wounded 5-12-1864 at Spotsylvania CH, VA.] 1906. Pompton Reformed Church Cemetery, Pompton Lakes, Passaic County.

BLACK*, WILLIAM H. Pvt, B, 54th IN Inf, 6-17-1924. Bayview-New York Bay Cemetery, Jersey City, Hudson County.

BLACKBURN, CHARLES Pvt, C, 22nd PA Inf, 5-22-1896. Cedar Grove Cemetery, Gloucester City, Camden County.

BLACKBURN, HENRY Pvt, E, 31st NJ Inf, 1-12-1901. Union Cemetery, Clinton, Hunterdon County.

BLACKBURN, J.L. Pvt, A, 2nd (Ashby's) TN Cav (CSA), 3-31-1864. Finn's Point National Cemetery, Pennsville, Salem County.

BLACKBURN, ROBERT Pvt, C, 12th NJ Inf, 1-8-1866. Methodist-Episcopal Cemetery, Glassboro, Gloucester County.

BLACKFAN*, JOHN W. Asst Surg, 1st NJ Cav 6-8-1881. Reformed Church Cemetery, Lebanon, Hunterdon County.

BLACKFORD, GEORGE R. Pvt, I, 38th NJ Inf, 8-5-1866. Riverview Cemetery, Trenton, Mercer County.

BLACKFORD, PHILIP Pvt, D, 15th NJ Inf, 1925. Balesville Cemetery, Balesville, Sussex County.

BLACKHURST, ELIJAH (aka: Blackhurst, William) Pvt, B, 1st NY Eng, DoD Unknown. Grove Church Cemetery, North Bergen, Hudson County.

BLACKHURST, WILLIAM (see: Blackhurst, Elijah) Grove Church Cemetery, North Bergen, Hudson County.

BLACKLEDGE, ISAAC N. Pvt, C, 22nd NJ Inf, DoD Unknown. Hackensack Cemetery, Hackensack, Bergen County.

BLACKMAN, EDWIN C. Pvt, G, 26th NJ Inf, 5-21-1912. Rosedale Cemetery, Orange, Essex County.

BLACKMAN, ELMER E. 1st Sgt, B, 12th NJ Inf, 4-16-1899. Atlantic City Cemetery, Pleasantville, Atlantic County.

BLACKMAN, ENOCH Pvt, Btty F, 1st PA Light Art, 8-22-1890. Oceanville Cemetery, Oceanville, Atlantic County.

BLACKMAN, JAMES G. (see: Blackmore, James G.) Finn's Point National Cemetery, Pennsville, Salem County.

BLACKMAN, THEODORE Pvt, C, 7th NJ Inf, 1-25-1862. Rosedale Cemetery, Orange, Essex County.

BLACKMAN, THOMAS Corp, K, 23rd NJ Inf, 12-25-1912. Greenwood Cemetery, Tuckerton, Ocean County.

BLACKMON, JOHN E. Sgt, E, 12th SC Inf (CSA), [Captured 5-12-1864 at Spotsylvania CH, VA. Died of typhoid.] 8-3-1864. Finn's Point National Cemetery, Pennsville, Salem County.

Our Brothers Gone Before

BLACKMORE, JAMES G. (aka: Blackman, James G.) 1st Lt, B, Waul's Legion TX Inf (CSA), 1-1-1865. Finn's Point National Cemetery, Pennsville, Salem County.

BLACKNEY, J. ALFORD Pvt, I, 26th AL Inf (CSA), [Captured 7-1-1863 at Gettysburg, PA. Died of chronic diarrhea.] 2-19-1864. Finn's Point National Cemetery, Pennsville, Salem County.

BLACKSHAW, JAMES F. Pvt, G, 21st NJ Inf, 1-8-1916. Bayview-New York Bay Cemetery, Jersey City, Hudson County.

BLACKWELL, HENRY Pvt, G, 1st NY Inf, 5-16-1891. Cedar Lawn Cemetery, Paterson, Passaic County.

BLACKWELL, ISAAC V.D. Pvt, F, 9th NJ Inf, [Cenotaph. Killed in action at Roanoke Island, NC.] 2-8-1862. Brainerd Cemetery, Cranbury, Middlesex County.

BLACKWELL, JOHN Pvt, A, 33rd NJ Inf, 3-28-1886. Bayview-New York Bay Cemetery, Jersey City, Hudson County.

BLACKWELL, JOHN Pvt, G, 23rd VA Inf (CSA), 7-6-1864. Finn's Point National Cemetery, Pennsville, Salem County.

BLACKWELL, JOHN C.S. Corp, A, 6th NJ Inf, 8-6-1907. Riverview Cemetery, Trenton, Mercer County.

BLACKWELL, RICHIE Pvt, G, 39th NY Inf, 8-1-1901. Hillside Cemetery, Lyndhurst, Bergen County.

BLACKWOOD, JAMES C. Com Sgt, K, 2nd NJ Cav, 1934. Baptist Church Cemetery, Alloway, Salem County.

BLACKWOOD, THOMAS Sgt, C, 11th NJ Inf, 3-3-1899. Greenwood Cemetery, Hamilton, Mercer County.

BLACKWOOD*, WILLIAM H. Pvt, C, 3rd NJ Inf, 4-21-1890. 1st Baptist Church Cemetery, Moorestown, Burlington County.

BLAESE, JOHN A. (aka: Blassie, John) Pvt, C, 21st PA Inf, 2-17-1907. Berlin Cemetery, Berlin, Camden County.

BLAGG, JOHN WESLEY Pvt, D, 1st MS Cav (CSA), 4-17-1865. Finn's Point National Cemetery, Pennsville, Salem County.

BLAICH, CHARLES F. Coal Heaver, U.S. Navy, USS Richmond, 3-23-1897. Palisade Cemetery, North Bergen, Hudson County.

BLAICHER, CHRISTIAN J. Pvt, Btty A, 1st NJ Light Art, 5-14-1913. Woodland Cemetery, Newark, Essex County.

BLAIN, JACOB 2-15-1890. United Methodist Church Cemetery, Pattenburg, Hunterdon County.

BLAIN, MILTON W. Pvt, G, 38th MS Inf (CSA), 6-18-1863. Finn's Point National Cemetery, Pennsville, Salem County.

BLAINE, WILLIAM (aka: Blair, William) Pvt, C, 27th NJ Inf, 1920. Congregational Church Cemetery, Chester, Morris County.

BLAIR, DAVID Pvt, F, 28th NJ Inf, 10-28-1886. Presbyterian Church Cemetery, Woodbridge, Middlesex County.

BLAIR, GEORGE (see: Bleyer, George H.) Arlington Cemetery, Pennsauken, Camden County.

BLAIR, GEORGE H. Pvt, F, 1st NJ Cav, 7-3-1888. Methodist Church Cemetery, Juliustown, Burlington County.

BLAIR, JAMES Pvt, C, 26th NJ Inf, 1879. Franklin Reformed Church Cemetery, Nutley, Essex County.

BLAIR, JAMES Pvt, A, 19th AR Inf (CSA), [Captured 5-17-1863 at Big Black River Bridge, MS.] 9-24-1863. Finn's Point National Cemetery, Pennsville, Salem County.

BLAIR, JOHN C. Corp, D, 6th NY Inf, 11-20-1888. United Methodist Church Cemetery, Little Silver, Monmouth County.

BLAIR, JOSEPH Pvt, A, 2nd NJ Cav, DoD Unknown. Methodist Church Cemetery, Fairmount, Hunterdon County.

New Jersey Civil War Burials

BLAIR*, ROBERT Pvt, D, 2nd NJ Inf, 11-14-1887. Newton Cemetery, Newton, Sussex County.

BLAIR*, ROBERT H. Pvt, D, 15th NJ Inf, 2-8-1918. Rosedale Cemetery, Orange, Essex County.

BLAIR, WILLIAM Pvt, G, 118th PA Inf, [Wounded 9-20-1862 at Shepherdstown, VA.] 5-10-1912. Evergreen Cemetery, Camden, Camden County.

BLAIR, WILLIAM (see: Blaine, William) Congregational Church Cemetery, Chester, Morris County.

BLAIR, WILLIAM S. Pvt, D, 1st NJ Militia, 1-27-1882. Fairmount Cemetery, Newark, Essex County.

BLAISCH, CHRISTIAN F. Pvt, Btty A, 1st NJ Light Art, DoD Unknown. Jersey City Cemetery, Jersey City, Hudson County.

BLAKE, ALFRED Pvt, K, 5th NJ Inf, [Died at Hightstown, NJ of wounds received at Williamsburg, VA.] 12-11-1862. Cedar Hill Cemetery, Hightstown, Mercer County.

BLAKE, ALFRED Pvt, I, 38th NJ Inf, 1-29-1904. Cedar Hill Cemetery, Hightstown, Mercer County.

BLAKE, ALLAN Pvt, E, 26th NJ Inf, DoD Unknown. Clinton Cemetery, Irvington, Essex County.

BLAKE, CALEB Pvt, H, 3rd NJ Cav, 4-22-1886. Highland Cemetery, Hopewell Boro, Mercer County.

BLAKE, CALEB C. Pvt, C, 3rd NJ Militia, 3-5-1902. Greenwood Cemetery, Hamilton, Mercer County.

BLAKE, CHARLES Pvt, K, 1st NJ Cav, 2-7-1907. Baptist Church Cemetery, Penns Neck, Mercer County.

BLAKE, CHRISTOPHER Sgt, U.S. Marine Corps, 3-26-1896. Clinton Cemetery, Irvington, Essex County.

BLAKE, DUNCAN W. Asst Surg, 4th NJ Inf 1-28-1931. Cedar Grove Cemetery, Gloucester City, Camden County.

BLAKE*, EDWARD Pvt, F, 27th NJ Inf, 2-6-1880. Holy Sepulchre Cemetery, East Orange, Essex County.

BLAKE, FRANK M. Pvt, K, 26th NJ Inf, 2-2-1873. Rosedale Cemetery, Orange, Essex County.

BLAKE, GEORGE Pvt, C, 156th NY Inf, 1-11-1914. Fairmount Cemetery, Newark, Essex County.

BLAKE*, GEORGE Pvt, A, 91st PA Inf, [Wounded 6-18-1864 at Petersburg, VA.] 6-13-1886. Cedar Green Cemetery, Clayton, Gloucester County.

BLAKE, HENRY L. Pvt, B, 11th ME Inf, [Died of wounds received 8-16-1864 at Deep Run, VA.] 9-4-1864. Beverly National Cemetery, Edgewater Park, Burlington County.

BLAKE, HENRY R. Pvt, E, 15th NJ Inf, [Wounded in action.] 3-8-1919. Elmwood Cemetery, New Brunswick, Middlesex County.

BLAKE, JAMES H. Pvt, Btty D, 1st NJ Light Art, 3-31-1901. Union Cemetery, Washington, Morris County.

BLAKE, JOHN H. Steward, U.S. Navy, USS Allegheny, 5-31-1896. Johnson Cemetery, Camden, Camden County.

BLAKE, JOHN J. Pvt, Btty F, 4th U.S. Art, 8-22-1918. Phillipsburg Cemetery, Phillipsburg, Warren County.

BLAKE, JOHN W. Pvt, K, 39th NJ Inf, 8-20-1873. Fairmount Cemetery, Newark, Essex County.

BLAKE, JOSEPH Sgt, G, 12th NJ Inf, 5-21-1890. New Camden Cemetery, Camden, Camden County.

BLAKE, JOSEPH Corp, E, 22nd U.S. CT, 12-13-1891. Chestnut Cemetery, Greenwich, Cumberland County.

Our Brothers Gone Before

BLAKE, PETER Pvt, D, 71st NY Inf, 7-2-1901. Holy Sepulchre Cemetery, East Orange, Essex County.
BLAKE, PRICE P. Pvt, F, 1st NJ Inf, [Cenotaph. Killed in action at Spotsylvania CH, VA.] 5-9-1864. Brainerd Cemetery, Cranbury, Middlesex County.
BLAKE*, RICHARD M. Pvt, K, 7th U.S. Hancock Corps, 11-7-1897. Holy Sepulchre Cemetery, East Orange, Essex County.
BLAKE, SPENCER Pvt, F, 24th U.S. CT, 2-24-1892. Spencer African Methodist Church Cemetery, Woodstown, Salem County.
BLAKE, STEPHEN J. Sgt, E, 26th NJ Inf, DoD Unknown. Clinton Cemetery, Irvington, Essex County.
BLAKE*, WALTER H. Pvt, Btty G, 1st NH Heavy Art, 11-10-1935. Siloam Cemetery, Vineland, Cumberland County.
BLAKE, WILLIAM DoD Unknown. Greenwood Cemetery, Hamilton, Mercer County.
BLAKE, WILLIAM DoD Unknown. Mount Pleasant Cemetery, Newark, Essex County.
BLAKE*, WILLIAM B. Corp, B, 12th NJ Inf, [Wounded in action.] 7-27-1893. Methodist Cemetery, Haddonfield, Camden County.
BLAKE, WILLIAM H. Landsman, U.S. Navy, USS North Carolina, 8-20-1929. Bloomfield Cemetery, Bloomfield, Essex County.
BLAKE, WILLIAM W. Pvt, K, 38th NJ Inf, 11-29-1891. Riverview Cemetery, Trenton, Mercer County.
BLAKELY, GEORGE DoD Unknown. Methodist Cemetery, Newfoundland, Morris County.
BLAKELY, JOHN W. Pvt, A, 22nd NY Inf, 7-23-1926. Evergreen Cemetery, Hillside, Union County.
BLAKENEY, MOSES COE Sgt, B, 9th NJ Inf, 4-6-1907. Elmwood Cemetery, New Brunswick, Middlesex County.
BLAKESLEE*, JOEL (aka: Blakesley, Joel) Pvt, E, 2nd NJ Cav, 11-4-1900. Riverview Cemetery, Trenton, Mercer County.
BLAKESLEY, JOEL (see: Blakeslee, Joel) Riverview Cemetery, Trenton, Mercer County.
BLAKINS, GEORGE Pvt, H, 127th U.S. CT, 12-4-1887. Methodist Church Cemetery, Asbury, Warren County.
BLAKINS, NELSON Pvt, H, 127th U.S. CT, DoD Unknown. Methodist Church Cemetery, Asbury, Warren County.
BLALOCK, W.F. (aka: Blaylock, W.F.) Pvt, F, 43rd GA Inf (CSA), [Captured 5-16-1863 at Baker's Creek, MS.] 6-27-1863. Finn's Point National Cemetery, Pennsville, Salem County.
BLANCHARD, BRADNER Pvt, B, 3rd NJ Cav, 3-13-1900. Newton Cemetery, Newton, Sussex County.
BLANCHARD, CHARLES H. Blacksmith, K, 2nd NJ Cav, 11-16-1878. Evergreen Cemetery, Morristown, Morris County.
BLANCHARD, DAVID Pvt, I, 4th ME Inf, 9-15-1919. New Camden Cemetery, Camden, Camden County.
BLANCHARD, FREDERICK Pvt, F, 13th NJ Inf, DoD Unknown. Evergreen Cemetery, Morristown, Morris County.
BLANCHARD, GEORGE H. Pvt, I, 3rd NJ Inf, 1940. Presbyterian Cemetery, New Vernon, Morris County.
BLANCHARD, HIRAM Pvt, F, 37th NJ Inf, 11-25-1924. Cedar Lawn Cemetery, Paterson, Passaic County.
BLANCHARD, JACOB H. Corp, L, 27th NJ Inf, 4-12-1893. Stanhope-Union Cemetery, Netcong, Morris County.
BLANCHARD, JOSEPH A. 1st Lt, E, 1st NY Mounted Rifles, 1909. Evergreen Cemetery, Morristown, Morris County.
BLANCHARD, MANNING Pvt, L, 27th NJ Inf, 5-13-1910. Savage Cemetery, Denville, Morris County.

New Jersey Civil War Burials

BLANCHARD, SAMUEL S. Pvt, E, 58th PA Inf, [Wounded in action 9-22-1864.] 9-20-1930. Fairview Cemetery, Wantage, Sussex County.
BLANCHARD, THEODORE Pvt, Btty B, 5th U.S. Art, 2-14-1900. Presbyterian Church Cemetery, Rockaway, Morris County.
BLANCHARD, THEODORE C.E. Pvt, G, 37th NJ Inf, 8-7-1916. Fairmount Cemetery, Newark, Essex County.
BLANCHARD, THERON Corp, K, 44th MA Inf, 3-28-1895. Evergreen Cemetery, Camden, Camden County.
BLANCHET, AUGUSTE DUREST Maj, 27th NJ Inf 1896. St. Vincent Martyr Cemetery, Madison, Morris County.
BLANCK, EDWARD Musc, L, 51st PA Militia, 1-19-1905. Evergreen Cemetery, Camden, Camden County.
BLANCK, WILLIAM (SR.) 1st Lt, H, 23rd PA Inf, 1-9-1891. Evergreen Cemetery, Camden, Camden County.
BLANEY, DANIEL Pvt, K, 30th NJ Inf, 12-27-1887. Griggstown Cemetery, Griggstown, Somerset County.
BLANEY, HUGH Seaman, U.S. Navy, DoD Unknown. Holy Name Cemetery, Jersey City, Hudson County.
BLANK, GEORGE (see: Blenck, George W.) Evergreen Cemetery, Camden, Camden County.
BLANKENSHIP, JOHN T. Pvt, A, 2nd (Ashby's) TN Cav (CSA), 5-8-1864. Finn's Point National Cemetery, Pennsville, Salem County.
BLANKENSHIP, SMITH Pvt, E, 22nd (Barteau's) TN Cav (CSA), 2-26-1864. Finn's Point National Cemetery, Pennsville, Salem County.
BLANKINSHIP, J.H. Pvt, D, 13th GA Cav (CSA), 1-31-1865. Finn's Point National Cemetery, Pennsville, Salem County.
BLANKMYER, VICTOR Pvt, I, 8th NJ Inf, 8-15-1873. Fairmount Cemetery, Newark, Essex County.
BLANVELT, WILLIAM (see: Blauvelt, William S.) Greengrove Cemetery, Keyport, Monmouth County.
BLASBERG, PAUL E. 1905. Evergreen Cemetery, Hillside, Union County.
BLASSIE, JOHN (see: Blaese, John A.) Berlin Cemetery, Berlin, Camden County.
BLATCHLEY, JOHN 10-10-1885. Atlantic Reformed Cemetery, Colts Neck, Monmouth County.
BLATCHLEY, MILLER Pvt, D, 140th PA Inf, [Died at Beverly, NJ.] 10-4-1864. Beverly National Cemetery, Edgewater Park, Burlington County.
BLATT, CHARLES Pvt, Btty B, 5th PA Heavy Art, 8-8-1900. Evergreen Cemetery, Hillside, Union County.
BLATTNER, EUGENE J. 2-12-1886. Presbyterian Church Cemetery, Cold Spring, Cape May County.
BLAUROCK, HENRY Pvt, H, 26th NJ Inf, 6-21-1918. Rosedale Cemetery, Orange, Essex County.
BLAUSCHER, HENRY MAGNUS Capt, K, 156th NY Inf, 8-31-1896. Edgewater Cemetery, Edgewater, Bergen County.
BLAUTH, ADAM 1866. Mercer Cemetery, Trenton, Mercer County.
BLAUVELT, ABRAHAM D. Pvt, D, 22nd NJ Inf, 3-3-1883. Old Hook Cemetery, Westwood, Bergen County.
BLAUVELT, ABRAHAM J. (aka: Blauvett, Abraham) Pvt, C, 102nd NY Inf, 3-10-1880. Old Hook Cemetery, Westwood, Bergen County.
BLAUVELT, CORNELIUS Pvt, G, 6th NY Inf, 9-21-1872. Blauvelt Cemetery, Harrington Park, Bergen County.
BLAUVELT, DANIEL D. 4-20-1873. Blauvelt Cemetery, Harrington Park, Bergen County.

Our Brothers Gone Before

BLAUVELT, DANIEL (JR.) Capt, I, 8th NJ Inf, [Killed in action at Atley's Station, VA.] 5-31-1864. 1st Reformed Church Cemetery, Pompton Plains, Morris County.

BLAUVELT, DAVID C. Sgt, C, 22nd NJ Inf, 6-8-1896. Old Hook Cemetery, Westwood, Bergen County.

BLAUVELT, DAVID D. DoD Unknown. Mount Pleasant Cemetery, Newark, Essex County.

BLAUVELT, DAVID DANIEL Capt, H, 22nd NJ Inf, 12-30-1879. Old Hook Cemetery, Westwood, Bergen County.

BLAUVELT, DAVID DEMAREST 1st Sgt, C, 22nd NJ Inf, 2-7-1905. Woodside Cemetery, Dumont, Bergen County.

BLAUVELT, EDWIN JAMES Pvt, D, 128th NY Inf, [Wounded 9-22-1864 at Fishers Hill, VA.] 4-28-1905. Hackensack Cemetery, Hackensack, Bergen County.

BLAUVELT, HENRY J. Pvt, A, 7th NJ Inf, 10-23-1903. Fairmount Cemetery, Newark, Essex County.

BLAUVELT, J.W. Pvt, A, 22nd NJ Inf, DoD Unknown. Cedar Lawn Cemetery, Paterson, Passaic County.

BLAUVELT, JACOB C. 6-30-1888. Old Hook Cemetery, Westwood, Bergen County.

BLAUVELT, JOHN 6-30-1912. Brookside Cemetery, Englewood, Bergen County.

BLAUVELT, JOHN C. 1st Sgt, C, 102nd NY Inf, 7-24-1893. Westwood Cemetery, Westwood, Bergen County.

BLAUVELT, JOHN J. Pvt, D, 22nd NJ Inf, 4-22-1911. Old Hook Cemetery, Westwood, Bergen County.

BLAUVELT, JOHN T. Pvt, B, 37th NJ Inf, 9-11-1906. Arlington Cemetery, Kearny, Hudson County.

BLAUVELT, JOHN T. Pvt, A, 22nd NJ Inf, 2-28-1895. Cedar Lawn Cemetery, Paterson, Passaic County.

BLAUVELT, LUCAS C. Pvt, D, 22nd NJ Inf, [Wounded in action.] 1928. Westwood Cemetery, Westwood, Bergen County.

BLAUVELT, RALPH Pvt, F, 82nd NY Inf, 10-11-1917. Arlington Cemetery, Kearny, Hudson County.

BLAUVELT, WILLIAM J. Pvt, D, 22nd NJ Inf, 4-9-1908. Old Hook Cemetery, Westwood, Bergen County.

BLAUVELT, WILLIAM S. (aka: Blanvelt, William) Corp, F, 1st MD Cav (PHB), 3-21-1887. Greengrove Cemetery, Keyport, Monmouth County.

BLAUVETT, ABRAHAM (see: Blauvelt, Abraham J.) Old Hook Cemetery, Westwood, Bergen County.

BLAYLOCK, W.F. (see: Blalock, W.F.) Finn's Point National Cemetery, Pennsville, Salem County.

BLAZIER, JOHN H. Pvt, I, 30th NJ Inf, 10- -1898. Evergreen/Bishop Jaynes Cemetery, Basking Ridge, Somerset County.

BLAZURE, ETHELBERT C. Pvt, I, 30th NJ Inf, 12-27-1914. Presbyterian Church Cemetery, Mendham, Morris County.

BLAZURE, JAMES 5-20-1899. Peapack Reformed Church Cemetery, Gladstone, Somerset County.

BLECKLY, JOHN M. Pvt, D, 8th NJ Inf, 8-28-1874. Fairmount Cemetery, Newark, Essex County.

BLEDSOE, JOHN Pvt, D, 2nd TX Inf (CSA), 7-8-1864. Finn's Point National Cemetery, Pennsville, Salem County.

BLEE, JACOB Pvt, H, 57th NY Inf, 11-9-1918. Riverview Cemetery, Trenton, Mercer County.

BLEECKER, JOHN VANBENTHUYSEN Actg Midshipman, U.S. Navy, 1922. Evergreen Cemetery, Morristown, Morris County.

BLEEKMAN*, GEORGE R. Pvt, D, 97th NY Inf, 2-1-1904. Greengrove Cemetery, Keyport, Monmouth County.

New Jersey Civil War Burials

BLEEM*, SAMUEL Landsman, U.S. Navy, USS Kansas, 7-11-1907. Johnson Cemetery, Camden, Camden County.
BLEESCH, HENRY DoD Unknown. New Camden Cemetery, Camden, Camden County.
BLEILER, JOSEPH Pvt, Btty A, 1st NJ Light Art, 12-16-1920. Flower Hill Cemetery, North Bergen, Hudson County.
BLEIM, JOHN C. 11-14-1894. Flower Hill Cemetery, North Bergen, Hudson County.
BLENCK, GEORGE W. (aka: Blank, George) Musc, B, 23rd PA Inf, 4-10-1922. Evergreen Cemetery, Camden, Camden County.
BLENKENHIEN*, CHRISTIAN Pvt, C, 34th NJ Inf, 11-25-1902. St. Paul's Lutheran Church Cemetery, Hainesport, Burlington County.
BLENKOW, DAVID Capt, F, 25th NJ Inf, 4-5-1877. Methodist-Episcopal Church Cemetery, South Dennis, Cape May County.
BLESSING, MAX Pvt, H, 174th PA Inf, 1918. Hazen Cemetery, Hazen, Warren County.
BLEVON, JOHN DoD Unknown. Old Camden Cemetery, Camden, Camden County.
BLEW, WILLIAM HOWARD Pvt, H, 24th NJ Inf, 12-28-1925. Presbyterian Church Cemetery, Upper Deerfield, Cumberland County.
BLEWETT, WILLIAM E. 1st Lt, F, 2nd NJ Inf, [Wounded in action.] 1-15-1913. Mount Pleasant Cemetery, Newark, Essex County.
BLEYER, GEORGE H. (aka: Blair, George) Pvt, Btty A, 3rd PA Heavy Art, 3-21-1918. Arlington Cemetery, Pennsauken, Camden County.
BLEYTHING, EUGENE A. Capt, H, 2nd DC Inf, 4-24-1909. Rosedale Cemetery, Orange, Essex County.
BLIENDT, FREDERICK (aka: Blint, Frederick) Pvt, B, 24th NJ Inf, 8-15-1911. United Methodist Church Cemetery, Port Elizabeth, Cumberland County.
BLINT, FREDERICK (see: Bliendt, Frederick) United Methodist Church Cemetery, Port Elizabeth, Cumberland County.
BLISS, ELI P. Corp, K, 24th NJ Inf, 8-8-1906. United Methodist Church Cemetery, Hainesneck, Salem County.
BLISS, FRANK H. (SR.) QM Sgt, 6th NY Ind Btty 5-5-1919. Rosedale Cemetery, Linden, Union County.
BLIVEN, ARTHUR J. Sgt, D, 2nd MA Inf, 7-4-1900. Fairview Cemetery, Westfield, Union County.
BLIVEN, CHARLES H. Capt, H, 13th NJ Inf, 9-20-1885. Rahway Cemetery, Rahway, Union County.
BLIZZARD*, BENJAMIN F. Pvt, B, 111th PA Inf, 1-12-1923. Evergreen Cemetery, Camden, Camden County.
BLIZZARD, CHARLES Pvt, B, 31st PA Inf, DoD Unknown. Hope Christian Church Cemetery, Marlton, Burlington County.
BLIZZARD, FIRMAN Pvt, 4th NY Ind Btty 1888. Methodist-Episcopal Church Cemetery, South Dennis, Cape May County.
BLIZZARD, JOHN Pvt, D, 25th NJ Inf, DoD Unknown. Methodist Church Cemetery, Haleyville, Cumberland County.
BLIZZARD, JOHN W. Pvt, G, 24th NJ Inf, 2-15-1883. Methodist Church Cemetery, Haleyville, Cumberland County.
BLIZZARD, WILLIAM Corp, A, 158th PA Inf, 10-9-1920. Soldier's Home Cemetery, Vineland, Cumberland County.
BLOCK, JOHN Pvt, Btty A, 1st NJ Light Art, 1906. Highland Cemetery, Hopewell Boro, Mercer County.
BLOCKER, WILLIAM Pvt, F, 20th OH Inf, 12-24-1923. Laurel Grove Cemetery, Totowa, Passaic County.
BLOMLEY, ARTHER (aka: Bloomley, Arthur) Corp, A, 91st PA Inf, [Wounded 6-18-1864 at Petersburg, VA.] 11-13-1905. Methodist Church Cemetery, Heislerville, Cumberland County.

Our Brothers Gone Before

BLON, HENRY Pvt, Btty G, 5th U.S. Art, 3-18-1912. Woodland Cemetery, Newark, Essex County.
BLOODGOOD, ALBERT Sgt, H, 81st NY Inf, 3-4-1886. Fairmount Cemetery, Newark, Essex County.
BLOODGOOD, ANDREW 12-24-1885. Rose Hill Cemetery, Matawan, Monmouth County.
BLOODGOOD, AUGUSTUS B. Pvt, A, 11th NJ Inf, 8-17-1922. Bayview-New York Bay Cemetery, Jersey City, Hudson County.
BLOODGOOD*, BENJAMIN CROW Pvt, H, 5th NJ Inf, [Wounded 8-29-1862 at 2nd Bull Run, VA.] 5-19-1926. Presbyterian Church Cemetery, Woodbridge, Middlesex County.
BLOODGOOD, MICHAEL Pvt, K, 28th NJ Inf, DoD Unknown. Christ Church Cemetery, Morgan, Middlesex County.
BLOODGOOD, PETER Pvt, K, 28th NJ Inf, 2-2-1893. Christ Church Cemetery, Morgan, Middlesex County.
BLOODGOOD*, PHINEOS F. Wagoner, F, 35th NJ Inf, [Wounded accidently.] 11-22-1898. Riverview Cemetery, Trenton, Mercer County.
BLOODGOOD, ROBERT P. Fireman, U.S. Navy, USS Daylight, 4-1-1900. Van Liew Cemetery, North Brunswick, Middlesex County.
BLOODGOOD*, THOMAS J. Pvt, K, 97th NY Inf, 2-16-1897. Ramapo Reformed Church Cemetery, Mahwah, Bergen County.
BLOODGOOD, WILLIAM H.H. Corp, F, 28th NJ Inf, 3-20-1915. Evergreen Cemetery, Hillside, Union County.
BLOODGOOD, WILLIAM R. Pvt, A, 28th NJ Inf, 4-2-1896. Old Mount Pleasant Cemetery, Matawan, Monmouth County.
BLOOM*, DAVID A. Corp, I, 2nd NJ Cav, 6-3-1883. Methodist-Episcopal Cemetery, Whitehouse, Hunterdon County.
BLOOM, ISAAC Pvt, F, 31st NJ Inf, 5-3-1864. Unitarian Church Cemetery, Kingwood, Hunterdon County.
BLOOM, JOHN Pvt, E, 23rd NJ Inf, 3-12-1904. Baptist Cemetery, Pemberton, Burlington County.
BLOOM, PETER A. Pvt, B, 6th NJ Inf, 1-16-1919. New Camden Cemetery, Camden, Camden County.
BLOOM*, WILLIAM C. Corp, Btty D, 2nd MA Heavy Art, 7-14-1927. Presbyterian Church Cemetery, Hampton, Hunterdon County.
BLOOMER, ANDREW J. Pvt, G, 5th NY Inf, 9-2-1912. 1st Presbyterian Union Cemetery, Ramsey, Bergen County.
BLOOMER, CHARLES A. Pvt, C, 24th PA Inf, 12-14-1903. Mount Calvary Cemetery, Mount Calvary, Atlantic County.
BLOOMER, DENNIS P. (aka: Horton, Harry) Pvt, B, 106th NY Inf, [Wounded in action.] 6-3-1925. New Presbyterian Cemetery, Hanover, Morris County.
BLOOMER, JOHN Pvt, Btty D, 1st NJ Light Art, 6- -1865. Mount Hope Presbyterian Cemetery, Lambertville, Hunterdon County.
BLOOMFIELD, EDWIN AUGUSTUS Pvt, F, 28th NJ Inf, 3-6-1914. Evergreen Cemetery, Hillside, Union County.
BLOOMFIELD*, LOTT 1st Lt, B, 11th NJ Inf, [Killed in action at Chancellorsville, VA.] 5-3-1863. Presbyterian Church Cemetery, Metuchen, Middlesex County.
BLOOMFIELD, TIMOTHY Pvt, E, 8th NJ Inf, [Killed in action at Williamsburg, VA.] 5-5-1862. Presbyterian Church Cemetery, Metuchen, Middlesex County.
BLOOMINGDALE, ROBERT G. Pvt, Btty K, 1st NY Light Art, 9-15-1889. Rosehill Cemetery, Newfield, Gloucester County.
BLOOMLEY, ARTHUR (see: Blomley, Arther) Methodist Church Cemetery, Heislerville, Cumberland County.

New Jersey Civil War Burials

BLOOMSBURG*, JOHN 1st Asst Eng, U.S. Navy, USS Victoria, 4-13-1883. Bordentown/Old St. Mary's Catholic Cemetery, Bordentown, Burlington County.

BLOOMSBURG, JOSEPH Q. Actg 2nd Asst Eng, U.S. Navy, USS Neptune, 1-16-1905. Bordentown/Old St. Mary's Catholic Cemetery, Bordentown, Burlington County.

BLORE, JOHN C. Pvt, Btty D, 1st NJ Light Art, 12-4-1918. Rahway Cemetery, Rahway, Union County.

BLOSS, HENRY (see: Eckert, William) Methodist Cemetery, Southard, Monmouth County.

BLOTH, WILLIAM Sgt, E, 14th NJ Inf, 11-20-1873. Fairmount Cemetery, Newark, Essex County.

BLOWER, WILLIAM H. Pvt, G, 14th NJ Inf, [Wounded in action.] 6-26-1916. Methodist Cemetery, Hamilton, Monmouth County.

BLOWERS, CHARLES E. Pvt, G, 27th NJ Inf, 9-26-1920. Reformed Church Cemetery, Montville, Morris County.

BLOWERS, WILLIAM H. Pvt, F, 35th NJ Inf, 3-31-1899. Evergreen Cemetery, New Brunswick, Middlesex County.

BLUE, ABRAM O. Pvt, E, 4th NJ Inf, DoD Unknown. Presbyterian Church Cemetery, Bridgeton, Cumberland County.

BLUE, ALBERT L. 1st Lt, I, 1st NJ Inf, 2-12-1883. Elmwood Cemetery, New Brunswick, Middlesex County.

BLUE, HENRY MARTIN Lt Commander, U.S. Navy, USS Tacony, [Died at Charleston, SC.] 8-22-1866. Mount Hope Presbyterian Cemetery, Lambertville, Hunterdon County.

BLUE, ROBERT D. Pvt, A, 54th OH Inf, 2-4-1901. Presbyterian Church Cemetery, Kingston, Somerset County.

BLUE, SAMUEL Pvt, C, 4th NJ Inf, [Missing in action at Spotsylvania CH, VA. Recorded as died that date.] 5-12-1864. Princeton Cemetery, Princeton, Mercer County.

BLUEM, FRIEDRICH (aka: Blueman, Frederick) Pvt, G, 68th NY Inf, 5-2-1905. Weehawken Cemetery, North Bergen, Hudson County.

BLUEMAN, FREDERICK (see: Bluem, Friedrich) Weehawken Cemetery, North Bergen, Hudson County.

BLUHM, EDWARD Pvt, I, 54th NY Inf, 12-14-1896. Weehawken Cemetery, North Bergen, Hudson County.

BLUM, G.F. (see: Blumm, George F.) Woodlawn Cemetery, Lakewood, Ocean County.

BLUM, GEORGE FLORIAN DoD Unknown. Trinity United Methodist Church Cemetery, Bayville, Ocean County.

BLUM, HENRY Pvt, A, 20th NY Inf, 3-1-1901. Hoboken Cemetery, North Bergen, Hudson County.

BLUMENBERG, C.F. 6-6-1894. Grove Church Cemetery, North Bergen, Hudson County.

BLUMM, GEORGE F. (aka: Blum, G.F.) Pvt, C, 14th PA Militia, 12-7-1919. Woodlawn Cemetery, Lakewood, Ocean County.

BLUNDELL, WILLIAM Asst Surg, 5th NJ Inf 6-30-1916. Cedar Lawn Cemetery, Paterson, Passaic County.

BLUNER, CHARLES (see: Benney, Charles E.) Oddfellows Cemetery, Burlington, Burlington County.

BOALER, GEORGE (see: Baulig, George) Egg Harbor Cemetery, Egg Harbor, Atlantic County.

BOALS, C.M. (aka: Bolls, C.N.) Pvt, Morphis', MS Ind Scouts (CSA), 8-10-1864. Finn's Point National Cemetery, Pennsville, Salem County.

BOARDMAN, VERUS N. Pvt, I, 187th PA Inf, [Died at Beverly, NJ.] 8-14-1864. Beverly National Cemetery, Edgewater Park, Burlington County.

BOARDMAN, WILLIAM J. Pvt, H, 25th NJ Inf, 12-23-1920. Methodist-Episcopal Cemetery, Midland Park, Bergen County.

Our Brothers Gone Before

BOATWRIGHT, BENJAMIN Pvt, A, 8th FL Inf (CSA), [Captured 7-2-1863 at Gettysburg, PA. Died of debility.] 8-24-1863. Finn's Point National Cemetery, Pennsville, Salem County.

BOCK, MICHAEL Pvt, E, 13th NJ Inf, 5-16-1893. St. Mary's Cemetery, East Orange, Essex County.

BOCKINS, WILLIAM H. (aka: Buckious, William) Pvt, A, 72nd PA Inf, 5-15-1912. Arlington Cemetery, Kearny, Hudson County.

BODDIE, ELIJAH 1st Lt, C, 7th TN Inf (CSA), 3-17-1865. Finn's Point National Cemetery, Pennsville, Salem County.

BODE, CHARLES 1st Cl Musc, 1st NJ Brigade Band 12-1-1903. Woodland Cemetery, Newark, Essex County.

BODE, JOHN Landsman, U.S. Navy, USS Hornet, 1-30-1897. Fairmount Cemetery, Newark, Essex County.

BODENHAMER, J.P. Pvt, K, 48th NC Inf (CSA), [Captured 9-17-1862 at Sharpsburg, MD.] 10-14-1862. Finn's Point National Cemetery, Pennsville, Salem County.

BODENHEIMER, JOHN Pvt, B, 30th NJ Inf, DoD Unknown. Presbyterian Cemetery, North Plainfield, Somerset County.

BODENSTEIN, FREDERICK (aka: Bordenstein, Frederick) Pvt, B, 27th PA Inf, 3-27-1893. Greenwood Cemetery, Hamilton, Mercer County.

BODENSTEIN, WILLIAM Pvt, C, 124th NY Inf, [Wounded 5-3-1863 at Chancellorsville, VA.] 12-26-1917. Laurel Grove Cemetery, Totowa, Passaic County.

BODENWEISER, JACOB Pvt, G, 1st NJ Cav, 11-23-1901. Temple Sharey Tefilo Cemetery, Orange, Essex County.

BODINE, ALONZO M. Pvt, C, 23rd NJ Inf, 4-30-1903. Baptist/St. Andrew's Cemetery, Mount Holly, Burlington County.

BODINE, BUDD S. 1st Lt, B, 14th NJ Inf, 8-28-1897. Mercer Cemetery, Trenton, Mercer County.

BODINE, DAVID 12-3-1921. Christian Church Cemetery, Locktown, Hunterdon County.

BODINE, HART W. 2nd Lt, A, 6th NJ Inf, 1911. Cedar Hill Cemetery, Hightstown, Mercer County.

BODINE, HENRY F. Pvt, B, 103rd PA Inf, 1909. Christian Church Cemetery, Locktown, Hunterdon County.

BODINE, JESSE L. Pvt, B, 192nd PA Inf, 3-18-1913. Methodist-Episcopal Church Cemetery, Penns Grove, Salem County.

BODINE, JOHN F. 1895. Sandy Ridge Cemetery, Sandy Ridge, Hunterdon County.

BODINE, JOHN F. Pvt, H, 6th NJ Inf, 6-4-1908. Riverview Cemetery, Trenton, Mercer County.

BODINE, JOHN WESLEY 1st Sgt, H, 3rd NJ Inf, [Wounded 9-14-1862 at Crampton's Pass, MD.] 3-6-1917. Baptist/St. Andrew's Cemetery, Mount Holly, Burlington County.

BODINE, LAMBERT 12-20-1863. Sandy Ridge Cemetery, Sandy Ridge, Hunterdon County.

BODINE, ROBERT M. Pvt, B, 31st NJ Inf, 10-8-1904. Presbyterian Church Cemetery, Hampton, Hunterdon County.

BODINE, THOMAS Pvt, H, 24th NJ Inf, 11-8-1895. 1st United Methodist Church Cemetery, Bridgeton, Cumberland County.

BODINE, WILLIAM Pvt, H, 24th NJ Inf, 2-22-1914. Soldier's Home Cemetery, Vineland, Cumberland County.

BODINE*, WILLIAM F. Pvt, I, 4th NJ Inf, [Wounded 6-27-1862 at Gaines' Farm, VA.] 6-4-1874. Oddfellows Cemetery, Burlington, Burlington County.

BODINE, WILLIAM J. Pvt, H, 15th NJ Inf, [Killed in action at Spotsylvania CH, VA.] 5-12-1864. Mansfield/Washington Cemetery, Washington, Warren County.

BODWELL, GRANTVILLE (see: Bodwell, Granville White) Rosedale Cemetery, Orange, Essex County.

New Jersey Civil War Burials

BODWELL, GRANVILLE WHITE (aka: Bodwell, Grantville) 1st Lt, I, 13th NJ Inf, 8-16-1887. Rosedale Cemetery, Orange, Essex County.
BODWELL*, JAMES L. Capt, E, 14th NJ Inf, [Wounded in action.] 2-6-1903. Rahway Cemetery, Rahway, Union County.
BOE, WILLIAM (aka: Bowes, William) Sgt, 13th NY Ind Btty DoD Unknown. Baptist Cemetery, South Plainfield, Middlesex County.
BOECKEL, FREDERICK Sgt, F, 55th NY Inf, 6-16-1866. Bayview-New York Bay Cemetery, Jersey City, Hudson County.
BOECKEL, WILLIAM W. Pvt, K, 1st NY Marine Art, 1925. Fairview Cemetery, Fairview, Monmouth County.
BOEGER, CHARLES A. 1-7-1895. Laurel Grove Cemetery, Totowa, Passaic County.
BOEHM*, ALOIS Pvt, Unassigned, 33rd NJ Inf, 2-1-1874. New Dutch Reformed/Neshanic Cemetery, Neshanic, Somerset County.
BOEHM, CHRISTIAN (aka: Boehme, Christian) Pvt, E, 2nd NJ Inf, [Wounded 5-8-1864 at Spotsylvania CH, VA.] 1-31-1893. Woodland Cemetery, Newark, Essex County.
BOEHM, EDWARD D. Pvt, D, 39th NJ Inf, 11-28-1933. New Dutch Reformed/Neshanic Cemetery, Neshanic, Somerset County.
BOEHM*, HENRY (aka: Bohem, Henry) Pvt, F, 3rd NJ Cav, 12-14-1921. Woodland Cemetery, Newark, Essex County.
BOEHM*, LOUIS Corp, 3rd NY Ind Btty 3-22-1921. Fairmount Cemetery, Newark, Essex County.
BOEHM, WILLIAM Pvt, H, 29th PA Inf, [Wounded in action 5-28-1864.] 6-22-1926. Atlantic City Cemetery, Pleasantville, Atlantic County.
BOEHME, CHRISTIAN (see: Boehm, Christian) Woodland Cemetery, Newark, Essex County.
BOEMAN, LAMBERT Actg Col, 10th NJ Inf [Killed in action at Cedar Creek, VA.] 10-19-1864. Presbyterian Church Cemetery, Flemington, Hunterdon County.
BOESE, HENRY Pvt, C, 11th NY Inf, 1874. Fairmount Cemetery, Newark, Essex County.
BOESEL, GUSTAVUS Sgt, F, 39th NJ Inf, 3-5-1872. Woodland Cemetery, Newark, Essex County.
BOESH, EDWARD Pvt, B, 35th NJ Inf, 7-27-1876. Holy Sepulchre Cemetery, East Orange, Essex County.
BOETTINGER, JOSEPH Pvt, H, 41st NY Inf, 1-2-1909. Woodland Cemetery, Newark, Essex County.
BOGAR, WILLIAM Pvt, D, 35th NJ Inf, DoD Unknown. Friendship United Methodist Church Cemetery, Landisville, Atlantic County.
BOGARDUS, ANTHONY Pvt, D, 120th NY Inf, 5-17-1906. Greengrove Cemetery, Keyport, Monmouth County.
BOGARDUS, FREDERICK Pvt, D, 168th NY Inf, 6-25-1905. Fairmount Cemetery, Newark, Essex County.
BOGARDUS, STEPHEN W. 1st Lt, E, 15th NJ Inf, 8-5-1890. Rose Hill Cemetery, Matawan, Monmouth County.
BOGART, ABRAHAM Pvt, K, 28th NJ Inf, 12-22-1897. Rose Hill Cemetery, Matawan, Monmouth County.
BOGART, ALBERT D. Corp, C, 30th NJ Inf, 1928. Clinton Cemetery, Irvington, Essex County.
BOGART, CHARLES C. DoD Unknown. Old South Church Cemetery, Bergenfield, Bergen County.
BOGART*, CHARLES C. Pvt, G, 1st NJ Inf, [Wounded in action.] 2-23-1911. Presbyterian Church Cemetery, Pennington, Mercer County.
BOGART, CORNELIUS D. Pvt, A, 22nd NJ Inf, [Wounded in action.] 1899. Valleau Cemetery, Ridgewood, Bergen County.
BOGART, DAVID A.L. Pvt, C, 13th NJ Inf, 3-7-1896. Valleau Cemetery, Ridgewood, Bergen County.

Our Brothers Gone Before

BOGART, GILLIAM DoD Unknown. Old South Church Cemetery, Bergenfield, Bergen County.
BOGART, ISAAC C. Pvt, C, 13th NJ Inf, 3-7-1885. Laurel Grove Cemetery, Totowa, Passaic County.
BOGART, ISAAC E. Pvt, F, 10th NJ Inf, 11-15-1892. Maple Grove Cemetery, Hackensack, Bergen County.
BOGART, JACOB D. Corp, A, 22nd NJ Inf, [Died of typhoid at Aquia Creek, VA.] 5-7-1863. Old South Church Cemetery, Bergenfield, Bergen County.
BOGART*, JAMES Pvt, B, 1st NJ Cav, [Wounded in action.] 9-19-1905. Union Cemetery, Gloucester City, Camden County.
BOGART, JAMES S. Corp, C, 22nd NJ Inf, 1905. Old South Church Cemetery, Bergenfield, Bergen County.
BOGART, JEROME B. Pvt, E, 3rd NJ Militia, 10-7-1883. Phillipsburg Cemetery, Phillipsburg, Warren County.
BOGART, JOHN AUGUSTUS 9-30-1900. Valleau Cemetery, Ridgewood, Bergen County.
BOGART, JOSEPH Pvt, I, 8th NJ Inf, 10-24-1909. Riverside Cemetery, Toms River, Ocean County.
BOGART, JOSEPH N. Pvt, I, 31st NJ Inf, 10-14-1918. Hillside Cemetery, Scotch Plains, Union County.
BOGART, MATTHEW D. DoD Unknown. Old South Church Cemetery, Bergenfield, Bergen County.
BOGART, PETER S. 7-29-1906. Mercer Cemetery, Trenton, Mercer County.
BOGART, STEPHEN F. Pvt, E, 37th NJ Inf, 10-1-1901. Rosedale Cemetery, Orange, Essex County.
BOGART*, WILLIAM M. Pvt, G, 213th PA Inf, DoD Unknown. Valleau Cemetery, Ridgewood, Bergen County.
BOGER, ELISHA (see: Boyer, Elisha) Baptist Cemetery, Pemberton, Burlington County.
BOGERT, AARON D. Pvt, Btty D, 1st NJ Light Art, 8-23-1900. Methodist-Episcopal Cemetery, Midland Park, Bergen County.
BOGERT, AARON J. Pvt, K, 22nd NJ Inf, 5-18-1918. Cedar Lawn Cemetery, Paterson, Passaic County.
BOGERT, ABRAHAM B. Pvt, D, 22nd NJ Inf, 4-12-1925. Westwood Cemetery, Westwood, Bergen County.
BOGERT, ABRAM HENRY 3-18-1879. Valleau Cemetery, Ridgewood, Bergen County.
BOGERT, ALBERT C. Pvt, A, 22nd NJ Inf, 2-19-1994. Hackensack Cemetery, Hackensack, Bergen County.
BOGERT, CORNELIUS Pvt, A, 22nd NJ Inf, 12-4-1896. Old 1st Reformed Church Cemetery, Hackensack, Bergen County.
BOGERT, CORNELIUS C. Pvt, H, 25th NJ Inf, 4-5-1928. Valleau Cemetery, Ridgewood, Bergen County.
BOGERT, DAVID Corp, I, 22nd NJ Inf, [Died of typhoid at Belle Plain, VA.] 4-5-1863. Old South Church Cemetery, Bergenfield, Bergen County.
BOGERT, DAVID C. Sgt, H, 25th NJ Inf, 3-27-1919. Cedar Lawn Cemetery, Paterson, Passaic County.
BOGERT*, GILBERT D. 1st Lt, H, 22nd NJ Inf, 12-1-1913. Cedar Lawn Cemetery, Paterson, Passaic County.
BOGERT, ISAAC D. Sgt, D, 22nd NJ Inf, 5-7-1918. Old Hook Cemetery, Westwood, Bergen County.
BOGERT, JACOB Capt, K, 2nd NJ Inf, [Killed in action at Wilderness, VA.] 5-6-1864. True Reformed at Washington Memorial Cemetery, Paramus, Bergen County.
BOGERT, JAMES M. Corp, D, 22nd NJ Inf, 11-12-1907. Westwood Cemetery, Westwood, Bergen County.

New Jersey Civil War Burials

BOGERT, JOHN (aka: Bigot, John) Pvt, B, 3rd NJ Cav, [Wounded in action.] 8-29-1898. Redeemer Cemetery, Mahwah, Bergen County.
BOGERT, JOHN C. Sgt, F, 3rd NJ Cav, [Killed in action at Taylors Plantation, VA.] 4-3-1865. Cedar Lawn Cemetery, Paterson, Passaic County.
BOGERT, JOHN H. Pvt, H, 22nd NJ Inf, 3-16-1877. Edgewater Cemetery, Edgewater, Bergen County.
BOGERT, JOHN W. Pvt, H, 198th PA Inf, 6-3-1913. Locust Hill Cemetery, Dover, Morris County.
BOGERT, PETER R. (JR.) 1-6-1909. Maple Grove Cemetery, Hackensack, Bergen County.
BOGERT, SAMUEL B. Pvt, C, 22nd NJ Inf, 6-18-1892. Old South Church Cemetery, Bergenfield, Bergen County.
BOGERT, WILLIAM PELL Pvt, K, 25th NJ Inf, 11-22-1909. Valleau Cemetery, Ridgewood, Bergen County.
BOGGS, ALONZO Coal Heaver, U.S. Navy, USS Princeton, 12-9-1909. New Camden Cemetery, Camden, Camden County.
BOGGS, CHARLES EDWARD Actg Asst Paymaster, U.S. Navy, USS Cyane, 10-1-1880. Christ Episcopal Church Cemetery, New Brunswick, Middlesex County.
BOGGS, CHARLES M. Pvt, I, 63rd IL Inf, DoD Unknown. Baptist Cemetery, Hopewell Boro, Mercer County.
BOGGS, CHARLES STUART Captain, U.S. Navy, USS Juniata, 4-22-1888. Christ Episcopal Church Cemetery, New Brunswick, Middlesex County.
BOGGS, ISAAC E. 1-22-1912. Old Camden Cemetery, Camden, Camden County.
BOGGS, ROBERT M. 1st Lt, G, 1st NJ Inf, [Died of typhoid at Harrisons Landing, VA.] 8-6-1862. Christ Episcopal Church Cemetery, New Brunswick, Middlesex County.
BOGGS*, WILLIAM GILBERT Capt, A, 33rd NJ Inf, [Died of wounds received 11-23-1863 at Chattanooga, TN.] 12-14-1863. Fairmount Cemetery, Newark, Essex County.
BOGLE, JAMES Pvt, E, 2nd U.S. Cav, 7-17-1891. Fairmount Cemetery, Newark, Essex County.
BOGLE, JOHN A. Pvt, C, 145th PA Inf, DoD Unknown. Tabernacle Cemetery, Tabernacle, Burlington County.
BOGNER, JOSEPH H. Pvt, G, 2nd NJ Cav, 8-8-1895. Woodland Cemetery, Newark, Essex County.
BOHAN, HENRY Pvt, D, Merritt's Bttn AR Inf (CSA), 4-10-1864. Finn's Point National Cemetery, Pennsville, Salem County.
BOHEM, HENRY (see: Boehm, Henry) Woodland Cemetery, Newark, Essex County.
BOHEMUS, JAMES (see: Polhemus, James H.) White Ridge Cemetery, Eatontown, Monmouth County.
BOHEN*, JOHN Pvt, F, 2nd NJ Inf, 6-16-1901. Holy Sepulchre Cemetery, East Orange, Essex County.
BOHLER, WILHELM Pvt, A, 41st NY Inf, 5-12-1912. Clinton Cemetery, Irvington, Essex County.
BOHNENBERGER, GEORGE (aka: Bonnenburgher, George) Musc, F, 83rd NY Inf, 2-1-1907. Fairmount Cemetery, Newark, Essex County.
BOHR, ADAM Pvt, D, 133rd NY Inf, 11-14-1893. Bloomfield Cemetery, Bloomfield, Essex County.
BOHR, MICHAEL Pvt, H, 2nd DC Inf, 4-1-1888. Fairmount Cemetery, Newark, Essex County.
BOHR, NICHOLAS Pvt, D, 9th NJ Inf, 6-8-1899. Fairmount Cemetery, Newark, Essex County.
BOHRER, PHILLIP Corp, D, 2nd NJ Inf, 12-11-1870. Fairmount Cemetery, Newark, Essex County.

Our Brothers Gone Before

BOICE, CHARLES Pvt, B, 14th NJ Inf, 3-11-1891. Cedar Hill Cemetery, Hightstown, Mercer County.
BOICE, CHARLES 1924. Fields Family Cemetery, Eatontown, Monmouth County.
BOICE, CLARKSON Pvt, H, 40th NJ Inf, 1911. Rose Hill Cemetery, Matawan, Monmouth County.
BOICE, DANIEL H. Pvt, D, 39th NJ Inf, 10-10-1892. Evergreen Cemetery, Hillside, Union County.
BOICE, DANIEL R. Bvt Col, 3rd NJ Cav 1-22-1911. Elmwood Cemetery, New Brunswick, Middlesex County.
BOICE, DAVID Pvt, C, 38th NJ Inf, 7-5-1911. Presbyterian Church Cemetery, Bridgeton, Cumberland County.
BOICE, GEORGE C. 2nd Lt, G, 11th NJ Inf, [Killed in action at Petersburg, VA.] 10-8-1864. Baptist Cemetery, South Plainfield, Middlesex County.
BOICE, GEORGE D. Pvt, C, 28th NJ Inf, [Cenotaph. Killed in action at Fredericksburg, VA.] 12-13-1862. 1st Baptist Church Cemetery, Stelton, Middlesex County.
BOICE, JAMES T. Pvt, A, 28th NJ Inf, 12-13-1897. Rosedale Cemetery, Orange, Essex County.
BOICE, JOHN 11-18-1876. Christ Episcopal Church Cemetery, New Brunswick, Middlesex County.
BOICE, JOHN Pvt, D, 38th NJ Inf, 6-21-1911. Old Scots Cemetery, Marlboro, Monmouth County.
BOICE, JOHN H. Pvt, E, 29th NJ Inf, 12-25-1898. Tennent Church Cemetery, Tennent, Monmouth County.
BOICE, MATHAIS A. Pvt, E, 29th NJ Inf, DoD Unknown. Rose Hill Cemetery, Matawan, Monmouth County.
BOICE, MATHIAS A. 6-20-1887. Adelphia Cemetery, Adelphia, Monmouth County.
BOICE*, URIAH Corp, K, 2nd NJ Inf, 2-12-1913. Chestnut Hill Cemetery, East Brunswick, Middlesex County.
BOILEAU, JOHN K. Sgt, L, 20th PA Cav, 1902. Union Cemetery, Frenchtown, Hunterdon County.
BOKER, CHARLES (see: Baker, Charles) Atlantic View Cemetery, Manasquan, Monmouth County.
BOLAND, MICHAEL Pvt, G, 11th NJ Inf, DoD Unknown. Holy Sepulchre Cemetery, East Orange, Essex County.
BOLAND*, PATRICK Pvt, Unassigned, 33rd NJ Inf, 4-7-1895. Holy Sepulchre Cemetery, East Orange, Essex County.
BOLD, PETER Seaman, U.S. Navy, 6-20-1937. Holy Sepulchre Cemetery, Totowa, Passaic County.
BOLD, ROBERT (see: Booth, Robert B.) Old Bergen Church Cemetery, Jersey City, Hudson County.
BOLDIN, GEORGE W. (aka: Baldin, George) Pvt, A, 8th U.S. CT, 8-19-1916. AME Cemetery, Pennington, Mercer County.
BOLDON, WILLIAM Pvt, Btty A, 1st NJ Light Art, 12-10-1893. St. Mary's Cemetery, Boonton, Morris County.
BOLDS, THOMAS (see: Bowles, Thomas F.) White Ridge Cemetery, Eatontown, Monmouth County.
BOLEN, ELIAS A. Pvt, F, 13th NJ Inf, 11-7-1892. Fairmount Cemetery, Newark, Essex County.
BOLEN, MILEM Pvt, D, 7th TN Inf (CSA), 6-7-1865. Finn's Point National Cemetery, Pennsville, Salem County.
BOLEN*, OWEN Pvt, B, 15th NJ Inf, DoD Unknown. Holy Sepulchre Cemetery, East Orange, Essex County.
BOLES, WARREN H. Pvt, Oneida NY Inf 12-13-1909. Arlington Cemetery, Kearny, Hudson County.

New Jersey Civil War Burials

BOLEY, DAVID 1898. Chestnut Cemetery, Greenwich, Cumberland County.

BOLIN, THOMAS (see: Bowlin, Thomas) Finn's Point National Cemetery, Pennsville, Salem County.

BOLING, CHARLES Pvt, B, 25th U.S. CT, 1918. Boling Cemetery, Clarks Mill, Atlantic County.

BOLING, JOSIAH Pvt, B, 25th U.S. CT, 5-28-1909. Boling Cemetery, Clarks Mill, Atlantic County.

BOLLER*, GEORGE (aka: Buller, George) Corp, E, 7th NJ Inf, 5-17-1906. Fairmount Cemetery, Newark, Essex County.

BOLLES, JOHN A. 6-26-1878. Evergreen Cemetery, Farmingdale, Monmouth County.

BOLLIGER, HENRY Pvt, C, 1st NJ Cav, 4-5-1906. Arlington Cemetery, Kearny, Hudson County.

BOLLING, HENRY Pvt, K, 1st NJ Inf, 5-29-1891. Fairmount Cemetery, Newark, Essex County.

BOLLING, JOHN __, B, 14th __ Inf, DoD Unknown. Holy Name Cemetery, Jersey City, Hudson County.

BOLLINGER, HENRY Pvt, Btty H, 15th NY Heavy Art, 10-29-1927. New Presbyterian Cemetery, Bound Brook, Somerset County.

BOLLS, C.N. (see: Boals, C.M.) Finn's Point National Cemetery, Pennsville, Salem County.

BOLMER, ALBERT Musc, A, 31st NJ Inf, 11-30-1918. Alpine Cemetery, Perth Amboy, Middlesex County.

BOLSFORD*, CHARLES J. (aka: Botsford, Charles) Pvt, F, 34th MA Inf, 10-19-1910. Presbyterian Church Cemetery, Flemington, Hunterdon County.

BOLT, SAMUEL G. Pvt, I, 14th LA Inf (CSA), [Captured 7-4-1863 at Gettysburg, PA.] 2-1-1864. Finn's Point National Cemetery, Pennsville, Salem County.

BOLTE, FREDERICK Pvt, H, 7th NH Inf, 8-24-1918. Rose Hill Cemetery, Matawan, Monmouth County.

BOLTON, GEORGE Pvt, M, 5th NY Cav, 3-26-1892. Laurel Grove Cemetery, Totowa, Passaic County.

BOLTON*, HENRY Pvt, A, 2nd RI Inf, 4-16-1914. St. Nicholas Cemetery, Lodi, Bergen County.

BOLTON, HILRY Pvt, E, 38th VA Inf (CSA), [Captured 7-4-1863 at Gettysburg, PA. Died of diarrhea.] 8-17-1863. Finn's Point National Cemetery, Pennsville, Salem County.

BOLTON, JAMES M. Pvt, E, 62nd (Rowan's) TN Inf (CSA), 8-25-1863. Finn's Point National Cemetery, Pennsville, Salem County.

BOLTON, JOHN F. Corp, H, 104th NY Inf, 4-4-1931. Arlington Cemetery, Kearny, Hudson County.

BOLTON, LEWIS Pvt, I, 132nd NY Inf, 8-7-1900. Greenlawn Cemetery, West Long Branch, Monmouth County.

BOLTON, ORRA C. Pvt, C, 31st MA Inf, 1923. Mount Pleasant Cemetery, Millville, Cumberland County.

BOLTON, SAMUEL HENRY Capt, K, 34th NJ Inf, [Died at St. Marys Hospital Montgomery, AL.] 9-7-1865. Presbyterian Church Cemetery, Bridgeton, Cumberland County.

BOLTON, WILLIAM M. 2nd Lt, A, 15th GA Inf (CSA), [Captured 7-2-1863 at Gettysburg, PA.] 10-8-1863. Finn's Point National Cemetery, Pennsville, Salem County.

BOLTZ, JOHN 8-8-1882. Edgewater Cemetery, Edgewater, Bergen County.

BOMAN, THEODORE Pvt, H, 1st CT Inf, DoD Unknown. Grove Church Cemetery, North Bergen, Hudson County.

BOMFORD*, GEORGE N. Lt Col, 42nd NY Inf [Wounded 9-17-1862 at Antietam, MD.] 9-5-1897. Evergreen Cemetery, Hillside, Union County.

Our Brothers Gone Before

BOMFORD, JAMES VOTE' Bvt Brig Gen, [Wounded in action at Perryville, KY. Colonel, 8th United States Infantry.] 1-6-1892. Evergreen Cemetery, Hillside, Union County.
BOMM, CHARLES H. (aka: Bahnmuller, Charles) Pvt, K, 86th NY Inf, 11-3-1872. Fairmount Cemetery, Newark, Essex County.
BOMO*, DOMENICO Corp, D, 7th NJ Inf, 1896. Greenmount Cemetery, Hammonton, Atlantic County.
BOND, ABRAM H. Musc, B, 17th MA Inf, 6-30-1930. Zion Methodist Church Cemetery, Bargaintown, Atlantic County.
BOND, ASA Pvt, D, 38th NJ Inf, 7-24-1900. Evergreen Cemetery, Camden, Camden County.
BOND, CHARLES C. Pvt, K, 20th PA Cav, [Cenotaph. Died while prisoner at Andersonville, GA.] 11-18-1864. Sandy Ridge Cemetery, Sandy Ridge, Hunterdon County.
BOND, CHARLES W.P. Pvt, D, 26th NJ Inf, 12-1-1919. South Orange Cemetery, South Orange, Essex County.
BOND, HERBERT T. (aka: Bond, Robert) Pvt, E, Ind Bttn NY Inf, [Enfans Perdus. Cenotaph. Died at Beaufort, SC. of wounds received at Fort Wagner, SC.] 8-11-1863. Boonton Cemetery, Boonton, Morris County.
BOND, JAMES Pvt, K, 47th NY Inf, 3-14-1914. Fairmount Cemetery, Newark, Essex County.
BOND, JOHN Pvt, D, 38th NJ Inf, 11-6-1867. Methodist Episcopal/Methodist Protestant Cemetery, Bridgeport, Gloucester County.
BOND, JOHN H. Pvt, B, 40th NJ Inf, 11-9-1914. New Camden Cemetery, Camden, Camden County.
BOND, JOSEPH Corp, I, 45th U.S. CT, 10-18-1872. Presbyterian Church Cemetery, Bridgeton, Cumberland County.
BOND, ROBERT (see: Bond, Herbert T.) Boonton Cemetery, Boonton, Morris County.
BOND, WILLIAM Pvt, C, 22nd U.S. CT, 12-18-1901. Mount Zion AME Cemetery, Swedesboro, Gloucester County.
BOND, WILLIAM DoD Unknown. Mercer Cemetery, Trenton, Mercer County.
BOND, WILLIAM Pvt, F, 10th NJ Inf, 10-22-1868. Huntsville Cemetery, Huntsville, Sussex County.
BOND, WILLIAM R. Pvt, D, 14th NJ Inf, 12-29-1916. Methodist-Episcopal Cemetery, Glendola, Monmouth County.
BONDGOUST*, IGNATZ Pvt, B, 2nd NJ Cav, 6-28-1879. Holy Sepulchre Cemetery, East Orange, Essex County.
BONDS, PATRICK D. Pvt, B, 5th Bttn AL Inf (CSA), 10-30-1863. Finn's Point National Cemetery, Pennsville, Salem County.
BONE*, JOHN F. Pvt, E, 5th NY Vet Inf, [Wounded 6-27-1862 at Gaines' Mill, VA.] 11-19-1876. Christ Episcopal Church Cemetery, New Brunswick, Middlesex County.
BONES, JOHN (see: Bowes, John) Holy Sepulchre Cemetery, Totowa, Passaic County.
BONES, JOHN W. 1st Sgt, D, 79th PA Inf, 9-26-1897. Evergreen Cemetery, Hillside, Union County.
BONET, AUGUST Pvt, B, 9th NJ Inf, 11-1-1882. Fairmount Cemetery, Newark, Essex County.
BONHAM, JOHN B. Pvt, K, 12th NJ Inf, 1917. 7th Day Baptist Church Cemetery, Shiloh, Cumberland County.
BONHAM, JONATHAN W. Pvt, F, 24th NJ Inf, 6-30-1908. 7th Day Baptist Church Cemetery, Shiloh, Cumberland County.
BONHAM, LUCIUS C. Capt, A, 9th NJ Inf, 2-15-1879. 7th Day Baptist Church Cemetery, Shiloh, Cumberland County.

New Jersey Civil War Burials

BONHAM, W.C. Pvt, E, 13th SC Inf (CSA), [Captured 7-5-1863 at Gettysburg, PA. Died of typhoid.] 9-18-1863. Finn's Point National Cemetery, Pennsville, Salem County.

BONHEIMER, GEORGE (see: Bernhammer, George F.) Grove Church Cemetery, North Bergen, Hudson County.

BONI, PAOLO Pvt, C, 39th NY Inf, [Died of wounds received 7-2-1863 at Gettysburg, PA.] 10-9-1863. Fairmount Cemetery, Newark, Essex County.

BONIFACE, JOHN K. 1927. Evergreen Cemetery, Morristown, Morris County.

BONKER, JOHN (JR.) Pvt, K, 27th NJ Inf, 1912. Presbyterian Church Cemetery, Sparta, Sussex County.

BONKER, WILLIAM B. Corp, K, 35th NY Inf, 1923. Methodist Church Cemetery, Sparta, Sussex County.

BONN, JOHN (see: Bunn, John R.) Trinity Episcopal Church Cemetery, Woodbridge, Middlesex County.

BONNELL, AARON EDWARD Pvt, K, 2nd DC Inf, 10-30-1885. Walnut Grove Cemetery, Mount Freedom, Morris County.

BONNELL*, ALEXANDER V. Capt, D, 31st NJ Inf, 8-13-1872. Presbyterian Church Cemetery, Flemington, Hunterdon County.

BONNELL, CHARLES P. Pvt, G, 26th NJ Inf, 1911. St. Mark's Cemetery, Orange, Essex County.

BONNELL, DAVID Pvt, K, 2nd DC Inf, DoD Unknown. Walnut Grove Cemetery, Mount Freedom, Morris County.

BONNELL, EDWARD C. Corp, A, 1st NJ Inf, 2-6-1914. Evergreen Cemetery, Hillside, Union County.

BONNELL, GEORGE C. Artificer, E, 1st NY Eng, 2-19-1904. Connecticut Farms Cemetery, Union, Union County.

BONNELL, GEORGE WESLEY Pvt, G, 40th NJ Inf, 1923. Presbyterian/Methodist-Episcopal Cemetery, Succasunna, Morris County.

BONNELL*, ISAAC Pvt, B, 11th NJ Inf, 1-16-1880. Fairmount Cemetery, Newark, Essex County.

BONNELL, JOHN DoD Unknown. United Methodist Church Cemetery, Vernon, Sussex County.

BONNELL, JOHN WESLEY Musc, 7th NJ Inf Band 1890. 1st Presbyterian Church Cemetery, Orange, Essex County.

BONNELL, JONATHAN (aka: Bunnell, John) Pvt, A, 26th NJ Inf, 5-2-1892. Evergreen Cemetery, Hillside, Union County.

BONNELL, JOSEPH W. Pvt, G, 26th NJ Inf, 5-16-1873. Rosedale Cemetery, Orange, Essex County.

BONNELL, MAHLON Pvt, B, 38th NJ Inf, 7-1-1901. Union Cemetery, Frenchtown, Hunterdon County.

BONNELL, ROSWELL V. Sgt, F, 19th U.S. Inf, 12-3-1916. Rosedale Cemetery, Linden, Union County.

BONNELL, STEPHEN M. Pvt, F, 12th MI Inf, [Cenotaph. Killed in action at Shiloh, TN.] 4-6-1862. Evergreen Cemetery, Hillside, Union County.

BONNELL, WILLIAM Pvt, H, 5th NJ Inf, 3-4-1899. Alpine Cemetery, Perth Amboy, Middlesex County.

BONNELL, WILLIAM Pvt, C, 14th NJ Inf, 2-23-1873. Presbyterian Church Cemetery, Mount Freedom, Morris County.

BONNELL, WILLIAM P. Pvt, F, 27th NJ Inf, 6-15-1910. Mount Pleasant Cemetery, Newark, Essex County.

BONNELL*, WILLIAM P. Artificer, E, 1st NY Eng, 6-20-1911. Evergreen Cemetery, Hillside, Union County.

BONNELL, WILLIAM W. Pvt, I, 26th NJ Inf, [Died of wounds received 5-4-1863 at Bank's Ford, VA.] 6-7-1863. Presbyterian Cemetery, Springfield, Union County.

Our Brothers Gone Before

BONNENBURGHER, GEORGE (see: Bohnenberger, George) Fairmount Cemetery, Newark, Essex County.
BONNER, JOHN Pvt, C, 1st DE Cav, 7-18-1911. Beverly National Cemetery, Edgewater Park, Burlington County.
BONNETT, DANIEL BLAKE Pvt, C, 7th NY State Militia, 1-26-1938. Evergreen Cemetery, Hillside, Union County.
BONNEY, CHARLES FORD 2nd Lt, E, 9th NJ Inf, 4-24-1905. Cedar Lawn Cemetery, Paterson, Passaic County.
BONSALL, JAMES M. Corp, E, PA Emerg NJ Militia, 10-12-1885. Presbyterian Church Cemetery, Rockaway, Morris County.
BONSTEAD, JOSEPH E. Pvt, F, 4th NJ Inf, 5-6-1896. Evergreen Cemetery, Camden, Camden County.
BONTEMPS, JOSEPH Corp, L, 15th PA Cav, 1877. Evergreen Cemetery, Camden, Camden County.
BOODY, DAVID Pvt, F, 12th NJ Inf, [Died of disease at Ellicotts Mills, MD.] 11-13-1862. Methodist-Episcopal Cemetery, Mullica Hill, Gloucester County.
BOODY, GEORGE W. Pvt, G, 2nd NJ Cav, DoD Unknown. Chickory Chapel Baptist Church Cemetery, Elk, Gloucester County.
BOODY, JOHN H. Pvt, G, 3rd NJ Cav, 3-9-1923. New Camden Cemetery, Camden, Camden County.
BOODY, JOHN H. Pvt, E, 24th NJ Inf, 8-21-1899. Eglington Cemetery, Clarksboro, Gloucester County.
BOODY, OLIVER C. 2-27-1910. Eglington Cemetery, Clarksboro, Gloucester County.
BOOFMAN, JACOB H. Pvt, A, 3rd NJ Cav, 2-7-1910. Bayview-New York Bay Cemetery, Jersey City, Hudson County.
BOOGAR, JEFFERSON G. 6-22-1935. Berlin Cemetery, Berlin, Camden County.
BOOKER, R.R. Cook, A, 8th U.S. Inf, DoD Unknown. Rosedale Cemetery, Orange, Essex County.
BOOKER, WILLIAM (see: Bowker, William R.) Methodist Cemetery, Crosswicks, Burlington County.
BOOKSTAVER, FRANCIS H. 2nd Lt, B, 21st NJ Inf, 11-5-1889. Macphelah Cemetery, North Bergen, Hudson County.
BOOKSTAVER*, JOHN H. Pvt, B, 21st NJ Inf, 8-4-1897. Arlington Cemetery, Kearny, Hudson County.
BOON, JOHN J. Pvt, A, 12th NJ Inf, 2-20-1931. Presbyterian Church Cemetery, Bridgeton, Cumberland County.
BOON, W.C. Pvt, C, 8th (Wade's) Confederate States Cav (CSA), 9-24-1863. Finn's Point National Cemetery, Pennsville, Salem County.
BOONE, HORACE Pvt, D, 71st NY Inf, [Wounded 7-2-1863 at Gettysburg, PA.] 1-16-1902. Hoboken Cemetery, North Bergen, Hudson County.
BOONE, JAMES Corp, I, 6th PA Cav, 11-4-1902. Evergreen Cemetery, Camden, Camden County.
BOONE, JOHN D. Pvt, H, 24th NJ Inf, 3-30-1911. Presbyterian Church Cemetery, Bridgeton, Cumberland County.
BOONE, JOHN H. Pvt, A, 24th NJ Inf, 12-2-1890. Baptist Church Cemetery, Canton, Salem County.
BOONE, WILLIAM E. Pvt, A, 37th NJ Inf, 10-27-1901. Arlington Cemetery, Kearny, Hudson County.
BOONEY, JAMES Pvt, A, 70th NY Inf, DoD Unknown. Holy Sepulchre Cemetery, East Orange, Essex County.
BOORAEM, HENRY Sgt, U.S. Army, [General Service.] DoD Unknown. 1st Reformed Church Cemetery, New Brunswick, Middlesex County.
BOORMAN, CORNELIUS Pvt, H, 14th NJ Inf, [Killed in action at Locust Grove, VA.] 11-27-1863. Brainerd Cemetery, Cranbury, Middlesex County.

New Jersey Civil War Burials

BOORMAN, FREDERICK Corp, C, 6th NJ Inf, [Wounded 7-2-1863 at Gettysburg, PA.] 2-24-1914. Bayview-New York Bay Cemetery, Jersey City, Hudson County.

BOORMAN, GEORGE Corp, K, 2nd NJ Militia, 7-12-1887. Hillside Cemetery, Oxford, Warren County.

BOORMAN, GEORGE P. Corp, K, 2nd NJ Militia, 2-27-1913. Old Bergen Church Cemetery, Jersey City, Hudson County.

BOOS, PHILIP Pvt, H, 14th IN Inf, [Died of natural causes.] 9-8-1862. Fairmount Cemetery, Newark, Essex County.

BOOTEYET, CHARLES Pvt, K, 1st NJ Militia, 4-12-1893. Fairmount Cemetery, Newark, Essex County.

BOOTH, BENJAMIN Pvt, C, 15th NJ Inf, 6-5-1882. Presbyterian Church Cemetery, Newton, Sussex County.

BOOTH, CHARLES Pvt, H, 67th PA Inf, 1-15-1912. St. Mary's Cemetery, Hamilton, Mercer County.

BOOTH, ELISHA Pvt, D, 58th VA Inf (CSA), [Captured 5-12-1864 at Spotsylvania CH, VA. Died of smallpox.] 8-12-1864. Finn's Point National Cemetery, Pennsville, Salem County.

BOOTH, ENOCH Corp, G, 39th NJ Inf, 8-7-1879. Vincent Methodist-Episcopal Cemetery, Nutley, Essex County.

BOOTH, JAMES Pvt, I, 27th NJ Inf, 4-22-1866. Evergreen Cemetery, Morristown, Morris County.

BOOTH, JOHN C. 1st Lt, B, 14th NJ Inf, 5-3-1891. Evergreen Cemetery, Hillside, Union County.

BOOTH, JOHN P. Pvt, E, 175th PA Inf, 6-10-1884. Newton Cemetery, Newton, Sussex County.

BOOTH, JOHN R. Musc, H, 4th NJ Militia, 1-1-1900. Cedar Grove Cemetery, Gloucester City, Camden County.

BOOTH, JONATHAN Pvt, I, 26th NJ Inf, DoD Unknown. Christ Church Cemetery, Belleville, Essex County.

BOOTH, ROBERT B. (aka: Bold, Robert) Pvt, B, 84th NY Inf, DoD Unknown. Old Bergen Church Cemetery, Jersey City, Hudson County.

BOOTH, SAMUEL Pvt, G, 1st NJ Cav, 9-26-1898. Chestnut Cemetery, Dover, Morris County.

BOOTH, THOMAS (SR.) Corp, A, 1st NJ Militia, 5-4-1876. Fairmount Cemetery, Newark, Essex County.

BOOTH, WILLIAM S. Sgt, K, 1st NJ Cav, 12-19-1892. Mercer Cemetery, Trenton, Mercer County.

BOOZ, ALFRED Pvt, A, 35th NJ Inf, 3-26-1903. Riverview Cemetery, Trenton, Mercer County.

BOOZ, HENRY N. Pvt, E, 88th PA Inf, 1906. Harleigh Cemetery, Camden, Camden County.

BOOZ, HENRY N. Pvt, G, 34th NJ Inf, 8-29-1893. Greenwood Cemetery, Hamilton, Mercer County.

BOOZ, WILLIAM H. Sgt, H, 37th NJ Inf, 6-5-1892. Greenwood Cemetery, Hamilton, Mercer County.

BOOZE*, JACOB V. Principal Musc, 38th NJ Inf 8-7-1909. Mercer Cemetery, Trenton, Mercer County.

BOPP, CHARLES E. Pvt, K, 7th Bttn DC Militia, 1913. Locust Hill Cemetery, Dover, Morris County.

BOPP, LENDHART (aka: Bopp, Leonard) Pvt, C, 30th NJ Inf, 6-22-1915. Evergreen Cemetery, Hillside, Union County.

BOPP, LEONARD (see: Bopp, Lendhart) Evergreen Cemetery, Hillside, Union County.

BORAFF, JOHN (see: Burov, John) Laurel Hill Cemetery, Elwood, Atlantic County.

Our Brothers Gone Before

BORDAN, JOHN A. Pvt, K, 29th NJ Inf, 5-3-1925. Mount Prospect Cemetery, Neptune, Monmouth County.
BORDEL, CONRAD (see: Bardell, Conrad) Fairmount Cemetery, Newark, Essex County.
BORDEN, ALEXANDER Pvt, G, 11th NJ Inf, 10-24-1889. Woodlane Graveyard Cemetery, Westampton, Burlington County.
BORDEN, CHARLES Pvt, F, 6th NJ Inf, 4-7-1895. Fairmount Cemetery, Newark, Essex County.
BORDEN, CHARLES 4-2-1923. Oddfellows Cemetery, Burlington, Burlington County.
BORDEN, CHARLES A. Pvt, H, 29th NJ Inf, 5-25-1912. Riverside Cemetery, Toms River, Ocean County.
BORDEN, DANIEL S. Pvt, K, 29th NJ Inf, 10-14-1918. Evergreen Cemetery, Farmingdale, Monmouth County.
BORDEN*, EDWARD Musc, K, 24th U.S. VRC, 5-26-1920. Methodist Church Cemetery, Groveville, Mercer County.
BORDEN, FRANCIS Pvt, A, 1st NJ Cav, DoD Unknown. Presbyterian Cemetery, Allentown, Monmouth County.
BORDEN, JONATHAN Pvt, K, 12th NJ Inf, DoD Unknown. 1st United Methodist Church Cemetery, Bridgeton, Cumberland County.
BORDEN, JONATHAN Pvt, G, 25th NJ Inf, 2-26-1882. Methodist Cemetery, Malaga, Gloucester County.
BORDEN, PARKER S. 1st Sgt, G, 11th NJ Inf, [Wounded in action.] 3-30-1910. Presbyterian Cemetery, Allentown, Monmouth County.
BORDEN, RICHARD Sgt, D, 14th NJ Inf, 6-22-1918. Fairview Cemetery, Fairview, Monmouth County.
BORDEN, SAMUEL R. Pvt, I, 4th NJ Inf, 11-15-1893. Methodist Church Cemetery, Juliustown, Burlington County.
BORDEN, THOMAS Corp, K, 29th NJ Inf, 5-3-1901. Fairmount Cemetery, Newark, Essex County.
BORDENSTEIN, FREDERICK (see: Bodenstein, Frederick) Greenwood Cemetery, Hamilton, Mercer County.
BORGAT, JOHN (aka: Borgman, John) Pvt, Btty D, 15th NY Heavy Art, 2-7-1894. Woodland Cemetery, Newark, Essex County.
BORGMAN, JOHN (see: Borgat, John) Woodland Cemetery, Newark, Essex County.
BORGQUIST*, JOHN P.F. (aka: Bergquist, John P.F.) Seaman, U.S. Navy, USS Vermont, 6-14-1910. Holy Name Cemetery, Jersey City, Hudson County.
BORLAND, CHARLES T. Sgt, I, 27th NJ Inf, 8-22-1901. Evergreen Cemetery, Morristown, Morris County.
BORMANN, ADOLPH Pvt, L, 1st NY Cav, 11-12-1896. Flower Hill Cemetery, North Bergen, Hudson County.
BORNE, JOHN W. Pvt, F, 27th NJ Inf, 1-14-1901. St. Stephen's Cemetery, Millburn, Essex County.
BORNEMANN, CARL 1st Lt, A, 41st NY Inf, 6-18-1922. Weehawken Cemetery, North Bergen, Hudson County.
BORNER, FRANK (see: Borner, Franz) St. John's Evangelical Church Cemetery, Orange, Essex County.
BORNER*, FRANZ (aka: Berner, Franz or Borner, Frank) Pvt, Btty A, 1st NJ Light Art, 8-30-1898. St. John's Evangelical Church Cemetery, Orange, Essex County.
BORNEYCUMPER, H. 8-21-1891. Laurel Grove Cemetery, Totowa, Passaic County.
BORNGESSER, HENRY (see: Bornkessel, George Henry Cedar Lawn Cemetery, Paterson, Passaic County.
BORNKESSEL, GEORGE HENRY (aka: Borngesser, Henry) Sgt, C, 56th NY National Guard, 11-28-1909. Cedar Lawn Cemetery, Paterson, Passaic County.
BORST, HENRY (see: Post, Theodore H.) Evergreen Cemetery, Camden, Camden County.

New Jersey Civil War Burials

BORTIC, WILLIAM NEWTON (aka: Bortie, William) 1st Sgt, C, 102nd NY Inf, 2-21-1912. Valleau Cemetery, Ridgewood, Bergen County.

BORTIE, WILLIAM (see: Bortic, William Newton) Valleau Cemetery, Ridgewood, Bergen County.

BORTON, ALFRED Corp, D, 23rd NJ Inf, 9-23-1930. Beverly National Cemetery, Edgewater Park, Burlington County.

BORTON, BENJAMIN Pvt, A, 24th NJ Inf, 1913. 1st Baptist Church Cemetery, Woodstown, Salem County.

BORTON, DAVID Sgt, F, 12th NJ Inf, 7-1-1914. Friends Cemetery, Mullica Hill, Gloucester County.

BORTON, JOSEPH E. Pvt, D, 95th PA Inf, 8-13-1895. Berlin Cemetery, Berlin, Camden County.

BORTON, NICHOLAS (see: Boston, Nicholas A.) Mount Prospect Cemetery, Neptune, Monmouth County.

BORTON, RICHARD Pvt, F, 12th NJ Inf, [Killed in action at Chancellorsville, VA.] 5-3-1863. Friends Cemetery, Mullica Hill, Gloucester County.

BORTON, SAMUEL Pvt, K, 109th PA Inf, 2-20-1879. Baptist/St. Andrew's Cemetery, Mount Holly, Burlington County.

BORTS, ISAAC (aka: Bortz, Isaac) Pvt, F, 13th PA Cav, 6-8-1928. Soldier's Home Cemetery, Vineland, Cumberland County.

BORTZ, ISAAC (see: Borts, Isaac) Soldier's Home Cemetery, Vineland, Cumberland County.

BOSENBERRY, JOHN Pvt, D, 31st NJ Inf, 4-15-1905. Evergreen Cemetery, Clinton, Hunterdon County.

BOSENBERY, HOLLOWAY W. (aka: Bozenberry, Halloway W.) Pvt, B, 2nd NJ Cav, 11-30-1882. United Methodist Church Cemetery, Pattenburg, Hunterdon County.

BOSENBURY*, DAVID M. Pvt, B, 2nd NJ Cav, 1906. Methodist-Episcopal Cemetery, Whitehouse, Hunterdon County.

BOSHIER, SAMUEL (aka: Bozeyer, Samuel) Pvt, E, 11th NJ Inf, DoD Unknown. Good Luck Cemetery, Murray Grove, Ocean County.

BOSLEY, J. (see: Boswell, Jethro) Finn's Point National Cemetery, Pennsville, Salem County.

BOSS, ABRAHAM W. Pvt, D, 31st NJ Inf, 7-17-1914. Prospect Hill Cemetery, Flemington, Hunterdon County.

BOSS, ABRAM Pvt, B, 3rd NJ Cav, 5-23-1915. Presbyterian Church Cemetery, Sparta, Sussex County.

BOSS, DAVID 8-23-1886. Baptist Church Cemetery, Port Murray, Warren County.

BOSS, DAVID S. Corp, A, 31st NJ Inf, 2-4-1896. Prospect Hill Cemetery, Flemington, Hunterdon County.

BOSS, DAVID S. 8-11-1872. Methodist Church Cemetery, Lebanon, Hunterdon County.

BOSS, JACOB (aka: Bass, Jacob) Corp, I, 30th NJ Inf, [Died of typhoid at Belle Plain, VA.] 3-31-1863. Evergreen Cemetery, Morristown, Morris County.

BOSS, JOHN 1883. Amwell Ridge Cemetery, Larisons Corner, Hunterdon County.

BOSS, JOHN BEDELL 6-8-1877. Presbyterian Church Cemetery, Sparta, Sussex County.

BOSSENT, PETER K. (aka: Bossuot, Peter K.) Pvt, B, 35th NY Inf, 8-11-1895. Fairview Cemetery, Fairview, Bergen County.

BOSSET, PETER Pvt, E, 77th NY National Guard, 10-8-1931. Holy Sepulchre Cemetery, East Orange, Essex County.

BOSSUOT, PETER K. (see: Bossent, Peter K.) Fairview Cemetery, Fairview, Bergen County.

BOSTEDO, CHARLES Corp, B, 95th NY Inf, 3-26-1913. Union Cemetery, Marcella, Morris County.

BOSTELL*, THEODORE Pvt, E, 20th MA Inf, [Wounded 5- -1864.] 4-14-1912. Fairmount Cemetery, Newark, Essex County.

Our Brothers Gone Before

BOSTICK, JOHN C. Pvt, B, 3rd NC Inf (CSA), [Wounded 9-17-1862 at Sharpsburg, MD. and 7-2-1863 at Gettysburg, PA. Captured 7-3-1863 at Gettysburg, PA. Died of diarrhea.] 8-2-1863. Finn's Point National Cemetery, Pennsville, Salem County.
BOSTON, NICHOLAS A. (aka: Borton, Nicholas) Pvt, K, 22nd U.S. CT, 4-15-1889. Mount Prospect Cemetery, Neptune, Monmouth County.
BOSTWICK*, DAVID Pvt, E, 152nd NY Inf, 2-4-1897. Rosehill Cemetery, Newfield, Gloucester County.
BOSWELL, CHARLES Ord Seaman, U.S. Navy, USS Niagra, 1-4-1902. Old 1st Methodist Church Cemetery, West Long Branch, Monmouth County.
BOSWELL, EUGENE (aka: Bagwell, Eugene) Pvt, H, 7th U.S. CT, 1919. Soldier's Home Cemetery, Vineland, Cumberland County.
BOSWELL*, JAMES (aka: Bidwell, James) Sgt, H, 162nd NY Inf, 4-19-1904. Fairmount Cemetery, Newark, Essex County.
BOSWELL, JETHRO (aka: Bosley, J.) Pvt, A, 55th NC Inf (CSA), [Captured 7-1-1863 at Gettysburg, PA. Died of chronic diarrhea.] 11-22-1863. Finn's Point National Cemetery, Pennsville, Salem County.
BOSWELL, JOSHUA J. Pvt, C, 18th NC Inf (CSA), [Captured 7-3-1863 at Gettysburg, PA. Died of typhoid.] 9-4-1863. Finn's Point National Cemetery, Pennsville, Salem County.
BOSWELL, NAPOLEON BONAPARTE Pvt, G, 3rd MS Inf (CSA), 6-27-1863. Finn's Point National Cemetery, Pennsville, Salem County.
BOSWELL, THOMAS Pvt, B, 4th NC Cav (CSA), [Captured 7-4-1863 at South Mountain, MD.] 8-24-1863. Finn's Point National Cemetery, Pennsville, Salem County.
BOTHNER, WILLIAM (see: Bennett, William A.) Princeton Cemetery, Princeton, Mercer County.
BOTSFORD, CHARLES (see: Bolsford, Charles J.) Presbyterian Church Cemetery, Flemington, Hunterdon County.
BOTSFORD, EDWARD Pvt, Btty I, 2nd CT Heavy Art, [Wounded 9-19-1864 at Winchester, VA.] 11-19-1907. Fairmount Cemetery, Newark, Essex County.
BOTT, FREDERICK Corp, A, 25th NJ Inf, DoD Unknown. Holy Sepulchre Cemetery, Totowa, Passaic County.
BOTT, JOHN Pvt, L, 3rd NJ Cav, [Killed in action at Petersburg, VA.] 7-25-1864. Speer Cemetery, Jersey City, Hudson County.
BOTT, THOMAS 1879. Whitehall Cemetery, Towaco, Morris County.
BOTT, WILLIAM M. 5-7-1889. Whitehall Cemetery, Towaco, Morris County.
BOTTELBERGER, GEORGE (see: Gottelberk, George C.) Clinton Cemetery, Irvington, Essex County.
BOTTELBERGER, GEORGE C. Pvt, F, 8th NJ Inf, 10-27-1908. Clinton Cemetery, Irvington, Essex County.
BOTTLES, WILLIAM J. Pvt, E, 21st NJ Inf, 1870. Baptist Church Cemetery, Hamilton Square, Mercer County.
BOTTS, GEORGE L. Pvt, H, 37th NJ Inf, 6-23-1926. Greenwood Cemetery, Hamilton, Mercer County.
BOUCH*, JOSEPH Pvt, B, 105th PA Inf, [Died at Beverly, NJ.] 9-29-1864. Beverly National Cemetery, Edgewater Park, Burlington County.
BOUCHER, ABRAHAM D. Pvt, U.S. Marine Corps, 5-16-1913. Brotherhood Cemetery, Hainesport, Burlington County.
BOUCHER, CHARLES Pvt, Btty F, 10th NY Heavy Art, 8-16-1864. Beverly National Cemetery, Edgewater Park, Burlington County.
BOUCHER, CHARLES C. 3-6-1926. Hillside Cemetery, Scotch Plains, Union County.
BOUCHER, HENRY Pvt, I, 9th NJ Inf, 9-15-1862. Fairmount Cemetery, Newark, Essex County.
BOUCHER, JAMES Pvt, E, 3rd NJ Cav, DoD Unknown. Holy Sepulchre Cemetery, East Orange, Essex County.

New Jersey Civil War Burials

BOUCHER, ROBERT Pvt, Btty C, 16th NY Heavy Art, [Died of disease at Beverly, NJ.] 8-19-1864. Beverly National Cemetery, Edgewater Park, Burlington County.
BOUD, RICHARD 9-12-1881. Adelphia Cemetery, Adelphia, Monmouth County.
BOUDE, JOHN H. 11-10-1915. New Camden Cemetery, Camden, Camden County.
BOUDE, JOHN H. Pvt, K, 29th NJ Inf, DoD Unknown. Adelphia Cemetery, Adelphia, Monmouth County.
BOUDINOT, WILLIAM B. Pvt, B, 9th NJ Inf, 7-22-1897. Evergreen Cemetery, New Brunswick, Middlesex County.
BOUGHER, MICHAEL Corp, F, 153rd PA Inf, 3-6-1914. Mount Holly Cemetery, Mount Holly, Burlington County.
BOUGHTON, STEPHEN E. Pvt, A, 1st NJ Inf, 2-13-1906. Evergreen Cemetery, Hillside, Union County.
BOULES, CHARLES (see: Bowles, Charles) Mount Moriah Cemetery, Hainesport, Burlington County.
BOULTINGHOUSE*, WILLIAM H. Pvt, K, 2nd NJ Cav, 5-27-1919. Methodist Church Cemetery, Sharptown, Salem County.
BOULTON, EDWARD (see: Bouton, Edwin H.) Cedar Ridge Cemetery, Blairstown, Warren County.
BOULTON, HENRY B. Pvt, A, 90th NY Inf, 5-29-1897. Evergreen Cemetery, Hillside, Union County.
BOULTON, JOHN R. Corp, A, 23rd NJ Inf, 10-2-1866. Baptist Cemetery, Burlington, Burlington County.
BOUND, THEODORE (see: Bowne, Theodore) Greenwood Cemetery, Hamilton, Mercer County.
BOUNDS, EDWARD F. Pvt, I, 8th U.S. CT, 2-7-1920. White Ridge Cemetery, Eatontown, Monmouth County.
BOURST*, DAVID Pvt, B, 77th NY Inf, DoD Unknown. Mount Pleasant Cemetery, Millville, Cumberland County.
BOUTELL, SAMUEL A. 3-3-1884. Oak Hill Cemetery, Vineland, Cumberland County.
BOUTELLETTE, JOSEPH H. Pvt, F, 8th NJ Inf, 4-23-1904. Fairmount Cemetery, Newark, Essex County.
BOUTON, EDWIN H. (aka: Boulton, Edward) Corp, B, 11th NY Cav, 1928. Cedar Ridge Cemetery, Blairstown, Warren County.
BOVELL, WILLIAM S. Pvt, C, 183rd PA Inf, 4-19-1920. Evergreen Cemetery, Camden, Camden County.
BOVEY*, JULES B. Landsman, U.S. Navy, USS Roanoke, 5-16-1904. Hillside Cemetery, Scotch Plains, Union County.
BOWDEN*, CHARLES J. Pvt, D, 2nd NJ Inf, 1-30-1887. Fairmount Cemetery, Newark, Essex County.
BOWDEN, GEORGE Pvt, Btty D, 1st NJ Light Art, 8-6-1889. Evergreen Cemetery, Hillside, Union County.
BOWDEN, GEORGE R. Pvt, G, 26th NJ Inf, 10-19-1907. Rosedale Cemetery, Orange, Essex County.
BOWDEN, ISAAC Pvt, E, 174th PA Inf, 8-13-1863. Sandy Ridge Cemetery, Sandy Ridge, Hunterdon County.
BOWDEN, JOHN Pvt, B, 38th NJ Inf, 6-7-1917. Holy Sepulchre Cemetery, East Orange, Essex County.
BOWDEN, JOHN T. Pvt, D, 11th MD Inf, 1920. 7th Day Baptist Church Cemetery, Shiloh, Cumberland County.
BOWDEN, PETER LEE Pvt, K, 2nd RI Inf, 1912. Prospect Hill Cemetery, Caldwell, Essex County.
BOWDEN, RICHARD A. Pvt, G, 38th NJ Inf, 4-8-1905. Rosemont Cemetery, Rosemont, Hunterdon County.

Our Brothers Gone Before

BOWE, MICHAEL Pvt, F, 177th NY Inf, 9-22-1913. Old St. Mary's Cemetery, Gloucester City, Camden County.

BOWE*, MICHAEL Pvt, B, 5th NJ Inf, 4-22-1884. Holy Name Cemetery, Jersey City, Hudson County.

BOWEN, BENJAMIN F. Pvt, I, 8th NJ Inf, 2-24-1893. Holy Name Cemetery, Jersey City, Hudson County.

BOWEN, DARIUS Pvt, H, 24th NJ Inf, DoD Unknown. Overlook Cemetery, Bridgeton, Cumberland County.

BOWEN, DAVID Pvt, F, 24th NJ Inf, 12-31-1923. Riverview Cemetery, Penns Grove, Salem County.

BOWEN, DAVID M. Pvt, F, 24th NJ Inf, 11-13-1919. Presbyterian Church Cemetery, Bridgeton, Cumberland County.

BOWEN, EDWARD Sgt, B, 47th NY Inf, 1898. Christ Church Cemetery, Belleville, Essex County.

BOWEN, FRANK Sgt, E, 22nd NJ Inf, 3-16-1914. Arlington Cemetery, Kearny, Hudson County.

BOWEN, FREDERICK Pvt, H, 24th NJ Inf, 4-8-1888. Presbyterian Church Cemetery, Bridgeton, Cumberland County.

BOWEN, GEORGE Pvt, I, 33rd NJ Inf, 4-15-1900. Cedar Green Cemetery, Clayton, Gloucester County.

BOWEN, GEORGE A. Capt, C, 12th NJ Inf, 3-26-1917. Presbyterian Church Cemetery, Bridgeton, Cumberland County.

BOWEN, GEORGE K. Lt Col, 188th PA Inf 10-23-1902. Morgan Cemetery, Cinnaminson, Burlington County.

BOWEN, GEORGE W. Sgt, H, 10th NJ Inf, 9-9-1923. Presbyterian Church Cemetery, Bridgeton, Cumberland County.

BOWEN, H. Pvt, G, 4th TN Cav (CSA), 1-5-1864. Finn's Point National Cemetery, Pennsville, Salem County.

BOWEN, ISAAC H. Pvt, H, 24th NJ Inf, 7-31-1884. Baptist Church Cemetery, Bridgeton, Cumberland County.

BOWEN, ISAAC S. 10-2-1896. United Methodist Church Cemetery, Smithville, Atlantic County.

BOWEN*, JOHN BUCK Surg, 34th NJ Inf [On staff of General Prince.] 12- -1888. Presbyterian Church Cemetery, Bridgeton, Cumberland County.

BOWEN, JOHN G. Corp, D, 10th NJ Inf, 8-21-1919. Friends Cemetery, Moorestown, Burlington County.

BOWEN, JOSIAH E. Pvt, E, 9th NJ Inf, 1885. Mount Pleasant Methodist Cemetery, Pleasantville, Atlantic County.

BOWEN, PURNEL Pvt, B, 25th NJ Inf, 5-6-1886. Mount Pleasant Methodist Cemetery, Pleasantville, Atlantic County.

BOWEN, WESLEY Pvt, D, 22nd IN Inf, 3-24-1899. United Methodist Church Cemetery, Smithville, Atlantic County.

BOWER, EPHRIAM V. 1st Sgt, E, 14th NJ Inf, 8-10-1899. Presbyterian Cemetery, Allentown, Monmouth County.

BOWER, FRANCIS Pvt, B, 11th OH Inf, 2-26-1867. Holy Sepulchre Cemetery, East Orange, Essex County.

BOWER, FREDERICK Pvt, K, 4th NJ Inf, 6-30-1919. New Camden Cemetery, Camden, Camden County.

BOWER, JOHN (aka: Brower, John) Pvt, H, 22nd NJ Inf, 4-15-1905. Brookside Cemetery, Englewood, Bergen County.

BOWER, JOHN (see: Bauer, John) Woodland Cemetery, Newark, Essex County.

BOWER, JOSEPH C. Pvt, K, 39th NJ Inf, 12-29-1903. Fairmount Cemetery, Chatham, Morris County.

New Jersey Civil War Burials

BOWER, JOSEPH H. Pvt, A, 5th NJ Inf, [Died at Fort Monroe, VA. of wounds received 5-5-1862 at Williamsburg, VA.] 5-17-1862. Baptist Church Cemetery, Haddonfield, Camden County.

BOWERBANK, __?__ 2-9-1923. Jersey City Cemetery, Jersey City, Hudson County.

BOWERS, ADAM (see: Bauer, Adam) Riverside Cemetery, Riverside, Burlington County.

BOWERS, ANDREW Q. Pvt, F, 14th NJ Inf, 1894. Baptist Cemetery, Pemberton, Burlington County.

BOWERS, BARZILLA P. (see: Dowers, Brizala) Princeton Cemetery, Princeton, Mercer County.

BOWERS, CHARLES Pvt, D, 35th NJ Inf, DoD Unknown. New Somerville Cemetery, Somerville, Somerset County.

BOWERS, CHARLES A. Sgt, E, 62nd NY Inf, 4-8-1920. Bayview-New York Bay Cemetery, Jersey City, Hudson County.

BOWERS, CHARLES F. Capt, F, 8th NJ Inf, 3-27-1889. Fairmount Cemetery, Newark, Essex County.

BOWERS, CHARLES S. Pvt, K, 22nd U.S. CT, 1-19-1877. Holy Name Cemetery, Jersey City, Hudson County.

BOWERS, ELIJAH Pvt, D, 48th NY Inf, 11-21-1934. Methodist Church Cemetery, Groveville, Mercer County.

BOWERS, EUGENE W. Landsman, U.S. Navy, USS Catskill, 7-15-1893. Cedar Grove Cemetery, Gloucester City, Camden County.

BOWERS*, GEORGE Pvt, F, 8th NJ Inf, 5-2-1913. Bordentown/Old St. Mary's Catholic Cemetery, Bordentown, Burlington County.

BOWERS, GEORGE Pvt, A, 34th NJ Inf, 8-29-1896. Oak Grove Cemetery, Hammonton, Atlantic County.

BOWERS, HARRY Pvt, D, 12th __ Inf, DoD Unknown. Evergreen Cemetery, Camden, Camden County.

BOWERS, ISAAC M. 3-10-1871. Fairview Cemetery, Fairview, Monmouth County.

BOWERS, JACOB (see: Bauer, Jacob) Weehawken Cemetery, North Bergen, Hudson County.

BOWERS, JACOB B. Pvt, B, 7th NJ Inf, 1-11-1892. Evergreen Cemetery, Camden, Camden County.

BOWERS*, JACOB G. Pvt, G, 8th NJ Inf, 6-30-1911. Manahath Cemetery, Glassboro, Gloucester County.

BOWERS, JAMES Sgt, H, 30th U.S. CT, 10-13-1900. Jacob's Chapel AME Church Cemetery, Colemantown, Burlington County.

BOWERS, JOHN Pvt, G, 52nd PA Inf, 5-21-1908. Bethel Cemetery, Pennsauken, Camden County.

BOWERS, JOHN Pvt, K, 1st NJ Inf, 1915. New Somerville Cemetery, Somerville, Somerset County.

BOWERS, JOHN Pvt, H, 29th NJ Inf, 10-19-1912. Reevestown Cemetery, Reevestown, Ocean County.

BOWERS, JOHN C. Pvt, G, 23rd NJ Inf, 9-16-1906. Monument Cemetery, Edgewater Park, Burlington County.

BOWERS, JOHN ZIEGLER (aka: Ziegler, John) Pvt, G, 12th NH Inf, 6-20-1884. Zion Methodist Church Cemetery, Bargaintown, Atlantic County.

BOWERS, JOSEPH Pvt, D, 38th NJ Inf, 1895. Methodist Church Cemetery, Groveville, Mercer County.

BOWERS, LEWIS Pvt, D, 2nd NJ Cav, 8-31-1893. Cedar Green Cemetery, Clayton, Gloucester County.

BOWERS, MARTIN Pvt, H, 38th NJ Inf, 9-11-1905. Arlington Cemetery, Kearny, Hudson County.

BOWERS, PAUL Pvt, D, 9th NJ Inf, 1926. Cedar Green Cemetery, Clayton, Gloucester County.

Our Brothers Gone Before

BOWERS, WILLIAM 1st Sgt, E, 1st NJ Militia, 8-24-1927. Arlington Cemetery, Kearny, Hudson County.

BOWERS, WILLIAM 1st Lt, G, 31st NJ Inf, 6-19-1916. Ramseyburg Cemetery, Ramseyburg, Warren County.

BOWERS, WILLIAM H. 10-25-1916. Methodist Church Cemetery, Groveville, Mercer County.

BOWERS, WILLIAM H. Pvt, PA Emerg NJ Light Art [Chapin's Battery.] 1925. Union Cemetery, Hope, Warren County.

BOWES, CHARLES M. Pvt, I, 69th NY State Militia, 9-5-1917. St. Nicholas Cemetery, Lodi, Bergen County.

BOWES, JOHN (aka: Bones, John) Sgt, I, 70th NY Inf, 12-3-1902. Holy Sepulchre Cemetery, Totowa, Passaic County.

BOWES, JOHN J. Pvt, I, 69th NY State Militia, DoD Unknown. St. Nicholas Cemetery, Lodi, Bergen County.

BOWES*, MICHAEL Pvt, I, 1st NJ Inf, 3-5-1906. Holy Name Cemetery, Jersey City, Hudson County.

BOWES, WILLIAM (see: Boe, William) Baptist Cemetery, South Plainfield, Middlesex County.

BOWKER, ALFRED D. Musc, D, 34th NJ Inf, 10-22-1909. Berlin Cemetery, Berlin, Camden County.

BOWKER, CHARLES P. (aka: Bowrer, Charles) QM Sgt, L, 15th PA Cav, 1-24-1916. Evergreen Cemetery, Camden, Camden County.

BOWKER, DANIEL Pvt, D, 34th NJ Inf, 11-17-1900. Methodist-Episcopal Cemetery, Pointville, Burlington County.

BOWKER, EARL P. Pvt, E, 2nd NJ Militia, DoD Unknown. Masonic Cemetery, Barnegat, Ocean County.

BOWKER, GARRAT Pvt, D, 34th NJ Inf, DoD Unknown. St. Mark's Baptist Church Cemetery, Browns Mills, Burlington County.

BOWKER, GEORGE W. Coal Heaver, U.S. Navy, USS Princeton, 1931. Oddfellows-Friends Cemetery, Medford, Burlington County.

BOWKER, JEROME L. Pvt, F, 25th NJ Inf, 11-25-1911. Methodist Church Cemetery, Goshen, Cape May County.

BOWKER, JONATHAN G. Corp, F, 23rd NJ Inf, 6-10-1907. Methodist Cemetery, Haddonfield, Camden County.

BOWKER, JOSEPH C. 1st Lt, D, 9th NJ Inf, 2-17-1908. Presbyterian Cemetery, Salem, Salem County.

BOWKER, JOSEPH F. Pvt, C, 34th NJ Inf, 3-9-1889. Baptist Cemetery, Vincentown, Burlington County.

BOWKER, LEVI Pvt, C, 34th NJ Inf, 8-20-1888. Methodist-Episcopal Cemetery, Vincentown, Burlington County.

BOWKER, LORENZO D. Pvt, F, 16th U.S. VRC, 2-24-1911. Oddfellows-Friends Cemetery, Medford, Burlington County.

BOWKER, URIAH Corp, C, 10th NJ Inf, 7-8-1890. Methodist-Episcopal Cemetery, Pointville, Burlington County.

BOWKER, WILLIAM H. Pvt, F, 23rd NJ Inf, 12-12-1886. Baptist Cemetery, Pemberton, Burlington County.

BOWKER, WILLIAM H. 4-2-1905. Methodist-Episcopal Cemetery, Vincentown, Burlington County.

BOWKER, WILLIAM R. (aka: Booker, William) Pvt, H, 37th NJ Inf, 2-7-1895. Methodist Cemetery, Crosswicks, Burlington County.

BOWLBY, EDGAR H. Pvt, D, 30th NJ Inf, [Died of convulsions at Washington, DC.] 2-6-1863. Presbyterian Church Cemetery, Hampton, Hunterdon County.

BOWLBY, ELISHA Pvt, H, 8th NJ Inf, 1928. Presbyterian Church Cemetery, Hampton, Hunterdon County.

New Jersey Civil War Burials

BOWLBY, HAMILTON Pvt, H, 8th NJ Inf, 2-23-1903. Presbyterian Church Cemetery, Hampton, Hunterdon County.

BOWLBY, LEVI H. 4-24-1906. Mansfield/Washington Cemetery, Washington, Warren County.

BOWLBY*, LUTHER C. Surg, 23rd NJ Inf [Also: Asst Surg,4th NJ Inf.] 10-15-1874. Union Cemetery, Washington, Morris County.

BOWLBY, STEWART Pvt, Btty B, 1st NJ Light Art, 5-27-1927. Presbyterian Church Cemetery, Hampton, Hunterdon County.

BOWLBY, STEWART C. 1878. Mansfield/Washington Cemetery, Washington, Warren County.

BOWLBY, WHITFIELD W. Pvt, B, 31st NJ Inf, DoD Unknown. Mansfield/Washington Cemetery, Washington, Warren County.

BOWLBY*, WHITFIELD W. Surg, 3rd NJ Cav [Also: Asst Surg, 26th NJ Inf, and Asst Surg, 2nd NJ Cav.] 9-11-1886. Union Cemetery, Washington, Morris County.

BOWLBY, WILLIAM M. Pvt, H, 8th NJ Inf, 4-10-1885. Presbyterian Church Cemetery, Hampton, Hunterdon County.

BOWLES, CHARLES (aka: Boules, Charles) 1st Sgt, B, 22nd U.S. CT, 6-10-1897. Mount Moriah Cemetery, Hainesport, Burlington County.

BOWLES, GEORGE H. (aka: Boyles, George) Pvt, B, 22nd U.S. CT, 1929. Pinebrook Cemetery, Macedonia, Monmouth County.

BOWLES, JAMES Pvt, B, 41st U.S. CT, 8-4-1916. Cedar View Cemetery, Lincroft, Monmouth County.

BOWLES, THOMAS F. (aka: Bolds, Thomas) Pvt, G, 127th U.S. CT, 1-4-1890. White Ridge Cemetery, Eatontown, Monmouth County.

BOWLIN, THOMAS (aka: Bolin, Thomas) Pvt, K, Hampton's Legion SC Inf (CSA), [Captured 10-29-1863 at Lookout Mountain, TN. Died of typhoid.] 7-28-1864. Finn's Point National Cemetery, Pennsville, Salem County.

BOWLING, DAVID Pvt, D, 45th VA Inf (CSA), [Captured 8-7-1864 at Hagerstown, MD. Died of pneumonia.] 2-18-1865. Finn's Point National Cemetery, Pennsville, Salem County.

BOWLSBY, GEORGE N. Pvt, B, 2nd NJ Cav, [Died of pleuritas at Memphis, TN.] 3-4-1864. Vail Presbyterian Cemetery, Parsippany, Morris County.

BOWMAN, ALEXANDER Landsman, U.S. Navy, 3-17-1923. Mount Peace Cemetery, Lawnside, Camden County.

BOWMAN, ANDREW Pvt, K, 30th NJ Inf, 3-20-1900. Cedar Hill Cemetery, East Millstone, Somerset County.

BOWMAN*, ANDREW W. Pvt, H, 39th NJ Inf, 3-28-1901. Prospect Hill Cemetery, Caldwell, Essex County.

BOWMAN*, CHARLES Pvt, E, 11th NJ Inf, [Wounded 7-2-1863 at Gettysburg, PA.] 4-12-1900. Eastview Cemetery, Salem, Salem County.

BOWMAN, CHARLES D.E. Pvt, G, 116th PA Inf, 5-28-1907. Soldier's Home Cemetery, Vineland, Cumberland County.

BOWMAN, FRANCIS E. Pvt, G, 29th NJ Inf, 6-3-1911. Old 1st Methodist Church Cemetery, West Long Branch, Monmouth County.

BOWMAN, ISAAC L. Pvt, D, 28th NJ Inf, [Wounded in action.] 12-7-1885. Van Liew Cemetery, North Brunswick, Middlesex County.

BOWMAN, JAMES Pvt, I, 55th NC Inf (CSA), [Captured 7-3-1863 at Gettysburg, PA. Died of diarrhea.] 9-17-1863. Finn's Point National Cemetery, Pennsville, Salem County.

BOWMAN, JAMES Capt, A, 30th NJ Inf, 6-19-1913. Reformed Church Cemetery, South Branch, Somerset County.

BOWMAN, JOHN Pvt, D, 12th NJ Inf, 2-28-1907. St. Paul's Methodist-Episcopal Church Cemetery, Thorofare, Gloucester County.

BOWMAN, JOHN 5-9-1891. Evergreen Cemetery, New Brunswick, Middlesex County.

Our Brothers Gone Before

BOWMAN, JOHN B. 6-26-1908. Prospect Hill Cemetery, Caldwell, Essex County.
BOWMAN, JOHN G. Pvt, I, 3rd NJ Inf, 3-13-1911. Berlin Cemetery, Berlin, Camden County.
BOWMAN, JONATHAN B. Pvt, D, 15th NJ Inf, 12-1-1897. Fairmount Cemetery, Newark, Essex County.
BOWMAN, JOSEPH Pvt, B, 27th NJ Inf, 4-17-1882. Presbyterian Church Cemetery, Pleasant Grove, Morris County.
BOWMAN, MARTIN Pvt, K, 7th MI Inf, [Died of disease at Newark, NJ.] 12-12-1862. Fairmount Cemetery, Newark, Essex County.
BOWMAN, OLIVER OTIS Pvt, A, 19th PA Militia, 12-5-1926. Riverview Cemetery, Trenton, Mercer County.
BOWMAN, WILLIAM Pvt, K, 50th VA Inf (CSA), [Captured 7-3-1863 at Gettysburg, PA.] 10-10-1863. Finn's Point National Cemetery, Pennsville, Salem County.
BOWMAN, WILLIAM (see: Cochran, William B.) Cedar Lawn Cemetery, Paterson, Passaic County.
BOWMAN, WILLIAM D.B. Pvt, B, 27th NJ Inf, 1-7-1899. Presbyterian Church Cemetery, Pleasant Grove, Morris County.
BOWMAN*, WILLIAM L. Pvt, B, 51st PA Inf, 4-12-1915. Hillside Cemetery, Scotch Plains, Union County.
BOWNE, CURTIS Pvt, K, 13th NJ Inf, [Died at Philadelphia, PA. of wounds received 9-17-1862 at Antietam, MD.] 3-13-1863. Cedar Lawn Cemetery, Paterson, Passaic County.
BOWNE, EDMUND C. (see: Bowne, Edward C.) Baptist Cemetery, Old Bridge, Middlesex County.
BOWNE, EDWARD Pvt, D, 29th NJ Inf, 1-26-1923. Fairview Cemetery, Fairview, Monmouth County.
BOWNE, EDWARD C. (aka: Bowne, Edmund C.) Pvt, H, 28th NJ Inf, DoD Unknown. Baptist Cemetery, Old Bridge, Middlesex County.
BOWNE, EMANUEL K. Pvt, B, 38th NJ Inf, DoD Unknown. Holcomb-Riverview Cemetery, Lambertville, Hunterdon County.
BOWNE, GEORGE A. Capt, M, 1st NJ Cav, 7-12-1922. Fairview Cemetery, Fairview, Monmouth County.
BOWNE, GEORGE W. Landsman, U.S. Navy, USS North Carolina, 12-26-1905. United Methodist Church Cemetery, Windsor, Mercer County.
BOWNE, JAMES D. Pvt, C, 1st NJ Inf, 3-11-1920. Fernwood Cemetery, Jamesburg, Middlesex County.
BOWNE, JOHN R. Pvt, I, 6th NY Cav, 2-20-1912. Fairmount Cemetery, Newark, Essex County.
BOWNE, THEODORE (aka: Bound, Theodore) Pvt, E, 21st NJ Inf, 8-20-1892. Greenwood Cemetery, Hamilton, Mercer County.
BOWNE, WILLIAM Corp, H, 128th NY Inf, 9-6-1881. Fairview Cemetery, Fairview, Monmouth County.
BOWRER, CHARLES (see: Bowker, Charles P.) Evergreen Cemetery, Camden, Camden County.
BOYAR, JOHN H. Pvt, H, 30th U.S. CT, 4-1-1896. Johnson Cemetery, Camden, Camden County.
BOYCE, HOLMES C. Pvt, D, 38th NJ Inf, 1922. Rose Hill Cemetery, Matawan, Monmouth County.
BOYCE, MARTIN Pvt, G, 22nd NJ Inf, 9-15-1900. Dutch Reformed Church Cemetery, Spotswood, Middlesex County.
BOYCE, MATTHIAS A. Pvt, E, 29th NJ Inf, 6-30-1887. Cedarwood Cemetery, Hazlet, Monmouth County.
BOYCE, MOSES M. 2nd Lt, C, 12th NY Cav, 7-15-1891. Siloam Cemetery, Vineland, Cumberland County.

New Jersey Civil War Burials

BOYD, AUGUSTUS Corp, H, 9th NJ Inf, 1-9-1908. Union Cemetery, Washington, Morris County.
BOYD, CHARLES S. 2nd Lt, C, 4th NJ Inf, 11-23-1901. Riverview Cemetery, Trenton, Mercer County.
BOYD, GEORGE 4-14-1893. Hillside Cemetery, Scotch Plains, Union County.
BOYD, GEORGE E. 8-27-1931. Bayview-New York Bay Cemetery, Jersey City, Hudson County.
BOYD, JAMES Pvt, B, 22nd NJ Inf, DoD Unknown. Cedar Lawn Cemetery, Paterson, Passaic County.
BOYD, JAMES L. Pvt, B, 31st NJ Inf, 1925. Mansfield/Washington Cemetery, Washington, Warren County.
BOYD, JOHN HOOK Pvt, A, 1st NY Cav, 7-12-1915. East Ridgelawn Cemetery, Clifton, Passaic County.
BOYD, JOHN S. 8-7-1900. Riverview Cemetery, Penns Grove, Salem County.
BOYD, JOHN W. Pvt, F, 95th PA Inf, 7-25-1883. Methodist Cemetery, Haddonfield, Camden County.
BOYD*, MATTHEW Pvt, A, 39th NJ Inf, 7-2-1901. Newton Cemetery, Newton, Sussex County.
BOYD, RANDOLPH Pvt, A, 6th AL Inf (CSA), [Captured at Gettysburg, PA. Died of typhoid.] 11-30-1863. Finn's Point National Cemetery, Pennsville, Salem County.
BOYD, ROBERT Pvt, B, 8th NJ Inf, 10-13-1866. Mount Pleasant Cemetery, Newark, Essex County.
BOYD, THOMAS J. Pvt, G, 42nd MS Inf (CSA), 10-20-1863. Finn's Point National Cemetery, Pennsville, Salem County.
BOYD, THOMAS S. Pvt, B, 27th NJ Inf, 7-20-1919. Chestnut Cemetery, Dover, Morris County.
BOYD*, WILLIAM B. Seaman, U.S. Navy, USS Moccasin, 7-14-1888. Evergreen Cemetery, New Brunswick, Middlesex County.
BOYD, WILLIAM W. Saddler, A, 1st NY Cav, 8-10-1913. United Methodist Church Cemetery, Millbrook, Morris County.
BOYDE, WILLIAM A. Pvt, C, 1st MA Cav, 7-29-1865. Old Camden Cemetery, Camden, Camden County.
BOYDELL, JOHN Pvt, G, 11th PA Cav, 1-19-1895. Riverview Cemetery, Trenton, Mercer County.
BOYDEN, OBADIAH S. Corp, K, 2nd NJ Inf, 12-8-1907. Mount Pleasant Cemetery, Newark, Essex County.
BOYER*, BENJAMIN FRANKLIN 2nd Lt, F, 202nd PA Inf, 1-3-1908. Harleigh Cemetery, Camden, Camden County.
BOYER*, CHARLES W. Pvt, C, 5th PA Cav, 1915. Alpine Cemetery, Perth Amboy, Middlesex County.
BOYER, EDWARD Pvt, C, 100th PA Inf, 5-7-1927. Old Camden Cemetery, Camden, Camden County.
BOYER, ELISHA (aka: Boger, Elisha) Pvt, F, 1st NJ Cav, 12-19-1898. Baptist Cemetery, Pemberton, Burlington County.
BOYER, HENRY Pvt, H, 127th U.S. CT, 1-9-1911. New Somerville Cemetery, Somerville, Somerset County.
BOYER, ISAAC Pvt, K, 8th U.S. CT, 6-26-1913. Spencer African Methodist Church Cemetery, Woodstown, Salem County.
BOYER, SAMUEL Pvt, D, 7th PA Cav, 7-21-1899. Fairmount Cemetery, Newark, Essex County.
BOYER, WILLIAM H. Pvt, E, 29th CT Inf, 7-8-1901. AME Cemetery, Pennington, Mercer County.
BOYET, W.H. Pvt, F, 35th MS Inf (CSA), 9-10-1863. Finn's Point National Cemetery, Pennsville, Salem County.

Our Brothers Gone Before

BOYETT, G.A. Pvt, I, 47th NC Inf (CSA), [Wounded 7-1-1863 and captured 7-5-1863 at Gettysburg, PA.] 10-1-1863. Finn's Point National Cemetery, Pennsville, Salem County.

BOYINGTON, AARON (see: Byington, Aaron H.) New Somerville Cemetery, Somerville, Somerset County.

BOYKIN, JOHN E. Pvt, A, 2nd SC Cav (CSA), [Captured 7-17-1863 at Martinsburg, WV.] 3-23-1864. Finn's Point National Cemetery, Pennsville, Salem County.

BOYLAN*, EDWARD Pvt, F, 33rd NJ Inf, 7-20-1881. Holy Sepulchre Cemetery, East Orange, Essex County.

BOYLAN, PATRICK Pvt, D, 6th NJ Inf, 3-3-1884. Old St. Mary's Cemetery, Gloucester City, Camden County.

BOYLAN, PATRICK J. Pvt, D, 2nd U.S. Inf, 3-6-1912. Holy Sepulchre Cemetery, East Orange, Essex County.

BOYLE, ANDREW Pvt, D, 4th NJ Inf, 11-14-1910. St. Paul's R.C. Church Cemetery, Princeton, Mercer County.

BOYLE, CHARLES JOHN Pvt, A, 71st NY Inf, DoD Unknown. Holy Sepulchre Cemetery, East Orange, Essex County.

BOYLE, CORNELIUS DoD Unknown. Woodlands Cemetery, Ocean View, Cape May County.

BOYLE, JAMES Pvt, D, 72nd PA Inf, 4-27-1915. Evergreen Cemetery, Camden, Camden County.

BOYLE, JAMES Pvt, G, 24th NJ Inf, 1918. Mount Pleasant Cemetery, Millville, Cumberland County.

BOYLE, JOHN Seaman, U.S. Navy, 5-15-1892. St. Peter's Cemetery, New Brunswick, Middlesex County.

BOYLE, JOHN (see: Boyne, John) Holy Name Cemetery, Jersey City, Hudson County.

BOYLE, JOHN H. Pvt, K, 69th NY State Militia, 1905. Bayview-New York Bay Cemetery, Jersey City, Hudson County.

BOYLE*, JOHN T. Pvt, G, 8th NJ Inf, 2-27-1905. Fairview Cemetery, Fairview, Bergen County.

BOYLE, JOHN T. 7-11-1900. Old Camden Cemetery, Camden, Camden County.

BOYLE, MICHAEL Pvt, D, 4th NJ Inf, 7-17-1871. St. Paul's R.C. Church Cemetery, Princeton, Mercer County.

BOYLE, PATRICK Pvt, B, 155th NY Inf, 10-30-1900. St. Peter's Cemetery, New Brunswick, Middlesex County.

BOYLE, ROBERT R. Pvt, A, 3rd NJ Inf, 12-23-1897. Evergreen Cemetery, Hillside, Union County.

BOYLE, THOMAS Pvt, F, 1st NJ Inf, 5-16-1893. Holy Sepulchre Cemetery, East Orange, Essex County.

BOYLE, THOMAS Pvt, G, 10th NJ Inf, 5-10-1888. Mount Olivet Cemetery, Newark, Essex County.

BOYLE, WILLIAM COOPER Sgt, B, 30th NJ Inf, 9-2-1900. Evergreen Cemetery, Hillside, Union County.

BOYLES, GEORGE (see: Bowles, George H.) Pinebrook Cemetery, Macedonia, Monmouth County.

BOYNE*, JOHN (aka: Boyle, John) Corp, C, 120th NY Inf, [Wounded 6-1-1862 at Fair Oaks, VA. and 11-5-1864 at Halifax Plank Road, VA.] 5-21-1903. Holy Name Cemetery, Jersey City, Hudson County.

BOZARTH*, ANDREW J. Pvt, G, 7th NJ Inf, 2-1-1903. Union Cemetery, Clarkstown, Atlantic County.

BOZARTH, BENJAMIN Pvt, I, 5th NJ Inf, 3-1-1920. Baptist/St. Andrew's Cemetery, Mount Holly, Burlington County.

BOZARTH, CHARLES 1923. Woodland Cemetery, Chatsworth, Burlington County.

New Jersey Civil War Burials

BOZARTH, CHARLES Pvt, L, 2nd NJ Cav, [Wounded in action.] 7-22-1924. Methodist-Episcopal Cemetery, Green Bank, Burlington County.

BOZARTH, CHARLES L. Pvt, I, 5th NJ Inf, [Died of typhoid at Washington, DC.] 6-21-1864. Baptist Cemetery, Medford, Burlington County.

BOZARTH, DAVID Pvt, U.S. Marine Corps, 8-14-1886. Evergreen Cemetery, Camden, Camden County.

BOZARTH, JEREMIAH (aka: Bozure, Jeremiah) Pvt, E, 23rd NJ Inf, 7-22-1889. Baptist Cemetery, Pemberton, Burlington County.

BOZARTH, JOHN C. 10-21-1880. Old Presbyterian Cemetery, Lakehurst, Ocean County.

BOZARTH, JOSEPH (aka: Bozearth, John) Corp, F, 110th PA Inf, 12-3-1907. Oddfellows Cemetery, Pemberton, Burlington County.

BOZARTH*, JOSEPH M. (aka: Bozearth, John) Corp, F, 110th PA Inf, 12-21-1900. Evergreen Cemetery, Camden, Camden County.

BOZARTH, MARK L. Pvt, F, 14th NJ Inf, 1920. Roadside Cemetery, Manchester Township, Ocean County.

BOZARTH, SAMUEL F. Corp, I, 5th NJ Inf, 3-22-1880. Baptist Cemetery, Medford, Burlington County.

BOZARTH, WILLIAM Pvt, E, 10th NJ Inf, 11-22-1895. Mount Pleasant Methodist Cemetery, Pleasantville, Atlantic County.

BOZARTH, WILLIAM Pvt, F, 23rd NJ Inf, 9-26-1902. St. Mark's Baptist Church Cemetery, Browns Mills, Burlington County.

BOZARTH, WILLIAM A. Pvt, H, 10th NJ Inf, [Died at Trenton, NJ.] 5-22-1864. Batsto/Pleasant Mills Methodist Church Cemetery, Pleasant Mills, Atlantic County.

BOZARTH*, WILLIAM HENRY Pvt, F, 15th NJ Inf, 7-15-1919. Baptist Cemetery, Pemberton, Burlington County.

BOZE, CHARLES S. Pvt, K, 22nd U.S. CT, 8-18-1875. Union Bethel Cemetery, Erma, Cape May County.

BOZEARTH, JOHN (see: Bozarth, Joseph) Oddfellows Cemetery, Pemberton, Burlington County.

BOZEARTH, JOHN (see: Bozarth, Joseph M.) Evergreen Cemetery, Camden, Camden County.

BOZENBERRY, HALLOWAY W. (see: Bosenbery, Holloway W.) United Methodist Church Cemetery, Pattenburg, Hunterdon County.

BOZEYER, SAMUEL (see: Boshier, Samuel) Good Luck Cemetery, Murray Grove, Ocean County.

BOZIER, HENRY C. Pvt, K, 91st PA Inf, 2-20-1906. Presbyterian Church Cemetery, Bridgeton, Cumberland County.

BOZURE, JEREMIAH (see: Bozarth, Jeremiah) Baptist Cemetery, Pemberton, Burlington County.

BRABBIN, MOSES Pvt, F, 1st NJ Inf, 3-17-1901. Fairmount Cemetery, Newark, Essex County.

BRABHAM, WILLIAM Pvt, I, 2nd VA Inf (CSA), [Captured 7-28-1863 at Harper's Ferry, WV. Died of diarrhea.] 5-15-1864. Finn's Point National Cemetery, Pennsville, Salem County.

BRACE, ALFRED S. 1897. Riverview Cemetery, Trenton, Mercer County.

BRACKEN, CHRISTOPHER (see: Smith, William) Fairview Cemetery, Fairview, Monmouth County.

BRACKEN, JAMES Pvt, G, 39th NJ Inf, 9-25-1904. Rosedale Cemetery, Orange, Essex County.

BRACKEN*, JAMES B. Seaman, U.S. Navy, USS Savannah, DoD Unknown. Rosedale Cemetery, Orange, Essex County.

BRACKEN, JAMES F. Pvt, Btty E, 1st NJ Light Art, 10-12-1925. Holy Name Cemetery, Jersey City, Hudson County.

Our Brothers Gone Before

BRACKEN, JOHN (see: Brocken, John) Holy Sepulchre Cemetery, East Orange, Essex County.

BRADA, GEORGE W. Pvt, B, 2nd NJ Cav, 10-30-1900. Bayview-New York Bay Cemetery, Jersey City, Hudson County.

BRADBURY, JONATHAN 1888. Presbyterian Church Cemetery, Andover, Sussex County.

BRADBURY, LOUIS Pvt, C, 5th NJ Inf, 2-3-1907. Bayview-New York Bay Cemetery, Jersey City, Hudson County.

BRADDOCK, ISAAC A. Pvt, A, MD Emerg NJ Militia, 1913. Baptist Church Cemetery, Haddonfield, Camden County.

BRADDOCK, WILLIAM D. Pvt, H, 25th NJ Inf, 10-19-1921. Preakness Reformed Church Cemetery, Wayne, Passaic County.

BRADEN, WILLIAM Seaman, U.S. Navy, 1-17-1880. Evergreen Cemetery, Hillside, Union County.

BRADENBACH, WILLIAM Pvt, I, 10th NJ Inf, 8-24-1880. Holy Sepulchre Cemetery, East Orange, Essex County.

BRADFIELD*, GEORGE E. Pvt, H, 11th MD Inf, [Accidently killed.] 5-29-1865. Finn's Point National Cemetery, Pennsville, Salem County.

BRADFORD, DAVID C. Pvt, B, 9th NJ Inf, 7-11-1897. Methodist Church Cemetery, Juliustown, Burlington County.

BRADFORD, ELBERT Pvt, F, 37th NJ Inf, 4-20-1895. Baptist Church Cemetery, Bridgeton, Cumberland County.

BRADFORD, GEORGE DoD Unknown. Presbyterian Church Cemetery, Metuchen, Middlesex County.

BRADFORD, GEORGE (see: Radford, George S.) Presbyterian Church Cemetery, Westfield, Union County.

BRADFORD*, GEORGE H. Pvt, I, 14th NJ Inf, [Wounded in action.] 7-15-1909. Elmwood Cemetery, New Brunswick, Middlesex County.

BRADFORD, HENRY H. Pvt, K, 12th NJ Inf, 3-20-1909. New Camden Cemetery, Camden, Camden County.

BRADFORD, JOHN W. Corp, H, 10th NJ Inf, 3-19-1909. Fairmount Cemetery, Newark, Essex County.

BRADFORD, JOSEPH Fireman, U.S. Navy, USS Miantonomah, 1-20-1911. Oak Hill Cemetery, Vineland, Cumberland County.

BRADFORD, JOSEPH C. Pvt, D, 25th NJ Inf, 3-13-1900. Bateman Memorial Cemetery, Newport, Cumberland County.

BRADFORD*, PETER Sgt, Btty M, 11th U.S. CHA, 5-17-1899. Laurel Grove Cemetery, Totowa, Passaic County.

BRADFORD, RICHARD J. Corp, B, 37th NJ Inf, 7-22-1876. Presbyterian Church Cemetery, Shrewsbury, Monmouth County.

BRADFORD*, WILLIAM S. Corp, F, 8th NJ Inf, [Died of diarrhea at Newark, NJ.] 10-24-1864. Methodist-Episcopal Church Cemetery, Aura, Gloucester County.

BRADFORD, WILLIAM S. Pvt, F, 8th NJ Inf, 12-9-1895. Arlington Cemetery, Kearny, Hudson County.

BRADLEY, ALBERT Pvt, E, 13th NJ Inf, [Wounded at Antietam, MD.] 2-7-1875. Rosedale Cemetery, Orange, Essex County.

BRADLEY, BERNARD Pvt, E, 34th NJ Inf, 4-25-1866. Cedar Lawn Cemetery, Paterson, Passaic County.

BRADLEY, HUGH Pvt, K, 40th NJ Inf, 2-1-1890. St. Peter's Cemetery, New Brunswick, Middlesex County.

BRADLEY, ISAAC (see: Beakley, Isaac H.) Mount Pleasant Cemetery, Millville, Cumberland County.

BRADLEY*, J. Pvt, Clinch's GA Light Art (CSA) 4-22-1865. Finn's Point National Cemetery, Pennsville, Salem County.

New Jersey Civil War Burials

BRADLEY, JAMES Pvt, D, 6th NJ Inf, 4-23-1886. Holy Sepulchre Cemetery, East Orange, Essex County.

BRADLEY, JAMES Artificer, A, 15th NY Eng, 5-11-1911. St. John's Cemetery, Hamilton, Mercer County.

BRADLEY*, JAMES Pvt, C, 1st Bttn MA Cav, 4-23-1886. Evergreen Cemetery, Hillside, Union County.

BRADLEY, JOHN __, __, __ NY Art, DoD Unknown. St. Joseph's Cemetery, Hackensack, Bergen County.

BRADLEY, JOHN Pvt, F, 37th NJ Inf, 2-2-1892. St. John's Cemetery, Hamilton, Mercer County.

BRADLEY, JOHN H. Pvt, D, 3rd NJ Cav, 3-14-1910. Laurel Grove Cemetery, Totowa, Passaic County.

BRADLEY, JOSEPH ABRAM Pvt, D, 22nd NJ Inf, 10-20-1900. Little Zion Methodist Cemetery, Upper Saddle River, Bergen County.

BRADLEY, MARTIN Pvt, I, 4th NJ Inf, 12-31-1881. St. Mary's Cemetery, Hainesport, Burlington County.

BRADLEY, MICHAEL Pvt, K, 7th NJ Inf, [Wounded in action.] 12-3-1867. St. Peter's Cemetery, New Brunswick, Middlesex County.

BRADLEY, ROBERT C. Pvt, D, 28th NJ Inf, 12-11-1935. Whitelawn Cemetery, Point Pleasant, Ocean County.

BRADLEY, ROBERT K. Pvt, Ahl's Btty, DE Heavy Art, 9-25-1863. Finn's Point National Cemetery, Pennsville, Salem County.

BRADLEY, THOMAS Pvt, G, 13th NJ Inf, 7-23-1886. Fairmount Cemetery, Newark, Essex County.

BRADLEY*, THOMAS Pvt, C, 2nd NJ Inf, 8-10-1874. St. Peter's Cemetery, New Brunswick, Middlesex County.

BRADLEY, WILLIAM H. Pvt, D, 28th NJ Inf, [Wounded in action.] 1918. Whitelawn Cemetery, Point Pleasant, Ocean County.

BRADSHAW*, ALBERT MORRIS Capt, U.S. Volunteers, [Acting Quartermaster.] 9-3-1915. Evergreen Cemetery, Lakewood, Ocean County.

BRADSHAW*, GEORGE W. Pvt, G, 2nd NJ Inf, 4-17-1903. Fairmount Cemetery, Newark, Essex County.

BRADSHAW, JAMES Pvt, H, 16th VA Cav (CSA), 3-22-1865. Finn's Point National Cemetery, Pennsville, Salem County.

BRADSHAW*, JAMES W. Pvt, K, 1st NJ Militia, 5-23-1915. Arlington Cemetery, Kearny, Hudson County.

BRADSHAW, WILLIAM M. Pvt, C, 11th NY Inf, 10-14-1896. Fairmount Cemetery, Newark, Essex County.

BRADSHAW, WILLIAM R. Seaman, U.S. Navy, USS Colorado, 1-25-1893. Fairmount Cemetery, Newark, Essex County.

BRADSHAW, WILSON Pvt, E, 4th NC Cav (CSA), 12-6-1863. Finn's Point National Cemetery, Pennsville, Salem County.

BRADT, SEBASTIAN (aka: Brath, Sebastian) Pvt, H, 6th NY Cav, [Wounded 8-13-1864 at Berryville, VA.] 4-12-1896. Bayview-New York Bay Cemetery, Jersey City, Hudson County.

BRADWAY, AARON R. (aka: Broadway, Aaron) Pvt, G, 24th NJ Inf, 1924. Presbyterian Church Cemetery, Bridgeton, Cumberland County.

BRADWAY, CHARLES H. Pvt, C, 24th NJ Inf, 5-25-1877. Baptist Cemetery, Salem, Salem County.

BRADWAY, EDWARD G. Musc, I, 12th NJ Inf, 10-10-1914. Presbyterian Church Cemetery, Bridgeton, Cumberland County.

BRADWAY, J. THOMAS DoD Unknown. Old Camden Cemetery, Camden, Camden County.

Our Brothers Gone Before

BRADWAY, JOHN P. Pvt, A, 19th PA Inf, 3-6-1908. Zion United Methodist Church Cemetery, Clarksboro, Gloucester County.
BRADWAY, JOSEPH S. Corp, C, 24th NJ Inf, 7-7-1918. 1st Baptist Church Cemetery, Woodstown, Salem County.
BRADY, ABNER Pvt, F, 33rd NJ Inf, 12-24-1885. Mount Pleasant Cemetery, Newark, Essex County.
BRADY, ANDREW Pvt, F, 26th NJ Inf, 12-16-1910. Mount Olivet Cemetery, Bloomfield, Essex County.
BRADY, CHARLES 11-10-1921. St. Nicholas Cemetery, Lodi, Bergen County.
BRADY, FRANK Musc, G, 39th NJ Inf, 6-28-1898. Lady of Lourdes/Holy Sepulchre Cemetery, Hamilton, Mercer County.
BRADY, GARRETT Capt, C, 2nd NJ Inf, [Wounded in action.] 7-18-1886. Holy Sepulchre Cemetery, East Orange, Essex County.
BRADY*, GEORGE W. Pvt, I, 35th NJ Inf, 4-13-1897. New Dutch Reformed/Neshanic Cemetery, Neshanic, Somerset County.
BRADY, HUGH Pvt, C, 3rd NJ Cav, 12-15-1910. Arlington Cemetery, Kearny, Hudson County.
BRADY, HUGH Pvt, I, 31st NY Inf, 7-3-1900. Mount Olivet Cemetery, Newark, Essex County.
BRADY, JAMES Sgt, E, 71st NY Inf, 3-28-1878. St. John's Evangelical Church Cemetery, Orange, Essex County.
BRADY, JAMES Bvt Col, 1st PA Light Art 1911. Mount Calvary Cemetery, Mount Calvary, Atlantic County.
BRADY, JAMES Pvt, Btty F, 4th NY Heavy Art, 12-25-1898. St. Mary's Cemetery, Hamilton, Mercer County.
BRADY, JAMES Pvt, I, 80th NY Inf, [Wounded 8-30-1862 at Manassas, VA.] 8-11-1863. St. Mary's Cemetery, South Amboy, Middlesex County.
BRADY, JOHN H. Corp, D, 5th NJ Inf, 3-3-1892. Baptist Cemetery, South Plainfield, Middlesex County.
BRADY*, JOSEPH Pvt, A, 10th ME Inf, 7-26-1897. Old St. Mary's Cemetery, Gloucester City, Camden County.
BRADY, JOSEPH H. Musc, E, 28th NJ Inf, 8-31-1914. Eglington Cemetery, Clarksboro, Gloucester County.
BRADY, LEVI S. Pvt, E, 153rd PA Inf, [Wounded 7-2-1863 at Gettysburg, PA.] 2-24-1887. Greenwood Cemetery, Hamilton, Mercer County.
BRADY, MICHAEL Pvt, D, 5th NJ Inf, 1-27-1901. Prospect Hill Cemetery, Caldwell, Essex County.
BRADY, NICHOLAS Pvt, D, 4th NJ Militia, 4-10-1871. Old St. Mary's Cemetery, Gloucester City, Camden County.
BRADY, PETER Pvt, B, 1st NJ Cav, 3-8-1879. Holy Sepulchre Cemetery, East Orange, Essex County.
BRADY, PHILIP Sgt, A, 40th NJ Inf, 4-23-1900. Reformed Church Cemetery, Pluckemin, Somerset County.
BRADY*, PHILIP Pvt, L, 1st NY Prov Cav, 1-12-1921. Mount Olivet Cemetery, Newark, Essex County.
BRADY, PHILIP Pvt, F, 30th NJ Inf, DoD Unknown. New Somerville Cemetery, Somerville, Somerset County.
BRADY, S.D. Pvt, F, 6th VA Cav (CSA), 4-20-1865. Finn's Point National Cemetery, Pennsville, Salem County.
BRADY, SILAS F. Pvt, Ind, Weaver's PA Militia, DoD Unknown. Egg Harbor Cemetery, Egg Harbor, Atlantic County.
BRADY, TERRENCE (CSA) DoD Unknown. Holy Name Cemetery, Jersey City, Hudson County.

New Jersey Civil War Burials

BRADY, THOMAS Pvt, Btty A, 1st MI Light Art, 12-12-1918. Arlington Cemetery, Kearny, Hudson County.

BRADY, THOMAS Pvt, Btty D, 1st NJ Light Art, 7-19-1895. Mount Olivet Cemetery, Newark, Essex County.

BRADY, THOMAS Pvt, B, 35th NJ Inf, 4-8-1873. Holy Sepulchre Cemetery, East Orange, Essex County.

BRADY, THOMAS T.C. Pvt, E, 153rd PA Inf, 1909. Greenwood Cemetery, Hamilton, Mercer County.

BRADY, WILLIAM Pvt, K, 38th PA Militia, 5-12-1888. Greenwood Cemetery, Hamilton, Mercer County.

BRADY, WILLIAM E. Pvt, F, 2nd NJ Inf, 4-29-1908. Holy Sepulchre Cemetery, East Orange, Essex County.

BRAEZLION, ARMAND (aka: Bressillon, Armand) Pvt, B, 3rd NJ Inf, 1908. New Camden Cemetery, Camden, Camden County.

BRAGDON, EUGENE Pvt, E, 11th ME Inf, [Died of wounds received 8-16-1864 at Deep Run, VA.] 8-27-1864. Beverly National Cemetery, Edgewater Park, Burlington County.

BRAGG, GEORGE H. Pvt, K, 23rd NJ Inf, 6-8-1899. Greenwood Cemetery, Tuckerton, Ocean County.

BRAGG, GEORGE L. 1st Lt, 8th PA Cav [Commissary of Subsistance. Killed in action at Deep Bottom, VA.] 8-16-1864. Mercer Cemetery, Trenton, Mercer County.

BRAGG, JOHN Pvt, F, 40th NJ Inf, 1919. Congregational Church Cemetery, Chester, Morris County.

BRAGG*, WILLIAM Corp, G, 8th NJ Inf, [Wounded in action.] 7-3-1907. Riverview Cemetery, Trenton, Mercer County.

BRAGG, WILLIAM M. Pvt, B, 43rd Bttn VA Cav (CSA), 3-26-1865. Finn's Point National Cemetery, Pennsville, Salem County.

BRAGGA*, CAMILLO (aka: Bragge, Camelia) Pvt, B, 48th NY Inf, [Wounded at Deep Bottom, VA.] 2-5-1915. Evergreen Cemetery, Hillside, Union County.

BRAGGE, CAMELIA (see: Bragga, Camillo) Evergreen Cemetery, Hillside, Union County.

BRAHM, WILLIAM Pvt, C, 6th NY State Militia, 3-1-1868. Berry Lawn Cemetery, Carlstadt, Bergen County.

BRAHN, EDWARD (see: Brandt, Edward) Methodist-Episcopal Cemetery, Glendola, Monmouth County.

BRAIDER, SIMON Sgt, I, 31st NJ Inf, 8-1-1917. Presbyterian Church Cemetery, New Providence, Union County.

BRAINARD, EDWARD (see: Bennard, Edward) Johnson Cemetery, Camden, Camden County.

BRAINARD, EDWARD F. Pvt, E, 8th NY National Guard, 2-4-1907. Cedar Lawn Cemetery, Paterson, Passaic County.

BRAISTED, GARRETT V. Pvt, K, 8th NJ Inf, 5-30-1894. Woodlawn Cemetery, Lakewood, Ocean County.

BRAISTED, GEORGE Corp, K, 8th NJ Inf, 8-11-1901. Bayview-New York Bay Cemetery, Jersey City, Hudson County.

BRAKELEY, ASHER 5-26-1911. Bordentown/Old St. Mary's Catholic Cemetery, Bordentown, Burlington County.

BRAMBLE, SAMUEL F. Corp, K, 12th NJ Inf, 6-27-1903. Baptist Church Cemetery, Canton, Salem County.

BRAMELL, WILLIAM B. Pvt, Ind, PA Militia, 5-28-1893. Methodist-Episcopal Church Cemetery, South Dennis, Cape May County.

BRAMHALL, WILLIAM 1st Lt, 6th NY Ind Btty 12-28-1913. Rahway Cemetery, Rahway, Union County.

Our Brothers Gone Before

BRAMMER, JOHN Pvt, A, 115th OH Inf, 1-22-1890. Riverview Cemetery, Trenton, Mercer County.
BRAMPTON, JOHN G. 5-16-1879. New Presbyterian Cemetery, Bound Brook, Somerset County.
BRAMPTON, ROBERT T. Landsman, U.S. Navy, USS Savannah, 8-5-1914. New Presbyterian Cemetery, Bound Brook, Somerset County.
BRANAGAN, FELIX W. 1st Sgt, B, 8th NJ Inf, 4-1-1892. Holy Sepulchre Cemetery, East Orange, Essex County.
BRAND, CHARLES M. Pvt, G, 9th MI Inf, 1922. Old 1st Methodist Church Cemetery, West Long Branch, Monmouth County.
BRAND*, FREDERICK Sgt, G, 9th NJ Inf, 3-2-1900. Fairmount Cemetery, Newark, Essex County.
BRAND, JAMES Pvt, E, 35th NJ Inf, 3-28-1889. Como Methodist Protestant Cemetery, Spring Lake, Monmouth County.
BRAND, OTTO (see: Brandt, Otto) Fairmount Cemetery, Newark, Essex County.
BRAND, ROBERT E. Landsman, U.S. Navy, USS Princeton, 10-11-1909. Mount Pleasant Cemetery, Newark, Essex County.
BRAND, WILLIAM O. Seaman, U.S. Navy, USS Rhode Island, 10-9-1921. Clinton Cemetery, Irvington, Essex County.
BRANDENSTEIN, GEORGE Pvt, H, 98th PA Inf, 4-10-1890. Evergreen Cemetery, Camden, Camden County.
BRANDER, FREDERICK Pvt, G, 9th NJ Inf, 4-16-1882. Fairmount Cemetery, Newark, Essex County.
BRANDES*, FREDERICK Pvt, H, 56th NY National Guard, 4-2-1915. Hoboken Cemetery, North Bergen, Hudson County.
BRANDIES, AUGUSTE Pvt, Btty A, 1st NJ Light Art, 5-17-1909. Rosedale Cemetery, Orange, Essex County.
BRANDIFF, AARON Pvt, C, 24th NJ Inf, 3-5-1903. 1st United Methodist Church Cemetery, Salem, Salem County.
BRANDON, JAMES C. Pvt, B, 4th NC Cav (CSA), [Captured 7-4-1863 at South Mountain, MD. Died of disease.] 10-3-1863. Finn's Point National Cemetery, Pennsville, Salem County.
BRANDON, MATTHEW H. 6-13-1907. Hillside Cemetery, Scotch Plains, Union County.
BRANDRETH, THOMAS L. Musc, H, 51st NY Inf, 9-3-1913. Prospect Hill Cemetery, Caldwell, Essex County.
BRANDRIFF, JOHN Corp, B, 10th NJ Inf, DoD Unknown. Mount Pleasant Cemetery, Millville, Cumberland County.
BRANDS, ORESTES M. Pvt, D, 8th NJ Inf, 3-18-1926. Laurel Grove Cemetery, Totowa, Passaic County.
BRANDT, EDWARD (aka: Brahn, Edward) Pvt, K, 29th NJ Inf, 12-3-1897. Methodist-Episcopal Cemetery, Glendola, Monmouth County.
BRANDT, HARVEY (see: Brunt, Harvey) Hazelwood Cemetery, Rahway, Union County.
BRANDT, HEINRICH (see: Brandt, Henry) Evergreen Cemetery, Hillside, Union County.
BRANDT, HENRY (aka: Brandt, Heinrich) 2nd Lt, I, 25th U.S. CT, 9-30-1912. Evergreen Cemetery, Hillside, Union County.
BRANDT*, LEWIS T. 2nd Lt, F, 8th NJ Inf, 1-20-1899. Fairmount Cemetery, Phillipsburg, Warren County.
BRANDT, OTTO (aka: Brand, Otto) Pvt, H, 68th NY Inf, 6-2-1921. Fairmount Cemetery, Newark, Essex County.
BRANIN, GEORGE S. Pvt, F, 23rd NJ Inf, 12-17-1914. Baptist Cemetery, Medford, Burlington County.
BRANIN, JAMES Capt, H, 13th NJ Inf, 7-17-1887. Fairmount Cemetery, Newark, Essex County.

New Jersey Civil War Burials

BRANIN, SAMUEL E. 1st Lt, B, 23rd NJ Inf, 1-18-1905. Riverview Cemetery, Trenton, Mercer County.
BRANNAGAN, THOMAS Pvt, D, 28th NJ Inf, 2-1-1879. St. Peter's Cemetery, New Brunswick, Middlesex County.
BRANNAN, JAMES MADISON 2nd Lt, B, 10th NJ Inf, [Killed at Washington, DC.] 9-9-1863. Holy Trinity Lutheran Church Cemetery, Manasquan, Monmouth County.
BRANNAN, JAMES N. 1st Sgt, K, 27th NJ Inf, 8-24-1905. Holy Sepulchre Cemetery, East Orange, Essex County.
BRANNAN, JOHN Pvt, Btty H, 1st U.S. Art, 3-19-1928. Holy Cross Cemetery, North Arlington, Bergen County.
BRANNAN, JOSEPH Pvt, B, 32nd U.S. CT, 8-30-1914. Mount Moriah Cemetery, Hainesport, Burlington County.
BRANNEN, TERRENCE (see: Brennan, Edward) Holy Sepulchre Cemetery, Totowa, Passaic County.
BRANNIGAN, PATRICK Pvt, C, 6th NJ Inf, 5-27-1884. Flower Hill Cemetery, North Bergen, Hudson County.
BRANNIN, ANDREW J. 1st Sgt, C, 15th NJ Inf, 8-19-1873. Presbyterian Church Cemetery, Rockaway, Morris County.
BRANNIN, HALSEY R. Pvt, C, 15th NJ Inf, 11-1-1882. Laurel Grove Cemetery, Totowa, Passaic County.
BRANNIN, JAMES Corp, E, 11th NJ Inf, 2-13-1931. United Methodist Church Cemetery, Millbrook, Morris County.
BRANNIN, JAMES Pvt, B, 21st NJ Inf, 12-21-1888. Holy Name Cemetery, Jersey City, Hudson County.
BRANNIN, JOHN Pvt, K, 26th NJ Inf, 11-3-1896. Fairmount Cemetery, Newark, Essex County.
BRANNIN, JOHN Pvt, C, 21st NJ Inf, 12-12-1880. St. Peter's Cemetery, Jersey City, Hudson County.
BRANNIN*, JOHN J. Pvt, A, 3rd NY Inf, 12-11-1920. Holy Sepulchre Cemetery, Totowa, Passaic County.
BRANNIN, JONATHAN Pvt, L, 27th NJ Inf, DoD Unknown. Presbyterian Church Cemetery, Rockaway, Morris County.
BRANNON, JAMES Landsman, U.S. Navy, USS Princeton, 6-21-1896. St. John's Evangelical Church Cemetery, Orange, Essex County.
BRANSON, CHARLES Pvt, F, 29th CT Inf, 12-13-1894. St. Matthew's Methodist-Episcopal Cemetery, Morrisville, Camden County.
BRANSON, HUDSON YATES Pvt, K, 10th NJ Inf, 6-29-1894. Giberson Cemetery, Whiting, Ocean County.
BRANSON, JAMES Pvt, C, 12th NJ Inf, 9-2-1922. Methodist-Episcopal Church Cemetery, Medford, Burlington County.
BRANSON*, JOHN Pvt, Btty L, 13th NY Heavy Art, 1-2-1915. Riverside Cemetery, Toms River, Ocean County.
BRANSON, JOSEPH Pvt, C, 10th NJ Inf, [Wounded in action.] 2-19-1911. Good Luck Cemetery, Murray Grove, Ocean County.
BRANSON, LEWIS W. Pvt, D, 23rd NJ Inf, 3-10-1910. Baptist Church Cemetery, Jacobstown, Burlington County.
BRANSON, SAMUEL Pvt, F, 23rd NJ Inf, 1-27-1904. Methodist-Episcopal Church Cemetery, Medford, Burlington County.
BRANSON, WILLIAM W. 1st Sgt, C, 1st NJ Cav, 5-19-1906. Hazelwood Cemetery, Rahway, Union County.
BRANT, AMOS A. 12-7-1913. Riverside Cemetery, Toms River, Ocean County.
BRANT, CHARLES Pvt, E, 27th NJ Inf, DoD Unknown. Hillside Cemetery, Madison, Morris County.

Our Brothers Gone Before

BRANT, EDMUND W. 7-6-1901. Evergreen Cemetery, Hillside, Union County.
BRANT, EDWARD M. Pvt, F, 29th NJ Inf, 12-3-1897. Old 1st Methodist Church Cemetery, West Long Branch, Monmouth County.
BRANT, ELIAS W. 1st Lt, B, 30th NJ Inf, DoD Unknown. Presbyterian Church Cemetery, Elizabeth, Union County.
BRANT, JOHN B. Pvt, H, 12th Consolidated TN Inf (CSA), 11-9-1863. Finn's Point National Cemetery, Pennsville, Salem County.
BRANT, JOHN M. Pvt, B, 1st NJ Militia, 11-20-1891. Mount Pleasant Cemetery, Newark, Essex County.
BRANT, JOHN T. Corp, F, 13th NJ Inf, [Killed in action at Antietam, MD.] 9-17-1862. Fairmount Cemetery, Newark, Essex County.
BRANT, JOSEPH (JR.) Pvt, A, 1st NJ Inf, 8-6-1922. Evergreen Cemetery, Hillside, Union County.
BRANT, WILLIAM (JR.) Bvt Capt, B, 1st NJ Inf, [Awarded the Medal of Honor.] 3-1-1898. Evergreen Cemetery, Hillside, Union County.
BRANT, WILLIAM W. Pvt, K, 7th NJ Inf, 9-2-1908. Evergreen Cemetery, Morristown, Morris County.
BRANTIGAM, FREDERICK Pvt, E, 2nd NJ Inf, 3-9-1897. Fairmount Cemetery, Newark, Essex County.
BRANTINGHAM, HENRY Sgt, C, 28th NJ Inf, [Cenotaph. Killed in action at Fredericksburg, VA.] 12-13-1862. 1st Baptist Church Cemetery, Stelton, Middlesex County.
BRANTLEY, HENRY C. Pvt, I, 49th GA Inf (CSA), [Captured 5-6-1864 at Wilderness, VA.] 2-27-1865. Finn's Point National Cemetery, Pennsville, Salem County.
BRANTLEY, JOSEPH J. Pvt, Abell's Btty, FL Light Art (CSA), 4-4-1864. Finn's Point National Cemetery, Pennsville, Salem County.
BRANTON, WILLIAM Pvt, B, 2nd NJ Militia, 4-30-1886. Hoboken Cemetery, North Bergen, Hudson County.
BRASIL, H. (see: Brazell, Henry) Finn's Point National Cemetery, Pennsville, Salem County.
BRASIL, J. (see: Brazell, Joel) Finn's Point National Cemetery, Pennsville, Salem County.
BRASSELL, WILLIAM (aka: Brossell, William) Pvt, D, 72nd PA Inf, 1-20-1865. Calvary Cemetery, Cherry Hill, Camden County.
BRASTED, DANIEL Pvt, K, 5th NJ Inf, 10-29-1911. St. James Cemetery, Jamesburg, Middlesex County.
BRATH, SEBASTIAN (see: Bradt, Sebastian) Bayview-New York Bay Cemetery, Jersey City, Hudson County.
BRATTON, GEORGE W. Pvt, Btty I, 2nd PA Heavy Art, 4-28-1898. Cedar Grove Cemetery, Gloucester City, Camden County.
BRATTON, SAMUEL Pvt, D, 4th MS Inf (CSA), 7-17-1863. Finn's Point National Cemetery, Pennsville, Salem County.
BRAUN*, CHRISTIAN H. (aka: Brown, Christian) Musc, H, 5th PA Cav, 2-10-1910. Riverview Cemetery, Trenton, Mercer County.
BRAUN, GEORGE Pvt, G, 9th NJ Inf, 1-30-1911. Evergreen Cemetery, Hillside, Union County.
BRAUN, LOUIS Asst Surg, 9th NJ Inf 9-30-1880. Evergreen Cemetery, Hillside, Union County.
BRAUNE, CARL F. (aka: Braune, Charles F.) 1st Lt, A, 2nd NJ Cav, 12-8-1910. Rosedale Cemetery, Linden, Union County.
BRAUNE, CHARLES F. (see: Braune, Carl F.) Rosedale Cemetery, Linden, Union County.
BRAUNER, CHARLES Pvt, Btty E, 2nd U.S. Art, 8-14-1884. Woodland Cemetery, Newark, Essex County.

New Jersey Civil War Burials

BRAUNINGER, HERMAN (see: Breuninger, Herman) Woodland Cemetery, Newark, Essex County.

BRAUTIGAM, BERNHARD (see: Brautigana, Henry) Bayview-New York Bay Cemetery, Jersey City, Hudson County.

BRAUTIGAN, JACOB 2-20-1906. Bayview-New York Bay Cemetery, Jersey City, Hudson County.

BRAUTIGANA, HENRY (aka: Brautigam, Bernhard) Pvt, K, 7th NY Inf, 8-24-1921. Bayview-New York Bay Cemetery, Jersey City, Hudson County.

BRAXMEIER, JOSEPH Corp, B, 41st NY Inf, 5-7-1904. Maple Grove Cemetery, Hackensack, Bergen County.

BRAY, ABRAHAM 5-9-1866. Lamington Colored Cemetery, Lamington, Somerset County.

BRAY, D.M. Pvt, D, 16th GA Inf (CSA), [Captured 7-2-1863 at Gettysburg, PA. Died of diarrhea.] 4-7-1864. Finn's Point National Cemetery, Pennsville, Salem County.

BRAY, FLETCHER Pvt, H, 34th NJ Inf, 4-26-1877. Union Cemetery, Frenchtown, Hunterdon County.

BRAY, FREDERICK Pvt, H, 6th KY Cav, DoD Unknown. Old Camden Cemetery, Camden, Camden County.

BRAY, JAMES Pvt, 5th, Unattached MA Militia, 7-5-1913. Laurel Grove Cemetery, Totowa, Passaic County.

BRAY, JOHN (JR.) Pvt, D, 27th NJ Inf, DoD Unknown. Balesville Cemetery, Balesville, Sussex County.

BRAY, JOHN W. Corp, D, 2nd NJ Cav, 4-27-1908. Fairmount Cemetery, Newark, Essex County.

BRAY, JOSEPH A. Pvt, G, 3rd NJ Militia, 2-5-1903. Glenwood Cemetery, West Long Branch, Monmouth County.

BRAY*, JOSEPH BUDD 1st Sgt, Btty B, 2nd U.S. Art, 1-2-1913. Rosedale Cemetery, Orange, Essex County.

BRAY*, NATHANIEL K. Maj, 33rd NJ Inf DoD Unknown. Branchville Cemetery, Branchville, Sussex County.

BRAY, ROBERT Pvt, H, 127th U.S. CT, 4-7-1894. Evergreen Cemetery, Hillside, Union County.

BRAYERTON, JOHN Pvt, A, 24th NJ Inf, 1914. Eastview Cemetery, Salem, Salem County.

BRAYNOR, WILLIAM (see: Burrough, William H.) Baptist Church Cemetery, Haddonfield, Camden County.

BRAYSHAW, JOHN Pvt, Btty B, 1st NJ Light Art, 2-12-1902. Fairmount Cemetery, Newark, Essex County.

BRAYTON, MICHAEL C. Pvt, A, 77th NY National Guard, 3-16-1893. St. Peter's Cemetery, New Brunswick, Middlesex County.

BRAZELL, HENRY (aka: Brasil, H.) Pvt, D, 12th SC Inf (CSA), [Captured 5-12-1864 at Spotsylvania CH, VA. Died of bowel inflammation.] 7-1-1864. Finn's Point National Cemetery, Pennsville, Salem County.

BRAZELL, JOEL (aka: Brasil, J.) Pvt, D, 12th SC Inf (CSA), [Captured 5-12-1864 at Spotsylvania CH, VA. Died of dropsy.] 8-30-1864. Finn's Point National Cemetery, Pennsville, Salem County.

BRAZINGTON, SAMUEL T. Pvt, C, 12th NJ Inf, 8-24-1912. Marlton Cemetery, Marlton, Burlington County.

BREAK, JAMES (aka: Breck, James) Pvt, H, 2nd NJ Cav, DoD Unknown. Mount Prospect Cemetery, Neptune, Monmouth County.

BREARLEY, ABRAHAM V.D. Pvt, F, 30th NJ Inf, [Died of typhoid at Belle Plain, VA.] 4-11-1863. Rocky Hill Cemetery, Rocky Hill, Somerset County.

BREARLEY, WILLIAM CONOVER Corp, H, 21st NJ Inf, 6-30-1916. Greenwood Cemetery, Hamilton, Mercer County.

Our Brothers Gone Before

BRECHT, MAX Pvt, C, 21st PA Inf, 8-3-1906. Bordentown/Old St. Mary's Catholic Cemetery, Bordentown, Burlington County.
BRECK, JAMES (see: Break, James) Mount Prospect Cemetery, Neptune, Monmouth County.
BREECE, GARRETT Pvt, I, 14th NJ Inf, 4-21-1904. Elmwood Cemetery, New Brunswick, Middlesex County.
BREECE, JOSEPH Pvt, I, 14th NJ Inf, [Died of wounds received 7-9-1864 at Monocacy, MD.] 8-26-1864. Van Liew Cemetery, North Brunswick, Middlesex County.
BREEDEN, CHARLES EDWIN Pvt, D, 7th NY State Militia, 8-22-1903. Rosedale Cemetery, Orange, Essex County.
BREEDEN, JOHN M. Pvt, B, 54th OH Inf, 3-18-1908. Mount Pleasant Cemetery, Millville, Cumberland County.
BREEDEN, WILLIAM B. Sgt, C, 39th NC Inf (CSA), [Wounded 9-19-1863 at Chickamauga, GA. Captured 2-18-1864 at Cherokee County, NC. Died of disease.] 3-6-1864. Finn's Point National Cemetery, Pennsville, Salem County.
BREEN, CORNELIUS 1907. Cedar Lawn Cemetery, Paterson, Passaic County.
BREEN, LEONARD 1921. Cedar Lawn Cemetery, Paterson, Passaic County.
BREEN, MICHAEL Pvt, D, 3rd NY Inf, 1-13-1912. Fairview Cemetery, Westfield, Union County.
BREESE, AARON Pvt, H, 22nd NJ Inf, 12-30-1890. Riverview Cemetery, Trenton, Mercer County.
BREESE, HENRY Pvt, B, 9th NJ Inf, 11-25-1898. Dayton Cemetery, Dayton, Middlesex County.
BREESE, JAMES BUCHANAN 2nd Lt, U.S. Marine Corps, 2-7-1887. Riverview Cemetery, Trenton, Mercer County.
BREESE, JAMES D. 2-1-1906. Presbyterian Church Cemetery, Kingston, Somerset County.
BREESE, JOHN Pvt, M, 2nd NJ Cav, 1904. Reformed Church Cemetery, Bedminster, Somerset County.
BREESE*, REUBEN J. Pvt, K, 40th NJ Inf, 8-18-1881. St. Barnabas Episcopal Cemetery, South Brunswick, Middlesex County.
BREESE, THOMAS L. Pvt, Btty D, Durell's Ind PA Art, 8-27-1893. Riverview Cemetery, Trenton, Mercer County.
BREESE, WILLIAM H.H. Pvt, F, 1st NJ Inf, DoD Unknown. Greenwood Cemetery, Hamilton, Mercer County.
BREEVORT, JACOB Z. (see: Brevort, Jacob Z.) Acquackanonk Church/Armory Park Cemetery, Passaic, Passaic County.
BREHM, LOUIS Pvt, H, 20th NY Inf, 3-19-1919. Palisade Cemetery, North Bergen, Hudson County.
BREINER, JAMES Pvt, D, 1st NJ Inf, 1919. Phillipsburg New Catholic Cemetery, Greenwich, Warren County.
BREINING, JACOB (aka: Breming, Jacob) Blacksmith, I, 3rd NJ Cav, 7-8-1890. Riverview Cemetery, Trenton, Mercer County.
BREINTNALL, JOHN HENRY HOBART (aka: Brintnall, John H.H.) Asst Surgeon, U.S. Navy, USS Crusader, 3-4-1895. Mount Pleasant Cemetery, Newark, Essex County.
BREINTNALL*, REGINAL HUBER QM Sgt, 39th NJ Inf 7-3-1925. Mount Pleasant Cemetery, Newark, Essex County.
BREITEL, MELCHIOR Pvt, I, 12th NJ Inf, 11-2-1890. New Presbyterian Church Cemetery, Daretown, Salem County.
BREM, FREDERICK Pvt, H, 9th NJ Inf, 3-5-1900. Fairmount Cemetery, Newark, Essex County.
BREMING, JACOB (see: Breining, Jacob) Riverview Cemetery, Trenton, Mercer County.

New Jersey Civil War Burials

BRENDEL, ADAM Corp, B, 45th NY Inf, 7-28-1911. Fairmount Cemetery, Newark, Essex County.

BRENNAN, BENJAMIN Pvt, A, 21st NJ Inf, 2-6-1887. Bayview-New York Bay Cemetery, Jersey City, Hudson County.

BRENNAN, EDWARD (aka: Brannen, Terrence) Pvt, K, 39th NJ Inf, 7-16-1878. Holy Sepulchre Cemetery, Totowa, Passaic County.

BRENNAN*, GEORGE Capt, Btty M, 14th NY Heavy Art, 4-24-1883. Presbyterian Church Cemetery, Metuchen, Middlesex County.

BRENNAN, JAMES Pvt, I, 11th NJ Inf, 12-13-1888. St. Peter's Cemetery, Jersey City, Hudson County.

BRENNAN*, JOHN Pvt, C, 9th NY Inf, 12-16-1873. Holy Sepulchre Cemetery, East Orange, Essex County.

BRENNAN, THOMAS (aka: Brinan, Thomas) Pvt, H, 21st NJ Inf, 10-4-1910. St. John's Cemetery, Hamilton, Mercer County.

BRENNAN, THOMAS F. Landsman, U.S. Navy, USS Princeton, 7-11-1929. St. John's Evangelical Church Cemetery, Orange, Essex County.

BRENNAN, TIMOTHY Pvt, U.S. Marine Corps, USS Advance, 5-16-1902. St. John's Evangelical Church Cemetery, Orange, Essex County.

BRENNAN, WALTER Corp, K, 4th NY Inf, 12-23-1897. Calvary Cemetery, Cherry Hill, Camden County.

BRENNER, GEORGE Pvt, I, 39th NJ Inf, 10-27-1889. Rosedale Cemetery, Orange, Essex County.

BRENNER, GEORGE D. 1921. Presbyterian Cemetery, North Plainfield, Somerset County.

BRENNFLECK, JOHN Sgt, B, 1st NY Eng, 4-20-1890. Fairmount Cemetery, Newark, Essex County.

BRENNING, JOHN L. (see: Breunig, John L.) Fairmount Cemetery, Newark, Essex County.

BRENNION, JOSEPH Pvt, Btty A, 1st NJ Light Art, 4-24-1882. Palisade Cemetery, North Bergen, Hudson County.

BRENS, WILLIAM Seaman, U.S. Navy, DoD Unknown. Bayview-New York Bay Cemetery, Jersey City, Hudson County.

BRENSINGER, JOHN (see: Brensinger, Joseph Henry) Phillipsburg Cemetery, Phillipsburg, Warren County.

BRENSINGER*, JOSEPH HENRY (aka: Brensinger, John) Pvt, G, 97th PA Inf, [Wounded in action.] 9-30-1924. Phillipsburg Cemetery, Phillipsburg, Warren County.

BRENTON, WILLIAM Seaman, U.S. Navy, 3-11-1874. St. Peter's Cemetery, Perth Amboy, Middlesex County.

BRESEE, WILLIAM H. Corp, D, 134th NY Inf, 10-12-1895. Fairmount Cemetery, Newark, Essex County.

BRESLIN, MORRIS Pvt, E, 9th NJ Inf, 1-18-1885. Methodist Church Cemetery, Liberty, Warren County.

BRESNAHAN, DANIEL (aka: Brisnaham, Daniel) Pvt, A, 6th NJ Inf, 1915. Windsor Burial Grounds Cemetery, East Windsor, Mercer County.

BRESSILLON, ARMAND (see: Braezlion, Armand) New Camden Cemetery, Camden, Camden County.

BRETON, LEWIS (see: Vere, Lewis Breton) Bayview-New York Bay Cemetery, Jersey City, Hudson County.

BRETWIG, JOHN Pvt, A, 13th NJ Inf, 11-24-1915. Holy Sepulchre Cemetery, East Orange, Essex County.

BREUNEMANN, PHILIP Landsman, U.S. Navy, USS Vermont, 12-18-1902. Rosedale Cemetery, Orange, Essex County.

Our Brothers Gone Before

BREUNIG, JOHN L. (aka: Brenning, John L.) Pvt, K, 1st NJ Cav, 3-1-1874. Fairmount Cemetery, Newark, Essex County.
BREUNINGER, HERMAN (aka: Brauninger, Herman) Pvt, H, 20th NY Inf, [Wounded 5-4-1863 at Salem Heights, VA.] 1-31-1896. Woodland Cemetery, Newark, Essex County.
BREVORT, JACOB Z. (aka: Breevort, Jacob Z.) Sgt, C, 13th NJ Inf, 4-28-1886. Acquackanonk Church/Armory Park Cemetery, Passaic, Passaic County.
BREWER, ANDREW A. (aka: Bruven, Andrew) Pvt, M, 16th PA Cav, 11-8-1916. Brotherhood Cemetery, Hainesport, Burlington County.
BREWER, C. 1915. Whitelawn Cemetery, Point Pleasant, Ocean County.
BREWER, CHARLES Surg, (CSA) [General Staff.] 1909. Siloam Cemetery, Vineland, Cumberland County.
BREWER, CHARLES W. Com Sgt, 4th NY Heavy Art 6-13-1906. Evergreen Cemetery, Farmingdale, Monmouth County.
BREWER, DAVID Pvt, E, 29th NJ Inf, 2-15-1907. Fairview Cemetery, Fairview, Monmouth County.
BREWER*, ELIAS Pvt, Btty F, 4th NY Heavy Art, 1909. Rose Hill Cemetery, Matawan, Monmouth County.
BREWER, ISAAC Pvt, D, 14th NJ Inf, 6-24-1892. Old Brick Reformed Church Cemetery, Marlboro, Monmouth County.
BREWER, JACOB Pvt, E, 29th NJ Inf, 9-16-1886. Old Brick Reformed Church Cemetery, Marlboro, Monmouth County.
BREWER, JOHN Pvt, A, Cobb's Legion GA Inf (CSA), 4-23-1864. Finn's Point National Cemetery, Pennsville, Salem County.
BREWER, JOHN C. Pvt, C, 3rd U.S. Inf, 6-29-1865. Greengrove Cemetery, Keyport, Monmouth County.
BREWER, JOHN L. 8-15-1912. Batsto/Pleasant Mills Methodist Church Cemetery, Pleasant Mills, Atlantic County.
BREWER, MARION (aka: Brewer, Masion) Pvt, A, Cobb's Legion GA Inf (CSA), 1-23-1864. Finn's Point National Cemetery, Pennsville, Salem County.
BREWER, MASION (see: Brewer, Marion) Finn's Point National Cemetery, Pennsville, Salem County.
BREWIN, CHARLES P. Pvt, H, 34th NJ Inf, 9-2-1929. Baptist/St. Andrew's Cemetery, Mount Holly, Burlington County.
BREWIN, JAMES H. 2nd Lt, B, 4th NJ Inf, 8-24-1909. Berlin Cemetery, Berlin, Camden County.
BREWIN, LEANDER 1st Lt, Adj, 4th NJ Inf 1886. Oddfellows Cemetery, Burlington, Burlington County.
BREWNER, SOLOMON (see: Bruner, Soloman H.) Baptist Church Cemetery, Jacobstown, Burlington County.
BREWSTER, ALBERT ABSALOM Sgt, Btty A, 6th NY Heavy Art, 3-2-1895. United Methodist Church Cemetery, Wayside, Monmouth County.
BREWSTER, CHARLES Pvt, C, 214th PA Inf, 11-14-1918. Evergreen Cemetery, Camden, Camden County.
BREWSTER*, DANIEL Corp, G, 1st NJ Inf, 1921. Oak Hill Cemetery, Vineland, Cumberland County.
BREWSTER, GEORGE Corp, B, 2nd NJ Cav, 5-14-1898. Fairmount Cemetery, Newark, Essex County.
BREWSTER, HENRY Pvt, D, 33rd NJ Inf, 1-9-1876. Rosedale Cemetery, Orange, Essex County.
BREWSTER, JAMES Pvt, F, 4th NJ Inf, 5-21-1911. Bloomfield Cemetery, Bloomfield, Essex County.
BREWSTER, JAMES K. Pvt, D, PA Emerg NJ Militia, 10-14-1898. Mount Hope Presbyterian Cemetery, Lambertville, Hunterdon County.

New Jersey Civil War Burials

BREWSTER, JOSEPH Pvt, D, 22nd U.S. CT, 11-19-1925. Mount Peace Cemetery, Lawnside, Camden County.

BREWSTER, JOSEPH Pvt, G, 99th PA Inf, [Wounded 5-30-1864 at Totopotomoy River, VA.] DoD Unknown. Mount Pleasant Cemetery, Millville, Cumberland County.

BREWSTER, WILLIAM H. Pvt, K, 2nd NJ Cav, 1-18-1929. Fairmount Cemetery, Newark, Essex County.

BREWTON*, JOSEPH H. Corp, B, 5th PA Cav, 1-5-1924. Presbyterian Church Cemetery, Cold Spring, Cape May County.

BREYER, JOHN Pvt, H, 10th NJ Inf, 9-20-1920. Harleigh Cemetery, Camden, Camden County.

BREZETTE, CHARLES Sgt, G, 27th NJ Inf, 3-28-1911. St. Mary's Cemetery, Boonton, Morris County.

BRIAD, DAVID L. 11-2-1884. Evergreen Cemetery, Hillside, Union County.

BRIAD, DAVID S. (aka: Briod, David) Pvt, F, 3rd NJ Inf, 12-8-1871. Evergreen Cemetery, Hillside, Union County.

BRIANT, CHARLES D. Pvt, C, 104th PA Inf, 7-23-1919. Presbyterian Church Cemetery, Mount Freedom, Morris County.

BRIANT, J. WELLINGTON (aka: Bryant, Wellington) Sgt, K, 1st NY Eng, 1929. Chestnut Cemetery, Dover, Morris County.

BRIANT, WILLIAM H. C. Pvt, G, 40th NJ Inf, 6-4-1910. Harleigh Cemetery, Camden, Camden County.

BRICK, EDWARD L. Corp, G, 12th NJ Inf, 8-17-1892. Methodist Church Cemetery, Hurffville, Gloucester County.

BRICK, EDWARD W. Pvt, C, 9th NJ Inf, 1-10-1915. Baptist Church Cemetery, Haddonfield, Camden County.

BRICK, JACOB P. 5-9-1897. Mount Pleasant Cemetery, Millville, Cumberland County.

BRICK, JAMES H. Corp, D, 2nd NJ Cav, 9-1-1878. Baptist Church Cemetery, Haddonfield, Camden County.

BRICK, THEODORE Corp, C, 12th NJ Inf, 2-1-1901. Cedar Grove Cemetery, Gloucester City, Camden County.

BRICKELL, SAMUEL C. Fireman, U.S. Navy, USS Emma, 6-3-1909. Riverview Cemetery, Trenton, Mercer County.

BRICKELL, WILLIAM A. Pvt, D, 71st NY State Militia, 6-14-1895. Bloomfield Cemetery, Bloomfield, Essex County.

BRICKEN, J.V. (aka: Brikeen, A.J.) Pvt, B, 3rd (Clack's) TN Inf (CSA), 10-8-1863. Finn's Point National Cemetery, Pennsville, Salem County.

BRICKHARDT, CONRAD (see: Bickhard, Conrad) Grove Church Cemetery, North Bergen, Hudson County.

BRIDEN, FRANK (SR.) Pvt, E, 39th NJ Inf, 8-26-1926. Hollywood Cemetery, Union, Union County.

BRIDGE, ROBERT Pvt, I, 6th NY Inf, 2-2-1907. Laurel Grove Cemetery, Totowa, Passaic County.

BRIDGE*, WILLIAM Pvt, C, 79th NY Inf, 6-2-1885. Cedar Lawn Cemetery, Paterson, Passaic County.

BRIDGEM, LEWIS H. (see: Bridgeman, Lewis H.) Fairmount Cemetery, Newark, Essex County.

BRIDGEMAN, LEWIS H. (aka: Bridgem, Lewis H.) Corp, A, 26th NJ Inf, [Wounded in action.] 10-6-1906. Fairmount Cemetery, Newark, Essex County.

BRIDGER, GEORGE E. Pvt, G, 23rd NJ Inf, 12- -1905. Oddfellows Cemetery, Burlington, Burlington County.

BRIDGER, THOMAS 7-25-1887. St. Mary's Episcopal Church Cemetery, Burlington, Burlington County.

Our Brothers Gone Before

BRIDGERS, EMORY A. Pvt, D, 4th NC Cav (CSA), [Captured 7-4-1863 at Gettysburg, PA. Died of typhoid.] 9-8-1863. Finn's Point National Cemetery, Pennsville, Salem County.
BRIDGES, DAVID A. Pvt, K, 112th NY Inf, 5-13-1906. Oak Hill Cemetery, Vineland, Cumberland County.
BRIDGES, PETER Pvt, F, 5th VA Inf (CSA), [Captured 5-12-1864 at Spotsylvania CH, VA. Died of smallpox.] 4-15-1865. Finn's Point National Cemetery, Pennsville, Salem County.
BRIDLEMAN, ALEXANDER Landsman, U.S. Navy, USS Ottowa, 9-15-1911. Evergreen Cemetery, Morristown, Morris County.
BRIEL, ALFRED Pvt, Btty I, 3rd PA Heavy Art, 3-21-1891. Riverview Cemetery, Trenton, Mercer County.
BRIEN, WILLIAM O. (see: O'Brien, William) Mount Pleasant Cemetery, Newark, Essex County.
BRIERLY, JOHN Pvt, C, 25th NJ Inf, 12-7-1900. Laurel Grove Cemetery, Totowa, Passaic County.
BRIEST, GEORGE DoD Unknown. Mercer Cemetery, Trenton, Mercer County.
BRIEST, LEWIS H. Musc, H, 1st NJ Inf, 10-1-1896. Riverview Cemetery, Trenton, Mercer County.
BRIEST, PETER S. Musc, B, 1st NJ Inf, 3-17-1870. Mercer Cemetery, Trenton, Mercer County.
BRIGGS, ALBERT L. Pvt, Btty G, 6th NY Heavy Art, 3-9-1895. Old Stone Church Cemetery, Fairton, Cumberland County.
BRIGGS, CHARLES F. Pvt, H, 45th MA Militia, 12-6-1903. Bayview-New York Bay Cemetery, Jersey City, Hudson County.
BRIGGS, CHARLES W. 1st Sgt, Btty H, 7th NY Heavy Art, 4-3-1910. Rahway Cemetery, Rahway, Union County.
BRIGGS, HENRY PETER Pvt, I, 93rd NY Inf, 11-18-1904. Mount Peace Cemetery, Lawnside, Camden County.
BRIGGS, HIRAM S. Pvt, I, 34th NJ Inf, 12-12-1908. Bayview-New York Bay Cemetery, Jersey City, Hudson County.
BRIGGS, HIRAM Y. Pvt, A, 6th PA Inf, 9-6-1915. Evergreen Cemetery, Camden, Camden County.
BRIGGS, JOHN Pvt, F, 72nd PA Inf, 1-15-1898. Baptist Church Cemetery, Palermo, Cape May County.
BRIGGS*, LEWIS W. Corp, A, 88th PA Inf, 10-1-1915. Evergreen Cemetery, Hillside, Union County.
BRIGGS, ROBERT M. Pvt, C, 26th NJ Inf, 3-17-1865. Mount Pleasant Cemetery, Newark, Essex County.
BRIGGS, ROLAND W. Pvt, C, 7th MA Inf, 1871. Boonton Cemetery, Boonton, Morris County.
BRIGGS, SALOMON R. Seaman, U.S. Navy, 1908. Bayview-New York Bay Cemetery, Jersey City, Hudson County.
BRIGGS, SAMUEL D. Pvt, A, 37th NJ Inf, 3-12-1867. Mount Pleasant Cemetery, Newark, Essex County.
BRIGGS*, STACY Pvt, F, 186th PA Inf, 7-18-1903. Brotherhood Cemetery, Hainesport, Burlington County.
BRIGGS, STEPHEN A. Pvt, Hummel's, Ind PA Cav, DoD Unknown. Cedar Grove Cemetery, Gloucester City, Camden County.
BRIGGS, WILLIAM Pvt, K, 31st NJ Inf, 1-17-1874. Fountain Grove Cemetery, Glen Gardner, Hunterdon County.
BRIGGS*, WILLIAM H. Pvt, Btty A, 1st NY Light Art, DoD Unknown. Bayview-New York Bay Cemetery, Jersey City, Hudson County.

New Jersey Civil War Burials

BRIGGS, WILLIAM M. Pvt, F, 4th NJ Inf, 7-25-1899. Presbyterian Church Cemetery, Bridgeton, Cumberland County.
BRIGHT, BENJAMIN T. Corp, H, 24th NJ Inf, DoD Unknown. Presbyterian Church Cemetery, Bridgeton, Cumberland County.
BRIGHT, GARDNER Pvt, I, 37th NJ Inf, 2-3-1911. Bayview-New York Bay Cemetery, Jersey City, Hudson County.
BRIGHT, ISAAC S. Pvt, K, 4th NJ Inf, [Died of fever.] 1-4-1862. Methodist-Episcopal Cemetery, Pennsville, Salem County.
BRIGHT*, JAMES Wagoner, F, 3rd NJ Inf, DoD Unknown. Presbyterian Church Cemetery, Bridgeton, Cumberland County.
BRIGHT, JOSEPH F. Pvt, K, 2nd NJ Cav, [Died of dysentery.] 6-4-1864. Methodist-Episcopal Cemetery, Pennsville, Salem County.
BRIGHT, M.D. Pvt, C, 46th AL Inf (CSA), 9-11-1863. Finn's Point National Cemetery, Pennsville, Salem County.
BRIGHT, MARTIN V.B. DoD Unknown. Washington Monumental Cemetery, South River, Middlesex County.
BRIGHT, SHAKESPEARE G. Musc, I, 37th NJ Inf, 3-1-1906. Bayview-New York Bay Cemetery, Jersey City, Hudson County.
BRIGHT, SMITH Pvt, B, 99th IN Inf, DoD Unknown. Presbyterian Cemetery, Salem, Salem County.
BRIGHT, WILLIAM D. Corp, I, 5th U.S. Inf, 10-17-1911. Atlantic City Cemetery, Pleasantville, Atlantic County.
BRIGHTON, CHARLES Pvt, E, 10th NJ Inf, [Wounded 5-14-1864 at Galt House, VA.] 1883. Methodist-Episcopal Cemetery, Vincentown, Burlington County.
BRIGHTON, WILLIAM Pvt, F, 23rd NJ Inf, DoD Unknown. Rose Hill Cemetery, Matawan, Monmouth County.
BRIGMAN, JESSE Pvt, I, 2nd LA Inf (CSA), [Captured 7-4-1863 at Gettysburg, PA.] 3-3-1865. Finn's Point National Cemetery, Pennsville, Salem County.
BRIKEEN, A.J. (see: Bricken, J.V.) Finn's Point National Cemetery, Pennsville, Salem County.
BRILEY, BENJAMIN P. Pvt, B, 13th GA Inf (CSA), [Captured 7-1-1863 at Gettysburg, PA. Died of smallpox.] 12-21-1863. Finn's Point National Cemetery, Pennsville, Salem County.
BRILL, ALBERT Pvt, I, 84th NY National Guard, 3-11-1908. Arlington Cemetery, Kearny, Hudson County.
BRILL*, ANTHONY C. Pvt, D, 8th NJ Inf, 12-29-1917. Fairmount Cemetery, Newark, Essex County.
BRILL, CONRAD Pvt, K, 12th NJ Inf, 1899. Methodist Church Cemetery, Friendship, Salem County.
BRILL, FREDERICK AMZI 2nd Lt, I, 5th NJ Inf, [Cenotaph. Killed in action at 2nd Bull Run, VA.] 8-29-1862. Rahway Cemetery, Rahway, Union County.
BRILL, HENRY Pvt, I, 24th NJ Inf, 12-11-1904. Berlin Cemetery, Berlin, Camden County.
BRILL, JACOB C. (aka: Brill, James) Pvt, A, 9th NY Inf, [Wounded 9-17-1862 at Antietam, MD.] 9-19-1924. Hollywood Cemetery, Union, Union County.
BRILL, JAMES (see: Brill, Jacob C.) Hollywood Cemetery, Union, Union County.
BRILL, JOHN C. Pvt, H, 12th NJ Inf, 9-14-1921. Fairview Cemetery, Fairview, Monmouth County.
BRILL*, JOHN N. Sgt, H, 3rd NY Inf, 11-7-1890. Bayview-New York Bay Cemetery, Jersey City, Hudson County.
BRINAN, PATRICK Pvt, H, 21st NJ Inf, 1-19-1890. St. Mary's Cemetery, Hamilton, Mercer County.
BRINAN, THOMAS (see: Brennan, Thomas) St. John's Cemetery, Hamilton, Mercer County.

Our Brothers Gone Before

BRINCKMANN, ADOLPH Sgt, D, 39th NY Inf, [Wounded 5-18-1864 at Landron House, VA.] DoD Unknown. Grove Church Cemetery, North Bergen, Hudson County.
BRINDLE, JACOB Pvt, A, 158th PA Inf, 5-27-1884. Flower Hill Cemetery, North Bergen, Hudson County.
BRINDLEY, CHARLES H. Pvt, F, 14th NJ Inf, 6-7-1898. Old 1st Methodist Church Cemetery, West Long Branch, Monmouth County.
BRINDLEY, SAMUEL W. Pvt, D, 9th NJ Inf, 4-25-1918. Riverside Cemetery, Toms River, Ocean County.
BRINING, ANTON Pvt, I, 3rd NJ Inf, 7-19-1887. Holy Sepulchre Cemetery, East Orange, Essex County.
BRINISCHOLTZ, FRANKLIN 1906. Old Camden Cemetery, Camden, Camden County.
BRINISCHOLTZ, JACOB Pvt, E, 1st NJ Inf, 6-14-1873. Old Camden Cemetery, Camden, Camden County.
BRINK, ALFRED M. 1931. Union Cemetery, Frenchtown, Hunterdon County.
BRINK, CHARLES A.K. Pvt, E, 95th PA Inf, 4-4-1903. New Presbyterian Church Cemetery, Daretown, Salem County.
BRINK*, DEWITT C. Pvt, I, 15th NJ Inf, 6-15-1907. Brink Cemetery, Colesville, Sussex County.
BRINK, JAMES MATTHEW Pvt, H, 27th NJ Inf, 1-11-1878. Brink Cemetery, Colesville, Sussex County.
BRINK, JOHN (see: Ring, John P.) New Camden Cemetery, Camden, Camden County.
BRINK, JOHN P. Pvt, B, 15th NJ Inf, 9-5-1888. Broadway Cemetery, Broadway, Warren County.
BRINK, MATTHEW Pvt, H, 27th NJ Inf, DoD Unknown. Brink Cemetery, Colesville, Sussex County.
BRINK, PETER Pvt, E, 8th NJ Inf, 1898. Minisink Reformed Church Cemetery, Montague, Sussex County.
BRINK, TYLER Pvt, 2nd Bttn U.S. VRC 12-15-1864. Fairmount Cemetery, Newark, Essex County.
BRINKERHOFF, ABRAHAM C. Pvt, C, 22nd NJ Inf, 3-25-1897. Woodside Cemetery, Dumont, Bergen County.
BRINKERHOFF, HENRY H. 1st Lt,QM, 2nd NJ Militia 2-13-1899. Old Bergen Church Cemetery, Jersey City, Hudson County.
BRINKERHOFF, JOHN D. (aka: Bunkerhoef, John) Pvt, I, 22nd NJ Inf, 10-24-1911. Fairview Cemetery, Westfield, Union County.
BRINKERHOFF, RALPH L. Pvt, C, 22nd NJ Inf, 8-8-1875. Woodside Cemetery, Dumont, Bergen County.
BRINKERHOFF, WILLIAM Pvt, I, 21st NJ Inf, 1-26-1931. Bayview-New York Bay Cemetery, Jersey City, Hudson County.
BRINKERNUFF*, SAMUEL (aka: Brinkniff, Samuel) Pvt, Btty G, 11th U.S. CHA, 4-10-1911. Laurel Grove Cemetery, Totowa, Passaic County.
BRINKLEY, HUGH G. 2nd Lt, I, 41st VA Inf (CSA), [Wounded 7-1-1862 at Malvern Hill, VA. Captured 7-15-1864 at Petersburg, VA. Died of pericarditis.] 12-26-1864. Finn's Point National Cemetery, Pennsville, Salem County.
BRINKLEY, JOSEPH Landsman, U.S. Navy, 2-2-1900. Fairmount Cemetery, Newark, Essex County.
BRINKNIFF, SAMUEL (see: Brinkernuff, Samuel) Laurel Grove Cemetery, Totowa, Passaic County.
BRINLEY, GEORGE HENRY Pvt, F, 3rd NJ Militia, 6-13-1862. Old 1st Methodist Church Cemetery, West Long Branch, Monmouth County.
BRINLEY, HOWARD A. Pvt, F, 38th NJ Inf, 4-2-1917. Old 1st Methodist Church Cemetery, West Long Branch, Monmouth County.
BRINSON, CHRISTOPHER Pvt, I, 66th NC Inf (CSA), 3-30-1865. Finn's Point National Cemetery, Pennsville, Salem County.

New Jersey Civil War Burials

BRINSON, ROBERT (see: Bimson, Robert) Cedar Lawn Cemetery, Paterson, Passaic County.
BRINTNALL, JOHN H.H. (see: Breintnall, John Henry Hobart) Mount Pleasant Cemetery, Newark, Essex County.
BRINTZINGHOFFER, JOHN Capt, A, 1st NJ Militia, 5-8-1889. Mount Pleasant Cemetery, Newark, Essex County.
BRIOD, DAVID (see: Briad, David S.) Evergreen Cemetery, Hillside, Union County.
BRISCO, ALEXANDER Pvt, C, 9th U.S. CT, 7-10-1899. Johnson Cemetery, Camden, Camden County.
BRISCO, JACOB Pvt, E, 25th U.S. CT, 2-17-1885. Johnson Cemetery, Camden, Camden County.
BRISCOE, JOHN Pvt, A, 127th U.S. CT, 5-18-1914. Butler Cemetery, Camden, Camden County.
BRISCOE, PETER Pvt, H, 35th NJ Inf, 11-23-1905. Holy Sepulchre Cemetery, East Orange, Essex County.
BRISKIE, WILLIAM D. Pvt, D, 29th NJ Inf, 1-12-1873. St. Joseph's Cemetery, Keyport, Monmouth County.
BRISNAHAM, DANIEL (see: Bresnahan, Daniel) Windsor Burial Grounds Cemetery, East Windsor, Mercer County.
BRISTOL*, ROBERT A. 2nd Lt, E, 39th NC Inf (CSA), [Wounded 5-4-1863 at Dowman's Hill, VA. Captured at Cherokee County, NC. Died of smallpox.] 2-8-1865. Finn's Point National Cemetery, Pennsville, Salem County.
BRISTOL, SAMUEL A. 1st Lt, Adj, 31st NJ Inf 1916. Presbyterian Cemetery, Asbury, Warren County.
BRITAIN, BENNETT (see: Britton, Bennett) Hillside Cemetery, Scotch Plains, Union County.
BRITLAND*, CHARLES J. Seaman, U.S. Navy, USS Constitution, 12-10-1918. Fairmount Cemetery, Newark, Essex County.
BRITT, GEORGE Pvt, K, 14th NJ Inf, 1-9-1883. Fairmount Cemetery, Newark, Essex County.
BRITTAIN, ALLEN E. (see: Britton, A.E.) Riverside Cemetery, Toms River, Ocean County.
BRITTAIN, JAMES Pvt, H, 79th NY Inf, 8-9-1909. Brotherhood Cemetery, Hainesport, Burlington County.
BRITTAIN, MILLER (see: Miller, Britten C.) Osbornville Protestant Church Cemetery, Breton Woods, Ocean County.
BRITTAIN, WILLIAM (aka: Britton, William) Pvt, B, 58th PA Inf, 7-20-1880. Fairmount Cemetery, Newark, Essex County.
BRITTAIN, WILLIAM J. Corp, K, 32nd PA Inf, [Killed in action at Antietam, MD.] 9-17-1862. Mercer Cemetery, Trenton, Mercer County.
BRITTAN*, EPHRIAM Pvt, C, 11th NJ Inf, 7-30-1905. Riverview Cemetery, Trenton, Mercer County.
BRITTEN, JAMES 10-29-1921. Holy Name Cemetery, Jersey City, Hudson County.
BRITTON, A.E. (aka: Brittain, Allen E.) Pvt, A, 211th PA Inf, DoD Unknown. Riverside Cemetery, Toms River, Ocean County.
BRITTON, BENJAMIN Pvt, D, 23rd NJ Inf, 7-28-1900. Mount Prospect Cemetery, Neptune, Monmouth County.
BRITTON, BENNETT (aka: Britain, Bennett) Pvt, B, 1st NY Cav, [102 years old at death.] 10-25-1915. Hillside Cemetery, Scotch Plains, Union County.
BRITTON, CHARLES Pvt, H, 53rd PA Inf, 11-15-1901. Riverview Cemetery, Trenton, Mercer County.
BRITTON, CHARLES (see: Britton, William F.) Oddfellows Cemetery, Burlington, Burlington County.

Our Brothers Gone Before

BRITTON, CLAYTON L. Pvt, K, 10th NJ Inf, 11-27-1920. Mount Holly Cemetery, Mount Holly, Burlington County.
BRITTON, CORNELIUS (JR.) Wagoner, B, 29th NJ Inf, 1-2-1913. Rose Hill Cemetery, Matawan, Monmouth County.
BRITTON*, DAVID S. Corp, B, 35th NJ Inf, 8-4-1900. Evergreen Cemetery, Hillside, Union County.
BRITTON, EDWARD M. Corp, F, 1st NJ Inf, 7-30-1913. Elmwood Cemetery, New Brunswick, Middlesex County.
BRITTON, ELI Pvt, A, 48th PA Inf, 3-14-1864. Union Cemetery, Frenchtown, Hunterdon County.
BRITTON*, HOLMES Pvt, E, 11th NJ Inf, 1908. Riverside Cemetery, Toms River, Ocean County.
BRITTON, JAMES Pvt, A, 28th NJ Inf, [Wounded in action.] 4-3-1926. Rose Hill Cemetery, Matawan, Monmouth County.
BRITTON, JAMES A. Sgt, I, 21st NJ Inf, 2-29-1916. Bayview-New York Bay Cemetery, Jersey City, Hudson County.
BRITTON, JAMES H. Seaman, U.S. Navy, 7-5-1918. Brotherhood Cemetery, Hainesport, Burlington County.
BRITTON, JOHN H. Pvt, K, 8th NJ Inf, 1907. Stanhope-Union Cemetery, Netcong, Morris County.
BRITTON, JOHN M. Sgt, K, 35th NJ Inf, 10-17-1890. Presbyterian Church Cemetery, Kingston, Somerset County.
BRITTON, JOHN S. Pvt, F, 37th NJ Inf, 1929. Greenwood Cemetery, Hamilton, Mercer County.
BRITTON, JOHN S. Pvt, F, 14th NJ Inf, [Died of erysipelas at Danville, VA.] 2-28-1865. Mount Pleasant Cemetery, Newark, Essex County.
BRITTON, JOHN W. Pvt, E, 38th NJ Inf, 11-23-1904. Riverview Cemetery, Trenton, Mercer County.
BRITTON, KENNETH DoD Unknown. Baptist Cemetery, Pemberton, Burlington County.
BRITTON, NATHANIEL Corp, A, 14th NJ Inf, 8-9-1923. Atlantic View Cemetery, Manasquan, Monmouth County.
BRITTON, NATHANIEL 5-12-1889. Belvidere/Catholic Cemetery, Belvidere, Warren County.
BRITTON, NATHANIEL F. Pvt, H, 2nd NJ Militia, 12-3-1876. Arlington Cemetery, Kearny, Hudson County.
BRITTON, RESTORE Pvt, E, 23rd NJ Inf, 3- -1863. Baptist Cemetery, Pemberton, Burlington County.
BRITTON, RICHARD J. Pvt, C, 9th VA Inf (CSA), [Captured 7-3-1863 at Gettysburg, PA. Died of disease.] 7-23-1863. Finn's Point National Cemetery, Pennsville, Salem County.
BRITTON, WILLIAM 1909. Union Cemetery, Frenchtown, Hunterdon County.
BRITTON, WILLIAM (aka: Britts, William) Pvt, A, 90th PA Inf, 3-16-1902. Bayview-New York Bay Cemetery, Jersey City, Hudson County.
BRITTON, WILLIAM Pvt, U.S. Marine Corps, USS Sophronia, 1-4-1911. Clinton Cemetery, Irvington, Essex County.
BRITTON, WILLIAM (see: Brittain, William) Fairmount Cemetery, Newark, Essex County.
BRITTON, WILLIAM C. Pvt, G, 37th NJ Inf, 8- -1888. Mount Holly Cemetery, Mount Holly, Burlington County.
BRITTON, WILLIAM F. (aka: Britton, Charles) Pvt, Btty F, 2nd PA Heavy Art, 12-9-1906. Oddfellows Cemetery, Burlington, Burlington County.
BRITTON, WILLIAM R. Pvt, D, 6th NJ Inf, 5-25-1902. Cedar Grove Cemetery, Gloucester City, Camden County.

New Jersey Civil War Burials

BRITTS, WILLIAM (see: Britton, William) Bayview-New York Bay Cemetery, Jersey City, Hudson County.

BRIXNER, JOHN (see: Brizner, John) Fairmount Cemetery, Newark, Essex County.

BRIZNER*, JOHN (aka: Brixner, John) Pvt, K, 1st NJ Militia, [President's Guard.] 3-7-1908. Fairmount Cemetery, Newark, Essex County.

BROADBENT, JOSEPH Landsman, U.S. Navy, USS Sabine, 4-11-1904. New Camden Cemetery, Camden, Camden County.

BROADFOOT, JOHN C. Pvt, Btty B, 1st NJ Light Art, 1-4-1892. Rahway Cemetery, Rahway, Union County.

BROADHURST, JAMES Landsman, U.S. Navy, 3-3-1917. United Methodist Church Cemetery, Leesburg, Cumberland County.

BROADWATER, GEORGE J. Corp, I, 24th NJ Inf, 3-29-1903. Baptist Church Cemetery, Haddonfield, Camden County.

BROADWATER*, WILLIAM Pvt, F, 2nd NJ Inf, 5-22-1901. New Camden Cemetery, Camden, Camden County.

BROADWATER, WILLIAM J. Pvt, K, 183rd PA Inf, 4-30-1908. Colestown Cemetery, Cherry Hill, Camden County.

BROADWAY, AARON (see: Bradway, Aaron R.) Presbyterian Church Cemetery, Bridgeton, Cumberland County.

BROADWAY, ALBERT (aka: Broadway, Alfred) Pvt, A, 22nd NJ Inf, DoD Unknown. English Neighborhood Reformed Church Cemetery, Ridgefield, Bergen County.

BROADWAY, ALFRED (see: Broadway, Albert) English Neighborhood Reformed Church Cemetery, Ridgefield, Bergen County.

BROADWAY, JOSEPH J. Pvt, F, 19th U.S. CT, 5-21-1895. Mount Salem Church Cemetery, Fenwick, Salem County.

BROADWELL, BURTIS M. Pvt, D, 5th NJ Inf, [Died of diarrhea at Beverly, NJ.] 10-5-1864. Chestnut Cemetery, Dover, Morris County.

BROADWELL, CALEB J. Sgt, K, 39th NJ Inf, 12-11-1909. Chestnut Cemetery, Dover, Morris County.

BROADWELL, JOHN A. Pvt, Btty D, 1st NJ Light Art, 1907. Clinton Cemetery, Irvington, Essex County.

BROADWELL, MANNING C. Pvt, E, 27th NJ Inf, 8-12-1905. Fairmount Cemetery, Chatham, Morris County.

BROADWELL, SILAS P. Pvt, Btty B, 1st NJ Light Art, 1-29-1887. Presbyterian Church Cemetery, Rockaway, Morris County.

BROADWELL, STEPHEN A. Pvt, K, 39th NJ Inf, 2-5-1888. Chestnut Cemetery, Dover, Morris County.

BROADWELL, WILLIAM E. Sgt, B, 15th NJ Inf, [Wounded 5-3-1863 at Salem Heights, VA.] 4-23-1907. Evergreen Cemetery, Morristown, Morris County.

BROBEN, HENRY Pvt, I, 39th NJ Inf, 9-3-1888. Fairmount Cemetery, Newark, Essex County.

BROBST, CHARLES Pvt, G, 143rd PA Inf, [Wounded 5-23-1864 at North Anna River, VA.] 4-29-1926. Cedar Lawn Cemetery, Paterson, Passaic County.

BROCAR, PETER Pvt, F, 29th CT Inf, DoD Unknown. Holy Sepulchre Cemetery, East Orange, Essex County.

BROCK, CHARLES L. Corp, F, 13th GA Cav (CSA), 7-28-1864. Finn's Point National Cemetery, Pennsville, Salem County.

BROCK, GEORGE H. Pvt, Btty D, 1st NJ Light Art, [Died of fever at Washington, DC.] 3-5-1864. Mercer Cemetery, Trenton, Mercer County.

BROCK*, GEORGE P. Pvt, G, 47th MA Militia, 12-29-1910. Holy Name Cemetery, Jersey City, Hudson County.

BROCK, JOHN W. Pvt, G, 55th NC Inf (CSA), [Captured 7-1-1863 at Gettysburg, PA.] 10-1-1863. Finn's Point National Cemetery, Pennsville, Salem County.

Our Brothers Gone Before

BROCK*, OLIVER S. Corp, B, 47th MA Militia, 9-9-1905. Bayview-New York Bay Cemetery, Jersey City, Hudson County.

BROCK, WILLIAM M. Pvt, K, 28th NJ Inf, 4-16-1874. St. Mary's Cemetery, South Amboy, Middlesex County.

BROCKEN, JOHN (aka: Bracken, John) Sgt, D, 71st NY Inf, [Wounded 5-7-1864 at Wilderness, VA.] 4-3-1884. Holy Sepulchre Cemetery, East Orange, Essex County.

BROCKHURST, BODLEY THOMAS Sgt, H, 1st NJ Inf, 7-24-1872. Bayview-New York Bay Cemetery, Jersey City, Hudson County.

BROCKINGTON, JOHN H. Pvt, I, 24th NJ Inf, 4-23-1886. Evergreen Cemetery, Camden, Camden County.

BROCKLEHURST, ROBERT (see: Brooks, Robert) Methodist-Episcopal Cemetery, Pennsville, Salem County.

BROCKSTEDT, HENRY 1-28-1932. Bayview-New York Bay Cemetery, Jersey City, Hudson County.

BROCKWAY*, JOHN Pvt, D, 54th PA Inf, 4-9-1888. Baptist Cemetery, Pemberton, Burlington County.

BROCKWAY, SAMUEL Sgt, F, 183rd PA Inf, 1-23-1915. Riverside Cemetery, Toms River, Ocean County.

BRODBECK, ERNEST A. Pvt, F, 9th U.S. Inf, 12-26-1919. Fairmount Cemetery, Newark, Essex County.

BRODEN, JAMES Pvt, K, 22nd U.S. CT, 5-12-1898. Mount Zion Methodist Church Cemetery, Lawnside, Camden County.

BRODERICK, VIRGIL Lt Col, 1st NJ Cav [Cenotaph. Killed in action at Brandy Station, VA.] 6-9-1863. Presbyterian Church Cemetery, Andover, Sussex County.

BRODLE*, THOMAS Sgt, C, 6th NJ Inf, 6-29-1869. St. Peter's Cemetery, Jersey City, Hudson County.

BROGAN*, JOHN Pvt, A, 40th NJ Inf, 2-16-1920. Holy Sepulchre Cemetery, East Orange, Essex County.

BROGAN, PETER Pvt, E, 8th NJ Inf, 11-1-1878. Holy Sepulchre Cemetery, East Orange, Essex County.

BROGAN, ROBERT Pvt, B, 42nd VA Inf (CSA), [Captured 7-3-1863 at Gettysburg, PA. Died of typhoid.] 10-3-1863. Finn's Point National Cemetery, Pennsville, Salem County.

BROKAW, GEORGE W. Seaman, U.S. Navy, 1906. Rahway Cemetery, Rahway, Union County.

BROKAW, GILBERT L. Pvt, A, 30th NJ Inf, 1906. Rural Hill Cemetery, Whitehouse, Hunterdon County.

BROKAW, ISAAC Pvt, I, 3rd NJ Inf, 1897. Baptist/Evergreen Methodist Cemetery, Plainfield, Union County.

BROKAW, ISAAC C. Sgt, C, 28th NJ Inf, 1890. Baptist/Evergreen Methodist Cemetery, Plainfield, Union County.

BROKAW, ISAAC P. Pvt, K, 30th NJ Inf, 1916. Old Somerville Cemetery, Somerville, Somerset County.

BROKAW, JEREMIAH F. Pvt, G, 8th NJ Inf, 1906. Methodist Cemetery, Southard, Monmouth County.

BROKAW, JOHN Q.A. Pvt, B, 6th NJ Inf, 2-6-1896. Baptist Church Cemetery, Mount Bethel, Somerset County.

BROKAW, OSCAR Corp, C, 15th NJ Inf, [Killed in action at Salem Heights, VA.] 5-3-1863. Rahway Cemetery, Rahway, Union County.

BROKAW, PETER H. 1879. Harlingen Cemetery, Belle Mead, Somerset County.

BROKAW, WILLIAM 3-6-1910. Reformed Church Cemetery, Lebanon, Hunterdon County.

New Jersey Civil War Burials

BROKAW, WILLIAM H. (JR.) Pvt, H, 21st NJ Inf, 12-30-1919. Greenwood Cemetery, Hamilton, Mercer County.

BROKER, WILLIAM W. (aka: Brown, William) Sgt, A, 90th NY Inf, 5-12-1895. Bayview-New York Bay Cemetery, Jersey City, Hudson County.

BROMLEY, THOMAS Pvt, F, 7th NJ Inf, 6-29-1919. Laurel Grove Cemetery, Totowa, Passaic County.

BRONDSTELLER, WILLIAM LEONARD (JR.) Pvt, G, 9th NJ Inf, [Wounded in action.] 4-24-1881. Evergreen Cemetery, Hillside, Union County.

BRONNER, AUGUST FREDERICK (aka: Brouner, August) Pvt, Btty C, 1st NY Light Art, [Awarded the Medal of Honor.] 10-31-1893. Fairmount Cemetery, Newark, Essex County.

BRONSON, OSCAR A. Pvt, B, 2nd NJ Inf, 11-20-1884. Deckertown-Union Cemetery, Papakating, Sussex County.

BROOK, JONATHAN Pvt, B, 51st PA Inf, 9-10-1871. Riverview Cemetery, Trenton, Mercer County.

BROOKER, CHRISTOPHER (aka: Cooker, Christopher) Pvt, I, 12th NJ Inf, 7-19-1865. Baptist Church Cemetery, Canton, Salem County.

BROOKER, REUBEN Pvt, Btty A, 16th NY Heavy Art, 10-2-1911. Elwood Rural Cemetery, Elwood, Atlantic County.

BROOKHOUSE, FREDERICK (see: Schlichter, Frederick) Evergreen Cemetery, Hillside, Union County.

BROOKINS, WILLIAM Pvt, B, 33rd NY Inf, 12-28-1894. Holy Name Cemetery, Jersey City, Hudson County.

BROOKS, A.W. Pvt, A, 50th NC Inf (CSA), [Captured at Savannah, GA.] 4-10-1865. Finn's Point National Cemetery, Pennsville, Salem County.

BROOKS, ABRAHAM Pvt, E, 9th NJ Inf, 12-22-1934. Mount Hebron Cemetery, Montclair, Essex County.

BROOKS, ALFRED J. Pvt, G, 3rd NJ Cav, [Wounded in action.] 3-9-1898. Siloam Cemetery, Vineland, Cumberland County.

BROOKS, BENJAMIN F. DoD Unknown. Elmwood Cemetery, New Brunswick, Middlesex County.

BROOKS, CHARLES H. Sgt, I, 10th NJ Inf, 2-5-1903. Bordentown/Old St. Mary's Catholic Cemetery, Bordentown, Burlington County.

BROOKS, DANIEL C. Pvt, F, 24th NJ Inf, 9-11-1925. Overlook Cemetery, Bridgeton, Cumberland County.

BROOKS, DAVID Corp, F, 2nd NJ Inf, 7-27-1899. Grove Church Cemetery, North Bergen, Hudson County.

BROOKS, ENOCH Pvt, H, 3rd NJ Cav, 3-30-1879. Presbyterian Church Cemetery, Bridgeton, Cumberland County.

BROOKS, GEORGE Pvt, Btty D, 1st NJ Light Art, DoD Unknown. East Ridgelawn Cemetery, Clifton, Passaic County.

BROOKS, GEORGE DoD Unknown. Old Camden Cemetery, Camden, Camden County.

BROOKS, GEORGE L. Asst Surg, 13th NJ Inf 12-14-1884. Grove Church Cemetery, North Bergen, Hudson County.

BROOKS, GEORGE O. 1st Lt, B, 4th NJ Inf, 10-2-1884. Hope Christian Church Cemetery, Marlton, Burlington County.

BROOKS*, GEORGE W. Pvt, L, 20th PA Cav, 2-7-1907. Presbyterian Cemetery, West Stewartsville, Warren County.

BROOKS, HARRIS Pvt, H, 24th NJ Inf, 4-17-1896. Evergreen Cemetery, Camden, Camden County.

BROOKS, HENRY Pvt, G, 124th NY Inf, 4-4-1873. Fernwood Cemetery, Jamesburg, Middlesex County.

BROOKS, HOMER Sgt, A, 37th NJ Inf, 5-3-1927. Bayview-New York Bay Cemetery, Jersey City, Hudson County.

Our Brothers Gone Before

BROOKS, JAMES H. Sgt, I, 70th NY Inf, 7-18-1898. Fairmount Cemetery, Newark, Essex County.
BROOKS, JAMES J. Pvt, H, 54th MA Inf, 4-13-1898. Mount Prospect Cemetery, Neptune, Monmouth County.
BROOKS, JOHN Pvt, G, 80th IL Inf, [Wounded in action.] 1921. Soldier's Home Cemetery, Vineland, Cumberland County.
BROOKS, JONATHAN 1-25-1885. Elmwood Cemetery, New Brunswick, Middlesex County.
BROOKS, JOSEPH C. Pvt, H, 24th NJ Inf, DoD Unknown. Presbyterian Church Cemetery, Bridgeton, Cumberland County.
BROOKS, JOSEPH H. Wagoner, G, 2nd NJ Cav, DoD Unknown. Methodist Church Cemetery, Sparta, Sussex County.
BROOKS, LEONARD Sgt, K, 1st NY Eng, 3-12-1908. Laurel Grove Cemetery, Totowa, Passaic County.
BROOKS, PHILIP (see: Bruch, Philip) Riverview Cemetery, Trenton, Mercer County.
BROOKS*, REUBEN H. Pvt, Btty D, 2nd U.S. Art, 7-23-1901. Deckertown-Union Cemetery, Papakating, Sussex County.
BROOKS, ROBERT (aka: Brocklehurst, Robert) Pvt, A, 116th PA Inf, 4-18-1884. Methodist-Episcopal Cemetery, Pennsville, Salem County.
BROOKS, SAMUEL Corp, K, 2nd DC Inf, 2-27-1867. Presbyterian Church Cemetery, Newton, Sussex County.
BROOKS, SAMUEL H. Pvt, A, 65th NY Inf, 10-11-1875. Walnut Grove Cemetery, Mount Freedom, Morris County.
BROOKS, THOMAS Pvt, G, 39th NJ Inf, 9-7-1911. Arlington Cemetery, Kearny, Hudson County.
BROOKS, W.T. Pvt, H, 21st VA Cav (CSA), 6-12-1864. Finn's Point National Cemetery, Pennsville, Salem County.
BROOKS, WILLIAM E. Pvt, H, 24th NJ Inf, 11-18-1919. Baptist Church Cemetery, Bridgeton, Cumberland County.
BROOKS, WILLIAM H. Sgt, E, 12th NJ Inf, 2-24-1912. Evergreen Cemetery, Camden, Camden County.
BROOM, ABEL Corp, G, PA Emerg NJ Militia, 3-14-1865. Baptist/St. Andrew's Cemetery, Mount Holly, Burlington County.
BROOM, JESSE E. Corp, K, 23rd NJ Inf, 12-17-1889. New Freedom Cemetery, New Freedom, Camden County.
BROOMALL*, JOSEPH W. Pvt, Btty G, 5th U.S. Art, 6-16-1890. 1st United Methodist Church Cemetery, Bridgeton, Cumberland County.
BROOME, WILLIAM M. Corp, B, 4th NJ Militia, 1918. Mount Holly Cemetery, Mount Holly, Burlington County.
BROOMELL*, WILLIAM C. Pvt, C, 124th PA Inf, 9-7-1904. Presbyterian Cemetery, Allentown, Monmouth County.
BROPHY, PATRICK Pvt, K, 38th NJ Inf, 4-25-1915. St. Mary's Cemetery, Hamilton, Mercer County.
BROPHY, THOMAS Pvt, D, 21st NJ Inf, 9-6-1867. St. Peter's Cemetery, Jersey City, Hudson County.
BROPHY*, WILLIAM Pvt, I, 13th NY Cav, 6-4-1929. Holy Sepulchre Cemetery, Totowa, Passaic County.
BROSIUS, PAXSON Pvt, A, 1st DE Cav, 6-8-1923. Rosehill Cemetery, Newfield, Gloucester County.
BROSS, ABRAM J. Pvt, C, 22nd NJ Inf, 8-10-1901. Old Hook Cemetery, Westwood, Bergen County.
BROSS, LOUIS Pvt, A, 13th NJ Inf, 6-15-1888. Fairmount Cemetery, Newark, Essex County.

New Jersey Civil War Burials

BROSS, MARTIN Pvt, A, 20th NY Inf, 1-24-1909. Fairmount Cemetery, Newark, Essex County.

BROSS, NICHOLAS Pvt, A, 22nd NJ Inf, 11-22-1893. Westwood Cemetery, Westwood, Bergen County.

BROSS, OLIVER L. Pvt, A, 1st NJ Cav, 9-23-1909. Brink Cemetery, Colesville, Sussex County.

BROSS, THOMAS Pvt, I, 15th NJ Inf, 6-14-1893. Brink Cemetery, Colesville, Sussex County.

BROSSELL, WILLIAM (see: Brassell, William) Calvary Cemetery, Cherry Hill, Camden County.

BROSTLER, GEORGE Pvt, H, 103rd NY Inf, 4-8-1925. Fairmount Cemetery, Newark, Essex County.

BROTHERS, ANDREW Pvt, H, 1st U.S. Inf, 12-26-1922. Greenwood Cemetery, Hamilton, Mercer County.

BROTHERTON, THOMAS Pvt, I, 1st NJ Cav, 8-18-1886. Fairmount Cemetery, Newark, Essex County.

BROTHINGTON, W.T. Pvt, Btty L, 1st CT Heavy Art, 12-2-1902. Fairmount Cemetery, Newark, Essex County.

BROTZMAN, WILLIAM Q. Musc, 47th PA Inf Band 8-10-1877. Mansfield/Washington Cemetery, Washington, Warren County.

BROUCH, JOSEPH (see: Bruch, Joseph) Phillipsburg Cemetery, Phillipsburg, Warren County.

BROUGHTON, CALVIN Pvt, I, 47th NC Inf (CSA), [Captured 7-1-1863 at Gettysburg, PA.] 10-2-1863. Finn's Point National Cemetery, Pennsville, Salem County.

BROUGHTON*, GEORGE Pvt, I, 51st NY Inf, 3-31-1891. Bayview-New York Bay Cemetery, Jersey City, Hudson County.

BROUGHTON, GRIMSHAW Sgt, I, 2nd NJ Inf, 1-25-1907. Cedar Lawn Cemetery, Paterson, Passaic County.

BROUNER, AUGUST (see: Bronner, August F.) Fairmount Cemetery, Newark, Essex County.

BROWER, ABRAHAM Pvt, C, 21st NJ Inf, 9-25-1891. Old Bergen Church Cemetery, Jersey City, Hudson County.

BROWER, ABRAHAM D. Pvt, H, 26th NJ Inf, 11-12-1864. Rosedale Cemetery, Orange, Essex County.

BROWER, ALFRED S. Landsman, U.S. Navy, [U.S. receiving ship.] 1-17-1867. Presbyterian Church Cemetery, Greenwich, Warren County.

BROWER, ANTHONY Pvt, F, 2nd NJ Cav, 3-21-1915. Osbornville Protestant Church Cemetery, Breton Woods, Ocean County.

BROWER, BURROUGH Pvt, C, 3rd NJ Cav, 5-30-1907. St. Paul's Methodist Church Cemetery, Port Republic, Atlantic County.

BROWER, CHARLES Pvt, K, 84th NY Inf, [Wounded 7-1-1863 at Gettysburg, PA.] 10-9-1905. Palisade Cemetery, North Bergen, Hudson County.

BROWER, CHARLES A. Pvt, D, 14th NJ Inf, [Wounded 6-1-1864 at Cold Harbor, VA.] 2-1-1903. Adelphia Cemetery, Adelphia, Monmouth County.

BROWER, DANIEL HARVEY Musc, A, 1st NJ Inf, [Died of typhoid at Camp Seminary, VA.] 9-6-1861. Rahway Cemetery, Rahway, Union County.

BROWER, DAVID 11-13-1863. Methodist Church Cemetery, Groveville, Mercer County.

BROWER, DAVID Pvt, E, 28th NJ Inf, [Wounded in action.] 6-5-1901. Greenville Cemetery, Lakewood, Ocean County.

BROWER, GEORGE W. Musc, K, 25th NJ Inf, 12-25-1916. Laurel Grove Cemetery, Totowa, Passaic County.

BROWER, GEORGE W. Pvt, B, 29th NJ Inf, 3-3-1887. Greengrove Cemetery, Keyport, Monmouth County.

BROWER, HENRY 10-17-1922. Fairmount Cemetery, Newark, Essex County.

Our Brothers Gone Before

BROWER, HENRY Pvt, A, 38th NJ Inf, DoD Unknown. Fairview Cemetery, Fairview, Monmouth County.

BROWER, JACOB Pvt, Btty D, 3rd NY Light Art, 7-19-1884. Weehawken Cemetery, North Bergen, Hudson County.

BROWER, JACOB M. Pvt, G, 1st NJ Cav, [Died of chronic diarrhea at Balls Cross Roads, VA.] 10-28-1861. Old 1st Methodist Church Cemetery, West Long Branch, Monmouth County.

BROWER*, JOEL Pvt, F, 2nd NJ Cav, 12-6-1929. Whitelawn Cemetery, Point Pleasant, Ocean County.

BROWER, JOHN (see: Bower, John) Brookside Cemetery, Englewood, Bergen County.

BROWER*, JOHN H. Corp, H, 2nd NJ Inf, 1-10-1920. Zion Methodist Church Cemetery, Bargaintown, Atlantic County.

BROWER, JOHN M. Sgt, H, 27th IN Inf, DoD Unknown. Finn's Point National Cemetery, Pennsville, Salem County.

BROWER, JOSEPH H. Pvt, B, 2nd NJ Inf, 2-2-1884. Old 1st Methodist Church Cemetery, West Long Branch, Monmouth County.

BROWER*, MATHIAS J. (aka: Brower, Matthew) Pvt, K, 22nd NJ Inf, 9-6-1911. Greengrove Cemetery, Keyport, Monmouth County.

BROWER, MATTHEW (see: Brower, Mathias J.) Greengrove Cemetery, Keyport, Monmouth County.

BROWER, NICHOLAS Pvt, D, 12th NJ Inf, DoD Unknown. Cedar Lawn Cemetery, Paterson, Passaic County.

BROWER, PETER T. Pvt, E, 12th U.S. VRC, 1928. Woodland Cemetery, Chatsworth, Burlington County.

BROWER, ROBERT DEWOLFE Pvt, H, 22nd NJ Inf, 1-6-1914. Bloomfield Cemetery, Bloomfield, Essex County.

BROWER*, SAMUEL S. 1st Lt, Adj, 82nd NY Inf 10-27-1907. Bayview-New York Bay Cemetery, Jersey City, Hudson County.

BROWER, STACY (see: Brown, Stacy L.) Laurel Grove Cemetery, Totowa, Passaic County.

BROWER, SYLVANUS 1924. Asbury Methodist-Episcopal Church Cemetery, Swainton, Cape May County.

BROWER, WILLIAM H. Pvt, Unassigned, 9th NJ Inf, 1922. Methodist Cemetery, Hamilton, Monmouth County.

BROWLES, ANDY __, __, __ Confederate States Cav (CSA), 9-3-1864. Finn's Point National Cemetery, Pennsville, Salem County.

BROWN*, A. BENSON Capt, C, 9th NJ Inf, 5-6-1875. Bordentown/Old St. Mary's Catholic Cemetery, Bordentown, Burlington County.

BROWN, AARON F. Pvt, I, 67th PA Inf, 7-10-1914. Greenwood Cemetery, Hamilton, Mercer County.

BROWN, ABRAHAM Pvt, F, 72nd NY Inf, 2-27-1870. Fairmount Cemetery, Newark, Essex County.

BROWN, ABRAHAM S. Corp, C, 12th NH Inf, [Wounded 5-3-1863 at Chancellorsville, VA.] 12-20-1908. Old 1st Methodist Church Cemetery, West Long Branch, Monmouth County.

BROWN, ABRAM 12-24-1892. Fairmount Cemetery, Newark, Essex County.

BROWN, ABRAM Pvt, Btty B, 1st NJ Light Art, 8-11-1916. Old Butler Cemetery, Butler, Morris County.

BROWN, ABRAM W. Pvt, H, 5th NJ Inf, [Wounded 5-5-1862 at Williamsburg, VA.] 11-8-1887. Presbyterian Church Cemetery, Woodbridge, Middlesex County.

BROWN, ADAM Pvt, G, 4th NJ Inf, DoD Unknown. Greengrove Cemetery, Keyport, Monmouth County.

BROWN, ALEXANDER Pvt, G, 34th NJ Inf, 3-8-1887. St. John's Cemetery, Hamilton, Mercer County.

New Jersey Civil War Burials

BROWN, ALEXANDER Wagoner, I, 29th NJ Inf, 10-10-1904. Rose Hill Cemetery, Matawan, Monmouth County.
BROWN, ALEXANDER Pvt, C, 25th NJ Inf, 12-25-1870. Cedar Lawn Cemetery, Paterson, Passaic County.
BROWN, ALEXANDER Pvt, A, 26th U.S. CT, 4-30-1902. Hillside Cemetery, Scotch Plains, Union County.
BROWN, ALFRED Sgt, B, 28th NJ Inf, 4-7-1889. Christ Church Cemetery, Morgan, Middlesex County.
BROWN, ALFRED B. Pvt, H, 2nd NJ Cav, 1-31-1887. Hoboken Cemetery, North Bergen, Hudson County.
BROWN, ALPHONZO C. Pvt, F, 7th ME Inf, 9-15-1862. Fairmount Cemetery, Newark, Essex County.
BROWN, AMBROSE Pvt, Btty D, 2nd NY Heavy Art, 1926. Mount Pleasant Cemetery, Millville, Cumberland County.
BROWN, AMOS Seaman, U.S. Navy, 10-21-1917. Cedar Hill Cemetery, Hightstown, Mercer County.
BROWN, AMOS F. Pvt, G, 26th NJ Inf, 8-2-1906. Hollywood Cemetery, Union, Union County.
BROWN, AMZI W. Pvt, C, 13th NJ Inf, 3-6-1882. Fairmount Cemetery, Newark, Essex County.
BROWN, ANDREW J. Pvt, F, 1st PA Prov Cav, 4-14-1919. Evergreen Cemetery, Camden, Camden County.
BROWN, ANDREW J. 9-9-1888. Cedar Green Cemetery, Clayton, Gloucester County.
BROWN, ANDREW J. Pvt, C, 25th U.S. CT, 1-14-1912. Arlington Cemetery, Kearny, Hudson County.
BROWN, ANDREW J. Pvt, F, 38th NJ Inf, 7-3-1911. Glenwood Cemetery, West Long Branch, Monmouth County.
BROWN, B. REED 3-26-1882. United Methodist Church Cemetery, Port Elizabeth, Cumberland County.
BROWN, BAILEY B. Bvt Maj, 1st NJ Inf [Wounded 5-12-1864 at Spotsylvania CH, VA.] 9-18-1890. Hoboken Cemetery, North Bergen, Hudson County.
BROWN, BENJAMIN F. Corp, E, 30th NJ Inf, 3-22-1899. New Presbyterian Cemetery, Bound Brook, Somerset County.
BROWN, BENJAMIN J. Seaman, U.S. Navy, 4-7-1918. Bayview-New York Bay Cemetery, Jersey City, Hudson County.
BROWN*, BENJAMIN S. Corp, E, 2nd NJ Cav, 1-3-1936. Riverview Cemetery, Trenton, Mercer County.
BROWN, BURLIN Pvt, C, 2nd NJ Militia, 11-29-1916. Bayview-New York Bay Cemetery, Jersey City, Hudson County.
BROWN, C. DoD Unknown. Methodist Church Cemetery, Springfield, Union County.
BROWN, CHARLES Pvt, F, 24th NJ Inf, 12-14-1879. Cohansey Baptist Church Cemetery, Bowentown, Cumberland County.
BROWN, CHARLES Pvt, K, 38th PA Inf, 10-17-1862. Fairmount Cemetery, Newark, Essex County.
BROWN, CHARLES Pvt, K, 1st NJ Militia, 4-17-1916. Fairmount Cemetery, Newark, Essex County.
BROWN, CHARLES Pvt, D, 38th NJ Inf, 7-4-1895. Eglington Cemetery, Clarksboro, Gloucester County.
BROWN, CHARLES Seaman, U.S. Navy, USS Vandalia, 5-31-1901. Weehawken Cemetery, North Bergen, Hudson County.
BROWN, CHARLES (see: Roome, Jacob P.) Bayview-New York Bay Cemetery, Jersey City, Hudson County.
BROWN, CHARLES (see: Buttell, Charles B.) Laurel Grove Cemetery, Totowa, Passaic County.

Our Brothers Gone Before

BROWN, CHARLES A. Pvt, B, 7th NH Inf, 8-13-1910. Phillipsburg Cemetery, Phillipsburg, Warren County.
BROWN, CHARLES E. Pvt, B, 9th NJ Inf, 9-6-1926. Mount Pleasant Cemetery, Newark, Essex County.
BROWN, CHARLES F. Pvt, G, 161st NY Inf, 5-20-1921. Cedar Lawn Cemetery, Paterson, Passaic County.
BROWN, CHARLES G. Pvt, D, 21st NJ Inf, 2-3-1913. Laurel Grove Cemetery, Totowa, Passaic County.
BROWN, CHARLES H. Pvt, F, 41st U.S. CT, 7-2-1891. Johnson Cemetery, Camden, Camden County.
BROWN, CHARLES H. Pvt, H, 2nd DC Inf, 5-25-1909. Fairmount Cemetery, Newark, Essex County.
BROWN, CHARLES H. Pvt, A, 29th NJ Inf, 1897. Old 1st Methodist Church Cemetery, West Long Branch, Monmouth County.
BROWN, CHARLES H. Pvt, D, 33rd NJ Inf, 6-29-1867. Pompton Reformed Church Cemetery, Pompton Lakes, Passaic County.
BROWN, CHARLES P. Capt, I, 12th NJ Inf, 11-27-1918. Riverview Cemetery, Trenton, Mercer County.
BROWN, CHRISTIAN 1897. Riverview Cemetery, Trenton, Mercer County.
BROWN, CHRISTIAN (see: Braun, Christian H.) Riverview Cemetery, Trenton, Mercer County.
BROWN, CLIFFORD I. Seaman, U.S. Navy, USS Marblehead, 11-22-1884. Evergreen Cemetery, Hillside, Union County.
BROWN, DANIEL L. Artificer, K, 1st NY Eng, 9-22-1903. Fairmount Cemetery, Chatham, Morris County.
BROWN, DAVID Capt, D, 79th NY Inf, [Killed in acton at 1st Bull Run, VA.] 7-21-1861. Bayview-New York Bay Cemetery, Jersey City, Hudson County.
BROWN, DAVID Pvt, E, 26th NJ Inf, 10-30-1892. Mount Pleasant Cemetery, Newark, Essex County.
BROWN*, DAVID B. Sgt, D, 3rd NJ Inf, 1-27-1887. Evergreen Cemetery, Camden, Camden County.
BROWN, DAVID O. Pvt, K, 73rd NY Inf, 8-8-1862. Presbyterian Church Cemetery, Elizabeth, Union County.
BROWN, DAVID POMROY Corp, C, 16th PA Cav, 7-21-1908. Bayview-New York Bay Cemetery, Jersey City, Hudson County.
BROWN, DAVID U. Pvt, D, 157th NY Inf, 1912. Laurel Hill Cemetery, Elwood, Atlantic County.
BROWN, DENNIS (aka: Bunn, Dennis) Pvt, K, 1st NJ Inf, [Missing in action at Wilderness, VA. Supposed dead.] 5-5-1864. Boonton Cemetery, Boonton, Morris County.
BROWN, DITMORE Pvt, A, 38th NJ Inf, 3-8-1883. Riverside Cemetery, Toms River, Ocean County.
BROWN, E. ___, ___, 2nd NJ ___, DoD Unknown. Laurel Grove Cemetery, Totowa, Passaic County.
BROWN, E. MARINER 1907. Chestnut Hill Cemetery, East Brunswick, Middlesex County.
BROWN, EDGAR 6-14-1912. Old Stone Church Cemetery, Fairton, Cumberland County.
BROWN, EDGAR S. Pvt, F, 24th NJ Inf, DoD Unknown. Presbyterian Church Cemetery, Greenwich, Cumberland County.
BROWN, EDWARD B. Pvt, D, 27th NJ Inf, 2-22-1877. Evergreen Cemetery, Camden, Camden County.
BROWN, EDWARD G. 1st Lt, I, 1st NJ Inf, 10-23-1895. Hoboken Cemetery, North Bergen, Hudson County.

New Jersey Civil War Burials

BROWN, EDWIN H. Pvt, F, 20th PA Cav, 5-10-1918. Riverview Cemetery, Trenton, Mercer County.

BROWN*, EDWIN N. Pvt, B, 15th NJ Inf, [Killed in action at Cold Harbor, VA.] 6-4-1864. Mount Pleasant Cemetery, Newark, Essex County.

BROWN, ELIAS Pvt, G, 28th NJ Inf, 4-17-1896. Mount Zion United Methodist Church Cemetery, Barnsboro, Gloucester County.

BROWN, ELIAS F. 8- -1869. Van Liew Cemetery, North Brunswick, Middlesex County.

BROWN, ELIJAH S. Sgt, A, 23rd NJ Inf, 4-26-1894. St. Mary's Episcopal Church Cemetery, Burlington, Burlington County.

BROWN, EVAN Pvt, B, 10th NJ Inf, 5-3-1895. Fairmount Cemetery, Newark, Essex County.

BROWN, FRANCIS Pvt, C, 34th NJ Inf, 12-8-1913. Bayview-New York Bay Cemetery, Jersey City, Hudson County.

BROWN, FRANCIS Pvt, K, 1st NJ Cav, 1-1-1918. Fairmount Cemetery, Newark, Essex County.

BROWN, FRANCIS Pvt, K, 34th NJ Inf, 8-23-1873. Mount Pleasant Cemetery, Newark, Essex County.

BROWN, FRANK B. Pvt, B, 32nd U.S. CT, 1866. Evergreen Cemetery, Morristown, Morris County.

BROWN, FURMAN Pvt, I, 2nd NJ Cav, 4-6-1898. United Presbyterian Church Cemetery, Perrineville, Monmouth County.

BROWN, FURMAN Pvt, C, 29th NJ Inf, 1907. Tennent Church Cemetery, Tennent, Monmouth County.

BROWN*, GARRETT Sgt, F, 1st NY Eng, 1-2-1872. Franklin Reformed Church Cemetery, Nutley, Essex County.

BROWN, GEORGE Pvt, C, 37th NJ Inf, 5-23-1881. Fairmount Cemetery, Newark, Essex County.

BROWN, GEORGE Pvt, F, 27th NJ Inf, 7-28-1901. Holy Sepulchre Cemetery, East Orange, Essex County.

BROWN, GEORGE Seaman, U.S. Navy, 12-23-1905. Flower Hill Cemetery, North Bergen, Hudson County.

BROWN, GEORGE Pvt, E, 40th NJ Inf, 6-16-1928. Zion Baptist Church Cemetery, New Egypt, Ocean County.

BROWN, GEORGE (see: Hobby, Charles E.) Presbyterian Cemetery, North Plainfield, Somerset County.

BROWN, GEORGE C. Lt Col, 23rd NJ Inf 2-1-1897. Baptist/St. Andrew's Cemetery, Mount Holly, Burlington County.

BROWN, GEORGE D. 1-12-1869. United Methodist Church Cemetery, Windsor, Mercer County.

BROWN*, GEORGE H. Pvt, I, 2nd NJ Cav, [Wounded 5-3-1863 at Salem Heights, VA.] 3-8-1907. Mount Pleasant Cemetery, Millville, Cumberland County.

BROWN, GEORGE H. Pvt, K, 22nd U.S. CT, 11-6-1915. Crystal Stream Cemetery, Navesink, Monmouth County.

BROWN*, GEORGE L. Pvt, I, 99th PA Inf, [Wounded in action 5-28-1864.] 1-20-1898. Brotherhood Cemetery, Hainesport, Burlington County.

BROWN, GEORGE M. Pvt, H, 22nd NJ Inf, 4-13-1863. Fairmount Cemetery, Newark, Essex County.

BROWN, GEORGE P. Pvt, F, 3rd NJ Cav, 8-7-1868. Mount Pleasant Cemetery, Newark, Essex County.

BROWN, GEORGE R. Pvt, A, 38th OH Inf, 5-21-1928. Riverview Cemetery, Trenton, Mercer County.

BROWN, GEORGE W. Pvt, K, 127th PA Inf, [Wounded 12-13-1862 at Fredericksburg, VA.] 8-16-1907. New Camden Cemetery, Camden, Camden County.

Our Brothers Gone Before

BROWN, GEORGE W. Pvt, K, 27th NJ Inf, 6-25-1898. Stanhope-Union Cemetery, Netcong, Morris County.
BROWN, GEORGE W. Pvt, H, 48th VA Inf (CSA), [Died of disease.] 12-31-1863. Finn's Point National Cemetery, Pennsville, Salem County.
BROWN, GEORGE W. Pvt, D, 23rd NJ Inf, 2-7-1918. Methodist Church Cemetery, Pemberton, Burlington County.
BROWN, GILBERT JAMES Sgt, B, 127th NY Inf, 1-17-1908. Methodist Cemetery, Newfoundland, Morris County.
BROWN, HARVEY Bvt Maj Gen, U.S. Army, 3-31-1874. Hazelwood Cemetery, Rahway, Union County.
BROWN, HENRY Pvt, A, 22nd U.S. CT, 2-4-1892. Bordentown/Old St. Mary's Catholic Cemetery, Bordentown, Burlington County.
BROWN*, HENRY Pvt, K, 38th NJ Inf, 2-2-1908. Tabernacle Baptist Church Cemetery, Erma, Cape May County.
BROWN, HENRY Pvt, I, 26th NJ Inf, 11-25-1903. Fairmount Cemetery, Newark, Essex County.
BROWN, HENRY Pvt, C, 2nd MO Cav, 5-3-1915. Rosedale Cemetery, Orange, Essex County.
BROWN, HENRY Pvt, C, 26th NJ Inf, 8-19-1900. Fairmount Cemetery, Newark, Essex County.
BROWN, HENRY Pvt, A, 7th NJ Inf, 6-12-1911. Arlington Cemetery, Kearny, Hudson County.
BROWN, HENRY 1921. Stillwater Cemetery, Stillwater, Sussex County.
BROWN, HENRY Corp, I, 2nd NH Inf, 12-27-1893. Baptist Church Cemetery, Scotch Plains, Union County.
BROWN, HENRY B. Corp, D, 12th NJ Inf, [Died of typhoid at Falmouth, VA.] 4-5-1863. Hedding Methodist-Episcopal Church Cemetery, Bellmawr, Camden County.
BROWN, HENRY C. Pvt, F, 3rd DE Inf, 3-5-1916. Shinn GAR Post Cemetery, Port Norris, Cumberland County.
BROWN, HENRY L. Pvt, C, 9th NJ Inf, 12-21-1904. Mount Pleasant Cemetery, Millville, Cumberland County.
BROWN, HENRY W. Pvt, F, 4th NJ Inf, 4-4-1923. Evergreen Cemetery, Camden, Camden County.
BROWN, HERMAN Sgt, A, 1st NY Mounted Rifles, DoD Unknown. Franklin Reformed Church Cemetery, Nutley, Essex County.
BROWN, HORACE Corp, E, 6th U.S. CT, 4-29-1885. Beverly National Cemetery, Edgewater Park, Burlington County.
BROWN, HUTCHINS Corp, G, 1st NJ Cav, 11-24-1890. Old 1st Methodist Church Cemetery, West Long Branch, Monmouth County.
BROWN, ISAAC Pvt, A, 67th OH Inf, [Died at New York, NY.] 11-4-1862. Fairmount Cemetery, Newark, Essex County.
BROWN, ISAAC J. 6-13-1885. Greengrove Cemetery, Keyport, Monmouth County.
BROWN, ISAAC S. 10-2-1895. United Methodist Church Cemetery, Smithville, Atlantic County.
BROWN*, ISHMAEL H. Landsman, U.S. Navy, USS Dan Smith, 2-24-1904. Riverview Cemetery, Trenton, Mercer County.
BROWN, ISRAEL Sgt, G, 2nd NJ Cav, 4-4-1908. Fairmount Cemetery, Newark, Essex County.
BROWN, J. (see: Stokes, Jessie A.) Methodist Church Cemetery, Titusville, Mercer County.
BROWN, J.M. Pvt, C, 46th AL Inf (CSA), 6-28-1863. Finn's Point National Cemetery, Pennsville, Salem County.
BROWN, JAMES Pvt, E, 23rd NJ Inf, 11-25-1890. Brotherhood Cemetery, Hainesport, Burlington County.

New Jersey Civil War Burials

BROWN, JAMES Pvt, F, 19th PA Inf, 5-18-1882. Colestown Cemetery, Cherry Hill, Camden County.
BROWN, JAMES Pvt, B, 2nd NJ Inf, 1923. Mount Pleasant Cemetery, Millville, Cumberland County.
BROWN, JAMES 9-10-1869. Methodist Cemetery, Cassville, Ocean County.
BROWN, JAMES Pvt, H, 29th NJ Inf, 5-1-1887. Riverside Cemetery, Toms River, Ocean County.
BROWN, JAMES Pvt, K, 22nd U.S. CT, 2-14-1885. Evergreen Cemetery, Hillside, Union County.
BROWN*, JAMES Pvt, G, 7th NJ Inf, [Wounded in action.] 7-4-1900. Chestnut Hill Cemetery, East Brunswick, Middlesex County.
BROWN, JAMES Pvt, B, 2nd NJ Inf, 1-30-1866. Mount Pleasant Cemetery, Newark, Essex County.
BROWN, JAMES B. 12-15-1884. Macphelah Cemetery, North Bergen, Hudson County.
BROWN*, JAMES B. Sgt, E, 30th NJ Inf, 6-6-1913. New Somerville Cemetery, Somerville, Somerset County.
BROWN*, JAMES D. Pvt, K, 6th NC Cav (CSA), [Died of smallpox.] 3-15-1864. Finn's Point National Cemetery, Pennsville, Salem County.
BROWN, JAMES H. Corp, K, 9th NJ Inf, 7-18-1900. Mount Pleasant Cemetery, Millville, Cumberland County.
BROWN, JAMES H. Corp, I, 2nd NJ Cav, 8-16-1897. United Presbyterian Church Cemetery, Perrineville, Monmouth County.
BROWN, JAMES H. Pvt, E, 37th NJ Inf, 12-7-1928. Fairmount Cemetery, Newark, Essex County.
BROWN, JAMES J. Pvt, G, 4th NJ Inf, DoD Unknown. Bethel Cemetery, Pennsauken, Camden County.
BROWN, JAMES J. Sgt, C, 7th NJ Inf, [Killed in action at Gettysburg, PA.] 7-2-1863. Evergreen Cemetery, Morristown, Morris County.
BROWN, JAMES L. Pvt, G, 14th NJ Inf, 6-10-1917. Glenwood Cemetery, West Long Branch, Monmouth County.
BROWN, JAMES M. Pvt, F, 11th NJ Inf, 7-25-1899. Princeton Cemetery, Princeton, Mercer County.
BROWN, JAMES M. DoD Unknown. Elmwood Cemetery, New Brunswick, Middlesex County.
BROWN, JAMES N. Corp, E, 1st MO Cav (CSA), 9-21-1863. Finn's Point National Cemetery, Pennsville, Salem County.
BROWN, JAMES W. Pvt, B, 1st NJ Cav, 3-14-1875. Bethlehem Presbyterian Church Cemetery, Grandin, Hunterdon County.
BROWN*, JASPER R. (aka: Smith, John) Pvt, A, 65th NY Inf, 1895. Methodist Cemetery, Cassville, Ocean County.
BROWN, JEREMIAH Pvt, A, 32nd U.S. CT, 2-19-1888. Chestnut Cemetery, Greenwich, Cumberland County.
BROWN, JEREMIAH Corp, A, 32nd U.S. CT, 12-15-1915. Mount Peace Cemetery, Lawnside, Camden County.
BROWN, JOB V. Corp, D, 11th NJ Inf, 2-5-1879. Fairmount Cemetery, Newark, Essex County.
BROWN, JOHN Ordinary Seaman, U.S. Navy, USS Vanderbilt, 1917. Atlantic City Cemetery, Pleasantville, Atlantic County.
BROWN, JOHN Pvt, D, 32nd U.S. CT, 1-11-1939. Trinity AME Church Cemetery, Wrightsville, Burlington County.
BROWN, JOHN Sgt, K, 8th U.S. Inf, 12-22-1898. New Camden Cemetery, Camden, Camden County.
BROWN, JOHN Pvt, B, 127th U.S. CT, 2-2-1905. Baptist Church Cemetery, Palermo, Cape May County.

Our Brothers Gone Before

BROWN, JOHN Corp, F, 38th NJ Inf, 1923. Old 1st Methodist Church Cemetery, West Long Branch, Monmouth County.

BROWN, JOHN Pvt, C, 60th (Crawford's) TN Mtd Inf (CSA), [Captured 5-17-1863 at Big Black River Bridge, MS.] 7-15-1863. Finn's Point National Cemetery, Pennsville, Salem County.

BROWN*, JOHN Pvt, B, 6th NJ Inf, 4-17-1920. New Presbyterian Cemetery, Bound Brook, Somerset County.

BROWN*, JOHN Seaman, U.S. Navy, USS Gem of the Sea, [Wounded in action.] 4-27-1905. Bloomfield Cemetery, Bloomfield, Essex County.

BROWN, JOHN Pvt, I, 35th NJ Inf, 11-17-1909. Rosedale Cemetery, Linden, Union County.

BROWN, JOHN A. Sgt, A, 3rd NJ Inf, 1910. Rahway Cemetery, Rahway, Union County.

BROWN, JOHN ALEXANDER Pvt, A, 20th MA Inf, 2-28-1931. Riverview Cemetery, Trenton, Mercer County.

BROWN, JOHN B. Pvt, E, 9th NJ Inf, 4-15-1868. Cedar Lawn Cemetery, Paterson, Passaic County.

BROWN, JOHN B. Corp, K, 70th NY Inf, 7-7-1871. Woodland Cemetery, Newark, Essex County.

BROWN, JOHN D. Sgt, A, 31st NJ Inf, 1901. Evergreen/Bishop Jaynes Cemetery, Basking Ridge, Somerset County.

BROWN*, JOHN F. Pvt, B, 124th NY Inf, [Wounded in action at Brandy Station, VA.] 10-20-1864. Beverly National Cemetery, Edgewater Park, Burlington County.

BROWN, JOHN F. Pvt, F, 14th NJ Inf, [Wounded in action.] 6-23-1915. Methodist Cemetery, Cassville, Ocean County.

BROWN, JOHN H. Pvt, D, 38th NJ Inf, 1912. Mount Pleasant Cemetery, Millville, Cumberland County.

BROWN, JOHN K. 9-14-1892. Fairmount Cemetery, Newark, Essex County.

BROWN, JOHN KELLEY Maj, 25th NJ Inf 7-16-1913. Evergreen Cemetery, Camden, Camden County.

BROWN, JOHN P. Pvt, C, 1st NJ Cav, 5-8-1883. Fairmount Cemetery, Newark, Essex County.

BROWN, JOHN P. Pvt, F, 4th NJ Inf, 4-30-1904. Manahath Cemetery, Glassboro, Gloucester County.

BROWN, JOHN R. Pvt, M, 2nd NJ Cav, 9-8-1917. Cedar Lawn Cemetery, Paterson, Passaic County.

BROWN*, JOHN W. Pvt, K, 83rd NY Inf, 2-13-1903. Riverview Cemetery, Trenton, Mercer County.

BROWN, JOHN W. Pvt, E, 8th NY State Militia, 10-2-1875. Evergreen Cemetery, Hillside, Union County.

BROWN, JOHN W. Capt, A, 1st NJ Inf, DoD Unknown. Evergreen Cemetery, Hillside, Union County.

BROWN, JOHN WILLIAM (JR.) Pvt, B, 5th NJ Inf, 2-20-1912. Bayview-New York Bay Cemetery, Jersey City, Hudson County.

BROWN, JONATHAN Pvt, D, 24th NJ Inf, 8-7-1910. 1st United Methodist Church Cemetery, Bridgeton, Cumberland County.

BROWN, JOSEPH Pvt, I, 4th NJ Inf, 7-24-1889. Christ Church Cemetery, Belleville, Essex County.

BROWN, JOSEPH Pvt, I, 6th NJ Inf, 6-18-1894. Methodist Church Cemetery, Ferrell, Gloucester County.

BROWN, JOSEPH 1-8-1895. Old 1st Methodist Church Cemetery, West Long Branch, Monmouth County.

BROWN, JOSEPH Corp, D, 14th NJ Inf, [Wounded in action.] 1915. Evergreen Cemetery, Farmingdale, Monmouth County.

New Jersey Civil War Burials

BROWN, JOSEPH Pvt, I, 26th NJ Inf, DoD Unknown. Fairmount Cemetery, Newark, Essex County.

BROWN, JOSEPH Pvt, K, 2nd NJ Militia, 1889. Mount Pleasant Cemetery, Newark, Essex County.

BROWN, JOSEPH B. Pvt, G, 28th NJ Inf, [Wounded in action.] 6-25-1882. Trinity Bible Church Cemetery, Glassboro, Gloucester County.

BROWN, JOSEPH E. Seaman, U.S. Navy, 3-9-1928. Greenwood Cemetery, Pleasantville, Atlantic County.

BROWN, JOSEPH F. Pvt, C, 38th NJ Inf, 1935. Manahath Cemetery, Glassboro, Gloucester County.

BROWN*, JOSEPH H. Seaman, U.S. Navy, USS Massachusetts, 1905. Presbyterian Church Cemetery, Bridgeton, Cumberland County.

BROWN, JOSEPH L. Pvt, I, 1st NJ Inf, 3-22-1912. Riverview Cemetery, Trenton, Mercer County.

BROWN*, JOSEPH R. Pvt, G, 7th NJ Inf, 2-18-1929. Methodist Cemetery, Cassville, Ocean County.

BROWN, JOSEPH W. Pvt, H, 1st NJ Inf, 10-26-1879. Evergreen Cemetery, Hillside, Union County.

BROWN, JOSHUA Pvt, B, 35th NJ Inf, DoD Unknown. Friendship United Methodist Church Cemetery, Landisville, Atlantic County.

BROWN*, JOSHUA M. Pvt, Btty E, 1st NJ Light Art, 1932. Batsto/Pleasant Mills Methodist Church Cemetery, Pleasant Mills, Atlantic County.

BROWN*, JOSIAH J. Pvt, G, 2nd NJ Inf, [Wounded in action.] 1-21-1936. Evergreen Cemetery, Hillside, Union County.

BROWN, JOSIAH W. Pvt, A, 42nd MS Inf (CSA), 3-28-1865. Finn's Point National Cemetery, Pennsville, Salem County.

BROWN, LEVI Pvt, D, PA Emerg NJ Militia, 11-1-1901. Holcomb-Riverview Cemetery, Lambertville, Hunterdon County.

BROWN, LEVI Pvt, D, 33rd NJ Inf, 1926. Old Butler Cemetery, Butler, Morris County.

BROWN, LEWIS 9-10-1862. St. John's Episcopal Church Cemetery, Salem, Salem County.

BROWN, LEWIS (see: Brown, Louis) Laurel Grove Cemetery, Totowa, Passaic County.

BROWN, LEWIS F. Pvt, L, 2nd NJ Cav, 2-28-1898. Baptist Church Cemetery, Jacobstown, Burlington County.

BROWN, LOUIS A. (aka: Brown, Lewis) Pvt, A, 68th NY Inf, 10-27-1913. Laurel Grove Cemetery, Totowa, Passaic County.

BROWN, LOUIS RICHARD Hosp Steward, 175th PA Inf 7-18-1901. Evergreen Cemetery, Hillside, Union County.

BROWN, LUCIEN B. Pvt, Charlottesville Btty, VA Light Art (CSA), [Captured 5-12-1864 at Spotsylvania CH, VA. Died of bowel or lung inflammation.] 7-21-1864. Finn's Point National Cemetery, Pennsville, Salem County.

BROWN, MARTIN Pvt, K, 185th NY Inf, 12-17-1895. Harmony Church Cemetery, Hopewell, Cumberland County.

BROWN, MARTIN A. Wagoner, C, 6th CT Inf, 1905. Fairview Cemetery, Westfield, Union County.

BROWN, MATTHEW Pvt, D, 29th NJ Inf, 3-23-1915. Bay View Cemetery, Leonardo, Monmouth County.

BROWN, MICHAEL 6-19-1888. St. John's Evangelical Church Cemetery, Orange, Essex County.

BROWN, MICHAEL Pvt, L, 1st NJ Cav, 12-2-1900. Fairmount Cemetery, Newark, Essex County.

BROWN, MILES S. Pvt, F, 11th NJ Inf, [Died of diarrhea at Washington, DC.] 2-7-1865. Methodist Church Cemetery, Mount Horeb, Somerset County.

Our Brothers Gone Before

BROWN*, NATHAN Pvt, C, 3rd U.S. VRC, 11-17-1907. Riverview Cemetery, Trenton, Mercer County.
BROWN, NATHANIEL Pvt, B, 22nd U.S. CT, 3-1-1912. Mount Pisgah Cemetery, Elsinboro, Salem County.
BROWN*, NELSON D. Pvt, D, 14th NJ Inf, 4-2-1876. Methodist-Episcopal Cemetery, Old Bridge, Middlesex County.
BROWN, NICHOLAS Pvt, E, 29th CT Inf, 8-5-1891. Beverly National Cemetery, Edgewater Park, Burlington County.
BROWN, NOAH Corp, K, 8th U.S. CT, 5-19-1921. Mount Salem Church Cemetery, Fenwick, Salem County.
BROWN, OLIVER Corp, F, 3rd NJ Cav, 6-27-1904. St. Nicholas Cemetery, Lodi, Bergen County.
BROWN, PHILIP Seaman, U.S. Navy, 7-10-1898. Fairmount Cemetery, Newark, Essex County.
BROWN, PHILIP A. __, C, 3rd NY __, 2-9-1899. New Somerville Cemetery, Somerville, Somerset County.
BROWN, PHILLIP Pvt, I, 35th NJ Inf, 2-24-1878. Fairmount Cemetery, Newark, Essex County.
BROWN, PHINEAS P. Pvt, Btty B, 1st NJ Light Art, 11-12-1896. Fairmount Cemetery, Newark, Essex County.
BROWN, PIERCE Pvt, F, 3rd U.S. CT, 5-24-1910. Mount Peace Cemetery, Lawnside, Camden County.
BROWN, RAHSELAH M. Pvt, F, 14th NJ Inf, [Killed in action at Cedar Creek, VA.] 10-19-1864. Methodist Cemetery, Cassville, Ocean County.
BROWN, RENWICK W. Pvt, D, 213th PA Inf, 5-14-1914. Evergreen Cemetery, Hillside, Union County.
BROWN, RICHARD E. 8-7-1903. Baptist/St. Andrew's Cemetery, Mount Holly, Burlington County.
BROWN, RICHARD H. Pvt, A, 1st NJ Militia, 4-29-1888. Evergreen Cemetery, Camden, Camden County.
BROWN, ROBERT M. Pvt, A, 34th NJ Inf, 8-19-1921. Mount Holly Cemetery, Mount Holly, Burlington County.
BROWN*, ROBERT P. Corp, A, 60th NC Inf (CSA), [Captured 7-3-1863 at Gettysburg, PA.] 8-30-1863. Finn's Point National Cemetery, Pennsville, Salem County.
BROWN, ROBERT S. 2nd Lt, A, 8th NJ Inf, 2-21-1912. Arlington Cemetery, Kearny, Hudson County.
BROWN, ROSTINE Musc, DoD Unknown. Bordentown/Old St. Mary's Catholic Cemetery, Bordentown, Burlington County.
BROWN, SAMUEL Pvt, A, 11th NY Cav, 4-9-1918. Evergreen Cemetery, Morristown, Morris County.
BROWN, SAMUEL B. Pvt, B, 80th NY Inf, 12-23-1896. South Orange Cemetery, South Orange, Essex County.
BROWN, SAMUEL C. Pvt, H, 9th NJ Inf, [Died of typhoid at Roanoke Island, NC.] 4-10-1862. Hainesburg Cemetery, Hainesburg, Warren County.
BROWN, SAMUEL F. Landsman, U.S. Navy, USS Allegheny, 10-20-1908. Mount Peace Cemetery, Lawnside, Camden County.
BROWN, SAMUEL G. Pvt, G, 11th AL Inf (CSA), 10-30-1863. Finn's Point National Cemetery, Pennsville, Salem County.
BROWN, SAMUEL K. Pvt, D, 7th NJ Inf, 10-6-1903. Oceanville Cemetery, Oceanville, Atlantic County.
BROWN, SANDY Pvt, C, 25th U.S. CT, 4-12-1895. Jordan Lawn Cemetery, Pennsauken, Camden County.
BROWN, SIMEON Pvt, K, 35th NJ Inf, 1908. Mount Pleasant Cemetery, Millville, Cumberland County.

New Jersey Civil War Burials

BROWN*, STACY L. (aka: Brower, Stacy) Pvt, G, 2nd NJ Cav, 6-22-1926. Laurel Grove Cemetery, Totowa, Passaic County.

BROWN, STEPHEN Pvt, C, 26th NJ Inf, 8-29-1893. Fairmount Cemetery, Newark, Essex County.

BROWN, STEPHEN N. Pvt, G, 24th U.S. CT, DoD Unknown. Jordan Lawn Cemetery, Pennsauken, Camden County.

BROWN, STUART SHARP Pvt, D, 5th VA Inf (CSA), [Captured 2-6-1864 at Morton's Ford, VA. Died of bronchitis.] 2-13-1865. Finn's Point National Cemetery, Pennsville, Salem County.

BROWN, THEODORE B. Pvt, D, 104th IL Inf, 2-7-1895. Greenmount Cemetery, Hammonton, Atlantic County.

BROWN, THEODORE C. Pvt, B, 37th NJ Inf, 9-13-1865. Evergreen Cemetery, Morristown, Morris County.

BROWN*, THOMAS (aka: Sherrill, Robert) Pvt, D, 2nd NJ Cav, 8-14-1899. Fairmount Cemetery, Newark, Essex County.

BROWN, THOMAS Pvt, C, 74th NY Inf, 2-21-1881. Hoboken Cemetery, North Bergen, Hudson County.

BROWN, THOMAS 1905. Princeton Cemetery, Princeton, Mercer County.

BROWN, THOMAS Pvt, D, 31st NJ Inf, 3-1-1905. St. Bernard's Cemetery, Bridgewater, Somerset County.

BROWN, THOMAS B. Pvt, Btty B, 1st NJ Light Art, DoD Unknown. New Episcopal Church Cemetery, Swedesboro, Gloucester County.

BROWN, THOMAS BENTON Actg 3rd Asst Eng, U.S. Navy, DoD Unknown. Arlington Cemetery, Kearny, Hudson County.

BROWN*, THOMAS C. (aka: Cruis, Thomas) Seaman, U.S. Navy, USS Pawnee, DoD Unknown. Presbyterian Church Cemetery, Greenwich, Cumberland County.

BROWN, THOMAS E. Landsman, U.S. Navy, USS Sumter, 10-6-1895. Holy Sepulchre Cemetery, East Orange, Essex County.

BROWN, THOMAS E. Pvt, G, 2nd DC Inf, 6-10-1883. Woodland Cemetery, Newark, Essex County.

BROWN, THOMAS FRANCIS Pvt, K, 1st NJ Cav, 1-1-1918. Fairmount Cemetery, Newark, Essex County.

BROWN, THOMAS H. Pvt, E, 60th (Crawford's) TN Mtd Inf (CSA), [Captured 5-17-1863 at Big Black River Bridge, MS.] 6-23-1863. Finn's Point National Cemetery, Pennsville, Salem County.

BROWN, THOMAS HACKETT Pvt, B, 9th NJ Inf, 6-25-1917. Woodland Cemetery, Newark, Essex County.

BROWN, THOMAS S. Pvt, Btty A, 2nd PA Heavy Art, 8- -1880. St. Mary's Episcopal Church Cemetery, Burlington, Burlington County.

BROWN, THOMAS T. Pvt, D, 12th NJ Inf, 12-25-1898. Methodist Church Cemetery, Hurffville, Gloucester County.

BROWN, THOMAS W. Pvt, C, 25th U.S. CT, 10-6-1922. Presbyterian Church Cemetery, Bridgeton, Cumberland County.

BROWN, TYLEE Pvt, K, 29th NJ Inf, 8-13-1898. Methodist-Episcopal Cemetery, Glendola, Monmouth County.

BROWN, URIAH Pvt, D, 2nd NJ Cav, 9-21-1898. Oak Hill Cemetery, Vineland, Cumberland County.

BROWN, VALENTINE W. Corp, F, 4th NJ Inf, 7-4-1875. Evergreen Cemetery, Camden, Camden County.

BROWN, WALTER P. Pvt, G, 1st NJ Cav, 11-9-1895. Mount Carmel Cemetery, West Long Branch, Monmouth County.

BROWN, WILLIAM Pvt, B, 2nd U.S. Cav, 8-24-1890. Methodist Church Cemetery, Pemberton, Burlington County.

Our Brothers Gone Before

BROWN, WILLIAM Pvt, G, 73rd NY Inf, [Died at Beverly, NJ.] 10-18-1864. Beverly National Cemetery, Edgewater Park, Burlington County.

BROWN*, WILLIAM Sgt, I, 37th NJ Inf, 4-11-1913. Evergreen Cemetery, Lumberton, Burlington County.

BROWN, WILLIAM Pvt, I, 8th PA Cav, 6-7-1904. Oddfellows Cemetery, Pemberton, Burlington County.

BROWN, WILLIAM 11-26-1906. Evergreen Cemetery, Camden, Camden County.

BROWN, WILLIAM (aka: Wiley, William) Pvt, I, 24th U.S. CT, 6-25-1931. St. Matthew's Methodist-Episcopal Cemetery, Morrisville, Camden County.

BROWN, WILLIAM 9-8-1905. Tabernacle Baptist Church Cemetery, Erma, Cape May County.

BROWN, WILLIAM Corp, M, 3rd NY Cav, 1-9-1863. 1st Presbyterian Church Cemetery, Orange, Essex County.

BROWN, WILLIAM 12-11-1923. Hoboken Cemetery, North Bergen, Hudson County.

BROWN*, WILLIAM 2nd Lt, I, 55th NY Inf, 1910. Presbyterian Church Cemetery, Mount Pleasant, Hunterdon County.

BROWN, WILLIAM Wagoner, D, 31st NJ Inf, 7-3-1915. Reformed Church Cemetery, Clover Hill, Somerset County.

BROWN, WILLIAM Landsman, U.S. Navy, USS Princeton, 1903. Hazelwood Cemetery, Rahway, Union County.

BROWN, WILLIAM 4-12-1868. Evergreen Cemetery, Hillside, Union County.

BROWN, WILLIAM (see: Banks, William) Holy Sepulchre Cemetery, East Orange, Essex County.

BROWN, WILLIAM (see: Broker, William W.) Bayview-New York Bay Cemetery, Jersey City, Hudson County.

BROWN*, WILLIAM A. Pvt, Unassigned, 33rd NJ Inf, 1-14-1878. Evergreen Cemetery, Camden, Camden County.

BROWN, WILLIAM A. Pvt, C, 13th NJ Inf, 4-10-1888. Methodist Church Cemetery, Stockholm, Sussex County.

BROWN*, WILLIAM B. Pvt, D, 2nd NJ Inf, 8-3-1902. Mount Pleasant Cemetery, Newark, Essex County.

BROWN, WILLIAM H. Pvt, F, 29th CT Inf, 2-14-1914. Oddfellows Cemetery, Burlington, Burlington County.

BROWN, WILLIAM H. Corp, B, 26th NJ Inf, 4-23-1903. Woodland Cemetery, Newark, Essex County.

BROWN, WILLIAM H. Pvt, H, 29th NJ Inf, 7-1-1910. Presbyterian Cemetery, Waretown, Ocean County.

BROWN, WILLIAM H. Seaman, U.S. Navy, USS Peoria, 9-4-1878. Masonic Cemetery, Barnegat, Ocean County.

BROWN, WILLIAM J. Pvt, E, 71st NY Inf, 1-20-1864. 1st Presbyterian Church Cemetery, Orange, Essex County.

BROWN, WILLIAM M. Pvt, D, 8th NJ Inf, 7-17-1887. Holy Name Cemetery, Jersey City, Hudson County.

BROWN, WILLIAM M. 10-27-1905. Mount Pleasant Cemetery, Newark, Essex County.

BROWN, WILLIAM P. Pvt, Btty E, 1st NJ Light Art, 7-22-1926. Tennent Church Cemetery, Tennent, Monmouth County.

BROWN*, WILLIAM S. Pvt, A, 8th NJ Inf, 4-26-1904. Mount Pleasant Cemetery, Newark, Essex County.

BROWN*, WILLIAM W. Sgt, C, 2nd DC Inf, 2-16-1904. Elmwood Cemetery, New Brunswick, Middlesex County.

BROWN, WILLIAM W. Pvt, I, 7th NJ Inf, DoD Unknown. Masonic Cemetery, Barnegat, Ocean County.

New Jersey Civil War Burials

BROWN, WILLIAM WASHINGTON Pvt, E, 31st GA Inf (CSA), [Captured 7-14-1863 at Williamsport, MD.] 11-1-1863. Finn's Point National Cemetery, Pennsville, Salem County.

BROWNELL, CHARLES E. Pvt, Btty L, 14th NY Heavy Art, [Wounded in action 6-1-1864.] 11-18-1925. Fairview Cemetery, Fairview, Monmouth County.

BROWNING, ABRAHAM M. Capt, H, 38th NJ Inf, 1-12-1880. Colestown Cemetery, Cherry Hill, Camden County.

BROWNING, J.H. Pvt, A, 1st AL Inf (CSA), 10-15-1863. Finn's Point National Cemetery, Pennsville, Salem County.

BROWNING, JAMES S. 8-23-1899. Bayview-New York Bay Cemetery, Jersey City, Hudson County.

BROWNING, JOHN C. Pvt, G, 3rd AL Inf (CSA), 10-2-1863. Finn's Point National Cemetery, Pennsville, Salem County.

BROWNING, WILLIAM H. Sgt, H, 1st NJ Inf, 2-17-1931. Bayview-New York Bay Cemetery, Jersey City, Hudson County.

BROWNING, WILLIAM T. Pvt, D, 10th NJ Inf, 9-21-1898. Hillside Cemetery, Madison, Morris County.

BROWNLEY, JOHN Capt, H, 13th MD Inf, 4-26-1894. Methodist-Episcopal Cemetery, Wrightstown, Burlington County.

BROWNLEY, WILLIAM W. Pvt, H, 13th NJ Inf, 10-21-1890. Bayview-New York Bay Cemetery, Jersey City, Hudson County.

BROWNLY, WILLIAM K. Pvt, G, 9th VA Inf (CSA), [Captured 7-3-1863 at Gettysburg, PA. Died of smallpox.] 11-6-1863. Finn's Point National Cemetery, Pennsville, Salem County.

BRUCE, A.J. Pvt, A, 31st GA Inf (CSA), [Captured 7-2-1863 at Hanover, PA. Died of lung inflammation.] 1-3-1864. Finn's Point National Cemetery, Pennsville, Salem County.

BRUCE, JOHN B. Pvt, C, 58th VA Inf (CSA), [Captured 5-12-1864 at Spotsylvania CH, VA. Died of smallpox.] 3-18-1865. Finn's Point National Cemetery, Pennsville, Salem County.

BRUCE, JOHN H. Corp, Btty B, 2nd CT Heavy Art, 12-14-1925. Brotherhood Cemetery, Hainesport, Burlington County.

BRUCH, JOSEPH (aka: Brouch, Joseph) Pvt, C, 54th PA Inf, [Wounded in action.] 8-9-1939. Phillipsburg Cemetery, Phillipsburg, Warren County.

BRUCH, PHILIP (aka: Brooks, Philip) Pvt, F, 3rd NJ Cav, 5-12-1881. Riverview Cemetery, Trenton, Mercer County.

BRUCHLE, GOTTFRIED Pvt, E, 2nd NJ Inf, [Wounded 8-27-1864 at Winchester, VA.] 1-30-1905. Fairmount Cemetery, Newark, Essex County.

BRUDEN, JOHN Pvt, E, 1st NJ Inf, 12-18-1902. Evergreen Cemetery, Camden, Camden County.

BRUEMMER, CHARLES G. Musc, E, 12th U.S. Inf, 12-12-1881. Woodland Cemetery, Newark, Essex County.

BRUEN, CHARLES HENRY Pvt, D, 1st DE Inf, 4-30-1928. East Ridgelawn Cemetery, Clifton, Passaic County.

BRUEN, ELIJAH DAVID Pvt, K, 7th NJ Inf, 6-7-1865. Hillside Cemetery, Madison, Morris County.

BRUEN*, JAMES HARVEY Pvt, D, 2nd NJ Inf, 5-19-1922. Clinton Cemetery, Irvington, Essex County.

BRUEN, JOHN NEWEL Pvt, K, 7th NJ Inf, 5-20-1908. Evergreen Cemetery, Morristown, Morris County.

BRUEN, MERRITT QM, 7th NJ Inf 8-25-1864. Hillside Cemetery, Madison, Morris County.

BRUEN, THEODORE WOOD Corp, K, 7th NJ Inf, 5-4-1879. Evergreen Cemetery, Hillside, Union County.

Our Brothers Gone Before

BRUEN, THOMAS Pvt, E, 37th NJ Inf, 2-5-1880. Fairmount Cemetery, Newark, Essex County.
BRUEN*, WILLIAM THOMAS Pvt, C, 20th U.S. VRC, 2-2-1920. Evergreen Cemetery, Hillside, Union County.
BRUERE, APOLLO MEIRS Pvt, E, 1st NJ Cav, 4-28-1904. Presbyterian Cemetery, Allentown, Monmouth County.
BRUGER, AUGUST Pvt, F, 52nd NY Inf, 4-14-1899. Fairmount Cemetery, Newark, Essex County.
BRUHN*, GEORGE E. Pvt, E, 26th IA Inf, 4-26-1894. Flower Hill Cemetery, North Bergen, Hudson County.
BRUHN, HENRY PETER Pvt, F, 97th PA Inf, 6-6-1924. New York/New Jersey Crematory Cemetery, North Bergen, Hudson County.
BRUHNE, WILLIAM Pvt, Btty E, 1st NJ Light Art, 11-2-1887. Bayview-New York Bay Cemetery, Jersey City, Hudson County.
BRULL, MICHAEL 2-4-1867. Grove Church Cemetery, North Bergen, Hudson County.
BRUMFIELD, ALONZO L. Corp, Btty M, 1st IL Light Art, 12-29-1924. Arlington Cemetery, Kearny, Hudson County.
BRUMLEY, JOHN DUANE Surg, US Volunteers [Chief Surgeon 1st Division, 4th Army Corps.] 1-8-1897. Fairmount Cemetery, Newark, Essex County.
BRUN, WILLIAM (aka: Burns, William) Pvt, A, 40th NY Inf, 7-20-1898. Flower Hill Cemetery, North Bergen, Hudson County.
BRUNDAGE*, JOHN E. Pvt, F, 3rd NJ Cav, [Wounded in action.] 7-27-1922. Rosedale Cemetery, Orange, Essex County.
BRUNDAGE, JOHN H. Pvt, C, 15th NJ Inf, 1-4-1886. Fairmount Cemetery, Newark, Essex County.
BRUNER, HENRY Pvt, E, 31st NJ Inf, 5-28-1890. Evergreen Cemetery, Clinton, Hunterdon County.
BRUNER, SOLOMAN H. (aka: Brewner, Solomon) Pvt, G, 28th NJ Inf, 1918. Baptist Church Cemetery, Jacobstown, Burlington County.
BRUNNER, GUSTAVE Pvt, G, 35th NJ Inf, 9-11-1902. Woodland Cemetery, Newark, Essex County.
BRUNNER, JOHN J. Pvt, K, 103rd NY Inf, 1-10-1898. Fairmount Cemetery, Newark, Essex County.
BRUNNER, JOHN W. Pvt, A, 2nd U.S. Inf, 7-7-1902. Weehawken Cemetery, North Bergen, Hudson County.
BRUNNER, JOSEPH Sgt, H, 29th NY Inf, 1-8-1901. Grove Church Cemetery, North Bergen, Hudson County.
BRUNO, EDWARD Pvt, F, 25th U.S. CT, 2-22-1905. Riverview Cemetery, Trenton, Mercer County.
BRUNS, HENRY LEE Pvt, Btty A, 1st SC Art (CSA), 4-13-1914. Hackensack Cemetery, Hackensack, Bergen County.
BRUNT, GEORGE W. Pvt, 6th NY Ind Btty 4-12-1915. Riverview Cemetery, Trenton, Mercer County.
BRUNT, HARVEY (aka: Brandt, Harvey) Pvt, 6th NY Ind Btty 5-6-1908. Hazelwood Cemetery, Rahway, Union County.
BRUNT, JAMES H. Pvt, I, 2nd DC Inf, 8-27-1906. Hazelwood Cemetery, Rahway, Union County.
BRUNT, ROBERT T. Pvt, U.S. Marine Corps, 5-28-1909. New Somerville Cemetery, Somerville, Somerset County.
BRUNT, WILLIAM Pvt, G, 71st PA Inf, 1-5-1903. St. Mary's Cemetery, Hamilton, Mercer County.
BRUQUIER, FRANCOIS Hosp Stew, Btty G, 5th U.S. Art, 12-24-1906. Fairmount Cemetery, Newark, Essex County.

New Jersey Civil War Burials

BRUSLE*, WILLIAM A. (JR.) Capt, H, 25th NY Cav, 3-3-1910. Jersey City Cemetery, Jersey City, Hudson County.
BRUSS, ABRAHAM DUMONT Pvt, B, 51st NY Inf, 1-4-1931. Hillside Cemetery, Scotch Plains, Union County.
BRUVEN, ANDREW (see: Brewer, Andrew A.) Brotherhood Cemetery, Hainesport, Burlington County.
BRYAN, CHRISTOPHER Pvt, K, 31st NJ Inf, 1925. Mansfield/Washington Cemetery, Washington, Warren County.
BRYAN, GEORGE Pvt, A, 2nd NJ Inf, 7-26-1914. Weller Cemetery, Willow Grove, Warren County.
BRYAN, GEORGE H. Corp, F, 14th NJ Inf, [Wounded in action.] 2-6-1910. Riverside Cemetery, Toms River, Ocean County.
BRYAN, JACOB F. Pvt, A, 15th NJ Inf, [Died of wounds received at Opequan, VA..] 9-19-1864. Old & New Lutheran Cemetery, Lebanon, Hunterdon County.
BRYAN, JAMES S. (JR.) Pvt, B, 4th U.S. Cav, DoD Unknown. Evergreen Cemetery, Hillside, Union County.
BRYAN, JOHN M. Pvt, K, 31st NJ Inf, 6-11-1894. Belvidere/Catholic Cemetery, Belvidere, Warren County.
BRYAN, JOHN W. Surg, 10th NJ Inf 6-20-1871. Monument Cemetery, Edgewater Park, Burlington County.
BRYAN, JOSEPH G. Pvt, B, 31st NJ Inf, 1932. Mansfield/Washington Cemetery, Washington, Warren County.
BRYAN, THOMAS Pvt, I, 95th PA Inf, 11-6-1897. Atlantic View Cemetery, Manasquan, Monmouth County.
BRYAN, WILLIAM Pvt, E, 6th U.S. VRC, 2-28-1891. Riverview Cemetery, Trenton, Mercer County.
BRYAN, WILLIAM Col, 10th NJ Inf 9-7-1874. Monument Cemetery, Edgewater Park, Burlington County.
BRYAN, WILLIAM E. Maj, 3rd NJ Inf 11-16-1893. Mount Holly Cemetery, Mount Holly, Burlington County.
BRYAN, WILLIAM H. Pvt, K, 2nd DC Inf, 3-12-1884. Fairmount Cemetery, Newark, Essex County.
BRYAN, WILLIAM H. (see: Byram, William H.) Locust Hill Cemetery, Dover, Morris County.
BRYAN*, WILLIAM P. 1st Sgt, F, 2nd NJ Inf, [Wounded 5-12-1864 at Spotsylvania CH, VA.] 1-9-1915. Presbyterian Church Cemetery, Rockaway, Morris County.
BRYANS, GREENBERRY S. (aka: Bryans, Greenbury) 4th Sgt, I, 44th GA Inf (CSA), [Captured 5-10-1864 at Spotsylvania CH, VA. Died of smallpox.] 2-8-1865. Finn's Point National Cemetery, Pennsville, Salem County.
BRYANS, GREENBURY (see: Bryans, Greenberry S.) Finn's Point National Cemetery, Pennsville, Salem County.
BRYANT, CHARLES H. Pvt, B, 24th U.S. CT, 4-5-1899. Siloam Cemetery, Vineland, Cumberland County.
BRYANT, CHARLES J. Pvt, I, 8th NJ Inf, 7-28-1884. Mount Pleasant Cemetery, Newark, Essex County.
BRYANT, DEMPSEY H. Pvt, E, 2nd FL Inf (CSA), [Wounded and captured 7-3-1863 at Gettysburg, PA.] 10-23-1863. Finn's Point National Cemetery, Pennsville, Salem County.
BRYANT, EDWARD Pvt, B, 31st NJ Inf, DoD Unknown. Evergreen Cemetery, Clinton, Hunterdon County.
BRYANT, FRANK N. 1901. Baptist/St. Andrew's Cemetery, Mount Holly, Burlington County.
BRYANT, GEORGE LYON 1st Lt, G, 9th NJ Inf, 7-24-1906. New Somerville Cemetery, Somerville, Somerset County.

BRYANT, JAMES Surg, 5th PA Cav [Also: Surgeon, U.S. Volunteers.] 11-5-1881. Evergreen Cemetery, Hillside, Union County.
BRYANT, JOHN W. Pvt, Btty K, 4th NY Heavy Art, 3-19-1922. Fairmount Cemetery, Newark, Essex County.
BRYANT, JOSEPH Pvt, D, 51st AL Cav (CSA), 10-8-1863. Finn's Point National Cemetery, Pennsville, Salem County.
BRYANT, RALPH B. Pvt, G, 15th NJ Inf, [Wounded in action.] 11-28-1868. Old & New Lutheran Cemetery, Lebanon, Hunterdon County.
BRYANT, T.C. Pvt, G, 19th (Biffle's) TN Cav (CSA), 7-26-1864. Finn's Point National Cemetery, Pennsville, Salem County.
BRYANT, WELLINGTON (see: Briant, J. Wellington) Chestnut Cemetery, Dover, Morris County.
BRYANT, WILLIAM B. Landsman, U.S. Navy, 3-7-1909. Chestnut Cemetery, Greenwich, Cumberland County.
BRYDEN, ROBERT Pvt, D, 7th NJ Inf, 12-13-1896. Alpine Cemetery, Perth Amboy, Middlesex County.
BRYSON, ALEXANDER Pvt, D, 4th NJ Militia, 9-16-1892. St. John's United Methodist Cemetery, Turnersville, Gloucester County.
BRYSON, R. Pvt, C, 22nd (Barteau's) TN Cav (CSA), 10-9-1863. Finn's Point National Cemetery, Pennsville, Salem County.
BRYSON, WILLIAM F. Pvt, D, 55th NC Inf (CSA), [Captured 7-1-1863 at Gettysburg, PA.] 10-15-1863. Finn's Point National Cemetery, Pennsville, Salem County.
BRYSON, WILLIAM H. Pvt, E, 37th NJ Inf, 2-9-1926. Fairmount Cemetery, Newark, Essex County.
BRZEZINSKI, ALEXANDER 6-6-1875. Old Somerville Cemetery, Somerville, Somerset County.
BUBSER, FREDERICK C. (aka: Busch, Frederick) Pvt, F, 9th NY Inf, 7-13-1875. Palisade Cemetery, North Bergen, Hudson County.
BUCHANAN, CORNELIUS W. Pvt, E, 31st NJ Inf, 4-18-1902. Riverview Cemetery, Trenton, Mercer County.
BUCHANAN*, GEORGE Pvt, A, 147th PA Inf, 10-28-1897. Greenmount Cemetery, Hammonton, Atlantic County.
BUCHANAN, GEORGE W. Pvt, D, 71st NY Inf, 3-13-1889. Macphelah Cemetery, North Bergen, Hudson County.
BUCHANAN, JOHN Pvt, D, 31st NJ Inf, 2-10-1907. Baptist Church Cemetery, Cherryville, Hunterdon County.
BUCHANAN, JOHN R. Pvt, B, 2nd NJ Cav, [Wounded in action.] 11-11-1913. Sergeant's Hill Cemetery, Sand Brook, Hunterdon County.
BUCHANAN, JOHN W. Pvt, I, 28th NJ Inf, 3-24-1893. Alpine Cemetery, Perth Amboy, Middlesex County.
BUCHANAN, JOSEPH W. Pvt, D, 30th NJ Inf, 7-28-1915. Prospect Hill Cemetery, Flemington, Hunterdon County.
BUCHANAN, MATTHIAS 12-5-1902. Barber's Burying Ground Cemetery, Dilts Corner, Hunterdon County.
BUCHANAN, NATHANIEL Pvt, C, 5th NJ Inf, [Wounded 1862 in action.] 3-17-1867. Jersey City Cemetery, Jersey City, Hudson County.
BUCHANAN, PETER Pvt, D, 30th NJ Inf, 1922. Sergeant's Hill Cemetery, Sand Brook, Hunterdon County.
BUCHANAN, SAMUEL A. Pvt, E, 5th VA Inf (CSA), [Died of disease.] 6-15-1865. Finn's Point National Cemetery, Pennsville, Salem County.
BUCHANAN, THOMAS Coal Heaver, U.S. Navy, 6-17-1917. Cedar Grove Cemetery, Gloucester City, Camden County.
BUCHANAN*, WILIIAM H. Pvt, I, 112th NY Inf, [Wounded 10-27-1864 at Darbytown Road, VA.] 9-6-1903. Deckertown-Union Cemetery, Papakating, Sussex County.

New Jersey Civil War Burials

BUCHANON, JOHN W. Pvt, G, 40th NJ Inf, 4-14-1900. Mount Prospect Cemetery, Neptune, Monmouth County.
BUCHELE, GOTTFRIED (see: Bugle, George) Fairmount Cemetery, Newark, Essex County.
BUCHER*, ESEK A. Pvt, Unassigned, 7th NY Heavy Art, 11-17-1899. Fairmount Cemetery, Newark, Essex County.
BUCHER, FRANZ H. Pvt, E, 103rd NY Inf, 1-25-1890. Holy Sepulchre Cemetery, East Orange, Essex County.
BUCHLEIN, HENRY (see: Buchlein, Jacob) Speer Cemetery, Jersey City, Hudson County.
BUCHLEIN, JACOB (aka: Buchlein, Henry) Pvt, A, 2nd NJ Militia, DoD Unknown. Speer Cemetery, Jersey City, Hudson County.
BUCHMAN, ERNST (see: Buckman, Ernst) Woodland Cemetery, Newark, Essex County.
BUCK, ANDREW 8-19-1927. Maplewood Cemetery, Freehold, Monmouth County.
BUCK, BENJAMIN F. Pvt, G, 3rd NJ Cav, 5-1-1936. Mount Pleasant Cemetery, Millville, Cumberland County.
BUCK*, BOWMAN H. Sgt, F, 3rd NJ Inf, 1-10-1908. Presbyterian Church Cemetery, Bridgeton, Cumberland County.
BUCK, CHARLES C. Pvt, H, 2nd NJ Cav, 6-7-1889. Locust Grove Cemetery, Quakertown, Hunterdon County.
BUCK, CHARLES W. Corp, H, 11th NJ Inf, [Died of debility at Washington, DC.] 3-13-1863. Presbyterian/Methodist-Episcopal Cemetery, Succasunna, Morris County.
BUCK, DANIEL R. 2nd Lt, L, 11th IL Cav, 11-25-1906. Evergreen Cemetery, Camden, Camden County.
BUCK*, DENNIS M. Sgt, D, 2nd U.S. Cav, 8-25-1896. Flower Hill Cemetery, North Bergen, Hudson County.
BUCK, EDMUND Seaman, U.S. Navy, USS Powhattan, 9-5-1863. Fairview Cemetery, Cape May Court House, Cape May County.
BUCK, EPHRIAM E. Pvt, H, 24th NJ Inf, 2-17-1904. Presbyterian Church Cemetery, Bridgeton, Cumberland County.
BUCK, FREDERICH Pvt, G, 41st NY Inf, 8-25-1902. Fairmount Cemetery, Newark, Essex County.
BUCK, FREDERICK (see: Buck, Fritz) Highland Cemetery, Hopewell Boro, Mercer County.
BUCK, FRITZ (aka: Buck, Frederick) Pvt, H, 15th NJ Inf, 12-27-1915. Highland Cemetery, Hopewell Boro, Mercer County.
BUCK, GEORGE (see: Burke, George W.) Bayview-New York Bay Cemetery, Jersey City, Hudson County.
BUCK, HENRY H. 1916. Washington Monumental Cemetery, South River, Middlesex County.
BUCK, HENRY O. 1- -1862. St. Stephen's Episcopal Church Cemetery, Beverly, Burlington County.
BUCK, ISAAC W. Actg 2nd Asst Eng, U.S. Navy, 1868. St. Stephen's Episcopal Church Cemetery, Beverly, Burlington County.
BUCK*, JAMES P. Pvt, K, 2nd U.S. Inf, 4-3-1906. Rosehill Cemetery, Newfield, Gloucester County.
BUCK, JONATHAN D. Pvt, G, 3rd NJ Cav, 4-3-1892. Mount Pleasant Cemetery, Millville, Cumberland County.
BUCK, JOSEPH P. Seaman, U.S. Navy, 5-30-1916. Riverview Cemetery, Trenton, Mercer County.
BUCK*, JULIUS M. Corp, Btty K, 1st VT Heavy Art, [Wounded 9-19-1864 at Opequan, VA.] 10-14-1919. Fairmount Cemetery, Newark, Essex County.

Our Brothers Gone Before

BUCK, MICHAEL H. Sgt, F, 174th PA Inf, 1-19-1902. Union Cemetery, Frenchtown, Hunterdon County.
BUCK, ROBERT J. Corp, F, 37th NJ Inf, DoD Unknown. Presbyterian Church Cemetery, Bridgeton, Cumberland County.
BUCK, SAMUEL L. Col, 2nd NJ Inf 2-5-1892. Fairmount Cemetery, Newark, Essex County.
BUCK*, THEODORE F. Sgt, F, 37th NJ Inf, DoD Unknown. Presbyterian Church Cemetery, Bridgeton, Cumberland County.
BUCKALEW, FRANK (aka: Bucklew, Frank) Pvt, C, 43rd U.S. CT, 6- -1895. Van Liew Cemetery, North Brunswick, Middlesex County.
BUCKALEW, FREDERICK Pvt, K, 14th NJ Inf, 3-15-1905. Evergreen Cemetery, New Brunswick, Middlesex County.
BUCKALEW, FREDERICK LEMUEL 1st Lt, Adj, 14th NJ Inf [Wounded 7-9-1864 at Monocacy, MD.] 3-8-1901. Fernwood Cemetery, Jamesburg, Middlesex County.
BUCKALEW*, GARRET Pvt, D, 109th PA Inf, 9-25-1895. Fairmount Cemetery, Newark, Essex County.
BUCKALEW, GEORGE Corp, G, 38th NJ Inf, 8-28-1917. Riverview Cemetery, Trenton, Mercer County.
BUCKALEW, JACOB Pvt, K, 14th NJ Inf, 7-21-1918. Christ Church Cemetery, Morgan, Middlesex County.
BUCKALEW, JOHN B. Pvt, G, 38th NJ Inf, 1-24-1918. Van Liew Cemetery, North Brunswick, Middlesex County.
BUCKALEW, WILLIAM Pvt, C, 29th NJ Inf, 1-23-1903. Emleys Hill United Methodist Church Cemetery, Upper Freehold, Monmouth County.
BUCKELEW, FRANCIS Pvt, C, 49th NY Inf, 9-15-1930. Christ Church Cemetery, Morgan, Middlesex County.
BUCKELEW, GEORGE H. Pvt, I, 29th NJ Inf, 1880. Chestnut Hill Cemetery, East Brunswick, Middlesex County.
BUCKELEW, JOHN H. Pvt, G, 38th NJ Inf, 2-2-1879. Tennent Church Cemetery, Tennent, Monmouth County.
BUCKELEW*, WILLIAM D. Pvt, K, 5th NJ Inf, 10-28-1910. Christ Church Cemetery, Morgan, Middlesex County.
BUCKEN*, CHARLES F. (aka: Bucken, Oliver) Sgt, G, 33rd NJ Inf, 4-12-1919. Bayview-New York Bay Cemetery, Jersey City, Hudson County.
BUCKEN, OLIVER (see: Bucken, Charles F.) Bayview-New York Bay Cemetery, Jersey City, Hudson County.
BUCKER, SAMUEL W. Pvt, H, 11th VA Cav (CSA), 4-29-1865. Finn's Point National Cemetery, Pennsville, Salem County.
BUCKEY, EDWIN 3-11-1865. Methodist Church Cemetery, Buttzville, Warren County.
BUCKHALTER, D. CLAUDE Pvt, A, 1st (Gregg's) SC Inf (CSA), [Captured 7-5-1863 at Gettysburg, PA. Died of chronic diarrhea.] 12-30-1863. Finn's Point National Cemetery, Pennsville, Salem County.
BUCKHUM, WILLIAM K. (aka: Buckman, William) Pvt, B, 4th NJ Inf, 2-7-1911. Riverview Cemetery, Trenton, Mercer County.
BUCKINGHAM, JOHN Pvt, H, 34th NJ Inf, 5-24-1886. Episcopal Church Cemetery, Shrewsbury, Monmouth County.
BUCKIOUS, WILLIAM (see: Bockins, William H.) Arlington Cemetery, Kearny, Hudson County.
BUCKLAND*, CHARLES Pvt, I, 9th NY Inf, 7-12-1871. Bayview-New York Bay Cemetery, Jersey City, Hudson County.
BUCKLAND, LEONARD R. 3-26-1906. Bloomfield Cemetery, Bloomfield, Essex County.
BUCKLEW, FRANK (see: Buckalew, Frank) Van Liew Cemetery, North Brunswick, Middlesex County.

New Jersey Civil War Burials

BUCKLEY, ALFRED Pvt, Stroud's, Ind PA Cav, 5-30-1903. Quaker Cemetery, Quaker Church, Warren County.
BUCKLEY*, DUNNING 2nd Cl Fireman, U.S. Navy, USS Dinsmore, 11-29-1920. Bordentown/Old St. Mary's Catholic Cemetery, Bordentown, Burlington County.
BUCKLEY, FRANCIS N. Pvt, H, 192nd PA Inf, 8-3-1912. Oddfellows Cemetery, Pemberton, Burlington County.
BUCKLEY, ISAAC Seaman, U.S. Navy, 1- -1915. Maplewood Cemetery, Freehold, Monmouth County.
BUCKLEY, JOHN Corp, G, 5th NJ Inf, [Wounded in action.] 2-3 -1903. Holy Name Cemetery, Jersey City, Hudson County.
BUCKLEY, JOHN F. Capt, A, 11th NJ Inf, 11-1-1913. Cedar Lawn Cemetery, Paterson, Passaic County.
BUCKLEY, JOSEPH Pvt, C, 25th NJ Inf, 6-29-1905. Cedar Lawn Cemetery, Paterson, Passaic County.
BUCKLEY, LAWRENCE I. 1st Sgt, G, 88th NY Inf, 2-12-1927. Holy Name Cemetery, Jersey City, Hudson County.
BUCKLEY, LEO F. DoD Unknown. Jersey City Cemetery, Jersey City, Hudson County.
BUCKLEY, RICHARD (aka: Tweedle, Richard B.) Musc, 11th PA Inf Band 1910. Arlington Cemetery, Kearny, Hudson County.
BUCKLEY, SAMUEL R. Corp, H, 9th NJ Inf, 12-25-1888. East Ridgelawn Cemetery, Clifton, Passaic County.
BUCKLEY, SAMUEL T. Pvt, B, 2nd NY Cav, 11-2-1910. East Ridgelawn Cemetery, Clifton, Passaic County.
BUCKLEY, WILLIAM J. Capt, I, 2nd NJ Inf, 10-12-1928. Cedar Lawn Cemetery, Paterson, Passaic County.
BUCKLIN*, LAWRENCE Corp, B, 32nd MA Inf, 2-20-1919. Arlington Cemetery, Kearny, Hudson County.
BUCKLISH*, WILLIAM 1st Lt, C, 13th NJ Inf, 1-5-1899. Evergreen Cemetery, Hillside, Union County.
BUCKMAN, ERNST (aka: Buchman, Ernst) Pvt, E, 39th NJ Inf, 1-1-1884. Woodland Cemetery, Newark, Essex County.
BUCKMAN, WILLIAM (see: Buckhum, William K.) Riverview Cemetery, Trenton, Mercer County.
BUCKMASTER, EZEKIEL Seaman, U.S. Navy, DoD Unknown. Methodist Church Cemetery, Haleyville, Cumberland County.
BUCKNUM, JOHN Musc, H, 40th NJ Inf, 6-9-1874. Pearson/Colonial Memorial Park Cemetery, Whitehorse, Mercer County.
BUCKRIDGE, WILLIAM H. Pvt, G, 162nd NY Inf, 8-21-1901. Holy Name Cemetery, Jersey City, Hudson County.
BUCKSBAUM, WILLIAM Pvt, D, 2nd NJ Inf, 11-8-1898. Fairmount Cemetery, Newark, Essex County.
BUCKSON, JARVIS B. Pvt, F, 9th DE Inf, 12-16-1916. Presbyterian Church Cemetery, Bridgeton, Cumberland County.
BUCKTER, WILLIAM (see: Butler, William H.) Arlington Cemetery, Kearny, Hudson County.
BUDD, ABRAHAM M. Pvt, E, 23rd NJ Inf, 6-25-1899. Riverview Cemetery, Trenton, Mercer County.
BUDD*, ENOS GOBLE 2nd Lt, 86, 2nd Bttn U.S. VRC, 2-10-1907. Baptist Church Cemetery, Mount Olive, Morris County.
BUDD, FRANCIS A. 6-6-1886. Methodist Church Cemetery, Pemberton, Burlington County.
BUDD*, RICHARD WILKINS Pvt, C, 12th NJ Inf, 7-8-1911. Baptist Church Cemetery, Haddonfield, Camden County.

Our Brothers Gone Before

BUDD, SAMUEL Pvt, G, 3rd DE Inf, DoD Unknown. Baptist Cemetery, Pemberton, Burlington County.
BUDD, WILLIAM H. Pvt, H, 3rd NJ Inf, 5-4-1914. Colestown Cemetery, Cherry Hill, Camden County.
BUDD, WILLIAM H. 1916. Baptist Church Cemetery, Mount Olive, Morris County.
BUDDEN*, ABRAHAM Pvt, H, 3rd NJ Inf, 7-17-1865. Baptist Cemetery, Pemberton, Burlington County.
BUDDEN*, JOSEPH Pvt, I, 37th NJ Inf, 2-25-1910. Baptist Cemetery, Pemberton, Burlington County.
BUDDEN, LEANDER Pvt, I, 2nd NJ Cav, 11-18-1872. Methodist-Episcopal Cemetery, Vincentown, Burlington County.
BUDDING, CHARLES Pvt, C, 9th NJ Inf, 3-20-1887. Evergreen Cemetery, Camden, Camden County.
BUDROW, CHARLES A. Seaman, U.S. Navy, 7-10-1893. Whippanong Cemetery, Whippany, Morris County.
BUECHLE, CARL FRITTS Pvt, F, 14th CT Inf, 6-3-1895. Pleasant Hill Cemetery, Pleasant Hill, Morris County.
BUEDEL, LOUIS Pvt, A, 35th NJ Inf, 4-18-1909. Fairview Cemetery, Westfield, Union County.
BUEHLER, CHARLES (aka: Beelher, Charles) Corp, I, 35th NJ Inf, 3-10-1913. Fairmount Cemetery, Newark, Essex County.
BUEHNER, LAWRENCE D. ___, I, ___ PA ___, 1905. Rosedale Cemetery, Linden, Union County.
BUERMANN, AUGUST (aka: Berman, August) Pvt, G, 9th NJ Inf, 11-2-1928. Fairmount Cemetery, Newark, Essex County.
BUFFER, AARON 11-22-1861. Union Cemetery, Frenchtown, Hunterdon County.
BUFFER, WILLIAM 1911. Union Cemetery, Frenchtown, Hunterdon County.
BUFFIN, CHARLES A. Pvt, F, 1st NJ Cav, [Wounded 12-2-1862 while on picket duty.] 5-22-1898. Columbus Cemetery, Columbus, Burlington County.
BUFFINGTON, EZEKIEL F. Pvt, F, 43rd GA Inf (CSA), [Captured 5-16-1863 at Baker's Creek, MS.] 7-8-1863. Finn's Point National Cemetery, Pennsville, Salem County.
BUGBEE, ALVIN N. Bvt Capt, G, 19th U.S. CT, 12-2-1903. Riverview Cemetery, Trenton, Mercer County.
BUGGINS, GEORGE Pvt, I, 70th NY Inf, [Cenotaph. Killed in action at Gettysburg, PA.] 7-2-1863. Whitehall Cemetery, Towaco, Morris County.
BUGLE*, GEORGE (aka: Buchele, Gottfried) Pvt, E, 2nd NJ Inf, [Wounded in action at Winchester, VA.] 1-30-1905. Fairmount Cemetery, Newark, Essex County.
BULL, JAMES HENRY (JR.) Pvt, I, 66th NY Inf, 4-25-1921. Evergreen Cemetery, Hillside, Union County.
BULL, JAMES HENRY (SR.) Lt Col, 66th NY Inf [Killed in action at Fredericksburg, VA.] 12-12-1862. Evergreen Cemetery, Hillside, Union County.
BULLARD*, BENJAMIN T. Pvt, H, 43rd NC Inf (CSA), [Captured 7-6-1863 at Gettysburg, PA. Died of typhoid.] 8-16-1863. Finn's Point National Cemetery, Pennsville, Salem County.
BULLARD, GEORGE W. Pvt, A, 51st AL Cav (CSA), 10-12-1863. Finn's Point National Cemetery, Pennsville, Salem County.
BULLARD, WILLIAM H. Pvt, H, 18th NC Inf (CSA), [Captured 7-3-1863 at Gettysburg, PA. Died of diarrhea.] 9-23-1863. Finn's Point National Cemetery, Pennsville, Salem County.
BULLARD, WILLIS F. Pvt, D, 41st GA Inf (CSA), [Captured 5-16-1863 at Baker's Creek, MS. Died of disease.] 7-7-1863. Finn's Point National Cemetery, Pennsville, Salem County.
BULLER, CYRUS W. Pvt, C, 38th NJ Inf, 8-31-1919. Baptist Church Cemetery, Mullica Hill, Gloucester County.

New Jersey Civil War Burials

BULLER, GEORGE Pvt, H, 1st PA Inf, 5-17-1906. Fairmount Cemetery, Newark, Essex County.
BULLER, GEORGE (see: Boller, George) Fairmount Cemetery, Newark, Essex County.
BULLER, JOHN Pvt, I, 58th NY Inf, 1-12-1900. Holy Sepulchre Cemetery, East Orange, Essex County.
BULLER, WILLIAM L. Corp, A, 3rd NJ Inf, [Died of disease at Baltimore, MD.] 7-6-1862. Methodist-Episcopal Cemetery, Mullica Hill, Gloucester County.
BULLIVANT, ISAAC H. Seaman, U.S. Navy, 2-8-1924. Fairmount Cemetery, Newark, Essex County.
BULLIVANT, JAMES Pvt, Btty F, 1st CT Heavy Art, 4-20-1903. Fairmount Cemetery, Newark, Essex County.
BULLIVANT, JOSIAH Seaman, U.S. Navy, USS Valley City, 6-14-1892. Evergreen Cemetery, Hillside, Union County.
BULLIVANT, THOMAS Pvt, G, 15th CT Inf, [Wounded 3-8-1865 at Kinston, NC.] 9-3-1888. Fairmount Cemetery, Newark, Essex County.
BULLIVANT*, THOMAS W. Pvt, G, 2nd NJ Inf, 11-21-1912. Fairmount Cemetery, Newark, Essex County.
BULLIVANT, WILLIAM Pvt, Btty B, 1st NJ Light Art, 6-9-1887. Fairmount Cemetery, Newark, Essex County.
BULLMAN, ISAAC Pvt, G, 22nd NJ Inf, DoD Unknown. Rocky Hill Cemetery, Rocky Hill, Somerset County.
BULLMAN, JAMES Corp, C, 14th NJ Inf, [Killed in action at Cold Harbor, VA.] 6-1-1864. Presbyterian Cemetery, North Plainfield, Somerset County.
BULLMAN, LEVI Corp, G, 76th NY Inf, [Died at Georgetown, DC of wounds received 8-28-1862 at Gainesville, VA.] 11-27-1862. Presbyterian Cemetery, North Plainfield, Somerset County.
BULLOCK, JAMES J. Capt, B, 15th NJ Inf, [Cenotaph. Lost on steamer General Lyon off Hatteras, NC.] 3-31-1865. Presbyterian Church Cemetery, Flemington, Hunterdon County.
BULLOCK, JOHN 9- -1870. Methodist Church Cemetery, Pemberton, Burlington County.
BULLOCK, THOMAS L. Pvt, C, 10th NJ Inf, [Died of typhoid at Washington, DC.] 3-6-1863. Methodist Church Cemetery, Pemberton, Burlington County.
BULLOCK, WILLIAM C. Pvt, B, 34th NJ Inf, [Died of diarrhea at Burlington, NJ.] 7-4-1865. Baptist Cemetery, Burlington, Burlington County.
BULMER, JOHN Pvt, A, 15th NJ Inf, 11-20-1900. Fairmount Cemetery, Newark, Essex County.
BULMER, JOHN F. Pvt, I, 3rd NJ Inf, 10-1-1908. Baptist/Evergreen Methodist Cemetery, Plainfield, Union County.
BUMFORD, THOMAS B. Pvt, K, 3rd U.S. CT, 3-14-1922. Greenwood Cemetery, Hamilton, Mercer County.
BUMS, ALEXANDER (see: Beatty, Alexander) Pearson/Colonial Memorial Park Cemetery, Whitehorse, Mercer County.
BUMSTEAD, ROBERT Capt, B, 13th NJ Inf, DoD Unknown. Holy Name Cemetery, Jersey City, Hudson County.
BUNCH, D.P. Pvt, Fry's Btty, VA Light Art (CSA), 9-7-1864. Finn's Point National Cemetery, Pennsville, Salem County.
BUNDY, WILLIAM H. Musc, B, 43rd U.S. CT, 5-20-1887. Holcomb-Riverview Cemetery, Lambertville, Hunterdon County.
BUNKERHOEF, JOHN (see: Brinkerhoff, John D.) Fairview Cemetery, Westfield, Union County.
BUNN*, DAVID J. Pvt, I, 2nd DC Inf, 6-28-1902. Rahway Cemetery, Rahway, Union County.
BUNN, DENNIS (see: Brown, Dennis) Boonton Cemetery, Boonton, Morris County.

Our Brothers Gone Before

BUNN, GEORGE A. Pvt, C, 8th NH Inf, 4-5-1903. Arlington Cemetery, Kearny, Hudson County.
BUNN, GEORGE T. Musc, I, 30th NJ Inf, 6-7-1914. Evergreen/Bishop Jaynes Cemetery, Basking Ridge, Somerset County.
BUNN, ISAAC A. Capt, E, 3rd NJ Inf, 1904. Rahway Cemetery, Rahway, Union County.
BUNN, JOHN R. (aka: Bonn, John) Sgt, 6th NY Ind Btty [Died at Washington, DC. of wounds received 5-28-1864 at Aenon Church (Hawe's Shop), VA.] 6-22-1864. Trinity Episcopal Church Cemetery, Woodbridge, Middlesex County.
BUNN, JONATHAN 6-17-1870. Methodist Cemetery, Pennington, Mercer County.
BUNN, MARION Pvt, B, 47th NC Inf (CSA), [Wounded 7-1-1863 and captured 7-5-1863 at Gettysburg, PA. Died of pneumonia.] 8-26-1863. Finn's Point National Cemetery, Pennsville, Salem County.
BUNN, MATTHIAS Pvt, E, 14th NJ Inf, 3-4-1916. Hazelwood Cemetery, Rahway, Union County.
BUNN, PHILIP W. Pvt, G, 3rd NJ Inf, DoD Unknown. Old Somerville Cemetery, Somerville, Somerset County.
BUNN, SAMUEL M. Pvt, M, 2nd NJ Cav, DoD Unknown. Frankford Plains Cemetery, Frankford, Sussex County.
BUNN, THOMAS G. 10-30-1905. Evergreen/Bishop Jaynes Cemetery, Basking Ridge, Somerset County.
BUNNELL, CHARLES R. Pvt, F, 14th CT Inf, [Wounded 5-3-1863 at Chancellorsville, VA.] 8-2-1911. Good Luck Cemetery, Murray Grove, Ocean County.
BUNNELL, CHARLES R. Corp, H, 29th NJ Inf, 8-27-1864. Old Methodist Cemetery, Toms River, Ocean County.
BUNNELL, ISAAC Corp, D, 30th NJ Inf, 5-15-1900. VanCampen Cemetery, Calno, Warren County.
BUNNELL, J.F. 1917. Cedar Ridge Cemetery, Blairstown, Warren County.
BUNNELL, JOHN (see: Bonnell, Jonathan) Evergreen Cemetery, Hillside, Union County.
BUNNISS, SAMUEL (see: Burriss, Samuel) Berlin Cemetery, Berlin, Camden County.
BUNTING, JOHN 3-20-1902. Methodist Cemetery, Allentown, Monmouth County.
BUNTING, THEODORE D. Pvt, B, 12th NJ Inf, 7-28-1915. Mount Holly Cemetery, Mount Holly, Burlington County.
BUNTING*, THOMAS GARDINER Sgt, B, 12th NJ Inf, 1911. Methodist Cemetery, Crosswicks, Burlington County.
BUNTING*, WASHINGTON Pvt, I, 2nd NJ Cav, 11-11-1884. Beverly National Cemetery, Edgewater Park, Burlington County.
BURBAGE, A.T. 6-9-1891. Atlantic City Cemetery, Pleasantville, Atlantic County.
BURBAGE, JOHN Pvt, H, 13th NJ Inf, [Wounded in action.] 8-9-1906. Sacred Heart Cemetery, Vineland, Cumberland County.
BURBANK, JAMES H. Pvt, F, 10th MA Inf, [Wounded 5-3-1863 at Salem Heights, VA.] 3-3-1909. Friendship United Methodist Church Cemetery, Landisville, Atlantic County.
BURBANK, ORRIN A. Musc, B, 4th NJ Inf, 6-29-1911. Greenwood Cemetery, Hamilton, Mercer County.
BURBECKER, ANDREW Artificer, B, 1st NY Eng, 12-7-1900. Fairmount Cemetery, Newark, Essex County.
BURBRIDGE*, RICHARD Pvt, E, 3rd NJ Inf, 11-6-1916. Arlington Cemetery, Kearny, Hudson County.
BURCH, ANDREW J. Pvt, F, 4th GA Inf (CSA), [Captured 5-10-1864 at Spotsylvania CH, VA. Died of diarrhea.] 2-22-1865. Finn's Point National Cemetery, Pennsville, Salem County.
BURCH, DAVID D. Sgt, C, 9th NJ Inf, 2-6-1929. 1st Baptist Cemetery, Cape May Court House, Cape May County.

New Jersey Civil War Burials

BURCH, GEORGE W. Pvt, H, 24th NJ Inf, [Died of consumption at Baltimore, MD.] 4-2-1863. 1st United Methodist Church Cemetery, Bridgeton, Cumberland County.

BURCH, JAMES W. Pvt, K, 23rd NC Inf (CSA), [Wounded 7-1-1862 at Malvern Hill, VA. Captured 7-1-1863 at Gettysburg, PA.] 10-14-1863. Finn's Point National Cemetery, Pennsville, Salem County.

BURCH, JOHN S. Pvt, C, 24th NJ Inf, 3-24-1893. Fairview Cemetery, Westfield, Union County.

BURCH, WILLIAM P. Corp, I, 9th NJ Inf, [Wounded in action.] 1-26-1899. Fairview Cemetery, Cape May Court House, Cape May County.

BURCHAM, AMAZIAH E. Pvt, D, 37th MA Inf, 3-22-1917. Mount Pleasant Cemetery, Millville, Cumberland County.

BURCHART, JOHN (see: Burkardt, John A.) Rosedale Cemetery, Orange, Essex County.

BURCHEL, JOHN J. 10-19-1911. Grove Church Cemetery, North Bergen, Hudson County.

BURCHELL, DANIEL Wagoner, C, 4th NJ Inf, 2-5-1909. Riverview Cemetery, Trenton, Mercer County.

BURCHELL, WILLIAM D. Wagoner, D, 5th NJ Inf, 8-27-1898. Riverview Cemetery, Trenton, Mercer County.

BURCHFIELD, WILLIAM WILSON Pvt, G, 26th AL Inf (CSA), [Wounded and captured 7-3-1863 at Gettysburg, PA. Died of chronic diarrhea.] 9-21-1863. Finn's Point National Cemetery, Pennsville, Salem County.

BURCHILL, JOHN (see: Burghill, John C.) Cedar Lawn Cemetery, Paterson, Passaic County.

BURD, DAVID B. Pvt, G, 30th NJ Inf, 1-30-1913. Holcomb-Riverview Cemetery, Lambertville, Hunterdon County.

BURD, ELIJAH C. Pvt, I, 31st NJ Inf, 1910. Hazen Cemetery, Hazen, Warren County.

BURD, ISAAC (see: Bird, Isaac) Baptist Church Cemetery, Mount Bethel, Somerset County.

BURD, JAMES M. Pvt, D, 3rd NJ Militia, 4-29-1887. Presbyterian Church Cemetery, Pennington, Mercer County.

BURD, JOHN E. Pvt, D, 3rd NJ Cav, 9-18-1889. Presbyterian Church Cemetery, Pennington, Mercer County.

BURD, JOHN M. Pvt, D, 15th NJ Inf, [Died of diarrhea at Harmony, NJ.] 6-13-1864. Montana Cemetery, Montana, Warren County.

BURD, LEONARD G. (aka: Bird, Leonard) Sgt, D, 31st NJ Inf, 9-26-1904. Prospect Hill Cemetery, Flemington, Hunterdon County.

BURD, SAMUEL W. Pvt, K, 31st NJ Inf, 10-10-1903. Fairmount Cemetery, Fairmount, Hunterdon County.

BURD, THOMAS (aka: Bird, Thomas) Corp, G, 1st NJ Cav, 1927. Fairmount Cemetery, Fairmount, Hunterdon County.

BURDEN, WILLIAM F. Pvt, K, 24th NJ Inf, 2-1-1904. Methodist Church Cemetery, Sharptown, Salem County.

BURDETT, JACOB D. Pvt, D, 15th NJ Inf, 6-23-1900. Belvidere/Catholic Cemetery, Belvidere, Warren County.

BURDETT, JOHN F. (JR.) Corp, K, 22nd NJ Inf, 1910. Rural Hill Cemetery, Whitehouse, Hunterdon County.

BURDETT, JOSEPH Pvt, B, 3rd NJ Cav, 1918. Methodist Church Cemetery, Mount Bethel, Warren County.

BURDGE, CHARLES Pvt, E, 28th NJ Inf, 1887. Methodist Cemetery, Cassville, Ocean County.

BURDGE, DAVID 1920. Methodist Church Cemetery, Liberty, Warren County.

BURDGE, DAVID H. Pvt, C, 4th NH Inf, DoD Unknown. Oak Hill Cemetery, Vineland, Cumberland County.

Our Brothers Gone Before

BURDGE, EDWARD T. Pvt, D, 29th NJ Inf, [Died of typhoid at Riceville, NJ.] 10-4-1862. Fairview Cemetery, Fairview, Monmouth County.
BURDGE, WILLIAM S. (aka: Burge, William) Pvt, G, 31st NJ Inf, 8-21-1905. Methodist Church Cemetery, Liberty, Warren County.
BURDICK, CHARLES W. Pvt, 29th Btty, Unattached MA Heavy Art, DoD Unknown. Holy Sepulchre Cemetery, East Orange, Essex County.
BURDON, JOHN WESLEY Pvt, A, 10th NJ Inf, DoD Unknown. Tabernacle Cemetery, Tabernacle, Burlington County.
BURDSALL, JOSEPH T. Pvt, E, 4th NJ Militia, 12-7-1888. Trinity Episcopal Church Cemetery, Moorestown, Burlington County.
BURDSELL, BARNET (aka: Birdsell, Barnet) 1st Lt, H, 3rd NJ Cav, [Killed in action at Warwick Bridge, VA.] 7-5-1864. 7th Day Baptist Church Cemetery, Shiloh, Cumberland County.
BURFORD, MITCHELL M. Pvt, D, 42nd MS Inf (CSA), 11-9-1863. Finn's Point National Cemetery, Pennsville, Salem County.
BURFORD, W.R. Pvt, F, 53rd GA Inf (CSA), 8-18-1863. Finn's Point National Cemetery, Pennsville, Salem County.
BURGE, WILLIAM (see: Burdge, William S.) Methodist Church Cemetery, Liberty, Warren County.
BURGER, ABRAHAM Pvt, K, 57th VA Inf (CSA), [Wounded 7-1-1862 at Malvern Hill, VA. Wounded and captured 7-3-1863 at Gettysburg, PA. Died of typhoid.] 9-22-1863. Finn's Point National Cemetery, Pennsville, Salem County.
BURGER, ALBERT Sgt, E, 25th NY Cav, 1918. Hillside Cemetery, Fairfield, Essex County.
BURGER, HIRAM (see: Berger, Hiram) Lutheran Cemetery, East Stewartsville, Warren County.
BURGER, REUBEN H. Pvt, G, 67th PA Inf, 4-25-1915. Presbyterian Cemetery, West Stewartsville, Warren County.
BURGESS, GARRETT Pvt, A, 1st NY Inf, 1-22-1915. Bayview-New York Bay Cemetery, Jersey City, Hudson County.
BURGESS, HARVEY D. Pvt, H, 42nd MS Inf (CSA), 10-23-1863. Finn's Point National Cemetery, Pennsville, Salem County.
BURGESS, WILLIAM H. 1st Lt, F, 53rd NY Inf, 2-26-1912. Brookside Cemetery, Englewood, Bergen County.
BURGESS, WILLIAM W. Sgt, B, 2nd NJ Cav, 5-16-1886. Fairmount Cemetery, Newark, Essex County.
BURGESSER, HENRY Pvt, U.S. Marine Corps, USS Flag, 3-21-1893. Fairmount Cemetery, Newark, Essex County.
BURGHARDT*, FEDOR Pvt, D, 178th NY Inf, 8-6-1866. St. Stephen's Cemetery, Millburn, Essex County.
BURGHILL, JOHN C. (aka: Burchill, John) Pvt, F, 1st NJ Cav, [Cenotaph.] DoD Unknown. Cedar Lawn Cemetery, Paterson, Passaic County.
BURGIN, JOSEPH 7-2-1866. Evergreen Cemetery, Camden, Camden County.
BURGMILLER, LOUIS 1898. United Methodist Church Cemetery, New Providence, Union County.
BURGNER, DANIEL W. Pvt, Ahl's Btty, DE Heavy Art, DoD Unknown. Finn's Point National Cemetery, Pennsville, Salem County.
BURGSTRESSER, ISRAEL (aka: Bergstresser, Israel) Pvt, C, 187th PA Inf, 2-13-1909. Riverview Cemetery, Trenton, Mercer County.
BURGSTRESSER, JOSEPH R. Pvt, B, 38th NJ Inf, 2-21-1917. Union Cemetery, Frenchtown, Hunterdon County.
BURK, ANDREW J. (see: Burke, Andrew J.) Finn's Point National Cemetery, Pennsville, Salem County.

New Jersey Civil War Burials

BURK, HENRY N. Pvt, B, 23rd NJ Inf, 9-16-1917. Methodist Church Cemetery, Groveville, Mercer County.

BURK, JOHN Fireman, U.S. Navy, 5-19-1908. Arlington Cemetery, Kearny, Hudson County.

BURK, JOHN 3-24-1893. Fairview Cemetery, Westfield, Union County.

BURK, JOHN 5-10-1870. Union Methodist Church Cemetery, Center Square, Gloucester County.

BURK, JOHN (see: Birck, John A.) Flower Hill Cemetery, North Bergen, Hudson County.

BURK, ROBERT K. Pvt, G, 12th NJ Inf, [Wounded in action.] 2-19-1912. Union Methodist Church Cemetery, Center Square, Gloucester County.

BURK, THOMAS Pvt, F, 41st U.S. CT, DoD Unknown. Holy Sepulchre Cemetery, East Orange, Essex County.

BURK, WILLIAM T. (see: Burke, William T.) Finn's Point National Cemetery, Pennsville, Salem County.

BURKARDT, JOHN A. (aka: Burchart, John) Pvt, Btty C, 1st NJ Light Art, 5-7-1898. Rosedale Cemetery, Orange, Essex County.

BURKART*, GEORGE Corp, F, 8th CA Inf, 2-5-1895. Holy Name Cemetery, Jersey City, Hudson County.

BURKE, ALEXANDER Pvt, H, 79th NY Inf, 1-20-1890. Macphelah Cemetery, North Bergen, Hudson County.

BURKE, ANDREW J. (aka: Burk, Andrew J.) Pvt, G, 26th NC Inf (CSA), [Wounded and captured 7-1-1863 at Gettysburg, PA.] 10-9-1863. Finn's Point National Cemetery, Pennsville, Salem County.

BURKE, EDWARD (aka: Burke, Patrick) Pvt, E, 5th CT Inf, 11-20-1903. Holy Name Cemetery, Jersey City, Hudson County.

BURKE, ENOCH Pvt, H, 12th TN Cav, 11-29-1918. Methodist Cemetery, Cassville, Ocean County.

BURKE, EPHRIAM Pvt, B, 8th NJ Inf, [Died of wounds received 9-23-1864 at Petersburg, VA.] 4-23-1865. Presbyterian Cemetery, Holmanville, Ocean County.

BURKE, GEORGE W. (aka: Buck, George) Pvt, G, 30th PA Inf, 7-31-1913. Bayview-New York Bay Cemetery, Jersey City, Hudson County.

BURKE, JAMES Pvt, A, 8th U.S. CT, 10-29-1902. Mount Peace Cemetery, Lawnside, Camden County.

BURKE, JAMES Pvt, E, 1st NJ Cav, 2-28-1885. Phillipsburg Cemetery, Phillipsburg, Warren County.

BURKE, JAMES (JR.) 9-21-1903. Holy Sepulchre Cemetery, Totowa, Passaic County.

BURKE, JOHN L. 1st Lt, Com, 13th PA Cav DoD Unknown. Siloam Cemetery, Vineland, Cumberland County.

BURKE, MARTIN Seaman, U.S. Navy, USS Osceola, 5-25-1867. St. Mary's Cemetery, South Amboy, Middlesex County.

BURKE, MICHAEL Corp, B, 102nd NY Inf, [Wounded in action.] 10-15-1894. St. Peter's Church Cemetery, Belleville, Essex County.

BURKE, MICHAEL J. Pvt, G, 7th NJ Inf, DoD Unknown. Holy Sepulchre Cemetery, Totowa, Passaic County.

BURKE, MILES Pvt, D, 23rd NJ Inf, 3-19-1916. Bordentown/Old St. Mary's Catholic Cemetery, Bordentown, Burlington County.

BURKE, PATRICK Pvt, I, 74th NY Inf, 2-6-1896. Holy Sepulchre Cemetery, East Orange, Essex County.

BURKE, PATRICK (see: Burke, Edward) Holy Name Cemetery, Jersey City, Hudson County.

BURKE, PATRICK F. Sgt, D, 21st NY Cav, 11-3-1920. Bayview-New York Bay Cemetery, Jersey City, Hudson County.

BURKE, PATRICK J. Fireman, U.S. Navy, USS North Carolina, 9-30-1896. Holy Name Cemetery, Jersey City, Hudson County.

Our Brothers Gone Before

BURKE*, RICHARD J. Pvt, K, 3rd NY Inf, DoD Unknown. Bayview-New York Bay Cemetery, Jersey City, Hudson County.
BURKE, RICHARD R. Pvt, F, 38th NJ Inf, 2-24-1892. Tabernacle Cemetery, Tabernacle, Burlington County.
BURKE, THOMAS Corp, I, 13th NJ Inf, 1928. 1st Baptist Cemetery, Cape May Court House, Cape May County.
BURKE, THOMAS Pvt, K, 21st NJ Inf, 11-7-1916. Holy Name Cemetery, Jersey City, Hudson County.
BURKE, THOMAS Pvt, H, 35th NJ Inf, 8-20-1896. St. Rose of Lima Cemetery, Freehold, Monmouth County.
BURKE, W. Pvt, C, 1st VA Cav (CSA), [Died of disease.] 2-21-1864. Finn's Point National Cemetery, Pennsville, Salem County.
BURKE, WILLIAM 11-27-1907. Holy Name Cemetery, Jersey City, Hudson County.
BURKE, WILLIAM H. Pvt, E, 8th PA Cav, 9-6-1907. Presbyterian Church Cemetery, Bridgeton, Cumberland County.
BURKE, WILLIAM T. (aka: Burk, William T.) Pvt, B, 4th NC Cav (CSA), [Captured 7-4-1863 at South Mountain, MD. Died of typhoid.] 9-6-1863. Finn's Point National Cemetery, Pennsville, Salem County.
BURKET, HENRY 2-4-1863. Union Cemetery, Frenchtown, Hunterdon County.
BURKETT, JACOB M. 11-23-1881. Presbyterian Cemetery, Woodbury, Gloucester County.
BURKETT, JOHN Pvt, H, 1st NJ Inf, 2-10-1915. Evergreen Cemetery, Camden, Camden County.
BURKETT, THEODORE F. Actg 3rd Asst Eng, U.S. Navy, USS Huron, 6-10-1924. Green Cemetery, Woodbury, Gloucester County.
BURKETT, THOMAS PETIT Pvt, G, 38th NJ Inf, 1888. Locust Grove Cemetery, Quakertown, Hunterdon County.
BURKHALTER, JOHN HENRY Pvt, H, 7th NY Inf, 1924. Bloomfield Cemetery, Bloomfield, Essex County.
BURKHARD, CARL (aka: Burkhardt, Carl) 8-15-1866. St. Stephen's Cemetery, Millburn, Essex County.
BURKHARDT, CARL (see: Burkhard, Carl) St. Stephen's Cemetery, Millburn, Essex County.
BURKHARDT, MICHAEL J. (aka: Bissert, Michael) Musc, A, 7th NY Inf, 12-13-1911. Old Camden Cemetery, Camden, Camden County.
BURKHART, ARCHIBALD 1911. Berlin Cemetery, Berlin, Camden County.
BURKHART, JOSEPH Pvt, I, 6th NJ Inf, DoD Unknown. Berlin Cemetery, Berlin, Camden County.
BURKLEY, FRANKLIN Pvt, H, 14th NJ Inf, [Killed in action at Cold Harbor, VA.] 6-1-1864. Brainerd Cemetery, Cranbury, Middlesex County.
BURLAND, GEORGE (see: Burlein, George M.) Grove Church Cemetery, North Bergen, Hudson County.
BURLEIN, GEORGE M. (aka: Burland, George) Pvt, Btty A, 1st NJ Light Art, 1-2-1898. Grove Church Cemetery, North Bergen, Hudson County.
BURLEW, JACOB Pvt, D, 13th NJ Inf, 1-28-1898. Cedarwood Cemetery, Hazlet, Monmouth County.
BURLEW, JAMES S. Fireman, U.S. Navy, USS Kanawha, 7-3-1901. Mercer Cemetery, Trenton, Mercer County.
BURLEW, JOHN C. (see: Berlew, John C.) Greengrove Cemetery, Keyport, Monmouth County.
BURLEW*, JOHN J.C. Pvt, D, 13th NJ Inf, DoD Unknown. Greengrove Cemetery, Keyport, Monmouth County.
BURLEY, ALEXANDER Pvt, I, 19th VA Inf (CSA), [Captured 7-3-1863 at Gettysburg, PA.] 10-3-1863. Finn's Point National Cemetery, Pennsville, Salem County.

New Jersey Civil War Burials

BURLEY, JOHN S. Pvt, C, 102nd PA Inf, 11-6-1910. Head of River Church Cemetery, Head of River, Atlantic County.

BURLIE, GEORGE (aka: Bamle, George) Pvt, E, 33rd NJ Inf, 1872. Fairmount Cemetery, Newark, Essex County.

BURLING, GEORGE CHILDS Bvt Brig Gen, U.S. Volunteers, [Colonel, 6th New Jersey Infantry.] 12-24-1885. Harleigh Cemetery, Camden, Camden County.

BURLINGHAM, HARVEY D. Surg, U.S. Navy, 3-7-1886. Baptist/Evergreen Methodist Cemetery, Plainfield, Union County.

BURLISON, JOHN B. Sgt, C, 156th NY Inf, [Wounded 9-19-1864 at Opequan, VA.] 1917. Mount Rest Cemetery, Butler, Morris County.

BURLOCK, SAMUEL S. Musc, Hasting's Btty, PA Light Art, 9-13-1921. New Dover United Methodist Church Cemetery, Edison, Middlesex County.

BURNBY, WILLIAM Pvt, H, 1st NJ Inf, 3-14-1929. Fairmount Cemetery, Newark, Essex County.

BURNER, ADAM Pvt, D, 5th OH Cav, 1-17-1935. Greenlawn Cemetery, West Long Branch, Monmouth County.

BURNES, JOHN (see: Byrnes, John Charles) Holy Name Cemetery, Jersey City, Hudson County.

BURNET, JAMES EDGAR Seaman, U.S. Navy, [Died at sea of yellow fever.] 8-30-1862. Hillside Cemetery, Madison, Morris County.

BURNETT, A.Y. Pvt, D, 3rd (Forrest's) TN Cav (CSA), 8-16-1864. Finn's Point National Cemetery, Pennsville, Salem County.

BURNETT, BENJAMIN P. 10-3-1868. United Methodist Church Cemetery, New Providence, Union County.

BURNETT, CHARLES (aka: Johnson, Charles) Pvt, K, 124th NY Inf, DoD Unknown. Arlington Cemetery, Kearny, Hudson County.

BURNETT, CHARLES A. Pvt, B, 11th NJ Inf, 4-12-1897. Mount Pleasant Cemetery, Newark, Essex County.

BURNETT, DANIEL Pvt, I, 2nd NY Cav, 1-2-1904. Mount Olivet Cemetery, Fairview, Monmouth County.

BURNETT*, JOHN Coal Heaver, U.S. Navy, USS Mount Vernon, 1-12-1895. Valleau Cemetery, Ridgewood, Bergen County.

BURNETT, JOHN Pvt, B, 9th (Malone's) AL Cav (CSA), 10-8-1863. Finn's Point National Cemetery, Pennsville, Salem County.

BURNETT, THOMAS W. Capt, B, 9th NJ Inf, 8-18-1875. St. Peter's Cemetery, New Brunswick, Middlesex County.

BURNETT, WILLIAM H. (aka: Barnett, William) Pvt, B, 15th NJ Inf, [Died at Alexandria, VA. of wounds received 6-2-1864 at Cold Harbor, VA.] 7-15-1864. Tranquility Cemetery, Tranquility, Sussex County.

BURNETT, WILLIAM H. Corp, G, 2nd NJ Inf, 1-18-1922. Mount Pleasant Cemetery, Newark, Essex County.

BURNEY, DAVID (see: Birney, David) German Valley Rural Cemetery, Naughright, Morris County.

BURNHAM, CORNELIUS Artificer, L, 1st NY Eng, 4-11-1899. Macphelah Cemetery, North Bergen, Hudson County.

BURNHAM, GEORGE Pvt, B, 33rd NJ Inf, 10-5-1869. Baptist Church Cemetery, Port Murray, Warren County.

BURNHAM, SILAS L. 10-19-1886. Atlantic City Cemetery, Pleasantville, Atlantic County.

BURNS*, CHARLES (aka: Burus, Charles) Pvt, C, 120th NY Inf, [Wounded in action.] 11-17-1895. St. John's Evangelical Church Cemetery, Orange, Essex County.

BURNS, CHARLES Pvt, A, 71st NY Inf, 7-14-1891. Holy Sepulchre Cemetery, East Orange, Essex County.

Our Brothers Gone Before

BURNS, CHARLES (see: Beirne, Charles) Holy Sepulchre Cemetery, Totowa, Passaic County.
BURNS, CHRISTOPHER Pvt, F, 28th NJ Inf, DoD Unknown. St. James Cemetery, Woodbridge, Middlesex County.
BURNS, CORNELIUS Pvt, K, 21st NJ Inf, 1-19-1900. Holy Name Cemetery, Jersey City, Hudson County.
BURNS, DAVID Pvt, I, 34th NJ Inf, DoD Unknown. 1st United Methodist Church Cemetery, Bridgeton, Cumberland County.
BURNS, DAVID 9-15-1871. Fairmount Cemetery, Newark, Essex County.
BURNS, JAMES Pvt, F, 1st NJ Inf, [Died at Philadelphia, PA. of wounds received 6-27-1862 at Gaines' Farm, VA.] 8-7-1862. St. James Cemetery, Woodbridge, Middlesex County.
BURNS, JAMES Pvt, K, 24th CT Inf, 3-13-1896. Holy Sepulchre Cemetery, East Orange, Essex County.
BURNS*, JAMES Seaman, U.S. Navy, USS Huntsville, 12-29-1908. Holy Sepulchre Cemetery, East Orange, Essex County.
BURNS, JEREMIAH (aka: Benson, Jeremiah) Pvt, B, 62nd NY Inf, DoD Unknown. St. James Cemetery, Woodbridge, Middlesex County.
BURNS, JOHN Pvt, A, 15th NJ Inf, [Wounded 5-12-1864 at Spotsylvania CH, VA.] 2-22-1923. Methodist Church Cemetery, Lebanon, Hunterdon County.
BURNS, JOHN Pvt, G, 1st NJ Inf, 4-15-1897. St. Mary's Cemetery, Clark, Union County.
BURNS, JOHN Pvt, D, 4th NJ Militia, 8-25-1878. Riverview Cemetery, Trenton, Mercer County.
BURNS, JOHN (see: Byrne, John (Sr.)) Holy Sepulchre Cemetery, East Orange, Essex County.
BURNS, JOHN (see: Byrnes, John) Holy Sepulchre Cemetery, East Orange, Essex County.
BURNS, JOHN J. Pvt, K, 11th (Bethel) NC Inf (CSA), [Wounded 12-16-1862 at White Hall, NC. Captured 7-1-1863 at Gettysburg, PA. Died of brain inflammation.] 3-3-1865. Finn's Point National Cemetery, Pennsville, Salem County.
BURNS, JOSEPH Pvt, F, 4th DE Inf, [Wounded in action.] 6-8-1884. Methodist-Episcopal Cemetery, Burlington, Burlington County.
BURNS, JOSEPH (aka: Gosney, Mark or Hooker, James) Seaman, U.S. Navy, USS Savannah, 2-7-1907. Holy Name Cemetery, Jersey City, Hudson County.
BURNS*, JOSEPH 1st Sgt, A, 11th NJ Inf, 11-11-1881. Alpine Cemetery, Perth Amboy, Middlesex County.
BURNS, MARTIN Pvt, D, 35th NJ Inf, 9-23-1889. St. John's Evangelical Church Cemetery, Orange, Essex County.
BURNS, MARTIN Pvt, Btty M, 15th NY Heavy Art, [Wounded in action.] 2-12-1910. Holy Sepulchre Cemetery, Totowa, Passaic County.
BURNS, MICHAEL Pvt, I, 8th NJ Inf, 1-28-1914. Arlington Cemetery, Kearny, Hudson County.
BURNS, OLIVER Pvt, C, 2nd MD Cav, 10-12-1924. Bayview-New York Bay Cemetery, Jersey City, Hudson County.
BURNS, PATRICK Pvt, I, 1st NJ Cav, 3-15-1885. St. Mary's Cemetery, Hamilton, Mercer County.
BURNS, PATRICK Seaman, U.S. Navy, USS Princeton, 3-8-1910. Holy Sepulchre Cemetery, East Orange, Essex County.
BURNS, PATRICK 4-19-1878. St. John's Evangelical Church Cemetery, Orange, Essex County.
BURNS, PATRICK (see: Byrnes, Patrick) Holy Sepulchre Cemetery, East Orange, Essex County.
BURNS*, PLUMMER W. Pvt, B, 11th MD Inf, 3-22-1924. Arlington Cemetery, Kearny, Hudson County.

New Jersey Civil War Burials

BURNS, ROBERT Com Sgt, F, 1st NJ Cav, 6-1-1917. Greenlawn Cemetery, West Long Branch, Monmouth County.

BURNS, THOMAS Pvt, D, 1st NJ Inf, [Wounded 6-27-1862 at Gaines' Farm, VA.] 1914. Mount Pleasant Cemetery, Newark, Essex County.

BURNS, WILLIAM (see: Brun, William) Flower Hill Cemetery, North Bergen, Hudson County.

BURNS, WILLIAM M. Pvt, G, 40th NJ Inf, 1-4-1890. Evergreen Cemetery, Camden, Camden County.

BURNSHOUSE, GEORGE 1st Sgt, I, 10th NJ Inf, 11-15-1910. Greenmount Cemetery, Hammonton, Atlantic County.

BURNSIDE, WILLIAM NELSON Pvt, F, 20th NY Cav, 6-14-1896. Phillipsburg Cemetery, Phillipsburg, Warren County.

BUROV*, JOHN (aka: Boraff, John) Pvt, G, 95th PA Inf, 5-31-1897. Laurel Hill Cemetery, Elwood, Atlantic County.

BURR, ABRAM P. Pvt, Btty H, 2nd U.S. Art, DoD Unknown. Hackensack Cemetery, Hackensack, Bergen County.

BURR, BENJAMIN ELI Pvt, I, 13th NJ Inf, 12-5-1898. Clinton Cemetery, Irvington, Essex County.

BURR*, BYRON MILTON Sgt, A, 14th NY Cav, 2-17-1914. Flower Hill Cemetery, North Bergen, Hudson County.

BURR, DAVID A. Pvt, G, 33rd NJ Inf, 1-2-1886. Congregational Church Cemetery, Chester, Morris County.

BURR, ELIAS Com Sgt, F, 1st NY Cav, 1924. Silverton Cemetery, Silverton, Ocean County.

BURR, EZRA 1st Cl Musc, 6th NJ Inf Band DoD Unknown. Baptist Cemetery, Burlington, Burlington County.

BURR, FRANK Seaman, U.S. Navy, USS Covington, 8-21-1909. Palisade Cemetery, North Bergen, Hudson County.

BURR, JAMES Pvt, I, 13th NJ Inf, 1912. Clinton Cemetery, Irvington, Essex County.

BURR, JAMES A. Corp, I, 33rd NJ Inf, 1926. Congregational Church Cemetery, Chester, Morris County.

BURR, JOHN M. Wagoner, F, 29th NJ Inf, 12-3-1872. Kettle Creek Cemetery, Silverton, Ocean County.

BURR, JOSEPH E. Pvt, B, 37th NJ Inf, DoD Unknown. Congregational Church Cemetery, Chester, Morris County.

BURR*, STEPHEN (JR.) Pvt, I, 13th NJ Inf, 6-6-1891. Fairmount Cemetery, Newark, Essex County.

BURR, WILLIAM H. Musc, 28th PA Inf Band 3-25-1884. New Camden Cemetery, Camden, Camden County.

BURRAGE*, JAMES F. Landsman, U.S. Navy, USS Commodore Read, 5-26-1905. Fairmount Cemetery, Newark, Essex County.

BURRELL, JAMES Pvt, C, 8th NJ Inf, [Died at 3rd Div., 2nd Corps hospital.] 1-20-1865. Hillside Cemetery, Madison, Morris County.

BURRELL, JAMES T. Pvt, A, 1st NJ Militia, 6-30-1913. Mount Pleasant Cemetery, Newark, Essex County.

BURRELL, JOHN T. Pvt, K, 1st NY Eng, 1893. Chestnut Cemetery, Dover, Morris County.

BURRELL, OSCAR F. 6-21-1864. Mount Pleasant Cemetery, Newark, Essex County.

BURRELL, THOMAS Pvt, G, 1st NJ Cav, 9-16-1896. Fairmount Cemetery, Newark, Essex County.

BURRILL, DAVID (see: Birrell, David A.) Fairmount Cemetery, Newark, Essex County.

BURRIS, CHARLES D. Pvt, C, 13th NJ Inf, 10-11-1898. Fairmount Cemetery, Newark, Essex County.

Our Brothers Gone Before

BURRIS, DAVID G. Pvt, E, 107th PA Inf, 4-23-1905. Evergreen Cemetery, Camden, Camden County.
BURRIS, DAVID H. Pvt, C, 13th NJ Inf, 1878. Valleau Cemetery, Ridgewood, Bergen County.
BURRIS, J.D. (see: Burroughs, J.D.) Finn's Point National Cemetery, Pennsville, Salem County.
BURRIS, JAMES P. Pvt, H, 25th NJ Inf, 7-31-1891. Laurel Grove Cemetery, Totowa, Passaic County.
BURRIS, THEODORE Pvt, M, 2nd NJ Cav, 1911. Union Cemetery, Washington, Morris County.
BURRIS*, THOMAS Pvt, Btty I, 11th U.S. CHA, 11-28-1899. Fairmount Cemetery, Newark, Essex County.
BURRISS, SAMUEL (aka: Bunniss, Samuel) Pvt, A, 20th PA Inf, 7-30-1885. Berlin Cemetery, Berlin, Camden County.
BURRITT, CONSTANTINE (see: Beuret, Constantine) Holy Sepulchre Cemetery, East Orange, Essex County.
BURROUGH, EDWARD (see: Burroughs, Edward) Old St. Mary's Cemetery, Gloucester City, Camden County.
BURROUGH, WILLIAM H. (aka: Braynor, William) Pvt, H, 169th PA Inf, 5-13-1893. Baptist Church Cemetery, Haddonfield, Camden County.
BURROUGHS, AMOS S. Corp, F, 22nd NJ Inf, 3-2-1923. Holcomb-Riverview Cemetery, Lambertville, Hunterdon County.
BURROUGHS, EDWARD (aka: Burrough, Edward) Pvt, A, 1st NJ Militia, DoD Unknown. Old St. Mary's Cemetery, Gloucester City, Camden County.
BURROUGHS*, GARRETT SCHANCK Corp, A, PA Emerg NJ Militia, 1867. Mercer Cemetery, Trenton, Mercer County.
BURROUGHS, GEORGE W. Pvt, A, 44th PA Militia, 2-16-1905. Evergreen Cemetery, Camden, Camden County.
BURROUGHS, HORATIO (see: Barrows, Horatio N.) Evergreen Cemetery, Hillside, Union County.
BURROUGHS, J.D. (aka: Burris, J.D.) Pvt, E, 1st AL Inf (CSA), 9-22-1863. Finn's Point National Cemetery, Pennsville, Salem County.
BURROUGHS, J.S. Pvt, A, 1st MO Cav (CSA), 10-13-1863. Finn's Point National Cemetery, Pennsville, Salem County.
BURROUGHS, JAMES DoD Unknown. Old Presbyterian Church Cemetery, Daretown, Salem County.
BURROUGHS*, JEHU A. Capt, U.S. Marine Corps, 11-28-1867. Baptist/St. Andrew's Cemetery, Mount Holly, Burlington County.
BURROUGHS*, JOHN R. QM Sgt, 24th NJ Inf 9-9-1874. New Presbyterian Church Cemetery, Daretown, Salem County.
BURROUGHS, TIMOTHY D. Sgt, K, 7th NJ Inf, 3-12-1908. Hillside Cemetery, Madison, Morris County.
BURROUGHS, WESLEY M. Pvt, A, 3rd NJ Cav, 8-20-1868. Baptist Cemetery, Hopewell Boro, Mercer County.
BURROUGHS*, WILLIAM S. Pvt, F, 1st PA Prov Cav, 1-18-1894. Riverview Cemetery, Trenton, Mercer County.
BURROW, JOHN FREDERICK M. 1st Lt, Adj, 3rd MD Inf 7-21-1909. Bayview-New York Bay Cemetery, Jersey City, Hudson County.
BURROW, PHILIP J. Pvt, H, 56th GA Inf (CSA), [Captured 5-16-1863 at Baker's Creek, MS. Died of diarrhea.] 11-26-1863. Finn's Point National Cemetery, Pennsville, Salem County.
BURROWES, EDWARD T. Sgt, H, 5th TX Cav (CSA), [Cenotaph. Killed in action at Glorietta Pass, NM.] 3-28-1862. Fairview Cemetery, Fairview, Monmouth County.

New Jersey Civil War Burials

BURROWS*, ALFRED T. Landsman, U.S. Navy, USS Princeton, 10-9-1895. Woodland Cemetery, Newark, Essex County.

BURROWS*, CHARLES Corp, C, 1st U.S. Vet Vol Inf, 3-17-1935. New York/New Jersey Crematory Cemetery, North Bergen, Hudson County.

BURROWS, EDWARD (see: Burrows, Edwin A.) Flower Hill Cemetery, North Bergen, Hudson County.

BURROWS, EDWIN A. (aka: Burrows, Edward) Pvt, H, 201st PA Inf, 9-21-1903. Flower Hill Cemetery, North Bergen, Hudson County.

BURROWS, HIRAM 1869. Brink Cemetery, Colesville, Sussex County.

BURROWS, JOSEPH Musc, 3rd RI Heavy Art 3-9-1898. Cedar Lawn Cemetery, Paterson, Passaic County.

BURROWS, WILLIAM B. Seaman, U.S. Navy, USS Columbus, 6-22-1890. Evergreen Cemetery, Camden, Camden County.

BURSTON, THOMAS B. Pvt, H, 4th MA Cav, 6-14-1913. Holy Sepulchre Cemetery, Totowa, Passaic County.

BURSTROM, ANDREW G. Pvt, I, 2nd NJ Inf, 2-8-1900. Fairmount Cemetery, Newark, Essex County.

BURT, ABRAM G. Pvt, E, 30th NJ Inf, DoD Unknown. New Somerville Cemetery, Somerville, Somerset County.

BURT, AMOS S. Corp, K, 12th NJ Inf, 4-3-1900. Old Stone Church Cemetery, Fairton, Cumberland County.

BURT, ASA R. Pvt, H, 12th NJ Inf, [Cenotaph. Died of wounds received 5-3-1863 at Chancellorsville, VA. Prisoner, buried on the field.] 5-3-1863. Old Presbyterian Church Cemetery, Daretown, Salem County.

BURT*, BENJAMIN DEAN Pvt, G, 58th MA Inf, 11-27-1914. Elmwood Cemetery, New Brunswick, Middlesex County.

BURT, CHARLES Pvt, K, 1st CT Cav, 2-23-1925. Arlington Cemetery, Kearny, Hudson County.

BURT*, FLOYD E. (aka: Burt, Loyd E.) Pvt, C, 8th NJ Inf, 7-18-1912. Van Liew Cemetery, North Brunswick, Middlesex County.

BURT, GEORGE E. Pvt, K, 9th VT Inf, 2-21-1916. Arlington Cemetery, Kearny, Hudson County.

BURT, JAMES C. Sgt, A, 141st NY Inf, [Died of wounds received 7-20-1864 at Peach Tree Creek, GA.] 7-26-1864. Brainerd Cemetery, Cranbury, Middlesex County.

BURT, JOHN WILLIAM Corp, A, 22nd NJ Inf, 3-28-1910. Hackensack Cemetery, Hackensack, Bergen County.

BURT, JOSEPH Sgt, H, 7th NJ Inf, [Died of congestion of the heart at Falmouth, VA.] 2-10-1863. Presbyterian Church Cemetery, Cedarville, Cumberland County.

BURT, LOYD E. (see: Burt, Floyd E.) Van Liew Cemetery, North Brunswick, Middlesex County.

BURT, ROBERT C. Pvt, D, 38th NJ Inf, 10-11-1904. Eglington Cemetery, Clarksboro, Gloucester County.

BURTCH*, SAMUEL S.W. Pvt, C, 139th PA Inf, [Wounded 5-12-1864 at Spotsylvania CH, VA.] 9-9-1907. Siloam Cemetery, Vineland, Cumberland County.

BURTIS*, AREUNAH MARTIN QM, 83rd NY Inf 3-16-1926. Rosedale Cemetery, Orange, Essex County.

BURTIS, BARNET Pvt, K, 1st NJ Militia, 12-5-1901. Mount Pleasant Cemetery, Newark, Essex County.

BURTON, BENJAMIN Pvt, G, 13th NJ Inf, 6-28-1883. Cedar Lawn Cemetery, Paterson, Passaic County.

BURTON, CHARLES H. Corp, A, 9th DE Inf, 1909. Arlington Cemetery, Pennsauken, Camden County.

BURTON, DAVID R. Pvt, E, 6th NJ Inf, 12-18-1895. Bordentown/Old St. Mary's Catholic Cemetery, Bordentown, Burlington County.

Our Brothers Gone Before

BURTON, ERNEST ALBERT Pvt, G, 134th NY Inf, 9-1-1932. Laurel Grove Cemetery, Totowa, Passaic County.
BURTON, GEORGE Pvt, C, 25th NJ Inf, 1920. Calvary Cemetery, Cherry Hill, Camden County.
BURTON, GEORGE M. Pvt, A, 25th NJ Inf, 1-24-1907. Cedar Lawn Cemetery, Paterson, Passaic County.
BURTON, JOHN (see: DeKolf, Peter C.) Presbyterian Church Cemetery, Hanover, Morris County.
BURTON, JOHN H. Pvt, (CSA) [Wounded in action.] 11-17-1892. Baptist/St. Andrew's Cemetery, Mount Holly, Burlington County.
BURTON, WEBSTER (aka: Benton, Webster) Sgt, D, 1st NY Mounted Rifles, 5-1-1896. Laurel Grove Cemetery, Totowa, Passaic County.
BURTRONE, RICHARD (see: Bertram, Richard S.) Fairmount Cemetery, Newark, Essex County.
BURTT, GEORGE Corp, K, 39th NJ Inf, 1917. Stanhope-Union Cemetery, Netcong, Morris County.
BURTT, WILLIAM W. Pvt, E, 13th AL Inf (CSA), 9-15-1863. Finn's Point National Cemetery, Pennsville, Salem County.
BURTZ, ANTON Pvt, E, 5th NJ Inf, 9-12-1893. Fairmount Cemetery, Newark, Essex County.
BURUS, CHARLES (see: Burns, Charles) St. John's Evangelical Church Cemetery, Orange, Essex County.
BUSBY, ANDREW Pvt, C, 5th PA Cav, 4-29-1910. Friendship United Methodist Church Cemetery, Landisville, Atlantic County.
BUSBY, SAMUEL Pvt, E, 4th NJ Inf, 9-28-1911. United Methodist Church Cemetery, Winslow, Camden County.
BUSBY, WILLIAM Com Sgt, C, 11th NY Cav, 4-21-1905. Beverly National Cemetery, Edgewater Park, Burlington County.
BUSCH, FREDERICK (see: Bubser, Frederick C.) Palisade Cemetery, North Bergen, Hudson County.
BUSCH, HENRY Corp, C, 54th NY Inf, DoD Unknown. Bayview-New York Bay Cemetery, Jersey City, Hudson County.
BUSCH, WILLIAM Pvt, Btty A, 1st NJ Light Art, 1-3-1898. Elmwood Cemetery, New Brunswick, Middlesex County.
BUSCHMANN, BRUNO Pvt, A, 4th NY Cav, 3-16-1882. Berry Lawn Cemetery, Carlstadt, Bergen County.
BUSER*, FREDERICK Musc, G, 3rd U.S. Vet Vol Inf, 5-6-1898. Evergreen Cemetery, Camden, Camden County.
BUSH, ABRAHAM A. Pvt, E, 9th NJ Inf, 5-9-1916. Fair Lawn Cemetery, Fair Lawn, Bergen County.
BUSH, ABRAHAM A. Pvt, K, 13th NJ Inf, 1-9-1922. Reformed Church Cemetery, Wyckoff, Bergen County.
BUSH, ABRAHAM P. Pvt, E, 22nd NJ Inf, 12-17-1924. Bayview-New York Bay Cemetery, Jersey City, Hudson County.
BUSH, CHARLES Pvt, A, 213th PA Inf, 2-20-1900. Evergreen Cemetery, Camden, Camden County.
BUSH, CORNELIUS VANNESS Pvt, Btty B, 1st NJ Light Art, [Wounded in action 7-2-1863 at Gettysburg, PA.] 7-16-1934. Reformed Church Cemetery, Fairfield, Essex County.
BUSH, EGBERT Pvt, Btty B, 1st NJ Light Art, 11-3-1899. Fairmount Cemetery, Newark, Essex County.
BUSH, ELIAS Pvt, C, 7th NJ Inf, 8-5-1880. Fairmount Cemetery, Newark, Essex County.
BUSH, GARRET D. Pvt, I, 13th NJ Inf, 7-23-1911. Saums Farm Cemetery, Hillsborough, Somerset County.

New Jersey Civil War Burials

BUSH*, GARRETT C. Pvt, C, 7th NJ Inf, 3-12-1918. Savage Cemetery, Denville, Morris County.
BUSH, GEORGE M. Pvt, D, 26th NJ Inf, DoD Unknown. Prospect Hill Cemetery, Caldwell, Essex County.
BUSH*, HARVEY Pvt, K, 124th NY Inf, 4-29-1909. Valleau Cemetery, Ridgewood, Bergen County.
BUSH, HENRY Pvt, K, 75th PA Inf, 3-25-1876. Cedar Grove Cemetery, Gloucester City, Camden County.
BUSH*, HENRY MORRISON Capt, D, 26th NJ Inf, 6-17-1911. Reformed Church Cemetery, Fairfield, Essex County.
BUSH, HERMAN Corp, __, 11th NY Inf, 7-1-1898. Lady of Lourdes/Holy Sepulchre Cemetery, Hamilton, Mercer County.
BUSH, JAMES K. Pvt, Btty D, 1st NJ Light Art, 6-23-1892. Mount Hebron Cemetery, Montclair, Essex County.
BUSH, JOHN Pvt, K, 13th NJ Inf, 5-23-1910. Cedar Lawn Cemetery, Paterson, Passaic County.
BUSH, JOHN 10-9-1887. Evergreen Cemetery, Hillside, Union County.
BUSH*, JOHN H. Pvt, H, 1st NJ Cav, 11-7-1926. Rural Hill Cemetery, Whitehouse, Hunterdon County.
BUSH, JOSEPH DoD Unknown. Cedar Grove Cemetery, Gloucester City, Camden County.
BUSH, LUKE W. 2nd Lt, E, 8th NJ Inf, 2-4-1869. Mount Hebron Cemetery, Montclair, Essex County.
BUSH, PETER DoD Unknown. Valleau Cemetery, Ridgewood, Bergen County.
BUSH, THOMAS Pvt, A, 7th NJ Inf, 3-2-1890. Presbyterian Church Cemetery, Cold Spring, Cape May County.
BUSH, WILLIAM (aka: Bush, Willis) Pvt, E, 2nd (Ashby's) TN Cav (CSA), 8-27-1864. Finn's Point National Cemetery, Pennsville, Salem County.
BUSH, WILLIS (see: Bush, William) Finn's Point National Cemetery, Pennsville, Salem County.
BUSHNELL, ALBERT E. Pvt, D, 71st NY National Guard, 1927. Presbyterian Cemetery, North Plainfield, Somerset County.
BUSS, DANIEL J. Pvt, H, 54th PA Inf, 7-11-1908. Phillipsburg Cemetery, Phillipsburg, Warren County.
BUSS, RICHARD Pvt, Btty C, 15th NY Heavy Art, 3-26-1914. Woodland Cemetery, Newark, Essex County.
BUSSE*, WILLIAM Pvt, B, 12th NY State Militia, 9-27-1906. Rahway Cemetery, Rahway, Union County.
BUSSING, EDWIN A. Pvt, M, 1st NY Cav, 2-9-1904. Fairview Cemetery, Westfield, Union County.
BUSSOM, BENJAMIN POINSETT Corp, D, 23rd NJ Inf, 2-27-1909. Baptist Church Cemetery, Jacobstown, Burlington County.
BUTCHER, EDMUND J. Pvt, Btty E, 2nd PA Heavy Art, 11-17-1890. Evergreen Cemetery, Camden, Camden County.
BUTCHER, GEORGE A. Pvt, 6th NY Ind Btty 5-18-1898. Presbyterian Cemetery, North Plainfield, Somerset County.
BUTCHER, I.K. 5-13-1932. Evergreen Cemetery, Camden, Camden County.
BUTCHER, JAMES 11-4-1901. Bayview-New York Bay Cemetery, Jersey City, Hudson County.
BUTCHER, JOHN Pvt, A, 32nd U.S. CT, 8-13-1899. Johnson Cemetery, Camden, Camden County.
BUTCHER, SAMUEL T. Pvt, I, 9th NJ Inf, 2-1-1924. Evergreen Cemetery, Camden, Camden County.

Our Brothers Gone Before

BUTCHER, SAMUEL T. 3-14-1916. Tennent Church Cemetery, Tennent, Monmouth County.
BUTCHER, SYLVESTER Pvt, C, 43rd U.S. CT, [Accidentally wounded 7-31-1864.] 8-28-1894. Johnson Cemetery, Camden, Camden County.
BUTCHER, WILLIAM A. Pvt, F, 4th NJ Inf, 2-18-1915. Evergreen Cemetery, Camden, Camden County.
BUTLER, ALFRED D. Pvt, I, 7th NJ Inf, 1917. Presbyterian Church Cemetery, Newton, Sussex County.
BUTLER, ALONZO Pvt, D, 8th NJ Inf, 4-10-1924. Union Cemetery, Frenchtown, Hunterdon County.
BUTLER, ARTHUR ANTHONY DoD Unknown. Fairmount Cemetery, Newark, Essex County.
BUTLER, CHARLES __, F, 19th NY __, DoD Unknown. Palisade Cemetery, North Bergen, Hudson County.
BUTLER, CLINTON Sgt, B, 6th U.S. CT, 12-25-1918. Maplewood Cemetery, Freehold, Monmouth County.
BUTLER, DAVID Pvt, E, 43rd U.S. CT, 11-21-1897. Lutheran Cemetery, East Stewartsville, Warren County.
BUTLER, EDWARD (see: Butler, Edwin) Bloomsbury Cemetery, Kennedy Mills, Warren County.
BUTLER*, EDWIN (aka: Butler, Edward) Pvt, H, 9th NJ Inf, 12-10-1903. Bloomsbury Cemetery, Kennedy Mills, Warren County.
BUTLER, FRANCIS E. Chaplain, 25th NJ Inf [Died of wounds received 5-3-1863 at Suffolk, VA.] 5-4-1863. Cedar Lawn Cemetery, Paterson, Passaic County.
BUTLER, FREDERICK Pvt, Btty D, 6th NY Heavy Art, 1-6-1903. Fairmount Cemetery, Newark, Essex County.
BUTLER, GEORGE Pvt, A, 8th NJ Inf, [Died of chronic diarrhea and wounds received in action at Deep Bottom, VA.] 11-23-1864. Christ Church Cemetery, Belleville, Essex County.
BUTLER, GEORGE Pvt, E, 1st U.S. Hancock Corps, 5-12-1901. Willow Grove Cemetery, New Brunswick, Middlesex County.
BUTLER, GEORGE J. 1925. Fairview Cemetery, Wantage, Sussex County.
BUTLER, GIDEON P. Pvt, A, 24th NJ Inf, 1924. Baptist Cemetery, Salem, Salem County.
BUTLER, HENRY E. Pvt, C, 31st NJ Inf, 7-2-1933. Mansfield/Washington Cemetery, Washington, Warren County.
BUTLER, HUGH Pvt, H, 138th PA Inf, 5-31-1905. Union Cemetery, Milford, Hunterdon County.
BUTLER, JACOB DoD Unknown. Bethel Cemetery, Pennsauken, Camden County.
BUTLER, JAMES Pvt, C, 2nd NJ Cav, [Died of fever at Mound City, IL.] 2-19-1864. St. Mary's Cemetery, Boonton, Morris County.
BUTLER, JAMES H. Pvt, B, 39th NJ Inf, 11-15-1910. Ramapo Reformed Church Cemetery, Mahwah, Bergen County.
BUTLER, JAMES H. Pvt, H, 7th NJ Inf, 7-11-1896. Methodist-Episcopal Church Cemetery, Aura, Gloucester County.
BUTLER, JAMES P. 2nd Lt, K, 24th NJ Inf, 2-24-1903. Methodist Church Cemetery, Sharptown, Salem County.
BUTLER, JOHN Pvt, B, 127th U.S. CT, 6-14-1907. Greenwood Cemetery, Pleasantville, Atlantic County.
BUTLER, JOHN Musc, G, 52nd NY National Guard, DoD Unknown. Christ Church Cemetery, Belleville, Essex County.
BUTLER, JOHN Pvt, E, 31st NJ Inf, 2-7-1910. Bethlehem Presbyterian Church Cemetery, Grandin, Hunterdon County.
BUTLER*, JOHN H. Pvt, Btty L, 7th NY Heavy Art, 6-18-1886. Chestnut Cemetery, Dover, Morris County.

New Jersey Civil War Burials

BUTLER, JOHN (JR.) Pvt, A, 15th NJ Inf, 10-4-1872. Riverview Cemetery, Trenton, Mercer County.
BUTLER*, JOHN (SR.) Pvt, A, 15th NJ Inf, 4-3-1897. Union Cemetery, Frenchtown, Hunterdon County.
BUTLER, JOHN T. Pvt, E, 11th NY Inf, 3-2-1920. Evergreen Cemetery, Hillside, Union County.
BUTLER, JOSIAH Pvt, E, 22nd NJ Inf, 12-24-1927. Union Cemetery, Frenchtown, Hunterdon County.
BUTLER, OSCEOLA 1st Cl Boy, U.S. Navy, 7-2-1917. Mount Peace Cemetery, Lawnside, Camden County.
BUTLER, PETER Pvt, D, 10th Confederate States Cav (CSA), 3-30-1864. Finn's Point National Cemetery, Pennsville, Salem County.
BUTLER, PETER J. Landsman, U.S. Navy, USS Monticello, 7-30-1889. Fairmount Cemetery, Chatham, Morris County.
BUTLER, SAMUEL Pvt, H, 25th U.S. CT, 11-27-1924. Trinity Episcopal Church Cemetery, Delran, Burlington County.
BUTLER, SAMUEL Corp, C, 32nd U.S. CT, 1931. Lake Park Cemetery, Swedesboro, Gloucester County.
BUTLER, SAMUEL L. Pvt, K, 62nd NC Inf (CSA), 8-8-1864. Finn's Point National Cemetery, Pennsville, Salem County.
BUTLER*, THOMAS Pvt, F, 1st WI Cav, 7-21-1885. Holy Sepulchre Cemetery, East Orange, Essex County.
BUTLER, THOMAS G. Pvt, E, 31st NJ Inf, 5-3-1888. Bethlehem Presbyterian Church Cemetery, Grandin, Hunterdon County.
BUTLER, WILLIAM Pvt, Btty A, Schaffer's Ind PA Heavy Art, 1-13-1864. Finn's Point National Cemetery, Pennsville, Salem County.
BUTLER, WILLIAM Pvt, E, 9th NJ Inf, 1-26-1867. Baptist Cemetery, Burlington, Burlington County.
BUTLER, WILLIAM G. 1929. Union Cemetery, Clinton, Hunterdon County.
BUTLER, WILLIAM H. Pvt, F, 47th NY Inf, 7-14-1911. Cedar Lawn Cemetery, Paterson, Passaic County.
BUTLER, WILLIAM H. (aka: Buckter, William) Pvt, L, 1st NJ Cav, 10-27-1910. Arlington Cemetery, Kearny, Hudson County.
BUTT*, ANDREW Musc, E, 61st VA Inf (CSA), [Captured 7-3-1863 at Gettysburg, PA. Died of bronchitis.] 9-28-1863. Finn's Point National Cemetery, Pennsville, Salem County.
BUTTELL*, CHARLES B. (aka: Brown, Charles) Corp, D, 2nd NH Inf, 7-20-1919. Laurel Grove Cemetery, Totowa, Passaic County.
BUTTELL, EDWARD W. Musc, A, 7th NY State Militia, 8-9-1885. Fairmount Cemetery, Newark, Essex County.
BUTTERFIELD, JAMES Capt, B, 5th CT Inf, 12-31-1907. Weehawken Cemetery, North Bergen, Hudson County.
BUTTERFIELD, LEVIN C. Pvt, K, 23rd NJ Inf, 9-14-1871. Baptist Cemetery, West Creek, Ocean County.
BUTTERWORTH, ABRAM Pvt, I, 6th NY Inf, 3-18-1893. Laurel Grove Cemetery, Totowa, Passaic County.
BUTTERWORTH, EDWARD Pvt, I, 1st NJ Inf, [Died of wounds received 5-3-1863 at Salem Heights, VA.] 5-29-1863. Grove Church Cemetery, North Bergen, Hudson County.
BUTTERWORTH, J.M. Pvt, F, 31st AL Inf (CSA), 6-16-1863. Finn's Point National Cemetery, Pennsville, Salem County.
BUTTERWORTH, JAMES P. Sgt, C, 79th NY Inf, 8-24-1884. Fairview Cemetery, Fairview, Monmouth County.

Our Brothers Gone Before

BUTTERWORTH, JOHN Pvt, K, 13th NJ Inf, 1-24-1902. Cedar Lawn Cemetery, Paterson, Passaic County.

BUTTERWORTH, JONATHAN Pvt, B, 9th NJ Inf, 6-12-1863. Elmwood Cemetery, New Brunswick, Middlesex County.

BUTTERWORTH, JOSEPH B. 1st Cl Musc, 1st NJ Inf Band 1900. Mount Holly Cemetery, Mount Holly, Burlington County.

BUTTNER, JOHN Musc, G, 54th NY Inf, 11-10-1888. Flower Hill Cemetery, North Bergen, Hudson County.

BUTTON, JOSEPH H. Pvt, I, 24th NJ Inf, 8-21-1884. 1st Methodist Church Cemetery, Williamstown, Gloucester County.

BUTTS, DANIEL (aka: Butz, Daniel) Pvt, I, 31st NJ Inf, 1-7-1864. Belvidere/Catholic Cemetery, Belvidere, Warren County.

BUTTS, JOHN H. Pvt, F, 129th PA Inf, [Died at Washington, DC of wounds received 12-13-1862 at Fredericksburg, VA.] 12-20-1862. Presbyterian Church Cemetery, Harmony, Warren County.

BUTTS, JOHN T. 3-2-1920. Evergreen Cemetery, Hillside, Union County.

BUTTS, MILES Pvt, B, 38th U.S. CT, 7-30-1899. Johnson Cemetery, Camden, Camden County.

BUTZ, DANIEL (see: Butts, Daniel) Belvidere/Catholic Cemetery, Belvidere, Warren County.

BUTZ, ENOS HENRY Pvt, K, 88th PA Inf, 6-10-1894. Ramseyburg Cemetery, Ramseyburg, Warren County.

BUXTON, DANIEL D. Pvt, I, 11th NJ Inf, 9-18-1912. Mount Prospect Cemetery, Neptune, Monmouth County.

BUXTON, JOHN T. Pvt, G, 9th VA Inf (CSA), [Captured 7-6-1863 at Greencastle, PA. Died of typhoid.] 8-16-1863. Finn's Point National Cemetery, Pennsville, Salem County.

BUZBY, CHARLES H. Pvt, H, 23rd NJ Inf, 12-22-1891. 1st Baptist Church Cemetery, Moorestown, Burlington County.

BUZBY, FRANKLIN W. Corp, H, 3rd NJ Cav, 1-3-1935. Arlington Cemetery, Kearny, Hudson County.

BUZBY, JOHN L. Pvt, G, 25th NJ Inf, 3-11-1923. United Methodist Church Cemetery, Tuckahoe, Cape May County.

BUZBY, JOSEPH Pvt, H, 28th NJ Inf, DoD Unknown. New Freedom Cemetery, New Freedom, Camden County.

BUZBY, RICHARD Pvt, H, 28th NJ Inf, 2-12-1887. Bates Mills Cemetery, Waterford Works, Camden County.

BUZINE, JOHN G. Pvt, G, 52nd PA Militia, 3- -1889. New Camden Cemetery, Camden, Camden County.

BUZZEE, AARON Musc, K, 28th NJ Inf, 1-14-1907. Elmwood Cemetery, New Brunswick, Middlesex County.

BUZZEE, ALEXANDER Pvt, G, 1st NJ Inf, 4-2-1870. Willow Grove Cemetery, New Brunswick, Middlesex County.

BUZZEE, GEORGE R. Musc, G, 1st NJ Inf, [Captured 5-6-1864 at Wilderness, VA. Died while prisoner at Florence, SC.] 12-16-1864. 1st Methodist-Episcopal Cemetery, New Brunswick, Middlesex County.

BUZZEE*, ISRAEL (aka: Buzzill, Israel) Landsman, U.S. Navy, USS Powhattan, 1-10-1893. Evergreen Cemetery, New Brunswick, Middlesex County.

BUZZEE, JACOB Pvt, K, 3rd NJ Militia, 4-23-1907. Elmwood Cemetery, New Brunswick, Middlesex County.

BUZZEE, JOHN Pvt, D, 28th NJ Inf, 12-19-1892. Evergreen Cemetery, New Brunswick, Middlesex County.

BUZZILL, ISRAEL (see: Buzzee, Israel) Evergreen Cemetery, New Brunswick, Middlesex County.

New Jersey Civil War Burials

BYARD, SAMUEL Pvt, C, 2nd NJ Cav, 2-19-1907. Greenlawn Cemetery, West Long Branch, Monmouth County.

BYARD*, SYLVESTER (aka: Baird, Sylvester) Corp, Btty I, 11th U.S. CHA, 11-22-1920. Laurel Grove Cemetery, Totowa, Passaic County.

BYDICK, JOHN A.F. (aka: Foster, John A.) Pvt, H, 66th NY Inf, 3-8-1899. Bayview-New York Bay Cemetery, Jersey City, Hudson County.

BYE, GIBBONS Pvt, E, 32nd U.S. CT, 12-31-1905. Mount Peace Cemetery, Lawnside, Camden County.

BYER*, ANDREW Pvt, A, 7th MA Inf, DoD Unknown. Methodist-Episcopal Cemetery, Midland Park, Bergen County.

BYER, MATTHEW (aka: Bayor, Matthew) Pvt, A, 40th NJ Inf, 3-9-1899. Fairmount Cemetery, Newark, Essex County.

BYERLEY, ROBERT L. 8-21-1894. Presbyterian Church Cemetery, Andover, Sussex County.

BYERS, JAMES Pvt, D, 4th NJ Militia, DoD Unknown. Old St. Mary's Cemetery, Gloucester City, Camden County.

BYERS, WILLIAM M. Pvt, E, 49th NC Inf (CSA), [Captured 7-1-1862 at Malvern Hill, VA. Died of typhoid.] 7-12-1862. Finn's Point National Cemetery, Pennsville, Salem County.

BYINGTON, AARON H. (aka: Boyington, Aaron) Saddler, I, 6th NY Cav, 4-27-1887. New Somerville Cemetery, Somerville, Somerset County.

BYINGTON, RODERICK 2-1-1904. Belvidere/Catholic Cemetery, Belvidere, Warren County.

BYLLESBY, DEWITT CLINTON 1891. Baptist/St. Andrew's Cemetery, Mount Holly, Burlington County.

BYRAM, JOB JOHNSON Pvt, K, 27th NJ Inf, DoD Unknown. Methodist Church Cemetery, Sparta, Sussex County.

BYRAM, SYDNEY S. (aka: Byron, Sydney) 1st Sgt, A, 27th NJ Inf, 8-9-1901. Presbyterian Church Cemetery, Sparta, Sussex County.

BYRAM, WILLIAM H. (aka: Bryan, William H.) Pvt, H, 22nd NY Cav, 1911. Locust Hill Cemetery, Dover, Morris County.

BYRAM, WILLIAM H. Corp, G, 14th NJ Inf, 1918. Hillside Cemetery, Madison, Morris County.

BYRD, HENRY W. Pvt, Btty A, 10th Bttn NC Heavy Art (CSA), [Captured 12-21-1864 at Savannah, GA. Died of pneumonia.] 5-28-1865. Finn's Point National Cemetery, Pennsville, Salem County.

BYRD, ISAAC Pvt, I, 33rd VA Inf (CSA), [Captured 5-12-1864 at Spotsylvania CH, VA. Died of smallpox.] 9-3-1864. Finn's Point National Cemetery, Pennsville, Salem County.

BYRD, THOMAS E. Corp, B, 176th NY Inf, 10-18-1885. Hackensack Cemetery, Hackensack, Bergen County.

BYRNE, CHARLES HUBERT Capt, H, Tucker's Confederate States Inf (CSA), 10-6-1908. Rosedale Cemetery, Orange, Essex County.

BYRNE, GARRETT SMOCK QM, 13th NJ Inf 10-15-1895. Rose Hill Cemetery, Matawan, Monmouth County.

BYRNE*, JOHN Sgt, E, 42nd NY Inf, 8-25-1877. St. John's Cemetery, Hamilton, Mercer County.

BYRNE, JOHN Landsman, U.S. Navy, 4-30-1894. Holy Sepulchre Cemetery, East Orange, Essex County.

BYRNE, JOHN (SR.) (aka: Burns, John) Pvt, C, 2nd NJ Inf, [Wounded 8-27-1862 at 2nd Bull Run, VA.] 8-20-1901. Holy Sepulchre Cemetery, East Orange, Essex County.

BYRNE, PATRICK 1943. St. Paul's R.C. Church Cemetery, Princeton, Mercer County.

BYRNE, THOMAS Pvt, G, 9th NJ Inf, 10-19-1879. Holy Sepulchre Cemetery, East Orange, Essex County.

Our Brothers Gone Before

BYRNES, CHARLES Pvt, K, 10th NJ Inf, DoD Unknown. St. Mary's Cemetery, South Amboy, Middlesex County.
BYRNES, JAMES Pvt, E, 71st NY Inf, DoD Unknown. St. John's Evangelical Church Cemetery, Orange, Essex County.
BYRNES, JOHN (aka: Burns, John) Pvt, C, 22nd NY Cav, 12-17-1913. Holy Sepulchre Cemetery, East Orange, Essex County.
BYRNES, JOHN CHARLES (aka: Burnes, John) Pvt, A, 71st NY Inf, 12-28-1894. Holy Name Cemetery, Jersey City, Hudson County.
BYRNES, MORGAN Sgt, G, 1st NY Eng, 5-26-1896. St. Cecelia's Cemetery, Rockaway, Morris County.
BYRNES, PATRICK Pvt, D, 4th NJ Militia, DoD Unknown. Holy Sepulchre Cemetery, East Orange, Essex County.
BYRNES, PATRICK Pvt, A, 20th NY Cav, 1-4-1914. Holy Sepulchre Cemetery, East Orange, Essex County.
BYRNES, PATRICK (aka: Burns, Patrick) Pvt, C, 2nd NJ Inf, 9-2-1888. Holy Sepulchre Cemetery, East Orange, Essex County.
BYRNES, RICHARD J. Pvt, A, 83rd NY Inf, 1-8-1884. Mount Olivet Cemetery, Newark, Essex County.
BYRNES, THOMAS Pvt, E, 13th NJ Inf, DoD Unknown. St. John's Evangelical Church Cemetery, Orange, Essex County.
BYRNES, THOMAS F. Seaman, U.S. Navy, 1-22-1909. Holy Sepulchre Cemetery, East Orange, Essex County.
BYRNES, WILLIAM D. Pvt, E, 12th NJ Inf, 7-13-1898. St. John's Cemetery, Allentown, Monmouth County.
BYRON, SYDNEY (see: Byram, Sydney S.) Presbyterian Church Cemetery, Sparta, Sussex County.
BYWATER, JOHN T. 1st Lt, B, 11th IN Inf, 4-16-1916. Fairmount Cemetery, Newark, Essex County.
CABEY, PETER (see: Geibig, Peter) St. Mary's Cemetery, Hainesport, Burlington County.
CABLES*, DANIEL C. Pvt, Btty D, 1st NJ Light Art, 4-30-1912. Reformed Church Cemetery, Fairfield, Essex County.
CACNER, AMOS 1906. Union Cemetery, Milford, Hunterdon County.
CADDELL, W.B. Sgt, A, 6th LA Inf (CSA), [Captured 7-3-1863 at Gettysburg, PA.] 9-21-1863. Finn's Point National Cemetery, Pennsville, Salem County.
CADDEN, BERNARD (aka: McCadden, Barney) Pvt, K, 70th NY Inf, 11-11-1862. Holy Sepulchre Cemetery, East Orange, Essex County.
CADE, ISAAC B. Pvt, A, 99th PA Inf, 4-8-1862. Methodist Cemetery, Haddonfield, Camden County.
CADLE, MATHEW Pvt, E, 14th VA Cav (CSA), 4-26-1864. Finn's Point National Cemetery, Pennsville, Salem County.
CADMES, ANDREW (see: Cadmus, Andrew) Clinton Cemetery, Irvington, Essex County.
CADMUS, AARON S. Pvt, K, 9th NJ Inf, 10-5-1880. Riverview Cemetery, Trenton, Mercer County.
CADMUS*, ABRAHAM H. 1st Sgt, G, 13th NJ Inf, 9-6-1867. Bloomfield Cemetery, Bloomfield, Essex County.
CADMUS*, ABRAM Pvt, C, 3rd NJ Cav, [Wounded in action.] 4-16-1898. Bloomfield Cemetery, Bloomfield, Essex County.
CADMUS, ALABAMA Pvt, H, 13th NJ Inf, 12-13-1880. Bayview-New York Bay Cemetery, Jersey City, Hudson County.
CADMUS, ANDREW (aka: Cadmes, Andrew) Pvt, 14th OH Ind Btty 1911. Clinton Cemetery, Irvington, Essex County.
CADMUS*, CALEB Sgt, C, 12th CT Inf, 4-20-1921. Fairmount Cemetery, Newark, Essex County.

New Jersey Civil War Burials

CADMUS, CORNELIUS Pvt, E, 1st NJ Militia, 11-7-1906. Fairmount Cemetery, Newark, Essex County.

CADMUS, FREDERICK Pvt, I, 14th NJ Inf, 4-6-1904. Presbyterian Cemetery, North Plainfield, Somerset County.

CADMUS, GEORGE M. Pvt, C, 74th NY Inf, 2-8-1914. Bloomfield Cemetery, Bloomfield, Essex County.

CADMUS, GEORGE W. Sgt, F, 26th NJ Inf, 9-21-1915. Bloomfield Cemetery, Bloomfield, Essex County.

CADMUS, HENRY S. Pvt, K, 2nd NJ Inf, 6-13-1885. Bloomfield Cemetery, Bloomfield, Essex County.

CADMUS, JAMES Pvt, F, 13th NJ Inf, 9-25-1924. Evergreen Cemetery, Hillside, Union County.

CADMUS, JAMES Pvt, C, 74th NY Inf, 7-28-1885. Bloomfield Cemetery, Bloomfield, Essex County.

CADMUS, JAMES HARVEY Pvt, F, 26th NJ Inf, 11-30-1880. Bloomfield Cemetery, Bloomfield, Essex County.

CADMUS*, JOHN A. Pvt, I, 21st NJ Inf, 4-23-1914. Bayview-New York Bay Cemetery, Jersey City, Hudson County.

CADMUS, JOHN A. Sgt, E, 2nd NJ Militia, DoD Unknown. Presbyterian Cemetery, North Plainfield, Somerset County.

CADMUS, PETER HOWARD Pvt, F, 26th NJ Inf, 6-24-1885. Bloomfield Cemetery, Bloomfield, Essex County.

CADMUS, STEPHEN V.C. (JR.) Pvt, K, 2nd NJ Inf, 1-27-1901. Mount Pleasant Cemetery, Newark, Essex County.

CADMUS, THEODORE 1st Sgt, F, 1st NJ Militia, 5-9-1916. Bloomfield Cemetery, Bloomfield, Essex County.

CADMUS, THOMAS J. Pvt, H, 26th NJ Inf, 7-8-1900. Rosedale Cemetery, Orange, Essex County.

CADMUS, WILLIAM H. Corp, E, 22nd NJ Inf, 11-25-1916. Cedar Lawn Cemetery, Paterson, Passaic County.

CADOTT, CHARLES Corp, F, 1st NJ Cav, 9-25-1914. Rosehill Cemetery, Linden, Union County.

CADWALDER, JAMES G. 4-20-1905. Greenwood Cemetery, Hamilton, Mercer County.

CADWALLADER, CYRUS Wagoner, E, 21st NJ Inf, 10-20-1912. Greenwood Cemetery, Hamilton, Mercer County.

CAFFERTY, GEORGE Pvt, H, 4th IA Cav, 3-26-1892. Fairmount Cemetery, Newark, Essex County.

CAFFERY*, ALEXANDER T. Pvt, D, 34th NJ Inf, 3-23-1907. Emleys Hill United Methodist Church Cemetery, Upper Freehold, Monmouth County.

CAFFERY*, CHARLES Corp, A, 2nd NJ Cav, 1868. Allenwood Church Cemetery, Allenwood, Monmouth County.

CAFFEY*, JOHN M. Corp, E, 174th PA Inf, 8-6-1907. Mount Hope Presbyterian Cemetery, Lambertville, Hunterdon County.

CAFFEY, WILLIAM Pvt, B, 3rd NJ Cav, 5-15-1917. Phillipsburg Cemetery, Phillipsburg, Warren County.

CAGNEY, MICHAEL Pvt, Btty F, 2nd NY Heavy Art, 5-20-1916. Holy Name Cemetery, Jersey City, Hudson County.

CAHILL*, ANDREW 1st Sgt, Btty I, 1st MN Heavy Art, 1-1-1898. St. Mary's Cemetery, Hamilton, Mercer County.

CAHILL, DANIEL Pvt, E, Cocke's AR Inf (CSA), [Captured 7-4-1863 at Helena, AR. Died of fever.] 12-22-1864. Finn's Point National Cemetery, Pennsville, Salem County.

CAHILL*, DENNIS Pvt, E, 6th U.S. VRC, 1-27-1892. Fairmount Cemetery, Newark, Essex County.

Our Brothers Gone Before

CAHILL, DENNIS Pvt, F, 28th NJ Inf, DoD Unknown. St. Peter's Cemetery, New Brunswick, Middlesex County.
CAHILL, EDWARD Pvt, B, 11th NY Inf, 1-4-1905. Holy Name Cemetery, Jersey City, Hudson County.
CAHILL, FRANCIS Pvt, B, 9th NJ Inf, 11-25-1899. St. Peter's Cemetery, New Brunswick, Middlesex County.
CAHILL, JAMES 12-14-1907. Holy Name Cemetery, Jersey City, Hudson County.
CAHILL*, JOHN J. Corp, G, 8th NJ Inf, 2-24-1912. Holy Sepulchre Cemetery, East Orange, Essex County.
CAHILL, PHILIP Corp, B, 14th U.S. Inf, DoD Unknown. Holy Sepulchre Cemetery, East Orange, Essex County.
CAHILL, THOMAS J. Pvt, G, 32nd PA Militia, 12-21-1900. Holy Name Cemetery, Jersey City, Hudson County.
CAHILL, WILLIAM Pvt, G, 41st NY Inf, 9-24-1915. Union Cemetery, Clarkstown, Atlantic County.
CAHILL, WILLIAM P. Pvt, G, 155th NY Inf, 6-12-1914. Holy Name Cemetery, Jersey City, Hudson County.
CAHOW, WILLIAM Pvt, D, 5th NJ Inf, [Died of consumption at Newark, NJ.] 5-9-1863. Presbyterian Church Cemetery, Elizabeth, Union County.
CAIN, DANIEL Pvt, H, 6th DE Inf, 2-23-1895. Evergreen Cemetery, Camden, Camden County.
CAIN, ENOS W. Pvt, H, 10th SC Inf (CSA), 12-30-1899. Evergreen Cemetery, Camden, Camden County.
CAIN, JAMES (aka: Kane, James) Pvt, I, 29th NJ Inf, 1890. St. Joseph's Cemetery, Keyport, Monmouth County.
CAIN*, JOSEPH Pvt, E, 10th NJ Inf, [Wounded in action.] 8-31-1889. Presbyterian Church Cemetery, Mays Landing, Atlantic County.
CAIN, JOSEPH Corp, A, 8th NJ Inf, [Wounded in action.] 10-26-1894. Presbyterian Church Cemetery, Oak Ridge, Passaic County.
CAIN, L.C. Pvt, G, 54th AL Inf (CSA), 7-22-1863. Finn's Point National Cemetery, Pennsville, Salem County.
CAIN, MICHAEL (see: Kane, Michael) Holy Name Cemetery, Jersey City, Hudson County.
CAIN, RUDOLPH P. Sgt, K, 35th NJ Inf, [Killed in action at Resaca, GA.] 5-15-1864. Mercer Cemetery, Trenton, Mercer County.
CAIN, RUDOLPH P. Musc, C, 3rd NJ Militia, DoD Unknown. North Crosswicks Cemetery, North Crosswicks, Mercer County.
CAIN*, WILLIAM Pvt, D, 11th PA Inf, 4-10-1875. Salem Cemetery, Pleasantville, Atlantic County.
CAIN, WILLIAM Pvt, I, 33rd MS Inf (CSA), 10-1-1863. Finn's Point National Cemetery, Pennsville, Salem County.
CAIN, WILLIAM H. Pvt, C, 4th NJ Inf, 3-30-1890. Fairmount Cemetery, Newark, Essex County.
CAIN, WILLIAM S. Pvt, U.S. Army, [General Service.] 8-16-1862. Finn's Point National Cemetery, Pennsville, Salem County.
CAIN, WILLIAM THOMAS Pvt, K, 23rd NJ Inf, 5-14-1928. Beverly National Cemetery, Edgewater Park, Burlington County.
CAINE, JOHN E. Pvt, K, 1st NY Vet Inf, 4-20-1902. New Camden Cemetery, Camden, Camden County.
CAIRNS, CHARLES L. Pvt, A, 37th NJ Inf, 2-8-1914. Rosedale Cemetery, Orange, Essex County.
CAIROLI, GEORGE A. Pvt, G, 4th NJ Militia, 1-8-1922. Harleigh Cemetery, Camden, Camden County.

New Jersey Civil War Burials

CAKE, JACOB F. Pvt, B, 24th NJ Inf, 5-27-1907. Friendship United Methodist Church Cemetery, Landisville, Atlantic County.

CAKE, LAWRENCE ELMER Pvt, I, 24th NJ Inf, [Killed in action at Fredericksburg, VA.] 12-13-1862. Trinity Bible Church Cemetery, Glassboro, Gloucester County.

CAKE, RICHARD C. Pvt, B, 23rd MO Inf, 2-22-1891. Evergreen Cemetery, Camden, Camden County.

CALDWELL, DANIEL Seaman, U.S. Navy, USS Keystone State, DoD Unknown. Jersey City Cemetery, Jersey City, Hudson County.

CALDWELL, DAVID L. DoD Unknown. Jersey City Cemetery, Jersey City, Hudson County.

CALDWELL, HUGH Pvt, H, 45th VA Inf (CSA), [Captured 3-2-1865 at Waynesboro, VA. Died of measles.] 4-26-1865. Finn's Point National Cemetery, Pennsville, Salem County.

CALDWELL, J.M. Pvt, I, 51st AL Cav (CSA), 11-10-1863. Finn's Point National Cemetery, Pennsville, Salem County.

CALDWELL, JOHN Pvt, B, 11th NJ Inf, 2-24-1890. Fairmount Cemetery, Newark, Essex County.

CALDWELL, JOHN T. Pvt, Btty D, 1st NJ Light Art, 10-10-1884. Whitesville Cemetery, Whitesville, Ocean County.

CALDWELL, R.W. Pvt, F, 57th NC Inf (CSA), [Captured 7-2-1863 at Gettysburg, PA.] 10-12-1863. Finn's Point National Cemetery, Pennsville, Salem County.

CALDWELL, ROBERT C. Landsman, U.S. Navy, 7-4-1875. Jersey City Cemetery, Jersey City, Hudson County.

CALDWELL, WASHINGTON C. Corp, I, 43rd U.S. CT, 1-23-1865. Jersey City Cemetery, Jersey City, Hudson County.

CALDWELL, WILLIAM B. (aka: Colwell, William) 1st Sgt, H, 66th NY Inf, 8-6-1873. Jersey City Cemetery, Jersey City, Hudson County.

CALE, WILLIAM Pvt, K, 40th NJ Inf, 4-2-1901. Baptist/St. Andrew's Cemetery, Mount Holly, Burlington County.

CALHEPP, JOHN (see: Kohlhepp, John K.) Elmwood Cemetery, New Brunswick, Middlesex County.

CALHOUN, J.M. Pvt, G, 9th AL Inf (CSA), 10-25-1863. Finn's Point National Cemetery, Pennsville, Salem County.

CALHOUN, JAMES Pvt, Btty B, 1st NJ Light Art, 12-19-1883. Franklin Reformed Church Cemetery, Nutley, Essex County.

CALHOUN, JAMES A. Pvt, E, 14th NJ Inf, 1872. Hazelwood Cemetery, Rahway, Union County.

CALHOUN*, JAMES THEODORE Asst Surg, U.S. Army, [Also: Surg, 74th NY Inf.] 7-19-1866. Hazelwood Cemetery, Rahway, Union County.

CALHOUN, JOSEPH Pvt, H, 26th NJ Inf, 1-23-1914. Rosedale Cemetery, Orange, Essex County.

CALHOUN, ROBERT 5-14-1899. Rosedale Cemetery, Orange, Essex County.

CALHOUN, SAMUEL Pvt, Btty B, 1st NJ Light Art, 12-5-1876. Rosedale Cemetery, Orange, Essex County.

CALKINS, A. (see: Anderson, George) New Camden Cemetery, Camden, Camden County.

CALL, JOSEPH S. Pvt, A, 93rd PA Inf, 9-3-1907. Phillipsburg Cemetery, Phillipsburg, Warren County.

CALL, SAMUEL W. Pvt, K, 124th NY Inf, 12-5-1904. Ramapo Reformed Church Cemetery, Mahwah, Bergen County.

CALL, WILLIAM R. Pvt, A, 41st PA Militia, 8-5-1899. Hillside Cemetery, Oxford, Warren County.

CALLAGAN, GEORGE Pvt, C, 5th NY Inf, [Wounded 8-30-1862 at 2nd Bull Run, VA.] 1-10-1904. Holy Name Cemetery, Jersey City, Hudson County.

Our Brothers Gone Before

CALLAGAN, THOMAS Pvt, B, 7th NJ Inf, DoD Unknown. St. Peter's Cemetery, New Brunswick, Middlesex County.

CALLAGHAN*, JOHN (aka: Callahan, John) Pvt, C, 23rd PA Inf, 5-28-1913. Holy Sepulchre Cemetery, East Orange, Essex County.

CALLAGHAN, PATRICK Pvt, Btty D, 1st NJ Light Art, DoD Unknown. St. Peter's Cemetery, New Brunswick, Middlesex County.

CALLAHAN, CHARLES Pvt, Btty A, 1st NY Light Art, 11-6-1900. Holy Name Cemetery, Jersey City, Hudson County.

CALLAHAN, EDWARD Pvt, A, 9th NY Inf, 12-4-1896. St. Peter's Cemetery, Jersey City, Hudson County.

CALLAHAN, EUGENE (aka: Callanan, Eugene) Pvt, F, 2nd NJ Inf, [Died of typhoid at Orange, NJ.] 3-18-1864. St. John's Evangelical Church Cemetery, Orange, Essex County.

CALLAHAN, GEORGE DoD Unknown. Finn's Point National Cemetery, Pennsville, Salem County.

CALLAHAN, JOHN Pvt, B, 3rd NJ Militia, 5-31-1896. Bayview-New York Bay Cemetery, Jersey City, Hudson County.

CALLAHAN*, JOHN Pvt, C, 23rd PA Inf, 3-12-1898. St. Mary's Cemetery, Clark, Union County.

CALLAHAN, JOHN (aka: Callanan, John) Sgt, D, 40th NY Inf, 1-31-1881. St. John's Evangelical Church Cemetery, Orange, Essex County.

CALLAHAN, JOHN Pvt, B, 71st NY State Militia, DoD Unknown. St. John's Evangelical Church Cemetery, Orange, Essex County.

CALLAHAN, JOHN (see: Callaghan, John) Holy Sepulchre Cemetery, East Orange, Essex County.

CALLAHAN, MICHAEL E. Pvt, D, 4th NJ Militia, 10-6-1885. Old St. Mary's Cemetery, Gloucester City, Camden County.

CALLAHAN, STEPHEN Pvt, K, 4th NJ Inf, 1-12-1883. Holy Name Cemetery, Jersey City, Hudson County.

CALLAHAN, THOMAS Pvt, K, 3rd NJ Inf, 6-10-1867. St. Mary's Cemetery, Elizabeth, Union County.

CALLAN, PATRICK Pvt, H, 6th NJ Inf, 9-2-1901. St. John's Cemetery, Lambertville, Hunterdon County.

CALLANAN, EUGENE (see: Callahan, Eugene) St. John's Evangelical Church Cemetery, Orange, Essex County.

CALLANAN, JOHN (see: Callahan, John) St. John's Evangelical Church Cemetery, Orange, Essex County.

CALLAWAY, ELISHA J. Pvt, H, 4th GA Inf (CSA), [Captured 5-10-1864 at Spotsylvania CH, VA.] 1-10-1865. Finn's Point National Cemetery, Pennsville, Salem County.

CALLAWAY, FREDERICK C. Landsman, U.S. Navy, 7-8-1899. Mount Pleasant Cemetery, Newark, Essex County.

CALLAWAY, JAMES P. Pvt, D, 25th NJ Inf, [Died of diphtheria at Fort Monroe, VA.] 5-25-1863. Hedding Methodist-Episcopal Church Cemetery, Bellmawr, Camden County.

CALLEN, EDWIN D. Sgt, F, 13th NJ Inf, [Died of wounds received at Antietam, MD.] 11-17-1867. Mount Pleasant Cemetery, Newark, Essex County.

CALLEN, HENRY H. Capt, H, 2nd NJ Inf, [Killed in action at Wilderness, VA.] 5-5-1864. Mount Pleasant Cemetery, Newark, Essex County.

CALLEN, LUTHER W. Pvt, K, 26th NJ Inf, 5-25-1896. Mount Pleasant Cemetery, Newark, Essex County.

CALLENDER, GEORGE E. Pvt, E, 49th MA Inf, [Wounded 5-27-1863 at Port Hudson, LA.] 8-7-1910. Old 1st Methodist Church Cemetery, West Long Branch, Monmouth County.

New Jersey Civil War Burials

CALLIGAN, JAMES Corp, H, 7th NJ Inf, 3-13-1894. Fairmount Cemetery, Newark, Essex County.

CALLIGAN, THOMAS J. Corp, A, 13th VT Inf, DoD Unknown. Holy Name Cemetery, Jersey City, Hudson County.

CALLIHAN, GEORGE Pvt, H, 3rd VA Inf (CSA), 7-21-1863. Finn's Point National Cemetery, Pennsville, Salem County.

CALLIS, ELIAS Pvt, F, 17th WV Inf, 3-17-1916. Riverview Cemetery, Trenton, Mercer County.

CALLOWAY, LUTHER Pvt, H, 1st NJ Cav, DoD Unknown. Elmwood Cemetery, New Brunswick, Middlesex County.

CALTON, NATHANIEL F. (aka: Kalton, Nathaniel) Pvt, I, 21st NJ Inf, 1899. Jersey City Cemetery, Jersey City, Hudson County.

CALVER, JAMES 2-28-1922. Flower Hill Cemetery, North Bergen, Hudson County.

CALVERLEY, JOHN (aka: Calverly, John) Pvt, B, 44th PA Militia, 1893. Atlantic City Cemetery, Pleasantville, Atlantic County.

CALVERLY, JOHN (see: Calverley, John) Atlantic City Cemetery, Pleasantville, Atlantic County.

CALVERT, GEORGE H. Pvt, B, 13th NJ Inf, 12-6-1890. Fairmount Cemetery, Newark, Essex County.

CAMBERON, WILLIAM 11-21-1899. Mount Pleasant Cemetery, Millville, Cumberland County.

CAMBREN, NATHAN Pvt, F, 5th NJ Inf, DoD Unknown. Mount Pleasant Cemetery, Millville, Cumberland County.

CAMBRON, SAMUEL B. Corp, A, 10th NJ Inf, 12-19-1915. Mount Pleasant Cemetery, Millville, Cumberland County.

CAMBURN, AARON (see: Cameron, Aaron) Mount Pleasant Cemetery, Millville, Cumberland County.

CAMBURN, AUGUSTUS F. Pvt, H, 29th NJ Inf, 11-10-1924. Presbyterian Cemetery, Waretown, Ocean County.

CAMBURN, BENJAMIN B. Pvt, C, 9th NJ Inf, 1930. Presbyterian Cemetery, Waretown, Ocean County.

CAMBURN*, CHARLES P. Pvt, D, 9th NJ Inf, 1901. Presbyterian Cemetery, Waretown, Ocean County.

CAMBURN*, FRANCIS E. Pvt, C, 9th NJ Inf, 8-18-1926. Riverside Cemetery, Toms River, Ocean County.

CAMBURN, HENRY A. Pvt, D, 9th NJ Inf, DoD Unknown. Cedar Grove Cemetery, Waretown, Ocean County.

CAMBURN, JOHN (aka: Camden, John) Pvt, F, 51st PA Inf, [Died at Washington, DC of wounds received 10-27-1864 at Hatchers Run, VA.] 11-23-1864. Presbyterian Cemetery, Waretown, Ocean County.

CAMDEN, JOHN (see: Camburn, John) Presbyterian Cemetery, Waretown, Ocean County.

CAMERON, AARON (aka: Camburn, Aaron) Pvt, B, 10th NJ Inf, 2-22-1899. Mount Pleasant Cemetery, Millville, Cumberland County.

CAMERON, ALEXANDER Pvt, I, 34th NJ Inf, 4-20-1880. St. Mary's Episcopal Church Cemetery, Burlington, Burlington County.

CAMERON, FRANKLIN (see: Kennemer, Franklin) Finn's Point National Cemetery, Pennsville, Salem County.

CAMERON, HUGH Pvt, F, 79th NY Inf, 1905. Cedar Lawn Cemetery, Paterson, Passaic County.

CAMERON, JOHN Pvt, D, 9th NJ Inf, 11-9-1903. Trinity United Methodist Church Cemetery, Bayville, Ocean County.

CAMERON, JOSEPH Pvt, B, 213th PA Inf, 11-14-1881. Evergreen Cemetery, Camden, Camden County.

Our Brothers Gone Before

CAMERON, JOSEPH L. Pvt, H, 6th U.S. Cav, 1-29-1904. Evergreen Cemetery, Camden, Camden County.
CAMERON, ROBERT E. Pvt, F, 5th PA Cav, 4-16-1923. Eglington Cemetery, Clarksboro, Gloucester County.
CAMIER, WILLIAM J. Pvt, K, 65th NY Inf, 1123-1914. Arlington Cemetery, Kearny, Hudson County.
CAMMAN, WALTER Maj, 30th NJ Inf 9-6-1869. Old Somerville Cemetery, Somerville, Somerset County.
CAMMANN, ALBERT 3-9-1868. Old Somerville Cemetery, Somerville, Somerset County.
CAMP, ABRAHAM Pvt, D, 24th NJ Inf, 5-21-1921. Presbyterian Church Cemetery, Bridgeton, Cumberland County.
CAMP, ELIAS Pvt, F, 25th NJ Inf, 5-25-1868. Little Joshua Baptist Cemetery, Steelmantown, Cape May County.
CAMP, EZEKIEL Pvt, B, 10th NJ Inf, DoD Unknown. Asbury Methodist-Episcopal Church Cemetery, Swainton, Cape May County.
CAMP, GILBERT M. Pvt, H, 14th NJ Inf, 4-30-1904. Fairmount Cemetery, Newark, Essex County.
CAMP, JOHN C. Pvt, H, 38th NJ Inf, 8-9-1895. Asbury Methodist-Episcopal Church Cemetery, Swainton, Cape May County.
CAMP, JOHN M. Corp, C, 29th NJ Inf, 1906. Cedar Hill Cemetery, Hightstown, Mercer County.
CAMP, JOSEPH Pvt, B, 24th NJ Inf, DoD Unknown. United Methodist Church Cemetery, Port Elizabeth, Cumberland County.
CAMP, REUBEN Pvt, I, 10th NJ Inf, 12-31-1906. Methodist Cemetery, Cassville, Ocean County.
CAMP, WILLIAM Pvt, U.S. Marine Corps, 1915. Bible Church Cemetery, Hardingville, Gloucester County.
CAMPBELL, ALBERT B. Pvt, K, 24th OH Inf, 1877. Old South Church Cemetery, Bergenfield, Bergen County.
CAMPBELL*, ALEXANDER (aka: Wilson, John) Pvt, F, 7th U.S. Vet Vol Inf, 9-15-1883. Mount Pleasant Cemetery, Newark, Essex County.
CAMPBELL*, ANDREW H. Pvt, D, 37th NY Inf, DoD Unknown. St. Mary's Cemetery, Clark, Union County.
CAMPBELL, ANDREW J. Pvt, G, 26th NJ Inf, 4-7-1899. Fairmount Cemetery, Newark, Essex County.
CAMPBELL, ARCHIBALD (JR.) Pvt, D, 25th NJ Inf, 12-1-1916. Shinn GAR Post Cemetery, Port Norris, Cumberland County.
CAMPBELL, ATWOOD Sgt, G, 37th NJ Inf, 1-13-1886. Rahway Cemetery, Rahway, Union County.
CAMPBELL, CALVIN Pvt, H, 10th (DeMoss') TN Cav (CSA), 5-15-1864. Finn's Point National Cemetery, Pennsville, Salem County.
CAMPBELL, CHARLES 1887. Mount Pleasant Cemetery, Newark, Essex County.
CAMPBELL, CHARLES E. Pvt, E, 32nd U.S. CT, 2-12-1915. Fairmount Cemetery, Newark, Essex County.
CAMPBELL, CHARLES F. Pvt, B, 1st NJ Inf, 8-12-1907. Baptist Church Cemetery, Palermo, Cape May County.
CAMPBELL, CHARLES W. Pvt, I, 8th NJ Inf, 6-11-1910. Fairmount Cemetery, Newark, Essex County.
CAMPBELL, DAVID Landsman, U.S. Navy, USS Supply, 4-20-1915. Atlantic City Cemetery, Pleasantville, Atlantic County.
CAMPBELL, DAVID K. Pvt, F, 3rd IA Cav, 1918. Reformed Church Cemetery, Readington, Hunterdon County.
CAMPBELL, ELIAS V. Pvt, Btty B, 1st NJ Light Art, 9-8-1872. Fairmount Cemetery, Newark, Essex County.

New Jersey Civil War Burials

CAMPBELL, FERRIS Pvt, G, 22nd NJ Inf, 1879. St. John's Cemetery, Hamilton, Mercer County.

CAMPBELL*, FREDERICK S. Pvt, E, 85th NY Inf, 11-6-1910. Arlington Cemetery, Kearny, Hudson County.

CAMPBELL, GARRET MYER 2nd Lt, A, 22nd NJ Inf, 12-13-1900. Hackensack Cemetery, Hackensack, Bergen County.

CAMPBELL, GEORGE S. Corp, G, 26th NJ Inf, 11-5-1893. Rosedale Cemetery, Orange, Essex County.

CAMPBELL, HENRY Pvt, K, 12th NJ Inf, 10-20-1920. Zion United Methodist Church Cemetery, Dividing Creek, Cumberland County.

CAMPBELL, HENRY Fireman, U.S. Navy, 11-15-1904. Bayview-New York Bay Cemetery, Jersey City, Hudson County.

CAMPBELL, HENRY Pvt, C, 3rd NY Inf, 12-23-1899. St. Joseph's Cemetery, Keyport, Monmouth County.

CAMPBELL, HENRY Pvt, I, 10th NJ Inf, 3-14-1919. Branchville Cemetery, Branchville, Sussex County.

CAMPBELL, HENRY L. (aka: Williams, Charles) Pvt, K, 1st CT Cav, 2-19-1903. Fairmount Cemetery, Newark, Essex County.

CAMPBELL, HEZEKIAH Pvt, C, 21st NJ Inf, 3-30-1915. Bayview-New York Bay Cemetery, Jersey City, Hudson County.

CAMPBELL, HIRAM H. Pvt, A, 38th NJ Inf, 4-7-1889. Harleigh Cemetery, Camden, Camden County.

CAMPBELL, J.A. Pvt, G, 22nd GA Inf (CSA), [Wounded and captured 7-2-1863 at Gettysburg, PA. Died of diarrhea.] 10-26-1863. Finn's Point National Cemetery, Pennsville, Salem County.

CAMPBELL, J.D. Pvt, D, 3rd (Forrest's) TN Cav (CSA), 11-2-1863. Finn's Point National Cemetery, Pennsville, Salem County.

CAMPBELL, J.P. Pvt, G, 51st VA Inf (CSA), [Captured 3-2-1865 at Waynesboro, VA. Died of lung inflammation.] 1865. Finn's Point National Cemetery, Pennsville, Salem County.

CAMPBELL, J.T. Pvt, Kirkpatrick's Btty, VA Light Art (CSA), 10-12-1863. Finn's Point National Cemetery, Pennsville, Salem County.

CAMPBELL, JACOB (aka: Campbell, John) Pvt, D, 102nd NY Inf, DoD Unknown. Alpine Cemetery, Perth Amboy, Middlesex County.

CAMPBELL, JACOB Pvt, Btty E, 1st NJ Light Art, 1-7-1888. Fairmount Cemetery, Newark, Essex County.

CAMPBELL, JACOB C. Pvt, B, 29th NJ Inf, 2-9-1917. Rose Hill Cemetery, Matawan, Monmouth County.

CAMPBELL, JAMES 1915. United Methodist Church Cemetery, Tuckahoe, Cape May County.

CAMPBELL, JAMES Pvt, M, 1st NJ Cav, 8-22-1902. Princeton Cemetery, Princeton, Mercer County.

CAMPBELL, JAMES Pvt, E, 29th NJ Inf, 5-31-1915. Glenwood Cemetery, West Long Branch, Monmouth County.

CAMPBELL, JOEL Pvt, I, 187th PA Inf, DoD Unknown. Hardyston Cemetery, North Church, Sussex County.

CAMPBELL, JOHN Sgt, F, 5th PA Cav, 5-5-1922. New Camden Cemetery, Camden, Camden County.

CAMPBELL, JOHN Sgt, F, 2nd NJ Inf, 8-10-1912. Christ Church Cemetery, Belleville, Essex County.

CAMPBELL, JOHN Pvt, H, 94th IL Inf, 11-12-1906. Holy Sepulchre Cemetery, East Orange, Essex County.

CAMPBELL, JOHN Pvt, H, 79th NY Inf, 12-20-1916. Flower Hill Cemetery, North Bergen, Hudson County.

Our Brothers Gone Before

CAMPBELL, JOHN Corp, E, 26th PA Inf, 9-30-1914. Bayview-New York Bay Cemetery, Jersey City, Hudson County.

CAMPBELL, JOHN Wagoner, A, 25th NJ Inf, DoD Unknown. Holy Sepulchre Cemetery, Totowa, Passaic County.

CAMPBELL, JOHN Pvt, D, 27th NJ Inf, 4-19-1915. Newton Cemetery, Newton, Sussex County.

CAMPBELL, JOHN (see: Campbell, Jacob) Alpine Cemetery, Perth Amboy, Middlesex County.

CAMPBELL, JOHN D. Pvt, H, 25th NJ Inf, 1-1-1902. Mount Pleasant Cemetery, Newark, Essex County.

CAMPBELL, JOHN EDGAR 1st Lt, E, 95th NY Inf, [Wounded 8-18-1864 at Weldon Railroad, VA.] 2-1-1908. Bayview-New York Bay Cemetery, Jersey City, Hudson County.

CAMPBELL*, JOHN FELIX Corp, E, 39th NJ Inf, 6-26-1932. Rosedale Cemetery, Orange, Essex County.

CAMPBELL, JOHN H. Pvt, F, 13th NJ Inf, [Died at Frederick City, MD. of wounds received 9-17-1862 at Antietam, MD.] 10-1-1862. Fairmount Cemetery, Newark, Essex County.

CAMPBELL*, JOHN HARVEY Pvt, C, 7th NJ Inf, 7-12-1902. Laurel Grove Cemetery, Totowa, Passaic County.

CAMPBELL, JOHN L.R. Sgt, G, 41st GA Inf (CSA), [Wounded 10-8-1862 at Perryville, KY. Captured 5-16-1863 at Baker's Creek, MS. Died of disease.] 6-18-1863. Finn's Point National Cemetery, Pennsville, Salem County.

CAMPBELL, JOHN M. (see: Campbell, Jonathan M.) Old Stone Church Cemetery, Fairton, Cumberland County.

CAMPBELL, JOHN W. Fireman, U.S. Navy, USS Princeton, 10-30-1907. Evergreen Cemetery, Camden, Camden County.

CAMPBELL, JONATHAN M. (aka: Campbell, John M.) Pvt, I, 6th MO Inf, 10-23-1883. Old Stone Church Cemetery, Fairton, Cumberland County.

CAMPBELL, JOSEPH D. Pvt, F, 31st NJ Inf, [Died near Fitzhugh House, VA.] 6-3-1863. Newton Cemetery, Newton, Sussex County.

CAMPBELL, KING Pvt, G, 1st NJ Cav, 2-22-1883. Princeton Cemetery, Princeton, Mercer County.

CAMPBELL, LEVI Pvt, A, 60th VA Inf (CSA), [Captured 3-2-1865 at Waynesboro, VA. Died of diarrhea.] 6-1-1865. Finn's Point National Cemetery, Pennsville, Salem County.

CAMPBELL, LEVI B. Pvt, A, 3rd NJ Cav, 7-28-1904. Bayview-New York Bay Cemetery, Jersey City, Hudson County.

CAMPBELL, LEWIS 9-15-1918. Baptist Church Cemetery, Dividing Creek, Cumberland County.

CAMPBELL, LEWIS Pvt, K, 9th NJ Inf, 1917. Presbyterian Church Cemetery, Metuchen, Middlesex County.

CAMPBELL*, MARTIN V.B. Artificer, Btty B, 1st NJ Light Art, 2-8-1902. Fairmount Cemetery, Newark, Essex County.

CAMPBELL, MICHAEL Pvt, D, 6th NJ Inf, 5-22-1877. Evergreen Cemetery, Lumberton, Burlington County.

CAMPBELL, MICHAEL Pvt, B, 10th NJ Inf, 10-24-1901. Presbyterian Church Cemetery, Cold Spring, Cape May County.

CAMPBELL*, OWEN Pvt, K, 2nd NJ Inf, 2-14-1918. St. John's Cemetery, Hamilton, Mercer County.

CAMPBELL, PATRICK Sgt, B, 3rd __ Cav, DoD Unknown. St. John's Cemetery, Lambertville, Hunterdon County.

CAMPBELL, PATRICK Sgt, C, 5th NJ Inf, 10-12-1869. St. John's Cemetery, Lambertville, Hunterdon County.

New Jersey Civil War Burials

CAMPBELL, PATRICK C. Blacksmith, C, 5th PA Cav, DoD Unknown. 1st Methodist Church Cemetery, Williamstown, Gloucester County.

CAMPBELL, PATRICK T. Pvt, D, 38th NJ Inf, 2-8-1896. St. Bernard's Cemetery, Bridgewater, Somerset County.

CAMPBELL, PETER Pvt, D, 25th NJ Inf, 2-23-1917. Bateman Memorial Cemetery, Newport, Cumberland County.

CAMPBELL, RICHARD H. Pvt, B, 4th NJ Inf, [Died of disease at Halifax CH, VA.] 4-26-1865. 1st Baptist Church Cemetery, Trenton, Mercer County.

CAMPBELL, ROBERT F. Pvt, F, 27th NJ Inf, 12-20-1910. Fairmount Cemetery, Newark, Essex County.

CAMPBELL, ROBERT F. 10-5-1886. Baptist Cemetery, Burlington, Burlington County.

CAMPBELL, ROBERT R. Pvt, G, 40th NJ Inf, 9-12-1919. Riverview Cemetery, Trenton, Mercer County.

CAMPBELL, THOMAS Pvt, F, 24th NJ Inf, 8-1-1870. Princeton Cemetery, Princeton, Mercer County.

CAMPBELL, THOMAS B. Pvt, K, 2nd NJ Cav, 1876. Cedar Grove Cemetery, Gloucester City, Camden County.

CAMPBELL, TIMOTHY 3-5-1906. Presbyterian Church Cemetery, Bridgeton, Cumberland County.

CAMPBELL, VALENTINE S. Corp, G, 60th VA Inf (CSA), [3rd Infantry, Wise' Legion.] 5-13-1900. Harleigh Cemetery, Camden, Camden County.

CAMPBELL, W.H. Pvt, C, 2nd KY Cav (CSA), 2-25-1865. Finn's Point National Cemetery, Pennsville, Salem County.

CAMPBELL, WARD Pvt, I, 148th NY Inf, [Died of diarrhea at Fort Monroe, VA.] 7-23-1864. Old South Church Cemetery, Bergenfield, Bergen County.

CAMPBELL, WILLIAM Pvt, H, 24th NJ Inf, 1921. Chickory Chapel Baptist Church Cemetery, Elk, Gloucester County.

CAMPBELL, WILLIAM Wagoner, D, 29th NJ Inf, 7-21-1900. Mansfield/Washington Cemetery, Washington, Warren County.

CAMPBELL, WILLIAM Pvt, Btty F, 7th NY Heavy Art, DoD Unknown. Arlington Cemetery, Kearny, Hudson County.

CAMPBELL, WILLIAM G. Pvt, B, 37th NJ Inf, 5-31-1919. Mount Pleasant Cemetery, Newark, Essex County.

CAMPBELL, WILLIAM H. Landsman, U.S. Navy, USS Commodore Morris, 1926. Pequest Union Cemetery, Great Meadows, Warren County.

CAMPBELL, WILLIAM (SR.) Pvt, B, 37th NJ Inf, DoD Unknown. Arlington Cemetery, Kearny, Hudson County.

CAMPION, STACY BUDD (JR.) Capt, K, 119th PA Inf, 4-25-1896. Evergreen Cemetery, Camden, Camden County.

CANADA*, JOSEPH Pvt, Btty G, 11th U.S. CHA, 1-27-1903. Princessville Cemetery, Princessville, Mercer County.

CANAN, PATRICK (aka: Cannair, Patrick) Pvt, C, 12th NJ Inf, [Wounded in action.] 3-12-1903. St. Joseph's Cemetery, Swedesboro, Gloucester County.

CANDY, MICHAEL R. Pvt, D, 71st PA Inf, DoD Unknown. Bayview-New York Bay Cemetery, Jersey City, Hudson County.

CANE, CHARLES (aka: Kene, Charles) Pvt, G, 10th NJ Inf, 9-2-1899. Holy Sepulchre Cemetery, East Orange, Essex County.

CANE*, MICHAEL Pvt, B, 3rd NY Inf, DoD Unknown. Holy Name Cemetery, Jersey City, Hudson County.

CANFIELD, ABRAM STOLL Corp, H, 33rd NJ Inf, 1912. Branchville Cemetery, Branchville, Sussex County.

CANFIELD, ALBERT 12-11-1887. Fairview Cemetery, Westfield, Union County.

Our Brothers Gone Before

CANFIELD*, CHARLES W. Capt, B, 2nd U.S. Cav, [Killed in action at Beverly Ford, VA.] 6-9-1863. St. Peter's Episcopal Church Cemetery, Morristown, Morris County.

CANFIELD, DAVID E. (JR.) 2nd Lt, B, 14th CT Inf, [Killed in action at Fredericksburg, VA.] 12-13-1862. 1st Presbyterian Church Cemetery, Newark, Essex County.

CANFIELD*, FERDINAND M. Pvt, H, 2nd NJ Inf, 2-12-1895. Evergreen Cemetery, Morristown, Morris County.

CANFIELD, HALSEY 1-20-1869. Mercer Cemetery, Trenton, Mercer County.

CANFIELD, JOSEPH 11-16-1884. Evergreen Cemetery, Morristown, Morris County.

CANFIELD, PATRICK Pvt, Btty B, 2nd CT Heavy Art, [Wounded 9-18-1864 at Winchester, VA.] 4-1-1893. Holy Name Cemetery, Jersey City, Hudson County.

CANFIELD, UZAL 1900. Baptist Church Cemetery, Port Murray, Warren County.

CANFIELD, WILLIAM H. Pvt, A, 33rd NJ Inf, 2-11-1922. Fairmount Cemetery, Newark, Essex County.

CANHUM, WILLIAM Pvt, C, 42nd U.S. CT, 6-14-1904. Edgewater Cemetery, Edgewater, Bergen County.

CANNAIR, PATRICK (see: Canan, Patrick) St. Joseph's Cemetery, Swedesboro, Gloucester County.

CANNING, JACOB N. Musc, H, 29th PA Inf, 3-14-1905. New Camden Cemetery, Camden, Camden County.

CANNING, JAMES Pvt, K, 13th PA Cav, 5-7-1911. Rosedale Cemetery, Orange, Essex County.

CANNON, B.S. Pvt, G, 53rd GA Inf (CSA), [Captured 7-1-1863 at Cashtown, PA. Died of smallpox.] 11-20-1863. Finn's Point National Cemetery, Pennsville, Salem County.

CANNON, BERNARD Seaman, U.S. Navy, DoD Unknown. Holy Name Cemetery, Jersey City, Hudson County.

CANNON, CORNELIUS Pvt, G, 9th NY Inf, 12-2-1902. Holy Sepulchre Cemetery, Totowa, Passaic County.

CANNON*, FREDERICK M. Pvt, Btty B, 3rd PA Heavy Art, 2-2-1897. Fairview Cemetery, Wantage, Sussex County.

CANNON, GEORGE W. Pvt, B, 7th NJ Inf, 6-1-1892. Fairmount Cemetery, Newark, Essex County.

CANNON, HENRY Pvt, B, 13th AL Inf (CSA), 8-3-1863. Finn's Point National Cemetery, Pennsville, Salem County.

CANNON, HENRY W. Musc, A, 124th NY Inf, 3-6-1929. Cedar Lawn Cemetery, Paterson, Passaic County.

CANNON, ISAAC S. Corp, K, 2nd NJ Cav, 2-12-1897. Methodist-Episcopal Cemetery, Pennsville, Salem County.

CANNON, J.M.F. Pvt, G, 24th GA Inf (CSA), [Captured 7-2-1863 at Gettysburg, PA.] 9-13-1863. Finn's Point National Cemetery, Pennsville, Salem County.

CANNON, JAMES Pvt, D, 21st NJ Inf, 12-12-1912. Cedar Hill Cemetery, Florence, Burlington County.

CANNON, JOHN Pvt, G, 8th U.S. Inf, 12-3-1914. Holy Sepulchre Cemetery, East Orange, Essex County.

CANNON, JOHN F. Landsman, U.S. Navy, USS Wissahickon, 2-13-1900. Beverly National Cemetery, Edgewater Park, Burlington County.

CANNON, JOHN N. Pvt, C, 51st AL Cav (CSA), 7-23-1863. Finn's Point National Cemetery, Pennsville, Salem County.

CANNON, JOHN P. Pvt, D, 1st MD Inf (ES), DoD Unknown. Old Camden Cemetery, Camden, Camden County.

CANNON, JOSEPH A. Pvt, Btty E, 4th NY Heavy Art, 1-5-1940. Evergreen Cemetery, Hillside, Union County.

CANNON, JOSEPH B. DoD Unknown. Valleau Cemetery, Ridgewood, Bergen County.

New Jersey Civil War Burials

CANNON, SOLOMON G. Pvt, H, 11th NJ Inf, 7-31-1929. Evergreen Cemetery, Morristown, Morris County.

CANNON, STEPHEN A. Pvt, K, 7th NJ Inf, 2-13-1908. Willow Grove Cemetery, New Brunswick, Middlesex County.

CANNON, THOMAS Pvt, D, 38th PA Inf, 8-13-1887. Holy Sepulchre Cemetery, East Orange, Essex County.

CANNON, WILLIAM W. Pvt, K, 184th OH Inf, [Wounded in action.] 4-31-1890. Fairmount Cemetery, Newark, Essex County.

CANNON, WILLIAM W. Pvt, C, 41st TN Inf (CSA), 8-5-1863. Finn's Point National Cemetery, Pennsville, Salem County.

CANOE, JOHN (see: Cornew, John) Lawrenceville Cemetery, Lawrenceville, Mercer County.

CANSDELL, HENRY W. Surg, 22nd WI Inf DoD Unknown. Siloam Cemetery, Vineland, Cumberland County.

CANSE, ALEXANDER Landsman, U.S. Navy, USS Niagra, 1873. Elmwood Cemetery, New Brunswick, Middlesex County.

CANTRELL, CALAWAY H. Pvt, A, 2nd MS Inf (CSA), [Captured 7-1-1863 at Gettysburg, PA. Died of scurvy.] 5-28-1865. Finn's Point National Cemetery, Pennsville, Salem County.

CANTRELL, T.A. Pvt, C, 51st AL Cav (CSA), 10-14-1863. Finn's Point National Cemetery, Pennsville, Salem County.

CANTWELL, MICHAEL Pvt, K, 34th NJ Inf, 6-19-1904. St. John's Cemetery, Hamilton, Mercer County.

CAPEHART, ROBERT A. Pvt, F, 4th GA Inf (CSA), [Wounded and captured 5-5-1864 at Wilderness, VA. Died of smallpox.] 12-23-1864. Finn's Point National Cemetery, Pennsville, Salem County.

CAPELL, CHARLES Pvt, Btty C, 1st PA Light Art, 5-25-1902. Evergreen Cemetery, Hillside, Union County.

CAPENS*, GEORGE P. 1st Sgt, M, 4th NY Cav, 12-9-1908. Oak Hill Cemetery, Vineland, Cumberland County.

CAPERN, THOMAS H. Pvt, E, 4th NJ Inf, 3-20-1907. Baptist Church Cemetery, Haddonfield, Camden County.

CAPEWELL, CHARLES B. Pvt, I, 13th PA Cav, 2-24-1893. New Camden Cemetery, Camden, Camden County.

CAPEWELL, DORCUS R. DoD Unknown. New Camden Cemetery, Camden, Camden County.

CAPNER, HUGH Pvt, B, 23rd NJ Inf, [Wounded in action.] 6-30-1885. Riverview Cemetery, Trenton, Mercer County.

CAPPEL, JOSEPH (see: Capple, Joseph) Riverview Cemetery, Trenton, Mercer County.

CAPPLE, JOSEPH (aka: Cappel, Joseph) Pvt, Detached, 54th PA Inf, 2-1-1910. Riverview Cemetery, Trenton, Mercer County.

CAPPS, LOUIS Pvt, E, 31st NY Inf, 4-24-1875. Fairmount Cemetery, Newark, Essex County.

CAPPS, WILLIAM J. Pvt, A, 31st AL Inf (CSA), 7-20-1863. Finn's Point National Cemetery, Pennsville, Salem County.

CARACIOLA, NAPOLEON B. Pvt, C, 30th NJ Inf, 2-13-1917. Presbyterian Church Cemetery, Woodbridge, Middlesex County.

CARAKER*, PETER Musc, B, 34th NJ Inf, 6-15-1884. Riverview Cemetery, Trenton, Mercer County.

CARALL, ELLIS (see: Carroll, Ellis) Finn's Point National Cemetery, Pennsville, Salem County.

CARBERRY, EDWARD Pvt, F, 73rd NY Inf, 4-4-1889. Holy Sepulchre Cemetery, East Orange, Essex County.

Our Brothers Gone Before

CARBEY, CORNELIUS (see: Corby, Cornelius) Canfield Cemetery, Cedar Grove, Essex County.
CARBIN, WILLIAM B. Coal Heaver, U.S. Navy, USS North Carolina, 7-26-1907. Erial Cemetery, Erial, Camden County.
CARD*, CLARK N. Corp, H, 80th NY Inf, 9-8-1927. Union Cemetery, Frenchtown, Hunterdon County.
CARD, ISRAEL Pvt, E, 33rd NJ Inf, 3-2-1922. Hardyston Cemetery, North Church, Sussex County.
CARD*, JOHN (JR.) Pvt, H, 2nd NJ Inf, 2-5-1895. Mosier Cemetery, Highland Lakes, Sussex County.
CARD, THOMAS Pvt, D, 29th NJ Inf, 6-10-1901. Bay View Cemetery, Leonardo, Monmouth County.
CARD, WILLIAM Pvt, I, 55th NC Inf (CSA), [Captured 7-1-1863 at Gettysburg, PA. Died of diarrhea.] 11-20-1863. Finn's Point National Cemetery, Pennsville, Salem County.
CARDER, WILLIAM Pvt, B, 52nd NY Inf, DoD Unknown. Prospect Hill Cemetery, Flemington, Hunterdon County.
CARDIPE, HERMAN Pvt, Btty E, 3rd U.S. Art, DoD Unknown. Holy Sepulchre Cemetery, East Orange, Essex County.
CARELS, HARRISON Musc, 3rd NJ Inf Band 3-9-1925. Evergreen Cemetery, Camden, Camden County.
CARELS, JOSEPH S. Pvt, D, 37th NJ Inf, 4-18-1918. Evergreen Cemetery, Camden, Camden County.
CAREY, DANIEL Corp, I, 10th NJ Inf, 1-10-1904. St. Mary's Cemetery, Boonton, Morris County.
CAREY*, DENNIS Pvt, H, 2nd NJ Cav, 2-22-1881. Holy Name Cemetery, Jersey City, Hudson County.
CAREY, GEORGE W. Pvt, H, 51st PA Inf, 4-17-1914. Phillipsburg Cemetery, Phillipsburg, Warren County.
CAREY*, JAMES H. Seaman, U.S. Navy, USS Wissahickon, 3-10-1934. Harleigh Cemetery, Camden, Camden County.
CAREY*, JOHN Actg 3rd Asst Eng, U.S. Navy, USS Penobscot, 7-26-1894. Evergreen Cemetery, Hillside, Union County.
CAREY, JOHN B. Pvt, G, 12th NJ Inf, 3-28-1915. Methodist Episcopal/Methodist Protestant Cemetery, Bridgeport, Gloucester County.
CAREY, JOHN E. Asst Surg, 22nd NJ Inf 1-8-1907. Methodist-Episcopal Cemetery, Lower Bank, Burlington County.
CAREY, PATRICK Pvt, K, 1st NJ Inf, [Missing in action at Wilderness, VA. Supposed dead.] 5-5-1864. Boonton Cemetery, Boonton, Morris County.
CAREY, PETER (aka: Cary, Peter) Pvt, G, 31st NJ Inf, DoD Unknown. Fairview Cemetery, Columbia, Warren County.
CAREY, TIMOTHY (JR.) (see: Carey, Tunis (Jr.)) Hillside Cemetery, Scotch Plains, Union County.
CAREY, TUNIS (JR.) (aka: Carey, Timothy (Jr.)) Pvt, A, 30th NJ Inf, 2-3-1904. Hillside Cemetery, Scotch Plains, Union County.
CAREY, WILLIAM Seaman, U.S. Navy, 3-22-1923. Jordan Lawn Cemetery, Pennsauken, Camden County.
CARFREY*, JAMES W. Pvt, I, 183rd PA Inf, 4-4-1886. Methodist Church Cemetery, New Albany, Burlington County.
CARGILL, GEORGE M. Pvt, K, 29th OH Inf, DoD Unknown. Finn's Point National Cemetery, Pennsville, Salem County.
CARHART, DANIEL AUMACK Sgt, A, 14th NJ Inf, [Died of diarrhea at Washington, DC.] 9-16-1864. Greengrove Cemetery, Keyport, Monmouth County.

New Jersey Civil War Burials

CARHART, GEORGE W. Pvt, H, 14th NJ Inf, [Cenotaph. Killed in action at Cold Harbor, VA.] 6-1-1864. Brainerd Cemetery, Cranbury, Middlesex County.
CARHART, JOHN W. Pvt, F, 6th NJ Inf, [Killed in action at Petersburg, VA.] 10-13-1864. Methodist-Episcopal Cemetery, Burlington, Burlington County.
CARHART, RICHARD K. Seaman, U.S. Navy, USS Southfield, 12-18-1895. Greengrove Cemetery, Keyport, Monmouth County.
CARHART, SAMUEL Capt, A, 31st NJ Inf, 8-8-1898. Phillipsburg Cemetery, Phillipsburg, Warren County.
CARHART, STEPHEN E. (aka: Cowhart, Stephen) Pvt, G, 53rd NY Inf, 8-4-1919. Greengrove Cemetery, Keyport, Monmouth County.
CARHART, THEODORE Pvt, D, 1st NJ Inf, 11-16-1883. Phillipsburg Cemetery, Phillipsburg, Warren County.
CARHART, THEODORE 9-24-1905. Belvidere/Catholic Cemetery, Belvidere, Warren County.
CARHART, THOMAS Pvt, D, 29th NJ Inf, 12-7-1872. Fairview Cemetery, Fairview, Monmouth County.
CARHART, WILLIAM M. Landsman, U.S. Navy, USS Ohio, 7-2-1910. Phillipsburg Cemetery, Phillipsburg, Warren County.
CARHUFF, ISAAC Pvt, Btty D, 1st NJ Light Art, 12- -1929. Presbyterian/Methodist-Episcopal Cemetery, Succasunna, Morris County.
CARKHUFF, ASA Pvt, H, 3rd NJ Militia, 1907. Reformed Church Cemetery, Readington, Hunterdon County.
CARKHUFF, JOHN G. 2-21-1865. Old Somerville Cemetery, Somerville, Somerset County.
CARKHUFF, PHILIP E. DoD Unknown. Reformed Church Cemetery, Readington, Hunterdon County.
CARKHUFF, PHILIP ENOCH Pvt, E, 30th NJ Inf, 5-30-1902. Evergreen Cemetery, Hillside, Union County.
CARKHUFF, WILLIAM ENOCH Pvt, E, 30th NJ Inf, 7-7-1919. Methodist Church Cemetery, Everittstown, Hunterdon County.
CARL, CHARLES (see: Carroll, Charles) Laurel Grove Cemetery, Totowa, Passaic County.
CARL, LOUIS A. Capt, I, 4th (new) MD Inf, 5-20-1885. Fairmount Cemetery, Newark, Essex County.
CARL, NICHOLAS (aka: Karl, Nicholas) Pvt, H, 97th NY Inf, 2-11-1878. Jersey City Cemetery, Jersey City, Hudson County.
CARLAN, BERNARD Pvt, C, 2nd NJ Inf, DoD Unknown. St. Peter's Cemetery, New Brunswick, Middlesex County.
CARLAW, WILLIAM (aka: Carter, William) Pvt, K, 10th IL Inf, 11-27-1865. Baptist Church Cemetery, Greenwich, Cumberland County.
CARLE, JOHN E. Pvt, I, 39th NJ Inf, 11-15-1913. Fairmount Cemetery, Newark, Essex County.
CARLIN, BENJAMIN Pvt, K, 54th PA Inf, 4-14-1927. Locustwood Cemetery, Cherry Hill, Camden County.
CARLIN*, OWEN Pvt, G, 7th NJ Inf, 11-26-1910. Holy Sepulchre Cemetery, East Orange, Essex County.
CARLING, CORNELIUS H. Sgt, K, 168th NY Inf, 8-18-1922. Holy Name Cemetery, Jersey City, Hudson County.
CARLING, DAVID S. Pvt, Btty D, 2nd U.S. Art, 4-19-1908. Phillipsburg Cemetery, Phillipsburg, Warren County.
CARLING, THEODORE 1st Sgt, D, 30th NJ Inf, 9-12-1899. Riverview Cemetery, Trenton, Mercer County.
CARLING, THEODORE T. 7-5-1914. Presbyterian Church Cemetery, Harmony, Warren County.

Our Brothers Gone Before

CARLISLE, CHARLES J. 4-28-1873. Macphelah Cemetery, North Bergen, Hudson County.
CARLISLE, FREDERICK QM Sgt, C, 1st CT Inf, 1-25-1908. Franklin Reformed Church Cemetery, Nutley, Essex County.
CARLISLE, JAMES S. (aka: Carlisle, Oliver) Pvt, E, 3rd NJ Cav, 5-4-1872. Macphelah Cemetery, North Bergen, Hudson County.
CARLISLE, JOHN Corp, F, 15th NJ Inf, [Wounded in action.] 1912. Pleasant Hill Cemetery, Pleasant Hill, Morris County.
CARLISLE, OLIVER (see: Carlisle, James S.) Macphelah Cemetery, North Bergen, Hudson County.
CARLISLE, SAMUEL Pvt, K, 38th NJ Inf, 1926. Soldier's Home Cemetery, Vineland, Cumberland County.
CARLL, RICHARD Pvt, A, 24th NJ Inf, 8-6-1897. Baptist Church Cemetery, Bridgeton, Cumberland County.
CARLL, SAMUEL M. Sgt, H, 24th NJ Inf, 10-12-1912. Baptist Church Cemetery, Bridgeton, Cumberland County.
CARLOCK, CORNELIUS (see: Carlough, Cornelius W.) Fair Lawn Cemetery, Fair Lawn, Bergen County.
CARLOCK, GEORGE Musc, A, 22nd NJ Inf, DoD Unknown. Bayview-New York Bay Cemetery, Jersey City, Hudson County.
CARLOCK, HENRY 12-3-1862. Old 1st Reformed Church Cemetery, Hackensack, Bergen County.
CARLOCK, JOHN J. 3-20-1903. Zion Lutheran Church Cemetery, Saddle River, Bergen County.
CARLOCK, MATTHIAS 3-8-1864. Old 1st Reformed Church Cemetery, Hackensack, Bergen County.
CARLOCK, ROBERT DoD Unknown. Old 1st Reformed Church Cemetery, Hackensack, Bergen County.
CARLOUGH, CORNELIUS W. (aka: Carlock, Cornelius) Pvt, B, 37th NJ Inf, 2-25-1918. Fair Lawn Cemetery, Fair Lawn, Bergen County.
CARLOUGH, GEORGE 1st Sgt, G, 27th NJ Inf, 7-16-1925. Boonton Cemetery, Boonton, Morris County.
CARLOUGH, GEORGE N. Pvt, H, 25th NJ Inf, 12-5-1906. Valleau Cemetery, Ridgewood, Bergen County.
CARLOUGH, JOHN J. Corp, K, 13th NJ Inf, 10- -1920. Cedar Lawn Cemetery, Paterson, Passaic County.
CARLOUGH, JOHN N. Corp, E, 9th NJ Inf, 5-29-1917. Laurel Grove Cemetery, Totowa, Passaic County.
CARLOUGH, JOHN R. 9-14-1903. Methodist-Episcopal Cemetery, Midland Park, Bergen County.
CARLOUGH, URIAH Pvt, K, 8th NJ Inf, 10-3-1893. Laurel Grove Cemetery, Totowa, Passaic County.
CARLOUGH*, WILLIAM H. Pvt, F, 10th NJ Inf, 9-2-1867. Laurel Grove Cemetery, Totowa, Passaic County.
CARLOUGH, WILLIAM J. Pvt, K, 13th NJ Inf, 3-11-1911. Ramapo Reformed Church Cemetery, Mahwah, Bergen County.
CARLSTEIN, WILHELM (see: Carlstrom, William) Fairmount Cemetery, Newark, Essex County.
CARLSTROM, WILLIAM (aka: Carlstein, Wilhelm) Pvt, Btty D, 5th NY Heavy Art, 12-23-1900. Fairmount Cemetery, Newark, Essex County.
CARLTON, ABSALOM C. Pvt, G, 18th NC Inf (CSA), [Captured 7-3-1863 at Gettysburg, PA. Died of disease.] 9-14-1863. Finn's Point National Cemetery, Pennsville, Salem County.

New Jersey Civil War Burials

CARLTON, JAMES C. DoD Unknown. Elmwood Cemetery, New Brunswick, Middlesex County.
CARLTON, R.W. Corp, B, 11th (Bethel) NC Inf (CSA), [Wounded 7-1-1863 and captured 7-2-1863 at Gettysburg, PA. Died of diarrhea.] 9-16-1863. Finn's Point National Cemetery, Pennsville, Salem County.
CARLTON, THOMAS 4-11-1874. Evergreen Cemetery, Hillside, Union County.
CARLTON, WILLIAM Pvt, B, 7th NJ Inf, 2-24-1895. Mount Pleasant Cemetery, Newark, Essex County.
CARLTON, WILLIAM JAMES Capt, D, 48th NY Inf, 7-18-1902. Evergreen Cemetery, Hillside, Union County.
CARMACK, R.P. Pvt, B, 12th TN Cav (CSA), 8-24-1864. Finn's Point National Cemetery, Pennsville, Salem County.
CARMADY, MICHAEL Pvt, G, 161st NY Inf, 8-14-1902. Fairview Cemetery, Wantage, Sussex County.
CARMAN, ALFRED Corp, H, 14th NJ Inf, [Killed in action at Locust Grove, VA.] 11-27-1863. Brainerd Cemetery, Cranbury, Middlesex County.
CARMAN, DANIEL V. Musc, H, 5th NJ Inf, 5-31-1862. Riverview Cemetery, Trenton, Mercer County.
CARMAN, DAVID H. Corp, E, 2nd NJ Cav, 1-18-1908. Greengrove Cemetery, Keyport, Monmouth County.
CARMAN, DAVID MARTIN Pvt, G, 24th NJ Inf, 11-25-1925. United Methodist Church Cemetery, Woodruff, Cumberland County.
CARMAN, EPHRIAM G. Pvt, G, 24th NJ Inf, 4-5-1909. Methodist Church Cemetery, Union Grove, Salem County.
CARMAN, GEORGE 1919. Brown Cemetery, Butler, Morris County.
CARMAN, GEORGE R. Pvt, A, 8th NJ Inf, 1-23-1923. Rosedale Cemetery, Orange, Essex County.
CARMAN, GEORGE W. Pvt, D, 9th NY Inf, 6-3-1927. Bordentown/Old St. Mary's Catholic Cemetery, Bordentown, Burlington County.
CARMAN, IRA CONDIT (JR.) Capt, F, 35th NJ Inf, 1-12-1899. Cedar Grove Cemetery, Middlebush, Somerset County.
CARMAN, JAMES H. Pvt, D, 29th NJ Inf, 3-26-1864. Bordentown/Old St. Mary's Catholic Cemetery, Bordentown, Burlington County.
CARMAN, JAMES L. 1st Lt, D, 13th NJ Inf, [Wounded 8-18-1864 at Atlanta, GA.] 6-23-1923. Presbyterian Church Cemetery, Metuchen, Middlesex County.
CARMAN*, JOHN S. Corp, I, 1st NJ Cav, 12-8-1913. New Presbyterian Cemetery, Bound Brook, Somerset County.
CARMAN, JOSEPH C. 9-27-1887. Bordentown/Old St. Mary's Catholic Cemetery, Bordentown, Burlington County.
CARMAN, JOSEPH J. 2-2-1934. Cedar Lawn Cemetery, Paterson, Passaic County.
CARMAN, LEWIS Pvt, Btty B, 1st NJ Light Art, 4-6-1919. Mount Rest Cemetery, Butler, Morris County.
CARMAN, LUKE K. Pvt, A, 9th NJ Inf, 11-26-1901. Brainerd Cemetery, Cranbury, Middlesex County.
CARMAN, PETER B. Pvt, G, 1st NJ Cav, [Wounded in action.] DoD Unknown. Maplewood Cemetery, Freehold, Monmouth County.
CARMAN, STEPHEN Pvt, G, 27th NJ Inf, DoD Unknown. Boonton Cemetery, Boonton, Morris County.
CARMAN, THOMAS Sgt, B, 1st NY Cav, 12-30-1912. Old 1st Methodist Church Cemetery, West Long Branch, Monmouth County.
CARMAN*, WILLIAM HENRY Actg 3rd Asst Eng, U.S. Navy, 3-26-1916. Old 1st Methodist Church Cemetery, West Long Branch, Monmouth County.
CARMAN, WILLIAM P. Pvt, K, 38th NJ Inf, 4-9-1906. Greenwood Cemetery, Hamilton, Mercer County.

Our Brothers Gone Before

CARMAN*, WILLIAM W. H. Pvt, A, 14th NJ Inf, 5-3-1890. Fairmount Cemetery, Newark, Essex County.
CARMELIA*, WILLIAM H. Pvt, A, 12th NJ Inf, 4-15-1912. Soldier's Home Cemetery, Vineland, Cumberland County.
CARMEN, PRIME (see: Carman, Prince) Hillside Cemetery, Scotch Plains, Union County.
CARMEN, PRINCE (aka: Carman, Prime) Pvt, A, 41st U.S. CT, 7-11-1902. Hillside Cemetery, Scotch Plains, Union County.
CARMEN, RICHARD DoD Unknown. Riverview Cemetery, Trenton, Mercer County.
CARMER, ABRAHAM 1-25-1886. Hainesville Cemetery, Hainesville, Sussex County.
CARMER, JACOB B. (aka: Crammer, Jacob) Pvt, H, 34th NJ Inf, 10-13-1880. Hainesville Cemetery, Hainesville, Sussex County.
CARMER, JAMES E. Pvt, B, 142nd NY Inf, [Wounded in action 1-15-1865 at Fort Fisher, NC.] 11-30-1866. Mettler Cemetery, Sandyston, Sussex County.
CARMER, OSCAR H. Pvt, C, 26th NJ Inf, 11-21-1914. Fairmount Cemetery, Newark, Essex County.
CARMICHAEL, JOHN Musc, G, 2nd NJ Cav, DoD Unknown. Evergreen Cemetery, Morristown, Morris County.
CARMICHAEL, ROBERT Pvt, E, 22nd NJ Inf, 7-26-1883. Fairmount Cemetery, Newark, Essex County.
CARMICHALL, JAMES Pvt, Btty G, 1st PA Light Art, 5-3-1908. Oddfellows Cemetery, Pemberton, Burlington County.
CARMODY, JOHN Pvt, F, 38th NJ Inf, 11-10-1906. St. John's Cemetery, Lambertville, Hunterdon County.
CARMODY, MICHAEL Pvt, F, 35th NJ Inf, 12-13-1905. St. John's Cemetery, Lambertville, Hunterdon County.
CARNALL, HERBERT (aka: Barker, Joseph) Pvt, I, 68th NY Inf, 10-13-1898. Greenwood Cemetery, Hamilton, Mercer County.
CARNES, JAMES ALBERT Pvt, K, 2nd MS Cav (CSA), 7-30-1864. Finn's Point National Cemetery, Pennsville, Salem County.
CARNEY, MARK L. Sgt, I, 9th NJ Inf, 7-12-1904. Baptist Church Cemetery, Greenwich, Cumberland County.
CARNEY, MARTIN Pvt, H, 1st NY Cav, 2-12-1893. St. Rose of Lima Cemetery, Freehold, Monmouth County.
CARNEY, WILLIAM Corp, D, 24th NJ Inf, 1915. Eastview Cemetery, Salem, Salem County.
CARNWRIGHT, ALONZO Pvt, D, 7th NY Cav, 4-27-1917. Fairmount Cemetery, Newark, Essex County.
CAROLAN, JOHN PATRICK Pvt, D, 28th NJ Inf, DoD Unknown. St. Peter's Cemetery, New Brunswick, Middlesex County.
CAROLINE, JOSEPH (see: Carrolen, Joseph C.) Holy Sepulchre Cemetery, East Orange, Essex County.
CAROTHERS, SAMUEL R. Sgt, H, 11th MS Inf (CSA), 1-4-1864. Finn's Point National Cemetery, Pennsville, Salem County.
CARPENDER, EDWARD W. Commodore, U.S. Navy, 5-16-1876. Episcopal Church Cemetery, Shrewsbury, Monmouth County.
CARPENTER, ABRAM O.S. 1st Lt, C, 31st NJ Inf, 6-20-1866. St. James Cemetery, Greenwich, Warren County.
CARPENTER, ALONZO FULLER Corp, F, 17th NY Inf, 2-10-1921. Arlington Cemetery, Kearny, Hudson County.
CARPENTER, CHARLES G. 10-7-1870. Evergreen Cemetery, Camden, Camden County.
CARPENTER*, CHARLES V. Pvt, M, 2nd NJ Cav, 1-29-1913. Union Cemetery, Washington, Morris County.

New Jersey Civil War Burials

CARPENTER*, DANIEL W. Corp, A, 76th NY Inf, [Wounded 8-29-1862 at 2nd Bull Run, VA.] 1913. Cedar Green Cemetery, Clayton, Gloucester County.

CARPENTER, DAVID P. Corp, 6th NY Ind Btty 1892. Hazelwood Cemetery, Rahway, Union County.

CARPENTER, EDWARD 3-4-1889. New Episcopal Church Cemetery, Swedesboro, Gloucester County.

CARPENTER, EDWIN ELVIDOR Pvt, Btty A, 3rd NY Light Art, DoD Unknown. Bayview-New York Bay Cemetery, Jersey City, Hudson County.

CARPENTER, ELIJAH H. Pvt, B, 143rd PA Inf, DoD Unknown. Greenmount Cemetery, Hammonton, Atlantic County.

CARPENTER, G.F. Pvt, C, 4th VA Cav (CSA), [Captured 1-31-1864 in Madison County, VA. Died of consumption.] 11-1-1864. Finn's Point National Cemetery, Pennsville, Salem County.

CARPENTER, GEORGE Pvt, G, 8th VA Inf (CSA), 9-24-1863. Finn's Point National Cemetery, Pennsville, Salem County.

CARPENTER, GEORGE H. Landsman, U.S. Navy, USS Princeton, 3-22-1906. Lutheran Cemetery, East Stewartsville, Warren County.

CARPENTER, HENRY Landsman, U.S. Navy, 1-25-1877. Rosedale Cemetery, Orange, Essex County.

CARPENTER, JAMES 3rd Cl Boy, U.S. Navy, USS Niagra, 1-6-1865. Evergreen Cemetery, Camden, Camden County.

CARPENTER, JAMES H. Landsman, U.S. Navy, [U.S. receiving ship at Cairo, IL.] 12-25-1920. Evergreen Cemetery, Hillside, Union County.

CARPENTER, JESSE N. Corp, A, 156th NY Inf, [Wounded in action.] 7-3-1917. Fairmount Cemetery, Newark, Essex County.

CARPENTER, JOHN Pvt, I, 47th NC Inf (CSA), [Captured 7-3-1863 at Gettysburg, PA. Died of pneumonia.] 8-3-1863. Finn's Point National Cemetery, Pennsville, Salem County.

CARPENTER, JOHN M. Pvt, G, 11th VA Inf (CSA), 10-16-1863. Finn's Point National Cemetery, Pennsville, Salem County.

CARPENTER, JOHN S. Capt, H, 95th PA Inf, 12- -1879. United Methodist Cemetery, Marlton, Burlington County.

CARPENTER, JONATHAN (see: Carpenter, Jotham) Arlington Cemetery, Kearny, Hudson County.

CARPENTER, JOSEPH Pvt, H, 47th VA Inf (CSA), 9-24-1863. Finn's Point National Cemetery, Pennsville, Salem County.

CARPENTER, JOSEPH E. Pvt, I, 58th PA Inf, 11-1-1875. St. Paul's Methodist-Episcopal Church Cemetery, Thorofare, Gloucester County.

CARPENTER, JOTHAM (aka: Carpenter, Jonathan) Pvt, F, 17th NY Inf, 3-15-1906. Arlington Cemetery, Kearny, Hudson County.

CARPENTER, LEWIS G. Landsman, U.S. Navy, DoD Unknown. Phillipsburg Cemetery, Phillipsburg, Warren County.

CARPENTER, LOUIS HENRY Lt Col, 5th U.S. Cav 1-21-1916. New Episcopal Church Cemetery, Swedesboro, Gloucester County.

CARPENTER, SAMUEL V. Corp, G, 10th MI Cav, 1-1-1902. New Somerville Cemetery, Somerville, Somerset County.

CARPENTER, SILAS M. Pvt, F, 29th CT Inf, 7-27-1912. Gethsemane Cemetery, Little Ferry, Bergen County.

CARPENTER, WALTON 1st Lt, B, 71st NY State Militia, 5-16-1885. Evergreen Cemetery, Hillside, Union County.

CARPENTER, WILBER F. Pvt, 7th NY Ind Btty 3-9-1886. Fairmount Cemetery, Newark, Essex County.

CARPENTER*, WILLIAM H. Pvt, B, 101st OH Inf, 5-11-1921. Evergreen Cemetery, Clinton, Hunterdon County.

Our Brothers Gone Before

CARPENTER, WILLIAM H. Pvt, B, 39th Bttn VA Cav (CSA), [Captured 7-4-1863 at Gettysburg, PA. Died of disease.] 9-15-1863. Finn's Point National Cemetery, Pennsville, Salem County.

CARPENTER*, WILLIAM R. Pvt, M, 2nd NJ Cav, 2-11-1914. Union Cemetery, Washington, Morris County.

CARPER, FRANKLIN Pvt, I, 39th U.S. CT, 1-22-1917. Mount Peace Cemetery, Lawnside, Camden County.

CARR, ANDREW Pvt, B, 8th NJ Inf, 3-18-1889. St. Peter's Cemetery, New Brunswick, Middlesex County.

CARR, ANDREW P. Corp, D, 23rd NJ Inf, 1929. Jacobstown Masonic Cemetery, Jacobstown, Burlington County.

CARR*, AUSTIN A. Pvt, F, 82nd NY Inf, 11-10-1907. Riverview Cemetery, Trenton, Mercer County.

CARR, CHARLES H. 10-15-1918. St. Mary's Cemetery, East Orange, Essex County.

CARR, EDWARD Pvt, H, 23rd NJ Inf, 8-5-1933. Cedar Hill Cemetery, Hightstown, Mercer County.

CARR, ELIJAH Pvt, K, 21st U.S. VRC, DoD Unknown. Emleys Hill United Methodist Church Cemetery, Upper Freehold, Monmouth County.

CARR, GEORGE Pvt, B, 4th NJ Inf, [Killed in action at Gaines' Farm, VA.] 6-27-1862. Dutch Reformed Church Cemetery, Spotswood, Middlesex County.

CARR, GEORGE J. Pvt, I, 11th NJ Inf, 10-25-1895. Riverview Cemetery, Trenton, Mercer County.

CARR, HARVEY 10-18-1884. Methodist Cemetery, Mantua, Gloucester County.

CARR, JAMES Pvt, E, 39th NJ Inf, 12-14-1893. Holy Sepulchre Cemetery, East Orange, Essex County.

CARR, JOHN Pvt, 28th NY Ind Btty 3-3-1920. Arlington Cemetery, Kearny, Hudson County.

CARR, JOHN DoD Unknown. Reformed Church Cemetery, Montville, Morris County.

CARR, JOHN H. Pvt, I, 99th PA Inf, 4-6-1891. Methodist Episcopal/Methodist Protestant Cemetery, Bridgeport, Gloucester County.

CARR, JOHN W. Sgt, B, 4th NJ Militia, 12-17-1879. Cedar Hill Cemetery, Florence, Burlington County.

CARR, LAWRENCE (see: Clark, George L.) St. Paul's Methodist Church Cemetery, Port Republic, Atlantic County.

CARR, MERRICK M. Pvt, H, 1st DE Inf, 5-27-1924. Hedding Methodist-Episcopal Church Cemetery, Bellmawr, Camden County.

CARR, PHILIP W. (aka: Karge, Philipp) Pvt, H, 3rd NJ Inf, 1-14-1916. Beverly National Cemetery, Edgewater Park, Burlington County.

CARR, RICHARD H. (aka: Carroll, Richard) Pvt, K, 11th MA Inf, 4-27-1903. Holy Name Cemetery, Jersey City, Hudson County.

CARR, SAMUEL Capt, C, 23rd NJ Inf, 1-30-1890. Mount Holly Cemetery, Mount Holly, Burlington County.

CARR, SAMUEL Pvt, A, 35th NJ Inf, 7-19-1890. Fairmount Cemetery, Newark, Essex County.

CARR*, SAMUEL M. Corp, I, 1st ME Vet Inf, [Wounded 7-12-1864 in the northern defences of Washington, DC.] DoD Unknown. Oak Hill Cemetery, Vineland, Cumberland County.

CARR, SYLVESTER B. Pvt, E, 1st NJ Cav, 7-27-1912. Presbyterian Church Cemetery, Rockaway, Morris County.

CARR*, THOMAS Pvt, A, 1st NJ Inf, 4-23-1882. Oddfellows Cemetery, Burlington, Burlington County.

CARR, THOMAS (aka: Coer, Thomas) Pvt, D, 5th NJ Inf, [Wounded in action.] 3-6-1910. Holy Sepulchre Cemetery, East Orange, Essex County.

New Jersey Civil War Burials

CARR, THOMAS A. Pvt, I, 29th NJ Inf, 3-31-1910. St. Mary's Cemetery, Wharton, Morris County.
CARR, VINCENT Pvt, 28th NY Ind Btty [Died of disease.] 1-4-1864. Old Woods Cemetery, Stockholm, Sussex County.
CARR, WILLIAM Pvt, K, 104th PA Inf, 4-11-1915. Riverview Cemetery, Trenton, Mercer County.
CARR, WILLIAM H. Pvt, K, 10th NJ Inf, DoD Unknown. Methodist Church Cemetery, Hurffville, Gloucester County.
CARR*, WILLIAM P. Pvt, F, 9th NJ Inf, 1899. United Methodist Church Cemetery, Richwood, Gloucester County.
CARR, WILLIAM (SR.) Pvt, C, 3rd NJ Inf, 5-28-1903. Monument Cemetery, Edgewater Park, Burlington County.
CARRAGAN, JOHN GEORGE Pvt, C, 21st NJ Inf, 1-19-1925. Bayview-New York Bay Cemetery, Jersey City, Hudson County.
CARRAGHER, JAMES Pvt, E, 12th U.S. Inf, [Wounded at Weldon Railroad, VA.] DoD Unknown. St. Peter's Church Cemetery, Belleville, Essex County.
CARREL, CHARLES H. Sgt, B, 2nd NJ Inf, [Died of typhoid at Point Lookout, MD.] 7-30-1862. Presbyterian Church Cemetery, Mount Freedom, Morris County.
CARRELL, JOHN HENRY (aka: Carroll, John H.) Pvt, E, 23rd NJ Inf, 10-8-1928. Methodist Church Cemetery, Pemberton, Burlington County.
CARRELL, JOSEPH Pvt, D, 40th NJ Inf, 8-3-1930. Holcomb-Riverview Cemetery, Lambertville, Hunterdon County.
CARRELL, SAMUEL A. 7-1-1911. Christian Church Cemetery, Locktown, Hunterdon County.
CARRELL, URIAH W. Pvt, D, 2nd NY Cav, DoD Unknown. Greenwood Cemetery, Boonton, Morris County.
CARRICK, JAMES Pvt, K, 70th NY Inf, 2-16-1917. Holy Sepulchre Cemetery, East Orange, Essex County.
CARRICK*, WILLIAM H. Sgt Maj, 214th PA Inf 2-16-1917. Glenwood Cemetery, West Long Branch, Monmouth County.
CARRIGAN, CHARLES M. Pvt, C, 12th MD Inf, DoD Unknown. Mount Prospect Cemetery, Neptune, Monmouth County.
CARRIGAN, EDWARD J. (aka: Corregan, Edward) Pvt, A, 70th NY Inf, 9-14-1893. Holy Sepulchre Cemetery, Totowa, Passaic County.
CARRIGAN, EUGENE Pvt, D, 28th NJ Inf, 12-17-1911. Van Liew Cemetery, North Brunswick, Middlesex County.
CARRIGAN, JAMES Pvt, K, 9th NJ Inf, 5-20-1899. New Camden Cemetery, Camden, Camden County.
CARRIGAN, JAMES DoD Unknown. Mount Olivet Cemetery, Bloomfield, Essex County.
CARRIGAN, JOHN Musc, E, 95th PA Inf, 6-23-1916. Methodist-Episcopal Church Cemetery, Medford, Burlington County.
CARRIGAN, JOHN 1919. Whitelawn Cemetery, Point Pleasant, Ocean County.
CARRIGAN, WYCKOFF P. (aka: Chamberlain, Wyckoff) Pvt, I, 40th NJ Inf, 12-14-1903. Evergreen Cemetery, New Brunswick, Middlesex County.
CARRINGTON, JOSEPH H. Pvt, G, 22nd NJ Inf, 12-6-1878. Mount Pleasant Cemetery, Newark, Essex County.
CARROLEN, JOSEPH C. (aka: Caroline, Joseph) Pvt, F, 11th NY Cav, 7-15-1900. Holy Sepulchre Cemetery, East Orange, Essex County.
CARROLL, ALFRED Pvt, D, 29th U.S. CT, DoD Unknown. Mount Zion Cemetery, Lower Cape May, Cape May County.
CARROLL, BRYAN Pvt, K, 25th NJ Inf, 6-5-1898. Mount Olivet Cemetery, Bloomfield, Essex County.
CARROLL, CHARLES Landsman, U.S. Navy, USS Princeton, 5-7-1876. Holy Sepulchre Cemetery, Totowa, Passaic County.

Our Brothers Gone Before

CARROLL, CHARLES (aka: Carl, Charles) Pvt, A, 165th NY Inf, [Wounded 5-27-1863 at Port Hudson, LA.] 4-27-1912. Laurel Grove Cemetery, Totowa, Passaic County.

CARROLL, ELLIS (aka: Carall, Ellis) Pvt, E, 9th AL Inf (CSA), 5-8-1864. Finn's Point National Cemetery, Pennsville, Salem County.

CARROLL, HAMILTON Pvt, K, 2nd NJ Inf, 11-22-1885. Fairmount Cemetery, Newark, Essex County.

CARROLL, JAMES 1st Lt, F, 175th NY Inf, DoD Unknown. Holy Name Cemetery, Jersey City, Hudson County.

CARROLL, JAMES Pvt, E, 1st NY Inf, 12-20-1884. Evergreen Cemetery, Hillside, Union County.

CARROLL, JAMES Pvt, D, 10th VT Inf, [Wounded 4-2-1865 at Petersburg, VA.] DoD Unknown. Mount Calvary Cemetery, Butler, Morris County.

CARROLL, JAMES H. Pvt, I, 1st DE Inf, 3-27-1892. Miller's Cemetery, New Gretna, Burlington County.

CARROLL, JOHN (see: Corbitt, Michael) Holy Sepulchre Cemetery, East Orange, Essex County.

CARROLL, JOHN H. (see: Carrell, John Henry) Methodist Church Cemetery, Pemberton, Burlington County.

CARROLL, MICHAEL Pvt, D, 5th NJ Inf, DoD Unknown. St. Peter's Cemetery, Jersey City, Hudson County.

CARROLL, PATRICK Seaman, U.S. Navy, 6-8-1904. Holy Name Cemetery, Jersey City, Hudson County.

CARROLL, PATRICK Landsman, U.S. Navy, USS Nansemond, 1-10-1918. St. John's Cemetery, Allentown, Monmouth County.

CARROLL, PATRICK Pvt, D, 33rd NJ Inf, 6-19-1894. Holy Sepulchre Cemetery, East Orange, Essex County.

CARROLL, PATRICK Landsman, U.S. Navy, 11-25-1919. Holy Name Cemetery, Jersey City, Hudson County.

CARROLL, PAUL 1st Sgt, K, 3rd NJ Inf, 4-23-1900. Mount Olivet Cemetery, Newark, Essex County.

CARROLL, PETER Pvt, I, 27th NJ Inf, 6-6-1877. United Methodist Church Cemetery, Vienna, Warren County.

CARROLL, RICHARD (see: Carr, Richard H.) Holy Name Cemetery, Jersey City, Hudson County.

CARROLL, ROBERT Pvt, K, 3rd NJ Inf, [Wounded 8-29-1862 at 2nd Bull Run, VA.] 1-22-1917. Mount Olivet Cemetery, Newark, Essex County.

CARROLL, ROBERT Pvt, F, 2nd NJ Cav, 1-7-1930. Greenlawn Cemetery, West Long Branch, Monmouth County.

CARROLL, THOMAS Pvt, F, 1st NJ Inf, 5-25-1910. Holy Name Cemetery, Jersey City, Hudson County.

CARSE*, HENRY Sgt, D, 147th PA Inf, 6-24-1887. Evergreen Cemetery, Camden, Camden County.

CARSNER*, EBEN Pvt, C, 1st MD Inf, 1926. Greenwood Cemetery, Hamilton, Mercer County.

CARSON, AARON S. Pvt, A, 3rd NJ Inf, 10-4-1921. Presbyterian Church Cemetery, Pennington, Mercer County.

CARSON, ANDREW DoD Unknown. Elmwood Cemetery, New Brunswick, Middlesex County.

CARSON, ANDREW Pvt, F, 38th NJ Inf, 11-15-1918. Greenlawn Cemetery, West Long Branch, Monmouth County.

CARSON, D.H. Pvt, G, 5th TX Inf (CSA), 10-6-1863. Finn's Point National Cemetery, Pennsville, Salem County.

CARSON, GEORGE (aka: Cassner, George) Pvt, F, 38th NJ Inf, 3-8-1903. Riverview Cemetery, Trenton, Mercer County.

New Jersey Civil War Burials

CARSON, GEORGE H. Pvt, E, 21st NJ Inf, 7-12-1911. Greenwood Cemetery, Hamilton, Mercer County.

CARSON*, JAMES R. Landsman, U.S. Navy, USS Princeton, 1897. Harleigh Cemetery, Camden, Camden County.

CARSON, JAMES T. Pvt, E, 21st NJ Inf, 11-13-1910. Methodist Church Cemetery, Groveville, Mercer County.

CARSON, JOHN Pvt, I, 91st PA Inf, 4-24-1897. St. Mary's Episcopal Church Cemetery, Burlington, Burlington County.

CARSON, JOHN F. Pvt, U.S. Marine Corps, 4-19-1889. Greenwood Cemetery, Hamilton, Mercer County.

CARSON, JOHN P. Pvt, H, 25th NY Cav, 3-16-1886. Reformed Church Cemetery, Pottersville, Somerset County.

CARSON, JOHN WESLEY Pvt, E, 2nd NJ Cav, [Died of diarrhea at Jefferson Barracks, MO.] 7-4-1864. Cedar Hill Cemetery, Hightstown, Mercer County.

CARSON, L.P. Capt, D, 35th TN Inf (CSA), [5th TN Mountain Rifle Regiment. Provisional Army.] 5-18-1865. Finn's Point National Cemetery, Pennsville, Salem County.

CARSON, MOSES Pvt, I, 22nd CT Inf, 4-3-1885. Macphelah Cemetery, North Bergen, Hudson County.

CARSON, PERMILLION (see: Corson, Parmenas) Mount Pleasant Cemetery, Millville, Cumberland County.

CARSON, PERRINE Pvt, I, 38th NJ Inf, 5-21-1866. Presbyterian Church Cemetery, Hamilton Square, Mercer County.

CARSON, SAMUEL Sgt, Btty E, 5th U.S. Art, 11-5-1908. Colestown Cemetery, Cherry Hill, Camden County.

CARSON, THOMAS S. Sgt, H, 37th NJ Inf, 1-19-1892. Baptist Cemetery, Burlington, Burlington County.

CARSON, WILLIAM C. Pvt, G, 12th SC Inf (CSA), [Captured 5-6-1864 at Wilderness, VA. Died of measles.] 8-20-1864. Finn's Point National Cemetery, Pennsville, Salem County.

CARSON, WILLIAM (JR.) Pvt, K, 11th NJ Inf, [Wounded 7-2-1863 at Gettysburg, PA.] 10-15-1882. Mount Pleasant Cemetery, Newark, Essex County.

CARSON, WILLIAM S. Pvt, B, 7th DE Inf, 5-4-1924. Hollywood Cemetery, Union, Union County.

CARSTENS, NICHOLAS (aka: Carstine, Nicholas) Corp, E, 40th NJ Inf, 3-3-1892. Flower Hill Cemetery, North Bergen, Hudson County.

CARSTINE, NICHOLAS (see: Carstens, Nicholas) Flower Hill Cemetery, North Bergen, Hudson County.

CARTER, AMOS C. Pvt, G, 28th NJ Inf, [Died of typhoid at Falmouth, VA.] 3-8-1863. Mount Zion United Methodist Church Cemetery, Barnsboro, Gloucester County.

CARTER, BENJAMIN S. Pvt, B, 14th NJ Inf, [Died of diarrhea at Fairfax Seminary, VA.] 11-8-1863. Mercer Cemetery, Trenton, Mercer County.

CARTER, CHARLES B. Pvt, G, 4th NJ Inf, 10-5-1868. Evergreen Cemetery, Camden, Camden County.

CARTER, DANIEL A. DoD Unknown. Bethel Cemetery, Pennsauken, Camden County.

CARTER, DANIEL A. 1st Cl Boy, U.S. Navy, USS Great Western, 1-3-1930. Colestown Cemetery, Cherry Hill, Camden County.

CARTER, DAVID Pvt, M, 2nd NJ Cav, 11-30-1883. Union Brick Cemetery, Blairstown, Warren County.

CARTER, DAVID J. Pvt, C, 9th NJ Inf, 11-7-1902. Riverview Cemetery, Trenton, Mercer County.

CARTER, DAVID S. Pvt, F, 9th NJ Inf, 1912. Cedar Green Cemetery, Clayton, Gloucester County.

CARTER, EDWARD Pvt, D, 8th NJ Inf, [Died of wounds.] 9-9-1862. Mount Pleasant Cemetery, Newark, Essex County.

Our Brothers Gone Before

CARTER, ELIAS H. Corp, E, 27th NJ Inf, 8-18-1875. Hillside Cemetery, Madison, Morris County.
CARTER, ENOCH Musc, B, 25th NJ Inf, 12-16-1917. Atlantic City Cemetery, Pleasantville, Atlantic County.
CARTER, GEORGE F. Pvt, I, 28th NJ Inf, 12-19-1903. Alpine Cemetery, Perth Amboy, Middlesex County.
CARTER, HARRISON Corp, A, 5th MA Colored Cav, 1-22-1866. Baptist Church Cemetery, Jacobstown, Burlington County.
CARTER, HENRY Corp, C, 31st NJ Inf, 10-17-1902. Evergreen Cemetery, Camden, Camden County.
CARTER, JACOB Pvt, F, 3rd NJ Cav, 5-4-1867. Clinton Cemetery, Irvington, Essex County.
CARTER, JAMES Pvt, H, 57th NY Inf, [Wounded 12-13-1862 at Fredericksburg, VA.] 3-16-1900. Oddfellows Cemetery, Burlington, Burlington County.
CARTER, JAMES Corp, B, 12th NJ Inf, [Died of disease at Ellicotts Mills, MD.] 11-6-1862. Baptist Church Cemetery, Jacobstown, Burlington County.
CARTER, JAMES W. Pvt, H, 58th VA Inf (CSA), [Captured 5-12-1864 at Spotsylvania CH, VA. Died of dysentery.] 5-24-1865. Finn's Point National Cemetery, Pennsville, Salem County.
CARTER, JOHN Pvt, H, 12th NJ Inf, 1922. Friends Cemetery, Woodstown, Salem County.
CARTER, JOHN DoD Unknown. Union Cemetery, Mantua, Gloucester County.
CARTER, JOHN H. Pvt, E, 1st MN Inf, 9-10-1862. Fairmount Cemetery, Newark, Essex County.
CARTER, JOHN H. Pvt, B, 9th NJ Inf, 6-30-1871. Fairmount Cemetery, Newark, Essex County.
CARTER, JOHN J. Pvt, F, 13th NJ Inf, 8-6-1879. Fairmount Cemetery, Newark, Essex County.
CARTER, JOHN J. Pvt, K, 39th NJ Inf, 3-11-1913. Fairmount Cemetery, Newark, Essex County.
CARTER, JOHNSON Pvt, I, 29th CT Inf, 2-9-1908. Mount Peace Cemetery, Lawnside, Camden County.
CARTER, JOSEPH M. Pvt, F, 12th NJ Inf, 2-12-1924. Methodist-Episcopal Church Cemetery, Aura, Gloucester County.
CARTER, JOSEPH S. Corp, B, 31st NJ Inf, 1919. Mansfield/Washington Cemetery, Washington, Warren County.
CARTER, LAFAYETTE Pvt, G, 4th NJ Inf, 12-12-1925. New Camden Cemetery, Camden, Camden County.
CARTER, NATHAN 1895. Colestown Cemetery, Cherry Hill, Camden County.
CARTER, NATHAN 2-22-1869. Bethel Cemetery, Pennsauken, Camden County.
CARTER, PHILIP W. Pvt, C, 38th NJ Inf, 1923. Mount Pleasant Cemetery, Millville, Cumberland County.
CARTER, RICHARD D. Pvt, Btty D, WV Light Art, 7-30-1885. Cedar Hill Cemetery, East Millstone, Somerset County.
CARTER, ROBERT O. Pvt, D, 8th VA Inf (CSA), [Captured 7-3-1863 at Gettysburg, PA. Died of diarrhea.] 9-21-1863. Finn's Point National Cemetery, Pennsville, Salem County.
CARTER, SAMUEL A. Pvt, H, 24th NJ Inf, 2-20-1923. Overlook Cemetery, Bridgeton, Cumberland County.
CARTER, SAMUEL B. Corp, G, 4th NJ Inf, [Died at Fredericksburg, VA. of wounds received 5-6-1864 at Wilderness, VA.] 5-17-1864. Old Camden Cemetery, Camden, Camden County.
CARTER, SARAH A. Nurse, 4-20-1891. Trinity Bible Church Cemetery, Glassboro, Gloucester County.

New Jersey Civil War Burials

CARTER, SHREVE H. Corp, B, 12th NJ Inf, 6-23-1908. Riverview Cemetery, Trenton, Mercer County.
CARTER, SINGLETON Pvt, C, 34th NJ Inf, 12-30-1882. Baptist Church Cemetery, Jacobstown, Burlington County.
CARTER, THOMAS (aka: Cotter, Thomas) Pvt, K, 69th PA Inf, [Killed in action at Antietam, MD.] 9-17-1862. Bordentown/Old St. Mary's Catholic Cemetery, Bordentown, Burlington County.
CARTER, THOMAS Pvt, K, 40th NJ Inf, 6-2-1909. Arlington Cemetery, Kearny, Hudson County.
CARTER, THOMAS E.D. Pvt, F, 4th NJ Militia, 1864. Methodist-Episcopal Church Cemetery, Blackwood, Camden County.
CARTER, THOMAS E.D. 1901. Hillside Cemetery, Madison, Morris County.
CARTER, WILLIAM Pvt, B, 2nd FL Cav (CSA), 6-13-1864. Finn's Point National Cemetery, Pennsville, Salem County.
CARTER, WILLIAM (see: Carlaw, William) Baptist Church Cemetery, Greenwich, Cumberland County.
CARTER, WILLIAM H. Pvt, Btty K, 13th NY Heavy Art, 1-14-1894. Laurel Grove Cemetery, Totowa, Passaic County.
CARTER*, WILLIAM H. Pvt, H, 23rd NJ Inf, 1-16-1916. Bordentown/Old St. Mary's Catholic Cemetery, Bordentown, Burlington County.
CARTER, WILLIAM (JR.) (aka: Miller, J.) Pvt, H, 8th MD Inf, 2- -1915. New Camden Cemetery, Camden, Camden County.
CARTER, WILLIAM M. Pvt, D, 25th NJ Inf, 6-19-1899. Mount Pleasant Cemetery, Millville, Cumberland County.
CARTER, WILLIAM R. Pvt, G, 12th NJ Inf, 5-22-1894. Pierce Cemetery, Almonessen, Gloucester County.
CARTER, WILLIAM T. 12-23-1900. Evergreen Cemetery, Camden, Camden County.
CARTEY, FRANCIS (see: Kellam, Francis) Bordentown/Old St. Mary's Catholic Cemetery, Bordentown, Burlington County.
CARTLEDGE, CYRUS C. Sgt, E, 91st PA Inf, [Wounded 7-2-1863 at Gettysburg, PA.] 3-5-1878. Baptist Church Cemetery, Haddonfield, Camden County.
CARTON, PATRICK Pvt, B, 43rd NY Inf, 5-5-1931. Mount Olivet Cemetery, Fairview, Monmouth County.
CARTWRIGHT, AMBROSE Pvt, H, 60th (Crawford's) TN Mtd Inf (CSA), [Captured 5-17-1863 at Big Black River Bridge, MS.] 11-6-1863. Finn's Point National Cemetery, Pennsville, Salem County.
CARTWRIGHT, GEORGE W. Col, 28th MA Inf [Wounded in action 8-30-1862 at 2nd Bull Run, VA. and 5-6-1864 at Wilderness, VA.] 3-20-1868. Fairmount Cemetery, Newark, Essex County.
CARTY, EDWARD Pvt, Btty B, 1st NJ Light Art, 5-10-1873. Berlin Cemetery, Berlin, Camden County.
CARTY, JOHN Pvt, B, 10th NJ Inf, [Died of measles at Beverly, NJ.] 12-24-1861. Beverly National Cemetery, Edgewater Park, Burlington County.
CARTY, JOHN (aka: Masterson, John) Pvt, B, 106th PA Inf, [Wounded in action.] 2-17-1900. Evergreen Cemetery, New Brunswick, Middlesex County.
CARTY, JOHN B. Pvt, B, 23rd NJ Inf, 1917. Columbus Cemetery, Columbus, Burlington County.
CARTY, NATHAN W. Coal Heaver, U.S. Navy, USS State of Georgia, 6-10-1894. Mount Holly Cemetery, Mount Holly, Burlington County.
CARTY, SUMPTER M. (see: McCarty, Somers H.) Evergreen Cemetery, Camden, Camden County.
CARTY, WILLIAM H. Pvt, A, 3rd NJ Cav, 1914. Columbus Cemetery, Columbus, Burlington County.

Our Brothers Gone Before

CARTY, WILLIAM L. Pvt, B, 12th NJ Inf, 4-29-1890. Fairmount Cemetery, Newark, Essex County.
CARUTHERS, NATHANIEL R. Pvt, G, 8th FL Inf (CSA), [Wounded 12-13-1862 at Fredericksburg, VA. Captured 7-3-1863 at Gettysburg, PA. Died of diarrhea.] 5-13-1864. Finn's Point National Cemetery, Pennsville, Salem County.
CARVER, ARTHUR D. Corp, A, 3rd U.S. CT, 4-25-1894. Fairmount Cemetery, Newark, Essex County.
CARVER, JOSEPH Pvt, H, 21st NJ Inf, 12-20-1909. Methodist Church Cemetery, Titusville, Mercer County.
CARVER, THEODORE Pvt, K, 8th U.S. CT, [Wounded in action.] 9-11-1910. Fairmount Cemetery, Newark, Essex County.
CARY, JOHN 4-22-1889. Mount Prospect Cemetery, Neptune, Monmouth County.
CARY*, JOHN E. Sgt, F, 2nd NY Mounted Rifles, 6-6-1915. Evergreen Cemetery, Hillside, Union County.
CARY, JOHN R. Pvt, A, 34th VA Inf (CSA), DoD Unknown. 1st United Methodist Church Cemetery, Bridgeton, Cumberland County.
CARY, JOHNSON W. Sgt, C, 173rd NY Inf, [Wounded 5-27-1863 at Port Hudson, LA.] 1-20-1903. Evergreen Cemetery, Hillside, Union County.
CARY, LITTLETON (aka: Littleton, Carey) Pvt, G, 19th U.S. CT, 8-30-1917. Fairview Cemetery, Fairview, Burlington County.
CARY, NATHAN J. Pvt, A, 1st NJ Cav, [Died of typhoid at Alexandria, VA.] 1-18-1864. Presbyterian Church Cemetery, Sparta, Sussex County.
CARY, PETER (see: Carey, Peter) Fairview Cemetery, Columbia, Warren County.
CARY, SAMUEL EDWIN 1st Lt, K, 13th MA Inf, 5-8-1927. Rosedale Cemetery, Orange, Essex County.
CARY, WILLIAM Pvt, A, 29th NJ Inf, 5-19-1905. Old 1st Methodist Church Cemetery, West Long Branch, Monmouth County.
CASE*, CHARLES P. Sgt, C, 2nd NJ Cav, 4-3-1903. Riverview Cemetery, Trenton, Mercer County.
CASE, EPHRIAM Pvt, L, 1st NJ Cav, 9-2-1905. Prospect Hill Cemetery, Flemington, Hunterdon County.
CASE, GEORGE M. 4-10-1877. Bayview-New York Bay Cemetery, Jersey City, Hudson County.
CASE, GEORGE M. Pvt, G, 30th NJ Inf, 7-9-1911. Riverview Cemetery, Trenton, Mercer County.
CASE*, GEORGE W. Pvt, G, 8th NJ Inf, 7-17-1910. Highland Cemetery, Hopewell Boro, Mercer County.
CASE, HENRY Wagoner, C, 27th NJ Inf, 3-14-1894. Fairmount Cemetery, Newark, Essex County.
CASE, JACOB Pvt, D, 30th NJ Inf, 5-2-1901. Union Cemetery, Frenchtown, Hunterdon County.
CASE, JACOB Pvt, I, 35th NJ Inf, 5-22-1905. Reformed Church Cemetery, Three Bridges, Hunterdon County.
CASE, JAMES G. Pvt, K, 2nd NJ Cav, 1915. Pleasant Hill Cemetery, Pleasant Hill, Morris County.
CASE*, JAMES M. Pvt, B, 83rd OH Inf, 12- -1887. Sandy Ridge Cemetery, Sandy Ridge, Hunterdon County.
CASE, JEREMIAH Pvt, F, 31st NJ Inf, 8-24-1885. Presbyterian Church Cemetery, Mount Pleasant, Hunterdon County.
CASE, JOHN H. 10-12-1865. Sandy Ridge Cemetery, Sandy Ridge, Hunterdon County.
CASE, JOHN H. Pvt, E, 30th NJ Inf, 1911. Old Somerville Cemetery, Somerville, Somerset County.
CASE*, JOHN V. 2nd Lt, H, 4th NJ Inf, 11-22-1919. Rosedale Cemetery, Orange, Essex County.

New Jersey Civil War Burials

CASE, MAHLON C. Pvt, Btty D, 1st NJ Light Art, 2-22-1915. Belvidere/Catholic Cemetery, Belvidere, Warren County.

CASE, OLIVER P. Pvt, C, 2nd NJ Cav, 2-27-1910. Phillipsburg Cemetery, Phillipsburg, Warren County.

CASE*, RUFUS K. Capt, U.S. Volunteers, [Acting Quartermaster.] 6-18-1898. Hillside Cemetery, Scotch Plains, Union County.

CASE*, SAMUEL Pvt, A, 15th NJ Inf, 4-2-1927. Prospect Hill Cemetery, Flemington, Hunterdon County.

CASE, SAMUEL P. 1-21-1880. Sandy Ridge Cemetery, Sandy Ridge, Hunterdon County.

CASE, SAMUEL P. Sgt, B, 6th NJ Inf, 2-28-1883. Hillside Cemetery, Scotch Plains, Union County.

CASE, SYLVESTER C. Pvt, E, 37th NJ Inf, 1-12-1894. Mount Pleasant Cemetery, Newark, Essex County.

CASE, WILLIAM Pvt, F, 38th NJ Inf, 9-7-1894. Presbyterian Church Cemetery, Mount Pleasant, Hunterdon County.

CASE, WILLIAM 1905. Presbyterian Church Cemetery, Greenwich, Warren County.

CASE, WILLIAM B. Pvt, E, 38th NJ Inf, 9-3-1909. Presbyterian Church Cemetery, Mount Pleasant, Hunterdon County.

CASE, WILLIAM B. (JR.) Musc, H, 138th PA Inf, 12-31-1894. Union Cemetery, Ringoes, Hunterdon County.

CASE, WILLIAM C. Pvt, F, 53rd PA Inf, 1-10-1882. Presbyterian/Methodist-Episcopal Cemetery, Succasunna, Morris County.

CASE, WILLIAM H. Corp, I, 15th NJ Inf, [Died at Washington, DC. of wounds received 5-12-1864 at Spotsylvania CH, VA.] 6-3-1864. Presbyterian/Methodist-Episcopal Cemetery, Succasunna, Morris County.

CASE, WILLIAM H. (SR.) Corp, E, 29th NJ Inf, 5-20-1903. Maplewood Cemetery, Freehold, Monmouth County.

CASEY*, JOHN B. Landsman, U.S. Navy, USS Princeton, 1913. Clinton Cemetery, Irvington, Essex County.

CASEY, THOMAS Pvt, C, 2nd NJ Inf, 8-24-1880. St. John's Evangelical Church Cemetery, Orange, Essex County.

CASEY, WILLIAM Pvt, G, 14th NJ Inf, 3-16-1911. Fairview Cemetery, Fairview, Monmouth County.

CASEY, WILLIAM Saddler, C, 5th PA Cav, 2-4-1894. 1st Baptist Church Cemetery, Pedricktown, Salem County.

CASH, JOHN P. Pvt, F, 19th U.S. Inf, [Wounded in action.] DoD Unknown. Holy Sepulchre Cemetery, East Orange, Essex County.

CASH, WILLIAM H. Pvt, I, 19th VA Inf (CSA), [Wounded 6-30-1862 at Darbytown Road, VA. Captured 7-3-1863 at Gettysburg, PA. Died of pericarditis.] 11-17-1863. Finn's Point National Cemetery, Pennsville, Salem County.

CASHIN, RICHARD T. Pvt, C, 133rd NY Inf, 12-15-1926. East Ridgelawn Cemetery, Clifton, Passaic County.

CASHION*, JAMES Pvt, I, 13th NJ Inf, [Died of consumption.] 2-7-1864. Fairmount Cemetery, Newark, Essex County.

CASHMAN, THOMAS Pvt, H, 6th TN Inf (CSA), 3-5-1864. Finn's Point National Cemetery, Pennsville, Salem County.

CASKEY*, JAMES 1st Sgt, K, 28th PA Inf, 8-8-1902. Cedar Grove Cemetery, Gloucester City, Camden County.

CASKEY, WILLIAM K. Corp, C, 27th NJ Inf, 8-11-1900. Presbyterian Church Cemetery, Andover, Sussex County.

CASKINS, WILLIAM A. DoD Unknown. Riverview Cemetery, Trenton, Mercer County.

CASLER, JACOB C. Pvt, B, 1st NJ Cav, 2-25-1926. Methodist Church Cemetery, Pleasant Grove, Ocean County.

Our Brothers Gone Before

CASLEY, HENRY (aka: Cosley, Henry) Pvt, Btty B, 2nd NY Heavy Art, DoD Unknown. Grove Church Cemetery, North Bergen, Hudson County.
CASNER, WILLIAM H. Corp, B, 30th NJ Inf, 8-28-1916. Evergreen Cemetery, Hillside, Union County.
CASON, WILLIAM J. Corp, I, 1st Bttn (Patton's) MS Inf (CSA), 11-14-1863. Finn's Point National Cemetery, Pennsville, Salem County.
CASPAR, FREDERICK C.H. (aka: Kneffner, Frederick) Pvt, Btty D, 16th NY Heavy Art, 5-4-1898. Presbyterian Cemetery, North Plainfield, Somerset County.
CASPER, JACOB Corp, D, 10th NJ Inf, [Died of typhoid at Georgetown, DC.] 8-12-1862. Lutheran Church Cemetery, Friesburg, Salem County.
CASPER, MOSES Pvt, D, 41st U.S. CT, 10-18-1902. Mount Pisgah Cemetery, Elsinboro, Salem County.
CASPERSON, EDWARD Pvt, F, 12th NJ Inf, 10-17-1923. Soldier's Home Cemetery, Vineland, Cumberland County.
CASS, JOHN Pvt, I, 97th NY Inf, 8-4-1886. Maplewood Cemetery, Freehold, Monmouth County.
CASSABOON, JAMES 7-6-1861. United Methodist Church Cemetery, Winslow, Camden County.
CASSABOON, JOHN (aka: Cossabone, John) Pvt, C, 2nd MD Inf (ES), DoD Unknown. Mount Pleasant Cemetery, Millville, Cumberland County.
CASSADAY, ANDREW Pvt, H, 58th VA Inf (CSA), [Captured 5-12-1864 at Spotsylvania CH, VA. Died of bowel inflammation.] 8-4-1864. Finn's Point National Cemetery, Pennsville, Salem County.
CASSADAY*, SAMUEL F. Pvt, D, 12th NJ Inf, 1900. Methodist Church Cemetery, Friendship, Salem County.
CASSADY, EDWARD Pvt, B, 2nd NY Cav, 2-14-1907. Hardyston Cemetery, North Church, Sussex County.
CASSADY, JOHN Pvt, H, 27th NJ Inf, 3-29-1866. Hardyston Cemetery, North Church, Sussex County.
CASSEL, JOHN C. 2nd Lt, A, 5th PA Cav, 1-19-1881. Presbyterian Church Cemetery, Upper Deerfield, Cumberland County.
CASSELMAN, RENSALLAER Pvt, Btty B, 1st NJ Light Art, [Cenotaph. Killed in action at Gettysburg, PA.] 7-2-1863. Fairmount Cemetery, Newark, Essex County.
CASSELMANN, CHRISTIAN Lt Col, Benton Hussars MO Cav 11-26-1861. Bayview-New York Bay Cemetery, Jersey City, Hudson County.
CASSERLY, THOMAS Pvt, B, 38th NY Inf, 11-7-1891. Holy Sepulchre Cemetery, East Orange, Essex County.
CASSIDY, ANDREW Pvt, B, 27th NY Inf, 4-6-1897. St. Peter's Cemetery, Jersey City, Hudson County.
CASSIDY, DAVID Corp, K, 15th NJ Inf, 9-14-1889. Hardyston Cemetery, North Church, Sussex County.
CASSIDY, JAMES Pvt, K, 4th NJ Inf, 3-6-1922. Eglington Cemetery, Clarksboro, Gloucester County.
CASSIDY, JOHN Pvt, B, 5th NJ Inf, 1897. St. Peter's Cemetery, Jersey City, Hudson County.
CASSIDY, LUKE Seaman, U.S. Navy, DoD Unknown. Holy Name Cemetery, Jersey City, Hudson County.
CASSIDY, LUKE J. (JR.) Pvt, C, 9th NY Inf, DoD Unknown. Holy Name Cemetery, Jersey City, Hudson County.
CASSIDY, RICHARD Sgt, G, 3rd NJ Inf, 8-17-1905. Bayview-New York Bay Cemetery, Jersey City, Hudson County.
CASSIDY*, WILLIAM (aka: Castle, William) Pvt, F, 84th NY Inf, 5-30-1900. Holy Sepulchre Cemetery, East Orange, Essex County.

New Jersey Civil War Burials

CASSIMORE, JOHN Pvt, M, 1st NJ Cav, [Died at Newark, NJ of wounds received at Fredericksburg, VA.] 9-5-1864. Fairmount Cemetery, Newark, Essex County.

CASSLER*, JOHN W. Pvt, F, 35th NJ Inf, 5-20-1872. Pitman Methodist-Episcopal Cemetery, New Brunswick, Middlesex County.

CASSLER, WILLIAM Pvt, A, 33rd NJ Inf, 2-18-1920. Fairmount Cemetery, Newark, Essex County.

CASSLER, WILLIAM 1st Sgt, I, 176th PA Inf, DoD Unknown. Pitman Methodist-Episcopal Cemetery, New Brunswick, Middlesex County.

CASSNER, GEORGE (see: Carson, George) Riverview Cemetery, Trenton, Mercer County.

CASTERLIN, BENJAMIN (aka: Casterline, Benjamin) Pvt, H, 27th NJ Inf, 4-28-1864. Mount Salem Cemetery, Mount Salem, Sussex County.

CASTERLIN, GEORGE C. (aka: Casterline, George C.) Pvt, K, 27th NJ Inf, 11-18-1895. Mount Salem Cemetery, Mount Salem, Sussex County.

CASTERLIN, WILLIAM B. (aka: Casterline, William B.) Pvt, H, 27th NJ Inf, 1-5-1915. Mount Salem Cemetery, Mount Salem, Sussex County.

CASTERLINE, BENJAMIN (see: Casterlin, Benjamin) Mount Salem Cemetery, Mount Salem, Sussex County.

CASTERLINE, GEORGE C. (see: Casterlin, George C.) Mount Salem Cemetery, Mount Salem, Sussex County.

CASTERLINE, JOHN 9-17-1898. Lodi Cemetery, Lodi, Bergen County.

CASTERLINE, JOHN Pvt, K, 27th NJ Inf, 6-11-1898. Methodist Church Cemetery, Sparta, Sussex County.

CASTERLINE, WILLIAM B. (see: Casterlin, William B.) Mount Salem Cemetery, Mount Salem, Sussex County.

CASTLE, LEWIS Seaman, U.S. Navy, DoD Unknown. Hackensack Cemetery, Hackensack, Bergen County.

CASTLE, WILLIAM Pvt, B, 17th ME Inf, [Died of wounds.] 9-30-1864. Beverly National Cemetery, Edgewater Park, Burlington County.

CASTLE, WILLIAM (see: Cassidy, William) Holy Sepulchre Cemetery, East Orange, Essex County.

CASTLEBURY, ISAAC Pvt, K, 32nd TN Inf (CSA), 6- -1865. Finn's Point National Cemetery, Pennsville, Salem County.

CASTLEMAN, CHAUNCEY Pvt, Btty E, 3rd NY Light Art, 2-2-1919. Bayview-New York Bay Cemetery, Jersey City, Hudson County.

CASTLER, ADAM (see: Kastner, Adam) Laurel Grove Cemetery, Totowa, Passaic County.

CASTLOW, BERNARD (see: Costello, Bernard) Holy Sepulchre Cemetery, East Orange, Essex County.

CASTMORE, CHARLES R. Pvt, E, 9th NJ Inf, 12-2-1877. Headley Cemetery, Milton, Morris County.

CASTMORE, HORACE B. Corp, A, 2nd NY Cav, 5-14-1893. Headley Cemetery, Milton, Morris County.

CASTMORE, SAMUEL Pvt, E, 9th NJ Inf, 10-15-1875. Headley Cemetery, Milton, Morris County.

CASTMORE, WILLIAM Corp, E, 9th NJ Inf, 10-25-1907. Presbyterian Church Cemetery, Sparta, Sussex County.

CASTNER*, CORNELIUS WYCKOFF Capt, B, 9th NJ Inf, [Wounded in action at Newbern, NC.] 12-12-1904. St. Peter's Cemetery, New Brunswick, Middlesex County.

CASTNER, JAMES J. Pvt, D, 28th NJ Inf, 11-1-1887. Elmwood Cemetery, New Brunswick, Middlesex County.

CASTNER, JESSE S. Sgt, H, 15th NJ Inf, 3-5-1892. Old & New Lutheran Cemetery, Lebanon, Hunterdon County.

Our Brothers Gone Before

CASTNER, THEODORE Pvt, K, 31st NJ Inf, 7-9-1922. Presbyterian Church Cemetery, Hampton, Hunterdon County.
CASTO, JAMES L. Pvt, H, 28th NJ Inf, 7-28-1901. New Freedom Cemetery, New Freedom, Camden County.
CASTO, JEREMIAH 1st Sgt, G, 12th NJ Inf, 1906. Eglington Cemetery, Clarksboro, Gloucester County.
CATERSON, JAMES H. Pvt, C, 11th NJ Inf, 3-20-1898. Atlantic City Cemetery, Pleasantville, Atlantic County.
CATHCART, ALAMANDA Pvt, K, 3rd NJ Militia, DoD Unknown. Elmwood Cemetery, New Brunswick, Middlesex County.
CATHCART, CHARLES (aka: Williams, Henry C.) Pvt, H, 4th NJ Inf, 11-15-1901. Baptist Cemetery, Pemberton, Burlington County.
CATHCART, MERRITT G. Corp, D, 28th NJ Inf, 2-28-1894. Elmwood Cemetery, New Brunswick, Middlesex County.
CATHCART, SAMUEL Pvt, E, 23rd NJ Inf, 3-24-1892. Riverview Cemetery, Trenton, Mercer County.
CATHCART, THOMAS Pvt, B, 23rd NJ Inf, 1-5-1871. Bordentown/Old St. Mary's Catholic Cemetery, Bordentown, Burlington County.
CATHCART, WILLIAM A. Sgt, U.S. Marine Corps, USS Morse, 2-23-1906. Arlington Cemetery, Pennsauken, Camden County.
CATHCART, WILLIAM WALLACE 2-19-1875. Presbyterian Church Cemetery, Metuchen, Middlesex County.
CATHEY, W.H. Pvt, G, 3rd MS Cav (CSA), 7-26-1864. Finn's Point National Cemetery, Pennsville, Salem County.
CATHRELL, ISAAC Pvt, A, 15th NJ Inf, [Died at Philadelphia, PA. of wounds received 7-3-1863 at Gettysburg, PA.] 7-13-1863. Mount Hope Presbyterian Cemetery, Lambertville, Hunterdon County.
CATLETT, BENJAMIN (aka: Catlette, Benjamin) Pvt, I, 55th NC Inf (CSA), [Captured 7-1-1863 at Gettysburg, PA. Died of typhoid.] 9-10-1863. Finn's Point National Cemetery, Pennsville, Salem County.
CATLETT, POSEY M. Pvt, G, 9th GA Inf (CSA), [Captured 7-3-1863 at Gettysburg, PA. Died of diarrhea.] 11-2-1863. Finn's Point National Cemetery, Pennsville, Salem County.
CATLETTE, BENJAMIN (see: Catlett, Benjamin) Finn's Point National Cemetery, Pennsville, Salem County.
CATLIN*, GEORGE LYNDE 1st Lt, A, 101st NY Inf, 12-14-1896. Cedar Lawn Cemetery, Paterson, Passaic County.
CATLING, WILLIAM Pvt, K, 24th NJ Inf, 1-25-1911. Eglington Cemetery, Clarksboro, Gloucester County.
CATO, WILLIAM Corp, G, 10th U.S. Vet Vol Inf, DoD Unknown. Arlington Cemetery, Kearny, Hudson County.
CATON, ANDREW J. Pvt, M, 2nd NJ Cav, 10-24-1911. Arlington Cemetery, Kearny, Hudson County.
CATTELL, ADON W. 1st Lt, A, 3rd NJ Inf, 1-10-1902. Green Cemetery, Woodbury, Gloucester County.
CATTELL*, EDWARD C. 1st Lt, E, 24th NJ Inf, [Wounded in action.] 9-2-1904. Eglington Cemetery, Clarksboro, Gloucester County.
CATTELL, GEORGE W. Pvt, E, 24th NJ Inf, 10-16-1895. Cattell Cemetery, Almonessen, Gloucester County.
CAUFIELD, CORNELIUS Seaman, U.S. Navy, 1-21-1907. St. Peter's Cemetery, Jersey City, Hudson County.
CAVALEER, JAMES (see: Cavalier, James H.) Presbyterian Church Cemetery, Westfield, Union County.

New Jersey Civil War Burials

CAVALIER, ISAAC Pvt, D, 28th NJ Inf, 4-16-1912. Arlington Cemetery, Kearny, Hudson County.

CAVALIER, JAMES H. (aka: Cavaleer, James) Pvt, E, 30th NJ Inf, [Died at Bridgewater, NJ. while on furlough.] 5-29-1863. Presbyterian Church Cemetery, Westfield, Union County.

CAVALIER, JOSEPH C. (aka: Cavileer, Joseph) Pvt, H, 30th NJ Inf, 1-5-1903. Fairview Cemetery, Westfield, Union County.

CAVALIER, SAMUEL (see: Cavileer, Samuel H.) St. Paul's Methodist Church Cemetery, Port Republic, Atlantic County.

CAVANAGH, DENNIS Pvt, H, 39th NJ Inf, 4-25-1893. Holy Sepulchre Cemetery, East Orange, Essex County.

CAVANAGH, JOHN Corp, B, 34th NJ Inf, DoD Unknown. Immaculate Conception Cemetery, Montclair, Essex County.

CAVANAUGH, BENJAMIN Landsman, U.S. Navy, USS North Carolina, 11-7-1911. New Camden Cemetery, Camden, Camden County.

CAVANAUGH, CHARLES Pvt, A, 8th NJ Inf, 10-13-1891. Mount Olivet Cemetery, Newark, Essex County.

CAVANAUGH, DANIEL (see: Kavanaugh, Daniel) Rosedale Cemetery, Linden, Union County.

CAVANAUGH, EDWARD (aka: Kavanaugh, Edward) Pvt, F, 10th NJ Inf, DoD Unknown. Holy Sepulchre Cemetery, Totowa, Passaic County.

CAVANAUGH, FRANCIS (see: Kavanagh, Francis J.) Holy Sepulchre Cemetery, East Orange, Essex County.

CAVANAUGH, JAMES Pvt, G, 7th NJ Inf, [Killed on picket duty at Petersburg, VA.] 9-1-1864. Holy Sepulchre Cemetery, Totowa, Passaic County.

CAVANAUGH*, JAMES Pvt, 34th NY Ind Btty 3-2-1900. St. Michael's Cemetery, Netcong, Morris County.

CAVANAUGH, JOHN Pvt, F, 10th NY Inf, [Died of disease at Beverly, NJ.] 3-13-1865. Beverly National Cemetery, Edgewater Park, Burlington County.

CAVANAUGH, JOHN Corp, H, 4th NJ Inf, 3-6-1893. Evergreen Cemetery, Camden, Camden County.

CAVANAUGH, JOHN Pvt, Btty H, 2nd U.S. Art, DoD Unknown. Mount Olivet Cemetery, Newark, Essex County.

CAVANAUGH, JOHN Pvt, C, 2nd NJ Inf, DoD Unknown. Holy Sepulchre Cemetery, East Orange, Essex County.

CAVANAUGH, PATRICK Pvt, E, 8th NJ Inf, 2-25-1883. Holy Rood Cemetery, Morristown, Morris County.

CAVANAUGH, THOMAS Pvt, A, 17th NY Inf, 11-17-1901. Holy Sepulchre Cemetery, East Orange, Essex County.

CAVANESS, J.W. Corp, A, 37th AR Inf (CSA), [Captured 7-4-1863 at Helena, AR. Died of bowel inflammation.] 4-15-1864. Finn's Point National Cemetery, Pennsville, Salem County.

CAVENDISH, JAMES W. Pvt, C, 22nd VA Inf (CSA), [Captured 11-6-1863 at Droop Mountain, WV. Died of measles.] 4-15-1864. Finn's Point National Cemetery, Pennsville, Salem County.

CAVILEER, GILBERT H. 1928. St. Paul's Methodist Church Cemetery, Port Republic, Atlantic County.

CAVILEER, JOSEPH (see: Cavalier, Joseph) Fairview Cemetery, Westfield, Union County.

CAVILEER, SAMUEL H. (aka: Cavalier, Samuel) 2nd Lt, C, 4th NJ Inf, DoD Unknown. St. Paul's Methodist Church Cemetery, Port Republic, Atlantic County.

CAW*, FLEMING Pvt, A, 90th PA Inf, [Wounded 8-10-1862 at Rappahannock Station, VA.] 1-14-1915. Oddfellows Cemetery, Burlington, Burlington County.

Our Brothers Gone Before

CAWLEY, ABRAHAM (aka: Colley, Abraham) Pvt, H, 6th U.S. CT, 7-7-1915. Bethel AME Cemetery, Cookstown, Burlington County.
CAWLEY*, JAMES S. 2nd Lt, K, 38th NJ Inf, 9-13-1893. New Presbyterian Cemetery, Bound Brook, Somerset County.
CAWLEY, ROGER 1892. Bordentown/Old St. Mary's Catholic Cemetery, Bordentown, Burlington County.
CAWLEY, WILLIAM H. Sgt, G, 15th NJ Inf, DoD Unknown. Union Cemetery, Frenchtown, Hunterdon County.
CAWMAN, ALBERT C. Pvt, I, 9th NJ Inf, 11-23-1877. Bateman Memorial Cemetery, Newport, Cumberland County.
CAWMAN*, DAVIP P. Sgt, B, 2nd NJ Inf, 9-20-1901. Mount Prospect Cemetery, Neptune, Monmouth County.
CAWMAN, GEORGE Pvt, H, 24th NJ Inf, DoD Unknown. Mount Pleasant Cemetery, Millville, Cumberland County.
CAZIER, WILLIAM S. Sgt, E, 10th NJ Inf, [Died of diarrhea and pneumonia at Baltimore, MD.] 8-19-1864. Salem Cemetery, Pleasantville, Atlantic County.
CEARS, SAMUEL (see: Kears, Samuel) Mount Pleasant Cemetery, Millville, Cumberland County.
CEASE, WILLIAM Pvt, C, 31st NJ Inf, 1891. Phillipsburg Cemetery, Phillipsburg, Warren County.
CHACE, IRA CLARENCE Hosp Steward, U.S. Army, 1898. Arlington Cemetery, Kearny, Hudson County.
CHADWICK, ANDREW W. Pvt, F, 72nd NY Inf, 7-30-1910. Fairmount Cemetery, Newark, Essex County.
CHADWICK, DANIEL 2-6-1892. Mount Pleasant Cemetery, Newark, Essex County.
CHADWICK, JAMES Seaman, U.S. Navy, USS Lafayette, 11-5-1923. Evergreen Cemetery, Camden, Camden County.
CHADWICK, JOHN 9-29-1866. Mount Pleasant Cemetery, Newark, Essex County.
CHADWICK, JOHN Pvt, F, 45th PA Militia, 10-14-1906. Mount Pleasant Cemetery, Newark, Essex County.
CHADWICK, JOHN J. Pvt, H, 190th PA Inf, 1-4-1915. Presbyterian Cemetery, Waretown, Ocean County.
CHADWICK*, JOSEPH A. Actg Ensign, U.S. Navy, USS Banshee, 2-26-1890. United Methodist Church Cemetery, Little Silver, Monmouth County.
CHADWICK*, JOSEPH P. Sgt, G, 14th NJ Inf, 11-10-1910. Greengrove Cemetery, Keyport, Monmouth County.
CHADWICK*, JOSEPH PARKER Pvt, H, 190th PA Inf, 4-24-1914. Fairview Cemetery, Fairview, Monmouth County.
CHADWICK, LEONARD A. (SR.) Pvt, I, 2nd NJ Inf, 10-6-1896. Holy Sepulchre Cemetery, Totowa, Passaic County.
CHADWICK, RICHARD H. Pvt, G, 27th MI Inf, 8-16-1881. Fairview Cemetery, Fairview, Monmouth County.
CHADWICK, SAMUEL Lt Col, 13th NJ Inf 1914. Mount Pleasant Cemetery, Newark, Essex County.
CHADWICK, TABER Fireman, U.S. Navy, USS Octorara, 1-27-1912. Greenlawn Cemetery, West Long Branch, Monmouth County.
CHADWICK, THOMAS Pvt, A, 7th PA Cav, 3-24-1911. Riverview Cemetery, Trenton, Mercer County.
CHADWICK*, WILLIAM H. Pvt, E, 33rd NJ Inf, 11-3-1904. Fairmount Cemetery, Newark, Essex County.
CHAFEY, CHARLES P. Pvt, D, 9th NJ Inf, 9-9-1882. Baptist Church Cemetery, Jacobstown, Burlington County.
CHAFEY, EDMUND R. Corp, F, 14th NJ Inf, 9-28-1875. Zion Baptist Church Cemetery, New Egypt, Ocean County.

New Jersey Civil War Burials

CHAFFER, RICHARD D. (aka: Shaffer, Richard) Pvt, I, 21st NJ Inf, 9-24-1904. Bayview-New York Bay Cemetery, Jersey City, Hudson County.

CHAFFEY, ANTHONY Wagoner, H, 35th NJ Inf, 3-22-1901. Tennent Church Cemetery, Tennent, Monmouth County.

CHAFFEY, ANTHONY C. Corp, K, 14th NJ Inf, 7-10-1916. Arlington Cemetery, Kearny, Hudson County.

CHAFFIN, ROBERT C. Pvt, I, 44th GA Inf (CSA), [Wounded 6-26-1862 at Ellison's Mill, VA. Captured 5-10-1864 at Spotsylvania CH, VA. Died of diarrhea.] 3-1-1865. Finn's Point National Cemetery, Pennsville, Salem County.

CHALLENDER, CHARLES P. Corp, G, 11th NJ Inf, 7-4-1912. Jacobstown Masonic Cemetery, Jacobstown, Burlington County.

CHALLENDER, LEVI Pvt, E, 40th NJ Inf, 6-10-1908. Riverview Cemetery, Trenton, Mercer County.

CHALLENDER, SAMUEL Pvt, D, 23rd NJ Inf, 3-16-1909. Jacobstown Masonic Cemetery, Jacobstown, Burlington County.

CHALLINOR, WILLIAM Seaman, U.S. Navy, 4-3-1901. Laurel Grove Cemetery, Totowa, Passaic County.

CHALLIS, WILLIAM M. Pvt, A, 34th NJ Inf, 5-21-1892. Fairmount Cemetery, Newark, Essex County.

CHALMERS, ANDREW Sgt, E, 19th IL Inf, 11-19-1894. Rosedale Cemetery, Orange, Essex County.

CHALMERS*, HUGH 2nd Lt, E, 146th NY Inf, [Died of wounds received 6-2-1864 at Cold Harbor, VA. Also wounded 6-27-1862 at Gaines' Mill, VA.] 6-9-1864. Rosedale Cemetery, Orange, Essex County.

CHALMERS, MATTHEW Pvt, B, 148th NY Inf, 1893. Rosedale Cemetery, Orange, Essex County.

CHAMBERLAIN, ANDREW L. 1st Lt, Adj, 74th NY Inf 12-21-1920. Epworth Methodist Cemetery, Palmyra, Burlington County.

CHAMBERLAIN, BENJAMIN A. Pvt, G, 59th MA Inf, [Died of disease at Beverly, NJ.] 12-10-1864. Beverly National Cemetery, Edgewater Park, Burlington County.

CHAMBERLAIN, CHARLES P. 1st Lt, CS, 20th PA Cav 11-28-1899. Bayview-New York Bay Cemetery, Jersey City, Hudson County.

CHAMBERLAIN, EDMUND DEFOE Pvt, A, 1st MA Inf, 6-1-1891. Fairview Cemetery, Westfield, Union County.

CHAMBERLAIN, EDWARD 7-26-1892. Baptist Cemetery, Salem, Salem County.

CHAMBERLAIN, FREDERICK M. Pvt, B, 2nd NJ Cav, 1-21-1925. Calvary Cemetery, Cherry Hill, Camden County.

CHAMBERLAIN, GABRIEL Pvt, F, 14th NJ Inf, 11-17-1901. Riverside Cemetery, Toms River, Ocean County.

CHAMBERLAIN, GEORGE W. Pvt, K, 4th NJ Inf, 1929. Methodist-Episcopal Cemetery, Glendola, Monmouth County.

CHAMBERLAIN, HENRY A. Sgt, E, 17th KS Cav (CSA), 8-24-1915. Bayview-New York Bay Cemetery, Jersey City, Hudson County.

CHAMBERLAIN, HENRY H. Pvt, E, 1st NJ Cav, 7-21-1918. Greenwood Cemetery, Hamilton, Mercer County.

CHAMBERLAIN, ISRAEL Corp, D, 40th NY Inf, 1-19-1885. Evergreen Cemetery, Hillside, Union County.

CHAMBERLAIN, JAMES B. Pvt, L, 1st NJ Cav, 1877. Baptist Church Cemetery, Jacobstown, Burlington County.

CHAMBERLAIN, JAMES M. Pvt, G, 3rd NJ Cav, 8-29-1913. Zion United Methodist Church Cemetery, Dividing Creek, Cumberland County.

CHAMBERLAIN, JOHN Pvt, A, 27th NY Inf, 3-27-1863. Fairmount Cemetery, Newark, Essex County.

Our Brothers Gone Before

CHAMBERLAIN, JOSEPH R. Pvt, G, 1st NJ Cav, 6-20-1882. Presbyterian Church Cemetery, Oak Ridge, Passaic County.
CHAMBERLAIN, JOSIAH Pvt, I, 5th NJ Inf, DoD Unknown. Methodist-Episcopal Church Cemetery, Medford, Burlington County.
CHAMBERLAIN, MARK Pvt, A, 12th NJ Inf, 12-9-1897. Maplewood Cemetery, Freehold, Monmouth County.
CHAMBERLAIN, REUBEN Pvt, F, 14th NJ Inf, 1-16-1908. Methodist Church Cemetery, Juliustown, Burlington County.
CHAMBERLAIN, REUBEN Pvt, E, 34th NJ Inf, 8-25-1886. Greenwood Cemetery, Hamilton, Mercer County.
CHAMBERLAIN, THOMAS Pvt, K, 12th NJ Inf, 11-14-1930. Cedar Lawn Cemetery, Paterson, Passaic County.
CHAMBERLAIN, WILLIAM Pvt, C, 93rd PA Inf, 9-28-1930. Baptist Cemetery, Vincentown, Burlington County.
CHAMBERLAIN, WILLIAM CONNER 7-6-1930. Hillside Cemetery, Scotch Plains, Union County.
CHAMBERLAIN, WILLIAM J. Pvt, D, 5th NJ Inf, 5-29-1906. Greenwood Cemetery, Hamilton, Mercer County.
CHAMBERLAIN, WYCKOFF (see: Carrigan, Wyckoff P.) Evergreen Cemetery, New Brunswick, Middlesex County.
CHAMBERLIN, ALFRED Sgt, B, 28th NJ Inf, [Wounded in action.] 3-9-1922. Brainerd Cemetery, Cranbury, Middlesex County.
CHAMBERLIN, ENOS Pvt, K, 153rd PA Inf, 1917. Methodist-Episcopal Cemetery, Columbia, Warren County.
CHAMBERLIN, EZEKIEL A. Sgt, C, 29th NJ Inf, 1876. Cedar Hill Cemetery, Hightstown, Mercer County.
CHAMBERLIN, FREDERICK M. 3-29-1884. United Methodist Church Cemetery, Absecon, Atlantic County.
CHAMBERLIN, ISAAC Pvt, H, 21st NJ Inf, 3-4-1913. Union Cemetery, Frenchtown, Hunterdon County.
CHAMBERLIN, JOHN C. Pvt, I, 15th NJ Inf, 9-19-1926. Fairmount Cemetery, Newark, Essex County.
CHAMBERLIN, JOHN M. 7-24-1896. Christian Church Cemetery, Locktown, Hunterdon County.
CHAMBERLIN*, THOMAS M. Corp, D, 33rd NJ Inf, [Wounded in action.] 1911. Maplewood Cemetery, Freehold, Monmouth County.
CHAMBERLIN, WILLIAM H. Pvt, H, 15th NJ Inf, 1-13-1900. Methodist Church Cemetery, Asbury, Warren County.
CHAMBERS, ALONZO Pvt, A, 38th NJ Inf, 1-22-1942. Riverside Cemetery, Toms River, Ocean County.
CHAMBERS, ANDERSON L. Pvt, B, 29th NJ Inf, 12-24-1885. Greengrove Cemetery, Keyport, Monmouth County.
CHAMBERS, ANDREW J. Pvt, E, 23rd NJ Inf, 7-2-1912. Columbus Cemetery, Columbus, Burlington County.
CHAMBERS, BENJAMIN Pvt, E, 25th U.S. CT, 12-17-1901. Bethel AME Cemetery, Cookstown, Burlington County.
CHAMBERS, BENJAMIN B. Pvt, F, 2nd NJ Cav, 7-28-1896. Baptist Cemetery, Pemberton, Burlington County.
CHAMBERS*, BENJAMIN L. Pvt, C, 2nd NJ Cav, 7-30-1893. United Methodist Church Cemetery, Little Silver, Monmouth County.
CHAMBERS, CHARLES Pvt, G, 25th U.S. CT, 9-17-1903. Mount Zion Methodist Church Cemetery, Lawnside, Camden County.
CHAMBERS, CHARLES H. Pvt, E, 23rd NJ Inf, 5-20-1897. Baptist Cemetery, Pemberton, Burlington County.

New Jersey Civil War Burials

CHAMBERS, CHARLES H. 4-23-1909. Riverview Cemetery, Trenton, Mercer County.

CHAMBERS, DANIEL Pvt, F, 25th NJ Inf, 2-21-1921. Methodist Church Cemetery, Eldora, Cape May County.

CHAMBERS, DANIEL (see: Chambers, David L.) Holy Sepulchre Cemetery, East Orange, Essex County.

CHAMBERS, DANIEL T. Pvt, I, 25th NJ Inf, 12-19-1900. Asbury Methodist-Episcopal Church Cemetery, Swainton, Cape May County.

CHAMBERS, DAVID L. (aka: Chambers, Daniel) Hosp Steward, M, 1st NY Mounted Rifles, 7-28-1887. Holy Sepulchre Cemetery, East Orange, Essex County.

CHAMBERS, EDWARD 7-16-1897. Mount Pleasant Cemetery, Newark, Essex County.

CHAMBERS, ELIAS A. Pvt, I, 38th NJ Inf, 11-23-1896. Cedar Grove Cemetery, Waretown, Ocean County.

CHAMBERS, GEORGE W. Pvt, D, 15th NJ Inf, 5-2-1907. Fairmount Cemetery, Newark, Essex County.

CHAMBERS, GERSHOM L. Pvt, E, 21st NJ Inf, 7-27-1888. Methodist Church Cemetery, Groveville, Mercer County.

CHAMBERS, HENRY W. Corp, B, 11th MS Inf (CSA), 9-21-1863. Finn's Point National Cemetery, Pennsville, Salem County.

CHAMBERS, ISAAC R. Pvt, E, 21st NJ Inf, 8-4-1898. Greenwood Cemetery, Hamilton, Mercer County.

CHAMBERS*, JAMES F. Pvt, K, 38th NJ Inf, 11-15-1897. Methodist Church Cemetery, Goshen, Cape May County.

CHAMBERS, JAMES T. 6-25-1878. Methodist Church Cemetery, Eldora, Cape May County.

CHAMBERS, JESSE Pvt, A, 6th NC Inf (CSA), [Wounded 7-1-1863 at Gettysburg, PA. Captured 7-4-1863 at South Mountain, MD.] 10-7-1863. Finn's Point National Cemetery, Pennsville, Salem County.

CHAMBERS, JOEL Pvt, F, 40th NJ Inf, 4-24-1919. Methodist Church Cemetery, Juliustown, Burlington County.

CHAMBERS, JOHN Pvt, I, 14th NJ Inf, 1925. Greenwood Cemetery, Hamilton, Mercer County.

CHAMBERS, JOHN H. Corp, F, 25th NJ Inf, [Wounded in action.] 11-4-1918. Methodist Church Cemetery, Eldora, Cape May County.

CHAMBERS, JOHN R. Pvt, F, 8th FL Inf (CSA), [Captured 7-5-1863 at Hillstown, PA. Died of diarrhea.] 5-10-1864. Finn's Point National Cemetery, Pennsville, Salem County.

CHAMBERS, JOHN S. Pvt, A, PA Emerg NJ Militia, 2-20-1911. Fairmount Cemetery, Newark, Essex County.

CHAMBERS, JOHN S. 2-24-1901. Presbyterian Church Cemetery, Ewing, Mercer County.

CHAMBERS, LEWIS Pvt, H, 40th NJ Inf, DoD Unknown. Baptist Cemetery, Pemberton, Burlington County.

CHAMBERS, LUCIUS Pvt, K, 12th SC Inf (CSA), 4-28-1910. Tabernacle Baptist Church Cemetery, Erma, Cape May County.

CHAMBERS, NEWMAN C. Pvt, D, 3rd NJ Inf, 7-23-1884. Presbyterian Church Cemetery, Newton, Sussex County.

CHAMBERS, ROBERT B. Pvt, D, 15th NJ Inf, [Died at Fort Schuyler, NY. of wounds received 6-1-1864 at Cold Harbor, VA.] 6-28-1864. Presbyterian Church Cemetery, Andover, Sussex County.

CHAMBERS, THOMAS Pvt, G, 6th U.S. CT, 7-17-1907. St. John's AME Cemetery, Chesilhurst, Camden County.

CHAMBERS*, WILLIAM Pvt, H, 13th MD Inf, 1-21-1901. Riverview Cemetery, Trenton, Mercer County.

Our Brothers Gone Before

CHAMBERS, WILLIAM Pvt, D, 3rd NJ Inf, 7-17-1901. Presbyterian Church Cemetery, Andover, Sussex County.
CHAMBERS, WILLIAM CLARK Landsman, U.S. Navy, USS Vermont, 6-20-1866. Cedar Grove Cemetery, Waretown, Ocean County.
CHAMBERS*, WILLIAM H. Landsman, U.S. Navy, USS North Carolina, 7-11-1923. Greengrove Cemetery, Keyport, Monmouth County.
CHAMBERS, WILSON M. Pvt, F, 22nd NJ Inf, [Died of typhoid at Belle Plain, VA.] 2-24-1863. Presbyterian Church Cemetery, Titusville, Mercer County.
CHAMBRE, HERBERT B. Asst Surg, 14th NJ Inf 8-13-1881. Chestnut Cemetery, Dover, Morris County.
CHAMPION, BENJAMIN O. Sgt, A, 72nd PA Inf, 5-10-1891. Mount Pleasant Cemetery, Millville, Cumberland County.
CHAMPION, ELIAS H. 2-23-1892. Cedar Green Cemetery, Clayton, Gloucester County.
CHAMPION, EZRA Pvt, G, 3rd NJ Cav, 1929. Mount Pleasant Cemetery, Millville, Cumberland County.
CHAMPION, JOHN Pvt, C, 61st PA Inf, 12-2-1887. Asbury United Methodist Church Cemetery, English Creek, Atlantic County.
CHAMPION, JOHN C. Pvt, I, 12th NJ Inf, 10-11-1863. Free Burying Ground Cemetery, Alloway, Salem County.
CHAMPION, JOHN G. Pvt, A, 20th U.S. CT, 10-26-1906. Evergreen Cemetery, Hillside, Union County.
CHAMPION, JOSEPH G. Pvt, C, 24th NJ Inf, 2-3-1878. Baptist Cemetery, Salem, Salem County.
CHAMPION, NATHAN (see: Champion, Nathaniel) Calvary Baptist Church Cemetery, Ocean View, Cape May County.
CHAMPION, NATHANIEL (aka: Champion, Nathan) Pvt, C, 38th NJ Inf, 4-19-1887. Calvary Baptist Church Cemetery, Ocean View, Cape May County.
CHAMPION, NICHOLAS S. Sgt, D, 9th NJ Inf, 12-28-1911. Atlantic City Cemetery, Pleasantville, Atlantic County.
CHAMPION, RICHARD Pvt, B, 2nd NJ Inf, 1930. Soldier's Home Cemetery, Vineland, Cumberland County.
CHAMPION, RICHARD C. Pvt, D, 55th NC Inf (CSA), [Wounded 7-1-1863 at Gettysburg, PA.] 10-31-1863. Finn's Point National Cemetery, Pennsville, Salem County.
CHAMPION, SOMERS T. Capt, B, 25th NJ Inf, 12-12-1924. Bay View Cemetery, Leonardo, Monmouth County.
CHAMPION, THOMAS S. Sgt, I, 12th NJ Inf, [Wounded 5-6-1864 at Wilderness, VA.] 1-30-1903. Mount Pleasant Cemetery, Millville, Cumberland County.
CHAMPION, WILLIAM H. 2nd Lt, I, 5th NJ Inf, 7-22-1898. Evergreen Cemetery, Camden, Camden County.
CHAMPLIN, ELIJAH B. Sgt, G, 61st NY Inf, [Died of disease.] 8-25-1862. Fairmount Cemetery, Newark, Essex County.
CHAMPLIN, HARRY W. Corp, H, 30th NJ Inf, 1-26-1918. Arlington Cemetery, Kearny, Hudson County.
CHANCE, CHARLES Pvt, E, 23rd NJ Inf, 12-3-1887. Columbus Cemetery, Columbus, Burlington County.
CHANCE, SPENCER 2-15-1871. Old Camden Cemetery, Camden, Camden County.
CHANCELLOR, THEODORE Landsman, U.S. Navy, USS Wyalusing, 1901. English Neighborhood Reformed Church Cemetery, Ridgefield, Bergen County.
CHANCY, CARY ALEXANDER Pvt, Charlottesville Btty, VA Light Art (CSA), [Captured 5-12-1864 at Spotsylvania CH, VA. Died of colic.] 11-10-1864. Finn's Point National Cemetery, Pennsville, Salem County.
CHANDLER, CORNELIUS V.W. Pvt, E, 47th NY State Militia, 10-31-1916. 1st Reformed Church Cemetery, Pompton Plains, Morris County.

New Jersey Civil War Burials

CHANDLER, DAVID M. Sgt, E, 1st NY Eng, 11-13-1913. Siloam Cemetery, Vineland, Cumberland County.

CHANDLER, DAVID W. Pvt, K, 8th MA Militia, 5-14-1898. New Presbyterian Cemetery, Bound Brook, Somerset County.

CHANDLER, EDWIN V. 5-25-1904. Evergreen Cemetery, Camden, Camden County.

CHANDLER, GEORGE C. Pvt, E, 39th NJ Inf, 4-12-1927. Prospect Hill Cemetery, Caldwell, Essex County.

CHANDLER, HENRY W. Pvt, K, 8th NJ Inf, 2-26-1932. Macphelah Cemetery, North Bergen, Hudson County.

CHANDLER, JAMES 11-4-1897. 1st Reformed Church Cemetery, Pompton Plains, Morris County.

CHANDLER*, JOHN QM Sgt, 2nd NJ Cav 10-5-1902. Union Cemetery, Frenchtown, Hunterdon County.

CHANDLER*, JOHN W. Pvt, H, 2nd NJ Inf, [Wounded in action.] 12-30-1917. Fairmount Cemetery, Newark, Essex County.

CHANDLER*, JOHN WESLEY 2nd Lt, A, 103rd NY Inf, 2-24-1923. Fairview Cemetery, Fairview, Monmouth County.

CHANDLER, JOSHUA G. Pvt, K, 27th PA Militia, 1-30-1898. Fairmount Cemetery, Newark, Essex County.

CHANDLER, LEWIS O. Pvt, F, 29th NJ Inf, 10-1-1926. Fairview Cemetery, Fairview, Monmouth County.

CHANDLER, NATHAN W. 1st Lt, H, 109th NY Inf, [Wounded 6-17-1864 at Petersburg, VA.] 1-10-1917. Evergreen Cemetery, Hillside, Union County.

CHANDLER, NATHANIEL Pvt, L, 1st IA Cav, 8-9-1896. Mount Pleasant Cemetery, Newark, Essex County.

CHANDLER, PETER Y. Pvt, E, 31st NJ Inf, 7-13-1928. Presbyterian Church Cemetery, Hampton, Hunterdon County.

CHANDLER, RICHARD N. Pvt, E, 10th Confederate States Cav (CSA), 3-23-1865. Finn's Point National Cemetery, Pennsville, Salem County.

CHANDLER, WALTER B. Pvt, E, 26th NJ Inf, 1909. Clinton Cemetery, Irvington, Essex County.

CHANDLER, WILLIAM D. Pvt, A, 8th NJ Inf, 4-3-1901. Laurel Grove Cemetery, Totowa, Passaic County.

CHANDLER, WILLIAM H. 12-12-1926. Fairview Cemetery, Fairview, Monmouth County.

CHANDLESS, CHARLES J. Corp, 20th NY Ind Btty 9-28-1922. Weehawken Cemetery, North Bergen, Hudson County.

CHANEY, WILLIAM Pvt, H, 3rd NJ Inf, 12-1-1862. Baptist/St. Andrew's Cemetery, Mount Holly, Burlington County.

CHANGEY, BARTHOLOMEW Seaman, U.S. Navy, 1-24-1889. Presbyterian Church Cemetery, Bridgeton, Cumberland County.

CHANNELL, WILLIAM A. Pvt, G, 4th NJ Inf, 4-10-1896. Mount Pleasant Methodist Cemetery, Pleasantville, Atlantic County.

CHAPLIN, ALFRED H. Fireman, U.S. Navy, USS Ohio, 6-3-1918. Hoboken Cemetery, North Bergen, Hudson County.

CHAPMAN, ALEXANDER Pvt, K, 5th NJ Inf, [Died at Freehold, NJ. of wounds received at Williamsburg, VA.] 7-5-1862. Adelphia Cemetery, Adelphia, Monmouth County.

CHAPMAN, ALEXANDER Corp, D, 70th NY Inf, 11-15-1870. Fairmount Cemetery, Newark, Essex County.

CHAPMAN, ARTHUR Pvt, E, 17th MI Inf, DoD Unknown. Evergreen Cemetery, Morristown, Morris County.

CHAPMAN, CHARLES Pvt, G, 56th NY Inf, 10-6-1874. Holy Sepulchre Cemetery, East Orange, Essex County.

Our Brothers Gone Before

CHAPMAN, CHARLES E. Pvt, I, 33rd NY Inf, [Died of typhoid at Newark, NJ.] 9-5-1862. Fairmount Cemetery, Newark, Essex County.
CHAPMAN, CHARLES H. Pvt, I, 33rd NJ Inf, 12-1-1920. Evergreen/Bishop Jaynes Cemetery, Basking Ridge, Somerset County.
CHAPMAN, CHARLES T. Pvt, B, 38th NJ Inf, 6-3-1889. New Somerville Cemetery, Somerville, Somerset County.
CHAPMAN, EDWARD DoD Unknown. Timbuctoo Cemetery, Timbuctoo, Burlington County.
CHAPMAN, EDWARD B. Pvt, G, 22nd U.S. CT, 8-2-1882. Colored Cemetery, Lumberton, Burlington County.
CHAPMAN, FRANK Pvt, D, 2nd NJ Inf, 12-9-1893. Fairmount Cemetery, Newark, Essex County.
CHAPMAN, FREDERICK Seaman, U.S. Navy, 1863. Whitehall Cemetery, Towaco, Morris County.
CHAPMAN, GEORGE W. Corp, B, 33rd NJ Inf, 10-27-1926. Rosedale Cemetery, Linden, Union County.
CHAPMAN*, HENRY C. Pvt, G, 61st NY Inf, [Wounded 6-1-1862 at Fair Oaks, VA.] 3-22-1906. Fairmount Cemetery, Newark, Essex County.
CHAPMAN, HIRAM Pvt, E, 93rd NY Inf, [Died of disease at Newark, NJ.] 9-6-1862. Fairmount Cemetery, Newark, Essex County.
CHAPMAN, JAMES Pvt, C, 97th NY Inf, [Died of disease at Newark, NJ.] 7-4-1863. Fairmount Cemetery, Newark, Essex County.
CHAPMAN, JOHN Corp, A, 24th NJ Inf, 4-13-1904. Presbyterian Church Cemetery, Bridgeton, Cumberland County.
CHAPMAN, JOSEPH 1912. Riverview Cemetery, Trenton, Mercer County.
CHAPMAN, MATTHEW Corp, B, 14th NJ Inf, 12-14-1900. Riverview Cemetery, Trenton, Mercer County.
CHAPMAN, THOMAS L. Pvt, A, 6th U.S. Cav, 1914. Prospect Hill Cemetery, Caldwell, Essex County.
CHAPMAN, WILLIAM G. Pvt, E, 56th PA Militia, 3-26-1915. Presbyterian Church Cemetery, Hamilton Square, Mercer County.
CHAPMAN, WILLIAM O. Pvt, K, 35th NJ Inf, 8-19-1900. Arlington Cemetery, Kearny, Hudson County.
CHAPMAN, WILLIAM W. 1st Lt, K, 51st NY Inf, 3-29-1865. Rahway Cemetery, Rahway, Union County.
CHAPMOND, W.J. Pvt, Page's Btty, VA Light Art (CSA), 9-13-1863. Finn's Point National Cemetery, Pennsville, Salem County.
CHAPPEL, JAMES 2-7-1887. Van Liew Cemetery, North Brunswick, Middlesex County.
CHAPPELL, HENRY Pvt, D, 1st NJ Cav, 12-30-1910. Riverview Cemetery, Trenton, Mercer County.
CHARAKER, JOSEPH Pvt, D, PA Emerg NJ Militia, 3-21-1890. Mount Hope Presbyterian Cemetery, Lambertville, Hunterdon County.
CHARAKER, MICHAEL Pvt, D, PA Emerg NJ Militia, 12-14-1889. Mount Hope Presbyterian Cemetery, Lambertville, Hunterdon County.
CHARDAVOYNE, AUGUSTA DoD Unknown. Cedar Lawn Cemetery, Paterson, Passaic County.
CHARDAVOYNE, STEPHEN R. Pvt, C, 2nd NJ Inf, [Died of typhoid at Hagerstown, MD.] 12-3-1862. Laurel Grove Cemetery, Totowa, Passaic County.
CHARLES, JOHN C. Corp, F, 1st NJ Cav, DoD Unknown. Phillipsburg Cemetery, Phillipsburg, Warren County.
CHARLES, MILTON Pvt, Btty C, 5th U.S. Art, DoD Unknown. Phillipsburg Cemetery, Phillipsburg, Warren County.
CHARLTON, JOHN Pvt, H, 11th NY Cav, 8-18-1918. Greenwood Cemetery, Boonton, Morris County.

New Jersey Civil War Burials

CHARLTON, JOSEPH A. Pvt, 4th NY Ind Btty DoD Unknown. Fernwood Cemetery, Jamesburg, Middlesex County.

CHARTREE, MITCHELL Pvt, B, 29th NJ Inf, 12-23-1907. Cedarwood Cemetery, Hazlet, Monmouth County.

CHASE, DANIEL Musc, A, 62nd NY Inf, 1898. Holy Sepulchre Cemetery, Totowa, Passaic County.

CHASE, HENRY E. Pvt, C, 3rd VT Inf, [Died of disease.] 8-24-1862. Fairmount Cemetery, Newark, Essex County.

CHASE, JOHN H. Pvt, E, 34th NJ Inf, DoD Unknown. Cedar Green Cemetery, Clayton, Gloucester County.

CHASE, LEVI Maj, 1st IA Cav 5-30-1906. Evergreen Cemetery, Morristown, Morris County.

CHASE, N.D. Pvt, D, 60th (Crawford's) TN Mtd Inf (CSA), [Captured 5-17-1863 at Big Black River Bridge, MS.] 8-26-1863. Finn's Point National Cemetery, Pennsville, Salem County.

CHASE, PETER P. Corp, A, 57th NY Inf, 2-27-1921. Bayview-New York Bay Cemetery, Jersey City, Hudson County.

CHASE*, SAMUEL W. Pvt, Btty K, 11th U.S. CHA, 3-21-1928. Oddfellows Cemetery, Burlington, Burlington County.

CHASEY, EDWARD A. Pvt, G, 34th NJ Inf, [Died of brain inflammation at Eastport, MS.] 1-31-1865. Greenwood Cemetery, Hamilton, Mercer County.

CHASEY, WILLIAM A. Sgt, C, 37th NJ Inf, [Died of debility at Hampton, VA.] 9-8-1864. Greenwood Cemetery, Hamilton, Mercer County.

CHATTEN, CHARLES Sgt, I, 38th NJ Inf, 10-31-1912. Highland Cemetery, Hopewell Boro, Mercer County.

CHATTEN, SMITH H. Pvt, D, 3rd NJ Militia, 12-28-1918. Christ Church Cemetery, Morgan, Middlesex County.

CHATTEN, WILLIAM B. Pvt, A, 38th VA Inf (CSA), [Wounded 7-3-1863 and captured 7-4-1863 at Gettysburg, PA. Died of variola.] 8-24-1863. Finn's Point National Cemetery, Pennsville, Salem County.

CHATTERTON, ENOCH Pvt, K, 1st NY Marine Art, 12-9-1921. Fairmount Cemetery, Newark, Essex County.

CHATTIN, WILLIAM WOOD Musc, E, 10th NJ Inf, 2-25-1895. Greenwood Cemetery, Tuckerton, Ocean County.

CHATTLE, THOMAS G. 10-20-1869. Old 1st Methodist Church Cemetery, West Long Branch, Monmouth County.

CHAZOTTE, ADOLPHUS T. 2nd Lt, F, 7th NJ Inf, [Killed in action at Seven Pines, VA.] 6-25-1862. Bayview-New York Bay Cemetery, Jersey City, Hudson County.

CHEATHAM, WILLIAM T. Pvt, D, 38th NY Inf, [Wounded 12-13-1862 at Fredericksburg, VA.] 10- -1875. Bayview-New York Bay Cemetery, Jersey City, Hudson County.

CHEATTLE, RUSSELL DoD Unknown. Riverview Cemetery, Trenton, Mercer County.

CHEDISTER, JOHN WESLEY (aka: Chiddester, J.W.) 1st Sgt, K, 1st NY Eng, 8-13-1921. Rosedale Cemetery, Orange, Essex County.

CHEESEMAN, ALFRED J. Pvt, C, 24th NJ Inf, 6-21-1873. United Methodist Church Cemetery, Alloway, Salem County.

CHEESEMAN, AUGUSTUS B. Pvt, K, 14th NJ Inf, 12-22-1890. Willow Grove Cemetery, New Brunswick, Middlesex County.

CHEESEMAN, CHALKEY Pvt, B, 58th PA Inf, DoD Unknown. Union Cemetery, Gloucester City, Camden County.

CHEESEMAN, CLINTON F. Sgt, K, 2nd NJ Cav, 8-10-1895. United Methodist Church Cemetery, Alloway, Salem County.

CHEESEMAN, DANIEL N. Pvt, H, 35th NJ Inf, 5-10-1888. Presbyterian Church Cemetery, Mays Landing, Atlantic County.

Our Brothers Gone Before

CHEESEMAN, GEORGE W. Pvt, A, MD Emerg NJ Militia, 10-17-1912. Cedar Grove Cemetery, Gloucester City, Camden County.
CHEESEMAN, GEORGE W. DoD Unknown. Phillipsburg Cemetery, Phillipsburg, Warren County.
CHEESEMAN, HENRY Pvt, I, 38th NJ Inf, 12-17-1914. Riverview Cemetery, Trenton, Mercer County.
CHEESEMAN, HIRAM Pvt, I, 38th NJ Inf, 7-25-1908. Riverview Cemetery, Trenton, Mercer County.
CHEESEMAN, JAMES Landsman, U.S. Navy, USS Atlanta, 11-13-1911. Arlington Cemetery, Kearny, Hudson County.
CHEESEMAN, JOHN Pvt, G, 6th NJ Inf, 4-7-1910. Cedar Grove Cemetery, Gloucester City, Camden County.
CHEESEMAN, JOHN F. Pvt, A, 23rd NJ Inf, 5-6-1877. Methodist-Episcopal Cemetery, Burlington, Burlington County.
CHEESEMAN, JOSEPH Pvt, K, 6th NJ Inf, 11-1-1891. Cedar Grove Cemetery, Gloucester City, Camden County.
CHEESEMAN, JOSEPH K. Pvt, K, 24th NJ Inf, 6-12-1913. Methodist-Episcopal Church Cemetery, Penns Grove, Salem County.
CHEESEMAN, PETER T. Pvt, A, 10th NJ Inf, 3-28-1910. Methodist-Episcopal Church Cemetery, Magnolia, Camden County.
CHEESEMAN, RICHARD Musc, G, 12th NJ Inf, 3-14-1913. Cedar Grove Cemetery, Gloucester City, Camden County.
CHEESEMAN, THEODORE 1902. Berlin Cemetery, Berlin, Camden County.
CHEESEMAN, THOMAS Pvt, G, 34th NJ Inf, DoD Unknown. Union Cemetery, Gloucester City, Camden County.
CHEESEMAN, THOMAS J. Pvt, I, 25th NJ Inf, DoD Unknown. Old Camden Cemetery, Camden, Camden County.
CHEESEMAN, WILLIAM Pvt, G, 23rd NJ Inf, 10-28-1904. Monument Cemetery, Edgewater Park, Burlington County.
CHEESEMAN, WILLIAM Pvt, I, 38th NJ Inf, 7-3-1911. Riverview Cemetery, Trenton, Mercer County.
CHEESEMAN, WILLIAM H. Pvt, I, 68th PA Inf, 1-2-1883. Fairmount Cemetery, Newark, Essex County.
CHEESMAN, DAVID AUGUSTUS Seaman, U.S. Navy, 10-17-1911. Washington Monumental Cemetery, South River, Middlesex County.
CHEESMAN*, HUGH L. Pvt, F, 1st U.S. Hancock Corps, 4-25-1888. Evergreen Cemetery, Camden, Camden County.
CHEESMAN, JAMES R. Pvt, H, 24th NJ Inf, 1926. Presbyterian Church Cemetery, Bridgeton, Cumberland County.
CHEESMAN, THOMAS J. Pvt, E, 3rd NJ Inf, [Wounded 9-14-1862 at Crampton's Pass, MD.] 3-21-1878. Evergreen Cemetery, Camden, Camden County.
CHEETHAM, CHARLES 1918. Siloam Cemetery, Vineland, Cumberland County.
CHEEVER, GEORGE A. Pvt, E, 32nd MA Inf, [Wounded 7-2-1863 at Gettysburg, PA.] 4-28-1907. Oak Hill Cemetery, Vineland, Cumberland County.
CHEEVERS, JOHN W. 4-19-1917. Fairview Cemetery, Fairview, Bergen County.
CHENEY, ANDREW Pvt, B, 19th WI Inf, 10-24-1877. Fairmount Cemetery, Newark, Essex County.
CHENOWETH, EPHRIAM Seaman, U.S. Navy, 8-29-1917. Evergreen Cemetery, Hillside, Union County.
CHERRY, GEORGE H. Pvt, C, 4th NJ Inf, [Wounded 9-14-1862 at Crampton's Pass, MD.] 9-9-1903. Riverview Cemetery, Trenton, Mercer County.
CHERRY*, JAMES C. Pvt, H, 61st VA Inf (CSA), [Died of diarrhea.] 8-24-1863. Finn's Point National Cemetery, Pennsville, Salem County.

New Jersey Civil War Burials

CHERRY, JOHN Pvt, B, 37th NY State Militia, 9-30-1923. Calvary Cemetery, Cherry Hill, Camden County.
CHERRY, NOAH Pvt, H, 36th U.S. CT, 3-17-1907. Devane's Cemetery, Burleigh, Cape May County.
CHERRY, WILLIAM Sgt, A, 26th NJ Inf, 3-18-1890. Fairmount Cemetery, Newark, Essex County.
CHERRY, WILLIAM M. 1st Lt, E, 1st NC Inf (US), DoD Unknown. Mount Prospect Cemetery, Neptune, Monmouth County.
CHESHIRE, JONAS W. (JR.) Sgt, C, 131st NY Inf, [Wounded 9-19-1864 at Opequan, VA.] DoD Unknown. Locust Hill Cemetery, Dover, Morris County.
CHESNEY, WILLIAM A. Pvt, E, 48th MS Inf (CSA), 9-5-1864. Finn's Point National Cemetery, Pennsville, Salem County.
CHESTER, GEORGE M. Sgt, G, 24th NJ Inf, 12-16-1903. Methodist Church Cemetery, Haleyville, Cumberland County.
CHESTER, JAMES Pvt, I, 25th NJ Inf, 5-22-1906. Methodist Church Cemetery, Goshen, Cape May County.
CHESTER, JAMES D. Corp, K, 4th NJ Inf, 1-6-1902. Evergreen Cemetery, Camden, Camden County.
CHESTER, JOSEPH C. 1929. 1st Baptist Cemetery, Cape May Court House, Cape May County.
CHESTER, REUBEN Pvt, K, 9th NJ Inf, 4-27-1865. Methodist Church Cemetery, Goshen, Cape May County.
CHESTER*, ROBERT M. Pvt, F, 2nd NJ Inf, 11-25-1925. Harleigh Cemetery, Camden, Camden County.
CHESTER, SAMUEL C. Pvt, A, 3rd NJ Inf, 1908. Methodist-Episcopal Cemetery, Glassboro, Gloucester County.
CHESTER, WILLIAM C. Corp, D, 48th NY Inf, 1913. Methodist-Episcopal Church Cemetery, Aura, Gloucester County.
CHETWOOD*, BRADBURY CHANDLER Lt Col, U.S. Army, [Assistant Inspector General.] 1-24-1916. Presbyterian Church Cemetery, Elizabeth, Union County.
CHEVANNE, HENRY (aka: Chevauney, Henry) Pvt, A, 1st NY Marine Art, 10-15-1912. Baptist Cemetery, Salem, Salem County.
CHEVAUNEY, HENRY (see: Chevanne, Henry) Baptist Cemetery, Salem, Salem County.
CHEW, ALBERT S. Seaman, U.S. Navy, DoD Unknown. Berlin Cemetery, Berlin, Camden County.
CHEW, ALONZO T. (aka: Chew, Alphonso) Corp, D, 24th NJ Inf, 10-22-1905. Eglington Cemetery, Clarksboro, Gloucester County.
CHEW, ALPHONSO (see: Chew, Alonzo T.) Eglington Cemetery, Clarksboro, Gloucester County.
CHEW, CHARLES W. Pvt, A, 5th DE Inf, 7-17-1914. Zion United Methodist Church Cemetery, Dividing Creek, Cumberland County.
CHEW, CHARLES W. Corp, G, 5th PA Cav, 5-31-1910. Manahath Cemetery, Glassboro, Gloucester County.
CHEW*, HENRY F. Maj, 12th NJ Inf 1910. Harleigh Cemetery, Camden, Camden County.
CHEW, ISRAEL E. Corp, B, 10th NJ Inf, DoD Unknown. St. Paul's Episcopal Cemetery, Atsion, Burlington County.
CHEW, JESSE C. Sgt, F, 58th PA Inf, 3-30-1911. Harleigh Cemetery, Camden, Camden County.
CHEW, LEWIS L. Pvt, E, 198th PA Inf, 4-11-1913. 1st Baptist Church Cemetery, Pedricktown, Salem County.
CHEW, MATTHIAS M. Musc, D, 24th NJ Inf, 1912. 1st Methodist Church Cemetery, Williamstown, Gloucester County.

Our Brothers Gone Before

CHEW, RICHARD Pvt, F, 34th NJ Inf, 11-16-1887. Fairmount Cemetery, Newark, Essex County.
CHEW, SINNOCKSON 6-26-1901. Evergreen Cemetery, Camden, Camden County.
CHEW, STEPHEN H. Pvt, H, 7th NJ Inf, 8-26-1920. Siloam Cemetery, Vineland, Cumberland County.
CHEW, WILLIAM H. Pvt, A, 9th NJ Inf, 10-11-1911. Methodist-Episcopal Cemetery, Glassboro, Gloucester County.
CHEW, WILLIAM H. (JR.) Pvt, D, 24th NJ Inf, 5-19-1915. Methodist Church Cemetery, Hurffville, Gloucester County.
CHEW, WILLIAM (JR.) Pvt, I, 24th NJ Inf, DoD Unknown. Oak Hill Cemetery, Vineland, Cumberland County.
CHEW, WILLIAM W. Coal Heaver, U.S. Navy, USS North Carolina, 1917. Chew Cemetery, Waterford, Camden County.
CHEWNING, A. Pvt, G, 18th VA Inf (CSA), 11-29-1863. Finn's Point National Cemetery, Pennsville, Salem County.
CHEWNING, B.F. Pvt, G, 18th VA Inf (CSA), 11-20-1863. Finn's Point National Cemetery, Pennsville, Salem County.
CHIDDESTER, J.W. (see: Chedister, John Wesley) Rosedale Cemetery, Orange, Essex County.
CHIDESTER*, DAVID N. Pvt, I, 2nd NJ Inf, 11-30-1934. Newton Cemetery, Newton, Sussex County.
CHIDESTER, GEORGE F. Pvt, H, 6th NJ Inf, 4-8-1896. Mount Hope Presbyterian Cemetery, Lambertville, Hunterdon County.
CHIDESTER*, JOHN H. Pvt, D, 38th NJ Inf, 10-23-1918. Mount Hope Presbyterian Cemetery, Lambertville, Hunterdon County.
CHILD, GARDNER D. Seaman, U.S. Navy, 10-23-1929. Arlington Cemetery, Kearny, Hudson County.
CHILD, JOSEPH WILLIAM 5-1-1900. Fairview Cemetery, Fairview, Monmouth County.
CHILDRESS, JAMES Pvt, E, 3rd AL Inf (CSA), 10-10-1863. Finn's Point National Cemetery, Pennsville, Salem County.
CHILDS, GEORGE H. Pvt, F, 38th NJ Inf, DoD Unknown. Arlington Cemetery, Kearny, Hudson County.
CHILDS, JOSHUA L. 1st Lt, C, 121st PA Inf, 10-29-1891. Evergreen Cemetery, Camden, Camden County.
CHILDS, ZADOC A. Pvt, I, 2nd NJ Cav, 5-7-1900. United Presbyterian Church Cemetery, Perrineville, Monmouth County.
CHILDS, ZENAS A. Pvt, I, 2nd NJ Cav, 3-26-1892. Methodist-Episcopal Church Cemetery, Clarksburg, Monmouth County.
CHILTON, THOMAS Fireman, U.S. Navy, USS Port Royal, DoD Unknown. 1st Baptist Church Cemetery, Trenton, Mercer County.
CHINERY, ISAAC H. Sgt, E, 71st NY State Militia, 3-22-1913. Cedarwood Cemetery, Hazlet, Monmouth County.
CHINOUTH, JAMES M. Pvt, E, 60th (Crawford's) TN Mtd Inf (CSA), [Captured 5-17-1863 at Big Black River Bridge, MS.] 7-13-1863. Finn's Point National Cemetery, Pennsville, Salem County.
CHIPMAN, CHARLES Sgt, G, 5th PA Cav, 7-14-1932. Manahath Cemetery, Glassboro, Gloucester County.
CHIPMAN*, THOMAS Pvt, I, 34th NJ Inf, 1-26-1916. Evergreen Cemetery, Camden, Camden County.
CHISHOLM, J.N. Capt, I, 9th AL Inf (CSA), 3-16-1865. Finn's Point National Cemetery, Pennsville, Salem County.
CHISHOLM, WILLIAM E. Pvt, B, 42nd MS Inf (CSA), 1-8-1864. Finn's Point National Cemetery, Pennsville, Salem County.

New Jersey Civil War Burials

CHISM, WILLIAM C. Pvt, C, 85th PA Inf, 4-15-1910. United Methodist Church Cemetery, Almonessen, Gloucester County.

CHISOM, GEORGE Seaman, U.S. Navy, 4-3-1911. Tabernacle Cemetery, Tabernacle, Burlington County.

CHISWELL, RICHARD 6-2-1869. Cedar Lawn Cemetery, Paterson, Passaic County.

CHITTENDEN*, OSWALD L. Corp, C, 156th NY Inf, 6-22-1894. Fairmount Cemetery, Newark, Essex County.

CHITTENDEN, WILLIAM J. Pvt, E, 13th IL Inf, 5-8-1914. Fairmount Cemetery, Newark, Essex County.

CHITTY, HENRY E. 2nd Lt, I, 10th CT Inf, [Wounded 12-14-1862 at Kingston, NC.] 7-24-1895. Cedar Lawn Cemetery, Paterson, Passaic County.

CHIVERAL, ALEXANDER Pvt, C, Purnell Legion MD Inf, 9-21-1863. Finn's Point National Cemetery, Pennsville, Salem County.

CHOLERTON, EDWARD Pvt, G, 109th PA Inf, 1893. Overlook Cemetery, Bridgeton, Cumberland County.

CHOLLHEPP, JOHN A. Pvt, F, 28th NJ Inf, 5-23-1896. St. Peter's Cemetery, New Brunswick, Middlesex County.

CHOYCE, RICHARD Corp, D, 31st NJ Inf, 8-14-1901. Presbyterian Church Cemetery, Flemington, Hunterdon County.

CHRISP, WILLIAM P. Pvt, I, 23rd VA Inf (CSA), [Captured 5-12-1864 at Spotsylvania CH, VA. Died of scurvy.] 1-4-1865. Finn's Point National Cemetery, Pennsville, Salem County.

CHRISPELL, PHILETUS L. Corp, C, 23rd NY Inf, [Wounded in action.] 12-5-1902. Presbyterian Church Cemetery, Andover, Sussex County.

CHRIST, GERTLER 7-8-1883. Riverside Cemetery, Riverside, Burlington County.

CHRIST, JOHN Pvt, A, 14th NY Cav, DoD Unknown. Madonna Cemetery, Leonia, Bergen County.

CHRISTIAN, CREISS (see: Kreis, Christian) Woodland Cemetery, Newark, Essex County.

CHRISTIAN, GEORGE T. Pvt, F, 4th GA Inf (CSA), [Wounded and captured 5-12-1864 at Spotsylvania CH, VA. Died of fever.] 9-1-1864. Finn's Point National Cemetery, Pennsville, Salem County.

CHRISTIAN, HENRY P. Pvt, F, 1st NJ Inf, 11-10-1895. Fairmount Cemetery, Newark, Essex County.

CHRISTIAN, JACK Pvt, B, 35th NJ Inf, 4-2-1881. Fairmount Cemetery, Newark, Essex County.

CHRISTIAN, LEVI Pvt, A, 3rd NJ Cav, DoD Unknown. Mount Pleasant Cemetery, Millville, Cumberland County.

CHRISTIE, ABRAM Pvt, E, 94th NY Inf, 1907. Ramapo Reformed Church Cemetery, Mahwah, Bergen County.

CHRISTIE, BENJAMIN Pvt, A, 22nd NJ Inf, 1-25-1917. Maple Grove Cemetery, Hackensack, Bergen County.

CHRISTIE, DANIEL (aka: Christy, Daniel) Corp, G, 13th NJ Inf, 7-10-1889. Fairmount Cemetery, Newark, Essex County.

CHRISTIE, DANIEL E. 1911. Maple Grove Cemetery, Hackensack, Bergen County.

CHRISTIE, ERASMUS Pvt, C, 22nd NJ Inf, 5-15-1901. Maple Grove Cemetery, Hackensack, Bergen County.

CHRISTIE*, HENRY C. Pvt, A, 6th NJ Inf, 1-8-1909. Laurel Grove Cemetery, Totowa, Passaic County.

CHRISTIE, JAMES Capt, K, 22nd NJ Inf, 11-26-1908. Maple Grove Cemetery, Hackensack, Bergen County.

CHRISTIE, JAMES A. 1-22-1878. Mount Pleasant Cemetery, Newark, Essex County.

CHRISTIE, JAMES J. Seaman, U.S. Navy, 1906. Riverside Cemetery, Riverside, Burlington County.

Our Brothers Gone Before

CHRISTIE, JAMES W. 1st Lt, H, 35th NJ Inf, DoD Unknown. St. Peter's Cemetery, New Brunswick, Middlesex County.

CHRISTIE, JOHN Pvt, G, 2nd CT Art, [Wounded 6-1-1864 at Cold Harbor, VA.] 1904. Maple Grove Cemetery, Hackensack, Bergen County.

CHRISTIE, JOHN Pvt, A, 22nd NJ Inf, 10-11-1889. Maple Grove Cemetery, Hackensack, Bergen County.

CHRISTIE, JOHN D. Corp, C, 22nd NJ Inf, 12-31-1889. Old South Church Cemetery, Bergenfield, Bergen County.

CHRISTIE, JOHN H. Musc, B, 40th NJ Inf, 1-21-1923. Stanhope-Union Cemetery, Netcong, Morris County.

CHRISTIE, JOHN HENRY Corp, K, 22nd NJ Inf, [Died of typhoid at Belle Plain, VA.] 3-29-1863. Maple Grove Cemetery, Hackensack, Bergen County.

CHRISTIE, JOHN S. Sgt, D, 8th NJ Inf, [Died of disease at Camp Parole Annapolis, MD.] 12-16-1864. Cedar Lawn Cemetery, Paterson, Passaic County.

CHRISTIE, WILLIAM 1874. Riverview Cemetery, Trenton, Mercer County.

CHRISTINE, HENRY G. Pvt, B, 1st NJ Cav, DoD Unknown. Mansfield/Washington Cemetery, Washington, Warren County.

CHRISTMAN, FREDERICK A. Pvt, G, 28th NJ Inf, 5-2-1890. Bethesda Methodist-Episcopal Church Cemetery, Swedesboro, Gloucester County.

CHRISTMANN, MICHAEL (aka: Kriegsmann, Michael) Pvt, B, 7th NY Inf, [Wounded 12-13-1862 at Fredericksburg, VA.] DoD Unknown. Laurel Grove Cemetery, Totowa, Passaic County.

CHRISTMAS, LEWIS Pvt, C, 29th U.S. CT, 8-27-1905. Mount Peace Cemetery, Lawnside, Camden County.

CHRISTOPH, THEODORE DoD Unknown. Mercer Cemetery, Trenton, Mercer County.

CHRISTOPHER, ERNEST DoD Unknown. Bethel Cemetery, Pennsauken, Camden County.

CHRISTOPHER, THOMAS J. Pvt, C, 6th U.S. Hancock Corps, 9-2-1887. Maplewood Cemetery, Freehold, Monmouth County.

CHRISTOPHER, WILLIAM J. Pvt, K, 42nd MS Inf (CSA), 2-12-1864. Finn's Point National Cemetery, Pennsville, Salem County.

CHRISTY, DANIEL (see: Christie, Daniel) Fairmount Cemetery, Newark, Essex County.

CHUBB, HENRY C. Seaman, U.S. Navy, 2-26-1927. Fairview Cemetery, Westfield, Union County.

CHUBBUCK, FRANCIS E.R. Chaplain, 31st MA Inf 1-2-1872. St Peter's Episcopal Church Cemetery, Mount Royal, Gloucester County.

CHUMAR, WILLIAM H. Corp, D, 4th NJ Inf, 2-28-1906. Riverview Cemetery, Trenton, Mercer County.

CHURCH, EDWIN H. Pvt, 10th MA Light Art 4-25-1910. New Camden Cemetery, Camden, Camden County.

CHURCH, HENRY B. Pvt, B, 190th PA Inf, 1931. Belvidere/Catholic Cemetery, Belvidere, Warren County.

CHURCH, JAMES P. Sgt, F, 4th OH Cav, 10-5-1920. Elmwood Cemetery, New Brunswick, Middlesex County.

CHURCH, RICHARD S. Pvt, E, 4th NJ Militia, 4-6-1921. Soldier's Home Cemetery, Vineland, Cumberland County.

CHURCH, SAMUEL S. (aka: Schurch, Samuel) Musc, D, 40th PA Militia, 8-12-1912. Wesley United Methodist Church Cemetery, Petersburg, Cape May County.

CHURCH, THEODORE Pvt, F, 25th NJ Inf, 9-26-1900. Tabernacle Baptist Church Cemetery, Erma, Cape May County.

CHURCH, WILLIAM D. 1904. Tennent Church Cemetery, Tennent, Monmouth County.

CHURCH, WILLIAM E. Pvt, B, 132nd NY Inf, 2-21-1924. Cedar Lawn Cemetery, Paterson, Passaic County.

New Jersey Civil War Burials

CHURCHWARD, GEORGE W. Pvt, D, 28th NJ Inf, [Wounded in action.] 8-7-1911. Elmwood Cemetery, New Brunswick, Middlesex County.

CHURCHWELL, SYLVESTER B. 2nd Lt, B, 49th NY Inf, [Wounded 5-10-1864 at Wilderness, VA.] 9-1-1897. Fairmount Cemetery, Newark, Essex County.

CIGLER, ANTHONY Pvt, A, 43rd U.S. CT, 3-10-1894. Bloomfield Cemetery, Bloomfield, Essex County.

CISCO, GEORGE (see: Sisco, George W.) St. Stephen's Cemetery, Millburn, Essex County.

CISCO, HERMAN (aka: Ciscoe, Harman) Pvt, E, 27th NJ Inf, 5-10-1890. Vail Presbyterian Cemetery, Parsippany, Morris County.

CISCO, JOHN (see: Sisco, John) Valleau Cemetery, Ridgewood, Bergen County.

CISCO, JOHN (see: Sisco, John E.) Brookside Cemetery, Englewood, Bergen County.

CISCO, LEWIS Pvt, I, 7th NJ Inf, 5-1-1882. Branchville Cemetery, Branchville, Sussex County.

CISCO*, ROBERT F. Pvt, F, 176th PA Inf, [Wounded in action.] 5-19-1895. Walpack Methodist Cemetery, Walpack, Sussex County.

CISCO, THOMAS (see: Sisco, Thomas) Gethsemane Cemetery, Little Ferry, Bergen County.

CISCO, WILLIAM H. Pvt, K, 80th NY Inf, 8-24-1925. 1st Reformed Church Cemetery, Pompton Plains, Morris County.

CISCOE, HARMAN (see: Cisco, Herman) Vail Presbyterian Cemetery, Parsippany, Morris County.

CITHCART*, STEPHEN Pvt, I, 4th NJ Inf, 1-7-1915. Brotherhood Cemetery, Hainesport, Burlington County.

CLADEK*, JOHN JULIUS Col, 35th NJ Inf 4-5-1884. Rahway Cemetery, Rahway, Union County.

CLAIR, CHARLES S. Pvt, D, 23rd NJ Inf, 1922. Columbus Cemetery, Columbus, Burlington County.

CLAIR, THEODORE R. Pvt, A, 23rd NJ Inf, 12-4-1898. St. Mary's Episcopal Church Cemetery, Burlington, Burlington County.

CLAIRVILLE, WILLIAM H. Pvt, Btty B, 1st NJ Light Art, 1-19-1910. Fairmount Cemetery, Newark, Essex County.

CLAMER, JOHN HENRY Seaman, U.S. Navy, USS Wabash, 10-8-1894. Evergreen Cemetery, Hillside, Union County.

CLANCEY, BARTLETT Pvt, F, 7th NJ Inf, 8-25-1893. Holy Name Cemetery, Jersey City, Hudson County.

CLARE, WILLIAM S. Corp, A, 3rd NJ Inf, 9-7-1891. Green Cemetery, Woodbury, Gloucester County.

CLAREY*, JOHN Corp, G, 8th NJ Inf, [Killed in action at Petersburg, VA.] 3-25-1865. Lady of Lourdes/Holy Sepulchre Cemetery, Hamilton, Mercer County.

CLARK, A. JUDSON Bvt Maj, Btty B, 1st NJ Light Art, 7-24-1913. Evergreen Cemetery, Hillside, Union County.

CLARK, A.M. Pvt, K, 7th MO Cav (CSA), 5-17-1864. Finn's Point National Cemetery, Pennsville, Salem County.

CLARK, AARON Pvt, D, 33rd NJ Inf, 6-6-1903. Fairmount Cemetery, Newark, Essex County.

CLARK, AARON B. Pvt, G, 25th NJ Inf, 4-14-1916. Trinity Methodist-Episcopal Church Cemetery, Marmora, Cape May County.

CLARK*, ALBERT H. Pvt, E, 84th NY Inf, 5-17-1907. Bayview-New York Bay Cemetery, Jersey City, Hudson County.

CLARK, ALEXANDER Musc, H, 35th NJ Inf, 8-3-1865. Old 1st Methodist Church Cemetery, West Long Branch, Monmouth County.

CLARK, ALEXANDER M. Pvt, B, 2nd NJ Inf, 9-8-1872. Tabernacle Baptist Church Cemetery, Erma, Cape May County.

Our Brothers Gone Before

CLARK*, ALFRED Pvt, D, 8th NJ Inf, [Wounded in action.] 12-7-1919. Arlington Cemetery, Kearny, Hudson County.
CLARK, ALFRED T. Sgt, K, 2nd NJ Inf, 7-5-1881. Fairmount Cemetery, Newark, Essex County.
CLARK, ALLEN Corp, K, 9th NJ Inf, 11-25-1919. Harleigh Cemetery, Camden, Camden County.
CLARK, ALMOND Pvt, C, 26th MI Inf, 10-31-1871. Old Church Cemetery, Holmanville, Ocean County.
CLARK, ALPHONSO Pvt, A, 26th ME Inf, 10-26-1862. Fairmount Cemetery, Newark, Essex County.
CLARK, ANDREW Pvt, C, 25th NJ Inf, 3-4-1884. Laurel Grove Cemetery, Totowa, Passaic County.
CLARK, BENJAMIN 3-3-1879. Chestnut Cemetery, Greenwich, Cumberland County.
CLARK, BENJAMIN C. Pvt, B, 30th NJ Inf, 7-20-1908. Baptist Church Cemetery, Scotch Plains, Union County.
CLARK, BENJAMIN G. Pvt, C, 23rd NJ Inf, 1925. Baptist/St. Andrew's Cemetery, Mount Holly, Burlington County.
CLARK, CALVIN C. Pvt, A, 22nd U.S. CT, 1-31-1907. Fairmount Cemetery, Newark, Essex County.
CLARK, CHARLES Corp, H, 3rd NJ Cav, 12-25-1885. 1st United Methodist Church Cemetery, Bridgeton, Cumberland County.
CLARK, CHARLES Pvt, A, 12th U.S. Inf, 1-22-1880. Woodland Cemetery, Newark, Essex County.
CLARK, CHARLES A. Pvt, I, 17th CT Inf, 6-8-1892. Maplewood Cemetery, Freehold, Monmouth County.
CLARK*, CHARLES C. Pvt, Unassigned, 33rd NJ Inf, DoD Unknown. Midvale Cemetery, Midvale, Passaic County.
CLARK*, CHARLES D. Pvt, I, 2nd NJ Inf, 7-27-1871. Presbyterian Church Cemetery, Westfield, Union County.
CLARK, CHARLES LEVI Pvt, Btty B, 1st NJ Light Art, 4-30-1922. Valleau Cemetery, Ridgewood, Bergen County.
CLARK, DANIEL 12-7-1906. Evergreen Cemetery, Hillside, Union County.
CLARK, DAVID Pvt, I, 6th NY Inf, 2-14-1887. Cedar Lawn Cemetery, Paterson, Passaic County.
CLARK, DAVID BROOKS Pvt, 6th NY Ind Btty [Wounded in action.] 6-27-1906. Rahway Cemetery, Rahway, Union County.
CLARK, DAVID C. Pvt, M, 2nd NJ Cav, 10-10-1881. United Methodist Church Cemetery, Absecon, Atlantic County.
CLARK, DAVID D. Pvt, E, 1st DE Inf, 12-28-1902. Methodist-Episcopal Cemetery, Burlington, Burlington County.
CLARK, DAVID E. Pvt, E, 10th NJ Inf, 12-29-1882. United Methodist Church Cemetery, Absecon, Atlantic County.
CLARK, DAVID P. Pvt, F, 3rd NJ Inf, 1912. Mount Pleasant Cemetery, Millville, Cumberland County.
CLARK, DAVID WILLIAM Pvt, D, 2nd NJ Cav, 12-22-1899. Fairmount Cemetery, Newark, Essex County.
CLARK, EDWARD Pvt, F, 84th NY National Guard, 2-16-1904. Rosedale Cemetery, Orange, Essex County.
CLARK, EDWARD C. 1st Sgt, Btty K, 1st CT Art, 10-5-1913. Baptist Cemetery, Medford, Burlington County.
CLARK, EDWARD P. 1st Lt, Btty B, 1st NJ Light Art, 7-30-1876. Evergreen Cemetery, Hillside, Union County.
CLARK, EDWIN Pvt, F, 8th NJ Inf, 12-29-1878. Fairmount Cemetery, Newark, Essex County.

New Jersey Civil War Burials

CLARK, EDWIN DoD Unknown. Bayview-New York Bay Cemetery, Jersey City, Hudson County.

CLARK, EDWIN F. Pvt, Btty E, 1st U.S. Art, 12-29-1893. Fairmount Cemetery, Newark, Essex County.

CLARK, ELISHA Pvt, C, 38th NJ Inf, 9-30-1915. Head of River Church Cemetery, Head of River, Atlantic County.

CLARK, FRANCIS D. Seaman, U.S. Navy, USS Union, 7-15-1899. Mount Pleasant Cemetery, Newark, Essex County.

CLARK, FRANCIS E. Sgt, Btty C, 1st WI Heavy Art, DoD Unknown. Mount Pleasant Methodist Cemetery, Pleasantville, Atlantic County.

CLARK, GARRET Pvt, E, 54th NY Inf, 1899. St. Paul's United Methodist Church Cemetery, Paulsboro, Gloucester County.

CLARK, GEORGE Pvt, K, 33rd NY Inf, [Died at Newark, NJ.] 10-19-1862. Fairmount Cemetery, Newark, Essex County.

CLARK, GEORGE Pvt, F, 29th CT Inf, 4-29-1920. Arlington Cemetery, Kearny, Hudson County.

CLARK, GEORGE Pvt, E, 28th NJ Inf, 7-14-1906. Arlington Cemetery, Kearny, Hudson County.

CLARK, GEORGE Seaman, U.S. Navy, USS Kansas, 12-18-1895. Mount Pisgah Cemetery, Elsinboro, Salem County.

CLARK, GEORGE Pvt, A, 4th NJ Inf, 3-27-1904. Lady of Lourdes/Holy Sepulchre Cemetery, Hamilton, Mercer County.

CLARK, GEORGE (see: Beegle, Jacob) Mount Hope Presbyterian Cemetery, Lambertville, Hunterdon County.

CLARK, GEORGE E. Pvt, A, 26th NJ Inf, 3-29-1915. Arlington Cemetery, Kearny, Hudson County.

CLARK, GEORGE E.A. Pvt, C, 188th PA Inf, 7-29-1891. Cedar Ridge Cemetery, Blairstown, Warren County.

CLARK, GEORGE L. (aka: Carr, Lawrence) Pvt, D, 12th TN Cav, 7-30-1908. St. Paul's Methodist Church Cemetery, Port Republic, Atlantic County.

CLARK, GEORGE P. Pvt, B, 1st NJ Militia, 1890. Green Cemetery, Woodbury, Gloucester County.

CLARK, GEORGE T. Capt, B, 91st IN Inf, 1911. New Somerville Cemetery, Somerville, Somerset County.

CLARK, GEORGE W. Seaman, U.S. Navy, USS Jamestown, 3-12-1886. Eglington Cemetery, Clarksboro, Gloucester County.

CLARK*, GEORGE W. Sgt, B, 12th NJ Inf, 11-10-1890. Eglington Cemetery, Clarksboro, Gloucester County.

CLARK, GEORGE WASHINGTON Pvt, I, 4th NJ Inf, [Died at Newark, NJ of wounds received in action.] 9-21-1864. Evergreen Cemetery, Lumberton, Burlington County.

CLARK*, GILBERT S. Bvt Maj, U.S. Volunteers, [Commissary of Subsistence.] 7-28-1882. Bayview-New York Bay Cemetery, Jersey City, Hudson County.

CLARK, HENRY Pvt, I, 40th NJ Inf, 7-22-1925. Harleigh Cemetery, Camden, Camden County.

CLARK, HENRY Pvt, K, 13th NJ Inf, 5-12-1914. Laurel Grove Cemetery, Totowa, Passaic County.

CLARK, HENRY Pvt, K, 25th NJ Inf, 3-31-1911. Holy Sepulchre Cemetery, Totowa, Passaic County.

CLARK*, HENRY CLAY Surg, 3rd NJ Inf [Also: Asst Surg, 2nd NJ Inf.] 12-24-1904. Eglington Cemetery, Clarksboro, Gloucester County.

CLARK, HENRY H. Pvt, H, 18th U.S. Inf, 10- -1924. Jersey City Cemetery, Jersey City, Hudson County.

Our Brothers Gone Before

CLARK, HENRY R. 2nd Lt, A, 5th NJ Inf, [Killed in action at Gettysburg, PA.] 7-2-1863. Mercer Cemetery, Trenton, Mercer County.
CLARK, HENRY S. DoD Unknown. Union Cemetery, Mantua, Gloucester County.
CLARK, ISAAC Sgt, B, 27th NJ Inf, 4-11-1914. Presbyterian Church Cemetery, Mount Freedom, Morris County.
CLARK, ISAAC Pvt, K, 13th NJ Inf, 4-6-1910. Laurel Grove Cemetery, Totowa, Passaic County.
CLARK, ISAAC JEFFERSON Pvt, B, 54th MA Inf, 1-12-1888. Methodist-Episcopal Church Cemetery, Aura, Gloucester County.
CLARK, JACOB Amb Driver, D, 6th NJ Inf, 10-29-1904. Mercer Cemetery, Trenton, Mercer County.
CLARK, JACOB E. Pvt, F, 13th NY Cav, DoD Unknown. Hackensack Cemetery, Hackensack, Bergen County.
CLARK, JAMES Pvt, E, 10th NJ Inf, [Killed in action at Galt House, VA.] 5-14-1864. Union Cemetery, Clarkstown, Atlantic County.
CLARK, JAMES Pvt, D, 24th U.S. CT, 8-28-1910. Mount Peace Cemetery, Lawnside, Camden County.
CLARK, JAMES Pvt, G, 22nd U.S. CT, 1-8-1916. St. John's Pentecostal Church Cemetery, Sheppards Mill, Cumberland County.
CLARK*, JAMES Pvt, B, 1st NJ Cav, DoD Unknown. St. John's Evangelical Church Cemetery, Orange, Essex County.
CLARK, JAMES Pvt, G, 2nd NJ Militia, DoD Unknown. Holy Name Cemetery, Jersey City, Hudson County.
CLARK, JAMES Landsman, U.S. Navy, USS Niagra, DoD Unknown. St. Mary's Cemetery, Plainfield, Union County.
CLARK, JAMES Corp, C, 15th NY Eng, 1893. Jersey City Cemetery, Jersey City, Hudson County.
CLARK, JAMES D. Pvt, C, 1st VA Inf (CSA), [Captured at Gettysburg, PA.] 7-22-1863. Finn's Point National Cemetery, Pennsville, Salem County.
CLARK, JAMES H. Pvt, G, 1st NJ Inf, 1-12-1865. Rahway Cemetery, Rahway, Union County.
CLARK, JAMES H. Pvt, A, 5th NJ Inf, [Missing in action at Wilderness, VA. Supposed dead.] 5-5-1864. Rahway Cemetery, Rahway, Union County.
CLARK, JAMES J. Landsman, U.S. Navy, USS Peoria, 11-27-1910. Phillipsburg Cemetery, Phillipsburg, Warren County.
CLARK, JAMES M. Pvt, H, 3rd NJ Cav, 9-26-1871. 1st United Methodist Church Cemetery, Bridgeton, Cumberland County.
CLARK, JAMES M. Pvt, K, 13th AL Inf (CSA), 9-22-1863. Finn's Point National Cemetery, Pennsville, Salem County.
CLARK, JAMES M. Sgt, C, 30th NJ Inf, 6-27-1907. Rahway Cemetery, Rahway, Union County.
CLARK*, JAMES V. Pvt, I, 9th NJ Inf, 9-30-1934. Presbyterian Church Cemetery, Cold Spring, Cape May County.
CLARK*, JAMISON Pvt, Btty L, 6th NY Heavy Art, 9-30-1913. Bayview-New York Bay Cemetery, Jersey City, Hudson County.
CLARK, JASPER V. Pvt, E, 55th MA Inf, DoD Unknown. Bloomfield Cemetery, Bloomfield, Essex County.
CLARK, JESSE H. Pvt, E, 10th NJ Inf, [Died at Richmond, VA.] 2-11-1865. Presbyterian Church Cemetery, Absecon, Atlantic County.
CLARK, JESSE L. Pvt, H, 57th NY Inf, [Wounded 9-17-1862 at Antietam, MD.] 7-15-1893. United Methodist Church Cemetery, Absecon, Atlantic County.
CLARK, JESSE W. Pvt, C, 30th NJ Inf, 3-21-1899. Rahway Cemetery, Rahway, Union County.

New Jersey Civil War Burials

CLARK, JOHN Pvt, E, 1st DE Cav, 6-30-1897. 1st United Methodist Church Cemetery, Bridgeton, Cumberland County.
CLARK, JOHN Pvt, B, 191st NY Inf, 3-6-1906. Old Bergen Church Cemetery, Jersey City, Hudson County.
CLARK, JOHN 9-3-1864. Trinity Episcopal Church Cemetery, Woodbridge, Middlesex County.
CLARK, JOHN Pvt, D, 79th NY Inf, [Wounded in action.] 2-25-1914. Old 1st Methodist Church Cemetery, West Long Branch, Monmouth County.
CLARK, JOHN Pvt, D, 48th NY Inf, [Cenotaph. Died while prisoner at Andersonville, GA.] 6-16-1864. Holy Sepulchre Cemetery, Totowa, Passaic County.
CLARK, JOHN Pvt, G, 42nd MS Inf (CSA), 11-13-1863. Finn's Point National Cemetery, Pennsville, Salem County.
CLARK, JOHN Pvt, E, 8th NJ Inf, 7-8-1889. St. Peter's Church Cemetery, Belleville, Essex County.
CLARK, JOHN Pvt, E, 71st NY Inf, 11-8-1886. Holy Sepulchre Cemetery, East Orange, Essex County.
CLARK, JOHN C. Pvt, L, 1st NJ Cav, 8-26-1922. Bloomfield Cemetery, Bloomfield, Essex County.
CLARK, JOHN E. Pvt, E, 1st DE Inf, 12-13-1887. Cedar Hill Cemetery, Florence, Burlington County.
CLARK, JOHN E. Corp, G, 7th NJ Inf, 11-15-1876. Cedar Lawn Cemetery, Paterson, Passaic County.
CLARK, JOHN G. Pvt, F, 2nd NJ Inf, 3-23-1914. Clinton Cemetery, Irvington, Essex County.
CLARK, JOHN G. Pvt, M, 3rd NJ Cav, [Died of typhoid at Trenton, NJ.] 1-17-1864. Riverview Cemetery, Trenton, Mercer County.
CLARK, JOHN H. Pvt, I, 8th U.S. CT, 1-9-1917. Evergreen Cemetery, Hillside, Union County.
CLARK, JOHN H. Pvt, I, 40th NJ Inf, 11-17-1926. Soldier's Home Cemetery, Vineland, Cumberland County.
CLARK, JOHN (JR.) Pvt, A, 28th NJ Inf, DoD Unknown. 1st Reformed Church Cemetery, New Brunswick, Middlesex County.
CLARK, JOHN K. Pvt, D, 34th NJ Inf, 11-6-1898. New Episcopal Church Cemetery, Swedesboro, Gloucester County.
CLARK, JOHN M. 1st Lt, Adj, 83rd PA Inf 9-5-1909. Atlantic City Cemetery, Pleasantville, Atlantic County.
CLARK, JOHN N. Corp, A, 31st NJ Inf, 1-28-1889. Mount Pleasant Cemetery, Newark, Essex County.
CLARK, JOHN R. Pvt, A, 22nd NJ Inf, 9-25-1899. Hackensack Cemetery, Hackensack, Bergen County.
CLARK, JOHN W. Pvt, H, 12th NJ Inf, 5-4-1899. Methodist Church Cemetery, Sharptown, Salem County.
CLARK, JOHN W. Pvt, K, 2nd NJ Cav, 1909. Presbyterian Church Cemetery, Andover, Sussex County.
CLARK, JOHNSON 3-14-1908. Christian Cemetery, Milford, Hunterdon County.
CLARK, JOHNSON M. Pvt, B, 27th NJ Inf, 8-27-1921. Presbyterian Church Cemetery, Mount Freedom, Morris County.
CLARK, JONAH N. Pvt, E, 10th NJ Inf, DoD Unknown. Presbyterian Church Cemetery, Absecon, Atlantic County.
CLARK, JONAS B. Pvt, A, 40th NY Inf, 1-25-1894. Evergreen Cemetery, Camden, Camden County.
CLARK, JOSEPH Pvt, H, 57th PA Inf, [Died at Beverly, NJ.] 10-22-1864. Beverly National Cemetery, Edgewater Park, Burlington County.

Our Brothers Gone Before

CLARK, JOSEPH Pvt, Btty M, 9th NY Heavy Art, 9-18-1901. Fairmount Cemetery, Newark, Essex County.
CLARK, JOSEPH Pvt, K, 1st NJ Inf, 8-16-1916. Baptist Church Cemetery, Scotch Plains, Union County.
CLARK, JOSEPH Pvt, Btty I, 7th NY Heavy Art, DoD Unknown. St. Peter's Church Cemetery, Belleville, Essex County.
CLARK*, JOSEPH Pvt, E, 8th NJ Inf, 9-17-1894. St. Peter's Church Cemetery, Belleville, Essex County.
CLARK, JOSEPH 11-4-1901. Mount Pleasant Cemetery, Newark, Essex County.
CLARK, JOSEPH CLAYPOOLE Bvt Lt Col, 4th U.S. Art 1906. Baptist/St. Andrew's Cemetery, Mount Holly, Burlington County.
CLARK, JOSHUA Pvt, G, 24th NJ Inf, 1-27-1889. United Methodist Church Cemetery, Woodruff, Cumberland County.
CLARK, JOSHUA P. 11-22-1901. 1st United Methodist Church Cemetery, Salem, Salem County.
CLARK, LEWIS D. Pvt, F, 150th OH Inf, 2-11-1908. Rosedale Cemetery, Orange, Essex County.
CLARK, LEWIS G. Pvt, F, 24th NJ Inf, 12-7-1886. 1st United Methodist Church Cemetery, Bridgeton, Cumberland County.
CLARK, MATHIAS Pvt, C, 71st NY National Guard, 6-23-1928. Fairview Cemetery, Westfield, Union County.
CLARK, MOSES P. Capt, 6th NY Ind Btty 1-3-1881. Christ Church Cemetery, Morgan, Middlesex County.
CLARK, NATHANIEL Corp, H, 11th NJ Inf, 2-22-1911. Walnut Grove Cemetery, Mount Freedom, Morris County.
CLARK*, NEHEMIAH Pvt, I, 2nd NJ Inf, 6-19-1897. Bible Church Cemetery, English Creek, Atlantic County.
CLARK, OLIVER G.H. Seaman, U.S. Navy, 4-15-1911. Mount Olivet Cemetery, Newark, Essex County.
CLARK, ORAN Sgt, F, 68th PA Inf, 3-17-1906. Eglington Cemetery, Clarksboro, Gloucester County.
CLARK, OWEN Pvt, Unassigned, 15th NJ Inf, DoD Unknown. St. John's Cemetery, Hamilton, Mercer County.
CLARK, PATRICK Pvt, K, 2nd DC Inf, 1-6-1888. Holy Sepulchre Cemetery, East Orange, Essex County.
CLARK, PEMBROKE S. Pvt, B, 30th NJ Inf, 2-7-1893. Evergreen Cemetery, Hillside, Union County.
CLARK, PETER Pvt, E, 22nd NJ Inf, 6-15-1906. Valleau Cemetery, Ridgewood, Bergen County.
CLARK, PETER Pvt, A, 7th PA Cav, 2-21-1893. Elmwood Cemetery, New Brunswick, Middlesex County.
CLARK, PHILIP Sgt, E, 7th NJ Inf, 9-5-1911. Phillipsburg Old Catholic Cemetery, Phillipsburg, Warren County.
CLARK, PHINEAS V. Corp, B, 101st PA Inf, 8-19-1896. Fairmount Cemetery, Newark, Essex County.
CLARK, R.C. 8-20-1864. Rahway Cemetery, Rahway, Union County.
CLARK, R. GRAHAM Pvt, F, 4th NJ Militia, 7-10-1903. Evergreen Cemetery, Camden, Camden County.
CLARK, REDMOND Pvt, C, 25th NJ Inf, DoD Unknown. Pompton Reformed Church Cemetery, Pompton Lakes, Passaic County.
CLARK*, RICHARD Pvt, Btty E, 11th U.S. CHA, 5-6-1876. Monument Cemetery, Edgewater Park, Burlington County.
CLARK, ROBERT Pvt, I, 8th NJ Inf, [Wounded in action.] 8-28-1889. United Methodist Church Cemetery, New Providence, Union County.

New Jersey Civil War Burials

CLARK, ROBERT Pvt, K, 2nd NJ Militia, 10-13-1865. Mount Pleasant Cemetery, Newark, Essex County.

CLARK, ROBERT C. DoD Unknown. Overlook Cemetery, Bridgeton, Cumberland County.

CLARK, ROBERT G. Pvt, K, 12th NJ Inf, DoD Unknown. Evergreen Cemetery, Camden, Camden County.

CLARK, RODERICK A. Corp, F, 14th NJ Inf, 11-9-1929. Whitelawn Cemetery, Point Pleasant, Ocean County.

CLARK, SAMUEL Sgt, A, 1st NY Eng, [Wounded in action 9-22-1863.] 8-16-1872. Cedar Lawn Cemetery, Paterson, Passaic County.

CLARK, SAMUEL Hosp Steward, 8th NJ Inf 12-28-1895. Fairmount Cemetery, Newark, Essex County.

CLARK, SAMUEL A. Pvt, K, 25th MA Inf, [Wounded 6-3-1864 at Cold Harbor, VA.] 5-28-1909. Fairmount Cemetery, Newark, Essex County.

CLARK, SAMUEL C. Pvt, G, 23rd NJ Inf, 1927. Greenwood Cemetery, Pleasantville, Atlantic County.

CLARK, SAMUEL C. Pvt, B, 30th NJ Inf, 8-25-1895. United Methodist Church Cemetery, New Providence, Union County.

CLARK, SAMUEL H. Pvt, D, 8th NJ Inf, 1904. Mount Pleasant Cemetery, Newark, Essex County.

CLARK, SAMUEL J. Seaman, U.S. Navy, USS Kansas, 2-12-1887. Mount Pisgah Cemetery, Elsinboro, Salem County.

CLARK, SAMUEL M. 8-9-1908. Evergreen Cemetery, Hillside, Union County.

CLARK*, SOLOMON Landsman, U.S. Navy, USS North Carolina, 9-3-1898. Johnson Cemetery, Camden, Camden County.

CLARK, STEPHEN F. Pvt, F, 13th NJ Inf, 11-29-1879. Bloomfield Cemetery, Bloomfield, Essex County.

CLARK, THEODORE Pvt, K, 2nd NJ Inf, 2-18-1910. Fairmount Cemetery, Newark, Essex County.

CLARK*, THERON B. Pvt, C, 189th NY Inf, 8-1-1924. Evergreen Cemetery, Hillside, Union County.

CLARK*, THOMAS Ordinary Seaman, U.S. Navy, USS Vermont, 5-26-1908. Oddfellows Cemetery, Pemberton, Burlington County.

CLARK, THOMAS Pvt, C, 13th NJ Inf, 2-17-1901. Fairmount Cemetery, Newark, Essex County.

CLARK, THOMAS 5-11-1914. Fairview Cemetery, Westfield, Union County.

CLARK, THOMAS (aka: Clarke, Thomas) Pvt, E, 14th NJ Inf, 2-23-1897. Hillside Cemetery, Scotch Plains, Union County.

CLARK, THOMAS S. Sgt, H, 28th NJ Inf, 10- -1909. Presbyterian Church Cemetery, Cold Spring, Cape May County.

CLARK, TIMOTHY Pvt, F, 34th NJ Inf, DoD Unknown. St. Mary's Cemetery, Hamilton, Mercer County.

CLARK, VINCENT B. Landsman, U.S. Navy, USS Lenapee, 3-28-1914. Fairmount Cemetery, Chatham, Morris County.

CLARK, WALLACE Corp, D, 95th NY Inf, [Wounded 5-7-1864 at Wilderness, VA. and 3-31-1865 at Hatchers Run, VA.] 8-15-1894. Deckertown-Union Cemetery, Papakating, Sussex County.

CLARK, WARREN H. Pvt, F, 1st IA Cav, 2-7-1884. Evergreen Cemetery, Lumberton, Burlington County.

CLARK, WILLIAM Pvt, H, 3rd NJ Cav, 8-7-1906. Overlook Cemetery, Bridgeton, Cumberland County.

CLARK, WILLIAM Pvt, A, 26th NJ Inf, 9-1-1903. Fairmount Cemetery, Newark, Essex County.

Our Brothers Gone Before

CLARK, WILLIAM Landsman, U.S. Navy, 6-20-1866. Cedar Grove Cemetery, Waretown, Ocean County.
CLARK, WILLIAM Pvt, B, 2nd NJ Inf, 1-26-1905. Mount Pleasant Cemetery, Newark, Essex County.
CLARK, WILLIAM Pvt, A, 9th NJ Inf, DoD Unknown. Mount Pleasant Cemetery, Newark, Essex County.
CLARK, WILLIAM Corp, K, 4th NJ Inf, DoD Unknown. Mount Pleasant Cemetery, Newark, Essex County.
CLARK*, WILLIAM A. Pvt, Btty I, 7th NY Heavy Art, [Wounded 6-3-1864 at Cold Harbor, VA.] 4-16-1906. Evergreen Cemetery, Hillside, Union County.
CLARK, WILLIAM B. Pvt, E, 1st DE Inf, 2-8-1926. Baptist Cemetery, Burlington, Burlington County.
CLARK, WILLIAM C. Pvt, DoD Unknown. Hardyston Cemetery, North Church, Sussex County.
CLARK, WILLIAM D. Pvt, A, 3rd NJ Inf, [Died at Washington, DC. of wounds received 5-5-1864 at Wilderness, VA.] 6-25-1864. Methodist-Episcopal Cemetery, Lake, Gloucester County.
CLARK, WILLIAM D. Pvt, C, 16th PA Cav, 6-27-1905. Baptist/Evergreen Methodist Cemetery, Plainfield, Union County.
CLARK, WILLIAM D. Pvt, A, 15th NJ Inf, 1876. Evergreen Cemetery, Hillside, Union County.
CLARK*, WILLIAM E. 1st Sgt, D, 2nd NJ Inf, 4-26-1899. Rahway Cemetery, Rahway, Union County.
CLARK, WILLIAM F. Pvt, D, 83rd NY Inf, 5-2-1903. New Somerville Cemetery, Somerville, Somerset County.
CLARK, WILLIAM H. Pvt, F, 34th NJ Inf, 4-16-1895. Eglington Cemetery, Clarksboro, Gloucester County.
CLARK, WILLIAM H.H. Pvt, C, 4th NJ Militia, 3-17-1901. Evergreen Cemetery, Camden, Camden County.
CLARK, WILLIAM J. Pvt, B, 2nd NJ Inf, 12-11-1886. Bethel Cemetery, Pennsauken, Camden County.
CLARK, WILLIAM J. Pvt, I, 12th NJ Inf, [Died at Philadelphia, PA.] 3-24-1863. Bethesda Methodist-Episcopal Church Cemetery, Swedesboro, Gloucester County.
CLARK, WILLIAM JACKSON Com Sgt, 5th IL Cav 9-9-1920. Evergreen Cemetery, Hillside, Union County.
CLARK, WILLIAM L. Pvt, M, 12th NY Cav, 5-3-1896. Bayview-New York Bay Cemetery, Jersey City, Hudson County.
CLARK, WILLIAM N. Pvt, E, 1st NJ Cav, 8-9-1910. Christian Cemetery, Milford, Hunterdon County.
CLARK, WILLIAM S. QM Sgt, 13th NJ Inf 8-23-1893. Fairmount Cemetery, Newark, Essex County.
CLARK, WILLIAM S. Pvt, C, 195th PA Inf, 5-18-1900. Union Methodist Church Cemetery, Center Square, Gloucester County.
CLARK*, WILLIAM T. Pvt, D, 2nd NJ Inf, 12-8-1899. Trinity Episcopal Church Cemetery, Woodbridge, Middlesex County.
CLARKE, CHARLES B. Pvt, A, 23rd NJ Inf, 12-1-1917. Coopertown Meeting House Cemetery, Edgewater Park, Burlington County.
CLARKE, ISAAC V. Pvt, K, 6th VA Cav (CSA), 4-21-1865. Finn's Point National Cemetery, Pennsville, Salem County.
CLARKE, JOHN F. Pvt, F, 2nd NJ Inf, 1915. Soldier's Home Cemetery, Vineland, Cumberland County.
CLARKE, JOHN S. 1st Sgt, B, 3rd NJ Inf, 1915. Soldier's Home Cemetery, Vineland, Cumberland County.

New Jersey Civil War Burials

CLARKE, THOMAS (see: Clark, Thomas) Hillside Cemetery, Scotch Plains, Union County.

CLARKE*, WILLIAM P. Pvt, H, 9th U.S. Vet Vol Inf, [Wounded 9-17-1862 at Antietam, MD.] 6-19-1906. Evergreen Cemetery, Camden, Camden County.

CLARKSON, JAMES B. Pvt, I, 5th NY Cav, 5-22-1914. Presbyterian Cemetery, North Plainfield, Somerset County.

CLARKSON, SAMUEL F. Pvt, G, 37th NY State Militia, 9-20-1909. Bayview-New York Bay Cemetery, Jersey City, Hudson County.

CLARY*, SILAS W. Pvt, F, 2nd DC Inf, 1-19-1894. Fairmount Cemetery, Newark, Essex County.

CLASEY, SAMUEL C. Seaman, U.S. Navy, 1900. Baptist/Evergreen Methodist Cemetery, Plainfield, Union County.

CLASS, GUSTAVE Artificer, B, 1st NY Eng, 5-7-1904. Flower Hill Cemetery, North Bergen, Hudson County.

CLASS, JOSEPH Pvt, L, 27th NJ Inf, [Drowned while crossing the Cumberland River, KY.] 5-6-1863. United Methodist Church Cemetery, Rockaway Valley, Morris County.

CLATTS, JOHN Pvt, I, 4th NJ Inf, 2-19-1907. Baptist Cemetery, Pemberton, Burlington County.

CLAUSEMAN, AUGUST Pvt, E, 5th NJ Inf, [Wounded at Fair Oaks, VA.] 2-8-1888. Greenwood Cemetery, Hamilton, Mercer County.

CLAUSEN*, MERWIN G. (aka: Clawson, Merwin) Pvt, B, 8th NJ Inf, 6-2-1886. Evergreen Cemetery, Hillside, Union County.

CLAUSON, WILLIAM (see: Clawson, William) Fairmount Cemetery, Fairmount, Hunterdon County.

CLAUSSEN, CHARLES E. 1st Lt, Btty K, 15th NY Heavy Art, 10-26-1890. Grove Church Cemetery, North Bergen, Hudson County.

CLAVE, ROBERT 3-5-1887. Boonton Cemetery, Boonton, Morris County.

CLAWGES*, WILLIAM R. Pvt, E, 8th NJ Inf, 7-3-1903. St. Mary's Episcopal Church Cemetery, Burlington, Burlington County.

CLAWSON, ANDERSON Pvt, F, 38th NJ Inf, [Wounded in action.] 5-28-1898. Sergeant's Hill Cemetery, Sand Brook, Hunterdon County.

CLAWSON, ANDREW C. Pvt, G, 2nd NJ Inf, 7-26-1922. Union Cemetery, Washington, Morris County.

CLAWSON, DANIEL Pvt, B, 7th NJ Inf, DoD Unknown. Methodist Church Cemetery, Fairmount, Hunterdon County.

CLAWSON, FREDERICK S. Pvt, C, 27th NJ Inf, DoD Unknown. Methodist Church Cemetery, Fairmount, Hunterdon County.

CLAWSON, JACOB S. Pvt, H, 11th NJ Inf, 10-2-1870. German Valley Rural Cemetery, Naughright, Morris County.

CLAWSON, JONATHAN F.R. Pvt, C, 28th NJ Inf, 1902. 7th Day Baptist Cemetery, Piscataway, Middlesex County.

CLAWSON, LACY DoD Unknown. Hillside Cemetery, Madison, Morris County.

CLAWSON, MERWIN (see: Clausen, Merwin G.) Evergreen Cemetery, Hillside, Union County.

CLAWSON, THOMAS J. Pvt, F, 9th NJ Inf, DoD Unknown. Evergreen Cemetery, Hillside, Union County.

CLAWSON*, WILLIAM (aka: Clauson, William) Pvt, M, 1st NJ Cav, [Wounded 6-25-1862 at Fair Oaks, VA.] 7-24-1907. Fairmount Cemetery, Fairmount, Hunterdon County.

CLAWSON, WILLIAM L. Seaman, U.S. Navy, USS Jamestown, 2-18-1926. Clinton Cemetery, Irvington, Essex County.

CLAWSON, WILLIAM R. Pvt, B, 15th NJ Inf, 1917. Union Cemetery, Washington, Morris County.

Our Brothers Gone Before

CLAXTON, GEORGE Pvt, K, 13th NJ Inf, 3-12-1884. Cedar Lawn Cemetery, Paterson, Passaic County.

CLAY, ABLY J. Corp, F, 13th MS Inf (CSA), 8-18-1864. Finn's Point National Cemetery, Pennsville, Salem County.

CLAY, ALBAN (SR.) Pvt, H, 50th PA Inf, 5-10-1927. Evergreen Cemetery, Camden, Camden County.

CLAY, HENRY Pvt, Btty A, 13th NY Heavy Art, 1-18-1885. Greenwood Cemetery, Hamilton, Mercer County.

CLAY, PETER Pvt, K, 118th U.S. CT, 1-12-1903. Riverview Cemetery, Trenton, Mercer County.

CLAYHUNCE, JOHN W. Pvt, G, 1st NJ Cav, [Wounded aboard ship on the Rappahannock River, VA.] 3-14-1893. Methodist Church Cemetery, Titusville, Mercer County.

CLAYPOOLE, CHARLES D. Capt, B, 10th NJ Inf, 9-3-1903. United Methodist Church Cemetery, Tuckahoe, Cape May County.

CLAYPOOLE, HENRY C. Corp, F, 2nd NJ Cav, 4-2-1909. Baptist/St. Andrew's Cemetery, Mount Holly, Burlington County.

CLAYPOOLE, JACOB B. (SR.) Musc, 3rd NJ Inf Band 1926. Baptist/St. Andrew's Cemetery, Mount Holly, Burlington County.

CLAYTON, ABRAM L. 6-15-1879. Methodist-Protestant Cemetery, Union Valley, Middlesex County.

CLAYTON, ARTHUR W. Pvt, F, 21st NJ Inf, 4-1-1915. Hoboken Cemetery, North Bergen, Hudson County.

CLAYTON, ASHER M. Pvt, F, 28th NJ Inf, 2-27-1913. Mount Olivet Cemetery, Newark, Essex County.

CLAYTON, AUTHER Seaman, U.S. Navy, USS Massachusetts, 8-25-1897. Baptist Church Cemetery, Port Murray, Warren County.

CLAYTON, AZARIAH Pvt, B, 34th NJ Inf, 4-3-1883. Riverview Cemetery, Trenton, Mercer County.

CLAYTON, CHARLES H. Pvt, F, 38th NJ Inf, 9-9-1869. Old 1st Methodist Church Cemetery, West Long Branch, Monmouth County.

CLAYTON, CHARLES T. Pvt, K, 29th NJ Inf, 12-3-1911. Atlantic View Cemetery, Manasquan, Monmouth County.

CLAYTON, CLARENCE 1894. Wall Church Cemetery, Wall, Monmouth County.

CLAYTON, CORLIS Pvt, H, 29th NJ Inf, 12-2-1927. Atlantic View Cemetery, Manasquan, Monmouth County.

CLAYTON, CORNELIUS C. Pvt, Btty L, 13th NY Heavy Art, 10-28-1913. Bayview-New York Bay Cemetery, Jersey City, Hudson County.

CLAYTON, CYRENUS J. Pvt, I, 29th NJ Inf, 10-4-1924. Old 1st Methodist Church Cemetery, West Long Branch, Monmouth County.

CLAYTON, DAVID C. Sgt, A, 9th NJ Inf, 12-5-1894. Laurel Grove Cemetery, Totowa, Passaic County.

CLAYTON, DAVID L. Pvt, C, 7th NJ Inf, 2-12-1907. Methodist Cemetery, Cassville, Ocean County.

CLAYTON, DAVID W. 1916. Maplewood Cemetery, Freehold, Monmouth County.

CLAYTON, EDWARD Pvt, D, 14th NJ Inf, 6-9-1912. Riverview Cemetery, Trenton, Mercer County.

CLAYTON, EDWARD 6-20-1879. Belvidere/Catholic Cemetery, Belvidere, Warren County.

CLAYTON*, EDWARD J. Corp, K, 146th NY Inf, 1-5-1885. Maplewood Cemetery, Freehold, Monmouth County.

CLAYTON, EDWARD W. Pvt, A, 3rd NJ Inf, 10-17-1908. Eglington Cemetery, Clarksboro, Gloucester County.

New Jersey Civil War Burials

CLAYTON, ELIAS Pvt, F, 2nd NJ Cav, 12-18-1916. Greengrove Cemetery, Keyport, Monmouth County.

CLAYTON, ELIAS J. 12-28-1925. Tennent Church Cemetery, Tennent, Monmouth County.

CLAYTON, EUGENE 9-20-1865. Whitelawn Cemetery, Point Pleasant, Ocean County.

CLAYTON, EUGENE C. Pvt, F, 14th NJ Inf, DoD Unknown. Old Methodist Cemetery, Point Pleasant, Ocean County.

CLAYTON, EZEKIEL Pvt, G, 29th NJ Inf, DoD Unknown. Atlantic Reformed Cemetery, Colts Neck, Monmouth County.

CLAYTON, FRANCIS R. Sgt, E, 28th NJ Inf, 6-5-1908. Adelphia Cemetery, Adelphia, Monmouth County.

CLAYTON, GEORGE W. Pvt, F, 71st PA Inf, 4-7-1895. Fairview Cemetery, Fairview, Monmouth County.

CLAYTON, GRANDIN L. 1-6-1918. Old Baptist Cemetery, Freehold, Monmouth County.

CLAYTON, ISAIAH Pvt, A, 38th NJ Inf, 2-21-1934. Greengrove Cemetery, Keyport, Monmouth County.

CLAYTON, JAMES 2-13-1882. Fairview Cemetery, Fairview, Monmouth County.

CLAYTON, JAMES S. Pvt, I, 11th PA Cav, 12-29-1886. Belvidere/Catholic Cemetery, Belvidere, Warren County.

CLAYTON, JOHN ATWOOD Pvt, D, 9th NJ Inf, 1-6-1920. Kettle Creek Cemetery, Silverton, Ocean County.

CLAYTON, JOHN B. Musc, G, 3rd NJ Militia, 4-19-1884. Asbury United Methodist Church Cemetery, English Creek, Atlantic County.

CLAYTON, JOHN M. Pvt, D, 9th NJ Inf, 12-6-1915. Kettle Creek Cemetery, Silverton, Ocean County.

CLAYTON, JOHN M. Pvt, I, 11th PA Cav, 12-27-1883. Belvidere/Catholic Cemetery, Belvidere, Warren County.

CLAYTON, JOHN T. Sgt, H, 48th NY Inf, [Died at Fort Schuyler, NY of wounds received in action.] 8-5-1863. Holmdel Cemetery, Holmdel, Monmouth County.

CLAYTON, JOHN V. Pvt, D, 14th NJ Inf, 7-11-1895. Riverview Cemetery, Trenton, Mercer County.

CLAYTON, JONATHAN B. Pvt, B, 14th NJ Inf, 4-29-1914. Riverview Cemetery, Trenton, Mercer County.

CLAYTON*, JOSEPH Corp, F, 3rd NJ Inf, [Wounded in action.] 11-18-1889. Brainerd Cemetery, Cranbury, Middlesex County.

CLAYTON, JOSEPH Pvt, E, 29th NJ Inf, 1873. Maplewood Cemetery, Freehold, Monmouth County.

CLAYTON, JOSEPH B. Sgt, F, 1st NJ Cav, 10-13-1908. Riverside Cemetery, Toms River, Ocean County.

CLAYTON, JOSEPH M. Wagoner, K, 29th NJ Inf, 1-27-1892. Adelphia Cemetery, Adelphia, Monmouth County.

CLAYTON, JOSHUA H. Pvt, A, 23rd NJ Inf, 3-8-1863. Coopertown Meeting House Cemetery, Edgewater Park, Burlington County.

CLAYTON, JOSHUA S. Pvt, C, 2nd MS Inf (CSA), [Wounded 6-27-1862 at Gaines' Mill, VA. Captured 7-1-1863 at Gettysburg, PA. Died of disease.] 10-2-1863. Finn's Point National Cemetery, Pennsville, Salem County.

CLAYTON, NICHOLAS 4-21-1910. Asbury United Methodist Church Cemetery, English Creek, Atlantic County.

CLAYTON, PATRICK Pvt, C, 14th NJ Inf, 3-4-1867. St. Mary's Cemetery, Elizabeth, Union County.

CLAYTON, SAMUEL Pvt, Btty E, 1st NJ Light Art, 4-18-1898. Fairmount Cemetery, Newark, Essex County.

CLAYTON, SAMUEL M. Musc, B, 14th NJ Inf, 7-9-1889. Riverview Cemetery, Trenton, Mercer County.

Our Brothers Gone Before

CLAYTON, STEPHEN N. Pvt, B, 76th OH Inf, [Wounded 5-15-1864 at Resaca, GA.] 3-30-1867. Old Oakhurst Cemetery, West Long Branch, Monmouth County.
CLAYTON, THOMAS Pvt, D, 14th NJ Inf, [Wounded in action.] 8-14-1897. Methodist Cemetery, Southard, Monmouth County.
CLAYTON, THOMAS J. Pvt, I, 10th NJ Inf, 9-19-1917. Tennent Church Cemetery, Tennent, Monmouth County.
CLAYTON, THOMAS O. Pvt, I, 14th NJ Inf, 10-10-1881. Greenwood Cemetery, Hamilton, Mercer County.
CLAYTON, WILLIAM Pvt, D, 14th NJ Inf, 11-12-1885. Adelphia Cemetery, Adelphia, Monmouth County.
CLAYTON, WILLIAM Pvt, F, 14th NJ Inf, [Wounded in action.] 1905. Methodist Cemetery, Southard, Monmouth County.
CLAYTON, WILLIAM 5-3-1918. Tennent Church Cemetery, Tennent, Monmouth County.
CLAYTON, WILLIAM B. Musc, A, 15th NJ Inf, 12-22-1902. Locust Grove Cemetery, Quakertown, Hunterdon County.
CLAYTON, WILLIAM B. DoD Unknown. Pitman Methodist-Episcopal Cemetery, New Brunswick, Middlesex County.
CLAYTON, WILLIAM B. 1906. Old Brick Reformed Church Cemetery, Marlboro, Monmouth County.
CLAYTON, WILLIAM H. Pvt, G, 1st NJ Inf, 11-12-1882. Pitman Methodist-Episcopal Cemetery, New Brunswick, Middlesex County.
CLAYTON, WILLIAM RANDOLPH Pvt, D, 9th NJ Inf, 12- -1890. Kettle Creek Cemetery, Silverton, Ocean County.
CLAYTON*, WILLIAM S. Pvt, K, 40th NJ Inf, 11-6-1908. Oddfellows Cemetery, Burlington, Burlington County.
CLEARE, WILLIAM H. Pvt, H, 71st PA Inf, 12-12-1907. Greenwood Cemetery, Hamilton, Mercer County.
CLEARMAN, CHARLES E. Pvt, K, 12th NY State Militia, 6-20-1914. Reformed Church Cemetery, Wyckoff, Bergen County.
CLEARMAN, ISAAC H. 3-25-1877. Mount Pleasant Cemetery, Newark, Essex County.
CLEARY, DANIEL Pvt, C, 6th NJ Inf, [Died at Jersey City, NJ of wounds received at Williamsburg, VA.] 6-22-1862. St. Peter's Cemetery, Jersey City, Hudson County.
CLEARY, JOHN Pvt, G, 133rd NY Inf, 4-9-1910. St. John's Cemetery, Hamilton, Mercer County.
CLEARY*, JOHN L. Capt, M, 13th NY Cav, 8-5-1896. Holy Name Cemetery, Jersey City, Hudson County.
CLEARY, MICHAEL Pvt, M, 3rd NJ Cav, 7-18-1906. St. Peter's Cemetery, Jersey City, Hudson County.
CLEAVER, C.H. DoD Unknown. Old Camden Cemetery, Camden, Camden County.
CLEGG, ABRAM Wagoner, H, 54th OH Inf, 7-27-1905. Cedar Lawn Cemetery, Paterson, Passaic County.
CLEGG*, GEORGE Sgt, C, 20th PA Cav, 4-14-1910. Baptist Church Cemetery, Haddonfield, Camden County.
CLEMENCE, BENJAMIN T. Pvt, E, 143rd NY Inf, 6-6-1909. Laurel Grove Cemetery, Totowa, Passaic County.
CLEMENS, ___?___ DoD Unknown. Macphelah Cemetery, North Bergen, Hudson County.
CLEMENS, BENJAMIN Sgt, K, 23rd U.S. CT, DoD Unknown. White Ridge Cemetery, Eatontown, Monmouth County.
CLEMENS, CHARLES Pvt, A, 34th NJ Inf, [Died of apoplexy at Newark, NJ.] 7-8-1865. Riverview Cemetery, Trenton, Mercer County.
CLEMENS, HENRY Pvt, H, 40th NJ Inf, 4-1-1906. Fairmount Cemetery, Newark, Essex County.

New Jersey Civil War Burials

CLEMENS*, JOHN Pvt, B, 4th NJ Inf, [Died of diarrhea at Philadelphia, PA.] 6-23-1864. Mercer Cemetery, Trenton, Mercer County.

CLEMENS, JOHN (see: Clements, John) Woodland Cemetery, Newark, Essex County.

CLEMENS*, JOHN G. Pvt, A, 14th NJ Inf, 4-4-1867. Fairmount Cemetery, Newark, Essex County.

CLEMENS, WILLIAM D.M. Pvt, H, 36th VA Inf (CSA), [Captured 3-2-1865 at Waynesboro, VA. Died of variola.] 5-12-1865. Finn's Point National Cemetery, Pennsville, Salem County.

CLEMENT, ALBERT Pvt, A, 4th NJ Inf, 8-4-1928. Bayview-New York Bay Cemetery, Jersey City, Hudson County.

CLEMENT, CHARLES W. Corp, E, 24th NJ Inf, 6-27-1903. Fairmount Cemetery, Newark, Essex County.

CLEMENT, HENRY E. Landsman, U.S. Navy, USS Jacob Bell, 9-27-1865. Mount Pleasant Cemetery, Newark, Essex County.

CLEMENT, THEODORE L. Sgt, E, 1st NJ Cav, 6-30-1908. Mount Pleasant Cemetery, Millville, Cumberland County.

CLEMENTS, F.C. Pvt, K, 63rd GA Inf (CSA), [Captured 2-22-1864 on Whitemarsh Island, GA. Died of pleurisy.] 7-12-1864. Finn's Point National Cemetery, Pennsville, Salem County.

CLEMENTS, HENRY Pvt, I, 35th NJ Inf, [Died at Savannah, GA.] 9-12-1864. Holy Sepulchre Cemetery, East Orange, Essex County.

CLEMENTS, ISAAC (aka: Hill, George A.) Pvt, G, 47th NY Inf, 7-30-1900. Mount Prospect Cemetery, Neptune, Monmouth County.

CLEMENTS, JOHN Corp, E, 12th NJ Inf, [Died of wounds received at Chancellorsville, VA.] 6-22-1863. Bethel Cemetery, Pennsauken, Camden County.

CLEMENTS, JOHN (aka: Clemens, John) Corp, K, 1st NJ Militia, 8-18-1912. Woodland Cemetery, Newark, Essex County.

CLEMENTS, JOHN P. ___, G, 31st ___ Inf, 7-3-1863. Holy Sepulchre Cemetery, East Orange, Essex County.

CLEMENTS, LANCE DoD Unknown. Mount Prospect Cemetery, Neptune, Monmouth County.

CLEMENTS, WILLIAM H. Pvt, I, 71st NY Inf, [Died of disease at Newark, NJ.] 12-11-1862. Fairmount Cemetery, Newark, Essex County.

CLEMM, AUGUST (see: Klemm, August) Oddfellows Cemetery, Burlington, Burlington County.

CLEMMER, JOHN C. Pvt, D, 5th VA Inf (CSA), [Wounded 7-3-1863 at Gettysburg, PA. Captured 5-12-1864 at Spotsylvania CH, VA. Died of erysipelas.] 3-20-1865. Finn's Point National Cemetery, Pennsville, Salem County.

CLENDENNING, CHARLES G. 7-23-1898. Phillipsburg Cemetery, Phillipsburg, Warren County.

CLENNON, JOHN Corp, E, 34th NJ Inf, 12-28-1899. Holy Sepulchre Cemetery, East Orange, Essex County.

CLERIHEW, PAUL (see: Clerihew, Peter J.) Laurel Grove Cemetery, Totowa, Passaic County.

CLERIHEW, PETER J. (aka: Clerihew, Paul) Pvt, C, 9th NY Inf, 12-23-1917. Laurel Grove Cemetery, Totowa, Passaic County.

CLERKIN, JOHN Pvt, B, 9th NJ Inf, 9-12-1913. St. Peter's Cemetery, New Brunswick, Middlesex County.

CLETUS, PAUL Corp, Btty D, 1st NJ Light Art, 3-31-1900. Mount Pleasant Cemetery, Newark, Essex County.

CLEVELAND, AUGUSTUS J. Pvt, Btty E, 1st U.S. Art, 12-16-1880. Mount Pleasant Cemetery, Newark, Essex County.

CLEVELAND, BENJAMIN F. Sgt, A, 51st NY Inf, 11-30-1930. Old 1st Reformed Church Cemetery, Hackensack, Bergen County.

Our Brothers Gone Before

CLEVELAND, FREDERICK C. Pvt, B, 26th NJ Inf, 3-2-1926. Arlington Cemetery, Kearny, Hudson County.
CLEVELAND, WILLIAM H. Pvt, C, 1st NJ Militia, 6-30-1893. Evergreen Cemetery, Hillside, Union County.
CLEVELAND, WILLIAM H. 10-3-1881. Mount Pleasant Cemetery, Newark, Essex County.
CLEVENGER, DANIEL W. 1st Sgt, G, 23rd NJ Inf, 12-15-1900. Baptist/St. Andrew's Cemetery, Mount Holly, Burlington County.
CLEVENGER, GEORGE W. Pvt, I, 4th NJ Inf, [Wounded in action.] 1-27-1915. Baptist Cemetery, Pemberton, Burlington County.
CLEVENGER, JOHN Musc, I, 23rd NJ Inf, 1926. Baptist Cemetery, Pemberton, Burlington County.
CLEVENGER, JOHN Sgt, H, 28th NJ Inf, 5-26-1890. Berlin Cemetery, Berlin, Camden County.
CLEVENGER, JONATHAN Pvt, E, 23rd NJ Inf, 1918. Cedar Hill Cemetery, Hightstown, Mercer County.
CLEVENGER, JOSEPH Corp, B, 12th NJ Inf, 1865. Giberson Cemetery, Whiting, Ocean County.
CLEVENGER, JOSHUA Pvt, E, 23rd NJ Inf, DoD Unknown. Baptist Cemetery, Pemberton, Burlington County.
CLEVENGER, SAMUEL G. Pvt, C, 23rd NJ Inf, 6-10-1919. Greenlawn Cemetery, West Long Branch, Monmouth County.
CLEVINGER*, JOHN C. Pvt, L, 1st NJ Cav, [Wounded in action.] 4-1-1922. Maplewood Cemetery, Freehold, Monmouth County.
CLICK, JOSEPH (see: Glick, Joseph) Holy Sepulchre Cemetery, Totowa, Passaic County.
CLIFF, JOHN L. Pvt, I, 9th NJ Inf, 8-20-1897. Cedar Green Cemetery, Clayton, Gloucester County.
CLIFFORD*, CHARLES H. Pvt, D, 35th NJ Inf, 4-10-1907. Eglington Cemetery, Clarksboro, Gloucester County.
CLIFFORD, CHARLES J. Seaman, U.S. Navy, USS Home, 3-2-1910. Evergreen Cemetery, Hillside, Union County.
CLIFFORD, CHARLES W. Pvt, D, 15th MA Inf, 1-29-1898. Oak Hill Cemetery, Vineland, Cumberland County.
CLIFFORD, HENRY Pvt, E, 12th MD Inf, 12-1-1910. Cedar Green Cemetery, Clayton, Gloucester County.
CLIFFORD, J.B. 1910. Bevans Church Cemetery, Peters Valley, Sussex County.
CLIFFORD, JOHN W. Pvt, K, 11th IL Cav, 12-4-1883. 1st Methodist-Episcopal Cemetery, New Brunswick, Middlesex County.
CLIFFORD, NATHAN Pvt, C, 17th ME Inf, [Died of disease.] 10-5-1864. Beverly National Cemetery, Edgewater Park, Burlington County.
CLIFT, ELLIS Corp, B, 23rd NJ Inf, 3-5-1906. Bordentown/Old St. Mary's Catholic Cemetery, Bordentown, Burlington County.
CLIFT*, JOEL W. Capt, B, 12th NJ Inf, 11-18-1888. Bordentown/Old St. Mary's Catholic Cemetery, Bordentown, Burlington County.
CLIFT, JOHN A. Corp, C, 15th NJ Inf, 4-17-1906. Evergreen Cemetery, Morristown, Morris County.
CLIFT, THOMAS JAMES Pvt, PA Eng 1923. Stanhope-Union Cemetery, Netcong, Morris County.
CLIFTON, GEORGE 3-20-1918. Atlantic City Cemetery, Pleasantville, Atlantic County.
CLINCH, GEORGE W. Corp, I, 8th NY State Militia, DoD Unknown. Presbyterian Church Cemetery, Woodbridge, Middlesex County.
CLINCH, WILLIAM MAXTED (aka: Smith, William) __, __, __ OH __, 1926. Woodlawn Cemetery, Lakewood, Ocean County.

New Jersey Civil War Burials

CLINE, ANDREW B. Corp, C, 9th NJ Inf, 1-26-1902. Baptist Cemetery, Vincentown, Burlington County.
CLINE, BENJAMIN W. Pvt, I, 5th NJ Inf, 5-27-1912. St. Mary's Cemetery, Hainesport, Burlington County.
CLINE, DANIEL Pvt, G, 47th AL Inf (CSA), 9-19-1863. Finn's Point National Cemetery, Pennsville, Salem County.
CLINE, DAVID Pvt, E, 10th NJ Inf, 9-2-1881. 1st United Methodist Church Cemetery, Bridgeton, Cumberland County.
CLINE, ELIHU C. Pvt, F, 14th TN Inf (CSA), 10-5-1863. Finn's Point National Cemetery, Pennsville, Salem County.
CLINE*, GEORGE H. Pvt, Btty B, 1st NJ Light Art, [Wounded in action.] 8-2-1892. Mansfield/Washington Cemetery, Washington, Warren County.
CLINE, JAMES R. Pvt, K, 13th AL Inf (CSA), 6-13-1865. Finn's Point National Cemetery, Pennsville, Salem County.
CLINE, JOHN Pvt, C, 1st NJ Cav, 12-24-1896. Fairmount Cemetery, Newark, Essex County.
CLINE, JOHN Pvt, B, 38th NJ Inf, 12-7-1898. Union Cemetery, Frenchtown, Hunterdon County.
CLINE, JOHN H. Pvt, I, 4th NJ Inf, [Killed in action at Spotsylvania CH, VA.] 5-12-1864. Grove Church Cemetery, North Bergen, Hudson County.
CLINE, JOHN W. 3-8-1904. Calvary Community Church Cemetery, Harmony, Warren County.
CLINE, JONATHAN Pvt, F, 23rd NJ Inf, 4-13-1912. Arlington Cemetery, Kearny, Hudson County.
CLINE, JOSEPH Pvt, C, 9th NJ Inf, 5-16-1923. Evergreen Cemetery, Camden, Camden County.
CLINE, JOSEPH Pvt, Btty B, 1st NJ Light Art, 9-12-1871. Mansfield/Washington Cemetery, Washington, Warren County.
CLINE, JOSEPH C. Corp, I, 5th NJ Inf, [Died of wounds received 10-13-1863 at McLean's Ford, VA.] 10-23-1863. Colestown Cemetery, Cherry Hill, Camden County.
CLINE, MARK Pvt, K, 8th MI Inf, 6-8-1870. Mansfield/Washington Cemetery, Washington, Warren County.
CLINE, PETER (aka: Kline, Peter) Pvt, G, 9th PA Cav, 10-24-1908. Grove Church Cemetery, North Bergen, Hudson County.
CLINE, SINNICKSON Pvt, E, 3rd U.S. CT, 6-1-1904. Mount Hope United Methodist Church Cemetery, Salem, Salem County.
CLINE, THOMAS J. Pvt, K, 151st OH Inf, 8-8-1881. Mount Holly Cemetery, Mount Holly, Burlington County.
CLINGER, JAMES H. Pvt, Btty E, 2nd PA Heavy Art, 5-25-1926. Arlington Cemetery, Pennsauken, Camden County.
CLINTOCK, FERDINAND (see: McClintock, Ferdinand) Prospect Hill Cemetery, Caldwell, Essex County.
CLINTOCK, WILLIAM R. Corp, E, 33rd NJ Inf, 4-2-1878. Clinton Cemetery, Irvington, Essex County.
CLINTON, BENJAMIN Pvt, C, 9th NJ Inf, [Wounded in action at Roanoke Island, NC.] 4-10-1882. Beverly National Cemetery, Edgewater Park, Burlington County.
CLINTON, CHARLES T.J. Pvt, D, 56th NY Inf, 10-7-1920. Cedar Lawn Cemetery, Paterson, Passaic County.
CLINTON, FRANCIS H. Corp, G, 40th NJ Inf, 2-14-1890. Bordentown/Old St. Mary's Catholic Cemetery, Bordentown, Burlington County.
CLIVER, CHARLES H. Corp, E, 23rd NJ Inf, 8-26-1918. Baptist Cemetery, Pemberton, Burlington County.

Our Brothers Gone Before

CLIVER, DANIEL Pvt, F, 1st NJ Cav, 2-16-1870. Bordentown/Old St. Mary's Catholic Cemetery, Bordentown, Burlington County.

CLIVER, DANIEL L. Pvt, E, 2nd NJ Cav, 7-12-1923. Riverview Cemetery, Trenton, Mercer County.

CLIVER, HENRY Pvt, I, 1st NJ Cav, DoD Unknown. Bordentown/Old St. Mary's Catholic Cemetery, Bordentown, Burlington County.

CLIVER, JAMES Farrier, F, 1st NJ Cav, 6-28-1920. St. Mark's Baptist Church Cemetery, Browns Mills, Burlington County.

CLIVER, JONATHAN P. Pvt, E, 23rd NJ Inf, 12-1-1881. Methodist Church Cemetery, Juliustown, Burlington County.

CLIVER, JONATHAN R. Pvt, G, 25th NJ Inf, 7-25-1885. Presbyterian Church Cemetery, Cold Spring, Cape May County.

CLIVER, JOSEPH A. Pvt, 51st, 2nd Bttn U.S. VRC, 10-3-1928. Methodist Church Cemetery, Groveville, Mercer County.

CLIVER, JOSEPH KING Pvt, D, 23rd NJ Inf, 12-16-1906. Methodist-Episcopal Cemetery, Pointville, Burlington County.

CLIVER, THOMAS A. Pvt, D, 23rd NJ Inf, 11-23-1891. Baptist Church Cemetery, Jacobstown, Burlington County.

CLIVER, WALTER H. 6-1-1889. Oddfellows Cemetery, Burlington, Burlington County.

CLIVER, WILLIAM H. Pvt, H, 37th NJ Inf, 8-23-1886. Baptist Cemetery, Burlington, Burlington County.

CLIVER, WILLIAM H. Sgt, E, 69th OH Inf, 10-22-1905. Springfield-Upper Springfield-Friends Cemetery, Springfield, Burlington County.

CLOCK, CHARLES 1-9-1928. Presbyterian Church Cemetery, Andover, Sussex County.

CLODFELTER, GEORGE Pvt, G, 2nd Bttn NC Inf (CSA), [Captured 7-3-1863 at Gettysburg, PA. Died of smallpox.] 11-6-1863. Finn's Point National Cemetery, Pennsville, Salem County.

CLODFELTER, H.L. Pvt, B, 57th NC Inf (CSA), [Captured 7-2-1863 at Gettysburg, PA. Died of pneumonia.] 8-20-1863. Finn's Point National Cemetery, Pennsville, Salem County.

CLOHOSEY*, THOMAS Pvt, B, 72nd PA Inf, 10-20-1869. Oak Grove Cemetery, Hammonton, Atlantic County.

CLOKE*, ALBERT S. Capt, B, 3rd NJ Cav, DoD Unknown. Jersey City Cemetery, Jersey City, Hudson County.

CLOKE, WILLIAM H. Sgt, A, 82nd VA Militia (CSA), DoD Unknown. Hazelwood Cemetery, Rahway, Union County.

CLORAN, JOHN (aka: Cloren, John) Pvt, D, 6th NJ Inf, [Died of typhoid at Tenallytown, MD.] 10-11-1862. Old St. Mary's Cemetery, Gloucester City, Camden County.

CLORAN, TIMOTHY (aka: Cloren, Timothy) Pvt, D, 6th NJ Inf, [Died of disease at Williamsburg, VA.] 5-5-1862. Old St. Mary's Cemetery, Gloucester City, Camden County.

CLOREN, JOHN (see: Cloran, John) Old St. Mary's Cemetery, Gloucester City, Camden County.

CLOREN, TIMOTHY (see: Cloran, Timothy) Old St. Mary's Cemetery, Gloucester City, Camden County.

CLOS, JOHN Pvt, H, 2nd NJ Cav, 8-29-1921. Jersey City Cemetery, Jersey City, Hudson County.

CLOSE, FREDERICK 2nd Lt, B, 35th NJ Inf, 6-13-1885. Rahway Cemetery, Rahway, Union County.

CLOSE, JAMES B. Pvt, E, 2nd NJ Militia, 6-10-1896. Bayview-New York Bay Cemetery, Jersey City, Hudson County.

CLOSE, JOSEPH DoD Unknown. Laurel Grove Cemetery, Totowa, Passaic County.

CLOSE, WILLIAM 8-28-1861. Laurel Grove Cemetery, Totowa, Passaic County.

New Jersey Civil War Burials

CLOSSEN*, MORDECAI Sgt, D, 34th NJ Inf, 1-18-1892. Beverly National Cemetery, Edgewater Park, Burlington County.

CLOSSON, THEODORE Pvt, U.S. Marine Corps, 10-4-1884. Mercer Cemetery, Trenton, Mercer County.

CLOUD, BENJAMIN (JR.) Pvt, G, 5th MD Inf, 11-21-1872. Green Cemetery, Woodbury, Gloucester County.

CLOUD, ISAAC W. Pvt, I, 38th NJ Inf, 1882. Methodist Church Cemetery, Groveville, Mercer County.

CLOUD, WILLIAM 1st Sgt, K, 91st PA Inf, 1-16-1907. Maple Grove Cemetery, Hackensack, Bergen County.

CLOUGHLEY, ALFRED Pvt, F, 8th NY State Militia, 12-4-1899. Glenwood Cemetery, West Long Branch, Monmouth County.

CLOW, ROBERT Musc, A, 4th NJ Inf, 11-1-1899. Riverview Cemetery, Trenton, Mercer County.

CLOYD, CHARLES H. Pvt, I, 29th NJ Inf, 1923. Mount Pleasant Cemetery, Newark, Essex County.

CLUGSTON, JAMES B. Wagoner, H, 7th NJ Inf, 5-8-1911. Riverview Cemetery, Trenton, Mercer County.

CLUGSTON, JOHN C. Pvt, C, PA Emerg NJ Militia, 4-11-1900. Riverview Cemetery, Trenton, Mercer County.

CLUM, CHAUNCEY Pvt, A, 1st NJ Inf, 9-16-1872. Evergreen Cemetery, Hillside, Union County.

CLUNN, ADRIAN Pvt, I, 24th NJ Inf, 1894. Riverview Cemetery, Penns Grove, Salem County.

CLUNN, CHARLES P. Sgt, G, 3rd NJ Cav, 11-16-1909. Mount Pleasant Cemetery, Millville, Cumberland County.

CLUNN, WILLIAM E. Com Sgt, G, 3rd NJ Cav, 4-11-1911. Mount Pleasant Cemetery, Millville, Cumberland County.

CLUSS, PETER PHILIP Pvt, C, 22nd NJ Inf, 2-27-1927. Valleau Cemetery, Ridgewood, Bergen County.

CLUSTER, JAMES Pvt, D, 8th NY Cav, 12-24-1915. Holy Name Cemetery, Jersey City, Hudson County.

CLUTE*, PETER H. 2nd Lt, H, 39th NJ Inf, 1-30-1893. Rosedale Cemetery, Orange, Essex County.

CLYMER, EDWARD S. Pvt, C, 26th NJ Inf, 11-15-1916. Fairmount Cemetery, Newark, Essex County.

CLYMER, ISAAC Pvt, B, 3rd NJ Cav, 9-28-1866. St. James Cemetery, Greenwich, Warren County.

CLYMER, JOHN N. Corp, B, 23rd NJ Inf, 6-8-1922. Methodist Church Cemetery, Groveville, Mercer County.

CLYMER, ROBERT G. Pvt, H, 3rd NJ Cav, DoD Unknown. 1st United Methodist Church Cemetery, Bridgeton, Cumberland County.

CLYNES, THOMAS H. Capt, C, 72nd NY State Militia, 8-10-1886. Bayview-New York Bay Cemetery, Jersey City, Hudson County.

COAKLEY, SAMUEL Pvt, A, 16th U.S. Inf, 7-2-1909. Arlington Cemetery, Kearny, Hudson County.

COATES, COLLINS (see: Coults, Collins) Evergreen Cemetery, Camden, Camden County.

COATES, JAMES Pvt, D, 27th NJ Inf, DoD Unknown. Presbyterian Church Cemetery, Andover, Sussex County.

COATES, JOHN (see: Coats, John) Harleigh Cemetery, Camden, Camden County.

COATES, JOHN H. Pvt, F, 2nd NJ Inf, 10-4-1904. Cedar Lawn Cemetery, Paterson, Passaic County.

Our Brothers Gone Before

COATES, JOHN W. Pvt, B, 3rd NJ Inf, 2-27-1899. Baptist/Evergreen Methodist Cemetery, Plainfield, Union County.

COATES, JOHN W. (see: Coats, John William) Harleigh Cemetery, Camden, Camden County.

COATES, RICHARD Pvt, D, 13th OH Cav, 1-3-1921. Methodist Church Cemetery, New Albany, Burlington County.

COATES, SEWELL Pvt, A, 12th KY Inf, 5-8-1865. Fairmount Cemetery, Newark, Essex County.

COATES, THOMAS Pvt, D, 30th NJ Inf, 1905. Locust Grove Cemetery, Quakertown, Hunterdon County.

COATES, WILLIAM Pvt, C, 1st NY Inf, 8-18-1920. Cedar Lawn Cemetery, Paterson, Passaic County.

COATES*, WILLIAM N. Pvt, B, 38th NJ Inf, 1-17-1921. Sandy Ridge Cemetery, Sandy Ridge, Hunterdon County.

COATS, JOHN (aka: Coates, John) Capt, I, 10th NJ Inf, 1-28-1903. Harleigh Cemetery, Camden, Camden County.

COATS, JOHN WILLIAM (aka: Coates, John W.) Pvt, E, 3rd NJ Inf, 2-28-1899. Harleigh Cemetery, Camden, Camden County.

COATS, LEWIS Pvt, I, 10th NJ Inf, 10-20-1925. Harleigh Cemetery, Camden, Camden County.

COBB, ALFRED S. Pvt, G, 24th NJ Inf, [Died of typhoid at Chain Bridge, VA.] 11-14-1862. Mount Pleasant Cemetery, Millville, Cumberland County.

COBB, CALEB Pvt, G, 24th NJ Inf, DoD Unknown. Mount Pleasant Cemetery, Millville, Cumberland County.

COBB, CHARLES E. Pvt, D, 26th NJ Inf, 3-25-1922. Rosedale Cemetery, Orange, Essex County.

COBB, CHARLES P. Pvt, C, 38th NJ Inf, 8-18-1913. Mount Pleasant Cemetery, Millville, Cumberland County.

COBB*, DAVID W. 1st Sgt, C, 12th NJ Inf, 3-15-1894. Mount Holly Cemetery, Mount Holly, Burlington County.

COBB, EDWARD Sgt, G, 10th NJ Inf, 4-18-1903. Evergreen Cemetery, Hillside, Union County.

COBB*, EDWARD L. Sgt, A, 83rd NY Inf, 5-30-1913. Harleigh Cemetery, Camden, Camden County.

COBB, ELIJAH C. Pvt, G, 19th (Dockery's) AR Inf (CSA), [Captured 5-16-1863 at Big Black River Bridge, MS.] 8-20-1863. Finn's Point National Cemetery, Pennsville, Salem County.

COBB, GEORGE Pvt, E, 6th NJ Inf, 8-2-1902. Columbus Cemetery, Columbus, Burlington County.

COBB, GEORGE B. 11-20-1908. Mount Pleasant Cemetery, Newark, Essex County.

COBB, JACOB P. Corp, G, 24th NJ Inf, 10-17-1895. Mount Pleasant Cemetery, Millville, Cumberland County.

COBB, JAMES D. Corp, A, 13th NJ Inf, 4-20-1921. Fairmount Cemetery, Newark, Essex County.

COBB, JAMES R. Pvt, K, 23rd NJ Inf, 3-11-1889. Methodist-Episcopal Cemetery, Green Bank, Burlington County.

COBB*, JESSE T. 1st Sgt, E, 5th NH Inf, 7-30-1915. Oak Hill Cemetery, Vineland, Cumberland County.

COBB, JOHN (see: Corb, John) Vincent Methodist-Episcopal Cemetery, Nutley, Essex County.

COBB, JOHN W. Corp, G, 24th NJ Inf, 11-16-1905. Methodist Church Cemetery, Haleyville, Cumberland County.

COBB, JOSEPH W. Pvt, G, 24th NJ Inf, 8-24-1911. Mount Pleasant Cemetery, Millville, Cumberland County.

New Jersey Civil War Burials

COBB*, REUBEN W. Pvt, D, 26th NJ Inf, DoD Unknown. Methodist Church Cemetery, Roseland, Essex County.
COBB, SAMUEL D. Pvt, E, 1st NY Eng, 9-25-1911. Fairmount Cemetery, Newark, Essex County.
COBB*, WILLIAM Pvt, D, 25th NJ Inf, [Wounded in action.] DoD Unknown. Evergreen Cemetery, Hillside, Union County.
COBB, WILLIAM Pvt, U.S. Army, [Signal Corps, Paines Company.] DoD Unknown. Hillside Cemetery, Oxford, Warren County.
COBB, WILLIAM L. 1928. Methodist-Episcopal Cemetery, Port Norris, Cumberland County.
COBB*, WILLIAM T. 1st Sgt, F, 5th NJ Inf, 1-14-1913. Greenlawn Cemetery, West Long Branch, Monmouth County.
COBBLE, LOUIS Pvt, C, 60th (Crawford's) TN Mtd Inf (CSA), [Captured 5-17-1863 at Big Black River Bridge, MS.] 9-18-1863. Finn's Point National Cemetery, Pennsville, Salem County.
COBEL, WILLIAM Pvt, G, 153rd PA Inf, 1910. Locust Hill Cemetery, Dover, Morris County.
COBINE*, JOSEPH S. Pvt, G, 8th NJ Inf, 2-10-1907. Riverview Cemetery, Trenton, Mercer County.
COBLE, GEORGE G. Pvt, I, 57th NC Inf (CSA), [Captured 5-3-1863 at Chancellorsville, VA.] 6-19-1863. Finn's Point National Cemetery, Pennsville, Salem County.
COBLENZER, JOHN Pvt, E, 2nd NJ Inf, 10-31-1888. Fairmount Cemetery, Newark, Essex County.
COBURN, CHARLES A. Pvt, B, 9th NJ Inf, 3-10-1929. Washington Monumental Cemetery, South River, Middlesex County.
COBURN*, JOHN Pvt, E, 7th NJ Inf, 5-4-1895. Riverview Cemetery, Trenton, Mercer County.
COBURN, JOHN C. Pvt, F, 11th NJ Inf, 4-1-1902. Washington Monumental Cemetery, South River, Middlesex County.
COCHRAN, JOHN E. Pvt, C, 91st PA Inf, 3-5-1897. Evergreen Cemetery, Camden, Camden County.
COCHRAN, JOHN E. 1st Sgt, D, 72nd PA Inf, 11-21-1904. 1st Baptist Cemetery, Cape May Court House, Cape May County.
COCHRAN, M.F. Pvt, I, 19th VA Cav (CSA), 6-18-1864. Finn's Point National Cemetery, Pennsville, Salem County.
COCHRAN*, SAMUEL W Pvt, G, 7th NJ Inf, 1921. Mount Hope Presbyterian Cemetery, Lambertville, Hunterdon County.
COCHRAN*, WILLIAM B. (aka: Bowman, William) Pvt, C, 142nd NY Inf, [Wounded in action 10-17-1864.] 1916. Cedar Lawn Cemetery, Paterson, Passaic County.
COCHRAN, WILLIAM HENRY Sgt, G, 61st PA Inf, [Wounded 5-12-1864 at Spotsylvania CH, VA.] 10-20-1897. 1st Baptist Cemetery, Cape May Court House, Cape May County.
COCHRANE, HENRY H. Pvt, E, 4th NJ Inf, 3-25-1914. Bloomfield Cemetery, Bloomfield, Essex County.
COCHRANE, HUGH K. Seaman, U.S. Navy, USS Saranac, 2-17-1911. Arlington Cemetery, Kearny, Hudson County.
COCHRANE, JOHN Pvt, H, 1st NJ Cav, 12-4-1890. St. Peter's Cemetery, New Brunswick, Middlesex County.
COCHRANE, WILLIAM H. Capt, G, 33rd NJ Inf, [Killed in action at Pine Knob, GA.] 6-16-1864. Presbyterian Church Cemetery, New Providence, Union County.
COCKEFAIR, EPHRIAM Pvt, F, 26th NJ Inf, 12-4-1878. Bloomfield Cemetery, Bloomfield, Essex County.
COCKEFAIR*, JOHN HENRY Corp, F, 26th NJ Inf, 11-6-1914. Bloomfield Cemetery, Bloomfield, Essex County.

Our Brothers Gone Before

COCKEFAIR, JOSEPH B. 5-30-1874. Bloomfield Cemetery, Bloomfield, Essex County.
COCKER, THOMAS W. Corp, G, 7th NJ Inf, 7-30-1918. Laurel Grove Cemetery, Totowa, Passaic County.
COCKROFT, WILLIAM Corp, K, 70th NY Inf, [Wounded 11-27-1863 at Locust Grove, VA.] 9-16-1873. Fairmount Cemetery, Newark, Essex County.
COCKS, ANDREW (see: Cox, Andrew) Cedar Hill Cemetery, East Millstone, Somerset County.
COCOKORO, JACOB Pvt, C, 13th NJ Inf, 1-19-1900. Laurel Grove Cemetery, Totowa, Passaic County.
CODDINGTON*, DAVID M. Pvt, I, 47th GA Inf (CSA), 4-25-1914. Trinity Episcopal Church Cemetery, Woodbridge, Middlesex County.
CODDINGTON, DAVID N. Pvt, K, 3rd NJ Militia, 9-15-1871. Van Liew Cemetery, North Brunswick, Middlesex County.
CODDINGTON, HARRISON Pvt, K, 92nd IL Inf, 1928. Baptist/Evergreen Methodist Cemetery, Plainfield, Union County.
CODDINGTON, JOB Pvt, I, 5th NY Cav, 4-9-1927. Methodist Church Cemetery, Mount Horeb, Somerset County.
CODDINGTON, JOHN Corp, E, 15th U.S. Vet Vol Inf, 7-19-1910. Methodist Cemetery, Haddonfield, Camden County.
CODDINGTON, JOHN Pvt, B, 80th NY Inf, 11-24-1875. Methodist-Episcopal Cemetery, Burlington, Burlington County.
CODDINGTON, JOHN W. 2-26-1897. Methodist Church Cemetery, Mount Horeb, Somerset County.
CODDINGTON*, JOHN WORTH Corp, G, 1st NY Mounted Rifles, 5-2-1924. Hillside Cemetery, Scotch Plains, Union County.
CODDINGTON, JONATHAN P. Pvt, G, 1st NJ Militia, 7-21-1903. Woodland Cemetery, Newark, Essex County.
CODDINGTON, MARTIN S. Pvt, D, 28th NJ Inf, 6-8-1877. Willow Grove Cemetery, New Brunswick, Middlesex County.
CODDINGTON, SAMUEL R. Pvt, H, 5th NJ Inf, 6-2-1917. Alpine Cemetery, Perth Amboy, Middlesex County.
CODDINGTON, WILLIAM Pvt, C, 30th NJ Inf, 4-22-1913. Greenwood Cemetery, Hamilton, Mercer County.
CODDINGTON, WILLIAM C. Pvt, I, 11th NJ Inf, 7-1-1896. Willow Grove Cemetery, New Brunswick, Middlesex County.
CODDINGTON*, WILLIAM R. 1st Lt, F, 6th U.S. VRC, [Wounded 5-3-1863 at Chancellorsville, VA.] 1896. Alpine Cemetery, Perth Amboy, Middlesex County.
CODE, NICHOLAS Pvt, I, 12th NJ Inf, 5-9-1867. St. John's Evangelical Church Cemetery, Orange, Essex County.
CODEY*, PETER Pvt, K, 15th NJ Inf, 8-15-1867. St. John's Evangelical Church Cemetery, Orange, Essex County.
CODIN, JOHN ___, C, 39th NY Inf, 1881. Oak Hill Cemetery, Vineland, Cumberland County.
CODINGHAM, WILLIAM (see: Cottingham, William) Woodland Cemetery, Newark, Essex County.
CODINGTON, WESLEYAN 1864. Baptist Church Cemetery, Mount Bethel, Somerset County.
COE, BERNARD V. Pvt, I, 8th OH Cav, 2-5-1904. Siloam Cemetery, Vineland, Cumberland County.
COE, ELI PERRY Pvt, C, 50th NY Eng, 10-11-1891. Elwood Rural Cemetery, Elwood, Atlantic County.
COE, GEORGE B. 1st Sgt, D, 35th NJ Inf, 5-13-1916. Oak Hill Cemetery, Vineland, Cumberland County.

New Jersey Civil War Burials

COE, HENRY Pvt, B, 29th NJ Inf, 11- -1888. Laurel Grove Cemetery, Totowa, Passaic County.

COE, THOMAS J. Pvt, B, 7th NJ Inf, 3-10-1885. Fairmount Cemetery, Newark, Essex County.

COEN*, JOSEPH (aka: Coin, James) Pvt, F, 34th GA Inf (CSA), [Captured 5-16-1863 at Baker's Creek, MS.] 6-21-1863. Finn's Point National Cemetery, Pennsville, Salem County.

COEN, MOORE G. Pvt, H, 15th NJ Inf, 1-18-1875. Wesley Chapel Cemetery, Belvidere, Warren County.

COER, JOSEPH SMITH Sgt, C, 3rd NJ Inf, 6-27-1906. Oddfellows Cemetery, Burlington, Burlington County.

COER, THOMAS (see: Carr, Thomas) Holy Sepulchre Cemetery, East Orange, Essex County.

COEYMAN, JOSEPH O. Pvt, B, 9th NJ Inf, 4-1-1893. Fairmount Cemetery, Newark, Essex County.

COEYMAN*, WILLIAM A. (aka: Freeman, William) Pvt, A, 3rd U.S. VRC, 6-23-1917. Evergreen Cemetery, Hillside, Union County.

COFF, JOSEPH D. 1-30-1874. Eglington Cemetery, Clarksboro, Gloucester County.

COFFEE, CHARLES A. Pvt, E, 1st PA Inf, 2-16-1917. Monument Cemetery, Edgewater Park, Burlington County.

COFFEE, PATRICK Pvt, I, 29th NJ Inf, 6-6-1907. St. Rose of Lima Cemetery, Freehold, Monmouth County.

COFFEE, ROBERT Pvt, B, 13th TN Inf (CSA), 11-9-1863. Finn's Point National Cemetery, Pennsville, Salem County.

COFFEE, THOMAS Pvt, C, 33rd NJ Inf, DoD Unknown. St. John's Evangelical Church Cemetery, Orange, Essex County.

COFFER, JACOB Landsman, U.S. Navy, 8-2-1917. Mount Olivet Cemetery, Fairview, Monmouth County.

COFFEY, JAMES Pvt, G, 6th PA Cav, [Wounded in action 6-11-1864 and 9-1-1864.] 1902. St. John's Cemetery, Allentown, Monmouth County.

COFFIELD, SILLERY Pvt, H, 8th Confederate States Cav (CSA), 11-13-1863. Finn's Point National Cemetery, Pennsville, Salem County.

COFFIN, EDWARD WINSLOW Bvt Maj, U.S. Volunteers, [Commissary of Subsistence.] 12-12-1912. Colestown Cemetery, Cherry Hill, Camden County.

COFFIN, GEORGE H. Sgt, C, 13th NY Inf, 1909. Mount Prospect Cemetery, Neptune, Monmouth County.

COFFIN, URIAH H. 1st Lt,RQM, 120th NY Inf 4-4-1919. Bayview-New York Bay Cemetery, Jersey City, Hudson County.

COFFMAN, JAMES Pvt, K, 59th GA Inf (CSA), [Wounded and captured 7-2-1863 at Gettysburg, PA. Died of smallpox.] 10-17-1863. Finn's Point National Cemetery, Pennsville, Salem County.

COFFY, JOHN (aka: Cosley, John) Pvt, I, 3rd U.S. CT, 12-21-1907. Flower Hill Cemetery, North Bergen, Hudson County.

COGAN, ELEAZER THOMAS Pvt, Btty E, 1st NJ Light Art, 12-21-1869. Fairmount Cemetery, Newark, Essex County.

COGAN, RICHARD E. 2nd Lt, B, 9th NJ Inf, 10-25-1924. Baptist Church Cemetery, Haddonfield, Camden County.

COGAN, THOMAS Pvt, G, 21st NJ Inf, 6-4-1896. Holy Sepulchre Cemetery, East Orange, Essex County.

COGER, JOHN J. Sgt, G, 7th NY Inf, 3-11-1909. Fairview Cemetery, Westfield, Union County.

COGGEI, BENJAMIN (see: Cogger, Benjamin Franklin) Prospect Hill Cemetery, Caldwell, Essex County.

Our Brothers Gone Before

COGGER*, BENJAMIN FRANKLIN (aka: Coggei, Benjamin) Pvt, K, 153rd IL Inf, 2-28-1906. Prospect Hill Cemetery, Caldwell, Essex County.

COGGIN, GEORGE W. Sgt, K, 34th NC Inf (CSA), [Captured 7-3-1863 at Gettysburg, PA.] 9-29-1863. Finn's Point National Cemetery, Pennsville, Salem County.

COGGIN, JEREMIAH 2nd Lt, C, 23rd NC Inf (CSA), [Wounded 5-31-1862 at Seven Pines, VA. and 9-17-1862 at Sharpsburg, MD. Captured 7-1-1863 at Gettysburg, PA. Died of diarrhea.] 3-15-1865. Finn's Point National Cemetery, Pennsville, Salem County.

COGGINS, DAVID C. Pvt, D, 8th AL Inf (CSA), 10-17-1863. Finn's Point National Cemetery, Pennsville, Salem County.

COGILL, WILLIAM G. Pvt, C, 12th U.S. Inf, 7-24-1901. Atlantic City Cemetery, Pleasantville, Atlantic County.

COGSWELL, ANDREW K. Pvt, E, 7th NY State Militia, 2-13-1887. Willow Grove Cemetery, New Brunswick, Middlesex County.

COGSWELL, FRANK W. Capt, C, 127th U.S. CT, 8-21-1881. Evergreen Cemetery, Camden, Camden County.

COGSWELL*, JESSE W. Capt, C, 34th NJ Inf, 5-30-1909. Evergreen Cemetery, Camden, Camden County.

COHEN, HENRY Pvt, E, 4th NJ Inf, 1895. Newton Cemetery, Newton, Sussex County.

COHEN, JOHN DoD Unknown. Holy Sepulchre Cemetery, East Orange, Essex County.

COHNHEIM*, MAX Capt, H, 41st NY Inf, 11-27-1904. Fairmount Cemetery, Newark, Essex County.

COHR, WILLIAM S. 9-7-1909. Rosedale Cemetery, Orange, Essex County.

COILE, MORRIS (see: Coyle, Morris) Mansfield/Washington Cemetery, Washington, Warren County.

COIN, JAMES (see: Coen, Joseph) Finn's Point National Cemetery, Pennsville, Salem County.

COINER, PRESTON H. Pvt, E, 1st VA Cav (CSA), [Died of disease.] 8-31-1863. Finn's Point National Cemetery, Pennsville, Salem County.

COKELET, ISAAC (aka: Cokelt, Isaac D.) Pvt, A, 106th NY Inf, DoD Unknown. Cedarwood Cemetery, Hazlet, Monmouth County.

COKELT, ISAAC D. (see: Cokelet, Isaac) Cedarwood Cemetery, Hazlet, Monmouth County.

COLAMINE, ALEXANDER Pvt, A, 39th U.S. CT, 4-4-1865. Beverly National Cemetery, Edgewater Park, Burlington County.

COLBATH, ALEXANDER B. 10-11-1905. Bayview-New York Bay Cemetery, Jersey City, Hudson County.

COLBATH, GEORGE Pvt, C, 1st PA Inf, 1907. Soldier's Home Cemetery, Vineland, Cumberland County.

COLBERT, HENRY Pvt, H, 4th NJ Inf, 4-21-1919. Soldier's Home Cemetery, Vineland, Cumberland County.

COLBERT, JOHN Pvt, B, 33rd VA Inf (CSA), [Wounded and captured 3-23-1862 at Kernstown, VA.] 6-11-1862. Finn's Point National Cemetery, Pennsville, Salem County.

COLBY, AARON Pvt, D, 3rd NJ Militia, 11-24-1883. Presbyterian Church Cemetery, Kingston, Somerset County.

COLBY, ALAN F.G. Pvt, B, 28th NJ Inf, [Wounded 12-13-1862 at Fredericksburg, VA.] 9-11-1895. Presbyterian Church Cemetery, Kingston, Somerset County.

COLBY, MARTIN Pvt, G, 39th NJ Inf, 6-1-1865. Holy Sepulchre Cemetery, East Orange, Essex County.

COLD, WILLIAM Seaman, U.S. Navy, USS Cumberland, 7-18-1877. Trinity Episcopal Church Cemetery, Moorestown, Burlington County.

COLE, A.P. Pvt, K, 42nd MS Inf (CSA), 9-2-1863. Finn's Point National Cemetery, Pennsville, Salem County.

New Jersey Civil War Burials

COLE, ABRAHAM Pvt, A, 30th NJ Inf, DoD Unknown. Peapack Reformed Church Cemetery, Gladstone, Somerset County.

COLE, ABRAHAM V. 4-11-1891. Grove Methodist Church Cemetery, Readington, Hunterdon County.

COLE, ABRAM A. Pvt, I, 22nd NJ Inf, 3-10-1908. Old South Church Cemetery, Bergenfield, Bergen County.

COLE, ALANSON Pvt, E, 9th NJ Inf, [Wounded in action.] 3-18-1897. Canistear Cemetery, Vernon, Sussex County.

COLE, ALANSON S. Pvt, Btty L, 5th NY Heavy Art, 4-8-1928. Fairmount Cemetery, Newark, Essex County.

COLE, ALBERT Pvt, F, 214th PA Inf, 11-2-1865. Christian Cemetery, Milford, Hunterdon County.

COLE, ALONZO A. 9-4-1906. English Neighborhood Reformed Church Cemetery, Ridgefield, Bergen County.

COLE, ANDREW J. Pvt, B, 95th PA Inf, 2-27-1916. Union Cemetery, Milford, Hunterdon County.

COLE, BENJAMIN Pvt, I, 83rd NY Inf, [Wounded 9-17-1862 at Antietam, MD.] 8-22-1882. Grove Church Cemetery, North Bergen, Hudson County.

COLE, C.N.J. Pvt, H, 16th GA Inf (CSA), [Captured 7-2-1863 at Gettysburg, PA. Died of smallpox.] 9-1-1863. Finn's Point National Cemetery, Pennsville, Salem County.

COLE, CHARLES M. Pvt, D, 48th NY Inf, [Died at Fort Schuyler, NY of wounds received 7-18-1863 at Fort Wagner, SC.] 8-3-1863. Congregational Church Cemetery, Chester, Morris County.

COLE, CHARLES P. Pvt, C, 24th NJ Inf, 1918. 1st United Methodist Church Cemetery, Salem, Salem County.

COLE, CHARLES W. 1st Cl Fireman, U.S. Navy, USS Alabama, 4-24-1925. Phillipsburg Cemetery, Phillipsburg, Warren County.

COLE, CHRIS JOHN Pvt, I, 31st NJ Inf, 1922. Hazen Cemetery, Hazen, Warren County.

COLE, DAVID L. 2-4-1916. Methodist Church Cemetery, Sparta, Sussex County.

COLE, EDWARD Pvt, E, 90th PA Inf, [Died at Warrenton, VA.] 7-9-1862. Old St. Mary's Cemetery, Gloucester City, Camden County.

COLE, EDWARD Pvt, C, 8th NJ Inf, DoD Unknown. United Methodist Church Cemetery, Port Elizabeth, Cumberland County.

COLE, FRANCIS W. Pvt, E, 2nd NJ Cav, 6-2-1901. Riverview Cemetery, Trenton, Mercer County.

COLE*, FRANCIS W. Pvt, E, 2nd NJ Cav, 6-2-1901. Cedar Hill Cemetery, Hightstown, Mercer County.

COLE, FRANK O. Sgt, E, 30th MA Inf, [Wounded 10-19-1864 at Cedar Creek, VA.] 10-7-1930. Bayview-New York Bay Cemetery, Jersey City, Hudson County.

COLE, GEORGE W. 10-21-1910. Harleigh Cemetery, Camden, Camden County.

COLE, GEORGE W. Pvt, G, 38th NJ Inf, 1927. Vail Presbyterian Cemetery, Parsippany, Morris County.

COLE, GEORGE W. Sgt, C, 12th NY Inf, 2-4-1921. Laurel Grove Cemetery, Totowa, Passaic County.

COLE, HENRY CLAY Pvt, A, 41st U.S. CT, 7-27-1915. Bordentown/Old St. Mary's Catholic Cemetery, Bordentown, Burlington County.

COLE, HENRY W. Pvt, B, 15th NJ Inf, [Killed in action at Fredericksburg, VA.] 12-13-1862. Mansfield/Washington Cemetery, Washington, Warren County.

COLE, ISAAC Pvt, D, 22nd NJ Inf, 9-17-1928. Bayview-New York Bay Cemetery, Jersey City, Hudson County.

COLE*, ISAAC A. Landsman, U.S. Navy, USS Princeton, 11-16-1927. Evergreen Cemetery, Hillside, Union County.

COLE, ISAAC B. Pvt, H, 15th NJ Inf, 6-23-1881. Mansfield/Washington Cemetery, Washington, Warren County.

Our Brothers Gone Before

COLE, ISAAC I. Pvt, D, 133rd NY Inf, 1-26-1895. Adelphia Cemetery, Adelphia, Monmouth County.
COLE, JABEZ G. Pvt, I, 52nd PA Inf, 4-5-1925. Evergreen Cemetery, Hillside, Union County.
COLE, JACOB Pvt, E, 30th NJ Inf, 3-16-1871. Grove Methodist Church Cemetery, Readington, Hunterdon County.
COLE*, JACOB H. Pvt, A, 57th NY Inf, [Wounded 7-2-1863 at Gettysburg, PA.] 4-22-1929. Laurel Grove Cemetery, Totowa, Passaic County.
COLE, JACOB H. Pvt, I, 30th NJ Inf, 1914. Presbyterian Church Cemetery, Liberty Corners, Somerset County.
COLE*, JAMES D. 2nd Lt, E, 13th NJ Inf, 9-22-1916. Arlington Cemetery, Kearny, Hudson County.
COLE, JAMES G. Pvt, C, 7th NJ Inf, 5-15-1868. Presbyterian Church Cemetery, Oak Ridge, Passaic County.
COLE, JOHN Pvt, A, 14th NJ Inf, [Wounded 6-1-1864 at Cold Harbor, VA.] 1-12-1895. Methodist Church Cemetery, Pleasant Grove, Ocean County.
COLE, JOHN 8-27-1872. Cedar Hill Cemetery, Hightstown, Mercer County.
COLE, JOHN A. Pvt, C, 4th NY Cav, 6-16-1903. Evergreen Cemetery, Hillside, Union County.
COLE, JOHN F. Pvt, G, 121st NY Inf, 4-13-1913. Fairview Cemetery, Fairview, Bergen County.
COLE, JOHN HARRIS 1st Sgt, H, 37th NY National Guard, 11-14-1918. Glenwood Cemetery, West Long Branch, Monmouth County.
COLE, JOHN S. Sgt, G, 25th NJ Inf, 12-24-1872. Calvary Baptist Church Cemetery, Ocean View, Cape May County.
COLE, LARKIN Pvt, C, 11th MS Inf (CSA), 9-30-1863. Finn's Point National Cemetery, Pennsville, Salem County.
COLE, LEMUEL Pvt, I, 11th NJ Inf, [Died of typhoid at Washington, DC.] 1-11-1863. Hazen Cemetery, Hazen, Warren County.
COLE, LEVI B. Pvt, U.S. Marine Corps, USS Iosco, 1934. Evergreen Cemetery, Camden, Camden County.
COLE, LEWIS Pvt, C, __ U.S. Cav, 9-10-1891. Riverview Cemetery, Trenton, Mercer County.
COLE, MAJOR P. Pvt, C, 8th NJ Inf, 2-16-1881. Fairmount Cemetery, Newark, Essex County.
COLE, MICHAEL Pvt, H, 22nd U.S. CT, 10-15-1881. Hamilton Cemetery, Allentown, Monmouth County.
COLE, PAUL K. Pvt, G, 30th NJ Inf, 1912. Reformed Church Cemetery, Three Bridges, Hunterdon County.
COLE, REUBEN B. Hosp Steward, 1st NJ Cav 6-12-1912. Evergreen Cemetery, Camden, Camden County.
COLE, RICHARD H. Seaman, U.S. Navy, DoD Unknown. Presbyterian Church Cemetery, Bridgeton, Cumberland County.
COLE, SAMUEL W. Pvt, H, 9th NJ Inf, 1-13-1892. Methodist Church Cemetery, Summerfield, Warren County.
COLE, SIMON H. Corp, C, 7th NJ Inf, 1904. Presbyterian Church Cemetery, Rockaway, Morris County.
COLE*, STEPHEN B. Corp, I, 3rd NJ Inf, 1-19-1910. Fairmount Cemetery, Newark, Essex County.
COLE, THOMAS C. Corp, K, 31st NJ Inf, 7-28-1925. Elmwood Cemetery, New Brunswick, Middlesex County.
COLE, THOMAS P. Pvt, E, 35th IN Inf, 3-31-1913. Phillipsburg Cemetery, Phillipsburg, Warren County.

New Jersey Civil War Burials

COLE*, WILLIAM Pvt, E, 7th NJ Inf, 5-12-1905. Presbyterian/Methodist-Episcopal Cemetery, Succasunna, Morris County.

COLE, WILLIAM Pvt, B, 3rd NJ Cav, DoD Unknown. Brink Cemetery, Colesville, Sussex County.

COLE, WILLIAM Pvt, F, 22nd NJ Inf, 11-28-1900. St. Mary's Cemetery, Hamilton, Mercer County.

COLE, WILLIAM D. Pvt, B, 142nd NY Inf, [Wounded in action.] 2-11-1904. Fairmount Cemetery, Newark, Essex County.

COLE, WILLIAM H. Pvt, C, 8th DE Inf, 6-25-1913. New Camden Cemetery, Camden, Camden County.

COLE, WILLIAM H. Pvt, C, 34th NJ Inf, 8-24-1910. Good Luck Cemetery, Murray Grove, Ocean County.

COLE*, WILLIAM H. Pvt, C, 1st U.S. Cav, 2-25-1896. Laurel Grove Cemetery, Totowa, Passaic County.

COLE, WILLIAM H. Corp, B, 71st NY Inf, 7-3-1911. Fairmount Cemetery, Newark, Essex County.

COLE, WILLIAM T. Sgt, A, 38th NJ Inf, 1920. Fairview Cemetery, Fairview, Monmouth County.

COLEMAN, ABEL Pvt, F, 29th NJ Inf, 9-11-1913. Presbyterian Church Cemetery, Shrewsbury, Monmouth County.

COLEMAN, ALEXANDER Pvt, F, 31st GA Inf (CSA), [Wounded 12-13-1862 at Fredericksburg, VA and 7-2-1863 at Gettysburg, PA. Captured 7-4-1863 at Williamsport, MD. Died of lung inflammation.] 9-17-1863. Finn's Point National Cemetery, Pennsville, Salem County.

COLEMAN, AMBROSE 1901. United Methodist Church Cemetery, Windsor, Mercer County.

COLEMAN, ANTHONY Pvt, I, 2nd NJ Cav, 12-22-1888. Cedar Hill Cemetery, Hightstown, Mercer County.

COLEMAN, B.F. Pvt, B, 30th VA Inf (CSA), 1-4-1864. Finn's Point National Cemetery, Pennsville, Salem County.

COLEMAN, DAVID Pvt, A, 3rd NJ Cav, [Wounded in action.] 5-21-1921. Batsto/Pleasant Mills Methodist Church Cemetery, Pleasant Mills, Atlantic County.

COLEMAN, DAVID C. Corp, A, 1st Va Inf (US), [1st Eastern Virginia Loyal Infantry.] 10-12-1896. Presbyterian Church Cemetery, Mays Landing, Atlantic County.

COLEMAN, ENOCH Pvt, F, 38th NJ Inf, 10-20-1901. Cedar Hill Cemetery, Hightstown, Mercer County.

COLEMAN, GEORGE W. Pvt, C, 56th NY Inf, 6-7-1913. Fair Lawn Cemetery, Fair Lawn, Bergen County.

COLEMAN, HENRY Pvt, K, 4th NJ Inf, 1922. Baptist Church Cemetery, Canton, Salem County.

COLEMAN, HENRY Musc, G, 96th NY Inf, 12-6-1903. Fairmount Cemetery, Newark, Essex County.

COLEMAN, HENRY W. 1st Lt, H, Miles' Legion LA Inf (CSA), [Captured 7-9-1863 at Port Hudson, LA. Died of lung inflammation.] 5-20-1865. Finn's Point National Cemetery, Pennsville, Salem County.

COLEMAN, JAMES Sgt, K, 18th PA Cav, [Cenotaph. Died while prisoner at Andersonville, GA.] 7-7-1864. Old Camden Cemetery, Camden, Camden County.

COLEMAN, JAMES Pvt, K, 6th NJ Inf, 7-17-1903. Calvary Cemetery, Cherry Hill, Camden County.

COLEMAN, JAMES H. 3-7-1870. Fairmount Cemetery, Newark, Essex County.

COLEMAN*, JEREMIAH Pvt, C, 5th CT Inf, [Wounded 7-20-1864 at Peach Tree Creek, GA.] 5-20-1900. St. Peter's Cemetery, New Brunswick, Middlesex County.

COLEMAN, JOHN Pvt, D, 25th NJ Inf, [Wounded in action.] 1920. Cedar Green Cemetery, Clayton, Gloucester County.

Our Brothers Gone Before

COLEMAN, JOHN Pvt, B, 88th NY Inf, DoD Unknown. Holy Name Cemetery, Jersey City, Hudson County.
COLEMAN, JOHN Landsman, U.S. Navy, USS Lackawanna, 1910. White Ridge Cemetery, Eatontown, Monmouth County.
COLEMAN, JOHN Pvt, A, 1st NJ Cav, DoD Unknown. Holy Sepulchre Cemetery, Totowa, Passaic County.
COLEMAN, JOHN Pvt, C, 72nd NY Inf, 5-2-1903. Holy Sepulchre Cemetery, East Orange, Essex County.
COLEMAN, JOHN T. Pvt, A, 19th MS Inf (CSA), 12-6-1863. Finn's Point National Cemetery, Pennsville, Salem County.
COLEMAN, JOHN W. Pvt, K, 20th PA Militia, 2-11-1935. Arlington Cemetery, Pennsauken, Camden County.
COLEMAN, MADISON W. Sgt, M, 1st NJ Cav, 12-18-1917. Oak Hill Cemetery, Vineland, Cumberland County.
COLEMAN, MADISON W. 1880. St. Mary's Cemetery, South Amboy, Middlesex County.
COLEMAN, MAGER (aka: Coleman, Major) Pvt, H, 119th U.S. CT, 7-11-1909. Cedar View Cemetery, Lincroft, Monmouth County.
COLEMAN, MAJOR (see: Coleman, Mager) Cedar View Cemetery, Lincroft, Monmouth County.
COLEMAN, MICHAEL 12-4-1921. Holy Name Cemetery, Jersey City, Hudson County.
COLEMAN, PATRICK Pvt, B, 88th NY Inf, 12-22-1907. Holy Name Cemetery, Jersey City, Hudson County.
COLEMAN, REUBEN Pvt, A, 3rd NJ Cav, 3-19-1895. Siloam Cemetery, Vineland, Cumberland County.
COLEMAN, ROBERT F. Sgt, H, 3rd NJ Inf, 3-13-1895. Baptist/St. Andrew's Cemetery, Mount Holly, Burlington County.
COLEMAN, SILAS A. Pvt, K, 4th NJ Militia, 3-10-1865. Methodist-Episcopal Cemetery, Burlington, Burlington County.
COLEMAN, THOMAS Pvt, Btty F, 3rd NC Light Art (CSA), [Lawrence's battery.] 10-10-1862. Finn's Point National Cemetery, Pennsville, Salem County.
COLEMAN, THOMAS J. Pvt, C, 15th AL Inf (CSA), [Captured at Gettysburg, PA.] 6-29-1864. Finn's Point National Cemetery, Pennsville, Salem County.
COLEMAN*, WILLIAM Pvt, D, 11th NJ Inf, 12-22-1865. Fairmount Cemetery, Newark, Essex County.
COLEMAN, WILLIAM A. Pvt, Btty F, 2nd NY Heavy Art, DoD Unknown. Bayview-New York Bay Cemetery, Jersey City, Hudson County.
COLEMAN, WILLIAM D. Pvt, H, 31st NJ Inf, 7-15-1917. Fairmount Cemetery, Newark, Essex County.
COLEMAN, WILLIAM MERRITT Corp, D, 17th MI Inf, [Wounded 5-6-1864 at Wilderness, VA.] 12-23-1929. Fairview Cemetery, Fairview, Bergen County.
COLES, AARON Corp, D, 48th NY Inf, [Wounded 7-10-1863 at Morris Island, SC.] 1910. Friends Cemetery, Woodstown, Salem County.
COLES, ALONZO W. Pvt, D, 173rd NY Inf, 1-17-1885. United Methodist Cemetery, Gladstone, Somerset County.
COLES, BENJAMIN Corp, E, 146th OH Inf, 7-23-1897. Greenlawn Cemetery, West Long Branch, Monmouth County.
COLES*, EDWIN Pvt, D, 8th NJ Inf, 8-5-1906. Evergreen Cemetery, Hillside, Union County.
COLES, ELLIS B. Pvt, C, 23rd NJ Inf, 8-31-1889. Baptist/St. Andrew's Cemetery, Mount Holly, Burlington County.
COLES, FRANKLIN H. 1st Lt, A, 3rd NJ Inf, 1897. Baptist Church Cemetery, Mullica Hill, Gloucester County.
COLES*, FREDERICK Pvt, D, 8th NJ Inf, 10-16-1882. Fairmount Cemetery, Newark, Essex County.

New Jersey Civil War Burials

COLES, GEORGE H. Pvt, E, 21st NJ Inf, 2-25-1912. Eglington Cemetery, Clarksboro, Gloucester County.
COLES, ISAIAH I. 1895. Colestown Cemetery, Cherry Hill, Camden County.
COLES, JACOB L. Pvt, G, 2nd NJ Inf, 1-15-1903. Mount Pleasant Cemetery, Newark, Essex County.
COLES, JAMES P. Pvt, G, 13th NJ Inf, 4-12-1925. Christ Church Cemetery, Belleville, Essex County.
COLES, JOHN Pvt, G, 2nd NJ Inf, 1-25-1896. Fairmount Cemetery, Newark, Essex County.
COLES*, JOHN Pvt, F, 13th NJ Inf, 12-27-1901. Greenwood Cemetery, Hamilton, Mercer County.
COLES, JOHN A. Landsman, U.S. Navy, USS Pensacola, 10-3-1889. Fairmount Cemetery, Newark, Essex County.
COLES, JOHN ACKERMAN Landsman, U.S. Navy, USS Pensacola, DoD Unknown. Willow Grove Cemetery, New Brunswick, Middlesex County.
COLES, JOHN WOOLSTON Asst Surg, U.S. Navy, 4-6-1895. Colestown Cemetery, Cherry Hill, Camden County.
COLES, JOSEPH L. Pvt, I, 23rd NJ Inf, 1-17-1881. Evergreen Cemetery, Camden, Camden County.
COLES, JOSEPH S. Pvt, F, 37th NJ Inf, 3-3-1906. Baptist Church Cemetery, Slabtown, Salem County.
COLES, SAMUEL Corp, I, 13th PA Cav, 9-29-1890. Evergreen Cemetery, Camden, Camden County.
COLES, THOMAS P. Pvt, F, 3rd NJ Inf, [Wounded in action.] 7-11-1915. Presbyterian Church Cemetery, Bridgeton, Cumberland County.
COLES, WILLIAM J. Pvt, D, 4th NJ Militia, DoD Unknown. Cedar Grove Cemetery, Gloucester City, Camden County.
COLEY, BENJAMIN D. Capt, I, 6th NJ Inf, 6-8-1899. Evergreen Cemetery, Camden, Camden County.
COLEY, CONSTANCE Pvt, H, 5th NJ Inf, [Died of typhoid at Lower Potomac, VA.] 3-4-1862. St. Mary's Cemetery, Perth Amboy, Middlesex County.
COLEY, HARRISON Pvt, A, 13th TN Cav (CSA), 6-19-1864. Finn's Point National Cemetery, Pennsville, Salem County.
COLFAX, HARRISON Artificer, A, 1st NY Eng, 6-4-1919. Fairmount Cemetery, Newark, Essex County.
COLFAX, RICHARD H. 12-16-1871. Methodist-Episcopal Cemetery, Midland Park, Bergen County.
COLFAX, WILLIAM W. 8-8-1878. Pompton Reformed Church Cemetery, Pompton Lakes, Passaic County.
COLFER, JAMES Pvt, H, 9th NJ Inf, 6-17-1903. Holy Sepulchre Cemetery, East Orange, Essex County.
COLGAN, ALFRED E. Capt, I, 28th PA Inf, [Wounded 5-3-1863 at Chancellorsville, VA. and 6-15-1864 at Pine Knob, GA.] 7-30-1906. Evergreen Cemetery, Camden, Camden County.
COLGAN, JOHN Pvt, A, 88th NY Inf, 9-7-1885. Holy Name Cemetery, Jersey City, Hudson County.
COLIE, DANIEL F. Corp, H, 30th NJ Inf, 9-12-1882. Rosedale Cemetery, Orange, Essex County.
COLIE, ROBERT Pvt, D, 39th NJ Inf, 4-11-1910. Evergreen Cemetery, Hillside, Union County.
COLKITT, BENJAMIN D. Wagoner, A, 34th NJ Inf, 5-3-1868. Baptist/St. Andrew's Cemetery, Mount Holly, Burlington County.
COLKITT, WILLIAM C. Pvt, I, 37th NJ Inf, 5-31-1895. Brotherhood Cemetery, Hainesport, Burlington County.

Our Brothers Gone Before

COLL, JOHN Pvt, B, 21st NJ Inf, 5-26-1901. St. Peter's Cemetery, Jersey City, Hudson County.
COLLARD, DAVID B. Pvt, D, 13th NJ Inf, 1924. Bloomfield Cemetery, Bloomfield, Essex County.
COLLARD, JAMES H. Pvt, L, 27th NJ Inf, [Died of typhoid at Washington, DC.] 1-8-1863. Union Cemetery, Marcella, Morris County.
COLLERD, JAMES E. Pvt, B, 7th NJ Inf, 1881. Mount Pleasant Cemetery, Newark, Essex County.
COLLEY, ABRAHAM (see: Cawley, Abraham) Bethel AME Cemetery, Cookstown, Burlington County.
COLLEY, HENRY D. 2-19-1864. Mount Pleasant Cemetery, Newark, Essex County.
COLLIER*, ALFRED 1st Sgt, E, 37th NJ Inf, 4-8-1907. Fairmount Cemetery, Newark, Essex County.
COLLIER, ASA Pvt, E, 6th MA Militia, 3-11-1919. Hillside Cemetery, Scotch Plains, Union County.
COLLIGAN, JAMES Pvt, L, 27th NJ Inf, 6-13-1910. St. Mary's Cemetery, Wharton, Morris County.
COLLIGAN, JAMES Corp, B, 7th NJ Inf, 3-14-1894. Fairmount Cemetery, Newark, Essex County.
COLLIGNON*, AUGUSTUS M. 1st Lt, G, 56th NY National Guard, 1921. Old Hook Cemetery, Westwood, Bergen County.
COLLIGNON, NICHOLAS 2nd Lt, D, 22nd NJ Inf, 6-25-1879. Old Hook Cemetery, Westwood, Bergen County.
COLLINS, ALBERT L. Seaman, U.S. Navy, USS Tacony, 1918. Methodist-Episcopal Church Cemetery, South Dennis, Cape May County.
COLLINS, ALFRED Pvt, B, 37th NJ Inf, 2-28-1911. Woodland Cemetery, Newark, Essex County.
COLLINS, ANDERSON Pvt, D, 29th TN Inf (CSA), 5-7-1864. Finn's Point National Cemetery, Pennsville, Salem County.
COLLINS, BENJAMIN A. Sgt, I, 22nd U.S. CT, 12-28-1915. Jordan Lawn Cemetery, Pennsauken, Camden County.
COLLINS, DANIEL Pvt, C, 23rd NJ Inf, 10-18-1903. Holy Sepulchre Cemetery, East Orange, Essex County.
COLLINS*, DANIEL Corp, B, 7th NJ Inf, 9-9-1886. Holy Sepulchre Cemetery, East Orange, Essex County.
COLLINS, DEMPS Pvt, E, 43rd U.S. CT, 12-10-1875. Asbury United Methodist Church Cemetery, English Creek, Atlantic County.
COLLINS, FREDERICK S. Musc, F, 26th NJ Inf, 1933. Bloomfield Cemetery, Bloomfield, Essex County.
COLLINS, G.B. Pvt, C, 60th GA Inf (CSA), [Captured 9-17-1862 at Sharpsburg, MD.] 10-6-1863. Finn's Point National Cemetery, Pennsville, Salem County.
COLLINS*, GEORGE Pvt, C, 3rd NJ Inf, 6-9-1902. Mount Holly Cemetery, Mount Holly, Burlington County.
COLLINS, GEORGE Pvt, B, 29th PA Inf, 12-8-1913. Harleigh Cemetery, Camden, Camden County.
COLLINS, GEORGE Pvt, E, 25th U.S. CT, 6-2-1913. Jordan Lawn Cemetery, Pennsauken, Camden County.
COLLINS, GEORGE H. Pvt, A, 29th CT Inf, 7-21-1883. Pinebrook Cemetery, Macedonia, Monmouth County.
COLLINS, GIDEON W. Pvt, A, 5th NH Inf, 10-19-1862. Fairmount Cemetery, Newark, Essex County.
COLLINS, HENRY Pvt, B, 33rd NJ Inf, 1-26-1876. Holy Sepulchre Cemetery, East Orange, Essex County.

New Jersey Civil War Burials

COLLINS*, ISAAC Pvt, D, 33rd NJ Inf, 11-14-1909. Oddfellows Cemetery, Burlington, Burlington County.
COLLINS, J.H. Pvt, K, 18th GA Inf (CSA), [Captured 7-3-1863 at Gettysburg, PA.] 10-8-1863. Finn's Point National Cemetery, Pennsville, Salem County.
COLLINS, JAMES 10-14-1916. Tennent Church Cemetery, Tennent, Monmouth County.
COLLINS, JAMES T. Pvt, Btty B, 1st NJ Light Art, 2-12-1905. Federated Baptist Church Cemetery, Livingston, Essex County.
COLLINS, JAMES W. Pvt, A, 1st NJ Cav, 4-19-1931. Pompton Reformed Church Cemetery, Pompton Lakes, Passaic County.
COLLINS, JASPER N. Pvt, A, 43rd TN Inf (CSA), [5th East Tennessee Volunteers (Gillespie's).] 8-3-1863. Finn's Point National Cemetery, Pennsville, Salem County.
COLLINS, JEFFERY W. Capt, D, 21st NJ Inf, 6-11-1882. Holy Name Cemetery, Jersey City, Hudson County.
COLLINS, JEHU Pvt, G, 25th NJ Inf, 2-21-1899. Old Camden Cemetery, Camden, Camden County.
COLLINS, JESSE T. Pvt, H, 25th NJ Inf, 9-28-1922. Cedar Lawn Cemetery, Paterson, Passaic County.
COLLINS, JOHN Pvt, G, 25th NJ Inf, 1-24-1904. Calvary Baptist Church Cemetery, Ocean View, Cape May County.
COLLINS, JOHN DoD Unknown. St. Barnabas Episcopal Cemetery, South Brunswick, Middlesex County.
COLLINS, JOHN Pvt, C, 14th NJ Inf, DoD Unknown. Holy Name Cemetery, Jersey City, Hudson County.
COLLINS, JOHN Pvt, F, 26th NJ Inf, 11-22-1906. Bloomfield Cemetery, Bloomfield, Essex County.
COLLINS, JOHN H. Pvt, C, 24th NJ Inf, 9-23-1916. Baptist Cemetery, Salem, Salem County.
COLLINS, JOHN J. Landsman, U.S. Navy, USS Mystic, 5-28-1891. Berlin Cemetery, Berlin, Camden County.
COLLINS, JOHN S. Pvt, A, 34th NJ Inf, 1-18-1910. New Camden Cemetery, Camden, Camden County.
COLLINS, JOHN W. 2-22-1918. Rosedale Cemetery, Linden, Union County.
COLLINS, JOHN W. Pvt, G, 2nd NJ Inf, 2-3-1902. Fairmount Cemetery, Newark, Essex County.
COLLINS, JONATHAN M. Pvt, H, 3rd (Howard's) Confederate States Cav (CSA), 11-26-1863. Finn's Point National Cemetery, Pennsville, Salem County.
COLLINS, JOSEPH Pvt, G, 25th NJ Inf, 4-26-1904. Calvary Baptist Church Cemetery, Ocean View, Cape May County.
COLLINS, JOSEPH B. Pvt, H, 25th U.S. CT, 6-1-1880. Oak Hill Cemetery, Vineland, Cumberland County.
COLLINS, JOSEPH C. Pvt, A, 10th NJ Inf, 12-5-1898. Reevestown Cemetery, Reevestown, Ocean County.
COLLINS, JOSEPH T. Pvt, K, 26th U.S. CT, 3-7-1897. Johnson Cemetery, Camden, Camden County.
COLLINS, LEMUEL A. Pvt, F, 15th IL Inf, 6-22-1914. Riverview Cemetery, Trenton, Mercer County.
COLLINS, LOUIS S. Pvt, D, 2nd U.S. Colored Cav, 6-23-1918. Oak Hill Cemetery, Vineland, Cumberland County.
COLLINS, MARK Pvt, G, 39th NJ Inf, 4-21-1875. Holy Sepulchre Cemetery, East Orange, Essex County.
COLLINS*, MATTHEW G. Pvt, C, 54th PA Inf, 9-27-1896. Evergreen Cemetery, Camden, Camden County.

Our Brothers Gone Before

COLLINS, MICHAEL (aka: Maloney, Richard) Pvt, K, 39th NY Inf, [Died at Davids Island, NY.] 8-8-1864. Holy Name Cemetery, Jersey City, Hudson County.
COLLINS*, OLIVER K Corp, I, 6th NJ Inf, 9-5-1913. Evergreen Cemetery, Camden, Camden County.
COLLINS, SAMUEL H. Pvt, H, 25th NJ Inf, 10-15-1903. Cedar Lawn Cemetery, Paterson, Passaic County.
COLLINS, SIDNEY DoD Unknown. Evergreen Cemetery, Morristown, Morris County.
COLLINS, SIDNEY B. 4-8-1891. Greengrove Cemetery, Keyport, Monmouth County.
COLLINS, SIMON C. Sgt, I, 6th U.S. CT, 5-12-1917. Atlantic City Cemetery, Pleasantville, Atlantic County.
COLLINS, THOMAS Landsman, U.S. Navy, USS Estrella, 4-8-1895. Fairmount Cemetery, Newark, Essex County.
COLLINS, THOMAS Pvt, F, 13th NJ Inf, 1-30-1876. Holy Sepulchre Cemetery, East Orange, Essex County.
COLLINS, THOMAS S. Sgt, H, 3rd NJ Inf, 9-2-1898. Brotherhood Cemetery, Hainesport, Burlington County.
COLLINS, WILLIAM Pvt, F, 11th NJ Inf, 8-10-1895. Evergreen Cemetery, New Brunswick, Middlesex County.
COLLINS, WILLIAM H. Corp, H, 3rd NJ Inf, 9-27-1868. Baptist/St. Andrew's Cemetery, Mount Holly, Burlington County.
COLLINS, WILLIAM MORRIS Pvt, G, 38th NJ Inf, 1-18-1942. St. Barnabas Episcopal Cemetery, South Brunswick, Middlesex County.
COLLINS, WILLIAM T. Sgt, D, 21st NJ Inf, 11-8-1867. Holy Name Cemetery, Jersey City, Hudson County.
COLLINS, ZEBULON Pvt, A, 40th NJ Inf, 10-27-1900. Giberson Cemetery, Whiting, Ocean County.
COLLINSON, JESSE ROBERT H. Pvt, B, 24th MI Inf, 1-29-1897. Fairview Cemetery, Fairview, Monmouth County.
COLLIOUD, SAMUEL Pvt, H, 97th PA Inf, [Wounded 5-20-1864 at Bermuda Hundred, VA.] 6-17-1897. Fairmount Cemetery, Newark, Essex County.
COLLIVER, ORLANDO Pvt, D, 39th NJ Inf, 2-4-1923. Arlington Cemetery, Kearny, Hudson County.
COLLOM, ANDREW H. (aka: Crawford, Andrew) Pvt, F, 104th PA Inf, [Last member of the GAR in Burlington County.] 4-17-1940. Monument Cemetery, Edgewater Park, Burlington County.
COLLOM, HOWARD M. Pvt, I, 23rd NJ Inf, DoD Unknown. Baptist Cemetery, Pemberton, Burlington County.
COLLOMY, J. Pvt, Page's Btty, VA Light Art (CSA), 2-11-1865. Finn's Point National Cemetery, Pennsville, Salem County.
COLLVER, CHARLES H. Pvt, M, 1st NJ Cav, 1-17-1931. Fairmount Cemetery, Newark, Essex County.
COLLVER, EDWARD A. Pvt, B, 2nd NY Cav, 1-17-1928. Fairmount Cemetery, Newark, Essex County.
COLLYER, J.GEORGE Corp, C, 102nd NY National Guard, 8-2-1916. Cedar Lawn Cemetery, Paterson, Passaic County.
COLLYER, SAMUEL D. Pvt, A, 30th NJ Inf, 1-19-1911. Reformed Church Cemetery, Pluckemin, Somerset County.
COLSTON, JOHN Pvt, C, 127th U.S. CT, 4-7-1907. Princeton Cemetery, Princeton, Mercer County.
COLT, THOMAS A. Lt Col, 26th NJ Inf 10-10-1885. Rosedale Cemetery, Orange, Essex County.
COLTER, HENRY Pvt, K, 4th CA Inf, 10-13-1909. Fairmount Cemetery, Newark, Essex County.

New Jersey Civil War Burials

COLTHAR, NELSON Pvt, D, 8th NJ Inf, 3-15-1871. Baptist/Evergreen Methodist Cemetery, Plainfield, Union County.

COLTO, LEWIS Seaman, U.S. Navy, USS Potomac, 2-29-1888. Hackensack Cemetery, Hackensack, Bergen County.

COLTON, JOHN (SR.) Pvt, D, 5th NJ Inf, 12-27-1934. Holcomb-Riverview Cemetery, Lambertville, Hunterdon County.

COLTON, NATHANIEL W. Pvt, F, 10th MA Inf, DoD Unknown. Jersey City Cemetery, Jersey City, Hudson County.

COLTON, WILLIAM R. Pvt, I, 99th PA Inf, 6-8-1908. Presbyterian Church Cemetery, Bridgeton, Cumberland County.

COLTRA, JOHN M. 2-26-1896. Fairview Cemetery, Fairview, Monmouth County.

COLVER, NATHAN Pvt, D, 27th NJ Inf, 6-1-1885. Lafayette Cemetery, Lafayette, Sussex County.

COLVIN, HENRY Pvt, L, 10th VA Inf (CSA), [Captured 7-3-1863 at Gettysburg, PA. Died of lung infection.] 10-20-1863. Finn's Point National Cemetery, Pennsville, Salem County.

COLVIN, JAMES J. Pvt, G, 54th AL Inf (CSA), 6-28-1863. Finn's Point National Cemetery, Pennsville, Salem County.

COLVIN*, WILSON B. Pvt, F, 16th PA Cav, 1-28-1919. Cedar Hill Cemetery, Cedarville, Cumberland County.

COLWELL, JOHN Pvt, E, 118th NY Inf, 12-10-1873. Macphelah Cemetery, North Bergen, Hudson County.

COLWELL, WILLIAM (see: Caldwell, William B.) Jersey City Cemetery, Jersey City, Hudson County.

COLYER, EZRA 3-14-1892. 1st Reformed Church Cemetery, Pompton Plains, Morris County.

COLYER, JOSEPH B. Pvt, B, 26th NJ Inf, 1-1-1916. Arlington Cemetery, Kearny, Hudson County.

COLYER*, JOSEPH (JR.) Pvt, D, 13th NJ Inf, [Wounded 7-30-1864 at Atlanta, GA. On duty at Fords Theater, Washington, when Lincoln was shot.] 8-19-1906. Fairmount Cemetery, Newark, Essex County.

COLYER, THOMAS S. DoD Unknown. Reformed Church Cemetery, Fairfield, Essex County.

COMBE, HAMILTON R. Capt, I, 12th NY Inf, 4-15-1866. Greenmount Cemetery, Hammonton, Atlantic County.

COMBES, WILLIAM (see: Combs, William W.) Tennent Church Cemetery, Tennent, Monmouth County.

COMBS, ADAM PEASE Corp, E, 29th NJ Inf, [Cenotaph. Died of typhoid at Belle Plain, VA.] 4-18-1863. Tennent Church Cemetery, Tennent, Monmouth County.

COMBS, CHARLES H. Pvt, G, 25th NJ Inf, DoD Unknown. Christ Church Cemetery, Morgan, Middlesex County.

COMBS*, COOK Landsman, U.S. Navy, USS Wyandank, 8-25-1904. Atlantic View Cemetery, Manasquan, Monmouth County.

COMBS, GODFREY F. Pvt, K, 2nd NJ Cav, 2-2-1879. Coopertown Meeting House Cemetery, Edgewater Park, Burlington County.

COMBS*, RUFUS (aka: Coombs, R.) Pvt, K, 146th NY Inf, DoD Unknown. Bayview-New York Bay Cemetery, Jersey City, Hudson County.

COMBS, WILLIAM H. 3-3-1912. Bordentown/Old St. Mary's Catholic Cemetery, Bordentown, Burlington County.

COMBS, WILLIAM S. Asst Surg, 38th NJ Inf 8-15-1915. Maplewood Cemetery, Freehold, Monmouth County.

COMBS, WILLIAM W. (aka: Combes, William) Pvt, E, 29th NJ Inf, 9-9-1881. Tennent Church Cemetery, Tennent, Monmouth County.

Our Brothers Gone Before

COMER, GEORGE H. Pvt, C, 13th NJ Inf, 3-10-1899. Laurel Grove Cemetery, Totowa, Passaic County.

COMER, JOHN Pvt, C, 6th NJ Inf, 2-20-1919. Holy Name Cemetery, Jersey City, Hudson County.

COMER, JOHN Pvt, B, 30th VA Inf (CSA), 4-6-1865. Finn's Point National Cemetery, Pennsville, Salem County.

COMER, JOSEPH C. Pvt, I, 24th NJ Inf, 7-6-1900. Mount Pleasant Cemetery, Millville, Cumberland County.

COMER, M. Pvt, C, 36th VA Cav (CSA), 9-17-1863. Finn's Point National Cemetery, Pennsville, Salem County.

COMER*, MICHAEL Pvt, F, 8th NJ Inf, 7-11-1881. St. Peter's Cemetery, Jersey City, Hudson County.

COMER, MICHAEL (see: Cormer, Michael) St. Peter's Cemetery, Jersey City, Hudson County.

COMER, NATHAN Pvt, I, 24th NJ Inf, [Wounded 12-13-1862 at Fredericksburg, VA.] 1903. Mount Pleasant Cemetery, Millville, Cumberland County.

COMER, REUBEN Pvt, H, 33rd VA Inf (CSA), [Wounded 11-19-1862, Captured 5-12-1864 at Spotsylvania CH, VA, Died of lung inflammation.] 10-28-1864. Finn's Point National Cemetery, Pennsville, Salem County.

COMER, SAMUEL L. Corp, K, 31st NJ Inf, [Died of typhoid pneumonia at Belle Plain, VA.] 3-2-1863. Evergreen Cemetery, Clinton, Hunterdon County.

COMFORT, WILLIAM E.H. Pvt, D, 35th NJ Inf, 4-14-1880. Pearson/Colonial Memorial Park Cemetery, Whitehorse, Mercer County.

COMINGER, JOHN B. (aka: Gorninger, John B.) Pvt, E, 21st NJ Inf, 9-9-1912. Bordentown/Old St. Mary's Catholic Cemetery, Bordentown, Burlington County.

COMINGS*, GEORGE T. (aka: Cummings, George) Pvt, C, 14th NJ Inf, 2-12-1901. Alpine Cemetery, Perth Amboy, Middlesex County.

COMISKY, FRANK (aka: McCamiskey, Francis) Pvt, A, 25th NJ Inf, DoD Unknown. Holy Sepulchre Cemetery, Totowa, Passaic County.

COMITTI, JOSEPH 1st Sgt, A, 75th PA Inf, [Wounded 8-24-1862 at White Sulphur Springs, VA.] 3-31-1906. Oak Hill Cemetery, Vineland, Cumberland County.

COMLEY, BENJAMIN F. Pvt, C, 12th NJ Inf, 4-29-1922. Atlantic City Cemetery, Pleasantville, Atlantic County.

COMLEY, JONATHAN T. Pvt, K, 38th NJ Inf, 8-21-1865. Presbyterian Church Cemetery, Ewing, Mercer County.

COMMANDER, JAMES L. Pvt, L, 2nd MS Inf (CSA), [Captured 7-1-1863 at Gettysburg, PA. Died of typhoid.] 9-12-1863. Finn's Point National Cemetery, Pennsville, Salem County.

COMMANDER, WILLIAM Pvt, B, 8th U.S. CT, 11-8-1922. Bordentown/Old St. Mary's Catholic Cemetery, Bordentown, Burlington County.

COMMONS, JACKSON W. (aka: Cummins, John Wesley) Corp, H, 4th DE Inf, 6-2-1895. Zion Baptist Church Cemetery, New Egypt, Ocean County.

COMPTON, CEPHAS Pvt, I, 8th NJ Inf, [Died of diarrhea at 2nd Corps hospital.] 7-8-1865. Beemerville Cemetery, Beemerville, Sussex County.

COMPTON*, CHARLES H. Pvt, A, 5th NJ Inf, 5-20-1905. Greenwood Cemetery, Hamilton, Mercer County.

COMPTON*, CHRISTOPHER Pvt, C, 11th NJ Inf, 2-24-1864. Mercer Cemetery, Trenton, Mercer County.

COMPTON, DAVID L. Pvt, A, 6th NJ Inf, 6-5-1918. Arlington Cemetery, Kearny, Hudson County.

COMPTON, DAVID L. 11-26-1865. Princeton Cemetery, Princeton, Mercer County.

COMPTON, EZEKIEL Pvt, G, 22nd NJ Inf, 1910. Fernwood Cemetery, Jamesburg, Middlesex County.

New Jersey Civil War Burials

COMPTON, FREDERICK 1st Lt, C, 2nd NY Cav, [Killed in action at 2nd Bull Run, VA.] 8-29-1862. Mount Pleasant Cemetery, Newark, Essex County.
COMPTON, GEORGE 5-27-1914. Greenwood Cemetery, Hamilton, Mercer County.
COMPTON, GEORGE S. 1905. Princeton Cemetery, Princeton, Mercer County.
COMPTON*, HARVEY P. Pvt, A, 10th NY Inf, [Killed in action at 2nd Bull Run, VA. Wounded 6-27-1862 at Gaines' Mill, VA.] 8-29-1862. Mount Pleasant Cemetery, Newark, Essex County.
COMPTON, ISRAEL Pvt, C, 28th NJ Inf, 1-22-1911. Hillside Cemetery, Scotch Plains, Union County.
COMPTON, J.R. Pvt, F, 3rd SC Cav (CSA), [Captured 8-17-1864 at South Newport, GA. Died of typhoid.] 4-29-1865. Finn's Point National Cemetery, Pennsville, Salem County.
COMPTON, JAMES Pvt, A, 28th NJ Inf, 8-4-1873. Alpine Cemetery, Perth Amboy, Middlesex County.
COMPTON, JAMES L. 6-20-1904. St. Peter's Cemetery, Perth Amboy, Middlesex County.
COMPTON, JAMES S. Sgt, A, 1st NJ Militia, 11-24-1891. Mount Pleasant Cemetery, Newark, Essex County.
COMPTON, JOHN Sgt, I, 14th NJ Inf, [Cenotaph. Died of wounds received 7-9-1864 at Monocacy, MD.] 7-23-1864. Brainerd Cemetery, Cranbury, Middlesex County.
COMPTON, JOSEPH Pvt, A, 1st NJ Militia, 11-15-1893. Fairmount Cemetery, Newark, Essex County.
COMPTON, NATHAN V. Pvt, H, 30th NJ Inf, 1-29-1917. Evergreen Cemetery, Hillside, Union County.
COMPTON, NATHANIEL V. Pvt, H, 30th NJ Inf, 12-11-1882. Presbyterian Church Cemetery, Liberty Corners, Somerset County.
COMPTON, THOMAS Pvt, D, 29th NJ Inf, 1917. Greengrove Cemetery, Keyport, Monmouth County.
COMPTON, THOMAS (aka: Crompton, Thomas) Pvt, A, 40th GA Inf (CSA), [Captured 5-16-1863 at Baker's Creek, MS. Died of typhoid.] 6-18-1863. Finn's Point National Cemetery, Pennsville, Salem County.
COMPTON, WILLIAM D. 1920. Evergreen/Bishop Jaynes Cemetery, Basking Ridge, Somerset County.
COMSTOCK, CHARLES H. Pvt, I, 33rd NY Inf, 2-25-1914. Woodlawn Cemetery, Lakewood, Ocean County.
COMSTOCK, MERRITT A. 2nd Lt, C, 26th CT Inf, 2- -1917. New Camden Cemetery, Camden, Camden County.
CONANT, DANIEL M. Pvt, C, 9th MA Inf, 11-26-1900. Fairmount Cemetery, Newark, Essex County.
CONARY, THOMAS J. DoD Unknown. Vincent Methodist-Episcopal Cemetery, Nutley, Essex County.
CONAWAY, GILLEY JAMES Pvt, K, 1st DE Inf, 10-16-1930. Eglington Cemetery, Clarksboro, Gloucester County.
CONAWAY, TURNER Pvt, H, 22nd GA Inf (CSA), [Captured 7-2-1863 at Gettysburg, PA. Died of disease.] 5-23-1864. Finn's Point National Cemetery, Pennsville, Salem County.
CONAWAY, WINGATE Seaman, U.S. Navy, 2-24-1904. Evergreen Cemetery, Hillside, Union County.
CONAWEAY, JOHN 2-19-1903. St. James Episcopal Church Cemetery, Piscatawaytown, Middlesex County.
CONCANNON, THOMAS Pvt, B, 175th NY Inf, 6-6-1903. Mount Olivet Cemetery, Bloomfield, Essex County.
CONDELLY, PATRICK Pvt, K, 9th NJ Inf, 11-13-1867. St. Mary's Cemetery, Elizabeth, Union County.

Our Brothers Gone Before

CONDICT, ALFRED HENRY Capt, I, 27th NJ Inf, 3-16-1904. Evergreen Cemetery, Morristown, Morris County.
CONDICT, WALTER Corp, I, 27th NJ Inf, 10-24-1888. Presbyterian Church Cemetery, Morristown, Morris County.
CONDIT, CHARLES Pvt, D, 14th NJ Inf, 1-18-1895. Fairmount Cemetery, Fairmount, Hunterdon County.
CONDIT, CHILIAN C. Pvt, Btty A, 1st NJ Light Art, 1-29-1880. Jersey City Cemetery, Jersey City, Hudson County.
CONDIT, DANIEL H. Pvt, H, 2nd NJ Inf, 5-7-1906. Rosedale Cemetery, Orange, Essex County.
CONDIT, DANIEL H. Pvt, H, 2nd NJ Inf, 3-3-1908. Evergreen Cemetery, Camden, Camden County.
CONDIT, FRANCIS Pvt, D, 26th NJ Inf, 8-24-1925. Rosedale Cemetery, Orange, Essex County.
CONDIT, GEORGE W. Pvt, M, 2nd NJ Cav, 7-29-1883. Fairmount Cemetery, Newark, Essex County.
CONDIT, REUBEN MUNSON Pvt, D, 26th NJ Inf, 3-11-1928. Prospect Hill Cemetery, Caldwell, Essex County.
CONDIT, WILLIAM Pvt, L, 2nd NY Mounted Rifles, 5-23-1901. Jersey City Cemetery, Jersey City, Hudson County.
CONDIT, WILLIAM H. Pvt, C, 7th NJ Inf, DoD Unknown. Methodist Church Cemetery, Roseland, Essex County.
CONDIT, WILLIAM HENRY HARRISON 1st Lt, H, 7th NJ Inf, 3-2-1939. Prospect Hill Cemetery, Caldwell, Essex County.
CONDRA, COLUMBUS C. Pvt, H, 3rd (Clack's) TN Inf (CSA), 7-31-1864. Finn's Point National Cemetery, Pennsville, Salem County.
CONDROY, HENRY E. 7-30-1908. Laurel Grove Cemetery, Totowa, Passaic County.
CONE, ANDREW J. 5th Sgt, K, 4th GA Inf (CSA), [Captured 5-10-1864 at Spotsylvania CH, VA. Died of smallpox.] 1-19-1865. Finn's Point National Cemetery, Pennsville, Salem County.
CONE, FRANCIS STEPHEN Pvt, Btty M, 15th NY Heavy Art, 1-23-1908. Bayview-New York Bay Cemetery, Jersey City, Hudson County.
CONE, ORSON C. 3-26-1868. New Presbyterian Cemetery, Bound Brook, Somerset County.
CONE*, WALTER N. Pvt, C, 3rd NJ Inf, 9-4-1910. Arlington Cemetery, Kearny, Hudson County.
CONEY, GEORGE R. 2nd Lt, C, 9th ME Inf, 1879. Ramapo Reformed Church Cemetery, Mahwah, Bergen County.
CONFROY*, EDWARD ALOYSIUS Pvt, I, 17th CT Inf, [Wounded 9-17-1862 at Antietam, MD. and at New Bern, NC.] 12-27-1889. Holy Sepulchre Cemetery, East Orange, Essex County.
CONGAR, CHARLES H. Corp, C, 28th NJ Inf, 1903. Baptist Cemetery, South Plainfield, Middlesex County.
CONGAR, JACOB Pvt, D, 10th NJ Inf, 1915. Elmwood Cemetery, New Brunswick, Middlesex County.
CONGAR, JOHN Y. Pvt, B, 19th PA Inf, DoD Unknown. Friends United Methodist-Episcopal Church Cemetery, Linwood, Atlantic County.
CONGDON, JOSEPH W. 1914. Cedar Lawn Cemetery, Paterson, Passaic County.
CONGER, ELIAS E. Pvt, K, 30th NJ Inf, 1-2-1917. Elmwood Cemetery, New Brunswick, Middlesex County.
CONGER, HARVEY Pvt, B, 1st NY Cav, DoD Unknown. Holy Name Cemetery, Jersey City, Hudson County.
CONGER, JACOB P. Pvt, D, 10th NJ Inf, 8-23-1915. Evergreen Cemetery, New Brunswick, Middlesex County.

New Jersey Civil War Burials

CONGER, JOHN H. Pvt, A, 2nd NJ Inf, [Wounded in action.] 1-15-1935. Elmwood Cemetery, New Brunswick, Middlesex County.
CONGER, JOHN H. 8-23-1915. Evergreen Cemetery, New Brunswick, Middlesex County.
CONGER, JOSEPH Pvt, I, 8th NJ Inf, 4-26-1875. Hazelwood Cemetery, Rahway, Union County.
CONGER, THOMAS B. Corp, C, 26th CT Inf, [Wounded 5-27-1863 at Port Hudson, LA.] 1909. Baptist Church Cemetery, Scotch Plains, Union County.
CONGER*, WILLIAM Pvt, 6th NY Ind Btty 1-3-1928. Rahway Cemetery, Rahway, Union County.
CONGER, WILLIAM H. Corp, G, 38th NJ Inf, 2-10-1930. Elmwood Cemetery, New Brunswick, Middlesex County.
CONGLETON, JOHN E. Sgt, D, 27th NJ Inf, 6-23-1879. Hardyston Cemetery, North Church, Sussex County.
CONGLETON, THOMAS G. Pvt, D, 77th OH Inf, 11-4-1918. Laurel Grove Cemetery, Totowa, Passaic County.
CONGO*, WILLIAM Pvt, Btty K, 11th U.S. CHA, 1920. Soldier's Home Cemetery, Vineland, Cumberland County.
CONINE, HENRY J. Capt, A, 14th NJ Inf, [Cenotaph. Killed in action at Monocacy, MD.] 7-9-1864. Adelphia Cemetery, Adelphia, Monmouth County.
CONINE*, JOHN NEWTON Musc, B, 38th NJ Inf, 5-1-1894. Holcomb-Riverview Cemetery, Lambertville, Hunterdon County.
CONK, ARCHIBALD JACKSON Pvt, H, 14th NJ Inf, 2-14-1889. Adelphia Cemetery, Adelphia, Monmouth County.
CONK, BENJAMIN P. Ordinary Seaman, U.S. Navy, USS New Ironsides, 9-30-1890. Greenlawn Cemetery, West Long Branch, Monmouth County.
CONK, GEORGE Pvt, F, 29th NJ Inf, 1911. Mount Olivet Cemetery, Fairview, Monmouth County.
CONK, JACKSON Sgt, D, 14th NJ Inf, 7-29-1876. Adelphia Cemetery, Adelphia, Monmouth County.
CONK, JOHN H. Pvt, A, 29th NJ Inf, 11-22-1880. Greenlawn Cemetery, West Long Branch, Monmouth County.
CONK, JOSEPH Wagoner, F, 7th NJ Inf, 12-1-1883. Old Bergen Church Cemetery, Jersey City, Hudson County.
CONK, PETER Seaman, U.S. Navy, 4-16-1870. Old 1st Methodist Church Cemetery, West Long Branch, Monmouth County.
CONK, SAMUEL Sgt, D, 8th NJ Inf, 12-25-1875. Adelphia Cemetery, Adelphia, Monmouth County.
CONK, STEPHEN G. Pvt, I, 11th NJ Inf, [Wounded in action at Petersburg, VA.] 1895. Adelphia Cemetery, Adelphia, Monmouth County.
CONK, THOMAS 2nd Lt, K, 28th NJ Inf, 3-7-1884. Adelphia Cemetery, Adelphia, Monmouth County.
CONK, WILLIAM H. 1st Lt, E, 29th NJ Inf, 12-4-1904. Maplewood Cemetery, Freehold, Monmouth County.
CONKLIN, ABRAM Pvt, D, 26th NJ Inf, DoD Unknown. Methodist Church Cemetery, Roseland, Essex County.
CONKLIN, ALEXANDER Pvt, L, 1st NJ Cav, 5-27-1878. Elmwood Cemetery, New Brunswick, Middlesex County.
CONKLIN*, ALFRED Pvt, Btty D, 6th NY Heavy Art, 1-5-1895. Bayview-New York Bay Cemetery, Jersey City, Hudson County.
CONKLIN, ALLEN Pvt, D, 33rd NJ Inf, 10-21-1903. Midvale Cemetery, Midvale, Passaic County.
CONKLIN, AMBI Pvt, C, 33rd NJ Inf, DoD Unknown. Midvale Cemetery, Midvale, Passaic County.

Our Brothers Gone Before

CONKLIN, ANDREW Pvt, K, 25th NJ Inf, DoD Unknown. Midvale Cemetery, Midvale, Passaic County.
CONKLIN, CHARLES Pvt, K, 2nd DC Inf, 12-9-1919. United Methodist Church Cemetery, Rockaway Valley, Morris County.
CONKLIN, CHARLES A. Pvt, K, 7th NJ Inf, 1-25-1907. Mount Pleasant Cemetery, Newark, Essex County.
CONKLIN, CLAUDIUS R. Pvt, A, 9th NJ Inf, 7-22-1870. Bayview-New York Bay Cemetery, Jersey City, Hudson County.
CONKLIN, DAVID DoD Unknown. Cedar Grove Cemetery, Gloucester City, Camden County.
CONKLIN, DAVID L. Pvt, B, 127th NY Inf, 1-9-1916. Woodlawn Cemetery, Lakewood, Ocean County.
CONKLIN, EDGAR W. (aka: Conklin, Edward) Pvt, Btty D, 2nd CT Heavy Art, [Wounded 9-22-1864 at Strasburg, VA.] 1923. Valleau Cemetery, Ridgewood, Bergen County.
CONKLIN, EDWARD Pvt, B, 14th U.S. Inf, 12-26-1891. Mount Carmel Cemetery, West Moorestown, Burlington County.
CONKLIN, EDWARD (see: Conklin, Edgar W.) Valleau Cemetery, Ridgewood, Bergen County.
CONKLIN, EDWARD L. Corp, G, 2nd NJ Inf, 3-4-1912. Rosedale Cemetery, Orange, Essex County.
CONKLIN, GEORGE E. Pvt, E, 25th NJ Inf, 3-11-1869. Cedar Lawn Cemetery, Paterson, Passaic County.
CONKLIN, HARMON (aka: Conklin, Herman) Pvt, Btty E, 6th NY Heavy Art, DoD Unknown. Midvale Cemetery, Midvale, Passaic County.
CONKLIN, HENRY B. Mate, U.S. Navy, 3-25-1876. Bordentown/Old St. Mary's Catholic Cemetery, Bordentown, Burlington County.
CONKLIN, HENRY W. Pvt, Btty L, 15th NY Heavy Art, DoD Unknown. Bordentown/Old St. Mary's Catholic Cemetery, Bordentown, Burlington County.
CONKLIN, HERMAN (see: Conklin, Harmon) Midvale Cemetery, Midvale, Passaic County.
CONKLIN, JAMES DoD Unknown. Midvale Cemetery, Midvale, Passaic County.
CONKLIN, JAMES S. Pvt, C, 22nd NJ Inf, 1909. Balesville Cemetery, Balesville, Sussex County.
CONKLIN, JOHN L. Pvt, D, 26th NJ Inf, 8-8-1911. Methodist Church Cemetery, Roseland, Essex County.
CONKLIN, JOHN L. Corp, B, 37th NJ Inf, 4-17-1924. Bayview-New York Bay Cemetery, Jersey City, Hudson County.
CONKLIN, JOHN L. Pvt, M, 1st NJ Cav, 6-19-1919. Cedar Lawn Cemetery, Paterson, Passaic County.
CONKLIN, JOHN L. 6-27-1882. Laurel Grove Cemetery, Totowa, Passaic County.
CONKLIN, JOHN S. Pvt, K, 80th NY Inf, 5-8-1919. United Methodist Church Cemetery, Vernon, Sussex County.
CONKLIN, JOHN T. Pvt, D, 38th NJ Inf, 1912. New Somerville Cemetery, Somerville, Somerset County.
CONKLIN, LEVI Pvt, K, 25th NJ Inf, DoD Unknown. Midvale Cemetery, Midvale, Passaic County.
CONKLIN, MATHEW H. Musc, K, 1st NJ Inf, DoD Unknown. Hoboken Cemetery, North Bergen, Hudson County.
CONKLIN*, MATTHEW R. Pvt, D, 71st NY Inf, [Wounded 8-27-1862 at Bristoe Station, VA. and 7-2-1863 at Gettysburg, PA.] 2-16-1915. Bloomfield Cemetery, Bloomfield, Essex County.
CONKLIN, MOSES J. Pvt, Btty L, 13th NY Heavy Art, 8-30-1910. Holy Name Cemetery, Jersey City, Hudson County.

New Jersey Civil War Burials

CONKLIN, NEHEMIAH Pvt, G, 33rd NJ Inf, 1894. Cedar Run/Greenwood Cemetery, Manahawkin, Ocean County.
CONKLIN, PETER L. 2nd Lt, C, 22nd NJ Inf, 10-20-1900. Maple Grove Cemetery, Hackensack, Bergen County.
CONKLIN, PHILETUS Pvt, K, 13th NJ Inf, 7-22-1885. Cedar Lawn Cemetery, Paterson, Passaic County.
CONKLIN*, SAMUEL H. 1st Lt, M, 16th PA Cav, DoD Unknown. Cedar Grove Cemetery, Gloucester City, Camden County.
CONKLIN*, SAMUEL J. Pvt, G, 40th NY Inf, DoD Unknown. Midvale Cemetery, Midvale, Passaic County.
CONKLIN, SAMUEL J. Pvt, E, 25th NJ Inf, 2-27-1904. United Methodist Church Cemetery, Vernon, Sussex County.
CONKLIN, STEPHEN H. Pvt, C, 79th NY Inf, DoD Unknown. Hoboken Cemetery, North Bergen, Hudson County.
CONKLIN, THOMAS Pvt, D, 26th NJ Inf, 5-20-1884. Methodist Church Cemetery, Roseland, Essex County.
CONKLIN, WALTER Pvt, K, 25th NJ Inf, 6-4-1912. Laurel Grove Cemetery, Totowa, Passaic County.
CONKLIN, WARREN Musc, I, 1st NJ Inf, 1922. Fairview Cemetery, Fairview, Monmouth County.
CONKLIN, WESLEY Pvt, D, 33rd NJ Inf, 11-11-1916. Arlington Cemetery, Kearny, Hudson County.
CONKLIN, WILLIAM A. __, __, __ NY __, 1923. Bay View Cemetery, Leonardo, Monmouth County.
CONKLIN, WILLIAM B. Musc, D, 9th NJ Inf, 7-13-1866. New 1st Methodist Meeting House Cemetery, Manahawkin, Ocean County.
CONKLIN*, WILLIAM H. Pvt, B, 32nd MA Inf, 8-31-1902. Alpine Cemetery, Perth Amboy, Middlesex County.
CONKLIN, WILLIAM H. 3-16-1908. Elmwood Cemetery, New Brunswick, Middlesex County.
CONKLIN, WILLIAM H. Pvt, G, 27th NJ Inf, 6-19-1871. Fredericks Cemetery, Brook Valley, Morris County.
CONKLIN, WILLIAM S. Pvt, H, 24th NJ Inf, 3-29-1895. Presbyterian Church Cemetery, Bridgeton, Cumberland County.
CONKLING, ALBERT B. Corp, E, 22nd NJ Inf, 9-7-1922. Cedar Lawn Cemetery, Paterson, Passaic County.
CONKLING, OSCAR 2nd Lt, B, 30th NJ Inf, 3-5-1892. Evergreen/Bishop Jaynes Cemetery, Basking Ridge, Somerset County.
CONKRIGHT, JOSEPH A. Corp, E, 17th IL Cav, 6-3-1918. Bayview-New York Bay Cemetery, Jersey City, Hudson County.
CONLAN, JOHN (aka: Conley, John) Pvt, K, 2nd DC Inf, 8-15-1894. St. Mary's Cemetery, Boonton, Morris County.
CONLEY, DAVID (aka: Connelly, Daniel) Pvt, D, 12th NJ Inf, DoD Unknown. Mount Pleasant Cemetery, Millville, Cumberland County.
CONLEY, GEORGE (aka: Connelly, George) Pvt, D, 12th NJ Inf, 2-29-1880. Mount Pleasant Cemetery, Millville, Cumberland County.
CONLEY, GEORGE (aka: Conly, George) Pvt, I, 24th NJ Inf, 2-9-1898. Methodist-Episcopal Church Cemetery, South Dennis, Cape May County.
CONLEY, GEORGE A. Corp, H, 83rd NY Inf, 9-24-1909. New York/New Jersey Crematory Cemetery, North Bergen, Hudson County.
CONLEY, JAMES (aka: Connolly, James) Pvt, B, 30th NJ Inf, 9-30-1915. Evergreen Cemetery, Hillside, Union County.

Our Brothers Gone Before

CONLEY, JAMES A. (aka: Connoly, James A.) Pvt, K, 6th LA Inf (CSA), [Captured 6-7-1862 at Strasburg, VA.] 4-1-1865. Finn's Point National Cemetery, Pennsville, Salem County.
CONLEY, JOHN Pvt, C, 12th NJ Inf, 1875. New Camden Cemetery, Camden, Camden County.
CONLEY, JOHN Seaman, U.S. Navy, 12-5-1905. St. Rose of Lima Cemetery, Millburn, Essex County.
CONLEY, JOHN (see: Conlan, John) St. Mary's Cemetery, Boonton, Morris County.
CONLEY, OWEN J. Pvt, L, 27th NJ Inf, 1920. St. Mary's Cemetery, Wharton, Morris County.
CONLEY*, THOMAS L. Sr Master Mate, U.S. Navy, USS North Carolina, 2-14-1899. New Camden Cemetery, Camden, Camden County.
CONLY, ___?___ DoD Unknown. Old Camden Cemetery, Camden, Camden County.
CONLY, GEORGE (see: Conley, George) Methodist-Episcopal Church Cemetery, South Dennis, Cape May County.
CONN, HARRY 1908. Boonton Cemetery, Boonton, Morris County.
CONN, J. Pvt, G, 8th KY Cav (CSA), 8-12-1864. Finn's Point National Cemetery, Pennsville, Salem County.
CONN, JAMES Pvt, B, 49th PA Militia, DoD Unknown. Marlton Cemetery, Marlton, Burlington County.
CONN, JAMES Pvt, F, 9th KS Cav, 11-14-1909. Presbyterian Church Cemetery, Andover, Sussex County.
CONN, JAMES Pvt, A, 1st NJ Cav, [Died of disease at Camp Mercer, VA.] 10-24-1861. Phillipsburg Cemetery, Phillipsburg, Warren County.
CONN, JOHN Pvt, D, 24th MS Inf (CSA), 11-28-1863. Finn's Point National Cemetery, Pennsville, Salem County.
CONNAUGHTON, MICHAEL Pvt, G, 21st NJ Inf, 6-2-1890. Old Bergen Church Cemetery, Jersey City, Hudson County.
CONNEGAN, PATRICK (see: Cunningham, Patrick) Mount Olivet Cemetery, Bloomfield, Essex County.
CONNELL*, EDWARD Pvt, F, 36th NY Inf, 1926. Soldier's Home Cemetery, Vineland, Cumberland County.
CONNELL, JOHN Pvt, D, 33rd NJ Inf, 3-8-1903. Holy Sepulchre Cemetery, East Orange, Essex County.
CONNELL, JOSEPH Pvt, I, 33rd NJ Inf, DoD Unknown. Holy Sepulchre Cemetery, East Orange, Essex County.
CONNELL, PATRICK Pvt, K, 33rd NJ Inf, DoD Unknown. Holy Sepulchre Cemetery, East Orange, Essex County.
CONNELLAN, THOMAS Pvt, A, 7th NJ Inf, [Wounded in action 11-18-1864.] 10-17-1870. Fairmount Cemetery, Newark, Essex County.
CONNELLY, BENJAMIN 1st Sgt, C, 4th NJ Militia, 1917. Morgan Cemetery, Cinnaminson, Burlington County.
CONNELLY, DANIEL (see: Conley, David) Mount Pleasant Cemetery, Millville, Cumberland County.
CONNELLY*, EPHRIAM Pvt, I, 2nd NJ Inf, 4-12-1918. United Methodist Church Cemetery, Absecon, Atlantic County.
CONNELLY, GEORGE (see: Conley, George) Mount Pleasant Cemetery, Millville, Cumberland County.
CONNELLY, JAMES (see: Connelly, Joseph) Hoboken Cemetery, North Bergen, Hudson County.
CONNELLY, JAMES F. Pvt, I, 35th NJ Inf, 2-2-1917. Holy Sepulchre Cemetery, East Orange, Essex County.
CONNELLY, JOHN Pvt, K, 22nd NJ Inf, 2-7-1910. Arlington Cemetery, Kearny, Hudson County.

New Jersey Civil War Burials

CONNELLY*, JOHN Pvt, E, 10th NJ Inf, DoD Unknown. Mount Pleasant Cemetery, Newark, Essex County.

CONNELLY, JOSEPH (aka: Connelly, James) Pvt, A, 165th NY Inf, DoD Unknown. Hoboken Cemetery, North Bergen, Hudson County.

CONNELLY, JOSEPH B. Pvt, C, 11th NJ Inf, 1-16-1898. Fairmount Cemetery, Newark, Essex County.

CONNELLY, JOSEPH B. DoD Unknown. Holy Name Cemetery, Jersey City, Hudson County.

CONNELLY, JOSEPH M. Pvt, H, 192nd PA Inf, 12-17-1920. New Camden Cemetery, Camden, Camden County.

CONNELLY, MARTIN Quartermaster, U.S. Navy, DoD Unknown. St. Peter's Cemetery, New Brunswick, Middlesex County.

CONNELLY, MICHAEL Pvt, D, 40th NJ Inf, 4-28-1889. Fairmount Cemetery, Newark, Essex County.

CONNELLY, PATRICK J. Corp, D, 71st NY Inf, 10-26-1890. Holy Sepulchre Cemetery, East Orange, Essex County.

CONNELY, JAMES Pvt, G, 12th NJ Inf, 9-24-1898. Evergreen Cemetery, Camden, Camden County.

CONNER, CHRISTOPHER C. Pvt, F, 41st GA Inf (CSA), [Captured 5-16-1863 at Baker's Creek, MS. Died of disease.] 7-20-1863. Finn's Point National Cemetery, Pennsville, Salem County.

CONNER, DANIEL T. [Died in U.S. Army Hospital, VA.] 8-4-1865. Presbyterian Church Cemetery, Cedarville, Cumberland County.

CONNER, DAVID Pvt, E, 22nd NJ Inf, 9-28-1919. Laurel Grove Cemetery, Totowa, Passaic County.

CONNER, FAYETTE Y. Pvt, E, 27th VA Inf (CSA), [Wounded 11-27-1863 at Payne's Farm, VA. Captured 5-12-1864 at Spotsylvania CH, VA. Died of diarrhea.] 4-14-1865. Finn's Point National Cemetery, Pennsville, Salem County.

CONNER, HARRIS (see: Tommer, Harris) Old & New Lutheran Cemetery, Lebanon, Hunterdon County.

CONNER, HENRY P. 9-9-1919. Mount Hebron Cemetery, Montclair, Essex County.

CONNER, JOHN Pvt, D, 4th MS Inf (CSA), 7-7-1863. Finn's Point National Cemetery, Pennsville, Salem County.

CONNER, MATTHEW Pvt, H, 21st NJ Inf, 1898. St. Mary's Cemetery, Hamilton, Mercer County.

CONNER, THOMAS Pvt, I, 1st NJ Cav, 12-29-1914. Elmwood Cemetery, New Brunswick, Middlesex County.

CONNERS, EDWARD Landsman, U.S. Navy, 7-9-1885. St. John's Evangelical Church Cemetery, Orange, Essex County.

CONNERS, HENRY Pvt, C, 7th NJ Inf, 3-8-1874. St. John's Evangelical Church Cemetery, Orange, Essex County.

CONNERS, THOMAS Landsman, U.S. Navy, DoD Unknown. St. John's Evangelical Church Cemetery, Orange, Essex County.

CONNERTY, JOHN Landsman, U.S. Navy, USS Emma Henry, 7-23-1890. Lady of Lourdes/Holy Sepulchre Cemetery, Hamilton, Mercer County.

CONNET*, ANDREW T. 2nd Lt, D, 31st NJ Inf, 8-2-1913. Prospect Hill Cemetery, Flemington, Hunterdon County.

CONNETT, FRAZEE (aka: Connitt,Frazer), Pvt, H, 39th NJ Inf, 11-23-1912. Hillside Cemetery, Scotch Plains, Union County.

CONNETT, HENRY Corp, D, 6th IN Inf, [Wounded in action at Resaca, GA.] 2-6-1907. Mount Hebron Cemetery, Montclair, Essex County.

CONNETT, ISAAC S. Sgt, E, 27th NJ Inf, 12-21-1913. Rahway Cemetery, Rahway, Union County.

Our Brothers Gone Before

CONNETT, JONATHAN T. Corp, H, 30th NJ Inf, 4-20-1890. Rahway Cemetery, Rahway, Union County.
CONNIFF*, THOMAS Corp, K, 35th NJ Inf, DoD Unknown. St. John's Cemetery, Lambertville, Hunterdon County.
CONNINE, JOHN W. 1922. Arlington Cemetery, Pennsauken, Camden County.
CONNITT, FRAZER (see: Connett,Frazee), Hillside Cemetery, Scotch Plains, Union County.
CONNOLLY, ABNER C. Pvt, B, 34th NJ Inf, [Died of diarrhea at Paducah, KY.] 1-11-1865. Riverview Cemetery, Trenton, Mercer County.
CONNOLLY, FRANCIS Pvt, U.S. Marine Corps, 8-3-1898. Grove Church Cemetery, North Bergen, Hudson County.
CONNOLLY, HENRY C. Pvt, B, 14th NJ Inf, [Died of diarrhea while prisoner at Belle Isle, VA.] 1-24-1864. Riverview Cemetery, Trenton, Mercer County.
CONNOLLY, JAMES Pvt, C, 37th NY Inf, [Wounded 5-30-1862 at Fair Oaks, VA.] 4-30-1915. Mount Olivet Cemetery, Newark, Essex County.
CONNOLLY, JAMES (see: Conley, James) Evergreen Cemetery, Hillside, Union County.
CONNOLLY, JOHN Fireman, U.S. Navy, USS Nina, DoD Unknown. Mount Pleasant Cemetery, Newark, Essex County.
CONNOLLY, JOHN Pvt, B, 14th NJ Inf, [Wounded 11-27-1863 at Locust Grove, VA.] 3--1866. Fairview Cemetery, Fairview, Monmouth County.
CONNOLLY, JOHN Landsman, U.S. Navy, USS Nipsic, 5-8-1913. Fairmount Cemetery, Newark, Essex County.
CONNOLLY, MICHAEL Pvt, G, 9th NJ Inf, 4-22-1903. Holy Sepulchre Cemetery, East Orange, Essex County.
CONNOLLY*, MICHAEL H. Musc, G, 57th NY Inf, [Wounded 6-18-1864 at Weldon Railroad, VA. and 11-5-1864 at Fort Sedgwick, VA.] 10-24-1932. St. Peter's Cemetery, New Brunswick, Middlesex County.
CONNOLLY, THOMAS Seaman, U.S. Navy, 6-26-1905. Arlington Cemetery, Kearny, Hudson County.
CONNOLLY, THOMAS Pvt, C, 26th NJ Inf, 2-12-1900. St. Peter's Church Cemetery, Belleville, Essex County.
CONNOLLY, THOMAS Pvt, E, 71st NY Inf, [Wounded 8-29-1863 at 2nd Bull Run, VA.] DoD Unknown. St. Peter's Church Cemetery, Belleville, Essex County.
CONNOLLY, WILLIAM D. 2nd Lt, H, 14th NJ Inf, 4-4-1863. Maplewood Cemetery, Freehold, Monmouth County.
CONNOLLY, WILLIAM G.D. 2nd Lt, H, 14th NJ Inf, 4-4-1863. Maplewood Cemetery, Freehold, Monmouth County.
CONNOLY, JAMES A. (see: Conley, James A.) Finn's Point National Cemetery, Pennsville, Salem County.
CONNOR, GEORGE S. Capt, A, 104th PA Inf, 1928. Evergreen Cemetery, Camden, Camden County.
CONNOR, JAMES Pvt, B, 4th NJ Inf, 1910. St. John's Cemetery, Hamilton, Mercer County.
CONNOR, JAMES Sgt, I, 33rd NJ Inf, 3-28-1905. Holy Sepulchre Cemetery, East Orange, Essex County.
CONNOR*, JOHN Pvt, H, 59th NY Inf, 4-11-1923. Holy Name Cemetery, Jersey City, Hudson County.
CONNOR, JOHN Pvt, D, 4th NJ Inf, [Wounded in action.] 9-7-1871. St. John's Cemetery, Hamilton, Mercer County.
CONNOR, JONATHAN M. Pvt, G, 38th NJ Inf, 5-5-1903. Rosemont Cemetery, Rosemont, Hunterdon County.
CONNOR, MICHAEL Pvt, A, 35th NJ Inf, 7-20-1867. Mount Olivet Cemetery, Fairview, Monmouth County.

New Jersey Civil War Burials

CONNOR, ORLANDO P. Corp, K, 38th NJ Inf, 3-1-1906. Riverview Cemetery, Trenton, Mercer County.
CONNOR, PATRICK H. Landsman, U.S. Navy, USS Princeton, 9-30-1868. St. John's Cemetery, Hamilton, Mercer County.
CONNOR, THOMAS Pvt, F, 8th NJ Inf, 5-1-1872. Holy Sepulchre Cemetery, East Orange, Essex County.
CONNOR*, THOMAS G. Fireman, U.S. Navy, USS Agawam, 2-13-1870. Old Camden Cemetery, Camden, Camden County.
CONNOR, WILLIAM Pvt, F, 2nd NJ Cav, 5-10-1912. New Somerville Cemetery, Somerville, Somerset County.
CONNOR, WILLIAM D. Pvt, H, 118th PA Inf, 12-2-1887. Baptist Cemetery, Pemberton, Burlington County.
CONNORS, DOMINICK JOHN Pvt, Btty A, 5th NY Heavy Art, 6-9-1896. Holy Sepulchre Cemetery, East Orange, Essex County.
CONNORS, JAMES Pvt, E, 45th PA Inf, 3-19-1907. Oddfellows Cemetery, Pemberton, Burlington County.
CONNORS, JOHN Pvt, B, 77th NY Inf, [Wounded 5-6-1864 at Wilderness, VA.] 5-9-1908. Fairmount Cemetery, Newark, Essex County.
CONNORS, PATRICK Pvt, H, 2nd NJ Cav, 7-1-1910. Fairmount Cemetery, Newark, Essex County.
CONNORS, PATRICK Pvt, F, 28th NJ Inf, 11-3-1872. St. Peter's Cemetery, New Brunswick, Middlesex County.
CONNORS, THOMAS Pvt, K, 30th NJ Inf, 11-8-1895. St. Peter's Cemetery, New Brunswick, Middlesex County.
CONOVER, A. DoD Unknown. Old Camden Cemetery, Camden, Camden County.
CONOVER, A.V.F. 3-6-1927. Old 1st Methodist Church Cemetery, West Long Branch, Monmouth County.
CONOVER, ABRAHAM B. Pvt, F, 30th NJ Inf, 10-11-1903. Rocky Hill Cemetery, Rocky Hill, Somerset County.
CONOVER, ABRAHAM C. Pvt, K, 1st NJ Inf, 1923. Holmdel Cemetery, Holmdel, Monmouth County.
CONOVER, ADAM Pvt, K, 186th PA Inf, 2-1-1911. Atlantic City Cemetery, Pleasantville, Atlantic County.
CONOVER, ALEXANDER S. Pvt, G, 38th NJ Inf, 4-5-1932. Evergreen Cemetery, New Brunswick, Middlesex County.
CONOVER, BENJAMIN Pvt, I, 25th NJ Inf, 5-4-1906. 1st Baptist Cemetery, Cape May Court House, Cape May County.
CONOVER, BENJAMIN R. Pvt, E, 10th NJ Inf, 1-28-1920. Presbyterian Church Cemetery, Absecon, Atlantic County.
CONOVER, BURRIS Pvt, E, 10th NJ Inf, DoD Unknown. Presbyterian Church Cemetery, Absecon, Atlantic County.
CONOVER, C. 10-6-1864. Bayview-New York Bay Cemetery, Jersey City, Hudson County.
CONOVER, CHARLES DoD Unknown. Bordentown/Old St. Mary's Catholic Cemetery, Bordentown, Burlington County.
CONOVER, CHARLES A. 11-2-1882. Maplewood Cemetery, Freehold, Monmouth County.
CONOVER, CHARLES H. Pvt, F, 30th NJ Inf, 5-29-1919. New Somerville Cemetery, Somerville, Somerset County.
CONOVER*, CHARLES S. Pvt, B, 1st NJ Inf, 12-20-1891. Elmwood Cemetery, New Brunswick, Middlesex County.
CONOVER, CORNELIUS N. 8-3-1861. Cedar Hill Cemetery, East Millstone, Somerset County.
CONOVER, EDWARD (aka: Conover, Edwin) Corp, B, 28th NJ Inf, 12-7-1918. Brainerd Cemetery, Cranbury, Middlesex County.

Our Brothers Gone Before

CONOVER, EDWIN (see: Conover, Edward) Brainerd Cemetery, Cranbury, Middlesex County.
CONOVER, FRANCIS STEVENS Actg Lt, U.S. Navy, 4-9-1901. Princeton Cemetery, Princeton, Mercer County.
CONOVER, G. W. Sgt, I, 3rd __ __, 10-31-1865. Bordentown/Old St. Mary's Catholic Cemetery, Bordentown, Burlington County.
CONOVER*, GARRET S. Pvt, E, 15th NJ Inf, 5-4-1886. Baptist Cemetery, Hopewell Boro, Mercer County.
CONOVER, GARRET W. Pvt, I, 29th NJ Inf, 1877. Mount Pleasant Cemetery, Newark, Essex County.
CONOVER, GEORGE Sgt, I, 14th NJ Inf, 6-27-1867. Elmwood Cemetery, New Brunswick, Middlesex County.
CONOVER, GEORGE H. Pvt, C, 3rd NJ Inf, [Killed in action at Spotsylvania CH, VA.] 5-10-1864. Presbyterian Church Cemetery, Flemington, Hunterdon County.
CONOVER, GEORGE W. Corp, K, 40th NJ Inf, 1926. Cedar Hill Cemetery, Hightstown, Mercer County.
CONOVER, GEORGE W. Pvt, C, 1st NJ Inf, [Died of wounds receiver 5-3-1863 at Salem Heights, VA.] 5-4-1863. Brainerd Cemetery, Cranbury, Middlesex County.
CONOVER, HARVEY GILLINGHAM 2nd Lt, H, 14th NJ Inf, 6-29-1904. Fairview Cemetery, Fairview, Monmouth County.
CONOVER, HENRY Corp, B, 8th U.S. CT, 9-10-1896. Evergreen Cemetery, Morristown, Morris County.
CONOVER, HOWARD A. Pvt, B, 38th NJ Inf, 1914. Mount Hope Presbyterian Cemetery, Lambertville, Hunterdon County.
CONOVER, ISAAC A. 1st Cl Fireman, U.S. Navy, USS Passaic, 1921. Methodist Cemetery, Woodstown, Salem County.
CONOVER, JACOB Pvt, G, 9th NJ Inf, 6-30-1902. Princeton Cemetery, Princeton, Mercer County.
CONOVER, JAMES Pvt, E, 10th NJ Inf, 11-2-1931. Salem Cemetery, Pleasantville, Atlantic County.
CONOVER, JAMES DoD Unknown. Old Camden Cemetery, Camden, Camden County.
CONOVER, JAMES PITMAN DoD Unknown. Presbyterian Church Cemetery, Absecon, Atlantic County.
CONOVER, JAMES W. Capt, D, 14th NJ Inf, [Died at Frederick City, MD. of wounds received 7-9-1864 at Monocacy, MD.] 8-4-1864. Maplewood Cemetery, Freehold, Monmouth County.
CONOVER, JOHN Pvt, G, 38th NJ Inf, 6-13-1891. Old Bethel Cemetery, Plainsboro, Middlesex County.
CONOVER*, JOHN Pvt, B, 2nd U.S. Cav, [Killed in action at Berryville, VA.] 8-10-1864. Brainerd Cemetery, Cranbury, Middlesex County.
CONOVER*, JOHN Pvt, C, 33rd NJ Inf, 4-12-1893. Methodist Cemetery, Woodstown, Salem County.
CONOVER, JOHN Pvt, E, 30th NJ Inf, 6-29-1863. Harlingen Cemetery, Belle Mead, Somerset County.
CONOVER, JOHN JACOB Pvt, M, 6th PA Cav, 9-23-1901. Riverview Cemetery, Trenton, Mercer County.
CONOVER, JOHN M. Pvt, E, 2nd NJ Cav, [Wounded in action.] 4-4-1925. Cedar Grove Cemetery, Gloucester City, Camden County.
CONOVER, JOHN N. Pvt, D, 48th NY Inf, [Died of dysentery at Fort Pulaski, GA.] 7-5-1862. Old Brick Reformed Church Cemetery, Marlboro, Monmouth County.
CONOVER, JOHN W. Corp, B, 1st NJ Cav, 3-19-1919. Salem Cemetery, Pleasantville, Atlantic County.
CONOVER, JOSEPH Pvt, H, 23rd NJ Inf, 2-3-1921. Methodist Cemetery, Bridgeboro, Burlington County.

New Jersey Civil War Burials

CONOVER, JOSEPH A. Pvt, H, 23rd NJ Inf, 9-1-1930. Tennent Church Cemetery, Tennent, Monmouth County.
CONOVER, JOSEPH C. Pvt, E, 28th PA Inf, 1-2-1883. St. John's United Methodist Cemetery, Turnersville, Gloucester County.
CONOVER, JOSEPH J. Pvt, K, 23rd NJ Inf, [Wounded in action.] 3-12-1905. Presbyterian Church Cemetery, Absecon, Atlantic County.
CONOVER, LAWRENCE T. Pvt, F, 30th NJ Inf, 1915. Rocky Hill Cemetery, Rocky Hill, Somerset County.
CONOVER, LEONARD Pvt, A, 9th NJ Inf, 6-30-1912. Riverview Cemetery, Trenton, Mercer County.
CONOVER, LEWIS I. Pvt, H, 127th U.S. CT, 1-6-1916. St. James AME Church Cemetery, Woodville, Monmouth County.
CONOVER, MARTIN Pvt, E, 14th NJ Inf, 3-15-1921. Presbyterian Cemetery, New Vernon, Morris County.
CONOVER, MATTHEW D. Farrier, L, 1st NJ Cav, 5-9-1905. Hillside Cemetery, Metuchen, Middlesex County.
CONOVER, MICAJAH Pvt, I, 25th NJ Inf, 4-27-1902. Methodist-Episcopal Church Cemetery, Green Creek, Cape May County.
CONOVER, NICHOLAS Pvt, E, 15th NJ Inf, [Killed in action at Spotsylvania CH, VA.] 5-12-1864. New Presbyterian Cemetery, Bound Brook, Somerset County.
CONOVER, OLIVER 7-11-1901. Atlantic City Cemetery, Pleasantville, Atlantic County.
CONOVER, PETER H. Pvt, A, 30th NJ Inf, 9-22-1900. Tennent Church Cemetery, Tennent, Monmouth County.
CONOVER*, PHINEAS W. Sgt, G, 33rd NJ Inf, 1-13-1890. Fairmount Cemetery, Newark, Essex County.
CONOVER, RALPH M. Pvt, C, 1st NJ Inf, [Wounded in action.] 3-12-1902. Bordentown/Old St. Mary's Catholic Cemetery, Bordentown, Burlington County.
CONOVER*, RICHARD S. Pvt, B, 38th NJ Inf, 3-28-1902. Sandy Ridge Cemetery, Sandy Ridge, Hunterdon County.
CONOVER, RUNEY D. 9-28-1918. Brainerd Cemetery, Cranbury, Middlesex County.
CONOVER, SAMUEL Landsman, U.S. Navy, USS Glaucus, [Navy yard at Norfolk, VA.] 9-23-1906. Bordentown/Old St. Mary's Catholic Cemetery, Bordentown, Burlington County.
CONOVER, SAMUEL S. Pvt, B, 54th IN Inf, 6-20-1891. Rahway Cemetery, Rahway, Union County.
CONOVER, SOMERS Pvt, E, 10th NJ Inf, 10-10-1927. Elwood Rural Cemetery, Elwood, Atlantic County.
CONOVER, STEVEN F. Pvt, H, 127th U.S. CT, DoD Unknown. St. James AME Church Cemetery, Woodville, Monmouth County.
CONOVER, SUYDAM __, __, __ __ Cav, 10-15-1909. Holmdel Cemetery, Holmdel, Monmouth County.
CONOVER, THOMAS DoD Unknown. Union Cemetery, Gloucester City, Camden County.
CONOVER, THOMAS Corp, C, 1st NJ Inf, [Killed in action at Spotsylvania CH, VA.] 5-12-1864. Brainerd Cemetery, Cranbury, Middlesex County.
CONOVER, THOMAS H. Pvt, G, 12th NJ Inf, 4-18-1917. Cedar Hill Cemetery, Cedarville, Cumberland County.
CONOVER, THOMAS J. Pvt, C, 127th U.S. CT, 8-21-1885. Princeton Cemetery, Princeton, Mercer County.
CONOVER, VINCENT Pvt, F, 22nd NJ Inf, 8-16-1912. Cedar Hill Cemetery, Hightstown, Mercer County.
CONOVER, WILLIAM Sgt, C, 14th NY Cav, 1-4-1900. Evergreen Cemetery, Hillside, Union County.

Our Brothers Gone Before

CONOVER, WILLIAM C. 1st Lt, Com, 1st NJ Cav 1-8-1920. Tennent Church Cemetery, Tennent, Monmouth County.

CONOVER, WILLIAM H. Pvt, G, 28th NJ Inf, [Wounded in action.] 4-26-1893. Lake Park Cemetery, Swedesboro, Gloucester County.

CONOVER, WILLIAM H. Pvt, B, 1st NJ Cav, 5-21-1914. Arlington Cemetery, Kearny, Hudson County.

CONOVER, WILLIAM H. Pvt, E, 28th NJ Inf, [Wounded in action.] 1-1-1903. Methodist Church Cemetery, Harmony, Ocean County.

CONOVER, WILLIAM L. Sgt, A, 28th NJ Inf, 5-28-1934. Tennent Church Cemetery, Tennent, Monmouth County.

CONOVER, WILLIAM S. 2nd Lt, F, 14th NJ Inf, [Wounded in action.] 1908. Whitelawn Cemetery, Point Pleasant, Ocean County.

CONOVER, WILLIAM W. Pvt, I, 83rd PA Inf, [Wounded in action.] 1908. Bethlehem Presbyterian Church Cemetery, Grandin, Hunterdon County.

CONOVER, WILLIAM W. Capt, G, 14th NJ Inf, 8-3-1921. Fairview Cemetery, Fairview, Monmouth County.

CONOVER, WILLIAM W. 1913. Holmdel Cemetery, Holmdel, Monmouth County.

CONOWAY, WILLIAM H. Pvt, D, 11th MD Inf, DoD Unknown. Finn's Point National Cemetery, Pennsville, Salem County.

CONRAD, CHARLES Pvt, A, 34th NJ Inf, 7-6-1876. Locust Hill Cemetery, Trenton, Mercer County.

CONRAD, FREDERICK Pvt, F, 28th PA Inf, 2-20-1875. Berlin Cemetery, Berlin, Camden County.

CONRAD, GEORGE W. 5-26-1871. Evergreen Cemetery, Hillside, Union County.

CONRAD*, JOSEPH C. Pvt, A, 3rd NJ Inf, 6-18-1928. Harleigh Cemetery, Camden, Camden County.

CONRAD, LEWIS Pvt, G, 9th NJ Inf, 10-15-1930. Evergreen Cemetery, Hillside, Union County.

CONRAD, OTTO Landsman, U.S. Navy, USS South Carolina, 1-10-1913. Bayview-New York Bay Cemetery, Jersey City, Hudson County.

CONRAD, TOWNSEND N. Pvt, Chapman's Btty, VA Light Art (CSA), 12-5-1907. Greenwood Cemetery, Hamilton, Mercer County.

CONRAD, WILLIAM (aka: Cunard, William) Pvt, D, 6th NJ Inf, 2-25-1894. Fairmount Cemetery, Newark, Essex County.

CONRAD, WILLIAM (see: Goward, William S.) Arlington Cemetery, Pennsauken, Camden County.

CONRADE*, CHARLES G. Pvt, C, 53rd NY Inf, 7-11-1884. Flower Hill Cemetery, North Bergen, Hudson County.

CONROE, JAMES M. (see: Conrow, James M.) Old 1st Methodist Church Cemetery, West Long Branch, Monmouth County.

CONROW, CHARLES H. Pvt, D, 21st NJ Inf, 1900. Greengrove Cemetery, Keyport, Monmouth County.

CONROW, CHARLES M. Sgt, G, 14th NJ Inf, 1- -1879. Fairview Cemetery, Fairview, Monmouth County.

CONROW, JAMES M. (aka: Conroe, James M.) Pvt, I, 49th NY Inf, 6-10-1908. Old 1st Methodist Church Cemetery, West Long Branch, Monmouth County.

CONROW, JOHN M. Pvt, C, 1st NJ Cav, 1923. Baptist Cemetery, Vincentown, Burlington County.

CONROW, JOHN S. Pvt, A, 29th NJ Inf, 3-27-1910. Glenwood Cemetery, West Long Branch, Monmouth County.

CONROW*, LUKE Corp, A, 29th NJ Inf, 4-19-1905. Old 1st Methodist Church Cemetery, West Long Branch, Monmouth County.

CONROW, STACEY H. Pvt, C, 34th NJ Inf, 12-27-1870. St. Mary's Episcopal Church Cemetery, Burlington, Burlington County.

New Jersey Civil War Burials

CONROW, WILLIAM J. Corp, F, 1st NJ Cav, 9-16-1914. Old 1st Methodist Church Cemetery, West Long Branch, Monmouth County.

CONROY, ANN E. Nurse, 9-5-1912. Evergreen Cemetery, Hillside, Union County.

CONROY, DENNIS Pvt, K, 27th NJ Inf, 4-23-1872. Mount Olivet Cemetery, Bloomfield, Essex County.

CONROY, GEORGE Musc, G, 21st NJ Inf, 2-9-1892. Holy Name Cemetery, Jersey City, Hudson County.

CONROY, JAMES Pvt, H, 27th NJ Inf, 1925. St. John's Evangelical Church Cemetery, Orange, Essex County.

CONROY, JOHN Pvt, K, 9th NJ Inf, 2-10-1895. Evergreen Cemetery, Hillside, Union County.

CONROY, JOHN DoD Unknown. Mount Carmel Cemetery, West Moorestown, Burlington County.

CONROY, JOHN M. Pvt, H, 65th NY Inf, [Wounded 5-3-1863 at Salem Heights, VA.] 1-15-1896. Holy Sepulchre Cemetery, Totowa, Passaic County.

CONROY, MICHAEL Pvt, C, 11th NJ Inf, 3-29-1865. St. Peter's Cemetery, New Brunswick, Middlesex County.

CONROY*, PATRICK Landsman, U.S. Navy, USS Vincennes, 3-25-1900. St. John's Evangelical Church Cemetery, Orange, Essex County.

CONROY, THOMAS J. Pvt, F, 39th NJ Inf, 2-4-1925. Elm Ridge Cemetery, North Brunswick, Middlesex County.

CONROY, WILLIAM Pvt, E, 8th NJ Inf, 8-14-1896. St. Peter's Church Cemetery, Belleville, Essex County.

CONSELYEA, IRA W. Corp, D, 13th NJ Inf, [Cenotaph. Wounded 9-17-1862 at Antietam, MD.] DoD Unknown. Mount Pleasant Cemetery, Newark, Essex County.

CONSELYEA, J. Seaman, U.S. Navy, 1874. Laurel Grove Cemetery, Totowa, Passaic County.

CONSELYEA, JAMES 1-12-1894. Prospect Hill Cemetery, Caldwell, Essex County.

CONSOLOY, LEWIS Pvt, B, 4th NJ Inf, 12-12-1889. Riverview Cemetery, Trenton, Mercer County.

CONTER*, ENOS Pvt, Btty C, 1st NJ Light Art, 2-1-1882. St. John's Evangelical Church Cemetery, Orange, Essex County.

CONVERSE, CHARLES S. Pvt, I, 1st VA Reserve Inf (CSA), [Richmond Home Guards.] 6-28-1905. Connecticut Farms Cemetery, Union, Union County.

CONVERY, JOHN Pvt, H, 40th NJ Inf, 9-27-1885. St. John's Cemetery, Hamilton, Mercer County.

CONVEY, JAMES Pvt, B, 27th NJ Inf, DoD Unknown. Holy Sepulchre Cemetery, East Orange, Essex County.

CONWAY*, ANDREW Pvt, E, 2nd PA Cav, 4-5-1901. Phillipsburg Old Catholic Cemetery, Phillipsburg, Warren County.

CONWAY, BARTHOLOMEW Corp, A, 69th PA Inf, [Wounded 12-13-1862 at Fredericksburg, VA.] 10-11-1905. Mount Calvary Cemetery, Mount Calvary, Atlantic County.

CONWAY, BENJAMIN DoD Unknown. St. James Episcopal Church Cemetery, Piscatawaytown, Middlesex County.

CONWAY, JAMES Pvt, G, 9th NY Inf, [Cenotaph. Killed in action at Antietam, MD.] 9-17-1862. Madonna Cemetery, Leonia, Bergen County.

CONWAY, JOHN Pvt, A, 9th NJ Inf, 1880. St. Mary's Cemetery, Hamilton, Mercer County.

CONWAY, ROBERT 1895. Baptist/Evergreen Methodist Cemetery, Plainfield, Union County.

CONWAY, WILLIAM Pvt, G, 17th NY Inf, DoD Unknown. Hoboken Cemetery, North Bergen, Hudson County.

Our Brothers Gone Before

CONWAY, WILLIAM (JR.) 1864. Madonna Cemetery, Leonia, Bergen County.
CONYARD, JASPER (CSA) [Black Confederate soldier or conscript in the Confederate Army.] 3-29-1906. Rosehill Cemetery, Linden, Union County.
CONZELMAN, CONRAD Pvt, Btty E, 1st NJ Light Art, 1-9-1889. Rahway Cemetery, Rahway, Union County.
COOK, ABRAHAM N. 1880. Union Cemetery, Hope, Warren County.
COOK, ABRAM A. Pvt, H, 161st NY Inf, [Wounded in action 5-28-1863 at Port Hudson, LA.] 6-10-1915. Evergreen Cemetery, New Brunswick, Middlesex County.
COOK, ABRAM N. Pvt, D, 14th NJ Inf, 1-4-1868. Evergreen Cemetery, New Brunswick, Middlesex County.
COOK, ABRAM N. Pvt, D, 14th NJ Inf, [Wounded in action.] 8-27-1885. Atlantic View Cemetery, Manasquan, Monmouth County.
COOK*, ALBERT B. Pvt, K, 6th NC Cav (CSA), [Died of smallpox.] 8-5-1864. Finn's Point National Cemetery, Pennsville, Salem County.
COOK*, ALEXANDER Corp, G, 34th NJ Inf, 10-29-1898. Evergreen Cemetery, Camden, Camden County.
COOK, ALEXANDER Seaman, U.S. Navy, 8-25-1883. Presbyterian Cemetery, Woodbury, Gloucester County.
COOK, ALFORD B. Corp, I, 2nd DC Inf, [Wounded in action.] 1-29-1921. Rahway Cemetery, Rahway, Union County.
COOK, AMAZIAH R. Sgt, A, 51st AL Cav (CSA), 12-30-1863. Finn's Point National Cemetery, Pennsville, Salem County.
COOK, ANDREW J. Pvt, D, 84th NY Inf, 2-26-1882. Fairmount Cemetery, Newark, Essex County.
COOK, ANDREW J. Pvt, D, 14th NJ Inf, DoD Unknown. Bay View Cemetery, Leonardo, Monmouth County.
COOK, APOLLO E. Pvt, G, 11th NJ Inf, 1905. Baptist Church Cemetery, Jacobstown, Burlington County.
COOK, ASA T. Pvt, G, 27th NJ Inf, 1-5-1920. United Methodist Church Cemetery, Rockaway Valley, Morris County.
COOK*, AUGUSTUS P. Pvt, I, 18th NY Cav, 12-11-1907. Rosedale Cemetery, Orange, Essex County.
COOK, BENJAMIN F. Pvt, M, 8th IL Inf, 11-30-1889. Oak Hill Cemetery, Vineland, Cumberland County.
COOK*, CHARLES E. Pvt, D, 13th NJ Inf, 3-26-1918. Fairmount Cemetery, Newark, Essex County.
COOK, CHARLES R. Pvt, E, 21st NJ Inf, 7-24-1926. Riverview Cemetery, Trenton, Mercer County.
COOK, CHARLES Y. Pvt, B, 27th NJ Inf, 7-11-1913. Presbyterian Church Cemetery, Rockaway, Morris County.
COOK, CURTIS Pvt, Btty L, 10th NY Heavy Art, [Died of disease.] 2-17-1865. Fairmount Cemetery, Newark, Essex County.
COOK, CYRUS E. Sgt, F, 1st NJ Cav, 4-1-1926. Presbyterian/Methodist-Episcopal Cemetery, Succasunna, Morris County.
COOK, DANIEL A. Pvt, E, 28th NJ Inf, [Cenotaph. Died of typhoid at Falmouth, VA.] 1-16-1863. Methodist Church Cemetery, Harmony, Ocean County.
COOK, DANIEL JUDSON Hosp Steward, 27th NJ Inf 4-15-1894. Presbyterian/Methodist-Episcopal Cemetery, Succasunna, Morris County.
COOK, EDWARD Pvt, F, 21st NJ Inf, 2-28-1910. Arlington Cemetery, Kearny, Hudson County.
COOK, EDWARD Pvt, I, 38th NJ Inf, 7-3-1912. Riverview Cemetery, Trenton, Mercer County.

New Jersey Civil War Burials

COOK, EDWARD Pvt, D, 10th NJ Inf, [Died at New York, NY of wounds received 5-14-1864 at Galt House, VA.] 7-31-1864. New Presbyterian Cemetery, Hanover, Morris County.

COOK, ELLIS L. Landsman, U.S. Navy, USS North Carolina, 2-3-1919. Rahway Cemetery, Rahway, Union County.

COOK, EPHRIAM REZZIAN 8-8-1910. Riverview Cemetery, Trenton, Mercer County.

COOK, EUGENE W. Coal Heaver, U.S. Navy, USS Brittainia, 4- -1887. Riverside Cemetery, Toms River, Ocean County.

COOK, FRANCIS C. 2nd Lt, H, 12th NJ Inf, 2-24-1869. 1st Baptist Church Cemetery, Woodstown, Salem County.

COOK*, FRANCIS E. Pvt, F, 3rd NJ Cav, DoD Unknown. Mount Calvary Cemetery, Butler, Morris County.

COOK, FRANCIS F. 3rd Asst Eng, U.S. Navy, 2-22-1901. St. Mary's Cemetery, Hainesport, Burlington County.

COOK, G.P. Pvt, Ahl's Btty, DE Heavy Art, 10-20-1863. Finn's Point National Cemetery, Pennsville, Salem County.

COOK, GARRET F. 2-25-1892. Ramseyburg Cemetery, Ramseyburg, Warren County.

COOK, GARRETT F. Pvt, H, 21st NJ Inf, 4-13-1909. Presbyterian Church Cemetery, Pennington, Mercer County.

COOK, GEORGE Pvt, C, 2nd CT Inf, 1-27-1914. Soldier's Home Cemetery, Vineland, Cumberland County.

COOK, GEORGE Pvt, K, 24th NJ Inf, 1896. Methodist-Episcopal Church Cemetery, Penns Grove, Salem County.

COOK, GEORGE C. Sgt, F, 3rd NJ Cav, 2-6-1888. Arlington Cemetery, Kearny, Hudson County.

COOK, GEORGE S. Pvt, G, 27th NJ Inf, 6-18-1910. Fairmount Cemetery, Newark, Essex County.

COOK, GREEN C. 3-9-1896. Presbyterian Church Cemetery, Andover, Sussex County.

COOK*, HENRY Pvt, K, 9th NJ Inf, 1-28-1913. Evergreen Cemetery, Hillside, Union County.

COOK, HENRY 3-28-1878. Methodist-Episcopal Cemetery, Burlington, Burlington County.

COOK, HENRY (see: Jones, Henry Phineas) Mount Pleasant Cemetery, Newark, Essex County.

COOK, HIRAM Capt, D, 5th NJ Inf, 3-7-1911. Prospect Hill Cemetery, Caldwell, Essex County.

COOK, HUGH Musc, I, 2nd NJ Cav, [Wounded in action.] 12-2-1902. Fairmount Cemetery, Newark, Essex County.

COOK, ISAAC B. Pvt, G, 4th NJ Inf, [Wounded in action.] 10-14-1933. St. James Episcopal Church Cemetery, Piscatawaytown, Middlesex County.

COOK, ISAAC J. 1st Lt, K, 175th PA Inf, 8-3-1897. Phillipsburg Cemetery, Phillipsburg, Warren County.

COOK, J. CORLIES 12-18-1915. Old 1st Methodist Church Cemetery, West Long Branch, Monmouth County.

COOK, JACOB Pvt, B, 33rd NJ Inf, 8-21-1868. Fairmount Cemetery, Newark, Essex County.

COOK, JAMES 5-18-1902. Fairmount Cemetery, Newark, Essex County.

COOK, JAMES Pvt, K, 9th NJ Inf, 3-25-1887. St. Peter's Cemetery, New Brunswick, Middlesex County.

COOK, JAMES Corp, I, 2nd NJ Inf, 9-14-1879. Cedar Lawn Cemetery, Paterson, Passaic County.

COOK, JAMES Pvt, A, 9th NJ Inf, 6-28-1870. Evergreen Cemetery, Hillside, Union County.

Our Brothers Gone Before

COOK, JAMES H. Pvt, G, 27th NJ Inf, 11-27-1902. 1st Reformed Church Cemetery, Pompton Plains, Morris County.
COOK, JAMES HERVEY 7-21-1905. United Methodist Church Cemetery, Waterloo, Sussex County.
COOK, JAMES M. Pvt, F, 12th NJ Inf, 6-5-1899. Methodist-Episcopal Church Cemetery, Penns Grove, Salem County.
COOK, JOHN Pvt, K, 79th PA Inf, 9-30-1888. Presbyterian Church Cemetery, Bridgeton, Cumberland County.
COOK, JOHN DoD Unknown. Bayview-New York Bay Cemetery, Jersey City, Hudson County.
COOK, JOHN Pvt, B, 45th U.S. CT, 8-20-1916. Riverview Cemetery, Trenton, Mercer County.
COOK, JOHN Pvt, D, 21st NJ Inf, 11-20-1864. Mount Pleasant Cemetery, Newark, Essex County.
COOK, JOHN 2nd Lt, G, 10th U.S. Inf, 11-4-1894. Mount Pleasant Cemetery, Newark, Essex County.
COOK, JOHN A. Pvt, U.S. Marine Corps, 3-21-1922. Monument Cemetery, Edgewater Park, Burlington County.
COOK, JOHN ELIHU Lt Col, 76th NY Inf [Wounded 7-1-1863 at Gettysburg, PA; 5-5-1864 at Wilderness, VA; 10-7-1864 at Hatchers Run, VA.] 4-4-1899. Berry Lawn Cemetery, Carlstadt, Bergen County.
COOK, JOHN H. Pvt, F, 14th NJ Inf, 2-20-1931. Woodlawn Cemetery, Lakewood, Ocean County.
COOK, JOHN S. Pvt, C, 15th NJ Inf, 5-17-1910. Greenwood Cemetery, Boonton, Morris County.
COOK, JOHN W. Corp, H, 2nd NJ Cav, 8-17-1904. Whitelawn Cemetery, Point Pleasant, Ocean County.
COOK, JOHN W. Pvt, I, 44th GA Inf (CSA), [Captured 5-10-1864 at Spotsylvania CH, VA. Died of brain inflammation.] 10-24-1864. Finn's Point National Cemetery, Pennsville, Salem County.
COOK, JOHN WATSON Pvt, H, 2nd NJ Cav, 2-28-1908. Union Brick Cemetery, Blairstown, Warren County.
COOK, JOSEPH Pvt, F, 14th NJ Inf, 1921. Harleigh Cemetery, Camden, Camden County.
COOK, JOSEPH Pvt, A, 2nd DC Inf, 10-11-1885. Fairmount Cemetery, Newark, Essex County.
COOK, JOSEPH C. 1915. Pequest Union Cemetery, Great Meadows, Warren County.
COOK, JOSEPH C. Pvt, E, 3rd NJ Cav, 10-22-1900. Montana Cemetery, Montana, Warren County.
COOK, JOSEPH S. Asst Surg, 31st NJ Inf 1903. Mansfield/Washington Cemetery, Washington, Warren County.
COOK, LEWIS H. Pvt, K, 39th NJ Inf, 6-14-1919. Evergreen Cemetery, Morristown, Morris County.
COOK, LUTHER Pvt, B, 132nd NY Inf, [Died while a prisoner at Richmond, VA.] 4-11-1864. New Presbyterian Cemetery, Hanover, Morris County.
COOK, LYDIA C. Nurse, 1-20-1884. New Episcopal Church Cemetery, Swedesboro, Gloucester County.
COOK, MARTIN Pvt, D, 33rd NJ Inf, DoD Unknown. Reformed Church Cemetery, Pluckemin, Somerset County.
COOK, MARTIN (see: Kuck, Martin) Greenmount Cemetery, Hammonton, Atlantic County.
COOK, MARTIN Pvt, E, 25th NJ Inf, 4-29-1933. Old Butler Cemetery, Butler, Morris County.
COOK, MATTHEW Pvt, B, 33rd NJ Inf, 1904. Mount Pleasant Cemetery, Newark, Essex County.

New Jersey Civil War Burials

COOK, MICHAEL M. (aka: Cook, William A.) Hosp Steward, 29th NJ Inf 3-15-1893. Greenlawn Cemetery, West Long Branch, Monmouth County.

COOK, MILLER HENRY Corp, C, 1st NJ Inf, DoD Unknown. Harleigh Cemetery, Camden, Camden County.

COOK, MINARD F. (see: Cook, Miner) New Presbyterian Cemetery, Hanover, Morris County.

COOK, MINER (aka: Cook, Minard F.) Corp, K, 3rd MI Cav, 1911. New Presbyterian Cemetery, Hanover, Morris County.

COOK, NOAH DoD Unknown. Jordan Lawn Cemetery, Pennsauken, Camden County.

COOK, NOAH Pvt, H, 25th U.S. CT, 2-22-1916. St. Matthew's Methodist-Episcopal Cemetery, Morrisville, Camden County.

COOK, P.J. Pvt, I, 40th MS Inf (CSA), 10-21-1863. Finn's Point National Cemetery, Pennsville, Salem County.

COOK, PATRICK S. DoD Unknown. Eastview Cemetery, Salem, Salem County.

COOK, PHILIP 9- -1880. Speer Cemetery, Jersey City, Hudson County.

COOK, PHILIP Pvt, C, 145th IL Inf, 12-19-1893. Amwell Ridge Cemetery, Larisons Corner, Hunterdon County.

COOK, PHILIP C. Pvt, C, 8th NJ Inf, 6-12-1925. Fairmount Cemetery, Phillipsburg, Warren County.

COOK, RICHARD Pvt, K, 21st NJ Inf, 3-1-1909. Arlington Cemetery, Kearny, Hudson County.

COOK, RICHARD Pvt, K, 15th NJ Inf, 2-4-1904. Glenwood Cemetery, Glenwood, Sussex County.

COOK, ROBERT Pvt, I, 4th GA Inf (CSA), [Captured 5-10-1864 at Spotsylvania CH, VA.] 1-6-1865. Finn's Point National Cemetery, Pennsville, Salem County.

COOK, SAMUEL Pvt, D, 14th NJ Inf, [Wounded in action.] 2-28-1903. Adelphia Cemetery, Adelphia, Monmouth County.

COOK, SAMUEL Pvt, F, 1st NJ Inf, 3-28-1868. Union Cemetery, Hope, Warren County.

COOK, SAMUEL J. Corp, A, 40th NY Inf, [Wounded in action 5- -1864.] 6-12-1897. Evergreen Cemetery, Camden, Camden County.

COOK, SAMUEL WARD Pvt, B, 34th NJ Inf, 5-10-1925. Riverside Cemetery, Toms River, Ocean County.

COOK, SARAH Volunteer Nurse, 35th NJ Inf 12-13-1889. Riverview Cemetery, Trenton, Mercer County.

COOK, SILAS S. Pvt, F, 23rd NJ Inf, DoD Unknown. Baptist Cemetery, Medford, Burlington County.

COOK, SYLVESTER A. Corp, K, 44th NY Inf, [Wounded 7-1-1862 at Malvern Hill, VA.] 9-26-1919. Siloam Cemetery, Vineland, Cumberland County.

COOK, THOMAS Pvt, K, 1st NJ Inf, [Missing in action at Wilderness, VA. Supposed dead.] 5-5-1864. Boonton Cemetery, Boonton, Morris County.

COOK, THOMAS F. Pvt, H, 25th NJ Inf, 10-15-1887. Cedar Lawn Cemetery, Paterson, Passaic County.

COOK, THOMAS VERMILYEA Corp, D, 39th NJ Inf, 11-21-1875. Fairmount Cemetery, Newark, Essex County.

COOK, URBANE S. 1st Lt, Btty M, 2nd PA Heavy Art, [Died at Fort Delaware.] 10-17-1862. Finn's Point National Cemetery, Pennsville, Salem County.

COOK*, WILLIAM Pvt, D, 2nd NJ Inf, 1884. Holy Rood Cemetery, Morristown, Morris County.

COOK, WILLIAM Pvt, H, 27th MI Inf, 12-31-1864. Vail Presbyterian Cemetery, Parsippany, Morris County.

COOK, WILLIAM A. Pvt, D, 71st NY Inf, 3-15-1896. Greenlawn Cemetery, West Long Branch, Monmouth County.

COOK, WILLIAM A. (see: Cook, Michael M.) Greenlawn Cemetery, West Long Branch, Monmouth County.

Our Brothers Gone Before

COOK, WILLIAM E. Pvt, E, 132nd NY Inf, 9-24-1894. Prospect Hill Cemetery, Caldwell, Essex County.

COOK, WILLIAM H. Surg, 23rd NJ Inf 10-5-1864. Bordentown/Old St. Mary's Catholic Cemetery, Bordentown, Burlington County.

COOK, WILLIAM H. Pvt, K, 1st NJ Cav, 9-20-1923. United Methodist Church Cemetery, Rockaway Valley, Morris County.

COOK, WILLIAM H. Pvt, F, 26th U.S. CT, 4-5-1914. Evergreen Cemetery, Hillside, Union County.

COOK, WILLIAM H. Pvt, E, 23rd NJ Inf, 9-5-1899. Methodist-Episcopal Cemetery, Wrightstown, Burlington County.

COOK, WILLIAM H. DoD Unknown. Old Cook Cemetery, Denville, Morris County.

COOK, WILLIAM H. Pvt, C, 21st NJ Inf, DoD Unknown. Baptist Church Cemetery, Laurelton, Ocean County.

COOK, WILLIAM H. 12-15-1875. Mount Pleasant Cemetery, Newark, Essex County.

COOK, WILLIAM J. 2nd Lt, D, 28th NJ Inf, 6-9-1888. Van Liew Cemetery, North Brunswick, Middlesex County.

COOK*, WILLIAM L. Pvt, C, 5th NJ Inf, 9-26-1905. Riverside Cemetery, Toms River, Ocean County.

COOK, WILLIAM M. Pvt, I, 44th GA Inf (CSA), [Captured 5-10-1864 at Spotsylvania CH, VA. Died of smallpox.] 2-16-1865. Finn's Point National Cemetery, Pennsville, Salem County.

COOK, WILLIAM M. Pvt, G, 2nd PA Cav, 6-25-1906. Mansfield/Washington Cemetery, Washington, Warren County.

COOK, WILLIAM R. Pvt, G, 37th NJ Inf, 3-3-1914. Presbyterian Church Cemetery, Woodbridge, Middlesex County.

COOKE, ANDREW C. 2-23-1923. Methodist-Episcopal Cemetery, Pennsville, Salem County.

COOKE, DANIEL Sgt, Btty E, 3rd U.S. Art, 12-19-1905. Harleigh Cemetery, Camden, Camden County.

COOKE, DAVID Pvt, B, 123rd PA Inf, 1884. Baptist Cemetery, Burlington, Burlington County.

COOKE, EDWIN FRANCIS Bvt Brig Gen, U.S. Volunteers, [Major, 2nd New York Cavalry.] 8-6-1867. Clove Cemetery, Wantage, Sussex County.

COOKE, FREDERICK A. 1st Sgt, M, 2nd NJ Cav, [Died of chronic diarrhea at Port Jervis, NY.] 6-13-1864. Clove Cemetery, Wantage, Sussex County.

COOKE, GEORGE W. 1st Lt, F, 27th NJ Inf, 12-5-1901. Rosedale Cemetery, Orange, Essex County.

COOKE, GILBERT SNOWDEN Pvt, F, 37th NJ Inf, 4-3-1903. New Somerville Cemetery, Somerville, Somerset County.

COOKE, HENRY GANSEVOORT Surg, 29th NJ Inf 12-2-1919. Old Brick Reformed Church Cemetery, Marlboro, Monmouth County.

COOKE, LESLIE ERWIN 1926. Union Cemetery, Washington, Morris County.

COOKE, R.D. DoD Unknown. New Somerville Cemetery, Somerville, Somerset County.

COOKE*, WILLIAM H. Pvt, E, 83rd NY Inf, 10-24-1918. Arlington Cemetery, Kearny, Hudson County.

COOKER, CHRISTOPHER (see: Brooker, Christopher) Baptist Church Cemetery, Canton, Salem County.

COOKES, JAMES M. Pvt, I, 66th OH Inf, [Killed in action at Port Republic, VA.] 6-9-1862. Finn's Point National Cemetery, Pennsville, Salem County.

COOL, AARON R. Pvt, M, 1st NJ Cav, 1924. Calvary Community Church Cemetery, Harmony, Warren County.

COOL, HARVEY S. (aka: Ryker, John) Pvt, Btty L, 1st CT Heavy Art, 1911. German Valley Rural Cemetery, Naughright, Morris County.

New Jersey Civil War Burials

COOL, JAMES P. (aka: Polk, James) Pvt, K, 135th IL Inf, 10-18-1913. Fairview Cemetery, Knowlton, Warren County.

COOLEN, JOHN JOSEPH Pvt, E, 133rd NY Inf, DoD Unknown. Holy Sepulchre Cemetery, Totowa, Passaic County.

COOLEY, EDWARD Pvt, B, 22nd NJ Inf, 7-4-1863. Presbyterian Church Cemetery, West Milford, Passaic County.

COOLEY, EDWARD H. Musc, 8th NJ Inf Band 6-5-1862. Christian Cemetery, Milford, Hunterdon County.

COOLEY, JAMES Landsman, U.S. Navy, USS Princeton, 3-9-1910. Oak Grove Cemetery, Hammonton, Atlantic County.

COOLEY, PATRICK Landsman, U.S. Navy, USS Indiana, 10-11-1901. Old Catholic Cemetery, Newton, Sussex County.

COOLEY, WILLIAM DoD Unknown. United Methodist Church Cemetery, Willow Grove, Salem County.

COOMBS, ALBERT Pvt, A, 12th NJ Inf, [Died of typhoid at Washington, DC.] 4-27-1863. Old Presbyterian Church Cemetery, Daretown, Salem County.

COOMBS, JAMES Pvt, A, 23rd NJ Inf, 11-11-1886. Methodist-Episcopal Cemetery, Burlington, Burlington County.

COOMBS, MATTHEW 1st Sgt, I, 12th NJ Inf, 10-16-1922. Evergreen Cemetery, Camden, Camden County.

COOMBS, R. (see: Combs, Rufus) Bayview-New York Bay Cemetery, Jersey City, Hudson County.

COOMBS, WILLIAM H. Pvt, G, 21st NJ Inf, 8-10-1891. Fairmount Cemetery, Newark, Essex County.

COOMBS, WILLIAM H.H. Pvt, D, 2nd DE Inf, 5-23-1895. New Camden Cemetery, Camden, Camden County.

COON, CHARLES (see: Kuhne, Charles) Arlington Cemetery, Kearny, Hudson County.

COON, CHARLES B. Pvt, B, 1st NJ Inf, DoD Unknown. Sandy Ridge Cemetery, Sandy Ridge, Hunterdon County.

COON, EPHRIAM P. Seaman, U.S. Navy, 6-10-1893. Flower Hill Cemetery, North Bergen, Hudson County.

COON, JACOB Pvt, I, 2nd NJ Cav, 12-21-1906. Oddfellows Cemetery, Pemberton, Burlington County.

COON, JOHN C. 1st Lt, D, 31st NJ Inf, 10-10-1887. Newton Cemetery, Newton, Sussex County.

COON, NATHAN Pvt, H, 8th NJ Inf, 2-18-1891. Evergreen Cemetery, Morristown, Morris County.

COON, OLIVER (aka: Coon, Orville W.) Pvt, G, Ind PA Inf, 11-23-1876. Union Cemetery, Washington, Morris County.

COON, ORVILLE W. (see: Coon, Oliver) Union Cemetery, Washington, Morris County.

COON*, PETER Pvt, E, 1st NJ Cav, 2-21-1893. Newton Cemetery, Newton, Sussex County.

COON, THOMAS 1878. Newton Cemetery, Newton, Sussex County.

COONER, JOHN Pvt, H, 51st AL Cav (CSA), 9-27-1863. Finn's Point National Cemetery, Pennsville, Salem County.

COONEY, JAMES Pvt, U.S. Marine Corps, 6-21-1886. Old St. Mary's Cemetery, Gloucester City, Camden County.

COONEY, JOHN Pvt, Btty E, 1st NJ Light Art, 3-4-1904. Holy Sepulchre Cemetery, East Orange, Essex County.

COONEY, MICHAEL Corp, I, 11th NJ Inf, 5-29-1865. St. Peter's Cemetery, New Brunswick, Middlesex County.

COONRADT, JOSEPH Pvt, H, 188th NY Inf, 1-2-1901. Fairmount Cemetery, Newark, Essex County.

Our Brothers Gone Before

COONROD, FRANCIS Pvt, B, 8th NJ Inf, 1-2-1903. Chestnut Cemetery, Dover, Morris County.

COONROD, JABEZ V.P. Pvt, K, 39th NJ Inf, 4-12-1903. Locust Hill Cemetery, Dover, Morris County.

COONS, JACOB P. Pvt, U.S. Marine Corps, 7-14-1908. Arlington Cemetery, Kearny, Hudson County.

COOPAY, SAMUEL (see: Coppy, Samuel) Washington Monumental Cemetery, South River, Middlesex County.

COOPER, ALVIN Corp, I, 13th PA Cav, 4-23-1907. Arlington Cemetery, Kearny, Hudson County.

COOPER, ASBERRY H. Pvt, L, 3rd GA Inf (CSA), [Wounded and captured 7-3-1863 at Gettysburg, PA. Died of typhoid.] 10-27-1863. Finn's Point National Cemetery, Pennsville, Salem County.

COOPER, BENJAMIN P. Pvt, I, 29th NJ Inf, 7-23-1891. Old Mount Pleasant Cemetery, Matawan, Monmouth County.

COOPER, CALVIN Pvt, B, 196th PA Inf, 9-25-1897. Mount Hope Presbyterian Cemetery, Lambertville, Hunterdon County.

COOPER, CHARLES ELIAS ___, ___, ___ PA ___, 1932. Clove Cemetery, Wantage, Sussex County.

COOPER, CREED Pvt, F, 22nd VA Inf (CSA), [Captured 11-6-1863 at Droop Mountain, WV. Died of lung inflammation.] 6-1-1865. Finn's Point National Cemetery, Pennsville, Salem County.

COOPER, DAVID E. Pvt, B, 27th NJ Inf, 5-20-1901. Presbyterian Church Cemetery, Oak Ridge, Passaic County.

COOPER, E.L. 5-27-1900. Hillside Cemetery, Scotch Plains, Union County.

COOPER, EDWARD J. Pvt, C, 8th NJ Inf, 11-16-1908. Fairmount Cemetery, Newark, Essex County.

COOPER, FREDERICK Bvt Col, 7th NJ Inf 2-14-1874. Holy Name Cemetery, Jersey City, Hudson County.

COOPER, GEORGE Corp, E, 22nd U.S. CT, [Died at Newark, NJ. of wounds received 6-15-1864 at Petersburg, VA.] 7-30-1864. Fairmount Cemetery, Newark, Essex County.

COOPER, GEORGE L. Pvt, G, 7th CT Inf, 6-14-1876. Oak Hill Cemetery, Vineland, Cumberland County.

COOPER, HENRY 2-23-1907. Brookside Cemetery, Englewood, Bergen County.

COOPER, HENRY C. Sgt, C, 9th NJ Inf, 2-7-1900. Cedar Lawn Cemetery, Paterson, Passaic County.

COOPER, HOWARD Pvt, D, 95th PA Inf, 6-27-1894. New Camden Cemetery, Camden, Camden County.

COOPER, IRA C. Pvt, B, 27th NJ Inf, 3-22-1883. Presbyterian Church Cemetery, Oak Ridge, Passaic County.

COOPER, J.D. Pvt, A, 35th VA Cav (CSA), 7-12-1864. Finn's Point National Cemetery, Pennsville, Salem County.

COOPER, JACOB EDWARD Chaplain, 3rd KY Inf 1-31-1904. Evergreen Cemetery, New Brunswick, Middlesex County.

COOPER, JAMES Pvt, I, 1st NJ Cav, 1-4-1882. Riverview Cemetery, Trenton, Mercer County.

COOPER, JAMES (see: Cooper, John) Fairview Cemetery, Fairview, Bergen County.

COOPER, JAMES F. DoD Unknown. Bayview-New York Bay Cemetery, Jersey City, Hudson County.

COOPER, JAMES W. Pvt, D, 11th MS Inf (CSA), 4-5-1864. Finn's Point National Cemetery, Pennsville, Salem County.

COOPER, JOHN Pvt, C, 28th U.S. CT, 4-5-1903. Evergreen Cemetery, Morristown, Morris County.

New Jersey Civil War Burials

COOPER*, JOHN (aka: Cooper, James) Pvt, I, 121st NY Inf, 12-21-1914. Fairview Cemetery, Fairview, Bergen County.

COOPER, JOHN Pvt, C, 4th NJ Inf, 4-21-1873. Holy Sepulchre Cemetery, East Orange, Essex County.

COOPER, JOHN C. Pvt, C, 69th PA Inf, 11-5-1913. New Camden Cemetery, Camden, Camden County.

COOPER, JOHN D. Corp, H, 4th NJ Inf, 3-4-1905. Old Camden Cemetery, Camden, Camden County.

COOPER, JOHN J. Pvt, K, 104th PA Inf, 12-4-1876. Mount Hope Presbyterian Cemetery, Lambertville, Hunterdon County.

COOPER, JOHN K. Pvt, A, 2nd NJ Cav, 8-24-1921. Locust Hill Cemetery, Dover, Morris County.

COOPER*, JOHN L. Pvt, I, 112th NY Inf, 4-26-1896. Glenwood Cemetery, Glenwood, Sussex County.

COOPER*, JOHN OWEN Pvt, Btty C, 5th U.S. Art, [Wounded in action.] 8-24-1907. Holcomb-Riverview Cemetery, Lambertville, Hunterdon County.

COOPER, JONAS F. Pvt, H, 38th NJ Inf, 12-10-1912. 2nd Presbyterian Church Cemetery, Mount Airy, Hunterdon County.

COOPER, JOSEPH Pvt, C, 28th NJ Inf, 4-7-1918. Arlington Cemetery, Kearny, Hudson County.

COOPER, JOSHUA W. Pvt, H, 25th U.S. CT, DoD Unknown. Cedar Lawn Cemetery, Paterson, Passaic County.

COOPER, NELSON Pvt, G, 14th NJ Inf, 2-25-1909. Evergreen Cemetery, Farmingdale, Monmouth County.

COOPER, PHILLIP HENRY Actg Ensign, U.S. Navy, 12-29-1912. Evergreen Cemetery, Morristown, Morris County.

COOPER, RICHARD 1st Lt, F, 7th NJ Inf, 4-25-1908. Bayview-New York Bay Cemetery, Jersey City, Hudson County.

COOPER, SAMUEL Pvt, I, 2nd NJ Inf, 1-25-1871. Laurel Grove Cemetery, Totowa, Passaic County.

COOPER, SHERMAN Surg, 6th NH Inf 8-9-1920. Fairview Cemetery, Westfield, Union County.

COOPER, SILAS B. Hosp Steward, 7th NJ Inf 11-6-1886. Evergreen Cemetery, Morristown, Morris County.

COOPER, STEPHEN A. Pvt, G, 27th NJ Inf, 8-26-1899. Whitehall Cemetery, Towaco, Morris County.

COOPER, STEPHEN L. Pvt, I, 27th NJ Inf, 1-13-1913. Arlington Cemetery, Kearny, Hudson County.

COOPER, THOMAS F.G. 1st Lt, Adj, 24th NJ Inf 4-23-1896. Methodist Cemetery, Mantua, Gloucester County.

COOPER, THOMAS H. Pvt, F, 37th NJ Inf, [Died of typhoid at 10th Army Corps hospital.] 8-24-1864. United Methodist Church Cemetery, Vienna, Warren County.

COOPER, WILLIAM Pvt, A, 22nd NJ Inf, DoD Unknown. Hackensack Cemetery, Hackensack, Bergen County.

COOPER, WILLIAM DoD Unknown. Bayview-New York Bay Cemetery, Jersey City, Hudson County.

COOPER, WILLIAM (see: Crane, Ward) Fairview Cemetery, Fairview, Monmouth County.

COOPER, WILLIAM C. Landsman, U.S. Navy, DoD Unknown. Monument Cemetery, Edgewater Park, Burlington County.

COOPER*, WILLIAM C. Pvt, B, 5th NJ Inf, 9-12-1909. Greenwood Cemetery, Hamilton, Mercer County.

Our Brothers Gone Before

COOPER, WILLIAM H. Corp, I, 32nd PA Inf, 2-17-1902. Harleigh Cemetery, Camden, Camden County.
COPASS, JOHN V. Pvt, E, 60th (Crawford's) TN Mtd Inf (CSA), [Captured 5-17-1863 at Big Black River Bridge, MS.] 10-4-1863. Finn's Point National Cemetery, Pennsville, Salem County.
COPE, CHARLES P. Pvt, H, 20th PA Inf, 6-14-1893. Evergreen Cemetery, Camden, Camden County.
COPE, ROBERT E. Pvt, A, 210th PA Inf, 1886. Bayview-New York Bay Cemetery, Jersey City, Hudson County.
COPLE, JOSEPH H. 11-15-1904. Holy Name Cemetery, Jersey City, Hudson County.
COPLEY, IRA K. 1st Lt, F, 5th WV Inf, 1890. Clinton Cemetery, Irvington, Essex County.
COPP*, GEORGE N. Capt, B, 25th U.S. CT, 5-22-1905. Rosehill Cemetery, Newfield, Gloucester County.
COPPERS*, GEORGE Pvt, F, 21st NJ Inf, 12-1-1908. Hoboken Cemetery, North Bergen, Hudson County.
COPPUCK, BENJAMIN A. Pvt, A, 12th PA Cav, 3-21-1862. Mount Holly Cemetery, Mount Holly, Burlington County.
COPPUCK, JOSEPH Pvt, G, PA Emerg NJ Militia, 1890. Baptist/St. Andrew's Cemetery, Mount Holly, Burlington County.
COPPY, SAMUEL (aka: Coopay, Samuel) Pvt, F, 11th NJ Inf, 4-11-1873. Washington Monumental Cemetery, South River, Middlesex County.
CORB*, JOHN (aka: Cobb, John) Pvt, H, 39th NJ Inf, 1900. Vincent Methodist-Episcopal Cemetery, Nutley, Essex County.
CORBET, JOHN (aka: Corbit, John) Pvt, L, 1st NJ Cav, DoD Unknown. Baptist Cemetery, Pemberton, Burlington County.
CORBETT, EDWARD W. Artificer, K, 1st NY Eng, 12-2-1887. Evergreen Cemetery, Morristown, Morris County.
CORBETT, PATRICK Seaman, U.S. Navy, USS Maratanza, 10-14-1902. Holy Sepulchre Cemetery, Totowa, Passaic County.
CORBETT, WILLIAM Seaman, U.S. Navy, USS Onondaga, 3-8-1904. Holy Name Cemetery, Jersey City, Hudson County.
CORBETT, WILLIAM M. Pvt, E, 9th FL Inf (CSA), [Captured 2-7-1864 at Jacksonville, FL. Died of disease.] 6-28-1864. Finn's Point National Cemetery, Pennsville, Salem County.
CORBEY, MARTIN P. Pvt, I, 1st NJ Cav, 3-2-1880. Holy Sepulchre Cemetery, East Orange, Essex County.
CORBEY, MOSES (see: Corby, Moses) United Methodist Church Cemetery, Millbrook, Morris County.
CORBIT, JOHN (see: Corbet, John) Baptist Cemetery, Pemberton, Burlington County.
CORBITT*, MICHAEL (aka: Carroll, John) Pvt, A, 2nd CA Inf, 5-30-1913. Holy Sepulchre Cemetery, East Orange, Essex County.
CORBY, CALEB Pvt, K, 39th NJ Inf, 2-9-1907. United Methodist Church Cemetery, Millbrook, Morris County.
CORBY, CORNELIUS (aka: Carbey, Cornelius) Pvt, Btty G, 5th NY Heavy Art, 5-4-1903. Canfield Cemetery, Cedar Grove, Essex County.
CORBY*, HARRISON Pvt, C, 39th NJ Inf, DoD Unknown. Rosedale Cemetery, Orange, Essex County.
CORBY, HENRY A. Pvt, F, 26th NJ Inf, 9-3-1872. Mount Hebron Cemetery, Montclair, Essex County.
CORBY, ISAAC (see: Ward, John) Prospect Hill Cemetery, Caldwell, Essex County.
CORBY, JOHN MUSON Corp, F, 26th NJ Inf, 4-10-1925. Rosedale Cemetery, Orange, Essex County.
CORBY, JOSEPH L. Pvt, H, 26th NJ Inf, 6-11-1911. Rosedale Cemetery, Orange, Essex County.

New Jersey Civil War Burials

CORBY, MOSES (aka: Corbey, Moses) Artificer, K, 1st NY Eng, 10-19-1873. United Methodist Church Cemetery, Millbrook, Morris County.

CORBY, WESLEY B. 2nd Lt, F, 1st NY Mounted Rifles, 7-26-1896. Bloomfield Cemetery, Bloomfield, Essex County.

CORBY, WILLIAM H. Pvt, F, 26th NJ Inf, 4-18-1899. Mount Hebron Cemetery, Montclair, Essex County.

CORCORAN, JOHN Sgt, H, 1st NJ Cav, 12-3-1890. St. Peter's Cemetery, New Brunswick, Middlesex County.

CORCORAN*, MICHAEL Pvt, K, 6th NJ Inf, 9-18-1886. Old St. Mary's Cemetery, Gloucester City, Camden County.

CORCORAN, THOMAS Pvt, F, 2nd NJ Militia, 4- -1890. St. Peter's Cemetery, Jersey City, Hudson County.

CORDERY, CHARLES H. Pvt, Btty B, 2nd PA Heavy Art, DoD Unknown. Cedar Grove Cemetery, Gloucester City, Camden County.

CORDERY, CLEMENT C. Pvt, K, 23rd NJ Inf, 5-14-1917. United Methodist Church Cemetery, Absecon, Atlantic County.

CORDERY, ENOCH Sgt, K, 4th NJ Inf, 4-10-1891. United Methodist Church Cemetery, Absecon, Atlantic County.

CORDES, HENRY Corp, Btty C, 5th NY Heavy Art, [Wounded 6-18-1864 at Lynchburg, VA.] 7-6-1888. 3rd Reformed Church/Outwater Cemetery, Carlstadt, Bergen County.

CORDREY, ENOCH Pvt, I, 9th NJ Inf, 6-9-1914. Oak Grove Cemetery, Hammonton, Atlantic County.

CORDUAN, EDWARD F. Sgt, I, 1st NJ Militia, 3-30-1882. Mount Pleasant Cemetery, Newark, Essex County.

CORE, JOEL M.D. Pvt, B, 4th NJ Militia, 9-11-1900. Baptist/St. Andrew's Cemetery, Mount Holly, Burlington County.

COREY, JAMES WILSON Sgt, B, 2nd NJ Cav, 8-23-1895. Mount Pleasant Cemetery, Newark, Essex County.

COREY, SAMUEL A. Pvt, C, 8th NJ Inf, 1927. New Presbyterian Cemetery, Hanover, Morris County.

COREY, SILAS J. Pvt, D, 90th NY Inf, 5-4-1914. Baptist Church Cemetery, Scotch Plains, Union County.

COREY, WILLIAM E. Pvt, E, 34th NJ Inf, 11-24-1885. Fairmount Cemetery, Newark, Essex County.

COREY, WILLIAM E. 12-1-1913. Mount Pleasant Cemetery, Newark, Essex County.

CORIELL, ISAIAH 11-12-1902. Methodist Church Cemetery, Mount Horeb, Somerset County.

CORIELL, WILLIAM WALLACE Asst Surg, 13th NJ Inf 5-25-1881. Baptist/Evergreen Methodist Cemetery, Plainfield, Union County.

CORIELL*, WILLIAM WALLACE (JR.) (aka: Corriell, William) Sgt, B, 6th NJ Inf, 5-28-1915. Baptist/Evergreen Methodist Cemetery, Plainfield, Union County.

CORIEM, FRANCIS (see: Corwin, Francis N.W.) Rosedale Cemetery, Orange, Essex County.

CORLEY, R.C. Pvt, F, 3rd SC Cav (CSA), [Captured 8-17-1864 at South Newport, GA. Died of chronic diarrhea.] 2-2-1865. Finn's Point National Cemetery, Pennsville, Salem County.

CORLIES, JAMES COOK Corp, A, 29th NJ Inf, 4-11-1926. Old 1st Methodist Church Cemetery, West Long Branch, Monmouth County.

CORLIES, SAMUEL Pvt, G, 1st NJ Cav, [Died at Washington, DC.] 3-26-1863. Old 1st Methodist Church Cemetery, West Long Branch, Monmouth County.

CORLIS, WILLIAM J. Pvt, H, 29th NJ Inf, 11-25-1915. Cedar Grove Cemetery, Waretown, Ocean County.

Our Brothers Gone Before

CORLISS, REUBEN C. Pvt, C, 24th MA Inf, 1908. Reevestown Cemetery, Reevestown, Ocean County.
CORLISS, SAMUEL Pvt, H, 29th NJ Inf, 1919. New 1st Methodist Meeting House Cemetery, Manahawkin, Ocean County.
CORLISS, WILLIAM FISK 1928. Brookside Cemetery, Englewood, Bergen County.
CORLISS, WILLIAM P. Pvt, I, 9th NJ Inf, 10-16-1896. Evergreen Cemetery, Camden, Camden County.
CORMER*, MICHAEL (aka: Comer, Michael) Pvt, F, 8th NJ Inf, 7-12-1882. St. Peter's Cemetery, Jersey City, Hudson County.
CORNELISON, JAMES Pvt, B, Hunter's MO Cav (CSA), 7-11-1864. Finn's Point National Cemetery, Pennsville, Salem County.
CORNELIUS, ABRAM 1-17-1914. Brookside Cemetery, Englewood, Bergen County.
CORNELIUS, GEORGE W. Pvt, C, 19th (Burford's) TX Cav (CSA), 1-16-1865. Finn's Point National Cemetery, Pennsville, Salem County.
CORNELIUS, GEORGE WILLIAM Pvt, I, 4th NY Inf, 4-3-1865. Old Methodist Cemetery, Toms River, Ocean County.
CORNELIUS, HENRY Pvt, I, 31st U.S. CT, 5-20-1903. White Ridge Cemetery, Eatontown, Monmouth County.
CORNELIUS, JAMES Pvt, K, 1st NJ Cav, 12-4-1907. Cedar Lawn Cemetery, Paterson, Passaic County.
CORNELIUS, JESSE Pvt, D, 33rd NJ Inf, 6-16-1876. Trinity United Methodist Church Cemetery, Bayville, Ocean County.
CORNELIUS, JOHN H. Pvt, D, 9th NJ Inf, 4-7-1900. Good Luck Cemetery, Murray Grove, Ocean County.
CORNELIUS, SAMUEL Pvt, K, 22nd U.S. CT, 11-5-1902. White Ridge Cemetery, Eatontown, Monmouth County.
CORNELIUS, SYDNEY Pvt, I, 8th NJ Inf, 1-1-1903. Riverside Cemetery, Toms River, Ocean County.
CORNELL, AARON COOK Pvt, H, 6th NJ Inf, 4-3-1922. Union Cemetery, Ringoes, Hunterdon County.
CORNELL, BIRDSALL 1st Lt, I, 1st NJ Cav, 6-25-1916. Soldier's Home Cemetery, Vineland, Cumberland County.
CORNELL, CHARLES T. Pvt, H, 48th NY Inf, [Wounded 6-2-1864 at Cold Harbor, VA.] 5-25-1869. Fairmount Cemetery, Newark, Essex County.
CORNELL, EMANUEL (aka: Cornels, Manuel) Pvt, G, 95th OH Inf, 5-10-1905. Elmwood Cemetery, New Brunswick, Middlesex County.
CORNELL, GEORGE H. Pvt, E, 71st NY State Militia, DoD Unknown. East Ridgelawn Cemetery, Clifton, Passaic County.
CORNELL, JAMES (see: Cornwall, James) 1st United Methodist Church Cemetery, Bridgeton, Cumberland County.
CORNELL, JAMES (see: Cornell, John H.) St. Peter's Cemetery, Perth Amboy, Middlesex County.
CORNELL, JAMES H. Pvt, I, 11th NJ Inf, 4-25-1907. Elmwood Cemetery, New Brunswick, Middlesex County.
CORNELL*, JAMES V.N. Pvt, E, 15th NJ Inf, [Wounded in action.] 6-18-1909. Reformed Church Cemetery, Readington, Hunterdon County.
CORNELL, JOHN H. (aka: Cornell, James) Pvt, F, 11th NJ Inf, 4-19-1905. St. Peter's Cemetery, Perth Amboy, Middlesex County.
CORNELL, NICHOLAS Pvt, A, 2nd NJ Cav, 1-25-1889. New Presbyterian Cemetery, Bound Brook, Somerset County.
CORNELL, WILLIAM Actg 2nd Asst Eng, U.S. Navy, 2-5-1913. Bayview-New York Bay Cemetery, Jersey City, Hudson County.
CORNELS, MANUEL (see: Cornell, Emanuel) Elmwood Cemetery, New Brunswick, Middlesex County.

New Jersey Civil War Burials

CORNEW, JOHN (aka: Canoe, John) Pvt, H, 21st NJ Inf, 10-3-1892. Lawrenceville Cemetery, Lawrenceville, Mercer County.

CORNEY, HENRY Landsman, U.S. Navy, 9-21-1919. St. Matthew's Methodist-Episcopal Cemetery, Morrisville, Camden County.

CORNIS, JOHN Pvt, A, 46th IN Inf, DoD Unknown. Elmwood Cemetery, New Brunswick, Middlesex County.

CORNISH, WILLIAM H. Pvt, D, 17th NY Inf, 8-9-1905. Presbyterian Cemetery, New Vernon, Morris County.

CORNISH*, WILLIAM T. Maj, 39th NJ Inf 7-30-1885. Presbyterian Church Cemetery, Hampton, Hunterdon County.

CORNWALL, JAMES (aka: Cornell, James) Pvt, G, 24th NJ Inf, 9-8-1891. 1st United Methodist Church Cemetery, Bridgeton, Cumberland County.

CORRAZ, VICTOR A. Pvt, D, 3rd NJ Cav, 4-1-1917. Prospect Hill Cemetery, Caldwell, Essex County.

CORREGAN, EDWARD (see: Carrigan, Edward J.) Holy Sepulchre Cemetery, Totowa, Passaic County.

CORRIELL, WILLIAM (see: Coriell, William Wallace (Jr.)) Baptist/Evergreen Methodist Cemetery, Plainfield, Union County.

CORRIGAN, ANTHONY G. Pvt, I, 79th NY Inf, DoD Unknown. Holy Sepulchre Cemetery, Totowa, Passaic County.

CORRIGAN, BARNEY (aka: Corrigan, Bernard) Pvt, A, 11th NY Inf, 5-27-1884. Flower Hill Cemetery, North Bergen, Hudson County.

CORRIGAN, BERNARD (see: Corrigan, Barney) Flower Hill Cemetery, North Bergen, Hudson County.

CORRIGAN*, JOHN (aka: Corrington, John) Pvt, Btty B, 1st NJ Light Art, 2-15-1909. Soldier's Home Cemetery, Vineland, Cumberland County.

CORRIGAN, JOHN Corp, D, 33rd NJ Inf, 3-26-1882. Holy Sepulchre Cemetery, Totowa, Passaic County.

CORRIGAN, JOHN 3-26-1897. Holy Sepulchre Cemetery, Totowa, Passaic County.

CORRIGAN, OWEN Pvt, A, 9th FL Inf (CSA), [Captured 2-7-1864 at Camp Finegan, FL. Died of lung inflammation.] 3-26-1864. Finn's Point National Cemetery, Pennsville, Salem County.

CORRIGAN*, THOMAS (aka: Korrigan, Thomas) Pvt, G, 6th NY Inf, 5-18-1898. Holy Name Cemetery, Jersey City, Hudson County.

CORRIGAN, THOMAS Pvt, G, 37th MA Inf, 10-16-1925. St. Peter's Cemetery, New Brunswick, Middlesex County.

CORRINGTON, JOHN (see: Corrigan, John) Soldier's Home Cemetery, Vineland, Cumberland County.

CORRY, ALEXANDER (aka: Kanup, A.) Pvt, K, 5th NC Inf (CSA), [Captured 7-1-1863 at Gettysburg, PA. Died of typhoid.] 9-16-1863. Finn's Point National Cemetery, Pennsville, Salem County.

CORSOFF*, RUDOLPH Pvt, B, 3rd NJ Cav, 10-8-1865. Willow Grove Cemetery, New Brunswick, Middlesex County.

CORSON, ABIJAH Sgt, E, 3rd DE Inf, [Cenotaph. Killed in action at Petersburg, VA.] 6-23-1864. Calvary Baptist Church Cemetery, Ocean View, Cape May County.

CORSON, ALEXANDER Pvt, I, 25th NJ Inf, 9-11-1907. Cedar Hill Cemetery, Cedarville, Cumberland County.

CORSON, ALEXANDER V. DoD Unknown. Evergreen Cemetery, Camden, Camden County.

CORSON, CHARLES H. Corp, G, 25th NJ Inf, 1909. Rosehill Cemetery, Newfield, Gloucester County.

CORSON, EDWIN 9-30-1899. Morgan Cemetery, Cinnaminson, Burlington County.

CORSON, GEORGE W. Pvt, I, 25th NJ Inf, 1908. Mount Pleasant Cemetery, Millville, Cumberland County.

Our Brothers Gone Before

CORSON, GEORGE W. DoD Unknown. 1st United Methodist Church Cemetery, Bridgeton, Cumberland County.

CORSON, GERMAN Blacksmith, A, 3rd NJ Cav, 10-12-1898. Calvary Baptist Church Cemetery, Ocean View, Cape May County.

CORSON, ISAAC Pvt, E, 1st NY Inf, 1930. Shinn GAR Post Cemetery, Port Norris, Cumberland County.

CORSON, ISAAC B. 5-28-1884. Baptist Church Cemetery, Palermo, Cape May County.

CORSON, JEREMIAH Pvt, L, 62nd PA Inf, [Killed in action at Gaines' Mill, VA.] 6-27-1862. Mount Pleasant Cemetery, Millville, Cumberland County.

CORSON, JOHN WESLEY Corp, F, 25th NJ Inf, 11-24-1910. Presbyterian Church Cemetery, Cold Spring, Cape May County.

CORSON, JOSEPH Pvt, G, 9th NJ Inf, 2-2-1896. Methodist-Episcopal Church Cemetery, South Dennis, Cape May County.

CORSON, LUCIEN B. Pvt, G, 25th NJ Inf, 10-13-1907. Presbyterian Church Cemetery, Mays Landing, Atlantic County.

CORSON, LUCIUS E. Quartermaster, U.S. Navy, USS Anemone, 1917. Trinity Methodist-Episcopal Church Cemetery, Marmora, Cape May County.

CORSON, LUCIUS E.P. Ordinary Seaman, U.S. Navy, USS Princeton, 2-2-1907. Trinity Methodist-Episcopal Church Cemetery, Marmora, Cape May County.

CORSON, MILES 10-18-1887. 1st Baptist Cemetery, Cape May Court House, Cape May County.

CORSON*, MULFORD Seaman, U.S. Navy, USS Anemone, 7-8-1889. Baptist Church Cemetery, Palermo, Cape May County.

CORSON, NICHOLAS 2nd Lt, G, 25th NJ Inf, 11-15-1909. Calvary Baptist Church Cemetery, Ocean View, Cape May County.

CORSON, PARMENAS (aka: Carson, Permillion) Pvt, L, 11th IL Cav, 12-19-1898. Mount Pleasant Cemetery, Millville, Cumberland County.

CORSON, PARMENAS (see: Corson, Parmenus) Baptist Church Cemetery, Palermo, Cape May County.

CORSON, PARMENUS (aka: Corson, Parmenas) Pvt, F, 138th OH Inf, 12-12-1904. Baptist Church Cemetery, Palermo, Cape May County.

CORSON, RICHARD L.W. 1918. Mount Pleasant Cemetery, Millville, Cumberland County.

CORSON, ROBERT Pvt, C, 38th NJ Inf, 1916. Mount Pleasant Cemetery, Millville, Cumberland County.

CORSON, THOMAS Pvt, F, 69th PA Inf, 10-28-1907. Arlington Cemetery, Pennsauken, Camden County.

CORSON, WILLETS Pvt, A, 3rd NJ Cav, [Died at Washington, DC.] 6-9-1864. Baptist Church Cemetery, Palermo, Cape May County.

CORSON, WILLIAM A. Pvt, G, 37th NJ Inf, 3-4-1919. Rahway Cemetery, Rahway, Union County.

CORSON, WILLIAM S. Pvt, G, 24th NJ Inf, [Died of wounds received 12-13-1862 at Fredericksburg, VA.] 12-22-1862. Methodist-Episcopal Cemetery, Glassboro, Gloucester County.

CORSON, WILLIAM S. Pvt, D, 6th PA Cav, 10-26-1909. Methodist-Episcopal Cemetery, Glassboro, Gloucester County.

CORT*, GEORGE (aka: Court, George) Pvt, G, 37th NJ Inf, 8-17-1902. Fairmount Cemetery, Newark, Essex County.

CORT*, HENRY (aka: Court, Harry) Pvt, G, 37th NJ Inf, 7-3-1917. Fairmount Cemetery, Newark, Essex County.

CORTELYOU, JOHN S. Pvt, A, 27th NJ Inf, 8-31-1889. Newton Cemetery, Newton, Sussex County.

CORTELYOU, WILLIAM Corp, A, 27th NJ Inf, 1-10-1873. Newton Cemetery, Newton, Sussex County.

New Jersey Civil War Burials

CORTIN, DAVID (see: Costine, David) Jacob's Chapel AME Church Cemetery, Colemantown, Burlington County.

CORTRIGHT, GEORGE N. (see: Courtright, George N.) Hillside Cemetery, Scotch Plains, Union County.

CORTRIGHT, SOLOMON Corp, I, 15th NJ Inf, [Killed in action at Salem Heights, VA.] 5-3-1863. Minisink Reformed Church Cemetery, Montague, Sussex County.

CORTWRIGHT, GEORGE Pvt, I, 9th NJ Inf, 9-21-1918. Stanhope-Union Cemetery, Netcong, Morris County.

CORVATT*, LAWRENCE (aka: Cravatt, Lawrence) Pvt, H, 15th NJ Inf, 1914. Methodist Church Cemetery, Lebanon, Hunterdon County.

CORWIN, FRANCIS N.W. (aka: Coriem, Francis) Pvt, H, 26th NJ Inf, 4-11-1904. Rosedale Cemetery, Orange, Essex County.

CORY, ABRAHAM MORRELL Surg, U.S. Volunteers, 1908. United Methodist Church Cemetery, New Providence, Union County.

CORY, CALEB A. Pvt, I, 27th NJ Inf, 3-19-1866. Whippanong Cemetery, Whippany, Morris County.

CORY, IRA W. Capt, H, 11th NJ Inf, 3-2-1904. Evergreen Cemetery, Morristown, Morris County.

CORY, JONATHAN Landsman, U.S. Navy, USS Princeton, DoD Unknown. Mount Pleasant Cemetery, Newark, Essex County.

CORY, WILLIAM 9-11-1873. United Methodist Church Cemetery, New Providence, Union County.

CORYELL, JOHN L. [U.S. Army Construction Corps.] 10-15-1911. Mount Hope Presbyterian Cemetery, Lambertville, Hunterdon County.

CORYELL, TORBERT Pvt, D, PA Emerg NJ Militia, 4-18-1912. Mount Hope Presbyterian Cemetery, Lambertville, Hunterdon County.

COSBY, JOHN H. Pvt, E, 4th GA Inf (CSA), [Captured 5-10-1864 at Spotsylvania CH, VA.] 7-7-1864. Finn's Point National Cemetery, Pennsville, Salem County.

COSGROVE, DANIEL Pvt, B, 9th NJ Inf, 12-27-1911. Presbyterian Church Cemetery, Cold Spring, Cape May County.

COSGROVE*, HENRY Corp, Btty M, 6th NY Heavy Art, 3-31-1904. Holy Name Cemetery, Jersey City, Hudson County.

COSGROVE, JAMES Pvt, I, 133rd NY Inf, [Wounded in action.] 5-27-1901. Baptist Cemetery, South Plainfield, Middlesex County.

COSGROVE*, JOHN Seaman, U.S. Navy, USS Princeton, 5-31-1907. St. John's Evangelical Church Cemetery, Orange, Essex County.

COSGROVE, LAWRENCE Pvt, Btty D, 1st CT Heavy Art, DoD Unknown. St. Peter's Cemetery, New Brunswick, Middlesex County.

COSGROVE, PATRICK Pvt, F, 2nd NJ Cav, 6-1-1875. Holy Name Cemetery, Jersey City, Hudson County.

COSGROVE, PATRICK Pvt, O, 198th PA Inf, 8-5-1902. Holy Sepulchre Cemetery, Totowa, Passaic County.

COSGROVE, THOMAS DoD Unknown. St. Mary's Cemetery, Wharton, Morris County.

COSGROVE*, THOMAS Pvt, A, 7th U.S. Vet Vol Inf, 10-4-1894. St. John's Evangelical Church Cemetery, Orange, Essex County.

COSGROVE, THOMAS P. 1865. Mount Pleasant Cemetery, Newark, Essex County.

COSIER, GEORGE C. (aka: Crosier, George) Corp, D, 25th NJ Inf, 8-10-1912. Methodist Church Cemetery, Newport, Cumberland County.

COSINE, WALTER Pvt, I, 22nd NJ Inf, 8-6-1917. Macphelah Cemetery, North Bergen, Hudson County.

COSKER, FELIX (see: McCosker, Felix A.) Old Hook Cemetery, Westwood, Bergen County.

COSKREY, JAMES L. Pvt, C, 44th AL Inf (CSA), [Captured in Tennessee.] 4-5-1864. Finn's Point National Cemetery, Pennsville, Salem County.

Our Brothers Gone Before

COSLEY, HENRY (see: Casley, Henry) Grove Church Cemetery, North Bergen, Hudson County.

COSLEY, JOHN (see: Coffy, John) Flower Hill Cemetery, North Bergen, Hudson County.

COSSABONE, JOHN (see: Cassaboon, John) Mount Pleasant Cemetery, Millville, Cumberland County.

COSSABOON, BENJAMIN Pvt, B, 24th NJ Inf, 1911. Mount Pleasant Cemetery, Millville, Cumberland County.

COSSABOON, JOHN M. Pvt, C, 2nd MD Inf (E.S.), DoD Unknown. Mount Pleasant Cemetery, Millville, Cumberland County.

COSSABOONE, JESSE Pvt, B, 24th NJ Inf, 1-11-1903. Methodist Church Cemetery, Newport, Cumberland County.

COSTELLE, PATRICK (see: Costello, Patrick) St. Peter's Cemetery, Jersey City, Hudson County.

COSTELLO, BERNARD (aka: Castlow, Bernard) Pvt, K, 9th NJ Inf, DoD Unknown. Holy Sepulchre Cemetery, East Orange, Essex County.

COSTELLO, EDWARD Pvt, F, 2nd NJ Inf, [Wounded 5-5-1862 at Williamsburg, VA.] 1-24-1903. Holy Sepulchre Cemetery, East Orange, Essex County.

COSTELLO*, EDWARD Pvt, C, 8th NJ Inf, 11-20-1878. Holy Sepulchre Cemetery, East Orange, Essex County.

COSTELLO, EDWARD (aka: Higgins, Edward) Pvt, H, 1st NY Cav, 12-31-1917. Holy Name Cemetery, Jersey City, Hudson County.

COSTELLO*, HUGH Pvt, Unassigned, 33rd NJ Inf, 4-14-1911. New Dutch Reformed/Neshanic Cemetery, Neshanic, Somerset County.

COSTELLO, JAMES Corp, D, 26th NJ Inf, 11-4-1871. Holy Sepulchre Cemetery, East Orange, Essex County.

COSTELLO, JOHN Pvt, A, 77th NY National Guard, 11-17-1887. St. Peter's Cemetery, New Brunswick, Middlesex County.

COSTELLO, PATRICK Musc, B, 13th NJ Inf, 7-11-1919. Laurel Grove Cemetery, Totowa, Passaic County.

COSTELLO, PATRICK (aka: Costelle, Patrick) Pvt, Lee Btty, Hardwicke's VA Light Art (CSA), 8-16-1863. St. Peter's Cemetery, Jersey City, Hudson County.

COSTELLO, PATRICK F. Corp, Btty B, 1st NJ Light Art, 8-31-1870. St. John's Evangelical Church Cemetery, Orange, Essex County.

COSTELLO, WILLIAM H. Pvt, K, 198th PA Inf, 11-8-1934. Berlin Cemetery, Berlin, Camden County.

COSTILL, ELWOOD S. Pvt, H, 12th NJ Inf, [Wounded in action.] 10-15-1914. Cedar Green Cemetery, Clayton, Gloucester County.

COSTILL, GEORGE N. Pvt, F, 2nd NJ Cav, 5-14-1874. Evergreen Cemetery, Lumberton, Burlington County.

COSTILL*, URIAH Pvt, E, 8th NJ Inf, [Died of diarrhea at Annapolis, MD.] 2-12-1865. Evergreen Cemetery, Lumberton, Burlington County.

COSTINE, DAVID (aka: Cortin, David) Pvt, K, 6th U.S. CT, 11-28-1891. Jacob's Chapel AME Church Cemetery, Colemantown, Burlington County.

COSTNER, JOHN F. Pvt, U.S. Marine Corps, 1889. Greenwood Cemetery, Hamilton, Mercer County.

COSTNER, WILLIAM S. Pvt, Btty B, 5th NY Heavy Art, 4-23-1896. Palmer-Wood Cemetery, Keansburg, Monmouth County.

COTHERMAN, NATHANIEL (see: Cothren, Nathaniel) Glenwood Cemetery, West Long Branch, Monmouth County.

COTHREN, NATHANIEL (aka: Cotherman, Nathaniel) Pvt, B, 29th PA Inf, 6-5-1901. Glenwood Cemetery, West Long Branch, Monmouth County.

COTNER, JOHN W. Pvt, F, 4th NJ Inf, 12-10-1909. Arlington Cemetery, Pennsauken, Camden County.

New Jersey Civil War Burials

COTRELL*, THOMAS Pvt, F, 3rd NJ Inf, 2-19-1920. New Camden Cemetery, Camden, Camden County.
COTTE, LOUIS Seaman, U.S. Navy, USS Potomac, 2-29-1888. Hackensack Cemetery, Hackensack, Bergen County.
COTTE, LOUIS C. Pvt, A, 22nd NJ Inf, 7-6-1925. Hackensack Cemetery, Hackensack, Bergen County.
COTTER, EDMUND Pvt, B, 24th PA Inf, 11-11-1906. Bordentown/Old St. Mary's Catholic Cemetery, Bordentown, Burlington County.
COTTER, JOHN Landsman, U.S. Navy, USS New Hampshire, 7-31-1863. St. John's Evangelical Church Cemetery, Orange, Essex County.
COTTER, THOMAS (see: Carter, Thomas) Bordentown/Old St. Mary's Catholic Cemetery, Bordentown, Burlington County.
COTTINGHAM, WILLIAM (aka: Codingham, William) Pvt, B, 139th NY Inf, 7-3-1886. Woodland Cemetery, Newark, Essex County.
COTTRELL, CHARLES H. Pvt, I, 7th NJ Inf, 4-9-1933. Methodist Church Cemetery, Harmony, Ocean County.
COTTRELL, DAVID S. [Wounded in action.] 1865. St. James Episcopal Church Cemetery, Piscatawaytown, Middlesex County.
COTTRELL, DAVID S. Pvt, G, 14th NJ Inf, [Wounded in action.] 1-20-1892. Adelphia Cemetery, Adelphia, Monmouth County.
COTTRELL*, GEORGE T. Corp, K, 38th OH Inf, [Wounded 11-25-1863 at Missionary Ridge, TN.] 7-9-1872. Oak Hill Cemetery, Vineland, Cumberland County.
COTTRELL, GERSHAM M. Pvt, G, 14th NJ Inf, [Wounded in action.] 11-19-1907. Old Mount Pleasant Cemetery, Matawan, Monmouth County.
COTTRELL, GORDON H. Sgt, E, 29th NJ Inf, 10-29-1911. Maplewood Cemetery, Freehold, Monmouth County.
COTTRELL, GRANDON L. 5-29-1903. Maplewood Cemetery, Freehold, Monmouth County.
COTTRELL, HENRY Sgt, K, 29th NJ Inf, 1920. Evergreen Cemetery, Farmingdale, Monmouth County.
COTTRELL, HIRAM Pvt, F, 38th NJ Inf, 1911. United Presbyterian Church Cemetery, Perrineville, Monmouth County.
COTTRELL, JAMES Pvt, A, 14th NJ Inf, 10-21-1901. Old 1st Methodist Church Cemetery, West Long Branch, Monmouth County.
COTTRELL, JOHN C. Pvt, H, 40th NJ Inf, 4-5-1921. Baptist/St. Andrew's Cemetery, Mount Holly, Burlington County.
COTTRELL, JOHN HENRY Pvt, C, 141st IL Inf, 3-25-1875. Oak Hill Cemetery, Vineland, Cumberland County.
COTTRELL, JOHN L. 6-24-1864. Ardena Baptist Church Cemetery, Adelphia, Monmouth County.
COTTRELL, JOHN N. 1st Lt, I, 29th NJ Inf, 1910. Mount Prospect Cemetery, Neptune, Monmouth County.
COTTRELL*, JOHN T. 1st Lt, K, 5th NJ Inf, 11-30-1898. Old Baptist Cemetery, Freehold, Monmouth County.
COTTRELL, ORSAMUS S. Pvt, I, 29th NJ Inf, 5-22-1900. Rose Hill Cemetery, Matawan, Monmouth County.
COTTRELL, RICHARD Pvt, K, 5th NJ Inf, 2-1-1871. United Presbyterian Church Cemetery, Perrineville, Monmouth County.
COTTRELL, SAMUEL Pvt, F, 38th NJ Inf, 5-28-1883. United Presbyterian Church Cemetery, Perrineville, Monmouth County.
COTTRELL, THOMAS Pvt, K, 29th NJ Inf, 11-25-1889. Ardena Baptist Church Cemetery, Adelphia, Monmouth County.
COTTRELL, WALTER Pvt, K, 158th PA Inf, 12-7-1917. Jacobstown Masonic Cemetery, Jacobstown, Burlington County.

Our Brothers Gone Before

COTTRELL, WILLIAM Sgt, F, 23rd NJ Inf, 3-7-1896. Methodist-Episcopal Church Cemetery, Medford, Burlington County.
COTTRELL, WILLIAM B. Color Sgt, A, 14th NJ Inf, [Killed in action at Monocacy, MD.] 7-9-1864. Adelphia Cemetery, Adelphia, Monmouth County.
COTTRELL, WILLIAM C. Pvt, D, 29th NJ Inf, 7-5-1919. Fairview Cemetery, Fairview, Monmouth County.
COTTRELL*, WILLIAM H. Pvt, Btty D, 1st NJ Light Art, [Died of fever at Washington, DC.] 12-21-1863. Maplewood Cemetery, Freehold, Monmouth County.
COTTRELL, WILLIAM J. Pvt, K, 29th NJ Inf, 6-9-1897. Ardena Baptist Church Cemetery, Adelphia, Monmouth County.
COTTRELL, WILLIAM M. 8-5-1895. Old Mount Pleasant Cemetery, Matawan, Monmouth County.
COTTRILL, PATRICK Pvt, I, 37th NJ Inf, 7-12-1895. Mount Olivet Cemetery, Newark, Essex County.
COUCH, HENRY Pvt, D, 91st PA Inf, 11-1-1923. Zion Methodist Church Cemetery, Bargaintown, Atlantic County.
COUCH, JAMES H. Sgt, D, 6th NY Inf, 1907. Presbyterian Church Cemetery, Yellow Frame, Warren County.
COUCH, JOSEPH A. Landsman, U.S. Navy, USS Manwaski, 1902. Union Cemetery, Clarkstown, Atlantic County.
COUGHLAN, DANIEL 3-22-1877. St. Mary's Cemetery, Whippany, Morris County.
COUGHLIN*, NICHOLAS B. Pvt, Unassigned, 33rd NJ Inf, 7-3-1906. Arlington Cemetery, Kearny, Hudson County.
COUGLE, JAMES C. Pvt, H, 9th NJ Inf, 1-10-1935. Bloomsbury Cemetery, Kennedy Mills, Warren County.
COUGLE, JOHN H. Pvt, B, 15th NJ Inf, 10-7-1870. Union Cemetery, Washington, Morris County.
COUILLARD*, ELIJAH E. Corp, C, 35th MA Inf, 3-14-1894. Flower Hill Cemetery, North Bergen, Hudson County.
COULL, FRANCIS W. Pvt, B, 3rd NJ Inf, [Wounded 6-27-1862 at Gaines' Farm, VA.] 1-20-1910. Trinity Bible Church Cemetery, Glassboro, Gloucester County.
COULSON, JOSEPH Pvt, I, 2nd MA Inf, 6-17-1927. Cedar Lawn Cemetery, Paterson, Passaic County.
COULTER, CHARLES R. Pvt, F, 24th NJ Inf, DoD Unknown. 1st United Methodist Church Cemetery, Bridgeton, Cumberland County.
COULTER, PATRICK Pvt, H, 58th IL Inf, 2-6-1904. Old St. Mary's Cemetery, Gloucester City, Camden County.
COULTER, REEVES Pvt, K, 12th NJ Inf, 1926. Baptist Church Cemetery, Dividing Creek, Cumberland County.
COULTER, WILLIAM Corp, C, 28th NJ Inf, 7-30-1920. Hillside Cemetery, Scotch Plains, Union County.
COULTER, WILLIAM 11-12-1884. Fairmount Cemetery, Newark, Essex County.
COULTS, COLLINS (aka: Coates, Collins) Pvt, A, 192nd PA Inf, 4-7-1910. Evergreen Cemetery, Camden, Camden County.
COUNSELLOR, BENJAMIN Pvt, I, 24th U.S. CT, 1-28-1897. Fairmount Cemetery, Newark, Essex County.
COUNSELLOR, HENRY C. Pvt, K, 9th NJ Inf, 1-27-1901. Eastview Cemetery, Salem, Salem County.
COUNTRYMAN, JOSEPH W. Pvt, A, 199th PA Inf, 5-28-1882. Evergreen Cemetery, Camden, Camden County.
COUNTS, GEORGE W. Pvt, H, 1st (Turney's) TN Inf (CSA), 7-1-1864. Finn's Point National Cemetery, Pennsville, Salem County.
COURSEN, JOHN E. Pvt, I, 15th NJ Inf, 4-27-1913. Hainesville Cemetery, Hainesville, Sussex County.

New Jersey Civil War Burials

COURSEN, SAMUEL J. Pvt, G, 2nd NJ Cav, 3-23-1915. Methodist Church Cemetery, Sparta, Sussex County.
COURSEN, WILLIAM H. Pvt, D, 27th NJ Inf, [Died of diarrhea at Falmouth, VA.] 12-29-1862. Old Beemer Church Cemetery, Roys, Sussex County.
COURSEN, WILLIAM P. 8-23-1918. Presbyterian Church Cemetery, Yellow Frame, Warren County.
COURSEY, JOHN H. Corp, I, 3rd U.S. CT, 3-10-1915. Presbyterian Church Cemetery, Bridgeton, Cumberland County.
COURSON, WALTER H. Pvt, E, 8th NJ Inf, 7-23-1896. Fairmount Cemetery, Newark, Essex County.
COURT, GEORGE (see: Cort, George) Fairmount Cemetery, Newark, Essex County.
COURT, HARRY (see: Court, Henry) Fairmount Cemetery, Newark, Essex County.
COURTER, CHARLES Pvt, D, 26th NJ Inf, 12-6-1915. Hillside Cemetery, Fairfield, Essex County.
COURTER*, DANIEL C. Pvt, D, 13th NJ Inf, 2-28-1907. Presbyterian Church Cemetery, Rockaway, Morris County.
COURTER, DAVID Pvt, I, 2nd NJ Inf, 9-17-1897. Cedar Lawn Cemetery, Paterson, Passaic County.
COURTER, EMMONS Pvt, D, 13th NJ Inf, 11-12-1888. Fairmount Cemetery, Newark, Essex County.
COURTER, GEORGE W. Pvt, B, 7th NJ Inf, 8-14-1875. Fairmount Cemetery, Newark, Essex County.
COURTER, GEORGE W.D. Sgt, G, 27th NJ Inf, DoD Unknown. Methodist Church Cemetery, Springfield, Union County.
COURTER*, HENRY Pvt, E, 7th NJ Inf, 1913. Boonton Cemetery, Boonton, Morris County.
COURTER*, JOHN Com Sgt, E, 9th NY Cav, 3-30-1911. Presbyterian Church Cemetery, Rockaway, Morris County.
COURTER, JOSEPH Pvt, A, 12th U.S. Inf, 12-30-1865. Prospect Hill Cemetery, Caldwell, Essex County.
COURTER, THOMAS J. Corp, D, 26th NJ Inf, 5-17-1923. Prospect Hill Cemetery, Caldwell, Essex County.
COURTER, WARD C. Pvt, F, 43rd OH Inf, [Wounded in action.] 4-21-1916. Methodist Church Cemetery, Roseland, Essex County.
COURTER, WILLIAM H. Pvt, A, 22nd NJ Inf, 5-22-1909. Arlington Cemetery, Kearny, Hudson County.
COURTER*, WILLIAM H. Pvt, K, 124th NY Inf, 1-28-1923. Cedar Lawn Cemetery, Paterson, Passaic County.
COURTER, WILLIAM H. 1st Lt, F, 8th NJ Inf, 3-3-1889. Fairmount Cemetery, Newark, Essex County.
COURTER, WILLIAM M. 12-11-1921. Mount Pleasant Cemetery, Newark, Essex County.
COURTER, WILLIAM MARTIN Corp, B, 39th NJ Inf, 4-22-1928. Reformed Church Cemetery, Wyckoff, Bergen County.
COURTLAND, EDWIN P. 6-15-1864. Baptist Church Cemetery, Penns Neck, Mercer County.
COURTOIS, CHARLES J. Capt, D, 33rd NJ Inf, 9-30-1887. Mount Pleasant Cemetery, Newark, Essex County.
COURTOIS*, LOUIS Pvt, C, 1st NJ Cav, 10-9-1923. Riverview Cemetery, Trenton, Mercer County.
COURTRIGHT, AENOS (see: Courtright, Enoch) Brink Cemetery, Colesville, Sussex County.
COURTRIGHT, DANIEL C. Pvt, D, 33rd NJ Inf, 3-3-1900. Frankford Plains Cemetery, Frankford, Sussex County.

Our Brothers Gone Before

COURTRIGHT, ELISHA B. Corp, M, 2nd NJ Cav, 1912. Beemerville Cemetery, Beemerville, Sussex County.
COURTRIGHT, ENOCH (aka: Courtright, Aenos) Pvt, H, 27th NJ Inf, 6-28-1895. Brink Cemetery, Colesville, Sussex County.
COURTRIGHT, GEORGE N. (aka: Cortright, George N.) Corp, D, 3rd NJ Inf, 6-7-1901. Hillside Cemetery, Scotch Plains, Union County.
COURTRIGHT, HORACE Pvt, D, 3rd NJ Cav, 9-5-1873. Brink Cemetery, Colesville, Sussex County.
COURTRIGHT, JOHN Pvt, H, 27th NJ Inf, 5-17-1902. Clove Cemetery, Wantage, Sussex County.
COURTRIGHT*, SANFORD J. Pvt, A, 2nd NY Cav, [Wounded 6-28-1863 at Aldie, VA.] 9-2-1873. Beemerville Cemetery, Beemerville, Sussex County.
COURTWRIGHT, THOMAS J. Pvt, D, 7th KS Cav, 2-19-1878. Fairmount Cemetery, Newark, Essex County.
COURVOISIER, P.FREDERICK L. Capt, D, 93rd IN Inf, 1895. Grove Church Cemetery, North Bergen, Hudson County.
COUSE, JOSEPH P. Capt, I, 33rd NJ Inf, 4-13-1900. Hardyston Cemetery, North Church, Sussex County.
COUSE, PETER 6-24-1888. Deckertown-Union Cemetery, Papakating, Sussex County.
COUZZANS, BENJAMIN (see: Cuzins, Benjamin) United Methodist Church Cemetery, Tuckahoe, Cape May County.
COVENTRY, WILLIAM A. Sgt, F, 10th NJ Inf, 1878. Laurel Grove Cemetery, Totowa, Passaic County.
COVERLY, JOB Pvt, I, 5th NJ Inf, 7-15-1862. Methodist-Episcopal Cemetery, Vincentown, Burlington County.
COVERSTON, W. Pvt, A, 41st VA Inf (CSA), 5-18-1864. Finn's Point National Cemetery, Pennsville, Salem County.
COVERT, ARTHUR Pvt, K, 48th PA Inf, 7-7-1888. Riverview Cemetery, Trenton, Mercer County.
COVERT, BENJAMIN B. Pvt, H, 21st NJ Inf, 3-20-1897. Greenwood Cemetery, Hamilton, Mercer County.
COVERT, ELIAS Corp, A, 3rd NJ Cav, 1868. Riverview Cemetery, Trenton, Mercer County.
COVERT, GEORGE W. Pvt, D, 29th NJ Inf, [Died of typhoid at Tennallytown, DC.] 11-26-1862. Fairview Cemetery, Fairview, Monmouth County.
COVERT, HENRY H. Sgt, I, 1st NJ Cav, 1-20-1907. Reformed Church Cemetery, Blawenburg, Somerset County.
COVERT, HENRY LAMBERTSON Pvt, D, 29th NJ Inf, 5-31-1897. Halsey Cemetery, Belford, Monmouth County.
COVERT, ISAAC Pvt, D, 31st PA Inf, DoD Unknown. Methodist Church Cemetery, Goshen, Cape May County.
COVERT, JAMES Pvt, G, 29th NJ Inf, 7-20-1917. Atlantic Reformed Cemetery, Colts Neck, Monmouth County.
COVERT, JOHN L. Pvt, D, 29th NJ Inf, 3-6-1924. Fairview Cemetery, Fairview, Monmouth County.
COVERT, JOHN P. Sgt, I, 9th LA Inf (CSA), 1-20-1903. Mount Pleasant Cemetery, Newark, Essex County.
COVERT, JOSIAH Pvt, G, 1st NJ Cav, 4-9-1881. Riverview Cemetery, Trenton, Mercer County.
COVERT, LEVI T. 1883. Harlingen Cemetery, Belle Mead, Somerset County.
COVERT, MATTHEW R. Pvt, B, 3rd NJ Cav, 10-28-1901. United Methodist Church Cemetery, Wayside, Monmouth County.
COVERT, NATHAN B. Pvt, B, 1st NJ Inf, 6-16-1920. Riverview Cemetery, Trenton, Mercer County.

New Jersey Civil War Burials

COVERT, WILLIAM H. Pvt, A, 38th NJ Inf, DoD Unknown. United Methodist Church Cemetery, Wayside, Monmouth County.

COVINGTON, EDWARD J. Pvt, F, 45th NC Inf (CSA), [Captured 7-6-1863 at Fairfield, PA.] 10-11-1863. Finn's Point National Cemetery, Pennsville, Salem County.

COVINGTON, GEORGE W. Pvt, F, 8th (Smith's) TN Cav (CSA), 2-14-1865. Finn's Point National Cemetery, Pennsville, Salem County.

COWAN, GILBERT Pvt, B, 119th PA Inf, [Wounded 5-10-1864 at Spotsylvania CH, VA.] 4-3-1917. Evergreen Cemetery, Camden, Camden County.

COWAN*, JACOB Pvt, G, 8th NJ Inf, 4-13-1913. Harleigh Cemetery, Camden, Camden County.

COWAN, JAMES Pvt, I, 6th NY Inf, 4-25-1911. Cedar Lawn Cemetery, Paterson, Passaic County.

COWAN, JAMES JOSEPH Pvt, K, 5th U.S. Hancock Corps, 2-1-1934. Fairmount Cemetery, Newark, Essex County.

COWAN, LEMUEL C. Mate, U.S. Navy, 2-25-1870. Mercer Cemetery, Trenton, Mercer County.

COWAN, MARTIN 3rd Cl Musc, 1st NJ Inf Band 9-23-1913. Harleigh Cemetery, Camden, Camden County.

COWARD, ABNER DoD Unknown. Bordentown/Old St. Mary's Catholic Cemetery, Bordentown, Burlington County.

COWARD, CALEB Pvt, A, 24th U.S. CT, 2-16-1902. Riverview Cemetery, Trenton, Mercer County.

COWARD, CHARLES A. Pvt, G, 10th NJ Inf, [Shot by a guard in the rebel prison at Lynchburg, VA.] 10-1-1864. Cedar Hill Cemetery, Hightstown, Mercer County.

COWARD, JOHN Sgt, A, 35th NJ Inf, 2-27-1896. Riverview Cemetery, Trenton, Mercer County.

COWARD*, JOSEPH B. Corp, Manns, PA Militia, 7-25-1907. Hillside Cemetery, Scotch Plains, Union County.

COWARD, RILEY 5-4-1922. Bordentown/Old St. Mary's Catholic Cemetery, Bordentown, Burlington County.

COWARD, THOMAS Pvt, A, 6th NJ Inf, 2-1-1894. Cedar Hill Cemetery, Hightstown, Mercer County.

COWARD, THOMAS N. (see: Cowart, Thomas N.) Finn's Point National Cemetery, Pennsville, Salem County.

COWARD*, WILLIAM D. 1st Sgt, E, 106th PA Inf, 11-22-1888. Mercer Cemetery, Trenton, Mercer County.

COWARD, WILLIAM G. Corp, A, 22nd U.S. CT, 10-26-1887. Mount Peace Cemetery, Lawnside, Camden County.

COWART, ENOCH LLOYD QM, 14th NJ Inf 4-17-1889. Tennent Church Cemetery, Tennent, Monmouth County.

COWART, THOMAS N. (aka: Coward, Thomas N.) Pvt, C, 43rd GA Inf (CSA), [Captured 5-16-1863 at Baker's Creek, MS.] 6-24-1863. Finn's Point National Cemetery, Pennsville, Salem County.

COWDRICK, AUGUSTUS 1905. Barber's Burying Ground Cemetery, Dilts Corner, Hunterdon County.

COWDRICK, SILAS Corp, E, 38th NJ Inf, 12-4-1918. Rosemont Cemetery, Rosemont, Hunterdon County.

COWELL, DANIEL Pvt, I, 12th NJ Inf, 9-27-1901. Mansfield/Washington Cemetery, Washington, Warren County.

COWELL, GEORGE W. 2-10-1887. Presbyterian Church Cemetery, Greenwich, Warren County.

COWELL, JACOB S. 1-27-1869. Presbyterian Church Cemetery, Greenwich, Warren County.

Our Brothers Gone Before

COWELL, LEWIS A. Pvt, C, 11th NJ Inf, 12-1-1902. Fairmount Cemetery, Newark, Essex County.
COWGILL, CHARLES Pvt, E, 24th NJ Inf, 7-20-1911. Eglington Cemetery, Clarksboro, Gloucester County.
COWGILL, ISAAC J. Sgt, E, 24th NJ Inf, 3-9-1900. St. Paul's United Methodist Church Cemetery, Paulsboro, Gloucester County.
COWGILL, STEPHEN M. 1st Sgt, A, 7th NJ Inf, 4-19-1904. Evergreen Cemetery, Camden, Camden County.
COWHART, STEPHEN (see: Carhart, Stephen E.) Greengrove Cemetery, Keyport, Monmouth County.
COWIE, GEORGE W. Actg 2nd Asst Eng, U.S. Navy, 5-23-1902. Hazelwood Cemetery, Rahway, Union County.
COWMAN, JOHN WESLEY Pvt, G, 3rd NJ Cav, 10-19-1902. Mount Pleasant Cemetery, Millville, Cumberland County.
COWPERTHWAIT, JAMES P. 2-27-1896. Riverside Cemetery, Toms River, Ocean County.
COWPERTHWAIT, JOSEPH Pvt, H, 28th NJ Inf, DoD Unknown. Finn's Point National Cemetery, Pennsville, Salem County.
COWPERTHWAITE, CHARLES T. Corp, L, 1st NJ Cav, [Died at Washington, DC. of wounds received 10-2-1863 at Sulphur Springs, VA.] 1-6-1864. Jacobstown Masonic Cemetery, Jacobstown, Burlington County.
COWPERTHWAITE, DILWYN R. 1st Sgt, C, 9th NJ Inf, [Died at Hampton, VA. of wounds received at Drewry's Bluff, VA.] 7-15-1864. Evergreen Cemetery, Camden, Camden County.
COWPERTHWAITE, WARDELL Pvt, I, 23rd NJ Inf, 4-10-1877. Baptist/St. Andrew's Cemetery, Mount Holly, Burlington County.
COX, ABIJAH Pvt, H, 21st NJ Inf, 5-5-1888. Riverview Cemetery, Trenton, Mercer County.
COX, ALBERT Corp, C, 1st NJ Cav, 4-4-1894. Evergreen Cemetery, Camden, Camden County.
COX, ALBERT F. Pvt, D, 1st VT Cav, [Wounded 6-23-1864 at Nottoway CH, VA.] 5-5-1870. Grove Church Cemetery, North Bergen, Hudson County.
COX, ANDREW (aka: Cocks, Andrew) Pvt, B, 1st NJ Inf, 3-24-1907. Cedar Hill Cemetery, East Millstone, Somerset County.
COX, ANDREW P. Pvt, C, 1st (Orr's) SC Rifles (CSA), [Captured 5-12-1864 at Spotsylvania CH, VA. Died of pneumonia.] 1-27-1865. Finn's Point National Cemetery, Pennsville, Salem County.
COX, B. Pvt, A, 5th KY Cav (CSA), 7-31-1864. Finn's Point National Cemetery, Pennsville, Salem County.
COX, CHARLES Sgt, K, 22nd U.S. CT, [Wounded in action.] 2-18-1913. Union Bethel Cemetery, Erma, Cape May County.
COX*, CHARLES A. Pvt, F, 8th PA Cav, 1898. Atlantic City Cemetery, Pleasantville, Atlantic County.
COX, CHARLES M. Corp, D, 83rd PA Inf, 12-18-1905. Riverview Cemetery, Trenton, Mercer County.
COX, CORNELIUS L. Pvt, A, 21st NJ Inf, 1-15-1914. Bayview-New York Bay Cemetery, Jersey City, Hudson County.
COX, CORNELIUS T. Capt, E, 30th NJ Inf, 9-26-1871. New Somerville Cemetery, Somerville, Somerset County.
COX, DAVID H. Pvt, F, 1st NY Eng, 5-27-1909. Hazelwood Cemetery, Rahway, Union County.
COX, DUNCAN S. Pvt, H, 29th NJ Inf, 1-3-1915. Riverside Cemetery, Toms River, Ocean County.

New Jersey Civil War Burials

COX, EDWARD W. Pvt, G, 1st NJ Cav, DoD Unknown. St. Mary's Cemetery, Hamilton, Mercer County.
COX, GEORGE F. 5-14-1900. Grove Church Cemetery, North Bergen, Hudson County.
COX, GEORGE M. 1933. Baptist Cemetery, West Creek, Ocean County.
COX, GEORGE M. DoD Unknown. Greenwood Cemetery, Tuckerton, Ocean County.
COX, GEORGE W. 1902. Rosedale Cemetery, Orange, Essex County.
COX*, GEORGE W. Sgt, H, 40th NJ Inf, 1-20-1886. Mercer Cemetery, Trenton, Mercer County.
COX, GUY P. 1st Sgt, A, 11th NJ Inf, [Died of wounds received at Chancellorsville, VA.] 5-15-1863. Presbyterian Church Cemetery, New Providence, Union County.
COX, HARVEY M. Pvt, B, 17th OH Inf, 12-3-1904. Evergreen Cemetery, Camden, Camden County.
COX, HENRY M. Pvt, A, 3rd NJ Cav, 11-5-1902. Mansfield/Washington Cemetery, Washington, Warren County.
COX, HENRY V.B. Pvt, K, 30th NJ Inf, 8-11-1925. Highland Cemetery, Hopewell Boro, Mercer County.
COX, ISRAEL Pvt, K, 22nd U.S. CT, 6-9-1884. Union Bethel Cemetery, Erma, Cape May County.
COX*, ISRAEL J. Pvt, I, 5th NJ Inf, 8-18-1884. Baptist Cemetery, Vincentown, Burlington County.
COX, J.A. Pvt, A, 20th VA Inf (CSA), 10-9-1863. Finn's Point National Cemetery, Pennsville, Salem County.
COX*, JAMES Pvt, F, 2nd NJ Cav, DoD Unknown. 1st United Methodist Church Cemetery, Bridgeton, Cumberland County.
COX, JAMES Pvt, K, 33rd NJ Inf, 7-9-1887. Holy Name Cemetery, Jersey City, Hudson County.
COX, JAMES Pvt, A, 35th NJ Inf, 6-2-1881. St. Mary's Cemetery, Hamilton, Mercer County.
COX, JAMES B. Pvt, G, 6th NJ Inf, 12-25-1891. Mount Pleasant Cemetery, Millville, Cumberland County.
COX, JAMES H. Pvt, L, 14th TN Inf (CSA), 7-12-1864. Finn's Point National Cemetery, Pennsville, Salem County.
COX, JAMES HOAGLAND Sgt, A, 21st NJ Inf, 1916. Pequest Union Cemetery, Great Meadows, Warren County.
COX, JAMES M. 5-30-1922. Sandy Ridge Cemetery, Sandy Ridge, Hunterdon County.
COX, JAMES R. Pvt, H, 51st GA Inf (CSA), [Captured 9-14-1862 at Fox's Gap, MD.] 10-21-1863. Finn's Point National Cemetery, Pennsville, Salem County.
COX, JAMESON 2- -1881. Brookside Cemetery, Englewood, Bergen County.
COX, JASON F. Pvt, I, 23rd NJ Inf, 7-21-1891. Cedar Hill Cemetery, Florence, Burlington County.
COX, JASPER 5-31-1905. Holy Sepulchre Cemetery, East Orange, Essex County.
COX, JOHN Corp, I, 25th NJ Inf, 7-4-1929. Evergreen Cemetery, Camden, Camden County.
COX*, JOHN Pvt, G, 5th NJ Inf, 10-17-1875. Atlantic Reformed Cemetery, Colts Neck, Monmouth County.
COX, JOHN 10-17-1872. New Dutch Reformed/Neshanic Cemetery, Neshanic, Somerset County.
COX, JOHN B. Corp, B, 2nd NJ Inf, 6-9-1901. Chestnut Cemetery, Dover, Morris County.
COX, JOHN SISBY Col, 23rd NJ Inf 10-9-1888. Baptist/St. Andrew's Cemetery, Mount Holly, Burlington County.
COX, JONATHAN G. Sgt, U.S. Marine Corps, 1917. Presbyterian Church Cemetery, Blackwood, Camden County.
COX, JOSEPH W. Pvt, K, 34th NJ Inf, 6-26-1901. Union Cemetery, Gloucester City, Camden County.

Our Brothers Gone Before

COX, LEWIS J. (SR.) Sgt, H, 27th NJ Inf, 1926. Newton Cemetery, Newton, Sussex County.
COX, LEWIS Y. Sgt, K, 22nd U.S. CT, 7-26-1926. Mount Zion Cemetery, Lower Cape May, Cape May County.
COX, LOUIS Pvt, A, 24th U.S. CT, 12-4-1904. Riverview Cemetery, Trenton, Mercer County.
COX, M.L. Pvt, A, 1st SC Cav (CSA), [Captured 7-5-1863 at Gettysburg, PA.] 6-30-1864. Finn's Point National Cemetery, Pennsville, Salem County.
COX, MORGAN R. Pvt, G, 70th IL Inf, 1-9-1886. Sandy Ridge Cemetery, Sandy Ridge, Hunterdon County.
COX*, RICHARD Pvt, B, 58th MA Inf, [Killed in action at Cold Harbor, VA.] 6-3-1864. Brainerd Cemetery, Cranbury, Middlesex County.
COX, RICHARD H. Pvt, C, 1st NJ Cav, 8-18-1908. Evergreen Cemetery, Lumberton, Burlington County.
COX, ROBERT T. Pvt, I, 3rd NJ Inf, 2-3-1888. Eglington Cemetery, Clarksboro, Gloucester County.
COX, ROWLAND Bvt Maj, U.S. Volunteers, [Acting Adjutant General.] 5-13-1900. Hillside Cemetery, Scotch Plains, Union County.
COX, SAMUEL B. Pvt, H, 33rd NJ Inf, 1910. Evergreen Cemetery, Lumberton, Burlington County.
COX, THOMAS S. 1st Lt, M, 1st NJ Cav, [Wounded in action.] 2-23-1869. Newton Cemetery, Newton, Sussex County.
COX, TOWNSEND Farrier, F, 1st NJ Cav, 12-7-1904. Bordentown/Old St. Mary's Catholic Cemetery, Bordentown, Burlington County.
COX, W.A. Pvt, G, 51st AL Cav (CSA), 9-10-1863. Finn's Point National Cemetery, Pennsville, Salem County.
COX, WHITFIELD H. Landsman, U.S. Navy, 5-17-1917. Evergreen Cemetery, Hillside, Union County.
COX, WILLIAM H. Corp, G, 11th NJ Inf, 11-24-1905. Baptist Cemetery, Burlington, Burlington County.
COX, WILLIAM H. Pvt, C, 3rd NJ Inf, 2-18-1914. Cedar Hill Cemetery, Florence, Burlington County.
COX, WILLIAM HENRY 1st Lt, G, 100th U.S. CT, 11-19-1869. Mount Laurel/Eldridge Cemetery, Mount Laurel, Burlington County.
COX*, WILLIAM M. Landsman, U.S. Navy, USS Ohio, 6-5-1912. Evergreen Cemetery, Camden, Camden County.
COX, WOODWARD Pvt, D, 6th NJ Inf, [Wounded in action.] 2-24-1917. Union Cemetery, Gloucester City, Camden County.
COXAN, JONATHAN (see: Coxon, Jonathan (Sr.)) Greenwood Cemetery, Hamilton, Mercer County.
COXNEY, JOHN (aka: Roxney, John) Pvt, Btty A, 2nd NY Heavy Art, 10-1-1864. Beverly National Cemetery, Edgewater Park, Burlington County.
COXON, JONATHAN (SR.) (aka: Coxan, Jonathan) Pvt, A, 21st NJ Inf, 9-21-1919. Greenwood Cemetery, Hamilton, Mercer County.
COXSON, WILLIAM HENRY Capt, I, 176th NY Inf, [Wounded 9-19-1864 at Winchester, VA.] 7-25-1891. Trinity Bible Church Cemetery, Glassboro, Gloucester County.
COY, JOHN Pvt, F, 22nd U.S. CT, 3-3-1884. Presbyterian Cemetery, Woodbury, Gloucester County.
COYE, ENIS (aka: Coyle, Enos) Pvt, H, 4th NJ Inf, DoD Unknown. Holy Sepulchre Cemetery, East Orange, Essex County.
COYLE, CHARLES Pvt, A, 71st NY Inf, 9-15-1872. Holy Sepulchre Cemetery, East Orange, Essex County.
COYLE, ENOS (see: Coye, Enis) Holy Sepulchre Cemetery, East Orange, Essex County.

New Jersey Civil War Burials

COYLE, FRANCIS Pvt, H, 13th NJ Inf, 1-5-1898. Holy Sepulchre Cemetery, East Orange, Essex County.
COYLE, GALOMB (aka: Coyle, John J.) Pvt, L, 6th U.S. Inf, 6-26-1900. Holy Name Cemetery, Jersey City, Hudson County.
COYLE, HENRY Pvt, C, 25th NJ Inf, 3-31-1911. Holy Sepulchre Cemetery, Totowa, Passaic County.
COYLE, JOHN Pvt, D, 39th NJ Inf, 11-6-1892. Fairmount Cemetery, Newark, Essex County.
COYLE, JOHN Pvt, A, 2nd NJ Militia, DoD Unknown. St. Peter's Cemetery, Jersey City, Hudson County.
COYLE, JOHN J. (see: Coyle, Galomb) Holy Name Cemetery, Jersey City, Hudson County.
COYLE, MARTIN (SR.) Pvt, E, 25th MA Inf, 4-29-1899. Old St. Mary's Cemetery, Gloucester City, Camden County.
COYLE, MICHAEL Pvt, G, 53rd MA Inf, [Wounded 6-14-1863 at Port Hudson, LA.] DoD Unknown. Old St. Mary's Cemetery, Gloucester City, Camden County.
COYLE, MORRIS (aka: Coile, Morris) Pvt, G, 15th NJ Inf, [Wounded in action.] 11-15-1906. Mansfield/Washington Cemetery, Washington, Warren County.
COYNE, FERDINAND Pvt, Btty A, 1st NJ Light Art, 5-10-1916. Rosedale Cemetery, Orange, Essex County.
COYNE, JOHN Pvt, I, 8th NJ Inf, 3-12-1893. Holy Sepulchre Cemetery, East Orange, Essex County.
COYNE, JOHN Pvt, H, 26th NJ Inf, 3-12-1893. Rosedale Cemetery, Orange, Essex County.
COYNE, PATRICK Pvt, B, 69th NY Inf, [Wounded in action.] 9-14-1888. Mount Olivet Cemetery, Fairview, Monmouth County.
COYNE, PATRICK Pvt, H, 26th NJ Inf, 1-11-1900. Rosedale Cemetery, Orange, Essex County.
COYNE, THOMAS Landsman, U.S. Navy, USS Vincennes, 1-4-1892. St. John's Evangelical Church Cemetery, Orange, Essex County.
COYNE*, THOMAS 2nd Lt, E, 10th NY Cav, [Wounded 6-9-1863 at Brandy Station, VA.] DoD Unknown. St. Rose of Lima Cemetery, Freehold, Monmouth County.
COYTE, BENJAMIN F. Pvt, 30th, NY Ind Militia, 2-5-1933. Maple Grove Cemetery, Hackensack, Bergen County.
COYTE, FREDERICK G. 1st Lt, Adj, 9th NJ Inf 11-9-1907. Woodland Cemetery, Englewood Cliffs, Bergen County.
COZENS, BENJAMIN F. Pvt, Btty C, 1st PA Light Art, 1-17-1909. Presbyterian Cemetery, Woodbury, Gloucester County.
COZENS, HENRY D. Pvt, D, 1st DE Inf, 11-7-1922. Fairmount Cemetery, Newark, Essex County.
COZENS, WILLIAM THACKARA Corp, E, 24th NJ Inf, 2-9-1923. Presbyterian Cemetery, Woodbury, Gloucester County.
COZINE, CORNELIUS DoD Unknown. Methodist-Episcopal Cemetery, Whitehouse, Hunterdon County.
COZINE, HENRY W. SAgt, A, 2nd NJ Inf, DoD Unknown. Methodist-Episcopal Cemetery, Whitehouse, Hunterdon County.
COZZENS, DANIEL W. 1st Sgt, A, 28th NJ Inf, 11-11-1897. St. Peter's Episcopal Church Cemetery, Spotswood, Middlesex County.
COZZENS, WILLIAM H. Sgt, A, 28th NJ Inf, 1-10-1918. Arlington Cemetery, Kearny, Hudson County.
CRABB, ROBERT C. Pvt, D, 7th TN Cav (CSA), 6-14-1865. Finn's Point National Cemetery, Pennsville, Salem County.
CRABBE, THOMAS Commodore, U.S. Navy, 6-29-1872. Princeton Cemetery, Princeton, Mercer County.

Our Brothers Gone Before

CRAFT*, EDWARD L. Pvt, K, 31st PA Inf, 1915. New Camden Cemetery, Camden, Camden County.
CRAFT, GEORGE H. Pvt, I, 34th NJ Inf, 1923. Columbus Cemetery, Columbus, Burlington County.
CRAFT, GERSHOM Pvt, F, 1st NJ Cav, DoD Unknown. Columbus Cemetery, Columbus, Burlington County.
CRAFT, HENRY T. Corp, I, 34th NJ Inf, 9-19-1910. Mercer Cemetery, Trenton, Mercer County.
CRAFT, HIRAM B. Pvt, D, 9th NJ Inf, 7-13-1908. Oddfellows Cemetery, Burlington, Burlington County.
CRAFT, ISAAC 5-23-1886. Haring Cemetery, Old Tappan, Bergen County.
CRAFT, JACOB (see: Kraft, Jacob) Arlington Cemetery, Pennsauken, Camden County.
CRAFT, JEREMIAH Corp, F, 22nd NJ Inf, 9-19-1884. Riverview Cemetery, Trenton, Mercer County.
CRAFT, JOSEPH Pvt, I, 6th NJ Inf, 9-27-1908. Methodist Church Cemetery, Hurffville, Gloucester County.
CRAFT, LEWIS Pvt, A, 23rd NJ Inf, 5-15-1906. Oddfellows Cemetery, Burlington, Burlington County.
CRAFT, NATHANIEL H. Pvt, H, 71st NY State Militia, 12-31-1890. Riverview Cemetery, Trenton, Mercer County.
CRAFT, PETER (aka: Kraft, Peter) Pvt, B, 1st NJ Cav, 11-30-1895. Atlantic City Cemetery, Pleasantville, Atlantic County.
CRAFT, SAMUEL T. Pvt, A, 23rd NJ Inf, 12-16-1903. Fairmount Cemetery, Newark, Essex County.
CRAFT, WILLIAM (aka: Johnson, James) Pvt, Btty G, 4th NY Heavy Art, DoD Unknown. Arlington Cemetery, Kearny, Hudson County.
CRAGIN, GEORGE K. Corp, B, 6th MA Militia, 9-24-1919. Harleigh Cemetery, Camden, Camden County.
CRAIG, ANDREW J. Sgt, A, 3rd NJ Inf, [Wounded in action.] 12-18-1907. Methodist Cemetery, Mantua, Gloucester County.
CRAIG, CASPER H. (aka: Cregg, Casper) Pvt, E, 10th NJ Inf, [Wounded in action.] 1-29-1935. Batsto/Pleasant Mills Methodist Church Cemetery, Pleasant Mills, Atlantic County.
CRAIG, DANIEL D. 1891. Evergreen/Bishop Jaynes Cemetery, Basking Ridge, Somerset County.
CRAIG, DRUMMOND H. 1916. Tennent Church Cemetery, Tennent, Monmouth County.
CRAIG, ELI Pvt, I, 24th NJ Inf, 3-5-1905. Greenmount Cemetery, Hammonton, Atlantic County.
CRAIG, GEORGE W. Sgt, A, 42nd VA Inf (CSA), [Captured 7-4-1863 at Gettysburg, PA. Died of debility.] 8-28-1863. Finn's Point National Cemetery, Pennsville, Salem County.
CRAIG, JAMES Pvt, F, 24th NJ Inf, 7-21-1912. Presbyterian Church Cemetery, Bridgeton, Cumberland County.
CRAIG, JAMES Pvt, C, 38th NJ Inf, 3-7-1878. Mount Pleasant Cemetery, Millville, Cumberland County.
CRAIG, JAMES Seaman, U.S. Navy, 11-4-1888. United Methodist Church Cemetery, Cross Keys, Gloucester County.
CRAIG, JAMES A. Pvt, K, 70th NY Inf, [Wounded 7-2-1863 at Gettysburg, PA.] 10-12-1889. Fairmount Cemetery, Newark, Essex County.
CRAIG*, JAMES G.D. Pvt, Btty E, 1st NJ Light Art, [Died of typhoid at Fort Monroe, VA.] 8-17-1864. New Presbyterian Church Cemetery, Daretown, Salem County.
CRAIG, JOHN (aka: Cregg, John) Pvt, E, 10th NJ Inf, 7-6-1899. Greenmount Cemetery, Hammonton, Atlantic County.

New Jersey Civil War Burials

CRAIG*, JOHN Coal Heaver, U.S. Navy, USS R.R. Cuyler, 11-19-1900. Bordentown/Old St. Mary's Catholic Cemetery, Bordentown, Burlington County.

CRAIG, JOHN D. Pvt, F, 24th NJ Inf, 7-23-1908. Tabernacle Baptist Church Cemetery, Erma, Cape May County.

CRAIG, JOSEPH F. Pvt, C, 9th NJ Inf, 12-29-1887. 1st Baptist Cemetery, Cape May Court House, Cape May County.

CRAIG*, ROBERT P. Pvt, Btty I, 1st U.S. Art, 3-17-1909. Presbyterian Church Cemetery, Cedarville, Cumberland County.

CRAIG, SAMUEL H. Corp, G, 5th NJ Inf, DoD Unknown. New Presbyterian Church Cemetery, Daretown, Salem County.

CRAIG, T.H. DoD Unknown. Acquackanonk Church/Armory Park Cemetery, Passaic, Passaic County.

CRAIG, WILLIAM H. Sgt, A, 105th OH Inf, [Killed in action at Chicamauga, GA.] 9-20-1863. Brainerd Cemetery, Cranbury, Middlesex County.

CRAIG, WILLIAM H. 1st Lt, D, 14th NJ Inf, [Wounded 7-9-1864 at Monocacy, MD.] 8-11-1898. Tennent Church Cemetery, Tennent, Monmouth County.

CRAIG, WILLIAM M. Pvt, K, 12th NJ Inf, DoD Unknown. Mount Pleasant Cemetery, Millville, Cumberland County.

CRAIGHT, JOHN C. Pvt, G, 37th NJ Inf, DoD Unknown. Holy Sepulchre Cemetery, East Orange, Essex County.

CRAIN, IRA Pvt, F, 23rd NJ Inf, DoD Unknown. Tabernacle Cemetery, Tabernacle, Burlington County.

CRAIN, JOHN Pvt, F, 170th NY Inf, [Wounded in action 10-24-1864.] DoD Unknown. Constable Hook Cemetery, Bayonne, Hudson County.

CRAIN*, MICHAEL Pvt, G, 7th NJ Inf, 2-5-1918. Oddfellows-Friends Cemetery, Medford, Burlington County.

CRAIN, MICHAEL (see: Crane, Michael) Oddfellows Cemetery, Burlington, Burlington County.

CRAMER, CHARLES Pvt, Btty E, 2nd PA Heavy Art, 11-29-1922. Beverly National Cemetery, Edgewater Park, Burlington County.

CRAMER, CYRUS P. Pvt, F, 57th PA Inf, 12-22-1930. Laurel Grove Cemetery, Totowa, Passaic County.

CRAMER, EDWARD 1st Sgt, E, 13th NJ Inf, 4-22-1900. Ramseyburg Cemetery, Ramseyburg, Warren County.

CRAMER, EDWARD 6-11-1918. Mount Pleasant Cemetery, Newark, Essex County.

CRAMER, GEORGE S. DoD Unknown. Tranquility Cemetery, Tranquility, Sussex County.

CRAMER, HIRAM Pvt, C, 12th NJ Inf, [Killed in action at Chancellorsville, VA.] 5-3-1863. Baptist Church Cemetery, Blackwood, Camden County.

CRAMER, JACOB F. Pvt, H, 34th NJ Inf, 1935. Mountain View Cemetery, Cokesbury, Hunterdon County.

CRAMER, JAMES 6-30-1883. Trinity Bible Church Cemetery, Glassboro, Gloucester County.

CRAMER, JAMES M. (see: Craner, James M.) Baptist Cemetery, Rio Grande, Cape May County.

CRAMER, JAMES MICHAEL 1-26-1898. Evergreen Cemetery, Hillside, Union County.

CRAMER, JESSE E. (see: Cranmer, Jesse E.) Old Somerville Cemetery, Somerville, Somerset County.

CRAMER, JOHN Pvt, E, 1st NJ Militia, 10-31-1918. Fairmount Cemetery, Newark, Essex County.

CRAMER, JOHN Pvt, G, 13th NJ Inf, 2-6-1869. Fairmount Cemetery, Newark, Essex County.

CRAMER, JOHN F. Pvt, B, 1st NY Cav, 6-8-1889. Mount Pleasant Cemetery, Newark, Essex County.

Our Brothers Gone Before

CRAMER, JOSEPH (aka: Cramer, William) Pvt, D, 11th NY Cav, 5-1-1910. Arlington Cemetery, Kearny, Hudson County.
CRAMER, LYMAN B. Pvt, E, 31st NJ Inf, 1914. Methodist Church Cemetery, Lebanon, Hunterdon County.
CRAMER, MATTHIAS J. Pvt, K, 31st NJ Inf, 6-12-1906. Methodist Church Cemetery, Lebanon, Hunterdon County.
CRAMER*, NOAH SHARP Pvt, H, 13th IL Inf, 11-21-1890. Methodist Church Cemetery, Asbury, Warren County.
CRAMER, PETER YATMAN 4-26-1898. Hillside Cemetery, Madison, Morris County.
CRAMER, VICTOR B. Pvt, E, 31st NJ Inf, 1874. Methodist Church Cemetery, Lebanon, Hunterdon County.
CRAMER, WILLIAM (see: Cramer, Joseph) Arlington Cemetery, Kearny, Hudson County.
CRAMER, WILLIAM A. Pvt, I, 31st NJ Inf, 12-5-1884. Belvidere/Catholic Cemetery, Belvidere, Warren County.
CRAMER, WILLIAM H. Pvt, A, 33rd NJ Inf, 2-3-1911. Fairmount Cemetery, Newark, Essex County.
CRAMMER, CHARLES Pvt, D, 23rd NJ Inf, 12-23-1904. Mount Prospect Cemetery, Neptune, Monmouth County.
CRAMMER*, ELI Pvt, H, 7th NJ Inf, 1-1-1902. Cedar Hill Cemetery, Florence, Burlington County.
CRAMMER, FRAZIER Pvt, H, 8th NJ Inf, 1873. Union Cemetery, Clarkstown, Atlantic County.
CRAMMER, FREDERICK L. Corp, H, 31st NJ Inf, 6-26-1883. Presbyterian Church Cemetery, Califon, Hunterdon County.
CRAMMER, JACOB (see: Carmer, Jacob B.) Hainesville Cemetery, Hainesville, Sussex County.
CRAMMER, JESSE C. Pvt, C, 2nd NJ Cav, 1-29-1916. Arlington Cemetery, Kearny, Hudson County.
CRAMMER, JOB L. Sgt, D, 9th NJ Inf, 1895. Baptist Cemetery, West Creek, Ocean County.
CRAMMER, JOSIAH M. Pvt, K, 10th NJ Inf, 10-15-1865. Methodist Cemetery, Tuckerton, Ocean County.
CRAMMER, SAMUEL B. Pvt, H, 29th NJ Inf, 3-13-1919. Baptist Cemetery, West Creek, Ocean County.
CRAMPTON, HENRY B. 2-24-1891. Evergreen Cemetery, Clinton, Hunterdon County.
CRAMPTON, HENRY B. Pvt, F, 15th NJ Inf, 9-4-1911. Cedar Lawn Cemetery, Paterson, Passaic County.
CRAMPTON, HENRY B. DoD Unknown. Locust Hill Cemetery, Dover, Morris County.
CRAMPTON, JOHN M. Pvt, I, 26th NJ Inf, 9-22-1892. Locust Hill Cemetery, Dover, Morris County.
CRAMPTON, JOSEPH M. Pvt, F, 15th NJ Inf, 9-10-1906. Locust Hill Cemetery, Dover, Morris County.
CRANDALL, JOHN S. Pvt, A, 125th NY Inf, [Wounded 7-3-1863 at Gettysburg, PA.] 1922. Bloomsbury Cemetery, Kennedy Mills, Warren County.
CRANDELL*, STEPHEN M. Corp, F, 83rd NY Inf, 1906. Mount Pleasant Cemetery, Newark, Essex County.
CRANDOL*, FREDERICK W. Pvt, H, 38th NJ Inf, 1-18-1899. Wesley United Methodist Church Cemetery, Petersburg, Cape May County.
CRANDOL, JAMES Pvt, I, 25th NJ Inf, 5-4-1907. Tabernacle Baptist Church Cemetery, Erma, Cape May County.
CRANDOL, RAYMOND D. Pvt, F, 3rd NJ Inf, [Died of smallpox at Shiloh, NJ.] 1-20-1863. Lutheran Church Cemetery, Friesburg, Salem County.

New Jersey Civil War Burials

CRANE, ALANSON S. Landsman, U.S. Navy, USS Miami, 3-27-1919. Fairmount Cemetery, Newark, Essex County.
CRANE, ALBERT G. Seaman, U.S. Navy, USS Mound City, 1-19-1904. New 1st Methodist Meeting House Cemetery, Manahawkin, Ocean County.
CRANE, ALFRED T. (SR.) Pvt, 6th NY Ind Btty 9-21-1934. Hazelwood Cemetery, Rahway, Union County.
CRANE, ALFRED W.B. Pvt, H, 2nd NJ Inf, 4-27-1919. 1st Reformed Church Cemetery, Pompton Plains, Morris County.
CRANE, AUGUSTUS B. Pvt, 6th NY Ind Btty 6-30-1903. Rahway Cemetery, Rahway, Union County.
CRANE*, BENJAMIN P. Pvt, B, 8th NJ Inf, 5-21-1912. Evergreen Cemetery, Hillside, Union County.
CRANE, CHARLES E. Sgt, F, 13th NJ Inf, 4-25-1869. Mount Pleasant Cemetery, Newark, Essex County.
CRANE, DANIEL W. Pvt, C, 14th NJ Inf, 12-18-1864. Presbyterian Cemetery, Springfield, Union County.
CRANE, EDWARD S. Pvt, G, 7th NY State Militia, 8-21-1917. Fairview Cemetery, Westfield, Union County.
CRANE, EUGENE A. Pvt, D, 9th NJ Inf, 2-4-1882. New 1st Methodist Meeting House Cemetery, Manahawkin, Ocean County.
CRANE, GEORGE 12-22-1893. Presbyterian Church Cemetery, Millbrook, Morris County.
CRANE, GEORGE Pvt, E, 39th NJ Inf, 1899. Reformed Church Cemetery, Montville, Morris County.
CRANE, GEORGE L. 10-15-1911. Fairview Cemetery, Fairview, Monmouth County.
CRANE, GEORGE M. Pvt, D, 39th NJ Inf, 1-17-1881. Fairmount Cemetery, Newark, Essex County.
CRANE, GEORGE W. Capt, E, 27th NJ Inf, 1864. Hillside Cemetery, Madison, Morris County.
CRANE, H.C. 4-15-1922. Fairmount Cemetery, Newark, Essex County.
CRANE, HARRIS (see: Crane, Horace M.) Mount Zion United Methodist Church Cemetery, Barnsboro, Gloucester County.
CRANE, HENRY D. Pvt, E, 1st NJ Militia, DoD Unknown. Rosedale Cemetery, Orange, Essex County.
CRANE, HENRY DURYEA Capt, C, 7th NJ Inf, 1906. Prospect Hill Cemetery, Caldwell, Essex County.
CRANE, HENRY M. Pvt, F, 26th NJ Inf, 6-18-1878. Mount Pleasant Cemetery, Newark, Essex County.
CRANE*, HORACE M. (aka: Crane, Harris) Pvt, B, 7th NJ Inf, 1-14-1918. Mount Zion United Methodist Church Cemetery, Barnsboro, Gloucester County.
CRANE, HORACE N. Pvt, C, 7th NJ Inf, 4-23-1908. Rosedale Cemetery, Orange, Essex County.
CRANE, ICHABOD LOSEY Pvt, E, 3rd NJ Cav, 2-17-1868. Rosedale Cemetery, Orange, Essex County.
CRANE, ISAAC A. Pvt, 6th NY Ind Btty 2-3-1918. Hazelwood Cemetery, Rahway, Union County.
CRANE, JAMES Pvt, L, 43rd GA Inf (CSA), [Captured 5-16-1863 at Baker's Creek, MS.] 6-22-1863. Finn's Point National Cemetery, Pennsville, Salem County.
CRANE, JAMES B. Pvt, F, 26th NJ Inf, 8-31-1880. Rosedale Cemetery, Orange, Essex County.
CRANE, JAMES H. Pvt, K, 1st NJ Inf, [Killed in action at Wilderness, VA.] 5-5-1864. Whitehall Cemetery, Towaco, Morris County.
CRANE, JOHN 1886. Mount Pleasant Cemetery, Newark, Essex County.

Our Brothers Gone Before

CRANE, JOHN B. Pvt, D, 23rd NJ Inf, [Died at Alexandria, VA of wounds received 12-13-1862 at Fredericksburg, VA.] 1-1-1863. Methodist-Episcopal Cemetery, Pointville, Burlington County.

CRANE, JOHN W. Musc, G, 27th NJ Inf, DoD Unknown. Whitehall Cemetery, Towaco, Morris County.

CRANE, JOHN W. 7-14-1874. United Methodist Church Cemetery, Rockaway Valley, Morris County.

CRANE*, JOHN WILLIAM Musc, K, 1st NJ Inf, 12-31-1913. Evergreen Cemetery, Hillside, Union County.

CRANE, JONATHAN T. 1st Lt, G, 37th NJ Inf, 8-25-1889. Rahway Cemetery, Rahway, Union County.

CRANE, JOSEPH P.T. Pvt, C, 30th NJ Inf, 12-18-1891. Rahway Cemetery, Rahway, Union County.

CRANE, JOSEPH W. Sgt, C, 7th NJ Inf, [Wounded in action at Williamsburg, VA.] 6-18-1908. Prospect Hill Cemetery, Caldwell, Essex County.

CRANE*, LEWIS M. Pvt, C, 14th NJ Inf, 5-27-1893. Fairmount Cemetery, Chatham, Morris County.

CRANE, MATTHIAS B.F. (JR.) Pvt, E, 8th NJ Inf, 7-20-1910. Evergreen Cemetery, Hillside, Union County.

CRANE*, MICHAEL (aka: Crain, Michael) Pvt, G, 7th NJ Inf, 2-5-1918. Oddfellows Cemetery, Burlington, Burlington County.

CRANE, MORRIS C. Pvt, C, 9th NJ Inf, 11-17-1911. Fairmount Cemetery, Newark, Essex County.

CRANE, ROBERT T. Pvt, A, 13th NY Cav, 5-31-1872. Fairmount Cemetery, Newark, Essex County.

CRANE*, SMITH B. Pvt, A, 26th NJ Inf, 3-24-1905. Fairmount Cemetery, Newark, Essex County.

CRANE, WARD (aka: Cooper, William) Pvt, H, 35th NJ Inf, 8-31-1922. Fairview Cemetery, Fairview, Monmouth County.

CRANE, WILLIAM L. Sgt, A, 1st NY Eng, 6-26-1887. Mansfield/Washington Cemetery, Washington, Warren County.

CRANER, CHARLES C. Pvt, F, 4th NJ Inf, 11-29-1909. Soldier's Home Cemetery, Vineland, Cumberland County.

CRANER, DAVID M. Pvt, D, 25th NJ Inf, 1883. Presbyterian Church Cemetery, Bridgeton, Cumberland County.

CRANER*, JAMES M. (aka: Cramer, James M.) Sgt, E, 12th NJ Inf, 6-23-1912. Baptist Cemetery, Rio Grande, Cape May County.

CRANEY, ANDREW Pvt, E, 15th NJ Inf, 6-2-1887. Holy Name Cemetery, Jersey City, Hudson County.

CRANMER, EZRA W. Pvt, D, 9th NJ Inf, [Died of typhoid at Newbern, NC. Wounded 3-14-1862 at Newbern, NC.] 4-12-1862. New 1st Methodist Meeting House Cemetery, Manahawkin, Ocean County.

CRANMER, ISAAC (see: Cranmer, Isaiah) New 1st Methodist Meeting House Cemetery, Manahawkin, Ocean County.

CRANMER, ISAIAH (aka: Cranmer, Isaac) Pvt, D, 9th NJ Inf, 8-12-1888. New 1st Methodist Meeting House Cemetery, Manahawkin, Ocean County.

CRANMER*, JARVIS Pvt, K, 2nd NJ Inf, 2-25-1866. Methodist Cemetery, Cassville, Ocean County.

CRANMER, JESSE (see: Gramer, Jesse E.) Old Somerville Cemetery, Somerville, Somerset County.

CRANMER, JESSE E. (aka: Cramer, Jesse E.) Pvt, E, 15th NJ Inf, DoD Unknown. Old Somerville Cemetery, Somerville, Somerset County.

New Jersey Civil War Burials

CRANMER, JOSEPH W. Corp, D, 9th NJ Inf, [Wounded 12-16-1862 at Walthall, NC.] 1-16-1920. New 1st Methodist Meeting House Cemetery, Manahawkin, Ocean County.

CRANMER, SAMUEL S. Pvt, H, 29th NJ Inf, 7-12-1909. Colestown Cemetery, Cherry Hill, Camden County.

CRANMER, WILLIAM Corp, H, 37th NJ Inf, 6-16-1924. Giberson Cemetery, Whiting, Ocean County.

CRANSTON, CHARLES K. Pvt, K, 26th CT Inf, 11-27-1920. Fairmount Cemetery, Newark, Essex County.

CRANSTON, JOHN O. Pvt, E, 28th NY National Guard, DoD Unknown. Presbyterian Cemetery, North Plainfield, Somerset County.

CRAPNELL, ROBERT (see: Crapnell, Thomas W.) Fairmount Cemetery, Newark, Essex County.

CRAPNELL, THOMAS W. (aka: Crapnell, Robert) Pvt, Btty E, 1st NJ Light Art, 4-4-1914. Fairmount Cemetery, Newark, Essex County.

CRASS, HENRY Sgt, B, 75th PA Inf, 10-10-1911. Presbyterian Church Cemetery, Bridgeton, Cumberland County.

CRATER, DENNIS Pvt, H, 11th NJ Inf, [Wounded in action at Spotsylvania CH, VA.] 10-30-1886. Pleasant Hill Cemetery, Pleasant Hill, Morris County.

CRATER, HENRY SUYDAM 1st Lt, G, 15th NJ Inf, 5-28-1876. Presbyterian Church Cemetery, Flemington, Hunterdon County.

CRATER, JOHN P. Bvt Maj, 15th NJ Inf 12-14-1872. Evergreen Cemetery, Morristown, Morris County.

CRATER, PETER A. 1910. Prospect Hill Cemetery, Flemington, Hunterdon County.

CRAULEY, CHRISTOPHER (aka: Crowley, Christopher) Corp, D, 27th PA Inf, 10-18-1904. Mount Pleasant Cemetery, Millville, Cumberland County.

CRAVATT, JEROME B. Pvt, F, 38th NJ Inf, 1925. Methodist-Episcopal Church Cemetery, Clarksburg, Monmouth County.

CRAVATT, LAWRENCE (see: Corvatt, Lawrence) Methodist Church Cemetery, Lebanon, Hunterdon County.

CRAVEN, CHARLES Pvt, D, 38th NJ Inf, 12-30-1868. Methodist-Episcopal Cemetery, Old Bridge, Middlesex County.

CRAVEN, HENRY Pvt, D, 25th NJ Inf, [Died of typhoid at Falmouth, VA.] 1-22-1863. 1st Methodist Church Cemetery, Williamstown, Gloucester County.

CRAVEN, JAMES L. Pvt, A, 28th NJ Inf, 5-21-1906. Methodist-Episcopal Cemetery, Old Bridge, Middlesex County.

CRAVEN, JOHN F. Pvt, A, 28th NJ Inf, [Died of sunstroke at Falmouth, VA.] 5-18-1863. Rose Hill Cemetery, Matawan, Monmouth County.

CRAVEN, THOMAS Pvt, A, 1st NJ Militia, 7-17-1881. Clinton Cemetery, Irvington, Essex County.

CRAVER, JOHN W. 6-13-1918. Chickory Chapel Baptist Church Cemetery, Elk, Gloucester County.

CRAVER, THOMAS Pvt, C, 7th PA Cav, DoD Unknown. St. John's Cemetery, Hamilton, Mercer County.

CRAWBACK, RICHARD V. (aka: Crawbuck, Richard) Blacksmith, I, 5th NY Cav, 7-10-1892. East Ridgelawn Cemetery, Clifton, Passaic County.

CRAWBUCK, RICHARD (see: Crawback, Richard V.) East Ridgelawn Cemetery, Clifton, Passaic County.

CRAWFORD, ANDREW (see: Collom, Andrew H.) Monument Cemetery, Edgewater Park, Burlington County.

CRAWFORD, CHARLES D.D. Pvt, G, 29th NJ Inf, 10-6-1874. Atlantic Reformed Cemetery, Colts Neck, Monmouth County.

CRAWFORD, DAVID Pvt, B, 24th NJ Inf, 11-8-1894. Siloam Cemetery, Vineland, Cumberland County.

Our Brothers Gone Before

CRAWFORD, GEORGE Pvt, D, 28th U.S. CT, 9-5-1913. Riverview Cemetery, Trenton, Mercer County.

CRAWFORD, GEORGE Pvt, K, 1st NJ Inf, [Killed in action at Wilderness, VA.] 5-5-1864. Greenwood Cemetery, Boonton, Morris County.

CRAWFORD, GEORGE W. 1921. Siloam Cemetery, Vineland, Cumberland County.

CRAWFORD, GEORGE W. Pvt, B, 28th NJ Inf, 10-15-1893. Dayton Cemetery, Dayton, Middlesex County.

CRAWFORD, GEORGE W. 1st Sgt, H, 2nd NJ Cav, 4-30-1908. Atlantic Reformed Cemetery, Colts Neck, Monmouth County.

CRAWFORD, GEORGE W. Landsman, U.S. Navy, USS Minnesota, 6-24-1923. Cedar Lawn Cemetery, Paterson, Passaic County.

CRAWFORD, GILBERT J. Corp, G, 29th NJ Inf, 1913. Atlantic Reformed Cemetery, Colts Neck, Monmouth County.

CRAWFORD, HENRY V. Sgt, C, 4th NY Cav, 3-5-1921. Rosedale Cemetery, Orange, Essex County.

CRAWFORD, ISAAC Pvt, F, 13th NJ Inf, [Wounded 9-17-1862 at Antietam, MD.] 1-28-1925. Bloomfield Cemetery, Bloomfield, Essex County.

CRAWFORD, JAMES Pvt, F, 22nd U.S. CT, DoD Unknown. Oak Hill Cemetery, Vineland, Cumberland County.

CRAWFORD, JAMES G. Pvt, G, 29th NJ Inf, 4-4-1893. Atlantic Reformed Cemetery, Colts Neck, Monmouth County.

CRAWFORD, JOEL Pvt, B, 29th NJ Inf, 9-1-1868. Greengrove Cemetery, Keyport, Monmouth County.

CRAWFORD, JOHN 3-20-1875. Green Cemetery, Woodbury, Gloucester County.

CRAWFORD, JOHN C. Pvt, C, 13th NJ Inf, 7-21-1906. Arlington Cemetery, Kearny, Hudson County.

CRAWFORD, JOHN H. Pvt, H, 5th NC Inf (CSA), [Captured 7-1-1863 at Gettysburg, PA. Died of smallpox.] 5-14-1864. Finn's Point National Cemetery, Pennsville, Salem County.

CRAWFORD, JOHN M. Pvt, G, 157th OH Inf, [Died at Fort Delaware.] 7-31-1864. Finn's Point National Cemetery, Pennsville, Salem County.

CRAWFORD, JOHN W. Corp, H, 12th NY Cav, 10-9-1894. Bayview-New York Bay Cemetery, Jersey City, Hudson County.

CRAWFORD, JOSEPH Pvt, E, 1st NJ Cav, 3-17-1902. Fairmount Cemetery, Newark, Essex County.

CRAWFORD, PAGE R. Pvt, I, 25th NJ Inf, 7-7-1918. Presbyterian Church Cemetery, Cold Spring, Cape May County.

CRAWFORD*, ROBERT Pvt, B, 2nd NJ Cav, 2-2-1868. Mount Pleasant Cemetery, Newark, Essex County.

CRAWFORD, ROBERT B. Pvt, K, 1st NY Inf, 4-30-1921. Laurel Grove Cemetery, Totowa, Passaic County.

CRAWFORD, ROBERT C. Pvt, Btty G, 2nd PA Heavy Art, 5-16-1913. New Camden Cemetery, Camden, Camden County.

CRAWFORD*, ROBERT C. Pvt, D, 2nd RI Inf, 5-25-1896. Fairmount Cemetery, Newark, Essex County.

CRAWFORD, ROBERT W. Pvt, I, 2nd NJ Inf, 7-20-1872. Cedar Lawn Cemetery, Paterson, Passaic County.

CRAWFORD*, RODERICK M. Corp, I, 2nd DE Inf, 3-21-1897. St. Paul's United Methodist Church Cemetery, Paulsboro, Gloucester County.

CRAWFORD, WILLIAM Pvt, B, 34th NJ Inf, 8-27-1901. Cedar Hill Cemetery, Florence, Burlington County.

CRAWFORD, WILLIAM Pvt, E, 4th NJ Inf, 9-27-1892. Macphelah Cemetery, North Bergen, Hudson County.

CRAWFORD, WILLIAM H. Corp, I, 5th CT Inf, 1917. Maplewood Cemetery, Freehold, Monmouth County.
CRAWFORD, WILLIAM K. Pvt, C, 1st NJ Cav, 3-13-1912. Evergreen Cemetery, Camden, Camden County.
CRAWFORD*, WILLIAM R. Pvt, F, 13th NJ Inf, 8-18-1887. Bloomfield Cemetery, Bloomfield, Essex County.
CRAWLEY, CHRISTIAN Pvt, B, 10th NJ Inf, 10-25-1906. Willow Grove Cemetery, New Brunswick, Middlesex County.
CRAWLEY, JAMES 10-25-1906. Willow Grove Cemetery, New Brunswick, Middlesex County.
CRAY, CORNELIUS 1907. Holcomb-Riverview Cemetery, Lambertville, Hunterdon County.
CRAY, CORNELIUS S. Wagoner, F, 30th NJ Inf, 7-6-1915. Princeton Cemetery, Princeton, Mercer County.
CRAY, JEREMIAH (see: Gray, Jeremiah) Unionville Cemetery, Dutchtown, Somerset County.
CRAYON, JOSEPH P. Pvt, Btty D, 1st NJ Light Art, 1-14-1908. John O'Neal Farm Cemetery, Franklin, Morris County.
CREAGER, GEORGE W. Pvt, E, 31st NJ Inf, 2-11-1906. Methodist Church Cemetery, Asbury, Warren County.
CREAMER, DANIEL Pvt, G, 25th NJ Inf, 6-6-1898. United Methodist Church Cemetery, Tuckahoe, Cape May County.
CREAMER, DAVID ANDREW Pvt, B, 3rd NJ Cav, 3-18-1901. Baptist Cemetery, Salem, Salem County.
CREAMER, FREDERICK Pvt, G, 25th NJ Inf, [Died of typhoid at Philadelphia, PA.] 3-2-1863. Little Joshua Baptist Cemetery, Steelmantown, Cape May County.
CREAMER, JAMES Pvt, B, 10th NJ Inf, 6-15-1902. Little Joshua Baptist Cemetery, Steelmantown, Cape May County.
CREAMER, JEREMIAH Pvt, G, 143rd NY Inf, 9-13-1925. Fairview Cemetery, Columbia, Warren County.
CREAMER, LEWIS PATRICK Pvt, G, 31st NJ Inf, DoD Unknown. Fairview Cemetery, Columbia, Warren County.
CREAMER, MILTON Pvt, F, 13th NJ Inf, 2-21-1909. Stanhope-Union Cemetery, Netcong, Morris County.
CREAMER, REUBEN Pvt, G, 25th NJ Inf, 6-12-1882. Little Joshua Baptist Cemetery, Steelmantown, Cape May County.
CREAMER, THOMAS M. Pvt, F, 25th NJ Inf, 9-11-1910. Methodist-Episcopal Church Cemetery, South Dennis, Cape May County.
CREASY, BENJAMIN M. Corp, G, 28th VA Inf (CSA), [Wounded 9-14-1862 at Boonsboro, MD. Captured 7-3-1863 at Gettysburg, PA. Died of rheumatism.] 10-27-1863. Finn's Point National Cemetery, Pennsville, Salem County.
CRECY, J. Pvt, Davis' Btty, VA Light Art (CSA), 8-24-1863. Finn's Point National Cemetery, Pennsville, Salem County.
CREE, WILLIAM J. 1st Lt, A, 2nd NJ Inf, 12-9-1869. Evergreen Cemetery, Hillside, Union County.
CREECH*, JOHN Corp, C, 3rd NY Inf, [Wounded 5-16-1864 at Drewry's Bluff, VA.] 4-30-1904. Jersey City Cemetery, Jersey City, Hudson County.
CREED, WILLIAM E. Pvt, I, 9th NJ Inf, 1-4-1871. Sergeant's Hill Cemetery, Sand Brook, Hunterdon County.
CREELY, JACOB (JR.) Pvt, H, 75th PA Inf, [Wounded 7-1-1863 at Gettysburg, PA.] 2-30-1895. New Camden Cemetery, Camden, Camden County.
CREGAR, JOHN D. (aka: Creiger, John) Pvt, H, 55th PA Inf, 8-18-1925. Union Cemetery, Clinton, Hunterdon County.

Our Brothers Gone Before

CREGAR, NAUM (aka: Cregur, Nahum) Pvt, A, 15th NJ Inf, 9-25-1929. Old & New Lutheran Cemetery, Lebanon, Hunterdon County.
CREGG, CASPER (see: Craig, Casper H.) Batsto/Pleasant Mills Methodist Church Cemetery, Pleasant Mills, Atlantic County.
CREGG, JOHN (see: Craig, John) Greenmount Cemetery, Hammonton, Atlantic County.
CREGUR, NAHUM (see: Cregar, Naum) Old & New Lutheran Cemetery, Lebanon, Hunterdon County.
CREIGER, JOHN (see: Cregar, John D.) Union Cemetery, Clinton, Hunterdon County.
CREIGHTON, ANDREW Pvt, G, 3rd PA Cav, 1917. Mount Olivet Cemetery, Fairview, Monmouth County.
CREIGHTON, DAVID J. (aka: Crenghton, David) Pvt, C, 1st NJ Inf, 6-5-1915. Fairmount Cemetery, Newark, Essex County.
CREIGHTON*, HUGH T. Pvt, A, 1st NJ Inf, 6-3-1893. Fairmount Cemetery, Newark, Essex County.
CREIMS, GEORGE DoD Unknown. Elmwood Cemetery, New Brunswick, Middlesex County.
CRELIN*, CHARLES E. Pvt, E, 4th U.S. Vet Vol Inf, 1-7-1902. Cedar Hill Cemetery, East Millstone, Somerset County.
CRELIN, PHILEMON B. Pvt, Btty D, 1st NJ Light Art, 1-27-1915. Arlington Cemetery, Kearny, Hudson County.
CRELIN, WILLIAM M. Pvt, I, 39th NJ Inf, 7-28-1914. Fairmount Cemetery, Newark, Essex County.
CRENEY, JAMES Pvt, B, 127th NY Inf, 2-3-1902. Fairmount Cemetery, Newark, Essex County.
CRENGHTON, DAVID (see: Creighton, David J.) Fairmount Cemetery, Newark, Essex County.
CRESS, EDMUND Pvt, F, 57th VA Inf (CSA), 9-17-1863. Finn's Point National Cemetery, Pennsville, Salem County.
CRESS*, SAMUEL S. Pvt, C, 73rd PA Inf, 2-25-1899. Monument Cemetery, Edgewater Park, Burlington County.
CRESSE, ANTHONY Corp, F, 25th NJ Inf, 3-27-1924. Presbyterian Church Cemetery, Cold Spring, Cape May County.
CRESSE*, EDMUND Pvt, D, 183rd PA Inf, 9-29-1909. 1st Baptist Cemetery, Cape May Court House, Cape May County.
CRESSE, GEORGE S. Musc, F, 25th NJ Inf, 6-9-1867. Presbyterian Church Cemetery, Cold Spring, Cape May County.
CRESSE, JOSEPH Pvt, K, 38th NJ Inf, 6-10-1922. Fairview Cemetery, Cape May Court House, Cape May County.
CRESSE, LEWIS H. Pvt, A, 7th NJ Inf, 6-27-1898. Presbyterian Church Cemetery, Cold Spring, Cape May County.
CRESSY*, OSCAR F. Pvt, K, 54th NY Inf, 11-7-1899. Bayview-New York Bay Cemetery, Jersey City, Hudson County.
CREVELING, EDWARD L. Corp, E, 7th NJ Inf, [Died of lung inflamation at Brandy Station, VA.] 1-26-1864. Phillipsburg Cemetery, Phillipsburg, Warren County.
CREVELING, FRANK 4-14-1908. Presbyterian Cemetery, Asbury, Warren County.
CREVELING, GEORGE R. Pvt, B, 31st NJ Inf, 4-10-1916. Fairmount Cemetery, Newark, Essex County.
CREVELING, JAMES ALVIN Pvt, C, 31st NJ Inf, 1912. Presbyterian Church Cemetery, Bloomsbury, Hunterdon County.
CREVELING, JOHN W. 1st Sgt, H, 9th NJ Inf, 2-24-1906. Presbyterian Church Cemetery, Bloomsbury, Hunterdon County.
CREVELING, JOSEPH B. Corp, G, 10th NJ Inf, [Cenotaph. Died of diarrhea while prisoner at Andersonville, GA.] 1-18-1865. Presbyterian Church Cemetery, Greenwich, Warren County.

New Jersey Civil War Burials

CREWS, HENRY T. (aka: Kruse, Henry) Sgt, G, 2nd Bttn NC Inf (CSA), [Captured 7-3-1863 at Gettysburg, PA. Died of hypertrophy of the heart.] 8-29-1863. Finn's Point National Cemetery, Pennsville, Salem County.

CREWS, L.S. Pvt, D, 58th VA Inf (CSA), [Captured 5-12-1864 at Spotsylvania CH, VA. Died of diarrhea.] 7-12-1864. Finn's Point National Cemetery, Pennsville, Salem County.

CREWS, SAMUEL Pvt, I, 8th FL Inf (CSA), [Captured 7-2-1863 at Gettysburg, PA. Died of fever.] 9-13-1863. Finn's Point National Cemetery, Pennsville, Salem County.

CREWS, THOMAS Pvt, I, 9th MO Inf (CSA), 3-23-1865. Finn's Point National Cemetery, Pennsville, Salem County.

CRICK, JOHN 1900. 1st Baptist Cemetery, Cape May Court House, Cape May County.

CRIGER, DAVID (aka: Kreiger, David) Pvt, K, 35th NJ Inf, 3-1-1911. Pequest Union Cemetery, Great Meadows, Warren County.

CRILL, MOORE Pvt, F, 27th NJ Inf, 2-12-1904. Locust Hill Cemetery, Dover, Morris County.

CRILLEY, THOMAS Landsman, U.S. Navy, USS North Carolina, 1-18-1920. Fairmount Cemetery, Newark, Essex County.

CRIPPEN, JAMES B. Corp, F, 6th U.S. CT, 4-14-1888. Riverview Cemetery, Trenton, Mercer County.

CRIPPS*, DANIEL E. Pvt, D, 5th NJ Inf, [Cenotaph. Killed in action at Wilderness, VA.] 5-6-1864. Peapack Reformed Church Cemetery, Gladstone, Somerset County.

CRIPPS, JAMES Pvt, D, 30th NJ Inf, 3-3-1924. Phillipsburg Cemetery, Phillipsburg, Warren County.

CRISDELL, SAMUEL (aka: Crisden, Samuel) Pvt, A, 41st U.S. CT, 9-3-1917. Mount Peace Cemetery, Lawnside, Camden County.

CRISDEN, SAMUEL (see: Crisdell, Samuel) Mount Peace Cemetery, Lawnside, Camden County.

CRISFIELD, DAVID Pvt, I, 7th U.S. CT, 11-30-1895. Riverview Cemetery, Trenton, Mercer County.

CRISMON, MICHAEL ___, B, 7th NY Inf, 10- -1903. Laurel Grove Cemetery, Totowa, Passaic County.

CRISP, JACOB (see: Crist, Jacob) Cedar Green Cemetery, Clayton, Gloucester County.

CRISP, JAMES M. Pvt, F, 39th NJ Inf, 5-19-1903. Riverview Cemetery, Trenton, Mercer County.

CRISP, PHILIP D. Com Sgt, 11th NJ Inf 4-19-1899. Greenwood Cemetery, Hamilton, Mercer County.

CRISPEN, BENJAMIN (see: Crispin, Benjamin F.) Huntsville Cemetery, Huntsville, Sussex County.

CRISPIN, BENJAMIN F. (aka: Crispen, Benjamin) Pvt, I, 7th IA Inf, [Wounded 11-7-1861 at Belmont, MO.] 1868. Huntsville Cemetery, Huntsville, Sussex County.

CRISPIN, CASPER W. Pvt, F, 37th NJ Inf, 1916. 1st Baptist Church Cemetery, Woodstown, Salem County.

CRISPIN, JOSIAH B. Pvt, H, 23rd NJ Inf, [Killed in action at Salem Heights, VA.] 5-3-1863. Riverview Cemetery, Trenton, Mercer County.

CRISPIN, RESTORE L. Pvt, E, 6th NJ Inf, 10-16-1897. New Camden Cemetery, Camden, Camden County.

CRISPIN*, THEODORE Corp, F, 40th NJ Inf, 8-31-1926. Chew's United Methodist Church Cemetery, Glendora, Camden County.

CRISSEY, CHARLES A. Pvt, M, 2nd NJ Cav, 10-10-1915. Glenwood Cemetery, Glenwood, Sussex County.

CRISSEY*, GEORGE C. Pvt, C, 2nd NJ Cav, 1914. Glenwood Cemetery, Glenwood, Sussex County.

Our Brothers Gone Before

CRISSEY, JOHN H. (aka: Crissy, John) Sgt, D, 1st NJ Militia, 4-26-1916. Riverview Cemetery, Trenton, Mercer County.
CRISSY, JOHN (see: Crissey, John H.) Riverview Cemetery, Trenton, Mercer County.
CRIST, JACOB (aka: Crisp, Jacob) Pvt, G, 10th NJ Inf, 1891. Cedar Green Cemetery, Clayton, Gloucester County.
CRIST, JOHN M. Corp, D, 3rd NJ Inf, 7-20-1915. Fairmount Cemetery, Newark, Essex County.
CRIST, JOHN P. Pvt, I, 9th NJ Inf, 6-25-1871. Cedar Green Cemetery, Clayton, Gloucester County.
CRITE, ROHAN 6-27-1919. Hillside Cemetery, Scotch Plains, Union County.
CRITSON, CHARLES F. Pvt, F, 214th PA Inf, DoD Unknown. Mount Zion United Methodist Church Cemetery, Barnsboro, Gloucester County.
CROASDALE, EDWARD H. Pvt, D, 48th NY Inf, [Wounded 5-7-1864 at Chester Hill, VA.] 4-5-1930. Holcomb-Riverview Cemetery, Lambertville, Hunterdon County.
CROASDALE*, JONAS PRESTON Pvt, D, 48th NY Inf, [Wounded 7-10-1863 at Morris Island, SC.] 6-29-1915. Greenwood Cemetery, Hamilton, Mercer County.
CROASDALE, ROBERT R. Wagoner, D, 48th NY Inf, 7-7-1910. Highland Cemetery, Hopewell Boro, Mercer County.
CROCK, CHARLES (see: Krock, Charles F.) Fairmount Cemetery, Newark, Essex County.
CROCK, HENRY (see: Krock, Henry E.) Fairmount Cemetery, Newark, Essex County.
CROCKER, CHARLES C. Corp, I, 2nd IA Cav, 7-20-1923. Flower Hill Cemetery, North Bergen, Hudson County.
CROCKER, HENRY H. Capt, F, 2nd MA Cav, [Awarded the Medal of Honor. Wounded 10-19-1864 at Cedar Creek, VA.] 1-1-1913. Mansfield/Washington Cemetery, Washington, Warren County.
CROCKER, J.M. Pvt, H, 11th (Holman's) TN Cav (CSA), 5-23-1864. Finn's Point National Cemetery, Pennsville, Salem County.
CROCKER, WILLIAM HAMILTON Corp, I, 9th VA Inf (CSA), [Captured 9-17-1862 at Frederick, MD.] 10-30-1862. Finn's Point National Cemetery, Pennsville, Salem County.
CROCKETT, ALONZO Pvt, B, 2nd NJ Cav, 5-26-1874. Evergreen Cemetery, Hillside, Union County.
CROCKETT, CHARLES N. Pvt, G, 192nd PA Inf, 6-4-1914. Atco Cemetery, Atco, Camden County.
CROCKETT, DAVID T. Coal Heaver, U.S. Navy, USS North Carolina, 9-8-1902. Mount Pleasant Cemetery, Newark, Essex County.
CROCKETT, GEORGE F. Pvt, Btty C, 2nd OH Heavy Art, 10-18-1918. Arlington Cemetery, Kearny, Hudson County.
CROCKETT, RICHARD Pvt, D, 55th MA Inf, DoD Unknown. Mount Holly Cemetery, Mount Holly, Burlington County.
CROCKETT, WILLIAM B. Pvt, E, 20th AR Inf (CSA), [Captured 5-16-1863 at Champion's Hill, MS.] 9-7-1863. Finn's Point National Cemetery, Pennsville, Salem County.
CROCKFORD, JOSEPH Sgt, A, 34th NJ Inf, 10-11-1910. Arlington Cemetery, Kearny, Hudson County.
CROFT, HENRY Pvt, B, 33rd NJ Inf, 2-12-1894. Fairmount Cemetery, Newark, Essex County.
CROFT*, HENRY H. (aka: Miller, John E.) Pvt, C, 26th NY Inf, 10-2-1919. Greenwood Cemetery, Blue Anchor, Camden County.
CROFT, WILLIAM A. Pvt, E, 25th NJ Inf, 3-1-1924. Zion Lutheran Church Cemetery, Saddle River, Bergen County.
CROFUT*, HENRY S. Pvt, K, 60th NY Inf, 5-9-1885. Fairmount Cemetery, Newark, Essex County.

New Jersey Civil War Burials

CROMACK, FREDERICK Pvt, C, 38th NJ Inf, 1890. Methodist Church Cemetery, Goshen, Cape May County.

CROMADY, JAMES MCKNIGHT (aka: Orumady, James) Pvt, I, 6th U.S. CT, DoD Unknown. Mount Prospect Cemetery, Neptune, Monmouth County.

CROMAN, JOHN C. Pvt, G, 38th NJ Inf, 6-24-1869. Elmwood Cemetery, New Brunswick, Middlesex County.

CROMARTIE, JUNIUS P. (aka: Cromarty, Junius) Pvt, Btty H, 2nd NC Light Art (CSA), 4-29-1865. Finn's Point National Cemetery, Pennsville, Salem County.

CROMARTY, JUNIUS (see: Cromartie, Junius P.) Finn's Point National Cemetery, Pennsville, Salem County.

CROMER, THOMAS N. Pvt, B, 15th GA Inf (CSA), [Captured 7-3-1863 at Gettysburg, PA. Died of lung inflammation.] 12-15-1863. Finn's Point National Cemetery, Pennsville, Salem County.

CROMIE, JOHN H. Pvt, I, 121st PA Inf, [Wounded 7-2-1863 at Gettysburg, PA. and 5-5-1864 at Wilderness, VA.] 5-19-1917. Harleigh Cemetery, Camden, Camden County.

CROMPTON, THOMAS (see: Compton, Thomas) Finn's Point National Cemetery, Pennsville, Salem County.

CROMWELL, ANDREW T. Pvt, G, 30th NJ Inf, 8-8-1904. Highland Cemetery, Hopewell Boro, Mercer County.

CROMWELL, ARTHUR (aka: Crummell, Arthur) Pvt, A, 22nd U.S. CT, 1-2-1919. Riverview Cemetery, Trenton, Mercer County.

CROMWELL, CHARLES Pvt, I, 29th CT Inf, 5-12-1895. White Ridge Cemetery, Eatontown, Monmouth County.

CROMWELL, EDWARD Pvt, F, 22nd NJ Inf, 2-1-1917. Pearson/Colonial Memorial Park Cemetery, Whitehorse, Mercer County.

CROMWELL, JOHN NELSON Col, 47th IL Inf [Killed in action at Jackson, MS.] 5-16-1863. Baptist/Evergreen Methodist Cemetery, Plainfield, Union County.

CROMWELL, OLIVER DALLAS Pvt, C, 1st NJ Cav, 7-25-1921. Rosehill Cemetery, Newfield, Gloucester County.

CROMWELL, SAMUEL Pvt, C, 29th NJ Inf, [Died of typhoid at Belle Plain, VA.] 2-25-1863. Methodist Cemetery, Pennington, Mercer County.

CROMWELL, SAMUEL (aka: Crummell, Samuel) Pvt, H, 6th U.S. CT, 4-31-1890. Fairmount Cemetery, Newark, Essex County.

CROMWELL*, WILLIAM H. Pvt, Btty H, 11th U.S. CHA, 7-17-1930. Bordentown/Old St. Mary's Catholic Cemetery, Bordentown, Burlington County.

CRON, WILHELM (see: Krohn, Wilhelm G.) Grove Church Cemetery, North Bergen, Hudson County.

CRONAN, JAMES 3-15-1877. St. John's Cemetery, Hamilton, Mercer County.

CRONAN, JOHN Pvt, __, __ U.S. VRC, 6-23-1913. Holy Sepulchre Cemetery, East Orange, Essex County.

CRONCE, AUGUSTUS Pvt, G, 15th NJ Inf, [Wounded 6-3-1864 at Cold Harbor, VA.] 12-19-1909. Union Cemetery, Frenchtown, Hunterdon County.

CRONCE, GEORGE W. Pvt, D, 30th NJ Inf, 7-14-1891. Prospect Hill Cemetery, Flemington, Hunterdon County.

CRONCE, JOHN C. 5-30-1903. Union Cemetery, Frenchtown, Hunterdon County.

CRONCE, LEONARD F. Pvt, F, 9th NJ Inf, 1910. Nixon Cemetery, Pittstown, Hunterdon County.

CRONCE, MARTIN DoD Unknown. Christian Cemetery, Milford, Hunterdon County.

CRONCE, PETER R. Pvt, F, 9th NJ Inf, 4-5-1870. Locust Grove Cemetery, Quakertown, Hunterdon County.

CRONCE, WILLIAM R. Pvt, D, 31st NJ Inf, 8-9-1882. Baptist Church Cemetery, Cherryville, Hunterdon County.

Our Brothers Gone Before

CRONIER, THOMAS J. (aka: Cronon, Thomas) Corp, G, 13th PA Cav, 1-10-1897. Holy Sepulchre Cemetery, Totowa, Passaic County.
CRONIN, TIMOTHY J. Pvt, B, 69th NY State Militia, 10-16-1907. Holy Sepulchre Cemetery, East Orange, Essex County.
CRONK, HENRY Pvt, C, 8th NJ Inf, 2-3-1914. Bloomfield Cemetery, Bloomfield, Essex County.
CRONK, JOSEPH Pvt, E, 25th NJ Inf, DoD Unknown. Midvale Cemetery, Midvale, Passaic County.
CRONK, LYMAN Seaman, U.S. Navy, USS Commodore Morris, 9-22-1922. Elmwood Cemetery, New Brunswick, Middlesex County.
CRONK, TUNIS 8- -1866. Midvale Cemetery, Midvale, Passaic County.
CRONK, VOLNEY O. Actg 2nd Asst Eng, U.S. Navy, USS Commodore Morris, 3-22-1877. Evergreen Cemetery, New Brunswick, Middlesex County.
CRONMILLER, JOHN B. (aka: Kaunmiller, John) Pvt, B, 27th NJ Inf, 11-10-1874. German Valley Rural Cemetery, Naughright, Morris County.
CRONON, THOMAS (see: Cronier, Thomas J.) Holy Sepulchre Cemetery, Totowa, Passaic County.
CROOK, EMANUEL Pvt, A, 45th PA Inf, [Died at Beverly, NJ.] 10-3-1864. Beverly National Cemetery, Edgewater Park, Burlington County.
CROOK*, HENRY 1st Sgt, K, 12th NJ Inf, 8-20-1889. Presbyterian Church Cemetery, Bridgeton, Cumberland County.
CROOK, HENRY (see: Krug, George Henry) Berry Lawn Cemetery, Carlstadt, Bergen County.
CROOK, JOHN WESLEY Pvt, C, 214th PA Inf, 12-29-1932. Mount Hope Presbyterian Cemetery, Lambertville, Hunterdon County.
CROOK, SAMUEL A. Pvt, K, 83rd PA Inf, 2-15-1922. Presbyterian Church Cemetery, Rockaway, Morris County.
CROOKER, AARON W. Pvt, B, 13th NY State Militia, 1-1-1921. Arlington Cemetery, Kearny, Hudson County.
CROOKES, JOHN EDWARD Pvt, B, 132nd NY Inf, 6-24-1880. Evergreen Cemetery, Hillside, Union County.
CROOKS, WHITFIELD (see: Crooks, William H.) Arlington Cemetery, Kearny, Hudson County.
CROOKS, WILLIAM H. (aka: Crooks, Whitfield) Pvt, I, 26th NJ Inf, 5-31-1909. Arlington Cemetery, Kearny, Hudson County.
CROOKSHANK, WILLIAM Pvt, B, 2nd DE Inf, [Died of typhoid at Newark, NJ.] 9-5-1862. Fairmount Cemetery, Newark, Essex County.
CROSBEY, RICHARD B. Pvt, F, 37th NJ Inf, 6-11-1911. Holy Sepulchre Cemetery, Totowa, Passaic County.
CROSBIE, JAMES (aka: Crosby, James) Artificer, Btty B, 1st NJ Light Art, 7-16-1883. Fairmount Cemetery, Newark, Essex County.
CROSBY*, ANDREW JACKSON (aka: Jackson, Andrew) Pvt, 3rd Btty, CT Light Art, 1-17-1890. Evergreen Cemetery, Morristown, Morris County.
CROSBY, CHARLES A. Landsman, U.S. Navy, USS North Carolina, 2-3-1906. Bayview-New York Bay Cemetery, Jersey City, Hudson County.
CROSBY, JACOB L. Corp, A, 8th NJ Inf, 12-18-1925. Fairmount Cemetery, Newark, Essex County.
CROSBY, JAMES Seaman, U.S. Navy, USS Decatur, 12-3-1915. Phillipsburg New Catholic Cemetery, Greenwich, Warren County.
CROSBY, JAMES (see: Crosbie, James) Fairmount Cemetery, Newark, Essex County.
CROSBY, JOHN DoD Unknown. Phillipsburg New Catholic Cemetery, Greenwich, Warren County.
CROSBY, ROBERT Pvt, I, 9th NY Inf, 1-3-1917. Evergreen Cemetery, Hillside, Union County.

New Jersey Civil War Burials

CROSIER, EDMOND R. Pvt, F, 3rd NJ Inf, 1871. 1st United Methodist Church Cemetery, Bridgeton, Cumberland County.

CROSIER, GEORGE (see: Cosier, George C.) Methodist Church Cemetery, Newport, Cumberland County.

CROSIER, HENRY (see: Grouser, Henry) Cedar Hill Cemetery, East Millstone, Somerset County.

CROSLAND, CHARLES S. Pvt, H, 6th PA Inf, 5-18-1904. Atlantic City Cemetery, Pleasantville, Atlantic County.

CROSLEY, JOHN R. Artificer, M, 1st NY Eng, 9-3-1924. Riverview Cemetery, Trenton, Mercer County.

CROSLEY, ROBERT Pvt, D, PA Emerg NJ Militia, 3-23-1889. Holcomb-Riverview Cemetery, Lambertville, Hunterdon County.

CROSLEY, THOMAS R. Pvt, K, 9th U.S. Inf, 1911. Baptist/Evergreen Methodist Cemetery, Plainfield, Union County.

CROSS, AUSTIN W. Pvt, I, 30th NJ Inf, 4-16-1913. Evergreen/Bishop Jaynes Cemetery, Basking Ridge, Somerset County.

CROSS, BENJAMIN (see: Lyon, Benjamin) Bloomfield Cemetery, Bloomfield, Essex County.

CROSS, BENJAMIN F. Pvt, I, 8th NJ Inf, 10-22-1900. Evergreen Cemetery, Hillside, Union County.

CROSS, CHARLES S. __, __, __ PA __, DoD Unknown. Finn's Point National Cemetery, Pennsville, Salem County.

CROSS, CONRAD Pvt, K, 3rd NJ Inf, 12-30-1875. Evergreen Cemetery, Hillside, Union County.

CROSS, HENRY Pvt, H, 50th MA Militia, 3-12-1911. Riverview Cemetery, Trenton, Mercer County.

CROSS, HOLCOMBE R. Corp, E, 2nd FL Inf (CSA), [Wounded 5-31-1862 at Seven Pines, VA. Captured 7-2-1863 at Gettysburg, PA.] 5-5-1864. Finn's Point National Cemetery, Pennsville, Salem County.

CROSS, JEREMIAH A. Volunteer Surgeon, U.S. Army, 3-30-1881. Fairmount Cemetery, Newark, Essex County.

CROSS*, JOEL Pvt, E, 34th NJ Inf, 1915. New Camden Cemetery, Camden, Camden County.

CROSS, JOSIAH W. Pvt, G, 16th ME Inf, 4-13-1893. Fairmount Cemetery, Newark, Essex County.

CROSS, JUDE 1896. Siloam Cemetery, Vineland, Cumberland County.

CROSS, POINSETT Musc, D, 23rd NJ Inf, 9-12-1920. Methodist-Episcopal Cemetery, Pointville, Burlington County.

CROSS, POMPEO DoD Unknown. Weehawken Cemetery, North Bergen, Hudson County.

CROSS, THOMAS Pvt, F, 1st NJ Cav, DoD Unknown. Methodist Church Cemetery, Pemberton, Burlington County.

CROSS, THOMAS H.P. Actg 3rd Asst Eng, U.S. Navy, 4-26-1878. Rose Hill Cemetery, Matawan, Monmouth County.

CROSS, WARNELL Pvt, D, 5th MD Inf, [Died of disease. Wounded 9-17-1862 at Antietam, MD.] 5-17-1864. Finn's Point National Cemetery, Pennsville, Salem County.

CROSS, WILLIAM J. Seaman, U.S. Navy, USS St. Louis, 12-28-1901. New Camden Cemetery, Camden, Camden County.

CROSSEN*, JAMES Pvt, B, 13th NJ Inf, DoD Unknown. Cedar Lawn Cemetery, Paterson, Passaic County.

CROSSLEY, ABRAHAM Pvt, B, 6th NJ Inf, 2-14-1905. Greenwood Cemetery, Hamilton, Mercer County.

Our Brothers Gone Before

CROSSLEY, ANDREW J. (SR.) Pvt, C, 1st Bttn U.S. Eng, 2-1-1888. Elmwood Cemetery, New Brunswick, Middlesex County.
CROSSLEY, GEORGE W. Pvt, I, 14th NJ Inf, 3-10-1913. Riverview Cemetery, Trenton, Mercer County.
CROSSLEY*, ROBERT Pvt, D, 9th NJ Inf, 3-29-1925. Evergreen Cemetery, Camden, Camden County.
CROSSLEY, SAMUEL Pvt, G, 8th NJ Inf, [Killed in action at Williamsburg, VA.] 5-5-1862. Fairmount Cemetery, Newark, Essex County.
CROSSMAN, EDWARD (see: Crossman, Edwin A.) Fairmount Cemetery, Newark, Essex County.
CROSSMAN, EDWARD S. Corp, G, 56th NY Inf, 5-26-1924. Rosedale Cemetery, Orange, Essex County.
CROSSMAN, EDWIN A. (aka: Crossman, Edward) 2nd Lt, A, 35th NJ Inf, 1-27-1910. Fairmount Cemetery, Newark, Essex County.
CROSSMAN, JAMES A. Actg Ensign, U.S. Navy, 1-8-1902. Bayview-New York Bay Cemetery, Jersey City, Hudson County.
CROSSMAN, NICHOLAS (see: Kruysman, Nicholas L.) Fairmount Cemetery, Newark, Essex County.
CROSSON, THOMAS H. Pvt, C, 30th NJ Inf, 3-15-1885. Hazelwood Cemetery, Rahway, Union County.
CROTHERS, JOHN H. 1st Lt, C, 32nd PA Inf, 3-24-1901. Riverview Cemetery, Trenton, Mercer County.
CROTSLEY, HENRY Wagoner, H, 15th NJ Inf, 10-13-1888. Methodist Church Cemetery, Asbury, Warren County.
CROTSLEY, WILLIAM Pvt, H, 15th NJ Inf, 8-29-1911. Mansfield/Washington Cemetery, Washington, Warren County.
CROTTS, JOSEPH Pvt, C, 55th NC Inf (CSA), [Captured 7-1-1863 at Gettysburg, PA. Died of typhoid.] 8-30-1863. Finn's Point National Cemetery, Pennsville, Salem County.
CROUGHAN, LUKE Pvt, C, 33rd NJ Inf, 9-7-1889. Holy Sepulchre Cemetery, East Orange, Essex County.
CROUPE, JONAS Pvt, E, 98th PA Inf, 7-12-1905. Cedar Ridge Cemetery, Blairstown, Warren County.
CROUSE, J.M. Pvt, C, 18th TN Inf (CSA), 5-15-1864. Finn's Point National Cemetery, Pennsville, Salem County.
CROUSE, JAMES 10-25-1878. Old Camden Cemetery, Camden, Camden County.
CROUTER, CORNELIUS P. (aka: Cruter, Cornelius) Pvt, D, 22nd NJ Inf, 1914. Valleau Cemetery, Ridgewood, Bergen County.
CROW, DAVID Pvt, H, 17th U.S. Inf, 10-1-1930. Arlington Cemetery, Kearny, Hudson County.
CROW, JOHN W. Sgt, K, 42nd MS Inf (CSA), 10-12-1863. Finn's Point National Cemetery, Pennsville, Salem County.
CROWELL, AARON Pvt, B, 26th NJ Inf, 4-2-1888. Reformed Church Cemetery, South Branch, Somerset County.
CROWELL*, CHARLES 1st Lt, F, 65th NY Inf, 10-8-1914. Mount Prospect Cemetery, Neptune, Monmouth County.
CROWELL, DANIEL F. Pvt, F, 25th NJ Inf, 12-29-1914. Presbyterian Church Cemetery, Cold Spring, Cape May County.
CROWELL, DAVID Sgt, A, 30th NJ Inf, 10-9-1907. Hazelwood Cemetery, Rahway, Union County.
CROWELL, DAVID S. 2nd Lt, A, 35th NJ Inf, 12-14-1893. Mount Pleasant Cemetery, Newark, Essex County.
CROWELL, EDWARD L. Corp, I, 24th NJ Inf, 1900. Clinton Cemetery, Irvington, Essex County.

CROWELL, JEREMIAH Corp, K, 9th NJ Inf, 9-29-1910. 1st Baptist Cemetery, Cape May Court House, Cape May County.

CROWELL, JOSEPH A. Seaman, U.S. Navy, 1-19-1881. Mount Pleasant Cemetery, Newark, Essex County.

CROWELL*, JOSEPH E. Pvt, K, 13th NJ Inf, 10-15-1919. Cedar Lawn Cemetery, Paterson, Passaic County.

CROWELL, JOSEPH LEE Capt, I, 28th NJ Inf, [Wounded 12-13-1862 at Fredericksburg, VA.] 6-14-1886. Alpine Cemetery, Perth Amboy, Middlesex County.

CROWELL, SAMUEL Pvt, M, 2nd NJ Cav, 3-10-1919. Cedar Lawn Cemetery, Paterson, Passaic County.

CROWELL, SAMUEL S. Wagoner, E, 9th NJ Inf, 5-18-1889. Preakness Reformed Church Cemetery, Wayne, Passaic County.

CROWELL, THOMAS LEE Pvt, C, 5th NJ Inf, 4-4-1887. Presbyterian Church Cemetery, Woodbridge, Middlesex County.

CROWELL, WILLIAM B. Pvt, D, 35th NJ Inf, 4-8-1881. Evergreen Cemetery, Morristown, Morris County.

CROWLER, THEODORE Pvt, Btty E, 4th NY Heavy Art, 2-22-1901. Evergreen Cemetery, Hillside, Union County.

CROWLEY, CHRISTIAN Pvt, B, 10th NJ Inf, 1883. Presbyterian Church Cemetery, Bridgeton, Cumberland County.

CROWLEY, CHRISTOPHER (see: Crauley, Christopher) Mount Pleasant Cemetery, Millville, Cumberland County.

CROWLEY, DAVID Pvt, G, 9th NY Inf, DoD Unknown. St. John's Evangelical Church Cemetery, Orange, Essex County.

CROWLEY, DENNIS D. Corp, U.S. Marine Corps, 8-14-1864. St. John's Evangelical Church Cemetery, Orange, Essex County.

CROWLEY, JAMES Pvt, A, 7th NJ Inf, 1-9-1881. Mount Olivet Cemetery, Bloomfield, Essex County.

CROWLEY, JEREMIAH Pvt, H, 2nd NJ Cav, 1-28-1913. Holy Sepulchre Cemetery, East Orange, Essex County.

CROWLEY, THOMAS Pvt, G, 9th NJ Inf, DoD Unknown. Batsto/Pleasant Mills Methodist Church Cemetery, Pleasant Mills, Atlantic County.

CROWLEY, WILLIAM H. Corp, G, 4th NJ Inf, 4-13-1868. Methodist-Episcopal Cemetery, Green Bank, Burlington County.

CROWN, JOHN Sgt, C, 12th U.S. Inf, [Wounded 6-27-1862 at Gaines' Mill, VA.] 9-18-1874. Laurel Grove Cemetery, Totowa, Passaic County.

CROWTHER, SYDNEY Pvt, E, 25th NJ Inf, 1925. Ramapo Reformed Church Cemetery, Mahwah, Bergen County.

CROXSON, CHARLES Pvt, A, 29th NJ Inf, 10-2-1871. Presbyterian Church Cemetery, Shrewsbury, Monmouth County.

CROXSON, FRANCIS Pvt, H, 33rd NJ Inf, 12-26-1904. Riverside Cemetery, Toms River, Ocean County.

CROZIER, GEORGE __, C, 2nd __ __, 6-9-1918. Flower Hill Cemetery, North Bergen, Hudson County.

CROZIER, JOSEPH Sgt, G, 10th NJ Inf, 8-21-1913. Oddfellows Cemetery, Burlington, Burlington County.

CRTE, JAMES Pvt, I, 53rd TN Inf (CSA), 6-23-1863. Finn's Point National Cemetery, Pennsville, Salem County.

CRUDEN*, ALEXANDER B. Pvt, B, 3rd NY Inf, 6-17-1932. English Neighborhood Reformed Church Cemetery, Ridgefield, Bergen County.

CRUE, CHARLES P. 4-30-1897. Evergreen/Bishop Jaynes Cemetery, Basking Ridge, Somerset County.

CRUGER, WILLIAM R. Pvt, H, 12th NY Inf, DoD Unknown. Windsor Burial Grounds Cemetery, East Windsor, Mercer County.
CRUIS, THOMAS (see: Brown, Thomas C.) Presbyterian Church Cemetery, Greenwich, Cumberland County.
CRUM, DAVID Pvt, K, 8th VA Cav (CSA), 1-24-1865. Finn's Point National Cemetery, Pennsville, Salem County.
CRUM, GEORGE L. Pvt, B, 161st NY Inf, 5-11-1914. Old 1st Methodist Church Cemetery, West Long Branch, Monmouth County.
CRUM, JACOB 4-17-1877. Cedar Green Cemetery, Clayton, Gloucester County.
CRUM, JACOB Pvt, K, 39th NJ Inf, 1931. St. Joseph's Cemetery, Echo Lake, Passaic County.
CRUM, JOHN (see: Krum, John H.) Mount Prospect Cemetery, Neptune, Monmouth County.
CRUM, WILLIAM Seaman, U.S. Navy, USS Princeton, 9-16-1866. Old 1st Methodist Church Cemetery, West Long Branch, Monmouth County.
CRUMBLEY, DANIEL Pvt, D, 4th NJ Inf, 12-15-1913. Riverview Cemetery, Trenton, Mercer County.
CRUMMELL, ARTHUR (see: Cromwell, Arthur) Riverview Cemetery, Trenton, Mercer County.
CRUMMELL, SAMUEL (see: Cromwell, Samuel) Fairmount Cemetery, Newark, Essex County.
CRUMP, ALBERT H. Capt, D, 2nd NJ Cav, DoD Unknown. Evergreen Cemetery, Camden, Camden County.
CRUMP, JAMES A. (JR.) Pvt, Btty C, 1st NJ Light Art, 5-1-1893. Evergreen Cemetery, Hillside, Union County.
CRUMP, JAMES A. (SR.) Pvt, I, 52nd MA Militia, 2-21-1889. Evergreen Cemetery, Hillside, Union County.
CRUSEN*, CHARLES W. Pvt, I, 2nd NJ Inf, 10-15-1896. Union Cemetery, Washington, Morris County.
CRUSER, CHARLES A. Pvt, F, 30th NJ Inf, [Died of typhoid at Belle Plain, VA.] 4-3-1863. Rocky Hill Cemetery, Rocky Hill, Somerset County.
CRUSER, JACOB Pvt, G, 31st NJ Inf, 1921. Methodist Church Cemetery, Hope, Warren County.
CRUSER, THEODORE Pvt, F, 30th NJ Inf, 10-10-1911. Greenwood Cemetery, Hamilton, Mercer County.
CRUTCHFIELD, AMERICUS Wagoner, E, 1st Bttn VA Inf (CSA), [Captured 3-23-1862 at Kernstown, VA. Died of disease.] 7-18-1862. Finn's Point National Cemetery, Pennsville, Salem County.
CRUTE, CHRISTOPHER C. Corp, C, 53rd VA Inf (CSA), [Captured 7-3-1863 at Gettysburg, PA. Died of rubeola.] 8-28-1863. Finn's Point National Cemetery, Pennsville, Salem County.
CRUTER, CORNELIUS (see: Crouter, Cornelius P.) Valleau Cemetery, Ridgewood, Bergen County.
CRUTZ, JOHN (see: Curtis, John V.) Brown Cemetery, Butler, Morris County.
CUBBERELEY, GEORGE W. (see: Cubberly, George W.) Baptist Church Cemetery, Hamilton Square, Mercer County.
CUBBERLEY, GEORGE D. Pvt, H, 37th NJ Inf, 1-19-1927. Methodist Church Cemetery, Groveville, Mercer County.
CUBBERLEY, JAMES M. DoD Unknown. Riverview Cemetery, Trenton, Mercer County.
CUBBERLEY, STACY 2-5-1905. United Methodist Church Cemetery, Windsor, Mercer County.
CUBBERLY, AZARIAH Pvt, E, 21st NJ Inf, 5-3-1910. Greenwood Cemetery, Hamilton, Mercer County.

New Jersey Civil War Burials

CUBBERLY, EDWARD C. Pvt, I, 14th NJ Inf, 1-19-1910. Lawrenceville Cemetery, Lawrenceville, Mercer County.
CUBBERLY*, GEORGE W. (aka: Cubbereley, George W.) Capt, I, 38th NJ Inf, 8-18-1897. Baptist Church Cemetery, Hamilton Square, Mercer County.
CUBBERLY, JACOB Pvt, H, 13th NJ Inf, 2-1-1913. Bayview-New York Bay Cemetery, Jersey City, Hudson County.
CUBBERLY*, NICHOLAS Pvt, K, 132nd NY Inf, 6-3-1913. Bayview-New York Bay Cemetery, Jersey City, Hudson County.
CUBBERLY, PIERSON AZARIAH Pvt, E, 21st NJ Inf, 8-16-1897. Baptist Church Cemetery, Hamilton Square, Mercer County.
CUBBLER*, GEORGE G. Pvt, C, 3rd NJ Cav, 12-27-1896. Cedar Grove Cemetery, Gloucester City, Camden County.
CUBROSS, ALEXANDER M. Pvt, K, 4th U.S. Inf, 10-24-1899. Laurel Grove Cemetery, Totowa, Passaic County.
CUDDINGTON, HENRY S. Pvt, C, 39th NJ Inf, 10-5-1900. Fairmount Cemetery, Newark, Essex County.
CUDGO, MOSES (see: Cudjo, Moses) Princeton Cemetery, Princeton, Mercer County.
CUDJO, MOSES (aka: Cudgo, Moses) Corp, K, 25th U.S. CT, [Cenotaph. Died at Barrancas, FL.] 8-14-1864. Princeton Cemetery, Princeton, Mercer County.
CUDNEY, JOHN (see: Gorduey, John) Presbyterian Church Cemetery, Ewing, Mercer County.
CUEMAN, JACOB 3-21-1901. Mount Hebron Cemetery, Montclair, Essex County.
CUEMAN, RICHARD V. Pvt, C, 26th NJ Inf, 11-4-1908. Fairmount Cemetery, Newark, Essex County.
CUFF, ELISHA Pvt, H, 127th U.S. CT, 6-29-1915. Cuff Cemetery, Canton, Salem County.
CUFF, JACOB W. Pvt, B, 6th NY Cav, 11-21-1892. Haring Cemetery, Old Tappan, Bergen County.
CUFF, JOSEPH Pvt, M, 2nd U.S. Colored Cav, 7-18-1919. Rosedale Cemetery, Orange, Essex County.
CUFF, REUBEN C. Seaman, U.S. Navy, 4-4-1916. Memorial Park Cemetery, Gouldtown, Cumberland County.
CULBERTSON, JOSEPH C. Sgt, F, 39th KY Inf, 3-22-1876. Riverview Cemetery, Trenton, Mercer County.
CULBERTSON, JOSEPH R. Asst Surg, 10th IN Cav DoD Unknown. Riverview Cemetery, Trenton, Mercer County.
CULL, AUGUST JOSEPH Pvt, H, 41st NY Inf, 7-21-1897. Woodland Cemetery, Newark, Essex County.
CULLEN, JAMES (aka: Cullen, Joseph) Pvt, A, 71st NY Inf, DoD Unknown. Holy Sepulchre Cemetery, East Orange, Essex County.
CULLEN, JOSEPH Pvt, A, 71st NY Inf, 5-20-1889. Holy Sepulchre Cemetery, East Orange, Essex County.
CULLEN, JOSEPH (see: Cullen, James) Holy Sepulchre Cemetery, East Orange, Essex County.
CULLEN, PATRICK Pvt, D, 12th NJ Inf, 9-7-1917. Holy Name Cemetery, Jersey City, Hudson County.
CULLEN, PATRICK Pvt, A, 37th NJ Inf, 1920. Holy Sepulchre Cemetery, East Orange, Essex County.
CULLEN, RICHARD H. Pvt, H, 5th NJ Inf, 9-14-1890. Rahway Cemetery, Rahway, Union County.
CULLEN, THOMAS F. 11-21-1877. Evergreen Cemetery, Camden, Camden County.
CULLIGAN, THOMAS J. Pvt, A, 13th VT Inf, 5-23-1903. St. Peter's Cemetery, Jersey City, Hudson County.
CULLIN, FRANCIS R. Landsman, U.S. Navy, USS Princeton, 12-28-1907. Bordentown/Old St. Mary's Catholic Cemetery, Bordentown, Burlington County.

Our Brothers Gone Before

CULLINGTON, JOHN (see: Cullington, William) Fairview Cemetery, Fairview, Monmouth County.
CULLINGTON, WILLIAM (aka: Cullington, John) 2-24-1918. Fairview Cemetery, Fairview, Monmouth County.
CULVER, AUGUSTUS Pvt, A, 28th NJ Inf, 3-3-1910. Evergreen Cemetery, Hillside, Union County.
CULVER*, CHARLES E. Pvt, B, 57th MA Inf, 11-15-1865. Christ Church Cemetery, Morgan, Middlesex County.
CULVER, GEORGE Pvt, K, 28th NJ Inf, 5-22-1905. Arlington Cemetery, Kearny, Hudson County.
CULVER, GEORGE MILTON Pvt, F, 3rd IN Cav, 10-2-1934. Locust Hill Cemetery, Dover, Morris County.
CULVER, JONATHAN Pvt, A, 28th NJ Inf, 5-13-1907. Christ Church Cemetery, Morgan, Middlesex County.
CULVER, LAWRENCE Pvt, H, 31st NJ Inf, 8-18-1903. Pleasant Hill Cemetery, Pleasant Hill, Morris County.
CUMINGS, JAMES H. Bvt Major, 15th NJ Inf 5-9-1902. Newton Cemetery, Newton, Sussex County.
CUMINS, ROBERT B. (see: Cummings, Robert B.) Finn's Point National Cemetery, Pennsville, Salem County.
CUMMING*, ALEXANDER M. Maj, 1st NJ Cav 7-16-1879. Princeton Cemetery, Princeton, Mercer County.
CUMMING, GILBERT WILLIAM Bvt Brig Gen, U.S. Volunteers, [Colonel, 51st Illinois Infantry.] 3-7-1877. Mount Pleasant Cemetery, Newark, Essex County.
CUMMING, THOMAS H. Pvt, M, 1st NY Cav, 1-3-1936. Hillside Cemetery, Scotch Plains, Union County.
CUMMINGS, ALEXANDER M. 1st Lt, H, 11th NJ Inf, 8-27-1924. Evergreen Cemetery, Hillside, Union County.
CUMMINGS, AMOS J. Sgt Maj, 26th NJ Inf [Awarded the Medal of Honor.] 5-2-1902. Clinton Cemetery, Irvington, Essex County.
CUMMINGS, CHARLES W. Corp, E, 26th NJ Inf, 10-22-1865. Clinton Cemetery, Irvington, Essex County.
CUMMINGS*, CHRISTIAN Pvt, B, 1st NJ Inf, 5-26-1900. Pequest Union Cemetery, Great Meadows, Warren County.
CUMMINGS*, CHRISTOPHER J. Pvt, C, 5th U.S. Cav, 3-7-1924. Riverside Cemetery, Toms River, Ocean County.
CUMMINGS, DANIEL GRIFFIN Pvt, L, 8th MS Cav (CSA), 1-30-1865. Finn's Point National Cemetery, Pennsville, Salem County.
CUMMINGS, FERDINAND Landsman, U.S. Navy, USS Sonoma, 4-27-1885. Rosedale Cemetery, Orange, Essex County.
CUMMINGS, FREDERICK Landsman, U.S. Navy, USS Monticello, 7-24-1904. Rosedale Cemetery, Orange, Essex County.
CUMMINGS, GEORGE (see: Comings, George T.) Alpine Cemetery, Perth Amboy, Middlesex County.
CUMMINGS, GEORGE B. Pvt, G, 27th NJ Inf, 12-23-1889. Whitehall Cemetery, Towaco, Morris County.
CUMMINGS, GEORGE C. Pvt, A, 3rd NJ Inf, 1932. Methodist Episcopal/Methodist Protestant Cemetery, Bridgeport, Gloucester County.
CUMMINGS*, GEORGE W. Sgt, B, 1st NY Mounted Rifles, 6-26-1925. Laurel Grove Cemetery, Totowa, Passaic County.
CUMMINGS*, JAMES C. Pvt, F, 7th NJ Inf, [Wounded 5-5-1862 at Williamsburg, VA.] 6-17-1911. Riverview Cemetery, Trenton, Mercer County.
CUMMINGS, JEREMIAH Pvt, Btty D, 1st NJ Light Art, 8-28-1893. Mount Olivet Cemetery, Newark, Essex County.

New Jersey Civil War Burials

CUMMINGS, JOHN F. 1st Sgt, A, 5th NH Inf, 1919. St. Rose of Lima Cemetery, Freehold, Monmouth County.

CUMMINGS, LORENZO (see: Cummins, Lorenzo C.) Presbyterian Church Cemetery, Newton, Sussex County.

CUMMINGS, MICHAEL Corp, E, 27th NJ Inf, DoD Unknown. St. Mary's Cemetery, Boonton, Morris County.

CUMMINGS, NATHANIEL Pvt, Btty B, 1st NJ Light Art, 12-15-1885. Pequest Union Cemetery, Great Meadows, Warren County.

CUMMINGS, RICHARD Pvt, H, 6th NJ Inf, DoD Unknown. Princeton Cemetery, Princeton, Mercer County.

CUMMINGS, ROBERT B. (aka: Cumins, Robert B.) Pvt, E, 39th GA Inf (CSA), [Captured 5-16-1863 at Baker's Creek, MS. Died of smallpox.] 1-2-1864. Finn's Point National Cemetery, Pennsville, Salem County.

CUMMINGS, SAMUEL S. Pvt, F, 25th NJ Inf, 10-19-1887. Presbyterian Church Cemetery, Cold Spring, Cape May County.

CUMMINGS, TIMOTHY Z. Pvt, H, 11th NJ Inf, [Died of dysentery at Fort Ellsworth, VA.] 10-25-1862. Methodist Cemetery, Bernardsville, Somerset County.

CUMMINGS, WALTER W. Corp, E, 13th NJ Inf, 12-5-1879. Rosedale Cemetery, Orange, Essex County.

CUMMINGS, WARREN B. Pvt, H, 58th IL Inf, 1-5-1916. Mount Hope Presbyterian Cemetery, Lambertville, Hunterdon County.

CUMMINGS, WILLIAM E. Pvt, H, 161st NY Inf, [Died of diarrhea at Baton Rouge, LA.] 8-5-1863. Methodist Cemetery, Bernardsville, Somerset County.

CUMMINGS, WILLIAM N. Pvt, Btty B, 1st NJ Light Art, 1915. Methodist Church Cemetery, Liberty, Warren County.

CUMMINS, JOHN WESLEY (see: Commons, Jackson W.) Zion Baptist Church Cemetery, New Egypt, Ocean County.

CUMMINS, LORENZO C. (aka: Cummings, Lorenzo) Pvt, E, 9th NJ Inf, 9-26-1876. Presbyterian Church Cemetery, Newton, Sussex County.

CUNARD, CHARLES H. Corp, A, 7th NJ Inf, 1892. Friends/Methodist-Episcopal Cemetery, Pedricktown, Salem County.

CUNARD, WILLIAM (see: Conrad, William) Fairmount Cemetery, Newark, Essex County.

CUNBALL, WILLIAM DoD Unknown. Elmwood Cemetery, New Brunswick, Middlesex County.

CUNDELL*, CHARLES H. 1st Lt, Btty G, 5th NY Heavy Art, 8-12-1915. Cedar Lawn Cemetery, Paterson, Passaic County.

CUNIFF, JAMES Pvt, H, 35th NJ Inf, [Wounded by guerrillas at Meridian, MS.] 11-11-1910. St. Gabriel's Cemetery, Bradevelt, Monmouth County.

CUNNINGHAM, ANDREW Pvt, B, 18th PA Inf, 4-15-1904. Riverview Cemetery, Trenton, Mercer County.

CUNNINGHAM, ANDREW J. Pvt, A, 3rd NJ Inf, [Wounded in action.] 11-6-1923. Atlantic City Cemetery, Pleasantville, Atlantic County.

CUNNINGHAM, CHARLES R. Pvt, F, 95th PA Inf, 3-26-1916. Presbyterian Church Cemetery, Bridgeton, Cumberland County.

CUNNINGHAM, DAVID Pvt, B, 2nd NJ Inf, 1-26-1905. Siloam Cemetery, Vineland, Cumberland County.

CUNNINGHAM, EDGAR W. Pvt, K, 26th ME Inf, 4-22-1925. Evergreen Cemetery, Hillside, Union County.

CUNNINGHAM, JAMES Pvt, Unassigned, 35th NJ Inf, 3-25-1892. Holy Name Cemetery, Jersey City, Hudson County.

CUNNINGHAM, JAMES Pvt, D, 14th NY Inf, 3-11-1893. Holy Name Cemetery, Jersey City, Hudson County.

Our Brothers Gone Before

CUNNINGHAM, JAMES Pvt, E, 12th NJ Inf, DoD Unknown. Arlington Cemetery, Kearny, Hudson County.
CUNNINGHAM, JEROME B. Pvt, C, 9th NJ Inf, 12-8-1887. Methodist Church Cemetery, Hope, Warren County.
CUNNINGHAM, JEROME JAMES Pvt, B, 4th NJ Inf, 8-22-1907. Arlington Cemetery, Kearny, Hudson County.
CUNNINGHAM, JOHN Pvt, B, 84th NY Inf, [Wounded 9-14-1862 at South Mountain, MD.] 1867. Franklin Reformed Church Cemetery, Nutley, Essex County.
CUNNINGHAM, JOHN J. Principal Musc, 3rd NY Inf 7-4-1928. Holy Cross Cemetery, North Arlington, Bergen County.
CUNNINGHAM*, JOHN R. Capt, H, 10th NJ Inf, DoD Unknown. Old Camden Cemetery, Camden, Camden County.
CUNNINGHAM, JOSEPH Pvt, B, 11th NJ Inf, 8-16-1883. Pitman Methodist-Episcopal Cemetery, New Brunswick, Middlesex County.
CUNNINGHAM, M.A. Pvt, F, 51st AL Cav (CSA), 10-30-1863. Finn's Point National Cemetery, Pennsville, Salem County.
CUNNINGHAM, NATHANIEL Pvt, H, 35th NJ Inf, 1-15-1893. Washington Monumental Cemetery, South River, Middlesex County.
CUNNINGHAM, NATHANIEL Pvt, I, 11th NJ Inf, 9-18-1892. Pitman Methodist-Episcopal Cemetery, New Brunswick, Middlesex County.
CUNNINGHAM, OLIVER C. Capt, B, 154th PA Inf, 9-12-1899. Harleigh Cemetery, Camden, Camden County.
CUNNINGHAM, PATRICK (aka: Connegan, Patrick) Pvt, K, 27th NJ Inf, 8-15-1892. Mount Olivet Cemetery, Bloomfield, Essex County.
CUNNINGHAM, THOMAS Capt, K, 38th NJ Inf, 12-14-1919. Greenwood Cemetery, Hamilton, Mercer County.
CUNNINGHAM, WILLIAM Pvt, H, 14th NJ Inf, 5-10-1901. Brotherhood Cemetery, Hainesport, Burlington County.
CUNNINGHAM, WILLIAM DoD Unknown. Pitman Methodist-Episcopal Cemetery, New Brunswick, Middlesex County.
CUNNINGHAM, WILLIAM J. Pvt, U.S. Marine Corps, 2-20-1902. Greenwood Cemetery, Hamilton, Mercer County.
CUNNINGHAM, WILLIAM P. Pvt, K, 118th PA Inf, 1892. Bethel Cemetery, Pennsauken, Camden County.
CUPPINGER, GOTTLIEB (see: Kuppinger, Gottlieb) Riverview Cemetery, Trenton, Mercer County.
CUPPLES, JOHN Pvt, I, 7th MI Cav, 1898. Presbyterian Church Cemetery, Williamstown, Gloucester County.
CURIE*, CHARLES Capt, A, 178th NY Inf, 5-9-1910. Cedar Lawn Cemetery, Paterson, Passaic County.
CURIE, HENRY Corp, F, 7th CT Inf, [Wounded 8-16-1864 at Deep Run, VA.] 10-14-1915. Hedding Methodist-Episcopal Church Cemetery, Bellmawr, Camden County.
CURL, DAVID DoD Unknown. Union Cemetery, Washington, Morris County.
CURL*, JOHN Pvt, K, 10th NJ Inf, 6-14-1908. Rockport Cemetery, Rockport, Warren County.
CURLEY, CHARLES Seaman, U.S. Navy, 3-1-1898. Holy Trinity Lutheran Church Cemetery, Manasquan, Monmouth County.
CURLEY, MARTIN Pvt, G, 118th PA Inf, [Wounded 9-20-1862 at Sheperdstown, WV.] 6-18-1892. St. John's Cemetery, Allentown, Monmouth County.
CURLEY, MICHAEL 4-27-1889. Fairmount Cemetery, Newark, Essex County.
CURLEY*, PATRICK Pvt, B, 18th NY Cav, 12-6-1888. Mount Olivet Cemetery, Newark, Essex County.

New Jersey Civil War Burials

CURLIS, RICHARD A. 1st Lt, C, 3rd NJ Inf, [Died at Fredericksburg, VA. of wounds received 5-12-1864 at Spotsylvania CH, VA.] 5-19-1864. Evergreen Cemetery, Camden, Camden County.

CURLIS, WILLIAM B. Lt Col, 9th NJ Inf 1-4-1903. Presbyterian Church Cemetery, Pennington, Mercer County.

CURLISS, WILLIAM H. Pvt, G, 1st MI Sharpshooters, 12-15-1906. Mount Pleasant Cemetery, Millville, Cumberland County.

CURRAN, FRANK A. Sgt, K, 2nd NJ Inf, 11-4-1887. Fairmount Cemetery, Newark, Essex County.

CURRAN*, JOHN Pvt, H, 66th NY Inf, [Wounded 9-17-1862 at Antietam, MD.] 6-23-1913. Holy Sepulchre Cemetery, East Orange, Essex County.

CURRAN, JOSIAH H. Pvt, H, 27th NJ Inf, 4-15-1919. Arlington Cemetery, Kearny, Hudson County.

CURRAN, PATRICK Pvt, C, 4th NJ Inf, 4-8-1890. Fairmount Cemetery, Newark, Essex County.

CURRAN, PHINEAS (aka: Curran, Phoenix) Pvt, G, 38th NJ Inf, 10-31-1909. Willow Grove Cemetery, New Brunswick, Middlesex County.

CURRAN, PHOENIX (see: Curran, Phineas) Willow Grove Cemetery, New Brunswick, Middlesex County.

CURRAN, WILLIAM Corp, L, 1st NJ Cav, 9-16-1911. St. Peter's Cemetery, New Brunswick, Middlesex County.

CURREDEN, BENJAMIN (see: Curriden, Benjamin) New Camden Cemetery, Camden, Camden County.

CURRENS, PATRICK Pvt, E, 33rd NJ Inf, DoD Unknown. Holy Sepulchre Cemetery, East Orange, Essex County.

CURREY, MICHAEL Pvt, C, 6th NJ Inf, 2-25-1914. St. Peter's Cemetery, New Brunswick, Middlesex County.

CURRIDEN*, BENJAMIN (aka: Curreden, Benjamin) Pvt, D, 23rd NJ Inf, 6-8-1914. New Camden Cemetery, Camden, Camden County.

CURRIDEN, MARTIN V. Corp, K, 4th NJ Inf, DoD Unknown. Free Burying Ground Cemetery, Pennsville, Salem County.

CURRIDEN, PHILIP Pvt, K, 40th NJ Inf, 1925. Methodist-Episcopal Church Cemetery, Penns Grove, Salem County.

CURRIE*, CHARLES F. Corp, H, 4th NJ Inf, 4-21-1913. Presbyterian Church Cemetery, Blackwood, Camden County.

CURRIE, FREDERICK Pvt, G, 5th PA Cav, [Wounded 6-17-1863 at Williamsburg, VA.] 1882. Atlantic City Cemetery, Pleasantville, Atlantic County.

CURRIE, GEORGE F. 2nd Cl Fireman, U.S. Navy, USS Kansas, 4-29-1914. Atlantic City Cemetery, Pleasantville, Atlantic County.

CURRIE, JOHN Pvt, B, 8th NJ Inf, 8-2-1888. Methodist-Episcopal Cemetery, Pennsville, Salem County.

CURRIE*, THOMAS W. Pvt, F, 1st NJ Inf, [Wounded in action.] 8-11-1891. Elmwood Cemetery, New Brunswick, Middlesex County.

CURRIER, BENJAMIN G. Pvt, K, 15th NH Inf, 1883. Presbyterian Cemetery, Salem, Salem County.

CURRIER, CHARLES E. Pvt, D, 44th MA Inf, 1926. Siloam Cemetery, Vineland, Cumberland County.

CURRIER, OSCEOLA Sgt, B, 26th NJ Inf, 9-20-1936. Rosedale Cemetery, Orange, Essex County.

CURRY, JOHN R. Pvt, D, 8th (Wade's) Confederate States Cav (CSA), 11-23-1863. Finn's Point National Cemetery, Pennsville, Salem County.

CURRY, JOSEPH M. Pvt, C, 68th PA Inf, 2-19-1884. Riverview Cemetery, Trenton, Mercer County.

Our Brothers Gone Before

CURRY, RICHARD Pvt, Btty A, 1st NJ Light Art, 12-12-1894. Grove Church Cemetery, North Bergen, Hudson County.
CURRY*, SAMUEL 2nd Lt, D, PA Emerg NJ Militia, 12-30-1902. Mount Hope Presbyterian Cemetery, Lambertville, Hunterdon County.
CURRY, THOMAS Pvt, B, 1st NJ Cav, 1-6-1888. Holy Sepulchre Cemetery, Totowa, Passaic County.
CURTIS, ABRAHAM T. Corp, F, 2nd NJ Cav, [Died of typhoid at Memphis, TN.] 4-10-1864. Mount Holly Cemetery, Mount Holly, Burlington County.
CURTIS, ALBERT ARTHUR Pvt, B, 7th NY State Militia, 6-3-1917. Hillside Cemetery, Scotch Plains, Union County.
CURTIS, AZNEZ R. Pvt, E, 9th KY Cav (CSA), [Captured on Morgan's Ohio raid.] 11-15-1863. Finn's Point National Cemetery, Pennsville, Salem County.
CURTIS, CHARLES Sgt, G, 29th NJ Inf, 1-5-1914. Fairview Cemetery, Fairview, Monmouth County.
CURTIS*, CHARLES H. Corp, D, 14th NJ Inf, DoD Unknown. Friends Cemetery, Wall, Monmouth County.
CURTIS, DAVID N. Pvt, K, 29th NJ Inf, 10-27-1904. Atlantic View Cemetery, Manasquan, Monmouth County.
CURTIS, EDWARD (see: Curtis, Edwin I.) Baptist Church Cemetery, Jacobstown, Burlington County.
CURTIS, EDWIN I. (aka: Curtis, Edward) Pvt, I, 55th PA Inf, 2-5-1868. Baptist Church Cemetery, Jacobstown, Burlington County.
CURTIS*, GEORGE G. Pvt, D, 2nd U.S. Cav, 9-19-1886. Atlantic View Cemetery, Manasquan, Monmouth County.
CURTIS, GEORGE S. Corp, G, 10th NJ Inf, [Died of wounds received 5-29-1864 at Hanover CH, VA.] 6-7-1864. Mercer Cemetery, Trenton, Mercer County.
CURTIS, HENRY H. Pvt, A, 55th NY Inf, [Wounded 5-31-1862 at Fair Oaks, VA.] 6-11-1902. United Methodist Church Cemetery, Little Silver, Monmouth County.
CURTIS, JOHN 3-18-1887. Presbyterian Church Cemetery, Shrewsbury, Monmouth County.
CURTIS, JOHN V. (aka: Crutz, John) Pvt, I, 31st NJ Inf, DoD Unknown. Brown Cemetery, Butler, Morris County.
CURTIS, MORRIS Landsman, U.S. Navy, USS Pensacola, 4-1-1925. New Camden Cemetery, Camden, Camden County.
CURTIS*, MORRIS R. Pvt, H, 34th NJ Inf, 10- -1918. Locust Grove Cemetery, Quakertown, Hunterdon County.
CURTIS, PETER 7-24-1885. Valleau Cemetery, Ridgewood, Bergen County.
CURTIS, RIDGWAY R. Sgt, D, 23rd NJ Inf, 11-18-1911. Methodist-Episcopal Cemetery, Pointville, Burlington County.
CURTIS, SAMUEL Actg Master, U.S. Navy, 1894. Old Baptist Church Cemetery, Manahawkin, Ocean County.
CURTIS, THOMAS Pvt, B, 2nd MI Inf, DoD Unknown. Beverly National Cemetery, Edgewater Park, Burlington County.
CURTIS, THOMAS S. 11-8-1894. Hoboken Cemetery, North Bergen, Hudson County.
CURTIS, WILIIAM A. Sgt, B, 57th NY Inf, 5-22-1865. Cedar Hill Cemetery, East Millstone, Somerset County.
CURTIS, WILLIAM S. Pvt, E, 28th NJ Inf, [Wounded 12-13-1862 at Fredericksburg, VA.] 3-20-1916. Woodlawn Cemetery, Lakewood, Ocean County.
CURTIS, WILLIAM W. Corp, I, 23rd NJ Inf, 10-3-1906. Mount Holly Cemetery, Mount Holly, Burlington County.
CURVEY, PETER Pvt, F, 26th U.S. CT, DoD Unknown. Laurel Grove Cemetery, Totowa, Passaic County.
CUSACK, PATRICK Pvt, C, 7th NJ Inf, 5-28-1882. St. John's Evangelical Church Cemetery, Orange, Essex County.

New Jersey Civil War Burials

CUSACK*, RICHARD S. Sgt, H, 39th NJ Inf, 12-9-1901. St. Mark's Cemetery, Orange, Essex County.
CUSHING, PATRICK Pvt, F, 28th NJ Inf, 8-17-1866. St. Peter's Cemetery, New Brunswick, Middlesex County.
CUSHMAN, HORATIO BENZIL 1-8-1918. New Presbyterian Cemetery, Bound Brook, Somerset County.
CUSHMAN, MARTIN G. Pvt, B, 1st LA Cav (US), 4-4-1903. United Methodist Cemetery, Gladstone, Somerset County.
CUSICK, JOHN Pvt, C, 7th NJ Inf, 9-25-1880. St. Mary's Cemetery, Boonton, Morris County.
CUSICK, THOMAS Pvt, K, 8th NJ Inf, 5-24-1905. Holy Sepulchre Cemetery, East Orange, Essex County.
CUSTER, ROBERT (aka: Guster, Bob) Pvt, C, 8th U.S. CT, 7-16-1915. Mount Peace Cemetery, Lawnside, Camden County.
CUSTIS, EDWARD Pvt, K, 2nd U.S. CT, 3-11-1892. Johnson Cemetery, Camden, Camden County.
CUTHBERT, HENRY CLAY Pvt, Ind Btty, Frishmuth's PA Light Art, 1902. Colestown Cemetery, Cherry Hill, Camden County.
CUTHBERT, WILLIAM S. Pvt, E, 15th NJ Inf, [Died of typhoid at Washington, DC.] 5-14-1865. Laurel Grove Cemetery, Totowa, Passaic County.
CUTLER, ALEXANDER R. Pvt, C, 15th PA Cav, 1-13-1903. Epworth Methodist Cemetery, Palmyra, Burlington County.
CUTLER, CHARLES Pvt, G, 9th NJ Inf, DoD Unknown. Holy Name Cemetery, Jersey City, Hudson County.
CUTLER, CHARLES (see: Kuttler, Charles) Holy Name Cemetery, Jersey City, Hudson County.
CUTLER, CHARLES D. Pvt, D, 1st MA Inf, 12-17-1924. Arlington Cemetery, Kearny, Hudson County.
CUTSHALL, JACOB A. Corp, H, 5th MN Inf, 1927. Berlin Cemetery, Berlin, Camden County.
CUTTER, ALEXANDER S. Seaman, U.S. Navy, USS San Jacinto, DoD Unknown. Presbyterian Church Cemetery, Woodbridge, Middlesex County.
CUZINS, BENJAMIN (aka: Couzzans, Benjamin) Pvt, H, 3rd NJ Cav, 4-12-1912. United Methodist Church Cemetery, Tuckahoe, Cape May County.
CYESTER, LEWIS H. Pvt, OH Light Art 6-26-1937. Evergreen Cemetery, Farmingdale, Monmouth County.
CYPHER, THEODORE Pvt, Btty C, 1st NJ Light Art, DoD Unknown. Prospect Hill Cemetery, Caldwell, Essex County.
CYPHERS, ALPHEUS Pvt, B, 31st NJ Inf, 2-2-1907. Mansfield/Washington Cemetery, Washington, Warren County.
CYPHERS, EDWARD Pvt, A, 5th NJ Inf, [Died of diarrhea at Beverly, NJ.] 9-29-1864. Beverly National Cemetery, Edgewater Park, Burlington County.
CYPHERS, HENRY Pvt, E, 37th NJ Inf, 6-14-1903. Mount Pleasant Cemetery, Newark, Essex County.
CYPHERS, JAMES H. Pvt, C, 15th NJ Inf, 1910. Mansfield/Washington Cemetery, Washington, Warren County.
CYPHERS, NICHOLAS T. Pvt, E, 37th NJ Inf, 9-17-1884. Mount Pleasant Cemetery, Newark, Essex County.
CYPHERS, PETER C. Pvt, M, 1st NJ Cav, 8-28-1871. Presbyterian Church Cemetery, Pleasant Grove, Morris County.
CYPHERS, PHILIP H. Pvt, M, 1st NJ Cav, 5-1-1885. Presbyterian Church Cemetery, Pleasant Grove, Morris County.
CYPHERS, WILLIAM Pvt, G, 31st NJ Inf, 3-12-1905. Pequest Union Cemetery, Great Meadows, Warren County.

Our Brothers Gone Before

D'ENGLESMAN, CORNELIUS Pvt, E, 22nd NJ Inf, 9-11-1879. Cedar Lawn Cemetery, Paterson, Passaic County.
DABB, ALBERT N. Pvt, C, 14th NJ Inf, 10-10-1872. Evergreen Cemetery, Hillside, Union County.
DABBS*, JOHN Pvt, A, 86th NY Inf, [Wounded 7-2-1863 at Gettysburg, PA.] 3-2-1906. Presbyterian Church Cemetery, Rockaway, Morris County.
DABNEY, MANUEL J. (see: Dabney, Maurice J.) St. Mary's Cemetery, Perth Amboy, Middlesex County.
DABNEY, MAURICE J. (aka: Dabney, Manuel J.) Ord Seaman, U.S. Navy, USS Princeton, 7-4-1912. St. Mary's Cemetery, Perth Amboy, Middlesex County.
DACE, EDWIN Pvt, D, 115th IL Inf, 1897. Roadside Cemetery, Manchester Township, Ocean County.
DACKERMANN, LEONARD D. Pvt, D, 2nd NJ Inf, 12-31-1882. Evergreen Cemetery, Hillside, Union County.
DADERLING*, AUGUST Pvt, H, 13th NJ Inf, 11-26-1880. Fairmount Cemetery, Newark, Essex County.
DAEBLER, JOHN W. Pvt, Btty A, 2nd PA Heavy Art, 3-1-1922. 1st Baptist Cemetery, Cape May Court House, Cape May County.
DAENTZER, JOHN (aka: Dentzer, John) Pvt, E, 98th PA Inf, 10-29-1891. Riverside Cemetery, Riverside, Burlington County.
DAFF, J. Pvt, Btty B, 1st MS Light Art (CSA), 7-25-1863. Finn's Point National Cemetery, Pennsville, Salem County.
DAFFNER, BERNARD Pvt, 13th NY Ind Btty 11-2-1915. Riverview Cemetery, Trenton, Mercer County.
DAFT, JOSEPH G. Pvt, C, 14th NJ Inf, 2-11-1882. Evergreen Cemetery, Hillside, Union County.
DAGAN, WILLIAM Pvt, B, 31st NJ Inf, 1903. Phillipsburg Cemetery, Phillipsburg, Warren County.
DAHMER, GEORGE Pvt, D, 31st NJ Inf, 1-4-1894. Elmwood Cemetery, New Brunswick, Middlesex County.
DAIBER*, CHARLES Pvt, H, 9th NJ Inf, 10-23-1895. Fairmount Cemetery, Newark, Essex County.
DAIBER, CHARLES (aka: Diebber, Charles) Pvt, C, 71st NY Inf, 11-13-1906. Soldier's Home Cemetery, Vineland, Cumberland County.
DAILEY, CHRISTOPHER Pvt, K, 35th NJ Inf, [Wounded in action.] 12-3-1896. Assumption R.C. Church Cemetery, New Egypt, Ocean County.
DAILEY, DANIEL Pvt, K, 34th NJ Inf, 1-16-1919. Holy Sepulchre Cemetery, East Orange, Essex County.
DAILEY, JAMES S. Pvt, F, 3rd NJ Inf, 3-8-1903. Baptist Church Cemetery, Palermo, Cape May County.
DAILEY, JOHN Fireman, U.S. Navy, USS Princeton, 7-19-1876. Broadway Cemetery, Broadway, Warren County.
DAILEY, JOHN A. Pvt, E, 14th IN Inf, 2-9-1922. Rosedale Cemetery, Orange, Essex County.
DAILEY*, JONATHAN R. Pvt, E, 10th NJ Inf, 11-10-1903. Batsto/Pleasant Mills Methodist Church Cemetery, Pleasant Mills, Atlantic County.
DAILEY, PATRICK (see: Daly, Patrick) Holy Sepulchre Cemetery, East Orange, Essex County.
DAILEY, PETER Pvt, D, 1st NJ Cav, 11-26-1894. Mercer Cemetery, Trenton, Mercer County.
DAILEY, WILLIAM 7-12-1894. Baptist Church Cemetery, Flemington, Hunterdon County.
DAILEY, WILSON 2nd Lt, K, 73rd IN Inf, 9-24-1909. Mansfield/Washington Cemetery, Washington, Warren County.

New Jersey Civil War Burials

DAILY, JOHN Musc, D, 12th NJ Inf, 9-15-1882. St. Peter's Cemetery, New Brunswick, Middlesex County.

DAILY, PATRICK (see: Doyle, Patrick) St. Paul's Church Cemetery, Burlington, Burlington County.

DAILY, WILLIAM (see: Daly, William P.) Holy Sepulchre Cemetery, East Orange, Essex County.

DAIR, THOMAS Pvt, Btty B, 1st NY Light Art, 1-16-1901. St. Joseph's Cemetery, Keyport, Monmouth County.

DAIRE*, ARMAND P. (aka: Dupont, Eugene) Pvt, H, 123rd NY Inf, 4-29-1935. St. Peter's Cemetery, New Brunswick, Middlesex County.

DAISEY, CHARLES H.C. Pvt, C, 1st DE Cav, 7-18-1904. Cedar Grove Cemetery, Gloucester City, Camden County.

DAISEY, THOMAS M. Pvt, C, 1st DE Cav, 7-28-1929. Cedar Grove Cemetery, Gloucester City, Camden County.

DAISEY, WILLIAM E. Pvt, F, 1st DE Inf, 10-29-1916. Union Cemetery, Gloucester City, Camden County.

DAISY, GEORGE W. Sgt, A, 183rd PA Inf, 4-10-1897. Cedar Grove Cemetery, Gloucester City, Camden County.

DALANE, MARTIN (aka: Delaney, Martin) Pvt, E, 48th PA Inf, 4-1-1894. New Camden Cemetery, Camden, Camden County.

DALE, WILLIAM Pvt, H, 1st NJ Militia, 9-14-1910. Fairmount Cemetery, Newark, Essex County.

DALEY, BERNARD (see: Daly, Bernard) Holy Sepulchre Cemetery, East Orange, Essex County.

DALEY, CHARLES WILLIAM Pvt, K, 13th CT Inf, [Wounded 3-26-1863 at Baton Rouge, LA.] 12-18-1888. Fairmount Cemetery, Newark, Essex County.

DALEY, GEORGE (aka: Baley, George) Pvt, K, 8th U.S. CT, 1-2-1912. Mount Peace Cemetery, Lawnside, Camden County.

DALLAS, BENJAMIN F. Pvt, I, 3rd NJ Militia, 11-16-1904. Riverview Cemetery, Trenton, Mercer County.

DALLAS, EDWARD Y. Pvt, F, 22nd NJ Inf, 10-19-1911. Methodist Church Cemetery, Titusville, Mercer County.

DALLAS, GEORGE M. Pvt, I, 38th NJ Inf, 3-18-1913. Presbyterian Church Cemetery, Pennington, Mercer County.

DALLAS, JAMES K. Pvt, G, 38th NJ Inf, 3-8-1923. Riverview Cemetery, Trenton, Mercer County.

DALLAS, WILLIAM Pvt, A, 214th PA Inf, 3-27-1919. Fairview Cemetery, Westfield, Union County.

DALLEY, EBENEZER S. Pvt, E, 30th NJ Inf, 1903. New Somerville Cemetery, Somerville, Somerset County.

DALLEY, JOHN Pvt, A, 8th NJ Inf, 1908. Sandy Ridge Cemetery, Sandy Ridge, Hunterdon County.

DALLEY, JOHN L. Pvt, E, 30th NJ Inf, 1895. Reformed Church Cemetery, Readington, Hunterdon County.

DALLEY, PETER J. 1914. Reformed Church Cemetery, Readington, Hunterdon County.

DALLUM, GEORGE (see: Datt, George) Siloam Cemetery, Vineland, Cumberland County.

DALLY*, CHARLES C. Capt, C, 7th NJ Inf, 4-3-1926. Presbyterian Church Cemetery, Woodbridge, Middlesex County.

DALLY, THOMAS J. Pvt, A, 7th NJ Inf, 1907. Presbyterian Church Cemetery, Woodbridge, Middlesex County.

DALLY, WILLIAM P. Pvt, I, 8th NY State Militia, 10-4-1886. Alpine Cemetery, Perth Amboy, Middlesex County.

Our Brothers Gone Before

DALRYMPLE, AARON P. Surg, 1st NY Eng 2-26-1894. Presbyterian Church Cemetery, Mount Freedom, Morris County.

DALRYMPLE*, ABRAM Pvt, H, 190th PA Inf, 5-4-1929. Presbyterian Church Cemetery, Bloomsbury, Hunterdon County.

DALRYMPLE, AMOS T. Wagoner, G, 30th NJ Inf, 1872. Rosemont Cemetery, Rosemont, Hunterdon County.

DALRYMPLE, ANDREW J. Farrier, F, 3rd NJ Cav, 4-12-1917. Presbyterian Church Cemetery, Bloomsbury, Hunterdon County.

DALRYMPLE, ASA Pvt, H, 3rd NJ Militia, 10-4-1907. Lower Amwell Cemetery, Headquarters, Hunterdon County.

DALRYMPLE, D. HUDSON Landsman, U.S. Navy, USS Princeton, 4-30-1918. Presbyterian/Methodist-Episcopal Cemetery, Succasunna, Morris County.

DALRYMPLE, ELIAS L. (see: Dalrymple, Elijah) Union Cemetery, Frenchtown, Hunterdon County.

DALRYMPLE, ELIJAH (aka: Dalrymple, Elias L.) Pvt, C, 34th NJ Inf, 11-4-1882. Union Cemetery, Frenchtown, Hunterdon County.

DALRYMPLE, EVAN SMITH Corp, F, 3rd NJ Inf, 5-11-1903. Baptist Church Cemetery, Bridgeton, Cumberland County.

DALRYMPLE, HENRY MELBOURNE Bvt Major, 1st NY Eng 1904. Evergreen Cemetery, Morristown, Morris County.

DALRYMPLE, JACOB B. Corp, F, 9th NJ Inf, 4-6-1915. Union Cemetery, Frenchtown, Hunterdon County.

DALRYMPLE, JACOB D. Pvt, H, 15th NJ Inf, [Wounded in action.] 1932. Union Cemetery, Ringoes, Hunterdon County.

DALRYMPLE, JAMES T. Pvt, C, 31st NJ Inf, 1930. Locust Grove Cemetery, Quakertown, Hunterdon County.

DALRYMPLE, JAMES T. 1907. Presbyterian Church Cemetery, Greenwich, Warren County.

DALRYMPLE, JAMES T. 2-13-1925. Locust Hill Cemetery, Dover, Morris County.

DALRYMPLE, JESSE 2nd Lt, D, 30th NJ Inf, 12-5-1899. New Presbyterian Cemetery, Bound Brook, Somerset County.

DALRYMPLE, JOHN Pvt, G, 38th NJ Inf, 1928. Union Cemetery, Frenchtown, Hunterdon County.

DALRYMPLE, JOHN MARDIN Pvt, I, 31st NJ Inf, 11-23-1917. Lutheran Cemetery, East Stewartsville, Warren County.

DALRYMPLE, JOSEPH S. 1909. Evergreen Cemetery, Clinton, Hunterdon County.

DALRYMPLE, LEVI 10-25-1898. Methodist Church Cemetery, Summerfield, Warren County.

DALRYMPLE, OSBUN L. 7-15-1871. Union Cemetery, Frenchtown, Hunterdon County.

DALRYMPLE, ROBERT T. 5-25-1903. Riverview Cemetery, Trenton, Mercer County.

DALRYMPLE*, SMITH Pvt, G, 95th PA Inf, DoD Unknown. Baptist Church Cemetery, Bridgeton, Cumberland County.

DALRYMPLE, SYLVESTER B. Corp, F, 31st NJ Inf, 1884. Locust Grove Cemetery, Quakertown, Hunterdon County.

DALRYMPLE, THOMSON 1903. Presbyterian Cemetery, West Stewartsville, Warren County.

DALRYMPLE, WILLIAM H. 1908. Union Cemetery, Frenchtown, Hunterdon County.

DALRYMPLE, WILLIAM H. 1924. United Methodist Cemetery, Gladstone, Somerset County.

DALRYMPLE, WILLIAM S. 3-20-1905. Van Liew Cemetery, North Brunswick, Middlesex County.

DALTON, EPHRIAM T. Pvt, H, 34th NJ Inf, 9-15-1885. Finesville Cemetery, Finesville, Warren County.

DALTON, JAMES (see: Arnold, James) Arlington Cemetery, Kearny, Hudson County.

New Jersey Civil War Burials

DALTON, JOHN Pvt, G, 9th NJ Inf, 1-30-1910. Beverly National Cemetery, Edgewater Park, Burlington County.

DALTON*, JOHN Pvt, C, 58th PA Inf, 2-5-1899. Union Cemetery, Milford, Hunterdon County.

DALTON, JOHN Pvt, F, 31st NJ Inf, DoD Unknown. Finesville Cemetery, Finesville, Warren County.

DALTON, JOHN J. Seaman, U.S. Navy, DoD Unknown. Holy Name Cemetery, Jersey City, Hudson County.

DALTON, PETER Pvt, Btty B, 1st NJ Light Art, 11-13-1894. Holy Sepulchre Cemetery, East Orange, Essex County.

DALTON, THOMAS Pvt, G, 37th NY Inf, [Wounded 5-31-1862 at Seven Days battles, VA.] 2-22-1901. Holy Name Cemetery, Jersey City, Hudson County.

DALTON, THOMAS Pvt, I, 15th NY Eng, 1-14-1902. Holy Name Cemetery, Jersey City, Hudson County.

DALTON, WILLIAM F. 1935. Presbyterian Cemetery, Cream Ridge, Monmouth County.

DALTON, WILLIAM H. Pvt, K, 21st NJ Inf, 8-16-1898. Holy Name Cemetery, Jersey City, Hudson County.

DALY, BERNARD (aka: Daley, Bernard) Pvt, A, 71st NY Inf, 3-28-1899. Holy Sepulchre Cemetery, East Orange, Essex County.

DALY, CHARLES W. Pvt, H, 173rd NY Inf, DoD Unknown. Fairmount Cemetery, Newark, Essex County.

DALY, JAMES Pvt, K, 2nd DC Inf, 1890. St. Vincent Martyr Cemetery, Madison, Morris County.

DALY, JAMES DoD Unknown. Old St. Mary's Cemetery, Gloucester City, Camden County.

DALY, JOHN Pvt, Btty G, 7th NY Heavy Art, 1-7-1916. Atlantic City Cemetery, Pleasantville, Atlantic County.

DALY, JOHN Seaman, U.S. Navy, 6-26-1905. Fairmount Cemetery, Newark, Essex County.

DALY, PATRICK Pvt, F, 8th NJ Inf, 5-8-1880. Holy Sepulchre Cemetery, East Orange, Essex County.

DALY, PATRICK (aka: Dailey, Patrick) 1st Lt, F, 33rd NJ Inf, DoD Unknown. Holy Sepulchre Cemetery, East Orange, Essex County.

DALY, THOMAS DoD Unknown. Willow Grove Cemetery, New Brunswick, Middlesex County.

DALY, WILLIAM P. (aka: Daily, William) Musc, I, 39th NJ Inf, 8-11-1909. Holy Sepulchre Cemetery, East Orange, Essex County.

DAM*, CARL JOHN Pvt, A, 12th NJ Inf, 4-6-1903. Palisade Cemetery, North Bergen, Hudson County.

DAMERON, RANDOLPH H. Pvt, M, 16th NC Inf (CSA), [Captured 7-3-1863 at Gettysburg, PA. Died of hemorrhoids.] 9-2-1863. Finn's Point National Cemetery, Pennsville, Salem County.

DAMM, LEWIS (aka: Daum, Lewis L.) Pvt, H, 2nd NJ Inf, 2-27-1862. Woodland Cemetery, Newark, Essex County.

DAMMAN, JOHN B. Pvt, A, 132nd NY Inf, 1-9-1906. Arlington Cemetery, Kearny, Hudson County.

DAMON, HENRY Sgt, F, 6th U.S. Hancock Corps, DoD Unknown. Speer Cemetery, Jersey City, Hudson County.

DAMOND, WILLIAM Pvt, D, 2nd MI Inf, 4-7-1889. Evergreen Cemetery, Hillside, Union County.

DAMPMAN, SAMUEL J. Corp, A, 14th PA Inf, 2-18-1914. Baptist Cemetery, Rio Grande, Cape May County.

DANA*, ROBERT S. Surg, 107th PA Inf 2-1-1915. Greenwood Cemetery, Hamilton, Mercer County.

Our Brothers Gone Before

DANABACKER, FRANCIS (see: Daunbacker, Francis) Bloomfield Cemetery, Bloomfield, Essex County.
DANBERG, LOUIS Seaman, U.S. Navy, DoD Unknown. Holy Name Cemetery, Jersey City, Hudson County.
DANBERRY, ASHER S. Pvt, A, 3rd NJ Cav, 2-16-1866. Amwell Ridge Cemetery, Larisons Corner, Hunterdon County.
DANBERRY, GEORGE W. Sgt, I, 8th NJ Inf, 1-16-1908. Elmwood Cemetery, New Brunswick, Middlesex County.
DANBERRY, JOHN Pvt, B, 9th NJ Inf, 12-13-1910. Mount Hope Presbyterian Cemetery, Lambertville, Hunterdon County.
DANBERRY, LAWRENCE V.S. Pvt, K, 30th NJ Inf, 11-21-1902. Mount Hope Presbyterian Cemetery, Lambertville, Hunterdon County.
DANBERRY, WILLIAM F. Corp, G, 1st NJ Inf, 5-21-1897. Elmwood Cemetery, New Brunswick, Middlesex County.
DANBURY, HENRY M. Pvt, B, 9th NJ Inf, [Wounded in action at Newbern, NC.] 11-2-1871. Elmwood Cemetery, New Brunswick, Middlesex County.
DANBURY*, ISAAC N. Pvt, A, 15th NJ Inf, [Wounded in action.] 2-28-1920. Baptist Church Cemetery, Flemington, Hunterdon County.
DANBURY, WILLIAM Pvt, B, 9th NJ Inf, 3-26-1870. Van Liew Cemetery, North Brunswick, Middlesex County.
DANCER, JOHN Pvt, G, 37th NJ Inf, 10-3-1923. Arlington Cemetery, Kearny, Hudson County.
DANCER, THOMAS L. Pvt, I, 20th MI Inf, [Wounded 5-6-1864 at Wilderness, VA.] 12-2-1911. Bloomfield Cemetery, Bloomfield, Essex County.
DANCER, WILLIAM (SR.) Pvt, G, 11th NJ Inf, 3-4-1863. Presbyterian Cemetery, Allentown, Monmouth County.
DANDY, JAMES H. Maj, 100th NY Inf [Killed in action at Fort Gregg, VA.] 4-2-1865. Alpine Cemetery, Perth Amboy, Middlesex County.
DANENHOWER, CHARLES Pvt, C, 12th NJ Inf, 1928. Harleigh Cemetery, Camden, Camden County.
DANFORTH, CHARLES (JR.) Capt, I, 2nd NJ Inf, [Killed in action at Gaines' Farm, VA.] 6-27-1862. Cedar Lawn Cemetery, Paterson, Passaic County.
DANFORTH, JOHN Maj, 37th NJ Inf 2-20-1886. Evergreen Cemetery, Hillside, Union County.
DANGERFIELD, JOSEPH L. Volunteer, U.S. Sanitary Commission, 1-4-1910. Atlantic City Cemetery, Pleasantville, Atlantic County.
DANGLER, DAVID Pvt, D, 27th NJ Inf, 1-17-1913. Glenwood Cemetery, West Long Branch, Monmouth County.
DANGLER, JAMES H. Pvt, B, 1st NY Cav, [Wounded 9-22-1864 at Fishers Hill, VA.] 3-15-1895. Old 1st Methodist Church Cemetery, West Long Branch, Monmouth County.
DANGLER, JEREMIAH Pvt, A, 38th NJ Inf, 12-28-1892. Methodist-Episcopal Cemetery, Glendola, Monmouth County.
DANGOOD, LEOPOLD (see: Dangood, Louis) Bayview-New York Bay Cemetery, Jersey City, Hudson County.
DANGOOD, LOUIS (aka: Dangood, Leopold) Pvt, D, 170th NY Inf, 3-25-1908. Bayview-New York Bay Cemetery, Jersey City, Hudson County.
DANIEL, PATTON C. Pvt, I, 61st (Pitts') TN Mtd Inf (CSA), 6-27-1863. Finn's Point National Cemetery, Pennsville, Salem County.
DANIELS, AUGUSTUS L. Pvt, K, 7th GA Cav (CSA), 4-19-1865. Finn's Point National Cemetery, Pennsville, Salem County.
DANIELS, EDWARD Pvt, U.S. Marine Corps, 11-21-1929. New Camden Cemetery, Camden, Camden County.

New Jersey Civil War Burials

DANIELS, JAMES E. Pvt, C, 8th FL Inf (CSA), [Captured 7-3-1863 at Gettysburg, PA. Died of disease.] 11-24-1863. Finn's Point National Cemetery, Pennsville, Salem County.

DANIELS, JAMES W. Corp, I, 9th NJ Inf, 10-14-1900. Presbyterian Church Cemetery, Greenwich, Cumberland County.

DANIELS*, JOHN J. Pvt, G, 8th NJ Inf, 11-3-1875. Methodist Cemetery, Malaga, Gloucester County.

DANIELS, JOHN J. 2nd Lt, E, 71st NY Inf, 5-31-1886. Rosedale Cemetery, Orange, Essex County.

DANIELS, LOGAN H. Pvt, H, 5th MO Inf (CSA), 11-15-1863. Finn's Point National Cemetery, Pennsville, Salem County.

DANIELSON, JAMES Pvt, I, 1st NJ Inf, 1922. Grove Church Cemetery, North Bergen, Hudson County.

DANLEY, ANDREW D. Pvt, D, 23rd NJ Inf, 4-27-1906. United Methodist Church Cemetery, Jacobstown, Burlington County.

DANLEY, EDWARD Pvt, B, 12th NJ Inf, [Wounded in action.] 3-28-1913. Brotherhood Cemetery, Hainesport, Burlington County.

DANLEY*, LEWIS (aka: Dannelly, Lewis) Pvt, D, 2nd NJ Cav, 12-23-1898. Baptist Cemetery, Pemberton, Burlington County.

DANLEY, SAMUEL B. Sgt, B, 15th NJ Inf, [Wounded in action at Wilderness, VA.] 1916. Hazen Cemetery, Hazen, Warren County.

DANLEY, WILLIAM H. Pvt, D, 23rd NJ Inf, 2-15-1873. Methodist-Episcopal Cemetery, Pointville, Burlington County.

DANNEBERGER*, ANTHONY J. Pvt, A, 2nd NJ Inf, 4-18-1915. Fairmount Cemetery, Newark, Essex County.

DANNEBERGER, JOHN J. Pvt, H, 4th NJ Inf, 2-27-1907. Rosedale Cemetery, Linden, Union County.

DANNELLY, LEWIS (see: Danley, Lewis) Baptist Cemetery, Pemberton, Burlington County.

DANNER, CHARLES L. Pvt, C, 30th NJ Inf, 9-3-1883. Rahway Cemetery, Rahway, Union County.

DANNER, WILLIAM EDWARD Pvt, C, 42nd MS Inf (CSA), 1-30-1864. Finn's Point National Cemetery, Pennsville, Salem County.

DANNON, CHRISTY Seaman, U.S. Navy, DoD Unknown. St. James Cemetery, Woodbridge, Middlesex County.

DANSBURY*, CHARLES A. Pvt, E, 1st NJ Cav, 8-22-1918. Mercer Cemetery, Trenton, Mercer County.

DANSBURY, JAMES DoD Unknown. Riverview Cemetery, Trenton, Mercer County.

DANSBURY, SAMUEL W. Pvt, B, PA Emerg NJ Militia, 10-14-1935. Greenwood Cemetery, Hamilton, Mercer County.

DANTZ, JOHN C. Pvt, F, 1st NJ Cav, 9-17-1923. Columbus Cemetery, Columbus, Burlington County.

DANZENBAKER, LEWIS H. Pvt, D, 10th NJ Inf, [Died of wounds received 6-1-1864 at Cold Harbor, VA.] 6-12-1864. Baptist Church Cemetery, Bridgeton, Cumberland County.

DARBY, JOHN (see: Darby, William) Miller's Cemetery, New Gretna, Burlington County.

DARBY*, WILLIAM (aka: Darby, John) Pvt, D, 162nd NY Inf, 2-27-1901. Miller's Cemetery, New Gretna, Burlington County.

DARCEY, ANDREW W. Pvt, B, 35th NJ Inf, 11-9-1895. Fairmount Cemetery, Newark, Essex County.

DARCY, JOHN Pvt, A, 35th NJ Inf, 1-7-1890. St. John's Evangelical Church Cemetery, Orange, Essex County.

DARCY, PATRICK Fireman, U.S. Navy, USS Hartford, 2-2-1919. St. John's Evangelical Church Cemetery, Orange, Essex County.

Our Brothers Gone Before

DARDEN, WILLIAM S. Pvt, H, 16th MS Inf (CSA), 9-15-1863. Finn's Point National Cemetery, Pennsville, Salem County.
DARE, AUGUSTUS Pvt, A, 8th NJ Inf, 12-6-1878. Methodist Cemetery, Haddonfield, Camden County.
DARE, CHARLES F. Hosp Steward, 118th PA Inf 5-16-1918. Presbyterian Church Cemetery, Bridgeton, Cumberland County.
DARE, CHARLES H. Pvt, G, 24th NJ Inf, 11-1-1918. Presbyterian Church Cemetery, Bridgeton, Cumberland County.
DARE, DONALD DoD Unknown. Friends Cemetery, Greenwich, Cumberland County.
DARE, EDMUND I. DoD Unknown. Cohansey Baptist Church Cemetery, Bowentown, Cumberland County.
DARE, EPHRIAM H. Drum Major, 10th NJ Inf 1910. 1st United Methodist Church Cemetery, Bridgeton, Cumberland County.
DARE, HENRY C. Pvt, H, 24th NJ Inf, 1-20-1911. Presbyterian Church Cemetery, Bridgeton, Cumberland County.
DARE, ISAAC M. Pvt, D, 10th NJ Inf, 3-22-1880. Cohansey Baptist Church Cemetery, Bowentown, Cumberland County.
DARE, JACOB Pvt, B, 2nd NJ Inf, 1921. Mount Pleasant Cemetery, Millville, Cumberland County.
DARE, SAMUEL M. DoD Unknown. Baptist Church Cemetery, Bridgeton, Cumberland County.
DARE, THEODORE A. Sgt, H, 3rd NJ Cav, 11-5-1921. Presbyterian Church Cemetery, Bridgeton, Cumberland County.
DARE, THOMAS Pvt, B, 10th NJ Inf, 11-3-1922. Siloam Cemetery, Vineland, Cumberland County.
DARE, WESLEY Pvt, H, 10th NJ Inf, 1-31-1906. New Camden Cemetery, Camden, Camden County.
DARE, WESLEY S. Pvt, E, 47th IL Inf, 3-20-1904. United Methodist Church Cemetery, Willow Grove, Salem County.
DARE, WILLIAM C. Pvt, G, 24th NJ Inf, 6-10-1902. Presbyterian Church Cemetery, Upper Deerfield, Cumberland County.
DARE, ZEPHANIAH W. Landsman, U.S. Navy, USS Princeton, 4-4-1904. United Methodist Church Cemetery, Willow Grove, Salem County.
DARGLE, GEORGE E. (aka: Diegle, George) Pvt, F, 6th NY Inf, 2-19-1917. St. Bernard's Cemetery, Bridgewater, Somerset County.
DARIGHTY, JOHN H. (see: Dougherty, John H.) Finn's Point National Cemetery, Pennsville, Salem County.
DARL, ISAAC Pvt, E, 4th DE Inf, 4-2-1907. Riverview Cemetery, Trenton, Mercer County.
DARLING, ANDREW (see: Garling, Andrew) Holy Name Cemetery, Jersey City, Hudson County.
DARLING, JAMES Pvt, H, 118th PA Inf, 1925. Evergreen Cemetery, Morristown, Morris County.
DARLING, JAMES A. Pvt, G, 2nd NH Inf, 9-14-1916. Siloam Cemetery, Vineland, Cumberland County.
DARLINGTON, EDWARD Sgt, K, 24th NJ Inf, 12-10-1907. Green Cemetery, Woodbury, Gloucester County.
DARLINGTON, JAMES H. Pvt, C, 34th NJ Inf, 3-16-1907. United Methodist Church Cemetery, Alloway, Salem County.
DARLINGTON, JOHN Wagoner, Btty F, 6th NY Heavy Art, 1906. Soldier's Home Cemetery, Vineland, Cumberland County.
DARNELL, JOHN W. Pvt, H, 28th NJ Inf, 6-1-1906. Evergreen Cemetery, Camden, Camden County.
DARR, ASA J.H. Pvt, C, 17th NY Inf, 4-26-1916. Bayview-New York Bay Cemetery, Jersey City, Hudson County.

New Jersey Civil War Burials

DARRAGH*, JOHN K. (aka: Darrah, John) Corp, A, 3rd NJ Cav, [Wounded in action.] 11-13-1920. Greenwood Cemetery, Boonton, Morris County.

DARRAH, CHARLES Pvt, E, 104th PA Inf, 3-3-1904. Riverview Cemetery, Trenton, Mercer County.

DARRAH, JOHN (see: Darragh, John K.) Greenwood Cemetery, Boonton, Morris County.

DARRAH, SOLOMON Sgt, H, 6th U.S. CT, 2-9-1897. Riverview Cemetery, Trenton, Mercer County.

DARRELL, VANDELINE (see: Dentel, Wendeline) St. Francis Cemetery, Trenton, Mercer County.

DARRESS, JOHN CHARLES Pvt, A, 37th NJ Inf, 11-30-1920. Mount Hebron Cemetery, Montclair, Essex County.

DARROW, SAMUEL G. Pvt, D, 1st NJ Cav, [Died of diarrhea at City Point, VA.] 10-26-1864. St. John's United Methodist Cemetery, Turnersville, Gloucester County.

DARWOOD, WILLIAM C. Pvt, F, 23rd NJ Inf, 1-23-1916. Baptist Cemetery, Vincentown, Burlington County.

DASEY, SIMON Pvt, I, 6th U.S. Inf, DoD Unknown. St. John's Cemetery, Hamilton, Mercer County.

DASHIELL, ALFRED HENRY Chaplain, 57th MA Inf 2-15-1908. Woodlawn Cemetery, Lakewood, Ocean County.

DASHIELL, ROBERT (see: Deshields, Robert H.) Jordan Lawn Cemetery, Pennsauken, Camden County.

DATOW, WILLIAM F. Pvt, U.S. Marine Corps, USS Illinois, 11-23-1891. Presbyterian Church Cemetery, Hanover, Morris County.

DATT, GEORGE (aka: Dallum, George) Musc, K, 210th PA Inf, 5-30-1904. Siloam Cemetery, Vineland, Cumberland County.

DAUB, JOHN G. Sgt, D, 12th PA Cav, 4-19-1886. Phillipsburg Cemetery, Phillipsburg, Warren County.

DAUBMAN, JULIUS N. 2-24-1926. New Camden Cemetery, Camden, Camden County.

DAUBNER, JOHN Pvt, A, 1st NJ Inf, [Wounded in action.] 9-30-1913. Mount Olivet Cemetery, Newark, Essex County.

DAUGHERTY, PATRICK Pvt, D, 49th NY Inf, [Died of disease.] 12-1-1862. Fairmount Cemetery, Newark, Essex County.

DAUGHERTY, WILLIAM Pvt, E, 2nd (Ashby's) TN Cav (CSA), 7-23-1862. Finn's Point National Cemetery, Pennsville, Salem County.

DAUGHTRY, REDDICK Pvt, I, 20th NC Inf (CSA), [Wounded 6-27-1862 at Gaines' Mill, VA. Captured 7-3-1863 at Gettysburg, PA.] 10-5-1863. Finn's Point National Cemetery, Pennsville, Salem County.

DAUM, LEWIS L. (see: Damm, Lewis) Woodland Cemetery, Newark, Essex County.

DAUM, PHILIP Pvt, H, 2nd NJ Inf, [Missing in action at Wilderness, VA. Supposed dead.] 5-6-1864. Federated Baptist Church Cemetery, Livingston, Essex County.

DAUNBACKER, FRANCIS (aka: Danabacker, Francis) 2nd Lt, F, 26th NJ Inf, 5-8-1912. Bloomfield Cemetery, Bloomfield, Essex County.

DAUSCH*, JOHN BAPTISTE Musc, 12th U.S. Inf Band 1911. Bayview-New York Bay Cemetery, Jersey City, Hudson County.

DAUTHADAY, JAMES Pvt, B, 34th NJ Inf, 4-2-1889. Riverview Cemetery, Trenton, Mercer County.

DAVENBURG, JEROME (see: Devinsburg, Jerome) Johnson Cemetery, Camden, Camden County.

DAVENPORT*, CHARLES Pvt, F, 15th NJ Inf, 1-15-1911. Presbyterian/Methodist-Episcopal Cemetery, Succasunna, Morris County.

DAVENPORT, CHARLES W. Pvt, E, 35th GA Inf (CSA), [Captured 7-3-1863 at Gettysburg, PA. Died of diarrhea.] 9-22-1863. Finn's Point National Cemetery, Pennsville, Salem County.

DAVENPORT*, EDWARD Corp, I, 39th NJ Inf, 1924. Locust Hill Cemetery, Dover, Morris County.

DAVENPORT*, GEORGE W. Pvt, D, 26th NJ Inf, 9-1-1926. Prospect Hill Cemetery, Caldwell, Essex County.

DAVENPORT*, HENRY H. Pvt, F, 82nd PA Inf, 1916. New Camden Cemetery, Camden, Camden County.

DAVENPORT, HUDSON Pvt, G, 27th NJ Inf, 2-22-1911. Presbyterian/Methodist-Episcopal Cemetery, Succasunna, Morris County.

DAVENPORT, JAMES Pvt, A, 1st NJ Cav, 1926. Arlington Cemetery, Kearny, Hudson County.

DAVENPORT, JAMES A. Pvt, I, 8th LA Inf (CSA), [Captured 7-4-1863 at South Mountain, MD. Died of typhoid.] 1-29-1864. Finn's Point National Cemetery, Pennsville, Salem County.

DAVENPORT, JOHN Pvt, B, 39th NJ Inf, DoD Unknown. Old Butler Cemetery, Butler, Morris County.

DAVENPORT, JOHN R. Sgt, H, 84th NY Inf, [Wounded 7-1-1863 at Gettysburg, PA.] 1-23-1914. Arlington Cemetery, Kearny, Hudson County.

DAVENPORT, JOHN W. Pvt, I, 2nd NJ Cav, 1928. Locust Grove Cemetery, Quakertown, Hunterdon County.

DAVENPORT, LORENZO D. Sgt, K, 15th NJ Inf, 9-8-1919. Holland Cemetery, Holland, Morris County.

DAVENPORT, PETER C. 5-7-1905. Van Liew Cemetery, North Brunswick, Middlesex County.

DAVENPORT, SAMUEL M. Pvt, G, 28th NJ Inf, DoD Unknown. Cedar Grove Cemetery, Gloucester City, Camden County.

DAVENPORT, WILLIAM H. Pvt, K, 1st NJ Cav, 2-5-1929. Presbyterian/Methodist-Episcopal Cemetery, Succasunna, Morris County.

DAVENPORT, WILLIAM H. Pvt, G, 27th NJ Inf, 2-15-1892. 1st Reformed Church Cemetery, Pompton Plains, Morris County.

DAVENPORT, WILLIAM H. Pvt, K, 25th NJ Inf, 1-29-1907. Laurel Grove Cemetery, Totowa, Passaic County.

DAVENPORT, WILLIAM R. Pvt, E, 26th MS Inf (CSA), 9-23-1863. Finn's Point National Cemetery, Pennsville, Salem County.

DAVENPORT, WILLIAM S. Sgt, A, 2nd NJ Inf, 12-24-1884. Evergreen Cemetery, Hillside, Union County.

DAVEY, FREDERICK 2-15-1900. New Presbyterian Cemetery, Bound Brook, Somerset County.

DAVEY, FREDERICK W. 9-2-1899. New Presbyterian Cemetery, Bound Brook, Somerset County.

DAVID, CHARLES Pvt, D, 39th NJ Inf, 5-22-1913. St. Peter's Cemetery, New Brunswick, Middlesex County.

DAVIDSON, EDWARD Pvt, B, 34th NY Inf, [Wounded 9-17-1862 at Antietam, MD.] 7-15-1920. Evergreen Cemetery, Hillside, Union County.

DAVIDSON, ENOS A. Pvt, D, 28th NJ Inf, 6-16-1866. 1st Methodist-Episcopal Cemetery, New Brunswick, Middlesex County.

DAVIDSON, GEORGE Pvt, B, 28th NJ Inf, [Wounded 12-13-1862 at Fredericksburg, VA.] 5-6-1889. Dayton Cemetery, Dayton, Middlesex County.

DAVIDSON*, GEORGE Pvt, K, 5th NY Inf, [Wounded 8-30-1862 at 2nd Bull Run, VA.] 1915. Siloam Cemetery, Vineland, Cumberland County.

DAVIDSON, GEORGE W. Pvt, I, 2nd NJ Inf, [Killed in action at Gaines' Farm, VA.] 6-27-1862. Cedar Lawn Cemetery, Paterson, Passaic County.

New Jersey Civil War Burials

DAVIDSON, JAMES Corp, H, 14th NJ Inf, [Wounded in action.] 2-22-1896. Dayton Cemetery, Dayton, Middlesex County.

DAVIDSON, JAMES 7-10-1866. Mansfield/Washington Cemetery, Washington, Warren County.

DAVIDSON, JOHN 1st Lt, Btty K, 6th NY Heavy Art, 6-5-1916. Fairmount Cemetery, Newark, Essex County.

DAVIDSON, JOHN Pvt, I, 12th NY State Militia, 4-14-1911. Evergreen Cemetery, Hillside, Union County.

DAVIDSON, JOHN W.E. Hosp Stew, 26th NJ Inf 11-27-1894. Rosedale Cemetery, Orange, Essex County.

DAVIDSON, JOSIAH KING Pvt, K, 2nd DC Inf, 3-2-1918. Boonton Cemetery, Boonton, Morris County.

DAVIDSON, JOSIAH STEWART Pvt, F, 27th PA Militia, DoD Unknown. Mansfield/Washington Cemetery, Washington, Warren County.

DAVIDSON, PETER Pvt, G, 2nd PA Cav, 3-22-1899. Mansfield/Washington Cemetery, Washington, Warren County.

DAVIDSON, SAMUEL Pvt, G, 6th NJ Inf, 4-6-1905. Baptist Church Cemetery, Haddonfield, Camden County.

DAVIDSON, T.M. Pvt, I, 14th AL Inf (CSA), 5-3-1864. Finn's Point National Cemetery, Pennsville, Salem County.

DAVIDSON, WALTER D. Pvt, A, 5th NJ Inf, [Died of apoplexy at Trenton, NJ.] 9-11-1862. Riverview Cemetery, Trenton, Mercer County.

DAVIDSON, WILLIAM Pvt, G, 28th NJ Inf, 12-22-1887. Mount Pleasant Cemetery, Millville, Cumberland County.

DAVIES, ALBERT E. Pvt, B, 29th NJ Inf, 1930. Siloam Cemetery, Vineland, Cumberland County.

DAVIES, GEORGE W. 1st Lt, RQM, 32nd NY Inf DoD Unknown. Elmwood Cemetery, New Brunswick, Middlesex County.

DAVIES, RICHARD O. Pvt, A, 8th NY State Militia, 1892. New Presbyterian Cemetery, Bound Brook, Somerset County.

DAVIES, SYDNEY A. 12-17-1924. Cedar Lawn Cemetery, Paterson, Passaic County.

DAVIES, THOMAS Seaman, U.S. Navy, 6-29-1910. Methodist Church Cemetery, Heislerville, Cumberland County.

DAVIES, WILLIAM C. (aka: Davis, William C.) Pvt, I, 22nd NJ Inf, 9-4-1917. Brookside Cemetery, Englewood, Bergen County.

DAVIS, AARON WILLIAMSON Sgt, G, 31st NJ Inf, 1911. Hazen Cemetery, Hazen, Warren County.

DAVIS, ADAM T. Pvt, G, 71st NY Inf, 6-1-1891. Evergreen Cemetery, Camden, Camden County.

DAVIS, ALBERT Pvt, F, 24th NJ Inf, 2-3-1907. 7th Day Baptist Church Cemetery, Shiloh, Cumberland County.

DAVIS*, ALBERT A. Corp, H, 10th NJ Inf, 2-28-1870. St. Paul's United Methodist Church Cemetery, Paulsboro, Gloucester County.

DAVIS, ALEXANDER W. Corp, A, 3rd NJ Inf, [Wounded in action.] 6-12-1902. Methodist Cemetery, Mantua, Gloucester County.

DAVIS, ALFRED T. Coal Heaver, U.S. Navy, USS Roanoke, 4-13-1936. Rosedale Cemetery, Orange, Essex County.

DAVIS, ANDREW S. Capt, H, 8th NJ Inf, [Died of wounds received 7-2-1863 at Gettysburg, PA.] 7-29-1863. Fairmount Cemetery, Newark, Essex County.

DAVIS, ARTHUR H. Pvt, B, 1st NY Cav, 7-16-1896. Fields Family Cemetery, Eatontown, Monmouth County.

DAVIS, AUGUSTUS Pvt, E, 13th NJ Inf, 11-21-1883. Fairmount Cemetery, Newark, Essex County.

Our Brothers Gone Before

DAVIS, BENJAMIN Pvt, K, 36th U.S. CT, 7-30-1916. Fairmount Cemetery, Newark, Essex County.
DAVIS, BENJAMIN C. Pvt, G, 28th NJ Inf, [Wounded 12-13-1862 at Fredericksburg, VA.] 9-19-1925. Eglington Cemetery, Clarksboro, Gloucester County.
DAVIS, BENJAMIN W. 4-10-1876. Presbyterian Church Cemetery, Lawrenceville, Mercer County.
DAVIS, BENJAMIN W. Pvt, H, 21st NJ Inf, [Wounded in action.] 4-10-1867. Riverview Cemetery, Trenton, Mercer County.
DAVIS, CHARLES Pvt, B, 4th NJ Inf, 10-10-1888. United Methodist Church Cemetery, Jacobstown, Burlington County.
DAVIS, CHARLES Pvt, F, 40th NJ Inf, 8-14-1898. Greenwood Cemetery, Hamilton, Mercer County.
DAVIS, CHARLES EDWARD LAW BALDWIN Cadet, U.S.M.A., 6-1-1925. Hillside Cemetery, Scotch Plains, Union County.
DAVIS, CHARLES H. Pvt, D, 24th NJ Inf, [Died of debility at Falmouth, VA.] 3-16-1863. Methodist-Episcopal Church Cemetery, Aura, Gloucester County.
DAVIS, CHARLES H. Pvt, C, 7th NJ Inf, 8-23-1915. Evergreen Cemetery, Morristown, Morris County.
DAVIS, CHARLES W. Pvt, G, 4th NJ Inf, 11-4-1880. Friends Hicksite Cemetery, Woodbury, Gloucester County.
DAVIS, COLLINS K. Capt, K, 3rd MI Inf, 3-29-1867. Baptist Church Cemetery, Haddonfield, Camden County.
DAVIS, DANIEL Pvt, K, 13th SC Inf (CSA), [Captured 7-5-1863 at Gettysburg, PA. Died of lung inflammation.] 11-26-1863. Finn's Point National Cemetery, Pennsville, Salem County.
DAVIS, DANIEL Pvt, F, 7th NJ Inf, 1-25-1914. Presbyterian Church Cemetery, Greenwich, Warren County.
DAVIS, DANIEL G. Pvt, K, 2nd NJ Inf, 4-26-1932. Hillcrest Memorial Park Cemetery, Hurffville, Gloucester County.
DAVIS, DAVID 4-16-1889. 7th Day Baptist Church Cemetery, Shiloh, Cumberland County.
DAVIS, DAVID Pvt, L, 27th NJ Inf, 3-25-1896. Fairmount Cemetery, Newark, Essex County.
DAVIS, DAVID Pvt, G, 4th NJ Militia, 2-23-1887. Schamp's Family Cemetery, Readington, Hunterdon County.
DAVIS, DAVID P. Pvt, F, 5th NY Inf, 3-29-1901. Bayview-New York Bay Cemetery, Jersey City, Hudson County.
DAVIS, DAVID R. Pvt, L, 1st NJ Cav, DoD Unknown. Elmwood Cemetery, New Brunswick, Middlesex County.
DAVIS, E. 1st Lt, Jackson's Bttn VA Inf (CSA) 12-25-1864. Finn's Point National Cemetery, Pennsville, Salem County.
DAVIS, EBENEZER W. Maj, 15th NJ Inf [Wounded 6-3-1864 at Cold Harbor, VA; 9-22-1864 at Fisher's Hill, VA; 10-19-1864 at Cedar Creek, VA.] 5-29-1907. Clinton Cemetery, Irvington, Essex County.
DAVIS, EDMUND TOMLINSON 3-5-1920. 7th Day Baptist Church Cemetery, Shiloh, Cumberland County.
DAVIS, EDWARD CHARLES Pvt, K, 2nd NJ Cav, [Wounded 1-2/3-1865 at Egypt Station, MS.] 3-31-1923. Oddfellows Cemetery, Burlington, Burlington County.
DAVIS, EDWARD H. 12-24-1935. Greenwood Cemetery, Hamilton, Mercer County.
DAVIS, EDWARD S. Pvt, C, 24th NJ Inf, 8-24-1914. 1st Baptist Church Cemetery, Woodstown, Salem County.
DAVIS, EDWIN PAGE Bvt Brig Gen, U.S. Volunteers, [Colonel, 153rd New York Infantry.] 10-22-1890. Baptist Church Cemetery, Haddonfield, Camden County.

New Jersey Civil War Burials

DAVIS, ELIJAH Pvt, B, 118th PA Inf, 9-15-1870. Union Cemetery, Clarkstown, Atlantic County.

DAVIS, ELIJAH T. Corp, F, 58th PA Inf, 7-13-1881. Old Camden Cemetery, Camden, Camden County.

DAVIS, ELWOOD P. Pvt, F, 12th NJ Inf, 1-24-1905. Methodist Cemetery, Woodstown, Salem County.

DAVIS, ERASTUS C. Corp, C, 6th NH Inf, 11-19-1915. Fairmount Cemetery, Newark, Essex County.

DAVIS*, ETHELBERT Sgt, E, 12th NJ Inf, 11-22-1907. Arlington Cemetery, Kearny, Hudson County.

DAVIS, FRANCIS Pvt, C, 22nd U.S. CT, 7-24-1885. Fairmount Cemetery, Newark, Essex County.

DAVIS, FRANCIS Pvt, E, 1st IL Cav, 1922. Methodist-Episcopal Church Cemetery, Aura, Gloucester County.

DAVIS, FRANCIS H. Pvt, Btty E, 2nd PA Heavy Art, DoD Unknown. Old Stone Church Cemetery, Fairton, Cumberland County.

DAVIS, FREDERICK Pvt, H, 8th NJ Inf, [Wounded in action.] 8-29-1906. Fairmount Cemetery, Newark, Essex County.

DAVIS, FREDERICK Pvt, F, 22nd U.S. CT, 6-23-1917. Mount Pisgah Cemetery, Elsinboro, Salem County.

DAVIS, FREDERICK C. 1st Lt, C, 5th VT Inf, 8-19-1924. Harmony Methodist-Episcopal Church Cemetery, Piney Hollow, Gloucester County.

DAVIS, GABRIEL L. Pvt, B, 2nd Bttn NC Inf (CSA), [Captured 7-3-1863 at Gettysburg, PA. Died of enteritis.] 8-11-1863. Finn's Point National Cemetery, Pennsville, Salem County.

DAVIS, GARRET W. Pvt, D, 39th NJ Inf, 10-30-1873. Flagtown Dutch Reformed Cemetery, Frankfort, Somerset County.

DAVIS, GEORGE Seaman, U.S. Navy, [U.S. receiving ship.] 2-6-1895. Evergreen Cemetery, Hillside, Union County.

DAVIS, GEORGE Pvt, D, 11th NJ Inf, 9-13-1895. Belvidere/Catholic Cemetery, Belvidere, Warren County.

DAVIS, GEORGE (see: Oakley, George W.) Methodist Church Cemetery, Springfield, Union County.

DAVIS, GEORGE B. Landsman, U.S. Navy, USS Mattabessett, 10-3-1899. Bay View Cemetery, Leonardo, Monmouth County.

DAVIS, GEORGE M. Pvt, M, 1st NJ Cav, 1906. New Camden Cemetery, Camden, Camden County.

DAVIS, GEORGE W. Pvt, F, 9th VA Inf (CSA), [Captured 7-3-1863 at Gettysburg, PA. Died of smallpox.] 11-17-1863. Finn's Point National Cemetery, Pennsville, Salem County.

DAVIS, GEORGE W. Pvt, A, 186th PA Inf, 8-15-1901. Presbyterian Church Cemetery, Mays Landing, Atlantic County.

DAVIS, GEORGE Y. Pvt, E, 24th NJ Inf, 7-16-1925. Union Cemetery, Gloucester City, Camden County.

DAVIS, GIDEON B. Pvt, A, 3rd NJ Cav, 3-18-1888. Holcomb-Riverview Cemetery, Lambertville, Hunterdon County.

DAVIS, GOMER S. Pvt, M, 11th PA Cav, 2-10-1919. Riverview Cemetery, Trenton, Mercer County.

DAVIS, GRIFFITH Pvt, H, 129th PA Inf, 3-10-1925. Baptist Church Cemetery, Haddonfield, Camden County.

DAVIS, HARRISON Musc, D, 22nd WI Inf, 3-25-1875. 7th Day Baptist Church Cemetery, Shiloh, Cumberland County.

DAVIS, HARRISON WELLS Pvt, A, 24th NJ Inf, 1926. 7th Day Baptist Church Cemetery, Shiloh, Cumberland County.

Our Brothers Gone Before

DAVIS, HENRY ALBERT Colored Cook, U.S. Navy, 1-7-1934. Mount Peace Cemetery, Lawnside, Camden County.
DAVIS, HENRY H. 1st Sgt, K, 11th ME Inf, 6-19-1913. Rosedale Cemetery, Orange, Essex County.
DAVIS*, HENRY N. Corp, A, 57th NY Inf, 3-28-1907. Van Liew Cemetery, North Brunswick, Middlesex County.
DAVIS, HEZEKIAH H. Pvt, C, 42nd MS Inf (CSA), 11-3-1863. Finn's Point National Cemetery, Pennsville, Salem County.
DAVIS, HORATIO H. Pvt, H, 30th NJ Inf, 4-23-1886. Presbyterian Church Cemetery, Rockaway, Morris County.
DAVIS*, HOWELL R. Pvt, G, 77th PA Inf, DoD Unknown. Cedar Grove Cemetery, Gloucester City, Camden County.
DAVIS, HUDSON B. Pvt, B, 31st IL Inf, DoD Unknown. Presbyterian Church Cemetery, Bridgeton, Cumberland County.
DAVIS, ISAAC Pvt, A, 175th PA Inf, 1920. Soldier's Home Cemetery, Vineland, Cumberland County.
DAVIS, ISAAC Corp, A, 2nd NJ Militia, DoD Unknown. 7th Day Baptist Church Cemetery, Shiloh, Cumberland County.
DAVIS, ISAAC C. Corp, E, 30th NJ Inf, 10-15-1911. New Dutch Reformed/Neshanic Cemetery, Neshanic, Somerset County.
DAVIS*, ISAAC L. Pvt, I, 156th NY Inf, [Wounded 4-12-1863 at Fort Bisland, LA.] 1-2-1874. Macphelah Cemetery, North Bergen, Hudson County.
DAVIS, J.G. Pvt, C, 5th U.S. Cav, DoD Unknown. Holy Sepulchre Cemetery, Totowa, Passaic County.
DAVIS, JAMES A. Landsman, U.S. Navy, USS Isonomia, 3-20-1897. Fairmount Cemetery, Newark, Essex County.
DAVIS, JAMES L. Pvt, I, 215th PA Inf, 4-26-1900. New Camden Cemetery, Camden, Camden County.
DAVIS, JAMES S.D. Pvt, H, 26th NJ Inf, 10-24-1878. Bloomfield Cemetery, Bloomfield, Essex County.
DAVIS, JAMES W. Pvt, D, 40th NJ Inf, 11-23-1912. Evergreen Cemetery, Camden, Camden County.
DAVIS, JAMES W. Pvt, B, 26th NJ Inf, 11-22-1904. Willow Grove Cemetery, New Brunswick, Middlesex County.
DAVIS, JEREMIAH A. Pvt, G, 24th NJ Inf, 5-3-1892. 7th Day Baptist Church Cemetery, Shiloh, Cumberland County.
DAVIS, JEREMIAH A. 1-27-1885. Baptist Cemetery, Salem, Salem County.
DAVIS, JESSE C. Sgt, G, 24th NJ Inf, DoD Unknown. Baptist Church Cemetery, Bridgeton, Cumberland County.
DAVIS, JOHN Pvt, G, 22nd U.S. CT, 12-26-1916. Mount Peace Cemetery, Lawnside, Camden County.
DAVIS, JOHN 1927. Methodist Church Cemetery, Goshen, Cape May County.
DAVIS, JOHN Pvt, F, 5th NJ Inf, 1-23-1899. Old Stone Church Cemetery, Fairton, Cumberland County.
DAVIS, JOHN Pvt, I, 40th NJ Inf, 2-22-1904. Flower Hill Cemetery, North Bergen, Hudson County.
DAVIS, JOHN Pvt, K, 162nd NY Inf, [Wounded 5-27-1863 at Port Hudson, LA.] 10-21-1924. Flower Hill Cemetery, North Bergen, Hudson County.
DAVIS, JOHN Pvt, D, 23rd NJ Inf, 6-1-1901. Methodist-Episcopal Cemetery, Pointville, Burlington County.
DAVIS, JOHN 2-19-1867. Presbyterian Church Cemetery, Lawrenceville, Mercer County.
DAVIS, JOHN Sgt, E, 62nd NY Inf, DoD Unknown. Holy Name Cemetery, Jersey City, Hudson County.

New Jersey Civil War Burials

DAVIS, JOHN B. Pvt, C, 1st CT Cav, 10-3-1916. Fairview Cemetery, Wantage, Sussex County.
DAVIS, JOHN B. Pvt, I, 96th PA Inf, [Wounded 9-14-1862 at Cramptons Pass, MD.] 8-6-1922. Evergreen Cemetery, Camden, Camden County.
DAVIS, JOHN H. Pvt, D, 25th ME Inf, 11-7-1907. Siloam Cemetery, Vineland, Cumberland County.
DAVIS, JOHN H. Pvt, K, 18th U.S. CT, 5-16-1911. Atlantic City Cemetery, Pleasantville, Atlantic County.
DAVIS, JOHN HARRISON 1-14-1905. Fairview Cemetery, Fairview, Monmouth County.
DAVIS, JOHN J. Pvt, D, 33rd NJ Inf, 1909. Presbyterian/Methodist-Episcopal Cemetery, Succasunna, Morris County.
DAVIS*, JOHN L. Corp, A, Thomas' Legion NC Inf (CSA), 9-12-1863. Finn's Point National Cemetery, Pennsville, Salem County.
DAVIS*, JOHN N. Pvt, I, 9th NJ Inf, 4-26-1899. Presbyterian Church Cemetery, Bridgeton, Cumberland County.
DAVIS, JOHN N. Pvt, B, 24th NJ Inf, DoD Unknown. Overlook Cemetery, Bridgeton, Cumberland County.
DAVIS, JOHN R. VA (CSA) 1-2-1906. Riverside Cemetery, Toms River, Ocean County.
DAVIS, JOHN W. Pvt, K, 10th NJ Inf, 1-7-1930. Monument Cemetery, Edgewater Park, Burlington County.
DAVIS, JOHN W. Pvt, A, 26th NJ Inf, 3-21-1892. Fairmount Cemetery, Newark, Essex County.
DAVIS, JOHN W. Pvt, D, 152nd OH Inf, 5-7-1915. Evergreen Cemetery, Hillside, Union County.
DAVIS, JOSEPH Corp, E, 21st NJ Inf, 1-20-1876. United Methodist Church Cemetery, Windsor, Mercer County.
DAVIS, JOSEPH Pvt, G, 143rd NY Inf, 5-11-1912. Riverside Cemetery, Toms River, Ocean County.
DAVIS, JOSEPH Seaman, U.S. Navy, 1908. Evergreen Cemetery, Hillside, Union County.
DAVIS, JOSEPH B. Pvt, H, 4th NJ Militia, DoD Unknown. Cedar Grove Cemetery, Gloucester City, Camden County.
DAVIS, JOSEPH K. Pvt, C, 27th NJ Inf, 4- -1890. Presbyterian/Methodist-Episcopal Cemetery, Succasunna, Morris County.
DAVIS, JOSEPH L. 1881. Free Burying Ground Cemetery, Pennsville, Salem County.
DAVIS, LAFFERD T. Pvt, B, 1st NJ Inf, 4-24-1870. Princeton Cemetery, Princeton, Mercer County.
DAVIS, LEWIS L. Corp, C, 15th NJ Inf, 12-16-1925. Evergreen Cemetery, Morristown, Morris County.
DAVIS, MAHLON DoD Unknown. 7th Day Baptist Church Cemetery, Shiloh, Cumberland County.
DAVIS, MICHAEL Pvt, G, 23rd NJ Inf, 6-21-1880. Monument Cemetery, Edgewater Park, Burlington County.
DAVIS, MITCHELL S. Pvt, C, 17th MS Inf (CSA), 10-21-1863. Finn's Point National Cemetery, Pennsville, Salem County.
DAVIS*, NATHAN Pvt, F, 22nd NJ Inf, 7-17-1929. United Methodist Church Cemetery, Windsor, Mercer County.
DAVIS, NEAL Pvt, C, 36th VA Inf (CSA), [Captured 3-2-1865 at Waynesboro, VA. Died of lung inflammation.] 4-11-1865. Finn's Point National Cemetery, Pennsville, Salem County.
DAVIS, NEHEMIAH Pvt, A, PA Emerg NJ Militia, 2-17-1898. Riverview Cemetery, Trenton, Mercer County.
DAVIS*, NEWTON H. Capt, I, 26th NY Cav, [Wounded 6-1-1864 at Cold Harbor, VA.] DoD Unknown. Rosehill Cemetery, Newfield, Gloucester County.

Our Brothers Gone Before

DAVIS, OBED S. Pvt, Hopkin's, 1st Bttn GA Cav (CSA), 2-2-1865. Finn's Point National Cemetery, Pennsville, Salem County.
DAVIS, P.A. Pvt, B, 1st MD Cav (CSA), 8-22-1863. Finn's Point National Cemetery, Pennsville, Salem County.
DAVIS, PHINEAS J. Pvt, B, 38th NJ Inf, 6-20-1885. Mount Hope Presbyterian Cemetery, Lambertville, Hunterdon County.
DAVIS, RICHARD Fireman, U.S. Navy, [U.S. receiving ship at New York, NY.] 1903. Tennent Church Cemetery, Tennent, Monmouth County.
DAVIS, RICHARD D. Pvt, E, 24th NJ Inf, 11-17-1913. St. Paul's United Methodist Church Cemetery, Paulsboro, Gloucester County.
DAVIS, RINEHART H. Pvt, K, 39th NJ Inf, 7-22-1865. Presbyterian Cemetery, Berkshire Valley, Morris County.
DAVIS, S.B. Pvt, F, 8th TN Inf (CSA), 4-12-1864. Finn's Point National Cemetery, Pennsville, Salem County.
DAVIS, SAMUEL B. 11-3-1896. Evergreen Cemetery, Camden, Camden County.
DAVIS, SAMUEL B. Pvt, M, 3rd NJ Cav, 2-18-1894. Presbyterian Church Cemetery, Upper Deerfield, Cumberland County.
DAVIS*, SAMUEL H. Pvt, H, 13th NJ Inf, 7-4-1899. Evergreen Cemetery, Camden, Camden County.
DAVIS, SAMUEL JOHNSTON Corp, Nield's Btty, DE Light Art, 1-10-1924. Fairmount Cemetery, Newark, Essex County.
DAVIS, SAMUEL S. Pvt, C, 1st NJ Militia, 10-19-1911. Mount Pleasant Cemetery, Newark, Essex County.
DAVIS, SAMUEL V. Pvt, H, 3rd NJ Cav, [Died of typhoid at Trenton, NJ.] 2-10-1864. 7th Day Baptist Church Cemetery, Shiloh, Cumberland County.
DAVIS, SHELDON S. Pvt, D, 183rd PA Inf, 2-1-1936. Oddfellows Cemetery, Burlington, Burlington County.
DAVIS, STEPHEN A. Pvt, Btty F, 10th NY Heavy Art, 7-26-1906. Evergreen Cemetery, Hillside, Union County.
DAVIS, THEODORE F. Pvt, F, 41st U.S. CT, 1902. 1st Baptist Cemetery, New Brunswick, Middlesex County.
DAVIS, THOMAS Pvt, B, 41st PA Inf, 8-18-1902. Van Liew Cemetery, North Brunswick, Middlesex County.
DAVIS, THOMAS Seaman, U.S. Navy, USS Bibb, 1-9-1909. Evergreen Cemetery, Hillside, Union County.
DAVIS*, THOMAS B. Pvt, Btty D, 2nd U.S. Art, 5-10-1900. Fairmount Cemetery, Newark, Essex County.
DAVIS, THOMAS G. Pvt, K, 1st NJ Inf, [Killed in action at Wilderness, VA.] 5-5-1864. St. Mary's Cemetery, Boonton, Morris County.
DAVIS, THOMAS J. Pvt, C, 18th MS Inf (CSA), 1-27-1864. Finn's Point National Cemetery, Pennsville, Salem County.
DAVIS, THOMAS L. Sgt, I, 69th PA Inf, [Wounded 6-16-1864 at Petersburg, VA.] 3-28-1890. Evergreen Cemetery, Camden, Camden County.
DAVIS, THOMAS LEONARD Pvt, D, 29th NJ Inf, 7-27-1932. Fairview Cemetery, Fairview, Monmouth County.
DAVIS, W.G. Pvt, B, 30th VA Inf (CSA), 6-28-1865. Finn's Point National Cemetery, Pennsville, Salem County.
DAVIS, WILLIAM Corp, G, 21st NJ Inf, [Died of typhoid at Belle Plain, VA.] 3-21-1863. Holy Name Cemetery, Jersey City, Hudson County.
DAVIS, WILLIAM Pvt, G, 10th NJ Inf, DoD Unknown. United Methodist Church Cemetery, Windsor, Mercer County.
DAVIS, WILLIAM Pvt, K, 27th NJ Inf, 2-5-1892. Presbyterian/Methodist-Episcopal Cemetery, Succasunna, Morris County.

DAVIS, WILLIAM Pvt, D, 26th NJ Inf, 12-5-1896. Whitehall Cemetery, Towaco, Morris County.
DAVIS, WILLIAM Pvt, G, 8th LA Inf (CSA), [Wounded 7-2-1863 and captured 7-3-1863 at Gettysburg, PA. Died of smallpox.] 11-14-1863. Finn's Point National Cemetery, Pennsville, Salem County.
DAVIS, WILLIAM 6-12-1902. Phillipsburg Cemetery, Phillipsburg, Warren County.
DAVIS, WILLIAM A. 2-29-1920. Manahath Cemetery, Glassboro, Gloucester County.
DAVIS, WILLIAM A.M. 1st Lt, B, 113th OH Inf, 7-10-1902. Mount Pleasant Cemetery, Newark, Essex County.
DAVIS, WILLIAM B. Pvt, C, 1st NJ Cav, 7-18-1910. Baptist Cemetery, Burlington, Burlington County.
DAVIS, WILLIAM B. Sgt, A, 7th NJ Inf, 10-30-1917. Soldier's Home Cemetery, Vineland, Cumberland County.
DAVIS, WILLIAM B. Pvt, C, 28th NJ Inf, 8-26-1929. Elmwood Cemetery, New Brunswick, Middlesex County.
DAVIS, WILLIAM C. Capt, H, 2nd DC Inf, [Died of typhoid at Washington, DC.] 11-9-1862. Rosedale Cemetery, Orange, Essex County.
DAVIS, WILLIAM C. Pvt, H, 21st NJ Inf, 9-3-1904. Lawrenceville Cemetery, Lawrenceville, Mercer County.
DAVIS, WILLIAM C. (see: Davies, William C.) Brookside Cemetery, Englewood, Bergen County.
DAVIS*, WILLIAM E. Corp, Btty B, 4th NY Heavy Art, 9-23-1899. Bayview-New York Bay Cemetery, Jersey City, Hudson County.
DAVIS, WILLIAM H. Pvt, B, 12th VA Inf (CSA), [Captured 9-14-1862 at Crampton's Gap, MD.] 10-7-1862. Finn's Point National Cemetery, Pennsville, Salem County.
DAVIS*, WILLIAM H. Pvt, C, 38th NJ Inf, 10-4-1910. Harmony Methodist-Episcopal Church Cemetery, Piney Hollow, Gloucester County.
DAVIS, WILLIAM H. Pvt, D, 22nd U.S. CT, 4-4-1914. Timbuctoo Cemetery, Timbuctoo, Burlington County.
DAVIS, WILLIAM H. 2-11-1896. Mount Pleasant Cemetery, Millville, Cumberland County.
DAVIS, WILLIAM H. 1912. Friends Hicksite Cemetery, Woodbury, Gloucester County.
DAVIS, WILLIAM H. 4-21-1894. Bayview-New York Bay Cemetery, Jersey City, Hudson County.
DAVIS*, WILLIAM H. Pvt, A, 6th NJ Inf, 1929. Fairview Cemetery, Fairview, Monmouth County.
DAVIS, WILLIAM H.H. Pvt, K, 8th U.S. CT, 4-1-1904. Mount Peace Cemetery, Lawnside, Camden County.
DAVIS, WILLIAM (JR.) 10-16-1898. Christ Church Cemetery, Morgan, Middlesex County.
DAVIS, WILLIAM L. Pvt, G, 1st NJ Inf, 12-5-1897. Christ Church Cemetery, Morgan, Middlesex County.
DAVIS, WILLIAM M. Pvt, K, 43rd GA Inf (CSA), [Captured 5-16-1863 at Baker's Creek, MS.] 7-7-1863. Finn's Point National Cemetery, Pennsville, Salem County.
DAVIS, WILLIAM S. Seaman, U.S. Navy, USS Periwinkle, 1-26-1913. New Camden Cemetery, Camden, Camden County.
DAVIS, WILLIS Musc, 95th PA Inf Band 4-20-1888. Evergreen Cemetery, Hillside, Union County.
DAVISON, ALEXANDER Corp, F, 2nd U.S. CT, 2-24-1905. Greenwood Cemetery, Pleasantville, Atlantic County.
DAVISON, DAVID A. Pvt, B, 28th NJ Inf, 1-6-1870. Dutch Reformed Church Cemetery, Spotswood, Middlesex County.
DAVISON, ISAAC 11-25-1899. Evergreen Cemetery, Camden, Camden County.

Our Brothers Gone Before

DAVISON, JOHN C. Landsman, U.S. Navy, USS Restless, 2-9-1906. Hainesburg Cemetery, Hainesburg, Warren County.

DAVISON, JOHN JOHNSON (JR.) 1st Sgt, B, 28th NJ Inf, 1-3-1911. Elmwood Cemetery, New Brunswick, Middlesex County.

DAVISON, LEWIS Pvt, F, 30th NJ Inf, 2-15-1894. New Dutch Reformed/Neshanic Cemetery, Neshanic, Somerset County.

DAVISON, LUKE Pvt, K, 9th NJ Inf, 11-30-1897. Princeton Cemetery, Princeton, Mercer County.

DAVISON, SAMUEL G. Corp, G, 29th NJ Inf, 1925. Tennent Church Cemetery, Tennent, Monmouth County.

DAVISON, WILLIAM Pvt, G, 1st AL Inf (CSA), 9-1-1863. Finn's Point National Cemetery, Pennsville, Salem County.

DAVISON, WILLIAM F. Pvt, E, 2nd NJ Cav, 3-10-1909. Baptist Church Cemetery, Jacobstown, Burlington County.

DAVISON, WILLIAM V.P. Corp, B, 28th NJ Inf, [Died of diarrhea at Washington, DC.] 2-17-1863. Dutch Reformed Church Cemetery, Spotswood, Middlesex County.

DAVITT, MARTIN Landsman, U.S. Navy, USS Ohio, 11-9-1889. Phillipsburg Old Catholic Cemetery, Phillipsburg, Warren County.

DAVITT, PATRICK (aka: Dewitt, Patrick) Pvt, 28th NY Ind Btty 1-3-1919. St. John's RC Church Cemetery, Lakehurst, Ocean County.

DAVLIN, CHARLES Corp, G, 3rd DE Inf, 1-1-1890. Old St. Mary's Cemetery, Gloucester City, Camden County.

DAVY, WILLIAM H. Corp, I, 7th NJ Inf, [Died of typhoid at Budds Ferry, MD.] 2-16-1862. Beemerville Cemetery, Beemerville, Sussex County.

DAWKINS, CHARLES C. Corp, A, 11th NJ Inf, 12-28-1896. Bloomfield Cemetery, Bloomfield, Essex County.

DAWSEY, JOSIAH (see: Dorsey, Josiah) Jericho/Oddfellows Cemetery, Deptford, Gloucester County.

DAWSON, DAVID Sgt, G, 27th NJ Inf, 5-21-1893. Greenwood Cemetery, Boonton, Morris County.

DAWSON, GEORGE W. Pvt, D, 1st Bttn U.S. Eng, 8-18-1883. Rosedale Cemetery, Orange, Essex County.

DAWSON, HOWARD __, I, 12th NY Inf, 1-7-1885. Old Camden Cemetery, Camden, Camden County.

DAWSON, JAMES F. Sgt, K, 7th VA Inf (CSA), [Captured 7-3-1863 at Gettysburg, PA. Died of dysentery.] 8-30-1863. Finn's Point National Cemetery, Pennsville, Salem County.

DAWSON, JOHN E. Pvt, A, 9th NJ Inf, 12-21-1910. Eglington Cemetery, Clarksboro, Gloucester County.

DAWSON, JOHN H. Pvt, C, 22nd NJ Inf, 2-12-1896. Maple Grove Cemetery, Hackensack, Bergen County.

DAWSON, JOSHUA Pvt, A, 12th NJ Inf, 7-9-1928. Eglington Cemetery, Clarksboro, Gloucester County.

DAWSON, RICHARD Pvt, G, 28th NJ Inf, 10-7-1913. Union Methodist Church Cemetery, Center Square, Gloucester County.

DAY, ANDREW J. Pvt, H, 26th PA Inf, 10-21-1902. Clinton Cemetery, Irvington, Essex County.

DAY*, ANDREW L. Sgt, G, 30th NJ Inf, 9-15-1866. Mount Hope Presbyterian Cemetery, Lambertville, Hunterdon County.

DAY, ASHER Pvt, Btty E, 4th U.S. Art, 2-22-1903. Clinton Cemetery, Irvington, Essex County.

DAY*, CHARLES M. Sgt, E, 8th NJ Inf, 1886. Clinton Cemetery, Irvington, Essex County.

New Jersey Civil War Burials

DAY, DANIEL C. Pvt, Btty A, 1st IL Light Art, 6-24-1906. Evergreen Cemetery, Hillside, Union County.

DAY, DAVID Pvt, E, 23rd NJ Inf, 6-9-1888. Baptist Cemetery, Medford, Burlington County.

DAY, DAVID C. Pvt, B, 8th NJ Inf, [Died at Fort Monroe, VA. of wounds received 5-5-1862 at Williamsburg, VA.] 5-14-1862. Evergreen Cemetery, Hillside, Union County.

DAY*, EDWARD J. Sgt, C, 86th NY Inf, 9-9-1876. Evergreen Cemetery, Hillside, Union County.

DAY, EZRA S. Corp, I, 30th NJ Inf, [Died of typhoid at Belle Plain, VA.] 2-18-1863. Presbyterian Church Cemetery, Mendham, Morris County.

DAY, GEORGE J. Pvt, U.S. Marine Corps, 3-30-1865. Berlin Cemetery, Berlin, Camden County.

DAY, GEORGE T. Musc, F, 13th NJ Inf, 11-2-1902. Mount Pleasant Cemetery, Newark, Essex County.

DAY*, GEORGE W. Capt, B, 38th NJ Inf, 6-5-1919. Harleigh Cemetery, Camden, Camden County.

DAY, HENRY Corp, H, 28th NJ Inf, 11-9-1905. Berlin Cemetery, Berlin, Camden County.

DAY, HENRY Pvt, G, 6th NJ Inf, 1885. Presbyterian Church Cemetery, Mendham, Morris County.

DAY, HORACE H. Pvt, F, 8th NJ Inf, 2-1-1918. Evergreen Cemetery, Hillside, Union County.

DAY, HORACE P. Pvt, E, 25th NJ Inf, 6-29-1898. Fairmount Cemetery, Newark, Essex County.

DAY, JAMES L. Musc, A, 8th NJ Inf, 3-18-1920. Fairmount Cemetery, Newark, Essex County.

DAY*, JAMES M. Pvt, A, 8th NJ Inf, [Wounded in action at Gettysburg, PA.] 9-8-1923. Arlington Cemetery, Kearny, Hudson County.

DAY*, JOHN Quartermaster, U.S. Navy, USS Miantonomah, 1-5-1905. Woodlands Cemetery, Ocean View, Cape May County.

DAY, JOSEPH L. Seaman, U.S. Navy, 1915. Colestown Cemetery, Cherry Hill, Camden County.

DAY, LAFAYETTE M. Landsman, U.S. Navy, USS Princeton, 3-18-1902. Berlin Cemetery, Berlin, Camden County.

DAY, MULFORD BROOKFIELD Pvt, C, 15th NJ Inf, 4-27-1886. United Methodist Church Cemetery, New Providence, Union County.

DAY*, OWEN HUNTINGTON Capt, I, 2nd NJ Inf, 11-24-1905. Greenwood Cemetery, Hamilton, Mercer County.

DAY, ROBERT (JR.) Pvt, C, 26th NJ Inf, 5-3-1903. Bloomfield Cemetery, Bloomfield, Essex County.

DAY, SAMUEL Pvt, G, 29th CT Inf, 2-15-1905. Fairmount Cemetery, Newark, Essex County.

DAY, SAMUEL Landsman, U.S. Navy, 4-19-1872. Fairmount Cemetery, Newark, Essex County.

DAY, STEPHEN B. Pvt, E, 8th NJ Inf, DoD Unknown. Clinton Cemetery, Irvington, Essex County.

DAY, THOMAS T. Pvt, E, 18th MS Inf (CSA), 3-29-1864. Finn's Point National Cemetery, Pennsville, Salem County.

DAY, WILLIAM H. Pvt, E, 8th NJ Inf, 2-5-1913. Clinton Cemetery, Irvington, Essex County.

DAY, WILLIAM H. Landsman, U.S. Navy, USS Princeton, DoD Unknown. Holy Sepulchre Cemetery, East Orange, Essex County.

DAY, WILLIAM H. Pvt, D, 100th IL Inf, 9-6-1926. Hillside Cemetery, Scotch Plains, Union County.

Our Brothers Gone Before

DAY, WILLIAM H. Pvt, Btty A, 1st IL Light Art, 4-4-1909. Holy Sepulchre Cemetery, East Orange, Essex County.

DAYMOND, WILLIAM Pvt, H, 6th NJ Inf, 4-7-1889. Evergreen Cemetery, Hillside, Union County.

DAYSPRING, GEORGE Pvt, F, 54th PA Inf, 10-19-1910. Holy Sepulchre Cemetery, Totowa, Passaic County.

DAYTON, ELI DoD Unknown. 1st United Methodist Church Cemetery, Bridgeton, Cumberland County.

DAYTON*, FERDINAND V. Surg, 2nd NJ Cav [Also: Asst Surg, 1st NJ Cav.] 11-1-1866. Riverview Cemetery, Trenton, Mercer County.

DAYTON, JAMES Pvt, F, 3rd U.S. CT, 2-3-1926. Jordan Lawn Cemetery, Pennsauken, Camden County.

DAYTON, JESSE Pvt, E, 10th NJ Inf, DoD Unknown. 1st Methodist Church Cemetery, Williamstown, Gloucester County.

DAYTON, JOHN Pvt, G, 25th NJ Inf, 5-6-1896. Evergreen/Bishop Jaynes Cemetery, Basking Ridge, Somerset County.

DAYTON, JOHN C. Pvt, C, 5th PA Cav, 2-25-1907. Cedar Grove Cemetery, Gloucester City, Camden County.

DAYTON, SAMUEL JAMES F. Pvt, K, 137th NY Inf, DoD Unknown. Holy Name Cemetery, Jersey City, Hudson County.

DAYTON, WILLIAM J. Ordinary Seaman, U.S. Navy, USS Neptune, 12-15-1915. Fairmount Cemetery, Newark, Essex County.

DAYTON, WILLIAM W. Pvt, Btty M, 1st CT Heavy Art, 1911. Mount Pleasant Cemetery, Millville, Cumberland County.

DEACHANT, JOHN (see: Koeber, John G.) Bloomfield Cemetery, Bloomfield, Essex County.

DEACON, BENJAMIN Seaman, U.S. Navy, USS Princeton, 2-20-1901. Woodlane Graveyard Cemetery, Westampton, Burlington County.

DEACON, CHARLES H. Sgt, G, 23rd NJ Inf, 8-30-1905. Mount Holly Cemetery, Mount Holly, Burlington County.

DEACON, GEORGE G. Pvt, C, 3rd NJ Inf, 6-26-1895. Oddfellows Cemetery, Burlington, Burlington County.

DEACON, JAPHET B. 1898. Mount Holly Cemetery, Mount Holly, Burlington County.

DEACON, JOSEPH 4-17-1888. Cedar Grove Cemetery, Princeton, Mercer County.

DEACON, JOSEPH D. Sgt, G, PA Emerg NJ Militia, 11-4-1864. Mount Holly Cemetery, Mount Holly, Burlington County.

DEADY, JOHN Pvt, B, 9th NJ Inf, 2-9-1900. St. Peter's Cemetery, New Brunswick, Middlesex County.

DEAGLE, JACOB (see: Deigle, Jacob) Mansfield/Washington Cemetery, Washington, Warren County.

DEAL, CHARLES H. (SR.) Pvt, B, 40th NJ Inf, 1891. Methodist-Episcopal Cemetery, Olivet, Salem County.

DEAL, JOHN (see: Deall, John) Macphelah Cemetery, North Bergen, Hudson County.

DEAL, SAMUEL H. 2nd Lt, D, 24th NJ Inf, 7-13-1898. Eglington Cemetery, Clarksboro, Gloucester County.

DEAL, WILLIAM Pvt, A, 22nd U.S. CT, 11-13-1917. Spencer African Methodist Church Cemetery, Woodstown, Salem County.

DEAL, ZACHARIAH Pvt, B, 51st GA Inf (CSA), 9-12-1863. Finn's Point National Cemetery, Pennsville, Salem County.

DEALING, NEWTON C. Pvt, H, 33rd NJ Inf, 1921. Mansfield/Washington Cemetery, Washington, Warren County.

DEALING, WILLIAM HENRY Pvt, F, 17th NY Inf, [Wounded 5-2-1863 at Chancellorsville, VA.] 10-19-1904. Bloomfield Cemetery, Bloomfield, Essex County.

New Jersey Civil War Burials

DEALL, JOHN (aka: Deal, John) Sgt, F, 125th NY Inf, 5-2-1904. Macphelah Cemetery, North Bergen, Hudson County.
DEAN, AARON Pvt, E, 2nd NJ Cav, 6-24-1901. Brotherhood Cemetery, Hainesport, Burlington County.
DEAN, CHARLES B. Pvt, A, 79th PA Inf, 1906. New Somerville Cemetery, Somerville, Somerset County.
DEAN, DAVID Pvt, D, 2nd NJ Cav, 1-31-1907. Arlington Cemetery, Pennsauken, Camden County.
DEAN, GEORGE D. Pvt, H, 2nd NJ Inf, 6-15-1905. Rosedale Cemetery, Orange, Essex County.
DEAN*, GILBERT E. Corp, G, 9th NY Inf, 9-13-1903. Hackensack Cemetery, Hackensack, Bergen County.
DEAN, HENRY S. 1st Cl Boy, U.S. Navy, USS Lackawanna, 1917. 1st Reformed Church Cemetery, Pompton Plains, Morris County.
DEAN, J. CHRISTOPHER Pvt, H, 97th PA Inf, 7-16-1923. New Episcopal Church Cemetery, Swedesboro, Gloucester County.
DEAN, JOHN Pvt, B, PA Emerg NJ Militia, 10-7-1918. Arlington Cemetery, Kearny, Hudson County.
DEAN, JOHN Pvt, I, 40th NJ Inf, 3-14-1921. Elmwood Cemetery, New Brunswick, Middlesex County.
DEAN, JOHN Sgt, A, 25th NJ Inf, 11-20-1900. Laurel Grove Cemetery, Totowa, Passaic County.
DEAN, JOHN J. 1st Sgt, C, 109th NY Inf, 8-6-1882. Old Somerville Cemetery, Somerville, Somerset County.
DEAN*, JOSEPH Wagoner, K, 38th NJ Inf, [Wounded 9-17-1862 at Antietam, MD.] 3-23-1913. Riverview Cemetery, Trenton, Mercer County.
DEAN, ROBERT Pvt, I, 24th NJ Inf, DoD Unknown. St. Mary's Episcopal Church Cemetery, Burlington, Burlington County.
DEAN, SILAS Pvt, E, 25th NY Inf, 5-22-1924. Arlington Cemetery, Kearny, Hudson County.
DEAN, WILLIAM A. Pvt, D, 35th IN Inf, 4-23-1916. Riverview Cemetery, Trenton, Mercer County.
DEAN, WILLIAM M. Pvt, A, 25th NJ Inf, 1924. Union Cemetery, Hope, Warren County.
DEARBORN, GEORGE S. Asst Surg, 15th NJ Inf 3-25-1906. Presbyterian Church Cemetery, Rockaway, Morris County.
DEARING, ALBERT G. Seaman, U.S. Navy, 6-5-1907. Bayview-New York Bay Cemetery, Jersey City, Hudson County.
DEARING, BENJAMIN M. Pvt, C, 9th MI Inf, 3-19-1935. St. Stephen's Cemetery, Millburn, Essex County.
DEARMAN, H.D. Pvt, D, 51st AL Cav (CSA), 2-16-1864. Finn's Point National Cemetery, Pennsville, Salem County.
DEARY, JAMES Pvt, E, 71st NY Inf, [Wounded in action.] 11-10-1876. St. John's Evangelical Church Cemetery, Orange, Essex County.
DEASE, AMOS R. Pvt, E, 128th PA Inf, 1-7-1916. Evergreen Cemetery, Camden, Camden County.
DEASE, WILLIAM (see: Birrell, William) Fairmount Cemetery, Newark, Essex County.
DEATS, EZRA (see: Deeths, Ezra) Cedar Lawn Cemetery, Paterson, Passaic County.
DEATS, JAMES Pvt, B, 38th NJ Inf, 1910. Baptist Church Cemetery, Flemington, Hunterdon County.
DEAVES, GEORGE T. Corp, K, 62nd PA Inf, 10-30-1910. Evergreen Cemetery, Camden, Camden County.
DEBACHER, JACOB 7-29-1898. Madonna Cemetery, Leonia, Bergen County.
DEBARRY, ALBERT Pvt, A, 82nd PA Inf, 12-21-1925. Greenwood Cemetery, Pleasantville, Atlantic County.

Our Brothers Gone Before

DEBARRY, JOHN Pvt, G, 91st PA Inf, 10-15-1914. Greenwood Cemetery, Pleasantville, Atlantic County.
DEBAUN, ABRAHAM Pvt, I, 22nd NJ Inf, [Died of typhoid at Belle Plain, VA.] 2-22-1863. Old Hook Cemetery, Westwood, Bergen County.
DEBAUN, GEORGE Pvt, F, 95th NY Inf, 2-15-1928. Hackensack Cemetery, Hackensack, Bergen County.
DEBAUN, ISAAC V.B. Pvt, B, 22nd NJ Inf, 3-5-1915. Ramapo Reformed Church Cemetery, Mahwah, Bergen County.
DEBAUN, JAMES A. 1919. Old Stone Reformed Church Cemetery, Upper Saddle River, Bergen County.
DEBAUN, JEREMIAH R. Pvt, G, 109th NY Inf, [Died of disease in Rhode Island.] 7-4-1864. Reformed Church Cemetery, Fairfield, Essex County.
DEBAUN, JOHN 1895. Reformed Church Cemetery, Fairfield, Essex County.
DEBBIE*, SIMON PETER (aka: Deppich, Simon) Pvt, D, 162nd NY Inf, 5-8-1929. St Mary's Cemetery, Watchung, Somerset County.
DEBEVOISE, ALFRED Pvt, A, 2nd NJ Militia, 6-26-1903. Grove Church Cemetery, North Bergen, Hudson County.
DEBEVOISE*, WILLIAM H. 2nd Lt, C, 21st NJ Inf, 5-21-1890. Maple Grove Cemetery, Hackensack, Bergen County.
DEBO, CHARLES (JR.) Corp, A, 1st NJ Inf, 5-8-1872. Evergreen Cemetery, Hillside, Union County.
DEBOLD*, CHARLES A. Pvt, K, 2nd NJ Inf, 6-14-1912. St. Mary's Cemetery, Clark, Union County.
DEBOLD, PETER Pvt, F, 28th NJ Inf, 1920. Alpine Cemetery, Perth Amboy, Middlesex County.
DEBOW, JAMES A. Pvt, K, 10th NJ Inf, DoD Unknown. Greenwood Cemetery, Tuckerton, Ocean County.
DEBOWMAN, CHARLES Pvt, G, 116th PA Inf, 1907. Soldier's Home Cemetery, Vineland, Cumberland County.
DEBUSK, J.E. Pvt, H, 27th Bttn VA Cav (CSA), 4-13-1864. Finn's Point National Cemetery, Pennsville, Salem County.
DECAMP, ALAMANZOR Pvt, G, 52nd PA Inf, 5-7-1890. Hillside Cemetery, Oxford, Warren County.
DECAMP, AUGUSTUS Pvt, D, 33rd NJ Inf, 3-22-1893. Fairmount Cemetery, Newark, Essex County.
DECAMP, CORNELIUS M. 1st Sgt, F, 30th NJ Inf, 5-22-1903. Evergreen Cemetery, Hillside, Union County.
DECAMP, EDWARD JANSEN Sgt, K, 1st NY Eng, 6-27-1917. Presbyterian/Methodist-Episcopal Cemetery, Succasunna, Morris County.
DECAMP, HARRISON Corp, D, 23rd NJ Inf, [Died of typhoid at Fredericksburg, VA.] 12-12-1862. Baptist Church Cemetery, Jacobstown, Burlington County.
DECAMP, JAMES L. Pvt, G, 38th NJ Inf, 1-19-1879. Presbyterian Cemetery, North Plainfield, Somerset County.
DECAMP, JAMES WOOD 2-18-1882. St. Mary's Episcopal Church Cemetery, Burlington, Burlington County.
DECAMP, JOHN Capt, U.S. Navy, 6-25-1875. Evergreen Cemetery, Morristown, Morris County.
DECAMP, JOHN Pvt, G, 2nd NJ Cav, 6-3-1882. Hillsborough Reformed Church Cemetery, Millstone, Somerset County.
DECAMP, JOHN COOPER Corp, D, 48th NY Inf, [Wounded 7-13-1863 at Morris Island, SC. and 5-7-1864 at Chester Hill, VA.] 1927. Pleasant Hill Cemetery, Pleasant Hill, Morris County.
DECAMP, JONATHAN W. Maj, 26th NJ Inf 10-13-1901. Pleasantdale Cemetery, West Orange, Essex County.

DECAMP, MAHLON Corp, A, 9th NJ Inf, 1-7-1914. Arlington Cemetery, Kearny, Hudson County.
DECAMP, WILBER W. 1st Sgt, D, 26th NJ Inf, 10-10-1903. Methodist Church Cemetery, Roseland, Essex County.
DECAMP*, WILLIAM H. Fireman, U.S. Navy, USS Rhode Island, 2-4-1904. Rahway Cemetery, Rahway, Union County.
DECASTRO, JOSEPH H. Sgt, F, 19th MA Inf, [Awarded the Medal of Honor.] 5-8-1892. Fairmount Cemetery, Newark, Essex County.
DECASTRO, JOSEPH W. Pvt, M, 1st NY Mounted Rifles, 2-4-1925. Arlington Cemetery, Kearny, Hudson County.
DECK, WILLIAM H. Pvt, Unassigned, 3rd PA Heavy Art, 2-8-1917. Atlantic City Cemetery, Pleasantville, Atlantic County.
DECKER, ALFRED Pvt, B, 36th NY Inf, 5-15-1900. Fairmount Cemetery, Newark, Essex County.
DECKER, AMOS A. Pvt, 6th NY Ind Btty 2-22-1910. Clinton Cemetery, Irvington, Essex County.
DECKER, ANDREW Pvt, E, 9th NJ Inf, 2- -1881. Harmony Methodist Church Cemetery, Stillwater, Sussex County.
DECKER*, BARNEY Sgt Maj, 33rd NJ Inf 7-23-1892. Pompton Reformed Church Cemetery, Pompton Lakes, Passaic County.
DECKER*, BENJAMIN (JR.) Pvt, E, 11th NY Inf, 2-12-1919. Greengrove Cemetery, Keyport, Monmouth County.
DECKER, CARVEY Pvt, F, 27th NJ Inf, 4-1-1884. United Methodist Church Cemetery, Vernon, Sussex County.
DECKER, CHARLES A. Pvt, C, 13th NJ Inf, 2-12-1907. Cedar Lawn Cemetery, Paterson, Passaic County.
DECKER, CHARLES S. 1-12-1919. East Ridgelawn Cemetery, Clifton, Passaic County.
DECKER, CHRISTOPHER (see: Jergus, Christopher) Old South Church Cemetery, Bergenfield, Bergen County.
DECKER, DANIEL WEBSTER Corp, B, 2nd NY Cav, DoD Unknown. Old Clove Church Cemetery, Wantage, Sussex County.
DECKER, EDMUND B. 1-3-1885. Hazelwood Cemetery, Rahway, Union County.
DECKER, ELWOOD (see: Arnold, Elwood) Whitelawn Cemetery, Point Pleasant, Ocean County.
DECKER, FREDERICK (see: Decker, Frederick) Washington Monumental Cemetery, South River, Middlesex County.
DECKER, GEORGE Pvt, A, 8th NJ Inf, 11-5-1896. Pompton Reformed Church Cemetery, Pompton Lakes, Passaic County.
DECKER, GEORGE 11-81-1881. Midvale Cemetery, Midvale, Passaic County.
DECKER, GEORGE M. Pvt, E, 9th NJ Inf, 12-3-1925. St. Vincent Martyr Cemetery, Madison, Morris County.
DECKER*, GEORGE W. Pvt, I, 67th NY Inf, [Wounded 5-31-1862 at Fair Oaks, VA.] 2-13-1922. Evergreen Cemetery, Hillside, Union County.
DECKER, HENRY Sgt, E, 25th NJ Inf, 2-9-1908. Mount Salem Cemetery, Mount Salem, Sussex County.
DECKER, HENRY E. Pvt, Btty E, 4th NY Heavy Art, 5-2-1927. Rahway Cemetery, Rahway, Union County.
DECKER*, HIRAM Pvt, D, 3rd NJ Inf, [Wounded in action.] 4-26-1915. Presbyterian Church Cemetery, Sparta, Sussex County.
DECKER, HUDSON Pvt, E, 1st NJ Cav, 1-12-1933. United Methodist Church Cemetery, Rockaway Valley, Morris County.
DECKER, ISAAC W. Pvt, I, 2nd DC Inf, 5-11-1909. New Camden Cemetery, Camden, Camden County.

Our Brothers Gone Before

DECKER, JAMES H. Pvt, C, 53rd PA Inf, [Died at City Point, VA.] 7-22-1864. Beemerville Cemetery, Beemerville, Sussex County.
DECKER, JAMES H. Pvt, Btty C, 4th NY Heavy Art, 12-17-1907. Evergreen Cemetery, Hillside, Union County.
DECKER, JAMES H. Pvt, Unassigned, 2nd NJ Cav, 9-22-1864. Branchville Cemetery, Branchville, Sussex County.
DECKER, JAMES I. Pvt, K, 15th NJ Inf, 11-14-1923. Pompton Reformed Church Cemetery, Pompton Lakes, Passaic County.
DECKER, JOEL Pvt, F, 27th NJ Inf, 9-3-1913. Glenwood Cemetery, Glenwood, Sussex County.
DECKER, JOHN Pvt, K, 1st NJ Cav, 1928. Pompton Reformed Church Cemetery, Pompton Lakes, Passaic County.
DECKER*, JOHN Pvt, Btty D, 1st NJ Light Art, 2-22-1882. Walpack Methodist Cemetery, Walpack, Sussex County.
DECKER, JOHN (see: Spiess, Charles) Methodist Church Cemetery, Springdale, Somerset County.
DECKER, JOHN C. (see: Vanderweg, Edward A.) Presbyterian Cemetery, North Plainfield, Somerset County.
DECKER, JOHN P. 2nd Lt, I, 13th NJ Inf, 6-6-1932. Evergreen Cemetery, Camden, Camden County.
DECKER, JOHN R. Pvt, A, 26th NJ Inf, 1-28-1913. Fairmount Cemetery, Newark, Essex County.
DECKER, JOSEPH L. Pvt, H, 11th NJ Inf, 12-12-1884. Balesville Cemetery, Balesville, Sussex County.
DECKER, LEVI Pvt, F, 27th NJ Inf, 5-7-1913. Mount Salem Cemetery, Mount Salem, Sussex County.
DECKER*, LEVI Pvt, K, 15th NJ Inf, 4-3-1901. Deckertown-Union Cemetery, Papakating, Sussex County.
DECKER, NELSON Musc, H, 27th NJ Inf, 2-19-1889. Fairmount Cemetery, Newark, Essex County.
DECKER, PHILIP (see: Fohs, Philip Decker) Fairmount Cemetery, Newark, Essex County.
DECKER, R. 7-21-1934. Atlantic View Cemetery, Manasquan, Monmouth County.
DECKER, RICHARD Corp, B, 11th NJ Inf, 6-13-1911. Evergreen Cemetery, Hillside, Union County.
DECKER, RICHARD Pvt, H, 30th NJ Inf, 3-30-1867. Baptist/Evergreen Methodist Cemetery, Plainfield, Union County.
DECKER, SAMUEL Sgt, A, 27th NJ Inf, 1-30-1867. Walpack Methodist Cemetery, Walpack, Sussex County.
DECKER, SYLVESTER 1917. Newton Cemetery, Newton, Sussex County.
DECKER, SYLVESTER B. Sgt, D, 3rd NJ Inf, 5-15-1864. Laurel Grove Cemetery, Totowa, Passaic County.
DECKER, THOMAS Pvt, D, 15th NJ Inf, 6-6-1914. Newton Cemetery, Newton, Sussex County.
DECKER, WILLIAM Sgt, H, 1st NY Mounted Rifles, 12-13-1922. United Methodist Church Cemetery, Rockaway Valley, Morris County.
DECKER, WILLIAM Pvt, Btty A, 1st NJ Light Art, 10-19-1877. Evergreen Cemetery, Hillside, Union County.
DECKER, WILLIAM A. Pvt, H, 11th NJ Inf, [Died at Washington, DC. of wounds received at Chancellorsville, VA.] 5-30-1863. Presbyterian/Methodist-Episcopal Cemetery, Succasunna, Morris County.
DECKER*, WILLIAM H. Pvt, E, 2nd NJ Inf, 9-30-1886. Christian Cemetery, Johnsonburg, Warren County.

New Jersey Civil War Burials

DECKER, WILLIAM HENRY Corp, A, 170th NY Inf, 2-12-1919. Greengrove Cemetery, Keyport, Monmouth County.

DECKERMAN, ANDREW Pvt, E, 35th NJ Inf, 4-26-1871. Evergreen Cemetery, Hillside, Union County.

DECKLENBERGER, FRANKLIN (see: Thacklinberg, Franklin) United Methodist Cemetery, Marlton, Burlington County.

DECLYNE, CHARLES Capt, Btty A, 15th NY Heavy Art, 11-5-1865. Flower Hill Cemetery, North Bergen, Hudson County.

DECOO, CHARLES (see: Decou, Charles H.) Harleigh Cemetery, Camden, Camden County.

DECOU, CHARLES H. (aka: Decoo, Charles) Pvt, H, 13th MI Inf, 1902. Harleigh Cemetery, Camden, Camden County.

DEDE, JOHN Pvt, I, 7th NJ Inf, 1-31-1901. Weehawken Cemetery, North Bergen, Hudson County.

DEDING, LOUIS Pvt, Btty K, 13th NY Heavy Art, 1-8-1910. St. Joseph's Cemetery, Hackensack, Bergen County.

DEE, JOHN Wagoner, F, 15th NJ Inf, [Wounded 5-6-1864 at Wilderness, VA.] 12-23-1885. Congregational Church Cemetery, Chester, Morris County.

DEEDRICH, CHARLES Pvt, I, 148th NY Inf, DoD Unknown. Manalapan Cemetery, Manalapan, Monmouth County.

DEEGAN, JAMES J. 1st Lt, H, 33rd NJ Inf, 7-30-1908. Holy Sepulchre Cemetery, East Orange, Essex County.

DEEGAN, MICHAEL Sgt, K, 3rd NJ Inf, 12-23-1866. Mount Olivet Cemetery, Newark, Essex County.

DEEM, WILLIAM Pvt, Btty M, 3rd PA Heavy Art, 7-14-1863. Finn's Point National Cemetery, Pennsville, Salem County.

DEETHS, BENJAMIN H. Pvt, F, 10th NJ Inf, 6-3-1918. Mount Hebron Cemetery, Montclair, Essex County.

DEETHS, EZRA (aka: Deats, Ezra) Pvt, A, 25th NJ Inf, 11-22-1921. Cedar Lawn Cemetery, Paterson, Passaic County.

DEETHS, HENRY (see: Deitch, Henry) Fairmount Cemetery, Newark, Essex County.

DEETHS, JOHN Pvt, K, 25th NJ Inf, 8-22-1888. Fairmount Cemetery, Newark, Essex County.

DEFEUER, BERNARD (see: Deffner, Bernard) Riverview Cemetery, Trenton, Mercer County.

DEFFNALL, E.J. Pvt, G, 5th GA Res Inf (CSA), 3-20-1865. Finn's Point National Cemetery, Pennsville, Salem County.

DEFFNER, BERNARD (aka: Defeuer, Bernard) Pvt, 13th NY Ind Btty 11-2-1915. Riverview Cemetery, Trenton, Mercer County.

DEFORD, HENRY Pvt, B, 3rd NJ Inf, 12-27-1894. Old Camden Cemetery, Camden, Camden County.

DEFORREST, AMIDEE Pvt, H, 9th NJ Inf, [Cenotaph. Died of typhoid at Roanoke Island, NC.] 2-25-1862. Hancock Cemetery, Florham Park, Morris County.

DEFREEST, LIVINGSTON Artificer, B, 15th NY Eng, [Died of meismatic disease at Washington, DC.] 7-8-1865. Bayview-New York Bay Cemetery, Jersey City, Hudson County.

DEFREITAS, JOSEPH Pvt, G, 114th IL Inf, 3-19-1889. Macphelah Cemetery, North Bergen, Hudson County.

DEGAN, BERNARD Pvt, E, 3rd NJ Inf, [Wounded 6-27-1862 at Gaines' Farm, VA.] DoD Unknown. Holy Name Cemetery, Jersey City, Hudson County.

DEGAN*, FRITZ Pvt, B, 7th NJ Inf, 5-7-1912. Holy Name Cemetery, Jersey City, Hudson County.

DEGELMANN, CHARLES Pvt, E, 9th NJ Inf, 5-5-1882. Cedar Lawn Cemetery, Paterson, Passaic County.

Our Brothers Gone Before

DEGELMANN, JOHN A. Pvt, E, 9th NJ Inf, 12-2-1864. Laurel Grove Cemetery, Totowa, Passaic County.
DEGENRING, JACOB Pvt, E, 1st MA Cav, [Wounded in action.] 1-1-1921. Fairview Cemetery, Fairview, Monmouth County.
DEGINS, JAMES (aka: Diggins, James) Pvt, A, 29th NJ Inf, 1898. Greenlawn Cemetery, West Long Branch, Monmouth County.
DEGINTHER, GEORGE Pvt, G, 20th PA Cav, 5-7-1900. Harleigh Cemetery, Camden, Camden County.
DEGNAN*, PATRICK Pvt, B, 5th NJ Inf, 5-8-1912. Holy Name Cemetery, Jersey City, Hudson County.
DEGRAFF, WILLIAM Pvt, E, 22nd U.S. CT, 11-20-1922. Mount Peace Cemetery, Lawnside, Camden County.
DEGRAW, CHARLES Pvt, B, 3rd NJ Cav, 10-28-1888. Laurel Grove Cemetery, Totowa, Passaic County.
DEGRAW, CHARLES DoD Unknown. Canfield Cemetery, Cedar Grove, Essex County.
DEGRAW*, CORNELIUS Pvt, C, 2nd NJ Inf, 11-6-1908. Pompton Reformed Church Cemetery, Pompton Lakes, Passaic County.
DEGRAW, DAVID Corp, L, 27th NJ Inf, 7-17-1925. Presbyterian Church Cemetery, Pleasant Grove, Morris County.
DEGRAW, ERASTUS Pvt, H, 33rd NJ Inf, 9-9-1900. United Methodist Church Cemetery, Vernon, Sussex County.
DEGRAW, ISAAC B. Corp, A, 11th NJ Inf, [Wounded in action at Chancellorsville, VA.] 1-14-1903. Midvale Cemetery, Midvale, Passaic County.
DEGRAW*, JOHN Corp, F, 65th NY Inf, 8-29-1908. Union Cemetery, Washington, Morris County.
DEGRAW, JOHN Pvt, K, 25th NJ Inf, 1922. Midvale Cemetery, Midvale, Passaic County.
DEGRAW, JOHN 11-13-1881. Hazelwood Cemetery, Rahway, Union County.
DEGRAW, LEMUEL Pvt, L, 27th NJ Inf, [Drowned while crossing the Cumberland River, KY.] 5-6-1863. United Methodist Church Cemetery, Rockaway Valley, Morris County.
DEGRAW, PETER Pvt, K, 25th NJ Inf, DoD Unknown. Midvale Cemetery, Midvale, Passaic County.
DEGRAW, WILLIAM Pvt, K, 39th NJ Inf, 10-1-1901. Methodist Church Cemetery, Stockholm, Sussex County.
DEGRAW, WILLIAM C. Pvt, I, 2nd NJ Inf, 3-9-1867. Rahway Cemetery, Rahway, Union County.
DEGROAT, HENRY Corp, C, 22nd U.S. CT, 11-22-1909. New Presbyterian Cemetery, Bound Brook, Somerset County.
DEGROFF, CHARLES Pvt, B, 20th IN Inf, 3-7-1900. Siloam Cemetery, Vineland, Cumberland County.
DEGROFF, GEORGE 1st Sgt, I, 28th NJ Inf, DoD Unknown. Alpine Cemetery, Perth Amboy, Middlesex County.
DEGROFFT, HIRAM H. Sgt, K, 24th NJ Inf, 4-20-1894. Methodist-Episcopal Church Cemetery, Penns Grove, Salem County.
DEGROOT, AARON S. Pvt, C, 7th NJ Inf, 12-7-1895. Evergreen Cemetery, Morristown, Morris County.
DEGROOT, EDWARD P. Pvt, B, 2nd NJ Cav, 6-26-1881. Evergreen Cemetery, Morristown, Morris County.
DEGROOTE, ALBERT Pvt, E, 1st NY Eng, 5-11-1913. Bayview-New York Bay Cemetery, Jersey City, Hudson County.
DEGROTE, JOHN Pvt, E, 1st NJ Cav, 11-20-1897. Cedar Lawn Cemetery, Paterson, Passaic County.
DEGRUCHY, ELIAS 7-5-1912. Bayview-New York Bay Cemetery, Jersey City, Hudson County.

New Jersey Civil War Burials

DEHART*, CORNELIUS Pvt, F, 2nd MI Inf, 3-6-1876. Willow Grove Cemetery, New Brunswick, Middlesex County.

DEHART, DAVID 11-2-1900. Mount Pleasant Cemetery, Millville, Cumberland County.

DEHART, DAVID B. Pvt, M, 9th NJ Inf, 6-27-1884. Elmwood Cemetery, New Brunswick, Middlesex County.

DEHART, EDWARD C. Pvt, I, 11th NJ Inf, 12-8-1896. Evergreen Cemetery, New Brunswick, Middlesex County.

DEHART, HENRY Sgt, E, 1st NJ Militia, 1884. Mount Pleasant Cemetery, Newark, Essex County.

DEHART, HENRY V. Capt, Btty M, 5th U.S. Art, [Died of wounds received 6-27-1862 at Gaines' Mill, VA.] 7-13-1862. Presbyterian Church Cemetery, Elizabeth, Union County.

DEHART, HORACE Pvt, F, 27th NJ Inf, 4-4-1900. St. Stephen's Cemetery, Millburn, Essex County.

DEHART, IRA S. Corp, G, 1st NJ Cav, 1866. Hillside Cemetery, Madison, Morris County.

DEHART, JACOB Sgt, A, 12th NJ Inf, 10-2-1910. Harleigh Cemetery, Camden, Camden County.

DEHART, JACOB S. Pvt, G, 1st NJ Inf, 6-29-1887. Van Liew Cemetery, North Brunswick, Middlesex County.

DEHART*, JAMES W. Corp, E, 34th NJ Inf, 8-15-1898. Willow Grove Cemetery, New Brunswick, Middlesex County.

DEHART, JOB W. Pvt, B, 160th NY Inf, [Died of diarrhea at New Orleans, LA.] 1-27-1864. Presbyterian Church Cemetery, Mount Freedom, Morris County.

DEHART, JOHN Pvt, B, 41st U.S. CT, 5-20-1873. Evergreen Cemetery, Hillside, Union County.

DEHART, JOHN SUMMERS Pvt, E, PA Emerg NJ Militia, 7-18-1914. Presbyterian Church Cemetery, Mount Freedom, Morris County.

DEHART*, JOHN W. Sgt, H, 8th NJ Inf, [Wounded in action.] 3-27-1908. Bloomsbury Cemetery, Kennedy Mills, Warren County.

DEHART, SAMUEL B. Pvt, G, 38th NJ Inf, 11-18-1887. Van Liew Cemetery, North Brunswick, Middlesex County.

DEHART*, THEODORE Sgt, B, 9th NJ Inf, 1888. Voorhees-Nevius Cemetery, Franklin Township, Somerset County.

DEHART, VOORHEES Pvt, G, 38th NJ Inf, 1886. Voorhees-Nevius Cemetery, Franklin Township, Somerset County.

DEHART, WILLIAM Pvt, G, 38th NJ Inf, 11-8-1898. Van Liew Cemetery, North Brunswick, Middlesex County.

DEHART, WILLIAM C. Seaman, U.S. Navy, 5-23-1922. Evergreen Cemetery, Hillside, Union County.

DEHART, WILLIAM H. Corp, B, 30th NJ Inf, 9-11-1865. Methodist Church Cemetery, Asbury, Warren County.

DEHART, WILLIAM S. Pvt, B, 1st NJ Inf, 9-5-1914. Elmwood Cemetery, New Brunswick, Middlesex County.

DEHNER, JOHN B. Sgt, A, 108th OH Inf, 11-6-1878. Green Cemetery, Woodbury, Gloucester County.

DEHOFF, RUDOLPH D. Pvt, A, 7th NY Inf, 6-23-1890. Arlington Cemetery, Kearny, Hudson County.

DEIGHAN, PETER (aka: Dieien, Peter) Sgt, I, 33rd NJ Inf, 2-4-1900. St. Peter's Church Cemetery, Belleville, Essex County.

DEIGHLEBOHR, JOSEPH (see: Bierkelbaugh, Jacob) Methodist Cemetery, Malaga, Gloucester County.

DEIGLE, JACOB (aka: Deagle, Jacob) Corp, H, 1st NJ Inf, 2-17-1868. Mansfield/Washington Cemetery, Washington, Warren County.

Our Brothers Gone Before

DEILY, VALENTINE (aka: Diley, Valentine) Pvt, D, 38th PA Militia, 2-28-1906. Riverview Cemetery, Trenton, Mercer County.
DEINER, FREDERICK (aka: Diner, Frederick) Corp, G, 7th PA Cav, 2-15-1930. Presbyterian Cemetery, Springfield, Union County.
DEIR, JACOB 2nd Lt, H, 8th NJ Inf, 10-25-1915. Fairmount Cemetery, Newark, Essex County.
DEISEL, JOHN Pvt, I, 31st NJ Inf, 1917. Belvidere/Catholic Cemetery, Belvidere, Warren County.
DEISZEROTH, GEORGE C. (aka: Deseroth, George) Pvt, D, 168th NY Inf, 3-16-1921. New York/New Jersey Crematory Cemetery, North Bergen, Hudson County.
DEITCH, HENRY (aka: Deeths, Henry) Pvt, K, 25th NJ Inf, 1-13-1887. Fairmount Cemetery, Newark, Essex County.
DEITH, CHARLES 1-16-1880. Evergreen Cemetery, Camden, Camden County.
DEITLER, MARTIN DoD Unknown. Elmwood Cemetery, New Brunswick, Middlesex County.
DEITMANN, HENRY Pvt, D, 7th NY Inf, 1-12-1896. Holy Sepulchre Cemetery, Totowa, Passaic County.
DEITZ, PHINEAS G. Pvt, M, 3rd NJ Cav, 4-10-1905. Mount Hope Presbyterian Cemetery, Lambertville, Hunterdon County.
DEKEISER, JOHN (see: DeKerzer, John) Maple Grove Cemetery, Hackensack, Bergen County.
DEKERZER, JOHN (aka: DeKeiser, John) Pvt, E, 22nd NJ Inf, 1903. Maple Grove Cemetery, Hackensack, Bergen County.
DEKOLF, PETER C. (aka: Burton, John) Pvt, Btty K, 2nd MO Light Art, 11-15-1890. Presbyterian Church Cemetery, Hanover, Morris County.
DELACOURT, JAMES CHARLES Pvt, G, 5th MD Inf, 11-14-1891. Evergreen Cemetery, Camden, Camden County.
DELACROIX, ALEXANDER Pvt, F, 27th NJ Inf, 2-22-1902. Methodist Church Cemetery, Springfield, Union County.
DELACROY, JOSEPH Pvt, Btty D, 1st NJ Light Art, 2-2-1882. Fairmount Cemetery, Newark, Essex County.
DELAMATER, ISRAEL 1-22-1897. Bayview-New York Bay Cemetery, Jersey City, Hudson County.
DELAMATER, JOHN S. Pvt, G, 91st PA Inf, 11-6-1921. Harleigh Cemetery, Camden, Camden County.
DELANCY, DAVID (see: Sparrow, Delancy D.) South Orange Cemetery, South Orange, Essex County.
DELANEY, FRANCIS Landsman, U.S. Navy, USS Nipsic, 1-9-1919. Holy Sepulchre Cemetery, East Orange, Essex County.
DELANEY, GEORGE Pvt, G, 2nd PA Cav, 8-23-1896. Riverview Cemetery, Trenton, Mercer County.
DELANEY, MARTIN (see: Dalane, Martin) New Camden Cemetery, Camden, Camden County.
DELANEY, WILLIAM Pvt, E, 13th NJ Inf, 2-12-1903. Holy Sepulchre Cemetery, East Orange, Essex County.
DELANEY, WILLIAM 1-5-1895. St. Teresa's Cemetery, Summit, Union County.
DELANO, ALBERT Hosp Steward, 13th NJ Inf 2-22-1904. Fairmount Cemetery, Newark, Essex County.
DELANO, DAVID Pvt, A, 13th OH Cav, [Died of diarrhea at Beverly, NJ.] 10-2-1864. Beverly National Cemetery, Edgewater Park, Burlington County.
DELANY, MICHAEL J. Pvt, B, 22nd CT Inf, 4-5-1914. Calvary Cemetery, Cherry Hill, Camden County.
DELANY, R.A. Pvt, F, 27th VA Inf (CSA), 6-26-1864. Finn's Point National Cemetery, Pennsville, Salem County.

New Jersey Civil War Burials

DELAROI, EUGENE Pvt, A, 26th IN Inf, 10-5-1910. Cedar Hill Cemetery, Florence, Burlington County.

DELATE, JOHN (aka: Dolan, John) Pvt, F, 4th NY Inf, DoD Unknown. Bayview-New York Bay Cemetery, Jersey City, Hudson County.

DELBOW, EDWARD (see: Dolbow, Edward R.) Methodist-Episcopal Church Cemetery, Penns Grove, Salem County.

DELHAGEN, CORNELIUS (aka: Dulhagen Cornelius) Pvt, F, 26th NJ Inf, 7-5-1920. Mount Hebron Cemetery, Montclair, Essex County.

DELL, ALFRED Musc, D, 33rd NJ Inf, 2-15-1905. Woodland Cemetery, Newark, Essex County.

DELL, GEORGE W. Corp, G, 31st NJ Inf, 3-5-1899. Methodist Church Cemetery, Liberty, Warren County.

DELLETT, DANIEL Corp, I, 5th NJ Inf, 3-23-1899. St. Mary of the Assumption Church Cemetery, Pleasant Mills, Atlantic County.

DELOREY, THOMAS (SR.) Pvt, F, 4th NY Cav, 2-14-1898. Phillipsburg Old Catholic Cemetery, Phillipsburg, Warren County.

DELP, WILLIAM Pvt, B, 104th PA Inf, 8-13-1922. Glenwood Cemetery, West Long Branch, Monmouth County.

DELUDE, JAMES Seaman, U.S. Navy, 3-16-1888. Fairmount Cemetery, Newark, Essex County.

DEMAREST, ABRAHAM GARRISON Col, 22nd NJ Inf 10-12-1900. Brookside Cemetery, Englewood, Bergen County.

DEMAREST, ABRAHAM S.D. 1914. Old 1st Reformed Church Cemetery, Hackensack, Bergen County.

DEMAREST, ABRAM A. G. Pvt, H, 25th NJ Inf, 4-16-1916. Woodside Cemetery, Dumont, Bergen County.

DEMAREST, CORNELIUS E. Pvt, D, 22nd NJ Inf, 1-9-1919. Spring Valley Cemetery, Paramus, Bergen County.

DEMAREST, CORNELIUS J. 6-29-1915. Brookside Cemetery, Englewood, Bergen County.

DEMAREST, DANIEL W. Sgt, C, 22nd NJ Inf, 6-21-1911. Maple Grove Cemetery, Hackensack, Bergen County.

DEMAREST, DAVID Pvt, I, 22nd NJ Inf, 10-6-1918. Woodside Cemetery, Dumont, Bergen County.

DEMAREST*, DAVID Corp, C, 5th NY Inf, [Wounded 8-30-1862 at 2nd Bull Run, VA.] 3-10-1898. Bayview-New York Bay Cemetery, Jersey City, Hudson County.

DEMAREST, DAVID A. Pvt, A, 5th NJ Inf, [Cenotaph. Died of scurvy while prisoner at Andersonville, GA.] 8-15-1864. Edgewater Cemetery, Edgewater, Bergen County.

DEMAREST, GARRET I. Sgt, I, 22nd NJ Inf, 4-25-1902. Woodside Cemetery, Dumont, Bergen County.

DEMAREST*, HARTMAN V. Pvt, A, 2nd NY Cav, [Cenotaph. Died while prisoner at Andersonville, GA.] 9-30-1864. Hillside Cemetery, Scotch Plains, Union County.

DEMAREST, HENRY G. Pvt, I, 22nd NJ Inf, 1910. Old Stone Reformed Church Cemetery, Upper Saddle River, Bergen County.

DEMAREST*, HENRY G. Pvt, F, 13th NY Cav, 9-8-1915. Old South Church Cemetery, Bergenfield, Bergen County.

DEMAREST, ISAAC D. Seaman, U.S. Navy, USS Crusader, 10-15-1897. Valleau Cemetery, Ridgewood, Bergen County.

DEMAREST, JACOB Pvt, A, 22nd NJ Inf, 11-28-1893. French Cemetery, New Milford, Bergen County.

DEMAREST, JAMES A. Pvt, C, 13th NJ Inf, 10-11-1890. Holy Sepulchre Cemetery, Totowa, Passaic County.

DEMAREST, JAMES B. Pvt, A, 1st NY Cav, 10-18-1913. Old 1st Reformed Church Cemetery, Hackensack, Bergen County.

Our Brothers Gone Before

DEMAREST, JAMES G. Sgt, K, 1st NY Marine Art, 1-21-1889. Woodside Cemetery, Dumont, Bergen County.
DEMAREST, JAMES H. Corp, H, 39th NJ Inf, 1911. Evergreen Cemetery, Hillside, Union County.
DEMAREST, JAMES HENRY Pvt, I, 22nd NJ Inf, 4-18-1891. English Neighborhood Reformed Church Cemetery, Ridgefield, Bergen County.
DEMAREST, JAMES J. Seaman, U.S. Navy, USS Allegheny, 4-17-1912. Laurel Grove Cemetery, Totowa, Passaic County.
DEMAREST*, JOHN Corp, A, 13th NJ Inf, 4-22-1907. Fairmount Cemetery, Newark, Essex County.
DEMAREST, JOHN A. Pvt, D, 22nd NJ Inf, 12-21-1891. Old South Church Cemetery, Bergenfield, Bergen County.
DEMAREST, JOHN H. __, G, 9th __ __, [Died at Fort Monroe, VA.] 12-18-1861. Old Hook Cemetery, Westwood, Bergen County.
DEMAREST, JOHN J. Pvt, D, 22nd NJ Inf, 8-7-1911. Pascack Reformed Cemetery, Park Ridge, Bergen County.
DEMAREST, JUSTIN 11-1-1878. Blauvelt Cemetery, Harrington Park, Bergen County.
DEMAREST, PETER J. Pvt, D, 22nd NJ Inf, 3-16-1912. Pascack Reformed Cemetery, Park Ridge, Bergen County.
DEMAREST, PETER J. Corp, A, 22nd NJ Inf, 10-1-1896. Valleau Cemetery, Ridgewood, Bergen County.
DEMAREST, RICHARD G. 1872. Woodside Cemetery, Dumont, Bergen County.
DEMAREST, SAMUEL D. Maj, 22nd NJ Inf 5-12-1879. Old South Church Cemetery, Bergenfield, Bergen County.
DEMAREST, THOMAS W. Sgt, D, 22nd NJ Inf, 12-31-1903. Old Hook Cemetery, Westwood, Bergen County.
DEMAREST, WILLIAM Pvt, H, 25th NJ Inf, 9-19-1905. Mount Pleasant Cemetery, Newark, Essex County.
DEMAREST, WILLIAM A. Pvt, H, 25th NJ Inf, 12-23-1894. Cedar Lawn Cemetery, Paterson, Passaic County.
DEMAREST, WILLIAM J. 1st Lt, C, 22nd NJ Inf, 10-20-1905. Maple Grove Cemetery, Hackensack, Bergen County.
DEMARIS, JAMES P. Pvt, G, 12th NJ Inf, 1910. Arlington Cemetery, Pennsauken, Camden County.
DEMARIS, WILLIAM FRANKLIN Corp, F, 24th NJ Inf, 4-4-1894. Cohansey Baptist Church Cemetery, Bowentown, Cumberland County.
DEMASS, JOHN LEWIS (aka: Demass, Lewis) Pvt, H, 28th PA Inf, 12-24-1910. Phillipsburg Cemetery, Phillipsburg, Warren County.
DEMASS, LEWIS (see: Demass, John Lewis) Phillipsburg Cemetery, Phillipsburg, Warren County.
DEMASURE*, LOUIS Capt, H, 38th NY Inf, [Wounded 5-31-1862 at Fair Oaks, VA.] 10-17-1895. Fairmount Cemetery, Newark, Essex County.
DEMBY, JOHN Pvt, G, 24th U.S. CT, 1-10-1919. Jordan Lawn Cemetery, Pennsauken, Camden County.
DEMEDUKE, EVAN 3-17-1918. New Camden Cemetery, Camden, Camden County.
DEMING, WILLIAM Corp, G, 7th MI Inf, [Died of disease at Beverly, NJ.] 10-5-1864. Beverly National Cemetery, Edgewater Park, Burlington County.
DEMONT, ISAIAH Pvt, K, 39th NJ Inf, 3-30-1867. Union Cemetery, Washington, Morris County.
DEMOTT, HENRY C. 10-9-1882. Union Cemetery, Frenchtown, Hunterdon County.
DEMOTT, HIRAM Pvt, E, 31st NJ Inf, 9-21-1910. Holcomb-Riverview Cemetery, Lambertville, Hunterdon County.
DEMOTT, JACOB H. 1914. Union Cemetery, Frenchtown, Hunterdon County.

New Jersey Civil War Burials

DEMOTT, JACOB K. (aka: Dermott, Jacob) Corp, A, 30th NJ Inf, 10-16-1923. New Presbyterian Cemetery, Bound Brook, Somerset County.

DEMOTT*, JAMES B. Corp, Btty B, 5th NY Heavy Art, [Wounded 3-4-1863 at Aldie, VA.] 12-16-1896. Maple Grove Cemetery, Hackensack, Bergen County.

DEMOTT, JAMES BLAUVELT (aka: DeMott, John) Pvt, I, 22nd NJ Inf, [Died of typhoid at Fort Alexandria, MD.] 11-22-1862. Woodside Cemetery, Dumont, Bergen County.

DEMOTT, JOHN (see: DeMott, James Blauvelt) Woodside Cemetery, Dumont, Bergen County.

DEMOTT, JOHN JACOB Pvt, A, 22nd NJ Inf, 10-1-1898. Woodside Cemetery, Dumont, Bergen County.

DEMOTT, JOHN JACOB 8-11-1917. Laurel Grove Cemetery, Totowa, Passaic County.

DEMOTT, NATHAN Pvt, 4th NY Ind Btty 3-22-1928. 1st Reformed Church Cemetery, Pompton Plains, Morris County.

DEMOTT, WALTER __, __, 3rd __ Inf, DoD Unknown. Evergreen Cemetery, Hillside, Union County.

DEMOUTH, CYRUS Pvt, L, 27th NJ Inf, 1-10-1887. Presbyterian Church Cemetery, Rockaway, Morris County.

DEMOUTH, JESSE Pvt, L, 27th NJ Inf, [Drowned while crossing the Cumberland River, KY.] 5-6-1863. United Methodist Church Cemetery, Rockaway Valley, Morris County.

DEMOUTH, THOMAS Pvt, L, 27th NJ Inf, [Died of typhoid at Washington, DC.] 1-26-1863. United Methodist Church Cemetery, Rockaway Valley, Morris County.

DEMOUTH, WILLIAM Pvt, L, 27th NJ Inf, [Died of diarrhea at Newport News, VA.] 3-1-1863. United Methodist Church Cemetery, Rockaway Valley, Morris County.

DEMPSEY, BARTHOLOMEW W. Corp, C, 7th NJ Inf, 3-20-1879. Holy Rood Cemetery, Morristown, Morris County.

DEMPSEY, JAMES E. Pvt, H, 65th NY Inf, [Wounded 5-6-1864 at Wilderness, VA.] 12-20-1906. Holy Name Cemetery, Jersey City, Hudson County.

DEMPSEY, JOHN Fireman, U.S. Navy, 11-19-1897. Greengrove Cemetery, Keyport, Monmouth County.

DEMPSEY, JOHN Pvt, Btty B, 1st NJ Light Art, 12-30-1901. Holy Sepulchre Cemetery, East Orange, Essex County.

DEMPSEY, JOHN A. Pvt, H, 7th NJ Inf, [Killed in action at Gettysburg, PA.] 7-2-1863. St. Mary's Cemetery, Boonton, Morris County.

DEMPSEY, LEVI J. Pvt, C, 7th VA Inf (CSA), [Wounded 6-30-1862 at Frayser's Farm, VA. Captured 7-3-1863 at Gettysburg, PA.] 10-3-1863. Finn's Point National Cemetery, Pennsville, Salem County.

DEMPSEY, MICHAEL Pvt, F, 10th NY Inf, 1-30-1897. Fairmount Cemetery, Newark, Essex County.

DEMPSEY, MICHAEL Pvt, F, 2nd NJ Militia, 9-1-1863. St. Peter's Cemetery, Jersey City, Hudson County.

DEMPSEY, PETER Pvt, G, 27th NJ Inf, DoD Unknown. St. Mary's Cemetery, Boonton, Morris County.

DEMPSEY, PETER Pvt, G, 26th NJ Inf, 9-11-1918. Holy Sepulchre Cemetery, East Orange, Essex County.

DEMPSEY*, THOMAS Pvt, B, 38th NJ Inf, 4-3-1899. St. John's Cemetery, Lambertville, Hunterdon County.

DEMPSEY, THOMAS 1st Lt, I, 44th NY Inf, [Accidently wounded 8-19-1863.] 1885. Mount Carmel Cemetery, West Long Branch, Monmouth County.

DEMPSEY*, WILLIAM H. Pvt, F, 123rd NY Inf, 1-4-1894. Riverside Cemetery, Toms River, Ocean County.

DEMPSTER, DAVID Pvt, Btty E, 1st U.S. Art, 10-24-1898. Grove Church Cemetery, North Bergen, Hudson County.

Our Brothers Gone Before

DEMPSTER*, WILLIAM Landsman, U.S. Navy, USS Florida, 5-19-1875. Phillipsburg Cemetery, Phillipsburg, Warren County.

DEMUNN, ISAIAH (aka: Dennon, Isaiah) Corp, A, 43rd U.S. CT, 4-18-1889. Van Liew Cemetery, North Brunswick, Middlesex County.

DENAWAY, JAMES F. (see: Dunaway, James F.) Finn's Point National Cemetery, Pennsville, Salem County.

DENEE*, DAVID L. Corp, I, 2nd NJ Inf, 11-4-1912. Union Cemetery, Washington, Morris County.

DENELSBECK, FREDERICK Pvt, D, 24th NJ Inf, 10-11-1917. Cohansey Baptist Church Cemetery, Bowentown, Cumberland County.

DENFY, JOHN (aka: Derofy, John) Pvt, Btty A, 1st NJ Light Art, 1-5-1875. Holy Name Cemetery, Jersey City, Hudson County.

DENGEL, JACOB (see: Dengel, John) Holy Sepulchre Cemetery, Totowa, Passaic County.

DENGEL, JOHN (aka: Dengel, Jacob) Pvt, I, 45th NY Inf, 6-7-1911. Holy Sepulchre Cemetery, Totowa, Passaic County.

DENGY, ELEASER (see: Dingee, Eleazer) Siloam Cemetery, Vineland, Cumberland County.

DENHOLM, CHARLES Corp, K, 25th NJ Inf, 6-31-1908. Cedar Lawn Cemetery, Paterson, Passaic County.

DENIKE, JACOB Corp, F, 2nd NJ Inf, 4-5-1897. Laurel Grove Cemetery, Totowa, Passaic County.

DENIKE, JOHN (see: Teneyck, John) Presbyterian Church Cemetery, Rockaway, Morris County.

DENISE, SAMUEL T. Pvt, F, 29th NJ Inf, 1903. Episcopal Church Cemetery, Shrewsbury, Monmouth County.

DENMAN, FRANK GEORGE (aka: Dinman, Francis) QM Sgt, I, 8th NY Cav, 2-13-1906. Fairview Cemetery, Fairview, Bergen County.

DENMAN*, JOHN Pvt, E, 7th NJ Inf, 1915. Evergreen Cemetery, Morristown, Morris County.

DENMAN, JULIUS R. Pvt, D, 106th NY Inf, 5-27-1916. Clinton Cemetery, Irvington, Essex County.

DENMAN, RICHARD L. Pvt, D, 22nd NY State Militia, DoD Unknown. Arlington Cemetery, Kearny, Hudson County.

DENMAN, THEODORE M. Pvt, K, 9th NJ Inf, [Died of typhoid at Newbern, NC.] 3-14-1862. Evergreen Cemetery, Hillside, Union County.

DENMEAD*, JOHN TENANT 2nd Lt, B, 13th NJ Inf, 10-22-1898. Jersey City Cemetery, Jersey City, Hudson County.

DENN, JARED Sgt, F, 2nd NJ Inf, 2-29-1879. Holy Sepulchre Cemetery, East Orange, Essex County.

DENNAN, MICHAEL Pvt, 5th NY Ind Btty 4-5-1907. Arlington Cemetery, Kearny, Hudson County.

DENNER, FREDERICK Pvt, F, 22nd NJ Inf, 8-23-1906. Riverview Cemetery, Trenton, Mercer County.

DENNETT, ADOLPHUS Actg Ensign, U.S. Navy, 6-15-1876. Cedar Green Cemetery, Clayton, Gloucester County.

DENNETT, HENRY CLAY 9-26-1913. Bayview-New York Bay Cemetery, Jersey City, Hudson County.

DENNETT, JOHN Actg Ensign, U.S. Navy, 1883. Princeton Cemetery, Princeton, Mercer County.

DENNETT, THOMAS Sgt, B, 30th NJ Inf, 2-6-1869. Evergreen Cemetery, Hillside, Union County.

DENNEY, FREDERICK Pvt, C, 28th PA Inf, 11-26-1876. Riverview Cemetery, Trenton, Mercer County.

New Jersey Civil War Burials

DENNING, GEORGE Pvt, F, 6th NJ Inf, 2-27-1917. Methodist Cemetery, Bridgeboro, Burlington County.

DENNING, JAMES Pvt, Btty D, 1st NJ Light Art, 1-23-1908. Fairmount Cemetery, Newark, Essex County.

DENNIS, ANDREW J. Pvt, H, 31st NJ Inf, 3-29-1897. Tranquility Cemetery, Tranquility, Sussex County.

DENNIS, ANTHONY E. Musc, A, 30th NJ Inf, 1866. United Methodist Cemetery, Gladstone, Somerset County.

DENNIS, CHARLES Pvt, D, 9th NJ Inf, 1-22-1872. Baptist Cemetery, Burlington, Burlington County.

DENNIS, CHARLES Pvt, D, 31st U.S. CT, 3-27-1922. Arlington Cemetery, Kearny, Hudson County.

DENNIS, CHARLES Corp, A, 6th U.S. CT, 12-3-1889. Hamilton Cemetery, Allentown, Monmouth County.

DENNIS*, CHARLES Landsman, U.S. Navy, USS Hartford, 9-28-1909. White Ridge Cemetery, Eatontown, Monmouth County.

DENNIS, CHARLES E. Pvt, L, 1st NJ Cav, 11-2-1907. Old 1st Methodist Church Cemetery, West Long Branch, Monmouth County.

DENNIS, EUGENE 1-13-1884. Mount Pleasant Cemetery, Newark, Essex County.

DENNIS*, EUGENE E. Corp, D, 39th NJ Inf, 12-16-1924. Fairmount Cemetery, Newark, Essex County.

DENNIS, FRANK W. Pvt, A, 13th NJ Inf, 12-15-1929. Holy Sepulchre Cemetery, East Orange, Essex County.

DENNIS*, GEORGE Pvt, G, 11th NJ Inf, 4-3-1916. Brotherhood Cemetery, Hainesport, Burlington County.

DENNIS, GEORGE W. Pvt, D, 25th VA Inf (CSA), [Captured 7-4-1863 at South Mountain, MD. died of erysipelas.] 10-16-1863. Finn's Point National Cemetery, Pennsville, Salem County.

DENNIS, GEORGE W. Pvt, Massie's Btty, Fluvanna VA Light Art (CSA), 4-14-1865. Finn's Point National Cemetery, Pennsville, Salem County.

DENNIS, H.G. Pvt, G, 30th VA Cav (CSA), 4-20-1864. Finn's Point National Cemetery, Pennsville, Salem County.

DENNIS, HARRY G. (see: Dennis, Henry G.) Oddfellows Cemetery, Burlington, Burlington County.

DENNIS, HENRY Pvt, G, 39th NY Inf, [Wounded 5-6-1864 at Wilderness, VA.] DoD Unknown. Flower Hill Cemetery, North Bergen, Hudson County.

DENNIS, HENRY DoD Unknown. Maplewood Cemetery, Freehold, Monmouth County.

DENNIS, HENRY Pvt, K, 27th NJ Inf, 6-13-1921. Minisink Reformed Church Cemetery, Montague, Sussex County.

DENNIS, HENRY G. (aka: Dennis, Harry G.) Sgt, A, 15th PA Cav, 10-13-1918. Oddfellows Cemetery, Burlington, Burlington County.

DENNIS, HORACE H. (see: Dennis, Horace S.) Evergreen Cemetery, Hillside, Union County.

DENNIS, HORACE S. (aka: Dennis, Horace H.) Pvt, C, 143rd PA Inf, 3-15-1884. Evergreen Cemetery, Hillside, Union County.

DENNIS, ISAIAH L. Pvt, C, 9th NJ Inf, 10-18-1924. Arlington Cemetery, Kearny, Hudson County.

DENNIS, JAMES M. Pvt, C, 8th NJ Inf, 8-8-1893. Fairview Cemetery, Wantage, Sussex County.

DENNIS, JOHN Pvt, C, 10th U.S. CT, 1-1-1911. Mount Peace Cemetery, Lawnside, Camden County.

DENNIS, JOHN Corp, C, 31st NJ Inf, 7-8-1920. Presbyterian Church Cemetery, Bloomsbury, Hunterdon County.

Our Brothers Gone Before

DENNIS, JOHN Pvt, F, 8th U.S. CT, 1-12-1932. Greenwood Cemetery, Hamilton, Mercer County.
DENNIS, JOHN Pvt, D, 3rd NJ Inf, 3-24-1884. Newton Cemetery, Newton, Sussex County.
DENNIS, JOHN H. Pvt, K, 2nd NJ Cav, 1932. Mount Hebron Cemetery, Montclair, Essex County.
DENNIS, JOHN W. Pvt, C, 9th NJ Inf, 2-12-1904. Baptist/St. Andrew's Cemetery, Mount Holly, Burlington County.
DENNIS, JOHN W. Pvt, D, 27th NJ Inf, 1923. Hardyston Cemetery, North Church, Sussex County.
DENNIS, JOSEPH H. Pvt, F, 29th NJ Inf, 4-20-1912. Fairview Cemetery, Fairview, Monmouth County.
DENNIS, JOSEPH H. Pvt, F, 29th NJ Inf, DoD Unknown. Episcopal Church Cemetery, Shrewsbury, Monmouth County.
DENNIS, LIPPINCOTT (aka: Lippincott, Dennis) Pvt, D, 5th U.S. Inf, 1-10-1897. Baptist/St. Andrew's Cemetery, Mount Holly, Burlington County.
DENNIS, MILTON H. (aka: Diemer, Milton H.) Pvt, G, 1st (Turney's) TN Inf (CSA), 9-10-1863. Finn's Point National Cemetery, Pennsville, Salem County.
DENNIS, NOAH Corp, G, 11th NJ Inf, 7-7-1911. Baptist Church Cemetery, Jacobstown, Burlington County.
DENNIS, NOAH B. (SR.) Pvt, C, 23rd NJ Inf, 7-1-1882. Baptist/St. Andrew's Cemetery, Mount Holly, Burlington County.
DENNIS, ROSTEEN Pvt, K, 35th NJ Inf, 4-2-1873. Mercer Cemetery, Trenton, Mercer County.
DENNIS, SAMUEL Capt, H, 27th NJ Inf, 4-21-1891. Deckertown-Union Cemetery, Papakating, Sussex County.
DENNIS*, SAMUEL Pvt, I, 9th VA Inf (CSA), 4-17-1891. Valleau Cemetery, Ridgewood, Bergen County.
DENNIS, THEODORE A. Pvt, E, 37th NJ Inf, 2-2-1926. Evergreen Cemetery, Hillside, Union County.
DENNIS, THOMAS Pvt, H, 3rd NJ Inf, 9-25-1894. Brotherhood Cemetery, Hainesport, Burlington County.
DENNIS, THOMAS JAMES Pvt, I, 37th NJ Inf, 1-16-1871. Mount Olivet Cemetery, Newark, Essex County.
DENNIS, WILLIAM Pvt, F, 29th NJ Inf, [Died of typhoid at Tennallytown, DC.] 11-10-1862. Fairview Cemetery, Fairview, Monmouth County.
DENNIS, WILLIAM Pvt, D, 9th NJ Inf, 4-4-1930. Roadside Cemetery, Manchester Township, Ocean County.
DENNIS, WILLIAM Pvt, G, 10th NJ Inf, 5-22-1912. Tabernacle Cemetery, Tabernacle, Burlington County.
DENNIS, WILLIAM A. Pvt, G, 34th NJ Inf, 4-23-1889. Methodist Church Cemetery, Groveville, Mercer County.
DENNISON, HARRY 11-4-1892. Arlington Cemetery, Kearny, Hudson County.
DENNISON, JAMES Pvt, B, 16th VA Cav (CSA), 3-19-1864. Finn's Point National Cemetery, Pennsville, Salem County.
DENNISON, RANSOM G. Pvt, B, 84th NY National Guard, 1929. Arlington Cemetery, Pennsauken, Camden County.
DENNISTON, C.A. 1-18-1911. Grove Church Cemetery, North Bergen, Hudson County.
DENNON, ISAIAH (see: DeMunn, Isaiah) Van Liew Cemetery, North Brunswick, Middlesex County.
DENNY*, SAMUEL M. Ordinary Seaman, U.S. Navy, USS Pawtuxet, 4-14-1932. Riverview Cemetery, Penns Grove, Salem County.
DENSEN, SAMUEL 3-5-1870. 1st Methodist-Episcopal Cemetery, New Brunswick, Middlesex County.

New Jersey Civil War Burials

DENSKY, JULIUS 5-1-1903. Flower Hill Cemetery, North Bergen, Hudson County.
DENSON, JOSEPH W. Corp, G, 15th NJ Inf, 9-27-1910. Holcomb-Riverview Cemetery, Lambertville, Hunterdon County.
DENT, MATTHEW M. (aka: Dent, W.M.) Pvt, D, 25th U.S. CT, 9-25-1912. Mount Salem Church Cemetery, Fenwick, Salem County.
DENT, W.M. (see: Dent, Matthew M.) Mount Salem Church Cemetery, Fenwick, Salem County.
DENTEL, WENDELINE (aka: Darrell, Vandeline) Pvt, G, 34th NJ Inf, 12-20-1918. St. Francis Cemetery, Trenton, Mercer County.
DENTON, ANTHONY WILLIAM Corp, G, 39th NJ Inf, 1-26-1905. Evergreen Cemetery, Hillside, Union County.
DENTON, BENJAMIN Pvt, U.S. Army, 1-18-1874. Fairmount Cemetery, Newark, Essex County.
DENTON, CHARLES C. Sgt, D, 28th NJ Inf, 1-25-1925. Elmwood Cemetery, New Brunswick, Middlesex County.
DENTON, CHARLES C. (SR.) Pvt, B, 9th NJ Inf, 1-11-1909. Evergreen Cemetery, Hillside, Union County.
DENTON, ELIAS Pvt, K, 37th VA Inf (CSA), [Captured 5-12-1864 at Spotsylvania CH, VA. Died of lung inflammation.] 8-6-1864. Finn's Point National Cemetery, Pennsville, Salem County.
DENTON, JAMES 1st Lt, A, 1st NJ Inf, 8-25-1888. Elmwood Cemetery, New Brunswick, Middlesex County.
DENTON, JAMES C. Seaman, U.S. Navy, 10-22-1909. Evergreen Cemetery, Hillside, Union County.
DENTON, JAMES O. Pvt, K, 37th VA Inf (CSA), [Captured 5-12-1864 at Spotsylvania CH, VA. Died of pneumonia.] 2-20-1865. Finn's Point National Cemetery, Pennsville, Salem County.
DENTON*, JOHN L. Corp, K, 7th NJ Inf, 4-20-1899. Presbyterian Church Cemetery, Mendham, Morris County.
DENTON, JOHN R. 3-14-1890. Woodlawn Cemetery, Lakewood, Ocean County.
DENTON, JOHN R.S. 4-8-1882. Woodland Cemetery, Newark, Essex County.
DENTON, REUBEN (see: Denton, Robert) Speer Cemetery, Jersey City, Hudson County.
DENTON, ROBERT (aka: Denton, Reuben) Pvt, C, 12th NJ Inf, 10-11-1865. Speer Cemetery, Jersey City, Hudson County.
DENTON, STEPHEN H. Pvt, B, 5th NY Inf, 1-14-1906. Mount Pleasant Cemetery, Newark, Essex County.
DENTZER, JOHN (see: Daentzer, John) Riverside Cemetery, Riverside, Burlington County.
DENYSE, AUGUSTUS M. Pvt, A, 21st NJ Inf, 11-12-1889. Rose Hill Cemetery, Matawan, Monmouth County.
DEOYNGEART, EMILE (see: DeWyngant, Emilio) St. Mary's Cemetery, East Orange, Essex County.
DEPEW, ABRAHAM Pvt, E, 26th U.S. CT, 10-10-1897. Evergreen Cemetery, Morristown, Morris County.
DEPEW, THOMAS Sgt, Btty E, 4th NY Heavy Art, 5-3-1935. Elmwood Cemetery, New Brunswick, Middlesex County.
DEPOE, JAMES H. Corp, K, 39th NJ Inf, 1930. Boonton Cemetery, Boonton, Morris County.
DEPOE, WILLIAM D. Pvt, I, 30th NJ Inf, 1907. Reformed Church Cemetery, Bedminster, Somerset County.
DEPPICH, SIMON (see: Debbie, Simon Peter) St Mary's Cemetery, Watchung, Somerset County.
DEPPISCH, STEPHEN (aka: Drodossky, John) Pvt, B, 175th NY Inf, DoD Unknown. Holy Name Cemetery, Jersey City, Hudson County.

Our Brothers Gone Before

DEPREAST, AMOS (aka: Prush, Amos) Pvt, A, 2nd AR Inf (CSA), [Captured 6-27-1863 at Hoover's Gap, TN.] 1-19-1864. Finn's Point National Cemetery, Pennsville, Salem County.

DEPREZ, JOHN Landsman, U.S. Navy, USS Sonora, 1-30-1912. Evergreen Cemetery, Hillside, Union County.

DEPUE, J.S. 1885. Greenmount Cemetery, Hammonton, Atlantic County.

DEPUE, MATTHEW E. Pvt, A, 27th NJ Inf, 10-31-1881. Hainesville Cemetery, Hainesville, Sussex County.

DEPUGH, JAMES E. (aka: James E. Pugh) Musc, 5th NJ Inf Band 5-7-1901. Baptist Cemetery, Salem, Salem County.

DERBY, DANIEL (aka: Derry, Daniel) Pvt, I, 8th U.S. CT, 5-3-1911. Mount Peace Cemetery, Lawnside, Camden County.

DEREAMER, GEORGE C. Pvt, H, 15th NJ Inf, 1-13-1904. Belvidere/Catholic Cemetery, Belvidere, Warren County.

DEREMER, GARDNER H. Corp, H, 15th NJ Inf, 1-24-1916. Broadway Cemetery, Broadway, Warren County.

DEREMER, ISAAC R. Pvt, H, 15th NJ Inf, 6-25-1893. Mansfield/Washington Cemetery, Washington, Warren County.

DEREMER*, JARED RUSSELL (aka: Deroemer, Russell) Pvt, C, 147th PA Inf, DoD Unknown. Union Brick Cemetery, Blairstown, Warren County.

DEREMER, PHILIP Pvt, B, 31st NJ Inf, 5-4-1914. Broadway Cemetery, Broadway, Warren County.

DEREMER, WILLIAM Sgt, H, 15th NJ Inf, 4-24-1904. Mansfield/Washington Cemetery, Washington, Warren County.

DERENGER, CHARLES Pvt, G, 132nd NY Inf, 4-29-1894. Reformed Church Cemetery, Three Bridges, Hunterdon County.

DERING, HENRY Pvt, A, 9th NJ Inf, 7-31-1910. Bayview-New York Bay Cemetery, Jersey City, Hudson County.

DERMER, MANNING Pvt, D, 3rd NJ Inf, 3-31-1870. Fairmount Cemetery, Newark, Essex County.

DERMOTT, JACOB (see: DeMott, Jacob K.) New Presbyterian Cemetery, Bound Brook, Somerset County.

DEROEMER, RUSSELL (see: Deremer, Jared Russell) Union Brick Cemetery, Blairstown, Warren County.

DEROFY, JOHN (see: Denfy, John) Holy Name Cemetery, Jersey City, Hudson County.

DEROUSSE, LOUIS THEODORE 8-27-1921. Harleigh Cemetery, Camden, Camden County.

DERREVERE, MATTHIAS Pvt, C, 30th NJ Inf, 2-8-1904. Hazelwood Cemetery, Rahway, Union County.

DERRICK*, JOHN Pvt, H, 10th MI Inf, 12-10-1903. Berlin Cemetery, Berlin, Camden County.

DERRIG, JOHN Pvt, F, 2nd NJ Inf, 8-26-1890. Holy Sepulchre Cemetery, East Orange, Essex County.

DERROM, ANDREW Col, 25th NJ Inf 7-14-1892. Cedar Lawn Cemetery, Paterson, Passaic County.

DERRY, DANIEL (see: Derby, Daniel) Mount Peace Cemetery, Lawnside, Camden County.

DERRY, JOHN Pvt, A, 5th PA Cav, 12-28-1906. Evergreen Cemetery, Camden, Camden County.

DERUSSY, THOMAS N. 8-28-1887. Christ Episcopal Church Cemetery, New Brunswick, Middlesex County.

DERVIR, JOHN (see: Devore, John) Cedar Lawn Cemetery, Paterson, Passaic County.

DESANGES*, ROBERT W.B. Col, 6th LA Inf (US) [African Descent Regiment.] 1-14-1894. Fairview Cemetery, Fairview, Monmouth County.

New Jersey Civil War Burials

DESCHRYVER, FRANCIS J. Capt, A, 145th PA Inf, 10-23-1899. Holy Sepulchre Cemetery, East Orange, Essex County.
DESEROTH, GEORGE (see: Deiszeroth, George C.) New York/New Jersey Crematory Cemetery, North Bergen, Hudson County.
DESHAZO, JOHN M. Pvt, B, 42nd MS Inf (CSA), 10-1-1863. Finn's Point National Cemetery, Pennsville, Salem County.
DESHIELDS, ROBERT H. (aka: Dashiell, Robert) Pvt, H, 19th U.S. CT, 6-20-1906. Jordan Lawn Cemetery, Pennsauken, Camden County.
DESHLER, E.B. (see: Dresler, John) Elmwood Cemetery, New Brunswick, Middlesex County.
DESMOND, DANIEL Pvt, C, 33rd NJ Inf, 9-17-1872. Fairmount Cemetery, Newark, Essex County.
DESMOND, JAMES (JR.) Pvt, E, 88th NY Inf, 3-25-1898. Holy Name Cemetery, Jersey City, Hudson County.
DESMOND, JOHN Pvt, D, 33rd NJ Inf, 2-1-1901. Holy Sepulchre Cemetery, East Orange, Essex County.
DESMOND, PATRICK Pvt, I, 29th NJ Inf, 2-28-1878. St. Rose of Lima Cemetery, Freehold, Monmouth County.
DETLEFSEN, HANS CHRISTIAN __, __, __ NY __, 11-3-1893. Berry Lawn Cemetery, Carlstadt, Bergen County.
DETTLINGER, GEORGE J. 2-5-1901. Greenlawn Cemetery, West Long Branch, Monmouth County.
DETZER, JOSEPH Corp, G, 1st NY Inf, 9-3-1905. Palisade Cemetery, North Bergen, Hudson County.
DEUEL, HENRY L. Pvt, D, 102nd NY National Guard, 3-1-1902. Washington Monumental Cemetery, South River, Middlesex County.
DEVAUL, ELWOOD Pvt, F, 25th NJ Inf, 5-8-1912. Methodist Church Cemetery, Seaville, Cape May County.
DEVAUSNA, JOHN (see: Devausney, John) Fairmount Cemetery, Newark, Essex County.
DEVAUSNEY, CHARLES (aka: Devorsoney, Charles) Pvt, H, 1st NJ Militia, 3-1-1914. Fairmount Cemetery, Newark, Essex County.
DEVAUSNEY, JOHN (aka: Devausna, John) Pvt, A, 13th NJ Inf, 11-9-1893. Fairmount Cemetery, Newark, Essex County.
DEVAUSNEY, JOHN S. Sgt, I, 13th NJ Inf, 9-22-1877. Fairmount Cemetery, Newark, Essex County.
DEVELIN, BARNEY (see: Devlin, Bernard) St. John's Cemetery, Hamilton, Mercer County.
DEVINE, CHRISTOPHER Pvt, I, 33rd NJ Inf, 8-26-1903. Holy Sepulchre Cemetery, East Orange, Essex County.
DEVINE, EDWARD M. Pvt, I, 37th NJ Inf, 8-7-1909. Baptist/Evergreen Methodist Cemetery, Plainfield, Union County.
DEVINE, HUGH Pvt, C, 25th NJ Inf, 12-13-1902. Laurel Grove Cemetery, Totowa, Passaic County.
DEVINE*, JAMES M. (aka: Devine, John) Pvt, D, 71st NY Inf, 9-30-1909. Holy Sepulchre Cemetery, East Orange, Essex County.
DEVINE, JOHN Pvt, C, 7th MO Inf, 3-10-1895. St. Rose of Lima Cemetery, Oxford, Warren County.
DEVINE, JOHN Pvt, K, 70th NY Inf, 4-2-1881. Holy Sepulchre Cemetery, East Orange, Essex County.
DEVINE, JOHN (see: Devine, James) Holy Sepulchre Cemetery, East Orange, Essex County.
DEVINE, JOHN J. Landsman, U.S. Navy, USS Hibiscus, 8-6-1894. Holy Sepulchre Cemetery, East Orange, Essex County.

Our Brothers Gone Before

DEVINE, PATRICK Pvt, G, 40th NJ Inf, 3-13-1888. Holy Name Cemetery, Jersey City, Hudson County.
DEVINE, PATRICK Pvt, K, 26th NJ Inf, DoD Unknown. Holy Sepulchre Cemetery, East Orange, Essex County.
DEVINE, PATRICK M. Pvt, C, 2nd NJ Inf, 7-13-1905. Holy Sepulchre Cemetery, East Orange, Essex County.
DEVINE, TERRENCE Landsman, U.S. Navy, USS Hibiscus, 9-10-1919. Holy Sepulchre Cemetery, East Orange, Essex County.
DEVINE, WILLIAM Pvt, C, 1st NJ Inf, 7-14-1919. Holy Name Cemetery, Jersey City, Hudson County.
DEVINNEY, ALEXANDER Pvt, E, 23rd NJ Inf, 10-6-1916. Brotherhood Cemetery, Hainesport, Burlington County.
DEVINNEY, MICHAEL E. Capt, D, 37th NJ Inf, 1-7-1925. Soldier's Home Cemetery, Vineland, Cumberland County.
DEVINSBURG, JEROME (aka: Davenburg, Jerome) Pvt, G, 41st U.S. CT, 3-6-1898. Johnson Cemetery, Camden, Camden County.
DEVLAN, CHARLES F. Pvt, K, 6th PA Cav, 10-6-1920. Evergreen Cemetery, Hillside, Union County.
DEVLIN*, BERNARD Pvt, B, 33rd NJ Inf, 3-7-1915. Holy Name Cemetery, Jersey City, Hudson County.
DEVLIN, BERNARD (aka: Develin, Barney) Pvt, I, 198th PA Inf, 2-8-1900. St. John's Cemetery, Hamilton, Mercer County.
DEVLIN, EDWARD Corp, H, 1st NJ Inf, 3-10-1924. Arlington Cemetery, Kearny, Hudson County.
DEVLIN, JAMES Pvt, D, 6th NJ Inf, DoD Unknown. St. Paul's R.C. Church Cemetery, Princeton, Mercer County.
DEVLIN, MICHAEL Pvt, G, 1st NJ Cav, DoD Unknown. Old St. Mary's Cemetery, Gloucester City, Camden County.
DEVLIN, WILLIAM Pvt, G, 22nd NJ Inf, 5-7-1873. St. Paul's R.C. Church Cemetery, Princeton, Mercer County.
DEVOE, ABRAHAM Pvt, C, 147th NY Inf, DoD Unknown. Hackensack Cemetery, Hackensack, Bergen County.
DEVOE, GEORGE (see: Devore, George) Cedar Lawn Cemetery, Paterson, Passaic County.
DEVOE, GEORGE H. Landsman, U.S. Navy, USS Jacob Bell, 5-26-1910. Fairmount Cemetery, Newark, Essex County.
DEVOE, GLENDORA Pvt, K, 104th PA Inf, 1927. Chestnut Grove Cemetery, Elmer, Salem County.
DEVOE, JOHN Pvt, M, 2nd NJ Cav, 8-16-1870. Bordentown/Old St. Mary's Catholic Cemetery, Bordentown, Burlington County.
DEVOE, PETER Pvt, D, 11th NJ Inf, 2-4-1872. Swayze Cemetery, Swayze's Mills, Warren County.
DEVOE, WILLIAM I. Corp, B, 29th NJ Inf, [Died at Camp Rappahannock, VA. of wounds received at Chancellorsville, VA.] 5-2-1863. Greengrove Cemetery, Keyport, Monmouth County.
DEVORE, BYRON Pvt, I, 39th NJ Inf, DoD Unknown. Cedar Lawn Cemetery, Paterson, Passaic County.
DEVORE, GEORGE (aka: Devoe, George) Pvt, F, 17th NY Inf, DoD Unknown. Cedar Lawn Cemetery, Paterson, Passaic County.
DEVORE, GEORGE S. Pvt, D, 15th NJ Inf, 1909. Newton Cemetery, Newton, Sussex County.
DEVORE, JOHN (aka: Dervir, John) Pvt, G, 7th NJ Inf, DoD Unknown. Cedar Lawn Cemetery, Paterson, Passaic County.

New Jersey Civil War Burials

DEVORSONEY, CHARLES (see: Devausney, Charles) Fairmount Cemetery, Newark, Essex County.

DEVOTO, JOHN (aka: Letter, John) Pvt, I, 85th PA Inf, 1-7-1933. Holy Redeemer Cemetery, South Plainfield, Middlesex County.

DEVOUR, WILLIAM Pvt, H, 25th NJ Inf, DoD Unknown. Cedar Lawn Cemetery, Paterson, Passaic County.

DEVRIES, NOMDO (see: Devries, Vombe Z.) Hillside Cemetery, Lyndhurst, Bergen County.

DEVRIES*, VOMBE Z. (aka: Devries, Nomdo) 2nd Lt, E, 6th NY Cav, DoD Unknown. Hillside Cemetery, Lyndhurst, Bergen County.

DEW, LEWIS Pvt, F, 30th NC Inf (CSA), [Captured 7-3-1863 at Gettysburg, PA. Died of scurvy.] 11-12-1863. Finn's Point National Cemetery, Pennsville, Salem County.

DEW, WYATT Pvt, E, 47th NC Inf (CSA), [Captured 7-3-1863 at Gettysburg, PA. Died of diarrhea.] 9-14-1863. Finn's Point National Cemetery, Pennsville, Salem County.

DEWEES, HOWARD DoD Unknown. Old Camden Cemetery, Camden, Camden County.

DEWER, JAMES Corp, H, 25th NJ Inf, 8-25-1903. Cedar Lawn Cemetery, Paterson, Passaic County.

DEWEY, JAMES H. Corp, H, 196th PA Inf, 10-17-1888. Evergreen Cemetery, Camden, Camden County.

DEWEY*, PERCIVAL E. Pvt, Btty B, 1st NJ Light Art, 9-2-1901. Fairmount Cemetery, Newark, Essex County.

DEWEY, ROBY Pvt, E, 29th OH Inf, 8-3-1894. Bayview-New York Bay Cemetery, Jersey City, Hudson County.

DEWEY, WALTER W. Pvt, F, 1st NH Cav, 4-4-1921. Trinity Episcopal Church Cemetery, Woodbridge, Middlesex County.

DEWEY, WILLIAM Pvt, I, 1st NJ Inf, DoD Unknown. Hoboken Cemetery, North Bergen, Hudson County.

DEWITT, ARCHIBALD MCINTYRE 1899. Reformed Church Cemetery, Montville, Morris County.

DEWITT, EBENEZER Pvt, H, 29th NJ Inf, DoD Unknown. Presbyterian Cemetery, Waretown, Ocean County.

DEWITT, JAMES M. Maj, 72nd PA Inf 1925. Presbyterian Church Cemetery, Clinton, Hunterdon County.

DEWITT, JOHN N. Pvt, E, 80th NY Inf, 7-17-1892. Roadside Cemetery, Manchester Township, Ocean County.

DEWITT, PATRICK (see: Davitt, Patrick) St. John's RC Church Cemetery, Lakehurst, Ocean County.

DEWITT, WALTER A. Actg Ensign, U.S. Navy, 12-3-1896. Grove Church Cemetery, North Bergen, Hudson County.

DEWOLF, WILLIAM H. Pvt, D, 8th NY State Militia, DoD Unknown. Hackensack Cemetery, Hackensack, Bergen County.

DEWORTH*, HENRY Pvt, C, 37th NJ Inf, 7-28-1910. Riverview Cemetery, Trenton, Mercer County.

DEWORTH, LAWRENCE HENRY Pvt, B, 23rd NJ Inf, 9-1-1917. Bordentown/Old St. Mary's Catholic Cemetery, Bordentown, Burlington County.

DEWSON, JOHN W. Pvt, K, 69th PA Inf, 7-19-1882. Methodist Church Cemetery, New Albany, Burlington County.

DEWYNGANT, EMILIO (aka: Deoyngeart, Emile) Pvt, B, 40th NY Inf, 4-3-1892. St. Mary's Cemetery, East Orange, Essex County.

DEXTER, WESLEY Pvt, Btty F, 16th NY Heavy Art, 1923. Van Liew Cemetery, North Brunswick, Middlesex County.

DEXTER, WILLIAM Corp, C, 21st NJ Inf, 5-29-1919. Clinton Cemetery, Irvington, Essex County.

Our Brothers Gone Before

DEY, CORNELIUS E. Pvt, A, 28th NJ Inf, 2-4-1897. Tennent Church Cemetery, Tennent, Monmouth County.
DEY, CORNELIUS H. Pvt, D, 26th NJ Inf, 3-21-1928. Reformed Church Cemetery, Fairfield, Essex County.
DEY, DANIEL E. Pvt, G, 38th NJ Inf, 10-4-1915. Van Liew Cemetery, North Brunswick, Middlesex County.
DEY, GEORGE M. Corp, A, 38th NJ Inf, 11-16-1942. Cedar Hill Cemetery, Hightstown, Mercer County.
DEY, JAMES F. Pvt, B, 40th NJ Inf, 5-31-1918. Presbyterian Church Cemetery, Dutch Neck, Mercer County.
DEY, JOHN Pvt, K, 25th U.S. CT, 1-3-1904. Fairmount Cemetery, Newark, Essex County.
DEY, JOHN B. Pvt, D, 26th NJ Inf, 12-19-1911. Fairmount Cemetery, Newark, Essex County.
DEY, JOSEPH N. Pvt, A, 14th NJ Inf, [Wounded in action.] 6-4-1911. Arlington Cemetery, Kearny, Hudson County.
DEY, LAWRENCE F. Pvt, C, 29th NJ Inf, 3-7-1870. Manalapan Cemetery, Manalapan, Monmouth County.
DEY, RICHARD C. Capt, K, 22nd NJ Inf, 4-16-1884. Westminster Cemetery, Cranbury, Middlesex County.
DEY, ROLAND A. Pvt, H, 14th NJ Inf, 2-18-1864. Tennent Church Cemetery, Tennent, Monmouth County.
DEY, THOMAS Pvt, G, 8th NJ Inf, 5-15-1886. Tennent Church Cemetery, Tennent, Monmouth County.
DEY, WALTER J. Pvt, B, 9th NJ Inf, [Wounded in action.] 3-11-1922. Elmwood Cemetery, New Brunswick, Middlesex County.
DEY, WILLIAM W. Pvt, C, 29th NJ Inf, 4-3-1876. United Presbyterian Church Cemetery, Perrineville, Monmouth County.
DEYEO, ROBERT (see: Deyo, Robert J.) Fairmount Cemetery, Newark, Essex County.
DEYER, CHARLES (see: Theuer, Charles W.) Woodland Cemetery, Newark, Essex County.
DEYO, ROBERT J. (aka: Deyeo, Robert) Artificer, Btty B, 1st NJ Light Art, 11-10-1905. Fairmount Cemetery, Newark, Essex County.
DEYO, WILLIAM B. Pvt, 6th NY Ind Btty 8-22-1923. Bayview-New York Bay Cemetery, Jersey City, Hudson County.
DIAL, MARTIN M. 2nd Corp, G, 35th GA Inf (CSA), [Captured 7-2-1863 at Gettysburg, PA. Died of typhoid.] 1-16-1864. Finn's Point National Cemetery, Pennsville, Salem County.
DIAMENT, EDWARD Y. Pvt, B, 3rd NJ Inf, [Died at Philadelphia, PA.] 12-9-1862. Old Stone Church Cemetery, Fairton, Cumberland County.
DIAMENT, ELMER Pvt, H, 7th NJ Inf, 12-8-1878. Chestnut Grove Cemetery, Elmer, Salem County.
DIAMENT, WILLIAM F. Corp, F, 37th NJ Inf, [Died of typhoid at 10th Army Corps hospital.] 9-8-1864. Old Stone Church Cemetery, Fairton, Cumberland County.
DIAMOND, JAMES Pvt, H, 1st NJ Inf, 2-3-1893. Lady of Lourdes/Holy Sepulchre Cemetery, Hamilton, Mercer County.
DIBLIN, TERTULLIS S. Sgt, G, 14th NJ Inf, 11-28-1902. Riverview Cemetery, Trenton, Mercer County.
DICK*, ALBERT R. Com Sgt, I, 20th PA Cav, 1924. Zion Methodist Church Cemetery, Bargaintown, Atlantic County.
DICK, ALEXANDER Pvt, D, 15th PA Inf, 10-13-1918. Evergreen Cemetery, Camden, Camden County.
DICK, E.F. Pvt, F, 5th NC Inf (CSA), [Captured 7-1-1863 at Gettysburg, PA.] 10-4-1863. Finn's Point National Cemetery, Pennsville, Salem County.

New Jersey Civil War Burials

DICK, JOHN Pvt, E, 4th NJ Inf, 2-4-1884. Riverside Cemetery, Riverside, Burlington County.

DICK*, LEWIS A. Pvt, K, 11th MD Inf, 4-19-1909. Fairmount Cemetery, Phillipsburg, Warren County.

DICKEL, CHRISTIAN FREDERICH Col, 4th NY Cav 9-18-1880. Maple Grove Cemetery, Hackensack, Bergen County.

DICKENSON, JOSHUA (see: Dixon, Joshua) Fairmount Cemetery, Newark, Essex County.

DICKENSON, SAMUEL Pvt, I, 12th NJ Inf, 6-10-1892. Methodist Church Cemetery, Newport, Cumberland County.

DICKERMAN, MICHAEL Pvt, F, 13th NJ Inf, 11-21-1915. Holy Sepulchre Cemetery, East Orange, Essex County.

DICKERSON, CHARLES Corp, A, 41st U.S. CT, DoD Unknown. Rahway Cemetery, Rahway, Union County.

DICKERSON, CHARLES H. (aka: Dickinson, Charles H.) Pvt, Btty C, 2nd NY Heavy Art, 1916. New Dover United Methodist Church Cemetery, Edison, Middlesex County.

DICKERSON, CHARLES W. Artificer, Btty D, 2nd PA Heavy Art, 7-28-1908. Berlin Cemetery, Berlin, Camden County.

DICKERSON, EDWARD S. Pvt, E, 39th NJ Inf, 8-27-1902. Rosedale Cemetery, Orange, Essex County.

DICKERSON, JAMES 11-8-1891. Mount Pleasant Cemetery, Newark, Essex County.

DICKERSON, JOHN Seaman, U.S. Navy, USS Wachusett, 12-19-1887. St. Mary's Cemetery, South Amboy, Middlesex County.

DICKERSON, JOHN A. Pvt, B, 7th NJ Inf, [Died of consumption at Falmouth, VA.] 3-20-1863. Presbyterian Church Cemetery, Hanover, Morris County.

DICKERSON, JOHN M. Pvt, C, 27th NJ Inf, DoD Unknown. Carey Cemetery, Carey, Morris County.

DICKERSON, JOSEPH E. Pvt, A, 2nd NY Cav, [Died of disease at Camp Palmer, VA.] 2-2-1862. Savage Cemetery, Denville, Morris County.

DICKERSON, JULIUS TRUMAN Pvt, F, 25th NY Cav, DoD Unknown. Cedar Lawn Cemetery, Paterson, Passaic County.

DICKERSON, LEVI F. Pvt, G, 47th NC Inf (CSA), [Captured 7-3-1863 at Gettysburg, PA. Died of diarrhea.] 9-13-1863. Finn's Point National Cemetery, Pennsville, Salem County.

DICKERSON*, PETER QM Sgt, Btty F, 11th U.S. CHA, 4- -1898. New Somerville Cemetery, Somerville, Somerset County.

DICKERSON, R.J. Pvt, H, 38th GA Inf (CSA), [Captured 7-3-1863 at Gettysburg, PA. Died of measles.] 8-21-1863. Finn's Point National Cemetery, Pennsville, Salem County.

DICKERSON, ROBERT Pvt, B, 3rd NJ Militia, 3-4-1903. Fairmount Cemetery, Newark, Essex County.

DICKERSON, WILLIAM H. 5-27-1867. Presbyterian Church Cemetery, Hanover, Morris County.

DICKERSON, WILLIAM MILLER Pvt, A, 31st NJ Inf, [Died of typhoid at Aquia Creek, VA.] 5-21-1863. New Germantown Cemetery, Oldwick, Hunterdon County.

DICKERT, ADAM Pvt, G, 9th NJ Inf, 11-26-1893. Mount Olivet Cemetery, Newark, Essex County.

DICKESON, SAMUEL 7-1-1889. 1st Baptist Church Cemetery, Woodstown, Salem County.

DICKESON, WILLIAM (see: Dickinson, William H.) 7th Day Baptist Church Cemetery, Shiloh, Cumberland County.

DICKEY, ELEAZER P. Pvt, K, 40th NJ Inf, 4-2-1913. Greenwood Cemetery, Hamilton, Mercer County.

Our Brothers Gone Before

DICKEY, J.B. (see: Dickie, James B.) Finn's Point National Cemetery, Pennsville, Salem County.
DICKEY, JOHN Wagoner, H, 9th NJ Inf, 6-25-1892. Belvidere/Catholic Cemetery, Belvidere, Warren County.
DICKEY, JOHN P. Pvt, I, 11th PA Cav, 12-19-1912. Belvidere/Catholic Cemetery, Belvidere, Warren County.
DICKEY, ROBERT Sgt, G, 9th NJ Inf, DoD Unknown. Riverview Cemetery, Trenton, Mercer County.
DICKIE, JAMES B. (aka: Dickey, J.B.) Sgt, B, 4th NC Cav (CSA), [Captured 7-4-1863 at South Mountain, MD. Died of dysentery.] 1-26-1864. Finn's Point National Cemetery, Pennsville, Salem County.
DICKINSON, CHARLES H. (see: Dickerson, Charles H.) New Dover United Methodist Church Cemetery, Edison, Middlesex County.
DICKINSON, DAVID (see: Harrison, David D.) Clinton Cemetery, Irvington, Essex County.
DICKINSON, HENRY B. Pvt, D, 24th NJ Inf, [Died of rubeola at Georgetown, DC.] 11-28-1862. Friends Cemetery, Mickleton, Gloucester County.
DICKINSON, JAMES J. Pvt, K, 8th U.S. CT, 4-24-1900. Princeton Cemetery, Princeton, Mercer County.
DICKINSON*, JOHN W. Sgt, I, 3rd NY Inf, 10-1-1916. Evergreen Cemetery, Hillside, Union County.
DICKINSON, JOSEPH E. Pvt, I, 25th NJ Inf, 8-5-1893. Tabernacle Baptist Church Cemetery, Erma, Cape May County.
DICKINSON*, SAMUEL MEREDITH Actg Asst Paymaster, U.S. Navy, USS Dale, 1-29-1905. Riverview Cemetery, Trenton, Mercer County.
DICKINSON, WALLACE 1st Lt, A, 10th MI Cav, 8-27-1887. Baptist Church Cemetery, Port Murray, Warren County.
DICKINSON, WESLEY B. Pvt, A, 24th NJ Inf, 2-6-1913. Shinn GAR Post Cemetery, Port Norris, Cumberland County.
DICKINSON, WILLIAM H. (aka: Dickeson, William) Pvt, K, 12th NJ Inf, 4-24-1924. 7th Day Baptist Church Cemetery, Shiloh, Cumberland County.
DICKISSON, JOHN V. (aka: Dickson, John) Pvt, I, 1st NJ Militia, 7-3-1881. Methodist-Episcopal Cemetery, Johnsonburg, Warren County.
DICKS, WILLIAM W. Pvt, Btty I, 2nd NC Light Art (CSA), [Wounded and captured 1-15-1865 at Fort Fisher, NC. Died of colic.] 3-29-1865. Finn's Point National Cemetery, Pennsville, Salem County.
DICKSON, ALEXANDER T. Pvt, K, 43rd MS Inf (CSA), 7-19-1863. Finn's Point National Cemetery, Pennsville, Salem County.
DICKSON, DARIUS M. Pvt, D, 27th NJ Inf, 8-20-1912. Newton Cemetery, Newton, Sussex County.
DICKSON, GEORGE (see: Dixon, George I.) Bordentown/Old St. Mary's Catholic Cemetery, Bordentown, Burlington County.
DICKSON, GEORGE B. Pvt, E, 9th NJ Inf, [Cenotaph. Died of wounds received 5-12-1864 at Drury's Bluff, VA.] 9-23-1864. Baptist Cemetery, Medford, Burlington County.
DICKSON, JOHN (see: Dickisson, John V.) Methodist-Episcopal Cemetery, Johnsonburg, Warren County.
DICKSON, MARTIN Pvt, M, 2nd NJ Cav, DoD Unknown. Union Cemetery, Washington, Morris County.
DICKSON, PHILIP (see: Dixon, Philip) Berlin Cemetery, Berlin, Camden County.
DICKSON, THOMAS Pvt, G, 10th NJ Inf, 4-14-1910. Whitelawn Cemetery, Point Pleasant, Ocean County.
DIEBBER, CHARLES (see: Daiber, Charles) Soldier's Home Cemetery, Vineland, Cumberland County.

New Jersey Civil War Burials

DIECKMAN, HENRY C. Musc, H, 10th NJ Inf, DoD Unknown. Evergreen Cemetery, Camden, Camden County.

DIEDRICH*, F.A. CHARLES Pvt, C, 7th NJ Inf, DoD Unknown. Grove Church Cemetery, North Bergen, Hudson County.

DIEDRICKS, HENRY A. Pvt, E, 30th MA Inf, 5-7-1906. Arlington Cemetery, Kearny, Hudson County.

DIEFENTHALER, VALENTINE 1st Sgt, I, 54th NY Inf, 11-26-1896. Hillside Cemetery, Scotch Plains, Union County.

DIEGLE, GEORGE (see: Dargle, George E.) St. Bernard's Cemetery, Bridgewater, Somerset County.

DIEHL, CHRISTIAN Pvt, A, 4th NJ Inf, 9-1-1904. Union Cemetery, Gloucester City, Camden County.

DIEHL, JOHAN DoD Unknown. Old Camden Cemetery, Camden, Camden County.

DIEIEN, PETER (see: Deighan, Peter) St. Peter's Church Cemetery, Belleville, Essex County.

DIEKER, CHARLES Seaman, U.S. Navy, 8-3-1926. Ernston Cemetery, Old Bridge, Middlesex County.

DIELKES, JOSEPH H. Sgt, I, 12th NJ Inf, 1908. Harleigh Cemetery, Camden, Camden County.

DIELMAN*, GEORGE W. 2nd Lt, G, 114th U.S. CT, 4-29-1911. Arlington Cemetery, Kearny, Hudson County.

DIELMAN, WILLIAM G. Seaman, U.S. Navy, 3-23-1898. Fairmount Cemetery, Newark, Essex County.

DIEMER, MILTON H. (see: Dennis, Milton H.) Finn's Point National Cemetery, Pennsville, Salem County.

DIERCKS*, CHRISTIAN (aka: Hansom, Charles) Pvt, D, 29th PA Inf, 4-23-1892. Palisade Cemetery, North Bergen, Hudson County.

DIERCOP, PETER Pvt, C, 2nd NJ Inf, 11-20-1897. Fairmount Cemetery, Newark, Essex County.

DIESLE, LEWIS Corp, C, 31st NJ Inf, 7-10-1903. Phillipsburg Cemetery, Phillipsburg, Warren County.

DIESTER, JOSEPH Pvt, B, 41st NY Inf, 3-7-1890. Fairmount Cemetery, Newark, Essex County.

DIESTERWAY, SAMUEL Pvt, A, 3rd NJ Militia, DoD Unknown. Locust Hill Cemetery, Dover, Morris County.

DIETAMPET, JACOB (see: Diettrich, Jacob) Fairmount Cemetery, Newark, Essex County.

DIETRICH, JOHN Special Agent, U.S. Treasury Department, 2-27-1910. Hillside Cemetery, Scotch Plains, Union County.

DIETRICH, JOHN NICHOLAS Sgt, H, 3rd CT Inf, 1-31-1908. Hoboken Cemetery, North Bergen, Hudson County.

DIETTRICH, JACOB (aka: Dietampet, Jacob) Pvt, B, 52nd NY Inf, [Wounded 7-16-1864 at Petersburg, VA.] 3-29-1926. Fairmount Cemetery, Newark, Essex County.

DIETZ, FRANCIS Pvt, C, 3rd NY Militia Cav, 10-21-1913. Flower Hill Cemetery, North Bergen, Hudson County.

DIETZ, FREDERICH Pvt, A, 29th NY Inf, 5-3-1910. Arlington Cemetery, Kearny, Hudson County.

DIETZ, GEORGE J. Pvt, E, 2nd DE Inf, 9-12-1907. Arlington Cemetery, Kearny, Hudson County.

DIETZ, JOHN Pvt, Btty A, Schaffer's Ind PA Heavy Art, DoD Unknown. Finn's Point National Cemetery, Pennsville, Salem County.

DIGGINS, JAMES (see: Degins, James) Greenlawn Cemetery, West Long Branch, Monmouth County.

Our Brothers Gone Before

DIKE*, GEORGE W. Wagoner, E, 20th NY Cav, 1-10-1904. Fairmount Cemetery, Newark, Essex County.

DILATUSH, JAMES THOMPSON (aka: Dilentush, James) Corp, K, 29th NJ Inf, 11-27-1906. Elmwood Cemetery, New Brunswick, Middlesex County.

DILATUSH, JOSEPH (aka: Dillentush, Joseph) Pvt, K, 29th NJ Inf, 5-16-1905. Adelphia Cemetery, Adelphia, Monmouth County.

DILCHER, GEORGE (aka: Doelger, George) Pvt, H, 45th NY Inf, 1906. Grove Church Cemetery, North Bergen, Hudson County.

DILDINE*, ALBERT C. Pvt, D, 38th NJ Inf, 11-9-1931. Belvidere/Catholic Cemetery, Belvidere, Warren County.

DILDINE, WILLIAM M. Corp, B, 38th NJ Inf, 2-11-1911. Mansfield/Washington Cemetery, Washington, Warren County.

DILENTUSH, JAMES (see: Dilatush, James T.) Elmwood Cemetery, New Brunswick, Middlesex County.

DILEY, VALENTINE (see: Deily, Valentine) Riverview Cemetery, Trenton, Mercer County.

DILG, HENRY Sgt, A, 4th NY Inf, DoD Unknown. Evergreen Cemetery, Hillside, Union County.

DILKES, JACOB C. Corp, G, 28th NJ Inf, 1915. Methodist Cemetery, Mantua, Gloucester County.

DILKS, BENJAMIN Corp, D, 24th NJ Inf, 9-24-1913. Methodist-Episcopal Cemetery, Glassboro, Gloucester County.

DILKS, BENJAMIN F. 12-17-1906. Riverview Cemetery, Penns Grove, Salem County.

DILKS, BENJAMIN H. Pvt, I, 147th PA Inf, 7-14-1909. Arlington Cemetery, Kearny, Hudson County.

DILKS, CHARLES F. Pvt, D, 24th NJ Inf, 12-9-1896. Methodist-Episcopal Cemetery, Glassboro, Gloucester County.

DILKS, GEORGE Pvt, H, 4th NJ Inf, [Wounded 9-14-1862 at Crampton's Pass, MD.] 4-14-1921. Zion United Methodist Church Cemetery, Dividing Creek, Cumberland County.

DILKS, GEORGE Pvt, B, 203rd PA Inf, 7-6-1899. Eglington Cemetery, Clarksboro, Gloucester County.

DILKS, ISAAC Wagoner, E, 1st NJ Cav, 9-8-1988. Baptist Church Cemetery, Greenwich, Cumberland County.

DILKS, ISRAEL Sgt, D, 7th NJ Inf, 12-22-1884. Elwood Rural Cemetery, Elwood, Atlantic County.

DILKS, JAMES Pvt, C, 12th NJ Inf, 8-16-1901. Eglington Cemetery, Clarksboro, Gloucester County.

DILKS, JOB Pvt, D, 25th NJ Inf, [Wounded in action at Fredericksburg, VA.] 2-15-1904. Old Stone Church Cemetery, Fairton, Cumberland County.

DILKS*, JOHN Pvt, F, 99th PA Inf, [Wounded 7-2-1863 at Gettysburg, PA.] 4-25-1923. Erial Cemetery, Erial, Camden County.

DILKS, JOHN W. Pvt, D, 2nd U.S. Cav, 3-19-1902. New Camden Cemetery, Camden, Camden County.

DILKS, SAMUEL J. Corp, K, 9th NJ Inf, DoD Unknown. Union Cemetery, Mantua, Gloucester County.

DILKS, SAMUEL W. Pvt, A, MD Emerg NJ Militia, 1920. Rosehill Cemetery, Newfield, Gloucester County.

DILKS, WILLIAM B. Musc, H, 28th NJ Inf, DoD Unknown. Methodist Church Cemetery, Sicklerville, Camden County.

DILKS, WILLIAM H. Pvt, E, 24th NJ Inf, 12-29-1878. Eglington Cemetery, Clarksboro, Gloucester County.

DILL, ALEXANDER S. Sgt, A, 119th PA Inf, 2-16-1915. Arlington Cemetery, Pennsauken, Camden County.

New Jersey Civil War Burials

DILL*, DANIEL M. Bvt Maj, 6th U.S. CT 6-9-1911. Rosedale Cemetery, Orange, Essex County.

DILL, HENRY A. 10-23-1871. Evergreen Cemetery, Camden, Camden County.

DILL, JACOB S. Pvt, G, 12th NJ Inf, [Died at Potomac Creek, VA., of wounds received 5-3-1863 at Chancellorsville, VA.] 5-15-1863. Baptist Church Cemetery, Haddonfield, Camden County.

DILL*, JOHN H. Pvt, G, 12th NJ Inf, 1-5-1929. Cedar Grove Cemetery, Gloucester City, Camden County.

DILL, STEPHEN D. Pvt, F, 8th LA Inf (CSA), [Captured 3-2-1865 at Waynesboro, VA. Died of smallpox.] 5-17-1865. Finn's Point National Cemetery, Pennsville, Salem County.

DILL, WILLIAM W. 2-21-1906. Evergreen Cemetery, Camden, Camden County.

DILL, WILLIAM W. Pvt, H, 28th NJ Inf, 4-20-1923. Rosedale Cemetery, Orange, Essex County.

DILLANE, AUGUST Seaman, U.S. Navy, 4-23-1874. Fairmount Cemetery, Newark, Essex County.

DILLARD, OSCAR P. Pvt, G, 19th VA Inf (CSA), [Captured 7-5-1863 at Gettysburg, PA. Died of diarrhea.] 9-13-1863. Finn's Point National Cemetery, Pennsville, Salem County.

DILLEN, DANIEL J. Sgt, F, 3rd NJ Inf, 1-7-1904. 1st United Methodist Church Cemetery, Bridgeton, Cumberland County.

DILLEN, DAVID D. Pvt, E, 1st DE Inf, 2-16-1913. Evergreen Cemetery, Camden, Camden County.

DILLEN, JOHN (see: Doolin, John) Holy Sepulchre Cemetery, East Orange, Essex County.

DILLENTUSH, JOSEPH (see: Dilatush, Joseph) Adelphia Cemetery, Adelphia, Monmouth County.

DILLER, FREDERICK Pvt, F, 8th NY Inf, 2-4-1901. Palisade Cemetery, North Bergen, Hudson County.

DILLETT, CLARENCE DoD Unknown. Overlook Cemetery, Bridgeton, Cumberland County.

DILLEY, DANIEL Pvt, A, 31st NJ Inf, [Died of typhoid at Washington, DC.] 4-30-1863. New Germantown Cemetery, Oldwick, Hunterdon County.

DILLEY, DAVID 1st Sgt, H, 48th OH Inf, 7-20-1918. Union Cemetery, Washington, Morris County.

DILLEY, TENEYCK C. Pvt, I, 37th NJ Inf, 11-23-1899. Rural Hill Cemetery, Whitehouse, Hunterdon County.

DILLIAN, MICHAEL (see: Dillon, Michael) Holy Name Cemetery, Jersey City, Hudson County.

DILLING, CHARLES (see: Dillon, Charles) Princeton Cemetery, Princeton, Mercer County.

DILLINGHAM, BENJAMIN Pvt, F, 154th NY Inf, 8-8-1907. Siloam Cemetery, Vineland, Cumberland County.

DILLON*, CHARLES (aka: Dilling, Charles) Pvt, Btty H, 11th U.S. CHA, 1-9-1889. Princeton Cemetery, Princeton, Mercer County.

DILLON, ELWOOD W. Pvt, F, 22nd U.S. CT, 4-4-1904. Princeton Cemetery, Princeton, Mercer County.

DILLON, GEORGE Pvt, I, 23rd U.S. CT, 6-15-1888. Moore's Farm Cemetery, Stoutsburg, Mercer County.

DILLON, HENRY Pvt, F, 2nd NJ Cav, 9-7-1897. Bayview-New York Bay Cemetery, Jersey City, Hudson County.

DILLON, HENRY Pvt, B, 10th NY Inf, 2-15-1913. Alpine Cemetery, Perth Amboy, Middlesex County.

Our Brothers Gone Before

DILLON, ISAIAH Pvt, A, 6th U.S. CT, 12-29-1913. Mount Moriah Cemetery, Hainesport, Burlington County.

DILLON*, JAMES Pvt, B, 3rd NJ Inf, 9-8-1907. Arlington Cemetery, Kearny, Hudson County.

DILLON, JOHN P. Pvt, I, 1st NJ Cav, 8-21-1896. Holy Name Cemetery, Jersey City, Hudson County.

DILLON*, MICHAEL (aka: Dillian, Michael) Wagoner, G, 21st NJ Inf, 7-18-1868. Holy Name Cemetery, Jersey City, Hudson County.

DILLON, PETER Pvt, H, 30th NJ Inf, 4-7-1887. Mount Olivet Cemetery, Newark, Essex County.

DILLON, ROBERT Pvt, F, 10th NJ Inf, [Died of dysentery at Paterson, NJ.] 7-7-1863. Holy Sepulchre Cemetery, Totowa, Passaic County.

DILLON, SAMUEL Pvt, H, 30th NJ Inf, 9-26-1906. Arlington Cemetery, Kearny, Hudson County.

DILLON, WILLIAM Corp, E, 33rd NJ Inf, 3-15-1893. Presbyterian Cemetery, Springfield, Union County.

DILLOUN, CHRISTOPHER J. Sgt, I, 8th NJ Inf, 7-20-1876. 1st Methodist-Episcopal Cemetery, New Brunswick, Middlesex County.

DILLOWAY, GODFREY G. Corp, I, 21st NJ Inf, 8-28-1929. Bayview-New York Bay Cemetery, Jersey City, Hudson County.

DILLSHAVER, JACOB Pvt, E, 1st NJ Inf, 8-1-1880. Lutheran Church Cemetery, Friesburg, Salem County.

DILMAN, LEWIS Sgt, G, 21st NJ Inf, 11-4-1906. Bayview-New York Bay Cemetery, Jersey City, Hudson County.

DILMORE, BENJAMIN H. Pvt, K, 9th NJ Inf, 1-27-1912. Evergreen Cemetery, Camden, Camden County.

DILMORE, SAMUEL 5-26-1906. Evergreen Cemetery, Camden, Camden County.

DILTS, CHARLES Musc, G, 11th NJ Inf, 5-21-1924. Presbyterian Church Cemetery, Titusville, Mercer County.

DILTS, DANIEL Sgt, G, 30th NJ Inf, DoD Unknown. Rosemont Cemetery, Rosemont, Hunterdon County.

DILTS, GEORGE S. Surg, 5th NY Heavy Art 12-8-1873. Presbyterian Church Cemetery, Pleasant Grove, Morris County.

DILTS*, GEORGE W. Hosp Steward, 7th NJ Inf 4-3-1892. Presbyterian Church Cemetery, Flemington, Hunterdon County.

DILTS, GODFREY Pvt, C, 11th NJ Inf, 2-25-1899. Riverview Cemetery, Trenton, Mercer County.

DILTS, HART 3-16-1863. Lower Amwell Cemetery, Headquarters, Hunterdon County.

DILTS, JAMES P. 6-5-1919. Rosemont Cemetery, Rosemont, Hunterdon County.

DILTS*, JOHN Pvt, E, 7th NJ Inf, 11-18-1908. Presbyterian/Methodist-Episcopal Cemetery, Succasunna, Morris County.

DILTS, JOHN Pvt, C, 31st NJ Inf, 10-1-1913. Lutheran Cemetery, East Stewartsville, Warren County.

DILTS*, JOHN W. Pvt, E, 7th NJ Inf, 1905. Saums Farm Cemetery, Hillsborough, Somerset County.

DILTS, JOHN W. (SR.) Pvt, D, 30th NJ Inf, 4-4-1882. Rosemont Cemetery, Rosemont, Hunterdon County.

DILTS, PAUL C. Pvt, H, 6th NJ Inf, [Wounded in action.] 4-12-1905. Presbyterian Church Cemetery, Pennington, Mercer County.

DILTS, READING M. Corp, G, 30th NJ Inf, 3-11-1916. Rosemont Cemetery, Rosemont, Hunterdon County.

DILTS, SAMUEL W. Pvt, D, 31st NJ Inf, 1919. Union Cemetery, Ringoes, Hunterdon County.

New Jersey Civil War Burials

DILTS, W. AUGUSTUS Pvt, E, 38th NJ Inf, [Last Civil War veteran in Hunterdon County.] 3-4-1943. Evergreen Cemetery, Clinton, Hunterdon County.

DILTS*, WILLIAM F. Wagoner, A, 3rd NJ Cav, 8-18-1914. Holcomb-Riverview Cemetery, Lambertville, Hunterdon County.

DILTS, WILLIAM J. Pvt, I, 21st NJ Inf, 11-2-1898. Reformed Church Cemetery, Readington, Hunterdon County.

DILTS, ZEPHANIAH C. Pvt, B, 2nd NY Cav, 1-10-1903. Sandy Ridge Cemetery, Sandy Ridge, Hunterdon County.

DILWORTH, JOHN 2-12-1922. Macphelah Cemetery, North Bergen, Hudson County.

DILWORTH*, RICHARD B. Pvt, A, 29th PA Inf, 4-13-1921. Laurel Grove Cemetery, Totowa, Passaic County.

DIMLER, DAVID Pvt, G, 9th NJ Inf, 7-13-1868. Evergreen Cemetery, Hillside, Union County.

DIMOCK, ANTHONY VAUGHN Pvt, E, 53rd MA Militia, 5-27-1872. Evergreen Cemetery, Hillside, Union County.

DIMOND*, JAMES Pvt, A, 9th NJ Inf, 11- -1904. Laurel Grove Cemetery, Totowa, Passaic County.

DIMOND*, PETER Pvt, G, 7th NJ Inf, 7-26-1879. Cedar Lawn Cemetery, Paterson, Passaic County.

DIMOND*, WILLIAM T. Pvt, B, 5th NJ Inf, 5-17-1888. Jersey City Cemetery, Jersey City, Hudson County.

DINER, FREDERICK (see: Deiner, Frederick) Presbyterian Cemetery, Springfield, Union County.

DINGEE, ELEAZER (aka: Dengy, Eleaser) Pvt, G, 53rd PA Inf, DoD Unknown. Siloam Cemetery, Vineland, Cumberland County.

DINGELDAY, CHARLES (see: Dingeldein, Charles) Bayview-New York Bay Cemetery, Jersey City, Hudson County.

DINGELDEIN, CHARLES (aka: Dingelday, Charles) Pvt, 30th NY Ind Btty 4-3-1871. Bayview-New York Bay Cemetery, Jersey City, Hudson County.

DINGLE, ISAAC Pvt, C, 7th U.S. CT, 12-29-1914. Mount Peace Cemetery, Lawnside, Camden County.

DINGLER*, EDWARD Capt, D, 7th NJ Inf, 6-11-1899. Jersey City Cemetery, Jersey City, Hudson County.

DINGLER, M.M. Pvt, Jeff Davis' AL Art (CSA) 1-4-1864. Finn's Point National Cemetery, Pennsville, Salem County.

DINGLER, MARCUS Pvt, E, 7th NJ Inf, 1-7-1889. Phillipsburg Cemetery, Phillipsburg, Warren County.

DINGMAN*, LEWIS B. Pvt, Btty G, 11th U.S. CHA, 4-16-1903. Riverview Cemetery, Trenton, Mercer County.

DINGNAN, MICHAEL JOHN Corp, I, 139th PA Inf, 1-10-1904. St. John's Evangelical Church Cemetery, Orange, Essex County.

DINGWALL, KENNETH Sgt, Btty K, 7th NY Heavy Art, 4-1-1887. Bayview-New York Bay Cemetery, Jersey City, Hudson County.

DINGWELL, CHARLES B. Pvt, G, 1st NJ Militia, 12-3-1907. Fairmount Cemetery, Newark, Essex County.

DINGWELL, GEORGE W. Pvt, K, 9th CT Inf, 11-17-1891. Fairmount Cemetery, Newark, Essex County.

DINKEL, WILHELM 11-4-1904. Weehawken Cemetery, North Bergen, Hudson County.

DINMAN, FRANCIS (see: Denman, Frank George) Fairview Cemetery, Fairview, Bergen County.

DINSMORE, ANDREW ALEXANDER 1920. Rosedale Cemetery, Orange, Essex County.

DINSMORE, EBENEZER A. Corp, B, 37th VA Inf (CSA), [Wounded 5-8-1862 at McDowell, VA. Captured 7-3-1863 at Gettysburg, PA. Died of dropsy.] 4-21-1864. Finn's Point National Cemetery, Pennsville, Salem County.

DINSMORE, WILLIAM Pvt, B, 37th VA Inf (CSA), [Wounded 8-9-1862 at Cedar Mountain, VA. Captured 7-4-1863 at Gettysburg, PA.] 10-15-1863. Finn's Point National Cemetery, Pennsville, Salem County.

DIPPEL, JOHN (aka: Dipple, John) Pvt, G, 4th NJ Inf, 9-23-1902. Flower Hill Cemetery, North Bergen, Hudson County.

DIPPLE, JOHN (see: Dippel, John) Flower Hill Cemetery, North Bergen, Hudson County.

DIRLAM*, JACOB Pvt, B, 40th NY Inf, 10-20-1912. Arlington Cemetery, Kearny, Hudson County.

DIRMITT, CHARLES H. 12-1-1929. Riverside Cemetery, Toms River, Ocean County.

DISBROW, ANDREW JOHN Sgt, G, 1st NJ Cav, 5-15-1876. Holy Trinity Lutheran Church Cemetery, Manasquan, Monmouth County.

DISBROW, COURTLAND Pvt, K, 28th NJ Inf, 9-17-1888. Christ Church Cemetery, Morgan, Middlesex County.

DISBROW, FERDINAND H. Pvt, B, 9th NJ Inf, [Cenotaph. Died of wounds received at Roanoke Island, NC.] 3-19-1862. Chestnut Hill Cemetery, East Brunswick, Middlesex County.

DISBROW, GEORGE H. Landsman, U.S. Navy, USS Montgomery, 2-22-1871. Riverview Cemetery, Trenton, Mercer County.

DISBROW, GEORGE W. Pvt, B, 30th NJ Inf, 4-10-1936. Hazelwood Cemetery, Rahway, Union County.

DISBROW, HARRISON 1st Lt, D, 49th NY Inf, [Wounded 6-27-1862 at Garnetts Farm, VA.] 4-18-1900. Christ Church Cemetery, Morgan, Middlesex County.

DISBROW, HEATHCOAT J. Capt, C, 4th NJ Inf, 12-25-1886. Mercer Cemetery, Trenton, Mercer County.

DISBROW, HENRY H. Pvt, D, 10th NJ Inf, 2-13-1903. Christ Church Cemetery, Morgan, Middlesex County.

DISBROW, J.F. Pvt, B, 30th NJ Inf, 6-20-1923. Rahway Cemetery, Rahway, Union County.

DISBROW*, J. HENRY Pvt, Btty C, 3rd U.S. Art, 2-13-1903. Cedar Hill Cemetery, Hightstown, Mercer County.

DISBROW, JACOB A. Landsman, U.S. Navy, USS Shokokon, 12-13-1909. Riverside Cemetery, Toms River, Ocean County.

DISBROW, JAMES R. Pvt, I, 14th NJ Inf, 8-1-1899. Riverview Cemetery, Trenton, Mercer County.

DISBROW, JOHN S. Sgt, G, 1st NJ Cav, 11-12-1887. Greenlawn Cemetery, West Long Branch, Monmouth County.

DISBROW, R. LEFFERTS Asst Surg, 14th NJ Inf 11-12-1912. Atlantic View Cemetery, Manasquan, Monmouth County.

DISBROW, SAMUEL W. Sgt, H, 2nd DC Inf, 7-17-1915. Fairmount Cemetery, Newark, Essex County.

DISBROW, SOLOMON Pvt, G, 14th NJ Inf, 1-17-1882. Methodist Cemetery, Hamilton, Monmouth County.

DISBROW, STACY J. Pvt, C, 1st NJ Inf, 4-16-1924. Bayview-New York Bay Cemetery, Jersey City, Hudson County.

DISBROW, STEPHEN M. Pvt, C, 37th NJ Inf, 5-27-1895. Chestnut Hill Cemetery, East Brunswick, Middlesex County.

DISCH, WILLIAM Pvt, Btty B, 6th NY Heavy Art, 5-1-1915. Bayview-New York Bay Cemetery, Jersey City, Hudson County.

DISMUKE, JOHN C. Pvt, B, 4th MS Inf (CSA), 7-22-1864. Finn's Point National Cemetery, Pennsville, Salem County.

New Jersey Civil War Burials

DISNEY*, GEORGE Actg 3rd Asst Eng, U.S. Navy, 1-11-1868. Monument Cemetery, Edgewater Park, Burlington County.
DITMAN, FREDERICK Corp, I, 12th NJ Inf, DoD Unknown. Vincent Methodist-Episcopal Cemetery, Nutley, Essex County.
DITMAR, JOHN __, __, __ U.S. CT, 3-8-1883. Evergreen Cemetery, Hillside, Union County.
DITMARS, FREDERICK A. Pvt, C, 39th NJ Inf, 7-24-1903. Rahway Cemetery, Rahway, Union County.
DITMARS, JOHN R. Pvt, A, 30th NJ Inf, 6-28-1928. New Somerville Cemetery, Somerville, Somerset County.
DITTLEBACK, HARTZ 12-2-1864. Evergreen Cemetery, Hillside, Union County.
DITTMAN, AUGUST Pvt, B, 17th NY Inf, 12-11-1885. Evergreen Cemetery, Hillside, Union County.
DITTMAR, FREDERICK Pvt, D, 20th NY Inf, 9-30-1919. Weller Cemetery, Willow Grove, Warren County.
DITTO, THOMAS P. Corp, E, 23rd (Martin's) TN Inf (CSA), 12-5-1863. Finn's Point National Cemetery, Pennsville, Salem County.
DIVERS, JOHN W. Pvt, A, 53rd PA Inf, 6-17-1913. Stillwater Cemetery, Stillwater, Sussex County.
DIX, CHARLES H. Pvt, G, 2nd NH Inf, 2-28-1914. Evergreen Cemetery, Lakewood, Ocean County.
DIX, HENRY Pvt, C, 14th GA Inf (CSA), [Wounded 5-3-1863 at Chancellorsville, VA. Captured 6-29-1863 at Hagerstown, MD. Died of pneumonia.] 10-27-1863. Finn's Point National Cemetery, Pennsville, Salem County.
DIX, JOHN L. Pvt, F, 6th NY Cav, 1919. Baptist/St. Andrew's Cemetery, Mount Holly, Burlington County.
DIX, NILETON Seaman, U.S. Navy, USS Princeton, 3-10-1891. Johnson Cemetery, Camden, Camden County.
DIX, VALENTINE Corp, G, 101st NY Inf, [Died at Newark, NJ.] 11-4-1862. Fairmount Cemetery, Newark, Essex County.
DIXEY, FRANCIS H. Seaman, U.S. Navy, 1912. Soldier's Home Cemetery, Vineland, Cumberland County.
DIXON, BENJAMIN Pvt, E, 43rd U.S. CT, 4-2-1892. Mount Peace Cemetery, Lawnside, Camden County.
DIXON, C.W. Pvt, B, 2nd KY Cav (CSA), 3-1-1865. Finn's Point National Cemetery, Pennsville, Salem County.
DIXON, EDWARD I. Pvt, H, 28th NJ Inf, 1-30-1899. Bible Church Cemetery, Hardingville, Gloucester County.
DIXON*, GEORGE I. (aka: Dickson, George) Corp, K, 10th NJ Inf, [Wounded in action.] 2-20-1902. Bordentown/Old St. Mary's Catholic Cemetery, Bordentown, Burlington County.
DIXON, JAMES Seaman, U.S. Navy, USS Macedonian, 4-18-1888. Methodist-Episcopal Cemetery, Burlington, Burlington County.
DIXON, JAMES W. Pvt, Btty D, 3rd NC Light Art (CSA), [Wounded and captured 1-15-1865 at Fort Fisher, NC. Died of brain inflammation.] 4-1-1865. Finn's Point National Cemetery, Pennsville, Salem County.
DIXON, JOHN J. Pvt, A, 2nd NJ Inf, [Wounded in action.] 4-7-1919. Evergreen Cemetery, Hillside, Union County.
DIXON, JONATHAN Pvt, G, 13th NJ Inf, 8-7-1908. Pine Brook Cemetery, Pine Brook, Morris County.
DIXON, JOSEPH L. Sgt, D, 85th OH Inf, DoD Unknown. Evergreen Cemetery, Hillside, Union County.

Our Brothers Gone Before

DIXON, JOSHUA (aka: Dickenson, Joshua) Pvt, D, 82nd NY Inf, [Died of wounds received 9-17-1862 at Antietam, MD.] 2-8-1863. Fairmount Cemetery, Newark, Essex County.

DIXON, MARCUS Pvt, G, 13th NJ Inf, 1-18-1899. Vail Presbyterian Cemetery, Parsippany, Morris County.

DIXON, PATRICK J. Pvt, E, 6th U.S. Inf, 8-22-1892. Flower Hill Cemetery, North Bergen, Hudson County.

DIXON, PHILIP (aka: Dickson, Philip) Pvt, B, 99th PA Inf, 7-16-1910. Berlin Cemetery, Berlin, Camden County.

DIXON, RICHARD 2-6-1922. Palisade Cemetery, North Bergen, Hudson County.

DIXON, THOMAS S. Pvt, H, 28th NJ Inf, 11-25-1883. Harmony Methodist-Episcopal Church Cemetery, Piney Hollow, Gloucester County.

DIXON, WALTER Pvt, B, 11th NJ Inf, 11-21-1922. Evergreen Cemetery, Hillside, Union County.

DIXON, WALTER Sgt, A, 149th NY Inf, 4-25-1917. Clinton Cemetery, Irvington, Essex County.

DIXON, WILLIAM H. Pvt, I, 158th NY Inf, 1-28-1903. Bayview-New York Bay Cemetery, Jersey City, Hudson County.

DOAK, JAMES VERNON Pvt, D, 196th PA Inf, 11-6-1938. Presbyterian Church Cemetery, Cold Spring, Cape May County.

DOAN, GEORGE P. (see: Doane, George P.) Riverview Cemetery, Trenton, Mercer County.

DOANE, GEORGE P. (aka: Doan, George P.) Capt, AQM, U.S. Volunteers, DoD Unknown. Riverview Cemetery, Trenton, Mercer County.

DOANE, HENRY R. Pvt, G, 37th MA Inf, 3-23-1873. Oak Hill Cemetery, Vineland, Cumberland County.

DOANE, TAPPEN D. Pvt, A, 47th NY State Militia, DoD Unknown. Laurel Grove Cemetery, Totowa, Passaic County.

DOANE*, THADEUS OSBORNE Corp, B, 11th NJ Inf, 12-3-1928. Hillside Cemetery, Scotch Plains, Union County.

DOBBINS, DAVID N. (see: Jacobus, David N.) Prospect Hill Cemetery, Caldwell, Essex County.

DOBBINS, EDWARD L. 1st Lt, D, 23rd NJ Inf, 1916. Mount Holly Cemetery, Mount Holly, Burlington County.

DOBBINS*, GEORGE Sgt, D, 2nd NJ Inf, 6-7-1914. Cedar Grove Cemetery, Gloucester City, Camden County.

DOBBINS, GEORGE S. Pvt, I, 37th NJ Inf, 9-29-1920. Mount Holly Cemetery, Mount Holly, Burlington County.

DOBBINS, HARVEY JOHN Pvt, F, 13th NJ Inf, [Wounded 9-17-1862 at Antietam, MD.] 4-15-1901. Prospect Hill Cemetery, Caldwell, Essex County.

DOBBINS, HENRY S. Pvt, B, 95th PA Inf, [Wounded 6-27-1862 at Gaines' Mill, VA.] 6-8-1889. New Camden Cemetery, Camden, Camden County.

DOBBINS, JAMES H. Pvt, Btty B, 1st NJ Light Art, 2-24-1904. Mount Pleasant Cemetery, Newark, Essex County.

DOBBINS, JEREMIAH B. Pvt, Btty B, 1st NJ Light Art, 11-26-1902. Evergreen Cemetery, Morristown, Morris County.

DOBBINS, JOHN Pvt, I, 70th NY Inf, DoD Unknown. Holy Sepulchre Cemetery, Totowa, Passaic County.

DOBBINS, JOHN Musc, I, 4th NJ Inf, 7-23-1871. Riverview Cemetery, Trenton, Mercer County.

DOBBINS, JOHN H. Wagoner, D, 26th NJ Inf, 4-11-1909. Prospect Hill Cemetery, Caldwell, Essex County.

DOBBINS, JOHN S. Pvt, Btty D, 1st NJ Light Art, 4-20-1887. Baptist Cemetery, Pemberton, Burlington County.

New Jersey Civil War Burials

DOBBINS, MATTHIAS CLARK Capt, D, 26th NJ Inf, 10-31-1909. Hillside Cemetery, Scotch Plains, Union County.

DOBBINS, SAMUEL A. Corp, I, 23rd NJ Inf, 1908. Mount Holly Cemetery, Mount Holly, Burlington County.

DOBBINS, WILLIAM A. Pvt, B, 124th PA Inf, 12-31-1915. Arlington Cemetery, Pennsauken, Camden County.

DOBBINS, WILLIAM A. Sgt, B, 34th NJ Inf, 3-1-1910. Riverview Cemetery, Trenton, Mercer County.

DOBBS, JOHN H. (SR.) Pvt, F, 1st NJ Militia, 3-1-1918. Holy Sepulchre Cemetery, East Orange, Essex County.

DOBBS, JOSEPH P. Pvt, K, 9th NJ Inf, 2-27-1890. Holy Sepulchre Cemetery, East Orange, Essex County.

DOBBS, RICHARD Pvt, A, 6th CA Inf, 4-22-1911. Bayview-New York Bay Cemetery, Jersey City, Hudson County.

DOBBS, THOMAS J. Seaman, U.S. Navy, 1-24-1917. Grove Church Cemetery, North Bergen, Hudson County.

DOBBS*, WARREN 1st Sgt, A, 37th NJ Inf, 4-20-1936. Bayview-New York Bay Cemetery, Jersey City, Hudson County.

DOBSON, GEORGE (SR.) Corp, A, 28th NJ Inf, 12-23-1916. Chestnut Hill Cemetery, East Brunswick, Middlesex County.

DOBSON, JOHN 1st Lt, A, 28th NJ Inf, 3-31-1891. Chestnut Hill Cemetery, East Brunswick, Middlesex County.

DOCHERTY, ISAAC NEWTON Pvt, U.S. Marine Corps, 1909. Highland Cemetery, Hopewell Boro, Mercer County.

DOCHERTY, JAMES Pvt, K, 79th PA Inf, 12-25-1869. Flagtown Dutch Reformed Cemetery, Frankfort, Somerset County.

DOCHERTY, JOHN M. Pvt, E, 3rd NJ Cav, 1900. Highland Cemetery, Hopewell Boro, Mercer County.

DOCHNAHL, CONRAD Corp, H, 5th NJ Inf, 9-20-1893. Rahway Cemetery, Rahway, Union County.

DOCK, ABRAHAM Corp, B, 9th NJ Inf, 1911. Soldier's Home Cemetery, Vineland, Cumberland County.

DOCK, ISAAC Wagoner, B, 9th NJ Inf, 10- -1865. Riverview Cemetery, Trenton, Mercer County.

DOCKERY, EDWARD Pvt, Btty A, 1st NJ Light Art, 10-11-1886. St. John's Evangelical Church Cemetery, Orange, Essex County.

DOCKERY*, ELISHA LOGAN Pvt, I, 6th NC Cav (CSA), [Captured 8-5-1863 at Clay County, NC. Died of smallpox.] 5-3-1864. Finn's Point National Cemetery, Pennsville, Salem County.

DOCKSTADER, CHARLES R. 10-20-1907. Atlantic City Cemetery, Pleasantville, Atlantic County.

DOD, ALBERT BALDWIN Capt, A, 15th U.S. Inf, 6-13-1880. Princeton Cemetery, Princeton, Mercer County.

DOD*, CHARLES HODGE Capt, U.S. Army, [General Hancocks staff.] 8-26-1864. Princeton Cemetery, Princeton, Mercer County.

DODD, AMZI P. Pvt, K, 25th NJ Inf, 11-8-1914. Laurel Grove Cemetery, Totowa, Passaic County.

DODD, BETHUEL LEWIS Volunteer Surgeon, [Ward U.S. Army Hospital, Newark, NJ.] 12-5-1908. Rosedale Cemetery, Orange, Essex County.

DODD, CHARLES BENJAMIN Pvt, G, 2nd NJ Inf, 2-19-1923. Bloomfield Cemetery, Bloomfield, Essex County.

DODD*, CHARLES E. Pvt, G, 11th NJ Inf, 2-4-1908. Rosedale Cemetery, Orange, Essex County.

Our Brothers Gone Before

DODD, EDWIN Pvt, F, 26th NJ Inf, 11-10-1878. Bloomfield Cemetery, Bloomfield, Essex County.

DODD, EDWIN FERDINAND Corp, F, 26th NJ Inf, 12-6-1929. Mount Hebron Cemetery, Montclair, Essex County.

DODD, GEORGE RAYMOND Sgt, D, 1st NJ Militia, 9-21-1885. Fairmount Cemetery, Newark, Essex County.

DODD*, GEORGE W. Pvt, C, 71st NY State Militia, 3-27-1914. Arlington Cemetery, Kearny, Hudson County.

DODD, HORACE Pvt, K, 1st NJ Inf, 1-29-1924. Mount Hebron Cemetery, Montclair, Essex County.

DODD, HORACE DoD Unknown. Whitehall Cemetery, Towaco, Morris County.

DODD, HORACE (JR.) Pvt, F, 26th NJ Inf, 1-29-1924. Bloomfield Cemetery, Bloomfield, Essex County.

DODD, IRA CONDIT Corp, H, 26th NJ Inf, 11-12-1923. Rosedale Cemetery, Orange, Essex County.

DODD, IRA SEYMOUR 1st Sgt, F, 26th NJ Inf, 8-3-1922. Mount Hebron Cemetery, Montclair, Essex County.

DODD, ISAAC B. 12-7-1865. Bloomfield Cemetery, Bloomfield, Essex County.

DODD, JAMES 7-18-1879. 1st Reformed Church Cemetery, Pompton Plains, Morris County.

DODD, JAMES H. 1879. Vincent Methodist-Episcopal Cemetery, Nutley, Essex County.

DODD, JOHN 2nd Lt, H, 26th NJ Inf, 1866. Mount Pleasant Cemetery, Newark, Essex County.

DODD, JOSHUA W. Corp, C, 26th NJ Inf, 10-17-1872. Vincent Methodist-Episcopal Cemetery, Nutley, Essex County.

DODD, ROBERT Pvt, Btty B, 1st NJ Light Art, 2-12-1912. Bloomfield Cemetery, Bloomfield, Essex County.

DODD, SAMUEL UZAL Capt, K, 26th NJ Inf, [Died of wounds received at Fredericksburg, VA.] 6-6-1863. Rosedale Cemetery, Orange, Essex County.

DODD, SAMUEL WALTER Pvt, F, 26th NJ Inf, 12-9-1878. Bloomfield Cemetery, Bloomfield, Essex County.

DODD, WILLIAM Pvt, B, 8th U.S. CT, 1908. Lamington Colored Cemetery, Lamington, Somerset County.

DODD, WILLIAM H. 3-11-1903. Hackensack Cemetery, Hackensack, Bergen County.

DODD, WILLIAM HENRY Pvt, H, 2nd DC Inf, [Died of lung inflammation at Georgetown, DC.] 3-4-1862. Rosedale Cemetery, Orange, Essex County.

DODD, WILLIAM HENRY Pvt, K, 4th NY Cav, 1908. Whitehall Cemetery, Towaco, Morris County.

DODD, WILLIAM HENRY Corp, D, 13th NJ Inf, 3-14-1903. Bloomfield Cemetery, Bloomfield, Essex County.

DODD, WILLIAM HENRY C. 3-1-1915. Bloomfield Cemetery, Bloomfield, Essex County.

DODGE, GEORGE SULLIVAN Bvt Brig Gen, U.S. Volunteers, [Colonel, Chief Quartermaster, Army of the James.] 8-24-1881. Newton Cemetery, Newton, Sussex County.

DODGE, JOSEPH C. Sgt, H, 177th NY Inf, 1-8-1927. Fairmount Cemetery, Newark, Essex County.

DODGE, JOSEPH H. Pvt, I, 6th MA Militia, [Died of disease at Fort Delaware.] 9-5-1864. Finn's Point National Cemetery, Pennsville, Salem County.

DODS, HENRY (JR.) Pvt, K, 22nd NJ Inf, 11-20-1917. Fairview Cemetery, Fairview, Bergen County.

DODSON, DAVID Colored Cook, B, 17th IL Inf, 3-1-1892. Mount Peace Cemetery, Lawnside, Camden County.

New Jersey Civil War Burials

DODSON, WILLIAM VANBUREN 1st Lt, C, 5th VA Cav (CSA), [Captured 5-11-1864 at Yellow Tavern, VA. Died of typhoid.] 6-1-1865. Finn's Point National Cemetery, Pennsville, Salem County.

DOE, ERASTUS A. Pvt, D, 1st ME Cav, 9-6-1911. Siloam Cemetery, Vineland, Cumberland County.

DOEHNHOF, JOHN Pvt, B, 52nd NY Inf, 12-7-1878. Castner-Compton Cemetery, Bridgewater, Somerset County.

DOELGER, GEORGE (see: Dilcher, George) Grove Church Cemetery, North Bergen, Hudson County.

DOELL, PHILIP Pvt, B, 40th NJ Inf, 4-3-1909. Egg Harbor Cemetery, Egg Harbor, Atlantic County.

DOERING, JOHN Corp, D, 48th NY Inf, 4-30-1926. Presbyterian/Methodist-Episcopal Cemetery, Succasunna, Morris County.

DOERR, JOHN (see: Dorr, John G.) Woodland Cemetery, Newark, Essex County.

DOERR, JOHN H. Pvt, D, 19th PA Inf, 11-14-1904. Harleigh Cemetery, Camden, Camden County.

DOGGETT, W. (see: Loggett, W.) Finn's Point National Cemetery, Pennsville, Salem County.

DOGUE, JOHN N. Pvt, Btty F, 3rd U.S. Art, 1-12-1890. Fairmount Cemetery, Newark, Essex County.

DOHERTY, JAMES Sgt, Btty C, 2nd NY Heavy Art, 8-11-1902. Phillipsburg Cemetery, Phillipsburg, Warren County.

DOHERTY*, JOHN (aka: Dougherty, John) Pvt, F, 6th PA Cav, [Wounded in action at Gettysburg, PA.] 9-14-1915. Cedar Lawn Cemetery, Paterson, Passaic County.

DOHERTY, NEIL Corp, B, 6th NY Cav, 10-3-1880. Holy Name Cemetery, Jersey City, Hudson County.

DOHERTY, PATRICK HENRY Pvt, K, 1st SC Cav (CSA), 8-13-1904. Mount Calvary Cemetery, Mount Calvary, Atlantic County.

DOHERTY, PETER (see: Dougherty, Peter) Holy Sepulchre Cemetery, East Orange, Essex County.

DOHERTY*, WILLIAM J. (aka: Thompson, William) Pvt, A, 163rd NY Inf, 12-28-1913. St. John's Evangelical Church Cemetery, Orange, Essex County.

DOHM*, GEORGE W. Pvt, F, 1st NJ Cav, 9-17-1895. Evergreen Cemetery, New Brunswick, Middlesex County.

DOHMEIR, BENJAMIN (see: Dohmyer, Benjamin C.) Bayview-New York Bay Cemetery, Jersey City, Hudson County.

DOHMYER, BENJAMIN C. (aka: Dohmeir, Benjamin) Corp, Btty B, 15th NY Heavy Art, 7-2-1919. Bayview-New York Bay Cemetery, Jersey City, Hudson County.

DOHMYER, CHARLES B. Pvt, B, 3rd NY Inf, 11-25-1911. Evergreen Cemetery, Hillside, Union County.

DOLAN, BERNHART Pvt, D, 4th NJ Inf, 4-12-1889. Riverview Cemetery, Trenton, Mercer County.

DOLAN, HENRY Pvt, F, 203rd PA Inf, DoD Unknown. Locust Hill Cemetery, Dover, Morris County.

DOLAN, JAMES Pvt, B, 2nd NJ Inf, DoD Unknown. Presbyterian/Methodist-Episcopal Cemetery, Succasunna, Morris County.

DOLAN, JOHN Sgt, C, 69th NY Inf, 8-13-1915. Holy Name Cemetery, Jersey City, Hudson County.

DOLAN, JOHN (see: Delate, John) Bayview-New York Bay Cemetery, Jersey City, Hudson County.

DOLAN, JOSEPH Pvt, B, 37th NJ Inf, 2-2-1900. Laurel Grove Cemetery, Totowa, Passaic County.

DOLAN*, MANNING H. Pvt, F, 65th NY Inf, 1-10-1922. Presbyterian/Methodist-Episcopal Cemetery, Succasunna, Morris County.

Our Brothers Gone Before

DOLAN, MICHAEL Pvt, K, 15th NJ Inf, DoD Unknown. St. Rose of Lima Cemetery, Freehold, Monmouth County.
DOLAN, MICHAEL E. Pvt, U.S. Marine Corps, 1-11-1864. St. John's Evangelical Church Cemetery, Orange, Essex County.
DOLAN, PATRICK Pvt, A, 28th NJ Inf, 9-12-1892. Old Calvary Cemetery, Sayreville, Middlesex County.
DOLAN, PATRICK H. (aka: Dolin, Patrick) Corp, F, 15th NY Eng, 5-3-1906. St. Peter's Cemetery, New Brunswick, Middlesex County.
DOLAN, PETER Blacksmith, M, 1st NJ Cav, 10-23-1906. Headley Cemetery, Milton, Morris County.
DOLAN, TERRANCE Corp, B, 33rd NJ Inf, 12-3-1896. Holy Sepulchre Cemetery, East Orange, Essex County.
DOLAN, WILLIAM Pvt, G, 39th NJ Inf, 1910. Holy Sepulchre Cemetery, East Orange, Essex County.
DOLAN*, WILLIAM Pvt, F, 12th NJ Inf, [Wounded in action at Chancellorsville, VA.] DoD Unknown. Baptist Church Cemetery, Mullica Hill, Gloucester County.
DOLAND, GEORGE Pvt, M, 1st NJ Cav, DoD Unknown. Hardyston Cemetery, North Church, Sussex County.
DOLAND, JOHN Corp, E, 4th NY Cav, 1-17-1907. Presbyterian Church Cemetery, Millbrook, Morris County.
DOLAND*, MENZIES Pvt, C, 2nd NJ Inf, 7-15-1877. Fairmount Cemetery, Newark, Essex County.
DOLAND, WILLIAM Sgt, D, 15th NJ Inf, 11-18-1878. Fairmount Cemetery, Newark, Essex County.
DOLAND, WILLIAM Pvt, B, 2nd NJ Inf, DoD Unknown. Hardyston Cemetery, North Church, Sussex County.
DOLAND, WILLIAM Pvt, K, 124th NY Inf, 2-13-1913. Union Cemetery, Wyckoff, Bergen County.
DOLBIER, EDWARD A. Corp, I, 8th NJ Inf, 7-14-1909. Evergreen Cemetery, Hillside, Union County.
DOLBIER*, JOHN V. 2nd Lt, C, 30th NJ Inf, 6-18-1882. Fairmount Cemetery, Newark, Essex County.
DOLBOW, CHARLES A. Corp, K, 4th NJ Inf, 1933. Methodist-Episcopal Church Cemetery, Penns Grove, Salem County.
DOLBOW, EDWARD R. (aka: Delbow, Edward) Pvt, Btty M, 3rd PA Heavy Art, DoD Unknown. Methodist-Episcopal Church Cemetery, Penns Grove, Salem County.
DOLBOW, JAMES F. Pvt, K, 24th NJ Inf, 10-3-1905. Methodist-Episcopal Church Cemetery, Penns Grove, Salem County.
DOLBOW, WILLIAM (aka: Dolby, William) Pvt, D, 12th NJ Inf, 2-23-1924. Riverview Cemetery, Penns Grove, Salem County.
DOLBY, WILLIAM (see: Dolbow, William) Riverview Cemetery, Penns Grove, Salem County.
DOLE, GEORGE A. Pvt, F, 3rd IA Cav, DoD Unknown. Old Beemerville Cemetery, Beemerville, Sussex County.
DOLIN, PATRICK (see: Dolan, Patrick H.) St. Peter's Cemetery, New Brunswick, Middlesex County.
DOLL, FREDERICK Pvt, I, 188th OH Inf, 1925. Glenwood Cemetery, West Long Branch, Monmouth County.
DOLL, JOHN A. Pvt, F, 12th IA Inf, 11-15-1927. Harleigh Cemetery, Camden, Camden County.
DOLLIVER, JAMES J. Sgt, 6th NY Ind Btty 4-4-1906. Reformed Church Cemetery, South Branch, Somerset County.
DOLLIVER, WILLIAM H. 1st Sgt, E, 15th NJ Inf, 3-27-1930. Reformed Church Cemetery, Readington, Hunterdon County.

New Jersey Civil War Burials

DOLPHIN, MARTIN Corp, I, 33rd NJ Inf, 10-22-1878. Holy Sepulchre Cemetery, East Orange, Essex County.

DOLPHIN, MICHAEL Pvt, A, 71st NY Inf, 11-26-1915. Holy Sepulchre Cemetery, East Orange, Essex County.

DOLSAY, JACKSON DoD Unknown. Hardyston Cemetery, North Church, Sussex County.

DOLSON, CHARLES MERRITT Pvt, H, 95th NY Inf, 1-16-1916. 1st Reformed Church Cemetery, Pompton Plains, Morris County.

DOLSON, WILLIAM Pvt, H, 4th NJ Inf, 5-7-1886. Evergreen Cemetery, Camden, Camden County.

DONAHOE, JOHN DoD Unknown. St. Magdalene's Cemetery, Flemington, Hunterdon County.

DONAHUE, JAMES Pvt, F, 23rd NJ Inf, 4-5-1897. Baptist Cemetery, Burlington, Burlington County.

DONAHUE, JEREMIAH Pvt, G, 90th IL Inf, 4-28-1897. St. Rose of Lima Cemetery, Oxford, Warren County.

DONAHUE, MARTIN Pvt, Btty B, 1st NJ Light Art, 1-1-1903. Holy Sepulchre Cemetery, Totowa, Passaic County.

DONAHUE, PATRICK Pvt, K, 7th NJ Inf, 1918. St. Peter's Church Cemetery, Belleville, Essex County.

DONAHUE, PATRICK Pvt, B, 27th NJ Inf, 8-6-1875. Holy Sepulchre Cemetery, East Orange, Essex County.

DONAHUE, PETER Pvt, E, 26th NJ Inf, 12-4-1873. Holy Sepulchre Cemetery, East Orange, Essex County.

DONAHUE, THOMAS Landsman, U.S. Navy, USS Princeton, DoD Unknown. Immaculate Conception Cemetery, Somerville, Somerset County.

DONAHUE, THOMAS Pvt, E, 33rd NJ Inf, DoD Unknown. Holy Sepulchre Cemetery, East Orange, Essex County.

DONAHUE, WILLIAM __, E, 2nd __ Inf, 1891. Presbyterian/Methodist-Episcopal Cemetery, Succasunna, Morris County.

DONALD, JOHN B. 1st Lt, E, 8th NJ Inf, 9-21-1869. Fairmount Cemetery, Newark, Essex County.

DONALD, ROBERT Pvt, E, 8th NJ Inf, [Wounded 5-5-1862 at Williamsburg, VA.] 1-21-1882. Fairmount Cemetery, Newark, Essex County.

DONALD, WILLIAM Pvt, E, 8th NJ Inf, 3-5-1890. Fairmount Cemetery, Newark, Essex County.

DONALD, WILLIAM B Pvt, B, 2nd WI Inf, 3-4-1919. Egg Harbor Cemetery, Egg Harbor, Atlantic County.

DONALDSON, DAVID Pvt, A, 6th NJ Inf, 10-16-1896. Adelphia Cemetery, Adelphia, Monmouth County.

DONALDSON, HENRY (see: Donelson, Henry) Baptist Church Cemetery, Canton, Salem County.

DONALDSON, JAMES Pvt, K, 5th NJ Inf, [Died at Freehold, NJ.] 9-26-1864. Adelphia Cemetery, Adelphia, Monmouth County.

DONALDSON, JAMES Pvt, I, 1st NJ Cav, 8-28-1907. Laurel Grove Cemetery, Totowa, Passaic County.

DONALDSON, JOHN Capt, G, 156th NY Inf, [Died of disease at Baton Rouge, LA.] 9-19-1863. Vincent Methodist-Episcopal Cemetery, Nutley, Essex County.

DONALDSON*, JOHN (JR.) Sgt, C, 7th NJ Inf, [Died of wounds received 5-5-1862 at Williamsburg, VA.] 5-17-1862. Fairmount Cemetery, Newark, Essex County.

DONALDSON, SYLVANUS Pvt, C, 9th NJ Inf, 7-3-1872. Adelphia Cemetery, Adelphia, Monmouth County.

Our Brothers Gone Before

DONALDSON, THOMAS Pvt, E, 13th OH Cav, [Died of wounds received 10-8-1864 at Vaughn and Squirrel Level Railroad, VA.] 10-29-1864. Beverly National Cemetery, Edgewater Park, Burlington County.

DONALDSON, WILLIAM Pvt, I, 2nd NJ Inf, 7-11-1888. Cedar Lawn Cemetery, Paterson, Passaic County.

DONAWAY, JOHN Captains Steward, U.S. Navy, USS Sciota, 10-12-1926. Atlantic City Cemetery, Pleasantville, Atlantic County.

DONEGAN, MICHAEL C. Pvt, B, 12th NJ Inf, 10-5-1874. Methodist-Episcopal Cemetery, Burlington, Burlington County.

DONELSON, HENRY (aka: Donaldson, Henry) Pvt, A, 24th NJ Inf, 3-6-1902. Baptist Church Cemetery, Canton, Salem County.

DONELY, JOHN Corp, __, __ PA __, DoD Unknown. Finn's Point National Cemetery, Pennsville, Salem County.

DONEVER*, OLIVER Pvt, Btty G, 2nd PA Heavy Art, 7-11-1901. Atlantic City Cemetery, Pleasantville, Atlantic County.

DONGAN, JOSEPH P. (aka: Duncan, Joseph) Pvt, D, 14th NJ Inf, DoD Unknown. Maplewood Cemetery, Freehold, Monmouth County.

DONGES, JOHN W. Pvt, H, 129th PA Inf, [Wounded 12-13-1862 at Fredericksburg, VA.] 2-5-1931. Harleigh Cemetery, Camden, Camden County.

DONKERSLEY, WILLIAM (see: Dunkerly, William B.) Cedar Lawn Cemetery, Paterson, Passaic County.

DONLON, JAMES Wagoner, B, 5th NJ Inf, 9-12-1900. St. John's Cemetery, Hamilton, Mercer County.

DONNEGAN*, JOHN (aka: Dunnavan, John) Pvt, F, 4th NY Cav, 8-28-1875. St. Peter's Cemetery, New Brunswick, Middlesex County.

DONNEGAN, JOHN (aka: Dunnigan, John) Pvt, F, 28th NJ Inf, 1-13-1876. St. Peter's Cemetery, New Brunswick, Middlesex County.

DONNEGAN*, MICHAEL Pvt, B, 12th NJ Inf, 1-24-1893. St. Peter's Cemetery, New Brunswick, Middlesex County.

DONNELL, CHARLES Pvt, A, 11th NJ Inf, 4-15-1906. St. Peter's Cemetery, Jersey City, Hudson County.

DONNELL, JOHN Pvt, I, 10th NJ Inf, 1918. Methodist Cemetery, Malaga, Gloucester County.

DONNELL, JOHN DoD Unknown. St. Peter's Cemetery, New Brunswick, Middlesex County.

DONNELL, JOHN (see: O'Donnell, John) Holy Name Cemetery, Jersey City, Hudson County.

DONNELL, JOHN W. 6-2-1902. Holy Rood Cemetery, Morristown, Morris County.

DONNELL, ROBERT L. Pvt, B, 27th NC State Troops (CSA), [Died at Chester, PA of wounds received 9-17-1862 at Antietam, MD.] 11-6-1862. Methodist-Episcopal Church Cemetery, Medford, Burlington County.

DONNELL, STEPHEN D. Pvt, C, 22nd NJ Inf, DoD Unknown. St. Joseph's Cemetery, Hackensack, Bergen County.

DONNELLY, ARTHUR B. Corp, C, 13th NJ Inf, 10-20-1896. Holy Sepulchre Cemetery, Totowa, Passaic County.

DONNELLY, BERNARD Pvt, I, 26th NJ Inf, 3-29-1893. Holy Sepulchre Cemetery, East Orange, Essex County.

DONNELLY, EDWARD J. 1st Sgt, C, 5th NJ Inf, 9-11-1922. St. Peter's Cemetery, Jersey City, Hudson County.

DONNELLY, JAMES Pvt, H, 40th NJ Inf, 7-27-1895. St. Paul's Church Cemetery, Burlington, Burlington County.

DONNELLY, JAMES Pvt, Btty B, 1st NJ Light Art, DoD Unknown. Holy Sepulchre Cemetery, East Orange, Essex County.

New Jersey Civil War Burials

DONNELLY, JAMES 2nd Lt, A, 15th NJ Inf, 4-18-1895. Mansfield/Washington Cemetery, Washington, Warren County.

DONNELLY, JOHN Pvt, A, 26th MO Inf, 10-2-1892. St. Joseph's Cemetery, Hackensack, Bergen County.

DONNELLY, JOHN Sgt, D, 57th MA Inf, [Died of rheumatic fever at Beverly, NJ.] 9-30-1864. Beverly National Cemetery, Edgewater Park, Burlington County.

DONNELLY, JOHN Pvt, C, 8th NJ Inf, 5-20-1902. Holy Sepulchre Cemetery, East Orange, Essex County.

DONNELLY*, JOHN Pvt, E, 9th NY Cav, 5-1-1906. St. Rose of Lima Cemetery, Oxford, Warren County.

DONNELLY, JOHN Pvt, C, 51st NY Inf, 9- -1914. Holy Sepulchre Cemetery, Totowa, Passaic County.

DONNELLY, JOHN Pvt, B, 33rd NJ Inf, 4-27-1895. Holy Sepulchre Cemetery, East Orange, Essex County.

DONNELLY, JOHN Seaman, U.S. Navy, USS Saint Mary's, 2- -1916. St. Stephen's Cemetery, Millburn, Essex County.

DONNELLY, JOHN E. Pvt, B, 21st NJ Inf, 1923. Elmwood Cemetery, New Brunswick, Middlesex County.

DONNELLY, JOHN M. (see: Bernardo, Carlos J.) Grove Church Cemetery, North Bergen, Hudson County.

DONNELLY, JOSEPH T. Pvt, G, 3rd NJ Cav, 4-7-1922. Oddfellows Cemetery, Burlington, Burlington County.

DONNELLY, PATRICK Pvt, B, 25th NY Inf, DoD Unknown. Holy Sepulchre Cemetery, East Orange, Essex County.

DONNELLY, RICHARD GRANT AUGUSTUS Sgt, I, 1st NJ Inf, [Wounded 6-27-1862 at Gaines' Farm, VA.] 2-27-1905. Greenwood Cemetery, Hamilton, Mercer County.

DONNELLY, WILLIAM W. Pvt, G, 9th NJ Inf, 5-21-1868. Evergreen Cemetery, Camden, Camden County.

DONNER*, DAVID Pvt, Btty D, 1st NJ Light Art, 2-15-1903. Evergreen Cemetery, Hillside, Union County.

DONNER, FREDERICK Pvt, F, 22nd NJ Inf, 8-23-1906. Riverview Cemetery, Trenton, Mercer County.

DONNINGTON, JOHN W. Corp, B, 7th NJ Inf, 1870. Mount Pleasant Cemetery, Newark, Essex County.

DONOHOE, CHARLES 9-15-1888. St. Mary's Cemetery, Plainfield, Union County.

DONOHOE, JOHN 4-8-1885. St. Mary's Cemetery, Plainfield, Union County.

DONOHUE, JAMES Pvt, C, 7th NJ Inf, 8-15-1917. Arlington Cemetery, Kearny, Hudson County.

DONOMORE, JAMES Pvt, A, 9th NJ Inf, 2-24-1915. St. James Episcopal Church Cemetery, Piscatawaytown, Middlesex County.

DONOVAN, JEREMIAH Pvt, D, 33rd NJ Inf, 1918. St. Peter's Cemetery, New Brunswick, Middlesex County.

DONOVAN, JOSEPH 1st Lt, A, 2nd NJ Inf, [Wounded in action.] 10-4-1901. Evergreen Cemetery, Hillside, Union County.

DONOVAN, PATRICK Pvt, H, 133rd NY Inf, DoD Unknown. Holy Name Cemetery, Jersey City, Hudson County.

DOODY, RICHARD Pvt, C, 24th NJ Inf, 3-10-1887. St. Mary's Cemetery, Salem, Salem County.

DOOLEY, JOHN Pvt, U.S. Marine Corps, 2-18-1886. St. James Cemetery, Woodbridge, Middlesex County.

DOOLEY, JOHN Pvt, A, 31st NJ Inf, 2-13-1903. Holy Name Cemetery, Jersey City, Hudson County.

Our Brothers Gone Before

DOOLEY, MICHAEL F. Sgt, B, 77th NY National Guard, 1-26-1912. Mount Olivet Cemetery, Newark, Essex County.
DOOLEY, WILLIAM Pvt, K, 35th NJ Inf, 6-10-1868. Holy Name Cemetery, Jersey City, Hudson County.
DOOLEY, WILLIAM (see: Dooling, William) Finn's Point National Cemetery, Pennsville, Salem County.
DOOLIN, JOHN (aka: Dillen, John) Pvt, F, 3rd NJ Cav, 9-14-1875. Holy Sepulchre Cemetery, East Orange, Essex County.
DOOLIN, JOHN S. Pvt, C, 9th NJ Inf, 5-24-1867. Baptist Cemetery, Burlington, Burlington County.
DOOLING, WILLIAM (aka: Dooley, William) Corp, E, 15th AL Inf (CSA), [Wounded at Sharpsburg, MD. Captured at Gettysburg, PA.] 11-27-1863. Finn's Point National Cemetery, Pennsville, Salem County.
DOOLITTLE, DAVID Pvt, G, 23rd NJ Inf, 10-7-1878. Coopertown Meeting House Cemetery, Edgewater Park, Burlington County.
DOONER, HUGH P. Corp, C, 2nd NJ Inf, 11-14-1893. Holy Sepulchre Cemetery, East Orange, Essex County.
DOPF, JOHN (aka: Topf, John) Pvt, L, 3rd NJ Cav, 2-27-1926. Woodland Cemetery, Newark, Essex County.
DOPSON, WILLIAM R. Pvt, A, 40th NJ Inf, 11-3-1930. Green Cemetery, Woodbury, Gloucester County.
DORAN, CHARLES H. Pvt, H, 3rd NJ Cav, 1923. Methodist Church Cemetery, Hurffville, Gloucester County.
DORAN*, GEORGE N. Pvt, K, 38th NJ Inf, 11-24-1908. Presbyterian Church Cemetery, Pennington, Mercer County.
DORAN*, HUGH Corp, B, 1st NJ Cav, 12-6-1899. Prospect Hill Cemetery, Flemington, Hunterdon County.
DORAN, JAMES Pvt, G, 14th NJ Inf, 1868. Mount Olivet Cemetery, Fairview, Monmouth County.
DORAN, JOHN (aka: Doren, John) Pvt, A, 99th NY Inf, 7-31-1895. Holy Sepulchre Cemetery, East Orange, Essex County.
DORAN, JOHN Pvt, A, 10th NJ Inf, 11-7-1931. Evergreen Cemetery, Hillside, Union County.
DORAN, JOHN D. Corp, D, 4th NJ Inf, DoD Unknown. Greenwood Cemetery, Hamilton, Mercer County.
DORAN, JOSEPH Pvt, K, 9th NJ Inf, 1-1-1925. Evergreen Cemetery, Hillside, Union County.
DORAN, MICHAEL 1894. St. Mary's Cemetery, Plainfield, Union County.
DORANS, WILLIAM DoD Unknown. Mercer Cemetery, Trenton, Mercer County.
DOREMUS, ABRAHAM 10-1-1891. Cedar Lawn Cemetery, Paterson, Passaic County.
DOREMUS, ABRAM Seaman, U.S. Navy, 3-11-1887. Laurel Grove Cemetery, Totowa, Passaic County.
DOREMUS, ALBERT C. Pvt, C, 25th NJ Inf, 4-25-1922. Cedar Lawn Cemetery, Paterson, Passaic County.
DOREMUS, ANDREW Sgt, C, 25th NJ Inf, 2-12-1920. Laurel Grove Cemetery, Totowa, Passaic County.
DOREMUS, CHARLES P. Pvt, E, 13th NJ Inf, 11-4-1911. Arlington Cemetery, Kearny, Hudson County.
DOREMUS, CORNELIUS Pvt, K, 27th NJ Inf, 1918. Hillside Cemetery, Lyndhurst, Bergen County.
DOREMUS, ELIJAH 1915. Rosedale Cemetery, Orange, Essex County.
DOREMUS, GOLINE Pvt, G, 26th NJ Inf, 6-8-1896. Cedar Lawn Cemetery, Paterson, Passaic County.

New Jersey Civil War Burials

DOREMUS, JAMES H. Corp, G, 27th NJ Inf, 11-12-1920. Reformed Church Cemetery, Montville, Morris County.

DOREMUS, JOHN H. Pvt, K, 13th NJ Inf, [Died of wounds received 9-17-1862 at Antietam, MD.] 12-9-1862. Laurel Grove Cemetery, Totowa, Passaic County.

DOREMUS, JOHN W. Sgt, E, 22nd NJ Inf, 11-11-1883. Cedar Lawn Cemetery, Paterson, Passaic County.

DOREMUS, RICHARD Pvt, F, 1st NJ Cav, DoD Unknown. Locust Hill Cemetery, Dover, Morris County.

DOREMUS, STEPHEN Pvt, C, 25th NJ Inf, 9-6-1891. Cedar Lawn Cemetery, Paterson, Passaic County.

DOREMUS, SYLVESTER Landsman, U.S. Navy, USS Restless, 8-17-1907. Rahway Cemetery, Rahway, Union County.

DOREMUS, THEODORE D. Corp, G, 5th NY Cav, 7-2-1913. Fairmount Cemetery, Newark, Essex County.

DOREMUS*, THOMAS B. Pvt, F, 72nd NY Inf, 9-28-1878. Mount Pleasant Cemetery, Newark, Essex County.

DOREMUS, THOMAS E. Pvt, C, 25th NJ Inf, 8-21-1866. Reformed Church Cemetery, Montville, Morris County.

DOREMUS, WILLIAM H. Corp, H, 2nd DC Inf, 2-26-1876. Fairmount Cemetery, Newark, Essex County.

DOREMUS, WILLIAM T. Pvt, B, 22nd NJ Inf, 1-6-1926. Cedar Lawn Cemetery, Paterson, Passaic County.

DOREN, JOHN (see: Doran, John) Holy Sepulchre Cemetery, East Orange, Essex County.

DOREY, WILLIAM Seaman, U.S. Navy, 6-21-1877. Fairmount Cemetery, Newark, Essex County.

DORING, HENRY Pvt, E, 22nd NJ Inf, 11-2-1898. Cedar Lawn Cemetery, Paterson, Passaic County.

DORLAND, HENRY C. 1902. New Somerville Cemetery, Somerville, Somerset County.

DORMAN, JAMES F. Sgt Maj, 73rd NY Inf DoD Unknown. Flower Hill Cemetery, North Bergen, Hudson County.

DORMAN, WILLIAM Pvt, D, 3rd NJ Inf, 3-17-1882. Old Catholic Cemetery, Franklin Boro, Sussex County.

DORMIDA*, THOMAS Pvt, D, 15th NJ Inf, 12-24-1912. Newton Cemetery, Newton, Sussex County.

DORN, GEORGE Corp, E, 50th PA Inf, DoD Unknown. Arlington Cemetery, Kearny, Hudson County.

DORN, HENRY G. Pvt, B, 13th NY Cav, DoD Unknown. Arlington Cemetery, Kearny, Hudson County.

DORNER, ANDREAS (see: Dorner, Andrew) Presbyterian Church Cemetery, Cold Spring, Cape May County.

DORNER*, ANDREW (aka: Dorner, Andreas) Pvt, K, 3rd NJ Cav, 2-14-1924. Presbyterian Church Cemetery, Cold Spring, Cape May County.

DORON, JOSEPH ALLEN 7-19-1898. Baptist Cemetery, Vincentown, Burlington County.

DORR, JOHN G. (aka: Doerr, John) Pvt, F, 39th NJ Inf, [Died of wounds received at Petersburg, VA.] 3-25-1865. Woodland Cemetery, Newark, Essex County.

DORRANCE*, GEORGE E. Pvt, C, 18th CT Inf, 12-18-1892. Fairmount Cemetery, Newark, Essex County.

DORRELL, JOSEPH Pvt, D, 2nd MD Inf (ES), 1-14-1915. Overlook Cemetery, Bridgeton, Cumberland County.

DORSETT, JAMES E. Seaman, U.S. Navy, USS North Carolina, DoD Unknown. Evergreen Cemetery, Farmingdale, Monmouth County.

DORSEY, ALEXANDER Corp, B, 30th U.S. CT, 2-16-1927. Jericho/Oddfellows Cemetery, Deptford, Gloucester County.

Our Brothers Gone Before

DORSEY, DANIEL DoD Unknown. Old Camden Cemetery, Camden, Camden County.
DORSEY, DECATUR 1st Sgt, B, 39th U.S. CT, [Awarded the Medal of Honor.] 7-11-1891. Flower Hill Cemetery, North Bergen, Hudson County.
DORSEY, ISAIAH Pvt, F, 3rd U.S. CT, 4-23-1904. Mount Peace Cemetery, Lawnside, Camden County.
DORSEY, JOSEPH B. Pvt, A, 32nd U.S. CT, 8-19-1917. Jericho/Oddfellows Cemetery, Deptford, Gloucester County.
DORSEY, JOSIAH (aka: Dawsey, Josiah) Pvt, E, 32nd U.S. CT, DoD Unknown. Jericho/Oddfellows Cemetery, Deptford, Gloucester County.
DORSEY, WILLIAM Pvt, I, 6th NJ Inf, DoD Unknown. Old Camden Cemetery, Camden, Camden County.
DORST, ANDREAS Pvt, Btty A, 1st NJ Light Art, 9-9-1882. Bayview-New York Bay Cemetery, Jersey City, Hudson County.
DORTCH, JOHN Pvt, D, 2nd FL Inf (CSA), [Wounded 6-27-1862 at Gaines' Farm, VA. Captured 7-3-1863 at Gettysburg, PA. Died of lung inflammation.] 12-22-1863. Finn's Point National Cemetery, Pennsville, Salem County.
DORTCH, NEWMAN J. Capt, H, 24th GA Inf (CSA), [Captured 6-1-1864 at Cold Harbor, VA. Died of disease.] 9-25-1864. Finn's Point National Cemetery, Pennsville, Salem County.
DORTON, JOHN S. Pvt, A, 2nd DC Inf, 10-6-1899. Fairmount Cemetery, Newark, Essex County.
DORWART, BENJAMIN Corp, G, 9th IL Inf, 10-7-1904. Baptist Church Cemetery, Scotch Plains, Union County.
DOSHANIS, JACOB (see: Duscheness, Jacob) B'nai Abraham Cemetery, Newark, Essex County.
DOSTER, GEORGE S. Pvt, A, 12th SC Inf (CSA), [Captured 7-5-1863 at Gettysburg, PA. Died of chronic diarrhea.] 10-2-1863. Finn's Point National Cemetery, Pennsville, Salem County.
DOTTERER, NEWBERRY 1912. Union Cemetery, Frenchtown, Hunterdon County.
DOTTS*, JOHN L. Sgt, A, 33rd PA Inf, 3-19-1920. New Camden Cemetery, Camden, Camden County.
DOTY*, DAVID W. Pvt, Btty D, 1st NJ Light Art, 6-10-1924. Branchville Cemetery, Branchville, Sussex County.
DOTY, EDWIN ALONZO Pvt, C, 15th NJ Inf, 4-4-1933. Evergreen Cemetery, Morristown, Morris County.
DOTY, GEORGE WOOD Pvt, E, 39th NJ Inf, 12-6-1906. Connecticut Farms Cemetery, Union, Union County.
DOTY, JAMES 3-28-1903. Evergreen/Bishop Jaynes Cemetery, Basking Ridge, Somerset County.
DOTY, JAMES C. Wagoner, A, 71st NY Inf, 3-4-1900. Fairmount Cemetery, Newark, Essex County.
DOTY, JOHN H. Pvt, B, 30th NJ Inf, 1-4-1937. Connecticut Farms Cemetery, Union, Union County.
DOTY, JOHN T. Corp, G, 39th NJ Inf, [Killed in action at Fort Mahone, VA.] 4-2-1865. Fairmount Cemetery, Newark, Essex County.
DOTY, JOSEPH D. Pvt, E, 3rd MO Inf, 1-18-1925. Evergreen Cemetery, Morristown, Morris County.
DOTY, JOSEPH L. Pvt, K, 1st NJ Cav, 11-19-1866. Evergreen Cemetery, Morristown, Morris County.
DOTY, JOSEPH L. 5-1-1880. Fairmount Cemetery, Newark, Essex County.
DOTY, MAHLON Sgt, B, 26th NJ Inf, 3-1-1888. Mount Pleasant Cemetery, Newark, Essex County.
DOTY*, SAMUEL D. Pvt, C, 15th NJ Inf, 1876. Evergreen/Bishop Jaynes Cemetery, Basking Ridge, Somerset County.

New Jersey Civil War Burials

DOTY, SAMUEL K. Pvt, G, 9th NJ Inf, 3-29-1895. Baptist/Evergreen Methodist Cemetery, Plainfield, Union County.

DOTY, STILLMAN R. Corp, I, 28th NJ Inf, 1896. Hillside Cemetery, Metuchen, Middlesex County.

DOTY, THOMAS E. Pvt, H, 22nd NJ Inf, 1882. 1st Reformed Church Cemetery, Pompton Plains, Morris County.

DOTY, WILLIAM Pvt, F, 28th NJ Inf, 6-1-1918. Cedar Lawn Cemetery, Paterson, Passaic County.

DOTY, WILLIAM Corp, H, 27th NJ Inf, [Died of fever at Camp Sumner, VA.] 1-28-1863. Slauson Cemetery, Wantage, Sussex County.

DOTY, WILLIAM H.H. Pvt, A, 26th NJ Inf, 4-13-1889. Arlington Cemetery, Kearny, Hudson County.

DOTY, WILLIAM H. H. Pvt, Btty G, 5th NY Heavy Art, [Wounded in action.] 7-21-1916. Arlington Cemetery, Kearny, Hudson County.

DOUD, CHARLES (see: Dowd, Charles) St. Peter's Cemetery, New Brunswick, Middlesex County.

DOUD, MILO G. Pvt, D, 11th PA Cav, 12-16-1911. Belvidere/Catholic Cemetery, Belvidere, Warren County.

DOUD, THOMAS Pvt, I, 29th NJ Inf, 8-9-1896. Mount Olivet Cemetery, Fairview, Monmouth County.

DOUDY*, JOSEPH (aka: Dowdy, Joseph) Pvt, Btty F, 11th U.S. CHA, 2-17-1901. Trinity AME Church Cemetery, Wrightsville, Burlington County.

DOUGHERTY*, ABNER Landsman, U.S. Navy, USS Dai-ching, [Wounded in action.] 9-7-1925. Bordentown/Old St. Mary's Catholic Cemetery, Bordentown, Burlington County.

DOUGHERTY, ALEXANDER N. Surg, 4th NJ Inf 11-28-1882. Mount Pleasant Cemetery, Newark, Essex County.

DOUGHERTY, ALFRED H. Pvt, C, 2nd U.S. Cav, 10-24-1887. Union Cemetery, Gloucester City, Camden County.

DOUGHERTY, CHARLES J. 5-28-1896. St. Mary's Cemetery, Hamilton, Mercer County.

DOUGHERTY, CHARLES R. 1st Lt, Adj, 7th NJ Inf [Wounded in action.] 7-21-1911. Oceanville Cemetery, Oceanville, Atlantic County.

DOUGHERTY, CHARLES W. Sgt, D, 33rd NJ Inf, 11-15-1873. Cedar Lawn Cemetery, Paterson, Passaic County.

DOUGHERTY, DANIEL Pvt, C, 34th NJ Inf, 3-28-1889. Flower Hill Cemetery, North Bergen, Hudson County.

DOUGHERTY, EDWARD G. Pvt, K, 24th NJ Inf, 11-14-1899. Methodist-Episcopal Church Cemetery, Penns Grove, Salem County.

DOUGHERTY, HENRY Wagoner, I, 30th NJ Inf, 2-9-1902. Fairview Cemetery, Westfield, Union County.

DOUGHERTY, ISAAC DoD Unknown. Old Camden Cemetery, Camden, Camden County.

DOUGHERTY, JAMES Pvt, C, 11th NJ Inf, 10-20-1889. Riverview Cemetery, Trenton, Mercer County.

DOUGHERTY, JAMES Pvt, H, ___ ___ ___, 11-9-1911. Presbyterian Church Cemetery, Andover, Sussex County.

DOUGHERTY, JAMES H. Pvt, G, 7th NJ Inf, 4-18-1877. Cedar Lawn Cemetery, Paterson, Passaic County.

DOUGHERTY, JOHN Pvt, I, 88th PA Inf, [Wounded 4-1-1865 at Five Forks, VA.] 8-26-1907. Methodist Church Cemetery, New Albany, Burlington County.

DOUGHERTY, JOHN Pvt, B, 8th NJ Inf, 5-27-1870. Fairmount Cemetery, Newark, Essex County.

Our Brothers Gone Before

DOUGHERTY, JOHN Pvt, C, 25th NJ Inf, DoD Unknown. Holy Sepulchre Cemetery, East Orange, Essex County.

DOUGHERTY, JOHN Pvt, A, 25th NY Inf, 11-17-1887. Holy Sepulchre Cemetery, East Orange, Essex County.

DOUGHERTY, JOHN Pvt, I, 30th NJ Inf, 8-10-1913. Presbyterian Church Cemetery, Liberty Corners, Somerset County.

DOUGHERTY, JOHN (see: Doherty, John) Cedar Lawn Cemetery, Paterson, Passaic County.

DOUGHERTY, JOHN H. (aka: Darighty, John H.) Pvt, E, 39th GA Inf (CSA), [Captured 5-16-1863 at Baker's Creek, MS.] 6-27-1863. Finn's Point National Cemetery, Pennsville, Salem County.

DOUGHERTY, LEWIS R. Pvt, D, 3rd NJ Militia, 7-26-1875. Fairmount Cemetery, Newark, Essex County.

DOUGHERTY, MICHAEL Pvt, I, 3rd NJ Inf, 7-30-1887. Evergreen Cemetery, Hillside, Union County.

DOUGHERTY, OWEN Pvt, C, 39th NJ Inf, [Wounded in action.] 4-20-1897. Holy Sepulchre Cemetery, East Orange, Essex County.

DOUGHERTY*, PATRICK Pvt, D, 7th NJ Inf, 1916. Head of River Church Cemetery, Head of River, Atlantic County.

DOUGHERTY, PATRICK J. Pvt, B, 1st NJ Militia, 6-27-1903. Holy Sepulchre Cemetery, East Orange, Essex County.

DOUGHERTY, PETER Pvt, G, 28th NJ Inf, DoD Unknown. St. Joseph's Cemetery, Swedesboro, Gloucester County.

DOUGHERTY, PETER (aka: Doherty, Peter) Pvt, H, 51st NY Inf, DoD Unknown. Holy Sepulchre Cemetery, East Orange, Essex County.

DOUGHERTY, PETER S. Pvt, B, 23rd NJ Inf, 2-27-1900. Bordentown/Old St. Mary's Catholic Cemetery, Bordentown, Burlington County.

DOUGHERTY, RICHARD Pvt, B, 26th NJ Inf, 8-22-1889. Fairmount Cemetery, Newark, Essex County.

DOUGHERTY, RODGER Pvt, G, 51st NY Inf, 3-6-1898. Mount Olivet Cemetery, Fairview, Monmouth County.

DOUGHERTY, SAMUEL 1st Sgt, K, 13th NJ Inf, 12-10-1870. Holy Sepulchre Cemetery, Totowa, Passaic County.

DOUGHERTY, SAMUEL HARRIS Sgt, C, 2nd DC Inf, 9-13-1923. Mount Pleasant Cemetery, Newark, Essex County.

DOUGHERTY, STEPHEN T. Pvt, A, 70th NY Inf, 5-26-1886. Cedar Lawn Cemetery, Paterson, Passaic County.

DOUGHERTY, SYLVANUS (see: Doughty, Sylvanus) 1st Methodist Church Cemetery, Williamstown, Gloucester County.

DOUGHERTY, THEODORE F. Corp, A, 26th NJ Inf, 9-4-1911. Mount Pleasant Cemetery, Newark, Essex County.

DOUGHERTY, THOMAS Pvt, I, 70th NY Inf, [Wounded 6-1-1862 at Fair Oaks, VA.] 9-2-1921. Laurel Grove Cemetery, Totowa, Passaic County.

DOUGHERTY, WILLIAM Pvt, B, 69th NY State Militia, 8-20-1877. Holy Name Cemetery, Jersey City, Hudson County.

DOUGHTEN, SAMUEL DoD Unknown. Old Camden Cemetery, Camden, Camden County.

DOUGHTY, ABIJAH Sgt, H, 4th NJ Inf, 9-11-1879. Methodist-Episcopal Cemetery, Lake, Gloucester County.

DOUGHTY, BENJAMIN Pvt, F, 29th NJ Inf, 3-23-1909. United Methodist Church Cemetery, Little Silver, Monmouth County.

DOUGHTY, BENJAMIN B. (JR.) Pvt, G, 4th NJ Inf, [Cenotaph. Died of typhoid at Mechanicsville, VA.] 6-6-1862. Batsto/Pleasant Mills Methodist Church Cemetery, Pleasant Mills, Atlantic County.

New Jersey Civil War Burials

DOUGHTY, BENJAMIN F. Pvt, A, 9th NJ Inf, 1-14-1914. Trinity Bible Church Cemetery, Glassboro, Gloucester County.

DOUGHTY, CHARLES H. Landsman, U.S. Navy, USS Macedonian, 3-16-1908. United Methodist Church Cemetery, Little Silver, Monmouth County.

DOUGHTY, DANIEL Pvt, K, 4th NJ Inf, 1-24-1913. Soldier's Home Cemetery, Vineland, Cumberland County.

DOUGHTY, DANIEL C. Pvt, E, 10th NJ Inf, [Died of wounds received at Cold Harbor, VA.] 3-12-1866. Batsto/Pleasant Mills Methodist Church Cemetery, Pleasant Mills, Atlantic County.

DOUGHTY, GEORGE T. 2nd Lt, B, 10th NJ Inf, 6-24-1900. Mount Pleasant Cemetery, Millville, Cumberland County.

DOUGHTY, J.N. Pvt, G, 51st AL Cav (CSA), 1-9-1864. Finn's Point National Cemetery, Pennsville, Salem County.

DOUGHTY, JOHN E. Capt, K, 4th NJ Inf, [Wounded 6-27-1864 at Gaines' Mill, VA.] 6-27-1921. Batsto/Pleasant Mills Methodist Church Cemetery, Pleasant Mills, Atlantic County.

DOUGHTY, JOHN H. Actg 3rd Asst Eng, U.S. Navy, USS Pocahontas, 6-30-1904. Harleigh Cemetery, Camden, Camden County.

DOUGHTY, JOSEPH G. 1921. Mount Pleasant Cemetery, Millville, Cumberland County.

DOUGHTY, RICHARD Pvt, F, Dale's Bttn PA Cav, 11-22-1897. Fairview Cemetery, Fairview, Monmouth County.

DOUGHTY, SYLVANUS (aka: Dougherty, Sylvanus) Pvt, D, 25th NJ Inf, 4-5-1915. 1st Methodist Church Cemetery, Williamstown, Gloucester County.

DOUGHTY, WILLIAM W. Pvt, G, 7th NJ Inf, 7-1-1905. Laurel Grove Cemetery, Totowa, Passaic County.

DOUGLAS, ALEXANDER Pvt, E, 38th NJ Inf, 8-16-1916. 1st Baptist Cemetery, Cape May Court House, Cape May County.

DOUGLAS, AUGUST (see: Hoff, Angus Douglass) Wesley United Methodist Church Cemetery, Petersburg, Cape May County.

DOUGLAS, C.C. DoD Unknown. Old South Church Cemetery, Bergenfield, Bergen County.

DOUGLAS, CHARLES F. Landsman, U.S. Navy, USS R.R. Cuyler, 1904. Arlington Cemetery, Pennsauken, Camden County.

DOUGLAS, HENRY Pvt, I, 2nd OH Cav, 12-17-1916. Holy Name Cemetery, Jersey City, Hudson County.

DOUGLAS, HUGH Pvt, E, 18th NY Inf, 1910. Bayview-New York Bay Cemetery, Jersey City, Hudson County.

DOUGLAS, JACOB M. Pvt, B, 13th NJ Inf, 5-11-1893. Maplewood Cemetery, Freehold, Monmouth County.

DOUGLAS, JOHN Pvt, G, 28th NJ Inf, [Wounded in action.] 7-21-1887. St. Joseph's Cemetery, Swedesboro, Gloucester County.

DOUGLAS, WILLIAM 10-14-1915. Old South Church Cemetery, Bergenfield, Bergen County.

DOUGLASS, ARMER A. Pvt, D, 1st DE Inf, 2-25-1907. Riverview Cemetery, Trenton, Mercer County.

DOUGLASS, CHARLES Pvt, K, 35th NJ Inf, 12-30-1920. Riverview Cemetery, Trenton, Mercer County.

DOUGLASS, CHARLES 12-16-1892. Fairmount Cemetery, Newark, Essex County.

DOUGLASS*, FRANK W. Sgt, C, 141st PA Inf, [Wounded 5-6-1864 at Wilderness, VA.] 6-24-1912. Evergreen Cemetery, Hillside, Union County.

DOUGLASS, FREDERICK H. Pvt, F, 23rd U.S. CT, 11-30-1904. Arlington Cemetery, Kearny, Hudson County.

DOUGLASS, GEORGE B. Principal Musc, 4th U.S. Inf 7-28-1867. Fairmount Cemetery, Newark, Essex County.

Our Brothers Gone Before

DOUGLASS, GEORGE W. Asst Surg, 39th NJ Inf 3-11-1876. Mount Pleasant Cemetery, Newark, Essex County.

DOUGLASS, HORACE Pvt, K, 118th U.S. CT, 5-15-1901. Evergreen Cemetery, Morristown, Morris County.

DOUGLASS, JACOB M. Pvt, B, 13th NJ Inf, 1-14-1873. Methodist-Episcopal Cemetery, Burlington, Burlington County.

DOUGLASS, JOHN 1904. Methodist-Episcopal Church Cemetery, South Dennis, Cape May County.

DOUGLASS, JOHN 2nd Lt, G, 7th NJ Inf, DoD Unknown. Laurel Grove Cemetery, Totowa, Passaic County.

DOUGLASS, JOHN N. Pvt, B, 26th NJ Inf, 8-23-1915. Mount Pleasant Cemetery, Newark, Essex County.

DOUGLASS, JOSIAH Pvt, A, 8th FL Inf (CSA), [Captured 7-3-1863 at Gettysburg, PA. Died of smallpox.] 11-9-1863. Finn's Point National Cemetery, Pennsville, Salem County.

DOUGLASS, ROBERT Corp, E, 48th NY Inf, [Wounded 7-18-1863 at Fort Wagner, SC.] 4-14-1910. Cedar Lawn Cemetery, Paterson, Passaic County.

DOUGLASS*, SAMUEL E. 1st Lt, I, 25th NJ Inf, 1-20-1901. 1st Baptist Cemetery, Cape May Court House, Cape May County.

DOUGLASS, SIMON Pvt, H, 33rd OH Inf, 3-8-1950. Fairview Cemetery, Fairview, Bergen County.

DOUGLASS, SYLVESTER D. Pvt, G, 2nd NJ Inf, 6-18-1936. Fairmount Cemetery, Newark, Essex County.

DOUGLASS, WILLIAM Corp, F, 2nd NJ Inf, 7-26-1920. Glendale Cemetery, Bloomfield, Essex County.

DOUGLASS, WILLIAM Pvt, H, 41st U.S. CT, DoD Unknown. Berrys Chapel Cemetery, Quinton, Salem County.

DOUGLASS, WILLIAM Pvt, L, 1st U.S. Cav, 3-9-1896. Mount Pleasant Cemetery, Newark, Essex County.

DOUGLASS, WILLIAM B. 10-15-1889. Mount Pleasant Cemetery, Newark, Essex County.

DOVE, RANSOM Pvt, L, 4th VA Inf (CSA), [Wounded and captured 7-3-1863 at Gettysburg, PA. Died of dysentery.] 11-8-1863. Finn's Point National Cemetery, Pennsville, Salem County.

DOW*, ALONZO Pvt, H, 15th NJ Inf, 11-6-1916. Methodist Cemetery, Crosswicks, Burlington County.

DOW, CLINTON Pvt, D, 14th NJ Inf, 1917. Tennent Church Cemetery, Tennent, Monmouth County.

DOW, EDWARD S. Corp, I, 5th NY Cav, 1901. Baptist/Evergreen Methodist Cemetery, Plainfield, Union County.

DOW, FOLKERT P. Pvt, H, 38th NJ Inf, 11-18-1890. Reformed Church Cemetery, Bedminster, Somerset County.

DOW, JOHN 10-9-1918. Presbyterian Church Cemetery, Shrewsbury, Monmouth County.

DOW, JOHN Pvt, H, 22nd NJ Inf, 3-12-1921. Laurel Grove Cemetery, Totowa, Passaic County.

DOWARS, RICHARD Pvt, B, 9th PA Inf, 12-11-1912. Baptist Church Cemetery, Jacobstown, Burlington County.

DOWD, CHARLES (aka: Doud, Charles) Pvt, F, 34th NJ Inf, 5-22-1913. St. Peter's Cemetery, New Brunswick, Middlesex County.

DOWD, JAMES Pvt, H, 35th NJ Inf, 1911. Mount Olivet Cemetery, Fairview, Monmouth County.

DOWD, MATTHEW Seaman, U.S. Navy, 9-26-1887. Evergreen Cemetery, Hillside, Union County.

New Jersey Civil War Burials

DOWD, MICHAEL Pvt, F, 8th NJ Inf, [Wounded in action.] 2-13-1870. Holy Sepulchre Cemetery, East Orange, Essex County.
DOWDNEY*, CHARLES B. Corp, I, 1st NJ Cav, 11-14-1908. Arlington Cemetery, Pennsauken, Camden County.
DOWDRIDGE*, JOHN Pvt, D, 25th NJ Inf, 7-19-1910. Methodist Cemetery, Haddonfield, Camden County.
DOWDY, JOSEPH (see: Doudy, Joseph) Trinity AME Church Cemetery, Wrightsville, Burlington County.
DOWDY, THOMAS W. Pvt, C, 57th VA Inf (CSA), [Captured 7-3-1863 at Gettysburg, PA. Died of diarrhea.] 9-12-1863. Finn's Point National Cemetery, Pennsville, Salem County.
DOWEN, WILLIAM Pvt, C, 77th NY Inf, 4-30-1921. Fairview Cemetery, Fairview, Monmouth County.
DOWER, GEORGE JOHN Pvt, G, 3rd NJ Cav, 11-21-1894. Flower Hill Cemetery, North Bergen, Hudson County.
DOWERS, BRIZALA (aka: Bowers, Barzilla P.) Pvt, Btty B, 1st VT Heavy Art, 7-18-1880. Princeton Cemetery, Princeton, Mercer County.
DOWGE, JOHN N. Pvt, Btty F, 5th U.S. Art, 1-13-1890. Fairmount Cemetery, Newark, Essex County.
DOWLING*, AARON Pvt, B, 3rd NJ Cav, [Wounded in action.] 7-25-1903. Oak Hill Cemetery, Vineland, Cumberland County.
DOWLING, CHRISTOPHER Corp, K, 6th NJ Inf, 11-28-1881. Old St. Mary's Cemetery, Gloucester City, Camden County.
DOWLING, ISAAC C. Pvt, B, 131st NY Inf, DoD Unknown. Lodi Cemetery, Lodi, Bergen County.
DOWLING, PETER J. Pvt, E, 165th NY Inf, 9-14-1883. St. Peter's Cemetery, New Brunswick, Middlesex County.
DOWLING, THOMAS Pvt, E, 73rd NY Inf, 3-16-1886. St. Peter's Cemetery, New Brunswick, Middlesex County.
DOWN, EPHRIAM Pvt, C, 29th NJ Inf, [Died of typhoid at Philadelphia, PA.] 12-28-1862. United Presbyterian Church Cemetery, Perrineville, Monmouth County.
DOWN, RUSLING Corp, A, 27th NJ Inf, 12-21-1881. Branchville Cemetery, Branchville, Sussex County.
DOWNAM*, WILLIAM E. Pvt, G, 12th NJ Inf, 5-17-1866. Methodist Church Cemetery, Newport, Cumberland County.
DOWNER, EDWIN F. Pvt, F, 5th VT Inf, 12-22-1901. Bloomfield Cemetery, Bloomfield, Essex County.
DOWNEY, DANIEL Corp, D, 24th PA Inf, 8-7-1906. Oak Hill Cemetery, Vineland, Cumberland County.
DOWNEY, HUGH Pvt, I, 11th NJ Inf, [Cenotaph. Died of ulcers while prisoner at Andersonville, GA.] 9-19-1864. Baptist Cemetery, South Plainfield, Middlesex County.
DOWNEY, JAMES Pvt, F, 106th NY Inf, 2-5-1916. Cedar Lawn Cemetery, Paterson, Passaic County.
DOWNEY, JAMES W. Pvt, F, 58th IN Inf, 5-1-1885. Holy Rood Cemetery, Morristown, Morris County.
DOWNEY, KEARIN (see: Downing, Keenan) Mount Olivet Cemetery, Newark, Essex County.
DOWNEY*, PATRICK Pvt, G, 7th NJ Inf, 9-13-1890. Holy Sepulchre Cemetery, East Orange, Essex County.
DOWNEY, WILLIAM Pvt, U.S. Marine Corps, 7-27-1900. New Camden Cemetery, Camden, Camden County.

Our Brothers Gone Before

DOWNIE, THOMAS S. Pvt, C, 1st NJ Inf, 1919. 1st United Methodist Church Cemetery, Bridgeton, Cumberland County.
DOWNING, CHARLES Pvt, E, 124th NY Inf, 5-9-1905. Arlington Cemetery, Kearny, Hudson County.
DOWNING, EDWARD R. Pvt, C, 6th MA Militia, DoD Unknown. Finn's Point National Cemetery, Pennsville, Salem County.
DOWNING*, JOHN N. Pvt, G, 13th NJ Inf, 1900. Mount Pleasant Cemetery, Newark, Essex County.
DOWNING, KEENAN (aka: Downey, Kearin) Pvt, K, 2nd NJ Cav, 9-28-1889. Mount Olivet Cemetery, Newark, Essex County.
DOWNING, ROBERT F. Pvt, H, 98th PA Inf, 12-20-1911. Evergreen Cemetery, Camden, Camden County.
DOWNS, ALBERT A. Pvt, G, 80th NY Inf, 2-11-1913. Arlington Cemetery, Kearny, Hudson County.
DOWNS, ALBERT B. Capt, I, 2nd CT Inf, 2-7-1905. Soldier's Home Cemetery, Vineland, Cumberland County.
DOWNS, CHARLES P. Pvt, H, 3rd NJ Inf, [Cenotaph. Died at Washington, DC. of wounds received 6-27-1862 at Gaines' Farm, VA.] 7-28-1862. Methodist Church Cemetery, Hurffville, Gloucester County.
DOWNS*, GEORGE H. Pvt, I, 2nd NJ Cav, 1918. United Presbyterian Church Cemetery, Perrineville, Monmouth County.
DOWNS, ISAAC W. Pvt, B, 24th NJ Inf, 6-6-1897. Mount Pleasant Cemetery, Millville, Cumberland County.
DOWNS, JACOB N. Musc, H, 31st NJ Inf, 12-25-1926. Evergreen Cemetery, Hillside, Union County.
DOWNS, JAMES Pvt, I, 14th NJ Inf, 1-2-1880. St. John's Cemetery, Hamilton, Mercer County.
DOWNS, JOHN Pvt, B, 35th NJ Inf, 5-5-1884. Fairmount Cemetery, Newark, Essex County.
DOWNS, JOHN Pvt, D, 51st NY Inf, 5-20-1900. Holy Name Cemetery, Jersey City, Hudson County.
DOWNS*, JOSEPH Corp, Btty L, 11th U.S. CHA, 9-5-1893. Oddfellows Cemetery, Burlington, Burlington County.
DOWNS, SAMUEL W. Capt, B, 40th NJ Inf, 1887. Greenwood Cemetery, Tuckerton, Ocean County.
DOWNS, THOMAS Seaman, U.S. Navy, 1-11-1919. St. Mary's Cemetery, Lower Cape May, Cape May County.
DOWNS, WALTER A. Pvt, E, 7th MI Inf, [Died at New York, NY.] 6-8-1863. Fairmount Cemetery, Newark, Essex County.
DOWNS, WILLIAM Pvt, F, 23rd NJ Inf, 2-16-1895. Old Presbyterian Cemetery, Lakehurst, Ocean County.
DOWNS*, WILLIAM A. Pvt, H, 6th U.S. Cav, 1-29-1905. Cedar Green Cemetery, Clayton, Gloucester County.
DOXEY, WILLIAM H. Pvt, D, 84th NY Inf, [Wounded 7-1-1863 at Gettysburg, PA.] 10-12-1918. Riverside Cemetery, Toms River, Ocean County.
DOYLE, ALEXANDER C. Pvt, F, 38th NJ Inf, 6-29-1908. Cedar Hill Cemetery, Hightstown, Mercer County.
DOYLE, HARVEY F. Pvt, F, 144th NY Inf, 10-6-1906. Rosedale Cemetery, Linden, Union County.
DOYLE, JAMES Pvt, F, 16th U.S. Inf, 10-24-1881. Holy Name Cemetery, Jersey City, Hudson County.
DOYLE, JAMES Pvt, G, 3rd NJ Inf, DoD Unknown. St. Paul's Church Cemetery, Burlington, Burlington County.

New Jersey Civil War Burials

DOYLE, JAMES W. Landsman, U.S. Navy, USS New Hampshire, DoD Unknown. Holy Name Cemetery, Jersey City, Hudson County.
DOYLE, MARTIN Sgt, G, 5th NJ Inf, 10- -1882. St. Peter's Cemetery, Jersey City, Hudson County.
DOYLE, MICHAEL Pvt, A, 11th ME Inf, [Died of wounds received 8-16-1864 at Deep Run, VA.] 9-14-1864. Beverly National Cemetery, Edgewater Park, Burlington County.
DOYLE, MICHAEL Seaman, U.S. Navy, 11-23-1923. Holy Name Cemetery, Jersey City, Hudson County.
DOYLE, PATRICK Pvt, D, 21st NJ Inf, 1896. Holy Name Cemetery, Jersey City, Hudson County.
DOYLE, PATRICK (aka: Daily, Patrick) Pvt, D, 3rd NJ Inf, 12-30-1896. St. Paul's Church Cemetery, Burlington, Burlington County.
DOYLE, THOMAS Seaman, U.S. Navy, 10-7-1933. Hillside Cemetery, Lyndhurst, Bergen County.
DOYLE, THOMAS Pvt, H, 55th NY Inf, 9-28-1916. Holy Name Cemetery, Jersey City, Hudson County.
DOYLE, THOMAS Pvt, A, 13th NJ Inf, [Killed in action at Chancellorsville, VA.] 5-3-1863. Bloomfield Cemetery, Bloomfield, Essex County.
DOYLE, WILLIAM S. Ordinary Seaman, U.S. Navy, USS Princeton, 1895. Immaculate Conception Cemetery, Montclair, Essex County.
DRAFFIN, JAMES (aka: Drefin, James) Pvt, E, 38th NJ Inf, 6-9-1892. Union Cemetery, Milford, Hunterdon County.
DRAKE*, ALBERT A. Pvt, A, 77th NY Inf, [Wounded 9-17-1862 at Antietam, MD.] 6-13-1897. Fairview Cemetery, Westfield, Union County.
DRAKE, ALBERT L. Pvt, B, 15th NJ Inf, 1899. Union Cemetery, Washington, Morris County.
DRAKE, ALEXANDER WILSON Pvt, B, 47th NY Inf, 2-4-1916. Mount Pleasant Cemetery, Newark, Essex County.
DRAKE*, ANDREW JACKSON Commander, U.S. Navy, USS Sassacus, 8-4-1875. Mount Pleasant Cemetery, Newark, Essex County.
DRAKE, CALVIN Pvt, C, 28th NJ Inf, DoD Unknown. Rosedale Cemetery, Orange, Essex County.
DRAKE, CHARLES Corp, H, 1st NJ Militia, 12-21-1896. Fairmount Cemetery, Newark, Essex County.
DRAKE, CHARLES Pvt, C, 30th NJ Inf, 5-5-1911. Rahway Cemetery, Rahway, Union County.
DRAKE*, CHARLES N. Pvt, Unassigned, 20th PA Cav, 5-5-1916. Connecticut Farms Cemetery, Union, Union County.
DRAKE, DANIEL Pvt, K, 38th NJ Inf, 7-20-1892. Princeton Cemetery, Princeton, Mercer County.
DRAKE, DANIEL W. Pvt, Unassigned, 33rd NJ Inf, 7-29-1909. Harleigh Cemetery, Camden, Camden County.
DRAKE, DANIEL W. Pvt, B, 13th NJ Inf, 1870. Quaker Cemetery, Quaker Church, Warren County.
DRAKE, EDWARD K. Pvt, I, 11th NJ Inf, 7-21-1920. Evergreen Cemetery, Hillside, Union County.
DRAKE, ELIAS J. Capt, K, 9th NJ Inf, 9-6-1891. Fairmount Cemetery, Newark, Essex County.
DRAKE, ELIJAH Pvt, F, 22nd NJ Inf, 12-22-1873. Baptist Cemetery, Hopewell Boro, Mercer County.
DRAKE, GEORGE F. Pvt, A, 31st NJ Inf, 4- -1872. Methodist Church Cemetery, Fairmount, Hunterdon County.

Our Brothers Gone Before

DRAKE, GEORGE M. Corp, C, 26th NJ Inf, 1-26-1910. Presbyterian Church Cemetery, Mount Freedom, Morris County.

DRAKE, GEORGE W. Corp, I, 15th NJ Inf, 12-31-1911. Fairmount Cemetery, Newark, Essex County.

DRAKE, GEORGE W. Pvt, G, 26th NJ Inf, DoD Unknown. South Orange Cemetery, South Orange, Essex County.

DRAKE, GEORGE WHITFIELD Hosp Steward, U.S. Navy, USS Arkansas, 6-7-1865. Evergreen Cemetery, Hillside, Union County.

DRAKE, HENRY C. Musc, C, 28th NJ Inf, 3-27-1906. Greenlawn Cemetery, West Long Branch, Monmouth County.

DRAKE, HENRY C. Corp, G, 35th NJ Inf, 4-26-1928. Hillside Cemetery, Scotch Plains, Union County.

DRAKE, ISAAC Corp, K, 28th NJ Inf, 11-23-1906. Elmwood Cemetery, New Brunswick, Middlesex County.

DRAKE, JACOB V. Pvt, E, 30th NJ Inf, 1-16-1872. New Somerville Cemetery, Somerville, Somerset County.

DRAKE, JAMES Pvt, 6th NY Ind Btty 2-28-1919. Rahway Cemetery, Rahway, Union County.

DRAKE, JAMES MADISON 1st Lt, K, 9th NJ Inf, [Awarded the Medal of Honor.] 11-28-1913. Evergreen Cemetery, Hillside, Union County.

DRAKE*, JOHN Pvt, D, 48th NY Inf, 5-14-1922. Riverview Cemetery, Trenton, Mercer County.

DRAKE, JOHN H. Wagoner, E, 15th NJ Inf, 1869. New Somerville Cemetery, Somerville, Somerset County.

DRAKE, JOHN H. Pvt, E, 47th NY Inf, 4-1-1905. Evergreen Cemetery, Lakewood, Ocean County.

DRAKE*, JOHN (JR.) Pvt, E, 2nd NJ Inf, [Wounded in action.] DoD Unknown. Layton Cemetery, Layton, Sussex County.

DRAKE, JONATHAN BAKER Hosp Steward, 30th NJ Inf 6-26-1904. Evergreen Cemetery, Hillside, Union County.

DRAKE, LEVI C. Sgt, G, 142nd PA Inf, 2-1-1923. Union Brick Cemetery, Blairstown, Warren County.

DRAKE*, NATHANIEL Corp, I, 15th NJ Inf, 1896. Presbyterian Church Cemetery, Andover, Sussex County.

DRAKE*, NATHANIEL 1st Sgt, E, 2nd NJ Inf, 1868. Quaker Cemetery, Quaker Church, Warren County.

DRAKE, NELSON H. Capt, C, 27th NJ Inf, 6-22-1889. Union Cemetery, Mount Olive, Morris County.

DRAKE*, NOAH Pvt, B, 73rd IL Inf, 9-25-1911. Hillside Cemetery, Scotch Plains, Union County.

DRAKE, ROBERT S. Pvt, F, 100th PA Inf, DoD Unknown. Siloam Cemetery, Vineland, Cumberland County.

DRAKE, SAMUEL WILSON Pvt, C, 7th MA Inf, [Died at Washington, DC.] 3-7-1863. Mansfield/Washington Cemetery, Washington, Warren County.

DRAKE, SILAS DOWNER Pvt, C, 14th NJ Inf, [Wounded at Winchester, VA.] 7-15-1908. Evergreen Cemetery, Hillside, Union County.

DRAKE, WALTER Corp, E, 10th NJ Inf, 12-19-1907. Fairmount Cemetery, Newark, Essex County.

DRAKE, WILLIAM Pvt, B, 8th NJ Inf, 6-9-1916. Holy Rood Cemetery, Morristown, Morris County.

DRAKE, WILLIAM A. Steward, U.S. Navy, USS Mingo, 11-12-1896. Johnson Cemetery, Camden, Camden County.

DRAKE, WILLIAM D. 2-11-1886. Presbyterian Church Cemetery, Andover, Sussex County.

New Jersey Civil War Burials

DRAKE, WILLIAM H.B. Pvt, I, 28th NJ Inf, 11-17-1902. Baptist/Evergreen Methodist Cemetery, Plainfield, Union County.
DRAKE*, WILLIAM HAMILTON Pvt, Btty D, 1st NJ Light Art, 1-29-1919. Rahway Cemetery, Rahway, Union County.
DRAKE, WILLIS SANFORD Gunner, U.S. Navy, USS Potomac, 2-7-1926. Evergreen Cemetery, Hillside, Union County.
DRAKE, ZEPHANIAH S. Corp, F, 30th NJ Inf, 1-11-1909. Baptist Cemetery, Hopewell Boro, Mercer County.
DRAPER, CHARLES Musc, F, 6th U.S. CT, 1-9-1893. Township Grounds #2 Cemetery, Mullica Hill, Gloucester County.
DRAPER, JOSEPH Pvt, K, 24th U.S. CT, 12-22-1896. Mount Pisgah Cemetery, Elsinboro, Salem County.
DRAPER, SOLOMON Pvt, D, 32nd (Lenoir Braves) NC Inf (CSA), [Captured 7-3-1863 at Gettysburg, PA. Died of disease.] 8-24-1863. Finn's Point National Cemetery, Pennsville, Salem County.
DREATLER, FREDERICK (see: Druetler, Frederick) Fairmount Cemetery, Newark, Essex County.
DREFIN, JAMES (see: Draffin, James) Union Cemetery, Milford, Hunterdon County.
DRENKLEBACH, JOHN Pvt, K, 5th MD Inf, 3-6-1894. Evergreen Cemetery, Camden, Camden County.
DRENNON*, WILLIAM Pvt, B, 2nd NJ Cav, 8-3-1910. St. Mary's Cemetery, Boonton, Morris County.
DRESCHER, JOHANN Pvt, D, 178th NY Inf, 10-31-1890. Brookside Cemetery, Englewood, Bergen County.
DRESCHER*, JOHN B. Pvt, A, 69th NY Inf, 1-20-1896. Fairmount Cemetery, Newark, Essex County.
DRESH*, FREDERICK (aka: Thresh, Frederick) Pvt, H, 3rd NJ Cav, 1-3-1910. Methodist Church Cemetery, Centre Grove, Cumberland County.
DRESLER, JOHN (aka: Deshler, E.B.) Pvt, B, 3rd NJ Militia, DoD Unknown. Elmwood Cemetery, New Brunswick, Middlesex County.
DRESSEL, LEONHARDT Pvt, E, 103rd NY Inf, 1884. Whippanong Cemetery, Whippany, Morris County.
DRESSER, GEORGE N. Pvt, C, 24th MA Inf, 12-11-1903. Evergreen Cemetery, Camden, Camden County.
DRESSER*, ROBERT (JR.) Pvt, D, 110th PA Inf, [Wounded 10-8-1864 at Petersburg, VA.] 8-19-1901. Evergreen Cemetery, Camden, Camden County.
DRESSER, ROBERT (SR.) Pvt, I, 10th NJ Inf, [Died of internal injuries at Washington, DC.] 1-25-1863. Evergreen Cemetery, Camden, Camden County.
DRESSER, WARWICK C. Pvt, U.S. Marine Corps, 12-19-1899. Evergreen Cemetery, Camden, Camden County.
DRESSLER, JOHN (see: Dresthler, John) Fairmount Cemetery, Newark, Essex County.
DRESTHLER, JOHN (aka: Dressler, John) Pvt, B, 8th NJ Inf, 1-19-1896. Fairmount Cemetery, Newark, Essex County.
DREW, ALEXANDER Pvt, C, 25th NJ Inf, 12-27-1919. Laurel Grove Cemetery, Totowa, Passaic County.
DREW*, BURTON 1st Lt, D, 38th U.S. CT, 11-9-1913. Rosedale Cemetery, Linden, Union County.
DREW, CHARLES Pvt, A, MD Emerg NJ Militia, 1887. Old Camden Cemetery, Camden, Camden County.
DREW, ELI Pvt, F, 26th NJ Inf, 8-14-1916. East Ridgelawn Cemetery, Clifton, Passaic County.
DREW, FRANCIS M. Pvt, D, 5th NJ Inf, [Died at Newark, NJ.] 12-1-1862. Fairmount Cemetery, Newark, Essex County.

Our Brothers Gone Before

DREW, JAMES B. Pvt, Btty B, 1st NJ Light Art, 3-9-1916. Bloomfield Cemetery, Bloomfield, Essex County.
DREW, JOHN W. Musc, F, 19th IL Inf, 1-12-1885. Cedar Lawn Cemetery, Paterson, Passaic County.
DREW, MARTIN R. Pvt, C, 25th NJ Inf, 5-26-1905. Cedar Lawn Cemetery, Paterson, Passaic County.
DREW, THOMAS P. Pvt, F, 2nd NJ Inf, 1865. Vincent Methodist-Episcopal Cemetery, Nutley, Essex County.
DREW, WILLIAM 1st Lt, E, 22nd NJ Inf, 7-20-1873. Old 1st Reformed Church Cemetery, Hackensack, Bergen County.
DREW, WILLIAM Pvt, F, 2nd NJ Inf, 5-23-1911. Fairmount Cemetery, Newark, Essex County.
DREW, WILLIAM Pvt, C, 33rd NJ Inf, DoD Unknown. Midvale Cemetery, Midvale, Passaic County.
DREWES, FRANK Pvt, D, 1st U.S. Hancock Corps, 3-28-1925. Palisade Cemetery, North Bergen, Hudson County.
DREY, HENRY Musc, 2nd NJ Inf Band 4-27-1875. Fairmount Cemetery, Newark, Essex County.
DREYER, CHARLES A. Quartermaster, U.S. Navy, DoD Unknown. Evergreen Cemetery, Hillside, Union County.
DREYER, FRANK 10-10-1912. Evergreen Cemetery, Hillside, Union County.
DRIGGERS, ANDERSON Pvt, E, 52nd NC Inf (CSA), [Captured 7-3-1863 at Gettysburg, PA. Died of disease.] 10-31-1863. Finn's Point National Cemetery, Pennsville, Salem County.
DRISCALL, EDWARD (see: Driscoll, Edward (Jr.)) Greenwood Cemetery, Tuckerton, Ocean County.
DRISCALL, THOMAS Pvt, K, 10th NJ Inf, 6-22-1925. Greenwood Cemetery, Tuckerton, Ocean County.
DRISCOLL, CORNELIUS Pvt, Btty E, 4th U.S. Art, 1-16-1886. Clinton Cemetery, Irvington, Essex County.
DRISCOLL, EDWARD (JR.) (aka: Driscall, Edward) Pvt, K, 10th NJ Inf, [Died at Tuckerton, NJ.] 3-11-1865. Greenwood Cemetery, Tuckerton, Ocean County.
DRISCOLL, JOHN Seaman, U.S. Navy, USS Wissahickon, 1928. Belvidere/Catholic Cemetery, Belvidere, Warren County.
DRISCOLL, JOHN A. Pvt, I, 2nd NJ Inf, 5- -1895. Laurel Grove Cemetery, Totowa, Passaic County.
DRIVER, JAMES R. 1st Sgt, C, 60th IL Inf, 11-18-1886. Methodist-Episcopal Church Cemetery, Blackwood, Camden County.
DRIVER, JOHN M. 1st Sgt, L, 1st NC Inf (US), 7-8-1904. Arlington Cemetery, Pennsauken, Camden County.
DRODOSSKY, JOHN (see: Deppisch, Stephen) Holy Name Cemetery, Jersey City, Hudson County.
DROS, FREDERICK WILLIAM Capt, I, 45th NY Inf, 5-25-1895. Berry Lawn Cemetery, Carlstadt, Bergen County.
DROSS, CHARLES Saddler, I, 1st NJ Cav, 10-4-1910. Laurel Grove Cemetery, Totowa, Passaic County.
DRUETLER, FREDERICK Pvt, C, 178th NY Inf, 11-25-1888. Fairmount Cemetery, Newark, Essex County.
DRUMGOULD, MICHAEL Pvt, A, 71st NY Inf, [Wounded 8-27-1862 at Bristoe Station, VA.] 5-22-1874. Holy Sepulchre Cemetery, East Orange, Essex County.
DRUMMOND*, GEORGE Pvt, F, 5th NJ Inf, 1-22-1918. Presbyterian Church Cemetery, Bridgeton, Cumberland County.
DRUMMOND, JAMES Pvt, F, 41st U.S. CT, 3-9-1896. Woodland Cemetery, Newark, Essex County.

New Jersey Civil War Burials

DRUMMOND*, JOHN Pvt, K, 4th NJ Inf, 3-25-1910. Baptist Cemetery, Salem, Salem County.

DRUMMOND, JOHN Corp, C, 14th NJ Inf, 3-29-1905. Presbyterian Cemetery, Springfield, Union County.

DRUMMONDS, WILLIAM Pvt, D, 12th CT Inf, 3-9-1932. Overlook Cemetery, Bridgeton, Cumberland County.

DRUMS, TERRENCE Fireman, U.S. Navy, 9-23-1908. Mount Olivet Cemetery, Newark, Essex County.

DRUREY, MICHAEL 9-29-1898. Holy Sepulchre Cemetery, Totowa, Passaic County.

DRURY, GEORGE F. Pvt, C, 16th ME Inf, 1-4-1918. Grove Church Cemetery, North Bergen, Hudson County.

DRURY*, HENRY S. Pvt, E, 4th NY Cav, 8-16-1886. Reformed Church Cemetery, Wyckoff, Bergen County.

DRURY, PETER Pvt, Btty A, 1st NJ Light Art, 4-14-1884. St. John's Evangelical Church Cemetery, Orange, Essex County.

DRURY, RICHARD A. Pvt, C, 12th IL Cav, 7-20-1904. Arlington Cemetery, Kearny, Hudson County.

DRY, GEORGE A. Pvt, I, 52nd NC Inf (CSA), [Captured 7-3-1863 at Gettysburg, PA. Died of disease.] 12-22-1863. Finn's Point National Cemetery, Pennsville, Salem County.

DRYDEN*, THOMAS S. Pvt, B, 33rd NJ Inf, 10-4-1890. Fairmount Cemetery, Newark, Essex County.

DRYFOUS*, JACOB Pvt, A, 71st PA Inf, 9-22-1890. New Camden Cemetery, Camden, Camden County.

DUBELL, GEORGE H. Pvt, G, 23rd NJ Inf, [Died of fever at White Oak Church, VA.] 12-26-1862. Woodlane Graveyard Cemetery, Westampton, Burlington County.

DUBELL, WILLIAM H. (aka: Duble, William) Sgt, B, 12th NJ Inf, [Wounded in action.] 5-19-1906. Baptist/St. Andrew's Cemetery, Mount Holly, Burlington County.

DUBELL, WILLIAM R. Corp, A, 23rd NJ Inf, 1925. Oddfellows Cemetery, Burlington, Burlington County.

DUBEN, GOTTLIEB Pvt, Btty D, 15th NY Heavy Art, 7-22-1891. Weehawken Cemetery, North Bergen, Hudson County.

DUBLE, WILLIAM (see: Dubell, William H.) Baptist/St. Andrew's Cemetery, Mount Holly, Burlington County.

DUBOIS, CHARLES D. (aka: DuBoise, Charles) Corp, A, 120th NY Inf, [Wounded 11-27-1863 at Mine Run, VA. and 5-5-1864 at Wilderness, VA.] 12-30-1914. Arlington Cemetery, Kearny, Hudson County.

DUBOIS, CHARLES H. Pvt, C, 1st NJ Cav, 12-2-1915. Glenwood Cemetery, West Long Branch, Monmouth County.

DUBOIS, EDMUND Maj, 12th NJ Inf 1888. Old Presbyterian Church Cemetery, Daretown, Salem County.

DUBOIS, EDWARD M. Maj, 12th NJ Inf 1906. Presbyterian Church Cemetery, Bridgeton, Cumberland County.

DUBOIS*, ELWOOD S. Pvt, H, 12th NJ Inf, 1910. Baptist Church Cemetery, Slabtown, Salem County.

DUBOIS, FRANCIS L. Asst Surg, U.S. Navy, 2-24-1895. Presbyterian Church Cemetery, Bridgeton, Cumberland County.

DUBOIS*, FRANCIS MARION Sgt Maj, 24th NJ Inf DoD Unknown. Presbyterian Church Cemetery, Bridgeton, Cumberland County.

DUBOIS, GARRETT N. Pvt, C, 1st MN Inf, 3-29-1874. Old Presbyterian Church Cemetery, Daretown, Salem County.

DUBOIS, GEORGE Sgt, C, 80th NY Inf, 7-8-1917. Grove Church Cemetery, North Bergen, Hudson County.

Our Brothers Gone Before

DUBOIS, GEORGE W. Corp, K, 145th NY Inf, 7-6-1885. Alpine Cemetery, Perth Amboy, Middlesex County.

DUBOIS, ISAAC A. Corp, H, 12th NJ Inf, 9-29-1905. Cedar Green Cemetery, Clayton, Gloucester County.

DUBOIS, JEREDIAH (aka: Dubois, Jeremiah) Pvt, Unassigned, 5th WI Inf, 1912. New Presbyterian Church Cemetery, Daretown, Salem County.

DUBOIS, JEREMIAH (see: Dubois, Jerediah) New Presbyterian Church Cemetery, Daretown, Salem County.

DUBOIS, JOHN Corp, G, 24th NJ Inf, 11-18-1900. Friendship United Methodist Church Cemetery, Upper Deerfield, Cumberland County.

DUBOIS, JOHN Pvt, B, 2nd MN Inf, 7-28-1882. Siloam Cemetery, Vineland, Cumberland County.

DUBOIS, JOHN T. Sgt, H, 12th NJ Inf, 1921. Cedar Green Cemetery, Clayton, Gloucester County.

DUBOIS, JOHN W. Pvt, I, 12th NJ Inf, [Died of typhoid.] 9-22-1862. New Presbyterian Church Cemetery, Daretown, Salem County.

DUBOIS, JOSEPH Pvt, B, 6th NY Cav, 1918. Brookside Cemetery, Englewood, Bergen County.

DUBOIS*, JOSIAH Pvt, I, 9th NJ Inf, 1926. Methodist-Episcopal Church Cemetery, Penns Grove, Salem County.

DUBOIS, MASKELL W. Pvt, D, 38th NJ Inf, 1928. Baptist Church Cemetery, Mullica Hill, Gloucester County.

DUBOIS*, PETER D. Pvt, H, 120th NY Inf, [Wounded 7-2-1863 at Gettysburg, PA.] 8-12-1908. Fairmount Cemetery, Newark, Essex County.

DUBOIS, ROBERT W. Sailmakers Mate, U.S. Navy, USS Powhattan, 1896. Methodist-Episcopal Cemetery, Port Norris, Cumberland County.

DUBOIS, WILLIAM Pvt, I, 28th NJ Inf, 1918. Alpine Cemetery, Perth Amboy, Middlesex County.

DUBOIS, WILLIAM H. Seaman, U.S. Navy, USS E.B. Hall, 1915. Cedar Green Cemetery, Clayton, Gloucester County.

DUBOIS, WILLIAM H. H. Pvt, Btty K, 16th NY Heavy Art, 11-13-1903. Fairmount Cemetery, Newark, Essex County.

DUBOIS, WILLIAM T. Steward, U.S. Navy, USS Itasca, 4-28-1900. Presbyterian Church Cemetery, Bridgeton, Cumberland County.

DUBOISE, CHARLES (see: DuBois, Charles D.) Arlington Cemetery, Kearny, Hudson County.

DUBON, WILLIAM Pvt, G, 38th NJ Inf, 3-24-1907. Union Cemetery, Frenchtown, Hunterdon County.

DUBY, JOSEPH Pvt, K, 147th IL Inf, 1907. Roadside Cemetery, Manchester Township, Ocean County.

DUCH, CORNELIUS (see: Dutch, Cornelius) United Methodist Church Cemetery, Absecon, Atlantic County.

DUCHWORTH, J.L. (see: Duckworth, Jonathan L.) Cav (CSA) Finn's Point National Cemetery, Pennsville, Salem County.

DUCK*, JOHN H. Pvt, F, 61st VA Inf (CSA), [Captured 7-3-1863 at Gettysburg, PA. Died of diarrhea.] 9-9-1863. Finn's Point National Cemetery, Pennsville, Salem County.

DUCKERY, JAMES H. Landsman, U.S. Navy, USS New Hampshire, 7-2-1904. Mount Peace Cemetery, Lawnside, Camden County.

DUCKETT, RICHARD Pvt, D, 82nd PA Inf, 11-7-1901. St. Rose of Lima Cemetery, Millburn, Essex County.

DUCKETT, THOMAS P. Pvt, I, 119th PA Inf, 11-7-1912. Harleigh Cemetery, Camden, Camden County.

New Jersey Civil War Burials

DUCKWORTH, ISAAC Pvt, F, 31st NJ Inf, 11-3-1875. Presbyterian Church Cemetery, Mount Pleasant, Hunterdon County.
DUCKWORTH, JOHN Pvt, G, 10th NJ Inf, 7-24-1874. Presbyterian Church Cemetery, Mount Pleasant, Hunterdon County.
DUCKWORTH*, JONATHAN L. (aka: Duchworth, J.L.) Pvt, B, 5th Bttn NC Cav (CSA), 4-3-1864. Finn's Point National Cemetery, Pennsville, Salem County.
DUCKWORTH, ROBEN P. (see: Duckworth, Robins) Evergreen Cemetery, Clinton, Hunterdon County.
DUCKWORTH*, ROBINS (aka: Duckworth, Roben P.) Pvt, I, 10th MO Cav, 5-10-1913. Evergreen Cemetery, Clinton, Hunterdon County.
DUDDY, JAMES A. 1st Sgt, H, 4th NJ Militia, DoD Unknown. Cedar Grove Cemetery, Gloucester City, Camden County.
DUDDY, MARTIN Pvt, B, 65th NY Inf, 9-11-1893. Holy Name Cemetery, Jersey City, Hudson County.
DUDLEY, EVAN DoD Unknown. Friends Cemetery, Colemantown, Burlington County.
DUDLEY, I. 2-5-1924. Rahway Cemetery, Rahway, Union County.
DUDLEY, JOHN T. Pvt, K, 33rd NJ Inf, 4-29-1914. Tennent Church Cemetery, Tennent, Monmouth County.
DUDLEY*, MICHAEL Pvt, I, 2nd U.S. VRC, 3-26-1885. St. Mary's Cemetery, Hamilton, Mercer County.
DUDLEY, MILTON 1st Sgt, I, 5th FL Inf (CSA), [Wounded 7-2-1863 and captured 7-5-1863 at Gettysburg, PA. Died of lung inflammation.] 4-15-1864. Finn's Point National Cemetery, Pennsville, Salem County.
DUDLEY, PETER (see: Glynn, John) Holy Name Cemetery, Jersey City, Hudson County.
DUDLEY, WILLIAM M. Pvt, A, 19th VA Inf (CSA), [Captured 7-3-1863 at Gettysburg, PA. Died of diarrhea.] 9-28-1863. Finn's Point National Cemetery, Pennsville, Salem County.
DUDLING, BENJAMIN Pvt, C, 28th NJ Inf, 4-1-1910. St. James Episcopal Church Cemetery, Piscatawaytown, Middlesex County.
DUEBEN, EMIL Sgt, Btty D, 3rd NY Light Art, DoD Unknown. Weehawken Cemetery, North Bergen, Hudson County.
DUELL, THOMAS W. Pvt, G, 70th IN Inf, 11-6-1869. Friends Cemetery, Mullica Hill, Gloucester County.
DUEMER, HENRY Pvt, K, 54th NY Inf, 3-6-1903. Grove Church Cemetery, North Bergen, Hudson County.
DUERR, JOHN J. (see: Durr, John J.) Bayview-New York Bay Cemetery, Jersey City, Hudson County.
DUETSCH, PHILIP (aka: Dutch, Philip) Pvt, D, 13th NJ Inf, 12-11-1891. St. Mary's Cemetery, East Orange, Essex County.
DUFF, JOSEPH Pvt, M, 2nd U.S. Colored Cav, DoD Unknown. Rosedale Cemetery, Orange, Essex County.
DUFFEE, CHARLES Ordinary Seaman, U.S. Navy, USS Pensacola, 10-26-1865. Evergreen Cemetery, Camden, Camden County.
DUFFEE, HENRY Seaman, U.S. Navy, 6-19-1902. Evergreen Cemetery, Camden, Camden County.
DUFFELL, CHARLES L. Asst Surg, 51st PA Inf 11-20-1912. 1st Methodist Church Cemetery, Williamstown, Gloucester County.
DUFFICY, BARNEY Pvt, G, 15th NJ Inf, [Wounded in action.] 1-3-1917. Union Cemetery, Frenchtown, Hunterdon County.
DUFFIELD, DAVID G. Pvt, F, 8th PA Cav, 1919. Mount Pleasant Cemetery, Millville, Cumberland County.
DUFFIELD, ENOCH A. Pvt, E, 12th NJ Inf, 4-15-1911. Presbyterian Church Cemetery, Upper Deerfield, Cumberland County.

Our Brothers Gone Before

DUFFIELD, FRANCIS T. Pvt, E, 15th NJ Inf, 1-30-1909. Riverview Cemetery, Trenton, Mercer County.

DUFFIELD, GEORGE E. Pvt, A, 15th PA Cav, 2-26-1904. Presbyterian Church Cemetery, Bridgeton, Cumberland County.

DUFFIELD, GEORGE W. Musc, 1st NJ Inf Band 2-16-1903. Cedar Green Cemetery, Clayton, Gloucester County.

DUFFIELD*, HENRY D. Pvt, K, 12th NJ Inf, 1-27-1874. Old Stone Church Cemetery, Fairton, Cumberland County.

DUFFIELD, HENRY W. Pvt, Btty E, 1st NJ Light Art, DoD Unknown. Cedar Hill Cemetery, Cedarville, Cumberland County.

DUFFIELD, JOHN L. 4-19-1904. Methodist-Episcopal Cemetery, Glassboro, Gloucester County.

DUFFIELD, JOSEPH S. Pvt, A, 40th NJ Inf, 3-1-1873. Trinity Bible Church Cemetery, Glassboro, Gloucester County.

DUFFIELD, JOSIAH D. Pvt, H, 4th PA Cav, 3-22-1907. Trinity Bible Church Cemetery, Glassboro, Gloucester County.

DUFFIELD, JOSIAH H. 4-3-1885. Methodist Cemetery, Woodstown, Salem County.

DUFFIELD, LORENZO Pvt, A, 2nd NJ Cav, 12-21-1913. Eglington Cemetery, Clarksboro, Gloucester County.

DUFFIELD, WILLIAM F. Corp, F, 24th NJ Inf, 2-10-1892. Zion United Methodist Church Cemetery, Dividing Creek, Cumberland County.

DUFFIELD, WILLIAM P. Pvt, E, 15th NJ Inf, 5-16-1905. Reformed Church Cemetery, Blawenburg, Somerset County.

DUFFILL, JAMES P. 1st Cl Fireman, U.S. Navy, USS Miami, 12-6-1883. Oak Grove Cemetery, Hammonton, Atlantic County.

DUFFIN, HENRY (see: Duffy, Henry F.) Holy Sepulchre Cemetery, Totowa, Passaic County.

DUFFIN, THOMAS (see: Duffy, Thomas) Holy Sepulchre Cemetery, East Orange, Essex County.

DUFFORD, BENJAMIN V. Pvt, E, 9th NJ Inf, 9-21-1881. Cedar Lawn Cemetery, Paterson, Passaic County.

DUFFY, CHRISTOPHER Pvt, H, 40th NJ Inf, 5-11-1910. Mount Hope Presbyterian Cemetery, Lambertville, Hunterdon County.

DUFFY, HENRY F. (aka: Duffin, Henry) Pvt, M, 2nd NJ Cav, 4-5-1888. Holy Sepulchre Cemetery, Totowa, Passaic County.

DUFFY, JAMES Seaman, U.S. Navy, DoD Unknown. Arlington Cemetery, Kearny, Hudson County.

DUFFY*, JAMES NICHOLSON Lt Col, 3rd NJ Inf 10-18-1901. Holy Sepulchre Cemetery, East Orange, Essex County.

DUFFY, JOHN Corp, D, 5th NJ Inf, 10-1-1924. St. Rose of Lima Cemetery, Millburn, Essex County.

DUFFY, JOHN F. Pvt, B, 37th NJ Inf, DoD Unknown. Holy Sepulchre Cemetery, East Orange, Essex County.

DUFFY, PATRICK Coal Heaver, U.S. Navy, USS Elk, 12-3-1892. Holy Sepulchre Cemetery, East Orange, Essex County.

DUFFY, RICHARD 2nd Lt, H, 3rd NJ Inf, [Killed in action at Spotsylvania CH, VA.] 5-12-1864. Holy Sepulchre Cemetery, East Orange, Essex County.

DUFFY, ROBERT Pvt, H, 2nd NJ Cav, DoD Unknown. Bayview-New York Bay Cemetery, Jersey City, Hudson County.

DUFFY, THOMAS Corp, I, 39th NJ Inf, 10-12-1873. Holy Sepulchre Cemetery, East Orange, Essex County.

DUFFY, THOMAS (aka: Duffin, Thomas) Pvt, C, 96th NY Inf, 1-7-1894. Holy Sepulchre Cemetery, East Orange, Essex County.

New Jersey Civil War Burials

DUFFY, WILLIAM Sgt, C, 2nd NJ Inf, 2-2-1892. Holy Sepulchre Cemetery, East Orange, Essex County.

DUFOUR*, JOSEPH L.M. (aka: Morgan, Joseph) Sgt, Ind, 97th PA Inf, 12-29-1920. New Presbyterian Cemetery, Bound Brook, Somerset County.

DUGAN, DANIEL Pvt, E, 56th MA Inf, [Died at Beverly, NJ. Wounded 5-27-1863 at Port Hudson, LA.] 10-8-1864. Beverly National Cemetery, Edgewater Park, Burlington County.

DUGAN, EDWARD Landsman, U.S. Navy, 2-24-1903. St. Peter's Cemetery, Jersey City, Hudson County.

DUGAN, JAMES Pvt, B, 31st NJ Inf, 6-12-1901. Broadway Cemetery, Broadway, Warren County.

DUGAN*, JOHN Pvt, C, 5th NJ Inf, 12-23-1887. St. Peter's Cemetery, Jersey City, Hudson County.

DUGAN, JOHN Ensign, F, 2nd NJ Militia, 5-20-1888. Holy Name Cemetery, Jersey City, Hudson County.

DUGAN, JOHN Seaman, U.S. Navy, 4-2-1910. Holy Sepulchre Cemetery, Totowa, Passaic County.

DUGAN, JOHN J. Ensign, F, 2nd NJ Militia, 11-3-1916. Mount Olivet Cemetery, Bloomfield, Essex County.

DUGAN, LAWRENCE Pvt, I, 2nd DC Inf, 1-25-1894. Holy Sepulchre Cemetery, East Orange, Essex County.

DUGAN, MATTHEW Pvt, E, 35th NJ Inf, DoD Unknown. Holy Name Cemetery, Jersey City, Hudson County.

DUGAN, PATRICK Pvt, B, 34th NJ Inf, 1-27-1895. St. Mary's Cemetery, Hamilton, Mercer County.

DUGAN, THOMAS Pvt, B, 40th NJ Inf, 6-13-1905. St. Mary's Cemetery, Hamilton, Mercer County.

DUGAN, THOMAS 5-8-1902. Brainerd Cemetery, Cranbury, Middlesex County.

DUGAN, THOMAS Pvt, A, 9th NJ Inf, [Cenotaph. Died of typhoid at Newbern, NC.] 4-30-1865. Brainerd Cemetery, Cranbury, Middlesex County.

DUGGER, WILLIAM Pvt, A, 8th FL Inf (CSA), [Wounded 5-4-1863 at Chancellorsville, VA. Captured 7-2-1863 at Gettysburg, PA. Died of smallpox.] 12-4-1863. Finn's Point National Cemetery, Pennsville, Salem County.

DUKE, FRANCIS K. 2nd Lt, F, 2nd DE Inf, 9-9-1908. Presbyterian Church Cemetery, Cold Spring, Cape May County.

DUKE, LYCURGUS Pvt, F, 9th (Ward's) TN Cav (CSA), 8-4-1864. Finn's Point National Cemetery, Pennsville, Salem County.

DUKIN, CHARLES Pvt, H, 15th NJ Inf, 10-12-1914. Stanhope-Union Cemetery, Netcong, Morris County.

DULEY, JOHN H. 4-27-1913. Evergreen Cemetery, New Brunswick, Middlesex County.

DULHAGEN, CORNELIUS (see: Delhagen Cornelius) Mount Hebron Cemetery, Montclair, Essex County.

DULHAGEN, ISAAC Pvt, F, 27th NJ Inf, 7-18-1912. Fairmount Cemetery, Newark, Essex County.

DULIN, JOHN Pvt, B, 26th NC Inf (CSA), [Wounded and captured 7-3-1863 at Gettysburg, PA. Died of wounds.] 9-16-1863. Finn's Point National Cemetery, Pennsville, Salem County.

DULL, A.L. Pvt, K, 38th AL Inf (CSA), 7-17-1863. Finn's Point National Cemetery, Pennsville, Salem County.

DUMONT, ABRAHAM Pvt, A, 30th NJ Inf, 6-1-1923. Reformed Church Cemetery, North Branch, Somerset County.

DUMONT, JOHN BROKAW 4-9-1928. Hillside Cemetery, Scotch Plains, Union County.

DUMONT, JOHN G. Pvt, E, 30th NJ Inf, 1922. Old Somerville Cemetery, Somerville, Somerset County.

Our Brothers Gone Before

DUMONT, WILLIAM S. Pvt, H, 21st NJ Inf, 1918. Lawrenceville Cemetery, Lawrenceville, Mercer County.

DUMPHREY, PETER (see: Dunphy, Peter) Holy Sepulchre Cemetery, East Orange, Essex County.

DUNAKIN, SAMUEL 1- -1907. Presbyterian Church Cemetery, Cold Spring, Cape May County.

DUNAWAY, B.T. Pvt, Milledge's Btty, GA Light Art (CSA), 4-5-1865. Finn's Point National Cemetery, Pennsville, Salem County.

DUNAWAY, JAMES F. (aka: Denaway, James F.) Pvt, E, 1st Confederate States Cav (CSA), 10-2-1863. Finn's Point National Cemetery, Pennsville, Salem County.

DUNBAR, BENJAMIN T. Pvt, F, 11th U.S. Inf, 11-1-1905. St. Mark's Baptist Church Cemetery, Browns Mills, Burlington County.

DUNBAR*, FREDERICK L. Corp, Btty G, 11th U.S. CHA, 2-27-1896. Mount Pleasant Cemetery, Newark, Essex County.

DUNBAR, MARY Nurse, 3-4-1887. Old 1st Methodist Church Cemetery, West Long Branch, Monmouth County.

DUNCAN, FRANCIS HERMAN (aka: Franks, Herman D.) Pvt, F, 7th ME Inf, 2-7-1908. Greenwood Cemetery, Hamilton, Mercer County.

DUNCAN, JOHN M. 3-30-1874. St. Paul's United Methodist Church Cemetery, Paulsboro, Gloucester County.

DUNCAN, JOSEPH Pvt, E, 4th GA Inf (CSA), [Captured 5-10-1864 at Spotsylvania CH, VA. Died of smallpox.] 1-5-1865. Finn's Point National Cemetery, Pennsville, Salem County.

DUNCAN, JOSEPH (see: Dongan, Joseph P.) Maplewood Cemetery, Freehold, Monmouth County.

DUNCAN, JOSEPH B. Pvt, B, 7th KY Inf (CSA), [Captured 5-16-1863 at Baker's Creek, MS.] 9-11-1863. Finn's Point National Cemetery, Pennsville, Salem County.

DUNCAN, JOSEPH P. Pvt, D, 14th NJ Inf, DoD Unknown. Maplewood Cemetery, Freehold, Monmouth County.

DUNCAN, OWEN Pvt, D, 20th NC Inf (CSA), [Wounded 5-3-1863 at Chancellorsville, VA. Captured 7-3-1863 at Gettysburg, PA. Died of disease.] 10-12-1863. Finn's Point National Cemetery, Pennsville, Salem County.

DUNCAN, ROBERT E. Corp, D, 14th NJ Inf, 9-7-1904. Maplewood Cemetery, Freehold, Monmouth County.

DUNCAN, SAMUEL AUGUSTUS Bvt Maj Gen, U.S. Volunteers, [Colonel, 4th United States Colored Troops.] 10-18-1895. Brookside Cemetery, Englewood, Bergen County.

DUNCAN*, THOMAS Pvt, I, 11th NJ Inf, 3-8-1902. Brainerd Cemetery, Cranbury, Middlesex County.

DUNCAN, THOMAS Pvt, B, 22nd U.S. CT, DoD Unknown. Presbyterian Church Cemetery, Greenwich, Warren County.

DUNCAN, THOMAS N. 1908. Baptist Church Cemetery, Penns Neck, Mercer County.

DUNCAN, THOMAS W. 11-28-1908. Mount Prospect Cemetery, Neptune, Monmouth County.

DUNCAN, USELMA Pvt, G, 71st NY State Militia, [Killed in action at 1st Bull Run, VA.] 7-21-1861. Brainerd Cemetery, Cranbury, Middlesex County.

DUNCAN, WILLIAM Pvt, I, 50th VA Inf (CSA), [Captured 7-3-1863 at Gettysburg, PA. Died of typhoid.] 9-17-1863. Finn's Point National Cemetery, Pennsville, Salem County.

DUNCAN, WILLIAM Pvt, F, 9th NY Inf, 5-29-1896. Bayview-New York Bay Cemetery, Jersey City, Hudson County.

DUNCAN, WILLIAM Pvt, C, 24th U.S. CT, 1-16-1898. Evergreen Cemetery, Morristown, Morris County.

DUNCAN, WILLIAM 3-7-1868. Evergreen Cemetery, Morristown, Morris County.

New Jersey Civil War Burials

DUNCAN, WILLIAM H. Corp, A, 28th NJ Inf, [Died of typhoid at Washington, DC.] 11-28-1862. Tennent Church Cemetery, Tennent, Monmouth County.

DUNCAN, WILLIAM S. (aka: Dunnegan, William) Pvt, E, 2nd DC Inf, 6-19-1903. St. Stephen's Cemetery, Millburn, Essex County.

DUNFEE, GEORGE Pvt, G, 10th NJ Inf, 12-19-1928. Baptist Church Cemetery, Jacobstown, Burlington County.

DUNFEE, GEORGE W. Pvt, D, 1st NJ Cav, 6-6-1912. Baptist Church Cemetery, Jacobstown, Burlington County.

DUNGAN, CHARLES Pvt, H, 197th PA Inf, 1-4-1922. Fairmount Cemetery, Newark, Essex County.

DUNGAN, EDMUND B. Pvt, D, 31st NJ Inf, 8- -1900. New Somerville Cemetery, Somerville, Somerset County.

DUNGAN*, WILLIAM B. 1st Sgt, A, 15th NJ Inf, [Wounded in action.] 1913. Pleasant Ridge Cemetery, East Amwell, Hunterdon County.

DUNHAM, ABRAHAM DoD Unknown. Baptist/Evergreen Methodist Cemetery, Plainfield, Union County.

DUNHAM*, ABRAM Pvt, D, 11th NJ Inf, 1917. Chestnut Hill Cemetery, East Brunswick, Middlesex County.

DUNHAM, ALFRED B. Pvt, H, 1st NJ Cav, 1-9-1889. Hillside Cemetery, Madison, Morris County.

DUNHAM, AMOS Pvt, E, 56th NY Inf, 1897. Presbyterian Cemetery, Springfield, Union County.

DUNHAM*, ANDREW M. 1st Sgt, F, 86th NY Inf, 5-14-1918. Fairmount Cemetery, Newark, Essex County.

DUNHAM, BERTHUNE P. Musc, I, 37th NJ Inf, DoD Unknown. Baptist Cemetery, South Plainfield, Middlesex County.

DUNHAM, CHARLES H. Asst Surg, [Harewood Hospital.] 10-16-1895. Mercer Cemetery, Trenton, Mercer County.

DUNHAM, CHESTER H. Sgt, G, 13th NJ Inf, 12-29-1917. Fairmount Cemetery, Newark, Essex County.

DUNHAM, CLARKSON F. Pvt, I, 11th NJ Inf, 3-11-1865. Alpine Cemetery, Perth Amboy, Middlesex County.

DUNHAM, CURTIS W. Pvt, H, 35th NJ Inf, [Killed in action at Big Shanty, GA.] 6-15-1864. Brainerd Cemetery, Cranbury, Middlesex County.

DUNHAM, FRANK A. Pvt, D, 2nd NJ Cav, 1919. New Presbyterian Church Cemetery, Daretown, Salem County.

DUNHAM, GEORGE A. Pvt, C, 28th NJ Inf, 5-2-1872. St. James Episcopal Church Cemetery, Piscatawaytown, Middlesex County.

DUNHAM, GEORGE A. 4-24-1868. Mount Pleasant Cemetery, Newark, Essex County.

DUNHAM, GEORGE W. 1921. Prospect Hill Cemetery, Flemington, Hunterdon County.

DUNHAM, JAMES M. Sgt, B, 9th NJ Inf, 3-1-1902. Elmwood Cemetery, New Brunswick, Middlesex County.

DUNHAM, JEREMIAH Pvt, C, 73rd NY Inf, 4-26-1899. Rahway Cemetery, Rahway, Union County.

DUNHAM, JEREMIAH H. Pvt, D, 11th NJ Inf, [Killed in action at Locust Grove, VA.] 11-27-1863. 7th Day Baptist Cemetery, Piscataway, Middlesex County.

DUNHAM, JOHN B. Pvt, E, 14th NJ Inf, [Died of diarrhea at Newark, NJ.] 1-18-1864. Alpine Cemetery, Perth Amboy, Middlesex County.

DUNHAM, JOHN R. 1-6-1906. Hillside Cemetery, Scotch Plains, Union County.

DUNHAM, JONATHAN P. Corp, A, 30th NJ Inf, [Died of typhoid at Millington, NJ.] 6-24-1863. Presbyterian Church Cemetery, Basking Ridge, Somerset County.

DUNHAM, JOSEPH Pvt, E, 29th CT Inf, [Wounded 9-30-1864 at Richmond, VA.] 1-26-1925. Hillside Cemetery, Scotch Plains, Union County.

Our Brothers Gone Before

DUNHAM, JOSEPH T. Pvt, I, 1st RI Militia, 9-12-1896. Hillside Cemetery, Scotch Plains, Union County.

DUNHAM, JOSHUA H. Corp, M, 15th PA Cav, 5-2-1886. Mount Pleasant Cemetery, Millville, Cumberland County.

DUNHAM, LEONARD W. Pvt, H, 35th NJ Inf, [Cenotaph. Died of dysentery while prisoner at Andersonville, GA.] 8-26-1864. Brainerd Cemetery, Cranbury, Middlesex County.

DUNHAM, NOAH W. Pvt, E, 15th NJ Inf, 8-20-1906. Cedar Lawn Cemetery, Paterson, Passaic County.

DUNHAM*, SAMUEL H. Pvt, C, 14th NJ Inf, 1-26-1902. Evergreen Cemetery, Hillside, Union County.

DUNHAM, SAMUEL S. Pvt, C, 28th NJ Inf, 6-8-1897. Old 1st Methodist Church Cemetery, West Long Branch, Monmouth County.

DUNHAM, SAMUEL S. 1865. Baptist/Evergreen Methodist Cemetery, Plainfield, Union County.

DUNHAM, SMITH Pvt, A, 32nd NY Inf, 2-5-1900. Mount Pleasant Cemetery, Millville, Cumberland County.

DUNHAM, SPRING P. Pvt, A, 30th NJ Inf, 11-16-1913. Riverview Cemetery, Trenton, Mercer County.

DUNHAM, WARREN N. Corp, A, 15th NJ Inf, [Killed in action at Salem Heights, VA.] 5-3-1863. Presbyterian Church Cemetery, Basking Ridge, Somerset County.

DUNHAM, WILLIAM H. Pvt, E, 14th NJ Inf, 1-12-1891. Rahway Cemetery, Rahway, Union County.

DUNHAM, WILLIAM HENRY S. Capt, D, 28th NJ Inf, 12-25-1889. Elmwood Cemetery, New Brunswick, Middlesex County.

DUNIGAN, GEORGE H. Pvt, D, 24th U.S. CT, 9-12-1887. Oak Hill Cemetery, Vineland, Cumberland County.

DUNK, THOMAS Pvt, H, 87th IL Inf, DoD Unknown. Midvale Cemetery, Midvale, Passaic County.

DUNKER, JOHN Pvt, K, 26th NJ Inf, 8-30-1902. Fairmount Cemetery, Newark, Essex County.

DUNKERLY, ENOCH Pvt, E, 9th NJ Inf, 10-8-1912. Laurel Grove Cemetery, Totowa, Passaic County.

DUNKERLY, JAMES Pvt, F, 6th NY Inf, 4-22-1901. Laurel Grove Cemetery, Totowa, Passaic County.

DUNKERLY, JOHN ROBERT Pvt, G, 7th NJ Inf, 12-10-1909. Laurel Grove Cemetery, Totowa, Passaic County.

DUNKERLY, JOSEPH 1871. Cedar Lawn Cemetery, Paterson, Passaic County.

DUNKERLY*, WILLIAM B. (aka: Donkersley, William) Pvt, I, 2nd NJ Inf, 10-4-1910. Cedar Lawn Cemetery, Paterson, Passaic County.

DUNKINS, FRANK H. Pvt, E, 24th U.S. CT, 4-28-1920. Baptist Cemetery, Burlington, Burlington County.

DUNKLE*, DANIEL Pvt, C, 12th NJ Inf, 1918. Mount Pleasant Cemetery, Millville, Cumberland County.

DUNKLE, GEORGE Pvt, C, 12th NJ Inf, [Wounded in action.] 1910. Trinity Bible Church Cemetery, Glassboro, Gloucester County.

DUNKLE, SOLOMON Pvt, C, 12th NJ Inf, 4-8-1872. Methodist Cemetery, Waterford, Camden County.

DUNKLIN, J.B. Pvt, K, 8th AL Inf (CSA), 8-7-1863. Finn's Point National Cemetery, Pennsville, Salem County.

DUNKUM, WILLIAM B. Pvt, A, 57th VA Inf (CSA), [Wounded and captured 7-3-1863 at Gettysburg, PA.] 10-26-1863. Finn's Point National Cemetery, Pennsville, Salem County.

New Jersey Civil War Burials

DUNLAP, A.S. Pvt, C, 12th SC Inf (CSA), [Captured 7-5-1863 at Gettysburg, PA. Died of typhoid.] 10-2-1863. Finn's Point National Cemetery, Pennsville, Salem County.

DUNLAP, GEORGE E. Capt, B, 24th NJ Inf, 2-29-1892. Mount Pleasant Cemetery, Millville, Cumberland County.

DUNLAP, GEORGE W. Pvt, F, 12th NJ Inf, 1926. New Episcopal Church Cemetery, Swedesboro, Gloucester County.

DUNLAP, HENRY N. Pvt, K, 27th NJ Inf, 6-12-1923. Newton Cemetery, Newton, Sussex County.

DUNLAP, JAMES Pvt, F, 127th NY Inf, 5-25-1878. Presbyterian Church Cemetery, Mendham, Morris County.

DUNLAP, JAMES Pvt, C, 28th NJ Inf, 1-24-1911. Rosedale Cemetery, Orange, Essex County.

DUNLAP, JOHN Pvt, B, 40th NJ Inf, 4-5-1895. Macphelah Cemetery, North Bergen, Hudson County.

DUNLAP, JOHN 7-30-1887. Mount Pleasant Cemetery, Newark, Essex County.

DUNLAP, JOSEPH M. Corp, K, 27th NJ Inf, 1928. Methodist Church Cemetery, Sparta, Sussex County.

DUNLEVY, CRAIG Pvt, I, 192nd PA Inf, 1-15-1915. Atlantic City Cemetery, Pleasantville, Atlantic County.

DUNMORE, EDWARD Pvt, A, 25th U.S. CT, 4-29-1879. Fairmount Cemetery, Newark, Essex County.

DUNN, ALMON Pvt, L, 2nd NJ Cav, 6- -1904. Tranquility Cemetery, Tranquility, Sussex County.

DUNN, ANDREW B. Pvt, A, 9th NJ Inf, 3-5-1895. Elmwood Cemetery, New Brunswick, Middlesex County.

DUNN, CHARLES A. 2nd Lt, D, 28th NJ Inf, 5-24-1903. Elmwood Cemetery, New Brunswick, Middlesex County.

DUNN*, CHRISTIAN Corp, I, 39th NJ Inf, 2-16-1885. Fairmount Cemetery, Newark, Essex County.

DUNN, DAVID R. Pvt, F, 11th NJ Inf, 8-12-1893. Elmwood Cemetery, New Brunswick, Middlesex County.

DUNN, EDWARD Pvt, A, 22nd NY Cav, 12-27-1890. Mount Carmel Cemetery, West Long Branch, Monmouth County.

DUNN, EDWARD T. Sgt, E, 15th NJ Inf, 12-9-1919. Hillside Cemetery, Scotch Plains, Union County.

DUNN, G.R. Landsman, U.S. Navy, 1-25-1899. Fairmount Cemetery, Newark, Essex County.

DUNN, GEORGE E. Pvt, C, 39th NJ Inf, 12-19-1898. Holy Sepulchre Cemetery, East Orange, Essex County.

DUNN, GEORGE W. Corp, C, 26th NJ Inf, 3-25-1903. Evergreen Cemetery, Hillside, Union County.

DUNN*, HENRY A. Pvt, G, 2nd NJ Inf, 6-9-1917. Fairmount Cemetery, Newark, Essex County.

DUNN, HENRY J. (aka: Durr, Henry) 1st Sgt, G, 65th NY Inf, [Wounded 5-10-1864 at Spotsylvania CH, VA.] 10-18-1903. Holy Sepulchre Cemetery, East Orange, Essex County.

DUNN, HENRY S. Pvt, A, 26th NJ Inf, 7-24-1891. Evergreen Cemetery, Hillside, Union County.

DUNN, ISAAC E. Sgt, D, 28th NJ Inf, 5-30-1913. Van Liew Cemetery, North Brunswick, Middlesex County.

DUNN, JAMES ___, ___, ___ MO ___, DoD Unknown. Riverview Cemetery, Trenton, Mercer County.

DUNN, JAMES B. Pvt, K, 21st NJ Inf, 10-7-1917. Elmwood Cemetery, New Brunswick, Middlesex County.

Our Brothers Gone Before

DUNN, JOHN DoD Unknown. Bayview-New York Bay Cemetery, Jersey City, Hudson County.
DUNN, JOHN Pvt, G, __ PA Inf, 2-18-1919. Lawrenceville Cemetery, Lawrenceville, Mercer County.
DUNN, JOHN A. Corp, H, 1st NJ Cav, 8-10-1897. Fairmount Cemetery, Newark, Essex County.
DUNN, JOHN H. Corp, F, 11th NJ Inf, DoD Unknown. Cedar Hill Cemetery, East Millstone, Somerset County.
DUNN, JOHN NELSON Corp, K, 15th NJ Inf, 2-17-1863. Methodist Church Cemetery, Stockholm, Sussex County.
DUNN*, JOSEPH Pvt, I, 7th NJ Inf, 2-3-1936. New Camden Cemetery, Camden, Camden County.
DUNN, JOSEPH Pvt, I, 5th NY Cav, [Died of disease at Washington, DC.] 4-12-1862. Baptist/Evergreen Methodist Cemetery, Plainfield, Union County.
DUNN, M.B. Pvt, B, 1st TN Cav (CSA), 7-24-1864. Finn's Point National Cemetery, Pennsville, Salem County.
DUNN*, MICHAEL W. Pvt, C, 14th NJ Inf, 3-30-1909. Mount Olivet Cemetery, Newark, Essex County.
DUNN, PETER Pvt, C, 119th PA Inf, 9-19-1908. St. Peter's Cemetery, New Brunswick, Middlesex County.
DUNN*, PETER Pvt, E, 7th NJ Inf, 1-7-1867. Holy Sepulchre Cemetery, East Orange, Essex County.
DUNN, REDMOND A. Pvt, E, 99th NY Inf, 5-6-1894. Holy Sepulchre Cemetery, East Orange, Essex County.
DUNN, RICHARD Sgt, H, 66th NY Inf, 3-10-1865. St. Peter's Cemetery, Jersey City, Hudson County.
DUNN, SIMEON Pvt, C, 1st OH Inf, DoD Unknown. Elmwood Cemetery, New Brunswick, Middlesex County.
DUNN, THEOPHILIUS C. Pvt, L, 9th RI Inf, 11-30-1918. Rosedale Cemetery, Orange, Essex County.
DUNN, THOMAS Pvt, C, 49th PA Militia, 9-17-1900. Holy Name Cemetery, Jersey City, Hudson County.
DUNN, THOMAS Seaman, U.S. Navy, USS Preston, 1890. St. Peter's Cemetery, New Brunswick, Middlesex County.
DUNN, THOMAS JEFFERSON 1st Sgt, I, 38th NJ Inf, 6-11-1926. Deckertown-Union Cemetery, Papakating, Sussex County.
DUNN*, WALTER GEORGE Pvt, D, 11th NJ Inf, 4-16-1866. Hillside Cemetery, Scotch Plains, Union County.
DUNN, WILLIAM Corp, E, 29th PA Inf, 1-12-1879. Macphelah Cemetery, North Bergen, Hudson County.
DUNN, WILLIAM Pvt, C, 14th NJ Inf, 6-30-1900. Mount Olivet Cemetery, Newark, Essex County.
DUNN, WILLIAM A. 1st Lt, E, 47th NC Inf (CSA), [Captured 10-27-1864 at Burgess' Mill, VA. Died of pneumonia and lung inflammation.] 2-20-1865. Finn's Point National Cemetery, Pennsville, Salem County.
DUNN, WILLIAM B. Pvt, I, 5th NY Cav, 9-24-1886. Presbyterian Cemetery, North Plainfield, Somerset County.
DUNN, WILLIAM H. Pvt, G, 23rd NJ Inf, 5-14-1919. Methodist Cemetery, Bridgeboro, Burlington County.
DUNN, WILLIAM H. 1906. Methodist Church Cemetery, Stockholm, Sussex County.
DUNN, WILLIAM H. 4-12-1919. Mount Pleasant Cemetery, Newark, Essex County.
DUNNAVAN, JOHN (see: Donnegan, John) St. Peter's Cemetery, New Brunswick, Middlesex County.

New Jersey Civil War Burials

DUNNAVANT, CHARLES FRANK Pvt, C, 9th VA Inf (CSA), [Captured 7-3-1863 at Gettysburg, PA. Died of diarrhea.] 9-15-1863. Finn's Point National Cemetery, Pennsville, Salem County.

DUNNEGAN, WILLIAM (see: Duncan, William S.) St. Stephen's Cemetery, Millburn, Essex County.

DUNNELL, JOSEPH A. 2nd Lt, G, 26th NJ Inf, 4-1-1904. New Camden Cemetery, Camden, Camden County.

DUNNIGAN, JOHN (see: Donnegan, John) St. Peter's Cemetery, New Brunswick, Middlesex County.

DUNNIGAN, MICHAEL Pvt, F, 28th NJ Inf, DoD Unknown. St. Peter's Cemetery, New Brunswick, Middlesex County.

DUNNING*, WILLIAM B. Capt, K, 11th NJ Inf, 6-19-1877. Bayview-New York Bay Cemetery, Jersey City, Hudson County.

DUNPHY, JAMES Gunner, U.S. Navy, USS Cayuga, 9-20-1901. St. James Cemetery, Woodbridge, Middlesex County.

DUNPHY, JAMES DoD Unknown. Holy Sepulchre Cemetery, East Orange, Essex County.

DUNPHY, JOHN Pvt, I, 2nd NJ Cav, 10-20-1886. Holy Sepulchre Cemetery, East Orange, Essex County.

DUNPHY*, PETER (aka: Dumphrey, Peter) 1st Sgt, F, 120th NY Inf, 1896. Holy Sepulchre Cemetery, East Orange, Essex County.

DUNSTER, GEORGE W. (aka: Dunston, George) Pvt, K, 7th NJ Inf, 1-10-1899. Evergreen Cemetery, Morristown, Morris County.

DUNSTON, GEORGE (see: Dunster, George W.) Evergreen Cemetery, Morristown, Morris County.

DUNWORTH, JOHN 11-13-1904. Phillipsburg Old Catholic Cemetery, Phillipsburg, Warren County.

DUNZ, MELCHIOR Pvt, D, 18th NY Cav, 11-8-1877. Woodland Cemetery, Newark, Essex County.

DUPELL, DAVID Musc, 4th NJ Inf Band 2-28-1893. St. Mary's Cemetery, Boonton, Morris County.

DUPONT, EUGENE (see: Daire, Armand P.) St. Peter's Cemetery, New Brunswick, Middlesex County.

DUPONT, WILFRED Asst Surg, 16th SC Inf (CSA) [Also on the General Staff.] 11-27-1897. Harleigh Cemetery, Camden, Camden County.

DUPONT, WILLIAM D. Chief Gunners Mate, U.S. Navy, 8-15-1914. Fairmount Cemetery, Newark, Essex County.

DUPOUSE, FREDERICK Seaman, U.S. Navy, 8-15-1907. Riverview Cemetery, Trenton, Mercer County.

DUPUY, LEVI Pvt, B, 38th NY Inf, 12-15-1917. Rosedale Cemetery, Orange, Essex County.

DURAND*, JAMES M. Pvt, Btty B, 1st NJ Light Art, 8-9-1895. Mount Pleasant Cemetery, Newark, Essex County.

DURAND, JAMES W. Pvt, H, 30th NJ Inf, 5-15-1899. Fairmount Cemetery, Newark, Essex County.

DURAND, JOHN 4-10-1868. Phillipsburg Cemetery, Phillipsburg, Warren County.

DURAND, JOSEPH Pvt, H, 9th NJ Inf, 3-9-1891. Holy Sepulchre Cemetery, East Orange, Essex County.

DURANT, JEAN Pvt, 1st Btty, SC Heavy Art (CSA), 9-20-1863. Finn's Point National Cemetery, Pennsville, Salem County.

DURANT, WILLIAM L. Pvt, A, 100th PA Inf, 4-25-1910. Greenwood Cemetery, Pleasantville, Atlantic County.

DURANT, YEA Pvt, Ahl's Btty, DE Heavy Art, DoD Unknown. Finn's Point National Cemetery, Pennsville, Salem County.

Our Brothers Gone Before

DURBAN, THEODORE Capt, D, 45th NY Inf, [Wounded in action.] 8-6-1902. Evergreen Cemetery, Hillside, Union County.

DUREN, GEORGE B. Musc, B, 26th MA Inf, 10-23-1917. Evergreen Cemetery, Hillside, Union County.

DURGET, JOSEPH A. 1-4-1894. Holy Sepulchre Cemetery, Totowa, Passaic County.

DURGIN, GEORGE WALTON Maj, 4th WI Cav 11-29-1888. Eglington Cemetery, Clarksboro, Gloucester County.

DURHAM, BENJAMIN COLLINS Corp, K, 1st NY Eng, 11-8-1915. Presbyterian Church Cemetery, Andover, Sussex County.

DURHAM*, JAMES Pvt, A, 16th VA Inf (CSA), [Captured 7-5-1863 at Chambersburg, PA.] 9-15-1863. Finn's Point National Cemetery, Pennsville, Salem County.

DURHAM, JOHN Corp, K, 103rd IL Inf, 11-8-1872. Willow Grove Cemetery, New Brunswick, Middlesex County.

DURHAM, THOMAS K. 1st Lt, M, 1st NY Eng, 1-5-1911. Episcopal Church Cemetery, Shrewsbury, Monmouth County.

DURIC, DAVID N. Corp, I, 22nd NJ Inf, 2-1-1898. Woodside Cemetery, Dumont, Bergen County.

DURIE, JAMES (see: Dwyre, James) Holy Sepulchre Cemetery, East Orange, Essex County.

DURIE*, JOHN D. Pvt, Btty B, 5th U.S. Art, 5-18-1925. Fairmount Cemetery, Chatham, Morris County.

DURIE*, WILLIAM BRITTEN Pvt, C, 39th NJ Inf, 1-16-1916. Fairmount Cemetery, Chatham, Morris County.

DURING, JOHN Pvt, B, 22nd NJ Inf, DoD Unknown. Immaculate Conception Cemetery, Montclair, Essex County.

DURKEE, JAMES Pvt, K, 1st CO Cav, 4-16-1913. Bloomfield Cemetery, Bloomfield, Essex County.

DURLING, ISAAC J. (JR.) Pvt, B, 2nd NJ Inf, 8-25-1886. Presbyterian Church Cemetery, Newton, Sussex County.

DURLING, THEODORE H. Pvt, A, 2nd NJ Inf, DoD Unknown. Old Somerville Cemetery, Somerville, Somerset County.

DURNING, JAMES Pvt, A, 77th OH Inf, DoD Unknown. Holy Sepulchre Cemetery, East Orange, Essex County.

DURR, HENRY (see: Dunn, Henry J.) Holy Sepulchre Cemetery, East Orange, Essex County.

DURR*, JOHN J. (aka: Duerr, John J.) Pvt, G, 7th NJ Inf, 10-23-1932. Bayview-New York Bay Cemetery, Jersey City, Hudson County.

DURRELL, ELWOOD Pvt, D, 40th NJ Inf, DoD Unknown. Cedar Hill Cemetery, Florence, Burlington County.

DURRELL, JOSEPH R. Corp, B, 5th PA Cav, 12-5-1916. Greenwood Cemetery, Hamilton, Mercer County.

DURRUA, WILLIAM Pvt, K, 132nd NY Inf, 5-27-1918. Alpine Cemetery, Perth Amboy, Middlesex County.

DURTON, DAVID R. Pvt, M, 9th (Malone's) AL Cav (CSA), 9-12-1863. Finn's Point National Cemetery, Pennsville, Salem County.

DURYEA, EDMUND A. Pvt, H, 2nd NJ Inf, 12-10-1925. Rosehill Cemetery, Linden, Union County.

DURYEA*, HENRY C. Pvt, Btty L, 7th NY Heavy Art, [Wounded 6-3-1864 at Cold Harbor, VA.] 1920. Greengrove Cemetery, Keyport, Monmouth County.

DURYEE, JOSEPH C. Pvt, 24th NY Ind Btty 9-27-1907. Hillside Cemetery, Scotch Plains, Union County.

DURYEE, WILLIAM RANKIN Chaplain, 1st KY Inf 1-20-1897. Mount Pleasant Cemetery, Newark, Essex County.

New Jersey Civil War Burials

DUSCHENESS, JACOB (aka: Doshanis, Jacob) Pvt, C, 71st NY Inf, [Wounded in action.] 3-24-1908. B'nai Abraham Cemetery, Newark, Essex County.

DUSENBERG, WILLIAM (see: Spieren, George H.) Arlington Cemetery, Kearny, Hudson County.

DUSENBERRY*, AUGUSTUS Capt, I, 35th NJ Inf, 3-13-1914. Mount Pleasant Cemetery, Newark, Essex County.

DUSENBERRY, CALEB C. Pvt, E, 26th NJ Inf, 5-25-1920. Clinton Cemetery, Irvington, Essex County.

DUSOLT, JOHN Pvt, E, 4th NJ Inf, 5-30-1886. Riverside Cemetery, Riverside, Burlington County.

DUSTER, JOSEPH Pvt, B, 41st NY Inf, 3-8-1890. Fairmount Cemetery, Newark, Essex County.

DUTCH, ALONZO 2nd Lt, E, 8th NY State Militia, 1-30-1922. Arlington Cemetery, Kearny, Hudson County.

DUTCH, CORNELIUS (aka: Duch, Cornelius) Pvt, E, 10th NJ Inf, [Wounded in action.] 8-29-1916. United Methodist Church Cemetery, Absecon, Atlantic County.

DUTCH, PHILIP (see: Duetsch, Philip) St. Mary's Cemetery, East Orange, Essex County.

DUTCHER, ANDREW GLOVER Pvt, C, 67th NY Inf, 12-24-1913. Evergreen Cemetery, Hillside, Union County.

DUTCHER, JAMES HENRY Artificer, B, 15th NY Eng, [Wounded at Fredericksburg, VA.] 3-15-1892. New Presbyterian Cemetery, Bound Brook, Somerset County.

DUTCHER, JOHN Pvt, H, 25th NJ Inf, 11-24-1904. Valleau Cemetery, Ridgewood, Bergen County.

DUTCHER, JOHN H. Pvt, I, 22nd NJ Inf, [Died of typhoid at Belle Plain, VA.] 3-30-1863. Sutjes Tave's Bergraven Cemetery, Demarest, Bergen County.

DUTCHER, SALEM G. Sgt, H, 7th VA Inf (CSA), 12-23-1917. Rahway Cemetery, Rahway, Union County.

DUTCHER*, WILLIAM H. Corp, E, 39th NJ Inf, 8-27-1903. Evergreen Cemetery, Hillside, Union County.

DUTLINGER, ALBERT Pvt, B, 8th NJ Inf, 5-25-1894. Fairmount Cemetery, Newark, Essex County.

DUTLINGER, KASPER Pvt, C, 28th NJ Inf, 6-30-1875. Old Somerville Cemetery, Somerville, Somerset County.

DUTROW, ADAM L. Artificer, 6th NY Ind Btty 12-9-1928. Rahway Cemetery, Rahway, Union County.

DUTTON*, JOSEPH H. Ordinary Seaman, U.S. Navy, USS Princeton, 3-27-1875. Old Camden Cemetery, Camden, Camden County.

DUTTON, RICHARD S. Pvt, I, 7th GA Inf (CSA), [Captured 7-3-1863 at Chambersburg, PA.] 10-7-1863. Finn's Point National Cemetery, Pennsville, Salem County.

DUVAL, AUGUST Pvt, H, 8th NY Inf, 3-15-1890. Palisade Cemetery, North Bergen, Hudson County.

DUVAL, ISAAC Artificer, L, 1st NY Eng, 11-28-1908. St. Bernard's Cemetery, Bridgewater, Somerset County.

DUVAL, JOHN Pvt, D, 8th NJ Inf, 2-19-1882. Mount Olivet Cemetery, Newark, Essex County.

DUVALL, W.H. Pvt, I, 7th MS Inf (CSA), 5-20-1862. Finn's Point National Cemetery, Pennsville, Salem County.

DUY, PHILIP M. Pvt, A, 31st NJ Inf, 1925. Fairmount Cemetery, Newark, Essex County.

DWIGHT, HENRY OTIS 1st Lt, Adj, 20th OH Inf 6-19-1917. Evergreen Cemetery, Hillside, Union County.

DWIGHT, JOHN H. Pvt, C, 1st U.S. Sharpshooters, 6-14-1896. Fairmount Cemetery, Newark, Essex County.

DWIGHT, LYMAN R. Pvt, F, 91st NY Inf, 11-20-1915. Arlington Cemetery, Kearny, Hudson County.

Our Brothers Gone Before

DWIRE, DANIEL Pvt, C, 2nd DC Inf, 9-30-1878. Holy Sepulchre Cemetery, East Orange, Essex County.

DWIRE, GEORGE W. Pvt, F, 9th LA Inf (CSA), [Captured 7-4-1863 at Gettysburg, PA. Died of chronic bronchitis.] 1-11-1864. Finn's Point National Cemetery, Pennsville, Salem County.

DWYER*, MICHAEL Sgt, E, 1st CA Inf, 5-7-1893. Holy Name Cemetery, Jersey City, Hudson County.

DWYER, MORRIS Pvt, D, 1st MD Cav, 5-6-1893. Holy Name Cemetery, Jersey City, Hudson County.

DWYER, PATRICK Pvt, F, 10th NJ Inf, DoD Unknown. St. John's Evangelical Church Cemetery, Orange, Essex County.

DWYER*, PATRICK J. Pvt, Btty K, 6th NY Heavy Art, 12-14-1912. Mount Olivet Cemetery, Newark, Essex County.

DWYRE, JAMES (aka: Durie, James) Pvt, F, 72nd NY Inf, DoD Unknown. Holy Sepulchre Cemetery, East Orange, Essex County.

DYCKMAN, WILLIAM H. Pvt, E, 22nd NJ Inf, [Died of brain inflammation at Belle Plain, VA.] 3-2-1863. Edgewater Cemetery, Edgewater, Bergen County.

DYE, EZEKIEL VOORHEES 1st Lt, L, 1st NJ Cav, [Cenotaph. Killed in action at Hawe's Shop, VA.] 5-28-1864. Cedar Hill Cemetery, Hightstown, Mercer County.

DYE, GEORGE R. Pvt, C, 37th NJ Inf, 1-1-1924. Riverview Cemetery, Trenton, Mercer County.

DYE, ISAAC S. Pvt, C, 4th NJ Inf, [Died of wounds received 5-6-1864 at Wilderness, VA.] 6-29-1864. Brainerd Cemetery, Cranbury, Middlesex County.

DYER, CHARLES Pvt, A, 80th NY Inf, 12-24-1903. Cedar Lawn Cemetery, Paterson, Passaic County.

DYER, EDWARD Pvt, G, 9th NJ Inf, 12-4-1896. Riverview Cemetery, Trenton, Mercer County.

DYER, GEORGE Pvt, C, 37th NY Inf, [Died of typhoid at Camp Michigan, VA.] 12-28-1861. St. Peter's Cemetery, Jersey City, Hudson County.

DYER, JAMES Pvt, B, 51st NY Inf, [Died at Newbern, NC of typhoid, and wounds received at Roanoke, NC.] 4-7-1862. St. Peter's Cemetery, Jersey City, Hudson County.

DYER, JOHN Seaman, U.S. Navy, USS North Carolina, 3-14-1916. Palmer-Wood Cemetery, Keansburg, Monmouth County.

DYER, JOHN G. Pvt, 28th NY Ind Btty 6-14-1916. Cedar Lawn Cemetery, Paterson, Passaic County.

DYER, WILLIAM H. Pvt, H, 38th NJ Inf, 2-8-1923. Riverview Cemetery, Trenton, Mercer County.

DYETT, ARTHUR 3-2-1906. English Neighborhood Reformed Church Cemetery, Ridgefield, Bergen County.

DYETT, HUGH Pvt, E, 28th NJ Inf, [Wounded in action.] DoD Unknown. Zion Baptist Church Cemetery, New Egypt, Ocean County.

DYKE, EDWARD Pvt, B, 51st PA Inf, 3-1-1925. Eglington Cemetery, Clarksboro, Gloucester County.

DYKES, BASIL Pvt, G, 2nd NJ Inf, [Killed in action at Wilderness, VA.] 5-6-1864. St. Mark's Cemetery, Orange, Essex County.

DYKES, JOHN 12-27-1896. Christ Church Cemetery, Morgan, Middlesex County.

EACHES, OWEN PHILLIPS 1st Sgt, A, 28th PA Militia, 1930. Baptist Church Cemetery, Haddonfield, Camden County.

EACRITT, AARON B. Pvt, F, 12th NJ Inf, 10-13-1924. Baptist Church Cemetery, Mullica Hill, Gloucester County.

EADES, JOHN Pvt, K, 35th NJ Inf, 3-17-1928. Riverview Cemetery, Trenton, Mercer County.

New Jersey Civil War Burials

EADLEY, PETER __, A, 1st __ Cav, 6-29-1923. Arlington Cemetery, Kearny, Hudson County.

EADS, THOMAS Pvt, F, 55th VA Inf (CSA), 10-7-1862. Finn's Point National Cemetery, Pennsville, Salem County.

EADY, L.W. Pvt, I, 5th AL Inf (CSA), 10-31-1863. Finn's Point National Cemetery, Pennsville, Salem County.

EAGAN, HENRY (see: Walsh, Lawrence) Holy Sepulchre Cemetery, East Orange, Essex County.

EAGAN, JOHN (see: Fagan, John B.) Holy Name Cemetery, Jersey City, Hudson County.

EAGAN, MICHAEL Pvt, B, 12th NY State Militia, 4-14-1898. Holy Name Cemetery, Jersey City, Hudson County.

EAGAN, PATRICK Pvt, K, 3rd NJ Inf, 12-14-1913. Holy Sepulchre Cemetery, East Orange, Essex County.

EAGAN, THOMAS Pvt, K, 6th NJ Inf, DoD Unknown. Old St. Mary's Cemetery, Gloucester City, Camden County.

EAGEN, JOHN Pvt, G, 37th NJ Inf, 1-1-1917. Holy Sepulchre Cemetery, East Orange, Essex County.

EAGLES*, DAVID Sgt, H, 40th NJ Inf, 8-25-1901. United Methodist Church Cemetery, Millbrook, Morris County.

EAGLES, ISAAC Pvt, K, 1st NY Eng, 11-3-1901. Presbyterian Church Cemetery, Millbrook, Morris County.

EAGLESON, JOHN Pvt, K, 26th NJ Inf, 2-20-1889. Fairmount Cemetery, Newark, Essex County.

EAGLESTON, JOHN Pvt, I, 5th MD Inf, [Died of disease.] 4-3-1864. Finn's Point National Cemetery, Pennsville, Salem County.

EAKERLY, LEMUEL (see: Eakley, Lemuel) Evergreen Cemetery, Morristown, Morris County.

EAKIN, JAMES M. Corp, H, 37th VA Inf (CSA), [Wounded 8-9-1862 at Cedar Mountain, VA. Captured 5-12-1864 at Spotsylvania CH, VA. Died of bronchitis.] 6-9-1865. Finn's Point National Cemetery, Pennsville, Salem County.

EAKINS, ROBERT Pvt, C, 25th NJ Inf, 12-21-1887. Reformed Church Cemetery, Wyckoff, Bergen County.

EAKINS, WILLIAM 2nd Lt, C, 25th NJ Inf, 5-31-1917. Laurel Grove Cemetery, Totowa, Passaic County.

EAKLEY, JOSEPH 6-21-1907. Evergreen Cemetery, Morristown, Morris County.

EAKLEY, LEMUEL (aka: Eakerly, Lemuel) Pvt, C, 56th NY Inf, 9-10-1922. Evergreen Cemetery, Morristown, Morris County.

EAKLEY, RUSSELL J. Pvt, __, 16th __ Inf, DoD Unknown. Evergreen Cemetery, Morristown, Morris County.

EAMES, JAMES Pvt, A, 77th NY Inf, DoD Unknown. Mount Pleasant Cemetery, Millville, Cumberland County.

EARES, GEORGE H. Pvt, E, 25th U.S. CT, DoD Unknown. Hampton Gate Cemetery, Hampton Gate, Burlington County.

EARHARDT, JOSEPH A. 3-1-1892. Bayview-New York Bay Cemetery, Jersey City, Hudson County.

EARHART*, DORSET Pvt, F, 7th NJ Inf, 1-18-1886. Fernwood Cemetery, Jamesburg, Middlesex County.

EARL, ABRAM Pvt, E, 12th NY State Militia, 3-24-1888. Valleau Cemetery, Ridgewood, Bergen County.

EARL, DANIEL Pvt, D, 22nd NJ Inf, 2-25-1899. Fair Lawn Cemetery, Fair Lawn, Bergen County.

EARL, EDWARD S. Pvt, H, 2nd NJ Inf, 7-7-1889. Rosedale Cemetery, Orange, Essex County.

Our Brothers Gone Before

EARL, ELI (JR.) Pvt, D, 25th NJ Inf, 7-14-1908. Cedar Hill Cemetery, Cedarville, Cumberland County.
EARL, J.D. 1st Cl Boy, U.S. Navy, 9-27-1886. Fairmount Cemetery, Newark, Essex County.
EARL, JOHN H. Pvt, E, 26th NJ Inf, 1-11-1906. Fairmount Cemetery, Newark, Essex County.
EARL, JOSEPH A. Corp, A, 21st NJ Inf, 1922. Fairview Cemetery, Westfield, Union County.
EARL, REUBEN W. Pvt, A, 39th NJ Inf, 2-10-1909. Fairmount Cemetery, Newark, Essex County.
EARL, SAMUEL B. 7-7-1913. Old 1st Methodist Church Cemetery, West Long Branch, Monmouth County.
EARLE, BARNEY V. Pvt, A, 22nd NJ Inf, 8-11-1906. Hackensack Cemetery, Hackensack, Bergen County.
EARLE*, CLEMENT G. Capt, A, 98th U.S. CT, [Wounded in action.] 3-12-1899. Atlantic City Cemetery, Pleasantville, Atlantic County.
EARLE, EDWARD Pvt, G, 124th NY Inf, 8-3-1904. Fairmount Cemetery, Newark, Essex County.
EARLE*, JAMES (aka: Early, James) Pvt, B, 9th CT Inf, 9-24-1886. Fairmount Cemetery, Newark, Essex County.
EARLE, SIMEON Artificer, K, 1st NY Eng, 6-10-1883. Walpack Reformed Cemetery, Flatbrookville, Sussex County.
EARLE, THOMPSON G. 2-11-1908. Riverview Cemetery, Trenton, Mercer County.
EARLE, WILLIAM H. Pvt, F, 27th NJ Inf, 12-13-1900. St. Stephen's Cemetery, Millburn, Essex County.
EARLE, WILLIAM J. Pvt, L, 1st NJ Cav, 9-25-1896. Presbyterian Church Cemetery, Rockaway, Morris County.
EARLE, WILLIAM WALLACE 12-29-1903. Hackensack Cemetery, Hackensack, Bergen County.
EARLEY, CHARLES Pvt, I, 1st NJ Cav, 11-30-1864. Bordentown/Old St. Mary's Catholic Cemetery, Bordentown, Burlington County.
EARLEY*, CHARLES Pvt, F, 8th NJ Inf, [Wounded in action.] 1919. Cedar Green Cemetery, Clayton, Gloucester County.
EARLEY, EDWARD H. Musc, C, 8th PA Cav, 1898. Atlantic City Cemetery, Pleasantville, Atlantic County.
EARLEY, HOWARD (see: Early, Howard) Baptist Cemetery, Pemberton, Burlington County.
EARLEY, JOHN I. Wagoner, K, 4th NJ Inf, 3-1-1898. Berlin Cemetery, Berlin, Camden County.
EARLIN, SAMUEL H. Pvt, Btty D, 1st NJ Light Art, [Wounded in action.] 10-9-1899. Bayview-New York Bay Cemetery, Jersey City, Hudson County.
EARLING, ELIJAH WESLEY Corp, H, 23rd NJ Inf, 1908. North Crosswicks Cemetery, North Crosswicks, Mercer County.
EARLY*, COURTNEY H. Sgt, Btty D, 2nd PA Heavy Art, 2-8-1897. Mount Hebron Cemetery, Montclair, Essex County.
EARLY, HOWARD (aka: Earley, Howard) Pvt, E, 34th NJ Inf, DoD Unknown. Baptist Cemetery, Pemberton, Burlington County.
EARLY, JAMES (see: Earle, James) Fairmount Cemetery, Newark, Essex County.
EARLY, RICHARD Pvt, E, 23rd NJ Inf, 7-24-1905. Baptist Cemetery, Pemberton, Burlington County.
EARLY, WILLIAM Corp, F, 6th NJ Inf, [Died of diarrhea at Burlington, NJ.] 12-28-1862. St. Mary's Episcopal Church Cemetery, Burlington, Burlington County.
EARLY, WILLIAM Pvt, I, 25th NJ Inf, 4-29-1922. Mount Holly Cemetery, Mount Holly, Burlington County.

New Jersey Civil War Burials

EARNEST, NATHANIEL C. Pvt, B, 10th NJ Inf, 5-3-1910. United Methodist Church Cemetery, Tuckahoe, Cape May County.

EARNEST, SEELEY (aka: Ernest, Seely) Pvt, F, 25th NJ Inf, 1914. Greenwood Cemetery, Millville, Cumberland County.

EARNSHAW, JOHN W.S. 9-24-1891. Monument Cemetery, Edgewater Park, Burlington County.

EARP, HARRIS 1st Lt, C, 24th NC Inf (CSA), [Wounded 9-17-1862 at Sharpsburg, MD. Captured 6-17-1864 at Petersburg, VA.] 3-21-1865. Finn's Point National Cemetery, Pennsville, Salem County.

EARP, WILLIAM Pvt, F, 6th CA Inf, 11-7-1903. Fairmount Cemetery, Newark, Essex County.

EASLEY, CHARLES (see: Eisele, Charles O.) Berlin Cemetery, Berlin, Camden County.

EASLEY, GEORGE B. (aka: Eesley, George B.) Ships Painter, U.S. Navy, USS Sabine, 11-18-1928. Fairmount Cemetery, Newark, Essex County.

EASLEY, PLEASANT L. Pvt, E, 2nd MS Inf (CSA), [Captured 7-1-1863 at Gettysburg, PA. Died of disease.] 8-26-1864. Finn's Point National Cemetery, Pennsville, Salem County.

EASLICK, WILLIAM 1862. Zion Baptist Church Cemetery, New Egypt, Ocean County.

EASON, JOHN Pvt, C, 30th TN Inf (CSA), 8-19-1863. Finn's Point National Cemetery, Pennsville, Salem County.

EAST, CHARLES (see: Easton, Charles J.) Newell Cemetery, Stanton Station, Hunterdon County.

EASTERLING, NELSON A. 1st Lt, F, 21st SC Inf (CSA), [Captured 8-21-1864 at Weldon Railroad, VA. Died of typhoid.] 12-3-1864. Finn's Point National Cemetery, Pennsville, Salem County.

EASTLACK, AMOS T. 4-16-1912. St. John's Methodist Church Cemetery, Harrisonville, Gloucester County.

EASTLACK, EDWARD H. Sgt, C, 9th NJ Inf, 5-4-1906. Lake Park Cemetery, Swedesboro, Gloucester County.

EASTLACK, FRANKLIN (aka: Estlack, Franklin) Pvt, F, 4th NJ Inf, DoD Unknown. Mount Pleasant Cemetery, Millville, Cumberland County.

EASTLACK, JESSE G. Pvt, H, 4th NJ Inf, [Died at Frederick, MD of wounds received 9-14-1862 at Crampton's Pass, MD.] 3-27-1863. Jesse Chew Cemetery, Sewell, Gloucester County.

EASTLACK, JOHN P. (aka: Estlack, John P.) Pvt, Btty I, Nevin's PA Light Art, 1-26-1884. Methodist Cemetery, Mantua, Gloucester County.

EASTLACK, JOSIAH (see: Estlack, Joseph F.) 1st United Methodist Church Cemetery, Salem, Salem County.

EASTLACK, OSCAR B. Pvt, B, 24th NJ Inf, 3-20-1878. Oak Hill Cemetery, Vineland, Cumberland County.

EASTLACK, WILLIAM E. Pvt, G, 6th NJ Inf, 2-2-1894. New Camden Cemetery, Camden, Camden County.

EASTLICK, SAMUEL Sgt, C, 10th NJ Inf, 4-10-1911. Riverview Cemetery, Trenton, Mercer County.

EASTON, CHARLES Musc, E, 1st DC Inf, 5-29-1921. Princeton Cemetery, Princeton, Mercer County.

EASTON, CHARLES J. (aka: East, Charles) Sgt, B, 5th U.S. Inf, 1909. Newell Cemetery, Stanton Station, Hunterdon County.

EASTON, EDWIN Pvt, A, 26th NJ Inf, 4-18-1902. Cedar Lawn Cemetery, Paterson, Passaic County.

EASTON, JOHN B. Pvt, M, 1st NJ Cav, 10-23-1889. Riverview Cemetery, Trenton, Mercer County.

EASTON, JOSEPH A. Seaman, U.S. Navy, USS Trenton, 2-6-1887. Presbyterian Church Cemetery, Rockaway, Morris County.

Our Brothers Gone Before

EASTWICK*, R. THEODORE Pvt, G, 61st PA Inf, [Wounded 5-8-1864 at Wilderness, VA.] 10-13-1907. Arlington Cemetery, Pennsauken, Camden County.

EASTWOOD, SAMUEL Pvt, B, 4th NJ Inf, [Died of diarrhea at Trenton, NJ.] 10-31-1864. Mercer Cemetery, Trenton, Mercer County.

EATON, AMHERST 1st Lt, I, 8th NJ Inf, 2-3-1869. Fairmount Cemetery, Newark, Essex County.

EATON, FRANK 12-31-1863. Baptist/Evergreen Methodist Cemetery, Plainfield, Union County.

EATON, GEORGE Pvt, C, 56th MA Inf, [Wounded 7-30-1864 at Petersburg, VA.] 5-8-1925. Evergreen Cemetery, Hillside, Union County.

EATON, HENRY Musc, G, 4th U.S. Cav, 4-10-1932. Fairmount Cemetery, Newark, Essex County.

EATON, HENRY L. Sgt Maj, 141st NY Inf 2-22-1874. Baptist/Evergreen Methodist Cemetery, Plainfield, Union County.

EATON*, JOHN Pvt, I, 74th PA Inf, 7-4-1894. Rahway Cemetery, Rahway, Union County.

EATON, JOHN H. Pvt, K, 5th NH Inf, [Died of disease at Newark, NJ.] 9-9-1862. Fairmount Cemetery, Newark, Essex County.

EATON, OSGOOD Pvt, A, 12th ME Inf, [Died at Fort Monroe, VA.] 1864. Atlantic View Cemetery, Manasquan, Monmouth County.

EATON, SAMUEL __, B, 21st __ Inf, DoD Unknown. Bayview-New York Bay Cemetery, Jersey City, Hudson County.

EATON*, THOMAS H. Corp, H, 33rd NJ Inf, 10-18-1913. Riverview Cemetery, Trenton, Mercer County.

EATON, THOMAS H. Corp, H, 33rd NJ Inf, 12-22-1920. Bordentown/Old St. Mary's Catholic Cemetery, Bordentown, Burlington County.

EAVES, WASHINGTON P. Pvt, C, 17th MS Inf (CSA), 6-7-1864. Finn's Point National Cemetery, Pennsville, Salem County.

EAYRE, GEORGE STRETCH Capt, McLains CO Ind Btty 11-22-1921. Baptist Cemetery, Vincentown, Burlington County.

EAYRE*, THOMAS W. Capt, AAG, U.S. Volunteers, [Killed in action at Spotsylvania CH, VA.] 5-12-1864. Grange/Friends Cemetery, Vincentown, Burlington County.

EBBECKE, CHARLES W. 5-1-1900. Fairmount Cemetery, Newark, Essex County.

EBEL, EDWARD Pvt, 34th NY Ind Btty [Died at Beverly, NJ. of wounds received 9-30-1864 at Pegram House, VA.] 10-6-1864. Beverly National Cemetery, Edgewater Park, Burlington County.

EBELING, JOHN Pvt, D, 8th CA Inf, 12-7-1885. Evergreen Cemetery, Camden, Camden County.

EBERBACH*, CHRISTIAN (aka: Eberbeck, Christian) Pvt, F, 7th NJ Inf, 9-14-1905. Arlington Cemetery, Kearny, Hudson County.

EBERBECK, CHRISTIAN (see: Eberbach, Christian) Arlington Cemetery, Kearny, Hudson County.

EBERHARD, FREDERICK Pvt, D, 2nd NJ Inf, 3-30-1900. Fairmount Cemetery, Newark, Essex County.

EBERHARDT, ALBERT H. 4-22-1931. Head of River Church Cemetery, Head of River, Atlantic County.

EBERHARDT, FREDERICK C. Pvt, A, 39th NJ Inf, DoD Unknown. Presbyterian Church Cemetery, Bridgeton, Cumberland County.

EBERHART, DAVID A. Pvt, B, 2nd NJ Inf, 1927. Presbyterian Church Cemetery, Mays Landing, Atlantic County.

EBERLE, JOHN (aka: Everle, John) Pvt, A, 33rd NJ Inf, 9-7-1863. Woodland Cemetery, Newark, Essex County.

EBERLY, JOHN J. Pvt, A, 9th NJ Inf, 6-2-1873. Fairmount Cemetery, Newark, Essex County.

New Jersey Civil War Burials

EBERT, PHILIP Pvt, I, 9th NJ Inf, 5-19-1907. Arlington Cemetery, Kearny, Hudson County.

EBINGER*, CHRISTIAN Pvt, C, 68th NY Inf, 5-22-1907. Berry Lawn Cemetery, Carlstadt, Bergen County.

EBLE, JACOB Pvt, E, 9th NJ Inf, 8-21-1893. Fairmount Cemetery, Newark, Essex County.

EBLIN, W.H. Pvt, A, 16th Bttn (Neal's) TN Cav (CSA), 5-28-1864. Finn's Point National Cemetery, Pennsville, Salem County.

EBNER, ARTHUR Corp, C, 27th NJ Inf, 6-23-1927. Presbyterian/Methodist-Episcopal Cemetery, Succasunna, Morris County.

EBNER, CHARLES Pvt, I, 19th U.S. Inf, 9-30-1907. Fairmount Cemetery, Newark, Essex County.

EBNER, KASSIMER Pvt, B, 1st NY Eng, 4-28-1907. Arlington Cemetery, Kearny, Hudson County.

ECHERT, JULIUS Landsman, U.S. Navy, USS E.B. Hale, 1-5-1923. Pleasantdale Cemetery, West Orange, Essex County.

ECHTON*, GUSTAVE Pvt, F, 15th NY Cav, 3-7-1881. Fairmount Cemetery, Newark, Essex County.

ECK, FRANCIS J. (see: Ecke, Frank) St. Joseph's Cemetery, Swedesboro, Gloucester County.

ECKARD, HENRY G. Seaman, U.S. Navy, USS Wyoming, 6-5-1913. New Camden Cemetery, Camden, Camden County.

ECKE*, EDWARD Corp, E, 162nd NY Inf, 7-19-1919. Arlington Cemetery, Kearny, Hudson County.

ECKE, EDWARD Sgt, G, 75th PA Inf, DoD Unknown. Old Camden Cemetery, Camden, Camden County.

ECKE, FRANZ JOSEPH (aka: Eck, Francis J.) Pvt, G, 98th PA Inf, 2-26-1912. St. Joseph's Cemetery, Swedesboro, Gloucester County.

ECKEL, AARON W. Pvt, K, 2nd NJ Militia, 8-15-1868. Presbyterian Church Cemetery, Mount Pleasant, Hunterdon County.

ECKER, FREDERICK W. Pvt, D, 2nd NJ Inf, 4-15-1892. Fairmount Cemetery, Newark, Essex County.

ECKER, PHILIP (see: Eckhardt, Philip) Berry Lawn Cemetery, Carlstadt, Bergen County.

ECKERSON, EDWARD D. Pvt, D, 22nd NJ Inf, 7-9-1912. Pascack Reformed Cemetery, Park Ridge, Bergen County.

ECKERSON, JACOB B. Pvt, D, 22nd NJ Inf, 6-12-1928. Eckerson Cemetery, Old Tappan, Bergen County.

ECKERSON, JOHN C. Pvt, D, 22nd NJ Inf, DoD Unknown. Zion Lutheran Church Cemetery, Saddle River, Bergen County.

ECKERSON, THOMAS 1st Sgt, B, 22nd NJ Inf, 7-16-1904. Zion Lutheran Church Cemetery, Saddle River, Bergen County.

ECKERSON, THOMAS HENRY 11-26-1863. Maple Grove Cemetery, Hackensack, Bergen County.

ECKERSON, WILLIAM Sgt, B, 73rd NY Inf, 1-2-1911. Evergreen Cemetery, Hillside, Union County.

ECKERT, CHARLES Pvt, Btty E, 15th NY Heavy Art, 8-29-1877. Hoboken Cemetery, North Bergen, Hudson County.

ECKERT, JACOB Pvt, Btty K, 3rd NY Light Art, 1-2-1896. Alpine Cemetery, Perth Amboy, Middlesex County.

ECKERT, JACOB 3-25-1867. Phillipsburg Cemetery, Phillipsburg, Warren County.

ECKERT, JOHN (aka: Ackert, John) Pvt, A, 2nd NJ Cav, 4-3-1891. Holy Sepulchre Cemetery, Totowa, Passaic County.

ECKERT, JOHN Pvt, A, 9th NJ Inf, 8-29-1878. Rosedale Cemetery, Orange, Essex County.

Our Brothers Gone Before

ECKERT, JOHN (see: Eckhart, John) Presbyterian Church Cemetery, Oak Ridge, Passaic County.
ECKERT, JOSEPH Pvt, A, 199th PA Inf, 4-7-1924. Baptist Cemetery, Pemberton, Burlington County.
ECKERT*, VALENTINE Pvt, B, 9th NJ Inf, 7-28-1882. Fairmount Cemetery, Newark, Essex County.
ECKERT, WILLIAM (aka: Bloss, Henry) Pvt, F, 6th MD Inf, [Wounded 4-6-1865 at Saylers Creek, VA.] 9-19-1925. Methodist Cemetery, Southard, Monmouth County.
ECKHARDT, CHARLES H. Pvt, K, 214th PA Inf, 6-1-1907. Bethel Cemetery, Pennsauken, Camden County.
ECKHARDT, PHILIP (aka: Ecker, Philip) Pvt, C, 68th NY Inf, DoD Unknown. Berry Lawn Cemetery, Carlstadt, Bergen County.
ECKHART, JOHN (aka: Eckert, John) Pvt, K, 80th NY Inf, 1936. Presbyterian Church Cemetery, Oak Ridge, Passaic County.
ECKLEY, MALACHI E. Pvt, I, 38th NJ Inf, 3-11-1887. Old 1st Methodist Church Cemetery, West Long Branch, Monmouth County.
ECKMAN, BRAZILLA 1893. Evergreen Cemetery, Lumberton, Burlington County.
ECKMAN, JOHN H. 3-30-1865. Mount Holly Cemetery, Mount Holly, Burlington County.
ECKSTEIN, FERDINAND Sgt, H, 68th NY Inf, 9-25-1896. Hoboken Cemetery, North Bergen, Hudson County.
ECTEL, JOHN Pvt, H, 1st NJ Cav, DoD Unknown. Elmwood Cemetery, New Brunswick, Middlesex County.
EDDINGTON, JOHN F. Pvt, I, 115th PA Inf, 9-24-1898. New Camden Cemetery, Camden, Camden County.
EDDLEMAN, HORATIO Sgt, C, 58th PA Inf, [Wounded in action 9-29-1864.] 1910. Baptist/St. Andrew's Cemetery, Mount Holly, Burlington County.
EDDY, FREDERICK G. Musc, I, 1st CT Cav, 4-1-1923. Fairmount Cemetery, Newark, Essex County.
EDDY, GEORGE H. QM Sgt, D, 12th NY Cav, DoD Unknown. Arlington Cemetery, Kearny, Hudson County.
EDDY, HOMER Pvt, D, 141st IL Inf, 1915. Calvary Baptist Church Cemetery, Ocean View, Cape May County.
EDDYBURN, CALVIN Pvt, A, 7th NY Inf, 9-18-1862. Fairmount Cemetery, Newark, Essex County.
EDELSTEIN*, JOHN Capt, A, 40th NJ Inf, 6-19-1903. Bayview-New York Bay Cemetery, Jersey City, Hudson County.
EDEN, JOHN R. Pvt, D, 8th NJ Inf, DoD Unknown. Van Liew Cemetery, North Brunswick, Middlesex County.
EDEN, MICHAEL Pvt, D, 60th (Crawford's) TN Mtd Inf (CSA), [Captured 5-17-1863 at Big Black River Bridge, MS.] 9-2-1863. Finn's Point National Cemetery, Pennsville, Salem County.
EDEN, ROBERT A. Pvt, A, 187th PA Inf, 3-11-1911. Van Liew Cemetery, North Brunswick, Middlesex County.
EDGAR, ALONZO Pvt, L, 1st NY Eng, 5-8-1895. Fairmount Cemetery, Newark, Essex County.
EDGAR, FRANCIS (aka: Edgar, Horace) Pvt, C, 1st NJ Inf, 4-11-1868. Fairmount Cemetery, Newark, Essex County.
EDGAR*, GEORGE P. Capt, AADC, U.S. Army, 1900. Hazelwood Cemetery, Rahway, Union County.
EDGAR, HORACE (see: Edgar, Francis) Fairmount Cemetery, Newark, Essex County.
EDGAR, JOHN BLANCHARD Pvt, C, 36th IL Inf, 12-27-1920. Hazelwood Cemetery, Rahway, Union County.

EDGAR, JOHN H. Pvt, A, 41st U.S. CT, 3-28-1899. Rahway Cemetery, Rahway, Union County.
EDGAR, MAHLON Pvt, C, 3rd U.S. CT, 10-17-1915. Rahway Cemetery, Rahway, Union County.
EDGAR, ROBERT Pvt, C, 53rd NY Inf, 9-25-1902. Grove Church Cemetery, North Bergen, Hudson County.
EDGAR, THEODORE F. Pvt, G, 71st NY National Guard, 12-30-1904. Hillside Cemetery, Metuchen, Middlesex County.
EDGAR, WILLIAM Pvt, H, 26th NJ Inf, 3-21-1902. Rosedale Cemetery, Orange, Essex County.
EDGARTON, ARTHUR R. Pvt, I, 13th NJ Inf, 2-12-1879. Fairmount Cemetery, Newark, Essex County.
EDGARTON, WARREN P. Maj, 1st OH Light Art 4-11-1906. Rosehill Cemetery, Newfield, Gloucester County.
EDGBERT, G.D. Seaman, U.S. Navy, 10-16-1892. Fairmount Cemetery, Newark, Essex County.
EDGE*, JOSIAH M. Musc, K, 86th NY Inf, 4-16-1913. Laurel Grove Cemetery, Totowa, Passaic County.
EDGE, NELSON JAMES H. Pvt, D, 7th SC Inf (CSA), 6-30-1930. Holy Name Cemetery, Jersey City, Hudson County.
EDGERTON*, AZEL Pvt, F, 2nd NJ Cav, 1897. Newton Cemetery, Newton, Sussex County.
EDGERTON, JAMES H. Pvt, K, 1st NJ Cav, 1917. Cedar Ridge Cemetery, Blairstown, Warren County.
EDGERTON, JUSTIN P. Pvt, B, 31st NJ Inf, 12-12-1913. Union Cemetery, Washington, Morris County.
EDGERTON*, WILLIAM A. Pvt, U.S. Marine Corps, USS Yankee, 7-30-1880. Evergreen Cemetery, Hillside, Union County.
EDGEWORTH, GEORGE B. Corp, G, 9th MI Cav, 8-30-1897. Fairmount Cemetery, Newark, Essex County.
EDIE, FRANKLIN (see: Edise, F.) St. Joseph's Cemetery, Hackensack, Bergen County.
EDISE, F. (aka: Edie, Franklin) Sgt, C, 81st NY Inf, [Wounded in action.] DoD Unknown. St. Joseph's Cemetery, Hackensack, Bergen County.
EDLER, ADOLPHUS S. Sgt, B, 1st PA Cav, 1920. Mount Pleasant Cemetery, Millville, Cumberland County.
EDMOND, THOMAS H. Corp, K, 68th OH Inf, 5-1-1928. Presbyterian Cemetery, Allentown, Monmouth County.
EDMOND*, WALTER H. Pvt, K, 4th NJ Inf, 3-11-1910. Riverview Cemetery, Trenton, Mercer County.
EDMONDS, ALVIN F. Corp, D, 67th PA Inf, 1912. Cedar Ridge Cemetery, Blairstown, Warren County.
EDMONDS, JOHN Pvt, H, 9th NJ Inf, 6-27-1903. Bayview-New York Bay Cemetery, Jersey City, Hudson County.
EDMONDS, PETER J. Pvt, G, 41st U.S. CT, 7-29-1890. Riverview Cemetery, Trenton, Mercer County.
EDMONDS, SAMUEL D. Pvt, E, 31st NJ Inf, 5-14-1886. Methodist Church Cemetery, Mount Horeb, Somerset County.
EDMONDS*, WILLIAM Landsman, U.S. Navy, USS Iosco, 1909. Old & New Lutheran Cemetery, Lebanon, Hunterdon County.
EDMONDSON, G.T. Pvt, E, 20th TN Inf (CSA), 2-21-1865. Finn's Point National Cemetery, Pennsville, Salem County.
EDMONSTON, AUGUSTUS Pvt, L, 11th NY Cav, 9-28-1902. Bayview-New York Bay Cemetery, Jersey City, Hudson County.

Our Brothers Gone Before

EDMONSTON, AUGUSTUS A. (see: Edmundson, Augustus A.) Maple Grove Cemetery, Hackensack, Bergen County.
EDMONSTON, CHARLES D. 1st Sgt, L, 11th NY Cav, 12-1-1889. Evergreen/Bishop Jaynes Cemetery, Basking Ridge, Somerset County.
EDMUNDS, ALBERT S. Sgt, F, 25th NJ Inf, [Killed in action at Fredericksburg, VA.] 12-13-1862. Presbyterian Church Cemetery, Cold Spring, Cape May County.
EDMUNDS, ELI D. Actg Master, U.S. Navy, USS Crusader, 6-22-1921. Presbyterian Church Cemetery, Cold Spring, Cape May County.
EDMUNDS, EVAN Pvt, F, 25th NJ Inf, 3-16-1885. Presbyterian Church Cemetery, Cold Spring, Cape May County.
EDMUNDS, EVENS B. Pvt, I, 33rd NJ Inf, 11-12-1918. Presbyterian Church Cemetery, Cold Spring, Cape May County.
EDMUNDSON, AUGUSTUS A. (aka: Edmonston, Augustus A.) Pvt, L, 11th NY Cav, DoD Unknown. Maple Grove Cemetery, Hackensack, Bergen County.
EDSALL, ABEL SMITH Corp, K, 22nd NJ Inf, 3-22-1893. English Neighborhood Reformed Church Cemetery, Ridgefield, Bergen County.
EDSALL, BENJAMIN H. Pvt, M, 1st NJ Cav, DoD Unknown. Newton Cemetery, Newton, Sussex County.
EDSALL, FOWLER H. Pvt, F, 27th NJ Inf, 8-12-1899. Fairmount Cemetery, Newark, Essex County.
EDSALL, HENRY F. Sgt, K, 22nd NJ Inf, 3-2-1913. English Neighborhood Reformed Church Cemetery, Ridgefield, Bergen County.
EDSALL, HENRY W. Pvt, K, 1st NJ Cav, 2-15-1922. Hardyston Cemetery, North Church, Sussex County.
EDSALL, JAMES 10-13-1886. Old Butler Cemetery, Butler, Morris County.
EDSALL, WILLIAM H. Capt, K, 15th NJ Inf, 4-19-1890. Baptist Church Cemetery, Hamburg, Sussex County.
EDSALL, WILLIAM R. Pvt, A, 33rd NJ Inf, 9-17-1909. United Methodist Church Cemetery, Vernon, Sussex County.
EDSON, JOHN HENRY Lt Col, 10th VT Inf 2-11-1914. Evergreen Cemetery, Hillside, Union County.
EDWARD, W.T. Pvt, D, 8th VA Cav (CSA), 4-18-1865. Finn's Point National Cemetery, Pennsville, Salem County.
EDWARDS*, ALBERT E. 2nd Lt, L, 1st NC Inf (US), 11-22-1887. Presbyterian Church Cemetery, Metuchen, Middlesex County.
EDWARDS, AMOS E. Pvt, D, 44th PA Inf, 1916. Baptist Church Cemetery, Blackwood, Camden County.
EDWARDS, ANDREW R. Pvt, C, 13th NJ Inf, 11-20-1913. Cedar Lawn Cemetery, Paterson, Passaic County.
EDWARDS, AUGUSTUS (aka: Edwards, Gustavus) Pvt, C, 104th PA Inf, 6-14-1884. Baptist Cemetery, Medford, Burlington County.
EDWARDS, BENJAMIN F. Pvt, A, 12th NJ Inf, 5-5-1915. Overlook Cemetery, Bridgeton, Cumberland County.
EDWARDS, CHARLES Pvt, A, 26th NJ Inf, 6-17-1894. Fairmount Cemetery, Newark, Essex County.
EDWARDS, CHARLES S. Sgt, H, 2nd NJ Cav, 1-1-1905. Oak Hill Cemetery, Vineland, Cumberland County.
EDWARDS, CLAYTON Pvt, C, 4th NJ Militia, 3-9-1882. New Camden Cemetery, Camden, Camden County.
EDWARDS*, CLAYTON Pvt, F, 58th PA Inf, DoD Unknown. Old Camden Cemetery, Camden, Camden County.
EDWARDS, DAVID Pvt, H, 24th NJ Inf, 8-16-1904. Oak Hill Cemetery, Vineland, Cumberland County.
EDWARDS, E.C. 12-4-1917. Berlin Cemetery, Berlin, Camden County.

New Jersey Civil War Burials

EDWARDS, EDWARD Landsman, U.S. Navy, USS Vandalia, 5-6-1894. Fairmount Cemetery, Newark, Essex County.

EDWARDS*, ELMER (aka: Edwards, Enoch) Corp, I, 10th NJ Inf, DoD Unknown. Methodist Church Cemetery, Goshen, Cape May County.

EDWARDS, ENOCH (see: Edwards, Elmer) Methodist Church Cemetery, Goshen, Cape May County.

EDWARDS, FREEMAN A. Sgt, K, 14th NJ Inf, 1-2-1903. Fairmount Cemetery, Newark, Essex County.

EDWARDS, GEORGE Pvt, F, 29th NJ Inf, 2-14-1914. Hackensack Cemetery, Hackensack, Bergen County.

EDWARDS, GEORGE A. Pvt, H, 3rd NJ Cav, 5-19-1902. Oak Hill Cemetery, Vineland, Cumberland County.

EDWARDS, GEORGE H. Pvt, B, 3rd VT Inf, [Died of disease.] 9-15-1862. Fairmount Cemetery, Newark, Essex County.

EDWARDS, GEORGE W. Corp, A, 124th NY Inf, 1917. Locust Hill Cemetery, Dover, Morris County.

EDWARDS, GEORGE W. 5-26-1892. Eastview Cemetery, Salem, Salem County.

EDWARDS, GRIFFITH W. Pvt, H, 21st PA Cav, 6-14-1901. Oddfellows Cemetery, Pemberton, Burlington County.

EDWARDS, GUSTAVUS (see: Edwards, Augustus) Baptist Cemetery, Medford, Burlington County.

EDWARDS, HERCULES Pvt, E, 27th NJ Inf, 3-6-1899. Fairmount Cemetery, Newark, Essex County.

EDWARDS, HORACE W. Pvt, C, 13th NJ Inf, DoD Unknown. Ponds Church Cemetery, Oakland, Bergen County.

EDWARDS, JACOB M. Landsman, U.S. Navy, [At Marine Hospital.] 1904. Manahath Cemetery, Glassboro, Gloucester County.

EDWARDS, JACOB O. Pvt, G, 52nd NC Inf (CSA), [Captured 7-3-1863 at Gettysburg, PA. Died of diarrhea.] 10-28-1863. Finn's Point National Cemetery, Pennsville, Salem County.

EDWARDS, JAMES L. Pvt, H, 48th NY Inf, 3-20-1890. Bordentown/Old St. Mary's Catholic Cemetery, Bordentown, Burlington County.

EDWARDS, JAMES LEWIS Corp, I, 38th PA Militia, 1911. Trinity Episcopal Church Cemetery, Moorestown, Burlington County.

EDWARDS, JAMES W. Pvt, B, 22nd NJ Inf, DoD Unknown. Ponds Church Cemetery, Oakland, Bergen County.

EDWARDS*, JAMES WELDON Pvt, H, 32nd (Lenoir Braves) NC Inf (CSA), [Captured 7-3-1863 at Gettysburg, PA.] 10-1-1863. Finn's Point National Cemetery, Pennsville, Salem County.

EDWARDS, JOB (JR.) Landsman, U.S. Navy, USS John Adams, 1918. Masonic Cemetery, Barnegat, Ocean County.

EDWARDS, JOB W. Landsman, U.S. Navy, USS John Adams, 1899. Old 1st Methodist Church Cemetery, West Long Branch, Monmouth County.

EDWARDS, JOHN 4-11-1879. Cedar Lawn Cemetery, Paterson, Passaic County.

EDWARDS, JOHN Pvt, C, 3rd NJ Militia, DoD Unknown. Presbyterian Church Cemetery, Oak Ridge, Passaic County.

EDWARDS, JOHN Sgt, I, 1st NJ Cav, [Died of smallpox at Camp Custis, VA.] 11-4-1861. Presbyterian Church Cemetery, Oak Ridge, Passaic County.

EDWARDS, JOHN C. Pvt, U.S. Marine Corps, 1-13-1902. Evergreen Cemetery, Camden, Camden County.

EDWARDS, JOHN E. Pvt, F, 1st NH Inf, 7-28-1898. Fairmount Cemetery, Newark, Essex County.

EDWARDS*, JOHN H. Pvt, Btty E, 1st NJ Light Art, 1889. 1st Baptist Church Cemetery, Woodstown, Salem County.

Our Brothers Gone Before

EDWARDS*, JONATHAN H. Pvt, F, 25th NJ Inf, 4-23-1873. Fairmount Cemetery, Newark, Essex County.

EDWARDS, JOSEPH H. Pvt, H, 12th NY State Militia, 3-21-1918. Fairview Cemetery, Westfield, Union County.

EDWARDS, JOSEPH W. Sgt, B, 73rd NY Inf, 5-5-1911. Evergreen Cemetery, Hillside, Union County.

EDWARDS, MARTIN Pvt, H, 24th NJ Inf, 12-5-1909. Green Cemetery, Woodbury, Gloucester County.

EDWARDS, MOSES Pvt, D, 15th NJ Inf, 10-22-1870. Northfield Baptist Cemetery, Livingston, Essex County.

EDWARDS, NELSON W. Bvt Maj, 15th IA Inf 11-30-1886. Bayview-New York Bay Cemetery, Jersey City, Hudson County.

EDWARDS, NOAH 5-29-1889. Methodist Cemetery, Haddonfield, Camden County.

EDWARDS, P.D. Pvt, G, 12th VA Inf (CSA), [Richmond Grey's. Captured 9-17-1862 at Antietam, MD.] 10-6-1862. Finn's Point National Cemetery, Pennsville, Salem County.

EDWARDS, PETER Pvt, D, 2nd NJ Cav, 2-6-1921. Newtonville Cemetery, Newtonville, Atlantic County.

EDWARDS, R.H. Pvt, D, 8th AL Inf (CSA), 8-28-1863. Finn's Point National Cemetery, Pennsville, Salem County.

EDWARDS, REUBEN B. Wagoner, C, 26th NJ Inf, 3-22-1900. Fairmount Cemetery, Newark, Essex County.

EDWARDS*, RUDOLPH Pvt, C, 38th NJ Inf, 12-14-1896. Mount Pleasant Cemetery, Millville, Cumberland County.

EDWARDS, SAMUEL B. Pvt, E, 25th NJ Inf, 1-11-1915. Newton Cemetery, Newton, Sussex County.

EDWARDS, STEPHEN W. Corp, C, 7th NJ Inf, 2-8-1920. Arlington Cemetery, Kearny, Hudson County.

EDWARDS, THADDEUS S. Pvt, C, 17th CT Inf, [Wounded 7-1-1863 at Gettysburg, PA.] 1-14-1878. Rosedale Cemetery, Orange, Essex County.

EDWARDS, THEODORE Pvt, K, 1st NJ Cav, [Died while prisoner at Libby Prison, VA.] 9-15-1864. Evergreen Cemetery, Morristown, Morris County.

EDWARDS, THEODORE D. 1906. Clinton Cemetery, Irvington, Essex County.

EDWARDS*, THOMAS Actg Volunteer Lt, U.S. Navy, USS Stockdale, 1866. Masonic Cemetery, Barnegat, Ocean County.

EDWARDS, THOMAS Pvt, E, 21st VA Inf (CSA), [Captured 5-12-1864 at Spotsylvania CH, VA. Died of bronchitis.] 12-8-1864. Finn's Point National Cemetery, Pennsville, Salem County.

EDWARDS, WILLIAM G. Pvt, D, 4th U.S. CT, 4-10-1886. Fairmount Cemetery, Newark, Essex County.

EDWARDS, WILLIAM H. Corp, B, 7th NJ Inf, 4-5-1911. Fairmount Cemetery, Newark, Essex County.

EDWARDS, WILLIAM L. Pvt, A, 29th NJ Inf, 11-5-1883. Greenlawn Cemetery, West Long Branch, Monmouth County.

EDWARDS*, WILLIAM W. Coal Heaver, U.S. Navy, USS Iroquois, 12-3-1901. Trinity Bible Church Cemetery, Glassboro, Gloucester County.

EESLEY, GEORGE B. (see: Easley, George B.) Fairmount Cemetery, Newark, Essex County.

EFENER, STEPHEN (see: Efner, Stephen O.) Fairmount Cemetery, Newark, Essex County.

EFFINGER, MARTIN Pvt, A, 4th NJ Inf, [Died of debility at Alexandria, VA.] 4-12-1862. Old Camden Cemetery, Camden, Camden County.

New Jersey Civil War Burials

EFFLER, JOHN Pvt, A, 60th (Crawford's) TN Mtd Inf (CSA), [Captured 5-17-1863 at Big Black River Bridge, MS.] 8-1-1863. Finn's Point National Cemetery, Pennsville, Salem County.

EFLINE, WILLIAM (see: Elpline, William) Baptist Cemetery, Salem, Salem County.

EFNER, STEPHEN O. (aka: Efener, Stephen) Pvt, H, 2nd NJ Cav, 10-5-1923. Fairmount Cemetery, Newark, Essex County.

EFNER, WILLIAM Pvt, M, 2nd NJ Cav, 4-2-1887. Fairmount Cemetery, Newark, Essex County.

EGAN, FRANK Corp, K, 2nd DC Inf, 2-28-1896. Evergreen Cemetery, Morristown, Morris County.

EGAN, JOHN Sgt, H, 2nd NJ Cav, 6-27-1882. Holy Sepulchre Cemetery, East Orange, Essex County.

EGAN, JOHN (aka: Egan, Thomas) Pvt, B, 4th NJ Inf, DoD Unknown. Holy Sepulchre Cemetery, East Orange, Essex County.

EGAN*, MICHAEL Capt, G, 88th NY Inf, 9-9-1878. Holy Name Cemetery, Jersey City, Hudson County.

EGAN, PATRICK Pvt, I, 69th NY Inf, 6-28-1894. Mount Olivet Cemetery, Newark, Essex County.

EGAN, PETER Pvt, A, 13th NJ Inf, 1-28-1911. Holy Sepulchre Cemetery, East Orange, Essex County.

EGAN, THOMAS (see: Egan, John) Holy Sepulchre Cemetery, East Orange, Essex County.

EGAN, THOMAS C. 2nd Lt, G, 31st NY Inf, DoD Unknown. St. John's Evangelical Church Cemetery, Orange, Essex County.

EGBERT, G.D. 10-9-1892. Fairmount Cemetery, Newark, Essex County.

EGBERT*, GEORGE Pvt, A, 8th NJ Inf, 8-20-1882. Woodland Cemetery, Newark, Essex County.

EGBERT, MOSES Artificer, F, 1st NY Eng, 8-23-1906. Arlington Cemetery, Kearny, Hudson County.

EGBERT, THEODORE H. Pvt, I, 27th NJ Inf, 12-15-1905. Fairmount Cemetery, Newark, Essex County.

EGBERT, TUNIS A. 4-12-1892. Evergreen Cemetery, Hillside, Union County.

EGBERT, WILLIAM H. Pvt, Btty D, 1st NJ Light Art, 1-29-1877. Fairmount Cemetery, Newark, Essex County.

EGEE, WILMER Pvt, E, 20th PA Militia, 12-26-1919. Lake Park Cemetery, Swedesboro, Gloucester County.

EGEL, FREDERICK 1866. Presbyterian Cemetery, North Plainfield, Somerset County.

EGERTER, JACOB (see: Egerton, Jacob) Methodist Church Cemetery, Asbury, Warren County.

EGERTON, JACOB (aka: Egerter, Jacob) Pvt, E, 11th NJ Inf, 12-28-1906. Methodist Church Cemetery, Asbury, Warren County.

EGGERS*, GEORGE Capt, C, 40th NJ Inf, 11-3-1890. Fairmount Cemetery, Newark, Essex County.

EGGERS, HERMAN Hosp Chaplain, U.S. Volunteers, 8-22-1879. Phillipsburg Cemetery, Phillipsburg, Warren County.

EGGERT, FRANCIS T. Pvt, C, 153rd PA Inf, 7-5-1889. Union Cemetery, Milford, Hunterdon County.

EGGERT, HENRY Farrier, 12-22-1933. Hoboken Cemetery, North Bergen, Hudson County.

EGGERT, JOACHIM C. Pvt, M, 6th PA Cav, 11-21-1894. Riverview Cemetery, Trenton, Mercer County.

EGGIE, EUSTACE Pvt, G, 28th NJ Inf, 10-25-1909. Methodist Cemetery, Mantua, Gloucester County.

Our Brothers Gone Before

EGGLER, JOHN C. Pvt, G, 2nd NY Mounted Rifles, 6-4-1915. Greenwood Cemetery, Pleasantville, Atlantic County.

EGGLETON, IRA HARDIN Pvt, F, 42nd VA Inf (CSA), [Wounded 9-17-1862 at Antietam, MD and 7-2-1863 at Gettysburg, PA. Captured 7-4-1863 at South Mountain, MD. Died of remittent fever.] 10-17-1863. Finn's Point National Cemetery, Pennsville, Salem County.

EGGMAN, SAMUEL QM Sgt, H, 6th PA Cav, DoD Unknown. Baptist Church Cemetery, Haddonfield, Camden County.

EGLE, SAMUEL Pvt, H, 132nd NY Inf, 1-8-1891. Baptist Cemetery, Pemberton, Burlington County.

EGLESTON, REUBEN Pvt, A, 1st MD Inf, 12-30-1925. Colestown Cemetery, Cherry Hill, Camden County.

EGNER*, PHILIP Pvt, F, 52nd NY Inf, 3-14-1888. Rosedale Cemetery, Orange, Essex County.

EGRET, JAMES H. 8-21-1909. Baptist Church Cemetery, Mullica Hill, Gloucester County.

EHILLMAN, JOHN M. DoD Unknown. Evergreen Cemetery, Camden, Camden County.

EHLERS, HENRY (aka: Meyer, Henry) Pvt, G, 140th NY Inf, 9-4-1907. Flower Hill Cemetery, North Bergen, Hudson County.

EHLY*, FRANKLIN (aka: Ely, Franklin) Pvt, K, 48th PA Inf, 6-1-1908. Phillipsburg Cemetery, Phillipsburg, Warren County.

EHNI, CHRISTOPHER Pvt, E, 30th NJ Inf, 9-30-1921. New Somerville Cemetery, Somerville, Somerset County.

EHRGOTT, FRANCIS (see: Airgott, Thomas) Laurel Grove Cemetery, Totowa, Passaic County.

EHRHARDT, LOUIS Corp, A, 45th NY Inf, 7-11-1897. Fairmount Cemetery, Newark, Essex County.

EHRHORN, JOHN C. Pvt, B, 148th PA Inf, 5-13-1915. Arlington Cemetery, Kearny, Hudson County.

EHRIGHT, RUDOLPH (see: Epright, Rudolph) Atlantic City Cemetery, Pleasantville, Atlantic County.

EICH, JEREMIAH LAMBERT Saddler, 7th PA Cav 1921. Cedar Ridge Cemetery, Blairstown, Warren County.

EICHELE, PETER Musc, 39th NY Inf Band 1-12-1915. Flower Hill Cemetery, North Bergen, Hudson County.

EICHLIN, JOHN S. Pvt, B, 51st PA Inf, 1910. Siloam Cemetery, Vineland, Cumberland County.

EICHMAN, JOHN E. Pvt, C, 7th NJ Inf, 9-16-1880. Bayview-New York Bay Cemetery, Jersey City, Hudson County.

EICHNER, CHRISTIAN Pvt, Btty A, 1st NJ Light Art, 1890. Hoboken Cemetery, North Bergen, Hudson County.

EICHNER*, THEODORE Pvt, L, 9th NY Cav, 1-19-1875. Hoboken Cemetery, North Bergen, Hudson County.

EICHOLZ, GOTLOB Pvt, K, 6th NH Inf, 5-2-1917. Woodland Cemetery, Newark, Essex County.

EICK, GARRET Pvt, K, 30th NJ Inf, 2-7-1903. Cedar Hill Cemetery, East Millstone, Somerset County.

EICK, GEORGE E. Pvt, A, 31st NJ Inf, 1907. Locust Grove Cemetery, Quakertown, Hunterdon County.

EICK*, JOHN Pvt, B, 55th PA Inf, 9-3-1916. Phillipsburg Cemetery, Phillipsburg, Warren County.

EIDSON, J.R. Corp, D, 15th AL Inf (CSA), [Wounded at Cross Keys, VA and Gettysburg, PA. Captured at Gettysburg, PA.] 10-3-1863. Finn's Point National Cemetery, Pennsville, Salem County.

EIFERT, GEORGE Pvt, G, 29th NJ Inf, 6-13-1925. Rose Hill Cemetery, Matawan, Monmouth County.
EIFERT, VALENTINE Pvt, G, 29th NJ Inf, 1918. Old Bethel Cemetery, Plainsboro, Middlesex County.
EIGER, JAMES G. 12-18-1890. Hoboken Cemetery, North Bergen, Hudson County.
EILENBERGER, ROBERT J. Pvt, G, 153rd PA Inf, 4-25-1882. Ramseyburg Cemetery, Ramseyburg, Warren County.
EISELE*, CHARLES O. (aka: Easley, Charles) Pvt, H, 4th NJ Inf, 6-21-1905. Berlin Cemetery, Berlin, Camden County.
EISELE, FRANCIS (see: Eisley, Francis) Phillipsburg Cemetery, Phillipsburg, Warren County.
EISELE, FREDERICK Pvt, E, 4th NJ Inf, 12-22-1908. Soldier's Home Cemetery, Vineland, Cumberland County.
EISELE, GEORGE F. Sgt, C, 10th MS Inf (CSA), 1918. Harleigh Cemetery, Camden, Camden County.
EISENBERG, HENRY Pvt, A, 20th NY Inf, [Wounded 9-17-1862 at Antietam, MD.] 11-21-1902. Rosedale Cemetery, Orange, Essex County.
EISENHARDT, GODFREY Pvt, A, 45th PA Inf, 2-29-1920. Calvary Cemetery, Cherry Hill, Camden County.
EISENHART, JOHN C. Pvt, B, 47th PA Inf, DoD Unknown. Evergreen Cemetery, Camden, Camden County.
EISENHART, JOHN C. Sgt, C, 13th NJ Inf, 6-25-1911. Arlington Cemetery, Kearny, Hudson County.
EISENHART, SIMON A. Pvt, M, 8th PA Cav, 10-31-1914. Union Cemetery, Frenchtown, Hunterdon County.
EISILE, ANDREW Pvt, E, 24th NJ Inf, 8-15-1915. Colestown Cemetery, Cherry Hill, Camden County.
EISLE, GUSTAV Pvt, G, 12th NJ Inf, 11-21-1891. Fairmount Cemetery, Newark, Essex County.
EISLEY*, FRANCIS (aka: Eisele, Francis) Pvt, K, 81st PA Inf, 1-10-1893. Phillipsburg Cemetery, Phillipsburg, Warren County.
EISMAN, STEPHEN Pvt, K, 46th NY Inf, 12-30-1898. Bayview-New York Bay Cemetery, Jersey City, Hudson County.
EITEL, JACOB Pvt, G, 2nd NJ Inf, DoD Unknown. Elmwood Cemetery, New Brunswick, Middlesex County.
EITING, JOHN Pvt, K, 98th PA Inf, 1-10-1916. Berlin Cemetery, Berlin, Camden County.
EKINGS, JOHN (JR.) 1862. Baptist/St. Andrew's Cemetery, Mount Holly, Burlington County.
EKINGS*, ROBERT M. Lt Col, 34th NJ Inf 7-25-1896. Cedar Lawn Cemetery, Paterson, Passaic County.
EKINGS, THOMAS K. 1st Lt, H, 3rd NJ Inf, [Killed while attempting to escape from rebel prison at Columbia, SC.] 11-25-1864. Baptist/St. Andrew's Cemetery, Mount Holly, Burlington County.
ELBERSON, ANDREW J. 2nd Lt, D, 9th NJ Inf, 8- -1896. Baptist Church Cemetery, Laurelton, Ocean County.
ELBERSON, JOB Landsman, U.S. Navy, USS Racer, 4-27-1891. Cedar Grove Cemetery, Gloucester City, Camden County.
ELBERSON, JOHN (aka: Elbertson, John) Corp, F, 4th NJ Inf, 4-10-1917. Arlington Cemetery, Pennsauken, Camden County.
ELBERSON #1, ___?___ DoD Unknown. Old Camden Cemetery, Camden, Camden County.
ELBERSON #2, ___?___ DoD Unknown. Old Camden Cemetery, Camden, Camden County.

Our Brothers Gone Before

ELBERTSON, CORNELIUS V. Pvt, K, 30th NJ Inf, 12-25-1906. Elmwood Cemetery, New Brunswick, Middlesex County.
ELBERTSON, ISAAC Pvt, C, 34th NJ Inf, DoD Unknown. Free Burial Ground Cemetery, Medford, Burlington County.
ELBERTSON, JOHN (see: Elberson, John) Arlington Cemetery, Pennsauken, Camden County.
ELBERTSON, SAMUEL C. Pvt, E, 12th NJ Inf, 1916. Harleigh Cemetery, Camden, Camden County.
ELDER, EPHRIAM C. Corp, Btty I, 2nd PA Heavy Art, 1-1-1914. 1st United Methodist Church Cemetery, Salem, Salem County.
ELDER, FREDERICK W. Pvt, C, 1st ME Cav, 1889. Cedar Ridge Cemetery, Blairstown, Warren County.
ELDER, GEORGE DoD Unknown. Old Camden Cemetery, Camden, Camden County.
ELDER, JOHN H. Corp, H, 9th OH Cav, 1912. Atlantic View Cemetery, Manasquan, Monmouth County.
ELDER, JOSEPH Pvt, C, 81st PA Inf, 2-9-1886. New Camden Cemetery, Camden, Camden County.
ELDER, JOSEPH T. Musc, F, 101st PA Inf, 6-24-1923. Bayview-New York Bay Cemetery, Jersey City, Hudson County.
ELDER, JULIUS R. Pvt, K, 85th PA Inf, 1913. Evergreen Cemetery, Lumberton, Burlington County.
ELDER, ROBERT B. Actg Ensign, U.S. Navy, USS Chicopee, 7-14-1905. Prospect Hill Cemetery, Caldwell, Essex County.
ELDRED, HIRAM W. Pvt, H, 13th MI Inf, [Died of diarrhea at Newark, NJ.] 5-1-1865. Fairmount Cemetery, Newark, Essex County.
ELDREDGE, GEORGE Pvt, K, 38th NJ Inf, 2-9-1929. 1st Baptist Cemetery, Cape May Court House, Cape May County.
ELDREDGE, GEORGE H. Pvt, F, 25th NJ Inf, 11-9-1886. Tabernacle Baptist Church Cemetery, Erma, Cape May County.
ELDREDGE, JAMES S. Pvt, F, 25th NJ Inf, 11-6-1919. Presbyterian Church Cemetery, Cold Spring, Cape May County.
ELDRIDGE, CHARLES Pvt, I, 2nd NJ Cav, 1912. Emleys Hill United Methodist Church Cemetery, Upper Freehold, Monmouth County.
ELDRIDGE, CORNELIUS R. Asst Surg, 214th PA Inf 1870. Atlantic City Cemetery, Pleasantville, Atlantic County.
ELDRIDGE, DANIEL B. Capt, 1894. Laurel Grove Cemetery, Totowa, Passaic County.
ELDRIDGE, DAVID E. Corp, G, 12th NJ Inf, [Wounded in action.] 12-28-1891. Mount Zion United Methodist Church Cemetery, Barnsboro, Gloucester County.
ELDRIDGE, GEORGE Pvt, C, 24th NJ Inf, 3-21-1933. Old Gloucester Burial Grounds Cemetery, Clarksboro, Gloucester County.
ELDRIDGE, GEORGE J. Pvt, F, 12th NJ Inf, [Died of apoplexy.] 3-5-1863. New Episcopal Church Cemetery, Swedesboro, Gloucester County.
ELDRIDGE, GEORGE R. Pvt, G, 1st NJ Cav, 12-20-1908. Methodist Church Cemetery, Norton, Hunterdon County.
ELDRIDGE*, ISAAC S. Pvt, G, 1st NJ Cav, 7-21-1893. Green Cemetery, Woodbury, Gloucester County.
ELDRIDGE, ISAAC S. Pvt, E, 31st NJ Inf, 7-15-1915. Fairmount Cemetery, Newark, Essex County.
ELDRIDGE, ISRAEL SMITH H. Corp, G, 11th NJ Inf, [Wounded 7-2-1863 at Gettysburg, PA.] 12-8-1905. Cedar Hill Cemetery, Hightstown, Mercer County.
ELDRIDGE, JOHN H. Corp, E, 27th NJ Inf, 4-4-1881. Hillside Cemetery, Madison, Morris County.
ELDRIDGE*, JOHN R. Pvt, Unassigned, 33rd NJ Inf, 6-21-1914. United Methodist Church Cemetery, Alloway, Salem County.

New Jersey Civil War Burials

ELDRIDGE, JOSEPH Seaman, U.S. Navy, 7-25-1868. Baptist Church Cemetery, Haddonfield, Camden County.

ELDRIDGE*, OBADIAH Wagoner, I, 2nd NJ Cav, 11-28-1868. Emleys Hill United Methodist Church Cemetery, Upper Freehold, Monmouth County.

ELDRIDGE, PETER K. Sgt Maj, 5th PA Cav 11-10-1919. New Camden Cemetery, Camden, Camden County.

ELDRIDGE, WILLIAM G. Pvt, F, 4th NJ Inf, [Died of typhoid at New York, NY.] 7-4-1862. Methodist Church Cemetery, Eldora, Cape May County.

ELFART, JOHN Pvt, I, 35th NJ Inf, 1-27-1883. Holy Sepulchre Cemetery, East Orange, Essex County.

ELFRETH, JOHN DoD Unknown. Evergreen Cemetery, Camden, Camden County.

ELFRETH, JOSIAH Pvt, L, 20th PA Inf, 1916. Evergreen Cemetery, Camden, Camden County.

ELGER, WILLIAM (see: Elkar, William) Woodland Cemetery, Newark, Essex County.

ELGRIM, WILLIAM Pvt, G, 29th NJ Inf, 5-12-1882. Atlantic Reformed Cemetery, Colts Neck, Monmouth County.

ELGRIM, WILLIAM H. Pvt, G, 29th NJ Inf, 12-15-1905. Mount Olivet Cemetery, Fairview, Monmouth County.

ELIAS*, CHARLES H. Sgt, D, 65th NY Inf, 4-25-1926. Van Liew Cemetery, North Brunswick, Middlesex County.

ELKAR, WILLIAM (aka: Elger, William) Pvt, H, 41st NY Inf, 9-2-1882. Woodland Cemetery, Newark, Essex County.

ELKIN, ISAAC L.F. 1st Lt, Adj, 1st NJ Inf 3-13-1908. Van Liew Cemetery, North Brunswick, Middlesex County.

ELKINGTON, CHARLES 1st Sgt, A, 3rd NJ Inf, 5-20-1876. Presbyterian Church Cemetery, Bridgeton, Cumberland County.

ELKINGTON, CHARLES (see: Elkins, Charles) Baptist Church Cemetery, Mullica Hill, Gloucester County.

ELKINGTON, JAMES M. Pvt, I, 9th NJ Inf, DoD Unknown. Overlook Cemetery, Bridgeton, Cumberland County.

ELKINS, CHARLES (aka: Elkington, Charles) 1st Sgt, A, 3rd NJ Inf, 11-4-1892. Baptist Church Cemetery, Mullica Hill, Gloucester County.

ELKINS, JAMES H. Corp, F, 48th NY Inf, [Wounded 5-7-1864 at Chester Hill, VA.] 4-8-1925. Fairmount Cemetery, Newark, Essex County.

ELLENBERGER, JACOB Pvt, D, 5th NJ Inf, 4-29-1909. Fairmount Cemetery, Newark, Essex County.

ELLENBERGER, JOHN Pvt, C, 7th NJ Inf, 2-8-1912. Fairmount Cemetery, Newark, Essex County.

ELLENBERGER, JOHN H. 4-5-1929. Union Cemetery, Frenchtown, Hunterdon County.

ELLER, FRANK 11-21-1905. St Mary's Cemetery, Watchung, Somerset County.

ELLER, JACOB F. Pvt, F, 58th NY Inf, DoD Unknown. Jersey City Cemetery, Jersey City, Hudson County.

ELLER, MATHIS Pvt, K, 53rd NC Inf (CSA), [Wounded 7-2-1863 at Gettysburg, PA. Captured 7-7-1863 at Williamsport, MD. Died of diarrhea.] 9-25-1863. Finn's Point National Cemetery, Pennsville, Salem County.

ELLER, PETER Artificer, 28th NY Ind Btty 1-22-1893. Jersey City Cemetery, Jersey City, Hudson County.

ELLETT, JOB C. (aka: Elliott, Job) Pvt, A, 2nd NJ Cav, 1915. Hainesville Cemetery, Hainesville, Sussex County.

ELLETT, WILLIAM T. Pvt, C, 9th VA Cav (CSA), [Captured at Gettysburg, PA. Died of diarrhea.] 8-23-1863. Finn's Point National Cemetery, Pennsville, Salem County.

ELLICKS, SAMUEL T. Pvt, K, 1st NJ Inf, 1931. Presbyterian Cemetery, New Vernon, Morris County.

Our Brothers Gone Before

ELLICOTT, CALVIN Pvt, G, 42nd NY Inf, 2-11-1905. Riverview Cemetery, Trenton, Mercer County.

ELLICOTT, GEORGE W. Pvt, C, 6th U.S. Cav, 5-6-1918. Greenwood Cemetery, Hamilton, Mercer County.

ELLIOT, GEORGE Pvt, A, 58th PA Inf, 1-6-1901. Greenwood Cemetery, Pleasantville, Atlantic County.

ELLIOT, ROBERT H. Corp, I, 35th NJ Inf, 11-6-1881. Holy Sepulchre Cemetery, East Orange, Essex County.

ELLIOTT, ABRAHAM F. Corp, F, 57th VA Inf (CSA), [Wounded and captured 7-3-1863 at Gettysburg, PA. Died of diarrhea.] 9-21-1863. Finn's Point National Cemetery, Pennsville, Salem County.

ELLIOTT, CLARK Pvt, F, 25th NJ Inf, 7-22-1897. Tabernacle Baptist Church Cemetery, Erma, Cape May County.

ELLIOTT*, HENRY Sgt, E, 91st PA Inf, 1919. Atlantic City Cemetery, Pleasantville, Atlantic County.

ELLIOTT, ISAAC Pvt, F, 183rd PA Inf, 1-17-1899. Bordentown/Old St. Mary's Catholic Cemetery, Bordentown, Burlington County.

ELLIOTT, JAMES Seaman, U.S. Navy, 9-15-1906. Grove Church Cemetery, North Bergen, Hudson County.

ELLIOTT, JAMES Corp, A, 6th NJ Inf, 2-14-1885. Tennent Church Cemetery, Tennent, Monmouth County.

ELLIOTT, JOB (see: Ellett, Job C.) Hainesville Cemetery, Hainesville, Sussex County.

ELLIOTT, JOHN P. Sgt, F, 29th NJ Inf, 4-2-1908. Fairview Cemetery, Fairview, Monmouth County.

ELLIOTT, JOHN R. Bvt Maj, 102nd NY Inf [Wounded 6-15-1864 at Pine Mountain, GA.] 1-28-1899. Mount Pleasant Cemetery, Newark, Essex County.

ELLIOTT, JOSEPH Pvt, F, 25th NJ Inf, DoD Unknown. Mount Pleasant Cemetery, Millville, Cumberland County.

ELLIOTT, THOMAS (see: Thompson, Thomas) Fairmount Cemetery, Newark, Essex County.

ELLIOTT, THOMAS E. (SR.) Pvt, E, 1st NJ Cav, 1891. Tennent Church Cemetery, Tennent, Monmouth County.

ELLIOTT, WILLIAM H. Musc, __, 2nd __ Cav, 4-16-1907. Harleigh Cemetery, Camden, Camden County.

ELLIOTT, WILLIAM (JR.) Corp, C, PA Emerg NJ Militia, 1-1-1873. Tennent Church Cemetery, Tennent, Monmouth County.

ELLIS, AARON Pvt, A, MD Emerg NJ Militia, DoD Unknown. Baptist Church Cemetery, Haddonfield, Camden County.

ELLIS, ALBERT M. Corp, 19th, Unattached MA Inf, 1871. Oak Grove Cemetery, Hammonton, Atlantic County.

ELLIS, ALFRED M. Pvt, E, 40th NJ Inf, 5-29-1880. Mount Hope Presbyterian Cemetery, Lambertville, Hunterdon County.

ELLIS, CHAUNCEY Pvt, H, 22nd NJ Inf, 1910. Riverview Cemetery, Trenton, Mercer County.

ELLIS, EDWARD B. Pvt, H, 4th NJ Inf, 7-4-1912. Cedar Grove Cemetery, Gloucester City, Camden County.

ELLIS, EDWARD S. Corp, E, 12th NJ Inf, 12-6-1923. New Camden Cemetery, Camden, Camden County.

ELLIS*, EDWIN S. Sgt, F, 7th NJ Inf, 8-14-1896. Riverview Cemetery, Trenton, Mercer County.

ELLIS, ELIJAH Pvt, I, 7th NJ Inf, [Killed in action at Spotsylvania CH, VA.] 5-12-1864. Beemerville Cemetery, Beemerville, Sussex County.

ELLIS, FRANCIS L. Corp, E, 82nd PA Inf, 1909. New Camden Cemetery, Camden, Camden County.

New Jersey Civil War Burials

ELLIS, GEORGE W. Pvt, F, 26th NJ Inf, 4-14-1909. Fairmount Cemetery, Newark, Essex County.

ELLIS, GEORGE W. Actg 3rd Asst Eng, U.S. Navy, USS Pinta, 1907. Union Cemetery, Washington, Morris County.

ELLIS, HAMILTON L. Pvt, F, 26th NJ Inf, 8-12-1901. Fairmount Cemetery, Newark, Essex County.

ELLIS, HENRY C. Sgt, E, 35th NJ Inf, 1901. Evergreen Cemetery, Hillside, Union County.

ELLIS, JAMES B. Musc, E, 1st NJ Cav, 10-4-1892. Riverview Cemetery, Trenton, Mercer County.

ELLIS, JOB B. Landsman, U.S. Navy, USS Susquehanna, 12-30-1905. Rosehill Cemetery, Newfield, Gloucester County.

ELLIS, JOHN (JR.) Corp, A, 8th CA Inf, 6-14-1906. Bayview-New York Bay Cemetery, Jersey City, Hudson County.

ELLIS, JOSEPH Pvt, E, 22nd NJ Inf, 5-14-1870. Old Lodi Cemetery, Lodi, Bergen County.

ELLIS, JOSEPH H. 1901. Trinity Bible Church Cemetery, Glassboro, Gloucester County.

ELLIS, MARION F. Sgt, F, 36th VA Inf (CSA), [Captured 12-21-1863 in Nicholas County, WV. Died of heart disease.] 5-1-1864. Finn's Point National Cemetery, Pennsville, Salem County.

ELLIS, MICAJAH Pvt, H, 23rd NJ Inf, [Wounded 12-13-1862 at Fredericksburg, VA.] 2-14-1928. Coopertown Meeting House Cemetery, Edgewater Park, Burlington County.

ELLIS, MILLER W. Pvt, C, 18th TX Inf (CSA), [Captured 6- -1863 at Richmond, LA.] 6-4-1864. Finn's Point National Cemetery, Pennsville, Salem County.

ELLIS, ROBERT (see: Thompson, Robert) Fairmount Cemetery, Newark, Essex County.

ELLIS, RUSSELL Corp, D, 19th U.S. CT, 12-25-1928. Mount Peace Cemetery, Lawnside, Camden County.

ELLIS, SAMUEL H. 2nd Lt, E, 4th NJ Inf, 1891. 1st Baptist Church Cemetery, Moorestown, Burlington County.

ELLIS, SAMUEL P. Pvt, Btty B, 2nd PA Heavy Art, 7-15-1926. Cedar Grove Cemetery, Gloucester City, Camden County.

ELLIS, T. Pvt, D, 1st (Turney's) TN Inf (CSA), 10-19-1863. Finn's Point National Cemetery, Pennsville, Salem County.

ELLIS, T.H. Pvt, H, 2nd (Ashby's) TN Cav (CSA), 5-14-1864. Finn's Point National Cemetery, Pennsville, Salem County.

ELLIS, THOMAS Pvt, U.S. Marine Corps, 12-25-1889. Old Lodi Cemetery, Lodi, Bergen County.

ELLIS, THOMAS M. Pvt, C, 23rd NJ Inf, 12-9-1919. Pearson/Colonial Memorial Park Cemetery, Whitehorse, Mercer County.

ELLIS, WILLIAM Pvt, A, 79th NY Inf, 10-16-1896. Holy Name Cemetery, Jersey City, Hudson County.

ELLIS, WILLIAM A. Seaman, U.S. Revenue Cutter Service, 9-15-1926. Evergreen Cemetery, Hillside, Union County.

ELLIS*, WILLIAM H. 1st Lt, K, 1st U.S. Vet Vol Inf, 4-16-1898. Holy Name Cemetery, Jersey City, Hudson County.

ELLIS, WILLIAM M. Pvt, I, 37th NJ Inf, 7-29-1877. Baptist/St. Andrew's Cemetery, Mount Holly, Burlington County.

ELLISON, ANTHONY Pvt, F, 2nd NJ Inf, 12-23-1886. Fairmount Cemetery, Newark, Essex County.

ELLISON, D.B. Pvt, I, 12th GA Cav (CSA), 1-12-1865. Finn's Point National Cemetery, Pennsville, Salem County.

ELLISON, JACOB Pvt, F, 1st NJ Cav, DoD Unknown. Evergreen Cemetery, Lakewood, Ocean County.

Our Brothers Gone Before

ELLISON, JOSEPH P. Pvt, H, 1st (Turney's) TN Inf (CSA), 9-20-1863. Finn's Point National Cemetery, Pennsville, Salem County.
ELLISON, THOMAS S. Pvt, D, 38th NJ Inf, 1908. Old Mount Pleasant Cemetery, Matawan, Monmouth County.
ELLOR, JOSEPH Pvt, B, 15th NY National Guard, 1-16-1902. Bloomfield Cemetery, Bloomfield, Essex County.
ELLSWORTH, DAVID Pvt, G, 31st ME Inf, [Died of disease.] 9-30-1864. Beverly National Cemetery, Edgewater Park, Burlington County.
ELLSWORTH, THOMAS H. Musc, A, 23rd U.S. CT, [Wounded in action.] 1-1-1891. Jersey City Cemetery, Jersey City, Hudson County.
ELLUM, JOSEPH Pvt, D, 9th NJ Inf, 12-27-1877. Old 1st Methodist Meeting House Cemetery, Manahawkin, Ocean County.
ELLYSON, A.B. Pvt, F, 2nd VA Cav (CSA), 3-12-1865. Finn's Point National Cemetery, Pennsville, Salem County.
ELMBARK, GEORGE DoD Unknown. Union Cemetery, Gloucester City, Camden County.
ELMENDORF, OLIVER Corp, K, 2nd NY Cav, 1892. Chestnut Cemetery, Dover, Morris County.
ELMER, AARON Corp, E, 28th NJ Inf, [Died of wounds received 12-13-1862 at Fredericksburg, VA.] 2-8-1863. Methodist Church Cemetery, Point Pleasant, Ocean County.
ELMER, ALFRED Pvt, F, 3rd NJ Cav, 1-30-1892. Baptist Church Cemetery, Laurelton, Ocean County.
ELMER, AMOS Pvt, I, 69th PA Inf, [Wounded in action 6-18-1864.] 5-27-1902. Tennent Church Cemetery, Tennent, Monmouth County.
ELMER, HORACE J. Ensign, U.S. Navy, USS Hartford, 1902. Evergreen Cemetery, Morristown, Morris County.
ELMER, HORACE J. Pvt, K, 2nd DC Inf, 1-22-1863. Evergreen Cemetery, Morristown, Morris County.
ELMER*, LUCIUS Q.C. Pvt, E, 12th NJ Inf, 1-5-1902. Monument Cemetery, Edgewater Park, Burlington County.
ELMER, ROBERT W. Asst Surg, 23rd NJ Inf 1885. Presbyterian Church Cemetery, Bridgeton, Cumberland County.
ELMER, SAMUEL A. Corp, G, 14th NJ Inf, 5-9-1890. Methodist Church Cemetery, Point Pleasant, Ocean County.
ELMER, WILLIAM B. Corp, H, 24th NJ Inf, [Died of wounds received 12-13-1862 at Fredericksburg, VA.] 12-21-1862. Old Stone Church Cemetery, Fairton, Cumberland County.
ELMER, WILLIAM J. Pvt, K, 29th NJ Inf, 1-10-1910. Methodist-Episcopal Cemetery, Glendola, Monmouth County.
ELMORE, DANIEL M. Capt, B, 102nd NY Inf, 11-22-1868. Bayview-New York Bay Cemetery, Jersey City, Hudson County.
ELMORE, JAMES Pvt, H, 30th AL Inf (CSA), 7-8-1863. Finn's Point National Cemetery, Pennsville, Salem County.
ELPLINE, WILLIAM (aka: Efline, William) Pvt, Btty M, 2nd PA Heavy Art, 1-21-1915. Baptist Cemetery, Salem, Salem County.
ELSAESSER*, JACOB Pvt, A, 12th NJ Inf, 5-20-1916. Woodland Cemetery, Newark, Essex County.
ELSASSER, CHARLES (see: Elsessor, Charles) Holy Name Cemetery, Jersey City, Hudson County.
ELSDEN, GEORGE Pvt, C, 9th NJ Inf, 2-4-1909. Fairmount Cemetery, Newark, Essex County.
ELSESSOR, CHARLES (aka: Elsasser, Charles) Pvt, E, 98th PA Inf, 6-9-1920. Holy Name Cemetery, Jersey City, Hudson County.

New Jersey Civil War Burials

ELSEY, ABRAHAM Pvt, C, 24th U.S. CT, 7-10-1898. Spencer African Methodist Church Cemetery, Woodstown, Salem County.

ELSEY*, GEORGE T. Landsman, U.S. Navy, USS Sebago, 1-30-1891. Fairmount Cemetery, Newark, Essex County.

ELSTON, JESSE K. 2nd Lt, K, 25th NJ Inf, 3-25-1914. Arlington Cemetery, Kearny, Hudson County.

ELSTON, LEMUEL O. Corp, E, 26th NJ Inf, 11-13-1896. Clinton Cemetery, Irvington, Essex County.

ELSTON, WILLIAM H. Pvt, F, 3rd NJ Cav, 1918. Baptist Church Cemetery, Scotch Plains, Union County.

ELSUM*, THOMAS Pvt, G, 1st NJ Cav, [Died of typhoid at Washington, DC.] 10-22-1862. Fairmount Cemetery, Newark, Essex County.

ELTON, MAURICE B. Pvt, I, 4th NJ Militia, 1892. Methodist Cemetery, Woodstown, Salem County.

ELTY, GEORGE Sgt, I, 5th PA Cav, 1-29-1910. New Camden Cemetery, Camden, Camden County.

ELVERSON, JAMES L. Musc, G, 2nd NJ Inf, 11-7-1903. Mount Pleasant Cemetery, Newark, Essex County.

ELVINS, THOMAS C. DoD Unknown. Oak Grove Cemetery, Hammonton, Atlantic County.

ELWELL, CHARLES S. Pvt, I, 25th NJ Inf, 8-30-1867. New Presbyterian Church Cemetery, Daretown, Salem County.

ELWELL, DAVID B. Corp, A, 12th NJ Inf, 1-27-1925. Chestnut Grove Cemetery, Elmer, Salem County.

ELWELL, GEORGE MAHLON DoD Unknown. Overlook Cemetery, Bridgeton, Cumberland County.

ELWELL, JACOB R. Pvt, H, 24th NJ Inf, DoD Unknown. Presbyterian Church Cemetery, Bridgeton, Cumberland County.

ELWELL, JOSEPH M. Corp, H, 24th NJ Inf, [Died of typhoid at Windmill Point, VA.] 1-27-1863. 1st United Methodist Church Cemetery, Bridgeton, Cumberland County.

ELWELL*, RICHARD E. Landsman, U.S. Navy, USS Princeton, 1927. Baptist Church Cemetery, Haddonfield, Camden County.

ELWELL, WILLIAM S. Sgt, E, 150th PA Inf, 10-28-1879. Presbyterian Church Cemetery, Williamstown, Gloucester County.

ELWOOD, JAMES Pvt, A, 1st NJ Inf, 1-2-1918. Evergreen Cemetery, Hillside, Union County.

ELWOOD, SAMUEL Pvt, Btty A, 2nd NY Heavy Art, 10-21-1883. Trinity Episcopal Church Cemetery, Woodbridge, Middlesex County.

ELY, EDWARD H. Pvt, G, 1st NJ Cav, 12-24-1904. Yellow Meeting House Cemetery, Imlaytown, Monmouth County.

ELY, FRANKLIN (see: Ehly, Franklin) Phillipsburg Cemetery, Phillipsburg, Warren County.

ELY*, GEORGE G. Pvt, Btty E, 1st NJ Light Art, 3-2-1929. Reformed Church Cemetery, Fairfield, Essex County.

ELY, JAMES J. Pvt, B, 38th MS Cav (CSA), DoD Unknown. Manalapan Cemetery, Manalapan, Monmouth County.

ELY, JOHN J. Pvt, E, 3rd NJ Militia, 1920. Tennent Church Cemetery, Tennent, Monmouth County.

ELY, JOSHUA Pvt, G, 38th NJ Inf, 12-13-1887. Windsor Burial Grounds Cemetery, East Windsor, Mercer County.

ELY*, PHINEAS Pvt, E, 3rd NJ Inf, 11-23-1904. Phillipsburg Cemetery, Phillipsburg, Warren County.

ELY, W. MERCY DoD Unknown. Old Camden Cemetery, Camden, Camden County.

Our Brothers Gone Before

ELY, WASHINGTON G. Pvt, B, 8th PA Cav, 5-23-1875. Methodist Episcopal/Methodist Protestant Cemetery, Bridgeport, Gloucester County.
ELY, WILLIAM H. Pvt, B, 8th NY State Militia, 7-21-1905. Fairmount Cemetery, Newark, Essex County.
ELYEA, DAYTON MEEKER Pvt, E, 95th NY Inf, [Wounded 7-1-1863 at Gettysburg, PA.] 8-19-1941. Glendale Cemetery, Bloomfield, Essex County.
EMBLEY, EDGAR Corp, C, 61st IL Inf, 9-25-1893. Cedar Hill Cemetery, Hightstown, Mercer County.
EMBREY, WILLIAM H. Pvt, A, 1st NJ Cav, 3-14-1914. New Somerville Cemetery, Somerville, Somerset County.
EMBRY, FELIX M. Pvt, H, 1st TX Inf (CSA), [Wounded 7-27-1862 at Gaines' Mill, VA and 9-17-1862 at Antietam, MD. Captured 7-2-1863 at Gettysburg, PA.] 11-2-1863. Finn's Point National Cemetery, Pennsville, Salem County.
EMBRY, WILLIAM B. Pvt, G, 42nd MS Inf (CSA), 3-4-1864. Finn's Point National Cemetery, Pennsville, Salem County.
EMDE, WILLIAM Pvt, Btty C, 1st NJ Light Art, 8-23-1869. Evergreen Cemetery, Hillside, Union County.
EMELY, JAMES Pvt, K, 34th NJ Inf, 3-17-1873. Old Camden Cemetery, Camden, Camden County.
EMENEKER, CHARLES Pvt, B, 119th PA Inf, [Wounded 5-6-1864 at Wilderness, VA.] 6-6-1925. Evergreen Cemetery, Camden, Camden County.
EMENS, JAMES H. (aka: Emmons, James) Corp, H, 14th NJ Inf, 5-13-1928. Fernwood Cemetery, Jamesburg, Middlesex County.
EMERSON, JAMES H. Pvt, H, 26th NJ Inf, 2-2-1898. Rosedale Cemetery, Orange, Essex County.
EMERSON, RICHARD FIRTH Pvt, A, 24th NJ Inf, 5-2-1912. Old Stone Church Cemetery, Fairton, Cumberland County.
EMERSON, WILLIAM Pvt, C, 2nd NJ Inf, 3-9-1909. Fairmount Cemetery, Newark, Essex County.
EMERY, FRANKLIN 2nd Lt, G, 7th MI Inf, [Killed in action at Fredericksburg, VA.] 12-11-1862. Mount Pleasant Cemetery, Newark, Essex County.
EMERY, GODFREY R. 1923. Bethlehem Presbyterian Church Cemetery, Grandin, Hunterdon County.
EMERY, JOHN Pvt, B, 23rd NJ Inf, 1889. Zion Baptist Church Cemetery, New Egypt, Ocean County.
EMERY, JOHN (JR.) Pvt, D, 15th NJ Inf, [Wounded 5-10-1864 at Spotsylvania CH, VA.] 10-22-1929. Newton Cemetery, Newton, Sussex County.
EMERY, JOHN RUNKLE 2nd Lt, A, 15th NJ Inf, 1-30-1916. Evergreen Cemetery, Morristown, Morris County.
EMERY, PHILIP Pvt, B, 23rd NJ Inf, 6-25-1928. Methodist Cemetery, Allentown, Monmouth County.
EMERY, ROBERT Sgt, F, 29th NJ Inf, 8-1-1906. United Methodist Church Cemetery, Little Silver, Monmouth County.
EMLEN, GEORGE H. Pvt, C, 1st NJ Cav, 9-10-1904. Arlington Cemetery, Kearny, Hudson County.
EMLEY, ABIAL (see: Imlay, Abiel) Old Methodist Cemetery, Toms River, Ocean County.
EMLEY, GEORGE P. Pvt, L, 1st NJ Cav, 12-17-1912. Baptist Church Cemetery, Jacobstown, Burlington County.
EMLEY, JOSEPH P. Pvt, E, 40th NJ Inf, 7-17-1871. Baptist Church Cemetery, Jacobstown, Burlington County.
EMLEY, THOMAS (see: Imlay, Thomas) Baptist Church Cemetery, Jacobstown, Burlington County.
EMMARICK, WILLIAM (see: Emmerich, William) Hollywood Cemetery, Union, Union County.

New Jersey Civil War Burials

EMMEL, ALBERT STOKES Pvt, H, 12th NJ Inf, 1912. Presbyterian Church Cemetery, Bridgeton, Cumberland County.
EMMEL, EDWARD R. Pvt, I, 12th NJ Inf, 3-5-1864. Free Burying Ground Cemetery, Alloway, Salem County.
EMMEL, HEYWARD G. Pvt, K, 7th NJ Inf, DoD Unknown. Walnut Grove Cemetery, Mount Freedom, Morris County.
EMMEL, WILLIAM Pvt, C, 24th NJ Inf, 5-24-1927. Grove Church Cemetery, North Bergen, Hudson County.
EMMEL*, WILLIAM Pvt, C, 34th NJ Inf, 6-19-1903. Methodist Church Cemetery, Aldine, Salem County.
EMMELL, HEYWARD G. Pvt, K, 7th NJ Inf, 5-20-1917. Presbyterian Church Cemetery, Morristown, Morris County.
EMMELL, JOHN Pvt, B, 1st NY Eng, 1-27-1927. Methodist Church Cemetery, Aldine, Salem County.
EMMENS, JAMES (JR.) (see: Emmons, James) Lodi Cemetery, Lodi, Bergen County.
EMMER, WILLIAM (aka: Immer, William) Pvt, C, 45th NY Inf, 2-7-1902. Grove Church Cemetery, North Bergen, Hudson County.
EMMERICH, ADAM Pvt, MO Home Guard [Booneville Reserve Corps Regiment.] 8-13-1896. Palisade Cemetery, North Bergen, Hudson County.
EMMERICH, WILLIAM (aka: Emmarick, William) Pvt, D, 2nd NJ Inf, 11-19-1917. Hollywood Cemetery, Union, Union County.
EMMETT, JOSEPH R. Pvt, D, 68th PA Inf, 6-30-1894. Presbyterian Church Cemetery, Bridgeton, Cumberland County.
EMMETT, WILLIAM COLVILLE Pvt, E, PA Emerg NJ Militia, 4-18-1901. Evergreen Cemetery, Morristown, Morris County.
EMMETT*, WILLIAM J. Pvt, H, 13th NJ Inf, DoD Unknown. Laurel Grove Cemetery, Totowa, Passaic County.
EMMONS, ANDREW J. Pvt, D, 8th NJ Inf, 8-20-1882. Saums Farm Cemetery, Hillsborough, Somerset County.
EMMONS, CHARLES HENRY Corp, K, 39th NJ Inf, 2-17-1916. Pleasant Hill Cemetery, Pleasant Hill, Morris County.
EMMONS, CLARK Pvt, G, 32nd NY Inf, 9-9-1896. Fairmount Cemetery, Newark, Essex County.
EMMONS, CONOVER Pvt, D, 48th NY Inf, [Wounded 6-1-1864 at Cold Harbor, VA.] 1923. Evergreen Cemetery, Farmingdale, Monmouth County.
EMMONS, CORLIES L. 12-22-1897. Adelphia Cemetery, Adelphia, Monmouth County.
EMMONS, CORNELIUS H. Capt, A, 29th NJ Inf, 10-17-1912. Glenwood Cemetery, West Long Branch, Monmouth County.
EMMONS, CORNELIUS S. Pvt, D, 31st NJ Inf, 12-5-1890. Newell Cemetery, Stanton Station, Hunterdon County.
EMMONS, DANIEL C. Pvt, A, 28th NJ Inf, 2-4-1935. Tennent Church Cemetery, Tennent, Monmouth County.
EMMONS, DAVID Sgt, A, 28th NJ Inf, 5-31-1916. Tennent Church Cemetery, Tennent, Monmouth County.
EMMONS, DAVID Pvt, C, 72nd NY Inf, [Cenotaph. Killed in action at Williamsburg, VA.] 5-5-1862. New Presbyterian Cemetery, Hanover, Morris County.
EMMONS, DAVID R. (JR.) Sgt, I, 27th NJ Inf, 1927. Congregational Church Cemetery, Chester, Morris County.
EMMONS, DAVID W. 2nd Lt, K, 29th NJ Inf, 10-31-1896. Ardena Baptist Church Cemetery, Adelphia, Monmouth County.
EMMONS, EDWARD H. 11-5-1921. Old 1st Methodist Church Cemetery, West Long Branch, Monmouth County.
EMMONS, ELIAS Pvt, C, 10th NJ Inf, 2-5-1917. Baptist Cemetery, Pemberton, Burlington County.

Our Brothers Gone Before

EMMONS, ELISHA Mate, U.S. Navy, USS Relief, 3-23-1918. Old 1st Methodist Church Cemetery, West Long Branch, Monmouth County.
EMMONS, EZRA S. Pvt, G, 30th NJ Inf, 5-4-1869. Methodist-Episcopal Cemetery, Whitehouse, Hunterdon County.
EMMONS, GEORGE Pvt, F, 22nd NJ Inf, 4-12-1897. Christ Church Cemetery, Morgan, Middlesex County.
EMMONS, GEORGE Pvt, D, 1st NJ Inf, 9-30-1897. Cedar Lawn Cemetery, Paterson, Passaic County.
EMMONS, GEORGE H. Pvt, F, 9th NJ Inf, [Wounded in action.] DoD Unknown. Congregational Church Cemetery, Chester, Morris County.
EMMONS, GORDON Pvt, A, 28th NJ Inf, 6-10-1873. Dutch Reformed Church Cemetery, Spotswood, Middlesex County.
EMMONS, ISAAC J. Pvt, A, 28th NJ Inf, 1909. Presbyterian Church Cemetery, Kingston, Somerset County.
EMMONS, ISAIAH W. Pvt, B, 31st NJ Inf, 12-2-1909. Mansfield/Washington Cemetery, Washington, Warren County.
EMMONS, JACOB Pvt, F, 40th NJ Inf, 3-4-1900. Tabernacle Cemetery, Tabernacle, Burlington County.
EMMONS, JAMES (aka: Emmens, James (Jr.)) Pvt, H, 10th NY Inf, DoD Unknown. Lodi Cemetery, Lodi, Bergen County.
EMMONS, JAMES (see: Emens, James H.) Fernwood Cemetery, Jamesburg, Middlesex County.
EMMONS, JAMES H. Corp, A, 28th NJ Inf, 5-31-1915. Tennent Church Cemetery, Tennent, Monmouth County.
EMMONS, JESSE Pvt, C, 29th NJ Inf, 12-16-1887. Cedar Hill Cemetery, Hightstown, Mercer County.
EMMONS, JOB E. 1913. Maplewood Cemetery, Freehold, Monmouth County.
EMMONS, JOHN Wagoner, A, 31st NJ Inf, 6-17-1908. New Germantown Cemetery, Oldwick, Hunterdon County.
EMMONS, JOHN Pvt, C, 10th NJ Inf, [Died of lung hemorrage at Philadelphia, PA.] 9-15-1863. Friends Cemetery, Arneys Mount, Burlington County.
EMMONS, JOHN H. Corp, A, 29th NJ Inf, 12-16-1921. Glenwood Cemetery, West Long Branch, Monmouth County.
EMMONS, JOSEPH Pvt, D, 2nd NJ Cav, 6-17-1902. Methodist-Episcopal Cemetery, Pointville, Burlington County.
EMMONS, LEVI S. Pvt, A, 38th NJ Inf, 12-18-1921. Rose Hill Cemetery, Matawan, Monmouth County.
EMMONS, MICHAEL T. Corp, G, 11th NJ Inf, [Wounded in action.] 5-26-1917. Methodist Cemetery, Allentown, Monmouth County.
EMMONS, RALPH C. Pvt, H, 38th NJ Inf, 10-20-1911. Tennent Church Cemetery, Tennent, Monmouth County.
EMMONS, READING (aka: Emmons,Redmond) Pvt, I, 10th NJ Inf, 9-8-1864. Friends Cemetery, Arneys Mount, Burlington County.
EMMONS, REDMOND (see: Emmons, Reading) Friends Cemetery, Arneys Mount, Burlington County.
EMMONS*, SILAS H. Capt, K, 2nd WV Cav, [Cenotaph.] 12-26-1902. Cedar Lawn Cemetery, Paterson, Passaic County.
EMMONS, SYLVANUS S. DoD Unknown. Rose Hill Cemetery, Matawan, Monmouth County.
EMMONS, SYLVANUS T. Pvt, G, 1st NJ Cav, 4-17-1930. Old 1st Methodist Church Cemetery, West Long Branch, Monmouth County.
EMMONS, WILLIAM Pvt, G, 11th NJ Inf, [Wounded in action.] DoD Unknown. Tennent Church Cemetery, Tennent, Monmouth County.

New Jersey Civil War Burials

EMMONS, WILLIAM DoD Unknown. Evergreen/Bishop Jaynes Cemetery, Basking Ridge, Somerset County.
EMMONS, WILLIAM H. Pvt, A, 38th NJ Inf, 4-21-1928. Maplewood Cemetery, Freehold, Monmouth County.
EMMONS, WILLIAM H.H. Corp, F, 15th NJ Inf, 12-13-1900. Evergreen Cemetery, Morristown, Morris County.
EMMONS, WILLIAM L. Pvt, A, 28th NJ Inf, 1909. Tennent Church Cemetery, Tennent, Monmouth County.
EMMONS*, WILLIAM N. Pvt, E, 7th NJ Inf, 5-20-1903. Woodland Cemetery, Newark, Essex County.
EMMONS*, WILLIAM N. Pvt, A, 14th NJ Inf, 6-19-1868. Methodist-Episcopal Cemetery, Englishtown, Monmouth County.
EMORY, GEORGE L. 2nd Lt, K, 31st NJ Inf, 1922. Reformed Church Cemetery, Lebanon, Hunterdon County.
EMORY, JOHN Corp, C, 25th U.S. CT, 8-18-1919. Mount Peace Cemetery, Lawnside, Camden County.
EMORY, NICHOLAS (see: Inlay, Nicholas) Old 1st Methodist Church Cemetery, West Long Branch, Monmouth County.
EMORY, WILLIAM S. Sgt, Btty I, 6th PA Heavy Art, 5-1-1890. Union Cemetery, Frenchtown, Hunterdon County.
EMSEY, JOHN Pvt, C, __ NY Eng, 6-11-1912. Methodist Cemetery, Allentown, Monmouth County.
ENDICOTT, FREDERICK Pvt, L, 3rd NJ Cav, 1923. United Methodist Church Cemetery, Tuckahoe, Cape May County.
ENDLICH, JOHN HENRY Pvt, F, 39th NJ Inf, 3-25-1892. Fairmount Cemetery, Newark, Essex County.
ENGARD, LOUIS Pvt, H, 28th NJ Inf, 6-10-1917. Methodist Church Cemetery, New Albany, Burlington County.
ENGEL*, CHARLES E. Musc, 9th PA Cav Band 2-29-1912. Greenwood Cemetery, Hamilton, Mercer County.
ENGEL, CHARLES EDMOND 1st Sgt, G, 2nd PA Cav, 5-12-1938. Harleigh Cemetery, Camden, Camden County.
ENGEL, FRANZ Pvt, G, 7th NY Inf, DoD Unknown. Holy Sepulchre Cemetery, East Orange, Essex County.
ENGEL, JOHN Sgt, B, 165th NY Inf, [Wounded in action.] 8-23-1903. Berry Lawn Cemetery, Carlstadt, Bergen County.
ENGEL, JOHN (aka: Engle, John) Sgt, Btty A, 2nd PA Heavy Art, 3- -1917. Monument Cemetery, Edgewater Park, Burlington County.
ENGELHARDT, JOHN Pvt, B, 28th U.S. Vet Vol Inf, 8-9-1900. Laurel Grove Cemetery, Totowa, Passaic County.
ENGENOCH, GEORGE Pvt, D, 1st NJ Cav, 5-22-1881. Riverview Cemetery, Trenton, Mercer County.
ENGLAND, DAVID C. Pvt, D, Morgan's KY Scouts (CSA), 8-24-1863. Finn's Point National Cemetery, Pennsville, Salem County.
ENGLAND, HENRY C. Sgt, E, 24th NJ Inf, 1910. Eglington Cemetery, Clarksboro, Gloucester County.
ENGLAND, HENRY H. Pvt, C, 26th PA Inf, 12-13-1922. Cedar Lawn Cemetery, Paterson, Passaic County.
ENGLAND, ISAAC W. Pvt, I, 139th OH Inf, 4-25-1885. Valleau Cemetery, Ridgewood, Bergen County.
ENGLE, ANDREW S. 1915. Arlington Cemetery, Kearny, Hudson County.
ENGLE*, ANDREW S. (JR.) Pvt, C, 97th NY Inf, 8-18-1915. English Neighborhood Reformed Church Cemetery, Ridgefield, Bergen County.

Our Brothers Gone Before

ENGLE, CHARLES L. Pvt, D, 39th NJ Inf, 1-11-1904. Fairmount Cemetery, Newark, Essex County.

ENGLE, FREDERICK Capt, U.S. Navy, 2-12-1868. St. Mary's Episcopal Church Cemetery, Burlington, Burlington County.

ENGLE, HENRY 1st Sgt, D, 7th NJ Inf, 2-8-1892. Phillipsburg Cemetery, Phillipsburg, Warren County.

ENGLE, JACOB Pvt, K, 13th NJ Inf, 12-15-1909. Laurel Grove Cemetery, Totowa, Passaic County.

ENGLE, JOHN Color Sgt, B, 165th NY Inf, [Wounded 4-23-1864 at Cane River Crossing, LA.] 1-8-1917. Maple Grove Cemetery, Hackensack, Bergen County.

ENGLE, JOHN (see: Engel, John) Monument Cemetery, Edgewater Park, Burlington County.

ENGLE, JOHN B. Pvt, K, 15th NJ Inf, 3-27-1899. Fairmount Cemetery, Newark, Essex County.

ENGLE, MARTIN 7-5-1910. Laurel Grove Cemetery, Totowa, Passaic County.

ENGLER, ANTON Pvt, K, 7th NY Inf, 9-12-1909. Weehawken Cemetery, North Bergen, Hudson County.

ENGLER*, JOHN (JR.) Sgt, A, 21st NJ Inf, 3-17-1922. Bayview-New York Bay Cemetery, Jersey City, Hudson County.

ENGLER, LAVINIA 12-14-1928. Bayview-New York Bay Cemetery, Jersey City, Hudson County.

ENGLES, EDWARD (aka: Inglis, Edward) Pvt, I, 170th NY Inf, 1-23-1872. Bayview-New York Bay Cemetery, Jersey City, Hudson County.

ENGLES, JAMES S. Capt, E, 10th CT Inf, 7-25-1887. Presbyterian Cemetery, Woodstown, Salem County.

ENGLIN, BENJAMIN Pvt, A, 22nd NJ Inf, 1922. Valleau Cemetery, Ridgewood, Bergen County.

ENGLIS, JOHN R. Pvt, A, 6th (Wharton, Stone's) TX Cav (CSA), 4-20-1864. Finn's Point National Cemetery, Pennsville, Salem County.

ENGLISH, ABEL Pvt, B, 25th NJ Inf, 1905. Asbury United Methodist Church Cemetery, English Creek, Atlantic County.

ENGLISH, ABRAM T. (JR.) Pvt, B, 13th MA Inf, 1925. Cedar Hill Cemetery, Florence, Burlington County.

ENGLISH, CHARLES B. Pvt, B, 25th NJ Inf, DoD Unknown. Asbury United Methodist Church Cemetery, English Creek, Atlantic County.

ENGLISH, CHARLES S. 1st Sgt, E, 3rd DE Inf, 1-5-1906. Riverview Cemetery, Penns Grove, Salem County.

ENGLISH, DANIEL E. Pvt, Btty E, 1st NJ Light Art, 7-3-1876. Asbury United Methodist Church Cemetery, English Creek, Atlantic County.

ENGLISH, EZEKIEL K. Pvt, D, 38th NJ Inf, 1896. Eglington Cemetery, Clarksboro, Gloucester County.

ENGLISH, GEORGE Pvt, K, 35th NJ Inf, 1-15-1893. Riverview Cemetery, Trenton, Mercer County.

ENGLISH, GEORGE W. Pvt, K, 38th NJ Inf, 4-29-1918. Evergreen Cemetery, New Brunswick, Middlesex County.

ENGLISH, GEORGE W. Pvt, E, 21st NJ Inf, 10-13-1884. Riverview Cemetery, Trenton, Mercer County.

ENGLISH, HENRY B. Pvt, A, 9th NJ Inf, 1929. Cedar Green Cemetery, Clayton, Gloucester County.

ENGLISH, JAMES 1-8-1881. Tennent Church Cemetery, Tennent, Monmouth County.

ENGLISH, JAMES Pvt, I, 3rd NJ Inf, [Wounded 8-29-1862 at 2nd Bull Run, VA.] 1869. St. Mary's Cemetery, Plainfield, Union County.

ENGLISH*, JAMES T. Pvt, I, 2nd NJ Inf, 1-8-1899. Mount Pleasant Methodist Cemetery, Pleasantville, Atlantic County.

New Jersey Civil War Burials

ENGLISH, JAMES T. 5-17-1873. Presbyterian Church Cemetery, Liberty Corners, Somerset County.

ENGLISH, JOHN RIDGWAY Pvt, H, 23rd NJ Inf, 2-7-1923. Bordentown/Old St. Mary's Catholic Cemetery, Bordentown, Burlington County.

ENGLISH, JOSEPH Pvt, Btty A, 2nd PA Heavy Art, 10-26-1887. Baptist Cemetery, Burlington, Burlington County.

ENGLISH, MIZEAL C. Corp, A, 12th NJ Inf, 8-6-1911. Cedar Green Cemetery, Clayton, Gloucester County.

ENGLISH*, OWEN Pvt, K, 9th NJ Inf, 11-7-1909. Holy Name Cemetery, Jersey City, Hudson County.

ENGLISH, PATRICK Landsman, U.S. Navy, 9-17-1908. Holy Sepulchre Cemetery, East Orange, Essex County.

ENGLISH, PHILETUS R. Com Sgt, 12th NJ Inf 1-25-1869. Riverview Cemetery, Trenton, Mercer County.

ENGLISH, SAMUEL Pvt, D, 6th NJ Inf, 3-20-1911. Cedar Grove Cemetery, Gloucester City, Camden County.

ENGLISH, SAMUEL W. Pvt, A, 9th NJ Inf, 9-20-1920. Cedar Green Cemetery, Clayton, Gloucester County.

ENGLISH, THOMAS DUNN 3-29-1902. Fairmount Cemetery, Newark, Essex County.

ENGLISH, WILLIAM Pvt, B, 22nd NJ Inf, 3-1-1919. Zion Lutheran Church Cemetery, Saddle River, Bergen County.

ENGSTER, JOHN J. Pvt, F, 1st NJ Inf, 3-9-1875. Fairmount Cemetery, Newark, Essex County.

ENNIS, GEORGE W. Pvt, C, 2nd NJ Inf, 7-3-1906. Rosedale Cemetery, Orange, Essex County.

ENNIS, HENRY (JR.) Musc, K, 26th NJ Inf, 5-5-1918. Fairmount Cemetery, Newark, Essex County.

ENNIS, JOHN Pvt, D, 38th NJ Inf, 10-20-1905. Evergreen Cemetery, Camden, Camden County.

ENNIS, JOHN H. Pvt, G, 12th U.S. Inf, 8-16-1868. Fairmount Cemetery, Newark, Essex County.

ENNIS, SAMUEL Sgt, Btty B, 1st NJ Light Art, 1-8-1916. Fairmount Cemetery, Newark, Essex County.

ENNIS, WILLIAM Pvt, C, 17th NY Inf, 5-9-1908. Evergreen Cemetery, Hillside, Union County.

ENO, BYRON EUGENE Pvt, I, 19th PA Inf, 11-21-1914. Good Luck Cemetery, Murray Grove, Ocean County.

ENSBRO, PATRICK (see: Ansbro, Patrick) St. Joseph's Cemetery, Keyport, Monmouth County.

ENSEL, JOHN (see: Ansel, John) Oak Hill Cemetery, Vineland, Cumberland County.

ENSIGN, CHARLES A. Pvt, G, 124th NY Inf, 6-30-1920. Rosedale Cemetery, Orange, Essex County.

ENSIGN, LEWIS Pvt, A, 35th NJ Inf, 1-15-1923. Jersey City Cemetery, Jersey City, Hudson County.

ENSLEE, WILLIAM H. 1922. Evergreen Cemetery, Morristown, Morris County.

ENT, HENRY S. Pvt, L, 6th U.S. Cav, 10-16-1907. Greenwood Cemetery, Hamilton, Mercer County.

ENT, LAMBERT Pvt, B, 38th NJ Inf, 4-22-1909. Riverview Cemetery, Trenton, Mercer County.

ENTREKIN, JOHN C. Pvt, A, 114th OH Inf, [Wounded 4-9-1865 at Fort Blakely, AL.] 1910. Siloam Cemetery, Vineland, Cumberland County.

ENTWISTLE, JAMES 2nd Asst Eng, U.S. Navy, 3-23-1910. Cedar Lawn Cemetery, Paterson, Passaic County.

Our Brothers Gone Before

ENTWISTLE, ROBERT Pvt, A, 70th NY Inf, 5-17-1908. St. John's Cemetery, Hamilton, Mercer County.
EPERSON, J.P. Pvt, C, 11th (Holman's) TN Cav (CSA), 8-5-1864. Finn's Point National Cemetery, Pennsville, Salem County.
EPLER, GEORGE L. Sgt Maj, 73rd PA Inf 2- -1928. 1st Baptist Cemetery, Cape May Court House, Cape May County.
EPPINGER, JOHN Pvt, F, 75th PA Inf, 3-29-1916. Fairview Cemetery, Fairview, Bergen County.
EPRIGHT*, RUDOLPH (aka: Ehright, Rudolph) Pvt, F, 82nd PA Inf, [Wounded in action.] 4-16-1903. Atlantic City Cemetery, Pleasantville, Atlantic County.
ERB, CHARLES H. Capt, L, 9th NJ Inf, DoD Unknown. St. Mary's Cemetery, Wharton, Morris County.
ERB, NICHOLAS Pvt, Btty L, 2nd PA Heavy Art, 2-4-1936. Berlin Cemetery, Berlin, Camden County.
ERBE, GEORGE Pvt, I, 40th NJ Inf, 5-12-1872. St. John's Cemetery, Hamilton, Mercer County.
ERBE, JACOB Pvt, B, 42nd IN Inf, 2-6-1872. Macphelah Cemetery, North Bergen, Hudson County.
ERDLE, CHRISTIAN Musc, E, 22nd NJ Inf, 3-18-1878. Berry Lawn Cemetery, Carlstadt, Bergen County.
ERDMAN, ALBERT Chaplain, 146th NY Inf 1-24-1918. Evergreen Cemetery, Morristown, Morris County.
ERDMAN, AUGUST Pvt, K, 20th NY Inf, 12-29-1889. Rosedale Cemetery, Orange, Essex County.
ERHARDT, CHRISTIAN Pvt, C, 11th NY National Guard, 11-29-1909. New York/New Jersey Crematory Cemetery, North Bergen, Hudson County.
ERHARDT, LOUIS Pvt, D, 54th NY Inf, 7-11-1897. Fairmount Cemetery, Newark, Essex County.
ERIC, C. 10-13-1895. Rahway Cemetery, Rahway, Union County.
ERICHSON, JAMES S. (aka: Erickson, James) Pvt, Btty B, 4th NY Heavy Art, 2-10-1920. Methodist Church Cemetery, Hurffville, Gloucester County.
ERICKSON, JAMES (see: Erichson, James S.) Methodist Church Cemetery, Hurffville, Gloucester County.
ERICKSON, MICHAEL BRIGHT Sgt, K, 29th PA Inf, 2-3-1936. Methodist Church Cemetery, Hurffville, Gloucester County.
ERLAND, GEORGE (SR.) Pvt, K, 194th OH Inf, 1927. Valleau Cemetery, Ridgewood, Bergen County.
ERLENKOTTER, CHARLES 5-20-1897. Hoboken Cemetery, North Bergen, Hudson County.
ERLENMYER, ALBRICHT Pvt, H, 5th NJ Inf, 8-9-1886. Evergreen Cemetery, Hillside, Union County.
ERNEST, JACOB Corp, H, 24th NJ Inf, 7-27-1896. Presbyterian Church Cemetery, Bridgeton, Cumberland County.
ERNEST, JOHN S. Pvt, H, 24th NJ Inf, 12-16-1908. Presbyterian Church Cemetery, Upper Deerfield, Cumberland County.
ERNEST, SEELY (see: Earnest, Seeley) Greenwood Cemetery, Millville, Cumberland County.
ERNST*, FRANCIS Pvt, K, 33rd NJ Inf, 4-9-1907. Evergreen Cemetery, Hillside, Union County.
ERNST, FRANK Pvt, E, 202nd PA Inf, 7-2-1900. Fairmount Cemetery, Newark, Essex County.
ERNST, GUSTAVE ADOLPH 1st Sgt, G, 29th NY Inf, 12-4-1922. Riverside Cemetery, Toms River, Ocean County.

New Jersey Civil War Burials

ERRICKSON, ANDREW Corp, C, 11th NJ Inf, 8-15-1882. Zion Baptist Church Cemetery, New Egypt, Ocean County.

ERRICKSON, BARZILLAR H. Pvt, B, 1st NJ Inf, [Killed in action at Petersburg, VA.] 4-2-1865. Zion Baptist Church Cemetery, New Egypt, Ocean County.

ERRICKSON*, CHARLES Pvt, H, 38th NJ Inf, 10-6-1910. United Methodist Church Cemetery, Tuckahoe, Cape May County.

ERRICKSON, CHARLES QM Sgt, 29th NJ Inf 12-24-1888. Adelphia Cemetery, Adelphia, Monmouth County.

ERRICKSON, CHARLES H. 1911. Presbyterian Cemetery, Cream Ridge, Monmouth County.

ERRICKSON, CHARLES P. Pvt, D, 24th NJ Inf, 1912. Soldier's Home Cemetery, Vineland, Cumberland County.

ERRICKSON, FULLER B. Pvt, D, 9th NJ Inf, 1920. Jacobstown Masonic Cemetery, Jacobstown, Burlington County.

ERRICKSON, GEORGE Pvt, I, 25th NJ Inf, 7-27-1919. Tennent Church Cemetery, Tennent, Monmouth County.

ERRICKSON, HORACE G. Pvt, D, 9th NJ Inf, 10-2-1915. Masonic Cemetery, Barnegat, Ocean County.

ERRICKSON, JACOB A. Musc, I, 3rd NJ Militia, 5-19-1871. Mount Hope Presbyterian Cemetery, Lambertville, Hunterdon County.

ERRICKSON, JAMES 1918. Methodist-Episcopal Church Cemetery, South Dennis, Cape May County.

ERRICKSON, JOHN Corp, D, 9th NJ Inf, [Wounded in action.] DoD Unknown. Zion Baptist Church Cemetery, New Egypt, Ocean County.

ERRICKSON, JOSEPH DoD Unknown. Colestown Cemetery, Cherry Hill, Camden County.

ERRICKSON, WILLIAM Pvt, F, 38th NJ Inf, 12-5-1908. Maplewood Cemetery, Freehold, Monmouth County.

ERTELL, EDWARD Pvt, I, 3rd NJ Cav, [Wounded in action.] 2-24-1918. Egg Harbor Cemetery, Egg Harbor, Atlantic County.

ERVEY, JAMES B. Musc, D, 15th NJ Inf, 11-24-1880. Harmony Methodist Church Cemetery, Stillwater, Sussex County.

ERVEY, JOHN N. Pvt, K, 27th NJ Inf, 2-27-1898. Locust Hill Cemetery, Dover, Morris County.

ERVIN, CHRISTOPHER C.P. (see: Irvin, P.C.) Finn's Point National Cemetery, Pennsville, Salem County.

ERVIN, FRANCIS Pvt, A, 3rd NC Inf (US), 8-16-1913. Arlington Cemetery, Kearny, Hudson County.

ERVIN, GEORGE (aka: Irvin, George) Pvt, I, 14th NJ Inf, 1-6-1904. Old Scots Cemetery, Marlboro, Monmouth County.

ERVIN, JACOB Pvt, D, 23rd NJ Inf, 8-18-1903. Riverview Cemetery, Trenton, Mercer County.

ERVIN, SCHUREMAN (aka: Irwin, Schureman) Pvt, A, 28th NJ Inf, DoD Unknown. Old Scots Cemetery, Marlboro, Monmouth County.

ERVING, WILLIAM (aka: Irvin, William) Pvt, K, 14th NJ Inf, 10-8-1892. Old Scots Cemetery, Marlboro, Monmouth County.

ERWIN, JOHN (see: Irwin, John H.) Baptist Cemetery, Burlington, Burlington County.

ERWIN, JOSEPH W. Corp, H, 14th NJ Inf, 4-10-1896. Christ Church Cemetery, Morgan, Middlesex County.

ERWIN, SAMUEL Pvt, A, 39th NJ Inf, 7-31-1869. Fairmount Cemetery, Newark, Essex County.

ERWIN, WILLIAM E. Pvt, B, 28th NJ Inf, 7-14-1921. New Camden Cemetery, Camden, Camden County.

Our Brothers Gone Before

ESCHER, FRANZ Pvt, K, 3rd NJ Inf, 6-6-1879. Fairmount Cemetery, Newark, Essex County.
ESIBILL, HERCULES Fireman, U.S. Navy, USS Princeton, 1884. United Methodist Church Cemetery, Willow Grove, Salem County.
ESKEW, JAMES M. Pvt, H, 42nd MS Inf (CSA), 12-3-1863. Finn's Point National Cemetery, Pennsville, Salem County.
ESLER, JOHN K. Pvt, K, 3rd PA Cav, 4-21-1918. Evergreen Cemetery, Camden, Camden County.
ESLER, THEODORE Corp, E, 8th NY Militia, 12-5-1908. Arlington Cemetery, Kearny, Hudson County.
ESLER, WILLIAM Corp, K, 30th NJ Inf, 1-5-1905. Cedar Hill Cemetery, East Millstone, Somerset County.
ESLICK, JOHN Pvt, C, 10th NJ Inf, 3-28-1917. Baptist Church Cemetery, Jacobstown, Burlington County.
ESPENSHADE, WILLIAM Pvt, E, 4th NJ Inf, 8-31-1876. Riverside Cemetery, Riverside, Burlington County.
ESPIE, GEORGE (see: Yorkston, George E.) Laurel Grove Cemetery, Totowa, Passaic County.
ESSER, JACOB Pvt, E, 2nd NJ Inf, 7-23-1889. Woodland Cemetery, Newark, Essex County.
ESSERT, HUBERT Pvt, A, 68th NY Inf, 10-11-1891. Flower Hill Cemetery, North Bergen, Hudson County.
ESSEX, DAVID Pvt, A, 2nd NJ Inf, 3-20-1927. Woodland Cemetery, Newark, Essex County.
ESSEX, EDWARD Pvt, A, 2nd NJ Inf, 3-21-1902. Fairmount Cemetery, Newark, Essex County.
ESTABROOK, HORATIO J. Sgt, C, 184th NY Inf, 9-19-1916. Bayview-New York Bay Cemetery, Jersey City, Hudson County.
ESTELL, BENJAMIN H. 1st Sgt, K, 5th NJ Inf, [Died at Washington, DC.] 5-19-1862. Old Baptist Cemetery, Freehold, Monmouth County.
ESTELL, BRITTON C. Pvt, A, 38th NJ Inf, 8-6-1909. Methodist Cemetery, Southard, Monmouth County.
ESTELL, JOHN (see: Estile, John B.) Vail Presbyterian Cemetery, Parsippany, Morris County.
ESTELL, JOHN (see: Estile, John W.) Vail Presbyterian Cemetery, Parsippany, Morris County.
ESTELL, JOHN B. Pvt, K, 29th NJ Inf, 8-17-1896. Lakewood-Hope Cemetery, Lakewood, Ocean County.
ESTELL*, JOHN S. 1st Cl Fireman, U.S. Navy, USS Minnesota, 2-28-1911. Methodist Cemetery, Southard, Monmouth County.
ESTELL, JOSEPH Q. Pvt, K, 29th NJ Inf, 2-15-1908. Ardena Baptist Church Cemetery, Adelphia, Monmouth County.
ESTELL, MATHIAS BARCALOW Pvt, C, 10th NJ Inf, 1-19-1913. Robbins-Covell Hill Cemetery, Upper Freehold, Monmouth County.
ESTELL, THOMAS H. 1st Sgt, K, 5th NJ Inf, [Died of disease at Georgetown, DC.] 2-3-1862. Old Baptist Cemetery, Freehold, Monmouth County.
ESTELL, WILLIAM T. Pvt, H, 1st NJ Cav, [Died of typhoid at Georgetown, DC.] 10-19-1861. Methodist Church Cemetery, Harmony, Ocean County.
ESTELLE, WILLIAM V. Wagoner, H, 29th NJ Inf, DoD Unknown. Methodist-Episcopal Cemetery, Glendola, Monmouth County.
ESTEN, GEORGE S. 1st Lt, G, 27th NJ Inf, 4-23-1899. Boonton Cemetery, Boonton, Morris County.
ESTEP, E. Pvt, F, 7th VA Inf (CSA), 4-11-1865. Finn's Point National Cemetery, Pennsville, Salem County.

New Jersey Civil War Burials

ESTERBROOK, EDWARD M. Musc, 1st ME Cav Band 12-24-1903. Evergreen Cemetery, Hillside, Union County.

ESTES, BENJAMIN L. Pvt, F, 13th AL Inf (CSA), [Wounded 5-3-1863 at Chancellorsville, VA. Captured 7-1-1863 at Gettysburg, PA.] 2-12-1864. Finn's Point National Cemetery, Pennsville, Salem County.

ESTES*, H. Pvt, F, 13th AL Inf (CSA), [Captured 7-1-1863 at Gettysburg, PA.] 9-9-1863. Finn's Point National Cemetery, Pennsville, Salem County.

ESTES, JOHN A. Pvt, E, Letcher's Bttn VA Inf (CSA), 12-9-1864. Finn's Point National Cemetery, Pennsville, Salem County.

ESTES, MILES H. Pvt, A, 10th Confederate States Cav (CSA), 4-10-1864. Finn's Point National Cemetery, Pennsville, Salem County.

ESTES*, MILO D. Pvt, F, 1st NY Mounted Rifles, 6-11-1917. Laurel Grove Cemetery, Totowa, Passaic County.

ESTES, MOSES E. Pvt, A, 10th TN Cav (CSA), 5-19-1864. Finn's Point National Cemetery, Pennsville, Salem County.

ESTILE, ALEXANDER L. Pvt, C, 23rd NJ Inf, 6-23-1864. Baptist/St. Andrew's Cemetery, Mount Holly, Burlington County.

ESTILE, DANIEL Pvt, C, 15th NJ Inf, [Died of typhoid at Brandy Station, VA.] 12-28-1863. Vail Presbyterian Cemetery, Parsippany, Morris County.

ESTILE, JOHN B. (aka: Estell, John) Pvt, K, 29th NJ Inf, DoD Unknown. Vail Presbyterian Cemetery, Parsippany, Morris County.

ESTILE, JOHN W. (aka: Estell, John) Pvt, Btty E, 1st NJ Light Art, 12-13-1863. Vail Presbyterian Cemetery, Parsippany, Morris County.

ESTILL, CHARLES H. Sgt, C, 23rd NJ Inf, 3-14-1914. Baptist/St. Andrew's Cemetery, Mount Holly, Burlington County.

ESTILL, H. Capt, Subsistence Dept (CSA) 4-26-1865. Finn's Point National Cemetery, Pennsville, Salem County.

ESTILL, WILLIAM F. Pvt, A, 38th NJ Inf, 11-11-1887. Methodist Cemetery, Cassville, Ocean County.

ESTILOW, BENJAMIN Pvt, I, 9th NJ Inf, 3-4-1885. Methodist-Episcopal Cemetery, Burlington, Burlington County.

ESTILOW, BENJAMIN DoD Unknown. Baptist Cemetery, Burlington, Burlington County.

ESTLACK, FRANKLIN (see: Eastlack, Franklin) Mount Pleasant Cemetery, Millville, Cumberland County.

ESTLACK, JOHN P. (see: Eastlack, John P.) Methodist Cemetery, Mantua, Gloucester County.

ESTLACK, JOSEPH F. (aka: Eastlack, Josiah) Corp, E, 1st NJ Cav, 7-14-1916. 1st United Methodist Church Cemetery, Salem, Salem County.

ESTLOW, JACOB Pvt, A, 6th U.S. Cav, [Wounded in action.] 1- -1896. Presbyterian Church Cemetery, Mays Landing, Atlantic County.

ESTLOW, JAMES L. Pvt, A, 3rd NJ Inf, 6-23-1917. Oddfellows Cemetery, Burlington, Burlington County.

ESTWORTHY, WILLIAM Pvt, G, 23rd NJ Inf, 12-15-1899. Monument Cemetery, Edgewater Park, Burlington County.

ETCHELL, SAMUEL H. Sgt, D, 1st NJ Cav, 4-17-1896. Cedar Lawn Cemetery, Paterson, Passaic County.

ETHERINGTON, JOSEPH O. Principal Musc, 111th PA Inf 4-28-1911. Presbyterian Church Cemetery, Bridgeton, Cumberland County.

ETIER, WILLIAM Pvt, K, 12th LA Inf (CSA), [Captured 5-16-1863 at Champion Hill, MS.] 6-19-1863. Finn's Point National Cemetery, Pennsville, Salem County.

ETSELL, LEWIS Pvt, E, 27th NJ Inf, 11-28-1926. Evergreen Cemetery, Morristown, Morris County.

Our Brothers Gone Before

ETTENGER, ISAAC A. (aka: Ettenger, Isacher) Pvt, K, 4th NJ Militia, 10-29-1862. Methodist-Episcopal Cemetery, Burlington, Burlington County.

ETTENGER, ISACHER (see: Ettenger, Isaac A.) Methodist-Episcopal Cemetery, Burlington, Burlington County.

ETTENGER, JOSEPH Pvt, I, 70th NY Inf, 3-23-1921. Cedar Lawn Cemetery, Paterson, Passaic County.

ETTER, DAVID C. Corp, G, 188th PA Inf, 2-12-1917. Old Camden Cemetery, Camden, Camden County.

EUKERS, GEORGE (see: Eukers, Jacob) Cedar Lawn Cemetery, Paterson, Passaic County.

EUKERS, JACOB (aka: Eukers, George) Pvt, K, 13th NJ Inf, 11-22-1869. Cedar Lawn Cemetery, Paterson, Passaic County.

EVAN, CARLTON 1906. Colestown Cemetery, Cherry Hill, Camden County.

EVANS, A. Pvt, C, 22nd VA Inf (CSA), 8-27-1864. Finn's Point National Cemetery, Pennsville, Salem County.

EVANS*, ALBERT W. Pvt, B, 54th NY Inf, 3-5-1908. Bayview-New York Bay Cemetery, Jersey City, Hudson County.

EVANS, BENJAMIN J. Pvt, I, 12th NY State Militia, 4-23-1902. Holy Name Cemetery, Jersey City, Hudson County.

EVANS, CHARLES H. 1923. Atlantic City Cemetery, Pleasantville, Atlantic County.

EVANS, CHARLES W. 1st Sgt, H, 27th IA Inf, 1921. Brookside Cemetery, Englewood, Bergen County.

EVANS*, DAVID S. Pvt, Btty E, 1st NJ Light Art, 12-24-1887. Jersey City Cemetery, Jersey City, Hudson County.

EVANS, GEORGE Pvt, Btty L, 2nd PA Heavy Art, [Died at Fort Delaware.] 7-17-1862. Finn's Point National Cemetery, Pennsville, Salem County.

EVANS, GEORGE Pvt, H, 21st NJ Inf, 6-18-1913. Greenwood Cemetery, Hamilton, Mercer County.

EVANS*, GEORGE H. Corp, H, 39th NJ Inf, 11-2-1899. Vail Presbyterian Cemetery, Parsippany, Morris County.

EVANS, J. STOKES DoD Unknown. Colestown Cemetery, Cherry Hill, Camden County.

EVANS, JACOB Pvt, B, 23rd U.S. CT, 8-11-1916. Riverview Cemetery, Trenton, Mercer County.

EVANS, JAMES Pvt, I, 2nd DC Inf, 11-7-1870. Chestnut Cemetery, Dover, Morris County.

EVANS, JAMES A. Pvt, D, 23rd NJ Inf, 5-30-1912. Methodist-Episcopal Cemetery, Pointville, Burlington County.

EVANS, JAMES ROBERT Musc, H, 62nd NY Inf, [Awarded the Medal of Honor.] 12-27-1918. 1st Reformed Church Cemetery, Pompton Plains, Morris County.

EVANS, JOHN Pvt, D, 1st NJ Cav, 11-3-1903. Baptist Church Cemetery, Haddonfield, Camden County.

EVANS, JOHN 12-9-1905. New Camden Cemetery, Camden, Camden County.

EVANS, JOHN Pvt, F, 99th PA Inf, [Wounded 11-7-1863 at Kellys Ford, VA.] 12-18-1897. Evergreen Cemetery, Camden, Camden County.

EVANS, JOHN Pvt, F, 155th NY Inf, 6-23-1892. Siloam Cemetery, Vineland, Cumberland County.

EVANS, JOHN Pvt, G, 1st NJ Militia, 4-27-1897. Fairmount Cemetery, Newark, Essex County.

EVANS, JOHN Corp, E, 12th NJ Inf, 6-11-1902. Woodland Cemetery, Newark, Essex County.

EVANS, JOHN 3-23-1900. Van Liew Cemetery, North Brunswick, Middlesex County.

EVANS, JOHN C. Pvt, D, 9th NY Inf, 4-18-1902. Flower Hill Cemetery, North Bergen, Hudson County.

EVANS, JOHN C. Pvt, A, 6th AL Inf (CSA), [Captured 7-3-1863 at Gettysburg, PA.] 9-29-1863. Finn's Point National Cemetery, Pennsville, Salem County.

EVANS, JOHN D. 1st Sgt, G, 8th NJ Inf, [Killed in action near Cold Harbor, VA.] 5-31-1864. Evergreen Cemetery, Morristown, Morris County.
EVANS, JOHN E. Pvt, F, 33rd NJ Inf, 12-8-1873. Van Liew Cemetery, North Brunswick, Middlesex County.
EVANS, JOHN H. Pvt, B, 35th NJ Inf, 11-17-1901. Evergreen Cemetery, Camden, Camden County.
EVANS, JOHN (JR.) Capt, E, 4th NJ Inf, 4-24-1897. Fairmount Cemetery, Newark, Essex County.
EVANS, JOHN W. Pvt, C, 2nd NJ Militia, 1909. Head of River Church Cemetery, Head of River, Atlantic County.
EVANS*, JONATHAN B. Sgt, D, 10th NJ Inf, 12-10-1915. Harleigh Cemetery, Camden, Camden County.
EVANS, JOSEPH Corp, K, 21st NJ Inf, 12-6-1886. Atlantic Reformed Cemetery, Colts Neck, Monmouth County.
EVANS, JOSEPH B. Corp, H, 5th NC Inf (CSA), [Captured 7-1-1863 at Gettysburg, PA. Died of smallpox.] 10-18-1863. Finn's Point National Cemetery, Pennsville, Salem County.
EVANS, JOSEPH H. Pvt, I, 68th PA Inf, 12-15-1896. Siloam Cemetery, Vineland, Cumberland County.
EVANS, JUDSON J. Pvt, D, 31st PA Militia, 1-3-1904. Friendship United Methodist Church Cemetery, Landisville, Atlantic County.
EVANS, JULIUS H. Pvt, A, 6th AL Inf (CSA), [Captured 5-13-1862 at Fair Oaks, VA.] 6-28-1862. Finn's Point National Cemetery, Pennsville, Salem County.
EVANS, LEMUEL E. Pvt, I, 2nd NJ Inf, 4-30-1925. Cedar Lawn Cemetery, Paterson, Passaic County.
EVANS, LEWIS Pvt, E, 42nd MS Inf (CSA), 12-9-1863. Finn's Point National Cemetery, Pennsville, Salem County.
EVANS, MARY Nurse, DoD Unknown. Methodist Church Cemetery, Pemberton, Burlington County.
EVANS, RACEY Pvt, G, 9th NJ Inf, 10-5-1930. Evergreen Cemetery, Hillside, Union County.
EVANS, THOMAS J. Pvt, D, 11th MS Inf (CSA), 1-21-1864. Finn's Point National Cemetery, Pennsville, Salem County.
EVANS, THOMAS (JR.) Pvt, C, 24th NJ Inf, 3-19-1900. Mount Pleasant Cemetery, Millville, Cumberland County.
EVANS, THOMAS M. Pvt, Btty H, 2nd PA Heavy Art, 10-22-1904. Berlin Cemetery, Berlin, Camden County.
EVANS, WALTER J. Pvt, G, 2nd NJ Militia, 4-8-1879. Cedar Lawn Cemetery, Paterson, Passaic County.
EVANS, WILLIAM C. Pvt, L, 1st NJ Cav, 11-26-1909. Harleigh Cemetery, Camden, Camden County.
EVANS, WILLIAM H. Pvt, E, 23rd NJ Inf, 9-5-1905. Methodist Church Cemetery, Pemberton, Burlington County.
EVANS, WILLIAM H.H. Pvt, F, 22nd NJ Inf, 8-28-1920. Presbyterian Church Cemetery, Titusville, Mercer County.
EVANS, WILLIAM JAMES Capt, B, 7th NJ Inf, [Cenotaph. Killed in action at Spotsylvania CH, VA.] 5-12-1864. Cedar Lawn Cemetery, Paterson, Passaic County.
EVANS, WILSON E. Pvt, B, 56th VA Inf (CSA), [Captured 7-3-1863 at Gettysburg, PA. Died of fever.] 11-4-1863. Finn's Point National Cemetery, Pennsville, Salem County.
EVARD, SAMUEL A. Pvt, I, 25th NJ Inf, 9-21-1867. Presbyterian Church Cemetery, Absecon, Atlantic County.

Our Brothers Gone Before

EVARTS, THOMAS M. (aka: Everetts, Thomas) Pvt, Btty B, 1st NJ Light Art, [Died of diarrhea at Fairfax, VA.] 10-17-1862. Boonton Cemetery, Boonton, Morris County.

EVATON, WILLIAM (see: Evertsen, William H.) Evergreen Cemetery, Hillside, Union County.

EVERDING, HENRY Sgt, G, 84th NY Inf, 7-6-1905. Fairview Cemetery, Fairview, Monmouth County.

EVERED*, JOSEPH G. Sgt, A, 5th MI Inf, 3-12-1911. Evergreen Cemetery, Camden, Camden County.

EVERETT, DAVID A. Pvt, A, 31st NJ Inf, 3-31-1905. Fairview Cemetery, Westfield, Union County.

EVERETT, DAVID R. Pvt, I, 7th NJ Inf, [Died of fever at Whitehouse, VA.] 5-26-1862. Branchville Cemetery, Branchville, Sussex County.

EVERETT, GERSHOM L. Pvt, F, 31st NJ Inf, 7-1-1911. Union Cemetery, Frenchtown, Hunterdon County.

EVERETT, JAMES M. Pvt, I, 10th NJ Inf, 2-27-1909. Arlington Cemetery, Kearny, Hudson County.

EVERETT, JOHN 1881. Harlingen Cemetery, Belle Mead, Somerset County.

EVERETT, JOSEPH __, D, 24th PA __, 8-2-1895. Free Burying Ground Cemetery, Alloway, Salem County.

EVERETT, JOSEPH C. Pvt, A, 15th NJ Inf, [Killed in action at Spotsylvania CH, VA.] 5-12-1864. Union Cemetery, Milford, Hunterdon County.

EVERETT*, LUCIUS T. Pvt, A, 11th NH Inf, 6-1-1914. Bayview-New York Bay Cemetery, Jersey City, Hudson County.

EVERETT, MARTIN Pvt, B, 124th NY Inf, [Wounded 5-12-1864 at Spotsylvania CH, VA.] 4-8-1895. Ponds Church Cemetery, Oakland, Bergen County.

EVERETT, RICHARD G. Pvt, G, 30th NJ Inf, [Died of exposure at Washington, DC.] 6-29-1863. Barber's Burying Ground Cemetery, Dilts Corner, Hunterdon County.

EVERETT, SEYMOUR V.D. Pvt, A, 37th NJ Inf, 2-9-1899. Rosedale Cemetery, Orange, Essex County.

EVERETT*, WALTER 1st Lt, H, 5th MA Militia, 9-5-1906. Cedar Lawn Cemetery, Paterson, Passaic County.

EVERETT, WILLIAM Pvt, A, 35th NJ Inf, 12-16-1901. Sergeant's Hill Cemetery, Sand Brook, Hunterdon County.

EVERETT, WILLIAM T. Pvt, B, 10th NJ Inf, 9-23-1910. Methodist Church Cemetery, Mount Bethel, Warren County.

EVERETTS, THOMAS (see: Evarts, Thomas M.) Boonton Cemetery, Boonton, Morris County.

EVERGAM, WILLIAM H. Pvt, B, 1st MD Cav (CSA), 8-29-1863. Finn's Point National Cemetery, Pennsville, Salem County.

EVERHAM, BENJAMIN S. Pvt, F, 23rd NJ Inf, 10-3-1913. Brotherhood Cemetery, Hainesport, Burlington County.

EVERHAM, GILBERT M. Pvt, D, 23rd NJ Inf, 9-29-1920. Riverview Cemetery, Trenton, Mercer County.

EVERHAM*, WILLIAM C. Corp, I, 23rd NJ Inf, [Died of typhoid at Portsmouth Grove, RI.] 1-26-1863. Evergreen Cemetery, Lumberton, Burlington County.

EVERHART, DAVID Pvt, B, 60th (Crawford's) TN Mtd Inf (CSA), [Captured 5-17-1863 at Big Black River Bridge, MS.] 7-23-1863. Finn's Point National Cemetery, Pennsville, Salem County.

EVERINGHAM, ALEXANDER L. Sgt, H, 14th NJ Inf, [Wounded in action.] 2-12-1909. Brainerd Cemetery, Cranbury, Middlesex County.

EVERINGHAM, BENJAMIN A. Pvt, H, 22nd NJ Inf, 1928. Mount Prospect Cemetery, Neptune, Monmouth County.

New Jersey Civil War Burials

EVERINGHAM, CHARLES M. Pvt, H, 14th NJ Inf, 4-30-1894. Windsor Burial Grounds Cemetery, East Windsor, Mercer County.

EVERINGHAM, CHARLES V. Pvt, B, 28th NJ Inf, 8-7-1923. Brainerd Cemetery, Cranbury, Middlesex County.

EVERINGHAM, DANIEL M. Pvt, G, 12th NJ Inf, 11-16-1910. Trinity Episcopal Church Cemetery, Delran, Burlington County.

EVERINGHAM, LEWIS J. Pvt, I, 14th NJ Inf, 5-15-1890. Holcomb-Riverview Cemetery, Lambertville, Hunterdon County.

EVERINGHAM, PETER Pvt, C, 29th NJ Inf, 2-23-1903. Fernwood Cemetery, Jamesburg, Middlesex County.

EVERINGHAM, WILLIAM H. Pvt, A, 6th NJ Inf, 4-27-1885. Mercer Cemetery, Trenton, Mercer County.

EVERITT, EDWARD C. 9-27-1870. Branchville Cemetery, Branchville, Sussex County.

EVERITT, GILBERT L. Pvt, F, 38th NJ Inf, 7-18-1896. Bethlehem Presbyterian Church Cemetery, Grandin, Hunterdon County.

EVERITT, JAMES MILTON Sgt Maj, 10th NJ Inf 1916. Union Cemetery, Washington, Morris County.

EVERLACKNER*, MICHAEL Pvt, D, 34th NJ Inf, DoD Unknown. Mount Pleasant Cemetery, Millville, Cumberland County.

EVERLE, JOHN (see: Eberle, John) Woodland Cemetery, Newark, Essex County.

EVERLY, EVAN Pvt, E, 4th OH Inf, [Died at Newark, NJ.] 12-10-1862. Fairmount Cemetery, Newark, Essex County.

EVERLY, STEPHEN Pvt, I, 26th NJ Inf, 3-29-1927. Fairmount Cemetery, Chatham, Morris County.

EVERMAN, DANIEL Pvt, M, 1st NJ Cav, DoD Unknown. Hardyston Cemetery, North Church, Sussex County.

EVERMAN, JOHN Pvt, K, 8th NJ Inf, DoD Unknown. Presbyterian Church Cemetery, Rockaway, Morris County.

EVERMAN, JOSEPH Pvt, K, 1st NJ Cav, 10-2-1918. Presbyterian Church Cemetery, Rockaway, Morris County.

EVERMAN, WILLIAM Pvt, M, 1st NJ Cav, 3-22-1898. Hardyston Cemetery, North Church, Sussex County.

EVERMENT*, HIRAM Pvt, K, 1st NJ Cav, 1910. Boonton Cemetery, Boonton, Morris County.

EVERNHAM, AARON J. Pvt, H, 138th PA Inf, 11-13-1919. Riverview Cemetery, Trenton, Mercer County.

EVERSFIELD, CHARLES Surg, U.S. Navy, 10-5-1873. Mount Pleasant Cemetery, Newark, Essex County.

EVERSON, ADOLPH Pvt, B, 12th CT Inf, 5-17-1898. Rosedale Cemetery, Orange, Essex County.

EVERSON, AUSTIN C. Musc, B, 88th NY Inf, 3-13-1890. Rahway Cemetery, Rahway, Union County.

EVERSON, BENJAMIN Pvt, D, 22nd NJ Inf, [Died of typhoid at Belle Plain, VA.] 2-23-1863. Union Cemetery, Wyckoff, Bergen County.

EVERSON, EDWARD Pvt, E, 8th NY State Militia, 1-20-1937. Grove Church Cemetery, North Bergen, Hudson County.

EVERSON, GEORGE O. Musc, F, 80th NY Inf, 2-13-1914. Arlington Cemetery, Kearny, Hudson County.

EVERSON, JEREMIAH (aka: Avison, Jeremiah) Pvt, A, 25th NJ Inf, 9-21-1897. Hackensack Cemetery, Hackensack, Bergen County.

EVERSON, MATTHIAS Pvt, C, 7th NJ Inf, DoD Unknown. Laurel Grove Cemetery, Totowa, Passaic County.

EVERSON, PETER (see: Everson, Willis) Macphelah Cemetery, North Bergen, Hudson County.

Our Brothers Gone Before

EVERSON, WILLIS (aka: Everson, Peter) Pvt, H, 80th NY Inf, DoD Unknown. Macphelah Cemetery, North Bergen, Hudson County.
EVERTSEN, WILLIAM H. (aka: Evaton, William) Corp, H, 1st NY Cav, 8-9-1869. Evergreen Cemetery, Hillside, Union County.
EVERTSON, ABRAM S. (see: Evertson, Edward S.) Fairmount Cemetery, Newark, Essex County.
EVERTSON, EDWARD S. (aka: Evertson, Abram S.) Pvt, H, 30th NJ Inf, 4-27-1902. Fairmount Cemetery, Newark, Essex County.
EVERTSON, HENRY H. Pvt, Btty A, 13th NY Heavy Art, 2-17-1916. Arlington Cemetery, Kearny, Hudson County.
EWALD*, FREDERICK Pvt, 31st NY Ind Btty 2-1-1899. Holy Sepulchre Cemetery, East Orange, Essex County.
EWALD, HENRY Corp, E, 14th NJ Inf, 6-22-1872. St. Rose of Lima Cemetery, Freehold, Monmouth County.
EWAN, JAMES (aka: Ewing, James) Corp, H, 24th NJ Inf, 3-17-1907. United Methodist Church Cemetery, Woodruff, Cumberland County.
EWAN, JOB Pvt, I, 23rd NJ Inf, 12-19-1918. Harleigh Cemetery, Camden, Camden County.
EWEN, SAMUEL M. Wagoner, G, 28th NJ Inf, 1916. Manahath Cemetery, Glassboro, Gloucester County.
EWING, FRANKLIN R. Pvt, I, 38th NJ Inf, 12-8-1895. Methodist Church Cemetery, Pleasant Grove, Ocean County.
EWING, ISAAC DoD Unknown. Methodist Church Cemetery, Pleasant Grove, Ocean County.
EWING, JAMES Pvt, F, 25th NJ Inf, 3-19-1916. Presbyterian Church Cemetery, Cold Spring, Cape May County.
EWING, JAMES (see: Ewan, James) United Methodist Church Cemetery, Woodruff, Cumberland County.
EWING, JOHN A. Pvt, D, 38th NJ Inf, 1903. New Presbyterian Church Cemetery, Daretown, Salem County.
EWING, JOSEPH F. Sgt, K, 9th NJ Inf, 1898. Ardena Baptist Church Cemetery, Adelphia, Monmouth County.
EWING, JOSEPH O. Pvt, M, 2nd NJ Cav, 1-18-1868. Lower Amwell Cemetery, Headquarters, Hunterdon County.
EWING, JUSTUS E. 5-7-1907. Glenwood Cemetery, West Long Branch, Monmouth County.
EWING, LIVINGSTONE (aka: Livingston, Ewing) Pvt, F, 25th NJ Inf, 1897. Presbyterian Church Cemetery, Cold Spring, Cape May County.
EWING, ROBERT P. Sgt, A, 20th IL Inf, 9-19-1867. Presbyterian Church Cemetery, Cold Spring, Cape May County.
EWING, SAMUEL W. Pvt, E, 99th PA Inf, 6-10-1913. New Camden Cemetery, Camden, Camden County.
EWING, THOMAS Capt, I, 3rd PA Cav, 5-16-1895. Overlook Cemetery, Bridgeton, Cumberland County.
EWING, WILLIAM BELFORD Sgt, E, 1st NJ Cav, [Died of disease.] 11-15-1862. Presbyterian Church Cemetery, Greenwich, Cumberland County.
EXTELL, HENRY Pvt, I, 25th U.S. CT, 3-20-1916. Arlington Cemetery, Kearny, Hudson County.
EYER, ELIJAH H. Pvt, F, 11th OH Inf, 5-6-1898. Fairview Cemetery, Columbia, Warren County.
EYRING, WILLIAM C. 9-9-1872. Reformed Church Cemetery, South Branch, Somerset County.
EYTH*, AUGUSTUS FREDERICK Pvt, F, 128th NY Inf, 10-22-1897. Grove Church Cemetery, North Bergen, Hudson County.

New Jersey Civil War Burials

EYTNIGE, SOLOMON 3-24-1905. Bayview-New York Bay Cemetery, Jersey City, Hudson County.
EZELL, JOHN Pvt, G, 144th IL Inf, 12-3-1909. Holy Name Cemetery, Jersey City, Hudson County.
FAAS, WILLIAM Pvt, F, 6th MD Inf, 11-1-1919. Mount Hebron Cemetery, Montclair, Essex County.
FABER, CHRISTIAN Pvt, H, 17th CT Inf, [Wounded 5-2-1863 at Chancellorsville, VA.] 3-26-1876. Palisade Cemetery, North Bergen, Hudson County.
FABRIEN, WALTER Seaman, U.S. Navy, USS Tacony, [Wounded in action.] 1898. Atlantic City Cemetery, Pleasantville, Atlantic County.
FACEMIRE, ABRAHAM (see: Myers, Abraham) Overlook Cemetery, Bridgeton, Cumberland County.
FACEMIRE, CHARLES H. Pvt, U.S. Marine Corps, 1923. Mount Pleasant Cemetery, Millville, Cumberland County.
FACEMIRE, HOSEA 1-29-1875. Methodist-Episcopal Cemetery, Olivet, Salem County.
FACEMYRE, JONATHAN H. Pvt, F, 3rd NJ Inf, 3-8-1911. Presbyterian Church Cemetery, Bridgeton, Cumberland County.
FACEMYRE, REUBEN B. Pvt, F, 11th MA Inf, [Wounded 7-2-1863 at Gettysburg, PA. and 11-27-1863 at Mine Run, VA.] 3-26-1874. Church of Christ Cemetery, Fairton, Cumberland County.
FACHS, JOSEPH (see: Fuchs, Joseph) Holy Sepulchre Cemetery, Totowa, Passaic County.
FACKENTHALL, JAMES C. Bvt Capt, E, 41st PA Inf, 3-17-1913. Atlantic City Cemetery, Pleasantville, Atlantic County.
FACKLER, CHARLES F. 1st Sgt, I, 24th NJ Inf, 3-14-1926. Greenwood Cemetery, Hamilton, Mercer County.
FACZEK, CHARLES A. Corp, G, 9th NJ Inf, 8-13-1870. Evergreen Cemetery, Hillside, Union County.
FADALEN, CHARLES P. (aka: Fidelin, Charles) Corp, C, 18th PA Inf, DoD Unknown. New Camden Cemetery, Camden, Camden County.
FADDE*, JOHN HENRY (aka: Fatti, John) Sgt, G, 9th NJ Inf, 9-23-1919. Mount Olivet Cemetery, Newark, Essex County.
FADELEY, ABRAHAM D. Pvt, D, 136th VA Militia (CSA), 1-2-1881. Old Camden Cemetery, Camden, Camden County.
FADER, JOSEPH (see: Frader, Joseph) Greenwood Cemetery, Hamilton, Mercer County.
FADER, LEWIS Pvt, G, 21st NJ Inf, 4-18-1895. Fairmount Cemetery, Newark, Essex County.
FAERBER, FRANCIS Pvt, D, 7th NJ Inf, 12-23-1917. Evergreen Cemetery, Hillside, Union County.
FAGAN, JOHN Pvt, B, 35th NJ Inf, 1897. Mount Olivet Cemetery, Newark, Essex County.
FAGAN, JOHN Pvt, I, 31st NJ Inf, 1906. Mansfield/Washington Cemetery, Washington, Warren County.
FAGAN*, JOHN B. (aka: Eagan, John) Pvt, B, 1st NJ Cav, 1-23-1923. Holy Name Cemetery, Jersey City, Hudson County.
FAGAN, JOHN EDWARD Pvt, D, 8th NJ Inf, 4-23-1901. Evergreen Cemetery, Camden, Camden County.
FAGAN, PATRICK Pvt, I, 26th NJ Inf, 12-30-1875. Holy Sepulchre Cemetery, East Orange, Essex County.
FAGAN, PETER Pvt, A, 28th PA Inf, 5-24-1901. Holy Sepulchre Cemetery, East Orange, Essex County.
FAGAN, THOMAS 2nd Lt, G, 7th NJ Inf, 7-12-1892. Phillipsburg Old Catholic Cemetery, Phillipsburg, Warren County.
FAGAN, WILLIAM Pvt, G, 39th NJ Inf, 2-24-1897. Holy Sepulchre Cemetery, East Orange, Essex County.

Our Brothers Gone Before

FAGAN, WILLIAM H. 6-6-1908. Methodist Church Cemetery, Groveville, Mercer County.
FAGINS, WILLIAM Pvt, I, 14th NJ Inf, 5-22-1907. Riverview Cemetery, Trenton, Mercer County.
FAGOLI, LAWRENCE Landsman, U.S. Navy, USS Ino, 12-22-1935. Riverview Cemetery, Trenton, Mercer County.
FAGOT, ISAAC M. __, __, 9th __ Inf, DoD Unknown. Bayview-New York Bay Cemetery, Jersey City, Hudson County.
FAHR, JULIUS Pvt, I, 7th NY Vet Inf, 11-27-1907. Bayview-New York Bay Cemetery, Jersey City, Hudson County.
FAHR, WILLIAM JOHN Pvt, H, 6th NY State Militia, 1-3-1890. Bayview-New York Bay Cemetery, Jersey City, Hudson County.
FAHRION, JOHN DoD Unknown. Old Camden Cemetery, Camden, Camden County.
FAIL, NATHANIEL Pvt, C, 23rd AL Inf (CSA), 7-7-1863. Finn's Point National Cemetery, Pennsville, Salem County.
FAIN, PATRICK Pvt, K, 8th NJ Inf, DoD Unknown. Holy Sepulchre Cemetery, Totowa, Passaic County.
FAIR, THOMAS Capt, I, 147th PA Inf, 1-4-1908. Greenwood Cemetery, Pleasantville, Atlantic County.
FAIRBAIRN, JAMES B. Sgt, C, 10th NJ Inf, 1922. Evergreen Cemetery, Lumberton, Burlington County.
FAIRBANKS, CHARLES H. 11-3-1913. Atlantic City Cemetery, Pleasantville, Atlantic County.
FAIRBANKS, CHARLES L. Pvt, 7th NY Ind Btty 4-16-1894. Arlington Cemetery, Kearny, Hudson County.
FAIRBROTHERS, JOHN Pvt, B, 25th NJ Inf, 11-15-1907. Salem Cemetery, Pleasantville, Atlantic County.
FAIRCHILD, EDMUND Pvt, K, 2nd NJ Inf, 12-2-1917. Rosedale Cemetery, Orange, Essex County.
FAIRCHILD, FREDERICK Pvt, F, 26th NJ Inf, 12-17-1903. Bloomfield Cemetery, Bloomfield, Essex County.
FAIRCHILD*, HENRY C. Pvt, B, 3rd VT Inf, [Wounded in action.] 3-12-1920. New Presbyterian Cemetery, Hanover, Morris County.
FAIRCHILD, J. EDSON Pvt, F, 26th NJ Inf, 1-9-1876. Bloomfield Cemetery, Bloomfield, Essex County.
FAIRCHILD*, JAMES (JR.) Pvt, E, 13th NJ Inf, 1884. Evergreen Cemetery, Morristown, Morris County.
FAIRCHILD, JESSE L. Pvt, M, 1st NJ Cav, 12-21-1897. Greenmount Cemetery, Hammonton, Atlantic County.
FAIRCHILD, JOHN Farrier, Btty B, 1st NJ Light Art, 2-6-1885. Fairmount Cemetery, Newark, Essex County.
FAIRCHILD, JOHN P. Pvt, H, 13th NJ Inf, 11-24-1916. Evergreen Cemetery, Hillside, Union County.
FAIRCHILD, JOSEPH R. Pvt, F, 13th NJ Inf, 10-8-1893. Fairmount Cemetery, Newark, Essex County.
FAIRCHILD, LUCIEN H. Pvt, M, 1st NJ Cav, 3-29-1904. Greenmount Cemetery, Hammonton, Atlantic County.
FAIRCHILD, NELSON H. Pvt, E, 115th NY Inf, 2-5-1898. Flower Hill Cemetery, North Bergen, Hudson County.
FAIRCHILD, WILLIAM Pvt, B, 37th NJ Inf, 1-31-1890. Fairmount Cemetery, Newark, Essex County.
FAIRCLO, CHARLES M. 1st Lt, B, 15th NJ Inf, 8-16-1895. Union Cemetery, Washington, Morris County.

New Jersey Civil War Burials

FAIRCLOUGH, HENRY Pvt, G, 80th NY Inf, 10-12-1918. Cedar Lawn Cemetery, Paterson, Passaic County.

FAIRFAX, J.F. Pvt, H, 15th VA Cav (CSA), 3-15-1865. Finn's Point National Cemetery, Pennsville, Salem County.

FAIRGRIEVE, GEORGE B. Pvt, H, 14th NJ Inf, 1-10-1886. Fernwood Cemetery, Jamesburg, Middlesex County.

FAIRLIE, GEORGE (aka: Farley, George) Pvt, G, 37th NJ Inf, 2-16-1930. Mount Pleasant Cemetery, Newark, Essex County.

FAIRSERVICE, THOMAS Sgt, K, 13th NH Inf, 9-11-1887. Arlington Cemetery, Kearny, Hudson County.

FAIRWEATHER, ROBERT O. Musc, U.S. Navy, DoD Unknown. Macphelah Cemetery, North Bergen, Hudson County.

FAITOUTE, JOHN 1864. Mount Pleasant Cemetery, Newark, Essex County.

FAITOUTE, JOSHUA F. Pvt, D, 13th NJ Inf, 3-21-1892. Mount Pleasant Cemetery, Newark, Essex County.

FAITOUTE, WILLIAM J. 7-6-1921. Mount Pleasant Cemetery, Newark, Essex County.

FALCONER, SYLVESTER Pvt, D, 33rd NJ Inf, 4-20-1929. Midvale Cemetery, Midvale, Passaic County.

FALES, PROSPER E. Pvt, 2nd Btty, VT Light Art, 1-17-1877. Fairmount Cemetery, Newark, Essex County.

FALK, JACOB Musc, B, 39th NJ Inf, 2-28-1873. St. Mary's Cemetery, East Orange, Essex County.

FALKENBURG, THOMAS B. (aka: Folkenburg, Thomas J.) Pvt, B, 17th IL Inf, 1901. Oddfellows Cemetery, Burlington, Burlington County.

FALKENBURG, WILLIAM HENRY H. Pvt, A, 23rd NJ Inf, 1924. Oddfellows Cemetery, Burlington, Burlington County.

FALKENBURGH, HAYS B. Pvt, A, 23rd NJ Inf, 11-18-1907. Oddfellows Cemetery, Burlington, Burlington County.

FALKINBURG, JAMES T. Pvt, B, 73rd PA Inf, 9-19-1927. Greenwood Cemetery, Tuckerton, Ocean County.

FALKINBURGH, THOMAS J. Capt, B, 17th IL Inf, 3-8-1873. Cedar Grove Cemetery, Waretown, Ocean County.

FALKNER, ALLEN (see: Faulkner, Allen) Finn's Point National Cemetery, Pennsville, Salem County.

FALLER, GEORGE Pvt, E, 13th NJ Inf, [Wounded in action.] 3-28-1900. Rosedale Cemetery, Orange, Essex County.

FALLON, JOHN Corp, F, 37th NY Inf, 6-24-1903. Holy Name Cemetery, Jersey City, Hudson County.

FALLON, JOHN Corp, I, 31st NJ Inf, 7-12-1906. Rosedale Cemetery, Orange, Essex County.

FALLON, MATTHEW C. (aka: Falyn, Matthew) Pvt, C, 71st NY Inf, DoD Unknown. Fairview Cemetery, Westfield, Union County.

FALLON*, THOMAS TIMOTHY Pvt, K, 37th NY Inf, [Awarded the Medal of Honor.] 8-29-1916. St. Rose of Lima Cemetery, Freehold, Monmouth County.

FALYN, MATTHEW (see: Fallon, Matthew C.) Fairview Cemetery, Westfield, Union County.

FANLEY, MICHAEL Corp, G, 10th NJ Inf, [Wounded 6-4-1864 at Cold Harbor, VA.] 8-29-1913. St. Mary's Cemetery, Hamilton, Mercer County.

FANNING, EDWARD (see: Fanning, Edwin) Holy Sepulchre Cemetery, Totowa, Passaic County.

FANNING, EDWIN (aka: Fanning, Edward) 1st Lt, G, 7th NJ Inf, DoD Unknown. Holy Sepulchre Cemetery, Totowa, Passaic County.

FANSHAW, EDWARD A. 6-2-1916. Cedar Hill Cemetery, Hightstown, Mercer County.

Our Brothers Gone Before

FANTICK, WILLIAM Pvt, Btty C, 1st NJ Light Art, 7-11-1892. Fairmount Cemetery, Newark, Essex County.

FARLEE, JOSEPH Q. 1-12-1903. Old Rock Church Cemetery, West Amwell, Hunterdon County.

FARLEY, ANDREW Seaman, U.S. Navy, USS Ottowa, 9-13-1927. Holy Sepulchre Cemetery, East Orange, Essex County.

FARLEY, BERNARD Seaman, U.S. Navy, 1-26-1931. Holy Sepulchre Cemetery, East Orange, Essex County.

FARLEY, CHARLES J. Capt, C, 5th NY Cav, [Wounded in action 10-19-1863 and 8-25-1864.] 7-7-1888. Macphelah Cemetery, North Bergen, Hudson County.

FARLEY, FREDERICK A. Corp, F, 37th MA Inf, [Wounded 8-21-1864 at Charlestown, VA.] DoD Unknown. Elmwood Cemetery, New Brunswick, Middlesex County.

FARLEY, GEORGE (see: Fairlie, George) Mount Pleasant Cemetery, Newark, Essex County.

FARLEY, GEORGE E. Corp, H, 14th OH Inf, DoD Unknown. Arlington Cemetery, Kearny, Hudson County.

FARLEY, JAMES Pvt, H, 1st NJ Inf, 1-1-1896. Holy Sepulchre Cemetery, East Orange, Essex County.

FARLEY, JOB Pvt, B, 38th NJ Inf, 8-14-1923. Old Rock Church Cemetery, West Amwell, Hunterdon County.

FARLEY, JOHN J. Seaman, U.S. Navy, DoD Unknown. Holy Sepulchre Cemetery, East Orange, Essex County.

FARLEY, MATTHEW Landsman, U.S. Navy, USS Princeton, DoD Unknown. Holy Sepulchre Cemetery, East Orange, Essex County.

FARLEY, MATTHEW Pvt, B, 79th NY Inf, DoD Unknown. Holy Sepulchre Cemetery, East Orange, Essex County.

FARLEY, MICHAEL Seaman, U.S. Navy, DoD Unknown. Holy Sepulchre Cemetery, East Orange, Essex County.

FARLEY, NICHOLAS Seaman, U.S. Navy, DoD Unknown. Holy Sepulchre Cemetery, East Orange, Essex County.

FARLEY, OWEN Pvt, E, 9th NJ Inf, 8-29-1925. Holy Sepulchre Cemetery, East Orange, Essex County.

FARLEY, PATRICK Pvt, K, 23rd NJ Inf, [Wounded 5-3-1863 at Salem Heights, VA.] 12-8-1907. New 1st Methodist Meeting House Cemetery, Manahawkin, Ocean County.

FARLEY, PATRICK J. Pvt, G, 39th NJ Inf, 3-21-1914. Holy Sepulchre Cemetery, East Orange, Essex County.

FARLEY*, PHILIP (aka: Paurling, Philip) Pvt, 15th NY Ind Btty DoD Unknown. Holy Sepulchre Cemetery, East Orange, Essex County.

FARLEY, PHILIP Pvt, K, 11th NJ Inf, 10-9-1883. Evergreen Cemetery, Morristown, Morris County.

FARLEY, PHILIP (see: Farrell, Philip) Mount Pleasant Cemetery, Newark, Essex County.

FARLEY, PHILIP L. Pvt, D, 10th NY Inf, 11-11-1916. Hackensack Cemetery, Hackensack, Bergen County.

FARLEY, PHILIP L. 1st Sgt, E, 176th NY Inf, DoD Unknown. St. John's Evangelical Church Cemetery, Orange, Essex County.

FARLEY, THOMAS Pvt, B, 4th NY Inf, DoD Unknown. Bayview-New York Bay Cemetery, Jersey City, Hudson County.

FARLEY, THOMAS Pvt, I, 38th NJ Inf, 12-27-1923. Riverview Cemetery, Trenton, Mercer County.

FARLEY, WILLIAM (SR.) DoD Unknown. Chestnut Grove Cemetery, Elmer, Salem County.

FARLOW, JOHN Pvt, K, 13th NJ Inf, 3-5-1893. Cedar Lawn Cemetery, Paterson, Passaic County.

New Jersey Civil War Burials

FARLOW*, THOMAS (aka: Jones, Thomas) Pvt, G, 12th NH Inf, [Wounded 5-14-1864 at Relay House, Fort Stevens, VA.] 1915. Presbyterian Church Cemetery, Rockaway, Morris County.

FARMER, ARNOLD V. 2-8-1911. Van Liew Cemetery, North Brunswick, Middlesex County.

FARMER, CHARLES H. Pvt, B, 15th MA Inf, 7-27-1915. Valleau Cemetery, Ridgewood, Bergen County.

FARMER, DAVID Pvt, C, 127th U.S. CT, 10-30-1917. Arlington Cemetery, Kearny, Hudson County.

FARMER, DAVID J. 5-6-1899. Evergreen Cemetery, Hillside, Union County.

FARMER, GEORGE Corp, B, 54th MA Inf, 7-31-1892. Mount Peace Cemetery, Lawnside, Camden County.

FARMER, IRVIN Seaman, U.S. Navy, 8-29-1902. Slauson Cemetery, Wantage, Sussex County.

FARMER, PATRICK Pvt, B, 28th MA Inf, [Died of disease at Beverly, NJ.] 10-8-1864. Beverly National Cemetery, Edgewater Park, Burlington County.

FARNER*, CHARLES P. Musc, G, 8th NJ Inf, 7- -1927. St. Mary's Episcopal Church Cemetery, Burlington, Burlington County.

FARNEY, JOSIAH S. Pvt, K, 4th NJ Inf, 11-1-1895. 1st United Methodist Church Cemetery, Salem, Salem County.

FARNSWORTH, RICHARD P. 2-1-1924. Zion Methodist Church Cemetery, Porchtown, Gloucester County.

FARQUIER, WILLIAM (see: Jarquin, Wilhelm) Fairmount Cemetery, Newark, Essex County.

FARR, PETER 4-25-1880. St. Mary's Cemetery, Wharton, Morris County.

FARR, STEWART A. Pvt, D, 71st NY Inf, 12-30-1907. Chestnut Cemetery, Dover, Morris County.

FARRAND, EDGAR S. Pvt, C, 15th NJ Inf, [Killed in action at Spotsylvania CH, VA.] 5-12-1864. United Methodist Church Cemetery, Rockaway Valley, Morris County.

FARRAND, SILAS F. Sgt, Btty B, 1st NJ Light Art, 7-9-1893. Bloomfield Cemetery, Bloomfield, Essex County.

FARRELL, DAVID B. Pvt, C, 72nd NY Inf, [Wounded 7-2-1862 at Malvern Hill, VA.] 10- -1890. Laurel Grove Cemetery, Totowa, Passaic County.

FARRELL, DENNIS Pvt, B, 15th KS Cav, 6- -1911. Holy Sepulchre Cemetery, Totowa, Passaic County.

FARRELL, JAMES Pvt, C, 6th NJ Inf, 6-15-1873. Holy Name Cemetery, Jersey City, Hudson County.

FARRELL, JAMES Pvt, U.S. Marine Corps, DoD Unknown. Holy Sepulchre Cemetery, East Orange, Essex County.

FARRELL, JAMES Pvt, G, 39th NJ Inf, DoD Unknown. Holy Sepulchre Cemetery, East Orange, Essex County.

FARRELL, JAMES E. Wagoner, F, 2nd NJ Inf, 2-11-1910. Bloomfield Cemetery, Bloomfield, Essex County.

FARRELL, JOHN Pvt, D, 25th U.S. CT, 7-23-1911. Mount Peace Cemetery, Lawnside, Camden County.

FARRELL, JOHN 2nd Lt, C, 37th NJ Inf, 6-18-1909. Riverview Cemetery, Trenton, Mercer County.

FARRELL*, JOHN Pvt, 3rd NY Ind Btty [Wounded in action 8-28-1864.] 9-15-1919. St. John's Evangelical Church Cemetery, Orange, Essex County.

FARRELL, JOHN J. Seaman, U.S. Navy, 11-17-1915. St. John's Evangelical Church Cemetery, Orange, Essex County.

FARRELL, JOHN J. (SR.) Pvt, 3rd NY Ind Btty [Wounded in action 8-28-1864.] 8-10-1937. Holy Name Cemetery, Jersey City, Hudson County.

Our Brothers Gone Before

FARRELL, LAWRENCE 1st Lt, H, 35th NJ Inf, 11-10-1905. St. John's Cemetery, Hamilton, Mercer County.

FARRELL, NICHOLAS HUGH Sgt, B, 69th PA Inf, [Wounded 12-13-62 at Fredericksburg, VA., 7-3-63 at Gettysburg, PA., and 5-6-64 at Wilderness, VA.] 11-4-1893. Holy Sepulchre Cemetery, East Orange, Essex County.

FARRELL, PATRICK 7-31-1875. Holy Name Cemetery, Jersey City, Hudson County.

FARRELL, PATRICK Pvt, H, 22nd NY Cav, 10-30-1889. Holy Sepulchre Cemetery, East Orange, Essex County.

FARRELL, PHILIP (aka: Farley, Philip) Pvt, F, 72nd NY Inf, 9-21-1862. Mount Pleasant Cemetery, Newark, Essex County.

FARRELL, ROBERT 1st Lt, H, 1st MI Sharpshooters, 7-8-1910. Mercer Cemetery, Trenton, Mercer County.

FARRELL, SAMUEL A. Corp, B, 4th NJ Inf, 1-15-1869. Riverview Cemetery, Trenton, Mercer County.

FARRELL, TERRENCE Pvt, C, 1st NJ Cav, 8-8-1876. Baptist/St. Andrew's Cemetery, Mount Holly, Burlington County.

FARRELL, THOMAS Musc, 2nd NJ Inf Band 12-21-1880. Fairmount Cemetery, Newark, Essex County.

FARRELL*, WILLIAM Pvt, K, 9th MA Inf, 1-30-1897. Holy Sepulchre Cemetery, East Orange, Essex County.

FARRELL, WILLIAM Pvt, C, 2nd NJ Inf, 9-28-1878. Holy Sepulchre Cemetery, East Orange, Essex County.

FARRELLY, WILLIAM S. Pvt, B, 72nd PA Inf, 12-15-1901. Evergreen Cemetery, Camden, Camden County.

FARRIER, GEORGE H. Capt, A, 21st NJ Inf, 4-26-1895. Arlington Cemetery, Kearny, Hudson County.

FARRIER, HENRY E. 2nd Lt, A, 21st NJ Inf, 1-24-1891. Bayview-New York Bay Cemetery, Jersey City, Hudson County.

FARRIER, JAMES B. Pvt, A, 21st NJ Inf, 8-14-1897. Bayview-New York Bay Cemetery, Jersey City, Hudson County.

FARRIER*, WILLIAM W. Pvt, G, 10th NJ Inf, 11-7-1898. Bayview-New York Bay Cemetery, Jersey City, Hudson County.

FARRINGTON, ABRAM B. Pvt, D, 6th CA Inf, 3-28-1905. Mount Prospect Cemetery, Neptune, Monmouth County.

FARRINGTON, STEPHEN R. Pvt, H, 128th NY Inf, 2-23-1906. Arlington Cemetery, Kearny, Hudson County.

FARRINGTON, WILLIAM F. Pvt, C, 37th NJ Inf, 1896. 1st Baptist Church Cemetery, Pedricktown, Salem County.

FARROATT*, THOMAS G. Actg 3rd Asst Eng, U.S. Navy, USS Larkspur, 2-10-1867. Alpine Cemetery, Perth Amboy, Middlesex County.

FARROR, HENRY (see: Hogarth, William H.F.) Laurel Grove Cemetery, Totowa, Passaic County.

FARROW, CHARLES __, K, 185th NY Inf, 2-19-1901. Bayview-New York Bay Cemetery, Jersey City, Hudson County.

FARROW, EDWIN T. 10-3-1862. Methodist Church Cemetery, Pemberton, Burlington County.

FARROW, FRANCIS L. Pvt, G, 6th NJ Inf, [Died of heart disease at Alexandria, VA.] 10-11-1862. Fairview Cemetery, Cape May Court House, Cape May County.

FARROW*, GEORGE W. Sgt, G, 6th NJ Inf, 2-1-1891. Methodist Church Cemetery, Pemberton, Burlington County.

FARROW, JOHN 8-4-1869. Fairview Cemetery, Cape May Court House, Cape May County.

FARROW, JOHN Corp, A, 26th NJ Inf, DoD Unknown. Mount Pleasant Cemetery, Newark, Essex County.

New Jersey Civil War Burials

FARROW, JOHN D. 5-1-1874. Methodist Church Cemetery, Pemberton, Burlington County.

FARROW, LEONIDAS H. Corp, H, 37th NJ Inf, 1-31-1892. Methodist Church Cemetery, Pemberton, Burlington County.

FARROW, ROBERT Pvt, C, 14th NJ Inf, [Killed in action at Locust Grove, VA.] 11-27-1863. Presbyterian Cemetery, Springfield, Union County.

FARROW*, WILLIAM B. Pvt, D, 39th NJ Inf, 10-12-1867. Methodist Church Cemetery, Pemberton, Burlington County.

FARRY, NELSON (aka: Frarey, Nelson) Pvt, M, 2nd NJ Cav, 1939. Locust Hill Cemetery, Dover, Morris County.

FASH, FRANCIS B. Musc, D, 15th NY Eng, 4-28-1883. St. Joseph's Cemetery, Washington, Warren County.

FASHOLZ, JOSEPH (see: Fasoli, Jacob) Woodland Cemetery, Newark, Essex County.

FASOLI, JACOB (aka: Fasholz, Joseph) Pvt, D, 73rd PA Inf, 4-20-1873. Woodland Cemetery, Newark, Essex County.

FASS, LUDWIG (aka: Fuss, Louis) Pvt, G, 7th NY Inf, 5-8-1906. Grove Church Cemetery, North Bergen, Hudson County.

FASS, MARTIN F. 10-21-1891. Flower Hill Cemetery, North Bergen, Hudson County.

FASSE, HEINRICH (see: Freese, Henry) Atlantic City Cemetery, Pleasantville, Atlantic County.

FASSELL, HENRY Landsman, U.S. Navy, USS North Carolina, DoD Unknown. Prospect Hill Cemetery, Caldwell, Essex County.

FASSETT, CHARLES (aka: Fossill, Charles) Pvt, B, 127th U.S. CT, 8-10-1910. Fairmount Cemetery, Newark, Essex County.

FASTNACHT, JACOB Pvt, E, 2nd NJ Inf, 11-4-1894. Fairmount Cemetery, Newark, Essex County.

FATE, JAMES Seaman, U.S. Navy, 1-13-1898. St. Peter's Cemetery, New Brunswick, Middlesex County.

FATE, PETER Pvt, B, 28th NJ Inf, 2-11-1914. Elmwood Cemetery, New Brunswick, Middlesex County.

FATTI, JOHN (see: Fadde, John Henry) Mount Olivet Cemetery, Newark, Essex County.

FAUBELL, MARTIN (aka: Faubil, Martin) Pvt, H, 27th PA Inf, 9-22-1900. 1st Methodist Church Cemetery, Williamstown, Gloucester County.

FAUBIAN, ABRAM 1-12-1892. Sandy Ridge Cemetery, Sandy Ridge, Hunterdon County.

FAUBIL, MARTIN (see: Faubell, Martin) 1st Methodist Church Cemetery, Williamstown, Gloucester County.

FAUCET, BENJAMIN F. Landsman, U.S. Navy, 10-25-1921. Mount Zion Methodist Church Cemetery, Lawnside, Camden County.

FAUCETT, JOHN FRANK Pvt, M, 15th PA Cav, 8-31-1904. Lake Park Cemetery, Swedesboro, Gloucester County.

FAUGHAN, JOHN (aka: Faughy, John) Pvt, B, 9th NJ Inf, DoD Unknown. Phillipsburg Old Catholic Cemetery, Phillipsburg, Warren County.

FAUGHY, JOHN (see: Faughan, John) Phillipsburg Old Catholic Cemetery, Phillipsburg, Warren County.

FAULK*, HENRY Landsman, U.S. Navy, USS Restless, 2-17-1924. Fairmount Cemetery, Newark, Essex County.

FAULKNER, ALLEN (aka: Falkner, Allen) Pvt, G, 23rd NC Inf (CSA), [Captured 7-1-1863 at Gettysburg, PA. Died of lung inflammation.] 12-31-1863. Finn's Point National Cemetery, Pennsville, Salem County.

FAULKNER, DAVID Pvt, G, 52nd NY Inf, 4-10-1911. Presbyterian Church Cemetery, Woodbridge, Middlesex County.

FAULKNER, JAMES N. Pvt, D, 13th OH Cav, 5-23-1928. Laurel Grove Cemetery, Totowa, Passaic County.

Our Brothers Gone Before

FAULKS, WILLIAM Pvt, H, 2nd NJ Inf, [Wounded at Gaines' Mill, VA.] 1-3-1929. Hillside Cemetery, Scotch Plains, Union County.
FAUNCE, ANSIL E. Pvt, B, 2nd NJ Inf, 3-19-1912. Salem Cemetery, Pleasantville, Atlantic County.
FAUNCE, WILLIAM DoD Unknown. Morgan Cemetery, Cinnaminson, Burlington County.
FAUNCE, WILLIAM ARMSTRONG Pvt, K, 23rd NJ Inf, 9-17-1890. Baptist Church Cemetery, Haddonfield, Camden County.
FAUROAT, SIMEON (aka: Ferote, Simeon) Pvt, D, 28th NJ Inf, 11-15-1898. Fairmount Cemetery, Newark, Essex County.
FAUROAT, WILLIAM S. (aka: Ferote, William) Pvt, D, 28th NJ Inf, 9-5-1916. All Saints Episcopal Church Cemetery, Navesink, Monmouth County.
FAUSSETT*, JOHN B. 1st Lt, C, 11th NJ Inf, 3-8-1899. Mercer Cemetery, Trenton, Mercer County.
FAUSSETT, ORRIN B. 1st Lt, C, 11th NJ Inf, 8-14-1881. Mercer Cemetery, Trenton, Mercer County.
FAUTH, BERNHARDT Pvt, A, 75th PA Inf, 3-8-1908. Riverview Cemetery, Trenton, Mercer County.
FAUVER, ROBERT A. Pvt, A, 46th IL Inf, 6-3-1907. 1st United Methodist Church Cemetery, Bridgeton, Cumberland County.
FAUX*, TILLMAN Pvt, E, 210th PA Inf, 1-29-1898. Fairmount Cemetery, Newark, Essex County.
FAY, CHARLES M. Paymaster's Clerk, U.S. Navy, USS Brooklyn, 4- -1868. Evergreen Cemetery, Hillside, Union County.
FAY, JAMES J. Landsman, U.S. Navy, USS Princeton, 9-7-1928. St. John's Cemetery, Hamilton, Mercer County.
FAY*, JULIUS AUGUSTUS (JR.) Bvt Lt Col, 40th NJ Inf 9-26-1891. Evergreen Cemetery, Hillside, Union County.
FAY, ROBERT Pvt, A, 29th NJ Inf, 3-26-1902. Old 1st Methodist Church Cemetery, West Long Branch, Monmouth County.
FAY*, WALDO L. Pvt, E, 2nd MA Cav, DoD Unknown. Rosedale Cemetery, Linden, Union County.
FAYLES, DAVID L. Corp, A, 21st U.S. VRC, 2-20-1896. Evergreen Cemetery, Camden, Camden County.
FEAREY, JABEZ Pvt, K, 2nd NJ Inf, [Wounded 9-14-1862 at Crampton's Pass, MD.] 11-16-1890. Fairmount Cemetery, Newark, Essex County.
FEARN, FREDERICK H. Seaman, U.S. Navy, 3-14-1904. Riverview Cemetery, Trenton, Mercer County.
FEARN, JOHN 1st Cl Boy, U.S. Navy, 6-17-1921. Baptist Church Cemetery, Haddonfield, Camden County.
FEASLER, JOSEPH A. Pvt, H, 27th NJ Inf, 7-29-1870. Old Beemer Church Cemetery, Roys, Sussex County.
FEASLER, JOSEPH J. Pvt, E, 9th NJ Inf, 11-28-1865. VanHorn Cemetery, Sparta, Sussex County.
FEASTER, JOHN Pvt, H, 1st NJ Cav, 1-27-1920. St. Peter's Cemetery, New Brunswick, Middlesex County.
FEASTER, JOHN 4-7-1892. Elmwood Cemetery, New Brunswick, Middlesex County.
FEATHERS, HENRY R. Pvt, H, 169th NY Inf, DoD Unknown. Mount Olivet Cemetery, Newark, Essex County.
FEATHERSTONE, PETER Seaman, U.S. Navy, 12-25-1882. Evergreen Cemetery, Hillside, Union County.
FECHNER, WILLIAM Artificer, D, 1st NY Eng, 8-15-1899. Hillside Cemetery, Scotch Plains, Union County.

New Jersey Civil War Burials

FECHT, FRANZ Pvt, A, 4th NJ Inf, 2-4-1908. Old St. Mary's Cemetery, Gloucester City, Camden County.

FEDIRHELLER, WILLIAM H. Pvt, E, 20th PA Inf, DoD Unknown. Monument Cemetery, Edgewater Park, Burlington County.

FEE, JAMES Pvt, A, 12th NJ Inf, 8-6-1908. St. John's Cemetery, Hamilton, Mercer County.

FEE, PATRICK Pvt, B, 6th NJ Inf, 9-21-1883. St. John's Cemetery, Hamilton, Mercer County.

FEE, THOMAS Pvt, B, 1st NJ Inf, DoD Unknown. Princeton Cemetery, Princeton, Mercer County.

FEE, THOMAS (see: Feehan, Thomas) St. Paul's R.C. Church Cemetery, Princeton, Mercer County.

FEE*, THOMAS J. Bvt 2nd Lt, A, 1st PA Prov Cav, 9-24-1908. Evergreen Cemetery, Hillside, Union County.

FEEDER, HENRY Pvt, K, 7th NJ Inf, 5-15-1872. Fairmount Cemetery, Newark, Essex County.

FEEHAN, THOMAS (aka: Fee, Thomas) Pvt, B, 1st NJ Inf, 1883. St. Paul's R.C. Church Cemetery, Princeton, Mercer County.

FEENEY, BENJAMIN Pvt, G, 7th NJ Inf, 2-28-1911. Holy Sepulchre Cemetery, Totowa, Passaic County.

FEENEY, JAMES Pvt, F, 2nd NJ Inf, 9-23-1892. Holy Sepulchre Cemetery, Totowa, Passaic County.

FEENEY, WILLIAM F. Pvt, B, 5th NY Vet Inf, 7-27-1911. Holy Name Cemetery, Jersey City, Hudson County.

FEENY, PETER 1886. Mount Olivet Cemetery, Fairview, Monmouth County.

FEES, CHARLES J. Pvt, H, 28th NJ Inf, 5-13-1923. New Camden Cemetery, Camden, Camden County.

FEHR, EDWARD Pvt, D, 1st NJ Inf, 1-3-1890. Mansfield/Washington Cemetery, Washington, Warren County.

FEHRING, ALBERT 11-12-1911. Madonna Cemetery, Leonia, Bergen County.

FEIGE, CHARLES Pvt, B, 6th NY Cav, 8-25-1914. Reformed Church Cemetery, Wyckoff, Bergen County.

FEILIO, HENRY C. (aka: Felis, Henry) Pvt, K, 2nd DC Inf, 1-8-1917. Holy Sepulchre Cemetery, Totowa, Passaic County.

FELDBUSCH, JOHN (aka: Feltbush, John) Pvt, E, 39th NJ Inf, 1-4-1878. Woodland Cemetery, Newark, Essex County.

FELDEN, JOHN P. (JR.) (aka: Feldon, John) Pvt, F, 5th PA Cav, DoD Unknown. Old Camden Cemetery, Camden, Camden County.

FELDEN, JOHN P. (SR.) Pvt, G, 6th PA Cav, DoD Unknown. Old Camden Cemetery, Camden, Camden County.

FELDMAN*, CASPAR C. 1st Lt, Btty K, 15th NY Heavy Art, 5-21-1909. Rosedale Cemetery, Orange, Essex County.

FELDMAN, FREDERICK Pvt, D, 4th U.S. Cav, DoD Unknown. Arlington Cemetery, Kearny, Hudson County.

FELDMEYER, GEORGE Pvt, Btty A, 1st NJ Light Art, 3-22-1905. Palisade Cemetery, North Bergen, Hudson County.

FELDOF, PETER 3-1-1922. Holy Name Cemetery, Jersey City, Hudson County.

FELDON, JOHN (see: Felden, John P. (Jr.)) Old Camden Cemetery, Camden, Camden County.

FELDPUSCH, HENRY CONRAD (aka: Veltpush, Henry) Pvt, F, 39th NJ Inf, 8-22-1936. Woodland Cemetery, Newark, Essex County.

FELDTMEYER, HENRY 4-8-1881. Riverview Cemetery, Trenton, Mercer County.

FELGER, ALEXANDER (aka: Fellgar, Alexander) Pvt, D, 15th NY Eng, 5-13-1904. Weehawken Cemetery, North Bergen, Hudson County.

Our Brothers Gone Before

FELGER, FREDERICK 1st Lt, A, 9th NJ Inf, 12-1-1917. Fairmount Cemetery, Newark, Essex County.
FELIS, HENRY (see: Feilio, Henry C.) Holy Sepulchre Cemetery, Totowa, Passaic County.
FELIX, AMBROSE Seaman, U.S. Navy, 9-27-1901. Cedar Lawn Cemetery, Paterson, Passaic County.
FELKER, LOUIS 11-29-1929. Grove Church Cemetery, North Bergen, Hudson County.
FELL, ADAM Pvt, K, 2nd U.S. Inf, 1-30-1904. Bayview-New York Bay Cemetery, Jersey City, Hudson County.
FELL*, JACOB P. Corp, G, 7th NJ Inf, 11-17-1880. Mercer Cemetery, Trenton, Mercer County.
FELL*, JOHN J. Pvt, C, 2nd NJ Inf, 1898. St. John's Evangelical Church Cemetery, Orange, Essex County.
FELL, LAWRENCE Seaman, U.S. Navy, 4-6-1903. St. John's Evangelical Church Cemetery, Orange, Essex County.
FELL*, WILLIAM H. Pvt, Stroud's, Ind PA Cav, 11-17-1919. Methodist Church Cemetery, Titusville, Mercer County.
FELLGAR, ALEXANDER (see: Felger, Alexander) Weehawken Cemetery, North Bergen, Hudson County.
FELLOWS, DANIEL (aka: Fieller, Daniel) Pvt, I, 30th NJ Inf, 1909. Peapack Reformed Church Cemetery, Gladstone, Somerset County.
FELMEY, ALBERT A. (SR.) Pvt, H, 26th PA Inf, 12-7-1901. Mount Pleasant Cemetery, Millville, Cumberland County.
FELMEY, THEODORE A. Pvt, F, 24th NJ Inf, 12-11-1913. Overlook Cemetery, Bridgeton, Cumberland County.
FELMEY, WILLIAM H. Pvt, G, 1st NJ Inf, 1-9-1909. Mount Pleasant Cemetery, Millville, Cumberland County.
FELMLEY, JONATHAN C. 7-23-1865. Reformed Church Cemetery, Pluckemin, Somerset County.
FELSING*, CHARLES Pvt, E, 5th NY National Guard, 10-19-1904. Fairmount Cemetery, Newark, Essex County.
FELTBUSH, JOHN (see: Feldpusch, John) Woodland Cemetery, Newark, Essex County.
FELTER, ALEXANDER Pvt, A, 22nd NJ Inf, 1-23-1890. Woodside Cemetery, Dumont, Bergen County.
FELTEY, JOSEPH Pvt, C, 7th NJ Inf, 1864. Prospect Hill Cemetery, Caldwell, Essex County.
FELTMAN, MICHAEL Pvt, A, 1st DC Inf, 1-20-1910. Eglington Cemetery, Clarksboro, Gloucester County.
FELTON, GEORGE G. Pvt, F, 52nd MA Inf, 7-7-1902. Harleigh Cemetery, Camden, Camden County.
FELTS, CETHE C. Pvt, C, 55th MA Inf, 1896. Memorial Park Cemetery, Gouldtown, Cumberland County.
FELTUS, WILLIAM Pvt, H, 30th NJ Inf, 2-24-1895. Evergreen Cemetery, Hillside, Union County.
FELTY, DAVID R. Seaman, U.S. Navy, USS Clifton, 7-4-1898. Rosedale Cemetery, Orange, Essex County.
FELVER, BENJAMIN Pvt, H, 31st NJ Inf, 9-2-1900. Baptist Church Cemetery, Port Murray, Warren County.
FELVER, CLARK Pvt, B, 31st NJ Inf, 2-20-1921. Mansfield/Washington Cemetery, Washington, Warren County.
FELVER, JOSEPH C. Capt, B, 31st NJ Inf, 7-9-1909. Locust Hill Cemetery, Dover, Morris County.
FELVER, PETER C. Pvt, B, 31st NJ Inf, 12-12-1919. Mansfield/Washington Cemetery, Washington, Warren County.

New Jersey Civil War Burials

FENDRICK*, KILLIAN Pvt, A, 34th NJ Inf, 1877. Presbyterian Church Cemetery, Bridgeton, Cumberland County.

FENIMORE, CHARLES Pvt, E, 6th NJ Inf, 6-22-1932. Bordentown/Old St. Mary's Catholic Cemetery, Bordentown, Burlington County.

FENIMORE, CHARLES (aka: Richardson, Lewis) Pvt, F, 10th NJ Inf, 2-1-1875. Friends Cemetery, Harmersville, Salem County.

FENIMORE, FRANCIS B. Corp, H, 23rd NJ Inf, 2-7-1879. Bordentown/Old St. Mary's Catholic Cemetery, Bordentown, Burlington County.

FENIMORE, GEORGE Pvt, Btty C, 2nd PA Heavy Art, 8-21-1906. Oddfellows Cemetery, Burlington, Burlington County.

FENIMORE, JACOB L. Pvt, U.S. Marine Corps, 1-12-1863. Monument Cemetery, Edgewater Park, Burlington County.

FENIMORE, JOHN W. Pvt, G, 23rd NJ Inf, 12-7-1899. Monument Cemetery, Edgewater Park, Burlington County.

FENIMORE, REUBEN Pvt, I, 82nd PA Inf, 9-12-1901. Baptist Cemetery, Vincentown, Burlington County.

FENIMORE, SAMUEL Pvt, D, 7th WV Cav, 1916. Baptist Church Cemetery, Haddonfield, Camden County.

FENIMORE*, WILLIAM A. Pvt, Btty C, 2nd PA Heavy Art, 3-19-1901. Bordentown/Old St. Mary's Catholic Cemetery, Bordentown, Burlington County.

FENIMORE, WILLIAM T. 2nd Lt, B, 2nd DE Inf, 2-28-1904. Monument Cemetery, Edgewater Park, Burlington County.

FENLE, JOHN (aka: Finley, John) Pvt, F, 24th NJ Inf, 6-30-1905. Soldier's Home Cemetery, Vineland, Cumberland County.

FENLIN, WILLIAM H. 1st Sgt, F, 88th PA Inf, [Wounded 12-13-1862 at Fredericksburg, VA.] 10-9-1922. Fairmount Cemetery, Newark, Essex County.

FENNELL, JAMES H. Pvt, G, 42nd MS Inf (CSA), 10-20-1863. Finn's Point National Cemetery, Pennsville, Salem County.

FENNELL, WILLIAM J. Pvt, D, 54th PA Inf, 1-10-1897. Evergreen Cemetery, Farmingdale, Monmouth County.

FENNEMAN, GEORGE W. (see: Finneman, George W.) Eglington Cemetery, Clarksboro, Gloucester County.

FENNER, AMOS Pvt, E, 30th NJ Inf, 1-7-1922. Reformed Church Cemetery, Pluckemin, Somerset County.

FENNER, JAMES Pvt, M, 5th NY Cav, 1924. Midvale Cemetery, Midvale, Passaic County.

FENNER*, JOHN D. Pvt, G, 48th NY Inf, [Wounded 6-1-1864 at Cold Harbor, VA.] 1900. East Ridgelawn Cemetery, Clifton, Passaic County.

FENNER, SAMUEL J. Sgt, F, 4th NJ Inf, 3-14-1900. Harleigh Cemetery, Camden, Camden County.

FENNER, WILLIAM Pvt, E, 196th PA Inf, 11-24-1934. Riverview Cemetery, Trenton, Mercer County.

FENNERMAN, LEWIS DoD Unknown. Oak Lawn Cemetery, Swedesboro, Gloucester County.

FENNIMORE, JAMES Pvt, Btty H, 1st PA Light Art, 8-8-1914. United Methodist Church Cemetery, Winslow, Camden County.

FENNIMORE, WILLIAM C. 2nd Lt, A, 10th NJ Inf, 12-28-1908. Mount Pleasant Cemetery, Millville, Cumberland County.

FENNING, CHARLES Pvt, F, 21st NJ Inf, 6-15-1910. Flower Hill Cemetery, North Bergen, Hudson County.

FENNON, JAMES (aka: Finnons, James) Pvt, I, 11th NJ Inf, [Wounded 7-2-1863 at Gettysburg, PA.] 2-8-1913. Bordentown/Old St. Mary's Catholic Cemetery, Bordentown, Burlington County.

FENTON*, ANDREW J. Seaman, U.S. Navy, USS Monitor, 4-18-1945. Overlook Cemetery, Bridgeton, Cumberland County.

Our Brothers Gone Before

FENTON*, CHARLES Pvt, A, 38th NJ Inf, 10-15-1914. Fairview Cemetery, Fairview, Monmouth County.

FENTON, CHARLES G. Corp, B, 23rd NJ Inf, 10-18-1907. Bordentown/Old St. Mary's Catholic Cemetery, Bordentown, Burlington County.

FENTON, CLEMENT T. Pvt, B, 23rd NJ Inf, 5-12-1921. Greenwood Cemetery, Hamilton, Mercer County.

FENTON, GEORGE G. Pvt, D, 23rd NJ Inf, 2-19-1915. Riverview Cemetery, Trenton, Mercer County.

FENTON, GEORGE H. Sgt, B, 23rd NJ Inf, 1894. Bordentown/Old St. Mary's Catholic Cemetery, Bordentown, Burlington County.

FENTON*, HENRY Sgt, G, 12th NJ Inf, 1908. New Camden Cemetery, Camden, Camden County.

FENTON, HENRY Pvt, I, 11th NJ Inf, 9-29-1909. Lower Springfield-Copany Meeting House Cemetery, Jacksonville, Burlington County.

FENTON, JAMES S. Pvt, H, 2nd DE Inf, 7-10-1905. St. George's Episcopal Church Cemetery, Pennsville, Salem County.

FENTON, JOHN (aka: Fiulon, John) Pvt, G, 69th NY State Militia, 3-6-1914. St. Peter's Cemetery, New Brunswick, Middlesex County.

FENTON*, JOHN Pvt, E, 2nd NJ Inf, 2-27-1910. Holy Sepulchre Cemetery, Totowa, Passaic County.

FENTON, JOHN Pvt, B, 21st NJ Inf, 10-14-1902. Flower Hill Cemetery, North Bergen, Hudson County.

FENTON, ROBERT 4-3-1927. Flower Hill Cemetery, North Bergen, Hudson County.

FENTON, THOMAS H. Pvt, F, 183rd PA Inf, 8-14-1882. Presbyterian Church Cemetery, Cold Spring, Cape May County.

FENTON, W.W. 3-3-1911. Oddfellows Cemetery, Burlington, Burlington County.

FENWICK, PETER B. Pvt, C, 48th NY Inf, [Cenotaph. Killed in action at Fort Wagner, SC.] 7-18-1863. Cedar Lawn Cemetery, Paterson, Passaic County.

FENWICK, ROBERT (SR.) Asst Surg, 146th NY Inf [Wounded 5-6-1864 at Wilderness, VA.] 4-10-1905. Presbyterian Church Cemetery, Hampton, Hunterdon County.

FERA, HENRY (aka: Ferra, Henry) Sgt Maj, 43rd IL Inf 2-21-1922. Mount Hebron Cemetery, Montclair, Essex County.

FERAT, CHARLES M. (aka: Ferot, Charles M.) Pvt, D, 114th PA Inf, DoD Unknown. Evergreen Cemetery, Camden, Camden County.

FERDON, ABRAHAM Pvt, I, 22nd NJ Inf, 4-2-1914. Old Hook Cemetery, Westwood, Bergen County.

FERDON, WILLIAM Corp, I, 22nd NJ Inf, 6-3-1891. Haring Cemetery, Old Tappan, Bergen County.

FERGUSON, A.I. (see: Fulkerson, A.I. Polk) Finn's Point National Cemetery, Pennsville, Salem County.

FERGUSON, ALEXANDER Pvt, U.S. Marine Corps, 4-2-1904. Cedar Grove Cemetery, Gloucester City, Camden County.

FERGUSON, DAVID Pvt, H, 126th IL Inf, 1-10-1910. Fairview Cemetery, Fairview, Bergen County.

FERGUSON, EDWARD Pvt, D, 28th NJ Inf, 1-8-1921. Elmwood Cemetery, New Brunswick, Middlesex County.

FERGUSON, GEORGE W. Corp, F, 52nd NY Inf, [Wounded 6-1-1862 at Fair Oaks, VA.] 4-13-1896. Harleigh Cemetery, Camden, Camden County.

FERGUSON, JAMES 1882. Fairview Cemetery, Westfield, Union County.

FERGUSON, JAMES G. Pvt, F, 43rd U.S. CT, 1905. Princeton Cemetery, Princeton, Mercer County.

FERGUSON, JAMES M. (aka: Ferguson, Joseph M.) Corp, C, 43rd GA Inf (CSA), [Captured 5-16-1863 at Baker's Creek, MS.] 7-23-1863. Finn's Point National Cemetery, Pennsville, Salem County.

New Jersey Civil War Burials

FERGUSON, JAMES S. Pvt, A, 90th NY Inf, 10-19-1893. Elmwood Cemetery, New Brunswick, Middlesex County.
FERGUSON, JOHN Seaman, U.S. Navy, 6-4-1912. Arlington Cemetery, Kearny, Hudson County.
FERGUSON*, JOHN SHAY Pvt, E, 7th NJ Inf, 6-4-1906. Phillipsburg Cemetery, Phillipsburg, Warren County.
FERGUSON, JOSEPH M. (see: Ferguson, James M.) Finn's Point National Cemetery, Pennsville, Salem County.
FERGUSON, JOSEPH W. Pvt, A, 1st NJ Militia, 2-1-1910. Evergreen Cemetery, Hillside, Union County.
FERGUSON, PHILIP T. Pvt, F, 1st NJ Inf, 5-28-1876. Pitman Methodist-Episcopal Cemetery, New Brunswick, Middlesex County.
FERGUSON*, WILLIAM Pvt, I, 8th NJ Inf, 3-29-1919. Van Liew Cemetery, North Brunswick, Middlesex County.
FERGUSON, WILLIAM Seaman, U.S. Navy, [Mississippi Squadron.] 3-16-1912. Laurel Grove Cemetery, Totowa, Passaic County.
FERGUSON*, WILLIAM G. Hosp Steward, 2nd NJ Cav 4-27-1901. Princeton Cemetery, Princeton, Mercer County.
FERGUSON, WILLIAM H. Pvt, B, 23rd NJ Inf, 8-3-1889. Flower Hill Cemetery, North Bergen, Hudson County.
FERKEL, HENRY Pvt, C, 6th U.S. Cav, 9-14-1896. Woodland Cemetery, Newark, Essex County.
FEROT, CHARLES M. (see: Ferat, Charles M.) Evergreen Cemetery, Camden, Camden County.
FEROTE, SIMEON (see: Fauroat, Simeon) Fairmount Cemetery, Newark, Essex County.
FEROTE, WILLIAM (see: Fauroat, William S.) All Saints Episcopal Church Cemetery, Navesink, Monmouth County.
FERRA, HENRY (see: Fera, Henry) Mount Hebron Cemetery, Montclair, Essex County.
FERRELL, JAMES W. Pvt, A, 55th NC Inf (CSA), [Captured 7-1-1863 at Gettysburg, PA.] 10-6-1863. Finn's Point National Cemetery, Pennsville, Salem County.
FERRELL, WILLIAM H. Corp, A, 90th NY Inf, 7-21-1921. Cedar Lawn Cemetery, Paterson, Passaic County.
FERRILL, JAMES Pvt, K, 24th NJ Inf, 11-2-1897. Eglington Cemetery, Clarksboro, Gloucester County.
FERRIS, EDWARD 3-19-1866. Old 1st Reformed Church Cemetery, Hackensack, Bergen County.
FERRIS, JOHN D. Actg 3rd Asst Eng, U.S. Navy, USS Mistletoe, 3-23-1867. Hillside Cemetery, Madison, Morris County.
FERRIS, JOHN W. Capt, U.S. Volunteers, [Acting Quartermaster.] 11-26-1897. Fairmount Cemetery, Newark, Essex County.
FERRIS, JOSIAH F. Musc, 72nd PA Inf Band 7-3-1903. Arlington Cemetery, Pennsauken, Camden County.
FERRIS, NATHANIEL Pvt, Unassigned, 10th U.S. CT, 1-23-1882. Locust Hill Cemetery, Trenton, Mercer County.
FERRIS, PATRICK Pvt, K, 2nd NJ Cav, 4-12-1912. St. Peter's Cemetery, New Brunswick, Middlesex County.
FERRIS*, SAMUEL Pvt, B, 35th NJ Inf, 1-30-1899. Frankford Plains Cemetery, Frankford, Sussex County.
FERRIS, WILLIS J. (see: Passwater, William J.) New Episcopal Church Cemetery, Swedesboro, Gloucester County.
FERRY, DANIEL Pvt, D, 2nd U.S. Inf, 5-10-1902. Old 1st Methodist Church Cemetery, West Long Branch, Monmouth County.
FERRY, JOHN B. (aka: Fery, John) Musc, D, Dale's Bttn PA Cav, 12-20-1897. Holy Name Cemetery, Jersey City, Hudson County.

Our Brothers Gone Before

FERRY, JOHN LEONARD Fireman, U.S. Navy, USS Ohio, DoD Unknown. Bordentown/Old St. Mary's Catholic Cemetery, Bordentown, Burlington County.

FERRY, LUTHER (see: Fountain, Luther S.) Rosedale Cemetery, Orange, Essex County.

FERY, JOHN (see: Ferry, John B.) Holy Name Cemetery, Jersey City, Hudson County.

FESMIER, CHARLES S. Pvt, H, 109th PA Inf, 5-14-1893. Beverly National Cemetery, Edgewater Park, Burlington County.

FESQ*, FRANK E. (aka: Fesq, Franz) Pvt, A, 40th NJ Inf, [Awarded the Medal of Honor.] 5-6-1920. Rosedale Cemetery, Orange, Essex County.

FESQ, FRANZ (see: Fesq, Frank E.) Rosedale Cemetery, Orange, Essex County.

FESSLER, JOSEPH Pvt, A, 20th NY Inf, 4-10-1897. Fairmount Cemetery, Newark, Essex County.

FESTER, ROBERT P. Pvt, G, 12th NY Inf, 6-24-1908. Woodland Cemetery, Newark, Essex County.

FETLER, DANIEL T. Pvt, G, 38th NJ Inf, 12-17-1877. Willow Grove Cemetery, New Brunswick, Middlesex County.

FETROW, WILLIAM F. Com Sgt, C, 5th PA Cav, [Wounded 5-7-1864 at Stony Creek, VA.] DoD Unknown. Baptist Church Cemetery, Blackwood, Camden County.

FETTER, THOMAS M. Capt, K, 4th NJ Inf, 12-22-1887. Evergreen Cemetery, Camden, Camden County.

FETTERS, CHARLES Pvt, B, 59th PA Militia, 6-6-1889. Old Camden Cemetery, Camden, Camden County.

FETTERS, JOHN A. Pvt, I, 24th NJ Inf, 7-31-1905. Baptist Cemetery, Salem, Salem County.

FEUERIGAL, WILLIAM (aka: Feuerriegel, William) Musc, C, 7th NJ Inf, 10-6-1887. Fairmount Cemetery, Newark, Essex County.

FEUERRIEGEL, WILLIAM (see: Feuerigal, William) Fairmount Cemetery, Newark, Essex County.

FEW, JOSEPH D. Pvt, H, 1st NJ Militia, DoD Unknown. Mount Pleasant Cemetery, Newark, Essex County.

FEW, JOSEPH M. Pvt, G, 42nd MS Inf (CSA), 3-2-1864. Finn's Point National Cemetery, Pennsville, Salem County.

FEWKES, GEORGE Pvt, I, 1st NJ Inf, 7-12-1903. Bayview-New York Bay Cemetery, Jersey City, Hudson County.

FEWREY, THOMAS Corp, D, 1st MI Cav, 11-17-1916. St. Rose of Lima Cemetery, Millburn, Essex County.

FICHE, CHARLES (see: Flattich, Charles) Hoboken Cemetery, North Bergen, Hudson County.

FICHER, FRANTZ (see: Fischer, Frank) Evergreen Cemetery, Hillside, Union County.

FICK, JACOB Seaman, U.S. Navy, USS Galatea, 4-24-1901. Bayview-New York Bay Cemetery, Jersey City, Hudson County.

FICKE, FRANK (aka: Fieckle, Frank) Pvt, K, 45th NY Inf, 3-23-1926. Flower Hill Cemetery, North Bergen, Hudson County.

FICKE, JOSEPH (see: Ficker, Theodore) Grove Church Cemetery, North Bergen, Hudson County.

FICKER, THEODORE (aka: Ficke, Joseph) Pvt, [Haddington Hospital, Philadelphia, PA.] 12-6-1900. Grove Church Cemetery, North Bergen, Hudson County.

FICKERT, FREDERICK T. Pvt, H, 39th NJ Inf, 2-28-1888. Fairmount Cemetery, Newark, Essex County.

FIDDLER, JONATHAN G. Corp, F, 25th NJ Inf, 2-12-1874. Methodist-Episcopal Church Cemetery, South Dennis, Cape May County.

FIDELIN, CHARLES (see: Fadalen, Charles P.) New Camden Cemetery, Camden, Camden County.

FIECKLE, FRANK (see: Ficke, Frank) Flower Hill Cemetery, North Bergen, Hudson County.

New Jersey Civil War Burials

FIELD, AARON L. Pvt, A, 30th NJ Inf, 1-28-1931. New Somerville Cemetery, Somerville, Somerset County.

FIELD, AMZI A. Landsman, U.S. Navy, USS William Badge, 4-1-1893. New Somerville Cemetery, Somerville, Somerset County.

FIELD, EDWARD Bvt Capt, Btty G, 4th U.S. Art, 8-15-1906. Princeton Cemetery, Princeton, Mercer County.

FIELD, EMANUEL Corp, A, 41st U.S. CT, 1903. New Somerville Cemetery, Somerville, Somerset County.

FIELD, HENDRICK 1912. Presbyterian Church Cemetery, Lamington, Somerset County.

FIELD, HENRY 1-7-1917. Fairview Cemetery, Fairview, Monmouth County.

FIELD, JACOB T. Actg Asst Surgeon, U.S. Navy, USS Choctaw, 1896. New Somerville Cemetery, Somerville, Somerset County.

FIELD, JEREMIAH R. Corp, C, 28th NJ Inf, [Cenotaph. Killed in action at Fredericksburg, VA.] 12-13-1862. 1st Baptist Church Cemetery, Stelton, Middlesex County.

FIELD, JOHN J. Pvt, C, 71st NY State Militia, 11-18-1896. Flower Hill Cemetery, North Bergen, Hudson County.

FIELD, JOHN S. Sgt, H, 173rd NY Inf, [Wounded 6-14-1863 at Port Hudson, LA.] 8-6-1887. Mount Prospect Cemetery, Neptune, Monmouth County.

FIELD, JOHN W. Pvt, D, 23rd NJ Inf, 2-11-1885. Bordentown/Old St. Mary's Catholic Cemetery, Bordentown, Burlington County.

FIELD, JOSEPH T. Maj, 29th NJ Inf 9-25-1920. Fairview Cemetery, Fairview, Monmouth County.

FIELD, JOSHUA C. Sgt, C, 9th NY Inf, 7-28-1898. Arlington Cemetery, Kearny, Hudson County.

FIELD, THEODORE F. Capt, H, 6th NJ Inf, 12-3-1918. Harleigh Cemetery, Camden, Camden County.

FIELD*, THEODORE H. Wagoner, H, 6th NJ Inf, 1902. Mount Hope Presbyterian Cemetery, Lambertville, Hunterdon County.

FIELD, THOMAS S. Pvt, M, 2nd NJ Cav, 1891. Fairview Cemetery, Fairview, Monmouth County.

FIELD, WILLIAM Seaman, U.S. Navy, DoD Unknown. Arlington Cemetery, Kearny, Hudson County.

FIELD, WILLIAM H. Com Sgt, L, 1st NJ Cav, 5-26-1895. New Camden Cemetery, Camden, Camden County.

FIELD, WILLIAM H. Hosp Steward, U.S. Army, 7-4-1902. Fairmount Cemetery, Newark, Essex County.

FIELDER, ALFRED Pvt, E, 29th NJ Inf, 11-13-1907. Glenwood Cemetery, West Long Branch, Monmouth County.

FIELDER, BENJAMIN H. Pvt, D, 14th NJ Inf, 5-30-1885. Jersey City Cemetery, Jersey City, Hudson County.

FIELDER, CHARLES P. 1909. Evergreen Cemetery, Lakewood, Ocean County.

FIELDER, DAVID P. Pvt, F, 14th NJ Inf, 12-29-1910. Adelphia Cemetery, Adelphia, Monmouth County.

FIELDER, FRANCIS A. Pvt, D, 48th NY Inf, 11-15-1933. Adelphia Cemetery, Adelphia, Monmouth County.

FIELDER, FREDERICK 10-27-1880. Macphelah Cemetery, North Bergen, Hudson County.

FIELDER, GEORGE BRAGG Sgt Maj, 21st NJ Inf 8-14-1906. Bayview-New York Bay Cemetery, Jersey City, Hudson County.

FIELDER, JOHN Pvt, K, 29th NJ Inf, 6-15-1883. Brewer Cemetery, Squankum, Monmouth County.

FIELDER, WILLIAM W. Pvt, B, 12th NJ Inf, 12-12-1890. Fairmount Cemetery, Newark, Essex County.

Our Brothers Gone Before

FIELDING, EDWARD DoD Unknown. Laurel Grove Cemetery, Totowa, Passaic County.
FIELDING*, ELISHA B. Pvt, E, 1st CT Cav, 3-1-1903. Fairmount Cemetery, Newark, Essex County.
FIELDING, GEORGE Pvt, L, 1st NC Inf (US), 5-21-1917. Arlington Cemetery, Kearny, Hudson County.
FIELDING, ISAAC Pvt, B, 4th NJ Inf, [Wounded in action.] 7-30-1920. Soldier's Home Cemetery, Vineland, Cumberland County.
FIELDING, JAMES 2-12-1877. Laurel Grove Cemetery, Totowa, Passaic County.
FIELDING, JOHN H. Pvt, E, 10th NJ Inf, [Wounded in action.] 1920. Green Cemetery, Woodbury, Gloucester County.
FIELDING, THOMAS Pvt, I, 2nd NJ Inf, 4-16-1879. Laurel Grove Cemetery, Totowa, Passaic County.
FIELDS, C.W. 2-14-1899. Evergreen Cemetery, Camden, Camden County.
FIELDS*, CHARLES Pvt, C, 34th NJ Inf, 12-8-1923. Brotherhood Cemetery, Hainesport, Burlington County.
FIELDS, CLAYTON Pvt, C, 34th NJ Inf, 1906. Glenwood Cemetery, West Long Branch, Monmouth County.
FIELDS*, CLAYTON Pvt, C, 34th NJ Inf, 1902. Greengrove Cemetery, Keyport, Monmouth County.
FIELDS*, HENRY D. Farrier, H, 2nd NJ Cav, 12-2-1871. Presbyterian Church Cemetery, Yellow Frame, Warren County.
FIELDS, ISAAC Sgt, E, Cocke's AR Inf (CSA), [Captured 7-4-1863 at Helena, AR. Died of lung inflammation.] 7-27-1864. Finn's Point National Cemetery, Pennsville, Salem County.
FIELDS, JAHIAL Sgt, F, 22nd U.S. CT, 1914. Reformed Church Cemetery, Pluckemin, Somerset County.
FIELDS, JOHN G. Pvt, I, 23rd NJ Inf, 2-23-1917. Baptist Cemetery, Pemberton, Burlington County.
FIELDS, PETER 2nd Lt, I, 13th NJ Inf, 4-15-1898. Cedar Lawn Cemetery, Paterson, Passaic County.
FIELDS, S.H. Sgt, F, 3rd (Howard's) Confederate States Cav (CSA), 7-24-1864. Finn's Point National Cemetery, Pennsville, Salem County.
FIELDS, THEODORE Corp, B, 29th NJ Inf, 5-11-1921. Atlantic View Cemetery, Manasquan, Monmouth County.
FIELDS, THOMAS Pvt, H, 37th NJ Inf, 3-15-1918. Maplewood Cemetery, Freehold, Monmouth County.
FIELDS, THOMAS D. Pvt, Btty G, 1st PA Light Art, 4-27-1879. Evergreen Cemetery, Camden, Camden County.
FIELDS, WILLIAM Pvt, H, 37th NJ Inf, 11-27-1922. Brotherhood Cemetery, Hainesport, Burlington County.
FIELDS*, WILLIAM H. Pvt, K, 8th NJ Inf, 3-19-1903. Holy Sepulchre Cemetery, Totowa, Passaic County.
FIELDS, WILLIAM JASON Capt, Fields', Partisan KY Rangers (CSA), [Captured 1863 in East Tennessee. Died of smallpox.] 7-2-1864. Finn's Point National Cemetery, Pennsville, Salem County.
FIELLER, DANIEL (see: Fellows, Daniel) Peapack Reformed Church Cemetery, Gladstone, Somerset County.
FIFER, BARTINE (see: Phifer, Bartine) Cedar Grove Methodist Church Cemetery, Toms River, Ocean County.
FIFER, JOSEPH Pvt, I, 23rd NJ Inf, 2-13-1894. Baptist Cemetery, Medford, Burlington County.
FIFER, THOMAS Pvt, I, 23rd NJ Inf, 5- -1880. Mount Pleasant Cemetery, Millville, Cumberland County.

New Jersey Civil War Burials

FIGNER*, WILLIAM C. Pvt, F, 8th NJ Inf, 7-9-1895. Evergreen Cemetery, Camden, Camden County.

FIGOTTS, GARDINER (see: Bailey, Gardiner) St. Peter's Cemetery, Perth Amboy, Middlesex County.

FIGUERA*, JOHN Seaman, U.S. Navy, USS North Carolina, 4-14-1911. St. Joseph's Cemetery, Keyport, Monmouth County.

FILE, ANDREW (see: Fyle, Andrew) Macphelah Cemetery, North Bergen, Hudson County.

FILER, ENOCH Pvt, D, 35th NJ Inf, 3-9-1896. Methodist Church Cemetery, Hurffville, Gloucester County.

FILER, JAMES B. Pvt, Btty A, 10th NY Heavy Art, 9-11-1877. Elwood Rural Cemetery, Elwood, Atlantic County.

FILER, JOSEPH KENNARD Pvt, C, 23rd NJ Inf, 12-15-1886. Baptist/St. Andrew's Cemetery, Mount Holly, Burlington County.

FILGER, ALEXANDER Pvt, D, 15th NY Eng, 5-13-1904. Palisade Cemetery, North Bergen, Hudson County.

FILLMAN, GEORGE N. 12-28-1899. Greenwood Cemetery, Hamilton, Mercer County.

FILLMAN, HENRY J. Com Sgt, 186th PA Inf 11-14-1899. Bordentown/Old St. Mary's Catholic Cemetery, Bordentown, Burlington County.

FILON, MARTIN 3-18-1931. Holy Name Cemetery, Jersey City, Hudson County.

FINARTY, MARTIN (see: Finnerty, Martin) Mount Olivet Cemetery, Bloomfield, Essex County.

FINCH, EDMOND J. (see: Leigh, Edmond J.) New Somerville Cemetery, Somerville, Somerset County.

FINCH, EDWIN H. Pvt, I, 15th NY Cav, 11-29-1877. English Neighborhood Reformed Church Cemetery, Ridgefield, Bergen County.

FINCH*, JAMES H. Pvt, H, 38th NJ Inf, 6-11-1907. Elmwood Cemetery, New Brunswick, Middlesex County.

FINCH, JOHN C. Pvt, F, 23rd NJ Inf, 2-22-1908. Methodist Church Cemetery, Hurffville, Gloucester County.

FINCH, JOHN HENRY Pvt, B, 22nd NJ Inf, 4-21-1897. Ramapo Reformed Church Cemetery, Mahwah, Bergen County.

FINCH, JOHN W. Pvt, F, 14th NJ Inf, 12-27-1913. New Camden Cemetery, Camden, Camden County.

FINCH, MINOR M. (aka: Fiske, Marcus M.) Pvt, H, 9th NJ Inf, 12-17-1918. Morgan Cemetery, Cinnaminson, Burlington County.

FINCKE, CHRISTOPHER __, __, __ NY __, 7-19-1905. Bayview-New York Bay Cemetery, Jersey City, Hudson County.

FINCLIFF, JOHN Pvt, G, 10th U.S. Inf, 11-27-1892. Maplewood Cemetery, Freehold, Monmouth County.

FINE, GEORGE P. Pvt, C, 25th NJ Inf, 1928. Finesville Cemetery, Finesville, Warren County.

FINE*, JARVIS Pvt, C, 14th NJ Inf, [Wounded 5-12-1864 at Spotsylvania CH, VA.] 7-10-1903. Evergreen Cemetery, Hillside, Union County.

FINE, JOHN Pvt, B, 28th NJ Inf, [Wounded 12-13-1862 at Fredericksburg, VA.] 11-2-1927. Van Liew Cemetery, North Brunswick, Middlesex County.

FINE, JOHN 1883. St. James Cemetery, Greenwich, Warren County.

FINE, JOHN H. Pvt, A, MD Emerg NJ Militia, 11-25-1898. Christ Church Cemetery, Morgan, Middlesex County.

FINE, RUSSELL Pvt, A, 60th (Crawford's) TN Mtd Inf (CSA), [Captured 5-17-1863 at Big Black River Bridge, MS.] 8-7-1863. Finn's Point National Cemetery, Pennsville, Salem County.

FINEGAN*, JAMES Pvt, K, 6th NJ Inf, DoD Unknown. St. Peter's Cemetery, New Brunswick, Middlesex County.

Our Brothers Gone Before

FINERTY, NEIL __, B, 5th NY Cav, DoD Unknown. Holy Name Cemetery, Jersey City, Hudson County.

FINGAR, JOHN W. 2-5-1884. Evergreen Cemetery, Morristown, Morris County.

FINGER, HEINRICH Pvt, A, 4th NJ Inf, 6-8-1913. Manahath Cemetery, Glassboro, Gloucester County.

FINGERS, JOHN Seaman, U.S. Navy, USS Montgomery, 1903. Methodist-Episcopal Cemetery, Glendola, Monmouth County.

FINK*, JAMES W. Pvt, K, 16th PA Cav, 3-7-1919. Fairview Cemetery, Westfield, Union County.

FINK*, JOHN H. Pvt, H, 96th PA Inf, [Cenotaph.] 1883. Eglington Cemetery, Clarksboro, Gloucester County.

FINK*, WILLIAM Pvt, K, 2nd U.S. Inf, 12-11-1925. Greenwood Cemetery, Hamilton, Mercer County.

FINKE, WILLIAM Pvt, H, 13th IN Inf, [Died of wounds received 5-20-1864 at Bermuda Hundred, VA.] 6-15-1864. Fairmount Cemetery, Newark, Essex County.

FINKELMEIER, JOHN N. QM, 73rd PA Inf 10-6-1895. Cedar Lawn Cemetery, Paterson, Passaic County.

FINLAYSON, DONALD Pvt, A, 9th NJ Inf, 3-28-1895. Bayview-New York Bay Cemetery, Jersey City, Hudson County.

FINLEY, A.N. Pvt, I, 4th (Clinch's) GA Cav (CSA), 4-20-1864. Finn's Point National Cemetery, Pennsville, Salem County.

FINLEY*, BENJAMIN FREEMAN Pvt, G, 5th NY Inf, 11-27-1905. Evergreen Cemetery, Hillside, Union County.

FINLEY, CHARLES Pvt, K, 10th NJ Inf, DoD Unknown. St. Mary's Cemetery, South Amboy, Middlesex County.

FINLEY, DENNIS Pvt, B, 80th NY Inf, 7-21-1903. Fairmount Cemetery, Newark, Essex County.

FINLEY, JAMES (see: McDermott, James) St. Nicholas Cemetery, Lodi, Bergen County.

FINLEY, JOHN (see: Fenle, John) Soldier's Home Cemetery, Vineland, Cumberland County.

FINLEY, JOHN I. Pvt, A, 127th NY Inf, 11-25-1923. St. Mary's Cemetery, Plainfield, Union County.

FINLEY, LEWIS R. Pvt, H, 3rd NJ Cav, DoD Unknown. Presbyterian Church Cemetery, Bridgeton, Cumberland County.

FINLEY, PATRICK (aka: Finnly, Patrick) Pvt, H, 39th NJ Inf, 10-3-1869. St. John's Evangelical Church Cemetery, Orange, Essex County.

FINLEY, WILLIAM Pvt, G, 14th SC Inf (CSA), [Captured 5-6-1864 at Wilderness, VA. Died of lung inflammation.] 5-7-1865. Finn's Point National Cemetery, Pennsville, Salem County.

FINN*, AUGUST Pvt, D, 2nd NJ Inf, 9-17-1913. Woodland Cemetery, Newark, Essex County.

FINN, CHARLES Pvt, D, 7th NJ Inf, 8-22-1899. Woodland Cemetery, Newark, Essex County.

FINN, HAMILTON T. Pvt, G, 14th NJ Inf, 10-21-1872. Fairmount Cemetery, Newark, Essex County.

FINN, JOHN Pvt, Btty D, 5th NY Heavy Art, 6-14-1874. Fairmount Cemetery, Newark, Essex County.

FINN, THOMAS Corp, B, 25th NY National Guard, 9-2-1905. Holy Name Cemetery, Jersey City, Hudson County.

FINNAMEN, CHARLES M. Pvt, H, 2nd U.S. CT, 9-27-1916. Union Bethel Cemetery, Erma, Cape May County.

FINNAMON, AARON S. Pvt, F, 41st U.S. CT, 9-16-1865. Mount Zion AME Cemetery, Swedesboro, Gloucester County.

New Jersey Civil War Burials

FINNEGAN, EDWARD Sgt, F, 1st NJ Inf, 12-17-1928. St. Peter's Cemetery, New Brunswick, Middlesex County.

FINNEGAN, JAMES Pvt, D, 4th NJ Militia, 1-15-1876. Old St. Mary's Cemetery, Gloucester City, Camden County.

FINNEGAN, JOHN Pvt, G, 1st NJ Cav, 7-7-1883. Mount Carmel Cemetery, West Long Branch, Monmouth County.

FINNEGAN*, JOHN C. Fireman, U.S. Navy, USS Merrimac, 10-30-1886. St. Rose of Lima Cemetery, Oxford, Warren County.

FINNEGAN, MATTHEW Pvt, K, 62nd NY Inf, DoD Unknown. Old St. Mary's Cemetery, Gloucester City, Camden County.

FINNEGAN*, PATRICK K. Coal Heaver, U.S. Navy, USS Nipsic, 6-12-1921. St. Peter's Cemetery, New Brunswick, Middlesex County.

FINNEGAN, THOMAS Pvt, F, 72nd NY Inf, 9-24-1876. Holy Sepulchre Cemetery, East Orange, Essex County.

FINNEMAN, GEORGE W. (aka: Fenneman, George W.) Pvt, D, 3rd U.S. CT, 12-7-1898. Eglington Cemetery, Clarksboro, Gloucester County.

FINNERN, JAMES Pvt, Btty A, 1st NJ Light Art, DoD Unknown. Holy Sepulchre Cemetery, East Orange, Essex County.

FINNERTY, DAVID Pvt, H, 94th NY Inf, DoD Unknown. Mount Olivet Cemetery, Bloomfield, Essex County.

FINNERTY, MARTIN (aka: Finarty, Martin) Pvt, H, 99th NY Inf, 9-18-1906. Mount Olivet Cemetery, Bloomfield, Essex County.

FINNERTY, PATRICK Corp, I, 36th NY Inf, 8-15-1897. Holy Sepulchre Cemetery, East Orange, Essex County.

FINNEY, PATRICK J. Pvt, C, 7th NJ Inf, 3-21-1903. St. Vincent Martyr Cemetery, Madison, Morris County.

FINNEY, THOMAS J. Pvt, Btty B, 2nd PA Heavy Art, 12-21-1909. Harleigh Cemetery, Camden, Camden County.

FINNLY, PATRICK (see: Finley, Patrick) St. John's Evangelical Church Cemetery, Orange, Essex County.

FINNONS, JAMES (see: Fennon, James) Bordentown/Old St. Mary's Catholic Cemetery, Bordentown, Burlington County.

FIRENG, JACOB E. Pay Steward, U.S. Navy, 5-24-1909. Beverly National Cemetery, Edgewater Park, Burlington County.

FIRENG, JOHN P. Seaman, U.S. Navy, 7-13-1917. Rosedale Cemetery, Orange, Essex County.

FIRENG, ROBERT Pvt, I, 34th NJ Inf, 8-12-1911. Monument Cemetery, Edgewater Park, Burlington County.

FIRMAN, ALFRED W. Pvt, E, 6th U.S. CT, 5-12-1892. Riverview Cemetery, Trenton, Mercer County.

FIRMAN, JACOB (aka: Firman, Josiah) Pvt, E, 6th U.S. CT, 11-2-1911. Atlantic City Cemetery, Pleasantville, Atlantic County.

FIRMAN, JOSIAH (see: Firman, Jacob) Atlantic City Cemetery, Pleasantville, Atlantic County.

FIRMAN, MARK (aka: Freeman, Mark) Pvt, C, 22nd U.S. CT, [Died in New Jersey.] 4-25-1864. Evergreen Cemetery, Morristown, Morris County.

FIRTH, ELMER Pvt, E, 2nd NJ Cav, 8-31-1876. Bordentown/Old St. Mary's Catholic Cemetery, Bordentown, Burlington County.

FIRTH*, JAMES Corp, K, 150th NY Inf, 2-28-1915. Hillside Cemetery, Lyndhurst, Bergen County.

FIRTH, JOHN Corp, K, 93rd OH Inf, [Died at Nashville, TN. of wounds received at Resaca, GA.] 5-15-1864. Laurel Grove Cemetery, Totowa, Passaic County.

FISCHER*, ERNEST (aka: Fisher, Ernest) Corp, E, 2nd NJ Inf, 6-24-1887. Woodland Cemetery, Newark, Essex County.

Our Brothers Gone Before

FISCHER, FRANK (aka: Ficher, Frantz) Artificer, B, 1st NY Eng, 8-14-1904. Evergreen Cemetery, Hillside, Union County.
FISCHER, HERMAN Pvt, E, 15th NJ Inf, 12-15-1895. Fairmount Cemetery, Newark, Essex County.
FISCHER*, JOHN GEORGE Pvt, I, 2nd DC Inf, 9-21-1892. Woodland Cemetery, Newark, Essex County.
FISCHINGER, LORENZ (aka: Fleshinger, Lawrence) Pvt, E, 103rd NY Inf, 6-25-1910. Fairmount Cemetery, Newark, Essex County.
FISH, CHARLES C. Pvt, A, 20th NY Cav, 12-1-1891. Fairmount Cemetery, Newark, Essex County.
FISH*, CHARLES F. Pvt, I, 14th NJ Inf, 2-22-1875. Mount Pleasant Cemetery, Newark, Essex County.
FISH, CHARLES N. Pvt, F, 4th NJ Inf, 6-9-1893. Evergreen Cemetery, Camden, Camden County.
FISH, CHARLES W. Pvt, I, 23rd NJ Inf, 2-19-1919. Evergreen Cemetery, Camden, Camden County.
FISH, DAVID C. Pvt, I, 14th NJ Inf, 4-28-1908. Mount Hope Presbyterian Cemetery, Lambertville, Hunterdon County.
FISH, GEORGE W. Pvt, H, 28th NJ Inf, 11-2-1920. New Camden Cemetery, Camden, Camden County.
FISH, HIRAM Pvt, E, 6th NJ Inf, 2-9-1898. Methodist Cemetery, Haddonfield, Camden County.
FISH*, ISRAEL L. Sgt, F, 37th NJ Inf, 12-20-1908. Harleigh Cemetery, Camden, Camden County.
FISH, JACOB T. Pvt, I, 24th NJ Inf, 1-18-1923. Harleigh Cemetery, Camden, Camden County.
FISH*, JAMES D. Pvt, C, 214th PA Inf, 11-27-1921. Monument Cemetery, Edgewater Park, Burlington County.
FISH, JOHN ALEXANDER Pvt, I, 24th NJ Inf, 2-18-1877. Methodist Cemetery, Haddonfield, Camden County.
FISH, JOSEPH B. Pvt, F, 23rd NJ Inf, 4-22-1924. Bethel Cemetery, Pennsauken, Camden County.
FISH, JOSIAH W. Pvt, G, 68th PA Inf, DoD Unknown. Methodist Cemetery, Haddonfield, Camden County.
FISH, LUCIUS M. 9-26-1898. Glenwood Cemetery, West Long Branch, Monmouth County.
FISH, LUCIUS W. Corp, A, 29th NJ Inf, 4-12-1909. Oak Hill Cemetery, Vineland, Cumberland County.
FISH, MESHECK P. Pvt, H, 10th NJ Inf, 1932. Eglington Cemetery, Clarksboro, Gloucester County.
FISH*, NELSON C. Pvt, I, 71st PA Inf, [Wounded 6-16-1864 at Petersburg, VA.] 2-19-1934. Monument Cemetery, Edgewater Park, Burlington County.
FISHBOUGH, ___?___ DoD Unknown. Hackensack Cemetery, Hackensack, Bergen County.
FISHBOUGH, PETER C. Pvt, B, 30th NJ Inf, 6-25-1899. Phillipsburg Cemetery, Phillipsburg, Warren County.
FISHER, ABRAM Pvt, D, 38th U.S. CT, 1-7-1919. Fairmount Cemetery, Newark, Essex County.
FISHER, ALBERT Corp, E, 4th NJ Inf, 1-15-1898. Presbyterian Church Cemetery, Bridgeton, Cumberland County.
FISHER*, ANDREW AUGUST Pvt, B, 3rd NJ Inf, 4-16-1911. Holy Sepulchre Cemetery, East Orange, Essex County.
FISHER, ARTHUR H. 1st Asst Eng, U.S. Navy, 12-9-1905. Evergreen Cemetery, Camden, Camden County.

New Jersey Civil War Burials

FISHER, BENJAMIN Colored Cook, H, 34th NJ Inf, 3-17-1912. Riverview Cemetery, Trenton, Mercer County.

FISHER, BENJAMIN Pvt, I, 8th NJ Inf, DoD Unknown. Baptist Cemetery, Osbornville, Ocean County.

FISHER, C. Pvt, I, 37th NJ Inf, DoD Unknown. Van Liew Cemetery, North Brunswick, Middlesex County.

FISHER*, CHARLES B. Pvt, E, 1st NJ Cav, 4-1-1893. Mount Hope Presbyterian Cemetery, Lambertville, Hunterdon County.

FISHER, CHARLES E. Pvt, Btty D, 1st NJ Light Art, 3-23-1913. Atlantic City Cemetery, Pleasantville, Atlantic County.

FISHER, CHARLES JOHN Pvt, G, 1st NJ Militia, 5-31-1883. Phillipsburg Cemetery, Phillipsburg, Warren County.

FISHER, CHRISTIAN Pvt, I, 107th OH Inf, [Died of wounds received 7-1-1863 at Gettysburg, PA.] 12-2-1863. Fairmount Cemetery, Newark, Essex County.

FISHER*, CLARK 1st Asst Eng, U.S. Navy, USS Agawam, 12-31-1903. Princeton Cemetery, Princeton, Mercer County.

FISHER, DAVID A. Pvt, K, 5th NJ Inf, 6-7-1867. Tennent Church Cemetery, Tennent, Monmouth County.

FISHER, DAVID H. Pvt, D, 31st NJ Inf, 11-19-1917. Highland Cemetery, Hopewell Boro, Mercer County.

FISHER, DAVID R. Sgt, I, 11th NJ Inf, 1872. Tennent Church Cemetery, Tennent, Monmouth County.

FISHER*, EDWARD L. Pvt, H, 12th NJ Inf, 3-20-1907. Old Camden Cemetery, Camden, Camden County.

FISHER*, ELIAS Pvt, B, 34th NJ Inf, 8-17-1919. Osbornville Protestant Church Cemetery, Breton Woods, Ocean County.

FISHER, ELWOOD Pvt, G, 3rd NJ Cav, 10-24-1905. Methodist-Episcopal Cemetery, Port Norris, Cumberland County.

FISHER, ERNEST (see: Fischer, Ernest) Woodland Cemetery, Newark, Essex County.

FISHER, FRANK S. DoD Unknown. Riverview Cemetery, Trenton, Mercer County.

FISHER, FREDERICK Pvt, A, 4th NJ Inf, 3-22-1873. Fairmount Cemetery, Newark, Essex County.

FISHER, FREDERICK DoD Unknown. Phillipsburg Cemetery, Phillipsburg, Warren County.

FISHER, GEORGE Musc, 84th NY Inf Band 3-8-1908. Laurel Grove Cemetery, Totowa, Passaic County.

FISHER, GEORGE H. Musc, G, 30th NJ Inf, 1925. Union Cemetery, Ringoes, Hunterdon County.

FISHER, GEORGE S. Pvt, H, 23rd NJ Inf, DoD Unknown. United Methodist Church Cemetery, Jacobstown, Burlington County.

FISHER, GEORGE W.P. Sgt, H, 6th NJ Inf, 11-11-1915. Mount Hope Presbyterian Cemetery, Lambertville, Hunterdon County.

FISHER, HENRY C. Corp, A, 9th NJ Inf, 8-2-1903. Mount Hope Presbyterian Cemetery, Lambertville, Hunterdon County.

FISHER, HOWARD (see: Fisler, Howard) 1st Methodist Church Cemetery, Williamstown, Gloucester County.

FISHER, ISAAC Pvt, K, 3rd NJ Militia, 2-28-1871. Christ Episcopal Church Cemetery, New Brunswick, Middlesex County.

FISHER, JACOB Pvt, C, 31st NJ Inf, 11-19-1922. New Somerville Cemetery, Somerville, Somerset County.

FISHER, JAMES D. Pvt, K, 44th VA Inf (CSA), [Wounded 12-13-1862 at Fredericksburg, VA and 5-3-1863 at Chancellorsville, VA. Captured 7-3-1863 at Gettysburg, PA. Died of diarrhea.] 8-11-1863. Finn's Point National Cemetery, Pennsville, Salem County.

Our Brothers Gone Before

FISHER, JAMES G. Pvt, A, 24th NJ Inf, 9-22-1866. Baptist Church Cemetery, Canton, Salem County.

FISHER, JAMES L. 1st Sgt, I, 14th NJ Inf, 6-24-1908. Elmwood Cemetery, New Brunswick, Middlesex County.

FISHER, JAMES S. (JR.) Musc, I, 38th NJ Inf, 12-21-1898. Prospect Hill Cemetery, Flemington, Hunterdon County.

FISHER, JAMES W. Landsman, U.S. Navy, USS North Carolina, 3-12-1881. Evergreen Cemetery, Hillside, Union County.

FISHER, JOHN Sgt, F, 45th U.S. CT, 7-11-1894. Mount Zion Methodist Church Cemetery, Lawnside, Camden County.

FISHER, JOHN Pvt, F, 101st NY Inf, [Died of consumption at Newark, NJ.] 2-29-1864. Fairmount Cemetery, Newark, Essex County.

FISHER, JOHN Pvt, B, 69th NY Inf, [Wounded in action.] 12-6-1905. Mount Olivet Cemetery, Bloomfield, Essex County.

FISHER, JOHN 11-14-1903. Phillipsburg Cemetery, Phillipsburg, Warren County.

FISHER, JOHN 3-7-1891. Phillipsburg Cemetery, Phillipsburg, Warren County.

FISHER, JOHN B. Pvt, K, 179th NY Inf, [Died of wounds received 9-30-1864 at Poplar Spring Church, VA.] 11-3-1864. Beverly National Cemetery, Edgewater Park, Burlington County.

FISHER, JOHN B. Pvt, D, 31st NJ Inf, 6-12-1910. Highland Cemetery, Hopewell Boro, Mercer County.

FISHER, JOHN D. Pvt, H, 28th NY Inf, [Wounded 8-9-1862 at Cedar Mountain, VA.] 3-20-1903. Fairmount Cemetery, Newark, Essex County.

FISHER, JOHN ENGLEBERT Landsman, U.S. Navy, USS St. Lawrence, 10-22-1905. Greenwood Cemetery, Hamilton, Mercer County.

FISHER, JOHN F. Corp, E, 1st NJ Inf, 12-25-1869. Old Camden Cemetery, Camden, Camden County.

FISHER, JOHN G. 2nd Lt, I, 14th NJ Inf, [Wounded 6-1-1864 at Cold Harbor, VA.] 8-9-1908. Rosedale Cemetery, Orange, Essex County.

FISHER, JOHN H. Musc, 7th NJ Inf Band 8-4-1920. Laurel Grove Cemetery, Totowa, Passaic County.

FISHER, JOHN L. 9-10-1862. Sergeant's Hill Cemetery, Sand Brook, Hunterdon County.

FISHER, JONATHAN Pvt, D, 10th NJ Inf, 10-24-1905. Mount Holly Cemetery, Mount Holly, Burlington County.

FISHER, JOSEPH Pvt, D, 10th NJ Inf, 10-9-1899. Presbyterian Church Cemetery, Bridgeton, Cumberland County.

FISHER, LEMUEL 1st Sgt, I, 1st NJ Cav, 11-10-1926. Bordentown/Old St. Mary's Catholic Cemetery, Bordentown, Burlington County.

FISHER, LEMUEL Corp, H, 3rd NJ Militia, 12-30-1906. Prospect Hill Cemetery, Flemington, Hunterdon County.

FISHER, LEWIS Pvt, F, 45th U.S. CT, 2-10-1895. Moore's Farm Cemetery, Stoutsburg, Mercer County.

FISHER, MICHAEL Pvt, B, 38th NJ Inf, 2-28-1907. Riverview Cemetery, Trenton, Mercer County.

FISHER, NATHAN Pvt, F, 22nd U.S. CT, [Died at Fort Monroe, VA.] 11-1-1864. Johnson Cemetery, Camden, Camden County.

FISHER, OTIS Bvt Maj, 8th U.S. Inf [Died of wounds received at Poplar Springs, VA.] 10-3-1864. Princeton Cemetery, Princeton, Mercer County.

FISHER, PATRICK Pvt, F, 7th NJ Inf, 12-18-1882. Holy Sepulchre Cemetery, East Orange, Essex County.

FISHER, PETER Corp, K, 7th NJ Inf, 4-2-1872. Belvidere/Catholic Cemetery, Belvidere, Warren County.

FISHER, SAMUEL B. 3-1-1930. Harleigh Cemetery, Camden, Camden County.

FISHER, SAMUEL B. Sgt, G, 4th NJ Inf, 9-20-1912. 1st Baptist Church Cemetery, Woodstown, Salem County.
FISHER, THOMAS Pvt, D, 82nd PA Inf, 7-12-1867. Head of River Church Cemetery, Head of River, Atlantic County.
FISHER, THOMAS J. Pvt, G, 14th NJ Inf, [Wounded in action.] 2-3-1928. Greenville Cemetery, Lakewood, Ocean County.
FISHER, THOMAS W. Pvt, H, 7th NJ Inf, 5-9-1914. Osbornville Protestant Church Cemetery, Breton Woods, Ocean County.
FISHER, WEON Pvt, D, 31st NJ Inf, 2-16-1910. Baptist/Evergreen Methodist Cemetery, Plainfield, Union County.
FISHER, WESLEY R. Pvt, A, 31st NJ Inf, 7-8-1904. Fairmount Cemetery, Fairmount, Hunterdon County.
FISHER, WILLIAM Pvt, B, 38th NJ Inf, 6-9-1885. Mount Hope Presbyterian Cemetery, Lambertville, Hunterdon County.
FISHER, WILLIAM Pvt, E, 21st NJ Inf, 4-26-1912. New Presbyterian Cemetery, Bound Brook, Somerset County.
FISHER, WILLIAM Sgt, E, 7th NJ Inf, 1-8-1888. Belvidere/Catholic Cemetery, Belvidere, Warren County.
FISHER, WILLIAM Pvt, I, 127th U.S. CT, 10-2-1893. Mount Pisgah Cemetery, Elsinboro, Salem County.
FISHER, WILLIAM C. Sgt, D, 34th NJ Inf, 8-11-1906. United Methodist Church Cemetery, Port Elizabeth, Cumberland County.
FISHER, WILLIAM F. Farrier, H, 11th PA Cav, 7-18-1891. Phillipsburg Cemetery, Phillipsburg, Warren County.
FISK, R.H. 4-4-1872. Presbyterian Church Cemetery, Ewing, Mercer County.
FISKE, FRANKLIN B. Capt, H, 4th IL Cav, 12-14-1888. Arlington Cemetery, Kearny, Hudson County.
FISKE, JOHN D. Sgt, Nim's Btty, 2nd MA Light Art, 4-1-1910. Greenwood Cemetery, Tuckerton, Ocean County.
FISKE, JOSEPH Pvt, A, 13th MA Inf, DoD Unknown. 1st United Methodist Church Cemetery, Bridgeton, Cumberland County.
FISKE, MARCUS M. Musc, H, 9th NJ Inf, 6-19-1895. Phillipsburg Cemetery, Phillipsburg, Warren County.
FISKE, MARCUS M. (see: Finch, Minor M.) Morgan Cemetery, Cinnaminson, Burlington County.
FISKE, MICHAEL (aka: Freshet, Michael) Pvt, K, 1st MI Inf, [Died of wounds received 8-30-1862 at 2nd Bull Run, VA.] 10-24-1864. Beverly National Cemetery, Edgewater Park, Burlington County.
FISLER*, HOWARD (aka: Fisher, Howard) Sgt, A, 10th NJ Inf, [Died at Winchester, VA. of wounds received 10-19-1864 at Cedar Creek, VA.] 11-12-1864. 1st Methodist Church Cemetery, Williamstown, Gloucester County.
FISLER, JOSEPH C. Pvt, E, 2nd NJ Cav, 1-25-1915. Cedar Green Cemetery, Clayton, Gloucester County.
FITCH, CLAYTON SHEPARD Seaman, U.S. Navy, 3-1-1911. Rosedale Cemetery, Orange, Essex County.
FITCH, EDWARD E. Pvt, K, 189th NY Inf, 4-18-1930. Calvary Baptist Church Cemetery, Ocean View, Cape May County.
FITCH*, GEORGE DRAKE Asst Surg, 2nd NJ Inf [Also: Asst Surg, 15th NJ Inf.] 1912. Methodist Church Cemetery, Hope, Warren County.
FITCH, THEODORE Pvt, A, 22nd NY Inf, 4-16-1912. Bloomfield Cemetery, Bloomfield, Essex County.
FITCH, WILLIAM Y. Corp, C, 21st NJ Inf, 5-2-1923. Old Bergen Church Cemetery, Jersey City, Hudson County.

Our Brothers Gone Before

FITCHETT, WILLIAM Pvt, I, 19th U.S. CT, 8-24-1897. Johnson Cemetery, Camden, Camden County.
FITHIAN, AARON B. Pvt, K, 10th NJ Inf, [Died of consumption at Bridgeton, NJ.] 2-5-1865. 1st United Methodist Church Cemetery, Bridgeton, Cumberland County.
FITHIAN, ALEXANDER H. Pvt, I, 90th PA Inf, 2-3-1916. Bordentown/Old St. Mary's Catholic Cemetery, Bordentown, Burlington County.
FITHIAN, AUSTIN M. Musc, 97th PA Inf Band 10-15-1892. Presbyterian Church Cemetery, Cedarville, Cumberland County.
FITHIAN, CHARLES C. Pvt, I, 12th NJ Inf, 4-28-1872. Cedar Grove Cemetery, Gloucester City, Camden County.
FITHIAN*, CHARLES C. Landsman, U.S. Navy, USS Princeton, 1915. Eastview Cemetery, Salem, Salem County.
FITHIAN, DAVID E. Pvt, E, 4th NJ Inf, 11-23-1907. Mount Pleasant Cemetery, Millville, Cumberland County.
FITHIAN, EDGAR M. Pvt, K, 12th NJ Inf, 2-16-1868. Evergreen Cemetery, Camden, Camden County.
FITHIAN, EDWIN Chief Eng, U.S. Navy, 8-29-1908. Presbyterian Church Cemetery, Bridgeton, Cumberland County.
FITHIAN, EPHRIAM B. Pvt, E, 1st NJ Cav, 2-1-1921. Evergreen Cemetery, Camden, Camden County.
FITHIAN, JAMES W. Corp, A, 10th NJ Inf, 1898. Mount Pleasant Cemetery, Millville, Cumberland County.
FITHIAN, JOEL A. DoD Unknown. Presbyterian Church Cemetery, Greenwich, Cumberland County.
FITHIAN, JOSEPH H. Sgt, H, 3rd NJ Cav, DoD Unknown. Presbyterian Church Cemetery, Bridgeton, Cumberland County.
FITHIAN, JOSHUA DANFORTH Sgt, G, 12th NJ Inf, DoD Unknown. Presbyterian Church Cemetery, Bridgeton, Cumberland County.
FITHIAN, JOSIAH P. Pvt, B, 109th PA Inf, 1902. Chestnut Grove Cemetery, Elmer, Salem County.
FITHIAN*, RICHARD V. Pvt, I, 12th NJ Inf, 6-5-1907. Arlington Cemetery, Kearny, Hudson County.
FITHIAN, SAMUEL R. QM, 24th NJ Inf 7- -1913. Presbyterian Church Cemetery, Greenwich, Cumberland County.
FITSCH, CHARLES Seaman, U.S. Navy, DoD Unknown. Bayview-New York Bay Cemetery, Jersey City, Hudson County.
FITSCHEN, ADOLPH J. 11-29-1895. Bayview-New York Bay Cemetery, Jersey City, Hudson County.
FITZER*, EDWARD F. Pvt, H, 4th NJ Inf, 1927. Evergreen Cemetery, Camden, Camden County.
FITZER, WILLIAM R. Pvt, B, 215th PA Inf, 5-16-1907. Presbyterian Church Cemetery, Mount Pleasant, Hunterdon County.
FITZGEORGE, CHARLES Pvt, G, 2nd NJ Militia, 1-19-1919. Greenwood Cemetery, Hamilton, Mercer County.
FITZGERALD, ASA V. Pvt, F, 60th (Crawford's) TN Mtd Inf (CSA), [Captured 5-17-1863 at Big Black River Bridge, MS.] 8-11-1863. Finn's Point National Cemetery, Pennsville, Salem County.
FITZGERALD, JOHN Pvt, D, 6th NJ Inf, [Died of disease at Newark, NJ.] 9-27-1862. Fairmount Cemetery, Newark, Essex County.
FITZGERALD, JOHN P. Landsman, U.S. Navy, USS Princeton, 3-20-1911. Butler Cemetery, Camden, Camden County.
FITZGERALD, MICHAEL Pvt, B, 90th NY Inf, 10-19-1867. St. Mary's Cemetery, Elizabeth, Union County.

New Jersey Civil War Burials

FITZGERALD, MICHAEL Pvt, D, 69th NY Inf, 9-4-1886. Holy Sepulchre Cemetery, East Orange, Essex County.

FITZGERALD, MICHAEL (see: Fitzgerald, Miles) Cedar Lawn Cemetery, Paterson, Passaic County.

FITZGERALD, MILES (aka: Fitzgerald, Michael) Pvt, G, 73rd NY Inf, 9-19-1895. Cedar Lawn Cemetery, Paterson, Passaic County.

FITZGERALD, PATRICK Pvt, G, 51st NY Inf, DoD Unknown. St. Thomas Cemetery, Ogdensburg, Sussex County.

FITZGERALD*, TIMOTHY Pvt, E, 2nd NJ Inf, 7-21-1913. Holy Rood Cemetery, Morristown, Morris County.

FITZGERALD, WILLIAM Pvt, M, 2nd NJ Cav, 1916. Union Cemetery, Washington, Morris County.

FITZGIBBON, JOHN 1st Sgt, I, 29th NJ Inf, 5-24-1872. St. Rose of Lima Cemetery, Freehold, Monmouth County.

FITZGYLES, WILLIAM Pvt, K, 24th U.S. CT, 3-13-1901. Greenwood Cemetery, Pleasantville, Atlantic County.

FITZHENRY, WILLIAM Pvt, I, 29th NJ Inf, 6-5-1903. Bayview-New York Bay Cemetery, Jersey City, Hudson County.

FITZMYER, JOHN Pvt, A, 9th NJ Inf, 2-11-1898. Fairmount Cemetery, Newark, Essex County.

FITZPATRICK, DANIEL (aka: Foster, Daniel) Pvt, I, 6th NY Cav, 6-20-1907. St. Joseph's Cemetery, Hackensack, Bergen County.

FITZPATRICK, GEORGE Pvt, G, 3rd NJ Cav, 3-12-1924. Holy Sepulchre Cemetery, East Orange, Essex County.

FITZPATRICK, JAMES Pvt, C, 8th NJ Inf, [Wounded in action.] 7-2-1887. Holy Sepulchre Cemetery, East Orange, Essex County.

FITZPATRICK, JOHN Corp, B, 37th NY Inf, 1-18-1899. Holy Sepulchre Cemetery, Totowa, Passaic County.

FITZPATRICK, JOHN W. Pvt, D, 61st NY Inf, 4-7-1899. Maple Grove Cemetery, Hackensack, Bergen County.

FITZPATRICK, MICHAEL W. Pvt, F, 77th PA Inf, 7-26-1922. Fairmount Cemetery, Phillipsburg, Warren County.

FITZPATRICK, PATRICK Seaman, U.S. Navy, 5-2-1873. St. John's Evangelical Church Cemetery, Orange, Essex County.

FITZPATRICK, THOMAS Pvt, G, 9th NJ Inf, 1-9-1885. Holy Sepulchre Cemetery, East Orange, Essex County.

FITZPATRICK*, THOMAS Seaman, U.S. Navy, USS Monongohela, 9-12-1917. Holy Sepulchre Cemetery, East Orange, Essex County.

FITZPATRICK*, WILLIAM Pvt, C, 4th NJ Inf, 9-7-1874. Baptist/St. Andrew's Cemetery, Mount Holly, Burlington County.

FITZPATRICK, WILLIAM Musc, C, 39th NJ Inf, 11-21-1882. St. John's Evangelical Church Cemetery, Orange, Essex County.

FITZRANDOLPH, AARON (aka: Randolph, Aaron F.) Pvt, H, 30th NJ Inf, [Died of fever at Belle Plain, VA.] 3-9-1863. Baptist Cemetery, South Plainfield, Middlesex County.

FITZSIMMONS, JAMES Pvt, B, 114th IL Inf, 6-14-1892. Fairmount Cemetery, Newark, Essex County.

FITZSIMMONS, MICHAEL Pvt, K, 1st NJ Inf, 10-16-1894. Holy Sepulchre Cemetery, East Orange, Essex County.

FITZSIMMONS, MICHAEL Pvt, D, 51st NY Inf, [Wounded 8-1-1864 at Petersburg, VA.] 8-31-1899. Bayview-New York Bay Cemetery, Jersey City, Hudson County.

FITZSIMMONS*, OWEN Pvt, C, 2nd NJ Inf, 10-6-1866. Holy Sepulchre Cemetery, East Orange, Essex County.

FITZSIMMONS, PATRICK 7-7-1883. Madonna Cemetery, Leonia, Bergen County.

Our Brothers Gone Before

FIULON, JOHN (see: Fenton, John) St. Peter's Cemetery, New Brunswick, Middlesex County.

FLAD, ANDREAS (aka: Flad, Andrew) Pvt, E, 14th NJ Inf, 1903. Immaculate Conception Cemetery, Somerville, Somerset County.

FLAD, ANDREW (see: Flad, Andreas) Immaculate Conception Cemetery, Somerville, Somerset County.

FLAHERTY, JOHN (see: Flattery, John) Holy Name Cemetery, Jersey City, Hudson County.

FLAHERTY, MICHAEL Landsman, U.S. Navy, USS Vandalia, 3-28-1898. St. Peter's Cemetery, Jersey City, Hudson County.

FLAHERTY, PATRICK JOHN Pvt, E, 14th ME Inf, 12-2-1912. St. Mary's Cemetery, Hamilton, Mercer County.

FLAHERTY, WILLIAM Pvt, C, 2nd NJ Inf, 5-31-1887. St. John's Evangelical Church Cemetery, Orange, Essex County.

FLAIRDEN, ALEXANDER (see: Flanders, Alexander) Beverly National Cemetery, Edgewater Park, Burlington County.

FLANAGAN, EDWARD Seaman, U.S. Navy, 5-23-1883. Holy Sepulchre Cemetery, Totowa, Passaic County.

FLANAGAN, FENTON Pvt, C, 34th OH Inf, 5-31-1900. Holy Sepulchre Cemetery, Totowa, Passaic County.

FLANAGAN, JAMES Seaman, U.S. Navy, 12-3-1891. Holy Sepulchre Cemetery, Totowa, Passaic County.

FLANAGAN, JOHN F. (aka: Flannigan, John) Pvt, I, 26th NJ Inf, 2-21-1907. Fairmount Cemetery, Newark, Essex County.

FLANAGAN, THOMAS Corp, B, 13th NJ Inf, 6-27-1906. Holy Name Cemetery, Jersey City, Hudson County.

FLANAGAN, THOMAS J. Fireman, U.S. Navy, USS Pawtucket, 4-4-1917. Mount Olivet Cemetery, Newark, Essex County.

FLANAGIN, HENRY M. Sgt, G, 5th PA Cav, 1-9-1905. Riverview Cemetery, Penns Grove, Salem County.

FLANDERS, ALEXANDER (aka: Flairden, Alexander) Pvt, Btty D, 1st NJ Light Art, [Died of wounds received 8-16-1864 at Malvern Hill, VA.] 9-15-1864. Beverly National Cemetery, Edgewater Park, Burlington County.

FLANIGAN, MICHAEL Pvt, A, 8th NJ Inf, 9-29-1873. Fairmount Cemetery, Newark, Essex County.

FLANIGAN, PATRICK (see: Flannagan, Patrick) St. John's Evangelical Church Cemetery, Orange, Essex County.

FLANIGAN, WILLIAM Pvt, A, 8th NJ Inf, 6-12-1912. St. Peter's Cemetery, New Brunswick, Middlesex County.

FLANIGAN, WILLIAM (see: Hester, William Flanigan) St. Peter's Cemetery, New Brunswick, Middlesex County.

FLANLEY, OWEN (aka: Flannelley, Owen) Pvt, G, 2nd NJ Militia, 11-21-1864. St. Peter's Cemetery, Jersey City, Hudson County.

FLANNAGAN, PATRICK (aka: Flanigan, Patrick) Sgt, B, 79th NY Inf, 3-13-1879. St. John's Evangelical Church Cemetery, Orange, Essex County.

FLANNELLEY, OWEN (see: Flanley, Owen) St. Peter's Cemetery, Jersey City, Hudson County.

FLANNELLY*, JOHN Pvt, E, 120th NY Inf, [Wounded 10-27-1864 at Boydton Plank Road, VA.] 4-27-1894. Holy Name Cemetery, Jersey City, Hudson County.

FLANNERY, THOMAS J. Pvt, B, 7th NJ Inf, 1896. Mount Olivet Cemetery, Bloomfield, Essex County.

FLANNIGAN, JAMES Pvt, Btty B, 1st NJ Light Art, 3-14-1894. Holy Sepulchre Cemetery, East Orange, Essex County.

New Jersey Civil War Burials

FLANNIGAN, JOHN (see: Flanagan, John F.) Fairmount Cemetery, Newark, Essex County.

FLATT, CHARLES Pvt, I, 31st NJ Inf, 1923. Methodist Church Cemetery, Buttzville, Warren County.

FLATT, GEORGE Pvt, I, 8th NJ Inf, 1894. Hazelwood Cemetery, Rahway, Union County.

FLATT, GEORGE W. Corp, E, 14th NJ Inf, [Killed in action at Monocacy, MD.] 7-9-1864. Hazelwood Cemetery, Rahway, Union County.

FLATT, WILLIAM Pvt, K, 31st NJ Inf, 4-24-1893. Evergreen Cemetery, Clinton, Hunterdon County.

FLATTERY, JOHN (aka: Flaherty, John) Pvt, F, 58th NY Inf, 1-4-1933. Holy Name Cemetery, Jersey City, Hudson County.

FLATTICH, CHARLES (aka: Fiche, Charles) Pvt, Btty C, 1st NJ Light Art, 1-23-1907. Hoboken Cemetery, North Bergen, Hudson County.

FLAVELL, JEREMIAH Pvt, K, 213th PA Inf, 1910. Eglington Cemetery, Clarksboro, Gloucester County.

FLAVELL, JOHN W. Pvt, I, 2nd NJ Inf, [Died at Fort Monroe, VA.] 8-25-1862. Cedar Lawn Cemetery, Paterson, Passaic County.

FLAVELL, WILLIAM A. 11-11-1886. Cedar Lawn Cemetery, Paterson, Passaic County.

FLECK, WILLIAM 10-27-1916. Fairview Cemetery, Fairview, Bergen County.

FLEET*, SAMUEL Pvt, E, 12th NJ Inf, [Died at Albany, NY.] 1-13-1864. Berlin Cemetery, Berlin, Camden County.

FLEET, WILLIAM W. (aka: Flett, William) Sgt, B, 29th NJ Inf, 3-25-1921. Glenwood Cemetery, West Long Branch, Monmouth County.

FLEETWOOD, MICHAEL J. Pvt, G, 28th NJ Inf, 9-13-1913. Mount Zion United Methodist Church Cemetery, Barnsboro, Gloucester County.

FLEIG*, ADOLPH Pvt, E, 68th NY Inf, 2-14-1887. Fairmount Cemetery, Newark, Essex County.

FLEIG, JOHN (aka: Pfleig, John) Corp, C, 75th PA Inf, 6-4-1884. Presbyterian Church Cemetery, Bridgeton, Cumberland County.

FLEISCHMAN, CHARLES Corp, F, 46th NY Inf, DoD Unknown. St. Joseph's Cemetery, Hackensack, Bergen County.

FLEMING, CHARLES EDWARD Lt Commander, U.S. Navy, 9-27-1867. Baptist/St. Andrew's Cemetery, Mount Holly, Burlington County.

FLEMING*, CHARLES H.C. Pvt, I, 11th NJ Inf, 8-27-1878. Maplewood Cemetery, Freehold, Monmouth County.

FLEMING, CHARLES W. Sgt, F, 14th NJ Inf, 3-13-1931. Whitelawn Cemetery, Point Pleasant, Ocean County.

FLEMING, CHRISTOPHER Pvt, F, 1st NJ Inf, DoD Unknown. St. Peter's Cemetery, New Brunswick, Middlesex County.

FLEMING, DAVID Sgt, H, 1st NJ Cav, 9-3-1891. Pequest Union Cemetery, Great Meadows, Warren County.

FLEMING, GODFREY Pvt, D, 1st NJ Inf, 3-26-1886. Methodist-Episcopal Cemetery, Whitehouse, Hunterdon County.

FLEMING, HARTSHORNE Pvt, A, 14th NJ Inf, 8-9-1868. Methodist Cemetery, Hamilton, Monmouth County.

FLEMING, JAMES A. Seaman, U.S. Navy, 1868. Holy Sepulchre Cemetery, Totowa, Passaic County.

FLEMING, JAMES L. Pvt, E, 55th NC Inf (CSA), [Captured 7-1-1863 at Gettysburg, PA. Died of typhoid.] 9-14-1863. Finn's Point National Cemetery, Pennsville, Salem County.

FLEMING*, JOSEPH W. Pvt, F, 14th NJ Inf, 12-23-1934. Whitelawn Cemetery, Point Pleasant, Ocean County.

FLEMING, MICHAEL Pvt, E, 33rd NJ Inf, 5-3-1865. Holy Sepulchre Cemetery, East Orange, Essex County.

Our Brothers Gone Before

FLEMING, PATRICK Pvt, E, 34th NJ Inf, 4-10-1914. St. Mary's Cemetery, Hamilton, Mercer County.
FLEMING, THOMAS Pvt, B, 26th NJ Inf, DoD Unknown. Holy Sepulchre Cemetery, East Orange, Essex County.
FLEMING*, THOMAS Pvt, A, 3rd NJ Cav, 6-1-1924. Presbyterian Church Cemetery, Mount Pleasant, Hunterdon County.
FLEMING, THOMAS B. Pvt, E, 23rd NC Inf (CSA), [Captured 7-1-1863 at Gettysburg, PA. Died of diptheria.] 10-5-1863. Finn's Point National Cemetery, Pennsville, Salem County.
FLEMING*, WILLIAM Corp, M, 2nd NJ Cav, 1921. Baptist Church Cemetery, Flemington, Hunterdon County.
FLEMING, WILLIAM Pvt, G, 30th NJ Inf, 1886. Presbyterian Church Cemetery, Mount Pleasant, Hunterdon County.
FLEMING*, WILLIAM F. 1st Lt, D, 192nd PA Inf, 6-8-1893. Atlantic City Cemetery, Pleasantville, Atlantic County.
FLEMING, WILLIAM H. Landsman, U.S. Navy, USS Princeton, 10-8-1924. Fairmount Cemetery, Fairmount, Hunterdon County.
FLENARD, ABEL R. Pvt, C, 23rd NJ Inf, 3-10-1919. Baptist/St. Andrew's Cemetery, Mount Holly, Burlington County.
FLENARD, GEORGE W. Corp, A, 213th PA Inf, 10-12-1900. Baptist Cemetery, Burlington, Burlington County.
FLENARD, JACOB Pvt, C, 23rd NJ Inf, 2-26-1890. Baptist/St. Andrew's Cemetery, Mount Holly, Burlington County.
FLESHINGER, LAWRENCE (see: Fischinger, Lorenz) Fairmount Cemetery, Newark, Essex County.
FLETCHER, ANDREW H. Pvt, Unassigned, 10th NJ Inf, DoD Unknown. Greenwood Cemetery, Lakewood, Ocean County.
FLETCHER, CHARLES M. 3-16-1887. Methodist-Episcopal Church Cemetery, Penns Grove, Salem County.
FLETCHER, FRANCIS Sgt, K, 15th NY Eng, 2-1-1914. Arlington Cemetery, Kearny, Hudson County.
FLETCHER, FRANK Chaplain, 134th NY Inf 6-28-1916. Hillside Cemetery, Scotch Plains, Union County.
FLETCHER, HANNAH Nurse, 11-22-1907. St. Mary's Episcopal Church Cemetery, Burlington, Burlington County.
FLETCHER, HENRY Corp, K, ___ PA Inf, 5-15-1916. Union Cemetery, Gloucester City, Camden County.
FLETCHER, HOWARD M. Pvt, H, 196th PA Inf, DoD Unknown. Monument Cemetery, Edgewater Park, Burlington County.
FLETCHER*, JACOB N. Pvt, Btty I, 1st PA Light Art, 4-18-1878. Elmwood Cemetery, New Brunswick, Middlesex County.
FLETCHER, JAMES 1st Lt, D, 14th NJ Inf, 4-18-1876. Elmwood Cemetery, New Brunswick, Middlesex County.
FLETCHER, JAMES Pvt, G, 7th NJ Inf, [Cenotaph. Died of wounds received at Gettysburg, PA.] 7-8-1863. Holy Sepulchre Cemetery, Totowa, Passaic County.
FLETCHER, JAMES A. Corp, G, 14th PA ___, [Wounded in action.] 5-14-1925. Elmwood Cemetery, New Brunswick, Middlesex County.
FLETCHER, JAMES A. 1878. Elmwood Cemetery, New Brunswick, Middlesex County.
FLETCHER, JOSEPH S. Corp, A, 12th NJ Inf, DoD Unknown. Evergreen Cemetery, Camden, Camden County.
FLETCHER, RICHARD 2nd Lt, C, 3rd MD Inf, DoD Unknown. Laurel Grove Cemetery, Totowa, Passaic County.
FLETCHER, RICHARD G. Pvt, A, 1st NJ Cav, DoD Unknown. Holy Sepulchre Cemetery, Totowa, Passaic County.

New Jersey Civil War Burials

FLETCHER, THOMAS Pvt, K, 35th NJ Inf, 12-23-1904. St. Mary's Episcopal Church Cemetery, Burlington, Burlington County.
FLETCHER, THOMAS DoD Unknown. Holy Sepulchre Cemetery, Totowa, Passaic County.
FLETCHER, VINSON C. Sgt, C, 36th AR Inf (CSA), [Captured 7-4-1863 at Helena, AR.] 3-2-1865. Finn's Point National Cemetery, Pennsville, Salem County.
FLETCHER, WILLIAM Pvt, A, 12th NJ Inf, [Died at Troy, NY.] 6-7-1865. Green Cemetery, Woodbury, Gloucester County.
FLETCHER, WILLIAM G 1st Sgt, C, 4th NJ Inf, 6-18-1879. Riverview Cemetery, Trenton, Mercer County.
FLETT, WILLIAM (see: Fleet, William W.) Glenwood Cemetery, West Long Branch, Monmouth County.
FLEW*, ALBERT Pvt, I, 99th PA Inf, 1-2-1897. Fairmount Cemetery, Newark, Essex County.
FLEXON, CHARLES Pvt, D, 12th NJ Inf, 1909. United Methodist Church Cemetery, Cross Keys, Gloucester County.
FLICK, CHRISTOPHER C. Pvt, D, 165th NY Inf, 2-14-1921. Glenwood Cemetery, West Long Branch, Monmouth County.
FLIGHA, WALTER 1887. Greenlawn Cemetery, West Long Branch, Monmouth County.
FLINN*, JAMES BART (aka: Flynn, James B.) Sgt, B, 33rd NJ Inf, 11-10-1912. Old 1st Methodist Church Cemetery, West Long Branch, Monmouth County.
FLINN, JOHN Pvt, D, 7th NJ Inf, 6-11-1869. Old 1st Methodist Church Cemetery, West Long Branch, Monmouth County.
FLINT, CHARLES L. Pvt, H, 4th MA Cav, 6-30-1915. Arlington Cemetery, Kearny, Hudson County.
FLINT, DAYTON E. Bvt Maj, 15th NJ Inf 10-17-1926. Union Cemetery, Washington, Morris County.
FLITCRAFT, HARVEY 2-5-1913. Evergreen Cemetery, Camden, Camden County.
FLOCK, JOHN H. Pvt, A, 94th IL Inf, [Cenotaph. Died at Carrollton, LA.] 9-3-1863. Methodist Cemetery, Allentown, Monmouth County.
FLOCK, SAMUEL Pvt, E, 2nd NJ Cav, 10-5-1891. Methodist Cemetery, Allentown, Monmouth County.
FLOHN, FRANCIS Pvt, E, 8th NJ Inf, 11-28-1883. Fairmount Cemetery, Newark, Essex County.
FLOHR, LEONARD Corp, E, 34th NJ Inf, 6-12-1909. Riverside Cemetery, Riverside, Burlington County.
FLOMERFELT*, DAVID NEIGHBOR (aka: Apgar, John) Pvt, C, 2nd NJ Cav, 1902. Fairmount Cemetery, Fairmount, Hunterdon County.
FLOOD, AUGUSTINE H. Pvt, D, 5th NY Inf, 10-28-1925. Presbyterian Church Cemetery, Woodbridge, Middlesex County.
FLOOD, JOSEPH N. Pvt, E, 27th PA Inf, 2-28-1899. St. Stephen Episcopal Cemetery, Florence, Burlington County.
FLOOD*, MICHAEL Pvt, A, 3rd NY Inf, DoD Unknown. Holy Sepulchre Cemetery, East Orange, Essex County.
FLOOD, PATRICK Pvt, I, 13th NJ Inf, 5-9-1887. Evergreen Cemetery, Hillside, Union County.
FLOOD, PATRICK A. 12-18-1884. St. Mary's Cemetery, East Orange, Essex County.
FLOOD*, PHILIP A. Pvt, I, 12th NJ Inf, DoD Unknown. Holy Sepulchre Cemetery, East Orange, Essex County.
FLOOD, PHILLIP Pvt, G, 33rd NJ Inf, 3-9-1904. Fairview Cemetery, Westfield, Union County.
FLOOD, THOMAS L. Pvt, D, 8th NJ Inf, 11-18-1871. Fairmount Cemetery, Newark, Essex County.

Our Brothers Gone Before

FLOOD, WILLIAM J. Pvt, E, 1st NJ Militia, 7-6-1901. Holy Sepulchre Cemetery, East Orange, Essex County.

FLORENCE, JAMES T. Pvt, E, 2nd Bttn NC Inf (CSA), [Captured 7-2-1863 at Gettysburg, PA. Died of diarrhea.] 10-27-1863. Finn's Point National Cemetery, Pennsville, Salem County.

FLORUS, JACOB FREDERICK Pvt, F, 3rd NJ Cav, 12-11-1907. Bloomfield Cemetery, Bloomfield, Essex County.

FLOUREY, AUGUSTUS Pvt, I, 47th AL Inf (CSA), 9-25-1863. Finn's Point National Cemetery, Pennsville, Salem County.

FLOWER, CHARLES Corp, A, 9th NJ Inf, 2-10-1915. St. Peter's Cemetery, New Brunswick, Middlesex County.

FLOWER, GEORGE Corp, A, 99th PA Inf, DoD Unknown. Presbyterian Church Cemetery, Bridgeton, Cumberland County.

FLOWERS, GEORGE W. Pvt, C, 52nd PA Inf, 8-11-1913. Mount Holly Cemetery, Mount Holly, Burlington County.

FLOWERS, JAMES W. Pvt, C, 9th NY Inf, 4-21-1902. Hoboken Cemetery, North Bergen, Hudson County.

FLOWERS, WILLIAM H. Pvt, G, 9th DE Inf, DoD Unknown. Finn's Point National Cemetery, Pennsville, Salem County.

FLOYD, EDMOND C. (see: Floyd, Edward) Cedar Lawn Cemetery, Paterson, Passaic County.

FLOYD, EDWARD (aka: Floyd, Edmond C.) Landsman, U.S. Navy, USS Wabash, 6-15-1924. Cedar Lawn Cemetery, Paterson, Passaic County.

FLOYD, GEORGE Pvt, H, 3rd NJ Inf, 2-10-1872. Baptist/St. Andrew's Cemetery, Mount Holly, Burlington County.

FLOYD, HENRY Pvt, F, 11th (Bethel) NC Inf (CSA), [Captured 7-3-1863 at Gettysburg, PA.] 10-6-1863. Finn's Point National Cemetery, Pennsville, Salem County.

FLOYD*, JOSEPH B. Pvt, A, 2nd Bttn FL Inf (CSA), [Captured 3-27-1863 at St. John's River, FL.] 10-3-1863. Finn's Point National Cemetery, Pennsville, Salem County.

FLOYD, SAMUEL 12-30-1910. New Camden Cemetery, Camden, Camden County.

FLOYD, WILLIAM Seaman, U.S. Navy, USS Powhattan, 4-1-1892. Johnson Cemetery, Camden, Camden County.

FLOYD, WILLIAM Pvt, I, 9th NJ Inf, 3-9-1888. Old 1st Baptist Cemetery, Auburn, Salem County.

FLUE, JOHN Pvt, C, 40th NY Inf, [Wounded 7-2-1863 at Gettysburg, PA.] 8-23-1878. Fairmount Cemetery, Newark, Essex County.

FLUERY, DAVID W. Pvt, F, 2nd NJ Cav, 6-7-1912. Evergreen Cemetery, Morristown, Morris County.

FLUKE, DAVID Pvt, C, 27th NJ Inf, 3-29-1869. Presbyterian/Methodist-Episcopal Cemetery, Succasunna, Morris County.

FLUMERFELT, JACOB B. 1-30-1903. Methodist Church Cemetery, Buttzville, Warren County.

FLYN, JOSEPH W. (see: Flynn, Joseph M.) Holy Rood Cemetery, Morristown, Morris County.

FLYNN, DAVID DoD Unknown. Lodi Cemetery, Lodi, Bergen County.

FLYNN, DAVID J. Pvt, C, 2nd NJ Inf, 2-18-1892. Holy Sepulchre Cemetery, East Orange, Essex County.

FLYNN, JAMES Pvt, E, 1st NY Eng, 8-11-1895. Holy Name Cemetery, Jersey City, Hudson County.

FLYNN, JAMES A. Pvt, U.S. Marine Corps, 3-6-1886. St. John's Evangelical Church Cemetery, Orange, Essex County.

FLYNN, JAMES B. (see: Flinn, James Bart) Old 1st Methodist Church Cemetery, West Long Branch, Monmouth County.

FLYNN, JEREMIAH Seaman, U.S. Navy, USS Chicopee, 5-30-1899. Holy Sepulchre Cemetery, Totowa, Passaic County.
FLYNN, JOHN J. Pvt, C, 6th NJ Inf, 7-27-1888. St. Paul's R.C. Church Cemetery, Princeton, Mercer County.
FLYNN*, JOSEPH Musc, E, 7th NY State Militia, 8-30-1911. Bayview-New York Bay Cemetery, Jersey City, Hudson County.
FLYNN, JOSEPH E. Pvt, E, 43rd GA Inf (CSA), [Captured 5-16-1863 at Baker's Creek, MS. Died of typhoid.] 7-8-1863. Finn's Point National Cemetery, Pennsville, Salem County.
FLYNN, JOSEPH M. (aka: Flyn, Joseph W.) Corp, B, 37th NJ Inf, 1-5-1910. Holy Rood Cemetery, Morristown, Morris County.
FLYNN, JOSEPH W. 8-5-1890. Monument Cemetery, Edgewater Park, Burlington County.
FLYNN, LAWRENCE Pvt, B, 35th NJ Inf, 4-13-1877. Holy Sepulchre Cemetery, East Orange, Essex County.
FLYNN, MARTIN Pvt, Btty B, 1st NJ Light Art, 5-11-1890. Lodi Cemetery, Lodi, Bergen County.
FLYNN, MICHAEL Landsman, U.S. Navy, USS Princeton, DoD Unknown. Flower Hill Cemetery, North Bergen, Hudson County.
FLYNN, MICHAEL A. Pvt, C, 2nd NJ Cav, 7-30-1888. Holy Name Cemetery, Jersey City, Hudson County.
FLYNN, NICHOLAS Pvt, C, 2nd NY Cav, 12-7-1918. Immaculate Conception Cemetery, Montclair, Essex County.
FLYNN, PATRICK Pvt, E, 35th NY Inf, 5-27-1884. Flower Hill Cemetery, North Bergen, Hudson County.
FLYNN*, PATRICK W. Corp, H, 13th NY Cav, 12-31-1871. Holy Name Cemetery, Jersey City, Hudson County.
FLYNN, PETER Pvt, N, 198th PA Inf, 8-5-1909. Mount Olivet Cemetery, Newark, Essex County.
FLYNN, RICHARD Pvt, Unassigned, 69th NY State Militia, 9-11-1903. Holy Sepulchre Cemetery, East Orange, Essex County.
FLYNN, THOMAS Sgt, B, 13th NJ Inf, 11-29-1879. Holy Name Cemetery, Jersey City, Hudson County.
FLYNN, THOMAS Pvt, D, 8th NJ Inf, 2-15-1900. Mount Olivet Cemetery, Newark, Essex County.
FLYNN*, WILLIAM Pvt, K, 3rd NJ Inf, 9-10-1898. Holy Name Cemetery, Jersey City, Hudson County.
FLYNN, WILLIAM H. Pvt, B, 5th NJ Inf, 9-29-1893. Jersey City Cemetery, Jersey City, Hudson County.
FOALKS, ALEXANDER (aka: Foalks, Thomas) Pvt, C, 25th NJ Inf, DoD Unknown. Holy Sepulchre Cemetery, Totowa, Passaic County.
FOALKS, THOMAS (see: Foalks, Alexander) Holy Sepulchre Cemetery, Totowa, Passaic County.
FOCER, JOSEPH C. 1-7-1894. Methodist-Episcopal Cemetery, Glassboro, Gloucester County.
FOERSTER, BERNHARD (aka: Barnard, George F.) Pvt, E, 150th NY Inf, 11-30-1931. Grove Church Cemetery, North Bergen, Hudson County.
FOGELSTRAND, OTTO Seaman, U.S. Navy, 8-11-1937. Laurel Grove Cemetery, Totowa, Passaic County.
FOGERTY, JOHN D. Pvt, K, 29th NJ Inf, 3-14-1895. Woodlawn Cemetery, Lakewood, Ocean County.
FOGG, JOHN H. Pvt, A, 24th NJ Inf, 2-2-1884. Baptist Church Cemetery, Canton, Salem County.

Our Brothers Gone Before

FOGG, JOHN M. 1st Lt, H, 12th NJ Inf, [Killed in action at Wilderness, VA.] 5-5-1864. Methodist Cemetery, Woodstown, Salem County.

FOGG, JOSEPH H. 9-28-1894. 7th Day Baptist Church Cemetery, Shiloh, Cumberland County.

FOGG, SMITH J Pvt, F, 3rd NJ Inf, [Died at Philadelphia, PA.] 6-1-1862. Presbyterian Church Cemetery, Bridgeton, Cumberland County.

FOGG, WILLIAM Sgt, I, ___ PA Inf, 5-14-1896. New Camden Cemetery, Camden, Camden County.

FOGTMAN, JOHN Pvt, E, 18th CT Inf, [Wounded 6-5-1864 at Piedmont, VA.] 9-9-1905. Laurel Grove Cemetery, Totowa, Passaic County.

FOHS, LOUIS 2nd Lt, C, 1st NJ Cav, 4-14-1884. Fairmount Cemetery, Newark, Essex County.

FOHS, PHILIP DECKER (aka: Decker, Philip) Pvt, F, 39th NJ Inf, 10-23-1885. Fairmount Cemetery, Newark, Essex County.

FOLAN, JOHN Pvt, I, 52nd PA Inf, 1-7-1871. Holy Name Cemetery, Jersey City, Hudson County.

FOLEY, DENNIS Pvt, F, 28th NJ Inf, 12-26-1912. St. Peter's Cemetery, New Brunswick, Middlesex County.

FOLEY, ELIAS Pvt, A, 25th NJ Inf, DoD Unknown. Crooked Pond Cemetery, Franklin Lakes, Bergen County.

FOLEY*, JEREMIAH Sgt, F, 15th NJ Inf, 9-22-1888. St. Mary's Cemetery, Wharton, Morris County.

FOLEY*, JOHN H. Pvt, L, 16th NY Cav, 2-26-1908. Holy Name Cemetery, Jersey City, Hudson County.

FOLEY, MICHAEL Pvt, G, 21st NJ Inf, 9-16-1905. Holy Name Cemetery, Jersey City, Hudson County.

FOLEY, PATRICK Pvt, Btty F, 4th NY Heavy Art, DoD Unknown. Holy Sepulchre Cemetery, East Orange, Essex County.

FOLEY, WILLIAM DoD Unknown. St. Mary's Cemetery, Perth Amboy, Middlesex County.

FOLEY, WILLIAM Pvt, I, 7th CT Inf, 8-12-1903. St. Mary's Cemetery, Boonton, Morris County.

FOLEY, WILLIAM DoD Unknown. St. Joseph's Cemetery, Bound Brook, Somerset County.

FOLEY, WILLIAM GREEN 3rd Corp, B, 51st GA Inf (CSA), 8-10-1863. Finn's Point National Cemetery, Pennsville, Salem County.

FOLK, JOHN P. 6-6-1916. Phillipsburg Cemetery, Phillipsburg, Warren County.

FOLKENBURG, THOMAS J. (see: Falkenburg, Thomas B.) Oddfellows Cemetery, Burlington, Burlington County.

FOLKES, GEORGE Musc, K, 45th U.S. CT, 7-23-1893. Beverly National Cemetery, Edgewater Park, Burlington County.

FOLKNER, JAMES M. Seaman, U.S. Navy, USS Nipsic, 1916. Tranquility Cemetery, Tranquility, Sussex County.

FOLKNER, JOHN Pvt, I, 31st NJ Inf, 10-26-1900. Tranquility Cemetery, Tranquility, Sussex County.

FOLL, FREDERICK Pvt, E, 214th PA Inf, 10-28-1912. New Camden Cemetery, Camden, Camden County.

FOLLEN, FREDERICK W. Seaman, U.S. Navy, USS Sarah Bruen, 11-21-1892. Bayview-New York Bay Cemetery, Jersey City, Hudson County.

FOLLEY, BRINKERHOFF D. Corp, H, 2nd DC Inf, 4-17-1907. Rosedale Cemetery, Orange, Essex County.

FOLLEY, JOHN B. Pvt, A, 25th NJ Inf, 3-9-1903. Crooked Pond Cemetery, Franklin Lakes, Bergen County.

New Jersey Civil War Burials

FOLLIN, WILLIAM R. Pvt, H, 8th VA Inf (CSA), [Captured 7-3-1863 at Gettysburg, PA. Died of fever.] 10-27-1863. Finn's Point National Cemetery, Pennsville, Salem County.

FOLSOM, WILLIAM (see: Folsome, William H.) Bayview-New York Bay Cemetery, Jersey City, Hudson County.

FOLSOME, WILLIAM H. (aka: Folsom, William) Pvt, E, 1st MI Sharpshooters, 3-26-1900. Bayview-New York Bay Cemetery, Jersey City, Hudson County.

FOLWELL, ROBERT C. (aka: Forwell, Robert) Corp, F, 8th PA Cav, 3- -1911. Friends Cemetery, Mullica Hill, Gloucester County.

FONSBURY, JOHN Pvt, K, 10th NJ Inf, [Killed in action at Cold Harbor, VA.] 6-3-1864. United Methodist Church Cemetery, Hainesneck, Salem County.

FOOR, GEORGE Pvt, A, 40th NY Inf, [Died of disease at Brandy Station, VA.] 12-22-1863. Christian Cemetery, Milford, Hunterdon County.

FOOS, RICHARD (see: Foryce, Richard C.) Prospect Hill Cemetery, Caldwell, Essex County.

FOOSE, JACOB Pvt, K, 15th NJ Inf, 7-30-1903. Fountain Grove Cemetery, Glen Gardner, Hunterdon County.

FOOSE, MARTIN J. Pvt, C, 31st NJ Inf, [Died of typhoid at Aquia Creek, VA.] 4-13-1863. Methodist Church Cemetery, Bloomsbury, Hunterdon County.

FOOSE, WILLIAM L. Pvt, C, 31st NJ Inf, [Died of fever at Philadelphia, PA.] 6-26-1863. Methodist Church Cemetery, Bloomsbury, Hunterdon County.

FOOSHEE, R.B. Pvt, E, 13th NC Inf (CSA), [Wounded 7-1-1863 at Gettysburg, PA. Died of bronchitis.] 9-7-1863. Finn's Point National Cemetery, Pennsville, Salem County.

FOOTE, EBENEZER H. Capt, K, 11th CT Inf, 1-19-1926. Oak Hill Cemetery, Vineland, Cumberland County.

FOOTE, JULIUS MERRILL 1st Sgt, H, 176th NY Inf, 9-4-1918. Fairmount Cemetery, Newark, Essex County.

FOOTE, ROBERT DoD Unknown. Evergreen Cemetery, Morristown, Morris County.

FOOTIT, WILLIAM N. Pvt, D, 4th NJ Inf, 3-17-1881. Riverview Cemetery, Trenton, Mercer County.

FORAN*, JAMES Pvt, G, 8th NJ Inf, [Wounded in action.] 12-29-1906. St. John's Cemetery, Lambertville, Hunterdon County.

FORAN, JOHN Pvt, Btty F, 1st MA Heavy Art, [Wounded 6-3-1864 at Cold Harbor, VA.] 11-10-1912. Prospect Hill Cemetery, Flemington, Hunterdon County.

FORAN, WILLIAM Pvt, F, 7th NJ Inf, 9-20-1873. Holy Name Cemetery, Jersey City, Hudson County.

FORBES, GEORGE 2nd Lt, F, 27th NJ Inf, DoD Unknown. 1st Reformed Church Cemetery, Pompton Plains, Morris County.

FORBES, HENRY T. (aka: Forbis, Henry T.) Pvt, K, 7th TN Inf (CSA), 11-6-1863. Finn's Point National Cemetery, Pennsville, Salem County.

FORBES, JOHN Pvt, F, 34th NJ Inf, 12-10-1886. St. Mary's Cemetery, Hainesport, Burlington County.

FORBES, JOSEPH 9-3-1892. Cedar Lawn Cemetery, Paterson, Passaic County.

FORBES, THOMAS (see: Forbis, Thomas L.) Soldier's Home Cemetery, Vineland, Cumberland County.

FORBES, THOMAS H. Pvt, D, 34th NJ Inf, 5-27-1870. Cedar Lawn Cemetery, Paterson, Passaic County.

FORBES, THOMAS H. Pvt, E, 1st NY Inf, DoD Unknown. Cedar Lawn Cemetery, Paterson, Passaic County.

FORBES, WILLIAM H. Fireman, U.S. Navy, USS Wynona, 3-29-1910. Evergreen Cemetery, Camden, Camden County.

FORBIS, HENRY T. (see: Forbes, Henry T.) Finn's Point National Cemetery, Pennsville, Salem County.

Our Brothers Gone Before

FORBIS, THOMAS L. (aka: Forbes, Thomas) Pvt, B, 40th NJ Inf, 8-28-1906. Soldier's Home Cemetery, Vineland, Cumberland County.
FORBUSH, ALBERT A. 1st Lt, K, 22nd NJ Inf, 1-1-1906. Evergreen Cemetery, Hillside, Union County.
FORCE, CHARLES E. Pvt, G, 26th NJ Inf, DoD Unknown. East Ridgelawn Cemetery, Clifton, Passaic County.
FORCE, CHARLES P. Pvt, K, 4th NJ Militia, 4-3-1862. Methodist-Episcopal Cemetery, Burlington, Burlington County.
FORCE, CHARLES R. Pvt, G, 13th NJ Inf, 5-20-1892. Bloomfield Cemetery, Bloomfield, Essex County.
FORCE, COLUMBUS Capt, G, 25th NJ Inf, 1-13-1895. Cedar Lawn Cemetery, Paterson, Passaic County.
FORCE*, CORYDON C. Pvt, C, 15th NJ Inf, DoD Unknown. Hillside Cemetery, Madison, Morris County.
FORCE, D.S. Pvt, K, 39th NJ Inf, DoD Unknown. Presbyterian Church Cemetery, Pleasant Grove, Morris County.
FORCE, DAVID Pvt, G, 4th U.S. Inf, 10-5-1864. Beverly National Cemetery, Edgewater Park, Burlington County.
FORCE, DEXTER N. 2nd Lt, G, 37th NY State Militia, 12-31-1928. Rosedale Cemetery, Orange, Essex County.
FORCE, GEORGE S. Sgt, G, 26th NJ Inf, DoD Unknown. South Orange Cemetery, South Orange, Essex County.
FORCE, JABEZ W. DoD Unknown. English Neighborhood Reformed Church Cemetery, Ridgefield, Bergen County.
FORCE, JAMES 8-17-1897. Bayview-New York Bay Cemetery, Jersey City, Hudson County.
FORCE, JOHN (JR.) Pvt, K, 4th NJ Militia, 9-13-1872. Mansfield/Washington Cemetery, Washington, Warren County.
FORCE, JOHN M. Pvt, Btty C, 2nd PA Heavy Art, 12-24-1864. Coopertown Meeting House Cemetery, Edgewater Park, Burlington County.
FORCE, JOHN R. Pvt, D, 26th NJ Inf, 5-21-1901. Methodist Church Cemetery, Roseland, Essex County.
FORCE, JONATHAN Pvt, D, 26th NJ Inf, 2-18-1912. Federated Baptist Church Cemetery, Livingston, Essex County.
FORCE, JOSEPH H. Pvt, B, 31st NJ Inf, 11-18-1868. Mansfield/Washington Cemetery, Washington, Warren County.
FORCE, JUSTICE L. Pvt, H, 15th NJ Inf, 2-1-1890. Methodist Church Cemetery, Summerfield, Warren County.
FORCE, LOUIS C. Musc, C, 27th NJ Inf, 1-6-1922. Presbyterian/Methodist-Episcopal Cemetery, Succasunna, Morris County.
FORCE, SAMUEL S. Pvt, F, 13th NJ Inf, DoD Unknown. Presbyterian Church Cemetery, Pleasant Grove, Morris County.
FORCE, SOBIESKI Pvt, K, 9th NJ Inf, 1906. Mount Hebron Cemetery, Montclair, Essex County.
FORCE, WILLIAM A. Pvt, E, 47th PA Inf, [Wounded 10-22-1862 at Pocotaligo, SC.] 2-12-1888. Phillipsburg Cemetery, Phillipsburg, Warren County.
FORCE, WILLIAM H. (aka: Krouse, William H.) Pvt, I, 37th NJ Inf, 1892. Mount Hebron Cemetery, Montclair, Essex County.
FORCE, WILLIAM HENRY Pvt, H, 97th PA Inf, 1-3-1917. Mount Pleasant Cemetery, Millville, Cumberland County.
FORCE, WILLIAM L. Pvt, B, 29th NJ Inf, 4-2-1891. Greengrove Cemetery, Keyport, Monmouth County.
FORCE, WILLIAM W. Pvt, Btty B, 1st NJ Light Art, 11-5-1904. Mansfield/Washington Cemetery, Washington, Warren County.

New Jersey Civil War Burials

FORD, AMIDEE B. Pvt, K, 39th NJ Inf, 6- -1873. Chestnut Cemetery, Dover, Morris County.

FORD, BENJAMIN Pvt, I, 1st PA Mtd Inf, 2-5-1894. Cedar Grove Cemetery, Gloucester City, Camden County.

FORD, BENJAMIN A. Sgt, H, 4th (Russell's) AL Cav (CSA), 7-3-1864. Finn's Point National Cemetery, Pennsville, Salem County.

FORD*, BENJAMIN F. Pvt, H, 24th NJ Inf, 5-5-1892. Presbyterian Church Cemetery, Bridgeton, Cumberland County.

FORD, BENJAMIN PIERSON Pvt, I, 27th NJ Inf, 2-2-1866. Evergreen Cemetery, Morristown, Morris County.

FORD, BERNARD Landsman, U.S. Navy, 4-1-1867. St. John's Evangelical Church Cemetery, Orange, Essex County.

FORD*, CHARLES E. Pvt, I, 1st NJ Inf, 5-1-1899. Holy Name Cemetery, Jersey City, Hudson County.

FORD, CHARLES M. Pvt, F, 9th NJ Inf, 8-12-1864. Cedar Hill Cemetery, Hightstown, Mercer County.

FORD, CHARLES P. Pvt, E, 1st (Gregg's) SC Inf (CSA), [Captured 7-4-1863 at Gettysburg, PA.] 10-7-1863. Finn's Point National Cemetery, Pennsville, Salem County.

FORD, CHARLES P. QM Sgt, 28th NJ Inf 4-14-1897. Elmwood Cemetery, New Brunswick, Middlesex County.

FORD, CHARLES R. 1st Lt, K, 76th IL Inf, 9-28-1878. Bordentown/Old St. Mary's Catholic Cemetery, Bordentown, Burlington County.

FORD, CONSTANT C. Pvt, K, 23rd NJ Inf, 1-18-1927. Cedar Green Cemetery, Clayton, Gloucester County.

FORD, DAVID J. Pvt, D, 14th NJ Inf, 4-24-1920. Emleys Hill United Methodist Church Cemetery, Upper Freehold, Monmouth County.

FORD, EDWARD Corp, E, 69th PA Inf, 2-4-1915. Old St. Mary's Cemetery, Gloucester City, Camden County.

FORD, EDWARD G. 1st Lt, I, 2nd NJ Inf, 1907. East Ridgelawn Cemetery, Clifton, Passaic County.

FORD, EZEKIEL Sgt, F, 6th NJ Inf, [Died at Burlington, NJ.] 8-29-1862. St. Mary's Episcopal Church Cemetery, Burlington, Burlington County.

FORD, GEORGE Pvt, K, 23rd NJ Inf, [Wounded in action.] 1-19-1908. Zion Methodist Church Cemetery, Bargaintown, Atlantic County.

FORD, GEORGE W. Pvt, E, 1st (Gregg's) SC Inf (CSA), [Captured 7-5-1863 at Gettysburg, PA. Died of abscess.] 11-29-1863. Finn's Point National Cemetery, Pennsville, Salem County.

FORD, GEORGE W. Maj, 50th NY Eng 1882. Rosedale Cemetery, Orange, Essex County.

FORD, GUSTAVUS Pvt, D, 5th U.S. Inf, 6-21-1899. Evergreen Cemetery, Camden, Camden County.

FORD, HENRY Pvt, F, 33rd NJ Inf, [Died of fits aboard the USS DeMolay.] 9-10-1863. Holy Sepulchre Cemetery, East Orange, Essex County.

FORD, ISHAM A. Pvt, K, 42nd MS Inf (CSA), 1-22-1864. Finn's Point National Cemetery, Pennsville, Salem County.

FORD, JAMES Corp, E, 40th NJ Inf, DoD Unknown. Maplewood Cemetery, Freehold, Monmouth County.

FORD, JAMES Pvt, F, 10th NJ Inf, DoD Unknown. St. Paul's Church Cemetery, Burlington, Burlington County.

FORD, JAMES Pvt, I, 2nd NJ Inf, [Died of diarrhea at Danville, VA.] 12-20-1864. Locust Hill Cemetery, Dover, Morris County.

FORD, JESSE Pvt, B, 24th NJ Inf, 1-10-1905. Mount Pleasant Cemetery, Millville, Cumberland County.

Our Brothers Gone Before

FORD, JOHN Pvt, C, 34th NJ Inf, 1911. Bordentown/Old St. Mary's Catholic Cemetery, Bordentown, Burlington County.

FORD, JOHN Pvt, G, 32nd WI Inf, 5-13-1894. Holy Sepulchre Cemetery, East Orange, Essex County.

FORD, JOHN (see: Wiseburn, John L.) Methodist Church Cemetery, Liberty, Warren County.

FORD, JOHN C. Seaman, U.S. Navy, USS Macedonian, 10-11-1937. Giberson Cemetery, Whiting, Ocean County.

FORD, JOHN E. Pvt, F, 22nd NJ Inf, 1-8-1919. Cedar Hill Cemetery, Hightstown, Mercer County.

FORD, JOHN EDGAR Corp, K, 1st NJ Cav, 10-19-1929. Arlington Cemetery, Kearny, Hudson County.

FORD, JOHN H. Pvt, C, 35th AL Inf (CSA), 7-15-1863. Finn's Point National Cemetery, Pennsville, Salem County.

FORD, JOHN R. Pvt, B, 12th NJ Inf, 2-27-1902. Presbyterian Church Cemetery, Bridgeton, Cumberland County.

FORD*, JOHN W. Pvt, E, 11th NJ Inf, 11-15-1895. Chestnut Cemetery, Dover, Morris County.

FORD, JOSEPH Pvt, G, 4th NJ Inf, 6-28-1866. Batsto/Pleasant Mills Methodist Church Cemetery, Pleasant Mills, Atlantic County.

FORD, MARCUS S. Pvt, E, 11th NJ Inf, 6-18-1889. Chestnut Cemetery, Dover, Morris County.

FORD, MAURICE 1926. Methodist-Episcopal Cemetery, Green Bank, Burlington County.

FORD, PATRICK Pvt, U.S. Marine Corps, 2-17-1897. St. John's Evangelical Church Cemetery, Orange, Essex County.

FORD, RICHARD B. Pvt, I, 23rd NJ Inf, 5-4-1922. Roadside Cemetery, Manchester Township, Ocean County.

FORD, SAMUEL Pvt, K, 23rd NJ Inf, 1-30-1892. Methodist-Episcopal Cemetery, Green Bank, Burlington County.

FORD, SAMUEL P. Pvt, K, 23rd NJ Inf, DoD Unknown. Methodist-Episcopal Cemetery, Green Bank, Burlington County.

FORD, SAMUEL W. Pvt, D, 20th MA Inf, [Died of disease at Alexandria, VA.] 8-24-1864. Presbyterian Church Cemetery, Metuchen, Middlesex County.

FORD, SAMUEL W. Corp, I, 144th IL Inf, 9-5-1904. Riverview Cemetery, Trenton, Mercer County.

FORD, W.L. Pvt, C, 4th (Neely's) TN Inf (CSA), 10-11-1863. Finn's Point National Cemetery, Pennsville, Salem County.

FORD, WILLIAM Pvt, G, 4th NJ Inf, 11-11-1881. Methodist-Episcopal Cemetery, Lower Bank, Burlington County.

FORD, WILLIAM Wagoner, A, 4th MA Militia, 12-29-1903. Greenwood Cemetery, Hamilton, Mercer County.

FORD, WILLIAM F. Sgt, K, 9th NJ Inf, 2-13-1910. Fairmount Cemetery, Chatham, Morris County.

FORD, WILLIAM H. Pvt, K, 23rd NJ Inf, 9-25-1904. Arlington Cemetery, Kearny, Hudson County.

FORD*, WILLIAM H. Pvt, K, 8th NJ Inf, [Wounded in action.] 4-28-1901. Presbyterian Cemetery, Springfield, Union County.

FORD, WILLIAM H. Pvt, K, 23rd NJ Inf, 8-8-1892. Methodist-Episcopal Cemetery, Green Bank, Burlington County.

FORDHAM, CHARLES F. Pvt, F, 37th NJ Inf, DoD Unknown. Hazelwood Cemetery, Rahway, Union County.

FORDHAM, STEPHEN C. Capt, A, 26th NJ Inf, 3-16-1897. Fairmount Cemetery, Newark, Essex County.

New Jersey Civil War Burials

FORDNER, SAMUEL (see: Fortney, Samuel T.) Monument Cemetery, Edgewater Park, Burlington County.
FOREMAN, CHARLES J. 1929. Harleigh Cemetery, Camden, Camden County.
FOREMAN, JAMES L. Pvt, D, 21st PA Cav, 1921. Rosemont Cemetery, Rosemont, Hunterdon County.
FORGARSON, DEWITT (aka: Forgeson, DeWitt) Wagonmaster, B, 2nd NJ Inf, [Died of lumbar abscess at Newark, NJ.] 7-13-1865. Deckertown-Union Cemetery, Papakating, Sussex County.
FORGE, JOSEPH L. Pvt, I, 3rd NJ Inf, [Died at Fredericksburg, VA. of wounds received at Spotsylvania CH, VA.] 5-15-1864. Presbyterian Cemetery, North Plainfield, Somerset County.
FORGESON, DEWITT (see: Forgarson, DeWitt) Deckertown-Union Cemetery, Papakating, Sussex County.
FORGUS, WILLIAM F. Pvt, B, 35th NJ Inf, 1-16-1916. Arlington Cemetery, Kearny, Hudson County.
FORKER, GEORGE Pvt, H, 3rd NJ Inf, 11-22-1867. Baptist/St. Andrew's Cemetery, Mount Holly, Burlington County.
FORKER*, JOHN W. Landsman, U.S. Navy, USS Minnesota, 2-21-1881. Baptist Church Cemetery, Flemington, Hunterdon County.
FORKER, NEHEMIAH B. Pvt, Btty H, 5th NY Heavy Art, 1-25-1868. Bloomfield Cemetery, Bloomfield, Essex County.
FORKER, SAMUEL Pvt, H, 3rd NJ Inf, 4-25-1897. Mount Holly Cemetery, Mount Holly, Burlington County.
FORMAN, DANIEL MCLEAN Surgeon's Steward, U.S. Navy, USS Rhode Island, 3-29-1909. Maplewood Cemetery, Freehold, Monmouth County.
FORMAN, JAMES H. Pvt, G, 38th NJ Inf, 1925. Evergreen Cemetery, New Brunswick, Middlesex County.
FORMAN*, SAMUEL R. Asst Surg, U.S. Navy, USS Circassian, 2-19-1900. Tennent Church Cemetery, Tennent, Monmouth County.
FORMAN, WILLIAM Corp, G, 3rd NJ Militia, 8-12-1870. Greenlawn Cemetery, West Long Branch, Monmouth County.
FORMAN, WILLIAM C. 12-28-1877. Brainerd Cemetery, Cranbury, Middlesex County.
FORNOFF, JACOB 1-21-1915. Bloomfield Cemetery, Bloomfield, Essex County.
FORRAN, WILLIAM Pvt, F, 7th NJ Inf, 9-20-1873. Holy Name Cemetery, Jersey City, Hudson County.
FORRESTER, ARCHIBALD 2nd Cl Fireman, U.S. Navy, USS Tallapoosa, 3-18-1906. Mansfield/Washington Cemetery, Washington, Warren County.
FORRESTER, WILLIAM Sgt, H, 15th NJ Inf, 1-26-1907. Mansfield/Washington Cemetery, Washington, Warren County.
FORSCHNER, JOHN 2nd Lt, G, 73rd PA Inf, 2-2-1915. Fairmount Cemetery, Newark, Essex County.
FORSHEE, JOHN C. Pvt, B, 26th NJ Inf, 3-15-1904. Fairmount Cemetery, Chatham, Morris County.
FORSYTH, ANDREW Sgt, K, 3rd NJ Inf, [Wounded 9-14-1862 at Crampton's Pass, MD. Killed in action at Salem Heights, VA.] 5-3-1863. Presbyterian Church Cemetery, Elizabeth, Union County.
FORSYTH, GEORGE 5-10-1898. Presbyterian Church Cemetery, Mendham, Morris County.
FORSYTH, GEORGE Pvt, E, 14th NJ Inf, 3-9-1882. St. Mary's Cemetery, Clark, Union County.
FORSYTH, GEORGE Pvt, A, 1st NJ Inf, 4-12-1868. Presbyterian Church Cemetery, Elizabeth, Union County.
FORSYTH, JAMES Landsman, U.S. Navy, 2-18-1901. New Camden Cemetery, Camden, Camden County.

Our Brothers Gone Before

FORT*, CHARLES H. Pvt, C, 12th NJ Inf, 12-25-1900. Fairmount Cemetery, Newark, Essex County.
FORT, ISAAC Pvt, E, 56th NY Inf, 7-19-1907. Fairmount Cemetery, Newark, Essex County.
FORT, WILLIAM Pvt, C, 12th NJ Inf, 11-6-1891. Fairmount Cemetery, Newark, Essex County.
FORT*, WILLIAM S. Asst Surg, U.S. Navy, USS Powhattan, [Cenotaph.] 3-24-1873. Mount Holly Cemetery, Mount Holly, Burlington County.
FORTINER*, ALFRED B. Pvt, G, 12th NJ Inf, 6-16-1878. Baptist Church Cemetery, Haddonfield, Camden County.
FORTMAN, CARSTEN E. Pvt, B, 68th NY Inf, DoD Unknown. Weehawken Cemetery, North Bergen, Hudson County.
FORTNER, J.M. Pvt, E, 1st (Carter's) TN Cav (CSA), 7-28-1864. Finn's Point National Cemetery, Pennsville, Salem County.
FORTNER, JAMES DoD Unknown. Baptist Church Cemetery, Haddonfield, Camden County.
FORTNEY, SAMUEL T. (aka: Fordner, Samuel) Pvt, C, 91st PA Inf, 1-17-1905. Monument Cemetery, Edgewater Park, Burlington County.
FORTUNE, S. DoD Unknown. Cedar Lawn Cemetery, Paterson, Passaic County.
FORWELL, ROBERT (see: Folwell, Robert C.) Friends Cemetery, Mullica Hill, Gloucester County.
FORYCE, RICHARD C. (aka: Foos, Richard) Pvt, B, 56th NY Inf, [Died at Harrisons Landing, VA of wounds received in action.] 9-18-1862. Prospect Hill Cemetery, Caldwell, Essex County.
FOSDICK*, GILBERT C. Corp, H, 86th NY Inf, 1-25-1900. Jersey City Cemetery, Jersey City, Hudson County.
FOSDICK, JOHN D. 7-15-1898. Bayview-New York Bay Cemetery, Jersey City, Hudson County.
FOSS, GEORGE 2nd Lt, F, 57th NY Inf, 6-24-1897. Hoboken Cemetery, North Bergen, Hudson County.
FOSS, LUDWIG (aka: Fuss, Ludwig) Pvt, G, 7th NY Inf, DoD Unknown. Grove Church Cemetery, North Bergen, Hudson County.
FOSSILL, CHARLES (see: Fassett, Charles) Fairmount Cemetery, Newark, Essex County.
FOSTER*, ABRAM Pvt, K, 97th NY Inf, 1-24-1912. Holy Sepulchre Cemetery, Totowa, Passaic County.
FOSTER*, AMARIAH E. Pvt, E, 1st NJ Cav, [Wounded 5-5-1864 at Wilderness, VA.] 9-3-1913. Presbyterian Church Cemetery, Cold Spring, Cape May County.
FOSTER, ANDREW J. Pvt, B, 4th NJ Inf, 4-4-1887. Fairmount Cemetery, Newark, Essex County.
FOSTER, BENJAMIN Seaman, U.S. Navy, 1928. Union Cemetery, Clarkstown, Atlantic County.
FOSTER, BENJAMIN J.M. Pvt, D, 31st GA Inf (CSA), [Captured 5-12-1864 at Spotsylvania CH, VA. Died of typhoid.] 7-18-1864. Finn's Point National Cemetery, Pennsville, Salem County.
FOSTER, CHARLES Pvt, Btty F, 2nd NY Heavy Art, 1907. Bayview-New York Bay Cemetery, Jersey City, Hudson County.
FOSTER, CHARLES Corp, A, 8th NJ Inf, 4-7-1876. Clinton Cemetery, Irvington, Essex County.
FOSTER, DANIEL (see: Fitzpatrick, Daniel) St. Joseph's Cemetery, Hackensack, Bergen County.
FOSTER, DAVID Landsman, U.S. Navy, USS Princeton, DoD Unknown. Bayview-New York Bay Cemetery, Jersey City, Hudson County.

New Jersey Civil War Burials

FOSTER, DAVID Pvt, F, 60th (Crawford's) TN Mtd Inf (CSA), [Captured 5-17-1863 at Big Black River Bridge, MS.] 9-12-1863. Finn's Point National Cemetery, Pennsville, Salem County.

FOSTER, EDWARD Pvt, B, 25th U.S. CT, 4-6-1914. Mount Peace Cemetery, Lawnside, Camden County.

FOSTER, FRANCIS Pvt, D, 28th NJ Inf, 2-17-1901. St. Peter's Cemetery, New Brunswick, Middlesex County.

FOSTER, FREDERICK 8-29-1922. Evergreen Cemetery, Hillside, Union County.

FOSTER, FREDERICK ELMER Pvt, D, 15th PA Cav, 2-12-1915. Greenwood Cemetery, Hamilton, Mercer County.

FOSTER, GEORGE Pvt, B, 2nd NJ Inf, 10-19-1886. Batsto/Pleasant Mills Methodist Church Cemetery, Pleasant Mills, Atlantic County.

FOSTER, GEORGE Pvt, C, 34th NJ Inf, 5-17-1914. Harleigh Cemetery, Camden, Camden County.

FOSTER, GEORGE W. Pvt, I, 22nd PA Inf, 4-14-1903. Oak Hill Cemetery, Vineland, Cumberland County.

FOSTER, GEORGE W. Musc, D, 5th OH Inf, 2-3-1912. Fairmount Cemetery, Newark, Essex County.

FOSTER, HENRY H. Pvt, D, 29th NJ Inf, 11-8-1902. Fairview Cemetery, Fairview, Monmouth County.

FOSTER, ISAAC MCKENDREE Corp, H, 46th NY Inf, 1915. Methodist-Episcopal Cemetery, Glendola, Monmouth County.

FOSTER, JAMES A. Pvt, F, 23rd NJ Inf, 10-5-1909. Methodist-Episcopal Church Cemetery, Medford, Burlington County.

FOSTER, JAMES Y. Pvt, F, 1st GA Cav (CSA), 7-3-1864. Finn's Point National Cemetery, Pennsville, Salem County.

FOSTER, JEREMIAH 1930. Methodist-Episcopal Church Cemetery, Green Creek, Cape May County.

FOSTER, JESSE DoD Unknown. Methodist Church Cemetery, Hurffville, Gloucester County.

FOSTER, JOEL D. (aka: Hawkins, Zeno Abel) Pvt, F, 15th NJ Inf, 5-1-1880. Presbyterian Church Cemetery, Rockaway, Morris County.

FOSTER, JOHN Pvt, C, 1st NJ Inf, 4-17-1892. Evergreen Cemetery, New Brunswick, Middlesex County.

FOSTER, JOHN A. (see: Bydick, John A.F.) Bayview-New York Bay Cemetery, Jersey City, Hudson County.

FOSTER, JOSIAH (JR.) Corp, G, 21st NJ Inf, 8-9-1905. Quaker Cemetery, Medford, Burlington County.

FOSTER, MARK Pvt, K, 10th NJ Inf, [Wounded in action.] DoD Unknown. Elwood Rural Cemetery, Elwood, Atlantic County.

FOSTER, MICHAEL Pvt, I, 12th NJ Inf, 8-2-1914. Riverview Cemetery, Trenton, Mercer County.

FOSTER, REUBEN Pvt, A, 3rd NJ Inf, 7-7-1880. 1st United Methodist Church Cemetery, Bridgeton, Cumberland County.

FOSTER, RICHARD Capt, K, 1st NJ Inf, [Died at Washington, DC. of wounds received at Spotsylvania CH, VA.] 6-14-1864. Boonton Cemetery, Boonton, Morris County.

FOSTER, SAMUEL B. Pvt, A, 9th NJ Inf, 2-18-1911. Soldier's Home Cemetery, Vineland, Cumberland County.

FOSTER, SAMUEL B. Pvt, A, 9th NJ Inf, 1917. Presbyterian Church Cemetery, Rockaway, Morris County.

FOSTER, STANFORD H. Pvt, E, 68th PA Inf, 9-1-1886. Cedar Grove Cemetery, Gloucester City, Camden County.

FOSTER, STEPHEN Pvt, D, 38th NJ Inf, 7-11-1896. St. Mary's Cemetery, Hamilton, Mercer County.

Our Brothers Gone Before

FOSTER, STEPHEN S. 10-13-1885. Presbyterian Church Cemetery, Yellow Frame, Warren County.
FOSTER, THOMAS S. Pvt, F, 25th NJ Inf, 11-2-1903. Methodist Church Cemetery, Eldora, Cape May County.
FOSTER, WILLIAM Pvt, H, 1st TX Inf (CSA), [Captured 7-2-1863 at Gettysburg, PA.] 10-13-1863. Finn's Point National Cemetery, Pennsville, Salem County.
FOSTER, WILLIAM H. Bvt Maj, 14th NJ Inf 8-14-1917. Atlantic Reformed Cemetery, Colts Neck, Monmouth County.
FOSTER, WILLIAM M. 1st Sgt, C, 99th NY Inf, 10-2-1911. Fairview Cemetery, Fairview, Monmouth County.
FOTHERGILL, JAMES 2nd Lt, I, 28th NJ Inf, 8-17-1915. Alpine Cemetery, Perth Amboy, Middlesex County.
FOTHERGILL, WILLIAM Pvt, I, 28th NJ Inf, DoD Unknown. Alpine Cemetery, Perth Amboy, Middlesex County.
FOULDS, ANDREW (JR.) Pvt, F, 8th NY Cav, 4-3-1933. Cedar Lawn Cemetery, Paterson, Passaic County.
FOULK, WILLIAM H. Pvt, C, 2nd NJ Cav, 10-12-1920. Baptist/St. Andrew's Cemetery, Mount Holly, Burlington County.
FOULKE, JOSEPH BRION 6-6-1900. Hillside Cemetery, Scotch Plains, Union County.
FOULKS, THOMAS (aka: Foutch, Thomas) Pvt, G, 11th NJ Inf, 4-30-1898. Roadside Cemetery, Manchester Township, Ocean County.
FOULKS, WILLIAM C. Pvt, K, 38th NJ Inf, 3-8-1923. Cedar Hill Cemetery, Florence, Burlington County.
FOULKS, WILLIAM W. Landsman, U.S. Navy, 12-6-1928. Evergreen Cemetery, Camden, Camden County.
FOUNTAIN, GEORGE A. 2nd Lt, F, 47th NY National Guard, 7-7-1910. Rose Hill Cemetery, Matawan, Monmouth County.
FOUNTAIN*, JOHN A. Pvt, H, 2nd NJ Cav, DoD Unknown. Rosedale Cemetery, Orange, Essex County.
FOUNTAIN, LUTHER S. (aka: Ferry, Luther) Pvt, E, 47th NY National Guard, 8-4-1935. Rosedale Cemetery, Orange, Essex County.
FOUNTAIN, WILLIAM A. Pvt, G, 3rd GA Inf (CSA), [Wounded 7-1-1862 at Malvern Hill, VA. Captured 7-6-1863 at Gettysburg, PA. Died of diarrhea.] 11-11-1863. Finn's Point National Cemetery, Pennsville, Salem County.
FOURATT*, ENOS Bvt Col, 33rd NJ Inf 7-23-1888. Elmwood Cemetery, New Brunswick, Middlesex County.
FOURRE, ANTONIO Corp, C, 13th WI Inf, 3-25-1889. Palisade Cemetery, North Bergen, Hudson County.
FOURRE, LEON A. Corp, C, 19th WI Inf, 7-1-1873. Palisade Cemetery, North Bergen, Hudson County.
FOUST, GEORGE N. Pvt, Hasting's Btty, PA Light Art, 1-30-1906. Harleigh Cemetery, Camden, Camden County.
FOUST, HENRY Sgt, G, 192nd PA Inf, 1-1-1890. New Camden Cemetery, Camden, Camden County.
FOUTCH, THOMAS (see: Foulks, Thomas) Roadside Cemetery, Manchester Township, Ocean County.
FOWLE*, ROBERT HOOKER Pvt, 6th NY Ind Btty [Wounded 6-9-1863 at Brandy Station, VA.] 1-31-1912. Bayview-New York Bay Cemetery, Jersey City, Hudson County.
FOWLER, AARON C. Pvt, D, 24th NJ Inf, 6-4-1878. United Methodist Church Cemetery, Little Silver, Monmouth County.
FOWLER, ALEXANDER Pvt, C, 38th NJ Inf, 4-9-1914. Mount Pleasant Cemetery, Millville, Cumberland County.

New Jersey Civil War Burials

FOWLER, BENJAMIN W. (SR.) Actg 2nd Asst Eng, U.S. Navy, USS Lancaster, 4-24-1914. Eglington Cemetery, Clarksboro, Gloucester County.

FOWLER, CHARLES Pvt, H, 28th NJ Inf, 8-26-1902. New Freedom Cemetery, New Freedom, Camden County.

FOWLER, CHARLES B. Pvt, B, 1st NJ Cav, 6-28-1914. Hillside Cemetery, Scotch Plains, Union County.

FOWLER, CURTIS Pvt, D, 4th NJ Inf, [Wounded in action.] 12-7-1917. Riverview Cemetery, Trenton, Mercer County.

FOWLER, DANIEL M. Pvt, F, 1st (Gregg's) SC Inf (CSA), [Captured 7-5-1863 at Gettysburg, PA. Died of chronic diarrhea.] 12-27-1863. Finn's Point National Cemetery, Pennsville, Salem County.

FOWLER, FRANCIS H. 3-18-1914. Harleigh Cemetery, Camden, Camden County.

FOWLER, GEORGE __, __, __ PA __, DoD Unknown. Finn's Point National Cemetery, Pennsville, Salem County.

FOWLER, GILBERT G. Pvt, F, 37th NJ Inf, 1-1-1865. Presbyterian Cemetery, Salem, Salem County.

FOWLER, HENRY Pvt, H, 37th NJ Inf, 11-20-1921. Baptist Church Cemetery, Jacobstown, Burlington County.

FOWLER, HENRY OGDEN 11-1-1874. Hardyston Cemetery, North Church, Sussex County.

FOWLER, HUGH Pvt, D, 25th NJ Inf, 8-8-1905. Methodist Church Cemetery, Heislerville, Cumberland County.

FOWLER, ISAAC L. Corp, E, 24th NJ Inf, 5-8-1921. Eglington Cemetery, Clarksboro, Gloucester County.

FOWLER, JAMES Pvt, U.S. Marine Corps, 12-9-1899. Eglington Cemetery, Clarksboro, Gloucester County.

FOWLER, JAMES 7-26-1891. Mount Pleasant Cemetery, Newark, Essex County.

FOWLER, JAMES H. Pvt, H, 23rd NJ Inf, 4-3-1901. Glenwood Cemetery, West Long Branch, Monmouth County.

FOWLER, JOHN 1st Lt, K, 15th NJ Inf, [Killed in action at Salem Heights, VA.] 5-3-1863. Hardyston Cemetery, North Church, Sussex County.

FOWLER, JOHN P. Sgt Maj, 15th NJ Inf [Killed in action at Fredericksburg, VA.] 12-13-1862. Baptist Church Cemetery, Hamburg, Sussex County.

FOWLER, JOSEPH Pvt, G, 11th NJ Inf, [Wounded 7-2-1863 at Gettysburg, PA.] 8-3-1899. Greengrove Cemetery, Keyport, Monmouth County.

FOWLER, JOSEPH H. Pvt, A, 4th NJ Militia, 5-10-1868. Bordentown/Old St. Mary's Catholic Cemetery, Bordentown, Burlington County.

FOWLER, JOSEPH H. Corp, K, 10th NJ Inf, 4-18-1908. Baptist Church Cemetery, Haddonfield, Camden County.

FOWLER, JOSEPH H. 8-14-1902. Evergreen Cemetery, Clinton, Hunterdon County.

FOWLER, JOSIAH Pvt, B, 95th PA Inf, 6-29-1908. Methodist-Episcopal Church Cemetery, Medford, Burlington County.

FOWLER, LOUIS C. Pvt, B, 8th NJ Inf, 7-25-1868. Fairmount Cemetery, Newark, Essex County.

FOWLER, LUCIAN D. Pvt, E, 1st IA Cav, 1-13-1898. Bayview-New York Bay Cemetery, Jersey City, Hudson County.

FOWLER, MURRAY Pvt, Wiggin's (2nd) Btty, AR Light Art (CSA), 4-19-1865. Finn's Point National Cemetery, Pennsville, Salem County.

FOWLER, OSCAR G. 12-21-1898. Greenlawn Cemetery, West Long Branch, Monmouth County.

FOWLER, SAMUEL Actg 3rd Asst Eng, U.S. Navy, 2-26-1923. Arlington Cemetery, Pennsauken, Camden County.

FOWLER, SAMUEL Col, 15th NJ Inf 1-14-1865. Hardyston Cemetery, North Church, Sussex County.

Our Brothers Gone Before

FOWLER, THADDEUS M. Pvt, A, 21st NY Inf, [Wounded 8-30-1862 at 2nd Bull Run, VA.] 3-17-1922. Riverview Cemetery, Trenton, Mercer County.
FOWLER, THEODORE Pvt, I, 4th NJ Inf, 9-20-1909. Baptist Church Cemetery, Jacobstown, Burlington County.
FOWLER, WILLIAM Pvt, D, 11th MA Inf, 11-4-1903. Holy Name Cemetery, Jersey City, Hudson County.
FOWLER, WILLIAM H. Pvt, D, 2nd NJ Cav, 11-15-1914. Baptist Church Cemetery, Haddonfield, Camden County.
FOWLER, WILLIAM HENRY Pvt, I, 24th NJ Inf, 1902. New Freedom Cemetery, New Freedom, Camden County.
FOWLKES, HIRAM O. Pvt, C, 18th VA Inf (CSA), [Captured 7-5-1863 at Monterey Springs, PA. Died of typhoid.] 9-6-1863. Finn's Point National Cemetery, Pennsville, Salem County.
FOWLKES, JAMES T. Pvt, C, 18th VA Inf (CSA), [Captured 7-3-1863 at Gettysburg, PA.] 10-6-1863. Finn's Point National Cemetery, Pennsville, Salem County.
FOX, ALEXANDER Corp, H, 155th PA Inf, [Died at Beverly, NJ.] 11-26-1864. Beverly National Cemetery, Edgewater Park, Burlington County.
FOX, ALEXANDER Pvt, F, 37th NC Inf (CSA), [Wounded 5-1-1863 at Chancellorsville, VA. Captured 7-3-1863 at Gettysburg, PA.] 9-13-1863. Finn's Point National Cemetery, Pennsville, Salem County.
FOX, AMBROSE P. Pvt, H, 24th NJ Inf, 3-4-1909. United Methodist Church Cemetery, Woodruff, Cumberland County.
FOX, ANDREW J. Pvt, G, 3rd NJ Cav, DoD Unknown. Mount Pleasant Cemetery, Millville, Cumberland County.
FOX, CHARLES J. Corp, M, 17th PA Cav, 10-2-1923. Fairview Cemetery, Westfield, Union County.
FOX, EDWARD D. Musc, E, 5th NJ Inf, 3-14-1931. Riverview Cemetery, Trenton, Mercer County.
FOX, ELIJAH J. Musc, F, 34th NJ Inf, 4-3-1886. Evergreen Cemetery, Lumberton, Burlington County.
FOX, EUGENE R. Pvt, D, 153rd NY Inf, 6-3-1919. Holcomb-Riverview Cemetery, Lambertville, Hunterdon County.
FOX, FRANCIS Pvt, K, 72nd NY Inf, [Wounded 6-16-1864 at Petersburg, VA.] 12-12-1920. Holy Name Cemetery, Jersey City, Hudson County.
FOX, GEORGE Corp, H, 24th NJ Inf, [Died of wounds received 12-13-1862 at Fredericksburg, VA.] 1-7-1863. United Methodist Church Cemetery, Woodruff, Cumberland County.
FOX, GEORGE 1st Sgt, I, 31st NJ Inf, 6-22-1891. Belvidere/Catholic Cemetery, Belvidere, Warren County.
FOX, GEORGE H. Musc, E, 40th NJ Inf, 1-27-1908. Evergreen Cemetery, Camden, Camden County.
FOX, GEORGE H. Pvt, G, 8th VA Inf (CSA), 5-6-1881. Old Stone Church Cemetery, Fairton, Cumberland County.
FOX*, GEORGE W. Musc, E, 8th NJ Inf, 4-17-1911. Riverview Cemetery, Trenton, Mercer County.
FOX, GEORGE W. 8-23-1904. Greenwood Cemetery, Hamilton, Mercer County.
FOX, JAMES (see: Walton, James F.) Harleigh Cemetery, Camden, Camden County.
FOX, JOHN F. Pvt, F, 13th AL Inf (CSA), [Wounded 5-3-1863 at Chancellorsville, VA. Captured 7-1-1863 at Gettysburg, PA.] 11-19-1863. Finn's Point National Cemetery, Pennsville, Salem County.
FOX, JOHN FRANCIS Pvt, A, 3rd PA Inf, 12-4-1920. Arlington Cemetery, Kearny, Hudson County.
FOX, JOHN P. Ordinary Seaman, U.S. Navy, USS Sabine, DoD Unknown. Mount Olivet Cemetery, Newark, Essex County.

New Jersey Civil War Burials

FOX, JOHN S. Pvt, G, 34th NJ Inf, 8-14-1908. Mount Pleasant Cemetery, Millville, Cumberland County.
FOX, JOSEPH Pvt, B, 12th NJ Inf, 12-25-1902. New Camden Cemetery, Camden, Camden County.
FOX, JOSEPH Pvt, A, 24th NJ Inf, 9-7-1898. Baptist Church Cemetery, Canton, Salem County.
FOX, JOSEPH B. Hosp Steward, U.S. Navy, USS Covington, 7-8-1918. Evergreen Cemetery, Camden, Camden County.
FOX*, JOSEPH P. Seaman, U.S. Navy, USS Brooklyn, 7-27-1878. Mount Olivet Cemetery, Newark, Essex County.
FOX, MARY JANE Nurse, 48th NY Inf 1-18-1911. Evergreen Cemetery, Camden, Camden County.
FOX, MATTHIAS Pvt, G, 24th NJ Inf, DoD Unknown. Friendship United Methodist Church Cemetery, Upper Deerfield, Cumberland County.
FOX, MICHAEL Pvt, D, 33rd NJ Inf, 1906. Holy Sepulchre Cemetery, East Orange, Essex County.
FOX, PETER J. Pvt, A, 82nd PA Inf, 11-1-1862. Fairmount Cemetery, Newark, Essex County.
FOX, SOLOMON J. Pvt, C, 2nd NJ Inf, DoD Unknown. Holy Sepulchre Cemetery, East Orange, Essex County.
FOX*, THOMAS Pvt, G, 8th NJ Inf, [Wounded 8-13-1862.] 5-25-1936. Mount Olivet Cemetery, Newark, Essex County.
FOX, THOMAS H. Pvt, A, 29th NJ Inf, 4-5-1916. Old 1st Methodist Church Cemetery, West Long Branch, Monmouth County.
FOX, VALENTINE Pvt, C, 11th NJ Inf, 7-8-1911. Arlington Cemetery, Kearny, Hudson County.
FOY, GEORGE Pvt, I, 88th NY Inf, DoD Unknown. Jersey City Cemetery, Jersey City, Hudson County.
FOY, JAMES M. DoD Unknown. Jersey City Cemetery, Jersey City, Hudson County.
FRACE, EZEKIEL A. Pvt, B, 27th NJ Inf, 8-3-1906. German Valley Rural Cemetery, Naughright, Morris County.
FRACE, GEORGE W. Corp, D, 27th NJ Inf, 12-13-1918. Newton Cemetery, Newton, Sussex County.
FRACE*, JOHN Sgt, D, 39th NJ Inf, 1-31-1897. United Methodist Church Cemetery, Vienna, Warren County.
FRADER, JOSEPH (aka: Fader, Joseph) Pvt, A, 3rd NJ Militia, 8-20-1922. Greenwood Cemetery, Hamilton, Mercer County.
FRAIN, WILLIAM J. Pvt, C, 38th NJ Inf, 1885. Mount Pleasant Cemetery, Millville, Cumberland County.
FRALEIGH*, WILLIAM H. Seaman, U.S. Navy, USS Shenandoah, 2-2-1895. Greengrove Cemetery, Keyport, Monmouth County.
FRALEY, ALFRED (aka: Froehlich, Alfred) Pvt, Btty A, 1st NJ Light Art, 12-28-1899. Elmwood Cemetery, New Brunswick, Middlesex County.
FRALEY, WILLIAM Corp, F, 31st NJ Inf, 5-17-1908. Holland Cemetery, Holland, Hunterdon County.
FRAMBES, ABRAHAM W. Corp, B, 25th NJ Inf, 4-3-1897. Asbury United Methodist Church Cemetery, English Creek, Atlantic County.
FRAMBES, NICHOLAS (see: Phrambes, Nicholas V.) Methodist Church Cemetery, Haleyville, Cumberland County.
FRAMBES, SAMUEL C. 2-8-1909. Eastview Cemetery, Salem, Salem County.
FRAMPES, AMOS (see: Frampus, Amos) Methodist-Episcopal Cemetery, Vincentown, Burlington County.
FRAMPUS, AMOS (aka: Frampes, Amos) Corp, G, 12th NJ Inf, 1876. Methodist-Episcopal Cemetery, Vincentown, Burlington County.

Our Brothers Gone Before

FRAMPUS, DAVID Pvt, I, 2nd NJ Cav, 3-10-1886. Methodist-Episcopal Cemetery, Vincentown, Burlington County.
FRAMPUS, JESSE B. Corp, A, 3rd NJ Inf, DoD Unknown. Overlook Cemetery, Bridgeton, Cumberland County.
FRAMPUS, JOSIAH DoD Unknown. Presbyterian Church Cemetery, Bridgeton, Cumberland County.
FRANCE, GEORGE F. Pvt, C, 58th PA Inf, 6-25-1876. Presbyterian Cemetery, Blairstown, Warren County.
FRANCE, HIRAM (aka: Francis, Hiram) Pvt, D, 35th NJ Inf, 7-1-1912. Cedar Ridge Cemetery, Blairstown, Warren County.
FRANCE*, IRA C. Pvt, B, 2nd NJ Cav, 1908. Cedar Ridge Cemetery, Blairstown, Warren County.
FRANCE, JACOB V. Sgt, C, 11th NY Cav, DoD Unknown. Cedar Ridge Cemetery, Blairstown, Warren County.
FRANCE, JAMES C. Corp, D, 35th NJ Inf, 1-21-1901. Cedar Ridge Cemetery, Blairstown, Warren County.
FRANCE, RICHARD 9-7-1868. Presbyterian Cemetery, Blairstown, Warren County.
FRANCES, WILLIAM (aka: Francis, William) Pvt, I, 2nd NJ Cav, 11-10-1890. Methodist Cemetery, Cassville, Ocean County.
FRANCINAL, ISAAC DoD Unknown. Rocky Hill Cemetery, Rocky Hill, Somerset County.
FRANCIS, ALEXANDER M. Pvt, A, 21st CT Inf, [Wounded 5-16-1864 at Drewrys Bluff, VA.] 3-13-1900. Mansfield/Washington Cemetery, Washington, Warren County.
FRANCIS, ASA Seaman, U.S. Navy, 3-1-1892. Woodlawn Cemetery, Lakewood, Ocean County.
FRANCIS, BERNARD Pvt, E, 1st NJ Cav, 3-8-1916. Holy Sepulchre Cemetery, East Orange, Essex County.
FRANCIS*, BRISTAR (aka: Francis, Brister) Pvt, Btty I, 11th U.S. CHA, 10-1-1908. Fairmount Cemetery, Newark, Essex County.
FRANCIS, BRISTER (see: Francis, Bristar) Fairmount Cemetery, Newark, Essex County.
FRANCIS, CHARLES Corp, B, 4th U.S. CT, DoD Unknown. Siloam Cemetery, Vineland, Cumberland County.
FRANCIS, CHARLES Pvt, G, 29th NJ Inf, 5-6-1922. Glenwood Cemetery, West Long Branch, Monmouth County.
FRANCIS, CHARLES H. 1st Cl Boy, U.S. Navy, USS Connecticut, 1-3-1917. White Ridge Cemetery, Eatontown, Monmouth County.
FRANCIS, CHARLES L. Pvt, D, 2nd DC Inf, DoD Unknown. Evergreen Cemetery, Hillside, Union County.
FRANCIS, EDWARD Pvt, G, 2nd DC Inf, 1-12-1870. Evergreen Cemetery, Hillside, Union County.
FRANCIS, ELIAS Pvt, D, 20th U.S. CT, 3-21-1917. Evergreen Cemetery, Hillside, Union County.
FRANCIS, GEORGE Ordinary Seaman, U.S. Navy, USS Ohio, 11-19-1871. Van Liew Cemetery, North Brunswick, Middlesex County.
FRANCIS, HENRY B. Actg Ensign, U.S. Navy, USS Mississippi, 1-30-1921. Harleigh Cemetery, Camden, Camden County.
FRANCIS, HIRAM (see: France, Hiram) Cedar Ridge Cemetery, Blairstown, Warren County.
FRANCIS, HOLMES C. Artificer, D, 1st NY Eng, 6-22-1866. Methodist Cemetery, Cassville, Ocean County.
FRANCIS, IRA H. Pvt, D, 1st NJ Militia, 12-3-1889. Fairmount Cemetery, Newark, Essex County.
FRANCIS, JOHN C. Pvt, Btty I, 2nd MA Light Art, 7-31-1889. Evergreen Cemetery, Hillside, Union County.

New Jersey Civil War Burials

FRANCIS, JOSEPH Pvt, G, 10th NJ Inf, 11-14-1876. Old Presbyterian Cemetery, Lakehurst, Ocean County.

FRANCIS, JOSEPH H. 1st Lt, D, 23rd Bttn TN Inf (CSA), [Newman's Battalion.] 11-28-1898. Cedar Lawn Cemetery, Paterson, Passaic County.

FRANCIS, RICHARD DoD Unknown. Baptist Church Cemetery, Jacobstown, Burlington County.

FRANCIS, THEODORE Corp, G, 29th NJ Inf, 1919. Fairview Cemetery, Fairview, Monmouth County.

FRANCIS, THOMAS Pvt, H, 29th CT Inf, 8-6-1898. Hackensack Cemetery, Hackensack, Bergen County.

FRANCIS, THOMAS J. Pvt, I, 43rd U.S. CT, 6-25-1903. Evergreen Cemetery, Camden, Camden County.

FRANCIS, W. Pvt, Montgomery's Bttn VA Inf (CSA) 12-30-1864. Finn's Point National Cemetery, Pennsville, Salem County.

FRANCIS, WILLIAM 7-11-1886. Methodist Cemetery, Cassville, Ocean County.

FRANCIS, WILLIAM (see: Frances, William) Methodist Cemetery, Cassville, Ocean County.

FRANCISCO*, GEORGE F. Landsman, U.S. Navy, USS Princeton, [Wounded in action.] 1-18-1911. Bloomfield Cemetery, Bloomfield, Essex County.

FRANCISCO, HENRY Pvt, K, 3rd U.S. CT, 12-15-1887. Bloomfield Cemetery, Bloomfield, Essex County.

FRANCISCO, JAMES H. Pvt, I, 26th NJ Inf, 12-20-1881. Fairmount Cemetery, Newark, Essex County.

FRANCISCO, SAMUEL (aka: Sisco, Samuel) Pvt, F, 4th U.S. Inf, 2-25-1907. Fairmount Cemetery, Newark, Essex County.

FRANCISCO, THOMAS ANGELO Pvt, I, 1st NJ Inf, 2-4-1920. Fairmount Cemetery, Newark, Essex County.

FRANCISCO, WILLIAM Pvt, Btty C, 2nd U.S. Art, 7-14-1895. Mount Pleasant Cemetery, Newark, Essex County.

FRANCK*, EMILE Pvt, D, 51st NY Inf, 12-20-1922. Rahway Cemetery, Rahway, Union County.

FRANCK, MARTIN Pvt, 13th NY Ind Btty 10-23-1905. Grove Church Cemetery, North Bergen, Hudson County.

FRANCKE, FREDERICK W. Pvt, B, 33rd NJ Inf, 5-16-1896. Arlington Cemetery, Kearny, Hudson County.

FRANEY, JAMES Pvt, G, 7th NJ Inf, 10-14-1900. Holy Sepulchre Cemetery, Totowa, Passaic County.

FRANK, AUGUST Pvt, H, 58th NY Inf, 11-15-1901. Jersey City Cemetery, Jersey City, Hudson County.

FRANK, CHARLES Pvt, F, 1st NJ Inf, 2-22-1904. Fairmount Cemetery, Newark, Essex County.

FRANK*, CORNELIUS Pvt, G, 15th NJ Inf, 9-23-1882. Holy Sepulchre Cemetery, East Orange, Essex County.

FRANK, FRANCIS 4-9-1903. Bayview-New York Bay Cemetery, Jersey City, Hudson County.

FRANK, FREDERICK Pvt, K, 35th NJ Inf, DoD Unknown. Rahway Cemetery, Rahway, Union County.

FRANK, GEORGE Pvt, E, 39th NJ Inf, 12-27-1891. Woodland Cemetery, Newark, Essex County.

FRANK, HENRY Pvt, A, 10th NJ Inf, 4-29-1909. Flower Hill Cemetery, North Bergen, Hudson County.

FRANK, JOHN Ordinary Seaman, U.S. Navy, 5-16-1913. Mount Peace Cemetery, Lawnside, Camden County.

Our Brothers Gone Before

FRANK, JOHN P. Pvt, H, 9th NJ Inf, 2-24-1902. Evergreen Cemetery, Hillside, Union County.
FRANK, JOSEPH CHARLES Pvt, A, 12th IN Inf, 12-27-1901. Mount Olivet Cemetery, Newark, Essex County.
FRANK, KARL HENRY 3-24-1914. Lodi Cemetery, Lodi, Bergen County.
FRANK, LOUIS Pvt, A, 10th NJ Inf, DoD Unknown. Van Liew Cemetery, North Brunswick, Middlesex County.
FRANK, LUDWIG (see: Funk, Ludwig) Hackensack Cemetery, Hackensack, Bergen County.
FRANK, PETER Musc, B, 69th NY Inf, 1-19-1903. Grove Church Cemetery, North Bergen, Hudson County.
FRANK, WILLIAM Pvt, D, 10th NJ Inf, DoD Unknown. 7th Day Baptist Church Cemetery, Marlboro, Salem County.
FRANK, WILLIAM Pvt, B, 1st NJ Militia, 5-1-1872. Mount Pleasant Cemetery, Newark, Essex County.
FRANKENFELD, ALBERT Pvt, U.S. Army, [Commissary Department, 19th Army Corps. Wounded 10-19-1864 at Cedar Creek, VA.] 6-22-1912. Bordentown/Old St. Mary's Catholic Cemetery, Bordentown, Burlington County.
FRANKLIN, BENJAMIN Pvt, B, 2nd DC Inf, DoD Unknown. Asbury Methodist-Episcopal Church Cemetery, Swainton, Cape May County.
FRANKLIN, BENJAMIN H. Musc, F, 85th NY Inf, 2-6-1901. Arlington Cemetery, Kearny, Hudson County.
FRANKLIN, FREDERICK H. Pvt, C, 14th NJ Inf, 2-20-1910. Evergreen Cemetery, Hillside, Union County.
FRANKLIN*, JOHN D. 2nd Lt, D, 14th NJ Inf, [Wounded in action.] 4-4-1893. Evergreen Cemetery, Hillside, Union County.
FRANKLIN, JOHN F. Pvt, E, 38th NJ Inf, 1901. Greenlawn Cemetery, West Long Branch, Monmouth County.
FRANKLIN, JOSEPH L. 2nd Lt, I, 3rd NJ Inf, DoD Unknown. Eglington Cemetery, Clarksboro, Gloucester County.
FRANKLIN, SAMUEL L. Corp, A, 24th U.S. CT, 1919. Eglington Cemetery, Clarksboro, Gloucester County.
FRANKLIN, T.J. Pvt, B, 40th PA Militia, DoD Unknown. Overlook Cemetery, Bridgeton, Cumberland County.
FRANKLIN, WILLIAM 2-26-1906. Old 1st Methodist Church Cemetery, West Long Branch, Monmouth County.
FRANKS, CHARLES BEYER (aka: Beyer, Charles) Musc, I, 9th NJ Inf, 11-8-1910. Fairmount Cemetery, Newark, Essex County.
FRANKS, HARRY HOUSTON Sgt, G, 25th NJ Inf, 1-1-1887. Evergreen Cemetery, Camden, Camden County.
FRANKS, HERMAN D. (see: Duncan, Francis Herman) Greenwood Cemetery, Hamilton, Mercer County.
FRANSCISCO, DAVID B. 1932. Old Butler Cemetery, Butler, Morris County.
FRANTZ, JOHN Capt, B, 3rd NJ Inf, 3-9-1894. Baptist/St. Andrew's Cemetery, Mount Holly, Burlington County.
FRANZ, WILLIAM F. 1897. Cedar Lawn Cemetery, Paterson, Passaic County.
FRAREY, NELSON (see: Farry, Nelson) Locust Hill Cemetery, Dover, Morris County.
FRASER, CHARLES B. Pvt, G, 4th NJ Militia, 3-11-1922. Evergreen Cemetery, Camden, Camden County.
FRASER, JESSE Corp, F, 21st NJ Inf, 12-29-1905. Flower Hill Cemetery, North Bergen, Hudson County.
FRASER, JOHN S. 2nd Cl Fireman, U.S. Navy, USS Ohio, 12-23-1903. Old Camden Cemetery, Camden, Camden County.

New Jersey Civil War Burials

FRATT, HENRY (see: Froat, Henry L.) Greenlawn Cemetery, West Long Branch, Monmouth County.

FRATZ, FRANCIS H. WILSON Seaman, U.S. Navy, USS Ohio, 1908. Bethel Cemetery, Pennsauken, Camden County.

FRAVEL, ISRAEL Pvt, I, 199th PA Inf, 3-28-1916. Harleigh Cemetery, Camden, Camden County.

FRAVEL*, JESSE Seaman, U.S. Navy, 1927. Baptist Church Cemetery, Penns Neck, Mercer County.

FRAZEE, ANDREW S. Pvt, A, 22nd PA Cav, 3-28-1904. Evergreen Cemetery, Camden, Camden County.

FRAZEE, DAVID D. Pvt, H, 57th NY Inf, 6-11-1882. Fairview Cemetery, Westfield, Union County.

FRAZEE, EDWIN S. Pvt, B, 26th NJ Inf, [Wounded 5-10-1863 at Fredericksburg, VA.] 8-1-1863. Mount Pleasant Cemetery, Newark, Essex County.

FRAZEE, HENRY Pvt, F, 28th NJ Inf, 2-10-1924. Hillside Cemetery, Scotch Plains, Union County.

FRAZEE, HENRY (JR.) Eng, U.S. Navy, USS Minnesota, 7-29-1868. 1st Methodist-Episcopal Cemetery, New Brunswick, Middlesex County.

FRAZEE, JOHN H.B. Chaplain, 3rd NJ Cav 2-20-1910. Mount Pleasant Cemetery, Newark, Essex County.

FRAZEE, MILTON J. Pvt, H, 30th NJ Inf, 9-6-1892. Fairview Cemetery, Westfield, Union County.

FRAZEE, PHINEAS FREEMAN (JR.) (aka: Frazee, Phineas H.) Pvt, A, 15th SC Inf (CSA), [Cenotaph. Died from an injury sustained in a fall from a wagon at New River Bridge near Hardeeville, SC.] 3-27-1862. Rahway Cemetery, Rahway, Union County.

FRAZEE, PHINEAS H. (see: Frazee, Phineas Freeman (Jr.)) Rahway Cemetery, Rahway, Union County.

FRAZEE, WILLIAM DoD Unknown. Van Liew Cemetery, North Brunswick, Middlesex County.

FRAZEE, WILLIAM DoD Unknown. Presbyterian Church Cemetery, Kingston, Somerset County.

FRAZEE, WILLIAM H. Pvt, C, 30th NJ Inf, 5-28-1912. Presbyterian Church Cemetery, New Providence, Union County.

FRAZEE, WILLIAM R. (aka: Frazy, William) Sgt, I, 33rd NJ Inf, 2-27-1907. Rahway Cemetery, Rahway, Union County.

FRAZER, CHARLES Pvt, K, 10th NJ Inf, 3-26-1870. Bordentown/Old St. Mary's Catholic Cemetery, Bordentown, Burlington County.

FRAZER, CHARLES P. Sgt, F, 5th NJ Inf, 8-3-1885. United Methodist Church Cemetery, Alloway, Salem County.

FRAZER, DAVID Pvt, D, 1st NJ Inf, 10-12-1876. Fairmount Cemetery, Newark, Essex County.

FRAZER, DAVID S. Pvt, Btty I, 1st PA Light Art, DoD Unknown. Methodist Church Cemetery, Aldine, Salem County.

FRAZER, GEORGE Pvt, A, 21st NJ Inf, 6-24-1898. Bayview-New York Bay Cemetery, Jersey City, Hudson County.

FRAZER, ISAAC N. Pvt, F, 5th NJ Inf, [Wounded in action.] 1906. United Methodist Church Cemetery, Alloway, Salem County.

FRAZER*, JACOB M. Pvt, F, 5th NJ Inf, 1936. Chestnut Grove Cemetery, Elmer, Salem County.

FRAZER, TOWNSEND 1913. Bible Church Cemetery, Hardingville, Gloucester County.

FRAZER, WILLIAM Pvt, F, 5th NJ Inf, [Died at Camp Seminary, VA. of wounds received at 2nd Bull Run, VA.] 9-11-1862. United Methodist Church Cemetery, Alloway, Salem County.

Our Brothers Gone Before

FRAZER, WILLIAM M. Corp, F, 95th NY Inf, 11-6-1910. Bayview-New York Bay Cemetery, Jersey City, Hudson County.
FRAZIER, CARL 12-23-1907. Old Camden Cemetery, Camden, Camden County.
FRAZIER, ELI Pvt, F, 38th NJ Inf, 1-11-1902. Union Cemetery, Milford, Hunterdon County.
FRAZIER, GEORGE W. Pvt, H, 31st NJ Inf, 11-26-1873. Presbyterian Church Cemetery, Marksboro, Warren County.
FRAZIER, JAMES Pvt, I, 61st (Pitts') TN Mtd Inf (CSA), 11-5-1863. Finn's Point National Cemetery, Pennsville, Salem County.
FRAZIER*, JAMES M. Pvt, G, 8th KS Inf, 1918. St. James Episcopal Church Cemetery, Piscatawaytown, Middlesex County.
FRAZIER, LEVI D. 1923. Cedar Hill Cemetery, Florence, Burlington County.
FRAZIER, WILLIAM B. Pvt, E, 10th NJ Inf, 2- -1873. Methodist Church Cemetery, Mays Landing, Atlantic County.
FRAZIER, WILLIAM C. DoD Unknown. United Methodist Church Cemetery, Winslow, Camden County.
FRAZIER, WILLIAM M. Pvt, F, 12th NJ Inf, [Wounded in action.] 3-19-1911. Evergreen Cemetery, Camden, Camden County.
FRAZOR, JOHN Pvt, A, 190th NY Inf, DoD Unknown. Soldier's Home Cemetery, Vineland, Cumberland County.
FRAZY, WILLIAM (see: Frazee, William R.) Rahway Cemetery, Rahway, Union County.
FREAM, JOHN G. Corp, E, 66th IL Inf, 6-27-1895. Maple Grove Cemetery, Hackensack, Bergen County.
FREAS, CHARLES H. Pvt, K, 4th NJ Inf, 1924. Baptist Church Cemetery, Alloway, Salem County.
FREAS, JACOB (aka: Fries, Jacob) Pvt, K, 2nd NJ Cav, 1885. Methodist Church Cemetery, Aldine, Salem County.
FREAS, JOHNSON 1887. Baptist Cemetery, Salem, Salem County.
FRECAUT, ANTONE (see: Frecont, Anton) Holy Sepulchre Cemetery, East Orange, Essex County.
FRECHE, GUSTAVUS (see: Fresche, Gustavus L.) Fairmount Cemetery, Newark, Essex County.
FRECK, CHRISTIAN Pvt, F, 68th PA Inf, 5-18-1924. Oddfellows Cemetery, Burlington, Burlington County.
FRECONT*, ANTON (aka: Frecaut, Antone) Pvt, B, 1st NJ Cav, DoD Unknown. Holy Sepulchre Cemetery, East Orange, Essex County.
FREDERICK, CHARLES F. Pvt, Btty B, 1st NJ Light Art, 3-5-1917. Mount Pleasant Cemetery, Newark, Essex County.
FREDERICK, DANIEL 2-28-1871. Mount Pleasant Cemetery, Newark, Essex County.
FREDERICK, JOHN H. 5-3-1871. Maple Grove Cemetery, Hackensack, Bergen County.
FREDERICK, JOSEPH (see: Friederichs, Joseph) Woodland Cemetery, Newark, Essex County.
FREDERICK, WILLIAM H. Corp, C, 25th NJ Inf, 8-2-1904. Brookside Cemetery, Englewood, Bergen County.
FREDERICK, WILLIAM H. Pvt, G, 9th NJ Inf, 10-19-1901. Rosedale Cemetery, Orange, Essex County.
FREDERICKS, CHARLES S. Pvt, Btty L, 15th NY Heavy Art, 10-18-1891. Evergreen Cemetery, Morristown, Morris County.
FREDERICKS, CHARLES W. Pvt, E, 6th NJ Inf, DoD Unknown. Laurel Grove Cemetery, Totowa, Passaic County.
FREDERICKS, DAVID J. Corp, B, 3rd NJ Cav, 8-7-1928. Midvale Cemetery, Midvale, Passaic County.
FREDERICKS, DAVID P. Pvt, A, 9th NJ Inf, 9-30-1881. Trinity Bible Church Cemetery, Glassboro, Gloucester County.

New Jersey Civil War Burials

FREDERICKS, EDWARD Pvt, F, 1st NJ Cav, 9-17-1904. Arlington Cemetery, Kearny, Hudson County.
FREDERICKS, GEORGE Pvt, A, 2nd NJ Inf, [Wounded 4-2-1865 at Petersburg, VA.] 1-15-1889. Presbyterian Church Cemetery, Rockaway, Morris County.
FREDERICKS, GODFREY Pvt, B, 3rd NJ Cav, 8-17-1864. Pompton Reformed Church Cemetery, Pompton Lakes, Passaic County.
FREDERICKS, GUSTAVE (see: Wilson, Frederick Gustave) Greengrove Cemetery, Keyport, Monmouth County.
FREDERICKS, HENRY Pvt, A, 9th NJ Inf, [Died of typhoid at Greensboro, NC.] 6-20-1865. Trinity Bible Church Cemetery, Glassboro, Gloucester County.
FREDERICKS, HENRY Pvt, C, 13th NJ Inf, DoD Unknown. Laurel Grove Cemetery, Totowa, Passaic County.
FREDERICKS, HENRY 1914. 1st Reformed Church Cemetery, Pompton Plains, Morris County.
FREDERICKS, HENRY I. Pvt, E, 25th NJ Inf, 3-16-1902. Methodist Church Cemetery, Stockholm, Sussex County.
FREDERICKS, JACOB Pvt, C, 25th NJ Inf, 1887. Vincent Methodist-Episcopal Cemetery, Nutley, Essex County.
FREDERICKS*, JAMES Pvt, D, 7th NJ Inf, 3-25-1919. Methodist-Episcopal Cemetery, Midland Park, Bergen County.
FREDERICKS*, JOHN Pvt, Btty C, 1st NJ Light Art, DoD Unknown. Jersey City Cemetery, Jersey City, Hudson County.
FREDERICKS, JOHN A. 11-20-1893. Christ Church Cemetery, Morgan, Middlesex County.
FREDERICKS, WILLIAM Pvt, K, 15th NJ Inf, 1933. Methodist Church Cemetery, Stockholm, Sussex County.
FREE, GERED (see: Free, Jared) Bayview-New York Bay Cemetery, Jersey City, Hudson County.
FREE, JARED (aka: Free, Gered) Pvt, E, 4th NY Cav, DoD Unknown. Bayview-New York Bay Cemetery, Jersey City, Hudson County.
FREELAND*, ABRAHAM N. Capt, A, 8th NJ Inf, 3-13-1920. Fairmount Cemetery, Newark, Essex County.
FREELAND, ABRAM (see: Vreeland, Abraham) Pompton Reformed Church Cemetery, Pompton Lakes, Passaic County.
FREELAND, GEORGE W. (aka: Vreeland, George) Saddler, A, 1st NY Mounted Rifles, 6-16-1922. Union Cemetery, Milford, Hunterdon County.
FREELAND, JAMES Pvt, H, 127th U.S. CT, 6-4-1914. Arlington Cemetery, Kearny, Hudson County.
FREELAND, JAMES (see: Vreeland, James P.) Cedar Lawn Cemetery, Paterson, Passaic County.
FREELAND, JOHN Pvt, E, 22nd NJ Inf, 8-7-1927. Lodi Cemetery, Lodi, Bergen County.
FREELAND, JOHN Pvt, C, 1st LA Cav (CSA), [Captured 7-31-1863 at Irvine, KY. Died of anemia.] 4-12-1864. Finn's Point National Cemetery, Pennsville, Salem County.
FREELAND, JOHN (see: Vreeland, John M.) Cedar Lawn Cemetery, Paterson, Passaic County.
FREELAND, JOHN M. Pvt, A, 8th NJ Inf, 8-22-1902. Fairmount Cemetery, Newark, Essex County.
FREELAND, LAWRENCE Pvt, B, 10th NY Inf, 4-21-1916. Fairmount Cemetery, Newark, Essex County.
FREELAND, WILLIAM H. Pvt, C, 25th NJ Inf, DoD Unknown. Laurel Grove Cemetery, Totowa, Passaic County.
FREEMAN, AARON Sgt, C, 1st DC Inf, 10-6-1879. Greengrove Cemetery, Keyport, Monmouth County.

FREEMAN, ALBERT DoD Unknown. Methodist Cemetery, Newfoundland, Morris County.
FREEMAN*, ALBERT T. Pvt, A, 11th NJ Inf, 2-4-1890. Presbyterian/Methodist-Episcopal Cemetery, Succasunna, Morris County.
FREEMAN, ALONZO DoD Unknown. Presbyterian/Methodist-Episcopal Cemetery, Succasunna, Morris County.
FREEMAN, AMOS G. Pvt, C, 4th NJ Inf, 2-1-1899. Presbyterian/Methodist-Episcopal Cemetery, Succasunna, Morris County.
FREEMAN, ANDREW A. Pvt, D, 56th MA Inf, [Died of disease at Beverly, NJ. Wounded 5-6-1864 at Wilderness, VA.] 10-31-1864. Beverly National Cemetery, Edgewater Park, Burlington County.
FREEMAN, BRAY Pvt, M, 2nd U.S. Colored Cav, 11-10-1899. Evergreen Cemetery, Hillside, Union County.
FREEMAN, CHARLES P. 1st Sgt, H, 31st NJ Inf, 6-8-1914. Rahway Cemetery, Rahway, Union County.
FREEMAN, EDWARD Pvt, C, 39th NJ Inf, 8-25-1912. Fairmount Cemetery, Newark, Essex County.
FREEMAN, EDWARD AUGUSTUS Pvt, C, 45th U.S. CT, 9-27-1926. Greenwood Cemetery, Hamilton, Mercer County.
FREEMAN, EDWARD S. Pvt, F, 2nd NJ Cav, 4-14-1903. Locust Hill Cemetery, Dover, Morris County.
FREEMAN, EDWIN H. Pvt, F, 26th NJ Inf, 12-4-1893. Bloomfield Cemetery, Bloomfield, Essex County.
FREEMAN, ELIJAH Pvt, K, 30th U.S. CT, 10-22-1907. Princeton Cemetery, Princeton, Mercer County.
FREEMAN, ELLMORE Corp, H, 20th U.S. CT, 12-30-1908. Fairmount Cemetery, Newark, Essex County.
FREEMAN, ENOS E. Corp, H, 22nd U.S. CT, 1-17-1879. Rahway Cemetery, Rahway, Union County.
FREEMAN, J.W. Pvt, C, 12th NC Inf (CSA), 10-1-1862. Finn's Point National Cemetery, Pennsville, Salem County.
FREEMAN, JACOB Pvt, D, 26th U.S. CT, 2-22-1926. Bloomfield Cemetery, Bloomfield, Essex County.
FREEMAN, JACOB Pvt, H, 26th NJ Inf, 1-1-1908. Rosedale Cemetery, Orange, Essex County.
FREEMAN, JACOB 7-9-1873. Hainesburg Cemetery, Hainesburg, Warren County.
FREEMAN, JAMES Pvt, Btty A, Schaffer's Ind PA Heavy Art, [Died at Fort Delaware.] 12-20-1863. Finn's Point National Cemetery, Pennsville, Salem County.
FREEMAN, JAMES B. Pvt, C, 28th NJ Inf, 4-13-1918. Elmwood Cemetery, New Brunswick, Middlesex County.
FREEMAN, JOHN J. Pvt, F, 28th NJ Inf, 3-9-1923. Hillside Cemetery, Scotch Plains, Union County.
FREEMAN, JOHN MILTON Pvt, H, 26th NJ Inf, 2-13-1925. Rosedale Cemetery, Orange, Essex County.
FREEMAN*, JOHN R. Pvt, H, 10th NJ Inf, 3-17-1894. Fairmount Cemetery, Newark, Essex County.
FREEMAN, JOHN W. Landsman, U.S. Navy, 2-20-1908. Fairmount Cemetery, Newark, Essex County.
FREEMAN, JOSEPH DoD Unknown. Rosedale Cemetery, Orange, Essex County.
FREEMAN*, JOSEPH ADDISON Asst Surg, U.S. Volunteers, [Died at Nashville, TN. Also: Surg, 13th NJ Inf.] 12-29-1864. Rosedale Cemetery, Orange, Essex County.
FREEMAN, JOSEPH L. DoD Unknown. Evergreen Cemetery, Morristown, Morris County.

New Jersey Civil War Burials

FREEMAN, LORENZO (see: Furman, Lorenzo) Evergreen Cemetery, Morristown, Morris County.

FREEMAN, LUKE Pvt, D, 33rd NJ Inf, 6-20-1908. Holy Sepulchre Cemetery, Totowa, Passaic County.

FREEMAN, MARK (see: Firman, Mark) Evergreen Cemetery, Morristown, Morris County.

FREEMAN*, MORRIS E. Pvt, D, 2nd DC Inf, 1897. Rosedale Cemetery, Orange, Essex County.

FREEMAN, OTIS Surgeon, 10th NJ Inf 6-8-1902. Maplewood Cemetery, Freehold, Monmouth County.

FREEMAN, PETER Sgt, E, 71st NY Inf, 9-10-1884. St. John's Evangelical Church Cemetery, Orange, Essex County.

FREEMAN, PETER EDMONDS Pvt, Btty B, 1st NJ Light Art, 11-4-1915. Savage Cemetery, Denville, Morris County.

FREEMAN, SAMUEL Pvt, B, 11th NJ Inf, 11-5-1881. Phillipsburg Cemetery, Phillipsburg, Warren County.

FREEMAN, SEYMOUR J.M. Pvt, Btty G, 15th NY Heavy Art, DoD Unknown. B'nai Abraham Cemetery, Newark, Essex County.

FREEMAN, SPENCER Landsman, U.S. Navy, USS Princeton, 3-14-1893. White Ridge Cemetery, Eatontown, Monmouth County.

FREEMAN, STEPHEN Pvt, D, 13th NJ Inf, [Wounded 9-17-1862 at Antietam, MD.] 5-28-1891. Fairmount Cemetery, Newark, Essex County.

FREEMAN, THOMAS B. Pvt, K, 28th NJ Inf, [Died of typhoid at Falmouth, VA.] 2-26-1863. Old School Baptist Cemetery, South River, Middlesex County.

FREEMAN, THOMAS W. Pvt, F, 11th MS Inf (CSA), 12-4-1863. Finn's Point National Cemetery, Pennsville, Salem County.

FREEMAN, UEL Pvt, 6th NY Ind Btty 10-19-1926. Rahway Cemetery, Rahway, Union County.

FREEMAN, WILLIAM (see: Coeyman, William A.) Evergreen Cemetery, Hillside, Union County.

FREESE*, GEORGE Pvt, K, 14th NJ Inf, 11-27-1894. Elmwood Cemetery, New Brunswick, Middlesex County.

FREESE, HENRY (aka: Fasse, Heinrich) Pvt, B, 8th NY Inf, 3-7-1898. Atlantic City Cemetery, Pleasantville, Atlantic County.

FREESE, JACOB R. Capt, AAG, NJ [Adjutant Generals Department.] 11-24-1885. Riverview Cemetery, Trenton, Mercer County.

FREESE, THEODORE W. 8-7-1891. Union Brick Cemetery, Blairstown, Warren County.

FREEZE, JACOB Pvt, H, 47th NC Inf (CSA), [Wounded and captured 7-3-1863 at Gettysburg, PA. Died of scurvy.] 10-21-1863. Finn's Point National Cemetery, Pennsville, Salem County.

FREEZER, CONRAD 8-1-1922. Van Liew Cemetery, North Brunswick, Middlesex County.

FREICK, GOTLIB (see: Frick, Gottlop) Grove Church Cemetery, North Bergen, Hudson County.

FREIDHOFFER, JOHN Pvt, B, 39th NJ Inf, 3-7-1891. Fairmount Cemetery, Newark, Essex County.

FREINSCHNER, PHILLIP Pvt, A, 20th NY Inf, 11-23-1879. Fairmount Cemetery, Newark, Essex County.

FREITAG, ALBERT Pvt, D, 2nd NJ Inf, [Wounded in action.] 6-16-1913. Woodland Cemetery, Newark, Essex County.

FREITAG, JOHN GEORGE Pvt, A, 20th NY Inf, 11-23-1918. Woodland Cemetery, Newark, Essex County.

FRENCH, ALFRED Pvt, A, MD Emerg NJ Militia, 4-8-1914. Friends Cemetery, Mullica Hill, Gloucester County.

Our Brothers Gone Before

FRENCH, BENJAMIN F. Pvt, A, 5th MA Inf, 4-1-1902. Cedar Lawn Cemetery, Paterson, Passaic County.
FRENCH, CHARLES Pvt, H, 12th NJ Inf, [Died of diarrhea at Philadelphia, PA.] 12-23-1863. Friends Cemetery, Mullica Hill, Gloucester County.
FRENCH, CORNELIUS V.N. Pvt, B, 28th NJ Inf, 7-7-1921. Glenwood Cemetery, West Long Branch, Monmouth County.
FRENCH, EDWARD B. Chaplain, 39th MA Inf 1907. Newton Cemetery, Newton, Sussex County.
FRENCH, EZRA G. Corp, H, 2nd U.S. Inf, [Died of wounds received 7-2-1863 at Gettysburg, PA.] 7-15-1863. Friends Cemetery, Mullica Hill, Gloucester County.
FRENCH, GEORGE W. Corp, F, 12th NJ Inf, 10- -1867. Friends Cemetery, Mullica Hill, Gloucester County.
FRENCH, HOWARD M. Pvt, G, 25th NJ Inf, 9-12-1916. Baptist Church Cemetery, Palermo, Cape May County.
FRENCH, JAMES G. Pvt, A, 9th NY Inf, 8-19-1913. Old 1st Methodist Church Cemetery, West Long Branch, Monmouth County.
FRENCH, JAMES W. Pvt, I, 5th NY Cav, 9-30-1865. Midvale Cemetery, Midvale, Passaic County.
FRENCH, JOHN E. Pvt, F, 9th NJ Inf, 3-21-1876. Presbyterian Church Cemetery, Greenwich, Cumberland County.
FRENCH, JOHN W. 9-26-1890. St. Stephen's Cemetery, Millburn, Essex County.
FRENCH*, LEWIS M. (aka: French, Louis M.) Pvt, K, 22nd MA Inf, 1909. Baptist Cemetery, Vincentown, Burlington County.
FRENCH, LOUIS M. (see: French, Lewis M.) Baptist Cemetery, Vincentown, Burlington County.
FRENCH, NATHAN C. Pvt, C, 27th NJ Inf, 5-2-1883. Fairmount Cemetery, Newark, Essex County.
FRENCH, PAUL H. Pvt, D, 4th NJ Inf, 8-15-1885. Saums Farm Cemetery, Hillsborough, Somerset County.
FRENCH*, PHILIP F. Corp, G, 3rd NJ Inf, 12-13-1917. Greenwood Cemetery, Hamilton, Mercer County.
FRENCH, RICHARD NEWTON Pvt, B, 30th NJ Inf, 7-18-1924. Fairview Cemetery, Westfield, Union County.
FRENCH, STEPHEN Pvt, G, 8th NJ Inf, 1903. Saums Farm Cemetery, Hillsborough, Somerset County.
FRENCH, THOMAS C. Pvt, Btty C, 5th NY Heavy Art, [Wounded 7-18-1864 at Nickers Gap, VA.] 1-21-1885. Alpine Cemetery, Perth Amboy, Middlesex County.
FRENCH, THOMAS J. Corp, H, 12th NJ Inf, 1911. Friends Cemetery, Mullica Hill, Gloucester County.
FRENCH, THOMAS M. Wagoner, A, 3rd NJ Inf, 5-9-1914. Baptist Church Cemetery, Mullica Hill, Gloucester County.
FRENCH, WILLIAM H. Pvt, A, 28th NJ Inf, 11-12-1896. Washington Monumental Cemetery, South River, Middlesex County.
FRENCH, WILLIAM W. DoD Unknown. Alpine Cemetery, Perth Amboy, Middlesex County.
FRESCHE*, GUSTAVUS L. (aka: Freche, Gustavus) 1st Lt, H, 40th NJ Inf, 8-15-1900. Fairmount Cemetery, Newark, Essex County.
FRESHET, MICHAEL (see: Fiske, Michael) Beverly National Cemetery, Edgewater Park, Burlington County.
FREUDENBERGER, LOUIS Pvt, D, 55th NY Inf, [Wounded 7-1-1862 at Malvern Hill, VA.] 2-15-1897. Hoboken Cemetery, North Bergen, Hudson County.
FREUND, AUGUSTUS Pvt, B, 39th NJ Inf, 5-12-1916. Fairmount Cemetery, Newark, Essex County.

New Jersey Civil War Burials

FREUND, GEORGE Pvt, I, 2nd DC Inf, 6-19-1886. Fairmount Cemetery, Newark, Essex County.
FREUND, GUSTAV Pvt, A, 39th NJ Inf, 3-4-1874. Fairmount Cemetery, Newark, Essex County.
FREUND, JOHN Pvt, C, 7th NY Inf, 3-9-1920. Arlington Cemetery, Kearny, Hudson County.
FREVERT*, WILLIAM H. Pvt, D, 40th NY Inf, [Wounded 7-2-1863 at Gettysburg, PA.] 12-27-1909. Bayview-New York Bay Cemetery, Jersey City, Hudson County.
FREW, SHAW W. Pvt, B, 205th PA Inf, 5-25-1916. Siloam Cemetery, Vineland, Cumberland County.
FREY, PETER A. (aka: Frye, Peter) Pvt, I, 31st NJ Inf, 4-21-1911. Belvidere/Catholic Cemetery, Belvidere, Warren County.
FREY, WILLIAM P. Pvt, Btty E, 1st NJ Light Art, 10-19-1913. Fairview Cemetery, Fairview, Monmouth County.
FRIANT, EPHRIAM H. Pvt, A, 24th NJ Inf, 10-21-1902. Eastview Cemetery, Salem, Salem County.
FRIANT, MATTHIAS B. Pvt, A, 24th NJ Inf, 5-27-1911. Mount Holly Cemetery, Mount Holly, Burlington County.
FRIANT, QUINTON G. Pvt, K, 215th PA Inf, 8-7-1936. Eastview Cemetery, Salem, Salem County.
FRICK, GOTTLOP (aka: Freick, Gotlib) Pvt, F, 96th NY Inf, 9-8-1909. Grove Church Cemetery, North Bergen, Hudson County.
FRICK, HENRY Corp, B, 35th NJ Inf, 7-3-1867. Holy Sepulchre Cemetery, East Orange, Essex County.
FRICK, JULIUS Sgt, A, 20th NY Inf, 12-24-1877. Fairmount Cemetery, Newark, Essex County.
FRICK, PHILLIPP Pvt, Btty A, 1st NJ Light Art, 7-23-1890. Grove Church Cemetery, North Bergen, Hudson County.
FRICKER, CHARLES (aka: Frickle, Charles) Pvt, A, 26th PA Inf, 9-12-1911. Arlington Cemetery, Kearny, Hudson County.
FRICKLE, CHARLES (see: Fricker, Charles) Arlington Cemetery, Kearny, Hudson County.
FRIDDLE, JOHN Pvt, I, 26th NC Inf (CSA), [Captured 7-3-1863 at Gettysburg, PA. Died of diarrhea.] 9-13-1863. Finn's Point National Cemetery, Pennsville, Salem County.
FRIEDEL*, GUSTAV Pvt, E, 2nd NJ Inf, 6-22-1891. Woodland Cemetery, Newark, Essex County.
FRIEDERICHS, JOSEPH (aka: Frederick, Joseph) Pvt, E, 2nd NJ Inf, 3-22-1889. Woodland Cemetery, Newark, Essex County.
FRIEDRICH, AUGUST Pvt, Btty B, 3rd NY Light Art, 11-22-1880. Weehawken Cemetery, North Bergen, Hudson County.
FRIEDRICH, GEORGE Pvt, F, 5th NY State Militia, 2-6-1893. Fairmount Cemetery, Newark, Essex County.
FRIEDRICH, GOTTLIEB Com Sgt, I, 1st NY Cav, 2-9-1893. Fairmount Cemetery, Newark, Essex County.
FRIEL, PATRICK Pvt, D, 1st CA Inf, DoD Unknown. St. John's Cemetery, Lambertville, Hunterdon County.
FRIEND*, FRANK Pvt, L, 3rd NY Prov Cav, 5-27-1913. Fairmount Cemetery, Newark, Essex County.
FRIES, FREDERICK Actg 3rd Asst Eng, U.S. Navy, 1908. Mount Prospect Cemetery, Neptune, Monmouth County.
FRIES, JACOB (see: Freas, Jacob) Methodist Church Cemetery, Aldine, Salem County.
FRIES, JOHN S. Sgt, K, 2nd NJ Cav, DoD Unknown. Presbyterian Church Cemetery, Bridgeton, Cumberland County.

Our Brothers Gone Before

FRIES, JOHN S. 4-27-1894. Manahath Cemetery, Glassboro, Gloucester County.
FRIES, WILHELM Pvt, F, 103rd NY Inf, 12-19-1912. Presbyterian Cemetery, North Plainfield, Somerset County.
FRISBY, DAVID Seaman, U.S. Navy, USS Massachusetts, 1-28-1873. Timbuctoo Cemetery, Timbuctoo, Burlington County.
FRISBY, EDWARD Wagoner, A, 22nd U.S. CT, 11-17-1899. Mount Salem Church Cemetery, Fenwick, Salem County.
FRISBY, RICHARD Pvt, F, 7th U.S. CT, 1-24-1902. AME Cemetery, Franklinville, Gloucester County.
FRISCH*, JOHN Pvt, C, 5th NJ Inf, 10-29-1864. Bayview-New York Bay Cemetery, Jersey City, Hudson County.
FRITH, HENRY H. Pvt, K, 8th AL Inf (CSA), 8-28-1863. Finn's Point National Cemetery, Pennsville, Salem County.
FRITSCHY, JOHN JACOB (JR.) 2nd Lt, B, 7th NJ Inf, [Died of wounds received 5-5-1862 at Williamsburg, VA.] 6-27-1862. Egg Harbor Cemetery, Egg Harbor, Atlantic County.
FRITSCHY, JOHN JACOB (SR.) Capt, D, 7th NJ Inf, 11-30-1890. Egg Harbor Cemetery, Egg Harbor, Atlantic County.
FRITTS, BENJAMIN Pvt, K, 31st NJ Inf, 5-13-1909. Old & New Lutheran Cemetery, Lebanon, Hunterdon County.
FRITTS, CONRAD A. Pvt, K, 31st NJ Inf, 8-12-1901. Old & New Lutheran Cemetery, Lebanon, Hunterdon County.
FRITTS, GEORGE F. (aka: Fritz, George) Corp, H, 62nd NY Inf, [Killed in action at Wilderness, VA.] 5-5-1864. Belvidere/Catholic Cemetery, Belvidere, Warren County.
FRITTS, HENRY S. Pvt, E, 30th NJ Inf, 10-9-1877. Old Somerville Cemetery, Somerville, Somerset County.
FRITTS, SAMUEL F. Corp, K, 31st NJ Inf, 5-7-1896. Old & New Lutheran Cemetery, Lebanon, Hunterdon County.
FRITZ, ADAM Corp, H, 152nd IL Inf, 12-25-1908. Laurel Grove Cemetery, Totowa, Passaic County.
FRITZ, CHRISTIAN F. (aka: Fritz, Christof) Corp, A, 103rd NY Inf, 2-8-1891. Fairmount Cemetery, Newark, Essex County.
FRITZ, CHRISTOF (see: Fritz, Christian F.) Fairmount Cemetery, Newark, Essex County.
FRITZ, GEORGE (see: Fritts, George F.) Belvidere/Catholic Cemetery, Belvidere, Warren County.
FRIZZELL, JOHN Pvt, A, 3rd NJ Cav, 1920. Old Rock Church Cemetery, West Amwell, Hunterdon County.
FROAT, HENRY L. (aka: Fratt, Henry) Pvt, K, 5th NJ Inf, 3-29-1899. Greenlawn Cemetery, West Long Branch, Monmouth County.
FROATE*, GERSHOM J. Pvt, K, 11th NJ Inf, 7-18-1885. Dutch Reformed Church Cemetery, Spotswood, Middlesex County.
FROCKENBROOK, ADOLPHUS Pvt, E, 22nd NJ Inf, 7-14-1886. Valleau Cemetery, Ridgewood, Bergen County.
FROEHLICH, ALFRED (see: Fraley, Alfred) Elmwood Cemetery, New Brunswick, Middlesex County.
FROEHLICH, CHARLES Pvt, I, 3rd NJ Cav, 8-19-1894. Fairmount Cemetery, Newark, Essex County.
FROMM, JOHN Pvt, H, 30th NJ Inf, 12-8-1912. Evergreen Cemetery, Hillside, Union County.
FROST, ALFRED 4-9-1872. Fairview Cemetery, Fairview, Bergen County.
FROST, ALFRED Pvt, B, 41st U.S. CT, DoD Unknown. Cedar View Cemetery, Lincroft, Monmouth County.

New Jersey Civil War Burials

FROST, DAVID Pvt, C, 41st U.S. CT, 12-22-1867. Evergreen Cemetery, Morristown, Morris County.
FROST, GEORGE HENRY 3-15-1917. Hillside Cemetery, Scotch Plains, Union County.
FROST, ISAAC N. Pvt, I, 39th NJ Inf, 6-27-1916. Bayview-New York Bay Cemetery, Jersey City, Hudson County.
FROST, JAMES D. Pvt, B, 47th NY Inf, 5-5-1904. Methodist Church Cemetery, Groveville, Mercer County.
FROST, JOHN W. Pvt, F, 25th U.S. CT, 2-11-1906. Crystal Stream Cemetery, Navesink, Monmouth County.
FROST, SAMUEL T. Sgt, D, 29th NJ Inf, 8-10-1914. Christ Church Cemetery, Morgan, Middlesex County.
FROST, WILLIAM 2-1-1894. White Ridge Cemetery, Eatontown, Monmouth County.
FRY, DAVID W. Pvt, F, 3rd NJ Inf, [Wounded 9-14-1862 at Crampton's Pass, MD.] DoD Unknown. 1st United Methodist Church Cemetery, Bridgeton, Cumberland County.
FRY, EDWIN (see: Fry, Francis H.) Baptist Cemetery, Burlington, Burlington County.
FRY, FRANCIS H. (aka: Fry, Edwin) Pvt, K, 72nd PA Inf, 9-29-1905. Baptist Cemetery, Burlington, Burlington County.
FRY, H. DoD Unknown. Trinity Bible Church Cemetery, Glassboro, Gloucester County.
FRY*, ISAAC S. Wagoner, H, 7th NJ Inf, 3-10-1900. Bible Church Cemetery, Hardingville, Gloucester County.
FRY, REINHART G. Pvt, D, 5th PA Cav, 8-5-1869. Baptist Cemetery, Burlington, Burlington County.
FRY, W.A. Sgt, A, 22nd VA Inf (CSA), 7-16-1864. Finn's Point National Cemetery, Pennsville, Salem County.
FRY, WHITNEY B. Pvt, D, 2nd NJ Cav, 1902. Bible Church Cemetery, Hardingville, Gloucester County.
FRY, WILLIAM C. [Cenotaph. Died while prisoner at Andersonville, GA.] 9-14-1864. 1st Methodist-Episcopal Cemetery, New Brunswick, Middlesex County.
FRY, WILLIAM ENGLISH Pvt, B, 3rd TN Inf (CSA), 11-4-1864. Finn's Point National Cemetery, Pennsville, Salem County.
FRYAR, JOHN W. Sgt, L, 2nd MS Inf (CSA), [Captured 7-1-1863 at Gettysburg, PA. Died of disease.] 10-31-1863. Finn's Point National Cemetery, Pennsville, Salem County.
FRYE, PETER (see: Frey, Peter A.) Belvidere/Catholic Cemetery, Belvidere, Warren County.
FRYER, JABEZ F. Corp, Btty F, 3rd PA Heavy Art, 4-3-1901. Cedar Green Cemetery, Clayton, Gloucester County.
FRYER*, WILLIAM Pvt, K, 145th NY Inf, 11-14-1909. Rosedale Cemetery, Orange, Essex County.
FUAREY, JAMES M. Pvt, C, 37th MA Inf, [Wounded 7-3-1863 at Gettysburg, PA.] 1-21-1906. Siloam Cemetery, Vineland, Cumberland County.
FUCHS, CHARLES Pvt, E, 9th NJ Inf, 4-21-1897. Holy Sepulchre Cemetery, East Orange, Essex County.
FUCHS, JACOB Pvt, A, 33rd NJ Inf, 1-10-1894. Woodland Cemetery, Newark, Essex County.
FUCHS, JOSEPH (aka: Fachs, Joseph) Corp, B, 6th WI Inf, [Wounded 8-28-1862 at Gainesville, VA. and 7-1-1863 at Gettysburg, PA.] 2-9-1903. Holy Sepulchre Cemetery, Totowa, Passaic County.
FUCHS, KASPER 1912. St Mary's Cemetery, Watchung, Somerset County.
FUGILL, JOHN R. Pvt, E, 2nd NY Mounted Rifles, 3-10-1913. Greenwood Cemetery, Hamilton, Mercer County.
FUHR, FREDERICK 1st Cl Musc, 1st NJ Brigade Band 10-31-1926. Fairview Cemetery, Fairview, Bergen County.

Our Brothers Gone Before

FUHR, FREDERICK Sgt, C, 2nd MO Inf, DoD Unknown. Arlington Cemetery, Kearny, Hudson County.

FUHRMAN, CHARLES Pvt, B, 191st NY Inf, 11-27-1915. Bayview-New York Bay Cemetery, Jersey City, Hudson County.

FULDING, P. 4-16-1879. Laurel Grove Cemetery, Totowa, Passaic County.

FULHEIM, WILLIAM Pvt, K, 8th NJ Inf, [Died at Philadelphia, PA. of wounds received in action.] 2-9-1864. St. Peter's Cemetery, Jersey City, Hudson County.

FULKERSON, A.I. POLK (aka: Ferguson, A.I.) Pvt, C, 60th (Crawford's) TN Mtd Inf (CSA), [Captured 5-17-1863 at Big Black River Bridge, MS.] 7-22-1863. Finn's Point National Cemetery, Pennsville, Salem County.

FULKERSON, JEREMIAH Pvt, E, 15th NJ Inf, 7-24-1886. Evergreen Cemetery, New Brunswick, Middlesex County.

FULKERSON, THOMAS N. Pvt, C, 60th (Crawford's) TN Mtd Inf (CSA), [Captured 5-17-1863 at Big Black River Bridge, MS.] 9-5-1863. Finn's Point National Cemetery, Pennsville, Salem County.

FULLBRIGHT, LENAS F. Pvt, F, 38th NC Inf (CSA), [Wounded 7-1-1863 at Gettysburg, PA. Captured 7-7-1863 at Williamsport, MD. Died of disease.] 9-17-1863. Finn's Point National Cemetery, Pennsville, Salem County.

FULLER, ALBERT S. (aka: Scandrett, Albert S.) Corp, D, 193rd PA Inf, DoD Unknown. Evergreen Cemetery, Camden, Camden County.

FULLER, BERRYMAN Pvt, B, 38th VA Inf (CSA), [Captured 7-3-1863 at Gettsburg, PA. Died of fever.] 9-25-1863. Finn's Point National Cemetery, Pennsville, Salem County.

FULLER, GEORGE Pvt, B, 39th NJ Inf, 3-12-1884. Holy Sepulchre Cemetery, East Orange, Essex County.

FULLER, GEORGE E. Pvt, I, 132nd PA Inf, 5-9-1899. Phillipsburg Cemetery, Phillipsburg, Warren County.

FULLER, JAMES E. Pvt, C, 43rd NY Inf, DoD Unknown. Arlington Cemetery, Kearny, Hudson County.

FULLER, JAMES H. Pvt, L, 27th NJ Inf, [Drowned while crossing the Cumberland River, KY.] 5-6-1863. Presbyterian Church Cemetery, Rockaway, Morris County.

FULLER, JAMES RICHARD Pvt, G, 1st VA Inf (CSA), [Captured at Gettysburg, PA.] 10-9-1863. Finn's Point National Cemetery, Pennsville, Salem County.

FULLER, JASON K.C. Pvt, A, 27th NJ Inf, 11-19-1907. Walpack Methodist Cemetery, Walpack, Sussex County.

FULLER, JOHN Pvt, F, 22nd NJ Inf, 1913. Methodist Church Cemetery, Titusville, Mercer County.

FULLER, JOHN B. Sgt, A, 27th NJ Inf, 1-8-1917. Walpack Methodist Cemetery, Walpack, Sussex County.

FULLER, OAKLEY B. Seaman, U.S. Navy, [U.S. Navy Yard at Brooklyn, NY.] 12-23-1888. Riverside Cemetery, Toms River, Ocean County.

FULLER*, WILLIAM LEE Pvt, B, 5th NY Vet Inf, 1889. Riverside Cemetery, Toms River, Ocean County.

FULLERTON, HUMPHREY Pvt, H, 33rd OH Inf, 7-3-1922. Mount Zion United Methodist Church Cemetery, Barnsboro, Gloucester County.

FULLERTON, J.O. DoD Unknown. Pompton Reformed Church Cemetery, Pompton Lakes, Passaic County.

FULLERTON, JOHN QUINCY ADAMS 2nd Lt, E, 34th OH Inf, 1916. Elm Ridge Cemetery, North Brunswick, Middlesex County.

FULLERTON, WILLIAM WISTER 5-2-1899. Presbyterian Cemetery, Woodbury, Gloucester County.

FULLINGTON, JAMES A. 2nd Lt, K, 9th AR Inf (CSA), [Captured 1-13-1864 at Natchez, MS.] 7-10-1864. Finn's Point National Cemetery, Pennsville, Salem County.

FULPER, ASHER 9-2-1895. Lower Amwell Cemetery, Headquarters, Hunterdon County.

New Jersey Civil War Burials

FULPER, DANIEL W. 1902. Prospect Hill Cemetery, Flemington, Hunterdon County.
FULTON, ISAAC 4-2-1897. Reformed Church Cemetery, Wyckoff, Bergen County.
FULTON, JOHN R. Pvt, A, 22nd NJ Inf, 12-7-1891. Cedar Lawn Cemetery, Paterson, Passaic County.
FULTON, WILLIAM H. Pvt, I, 2nd MS Cav (CSA), 8-2-1864. Finn's Point National Cemetery, Pennsville, Salem County.
FUNK, ALBERT (see: Funk, John Haus) Phillipsburg Cemetery, Phillipsburg, Warren County.
FUNK, BERNARD H. Seaman, U.S. Navy, USS Norfolk, 3-22-1903. Flower Hill Cemetery, North Bergen, Hudson County.
FUNK, JOHN Pvt, D, 183rd PA Inf, 12-13-1926. Baptist Cemetery, Medford, Burlington County.
FUNK, JOHN HAUS (aka: Funk, Albert) Pvt, Btty C, 1st NJ Light Art, DoD Unknown. Phillipsburg Cemetery, Phillipsburg, Warren County.
FUNK, LEOPOLD DoD Unknown. Hackensack Cemetery, Hackensack, Bergen County.
FUNK, LUDWIG (aka: Frank, Ludwig) Pvt, D, 51st NY Inf, 5-22-1922. Hackensack Cemetery, Hackensack, Bergen County.
FUREY, JAMES B. 2nd Lt, D, 150th NY Inf, 9-22-1896. Evergreen Cemetery, Hillside, Union County.
FURFEY, EDWARD ___, I, 7th ___ Art, 10-9-1918. Riverview Cemetery, Trenton, Mercer County.
FURGESON, WILLIAM Pvt, I, 8th NJ Inf, 3-27-1919. Elmwood Cemetery, New Brunswick, Middlesex County.
FURGUSON, ELDRIDGE F. Pvt, K, 11th VA Inf (CSA), [Wounded and captured 7-3-1863 at Gettysburg, PA. Died of anemia.] 9-26-1863. Finn's Point National Cemetery, Pennsville, Salem County.
FURGUSON, HUGH Pvt, E, 34th NJ Inf, DoD Unknown. 1st Baptist Church Cemetery, Florence, Burlington County.
FURLONG, JAMES Corp, Btty A, 1st NJ Light Art, DoD Unknown. Holy Sepulchre Cemetery, East Orange, Essex County.
FURLONG, WILLIAM Pvt, F, 28th NJ Inf, 9-4-1919. Arlington Cemetery, Kearny, Hudson County.
FURMAN, ALFRED H. Pvt, E, 34th NJ Inf, 5-12-1892. Riverview Cemetery, Trenton, Mercer County.
FURMAN, HENRY Pvt, H, 21st NJ Inf, 6-18-1904. Greenwood Cemetery, Hamilton, Mercer County.
FURMAN, JAMES Pvt, E, 54th MA Inf, 5-26-1907. Mansfield/Washington Cemetery, Washington, Warren County.
FURMAN, JOHN M. Pvt, E, 86th OH Inf, 12-11-1899. Belvidere/Catholic Cemetery, Belvidere, Warren County.
FURMAN, JOSHUA Pvt, G, 10th NJ Inf, 7-25-1899. Riverview Cemetery, Trenton, Mercer County.
FURMAN, LORENZO (aka: Freeman, Lorenzo) Pvt, A, 41st U.S. CT, DoD Unknown. Evergreen Cemetery, Morristown, Morris County.
FURMAN, WILLIAM H. Pvt, K, 28th NJ Inf, 1-19-1874. Elmwood Cemetery, New Brunswick, Middlesex County.
FURMAN, WILLIAM N. Pvt, D, 11th NJ Inf, 9-8-1918. Belvidere/Catholic Cemetery, Belvidere, Warren County.
FURNACE, WILLIAM S. (aka: Furness, William) Musc, 23rd PA Inf Band 1-29-1904. Fairmount Cemetery, Newark, Essex County.
FURNESS, WILLIAM Pvt, A, 8th NJ Inf, 7-18-1884. Mount Pleasant Cemetery, Newark, Essex County.
FURNESS, WILLIAM (see: Furnace, William S.) Fairmount Cemetery, Newark, Essex County.

Our Brothers Gone Before

FURNESS, WILLIAM T. Pvt, K, 28th NJ Inf, 1-3-1874. Elmwood Cemetery, New Brunswick, Middlesex County.
FURNEY, LUCIUS A. Capt, F, 45th U.S. CT, DoD Unknown. Grove Church Cemetery, North Bergen, Hudson County.
FURRY, ANDREW J. Corp, K, 23rd NJ Inf, 5-20-1900. Eglington Cemetery, Clarksboro, Gloucester County.
FURRY, PETER U. 1909. Baptist/St. Andrew's Cemetery, Mount Holly, Burlington County.
FURZE, THOMAS Corp, B, 8th NJ Inf, 5-2-1872. Fairmount Cemetery, Newark, Essex County.
FURZE, WILLIAM J. Landsman, U.S. Navy, 10-30-1909. Fairmount Cemetery, Newark, Essex County.
FUSS, ALEXANDER Pvt, F, 3rd NJ Cav, 3-3-1904. Fairmount Cemetery, Newark, Essex County.
FUSS, LOUIS (see: Fass, Ludwig) Grove Church Cemetery, North Bergen, Hudson County.
FUSS, LUDWIG (see: Foss, Ludwig) Grove Church Cemetery, North Bergen, Hudson County.
FUTRELL, DAVID Pvt, C, 20th MS Inf (CSA), 5-23-1864. Finn's Point National Cemetery, Pennsville, Salem County.
FUTRIAL, JOHN Pvt, G, 38th GA Inf (CSA), [Wounded 12-13-1862 at Fredericksburg, VA. Captured 5-12-1864 at Mine Run, VA. Died of bronchitis.] 7-3-1864. Finn's Point National Cemetery, Pennsville, Salem County.
FYLE, ANDREW (aka: File, Andrew) Pvt, H, 2nd NY Cav, [Wounded 4-1-1865 at Five Forks, VA.] 6-10-1894. Macphelah Cemetery, North Bergen, Hudson County.
FYRER, JOHN Pvt, K, 198th PA Inf, 1919. Cedar Hill Cemetery, Hightstown, Mercer County.
GABRIEL, CLARKSON Pvt, B, 28th NJ Inf, 3-18-1869. Dutch Reformed Church Cemetery, Spotswood, Middlesex County.
GABRIEL, HENRY (see: Gabrielle, Henry H.) Rahway Cemetery, Rahway, Union County.
GABRIELLE, HENRY H. (aka: Gabriel, Henry) Pvt, C, 30th NJ Inf, 2-6-1922. Rahway Cemetery, Rahway, Union County.
GADDIS, JAMES Pvt, E, 1st NJ Militia, 12-29-1871. Baptist Cemetery, Hopewell Boro, Mercer County.
GADDIS, SAMUEL L. Seaman, U.S. Navy, 8-24-1863. Fairmount Cemetery, Chatham, Morris County.
GADDIS, THOMAS Pvt, G, 79th NY Inf, [Wounded 9-17-1862 at Antietam, MD.] 1-6-1868. Macphelah Cemetery, North Bergen, Hudson County.
GAFFA, JULIUS (see: Juffa, Julius) Woodland Cemetery, Newark, Essex County.
GAFFEY, MICHAEL (see: Gaffney, Michael F.) Holy Sepulchre Cemetery, East Orange, Essex County.
GAFFNEY, JAMES Seaman, U.S. Navy, 5-30-1884. Flower Hill Cemetery, North Bergen, Hudson County.
GAFFNEY, MICHAEL F. (aka: Gaffey, Michael) Corp, F, 33rd PA Inf, 4-2-1938. Holy Sepulchre Cemetery, East Orange, Essex County.
GAFFNEY, PATRICK Pvt, Btty B, 1st NJ Light Art, 6-2-1870. St. Mary's Cemetery, Elizabeth, Union County.
GAFFNEY, PATRICK Landsman, U.S. Navy, USS Chimo, 11-18-1895. Holy Sepulchre Cemetery, East Orange, Essex County.
GAGE, GEORGE Capt, E, PA Emerg NJ Militia, 9-5-1868. Chestnut Cemetery, Dover, Morris County.
GAGE, GEORGE W. Pvt, F, 10th ME Inf, 1905. Oddfellows Cemetery, Burlington, Burlington County.

New Jersey Civil War Burials

GAGE*, JARED DANA Pvt, E, 15th IL Inf, 1-12-1868. Siloam Cemetery, Vineland, Cumberland County.
GAGE, JOHN 2-13-1878. Atlantic City Cemetery, Pleasantville, Atlantic County.
GAGE, RHOMANZA Pvt, K, 11th CT Inf, 5-14-1882. Rosedale Cemetery, Orange, Essex County.
GAGE, SMITH C. Pvt, C, 15th NJ Inf, [Died at Washington, DC. of wounds received 5-3-1863 at Salem Heights, VA.] 5-14-1863. Boonton Cemetery, Boonton, Morris County.
GAGE, THOMAS J. Pvt, Btty C, 5th NY Heavy Art, DoD Unknown. Presbyterian Church Cemetery, Woodbridge, Middlesex County.
GAGER, EDWIN V. Actg Master, U.S. Navy, 7-12-1914. Fairmount Cemetery, Newark, Essex County.
GAHAN*, SAMUEL W. 2nd Cl Fireman, U.S. Navy, USS Nereus, 7-19-1906. Evergreen Cemetery, Camden, Camden County.
GAHM, PETER Leader, 9th NJ Inf Band 5-14-1899. Holy Sepulchre Cemetery, East Orange, Essex County.
GAHN, HARRY JOSEPH Seaman, U.S. Navy, 5-11-1919. Columbus Cemetery, Columbus, Burlington County.
GAHN, LEON H. Seaman, U.S. Navy, DoD Unknown. Columbus Cemetery, Columbus, Burlington County.
GAILING, ANDREW (see: Garling, Andrew) Holy Name Cemetery, Jersey City, Hudson County.
GAINES, EDMOND P. Pvt, G, 3rd AL Cav (CSA), 8-25-1863. Finn's Point National Cemetery, Pennsville, Salem County.
GAINES, ISAAC H. Corp, K, 22nd U.S. CT, 6-16-1915. Mount Moriah Cemetery, Hainesport, Burlington County.
GAINES, JOHN W. Pvt, F, 54th MA Inf, [Wounded 7-18-1863 at Fort Wagner, SC.] 9-18-1909. Jordan Lawn Cemetery, Pennsauken, Camden County.
GAINES, MORRIS Pvt, C, 1st U.S. Colored Cav, 3-22-1918. Mount Moriah Cemetery, Hainesport, Burlington County.
GAINES, STANLEY 1st Lt, K, 7th NJ Inf, 9-17-1882. Reformed Church Cemetery, Montville, Morris County.
GAISBAUER, CHARLES Pvt, F, 1st NJ Inf, 5-18-1866. Willow Grove Cemetery, New Brunswick, Middlesex County.
GAISER, MICHAEL 1-27-1899. Riverview Cemetery, Trenton, Mercer County.
GAISER, SAMUEL (see: Geiser, Samuel) Woodland Cemetery, Newark, Essex County.
GAITHER, CALVIN Pvt, E, 33rd NC Inf (CSA), [Captured 7-3-1863 at Gettysburg, PA.] 10-1-1863. Finn's Point National Cemetery, Pennsville, Salem County.
GALABRASGE, SALVADOR Coal Heaver, U.S. Navy, USS Wyalusing, 8-10-1881. United Methodist Church Cemetery, Winslow, Camden County.
GALAGER, WILLIAM F. Sgt, F, 22nd NJ Inf, 1925. Presbyterian Church Cemetery, Pennington, Mercer County.
GALBAUGH, AUGUSTUS (see: Gilbaugh, Augustus) Prospect Hill Cemetery, Flemington, Hunterdon County.
GALBRAITH*, BENJAMIN (SR.) 2nd Lt, Btty B, 1st NJ Light Art, 7-2-1883. Mount Pleasant Cemetery, Newark, Essex County.
GALBRAITH, JAMES Pvt, F, 4th NJ Inf, 2-19-1907. New Camden Cemetery, Camden, Camden County.
GALBRAITH*, WILLIAM Pvt, F, 5th NY Vet Inf, DoD Unknown. Macphelah Cemetery, North Bergen, Hudson County.
GALBRAITH, WILLIAM L. Pvt, I, 24th NJ Inf, 8-26-1900. Oak Grove Cemetery, Hammonton, Atlantic County.
GALE, AMOS R. Pvt, K, 23rd NJ Inf, 7-6-1925. Greenwood Cemetery, Tuckerton, Ocean County.

Our Brothers Gone Before

GALE, EDWIN A. Pvt, K, 23rd NJ Inf, 8-14-1920. Greenwood Cemetery, Tuckerton, Ocean County.
GALE, FRANCIS (see: Gile, Francis A.) Hazelwood Cemetery, Rahway, Union County.
GALE, GABRIEL N.P. 1st Lt, 11th NY Ind Btty 11-25-1882. Evergreen Cemetery, Hillside, Union County.
GALE, JAMES R. Pvt, K, 10th NJ Inf, 6-23-1889. Greenwood Cemetery, Tuckerton, Ocean County.
GALE, JOSEPH Capt, B, 4th NJ Militia, 12-21-1870. Mount Holly Cemetery, Mount Holly, Burlington County.
GALE, OLIVER Pvt, K, 10th NJ Inf, 1865. Greenwood Cemetery, Tuckerton, Ocean County.
GALE, ROBERT A. 1st Sgt, I, 127th U.S. CT, 10-25-1896. Evergreen Cemetery, Morristown, Morris County.
GALE, SAMUEL A. Pvt, K, 23rd NJ Inf, 8-27-1914. Greenwood Cemetery, Tuckerton, Ocean County.
GALE, SAMUEL B. 1st Lt, B, 4th NJ Militia, 1919. Mount Holly Cemetery, Mount Holly, Burlington County.
GALE, WILLIAM Pvt, K, 10th NJ Inf, 8-4-1870. Greenwood Cemetery, Tuckerton, Ocean County.
GALE*, WILLIAM Actg Asst Surg, U.S. Navy, USS Guard, 4-15-1917. Fairview Cemetery, Westfield, Union County.
GALE, WILLIAM (aka: Gold, William) Corp, K, 40th NJ Inf, 4-2-1901. Baptist/St. Andrew's Cemetery, Mount Holly, Burlington County.
GALES, CHARLES T. Seaman, U.S. Navy, 9-21-1913. Laurel Grove Cemetery, Totowa, Passaic County.
GALES, ISAAC Pvt, K, 6th U.S. CT, 12-31-1894. Memorial Park Cemetery, Gouldtown, Cumberland County.
GALLAGHER, AMBROSE F. Pvt, F, 9th U.S. Inf, DoD Unknown. Phillipsburg Cemetery, Phillipsburg, Warren County.
GALLAGHER, EDWARD J. Pvt, U.S. Marine Corps, 12-24-1900. Holy Sepulchre Cemetery, East Orange, Essex County.
GALLAGHER, FRANCIS W. Pvt, G, 24th NJ Inf, 3-22-1885. Presbyterian Church Cemetery, Bridgeton, Cumberland County.
GALLAGHER*, HUGH Pvt, F, 9th NJ Inf, 1916. Phillipsburg New Catholic Cemetery, Greenwich, Warren County.
GALLAGHER, JAMES Pvt, B, 13th __ Inf, DoD Unknown. Holy Sepulchre Cemetery, East Orange, Essex County.
GALLAGHER, JAMES 2-24-1892. Eglington Cemetery, Clarksboro, Gloucester County.
GALLAGHER, JAMES A. Pvt, E, 30th NJ Inf, 11-4-1912. Evergreen Cemetery, Hillside, Union County.
GALLAGHER, JOHN Pvt, E, 24th NJ Inf, 11-3-1889. Eglington Cemetery, Clarksboro, Gloucester County.
GALLAGHER, JOHN Pvt, G, 5th NJ Inf, 5-9-1912. Holy Name Cemetery, Jersey City, Hudson County.
GALLAGHER, JOHN Sgt, D, 22nd NY Inf, 8-29-1895. St. Vincent Martyr Cemetery, Madison, Morris County.
GALLAGHER, JOSEPH S. 4-12-1877. Rosedale Cemetery, Orange, Essex County.
GALLAGHER*, PATRICK Pvt, I, 2nd NJ Inf, DoD Unknown. Mount Pleasant Cemetery, Newark, Essex County.
GALLAGHER, PATRICK D. Wagoner, G, 1st NJ Inf, DoD Unknown. St. Mary's Cemetery, Clark, Union County.
GALLAGHER*, SAMUEL D. Pvt, F, 37th NJ Inf, 6-10-1907. Presbyterian Church Cemetery, Bridgeton, Cumberland County.

New Jersey Civil War Burials

GALLAGHER, SAMUEL J. Pvt, E, 5th MO Inf (CSA), 1-15-1865. Finn's Point National Cemetery, Pennsville, Salem County.

GALLAGHER, THOMAS Pvt, K, 2nd U.S. Inf, 2-3-1894. Bayview-New York Bay Cemetery, Jersey City, Hudson County.

GALLAGHER, THOMAS Pvt, A, 155th NY Inf, 11-19-1906. Evergreen Cemetery, Hillside, Union County.

GALLAGHER, WILLIAM 12-4-1890. St. Peter's Church Cemetery, Belleville, Essex County.

GALLAGHER, WILLIAM H. Sgt, G, 2nd NJ Militia, 10-21-1871. Bayview-New York Bay Cemetery, Jersey City, Hudson County.

GALLARDO, JOSEPH DoD Unknown. Mount Pleasant Cemetery, Newark, Essex County.

GALLASPIE, ROBERT (see: Glaspey, Robert) 1st United Methodist Church Cemetery, Bridgeton, Cumberland County.

GALLAWAY, EDWIN H. Pvt, E, 13th NJ Inf, 6-27-1909. Mountain View Cemetery, Cokesbury, Hunterdon County.

GALLAWAY*, ROBERT 1st Sgt, K, 1st NJ Inf, DoD Unknown. Midvale Cemetery, Midvale, Passaic County.

GALLERY, BARTHOLOMEW Corp, B, 13th U.S. Inf, 7-1-1898. Holy Name Cemetery, Jersey City, Hudson County.

GALLIGAN*, EDWARD B. Pvt, Btty B, 5th U.S. Art, 8-3-1913. Phillipsburg Cemetery, Phillipsburg, Warren County.

GALLIGAN, JOHN Pvt, E, 37th NJ Inf, 5-9-1914. Holy Sepulchre Cemetery, East Orange, Essex County.

GALLIGAN, PETER (see: Giele, Peter) 1st Baptist Cemetery, Cape May Court House, Cape May County.

GALLIGHAN, JAMES Pvt, B, 34th NJ Inf, 4-15-1886. St. Peter's Cemetery, New Brunswick, Middlesex County.

GALLON, CHARLES Pvt, B, 157th PA Inf, DoD Unknown. Finn's Point National Cemetery, Pennsville, Salem County.

GALLOWAY, EDWIN T. Pvt, D, 56th PA Inf, [Wounded in action.] 8-9-1926. Hillside Cemetery, Lyndhurst, Bergen County.

GALLOWAY, JOSEPH D. 1st Lt, M, 3rd PA Cav, 4-22-1913. Siloam Cemetery, Vineland, Cumberland County.

GALLOWAY, RANSOM J. Pvt, G, 15th AL Inf (CSA), [Captured at Gettysburg, PA.] 8-31-1863. Finn's Point National Cemetery, Pennsville, Salem County.

GALLOWAY, ROBERT 1st Sgt, K, 1st NJ Inf, 11-27-1912. Arlington Cemetery, Kearny, Hudson County.

GALLUBA, CHARLES (see: Galuba, Charles A.) Fairmount Cemetery, Newark, Essex County.

GALUBA*, CHARLES A. (aka: Galluba, Charles) 1st Lt, A, 40th NJ Inf, 4-28-1886. Fairmount Cemetery, Newark, Essex County.

GALVIN, WILLIAM Pvt, K, 37th NY Inf, DoD Unknown. Holy Sepulchre Cemetery, East Orange, Essex County.

GAMBERTON, CHARLES P. Sgt, I, 58th NY Inf, [Wounded in action.] 1-25-1892. Fairmount Cemetery, Newark, Essex County.

GAMBLE, ADNEY W. (aka: Gamble, Alonzo) Pvt, A, 2nd NY Inf, 10-12-1917. Fairmount Cemetery, Newark, Essex County.

GAMBLE, ALONZO (see: Gamble, Adney W.) Fairmount Cemetery, Newark, Essex County.

GAMBLE, CHARLES Pvt, G, 10th NJ Inf, [Wounded in action.] 7-1-1875. Mercer Cemetery, Trenton, Mercer County.

GAMBLE, CHARLES W. Corp, D, 12th NJ Inf, [Died of typhoid at Stony Mountain, VA.] 1-13-1864. Methodist Church Cemetery, Friendship, Salem County.

Our Brothers Gone Before

GAMBLE, JAMES W. Pvt, A, 5th NJ Inf, [Killed in action at Cold Harbor, VA.] 5-31-1864. Bayview-New York Bay Cemetery, Jersey City, Hudson County.

GAMBLE, JOHN Capt, C, 5th NJ Inf, [Killed in action at Chancellorsville, VA.] 5-3-1863. Bayview-New York Bay Cemetery, Jersey City, Hudson County.

GAMBLE, THEODORE A. Pvt, H, 23rd NJ Inf, 3-8-1911. Methodist Church Cemetery, Groveville, Mercer County.

GAMBLE, WILLIAM Pvt, I, 106th PA Inf, 1-12-1863. Bayview-New York Bay Cemetery, Jersey City, Hudson County.

GAMBLE, WILLIAM H. Pvt, D, 28th NJ Inf, 7-9-1914. Evergreen Cemetery, New Brunswick, Middlesex County.

GAMBLE, WILLIAM M. Lt Commander, U.S. Navy, 10-19-1896. St. Peter's Episcopal Church Cemetery, Morristown, Morris County.

GAMBUCHLER, GEORGE (see: Gamlicher, George) Fairmount Cemetery, Newark, Essex County.

GAMIEL, SAMUEL Pvt, A, 36th __ Inf, 11-28-1913. Greenwood Cemetery, Hamilton, Mercer County.

GAMLICHER, GEORGE (aka: Gambuchler, George) Pvt, E, 2nd NJ Inf, 2-7-1869. Fairmount Cemetery, Newark, Essex County.

GAMMON, DREWRY Pvt, G, 45th VA Inf (CSA), [Captured 3-2-1865 at Waynesboro, VA. Died of bronchitis.] 4-30-1865. Finn's Point National Cemetery, Pennsville, Salem County.

GAMMON, THOMAS H. Pvt, H, 7th AL Inf (CSA), 6-30-1863. Finn's Point National Cemetery, Pennsville, Salem County.

GAMMONS, ISAIAH Pvt, B, 60th (Crawford's) TN Mtd Inf (CSA), [Captured 5-17-1863 at Big Black River Bridge, MS.] 9-27-1863. Finn's Point National Cemetery, Pennsville, Salem County.

GAMMONS, JAIRUS Pvt, D, 18th MA Inf, 2- -1905. Laurel Grove Cemetery, Totowa, Passaic County.

GAMMONS, JOHN W. Pvt, B, 60th (Crawford's) TN Mtd Inf (CSA), [Captured 5-17-1863 at Big Black River Bridge, MS.] 10-16-1863. Finn's Point National Cemetery, Pennsville, Salem County.

GAMO, JOHN F. Pvt, A, 31st NJ Inf, 1911. New Presbyterian Cemetery, Bound Brook, Somerset County.

GAND, WILLIAM Pvt, A, 62nd NY Inf, DoD Unknown. Grove Church Cemetery, North Bergen, Hudson County.

GANDENBERGER, VALENTINE Pvt, H, 7th NY Inf, 3-28-1908. Arlington Cemetery, Kearny, Hudson County.

GANDIBLUE, JOSEPH Pvt, F, 93rd PA Inf, 2-14-1894. Baptist Cemetery, Pemberton, Burlington County.

GANDRO, WILLIAM (see: Jandro, William) Laurel Grove Cemetery, Totowa, Passaic County.

GANDY, FRANKLIN Corp, D, 25th NJ Inf, 6-29-1912. Old Stone Church Cemetery, Fairton, Cumberland County.

GANDY*, GEORGE B. Pvt, K, 35th NJ Inf, 1928. Methodist Church Cemetery, Seaville, Cape May County.

GANDY, GEORGE E. Pvt, G, 25th NJ Inf, 5-12-1928. Methodist Church Cemetery, Seaville, Cape May County.

GANDY, LEWIS 10-15-1894. Mount Pleasant Cemetery, Millville, Cumberland County.

GANDY*, MAURICE (aka: Gandy, Morris) Steward, U.S. Navy, USS James Adger, 3-4-1930. United Methodist Church Cemetery, Tuckahoe, Cape May County.

GANDY, MORRIS (see: Gandy, Maurice) United Methodist Church Cemetery, Tuckahoe, Cape May County.

GANDY, NATHANIEL OSBOURNE Corp, I, 24th NJ Inf, 1-19-1910. Methodist-Episcopal Church Cemetery, Green Creek, Cape May County.

New Jersey Civil War Burials

GANDY, THOMAS ROBINSON Pvt, G, 25th NJ Inf, 2-21-1895. Calvary Baptist Church Cemetery, Ocean View, Cape May County.
GANNON, CHRISTOPHER Seaman, U.S. Navy, 5-30-1881. St. James Cemetery, Woodbridge, Middlesex County.
GANNON*, JAMES A. Corp, I, 39th NJ Inf, 8-2-1897. Presbyterian Cemetery, Springfield, Union County.
GANNON, JOHN DoD Unknown. Holy Sepulchre Cemetery, East Orange, Essex County.
GANNON, JOHN Pvt, C, 25th NJ Inf, 2-17-1905. Laurel Grove Cemetery, Totowa, Passaic County.
GANNON, JOHN P. Landsman, U.S. Navy, [U.S. receiving ship at Washington, DC.] 3-16-1876. Old Camden Cemetery, Camden, Camden County.
GANNON, PETER Pvt, A, 1st NY Eng, 2-14-1913. Arlington Cemetery, Kearny, Hudson County.
GANNON, PHILLIP Pvt, F, 4th MA Cav, 11-5-1890. Fairmount Cemetery, Newark, Essex County.
GANO, JOSEPH Corp, B, 38th NJ Inf, 9-23-1886. Union Cemetery, Frenchtown, Hunterdon County.
GANO*, JOSEPH W. Capt, G, 176th NY Inf, 4-3-1907. Arlington Cemetery, Kearny, Hudson County.
GANO, SAMUEL Pvt, H, 15th NJ Inf, 11-18-1925. New Dutch Reformed/Neshanic Cemetery, Neshanic, Somerset County.
GANON, JACOB W. (JR.) Pvt, G, 15th NJ Inf, DoD Unknown. Cedar Lawn Cemetery, Paterson, Passaic County.
GANONG, ALONZO T. Pvt, E, 40th NY Inf, [Wounded 6-1-1862 at Fair Oaks, VA. and 9-1-1862 at Chantilly, VA.] 7-13-1913. Fairmount Cemetery, Newark, Essex County.
GANT*, ABNER P. Pvt, F, 3rd NJ Cav, 2-28-1922. Baptist Church Cemetery, Laurelton, Ocean County.
GANT, CHARLES (aka: Gaunt, Charles) Pvt, K, 10th NJ Inf, 8-19-1871. Riverview Cemetery, Trenton, Mercer County.
GANT*, ELIAS M. Pvt, F, 3rd NJ Cav, 11-26-1919. Osbornville Protestant Church Cemetery, Breton Woods, Ocean County.
GANT, HANCE H. Pvt, D, 9th NJ Inf, 11-9-1882. Osbornville Protestant Church Cemetery, Breton Woods, Ocean County.
GANT, ISRAEL H. Pvt, E, 28th NJ Inf, 7-4-1911. Osbornville Protestant Church Cemetery, Breton Woods, Ocean County.
GANT, JEFFERSON Pvt, G, 52nd NC Inf (CSA), [Captured 7-3-1863 at Gettysburg, PA. Died of bronchitis.] 9-23-1863. Finn's Point National Cemetery, Pennsville, Salem County.
GANT, JOHN Pvt, E, 28th NJ Inf, 5-23-1911. Overlook Cemetery, Bridgeton, Cumberland County.
GANT*, JOHN E. Pvt, A, 38th NJ Inf, 8-15-1901. Osbornville Protestant Church Cemetery, Breton Woods, Ocean County.
GANT, JOSEPH A. Sgt, D, 12th NJ Inf, DoD Unknown. Overlook Cemetery, Bridgeton, Cumberland County.
GANT, ROBERT H. Pvt, D, 12th NJ Inf, [Died of wounds received 7-2-1863 at Gettysburg, PA.] 7-8-1863. St. John's United Methodist Cemetery, Turnersville, Gloucester County.
GANT, STEPHEN R. Pvt, D, 9th NJ Inf, 1928. Riverside Cemetery, Toms River, Ocean County.
GANT, ZACHARIAH Pvt, K, 29th NJ Inf, 4-25-1908. Methodist Cemetery, Southard, Monmouth County.
GANTRY, T.Y. (aka: Gantz, Frank F.) Pvt, C, 43rd MO Inf, 10-17-1897. Flower Hill Cemetery, North Bergen, Hudson County.

Our Brothers Gone Before

GANTZ, FRANK F. (see: Gantry, T.Y.) Flower Hill Cemetery, North Bergen, Hudson County.
GANZELL, ADOLPH Pvt, G, 20th NY Inf, 7-23-1893. Fairview Cemetery, Westfield, Union County.
GARA, LEMUEL 1st Sgt, I, 122nd PA Inf, 4- -1922. Monument Cemetery, Edgewater Park, Burlington County.
GARABRANT, GARRETT Pvt, K, 25th NJ Inf, 11-7-1873. Fairmount Cemetery, Newark, Essex County.
GARABRANT, JAMES E. Pvt, D, 13th NJ Inf, 8-9-1918. Fairmount Cemetery, Newark, Essex County.
GARBANATI*, FREDERICK J. 1st Lt, Btty E, 2nd NY Heavy Art, [Wounded in action.] 5-2-1917. Hazelwood Cemetery, Rahway, Union County.
GARBE, HENRY Corp, E, 4th NJ Inf, DoD Unknown. Riverside Cemetery, Riverside, Burlington County.
GARDINELLI, JOSEPH Pvt, E, 20th NY Inf, [Wounded 9-17-1862 at Antietam, MD.] 11-12-1884. Holy Sepulchre Cemetery, East Orange, Essex County.
GARDINER, ABRAM Q. Pvt, U.S. Marine Corps, 6-3-1915. Oddfellows Cemetery, Burlington, Burlington County.
GARDINER, CHARLES J. Pvt, I, 23rd NJ Inf, DoD Unknown. Marlton Cemetery, Marlton, Burlington County.
GARDINER, HERMAN Pvt, Btty E, 3rd U.S. Art, 1-10-1884. Holy Sepulchre Cemetery, East Orange, Essex County.
GARDINER*, JOEL E. Pvt, A, 21st NJ Inf, DoD Unknown. Bayview-New York Bay Cemetery, Jersey City, Hudson County.
GARDINER, JOHN Pvt, H, 21st NJ Inf, 10-18-1898. Arlington Cemetery, Kearny, Hudson County.
GARDINER, JOSEPH W. 10-4-1910. Bay View Cemetery, Leonardo, Monmouth County.
GARDINER, PETER Z. Pvt, U.S. Marine Corps, 1920. Oddfellows Cemetery, Burlington, Burlington County.
GARDINER, WILLIAM H. Pvt, I, 1st U.S. Hancock Corps, 12-18-1891. Old Camden Cemetery, Camden, Camden County.
GARDIPE, NELSON Pvt, C, 71st NY Inf, 9-7-1887. Holy Sepulchre Cemetery, East Orange, Essex County.
GARDNER, ANDREW J. Pvt, K, 38th NJ Inf, 6-7-1873. Speer Cemetery, Jersey City, Hudson County.
GARDNER, CHARLES H. Pvt, F, 38th NJ Inf, 9-20-1886. Old 1st Methodist Church Cemetery, West Long Branch, Monmouth County.
GARDNER, CHARLES R. 1864. Presbyterian Church Cemetery, Andover, Sussex County.
GARDNER, DANIEL Pvt, Unassigned, 4th NJ Inf, DoD Unknown. Evergreen Cemetery, Hillside, Union County.
GARDNER, DAVID C. Corp, I, 31st NJ Inf, 12-23-1918. Belvidere/Catholic Cemetery, Belvidere, Warren County.
GARDNER, DAVID H. Corp, L, 27th NJ Inf, 11-10-1882. Greenwood Cemetery, Boonton, Morris County.
GARDNER, EDWARD C. 1911. Berlin Cemetery, Berlin, Camden County.
GARDNER, FRANCIS Pvt, F, 28th NJ Inf, 5-6-1881. Trinity Episcopal Church Cemetery, Woodbridge, Middlesex County.
GARDNER, FRANK Pvt, C, 1st NJ Cav, 1897. Old Camden Cemetery, Camden, Camden County.
GARDNER, FRANK Pvt, C, 1st NJ Cav, 6-3-1905. Tabernacle Cemetery, Tabernacle, Burlington County.
GARDNER*, GEORGE Landsman, U.S. Navy, USS Eolus, 1-31-1905. Fairmount Cemetery, Newark, Essex County.

New Jersey Civil War Burials

GARDNER*, GEORGE HENRY Maj, 5th NY Cav 2-15-1888. Evergreen Cemetery, Hillside, Union County.

GARDNER*, GEORGE T. Pvt, C, 36th NY Inf, [Wounded 6-1-1862 at Fair Oaks, VA. and 7-1-1862 at Malvern Hill, VA.] 9-20-1918. Rosedale Cemetery, Orange, Essex County.

GARDNER, GEORGE W. 2-2-1911. Bayview-New York Bay Cemetery, Jersey City, Hudson County.

GARDNER, GEORGE W. Pvt, K, 42nd OH Inf, 10-10-1896. Mansfield/Washington Cemetery, Washington, Warren County.

GARDNER, JAMES (see: Garner, James Edward) Laurel Grove Cemetery, Totowa, Passaic County.

GARDNER, JAMES W. Corp, F, 38th NJ Inf, 1-12-1909. Atlantic View Cemetery, Manasquan, Monmouth County.

GARDNER, JOHN Pvt, D, 33rd NJ Inf, 12-27-1945. Laurel Grove Cemetery, Totowa, Passaic County.

GARDNER, JOHN Pvt, H, 12th NJ Inf, 7-3-1884. Belvidere/Catholic Cemetery, Belvidere, Warren County.

GARDNER, JOHN (see: Garner, John J.) Laurel Grove Cemetery, Totowa, Passaic County.

GARDNER, JOHN F. Pvt, F, 13th NJ Inf, 8-1-1916. Clinton Cemetery, Irvington, Essex County.

GARDNER*, JOHN JAMES Pvt, G, 6th NJ Inf, 2-6-1921. Atlantic City Cemetery, Pleasantville, Atlantic County.

GARDNER, JOHN R.S. Corp, D, 12th NJ Inf, [Died of typhoid at Falmouth, VA.] 3-24-1863. St. John's United Methodist Cemetery, Turnersville, Gloucester County.

GARDNER, JOHN S. Pvt, G, 3rd NJ Cav, 1928. Soldier's Home Cemetery, Vineland, Cumberland County.

GARDNER, JOHN S. 1929. Presbyterian Church Cemetery, Harmony, Warren County.

GARDNER, LEVI Landsman, U.S. Navy, USS Rhode Island, DoD Unknown. Clinton Cemetery, Irvington, Essex County.

GARDNER, MAITLAND 1st Sgt, G, 1st NJ Cav, 3-2-1909. Old 1st Methodist Church Cemetery, West Long Branch, Monmouth County.

GARDNER, STEPHEN AUGUSTUS Pvt, G, 83rd NY Inf, 2-8-1912. Evergreen Cemetery, Hillside, Union County.

GARDNER, THOMAS Pvt, D, 33rd NJ Inf, 1880. Valleau Cemetery, Ridgewood, Bergen County.

GARDNER, THOMAS C. Pvt, B, 9th NJ Inf, 5-25-1877. Fairmount Cemetery, Newark, Essex County.

GARDNER, WARREN D. Pvt, K, 4th RI Inf, [Wounded in action.] DoD Unknown. Presbyterian/Methodist-Episcopal Cemetery, Succasunna, Morris County.

GARDNER, WILLIAM Sgt, B, 7th NJ Inf, 6-5-1887. Fairmount Cemetery, Newark, Essex County.

GARDNER, WILLIAM D. Pvt, C, 34th NJ Inf, 6-2-1909. Brotherhood Cemetery, Hainesport, Burlington County.

GARDNER, WILLIAM G. Musc, K, 14th NJ Inf, 1-30-1884. Elmwood Cemetery, New Brunswick, Middlesex County.

GARDNER, WILLIAM H. Pvt, D, 2nd DC Inf, 7-12-1924. Evergreen Cemetery, Hillside, Union County.

GAREY, MARTIN P. Pvt, H, 15th NJ Inf, 12-2-1900. Mansfield/Washington Cemetery, Washington, Warren County.

GAREY, NELSON (see: Geary, Nelson) Union Cemetery, Milford, Hunterdon County.

GARFIELD, JAMES 3-24-1901. Fairmount Cemetery, Newark, Essex County.

Our Brothers Gone Before

GARIES, WILLIAM R. (aka: Gary, William) Pvt, D, 30th NJ Inf, 1912. Mount Hope Presbyterian Cemetery, Lambertville, Hunterdon County.
GARIS*, AARON Pvt, C, 20th PA Cav, 1-4-1917. Phillipsburg Cemetery, Phillipsburg, Warren County.
GARIS, GEORGE A. Pvt, F, 2nd NJ Cav, 4-12-1864. Walpack Reformed Cemetery, Flatbrookville, Sussex County.
GARLAND, JOSEPH Pvt, E, 8th NJ Inf, 9-6-1900. Soldier's Home Cemetery, Vineland, Cumberland County.
GARLAND*, PRESTON Seaman, U.S. Navy, 3-25-1906. Evergreen Cemetery, Morristown, Morris County.
GARLICK, JEPTHA Pvt, K, 12th NJ Inf, 1-2-1930. Cedar Lawn Cemetery, Paterson, Passaic County.
GARLICK, SETH Corp, C, 25th NJ Inf, 12-19-1922. Cedar Lawn Cemetery, Paterson, Passaic County.
GARLING, ANDREW (aka: Darling, Andrew) Pvt, B, 45th NY Inf, DoD Unknown. Holy Name Cemetery, Jersey City, Hudson County.
GARLING*, ANDREW (aka: Gailing, Andrew) Pvt, B, 58th NY Inf, 10-15-1889. Holy Name Cemetery, Jersey City, Hudson County.
GARLING, WILLIAM DoD Unknown. Eglington Cemetery, Clarksboro, Gloucester County.
GARMAN, PATRICK Pvt, C, 12th NJ Inf, DoD Unknown. Sandy Ridge Cemetery, Sandy Ridge, Hunterdon County.
GARMAN, THOMAS W. Corp, Btty G, 1st PA Light Art, 9-28-1912. Evergreen Cemetery, Camden, Camden County.
GARMO, CHARLES Pvt, A, 15th NJ Inf, DoD Unknown. Union Cemetery, Frenchtown, Hunterdon County.
GARMO, RICHARD Wagoner, A, 35th NJ Inf, 5-13-1897. Saums Farm Cemetery, Hillsborough, Somerset County.
GARNER, GEORGE Pvt, G, 9th (Malone's) AL Cav (CSA), 12-9-1863. Finn's Point National Cemetery, Pennsville, Salem County.
GARNER, JAMES E. Seaman, U.S. Navy, USS Mohawk, 12- -1901. Laurel Grove Cemetery, Totowa, Passaic County.
GARNER*, JAMES EDWARD (aka: Gardner, James) Pvt, F, 10th NJ Inf, 1895. Laurel Grove Cemetery, Totowa, Passaic County.
GARNER, JOHN J. (aka: Gardner, John) Corp, F, 10th NJ Inf, 10-28-1923. Laurel Grove Cemetery, Totowa, Passaic County.
GARNER, LOUIS (see: Garnier, Ludwig) Bloomfield Cemetery, Bloomfield, Essex County.
GARNER*, ROBERT HENRY Prin Musc, 86th NY Inf 1-10-1893. Pascack Reformed Church Cemetery, Park Ridge, Bergen County.
GARNIER, ALBERT L. Pvt, A, 2nd NJ Inf, 1-20-1908. Arlington Cemetery, Kearny, Hudson County.
GARNIER, LUDWIG (aka: Garner, Louis) Pvt, Btty E, 15th NY Heavy Art, 1922. Bloomfield Cemetery, Bloomfield, Essex County.
GARRA, JOHN Pvt, D, 76th PA Inf, 7-29-1872. St. John's Cemetery, Lambertville, Hunterdon County.
GARRABRANDT*, AARON M. Pvt, E, 95th NY Inf, 5-14-1900. Fairmount Cemetery, Newark, Essex County.
GARRABRANDT, ABRAM Pvt, E, 2nd NJ Militia, 4-26-1914. Bloomfield Cemetery, Bloomfield, Essex County.
GARRABRANDT, CHARLES Pvt, Btty B, 1st NJ Light Art, 4-1-1884. Fairmount Cemetery, Newark, Essex County.
GARRABRANDT, CHARLES Pvt, F, 1st NJ Militia, 4-17-1909. Mount Pleasant Cemetery, Newark, Essex County.

New Jersey Civil War Burials

GARRABRANDT, CHARLES 11-3-1905. Prospect Hill Cemetery, Caldwell, Essex County.
GARRABRANDT, CHARLES H. Musc, F, 26th NJ Inf, 7-27-1880. Presbyterian Church Cemetery, Rockaway, Morris County.
GARRABRANDT, CORNELIUS 9-23-1888. Rosedale Cemetery, Orange, Essex County.
GARRABRANDT, EDWARD G. Pvt, B, 9th NJ Inf, 11-11-1929. Rosedale Cemetery, Orange, Essex County.
GARRABRANDT, GEORGE (aka: Garrabrant, George) Pvt, I, 13th NJ Inf, 3-13-1881. Fairmount Cemetery, Newark, Essex County.
GARRABRANDT, GEORGE H. Pvt, K, 26th NJ Inf, 10-8-1903. Fairmount Cemetery, Newark, Essex County.
GARRABRANDT, JAMES E. Pvt, D, 13th NJ Inf, [Wounded in action.] 8-9-1918. Fairmount Cemetery, Newark, Essex County.
GARRABRANDT, JOHN B. Pvt, K, 13th NJ Inf, 1888. Mount Hebron Cemetery, Montclair, Essex County.
GARRABRANDT, JOHN B. Pvt, F, 1st NJ Militia, 8-5-1880. Fairmount Cemetery, Newark, Essex County.
GARRABRANDT, MINARD (aka: Garrabrants, Mindrit) Pvt, B, 9th NJ Inf, 6-24-1900. Woodland Cemetery, Newark, Essex County.
GARRABRANDT, MUNSON Pvt, H, 26th NJ Inf, 11-19-1884. 1st Presbyterian Church Cemetery, Orange, Essex County.
GARRABRANDT, RICHARD E. Sgt, E, 95th NY Inf, [Wounded 9-14-1862 at South Mountain, MD. and 6-17-1864 at Petersburg, VA.] 1-9-1908. Fairmount Cemetery, Newark, Essex County.
GARRABRANT, ABRAHAM Pvt, G, 4th NJ Inf, DoD Unknown. Methodist Cemetery, Hamilton, Monmouth County.
GARRABRANT, ELIAS P. Pvt, L, 56th NY Inf, 11-24-1922. 1st Presbyterian Union Cemetery, Ramsey, Bergen County.
GARRABRANT, GEORGE (see: Garrabrandt, George) Fairmount Cemetery, Newark, Essex County.
GARRABRANT, GEORGE Z. Pvt, K, 26th NJ Inf, 10-7-1903. Presbyterian Church Cemetery, Rockaway, Morris County.
GARRABRANT, HARVEY G. Pvt, Btty C, 6th NY Heavy Art, 4-26-1894. Cedar Lawn Cemetery, Paterson, Passaic County.
GARRABRANT, ISAAC Pvt, E, 29th NJ Inf, 9-29-1909. Methodist Cemetery, Hamilton, Monmouth County.
GARRABRANT, ISAAC H. Pvt, I, 70th NY Inf, 6-24-1912. Laurel Grove Cemetery, Totowa, Passaic County.
GARRABRANT, JAMES J. Sgt, A, 11th NJ Inf, 3-21-1910. Old 1st Methodist Church Cemetery, West Long Branch, Monmouth County.
GARRABRANT, JAMES J. Sgt, H, 39th NJ Inf, [Murdered at Newark, NJ while on furlough.] 1-13-1865. Laurel Grove Cemetery, Totowa, Passaic County.
GARRABRANT, JOHN Pvt, B, 39th NJ Inf, 4-24-1929. Presbyterian Church Cemetery, Rockaway, Morris County.
GARRABRANT, MOSES Pvt, I, 13th NJ Inf, DoD Unknown. Rosedale Cemetery, Orange, Essex County.
GARRABRANTS, ABRAHAM Musc, A, 7th NJ Inf, 2-2-1900. Mount Prospect Cemetery, Neptune, Monmouth County.
GARRABRANTS, MINDRIT (see: Garrabrandt, Minard) Woodland Cemetery, Newark, Essex County.
GARREN, ABRAHAM Sgt, K, 8th NJ Inf, [Died of wounds received 5-3-1863 at Chancellorsville, VA.] 5-17-1863. Union Cemetery, Frenchtown, Hunterdon County.

Our Brothers Gone Before

GARREN, HENRY Seaman, U.S. Navy, USS Kansas, 11-23-1913. Evergreen Cemetery, Camden, Camden County.
GARREN, ISRAEL Pvt, G, 3rd NJ Cav, 5-26-1901. Chestnut Grove Cemetery, Elmer, Salem County.
GARRETSON, ALBERT I. Pvt, F, 28th NJ Inf, 6-27-1871. Van Liew Cemetery, North Brunswick, Middlesex County.
GARRETSON*, DUMONT Corp, C, 4th NJ Inf, [Wounded in action.] 1-20-1901. Willow Grove Cemetery, New Brunswick, Middlesex County.
GARRETSON, ETHAN T. Capt, D, 25th NJ Inf, 1886. Church of Christ Cemetery, Fairton, Cumberland County.
GARRETSON, FIELD G. Corp, K, 30th NJ Inf, 12-4-1911. New Presbyterian Cemetery, Bound Brook, Somerset County.
GARRETSON, GARRET TERHUNE Pvt, F, 11th NJ Inf, [Died of typhoid at Falmouth, VA.] 12-27-1862. Cedar Hill Cemetery, East Millstone, Somerset County.
GARRETSON, JOHN Pvt, E, 15th NJ Inf, [Died of typhoid at White Oak Church, VA.] 3-9-1863. Old Somerville Cemetery, Somerville, Somerset County.
GARRETSON, JOHN 1917. Presbyterian Cemetery, North Plainfield, Somerset County.
GARRETSON, PETER V. Pvt, K, 30th NJ Inf, 4-5-1926. Cedar Hill Cemetery, East Millstone, Somerset County.
GARRETSON, SAMUEL Pvt, I, 28th NJ Inf, 3-1-1928. Alpine Cemetery, Perth Amboy, Middlesex County.
GARRETSON, THOMAS G. 1-7-1873. Old Somerville Cemetery, Somerville, Somerset County.
GARRETT, GREEN Pvt, G, 20th GA Inf (CSA), [Captured 7-2-1863 at Gettysburg, PA. Died of fever.] 9-22-1863. Finn's Point National Cemetery, Pennsville, Salem County.
GARRETT, JOHN Pvt, I, 24th NJ Inf, 9-1-1889. Eglington Cemetery, Clarksboro, Gloucester County.
GARRETT, KLEBER P. Pvt, F, 1st MO Cav (CSA), 7-3-1863. Finn's Point National Cemetery, Pennsville, Salem County.
GARRETT, THEOFFALEIS H. Pvt, B, 10th Confederate States Cav (CSA), 5-30-1865. Finn's Point National Cemetery, Pennsville, Salem County.
GARRETT, THOMAS J. Pvt, K, 31st GA Inf (CSA), [Captured 5-12-1864 at Spotsylvania CH, VA. Died of pneumonia.] 12-21-1864. Finn's Point National Cemetery, Pennsville, Salem County.
GARRETT, W.H. Corp, E, 4th TN Inf (CSA), 5-15-1864. Finn's Point National Cemetery, Pennsville, Salem County.
GARRETT, WILLIAM N. Pvt, E, 23rd NJ Inf, 12-18-1914. Baptist/St. Andrew's Cemetery, Mount Holly, Burlington County.
GARRETTSON*, JOHN D. Pvt, H, 38th NJ Inf, 12-25-1907. Willow Grove Cemetery, New Brunswick, Middlesex County.
GARRICK, RICHARD Pvt, G, 21st NJ Inf, 11-2-1910. Holy Name Cemetery, Jersey City, Hudson County.
GARRIGAN*, CHARLES M. Corp, B, 12th NJ Inf, DoD Unknown. Mount Prospect Cemetery, Neptune, Monmouth County.
GARRIGAN, JOHN Sgt, C, 9th NJ Inf, 9-13-1891. Bordentown/Old St. Mary's Catholic Cemetery, Bordentown, Burlington County.
GARRIGAN*, MICHAEL Pvt, B, 5th NJ Inf, DoD Unknown. Holy Name Cemetery, Jersey City, Hudson County.
GARRIGAN, THOMAS Pvt, Btty E, 4th NY Heavy Art, 10-16-1924. St. Peter's Cemetery, New Brunswick, Middlesex County.
GARRIGAN, THOMAS W. Pvt, H, 14th NJ Inf, DoD Unknown. Mount Prospect Cemetery, Neptune, Monmouth County.

New Jersey Civil War Burials

GARRIS, GEORGE DALLAS Pvt, F, 2nd NJ Cav, 6-28-1938. Stillwater Cemetery, Stillwater, Sussex County.

GARRIS, JASON Pvt, H, 9th NJ Inf, 1926. Belvidere/Catholic Cemetery, Belvidere, Warren County.

GARRIS, PETER S. 4-17-1906. Branchville Cemetery, Branchville, Sussex County.

GARRISON, ALLEN S. Pvt, B, 24th NJ Inf, 3-13-1873. United Methodist Church Cemetery, Willow Grove, Salem County.

GARRISON, AUGUSTUS F. Pvt, 4th KS Ind Btty 1917. New Episcopal Church Cemetery, Swedesboro, Gloucester County.

GARRISON, BENJAMIN L. Corp, A, 14th NJ Inf, 9-21-1913. Greenwood Cemetery, Brielle, Monmouth County.

GARRISON, CHARLES E. Pvt, C, 8th NJ Inf, DoD Unknown. Hillside Cemetery, Madison, Morris County.

GARRISON, CHARLES F. Pvt, F, 24th NJ Inf, [Died of wounds received 12-13-1862 at Fredericksburg, VA.] 12-21-1862. Baptist Church Cemetery, Dividing Creek, Cumberland County.

GARRISON, CHARLES P. Pvt, G, 3rd NJ Cav, 1929. Baptist Church Cemetery, Dividing Creek, Cumberland County.

GARRISON, CHARLES S. Pvt, A, 12th NJ Inf, [Died of erysipelas at Newark, NJ. Wounded in action at Gettysburg, PA.] 7-23-1863. Fairmount Cemetery, Newark, Essex County.

GARRISON, DAVID Sgt, F, 24th NJ Inf, 8-29-1913. Baptist Church Cemetery, Dividing Creek, Cumberland County.

GARRISON, DAVID C. Musc, E, 8th NJ Inf, 3-28-1890. Fairmount Cemetery, Newark, Essex County.

GARRISON, EBENEZER Pvt, F, 9th DE Inf, 1-21-1901. Harleigh Cemetery, Camden, Camden County.

GARRISON, EBENEZER D. Sgt, G, 34th NJ Inf, 4-7-1889. Fairmount Cemetery, Newark, Essex County.

GARRISON, ELI Pvt, C, 38th NJ Inf, 1916. Mount Pleasant Cemetery, Millville, Cumberland County.

GARRISON, ENOCH B. Pvt, H, 3rd NJ Cav, 11-6-1899. Cohansey Baptist Church Cemetery, Bowentown, Cumberland County.

GARRISON, ENOS Pvt, D, 12th NJ Inf, 2-4-1900. Siloam Cemetery, Vineland, Cumberland County.

GARRISON*, FURMAN M. Landsman, U.S. Navy, USS North Carolina, 1911. Oak Hill Cemetery, Vineland, Cumberland County.

GARRISON, GARRETT Pvt, H, 33rd NJ Inf, 9-5-1886. Laurel Grove Cemetery, Totowa, Passaic County.

GARRISON, GEORGE H. Pvt, E, 22nd NJ Inf, 9-14-1910. Arlington Cemetery, Kearny, Hudson County.

GARRISON, HENRY J. Corp, F, 7th NJ Inf, 1913. Lake Park Cemetery, Swedesboro, Gloucester County.

GARRISON, HUGH Pvt, L, 3rd NJ Cav, 1-31-1892. Hedding Methodist-Episcopal Church Cemetery, Bellmawr, Camden County.

GARRISON, ISAAC Corp, B, 15th NJ Inf, 8-10-1910. Cedar Lawn Cemetery, Paterson, Passaic County.

GARRISON, JACOB J. Pvt, A, 22nd NJ Inf, DoD Unknown. Hackensack Cemetery, Hackensack, Bergen County.

GARRISON, JAMES Pvt, H, 3rd NJ Cav, DoD Unknown. Presbyterian Church Cemetery, Bridgeton, Cumberland County.

GARRISON, JAMES N. Pvt, C, 127th NY Inf, [Cenotaph. Died of wounds received 12-6-1864 at Deveaux Neck, SC.] 12-17-1864. Presbyterian Church Cemetery, Titusville, Mercer County.

Our Brothers Gone Before

GARRISON, JAMES P. Pvt, C, 26th AL Inf (CSA), [Wounded 9-14-1862 at South Mountain, MD. Captured 7-3-1863 at Gettysburg, PA. Died of smallpox.] 11-20-1863. Finn's Point National Cemetery, Pennsville, Salem County.

GARRISON, JOEL O. 2-4-1922. Methodist Church Cemetery, Union Grove, Salem County.

GARRISON, JOHN Pvt, K, 12th NJ Inf, [Wounded 5-3-1863 at Chancellorsville, VA. and 9-15-1864 at Hatchers Run, VA.] 10-12-1912. Evergreen Cemetery, New Brunswick, Middlesex County.

GARRISON, JOHN C. Corp, F, 3rd NJ Inf, 1915. Shinn GAR Post Cemetery, Port Norris, Cumberland County.

GARRISON, JOHN H. Pvt, A, 70th NY Inf, 6-30-1912. Pompton Reformed Church Cemetery, Pompton Lakes, Passaic County.

GARRISON, JOHN W. Pvt, K, 52nd VA Inf (CSA), [Captured 7-3-1863 at Gettysburg, PA. Died of dysentery.] 10-9-1863. Finn's Point National Cemetery, Pennsville, Salem County.

GARRISON, JONATHAN C. Pvt, G, 24th NJ Inf, 5-2-1884. United Methodist Church Cemetery, Woodruff, Cumberland County.

GARRISON, JOSEPH Corp, F, 25th NJ Inf, 2-11-1931. Tabernacle Baptist Church Cemetery, Erma, Cape May County.

GARRISON, JOSEPH Pvt, C, 2nd NJ Inf, 5-24-1895. Cedar Lawn Cemetery, Paterson, Passaic County.

GARRISON, JOSEPH S. Corp, K, 2nd NJ Cav, 8-27-1932. Manahath Cemetery, Glassboro, Gloucester County.

GARRISON, JOSEPH W. 1st Sgt, K, 38th NJ Inf, 4-24-1911. Greenwood Cemetery, Hamilton, Mercer County.

GARRISON*, JOSIAH Pvt, C, 38th NJ Inf, 7-10-1909. Old Camden Cemetery, Camden, Camden County.

GARRISON, LEWIS Pvt, B, 25th NJ Inf, 6-10-1911. Mount Pleasant Cemetery, Millville, Cumberland County.

GARRISON, MENZIES Pvt, B, 9th NJ Inf, 9-11-1873. Hillside Cemetery, Madison, Morris County.

GARRISON, PETER 1890. Union Cemetery, Hope, Warren County.

GARRISON, PETER G. 1926. Methodist Church Cemetery, Liberty, Warren County.

GARRISON, PHILIP S. Pvt, I, 9th NJ Inf, 2-25-1893. Fairview Cemetery, Knowlton, Warren County.

GARRISON*, SAMUEL Sgt, E, 2nd NJ Cav, DoD Unknown. Bordentown/Old St. Mary's Catholic Cemetery, Bordentown, Burlington County.

GARRISON, THEODORE F. Pvt, E, 27th NJ Inf, DoD Unknown. Hillside Cemetery, Madison, Morris County.

GARRISON, WILLIAM Pvt, G, 3rd NJ Cav, 7-31-1893. Mount Pleasant Cemetery, Millville, Cumberland County.

GARRISON, WILLIAM Pvt, E, 27th NJ Inf, 11-8-1904. Bloomfield Cemetery, Bloomfield, Essex County.

GARRISON, WILLIAM R. Pvt, Btty B, 1st NJ Light Art, 3-17-1866. Old Quaker Cemetery, Squankum, Monmouth County.

GARRISON*, WILLIAM W. Pvt, G, 175th OH Inf, DoD Unknown. Overlook Cemetery, Bridgeton, Cumberland County.

GARRITY, DANIEL (aka: Gerrety, Daniel) Pvt, F, 33rd NJ Inf, 11-26-1889. Holy Sepulchre Cemetery, East Orange, Essex County.

GARROCK, ANDREW Corp, F, PA Emerg NJ Militia, 1877. Mount Pleasant Cemetery, Newark, Essex County.

GARRON, THOMAS Pvt, G, 25th NJ Inf, 4-10-1899. United Methodist Church Cemetery, Tuckahoe, Cape May County.

New Jersey Civil War Burials

GARROW, WILLIAM Corp, G, 24th NJ Inf, 11- -1910. Presbyterian Church Cemetery, Bridgeton, Cumberland County.

GARRY, JOHN Pvt, A, 9th NJ Inf, DoD Unknown. St. Peter's Cemetery, New Brunswick, Middlesex County.

GARTHWAITE, CHARLES B. Corp, G, 9th NJ Inf, 6-20-1894. Evergreen Cemetery, Hillside, Union County.

GARTHWAITE, GEORGE W. Actg Asst Paymaster, U.S. Navy, USS Sassacus, [Drowned off ship.] 4-5-1865. Mount Pleasant Cemetery, Newark, Essex County.

GARTHWAITE, SAMUEL S. Corp, C, 14th NJ Inf, 12-2-1909. Evergreen Cemetery, Hillside, Union County.

GARTLAND*, HUGH Pvt, E, 5th NY Vet Inf, DoD Unknown. Holy Sepulchre Cemetery, East Orange, Essex County.

GARTLAND, JOHN Pvt, Btty D, 1st NJ Light Art, DoD Unknown. Holy Sepulchre Cemetery, East Orange, Essex County.

GARTON, BENJAMIN Pvt, I, 119th PA Inf, DoD Unknown. Overlook Cemetery, Bridgeton, Cumberland County.

GARTON*, ISAAC T. Sgt, G, 8th NJ Inf, DoD Unknown. Presbyterian Church Cemetery, Bridgeton, Cumberland County.

GARTON, JACOB Pvt, H, 24th NJ Inf, DoD Unknown. Lutheran Church Cemetery, Friesburg, Salem County.

GARTON, SAMUEL P. Sgt, D, 10th NJ Inf, [Died of wounds received 6-1-1864 at Cold Harbor, VA.] 6-22-1864. Lutheran Church Cemetery, Friesburg, Salem County.

GARTON, SAMUEL S. 1910. Presbyterian Cemetery, Woodstown, Salem County.

GARVAN, JAMES Pvt, U.S. Army, DoD Unknown. South Orange Cemetery, South Orange, Essex County.

GARVEY, JAMES 2-21-1934. Brookside Cemetery, Englewood, Bergen County.

GARVEY, JOHN Pvt, G, 21st NJ Inf, 3-17-1897. Holy Name Cemetery, Jersey City, Hudson County.

GARVEY, PATRICK 1st Lt, H, 99th NY Inf, 4-14-1891. Fairmount Cemetery, Newark, Essex County.

GARVEY*, THOMAS Pvt, G, 8th NJ Inf, 9-15-1899. Baptist/St. Andrew's Cemetery, Mount Holly, Burlington County.

GARVIN, CORNELIUS Pvt, H, 8th NJ Inf, [Died of delirium tremens at Newark, NJ.] 4-7-1864. Old St. Mary's Cemetery, Clinton, Hunterdon County.

GARVIN*, DAVID W. Landsman, U.S. Navy, USS Alabama, 6-13-1902. Bayview-New York Bay Cemetery, Jersey City, Hudson County.

GARVIN, JOHN Pvt, K, 39th NJ Inf, DoD Unknown. Holy Sepulchre Cemetery, East Orange, Essex County.

GARVIN, OWEN (see: Gavin, Owen) Mount Olivet Cemetery, Newark, Essex County.

GARVIN*, THOMAS Pvt, I, 188th PA Inf, 12-2-1918. Sacred Heart Cemetery, Vineland, Cumberland County.

GARWOOD, ABRAM Pvt, C, 9th NJ Inf, 2-16-1904. Bordentown/Old St. Mary's Catholic Cemetery, Bordentown, Burlington County.

GARWOOD, CHARLES Pvt, G, 10th NJ Inf, 1893. Monument Cemetery, Edgewater Park, Burlington County.

GARWOOD, JOHN 7-31-1875. United Methodist Church Cemetery, Tuckahoe, Cape May County.

GARWOOD, JOHN C. Corp, D, 1st NJ Cav, 3-30-1909. Overlook Cemetery, Bridgeton, Cumberland County.

GARWOOD, JOHN C. 10-14-1892. Lake Park Cemetery, Swedesboro, Gloucester County.

GARWOOD, JOHN W. Pvt, A, 10th NJ Inf, 6-20-1901. Evergreen Cemetery, Camden, Camden County.

GARWOOD*, JOHN T. Capt, C, 24th NJ Inf, 1913. Eastview Cemetery, Salem, Salem County.

Our Brothers Gone Before

GARWOOD, JOSEPH B. Pvt, F, 4th NJ Militia, 2-19-1896. Berlin Cemetery, Berlin, Camden County.
GARWOOD, JOSIAH S. Pvt, A, 6th NJ Inf, 11-30-1907. Arlington Cemetery, Kearny, Hudson County.
GARWOOD, SAMUEL W. 1-21-1933. Monument Cemetery, Edgewater Park, Burlington County.
GARWOOD, THOMAS S. Pvt, I, 88th PA Inf, 7-10-1867. Baptist Cemetery, Burlington, Burlington County.
GARWOOD, WILLIAM H. Pvt, G, 23rd NJ Inf, 10-20-1892. Monument Cemetery, Edgewater Park, Burlington County.
GARWOOD*, WILLIAM S. 1st Sgt, A, 12th NJ Inf, 9-23-1875. Eglington Cemetery, Clarksboro, Gloucester County.
GARY, EDWIN Pvt, H, 5th MA Inf, 2-1-1905. United Methodist Church Cemetery, Wayside, Monmouth County.
GARY, JAMES S. Pvt, K, 31st NJ Inf, 6-16-1886. Amwell Ridge Cemetery, Larisons Corner, Hunterdon County.
GARY, JOHN W. Pvt, G, 6th CT Inf, 4-22-1889. Mount Prospect Cemetery, Neptune, Monmouth County.
GARY*, MILLER H. Pvt, E, 7th NJ Inf, 8-15-1915. Laurel Grove Cemetery, Totowa, Passaic County.
GARY, WILLIAM Pvt, D, 30th NJ Inf, 4-17-1891. Locust Grove Cemetery, Quakertown, Hunterdon County.
GARY, WILLIAM (see: Garies, William R.) Mount Hope Presbyterian Cemetery, Lambertville, Hunterdon County.
GARY, WILLIAM (see: Geary, William) Riverview Cemetery, Trenton, Mercer County.
GARY, WILLIAM (see: Geary, William W.) Greenwood Cemetery, Boonton, Morris County.
GASKELL, SAMUEL 1-20-1920. Riverview Cemetery, Trenton, Mercer County.
GASKILL, BENJAMIN Pvt, C, 1st NJ Cav, 7-7-1916. Mount Holly Cemetery, Mount Holly, Burlington County.
GASKILL, BENJAMIN F. Pvt, D, 25th NJ Inf, 4-8-1874. Methodist Church Cemetery, Newport, Cumberland County.
GASKILL, CHARLES EDWARD 6-10-1901. Pearson/Colonial Memorial Park Cemetery, Whitehorse, Mercer County.
GASKILL, DANIEL Corp, D, 12th NJ Inf, 8-13-1881. New Presbyterian Church Cemetery, Daretown, Salem County.
GASKILL, EDWIN F. Pvt, K, 40th NJ Inf, 8-11-1911. Methodist Cemetery, Eagleswood Village, Ocean County.
GASKILL, FRANKLIN S. Corp, E, 23rd NJ Inf, [Wounded 5-3-1863 at Salem Church, VA.] 9-16-1920. Methodist Church Cemetery, Pemberton, Burlington County.
GASKILL*, GEORGE Pvt, I, 2nd NJ Inf, 8-20-1887. Methodist Church Cemetery, Pemberton, Burlington County.
GASKILL, GEORGE B. Pvt, I, 4th NJ Inf, 4-18-1887. Cedar Hill Cemetery, Hightstown, Mercer County.
GASKILL, HENRY W. 1st Lt, K, 12th NJ Inf, 7-22-1911. Evergreen Cemetery, Camden, Camden County.
GASKILL, JAMES R. 1932. 1st Methodist Church Cemetery, Williamstown, Gloucester County.
GASKILL, JAMES R. Pvt, K, 10th NJ Inf, 7-2-1865. Methodist Cemetery, Tuckerton, Ocean County.
GASKILL, JEREMIAH Pvt, K, 10th NJ Inf, 6-27-1913. Greenwood Cemetery, Tuckerton, Ocean County.
GASKILL, JOB Pvt, B, 23rd NJ Inf, 5-21-1869. Bordentown/Old St. Mary's Catholic Cemetery, Bordentown, Burlington County.

New Jersey Civil War Burials

GASKILL, JOHN 9-5-1897. Methodist Church Cemetery, Newport, Cumberland County.
GASKILL, JOHN 1901. Cedar Hill Cemetery, Hightstown, Mercer County.
GASKILL, JOHN B. Sgt, I, 23rd NJ Inf, 1903. Harleigh Cemetery, Camden, Camden County.
GASKILL, JOHN R. Pvt, I, 5th NJ Inf, 12-17-1918. Baptist/St. Andrew's Cemetery, Mount Holly, Burlington County.
GASKILL, JOSEPH H. Pvt, K, 3rd NJ Cav, 8-31-1901. Oddfellows Cemetery, Pemberton, Burlington County.
GASKILL*, NORWOOD P. Pvt, H, 2nd NJ Inf, 1-28-1904. Atlantic City Cemetery, Pleasantville, Atlantic County.
GASKILL, SAMUEL B. Sgt, B, 12th NJ Inf, 3-27-1923. New Episcopal Church Cemetery, Swedesboro, Gloucester County.
GASKILL, STEPHEN 11-5-1873. Baptist Church Cemetery, Dividing Creek, Cumberland County.
GASKILL*, VARNEY W. Pvt, K, 12th NJ Inf, 12-21-1925. Presbyterian Church Cemetery, Bridgeton, Cumberland County.
GASKILL, WILLIAM F. Pvt, K, 23rd NJ Inf, 1918. Greenwood Cemetery, Tuckerton, Ocean County.
GASKILL, WILLIAM R. Pvt, K, 10th NJ Inf, 1926. Greenwood Cemetery, Tuckerton, Ocean County.
GASKINS, BENJAMIN W. Pvt, D, 14th NJ Inf, 1935. Methodist-Episcopal Cemetery, Glendola, Monmouth County.
GASSER, JOSEPH (aka: Gosser, Joseph) Pvt, D, 82nd PA Inf, 1-22-1913. Riverview Cemetery, Trenton, Mercer County.
GASSERT, CHARLES A. Pvt, G, 35th NJ Inf, 5-31-1896. Fairmount Cemetery, Newark, Essex County.
GASSERT, GEORGE (see: Gessert, George) Woodland Cemetery, Newark, Essex County.
GASSLER, VALENTINE Pvt, E, 39th NJ Inf, 7-15-1893. Fairmount Cemetery, Newark, Essex County.
GASSMAN, CHARLES Sgt, Btty M, 1st U.S. Art, DoD Unknown. Bayview-New York Bay Cemetery, Jersey City, Hudson County.
GASSMAN, GEORGE (see: Gosman, Gottlieb C.) Presbyterian Church Cemetery, Bridgeton, Cumberland County.
GASTON, FORMAN Pvt, A, 28th NJ Inf, 1912. Rose Hill Cemetery, Matawan, Monmouth County.
GASTON, JAMES Pvt, A, 30th NJ Inf, 1920. New Somerville Cemetery, Somerville, Somerset County.
GASTON, JOHN D. 11-13-1927. Old Somerville Cemetery, Somerville, Somerset County.
GASTON, JOHN S. 1-19-1898. Mansfield/Washington Cemetery, Washington, Warren County.
GASTON, JOHN WORTMAN Pvt, A, 30th NJ Inf, 1924. New Somerville Cemetery, Somerville, Somerset County.
GASTON, LOUIS DoD Unknown. St. Mary's Cemetery, Salem, Salem County.
GASTON, O.B. Capt, F, 4th (Russell's) AL Cav (CSA), 8-6-1864. Finn's Point National Cemetery, Pennsville, Salem County.
GASTON, ROBERT K. Pvt, B, 172nd PA Inf, 2-18-1878. Lutheran Cemetery, East Stewartsville, Warren County.
GASTON*, SAMUEL B. Pvt, D, 9th NJ Inf, 11-11-1906. Riverview Cemetery, Trenton, Mercer County.
GASTON, THOMAS C. Pvt, H, 15th NJ Inf, 10-23-1911. Presbyterian Church Cemetery, Mendham, Morris County.
GATELEY, JOHN (see: Gately, John) Holy Name Cemetery, Jersey City, Hudson County.
GATELY, JOHN (aka: Gateley, John) Pvt, Btty G, 13th NY Heavy Art, 8-18-1873. Holy Name Cemetery, Jersey City, Hudson County.

Our Brothers Gone Before

GATES, FRANK E. Capt, K, 157th NY Inf, [Wounded 7-2-1863 at Gettysburg, PA.] 9-30-1898. Baptist Church Cemetery, Haddonfield, Camden County.

GATES, GEORGE E. Pvt, I, 5th NY Inf, [Died of typhoid at Washington, DC.] 5-26-1862. Rosedale Cemetery, Orange, Essex County.

GATES, HENRY (see: Goetz, Henry L.) Bayview-New York Bay Cemetery, Jersey City, Hudson County.

GATES, HORATIO M. Pvt, D, 25th NJ Inf, 11-6-1875. Bateman Memorial Cemetery, Newport, Cumberland County.

GATES, JAMES F. Pvt, E, 149th NY Inf, [Wounded 6-27-1864 at Kenesaw Mountain, GA.] 4-24-1899. Siloam Cemetery, Vineland, Cumberland County.

GATES, SAMUEL CHIPMAN Pvt, A, 4th MA Cav, DoD Unknown. Holy Name Cemetery, Jersey City, Hudson County.

GATFIELD, HENRY Landsman, U.S. Navy, DoD Unknown. Holy Sepulchre Cemetery, East Orange, Essex County.

GATFIELD, HENRY (see: Jacobus, Henry) Boonton Cemetery, Boonton, Morris County.

GATFIELD, JAMES Pvt, K, 70th NY Inf, [Wounded 5-5-1862 at Williamsburg, VA.] 3-24-1901. Fairmount Cemetery, Newark, Essex County.

GATHERCOLE, GEORGE Pvt, K, 2nd NY Cav, 12-14-1910. Mount Hebron Cemetery, Montclair, Essex County.

GAUB, WILLIAM Pvt, B, 18th Bttn GA Inf (CSA), [State Guards.] DoD Unknown. Elmwood Cemetery, New Brunswick, Middlesex County.

GAUGHRAN, PHILIP Wagoner, K, 3rd NJ Inf, 11-13-1927. Mount Olivet Cemetery, Newark, Essex County.

GAUL, SAMUEL M. Capt, F, 4th NJ Inf, [Wounded 9-14-1862 at Crampton's Pass, MD.] 1895. Evergreen Cemetery, Camden, Camden County.

GAUL, W. FRANK Musc, G, 4th NJ Inf, DoD Unknown. Methodist-Episcopal Cemetery, Green Bank, Burlington County.

GAUN, JACOB L. Pvt, Btty I, 2nd PA Heavy Art, 9-2-1882. Mount Holly Cemetery, Mount Holly, Burlington County.

GAUN, WILLIAM F. 5-30-1910. Friendship United Methodist Church Cemetery, Upper Deerfield, Cumberland County.

GAUNT, ABNER H. Pvt, C, 12th NJ Inf, 2-6-1892. Mount Holly Cemetery, Mount Holly, Burlington County.

GAUNT, ALVIN Pvt, F, 37th NJ Inf, 1911. Cedar Green Cemetery, Clayton, Gloucester County.

GAUNT, AMOS Pvt, A, 10th NJ Inf, 1922. Head of River Church Cemetery, Head of River, Atlantic County.

GAUNT, BARCLAY Pvt, A, 12th NJ Inf, [Wounded in action at Cold Harbor, VA.] 7-9-1900. Eglington Cemetery, Clarksboro, Gloucester County.

GAUNT, CHARLES (see: Gant, Charles) Riverview Cemetery, Trenton, Mercer County.

GAUNT, JOHN Pvt, L, 2nd NJ Cav, 6-29-1918. Evergreen Cemetery, Lumberton, Burlington County.

GAUNT, JOSEPH H. Pvt, K, 12th NJ Inf, [Died of diarrhea at Newark, NJ.] 4-20-1865. Fairmount Cemetery, Newark, Essex County.

GAUNT, MOSES M. Pvt, D, 46th OH Inf, 10-19-1900. Evergreen Cemetery, Camden, Camden County.

GAUNT, RICHARD Corp, I, 25th NJ Inf, 2-8-1897. Evergreen Cemetery, Camden, Camden County.

GAUNT, SAMUEL M. (aka: Grant, Samuel) Pvt, C, 185th NY Inf, 11-17-1914. Fairview Cemetery, Fairview, Monmouth County.

GAUNTT*, BENJAMIN Pvt, C, 1st NJ Cav, 10-3-1901. Baptist Cemetery, Vincentown, Burlington County.

New Jersey Civil War Burials

GAUNTT, FRANKLIN Actg Asst Surg, U.S. Army, [Served under contract from 7-30-1864 to 3-9-1865.] 7-7-1900. St. Mary's Episcopal Church Cemetery, Burlington, Burlington County.

GAUNTT, SELAH Pvt, C, 34th NJ Inf, 10-3-1905. Evergreen Cemetery, Lumberton, Burlington County.

GAVEN, JAMES Pvt, H, 1st NH Cav, 2-18-1897. Holy Name Cemetery, Jersey City, Hudson County.

GAVIN, OWEN (aka: Garvin, Owen) Pvt, K, 3rd NJ Inf, 2-7-1886. Mount Olivet Cemetery, Newark, Essex County.

GAY, ALMARINE H. Pvt, D, 5th VA Inf (CSA), [Wounded 8-30-1862 at 2nd Bull Run, VA and 6-14-1863 at Winchester, VA. Captured 5-9-1864 at Spotsylvania CH, VA.] 7-4-1865. Finn's Point National Cemetery, Pennsville, Salem County.

GAY, THOMAS (see: Guy, Thomas) Riverview Cemetery, Trenton, Mercer County.

GAY, WILLIAM Pvt, D, 51st AL Cav (CSA), 1-22-1864. Finn's Point National Cemetery, Pennsville, Salem County.

GAY, WILLIAM A. Pvt, D, 140th IL Inf, 8-6-1926. Rahway Cemetery, Rahway, Union County.

GAYNOR, FREDERICK Pvt, K, 9th NY Inf, 8-6-1919. Rosedale Cemetery, Orange, Essex County.

GEARRY, MAX __, A, __ U.S. Inf, 3-26-1889. Greenwood Cemetery, Hamilton, Mercer County.

GEARY, NELSON (aka: Garey, Nelson) Sgt, B, 38th NJ Inf, 2-9-1921. Union Cemetery, Milford, Hunterdon County.

GEARY, WILLIAM (aka: Gary, William) Pvt, D, 30th NJ Inf, 1873. Riverview Cemetery, Trenton, Mercer County.

GEARY, WILLIAM W. (aka: Gary, William) Pvt, K, 1st NJ Inf, DoD Unknown. Greenwood Cemetery, Boonton, Morris County.

GEAYER, JACOB A. 1st Sgt, C, 9th NY Inf, 1-19-1892. Flower Hill Cemetery, North Bergen, Hudson County.

GEBAENTZ, AUGUST (see: Gebretz, August) Fairmount Cemetery, Newark, Essex County.

GEBART, THOMAS (see: Gebhard, Thomas) Methodist Cemetery, Waterford, Camden County.

GEBHARD, JOHN Pvt, F, 39th NJ Inf, 8-27-1916. Holy Sepulchre Cemetery, East Orange, Essex County.

GEBHARD, THOMAS (aka: Gebart, Thomas) Corp, C, 59th NY Inf, [Wounded 7-2-1863 at Gettysburg, PA.] 7-26-1895. Methodist Cemetery, Waterford, Camden County.

GEBICKER, AUGUST F. (aka: Schawager, August) Pvt, I, 33rd NJ Inf, [Died of wounds at Newark, NJ.] 9-17-1863. Woodland Cemetery, Newark, Essex County.

GEBRAETZ, JOHN Corp, H, 41st NY Inf, 4-5-1867. Fairmount Cemetery, Newark, Essex County.

GEBRETZ, AUGUST (aka: Gebaentz, August) Pvt, A, 1st MO Cav, 3-23-1888. Fairmount Cemetery, Newark, Essex County.

GECK, GEORGE Pvt, A, 23rd AL Inf (CSA), 6-24-1863. Finn's Point National Cemetery, Pennsville, Salem County.

GEDDES, ALEXANDER A. Corp, C, 6th NY Inf, DoD Unknown. Holy Trinity Lutheran Cemetery, Middletown, Monmouth County.

GEDDES, JOHN Pvt, F, 7th NY Cav, 11-16-1915. Holy Name Cemetery, Jersey City, Hudson County.

GEDDIS, GEORGE R. Corp, F, 15th NJ Inf, [Wounded 5-6-1864 at Wilderness, VA.] 1913. Congregational Church Cemetery, Chester, Morris County.

GEE, CHARLES Seaman, U.S. Navy, DoD Unknown. Evergreen Cemetery, Hillside, Union County.

Our Brothers Gone Before

GEE, FRANK A. Pvt, E, 5th __ Inf, 8-5-1877. Fairmount Cemetery, Newark, Essex County.

GEE*, JAMES S.W. Sgt, F, 21st MA Inf, [Wounded 11- -1863 at Knoxville, TN.] 3-22-1892. New Camden Cemetery, Camden, Camden County.

GEE, NEVIL Pvt, A, 5th NC Inf (CSA), [Captured 7-1-1863 at Gettysburg, PA.] 10-11-1863. Finn's Point National Cemetery, Pennsville, Salem County.

GEERY, RICHARD C. DoD Unknown. Flower Hill Cemetery, North Bergen, Hudson County.

GEFFINGER, PHILIP Pvt, E, 26th NJ Inf, 10-21-1885. Woodland Cemetery, Newark, Essex County.

GEGAN, JOHN Pvt, D, 2nd NJ Inf, 7-16-1892. Holy Sepulchre Cemetery, East Orange, Essex County.

GEGENHEIMER, FREDERICK Pvt, K, 26th NJ Inf, 6-18-1894. Woodland Cemetery, Newark, Essex County.

GEHRIG, GEORGE W. (aka: Gherig, George) Pvt, H, 2nd DC Inf, 5-18-1907. Fairmount Cemetery, Newark, Essex County.

GEHRIG, JOSEPH Pvt, C, 35th NJ Inf, 10-1-1878. Fairmount Cemetery, Newark, Essex County.

GEHRING, JACOB Pvt, D, 75th PA Inf, 12-28-1893. Atco Cemetery, Atco, Camden County.

GEHRING, JOHN E. Pvt, E, 9th NJ Inf, 2-8-1883. Rahway Cemetery, Rahway, Union County.

GEHWEILER, SUTON DoD Unknown. Old Camden Cemetery, Camden, Camden County.

GEIB, EDWIN V. Pvt, B, 53rd NY Inf, DoD Unknown. Evergreen Cemetery, Hillside, Union County.

GEIBIG*, PETER (aka: Cabey, Peter) Pvt, A, 68th PA Inf, 3-9-1921. St. Mary's Cemetery, Hainesport, Burlington County.

GEIBLE, LUDWIG Pvt, E, 103rd NY Inf, 8-2-1885. Fairmount Cemetery, Newark, Essex County.

GEICKLER, ADOLPH (see: Goeckler, Adolph) Speer Cemetery, Jersey City, Hudson County.

GEIGER, EDWARD 1896. St. Nicholas Cemetery, Lodi, Bergen County.

GEIGER, GEORGE O. 1927. Cedar Hill Cemetery, Cedarville, Cumberland County.

GEIGER, JACOB Sgt, A, 34th NJ Inf, 8-5-1874. Fairmount Cemetery, Newark, Essex County.

GEIGER, JOHN 1-28-1911. Mount Olivet Cemetery, Newark, Essex County.

GEIGER*, WILLIAM H.D. Pvt, B, 191st PA Inf, 9-25-1912. Green Cemetery, Woodbury, Gloucester County.

GEIMER, SIMON (aka: O'Brien, John) Pvt, D, 9th NJ Inf, 6-22-1917. New Catholic Cemetery, Newton, Sussex County.

GEIPEL, ADAM Corp, K, 14th NJ Inf, [Wounded at Cold Harbor, VA.] 3-1-1925. Elmwood Cemetery, New Brunswick, Middlesex County.

GEIS, JOHN N. DoD Unknown. Speer Cemetery, Jersey City, Hudson County.

GEISEL, PHILIP (aka: Grissel, Philip) Pvt, C, 54th NY Inf, [Wounded 7-2-1863 at Gettysburg, PA.] 5-20-1898. Weehawken Cemetery, North Bergen, Hudson County.

GEISER, SAMUEL (aka: Gaiser, Samuel) Pvt, I, 26th NJ Inf, 8-1-1895. Woodland Cemetery, Newark, Essex County.

GEISINGER, ANDREW Pvt, D, 7th NJ Inf, 9-20-1910. Head of River Church Cemetery, Head of River, Atlantic County.

GEISINGER, JACOB Pvt, D, 7th NJ Inf, 12-18-1862. United Methodist Church Cemetery, Winslow, Camden County.

New Jersey Civil War Burials

GEISINGER, JOHN (aka: Guysinger, John) Sgt, I, 5th OH Inf, 12-24-1893. Evergreen Cemetery, Hillside, Union County.

GEISKING*, FREDERICK Pvt, Btty B, 13th NY Heavy Art, 1-10-1870. Palisade Cemetery, North Bergen, Hudson County.

GENNETT, RICHARD Pvt, K, 110th PA Inf, 2-1-1934. Beverly National Cemetery, Edgewater Park, Burlington County.

GENT, GEORGE (aka: Gent, Patrick) Coal Heaver, U.S. Navy, USS Rhode Island, 2-23-1928. Fairview Cemetery, Fairview, Bergen County.

GENT, PATRICK (see: Gent, George) Fairview Cemetery, Fairview, Bergen County.

GENTRY, G.W. Pvt, L, 8th (Smith's) TN Cav (CSA), 6-26-1864. Finn's Point National Cemetery, Pennsville, Salem County.

GENTRY, JOSEPH R. Pvt, A, 26th NC Inf (CSA), [Wounded 7-3-1863 and captured 7-4-1863 at Gettysburg, PA. Died of typhoid.] 8-18-1863. Finn's Point National Cemetery, Pennsville, Salem County.

GENTZEL, JOHN D. Landsman, U.S. Navy, USS Nyack, 9-13-1920. St. Stephen's Cemetery, Millburn, Essex County.

GENUNG, ANDREW J. Pvt, C, 15th NJ Inf, [Killed in action at Spotsylvania CH, VA.] 5-12-1864. Hillside Cemetery, Madison, Morris County.

GENUNG, IRVIN M. Pvt, Btty B, 1st NJ Light Art, 11-21-1905. Rosedale Cemetery, Orange, Essex County.

GENUNG, SILAS P. Pvt, C, 15th NJ Inf, 1-15-1911. New Presbyterian Cemetery, Hanover, Morris County.

GEORGE, ADAM (aka: Jerges, Adam) Pvt, C, 19th U.S. Inf, 9-6-1926. Arlington Cemetery, Kearny, Hudson County.

GEORGE, ALFRED Pvt, D, 2nd U.S. Colored Cav, 12-7-1928. Fairmount Cemetery, Newark, Essex County.

GEORGE, HENRY (see: Henry, George S.) Soldier's Home Cemetery, Vineland, Cumberland County.

GEORGE, ISAAC PARKER Pvt, D, 29th CT Inf, 9-10-1910. Mount Peace Cemetery, Lawnside, Camden County.

GEORGE, JOHN Pvt, A, 22nd U.S. CT, 4-7-1909. Bordentown/Old St. Mary's Catholic Cemetery, Bordentown, Burlington County.

GEORGE, JOHN H. 2nd Lt, Btty D, 1st NJ Light Art, 11-10-1917. Fairmount Cemetery, Newark, Essex County.

GEORGE, MILTON Corp, D, 60th OH Inf, [Died at Beverly, NJ.] 10-24-1864. Beverly National Cemetery, Edgewater Park, Burlington County.

GEPHART, EDWARD 1st Lt, E, 7th NJ Inf, [Wounded 5-3-1863 at Chancellorsville, VA.] 5-23-1885. Phillipsburg Cemetery, Phillipsburg, Warren County.

GERALD, RICHARD M. Sgt, H, 51st AL Cav (CSA), 10-15-1863. Finn's Point National Cemetery, Pennsville, Salem County.

GERARD, CHARLES HENRY Corp, F, 128th NY Inf, [Wounded in action.] 8-1-1917. Lodi Cemetery, Lodi, Bergen County.

GERARD, DAVID Pvt, I, 2nd NJ Cav, 2-18-1923. Baptist Cemetery, Hampton, Hunterdon County.

GERBACH, JOHN (see: Gilbeck, John) Woodland Cemetery, Newark, Essex County.

GERCKE, AUGUST (see: Gerecke, August) Berry Lawn Cemetery, Carlstadt, Bergen County.

GERDING, AUGUSTUS Landsman, U.S. Navy, USS Mattabessett, 10-20-1918. Arlington Cemetery, Kearny, Hudson County.

GERECKE*, AUGUST (aka: Gercke, August) Corp, H, 52nd NY Inf, 5-1-1916. Berry Lawn Cemetery, Carlstadt, Bergen County.

GERECKE*, HENRY (aka: Gerke, Henry) Pvt, C, 54th NY Inf, 1878. Berry Lawn Cemetery, Carlstadt, Bergen County.

Our Brothers Gone Before

GERECKE, THEODORE Pvt, B, 5th NY State Militia, 7-2-1920. Berry Lawn Cemetery, Carlstadt, Bergen County.
GERHARD, JOHN B. Pvt, I, 1st NJ Inf, 6-27-1906. Hoboken Cemetery, North Bergen, Hudson County.
GERHARDT, FREDERICK G. Pvt, D, 28th NJ Inf, [Wounded 12-13-1862 at Fredericksburg, VA.] 10-1-1890. Elmwood Cemetery, New Brunswick, Middlesex County.
GERHART, ZACHARIAH Pvt, G, 179th PA Inf, 12-28-1933. Siloam Cemetery, Vineland, Cumberland County.
GERITY, THOMAS Pvt, B, 30th NJ Inf, 1903. Maplewood Cemetery, Freehold, Monmouth County.
GERKE, HENRY (see: Gerecke, Henry) Berry Lawn Cemetery, Carlstadt, Bergen County.
GERKE, REINHARD Capt, A, 75th PA Inf, 1-31-1904. Evergreen Cemetery, Hillside, Union County.
GERLACH*, LEWIS Pvt, F, 5th NJ Inf, 11-6-1909. Arlington Cemetery, Kearny, Hudson County.
GERLS, NATHAN (see: Jerrell, Nathan P.) Methodist Church Cemetery, Haleyville, Cumberland County.
GERMAN, CHARLES W. Sgt, C, 4th NJ Inf, 5-2-1894. Mount Hope Presbyterian Cemetery, Lambertville, Hunterdon County.
GERMAN, JAMES D. Pvt, D, 13th VT Inf, 8-16-1900. Phillipsburg Cemetery, Phillipsburg, Warren County.
GERMAN, JETHRO Sgt, K, 31st NJ Inf, 7-4-1910. Baptist Cemetery, Hampton, Hunterdon County.
GERMAN, JOSEPH A. Pvt, G, 30th NJ Inf, 9-20-1916. Mount Hope Presbyterian Cemetery, Lambertville, Hunterdon County.
GERMAN, PETER Pvt, E, 81st NY Inf, 5-23-1895. Weehawken Cemetery, North Bergen, Hudson County.
GERMER, CONRAD G. Pvt, E, 12th U.S. Inf, 7-27-1872. Woodland Cemetery, Newark, Essex County.
GERNAHLIG, FREDERICK Pvt, Btty A, 1st NJ Light Art, 2-3-1905. Maple Grove Cemetery, Hackensack, Bergen County.
GERNLER, CHARLES Pvt, H, 8th NJ Inf, [Wounded in action.] 10-5-1930. Flower Hill Cemetery, North Bergen, Hudson County.
GEROE, DANIEL B. Pvt, C, 9th NJ Inf, 10-12-1901. Laurel Grove Cemetery, Totowa, Passaic County.
GEROW, DANIEL J. Corp, G, 15th NY Eng, 1891. New Presbyterian Cemetery, Hanover, Morris County.
GERRETY, DANIEL (see: Garrity, Daniel) Holy Sepulchre Cemetery, East Orange, Essex County.
GERRITY, FRANCIS Pvt, Btty A, 1st NJ Light Art, 11-16-1883. Holy Sepulchre Cemetery, East Orange, Essex County.
GERRY, RICHARD G. (aka: Maury, Richard) Landsman, U.S. Navy, USS Bienville, 1-7-1915. Flower Hill Cemetery, North Bergen, Hudson County.
GERSEY, FERNANDO (see: Giese, Ferdinand) Rahway Cemetery, Rahway, Union County.
GERSHON, WILLIAM (see: Girsham, William) Riverview Cemetery, Trenton, Mercer County.
GERSTENACKER, JOHN Pvt, H, 5th NJ Inf, [Wounded in action at 2nd Bull Run, VA.] 5-9-1886. Fairmount Cemetery, Newark, Essex County.
GERTH, ROBERT G. Pvt, K, 9th NJ Inf, 4-27-1918. Fairmount Cemetery, Newark, Essex County.
GERVIN, GEORGE Pvt, H, 21st NJ Inf, DoD Unknown. Riverview Cemetery, Trenton, Mercer County.

New Jersey Civil War Burials

GESBOEKER, AUGUST Pvt, D, 131st NY Inf, [Wounded in action 5-27-1863.] 1-14-1888. Mount Olivet Cemetery, Newark, Essex County.
GESCH, LUDWIG Pvt, K, 41st NY Inf, 10-13-1889. St. John's Evangelical Church Cemetery, Orange, Essex County.
GESSERT, GEORGE (aka: Gassert, George) Pvt, A, 20th NY Inf, 11-26-1866. Woodland Cemetery, Newark, Essex County.
GESSLER*, CHARLES Pvt, I, 168th PA Inf, DoD Unknown. Chestnut Cemetery, Dover, Morris County.
GESSLER, JOHN M. Pvt, B, 19th PA Inf, 1906. Rose Hill Cemetery, Matawan, Monmouth County.
GESSLER*, THOMAS Pvt, H, 41st NY Inf, [Wounded 7-2-1863 at Gettysburg, PA.] 9-20-1915. Fairmount Cemetery, Newark, Essex County.
GESSNER, HENRY Pvt, D, 27th NJ Inf, DoD Unknown. Branchville Cemetery, Branchville, Sussex County.
GESTENMIER, MICHAEL Pvt, A, 9th NJ Inf, DoD Unknown. Holy Sepulchre Cemetery, East Orange, Essex County.
GETCHIUS, CHARLES F. Pvt, G, 2nd NJ Inf, 11-13-1916. Fairmount Cemetery, Newark, Essex County.
GETCHIUS, JAMES E. Corp, A, 13th NJ Inf, 2-25-1916. Fairmount Cemetery, Newark, Essex County.
GETHARD*, ANDREW (aka: Getherd, Andrew) Pvt, G, 3rd NJ Inf, 9-7-1864. Nixon Cemetery, Pittstown, Hunterdon County.
GETHARD, WILLIAM Pvt, D, 31st NJ Inf, 12-30-1904. Presbyterian Church Cemetery, Flemington, Hunterdon County.
GETHERD, ANDREW (see: Gethard, Andrew) Nixon Cemetery, Pittstown, Hunterdon County.
GETSINGER, CHRISTOPHER G. Pvt, F, 24th NJ Inf, DoD Unknown. Overlook Cemetery, Bridgeton, Cumberland County.
GETSINGER, EDWARD Musc, B, 2nd NJ Inf, DoD Unknown. Mount Pleasant Cemetery, Millville, Cumberland County.
GETSINGER, FRANCIS (JR.) Saddler, I, 2nd NJ Cav, 3-11-1924. Presbyterian Cemetery, Allentown, Monmouth County.
GETSINGER, SAMUEL Pvt, G, 3rd NJ Cav, 1-7-1871. Mount Pleasant Cemetery, Millville, Cumberland County.
GETTINGS, THOMAS DoD Unknown. St. Peter's Cemetery, New Brunswick, Middlesex County.
GETTLER, JACOB Pvt, C, 2nd NJ Cav, [Died of pneumonia at Trenton, NJ.] 3-31-1865. St. Francis Cemetery, Trenton, Mercer County.
GETTY, JOHN Seaman, U.S. Navy, DoD Unknown. Mount Pleasant Cemetery, Millville, Cumberland County.
GETTY, JOHN Pvt, C, 3rd NJ Inf, 5-13-1911. Green Cemetery, Woodbury, Gloucester County.
GETZ, MARTIN L. Pvt, G, 194th PA Inf, 8-21-1907. Maple Grove Cemetery, Hackensack, Bergen County.
GETZWEILLER, WILLIAM (see: Wheeler, William J.) Arlington Cemetery, Pennsauken, Camden County.
GEYER, JOHN Pvt, D, 51st PA Inf, 8-25-1891. Evergreen Cemetery, Hillside, Union County.
GHERIG, GEORGE (see: Gehrig, George W.) Fairmount Cemetery, Newark, Essex County.
GIBBON, LEONARD Capt, K, 19th MI Inf, [Killed in action at Averysboro, NC.] 3-16-1865. Cohansey Baptist Church Cemetery, Bowentown, Cumberland County.

Our Brothers Gone Before

GIBBONS, JOHN Pvt, U.S. Marine Corps, 1920. Locust Hill Cemetery, Dover, Morris County.
GIBBONS, JOHN W. Pvt, U.S. Marine Corps, 3-29-1929. St. Peter's Cemetery, New Brunswick, Middlesex County.
GIBBS, ABEL S. Pvt, I, 23rd NJ Inf, 4-8-1912. Baptist/St. Andrew's Cemetery, Mount Holly, Burlington County.
GIBBS, BENJAMIN T. 3-6-1895. Eglington Cemetery, Clarksboro, Gloucester County.
GIBBS*, CHARLES Pvt, C, 34th NJ Inf, 7-24-1890. Baptist Cemetery, Vincentown, Burlington County.
GIBBS, CHARLES B. Pvt, I, 23rd NJ Inf, 7-8-1907. Baptist/St. Andrew's Cemetery, Mount Holly, Burlington County.
GIBBS, GEORGE G. 6-17-1863. United Methodist Church Cemetery, Vienna, Warren County.
GIBBS, JAMES Pvt, K, 22nd U.S. CT, 3-15-1893. Union Bethel Cemetery, Erma, Cape May County.
GIBBS, JAMES H. (see: White, Henry Simmons) Fairview Cemetery, Fairview, Monmouth County.
GIBBS, JOSEPH Pvt, K, 22nd U.S. CT, 5-5-1911. Mount Peace Cemetery, Lawnside, Camden County.
GIBBS, ROBERT Musc, H, 71st PA Inf, 5-15-1928. Cedar Lawn Cemetery, Paterson, Passaic County.
GIBBS, ROBERT Pvt, E, 26th NJ Inf, 5-17-1877. Clinton Cemetery, Irvington, Essex County.
GIBBS, THEODORE Pvt, D, 9th U.S. CT, 5-12-1923. Mount Peace Cemetery, Lawnside, Camden County.
GIBBS, THEODORE B. Corp, G, 29th NJ Inf, 10-27-1909. Berlin Cemetery, Berlin, Camden County.
GIBBS, THOMAS Pvt, H, 4th NJ Inf, [Wounded in action at Winchester, VA.] DoD Unknown. Mount Pleasant Cemetery, Millville, Cumberland County.
GIBBS, WARNER Pvt, I, 29th CT Inf, 4-14-1906. Mount Peace Cemetery, Lawnside, Camden County.
GIBBS*, WILLIAM Pvt, I, 6th NY Inf, 11-16-1905. Laurel Grove Cemetery, Totowa, Passaic County.
GIBERSON, DAVID Pvt, B, 12th NJ Inf, 2-22-1923. Roadside Cemetery, Manchester Township, Ocean County.
GIBERSON, ENOCH Pvt, C, 29th NJ Inf, 10-5-1893. Robbins-Covell Hill Cemetery, Upper Freehold, Monmouth County.
GIBERSON, EZEKIEL COOPER Pvt, H, 29th NJ Inf, 8-10-1884. Riverside Cemetery, Toms River, Ocean County.
GIBERSON, GILBERT Pvt, G, 11th NJ Inf, DoD Unknown. Baptist Cemetery, Medford, Burlington County.
GIBERSON, HENRY DoD Unknown. Cedar Run/Greenwood Cemetery, Manahawkin, Ocean County.
GIBERSON, ISRAEL Pvt, D, 39th NJ Inf, 4-7-1901. Riverside Cemetery, Toms River, Ocean County.
GIBERSON, JAMES Pvt, I, 4th NJ Inf, 6-10-1895. Methodist Church Cemetery, Juliustown, Burlington County.
GIBERSON, JOHN Pvt, A, 3rd NJ Cav, 4-5-1894. Riverside Cemetery, Toms River, Ocean County.
GIBERSON, JOHN G. Pvt, B, 14th NJ Inf, 8-15-1886. New Freedom Cemetery, New Freedom, Camden County.
GIBERSON, JOSEPH H. Pvt, H, 29th NJ Inf, 6-30-1923. Cedar Run/Greenwood Cemetery, Manahawkin, Ocean County.

New Jersey Civil War Burials

GIBERSON*, JOSIAH Pvt, B, 8th NJ Inf, [Wounded in action.] 1-27-1903. New Freedom Cemetery, New Freedom, Camden County.

GIBERSON, MILLER J. Corp, B, 12th NJ Inf, 1922. Methodist Cemetery, Allentown, Monmouth County.

GIBERSON, ROBERT R. Pvt, K, 34th NJ Inf, 3-12-1899. Evergreen Cemetery, Camden, Camden County.

GIBLIN, JOHN Pvt, K, 24th NJ Inf, 1924. Methodist-Episcopal Church Cemetery, Penns Grove, Salem County.

GIBLIN, MICHAEL Pvt, I, 29th NJ Inf, 5-27-1910. St. Rose of Lima Cemetery, Freehold, Monmouth County.

GIBNEY, JAMES (see: Gibney, William) St. Joseph's Cemetery, Keyport, Monmouth County.

GIBNEY, MICHAEL Seaman, U.S. Navy, USS Penguin, 2-26-1903. Holy Sepulchre Cemetery, East Orange, Essex County.

GIBNEY, PATRICK Pvt, C, 2nd NJ Inf, 11-3-1869. Holy Sepulchre Cemetery, East Orange, Essex County.

GIBNEY, WILLIAM (aka: Gibney, James) Pvt, Btty C, 5th NY Heavy Art, 11-11-1893. St. Joseph's Cemetery, Keyport, Monmouth County.

GIBSON, BENJAMIN N. Pvt, H, 24th NJ Inf, 11-25-1924. Presbyterian Church Cemetery, Bridgeton, Cumberland County.

GIBSON, CHARLES (aka: Gibson, George) Pvt, I, 29th CT Inf, 4-26-1880. Presbyterian Cemetery, Woodbury, Gloucester County.

GIBSON, CORNELIUS Corp, A, 14th NJ Inf, [Wounded in action.] 8-27-1903. Adelphia Cemetery, Adelphia, Monmouth County.

GIBSON, DANIEL Corp, Btty K, 2nd PA Heavy Art, 3-1-1895. Oddfellows Cemetery, Burlington, Burlington County.

GIBSON, DAVID S. Corp, A, 3rd NJ Inf, [Died at Gaines' Heights, VA.] 6-4-1862. Baptist Church Cemetery, Mullica Hill, Gloucester County.

GIBSON, GEORGE (see: Gibson, Charles) Presbyterian Cemetery, Woodbury, Gloucester County.

GIBSON, HENRY C. Capt, B, 3rd NJ Inf, DoD Unknown. Evergreen Cemetery, Camden, Camden County.

GIBSON, JACOB Pvt, I, 10th NJ Inf, 11-11-1915. Old Stone Church Cemetery, Fairton, Cumberland County.

GIBSON, JACOB L. Corp, A, 10th AL Inf (CSA), 10-20-1863. Finn's Point National Cemetery, Pennsville, Salem County.

GIBSON, JAMES F. Pvt, E, 11th NJ Inf, [Died of diarrhea at Trenton, NJ. Wounded 7-2-1863 at Gettysburg, PA.] 3-4-1865. Greenwood Cemetery, Hamilton, Mercer County.

GIBSON, JOHN Pvt, D, 5th NJ Inf, 1-24-1869. Mount Holly Cemetery, Mount Holly, Burlington County.

GIBSON*, JOHN Pvt, Btty E, 1st NJ Light Art, 3-21-1866. Methodist Episcopal/Methodist Protestant Cemetery, Bridgeport, Gloucester County.

GIBSON, JOHN F. Pvt, D, 2nd NJ Cav, 1906. Soldier's Home Cemetery, Vineland, Cumberland County.

GIBSON, JOHN P. Pvt, I, 3rd (Clack's) TN Inf (CSA), 10-23-1863. Finn's Point National Cemetery, Pennsville, Salem County.

GIBSON, JOSEPH Seaman, U.S. Navy, USS Louisiana, 4-24-1887. Johnson Cemetery, Camden, Camden County.

GIBSON, JOSEPH Pvt, B, 6th U.S. CT, [Wounded in action.] 12-8-1901. Presbyterian Cemetery, Woodbury, Gloucester County.

GIBSON, LEVI Pvt, F, 79th NY Inf, 4-7-1925. Fairmount Cemetery, Newark, Essex County.

Our Brothers Gone Before

GIBSON, LORENZO DOW Pvt, F, 27th MA Inf, [Killed in action at Goldsboro, NC.] 12-17-1862. Greenwood Cemetery, Hamilton, Mercer County.
GIBSON, WALTER P. Pvt, E, 186th PA Inf, 4-5-1895. Brotherhood Cemetery, Hainesport, Burlington County.
GIBSON, WILLIAM HOWARD 1st Lt, E, 34th NJ Inf, 6-23-1881. All Saints Episcopal Church Cemetery, Navesink, Monmouth County.
GIBSON, WILLIAM Z. Pvt, A, MD Emerg NJ Militia, 1925. Baptist Church Cemetery, Mullica Hill, Gloucester County.
GICE, JOHN (see: Guise, John) Greengrove Cemetery, Keyport, Monmouth County.
GIDDINGS, ANDREW A. Pvt, C, 44th NY Inf, [Wounded 5-5-1864 at Wilderness, VA.] 1-22-1880. Oak Grove Cemetery, Hammonton, Atlantic County.
GIDDIS, EDWARD Pvt, I, 30th NJ Inf, 9-13-1863. Methodist Church Cemetery, Mount Horeb, Somerset County.
GIDEON*, WILLIAM Pvt, D, 99th PA Inf, 5-19-1884. Cedar Grove Cemetery, Gloucester City, Camden County.
GIDLOF, CONRAD E. 10-1-1922. Fairmount Cemetery, Newark, Essex County.
GIELE, PETER (aka: Galligan, Peter) Pvt, K, 9th PA Cav, 2-12-1900. 1st Baptist Cemetery, Cape May Court House, Cape May County.
GIER, LOUIS P. (aka: Martin, Louis) Landsman, U.S. Navy, USS Savannah, 12-3-1928. Fairview Cemetery, Fairview, Bergen County.
GIERTH, CHARLES Pvt, D, 8th NJ Inf, 12-23-1902. Fairmount Cemetery, Newark, Essex County.
GIESE, FERDINAND (aka: Gersey, Fernando) Pvt, A, 30th NJ Inf, 4-29-1919. Rahway Cemetery, Rahway, Union County.
GIFFIN, CHARLES H. Pvt, K, 23rd NJ Inf, 2-17-1882. Berlin Cemetery, Berlin, Camden County.
GIFFIN, URIAH (see: Griffin, Uriah) 1st Baptist Church Cemetery, Florence, Burlington County.
GIFFINS, JACOB Pvt, D, 24th NJ Inf, 11-19-1910. Berlin Cemetery, Berlin, Camden County.
GIFFINS, WILLIAM Pvt, D, 24th NJ Inf, 10-28-1904. Berlin Cemetery, Berlin, Camden County.
GIFFORD, ABSALOM Pvt, B, 25th NJ Inf, 10-4-1895. Asbury United Methodist Church Cemetery, English Creek, Atlantic County.
GIFFORD, ALFRED H. Pvt, B, 12th NJ Inf, 12-3-1918. Old Methodist Cemetery, Point Pleasant, Ocean County.
GIFFORD, BENJAMIN Pvt, E, 3rd NJ Cav, 1865. Old Methodist Cemetery, Point Pleasant, Ocean County.
GIFFORD, DAVID Corp, E, 10th NJ Inf, 1-10-1895. Presbyterian Church Cemetery, Absecon, Atlantic County.
GIFFORD*, EDWARD S. Pvt, B, 23rd PA Inf, 7-13-1890. Evergreen Cemetery, Camden, Camden County.
GIFFORD, ISAAC Pvt, G, 4th NJ Inf, 7-16-1904. United Methodist Church Cemetery, Absecon, Atlantic County.
GIFFORD, ISRAEL W. Corp, B, 10th NJ Inf, 9-28-1924. Little Joshua Baptist Cemetery, Steelmantown, Cape May County.
GIFFORD, JAMES 2nd Cl Fireman, U.S. Navy, USS Nereus, 6-16-1896. Old Camden Cemetery, Camden, Camden County.
GIFFORD, JOHN L. Pvt, E, 10th NJ Inf, 10-20-1919. Salem Cemetery, Pleasantville, Atlantic County.
GIFFORD, JOHN L. 2-17-1924. Mount Pleasant Cemetery, Newark, Essex County.
GIFFORD, OSCAR FARNUM Pvt, E, 3rd RI Cav, [Wounded in action.] 3-27-1907. Rosedale Cemetery, Orange, Essex County.
GIFFORD, ROLAND DoD Unknown. Riverview Cemetery, Trenton, Mercer County.

New Jersey Civil War Burials

GIFFORD*, SAMUEL A. Pvt, C, 33rd NJ Inf, 10-25-1916. Whitelawn Cemetery, Point Pleasant, Ocean County.

GIFFORD, SAMUEL H. Pvt, B, 10th NJ Inf, [Died of diarrhea at Newark, NJ.] 12-4-1864. Fairmount Cemetery, Newark, Essex County.

GIFFORD, THOMAS Pvt, B, 12th NJ Inf, 3-15-1914. Columbus Cemetery, Columbus, Burlington County.

GIFFORD, THOMAS CHAULKLEY Corp, B, 2nd NJ Inf, DoD Unknown. Greenwood Cemetery, Tuckerton, Ocean County.

GIFFORD, THOMAS M. Corp, B, 12th NJ Inf, 11-10-1900. Whitelawn Cemetery, Point Pleasant, Ocean County.

GIFFORD, WILLIAM H. Corp, K, 10th NJ Inf, 7-31-1871. Greenwood Cemetery, Tuckerton, Ocean County.

GIFORD, WILLIAM Corp, B, 2nd NJ Inf, DoD Unknown. Mount Pleasant Cemetery, Millville, Cumberland County.

GILAND, JEREMIAH DoD Unknown. Evergreen Cemetery, New Brunswick, Middlesex County.

GILBAUGH, AUGUSTUS (aka: Galbaugh, Augustus) 1st Lt, B, 1st MO Inf (CSA), 4-3-1901. Prospect Hill Cemetery, Flemington, Hunterdon County.

GILBECK, JOHN (aka: Gerbach, John) Pvt, H, 9th NJ Inf, 1-24-1893. Woodland Cemetery, Newark, Essex County.

GILBERT, ABRAHAM Pvt, G, 31st NJ Inf, 4-26-1871. Fairview Cemetery, Columbia, Warren County.

GILBERT, ALBERT Sgt, G, 25th NJ Inf, 3-30-1918. Harleigh Cemetery, Camden, Camden County.

GILBERT*, ASHER W. Pvt, F, 38th NJ Inf, 4-2-1936. Greenwood Cemetery, Hamilton, Mercer County.

GILBERT, CARY Corp, E, 25th U.S. CT, 7-6-1894. Jericho/Oddfellows Cemetery, Deptford, Gloucester County.

GILBERT, CHARLES Pvt, F, 4th NJ Militia, 10-25-1909. Brotherhood Cemetery, Hainesport, Burlington County.

GILBERT, EDWIN F. Corp, E, 34th NJ Inf, 10-15-1903. Baptist/St. Andrew's Cemetery, Mount Holly, Burlington County.

GILBERT, EPHRIAM Pvt, G, 31st NJ Inf, 4-15-1888. Fairview Cemetery, Columbia, Warren County.

GILBERT, FRANK W. Pvt, Btty E, 1st CT Heavy Art, 8-22-1864. Beverly National Cemetery, Edgewater Park, Burlington County.

GILBERT, GEORGE A. Pvt, I, 23rd NJ Inf, [Died of typhoid at Belle Plain, VA.] 12-7-1862. St. Mary's Episcopal Church Cemetery, Burlington, Burlington County.

GILBERT, GEORGE W. Pvt, G, 90th PA Inf, 10-24-1904. Riverview Cemetery, Trenton, Mercer County.

GILBERT, JOHN Pvt, G, 23rd NJ Inf, 7-8-1902. Beverly National Cemetery, Edgewater Park, Burlington County.

GILBERT*, JOHN H. Pvt, E, 11th NJ Inf, 12-16-1896. Mount Hope Presbyterian Cemetery, Lambertville, Hunterdon County.

GILBERT, JOHN S. 7-10-1905. Prospect Hill Cemetery, Caldwell, Essex County.

GILBERT, JOSEPH A. Pvt, E, 3rd AL Cav (CSA), 2-5-1864. Finn's Point National Cemetery, Pennsville, Salem County.

GILBERT, LESLIE Pvt, B, 1st NJ Militia, 1907. Reformed Church Cemetery, Fairfield, Essex County.

GILBERT, SAMUEL R. 1925. Oddfellows Cemetery, Burlington, Burlington County.

GILBERT, T.B. Pvt, H, 49th AL Inf (CSA), 1-9-1864. Finn's Point National Cemetery, Pennsville, Salem County.

Our Brothers Gone Before

GILBERT, THEODORE A. (aka: Gilbert, Thomas) Pvt, A, 23rd NJ Inf, 7-10-1903. Evergreen Cemetery, Camden, Camden County.

GILBERT, THOMAS Pvt, Btty C, 2nd PA Heavy Art, 6-27-1876. Baptist Cemetery, Burlington, Burlington County.

GILBERT, THOMAS (see: Gilbert, Theodore A.) Evergreen Cemetery, Camden, Camden County.

GILBREATH, JOHN W. Pvt, G, 2nd (Ashby's) TN Cav (CSA), 8-3-1864. Finn's Point National Cemetery, Pennsville, Salem County.

GILCHRIST*, WILLIAM Pvt, E, 71st NY Inf, [Wounded 8-27-1862 at Bristoe Station, VA, 5-12-1864 at Spotsylvania CH, VA, and 2-5-1865 at Hatchers Run, VA.] DoD Unknown. St. John's Evangelical Church Cemetery, Orange, Essex County.

GILDAY, ANTHONY Pvt, Btty D, 1st NJ Light Art, 1-3-1913. Holy Name Cemetery, Jersey City, Hudson County.

GILDEA, JOHN (see: Guire, John) Mercer Cemetery, Trenton, Mercer County.

GILDER, RICHARD WATSON Pvt, Landis' Btty, PA Light Art, 11-8-1909. Bordentown/Old St. Mary's Catholic Cemetery, Bordentown, Burlington County.

GILDER*, WILLIAM HENRY (JR.) Bvt Maj, 40th NY Inf [Wounded 7-2-1863 at Gettysburg, PA.] 2-5-1900. Bordentown/Old St. Mary's Catholic Cemetery, Bordentown, Burlington County.

GILDER, WILLIAM HENRY (SR.) Chaplain, 40th NY Inf [Died of disease at Brandy, VA.] 4-13-1864. Bordentown/Old St. Mary's Catholic Cemetery, Bordentown, Burlington County.

GILDNER, FRANK G. (aka: Gildner, Friedrich G.) Pvt, A, 20th NY Inf, [Wounded 5-3-1863 at Salem Heights, VA.] 4-14-1928. Hollywood Cemetery, Union, Union County.

GILDNER, FRIEDRICH G. (see: Gildner, Frank G.) Hollywood Cemetery, Union, Union County.

GILE*, FRANCIS A. (aka: Gale, Francis) Pvt, B, 16th NH Inf, 10-12-1908. Hazelwood Cemetery, Rahway, Union County.

GILES, ASA Pvt, C, 9th NJ Inf, [Died of disease at Trenton, NJ.] 3-15-1864. New Presbyterian Cemetery, Bound Brook, Somerset County.

GILES*, DAVID S. Pvt, K, 9th NJ Inf, 3-4-1912. Cedar Lawn Cemetery, Paterson, Passaic County.

GILES, ENOCH Pvt, A, 9th NJ Inf, 12-12-1892. Presbyterian Church Cemetery, Metuchen, Middlesex County.

GILES, GEORGE F. Pvt, C, 28th NJ Inf, [Wounded in action.] 12-31-1897. New Presbyterian Cemetery, Bound Brook, Somerset County.

GILES, HENRY Pvt, C, 28th NJ Inf, 3-19-1867. New Presbyterian Cemetery, Bound Brook, Somerset County.

GILES, JAMES Pvt, G, 15th NJ Inf, [Died of typhoid at Washington, DC.] 12-9-1862. Presbyterian Church Cemetery, Flemington, Hunterdon County.

GILES, JAMES K. Corp, C, 14th NJ Inf, 1-7-1908. New Presbyterian Cemetery, Bound Brook, Somerset County.

GILES, JOEL Musc, C, 28th NJ Inf, DoD Unknown. St. James Episcopal Church Cemetery, Piscatawaytown, Middlesex County.

GILES, JOHN Landsman, U.S. Navy, 5-26-1894. Presbyterian Church Cemetery, Flemington, Hunterdon County.

GILES, JOHN Landsman, U.S. Navy, USS Vandalia, 6-29-1936. Greenwood Cemetery, Hamilton, Mercer County.

GILES, JOHN H. 1st Sgt, H, 38th NJ Inf, 2-5-1873. Presbyterian Church Cemetery, Metuchen, Middlesex County.

GILES, JOSIAH C. Sgt, Btty F, 1st OH Light Art, 3-31-1911. Mount Pisgah Cemetery, Elsinboro, Salem County.

New Jersey Civil War Burials

GILES, MANLEY J. Pvt, C, 28th NJ Inf, [Wounded in action.] 1924. Baptist Cemetery, South Plainfield, Middlesex County.

GILES, MORRIS R. 1st Sgt, E, 30th NJ Inf, 12-12-1884. Evergreen Cemetery, Camden, Camden County.

GILES, RICHARD (see: Guile, Richard) Vincent Methodist-Episcopal Cemetery, Nutley, Essex County.

GILES, RUNYON V. Pvt, B, 9th NJ Inf, 7-21-1920. St. James Episcopal Church Cemetery, Piscatawaytown, Middlesex County.

GILES, WILLIAM H. Seaman, U.S. Navy, USS Kearsage, 12-17-1931. Dayton Cemetery, Dayton, Middlesex County.

GILFORT, ROBERT Pvt, B, 1st MO Cav, 10-27-1914. Rosedale Cemetery, Orange, Essex County.

GILHAM, JESSE M. (see: Gillam, Jesse M.) Finn's Point National Cemetery, Pennsville, Salem County.

GILHOOLEY, MICHAEL (see: Gilhooly, Michael) Holy Name Cemetery, Jersey City, Hudson County.

GILHOOLY*, MICHAEL (aka: Gilhooley, Michael) Pvt, C, 26th MA Inf, 12-20-1929. Holy Name Cemetery, Jersey City, Hudson County.

GILKAY, JOHN H. Pvt, G, 44th PA Inf, 1915. New Camden Cemetery, Camden, Camden County.

GILL, BENJAMIN Pvt, I, 9th NJ Inf, [Wounded in action.] 9-26-1911. Eglington Cemetery, Clarksboro, Gloucester County.

GILL, BENJAMIN RAMBO 1-17-1881. New Episcopal Church Cemetery, Swedesboro, Gloucester County.

GILL, GEORGE H. Pvt, K, 42nd MA Militia, 9-19-1912. Rosedale Cemetery, Orange, Essex County.

GILL, GEORGE W. Pvt, I, 71st NY National Guard, 9-22-1910. Flower Hill Cemetery, North Bergen, Hudson County.

GILL, HENRY E. Pvt, F, 29th NJ Inf, 10-30-1914. Fairview Cemetery, Fairview, Monmouth County.

GILL*, JACKSON Pvt, E, 47th GA Inf (CSA), [Captured 7-3-1863 at Gettysburg, PA. Died of smallpox.] 11-4-1863. Finn's Point National Cemetery, Pennsville, Salem County.

GILL, JAMES P. Pvt, K, 73rd NY Inf, 7-22-1889. Greengrove Cemetery, Keyport, Monmouth County.

GILL, JOHN Pvt, I, 11th NJ Inf, 2-9-1883. Cedar Lawn Cemetery, Paterson, Passaic County.

GILL, MARTIN Pvt, D, 2nd NJ Inf, 5-10-1885. Fairmount Cemetery, Newark, Essex County.

GILL, PETER Pvt, D, 16th PA Cav, 2-28-1915. Lady of Lourdes/Holy Sepulchre Cemetery, Hamilton, Mercer County.

GILL*, RICHARD Corp, C, 5th NJ Inf, 11-24-1894. Holy Name Cemetery, Jersey City, Hudson County.

GILL, WILLIAM A. Pvt, A, 97th NY Inf, 8-11-1896. Fairmount Cemetery, Newark, Essex County.

GILL, WILLIAM H. Pvt, E, 2nd NJ Cav, 12-30-1913. Bethel Cemetery, Pennsauken, Camden County.

GILL, WILLIAM H. Capt, U.S. Army, [Quartermasters Department.] 8-21-1886. Mount Olivet Cemetery, Newark, Essex County.

GILLAM, GERSHAM W. Pvt, D, 2nd NJ Cav, 10-14-1903. Presbyterian Church Cemetery, Newton, Sussex County.

GILLAM, JESSE M. (aka: Gilham, Jesse M.) Pvt, B, 8th (Wade's) Confederate States Cav (CSA), 11-9-1863. Finn's Point National Cemetery, Pennsville, Salem County.

Our Brothers Gone Before

GILLAM, JOSEPH (aka: Gillen, Joseph) Pvt, D, 72nd PA Inf, 3-3-1897. Riverview Cemetery, Trenton, Mercer County.
GILLAM, NATHANIEL Pvt, K, 39th NJ Inf, 11-17-1897. St. Teresa's Cemetery, Summit, Union County.
GILLAND, DAVID Pvt, K, 3rd NJ Militia, 5-1-1902. Willow Grove Cemetery, New Brunswick, Middlesex County.
GILLARD, DAVID Pvt, Btty G, 12th U.S. CHA, 5-2-1902. Johnson Cemetery, Camden, Camden County.
GILLELAND, THOMAS Pvt, A, 27th NJ Inf, 2-12-1897. Newton Cemetery, Newton, Sussex County.
GILLEN, ANDREW 2- -1902. Holy Sepulchre Cemetery, East Orange, Essex County.
GILLEN*, HUDSON H. Corp, H, 40th NJ Inf, 12-26-1871. Phillipsburg Cemetery, Phillipsburg, Warren County.
GILLEN, JAMES R. Pvt, H, 24th NJ Inf, 11-28-1908. Arlington Cemetery, Pennsauken, Camden County.
GILLEN, JAMES R. (aka: Gillen, John) Pvt, E, 131st NY Inf, 9-5-1920. Phillipsburg Cemetery, Phillipsburg, Warren County.
GILLEN, JOHN Landsman, U.S. Navy, USS South Carolina, 4-17-1893. Johnson Cemetery, Camden, Camden County.
GILLEN, JOHN (see: Gillen, James R.) Phillipsburg Cemetery, Phillipsburg, Warren County.
GILLEN, JOSEPH (see: Gillam, Joseph) Riverview Cemetery, Trenton, Mercer County.
GILLEN, LEONARD V. Corp, E, 11th NJ Inf, 8-16-1914. Chestnut Cemetery, Dover, Morris County.
GILLEN*, WILLIAM Pvt, Btty D, 1st NJ Light Art, 9-3-1914. Holy Sepulchre Cemetery, East Orange, Essex County.
GILLESPIE, GEORGE Pvt, F, 5th NY Vet Inf, 9-18-1889. Fairmount Cemetery, Newark, Essex County.
GILLESPIE, JOHN A. Pvt, I, 1st KY Inf (CSA), 7-29-1864. Finn's Point National Cemetery, Pennsville, Salem County.
GILLESPIE, MICAJAH L. Corp, 4th Btty, IN Light Art, 11-4-1911. Bayview-New York Bay Cemetery, Jersey City, Hudson County.
GILLESPIE*, SAMUEL Pvt, K, 33rd NJ Inf, 6-15-1894. Union Cemetery, Mount Olive, Morris County.
GILLESPY, WILLIAM W. 10-31-1894. Riverview Cemetery, Trenton, Mercer County.
GILLETT, ANDREW T. Musc, O, 198th PA Inf, 1893. Harleigh Cemetery, Camden, Camden County.
GILLETT*, FRANCIS Pvt, Btty A, 2nd MA Heavy Art, 5-23-1877. Old Camden Cemetery, Camden, Camden County.
GILLETT, WILLIAM J. Pvt, I, 104th OH Inf, 1863. Oak Hill Cemetery, Vineland, Cumberland County.
GILLETTE*, FIDELIO BUCKINGHAM Chief Surg, 2nd Div, 23rd Corps [Also: Surg, 9th NJ Inf.] 7-1-1895. 7th Day Baptist Church Cemetery, Shiloh, Cumberland County.
GILLETTE, FRANK H. Pvt, A, 76th NY Inf, 7-11-1906. Presbyterian Church Cemetery, Bridgeton, Cumberland County.
GILLEY, BRIGHT (aka: Gilley, R.G.) Pvt, E, 5th AL Inf (CSA), 8-29-1863. Finn's Point National Cemetery, Pennsville, Salem County.
GILLEY, R.G. (see: Gilley, Bright) Finn's Point National Cemetery, Pennsville, Salem County.
GILLIAM, GEORGE M. Pvt, E, 9th NJ Inf, 11-6-1885. Lodi Cemetery, Lodi, Bergen County.
GILLIAM, JOHN A. Pvt, Btty B, 1st NJ Light Art, 6-2-1917. Methodist Church Cemetery, Springfield, Union County.

New Jersey Civil War Burials

GILLIAM, JOSEPH M. Pvt, E, 9th NJ Inf, 1-18-1921. Cedar Lawn Cemetery, Paterson, Passaic County.

GILLIAN, JAMES R. Pvt, Ahl's Btty, DE Heavy Art, DoD Unknown. Finn's Point National Cemetery, Pennsville, Salem County.

GILLIG*, GEORGE A. 1st Sgt, H, 2nd DC Inf, 8-15-1909. Presbyterian/Methodist-Episcopal Cemetery, Succasunna, Morris County.

GILLIG, JAMES M. Pvt, K, 26th NJ Inf, [Died of typhoid at Camp Fairview, VA.] 4-8-1863. Mount Pleasant Cemetery, Newark, Essex County.

GILLIGAN, DANIEL Landsman, U.S. Navy, DoD Unknown. Sacred Heart Cemetery, Vineland, Cumberland County.

GILLIGAN, PATRICK Pvt, A, 1st NJ Cav, DoD Unknown. Holy Name Cemetery, Jersey City, Hudson County.

GILLIGAN, TIMOTHY 1915. St. Mary's Cemetery, Wharton, Morris County.

GILLILAND, B. Pvt, H, 9th (Malone's) AL Cav (CSA), 10-26-1863. Finn's Point National Cemetery, Pennsville, Salem County.

GILLILAND, JOHN Pvt, B, 24th NJ Inf, 11-25-1908. United Methodist Church Cemetery, Port Elizabeth, Cumberland County.

GILLILAND, WILLIAM M. Sgt, E, 3rd Bttn SC Inf (CSA), [Captured 7-3-1863 at Gettysburg, PA. Died of chronic diarrhea.] 3-24-1864. Finn's Point National Cemetery, Pennsville, Salem County.

GILLIN, ALEXANDER (JR.) Gunner, U.S. Navy, USS Potomac, 12-28-1924. Mount Pleasant Cemetery, Millville, Cumberland County.

GILLIN, CHRISTOPHER C. Corp, G, 37th NJ Inf, 2-3-1909. Fairmount Cemetery, Newark, Essex County.

GILLIN, JAMES Capt, H, 8th NJ Inf, 8-18-1906. Mount Pleasant Cemetery, Newark, Essex County.

GILLIN*, ROBERT F. 2nd Lt, K, 8th NJ Inf, 5-27-1904. Fairmount Cemetery, Newark, Essex County.

GILLING, WILLIAM E. Pvt, Btty H, 4th U.S. Art, 4-28-1900. Evergreen Cemetery, Camden, Camden County.

GILLIS, CHARLES P. Musc, G, 23rd NJ Inf, 9-24-1886. Coopertown Meeting House Cemetery, Edgewater Park, Burlington County.

GILLIS, GEORGE P. Pvt, G, 23rd NJ Inf, 8-28-1868. Methodist-Episcopal Cemetery, Burlington, Burlington County.

GILLIS, JOHN Ordinary Seaman, U.S. Navy, 5-4-1875. Trinity Episcopal Church Cemetery, Woodbridge, Middlesex County.

GILLIS, JOSEPH Pvt, A, 118th PA Inf, [Wounded 9-20-1862 at Sheperdstown, WV.] 3-9-1889. Riverside Cemetery, Toms River, Ocean County.

GILLIS, THOMAS C. Musc, H, 29th PA Inf, 5-5-1915. Monument Cemetery, Edgewater Park, Burlington County.

GILLMORE, DAVID F. 1st Sgt, E, 25th NJ Inf, 8-17-1902. Cedar Lawn Cemetery, Paterson, Passaic County.

GILLOGLEY, JOHN Pvt, Btty B, 1st NJ Light Art, 1-4-1887. Holy Sepulchre Cemetery, East Orange, Essex County.

GILLOM, JAMES H. Pvt, K, 14th NJ Inf, DoD Unknown. Presbyterian Cemetery, Allentown, Monmouth County.

GILLON, J. Pvt, D, 37th Bttn VA Res Inf (CSA), 10-22-1863. Finn's Point National Cemetery, Pennsville, Salem County.

GILMAN, CHARLES (see: Glimman, Charles) Beverly National Cemetery, Edgewater Park, Burlington County.

GILMAN, CHARLES D. Sgt, F, 28th NJ Inf, [Died of typhoid at Falmouth, VA.] 1-24-1863. Alpine Cemetery, Perth Amboy, Middlesex County.

GILMAN, DAMON T. Pvt, A, 12th NJ Inf, 11-10-1870. Presbyterian Cemetery, Woodstown, Salem County.

Our Brothers Gone Before

GILMAN, EDMUND R. (aka: Gilman, Edward) Pvt, H, 24th NJ Inf, [Died of typhoid at Camp Kearny, VA.] 10-24-1862. Baptist Church Cemetery, Bridgeton, Cumberland County.
GILMAN, EDWARD (see: Gilman, Edmund R.) Baptist Church Cemetery, Bridgeton, Cumberland County.
GILMAN, URIAH Asst Surg, 12th NJ Inf 3-24-1902. New Presbyterian Church Cemetery, Daretown, Salem County.
GILMAN, WILLIAM B. Pvt, H, 24th NJ Inf, 8-20-1905. Overlook Cemetery, Bridgeton, Cumberland County.
GILMAN, WILMER (aka: Gilmar, Wilmar) Pvt, H, 5th NJ Inf, [Wounded in action.] 10-20-1917. Presbyterian Church Cemetery, Woodbridge, Middlesex County.
GILMAR, WILMAR (see: Gilman, Wilmer) Presbyterian Church Cemetery, Woodbridge, Middlesex County.
GILMER, JOHN P. 4-30-1877. Old Stone Church Cemetery, Fairton, Cumberland County.
GILMORE, DANIEL L. Pvt, U.S. Marine Corps, 4-20-1895. Greenwood Cemetery, Hamilton, Mercer County.
GILMORE, JACOB H. Pvt, I, 6th NJ Inf, 5-1-1885. Evergreen Cemetery, Camden, Camden County.
GILMORE, MICHAEL Pvt, G, 7th NJ Inf, 5-14-1912. Holy Sepulchre Cemetery, Totowa, Passaic County.
GILPIN, CHARLES P. Pvt, C, 22nd NY State Militia, 7-14-1869. Fairview Cemetery, Westfield, Union County.
GILPIN*, GEORGE Pvt, F, 69th PA Inf, 6-22-1894. Evergreen Cemetery, Camden, Camden County.
GILROY, JAMES 7-16-1866. St. Mary's Cemetery, Elizabeth, Union County.
GILROY, JAMES 1866. Holy Sepulchre Cemetery, East Orange, Essex County.
GILROY, JOHN Landsman, U.S. Navy, USS Princeton, DoD Unknown. Holy Sepulchre Cemetery, East Orange, Essex County.
GILROY, LAWRENCE Pvt, G, 39th NJ Inf, 3-11-1930. Holy Sepulchre Cemetery, East Orange, Essex County.
GILROY, PATRICK Pvt, K, 26th NJ Inf, 10-11-1880. Holy Sepulchre Cemetery, East Orange, Essex County.
GILROY, STEPHEN JAMES Pvt, A, 33rd NJ Inf, 8-12-1886. Mount Olivet Cemetery, Newark, Essex County.
GILROY, WILLIAM (aka: Giroy, William) Pvt, H, 16th PA Inf, 7- -1921. Soldier's Home Cemetery, Vineland, Cumberland County.
GILSON, EDGAR T. Pvt, Btty D, 1st NJ Light Art, 8-14-1865. Rahway Cemetery, Rahway, Union County.
GILSON, GEORGE Capt, F, 38th NJ Inf, 9-6-1869. Old 1st Methodist Church Cemetery, West Long Branch, Monmouth County.
GILSON, JOHN Pvt, G, 26th NJ Inf, 3-8-1880. Cedar Lawn Cemetery, Paterson, Passaic County.
GILVANY, THOMAS Pvt, B, 2nd NJ Cav, 2-3-1895. St. Peter's Cemetery, Jersey City, Hudson County.
GIMBLE, ROBERT Pvt, I, 30th NJ Inf, 4-22-1892. Fairmount Cemetery, Newark, Essex County.
GIMMING, JACOB R.B. Corp, A, 33rd NJ Inf, 1-21-1879. Woodland Cemetery, Newark, Essex County.
GINDER, CONRAD 1883. Mercer Cemetery, Trenton, Mercer County.
GINDER, JOHN Pvt, B, 54th PA Inf, 5-26-1884. Mercer Cemetery, Trenton, Mercer County.
GINENBACK, DANIEL B. Corp, F, 3rd NJ Inf, 1898. Presbyterian Church Cemetery, Bridgeton, Cumberland County.

New Jersey Civil War Burials

GINGLEN, HUMPHREY Actg 3rd Asst Eng, U.S. Navy, USS Fort Morgan, 5-30-1868. Willow Grove Cemetery, New Brunswick, Middlesex County.

GINN, __?__ DoD Unknown. Cedar Grove Cemetery, Gloucester City, Camden County.

GIRAUD, FREDERICK Pvt, C, 150th NY Inf, 2-25-1892. Bayview-New York Bay Cemetery, Jersey City, Hudson County.

GIRAULT, ARTHUR N. Pvt, I, 3rd MD Cav, 6-10-1890. United Methodist Church Cemetery, Tuckahoe, Cape May County.

GIRGANOUS, W.D. Pvt, G, 51st AL Cav (CSA), 9-1-1863. Finn's Point National Cemetery, Pennsville, Salem County.

GIRODS, EMIL JULES Sgt, G, 2nd NJ Inf, 9-19-1889. Woodland Cemetery, Newark, Essex County.

GIROY, WILLIAM (see: Gilroy, William) Soldier's Home Cemetery, Vineland, Cumberland County.

GIRR, FREDERICK Pvt, I, 4th NY Cav, 12-27-1918. Arlington Cemetery, Kearny, Hudson County.

GIRSHAM, ANDREW Pvt, A, 11th NY Inf, 7-1-1916. Fairview Cemetery, Fairview, Bergen County.

GIRSHAM, WILLIAM (aka: Gershon, William) Pvt, F, 71st NY Inf, [Wounded 8-27-1863 at Bristoe Station, VA.] 1-28-1901. Riverview Cemetery, Trenton, Mercer County.

GISE, FURMAN HULLFISH (aka: Halfosh, Firman) Pvt, H, 37th NJ Inf, 4-21-1930. Hillside Cemetery, Scotch Plains, Union County.

GISMOND, EMANUEL G. Pvt, K, 22nd NJ Inf, 8-9-1887. Brookside Cemetery, Englewood, Bergen County.

GIST, J.J. Corp, B, 4th Bttn AR Inf (CSA), [Captured 7- -1863 at Jackson, MS. Died of erysipelas.] 5-3-1864. Finn's Point National Cemetery, Pennsville, Salem County.

GITHCART, JOSEPH Pvt, A, 10th NJ Inf, 8-7-1864. Colestown Cemetery, Cherry Hill, Camden County.

GITHENS, C.E. 1926. Berlin Cemetery, Berlin, Camden County.

GITHENS, CHARLES E. Pvt, G, 6th NJ Inf, [Died at Philadelphia, PA of wounds received 5-5-1862 at Williamsburg, VA.] 6-21-1862. Evergreen Cemetery, Camden, Camden County.

GITHENS, CHARLES H. Pvt, G, 25th NJ Inf, 8-14-1892. Evergreen Cemetery, Camden, Camden County.

GITHENS, CHARLES N. 3-23-1864. Methodist Cemetery, Haddonfield, Camden County.

GITHENS, EDWARD H. 4-23-1906. Methodist-Episcopal Cemetery, Olivet, Salem County.

GITHENS, JOHN A. 1-18-1886. Methodist Cemetery, Haddonfield, Camden County.

GITHENS, RICHARD Sgt, G, 25th NJ Inf, 1918. Berlin Cemetery, Berlin, Camden County.

GITTINGER, JOHN D. Pvt, H, 55th OH Inf, 3-11-1895. Fairmount Cemetery, Newark, Essex County.

GIVEANS*, ISAAC S. (aka: Givens, Isaac) Pvt, A, 2nd NJ Cav, 4-4-1887. Christian Cemetery, Johnsonburg, Warren County.

GIVEN*, DAVID B. Corp, C, 183rd PA Inf, 1904. Cedar Grove Cemetery, Gloucester City, Camden County.

GIVEN, JAMES B. Corp, K, 24th NJ Inf, DoD Unknown. Bethesda Methodist-Episcopal Church Cemetery, Swedesboro, Gloucester County.

GIVENS, ISAAC (see: Giveans, Isaac S.) Christian Cemetery, Johnsonburg, Warren County.

GIVENS, JOHN N. Capt, H, 2nd NJ Cav, 8-2-1882. Belvidere/Catholic Cemetery, Belvidere, Warren County.

GIVENS, WILLIAM Corp, D, 38th NJ Inf, 6-22-1871. Methodist Episcopal/Methodist Protestant Cemetery, Bridgeport, Gloucester County.

Our Brothers Gone Before

GLACKEN*, THOMAS Seaman, U.S. Navy, USS Wampanoag, 9-5-1880. Phillipsburg Cemetery, Phillipsburg, Warren County.
GLADDEN, CALEB Landsman, U.S. Navy, USS Wachusett, 3-7-1880. Rosedale Cemetery, Orange, Essex County.
GLADDEN, THOMAS Pvt, G, 6th NJ Inf, 12-17-1886. Hedding Methodist-Episcopal Church Cemetery, Bellmawr, Camden County.
GLADDING*, NORWOOD P. Sgt, F, 183rd PA Inf, 1931. Methodist-Episcopal Church Cemetery, Aura, Gloucester County.
GLADING, HENRY C. Pvt, A, 20th PA Inf, 1914. Harleigh Cemetery, Camden, Camden County.
GLADNEY, WILLIAM Y. Pvt, G, 12th NJ Inf, 11-8-1906. Arlington Cemetery, Pennsauken, Camden County.
GLASER, MATTHEW (aka: Glasser, Matthias) Pvt, K, 22nd NJ Inf, 9-3-1896. Holy Name Cemetery, Jersey City, Hudson County.
GLASIER, JACOB A. Pvt, A, 17th NY Inf, 5-14-1884. Rosedale Cemetery, Orange, Essex County.
GLASIER, JAMES H. 1-11-1899. Bloomfield Cemetery, Bloomfield, Essex County.
GLASPELL, ENOS E. Pvt, F, 24th NJ Inf, 6-5-1896. Presbyterian Church Cemetery, Bridgeton, Cumberland County.
GLASPEY, JOSEPH S. Sgt, F, 24th NJ Inf, DoD Unknown. Overlook Cemetery, Bridgeton, Cumberland County.
GLASPEY, ROBERT (aka: Gallaspie, Robert) Pvt, F, 3rd NJ Inf, 10-8-1866. 1st United Methodist Church Cemetery, Bridgeton, Cumberland County.
GLASS*, DANIEL Corp, H, 39th NJ Inf, 5-19-1927. Cedar Lawn Cemetery, Paterson, Passaic County.
GLASS, GEORGE Actg Ensign, U.S. Navy, DoD Unknown. Brotherhood Cemetery, Hainesport, Burlington County.
GLASS, GUSTAVE Pvt, B, 1st NY Eng, 3-7-1904. Flower Hill Cemetery, North Bergen, Hudson County.
GLASS, J.P. Pvt, B, 1st GA Cav (CSA), 4-19-1864. Finn's Point National Cemetery, Pennsville, Salem County.
GLASS*, JAMES Pvt, Btty C, 5th U.S. Art, 9-24-1888. St. Stephen Episcopal Cemetery, Florence, Burlington County.
GLASS, JOHN Pvt, Btty D, 1st NJ Light Art, 1901. Methodist Cemetery, Crosswicks, Burlington County.
GLASS, R.L. Pvt, C, 24th GA Inf (CSA), [Captured 7-2-1863 at Gettysburg, PA. Died of diarrhea.] 2-9-1865. Finn's Point National Cemetery, Pennsville, Salem County.
GLASS, REUBEN Pvt, I, 31st NJ Inf, 1894. Cedar Ridge Cemetery, Blairstown, Warren County.
GLASSCOCK, JAMES (JR.) Pvt, E, 14th VA Inf (CSA), [Captured 7-3-1863 at Gettysburg, PA. Died of disease.] 7-21-1863. Finn's Point National Cemetery, Pennsville, Salem County.
GLASSER, MATTHIAS (see: Glaser, Matthew) Holy Name Cemetery, Jersey City, Hudson County.
GLASSON*, PETER Sgt, A, 2nd U.S. Cav, 11-26-1884. Holy Sepulchre Cemetery, East Orange, Essex County.
GLASTER, ALFRED T. Pvt, H, 39th NJ Inf, DoD Unknown. Immaculate Conception Cemetery, Montclair, Essex County.
GLATTS, JOSEPH Wagoner, F, 23rd NJ Inf, 11-9-1914. Methodist Church Cemetery, Pemberton, Burlington County.
GLAZE, G.W. Pvt, K, 13th GA Inf (CSA), [Captured 7-4-1863 at Gettysburg, PA. Died of smallpox.] 10-20-1863. Finn's Point National Cemetery, Pennsville, Salem County.

New Jersey Civil War Burials

GLAZE, YOUNG RUFUS Pvt, K, 31st GA Inf (CSA), [Captured 7-3-1863 at Gettysburg, PA. Died of smallpox.] 11-21-1863. Finn's Point National Cemetery, Pennsville, Salem County.

GLAZIER, CHARLES L. Pvt, L, 1st NJ Cav, [Wounded in action.] 2-9-1922. Methodist Church Cemetery, Fairmount, Hunterdon County.

GLAZIER, JOHN A. 1st Lt, D, 1st NJ Militia, 3-15-1930. Arlington Cemetery, Kearny, Hudson County.

GLEASON, ISAAC (aka: Gleeson, Isaac) Pvt, G, 12th LA Inf (CSA), [Captured 5-16-1863 at Champion Hill, MS.] 7-16-1863. Finn's Point National Cemetery, Pennsville, Salem County.

GLEASON, JAMES 9-27-1894. Old 1st Methodist Church Cemetery, West Long Branch, Monmouth County.

GLEASON, JAMES Pvt, G, 91st NY Inf, DoD Unknown. Rosehill Cemetery, Linden, Union County.

GLEASON, JOHN Pvt, K, 4th NJ Inf, 2-13-1901. Cedar Grove Cemetery, Gloucester City, Camden County.

GLEASON, MICHAEL Pvt, C, 28th NJ Inf, 4-19-1906. St. Peter's Cemetery, New Brunswick, Middlesex County.

GLEASON*, WILLIAM Corp, K, 52nd PA Militia, 4-18-1896. Old Camden Cemetery, Camden, Camden County.

GLEASON, WILLIAM B. Corp, F, 12th NJ Inf, [Wounded in action.] 11-29-1902. Lake Park Cemetery, Swedesboro, Gloucester County.

GLEDHILL, WILLIAM Pvt, E, 1st NJ Cav, DoD Unknown. Grove Church Cemetery, North Bergen, Hudson County.

GLEESON, ISAAC (see: Gleason, Isaac) Finn's Point National Cemetery, Pennsville, Salem County.

GLEICH, GEORGE Pvt, F, 39th NJ Inf, 11-13-1894. Fairmount Cemetery, Newark, Essex County.

GLEISINGER, BENJAMIN (aka: Gleisner, Benjamin) Pvt, G, 9th NJ Inf, DoD Unknown. Methodist Cemetery, Malaga, Gloucester County.

GLEISNER, BENJAMIN (see: Gleisinger, Benjamin) Methodist Cemetery, Malaga, Gloucester County.

GLENDENNING, JOHN Capt, A, 79th NY Inf, 11-3-1904. Bayview-New York Bay Cemetery, Jersey City, Hudson County.

GLENN, CHARLES Pvt, E, 10th NJ Inf, 12-23-1902. Fairmount Cemetery, Newark, Essex County.

GLENN, GEORGE K. Pvt, I, 67th PA Inf, 12-19-1902. Berry Lawn Cemetery, Carlstadt, Bergen County.

GLENN, JACOB T. 1st Lt, I, 153rd IL Inf, 12-31-1892. Riverview Cemetery, Trenton, Mercer County.

GLENNON, JOHN Pvt, I, 29th NJ Inf, 8-5-1922. Mount Olivet Cemetery, Fairview, Monmouth County.

GLENUM, HENRY Com Sgt, E, 11th PA Cav, 1912. Berlin Cemetery, Berlin, Camden County.

GLIBBS, JOHN (see: Krebs, John) Mount Hope Cemetery, Deerfield, Cumberland County.

GLICK, JOSEPH (aka: Click, Joseph) Pvt, H, 1st NY Cav, 2-18-1891. Holy Sepulchre Cemetery, Totowa, Passaic County.

GLIDEWELL, LEWIS F. (aka: Glidewell, Louis F.) Pvt, B, 4th NC Cav (CSA), [Captured 7-4-1863 at South Mountain, MD. Died of typhoid.] 9-1-1863. Finn's Point National Cemetery, Pennsville, Salem County.

GLIDEWELL, LOUIS F. (see: Glidewell, Lewis F.) Finn's Point National Cemetery, Pennsville, Salem County.

Our Brothers Gone Before

GLIMMAN, CHARLES (aka: Gilman, Charles) Corp, Btty D, 15th NY Heavy Art, 10-3-1864. Beverly National Cemetery, Edgewater Park, Burlington County.

GLISSON, HENRY J. Pvt, F, 2nd FL Inf (CSA), [Captured 7-5-1863 at Gettysburg, PA. Died of lung inflammation.] 2-16-1864. Finn's Point National Cemetery, Pennsville, Salem County.

GLOBIG*, HENRY Pvt, E, 5th PA Cav, 4-2-1902. Fairmount Cemetery, Newark, Essex County.

GLOVER, CLARENCE DoD Unknown. Presbyterian Church Cemetery, Blackwood, Camden County.

GLOVER, DAVID Pvt, H, NY Marine Art, 3-20-1914. Laurel Grove Cemetery, Totowa, Passaic County.

GLOVER, EDMUND W. Pvt, Btty E, 3rd PA Heavy Art, 5-8-1926. Locustwood Cemetery, Cherry Hill, Camden County.

GLOVER, ELI Pvt, G, 4th GA Inf (CSA), [Captured 5-10-1864 at Spotsylvania CH, VA. Died of typhoid.] 7-24-1864. Finn's Point National Cemetery, Pennsville, Salem County.

GLOVER, JOSEPH Landsman, U.S. Navy, 8-3-1897. Holy Sepulchre Cemetery, East Orange, Essex County.

GLUTING, HENRY 12-29-1877. St. Peter's Cemetery, New Brunswick, Middlesex County.

GLYNN, JOHN (aka: Dudley, Peter) Corp, D, 20th MA Inf, 10-13-1905. Holy Name Cemetery, Jersey City, Hudson County.

GNADE, AUGUST Pvt, Btty A, Schaffer's Ind PA Heavy Art, [Drowned at Fort Delaware.] 5-15-1864. Finn's Point National Cemetery, Pennsville, Salem County.

GOARCKE, HENRY A. Pvt, H, 15th NJ Inf, 7-15-1900. Methodist Church Cemetery, Liberty, Warren County.

GOARCKE, WILLIAM S. (aka: Goarkee, William) Corp, H, 11th NJ Inf, 1-21-1918. Locust Hill Cemetery, Dover, Morris County.

GOARKEE, WILLIAM (see: Goarcke, William S.) Locust Hill Cemetery, Dover, Morris County.

GOBLE, ALANSON Pvt, K, 27th NJ Inf, DoD Unknown. Methodist Church Cemetery, Sparta, Sussex County.

GOBLE, ALLEN 1924. Whitelawn Cemetery, Point Pleasant, Ocean County.

GOBLE, CHARLES C. 11-25-1891. Riverside Cemetery, Toms River, Ocean County.

GOBLE, CHARLES H. Pvt, Btty E, 1st NJ Light Art, 3-2-1893. Presbyterian Cemetery, New Vernon, Morris County.

GOBLE, CHILEON Pvt, I, 27th NJ Inf, 10-28-1869. Presbyterian Cemetery, New Vernon, Morris County.

GOBLE, DANIEL W. Sgt, B, 3rd NJ Cav, 1-29-1909. Presbyterian Church Cemetery, Andover, Sussex County.

GOBLE, EPHRIAM Pvt, Btty M, 2nd NY Heavy Art, 1866. Maplewood Cemetery, Freehold, Monmouth County.

GOBLE, GEORGE W. Pvt, K, 2nd NJ Cav, DoD Unknown. Methodist Church Cemetery, Sparta, Sussex County.

GOBLE, JONATHAN W. 2nd Lt, H, 2nd NJ Cav, 1915. Whitelawn Cemetery, Point Pleasant, Ocean County.

GOBLE, LEWIS Pvt, B, 3rd NJ Cav, 10-11-1922. Presbyterian Church Cemetery, Andover, Sussex County.

GOBLE, NICHOLAS M. Pvt, I, 27th NJ Inf, 3-18-1885. Presbyterian Cemetery, New Vernon, Morris County.

GOBLE, SYDNEY Pvt, B, 12th NJ Inf, 1-10-1892. Methodist Church Cemetery, Point Pleasant, Ocean County.

GODBEER, WILLIAM Pvt, H, 23rd NJ Inf, 8-31-1875. Trinity Episcopal Church Cemetery, Moorestown, Burlington County.

New Jersey Civil War Burials

GODBER, WILLIAM Pvt, A, 26th NJ Inf, 5-27-1909. Clinton Cemetery, Irvington, Essex County.
GODDEN, THOMAS O. Pvt, A, 187th PA Inf, [Died at Philadelphia, PA.] 8-25-1864. Beverly National Cemetery, Edgewater Park, Burlington County.
GODEKA, AUGUST (see: Goedecke, August B.) Woodland Cemetery, Newark, Essex County.
GODFREY, AUGUST (see: Ang, Godfrey) Atlantic City Cemetery, Pleasantville, Atlantic County.
GODFREY, G. TOWNSEND 5-2-1901. Tabernacle Baptist Church Cemetery, Erma, Cape May County.
GODFREY, GEORGE W. Pvt, Btty M, 2nd NY Heavy Art, 6-12-1912. Rosedale Cemetery, Orange, Essex County.
GODFREY, HAROLD DoD Unknown. St. Mary's Cemetery, Plainfield, Union County.
GODFREY*, JAMES Landsman, U.S. Navy, USS Marion, 6-27-1897. Atlantic City Cemetery, Pleasantville, Atlantic County.
GODFREY*, JAMES Pvt, C, 13th NJ Inf, 6-2-1917. Evergreen Cemetery, Camden, Camden County.
GODFREY, JAMES A. Pvt, I, 4th NY Inf, 3-3-1878. Atco Cemetery, Atco, Camden County.
GODFREY, JESSE S. Corp, F, 25th NJ Inf, 2-2-1885. Calvary Baptist Church Cemetery, Ocean View, Cape May County.
GODFREY, JOHN Pvt, D, 53rd NC Inf (CSA), 1923. Atlantic City Cemetery, Pleasantville, Atlantic County.
GODFREY*, THOMAS C. Capt, F, 5th NJ Inf, 6-13-1867. United Methodist Church Cemetery, Alloway, Salem County.
GODFREY, WILLIAM Pvt, G, 9th NJ Inf, 7-7-1892. Evergreen Cemetery, Hillside, Union County.
GODFREY, WILLIAM T. 2-20-1914. Evergreen Cemetery, Camden, Camden County.
GODSHALK, SAMUEL Pvt, E, 7th NJ Inf, 5-23-1907. Fairview Cemetery, Westfield, Union County.
GODWOLD, CHARLES Pvt, A, 12th NJ Inf, 11-27-1917. Cedar Lawn Cemetery, Paterson, Passaic County.
GOECKLER*, ADOLPH (aka: Geickler, Adolph) Pvt, C, 107th NY Inf, 7-27-1871. Speer Cemetery, Jersey City, Hudson County.
GOECKLER, GOTTLIEB Pvt, Btty C, 1st NJ Light Art, 12-2-1894. Speer Cemetery, Jersey City, Hudson County.
GOEDECKE, AUGUST B. (aka: Godeka, August) Pvt, F, 8th NJ Inf, 2-1-1918. Woodland Cemetery, Newark, Essex County.
GOERNER, FRANK 4-18-1899. New Somerville Cemetery, Somerville, Somerset County.
GOETCHINS, JOHN (see: Goetchius, John J.) Holy Sepulchre Cemetery, Totowa, Passaic County.
GOETCHIUS, JOHN J. (aka: Goetchins, John) Pvt, C, 176th NY Inf, 4-20-1912. Holy Sepulchre Cemetery, Totowa, Passaic County.
GOETHE, FRANZ (aka: Grothe, Franz) Pvt, G, 33rd NJ Inf, 5-16-1875. Palisade Cemetery, North Bergen, Hudson County.
GOETSCHINS, EDWARD W. DoD Unknown. Grove Church Cemetery, North Bergen, Hudson County.
GOETSCHIUS, BENJAMIN FRANKLIN Corp, H, 120th NY Inf, [Wounded 7-2-1863 at Gettysburg, Pa.] 11-18-1918. Bayview-New York Bay Cemetery, Jersey City, Hudson County.
GOETZ, GEORGE Pvt, H, 10th MD Inf, 1-29-1896. Holy Sepulchre Cemetery, East Orange, Essex County.
GOETZ, HENRY L. (aka: Gates, Henry) Pvt, Btty E, 6th NY Heavy Art, 8-19-1909. Bayview-New York Bay Cemetery, Jersey City, Hudson County.

Our Brothers Gone Before

GOETZ, JOHN Pvt, H, 46th NY Inf, 10-28-1864. Beverly National Cemetery, Edgewater Park, Burlington County.
GOETZ, JOHN P. Artificer, B, 1st NY Eng, 8-19-1884. Laurel Grove Cemetery, Totowa, Passaic County.
GOETZ, WENZEL Pvt, A, 20th NY Inf, 8-10-1902. Fairmount Cemetery, Newark, Essex County.
GOFF, ELBRIDGE G. Pvt, F, 25th NJ Inf, 11-3-1894. Methodist Church Cemetery, Eldora, Cape May County.
GOFF, JOHN F. 1st Sgt, F, 25th NJ Inf, 5- -1896. Methodist Church Cemetery, Eldora, Cape May County.
GOFF, JOSEPH D. Pvt, B, 3rd PA Cav, 1-30-1874. Eglington Cemetery, Clarksboro, Gloucester County.
GOFF, SAMUEL Pvt, I, 10th NJ Inf, 1-21-1892. Methodist Cemetery, Waterford, Camden County.
GOFF, SAMUEL B. 1921. Wenonah Cemetery, Mantua, Gloucester County.
GOFF*, SAMUEL H. (aka: Gough, Samuel) Pvt, Btty E, 1st NJ Light Art, 4-18-1910. St. Mark's Baptist Church Cemetery, Browns Mills, Burlington County.
GOFF, WILLIAM Pvt, G, 4th NJ Inf, 2-8-1920. Atlantic City Cemetery, Pleasantville, Atlantic County.
GOFORTH, CHARLES G.P. Sgt, E, 6th NJ Inf, [Died at Camden, NJ. of wounds received 7-2-1863 at Gettysburg, PA.] 9-1-1864. Evergreen Cemetery, Camden, Camden County.
GOFORTH, WILLIAM Pvt, B, 2nd (Ashby's) TN Cav (CSA), 5-8-1865. Finn's Point National Cemetery, Pennsville, Salem County.
GOFORTH, WILLIAM M. Pvt, I, 10th MO Inf (CSA), 7-22-1864. Finn's Point National Cemetery, Pennsville, Salem County.
GOIN, ALFORD (see: Gowins, Alfred) Finn's Point National Cemetery, Pennsville, Salem County.
GOLD*, SAMUEL FAY 1st Sgt, K, 13th NY National Guard, 1907. Brookside Cemetery, Englewood, Bergen County.
GOLD, WILLIAM (see: Gale, William) Baptist/St. Andrew's Cemetery, Mount Holly, Burlington County.
GOLDE, PHILLIP HENRY Pvt, Btty D, 2nd CT Heavy Art, [Wounded 9-9-1864 at Winchester, VA.] 4-4-1872. Fairmount Cemetery, Newark, Essex County.
GOLDEN, GARRET C. Pvt, B, 3rd NJ Cav, 8-16-1940. Wall Church Cemetery, Wall, Monmouth County.
GOLDEN, GEORGE W. Pvt, F, 27th AL Inf (CSA), 7-16-1863. Finn's Point National Cemetery, Pennsville, Salem County.
GOLDEN, JOSEPH A. Pvt, G, 29th NJ Inf, 9-30-1911. Atlantic Reformed Cemetery, Colts Neck, Monmouth County.
GOLDEN*, MICHAEL C. (aka: Hogan, Charles) Pvt, F, 6th NH Inf, 6-21-1876. Holy Name Cemetery, Jersey City, Hudson County.
GOLDER, SAMUEL (JR.) Pvt, F, 24th NJ Inf, 8-4-1902. Baptist Church Cemetery, Bridgeton, Cumberland County.
GOLDING, STEPHEN Pvt, C, 61st MA Inf, 11-14-1908. Fairmount Cemetery, Newark, Essex County.
GOLDSBORO, ROBERT (see: Goldsborough, Robert) Memorial Park Cemetery, Gouldtown, Cumberland County.
GOLDSBORO, THOMAS Pvt, C, 39th U.S. CT, DoD Unknown. Jersey City Cemetery, Jersey City, Hudson County.
GOLDSBORO, WILLIAM (aka: Goldsborough, William) Pvt, H, 22nd U.S. CT, 8-12-1887. Mount Zion Methodist Church Cemetery, Lawnside, Camden County.
GOLDSBORO, WILLIAM (see: Goldsborough, William) Memorial Park Cemetery, Gouldtown, Cumberland County.

New Jersey Civil War Burials

GOLDSBOROUGH, CHARLES Pvt, K, 22nd U.S. CT, 9-11-1916. Memorial Park Cemetery, Gouldtown, Cumberland County.

GOLDSBOROUGH, E.Y. Pvt, C, 2nd Bttn MD Cav (CSA), 2-21-1865. Finn's Point National Cemetery, Pennsville, Salem County.

GOLDSBOROUGH, F.F. Pvt, F, 7th VA Inf (CSA), 8-9-1864. Finn's Point National Cemetery, Pennsville, Salem County.

GOLDSBOROUGH, ROBERT (aka: Goldsboro, Robert) Pvt, H, 22nd U.S. CT, 8-15-1888. Memorial Park Cemetery, Gouldtown, Cumberland County.

GOLDSBOROUGH, WILLIAM (aka: Goldsboro, William) Pvt, H, 22nd U.S. CT, 7--1885. Memorial Park Cemetery, Gouldtown, Cumberland County.

GOLDSBOROUGH, WILLIAM (see: Goldsboro, William) Mount Zion Methodist Church Cemetery, Lawnside, Camden County.

GOLDSCHMIDT, LEOPOLD (see: Goldsmith, Leopold) Cedar Lawn Cemetery, Paterson, Passaic County.

GOLDSMITH, LEOPOLD (aka: Goldschmidt, Leopold) Pvt, C, 71st NY Inf, [Died of disease at Philadelphia, PA.] 12-25-1862. Cedar Lawn Cemetery, Paterson, Passaic County.

GOLDSMITH, WILLIAM A. Corp, H, 1st PA Inf, 3- -1918. Monument Cemetery, Edgewater Park, Burlington County.

GOLDSPINK, DANIEL L. Pvt, G, 21st NJ Inf, 8-20-1896. Bayview-New York Bay Cemetery, Jersey City, Hudson County.

GOLDTHORP, GEORGE Fireman, U.S. Navy, USS Tulip, 3-18-1912. Harleigh Cemetery, Camden, Camden County.

GOLDY, CHARLES Pvt, H, 29th NJ Inf, 7-6-1885. Baptist Cemetery, Pemberton, Burlington County.

GOLDY, JOHN L. Sgt, G, 3rd DE Inf, 4-27-1887. Methodist Church Cemetery, Pemberton, Burlington County.

GOLLEHON, J.M. 1st Lt, A, 23rd Bttn VA Cav (CSA), 7-18-1865. Finn's Point National Cemetery, Pennsville, Salem County.

GOLTRA, NEWTON P. (aka: Golty, Newton) Pvt, B, 12th WV Inf, 7-24-1903. Methodist Church Cemetery, Springdale, Somerset County.

GOLTY, NEWTON (see: Goltra, Newton P.) Methodist Church Cemetery, Springdale, Somerset County.

GOMER, WILLIAM D. Sgt, I, 26th NJ Inf, 7-22-1895. Fairmount Cemetery, Newark, Essex County.

GOMERSALL, DANIEL H. Sgt, G, 36th PA Inf, 6-1-1921. Evergreen Cemetery, Camden, Camden County.

GOOD, EDWIN R. 1882. Hoboken Cemetery, North Bergen, Hudson County.

GOOD, EDWIN R. 1st Lt, F, 11th NJ Inf, [Wounded in action at Chancellorsville, VA. and 7-2-1863 at Gettysburg, PA. (three times).] 9-1-1916. Greenwood Cemetery, Hamilton, Mercer County.

GOOD, JACOB Pvt, C, 7th NY Inf, 9-8-1910. Holcomb-Riverview Cemetery, Lambertville, Hunterdon County.

GOOD, JOHN HOFFMAN Corp, K, 9th NJ Inf, 10-23-1927. Evergreen Cemetery, Hillside, Union County.

GOOD, JOHN M. Pvt, F, Collins' MS Cav (CSA), 2-21-1865. Finn's Point National Cemetery, Pennsville, Salem County.

GOOD, LOUIS (aka: Good, Lucas) Pvt, D, 7th NJ Inf, 1888. Berlin Cemetery, Berlin, Camden County.

GOOD, LUCAS (see: Good, Louis) Berlin Cemetery, Berlin, Camden County.

GOOD, THOMAS Pvt, D, 5th PA Cav, 6-22-1916. Holcomb-Riverview Cemetery, Lambertville, Hunterdon County.

GOOD, WILLIAM H. Sgt, E, 1st NJ Inf, DoD Unknown. Holy Sepulchre Cemetery, East Orange, Essex County.

Our Brothers Gone Before

GOODE, SYLVANUS S. Pvt, Kirkpatrick's Btty, VA Light Art (CSA), 7-1-1865. Finn's Point National Cemetery, Pennsville, Salem County.

GOODELL, ABNER A. Pvt, A, 190th PA Inf, 4-13-1918. Arlington Cemetery, Kearny, Hudson County.

GOODELL, HORACE Pvt, A, 85th NY Inf, [Wounded in action 12-14-1862 at Kingston, NC.] 4-2-1907. Lodi Cemetery, Lodi, Bergen County.

GOODENOUGH, JOHN W. Bvt Maj, 40th NJ Inf 10- -1876. Oddfellows Cemetery, Burlington, Burlington County.

GOODEY, J.N. Pvt, K, 1st (Butler's) KY Cav (CSA), 10-7-1863. Finn's Point National Cemetery, Pennsville, Salem County.

GOODFELLOW, CHARLES M. Sgt, E, 8th U.S. Inf, 10-14-1912. Holcomb-Riverview Cemetery, Lambertville, Hunterdon County.

GOODFELLOW, JAMES Pvt, F, 22nd NJ Inf, 12-20-1918. Arlington Cemetery, Kearny, Hudson County.

GOODFELLOW, PRESTON B. Corp, I, 3rd NJ Militia, 2-1-1920. Hillside Cemetery, Scotch Plains, Union County.

GOODFELLOW*, SAMUEL Pvt, D, 9th NJ Inf, 1916. Locust Grove Cemetery, Quakertown, Hunterdon County.

GOODHEART, PHILIP Pvt, G, 3rd NJ Inf, 11-11-1864. 1st Methodist-Episcopal Cemetery, New Brunswick, Middlesex County.

GOODMAN, MOSES 2nd Lt, A, 109th IL Inf, 11-3-1882. Riverview Cemetery, Trenton, Mercer County.

GOODRICH*, ALLEN O. Pvt, C, 1st MI Inf, 5-23-1891. Holy Sepulchre Cemetery, East Orange, Essex County.

GOODRICH, BETHUEL Pvt, F, 1st NJ Militia, 5-20-1895. Fairmount Cemetery, Newark, Essex County.

GOODRICH, EDWARD Pvt, F, 8th NY Inf, 1-11-1888. Mount Prospect Cemetery, Neptune, Monmouth County.

GOODRICH*, LEONARD Pvt, A, 3rd NY Inf, 6-11-1900. Mount Prospect Cemetery, Neptune, Monmouth County.

GOODSELL, JOHN F. 1st Sgt, E, 18th Bttn GA Inf (CSA), [State Guards.] 2-14-1892. Fairmount Cemetery, Newark, Essex County.

GOODSON, W.D. Corp, F, 13th GA Cav (CSA), 4-21-1864. Finn's Point National Cemetery, Pennsville, Salem County.

GOODWIN, A.J. Pvt, K, 13th SC Inf (CSA), [Captured 5-12-1864 at Spotsylvania CH, VA. Died of measles.] 8-15-1864. Finn's Point National Cemetery, Pennsville, Salem County.

GOODWIN, CHARLES P 1st Sgt, I, 9th NJ Inf, 1921. Cedar Green Cemetery, Clayton, Gloucester County.

GOODWIN, CHARLES R. Pvt, K, 28th PA Inf, 2-21-1907. New Camden Cemetery, Camden, Camden County.

GOODWIN, DEXTER Sgt, Btty E, 1st ME Heavy Art, 9-29-1864. Beverly National Cemetery, Edgewater Park, Burlington County.

GOODWIN*, EUGENE B. Sgt, F, 99th NY Inf, 11-15-1917. Mount Pleasant Cemetery, Millville, Cumberland County.

GOODWIN, FRANKLIN 5-13-1882. Episcopal Church Cemetery, Shrewsbury, Monmouth County.

GOODWIN, GEORGE Pvt, D, 35th NJ Inf, 4-17-1898. Fairview Cemetery, Westfield, Union County.

GOODWIN, GEORGE W. Pvt, I, 12th NJ Inf, 10-15-1929. Presbyterian Church Cemetery, Bridgeton, Cumberland County.

GOODWIN, HARVEY B. Pvt, F, 4th NJ Militia, 12-13-1866. Evergreen Cemetery, Camden, Camden County.

New Jersey Civil War Burials

GOODWIN, JOHN A. (aka: Zuckworth, John or Zuckschwart, John) Pvt, B, 11th NJ Inf, 1925. Flower Hill Cemetery, North Bergen, Hudson County.

GOODWIN, JOHN F. Pvt, B, 27th MO Inf, 5-18-1906. Beverly National Cemetery, Edgewater Park, Burlington County.

GOODWIN, JOHN H. 1st Sgt, F, 14th NH Inf, 6-27-1881. Fairmount Cemetery, Newark, Essex County.

GOODWIN, JOHN S. Corp, D, 97th PA Inf, [Wounded 5-20-1864 at Bermuda Hundred, VA.] 6-9-1913. Riverview Cemetery, Trenton, Mercer County.

GOODWIN, MICHAEL Pvt, B, 102nd NY Inf, 7-30-1880. Holy Sepulchre Cemetery, East Orange, Essex County.

GOODWIN, OLIVER W. 2-4-1874. Evergreen Cemetery, Camden, Camden County.

GOODWIN*, ROBERT J. Corp, B, 14th NJ Inf, 7-21-1914. Greenwood Cemetery, Hamilton, Mercer County.

GOODWIN, WILLIAM Musc, F, 35th NJ Inf, 8-28-1898. Elmwood Cemetery, New Brunswick, Middlesex County.

GOODWIN, WILLIAM Pvt, D, 23rd NJ Inf, 8-31-1893. Methodist-Episcopal Cemetery, Wrightstown, Burlington County.

GOODWIN*, WILLIAM WALLACE Actg Asst Paymaster, U.S. Navy, USS Fort Morgan, 10-6-1901. St. Mary's Episcopal Church Cemetery, Burlington, Burlington County.

GOODYEAR, JOHN EMORY Pvt, E, 1st (Gregg's) SC Inf (CSA), [Captured 7-5-1863 at Gettysburg, PA.] 8-25-1863. Finn's Point National Cemetery, Pennsville, Salem County.

GOON, E.P. 6-11-1893. Flower Hill Cemetery, North Bergen, Hudson County.

GORDEN, JOHN J. Sgt, A, 1st MO Cav (CSA), 7-26-1863. Finn's Point National Cemetery, Pennsville, Salem County.

GORDES, HEINRICH Pvt, C, 41st NY Inf, DoD Unknown. Edgewater Cemetery, Edgewater, Bergen County.

GORDON, ABRAHAM L. Pvt, L, 27th NJ Inf, 10-10-1876. Boonton Cemetery, Boonton, Morris County.

GORDON, ADDISON Pvt, C, 127th U.S. CT, 3-24-1913. Princeton Cemetery, Princeton, Mercer County.

GORDON, ALEXANDER 5-13-1921. Hillside Cemetery, Scotch Plains, Union County.

GORDON, CHARLTON HENRY Pvt, G, 15th SC Inf (CSA), [Captured 7-3-1863 at Gettysburg, PA. Died of scurvy.] 6-9-1865. Finn's Point National Cemetery, Pennsville, Salem County.

GORDON, DEMAREST Musc, D, 30th NJ Inf, 2-10-1911. Union Cemetery, Frenchtown, Hunterdon County.

GORDON, EVERITT Sgt, C, 8th NJ Inf, 4-20-1923. Presbyterian Church Cemetery, Hampton, Hunterdon County.

GORDON, HENDRICK CONOVER Pvt, I, 29th NJ Inf, 11-19-1881. Old Brick Reformed Church Cemetery, Marlboro, Monmouth County.

GORDON, ISAAC Slave, [Provided information to U.S. troops that helped to repulse a rebel attack in North Carolina.] 4-8-1917. Hillside Cemetery, Madison, Morris County.

GORDON, JAMES 1st Lt, H, 3rd NJ Militia, 7-4-1912. Greenwood Cemetery, Hamilton, Mercer County.

GORDON, JOHN Pvt, A, 25th NJ Inf, 2-28-1904. Fairmount Cemetery, Newark, Essex County.

GORDON, JOHN Corp, B, 38th NJ Inf, 1912. Locust Grove Cemetery, Quakertown, Hunterdon County.

GORDON, JOHN A. Corp, B, 3rd NJ Cav, 11-13-1883. Newton Cemetery, Newton, Sussex County.

Our Brothers Gone Before

GORDON, JOHN C. Pvt, E, 9th NJ Inf, 2-28-1934. Presbyterian/Methodist-Episcopal Cemetery, Succasunna, Morris County.
GORDON*, JOHN V. Pvt, G, 15th NJ Inf, 7-9-1898. Union Cemetery, Frenchtown, Hunterdon County.
GORDON, RANSON SAMUEL Wagoner, E, 72nd NY Inf, 5-25-1900. Greenwood Cemetery, Boonton, Morris County.
GORDON, SAMUEL R. Sgt, C, 1st NJ Cav, 3-1-1904. Evergreen Cemetery, Camden, Camden County.
GORDON, SAMUEL W. Pvt, H, 26th NJ Inf, 11-27-1900. Fairmount Cemetery, Newark, Essex County.
GORDON, STEPHEN WARD Pvt, I, 15th NJ Inf, 10-24-1923. Fairmount Cemetery, Newark, Essex County.
GORDON, THOMAS Sgt, A, 12th NJ Inf, 2- -1904. Laurel Grove Cemetery, Totowa, Passaic County.
GORDON, THOMAS J. Pvt, E, 12th NJ Inf, 4-25-1887. Prospect Hill Cemetery, Caldwell, Essex County.
GORDON, WILLIAM Pvt, G, 10th NJ Inf, 10-15-1912. Riverview Cemetery, Trenton, Mercer County.
GORDON, WILLIAM F. Pvt, A, 35th NJ Inf, 8-8-1926. Phillipsburg Cemetery, Phillipsburg, Warren County.
GORDON, WILLIAM S. Landsman, U.S. Navy, USS Conemaugh, 8-16-1891. Princeton Cemetery, Princeton, Mercer County.
GORDON, WILLIAM WEST Pvt, Unassigned, 21st NY Cav, 11-11-1909. Greenwood Cemetery, Hamilton, Mercer County.
GORDUEY, JOHN (aka: Cudney, John) Corp, D, 80th NY Inf, [Wounded 7-1-1863 at Gettysburg, PA.] 1-6-1916. Presbyterian Church Cemetery, Ewing, Mercer County.
GORE, EDWARD E. Pvt, A, 70th NY Inf, 4-28-1881. Cedar Lawn Cemetery, Paterson, Passaic County.
GORENFLO, EDWARD Pvt, I, 68th NY Inf, 12-28-1896. Palisade Cemetery, North Bergen, Hudson County.
GORHAM, CHARLES H. Pvt, B, 38th NY Inf, 9-11-1909. Rosedale Cemetery, Linden, Union County.
GORHAM, RUFUS ALLEN Pvt, B, 47th NY State Militia, 4-24-1917. Brookside Cemetery, Englewood, Bergen County.
GORLEY, WILLIAM Pvt, F, 10th NJ Inf, 12-4-1911. Laurel Grove Cemetery, Totowa, Passaic County.
GORMAN, DANIEL Pvt, E, 5th PA Cav, 10-11-1915. St. Mary's Cemetery, Hainesport, Burlington County.
GORMAN, JAMES PATRICK Pvt, M, 8th PA Cav, 2-26-1928. Fairmount Cemetery, Newark, Essex County.
GORMAN, JOHN Pvt, F, 71st NY Inf, 3-10-1872. St. John's Evangelical Church Cemetery, Orange, Essex County.
GORMAN, JOHN H. Pvt, F, 34th NJ Inf, 2-23-1880. St. Peter's Cemetery, Jersey City, Hudson County.
GORMLEY, JAMES M. Pvt, C, 25th NY Inf, 9-30-1886. Holy Name Cemetery, Jersey City, Hudson County.
GORMLY, THOMAS H. Sgt, E, 25th NJ Inf, 2-17-1914. Fairmount Cemetery, Newark, Essex County.
GORNINGER, JOHN B. (see: Cominger, John B.) Bordentown/Old St. Mary's Catholic Cemetery, Bordentown, Burlington County.
GORRIS, JAMES 1904. Clinton Cemetery, Irvington, Essex County.
GORRY, THOMAS Sgt, C, 127th NY Inf, 7-15-1899. Arlington Cemetery, Kearny, Hudson County.

New Jersey Civil War Burials

GOSGER, JACOB Pvt, E, 22nd NJ Inf, 12-21-1890. Fairmount Cemetery, Newark, Essex County.

GOSLINE, THOMAS R. Pvt, C, 95th PA Inf, 2-28-1897. Oddfellows-Friends Cemetery, Medford, Burlington County.

GOSMAN, GOTTLIEB C. (aka: Gassman, George) Pvt, G, 188th PA Inf, 5-18-1915. Presbyterian Church Cemetery, Bridgeton, Cumberland County.

GOSNEY, MARK OR HOOKER (see: Burns, Joseph) Holy Name Cemetery, Jersey City, Hudson County.

GOSSER, JOSEPH (see: Gasser, Joseph) Riverview Cemetery, Trenton, Mercer County.

GOSSON*, LOUIS C. Pvt, F, 7th NJ Inf, 5-11-1912. Riverview Cemetery, Trenton, Mercer County.

GOSSWEILER, JOHN H. Pvt, K, 41st NY Inf, 4-15-1886. Woodland Cemetery, Newark, Essex County.

GOTTA, ALEXANDER C. (aka: Gotte, Alexander) Pvt, H, 57th NY Inf, 4-26-1924. Oddfellows Cemetery, Burlington, Burlington County.

GOTTE, ALEXANDER (see: Gotta, Alexander C.) Oddfellows Cemetery, Burlington, Burlington County.

GOTTELBERK, GEORGE C. (aka: Bottelberger, George) Pvt, F, 8th NJ Inf, DoD Unknown. Clinton Cemetery, Irvington, Essex County.

GOTTHEINER, ISAAC 1922. Temple Sharey Tefilo Cemetery, Orange, Essex County.

GOTTLIEB, JOHN Pvt, G, 20th NY Inf, 3-10-1878. Woodland Cemetery, Newark, Essex County.

GOTTSCHALK, JOHN F. Pvt, F, 26th NJ Inf, 7-9-1888. Bloomfield Cemetery, Bloomfield, Essex County.

GOUERDEROI, JAMES DoD Unknown. Presbyterian Church Cemetery, Greenwich, Cumberland County.

GOUGARTY, MICHAEL Seaman, U.S. Navy, USS Potomac, 5-14-1900. Holy Sepulchre Cemetery, East Orange, Essex County.

GOUGE, WILLIAM O. Sgt, C, 13th NJ Inf, 12-1-1896. Fairmount Cemetery, Newark, Essex County.

GOUGER, JOSEPH Pvt, B, 2nd NJ Cav, 2-28-1913. Belvidere/Catholic Cemetery, Belvidere, Warren County.

GOUGH, JAMES B. Corp, C, 13th NJ Inf, 5-17-1912. Holy Sepulchre Cemetery, East Orange, Essex County.

GOUGH, JEREMIAH Pvt, H, 69th NY Inf, 11-7-1864. Beverly National Cemetery, Edgewater Park, Burlington County.

GOUGH, JOHN J. Pvt, C, 5th TX Inf (CSA), 3-13-1864. Finn's Point National Cemetery, Pennsville, Salem County.

GOUGH, SAMUEL (see: Goff, Samuel H.) St. Mark's Baptist Church Cemetery, Browns Mills, Burlington County.

GOUILARD, EDWARD Corp, 117, 2nd U.S. VRC, 3-14-1894. Flower Hill Cemetery, North Bergen, Hudson County.

GOUKLEAR, THOMAS H. Quartermaster, U.S. Navy, USS Louisville, 5-31-1905. Cedar Grove Cemetery, Gloucester City, Camden County.

GOULD, ALONZO (see: Gould, Lorenzo) Memorial Park Cemetery, Gouldtown, Cumberland County.

GOULD, CHANDLER Sgt, 10th MA Ind Btty [Died of disease at Beverly, NJ.] 10-5-1864. Beverly National Cemetery, Edgewater Park, Burlington County.

GOULD, DANIEL (SR.) Pvt, B, 69th PA Inf, [Wounded 9-17-1862 at Antietam, MD.] 6-22-1911. Lady of Lourdes/Holy Sepulchre Cemetery, Hamilton, Mercer County.

GOULD, FRANK H. 1st Lt, 16th NY Ind Btty DoD Unknown. Holy Name Cemetery, Jersey City, Hudson County.

GOULD, GEORGE C. Pvt, C, 9th NJ Inf, 7-1-1886. Cedar Lawn Cemetery, Paterson, Passaic County.

Our Brothers Gone Before

GOULD, JACOB C. Pvt, H, 27th NJ Inf, 1-10-1903. Beemerville Cemetery, Beemerville, Sussex County.
GOULD, JAMES Pvt, G, 22nd U.S. CT, 7-28-1882. Mount Hope United Methodist Church Cemetery, Salem, Salem County.
GOULD, JAMES Pvt, E, 35th NJ Inf, 1929. Hazen Cemetery, Hazen, Warren County.
GOULD, JAMES Pvt, H, 22nd U.S. CT, [Wounded in action.] DoD Unknown. Memorial Park Cemetery, Gouldtown, Cumberland County.
GOULD*, JOHN B. Corp, D, 168th NY Inf, 2-12-1897. Fairmount Cemetery, Newark, Essex County.
GOULD, JOHN R. Pvt, E, 35th NJ Inf, 4-26-1929. Riverview Cemetery, Trenton, Mercer County.
GOULD, JONATHAN A. Corp, E, 38th NJ Inf, 6-21-1889. Fairmount Cemetery, Newark, Essex County.
GOULD, JOSEPH Pvt, E, 6th U.S. CT, 8-24-1864. Fairmount Cemetery, Newark, Essex County.
GOULD, LORENZO (aka: Gould, Alonzo) Pvt, K, 22nd U.S. CT, 1920. Memorial Park Cemetery, Gouldtown, Cumberland County.
GOULD*, PETER J. Pvt, Btty B, 1st NJ Light Art, 11-24-1924. Reformed Church Cemetery, Montville, Morris County.
GOULD, ROBERT DoD Unknown. Mount Zion Cemetery, Kresson, Camden County.
GOULD, ROBERT Pvt, I, 3rd U.S. CT, 3-4-1902. Chestnut Cemetery, Greenwich, Cumberland County.
GOULD*, ROBERT S. Capt, E, 5th NJ Inf, 2-26-1895. Mercer Cemetery, Trenton, Mercer County.
GOULD, SILAS W. Pvt, B, 26th NJ Inf, 1-21-1913. Prospect Hill Cemetery, Caldwell, Essex County.
GOULD*, THOMAS Sgt, B, 80th NY Inf, 7-29-1911. Bloomfield Cemetery, Bloomfield, Essex County.
GOULD, WILLIAM Pvt, G, 27th NJ Inf, DoD Unknown. Midvale Cemetery, Midvale, Passaic County.
GOULD, WILLIAM 1-1-1889. Prospect Hill Cemetery, Caldwell, Essex County.
GOULD, WILLIAM H. Pvt, K, 22nd U.S. CT, 5-2-1911. Memorial Park Cemetery, Gouldtown, Cumberland County.
GOULDY, ISAAC Pvt, A, 95th PA Inf, [Wounded in action.] 1-17-1905. Atlantic City Cemetery, Pleasantville, Atlantic County.
GOULDY, THOMAS Corp, F, 1st NJ Cav, [Wounded in action.] 1927. Methodist Cemetery, Hamilton, Monmouth County.
GOURERTY, MICHAEL Landsman, U.S. Navy, 5-18-1900. Holy Sepulchre Cemetery, East Orange, Essex County.
GOURLEY, CHARLES S. Pvt, I, 7th IL Inf, 2-8-1923. Harleigh Cemetery, Camden, Camden County.
GOURLEY*, JOHN Fireman, U.S. Navy, USS Bermuda, DoD Unknown. Harleigh Cemetery, Camden, Camden County.
GOVE, CHARLES H. Pvt, I, 145th NY Inf, 1-16-1923. Fairview Cemetery, Fairview, Bergen County.
GOVERN, PATRICK Pvt, U.S. Marine Corps, USS Nipsic, 11-6-1892. Holy Sepulchre Cemetery, East Orange, Essex County.
GOWAN, BENJAMIN A. 2nd Lt, G, 51st NC Inf (CSA), [Captured 6-16-1864 at Petersburg, VA.] 3-22-1865. Finn's Point National Cemetery, Pennsville, Salem County.
GOWARD, WILLIAM S. (aka: Conrad, William) Pvt, A, 22nd PA Inf, 2-4-1909. Arlington Cemetery, Pennsauken, Camden County.
GOWDY, RALPH B. Capt, F, 14th NJ Inf, 4-18-1911. Riverside Cemetery, Toms River, Ocean County.

New Jersey Civil War Burials

GOWINS, ALFRED (aka: Goin, Alford) Pvt, A, 63rd (Fain's) TN Inf (CSA), 3-26-1864. Finn's Point National Cemetery, Pennsville, Salem County.

GOWRIE, JOSEPH Corp, I, 3rd NJ Inf, 10-26-1890. Fairmount Cemetery, Newark, Essex County.

GRAAF, BENJAMIN GOTTLIEB (aka: Greff, Benjamin) Pvt, F, 39th NJ Inf, 2-9-1890. Woodland Cemetery, Newark, Essex County.

GRABOW, JOHN H. 4-13-1903. Prospect Hill Cemetery, Flemington, Hunterdon County.

GRACE, ALBERT HAWKINS Pvt, F, 25th NJ Inf, 11-29-1870. Methodist-Episcopal Church Cemetery, South Dennis, Cape May County.

GRACE, GEORGE W. Carpenter's Mate, U.S. Navy, USS Spirea, 5-9-1900. 1st Baptist Cemetery, Cape May Court House, Cape May County.

GRACE, HUBERT Pvt, D, 28th NJ Inf, DoD Unknown. St. Peter's Cemetery, New Brunswick, Middlesex County.

GRACE, JESSE S. Pvt, I, 25th NJ Inf, 10-14-1906. Methodist Church Cemetery, Goshen, Cape May County.

GRACE, JOSEPH Pvt, Btty A, 1st CT Heavy Art, 9-27-1900. Mount Olivet Cemetery, Newark, Essex County.

GRACE, PATRICK __, C, 4th __ Inf, 12-17-1889. Holy Name Cemetery, Jersey City, Hudson County.

GRACE, PATRICK Pvt, Btty A, 1st NY Art, 9-25-1900. Mount Olivet Cemetery, Newark, Essex County.

GRACE, THOMAS P.K. Corp, F, 28th NJ Inf, 9-26-1897. St. James Cemetery, Woodbridge, Middlesex County.

GRACEY, GEORGE H. Sgt, K, 9th PA Cav, 7-19-1905. Mount Pleasant Methodist Cemetery, Pleasantville, Atlantic County.

GRADWELL*, RICHARD Pvt, G, 115th NY Inf, DoD Unknown. Laurel Grove Cemetery, Totowa, Passaic County.

GRADY, JOHN Pvt, G, 35th NJ Inf, 11-8-1920. Holy Sepulchre Cemetery, East Orange, Essex County.

GRADY, JOHN Pvt, G, 37th NJ Inf, DoD Unknown. Holy Sepulchre Cemetery, East Orange, Essex County.

GRADY, JOHN Pvt, G, 27th NJ Inf, 1918. Boonton Cemetery, Boonton, Morris County.

GRADY, JOHN H. DoD Unknown. Mount Olivet Cemetery, Bloomfield, Essex County.

GRADY, MARTIN Pvt, I, 23rd NJ Inf, 11-9-1910. St. Mary's Cemetery, Hainesport, Burlington County.

GRADY, MARTIN 12-9-1873. Mount Carmel Cemetery, West Moorestown, Burlington County.

GRADY, WILLIAM Pvt, B, 35th NJ Inf, 4-11-1866. St. Mary's Cemetery, Elizabeth, Union County.

GRAEBER, JACOB Pvt, E, 9th NJ Inf, 2-20-1900. Woodland Cemetery, Newark, Essex County.

GRAEF, FREDERICK (see: Graf, Frank) Flower Hill Cemetery, North Bergen, Hudson County.

GRAEFF, WILLIAM (see: Groft, William C.) Baptist Cemetery, Salem, Salem County.

GRAEME, EDWARD W.H. (aka: Graham, Edward) Pvt, C, 1st NJ Inf, 4-6-1918. Arlington Cemetery, Kearny, Hudson County.

GRAF, FRANK (aka: Graef, Frederick) 1st Sgt, Btty C, 1st NJ Light Art, 2-3-1898. Flower Hill Cemetery, North Bergen, Hudson County.

GRAF, HENRY (aka: Graff, Henry) Pvt, C, 2nd NY Cav, 5-10-1891. Woodland Cemetery, Newark, Essex County.

GRAFF, CHARLES HENRY Pvt, C, 7th NJ Inf, 12-27-1869. Baptist Church Cemetery, Haddonfield, Camden County.

Our Brothers Gone Before

GRAFF, CHRISTIAN Pvt, L, 9th NJ Inf, 1-25-1885. Fairmount Cemetery, Newark, Essex County.

GRAFF, EDMUND D. (aka: Graff, Ephriam D.) Pvt, I, 13th AR Inf (CSA), 2-6-1875. Baptist Church Cemetery, Haddonfield, Camden County.

GRAFF, EPHRIAM D. (see: Graff, Edmund D.) Baptist Church Cemetery, Haddonfield, Camden County.

GRAFF, EVERETT Sgt, Btty E, 4th NY Heavy Art (National Guard), 8-2-1898. Presbyterian Church Cemetery, Rockaway, Morris County.

GRAFF, FRANK Sgt, B, 10th NY Inf, [Wounded 5-6-1864 at Wilderness, VA.] 8-22-1928. Grove Church Cemetery, North Bergen, Hudson County.

GRAFF, GEORGE Pvt, F, 12th NY State Militia, 4-5-1904. Fairmount Cemetery, Newark, Essex County.

GRAFF, HENRY (see: Graf, Henry) Woodland Cemetery, Newark, Essex County.

GRAFF, JOHN Pvt, B, 28th NJ Inf, 12-21-1873. Brainerd Cemetery, Cranbury, Middlesex County.

GRAFF, JOHN (see: Grau, John) Bayview-New York Bay Cemetery, Jersey City, Hudson County.

GRAFFIN, HARRIS 2nd Lt, H, 6th PA Cav, 1901. Harleigh Cemetery, Camden, Camden County.

GRAFTON, JOSEPH Pvt, Btty A, 1st MS Light Art (CSA), 7-25-1863. Finn's Point National Cemetery, Pennsville, Salem County.

GRAGE*, HENRY Pvt, B, 10th NJ Inf, 5-10-1895. Rosedale Cemetery, Orange, Essex County.

GRAHAM, ABRAHAM Pvt, A, 20th U.S. CT, 7-31-1902. Fairmount Cemetery, Newark, Essex County.

GRAHAM, ADAM Capt, I, 12th GA Inf (CSA), [Died of wounds received 7-12-1864 at Washington, DC.] 4-23-1865. Finn's Point National Cemetery, Pennsville, Salem County.

GRAHAM, ARCHIBALD Capt, C, 25th NJ Inf, 12-9-1882. Cedar Lawn Cemetery, Paterson, Passaic County.

GRAHAM, EDWARD Coal Heaver, U.S. Navy, USS Cornubia, 1907. Arlington Cemetery, Pennsauken, Camden County.

GRAHAM, EDWARD (see: Graeme, Edward W.H.) Arlington Cemetery, Kearny, Hudson County.

GRAHAM, EDWARD A. Pvt, G, 69th IL Inf, 3-1-1908. Arlington Cemetery, Pennsauken, Camden County.

GRAHAM, FRANK DoD Unknown. Atlantic City Cemetery, Pleasantville, Atlantic County.

GRAHAM, GEORGE W. Pvt, E, 31st NJ Inf, 1898. New Presbyterian Cemetery, Bound Brook, Somerset County.

GRAHAM, HENRY M. Pvt, Btty G, Young's Ind PA Art, [Died at Fort Delaware.] 7-22-1863. Finn's Point National Cemetery, Pennsville, Salem County.

GRAHAM, J.W.W. Sgt, K, 12th GA Inf (CSA), 4-16-1865. Finn's Point National Cemetery, Pennsville, Salem County.

GRAHAM, JAMES DoD Unknown. Old Camden Cemetery, Camden, Camden County.

GRAHAM, JAMES Capt, C, 42nd NY Inf, DoD Unknown. Clinton Cemetery, Irvington, Essex County.

GRAHAM, JAMES 1st Lt, Adj, 34th NJ Inf DoD Unknown. Old Catholic Cemetery, Franklin Boro, Sussex County.

GRAHAM, JOHN 2nd Lt, K, 81st PA Inf, 6-20-1904. Cedar Grove Cemetery, Gloucester City, Camden County.

GRAHAM, JOHN Pvt, F, 2nd NJ Inf, 5-9-1898. Fairmount Cemetery, Newark, Essex County.

GRAHAM, JOHN R. 6-30-1909. Lake Park Cemetery, Swedesboro, Gloucester County.

New Jersey Civil War Burials

GRAHAM, MICHAEL (CSA) [Guard for Colonel Randolph.] 8-26-1883. Holy Sepulchre Cemetery, East Orange, Essex County.

GRAHAM*, ROBERT Landsman, U.S. Navy, USS Red Rover, 11-1-1899. Evergreen Cemetery, Hillside, Union County.

GRAHAM*, SAMUEL G. Seaman, U.S. Navy, 6-1-1879. Eglington Cemetery, Clarksboro, Gloucester County.

GRAHAM, THOMAS Pvt, C, 6th NJ Inf, [Died at Jersey City, NJ of wounds received 5-5-1862 at Williamsburg, VA.] 6-2-1862. Holy Name Cemetery, Jersey City, Hudson County.

GRAHAM, WALLACE 7-19-1931. Cedar Lawn Cemetery, Paterson, Passaic County.

GRAHAM, WALLACE S. Pvt, B, 37th NJ Inf, DoD Unknown. Rahway Cemetery, Rahway, Union County.

GRAHAM, WILLIAM Sgt, M, 3rd NJ Cav, DoD Unknown. Cedar Hill Cemetery, Florence, Burlington County.

GRAHAM, WILLIAM Corp, Nield's Btty, DE Light Art, 3-3-1902. Mount Prospect Cemetery, Neptune, Monmouth County.

GRAHAM, WILLIAM Pvt, E, 31st NJ Inf, 1896. New Presbyterian Cemetery, Bound Brook, Somerset County.

GRAHAM, WILLIAM (see: Grant, William) Free Burying Ground Cemetery, Alloway, Salem County.

GRAHAM, WILLIAM B.M. Musc, G, 9th FL Inf (CSA), [Captured 2-8-1864 at Baldwin, FL. Died of typhoid.] 11-3-1864. Finn's Point National Cemetery, Pennsville, Salem County.

GRAISBERRY, JOSEPH Pvt, D, 6th NJ Inf, 1905. Green Cemetery, Woodbury, Gloucester County.

GRAMLICH, ADAM Pvt, F, 39th NY Inf, 12-9-1879. Palisade Cemetery, North Bergen, Hudson County.

GRAMMELL, JOHN GEORGE Pvt, I, 24th NJ Inf, DoD Unknown. Methodist Cemetery, Malaga, Gloucester County.

GRAMMER*, CHARLES Pvt, A, 104th OH Inf, 1904. Mount Prospect Cemetery, Neptune, Monmouth County.

GRANBERG, JOHN B. 11-26-1895. St. Joseph's Cemetery, Woodstown, Salem County.

GRANGER, WILLIAM Pvt, F, 12th NY State Militia, 5-6-1910. Cedar Lawn Cemetery, Paterson, Passaic County.

GRANT, ASHER Pvt, I, 40th NJ Inf, 5-28-1904. Arlington Cemetery, Kearny, Hudson County.

GRANT, BARZILLA Pvt, B, 28th NJ Inf, 5-10-1894. Baptist Church Cemetery, Penns Neck, Mercer County.

GRANT, BARZILLA Pvt, A, 6th NJ Inf, [Wounded in action at Williamsburg, VA.] 7-21-1896. Methodist Cemetery, Hamilton, Monmouth County.

GRANT, GEORGE R. (see: Rosegrant, George W.) Arlington Cemetery, Kearny, Hudson County.

GRANT, HENRY Corp, E, 40th NJ Inf, 11-10-1921. Jacobstown Masonic Cemetery, Jacobstown, Burlington County.

GRANT, HOLMES C. Pvt, F, 35th NJ Inf, 8-7-1926. Woodlawn Cemetery, Lakewood, Ocean County.

GRANT*, HUGH Pvt, Btty G, 8th NY Heavy Art, 11-2-1903. Fairmount Cemetery, Newark, Essex County.

GRANT, J.B. Pvt, Carter's Btty, VA Light Art (CSA), 9-2-1864. Finn's Point National Cemetery, Pennsville, Salem County.

GRANT, JAMES GEORGE Pvt, L, 2nd NJ Cav, 7-8-1865. Riverside Cemetery, Toms River, Ocean County.

GRANT, JOB Pvt, K, 10th NJ Inf, 4-17-1925. Greenwood Cemetery, Tuckerton, Ocean County.

Our Brothers Gone Before

GRANT*, JOEL Pvt, E, 7th NJ Inf, [Killed on picket duty at Petersburg, VA.] 11-16-1864. Mercer Cemetery, Trenton, Mercer County.
GRANT, JOHN Pvt, K, 29th NJ Inf, 3-5-1874. Methodist Cemetery, Hamilton, Monmouth County.
GRANT, JOHN 2nd Lt, A, 38th NJ Inf, 11-12-1898. Good Luck Cemetery, Murray Grove, Ocean County.
GRANT, JOHN H. Pvt, D, 35th GA Inf (CSA), [Captured 7-3-1863 at Gettysburg, PA.] 9-20-1863. Finn's Point National Cemetery, Pennsville, Salem County.
GRANT, JOHN J. Pvt, K, 10th NJ Inf, 11-29-1905. Greenwood Cemetery, Tuckerton, Ocean County.
GRANT, JOHN P. Pvt, G, 4th NJ Inf, 12-15-1874. Old Camden Cemetery, Camden, Camden County.
GRANT, JOSEPH Pvt, C, 3rd U.S. CT, 1-20-1904. Riverside Cemetery, Toms River, Ocean County.
GRANT, LEMUEL F. Seaman, U.S. Navy, DoD Unknown. Bay View Cemetery, Leonardo, Monmouth County.
GRANT, NOAH E. Pvt, I, 1st NJ Inf, 10-6-1934. Rose Hill Cemetery, Matawan, Monmouth County.
GRANT, SAMUEL (see: Gaunt, Samuel M.) Fairview Cemetery, Fairview, Monmouth County.
GRANT, WILLIAM Corp, K, 27th NJ Inf, 4-25-1907. Presbyterian Church Cemetery, Rockaway, Morris County.
GRANT, WILLIAM (aka: Graham, William) Corp, F, 5th NJ Inf, 12-29-1884. Free Burying Ground Cemetery, Alloway, Salem County.
GRANT, WILLIAM H. Pvt, G, 2nd U.S. Inf, 2-23-1905. United Methodist Church Cemetery, Wayside, Monmouth County.
GRANT, WILLIAM W. Pvt, A, 2nd Bttn GA Inf (CSA), 4-27-1865. Finn's Point National Cemetery, Pennsville, Salem County.
GRAPE, THOMAS E. Sgt, F, 9th MD Inf, 1883. Old Stone Church Cemetery, Fairton, Cumberland County.
GRAPER, DIEDRICH HERMAN Pvt, G, 47th NY Inf, 4-12-1924. Bayview-New York Bay Cemetery, Jersey City, Hudson County.
GRAPES, MARTIN (aka: Krebs, Martin) Pvt, I, 39th NJ Inf, 1- -1899. Laurel Grove Cemetery, Totowa, Passaic County.
GRASS, LEWIS Pvt, B, 23rd NJ Inf, DoD Unknown. Bordentown/Old St. Mary's Catholic Cemetery, Bordentown, Burlington County.
GRASS, WILLIAM (see: Grasser, William) Woodland Cemetery, Newark, Essex County.
GRASSER, WILLIAM (aka: Grass, William) Pvt, B, 39th OH Inf, [Wounded 8-7-1864 at Atlanta, GA.] 12-23-1877. Woodland Cemetery, Newark, Essex County.
GRASSMAN, WILLIAM (see: Grossman, Wilhelm) Holy Sepulchre Cemetery, East Orange, Essex County.
GRATTIN, WILLIAM Musc, G, 67th PA Inf, 3-24-1926. Arlington Cemetery, Kearny, Hudson County.
GRAU*, AUGUSTUS Pvt, C, 176th PA Inf, 4-9-1894. Hainesville Cemetery, Hainesville, Sussex County.
GRAU, HEINRICH Pvt, E, 4th U.S. Hancock Corps, 1-26-1907. Hainesville Cemetery, Hainesville, Sussex County.
GRAU*, JOHN (aka: Graff, John) Pvt, I, 1st NY Mounted Rifles, 1-24-1915. Bayview-New York Bay Cemetery, Jersey City, Hudson County.
GRAUL, FREDERICK S. (see: Graul, Kindle) Cedar Lawn Cemetery, Paterson, Passaic County.
GRAUL*, JACOB H. Pvt, E, 3rd PA Cav, DoD Unknown. Oak Hill Cemetery, Vineland, Cumberland County.

New Jersey Civil War Burials

GRAUL, KINDLE (aka: Graul, Frederick S.) Corp, G, 7th NJ Inf, 12-14-1905. Cedar Lawn Cemetery, Paterson, Passaic County.

GRAVAT, HENRY E. Pvt, K, 38th NJ Inf, 1-17-1930. Methodist Cemetery, Hamilton, Monmouth County.

GRAVATT, BENJAMIN Pvt, E, 10th NY Inf, 3-21-1905. Elmwood Cemetery, New Brunswick, Middlesex County.

GRAVATT, CHARLES H. Pvt, E, 29th NJ Inf, 11-12-1914. Glenwood Cemetery, West Long Branch, Monmouth County.

GRAVATT, HENRY CLAY 1932. Yellow Meeting House Cemetery, Imlaytown, Monmouth County.

GRAVATT, JOHN Pvt, D, 14th NJ Inf, 9-30-1863. Christ Church Cemetery, Morgan, Middlesex County.

GRAVATT, LAWRENCE Pvt, I, 38th NJ Inf, 1913. United Methodist Church Cemetery, Ellisdale, Burlington County.

GRAVATT, M. PERRINE 2nd Lt, H, 29th NJ Inf, 10-16-1898. Riverside Cemetery, Toms River, Ocean County.

GRAVATT, SAMUEL H. 1906. Fairview Cemetery, Fairview, Monmouth County.

GRAVATT, THOMAS M. Pvt, B, 29th NJ Inf, 2-10-1898. Rose Hill Cemetery, Matawan, Monmouth County.

GRAVATT, WILLIAM LARUE Pvt, Btty K, 3rd PA Heavy Art, 10-7-1896. Cedar Hill Cemetery, Hightstown, Mercer County.

GRAVELIUS, GEORGE Pvt, H, 25th NJ Inf, 8-4-1896. Laurel Grove Cemetery, Totowa, Passaic County.

GRAVENER, JOHN Pvt, C, Zell's Bttn PA Inf, 1907. New Camden Cemetery, Camden, Camden County.

GRAVES, CHARLES 11-14-1902. Hillside Cemetery, Scotch Plains, Union County.

GRAVES, CHARLES C. Maj, 1st NC Inf (US) 7-22-1885. Bloomfield Cemetery, Bloomfield, Essex County.

GRAVES, JAMES Pvt, G, 5th NJ Inf, [Wounded in action.] 2-8-1913. Laurel Grove Cemetery, Totowa, Passaic County.

GRAVES, JOHN Pvt, K, 10th NJ Inf, 1-14-1892. Presbyterian Church Cemetery, Bridgeton, Cumberland County.

GRAVES, JOSHUA Pvt, Btty B, 2nd MA Heavy Art, 6-1-1930. Presbyterian Church Cemetery, Mays Landing, Atlantic County.

GRAVES, TAYLOR Pvt, G, 21st NJ Inf, 11-12-1863. Greengrove Cemetery, Keyport, Monmouth County.

GRAVES, THEODORE Pvt, B, 8th NJ Inf, 2-8-1920. Atlantic City Cemetery, Pleasantville, Atlantic County.

GRAVES, WILLIAM B. 7-22-1910. Hillside Cemetery, Lyndhurst, Bergen County.

GRAW, JACOB BENTLEY Chaplain, 10th NJ Inf 2-18-1901. Monument Cemetery, Edgewater Park, Burlington County.

GRAY, ALEXANDER Pvt, E, 39th IL Inf, [Died of wounds received 8-16-1864 at Deep Run, VA.] 9-10-1864. Beverly National Cemetery, Edgewater Park, Burlington County.

GRAY*, ANDREW Pvt, G, 39th NJ Inf, 3-13-1923. Arlington Cemetery, Kearny, Hudson County.

GRAY, ANDREW Pvt, F, 13th NJ Inf, 2-8-1881. Holy Sepulchre Cemetery, East Orange, Essex County.

GRAY, BENJAMIN Corp, E, 48th NY Inf, 11-19-1895. Laurel Grove Cemetery, Totowa, Passaic County.

GRAY, DAVID V.D. Pvt, B, 9th NJ Inf, 5-21-1902. Evergreen Cemetery, New Brunswick, Middlesex County.

GRAY, DEWITT C. 1st Lt, D, 2nd DC Inf, 3-9-1867. Rahway Cemetery, Rahway, Union County.

Our Brothers Gone Before

GRAY, EUGENE DOUGLAS Pvt, H, 1st NJ Cav, 7-19-1890. Elmwood Cemetery, New Brunswick, Middlesex County.

GRAY, FRANCIS Pvt, C, 2nd Bttn MD Inf (CSA), 9-6-1863. Finn's Point National Cemetery, Pennsville, Salem County.

GRAY*, FREEMAN Corp, H, 35th NJ Inf, 1-8-1896. Greenlawn Cemetery, West Long Branch, Monmouth County.

GRAY, GEORGE Col, 6th MI Cav 4-19-1892. Rosedale Cemetery, Orange, Essex County.

GRAY, GEORGE Pvt, E, 25th U.S. CT, 2-12-1912. Mount Pisgah Cemetery, Elsinboro, Salem County.

GRAY*, GEORGE Pvt, Btty M, 3rd U.S. Art, 7-20-1926. Rosedale Cemetery, Orange, Essex County.

GRAY, GEORGE A. Pvt, I, 31st NJ Inf, 2-27-1895. Methodist-Episcopal Cemetery, Johnsonburg, Warren County.

GRAY, GEORGE A. Pvt, Btty D, 1st NJ Light Art, 1910. Mount Pleasant Cemetery, Newark, Essex County.

GRAY, HARVEY Pvt, E, 60th (Crawford's) TN Mtd Inf (CSA), [Captured 5-17-1863 at Big Black River Bridge, MS.] 7-20-1863. Finn's Point National Cemetery, Pennsville, Salem County.

GRAY, JAMES H. Pvt, A, 38th NJ Inf, 1-13-1878. Presbyterian Church Cemetery, Shrewsbury, Monmouth County.

GRAY, JEREMIAH (aka: Cray, Jeremiah) Pvt, F, 30th NJ Inf, 10-9-1916. Unionville Cemetery, Dutchtown, Somerset County.

GRAY, JEREMIAH S. Corp, D, 4th NJ Inf, 1925. Reformed Church Cemetery, South Branch, Somerset County.

GRAY, JOHN Pvt, F, 40th NJ Inf, 2-22-1906. Macphelah Cemetery, North Bergen, Hudson County.

GRAY, JOHN Pvt, K, 24th NJ Inf, 4-20-1909. Methodist Church Cemetery, Mount Bethel, Warren County.

GRAY, JOHN V. Pvt, K, 2nd NJ Inf, [Wounded in action.] 11-18-1903. Presbyterian Church Cemetery, Flemington, Hunterdon County.

GRAY, JOHN V. 12-29-1871. Old Presbyterian Cemetery, Lakehurst, Ocean County.

GRAY, JOHN W. Pvt, K, 24th NJ Inf, 7-11-1930. Harleigh Cemetery, Camden, Camden County.

GRAY, JOSEPH Seaman, U.S. Navy, USS Princeton, 12-15-1893. Mount Peace Cemetery, Lawnside, Camden County.

GRAY, MATTHEW Pvt, F, 9th NJ Inf, 6-9-1916. Evergreen Cemetery, Hillside, Union County.

GRAY, MATTHEW Pvt, H, 34th NJ Inf, DoD Unknown. Fairmount Cemetery, Newark, Essex County.

GRAY, MOSES Pvt, F, 2nd NJ Cav, 3-4-1891. United Methodist Church Cemetery, Vienna, Warren County.

GRAY, PHILANDER RAYMOND (SR.) 1st Lt,RQM, 121st PA Inf 9-15-1914. Evergreen Cemetery, Hillside, Union County.

GRAY, PHILIP V. Pvt, K, 97th PA Inf, 5-31-1891. Evergreen Cemetery, Camden, Camden County.

GRAY, ROBERT 9-27-1875. Macphelah Cemetery, North Bergen, Hudson County.

GRAY, ROBERT C. Pvt, U.S. Marine Corps, 4-3-1908. Balesville Cemetery, Balesville, Sussex County.

GRAY, ROBERT (JR.) 5-26-1905. Newton Cemetery, Newton, Sussex County.

GRAY, ROBERT M. Pvt, C, 15th NJ Inf, [Wounded in action.] 6-2-1883. Newton Cemetery, Newton, Sussex County.

GRAY*, SAMUEL Wagoner, F, 39th NJ Inf, 4-29-1895. Clinton Cemetery, Irvington, Essex County.

New Jersey Civil War Burials

GRAY, THEODORE B. Pvt, A, 1st NJ Cav, 1905. New Somerville Cemetery, Somerville, Somerset County.

GRAY, WILLIAM Pvt, D, 39th NJ Inf, 12-26-1900. Clinton Cemetery, Irvington, Essex County.

GRAY, WILLIAM (JR.) 5-24-1916. Mount Pleasant Cemetery, Newark, Essex County.

GRAY, WILLIAM K. Hosp Steward, 3rd NJ Cav 7-8-1896. Rosedale Cemetery, Orange, Essex County.

GRAY, WILLIAM L. Pvt, D, 25th NJ Inf, 1-21-1893. Mount Pleasant Cemetery, Millville, Cumberland County.

GRAY, WILLIAM L. DoD Unknown. Old Camden Cemetery, Camden, Camden County.

GRAY, WILLIAM W. Capt, C, 1st NJ Cav, [Wounded in action at Mine Run, VA.] 9-7-1923. St. Stephen Episcopal Cemetery, Florence, Burlington County.

GRAYBACK, ROBERT Pvt, K, 2nd NJ Inf, [Wounded 9-14-1862 at Crampton's Pass, MD.] 8-31-1872. Fairmount Cemetery, Newark, Essex County.

GRAYBILL, ABRAHAM W. Pvt, D, 1st MD Cav (CSA), 8-22-1863. Finn's Point National Cemetery, Pennsville, Salem County.

GRAYDON, JAMES W. Musc, D, 7th IN Cav, 9-6-1914. Arlington Cemetery, Kearny, Hudson County.

GRAYDON, W.L. Pvt, E, 10th GA Inf (CSA), [Captured 7-4-1863 at Gettysburg, PA. Died of disease.] 9-22-1863. Finn's Point National Cemetery, Pennsville, Salem County.

GREANEY, CORNELIUS C. Pvt, G, 34th NJ Inf, 7-2-1899. Harleigh Cemetery, Camden, Camden County.

GREANEY, JOHN C. Landsman, U.S. Navy, DoD Unknown. Harleigh Cemetery, Camden, Camden County.

GREAR, JOHN H. (see: Greer, John H.) Cedar Lawn Cemetery, Paterson, Passaic County.

GREATHEAD, WILLIAM Pvt, B, 9th NJ Inf, 7-29-1890. Mount Pleasant Cemetery, Newark, Essex County.

GREAVES, FRANCIS M. Pvt, G, 1st PA Cav, 1873. Laurel Grove Cemetery, Totowa, Passaic County.

GREAVES, FRANCIS N. Pvt, E, 2nd PA Inf, 1-30-1871. Presbyterian Church Cemetery, Metuchen, Middlesex County.

GREBE, CHRISTIAN (aka: Grepe, Christian) Pvt, E, 39th NJ Inf, 8-24-1886. Fairmount Cemetery, Newark, Essex County.

GREELIN, CORNELIUS Pvt, C, 8th NJ Inf, 1-7-1902. Cedar Hill Cemetery, East Millstone, Somerset County.

GREEN*, AARON Pvt, D, 13th NJ Inf, 4-23-1890. St. Mary's Cemetery, East Orange, Essex County.

GREEN, AARON L. 1918. Princeton Cemetery, Princeton, Mercer County.

GREEN, ALEXANDER 10-8-1893. Baptist Church Cemetery, Haddonfield, Camden County.

GREEN, ALEXANDER Sgt, I, 14th NJ Inf, [Killed in action at Monocacy, MD.] 7-9-1864. Presbyterian Church Cemetery, Ewing, Mercer County.

GREEN, ALFRED Pvt, C, 1st NJ Cav, 5-17-1909. Evergreen Cemetery, Lumberton, Burlington County.

GREEN, ALFRED Pvt, F, 37th NJ Inf, 7-26-1905. Presbyterian Church Cemetery, Bridgeton, Cumberland County.

GREEN, AMER I. Pvt, U.S. Marine Corps, DoD Unknown. New Camden Cemetery, Camden, Camden County.

GREEN, ANDREW Pvt, A, 35th NJ Inf, 10-2-1888. New Camden Cemetery, Camden, Camden County.

GREEN, ANDREW Corp, A, 1st U.S. CT, 9-23-1896. Rosedale Cemetery, Orange, Essex County.

Our Brothers Gone Before

GREEN, AUGUSTUS P. Capt, A, 5th NY Cav, DoD Unknown. Cedar Lawn Cemetery, Paterson, Passaic County.

GREEN, BENJAMIN C. Pvt, A, 6th U.S. CT, 4-16-1913. Greenwood Cemetery, Pleasantville, Atlantic County.

GREEN, CHARLES Sgt, G, 22nd NJ Inf, 1919. Harleigh Cemetery, Camden, Camden County.

GREEN, CHARLES Fireman, U.S. Navy, USS Union, 9-9-1895. Christ Church Cemetery, Morgan, Middlesex County.

GREEN, CHARLES 4-4-1906. Presbyterian Church Cemetery, Kingston, Somerset County.

GREEN, CHARLES A. Pvt, A, 6th U.S. CT, 1914. Bordentown/Old St. Mary's Catholic Cemetery, Bordentown, Burlington County.

GREEN, CHARLES B. Pvt, G, 6th NJ Inf, 10-8-1886. Evergreen Cemetery, Camden, Camden County.

GREEN, CHARLES E Pvt, G, 10th MA Inf, 3-28-1907. Oak Hill Cemetery, Vineland, Cumberland County.

GREEN, CHARLES G. Pvt, A, 34th NJ Inf, 2-11-1904. New Camden Cemetery, Camden, Camden County.

GREEN*, CHARLES H. Pvt, U.S. Marine Corps, 2-13-1924. Evergreen Cemetery, Camden, Camden County.

GREEN, CHARLES H. Musc, E, PA Emerg NJ Militia, 4-28-1907. Evergreen Cemetery, Morristown, Morris County.

GREEN, CHESTER Pvt, E, 24th NJ Inf, 10-27-1895. Eglington Cemetery, Clarksboro, Gloucester County.

GREEN, CHRISTIAN Pvt, I, 1st NJ Cav, [Died at Newark, NJ.] 6-29-1864. Fairmount Cemetery, Newark, Essex County.

GREEN, CLARENCE (aka: Green, Clarendo) Pvt, C, 28th NJ Inf, [Cenotaph. Killed in action at Fredericksburg, VA.] 12-13-1862. 1st Baptist Church Cemetery, Stelton, Middlesex County.

GREEN, CLARENCE W. Pvt, D, 185th NY Inf, [Wounded 3-29-1865 at Quaker Road, VA.] 2-25-1919. Bayview-New York Bay Cemetery, Jersey City, Hudson County.

GREEN, CLARENDO (see: Green, Clarence) 1st Baptist Church Cemetery, Stelton, Middlesex County.

GREEN, DANIEL Pvt, A, 34th NJ Inf, 8-19-1901. Siloam Cemetery, Vineland, Cumberland County.

GREEN, DANIEL 11-28-1892. Methodist Church Cemetery, Liberty, Warren County.

GREEN, DENNIS Pvt, E, 23rd NJ Inf, 9-11-1898. St. Mary's Cemetery, Hainesport, Burlington County.

GREEN, EDWARD H. 1st Lt, C, 9th NJ Inf, 1924. Friends/Methodist-Episcopal Cemetery, Pedricktown, Salem County.

GREEN, EDWIN D. Pvt, A, 3rd NJ Cav, 2-22-1870. Vail Presbyterian Cemetery, Parsippany, Morris County.

GREEN, ELDRIDGE Pvt, I, 3rd NJ Militia, 3-30-1898. Rosemont Cemetery, Rosemont, Hunterdon County.

GREEN, ELDRIDGE C. Pvt, E, 31st NJ Inf, 8-6-1928. Prospect Hill Cemetery, Flemington, Hunterdon County.

GREEN, EVIN JACKSON Pvt, A, 15th NJ Inf, [Died of diarrhea at Portsmouth Grove, RI.] 5-14-1864. Methodist-Episcopal Church Cemetery, Sergeantsville, Hunterdon County.

GREEN, FRANCIS M. Pvt, B, 34th NC Inf (CSA), [Wounded 6-27-1862 at Gaines' Mill, VA. Captured 7-1-1863 at Gettysburg, PA.] 9-21-1863. Finn's Point National Cemetery, Pennsville, Salem County.

GREEN*, FRANCIS W. Pvt, E, 25th NY Inf, 6-21-1901. Fairmount Cemetery, Newark, Essex County.

New Jersey Civil War Burials

GREEN*, FREDERICK Pvt, F, 5th NJ Inf, 10-2-1875. Chickory Chapel Baptist Church Cemetery, Elk, Gloucester County.

GREEN, GARRET C. Pvt, U.S. Marine Corps, USS Susquehanna, 1916. Fairview Cemetery, Fairview, Monmouth County.

GREEN, GEORGE Pvt, K, 23rd NJ Inf, 8-19-1898. Batsto/Pleasant Mills Methodist Church Cemetery, Pleasant Mills, Atlantic County.

GREEN*, GEORGE Seaman, U.S. Navy, USS Vanderbilt, 3-25-1897. Rosedale Cemetery, Orange, Essex County.

GREEN, GEORGE GILL 1925. Eglington Cemetery, Clarksboro, Gloucester County.

GREEN*, GEORGE H. Capt, A, 29th NJ Inf, 6-30-1914. Old 1st Methodist Church Cemetery, West Long Branch, Monmouth County.

GREEN, GEORGE W. Pvt, C, 88th PA Inf, 6-23-1914. Oak Grove Cemetery, Hammonton, Atlantic County.

GREEN, GEORGE W. Pvt, F, 5th NJ Inf, 1917. Chestnut Grove Cemetery, Elmer, Salem County.

GREEN, HENRY Pvt, A, 38th NJ Inf, 12-20-1872. Old 1st Methodist Church Cemetery, West Long Branch, Monmouth County.

GREEN, HENRY A. Pvt, E, 31st NJ Inf, 1-4-1917. New Somerville Cemetery, Somerville, Somerset County.

GREEN, HOWARD (aka: Howard, Greene) Pvt, C, 51st GA Inf (CSA), 9-9-1863. Finn's Point National Cemetery, Pennsville, Salem County.

GREEN, J. Pvt, B, 9th (Ward's) TN Cav (CSA), 4-6-1864. Finn's Point National Cemetery, Pennsville, Salem County.

GREEN*, JACOB Pvt, I, 5th NJ Inf, 9-15-1890. Methodist Church Cemetery, Pemberton, Burlington County.

GREEN, JAMES Wagonmaster, U.S. Army, 1863. Old 1st Methodist Church Cemetery, West Long Branch, Monmouth County.

GREEN, JAMES 6-29-1892. Rosedale Cemetery, Orange, Essex County.

GREEN, JAMES F. 2nd Lt, G, 31st NJ Inf, 10-15-1901. Fairview Cemetery, Columbia, Warren County.

GREEN, JAMES H. 1904. Presbyterian Cemetery, Springfield, Union County.

GREEN, JAMES K. Pvt, H, 25th NY Cav, 2-9-1907. United Methodist Church Cemetery, Willow Grove, Salem County.

GREEN, JAMES O. 11-24-1916. Old 1st Methodist Church Cemetery, West Long Branch, Monmouth County.

GREEN, JAMES W. Pvt, M, 2nd FL Inf (CSA), [Captured 7-3-1863 at Gettysburg, PA. Died of disease.] 4-20-1864. Finn's Point National Cemetery, Pennsville, Salem County.

GREEN*, JEREMIAH M. 2nd Lt, 13th Btty, IN Light Art, 10-22-1889. Fairmount Cemetery, Newark, Essex County.

GREEN, JOEL 7-31-1913. Hoboken Cemetery, North Bergen, Hudson County.

GREEN, JOHN Pvt, G, 11th NJ Inf, 9-24-1924. Methodist Church Cemetery, Pemberton, Burlington County.

GREEN, JOHN Pvt, A, 3rd NJ Inf, 1913. United Methodist Church Cemetery, Port Elizabeth, Cumberland County.

GREEN, JOHN Pvt, I, 48th GA Inf (CSA), [Captured 7-2-1863 at Gettysburg, PA. Died of smallpox.] 11-27-1863. Finn's Point National Cemetery, Pennsville, Salem County.

GREEN, JOHN G. 1913. Methodist-Episcopal Cemetery, Whitehouse, Hunterdon County.

GREEN, JOHN H. Corp, K, 8th U.S. CT, 6-19-1918. Zion AME Church Cemetery, Marshalltown, Salem County.

GREEN, JOHN H. Pvt, G, 29th CT Inf, 3-24-1903. Evergreen Cemetery, Hillside, Union County.

GREEN, JOHN HALE 3-27-1909. Riverview Cemetery, Trenton, Mercer County.

Our Brothers Gone Before

GREEN, JOHN J. Musc, 8th NJ Inf Band 1909. Mount Hope Presbyterian Cemetery, Lambertville, Hunterdon County.

GREEN, JOHN R. Pvt, K, 8th U.S. CT, 12-7-1888. Johnson Cemetery, Camden, Camden County.

GREEN, JOHN S. Pvt, A, 15th NJ Inf, 8-6-1927. Arlington Cemetery, Kearny, Hudson County.

GREEN, JOHN W. Pvt, I, 33rd NJ Inf, 8-1-1917. Fairmount Cemetery, Newark, Essex County.

GREEN, JOHN WESLEY Pvt, G, 22nd NJ Inf, 3-15-1888. Princeton Cemetery, Princeton, Mercer County.

GREEN, JOSEPH Seaman, U.S. Navy, USS Franklin, 3-1 6-1924. Old St. Mary's Cemetery, Gloucester City, Camden County.

GREEN, JOSEPH H. Pvt, H, 4th NJ Inf, 1911. Methodist Church Cemetery, Everittstown, Hunterdon County.

GREEN, LEWIS H. Pvt, E, 29th U.S. CT, 4-6-1936. Mount Peace Cemetery, Lawnside, Camden County.

GREEN, LORENZO Pvt, B, 7th NJ Inf, 11-9-1928. Mount Pleasant Cemetery, Millville, Cumberland County.

GREEN, MARTIN LUTHER 7-5-1904. Maplewood Cemetery, Freehold, Monmouth County.

GREEN, MOSES W. Pvt, G, 5th NJ Inf, 5-1-1896. Fairmount Cemetery, Newark, Essex County.

GREEN, N.M. Pvt, C, 21st NC Inf (CSA), [Captured 7-3-1863 at Gettysburg, PA. Died of scurvy.] 1-5-1864. Finn's Point National Cemetery, Pennsville, Salem County.

GREEN, NATHANIEL Pvt, C, 196th PA Inf, 2-5-1916. Chestnut Grove Cemetery, Elmer, Salem County.

GREEN, NATHANIEL (SR.) Pvt, A, 1st NJ Inf, 3-6-1904. Evergreen Cemetery, Hillside, Union County.

GREEN, NEHEMIAH Musc, 8th NJ Inf Band 9-30-1892. Holcomb-Riverview Cemetery, Lambertville, Hunterdon County.

GREEN, PETER Pvt, C, 10th NJ Inf, 1-22-1894. Methodist-Episcopal Cemetery, Whitehouse, Hunterdon County.

GREEN, PETER D. Pvt, H, 21st NJ Inf, 1873. Princeton Cemetery, Princeton, Mercer County.

GREEN, RICHARD Coal Passer, U.S. Navy, USS Pink, 8-23-1907. Mount Peace Cemetery, Lawnside, Camden County.

GREEN, ROBERT Pvt, E, PA Emerg NJ Militia, 1928. Boonton Cemetery, Boonton, Morris County.

GREEN, SAMUEL Pvt, C, 25th U.S. CT, [Wounded in action.] 3-5-1899. Hillside Cemetery, Scotch Plains, Union County.

GREEN, SAMUEL S. Pvt, D, 12th NJ Inf, 1875. Methodist-Episcopal Cemetery, Whitehouse, Hunterdon County.

GREEN, THEODORE J. 1st Lt, I, 14th NJ Inf, [Killed in action at Opequan, VA.] 9-19-1864. Presbyterian Church Cemetery, Ewing, Mercer County.

GREEN, THOMAS 1907. 1st Baptist Church Cemetery, Woodstown, Salem County.

GREEN, THOMAS S. Pvt, K, 12th NJ Inf, DoD Unknown. 1st United Methodist Church Cemetery, Bridgeton, Cumberland County.

GREEN, TIMOTHY Pvt, H, 3rd VT Inf, [Died of disease.] 8-21-1862. Fairmount Cemetery, Newark, Essex County.

GREEN, WESLEY B. 1919. Methodist Church Cemetery, Liberty, Warren County.

GREEN, WILLIAM Farrier, C, 1st NJ Cav, 1-5-1904. Cedar Grove Cemetery, Gloucester City, Camden County.

GREEN, WILLIAM Pvt, A, 22nd U.S. CT, 3-25-1883. Johnson Cemetery, Camden, Camden County.

GREEN, WILLIAM Pvt, C, 10th Confederate States Cav (CSA), 2-20-1865. Finn's Point National Cemetery, Pennsville, Salem County.
GREEN, WILLIAM F. Pvt, K, 33rd NJ Inf, [Killed in action at Peach Tree Creek, GA.] 7-20-1864. Midvale Cemetery, Midvale, Passaic County.
GREEN, WILLIAM H. Pvt, A, 8th NJ Inf, 8-14-1936. Rosedale Cemetery, Orange, Essex County.
GREEN, WILLIAM H. Pvt, C, 82nd NY Inf, 2-7-1905. Arlington Cemetery, Kearny, Hudson County.
GREEN*, WILLIAM H. Corp, E, 2nd NJ Inf, 6-14-1908. Holcomb-Riverview Cemetery, Lambertville, Hunterdon County.
GREEN, WILLIAM H. Pvt, A, 62nd NY Inf, [Wounded in action.] 2-3-1917. Evergreen Cemetery, Hillside, Union County.
GREEN, WILLIAM J. Pvt, I, 13th AL Inf (CSA), 12-24-1863. Finn's Point National Cemetery, Pennsville, Salem County.
GREEN, WILLIAM M. Pvt, B, 25th U.S. CT, 5-18-1926. Union Bethel Cemetery, Erma, Cape May County.
GREENBALGH, JAMES __, __, 13th __ Inf, 5-20-1895. Palisade Cemetery, North Bergen, Hudson County.
GREENBANCK, JOHN (see: Greenbank, John) Bloomfield Cemetery, Bloomfield, Essex County.
GREENBANK, JOHN (aka: Greenbanck, John) Pvt, U.S. Marine Corps, USS Seneca, 1909. Bloomfield Cemetery, Bloomfield, Essex County.
GREENBERG, SOLOMON 1-23-1897. B'nai Abraham Cemetery, Newark, Essex County.
GREENE, ABRAHAM 8-1-1902. Berlin Cemetery, Berlin, Camden County.
GREENE, JAMES GARDNER Pvt, F, 118th NY Inf, 7-9-1924. Evergreen Cemetery, Hillside, Union County.
GREENER, IGNATZ (aka: Greiner, Enos) Pvt, B, 33rd NJ Inf, 5-21-1875. Fairmount Cemetery, Newark, Essex County.
GREENGROVE*, MARK Pvt, E, 8th NJ Inf, 7-22-1898. Fairmount Cemetery, Newark, Essex County.
GREENHALGH, JAMES (aka: Greenly, James) Pvt, C, 3rd NJ Cav, 8-9-1896. Hoboken Cemetery, North Bergen, Hudson County.
GREENLEAF*, ABRAHAM D. Pvt, A, 2nd NJ Cav, DoD Unknown. English Neighborhood Reformed Church Cemetery, Ridgefield, Bergen County.
GREENLEAF, ROBERT Pvt, I, 21st NJ Inf, DoD Unknown. English Neighborhood Reformed Church Cemetery, Ridgefield, Bergen County.
GREENLY, JAMES (see: Greenhalgh, James) Hoboken Cemetery, North Bergen, Hudson County.
GREENSWICK, WILLIAM Pvt, D, 5th NJ Inf, [Died of diarrhea at Newark, NJ.] 10-8-1864. Fairmount Cemetery, Newark, Essex County.
GREENWALT, CHRISTOPHER Pvt, I, 35th NJ Inf, 4-26-1900. Holy Sepulchre Cemetery, East Orange, Essex County.
GREENWOOD, BERRY (aka: Berry, Greene) Pvt, A, 41st U.S. CT, DoD Unknown. Bethel AME Cemetery, Cookstown, Burlington County.
GREENWOOD, CHARLES Pvt, K, 26th NJ Inf, 6-9-1893. Fairmount Cemetery, Newark, Essex County.
GREENWOOD, GEORGE W. Actg 3rd Asst Eng, U.S. Navy, USS Circassian, 12-12-1875. Cedar Lawn Cemetery, Paterson, Passaic County.
GREENWOOD, RICHARD J. Pvt, A, 3rd PA Cav, 11-3-1892. Cedar Grove Cemetery, Gloucester City, Camden County.
GREENWOOD, WILLIAM Pvt, G, 10th NJ Inf, 11-11-1905. Phillipsburg Cemetery, Phillipsburg, Warren County.
GREENWOOD, WILLIAM A. 1899. Tennent Church Cemetery, Tennent, Monmouth County.

Our Brothers Gone Before

GREER, JOHN H. (aka: Grear, John H.) Pvt, G, 8th NY State Militia, 7-3-1915. Cedar Lawn Cemetery, Paterson, Passaic County.

GREER, JOSEPH (aka: Greer, Joshua) Coal Heaver, U.S. Navy, USS New Ironsides, 3-26-1903. Macphelah Cemetery, North Bergen, Hudson County.

GREER, JOSHUA (see: Greer, Joseph) Macphelah Cemetery, North Bergen, Hudson County.

GREER, R. Pvt, L, 2nd FL Inf (CSA), [Captured 7-5-1863 at Gettysburg, PA. Died of disease.] 11-24-1864. Finn's Point National Cemetery, Pennsville, Salem County.

GREER, THOMAS H. Pvt, C, 13th NJ Inf, DoD Unknown. Laurel Grove Cemetery, Totowa, Passaic County.

GREER, WILLIAM F. Pvt, E, 9th AR Inf (CSA), [Captured 5-17-1863 at Champion's Hill, MS. Died of diarrhea.] 9-24-1863. Finn's Point National Cemetery, Pennsville, Salem County.

GREFE, PETER N. Pvt, G, 1st NY Mounted Rifles, 3-28-1914. Hoboken Cemetery, North Bergen, Hudson County.

GREFF, BENJAMIN (see: Graaf, Benjamin Gottlieb) Woodland Cemetery, Newark, Essex County.

GREGG*, ABRAHAM Coal Heaver, U.S. Navy, USS New Hampshire, 3-3-1908. Berlin Cemetery, Berlin, Camden County.

GREGG, EDWARD A. Corp, C, 15th PA Inf, 5-29-1930. Mount Hope Presbyterian Cemetery, Lambertville, Hunterdon County.

GREGG, THOMAS Sgt, I, 104th NY Inf, 3-29-1915. Harleigh Cemetery, Camden, Camden County.

GREGLETTI*, RICHARD D. Corp, G, 7th NJ Inf, 1-13-1886. Mount Holly Cemetery, Mount Holly, Burlington County.

GREGOR, RUDOLPH (see: Gregorovius, Richard Rudolph) Flower Hill Cemetery, North Bergen, Hudson County.

GREGOROVIUS, RICHARD RUDOLPH (aka: Gregor, Rudolph) Pvt, E, 28th NY National Guard, 8-27-1916. Flower Hill Cemetery, North Bergen, Hudson County.

GREGORY, CHARLES Sgt, G, 38th NJ Inf, 3-10-1893. St. Peter's Cemetery, New Brunswick, Middlesex County.

GREGORY, CHARLES (see: Gregory, Frederick J.) Deckertown-Union Cemetery, Papakating, Sussex County.

GREGORY, FREDERICK J. (aka: Gregory, Charles) Pvt, I, 11th NY Inf, [Wounded 7-21-1861 at 1st Bull Run, VA.] 9-29-1908. Deckertown-Union Cemetery, Papakating, Sussex County.

GREGORY*, LEWIS F. Pvt, M, 2nd NJ Cav, 12-15-1863. Evergreen Cemetery, Morristown, Morris County.

GREGORY, MILTON A. Corp, E, 31st NJ Inf, 2-16-1910. Fairmount Cemetery, Newark, Essex County.

GREGORY, PATRICK Pvt, F, 28th NJ Inf, 8-8-1868. St. Peter's Cemetery, New Brunswick, Middlesex County.

GREGORY, THOMAS R. Musc, A, 15th NJ Inf, 1905. Baptist/Evergreen Methodist Cemetery, Plainfield, Union County.

GREIB, ANDREAS 1st Sgt, G, 12th MO Inf, 2-5-1905. Mount Prospect Cemetery, Neptune, Monmouth County.

GREIB, GEORGE (aka: Grieb, George) Corp, B, 23rd NJ Inf, 12-7-1891. Bordentown/Old St. Mary's Catholic Cemetery, Bordentown, Burlington County.

GREINER, ENOS (see: Greener, Ignatz) Fairmount Cemetery, Newark, Essex County.

GREINER, FREDERICK Pvt, A, 8th NJ Inf, 4-17-1880. Grove Church Cemetery, North Bergen, Hudson County.

GREINOR, GEORGE Pvt, B, 33rd NJ Inf, 5-4-1880. Fairmount Cemetery, Newark, Essex County.

New Jersey Civil War Burials

GREPE, CHRISTIAN (see: Grebe, Christian) Fairmount Cemetery, Newark, Essex County.
GRESSETT, WILLIAM Sgt, C, 10th NJ Inf, 10-15-1890. New Camden Cemetery, Camden, Camden County.
GRETHER, LUTHER (see: Grethler, Lutiker) Princeton Cemetery, Princeton, Mercer County.
GRETHLER, LUTIKER (aka: Grether, Luther) Pvt, G, 22nd NJ Inf, 1920. Princeton Cemetery, Princeton, Mercer County.
GREY, HENRY (see: Guy, Harry) New Camden Cemetery, Camden, Camden County.
GRIBBLE, JOHN Corp, C, 42nd NY Inf, 3-13-1906. Presbyterian Church Cemetery, Rockaway, Morris County.
GRICE, JOSHUA C. Corp, F, 12th NJ Inf, 10-13-1924. Chestnut Grove Cemetery, Elmer, Salem County.
GRIEB, GEORGE (see: Greib, George) Bordentown/Old St. Mary's Catholic Cemetery, Bordentown, Burlington County.
GRIEBEL, JOHN B. Pvt, D, 12th NJ Inf, 7-26-1900. Cedar Lawn Cemetery, Paterson, Passaic County.
GRIESER, JOHN BLASIUS Pvt, U.S. Marine Corps, 10-16-1904. Holy Sepulchre Cemetery, East Orange, Essex County.
GRIEVES, ROBERT 5-13-1879. Rahway Cemetery, Rahway, Union County.
GRIFFEE*, JAMES Pvt, C, 20th PA Cav, 12-4-1917. Arlington Cemetery, Pennsauken, Camden County.
GRIFFEE, JAMES DoD Unknown. Old Camden Cemetery, Camden, Camden County.
GRIFFEN, JOEL Pvt, H, 5th U.S. Cav, DoD Unknown. Elmwood Cemetery, New Brunswick, Middlesex County.
GRIFFEN, MICAJAH (aka: Griffith, Micajah) Capt, A, 9th (Ward's) TN Cav (CSA), 8-4-1864. Finn's Point National Cemetery, Pennsville, Salem County.
GRIFFEY, SAMUEL (see: Griffith, Samuel) Evergreen Cemetery, Lumberton, Burlington County.
GRIFFEY, SAMUEL J. Pvt, F, 2nd NJ Cav, 12-2-1878. Old Camden Cemetery, Camden, Camden County.
GRIFFIN, ALLEN S. Pvt, Btty F, 6th NY Heavy Art, 10-12-1883. Old Hook Cemetery, Westwood, Bergen County.
GRIFFIN, CARLETON L. 12-9-1918. Bayview-New York Bay Cemetery, Jersey City, Hudson County.
GRIFFIN, CHARLES DoD Unknown. Cedar Lawn Cemetery, Paterson, Passaic County.
GRIFFIN, CHARLES H. Pvt, 7th, Unattached MA Militia, 4-26-1917. Arlington Cemetery, Kearny, Hudson County.
GRIFFIN, CHRISTIAN Pvt, K, 4th NJ Militia, 12-31-1913. Baptist Cemetery, Burlington, Burlington County.
GRIFFIN, DANIEL D. Landsman, U.S. Navy, USS Princeton, 8-20-1909. Valleau Cemetery, Ridgewood, Bergen County.
GRIFFIN, EDWARD M. Corp, C, 25th NY Cav, 1-16-1896. Jersey City Cemetery, Jersey City, Hudson County.
GRIFFIN, EDWARD PATRICK Musc, C, 2nd NJ Cav, [Cenotaph.] 7-18-1914. Cedar Lawn Cemetery, Paterson, Passaic County.
GRIFFIN, GABRIEL B. Pvt, B, 5th Bttn AL Inf (CSA), 10-15-1863. Finn's Point National Cemetery, Pennsville, Salem County.
GRIFFIN, GEORGE E. Pvt, A, 11th NJ Inf, 7-20-1865. Riverview Cemetery, Trenton, Mercer County.
GRIFFIN, GEORGE W. Pvt, I, 26th NJ Inf, 1-23-1921. Bloomfield Cemetery, Bloomfield, Essex County.
GRIFFIN*, JACOB W. Pvt, I, 9th NY Inf, 4-19-1914. Masonic Cemetery, Barnegat, Ocean County.

Our Brothers Gone Before

GRIFFIN*, JOHN Pvt, C, 90th IL Inf, 12-9-1910. Holy Name Cemetery, Jersey City, Hudson County.
GRIFFIN*, JOHN C. Landsman, U.S. Navy, USS Mohawk, 9-29-1897. Mount Zion AME Cemetery, Swedesboro, Gloucester County.
GRIFFIN, JOHN S. Pvt, D, 13th NJ Inf, 8-15-1899. Fairmount Cemetery, Newark, Essex County.
GRIFFIN, LAWRENCE Pvt, G, 20th MA Inf, [Wounded 9-17-1862 at Antietam, MD.] 11-8-1914. Grove Church Cemetery, North Bergen, Hudson County.
GRIFFIN, LAWRENCE Pvt, B, 39th NJ Inf, 1-9-1878. Holy Sepulchre Cemetery, East Orange, Essex County.
GRIFFIN, MICHAEL J. Pvt, C, 33rd NJ Inf, 12-21-1897. Holy Name Cemetery, Jersey City, Hudson County.
GRIFFIN, SAMUEL Pvt, I, 26th NJ Inf, 10-19-1902. Fairmount Cemetery, Newark, Essex County.
GRIFFIN, THOMAS Pvt, G, 29th U.S. CT, 6-26-1907. Mount Zion Cemetery, Lower Cape May, Cape May County.
GRIFFIN, URIAH (aka: Giffin, Uriah) Corp, Btty E, 1st RI Light Art, 10-5-1886. 1st Baptist Church Cemetery, Florence, Burlington County.
GRIFFIN, WILLIAM Pvt, F, 26th NJ Inf, 11-21-1889. Bloomfield Cemetery, Bloomfield, Essex County.
GRIFFIN, WILLIAM 5-20-1935. Fairmount Cemetery, Newark, Essex County.
GRIFFIN*, WILLIAM H. Pvt, A, 12th NJ Inf, 8-26-1895. Evergreen Cemetery, Camden, Camden County.
GRIFFIN, WILLIAM H. QM Sgt, A, 2nd NJ Cav, 12-2-1906. Bayview-New York Bay Cemetery, Jersey City, Hudson County.
GRIFFIN, WILLIAM S. Corp, G, 69th NY Inf, 11-24-1936. Greengrove Cemetery, Keyport, Monmouth County.
GRIFFING, AUGUSTUS W. Pvt, F, 7th NJ Inf, 2-3-1918. Rosedale Cemetery, Orange, Essex County.
GRIFFING, AUGUSTUS W. DoD Unknown. Jersey City Cemetery, Jersey City, Hudson County.
GRIFFIS, GEORGE W. Corp, D, 53rd NC Inf (CSA), [Wounded and captured 7-3-1863 at Gettysburg, PA. Died of erysipelas.] 4-20-1864. Finn's Point National Cemetery, Pennsville, Salem County.
GRIFFITH, BENJAMIN S. Pvt, B, 2nd NJ Cav, DoD Unknown. Baptist Church Cemetery, Flemington, Hunterdon County.
GRIFFITH, CALIBORN D. Pvt, D, 28th Consolidated TN Inf (CSA), 3-27-1864. Finn's Point National Cemetery, Pennsville, Salem County.
GRIFFITH, CHARLES Pvt, H, 8th NJ Inf, 9-3-1918. Baptist Cemetery, Vincentown, Burlington County.
GRIFFITH, CHARLES E. Pvt, B, 37th NY National Guard, 8-29-1889. Hillside Cemetery, Lyndhurst, Bergen County.
GRIFFITH, DENNIS (aka: Griffith, William) Pvt, B, 60th (Crawford's) TN Mtd Inf (CSA), [Captured 5-17-1863 at Big Black River Bridge, MS.] 8-16-1863. Finn's Point National Cemetery, Pennsville, Salem County.
GRIFFITH, EBENEZER Pvt, D, 10th NJ Inf, [Died of typhoid at Frederick City, MD.] 8-26-1864. New Presbyterian Cemetery, Hanover, Morris County.
GRIFFITH*, ENOCH S. Musc, Btty L, 6th NY Heavy Art, 2-22-1887. Rose Hill Cemetery, Matawan, Monmouth County.
GRIFFITH, GEORGE Capt, I, 2nd NJ Inf, 1-5-1875. Cedar Lawn Cemetery, Paterson, Passaic County.
GRIFFITH, JAMES Pvt, Btty G, Young's Ind PA Art, [Died at Fort Delaware.] 10-10-1862. Finn's Point National Cemetery, Pennsville, Salem County.

New Jersey Civil War Burials

GRIFFITH, JAMES W. Pvt, G, 62nd NY Inf, [Wounded 5-5-1862 at Williamsburg, VA.] 12-25-1887. Elmwood Cemetery, New Brunswick, Middlesex County.
GRIFFITH, JAMES W. Pvt, D, 31st GA Inf (CSA), [Captured 5-12-1864 at Spotsylvania CH, VA. Died of smallpox.] 1-1-1865. Finn's Point National Cemetery, Pennsville, Salem County.
GRIFFITH, JOHN S. Corp, E, 1st NJ Cav, 4-24-1894. Baptist Church Cemetery, Canton, Salem County.
GRIFFITH, M. Pvt, I, 50th VA Inf (CSA), [Captured 7-4-1863 at Gettysburg, PA. Died of fever.] 10-22-1863. Finn's Point National Cemetery, Pennsville, Salem County.
GRIFFITH, NATHAN RAYMOND W. 1st Sgt, F, 14th CT Inf, 1-4-1932. Presbyterian/Methodist-Episcopal Cemetery, Succasunna, Morris County.
GRIFFITH, SAMUEL Pvt, Btty E, 2nd PA Heavy Art, 10-23-1886. Union Cemetery, Gloucester City, Camden County.
GRIFFITH, SAMUEL (aka: Griffey, Samuel) Pvt, F, 2nd NJ Cav, 6-23-1913. Evergreen Cemetery, Lumberton, Burlington County.
GRIFFITH*, SMITH Pvt, Btty M, 7th NY Heavy Art, [Wounded 6-9-1863 at Yorktown, VA.] 1902. Methodist Church Cemetery, Eldora, Cape May County.
GRIFFITH*, THOMAS Pvt, B, 124th NY Inf, [Wounded 10-27-1864 at Boydton Plank Road, VA.] 2-3-1896. Fairmount Cemetery, Newark, Essex County.
GRIFFITH, WILLIAM Seaman, U.S. Navy, 11-23-1903. Bayview-New York Bay Cemetery, Jersey City, Hudson County.
GRIFFITH, WILLIAM (see: Griffith, Dennis) Finn's Point National Cemetery, Pennsville, Salem County.
GRIFFITH, WILLIAM H. Corp, A, 13th NJ Inf, 4-13-1905. Fairmount Cemetery, Newark, Essex County.
GRIFFITH*, WILLIAM P. Corp, L, 102nd PA Inf, 2-16-1936. Christ Church Cemetery, Morgan, Middlesex County.
GRIFFITHS, E.M. Pvt, H, PA Emerg NJ Militia, 11-8-1910. Fairmount Cemetery, Newark, Essex County.
GRIFFITHS, HENRY R. Corp, G, 3rd NJ Cav, 1923. Mount Pleasant Cemetery, Millville, Cumberland County.
GRIFFITHS, MAHLON H. Pvt, B, 26th NJ Inf, 1-10-1896. Bloomfield Cemetery, Bloomfield, Essex County.
GRIGG, WILLIAM T. Sgt, H, 192nd PA Inf, 1-15-1904. Evergreen Cemetery, Camden, Camden County.
GRIGGS, ABRAHAM P. Farrier, B, 1st NJ Cav, 10-17-1903. Prospect Hill Cemetery, Flemington, Hunterdon County.
GRIGGS, ALFRED H. Corp, K, 27th NJ Inf, 5-21-1898. Fairmount Cemetery, Newark, Essex County.
GRIGGS, BENJAMIN Pvt, F, 30th NJ Inf, 4-30-1869. Cedar Hill Cemetery, East Millstone, Somerset County.
GRIGGS, GEORGE V. Capt, K, 2nd NY Cav, [Killed in action at Culpepper, VA.] 10-11-1863. Presbyterian Church Cemetery, Newton, Sussex County.
GRIGGS, REUBEN Pvt, B, 28th NJ Inf, 6-6-1919. Brainerd Cemetery, Cranbury, Middlesex County.
GRIGGS, VANWICKLE Pvt, H, 14th NJ Inf, [Cenotaph. Died of diarrhea at Danville Prison, VA.] 12-15-1864. Brainerd Cemetery, Cranbury, Middlesex County.
GRIGGS, WILLIAM F. Pvt, H, 2nd NJ Inf, 9-14-1876. Clinton Cemetery, Irvington, Essex County.
GRIGGS, WILLIAM T. Pvt, K, 93rd IL Inf, 10-14-1887. Dayton Cemetery, Dayton, Middlesex County.
GRIGLIETTI, NOBLE 1st Lt, K, 21st NJ Inf, 11-18-1921. Arlington Cemetery, Kearny, Hudson County.

Our Brothers Gone Before

GRILLS, WILLIAM J. Sgt, E, 1st (Carter's) TN Cav (CSA), 7-5-1864. Finn's Point National Cemetery, Pennsville, Salem County.

GRIMES, JOHN A. Pvt, G, 30th NJ Inf, DoD Unknown. Baptist Church Cemetery, Port Murray, Warren County.

GRIMES, JOSIAH QUINCY Pvt, C, 15th NJ Inf, [Died of diarrhea at Warrenton, VA.] 9-8-1863. Vail Presbyterian Cemetery, Parsippany, Morris County.

GRIMES, ROBERT Pvt, H, 5th LA Inf (CSA), [Captured 7-7-1863 in Washington County, MD. Died of lung inflammation.] 1-28-1864. Finn's Point National Cemetery, Pennsville, Salem County.

GRIMES, THOMAS Pvt, F, 95th NY Inf, 3-2-1900. Holy Sepulchre Cemetery, East Orange, Essex County.

GRIMES, WILLIAM P. Pvt, C, 30th AR Inf (CSA), [Captured 9-11-1863 at White River, AR. Died of scurvy.] 7-12-1864. Finn's Point National Cemetery, Pennsville, Salem County.

GRIMM, CHARLES W. Ordinary Seaman, U.S. Navy, USS Princeton, 11-7-1926. Maple Grove Cemetery, Hackensack, Bergen County.

GRIMM, CHARLES W. 2nd Lt, B, 12th IL Cav, 3-25-1913. Evergreen Cemetery, Camden, Camden County.

GRIMM, LEONARD Pvt, I, 6th U.S. Inf, 11-7-1899. Fairmount Cemetery, Newark, Essex County.

GRIMSTEAD*, JAMES A. Pvt, C, 14th NJ Inf, 9-7-1925. Hillside Cemetery, Metuchen, Middlesex County.

GRINAGE, LEVI Pvt, E, 22nd U.S. CT, 3-16-1895. Chestnut Cemetery, Greenwich, Cumberland County.

GRINAGE, PETER D. Seaman, U.S. Navy, USS Glaucus, 6-20-1899. Presbyterian Church Cemetery, Bridgeton, Cumberland County.

GRINDER, JOHN F. Pvt, E, 10th NJ Inf, [Died of phthisis at Millville, NJ.] 9-3-1863. Mount Pleasant Cemetery, Millville, Cumberland County.

GRINDER, NICHOLAS (see: Griner, Nicholas) Mount Pleasant Cemetery, Millville, Cumberland County.

GRINDROD*, JAMES Corp, F, 22nd NJ Inf, 10-3-1891. Riverview Cemetery, Trenton, Mercer County.

GRINER, HENRY R. Pvt, H, 24th NJ Inf, 2-16-1888. Presbyterian Church Cemetery, Bridgeton, Cumberland County.

GRINER*, NICHOLAS (aka: Grinder, Nicholas) Pvt, C, 38th NJ Inf, 1929. Mount Pleasant Cemetery, Millville, Cumberland County.

GRISCHELE, RUDOLPH Gunner, U.S. Navy, [Wounded in action.] 9-3-1903. Hoboken Cemetery, North Bergen, Hudson County.

GRISCOM, ALEXANDER H. Pvt, H, 23rd NJ Inf, 10-22-1909. Harleigh Cemetery, Camden, Camden County.

GRISCOM, ELLWOOD 1st Lt, E, 12th NJ Inf, 1930. Friends Cemetery, Moorestown, Burlington County.

GRISCOM, ROBERT Pvt, D, 23rd NJ Inf, 8-18-1897. Methodist-Episcopal Cemetery, Pointville, Burlington County.

GRISCOMB, JOHN (see: Grissom, John) Baptist/St. Andrew's Cemetery, Mount Holly, Burlington County.

GRISHAM, G.W. Pvt, A, 18th GA Inf (CSA), [Captured 7-3-1863 at Gettysburg, PA. Died of lung inflammation.] 4-1-1864. Finn's Point National Cemetery, Pennsville, Salem County.

GRISHAM, JOHN M. Pvt, K, 43rd TN Inf (CSA), [5th East Tennessee Volunteers (Gillespie's).] 7-12-1864. Finn's Point National Cemetery, Pennsville, Salem County.

GRISSEL, PHILIP (see: Geisel, Philip) Weehawken Cemetery, North Bergen, Hudson County.

New Jersey Civil War Burials

GRISSOM, JOHN (aka: Griscomb, John) Pvt, I, 5th NJ Inf, 9-17-1908. Baptist/St. Andrew's Cemetery, Mount Holly, Burlington County.

GRISSOM, THOMAS Pvt, I, 23rd NJ Inf, 6-23-1875. Mount Holly Cemetery, Mount Holly, Burlington County.

GRISWOLD, ALEXANDER (see: Low, Louis J.) Arlington Cemetery, Kearny, Hudson County.

GRISWOLD, JOHN MILTON Capt, B, 44th MA Inf, 1925. Tennent Church Cemetery, Tennent, Monmouth County.

GRISWOLD, JOSEPH Pvt, A, 11th IN Inf, 1892. Fairview Cemetery, Wantage, Sussex County.

GROAT, FREDERICK THOMAS Pvt, F, 29th NJ Inf, 7-26-1867. Halsey Cemetery, Belford, Monmouth County.

GROAT, HENRY WILLIAM Pvt, F, 29th NJ Inf, 7-29-1867. Halsey Cemetery, Belford, Monmouth County.

GROAT, JAMES ELLIOTT Pvt, E, 84th IL Inf, 5-9-1936. New York/New Jersey Crematory Cemetery, North Bergen, Hudson County.

GROBELS, WILHELM Pvt, Btty A, 1st NJ Light Art, 1-29-1869. Flower Hill Cemetery, North Bergen, Hudson County.

GROBLER*, AUGUSTUS W. 1st Lt, H, 34th NJ Inf, 5-20-1901. Baptist Cemetery, Pemberton, Burlington County.

GROCE*, WILLIAM H. Pvt, Btty H, 11th U.S. CHA, 1-3-1900. Beverly National Cemetery, Edgewater Park, Burlington County.

GROELL*, CHARLES G. Corp, B, 114th OH Inf, 3-16-1917. St. Mary's Cemetery, East Orange, Essex County.

GROENDYKE, DANIEL J. Corp, H, 2nd NJ Cav, 9-29-1887. Mansfield/Washington Cemetery, Washington, Warren County.

GROESSEL, LOUIS Musc, E, 20th NY Inf, [Died of disease.] 3-16-1862. Mount Olivet Cemetery, Newark, Essex County.

GROESSER, GEORGE Corp, G, 20th NY Inf, 9-2-1872. Fairmount Cemetery, Newark, Essex County.

GROFF, CHARLES 6-15-1864. 1st United Methodist Church Cemetery, Salem, Salem County.

GROFF, JOHN H. 1st Sgt, H, 12th NJ Inf, 6-19-1901. Riverview Cemetery, Penns Grove, Salem County.

GROFF, SYLVESTER Corp, E, 31st NJ Inf, 4-2-1920. Mansfield/Washington Cemetery, Washington, Warren County.

GROFT, WILLIAM C. (aka: Graeff, William) 2nd Lt, B, 107th PA Inf, 1916. Baptist Cemetery, Salem, Salem County.

GROGAN, JOHN 1905. Mount Carmel Cemetery, West Long Branch, Monmouth County.

GROGAN, PETER Artificer, A, 1st NY Eng, 7-21-1902. Laurel Hill Cemetery, Burlington, Burlington County.

GROGAN, THOMAS R. Pvt, G, 83rd NY Inf, [Died of wounds received 9-17-1862 at Antietam, MD.] 9-27-1862. Bayview-New York Bay Cemetery, Jersey City, Hudson County.

GROGAN, WILLIAM Pvt, Btty C, 5th U.S. Art, 6-11-1872. Fairmount Cemetery, Newark, Essex County.

GROISSETTE, CHARLES A. 7-19-1925. Evergreen Cemetery, Camden, Camden County.

GROOM, BERNARD A. Pvt, E, 3rd VA Inf (CSA), 1-5-1864. Finn's Point National Cemetery, Pennsville, Salem County.

GROOM, CHARLES W. Pvt, I, 4th NJ Inf, 12-26-1883. Baptist/St. Andrew's Cemetery, Mount Holly, Burlington County.

GROOM, JOSEPH S. Pvt, C, 23rd NJ Inf, 11-30-1912. Baptist/St. Andrew's Cemetery, Mount Holly, Burlington County.

Our Brothers Gone Before

GROOME, EDWARD Pvt, F, 33rd NJ Inf, 4-19-1903. Baptist/St. Andrew's Cemetery, Mount Holly, Burlington County.
GROOME, EDWARD F. 4-29-1908. Fairmount Cemetery, Newark, Essex County.
GROOMS, EDWARD Pvt, B, Purnell Legion MD Inf, 9-3-1863. Finn's Point National Cemetery, Pennsville, Salem County.
GROOT, THEODORE (aka: Groote, Theodore) Pvt, I, 15th ME Inf, 11-26-1912. Mercer Cemetery, Trenton, Mercer County.
GROOTE, THEODORE (see: Groot, Theodore) Mercer Cemetery, Trenton, Mercer County.
GROOVER, JOHN W. (aka: Gruver, John) Pvt, H, 31st NJ Inf, 11-15-1900. Methodist Church Cemetery, Mount Bethel, Warren County.
GROSCUP, ALBANER H. (aka: Grosscup, Albanus) Pvt, F, 5th NJ Inf, 1-19-1904. Baptist Cemetery, Salem, Salem County.
GROSCUP, WILLIAM T. Pvt, A, 24th NJ Inf, 10-17-1879. Baptist Church Cemetery, Canton, Salem County.
GROSER, ALEXANDER T. Pvt, H, 71st NY State Militia, 2-20-1884. Cedar Lawn Cemetery, Paterson, Passaic County.
GROSS, AUGUSTUS Pvt, D, 14th CT Inf, [Wounded 9-17-1862 at Antietam, MD. and 12-13-1862 at Fredericksburg, VA.] 8-22-1896. Christian Church Cemetery, Locktown, Hunterdon County.
GROSS, BALTHAZAR Pvt, H, 1st NJ Cav, 3-5-1908. Arlington Cemetery, Kearny, Hudson County.
GROSS, CONRAD Pvt, K, 3rd NJ Inf, 12-30-1875. Evergreen Cemetery, Hillside, Union County.
GROSS, EUGENE A. 3-14-1900. Hillside Cemetery, Scotch Plains, Union County.
GROSS, ISAIAH Pvt, F, 22nd U.S. CT, 6-18-1889. Mount Peace Cemetery, Lawnside, Camden County.
GROSS, JACOB Pvt, C, 52nd NY Inf, 11-11-1913. 1st Presbyterian Union Cemetery, Ramsey, Bergen County.
GROSS*, JOHN Pvt, B, 97th PA Inf, 3-12-1904. Hillside Cemetery, Oxford, Warren County.
GROSS, JOHN Pvt, I, 47th PA Inf, [Wounded 10-19-1864 at Cedar Creek, VA.] 10-29-1900. Mansfield/Washington Cemetery, Washington, Warren County.
GROSS, JOSEPH Pvt, Btty D, 1st NJ Light Art, 11-27-1897. Oddfellows Cemetery, Burlington, Burlington County.
GROSS, JOSEPH S. Pvt, Btty E, 1st NJ Light Art, 6-24-1915. Mansfield/Washington Cemetery, Washington, Warren County.
GROSSCUP, ALBANUS (see: Groscup, Albaner H.) Baptist Cemetery, Salem, Salem County.
GROSSCUP, EDWARD (see: Grosscup, Eldorando H.) Presbyterian Church Cemetery, Bridgeton, Cumberland County.
GROSSCUP, ELDORANDO H. (aka: Grosscup, Edward) Pvt, F, 3rd NJ Inf, 1925. Presbyterian Church Cemetery, Bridgeton, Cumberland County.
GROSSCUP, ROBERT F. Pvt, A, 24th NJ Inf, 12-1-1907. Baptist Church Cemetery, Canton, Salem County.
GROSSMAN, MARTIN (aka: Grozing, Martin) Sgt, E, 33rd NJ Inf, 3- -1868. Cedar Lawn Cemetery, Paterson, Passaic County.
GROSSMAN, MATTHIAS (see: Grossner, Mattias) Woodland Cemetery, Newark, Essex County.
GROSSMAN, WILHELM (aka: Grassman, William) Pvt, H, 68th NY Inf, [Wounded 8-30-1862 at 2nd Bull Run, VA.] DoD Unknown. Holy Sepulchre Cemetery, East Orange, Essex County.

New Jersey Civil War Burials

GROSSNER, MATTIAS (aka: Grossman, Matthias) Pvt, I, 36th NY Inf, [Wounded 7-1-1862 at Malvern Hill, VA.] 12-27-1918. Woodland Cemetery, Newark, Essex County.

GROSVENOR, CHARLES H. Sgt, H, 13th CT Inf, 4-19-1910. Laurel Grove Cemetery, Totowa, Passaic County.

GROTEGLOSS, WILLIAM G. Pvt, C, 37th NY State Militia, 1908. Cedar Lawn Cemetery, Paterson, Passaic County.

GROTHE, FRANZ (see: Goethe, Franz) Palisade Cemetery, North Bergen, Hudson County.

GROUSER, HENRY (aka: Crosier, Henry) Pvt, K, 30th NJ Inf, 1912. Cedar Hill Cemetery, East Millstone, Somerset County.

GROVENDYKE, ABERNETHY (see: Grundyke, Abernetha) Sandy Ridge Cemetery, Sandy Ridge, Hunterdon County.

GROVER, BARZILLA Pvt, K, 5th NJ Inf, 1907. Methodist-Episcopal Cemetery, Glendola, Monmouth County.

GROVER, CHARLES W. 2nd Lt, A, 9th NJ Inf, 12-1-1927. Elmwood Cemetery, New Brunswick, Middlesex County.

GROVER, CORNELIUS S. Pvt, D, 9th NJ Inf, 10-25-1910. Whitesville Cemetery, Whitesville, Ocean County.

GROVER, EDWARD Pvt, F, 1st NJ Cav, DoD Unknown. Presbyterian Church Cemetery, Andover, Sussex County.

GROVER, EDWARD DoD Unknown. Hardyston Cemetery, North Church, Sussex County.

GROVER, JACOB 3-12-1903. Harmony Methodist Church Cemetery, Stillwater, Sussex County.

GROVER, JAMES W. Pvt, A, 14th NJ Inf, 5-24-1920. Whitesville Cemetery, Whitesville, Ocean County.

GROVER, JAMES W. 8-1-1905. Mount Pleasant Cemetery, Newark, Essex County.

GROVER, JOHN Pvt, F, 1st NJ Cav, 1892. Presbyterian Church Cemetery, Andover, Sussex County.

GROVER, JOHN Sgt, F, 14th NJ Inf, [Wounded deliberately by rebels after capture at Petersburg, VA.] 1-12-1916. Riverview Cemetery, Trenton, Mercer County.

GROVER, JOHN B. Pvt, B, 7th NJ Inf, 2-17-1892. Riverview Cemetery, Trenton, Mercer County.

GROVER*, JOHN B. Pvt, F, 14th NJ Inf, DoD Unknown. Methodist Cemetery, Cassville, Ocean County.

GROVER, JOHN W. Pvt, A, 14th NJ Inf, 10-3-1912. Methodist Cemetery, Southard, Monmouth County.

GROVER, JOHN W. (JR.) Sgt, F, 14th NJ Inf, [Wounded 4-2-1865 at Petersburg, VA.] 4-3-1926. Mount Pleasant Cemetery, Newark, Essex County.

GROVER, JOSEPH Pvt, D, 29th NJ Inf, 10-9-1935. Fairview Cemetery, Fairview, Monmouth County.

GROVER*, JOSEPH K. Pvt, D, 2nd U.S. Cav, [Wounded in action at Wilderness, VA.] 6-22-1906. Whitesville Cemetery, Whitesville, Ocean County.

GROVER, LEWIS CONGER (JR.) 2nd Lt, E, 37th NJ Inf, 3-1-1896. Mount Pleasant Cemetery, Newark, Essex County.

GROVER, MASON G. Pvt, H, 48th NY Inf, 12-29-1881. Methodist Cemetery, Cassville, Ocean County.

GROVER, SAMUEL Pvt, F, 14th NJ Inf, [Cenotaph. Died of a lung abcess at Frederick City, MD.] 11-7-1862. Dayton Cemetery, Dayton, Middlesex County.

GROVER, WILLIAM Pvt, B, 4th NJ Militia, 1-27-1886. Methodist Church Cemetery, Pemberton, Burlington County.

GROVER, WILLIAM A. (aka: Grow, George) Pvt, I, 68th NY Inf, 11-4-1918. Riverview Cemetery, Trenton, Mercer County.

Our Brothers Gone Before

GROVER, WILLIAM B. Hosp Steward, U.S. Army, 8-20-1885. Prospect Hill Cemetery, Caldwell, Essex County.

GROVER*, WILLIAM V. Pvt, G, 14th NJ Inf, 11-27-1898. Fairview Cemetery, Fairview, Monmouth County.

GROVES, EDWARD 10-6-1896. Evergreen Cemetery, Hillside, Union County.

GROVES, HENRY Pvt, H, 38th NJ Inf, 4-24-1913. Riverview Cemetery, Trenton, Mercer County.

GROVES, JAMES Pvt, D, 6th NJ Inf, 12-22-1867. Cedar Grove Cemetery, Gloucester City, Camden County.

GROVES, LUTHER M. Pvt, F, 22nd NJ Inf, 4-7-1882. Cedar Hill Cemetery, Hightstown, Mercer County.

GROVES, REUBEN D. Pvt, E, 5th NJ Inf, [Killed in action at Malvern Hill, Va.] 7-2-1862. Presbyterian Cemetery, Holmanville, Ocean County.

GROVES*, WILLIAM N. Pvt, G, 8th NJ Inf, [Wounded in action at Petersburg, VA.] 11-18-1865. Cedar Grove Cemetery, Gloucester City, Camden County.

GROW, GEORGE (see: Grover, William A.) Riverview Cemetery, Trenton, Mercer County.

GROWNEY, HENRY K. Pvt, H, 26th NJ Inf, 7-24-1875. Rosedale Cemetery, Orange, Essex County.

GROWS, DAVID Pvt, D, 25th U.S. CT, 3-28-1900. Spencer African Methodist Church Cemetery, Woodstown, Salem County.

GROZING, MARTIN Sgt, E, 33rd NJ Inf, DoD Unknown. Laurel Grove Cemetery, Totowa, Passaic County.

GROZING, MARTIN (see: Grossman, Martin) Cedar Lawn Cemetery, Paterson, Passaic County.

GRUB, PHILIP Pvt, F, 33rd NJ Inf, 1-4-1909. Fairmount Cemetery, Newark, Essex County.

GRUBB, CALVIN Pvt, F, 9th U.S. CT, 6-19-1904. Mount Peace Cemetery, Lawnside, Camden County.

GRUBB, EDWARD BURD Bvt Brig Gen, U.S. Volunteers, [Colonel, 23rd and 37th New Jersey Infantries.] 7-7-1913. St. Mary's Episcopal Church Cemetery, Burlington, Burlington County.

GRUBB, EVAN P. 1904. Harleigh Cemetery, Camden, Camden County.

GRUBB, PARKER 1st Lt, Adj, 37th NJ Inf [Died of typhoid at Spring Hill, VA.] 8-11-1864. St. Mary's Episcopal Church Cemetery, Burlington, Burlington County.

GRUBBINS, JOHN H. Pvt, A, 3rd NJ Inf, 11-10-1897. Methodist Cemetery, Malaga, Gloucester County.

GRUBER, MARTIN Pvt, A, 13th NJ Inf, 7-6-1903. Holy Sepulchre Cemetery, East Orange, Essex County.

GRUCKENBERGER*, JOHN Pvt, Btty I, 2nd PA Heavy Art, 3-3-1887. Riverside Cemetery, Riverside, Burlington County.

GRUDER, CORNELIUS P. 1914. Valleau Cemetery, Ridgewood, Bergen County.

GRUENZWEIG, JOHANN Pvt, A, 103rd NY Inf, 5-10-1892. Palisade Cemetery, North Bergen, Hudson County.

GRUETT, FREDERICK T.R. Capt, K, 70th NY Inf, 7-9-1911. Mount Pleasant Cemetery, Newark, Essex County.

GRUFF*, GEORGE Pvt, C, 11th PA Inf, 8-8-1924. Union Cemetery, Gloucester City, Camden County.

GRUFF, WILLIAM Pvt, G, 25th NJ Inf, 1914. Methodist Church Cemetery, Heislerville, Cumberland County.

GRUMIUR, ALEXANDER DoD Unknown. Brewer Cemetery, Squankum, Monmouth County.

New Jersey Civil War Burials

GRUMMAN, JOSIAH M. 2nd Lt, H, 84th NY Inf, [Died at Washington, DC of wounds received 8-29-1862 at 2nd Bull Run, VA.] 9-19-1862. Evergreen Cemetery, Hillside, Union County.
GRUMMAN, WILLIAM 1913. Evergreen Cemetery, Hillside, Union County.
GRUNDLER, ALFRED Pvt, Btty A, 1st NJ Light Art, 8-31-1881. Woodland Cemetery, Newark, Essex County.
GRUNDNER, STEPHEN Corp, G, 173rd NY Inf, 12-21-1907. Arlington Cemetery, Kearny, Hudson County.
GRUNDY, FREDERICK Musc, Btty H, 13th NY Heavy Art, 3-14-1900. New Camden Cemetery, Camden, Camden County.
GRUNDYKE, ABERNETHA (aka: Grovendyke, Abernethy) Pvt, G, 15th NJ Inf, 5-25-1865. Sandy Ridge Cemetery, Sandy Ridge, Hunterdon County.
GRUNEWALD, OTTO Pvt, D, 68th NY Inf, DoD Unknown. Greenwood Cemetery, Boonton, Morris County.
GRUNNALD, OTTO (see: Grunwaldt, Otto) Palisade Cemetery, North Bergen, Hudson County.
GRUNOW, CHARLES Pvt, D, 7th NJ Inf, [Wounded 5-5-1862 at Williamsburg, VA.] 12-16-1904. Germania Cemetery, Galloway, Atlantic County.
GRUNWALDT, OTTO (aka: Grunnald, Otto) Corp, C, 175th NY Inf, 9-7-1881. Palisade Cemetery, North Bergen, Hudson County.
GRUVER, JOHN (see: Groover, John W.) Methodist Church Cemetery, Mount Bethel, Warren County.
GSHWINTER, WILLIAM (see: Reuther, William) Fairmount Cemetery, Newark, Essex County.
GUDNIAWECZ, PAUL __, K, 19th U.S. Inf, DoD Unknown. Holy Sepulchre Cemetery, East Orange, Essex County.
GUENTHER, CHARLES (see: Guenther, Gustavous Charles) Atlantic City Cemetery, Pleasantville, Atlantic County.
GUENTHER, CHRISTIAN Pvt, E, 1st NY Eng, 2-18-1909. Riverview Cemetery, Trenton, Mercer County.
GUENTHER*, GUSTAVOUS CHARLES (aka: Guenther, Charles) Pvt, A, 7th NY Vet Inf, [Wounded 5-18-1864 at Po River, VA.] 12-31-1920. Atlantic City Cemetery, Pleasantville, Atlantic County.
GUERARD, JOHN JACOB 1st Lt, C, 11th SC Inf (CSA), [Captured 9-5-1864 at Petersburg, VA. Died of chronic diarrhea.] 9-14-1864. Finn's Point National Cemetery, Pennsville, Salem County.
GUERIN, CHARLES H. Sgt, C, 15th NJ Inf, 2-17-1917. Evergreen Cemetery, Morristown, Morris County.
GUERIN, CHARLES M. Pvt, E, 39th NJ Inf, 3-14-1916. Arlington Cemetery, Kearny, Hudson County.
GUERIN*, ORLANDO K. 1st Lt, A, 33rd NJ Inf, 10-19-1881. Evergreen Cemetery, Morristown, Morris County.
GUERIN, SILAS J. Pvt, C, 15th NJ Inf, 3-12-1911. Arlington Cemetery, Kearny, Hudson County.
GUEST, B.G. Pvt, E, 1st (Symon's) GA Res Inf (CSA), 3-28-1865. Finn's Point National Cemetery, Pennsville, Salem County.
GUEST, CHARLES J. Sgt, D, 3rd NJ Inf, 11- -1865. Presbyterian Church Cemetery, Andover, Sussex County.
GUEST, ISAAC Pvt, A, 30th NJ Inf, 1917. Locust Hill Cemetery, Dover, Morris County.
GUEST, JACOB Pvt, F, 15th NJ Inf, 9-13-1897. German Valley Rural Cemetery, Naughright, Morris County.
GUEST, JACOB 1904. United Methodist Cemetery, Gladstone, Somerset County.
GUEST, MARK H. Pvt, K, 24th NJ Inf, 3-15-1919. Harleigh Cemetery, Camden, Camden County.

Our Brothers Gone Before

GUEST, WILLIAM E. Pvt, K, 24th NJ Inf, DoD Unknown. Friends/Methodist-Episcopal Cemetery, Pedricktown, Salem County.

GUGEL, HENRY Corp, A, 29th NJ Inf, 1905. Old 1st Methodist Church Cemetery, West Long Branch, Monmouth County.

GUGEL, JOHN I. 1915. Old 1st Methodist Church Cemetery, West Long Branch, Monmouth County.

GUICE, CHARLES (see: Guise, Charles W.) Evergreen Cemetery, Lakewood, Ocean County.

GUICE, JAMES Pvt, D, 24th NJ Inf, 1-15-1912. Greenwood Cemetery, Pleasantville, Atlantic County.

GUIE, GEORGE Q. (aka: Guil, George) Pvt, F, 104th PA Inf, 5-16-1916. Riverview Cemetery, Trenton, Mercer County.

GUIE, WILLIAM (see: Guye, William) Fairview Cemetery, Fairview, Monmouth County.

GUIGAN, THOMAS DoD Unknown. Old St. Mary's Cemetery, Gloucester City, Camden County.

GUIL, GEORGE (see: Guie, George Q.) Riverview Cemetery, Trenton, Mercer County.

GUILDERSLEEVE, HENRY C. Pvt, A, 22nd NJ Inf, 3-28-1883. Hackensack Cemetery, Hackensack, Bergen County.

GUILE, RICHARD (aka: Giles, Richard) Pvt, M, 2nd NY Cav, 2-4-1898. Vincent Methodist-Episcopal Cemetery, Nutley, Essex County.

GUILE, ROBERT Pvt, B, 39th NJ Inf, DoD Unknown. Vincent Methodist-Episcopal Cemetery, Nutley, Essex County.

GUILKEY*, JAMES E. Pvt, C, 12th NJ Inf, 3-25-1877. Baptist Cemetery, Medford, Burlington County.

GUINAN, JOHN 12-19-1887. Mount Olivet Cemetery, Newark, Essex County.

GUIRE, JOHN (aka: Gildea, John) Corp, B, 4th NJ Inf, [Died of consumption at Trenton, NJ.] 4-11-1865. Mercer Cemetery, Trenton, Mercer County.

GUISE*, CHARLES W. (aka: Guice, Charles) Pvt, C, 34th NJ Inf, 3-12-1900. Evergreen Cemetery, Lakewood, Ocean County.

GUISE, JOHN (aka: Gice, John) Pvt, K, 14th NJ Inf, 12-8-1911. Greengrove Cemetery, Keyport, Monmouth County.

GULDEN*, JOHN H. Pvt, G, 24th VA Cav (CSA), 7-19-1904. Riverview Cemetery, Trenton, Mercer County.

GULICK, ABRAM Pvt, K, 2nd DC Inf, 5-13-1893. Mansfield/Washington Cemetery, Washington, Warren County.

GULICK, ALEXANDER Pvt, G, 193rd OH Inf, 3-31-1884. Presbyterian Church Cemetery, Kingston, Somerset County.

GULICK, CORNELIUS 12-17-1889. Van Liew Cemetery, North Brunswick, Middlesex County.

GULICK*, CORNELIUS Wagoner, M, 2nd NJ Cav, 3- -1885. Methodist Church Cemetery, Mount Bethel, Warren County.

GULICK, ELIAS WYCKOFF Pvt, D, 31st NJ Inf, [Died of fever at Washington, DC.] 12-26-1862. Baptist Church Cemetery, Flemington, Hunterdon County.

GULICK, EZRA P. Pvt, E, 27th NJ Inf, 1917. Union Cemetery, Washington, Morris County.

GULICK, GEORGE E. Pvt, K, 30th NJ Inf, [Died of typhoid at Belle Plain, VA.] 3-6-1863. Pleasant Plains Cemetery, Franklin Park, Somerset County.

GULICK, GEORGE W. Pvt, B, 11th NJ Inf, [Died at Washington, DC. of wounds received in action.] 4-3-1865. Reformed Church Cemetery, Lebanon, Hunterdon County.

GULICK, HORATIO E. 3-21-1870. Riverside Cemetery, Toms River, Ocean County.

GULICK, JACOB F. 1912. Union Cemetery, Washington, Morris County.

GULICK, JAMES CLARK Pvt, E, 31st NJ Inf, 1910. Evergreen Cemetery, Clinton, Hunterdon County.

New Jersey Civil War Burials

GULICK, JOACHIM Pvt, G, 3rd NJ Inf, 1907. Rural Hill Cemetery, Whitehouse, Hunterdon County.
GULICK, PETER Pvt, C, 26th MA Inf, 12-12-1913. Evergreen Cemetery, Morristown, Morris County.
GULICK, SPENCER E. Corp, B, 28th NJ Inf, 1-17-1900. Tennent Church Cemetery, Tennent, Monmouth County.
GULICK, WESLEY Pvt, F, 23rd NJ Inf, 3-25-1904. Harleigh Cemetery, Camden, Camden County.
GULICK, WILLIAM Sgt, U.S. Marine Corps, 5-13-1908. Mount Holly Cemetery, Mount Holly, Burlington County.
GULICK, WILLIAM Pvt, F, 15th NJ Inf, DoD Unknown. Methodist Church Cemetery, Fairmount, Hunterdon County.
GULICK*, WILLIAM Pvt, F, 2nd NJ Inf, 1881. Fairmount Cemetery, Fairmount, Hunterdon County.
GULICK*, WILLIAM ARMSTEAD 1st Lt, Adj, 28th NJ Inf 11-8-1884. Presbyterian Church Cemetery, Kingston, Somerset County.
GULLEDGE, GEORGE S. Corp, H, 13th AL Inf (CSA), 2-5-1864. Finn's Point National Cemetery, Pennsville, Salem County.
GULLICK, FRANCIS A. Pvt, A, 31st NJ Inf, 7-18-1902. Soldier's Home Cemetery, Vineland, Cumberland County.
GUM, WILLIAM G. Pvt, F, 62nd VA Inf (CSA), [Died of dysentery.] 10-16-1863. Finn's Point National Cemetery, Pennsville, Salem County.
GUMBLE, ISAAC V.A. Pvt, E, 30th NJ Inf, 3-9-1936. New Somerville Cemetery, Somerville, Somerset County.
GUMBLE, JACOB H. Pvt, E, 30th NJ Inf, 1912. New Somerville Cemetery, Somerville, Somerset County.
GUNDELL*, PHILLIP 2nd Lt, L, 1st NJ Cav, 4-30-1912. Fairmount Cemetery, Newark, Essex County.
GUNDENRATH, WILLIAM Actg 3rd Asst Eng, U.S. Navy, 5-14-1893. Flower Hill Cemetery, North Bergen, Hudson County.
GUNDERMAN, JACOB (aka: Gundryman, Jacob) Pvt, G, 31st NJ Inf, 7-2-1903. Mansfield/Washington Cemetery, Washington, Warren County.
GUNDERMAN, JAMES E. Corp, M, 1st NJ Cav, [Wounded in action.] 11-12-1894. Vaughn Cemetery, Ackerson, Sussex County.
GUNDERMAN, PETER S. Sgt, D, 15th NJ Inf, 5-28-1910. Presbyterian Church Cemetery, Sparta, Sussex County.
GUNDERSDORFF, AUGUSTUS Pvt, A, 12th MD Inf, 10-26-1905. Flower Hill Cemetery, North Bergen, Hudson County.
GUNDLING, JOHN L. Pvt, A, 4th NJ Inf, 5-27-1896. Chickory Chapel Baptist Church Cemetery, Elk, Gloucester County.
GUNDRYMAN, JACOB (see: Gunderman, Jacob) Mansfield/Washington Cemetery, Washington, Warren County.
GUNKE, JOSEPH F. Pvt, A, 4th NY Cav, 5-28-1933. Hoboken Cemetery, North Bergen, Hudson County.
GUNN, HENRY ALEXANDER Corp, C, 2nd NY Cav, 9-9-1895. Newton Cemetery, Newton, Sussex County.
GUNN, JAMES Pvt, C, 14th NJ Inf, [Wounded 10-19-1864 at Cedar Creek, VA.] 7-24-1885. Presbyterian Cemetery, North Plainfield, Somerset County.
GUNN, WILSON C. Pvt, M, 1st NJ Cav, 1919. Hainesville Cemetery, Hainesville, Sussex County.
GUNNELE, ENOCH W. (aka: Gwennell, Enoch) Corp, Btty E, 1st CT Heavy Art, DoD Unknown. Bayview-New York Bay Cemetery, Jersey City, Hudson County.
GUNTHER, GUSTAVUS Corp, C, 28th NJ Inf, 11-28-1922. Elm Ridge Cemetery, North Brunswick, Middlesex County.

Our Brothers Gone Before

GUNTHER*, VALENTINE Pvt, G, 7th NJ Inf, DoD Unknown. Arlington Cemetery, Kearny, Hudson County.

GUPTON, JESSE Pvt, G, 8th (Wade's) Confederate States Cav (CSA), 10-13-1863. Finn's Point National Cemetery, Pennsville, Salem County.

GURDINIER, NELSON Pvt, H, 22nd NJ Inf, [Died of typhoid at Belle Plain, VA.] 3-15-1863. Alpine Cemetery, Alpine, Bergen County.

GURLY, J.I. Pvt, C, 51st AL Cav (CSA), 10-25-1863. Finn's Point National Cemetery, Pennsville, Salem County.

GURNSEY, SILAS Pvt, F, 1st NJ Inf, 4-4-1924. Riverview Cemetery, Trenton, Mercer County.

GURTLER, JOHN Corp, B, 83rd NY Inf, 4-3-1888. Fairmount Cemetery, Newark, Essex County.

GURTON, WILLIAM 3-12-1922. Evergreen Cemetery, Morristown, Morris County.

GUSHEE, WARREN Pvt, Unassigned, 26th MA Militia, 11-4-1905. Laurel Grove Cemetery, Totowa, Passaic County.

GUSTAVUS, OTTO (see: Otto, Gustave) Fairmount Cemetery, Newark, Essex County.

GUSTER, BOB (see: Custer, Robert) Mount Peace Cemetery, Lawnside, Camden County.

GUSTIN, JAMES S. Corp, I, 7th NJ Inf, [Killed in action at Williamsburg, VA.] 5-5-1862. Branchville Cemetery, Branchville, Sussex County.

GUSTIN, JOHN M. Pvt, K, 1st NY Eng, 4-1-1924. Presbyterian Church Cemetery, Rockaway, Morris County.

GUTERL, JACOB 6-14-1898. Holy Name Cemetery, Jersey City, Hudson County.

GUTH, WILLIAM Pvt, G, MO Inf, [1st U.S. Reserve Corps] 12-27-1884. Palisade Cemetery, North Bergen, Hudson County.

GUTHRIE, EDMUND J. DoD Unknown. Riverview Cemetery, Trenton, Mercer County.

GUTHRIE, JOHN BRANDON 2nd Lt, C, 1st KY Inf, 1-12-1900. Princeton Cemetery, Princeton, Mercer County.

GUTHRIE, OLIVER S. Pvt, G, 186th PA Inf, 12-16-1911. Evergreen Cemetery, Camden, Camden County.

GUTHRIE, WILLIAM LILLIOUS Capt, I, 23rd VA Inf (CSA), [Captured 5-12-1864 at Spotsylvania CH, VA. Died of scurvy.] 3-22-1865. Finn's Point National Cemetery, Pennsville, Salem County.

GUTTERSON, ABEL F. 1st Sgt, C, 4th NH Inf, 1-28-1923. Siloam Cemetery, Vineland, Cumberland County.

GUY, HARRY (aka: Grey, Henry) Pvt, D, 31st PA Inf, [Wounded in action at Gettysburg, PA.] 1911. New Camden Cemetery, Camden, Camden County.

GUY, THOMAS 11-18-1927. Bloomfield Cemetery, Bloomfield, Essex County.

GUY, THOMAS (aka: Gay, Thomas) Pvt, G, 68th PA Inf, 6-8-1919. Riverview Cemetery, Trenton, Mercer County.

GUYE, WILLIAM (aka: Guie, William) Corp, F, 29th NJ Inf, 3-31-1904. Fairview Cemetery, Fairview, Monmouth County.

GUYER, HENRY Capt, F, 13th NJ Inf, 11-30-1885. Mount Pleasant Cemetery, Newark, Essex County.

GUYER, JOHN 2nd Cl Fireman, U.S. Navy, [U.S. receiving ship at New York, NY.] 1888. Mercer Cemetery, Trenton, Mercer County.

GUYON, J.H. Pvt, G, 127th NY Inf, [Wounded 11-30-1864 at Honey Hill, SC.] 12-22-1903. Fairmount Cemetery, Newark, Essex County.

GUYRE, PEYTON R. Pvt, H, 12th NY State Militia, DoD Unknown. Grove Church Cemetery, North Bergen, Hudson County.

GUYSINGER, JOHN (see: Geisinger, John) Evergreen Cemetery, Hillside, Union County.

GWENNELL, ENOCH (see: Gunnele, Enoch W.) Bayview-New York Bay Cemetery, Jersey City, Hudson County.

New Jersey Civil War Burials

GWIN*, WILLIAM Lt Commander, U.S. Navy, USS Benton, [Died of wounds received 12-27-1862 at Haynes Bluff (Yazoo River), MS.] 1-3-1863. Mount Pleasant Cemetery, Newark, Essex County.

GWINN, W.W. (see: Gwynn, W.W.) Finn's Point National Cemetery, Pennsville, Salem County.

GWINN, WILLIAM A. Sgt, C, 22nd VA Inf (CSA), [Captured 11-6-1863 at Droop Mountain, WV. Died of typhoid.] 7-2-1864. Finn's Point National Cemetery, Pennsville, Salem County.

GWYNN, W.W. (aka: Gwinn, W.W.) Pvt, K, 2nd FL Cav (CSA), [Captured 2-16-1864 at Jacksonville, FL. Died of measles.] 9-25-1864. Finn's Point National Cemetery, Pennsville, Salem County.

GWYNN, WILLIAM Landsman, U.S. Navy, USS Savannah, 4-20-1887. Princeton Cemetery, Princeton, Mercer County.

HAACKE*, AUGUSTUS FRANCIS W. (aka: Haacke, William) Pvt, C, 24th WI Inf, [Wounded 11-25-1863 at Missionary Ridge, TN.] 1893. Holy Name Cemetery, Jersey City, Hudson County.

HAACKE, WILLIAM (see: Haacke, Augustus Francis W.) Holy Name Cemetery, Jersey City, Hudson County.

HAAG, JOHN BRUNO (aka: Hagg, John B.) Pvt, E, 27th NJ Inf, 10-4-1906. St. John's Evangelical Church Cemetery, Orange, Essex County.

HAAG, LOUIS Sgt, A, 7th NJ Inf, 4-3-1876. Bayview-New York Bay Cemetery, Jersey City, Hudson County.

HAAS, BERNHARD (see: Hass, Bernard) Holy Sepulchre Cemetery, East Orange, Essex County.

HAAS*, CHRISTIAN Pvt, 6th NY Ind Btty 7-31-1873. Bloomfield Cemetery, Bloomfield, Essex County.

HAAS, GEORGE Musc, E, 103rd NY Inf, 3-27-1929. Fairmount Cemetery, Newark, Essex County.

HAAS*, HENRY Corp, G, 37th NJ Inf, 6-21-1896. Fairmount Cemetery, Newark, Essex County.

HAAS*, JACOB Pvt, C, 6th CT Inf, 12-8-1892. Willow Grove Cemetery, New Brunswick, Middlesex County.

HAAS, JOHN Pvt, D, 39th NJ Inf, 2-19-1884. Woodland Cemetery, Newark, Essex County.

HAAS, JOSEPH Pvt, B, 9th NJ Inf, 9-17-1885. Fairmount Cemetery, Newark, Essex County.

HAAS, NELSON 1st Lt, B, 215th PA Inf, DoD Unknown. Hackensack Cemetery, Hackensack, Bergen County.

HAASE, HENRY Pvt, C, 11th NY State Militia, 1-27-1904. Bayview-New York Bay Cemetery, Jersey City, Hudson County.

HABACHAN, AUGUST (aka: Haberghan, Gustavus) Corp, G, 1st NJ Cav, DoD Unknown. Washington Monumental Cemetery, South River, Middlesex County.

HABERGHAN, GUSTAVUS (see: Habachan, August) Washington Monumental Cemetery, South River, Middlesex County.

HABERLANDT, ROBERT W. Landsman, U.S. Navy, 1-17-1921. Clinton Cemetery, Irvington, Essex County.

HABERSTROH, CHARLES Pvt, H, 41st NY Inf, 11-21-1896. Fairmount Cemetery, Newark, Essex County.

HABIG, FRANCIS Pvt, A, 9th NJ Inf, 11-7-1883. Holy Sepulchre Cemetery, East Orange, Essex County.

HACKBARTH*, JULIUS A.G. 1st Lt, Btty G, 2nd MO Light Art, 6-1-1893. Weehawken Cemetery, North Bergen, Hudson County.

HACKENBOIG, JOHN (aka: Hagenbucher, John) Pvt, I, 3rd NJ Cav, 1-14-1891. Flower Hill Cemetery, North Bergen, Hudson County.

Our Brothers Gone Before

HACKER, BERNHARD 1st Sgt, E, 54th NY Inf, DoD Unknown. Palisade Cemetery, North Bergen, Hudson County.

HACKET, NATHANIEL Pvt, Unassigned, 25th NY Cav, DoD Unknown. Phillipsburg Cemetery, Phillipsburg, Warren County.

HACKETT, JOHN Pvt, C, 11th NJ Inf, 9-19-1912. Reformed Church Cemetery, Lebanon, Hunterdon County.

HACKETT, JOHN H. Pvt, B, 25th NJ Inf, 1905. United Methodist Church Cemetery, Absecon, Atlantic County.

HACKETT, JONATHAN A. Pvt, B, 118th PA Inf, 1924. Zion Methodist Church Cemetery, Bargaintown, Atlantic County.

HACKETT, JOSEPH Pvt, K, 3rd NJ Inf, 8-12-1904. Holy Sepulchre Cemetery, Totowa, Passaic County.

HACKETT, LEVI B. Pvt, A, 14th PA Cav, 1-22-1928. New Camden Cemetery, Camden, Camden County.

HACKETT, MICHAEL H. Pvt, U.S. Army, [General service.] 8-3-1910. Holy Name Cemetery, Jersey City, Hudson County.

HACKETT, PETER HENRY Pvt, B, 25th NJ Inf, 3-26-1921. Zion Methodist Church Cemetery, Bargaintown, Atlantic County.

HACKETT, THOMAS Pvt, Btty B, 4th U.S. Art, 5- -1865. Bayview-New York Bay Cemetery, Jersey City, Hudson County.

HACKNEY, JOHN Corp, B, 25th NJ Inf, 7-16-1865. Mount Pleasant Methodist Cemetery, Pleasantville, Atlantic County.

HACKNEY, MAHLON Pvt, D, 7th NJ Inf, [Wounded in action.] 11-16-1913. Fairview Cemetery, Cape May Court House, Cape May County.

HACKNEY, WESLEY Pvt, B, 25th NJ Inf, DoD Unknown. Mount Pleasant Methodist Cemetery, Pleasantville, Atlantic County.

HACKWORTH, GEORGE D. Pvt, B, 14th VA Inf (CSA), [Captured 7-3-1863 at Gettysburg, PA. Died of liver inflammation.] 5-21-1864. Finn's Point National Cemetery, Pennsville, Salem County.

HADDEN, GEORGE W. (SR.) Actg Ensign, U.S. Navy, 7-7-1893. Jersey City Cemetery, Jersey City, Hudson County.

HADDEN, WILLIAM H. Pvt, A, 8th NJ Inf, 4- -1924. Presbyterian Church Cemetery, Millbrook, Morris County.

HADDOCK, WILLIAM A. Pvt, F, 5th FL Inf (CSA), [Captured 7-3-1863 at Gettysburg, PA. Died of diarrhea.] 1-10-1864. Finn's Point National Cemetery, Pennsville, Salem County.

HADDOCK, WILLIAM J. Musc, D, 46th IA Inf, 6-26-1923. Greenwood Cemetery, Hamilton, Mercer County.

HADDON, ROBERT (aka: Haddow, Robert) Pvt, 8th NY Ind Btty 10-31-1914. Mount Hebron Cemetery, Montclair, Essex County.

HADDOW, ROBERT (see: Haddon, Robert) Mount Hebron Cemetery, Montclair, Essex County.

HADFIELD*, FREDERICK J. Pvt, C, 86th NY Inf, 8-15-1873. St. Stephen's Cemetery, Millburn, Essex County.

HADFIELD*, JOHN Pvt, C, 10th NJ Inf, 12-26-1888. Fairmount Cemetery, Newark, Essex County.

HADLEY, EDMUND V. Corp, E, 25th NJ Inf, DoD Unknown. Laurel Grove Cemetery, Totowa, Passaic County.

HADLEY*, JACOB Pvt, H, 9th NJ Inf, 6-18-1909. Methodist Church Cemetery, Hope, Warren County.

HADLEY, LEONARD Corp, A, 2nd NY Cav, 5-2-1921. Bayview-New York Bay Cemetery, Jersey City, Hudson County.

HADLEY, PETER Pvt, H, 1st NJ Cav, 6-29-1923. Arlington Cemetery, Kearny, Hudson County.

New Jersey Civil War Burials

HADON, WILLIAM (see: Hayden, William) Holy Sepulchre Cemetery, Totowa, Passaic County.

HADWIN, JOHN E. Pvt, F, 3rd SC Cav (CSA), [Captured 8-17-1864 at South Newport, GA. Died of chronic diarrhea.] 5-18-1865. Finn's Point National Cemetery, Pennsville, Salem County.

HAEATON, ERASTUS M. (see: Heaton, Erastus M.) Evergreen Cemetery, Hillside, Union County.

HAEFELE, JOHN Pvt, U.S. Marine Corps, 3-30-1876. Palisade Cemetery, North Bergen, Hudson County.

HAEFFLE*, WILLIAM Pvt, B, 24th IL Inf, 11-26-1897. Fairmount Cemetery, Newark, Essex County.

HAEGELE, WILLIAM H. Pvt, A, 82nd PA Inf, 1930. Soldier's Home Cemetery, Vineland, Cumberland County.

HAEGER, JUDAS J. (see: Jaeger, Julius) Fairmount Cemetery, Newark, Essex County.

HAEHR, BERNHARDT Pvt, Btty C, 1st NJ Light Art, 8-13-1888. Palisade Cemetery, North Bergen, Hudson County.

HAERING, MARTIN ANTOINE (aka: Herring, Antone) Artificer, M, 1st NY Eng, 9-21-1892. Oak Hill Cemetery, Vineland, Cumberland County.

HAESELER, FRANCIS S. 2nd Lt, H, 194th PA Inf, 1926. Harleigh Cemetery, Camden, Camden County.

HAFFER, JOHN J. Pvt, E, 34th NJ Inf, 5-4-1932. Cedar Lawn Cemetery, Paterson, Passaic County.

HAFFNER, FREDERICK J. Pvt, H, 4th DE Inf, 6-14-1892. Fairview Cemetery, Westfield, Union County.

HAFLEY, JOSEPH [Lost in the last days.] 1865. Madonna Cemetery, Leonia, Bergen County.

HAGADORN*, MOSES C. 1st Lt, G, 1st NY Inf, [Wounded 8-29-1862 at 2nd Bull Run, VA.] 1872. Clinton Cemetery, Irvington, Essex County.

HAGAMAN, AARON (aka: Higgaman, Aaron) Pvt, B, 45th U.S. CT, 7-22-1888. Riverview Cemetery, Trenton, Mercer County.

HAGAMAN, ASHER (see: Hagerman, Asher) Batchellor Farm Cemetery, Hillsborough, Somerset County.

HAGAMAN*, EDWARD I. Pvt, K, 2nd NJ Inf, 4-4-1873. Methodist Cemetery, Cassville, Ocean County.

HAGAMAN, JAMES MONROE Pvt, F, 30th NJ Inf, 6-9-1917. Barber's Burying Ground Cemetery, Dilts Corner, Hunterdon County.

HAGAMAN, JOHN H. Pvt, A, 29th NJ Inf, 3-10-1870. Adelphia Cemetery, Adelphia, Monmouth County.

HAGAMAN, JOSEPH H. 1904. Barber's Burying Ground Cemetery, Dilts Corner, Hunterdon County.

HAGAMAN, JOSEPH H. Pvt, F, 30th NJ Inf, 5-20-1902. New Dutch Reformed/Neshanic Cemetery, Neshanic, Somerset County.

HAGAMAN, NICHOLAS Pvt, D, 14th NJ Inf, DoD Unknown. Ardena Baptist Church Cemetery, Adelphia, Monmouth County.

HAGAMAN, WILLIAM C. Pvt, A, 38th NJ Inf, 11-12-1931. Methodist Cemetery, Cassville, Ocean County.

HAGAMAN, WILLIAM H. Corp, Btty H, 2nd PA Heavy Art, 5-5-1913. Bloomsbury Cemetery, Kennedy Mills, Warren County.

HAGAMEN, JAMES G. Pvt, F, 30th NJ Inf, 1929. Rocky Hill Cemetery, Rocky Hill, Somerset County.

HAGAN, DAVID O. (aka: Hager, David) Pvt, F, 31st NJ Inf, DoD Unknown. St. Peter's Church Cemetery, Belleville, Essex County.

HAGAN, DAVIS Pvt, I, 38th NJ Inf, 8-11-1913. Princeton Cemetery, Princeton, Mercer County.

Our Brothers Gone Before

HAGAN, FREDERICH Pvt, C, 58th NY Inf, 11-25-1870. Fairmount Cemetery, Newark, Essex County.
HAGAN, MARK 7-27-1875. St. Peter's Church Cemetery, Belleville, Essex County.
HAGAN, PETER (see: Hager, Peter H.) Phillipsburg Cemetery, Phillipsburg, Warren County.
HAGEDORN, RUDOLPH 10-15-1915. Flower Hill Cemetery, North Bergen, Hudson County.
HAGEL*, ANDREW (aka: Petters, John) Pvt, Btty K, 15th NY Heavy Art, 10-29-1876. Holy Sepulchre Cemetery, East Orange, Essex County.
HAGELE, MARTIN Pvt, A, 39th NJ Inf, 9-28-1880. Rahway Cemetery, Rahway, Union County.
HAGEMAN, ELBERT N. Corp, E, 26th NJ Inf, 10-28-1903. Clinton Cemetery, Irvington, Essex County.
HAGEMAN, JOHN V. Pvt, E, 26th NJ Inf, 3-2-1912. Clinton Cemetery, Irvington, Essex County.
HAGEN, ALEXANDER Pvt, A, 25th NJ Inf, 11-14-1888. Fairmount Cemetery, Newark, Essex County.
HAGEN, JAMES Pvt, B, 11th NJ Inf, 12-3-1881. Holy Sepulchre Cemetery, East Orange, Essex County.
HAGEN, SEBASTIAN 1-7-1909. Bloomfield Cemetery, Bloomfield, Essex County.
HAGENBUCHER, JOHN (see: Hackenboig, John) Flower Hill Cemetery, North Bergen, Hudson County.
HAGER, DAVID (see: Hagan, David O.) St. Peter's Church Cemetery, Belleville, Essex County.
HAGER, DAVID O. Pvt, F, 31st NJ Inf, 2-25-1906. Holland Cemetery, Holland, Hunterdon County.
HAGER, JACOB Pvt, Btty A, 1st NJ Light Art, 7-11-1882. Fairmount Cemetery, Newark, Essex County.
HAGER, PETER (see: Hagerty, Peter H.) Phillipsburg Cemetery, Phillipsburg, Warren County.
HAGER, PETER H. (aka: Hagan, Peter) Pvt, L, 2nd NJ Cav, 9-13-1933. Phillipsburg Cemetery, Phillipsburg, Warren County.
HAGERMAN, ASHER (aka: Hagaman, Asher) Pvt, H, 127th U.S. CT, 4-19-1888. Batchellor Farm Cemetery, Hillsborough, Somerset County.
HAGERMAN, CHARLES H. Sgt, B, 4th NJ Inf, 8-23-1914. Arlington Cemetery, Kearny, Hudson County.
HAGERMAN, DANIEL Corp, K, 29th NJ Inf, 11-15-1874. Methodist Cemetery, Hamilton, Monmouth County.
HAGERMAN, HENRY Pvt, A, 1st NJ Cav, 11-9-1890. Union Cemetery, Frenchtown, Hunterdon County.
HAGERMAN*, JAMES E. Corp, H, 38th NJ Inf, 12-9-1926. Maplewood Cemetery, Freehold, Monmouth County.
HAGERMAN, JOHN H. 1st Sgt, K, 29th NJ Inf, 9-14-1904. Mount Prospect Cemetery, Neptune, Monmouth County.
HAGERMAN, PHILIP Pvt, B, 14th NJ Inf, 2-11-1918. Riverview Cemetery, Trenton, Mercer County.
HAGERMAN, WILLIAM E. (JR.) Pvt, I, 24th NJ Inf, 3-11-1925. Methodist Cemetery, Malaga, Gloucester County.
HAGERMAN, WILLIAM M. Sgt, B, 14th NJ Inf, 7-19-1884. Mercer Cemetery, Trenton, Mercer County.
HAGERMAN, WILLIAM P. Corp, D, 91st PA Inf, [Wounded 5-3-1863 at Chancellorsville, VA.] 5-13-1897. Methodist Church Cemetery, Hope, Warren County.

New Jersey Civil War Burials

HAGERTY, DANIEL Pvt, B, 9th NJ Inf, 5-7-1872. St. Peter's Cemetery, New Brunswick, Middlesex County.

HAGERTY, JAMES Sgt, G, 2nd NJ Militia, 10-10-1909. Bayview-New York Bay Cemetery, Jersey City, Hudson County.

HAGERTY, PETER H. (aka: Hager, Peter) Pvt, C, 31st NJ Inf, 3-14-1928. Phillipsburg Cemetery, Phillipsburg, Warren County.

HAGERTY, THOMAS Sgt, F, 24th PA Inf, 3-26-1890. Pesseltown/St. Anthony's Cemetery, Waterford, Camden County.

HAGERTY, THOMAS L. Pvt, C, 1st NJ Militia, DoD Unknown. Mount Pleasant Cemetery, Newark, Essex County.

HAGERTY, WARREN Sgt, K, 31st NJ Inf, 5-16-1890. Union Cemetery, Washington, Morris County.

HAGG, JOHN B. (see: Haag, John Bruno) St. John's Evangelical Church Cemetery, Orange, Essex County.

HAGG*, MATTHIAS Pvt, A, 39th NJ Inf, 7-13-1894. Woodland Cemetery, Newark, Essex County.

HAGGERTY, BERNARD Sgt, F, 1st NJ Inf, 1-5-1890. St. Peter's Cemetery, New Brunswick, Middlesex County.

HAGGERTY, CHARLES Pvt, G, 57th NY Inf, [Wounded 12-13-1862 at Fredericksburg, VA. and 6-16-1864 at Petersburg, VA.] 8-8-1905. Fairmount Cemetery, Newark, Essex County.

HAGGERTY, CHARLES A. Corp, E, 14th NJ Inf, 1-29-1910. Alpine Cemetery, Perth Amboy, Middlesex County.

HAGGERTY, ISAAC W. Pvt, H, 9th NJ Inf, 3-17-1866. Phillipsburg Cemetery, Phillipsburg, Warren County.

HAGGERTY, JAMES Pvt, A, 37th NJ Inf, 6-22-1892. Holy Name Cemetery, Jersey City, Hudson County.

HAGGERTY, JAMES Pvt, D, 28th NJ Inf, 11-11-1888. St. Peter's Cemetery, New Brunswick, Middlesex County.

HAGGERTY, JAMES (see: Hogarty, James R.) St. Paul's R.C. Church Cemetery, Princeton, Mercer County.

HAGGERTY, JAMES R. Pvt, B, 3rd NJ Cav, DoD Unknown. Branchville Cemetery, Branchville, Sussex County.

HAGGERTY, JOHN M. Com Sgt, B, 2nd NY Cav, 12-25-1887. Newton Cemetery, Newton, Sussex County.

HAGGERTY*, JOSEPH W. Pvt, D, 3rd NJ Inf, 11-27-1898. Newton Cemetery, Newton, Sussex County.

HAGGERTY, NOAH C. Pvt, C, 1st NJ Inf, 5- -1867. Chestnut Cemetery, Dover, Morris County.

HAGGERTY, PETER JACOB Pvt, E, 47th PA Inf, 5-12-1899. Flower Hill Cemetery, North Bergen, Hudson County.

HAGGERTY, WILLIAM R. Pvt, A, 9th NJ Inf, 1-10-1869. Fairmount Cemetery, Newark, Essex County.

HAGIS, L. Pvt, G, 3rd MS Inf (CSA), 5-9-1864. Finn's Point National Cemetery, Pennsville, Salem County.

HAHN, CHARLES Pvt, H, 8th NJ Inf, 2-8-1923. Arlington Cemetery, Kearny, Hudson County.

HAHN, DANIEL W. 4-24-1934. Bayview-New York Bay Cemetery, Jersey City, Hudson County.

HAHN, ELIAS Pvt, C, 5th VA Inf (CSA), [Captured 5-12-1864 at Spotsylvania CH, VA. Died of dysentery.] 3-6-1865. Finn's Point National Cemetery, Pennsville, Salem County.

HAHN, GEORGE W. Pvt, A, 31st NJ Inf, 6-8-1896. Mansfield/Washington Cemetery, Washington, Warren County.

Our Brothers Gone Before

HAHN, HENRY Pvt, B, 26th NJ Inf, 12-14-1907. Fairmount Cemetery, Newark, Essex County.
HAHN, JOHN Pvt, H, 11th NJ Inf, 1883. Fairview Cemetery, Fairview, Bergen County.
HAHN, NICHOLAS (see: Ham, Nicholas) Riverview Cemetery, Trenton, Mercer County.
HAHN, NICHOLAS (see: Hannes, Nicholas) St. Mary's Cemetery, Hamilton, Mercer County.
HAIGH, EDWIN D. Pvt, E, 84th NY Inf, 10-6-1898. Rosedale Cemetery, Orange, Essex County.
HAIGH, THOMAS (see: Hough, Thomas) Cedar Lawn Cemetery, Paterson, Passaic County.
HAIGHT, CHARLES Brig Gen, NJ State Militia 8-1-1891. Maplewood Cemetery, Freehold, Monmouth County.
HAIGHT, JAMES A. 3-17-1889. Methodist-Episcopal Cemetery, Glassboro, Gloucester County.
HAIGHT, JAMES W. 1st Sgt, C, 82nd NY Inf, [Died at New York, NY.] 11-19-1862. Bayview-New York Bay Cemetery, Jersey City, Hudson County.
HAIGHT, JOHN (see: Height, John T.) Atlantic View Cemetery, Manasquan, Monmouth County.
HAIGHT, JOHN T. Pvt, K, 29th NJ Inf, 1865. Mount Hebron Cemetery, Montclair, Essex County.
HAIGHT, THOMAS A. Pvt, C, 82nd NY Inf, 12-20-1862. Bayview-New York Bay Cemetery, Jersey City, Hudson County.
HAIGHT, WILLIAM H. Pvt, E, 12th NJ Inf, 11- -1902. Laurel Grove Cemetery, Totowa, Passaic County.
HAILEY, J.W. Corp, K, 23rd VA Inf (CSA), [Captured 5-12-1864 at Spotsylvania CH, VA. Died of diarrhea.] 9-3-1864. Finn's Point National Cemetery, Pennsville, Salem County.
HAINES, A. JACKSON Pvt, K, 36th MS Inf (CSA), 8-11-1863. Finn's Point National Cemetery, Pennsville, Salem County.
HAINES, AARON W. DoD Unknown. Presbyterian Cemetery, New Vernon, Morris County.
HAINES, AARON WILLIS Corp, E, 23rd NJ Inf, 5-4-1916. Rosedale Cemetery, Orange, Essex County.
HAINES, ALANSON AUSTIN Chaplain, 15th NJ Inf 12-11-1891. Hardyston Cemetery, North Church, Sussex County.
HAINES, ALBERT L. Pvt, H, 40th NJ Inf, 1917. Baptist Cemetery, Vincentown, Burlington County.
HAINES, ALEXANDER Pvt, K, 34th NJ Inf, [Wounded 4-6-1865 at Fort Blakely, AL.] 12-2-1898. Baptist Cemetery, Vincentown, Burlington County.
HAINES, AMITY Pvt, H, 2nd NJ Inf, 5-28-1922. Fairmount Cemetery, Newark, Essex County.
HAINES, ASA Pvt, D, 118th PA Inf, 9-5-1917. 1st Baptist Church Cemetery, Moorestown, Burlington County.
HAINES, CHARLES Corp, F, 23rd NJ Inf, 8-1-1909. Brotherhood Cemetery, Hainesport, Burlington County.
HAINES, CHARLES 4-6-1924. Old Gloucester Burial Grounds Cemetery, Clarksboro, Gloucester County.
HAINES, CHARLES FURMAN Pvt, I, 23rd NJ Inf, 6-18-1906. Colestown Cemetery, Cherry Hill, Camden County.
HAINES*, CHARLES G. Corp, E, 4th U.S. Vet Vol Inf, 12-10-1902. Soldier's Home Cemetery, Vineland, Cumberland County.
HAINES, CHARLES H. Pvt, I, 4th NJ Inf, 1894. Mount Holly Cemetery, Mount Holly, Burlington County.

HAINES, CHARLES P. Musc, 3rd NJ Inf Band 8-1-1902. Baptist/St. Andrew's Cemetery, Mount Holly, Burlington County.
HAINES, EDWARD B. Pvt, Unassigned, 54th IL Inf, 5-3-1911. Cedar Lawn Cemetery, Paterson, Passaic County.
HAINES, ELEAZER C. (aka: Haines, Eli) Pvt, E, 4th NJ Inf, 4-9-1923. Harleigh Cemetery, Camden, Camden County.
HAINES, ELI (see: Haines, Eleazer C.) Harleigh Cemetery, Camden, Camden County.
HAINES, ELI W. Pvt, E, 4th NJ Inf, 4-9-1919. Oddfellows-Friends Cemetery, Medford, Burlington County.
HAINES, ELLIS W. Sgt, I, 34th NJ Inf, 10-24-1918. Baptist Cemetery, Vincentown, Burlington County.
HAINES, FRANKLIN J. Pvt, F, 23rd NJ Inf, 2-28-1901. Oddfellows-Friends Cemetery, Medford, Burlington County.
HAINES, GEORGE W. Pvt, E, 23rd NJ Inf, 4-12-1887. Methodist Church Cemetery, Juliustown, Burlington County.
HAINES, GEORGE W. Pvt, D, 1st NJ Cav, DoD Unknown. Baptist Cemetery, Medford, Burlington County.
HAINES, HENRY L. Pvt, C, 34th NJ Inf, 2-14-1894. Evergreen Cemetery, Camden, Camden County.
HAINES, HEZEKIAH Pvt, G, 214th PA Inf, 1-5-1880. Coopertown Meeting House Cemetery, Edgewater Park, Burlington County.
HAINES*, HORACE L. Pvt, G, 6th NJ Inf, 12-19-1885. Evergreen Cemetery, Camden, Camden County.
HAINES, ISAAC REUBEN Pvt, H, 99th PA Inf, 1-16-1931. Colestown Cemetery, Cherry Hill, Camden County.
HAINES, J. WOOD Pvt, I, 23rd NJ Inf, DoD Unknown. Mount Holly Cemetery, Mount Holly, Burlington County.
HAINES, JAPHET Pvt, I, 23rd NJ Inf, 7-19-1887. Epworth Methodist Cemetery, Palmyra, Burlington County.
HAINES, JOHN R. Pvt, C, 12th NJ Inf, 9-27-1895. Marlton Cemetery, Marlton, Burlington County.
HAINES, JOSEPH L. Pvt, C, 73rd NY Inf, [Died of typhoid fever at Yorktown, VA.] 6-7-1862. Hazelwood Cemetery, Rahway, Union County.
HAINES*, JOSEPH T. 1st Lt, H, 38th NJ Inf, 1918. Friends United Methodist-Episcopal Church Cemetery, Linwood, Atlantic County.
HAINES, JOSHUA D. Pvt, I, 9th NJ Inf, 12-2-1901. Evergreen Cemetery, Camden, Camden County.
HAINES, LEWIS Pvt, C, 11th NJ Inf, 2-22-1906. Fairmount Cemetery, Newark, Essex County.
HAINES, LORENZO Pvt, H, 32nd U.S. CT, 11-18-1901. Jordan Lawn Cemetery, Pennsauken, Camden County.
HAINES, MARTIN L. Capt, C, 34th NJ Inf, 1905. Baptist Cemetery, Vincentown, Burlington County.
HAINES, MARTIN V. Pvt, D, 24th NJ Inf, [Wounded 12-13-1862 at Fredericksburg, VA.] 6-4-1924. Chestnut Grove Cemetery, Elmer, Salem County.
HAINES, RICHARD C. Corp, I, 6th NJ Inf, DoD Unknown. Mount Pleasant Cemetery, Millville, Cumberland County.
HAINES*, SAMUEL Corp, E, 7th NJ Inf, 3-14-1906. Pleasant Ridge Cemetery, East Amwell, Hunterdon County.
HAINES, SAMUEL B. Pvt, B, 95th PA Inf, 1-8-1916. Colestown Cemetery, Cherry Hill, Camden County.
HAINES, SAMUEL E. Pvt, Btty C, 2nd PA Heavy Art, 6-12-1927. Arlington Cemetery, Pennsauken, Camden County.

Our Brothers Gone Before

HAINES, THEODORE B. Pvt, C, 23rd NJ Inf, 1918. Mount Holly Cemetery, Mount Holly, Burlington County.
HAINES*, THEODORE S. Sgt, C, 34th NJ Inf, 11-7-1909. Baptist Cemetery, Vincentown, Burlington County.
HAINES, THOMAS Seaman, U.S. Navy, 4-14-1925. Laurel Grove Cemetery, Totowa, Passaic County.
HAINES,.THOMAS E. 1874. Mount Holly Cemetery, Mount Holly, Burlington County.
HAINES, THOMAS RYERSON Capt, M, 1st NJ Cav, [Killed in action at Harrisonburg, VA.] 6-6-1862. Hardyston Cemetery, North Church, Sussex County.
HAINES, WILLIAM Pvt, B, 4th U.S. Cav, 11-11-1898. Washington Monumental Cemetery, South River, Middlesex County.
HAINES, WILLIAM H.H. Pvt, I, 27th NJ Inf, [Died of typhoid at Fort Monroe, VA.] 3-7-1863. Presbyterian Cemetery, New Vernon, Morris County.
HAINES*, WILLIAM R. Pvt, K, 34th NJ Inf, 1904. Baptist/St. Andrew's Cemetery, Mount Holly, Burlington County.
HAIPT, JOSEPH (aka: Hipe, Joseph) Pvt, Unassigned, 69th NY Inf, 8-11-1894. Woodland Cemetery, Newark, Essex County.
HAIRE, ROBERT Sgt, H, 4th MI Inf, 12-15-1901. Bayview-New York Bay Cemetery, Jersey City, Hudson County.
HAIRES, DANIEL Pvt, K, 8th LA Inf (CSA), [Captured 7-3-1863 at Gettysburg, PA. Died of typhoid.] 3-22-1864. Finn's Point National Cemetery, Pennsville, Salem County.
HAIZLIP, JEFFERSON (aka: Hayslip, Jefferson) Pvt, D, 57th VA Inf (CSA), [Wounded and captured 7-3-1863 at Gettysburg, PA. Died of typhoid.] 9-25-1863. Finn's Point National Cemetery, Pennsville, Salem County.
HALE, EDWARD C. Pvt, K, 9th NJ Inf, 5-11-1891. Evergreen Cemetery, Camden, Camden County.
HALE, EDWARD M. Pvt, E, 39th MA Inf, 5-7-1920. Cedar Lawn Cemetery, Paterson, Passaic County.
HALE, FRANK B. Pvt, H, 2nd OH Cav, DoD Unknown. Hackensack Cemetery, Hackensack, Bergen County.
HALE, JOHN A. Pvt, C, 60th (Crawford's) TN Mtd Inf (CSA), [Captured 5-17-1863 at Big Black River Bridge, MS.] 9-7-1863. Finn's Point National Cemetery, Pennsville, Salem County.
HALE*, JOSEPH Pvt, Btty D, 1st NJ Light Art, [Wounded 5-5-1862 at Williamsburg, VA.] 10-16-1895. Evergreen Cemetery, Farmingdale, Monmouth County.
HALE, JOSEPH 1st Lt, B, 3rd U.S. Inf, 10-12-1898. Cedar Lawn Cemetery, Paterson, Passaic County.
HALE, WILLIAM R. Pvt, E, 60th (Crawford's) TN Mtd Inf (CSA), [Captured 5-17-1863 at Big Black River Bridge, MS.] 9-28-1863. Finn's Point National Cemetery, Pennsville, Salem County.
HALES, EDWARD Pvt, C, 133rd NY Inf, 11-16-1918. Hoboken Cemetery, North Bergen, Hudson County.
HALEY, CHARLES Corp, F, 24th NJ Inf, 1926. Zion United Methodist Church Cemetery, Dividing Creek, Cumberland County.
HALEY, DALLAS T. Corp, G, 24th NJ Inf, DoD Unknown. Methodist Church Cemetery, Haleyville, Cumberland County.
HALEY, GEORGE Pvt, E, 116th NY Inf, [Accidently wounded 6-15-1863.] 1-2-1923. Evergreen Cemetery, Camden, Camden County.
HALEY, GEORGE W. Musc, B, 7th NJ Inf, 3-25-1900. Fairmount Cemetery, Newark, Essex County.
HALEY, JAMES Pvt, B, 1st NJ Inf, 1-15-1917. Riverview Cemetery, Trenton, Mercer County.

New Jersey Civil War Burials

HALEY, JAMES (see: Healey, Bernard) Holy Sepulchre Cemetery, Totowa, Passaic County.

HALEY, JAMES W. Pvt, A, 13th NJ Inf, 5-23-1884. Holy Sepulchre Cemetery, East Orange, Essex County.

HALEY, JOHN (see: Hallar, John E.) Trinity United Methodist Church Cemetery, Bayville, Ocean County.

HALEY, JOHN H. Pvt, K, 7th NJ Inf, DoD Unknown. New Vernon Cemetery, New Vernon, Morris County.

HALEY, MARTIN Pvt, I, 57th MA Inf, [Died of diarrhea at Beverly, NJ. Wounded 5-12-1864 at Spotsylvania CH, VA.] 10-16-1864. Beverly National Cemetery, Edgewater Park, Burlington County.

HALEY, NELSON Pvt, G, 24th NJ Inf, 5-2-1885. Methodist Church Cemetery, Haleyville, Cumberland County.

HALEY, PATRICK Pvt, I, 1st NY Eng, 1878. Holy Name Cemetery, Jersey City, Hudson County.

HALEY, PATRICK Pvt, A, 14th NJ Inf, 11-16-1899. St. John's Cemetery, Lambertville, Hunterdon County.

HALEY, PATRICK Pvt, K, 1st NJ Inf, 1-21-1888. St. Joseph's Cemetery, Mendham, Morris County.

HALEY, THOMAS Corp, B, 133rd NY Inf, 11-3-1909. Laurel Grove Cemetery, Totowa, Passaic County.

HALFORD, JOSEPH Pvt, D, 71st NY Inf, 12-21-1877. Fairmount Cemetery, Newark, Essex County.

HALFORD, MICHAEL Pvt, F, 22nd NJ Inf, 1-9-1916. St. Mary's Cemetery, Hamilton, Mercer County.

HALFOSH, FIRMAN (see: Gise, Furman Hullfish) Hillside Cemetery, Scotch Plains, Union County.

HALL, ANTHONY Pvt, B, 25th U.S. CT, 8-29-1907. Evergreen Cemetery, Hillside, Union County.

HALL, ANTHONY A. Pvt, H, 11th PA Cav, 10-9-1886. Baptist/St. Andrew's Cemetery, Mount Holly, Burlington County.

HALL*, BARNABUS K. (aka: Hall, Stephen K.) Pvt, E, 1st NJ Cav, 10-28-1881. Presbyterian Church Cemetery, Rockaway, Morris County.

HALL, BENJAMIN (see: Wall, Benjamin) Mount Olivet Cemetery, Newark, Essex County.

HALL, BENJAMIN F. 9-28-1915. 1st Baptist Cemetery, Cape May Court House, Cape May County.

HALL, CHARLES Capt, E, 4th NJ Inf, 1899. Morgan Cemetery, Cinnaminson, Burlington County.

HALL, CHARLES Pvt, F, 14th NJ Inf, DoD Unknown. Osbornville Protestant Church Cemetery, Breton Woods, Ocean County.

HALL, CHARLES A. Teamster, B, 15th NY Eng, 5-16-1918. Clinton Cemetery, Irvington, Essex County.

HALL*, CHARLES E. Surg, 40th NJ Inf [Also: Asst Surg, 15th NJ Inf.] 12-5-1922. Maplewood Cemetery, Freehold, Monmouth County.

HALL, DENNIS S. 1925. Reformed Church Cemetery, Readington, Hunterdon County.

HALL*, DENNISON C. Pvt, Btty C, 2nd CT Heavy Art, 1-19-1902. Holcomb-Riverview Cemetery, Lambertville, Hunterdon County.

HALL, EBENEZER Corp, B, 9th NJ Inf, 8-7-1881. Evergreen Cemetery, New Brunswick, Middlesex County.

HALL, EDWARD C. Pvt, K, 12th NJ Inf, 12-28-1877. Old Stone Church Cemetery, Fairton, Cumberland County.

HALL, EDWIN Sgt, C, 7th NJ Inf, 4-15-1925. Locust Hill Cemetery, Dover, Morris County.

Our Brothers Gone Before

HALL, ENOCH W. Pvt, H, 71st NY Inf, 10-15-1896. Presbyterian Church Cemetery, Rockaway, Morris County.

HALL, EPHRIAM F. 2nd Lt, K, 1st NJ Militia, 7-14-1914. Locust Hill Cemetery, Dover, Morris County.

HALL, EZRA GEORGE Pvt, C, 37th NY Inf, 5-1-1921. Glendale Cemetery, Bloomfield, Essex County.

HALL, FARRIS H. (aka: Hall, Paris) Corp, E, 22nd U.S. CT, 1-23-1902. Oak Hill Cemetery, Vineland, Cumberland County.

HALL, FERDINAND (aka: Hall, Frederick) Pvt, A, 132nd NY Inf, 11-7-1898. Alpine Cemetery, Perth Amboy, Middlesex County.

HALL, FRANCIS Pvt, U.S. Marine Corps, USS Colorado, DoD Unknown. Presbyterian/Methodist-Episcopal Cemetery, Succasunna, Morris County.

HALL, FRANCIS Pvt, A, 40th NJ Inf, DoD Unknown. Cedar Hill Cemetery, Cedarville, Cumberland County.

HALL, FRANCIS B. (aka: Bickel, Francis) Pvt, D, 5th NY Inf, [Wounded 8-30-1862 at 2nd Bull Run, VA.] 11-5-1881. Bayview-New York Bay Cemetery, Jersey City, Hudson County.

HALL, FREDERICK (see: Hall, Ferdinand) Alpine Cemetery, Perth Amboy, Middlesex County.

HALL, GEORGE Pvt, B, 142nd NY Inf, 1-14-1927. Pearson/Colonial Memorial Park Cemetery, Whitehorse, Mercer County.

HALL*, GEORGE B. Musc, Btty E, 11th U.S. CHA, 10-15-1917. Evergreen Cemetery, Hillside, Union County.

HALL, GEORGE M. Pvt, H, 5th DE Inf, 1924. Eastview Cemetery, Salem, Salem County.

HALL, GEORGE R. Pvt, F, 15th NJ Inf, 2-14-1914. Presbyterian Church Cemetery, Rockaway, Morris County.

HALL*, GEORGE W. 2nd Asst Eng, U.S. Navy, [Special duty at NewYork, NY.] 3-12-1920. Fairmount Cemetery, Newark, Essex County.

HALL, GEORGE W. Pvt, A, 29th NJ Inf, 7-3-1881. Old 1st Methodist Church Cemetery, West Long Branch, Monmouth County.

HALL, GEORGE W. Pvt, F, 56th VA Inf (CSA), [Wounded 6-27-1862 at Gaines' Mill, VA. Captured 7-3-1863 at Gettysburg, PA.] 10-5-1863. Finn's Point National Cemetery, Pennsville, Salem County.

HALL*, GEORGE W. Sgt, F, 8th NJ Inf, DoD Unknown. Presbyterian Church Cemetery, Bridgeton, Cumberland County.

HALL, GEORGE W. Pvt, D, 25th NJ Inf, 10-16-1903. Overlook Cemetery, Bridgeton, Cumberland County.

HALL, GORDON N. Pvt, A, 6th NJ Inf, 1875. Maplewood Cemetery, Freehold, Monmouth County.

HALL, GUADALOUPE (see: Holl, George K.) Evergreen Cemetery, Camden, Camden County.

HALL, HENRY Pvt, H, 127th U.S. CT, 9-26-1882. New Presbyterian Cemetery, Bound Brook, Somerset County.

HALL, HENRY Pvt, E, 30th NJ Inf, 1-4-1899. Cedar Hill Cemetery, East Millstone, Somerset County.

HALL, HIRAM Pvt, H, 34th NJ Inf, 1-4-1888. Fairmount Cemetery, Newark, Essex County.

HALL, HORATIO A. Pvt, D, 18th CT Inf, 8-18-1891. Fairmount Cemetery, Newark, Essex County.

HALL, HOWARD Pvt, C, 22nd U.S. CT, [Wounded in action.] DoD Unknown. Chestnut Cemetery, Greenwich, Cumberland County.

HALL, IRA J. Pvt, H, 84th NY National Guard, 12-26-1900. Evergreen Cemetery, Hillside, Union County.

New Jersey Civil War Burials

HALL, ISAAC BRADSHAW 1st Lt, Btty A, 1st NY Light Art, 4-25-1918. Rosedale Cemetery, Orange, Essex County.

HALL, ISAAC H. Pvt, A, 7th NJ Inf, [Wounded in action.] 10-15-1866. Presbyterian Church Cemetery, Cold Spring, Cape May County.

HALL, JAMES Ensign, U.S. Navy, USS North Carolina, 9-20-1884. Evergreen Cemetery, Hillside, Union County.

HALL, JAMES B. 9-24-1890. Evergreen Cemetery, Hillside, Union County.

HALL*, JAMES H. Pvt, E, 5th NY Vet Inf, 5-3-1892. Fairmount Cemetery, Newark, Essex County.

HALL, JAMES K. Pvt, F, 48th GA Inf (CSA), [Captured 7-2-1863 at Gettysburg, PA. Died of disease.] 10-13-1863. Finn's Point National Cemetery, Pennsville, Salem County.

HALL, JESSE B. Pvt, C, 61st (Pitts') TN Mtd Inf (CSA), 7-8-1863. Finn's Point National Cemetery, Pennsville, Salem County.

HALL, JOHN Pvt, D, 27th VA Inf (CSA), [Captured 5-12-1864 at Spotsylvania CH, VA. Died of diarrhea.] 3-25-1865. Finn's Point National Cemetery, Pennsville, Salem County.

HALL, JOHN Pvt, I, 8th NJ Inf, 8-14-1871. Reformed Church Cemetery, Lebanon, Hunterdon County.

HALL, JOHN Pvt, G, 1st NJ Cav, 4-4-1894. Presbyterian Church Cemetery, Woodbridge, Middlesex County.

HALL, JOHN Pvt, B, 7th TN Inf (CSA), 10-19-1863. Finn's Point National Cemetery, Pennsville, Salem County.

HALL, JOHN Sgt, G, 12th NJ Inf, 2-14-1883. Phillipsburg Cemetery, Phillipsburg, Warren County.

HALL, JOHN (see: Stain, John C.) Arlington Cemetery, Pennsauken, Camden County.

HALL, JOHN A. Pvt, H, 26th AL Inf (CSA), [Captured at Gettysburg, PA. Died of lung inflammation.] 3-16-1864. Finn's Point National Cemetery, Pennsville, Salem County.

HALL, JOHN B. Pvt, H, 26th NJ Inf, [Wounded in action.] 8-14-1904. South Orange Cemetery, South Orange, Essex County.

HALL, JOHN F. Pvt, F, 60th VA Inf (CSA), [Captured 3-2-1865 at Waynesboro, VA. Died of measles.] 4-17-1865. Finn's Point National Cemetery, Pennsville, Salem County.

HALL, JOHN H. Pvt, C, 7th NJ Inf, 3-29-1934. Presbyterian Church Cemetery, Rockaway, Morris County.

HALL, JOHN H. Pvt, F, 38th NJ Inf, 6-21-1929. Greenville Cemetery, Lakewood, Ocean County.

HALL, JOHN L. Pvt, F, 15th NJ Inf, [Wounded in action.] 6-13-1889. Presbyterian Church Cemetery, Rockaway, Morris County.

HALL, JOHN N. Pvt, E, 30th NJ Inf, 1925. New Somerville Cemetery, Somerville, Somerset County.

HALL, JOHN T. Pvt, D, 1st MO Cav (CSA), 10-2-1863. Finn's Point National Cemetery, Pennsville, Salem County.

HALL, JOHN T.S. Pvt, K, 29th NJ Inf, 1920. Evergreen Cemetery, Farmingdale, Monmouth County.

HALL, JOHN W. Sgt, H, 29th CT Inf, 3-24-1894. St. Paul's Church Cemetery, Burlington, Burlington County.

HALL*, JOHN W. Pvt, C, 7th CT Inf, 4-23-1909. Fairmount Cemetery, Newark, Essex County.

HALL, JOSEPH G. Pvt, D, 2nd U.S. Cav, 5-2-1885. Holcomb-Riverview Cemetery, Lambertville, Hunterdon County.

HALL, JOSEPH H. Pvt, L, 1st NJ Cav, 4-11-1912. Cedar Hill Cemetery, Hightstown, Mercer County.

Our Brothers Gone Before

HALL, JOSEPH (SR.) 6-21-1897. Presbyterian Church Cemetery, Cold Spring, Cape May County.
HALL*, LEVI Corp, G, 7th NJ Inf, [Wounded in action.] 1-15-1895. Fairmount Cemetery, Newark, Essex County.
HALL*, LORENZO Pvt, E, 17th ME Inf, 11-28-1880. Greenmount Cemetery, Hammonton, Atlantic County.
HALL, MATTHEW WHILDIN Pvt, F, 25th NJ Inf, 2-19-1874. Presbyterian Church Cemetery, Cold Spring, Cape May County.
HALL, MICHAEL Pvt, Btty D, 1st NJ Light Art, DoD Unknown. St. Rose of Lima Cemetery, Millburn, Essex County.
HALL, MOSES J. Pvt, B, Thomas' Legion (Walker's Bttn) NC Inf (CSA), 3-31-1864. Finn's Point National Cemetery, Pennsville, Salem County.
HALL, NATHAN Pvt, C, 4th NC Cav (CSA), [Captured at Monterey, PA. Died of diarrhea.] 9-28-1863. Finn's Point National Cemetery, Pennsville, Salem County.
HALL, NATHAN C. Pvt, F, 52nd NC Inf (CSA), [Wounded and captured 7-1-1863 at Gettysburg, PA. Died of wounds.] 12-10-1863. Finn's Point National Cemetery, Pennsville, Salem County.
HALL, NATHANIEL (see: Haller, Nathaniel) Spencer African Methodist Church Cemetery, Woodstown, Salem County.
HALL, OLIVER R.C. Pvt, H, 42nd MS Inf (CSA), 10-3-1863. Finn's Point National Cemetery, Pennsville, Salem County.
HALL, ORIN S. (aka: Hall, Orwin) Pvt, Btty D, 4th NY Heavy Art, [Died of disease at Beverly, NJ.] 3-13-1865. Beverly National Cemetery, Edgewater Park, Burlington County.
HALL, ORWIN (see: Hall, Orin S.) Beverly National Cemetery, Edgewater Park, Burlington County.
HALL, PARIS (see: Hall, Farris H.) Oak Hill Cemetery, Vineland, Cumberland County.
HALL, PETER M. Pvt, F, 22nd NY Inf, 8-29-1913. Rosedale Cemetery, Orange, Essex County.
HALL, PHILIP Corp, E, 45th U.S. CT, 2-10-1911. Memorial Park Cemetery, Gouldtown, Cumberland County.
HALL, REUBEN Pvt, B, 9th NJ Inf, 7-14-1875. Willow Grove Cemetery, New Brunswick, Middlesex County.
HALL, ROBERT B. Musc, A, 30th NJ Inf, 1925. Methodist-Episcopal Cemetery, Whitehouse, Hunterdon County.
HALL, SAMUEL (aka: VanHalle, Soloman) Pvt, B, 81st NY Inf, 4-14-1908. Fairview Cemetery, Fairview, Bergen County.
HALL, SAMUEL Actg Master, U.S. Navy, 5-13-1920. Arlington Cemetery, Kearny, Hudson County.
HALL, SAMUEL Pvt, C, 11th NJ Inf, 10-16-1868. Pequest Union Cemetery, Great Meadows, Warren County.
HALL, SAMUEL B. 5-21-1901. Siloam Cemetery, Vineland, Cumberland County.
HALL, SAMUEL D. Corp, A, 30th NJ Inf, 3-5-1896. Reformed Church Cemetery, Readington, Hunterdon County.
HALL, SAMUEL T. Corp, E, 30th NJ Inf, 5-19-1913. Reformed Church Cemetery, Three Bridges, Hunterdon County.
HALL, STEPHEN Pvt, E, 1st NJ Cav, 7-7-1905. Methodist-Episcopal Cemetery, Old Bridge, Middlesex County.
HALL, STEPHEN D. Pvt, C, 7th NJ Inf, 3-11-1881. United Methodist Church Cemetery, Rockaway Valley, Morris County.
HALL, STEPHEN K. (see: Hall, Barnabas K.) Presbyterian Church Cemetery, Rockaway, Morris County.
HALL, SYLVESTER Corp, H, 29th NJ Inf, 1924. Evergreen Cemetery, Farmingdale, Monmouth County.

New Jersey Civil War Burials

HALL, T.A. Actg Master, U.S. Navy, USS Nipsic, 5-28-1866. Mount Pleasant Cemetery, Newark, Essex County.
HALL, THEOPHILUS B. Pvt, B, 42nd MS Inf (CSA), 11-20-1863. Finn's Point National Cemetery, Pennsville, Salem County.
HALL, TOWNSEND Landsman, U.S. Navy, USS Nipsic, 1-26-1896. Cedar Hill Cemetery, Hightstown, Mercer County.
HALL, WILLIAM Pvt, F, 6th NJ Inf, 2-25-1873. St. Mary's Episcopal Church Cemetery, Burlington, Burlington County.
HALL, WILLIAM Sgt, A, 47th PA Inf, 11-13-1914. Pequest Union Cemetery, Great Meadows, Warren County.
HALL, WILLIAM Pvt, C, 34th NJ Inf, 1900. Fairview Cemetery, Fairview, Monmouth County.
HALL, WILLIAM A. Pvt, F, 48th GA Inf (CSA), [Captured 7-2-1863 at Gettysburg, PA.] 8-31-1863. Finn's Point National Cemetery, Pennsville, Salem County.
HALL, WILLIAM E. 1st Lt, F, 57th NY Inf, [Wounded 7-3-1863 at Gettysburg, PA and 5-18-1864 at Spotsylvania CH, VA.] 9-10-1880. Hoboken Cemetery, North Bergen, Hudson County.
HALL, WILLIAM F. Pvt, B, 2nd RI Inf, 3-14-1914. Bayview-New York Bay Cemetery, Jersey City, Hudson County.
HALL, WILLIAM H. Sgt, H, 6th U.S. CT, 1-31-1900. Johnson Cemetery, Camden, Camden County.
HALL, WILLIAM H. Pvt, F, 14th NJ Inf, 1-2-1900. Osbornville Protestant Church Cemetery, Breton Woods, Ocean County.
HALL*, WILLIAM H. Pvt, H, 63rd NY Inf, 6-14-1901. Fairmount Cemetery, Newark, Essex County.
HALL*, WILLIAM HENRY Pvt, I, 146th NY Inf, 12-8-1923. Rosedale Cemetery, Orange, Essex County.
HALLAGAN, MARTIN Pvt, E, 22nd MA Inf, 9-2-1893. Holy Sepulchre Cemetery, East Orange, Essex County.
HALLAR, JOHN E. (aka: Haley, John) Pvt, H, 20th ME Inf, DoD Unknown. Trinity United Methodist Church Cemetery, Bayville, Ocean County.
HALLECK, DEBOISE H. Pvt, D, 26th U.S. CT, 12-14-1894. Bayview-New York Bay Cemetery, Jersey City, Hudson County.
HALLECK, HENRY L. Pvt, G, 95th NY Inf, [Wounded in action.] 5-31-1905. Arlington Cemetery, Kearny, Hudson County.
HALLECK, JOHN Pvt, H, 2nd U.S. CT, DoD Unknown. Arlington Cemetery, Kearny, Hudson County.
HALLER*, NATHANIEL (aka: Hall, Nathaniel) Pvt, Btty M, 11th U.S. CHA, 8-19-1911. Spencer African Methodist Church Cemetery, Woodstown, Salem County.
HALLGRING, AUGUSTUS W. Musc, A, 7th NJ Inf, 3-15-1904. Fairmount Cemetery, Newark, Essex County.
HALLIDAY, ADAM M. Pvt, K, 2nd DC Inf, DoD Unknown. Vincent Methodist-Episcopal Cemetery, Nutley, Essex County.
HALLINBECK, STEPHEN (see: Haullenbeck, Stephen) Rosedale Cemetery, Orange, Essex County.
HALLINBECK, STEPHEN I. (aka: Haulenbeck. Stephen) Pvt, H, 26th NJ Inf, 5-30-1880. Rosedale Cemetery, Orange, Essex County.
HALLINWAY, C. 5-2-1884. Cedar Lawn Cemetery, Paterson, Passaic County.
HALLIWELL, JOSEPH (aka: Hollowell, Joseph) Pvt, C, 9th NY Inf, 10-19-1884. Cedar Lawn Cemetery, Paterson, Passaic County.
HALLIWELL, THOMAS J. Pvt, E, 9th NJ Inf, 11-27-1889. Cedar Lawn Cemetery, Paterson, Passaic County.
HALLOCK, ALFRED Pvt, D, 2nd DC Inf, [Died of typhoid at Camp Wadsworth, VA.] 7-10-1862. Rosedale Cemetery, Orange, Essex County.

Our Brothers Gone Before

HALLORAN, PATRICK Seaman, U.S. Navy, 7-23-1905. Holy Name Cemetery, Jersey City, Hudson County.

HALLORAN, THOMAS (see: O'Halloran, Thomas) Holy Name Cemetery, Jersey City, Hudson County.

HALLOWAY, RICHARD Musc, B, 33rd NJ Inf, 1-7-1901. Evergreen Cemetery, Hillside, Union County.

HALLUM, J.N. Pvt, A, 27th AL Inf (CSA), 6-23-1863. Finn's Point National Cemetery, Pennsville, Salem County.

HALLY, CORNELIUS (aka: Hully, Cornelius) Pvt, A, 35th NJ Inf, 1-23-1911. Holy Rood Cemetery, Morristown, Morris County.

HALLY, JOHN Pvt, Btty D, 1st NJ Light Art, 8-15-1886. St. Mary's Cemetery, Clark, Union County.

HALPIN, JOHN Pvt, C, 29th NJ Inf, 12-21-1914. Baptist Church Cemetery, Jacobstown, Burlington County.

HALPIN, PETER Pvt, H, 6th NJ Inf, DoD Unknown. St. John's Cemetery, Lambertville, Hunterdon County.

HALPS, CHARLES (see: Herpst, Karl) Woodland Cemetery, Newark, Essex County.

HALSEY, ABRAHAM W. Corp, C, 102nd NY Inf, 3-2-1903. Holy Name Cemetery, Jersey City, Hudson County.

HALSEY, ALEXANDER Pvt, K, 27th NJ Inf, 12-25-1910. Lady of Lourdes/Holy Sepulchre Cemetery, Hamilton, Mercer County.

HALSEY, ANDREW C. Corp, K, 7th NJ Inf, [Died of wounds.] 6-20-1864. Presbyterian Church Cemetery, Morristown, Morris County.

HALSEY*, CHARLES L. Pvt, I, 39th NJ Inf, 1867. Mount Pleasant Cemetery, Newark, Essex County.

HALSEY, DANIEL S. Pvt, I, 26th NJ Inf, 6-23-1923. Mount Pleasant Cemetery, Newark, Essex County.

HALSEY, DANIEL S. (SR.) Pvt, I, 26th NJ Inf, 1872. Presbyterian Cemetery, Springfield, Union County.

HALSEY, EDMUND DRAKE 1st Lt, Adj, 15th NJ Inf 10-15-1896. Presbyterian Church Cemetery, Rockaway, Morris County.

HALSEY, GEORGE (see: Horsey, George) Spencer African Methodist Church Cemetery, Woodstown, Salem County.

HALSEY, HORACE A. Pvt, C, 2nd NJ Militia, 3-15-1901. Fairmount Cemetery, Newark, Essex County.

HALSEY, JAMES HARVEY Musc, I, 35th NJ Inf, 2-6-1898. Mount Pleasant Cemetery, Newark, Essex County.

HALSEY, JEREMIAH Pvt, H, 30th NJ Inf, DoD Unknown. St. Mary's Cemetery, Plainfield, Union County.

HALSEY, JOHN H. Pvt, H, 67th NY Inf, [Wounded 5-31-1862 at Seven Pines, VA.] 1930. Maple Grove Cemetery, Hackensack, Bergen County.

HALSEY*, LUTHER FOSTER Asst Surg, 2nd NJ Inf [Wounded in action. Also: Asst Surg, 7th NJ Inf.] 7-7-1895. New Episcopal Church Cemetery, Swedesboro, Gloucester County.

HALSEY, NELSON S. Pvt, E, 38th NJ Inf, 4-4-1885. Presbyterian Church Cemetery, Mount Pleasant, Hunterdon County.

HALSEY, NORWOOD A. 1st Lt, D, 10th NY Inf, 5-10-1906. Rosedale Cemetery, Orange, Essex County.

HALSEY, THOMAS J. Maj, 11th NJ Inf [Wounded 5-3-1863 at Chancellorsville, VA.] 1-20-1893. Chestnut Cemetery, Dover, Morris County.

HALSEY, WILLIAM F. 2nd Lt, E, 40th NY Inf, [Wounded in action 5- -1864.] 6-4-1921. Fairmount Cemetery, Newark, Essex County.

HALSEY*, WILLIAM S. Pvt, F, 5th NY Inf, 10-1-1904. Bayview-New York Bay Cemetery, Jersey City, Hudson County.

New Jersey Civil War Burials

HALSEY, WILLIAM V.H. Capt, B, 26th NJ Inf, 1901. Mount Pleasant Cemetery, Newark, Essex County.

HALSTEAD*, DAVID W. Pvt, K, 21st U.S. VRC, 7-2-1895. Methodist Cemetery, Newfoundland, Morris County.

HALSTEAD, GEORGE G. 1891. Cedar Lawn Cemetery, Paterson, Passaic County.

HALSTEAD, GEORGE W. Pvt, C, 14th NJ Inf, 4-29-1890. Evergreen Cemetery, Hillside, Union County.

HALSTEAD*, ISAAC S. Corp, H, 7th NJ Inf, 12-11-1892. Bayview-New York Bay Cemetery, Jersey City, Hudson County.

HALSTEAD, ISAAC W. Pvt, A, 1st NJ Inf, [Died at Alexandria, VA.] 12-31-1862. Evergreen Cemetery, Hillside, Union County.

HALSTEAD, JAMES Corp, I, 14th IN Inf, [Died of typhoid at Newark, NJ.] 10-11-1862. Fairmount Cemetery, Newark, Essex County.

HALSTEAD, JAMES 1st Sgt, I, 70th NY Inf, 6-13-1869. Cedar Lawn Cemetery, Paterson, Passaic County.

HALSTEAD, OLIVER (see: Halsted, Oliver Spencer (Jr.)) Presbyterian Church Cemetery, Elizabeth, Union County.

HALSTEAD, THOMAS K. Pvt, H, 13th NY Inf, 8-14-1913. Bayview-New York Bay Cemetery, Jersey City, Hudson County.

HALSTEAD, WILLIAM Pvt, K, 8th NJ Inf, [Died of wounds received 5-3-1863 at Chancellorsville, VA.] 5-18-1863. Laurel Grove Cemetery, Totowa, Passaic County.

HALSTED, ALBERT H. Pvt, G, 5th NJ Inf, 10-23-1883. Cedar Lawn Cemetery, Paterson, Passaic County.

HALSTED, AMMI B. Pvt, Btty B, 3rd NY Light Art, 1897. Valleau Cemetery, Ridgewood, Bergen County.

HALSTED*, FRANCIS WILLIAM Actg Ensign, U.S. Navy, USS General Pillow, 1876. Presbyterian Church Cemetery, Elizabeth, Union County.

HALSTED, NATHANIEL NORRIS Lt Col, NJ [Aide-de-Camp to Governer Olden 1861-1863. Brig Gen Commanding Trenton Rendezvous August 20, 1862.] 5-6-1884. Presbyterian Church Cemetery, Elizabeth, Union County.

HALSTED, OLIVER SPENCER (JR.) (aka: Halstead, Oliver) 1st Lt, G, 68th IN Inf, 1871. Presbyterian Church Cemetery, Elizabeth, Union County.

HALSTED, WILLIAM Col, 1st NJ Cav 3-4-1878. Riverview Cemetery, Trenton, Mercer County.

HALSTED, WILLIAM A. 1st Lt, E, PA Emerg NJ Militia, 8-30-1898. Evergreen Cemetery, Morristown, Morris County.

HALTER*, ALFRED P. Pvt, F, 5th NJ Inf, 2-6-1918. Lutheran Church Cemetery, Friesburg, Salem County.

HALTER, DAVID A. Pvt, F, 5th NJ Inf, 1904. Lutheran Church Cemetery, Friesburg, Salem County.

HALTER, JAMES Pvt, I, 2nd DE Inf, 10-17-1908. Riverview Cemetery, Penns Grove, Salem County.

HALTER, JOHN Pvt, I, 2nd DE Inf, [Cenotaph. Died of diarrhea at Philadelphia, PA.] 8-18-1862. Methodist-Episcopal Church Cemetery, Penns Grove, Salem County.

HALTER, JOHN G. 3-8-1864. Lutheran Church Cemetery, Friesburg, Salem County.

HAM, EPHRIAM Pvt, K, 1st NJ Militia, 6-17-1878. Fairmount Cemetery, Newark, Essex County.

HAM*, NICHOLAS (aka: Hahn, Nicholas) Corp, F, 11th NJ Inf, 9-16-1901. Riverview Cemetery, Trenton, Mercer County.

HAMBERGER, JOHN Pvt, B, 3rd NJ Inf, 2-19-1900. Cedar Lawn Cemetery, Paterson, Passaic County.

HAMBERLIN, WILLIAM A. Pvt, E, 46th MS Inf (CSA), 9-15-1863. Finn's Point National Cemetery, Pennsville, Salem County.

Our Brothers Gone Before

HAMBRICK, JOSEPH Pvt, F, 60th (Crawford's) TN Mtd Inf (CSA), [Captured 5-17-1863 at Big Black River Bridge, MS.] 6-29-1863. Finn's Point National Cemetery, Pennsville, Salem County.

HAMBRICK, PAUL R. Bvt Maj, 23rd NJ Inf 3-16-1888. Fairmount Cemetery, Newark, Essex County.

HAMBY, ISAAC Pvt, G, 9th (Malone's) AL Cav (CSA), 9-15-1863. Finn's Point National Cemetery, Pennsville, Salem County.

HAMBY, JEREMIAH B. Pvt, F, 42nd GA Inf (CSA), [Captured 5-16-1863 at Baker's Creek, MS.] 7-25-1863. Finn's Point National Cemetery, Pennsville, Salem County.

HAMELL*, BENJAMIN F. Actg Asst Surg, U.S. Navy, USS Shokokon, 8-26-1869. Evergreen Cemetery, Camden, Camden County.

HAMELL, DAVID D. 1st Sgt, F, 4th NJ Inf, 4-9-1885. Evergreen Cemetery, Camden, Camden County.

HAMER, JAMES Pvt, I, 38th NJ Inf, 12-8-1916. Riverview Cemetery, Trenton, Mercer County.

HAMER*, WILLIAM T. 1st Sgt, I, 36th MA Inf, [Cenotaph. Killed in action at Spotsylvania CH, VA.] 5-12-1864. Cedar Lawn Cemetery, Paterson, Passaic County.

HAMET, ROSS M. Pvt, E, 60th (Crawford's) TN Mtd Inf (CSA), [Captured 5-17-1863 at Big Black River Bridge, MS.] 8-23-1863. Finn's Point National Cemetery, Pennsville, Salem County.

HAMET, ZACHARIAH Pvt, E, 60th (Crawford's) TN Mtd Inf (CSA), [Captured 5-17-1863 at Big Black River Bridge, MS.] 6-30-1863. Finn's Point National Cemetery, Pennsville, Salem County.

HAMILL, THOMAS Pvt, F, 57th NY Inf, [Wounded 12-13-1862 at Fredericksburg, VA.] 10-5-1899. Fairmount Cemetery, Newark, Essex County.

HAMILTON*, ADAM G. 1st Lt, I, 25th VA Inf (CSA), [Captured 5-10-1864 at Spotsylvania CH, VA. Died of smallpox.] 7-28-1864. Finn's Point National Cemetery, Pennsville, Salem County.

HAMILTON, BENJAMIN Pvt, I, 39th NJ Inf, 1917. Tranquility Cemetery, Tranquility, Sussex County.

HAMILTON, CHARLES H. Seaman, U.S. Navy, 7-1-1892. Tennent Church Cemetery, Tennent, Monmouth County.

HAMILTON, EDGAR AUGUSTUS Maj, 1st NY Mounted Rifles 6-25-1926. Fairview Cemetery, Wantage, Sussex County.

HAMILTON, EDWARD C. Pvt, B, 157th OH Inf, [Died at Fort Delaware.] 7-14-1864. Finn's Point National Cemetery, Pennsville, Salem County.

HAMILTON, ELI Pvt, E, 5th NJ Inf, [Wounded in action.] 1916. Amwell Ridge Cemetery, Larisons Corner, Hunterdon County.

HAMILTON, ELLIS Capt, F, 15th NJ Inf, [Died of wounds received 5-12-1864 at Spotsylvania CH, VA.] 5-16-1864. Mercer Cemetery, Trenton, Mercer County.

HAMILTON, GAVIN Musc, C, 23rd NJ Inf, 7-15-1891. Mount Holly Cemetery, Mount Holly, Burlington County.

HAMILTON, GEORGE H. Pvt, A, 5th MA Colored Cav, 10-10-1873. Fairmount Cemetery, Newark, Essex County.

HAMILTON, GEORGE H. DoD Unknown. Baptist Church Cemetery, Hamburg, Sussex County.

HAMILTON*, HORACE E. Pvt, L, 1st NJ Cav, 1921. Presbyterian Church Cemetery, Andover, Sussex County.

HAMILTON, JAMES Pvt, G, 9th NJ Inf, 10-17-1897. Castner-Compton Cemetery, Bridgewater, Somerset County.

HAMILTON*, JAMES S. Pvt, I, 55th MA Inf, 12-9-1928. Greenwood Cemetery, Hamilton, Mercer County.

New Jersey Civil War Burials

HAMILTON, JOHN Pvt, L, 27th NJ Inf, 8-8-1930. Chestnut Cemetery, Dover, Morris County.

HAMILTON, JOHN Pvt, E, 71st NY Inf, DoD Unknown. St. John's Evangelical Church Cemetery, Orange, Essex County.

HAMILTON, JOHN P. Pvt, Btty A, 1st NJ Light Art, 7-15-1918. Glenwood Cemetery, West Long Branch, Monmouth County.

HAMILTON, JOSEPH Pvt, D, 4th NJ Inf, 5-5-1897. Mercer Cemetery, Trenton, Mercer County.

HAMILTON, LAWRENCE Pvt, C, 2nd NJ Inf, 11-6-1876. Holy Sepulchre Cemetery, East Orange, Essex County.

HAMILTON, LEWIS Pvt, L, 27th NJ Inf, 11-26-1875. Union Cemetery, Washington, Morris County.

HAMILTON, LYCIDIOUS (aka: Hamilton, Lyeidas) Corp, H, 9th NJ Inf, 1-20-1880. Greenwood Cemetery, Hamilton, Mercer County.

HAMILTON, LYEIDAS (see: Hamilton, Lycidious) Greenwood Cemetery, Hamilton, Mercer County.

HAMILTON, MARCUS A. Pvt, K, 1st NJ Cav, 12-19-1894. Fairview Cemetery, Wantage, Sussex County.

HAMILTON, N.J. Pvt, L, 43rd MS Inf (CSA), 6-26-1863. Finn's Point National Cemetery, Pennsville, Salem County.

HAMILTON, RICHARD Coal Heaver, U.S. Navy, USS Shamrock, [Awarded the Medal of Honor.] 7-6-1881. Evergreen Cemetery, Camden, Camden County.

HAMILTON, RICHARD (SR.) 1st Lt, B, 1st NJ Cav, 10-12-1903. Cedar Hill Cemetery, Florence, Burlington County.

HAMILTON, ROBERT 2nd Lt, B, 2nd NJ Cav, 1-17-1888. Old 1st Methodist Church Cemetery, West Long Branch, Monmouth County.

HAMILTON, ROBERT F. Seaman, U.S. Navy, USS Tallapoosa, 12- -1876. Old 1st Methodist Church Cemetery, West Long Branch, Monmouth County.

HAMILTON, THOMAS Pvt, D, 8th U.S. Inf, 10-16-1905. Holy Name Cemetery, Jersey City, Hudson County.

HAMILTON*, WILLIAM Actg Lt Commander, U.S. Navy, USS A. Dinsmore, 5- -1873. Jersey City Cemetery, Jersey City, Hudson County.

HAMILTON*, WILLIAM C. Pvt, Unassigned, 15th NY Eng, 5-25-1900. Jersey City Cemetery, Jersey City, Hudson County.

HAMILTON, WILLIAM M. Pvt, F, 48th AL Inf (CSA), [Captured at Gettysburg, PA.] 10-16-1863. Finn's Point National Cemetery, Pennsville, Salem County.

HAMLER, ABNER B. Pvt, K, 9th NJ Inf, 4-2-1884. Tranquility Cemetery, Tranquility, Sussex County.

HAMLER, ANDREW H. Pvt, A, 27th NJ Inf, 1930. Tranquility Cemetery, Tranquility, Sussex County.

HAMLER, WILLIAM H. Pvt, K, 9th NJ Inf, 11-11-1906. Presbyterian/Methodist-Episcopal Cemetery, Succasunna, Morris County.

HAMLIN, GEORGE F. Pvt, G, 9th NJ Inf, 4-20-1929. Baptist Church Cemetery, Scotch Plains, Union County.

HAMLIN, WILLIAM T. Pvt, K, 102nd NY National Guard, DoD Unknown. Oak Hill Cemetery, Vineland, Cumberland County.

HAMM, LOUIS Pvt, K, 25th NJ Inf, 12-1-1915. Holy Sepulchre Cemetery, Totowa, Passaic County.

HAMMA, ELIJAH B. Corp, G, 27th NJ Inf, 1907. Boonton Cemetery, Boonton, Morris County.

HAMMA, WILLIAM Pvt, I, 30th NJ Inf, 4-4-1900. Reformed Church Cemetery, Montville, Morris County.

HAMMAN, JOHN Corp, I, 25th NJ Inf, [Wounded 12-13-1862 at Fredericksburg, VA.] 8-27-1897. Fairmount Cemetery, Newark, Essex County.

Our Brothers Gone Before

HAMMAN, WILLIAM (aka: Hammond, William) Pvt, D, 34th NJ Inf, 4-13-1914. Arlington Cemetery, Kearny, Hudson County.
HAMMEL, FRANKLIN QM Sgt, 1st NJ Cav 12-18-1900. Fairmount Cemetery, Newark, Essex County.
HAMMEL, GEORGE 2nd Lt, D, 59th U.S. CT, 6-26-1890. Holy Sepulchre Cemetery, East Orange, Essex County.
HAMMELL, BENJAMIN F. DoD Unknown. Old Camden Cemetery, Camden, Camden County.
HAMMELL, CHARLES 2nd Cl Fireman, U.S. Navy, USS Juniata, 4-20-1890. Presbyterian Church Cemetery, Absecon, Atlantic County.
HAMMELL, CHARLES DoD Unknown. Elmwood Cemetery, New Brunswick, Middlesex County.
HAMMELL, CHARLES WESLEY Pvt, K, 38th NJ Inf, 2-7-1890. Riverview Cemetery, Trenton, Mercer County.
HAMMELL, CHRISTOPHER Pvt, D, 2nd NJ Inf, DoD Unknown. Cedar Lawn Cemetery, Paterson, Passaic County.
HAMMELL, DANIEL F. 1st Sgt, E, 122nd NY Inf, 9-20-1913. St. Mary's Episcopal Church Cemetery, Burlington, Burlington County.
HAMMELL, GEORGE W. Pvt, B, 157th PA Inf, 5-5-1872. Old Camden Cemetery, Camden, Camden County.
HAMMELL, JOHN F. Pvt, B, 28th NJ Inf, DoD Unknown. Pitman Methodist-Episcopal Cemetery, New Brunswick, Middlesex County.
HAMMELL, JOHN SWEENEY Bvt Brig Gen, U.S. Volunteers, [Lt. Colonel, 66th New York Infantry.] 1-31-1873. Mercer Cemetery, Trenton, Mercer County.
HAMMELL, JOSEPH L. Corp, A, 15th PA Cav, 12-7-1915. Coopertown Meeting House Cemetery, Edgewater Park, Burlington County.
HAMMELL, PATRICK Pvt, E, 3rd NJ Militia, 8-27-1873. St. John's Cemetery, Lambertville, Hunterdon County.
HAMMELL, RICHARD E. Landsman, U.S. Navy, USS Vandalia, 1-3-1913. New Camden Cemetery, Camden, Camden County.
HAMMELL, RICHARD W. Pvt, F, 15th PA Cav, 3-21-1922. Monument Cemetery, Edgewater Park, Burlington County.
HAMMELL, SAMUEL 2-5-1878. Fairview Cemetery, Fairview, Monmouth County.
HAMMELL, WILLIAM Pvt, C, 10th NJ Inf, 1-10-1887. Hoboken Cemetery, North Bergen, Hudson County.
HAMMELL, WILLIAM Sgt, K, 29th NY Inf, [Wounded 5-2-1863 at Chancellorsville, VA.] 1-16-1918. Arlington Cemetery, Pennsauken, Camden County.
HAMMELL, WILLIAM Sgt, B, 4th NJ Inf, 12-2-1898. Riverview Cemetery, Trenton, Mercer County.
HAMMER, JOHN Pvt, K, 20th NY Inf, [Wounded 9-17-1862 at Antietam, MD.] 11-5-1884. Fairmount Cemetery, Newark, Essex County.
HAMMER, JOHN J. Pvt, A, 8th NJ Inf, [Died at Washington, DC of wounds received 5-5-1864 at Wilderness, VA.] 5-17-1864. Holy Sepulchre Cemetery, East Orange, Essex County.
HAMMER, WILLIAM A. Pvt, A, 27th PA Militia, 2-24-1899. Woodland Cemetery, Newark, Essex County.
HAMMERSCHLAG, SIEGFRIED Pvt, 5th Bttn DC Inf [Degges Company.] 10-23-1896. Hoboken Cemetery, North Bergen, Hudson County.
HAMMESFAHR, CHARLES Pvt, D, 2nd NJ Inf, 1-26-1892. Fairmount Cemetery, Newark, Essex County.
HAMMETT, ELIJAH Pvt, H, 45th U.S. CT, 6-30-1904. Atlantic City Cemetery, Pleasantville, Atlantic County.
HAMMIL, SIMEON Pvt, I, 10th NJ Inf, 7-21-1890. New Camden Cemetery, Camden, Camden County.

New Jersey Civil War Burials

HAMMILL, JOHN Pvt, K, 70th NY Inf, [Wounded 5-5-1862 at Williamsburg, VA.] 12-4-1905. Holy Sepulchre Cemetery, East Orange, Essex County.

HAMMILL, THOMAS Pvt, Btty B, 1st NJ Light Art, 4-25-1904. Evergreen Cemetery, Hillside, Union County.

HAMMITT, JOSEPH H. Pvt, I, 23rd NJ Inf, 1889. Colestown Cemetery, Cherry Hill, Camden County.

HAMMOND, ALBERT V. Pvt, I, 6th NY Cav, 7-20-1931. Union Cemetery, Washington, Morris County.

HAMMOND*, ALFRED R. Pvt, A, 82nd NY Inf, 1924. Maple Grove Cemetery, Hackensack, Bergen County.

HAMMOND, BENJAMIN (aka: Hemingway, Benjamin) 5-22-1884. Cedar Lawn Cemetery, Paterson, Passaic County.

HAMMOND, EDWARD W. Wagoner, I, 3rd DE Inf, 9-18-1919. Evergreen Cemetery, Camden, Camden County.

HAMMOND, GARRETT H. Pvt, I, 70th NY Inf, DoD Unknown. Laurel Grove Cemetery, Totowa, Passaic County.

HAMMOND, HENRY CLAY Pvt, I, 1st MD Cav, 1893. Presbyterian Church Cemetery, Flemington, Hunterdon County.

HAMMOND*, JAMES Pvt, Btty L, 1st U.S. Art, 4-26-1879. Riverview Cemetery, Penns Grove, Salem County.

HAMMOND, JOHN 8-24-1897. Fairmount Cemetery, Newark, Essex County.

HAMMOND, NATHAN R. Corp, D, 24th NJ Inf, 5-2-1901. 1st United Methodist Church Cemetery, Bridgeton, Cumberland County.

HAMMOND, ORRIN B. Pvt, 11th MA Light Art 5-14-1890. Rosedale Cemetery, Orange, Essex County.

HAMMOND, PAUL Pvt, E, 24th U.S. CT, 8-7-1901. Mount Peace Cemetery, Lawnside, Camden County.

HAMMOND*, THOMAS R. Pvt, G, 94th IL Inf, 1-10-1885. Riverview Cemetery, Trenton, Mercer County.

HAMMOND, WILLIAM (see: Hamman, William) Arlington Cemetery, Kearny, Hudson County.

HAMMOND, WILLIAM D. Pvt, C, 127th NY Inf, 4-16-1929. Jersey City Cemetery, Jersey City, Hudson County.

HAMMOND, WILLIAM G. Pvt, D, 34th NJ Inf, 12-15-1925. Riverview Cemetery, Trenton, Mercer County.

HAMOND, OLIVER B. Pvt, D, 1st MD Cav (CSA), 3-4-1864. Finn's Point National Cemetery, Pennsville, Salem County.

HAMPSON, JAMES E. Pvt, G, 39th NJ Inf, 2-10-1911. Fairmount Cemetery, Newark, Essex County.

HAMPSON, SAMUEL Pvt, G, 39th NJ Inf, 4-7-1897. Fairmount Cemetery, Newark, Essex County.

HAMPTON, CHARLES G. Capt, H, 15th NY Cav, [Wounded 2-20-1864 at Upperville, VA.] 2-22-1895. Presbyterian Church Cemetery, Bridgeton, Cumberland County.

HAMPTON, DAVID H. Sgt, F, 127th U.S. CT, DoD Unknown. Jamison/Midway Green Cemetery, Aberdeen, Monmouth County.

HAMPTON, EDWARD Pvt, I, 6th U.S. CT, [Wounded in action.] 10-24-1909. Fairmount Cemetery, Newark, Essex County.

HAMPTON, GRANDIN Corp, D, 14th NJ Inf, 1-4-1892. Old 1st Methodist Church Cemetery, West Long Branch, Monmouth County.

HAMPTON, JAMES H. Pvt, A, 14th NJ Inf, 1923. Evergreen Cemetery, Farmingdale, Monmouth County.

HAMPTON, JOHN G. Pvt, I, 2nd NJ Cav, 12-12-1898. Cedar Hill Cemetery, Hightstown, Mercer County.

Our Brothers Gone Before

HAMPTON, JOHN R.S. Sgt, M, 2nd NJ Cav, 1-5-1868. Phillipsburg Cemetery, Phillipsburg, Warren County.

HAMPTON, JOHN S. Corp, I, 9th NJ Inf, 3-30-1901. Friends/Methodist-Episcopal Cemetery, Pedricktown, Salem County.

HAMPTON, PETER (aka: Harrington, Peter B.) Pvt, G, 4th DE Inf, 5-1-1895. Fairmount Cemetery, Newark, Essex County.

HAMPTON, PLEASANT R. Pvt, K, 1st (Turney's) TN Inf (CSA), 11-23-1863. Finn's Point National Cemetery, Pennsville, Salem County.

HAMPTON*, RUSSELL Corp, D, 2nd NJ Inf, 4-9-1903. Evergreen Cemetery, Farmingdale, Monmouth County.

HAMPTON, THOMAS Pvt, K, 5th NJ Inf, [Wounded 7-2-1863 at Gettysburg, PA.] 1907. Manalapan Cemetery, Manalapan, Monmouth County.

HAMPTON, WILLIAM Pvt, K, 6th NJ Inf, 4-13-1873. Old Camden Cemetery, Camden, Camden County.

HAMPTON, WILLIAM H. Pvt, E, 23rd NJ Inf, 1923. Methodist Church Cemetery, Pemberton, Burlington County.

HAMTRAMCK, SELBY M. Pvt, B, 2nd VA Inf (CSA), [Captured 3-23-1862 at Kernstown, VA.] 6-9-1862. Finn's Point National Cemetery, Pennsville, Salem County.

HANCE, HENRY C. Pvt, K, 12th NJ Inf, 12-8-1898. Cedar Green Cemetery, Clayton, Gloucester County.

HANCE, ISAAC Pvt, A, 2nd U.S. Cav, 3-28-1914. Oddfellows Cemetery, Pemberton, Burlington County.

HANCE, ISAAC Pvt, F, 14th NJ Inf, [Wounded in action.] 8-19-1884. Friends Cemetery, Shrewsbury, Monmouth County.

HANCE, JOHN Pvt, B, 40th NJ Inf, 1933. Methodist-Episcopal Cemetery, Pointville, Burlington County.

HANCE, SILAS W. Pvt, M, 1st NJ Cav, 1-15-1911. Union Cemetery, Washington, Morris County.

HANCE, WILLIAM M. Landsman, U.S. Navy, USS Connemaugh, 7-12-1934. Presbyterian/Methodist-Episcopal Cemetery, Succasunna, Morris County.

HANCOCK*, ASBURY W. Pvt, Bowen's Chulahoma MS Cav (CSA) 7-13-1892. Brotherhood Cemetery, Hainesport, Burlington County.

HANCOCK, BENJAMIN 1st Sgt, F, 24th NJ Inf, DoD Unknown. Overlook Cemetery, Bridgeton, Cumberland County.

HANCOCK, BENJAMIN L. Corp, A, 23rd NJ Inf, 11-8-1909. Oddfellows Cemetery, Burlington, Burlington County.

HANCOCK, CORNELIA Nurse, 12-31-1927. Friends Cemetery, Harmersville, Salem County.

HANCOCK, DANIEL F. Pvt, A, 23rd NJ Inf, 10-14-1893. Baptist Church Cemetery, Canton, Salem County.

HANCOCK, ELIJAH C. Pvt, F, 13th AL Inf (CSA), 12-21-1863. Finn's Point National Cemetery, Pennsville, Salem County.

HANCOCK, GODFREY E. 8-4-1901. Eastview Cemetery, Salem, Salem County.

HANCOCK*, ROBERT D. Pvt, E, 8th NJ Inf, 3-10-1874. Methodist-Episcopal Cemetery, Burlington, Burlington County.

HANCOCK, THOMAS S. Pvt, A, 9th NJ Inf, DoD Unknown. Methodist-Episcopal Cemetery, Burlington, Burlington County.

HANCOCK, WILLIAM Corp, K, 1st CT Cav, 4-9-1932. Methodist Church Cemetery, Juliustown, Burlington County.

HANCOCK, WILLIAM N. 1st Lt, C, 24th NJ Inf, 10-2-1911. Friends Cemetery, Harmersville, Salem County.

HANCY, JOHN V. (aka: Haughey, John) Pvt, E, 3rd NJ Cav, 8-25-1899. Methodist Church Cemetery, Groveville, Mercer County.

New Jersey Civil War Burials

HAND, ALONZO Corp, I, 37th NJ Inf, 1919. Bay View Cemetery, Leonardo, Monmouth County.
HAND*, CHARLES Sgt, K, 1st NY Cav, 7-31-1884. St. Vincent Martyr Cemetery, Madison, Morris County.
HAND, CHARLES Pvt, B, 15th NJ Inf, 4-2-1904. Tranquility Cemetery, Tranquility, Sussex County.
HAND, DANIEL Pvt, C, 7th NJ Inf, DoD Unknown. Presbyterian Cemetery, New Vernon, Morris County.
HAND, DAVID E. Pvt, F, 25th NJ Inf, [Died of typhoid at Newark, NJ.] 1-26-1863. Presbyterian Church Cemetery, Cold Spring, Cape May County.
HAND, ELDRIDGE Pvt, D, 25th NJ Inf, 6-23-1910. Bateman Memorial Cemetery, Newport, Cumberland County.
HAND, ELIAS Pvt, I, 25th NJ Inf, 12-12-1900. 1st Baptist Cemetery, Cape May Court House, Cape May County.
HAND, ELLIS H. 1905. Methodist-Episcopal Cemetery, Port Norris, Cumberland County.
HAND, ENOCH WILLETTS Pvt, C, 9th NJ Inf, [Wounded in action.] 3-19-1918. Presbyterian Church Cemetery, Cold Spring, Cape May County.
HAND, FRANKLIN E. Pvt, G, 24th NJ Inf, 1916. Harleigh Cemetery, Camden, Camden County.
HAND, FRANKLIN E. Pvt, H, 6th NJ Inf, 11-1-1887. Fairview Cemetery, Cape May Court House, Cape May County.
HAND, FURMAN 4-17-1905. Evergreen Cemetery, Camden, Camden County.
HAND, GEORGE W. 1-29-1868. Newton Cemetery, Newton, Sussex County.
HAND, HENRY Corp, B, 11th NJ Inf, 1905. Baptist Church Cemetery, Scotch Plains, Union County.
HAND, HENRY W. Actg Master, U.S. Navy, USS Vermont, 3-15-1898. Fairview Cemetery, Cape May Court House, Cape May County.
HAND*, IRA Pvt, C, 14th NJ Inf, 5-31-1903. Evergreen Cemetery, Hillside, Union County.
HAND, JACOB G. 10- -1910. Fairview Cemetery, Cape May Court House, Cape May County.
HAND*, JAMES Pvt, Btty D, 1st NJ Light Art, 6-10-1916. Holy Sepulchre Cemetery, Totowa, Passaic County.
HAND, JAMES (aka: Hencliff, James) Pvt, K, 25th NJ Inf, 5-17-1895. Laurel Grove Cemetery, Totowa, Passaic County.
HAND, JAMES 11-11-1916. St. Vincent Martyr Cemetery, Madison, Morris County.
HAND, JAMES K. Pvt, K, 6th PA Inf, 1-10-1892. Baptist Cemetery, Pemberton, Burlington County.
HAND, JAMES L. Pvt, D, 87th NY Inf, [Killed in action at Fair Oaks, VA.] 5-31-1862. Holy Sepulchre Cemetery, East Orange, Essex County.
HAND, JAMES W. Pvt, F, 33rd NJ Inf, [Died of dysentery at Tunnel Hill, GA.] 1-29-1865. Mount Pleasant Cemetery, Millville, Cumberland County.
HAND, JEREMIAH S. Pvt, K, 12th NJ Inf, 9-8-1908. Presbyterian Church Cemetery, Cold Spring, Cape May County.
HAND, JOHN Corp, I, 3rd NJ Inf, [Killed in action at Munsons Hill, VA.] 8-31-1861. Baptist Church Cemetery, Scotch Plains, Union County.
HAND, JOHN Pvt, H, 6th NY Inf, DoD Unknown. St. Vincent Martyr Cemetery, Madison, Morris County.
HAND, JOHN S. Pvt, B, 2nd NY Cav, [Died of disease at Georgetown, DC.] 12-31-1861. Newton Cemetery, Newton, Sussex County.
HAND, JOHN WILEY Pvt, A, 3rd NJ Cav, 12-29-1901. Baptist Cemetery, Rio Grande, Cape May County.
HAND, JOSEPH Pvt, F, 4th NJ Inf, 8-2-1930. Presbyterian Church Cemetery, Cold Spring, Cape May County.
HAND, JOSEPH H. 11-13-1896. Evergreen Cemetery, Camden, Camden County.

Our Brothers Gone Before

HAND, JUDSON Pvt, E, 1st NJ Cav, 12-12-1930. Cedar Lawn Cemetery, Paterson, Passaic County.

HAND, PATRICK Pvt, G, 26th NJ Inf, 7-7-1914. Holy Sepulchre Cemetery, East Orange, Essex County.

HAND, PETER J. Pvt, K, 12th NJ Inf, 1-20-1923. Fairview Cemetery, Cape May Court House, Cape May County.

HAND, PHILIP (JR.) Pvt, F, 25th NJ Inf, 12-7-1888. Presbyterian Church Cemetery, Cold Spring, Cape May County.

HAND, RANDOLPH Pvt, Btty F, 2nd U.S. Art, [Died of wounds received 10- -1862 at Corinth, MS.] 10-6-1862. Newton Cemetery, Newton, Sussex County.

HAND*, SETH L. Landsman, U.S. Navy, USS Princeton, 3-10-1886. Fairview Cemetery, Cape May Court House, Cape May County.

HAND, SETH L. Pvt, F, 25th NJ Inf, 1912. Methodist Church Cemetery, Eldora, Cape May County.

HAND, THOMAS PIERSON Pvt, F, 25th NJ Inf, [Died of diarrhea at Fort Monroe, VA.] 5-3-1863. Presbyterian Church Cemetery, Cold Spring, Cape May County.

HAND, WILLIAM Pvt, G, 3rd NJ Cav, 3-19-1908. Methodist Cemetery, Malaga, Gloucester County.

HAND, WILLIAM 2nd Lt, I, 11th NJ Inf, 2-14-1916. Presbyterian Cemetery, North Plainfield, Somerset County.

HANDLETON, GEORGE W. Pvt, B, 95th PA Inf, 5-7-1907. Baptist/St. Andrew's Cemetery, Mount Holly, Burlington County.

HANDLEY, DANIEL Corp, G, 2nd NJ Cav, 12-20-1916. Baptist Cemetery, Burlington, Burlington County.

HANDY, ABRAM (aka: Hardy, Abraham) Pvt, A, 10th NJ Inf, 1908. Newton Cemetery, Newton, Sussex County.

HANDY*, DAVIS N. Corp, K, 18th CT Inf, [Wounded 6-5-1864 at Piedmont, VA.] 11-4-1901. Fairmount Cemetery, Newark, Essex County.

HANDY, FRANCIS E. Pvt, C, 22nd U.S. CT, 12-5-1909. Mount Peace Cemetery, Lawnside, Camden County.

HANDY, JOHN Pvt, F, 22nd U.S. CT, 2-25-1875. Presbyterian Cemetery, Woodbury, Gloucester County.

HANES, JOHN Pvt, D, 25th NJ Inf, 8-5-1913. Old Stone Church Cemetery, Fairton, Cumberland County.

HANES, JOSEPH H. 3-20-1929. Presbyterian Church Cemetery, Cold Spring, Cape May County.

HANEY, HENRY Pvt, F, 25th U.S. CT, 1-1-1904. Mount Zion Methodist Church Cemetery, Lawnside, Camden County.

HANEY*, JOHN Sgt, F, 7th NJ Inf, 5-26-1900. Dayton Cemetery, Dayton, Middlesex County.

HANEY, WILLIAM M. Pvt, H, 1st NJ Militia, 7-23-1900. Clinton Cemetery, Irvington, Essex County.

HANILY, JOHN J. Pvt, G, 39th NJ Inf, 6-17-1917. St. Peter's Church Cemetery, Belleville, Essex County.

HANKE, PHILIP B. Sgt, E, 30th PA Inf, 12-14-1908. Evergreen Cemetery, Camden, Camden County.

HANKERSON, CHARLES C. Pvt, D, 54th MA Inf, [Wounded 11-30-1864 at Honey Hill, SC.] 8-21-1906. Mount Zion Methodist Church Cemetery, Lawnside, Camden County.

HANKINS, BENJAMIN A. Pvt, K, 38th NJ Inf, 3-6-1915. Fairview Cemetery, Cape May Court House, Cape May County.

HANKINS, CHARLES Pvt, G, 3rd NJ Cav, 3-1-1910. Mount Pleasant Cemetery, Millville, Cumberland County.

New Jersey Civil War Burials

HANKINS, CHARLES H. Pvt, C, 11th NJ Inf, [Wounded in action.] 8-25-1885. Zion Baptist Church Cemetery, New Egypt, Ocean County.

HANKINS, CHARLES W. Musc, G, 26th NJ Inf, 10-14-1902. Soldier's Home Cemetery, Vineland, Cumberland County.

HANKINS, DAVID C. Corp, D, 9th NJ Inf, 1907. Baptist Church Cemetery, Jacobstown, Burlington County.

HANKINS, DAVID V. Corp, E, 14th NJ Inf, 1-14-1884. Riverview Cemetery, Trenton, Mercer County.

HANKINS, EDWARD H. Pvt, K, 23rd VA Inf (CSA), [Captured 3-23-1862 at Kernstown, VA.] 4-18-1862. Finn's Point National Cemetery, Pennsville, Salem County.

HANKINS*, ELEAZER F. Sgt, K, 38th NJ Inf, 10-13-1906. Fairview Cemetery, Cape May Court House, Cape May County.

HANKINS, ELIAS S. Pvt, E, 28th NJ Inf, 3-10-1879. Rose Hill Cemetery, Matawan, Monmouth County.

HANKINS*, FRANCIS G. (aka: Hankins, Franklin) Sgt, C, 38th NJ Inf, 10-14-1913. United Methodist Church Cemetery, Leesburg, Cumberland County.

HANKINS, FRANKLIN (see: Hankins, Francis G.) United Methodist Church Cemetery, Leesburg, Cumberland County.

HANKINS, GEORGE Pvt, F, 29th NJ Inf, [Died of disease at Tinton Falls, NJ.] 10-29-1862. Presbyterian Church Cemetery, Shrewsbury, Monmouth County.

HANKINS, GILBERT P. Pvt, E, 28th NJ Inf, 4-18-1884. Fairview Cemetery, Fairview, Monmouth County.

HANKINS, HENRY H. Pvt, F, 14th NJ Inf, [Wounded in action.] 8-31-1916. Presbyterian Cemetery, Cream Ridge, Monmouth County.

HANKINS, JACOB B. Pvt, K, 4th NJ Inf, 12-11-1891. Presbyterian Church Cemetery, Bridgeton, Cumberland County.

HANKINS, JAMES P. Pvt, A, 11th AL Inf (CSA), 12-13-1863. Finn's Point National Cemetery, Pennsville, Salem County.

HANKINS, JOHN W. Corp, E, 28th NJ Inf, 3-1-1915. Lakewood-Hope Cemetery, Lakewood, Ocean County.

HANKINS, JOSEPH Sgt, E, 28th NJ Inf, 1913. Whitesville Cemetery, Whitesville, Ocean County.

HANKINS, JOSEPH 12-23-1888. Columbus Cemetery, Columbus, Burlington County.

HANKINS, JOSEPH R. Sgt, F, 14th NJ Inf, DoD Unknown. Presbyterian Cemetery, Holmanville, Ocean County.

HANKINS, JOSHUA R. Corp, F, 29th NJ Inf, 1-12-1885. Presbyterian Church Cemetery, Shrewsbury, Monmouth County.

HANKINS, RICHARD D. Pvt, L, 3rd NY Cav, 9-7-1915. Rose Hill Cemetery, Matawan, Monmouth County.

HANKINS, RICHARD W. Pvt, I, 6th NJ Inf, [Wounded in action at Fair Oaks, VA.] DoD Unknown. Baptist/St. Andrew's Cemetery, Mount Holly, Burlington County.

HANKINS, SAMUEL Farrier, C, 5th MA Colored Cav, 1-15-1888. Johnson Cemetery, Camden, Camden County.

HANKINS*, SAMUEL W. Pvt, D, 9th NJ Inf, 1931. Zion Baptist Church Cemetery, New Egypt, Ocean County.

HANKINS*, STEPHEN (aka: Hawkins, Stephen) Corp, D, 34th NJ Inf, [Wounded in action.] 1-7-1901. Mount Holly Cemetery, Mount Holly, Burlington County.

HANKINS, WILLIAM Pvt, K, 15th NJ Inf, 11-23-1916. Arlington Cemetery, Kearny, Hudson County.

HANKINS, WILLIAM H. Pvt, E, 28th NJ Inf, 3-21-1919. Whitelawn Cemetery, Point Pleasant, Ocean County.

HANKINS, WILLIAM H. 9-1-1875. Methodist Church Cemetery, Harmony, Ocean County.

Our Brothers Gone Before

HANKINS, WILLIAM HENRY DoD Unknown. Van Liew Cemetery, North Brunswick, Middlesex County.

HANKINS, ZACHARIAH Pvt, F, 22nd NJ Inf, 11-19-1905. Methodist Church Cemetery, Harmony, Ocean County.

HANKINS, ZACHARIAH Corp, B, 1st NJ Inf, [Wounded in action.] 4-20-1894. Zion Baptist Church Cemetery, New Egypt, Ocean County.

HANKINSON, HENRY REMSEN Landsman, U.S. Navy, 6-28-1866. Old Baptist Church Cemetery, Manahawkin, Ocean County.

HANKINSON, JAMES W. Pvt, B, 6th NJ Inf, 9-3-1903. Congregational Church Cemetery, Chester, Morris County.

HANKINSON, JOHN L. Pvt, D, 27th NJ Inf, 10-29-1917. Presbyterian Church Cemetery, Rockaway, Morris County.

HANKINSON, SIMEON G. DoD Unknown. Newton Cemetery, Newton, Sussex County.

HANKINSON, WILLIAM A. Pvt, A, 12th NJ Inf, 8-24-1934. Maplewood Cemetery, Freehold, Monmouth County.

HANKS, EDMUND F. (see: Hanks, Edward F.) Valleau Cemetery, Ridgewood, Bergen County.

HANKS, EDWARD F. (aka: Hanks, Edmund F.) 1st Lt, A, 56th NC Inf (CSA), [Wounded at Ware Bottom Church, VA.] 1-15-1916. Valleau Cemetery, Ridgewood, Bergen County.

HANLEY*, GOTTLIEB Pvt, F, 13th NJ Inf, [Wounded 5-3-1863 at Chancellorsville, VA.] 3-2-1916. Fairmount Cemetery, Newark, Essex County.

HANLEY, JOHN Pvt, K, 1st NJ Cav, 11-13-1909. Union Cemetery, Washington, Morris County.

HANLEY, JOHN H. Pvt, F, 5th NY Vet Inf, DoD Unknown. Savage Cemetery, Denville, Morris County.

HANLEY, MICHAEL 8-1-1908. St. Mary's Cemetery, Hamilton, Mercer County.

HANLEY, MICHAEL Pvt, H, 35th NJ Inf, DoD Unknown. St. Rose of Lima Cemetery, Freehold, Monmouth County.

HANLEY, MICHAEL A. Pvt, C, 8th NJ Inf, 8-15-1908. Holy Name Cemetery, Jersey City, Hudson County.

HANLEY, MICHAEL F. Seaman, U.S. Navy, USS Penobscot, 9-23-1888. St. John's Evangelical Church Cemetery, Orange, Essex County.

HANLEY, THOMAS Pvt, G, 5th NJ Inf, 3-31-1870. St. John's Evangelical Church Cemetery, Orange, Essex County.

HANLEY, THOMAS J. Pvt, D, 33rd NJ Inf, 12-12-1890. Holy Sepulchre Cemetery, East Orange, Essex County.

HANLON, JAMES J. Pvt, E, 71st NY Inf, DoD Unknown. St. James Cemetery, Woodbridge, Middlesex County.

HANN, ALBERT J. 7-12-1919. Rosemont Cemetery, Rosemont, Hunterdon County.

HANN, ANDREW Pvt, H, 12th NJ Inf, 8-17-1887. New Presbyterian Church Cemetery, Daretown, Salem County.

HANN, CORNELIUS A. Pvt, G, 30th NJ Inf, 4-17-1889. Prospect Hill Cemetery, Flemington, Hunterdon County.

HANN, ENOS F. Pvt, H, 12th NJ Inf, 12-6-1936. Atlantic City Cemetery, Pleasantville, Atlantic County.

HANN, HENRY Pvt, B, 27th NJ Inf, DoD Unknown. Union Cemetery, Washington, Morris County.

HANN, IRA L. Pvt, C, 7th NJ Inf, 5-23-1912. Methodist Church Cemetery, Hope, Warren County.

HANN, JAPHET E. Corp, G, 24th NJ Inf, 5-2-1915. United Methodist Church Cemetery, Tuckahoe, Cape May County.

HANN, JEREMIAH 5-4-1870. Union Cemetery, Hope, Warren County.

New Jersey Civil War Burials

HANN, JEREMIAH Pvt, F, 24th NJ Inf, 1-27-1923. Presbyterian Church Cemetery, Bridgeton, Cumberland County.

HANN, MORRIS S. 2nd Lt, F, 15th NJ Inf, 3-13-1920. Evergreen Cemetery, Hillside, Union County.

HANN, MOSES F. Pvt, K, 31st NJ Inf, DoD Unknown. Presbyterian Church Cemetery, Greenwich, Warren County.

HANN, RICHARD (aka: Hawn, Richard) Pvt, F, 3rd NJ Cav, 5-7-1909. United Methodist Church Cemetery, Port Elizabeth, Cumberland County.

HANNA, JAMES G. Seaman, U.S. Navy, USS Mohican, 1924. New Somerville Cemetery, Somerville, Somerset County.

HANNA, ROBERT Pvt, Btty M, 9th NY Heavy Art, 2-7-1910. Oak Hill Cemetery, Vineland, Cumberland County.

HANNA*, THOMAS L. 1st Lt, G, 51st U.S. CT, [Wounded 9-17-1862 at Antietam, MD. and 7-3-1863 at Gettysburg, PA.] 10-20-1908. Bloomfield Cemetery, Bloomfield, Essex County.

HANNAH, CHARLES Pvt, C, 24th NJ Inf, 4-18-1896. Evergreen Cemetery, Camden, Camden County.

HANNAH*, SAMUEL Pvt, F, 105th PA Inf, DoD Unknown. Presbyterian Church Cemetery, Greenwich, Cumberland County.

HANNAKA*, AUGUSTUS (aka: Henneke, Augustus) Pvt, F, 2nd NJ Inf, 11-8-1901. St. Mary's Cemetery, Wharton, Morris County.

HANNAKA*, CHARLES Pvt, H, 2nd PA Cav, [Wounded in action.] 10-16-1905. Locust Hill Cemetery, Dover, Morris County.

HANNAN, MADISON (aka: Harmon, Madison) Pvt, G, 45th VA Inf (CSA), [Captured 8-7-1864 at Hagerstown, MD.] 3-7-1865. Finn's Point National Cemetery, Pennsville, Salem County.

HANNAS, LUCIUS P. (aka: Harmas, Lucius) Musc, I, 27th NJ Inf, 4-9-1920. Evergreen Cemetery, Morristown, Morris County.

HANNES, NICHOLAS (aka: Hahn, Nicholas) Pvt, D, 3rd NJ Militia, 1896. St. Mary's Cemetery, Hamilton, Mercer County.

HANNIGAN*, THOMAS Pvt, H, 7th NJ Inf, DoD Unknown. St. John's Cemetery, Hamilton, Mercer County.

HANNING, CHARLES Sgt, I, 81st PA Inf, DoD Unknown. Fairmount Cemetery, Newark, Essex County.

HANNOLD, BENJAMIN D. 1908. St. Paul's United Methodist Church Cemetery, Paulsboro, Gloucester County.

HANNOLD, FREDERICK 12-7-1882. St. Paul's United Methodist Church Cemetery, Paulsboro, Gloucester County.

HANNOLD, GEORGE W. Corp, E, 24th NJ Inf, [Died of wounds received 12-13-1862 at Fredericksburg, VA.] 12-26-1862. St. Paul's United Methodist Church Cemetery, Paulsboro, Gloucester County.

HANNOLD, JOHN WOOD Pvt, E, 24th NJ Inf, 5-11-1920. Eglington Cemetery, Clarksboro, Gloucester County.

HANNOLD, THOMAS C. Pvt, A, 7th NJ Inf, 6-17-1896. Eglington Cemetery, Clarksboro, Gloucester County.

HANNOLD, THOMPSON DoD Unknown. St. Paul's United Methodist Church Cemetery, Paulsboro, Gloucester County.

HANNON, JAMES H. Seaman, U.S. Navy, DoD Unknown. Holy Name Cemetery, Jersey City, Hudson County.

HANNON*, JOHN Pvt, A, 1st NJ Militia, 12-4-1882. Holy Name Cemetery, Jersey City, Hudson County.

HANNON, JOHN (aka: Harmon, John) Pvt, E, 22nd U.S. CT, 10-9-1910. Beverly National Cemetery, Edgewater Park, Burlington County.

Our Brothers Gone Before

HANNUM, PHILIP E. 1st Sgt, D, 97th PA Inf, [Wounded 5-18-1864 at Bermuda Hundred, VA.] 4-13-1919. Methodist Cemetery, Weymouth, Atlantic County.
HANSEL, ISAAC Pvt, B, 8th NJ Inf, 11-14-1894. Fairmount Cemetery, Newark, Essex County.
HANSELL, JAMES A. 8-11-1884. Elmwood Cemetery, New Brunswick, Middlesex County.
HANSELL, JOHN B. Pvt, I, 116th PA Inf, [Wounded in action.] 10-17-1889. Elmwood Cemetery, New Brunswick, Middlesex County.
HANSELL, MILTON Pvt, I, 61st PA Inf, 5-21-1893. Monument Cemetery, Edgewater Park, Burlington County.
HANSELL, WILLIAM C. Musc, F, 51st PA Inf, DoD Unknown. Evergreen Cemetery, Camden, Camden County.
HANSEN, ALEXANDER Actg Ensign, U.S. Navy, 12-23-1902. Evergreen Cemetery, Morristown, Morris County.
HANSEN, FREDERICK Pvt, B, 9th NY Inf, 11-22-1902. Hoboken Cemetery, North Bergen, Hudson County.
HANSEN, JULIUS Pvt, Btty C, 1st NJ Light Art, 9-6-1891. Lodi Cemetery, Lodi, Bergen County.
HANSEN, PETER Pvt, Btty A, 1st NJ Light Art, 12-30-1880. Palisade Cemetery, North Bergen, Hudson County.
HANSOM, CHARLES (see: Diercks, Christian) Palisade Cemetery, North Bergen, Hudson County.
HANSON*, CHARLES Pvt, B, 7th U.S. Hancock Corps, 7-10-1913. Riverview Cemetery, Trenton, Mercer County.
HANSON, CHARLES P. 1st Lt, H, 145th NY Inf, 4-2-1909. Hoboken Cemetery, North Bergen, Hudson County.
HANSON, JAMES Pvt, Btty C, 1st PA Light Art, 9-25-1909. Harleigh Cemetery, Camden, Camden County.
HANSON*, JAMES EAGLETON Seaman, U.S. Navy, USS North Carolina, 8-27-1908. Riverview Cemetery, Trenton, Mercer County.
HANSON, JOHN Landsman, U.S. Navy, USS Princeton, 1888. Greenwood Cemetery, Tuckerton, Ocean County.
HANSOTTER, GERHARDT Sgt, C, 20th NY Inf, 10- -1897. Hoboken Cemetery, North Bergen, Hudson County.
HANVILLE, ALVAH W. Corp, K, 1st NY Eng, 5-12-1892. Presbyterian Cemetery, New Vernon, Morris County.
HAPPAUGH, HORACE Pvt, M, 1st NJ Cav, DoD Unknown. Prospect Hill Cemetery, Caldwell, Essex County.
HAPPOCK, E.H. Pvt, G, 5th U.S. Cav, DoD Unknown. Clinton Cemetery, Irvington, Essex County.
HARBEIN, WILLIAM 5-26-1880. Hoboken Cemetery, North Bergen, Hudson County.
HARBERT, ASA K. Musc, I, 9th NJ Inf, DoD Unknown. Overlook Cemetery, Bridgeton, Cumberland County.
HARBERT, GEORGE (see: Harbourt, George) Methodist Church Cemetery, Titusville, Mercer County.
HARBERT, THOMAS G. Corp, H, 57th NY Inf, 2-26-1891. Mount Holly Cemetery, Mount Holly, Burlington County.
HARBIN, W.F. Pvt, C, 4th NC Inf (CSA), 9-20-1863. Finn's Point National Cemetery, Pennsville, Salem County.
HARBISON, CHRISTOPHER C. Sgt, D, 48th NY Inf, [Wounded 6-2-1864 at Cold Harbor, VA.] 6-20-1917. St. John's Methodist Church Cemetery, Harrisonville, Gloucester County.
HARBISON, JOHN W. Pvt, I, 9th NJ Inf, 7-2-1919. Lake Park Cemetery, Swedesboro, Gloucester County.

New Jersey Civil War Burials

HARBISON*, SAMUEL B. Sgt, I, 9th NJ Inf, DoD Unknown. Old Camden Cemetery, Camden, Camden County.

HARBOURT, ALFRED Pvt, B, 34th NJ Inf, DoD Unknown. Methodist Church Cemetery, Titusville, Mercer County.

HARBOURT, GEORGE (aka: Harbert, George) Pvt, H, 21st NJ Inf, DoD Unknown. Methodist Church Cemetery, Titusville, Mercer County.

HARBOURT, THEODORE S. Pvt, F, 22nd NJ Inf, [Died of pneumonia at Washington, DC.] 1-21-1863. Presbyterian Church Cemetery, Titusville, Mercer County.

HARBRIDGE, GEORGE Pvt, E, 26th NJ Inf, 10-15-1912. Clinton Cemetery, Irvington, Essex County.

HARBUT, THOMAS (see: Herbert, Thomas G.) Mount Holly Cemetery, Mount Holly, Burlington County.

HARCINGER, ADAM (see: Herzinger, Adam) Woodland Cemetery, Newark, Essex County.

HARDCASTLE, EDWARD Pvt, G, 99th PA Inf, 9-19-1917. St. Paul's Methodist Church Cemetery, Port Republic, Atlantic County.

HARDCASTLE, JAMES Pvt, C, 25th U.S. CT, 8-29-1910. Butler Cemetery, Camden, Camden County.

HARDCASTLE, JOHN R. Pvt, H, 36th (Broyle's) GA Inf (CSA), [Captured 5-16-1863 at Baker's Creek, MS.] 7-16-1863. Finn's Point National Cemetery, Pennsville, Salem County.

HARDCASTLE, PETER V.D. Pvt, E, 15th NJ Inf, DoD Unknown. New Somerville Cemetery, Somerville, Somerset County.

HARDEE, JOEL Pvt, F, 1st (Gregg's) SC Inf (CSA), [Captured 7-5-1863 at Gettysburg, PA. Died of remittent fever.] 9-21-1863. Finn's Point National Cemetery, Pennsville, Salem County.

HARDEN, ALEXANDER Sgt, M, 2nd NJ Cav, 10-2-1911. Methodist Church Cemetery, Mount Hermon, Warren County.

HARDEN, CHRISTOPHER Pvt, K, 62nd NY Inf, 2-12-1927. Fairview Cemetery, Westfield, Union County.

HARDEN, J.P. (see: Harding, James P.) Finn's Point National Cemetery, Pennsville, Salem County.

HARDEN, MAHLON Pvt, B, 3rd NJ Inf, 5-15-1907. Evergreen Cemetery, Camden, Camden County.

HARDEN, PETER B. Pvt, G, 5th AL Cav (CSA), 8-24-1863. Finn's Point National Cemetery, Pennsville, Salem County.

HARDENBERG, DANIEL S. Asst Surg, 56th NY Inf 1-1-1908. Old Bergen Church Cemetery, Jersey City, Hudson County.

HARDESTY, JAMES N. Pvt, A, 1st (Butler's) KY Cav (CSA), [Captured 6-6-1863 at Liberty, TN.] 11-7-1863. Finn's Point National Cemetery, Pennsville, Salem County.

HARDGROVE, WILLIAM 1921. New Somerville Cemetery, Somerville, Somerset County.

HARDGROVE, WILLIAM E. Pvt, B, 13th Bttn U.S. Guards, 10-2-1918. Clinton Cemetery, Irvington, Essex County.

HARDHAM, JOHN Pvt, Btty B, 1st NJ Light Art, 6-12-1905. Bloomfield Cemetery, Bloomfield, Essex County.

HARDICK*, LEMUEL Pvt, E, 2nd NJ Inf, [Wounded in action.] 1931. Stillwater Cemetery, Stillwater, Sussex County.

HARDICK*, NELSON S. Pvt, I, 15th NJ Inf, 6-11-1901. Newton Cemetery, Newton, Sussex County.

HARDICK, URIAH Pvt, I, 15th NJ Inf, 8-13-1900. Union Cemetery, Washington, Morris County.

Our Brothers Gone Before

HARDIGREE, JOHN S. Pvt, L, 3rd GA Inf (CSA), [Wounded and captured 7-2-1863 at Gettysburg, PA. Died of measles.] 9-13-1863. Finn's Point National Cemetery, Pennsville, Salem County.

HARDIN, CHARLES 4-8-1902. Newton Cemetery, Newton, Sussex County.

HARDIN, JOHN SMITH Corp, H, 11th NJ Inf, [Died of brain congestion at Fort Ellsworth, VA.] 10-9-1862. Deckertown-Union Cemetery, Papakating, Sussex County.

HARDIN, SYLVESTER J. 1-26-1885. Newton Cemetery, Newton, Sussex County.

HARDIN, WILLIAM S. Pvt, G, 30th NJ Inf, 3-25-1908. Old Rock Church Cemetery, West Amwell, Hunterdon County.

HARDING, CHARLES A. Pvt, B, 81st OH Inf, 5-12-1905. Newton Cemetery, Newton, Sussex County.

HARDING, FREDERICK Pvt, Btty H, 1st CT Heavy Art, 8-31-1907. Cedar Lawn Cemetery, Paterson, Passaic County.

HARDING, GEORGE Landsman, U.S. Navy, USS Princeton, 1-6-1907. Mount Peace Cemetery, Lawnside, Camden County.

HARDING, JAMES Pvt, Btty H, 1st CT Heavy Art, 1-31-1910. Fairmount Cemetery, Newark, Essex County.

HARDING, JAMES F. Pvt, F, 24th NJ Inf, 1914. Baptist Church Cemetery, Greenwich, Cumberland County.

HARDING, JAMES P. (aka: Harden, J.P.) Pvt, M, 9th (Malone's) AL Cav (CSA), 8-22-1863. Finn's Point National Cemetery, Pennsville, Salem County.

HARDING, JOHN B. Pvt, F, 22nd NJ Inf, 2-25-1906. Riverview Cemetery, Trenton, Mercer County.

HARDING, JOSEPH Corp, A, 4th NJ Inf, 5-3-1883. Cedar Lawn Cemetery, Paterson, Passaic County.

HARDING*, JUNIUS W. Pvt, F, 53rd VA Inf (CSA), [Captured 7-3-1863 at Gettysburg, PA. Died of diarrhea.] 9-23-1863. Finn's Point National Cemetery, Pennsville, Salem County.

HARDING, THOMAS 9-10-1868. Old Presbyterian Church Cemetery, Daretown, Salem County.

HARDING, THOMAS J. Pvt, H, 7th NJ Inf, 1-15-1872. Trinity Bible Church Cemetery, Glassboro, Gloucester County.

HARDMAN, JOB Pvt, A, 13th NJ Inf, 9-6-1894. Presbyterian Cemetery, Springfield, Union County.

HARDMAN, THOMAS (see: Hartman, Thomas A.) Clinton Cemetery, Irvington, Essex County.

HARDON, JOHN R. Pvt, B, 38th NJ Inf, 7-7-1917. Union Cemetery, Frenchtown, Hunterdon County.

HARDWICK, THEODORE (aka: Hartwick, Theodore) Pvt, A, 2nd NY Cav, DoD Unknown. South Orange Cemetery, South Orange, Essex County.

HARDY, ABRAHAM (see: Handy, Abram) Newton Cemetery, Newton, Sussex County.

HARDY*, ADOLPHUS C. Pvt, Btty I, 4th U.S. Art, 2-25-1921. Evergreen Cemetery, Morristown, Morris County.

HARDY*, DANIEL PYATT Pvt, H, 1st NJ Cav, [Wounded in action.] 9-14-1909. Evergreen Cemetery, New Brunswick, Middlesex County.

HARDY, FRANK Pvt, F, 2nd NJ Inf, 7-24-1901. Rosedale Cemetery, Orange, Essex County.

HARDY*, GEORGE Corp, D, 150th NY Inf, 9-28-1904. Van Liew Cemetery, North Brunswick, Middlesex County.

HARDY*, GEORGE Pvt, G, 190th PA Inf, 7-18-1919. St. Gabriel's Cemetery, Bradevelt, Monmouth County.

HARDY, GEORGE G. Pvt, F, 190th PA Inf, 7-19-1892. Mount Pleasant Cemetery, Newark, Essex County.

New Jersey Civil War Burials

HARDY, GODFREY H. Pvt, K, 31st NJ Inf, 2-7-1897. Presbyterian Church Cemetery, Hampton, Hunterdon County.

HARDY, HENRY Pvt, E, 29th NJ Inf, 11-21-1927. St. Rose of Lima Cemetery, Freehold, Monmouth County.

HARDY, HUGH Pvt, B, 21st NJ Inf, [Died of typhoid at Falmouth, VA.] 3-7-1863. Hoboken Cemetery, North Bergen, Hudson County.

HARDY*, JACOB Pvt, K, 14th NJ Inf, 7-3-1891. Elmwood Cemetery, New Brunswick, Middlesex County.

HARDY*, JAMES Corp, K, 14th NJ Inf, 1-17-1918. Elmwood Cemetery, New Brunswick, Middlesex County.

HARDY, JOHN (see: Harty, John) Midvale Cemetery, Midvale, Passaic County.

HARDY, JOHN S. 9-22-1867. Mansfield/Washington Cemetery, Washington, Warren County.

HARDY, JOSEPH DoD Unknown. Ponds Church Cemetery, Oakland, Bergen County.

HARDY, THOMAS Corp, C, 13th NJ Inf, 6-17-1916. Laurel Grove Cemetery, Totowa, Passaic County.

HARDY, WILLIAM B. Pvt, E, 31st NJ Inf, 7-21-1885. Evergreen Cemetery, Clinton, Hunterdon County.

HARDY*, WILLIAM H. 1st Sgt, A, 57th NY Inf, [Wounded in action.] 12-10-1907. Willow Grove Cemetery, New Brunswick, Middlesex County.

HARFORD, REUBEN B. Landsman, U.S. Navy, USS Lenapee, 7-3-1868. Evergreen Cemetery, Hillside, Union County.

HARGEST, ROBERT Pvt, G, 20th U.S. CT, 6-17-1907. Mount Peace Cemetery, Lawnside, Camden County.

HARGOUS, CHARLES EMELIO Capt, B, 15th NY Eng, 3-10-1891. St. Mary's Cemetery, Hamilton, Mercer County.

HARGOUS, PETER J. Actg Master, U.S. Navy, USS Congress, 10- -1907. St. Mary's Cemetery, Hamilton, Mercer County.

HARGRAVES, JOHN E. Pvt, C, 37th NJ Inf, 11-28-1889. Greenwood Cemetery, Hamilton, Mercer County.

HARGREAVES, ADAM Pvt, Btty D, 5th RI Heavy Art, 2-2-1907. Cedar Lawn Cemetery, Paterson, Passaic County.

HARGREAVES, JOHN S. Pvt, D, 13th NJ Inf, 4-9-1897. Fairmount Cemetery, Newark, Essex County.

HARGROVE, ELIAS (aka: Hartsgrove, Elias) Pvt, C, 23rd NJ Inf, 2-21-1897. Brotherhood Cemetery, Hainesport, Burlington County.

HARGROVE, JEFFERSON (aka: Hartsgrove, Jefferson) Pvt, E, 23rd NJ Inf, 10-19-1873. Friends Cemetery, Arneys Mount, Burlington County.

HARGROVE, MARTIN V. 1st Sgt, E, 23rd NJ Inf, 8-5-1892. Baptist Cemetery, Pemberton, Burlington County.

HARGROVE, THADDEUS L. Pvt, H, 30th AL Inf (CSA), 7-11-1863. Finn's Point National Cemetery, Pennsville, Salem County.

HARGROVES, THOMAS JUDSON Sgt Maj, A, 3rd GA Inf (CSA), [Captured 7-2-1863 at Gettysburg, PA. Died of smallpox.] 9-29-1863. Finn's Point National Cemetery, Pennsville, Salem County.

HARING, ABRAHAM P. (aka: Herring, Abraham) Pvt, D, 22nd NJ Inf, 6-11-1907. Haring Cemetery, Old Tappan, Bergen County.

HARING, DANIEL J. (aka: Herring, Daniel) Pvt, D, 22nd NJ Inf, 5-12-1928. Valleau Cemetery, Ridgewood, Bergen County.

HARING, DAVID E. Pvt, I, 22nd NJ Inf, 1920. Pascack Reformed Cemetery, Park Ridge, Bergen County.

HARING, HENRY C. Sgt, C, 1st CA Inf, 5-14-1900. Valleau Cemetery, Ridgewood, Bergen County.

Our Brothers Gone Before

HARING, HENRY J. Pvt, C, 22nd NJ Inf, DoD Unknown. Hackensack Cemetery, Hackensack, Bergen County.

HARING, JOHN H. Pvt, I, 22nd NJ Inf, 12-18-1904. Old South Church Cemetery, Bergenfield, Bergen County.

HARING, JOHN P. (aka: Herring, John) Pvt, D, 22nd NJ Inf, [Died of typhoid at Washington, DC.] 3-26-1863. Pascack Reformed Cemetery, Park Ridge, Bergen County.

HARKENS, ALBERT (see: Harkins, Albert) Cedar Hill Cemetery, Florence, Burlington County.

HARKER, CHARLES GARRISON Brig Gen, U.S. Army, [Killed in action at Kenesaw Mountain, GA.] 6-27-1864. New Episcopal Church Cemetery, Swedesboro, Gloucester County.

HARKER, DANIEL Pvt, F, 40th NJ Inf, 4-5-1917. Evergreen Cemetery, Camden, Camden County.

HARKER, EDWARD B. Pvt, C, 154th PA Inf, 8-1-1915. Evergreen Cemetery, Camden, Camden County.

HARKER, JAMES M. Pvt, A, 27th NJ Inf, 12-4-1883. Harmony Methodist Church Cemetery, Stillwater, Sussex County.

HARKER, JAMES W. Pvt, K, 24th NJ Inf, 6-15-1869. Methodist Cemetery, Woodstown, Salem County.

HARKER, JOSEPH S. Pvt, F, 12th NJ Inf, 1931. Baptist Church Cemetery, Mullica Hill, Gloucester County.

HARKER, L.H. DoD Unknown. Evergreen Cemetery, Camden, Camden County.

HARKER, WILLIAM H. Corp, C, 33rd NJ Inf, [Killed in action at Pine Knob, GA.] 6-16-1864. Adelphia Cemetery, Adelphia, Monmouth County.

HARKER, WILLIAM S. Pvt, H, 12th NJ Inf, [Killed in action at Gettysburg, PA.] 7-2-1863. Methodist Cemetery, Woodstown, Salem County.

HARKINS, ALBERT (aka: Harkens, Albert) Pvt, I, 32nd PA Inf, 6-9-1917. Cedar Hill Cemetery, Florence, Burlington County.

HARKINS, HUGH Pvt, G, 38th NJ Inf, 9-4-1877. Van Liew Cemetery, North Brunswick, Middlesex County.

HARKINS, JOHN P. Sgt, Btty K, 6th NY Heavy Art, 1-11-1876. Cedar Lawn Cemetery, Paterson, Passaic County.

HARKINS, WILLIAM Pvt, B, 104th PA Inf, 7-24-1909. Colestown Cemetery, Cherry Hill, Camden County.

HARLAN, JAMES V. Pvt, D, 13th AL Inf (CSA), 9-24-1863. Finn's Point National Cemetery, Pennsville, Salem County.

HARLEY, GEORGE Pvt, D, 25th NJ Inf, DoD Unknown. Methodist-Episcopal Church Cemetery, Magnolia, Camden County.

HARLEY, HENRY M. Pvt, D, 6th NJ Inf, DoD Unknown. Harleigh Cemetery, Camden, Camden County.

HARLEY, JOSIAH G.G. Pvt, C, 4th NJ Militia, 3-2-1897. Berlin Cemetery, Berlin, Camden County.

HARLOW, GEORGE K. Pvt, D, 23rd VA Inf (CSA), [Captured 5-12-1864 at Spotsylvania CH, VA. Died of diarrhea.] 4-11-1865. Finn's Point National Cemetery, Pennsville, Salem County.

HARLOW, JOB J. Com Sgt, B, 115th NY Inf, [Wounded 12-13-1862 at Fredericksburg, VA.] 7-10-1925. Yellow Meeting House Cemetery, Imlaytown, Monmouth County.

HARMAN, GEORGE Pvt, D, ___ PA Inf, 6-27-1910. Evergreen Cemetery, Camden, Camden County.

HARMAN, GEORGE W. Corp, D, 41st U.S. CT, 6-25-1909. Atlantic City Cemetery, Pleasantville, Atlantic County.

New Jersey Civil War Burials

HARMAN, HENRY (see: Harmon, Robert) Manahath Cemetery, Glassboro, Gloucester County.

HARMAN, SAMUEL Pvt, I, 33rd VA Inf (CSA), [Captured 5-12-1864 at Spotsylvania CH, VA. Died of lung inflammation.] 1-12-1865. Finn's Point National Cemetery, Pennsville, Salem County.

HARMAN, THOMAS Pvt, A, 5th MD Inf, [Wounded in action at Antietam, MD.] 10-22-1900. Harleigh Cemetery, Camden, Camden County.

HARMAS, LUCIUS (see: Hannas, Lucius P.) Evergreen Cemetery, Morristown, Morris County.

HARMER, SAMUEL W. Pvt, U.S. Marine Corps, 7-13-1899. Bethel Cemetery, Pennsauken, Camden County.

HARMER, WILLIAM L. Corp, A, 118th PA Inf, 2-4-1925. Harleigh Cemetery, Camden, Camden County.

HARMON, DOCTOR F. Pvt, C, 55th NC Inf (CSA), [Captured 7-1-1863 at Gettysburg, PA. Died of diarrhea.] 11-9-1863. Finn's Point National Cemetery, Pennsville, Salem County.

HARMON, JOHN (see: Hannon, John) Beverly National Cemetery, Edgewater Park, Burlington County.

HARMON, JOHN EDWARD Pvt, K, 29th CT Inf, 7-8-1930. Mount Moriah Cemetery, Hainesport, Burlington County.

HARMON, MADISON (see: Hannan, Madison) Finn's Point National Cemetery, Pennsville, Salem County.

HARMON, ROBERT (aka: Harman, Henry) Pvt, C, 40th NJ Inf, 1-19-1907. Manahath Cemetery, Glassboro, Gloucester County.

HARMOUR, PETER ALLDER (aka: Allder, Peter) Sgt, B, 2nd NJ Cav, 2-8-1908. Princeton Cemetery, Princeton, Mercer County.

HARMS, JOHN Pvt, F, 2nd U.S. Inf, 12-27-1898. Greenwood Cemetery, Tuckerton, Ocean County.

HARMS, WILLIAM (see: Harris, William) Fairmount Cemetery, Newark, Essex County.

HARNED, ELLIS Musc, H, 5th NJ Inf, 7-18-1892. Evergreen Cemetery, New Brunswick, Middlesex County.

HARNED, FRANK Fireman, U.S. Navy, USS Daylight, 6-21-1885. Alpine Cemetery, Perth Amboy, Middlesex County.

HARNED, GEORGE D. 2-12-1865. Sergeant's Hill Cemetery, Sand Brook, Hunterdon County.

HARNEY, BENJAMIN A. 1st Sgt, E, 59th NY Inf, 9-1-1883. Bayview-New York Bay Cemetery, Jersey City, Hudson County.

HARNEY*, FRANCIS W. Pvt, B, 8th NJ Inf, [Wounded in action.] 11-3-1910. Fairmount Cemetery, Newark, Essex County.

HARNEY, JOHN 7-17-1890. St. Peter's Cemetery, Jersey City, Hudson County.

HARNEY, PATRICK Pvt, H, 1st NJ Inf, 6-12-1893. St. Peter's Cemetery, Jersey City, Hudson County.

HARNING, THEODORE W. Corp, A, 84th NY Inf, 7-18-1864. Bayview-New York Bay Cemetery, Jersey City, Hudson County.

HAROLD, JAMES H. Bvt Capt, I, 1st NY Eng, 9-2-1902. Presbyterian Cemetery, North Plainfield, Somerset County.

HAROLD, JAMES L. Pvt, K, 40th MS Inf (CSA), 6-14-1863. Finn's Point National Cemetery, Pennsville, Salem County.

HAROLD, LOUIS F.A. (aka: Herold, F. A.) Pvt, E, 4th U.S. Cav, 2-15-1932. Woodland Cemetery, Newark, Essex County.

HARP, GEORGE W. Pvt, A, 26th MS Inf (CSA), 5-2-1865. Finn's Point National Cemetery, Pennsville, Salem County.

HARP, HENRY 1922. Old Brick Reformed Church Cemetery, Marlboro, Monmouth County.

Our Brothers Gone Before

HARP, JOHN Pvt, G, 23rd NC Inf (CSA), [Captured 7-3-1863 at Gettysburg, PA.] 9-20-1863. Finn's Point National Cemetery, Pennsville, Salem County.
HARP, JOSEPH Pvt, F, 64th OH Inf, 7-14-1895. Fairmount Cemetery, Newark, Essex County.
HARPER, CANDY Pvt, G, 7th NY State Militia, 8-26-1910. Fairmount Cemetery, Newark, Essex County.
HARPER, GEORGE 11-23-1891. Presbyterian Church Cemetery, Rockaway, Morris County.
HARPER, GEORGE H. 2-17-1938. Clinton Cemetery, Irvington, Essex County.
HARPER*, H.W. Corp, B, 8th FL Inf (CSA), [Wounded 12-13-1862 at Fredericksburg, VA. Died of erysipelas.] 11-1-1863. Finn's Point National Cemetery, Pennsville, Salem County.
HARPER, JOHN W. (see: Herbert, John W.) Bordentown/Old St. Mary's Catholic Cemetery, Bordentown, Burlington County.
HARPER, SIMON O. Ordinary Seaman, U.S. Navy, USS Hartford, 5-23-1901. Bayview-New York Bay Cemetery, Jersey City, Hudson County.
HARPER, WILLETT R. (aka: Harper, William) Pvt, F, 197th PA Inf, 1-16-1906. Harleigh Cemetery, Camden, Camden County.
HARPER, WILLIAM (see: Harper, Willett R.) Harleigh Cemetery, Camden, Camden County.
HARPER, WILLIAM W. Corp, A, 22nd NJ Inf, 1-30-1903. Old 1st Reformed Church Cemetery, Hackensack, Bergen County.
HARPERMAN, JOHN J. Seaman, U.S. Navy, DoD Unknown. Holy Name Cemetery, Jersey City, Hudson County.
HARR, DAVID Pvt, E, 104th PA Inf, 1890. Union Cemetery, Milford, Hunterdon County.
HARRAD, A.R. (see: Howard, A.R.) Finn's Point National Cemetery, Pennsville, Salem County.
HARRELL, B.S. Pvt, H, 6th VA Cav (CSA), 5-6-1865. Finn's Point National Cemetery, Pennsville, Salem County.
HARRELL, REUBEN Pvt, I, 9th VA Inf (CSA), [Captured 7-3-1863 at Gettysburg, PA. Died of diarrhea.] 9-9-1863. Finn's Point National Cemetery, Pennsville, Salem County.
HARRIMAN, RODNEY C. Pvt, F, 11th ME Inf, [Died of wounds received 8-16-1864 at Deep Run, VA.] 9-26-1864. Beverly National Cemetery, Edgewater Park, Burlington County.
HARRING, HENRY (see: Herring, Henry J.) Pascack Reformed Cemetery, Park Ridge, Bergen County.
HARRING, JOHN F. (see: Hering, John F.) Old Hook Cemetery, Westwood, Bergen County.
HARRINGTON, CHARLES Pvt, I, 11th NY Inf, 10-5-1862. Adelphia Cemetery, Adelphia, Monmouth County.
HARRINGTON*, CHARLES F. Sgt, A, 18th NH Inf, 9-29-1904. Hillside Cemetery, Lyndhurst, Bergen County.
HARRINGTON, HENRY B. Corp, D, 79th NY Inf, 1-10-1885. Cedar Hill Cemetery, East Millstone, Somerset County.
HARRINGTON, HIRAM (see: Harrington, John) Prospect Hill Cemetery, Caldwell, Essex County.
HARRINGTON, JEREMIAH Landsman, U.S. Navy, 12-29-1914. Oak Grove Cemetery, Hammonton, Atlantic County.
HARRINGTON, JOHN (aka: Harrington, Hiram) Corp, A, 140th IN Inf, 1-26-1893. Prospect Hill Cemetery, Caldwell, Essex County.
HARRINGTON, JOSEPH Pvt, B, 4th NJ Inf, 2-24-1910. Mount Pleasant Cemetery, Newark, Essex County.

New Jersey Civil War Burials

HARRINGTON, PATRICK Pvt, E, 8th NJ Inf, 5-8-1876. Fairmount Cemetery, Newark, Essex County.

HARRINGTON, PETER B. (see: Hampton, Peter) Fairmount Cemetery, Newark, Essex County.

HARRIOTT*, ROBERT Pvt, B, 33rd NJ Inf, 11-19-1878. Holy Name Cemetery, Jersey City, Hudson County.

HARRIS, ___?___ DoD Unknown. Old Camden Cemetery, Camden, Camden County.

HARRIS, ABBIE J. Nurse, 1925. Baptist Church Cemetery, Canton, Salem County.

HARRIS, ABEL Pvt, G, 42nd MS Inf (CSA), 2-6-1864. Finn's Point National Cemetery, Pennsville, Salem County.

HARRIS, ABRAHAM R. (JR.) Sgt, I, 1st NJ Cav, 4-15-1895. Mercer Cemetery, Trenton, Mercer County.

HARRIS, ABRAM Ordinary Seaman, U.S. Navy, USS Princeton, 1-13-1910. Presbyterian Church Cemetery, Kingston, Somerset County.

HARRIS, ABRAM Musc, H, 30th NJ Inf, DoD Unknown. Presbyterian Church Cemetery, Rockaway, Morris County.

HARRIS, ABRAM M. Corp, D, 13th NJ Inf, [Wounded 9-17-1862 at Antietam, MD.] 1-19-1909. Presbyterian Church Cemetery, Rockaway, Morris County.

HARRIS, ALEXANDER Pvt, ___, 1st VA Light Art (CSA), 10-23-1863. Finn's Point National Cemetery, Pennsville, Salem County.

HARRIS, ALFRED Pvt, G, 24th NJ Inf, 2-15-1867. Methodist Church Cemetery, Haleyville, Cumberland County.

HARRIS, ANANIAS 1-22-1864. Presbyterian Church Cemetery, Upper Deerfield, Cumberland County.

HARRIS, ANDREW Pvt, C, 39th NJ Inf, 3-23-1925. Mount Hebron Cemetery, Montclair, Essex County.

HARRIS, ANDREW Corp, A, 41st U.S. CT, 3-29-1896. Cedar Hill Cemetery, East Millstone, Somerset County.

HARRIS, BARON DEKALB Corp, K, 10th NJ Inf, [Died of sunstroke at Relay House, MD.] 8-4-1864. Baptist Church Cemetery, Bridgeton, Cumberland County.

HARRIS, BENJAMIN C. Pvt, C, 38th NJ Inf, 1-28-1907. Cedar Green Cemetery, Clayton, Gloucester County.

HARRIS, BENJAMIN H. Corp, E, 1st NJ Inf, 1-3-1917. Old Camden Cemetery, Camden, Camden County.

HARRIS, CHARLES F. 1894. 1st United Methodist Church Cemetery, Salem, Salem County.

HARRIS, CHARLES P. Coal Heaver, U.S. Navy, USS Mohican, 12-27-1896. Grove Church Cemetery, North Bergen, Hudson County.

HARRIS, CHAUNCEY Bvt Lt Col, 14th NJ Inf [Wounded 7-9-1864 at Monocacy, MD.] 3-20-1911. Evergreen Cemetery, Hillside, Union County.

HARRIS, CICERO F. Pvt, Btty B, 10th Bttn NC Heavy Art (CSA), [Captured 12-21-1864 at Savannah, GA. Died of fever.] 4-12-1865. Finn's Point National Cemetery, Pennsville, Salem County.

HARRIS*, CUNNINGHAM Pvt, I, 2nd NJ Cav, 1920. Methodist-Episcopal Cemetery, Pointville, Burlington County.

HARRIS*, DANIEL BURT Pvt, K, 12th NJ Inf, 12-13-1909. Mount Pleasant Cemetery, Millville, Cumberland County.

HARRIS, DAVID Pvt, G, 3rd NJ Cav, 1918. Mount Pleasant Cemetery, Millville, Cumberland County.

HARRIS, DAVID M. Pvt, F, 1st NJ Militia, 9-16-1922. Fairmount Cemetery, Newark, Essex County.

HARRIS, DAVID S. Pvt, F, 4th NJ Inf, DoD Unknown. Mount Pleasant Cemetery, Millville, Cumberland County.

Our Brothers Gone Before

HARRIS, EDWARD Pvt, D, 8th PA Cav, 4-18-1898. New Camden Cemetery, Camden, Camden County.
HARRIS, EDWARD B. 12-10-1862. Mount Pleasant Cemetery, Newark, Essex County.
HARRIS, EDWARD L. Corp, L, 1st NJ Cav, [Wounded in action.] 5-24-1887. Presbyterian Church Cemetery, Kingston, Somerset County.
HARRIS, EDWARD P. Pvt, E, 12th NJ Inf, 8-9-1894. Morgan Cemetery, Cinnaminson, Burlington County.
HARRIS, ELIAS Pvt, M, 2nd NJ Cav, 1931. Presbyterian Church Cemetery, LaBarre, Warren County.
HARRIS*, EPHRIAM B. Pvt, Btty B, 1st NJ Light Art, DoD Unknown. Arlington Cemetery, Kearny, Hudson County.
HARRIS, ETHAN T. Maj, 3rd NJ Cav 1-8-1868. 1st United Methodist Church Cemetery, Bridgeton, Cumberland County.
HARRIS, EUGENE DoD Unknown. Presbyterian/Methodist-Episcopal Cemetery, Succasunna, Morris County.
HARRIS, FRANCIS B. Corp, A, 12th NJ Inf, 6-5-1894. Harleigh Cemetery, Camden, Camden County.
HARRIS, FRANCIS M. Pvt, H, 24th NJ Inf, 1921. 1st United Methodist Church Cemetery, Bridgeton, Cumberland County.
HARRIS, FREDERICK HALSEY Bvt Col, 13th NJ Inf 3-16-1899. Rosedale Cemetery, Orange, Essex County.
HARRIS*, GABRIEL Corp, Btty D, 11th U.S. CHA, 1902. New Somerville Cemetery, Somerville, Somerset County.
HARRIS, GEORGE Pvt, I, 6th U.S. CT, 7-4-1887. Princeton Cemetery, Princeton, Mercer County.
HARRIS, GEORGE Pvt, G, 31st NJ Inf, 3-26-1912. Methodist Church Cemetery, Liberty, Warren County.
HARRIS, GEORGE A. Pvt, K, 12th NJ Inf, [Wounded in action.] 2-5-1903. Presbyterian Church Cemetery, Bridgeton, Cumberland County.
HARRIS, GEORGE E. Pvt, A, 51st PA Militia, 3- -1898. 1st United Methodist Church Cemetery, Bridgeton, Cumberland County.
HARRIS, GEORGE L. Clerk, U.S. Navy, USS Restless, 1-19-1916. Fairmount Cemetery, Newark, Essex County.
HARRIS, GEORGE M. Capt, E, 33rd NJ Inf, [Wounded in action.] 6-27-1901. St. Paul's Methodist Church Cemetery, Port Republic, Atlantic County.
HARRIS, GEORGE W. Pvt, H, 25th NJ Inf, 1-4-1891. Fairmount Cemetery, Newark, Essex County.
HARRIS, GEORGE W. Pvt, G, 4th NJ Inf, DoD Unknown. Cedar Green Cemetery, Clayton, Gloucester County.
HARRIS, GEORGE W. 6-18-1894. Flower Hill Cemetery, North Bergen, Hudson County.
HARRIS, GEORGE WASHINGTON Sgt, K, 39th NJ Inf, 2-12-1899. Newton Cemetery, Newton, Sussex County.
HARRIS, GILES N. Landsman, U.S. Navy, USS Neptune, 5-3-1925. Evergreen Cemetery, Hillside, Union County.
HARRIS, HENRY Sgt, D, 2nd U.S. CT, 1-7-1919. Atlantic City Cemetery, Pleasantville, Atlantic County.
HARRIS, HENRY Corp, K, 4th NY Inf, 5-2-1909. Fairmount Cemetery, Newark, Essex County.
HARRIS, HENRY Corp, D, 4th NJ Inf, [Killed in action at Gaines' Farm, VA.] 6-27-1862. Fairmount Cemetery, Newark, Essex County.
HARRIS, HENRY H. Pvt, B, 25th U.S. CT, 4-28-1895. Johnson Cemetery, Camden, Camden County.
HARRIS, HENRY H. Pvt, G, 24th NJ Inf, 7-8-1900. Methodist Church Cemetery, Haleyville, Cumberland County.

New Jersey Civil War Burials

HARRIS, HUDSON W. Pvt, F, 47th NC Inf (CSA), [Wounded and captured 7-3-1863 at Gettysburg, PA. Died of wounds.] 7-31-1863. Finn's Point National Cemetery, Pennsville, Salem County.

HARRIS, IRA Ensign, U.S. Navy, 6-21-1925. Hackensack Cemetery, Hackensack, Bergen County.

HARRIS, IRA (aka: Kennedy, William) Pvt, K, 5th NY Cav, 3-9-1920. Holy Sepulchre Cemetery, East Orange, Essex County.

HARRIS, ISAAC Corp, F, 56th NY Inf, 4-15-1899. Cedar Lawn Cemetery, Paterson, Passaic County.

HARRIS, ISAAC 2nd Lt, F, 2nd NJ Inf, 9-4-1913. Newton Cemetery, Newton, Sussex County.

HARRIS, ISAAC (SR.) Pvt, I, 10th NJ Inf, 1910. Manahath Cemetery, Glassboro, Gloucester County.

HARRIS, ISHMAEL P. Pvt, D, 21st NJ Inf, 1896. North Crosswicks Cemetery, North Crosswicks, Mercer County.

HARRIS, JACOB I. 1907. Cedar Ridge Cemetery, Blairstown, Warren County.

HARRIS, JAMES Corp, Btty E, 2nd PA Heavy Art, 1930. Cedar Green Cemetery, Clayton, Gloucester County.

HARRIS, JAMES J. Pvt, I, 9th NJ Inf, 3-24-1905. Riverview Cemetery, Penns Grove, Salem County.

HARRIS, JOHN Pvt, C, 2nd NJ Cav, 1917. United Methodist Church Cemetery, Ellisdale, Burlington County.

HARRIS*, JOHN Pvt, F, 2nd NJ Inf, DoD Unknown. Presbyterian/Methodist-Episcopal Cemetery, Succasunna, Morris County.

HARRIS*, JOHN NILES Pvt, F, 11th ME Inf, 1-25-1909. Van Liew Cemetery, North Brunswick, Middlesex County.

HARRIS, JOHN T. 10-5-1898. Overlook Cemetery, Bridgeton, Cumberland County.

HARRIS, JOHN W. Pvt, C, 29th CT Inf, 12-31-1894. White Ridge Cemetery, Eatontown, Monmouth County.

HARRIS*, LAWRENCE Musc, Btty K, 14th NY Heavy Art, 1-20-1913. Fairmount Cemetery, Newark, Essex County.

HARRIS, LEWIS Pvt, C, 28th NJ Inf, 1919. Baptist Cemetery, South Plainfield, Middlesex County.

HARRIS, LEWIS Musc, K, 10th NJ Inf, 11-20-1893. Mount Prospect Cemetery, Neptune, Monmouth County.

HARRIS, M. Pvt, A, __ Bttn MS Cav (CSA), 7-17-1864. Finn's Point National Cemetery, Pennsville, Salem County.

HARRIS, MARK DoD Unknown. Harmony Methodist-Episcopal Church Cemetery, Piney Hollow, Gloucester County.

HARRIS, MONROE M. Pvt, B, 42nd MS Inf (CSA), 6-26-1865. Finn's Point National Cemetery, Pennsville, Salem County.

HARRIS, PETER W. Sgt, E, 40th NY Inf, 4-25-1881. Mount Pleasant Cemetery, Newark, Essex County.

HARRIS, R. Pvt, D, 5th VA Inf (CSA), 4-27-1865. Finn's Point National Cemetery, Pennsville, Salem County.

HARRIS, RICHARD H. Pvt, 9th OH Light Art 3-21-1903. Fairmount Cemetery, Newark, Essex County.

HARRIS, ROBERT Sgt, D, 79th NY Inf, 11-9-1894. Macphelah Cemetery, North Bergen, Hudson County.

HARRIS, ROBERT Corp, A, 12th NJ Inf, 10-14-1872. Baptist Church Cemetery, Slabtown, Salem County.

HARRIS*, SAMUEL Capt, F, 24th NJ Inf, 1-8-1889. Presbyterian Church Cemetery, Bridgeton, Cumberland County.

Our Brothers Gone Before

HARRIS, SAMUEL S. Pvt, B, 76th PA Inf, 9-6-1928. Methodist-Episcopal Cemetery, Olivet, Salem County.
HARRIS, TERREL S. Pvt, B, 2nd MS Inf (CSA), [Wounded and captured 7-1-1863 at Gettysburg, PA. Died of disease.] 6-30-1864. Finn's Point National Cemetery, Pennsville, Salem County.
HARRIS, THEODORE Seaman, U.S. Navy, 2-13-1914. Butler Cemetery, Camden, Camden County.
HARRIS, THEODORE (see: Sinclair, Theodore) Union Cemetery, Frenchtown, Hunterdon County.
HARRIS, THOMAS Mate, U.S. Navy, 1880. Hazelwood Cemetery, Rahway, Union County.
HARRIS, THOMAS A. Sgt, G, 24th NJ Inf, 7-22-1903. Methodist Church Cemetery, Haleyville, Cumberland County.
HARRIS, THOMAS MARTIN 1913. Greenwood Cemetery, Pleasantville, Atlantic County.
HARRIS, THOMAS W. Capt, F, 174th PA Inf, 1885. Siloam Cemetery, Vineland, Cumberland County.
HARRIS, WALTER L. Sgt, E, 3rd PA Inf, 7-18-1912. Greenwood Cemetery, Pleasantville, Atlantic County.
HARRIS, WILBER Pvt, Btty C, 5th NY Heavy Art, 1- -1894. Laurel Grove Cemetery, Totowa, Passaic County.
HARRIS, WILLIAM 12-3-1870. United Methodist Church Cemetery, Winslow, Camden County.
HARRIS, WILLIAM 2-5-1915. Mount Peace Cemetery, Lawnside, Camden County.
HARRIS, WILLIAM Sgt, H, 2nd MA Inf, [Wounded 5-25-1862 at Winchester, VA.] 5-9-1904. Fairmount Cemetery, Newark, Essex County.
HARRIS, WILLIAM Pvt, F, 41st U.S. CT, 7-16-1922. Mount Vernon Cemetery, Paulsboro, Gloucester County.
HARRIS, WILLIAM (aka: Harms, William) Pvt, B, 33rd NJ Inf, 12-4-1899. Fairmount Cemetery, Newark, Essex County.
HARRIS, WILLIAM Chaplain, 3-23-1885. Princeton Cemetery, Princeton, Mercer County.
HARRIS, WILLIAM F. Pvt, C, 24th NJ Inf, 1924. Soldier's Home Cemetery, Vineland, Cumberland County.
HARRIS, WILLIAM F. Pvt, B, 24th NJ Inf, DoD Unknown. 1st United Methodist Church Cemetery, Bridgeton, Cumberland County.
HARRIS, WILLIAM H. Seaman, U.S. Navy, USS Aries, 12-7-1898. White Ridge Cemetery, Eatontown, Monmouth County.
HARRIS, WILLIAM H. Pvt, I, 9th NJ Inf, 3-1-1885. Riverview Cemetery, Penns Grove, Salem County.
HARRIS, WILLIAM H. Landsman, U.S. Navy, 4-15-1908. Rosedale Cemetery, Linden, Union County.
HARRIS, WILLIS Pvt, G, 23rd NC Inf (CSA), [Wounded 6-27-1862 at Gaines' Mill, VA. Captured 7-1-1863 at Gettysburg, PA. Died of fever.] 4-1-1864. Finn's Point National Cemetery, Pennsville, Salem County.
HARRIS, WINFIELD S. Pvt, C, 35th NJ Inf, DoD Unknown. Greenwood Cemetery, Millville, Cumberland County.
HARRISON, ABRAHAM H. Pvt, B, 43rd U.S. CT, 4-14-1900. Mount Zion Methodist Church Cemetery, Lawnside, Camden County.
HARRISON, ABRAHAM H. 11-20-1873. Phillipsburg Cemetery, Phillipsburg, Warren County.
HARRISON, ALBERT C. Sgt, G, 14th NJ Inf, 9-10-1925. United Methodist Church Cemetery, Little Silver, Monmouth County.

New Jersey Civil War Burials

HARRISON, AZARIAH Steward, U.S. Navy, USS Proteus, 11-12-1910. Fairmount Cemetery, Newark, Essex County.

HARRISON, CALEB H. Corp, Btty B, 1st NJ Light Art, 7-2-1902. Evergreen Cemetery, Hillside, Union County.

HARRISON, CHARLES H. 2nd Lt, H, PA Emerg NJ Militia, 10-9-1904. Rosedale Cemetery, Orange, Essex County.

HARRISON, DANIEL Landsman, U.S. Navy, 1-22-1881. Holy Sepulchre Cemetery, East Orange, Essex County.

HARRISON, DAVID Pvt, G, 1st NY Eng, 6-10-1908. Ponds Church Cemetery, Oakland, Bergen County.

HARRISON, DAVID 10-26-1897. Fairmount Cemetery, Newark, Essex County.

HARRISON, DAVID Pvt, Btty C, 1st NJ Light Art, 8-30-1906. Presbyterian Church Cemetery, Greenwich, Warren County.

HARRISON*, DAVID D. (aka: Dickinson, David) Pvt, Btty K, 16th NY Heavy Art, 9-7-1904. Clinton Cemetery, Irvington, Essex County.

HARRISON, DOMINICK Pvt, U.S. Marine Corps, USS Isonomia, 6-16-1872. St. John's Evangelical Church Cemetery, Orange, Essex County.

HARRISON, EBENEZER Corp, K, 26th NJ Inf, 1-15-1905. Fairmount Cemetery, Newark, Essex County.

HARRISON, EDMOND Corp, F, 18th WI Inf, 9-7-1894. Arlington Cemetery, Kearny, Hudson County.

HARRISON*, ENOCH 1st Lt, A, 63rd NY Inf, 4- -1900. 1st United Methodist Church Cemetery, Bridgeton, Cumberland County.

HARRISON, FRANK 2nd Lt, D, ___ ___ ___, 3-14-1893. St. John's Evangelical Church Cemetery, Orange, Essex County.

HARRISON*, FREDERIC M. 1st Sgt, A, 39th NJ Inf, 8-23-1895. Fairmount Cemetery, Newark, Essex County.

HARRISON*, GEORGE W. Capt, H, 39th NJ Inf, [Killed in action at Petersburg, VA.] 4-2-1865. Rosedale Cemetery, Orange, Essex County.

HARRISON, GODFREY 1908. Harleigh Cemetery, Camden, Camden County.

HARRISON, HENRY (see: Neely, Theodore H.) Mount Holly Cemetery, Mount Holly, Burlington County.

HARRISON, HENRY F. Corp, D, 13th NJ Inf, [Wounded 9-17-1862 at Antietam, MD.] 1-22-1921. Prospect Hill Cemetery, Caldwell, Essex County.

HARRISON, JACOB Pvt, B, 21st NJ Inf, DoD Unknown. Bayview-New York Bay Cemetery, Jersey City, Hudson County.

HARRISON, JAMES Pvt, D, 9th LA Inf (CSA), [Captured 7-8-1863 at Hancock, VA. Died of joint infection.] 9-5-1863. Finn's Point National Cemetery, Pennsville, Salem County.

HARRISON, JAMES H. Sgt, C, 7th NJ Inf, [Killed in action at Gettysburg, PA.] 7-2-1863. Prospect Hill Cemetery, Caldwell, Essex County.

HARRISON, JAMES P. Pvt, D, 2nd VA Inf (CSA), 1-29-1864. Finn's Point National Cemetery, Pennsville, Salem County.

HARRISON, JOHN C. Pvt, G, 37th NJ Inf, 8-11-1915. Mount Hebron Cemetery, Montclair, Essex County.

HARRISON, JOHN T. Corp, B, 15th GA Inf (CSA), [Wounded and captured 7-3-1863 at Gettysburg, PA. Died of fever.] 9-30-1863. Finn's Point National Cemetery, Pennsville, Salem County.

HARRISON, JOHN W. Pvt, I, 4th NJ Inf, 8-30-1889. Arlington Cemetery, Kearny, Hudson County.

HARRISON, JOSEPH H. 2nd Lt, A, 80th NY Inf, 1920. Rosedale Cemetery, Orange, Essex County.

HARRISON, JOSIAH Q. 7-4-1922. Mount Prospect Cemetery, Neptune, Monmouth County.

Our Brothers Gone Before

HARRISON, JOSIAH W. 2-28-1898. Macphelah Cemetery, North Bergen, Hudson County.
HARRISON, M. Pvt, E, 22nd VA Cav (CSA), 4-23-1865. Finn's Point National Cemetery, Pennsville, Salem County.
HARRISON, PATRICK Pvt, U.S. Marine Corps, DoD Unknown. St. John's Evangelical Church Cemetery, Orange, Essex County.
HARRISON, PRINCE A. Sgt, B, 25th U.S. CT, 5-10-1911. Fairmount Cemetery, Newark, Essex County.
HARRISON, RICHARD S. Capt, A, 88th NY Inf, [Wounded 9-17-1862 at Antietam, MD.] 7-23-1921. Macphelah Cemetery, North Bergen, Hudson County.
HARRISON*, ROBERT J. Pvt, I, 33rd NJ Inf, 8-3-1904. Fairmount Cemetery, Newark, Essex County.
HARRISON, SAMUEL B. Pvt, K, 2nd DC Inf, 6-14-1881. Vail Presbyterian Cemetery, Parsippany, Morris County.
HARRISON, STEPHEN W. Seaman, U.S. Navy, USS Badger, 12-13-1914. Rosedale Cemetery, Orange, Essex County.
HARRISON, T.F. DoD Unknown. Vincent Methodist-Episcopal Cemetery, Nutley, Essex County.
HARRISON, THOMAS Pvt, A, 51st GA Inf (CSA), [Captured 7-2-1863 at Gettysburg, PA.] 10-29-1863. Finn's Point National Cemetery, Pennsville, Salem County.
HARRISON, THOMAS D. Pvt, F, 37th NY National Guard, 1-23-1891. Mount Pleasant Cemetery, Newark, Essex County.
HARRISON, THOMAS M. Pvt, D, 5th NJ Inf, 11-24-1895. Fairmount Cemetery, Newark, Essex County.
HARRISON*, THOMAS M. Pvt, G, 12th NJ Inf, 9-28-1896. Mount Pleasant Cemetery, Newark, Essex County.
HARRISON, VINCENT A. 3-16-1865. Mount Pleasant Cemetery, Newark, Essex County.
HARRISON, W. M. Pvt, D, 51st AL Cav (CSA), 2-19-1864. Finn's Point National Cemetery, Pennsville, Salem County.
HARRISON, WILLIAM B. Pvt, B, 21st NJ Inf, 7-28-1921. Arlington Cemetery, Kearny, Hudson County.
HARRISON, WILLIAM H. Pvt, A, 2nd FL Inf (CSA), [Wounded and captured 7-2-1863 at Gettysburg, PA.] 12-25-1864. Finn's Point National Cemetery, Pennsville, Salem County.
HARRISON, WILLIAM H. Pvt, C, 37th TN Inf (CSA), 10-3-1863. Finn's Point National Cemetery, Pennsville, Salem County.
HARRISON*, WILLIAM H. Pvt, E, 39th NJ Inf, [Wounded in action.] 12-24-1903. Presbyterian Church Cemetery, Bridgeton, Cumberland County.
HARRISON, WILLIAM H. Corp, D, 39th NJ Inf, DoD Unknown. New Presbyterian Cemetery, Hanover, Morris County.
HARRISON, WILLIAM H. 12-13-1898. Mount Pleasant Cemetery, Newark, Essex County.
HARRISON*, WILLIAM J. Capt, K, 15th U.S. CT, 5-8-1909. Prospect Hill Cemetery, Caldwell, Essex County.
HARRISON, WILLIAM LAWRENCE 9-27-1889. Rosedale Cemetery, Orange, Essex County.
HARRISON, WILLIAM S. Pvt, A, 2nd NJ Militia, 1914. Rosehill Cemetery, Newfield, Gloucester County.
HARRISON, WILLIAM V. Pvt, C, 72nd PA Inf, 10-29-1862. Fairmount Cemetery, Newark, Essex County.
HARRISON, WILLIAM W. Pvt, G, 26th NJ Inf, 5-3-1865. Rosedale Cemetery, Orange, Essex County.
HARROLD*, CHRISTOPHER Pvt, Btty D, 1st NJ Light Art, DoD Unknown. Rosedale Cemetery, Orange, Essex County.

New Jersey Civil War Burials

HARROLD, SAMUEL B. Pvt, A, 35th NJ Inf, 1-12-1894. Riverview Cemetery, Trenton, Mercer County.

HARROP, ALEXANDER Sgt, E, 71st NY Inf, [Killed in action at Bristoe Station, VA.] 8-27-1862. Rosedale Cemetery, Orange, Essex County.

HARROP, FRANK 10-6-1933. Woodland Cemetery, Newark, Essex County.

HARROP, HARVEY Corp, D, 37th NJ Inf, 12-5-1899. Bethel Cemetery, Pennsauken, Camden County.

HARROP, THOMAS Sgt, H, 107th PA Inf, 5-22-1917. Arlington Cemetery, Kearny, Hudson County.

HARROP, THOMAS Pvt, H, 38th NJ Inf, 12-11-1907. Rosedale Cemetery, Orange, Essex County.

HART*, ABNER P. Pvt, F, 38th NJ Inf, 1868. Presbyterian Church Cemetery, Pennington, Mercer County.

HART, ABSALOM Pvt, E, 21st NJ Inf, 2-26-1905. United Methodist Church Cemetery, Windsor, Mercer County.

HART, ALFRED Pvt, D, 36th U.S. CT, 2-15-1907. Trinity AME Church Cemetery, Wrightsville, Burlington County.

HART, ANDREW Pvt, L, 58th NC Inf (CSA), [Captured in Hawkins County, TN. Died of typhoid.] 9-2-1863. Finn's Point National Cemetery, Pennsville, Salem County.

HART, CHARLES Pvt, G, 174th PA Inf, 2-28-1914. Riverview Cemetery, Trenton, Mercer County.

HART, CHARLES F. Pvt, L, 3rd NJ Cav, 8-23-1919. Prospect Hill Cemetery, Flemington, Hunterdon County.

HART, DAVID Pvt, H, 31st NJ Inf, 6-12-1890. Fountain Grove Cemetery, Glen Gardner, Hunterdon County.

HART, FRANCIS Pvt, E, 66th NY Inf, 4-17-1889. Egg Harbor Cemetery, Egg Harbor, Atlantic County.

HART, ISRAEL Asst Surg, 38th NJ Inf 1907. Presbyterian Church Cemetery, Pennington, Mercer County.

HART, JACOB Pvt, A, 1st NJ Cav, 7-6-1918. Presbyterian Church Cemetery, Shrewsbury, Monmouth County.

HART, JACOB C. Pvt, A, 3rd NJ Cav, 5-24-1918. Union Cemetery, Washington, Morris County.

HART, JACOB J. Pvt, K, 4th U.S. Cav, 11-27-1910. Union Cemetery, Washington, Morris County.

HART, JAMES H. Pvt, K, 25th U.S. CT, 11-19-1916. Mount Peace Cemetery, Lawnside, Camden County.

HART, JAMES L. Pvt, A, 1st CA Inf, 2- -1913. Monument Cemetery, Edgewater Park, Burlington County.

HART, JEREMIAH Musc, C, 28th MA Inf, 10-27-1907. Holy Name Cemetery, Jersey City, Hudson County.

HART, JOHN Pvt, I, 28th NJ Inf, [Wounded 12-13-1862 at Fredericksburg, VA.] 1929. Methodist-Episcopal Cemetery, Glendola, Monmouth County.

HART, JOHN H. Pvt, K, 35th NJ Inf, 11-16-1917. Greenwood Cemetery, Hamilton, Mercer County.

HART, JOHN R. 2-4-1916. Presbyterian Church Cemetery, Shrewsbury, Monmouth County.

HART, JOHN R. 1st Sgt, C, 5th FL Inf (CSA), [Captured 7-5-1863 at Gettysburg, PA. Died of lung inflammation.] 1-21-1864. Finn's Point National Cemetery, Pennsville, Salem County.

HART, JOHN S. Pvt, D, 12th NJ Inf, 4-4-1910. Elmwood Cemetery, New Brunswick, Middlesex County.

HART, JOHN W. Pvt, E, 4th NJ Militia, 8-22-1906. Old Camden Cemetery, Camden, Camden County.

Our Brothers Gone Before

HART, JOHN W. Corp, F, 22nd NJ Inf, 2-25-1881. Methodist Church Cemetery, Titusville, Mercer County.

HART, JOSEPH Pvt, L, 58th NC Inf (CSA), [Captured in Hawkins County, TN.] 8-26-1863. Finn's Point National Cemetery, Pennsville, Salem County.

HART, JOSEPH Pvt, H, 15th NJ Inf, 1917. Methodist Church Cemetery, Mount Bethel, Warren County.

HART, JOSEPH A. 3-19-1881. United Methodist Church Cemetery, Pattenburg, Hunterdon County.

HART, JOSEPH T. Sgt, A, 104th PA Inf, 3-10-1920. Holcomb-Riverview Cemetery, Lambertville, Hunterdon County.

HART, MATHIAS Pvt, I, 31st NJ Inf, 4-17-1891. Fairmount Cemetery, Newark, Essex County.

HART, MATTHEW (see: Bart, Matthew S.) Fairmount Cemetery, Newark, Essex County.

HART, NICHOLAS Pvt, G, 15th NJ Inf, 2-6-1888. Presbyterian Church Cemetery, Rockaway, Morris County.

HART, NOAH L. Pvt, B, 28th NJ Inf, 1909. Brainerd Cemetery, Cranbury, Middlesex County.

HART, PETER Pvt, K, 21st NJ Inf, 3-3-1889. Fairmount Cemetery, Newark, Essex County.

HART, PETER Capt, F, 31st NJ Inf, 3-18-1896. Finesville Cemetery, Finesville, Warren County.

HART*, RICHARD B. Corp, A, 49th PA Militia, 10-9-1903. Presbyterian Church Cemetery, Woodbridge, Middlesex County.

HART, RILEY Pvt, L, 58th NC Inf (CSA), [Captured in Hawkins County, TN. Died of rubella.] 8-26-1863. Finn's Point National Cemetery, Pennsville, Salem County.

HART, ROBERT Corp, D, 20th MA Inf, [Wounded 12-11-1862 at Fredericksburg, VA. and 6-19-1864 at Petersburg, VA.] 5-26-1914. St. Mary's Cemetery, Plainfield, Union County.

HART, SAMUEL Pvt, A, 43rd U.S. CT, 6-27-1897. Atlantic City Cemetery, Pleasantville, Atlantic County.

HART, SAMUEL Pvt, I, 2nd NJ Cav, DoD Unknown. Presbyterian Church Cemetery, Lawrenceville, Mercer County.

HART, SAMUEL C. Pvt, G, 23rd PA Inf, 2-12-1889. Trinity Episcopal Church Cemetery, Moorestown, Burlington County.

HART, SAMUEL L. Pvt, K, 33rd PA Militia, 7-28-1925. Prospect Hill Cemetery, Flemington, Hunterdon County.

HART*, SAMUEL S. Pvt, I, 2nd NJ Cav, 12-6-1897. Bayview-New York Bay Cemetery, Jersey City, Hudson County.

HART, STEPHEN P. Sgt, H, 17th ME Inf, [Wounded in action.] 1917. Mount Hebron Cemetery, Montclair, Essex County.

HART, THOMAS Pvt, D, 4th NJ Inf, 1904. Baptist Church Cemetery, Jacobstown, Burlington County.

HART, WILLIAM Pvt, I, 28th NJ Inf, 9-1-1912. Alpine Cemetery, Perth Amboy, Middlesex County.

HART, WILLIAM Pvt, F, 104th PA Inf, [Died while prisoner at Fair Oaks, VA.] 7-2-1862. Methodist Cemetery, Allentown, Monmouth County.

HART, WILLIAM Pvt, E, 18th PA Inf, 1-18-1920. Harleigh Cemetery, Camden, Camden County.

HART, WILLIAM H. Sgt, G, 3rd NJ Militia, 4-30-1888. Maplewood Cemetery, Freehold, Monmouth County.

HART, WILLIAM H. Pvt, Btty B, 3rd PA Heavy Art, DoD Unknown. Finn's Point National Cemetery, Pennsville, Salem County.

HART, WILLIAM M. Pvt, I, 2nd NJ Cav, 3-15-1901. Riverview Cemetery, Trenton, Mercer County.

New Jersey Civil War Burials

HART, WILLIAM P. Pvt, K, 39th NJ Inf, 2-14-1912. St. Mary's Cemetery, Hamilton, Mercer County.

HARTELL*, JAMES Pvt, B, 8th NJ Inf, 3-10-1911. Fairmount Cemetery, Newark, Essex County.

HARTENSTEIN, PETER Corp, A, 32nd PA Inf, 8-15-1897. Holy Sepulchre Cemetery, East Orange, Essex County.

HARTER, FREDERICK C. Pvt, K, 1st NJ Militia, 5-4-1894. Fairmount Cemetery, Newark, Essex County.

HARTGROVE, WILLIAM 2-23-1879. Evergreen Cemetery, Camden, Camden County.

HARTH, GUSTAV Pvt, F, 39th NJ Inf, 2-28-1929. Princeton Cemetery, Princeton, Mercer County.

HARTIGAN, WILLIAM Pvt, D, 10th Confederate States Cav (CSA), 5-10-1865. Finn's Point National Cemetery, Pennsville, Salem County.

HARTKOFT, AUGUST (see: Hartkopf, August) Evergreen Cemetery, Hillside, Union County.

HARTKOPF, AUGUST (aka: Hartkoft, August) Pvt, D, 2nd NJ Inf, 9-7-1891. Evergreen Cemetery, Hillside, Union County.

HARTLESS, BENJAMIN Pvt, I, 19th VA Inf (CSA), [Captured 7-3-1863 at Gettysburg, PA. Died of rheumatism.] 10-30-1863. Finn's Point National Cemetery, Pennsville, Salem County.

HARTLESS, ISAIAH Pvt, A, 41st U.S. CT, 11-15-1911. Presbyterian Church Cemetery, Titusville, Mercer County.

HARTLESS, ISAIAH (aka: Hartley, Isaiah) Pvt, G, 40th NJ Inf, 1-6-1883. Belvidere/Catholic Cemetery, Belvidere, Warren County.

HARTLEY, CHARLES (see: Scull, Thomas W.) Oak Hill Cemetery, Vineland, Cumberland County.

HARTLEY*, GEORGE A. Pvt, A, 2nd Bttn FL Inf (CSA), [Captured 3-27-1863 at St. John's River, FL. Died of rubella.] 8-28-1863. Finn's Point National Cemetery, Pennsville, Salem County.

HARTLEY, ISAIAH (see: Hartless, Isaiah) Belvidere/Catholic Cemetery, Belvidere, Warren County.

HARTLEY, JAMES Sgt, G, 114th PA Inf, 1902. Morgan Cemetery, Cinnaminson, Burlington County.

HARTLEY, JOHN Pvt, C, 13th NJ Inf, DoD Unknown. Laurel Grove Cemetery, Totowa, Passaic County.

HARTLEY, JOSEPH Wagoner, I, 2nd NJ Inf, 12-8-1920. Holy Sepulchre Cemetery, Totowa, Passaic County.

HARTLEY, NICHOLAS B. Pvt, A, 201st PA Inf, 11-13-1916. Arlington Cemetery, Pennsauken, Camden County.

HARTLEY, WILLIAM H. Pvt, C, 3rd NJ Militia, 2-9-1912. Glendale Cemetery, Bloomfield, Essex County.

HARTMAN, ANTHONY Pvt, D, 23rd NJ Inf, DoD Unknown. Springfield-Upper Springfield-Friends Cemetery, Springfield, Burlington County.

HARTMAN, CHARLES L. Pvt, D, 2nd NJ Cav, 12-20-1920. Union Cemetery, Clarkstown, Atlantic County.

HARTMAN, CHRISTOPHER (see: Hartrum, Christopher C.) Mountain View Cemetery, Cokesbury, Hunterdon County.

HARTMAN, FREDERICK Pvt, B, 1st NY Mounted Rifles, 7-7-1910. Hoboken Cemetery, North Bergen, Hudson County.

HARTMAN, GEORGE W. 10-15-1866. Amwell Ridge Cemetery, Larisons Corner, Hunterdon County.

HARTMAN, GEORGE W. 1885. Union Cemetery, Hope, Warren County.

HARTMAN, GUSTAVE Pvt, K, 33rd NJ Inf, 6-5-1887. Palisade Cemetery, North Bergen, Hudson County.

Our Brothers Gone Before

HARTMAN, JOHN (aka: Hootman, John) Pvt, C, 18th NC Inf (CSA), [Wounded 12-13-1862 at Fredericksburg, VA. Captured 7-7-1863 at Williamsport, MD. Died of chronic dysentery.] 8-24-1863. Finn's Point National Cemetery, Pennsville, Salem County.

HARTMAN, REUBEN M. 1st Sgt, H, 23rd NJ Inf, 12-1-1917. Holcomb-Riverview Cemetery, Lambertville, Hunterdon County.

HARTMAN, SAMUEL M. Pvt, B, 23rd NJ Inf, 12-14-1894. Cedar Run/Greenwood Cemetery, Manahawkin, Ocean County.

HARTMAN, THOMAS A. (aka: Hardman, Thomas) Pvt, L, 8th NY Cav, 8-10-1927. Clinton Cemetery, Irvington, Essex County.

HARTMAN, URIAH S. Pvt, U.S. Marine Corps, USS Vermont, 1914. Rosehill Cemetery, Newfield, Gloucester County.

HARTMAN*, WILLIAM Pvt, F, 8th NJ Inf, 4-13-1870. Methodist Church Cemetery, Groveville, Mercer County.

HARTMAN, WILLIAM L. Pvt, E, 1st NJ Inf, 11-27-1922. New Camden Cemetery, Camden, Camden County.

HARTMANN, CHARLES 2nd Lt, I, 54th NY Inf, 10-21-1872. Arlington Cemetery, Kearny, Hudson County.

HARTMANN, GUSTAV Pvt, A, 8th NY Inf, DoD Unknown. Atlantic City Cemetery, Pleasantville, Atlantic County.

HARTMANN, HUGO 8-15-1903. Evergreen Cemetery, Hillside, Union County.

HARTPENCE, APPENITUS (see: Hartpence, Eppendtus) Sandy Ridge Cemetery, Sandy Ridge, Hunterdon County.

HARTPENCE, ENOCH C. Pvt, K, 31st NJ Inf, 4-14-1914. Presbyterian Church Cemetery, Mount Pleasant, Hunterdon County.

HARTPENCE, EPPENDTUS (aka: Hartpence, Appenitus) Pvt, 8th OH Ind Btty 7-13-1866. Sandy Ridge Cemetery, Sandy Ridge, Hunterdon County.

HARTPENCE*, FORMAN V. Pvt, Btty D, 1st NJ Light Art, 7-4-1868. Pitman Methodist-Episcopal Cemetery, New Brunswick, Middlesex County.

HARTPENCE*, JONATHAN Coal Heaver, U.S. Navy, USS Lehigh, 3-14-1898. Prospect Hill Cemetery, Flemington, Hunterdon County.

HARTPENCE, PETER R. Corp, F, 35th NJ Inf, [Died at Quakertown, NJ.] 3-14-1865. Locust Grove Cemetery, Quakertown, Hunterdon County.

HARTPENCE, RICHARD S. Pvt, Btty D, 3rd PA Heavy Art, 7-29-1918. Rosemont Cemetery, Rosemont, Hunterdon County.

HARTPENCE, SAMUEL B. Pvt, H, 30th NJ Inf, 8-12-1881. Locust Grove Cemetery, Quakertown, Hunterdon County.

HARTPENCE, SAMUEL B. Pvt, H, 31st NJ Inf, 4-9-1882. Mansfield/Washington Cemetery, Washington, Warren County.

HARTPENCE, WILLIAM W. 1913. Sandy Ridge Cemetery, Sandy Ridge, Hunterdon County.

HARTRANFT, CHARLES R. Chaplain, 38th NJ Inf DoD Unknown. Methodist-Episcopal Church Cemetery, Penns Grove, Salem County.

HARTRANFT*, HENRY A. Pvt, Btty C, 1st U.S. Art, 3-26-1926. Harleigh Cemetery, Camden, Camden County.

HARTRANFT*, HENRY A. Pvt, D, 9th NJ Inf, DoD Unknown. Methodist-Episcopal Church Cemetery, Penns Grove, Salem County.

HARTRAUFT, WILLIAM Pvt, Unassigned, 24th MI Inf, DoD Unknown. Methodist-Episcopal Church Cemetery, Penns Grove, Salem County.

HARTRUM, ALFRED Pvt, Btty C, 1st NJ Light Art, 12-27-1898. Old & New Lutheran Cemetery, Lebanon, Hunterdon County.

HARTRUM, CHRISTOPHER C. (aka: Hartman, Christopher) Corp, K, 31st NJ Inf, 1917. Mountain View Cemetery, Cokesbury, Hunterdon County.

New Jersey Civil War Burials

HARTSELL, NIMROD Pvt, E, 4th NC Cav (CSA), [Captured 7-5-1863 at Monterey, PA.] 10-3-1863. Finn's Point National Cemetery, Pennsville, Salem County.

HARTSGROVE, ELIAS (see: Hargrove, Elias) Brotherhood Cemetery, Hainesport, Burlington County.

HARTSGROVE, GEORGE Pvt, G, 29th NJ Inf, 10-28-1916. All Saints Episcopal Church Cemetery, Navesink, Monmouth County.

HARTSGROVE, JEFFERSON Pvt, E, 23rd NJ Inf, DoD Unknown. Friends Cemetery, Arneys Mount, Burlington County.

HARTSGROVE, JOSEPH B. Pvt, C, 10th NJ Inf, 8-20-1882. Grange/Friends Cemetery, Vincentown, Burlington County.

HARTSHORN, HENRY L. 1st Lt, B, 24th MA Inf, 4-30-1914. Harleigh Cemetery, Camden, Camden County.

HARTUNG*, WILLIAM J. Pvt, 29th NY Ind Btty 5-26-1880. Hoboken Cemetery, North Bergen, Hudson County.

HARTWELL, ALLEN L. Capt, D, 199th PA Inf, 3-2-1892. Greenmount Cemetery, Hammonton, Atlantic County.

HARTWICK, BARNEY Seaman, U.S. Navy, 7-29-1892. Pitman Methodist-Episcopal Cemetery, New Brunswick, Middlesex County.

HARTWICK, JOHN (JR.) Pvt, E, 37th NJ Inf, [Died of typhoid at Fort Monroe, VA.] 8-25-1864. Fairmount Cemetery, Newark, Essex County.

HARTWICK, THEODORE (see: Hardwick, Theodore) South Orange Cemetery, South Orange, Essex County.

HARTY*, JAMES (aka: Hearty, James) Pvt, I, 14th CT Inf, [Wounded 12-13-1862 at Fredericksburg, VA.] 1932. Mount Carmel Cemetery, West Moorestown, Burlington County.

HARTY, JOHN (aka: Hardy, John) Pvt, K, 25th NJ Inf, 1-18-1902. Midvale Cemetery, Midvale, Passaic County.

HARTZ, PETER 1-17-1913. Hillside Cemetery, Lyndhurst, Bergen County.

HARTZELL, PETER Pvt, E, 7th NJ Inf, 8-17-1913. Union Cemetery, Milford, Hunterdon County.

HARVELL, G.H. Pvt, E, 52nd NC Inf (CSA), [Wounded and captured 7-3-1863 at Gettysburg, PA. Died of disease.] 11-3-1863. Finn's Point National Cemetery, Pennsville, Salem County.

HARVEY, AMBROSE F. Pvt, F, 26th NJ Inf, 3-5-1880. Bloomfield Cemetery, Bloomfield, Essex County.

HARVEY, CORNELIUS B. Principal Musc, 14th NJ Inf 10-4-1902. Brookside Cemetery, Englewood, Bergen County.

HARVEY, EDWARD Landsman, U.S. Navy, 12-3-1879. Fairmount Cemetery, Newark, Essex County.

HARVEY, EDWARD W. Pvt, K, 198th PA Inf, [Killed in action at Lewis Farm, VA.] 3-29-1865. Eglington Cemetery, Clarksboro, Gloucester County.

HARVEY, ELIAS C. Pvt, F, 40th NJ Inf, 3-12-1899. Evergreen Cemetery, Hillside, Union County.

HARVEY*, H.H. Pvt, E, 9th GA Inf (CSA), [Captured 7-3-1863 at Gettysburg, PA. Died of diarrhea.] 9-23-1863. Finn's Point National Cemetery, Pennsville, Salem County.

HARVEY*, JACOB V. Pvt, A, 12th NJ Inf, 2-13-1912. Presbyterian Church Cemetery, Bridgeton, Cumberland County.

HARVEY, JAMES Pvt, B, 23rd NJ Inf, 1-17-1890. Fairmount Cemetery, Newark, Essex County.

HARVEY, JAMES K. Pvt, E, 2nd NJ Cav, 3-15-1936. Mount Pleasant Cemetery, Millville, Cumberland County.

HARVEY, JOHN F. 9-26-1916. Bayview-New York Bay Cemetery, Jersey City, Hudson County.

HARVEY*, JOHN H. Pvt, I, 9th NJ Inf, 1912. Eastview Cemetery, Salem, Salem County.

Our Brothers Gone Before

HARVEY*, JOHN H. Sgt, E, 14th NJ Inf, 6-24-1905. Rahway Cemetery, Rahway, Union County.
HARVEY, JOHN H. (JR.) Pvt, I, 8th PA Cav, 4-14-1880. Eglington Cemetery, Clarksboro, Gloucester County.
HARVEY, JOHN H. (SR.) Pvt, A, 69th PA Inf, [Died at Alexandria, VA.] 11-15-1863. Eglington Cemetery, Clarksboro, Gloucester County.
HARVEY, JOHN W. Corp, F, 38th NJ Inf, 5-2-1919. Old 1st Methodist Church Cemetery, West Long Branch, Monmouth County.
HARVEY, LEMUEL D. Pvt, K, 24th NJ Inf, 4-15-1911. Old Friends Cemetery, Salem, Salem County.
HARVEY, STEPHEN L. Pvt, B, 13th NJ Inf, 3-28-1913. Arlington Cemetery, Kearny, Hudson County.
HARVEY, THOMAS Pvt, D, 4th NJ Inf, 1881. Old Catholic Cemetery, Newton, Sussex County.
HARVEY, WILLIAM Pvt, B, 53rd PA Inf, 11-30-1861. Eglington Cemetery, Clarksboro, Gloucester County.
HARVEY*, WILLIAM Pvt, F, 91st PA Inf, [Wounded 7-27-1864 at Petersburg, VA.] 10-6-1894. Riverview Cemetery, Trenton, Mercer County.
HARVEY, WILLIAM W. Pvt, E, 9th (Malone's) AL Cav (CSA), 8-9-1864. Finn's Point National Cemetery, Pennsville, Salem County.
HASH, MARTIN W. Pvt, C, 45th VA Inf (CSA), [Captured 3-5-1865 at Mount Jackson, VA. Died of lung inflammation.] 4-2-1865. Finn's Point National Cemetery, Pennsville, Salem County.
HASKARD, CHARLES Pvt, A, 1st NJ Inf, [Wounded in action.] 10-15-1896. Evergreen Cemetery, Hillside, Union County.
HASKARD, JOHN R. 1885. Baptist Church Cemetery, Scotch Plains, Union County.
HASKARD, THOMAS Pvt, A, 1st NJ Inf, 5-15-1913. Baptist Church Cemetery, Scotch Plains, Union County.
HASKELL, WARNER (aka: Haskell, Warren) Pvt, K, 24th MA Inf, [Died of wounds received 8-16-1864 at Deep Run, VA.] 8-29-1864. Beverly National Cemetery, Edgewater Park, Burlington County.
HASKELL, WARREN (see: Haskell, Warner) Beverly National Cemetery, Edgewater Park, Burlington County.
HASKELL, WILLIAM H. Sgt, K, 2nd NJ Inf, 1901. Clinton Cemetery, Irvington, Essex County.
HASKINS, GEORGE H. Pvt, U.S. Army, [Quartermaster Corps.] DoD Unknown. Fairview Cemetery, Westfield, Union County.
HASKINS, JAMES Ordinary Seaman, U.S. Navy, 4-21-1863. Fairmount Cemetery, Newark, Essex County.
HASKINS, JOHN Pvt, B, 21st NJ Inf, 1-26-1895. Holy Name Cemetery, Jersey City, Hudson County.
HASKINS, WILLIAM Pvt, A, 73rd NY Inf, [Wounded in action.] 5-29-1922. Holy Sepulchre Cemetery, East Orange, Essex County.
HASLEM, NICHOLAS (see: Hausler, Nicholas) Ardena Baptist Church Cemetery, Adelphia, Monmouth County.
HASLEM, THOMAS Farrier, M, 3rd NJ Cav, 11-8-1889. New Camden Cemetery, Camden, Camden County.
HASLER, CARL R. (see: Hasler, Charles R.) Prospect Hill Cemetery, Caldwell, Essex County.
HASLER, CHARLES R. (aka: Hasler, Carl R.) Pvt, A, 8th Bttn DC Inf, [Wounded at Seneca Mills, MD.] 1-1-1901. Prospect Hill Cemetery, Caldwell, Essex County.
HASLINGER, CHARLES Hosp Steward, U.S. Army, 6-30-1901. Union Cemetery, Washington, Morris County.

New Jersey Civil War Burials

HASS, BERNARD (aka: Haas, Bernhard) 3rd Cl Musc, 1st NJ Brigade Band 11-9-1884. Holy Sepulchre Cemetery, East Orange, Essex County.

HASSELL, ALEXANDER 8-9-1868. Bayview-New York Bay Cemetery, Jersey City, Hudson County.

HASSELL, ISAIAH Pvt, A, 15th NJ Inf, [Died of disease at Tennallytown, DC.] 10-28-1863. Newell Cemetery, Stanton Station, Hunterdon County.

HASSELL, JAMES Pvt, E, 13th NY State Militia, 6-15-1894. Cedar Lawn Cemetery, Paterson, Passaic County.

HASSET, PATRICK Pvt, D, 15th NY Eng, 4-27-1886. St. John's Evangelical Church Cemetery, Orange, Essex County.

HASSETT, JOHN Landsman, U.S. Navy, USS Hartford, 2-27-1903. Holy Name Cemetery, Jersey City, Hudson County.

HASSINGER*, STACY C. Sgt, U.S. Army, [Signal Corps.] 11-10-1912. Oddfellows Cemetery, Burlington, Burlington County.

HASSLER, CHARLES W. 2-19-1888. Brookside Cemetery, Englewood, Bergen County.

HASTIE, WILLIAM Sgt, E, 79th NY Inf, 12-14-1878. Woodland Cemetery, Newark, Essex County.

HASTINGS*, ALEXANDER S. Pvt, Unassigned, 33rd NJ Inf, 6-7-1911. Fairmount Cemetery, Newark, Essex County.

HASTINGS, AMBROSE Pvt, E, 37th NJ Inf, 2-28-1906. Fairmount Cemetery, Newark, Essex County.

HASTINGS, GEORGE Pvt, I, 39th NJ Inf, 3-31-1890. Fairmount Cemetery, Newark, Essex County.

HATCH, CHARLES HOLLINGSHEAD 2nd Lt, H, 4th NJ Inf, [Wounded 6-27-1862 at Gaines' Farm, VA.] 3-7-1907. Evergreen Cemetery, Camden, Camden County.

HATCH, COOPER S. (aka: Hatch, Cowper) Pvt, L, 1st MD Cav, 2-15-1922. Evergreen Cemetery, Camden, Camden County.

HATCH, COWPER (see: Hatch, Cooper S.) Evergreen Cemetery, Camden, Camden County.

HATCH*, WILLIAM B. Col, 4th NJ Inf [Died of wounds received 12-13-1862 at Fredericksburg, VA.] 12-15-1862. Evergreen Cemetery, Camden, Camden County.

HATCHER, SAMUEL L. Pvt, I, 38th NJ Inf, 8-29-1914. Methodist Church Cemetery, Groveville, Mercer County.

HATCHER, THOMAS W. Pvt, D, 7th TN Inf (CSA), 2-4-1864. Finn's Point National Cemetery, Pennsville, Salem County.

HATFIELD, AUGUSTUS 1st Lt, D, 28th NJ Inf, 4-3-1891. Willow Grove Cemetery, New Brunswick, Middlesex County.

HATFIELD, CHARLES Corp, F, 13th NJ Inf, 10-25-1897. Fairmount Cemetery, Newark, Essex County.

HATFIELD, CHARLES DoD Unknown. St. Bernard's Cemetery, Bridgewater, Somerset County.

HATFIELD, DAVID Maj, 1st NJ Inf [Died at Elizabeth, NJ. of wounds received 6-27-1862 at Gaines' Mill, VA.] 7-30-1862. Evergreen Cemetery, Hillside, Union County.

HATFIELD, EDMUND S. Pvt, C, 30th NJ Inf, [Died of typhoid at Washington, DC.] 6-3-1863. Rahway Cemetery, Rahway, Union County.

HATFIELD, JOHN V.B. 2nd Cl Boy, U.S. Navy, 10-16-1929. Greenwood Cemetery, Hamilton, Mercer County.

HATFIELD, SAMUEL L. Pvt, B, 30th NJ Inf, 12-23-1897. Rahway Cemetery, Rahway, Union County.

HATFIELD, WILLIAM M. Pvt, K, 26th NJ Inf, 12-29-1909. Fairmount Cemetery, Newark, Essex County.

HATHAWAY, CHARLES W. Pvt, G, 26th NJ Inf, 9-12-1874. Fairmount Cemetery, Newark, Essex County.

Our Brothers Gone Before

HATHAWAY, CHRISTOPHER Pvt, C, 32nd U.S. CT, 12-21-1907. Fairmount Cemetery, Newark, Essex County.
HATHAWAY, JAMES H. Pvt, C, 15th NJ Inf, 1-6-1903. Presbyterian Cemetery, New Vernon, Morris County.
HATHAWAY, JOHN Pvt, Btty B, 1st NJ Light Art, 9-12-1874. Clinton Cemetery, Irvington, Essex County.
HATHAWAY, JOHN H. Pvt, I, 177th NY Inf, 10-3-1909. Arlington Cemetery, Kearny, Hudson County.
HATHAWAY, WILLIAM 10-6-1901. Old 1st Methodist Church Cemetery, West Long Branch, Monmouth County.
HATHAWAY, WILLIAM L. Pvt, I, 27th NJ Inf, 3-30-1899. Evergreen Cemetery, Morristown, Morris County.
HATHCOCK, JOSEPH J. (see: HItchcock, H.P.J.) Finn's Point National Cemetery, Pennsville, Salem County.
HATT, JOEL W. Sgt, K, 26th NJ Inf, 8-1-1914. Rosedale Cemetery, Orange, Essex County.
HATT, JOHN H. Corp, H, 26th NJ Inf, 9-13-1886. Rosedale Cemetery, Orange, Essex County.
HATTAWAY, THOMAS B. Pvt, Santee (Gaillard's) SC Light Art (CSA) [Captured 10-15-1864 at Santee River, SC. Died of diarrhea.] 3-9-1865. Finn's Point National Cemetery, Pennsville, Salem County.
HATTEMER, JOHN Pvt, F, 58th NY Inf, [Wounded 5-2-1863 at Chancellorsville, VA.] 4-11-1911. Arlington Cemetery, Kearny, Hudson County.
HATTERSLEY*, JOSEPH Pvt, H, 82nd PA Inf, 2-19-1915. Mount Pleasant Cemetery, Newark, Essex County.
HATTMAN, HENRY B. Pvt, A, 99th PA Inf, [Wounded 7-2-1863 at Gettysburg, PA. and 7-30-1864 at Petersburg, VA.] 10-2-1921. Harleigh Cemetery, Camden, Camden County.
HATTON, MATTHEW Pvt, K, 27th NJ Inf, 8-12-1894. Old Catholic Cemetery, Newton, Sussex County.
HAUCK, CARL (aka: Houck, Karl) Pvt, D, 56th NY Inf, 5-10-1898. Fairmount Cemetery, Newark, Essex County.
HAUCK, FRANZ 7-9-1882. Palisade Cemetery, North Bergen, Hudson County.
HAUCK, PETER (aka: Hauk, Peter) Pvt, K, 3rd NJ Inf, [Wounded 9-14-1862 at Crampton's Pass, MD.] 11-9-1888. Mount Olivet Cemetery, Newark, Essex County.
HAUCK, WILLIAM Pvt, F, 20th NY Inf, 6-19-1926. Hillside Cemetery, Lyndhurst, Bergen County.
HAUFF, GUSTAVE WILLIAM Pvt, Btty A, 1st NJ Light Art, 5-27-1895. Fairmount Cemetery, Newark, Essex County.
HAUFLER, GEORGE FREDERICK Pvt, Btty E, 1st NJ Light Art, 1-31-1903. Woodland Cemetery, Newark, Essex County.
HAUFLER, JACOB F. Pvt, D, 75th PA Inf, 12-8-1897. Monument Cemetery, Edgewater Park, Burlington County.
HAUGHEY, JOHN (see: Hancy, John V.) Methodist Church Cemetery, Groveville, Mercer County.
HAUGHWOUT, PETER S. Pvt, F, 31st NJ Inf, 12-19-1901. Holland Cemetery, Holland, Hunterdon County.
HAUGHWOUT, WILLIAM B. Pvt, B, 15th NY Eng, 4-19-1916. Evergreen Cemetery, Hillside, Union County.
HAUK, PETER (see: Hauck, Peter) Mount Olivet Cemetery, Newark, Essex County.
HAULENBECK, GARRET H. Seaman, U.S. Navy, 11-18-1905. Cedar Lawn Cemetery, Paterson, Passaic County.

New Jersey Civil War Burials

HAULENBECK, HENRY (see: Hollenback, Henry (Jr.)) Holy Sepulchre Cemetery, East Orange, Essex County.

HAULENBECK*, HENRY (SR.) Pvt, G, 13th NJ Inf, 4-9-1882. Holy Sepulchre Cemetery, East Orange, Essex County.

HAULENBECK, JOHN R. Pvt, G, 2nd NJ Inf, 8-10-1872. Rosedale Cemetery, Orange, Essex County.

HAULER, JAMES Seaman, U.S. Navy, USS Grand Gulf, 2-29-1914. Cedar Hill Cemetery, Hightstown, Mercer County.

HAULLENBECK, STEPHEN (see: Hallinbeck, Stephen I.) Rosedale Cemetery, Orange, Essex County.

HAUN, JEREMIAH Pvt, K, 25th NJ Inf, 5-21-1895. Laurel Grove Cemetery, Totowa, Passaic County.

HAUPT, WILLIAM MAX Corp, Btty A, 1st NJ Light Art, 11-26-1904. Flower Hill Cemetery, North Bergen, Hudson County.

HAUS, ALBERT Pvt, K, 3rd NJ Cav, 5-18-1906. Phillipsburg Cemetery, Phillipsburg, Warren County.

HAUS, PETER Pvt, K, 3rd NJ Cav, 6-6-1904. Phillipsburg Cemetery, Phillipsburg, Warren County.

HAUS, THOMAS J. Pvt, C, 50th PA Inf, 3-22-1917. New Camden Cemetery, Camden, Camden County.

HAUSER, JOHN Pvt, H, 13th NJ Inf, 8-25-1888. Fairmount Cemetery, Newark, Essex County.

HAUSERMAN, CHRISTOPHER Pvt, E, 39th NJ Inf, 5-24-1895. Fairmount Cemetery, Newark, Essex County.

HAUSETTER, T.M. 1895. Hoboken Cemetery, North Bergen, Hudson County.

HAUSHALTER, FREDERICK Pvt, B, 37th NJ Inf, 2-27-1894. Mount Pleasant Cemetery, Newark, Essex County.

HAUSLER, NICHOLAS (aka: Haslem, Nicholas) Pvt, B, 131st NY Inf, [Wounded 10-19-1864 at Cedar Creek, VA.] 1890. Ardena Baptist Church Cemetery, Adelphia, Monmouth County.

HAUSMAN*, WILLIAM Pvt, E, 4th U.S. Hancock Corps, [Wounded in action.] 11-30-1919. Fernwood Cemetery, Jamesburg, Middlesex County.

HAUX, CHARLES F. Pvt, F, 45th PA Inf, 3-24-1882. Fairmount Cemetery, Newark, Essex County.

HAVEN, GARRETT DoD Unknown. Riverview Cemetery, Trenton, Mercer County.

HAVEN*, HENRY R. Landsman, U.S. Navy, USS Ohio, 5-15-1914. Riverview Cemetery, Trenton, Mercer County.

HAVENS, CALVIN C. Pvt, F, 48th NY Inf, 7-18-1890. Riverside Cemetery, Toms River, Ocean County.

HAVENS*, CHARLES Pvt, E, 40th NJ Inf, 11-21-1898. Methodist-Episcopal Cemetery, Wrightstown, Burlington County.

HAVENS, CHARLES F. Pvt, C, 3rd NJ Inf, [Died of disease at New York, NY.] 11-22-1862. St. Mary's Episcopal Church Cemetery, Burlington, Burlington County.

HAVENS, DAVID 1913. Greengrove Cemetery, Keyport, Monmouth County.

HAVENS, EDWIN L. Pvt, G, 14th NJ Inf, 3-13-1911. United Methodist Church Cemetery, Wayside, Monmouth County.

HAVENS, GEORGE Pvt, K, 35th NJ Inf, 1-23-1919. Methodist Church Cemetery, Juliustown, Burlington County.

HAVENS, HENRY CLAY 1st Sgt, F, 14th NJ Inf, [Killed in action at Monocacy, MD.] 7-9-1864. Baptist Church Cemetery, Laurelton, Ocean County.

HAVENS, HERBERT Pvt, F, 14th NJ Inf, [Wounded in action.] 1920. Methodist Church Cemetery, Point Pleasant, Ocean County.

Our Brothers Gone Before

HAVENS, HORACE Pvt, E, 9th NJ Inf, 5-25-1883. Methodist Church Cemetery, Stockholm, Sussex County.

HAVENS, JACOB Pvt, F, 14th NJ Inf, DoD Unknown. Methodist Church Cemetery, Point Pleasant, Ocean County.

HAVENS, JAMES HENRY Pvt, E, 28th NJ Inf, 7-6-1929. Allenwood Church Cemetery, Allenwood, Monmouth County.

HAVENS, JOHN R. Pvt, C, 9th NY Inf, 1-7-1907. Hoboken Cemetery, North Bergen, Hudson County.

HAVENS, JOSEPH P. Pvt, B, 12th NJ Inf, 12-24-1900. Baptist Cemetery, Osbornville, Ocean County.

HAVENS, MARTIN Pvt, I, 26th IA Inf, [Died of disease at St. Louis, MO.] 5-24-1863. Deckertown-Union Cemetery, Papakating, Sussex County.

HAVENS, READING Pvt, D, 23rd NJ Inf, [Died of wounds received 5-3-1863 at Salem Heights, VA.] 5-10-1863. Baptist/St. Andrew's Cemetery, Mount Holly, Burlington County.

HAVENS, RICHARD C. Pvt, I, 28th PA Inf, DoD Unknown. Baptist/St. Andrew's Cemetery, Mount Holly, Burlington County.

HAVENS, SILAS M. Pvt, F, 6th NJ Inf, [Died of diarrhea at Burlington, NJ.] 1-6-1864. St. Mary's Episcopal Church Cemetery, Burlington, Burlington County.

HAVENS, TABER C. Pvt, B, 12th NJ Inf, 9-22-1910. Allenwood Church Cemetery, Allenwood, Monmouth County.

HAVENS, THOMAS Pvt, D, 23rd NJ Inf, 12-24-1908. Greenlawn Cemetery, West Long Branch, Monmouth County.

HAVENS, THOMAS Pvt, A, 38th NJ Inf, 3-7-1917. Methodist Church Cemetery, Point Pleasant, Ocean County.

HAVENS, URIAH Pvt, D, 23rd NJ Inf, 11-6-1891. Methodist-Episcopal Cemetery, Pointville, Burlington County.

HAVENS, WILLIAM A. Sgt, F, 21st NJ Inf, 4-20-1920. Arlington Cemetery, Kearny, Hudson County.

HAVENS, WILLIAM T. Pvt, M, 9th IN Cav, 8-15-1938. Mansfield/Washington Cemetery, Washington, Warren County.

HAVER, JOHN R. Pvt, A, 31st NJ Inf, 1925. Reformed Church Cemetery, Lebanon, Hunterdon County.

HAVERSTICK, JOHN Pvt, I, 12th NJ Inf, 12-31-1902. Monument Cemetery, Edgewater Park, Burlington County.

HAVILAND, AARON 12-8-1870. Evergreen Cemetery, Hillside, Union County.

HAVILAND, HENRY S. Pvt, I, 2nd PA Cav, 1912. Harleigh Cemetery, Camden, Camden County.

HAVILAND, JAMES F. Capt, H, 127th NY Inf, 4-14-1895. Evergreen Cemetery, Hillside, Union County.

HAVILAND*, JAMES J. (aka: Herlin, James) Pvt, A, 78th NY Inf, 9-18-1893. Fairmount Cemetery, Newark, Essex County.

HAVILAND, JOSEPH T. Pvt, D, 28th NJ Inf, 9-21-1893. Fairmount Cemetery, Newark, Essex County.

HAVILAND, WILLIAM F. QM Sgt, 5th NY Cav 3-13-1882. Evergreen Cemetery, Hillside, Union County.

HAWES, WILLIAM H.H. Corp, Btty D, 1st NJ Light Art, 1923. Methodist Church Cemetery, Groveville, Mercer County.

HAWK*, CHARLES E. Pvt, C, 2nd NJ Inf, 1926. Presbyterian Church Cemetery, Sparta, Sussex County.

HAWK, ISAAC Landsman, U.S. Navy, USS Sonoma, 5-1-1898. Presbyterian Church Cemetery, Greenwich, Warren County.

HAWK, JACOB Pvt, H, 21st NJ Inf, 5-29-1929. Riverview Cemetery, Trenton, Mercer County.

New Jersey Civil War Burials

HAWK, JACOB L. 1st Lt, H, 9th NJ Inf, [Wounded in action.] 8-7-1911. Arlington Cemetery, Kearny, Hudson County.
HAWK, JAMES W. Corp, D, 30th NJ Inf, 8-29-1906. Union Cemetery, Frenchtown, Hunterdon County.
HAWK, JOSEPH H. 9-8-1919. Presbyterian Cemetery, Asbury, Warren County.
HAWK, JOSEPH J. Capt, I, 14th NJ Inf, [Wounded 7-9-1864 at Monocacy, MD.] 11-21-1901. Reformed Church Cemetery, Blawenburg, Somerset County.
HAWK, WESLEY I. Pvt, Btty I, 6th PA Heavy Art, 1914. Cedar Green Cemetery, Clayton, Gloucester County.
HAWK, WILLIAM HENRY Corp, C, 3rd OH Inf, 1909. Atlantic City Cemetery, Pleasantville, Atlantic County.
HAWKER*, JAMES H. (aka: Hawkins, James) Pvt, G, 39th NY Inf, 8-5-1882. Evergreen Cemetery, Camden, Camden County.
HAWKEY, C.G. Landsman, U.S. Navy, DoD Unknown. St. John's Evangelical Church Cemetery, Orange, Essex County.
HAWKEY, CHARLES A. Seaman, U.S. Navy, 9-11-1890. Mount Pleasant Cemetery, Newark, Essex County.
HAWKEY, GEORGE W. Pvt, C, 22nd NJ Inf, 8-25-1895. Fairmount Cemetery, Newark, Essex County.
HAWKEY, OLIVER Pvt, K, 12th NJ Inf, 10-7-1902. Cedar Green Cemetery, Clayton, Gloucester County.
HAWKEY, ROBERT Pvt, A, 192nd PA Inf, 9-19-1915. Oddfellows Cemetery, Burlington, Burlington County.
HAWKHORST, CHARLES H. (aka: Hawxhurst, Charles) Pvt, A, 90th NY Inf, 1920. Tennent Church Cemetery, Tennent, Monmouth County.
HAWKINS, CHARLES R.H. Pvt, K, 3rd U.S. CT, 8-20-1924. Evergreen Cemetery, Hillside, Union County.
HAWKINS, CORNELIUS HENRY Pvt, A, 28th NJ Inf, 3-14-1920. Presbyterian Church Cemetery, Califon, Hunterdon County.
HAWKINS, EDWARD P. 10-3-1866. St. Mary's Episcopal Church Cemetery, Burlington, Burlington County.
HAWKINS, GEORGE V. Pvt, C, 38th NJ Inf, 11-19-1900. Methodist Church Cemetery, Heislerville, Cumberland County.
HAWKINS, ISRAEL (see: Hoffman, Israel) 1st Methodist Church Cemetery, Williamstown, Gloucester County.
HAWKINS, JAMES (see: Hawker, James H.) Evergreen Cemetery, Camden, Camden County.
HAWKINS, JAMES MAGEE Pvt, E, 29th NJ Inf, 1923. Holmdel Cemetery, Holmdel, Monmouth County.
HAWKINS, JOHN R. Corp, E, 47th NY Inf, 3-5-1920. New Camden Cemetery, Camden, Camden County.
HAWKINS, JOSEPH 3-18-1927. Lakeview Cemetery, New Albany, Burlington County.
HAWKINS*, JOSEPH R. Pvt, I, 140th NY Inf, 3-31-1921. Cedar Lawn Cemetery, Paterson, Passaic County.
HAWKINS, MICHAEL S. Pvt, C, 42nd NY Inf, 1889. Methodist Church Cemetery, Mount Horeb, Somerset County.
HAWKINS, RICHARD Pvt, E, 38th NJ Inf, 1-6-1924. Old Scots Cemetery, Marlboro, Monmouth County.
HAWKINS, SAMUEL T. Pvt, C, 37th NJ Inf, 1-30-1931. Greenwood Cemetery, Hamilton, Mercer County.
HAWKINS, STEPHEN (see: Hankins, Stephen) Mount Holly Cemetery, Mount Holly, Burlington County.
HAWKINS, THOMAS H. Pvt, I, 47th MA Inf, 2-2-1890. Siloam Cemetery, Vineland, Cumberland County.

Our Brothers Gone Before

HAWKINS, THOMAS J. Pvt, A, 2nd NJ Militia, 5-17-1914. Episcopal Church Cemetery, Shrewsbury, Monmouth County.

HAWKINS, THOMAS J. Com Sgt, H, 5th FL Inf (CSA), [Captured 7-5-1863 at Gettysburg, PA. Died of diarrhea.] 8-22-1863. Finn's Point National Cemetery, Pennsville, Salem County.

HAWKINS, WILLIAM H. Pvt, K, 29th CT Inf, 6-26-1903. Woodland Cemetery, Newark, Essex County.

HAWKINS, ZENO ABEL (see: Foster, Joel D.) Presbyterian Church Cemetery, Rockaway, Morris County.

HAWKYARD, AARON Landsman, U.S. Navy, [U.S. receiving ship at Washington, DC.] 8-8-1901. Riverview Cemetery, Trenton, Mercer County.

HAWLEY, JAMES A. Pvt, H, 30th NJ Inf, 5-28-1914. Rosehill Cemetery, Linden, Union County.

HAWLEY, SETH E. Pvt, H, 15th NJ Inf, [Wounded in action.] 1-8-1898. Greenmount Cemetery, Hammonton, Atlantic County.

HAWN, ISAAC M. Pvt, K, 1st DE Inf, 1927. Baptist Church Cemetery, Canton, Salem County.

HAWN, RICHARD (see: Hann, Richard) United Methodist Church Cemetery, Port Elizabeth, Cumberland County.

HAWNE, MICHAEL Pvt, H, 53rd NY Inf, DoD Unknown. Holy Sepulchre Cemetery, East Orange, Essex County.

HAWS, PETER Pvt, B, 34th NJ Inf, 5-24-1917. Riverview Cemetery, Trenton, Mercer County.

HAWS, SAMUEL (see: Hewes, Samuel A.) New Episcopal Church Cemetery, Swedesboro, Gloucester County.

HAWTHORN, ASBERRY G. Pvt, A, 14th GA Inf (CSA), [Captured 7-3-1863 at Gettysburg, PA.] 10-5-1863. Finn's Point National Cemetery, Pennsville, Salem County.

HAWTHORN, M.D. Pvt, F, 37th VA Inf (CSA), [Wounded 7-3-1863 at Gettysburg, PA. Captured 5-12-1864 at Spotsylvania CH, VA. Died of dysentery.] 9-14-1864. Finn's Point National Cemetery, Pennsville, Salem County.

HAWTHORN, WILLIAM Pvt, B, 2nd NY Cav, 9-7-1896. Hardyston Cemetery, North Church, Sussex County.

HAWTHORNE, JOHN Sgt, C, 26th NJ Inf, 3-3-1893. Woodland Cemetery, Newark, Essex County.

HAWTHORNE, WILLIAM Pvt, Btty I, 5th U.S. Art, 10-28-1907. Siloam Cemetery, Vineland, Cumberland County.

HAWXHURST, CHARLES (see: Hawkhorst, Charles H.) Tennent Church Cemetery, Tennent, Monmouth County.

HAY, ARTHUR C. Pvt, A, 73rd NY Inf, [Wounded 5-12-1864 at Spotsylvania CH, VA.] 9-15-1910. Greengrove Cemetery, Keyport, Monmouth County.

HAY, WILLIAM 1895. Grove Church Cemetery, North Bergen, Hudson County.

HAYCOCK, AMOS 2-17-1925. Evergreen Cemetery, Morristown, Morris County.

HAYCOCK, MAHLON Pvt, C, 25th NJ Inf, DoD Unknown. Pompton Reformed Church Cemetery, Pompton Lakes, Passaic County.

HAYCOCK, NATHANIEL Pvt, E, 27th NJ Inf, DoD Unknown. Laurel Grove Cemetery, Totowa, Passaic County.

HAYCOCK, PETER Pvt, H, 25th NJ Inf, 8-1-1898. Laurel Grove Cemetery, Totowa, Passaic County.

HAYDEN, GEORGE H. Seaman, U.S. Navy, 4-2-1917. Mount Hebron Cemetery, Montclair, Essex County.

HAYDEN, JAMES M. Pvt, E, 5th NY Inf, 4-13-1896. Old 1st Methodist Church Cemetery, West Long Branch, Monmouth County.

New Jersey Civil War Burials

HAYDEN, THOMAS Pvt, I, 33rd NJ Inf, 8-21-1871. Holy Sepulchre Cemetery, East Orange, Essex County.

HAYDEN, THOMAS Pvt, I, 187th PA Inf, 9-14-1896. St. John's Evangelical Church Cemetery, Orange, Essex County.

HAYDEN, THOMAS H. Pvt, I, 8th NY State Militia, 4-3-1909. Cedar Lawn Cemetery, Paterson, Passaic County.

HAYDEN, WILLIAM (aka: Hadon, William) Pvt, B, 37th NJ Inf, DoD Unknown. Holy Sepulchre Cemetery, Totowa, Passaic County.

HAYDEN, WILLIAM Pvt, K, 33rd NJ Inf, DoD Unknown. Holy Sepulchre Cemetery, Totowa, Passaic County.

HAYDEN, WILLIAM H. Pvt, U.S. Marine Corps, USS Constitution, 8-10-1903. Holy Sepulchre Cemetery, East Orange, Essex County.

HAYES, ANDREW J. Corp, E, 7th NJ Inf, 10-2-1896. Belvidere/Catholic Cemetery, Belvidere, Warren County.

HAYES, CHARLES A. Pvt, H, 37th NJ Inf, 7-9-1927. Oddfellows Cemetery, Burlington, Burlington County.

HAYES, CHARLES H. Pvt, A, 14th NJ Inf, 12-17-1915. Old 1st Methodist Church Cemetery, West Long Branch, Monmouth County.

HAYES, CHARLES K. Capt, A, 9th NJ Inf, 3-10-1896. Bloomfield Cemetery, Bloomfield, Essex County.

HAYES, CHARLES S. Seaman, U.S. Navy, DoD Unknown. Jersey City Cemetery, Jersey City, Hudson County.

HAYES*, DAVID L. Pvt, B, 15th NJ Inf, 1914. Christian Cemetery, Milford, Hunterdon County.

HAYES, EDWARD Pvt, D, 3rd NJ Cav, 1905. Belvidere/Catholic Cemetery, Belvidere, Warren County.

HAYES*, EDWIN LEWIS Bvt Brig Gen, U.S. Volunteers, [Colonel, 100th Ohio Infantry.] 12-31-1916. Bloomfield Cemetery, Bloomfield, Essex County.

HAYES, EUGENE M. Sgt, B, 9th NJ Inf, [Drowned at the foot of Barclay Street in New York City.] 10-24-1863. 1st Methodist-Episcopal Cemetery, New Brunswick, Middlesex County.

HAYES, GEORGE Pvt, Btty D, 1st NJ Light Art, 10-30-1882. Fairmount Cemetery, Newark, Essex County.

HAYES, GEORGE B. Pvt, F, 3rd NJ Cav, 6-12-1908. Fairmount Cemetery, Newark, Essex County.

HAYES, HENRY HILL Pvt, F, 26th NC Inf (CSA), [Wounded and captured 7-1-1863 at Gettysburg, PA. Died of wounds.] 10-6-1863. Finn's Point National Cemetery, Pennsville, Salem County.

HAYES, ISAAC Pvt, H, 10th NJ Inf, 1919. Baptist/St. Andrew's Cemetery, Mount Holly, Burlington County.

HAYES, JACOB M. Pvt, D, 91st NY Inf, 8-16-1906. Clinton Cemetery, Irvington, Essex County.

HAYES, JAMES Corp, G, 8th NJ Inf, 9-25-1897. Presbyterian Church Cemetery, Bridgeton, Cumberland County.

HAYES, JAMES M. Pvt, H, 37th NC Inf (CSA), [Captured 11-25-1863 at Clinch Mountain, TN. Died of diarrhea.] 4-11-1865. Finn's Point National Cemetery, Pennsville, Salem County.

HAYES, JOHN (see: Hays, John) Holy Name Cemetery, Jersey City, Hudson County.

HAYES, JOHN M. 10-8-1871. Mount Pleasant Cemetery, Millville, Cumberland County.

HAYES, JOSEPH Capt, F, 6th NJ Inf, 7-16-1895. Fairmount Cemetery, Newark, Essex County.

HAYES, JOSEPH T. Pvt, K, 38th NJ Inf, 12-14-1892. St. Mary's Cemetery, Hamilton, Mercer County.

HAYES, THOMAS 1-23-1898. Tranquility Cemetery, Tranquility, Sussex County.

Our Brothers Gone Before

HAYES, WILLIAM 1st Lt, C, 13th NJ Inf, DoD Unknown. Cedar Lawn Cemetery, Paterson, Passaic County.

HAYGOOD, WYATT J.M. Pvt, H, 4th GA Inf (CSA), [Captured 5-10-1864 at Spotsylvania CH, VA. Died of typhoid.] 6-25-1864. Finn's Point National Cemetery, Pennsville, Salem County.

HAYNES, DUDLEY W. Bvt Maj, 139th NY Inf [Wounded in action.] 9-27-1907. Rosedale Cemetery, Orange, Essex County.

HAYNES, FREDERICK (see: Heintz, Frederick) Evergreen Cemetery, Hillside, Union County.

HAYNES, GEORGE O. Corp, K, 15th NJ Inf, 4-14-1906. Arlington Cemetery, Kearny, Hudson County.

HAYNES, HENRY C. Pvt, G, 23rd VA Inf (CSA), [Captured 5-12-1864 at Spotsylvania CH, VA. Died of dysentery.] 7-11-1864. Finn's Point National Cemetery, Pennsville, Salem County.

HAYNES, JOHN Pvt, K, 36th MS Inf (CSA), 9-17-1863. Finn's Point National Cemetery, Pennsville, Salem County.

HAYNES*, JOHN M. Sgt, C, 7th NJ Inf, 11-21-1904. Evergreen Cemetery, Morristown, Morris County.

HAYNES, WILLIAM H. Pvt, B, 26th NJ Inf, 5-11-1876. Fairmount Cemetery, Newark, Essex County.

HAYS, ADDIS Hosp Steward, 1st KY Inf 10-7-1880. Baptist Cemetery, Burlington, Burlington County.

HAYS, GEORGE H. Pvt, G, 7th KY Cav (CSA), 4-12-1864. Finn's Point National Cemetery, Pennsville, Salem County.

HAYS, GODFREY H. Pvt, Btty D, __ __ __, 6-26-1876. Baptist Cemetery, Burlington, Burlington County.

HAYS, HENRY Pvt, D, 45th U.S. CT, 11-19-1922. Old Brick Reformed Church Cemetery, Marlboro, Monmouth County.

HAYS, JACOB 10-7-1880. Baptist Cemetery, Burlington, Burlington County.

HAYS, JAMES L. Pvt, K, 2nd DC Inf, 6-1-1916. Mount Pleasant Cemetery, Newark, Essex County.

HAYS*, JOHN (aka: Hayes, John) Pvt, K, 33rd NJ Inf, 12-17-1900. Holy Name Cemetery, Jersey City, Hudson County.

HAYS, JOHN Pvt, A, 3rd (Howard's) Confederate States Cav (CSA), 11-13-1863. Finn's Point National Cemetery, Pennsville, Salem County.

HAYS, JOSEPH L. 8-14-1863. Baptist Cemetery, Burlington, Burlington County.

HAYS, M.R. Pvt, H, 14th AL Inf (CSA), [Wounded 9-17-1862 at Sharpsburg, MD.] 12-31-1863. Finn's Point National Cemetery, Pennsville, Salem County.

HAYS, PATRICK Pvt, I, 29th NJ Inf, 1914. Methodist-Episcopal Cemetery, Whitehouse, Hunterdon County.

HAYS*, RICHARD Musc, A, 38th NJ Inf, 1-29-1913. Arlington Cemetery, Kearny, Hudson County.

HAYS, SILAS Pvt, E, 43rd TN Inf (CSA), [5th East Tennessee Volunteers (Gillespie's).] 8-10-1864. Finn's Point National Cemetery, Pennsville, Salem County.

HAYSLIP, JEFFERSON (see: Haizlip, Jefferson) Finn's Point National Cemetery, Pennsville, Salem County.

HAYWARD, ANTHONY Pvt, C, 27th NJ Inf, 7-8-1913. Pompton Reformed Church Cemetery, Pompton Lakes, Passaic County.

HAYWARD, CHARLES H. Pvt, H, 39th NJ Inf, 5-11-1890. Fairmount Cemetery, Newark, Essex County.

HAYWARD, GEORGE W. Pvt, C, 7th NJ Inf, 1915. Northfield Baptist Cemetery, Livingston, Essex County.

HAYWARD*, LEWIS E. Corp, H, 39th NJ Inf, 4-3-1904. Fairmount Cemetery, Newark, Essex County.

New Jersey Civil War Burials

HAYWOOD*, GEORGE WILLIAM Pvt, K, 146th NY Inf, 4-21-1913. Arlington Cemetery, Kearny, Hudson County.
HAYWOOD, JAMES C. Pvt, K, 6th MI Cav, 6-21-1917. New 1st Methodist Meeting House Cemetery, Manahawkin, Ocean County.
HAYWOOD, SAMUEL Pvt, D, 24th NJ Inf, 5-3-1895. Trinity Bible Church Cemetery, Glassboro, Gloucester County.
HAZARD, THOMAS TILLEY 7-8-1911. Evergreen Cemetery, Hillside, Union County.
HAZELTINE*, ROBERT Pvt, M, 1st U.S. Cav, 1911. Riverview Cemetery, Trenton, Mercer County.
HAZELTON, ELMORE J. Pvt, B, 42nd MA Militia, 1-7-1916. Arlington Cemetery, Kearny, Hudson County.
HAZEN, JACOB (aka: Hazen, Jeremiah) Pvt, C, 1st NY Mounted Rifles, DoD Unknown. Weehawken Cemetery, North Bergen, Hudson County.
HAZEN, JEREMIAH (see: Hazen, Jacob) Weehawken Cemetery, North Bergen, Hudson County.
HAZEN, JOHN S. Pvt, E, 2nd NJ Cav, 1884. Union Cemetery, Washington, Morris County.
HAZEN, PHINEAS K. Corp, I, 31st NJ Inf, 10-1-1917. Holcomb-Riverview Cemetery, Lambertville, Hunterdon County.
HAZEN, THEODORE F. Pvt, E, 2nd NJ Cav, 10-16-1877. Union Cemetery, Washington, Morris County.
HAZEN, WILLIAM M. 1909. Methodist Church Cemetery, Fairmount, Hunterdon County.
HAZEN, WILLIAM M. Pvt, M, 2nd NJ Cav, 1896. Tranquility Cemetery, Tranquility, Sussex County.
HAZLETON, JARVIS T. Landsman, U.S. Navy, USS Water Witch, [Wounded in action.] 3-13-1896. Morgan Cemetery, Cinnaminson, Burlington County.
HAZLETON, THOMAS Sgt, D, 9th NJ Inf, DoD Unknown. Old Baptist Church Cemetery, Manahawkin, Ocean County.
HAZLETT, GEORGE W. Pvt, B, 29th NJ Inf, 4-4-1897. Siloam Cemetery, Vineland, Cumberland County.
HAZLETT*, JOHN Pvt, K, 35th NJ Inf, 7-24-1901. Riverview Cemetery, Trenton, Mercer County.
HAZLETT, WILLIAM Pvt, B, 1st (Carter's) TN Cav (CSA), 4-14-1864. Finn's Point National Cemetery, Pennsville, Salem County.
HAZZARD, SAMUEL J. Pvt, Btty A, 1st MS Light Art (CSA), 6-16-1863. Finn's Point National Cemetery, Pennsville, Salem County.
HAZZARD, THEODORE Pvt, E, 11th MD Inf, 6-11-1892. Evergreen Cemetery, Camden, Camden County.
HAZZARD, W.H. 2nd Lt, E, 1st (Symon's) GA Res Inf (CSA), 3-6-1865. Finn's Point National Cemetery, Pennsville, Salem County.
HEAD, PENROSE BARNETT 1st Sgt, H, 114th PA Inf, [Killed in action at Chancellorsville, VA.] 5-3-1863. Baptist/St. Andrew's Cemetery, Mount Holly, Burlington County.
HEADDEN, C.S. 1880. Quaker Cemetery, Quaker Church, Warren County.
HEADLAND, THOMAS Pvt, K, 1st NJ Inf, 3-25-1909. Locust Hill Cemetery, Dover, Morris County.
HEADLEY, CHARLES E. Pvt, A, 24th NJ Inf, DoD Unknown. Baptist Church Cemetery, Canton, Salem County.
HEADLEY, GEORGE F. Pvt, B, 24th NJ Inf, 8-12-1893. Mount Pleasant Cemetery, Millville, Cumberland County.
HEADLEY*, HEZEKIAH (aka: Heddy, Hezekiah) Pvt, D, 112th NY Inf, 12-2-1905. Glenwood Cemetery, Glenwood, Sussex County.

Our Brothers Gone Before

HEADLEY*, JAMES BOYD Pvt, F, 7th NJ Inf, 8-6-1870. Evergreen Cemetery, Morristown, Morris County.
HEADLEY, JOHN C. Sgt, Btty A, 2nd NY Heavy Art, 11-24-1910. Phillipsburg Cemetery, Phillipsburg, Warren County.
HEADLEY, JOSEPH E. Pvt, C, 38th NJ Inf, 9-20-1903. Lake Park Cemetery, Swedesboro, Gloucester County.
HEADLEY, LEWIS PIERSON Pvt, C, 45th IA Inf, 1894. Connecticut Farms Cemetery, Union, Union County.
HEADLEY, MOSES R. 12-6-1901. Cedar Grove Cemetery, Waretown, Ocean County.
HEADLEY, SAMUEL Pvt, H, 12th NJ Inf, 9-4-1905. 1st Baptist Church Cemetery, Woodstown, Salem County.
HEADLEY, SOLOMON R. Pvt, D, 11th NJ Inf, 1-11-1936. Mount Holly Cemetery, Mount Holly, Burlington County.
HEADLEY, THOMAS Gunner, U.S. Navy, USS New Era, DoD Unknown. Old Methodist Cemetery, Point Pleasant, Ocean County.
HEADLEY, WICKLIFF (aka: Headley, Wyclyffe) 1-26-1902. St. Stephen's Cemetery, Millburn, Essex County.
HEADLEY, WYCLYFFE (see: Headley, Wickliff) St. Stephen's Cemetery, Millburn, Essex County.
HEADY*, GEORGE Pvt, I, 112th NY Inf, 1912. Fairview Cemetery, Wantage, Sussex County.
HEAL, JAMES Corp, G, 40th NJ Inf, 1890. 1st Baptist Church Cemetery, Moorestown, Burlington County.
HEALEY, BERNARD (aka: Haley, James) Pvt, I, 70th NY Inf, DoD Unknown. Holy Sepulchre Cemetery, Totowa, Passaic County.
HEALEY, JACOB (see: Hesley, Jacob) Christ Episcopal Church Cemetery, Bordentown, Burlington County.
HEALEY, JAMES Pvt, I, 8th NJ Inf, [Killed in action at Williamsburg, VA.] 5-5-1862. St. Mary's Cemetery, Clark, Union County.
HEALEY*, JAMES W. Pvt, F, 20th CT Inf, DoD Unknown. Holy Sepulchre Cemetery, East Orange, Essex County.
HEALEY, PATRICK Pvt, H, 40th NJ Inf, 11-16-1899. St. John's Cemetery, Lambertville, Hunterdon County.
HEALY, ALFRED S. Musc, D, 37th NY State Militia, 3-14-1910. Fairview Cemetery, Fairview, Bergen County.
HEALY, DANIEL __, E, 20th __ Inf, 9-11-1889. Holy Name Cemetery, Jersey City, Hudson County.
HEALY, GEORGE Pvt, G, 6th MA Militia, 6-24-1915. Fairmount Cemetery, Newark, Essex County.
HEALY, MARTIN J. 1901. St. John's Evangelical Church Cemetery, Orange, Essex County.
HEALY*, MAURICE Pvt, Btty G, 1st NY Light Art, 9-1-1866. St. Peter's Cemetery, Jersey City, Hudson County.
HEALY, PATRICK Pvt, E, 11th NJ Inf, 12-16-1867. St. Peter's Cemetery, Jersey City, Hudson County.
HEANY, PATRICK H. Pvt, Btty B, 1st NJ Light Art, DoD Unknown. Holy Sepulchre Cemetery, East Orange, Essex County.
HEARD, JOHN S. Seaman, U.S. Navy, USS Princeton, 12-17-1912. New Camden Cemetery, Camden, Camden County.
HEARIE, PHILIP (see: Heery, Philip) Phillipsburg Old Catholic Cemetery, Phillipsburg, Warren County.
HEARN, HARVEY C. Pvt, F, 45th VA Inf (CSA), [Captured 3-2-1865 at Waynesboro, VA. Died of lung inflammation.] 4-27-1865. Finn's Point National Cemetery, Pennsville, Salem County.

HEARN, JAMES D. Pvt, D, 7th TN Inf (CSA), 8-28-1863. Finn's Point National Cemetery, Pennsville, Salem County.
HEARON, SAMUEL Pvt, E, 9th NJ Inf, 5-8-1903. Methodist Church Cemetery, Goshen, Cape May County.
HEARTY, JAMES (see: Harty, James) Mount Carmel Cemetery, West Moorestown, Burlington County.
HEATER, GEORGE M. Pvt, M, 2nd NJ Cav, 9-8-1907. Phillipsburg Cemetery, Phillipsburg, Warren County.
HEATER, H. 1st Lt, E, 7th VA Cav (CSA), 3-18-1865. Finn's Point National Cemetery, Pennsville, Salem County.
HEATER, HENRY Sgt, K, 1st NJ Cav, [Wounded in action.] 9-14-1916. Hardyston Cemetery, North Church, Sussex County.
HEATER, JACOB Pvt, D, 27th NJ Inf, 11-9-1898. Evergreen Cemetery, Camden, Camden County.
HEATER, JOHN C. Pvt, K, 1st NJ Cav, 4-13-1899. Phillipsburg Cemetery, Phillipsburg, Warren County.
HEATH, ANDREW 8-21-1871. Evergreen Cemetery, Camden, Camden County.
HEATH, CHARLES A. Pvt, A, 15th NJ Inf, 4-29-1863. Sandy Ridge Cemetery, Sandy Ridge, Hunterdon County.
HEATH, EDWARD M. 1916. Christian Church Cemetery, Locktown, Hunterdon County.
HEATH, GEORGE Pvt, E, 14th NJ Inf, 11-24-1892. Rahway Cemetery, Rahway, Union County.
HEATH, ISAAC S. Pvt, D, 11th NJ Inf, 9-29-1912. Union Cemetery, Washington, Morris County.
HEATH, JOHN Pvt, E, 37th NY Inf, 4-11-1890. Mount Olivet Cemetery, Newark, Essex County.
HEATH, JOHN C. Corp, A, 5th NJ Inf, 12-31-1883. Union Cemetery, Frenchtown, Hunterdon County.
HEATH, JOHN O. Pvt, E, 15th NJ Inf, 1870. Presbyterian Church Cemetery, Basking Ridge, Somerset County.
HEATH, LEWIS P. Ordinary Seaman, U.S. Navy, 1-14-1901. Harleigh Cemetery, Camden, Camden County.
HEATH*, MILLWARD WARREN Pvt, A, 27th SC Inf (CSA), [Wounded 6-16-1864 at Petersburg, VA.] 9-22-1908. Hackensack Cemetery, Hackensack, Bergen County.
HEATH, PETER Landsman, U.S. Navy, USS Brandywine, 11-3-1904. Mount Peace Cemetery, Lawnside, Camden County.
HEATH, PETER V. Pvt, D, 11th NJ Inf, 4-10-1896. Presbyterian Church Cemetery, Hampton, Hunterdon County.
HEATH, RICHARD Pvt, B, 38th NJ Inf, 1-2-1891. Union Cemetery, Frenchtown, Hunterdon County.
HEATH, RICHARD DoD Unknown. Sandy Ridge Cemetery, Sandy Ridge, Hunterdon County.
HEATH, SAMUEL B. Wagoner, B, 15th NJ Inf, 9-16-1919. Evergreen Cemetery, Morristown, Morris County.
HEATH, SYLVESTER W. Pvt, C, 8th NJ Inf, 12-28-1910. Locust Hill Cemetery, Dover, Morris County.
HEATH, SYLVESTER W. 12-2-1888. Mount Pleasant Cemetery, Newark, Essex County.
HEATH, WILLIAM A. Pvt, H, 8th NJ Inf, 1915. Bayview-New York Bay Cemetery, Jersey City, Hudson County.
HEATH, WILLIAM H. 2-5-1882. Sandy Ridge Cemetery, Sandy Ridge, Hunterdon County.
HEATH, WILLIAM R. Pvt, H, 34th NJ Inf, 1-1-1921. Rosemont Cemetery, Rosemont, Hunterdon County.

Our Brothers Gone Before

HEATON, ERASTUS M. (aka: Haeaton, Erastus M.) Pvt, A, 102nd NY Inf, [Wounded 5-26-1864 at Dallas, GA.] 11-23-1929. Evergreen Cemetery, Hillside, Union County.
HEATON, JOHN W. 1-25-1926. Mount Pleasant Cemetery, Newark, Essex County.
HEATON, LEVI H. Corp, C, 1st NJ Cav, 12-5-1931. Eglington Cemetery, Clarksboro, Gloucester County.
HEAVENER, JEREMIAH Pvt, C, 55th NC Inf (CSA), [Captured 7-1-1863 at Gettysburg, PA.] 10-5-1863. Finn's Point National Cemetery, Pennsville, Salem County.
HEAVILAND, JOHN HENRY Musc, C, 3rd NJ Inf, 12-19-1901. Mount Holly Cemetery, Mount Holly, Burlington County.
HEAVILAND, JOSHUA A. Pvt, B, 4th NJ Militia, 1-9-1891. Mount Holly Cemetery, Mount Holly, Burlington County.
HEBERLE, THOMAS Pvt, G, 35th NJ Inf, 5-5-1887. Fairmount Cemetery, Newark, Essex County.
HEBERTON, GEORGE A. 1st Lt, K, 110th PA Inf, 1-20-1917. Jacobstown Masonic Cemetery, Jacobstown, Burlington County.
HEBLER, CONRAD Coal Heaver, U.S. Navy, 8-16-1909. Woodland Cemetery, Newark, Essex County.
HEBLER, EUSTACE (aka: Hebler, Justus) Pvt, K, 54th NY Inf, 6-21-1868. Woodland Cemetery, Newark, Essex County.
HEBLER, HENRY (aka: Hobeler, Heinrich) Pvt, F, 54th NY Inf, [Cenotaph.] 1864. Woodland Cemetery, Newark, Essex County.
HEBLER, JUSTUS (see: Hebler, Eustace) Woodland Cemetery, Newark, Essex County.
HEBNER, JOSEPH Pvt, H, 7th NJ Inf, 6-5-1925. Arlington Cemetery, Kearny, Hudson County.
HEBRING, THEODORE 9-8-1886. Mount Pleasant Cemetery, Newark, Essex County.
HECHT, EPHRIAM M. Musc, 7th IA Inf Band 8-9-1907. B'nai Abraham Cemetery, Newark, Essex County.
HECHT, GOTTLIEB Pvt, G, 2nd PA Cav, 10-13-1903. Bethel Cemetery, Pennsauken, Camden County.
HECK, GEORGE (JR.) Pvt, Btty A, 1st NJ Light Art, 5-14-1887. Palisade Cemetery, North Bergen, Hudson County.
HECK, GEORGE (SR.) Pvt, Btty A, 1st NJ Light Art, 11-12-1872. Grove Church Cemetery, North Bergen, Hudson County.
HECK*, HENRY (aka: Hicks, Henry) Pvt, I, 5th NY Cav, [Wounded in action.] 10-27-1918. Old Hook Cemetery, Westwood, Bergen County.
HECK, SAMUEL Pvt, K, 18th NY Inf, 4-29-1928. Mount Prospect Cemetery, Neptune, Monmouth County.
HECKER, CASPER (see: Schillinger, Casper) 1st Baptist Cemetery, Cape May Court House, Cape May County.
HECKER, CHARLES F. Bandmaster, 5th U.S. Cav 11-9-1917. Zion Methodist Church Cemetery, Bargaintown, Atlantic County.
HECKEROTH, CONRAD Pvt, I, 20th NY Inf, 12-25-1894. Rosedale Cemetery, Orange, Essex County.
HECKMAN, ADAM Musc, B, 26th NJ Inf, 11-17-1930. Woodland Cemetery, Newark, Essex County.
HECKMAN, JOHN Corp, I, 2nd DC Inf, 9-19-1892. Woodland Cemetery, Newark, Essex County.
HECKMAN, WILLIAM SAMUEL 11-24-1904. Presbyterian Church Cemetery, Kingston, Somerset County.
HECTOR, GEORGE 2-11-1915. Evergreen Cemetery, Hillside, Union County.
HEDDEN, ALONZO Corp, F, 15th NJ Inf, 10-11-1915. Presbyterian/Methodist-Episcopal Cemetery, Succasunna, Morris County.
HEDDEN, CHARLES B. 1908. New Somerville Cemetery, Somerville, Somerset County.

New Jersey Civil War Burials

HEDDEN, DANIEL Pvt, G, 13th NJ Inf, 4-1-1900. Fairmount Cemetery, Newark, Essex County.

HEDDEN*, EDWIN H. 2nd Lt, B, 40th NJ Inf, 2-4-1923. Fairmount Cemetery, Newark, Essex County.

HEDDEN, GEORGE E. Pvt, I, 12th NJ Inf, 12-4-1916. Siloam Cemetery, Vineland, Cumberland County.

HEDDEN, GEORGE W. Sgt, H, 11th NJ Inf, 1-24-1923. Arlington Cemetery, Kearny, Hudson County.

HEDDEN, GEORGE W. 4-9-1924. Fairmount Cemetery, Newark, Essex County.

HEDDEN, JOTHAM E. Pvt, H, 71st NY State Militia, 4-5-1899. Rosedale Cemetery, Orange, Essex County.

HEDDEN, THEODORE A. Pvt, B, 8th NJ Inf, 7-10-1907. Mansfield/Washington Cemetery, Washington, Warren County.

HEDDEN, WILLIAM Sgt, I, 3rd NJ Inf, 2-16-1913. Hillside Cemetery, Scotch Plains, Union County.

HEDDRICK, JOHN Corp, B, 35th NJ Inf, 1-21-1924. Mount Olivet Cemetery, Newark, Essex County.

HEDDY, HEZEKIAH (see: Headley, Hezekiah) Glenwood Cemetery, Glenwood, Sussex County.

HEDENBERG, WATSON S. 1885. Mount Pleasant Cemetery, Newark, Essex County.

HEDGEPATH, WILLIAM Pvt, D, 1st GA Cav (CSA), 3-13-1864. Finn's Point National Cemetery, Pennsville, Salem County.

HEDGER, HARVEY Pvt, K, 12th NY Inf, 8-5-1896. Fairmount Cemetery, Newark, Essex County.

HEDGES, FLETCHER Sgt, G, 107th IL Inf, 5-19-1911. Fairmount Cemetery, Newark, Essex County.

HEDRICK, GEORGE M. Pvt, D, 119th NY Inf, [Wounded 5-2-1863 at Chancellorsville, VA. and 5-15-1864 at Resaca, GA.] 3-24-1895. Fairmount Cemetery, Newark, Essex County.

HEED, EDWARD B. Pvt, H, 31st NJ Inf, 6-10-1894. Union Cemetery, Washington, Morris County.

HEED, HENRY J.V. Pvt, B, 15th NJ Inf, 1923. Belvidere/Catholic Cemetery, Belvidere, Warren County.

HEEGE*, JACOB Pvt, A, 7th OH Inf, 2-9-1917. Evergreen Cemetery, Hillside, Union County.

HEENAN, CONSTANT (aka: Herman, Constant) Pvt, G, 48th NY Inf, [Wounded in action.] DoD Unknown. Old Hook Cemetery, Westwood, Bergen County.

HEENAN, MARTIN Pvt, K, 28th NJ Inf, DoD Unknown. Christ Church Cemetery, Morgan, Middlesex County.

HEERY, PHILIP (aka: Hearie, Philip) Pvt, D, 1st NJ Inf, 12-22-1892. Phillipsburg Old Catholic Cemetery, Phillipsburg, Warren County.

HEFELE, JOSEPH Pvt, E, 3rd NJ Cav, 2-17-1890. Fairmount Cemetery, Newark, Essex County.

HEFERN, DENNIS (see: Heffernan, John) Holy Name Cemetery, Jersey City, Hudson County.

HEFFELFINGER, LEVI P. Musc, K, 138th PA Inf, 5-7-1908. Harleigh Cemetery, Camden, Camden County.

HEFFERNAN, JOHN (aka: Hefern, Dennis) Pvt, C, 15th NJ Inf, 7-3-1919. Holy Name Cemetery, Jersey City, Hudson County.

HEFFERNAN, THOMAS Pvt, Btty B, 1st CT Heavy Art, 7-5-1887. Holy Sepulchre Cemetery, East Orange, Essex County.

HEFFERON*, WILLIAM Pvt, Btty D, 2nd U.S. Art, 10-1-1881. New Camden Cemetery, Camden, Camden County.

Our Brothers Gone Before

HEFFLER, R.H. Pvt, McRae's Bttn NC Cav (CSA) [Died of rubella.] 8-1-1863. Finn's Point National Cemetery, Pennsville, Salem County.

HEFFRAN, JAMES Pvt, C, 2nd NJ Inf, 7-10-1879. Fairmount Cemetery, Newark, Essex County.

HEFLEY, JAMES F. Pvt, I, 90th PA Inf, 4-8-1890. Methodist Cemetery, Tuckerton, Ocean County.

HEFNER, ANDREW Pvt, F, 9th (Malone's) AL Cav (CSA), 10-1-1863. Finn's Point National Cemetery, Pennsville, Salem County.

HEFT, DANIEL Com Sgt, G, 1st NY Cav, 4-7-1883. Grove Church Cemetery, North Bergen, Hudson County.

HEGAMIN, WILLIAM W. Ordinary Seaman, U.S. Navy, USS Princeton, 8-14-1901. Mount Peace Cemetery, Lawnside, Camden County.

HEGEMAN, JOHN Pvt, E, 139th NY Inf, 11-20-1928. Evergreen Cemetery, Morristown, Morris County.

HEGI, LOUIS G. Pvt, D, 6th NY National Guard, 5-5-1912. Atlantic City Cemetery, Pleasantville, Atlantic County.

HEIDMAN, ERNEST Pvt, F, 39th NJ Inf, 9-26-1894. Fairmount Cemetery, Newark, Essex County.

HEIDWEILER, HENRY K. Pvt, B, 1st NJ Inf, 1883. Greenwood Cemetery, Hamilton, Mercer County.

HEIGHT, BRITTEN R. Sgt, G, 1st NJ Cav, 12-6-1879. Methodist-Episcopal Cemetery, Glendola, Monmouth County.

HEIGHT, CHARLES Pvt, E, 15th NJ Inf, 1900. Reformed Church Cemetery, Blawenburg, Somerset County.

HEIGHT, JOHN T. (aka: Haight, John) Pvt, K, 29th NJ Inf, 1895. Atlantic View Cemetery, Manasquan, Monmouth County.

HEIGHT, THOMAS B. Musc, K, 29th NJ Inf, 7-10-1897. Methodist Cemetery, Hamilton, Monmouth County.

HEIL, HENRY Pvt, F, 5th NY National Guard, 8-15-1905. Bayview-New York Bay Cemetery, Jersey City, Hudson County.

HEILEMAN, FREDERICK Corp, F, 162nd NY Inf, 2-8-1912. Evergreen Cemetery, New Brunswick, Middlesex County.

HEIM*, CHARLES Pvt, Btty A, 1st NJ Light Art, 1-11-1889. Flower Hill Cemetery, North Bergen, Hudson County.

HEIM, JOSEPH Pvt, C, 20th MA Inf, [Wounded 12-11-1862 at Fredericksburg, VA. and 6-18-1864 at Petersburg, VA.] 3-26-1898. Palisade Cemetery, North Bergen, Hudson County.

HEIMAN, HENRY Pvt, E, 31st NY Inf, 1898. New Camden Cemetery, Camden, Camden County.

HEIMBOLD, FRANCIS Pvt, A, 3rd NJ Cav, 9-20-1893. St. John's Cemetery, Lambertville, Hunterdon County.

HEIN, JOHN (aka: Hines, John) Pvt, D, 35th NJ Inf, 11-10-1898. Holy Name Cemetery, Jersey City, Hudson County.

HEINECKE, CHARLES Pvt, A, 6th U.S. Cav, [Wounded in action.] 12-19-1893. Batsto/Pleasant Mills Methodist Church Cemetery, Pleasant Mills, Atlantic County.

HEINECKE*, HERMAN Pvt, G, 61st NY Inf, 9-2-1908. Fairview Cemetery, Fairview, Bergen County.

HEINER, CHARLES (aka: Hiner, Charles) Pvt, D, 39th NJ Inf, 10-7-1906. Fairmount Cemetery, Newark, Essex County.

HEINHOLD, LOUIS (aka: Heinold, Lewis) Corp, D, 2nd NJ Inf, 1-8-1911. Fairmount Cemetery, Newark, Essex County.

HEINISCH, ROCHUS 1st Lt, A, 26th NJ Inf, 7-28-1898. Mount Pleasant Cemetery, Newark, Essex County.

HEINLEY, ABRAHAM E. (aka: Hinley, Abraham) Sgt, C, 31st NJ Inf, 1-17-1890. Phillipsburg Cemetery, Phillipsburg, Warren County.

HEINOLD, LEWIS (see: Heinhold, Louis) Fairmount Cemetery, Newark, Essex County.

HEINRICH, J.F. 1-27-1868. Bayview-New York Bay Cemetery, Jersey City, Hudson County.

HEINRICH, OTTO Landsman, U.S. Navy, 7-15-1902. Fairmount Cemetery, Newark, Essex County.

HEINS, HERMAN Pvt, H, 3rd NY Inf, 1-11-1899. Fairmount Cemetery, Newark, Essex County.

HEINS, JACOB (aka: Hines, Jacob) Pvt, E, 3rd NJ Militia, 12-6-1928. Mount Hope Presbyterian Cemetery, Lambertville, Hunterdon County.

HEINSBERGER, CHARLES Pvt, E, 31st NY Inf, 4-26-1916. Evergreen Cemetery, Hillside, Union County.

HEINTZ*, FREDERICK (aka: Haynes, Frederick) Pvt, H, 40th NJ Inf, 2-6-1889. Evergreen Cemetery, Hillside, Union County.

HEINTZ, FREDERICK Pvt, G, 24th NJ Inf, 2-5-1902. Church of Christ Cemetery, Fairton, Cumberland County.

HEINTZ, JOHN F. Pvt, G, 24th NJ Inf, 1-5-1907. Church of Christ Cemetery, Fairton, Cumberland County.

HEINTZ, WILLIAM C. Pvt, K, 190th PA Inf, DoD Unknown. Presbyterian Church Cemetery, Bridgeton, Cumberland County.

HEINZ, JULIUS (aka: Hintzy, Julius) Pvt, F, 12th RI Inf, [Wounded 12-13-1862 at Fredericksburg, VA.] DoD Unknown. Bayview-New York Bay Cemetery, Jersey City, Hudson County.

HEIREAGLE, JOSEPH (see: Hellrigle, Joshua) Fairmount Cemetery, Newark, Essex County.

HEIRMIER, JACOB 1903. Evergreen Cemetery, Hillside, Union County.

HEISLER, CHARLES 10-4-1906. Fairmount Cemetery, Newark, Essex County.

HEISLER, CHARLES Sgt, E, 23rd NJ Inf, 1926. Baptist Cemetery, Pemberton, Burlington County.

HEISLER, CHARLES W. Pvt, F, 25th NJ Inf, 1923. Mount Holly Cemetery, Mount Holly, Burlington County.

HEISLER*, GEORGE 2nd Lt, U.S. Marine Corps, [Died at Memphis, TN. of wounds received at New Orleans, LA.] 7-12-1862. Methodist Church Cemetery, Pemberton, Burlington County.

HEISLER, GEORGE H. (aka: Hissler, George) Pvt, U.S. Marine Corps, 8-29-1912. New Camden Cemetery, Camden, Camden County.

HEISLER, ISAAC SHARP Corp, G, 23rd NJ Inf, [Died of pneumonia at White Oak Church, VA.] 2-15-1863. Coopertown Meeting House Cemetery, Edgewater Park, Burlington County.

HEISLER, JOHN S. 5-17-1907. Princeton Cemetery, Princeton, Mercer County.

HEISLEY, CHARLES WESLEY Chaplain, 28th PA Inf 3-1-1916. Evergreen Cemetery, Farmingdale, Monmouth County.

HEISS, PHILIP Pvt, F, 39th NJ Inf, 9-9-1902. Woodland Cemetery, Newark, Essex County.

HEIST, CHARLES F. Pvt, Btty C, 1st NJ Light Art, 11-9-1904. Phillipsburg Cemetery, Phillipsburg, Warren County.

HEISTAND, JOHN W. Pvt, F, 9th PA Cav, 7-31-1887. Evergreen Cemetery, Camden, Camden County.

HEITMAN, CHARLES Pvt, A, 4th NJ Inf, 9-23-1894. Fairmount Cemetery, Newark, Essex County.

HEITMAN, HENRY C. (aka: Hidman, Henry) Pvt, F, 176th NY Inf, 7-22-1885. Greengrove Cemetery, Keyport, Monmouth County.

Our Brothers Gone Before

HEITMANN, ROBERT Pvt, C, 26th NJ Inf, 5-26-1930. Holy Sepulchre Cemetery, East Orange, Essex County.
HEITSMAN, CHARLES Pvt, H, 11th PA Cav, 1909. Union Cemetery, Milford, Hunterdon County.
HEITZMAN, GEORGE (aka: Heitzmann, George) Pvt, B, 149th NY Inf, 2-9-1911. Phillipsburg Cemetery, Phillipsburg, Warren County.
HEITZMAN, WILLIAM H. Pvt, A, 215th PA Inf, 2-11-1913. Phillipsburg Cemetery, Phillipsburg, Warren County.
HEITZMANN, GEORGE (see: Heitzman, George) Phillipsburg Cemetery, Phillipsburg, Warren County.
HELBIG*, FREDERICK WILLIAM Pvt, E, 7th NJ Inf, 7-10-1899. Fairmount Cemetery, Newark, Essex County.
HELBIG, GEORGE W. Pvt, Unassigned, 5th NY Heavy Art, 5-8-1907. Madonna Cemetery, Leonia, Bergen County.
HELD, ADOLPHUS A. Pvt, H, 139th NY Inf, [Wounded 6-2-1864 at Cold Harbor, VA.] 8-24-1910. Riverside Cemetery, Toms River, Ocean County.
HELF*, JACOB Pvt, B, 102nd NY Inf, 2-17-1886. Fairmount Cemetery, Newark, Essex County.
HELLEMUTH, ANTON Pvt, G, 35th NJ Inf, 4-16-1878. Fairmount Cemetery, Newark, Essex County.
HELLER, AUGUST Corp, K, 8th NY Inf, [Killed in action at Cross Keys, VA.] 6-8-1862. Mount Pleasant Cemetery, Newark, Essex County.
HELLER, CARL (see: Heller, Charles) Weehawken Cemetery, North Bergen, Hudson County.
HELLER, CHARLES 1922. Evergreen Cemetery, Clinton, Hunterdon County.
HELLER, CHARLES (aka: Heller, Carl) 1st Sgt, I, 54th NY Inf, 5-19-1906. Weehawken Cemetery, North Bergen, Hudson County.
HELLER, EDWARD Pvt, K, 18th PA Cav, 4-3-1906. Christian Church Cemetery, Locktown, Hunterdon County.
HELLER, FREDERICK Pvt, D, 8th NJ Inf, 1885. Cedar Lawn Cemetery, Paterson, Passaic County.
HELLER, JOHN Pvt, B, 8th NJ Inf, 6-16-1912. Evergreen Cemetery, Hillside, Union County.
HELLER, JOHN G. Pvt, A, 9th NJ Inf, 1-11-1915. Hoboken Cemetery, North Bergen, Hudson County.
HELLER, LOUIS 1905. Bayview-New York Bay Cemetery, Jersey City, Hudson County.
HELLER, MATTHIAS Pvt, E, 29th NY Inf, 4-9-1923. Atlantic City Cemetery, Pleasantville, Atlantic County.
HELLER, PETER J. 2-21-1924. Mount Hebron Cemetery, Montclair, Essex County.
HELLER, SAMUEL B. Pvt, A, 2nd NJ Cav, 1-27-1910. Phillipsburg Cemetery, Phillipsburg, Warren County.
HELLERMANN, CARL 1920. Princeton Cemetery, Princeton, Mercer County.
HELLINA, PHILIP Sgt, F, 183rd PA Inf, 1915. Chestnut Grove Cemetery, Elmer, Salem County.
HELLINGER, JOSEPH Pvt, F, 9th NJ Inf, 3-23-1935. Highland Cemetery, Hopewell Boro, Mercer County.
HELLM, CHARLES (see: Helms, Charles A.) Cedar Lawn Cemetery, Paterson, Passaic County.
HELLMAN, AUGUST Pvt, E, 3rd NY Cav, 11-19-1878. Fairmount Cemetery, Newark, Essex County.
HELLMUTH, PHILIP Pvt, Btty A, 1st NJ Light Art, 2-27-1903. Riverview Cemetery, Trenton, Mercer County.

New Jersey Civil War Burials

HELLRIGLE, JOSHUA (aka: Heireagle, Joseph) Pvt, F, 39th IL Inf, [Died at Newark, NJ. of wounds received in action.] 7-1-1864. Fairmount Cemetery, Newark, Essex County.

HELLSTERN*, JOHN (aka: Helstein, John) Pvt, B, 4th NJ Inf, 12-3-1899. Grove Church Cemetery, North Bergen, Hudson County.

HELLWIG, JOHN Sgt, G, 125th PA Inf, 2-26-1917. Fairmount Cemetery, Newark, Essex County.

HELM*, CHARLES (aka: Helmers, Charles) Pvt, F, 8th NJ Inf, 6-8-1910. Harleigh Cemetery, Camden, Camden County.

HELM, DAVID D. Sgt, C, 4th NJ Militia, 8-4-1893. Harleigh Cemetery, Camden, Camden County.

HELM, JAMES Pvt, C, 26th NJ Inf, 9-6-1904. Hancock Cemetery, Florham Park, Morris County.

HELM*, JOHN Asst Surg, 3rd NJ Cav [Also: Asst Surg, 2nd NJ Inf.] 11-7-1898. Willow Grove Cemetery, New Brunswick, Middlesex County.

HELM*, LOUIS Pvt, C, 102nd NY Inf, 3-3-1916. Arlington Cemetery, Kearny, Hudson County.

HELM, ROBERT JAMES Pvt, C, 26th NJ Inf, 10-10-1895. Hancock Cemetery, Florham Park, Morris County.

HELM, WILLIAM DoD Unknown. Hancock Cemetery, Florham Park, Morris County.

HELMBOLD, JOHN W. Pvt, E, 213th PA Inf, 1-8-1901. Evergreen Cemetery, Camden, Camden County.

HELME, GEORGE W. Capt, G, 24th LA Inf (CSA), [Crescent Regiment.] 6-13-1893. Fernwood Cemetery, Jamesburg, Middlesex County.

HELMER*, LOUIS H. (aka: Louis, Helmer) Capt, G, 35th NJ Inf, 8-29-1890. Woodland Cemetery, Newark, Essex County.

HELMERS, CHARLES (see: Helm, Charles) Harleigh Cemetery, Camden, Camden County.

HELMLINGER, FREDERICK Pvt, L, 1st NJ Cav, 1-11-1906. Rosedale Cemetery, Orange, Essex County.

HELMS, AARON S. Pvt, F, 114th PA Inf, [Wounded 7-3-1863 at Gettysburg, PA.] 4-21-1897. Harleigh Cemetery, Camden, Camden County.

HELMS, BENAJAH Pvt, I, 4th NJ Militia, 4-9-1932. 1st United Methodist Church Cemetery, Salem, Salem County.

HELMS, CHARLES A. (aka: Hellm, Charles) Pvt, E, 158th NY Inf, 12-25-1918. Cedar Lawn Cemetery, Paterson, Passaic County.

HELMS, CHARLES W. Pvt, D, 8th NJ Inf, 1-13-1905. Cedar Lawn Cemetery, Paterson, Passaic County.

HELMS, ENOS Pvt, B, 68th PA Inf, 8-22-1885. Methodist-Episcopal Church Cemetery, Medford, Burlington County.

HELMS, SAMUEL J. Pvt, Btty K, 2nd PA Heavy Art, 9-2-1912. Evergreen Cemetery, Camden, Camden County.

HELMUS, JOHN Pvt, C, 77th NY State Militia, 3-25-1926. Woodland Cemetery, Newark, Essex County.

HELMUTH*, CHARLES Fireman, U.S. Navy, USS Donegal, DoD Unknown. Old Camden Cemetery, Camden, Camden County.

HELMUTH, WILLIAM Pvt, E, 4th NJ Militia, 1-5-1891. Old Camden Cemetery, Camden, Camden County.

HELSLEY, NICHOLAS Pvt, E, 33rd VA Inf (CSA), [Captured 7-4-1863 at Gettysburg, PA. Died of remittent fever.] 7-14-1863. Finn's Point National Cemetery, Pennsville, Salem County.

HELSTEIN, JOHN (see: Hellstern, John) Grove Church Cemetery, North Bergen, Hudson County.

Our Brothers Gone Before

HELTBRANT, DAVID Pvt, H, 8th NJ Inf, 6-21-1885. Newton Cemetery, Newton, Sussex County.
HELTON, ANDREW J. Pvt, D, 57th GA Inf (CSA), [Captured 5-16-1863 at Baker's Creek, MS.] 7-10-1863. Finn's Point National Cemetery, Pennsville, Salem County.
HELTON, J.M. Pvt, A, 7th MS Inf (CSA), 5-2-1865. Finn's Point National Cemetery, Pennsville, Salem County.
HELTON, JONATHAN Pvt, G, 61st (Pitts') TN Mtd Inf (CSA), 9-1-1863. Finn's Point National Cemetery, Pennsville, Salem County.
HELY, DANIEL F. Pvt, A, 2nd U.S. Cav, 1908. St. Mary's Cemetery, Clark, Union County.
HEMENWAY, FRANK F. Pvt, B, 53rd MA Inf, [Wounded 6-14-1863 at Port Hudson, LA.] 10-14-1898. Arlington Cemetery, Kearny, Hudson County.
HEMINGWAY, BENJAMIN (see: Hammond, Benjamin) Cedar Lawn Cemetery, Paterson, Passaic County.
HEMINGWAY, GEORGE 10-20-1913. Arlington Cemetery, Pennsauken, Camden County.
HEMINGWAY, WASHINGTON Pvt, F, 24th CT Inf, 4-18-1908. Tabernacle Baptist Church Cemetery, Erma, Cape May County.
HEMINOVER, JOHN T. Pvt, E, 3rd NJ Cav, [Died of diarrhea at Salisbury, NC.] 12-4-1863. Union Cemetery, Marcella, Morris County.
HEMINOVER, WILLIAM Pvt, G, 1st NJ Cav, 2-8-1863. Union Cemetery, Marcella, Morris County.
HEMINSLEY, SIDNEY Pvt, H, 20th CT Inf, 1-20-1894. Cedar Lawn Cemetery, Paterson, Passaic County.
HEMINWAY, AMENZO B. Pvt, E, 136th NY Inf, 11-26-1916. Rosehill Cemetery, Newfield, Gloucester County.
HEMMENGER, FREDERICK (see: Hemminger, Frederick) Lodi Cemetery, Lodi, Bergen County.
HEMMENWAY*, CHARLES B. Pvt, G, 13th NJ Inf, 2-11-1909. Arlington Cemetery, Kearny, Hudson County.
HEMMER, GEORGE DoD Unknown. Old Camden Cemetery, Camden, Camden County.
HEMMER, PETER Corp, C, 1st NY Eng, DoD Unknown. Holy Sepulchre Cemetery, East Orange, Essex County.
HEMMER, WILLIAM Pvt, C, 1st NY Eng, 1-10-1880. Holy Sepulchre Cemetery, East Orange, Essex County.
HEMMINGER, FREDERICK (aka: Hemmenger, Frederick) Pvt, A, 11th NJ Inf, 12-1-1886. Lodi Cemetery, Lodi, Bergen County.
HEMMINGWAY, SAMUEL M. Pvt, D, 3rd NJ Cav, 2-9-1904. Cedar Lawn Cemetery, Paterson, Passaic County.
HEMPHILL, JAMES Pvt, I, 12th NJ Inf, 7-6-1903. Cedar Hill Cemetery, Cedarville, Cumberland County.
HEMPSTEAD, JOHN G. Wagoner, I, 27th NJ Inf, 3-31-1907. Evergreen Cemetery, Morristown, Morris County.
HEMSING, WILLIAM H. Capt, E, 6th NJ Inf, 8-27-1899. Riverview Cemetery, Trenton, Mercer County.
HEN, HUBBARD (see: Hendrickson, Hubbard) Fairview Cemetery, Fairview, Monmouth County.
HENBEL, ALBERT Capt, H, 186th PA Inf, DoD Unknown. Evergreen Cemetery, Camden, Camden County.
HENCLIFF, JAMES (see: Hand, James) Laurel Grove Cemetery, Totowa, Passaic County.
HENDBERG, F. DoD Unknown. Fairview Cemetery, Fairview, Bergen County.
HENDBERG*, MAURICE (aka: Hendenberg, Mauritz) Pvt, E, 2nd NJ Inf, 5-17-1918. New York/New Jersey Crematory Cemetery, North Bergen, Hudson County.

New Jersey Civil War Burials

HENDENBERG, MAURITZ (see: Hendberg, Maurice) New York/New Jersey Crematory Cemetery, North Bergen, Hudson County.
HENDERSHOT*, ANDREW J. Pvt, D, 15th NJ Inf, [Wounded in action.] DoD Unknown. Balesville Cemetery, Balesville, Sussex County.
HENDERSHOT, DAVID D. Pvt, A, 15th NJ Inf, 12-2-1894. Old & New Lutheran Cemetery, Lebanon, Hunterdon County.
HENDERSHOT, GEORGE Pvt, Btty E, 1st NJ Light Art, 11-10-1902. Mansfield/Washington Cemetery, Washington, Warren County.
HENDERSHOT, GEORGE T. Pvt, A, 27th NJ Inf, 5-24-1863. Presbyterian Church Cemetery, Newton, Sussex County.
HENDERSHOT*, HENRY J. Pvt, E, 2nd NJ Inf, 2-16-1885. Mercer Cemetery, Trenton, Mercer County.
HENDERSHOT, JACOB B. Sgt, D, 3rd NJ Inf, 11-4-1914. Newton Cemetery, Newton, Sussex County.
HENDERSHOT, JAMES Corp, D, 15th NJ Inf, 1907. Hardyston Cemetery, North Church, Sussex County.
HENDERSHOT, JOHN 3-17-1891. Newton Cemetery, Newton, Sussex County.
HENDERSHOT, JOHN B. Musc, A, 27th NJ Inf, 12-11-1893. Fairmount Cemetery, Newark, Essex County.
HENDERSHOT, JOHN M. Sgt, K, 1st NJ Cav, 4-17-1885. Union Cemetery, Hope, Warren County.
HENDERSHOT*, JOHN S. Pvt, F, 2nd NJ Inf, 5-24-1867. Presbyterian Church Cemetery, Newton, Sussex County.
HENDERSHOT, JOSEPH H. Pvt, A, 31st NJ Inf, DoD Unknown. Methodist-Episcopal Cemetery, Whitehouse, Hunterdon County.
HENDERSHOT*, JOSIAH Pvt, E, 7th NJ Inf, 4-28-1900. Cedar Ridge Cemetery, Blairstown, Warren County.
HENDERSHOT, OBADIAH Pvt, F, 9th NJ Inf, 12-25-1898. Newton Cemetery, Newton, Sussex County.
HENDERSHOT*, PHILLIP Pvt, F, 9th NJ Inf, 3-23-1914. Presbyterian Church Cemetery, Hampton, Hunterdon County.
HENDERSHOT*, WILLIAM W. Pvt, F, 9th NJ Inf, [Wounded in action.] 6-20-1897. New Germantown Cemetery, Oldwick, Hunterdon County.
HENDERSON, AARON Pvt, A, 8th NJ Inf, 3-20-1920. Union Cemetery, Marcella, Morris County.
HENDERSON, AARON Pvt, C, 8th NJ Inf, 8-17-1867. Methodist Church Cemetery, Buttzville, Warren County.
HENDERSON, ANDREW S. Pvt, A, 31st NJ Inf, 2-27-1876. Presbyterian Cemetery, Cokesbury, Hunterdon County.
HENDERSON*, ARCHIBALD Sgt, E, 86th NY Inf, [Wounded 8-14-1864 at Deep Bottom, VA.] 2-1-1904. Evergreen Cemetery, Hillside, Union County.
HENDERSON, AUGUSTUS (aka: Hendrickson, Augustus) Pvt, H, 45th U.S. CT, 10-26-1865. Princeton Cemetery, Princeton, Mercer County.
HENDERSON, DANIEL K. Corp, B, 27th NJ Inf, DoD Unknown. Little Valley Cemetery, Middle Valley, Morris County.
HENDERSON, DANIEL S. Corp, H, 47th MA Inf, 9-22-1894. Riverview Cemetery, Trenton, Mercer County.
HENDERSON, DAVID Pvt, B, 2nd NJ Inf, 1-27-1908. Bethel Cemetery, Pennsauken, Camden County.
HENDERSON, EDWARD L. 7-21-1911. Mount Pleasant Cemetery, Millville, Cumberland County.
HENDERSON, J.C.B. Pvt, G, 9th AL Inf (CSA), 10-4-1863. Finn's Point National Cemetery, Pennsville, Salem County.

Our Brothers Gone Before

HENDERSON, JAMES Pvt, F, 187th PA Inf, 11-18-1892. Evergreen Cemetery, Camden, Camden County.

HENDERSON, JAMES Coal Heaver, U.S. Navy, USS Ossipee, 9-16-1911. Fairmount Cemetery, Newark, Essex County.

HENDERSON, JAMES Musc, E, 90th NY Inf, 4-10-1917. Bayview-New York Bay Cemetery, Jersey City, Hudson County.

HENDERSON, JAMES Pvt, E, 11th NJ Inf, 1922. Methodist Cemetery, Hurdtown, Morris County.

HENDERSON, JAMES 6-5-1902. Zion Baptist Church Cemetery, New Egypt, Ocean County.

HENDERSON, JAMES P. Pvt, G, 36th VA Inf (CSA), [Captured 3-2-1865 at Waynesboro, VA. Died of lung inflammation.] 5-20-1865. Finn's Point National Cemetery, Pennsville, Salem County.

HENDERSON, JOHN Pvt, G, 22nd NJ Inf, 6-4-1874. Princeton Cemetery, Princeton, Mercer County.

HENDERSON, JOHN __, __, __ DE __, DoD Unknown. Finn's Point National Cemetery, Pennsville, Salem County.

HENDERSON, JOHN Pvt, I, 30th NJ Inf, 3-5-1884. New Somerville Cemetery, Somerville, Somerset County.

HENDERSON, JOHN Pvt, H, 10th NJ Inf, 1922. Hardyston Cemetery, North Church, Sussex County.

HENDERSON, JOHN B. 10-26-1866. Baptist Church Cemetery, Haddonfield, Camden County.

HENDERSON, JOHN M. Pvt, B, 24th NJ Inf, DoD Unknown. United Methodist Church Cemetery, Port Elizabeth, Cumberland County.

HENDERSON, JOHN M. Pvt, F, 4th NJ Militia, 10-27-1909. Eglington Cemetery, Clarksboro, Gloucester County.

HENDERSON, JOSEPH Sgt, G, 10th NJ Inf, 3-3-1879. Princeton Cemetery, Princeton, Mercer County.

HENDERSON, JOSEPH Corp, L, 15th AL Inf (CSA), [Captured at Gettysburg, PA.] 6-4-1864. Finn's Point National Cemetery, Pennsville, Salem County.

HENDERSON, JOSEPH B. Pvt, A, 31st NJ Inf, 4-5-1914. Presbyterian Church Cemetery, Califon, Hunterdon County.

HENDERSON, MATTHIAS Pvt, E, 11th NJ Inf, DoD Unknown. Union Cemetery, Marcella, Morris County.

HENDERSON, MATTHIAS Pvt, Btty D, 1st NJ Light Art, 7-26-1914. Holland Cemetery, Holland, Morris County.

HENDERSON, PETER Corp, H, 47th NY Inf, DoD Unknown. Holy Sepulchre Cemetery, East Orange, Essex County.

HENDERSON, PETER D. Pvt, E, 11th NJ Inf, 8-3-1902. Union Cemetery, Marcella, Morris County.

HENDERSON, R.B. Pvt, G, 5th TX Inf (CSA), 2-4-1864. Finn's Point National Cemetery, Pennsville, Salem County.

HENDERSON, ROBERT Pvt, H, 22nd NJ Inf, 12-3-1908. Jersey City Cemetery, Jersey City, Hudson County.

HENDERSON, ROBERT 2nd Lt, A, 84th NY Inf, 10-7-1877. Palisade Cemetery, North Bergen, Hudson County.

HENDERSON, ROBERT C. Pvt, G, 33rd NJ Inf, 5-19-1911. Arlington Cemetery, Kearny, Hudson County.

HENDERSON, SAMUEL Pvt, E, 1st NJ Cav, 7-13-1932. Union Cemetery, Marcella, Morris County.

HENDERSON, SAMUEL M. Corp, A, 8th NJ Inf, DoD Unknown. Union Cemetery, Marcella, Morris County.

New Jersey Civil War Burials

HENDERSON, THOMAS 1st Lt, 5th NY Ind Btty 2-2-1902. Bloomfield Cemetery, Bloomfield, Essex County.

HENDERSON, THOMAS B. Corp, C, 47th NY Inf, 4-30-1909. Presbyterian Cemetery, Springfield, Union County.

HENDERSON, WILLIAM Pvt, Ind, 1st U.S. Pontoniers, 1-3-1907. Tabernacle Baptist Church Cemetery, Erma, Cape May County.

HENDERSON, WILLIAM Pvt, G, 1st NJ Inf, 4-21-1874. Princeton Cemetery, Princeton, Mercer County.

HENDERSON, WILLIAM Pvt, B, 39th NJ Inf, 12-3-1890. Methodist Cemetery, Hurdtown, Morris County.

HENDERSON, WILLIAM Corp, A, 1st NJ Inf, 9-10-1892. Riverview Cemetery, Trenton, Mercer County.

HENDERSON, WILLIAM (see: Hendrickson, William Edgar) Old Somerville Cemetery, Somerville, Somerset County.

HENDERSON, WILLIAM A. Pvt, D, 102nd NY Inf, 4-27-1930. Greengrove Cemetery, Keyport, Monmouth County.

HENDERSON, WILLIAM H. Pvt, G, 12th NJ Inf, 4-1-1909. Old Stone Church Cemetery, Fairton, Cumberland County.

HENDERSON, WILLIAM H. Pvt, K, 26th NJ Inf, 4-15-1903. Fairmount Cemetery, Newark, Essex County.

HENDERSON, WILLIAM J. Pvt, G, 2nd (Ashby's) TN Cav (CSA), 7-15-1864. Finn's Point National Cemetery, Pennsville, Salem County.

HENDERSON, WILLIAM (JR.) Pvt, K, 31st NJ Inf, 1-29-1934. Evergreen Cemetery, Clinton, Hunterdon County.

HENDERSON, WILLIAM W. Pvt, C, 28th NJ Inf, 5-22-1899. Fountain Grove Cemetery, Glen Gardner, Hunterdon County.

HENDLEY, JAMES Pvt, B, 8th NY State Militia, 1891. Greenwood Cemetery, Hamilton, Mercer County.

HENDRA, WILLIAM DoD Unknown. Hardyston Cemetery, North Church, Sussex County.

HENDRICK, OREN A. Maj, 36th U.S. CT 2-24-1890. Mount Pleasant Cemetery, Newark, Essex County.

HENDRICKS, CHARLES SOLLIDAY Com Sgt, A, 3rd NJ Cav, [Wounded 4-4-1865 at Five Forks, VA.] 3-8-1920. Sandy Ridge Cemetery, Sandy Ridge, Hunterdon County.

HENDRICKS*, GEORGE WASHINGTON (aka: Hendrickson, George W.) Pvt, D, 28th NJ Inf, 2-18-1900. Van Liew Cemetery, North Brunswick, Middlesex County.

HENDRICKS, ISAAC Pvt, K, 14th NJ Inf, 2-9-1913. Van Liew Cemetery, North Brunswick, Middlesex County.

HENDRICKS, JOHN Pvt, U.S. Marine Corps, 1919. Evergreen Cemetery, New Brunswick, Middlesex County.

HENDRICKS, SEABORN W. Pvt, H, 42nd MS Inf (CSA), 10-29-1863. Finn's Point National Cemetery, Pennsville, Salem County.

HENDRICKS*, WILLIAM Pvt, H, 12th NJ Inf, 8-30-1863. Methodist Church Cemetery, Sharptown, Salem County.

HENDRICKSON, AUGUSTUS (see: Henderson, Augustus) Princeton Cemetery, Princeton, Mercer County.

HENDRICKSON, BARKALOW Pvt, H, 48th NY Inf, 2-1-1911. Greenlawn Cemetery, West Long Branch, Monmouth County.

HENDRICKSON, BARZILLA Corp, F, 29th NJ Inf, 8-20-1912. Maplewood Cemetery, Freehold, Monmouth County.

HENDRICKSON, CHARLES Pvt, E, 25th U.S. CT, DoD Unknown. Johnson Cemetery, Matawan, Monmouth County.

Our Brothers Gone Before

HENDRICKSON, CHARLES G. Pvt, G, 28th NJ Inf, DoD Unknown. New Episcopal Church Cemetery, Swedesboro, Gloucester County.
HENDRICKSON, CHARLES H. (see: Hendrickson, William) Bethel AME Cemetery, Freehold, Monmouth County.
HENDRICKSON, COMBS S. Musc, E, 28th NJ Inf, 7-2-1918. Methodist Cemetery, Cassville, Ocean County.
HENDRICKSON, DANIEL G. Pvt, C, 9th NJ Inf, 1-12-1886. Greenwood Cemetery, Hamilton, Mercer County.
HENDRICKSON, DANIEL T. Pvt, F, 13th NJ Inf, 1-24-1919. Fairmount Cemetery, Newark, Essex County.
HENDRICKSON, DAVID H. Pvt, G, 10th NJ Inf, DoD Unknown. Friendship United Methodist Church Cemetery, Landisville, Atlantic County.
HENDRICKSON*, GARRET C. Pvt, A, 7th NJ Inf, 10-28-1907. Fairview Cemetery, Fairview, Monmouth County.
HENDRICKSON, GEORGE C. Capt, E, 28th NJ Inf, 10-19-1892. Methodist Church Cemetery, Harmony, Ocean County.
HENDRICKSON, GEORGE M. Pvt, G, 1st NJ Inf, [Died of consumption at Fairfax Seminary, VA.] 4-22-1862. Princeton Cemetery, Princeton, Mercer County.
HENDRICKSON, GEORGE W. (see: Hendricks, George Washington) Van Liew Cemetery, North Brunswick, Middlesex County.
HENDRICKSON, HENRY B. Pvt, G, 28th NJ Inf, 3-29-1898. Eglington Cemetery, Clarksboro, Gloucester County.
HENDRICKSON, HUBBARD (aka: Hen, Hubbard) Pvt, A, 5th PA Inf, 11-21-1891. Fairview Cemetery, Fairview, Monmouth County.
HENDRICKSON, JAMES H. Pvt, E, 28th NJ Inf, DoD Unknown. Methodist Church Cemetery, Harmony, Ocean County.
HENDRICKSON, JASPER W. Pvt, G, 22nd NJ Inf, [Died of paralysis at Philadelphia, PA.] 6-23-1863. Presbyterian Church Cemetery, Dutch Neck, Mercer County.
HENDRICKSON, JEHU (see: Hendrickson, John) Baptist Church Cemetery, Haddonfield, Camden County.
HENDRICKSON, JOHN (aka: Hendrickson, Jehu) Corp, C, 12th NJ Inf, 9-6-1887. Baptist Church Cemetery, Haddonfield, Camden County.
HENDRICKSON, JOHN H. Pvt, B, 8th NJ Inf, 5-27-1904. Emleys Hill United Methodist Church Cemetery, Upper Freehold, Monmouth County.
HENDRICKSON, JOHN H. 12-4-1873. Methodist Cemetery, Cassville, Ocean County.
HENDRICKSON, JOSEPH C. Musc, G, 28th NJ Inf, 5-26-1921. Lake Park Cemetery, Swedesboro, Gloucester County.
HENDRICKSON, JOSEPH H. Pvt, A, 1st NJ Militia, 4-1-1887. Fairmount Cemetery, Newark, Essex County.
HENDRICKSON, JOSEPH T. Sgt, C, 29th NJ Inf, 3-18-1898. United Presbyterian Church Cemetery, Perrineville, Monmouth County.
HENDRICKSON, LEWIS C. Pvt, C, 95th PA Inf, 3-19-1880. Evergreen Cemetery, Camden, Camden County.
HENDRICKSON, PETER J. QM, 29th NJ Inf 1-5-1870. Fairview Cemetery, Fairview, Monmouth County.
HENDRICKSON, RANDALL Pvt, G, 28th NJ Inf, [Wounded in action.] 1921. Cedar Green Cemetery, Clayton, Gloucester County.
HENDRICKSON, SAMUEL Pvt, K, 10th NJ Inf, 7-24-1920. Riverview Cemetery, Trenton, Mercer County.
HENDRICKSON, SAMUEL G. Pvt, H, 3rd NJ Inf, [Wounded 5-10-1864 at Spotsylvania CH, VA.] 7-2-1898. Riverview Cemetery, Trenton, Mercer County.
HENDRICKSON, THOMAS Pvt, B, 23rd NJ Inf, 9-16-1902. Bordentown/Old St. Mary's Catholic Cemetery, Bordentown, Burlington County.

New Jersey Civil War Burials

HENDRICKSON, WILLIAM (aka: Hendrickson, Charles H.) Pvt, H, 127th U.S. CT, 7-4-1889. Bethel AME Cemetery, Freehold, Monmouth County.
HENDRICKSON, WILLIAM E. Pvt, H, 23rd NJ Inf, 7-21-1875. Baptist Church Cemetery, Haddonfield, Camden County.
HENDRICKSON, WILLIAM E. Pvt, A, 14th NJ Inf, 2-23-1866. Yellow Meeting House Cemetery, Imlaytown, Monmouth County.
HENDRICKSON, WILLIAM EDGAR (aka: Henderson, William) Corp, K, 1st NY Mounted Rifles, 6-10-1894. Old Somerville Cemetery, Somerville, Somerset County.
HENDRY*, BOWMAN Asst Surg, 4th NJ Inf [Also: Asst Surg, 6th NJ Inf.] 11-1-1904. Colestown Cemetery, Cherry Hill, Camden County.
HENDRY, THOMAS G. (SR.) Pvt, B, 165th NY Inf, 4-27-1877. Clinton Cemetery, Irvington, Essex County.
HENDRY, WILLIAM Pvt, E, 22nd NJ Inf, 6-4-1918. Laurel Grove Cemetery, Totowa, Passaic County.
HENDZEL, VALENTINE (aka: Hensel, Valentine) Corp, C, 31st NY Inf, 5-23-1889. New Somerville Cemetery, Somerville, Somerset County.
HENEMAN, HENRY (see: Hering, Henry) Riverview Cemetery, Trenton, Mercer County.
HENESY, JOHN Pvt, F, 23rd NJ Inf, 12-4-1906. Oddfellows-Friends Cemetery, Medford, Burlington County.
HENFT, BENJAMIN (see: Hutt, Benjamin) Johnson Cemetery, Camden, Camden County.
HENGER, JACOB Pvt, E, 39th NJ Inf, 10-7-1883. Fairmount Cemetery, Newark, Essex County.
HENHOEFER, ALEXANDER (aka: Henhofer, Ellis) Pvt, Btty A, Schaffer's Ind PA Heavy Art, [Died at Fort Delaware.] 5-8-1864. Finn's Point National Cemetery, Pennsville, Salem County.
HENHOFER, ELLIS (see: Henhoefer, Alexander) Finn's Point National Cemetery, Pennsville, Salem County.
HENING, NEWTON I. (see: Herring, Newton J.) Finn's Point National Cemetery, Pennsville, Salem County.
HENION, GARRETT G. Pvt, B, 22nd NJ Inf, 12-1-1894. Ramapo Reformed Church Cemetery, Mahwah, Bergen County.
HENKLE, JAMES R. Corp, B, 1st WV Inf, 2-7-1940. Evergreen Cemetery, Hillside, Union County.
HENLEY, THOMAS (see: Hurley, Thomas P.) 1st Methodist Church Cemetery, Williamstown, Gloucester County.
HENN, GEORGE F. Pvt, E, 3rd NJ Cav, 10-14-1894. Phillipsburg Cemetery, Phillipsburg, Warren County.
HENNARD, FRANKLIN E. 5-18-1866. Green Cemetery, Woodbury, Gloucester County.
HENNEKE, AUGUSTUS (see: Hannaka, Augustus) St. Mary's Cemetery, Wharton, Morris County.
HENNER, LEOPOLD Pvt, E, 2nd NJ Inf, DoD Unknown. Holy Sepulchre Cemetery, East Orange, Essex County.
HENNESEE, OWEN Pvt, C, 33rd NJ Inf, 6-18-1873. Holy Sepulchre Cemetery, East Orange, Essex County.
HENNESSEY, E.F. Pvt, B, 6th U.S. Cav, DoD Unknown. Cedar Green Cemetery, Clayton, Gloucester County.
HENNESSEY, EDWARD Sgt, B, 21st NJ Inf, 10-7-1881. St. Peter's Cemetery, Jersey City, Hudson County.
HENNESSEY, JAMES Pvt, B, 10th NJ Inf, DoD Unknown. Holy Name Cemetery, Jersey City, Hudson County.
HENNESSEY, JOSEPH J. 1918. Holy Sepulchre Cemetery, East Orange, Essex County.

Our Brothers Gone Before

HENNESSEY*, MANASSAS S. 3rd Lt, K, 6th NC Cav (CSA), 4-8-1864. Finn's Point National Cemetery, Pennsville, Salem County.

HENNESSEY*, THOMAS Pvt, E, 7th NJ Inf, 5-14-1903. St. Peter's Cemetery, Jersey City, Hudson County.

HENNESSY, GEORGE I. Pvt, A, 2nd NJ Cav, 6-11-1924. Fairview Cemetery, Fairview, Bergen County.

HENNESSY, JAMES Coal Heaver, U.S. Navy, USS Bienville, 7-26-1904. Mount Olivet Cemetery, Newark, Essex County.

HENNING, LEONARD 1st Lt, C, 14th NJ Inf, 6-5-1872. Evergreen Cemetery, Hillside, Union County.

HENNINGS, JOHN (aka: Herning, John) Pvt, G, 9th NJ Inf, 3-31-1906. Berry Lawn Cemetery, Carlstadt, Bergen County.

HENNION, ANDREW (JR.) Pvt, B, 22nd NJ Inf, [Wounded in action.] 7-17-1916. 1st Presbyterian Union Cemetery, Ramsey, Bergen County.

HENNION, CHESTER N. Pvt, A, 26th NJ Inf, 6-12-1920. Mount Pleasant Cemetery, Newark, Essex County.

HENNION, DAVID Pvt, G, 1st NY Eng, 10-10-1908. Laurel Grove Cemetery, Totowa, Passaic County.

HENNION, GEORGE W. Pvt, B, 9th NJ Inf, 11-4-1915. Old Butler Cemetery, Butler, Morris County.

HENNION, JOHN H. Pvt, F, 26th NJ Inf, 2-16-1924. Prospect Hill Cemetery, Caldwell, Essex County.

HENNION, PETER Pvt, F, 2nd DC Inf, [Wounded in action.] 10-9-1914. Pompton Reformed Church Cemetery, Pompton Lakes, Passaic County.

HENNION, PETER (aka: Henyon, Peter) Corp, K, 1st NJ Cav, 5-29-1902. Presbyterian Church Cemetery, Sparta, Sussex County.

HENNION, WILLIAM (aka: Henyon, William) Pvt, K, 39th NJ Inf, 1-12-1895. United Methodist Church Cemetery, Millbrook, Morris County.

HENNIWELL, WILLIAM H. (see: Hunniwell, William H.) Clinton Cemetery, Irvington, Essex County.

HENRIE, FRANK (see: Henry, Frank J.) Brookside Cemetery, Englewood, Bergen County.

HENRIQUES, OTTO R. Paymaster, U.S. Navy, USS Wabash, 3-31-1907. Rosehill Cemetery, Linden, Union County.

HENRY, A. RICHMOND Pvt, C, 38th NJ Inf, 2-25-1899. Manahath Cemetery, Glassboro, Gloucester County.

HENRY, ABRAM Corp, A, 25th U.S. CT, 11-17-1907. Baptist/Evergreen Methodist Cemetery, Plainfield, Union County.

HENRY, ALEXANDER Pvt, H, 30th NJ Inf, 1-9-1905. Evergreen Cemetery, Hillside, Union County.

HENRY, ALFRED Pvt, G, 31st NJ Inf, DoD Unknown. Ramseyburg Cemetery, Ramseyburg, Warren County.

HENRY*, ANDREW F. Sgt, G, 2nd NJ Inf, [Wounded in action.] 5-22-1900. Union Cemetery, Ringoes, Hunterdon County.

HENRY, CHARLES Pvt, D, 25th NJ Inf, 12-3-1879. 1st Baptist Church Cemetery, Moorestown, Burlington County.

HENRY*, CHARLES Pvt, I, 170th NY Inf, [Wounded 5-24-1864 at North Anna River, VA.] 12-5-1905. Mount Carmel Cemetery, Tenafly, Bergen County.

HENRY, CHARLES C. Pvt, K, 13th NJ Inf, 1923. Old South Church Cemetery, Bergenfield, Bergen County.

HENRY*, DAVID M. Pvt, E, 150th PA Inf, 12-25-1913. Old Camden Cemetery, Camden, Camden County.

HENRY, FRANCIS Pvt, F, 22nd U.S. CT, 4-20-1897. United Methodist Church Cemetery, Vienna, Warren County.

New Jersey Civil War Burials

HENRY*, FRANK J. (aka: Henrie, Frank) Pvt, K, 4th NY Inf, [Wounded 12-13-1862 at Fredericksburg, VA.] 5-21-1913. Brookside Cemetery, Englewood, Bergen County.

HENRY, GEORGE Pvt, A, 3rd NJ Cav, 3-8-1903. Amwell Ridge Cemetery, Larisons Corner, Hunterdon County.

HENRY*, GEORGE Seaman, U.S. Navy, USS Mohican, 10-28-1915. Christ Church Cemetery, Morgan, Middlesex County.

HENRY, GEORGE S. (aka: George, Henry) Pvt, A, 73rd NY Inf, 1914. Soldier's Home Cemetery, Vineland, Cumberland County.

HENRY, ISAAC C. Musc, D, 5th NJ Inf, 1-10-1925. Fairmount Cemetery, Newark, Essex County.

HENRY, JACOB 6-3-1913. Cedar Lawn Cemetery, Paterson, Passaic County.

HENRY, JACOB S. 12-11-1912. Evergreen Cemetery, Camden, Camden County.

HENRY, JAMES DoD Unknown. Colestown Cemetery, Cherry Hill, Camden County.

HENRY, JAMES WILLIAM Sgt, E, 185th NY Inf, 4-22-1905. Hoboken Cemetery, North Bergen, Hudson County.

HENRY, JESSE Pvt, D, 174th PA Inf, 8-30-1897. St. Peter's Cemetery, New Brunswick, Middlesex County.

HENRY, JOHN Pvt, C, 39th NJ Inf, 6-12-1909. Arlington Cemetery, Pennsauken, Camden County.

HENRY*, JOHN R. Pvt, I, 2nd NJ Inf, 12-2-1882. Rural Hill Cemetery, Whitehouse, Hunterdon County.

HENRY, JONATHAN C. Pvt, A, 30th NJ Inf, 1908. New Somerville Cemetery, Somerville, Somerset County.

HENRY, JOSEPH J. Capt, H, 9th NJ Inf, [Killed in action at Roanoke Island, NC. (First NJ officer killed in the Civil War.)] 2-8-1862. Belvidere/Catholic Cemetery, Belvidere, Warren County.

HENRY, JOSIAH Pvt, D, 9th U.S. CT, 11-25-1881. Mount Zion Cemetery, Kresson, Camden County.

HENRY, OLIVER Pvt, K, 31st NJ Inf, 1908. Pleasant Hill Cemetery, Pleasant Hill, Morris County.

HENRY, PRINCE DoD Unknown. Mount Pisgah Cemetery, Elsinboro, Salem County.

HENRY, ROBERT L. 2nd Lt, A, 1st NJ Cav, 11-12-1933. Union Cemetery, Frenchtown, Hunterdon County.

HENRY, S.M. Pvt, H, 27th GA Inf (CSA), 7-9-1862. Finn's Point National Cemetery, Pennsville, Salem County.

HENRY, SAMUEL Seaman, U.S. Navy, USS Princeton, 3-9-1909. Evergreen Cemetery, Camden, Camden County.

HENRY, SAMUEL Pvt, K, 35th NJ Inf, 1869. Mount Pleasant Cemetery, Newark, Essex County.

HENRY, THOMAS (aka: Huss, Thomas) Pvt, A, 5th MO Inf (CSA), 9-4-1863. Finn's Point National Cemetery, Pennsville, Salem County.

HENRY, THOMAS S. 3-17-1934. Mount Pleasant Cemetery, Newark, Essex County.

HENRY*, WALTER M. Corp, F, 1st NJ Inf, 2-1-1908. Van Liew Cemetery, North Brunswick, Middlesex County.

HENRY, WILLIAM Pvt, F, 22nd NJ Inf, 1-27-1868. Cedar Hill Cemetery, Hightstown, Mercer County.

HENRY, WILLIAM Pvt, C, 14th NJ Inf, [Wounded in action.] 4-26-1906. Evergreen Cemetery, Hillside, Union County.

HENRY, WILLIAM A. Bvt Col, 35th NJ Inf 1-8-1868. Fairmount Cemetery, Newark, Essex County.

HENRY, WILLIAM (JR.) Lt Col, 1st NJ Inf 3-16-1889. Belvidere/Catholic Cemetery, Belvidere, Warren County.

HENSCHALL, OTTO W. Com Sgt, M, 16th NY Cav, 5-26-1902. Hoboken Cemetery, North Bergen, Hudson County.

Our Brothers Gone Before

HENSCHKEL, FREDERICK Pvt, Btty A, 1st NJ Light Art, 8-1-1910. Fairmount Cemetery, Newark, Essex County.
HENSE, FRANK Pvt, I, 1st GA Inf (CSA), 7-25-1862. Finn's Point National Cemetery, Pennsville, Salem County.
HENSEL, VALENTINE (see: Hendzel, Valentine) New Somerville Cemetery, Somerville, Somerset County.
HENSHAW, BENJAMIN FRANKLIN Pvt, A, 42nd __ Inf, 11-18-1917. Greenmount Cemetery, Hammonton, Atlantic County.
HENSLEY, FRANCIS Pvt, H, 48th VA Inf (CSA), [Captured 7-3-1863 at Gettysburg, PA. Died of typhoid] 11-19-1863. Finn's Point National Cemetery, Pennsville, Salem County.
HENSLEY, WILLIAM J. Pvt, B, 4th NC Cav (CSA), [Captured 7-4-1863 at South Mountain, MD.] 10-6-1863. Finn's Point National Cemetery, Pennsville, Salem County.
HENSON, HENRY Pvt, K, 8th U.S. CT, 1-22-1909. Spencer African Methodist Church Cemetery, Woodstown, Salem County.
HENTHORNE*, ISAAC Pvt, B, 162nd NY Inf, 12-1-1906. St. Stephen's Cemetery, Millburn, Essex County.
HENYON, HENRY H. Pvt, K, 1st NJ Cav, 10-28-1900. Presbyterian Church Cemetery, Sparta, Sussex County.
HENYON, PETER (see: Hennion, Peter) Presbyterian Church Cemetery, Sparta, Sussex County.
HENYON, WILLIAM (see: Hennion, William) United Methodist Church Cemetery, Millbrook, Morris County.
HEPPARD, JOHN Sgt, A, 46th OH Inf, [Wounded 4-6-1862 at Shiloh, TN.] 7-21-1895. Eglington Cemetery, Clarksboro, Gloucester County.
HEPPENHEIMER, FREDERICK Capt, F, 5th NY State Militia, 4-20-1878. Hoboken Cemetery, North Bergen, Hudson County.
HEPPENSTILL, WILLIAM G. 1st Sgt, A, 99th NY Inf, [Wounded 5-1-1863 at South Quay Bridge, VA.] DoD Unknown. St. Mary's Cemetery, Perth Amboy, Middlesex County.
HERA, JAMES WILSON Pvt, Btty K, 1st U.S. Art, 1931. Methodist-Episcopal Church Cemetery, Aura, Gloucester County.
HERAN, E. (see: Herne, Elisha) Finn's Point National Cemetery, Pennsville, Salem County.
HERBERT, AARON IRVINS 1st Sgt, D, 23rd NJ Inf, 12-12-1909. Mercer Cemetery, Trenton, Mercer County.
HERBERT, ABRAHAM A. 10-9-1919. Glenwood Cemetery, West Long Branch, Monmouth County.
HERBERT, ABRAM A. Pvt, D, 34th NJ Inf, [Wounded in action.] 1915. Old Methodist Cemetery, Point Pleasant, Ocean County.
HERBERT, BENJAMIN (see: Herbert, Franklin) Mount Prospect Cemetery, Neptune, Monmouth County.
HERBERT, BENJAMIN F. Pvt, D, 34th NJ Inf, 2-26-1911. Tennent Church Cemetery, Tennent, Monmouth County.
HERBERT*, DAVID Corp, F, 8th NJ Inf, 8-13-1923. Bordentown/Old St. Mary's Catholic Cemetery, Bordentown, Burlington County.
HERBERT, FRANKLIN (aka: Herbert, Benjamin) Pvt, D, 34th NJ Inf, 1940. Mount Prospect Cemetery, Neptune, Monmouth County.
HERBERT, GEORGE Pvt, B, 29th NJ Inf, 1-16-1912. Maplewood Cemetery, Freehold, Monmouth County.
HERBERT, GEORGE 1895. Clinton Cemetery, Irvington, Essex County.
HERBERT, GEORGE W. Pvt, B, 23rd NJ Inf, 7-8-1922. Bordentown/Old St. Mary's Catholic Cemetery, Bordentown, Burlington County.

New Jersey Civil War Burials

HERBERT, GIDEON Pvt, F, 4th DE Inf, 4-24-1914. Evergreen Cemetery, Camden, Camden County.

HERBERT, HARRY (see: Herbert, Henry) Columbus Cemetery, Columbus, Burlington County.

HERBERT*, HENRY (aka: Herbert, Harry) Pvt, E, 14th NJ Inf, 12-19-1914. Columbus Cemetery, Columbus, Burlington County.

HERBERT, JACOB V.W. Paymaster, U.S. Volunteers, 6-9-1899. New Presbyterian Cemetery, Bound Brook, Somerset County.

HERBERT*, JAMES Pvt, F, 14th NJ Inf, DoD Unknown. Fairview Cemetery, Fairview, Monmouth County.

HERBERT, JAMES D. Pvt, G, 3rd NJ Militia, DoD Unknown. Tennent Church Cemetery, Tennent, Monmouth County.

HERBERT, JAMES H. Artificer, E, 1st NY Eng, DoD Unknown. Old 1st Methodist Church Cemetery, West Long Branch, Monmouth County.

HERBERT*, JOHN Pvt, E, 14th NJ Inf, 9-4-1906. Columbus Cemetery, Columbus, Burlington County.

HERBERT, JOHN Pvt, A, 119th PA Inf, DoD Unknown. Evergreen Cemetery, Camden, Camden County.

HERBERT, JOHN B. Pvt, B, 23rd NJ Inf, 5-31-1883. Bordentown/Old St. Mary's Catholic Cemetery, Bordentown, Burlington County.

HERBERT, JOHN OSBORN Pvt, 28th NY Ind Btty 1931. Atlantic View Cemetery, Manasquan, Monmouth County.

HERBERT, JOHN W. (aka: Harper, John W.) Pvt, K, 10th TN Cav, 10-28-1894. Bordentown/Old St. Mary's Catholic Cemetery, Bordentown, Burlington County.

HERBERT*, JOSEPH Pvt, F, 8th NJ Inf, 10-27-1923. Bordentown/Old St. Mary's Catholic Cemetery, Bordentown, Burlington County.

HERBERT, JOSEPH Pvt, G, 8th NJ Inf, 1-1-1921. Whitelawn Cemetery, Point Pleasant, Ocean County.

HERBERT, JOSIAH DoD Unknown. Old 1st Methodist Church Cemetery, West Long Branch, Monmouth County.

HERBERT*, LOUIS Pvt, F, 14th NJ Inf, 1-26-1892. Whitelawn Cemetery, Point Pleasant, Ocean County.

HERBERT, ROBERT Landsman, U.S. Navy, 7-8-1902. Fairmount Cemetery, Newark, Essex County.

HERBERT, THEODORE C. Sailmaker, U.S. Navy, USS Congress, 7-4-1890. Monument Cemetery, Edgewater Park, Burlington County.

HERBERT, THOMAS 3-9-1873. Evergreen Cemetery, Camden, Camden County.

HERBERT, THOMAS G. (aka: Harbut, Thomas) Corp, H, 57th NY Inf, 2-26-1891. Mount Holly Cemetery, Mount Holly, Burlington County.

HERBERT, WILLIAM Pvt, I, 33rd NJ Inf, 2-11-1914. Riverside Cemetery, Toms River, Ocean County.

HERBERT, WILLIAM 7-23-1903. Old 1st Methodist Church Cemetery, West Long Branch, Monmouth County.

HERBERT, WILLIAM D. DoD Unknown. Tennent Church Cemetery, Tennent, Monmouth County.

HERBERT*, WILLIAM H.H. Pvt, D, 34th NJ Inf, [Wounded in action.] 10-4-1911. Allenwood Church Cemetery, Allenwood, Monmouth County.

HERBERT, WILLIAM S. Pvt, I, 4th NJ Inf, 2-3-1878. Methodist Church Cemetery, Groveville, Mercer County.

HERBIG, MARCUS Pvt, Btty G, 1st NY Light Art, 7-4-1912. Arlington Cemetery, Kearny, Hudson County.

HERDE, FRANZ JOSEPH (aka: Herte, Francis) Pvt, F, 62nd NY Inf, 10-21-1915. Bayview-New York Bay Cemetery, Jersey City, Hudson County.

Our Brothers Gone Before

HERDMAN*, JOHN Pvt, D, 2nd NJ Inf, 2-6-1912. Fairmount Cemetery, Newark, Essex County.

HERHLE, AUGUST 5-28-1914. Macphelah Cemetery, North Bergen, Hudson County.

HERIG, RUDOLPH Pvt, G, 20th NY Inf, 3-2-1917. Cedar Lawn Cemetery, Paterson, Passaic County.

HERING, HENRY (aka: Heneman, Henry) Pvt, E, 3rd NJ Cav, 1903. Riverview Cemetery, Trenton, Mercer County.

HERING, JOHN F. (aka: Harring, John F.) Corp, D, 22nd NJ Inf, 11-18-1911. Old Hook Cemetery, Westwood, Bergen County.

HERING, MAURICE 10-21-1932. Fairview Cemetery, Wantage, Sussex County.

HERITAGE, GILBERT R. Sgt, B, 24th NJ Inf, DoD Unknown. Mount Pleasant Cemetery, Millville, Cumberland County.

HERITAGE, ISAAC Corp, K, 38th NJ Inf, [Wounded in action.] 9-15-1870. 1st Baptist Cemetery, Cape May Court House, Cape May County.

HERITAGE, JOB Pvt, C, 9th NJ Inf, 9-9-1920. Evergreen Cemetery, Camden, Camden County.

HERITAGE, JOHN DOWN Asst Surg, 11th NJ Inf 1918. Methodist Church Cemetery, Hurffville, Gloucester County.

HERITAGE, WILLIAM H. Pvt, K, 38th NJ Inf, 11-3-1933. Fairview Cemetery, Cape May Court House, Cape May County.

HERLIN, JAMES (see: Haviland, James J.) Fairmount Cemetery, Newark, Essex County.

HERLING, MARTIN (aka: Hurling, Martin) Pvt, A, 41st U.S. CT, 11-13-1907. Hillside Cemetery, Scotch Plains, Union County.

HERMAN, CONSTANT (see: Heenan, Constant) Old Hook Cemetery, Westwood, Bergen County.

HERMAN, EMIL O. Musc, E, 2nd NJ Inf, 2-21-1923. Fairmount Cemetery, Newark, Essex County.

HERMAN, HENRY Pvt, F, 8th NJ Inf, 3-15-1914. Presbyterian Church Cemetery, Harmony, Warren County.

HERMAN, JACOB (see: Herrmann, Jacob F.) Fairmount Cemetery, Newark, Essex County.

HERMAN, JOSEPH Pvt, K, 35th NJ Inf, 1882. Berry Lawn Cemetery, Carlstadt, Bergen County.

HERMAN, THOMAS N. Pvt, L, 7th PA Cav, 1913. Alpine Cemetery, Perth Amboy, Middlesex County.

HERMANCE, JAMES M. Pvt, C, 3rd CT Inf, 7-21-1923. Fairmount Cemetery, Newark, Essex County.

HERMANN, AUGUST Pvt, Btty E, 1st NJ Light Art, 5-21-1888. Fairmount Cemetery, Newark, Essex County.

HERMANN, CHARLES Fireman, U.S. Navy, USS Princeton, 10-10-1911. Methodist-Episcopal Church Cemetery, South Dennis, Cape May County.

HERMES, MICHAEL Pvt, C, 30th NJ Inf, 5-29-1913. Rahway Cemetery, Rahway, Union County.

HERMES*, PETER Pvt, A, 9th NJ Inf, 10-16-1917. Phillipsburg Cemetery, Phillipsburg, Warren County.

HERN, HANDY Sgt, F, 43rd U.S. CT, 5-21-1896. Presbyterian Cemetery, Woodbury, Gloucester County.

HERNDON, HANSFORD Pvt, F, 5th FL Inf (CSA), [Wounded 9-17-1862 at Antietam, MD and 5-3-1863 at Chancellorsville, VA. Wounded and captured 7-3-1863 at Gettysburg, PA.] 1-27-1864. Finn's Point National Cemetery, Pennsville, Salem County.

HERNE, ELISHA (aka: Heran, E.) Pvt, G, 15th LA Inf (CSA), [Captured 7-3-1863 at Gettysburg, PA.] 9-19-1863. Finn's Point National Cemetery, Pennsville, Salem County.

New Jersey Civil War Burials

HERNING, JOHN (see: Hennings, John) Berry Lawn Cemetery, Carlstadt, Bergen County.

HEROLD, F. A. (see: Harold, Louis F.A.) Woodland Cemetery, Newark, Essex County.

HERON, EDWARD DEVERE 4-1-1870. Evergreen/Bishop Jaynes Cemetery, Basking Ridge, Somerset County.

HERPST, KARL (aka: Halps, Charles) Pvt, A, 35th NJ Inf, 11-3-1885. Woodland Cemetery, Newark, Essex County.

HERREN, WILLIAM Pvt, H, 35th GA Inf (CSA), [Captured 7-1-1863 at Gettysburg, PA. Died of lung inflammation.] 7-19-1863. Finn's Point National Cemetery, Pennsville, Salem County.

HERRICK*, BENJAMIN F. Pvt, F, 3rd NY Inf, DoD Unknown. Newton Cemetery, Newton, Sussex County.

HERRICK, WILLIAM H. 1st Sgt, F, 3rd NY Inf, 6-10-1907. Rosehill Cemetery, Linden, Union County.

HERRIN, JOHN Pvt, Btty A, Schaffer's Ind PA Heavy Art, [Died at Fort Delaware.] 1-12-1864. Finn's Point National Cemetery, Pennsville, Salem County.

HERRING, ABRAHAM (see: Haring, Abraham P.) Haring Cemetery, Old Tappan, Bergen County.

HERRING, ANTONE (see: Haering, Martin Antoine) Oak Hill Cemetery, Vineland, Cumberland County.

HERRING, DANIEL (see: Haring, Daniel J.) Valleau Cemetery, Ridgewood, Bergen County.

HERRING, HENRY J. (aka: Harring, Henry) Pvt, I, 22nd NJ Inf, 2-15-1934. Pascack Reformed Cemetery, Park Ridge, Bergen County.

HERRING, JACOB C. Corp, I, 22nd NJ Inf, 10-24-1900. Woodside Cemetery, Dumont, Bergen County.

HERRING, JOHN (see: Haring, John P.) Pascack Reformed Cemetery, Park Ridge, Bergen County.

HERRING, LEWIS Pvt, F, 26th NJ Inf, 3-5-1918. Bloomfield Cemetery, Bloomfield, Essex County.

HERRING, NEWTON J. (aka: Hening, Newton I.) Sgt, A, 16th GA Inf (CSA), [Captured 7-5-1863 at Gettysburg, PA. Died of disease.] 11-17-1863. Finn's Point National Cemetery, Pennsville, Salem County.

HERRING, RICHARD N. 2nd Lt, I, 10th NJ Inf, 4-18-1896. St. John's Episcopal Church Cemetery, Chews Landing, Camden County.

HERRING, WALTER Pvt, H, 30th NJ Inf, 8-1-1880. Presbyterian Cemetery, North Plainfield, Somerset County.

HERRING, WILLIAM C. Sgt, I, 22nd NJ Inf, 7-25-1917. Haring Cemetery, Old Tappan, Bergen County.

HERRMAN, AMBROSE Pvt, H, 41st NY Inf, 5-24-1888. Fairmount Cemetery, Newark, Essex County.

HERRMAN, CHARLES D. Capt, C, 131st OH Inf, 1909. Vincent Methodist-Episcopal Cemetery, Nutley, Essex County.

HERRMAN, JOHN Pvt, E, 30th NJ Inf, 1-7-1910. New Presbyterian Cemetery, Bound Brook, Somerset County.

HERRMAN*, JOHN C. Sgt, I, 7th NJ Inf, 10-21-1889. Riverview Cemetery, Trenton, Mercer County.

HERRMANN, AUGUST Pvt, C, 20th NY Inf, [Wounded 9-17-1862 at Antietam, MD.] 5-18-1922. Fairmount Cemetery, Newark, Essex County.

HERRMANN, FERDINAND Capt, D, 58th NY Inf, 10-21-1877. Hoboken Cemetery, North Bergen, Hudson County.

HERRMANN, JACOB F. (aka: Herman, Jacob) Corp, G, 5th IL Cav, 3-19-1922. Fairmount Cemetery, Newark, Essex County.

Our Brothers Gone Before

HERRON, BERNARD (aka: O'Harron, Bernard) Corp, A, 192nd PA Inf, 10-11-1899. Bordentown/Old St. Mary's Catholic Cemetery, Bordentown, Burlington County.

HERRON, CHARLES Pvt, E, 39th NJ Inf, 10-11-1880. Holy Sepulchre Cemetery, East Orange, Essex County.

HERRON, JAMES Pvt, D, 6th NJ Inf, 10-22-1863. Cedar Grove Cemetery, Gloucester City, Camden County.

HERRON*, JOHN Pvt, E, 213th PA Inf, 2-8-1869. Cedar Grove Cemetery, Gloucester City, Camden County.

HERRON, MICHAEL Landsman, U.S. Navy, USS Naiad, 1-26-1917. Bordentown/Old St. Mary's Catholic Cemetery, Bordentown, Burlington County.

HERRON, WILLIAM REEP Corp, B, 28th NJ Inf, [Died of wounds received 12-13-1862 at Fredericksburg, VA.] 1-4-1863. Brainerd Cemetery, Cranbury, Middlesex County.

HERSEY, SAMUEL E. Pvt, E, 54th MA Inf, 2-20-1908. Mount Pisgah Cemetery, Elsinboro, Salem County.

HERT*, CHARLES H. Pvt, H, 7th NJ Inf, 5-2-1927. Methodist-Episcopal Cemetery, Lake, Gloucester County.

HERTE, FRANCIS (see: Herde, Franz Joseph) Bayview-New York Bay Cemetery, Jersey City, Hudson County.

HERTEL, FERDINAND Pvt, Btty A, 1st NJ Light Art, 1-8-1890. Palisade Cemetery, North Bergen, Hudson County.

HERTENSTEIN, CHRISTIAN Pvt, I, 3rd NJ Cav, 2-19-1913. Fairmount Cemetery, Newark, Essex County.

HERTZBERG, FRIEDRICH (see: Herzberg, Frederick) Palisade Cemetery, North Bergen, Hudson County.

HERTZEL, PETER 6-10-1906. St. James Lutheran Church Cemetery, Folsom, Atlantic County.

HERTZMAN, JOHN 1888. Riverview Cemetery, Trenton, Mercer County.

HERTZOG, PAUL T. Seaman, U.S. Navy, 5-22-1929. Fairmount Cemetery, Newark, Essex County.

HERVEY*, DANIEL EDWARD Coal Heaver, U.S. Navy, USS Portsmouth, 12-26-1914. Christ Church Cemetery, Belleville, Essex County.

HERZBERG, FREDERICK (aka: Hertzberg, Friedrich) 1st Lt, E, 66th NY Inf, 2-16-1884. Palisade Cemetery, North Bergen, Hudson County.

HERZINGER*, ADAM (aka: Harciger, Adam) Sgt, E, 39th NJ Inf, 3-30-1904. Woodland Cemetery, Newark, Essex County.

HERZOG, CHRISTIAN Pvt, K, 2nd NJ Inf, 11-20-1916. Arlington Cemetery, Kearny, Hudson County.

HESLEY, JACOB (aka: Healey, Jacob) Pvt, C, 9th NJ Inf, 12-25-1889. Christ Episcopal Church Cemetery, Bordentown, Burlington County.

HESS, CASPAR Pvt, G, 4th (old) MD Inf, 8-12-1863. Finn's Point National Cemetery, Pennsville, Salem County.

HESS, CHARLES (see: Hesse, Christian) Clinton Cemetery, Irvington, Essex County.

HESS, CHRISTIAN Pvt, Btty A, 2nd PA Heavy Art, 5-9-1885. Old Camden Cemetery, Camden, Camden County.

HESS, DAYTON L.V. Pvt, C, 38th NJ Inf, 1914. United Methodist Church Cemetery, Cumberland, Cumberland County.

HESS, EDWARD KNIGHT Sgt, F, 150th PA Inf, [Wounded 7-1-1863 at Gettysburg, PA.] 10-28-1910. Methodist Church Cemetery, Hurffville, Gloucester County.

HESS, EDWIN C. Pvt, E, 202nd PA Inf, 4-27-1906. Evergreen Cemetery, Camden, Camden County.

HESS, JACOB Pvt, H, 1st PA Mtd Inf, 5-27-1914. Methodist Church Cemetery, Groveville, Mercer County.

New Jersey Civil War Burials

HESS, JOHN L. Pvt, B, 24th NJ Inf, 1-4-1918. Methodist Church Cemetery, Seaville, Cape May County.

HESS, PETER Pvt, Unassigned, 8th NJ Inf, 2-9-1899. Fairmount Cemetery, Newark, Essex County.

HESS, SAMUEL Pvt, B, 24th NJ Inf, 1930. Greenwood Cemetery, Millville, Cumberland County.

HESS, STEPHEN G. Pvt, C, 38th WI Inf, [Died of disease.] 8-30-1864. Beverly National Cemetery, Edgewater Park, Burlington County.

HESS, WILLIAM Corp, D, 2nd NJ Militia, 9-1-1898. Tennent Church Cemetery, Tennent, Monmouth County.

HESSDORFER, JOSEPH Corp, C, 33rd NJ Inf, 9-9-1910. Mount Olivet Cemetery, Bloomfield, Essex County.

HESSE, CHRISTIAN (aka: Hess, Charles) Pvt, G, 4th NY Inf, [Missing in action at Fredericksburg, VA. Supposed killed.] 12-13-1862. Clinton Cemetery, Irvington, Essex County.

HESSELL*, JOHN Ordinary Seaman, U.S. Navy, USS Arkansas, 4-30-1890. Hillside Cemetery, Oxford, Warren County.

HESSER, JOHN W. Pvt, A, 129th PA Inf, 3-16-1913. Harleigh Cemetery, Camden, Camden County.

HESSEY, GEORGE Musc, 7th NJ Inf Band 1928. Boonton Cemetery, Boonton, Morris County.

HESSEY, WILLIAM Chief Bugler, 2nd NJ Cav 11-19-1931. Evergreen Cemetery, Morristown, Morris County.

HESTER, DAVID DoD Unknown. 1st Baptist Cemetery, Cape May Court House, Cape May County.

HESTER, GOODMAN W. Pvt, H, 3rd MS Inf (CSA), 6-14-1863. Finn's Point National Cemetery, Pennsville, Salem County.

HESTER, JOHN W. Pvt, B, 198th PA Inf, 2-27-1909. Greenwood Cemetery, Hamilton, Mercer County.

HESTER, ROBERT U.O. 6-28-1886. Mercer Cemetery, Trenton, Mercer County.

HESTER, RUFUS Pvt, C, 7th TN Inf (CSA), 12-28-1863. Finn's Point National Cemetery, Pennsville, Salem County.

HESTER, WILLIAM FLANIGAN (aka: Flanigan, William) Pvt, K, 15th NJ Inf, 6-12-1912. St. Peter's Cemetery, New Brunswick, Middlesex County.

HESTON, JOHN L. 4-20-1924. Old Camden Cemetery, Camden, Camden County.

HESTONBRITTLE*, DEIDRITCH (aka: Histanbrittle, Dedrick) Pvt, I, 140th NY Inf, 4-26-1875. Fairmount Cemetery, Newark, Essex County.

HETFIELD, DAVID B. Pvt, B, 30th NJ Inf, 7-19-1911. Hazelwood Cemetery, Rahway, Union County.

HETFIELD, SAMUEL I. Pvt, B, 30th NJ Inf, 12-23-1897. Rahway Cemetery, Rahway, Union County.

HETHERINGTON*, JOSEPH S. Pvt, F, 42nd MA Inf, 11-26-1921. Elmwood Cemetery, New Brunswick, Middlesex County.

HETRICK, JOEL W. Corp, K, 22nd OH Inf, 8-27-1899. Mount Prospect Cemetery, Neptune, Monmouth County.

HETTINGER, J. WILLIAM Pvt, Btty K, 5th NY Heavy Art, 9-21-1899. Beverly National Cemetery, Edgewater Park, Burlington County.

HETZEL, JACOB Pvt, H, 2nd DC Inf, 2-15-1897. Fairmount Cemetery, Newark, Essex County.

HETZEL, JACOB N. Pvt, D, 13th NJ Inf, 8-8-1907. Greenwood Cemetery, Hamilton, Mercer County.

HETZELL, CHARLES E. Pvt, A, 38th NJ Inf, 2-26-1914. United Methodist Church Cemetery, Upper Deerfield, Cumberland County.

Our Brothers Gone Before

HEUBEL, ALBERT Capt, H, 186th PA Inf, 10-6-1883. Evergreen Cemetery, Camden, Camden County.

HEULINGS, WILLIAM H.H. Pvt, A, 10th NJ Inf, 6-18-1891. Colestown Cemetery, Cherry Hill, Camden County.

HEULITT, THOMAS Pvt, K, 29th NJ Inf, 6-24-1894. Atlantic View Cemetery, Manasquan, Monmouth County.

HEURER, WILLIAM S. Pvt, H, 5th KY Inf, 5-9-1905. Presbyterian Church Cemetery, Cold Spring, Cape May County.

HEVENER, ROBERT Pvt, B, 51st NY Inf, [Wounded 5-12-1864 at Spotsylvania CH, VA.] 6-17-1891. Fairmount Cemetery, Newark, Essex County.

HEVEY, FRANCIS 1st Sgt, C, 170th NY Inf, 12-16-1898. Holy Sepulchre Cemetery, East Orange, Essex County.

HEWARD, FRANCIS Pvt, F, 1st NJ Inf, [Died at Alexandria, VA.] 4-15-1862. Elmwood Cemetery, New Brunswick, Middlesex County.

HEWARD, JOHN J. Corp, G, 3rd NJ Militia, 3-26-1888. Cedar Hill Cemetery, Hightstown, Mercer County.

HEWELL, PHILIP W. Pvt, H, 38th GA Inf (CSA), [Captured 7-3-1863 at Gettysburg, PA. Died of smallpox.] 11-16-1863. Finn's Point National Cemetery, Pennsville, Salem County.

HEWES, BENJAMIN B. Pvt, C, 38th NJ Inf, 1926. St. John's Methodist Church Cemetery, Harrisonville, Gloucester County.

HEWES, CHARLES A. Pvt, I, 6th ME Inf, 1926. Soldier's Home Cemetery, Vineland, Cumberland County.

HEWES, FLETCHER WILLIS 1st Lt, D, 10th MI Inf, 2-19-1911. Bloomfield Cemetery, Bloomfield, Essex County.

HEWES, SAMUEL A. (aka: Haws, Samuel) Pvt, B, 1st PA Cav, [Killed in action at Hawe's Shop, VA.] 5-28-1864. New Episcopal Church Cemetery, Swedesboro, Gloucester County.

HEWETT, ANTHONY B. Pvt, Btty E, 1st NJ Light Art, 11-11-1907. Baptist Church Cemetery, Canton, Salem County.

HEWETT, GEORGE Pvt, D, 2nd NJ Cav, 5-12-1920. Union Cemetery, Gloucester City, Camden County.

HEWITT, AARON Pvt, I, 25th NJ Inf, 5-13-1876. 1st Baptist Cemetery, Cape May Court House, Cape May County.

HEWITT*, BENJAMIN W. Pvt, C, 12th NJ Inf, [Wounded in action.] 7-3-1904. Eglington Cemetery, Clarksboro, Gloucester County.

HEWITT, CLARK Pvt, K, 23rd NJ Inf, 1919. Salem Cemetery, Pleasantville, Atlantic County.

HEWITT, DAVID Pvt, K, 23rd NJ Inf, 12-10-1864. St. Paul's Methodist Church Cemetery, Port Republic, Atlantic County.

HEWITT, ELMER Pvt, Btty E, 1st NJ Light Art, 5-2-1897. 7th Day Baptist Church Cemetery, Marlboro, Salem County.

HEWITT, FRANKLIN Pvt, H, 34th NJ Inf, 3-1-1922. Union Cemetery, Gloucester City, Camden County.

HEWITT, FREELING F. Pvt, I, 25th NJ Inf, 1923. 1st Baptist Cemetery, Cape May Court House, Cape May County.

HEWITT, GEORGE Pvt, I, 25th NJ Inf, 3-9-1888. 1st Baptist Cemetery, Cape May Court House, Cape May County.

HEWITT, GEORGE T. 2-27-1894. Evergreen Cemetery, Camden, Camden County.

HEWITT, GEORGE W. Pvt, C, 34th NJ Inf, 9-7-1908. Oddfellows-Friends Cemetery, Medford, Burlington County.

HEWITT, GIDEON R. Sgt, K, 16th NY Inf, 12-15-1869. Presbyterian Church Cemetery, Millbrook, Morris County.

New Jersey Civil War Burials

HEWITT*, HENRY Seaman, U.S. Navy, USS Colorado, DoD Unknown. New 1st Methodist Meeting House Cemetery, Manahawkin, Ocean County.

HEWITT, JESSE Pvt, C, 199th PA Inf, 5-24-1936. Laurel Memorial Cemetery, Upper Deerfield, Cumberland County.

HEWITT, JOHN Corp, C, 34th NJ Inf, 2-3-1871. Baptist/St. Andrew's Cemetery, Mount Holly, Burlington County.

HEWITT, JOHN Pvt, I, 25th NJ Inf, DoD Unknown. 1st Baptist Cemetery, Cape May Court House, Cape May County.

HEWITT, JOHN E. Pvt, G, 21st NJ Inf, 1-24-1901. Holy Name Cemetery, Jersey City, Hudson County.

HEWITT, JOSEPH Pvt, K, 4th NJ Inf, 1-28-1898. Presbyterian Church Cemetery, Bridgeton, Cumberland County.

HEWITT*, RICHARD Sgt, G, 8th NJ Inf, 5-15-1876. Fairmount Cemetery, Newark, Essex County.

HEWITT, ROBERT C. 4-14-1906. Bayview-New York Bay Cemetery, Jersey City, Hudson County.

HEWITT, SAMUEL Pvt, H, 4th PA Cav, 11-16-1893. Old St. Thomas Cemetery, Glassboro, Gloucester County.

HEWITT, WESLEY Corp, A, 5th PA Cav, 1911. 1st Baptist Church Cemetery, Pedricktown, Salem County.

HEWITT, WILLIAM Pvt, A, 12th NJ Inf, 8-24-1894. Oddfellows-Friends Cemetery, Medford, Burlington County.

HEWITT, WILLIAM DoD Unknown. Union Cemetery, Mantua, Gloucester County.

HEWITT, WILLIAM N. 12-1-1913. Harleigh Cemetery, Camden, Camden County.

HEWITT, WILLIAM N. 1st Sgt, E, 24th NJ Inf, DoD Unknown. Presbyterian Church Cemetery, Bridgeton, Cumberland County.

HEWLETT, REUBEN (see: Hulit, Reuben V.) Highland Cemetery, Hopewell Boro, Mercer County.

HEWLINGS, JOHN Pvt, H, 12th NJ Inf, [Died of heart disease at Washington, DC.] 12-22-1863. St. Paul's United Methodist Church Cemetery, Paulsboro, Gloucester County.

HEWLINGS*, PETER D. Pvt, H, 12th NJ Inf, DoD Unknown. Cedar Grove Cemetery, Gloucester City, Camden County.

HEWS, JAMES E. Pvt, I, 25th NJ Inf, DoD Unknown. Old Camden Cemetery, Camden, Camden County.

HEXAMER, WILLIAM Capt, Btty A, 1st NJ Light Art, 6-8-1870. Grove Church Cemetery, North Bergen, Hudson County.

HEYER, JOHN A. Pvt, G, 29th NJ Inf, 5-1-1917. Old 1st Methodist Church Cemetery, West Long Branch, Monmouth County.

HEYER, JOHN HENRY Capt, G, 29th NJ Inf, 5-6-1905. Holmdel Cemetery, Holmdel, Monmouth County.

HEYER, PETER V. Pvt, G, 29th NJ Inf, 3-13-1899. Holmdel Cemetery, Holmdel, Monmouth County.

HEYER, WILLIAM DANIEL 1st Sgt, I, 18th LA Inf (CSA), 2-5-1916. Woodland Cemetery, Newark, Essex County.

HEYERS, GILBERT H. (see: Hyers, Gilbert H.) Riverside Cemetery, Toms River, Ocean County.

HEYL, FREDERICK Pvt, Btty A, 1st NJ Light Art, 11-16-1903. Van Liew Cemetery, North Brunswick, Middlesex County.

HEYLER, ROBERT DoD Unknown. Stanhope-Union Cemetery, Netcong, Morris County.

HIBBETTS, PETER S. Pvt, G, 22nd NJ Inf, DoD Unknown. Princeton Cemetery, Princeton, Mercer County.

HIBBLER, JACOB Pvt, D, 15th NJ Inf, 11-13-1880. Fairmount Cemetery, Newark, Essex County.

Our Brothers Gone Before

HIBBLER, WHITFIELD 1st Sgt, C, 2nd NY Cav, [Wounded in action.] 10-3-1930. Fairmount Cemetery, Newark, Essex County.
HIBBS*, ALBERTUS K. Pvt, E, 5th NJ Inf, 12-15-1896. Riverview Cemetery, Trenton, Mercer County.
HIBBS, JOHN Pvt, H, 23rd NJ Inf, 6-27-1914. Greenwood Cemetery, Hamilton, Mercer County.
HIBBS, JOSEPH Pvt, G, 30th NJ Inf, 1922. Union Cemetery, Ringoes, Hunterdon County.
HIBBS*, JOSEPH H. Pvt, A, 116th PA Inf, 9-15-1921. Riverview Cemetery, Trenton, Mercer County.
HIBBS, WILLIAM A. Pvt, D, 3rd NJ Militia, 1-1-1919. Riverview Cemetery, Trenton, Mercer County.
HIBLER, ANDREW H. Pvt, H, 31st NJ Inf, 1909. Pequest Union Cemetery, Great Meadows, Warren County.
HICE*, JAMES N. (aka: Hise, James N.) Sgt, K, 38th NJ Inf, 9-9-1896. Union Cemetery, Milford, Hunterdon County.
HICK, JOHN Seaman, U.S. Navy, 12-23-1892. Flower Hill Cemetery, North Bergen, Hudson County.
HICKEY, DANIEL JOHN Pvt, A, 69th PA Inf, 2-16-1920. St. Mary's Cemetery, Hamilton, Mercer County.
HICKEY, EDWARD Pvt, H, 22nd NJ Inf, 1-29-1904. Mount Carmel Cemetery, Tenafly, Bergen County.
HICKEY, JAMES Landsman, U.S. Navy, 3-4-1921. St. Peter's Cemetery, New Brunswick, Middlesex County.
HICKEY, JOHN Pvt, Btty B, 1st NJ Light Art, DoD Unknown. Holy Sepulchre Cemetery, East Orange, Essex County.
HICKEY, JOSEPH P. Pvt, C, 6th U.S. Cav, 1-12-1923. St. Mary's Cemetery, Hamilton, Mercer County.
HICKEY, PATRICK 2nd Lt, C, 33rd NJ Inf, 1918. St. Bridget's Cemetery, Glassboro, Gloucester County.
HICKEY, TERRANCE Seaman, U.S. Navy, 5-14-1892. St. Peter's Cemetery, New Brunswick, Middlesex County.
HICKEY, THOMAS Pvt, D, 28th NJ Inf, 2-21-1902. St. Gabriel's Cemetery, Bradevelt, Monmouth County.
HICKEY, THOMAS Pvt, F, 1st NJ Inf, DoD Unknown. St. Peter's Cemetery, New Brunswick, Middlesex County.
HICKEY, THOMAS C. Pvt, G, 1st TX Inf (CSA), [Captured 7-30-1863 at Hagerstown, MD. Died of acute dysentery.] 6-19-1864. Finn's Point National Cemetery, Pennsville, Salem County.
HICKMAN, D. THOMAS 3-4-1921. Evergreen Cemetery, Camden, Camden County.
HICKMAN, JAMES Pvt, E, 9th NJ Inf, 2-20-1884. Fairmount Cemetery, Newark, Essex County.
HICKMAN*, JEREMIAH R. Pvt, I, 8th NJ Inf, 12-15-1887. Fairmount Cemetery, Newark, Essex County.
HICKMAN, SAMUEL Pvt, G, 4th NJ Militia, 5-1-1926. Tennent Church Cemetery, Tennent, Monmouth County.
HICKMAN, SAMUEL G. Pvt, G, 99th PA Inf, 9-11-1895. Evergreen Cemetery, Camden, Camden County.
HICKMAN, THOMAS Pvt, E, 45th U.S. CT, 9-20-1900. Fairmount Cemetery, Newark, Essex County.
HICKMAN, THOMAS 12-20-1908. Bayview-New York Bay Cemetery, Jersey City, Hudson County.
HICKOK, WILLIAM (JR.) Pvt, L, 56th NY Inf, 1884. Clinton Cemetery, Irvington, Essex County.

New Jersey Civil War Burials

HICKS, ASHER N. Principal Musc, 8th NJ Inf 4-27-1895. Fairmount Cemetery, Newark, Essex County.
HICKS, CHARLES Seaman, U.S. Navy, USS James Adger, 11-15-1897. Fairmount Cemetery, Newark, Essex County.
HICKS, DAVID EUGENE Color Sgt, A, 15th NJ Inf, [Killed in action at Salem Heights, VA.] 5-3-1863. Presbyterian Cemetery, Asbury, Warren County.
HICKS, EDWARD Musc, D, 8th NJ Inf, 10-9-1929. Fairmount Cemetery, Newark, Essex County.
HICKS, EDWARD D. Musc, B, 8th NJ Inf, 12-31-1915. Jersey City Cemetery, Jersey City, Hudson County.
HICKS, GEORGE Musc, I, 8th NJ Inf, 4-29-1895. Fairmount Cemetery, Newark, Essex County.
HICKS, HENRY (see: Heck, Henry) Old Hook Cemetery, Westwood, Bergen County.
HICKS, JAMES E. Pvt, B, 126th NY Inf, [Wounded 9-15-1862 at Harpers Ferry, VA.] 6-19-1924. Overlook Cemetery, Bridgeton, Cumberland County.
HICKS, JOHN Pvt, D, 33rd NJ Inf, 2-16-1883. Holy Sepulchre Cemetery, Totowa, Passaic County.
HICKS, JOHN H. Pvt, F, 41st U.S. CT, 1917. Pinebrook Cemetery, Macedonia, Monmouth County.
HICKS, JOHN W. Sgt, E, 22nd U.S. CT, 5-10-1905. Greens Cemetery, Janvier, Gloucester County.
HICKS, JOSEPH SISCO Landsman, U.S. Navy, USS Atlanta, 7-9-1901. Alpine Cemetery, Perth Amboy, Middlesex County.
HICKS, PETER J. Pvt, G, 19th (Biffle's) TN Cav (CSA), 9-17-1864. Finn's Point National Cemetery, Pennsville, Salem County.
HICKS, QUIMBY Pvt, G, 26th NC Inf (CSA), [Captured 7-5-1863 at Gettysburg, PA.] 10-12-1863. Finn's Point National Cemetery, Pennsville, Salem County.
HICKS*, SAMUEL Pvt, E, 14th NJ Inf, 4-11-1914. Cedar Hill Cemetery, Hightstown, Mercer County.
HICKS, SAMUEL D. Pvt, Carter's Btty, VA Light Art (CSA), 3-14-1864. Finn's Point National Cemetery, Pennsville, Salem County.
HICKS, SHADRICK J. Pvt, E, 5th FL Inf (CSA), [Captured 7-2-1863 at Gettysburg, PA. Died of diarrhea.] 9-12-1863. Finn's Point National Cemetery, Pennsville, Salem County.
HICKS, WILLIAM Pvt, C, 4th TN Cav (CSA), 6-2-1864. Finn's Point National Cemetery, Pennsville, Salem County.
HICKS, WILLIAM 12-17-1908. Mount Pleasant Cemetery, Newark, Essex County.
HICKS, WILLIAM A. Pvt, H, 38th AL Inf (CSA), 12-30-1863. Finn's Point National Cemetery, Pennsville, Salem County.
HICKSON, WILLIAM Pvt, Btty G, 1st NY Light Art, [Wounded in action.] 10-10-1892. Mount Carmel Cemetery, Tenafly, Bergen County.
HIDER, ISAAC 1874. St. John's Episcopal Church Cemetery, Chews Landing, Camden County.
HIDER, WILLIAM Pvt, D, 9th NJ Inf, [Died of disease at Greensborough, NC.] 7-11-1865. 1st United Methodist Church Cemetery, Bridgeton, Cumberland County.
HIDMAN, HENRY (see: Heitman, Henry C.) Greengrove Cemetery, Keyport, Monmouth County.
HIEBER, JOSEPH A. 10-6-1910. Bayview-New York Bay Cemetery, Jersey City, Hudson County.
HIERS, HENRY Pvt, B, 29th NJ Inf, 10-13-1867. St. Joseph's Cemetery, Keyport, Monmouth County.
HIGBEE, DAVID 6-14-1913. Mount Prospect Cemetery, Neptune, Monmouth County.

Our Brothers Gone Before

HIGBEE, GEORGE L. Pvt, B, 8th NY State Militia, 12-17-1864. Rosedale Cemetery, Orange, Essex County.
HIGBEE, HENRY Pvt, E, 10th NJ Inf, 3-14-1902. Atlantic City Cemetery, Pleasantville, Atlantic County.
HIGBEE, HENRY H. 2nd Lt, H, 57th NY Inf, [Killed in action at Antietam, MD.] 9-17-1862. St. Mary's Episcopal Church Cemetery, Burlington, Burlington County.
HIGBEE, JAMES T. Pvt, K, 23rd NJ Inf, 8-23-1863. United Methodist Church Cemetery, Smithville, Atlantic County.
HIGBEE, JOSEPH S. Pvt, F, 25th NJ Inf, 1916. Mount Pleasant Cemetery, Millville, Cumberland County.
HIGBEE, WILLIAM L. Pvt, H, 26th NJ Inf, 10-14-1923. Rosedale Cemetery, Orange, Essex County.
HIGBID, EDWARD Sgt, I, 2nd NJ Inf, 5-5-1904. Cedar Lawn Cemetery, Paterson, Passaic County.
HIGBY, GEORGE W. Pvt, I, 123rd NY Inf, [Wounded 7-20-1864 at Peach Tree Creek, GA.] 4-14-1891. Fairmount Cemetery, Newark, Essex County.
HIGDON*, AMOS DANIEL Pvt, G, 5th Bttn FL Cav (CSA), 4-25-1864. Finn's Point National Cemetery, Pennsville, Salem County.
HIGGAMAN, AARON (see: Hagaman, Aaron) Riverview Cemetery, Trenton, Mercer County.
HIGGENBOTHAM, MARCUS (see: Higginbotham, Marcus) Bayview-New York Bay Cemetery, Jersey City, Hudson County.
HIGGENBOTTOM, WILLIAM Pvt, E, 71st NY Inf, 7-2-1890. Fairmount Cemetery, Newark, Essex County.
HIGGINBOTHAM, HENRY Pvt, Btty B, 2nd PA Heavy Art, 6-24-1924. Cedar Grove Cemetery, Gloucester City, Camden County.
HIGGINBOTHAM, MARCUS (aka: Higgenbotham, Marcus) 1st Lt, K, 12th NY National Guard, 8-13-1924. Bayview-New York Bay Cemetery, Jersey City, Hudson County.
HIGGINS, ALBERT F. Pvt, K, 99th PA Inf, [Wounded 4-6-1865 at Saylers Creek, VA.] 3-18-1922. Atlantic City Cemetery, Pleasantville, Atlantic County.
HIGGINS, BARTON G. Musc, F, 9th NJ Inf, 3-14-1907. Baptist Church Cemetery, Flemington, Hunterdon County.
HIGGINS, DAVID Pvt, K, 20th U.S. CT, 3-20-1883. Bethel AME Cemetery, Freehold, Monmouth County.
HIGGINS, EDWARD Musc, A, 26th NJ Inf, 6-12-1908. Holy Sepulchre Cemetery, East Orange, Essex County.
HIGGINS, EDWARD Pvt, D, 4th NJ Inf, DoD Unknown. Holy Name Cemetery, Jersey City, Hudson County.
HIGGINS, EDWARD (see: Costello, Edward) Holy Name Cemetery, Jersey City, Hudson County.
HIGGINS, FRANCIS H. Capt, B, 23rd NJ Inf, 11-2-1911. Bordentown/Old St. Mary's Catholic Cemetery, Bordentown, Burlington County.
HIGGINS, HENRY Pvt, I, 1st NJ Cav, [Died of pneumonia at Washington, DC.] 5-29-1864. St. Peter's Cemetery, New Brunswick, Middlesex County.
HIGGINS, ISRAEL (JR.) Pvt, F, 30th NJ Inf, DoD Unknown. Baptist Cemetery, Wertsville, Hunterdon County.
HIGGINS*, JAMES Sgt, E, 86th NY Inf, DoD Unknown. Holy Sepulchre Cemetery, East Orange, Essex County.
HIGGINS, JAMES Corp, B, 69th NY Inf, DoD Unknown. Holy Sepulchre Cemetery, Totowa, Passaic County.
HIGGINS*, JAMES Pvt, F, 7th NJ Inf, 10-25-1890. Dayton Cemetery, Dayton, Middlesex County.

New Jersey Civil War Burials

HIGGINS, JOHN QM Sgt, Btty B, 1st NJ Light Art, DoD Unknown. Holy Sepulchre Cemetery, East Orange, Essex County.

HIGGINS, JOHN Pvt, G, 38th NJ Inf, 9-12-1892. Dayton Cemetery, Dayton, Middlesex County.

HIGGINS, JOHN Pvt, I, 10th NY Inf, 7-13-1924. Holy Sepulchre Cemetery, Totowa, Passaic County.

HIGGINS, JOHN Pvt, D, 5th NJ Inf, 1905. Immaculate Conception Cemetery, Montclair, Essex County.

HIGGINS*, JOHN C. Sgt, A, 35th NJ Inf, [Wounded in action at Fair Oaks, VA.] 1917. Harlingen Cemetery, Belle Mead, Somerset County.

HIGGINS, JOSEPH DoD Unknown. Holy Sepulchre Cemetery, Totowa, Passaic County.

HIGGINS, JOSEPH G. Musc, A, 115th PA Inf, DoD Unknown. Old Camden Cemetery, Camden, Camden County.

HIGGINS, LEMUEL S. (aka: Higgins, Samuel L.) Pvt, D, 1st VT Cav, 1910. Sandy Ridge Cemetery, Sandy Ridge, Hunterdon County.

HIGGINS, MICHAEL Pvt, I, 36th IN Inf, 5-20-1893. Holy Sepulchre Cemetery, East Orange, Essex County.

HIGGINS, MICHAEL M. Sgt, C, 33rd NJ Inf, 10-27-1877. Presbyterian Cemetery, Springfield, Union County.

HIGGINS, SAMUEL L. (see: Higgins, Lemuel S.) Sandy Ridge Cemetery, Sandy Ridge, Hunterdon County.

HIGGINS, THOMAS Pvt, E, 95th NY Inf, 11-6-1911. Holy Sepulchre Cemetery, East Orange, Essex County.

HIGGINS, THOMAS Pvt, F, 54th MA Inf, [Wounded 7-18-1863 at Fort Wagner, SC.] 12-1-1907. 1st Baptist Cemetery, New Brunswick, Middlesex County.

HIGGINS, THOMAS 11-18-1895. Mount Olivet Cemetery, Newark, Essex County.

HIGGINS, THOMAS Actg Asst Paymaster, U.S. Navy, USS North Carolina, 10-13-1871. Holy Sepulchre Cemetery, East Orange, Essex County.

HIGGINS, THOMAS F. Pvt, H, 8th NJ Inf, [Wounded in action at Williamsburg, VA.] 7--1869. Monument Cemetery, Edgewater Park, Burlington County.

HIGGINS*, TIMOTHY E. Pvt, B, 40th NY Inf, [Wounded in action.] 6-3-1910. Mount Olivet Cemetery, Newark, Essex County.

HIGGINS, WILLIAM Sgt, C, 5th CT Inf, DoD Unknown. Finn's Point National Cemetery, Pennsville, Salem County.

HIGGINS, WILLIAM AUGUSTUS N. Pvt, I, 11th NJ Inf, 4-9-1886. Baptist Church Cemetery, Jacobstown, Burlington County.

HIGGINS, WILLIAM J. Pvt, I, 3rd U.S. CT, 10-4-1897. Mount Pisgah Cemetery, Elsinboro, Salem County.

HIGGINS, WILLIAM L. Pvt, A, 15th NJ Inf, 1-15-1890. Greenwood Cemetery, Hamilton, Mercer County.

HIGGINS*, WILLIAM T. Corp, B, 13th NJ Inf, 11-9-1899. Bordentown/Old St. Mary's Catholic Cemetery, Bordentown, Burlington County.

HIGGINSON*, JOHN H. Capt, I, 26th NJ Inf, 9-8-1910. Mount Pleasant Cemetery, Newark, Essex County.

HIGGINSON, MICHAEL W. Pvt, A, 8th NY State Militia, 2-6-1916. Evergreen Cemetery, Hillside, Union County.

HIGGINSON, RICHARD B. Sgt, A, 8th NY State Militia, 1880. Evergreen Cemetery, Hillside, Union County.

HIGGS, THOMAS W. 1st Lt, L, 83rd NY Inf, 12-21-1882. Grove Church Cemetery, North Bergen, Hudson County.

HIGH, DANIEL A. (aka: High, David) Pvt, 6th NY Ind Btty 3-19-1897. Rahway Cemetery, Rahway, Union County.

HIGH, DAVID (see: High, Daniel A.) Rahway Cemetery, Rahway, Union County.

HIGH, JOHN Pvt, I, 30th NJ Inf, 3-14-1901. Fairmount Cemetery, Newark, Essex County.

Our Brothers Gone Before

HIGH, JOHN C. Pvt, E, 9th NJ Inf, 12-26-1926. Methodist Church Cemetery, Goshen, Cape May County.

HIGH, JOHN H. Pvt, H, 47th NY Inf, 11-18-1865. Bloomfield Cemetery, Bloomfield, Essex County.

HIGH, MALACHI Corp, I, 25th NJ Inf, 5-9-1905. Methodist Church Cemetery, Goshen, Cape May County.

HIGHLAND, JAMES 1st Sgt, C, 5th NY Cav, 12-4-1888. Holy Sepulchre Cemetery, Totowa, Passaic County.

HIGHLAND, JOHN (see: Hyland, John) Mount Olivet Cemetery, Fairview, Monmouth County.

HIGHT, ELIAS H. Pvt, M, 2nd NJ Cav, 5-27-1906. Prospect Hill Cemetery, Flemington, Hunterdon County.

HIGHTOWER, THOMAS Pvt, E, 3rd MS Inf (CSA), 10-25-1863. Finn's Point National Cemetery, Pennsville, Salem County.

HIGNAN, WILLIAM Actg 2nd Asst Eng, U.S. Navy, USS Anemone, 10-28-1911. Evergreen Cemetery, Camden, Camden County.

HILD, AUGUST Pvt, A, 52nd NY Inf, 2-26-1904. Speer Cemetery, Jersey City, Hudson County.

HILDABRANT, HORACE G. Pvt, K, 31st NJ Inf, 1919. Union Cemetery, Clinton, Hunterdon County.

HILDEBRAND, AUGUSTUS Pvt, F, 29th NJ Inf, 8-17-1897. Fairmount Cemetery, Newark, Essex County.

HILDEBRANT, GEORGE Pvt, E, 35th NJ Inf, [Wounded in action.] 1924. Methodist Church Cemetery, Fairmount, Hunterdon County.

HILDEBRANT, NATHAN Pvt, A, 31st NJ Inf, 1-9-1896. Methodist Church Cemetery, Lebanon, Hunterdon County.

HILDENBRAND*, JULIUS P. Pvt, Btty L, 5th U.S. Art, 1905. Greenwood Cemetery, Brielle, Monmouth County.

HILDRETH, DAVID Corp, I, 25th NJ Inf, [Died of typhoid at Washington, DC.] 12-29-1862. 1st Baptist Cemetery, Cape May Court House, Cape May County.

HILER, GEORGE W. Pvt, C, 15th NJ Inf, 5-16-1905. Greenwood Cemetery, Boonton, Morris County.

HILER, JAMES N. Pvt, F, 33rd NJ Inf, 5-2-1910. Fairmount Cemetery, Newark, Essex County.

HILER, SAMUEL RICHTER Pvt, E, 1st NJ Cav, 5-8-1920. Presbyterian Church Cemetery, Rockaway, Morris County.

HILES, ANDREW Pvt, G, 3rd NJ Cav, DoD Unknown. Mount Pleasant Cemetery, Millville, Cumberland County.

HILES, GEORGE F. Pvt, C, 3rd NJ Cav, DoD Unknown. Siloam Cemetery, Vineland, Cumberland County.

HILES, GEORGE W. (aka: Hoile, George) Corp, C, 1st NJ Cav, 9-27-1899. Zion Methodist Church Cemetery, Porchtown, Gloucester County.

HILES, JOB Pvt, C, 38th NJ Inf, 6-29-1900. Mount Pleasant Cemetery, Millville, Cumberland County.

HILES, WINFIELD SCOTT Pvt, A, 82nd PA Inf, 6-14-1884. Eastview Cemetery, Salem, Salem County.

HILGAR, PHILIP Pvt, G, 33rd NJ Inf, 1-31-1906. Speer Cemetery, Jersey City, Hudson County.

HILIMONGEN, FRANK 6-7-1884. Flower Hill Cemetery, North Bergen, Hudson County.

HILL, ABRAM Pvt, ___, ___ U.S. Hancock Corps, 1909. New Somerville Cemetery, Somerville, Somerset County.

HILL, ADAM Pvt, K, 1st NY Eng, [(Cenotaph) Died of disease at Hilton Head, SC.] 6-25-1863. Newton Cemetery, Newton, Sussex County.

New Jersey Civil War Burials

HILL*, **ALPHONSO S.** Pvt, E, 2nd NJ Cav, 2-26-1905. Riverview Cemetery, Trenton, Mercer County.

HILL, **AMOS** Pvt, Ahl's Btty, DE Heavy Art, DoD Unknown. Finn's Point National Cemetery, Pennsville, Salem County.

HILL, **ANDREW** Pvt, E, 1st NJ Cav, DoD Unknown. St. John's Episcopal Church Cemetery, Salem, Salem County.

HILL, **ANDREW G.** Pvt, A, 27th NJ Inf, 1882. Presbyterian Church Cemetery, Marksboro, Warren County.

HILL, **BENJAMIN F.** Corp, A, 12th NJ Inf, 5-18-1906. Bayview-New York Bay Cemetery, Jersey City, Hudson County.

HILL, **BENJAMIN W.** 1st Sgt, C, 3rd U.S. Cav, DoD Unknown. Cedar Grove Cemetery, Gloucester City, Camden County.

HILL, **CALVIN H.** Pvt, B, 35th NJ Inf, 1-23-1916. Presbyterian Church Cemetery, Califon, Hunterdon County.

HILL, **CHARLES** Seaman, U.S. Navy, USS Aries, 3-7-1909. St. Joseph's Cemetery, Keyport, Monmouth County.

HILL, **CHARLES B.** Pvt, A, 35th NJ Inf, [Died of diarrhea at Marietta, GA.] 8-4-1864. Riverview Cemetery, Trenton, Mercer County.

HILL, **CHARLES E.** Corp, F, 5th PA Cav, 7-6-1915. Methodist Cemetery, Mantua, Gloucester County.

HILL, **CHARLES EDWARD** Chaplain, 118th PA Inf 10-14-1908. Fairview Cemetery, Fairview, Monmouth County.

HILL*, **CHARLES H.** Sgt, I, 4th NJ Inf, DoD Unknown. Harleigh Cemetery, Camden, Camden County.

HILL, **CHARLES J.** 4-22-1891. Rancocas Quaker Cemetery, Westampton, Burlington County.

HILL, **CHARLES S.** Pvt, G, 3rd NJ Inf, 9-4-1884. Willow Grove Cemetery, New Brunswick, Middlesex County.

HILL, **CHARLES W.** Corp, A, 115th IL Inf, 1-31-1928. Bayview-New York Bay Cemetery, Jersey City, Hudson County.

HILL, **CHRISTOPHER S.** Pvt, C, 99th PA Inf, [Wounded 10-27-1864 at Boydton Plank Road, VA. and 3-25-1865 at Petersburg, VA.] 5-9-1893. Old Camden Cemetery, Camden, Camden County.

HILL*, **EDWARD L.** Pvt, G, 15th NJ Inf, 1925. Soldier's Home Cemetery, Vineland, Cumberland County.

HILL, **EZEKIEL** Pvt, B, 8th (Wade's) Confederate States Cav (CSA), 3-4-1864. Finn's Point National Cemetery, Pennsville, Salem County.

HILL*, **EZRA** Pvt, G, 38th NJ Inf, 11-29-1900. New Somerville Cemetery, Somerville, Somerset County.

HILL, **EZRA H.** Pvt, K, 1st NJ Inf, 2-3-1891. Greenwood Cemetery, Boonton, Morris County.

HILL, **FRANK T.** Pvt, C, 11th NJ Inf, 11-20-1911. Siloam Cemetery, Vineland, Cumberland County.

HILL, **GEORGE A.** (see: Clements, Isaac) Mount Prospect Cemetery, Neptune, Monmouth County.

HILL, **HENRY A.** Pvt, F, 61st GA Inf (CSA), [Captured 7-1-1863 at Gettysburg, PA.] 12-6-1863. Finn's Point National Cemetery, Pennsville, Salem County.

HILL, **HENRY JUDSON** Pvt, G, 27th NJ Inf, 10-14-1908. Greenwood Cemetery, Boonton, Morris County.

HILL, **HENRY P.** Pvt, K, 34th NJ Inf, 2-15-1924. Union Cemetery, Gloucester City, Camden County.

HILL, **ISAAC J.** Pvt, D, 29th CT Inf, 10-17-1882. Presbyterian Cemetery, Woodbury, Gloucester County.

Our Brothers Gone Before

HILL, JACOB M. Landsman, U.S. Navy, USS Roanoke, 1917. Pequest Union Cemetery, Great Meadows, Warren County.
HILL, JAMES Pvt, B, 79th NY Inf, 4-17-1876. Macphelah Cemetery, North Bergen, Hudson County.
HILL, JAMES Pvt, F, 37th NJ Inf, 1-3-1899. Laurel Grove Cemetery, Totowa, Passaic County.
HILL, JAMES F. Corp, H, 29th CT Inf, 10-24-1884. Fairmount Cemetery, Newark, Essex County.
HILL, JAMES W. 1st Sgt, G, 14th NJ Inf, DoD Unknown. Cedarwood Cemetery, Hazlet, Monmouth County.
HILL, JOHN Pvt, E, 4th NJ Militia, 8-17-1900. New Camden Cemetery, Camden, Camden County.
HILL, JOHN Pvt, G, 25th NJ Inf, 1-9-1887. Evergreen Cemetery, Camden, Camden County.
HILL, JOHN Corp, Btty A, 1st NJ Light Art, 1-10-1890. Holy Name Cemetery, Jersey City, Hudson County.
HILL, JOHN Sgt, B, 79th NY Inf, 8-13-1866. Macphelah Cemetery, North Bergen, Hudson County.
HILL, JOHN Pvt, E, 35th NJ Inf, 5-17-1867. Macphelah Cemetery, North Bergen, Hudson County.
HILL, JOHN Corp, H, 35th NJ Inf, [Died of wounds received at Atlanta, GA.] 7-29-1864. Manalapan Cemetery, Manalapan, Monmouth County.
HILL, JOHN A. Actg 1st Asst Eng, U.S. Navy, 8-27-1902. Bayview-New York Bay Cemetery, Jersey City, Hudson County.
HILL, JOHN C. (aka: Hills, John C.) Pvt, A, 42nd PA Inf, [Wounded 12-13-1862 at Fredericksburg, VA.] 5-13-1929. Greenwood Cemetery, Hamilton, Mercer County.
HILL*, JOHN D. Pvt, F, 34th NJ Inf, DoD Unknown. Reformed Church Cemetery, Lebanon, Hunterdon County.
HILL, JOHN M. 1-6-1889. Stillwater Cemetery, Stillwater, Sussex County.
HILL, JOHN R. Pvt, F, 3rd NJ Inf, 1-7-1919. St. Joseph's Cemetery, Keyport, Monmouth County.
HILL*, JOHN T. Maj, 12th NJ Inf 3-1-1891. Elmwood Cemetery, New Brunswick, Middlesex County.
HILL, JOSEPH P. 11-10-1871. Huntsville Cemetery, Huntsville, Sussex County.
HILL, JOSEPH W. Pvt, A, 37th NJ Inf, 4-24-1903. Jersey City Cemetery, Jersey City, Hudson County.
HILL, JOSHUA (JR.) DoD Unknown. Huntsville Cemetery, Huntsville, Sussex County.
HILL, LEONIDAS H. Pvt, G, 145th PA Inf, [Died at Washington, DC.] 10-15-1864. Beverly National Cemetery, Edgewater Park, Burlington County.
HILL, LUTHER DoD Unknown. Huntsville Cemetery, Huntsville, Sussex County.
HILL, NICHOLAS Corp, K, 2nd DC Inf, DoD Unknown. Greenwood Cemetery, Boonton, Morris County.
HILL*, RALPH Seaman, U.S. Navy, USS Potomac, 3-31-1913. Riverview Cemetery, Trenton, Mercer County.
HILL, RICHARD J. 3-15-1906. Bayview-New York Bay Cemetery, Jersey City, Hudson County.
HILL, ROBERT Pvt, I, 15th NJ Inf, 3-26-1887. Macphelah Cemetery, North Bergen, Hudson County.
HILL, ROBERT B. Pvt, F, 129th PA Inf, 9-15-1880. Union Cemetery, Washington, Morris County.
HILL, ROBERT R. DoD Unknown. Mount Salem Church Cemetery, Fenwick, Salem County.

New Jersey Civil War Burials

HILL, SAMUEL Musc, A, 4th NJ Inf, 6-26-1918. Riverview Cemetery, Trenton, Mercer County.
HILL, SAMUEL B. Pvt, Gossin's Co., Jones' Ind Bttn OH Inf, 9-11-1909. Soldier's Home Cemetery, Vineland, Cumberland County.
HILL, SAMUEL C. Pvt, A, 35th NJ Inf, 11-28-1913. Greenwood Cemetery, Hamilton, Mercer County.
HILL*, SILAS WELLS Corp, F, 6th NH Inf, 5-9-1901. Hillside Cemetery, Scotch Plains, Union County.
HILL, THOMAS Sgt, A, 12th U.S. Inf, 4-2-1903. Holy Sepulchre Cemetery, East Orange, Essex County.
HILL, THOMAS E. Pvt, D, 22nd NJ Inf, 5-7-1924. Pascack Reformed Cemetery, Park Ridge, Bergen County.
HILL, W.L. Pvt, E, 14th AL Inf (CSA), 10-21-1863. Finn's Point National Cemetery, Pennsville, Salem County.
HILL, WILLIAM Pvt, C, 132nd NY Inf, 12-12-1919. Jersey City Cemetery, Jersey City, Hudson County.
HILL, WILLIAM B. 2-18-1889. Evergreen Cemetery, Morristown, Morris County.
HILL, WILLIAM E. Pvt, 6th MA Light Art 2-1-1913. Evergreen Cemetery, Hillside, Union County.
HILL*, WILLIAM HENRY Capt, AAG, U.S. Volunteers, 9-9-1881. Evergreen Cemetery, Camden, Camden County.
HILL, WILLIAM HENRY Corp, G, 22nd NJ Inf, 9-13-1911. Princeton Cemetery, Princeton, Mercer County.
HILL*, WILLIAM HENRY Pvt, C, 7th NJ Inf, 7-26-1920. Riverview Cemetery, Trenton, Mercer County.
HILL, WILLIAM T. Corp, K, 1st NY Eng, DoD Unknown. Newton Cemetery, Newton, Sussex County.
HILL, WINFIELD S. Pvt, G, 4th NJ Inf, 1-16-1926. Baptist Cemetery, Vincentown, Burlington County.
HILLAN, CHARLES PATRICK Pvt, C, 29th NJ Inf, 12-3-1913. St. Joseph's Church Cemetery, Perrineville, Monmouth County.
HILLAS, JOSHUA Pvt, G, 27th NJ Inf, 12-16-1881. Boonton Cemetery, Boonton, Morris County.
HILLER, FREDERICK Sgt, A, 41st NY Inf, 6-12-1902. Evergreen Cemetery, Hillside, Union County.
HILLERMAN, FREDERICK Pvt, E, 10th NJ Inf, 1-13-1893. New Camden Cemetery, Camden, Camden County.
HILLERY, HENRY Pvt, F, 32nd U.S. CT, 10-7-1914. Fairmount Cemetery, Newark, Essex County.
HILLEY, WILLIAM Pvt, C, 16th GA Inf (CSA), [Captured 7-2-1863 at Gettysburg, PA.] 11-1-1863. Finn's Point National Cemetery, Pennsville, Salem County.
HILLIARD*, FRANKLIN STOCKTON Pvt, B, 12th OH Cav, 10-7-1912. Baptist Cemetery, Vincentown, Burlington County.
HILLIARD, JOSEPH B. Pvt, F, 12th NJ Inf, 11-9-1922. Presbyterian Church Cemetery, Cedarville, Cumberland County.
HILLIARD*, WILLIAM IRICK 2nd Lt, A, 2 MA Cav, 7-19-1918. Baptist/St. Andrew's Cemetery, Mount Holly, Burlington County.
HILLIER, HERMAN Pvt, B, 11th NJ Inf, 2-24-1897. Laurel Grove Cemetery, Totowa, Passaic County.
HILLIER, JOHN H. 8-30-1894. Oddfellows Cemetery, Burlington, Burlington County.
HILLMAN, GEORGE Pvt, G, 3rd NJ Cav, 2-22-1907. Evergreen Cemetery, Camden, Camden County.
HILLMAN, JOHN D. 1896. Methodist Church Cemetery, Sharptown, Salem County.

Our Brothers Gone Before

HILLMAN, ROBERT M. Sgt, E, 10th NJ Inf, 12-30-1922. Harleigh Cemetery, Camden, Camden County.
HILLMAN, WILLIAM H. Pvt, Btty E, 2nd PA Heavy Art, [Wounded in action.] 6-3-1917. Green Cemetery, Woodbury, Gloucester County.
HILLMANN*, JOSEPH H. 1st Sgt, H, 7th NJ Inf, 10-5-1911. Holy Sepulchre Cemetery, Totowa, Passaic County.
HILLS, F. EUGENE Pvt, D, 189th NY Inf, 1887. United Methodist Church Cemetery, Woodruff, Cumberland County.
HILLS, JOHN C. (see: Hill, John C.) Greenwood Cemetery, Hamilton, Mercer County.
HILLYER, CHARLES DoD Unknown. Vincent Methodist-Episcopal Cemetery, Nutley, Essex County.
HILLYER, ISAAC Sgt, C, 28th NJ Inf, 1895. Baptist/Evergreen Methodist Cemetery, Plainfield, Union County.
HILLYER, WILLIAM SILLIMAN Bvt Brig Gen, U.S. Volunteers, [Colonel, Provost Marshal General, Department of the Tennessee.] 7-12-1874. Mount Pleasant Cemetery, Newark, Essex County.
HILSER, JOSEPH Sgt, Btty E, 15th NY Heavy Art, 8-18-1886. Woodland Cemetery, Newark, Essex County.
HILSON, CLEAVELAND 7-23-1892. Riverview Cemetery, Trenton, Mercer County.
HILTON*, JOHN R. Asst Surg, 2nd NJ Inf [Died of typhoid at White Oak Church, VA.] 3-17-1863. Belvidere/Catholic Cemetery, Belvidere, Warren County.
HILTON, JOHN T. Pvt, H, 25th NJ Inf, 3-14-1922. Cedar Lawn Cemetery, Paterson, Passaic County.
HILYARD, ALBERT 4- -1919. 1st Methodist Church Cemetery, Williamstown, Gloucester County.
HILYARD, JOHN W. Pvt, I, 9th NJ Inf, 1926. Presbyterian Church Cemetery, Upper Deerfield, Cumberland County.
HIME, JACOB Pvt, G, 30th NJ Inf, 7-29-1887. Evergreen Cemetery, Hillside, Union County.
HIME, SAMUEL V. Pvt, C, 8th NJ Inf, 4-7-1899. Fairmount Cemetery, Newark, Essex County.
HIMES, GEORGE W. Musc, G, 3rd NJ Inf, 1-24-1885. Evergreen Cemetery, Hillside, Union County.
HINCHCLIFFE, JOHN 9-1-1886. Holy Sepulchre Cemetery, Totowa, Passaic County.
HINCHMAN, BENJAMIN Pvt, H, 28th NJ Inf, 12-6-1892. Riverview Cemetery, Penns Grove, Salem County.
HINCHMAN, EDWARD Pvt, H, 23rd NJ Inf, 5-22-1906. Colestown Cemetery, Cherry Hill, Camden County.
HINCHMAN*, ISAAC E. Pvt, D, 147th PA Inf, 8-2-1903. Baptist Church Cemetery, Haddonfield, Camden County.
HINCHMAN, JACOB Pvt, E, 12th NJ Inf, 4-25-1913. Evergreen Cemetery, Camden, Camden County.
HINCKE, CHARLES (aka: Hinkey, Charles) Pvt, A, 26th NJ Inf, [Wounded in action.] 4-17-1898. Fairmount Cemetery, Newark, Essex County.
HINCKEN, CARSTEN H. 3-2-1899. Hoboken Cemetery, North Bergen, Hudson County.
HINCKLEY, FREDERICK A. Pvt, C, 29th NJ Inf, 1915. Rosehill Cemetery, Newfield, Gloucester County.
HINCKLEY, JOHN Pvt, D, 31st NJ Inf, DoD Unknown. Presbyterian Church Cemetery, Flemington, Hunterdon County.
HINDLE*, GEORGE Pvt, E, 22nd NJ Inf, 2-9-1911. Laurel Grove Cemetery, Totowa, Passaic County.
HINDLE, JAMES A. Sgt, A, 11th NJ Inf, 2-18-1873. Cedar Lawn Cemetery, Paterson, Passaic County.
HINDLEY, GEORGE A. 2-5-1907. Riverview Cemetery, Trenton, Mercer County.

New Jersey Civil War Burials

HINELINE, MORGAN L. Pvt, I, 31st NJ Inf, 2-6-1864. United Methodist Church Cemetery, Montana, Warren County.

HINELINE, SAMUEL V. 1-19-1903. Presbyterian Church Cemetery, Harmony, Warren County.

HINELY, EDWARD S. Pvt, D, 5th FL Inf (CSA), [Wounded and captured 7-3-1863 at Gettysburg, PA. Died of scurvy.] 11-2-1863. Finn's Point National Cemetery, Pennsville, Salem County.

HINER, CHARLES (see: Heiner, Charles) Fairmount Cemetery, Newark, Essex County.

HINES, ANDREW 8-18-1866. Monument Cemetery, Edgewater Park, Burlington County.

HINES, F.J. Seaman, U.S. Navy, 12-18-1890. Holy Sepulchre Cemetery, Totowa, Passaic County.

HINES, HENRY D. Pvt, D, 25th NJ Inf, 11-15-1901. Bateman Memorial Cemetery, Newport, Cumberland County.

HINES*, HENRY P. Pvt, D, 10th MA Inf, [Wounded in action 1862.] 5-19-1906. Cedar Hill Cemetery, Hightstown, Mercer County.

HINES, HUGH Pvt, D, 38th NJ Inf, 4-13-1885. Old St. Mary's Cemetery, Gloucester City, Camden County.

HINES, JACOB (see: Heins, Jacob) Mount Hope Presbyterian Cemetery, Lambertville, Hunterdon County.

HINES, JOHN (see: Hein, John) Holy Name Cemetery, Jersey City, Hudson County.

HINES, JOHN O. Pvt, C, 3rd NJ Cav, 1904. Harleigh Cemetery, Camden, Camden County.

HINES, JOSEPH B. Pvt, K, 34th NJ Inf, 3-1-1926. Beverly National Cemetery, Edgewater Park, Burlington County.

HINES, JOSEPH W. Telegraph Operator, U.S. Army, [On detached service.] 7-22-1899. Mount Carmel Cemetery, West Long Branch, Monmouth County.

HINES, ORRIN H. Corp, K, 122nd NY Inf, [Wounded 5-6-1864 at Wilderness, VA.] 9-29-1914. Bayview-New York Bay Cemetery, Jersey City, Hudson County.

HINES, THOMAS Pvt, F, 2nd NJ Inf, 4-30-1901. Holy Name Cemetery, Jersey City, Hudson County.

HINES, THOMAS Pvt, G, 3rd NJ Inf, 2-2-1880. St. John's Cemetery, Hamilton, Mercer County.

HINES, THOMAS G. Seaman, U.S. Navy, 12-19-1890. Holy Sepulchre Cemetery, Totowa, Passaic County.

HINES, THOMAS H. Pvt, E, 24th U.S. CT, 3-5-1912. Mount Peace Cemetery, Lawnside, Camden County.

HINES, WILLIAM B. 1st Sgt, K, 12th NJ Inf, 1-15-1923. Bateman Memorial Cemetery, Newport, Cumberland County.

HINHOLD, JAMES (see: Arnold, James A.) Mount Pleasant Cemetery, Newark, Essex County.

HINKEY, CHARLES (see: Hincke, Charles) Fairmount Cemetery, Newark, Essex County.

HINKEY*, JULIUS Pvt, Btty C, 2nd CT Heavy Art, [Wounded 2-6-1864 at Mortons Ford, VA.] 3-7-1906. Elmwood Cemetery, New Brunswick, Middlesex County.

HINKLE, E.H. Seaman, U.S. Navy, 6-10-1903. Union Cemetery, Frenchtown, Hunterdon County.

HINKLE, HIRAM 10-7-1914. Union Cemetery, Frenchtown, Hunterdon County.

HINKLEY, CHARLES Pvt, H, 1st NJ Cav, 10-7-1910. Princeton Cemetery, Princeton, Mercer County.

HINLEY, ABRAHAM (see: Heinley, Abraham E.) Phillipsburg Cemetery, Phillipsburg, Warren County.

HINLEY, JOHN W. Musc, B, 4th NJ Inf, 8-15-1911. Riverview Cemetery, Trenton, Mercer County.

Our Brothers Gone Before

HINMAN, WILLIAM Pvt, H, 2nd NJ Militia, 1-1-1897. Greenwood Cemetery, Hamilton, Mercer County.
HINNAN, CALEB Pvt, C, 3rd ___ ___, 2-1-1910. Riverview Cemetery, Trenton, Mercer County.
HINNEN, GOTTLIEB 1st Sgt, B, 41st NY Inf, 8-22-1916. Bayview-New York Bay Cemetery, Jersey City, Hudson County.
HINSCH, CHARLES Pvt, Btty C, 2nd OH Heavy Art, 3-15-1915. Flower Hill Cemetery, North Bergen, Hudson County.
HINSDALE*, SAMUEL BURRITT Corp, H, 151st IL Inf, 12-28-1903. Presbyterian Church Cemetery, Woodbridge, Middlesex County.
HINSON, GEORGE Pvt, E, 7th U.S. CT, 12-24-1914. Mount Peace Cemetery, Lawnside, Camden County.
HINSON, JOHN C. Pvt, G, 51st VA Inf (CSA), [Captured 3-2-1865 at Waynesboro, VA. Died of diarrhea.] 4-12-1865. Finn's Point National Cemetery, Pennsville, Salem County.
HINSON, JOHN Q. Pvt, K, 45th GA Inf (CSA), [Captured 4-2-1865 at Petersburg, VA. Died of malarial fever.] 5-11-1865. Finn's Point National Cemetery, Pennsville, Salem County.
HINTON, THOMAS Pvt, I, 3rd NJ Inf, [Died of typhoid at Newark, NJ.] 9-12-1862. Fairmount Cemetery, Newark, Essex County.
HINTON, WILLIAM Musc, A, 9th NJ Inf, 11-6-1888. Fairmount Cemetery, Newark, Essex County.
HINTZE, JULIUS Pvt, E, 12th RI Inf, 4-29-1904. Bayview-New York Bay Cemetery, Jersey City, Hudson County.
HINTZY, JULIUS (see: Heinz, Julius) Bayview-New York Bay Cemetery, Jersey City, Hudson County.
HIPE, JOSEPH (see: Haipt, Joseph) Woodland Cemetery, Newark, Essex County.
HIRES, CHARLES Pvt, G, 6th NJ Inf, 3-17-1880. Harmony Methodist-Episcopal Church Cemetery, Piney Hollow, Gloucester County.
HIRES*, GERSHOM C. Hosp Steward, U.S. Army, 1915. Prospect Hill Cemetery, Flemington, Hunterdon County.
HIRES, ISAAC E. Coal Heaver, U.S. Navy, USS Rocket, 8-22-1922. Harleigh Cemetery, Camden, Camden County.
HIRES, LEWIS C. Pvt, H, 10th NJ Inf, 6-15-1893. Oak Hill Cemetery, Vineland, Cumberland County.
HIRSCH*, CHARLES Pvt, I, 175th NY Inf, 6-8-1896. Greenlawn Cemetery, West Long Branch, Monmouth County.
HIRSCH, GEORGE Corp, C, 41st NY Inf, 5-2-1892. Fairmount Cemetery, Newark, Essex County.
HIRSCH, JACOB Pvt, A, 4th NJ Inf, DoD Unknown. Old Camden Cemetery, Camden, Camden County.
HIRSCHMAN, ANTON Pvt, Btty B, Bushaman's Bttn SC Light Art (CSA), [Hampton's Legion.] 5-22-1920. Bayview-New York Bay Cemetery, Jersey City, Hudson County.
HIRSCHY*, FREDERICK L. Pvt, Btty L, 5th U.S. Art, 1901. Maplewood Cemetery, Freehold, Monmouth County.
HIRST, JOSEPH 1-12-1887. Bayview-New York Bay Cemetery, Jersey City, Hudson County.
HISE, JAMES N. (see: Hice, James N.) Union Cemetery, Milford, Hunterdon County.
HISER*, CHRISTOPHER Pvt, C, 9th NJ Inf, [Wounded in action.] 4-25-1911. Old Baptist Cemetery, Freehold, Monmouth County.
HISSLER, GEORGE (see: Heisler, George H.) New Camden Cemetery, Camden, Camden County.

New Jersey Civil War Burials

HISTANBRITTLE, DEDRICK (see: Hestonbrittle, Deidritch) Fairmount Cemetery, Newark, Essex County.

HITCHCOCK, DAVID Sgt, K, 70th NY Inf, [Wounded 7-2-1863 at Gettysburg, PA.] 7-9-1901. Mount Prospect Cemetery, Neptune, Monmouth County.

HITCHCOCK, H.P.J. (aka: Hathcock, Joseph J.) Pvt, A, 19th TN Inf (CSA), 11-18-1864. Finn's Point National Cemetery, Pennsville, Salem County.

HITCHCOCK, JAMES H. Landsman, U.S. Navy, 12-13-1920. Fairmount Cemetery, Newark, Essex County.

HITCHINS, WILLIAM Pvt, B, 1st NJ Cav, [Died of pneumonia and brain inflammation.] 2-1-1864. Friends United Methodist-Episcopal Church Cemetery, Linwood, Atlantic County.

HITESMAN, GEORGE __, C, 3rd __ __, 7-30-1897. Greenwood Cemetery, Hamilton, Mercer County.

HIXSON, GEORGE W. 1st Lt, G, 26th NJ Inf, 5-19-1929. South Orange Cemetery, South Orange, Essex County.

HIZER*, HIRAM Pvt, C, 111th PA Inf, 3-7-1915. Evergreen Cemetery, Camden, Camden County.

HOADLEY, JONAS (aka: Hudley, Jonas) Pvt, D, 28th PA Inf, DoD Unknown. St. James Cemetery, Greenwich, Warren County.

HOAGE, MOSES A. (aka: Hogge, Moses) 2nd Lt, D, 26th NJ Inf, 8-20-1911. Prospect Hill Cemetery, Caldwell, Essex County.

HOAGE, THOMAS (aka: Hogge, Thomas) Pvt, D, 26th NJ Inf, 10-7-1920. Prospect Hill Cemetery, Caldwell, Essex County.

HOAGLAND, ASA P. Pvt, F, 9th NJ Inf, 1-18-1885. Presbyterian Church Cemetery, Pennington, Mercer County.

HOAGLAND*, CHARLES M. 1st Sgt, F, 8th NJ Inf, 2-25-1909. Harleigh Cemetery, Camden, Camden County.

HOAGLAND*, CORNELIUS A. Pvt, E, 15th NJ Inf, 9-2-1868. Cedar Grove Cemetery, Middlebush, Somerset County.

HOAGLAND, CORNELIUS B. Sgt, A, 9th NJ Inf, 3-20-1915. Brainerd Cemetery, Cranbury, Middlesex County.

HOAGLAND, GEORGE W. Pvt, K, 3rd NJ Militia, 9-2-1872. 1st Baptist Cemetery, New Brunswick, Middlesex County.

HOAGLAND, HENRY C. Pvt, G, 1st NJ Inf, DoD Unknown. Elmwood Cemetery, New Brunswick, Middlesex County.

HOAGLAND, HENRY H. Corp, E, 30th NJ Inf, 9-8-1871. New Dutch Reformed/Neshanic Cemetery, Neshanic, Somerset County.

HOAGLAND*, HENRY LIVINGSTON Coal Heaver, U.S. Navy, USS Chenango, [Killed aboard ship in New York harbor when the port boiler exploded.] 4-15-1864. Christ Church Cemetery, Morgan, Middlesex County.

HOAGLAND, HERMAN J. Pvt, E, 30th NJ Inf, 4-11-1885. Elmwood Cemetery, New Brunswick, Middlesex County.

HOAGLAND, JACOB M. Corp, I, 38th NJ Inf, 8-6-1900. Pleasant Ridge Cemetery, East Amwell, Hunterdon County.

HOAGLAND, JACOB W. Pvt, B, 38th NJ Inf, 6-25-1899. Union Cemetery, Frenchtown, Hunterdon County.

HOAGLAND, JAMES ROMEYN Capt, G, 24th NJ Inf, 5-26-1914. Presbyterian Church Cemetery, Bridgeton, Cumberland County.

HOAGLAND, JOHN E. Pvt, A, 31st NJ Inf, 3-23-1915. Reformed Church Cemetery, Readington, Hunterdon County.

HOAGLAND, JOHN HENRY Corp, F, 1st NY Cav, [Killed in action at Mt. Jackson, WV.] 11-16-1863. Reformed Church Cemetery, South Branch, Somerset County.

HOAGLAND, JOHN Y. Pvt, E, 29th PA Inf, 7-23-1897. Riverview Cemetery, Trenton, Mercer County.

Our Brothers Gone Before

HOAGLAND, JOSEPH L. Pvt, B, 38th NJ Inf, 6-30-1916. Union Cemetery, Frenchtown, Hunterdon County.
HOAGLAND, JOSIAH Q. Corp, E, 30th NJ Inf, 1922. Reformed Church Cemetery, Readington, Hunterdon County.
HOAGLAND*, LEMUEL Pvt, A, 5th NJ Inf, 3-23-1902. Pleasant Ridge Cemetery, East Amwell, Hunterdon County.
HOAGLAND, MORRIS S. 7-5-1876. Rural Hill Cemetery, Whitehouse, Hunterdon County.
HOAGLAND, MOSES Pvt, G, 25th U.S. CT, 1-24-1891. Riverview Cemetery, Trenton, Mercer County.
HOAGLAND, PETER Corp, H, 30th NJ Inf, 1901. Holcomb-Riverview Cemetery, Lambertville, Hunterdon County.
HOAGLAND, PETER K. Pvt, B, 25th U.S. CT, 5-20-1891. Presbyterian Cemetery, North Plainfield, Somerset County.
HOAGLAND, PETER W. 6-22-1886. Mount Pleasant Cemetery, Newark, Essex County.
HOAGLAND, SAMUEL S. 1906. Christ Church Cemetery, Morgan, Middlesex County.
HOAGLAND, SILAS (aka: Hugland, Silas) Corp, I, 22nd U.S. CT, 3-27-1907. Fernwood Cemetery, Jamesburg, Middlesex County.
HOAGLAND, WYCKOFF V. Pvt, F, 1st NJ Inf, 11-21-1919. Elmwood Cemetery, New Brunswick, Middlesex County.
HOBART, DAVID 1901. Old Brick Reformed Church Cemetery, Marlboro, Monmouth County.
HOBBIS, THOMAS (JR.) Pvt, G, 8th NJ Inf, 1-22-1908. Fairmount Cemetery, Newark, Essex County.
HOBBS, GEORGE Seaman, U.S. Navy, 9-13-1900. Cedar Lawn Cemetery, Paterson, Passaic County.
HOBBS, GEORGE W. Pvt, K, 12th SC Inf (CSA), [Captured 7-5-1863 at Gettysburg, PA. Died of remittent fever.] 9-18-1863. Finn's Point National Cemetery, Pennsville, Salem County.
HOBBS, GEORGE W. Pvt, C, 1st NJ Cav, 2-18-1905. St. Stephen Episcopal Cemetery, Florence, Burlington County.
HOBBS, JAMES 1908. Halsey Cemetery, Belford, Monmouth County.
HOBBS, WILLIAM 1-13-1873. Evergreen Cemetery, Morristown, Morris County.
HOBBY*, CHARLES E. (aka: Brown, George) Pvt, E, 6th NH Inf, 9-10-1889. Presbyterian Cemetery, North Plainfield, Somerset County.
HOBELER, HEINRICH (see: Hebler, Henry) Woodland Cemetery, Newark, Essex County.
HOBEN, NICHOLAS Pvt, K, 38th NJ Inf, 3-11-1891. St. John's Cemetery, Hamilton, Mercer County.
HOBENSACK*, CHARLES Pvt, K, 35th NJ Inf, DoD Unknown. Evergreen Cemetery, New Brunswick, Middlesex County.
HOBSON, HENRY Pvt, B, 7th NJ Inf, 1924. Mount Hebron Cemetery, Montclair, Essex County.
HOBSON, WILLIAM H. Pvt, B, 37th NJ Inf, 7-31-1908. Laurel Grove Cemetery, Totowa, Passaic County.
HOCH, JOHN FREDERICK 5-31-1883. Eglington Cemetery, Clarksboro, Gloucester County.
HOCHKINS*, CHARLES E. Pvt, B, 11th NJ Inf, 6-22-1906. Fairmount Cemetery, Newark, Essex County.
HOCKENBURY, ANDREW Pvt, B, 27th NJ Inf, 7-5-1897. Presbyterian Church Cemetery, Rockaway, Morris County.
HOCKENBURY, COONROD Pvt, A, 5th NJ Inf, 1-8-1895. Fairmount Cemetery, Newark, Essex County.

New Jersey Civil War Burials

HOCKENBURY, LEMUEL Pvt, A, 15th NJ Inf, [Cenotaph. Died at Fredericksburg, VA of wounds received 5-12-1864 at Spotsylvania CH, VA.] 5-20-1864. Presbyterian Church Cemetery, Flemington, Hunterdon County.

HOCKENBURY, WILLIAM H. Pvt, D, 143rd PA Inf, 6-25-1898. Presbyterian Church Cemetery, Flemington, Hunterdon County.

HOCKETT*, JONATHAN W. Actg 2nd Asst Eng, U.S. Navy, USS Quaker City, 5-27-1904. Cedar Lawn Cemetery, Paterson, Passaic County.

HODGDON, HENRY C. Capt, U.S. Volunteers, [Commissary of Subsistence.] 8-9-1916. Mount Pleasant Cemetery, Newark, Essex County.

HODGE, JAMES Pvt, A, 25th NJ Inf, 1-10-1909. Laurel Grove Cemetery, Totowa, Passaic County.

HODGE, JOHN Pvt, I, 26th NJ Inf, 10-26-1881. Fairmount Cemetery, Newark, Essex County.

HODGE, JOHN B. 2nd Lt, F, 10th NJ Inf, 10-1-1888. Christ Church Cemetery, Morgan, Middlesex County.

HODGE, W.D. Pvt, K, 46th AL Inf (CSA), 6-30-1863. Finn's Point National Cemetery, Pennsville, Salem County.

HODGE*, WILLIAM M. Corp, E, 146th NY Inf, [Wounded 5-5-1864 at Wilderness, VA.] 9-23-1926. Grove Church Cemetery, North Bergen, Hudson County.

HODGES, ALFRED M. Pvt, B, 11th TX Cav (CSA), [Captured 6-22-1863 at Bridgeville, TN. Died of liver infection.] 5-31-1864. Finn's Point National Cemetery, Pennsville, Salem County.

HODGES, R. Pvt, D, 16th VA Cav (CSA), 6-24-1864. Finn's Point National Cemetery, Pennsville, Salem County.

HODGINS*, GEORGE Corp, A, 88th NY Inf, DoD Unknown. Mount Olivet Cemetery, Newark, Essex County.

HODGKINS, JOSEPH B. Pvt, H, 2nd NJ Inf, [Wounded 9-14-1862 at Crampton's Pass, MD.] 11-23-1918. Greenwood Cemetery, Boonton, Morris County.

HODGKINSON, THOMAS H. Pvt, D, 7th NY State Militia, 2-6-1908. Rosedale Cemetery, Orange, Essex County.

HODGKISS, HENRY (see: Hotchkiss, Henry E.) Oak Hill Cemetery, Vineland, Cumberland County.

HODGSON, WILLIAM H. Pvt, I, 27th NJ Inf, 4-23-1870. Evergreen Cemetery, Morristown, Morris County.

HODSON, CHARLES B. Pvt, I, 4th NJ Inf, [Wounded in action.] 10-12-1893. Mount Holly Cemetery, Mount Holly, Burlington County.

HODSON, JAMES C. Pvt, A, 106th PA Inf, [Died of wounds received at Wilderness, VA.] 5-20-1864. Mount Holly Cemetery, Mount Holly, Burlington County.

HOE, CHARLES Musc, C, 4th NJ Militia, DoD Unknown. Grove Church Cemetery, North Bergen, Hudson County.

HOE, THOMAS Corp, E, 2nd U.S. CT, 4-25-1914. White Ridge Cemetery, Eatontown, Monmouth County.

HOEBER, FREDERICK C. 2nd Lt, K, 1st NJ Inf, 11-9-1871. Hoboken Cemetery, North Bergen, Hudson County.

HOEFLE*, FREDERICK Pvt, Btty E, 1st NJ Light Art, 11-9-1881. Hoboken Cemetery, North Bergen, Hudson County.

HOEHING, GEORGE (aka: Hohing, George) Pvt, A, 13th NJ Inf, 4-15-1906. Woodland Cemetery, Newark, Essex County.

HOEHLE, JOHN H. Sgt, H, 5th NJ Inf, 4-4-1886. Rahway Cemetery, Rahway, Union County.

HOEHNE, HENRY (aka: Mooney, Henry) Pvt, Btty B, 1st NJ Light Art, 7-8-1890. Palisade Cemetery, North Bergen, Hudson County.

HOELZEL, JOHN Pvt, A, 9th NJ Inf, 12-2-1899. Evergreen Cemetery, Hillside, Union County.

Our Brothers Gone Before

HOERMAN, GEORGE 1st Lt, F, 31st NY Inf, 6-5-1915. Rosedale Cemetery, Orange, Essex County.
HOEY*, ANDREW JACKSON Capt of the Hold, U.S. Navy, USS Princeton, 4-21-1900. Baptist Church Cemetery, Haddonfield, Camden County.
HOEY*, ISAAC N. (aka: Hoy, Isaac) Pvt, B, 81st PA Inf, 5-21-1911. Baptist Church Cemetery, Haddonfield, Camden County.
HOEY, JOHN Pvt, I, 8th NJ Inf, 2-1-1907. Rosedale Cemetery, Orange, Essex County.
HOEY, JOHN N. Pvt, I, 186th PA Inf, DoD Unknown. Old Camden Cemetery, Camden, Camden County.
HOEY, JOHN W. Sgt, G, 5th NJ Inf, DoD Unknown. Bayview-New York Bay Cemetery, Jersey City, Hudson County.
HOEY, WILLIAM E. Pvt, C, 186th PA Inf, 9-16-1871. Baptist Church Cemetery, Haddonfield, Camden County.
HOEZLE, FELIX Pvt, F, 7th NJ Inf, DoD Unknown. Holy Sepulchre Cemetery, East Orange, Essex County.
HOFF*, ANGUS DOUGLASS (aka: Douglas, August) Pvt, Btty E, 2nd PA Heavy Art, 6-12-1911. Wesley United Methodist Church Cemetery, Petersburg, Cape May County.
HOFF, CHARLES Pvt, K, 40th NJ Inf, 11-16-1913. Greenwood Cemetery, Hamilton, Mercer County.
HOFF, JACOB H. Pvt, E, 4th NJ Inf, 8-5-1915. Union Cemetery, Frenchtown, Hunterdon County.
HOFF, JAMES 11-4-1869. Greengrove Cemetery, Keyport, Monmouth County.
HOFF, JAMES B. Pvt, D, 29th NJ Inf, 1878. Eastmond Cemetery, Port Monmouth, Monmouth County.
HOFF*, JAMES V. Pvt, E, 2nd NJ Inf, 1884. Harlingen Cemetery, Belle Mead, Somerset County.
HOFF, JEREMIAH J. Sgt, A, 31st NJ Inf, 6-28-1905. Presbyterian Cemetery, Springfield, Union County.
HOFF, JOHN Pvt, B, 9th NJ Inf, 2-17-1888. Rahway Cemetery, Rahway, Union County.
HOFF, JOHN L. 1-18-1916. Washington Monumental Cemetery, South River, Middlesex County.
HOFF, JOSEPH Pvt, Btty H, 4th NY Heavy Art, 9-16-1901. Grove Church Cemetery, North Bergen, Hudson County.
HOFF, LEWIS B. 1st Sgt, H, 30th NJ Inf, 5-7-1878. Rahway Cemetery, Rahway, Union County.
HOFF, RUTLEDGE T. (aka: Huck, Rutledge) Pvt, B, 196th PA Inf, 5-25-1907. Riverview Cemetery, Trenton, Mercer County.
HOFF, SAMUEL Corp, G, 15th NJ Inf, [Wounded in action.] 12-30-1908. Presbyterian Church Cemetery, Mount Pleasant, Hunterdon County.
HOFF, THOMAS DoD Unknown. Cedar Grove Cemetery, Gloucester City, Camden County.
HOFF, WILLIAM Pvt, D, 4th NJ Inf, 7-22-1893. Presbyterian Church Cemetery, Harmony, Warren County.
HOFF, WILLIAM H. 1-15-1863. Baptist Church Cemetery, Baptistown, Hunterdon County.
HOFFER, FREDERICK F. 1-10-1915. Holy Sepulchre Cemetery, Totowa, Passaic County.
HOFFLER, JOHN F. Pvt, A, 46th NY Inf, 8-5-1911. Fairmount Cemetery, Newark, Essex County.
HOFFLINGER, ERASTUS S. Pvt, D, 23rd NJ Inf, 12-28-1901. Windsor Burial Grounds Cemetery, East Windsor, Mercer County.
HOFFLINGER*, JOSEPH Pvt, E, 8th NJ Inf, 7-20-1907. Arlington Cemetery, Pennsauken, Camden County.

New Jersey Civil War Burials

HOFFLINGER, WILLIAM C. 9-16-1866. Evergreen Cemetery, Camden, Camden County.

HOFFLINGER, WILLIAM C. Pvt, B, 40th NJ Inf, 1-21-1902. Presbyterian Church Cemetery, Bridgeton, Cumberland County.

HOFFMAN, AARON Sgt, H, 8th NJ Inf, 1921. Atlantic View Cemetery, Manasquan, Monmouth County.

HOFFMAN, ABRAHAM H. Pvt, H, 8th NJ Inf, [Wounded in action.] 12-1-1902. Presbyterian Church Cemetery, Pleasant Grove, Morris County.

HOFFMAN, ABRAM S. 1897. Newell Cemetery, Stanton Station, Hunterdon County.

HOFFMAN, ALFRED Sgt, B, 4th NJ Inf, 11-23-1898. Riverview Cemetery, Trenton, Mercer County.

HOFFMAN, ARNOLD G. DoD Unknown. Friendship United Methodist Church Cemetery, Upper Deerfield, Cumberland County.

HOFFMAN, ARTHUR Pvt, G, 28th NJ Inf, DoD Unknown. Mount Zion United Methodist Church Cemetery, Barnsboro, Gloucester County.

HOFFMAN, BENJAMIN Pvt, D, 24th NJ Inf, 9-24-1881. Cedar Green Cemetery, Clayton, Gloucester County.

HOFFMAN, BENJAMIN 1894. Cedar Lawn Cemetery, Paterson, Passaic County.

HOFFMAN, BENJAMIN (see: Hoffner, Benjamin A.) Mount Pleasant Cemetery, Millville, Cumberland County.

HOFFMAN, CARL GUSTAVE (aka: Hoffman, Charles G.) Pvt, D, 124th NY Inf, [Wounded 5-3-1863 at Chancellorsville, VA. and 5-6-1864 at Wilderness, VA.] 3-26-1915. Fairmount Cemetery, Newark, Essex County.

HOFFMAN, CARL P. 1930. Mount Hope Presbyterian Cemetery, Lambertville, Hunterdon County.

HOFFMAN, CHARLES Pvt, Unassigned, 6th NJ Inf, 9-5-1923. Old Gloucester Burial Grounds Cemetery, Clarksboro, Gloucester County.

HOFFMAN, CHARLES DoD Unknown. Bethesda Methodist-Episcopal Church Cemetery, Swedesboro, Gloucester County.

HOFFMAN, CHARLES G. (see: Hoffman, Carl Gustave) Fairmount Cemetery, Newark, Essex County.

HOFFMAN, CHARLES L. Pvt, D, 10th NJ Inf, [Died of typhoid at Washington, DC.] 5-14-1862. Methodist Church Cemetery, New Albany, Burlington County.

HOFFMAN, CHAUNCEY C. Pvt, L, 25th NY Cav, 3-19-1900. Baptist Cemetery, Vincentown, Burlington County.

HOFFMAN, CHRISTOPHER Pvt, B, 1st NY Eng, 1-16-1907. Hoboken Cemetery, North Bergen, Hudson County.

HOFFMAN, CLEMENS Pvt, E, 103rd NY Inf, DoD Unknown. Holy Sepulchre Cemetery, East Orange, Essex County.

HOFFMAN, CONRAD Sgt, H, 45th NY Inf, [Wounded 5-2-1863 at Chancellorsville, VA.] 1919. Maple Grove Cemetery, Hackensack, Bergen County.

HOFFMAN, DAVID Pvt, H, 15th NJ Inf, 1-6-1902. Methodist Church Cemetery, Mount Bethel, Warren County.

HOFFMAN, DAVID DoD Unknown. Presbyterian Church Cemetery, Bridgeton, Cumberland County.

HOFFMAN, ELIAS Pvt, H, 8th NJ Inf, [Wounded in action.] 3-1-1922. Mansfield/Washington Cemetery, Washington, Warren County.

HOFFMAN, FREDERICK Pvt, I, 4th NJ Inf, 5-8-1914. Baptist Cemetery, Pemberton, Burlington County.

HOFFMAN, FREDERICK Capt, H, 68th NY Inf, 1897. Bayview-New York Bay Cemetery, Jersey City, Hudson County.

HOFFMAN, FREDERICK Pvt, Btty A, 1st NJ Light Art, 1927. New Presbyterian Cemetery, Hanover, Morris County.

HOFFMAN, FREDERICK 12-19-1922. Rosedale Cemetery, Orange, Essex County.

Our Brothers Gone Before

HOFFMAN, GARRETT C. Pvt, K, 31st NJ Inf, 8-2-1902. Evergreen Cemetery, Clinton, Hunterdon County.

HOFFMAN, GEORGE Pvt, H, 9th NJ Inf, 4-4-1889. Fairmount Cemetery, Newark, Essex County.

HOFFMAN, GEORGE Pvt, E, 30th NJ Inf, 1907. Reformed Church Cemetery, Readington, Hunterdon County.

HOFFMAN, GEORGE Maj, 8th NJ Inf 8-9-1886. Presbyterian Cemetery, Asbury, Warren County.

HOFFMAN, GEORGE Pvt, H, 11th NJ Inf, 3-8-1905. Mansfield/Washington Cemetery, Washington, Warren County.

HOFFMAN, GEORGE DoD Unknown. Union Cemetery, Gloucester City, Camden County.

HOFFMAN, GEORGE H. Corp, C, 50th PA Inf, 1-22-1903. Eastview Cemetery, Salem, Salem County.

HOFFMAN, GEORGE M. Pvt, I, 23rd NJ Inf, 10-9-1897. Baptist/St. Andrew's Cemetery, Mount Holly, Burlington County.

HOFFMAN, GEORGE S. Pvt, C, 2nd NJ Militia, 1929. Fairmount Cemetery, Fairmount, Hunterdon County.

HOFFMAN, GEORGE W. Corp, H, 4th NJ Inf, [Wounded in action.] 4-15-1924. Cedar Hill Cemetery, Florence, Burlington County.

HOFFMAN*, GUSTAV 2nd Lt, E, 45th U.S. CT, DoD Unknown. Rosedale Cemetery, Linden, Union County.

HOFFMAN, HENRY Pvt, D, 11th NJ Inf, DoD Unknown. Bloomfield Cemetery, Bloomfield, Essex County.

HOFFMAN, HENRY 12-18-1908. Presbyterian Church Cemetery, Califon, Hunterdon County.

HOFFMAN, HENRY Pvt, B, 33rd VA Inf (CSA), [Wounded 5-3-1863 at Chancellorsville, VA. Captured 5-12-1864 at Spotsylvania CH, VA. Died of lung inflammation.] 11-24-1864. Finn's Point National Cemetery, Pennsville, Salem County.

HOFFMAN, HENRY H. Pvt, B, 15th NJ Inf, 6-18-1912. Fairmount Cemetery, Newark, Essex County.

HOFFMAN, HENRY H. (JR.) Pvt, F, 26th NJ Inf, [Died at Potomac Creek, VA. of wounds received 5-4-1863 at Banks Ford, VA.] 5-18-1863. Bloomfield Cemetery, Bloomfield, Essex County.

HOFFMAN*, HEZEKIAH Pvt, H, 15th NJ Inf, 3-11-1910. Mount Lebanon Cemetery, Mount Lebanon, Hunterdon County.

HOFFMAN, HORACE J. Sgt, B, 10th WI Inf, 4-16-1915. Bayview-New York Bay Cemetery, Jersey City, Hudson County.

HOFFMAN, ISAAC H. Pvt, G, 30th NJ Inf, DoD Unknown. Christian Church Cemetery, Locktown, Hunterdon County.

HOFFMAN, ISRAEL (aka: Hawkins, Israel) Pvt, I, 2nd NJ Cav, 8-9-1915. 1st Methodist Church Cemetery, Williamstown, Gloucester County.

HOFFMAN, JACOB A. Pvt, K, 31st NJ Inf, 1921. Mountain View Cemetery, Cokesbury, Hunterdon County.

HOFFMAN, JACOB H. 1st Lt, M, 2nd NJ Cav, 12-9-1895. Greenwood Cemetery, Boonton, Morris County.

HOFFMAN, JACOB T. Pvt, F, 17th PA Inf, 2-16-1916. Rosehill Cemetery, Linden, Union County.

HOFFMAN*, JAMES Pvt, H, 9th NJ Inf, 7-4-1926. Bordentown/Old St. Mary's Catholic Cemetery, Bordentown, Burlington County.

HOFFMAN, JAMES 8-19-1870. Methodist Church Cemetery, Mount Bethel, Warren County.

HOFFMAN*, JAMES Pvt, I, 2nd NJ Inf, 8-24-1874. Rockport Cemetery, Rockport, Warren County.

New Jersey Civil War Burials

HOFFMAN, JEREMIAH K. Pvt, H, 8th NJ Inf, 1908. Presbyterian Church Cemetery, Clinton, Hunterdon County.

HOFFMAN, JOHN Pvt, B, 9th NJ Inf, 1-4-1870. Rahway Cemetery, Rahway, Union County.

HOFFMAN, JOHN 2-9-1876. Fairview Cemetery, Westfield, Union County.

HOFFMAN, JOHN ADAM Pvt, H, 10th NJ Inf, 3-4-1911. Berlin Cemetery, Berlin, Camden County.

HOFFMAN, JOHN B. 2nd Lt, H, 10th NJ Inf, 1921. 7th Day Baptist Church Cemetery, Shiloh, Cumberland County.

HOFFMAN, JOHN EDWARD Sgt, E, 34th NJ Inf, 1-20-1932. Mount Hope Presbyterian Cemetery, Lambertville, Hunterdon County.

HOFFMAN, JOHN HENRY Pvt, C, 1st MA Inf, [Wounded 5-2-1863 at Chancellorsville, VA. and 5-12-1864 at Spotsylvania CH, VA.] 1-28-1883. Chestnut Hill Cemetery, East Brunswick, Middlesex County.

HOFFMAN, JOHN J. Pvt, C, 9th NJ Inf, 2-3-1896. Methodist-Episcopal Church Cemetery, Aura, Gloucester County.

HOFFMAN, JOHN J. 8-22-1881. Newell Cemetery, Stanton Station, Hunterdon County.

HOFFMAN, JOHN L. Pvt, D, 8th NJ Inf, [Wounded in action.] 2-2-1882. Presbyterian Cemetery, Cokesbury, Hunterdon County.

HOFFMAN, JOHN T. Pvt, F, 25th NJ Inf, 1916. Mount Pleasant Cemetery, Millville, Cumberland County.

HOFFMAN, JOHN T. 2-6-1916. Woodland Cemetery, Newark, Essex County.

HOFFMAN, JOHN W. Pvt, D, 5th NJ Inf, [Wounded in action.] 2-18-1924. Laurel Grove Cemetery, Totowa, Passaic County.

HOFFMAN, LEMUEL H. Pvt, B, 27th NJ Inf, DoD Unknown. Presbyterian Church Cemetery, Pleasant Grove, Morris County.

HOFFMAN, LEVI W. Pvt, I, 7th NJ Inf, 3-3-1870. Reformed Church Cemetery, Lebanon, Hunterdon County.

HOFFMAN, LEWIS Pvt, A, 31st NJ Inf, 3-21-1865. Reformed Church Cemetery, Lebanon, Hunterdon County.

HOFFMAN, LEYBRAND (see: Hufman, Lybrand) Harleigh Cemetery, Camden, Camden County.

HOFFMAN, LOUIS A. 2nd Lt, K, 14th NJ Inf, 9-1-1884. Maplewood Cemetery, Freehold, Monmouth County.

HOFFMAN, MARTIN Sgt, A, 31st NJ Inf, 7-18-1902. Reformed Church Cemetery, Lebanon, Hunterdon County.

HOFFMAN, MORRIS Pvt, H, 8th NJ Inf, [Wounded 5-5-1862 at Williamsburg, VA.] 10-18-1890. Methodist Church Cemetery, Asbury, Warren County.

HOFFMAN, NOAH Pvt, C, 90th NY Inf, 3-29-1910. Evergreen Cemetery, Clinton, Hunterdon County.

HOFFMAN, PETER P. Pvt, H, 2nd NJ Cav, 7-26-1898. Presbyterian Cemetery, Cokesbury, Hunterdon County.

HOFFMAN, PHILIP H. 4-9-1924. Presbyterian Church Cemetery, Mendham, Morris County.

HOFFMAN, SAMUEL C. Pvt, H, 4th NJ Inf, 9-13-1882. Presbyterian Church Cemetery, Pleasant Grove, Morris County.

HOFFMAN, SAMUEL M. 7-18-1881. Bayview-New York Bay Cemetery, Jersey City, Hudson County.

HOFFMAN, SILAS Pvt, I, 10th NJ Inf, [Wounded in action.] 11-29-1904. Tabernacle Baptist Church Cemetery, Erma, Cape May County.

HOFFMAN, THEODORE Pvt, A, 31st NJ Inf, 7-25-1887. Reformed Church Cemetery, Lebanon, Hunterdon County.

HOFFMAN, THEODORE J. Pvt, E, 8th NJ Inf, 9-28-1917. New Somerville Cemetery, Somerville, Somerset County.

Our Brothers Gone Before

HOFFMAN*, WILLIAM Pvt, Btty B, 1st NJ Light Art, 5-16-1911. Oddfellows Cemetery, Burlington, Burlington County.
HOFFMAN, WILLIAM Pvt, K, 38th NJ Inf, 11-19-1892. Methodist-Episcopal Church Cemetery, South Dennis, Cape May County.
HOFFMAN, WILLIAM (aka: Taufman, William) Pvt, A, 8th NJ Inf, 2-11-1872. Woodland Cemetery, Newark, Essex County.
HOFFMAN, WILLIAM D. Seaman, U.S. Navy, 1874. Christ Church Cemetery, Morgan, Middlesex County.
HOFFMAN, WILLIAM E. Pvt, B, 30th NJ Inf, DoD Unknown. Bayview-New York Bay Cemetery, Jersey City, Hudson County.
HOFFMAN, WILLIAM G. Pvt, Btty D, 1st NJ Light Art, 5-30-1900. Fairmount Cemetery, Newark, Essex County.
HOFFMAN, WILLIAM H. 10-23-1867. Reformed Church Cemetery, Lebanon, Hunterdon County.
HOFFMAN, WILLIAM H. Pvt, I, 8th NJ Inf, [Died of wounds received at Hatchers Run, VA.] 2-7-1865. United Methodist Cemetery, Gladstone, Somerset County.
HOFFMAN*, WILLIAM O. Ord Seaman, U.S. Navy, USS Acacia, 1-10-1904. Woodland Cemetery, Newark, Essex County.
HOFFMAN, WILLIAM P. Pvt, G, 10th WI Inf, [Wounded in action at Peach Tree Creek, GA.] 10-23-1918. Arlington Cemetery, Kearny, Hudson County.
HOFFMANN, CLEMENT Pvt, E, 103rd NY Inf, 1897. Holy Sepulchre Cemetery, East Orange, Essex County.
HOFFMANN, ERNST Pvt, G, 45th NY Inf, 12-5-1890. Palisade Cemetery, North Bergen, Hudson County.
HOFFMIRE, G. EDWARD Pvt, H, 29th NJ Inf, 1-3-1911. Riverside Cemetery, Toms River, Ocean County.
HOFFNEGEL, JOHN M. (aka: Hofnagle, John) Pvt, E, 1st NJ Militia, 12-21-1865. Woodland Cemetery, Newark, Essex County.
HOFFNER*, BENJAMIN A. (aka: Hoffman, Benjamin) Pvt, K, 191st PA Inf, 1927. Mount Pleasant Cemetery, Millville, Cumberland County.
HOFFNER, JACOB D. Pvt, U.S. Marine Corps, 3-1-1923. Oddfellows Cemetery, Burlington, Burlington County.
HOFFSASS, CARL (see: Hofsachs, Carl) Fairmount Cemetery, Newark, Essex County.
HOFKER, JOHN Seaman, U.S. Navy, USS Aroostook, 3-16-1899. Bloomfield Cemetery, Bloomfield, Essex County.
HOFLER, JACOB Pvt, C, 52nd NC Inf (CSA), [Captured 7-3-1863 at Gettysburg, PA.] 11-3-1863. Finn's Point National Cemetery, Pennsville, Salem County.
HOFLER, JOHN F. Pvt, A, 46th NY Inf, 8-2-1911. Fairmount Cemetery, Newark, Essex County.
HOFMEISTER, JACOB Pvt, Btty A, 1st NJ Light Art, 4-11-1887. Grove Church Cemetery, North Bergen, Hudson County.
HOFNAGLE, JOHN (see: Hoffnegel, John M.) Woodland Cemetery, Newark, Essex County.
HOFSACHS, CARL (aka: Hoffsass, Carl) Pvt, E, 103rd NY Inf, 11-11-1890. Fairmount Cemetery, Newark, Essex County.
HOFT, HENRY Pvt, F, 1st NJ Cav, [Died of consumption at Burkville, VA.] 4-25-1865. Bergen Iron Works Cemetery, Lakewood, Ocean County.
HOFT, HERMAN Pvt, F, 1st NJ Cav, 6-15-1892. Woodlawn Cemetery, Lakewood, Ocean County.
HOGAN, CHARLES (see: Golden, Michael C.) Holy Name Cemetery, Jersey City, Hudson County.
HOGAN, CLAYBURN Corp, E, 40th NJ Inf, [Wounded 4-2-1865 at Petersburg, VA.] 10-17-1871. Fairmount Cemetery, Newark, Essex County.

New Jersey Civil War Burials

HOGAN, CORDY W. Pvt, G, 35th GA Inf (CSA), [Captured 7-3-1863 at Gettysburg, PA. Died of diarrhea.] 2-21-1864. Finn's Point National Cemetery, Pennsville, Salem County.

HOGAN*, COUNT DE GRACE (aka: Hogan, Grasse) Corp, E, 6th NJ Inf, 5-20-1895. Evergreen Cemetery, Camden, Camden County.

HOGAN*, EDMOND Pvt, E, 35th NJ Inf, 2-22-1879. Old Catholic Cemetery, Newton, Sussex County.

HOGAN, GARRETT Corp, A, 15th NJ Inf, 4-2-1881. St. John's Cemetery, Lambertville, Hunterdon County.

HOGAN, GEORGE F. Pvt, G, 3rd NJ Cav, 1923. Mount Pleasant Cemetery, Millville, Cumberland County.

HOGAN, GEORGE W. DoD Unknown. Van Liew Cemetery, North Brunswick, Middlesex County.

HOGAN, GEORGE W. Corp, A, 52nd GA Inf (CSA), [Captured 5-16-1863 at Baker's Creek, MS. Died of fever.] 7-8-1863. Finn's Point National Cemetery, Pennsville, Salem County.

HOGAN, GRASSE (see: Hogan, Count de Grace) Evergreen Cemetery, Camden, Camden County.

HOGAN, HARRY A. Pvt, I, 37th NJ Inf, 10-30-1888. Baptist/St. Andrew's Cemetery, Mount Holly, Burlington County.

HOGAN, JAMES 4-14-1885. Holy Name Cemetery, Jersey City, Hudson County.

HOGAN, JAMES (aka: Monahan, James) Pvt, F, 35th NJ Inf, 12-4-1915. St. Rose of Lima Cemetery, Freehold, Monmouth County.

HOGAN, JAMES Pvt, B, 8th NJ Inf, DoD Unknown. Holy Sepulchre Cemetery, East Orange, Essex County.

HOGAN, JOHN Pvt, F, 2nd NJ Militia, DoD Unknown. Holy Sepulchre Cemetery, East Orange, Essex County.

HOGAN, JOHN Pvt, D, 71st PA Inf, DoD Unknown. Arlington Cemetery, Kearny, Hudson County.

HOGAN, JOHN Pvt, G, 2nd NJ Militia, 8-12-1900. Bayview-New York Bay Cemetery, Jersey City, Hudson County.

HOGAN, JOHN Pvt, H, 31st NJ Inf, 6-16-1906. Old Catholic Cemetery, Newton, Sussex County.

HOGAN, JOHN Pvt, H, 66th NY Inf, 5-28-1881. Holy Name Cemetery, Jersey City, Hudson County.

HOGAN, JOHN Pvt, H, 31st NJ Inf, 6-24-1899. Bloomfield Cemetery, Bloomfield, Essex County.

HOGAN, MARTIN Pvt, G, 91st NY Inf, 5-1-1916. Holy Sepulchre Cemetery, Totowa, Passaic County.

HOGAN, MATTHEW Corp, B, 88th NY Inf, [Wounded 12-13-1862 at Fredericksburg, VA. and 5-12-1864 at Po River, VA.] 9-5-1907. Holy Name Cemetery, Jersey City, Hudson County.

HOGAN, THADDEUS 3-18-1918. St. John's Cemetery, Hamilton, Mercer County.

HOGARTH, WILLIAM H.F. (aka: Farror, Henry) Pvt, M, 4th PA Cav, 1-19-1890. Laurel Grove Cemetery, Totowa, Passaic County.

HOGARTY, JAMES R. (aka: Haggerty, James) Pvt, B, 3rd NJ Cav, 3-7-1914. St. Paul's R.C. Church Cemetery, Princeton, Mercer County.

HOGATE, SAMUEL Pvt, I, 4th NJ Militia, 2-21-1899. Eastview Cemetery, Salem, Salem County.

HOGATE, WILLIAM G. Pvt, F, 12th NJ Inf, 2-2-1906. Baptist Cemetery, Salem, Salem County.

HOGBEN, ELMER E. Pvt, D, 25th NJ Inf, 7-27-1915. Old Stone Church Cemetery, Fairton, Cumberland County.

Our Brothers Gone Before

HOGENCAMP, JAMES Pvt, D, 33rd NJ Inf, 8-31-1921. Cedar Lawn Cemetery, Paterson, Passaic County.

HOGENCAMP*, MARTIN Pvt, I, 142nd IN Inf, 5-25-1885. Valleau Cemetery, Ridgewood, Bergen County.

HOGG, ALEXANDER Pvt, B, 65th NY Inf, [Wounded 10-19-1864 at Cedar Creek, VA.] 3-1-1898. Evergreen Cemetery, Hillside, Union County.

HOGGE, MOSES (see: Hoage, Moses A.) Prospect Hill Cemetery, Caldwell, Essex County.

HOGGE, THOMAS (see: Hoage, Thomas) Prospect Hill Cemetery, Caldwell, Essex County.

HOHING, GEORGE (see: Hoehing, George) Woodland Cemetery, Newark, Essex County.

HOHL*, GEORGE Pvt, Btty D, 1st NJ Light Art, 12-20-1895. Presbyterian Cemetery, Allentown, Monmouth County.

HOHL, JOHN Pvt, D, 7th NJ Inf, 1-10-1897. St. Mary's Cemetery, East Orange, Essex County.

HOHNEISEN, WILLIAM CONRAD Pvt, G, 119th NY Inf, 1922. Egg Harbor Cemetery, Egg Harbor, Atlantic County.

HOHWEILLER*, GEORGE Pvt, H, 7th NJ Inf, 6-22-1893. Fairmount Cemetery, Newark, Essex County.

HOILE, GEORGE (see: Hiles, George W.) Zion Methodist Church Cemetery, Porchtown, Gloucester County.

HOLAHAN, RICHARD Corp, H, 1st U.S. Inf, DoD Unknown. Holy Sepulchre Cemetery, East Orange, Essex County.

HOLBERT*, CORNELIUS H. Pvt, D, 124th NY Inf, 9-6-1910. Laurel Grove Cemetery, Totowa, Passaic County.

HOLBROOK*, ROBERT Pvt, I, 99th PA Inf, 6-1-1900. Mount Prospect Cemetery, Neptune, Monmouth County.

HOLCOMB, ALFRED B. Pvt, F, 22nd NJ Inf, DoD Unknown. 2nd Presbyterian Church Cemetery, Mount Airy, Hunterdon County.

HOLCOMB, DAVID H. Musc, A, 10th NJ Inf, DoD Unknown. Arlington Cemetery, Kearny, Hudson County.

HOLCOMB, DAVID HIRAM 9-3-1923. Sandy Ridge Cemetery, Sandy Ridge, Hunterdon County.

HOLCOMBE, ALFRED Pvt, F, 22nd NJ Inf, 2-3-1889. Methodist Church Cemetery, Titusville, Mercer County.

HOLCOMBE, ELISHA D. Pvt, H, 4th GA Inf (CSA), [Captured 5-10-1864 at Spotsylvania CH, VA. Died of pneumonia.] 1-19-1865. Finn's Point National Cemetery, Pennsville, Salem County.

HOLCOMBE, HENRY Corp, B, 22nd U.S. CT, 3-9-1891. Riverview Cemetery, Trenton, Mercer County.

HOLCOMBE, ISAAC W. Pvt, B, 38th NJ Inf, 8-28-1914. Mount Hope Presbyterian Cemetery, Lambertville, Hunterdon County.

HOLCOMBE, JESSE A. Corp, I, 14th NJ Inf, 5-21-1913. Methodist Church Cemetery, Titusville, Mercer County.

HOLCOMBE, THEOPHILUS MOORE Pvt, D, 28th NJ Inf, [Died of fever at New Brunswick, NJ.] 4-1-1863. Christ Episcopal Church Cemetery, New Brunswick, Middlesex County.

HOLDCRAFT, ASA G. Pvt, F, 12th NJ Inf, 11-19-1883. Methodist Cemetery, Mantua, Gloucester County.

HOLDCRAFT, SAMUEL O. Coal Heaver, U.S. Navy, USS Brooklyn, 11-14-1872. New Episcopal Church Cemetery, Swedesboro, Gloucester County.

HOLDEN, ABIJAH M. Sgt, K, 15th NJ Inf, 7-28-1898. Deckertown-Union Cemetery, Papakating, Sussex County.

HOLDEN*, EDGAR Surg, U.S. Navy, USS Sassacus, 7-16-1909. Mount Pleasant Cemetery, Newark, Essex County.

New Jersey Civil War Burials

HOLDEN, HAVILAH H. Pvt, C, 8th NJ Inf, 11-22-1904. Arlington Cemetery, Kearny, Hudson County.
HOLDEN, HENRY Seaman, U.S. Navy, 3-26-1916. Atlantic City Cemetery, Pleasantville, Atlantic County.
HOLDEN, HENRY S. Pvt, H, 21st NJ Inf, 11-10-1863. Mount Pleasant Cemetery, Newark, Essex County.
HOLDEN, JAMES Pvt, B, 7th NJ Inf, 1905. Presbyterian Church Cemetery, Hampton, Hunterdon County.
HOLDEN, JONATHAN (aka: Holdner, Jonathan) Pvt, E, 38th NJ Inf, 1-26-1934. Riverview Cemetery, Trenton, Mercer County.
HOLDEN, JOSEPH H. 1919. Union Cemetery, Milford, Hunterdon County.
HOLDEN, SAMUEL L. Pvt, G, 153rd PA Inf, 1-1-1905. Mansfield/Washington Cemetery, Washington, Warren County.
HOLDEN, WILLIAM 8-16-1885. Bayview-New York Bay Cemetery, Jersey City, Hudson County.
HOLDEN, WILLIAM Pvt, K, 4th (Russell's) AL Cav (CSA), 10-24-1863. Finn's Point National Cemetery, Pennsville, Salem County.
HOLDER, JOHN M. Pvt, G, 44th GA Inf (CSA), [Captured 5-10-1864 at Spotsylvania CH, VA. Died of smallpox.] 7-10-1864. Finn's Point National Cemetery, Pennsville, Salem County.
HOLDING, JOHN H. 1910. Mount Pleasant Cemetery, Millville, Cumberland County.
HOLDNER, JONATHAN (see: Holden, Jonathan) Riverview Cemetery, Trenton, Mercer County.
HOLDOFFER, ANDREW Pvt, H, 28th PA Inf, DoD Unknown. Mount Pleasant Cemetery, Millville, Cumberland County.
HOLDRIDGE, LOREN Pvt, B, 21st NY Cav, 8-22-1933. Riverview Cemetery, Trenton, Mercer County.
HOLDRUM, ABRAM G. 3-24-1909. Old Hook Cemetery, Westwood, Bergen County.
HOLDZKOM, WILLIAM 4-25-1903. Atlantic City Cemetery, Pleasantville, Atlantic County.
HOLEBROOK, HENRY B. Sgt Maj, 98th NY Inf 1915. Evergreen Cemetery, Morristown, Morris County.
HOLEMAN, GEORGE Pvt, B, 23rd NJ Inf, 7-17-1891. Methodist Church Cemetery, Groveville, Mercer County.
HOLEMAN, REUBEN P. Corp, D, 31st NJ Inf, DoD Unknown. Reformed Church Cemetery, Clover Hill, Somerset County.
HOLEMAN*, WILLIAM H. (aka: Holman, William H.) Pvt, A, 6th NJ Inf, 11-15-1892. Presbyterian Church Cemetery, Hampton, Hunterdon County.
HOLETON, JESSE Pvt, K, 24th NJ Inf, 11-9-1899. Methodist-Episcopal Church Cemetery, Penns Grove, Salem County.
HOLETON, JOSIAH (aka: Holton, Josiah) Pvt, I, 12th NJ Inf, 7-19-1901. Methodist-Episcopal Church Cemetery, Penns Grove, Salem County.
HOLETON, WILLIAM Pvt, K, 24th NJ Inf, 5-20-1865. Methodist-Episcopal Church Cemetery, Penns Grove, Salem County.
HOLGATE, FRANCIS Musc, K, 70th NY Inf, DoD Unknown. Fairmount Cemetery, Newark, Essex County.
HOLINGSHEAD, HENRY A. 4-2-1910. Evergreen Cemetery, Camden, Camden County.
HOLL, FREDERICK Pvt, I, 5th U.S. Inf, 7-6-1880. Beverly National Cemetery, Edgewater Park, Burlington County.
HOLL*, GEORGE K. (aka: Hall, Guadaloupe) Pvt, B, 95th PA Inf, [Wounded 5-14-1864 at Spotsylvania CH, VA.] 2-13-1917. Evergreen Cemetery, Camden, Camden County.
HOLL, L.F. DoD Unknown. Evergreen Cemetery, Camden, Camden County.

Our Brothers Gone Before

HOLLAHAN, MARTIN Pvt, B, 8th U.S. Inf, 7-13-1906. New Camden Cemetery, Camden, Camden County.
HOLLAND, ANDREW Pvt, B, 6th NJ Inf, [Died of wounds received at Wilderness, VA.] 7-26-1864. Methodist Church Cemetery, Everittstown, Hunterdon County.
HOLLAND, FRANKLIN Pvt, A, 44th PA Militia, 10-28-1910. Laurel Grove Cemetery, Totowa, Passaic County.
HOLLAND, FREDERICK Pvt, I, 33rd NJ Inf, 1-13-1881. Fairmount Cemetery, Newark, Essex County.
HOLLAND, GEORGE E. 3-2-1915. Hackensack Cemetery, Hackensack, Bergen County.
HOLLAND, GEORGE L. Pvt, L, 1st NJ Cav, 11-28-1904. Fairmount Cemetery, Newark, Essex County.
HOLLAND, GEORGE L. Pvt, D, 1st NJ Cav, 1-21-1909. Fairview Cemetery, Westfield, Union County.
HOLLAND, GEORGE W. Pvt, B, 8th NJ Inf, 9-2-1870. Fairmount Cemetery, Newark, Essex County.
HOLLAND, HENRY T. Pvt, D, 36th (Broyle's) GA Inf (CSA), [Captured 5-16-1863 at Baker's Creek, MS.] 7-26-1863. Finn's Point National Cemetery, Pennsville, Salem County.
HOLLAND, J.A. Pvt, C, 5th AL Inf (CSA), 7-12-1864. Finn's Point National Cemetery, Pennsville, Salem County.
HOLLAND, J.A. Pvt, C, 3rd LA Inf (CSA), [Captured 7-7-1863 atGettysburg, PA.] 9-24-1863. Finn's Point National Cemetery, Pennsville, Salem County.
HOLLAND, J.R. (aka: Holland, James K.) Pvt, I, 1st (Turney's) TN Inf (CSA), 11-22-1863. Finn's Point National Cemetery, Pennsville, Salem County.
HOLLAND, JAMES BALLARD Pvt, K, 50th VA Inf (CSA), [Captured 7-5-1863 at Waterloo, PA. Died of diarrhea.] 10-16-1863. Finn's Point National Cemetery, Pennsville, Salem County.
HOLLAND, JAMES H. Corp, L, 1st (Orr's) SC Rifles (CSA), [Captured 5-12-1864 at Spotsylvania CH, VA. Died of pleurisy.] 2-22-1865. Finn's Point National Cemetery, Pennsville, Salem County.
HOLLAND, JAMES K. (see: Holland, J.R.) Finn's Point National Cemetery, Pennsville, Salem County.
HOLLAND, JAMES M. Pvt, F, 41st U.S. CT, 1-6-1900. Evergreen Cemetery, Morristown, Morris County.
HOLLAND, JOHN 7-17-1876. Holy Name Cemetery, Jersey City, Hudson County.
HOLLAND, JOHN F. (see: Hollerd, John F.) Hillside Cemetery, Scotch Plains, Union County.
HOLLAND, R. Pvt, C, 13th VA Cav (CSA), 3-2-1865. Finn's Point National Cemetery, Pennsville, Salem County.
HOLLAND, ROBERT Seaman, U.S. Navy, 1-3-1905. Mount Prospect Cemetery, Neptune, Monmouth County.
HOLLAND*, SHEDRICK Landsman, U.S. Navy, USS Sagamore, 6-11-1915. Mount Moriah Cemetery, Hainesport, Burlington County.
HOLLAND, V.W. Pvt, Carter's Btty, VA Light Art (CSA), 4-2-1865. Finn's Point National Cemetery, Pennsville, Salem County.
HOLLAND, WILLIAM E. DoD Unknown. Elmwood Cemetery, New Brunswick, Middlesex County.
HOLLAND, YORK Corp, C, 41st U.S. CT, 12-29-1895. Fairmount Cemetery, Newark, Essex County.
HOLLEMBACK, SAMUEL (aka: Hollembeak, Samuel) Pvt, K, 4th NJ Militia, 2-8-1902. Methodist-Episcopal Cemetery, Burlington, Burlington County.
HOLLEMBEAK, SAMUEL (see: Hollemback, Samuel) Methodist-Episcopal Cemetery, Burlington, Burlington County.

New Jersey Civil War Burials

HOLLEN, ROBERT R. Pvt, Btty H, 1st U.S. Art, [Died of consumption.] 10-22-1861. Fairmount Cemetery, Newark, Essex County.

HOLLENBACK, HENRY Corp, B, 56th OH Inf, 11-3-1894. Baptist Cemetery, Burlington, Burlington County.

HOLLENBACK, HENRY (JR.) (aka: Haulenbeck, Henry) Pvt, G, 13th NJ Inf, DoD Unknown. Holy Sepulchre Cemetery, East Orange, Essex County.

HOLLENBECK, HENRY Saddler, A, 12th IL Cav, DoD Unknown. Holy Sepulchre Cemetery, East Orange, Essex County.

HOLLER*, VALENTINE Pvt, I, 13th NJ Inf, 6-11-1891. Fairmount Cemetery, Newark, Essex County.

HOLLERD, JOHN F. (aka: Holland, John F.) Pvt, Btty L, 4th NY Heavy Art, 9-7-1884. Hillside Cemetery, Scotch Plains, Union County.

HOLLEY, GEORGE Pvt, K, 11th NJ Inf, 1922. Holland Cemetery, Holland, Morris County.

HOLLEY, JAMES Pvt, G, 27th NJ Inf, 4-3-1900. 1st Reformed Church Cemetery, Pompton Plains, Morris County.

HOLLIDAY, HUGH C. Pvt, E, 2nd U.S. Cav, DoD Unknown. Vincent Methodist-Episcopal Cemetery, Nutley, Essex County.

HOLLINGER, FRANK Pvt, A, 1st NJ Militia, 8-30-1886. Fairmount Cemetery, Newark, Essex County.

HOLLINGS, JOHN 1-17-1864. Bayview-New York Bay Cemetery, Jersey City, Hudson County.

HOLLINGSHEAD, CALEB H. Pvt, B, 31st NJ Inf, 7-11-1915. Mansfield/Washington Cemetery, Washington, Warren County.

HOLLINGSHEAD, CHARLES Pvt, A, 32nd PA Militia, 5-13-1893. Evergreen Cemetery, Camden, Camden County.

HOLLINGSHEAD, CHARLES H. 1861. Baptist/St. Andrew's Cemetery, Mount Holly, Burlington County.

HOLLINGSHEAD, CLAYTON 2nd Lt, K, 4th NJ Inf, 8-12-1875. Friends Cemetery, Moorestown, Burlington County.

HOLLINGSHEAD, THOMAS Pvt, C, 213th PA Inf, 3-13-1916. Harleigh Cemetery, Camden, Camden County.

HOLLINGSWORTH, FRANCIS M. Sgt, D, 11th AL Inf (CSA), 6-1-1864. Finn's Point National Cemetery, Pennsville, Salem County.

HOLLINGSWORTH, JAMES Pvt, B, 3rd NJ Inf, [Died at Burkettsville, MD. of wounds received 9-14-1862 at Crampton's Pass, MD.] 10-30-1862. Old Camden Cemetery, Camden, Camden County.

HOLLINGSWORTH, SAMUEL H. Landsman, U.S. Navy, USS Midnight, 12-16-1915. Old Camden Cemetery, Camden, Camden County.

HOLLINSHEAD, JOHN R. Corp, G, 22nd NJ Inf, 11-20-1897. Evergreen/Bishop Jaynes Cemetery, Basking Ridge, Somerset County.

HOLLIS, AMARIAH C. Pvt, E, 24th NJ Inf, 12-28-1899. Eglington Cemetery, Clarksboro, Gloucester County.

HOLLIS, JOHN L. 11-9-1922. Evergreen Cemetery, Camden, Camden County.

HOLLIS, JOHN L. (aka: Hollise, John) Pvt, E, 2nd PA Cav, 8-22-1884. Evergreen Cemetery, Camden, Camden County.

HOLLISE, JOHN (see: Hollis, John L.) Evergreen Cemetery, Camden, Camden County.

HOLLISTER, WILLIAM C. Pvt, C, 1st __ Inf, 12-19-1911. Fairmount Cemetery, Newark, Essex County.

HOLLOWAY, CHARLES M. Pvt, E, PA Emerg NJ Militia, 3-12-1884. Evergreen Cemetery, Morristown, Morris County.

HOLLOWAY*, DAVID Pvt, F, 8th NJ Inf, [Wounded in action.] 1-14-1899. Bordentown/Old St. Mary's Catholic Cemetery, Bordentown, Burlington County.

Our Brothers Gone Before

HOLLOWAY, DAVID W. Pvt, C, 7th NJ Inf, 9-27-1883. Evergreen Cemetery, Morristown, Morris County.
HOLLOWAY, JAMES RICHARD Musc, B, 33rd NJ Inf, 4-30-1915. Evergreen Cemetery, Hillside, Union County.
HOLLOWAY, JOHN Pvt, K, 25th NJ Inf, 6-9-1881. Presbyterian Church Cemetery, Oak Ridge, Passaic County.
HOLLOWAY, JOHN M. 11-21-1913. Mount Pleasant Cemetery, Newark, Essex County.
HOLLOWAY, LEWIS P. Capt, C, 27th VA Inf (CSA), [Captured 3-23-1862 at Kerstown, VA. Died of disease.] 4-9-1862. Finn's Point National Cemetery, Pennsville, Salem County.
HOLLOWAY, OLIVER F. Pvt, G, 11th NJ Inf, 9-25-1887. Greenwood Cemetery, Hamilton, Mercer County.
HOLLOWAY, THOMAS Pvt, K, 20th PA Inf, 3-4-1906. Harleigh Cemetery, Camden, Camden County.
HOLLOWBUSH, HENRY Pvt, F, 32nd PA Militia, 10-7-1914. Fairmount Cemetery, Newark, Essex County.
HOLLOWELL, JOSEPH (see: Halliwell, Joseph) Cedar Lawn Cemetery, Paterson, Passaic County.
HOLLY, EDWARD W. Pvt, G, 2nd NJ Cav, 1905. Methodist Church Cemetery, Stockholm, Sussex County.
HOLLY, FRANCIS Seaman, U.S. Navy, 1911. Harleigh Cemetery, Camden, Camden County.
HOLLY, JAMES W. Corp, E, 54th NY Inf, 10-17-1921. Cedar Lawn Cemetery, Paterson, Passaic County.
HOLLY*, JOSEPH W. Pvt, K, 1st NJ Cav, 8-22-1864. Presbyterian Church Cemetery, Oak Ridge, Passaic County.
HOLLY, MICHAEL Pvt, F, 27th NJ Inf, 8-9-1884. Canistear Cemetery, Vernon, Sussex County.
HOLLY, MORDECAI W. Pvt, K, 15th NJ Inf, 1-31-1916. Beemerville Cemetery, Beemerville, Sussex County.
HOLLY, TIMOTHY J. Com Sgt, 33rd NJ Inf 8-30-1872. Branchville Cemetery, Branchville, Sussex County.
HOLLY, WILLIAM Blacksmith, G, 2nd NJ Cav, 6-11-1911. Arlington Cemetery, Kearny, Hudson County.
HOLMAN, B.O. Sgt Maj, 13th AL Inf (CSA) [Captured at Gettysburg, PA.] 1-24-1864. Finn's Point National Cemetery, Pennsville, Salem County.
HOLMAN, DAVID Pvt, F, 2nd U.S. Vet Vol Inf, 7-30-1864. Beverly National Cemetery, Edgewater Park, Burlington County.
HOLMAN, EMANUEL Sgt, K, 1st NJ Inf, 1-27-1902. Fairmount Cemetery, Newark, Essex County.
HOLMAN, GEORGE Pvt, D, 28th NJ Inf, 7-8-1911. Evergreen Cemetery, New Brunswick, Middlesex County.
HOLMAN*, HENRY Pvt, E, 7th NJ Inf, 8-18-1911. Soldier's Home Cemetery, Vineland, Cumberland County.
HOLMAN, JOSIAH Pvt, D, 35th NJ Inf, 7-8-1923. Methodist Cemetery, Allentown, Monmouth County.
HOLMAN, WILLIAM H. (see: Holeman, William H.) Presbyterian Church Cemetery, Hampton, Hunterdon County.
HOLME, JOHN GIBBONS 1st Sgt, A, 24th NJ Inf, DoD Unknown. Eastview Cemetery, Salem, Salem County.
HOLMER, ALFRED (see: Homler, Alfred L.) Baptist Church Cemetery, Port Murray, Warren County.
HOLMES, ANDREW Pvt, C, 11th NJ Inf, 2-23-1889. St. Mary's Cemetery, South Amboy, Middlesex County.

New Jersey Civil War Burials

HOLMES, AUGUSTUS Pvt, H, 15th AL Inf (CSA), [Captured at Gettysburg, PA.] 4-11-1864. Finn's Point National Cemetery, Pennsville, Salem County.

HOLMES, BENJAMIN PROCTOR Pvt, A, 8th NJ Inf, 1-20-1922. Fairmount Cemetery, Chatham, Morris County.

HOLMES, CHARLES Ordinary Seaman, U.S. Navy, 3-4-1898. Methodist Cemetery, Crosswicks, Burlington County.

HOLMES, CHARLES H. Pvt, A, 41st U.S. CT, 5-30-1889. Pinebrook Cemetery, Macedonia, Monmouth County.

HOLMES, DANIEL A. 3-18-1870. Presbyterian Church Cemetery, Shrewsbury, Monmouth County.

HOLMES, DAVID BOWEN Bvt Capt, E, 19th U.S. CT, 6-24-1898. Cohansey Baptist Church Cemetery, Bowentown, Cumberland County.

HOLMES, DAVID C. Landsman, U.S. Navy, USS Savannah, 1910. Mount Pleasant Cemetery, Millville, Cumberland County.

HOLMES, EDMUND T. Pvt, F, 39th NJ Inf, DoD Unknown. Christ Church Cemetery, Belleville, Essex County.

HOLMES, EDWARD Pvt, D, 14th NJ Inf, 7-21-1891. Presbyterian Church Cemetery, Dutch Neck, Mercer County.

HOLMES, EDWARD L. Saddler, D, 6th NY Cav, 1-15-1899. Methodist Church Cemetery, Asbury, Warren County.

HOLMES, EDWIN HENRY Pvt, A, 51st MA Inf, 4-18-1918. Hillside Cemetery, Scotch Plains, Union County.

HOLMES, FRANCIS G.D. 1st Lt, B, 15th NY Eng, 9-14-1898. Phillipsburg Cemetery, Phillipsburg, Warren County.

HOLMES, FRANKLIN Seaman, U.S. Navy, 1865. Boonton Cemetery, Boonton, Morris County.

HOLMES, GABRIEL H. Pvt, I, 25th NJ Inf, 3- -1904. Methodist-Episcopal Church Cemetery, Green Creek, Cape May County.

HOLMES, GEORGE H. Pvt, B, 95th PA Inf, 7-11-1905. Union Cemetery, Gloucester City, Camden County.

HOLMES, GEORGE W. Pvt, E, 5th IA Inf, 5-9-1910. Greenwood Cemetery, Boonton, Morris County.

HOLMES, HENRY Pvt, A, 41st U.S. CT, 12-4-1918. White Ridge Cemetery, Eatontown, Monmouth County.

HOLMES, HENRY E. Seaman, U.S. Navy, USS New Ironsides, 8-6-1906. Laurel Grove Cemetery, Totowa, Passaic County.

HOLMES, HENRY H. Seaman, U.S. Navy, USS Itasca, DoD Unknown. Atlantic City Cemetery, Pleasantville, Atlantic County.

HOLMES, HUDSON Pvt, D, 23rd CT Inf, DoD Unknown. Arlington Cemetery, Kearny, Hudson County.

HOLMES, JACOB Pvt, C, 17th MA Inf, 9-19-1862. Fairmount Cemetery, Newark, Essex County.

HOLMES, JAMES B. 1-12-1892. Mercer Cemetery, Trenton, Mercer County.

HOLMES, JAMES H. Seaman, U.S. Navy, USS Mattabessett, 4-27-1899. Tennent Church Cemetery, Tennent, Monmouth County.

HOLMES, JOHN M. Pvt, C, 6th NJ Inf, 1923. Evergreen/Bishop Jaynes Cemetery, Basking Ridge, Somerset County.

HOLMES, JOHN W. Bvt Lt Col, 72nd NY Inf [Wounded 5-3-1863 at Chancellorsville, VA.] 6-17-1881. Valleau Cemetery, Ridgewood, Bergen County.

HOLMES*, JOHN W. Pvt, E, 8th NJ Inf, 1-20-1910. Atlantic City Cemetery, Pleasantville, Atlantic County.

HOLMES, JONATHAN JARVIS Pvt, G, 29th NJ Inf, 4-29-1902. Fairview Cemetery, Fairview, Monmouth County.

Our Brothers Gone Before

HOLMES, JOSEPH Corp, G, 8th NJ Inf, 1898. Good Luck Cemetery, Murray Grove, Ocean County.
HOLMES, JOSEPH H. Sgt, F, 4th NJ Inf, 1906. Atlantic City Cemetery, Pleasantville, Atlantic County.
HOLMES*, JOSEPH H. 2nd Lt, F, 3rd NJ Cav, 5-19-1923. 1st Baptist Cemetery, Cape May Court House, Cape May County.
HOLMES, LEVI L. Pvt, A, 27th MA Inf, 1922. Old South Church Cemetery, Bergenfield, Bergen County.
HOLMES, LEWIS B. Pvt, D, 25th NJ Inf, DoD Unknown. Overlook Cemetery, Bridgeton, Cumberland County.
HOLMES, LEWIS F.R. Pvt, H, 87th NY Inf, 5-22-1896. Hackensack Cemetery, Hackensack, Bergen County.
HOLMES, MCADAM Pvt, H, 80th NY Inf, 10-29-1934. Laurel Grove Cemetery, Totowa, Passaic County.
HOLMES, MICHAEL B. (aka: Houseman, Michael) Pvt, I, 8th NJ Inf, 12-14-1907. Holy Name Cemetery, Jersey City, Hudson County.
HOLMES, MOSES BLOOMFIELD Sgt, K, 12th NJ Inf, [Died of wounds received 6-3-1864 at Cold Harbor, VA.] 6-4-1864. Presbyterian Church Cemetery, Bridgeton, Cumberland County.
HOLMES, NATHANIEL 1889. Fairview Cemetery, Fairview, Monmouth County.
HOLMES, SAMUEL Pvt, A, 29th NJ Inf, 12-29-1895. Old 1st Methodist Church Cemetery, West Long Branch, Monmouth County.
HOLMES, SAMUEL ADAMS DoD Unknown. Phillipsburg Cemetery, Phillipsburg, Warren County.
HOLMES, THOMAS Pvt, I, 91st NY Inf, 7-8-1919. Laurel Grove Cemetery, Totowa, Passaic County.
HOLMES, THOMAS Pvt, E, 79th NY Inf, 12-13-1909. Cedar Lawn Cemetery, Paterson, Passaic County.
HOLMES, THOMAS B. Pvt, C, 1st NJ Inf, 1-27-1909. Holy Name Cemetery, Jersey City, Hudson County.
HOLMES, THOMAS S. (SR.) 7-23-1913. Bayview-New York Bay Cemetery, Jersey City, Hudson County.
HOLMES, WILLIAM Pvt, F, 213th PA Inf, 1-21-1913. Union Cemetery, Gloucester City, Camden County.
HOLMS, ALEXANDER T. Capt, E, 25th NJ Inf, 10-1-1865. Monument Cemetery, Edgewater Park, Burlington County.
HOLSENGER, JOHN Pvt, K, 2nd NJ Cav, 10-29-1893. Palisade Cemetery, North Bergen, Hudson County.
HOLSHANER, ADAM (see: Holzhauer, Adam) Woodland Cemetery, Newark, Essex County.
HOLSTEIN, L.M. Sgt, Btty A, 1st PA Light Art, 3-5-1908. Belvidere/Catholic Cemetery, Belvidere, Warren County.
HOLSTMAN, SAMUEL (see: Holtzman, Samuel E.) Mount Pleasant Cemetery, Newark, Essex County.
HOLSTON*, ALFRED BENJAMIN (SR.) Landsman, U.S. Navy, USS Grand Gulf, 7-27-1901. Greengrove Cemetery, Keyport, Monmouth County.
HOLSTON*, JOHN M. Pvt, K, 9th NJ Inf, 1926. Cedar Green Cemetery, Clayton, Gloucester County.
HOLT, BENJAMIN Pvt, B, 39th NJ Inf, 5-11-1886. Bayview-New York Bay Cemetery, Jersey City, Hudson County.
HOLT*, CHAUNCEY 1st Lt, F, 40th NJ Inf, 10-26-1920. New Somerville Cemetery, Somerville, Somerset County.
HOLT, FRANCIS B. Capt, E, 1st NJ Inf, 6-7-1878. Evergreen Cemetery, Camden, Camden County.

New Jersey Civil War Burials

HOLT, FREDERICK V. Sgt, D, 127th NY Inf, 3-14-1909. Evergreen Cemetery, Camden, Camden County.
HOLT, HENRY Fireman, U.S. Navy, 7-11-1902. New Camden Cemetery, Camden, Camden County.
HOLT, HENRY D. 1894. New Somerville Cemetery, Somerville, Somerset County.
HOLT, HENRY L. Pvt, Page's Btty, VA Light Art (CSA), 11-3-1864. Finn's Point National Cemetery, Pennsville, Salem County.
HOLT, JAMES Pvt, H, 65th NY Inf, 1-25-1918. Rosehill Cemetery, Linden, Union County.
HOLT, JAMES H. Pvt, I, 13th NJ Inf, 12-9-1905. Arlington Cemetery, Kearny, Hudson County.
HOLT, JOHN Sgt, H, 5th FL Inf (CSA), [Wounded 7-3-1863 and captured 7-5-1863 at Gettysburg, PA.] 2-25-1864. Finn's Point National Cemetery, Pennsville, Salem County.
HOLT, WILLIAM Pvt, D, 23rd PA Inf, [Wounded 5-31-1862 at Fair Oaks, VA.] 7-27-1918. Mount Holly Cemetery, Mount Holly, Burlington County.
HOLT, WILLIAM Lt Col, 31st NJ Inf 1-6-1902. Union Cemetery, Washington, Morris County.
HOLT*, WILLIAM J. Pvt, C, 18th VA Inf (CSA), [Captured 7-3-1863 at Gettysburg, PA. Died of fever.] 9-5-1863. Finn's Point National Cemetery, Pennsville, Salem County.
HOLT, WILLIAM JAMES Pvt, K, 13th NJ Inf, 2-26-1891. Cedar Lawn Cemetery, Paterson, Passaic County.
HOLT, WOODBURY D. Capt, E, 31st NJ Inf, 7-5-1909. Greenwood Cemetery, Hamilton, Mercer County.
HOLTHUSEN, HERMAN Pvt, G, 17th IL Inf, 1908. Reformed Church Cemetery, Fairfield, Essex County.
HOLTON, JAMES MCKEEVER Landsman, U.S. Navy, USS Ironsides, 3-16-1929. Church of Christ Cemetery, Fairton, Cumberland County.
HOLTON, JOSIAH (see: Holeton, Josiah) Methodist-Episcopal Church Cemetery, Penns Grove, Salem County.
HOLTZ, JOHN Pvt, A, 74th PA Inf, 3-31-1895. Riverview Cemetery, Trenton, Mercer County.
HOLTZKNECHT, JOHN Pvt, C, 1st NJ Cav, [Wounded in action.] 11-12-1899. Brainerd Cemetery, Cranbury, Middlesex County.
HOLTZMAN, SAMUEL E. (aka: Holstman, Samuel) Surg, 58th IN Inf 5-7-1911. Mount Pleasant Cemetery, Newark, Essex County.
HOLTZWORTH, JAMES F. Pvt, D, 15th PA Cav, 10-11-1895. Bordentown/Old St. Mary's Catholic Cemetery, Bordentown, Burlington County.
HOLWELL, FRANCIS (see: Howell, Francis P.) Bayview-New York Bay Cemetery, Jersey City, Hudson County.
HOLWELL*, FRANCIS P. Musc, B, 76th NY Inf, 7-25-1930. Bayview-New York Bay Cemetery, Jersey City, Hudson County.
HOLZAPFEL*, JOHN Pvt, H, 5th NY Vet Inf, 2-4-1922. Van Liew Cemetery, North Brunswick, Middlesex County.
HOLZHAUER*, ADAM (aka: Holshaner, Adam) Pvt, F, 39th NJ Inf, 10-24-1897. Woodland Cemetery, Newark, Essex County.
HOLZHAUER, HENRY Pvt, A, 39th NJ Inf, 4-25-1919. Woodland Cemetery, Newark, Essex County.
HOLZMAN, GEORGE Pvt, A, 4th NJ Inf, 7-23-1884. St. Francis Cemetery, Trenton, Mercer County.
HOMAN*, AMOS C. Pvt, H, 12th NJ Inf, DoD Unknown. Arlington Cemetery, Kearny, Hudson County.
HOMAN, EDWARD A. Actg 3rd Asst Eng, U.S. Navy, DoD Unknown. Siloam Cemetery, Vineland, Cumberland County.

Our Brothers Gone Before

HOMAN, FRANKLIN T. 1st Sgt, D, 24th NJ Inf, DoD Unknown. Trinity Bible Church Cemetery, Glassboro, Gloucester County.

HOMAN, GEORGE D. Pvt, I, 23rd NJ Inf, 1898. Hope Christian Church Cemetery, Marlton, Burlington County.

HOMAN, GEORGE W. Pvt, I, 12th NJ Inf, 8-12-1918. Presbyterian Church Cemetery, Cold Spring, Cape May County.

HOMAN*, JOSEPH Pvt, G, 3rd NJ Inf, 12-26-1891. Riverview Cemetery, Trenton, Mercer County.

HOMAN, MAHLON Pvt, E, 10th NJ Inf, 1-15-1902. Fairmount Cemetery, Newark, Essex County.

HOMAN, MAHLON W. 11-1-1916. Baptist Cemetery, West Creek, Ocean County.

HOME, B.L. Pvt, E, 3rd VA Inf (CSA), 4-19-1862. Finn's Point National Cemetery, Pennsville, Salem County.

HOMER, MALACHI (see: Horner, Malachi) New Camden Cemetery, Camden, Camden County.

HOMER, THEODORE (see: Horner, Theodore) Cedar Grove Cemetery, Gloucester City, Camden County.

HOMER, WILLIAM H. Landsman, U.S. Navy, USS Princeton, 9-8-1909. Evergreen Cemetery, Camden, Camden County.

HOMES, JOHN J. Pvt, F, 170th NY Inf, 1898. Mount Prospect Cemetery, Neptune, Monmouth County.

HOMILLER, WILLIAM M. Seaman, U.S. Navy, 9-25-1914. Presbyterian Church Cemetery, Bridgeton, Cumberland County.

HOMLER, ALFRED L. (aka: Holmer, Alfred) Pvt, D, 1st NJ Cav, 12-19-1871. Baptist Church Cemetery, Port Murray, Warren County.

HOMMAINE, JOSEPH (see: Hommaire, Joseph) Fairmount Cemetery, Newark, Essex County.

HOMMAIRE*, JOSEPH (aka: Hommaine, Joseph) Corp, I, 1st NY Cav, 10-10-1893. Fairmount Cemetery, Newark, Essex County.

HONE, COLBRETH PERRY 1901. Evergreen Cemetery, Morristown, Morris County.

HONE, JOHN (JR.) Pvt, B, 2nd NJ Cav, 3-21-1915. Evergreen Cemetery, Morristown, Morris County.

HONEYMAN, AUGUSTUS A. Pvt, A, 30th NJ Inf, 1917. New Germantown Cemetery, Oldwick, Hunterdon County.

HONEYMAN*, NEVIUS K. Pvt, B, 3rd NJ Cav, 12-16-1919. Presbyterian Cemetery, New Vernon, Morris County.

HONEYMAN, ROBERT R. Lt Col, 31st NJ Inf 6-14-1873. New Germantown Cemetery, Oldwick, Hunterdon County.

HONIG, ELIAS Pvt, E, 39th NJ Inf, 2-24-1899. Fairmount Cemetery, Newark, Essex County.

HONIWELL, JOHN (aka: Hunniwell, John) Pvt, I, 13th NJ Inf, 2-17-1901. Rahway Cemetery, Rahway, Union County.

HONLIGAN, JAMES (aka: Houlighan, James) Pvt, F, 6th NH Inf, [Died of disease at Newark, NJ.] 11-17-1862. Fairmount Cemetery, Newark, Essex County.

HONN, SAMUEL H. Pvt, A, 7th NJ Inf, [Died of diarrhea at Washington, DC.] 1-13-1865. Methodist Church Cemetery, Eldora, Cape May County.

HONNERS*, AARON Landsman, U.S. Navy, USS Lodona, 9-1-1896. Old & New Lutheran Cemetery, Lebanon, Hunterdon County.

HONSEL*, HENRY C. (aka: Housell, Henry C.) Corp, A, 57th NY Inf, [Wounded 9-17-1862 at Antietam, MD.] 6-26-1910. Elmwood Cemetery, New Brunswick, Middlesex County.

HOOD, CHARLES L. Pvt, E, 24th NJ Inf, 11-19-1921. Evergreen Cemetery, Camden, Camden County.

New Jersey Civil War Burials

HOOD, EDWARD B. Pvt, I, 6th NJ Inf, 2-22-1905. Atlantic City Cemetery, Pleasantville, Atlantic County.

HOOK, BENJAMIN Pvt, C, 33rd NJ Inf, 2-27-1895. Cedar Lawn Cemetery, Paterson, Passaic County.

HOOKINGSON, SAMUEL 10-18-1930. Fairview Cemetery, Fairview, Bergen County.

HOOPER, JOHN W. Pvt, I, 4th NJ Inf, [Died at Philadelphia, PA. of wounds received 5-6-1864 at Wilderness, VA.] 8-31-1864. Baptist/St. Andrew's Cemetery, Mount Holly, Burlington County.

HOOPER, THOMAS R. Corp, C, 10th NJ Inf, 2-22-1909. Brotherhood Cemetery, Hainesport, Burlington County.

HOOPER, WILLIAM S. Sgt, A, 7th NJ Inf, 8-20-1896. Calvary Baptist Church Cemetery, Ocean View, Cape May County.

HOOPER, WILLIAM W. 1st Sgt, C, 9th NJ Inf, [Wounded in action.] 12-14-1894. Bordentown/Old St. Mary's Catholic Cemetery, Bordentown, Burlington County.

HOOPES*, FRANCIS D. Pvt, I, 99th PA Inf, 5-17-1879. Methodist Cemetery, Haddonfield, Camden County.

HOORNBECK, JACOB (see: Hornbeck, Jacob E.) Fairview Cemetery, Wantage, Sussex County.

HOOS, J. DoD Unknown. Rahway Cemetery, Rahway, Union County.

HOOSE*, CHARLES H. Pvt, H, 59th NY Inf, 10-17-1918. Flower Hill Cemetery, North Bergen, Hudson County.

HOOTEN, SAMUEL (see: Hutton, Samuel) Cedar Grove Cemetery, Gloucester City, Camden County.

HOOTS, ISAAC Pvt, I, 32nd (Lenoir Braves) NC Inf (CSA), [Captured 7-3-1863 at Gettysburg, PA. Died of disease.] 8-12-1863. Finn's Point National Cemetery, Pennsville, Salem County.

HOOVER, ARTHUR Sgt, C, 1st NJ Cav, 12-12-1919. St. Stephen Episcopal Cemetery, Florence, Burlington County.

HOOVER, FRANK W. Pvt, Btty A, 7th NY Heavy Art, 4- -1911. Laurel Grove Cemetery, Totowa, Passaic County.

HOOVER, HENRY E. Pvt, K, 5th NC Cav (CSA), [Captured 7-7-1863 at Williamsport, MD.] 10-31-1863. Finn's Point National Cemetery, Pennsville, Salem County.

HOOVER, HENRY J. Pvt, E, 30th PA Inf, 7-10-1893. Cedar Grove Cemetery, Gloucester City, Camden County.

HOOVER, JOHN W. Pvt, C, 38th NJ Inf, 1891. Mount Pleasant Cemetery, Millville, Cumberland County.

HOOVER*, MICHAEL Pvt, C, 1st NJ Cav, 1-22-1876. Methodist-Episcopal Cemetery, Burlington, Burlington County.

HOOVER, PETER Pvt, I, 1st NJ Cav, 10-16-1897. Evergreen Cemetery, Hillside, Union County.

HOOVER, SAMUEL Pvt, A, 23rd NJ Inf, 5-29-1926. Bordentown/Old St. Mary's Catholic Cemetery, Bordentown, Burlington County.

HOOVER, W.D. Pvt, A, 4th (Neely's) TN Inf (CSA), 9-24-1863. Finn's Point National Cemetery, Pennsville, Salem County.

HOOVER, WILLIAM D. Pvt, E, 10th NJ Inf, 4-10-1891. Union Cemetery, Clarkstown, Atlantic County.

HOOVER*, WILLIAM H. Pvt, F, 11th NJ Inf, DoD Unknown. Presbyterian Church Cemetery, Califon, Hunterdon County.

HOPE, AARON DUNHAM Pvt, D, 129th PA Inf, 1-10-1900. Presbyterian Church Cemetery, Clinton, Hunterdon County.

HOPE*, CORNELIUS 1st Sgt, A, 38th NJ Inf, 4-13-1890. Fairmount Cemetery, Newark, Essex County.

HOPE, CORNELIUS 1-2-1873. Tennent Church Cemetery, Tennent, Monmouth County.

Our Brothers Gone Before

HOPE, HIRAM Pvt, E, 30th NJ Inf, 9-29-1898. New Somerville Cemetery, Somerville, Somerset County.

HOPE, JOHN Pvt, G, 30th NJ Inf, 7-5-1884. Sandy Ridge Cemetery, Sandy Ridge, Hunterdon County.

HOPE, JOHN Pvt, H, 2nd NY Inf, 2-6-1902. Greenwood Cemetery, Hamilton, Mercer County.

HOPE, WHITFIELD D. Pvt, E, 30th NJ Inf, 1-17-1866. Old Somerville Cemetery, Somerville, Somerset County.

HOPE*, WILLIAM J. (aka: Murphy, James) Musc, I, 34th NJ Inf, 5-26-1909. Hollywood Cemetery, Union, Union County.

HOPKINS, ANDERSON (aka: Hopkins, Andrew) Pvt, B, 8th NJ Inf, DoD Unknown. Northfield Baptist Cemetery, Livingston, Essex County.

HOPKINS, ANDREW (see: Hopkins, Anderson) Northfield Baptist Cemetery, Livingston, Essex County.

HOPKINS, ANDREW J. Pvt, A, 4th NJ Inf, 2-28-1917. Hardyston Cemetery, North Church, Sussex County.

HOPKINS*, AUGUSTUS C. Pvt, I, 20th CT Inf, 3-14-1924. Evergreen Cemetery, Hillside, Union County.

HOPKINS, BENJAMIN F. Sgt, F, 5th (McKenzie's) TN Cav (CSA), 5-7-1864. Finn's Point National Cemetery, Pennsville, Salem County.

HOPKINS, CHARLES F. Pvt, I, 1st NJ Inf, [Awarded the Medal of Honor.] 2-14-1934. Greenwood Cemetery, Boonton, Morris County.

HOPKINS, CHARLES H. Wagoner, F, 2nd NJ Cav, DoD Unknown. Rose Hill Cemetery, Matawan, Monmouth County.

HOPKINS, CHARLES R. Pvt, G, 24th NJ Inf, 5-21-1928. Baptist Church Cemetery, Canton, Salem County.

HOPKINS, COWARD H. Pvt, G, 15th NJ Inf, 8-21-1865. Northfield Baptist Cemetery, Livingston, Essex County.

HOPKINS, DANIEL Pvt, E, 25th NJ Inf, [Wounded in action.] 1-7-1917. Laurel Grove Cemetery, Totowa, Passaic County.

HOPKINS, DANIEL H. Pvt, F, 14th NJ Inf, 3-17-1890. Jacobstown Masonic Cemetery, Jacobstown, Burlington County.

HOPKINS*, HARRISON Sgt, D, 4th NJ Inf, 3-29-1896. Mercer Cemetery, Trenton, Mercer County.

HOPKINS, JOHN A. Pvt, I, 27th NJ Inf, 1906. Union Cemetery, Marcella, Morris County.

HOPKINS, JOSEPH Pvt, F, 12th NJ Inf, 2-19-1913. Green Cemetery, Woodbury, Gloucester County.

HOPKINS, JOSEPH Pvt, H, 40th NJ Inf, 1902. Windsor Burial Grounds Cemetery, East Windsor, Mercer County.

HOPKINS, JOSEPH D. Landsman, U.S. Navy, USS Union, 3-26-1910. Clinton Cemetery, Irvington, Essex County.

HOPKINS, LLOYD Pvt, C, 132nd NY Inf, 2-20-1906. Fairmount Cemetery, Newark, Essex County.

HOPKINS, MICHAEL Pvt, Btty B, 1st NJ Light Art, 4-7-1912. Holy Sepulchre Cemetery, East Orange, Essex County.

HOPKINS, MITCHELL Pvt, G, 24th U.S. CT, 3-11-1892. Johnson Cemetery, Camden, Camden County.

HOPKINS, PHILIP Pvt, I, 31st NJ Inf, 1916. Methodist Church Cemetery, Liberty, Warren County.

HOPKINS, REUBEN S. Pvt, I, 60th VA Inf (CSA), [Captured 3-2-1865 at Waynesboro, VA. Died of pneumonia.] 4-1-1865. Finn's Point National Cemetery, Pennsville, Salem County.

New Jersey Civil War Burials

HOPKINS, SAMUEL Pvt, F, 14th NJ Inf, 1-29-1920. Presbyterian Cemetery, Cream Ridge, Monmouth County.

HOPKINS, SIMEON F. Pvt, B, 9th NJ Inf, 10-31-1880. St. Peter's Cemetery, New Brunswick, Middlesex County.

HOPKINS, WILLIAM Pvt, E, 5th U.S. Cav, 6-21-1917. Fairmount Cemetery, Newark, Essex County.

HOPKINSON, CHARLES B. Capt, C, 9th NJ Inf, 6-29-1870. Bordentown/Old St. Mary's Catholic Cemetery, Bordentown, Burlington County.

HOPKINSON, JOSEPH Surg, U.S. Volunteers, 7-11-1865. Christ Episcopal Church Cemetery, Bordentown, Burlington County.

HOPLER, ALEXANDER Pvt, A, 2nd NJ Cav, 3-24-1866. German Valley Rural Cemetery, Naughright, Morris County.

HOPLER, ALFRED B. Pvt, C, 15th NJ Inf, [Wounded 12-13-1862 at Fredericksburg, VA.] 9-2-1910. Boonton Cemetery, Boonton, Morris County.

HOPLER, JAMES H. Corp, Btty B, 1st NJ Light Art, 10-12-1922. Greenwood Cemetery, Boonton, Morris County.

HOPLER, PETER W. Pvt, E, 1st NJ Cav, DoD Unknown. Presbyterian Church Cemetery, Rockaway, Morris County.

HOPMAN, JAMES H. Pvt, B, 10th NJ Inf, DoD Unknown. Mount Pleasant Cemetery, Millville, Cumberland County.

HOPP, CONRAD Pvt, B, 151st PA Inf, 7-2-1901. Jersey City Cemetery, Jersey City, Hudson County.

HOPP, JOHN (JR.) Pvt, A, 9th NJ Inf, 2-2-1899. Fairmount Cemetery, Newark, Essex County.

HOPPAUGH, HENRY C. Pvt, K, 27th NJ Inf, 4-2-1907. Presbyterian Church Cemetery, Sparta, Sussex County.

HOPPAUGH, HORACE Pvt, M, 1st NJ Cav, DoD Unknown. Prospect Hill Cemetery, Caldwell, Essex County.

HOPPE, CHARLES Pvt, H, 20th NY State Militia, DoD Unknown. Arlington Cemetery, Kearny, Hudson County.

HOPPE, WILLIAM Pvt, Btty I, 5th NY Heavy Art, 2-19-1907. Alpine Cemetery, Perth Amboy, Middlesex County.

HOPPER, ABRAHAM A. Pvt, B, 39th NJ Inf, 1-17-1925. Reformed Church Cemetery, Wyckoff, Bergen County.

HOPPER, ABRAHAM H. Pvt, B, 22nd NJ Inf, 1-13-1889. Maple Grove Cemetery, Hackensack, Bergen County.

HOPPER, ABRAHAM H. Sgt, B, 22nd NJ Inf, 3-16-1923. Valleau Cemetery, Ridgewood, Bergen County.

HOPPER, ABRAHAM PULIS Pvt, K, 1st NJ Cav, 11-15-1879. Presbyterian Church Cemetery, Oak Ridge, Passaic County.

HOPPER, ABRAM A. Corp, D, 22nd NJ Inf, 5-10-1913. Westwood Cemetery, Westwood, Bergen County.

HOPPER, ALBERT G. Corp, B, 22nd NJ Inf, 3-14-1899. Valleau Cemetery, Ridgewood, Bergen County.

HOPPER, ANDREW J. Musc, H, 25th NJ Inf, 5-13-1920. Laurel Grove Cemetery, Totowa, Passaic County.

HOPPER, BYRON C. Pvt, D, 13th NJ Inf, [Died of wounds received 9-17-1862 at Antietam, MD.] 10-12-1862. Mount Pleasant Cemetery, Newark, Essex County.

HOPPER, DAVID CATHER Pvt, B, 22nd NJ Inf, 4-20-1928. Ponds Church Cemetery, Oakland, Bergen County.

HOPPER, EDWARD D. Capt, G, 5th NJ Inf, 3-28-1870. St. Peter's Cemetery, Jersey City, Hudson County.

HOPPER, EGBERT Pvt, C, 12th U.S. Inf, 8-11-1909. Old 1st Methodist Church Cemetery, West Long Branch, Monmouth County.

Our Brothers Gone Before

HOPPER, GEORGE C. Pvt, D, 5th NJ Inf, 11-25-1904. Fairmount Cemetery, Newark, Essex County.
HOPPER*, GEORGE D. Pvt, B, 28th MA Inf, DoD Unknown. Laurel Grove Cemetery, Totowa, Passaic County.
HOPPER, GEORGE W. Pvt, E, 3rd NJ Cav, 12-31-1891. Redeemer Cemetery, Mahwah, Bergen County.
HOPPER, HARRY C. Pvt, C, 49th IN Inf, 6-4-1888. Presbyterian Church Cemetery, Blackwood, Camden County.
HOPPER, HENRY 1st Lt, E, 9th NJ Inf, 11-18-1939. Fairmount Cemetery, Newark, Essex County.
HOPPER, HENRY G. Pvt, F, 7th NJ Inf, DoD Unknown. Cedar Lawn Cemetery, Paterson, Passaic County.
HOPPER, HENRY LEWIS Musc, B, 22nd NJ Inf, 9-24-1907. Ramapo Reformed Church Cemetery, Mahwah, Bergen County.
HOPPER, ISAAC ACKERMAN Pvt, E, 22nd NJ Inf, 1927. Valleau Cemetery, Ridgewood, Bergen County.
HOPPER, JACOB Pvt, H, 25th NJ Inf, DoD Unknown. Laurel Grove Cemetery, Totowa, Passaic County.
HOPPER, JACOB Pvt, K, 79th NY Inf, [Wounded 6-16-1862 at Secessionville, SC.] 11-15-1864. Reformed Church Cemetery, Wyckoff, Bergen County.
HOPPER, JACOB A. 8- -1861. Edgewater Cemetery, Edgewater, Bergen County.
HOPPER, JACOB B. Saddler, F, 1st NJ Cav, 1-18-1877. Presbyterian Church Cemetery, Oak Ridge, Passaic County.
HOPPER, JAMES Pvt, E, 12th NJ Inf, DoD Unknown. Redeemer Cemetery, Mahwah, Bergen County.
HOPPER, JOHN Capt, H, 66th NY Inf, DoD Unknown. St. Peter's Cemetery, Jersey City, Hudson County.
HOPPER, JOHN 1st Lt, B, 2nd NJ Militia, 5-15-1894. Episcopal Church Cemetery, Shrewsbury, Monmouth County.
HOPPER, JOHN A. 5-17-1911. Old Stone Reformed Church Cemetery, Upper Saddle River, Bergen County.
HOPPER, JOHN A. Pvt, E, 22nd NJ Inf, [Died of typhoid at Washington, DC.] 5-24-1863. Hopper Cemetery, Glen Rock, Bergen County.
HOPPER, JOHN C. Capt, AADC, U.S. Army, [Acting Aide-de-Camp to General Fremont.] 11-5-1910. Cedar Lawn Cemetery, Paterson, Passaic County.
HOPPER, JOHN E. 2-24-1918. Old Stone Reformed Church Cemetery, Upper Saddle River, Bergen County.
HOPPER, JOHN H. Pvt, Btty E, 1st NJ Light Art, 9-20-1895. Fairmount Cemetery, Newark, Essex County.
HOPPER, JOHN HINCHMAN Corp, D, 33rd NJ Inf, 10-27-1907. Maple Grove Cemetery, Hackensack, Bergen County.
HOPPER*, JOSEPH C. 1st Lt, Btty K, 6th NY Heavy Art, 7-16-1890. Cedar Lawn Cemetery, Paterson, Passaic County.
HOPPER, PETER G. Pvt, E, 22nd NJ Inf, 8-10-1904. Cedar Lawn Cemetery, Paterson, Passaic County.
HOPPER, RULIF F. 2nd Lt, A, 28th WI Inf, 8-15-1918. Old 1st Methodist Church Cemetery, West Long Branch, Monmouth County.
HOPPER, STEPHEN Pvt, C, 39th NJ Inf, 11-30-1897. Fairmount Cemetery, Newark, Essex County.
HOPPER, STEPHEN GOETSCHIUS 1st Lt, A, 22nd NJ Inf, 9-14-1894. Maple Grove Cemetery, Hackensack, Bergen County.
HOPPER, THOMAS A. Pvt, H, 25th NJ Inf, 12-1-1871. Redeemer Cemetery, Mahwah, Bergen County.

New Jersey Civil War Burials

HOPPER, WILLIAM Pvt, I, 6th NY Inf, DoD Unknown. Preakness Reformed Church Cemetery, Wayne, Passaic County.

HOPPER, WILLIAM T. Com Sgt, 29th NJ Inf 10-3-1904. Old 1st Methodist Church Cemetery, West Long Branch, Monmouth County.

HOPPING, AUGUSTUS STILES Corp, C, 15th NJ Inf, 8-10-1876. Presbyterian Church Cemetery, Hanover, Morris County.

HOPPING, EDWARD T. __, __, __ U.S. __, 5-10-1901. Fairview Cemetery, Fairview, Monmouth County.

HOPPING, WESLEY D. Pvt, K, 7th NJ Inf, 1927. New Presbyterian Cemetery, Hanover, Morris County.

HOPPING*, WILLIAM H. Pvt, E, 75th NY Inf, 1-16-1894. Oak Grove Cemetery, Hammonton, Atlantic County.

HOPPING, WILLIAM H. Musc, I, 38th NJ Inf, 7-5-1918. Riverview Cemetery, Trenton, Mercer County.

HOPPING, WILLIAM HUGH 3-25-1904. Fairmount Cemetery, Newark, Essex County.

HOPPOCK, PETER 1915. Christian Church Cemetery, Locktown, Hunterdon County.

HOPPOCK, SAMUEL Pvt, E, 31st NJ Inf, 5-4-1912. Baptist Church Cemetery, Port Murray, Warren County.

HOPPOCK, THOMAS Pvt, D, 31st NJ Inf, 1893. New Somerville Cemetery, Somerville, Somerset County.

HOPPOCK, WILLIAM Pvt, D, 31st NJ Inf, 2-4-1900. Prospect Hill Cemetery, Flemington, Hunterdon County.

HOPSON, HORACE (aka: Horton, Horace) Corp, F, 1st NY Eng, 10-31-1873. Hillside Cemetery, Madison, Morris County.

HOPSON, JOSEPH Pvt, I, 1st NJ Inf, DoD Unknown. Laurel Grove Cemetery, Totowa, Passaic County.

HORAN, JOHN J. Pvt, U.S. Marine Corps, 1923. St. Peter's Cemetery, New Brunswick, Middlesex County.

HORAN, MICHAEL (aka: Moran, Michael) Pvt, Btty A, 2nd NY Heavy Art, 6-21-1905. St. John's Evangelical Church Cemetery, Orange, Essex County.

HORAN, PATRICK Pvt, E, 26th NJ Inf, 8-30-1892. Holy Sepulchre Cemetery, East Orange, Essex County.

HORAY, WILLIAM Pvt, D, 5th CA Inf, 11-6-1876. Methodist-Episcopal Church Cemetery, Magnolia, Camden County.

HORIGAN, JEREMIAH Corp, E, 71st NY Inf, [Wounded 6-1-1862 at Fair Oaks, VA.] 7-4-1868. St. John's Evangelical Church Cemetery, Orange, Essex County.

HORN, ALBERT W. __, __, __ PA Heavy Art, DoD Unknown. Methodist-Episcopal Cemetery, Burlington, Burlington County.

HORN, AMOS N. 4-10-1911. Greenwood Cemetery, Hamilton, Mercer County.

HORN*, ANTHONY Pvt, Btty I, 1st U.S. Art, 1-10-1905. St. John's Evangelical Church Cemetery, Orange, Essex County.

HORN, ANTON Pvt, A, 54th NY Inf, 3-5-1901. St. Mark's Cemetery, Orange, Essex County.

HORN, CHARLES Corp, Btty M, 2nd PA Heavy Art, 1-5-1913. Oddfellows Cemetery, Burlington, Burlington County.

HORN, CHARLES Pvt, D, 2nd NJ Inf, [Wounded in action.] 5-24-1915. Fairmount Cemetery, Newark, Essex County.

HORN, CHARLES W. Corp, I, 33rd PA Militia, 4-26-1910. Arlington Cemetery, Kearny, Hudson County.

HORN, CHARLES W. Pvt, C, 40th NJ Inf, 8-3-1918. Riverview Cemetery, Trenton, Mercer County.

HORN, CONRAD Pvt, A, 7th NJ Inf, 5-25-1883. Greenwood Cemetery, Hamilton, Mercer County.

Our Brothers Gone Before

HORN*, ELIJAH W. Pvt, A, 15th NJ Inf, 7-29-1868. Mount Hope Presbyterian Cemetery, Lambertville, Hunterdon County.
HORN, GEORGE W. Pvt, B, 2nd U.S. Cav, 1935. Holcomb-Riverview Cemetery, Lambertville, Hunterdon County.
HORN, HENRY P. Pvt, I, 20th AL Inf (CSA), 6-14-1863. Finn's Point National Cemetery, Pennsville, Salem County.
HORN, JOHN D. Musc, C, 3rd NJ Inf, 3-27-1875. St. Mary's Episcopal Church Cemetery, Burlington, Burlington County.
HORN, JOHN V. Pvt, A, 7th NJ Inf, 8-23-1909. Oddfellows Cemetery, Burlington, Burlington County.
HORN, JOHN W. Pvt, E, 7th NJ Inf, 12-18-1868. Mount Hope Presbyterian Cemetery, Lambertville, Hunterdon County.
HORN, JOHN W. Pvt, G, 3rd NJ Cav, 7-16-1901. Riverview Cemetery, Trenton, Mercer County.
HORN, LUTHER S. Pvt, E, 47th PA Inf, 1-27-1909. Riverview Cemetery, Trenton, Mercer County.
HORN, PEARSON A. Corp, A, 104th PA Inf, [Wounded 9-1-1863 and 9-4-1863 at Morris Island, SC.] 4-9-1914. Arlington Cemetery, Kearny, Hudson County.
HORN, PETER Pvt, C, 1st NJ Cav, 2-20-1866. St. Mary's Episcopal Church Cemetery, Burlington, Burlington County.
HORN, RICHARD B. Pvt, B, 15th NJ Inf, 4-26-1893. St. Mary's Episcopal Church Cemetery, Burlington, Burlington County.
HORN, SAMUEL Pvt, B, 10th NJ Inf, 9-10-1907. Bible Church Cemetery, English Creek, Atlantic County.
HORN, SAMUEL Pvt, E, 187th PA Inf, 3-23-1925. Oddfellows Cemetery, Burlington, Burlington County.
HORN, THEODORE F. Corp, I, 40th NJ Inf, 10-18-1919. Oddfellows Cemetery, Burlington, Burlington County.
HORN, THOMAS Corp, F, 9th NJ Inf, 12-19-1919. Riverview Cemetery, Trenton, Mercer County.
HORN, WILLIAM Pvt, A, 23rd NJ Inf, 3-18-1873. St. Mary's Episcopal Church Cemetery, Burlington, Burlington County.
HORN, WILLIAM J. Pvt, A, 23rd NJ Inf, 7-2-1911. St. Mary's Episcopal Church Cemetery, Burlington, Burlington County.
HORNBAKER, WILLIAM H. Pvt, B, 31st NJ Inf, 9-1-1873. Mansfield/Washington Cemetery, Washington, Warren County.
HORNBECK, ALEXANDER Pvt, A, 1st NJ Cav, [Wounded in action.] 7-17-1906. Walpack Reformed Cemetery, Flatbrookville, Sussex County.
HORNBECK, JACOB E. (aka: Hoornbeck, Jacob) Pvt, C, 120th NY Inf, [Wounded 5-5-1864 at Wilderness, VA.] 1894. Fairview Cemetery, Wantage, Sussex County.
HORNBLOWER, JOHN TOWN DoD Unknown. Old Bergen Church Cemetery, Jersey City, Hudson County.
HORNE, JOHN Pvt, H, 45th NY Inf, 1912. Holy Sepulchre Cemetery, East Orange, Essex County.
HORNE, STEPHEN H. Pvt, E, 10th NJ Inf, 3-3-1874. Batsto/Pleasant Mills Methodist Church Cemetery, Pleasant Mills, Atlantic County.
HORNER*, AARON Pvt, I, 2nd NJ Inf, 3-5-1882. Beverly National Cemetery, Edgewater Park, Burlington County.
HORNER, ALFRED Pvt, H, 23rd NJ Inf, 2-16-1884. Evergreen Cemetery, Camden, Camden County.
HORNER, CHARLES 9-23-1863. Union Cemetery, Frenchtown, Hunterdon County.
HORNER, CHARLES (see: Koerner, Charles) Fairmount Cemetery, Newark, Essex County.

New Jersey Civil War Burials

HORNER, CHARLES COLLINS Pvt, B, 23rd NJ Inf, 8-4-1932. Greenwood Cemetery, Hamilton, Mercer County.
HORNER*, CHARLES F. Corp, K, 186th PA Inf, 1-7-1926. Atlantic City Cemetery, Pleasantville, Atlantic County.
HORNER*, CHARLES R. Pvt, A, 10th NJ Inf, 12-25-1885. Fairmount Cemetery, Newark, Essex County.
HORNER, CLARENCE Pvt, C, 34th NJ Inf, 4-19-1899. United Methodist Church Cemetery, Jacobstown, Burlington County.
HORNER, DANIEL Pvt, F, 23rd NJ Inf, DoD Unknown. Baptist Cemetery, Vincentown, Burlington County.
HORNER, DANIEL H. Pvt, E, 12th NJ Inf, 7-27-1912. Monument Cemetery, Edgewater Park, Burlington County.
HORNER*, FRANKLIN Corp, E, 8th NJ Inf, 10-24-1920. 1st Baptist Church Cemetery, Florence, Burlington County.
HORNER, GEORGE W. Sgt, G, 47th NC Inf (CSA), [Captured 7-3-1863 at Gettysburg, PA.] 7-31-1863. Finn's Point National Cemetery, Pennsville, Salem County.
HORNER, GEORGE W. Pvt, A, 23rd NJ Inf, 8-20-1871. Baptist Cemetery, Burlington, Burlington County.
HORNER, HENRY S. Corp, I, 186th PA Inf, 2-4-1914. New Camden Cemetery, Camden, Camden County.
HORNER, HIRAM M. Pvt, E, 38th NJ Inf, 1910. Christian Church Cemetery, Locktown, Hunterdon County.
HORNER, JAMES Pvt, I, 12th NJ Inf, 8-25-1910. Presbyterian Church Cemetery, Bridgeton, Cumberland County.
HORNER*, JAMES Pvt, E, 4th NY Inf, [Wounded 9-17-1862 at Antietam, MD.] 5-20-1899. Presbyterian Church Cemetery, New Providence, Union County.
HORNER, JAMES P. Pvt, E, 28th NJ Inf, 7-30-1894. Presbyterian Cemetery, Holmanville, Ocean County.
HORNER, JEREMIAH A. Pvt, K, 10th NJ Inf, 1908. Christian Church Cemetery, Locktown, Hunterdon County.
HORNER, JOHN (JR.) Pvt, D, 23rd NJ Inf, 10-23-1909. Methodist-Episcopal Cemetery, Pointville, Burlington County.
HORNER, JOSEPH B. 7-26-1864. Union Cemetery, Frenchtown, Hunterdon County.
HORNER, LAFAYETTE (JR.) Pvt, B, 4th NJ Inf, 3-31-1919. Riverview Cemetery, Trenton, Mercer County.
HORNER, MAHLON G. Pvt, I, 11th NJ Inf, 1908. Emleys Hill United Methodist Church Cemetery, Upper Freehold, Monmouth County.
HORNER, MALACHI (aka: Homer, Malachi) Pvt, F, 27th MA Inf, [Wounded 5-7-1864 at Port Walthall, VA. and 6-18-1864 at Petersburg, VA.] 3-3-1901. New Camden Cemetery, Camden, Camden County.
HORNER, REESE Pvt, D, 34th NJ Inf, 7-16-1903. Old Quaker Cemetery, Squankum, Monmouth County.
HORNER, RICHARD Pvt, G, 23rd NJ Inf, 8-7-1915. Monument Cemetery, Edgewater Park, Burlington County.
HORNER*, ROBERT N. Pvt, C, 15th U.S. Inf, 4-2-1877. Eglington Cemetery, Clarksboro, Gloucester County.
HORNER, SAMUEL Pvt, H, 7th MD Inf, 9-27-1899. Presbyterian Cemetery, Allentown, Monmouth County.
HORNER, THEODORE (aka: Homer, Theodore) Corp, Btty B, 2nd PA Heavy Art, 1-25-1890. Cedar Grove Cemetery, Gloucester City, Camden County.
HORNER*, THOMAS (aka: Huntley, Thomas) Seaman, U.S. Navy, USS Alleghany, 1-5-1918. St. Peter's Cemetery, Perth Amboy, Middlesex County.
HORNER, WESLEY H. 2nd Lt, I, 30th NJ Inf, 5-6-1899. New Dutch Reformed/Neshanic Cemetery, Neshanic, Somerset County.

Our Brothers Gone Before

HORNER, WESLEY H. 1st Sgt, F, 30th NJ Inf, DoD Unknown. Methodist-Episcopal Cemetery, Burlington, Burlington County.

HORNER, WESLEY (JR.) Capt, H, 57th NY Inf, 1910. Oddfellows Cemetery, Burlington, Burlington County.

HORNER, WILLIAM S. Corp, C, 40th MA Inf, 12-31-1888. Cedar Grove Cemetery, Gloucester City, Camden County.

HORNLE, JOHN B. (aka: Hornley, John) Pvt, G, 8th NJ Inf, [Wounded in action.] 2-11-1911. Woodland Cemetery, Newark, Essex County.

HORNLEIN, FREDERICK Pvt, D, 2nd NJ Inf, 4-5-1870. Fairmount Cemetery, Newark, Essex County.

HORNLEY, JOHN (see: Hornle, John B.) Woodland Cemetery, Newark, Essex County.

HORNOR, CHARLES Corp, E, 28th NJ Inf, 12-11-1923. Maplewood Cemetery, Freehold, Monmouth County.

HORNOR, GEORGE H. Pvt, I, 2nd NJ Cav, [Wounded in action.] 9-26-1911. Zion Baptist Church Cemetery, New Egypt, Ocean County.

HORNOR, WILLIAM S. Corp, C, 40th MA Inf, 4-13-1879. Rose Hill Cemetery, Matawan, Monmouth County.

HORNSBY, MOSES C. Pvt, K, 3rd AL Inf (CSA), 8-24-1863. Finn's Point National Cemetery, Pennsville, Salem County.

HORNUNG*, JOHN Pvt, L, 2nd NJ Cav, 2-8-1890. Palisade Cemetery, North Bergen, Hudson County.

HORSEFALL, CHARLES A. Capt, E, 12th NJ Inf, [Killed in action at Gettysburg, PA.] 7-2-1863. Evergreen Cemetery, Camden, Camden County.

HORSEMAN, HENRY F. Pvt, I, 1st NJ Cav, 9-26-1897. New Camden Cemetery, Camden, Camden County.

HORSEY*, GEORGE (aka: Holsey, George) Pvt, Btty H, 11th U.S. CHA, 10-24-1901. Spencer African Methodist Church Cemetery, Woodstown, Salem County.

HORSEY, MINUS Pvt, D, 25th U.S. CT, 10-14-1914. Jordan Lawn Cemetery, Pennsauken, Camden County.

HORSLEY*, JOHN Pvt, B, 3rd U.S. VRC, DoD Unknown. Finn's Point National Cemetery, Pennsville, Salem County.

HORSTMAN, FREDERICK WILLIAM Pvt, E, 1st NJ Militia, 2-29-1901. Arlington Cemetery, Kearny, Hudson County.

HORTEN, HUMPHREY (aka: Humphrey, Horton) Pvt, I, 25th NJ Inf, 8-25-1881. United Methodist Church Cemetery, Woodruff, Cumberland County.

HORTMAN, ENOCH Pvt, B, 38th NJ Inf, 10-14-1905. Holcomb-Riverview Cemetery, Lambertville, Hunterdon County.

HORTON, ALBERT Pvt, B, 25th NJ Inf, 3-19-1906. Atlantic City Cemetery, Pleasantville, Atlantic County.

HORTON, BENJAMIN O. Pvt, I, 2nd NY Cav, 12-6-1896. Evergreen Cemetery, Hillside, Union County.

HORTON, CHARLES P. DoD Unknown. Old Camden Cemetery, Camden, Camden County.

HORTON, DAVID L. 2-2-1919. Congregational Church Cemetery, Chester, Morris County.

HORTON, GEORGE W. Pvt, H, 11th NJ Inf, [Wounded in action.] 3-20-1918. Balesville Cemetery, Balesville, Sussex County.

HORTON, HARRY (see: Bloomer, Dennis P.) New Presbyterian Cemetery, Hanover, Morris County.

HORTON, HORACE (see: Hopson, Horace) Hillside Cemetery, Madison, Morris County.

HORTON, JOHN T. Pvt, I, 27th NJ Inf, 12-8-1906. Arlington Cemetery, Kearny, Hudson County.

HORTON, JOHN W. Pvt, K, 11th AL Inf (CSA), 11-3-1863. Finn's Point National Cemetery, Pennsville, Salem County.

New Jersey Civil War Burials

HORTON, MILTON G. Corp, L, 1st NJ Cav, 7-29-1899. Methodist Church Cemetery, Fairmount, Hunterdon County.
HORTON, SAMUEL Pvt, 3rd Btty, VT Light Art, [Died of disease.] 10-4-1864. Beverly National Cemetery, Edgewater Park, Burlington County.
HORTON, STEPHEN Pvt, G, 30th NJ Inf, 2-6-1902. Holcomb-Riverview Cemetery, Lambertville, Hunterdon County.
HORTON, WILLIAM H. Pvt, E, 7th NJ Inf, 9-24-1866. Bordentown/Old St. Mary's Catholic Cemetery, Bordentown, Burlington County.
HORWEDEL, FRANK Pvt, C, 6th NY National Guard, 10-30-1904. Holy Name Cemetery, Jersey City, Hudson County.
HOSEY*, ROBERT (aka: Smith, John) Pvt, E, 117th U.S. CT, 1-11-1940. Laurel Grove Cemetery, Totowa, Passaic County.
HOSKING, WILLIAM Pvt, I, 16th WI Inf, 4-20-1915. Old Butler Cemetery, Butler, Morris County.
HOSURE, STACY G. Pvt, E, 23rd NJ Inf, 10-2-1909. Columbus Cemetery, Columbus, Burlington County.
HOTALEN, LANSING M. Corp, B, 2nd NJ Inf, 5-25-1925. Minisink Reformed Church Cemetery, Montague, Sussex County.
HOTCHKISS, CHARLES A. Corp, 1st Btty, CT Light Art, 10-4-1897. Evergreen Cemetery, Camden, Camden County.
HOTCHKISS, CHARLES W. Pvt, F, 2nd NJ Inf, 12-5-1886. Fairmount Cemetery, Newark, Essex County.
HOTCHKISS, HENRY E. (aka: Hodgkiss, Henry) Sgt, G, 59th NY Inf, 7-30-1911. Oak Hill Cemetery, Vineland, Cumberland County.
HOTCHKISS, ORRIN A. 1st Lt, B, 83rd PA Inf, 1884. Siloam Cemetery, Vineland, Cumberland County.
HOTHAM, EDMOND S. Paymaster's Clerk, U.S. Navy, 8-10-1908. Rosedale Cemetery, Orange, Essex County.
HOTTBUM, GEORGE 5-5-1892. Methodist Church Cemetery, Cokesbury, Hunterdon County.
HOTTLE, PETER Pvt, A, 5th VA Inf (CSA), [Captured 5-12-1864 at Spotsylvania CH, VA. Died of fever.] 10-4-1864. Finn's Point National Cemetery, Pennsville, Salem County.
HOUCK, KARL (see: Hauck, Carl) Fairmount Cemetery, Newark, Essex County.
HOUG, JACOB (see: Hough, Jacob) Phillipsburg Cemetery, Phillipsburg, Warren County.
HOUGH, ALFRED LACEY Bvt Col, 19th U.S. Inf 4-28-1908. Friends Cemetery, Arneys Mount, Burlington County.
HOUGH, BENJAMIN M. Pvt, K, 15th NJ Inf, [Killed in action at Spotsylvania CH, VA.] 5-12-1864. Old Hough Cemetery, Colesville, Sussex County.
HOUGH, DEWITT C. Surg, 7th NJ Inf 8-25-1897. Union Cemetery, Milford, Hunterdon County.
HOUGH*, EDWARD B. Pvt, E, 13th NY Inf, 1916. Baptist Church Cemetery, Haddonfield, Camden County.
HOUGH, GEORGE W. Pvt, D, 7th LA Inf (CSA), [Captured 5-3-1863 at Fredericksburg, VA.] 11-3-1863. Finn's Point National Cemetery, Pennsville, Salem County.
HOUGH*, HENRY J. 2nd Lt, G, 26th CT Inf, [Wounded 2-8-1862 at Roanoke Island, NC.] DoD Unknown. Evergreen Cemetery, Farmingdale, Monmouth County.
HOUGH, JACOB (aka: Houg, Jacob) Pvt, I, 34th NJ Inf, DoD Unknown. Phillipsburg Cemetery, Phillipsburg, Warren County.
HOUGH, JOHN 6-17-1880. Macphelah Cemetery, North Bergen, Hudson County.
HOUGH, JOHN Pvt, K, 8th NJ Inf, 4-25-1915. Cedar Lawn Cemetery, Paterson, Passaic County.
HOUGH, JOSEPH Pvt, F, 202nd PA Inf, 6-5-1901. Phillipsburg Cemetery, Phillipsburg, Warren County.

Our Brothers Gone Before

HOUGH, THOMAS (aka: Haigh, Thomas) Pvt, I, 70th NY Inf, 3-30-1910. Cedar Lawn Cemetery, Paterson, Passaic County.

HOUGH, WILLIAM Pvt, H, 23rd PA Inf, 10-27-1878. Cedar Grove Cemetery, Gloucester City, Camden County.

HOUGHKERK, ISAAC F. Corp, I, 8th NJ Inf, [Died of consumption at Rahway, NJ.] 4-15-1862. Hazelwood Cemetery, Rahway, Union County.

HOUGHTALING, HENRY Pvt, K, 9th NJ Inf, 3-16-1896. Greenwood Cemetery, Hamilton, Mercer County.

HOUGHTALING*, LEANDER Sgt, G, 4th NJ Inf, 4-24-1896. New Camden Cemetery, Camden, Camden County.

HOUGHTALING, STEPHEN D. Drum Major, A, 20th NY State Militia, 12-19-1927. Fairmount Cemetery, Chatham, Morris County.

HOUGHTON, ABNER S. 4-11-1905. Greenwood Cemetery, Hamilton, Mercer County.

HOUGHTON, JESSE M. Pvt, I, 31st VA Inf (CSA), [Captured 7-3-1863 at Gettysburg, PA.] 10-1-1863. Finn's Point National Cemetery, Pennsville, Salem County.

HOUK, GEORGE Pvt, C, 9th NJ Inf, 9-21-1910. Laurel Grove Cemetery, Totowa, Passaic County.

HOULIGHAN, JAMES (see: Honligan, James) Fairmount Cemetery, Newark, Essex County.

HOULROYD, CHARLES A. Pvt, G, 15th NY Eng, 7-18-1914. Van Liew Cemetery, North Brunswick, Middlesex County.

HOUNSLOW, ALFRED W. Corp, G, 25th NJ Inf, 10-19-1903. Bordentown/Old St. Mary's Catholic Cemetery, Bordentown, Burlington County.

HOURIET, JULIEN (aka: Houriett, Julius) Corp, I, 1st NJ Inf, [Killed in action at Crampton's Pass, MD.] 9-14-1862. Hoboken Cemetery, North Bergen, Hudson County.

HOURIETT, JULIUS (see: Houriet, Julien) Hoboken Cemetery, North Bergen, Hudson County.

HOUSE*, ALEXANDER Pvt, C, 38th NC Inf (CSA), [Captured 7-3-1863 at Gettysburg, PA. Died of fever.] 9-15-1863. Finn's Point National Cemetery, Pennsville, Salem County.

HOUSE, EDWARD 4-13-1914. Hackensack Cemetery, Hackensack, Bergen County.

HOUSE, GEORGE V.W. Sgt, 22nd NY National Guard [Standard Bearer.] 3-24-1910. Fairview Cemetery, Fairview, Bergen County.

HOUSE, JAMES H. Pvt, Btty D, 1st NJ Light Art, 5-11-1888. Hillside Cemetery, Scotch Plains, Union County.

HOUSE, PETER A. Sgt, H, 27th NJ Inf, 9-18-1889. Minisink Reformed Church Cemetery, Montague, Sussex County.

HOUSE, WILLIAM Pvt, H, 8th NJ Inf, 5-2-1919. Phillipsburg Cemetery, Phillipsburg, Warren County.

HOUSEL, EDWARD Pvt, G, 30th NJ Inf, 6-10-1909. Sergeant's Hill Cemetery, Sand Brook, Hunterdon County.

HOUSEL*, JACOB Pvt, H, 15th NJ Inf, 2- -1928. Chestnut Cemetery, Dover, Morris County.

HOUSEL, JAMES B. 10-23-1866. Union Cemetery, Frenchtown, Hunterdon County.

HOUSEL, MOSES G. Pvt, A, 15th NJ Inf, 9-21-1883. Fountain Grove Cemetery, Glen Gardner, Hunterdon County.

HOUSEL, SAMUEL Pvt, E, 69th OH Inf, 1863. Mount Hope Presbyterian Cemetery, Lambertville, Hunterdon County.

HOUSEL, WILLIAM M. (aka: Housel, Wilson) Corp, G, 15th NJ Inf, 11-25-1908. Union Cemetery, Frenchtown, Hunterdon County.

HOUSEL, WILSON (see: Housel, William M.) Union Cemetery, Frenchtown, Hunterdon County.

New Jersey Civil War Burials

HOUSELL*, EDWARD E. Pvt, E, 132nd NY Inf, DoD Unknown. Hackensack Cemetery, Hackensack, Bergen County.
HOUSELL, HENRY Pvt, G, 1st NJ Cav, 1933. Presbyterian Church Cemetery, Greenwich, Warren County.
HOUSELL, HENRY C. (see: Honsel, Henry C.) Elmwood Cemetery, New Brunswick, Middlesex County.
HOUSELL, WILLIAM H.H. Pvt, F, 9th NJ Inf, [Cenotaph. Died of fever at Newbern, NC.] 5-27-1862. Amwell Ridge Cemetery, Larisons Corner, Hunterdon County.
HOUSEMAN, JOHN Corp, A, 150th PA Inf, 4-4-1914. Fairmount Cemetery, Newark, Essex County.
HOUSEMAN, MICHAEL (see: Holmes, Michael B.) Holy Name Cemetery, Jersey City, Hudson County.
HOUSER, JOHN Pvt, L, 13th PA Cav, 1912. Siloam Cemetery, Vineland, Cumberland County.
HOUSER, JONAS Pvt, G, 57th NC Inf (CSA), [Captured 7-10-1864 at Middletown, MD. Died of pneumonia.] 1-25-1865. Finn's Point National Cemetery, Pennsville, Salem County.
HOUSMAN, MICHAEL Pvt, I, 8th NJ Inf, 2-15-1905. Lutheran Cemetery, East Stewartsville, Warren County.
HOUSSELL, JOHN MANNERS Sgt, B, 4th NJ Inf, 8-15-1865. Greenwood Cemetery, Hamilton, Mercer County.
HOUSSER, CHARLES Pvt, E, 21st NJ Inf, 1919. Cedar Hill Cemetery, Hightstown, Mercer County.
HOUSTON*, CHARLES A. Pvt, K, 11th IN Inf, 1917. New Somerville Cemetery, Somerville, Somerset County.
HOUSTON, ISAAC Pvt, F, 1st NH Cav, 2-12-1918. Hillside Cemetery, Scotch Plains, Union County.
HOUSTON, JAMES Pvt, F, 10th MO Inf, 3-10-1911. Evergreen Cemetery, Hillside, Union County.
HOUSTON, JESSE E. (see: Huston, Jesse E.) Evergreen Cemetery, Camden, Camden County.
HOUTENVILLE*, WILLIAM B. Landsman, U.S. Navy, USS Princeton, 4-1-1912. Riverview Cemetery, Trenton, Mercer County.
HOWARD, A.R. (aka: Harrad, A.R.) Pvt, H, 3rd (Howard's) Confederate States Cav (CSA), 1-26-1864. Finn's Point National Cemetery, Pennsville, Salem County.
HOWARD*, ALBERT Pvt, I, 1st ME Cav, [Died of disease.] 9-7-1864. Beverly National Cemetery, Edgewater Park, Burlington County.
HOWARD, ALFRED C. Pvt, B, 21st NJ Inf, 10-7-1896. Jersey City Cemetery, Jersey City, Hudson County.
HOWARD, ANDREW J. Pvt, H, 26th NJ Inf, 8-11-1907. Rosedale Cemetery, Orange, Essex County.
HOWARD, BENJAMIN 6-21-1900. Glenwood Cemetery, West Long Branch, Monmouth County.
HOWARD, CHARLES P. Sgt, H, 96th IL Inf, [Wounded in action.] 5-8-1890. Fairmount Cemetery, Newark, Essex County.
HOWARD, CHARLES P. Pvt, 2nd Btty, IN Light Art, DoD Unknown. Reformed Church Cemetery, Montville, Morris County.
HOWARD, CORNELIUS Pvt, B, 22nd NJ Inf, 8-8-1880. Valleau Cemetery, Ridgewood, Bergen County.
HOWARD, DAVID Pvt, H, 26th NJ Inf, 9-21-1884. Rosedale Cemetery, Orange, Essex County.
HOWARD, EDWARD B. Pvt, H, 23rd U.S. CT, 10-16-1916. Fairmount Cemetery, Newark, Essex County.

Our Brothers Gone Before

HOWARD, EDWARD CHARLES N. Capt, G, 25th NY Cav, [Killed in action at Whitehouse Landing, VA.] 6-20-1864. Prospect Hill Cemetery, Caldwell, Essex County.

HOWARD, EDWARD R. Bvt Capt, I, 4th NJ Inf, 10-22-1893. Riverview Cemetery, Trenton, Mercer County.

HOWARD, FRANCIS Pvt, F, 8th NJ Inf, DoD Unknown. Elmwood Cemetery, New Brunswick, Middlesex County.

HOWARD, GEORGE Corp, H, 23rd NJ Inf, 10-28-1922. North Crosswicks Cemetery, North Crosswicks, Mercer County.

HOWARD, GEORGE E. Pvt, K, 3rd NC Inf (CSA), [Captured 7-3-1863 at Gettysburg, PA. Died of typhoid.] 10-18-1863. Finn's Point National Cemetery, Pennsville, Salem County.

HOWARD, GEORGE LAYTON Pvt, K, 124th NY Inf, [Wounded 4-6-1865 at Saylers Creek, VA.] 1-6-1932. Pompton Reformed Church Cemetery, Pompton Lakes, Passaic County.

HOWARD, GEORGE P. Pvt, I, 27th NJ Inf, 5-18-1890. Fairmount Cemetery, Newark, Essex County.

HOWARD, GEORGE W. Pvt, B, 4th NJ Inf, 4-21-1896. Riverview Cemetery, Trenton, Mercer County.

HOWARD, GREENE (see: Green, Howard) Finn's Point National Cemetery, Pennsville, Salem County.

HOWARD, JAMES Pvt, K, 10th CT Inf, [Died of wounds received 8-16-1864 at Deep Run, VA.] 9-2-1864. Beverly National Cemetery, Edgewater Park, Burlington County.

HOWARD*, JAMES Pvt, F, 9th CT Inf, 4-24-1894. Fairmount Cemetery, Newark, Essex County.

HOWARD, JAMES Pvt, A, 14th MS Inf (CSA), 10-4-1863. Finn's Point National Cemetery, Pennsville, Salem County.

HOWARD, JAMES C. Pvt, H, 7th NH Inf, [Wounded 7-18-1863 at Fort Wagner, SC.] 3-2-1900. Mount Olivet Cemetery, Bloomfield, Essex County.

HOWARD, JAMES W. Pvt, H, 26th NJ Inf, 3-7-1900. Fairmount Cemetery, Newark, Essex County.

HOWARD, JAMES W. DoD Unknown. Pine Brook Cemetery, Pine Brook, Morris County.

HOWARD, JOHN Pvt, I, 3rd (Forrest's) TN Cav (CSA), 10-25-1863. Finn's Point National Cemetery, Pennsville, Salem County.

HOWARD, JOHN Pvt, K, 23rd VA Inf (CSA), [Captured 3-23-1862 at Kernstown, VA. Died of disease.] 4-23-1862. Finn's Point National Cemetery, Pennsville, Salem County.

HOWARD, JOHN H. (see: Howard, Richard) Holy Sepulchre Cemetery, East Orange, Essex County.

HOWARD, JOHN R. Pvt, E, 6th U.S. Cav, 10-16-1902. Fairmount Cemetery, Newark, Essex County.

HOWARD, JOHN R. Pvt, H, 26th NJ Inf, 4-9-1906. Rosedale Cemetery, Orange, Essex County.

HOWARD, JOHN R. Pvt, H, 8th NJ Inf, [Wounded in action.] 9-25-1919. Arlington Cemetery, Kearny, Hudson County.

HOWARD, JOHN T. Pvt, K, 5th MA Colored Cav, 3-9-1898. Riverview Cemetery, Trenton, Mercer County.

HOWARD, JOSEPH J. Pvt, A, 6th AL Inf (CSA), 8-6-1863. Finn's Point National Cemetery, Pennsville, Salem County.

HOWARD, LEWIS T. Pvt, H, 30th NJ Inf, 11-10-1888. Methodist Church Cemetery, Springfield, Union County.

New Jersey Civil War Burials

HOWARD, MILLER Pvt, Unassigned, U.S. CT, 11-13-1909. North Crosswicks Cemetery, North Crosswicks, Mercer County.

HOWARD, MOSES 1920. Roadside Cemetery, Manchester Township, Ocean County.

HOWARD, NATHAN Pvt, E, 8th U.S. CT, [Wounded 2-20-1864 at Olustee, FL.] 8-19-1911. Spencer African Methodist Church Cemetery, Woodstown, Salem County.

HOWARD, PETER Pvt, B, 5th MA Colored Cav, 12-4-1913. Jordan Lawn Cemetery, Pennsauken, Camden County.

HOWARD, RICHARD Pvt, G, 2nd NJ Cav, DoD Unknown. Holy Sepulchre Cemetery, Totowa, Passaic County.

HOWARD, RICHARD (aka: Howard, John H.) Capt, F, 72nd NY Inf, 12-23-1893. Holy Sepulchre Cemetery, East Orange, Essex County.

HOWARD, ROBERT HUGHES Capt, F, Douglass' Bttn TN Partisan Rangers (CSA), 8-29-1863. Finn's Point National Cemetery, Pennsville, Salem County.

HOWARD, SAMUEL Pvt, A, 6th U.S. CT, DoD Unknown. Mount Moriah Cemetery, Hainesport, Burlington County.

HOWARD, THOMAS Pvt, A, 25th NJ Inf, DoD Unknown. Holy Sepulchre Cemetery, Totowa, Passaic County.

HOWARD, WILLIAM Pvt, H, 23rd U.S. CT, DoD Unknown. Jordan Lawn Cemetery, Pennsauken, Camden County.

HOWARD, WILLIAM Corp, F, 111th U.S. CT, 9-9-1891. Johnson Cemetery, Camden, Camden County.

HOWARD*, WILLIAM Pvt, G, 7th NJ Inf, 4-8-1891. Fairmount Cemetery, Newark, Essex County.

HOWARD, WILLIAM Pvt, I, 39th NJ Inf, 1918. Rahway Cemetery, Rahway, Union County.

HOWARD, WILLIAM H. 1-10-1893. 7th Day Baptist Church Cemetery, Shiloh, Cumberland County.

HOWARD, WILLIAM H. Pvt, K, 11th RI Inf, 12-25-1921. Bayview-New York Bay Cemetery, Jersey City, Hudson County.

HOWARD, WILLIAM H. Pvt, B, 29th NJ Inf, 6-3-1891. Greengrove Cemetery, Keyport, Monmouth County.

HOWARD, WILLIAM H. Corp, H, 15th NJ Inf, 1917. Presbyterian Cemetery, Asbury, Warren County.

HOWARD, WILLIAM H. Pvt, B, 8th NJ Inf, 1-24-1912. Pine Brook Cemetery, Pine Brook, Morris County.

HOWARD, WILLIAM P. Pvt, D, 13th NJ Inf, 7-15-1881. Fairmount Cemetery, Chatham, Morris County.

HOWARD, WILLIAM W. Pvt, F, 1st WV Inf, 1924. Soldier's Home Cemetery, Vineland, Cumberland County.

HOWART, WILLIAM (see: Howatt, William) Hillside Cemetery, Scotch Plains, Union County.

HOWARTH, EDWARD Corp, B, 175th NY Inf, 4-19-1911. Macphelah Cemetery, North Bergen, Hudson County.

HOWARTH, GEORGE 3-28-1883. Elmwood Cemetery, New Brunswick, Middlesex County.

HOWARTH, JAMES W. Pvt, K, 70th NY Inf, 3-14-1883. Fairmount Cemetery, Newark, Essex County.

HOWATT, WILLIAM (aka: Howart, William) Pvt, I, 3rd NJ Inf, 4-5-1903. Hillside Cemetery, Scotch Plains, Union County.

HOWCROFT, WILLIAM Pvt, A, 7th NJ Inf, 9-15-1884. Cedar Lawn Cemetery, Paterson, Passaic County.

HOWE, BAXTER Sgt, C, 12th NY State Militia, 11-18-1890. Evergreen Cemetery, Camden, Camden County.

Our Brothers Gone Before

HOWE, F. Sgt, B, 1st MA Cav, 10-1-1886. Fairmount Cemetery, Newark, Essex County.

HOWE*, GARDNER Pvt, A, 32nd MA Inf, 7-5-1898. Siloam Cemetery, Vineland, Cumberland County.

HOWE, MATTHEW Pvt, E, 141st PA Inf, 2-27-1925. Arlington Cemetery, Kearny, Hudson County.

HOWE*, PATRICK M. Pvt, G, 59th NY Inf, 6-1-1925. St. Mary's Cemetery, Perth Amboy, Middlesex County.

HOWE, THOMAS Seaman, U.S. Navy, USS Mattabassett, 3-16-1907. Bayview-New York Bay Cemetery, Jersey City, Hudson County.

HOWE, THOMAS Seaman, U.S. Navy, 11-2-1917. Holy Name Cemetery, Jersey City, Hudson County.

HOWE, WILLIAM W. Corp, G, 12th NJ Inf, 4-18-1885. Old Camden Cemetery, Camden, Camden County.

HOWELL, ABEL Pvt, H, 8th AL Inf (CSA), 11-25-1863. Finn's Point National Cemetery, Pennsville, Salem County.

HOWELL, ALEXANDER C. Pvt, F, 42nd NC Inf (CSA), 1902. Union Cemetery, Washington, Morris County.

HOWELL, ALFRED Pvt, C, 2nd NJ Cav, 1928. Fairmount Cemetery, Fairmount, Hunterdon County.

HOWELL, ARMITAGE G. Corp, B, 14th NJ Inf, 4-22-1902. Bordentown/Old St. Mary's Catholic Cemetery, Bordentown, Burlington County.

HOWELL, BENJAMIN F. Pvt, I, 34th NJ Inf, 11-15-1872. English Neighborhood Reformed Church Cemetery, Ridgefield, Bergen County.

HOWELL*, BENJAMIN FRANKLIN Sgt, K, 12th NJ Inf, 2-1-1933. Christ Church Cemetery, Morgan, Middlesex County.

HOWELL, BENJAMIN PASCHALL 3-10-1925. Eglington Cemetery, Clarksboro, Gloucester County.

HOWELL, BENJAMIN S. 6-26-1910. Elmwood Cemetery, New Brunswick, Middlesex County.

HOWELL, BYRON C. (SR.) Corp, C, 76th NY Inf, 1-6-1915. Fairview Cemetery, Westfield, Union County.

HOWELL, CALEB HENRY Wagoner, D, 48th NY Inf, 1904. Pleasant Hill Cemetery, Pleasant Hill, Morris County.

HOWELL, E.A. Pvt, G, 60th GA Inf (CSA), 2-23-1865. Finn's Point National Cemetery, Pennsville, Salem County.

HOWELL*, FRANCIS A. Capt, E, 131st NY Inf, 3-27-1898. English Neighborhood Reformed Church Cemetery, Ridgefield, Bergen County.

HOWELL*, FRANCIS P. (aka: Holwell, Francis) Musc, B, 76th NY Inf, 7-23-1930. Bayview-New York Bay Cemetery, Jersey City, Hudson County.

HOWELL, FRANKLIN A. Pvt, A, 54th PA Inf, 6-4-1914. Oddfellows Cemetery, Burlington, Burlington County.

HOWELL, FREDERICK P. Pvt, Btty B, 1st NJ Light Art, 2-9-1873. Presbyterian Church Cemetery, Fairmount, Hunterdon County.

HOWELL, GEORGE Wagoner, B, 48th NY Inf, DoD Unknown. Methodist Church Cemetery, Fairmount, Hunterdon County.

HOWELL, GEORGE W. 3-16-1904. Mount Pleasant Cemetery, Newark, Essex County.

HOWELL, GEORGE W. Sgt, D, 15th NJ Inf, 1926. Congregational Church Cemetery, Chester, Morris County.

HOWELL, HENRY Pvt, K, 12th NJ Inf, [Died of diarrhea at Falmouth, VA.] 3-23-1863. Old Stone Church Cemetery, Fairton, Cumberland County.

HOWELL, HENRY C. Sgt, B, 12th NJ Inf, 1-12-1915. Rosehill Cemetery, Linden, Union County.

HOWELL, HORACE B. Pvt, U.S. Marine Corps, 8-3-1862. Mercer Cemetery, Trenton, Mercer County.

New Jersey Civil War Burials

HOWELL, HORACE FORD Pvt, D, 10th NJ Inf, 7-30-1865. Hillside Cemetery, Madison, Morris County.

HOWELL, IRENIUS PRIME Corp, F, 13th NJ Inf, [Died at Brooke's Station, VA of wounds received 5-3-1863 at Chancellorsville, VA.] 5-22-1863. Mount Pleasant Cemetery, Newark, Essex County.

HOWELL, ISAAC Pvt, E, 83rd NY Inf, [Died of disease at Frederick, MD.] 12-13-1861. Bayview-New York Bay Cemetery, Jersey City, Hudson County.

HOWELL, ISAAC Sgt, D, 4th NJ Inf, 10-26-1900. Riverview Cemetery, Trenton, Mercer County.

HOWELL, JACOB Pvt, D, 25th U.S. CT, 7-9-1894. Mount Salem Church Cemetery, Fenwick, Salem County.

HOWELL, JAMES G. Pvt, D, 25th U.S. CT, 4-5-1882. Mount Salem Church Cemetery, Fenwick, Salem County.

HOWELL, JAMES H. Pvt, C, 4th NY Cav, 8-3-1911. Fairmount Cemetery, Newark, Essex County.

HOWELL, JAMSON (see: Howell, Samson O.) Union Cemetery, Washington, Morris County.

HOWELL, JOHN Pvt, D, 25th U.S. CT, 5-1-1911. Mount Salem Church Cemetery, Fenwick, Salem County.

HOWELL, JOHN C. Sgt, H, 27th NJ Inf, 1906. Newton Cemetery, Newton, Sussex County.

HOWELL, JOHN H. Pvt, M, 2nd NJ Cav, 6-5-1921. Calvary Community Church Cemetery, Harmony, Warren County.

HOWELL, JOHN J. Pvt, F, 11th MS Inf (CSA), 2-23-1865. Finn's Point National Cemetery, Pennsville, Salem County.

HOWELL, JOHN P. Pvt, C, 23rd NJ Inf, 1-11-1912. New Camden Cemetery, Camden, Camden County.

HOWELL, JOHN P. Pvt, D, 15th NJ Inf, 12-2-1903. Mount Pleasant Cemetery, Newark, Essex County.

HOWELL, JOSEPH WARREN Pvt, E, 39th NJ Inf, 8-25-1916. Fairmount Cemetery, Newark, Essex County.

HOWELL, JOSHUA BLACKWOOD Bvt Brig Gen, U.S. Army, [Died from injuries after a fall with his horse on 9-12-1864.] 9-14-1864. Eglington Cemetery, Clarksboro, Gloucester County.

HOWELL, NATHAN 3-10-1879. Fairmount Cemetery, Fairmount, Hunterdon County.

HOWELL, PHILIP F. Pvt, A, 7th IL Inf, DoD Unknown. Presbyterian Church Cemetery, Greenwich, Cumberland County.

HOWELL, RICHARD V. Pvt, C, 11th NJ Inf, 11-1-1932. Arlington Cemetery, Kearny, Hudson County.

HOWELL, ROBERT H. Maj, Pay Dept NJ [Paymaster.] 5-14-1901. Newton Cemetery, Newton, Sussex County.

HOWELL, S.W. Pvt, B, 8th Confederate States Cav (CSA), 11-29-1863. Finn's Point National Cemetery, Pennsville, Salem County.

HOWELL, SAMSON O. (aka: Howell, Jamson) Pvt, B, 15th NJ Inf, 8-10-1901. Union Cemetery, Washington, Morris County.

HOWELL, THOMAS B. Pvt, C, 38th NJ Inf, 2-5-1915. Friendship United Methodist Church Cemetery, Landisville, Atlantic County.

HOWELL, THOMAS JAMES 2nd Lt, I, 3rd NJ Inf, [Killed in action at Gaines' Farm, VA.] 6-27-1862. Evergreen Cemetery, Camden, Camden County.

HOWELL, THOMAS W. Saddler, M, 2nd NJ Cav, 9-11-1902. Mount Prospect Cemetery, Neptune, Monmouth County.

HOWELL, TILMAN Corp, K, 42nd MS Inf (CSA), 8-26-1864. Finn's Point National Cemetery, Pennsville, Salem County.

Our Brothers Gone Before

HOWELL, WILLIAM Pvt, B, 9th NJ Inf, 10-18-1876. Macphelah Cemetery, North Bergen, Hudson County.

HOWELL, WILLIAM Corp, L, 27th NJ Inf, [Died of typhoid at Baltimore, MD.] 4-11-1863. Presbyterian Church Cemetery, Rockaway, Morris County.

HOWELL, WILLIAM G. Seaman, U.S. Navy, 1-29-1899. Christ Church Cemetery, Morgan, Middlesex County.

HOWELL, WILLIAM H. Pvt, D, 27th NJ Inf, 1-16-1926. Branchville Cemetery, Branchville, Sussex County.

HOWELL, WILLIAM R. Pvt, K, 107th IL Inf, 4-29-1903. Mercer Cemetery, Trenton, Mercer County.

HOWENSTEIN, CASPER (see: Howenstine, Casper) Atlantic City Cemetery, Pleasantville, Atlantic County.

HOWENSTINE, CASPER (aka: Howenstein, Casper) Corp, D, 98th PA Inf, DoD Unknown. Atlantic City Cemetery, Pleasantville, Atlantic County.

HOWER, DAVID W. Pvt, E, 33rd NJ Inf, 11-22-1872. Fairmount Cemetery, Newark, Essex County.

HOWES, ALFRED Pvt, A, 8th CT Inf, 1923. Rosehill Cemetery, Newfield, Gloucester County.

HOWETH, JOHN 1st Lt, C, 6th NJ Inf, [Died at Washington, DC of wounds received 5-3-1863 at Chancellorsville, VA.] 5-15-1863. Bayview-New York Bay Cemetery, Jersey City, Hudson County.

HOWEY, BENJAMIN FRANKLIN Capt, G, 31st NJ Inf, 2-6-1893. New Episcopal Church Cemetery, Swedesboro, Gloucester County.

HOWEY, JAMES S. 1-9-1902. New Episcopal Church Cemetery, Swedesboro, Gloucester County.

HOWEY*, ROBERT Pvt, I, 77th IL Inf, 1-29-1911. Eglington Cemetery, Clarksboro, Gloucester County.

HOWLAND, BRITTON 10-29-1891. Old 1st Methodist Church Cemetery, West Long Branch, Monmouth County.

HOWLAND, EDGAR D. Pvt, Btty A, 1st IL Light Art, [Wounded in action.] 10-31-1905. Hackensack Cemetery, Hackensack, Bergen County.

HOWLAND, ESECK Pvt, G, 14th NJ Inf, [Wounded in action.] 4-2-1895. Methodist Cemetery, Hamilton, Monmouth County.

HOWLAND, J. BLOOMFIELD Pvt, A, 29th NJ Inf, 12-5-1922. Glendale Cemetery, Bloomfield, Essex County.

HOWLAND, JESSE Pvt, G, 1st NJ Cav, 2-4-1909. Greenlawn Cemetery, West Long Branch, Monmouth County.

HOWLAND, WILLIAM H. Pvt, A, 29th NJ Inf, 12-30-1910. Greenlawn Cemetery, West Long Branch, Monmouth County.

HOWLAND, ZENAS M. 1912. Old 1st Methodist Church Cemetery, West Long Branch, Monmouth County.

HOWLETT, FREDERICK Pvt, D, 8th NY Inf, 1910. Christ Church Cemetery, Morgan, Middlesex County.

HOXEY, WILLIAM A. DoD Unknown. Alpine Cemetery, Perth Amboy, Middlesex County.

HOXSEY, BENJAMIN WELLER Capt, A, 70th NY Inf, 12-8-1881. Cedar Lawn Cemetery, Paterson, Passaic County.

HOY, CHAUNCEY Pvt, E, 40th NY Inf, DoD Unknown. Holy Name Cemetery, Jersey City, Hudson County.

HOY, ISAAC (see: Hoey, Isaac N.) Baptist Church Cemetery, Haddonfield, Camden County.

HOY, THOMAS H. Corp, G, 25th NJ Inf, 1-11-1899. Evergreen Cemetery, Camden, Camden County.

HOYT, C.B. 2-23-1919. Hoboken Cemetery, North Bergen, Hudson County.

New Jersey Civil War Burials

HOYT, CHARLES EDWIN Pvt, Btty B, 5th NY Heavy Art, 2-23-1940. Mount Rest Cemetery, Butler, Morris County.
HOYT, DAVID N. Pvt, I, 28th NJ Inf, 2-3-1885. Alpine Cemetery, Perth Amboy, Middlesex County.
HOYT, EDWIN Sgt, D, 13th NJ Inf, 7-29-1913. Rosehill Cemetery, Linden, Union County.
HOYT*, ENOCH Pvt, L, 20th NY Cav, 4-29-1901. Reformed Church Cemetery, Lebanon, Hunterdon County.
HOYT, GEORGE W. Pvt, H, 27th NJ Inf, DoD Unknown. Jersey City Cemetery, Jersey City, Hudson County.
HOYT, HENRY R. 1st Lt, Btty H, 2nd CT Heavy Art, 11-4-1903. Methodist Church Cemetery, Hope, Warren County.
HOYT, JARED R. Sgt, A, 18th NY National Guard, 1886. Mount Salem Cemetery, Mount Salem, Sussex County.
HOYT, WILLIAM A. Pvt, D, 39th NJ Inf, 9-9-1909. Ramseyburg Cemetery, Ramseyburg, Warren County.
HOYWARD, GEORGE P. 5-15-1890. Fairmount Cemetery, Newark, Essex County.
HOZIER, DAVID P. 10- -1864. Woodlane Graveyard Cemetery, Westampton, Burlington County.
HOZIER*, WILLIAM H. Surg, 162nd NY Inf [Also: Surg, 174th NY Inf.] 2-7-1872. Presbyterian Church Cemetery, New Providence, Union County.
HUBBARD*, DAVID H. Pvt, Btty E, 11th U.S. CHA, 1-3-1898. Riverview Cemetery, Trenton, Mercer County.
HUBBARD, GEORGE Pvt, D, 37th NJ Inf, 4-7-1924. Old St. Mary's Cemetery, Gloucester City, Camden County.
HUBBARD, GEORGE Wagoner, A, 10th NJ Inf, 8-1-1920. Mount Pleasant Cemetery, Millville, Cumberland County.
HUBBARD, HARLAND Pvt, Btty D, 1st CT Heavy Art, 2-25-1932. Bayview-New York Bay Cemetery, Jersey City, Hudson County.
HUBBARD, HENRY Seaman, U.S. Navy, USS Constellation, 8-21-1921. Greenwood Cemetery, Hamilton, Mercer County.
HUBBARD, JAMES FRANKLIN Capt, H, 30th NJ Inf, 6-26-1905. Hillside Cemetery, Scotch Plains, Union County.
HUBBELL, FRANCIS Pvt, F, 38th NJ Inf, 5-2-1866. Old 1st Methodist Church Cemetery, West Long Branch, Monmouth County.
HUBBELL, FRANKLIN Pvt, H, 8th CT Inf, 4-1-1917. Riverside Cemetery, Toms River, Ocean County.
HUBBS, ALLEN Pvt, G, 23rd NJ Inf, 12-26-1896. Methodist Church Cemetery, New Albany, Burlington County.
HUBBS, GEORGE Pvt, H, 9th NJ Inf, 1-7-1898. Norton Church Cemetery, Norton, Hunterdon County.
HUBBS, JOHN L. Corp, G, 23rd NJ Inf, 5-14-1915. Overlook Cemetery, Bridgeton, Cumberland County.
HUBBS, SAMUEL G. Pvt, G, 23rd NJ Inf, 5-9-1913. Methodist Church Cemetery, New Albany, Burlington County.
HUBER, ADOLPHUS Pvt, D, 11th NJ Inf, 3-5-1896. Fairmount Cemetery, Newark, Essex County.
HUBER*, ALBERT Pvt, E, 13th NJ Inf, 6-3-1880. Fairmount Cemetery, Newark, Essex County.
HUBER, CARL Landsman, U.S. Navy, 12-27-1888. Fairmount Cemetery, Newark, Essex County.
HUBER, CHARLES Pvt, I, 98th PA Inf, 2-7-1902. Egg Harbor Cemetery, Egg Harbor, Atlantic County.
HUBER, JACOB Pvt, B, 35th NJ Inf, 10-16-1899. Palisade Cemetery, North Bergen, Hudson County.

Our Brothers Gone Before

HUBER, JOHN Pvt, Btty E, 4th U.S. Art, 3-30-1890. Bordentown/Old St. Mary's Catholic Cemetery, Bordentown, Burlington County.

HUBER, JOSEPH 9-20-1913. Edgewater Cemetery, Edgewater, Bergen County.

HUBER, JOSEPH Fireman, U.S. Navy, USS Isaac Smith, 1906. Berry Lawn Cemetery, Carlstadt, Bergen County.

HUBER, LOUIS Pvt, G, 35th NJ Inf, 10-13-1883. Fairmount Cemetery, Newark, Essex County.

HUBER, MICHAEL Pvt, M, 8th NY Cav, 2-14-1918. Mount Laurel/Eldridge Cemetery, Mount Laurel, Burlington County.

HUBER, VALENTINE Pvt, G, 94th NY Inf, [Died of disease at Camp Parole, VA.] 8-21-1864. Beverly National Cemetery, Edgewater Park, Burlington County.

HUBER, VALENTINE 3-15-1886. Speer Cemetery, Jersey City, Hudson County.

HUBERT, CHARLES Corp, D, 7th NJ Inf, 12-4-1922. Riverview Cemetery, Trenton, Mercer County.

HUBERT, JOSEPH C. Pvt, K, 9th NJ Inf, 1924. Presbyterian Church Cemetery, Andover, Sussex County.

HUCK, RUTLEDGE (see: Hoff, Rutledge T.) Riverview Cemetery, Trenton, Mercer County.

HUCKABEE, JAMES Pvt, D, 30th AL Inf (CSA), 6-23-1863. Finn's Point National Cemetery, Pennsville, Salem County.

HUCKE, JACOB Pvt, A, 4th NJ Inf, 11-17-1899. Eastview Cemetery, Salem, Salem County.

HUDDLER, JAMES (see: Hudler, James) Finn's Point National Cemetery, Pennsville, Salem County.

HUDDLESON, JOHN Pvt, E, 31st NJ Inf, 6-5-1891. Norton Church Cemetery, Norton, Hunterdon County.

HUDDLESTON, HENRY Sgt, I, 1st/4th Consolidated MO Inf (CSA), 10-17-1863. Finn's Point National Cemetery, Pennsville, Salem County.

HUDGINS, J.W. Pvt, A, 42nd VA Cav (CSA), 3-27-1865. Finn's Point National Cemetery, Pennsville, Salem County.

HUDLER, JAMES (aka: Huddler, James) Pvt, G, 33rd NC Inf (CSA), [Captured 7-3-1863 at Gettysburg, PA. Died of diarrhea.] 9-28-1863. Finn's Point National Cemetery, Pennsville, Salem County.

HUDLEY, JONAS (see: Hoadley, Jonas) St. James Cemetery, Greenwich, Warren County.

HUDNET, WILLIAM Corp, K, 28th NJ Inf, 3-2-1881. Cedar Hill Cemetery, Hightstown, Mercer County.

HUDNITE, JACOB Pvt, F, 20th CT Inf, 1-8-1927. Fairmount Cemetery, Phillipsburg, Warren County.

HUDSON, ABRAM D. 1st Lt, D, 2nd DC Inf, 2-11-1885. Mount Pleasant Cemetery, Newark, Essex County.

HUDSON, CHARLES Pvt, K, 172nd NY Inf, [Wounded 5-3-1864 at Spotsylvania CH, VA.] DoD Unknown. Laurel Grove Cemetery, Totowa, Passaic County.

HUDSON, GEORGE Pvt, C, 6th NJ Inf, 12-21-1926. Arlington Cemetery, Kearny, Hudson County.

HUDSON*, ISAAC A. Pvt, Btty B, Milton's Bttn FL Light Art (CSA), [Captured 2-28-1864 at Camp Finegan, FL. Died of erysipelas.] 6-8-1864. Finn's Point National Cemetery, Pennsville, Salem County.

HUDSON*, J.L. Pvt, A, 9th KY Cav (CSA), [Captured 6-15-1863 in Kentucky.] 10-15-1863. Finn's Point National Cemetery, Pennsville, Salem County.

HUDSON, JOHN Corp, I, 21st NJ Inf, 9-19-1902. Phillipsburg Cemetery, Phillipsburg, Warren County.

HUDSON, JOSEPH Pvt, C, 37th NJ Inf, 9-28-1901. Bordentown/Old St. Mary's Catholic Cemetery, Bordentown, Burlington County.

New Jersey Civil War Burials

HUDSON, M.B. Pvt, G, 51st VA Inf (CSA), [Captured 3-2-1865 at Waynesboro, VA. Died of measles.] 4-9-1865. Finn's Point National Cemetery, Pennsville, Salem County.

HUDSON, MILTON Sgt, B, 7th NJ Inf, 5-19-1925. Mount Pleasant Cemetery, Newark, Essex County.

HUDSON, RICHARD H. Pvt, E, 5th FL Inf (CSA), [Captured 7-2-1863 at Gettysburg, PA.] 12-20-1863. Finn's Point National Cemetery, Pennsville, Salem County.

HUDSON, SAMUEL T. Pvt, E, 47th PA Inf, 5-22-1870. St. John's Evangelical Church Cemetery, Orange, Essex County.

HUDSON, SHEPHARD S. Seaman, U.S. Navy, 6-7-1906. Union Cemetery, Clarkstown, Atlantic County.

HUDSON, THEODORE F. Pvt, F, 12th NJ Inf, DoD Unknown. St. John's Methodist Church Cemetery, Harrisonville, Gloucester County.

HUDSON*, WILLIAM 1st Sgt, H, 1st NJ Cav, 11-16-1903. St. Peter's Cemetery, New Brunswick, Middlesex County.

HUDSON, WILLIAM J. Hosp Steward, 6th NJ Inf 2-24-1912. Oddfellows Cemetery, Burlington, Burlington County.

HUDSON*, WILLIAM S. Capt, D, 49th NY Inf, [Wounded 5-18-1864 at Spotsylvania CH, VA. and 10-19-1864 at Cedar Creek, VA.] 4-25-1877. Cedar Lawn Cemetery, Paterson, Passaic County.

HUEBNER, MARTIN (aka: Wisner, Martin) Pvt, I, 199th PA Inf, 5-24-1897. Grove Church Cemetery, North Bergen, Hudson County.

HUELBIG, FREDERICK Pvt, Btty C, 1st NJ Light Art, 7-11-1900. Hoboken Cemetery, North Bergen, Hudson County.

HUEY, ISAAC H. Pvt, K, 9th NJ Inf, 1-14-1892. Evergreen Cemetery, Hillside, Union County.

HUFF, ABRAHAM T. 8-7-1907. New Dutch Reformed/Neshanic Cemetery, Neshanic, Somerset County.

HUFF, CHARLES Pvt, K, 25th U.S. CT, 9-3-1910. Fairmount Cemetery, Newark, Essex County.

HUFF, CHARLES W. 2-12-1898. Union Cemetery, Frenchtown, Hunterdon County.

HUFF, CHARLES W. Pvt, F, 2nd NJ Cav, 1900. Cedar Ridge Cemetery, Blairstown, Warren County.

HUFF, CHARLES W. 8-25-1900. Presbyterian Church Cemetery, Marksboro, Warren County.

HUFF, DAVID 1st Sgt, F, 20th U.S. CT, 6-12-1912. Evergreen Cemetery, Morristown, Morris County.

HUFF, EDEN Corp, G, 11th NJ Inf, 2-9-1923. Van Liew Cemetery, North Brunswick, Middlesex County.

HUFF, EDWARD W. Pvt, G, 38th NJ Inf, 2-7-1921. Presbyterian Church Cemetery, Mount Pleasant, Hunterdon County.

HUFF, ELMER 2-24-1920. Union Cemetery, Washington, Morris County.

HUFF, GEORGE V. Pvt, I, 15th NJ Inf, 3-27-1921. Union Cemetery, Washington, Morris County.

HUFF, JACOB E. Pvt, F, 2nd NJ Cav, 3-22-1913. Balesville Cemetery, Balesville, Sussex County.

HUFF, JAMES Coal Heaver, U.S. Navy, USS Princeton, 12-28-1926. Fairmount Cemetery, Newark, Essex County.

HUFF, JAMES Pvt, A, 20th U.S. CT, 2-11-1887. Fairmount Cemetery, Newark, Essex County.

HUFF, JOHN Corp, C, 12th NJ Inf, 1909. Marlton Cemetery, Marlton, Burlington County.

HUFF, JOHN A. QM Sgt, 20th U.S. CT 6-6-1922. Fairmount Cemetery, Newark, Essex County.

Our Brothers Gone Before

HUFF, JOHN L. Corp, E, 24th NJ Inf, 10-19-1876. St. Paul's United Methodist Church Cemetery, Paulsboro, Gloucester County.

HUFF, PHILIP W. Pvt, E, 2nd SC Inf (CSA), [Captured 7-5-1863 at Greencastle, PA. Died of typhoid.] 2-7-1864. Finn's Point National Cemetery, Pennsville, Salem County.

HUFF, RICHARD S. Musc, F, 84th OH Inf, 9-26-1893. Evergreen Cemetery, Camden, Camden County.

HUFF, SIMEON C. Pvt, C, 13th IL Inf, 4-25-1895. Phillipsburg Cemetery, Phillipsburg, Warren County.

HUFF, THOMAS H. Pvt, I, 15th NJ Inf, 1-24-1924. New Somerville Cemetery, Somerville, Somerset County.

HUFF, WILLIAM H. Pvt, G, 37th NJ Inf, 12-14-1876. Rahway Cemetery, Rahway, Union County.

HUFF, WILLIAM H. Pvt, Btty E, 1st NJ Light Art, 11-21-1917. Phillipsburg Cemetery, Phillipsburg, Warren County.

HUFFMAN, EDMIN (see: Huffman, Edmund) Sandy Ridge Cemetery, Sandy Ridge, Hunterdon County.

HUFFMAN, EDMUND (aka: Huffman, Edmin) Pvt, B, 3rd U.S. VRC, DoD Unknown. Sandy Ridge Cemetery, Sandy Ridge, Hunterdon County.

HUFFMAN, GEORGE (see: McCully, George Hoffman) Riverview Cemetery, Trenton, Mercer County.

HUFFMAN, ISAAC Pvt, G, 30th NJ Inf, 6-22-1935. Holcomb-Riverview Cemetery, Lambertville, Hunterdon County.

HUFFMAN, WILLIAM C. Pvt, C, 7th IL Cav, 10-14-1895. Presbyterian Church Cemetery, Clinton, Hunterdon County.

HUFMAN*, LYBRAND (aka: Hoffman, Leybrand) Chaplain, U.S. VRC 1926. Harleigh Cemetery, Camden, Camden County.

HUFSEY*, HIRAM Seaman, U.S. Navy, USS Glaucus, 8-3-1893. Cedar Green Cemetery, Clayton, Gloucester County.

HUFTELN*, BENNETT (aka: Huftelu, Bennett) Pvt, C, 1st NY Eng, 9-4-1901. Newton Cemetery, Newton, Sussex County.

HUFTELU, BENNETT (see: Hufteln, Bennett) Newton Cemetery, Newton, Sussex County.

HUFTY, SAMUEL Lt Col, 9th NJ Inf 6-9-1913. Harleigh Cemetery, Camden, Camden County.

HUGEE, BENJAMIN (see: Mansfield, Benjamin H.) Atlantic City Cemetery, Pleasantville, Atlantic County.

HUGERICH, GEORGE 12-4-1912. Palisade Cemetery, North Bergen, Hudson County.

HUGG, CALEB Pvt, A, 41st U.S. CT, DoD Unknown. Mount Peace Cemetery, Lawnside, Camden County.

HUGG*, CHARLES E. Sgt, H, 10th NJ Inf, [Died of consumption at Philadelphia, PA.] 2-13-1865. Berlin Cemetery, Berlin, Camden County.

HUGG, GEORGE W. 2nd Lt, A, 25th CT Militia, 7-30-1864. Trinity Episcopal Church Cemetery, Moorestown, Burlington County.

HUGG, ISAAC N. 1st Lt, I, 34th NJ Inf, 10-14-1904. Evergreen Cemetery, Camden, Camden County.

HUGG, ISAAC N. 4-5-1866. Brainerd Cemetery, Cranbury, Middlesex County.

HUGG, JAMES S. Capt, G, 34th NJ Inf, 1874. Berlin Cemetery, Berlin, Camden County.

HUGG, JAMES S. 9-10-1863. Methodist-Episcopal Cemetery, Burlington, Burlington County.

HUGG, JOHN 10-25-1880. Berlin Cemetery, Berlin, Camden County.

HUGG*, JOSEPH Asst Surg, U.S. Navy, [Naval Academy, MD.] 12-24-1889. Trinity Episcopal Church Cemetery, Moorestown, Burlington County.

HUGGINS, JOHN M. Pvt, G, 11th NJ Inf, [Died of typhoid at Falmouth, VA.] 1-3-1863. Baptist Church Cemetery, Jacobstown, Burlington County.

New Jersey Civil War Burials

HUGGINS, JOSEPH Pvt, H, 16th NC Inf (CSA), [Captured 7-3-1863 at Gettysburg, PA. Died of typhoid.] 10-16-1863. Finn's Point National Cemetery, Pennsville, Salem County.

HUGGO, ALEXANDER (see: Huggs, Alexander) Fairmount Cemetery, Newark, Essex County.

HUGGS, ALEXANDER (aka: Huggo, Alexander) Seaman, U.S. Navy, USS Huron, 9-20-1899. Fairmount Cemetery, Newark, Essex County.

HUGHES, ALBERT HENRY Pvt, K, 40th NJ Inf, 5- -1931. Presbyterian Church Cemetery, Cold Spring, Cape May County.

HUGHES, ALFRED Pvt, I, 38th NJ Inf, 3-9-1887. Greenwood Cemetery, Hamilton, Mercer County.

HUGHES, AMOS Pvt, H, 21st NJ Inf, 8-2-1891. Fairmount Cemetery, Newark, Essex County.

HUGHES*, ANDREW Landsman, U.S. Navy, USS Princeton, 10-8-1898. St. Peter's Cemetery, New Brunswick, Middlesex County.

HUGHES, ANDREW P. Pvt, K, 24th NJ Inf, 10-16-1900. Moose Cemetery, Perkintown, Salem County.

HUGHES, ARMITAGE D. 1st Cl Fireman, U.S. Navy, USS Penguin, 3-30-1914. Riverview Cemetery, Trenton, Mercer County.

HUGHES, BENJAMIN W. Pvt, H, 28th NJ Inf, 5-27-1875. Zion United Methodist Church Cemetery, Clarksboro, Gloucester County.

HUGHES, BENJAMIN W. Pvt, C, 30th NJ Inf, 5-31-1912. Rahway Cemetery, Rahway, Union County.

HUGHES, BERRY E. Corp, H, 28th NC Inf (CSA), [Captured 7-3-1863 at Gettysburg, PA.] 9-25-1863. Finn's Point National Cemetery, Pennsville, Salem County.

HUGHES, CHARLES M. Pvt, G, 8th NY State Militia, 2-18-1895. Holy Name Cemetery, Jersey City, Hudson County.

HUGHES, CHARLES R. Pvt, B, 29th NJ Inf, 5-17-1901. Evergreen Cemetery, Camden, Camden County.

HUGHES, DAVID MORGAN Seaman, U.S. Navy, DoD Unknown. Rahway Cemetery, Rahway, Union County.

HUGHES, EDWIN 2nd Lt, C, 6th NJ Inf, 10-6-1893. Bayview-New York Bay Cemetery, Jersey City, Hudson County.

HUGHES, ELI R. Pvt, H, 38th NJ Inf, 1909. Old 1st Methodist Church Cemetery, West Long Branch, Monmouth County.

HUGHES, GEORGE Pvt, E, 8th PA Cav, 10-5-1876. Mount Pleasant Cemetery, Millville, Cumberland County.

HUGHES, GEORGE B. Pvt, F, 47th AL Inf (CSA), 12-26-1863. Finn's Point National Cemetery, Pennsville, Salem County.

HUGHES, GEORGE W. Corp, I, 29th CT Inf, [Wounded 8-27-1864 at Petersburg, VA.] 12- -1870. Methodist-Episcopal Cemetery, Burlington, Burlington County.

HUGHES, GEORGE W. 1st Lt, H, 10th NJ Inf, 10-1-1910. Eglington Cemetery, Clarksboro, Gloucester County.

HUGHES, HENRY H. DoD Unknown. Zion United Methodist Church Cemetery, Clarksboro, Gloucester County.

HUGHES, HENRY H. Pvt, I, 24th NJ Inf, 1-31-1871. Baptist Church Cemetery, Slabtown, Salem County.

HUGHES, HENRY N. 5-21-1935. Arlington Cemetery, Kearny, Hudson County.

HUGHES, HENRY N. Pvt, A, 26th NJ Inf, 11-18-1904. Fairmount Cemetery, Newark, Essex County.

HUGHES, HIRAM Pvt, E, 21st NJ Inf, [Died of typhoid at White Oak Church, VA.] 2-16-1863. Presbyterian Church Cemetery, Hamilton Square, Mercer County.

HUGHES, HIRAM Capt, D, PA Emerg NJ Militia, DoD Unknown. Mount Hope Presbyterian Cemetery, Lambertville, Hunterdon County.

Our Brothers Gone Before

HUGHES, HUGH Pvt, A, 2nd NJ Inf, 6-3-1917. Rahway Cemetery, Rahway, Union County.
HUGHES, HUSTON P. Pvt, K, 43rd TN Inf (CSA), [5th East Tennessee Volunteers (Gillespie's).] 6-19-1863. Finn's Point National Cemetery, Pennsville, Salem County.
HUGHES, J.H. Pvt, C, 2nd SC Cav (CSA), [Captured 7-5-1863 at Gettysburg, PA. Died of typhoid.] 9-18-1863. Finn's Point National Cemetery, Pennsville, Salem County.
HUGHES, JACOB Pvt, K, 24th NJ Inf, 9-24-1887. Zion United Methodist Church Cemetery, Clarksboro, Gloucester County.
HUGHES, JACOB (see: Hughes, John) Eglington Cemetery, Clarksboro, Gloucester County.
HUGHES, JAMES Pvt, I, 13th NJ Inf, 8-11-1901. Holy Sepulchre Cemetery, East Orange, Essex County.
HUGHES, JAMES Pvt, F, 69th NY State Militia, 1-18-1909. Bayview-New York Bay Cemetery, Jersey City, Hudson County.
HUGHES, JAMES C. Pvt, C, 1st NJ Cav, 6-23-1883. Evergreen Cemetery, Lumberton, Burlington County.
HUGHES, JAMES G. (see: Hughes, M.) Finn's Point National Cemetery, Pennsville, Salem County.
HUGHES, JAMES H. Pvt, E, 24th NJ Inf, 3-11-1887. Eglington Cemetery, Clarksboro, Gloucester County.
HUGHES*, JAMES H. Capt, K, 21st NJ Inf, [Died of pneumonia at Hagerstown, MD.] 12-13-1862. Bayview-New York Bay Cemetery, Jersey City, Hudson County.
HUGHES*, JAMES H. Seaman, U.S. Navy, USS Princeton, 1-8-1921. Van Liew Cemetery, North Brunswick, Middlesex County.
HUGHES, JAMES P. Pvt, G, 3rd NJ Cav, 8-14-1876. Mount Pleasant Cemetery, Millville, Cumberland County.
HUGHES, JOHN Pvt, I, 70th NY Inf, 3-26-1927. Laurel Grove Cemetery, Totowa, Passaic County.
HUGHES, JOHN (aka: Hughes, Jacob) Pvt, K, 24th NJ Inf, DoD Unknown. Eglington Cemetery, Clarksboro, Gloucester County.
HUGHES, JOHN Landsman, U.S. Navy, USS Princeton, 12-11-1874. Holy Sepulchre Cemetery, East Orange, Essex County.
HUGHES, JOHN Pvt, C, 95th PA Inf, 3-10-1893. Eglington Cemetery, Clarksboro, Gloucester County.
HUGHES, JOHN B. Pvt, D, 38th NY Inf, [Wounded 12-13-1862 at Fredericksburg, VA.] DoD Unknown. Riverview Cemetery, Trenton, Mercer County.
HUGHES, JOHN C. Pvt, B, 2nd NJ Inf, 1-2-1917. Friendship United Methodist Church Cemetery, Landisville, Atlantic County.
HUGHES, JOHN H. (see: Hughs, John H.) Finn's Point National Cemetery, Pennsville, Salem County.
HUGHES, JOHN J. Landsman, U.S. Navy, USS Don, 3-28-1880. Old Stone Church Cemetery, Fairton, Cumberland County.
HUGHES, JONES C. Pvt, Ahl's Btty, DE Heavy Art, DoD Unknown. Finn's Point National Cemetery, Pennsville, Salem County.
HUGHES, JOSEPH Pvt, E, 40th NJ Inf, 1914. Mount Olivet Cemetery, Newark, Essex County.
HUGHES, JOSEPH B. Pvt, F, 25th NJ Inf, 7-29-1913. Presbyterian Church Cemetery, Cold Spring, Cape May County.
HUGHES, JOSEPH F. Pvt, H, 28th NJ Inf, 4-22-1898. Eglington Cemetery, Clarksboro, Gloucester County.
HUGHES*, JOSIAH C. Pvt, E, 12th NJ Inf, 9-6-1886. Evergreen Cemetery, Camden, Camden County.

New Jersey Civil War Burials

HUGHES*, M. (aka: Hughes, James G.) Pvt, F, 4th KY Cav (CSA), 9-15-1863. Finn's Point National Cemetery, Pennsville, Salem County.

HUGHES, NEWTON Pvt, E, 37th NJ Inf, 5-4-1891. Fairmount Cemetery, Newark, Essex County.

HUGHES, PRESMIL D. Corp, H, 12th NJ Inf, 5-14-1922. Eglington Cemetery, Clarksboro, Gloucester County.

HUGHES, ROBERT FERIDAY Pvt, Btty D, 1st NJ Light Art, 4-10-1882. Rahway Cemetery, Rahway, Union County.

HUGHES, ROBERT S.C. Pvt, E, 2nd MS Inf (CSA), [Wounded and captured 7-3-1863 at Gettysburg, PA.] 3-1-1864. Finn's Point National Cemetery, Pennsville, Salem County.

HUGHES, SAMUEL A. 1907. Siloam Cemetery, Vineland, Cumberland County.

HUGHES, SIMEON Pvt, F, 9th NJ Inf, 6-29-1883. Baptist Church Cemetery, Hamilton Square, Mercer County.

HUGHES, THEODORE Pvt, G, 11th IL Cav, 12-6-1905. Greenwood Cemetery, Hamilton, Mercer County.

HUGHES, THEODORE W. Pvt, G, 12th NJ Inf, 10-29-1908. Zion United Methodist Church Cemetery, Clarksboro, Gloucester County.

HUGHES*, THOMAS Sgt, G, 8th NJ Inf, DoD Unknown. Holy Sepulchre Cemetery, East Orange, Essex County.

HUGHES, THOMAS Landsman, U.S. Navy, USS Preston, 3-9-1922. Holy Sepulchre Cemetery, East Orange, Essex County.

HUGHES, THOMAS Seaman, U.S. Navy, USS Princeton, 2-11-1925. Arlington Cemetery, Kearny, Hudson County.

HUGHES, THOMAS H. Sgt, I, 35th NJ Inf, 9-8-1873. Holy Sepulchre Cemetery, East Orange, Essex County.

HUGHES, THOMAS J. (JR.) Sgt, A, 13th MS Inf (CSA), 8-22-1863. Finn's Point National Cemetery, Pennsville, Salem County.

HUGHES, WILLIAM Pvt, A, 3rd NJ Cav, [Died of heart disease at Camp Bayard, Trenton, NJ.] 3-5-1864. Methodist Church Cemetery, Hamilton Square, Mercer County.

HUGHES, WILLIAM 2-7-1890. Old 1st Methodist Church Cemetery, West Long Branch, Monmouth County.

HUGHES, WILLIAM Pvt, E, 102nd NY Inf, 8-29-1871. Holy Sepulchre Cemetery, East Orange, Essex County.

HUGHES, WILLIAM DoD Unknown. Methodist Cemetery, Mantua, Gloucester County.

HUGHES, WILLIAM H. Pvt, I, 8th NJ Inf, 10-26-1881. Fairmount Cemetery, Newark, Essex County.

HUGHES, WILLIAM H. Pvt, G, 2nd DC Inf, 10-20-1914. Fairmount Cemetery, Newark, Essex County.

HUGHES, WILLIAM H. Pvt, D, 1st NJ Inf, 10-22-1908. Riverview Cemetery, Trenton, Mercer County.

HUGHES, WILLIAM H. Pvt, I, 9th NJ Inf, [Died of congestive fever at Trenton, NJ.] 3-12-1864. Moose Cemetery, Perkintown, Salem County.

HUGHES, WILLIAM H. Pvt, 6th NY Ind Btty 9-21-1909. Rahway Cemetery, Rahway, Union County.

HUGHES, WILLIAM S. Pvt, F, 1st NJ Inf, 10-21-1868. Pitman Methodist-Episcopal Cemetery, New Brunswick, Middlesex County.

HUGHES, WILLIE A. Corp, B, 1st NJ Inf, [Wounded in action at Cold Harbor, VA.] 9--1871. Riverview Cemetery, Trenton, Mercer County.

HUGHES, WOODROW C. Pvt, I, 4th NJ Inf, [Wounded 6-27-1862 at Gaines' Mill, VA.] 10-9-1913. Mount Holly Cemetery, Mount Holly, Burlington County.

Our Brothers Gone Before

HUGHS, JOHN H. (aka: Hughes, John H.) Pvt, B, 3rd Bttn SC Inf (CSA), [Captured 7-2-1863 at Hagerstown, MD. Died of scurvy.] 9-20-1863. Finn's Point National Cemetery, Pennsville, Salem County.

HUGHS, SAMUEL Pvt, I, 2nd (Ashby's) TN Cav (CSA), 6-16-1864. Finn's Point National Cemetery, Pennsville, Salem County.

HUGHSON, CHARLES A. Pvt, K, 1st NJ Inf, [Died at Baltimore, MD of wounds received at Wilderness, VA.] 6-19-1864. Presbyterian Church Cemetery, Mount Freedom, Morris County.

HUGHSON, THEODORE P. Sgt, B, 11th NJ Inf, 4-10-1909. Mount Pleasant Cemetery, Newark, Essex County.

HUGLAND, SILAS (see: Hoagland, Silas) Fernwood Cemetery, Jamesburg, Middlesex County.

HUHN*, FRANK HENRY Pvt, D, 7th NJ Inf, 12-13-1907. Arlington Cemetery, Kearny, Hudson County.

HULBERT, GEORGE W. Pvt, B, 27th NJ Inf, 12-14-1903. Presbyterian Church Cemetery, Mount Freedom, Morris County.

HULBERT, SYLVESTER C. Corp, B, 27th NJ Inf, 2-28-1907. Fairmount Cemetery, Newark, Essex County.

HULETT, GEORGE 2-13-1899. Maplewood Cemetery, Freehold, Monmouth County.

HULETT, ROBERT 2-16-1897. Maplewood Cemetery, Freehold, Monmouth County.

HULFORD, THOMAS Musc, A, 1st NJ Cav, 11-21-1928. Fairmount Cemetery, Newark, Essex County.

HULICK, HENRY Pvt, F, 157th OH Inf, 10-17-1893. Hillsborough Reformed Church Cemetery, Millstone, Somerset County.

HULICK, HENRY (see: Hulick, Jeremiah S.) Cedar Hill Cemetery, East Millstone, Somerset County.

HULICK, JEREMIAH S. (aka: Hulick, Henry) Pvt, K, 30th NJ Inf, 9-2-1905. Cedar Hill Cemetery, East Millstone, Somerset County.

HULIN, STEPHEN MORRIS Pvt, A, 13th NJ Inf, 6-16-1904. Bloomfield Cemetery, Bloomfield, Essex County.

HULINGS, BENJAMIN Pvt, Btty D, 2nd PA Heavy Art, DoD Unknown. Presbyterian Church Cemetery, Bridgeton, Cumberland County.

HULINGS*, CHARLES Pvt, C, 3rd NJ Cav, DoD Unknown. Presbyterian Church Cemetery, Williamstown, Gloucester County.

HULINGS, CHARLES H. Pvt, H, 4th NJ Militia, DoD Unknown. Cedar Grove Cemetery, Gloucester City, Camden County.

HULINGS, WILLIAM Pvt, U.S. Marine Corps, 8-27-1922. Trinity Episcopal Church Cemetery, Delran, Burlington County.

HULIT, REUBEN V. (aka: Hewlett, Reuben) Pvt, H, 6th NJ Inf, 10-12-1901. Highland Cemetery, Hopewell Boro, Mercer County.

HULITT, JEROME Pvt, L, 1st NJ Cav, 2- -1903. Highland Cemetery, Hopewell Boro, Mercer County.

HULL, ALEXANDER Pvt, C, 7th NJ Inf, [Died of diarrhea at Alexandria, VA.] 9-3-1864. Pleasantdale Cemetery, West Orange, Essex County.

HULL, ALPHEUS G. Pvt, A, 27th NJ Inf, 5-15-1912. Fairmount Cemetery, Newark, Essex County.

HULL*, BENJAMIN Pvt, K, 9th NJ Inf, [Wounded in action.] 12-25-1906. Union Cemetery, Washington, Morris County.

HULL*, CHARLES F. Pvt, A, 5th NY Inf, 8-6-1906. Rahway Cemetery, Rahway, Union County.

HULL*, CHARLES H. Pvt, F, 7th NJ Inf, 1926. Presbyterian Church Cemetery, Rockaway, Morris County.

HULL, CHARLES H. Pvt, G, 26th NJ Inf, 11-28-1902. St. Mark's Cemetery, Orange, Essex County.

New Jersey Civil War Burials

HULL, CORNELIUS Pvt, C, 15th NJ Inf, 2-9-1873. Presbyterian Church Cemetery, Andover, Sussex County.
HULL, DAVID M. Pvt, B, 38th NY Inf, 8-9-1930. Arlington Cemetery, Kearny, Hudson County.
HULL, ELEAZER (JR.) 1st Sgt, I, 1st NJ Inf, 9-20-1909. Arlington Cemetery, Kearny, Hudson County.
HULL, FREDERICK L. Pvt, Btty D, 2nd IL Light Art, 6-6-1923. Bayview-New York Bay Cemetery, Jersey City, Hudson County.
HULL, GEORGE Sgt, C, 15th NJ Inf, 7-23-1918. Presbyterian Church Cemetery, Rockaway, Morris County.
HULL*, HENRY A. Pvt, D, 11th CT Inf, 3-5-1913. Cedar Hill Cemetery, East Millstone, Somerset County.
HULL, HENRY J. Com Sgt, 15th NJ Inf DoD Unknown. Union Cemetery, Washington, Morris County.
HULL, JEREMIAH (JR.) Pvt, G, 2nd NJ Inf, 5-16-1878. Fairmount Cemetery, Newark, Essex County.
HULL, JOHN Corp, E, 12th NJ Inf, 7-9-1873. Methodist Church Cemetery, Everittstown, Hunterdon County.
HULL*, JOHN C. Corp, F, 34th NJ Inf, 1-28-1912. Riverview Cemetery, Trenton, Mercer County.
HULL, JOHN O. Musc, D, PA Emerg NJ Militia, 2-4-1890. Mount Hope Presbyterian Cemetery, Lambertville, Hunterdon County.
HULL, JONAS F. 2nd Lt, H, 6th NJ Inf, DoD Unknown. Evergreen Cemetery, Camden, Camden County.
HULL, JOSEPH Pvt, E, 38th NJ Inf, 11-26-1881. Union Cemetery, Milford, Hunterdon County.
HULL, NATHAN S. 3-23-1897. Mount Pleasant Cemetery, Newark, Essex County.
HULL, STEPHEN Corp, H, 6th NJ Inf, [Wounded in action.] 12-19-1903. Holcomb-Riverview Cemetery, Lambertville, Hunterdon County.
HULL, WARNER Pvt, B, 35th NJ Inf, 3-8-1894. Fairmount Cemetery, Newark, Essex County.
HULL, WILLIAM Corp, C, 8th NJ Inf, 8-18-1900. Methodist-Episcopal Cemetery, Wrightstown, Burlington County.
HULLENER, HENRY 4-12-1890. New Germantown Cemetery, Oldwick, Hunterdon County.
HULLFISH, DAVID S. Pvt, G, 10th NJ Inf, 2-25-1901. Riverview Cemetery, Trenton, Mercer County.
HULLFISH, JOHN N. 2nd Lt, B, 1st NJ Inf, 2-8-1882. Princeton Cemetery, Princeton, Mercer County.
HULLINGS, CHARLES Wagoner, G, 23rd NJ Inf, 10-4-1928. Methodist Church Cemetery, New Albany, Burlington County.
HULLINGS, EZRA R. Corp, G, 23rd NJ Inf, 10-10-1895. Colestown Cemetery, Cherry Hill, Camden County.
HULLINGS, JOHN Pvt, U.S. Marine Corps, 5-7-1926. Evergreen Cemetery, Camden, Camden County.
HULLJOHN, WILLIAM Corp, G, 39th NJ Inf, 2-15-1900. Fairview Cemetery, Fairview, Monmouth County.
HULLY, CORNELIUS (see: Hally, Cornelius) Holy Rood Cemetery, Morristown, Morris County.
HULLY, JOHN Pvt, Btty D, 2nd U.S. Art, 10-12-1881. Fairmount Cemetery, Newark, Essex County.
HULME, JAMES S. (JR.) Pvt, G, PA Emerg NJ Militia, 1917. Baptist/St. Andrew's Cemetery, Mount Holly, Burlington County.

Our Brothers Gone Before

HULMES, CHARLES Pvt, D, 1st NJ Cav, 11-1-1880. Princeton Cemetery, Princeton, Mercer County.
HULMES, CHARLES Pvt, M, 1st NJ Cav, 8-10-1910. Laurel Grove Cemetery, Totowa, Passaic County.
HULMES, FREDERICK F. Pvt, L, 27th NJ Inf, 5-11-1901. Presbyterian Church Cemetery, Rockaway, Morris County.
HULMES*, JACOB Pvt, E, 7th NJ Inf, 5-27-1899. Fairmount Cemetery, Newark, Essex County.
HULMES, WILLIAM S. Pvt, K, 39th NJ Inf, 6-26-1908. Presbyterian/Methodist-Episcopal Cemetery, Succasunna, Morris County.
HULSE, ELIAS (aka: Hults, Elias) Pvt, D, 8th NJ Inf, 1890. Baptist Cemetery, Osbornville, Ocean County.
HULSE, JAMES Pvt, D, 9th NJ Inf, 1905. Baptist Church Cemetery, Jacobstown, Burlington County.
HULSE, JAMES 12-12-1913. Glenwood Cemetery, West Long Branch, Monmouth County.
HULSE, JOEL Pvt, D, 9th NJ Inf, [Died at Portsmouth, VA. of wounds received at Deep Creek, VA.] 3-8-1864. Osbornville Protestant Church Cemetery, Breton Woods, Ocean County.
HULSE, JOHN Pvt, G, 10th NJ Inf, 4-10-1910. Ardena Baptist Church Cemetery, Adelphia, Monmouth County.
HULSE, JOHN Pvt, E, 28th NJ Inf, 8-30-1921. Osbornville Protestant Church Cemetery, Breton Woods, Ocean County.
HULSE, JOHN W. (aka: Hulsert, John) Pvt, A, 38th NJ Inf, 12-25-1920. Maplewood Cemetery, Freehold, Monmouth County.
HULSE, SIDNEY DoD Unknown. Fairview Cemetery, Fairview, Monmouth County.
HULSE, WILLIAM Pvt, E, 28th NJ Inf, 2-14-1923. Osbornville Protestant Church Cemetery, Breton Woods, Ocean County.
HULSE, WILLIAM C. Pvt, E, 29th NJ Inf, 1923. Old Brick Reformed Church Cemetery, Marlboro, Monmouth County.
HULSEHART, CORNELIUS (JR.) Pvt, K, 28th NJ Inf, 11-18-1878. Rose Hill Cemetery, Matawan, Monmouth County.
HULSEHART, WILLIAM H. (aka: Hulshart, William H.) Pvt, I, 10th NJ Inf, 10-4-1915. Methodist-Episcopal Cemetery, Glendola, Monmouth County.
HULSEHART, WILLIAM H. Pvt, E, 28th NJ Inf, DoD Unknown. Rose Hill Cemetery, Matawan, Monmouth County.
HULSERT, JOHN (see: Hulse, John W.) Maplewood Cemetery, Freehold, Monmouth County.
HULSHART, ALFRED H. Pvt, E, 28th NJ Inf, 4-25-1896. Methodist Church Cemetery, Harmony, Ocean County.
HULSHART, JESSE R. 1st Sgt, D, 9th NJ Inf, 1930. Methodist Church Cemetery, Harmony, Ocean County.
HULSHART, WILLIAM H. (see: Hulsehart, William H.) Methodist-Episcopal Cemetery, Glendola, Monmouth County.
HULSHIZER*, GEORGE FREEMAN Pvt, B, 1st NJ Cav, 4-25-1924. Presbyterian Cemetery, West Stewartsville, Warren County.
HULSHIZER*, JAMES E. Pvt, D, 1st PA Inf, 4-2-1900. Presbyterian Cemetery, West Stewartsville, Warren County.
HULSIZER, AARON V. Pvt, I, 31st NJ Inf, 5-9-1926. Ramseyburg Cemetery, Ramseyburg, Warren County.
HULSIZER, JOHN W. Pvt, F, 9th NJ Inf, 3-29-1916. New Somerville Cemetery, Somerville, Somerset County.
HULSIZER, PETER Pvt, E, 31st NJ Inf, 4-14-1913. Prospect Hill Cemetery, Flemington, Hunterdon County.

New Jersey Civil War Burials

HULTS, ELIAS (see: Hulse, Elias) Baptist Cemetery, Osbornville, Ocean County.
HUMBERT*, AUGUST 2nd Lt, A, Zell's Bttn PA Inf, 1926. Mount Hebron Cemetery, Montclair, Essex County.
HUMBERT, PETER JOHN Pvt, Btty A, 15th NY Heavy Art, 4-24-1907. Flower Hill Cemetery, North Bergen, Hudson County.
HUMES, DAVID M. Pvt, A, 66th OH Inf, [Died at Fort Delaware.] 10-24-1862. Finn's Point National Cemetery, Pennsville, Salem County.
HUMES, WILLIAM Pvt, H, 2nd NJ Cav, 8-22-1892. Fairmount Cemetery, Newark, Essex County.
HUMMEL, CARL (aka: Hummel, Charles) Pvt, D, 2nd NJ Inf, 9-29-1880. Rosedale Cemetery, Orange, Essex County.
HUMMEL, CHARLES (see: Hummel, Carl) Rosedale Cemetery, Orange, Essex County.
HUMMEL, GEORGE W. Capt, H, 10th NJ Inf, 9-15-1910. 7th Day Baptist Church Cemetery, Shiloh, Cumberland County.
HUMMEL, WILHELM Pvt, H, 41st NY Inf, 11-12-1902. Woodland Cemetery, Newark, Essex County.
HUMMELL, CHRISTOPHER Pvt, D, 2nd NJ Inf, 3-9-1903. Cedar Lawn Cemetery, Paterson, Passaic County.
HUMMELL, GEORGE E. Sgt, I, 2nd NJ Cav, 7-12-1907. Presbyterian Church Cemetery, Hampton, Hunterdon County.
HUMMELL, JOHN Pvt, E, 51st PA Inf, 8-1-1922. New Camden Cemetery, Camden, Camden County.
HUMMELL*, SEBASTIAN Pvt, E, 12th PA Cav, 7-4-1895. Fairmount Cemetery, Newark, Essex County.
HUMMER, ADAM (SR.) Wagoner, C, 28th NJ Inf, 1923. Cedar Hill Cemetery, East Millstone, Somerset County.
HUMMER, JAMES C. Pvt, B, 31st NJ Inf, 10-27-1868. Broadway Cemetery, Broadway, Warren County.
HUMMER, JAMES H.T. Pvt, B, 38th NJ Inf, 3-21-1931. Rosemont Cemetery, Rosemont, Hunterdon County.
HUMMER, PETER Pvt, B, 31st NJ Inf, [Died of typhoid at Belle Plain, VA.] 4-8-1863. Broadway Cemetery, Broadway, Warren County.
HUMMER, WILLIAM Pvt, H, 9th NJ Inf, 5-19-1902. Presbyterian Church Cemetery, Hampton, Hunterdon County.
HUMMER*, WILLIAM Pvt, E, 38th NJ Inf, 8-28-1896. Prospect Hill Cemetery, Flemington, Hunterdon County.
HUMPHREVILLE, CHARLES Corp, C, 26th NJ Inf, 12-14-1898. Fairmount Cemetery, Newark, Essex County.
HUMPHREY, CHARLES H. Pvt, Btty D, 1st MN Heavy Art, 3-31-1887. St. Stephen's Cemetery, Millburn, Essex County.
HUMPHREY, HENRY CLAY Corp, D, 22nd NJ Inf, 2-18-1888. Westwood Cemetery, Westwood, Bergen County.
HUMPHREY, HORTON (see: Horten, Humphrey) United Methodist Church Cemetery, Woodruff, Cumberland County.
HUMPHREY, MOORE J. 11-21-1892. Holcomb-Riverview Cemetery, Lambertville, Hunterdon County.
HUMPHREYS, CHARLES F. Seaman, U.S. Navy, 1-3-1883. Evergreen Cemetery, Camden, Camden County.
HUMPHREYS*, HENRY L. Maj, 45th PA Militia 9-3-1898. Fairmount Cemetery, Newark, Essex County.
HUMPHREYS, MAY (JR.) (see: Humphries, May) Salem Cemetery, Pleasantville, Atlantic County.
HUMPHREYS, SAMUEL Musc, F, 24th NJ Inf, DoD Unknown. Overlook Cemetery, Bridgeton, Cumberland County.

Our Brothers Gone Before

HUMPHRIES, JEFF Pvt, G, 9th LA Inf (CSA), [Captured 7-3-1863 at Gettysburg, PA. Died of erysipelas.] 5-11-1864. Finn's Point National Cemetery, Pennsville, Salem County.
HUMPHRIES, MAY (aka: Humphreys, May (Jr.)) Pvt, Ind, Commonwealth PA Heavy Art, 11-12-1898. Salem Cemetery, Pleasantville, Atlantic County.
HUMPHRIES, PRINCE G. Pvt, B, 25th U.S. CT, 11-21-1923. Union Bethel Cemetery, Erma, Cape May County.
HUNCKLE, LEWIS (see: Hunkle, Lewis) Evergreen Cemetery, Hillside, Union County.
HUNDT, FRANK Pvt, Btty D, 2nd OH Heavy Art, 11-2-1897. Egg Harbor Cemetery, Egg Harbor, Atlantic County.
HUNEMOND, HENRY (aka: Hunermand, Henry) Pvt, B, 5th NY National Guard, 6-18-1910. Berry Lawn Cemetery, Carlstadt, Bergen County.
HUNERMAND, HENRY (see: Hunemond, Henry) Berry Lawn Cemetery, Carlstadt, Bergen County.
HUNKELE, ELIAS Pvt, F, 39th NJ Inf, 7-22-1911. Evergreen Cemetery, Hillside, Union County.
HUNKELE, HERMAN Musc, F, 39th NJ Inf, 6-26-1903. Fairmount Cemetery, Newark, Essex County.
HUNKELE, JOHN Capt, F, 39th NJ Inf, 1-8-1908. Woodland Cemetery, Newark, Essex County.
HUNKELE*, LEWIS (aka: Hunckle, Lewis) Pvt, C, 2nd NJ Cav, 1-14-1918. Evergreen Cemetery, Hillside, Union County.
HUNLEY, WIATT (see: Hunley, Wyatt) Finn's Point National Cemetery, Pennsville, Salem County.
HUNLEY, WYATT (aka: Hunley, Wiatt) Pvt, G, 53rd NC Inf (CSA), [Captured 7-5-1863 at Gettysburg, PA. Died of diarrhea.] 9-6-1863. Finn's Point National Cemetery, Pennsville, Salem County.
HUNNIWELL, GEORGE SPENCER Actg Master Mate, U.S. Navy, USS Itasca, 7-16-1911. Evergreen Cemetery, Camden, Camden County.
HUNNIWELL, JOHN (see: Honiwell, John) Rahway Cemetery, Rahway, Union County.
HUNNIWELL, WILLIAM F. Sgt, A, 1st NJ Militia, 12-5-1910. Arlington Cemetery, Kearny, Hudson County.
HUNNIWELL, WILLIAM H. (aka: Henniwell, William) Pvt, C, 39th NJ Inf, [Wounded in action.] 3-6-1923. Clinton Cemetery, Irvington, Essex County.
HUNSINGER, CHARLES G. Pvt, A, 51st PA Inf, 9-13-1914. Evergreen Cemetery, Camden, Camden County.
HUNSINGER, JOHN Corp, I, 10th NJ Inf, 11-8-1919. Arlington Cemetery, Kearny, Hudson County.
HUNSUCKER, S. PHILO Pvt, A, 12th NC Inf (CSA), [Wounded 7-1-1863 at Gettysburg, PA. Captured 11-8-1863 at Kelly's Ford, VA. Died of diarrhea.] 3-8-1865. Finn's Point National Cemetery, Pennsville, Salem County.
HUNT, A.P. 2-26-1895. New Somerville Cemetery, Somerville, Somerset County.
HUNT, ALEXANDER Sgt, Btty M, 15th NY Heavy Art, 4-23-1903. Evergreen Cemetery, Hillside, Union County.
HUNT, ANDREW Pvt, G, 38th NJ Inf, 9-29-1895. Branchville Cemetery, Branchville, Sussex County.
HUNT, CHARLES L. Pvt, F, 22nd NJ Inf, 5-24-1909. Presbyterian Church Cemetery, Titusville, Mercer County.
HUNT, CHARLES S. Pvt, B, 4th NJ Inf, 12-1-1915. Arlington Cemetery, Kearny, Hudson County.
HUNT, CLARKSON T. 1st Lt, G, 30th NJ Inf, 5-23-1929. Holcomb-Riverview Cemetery, Lambertville, Hunterdon County.
HUNT, EBENEZER Pvt, G, 38th NJ Inf, 1928. Soldier's Home Cemetery, Vineland, Cumberland County.

New Jersey Civil War Burials

HUNT, ELIAS A. Pvt, I, 1st NJ Cav, [Wounded in action.] 7-22-1897. Fairmount Cemetery, Newark, Essex County.
HUNT, EZRA M. Asst Surg, 29th NJ Inf 7-1-1894. Presbyterian Church Cemetery, Metuchen, Middlesex County.
HUNT, GEORGE Pvt, C, 60th (Crawford's) TN Mtd Inf (CSA), [Captured 5-17-1863 at Big Black River Bridge, MS.] 9-28-1863. Finn's Point National Cemetery, Pennsville, Salem County.
HUNT, GEORGE F.S. Pvt, C, 51st AL Cav (CSA), 8-22-1863. Finn's Point National Cemetery, Pennsville, Salem County.
HUNT, JOB Pvt, G, 10th NJ Inf, DoD Unknown. Presbyterian Church Cemetery, Kingston, Somerset County.
HUNT, JOSEPH Corp, C, 10th NJ Inf, 8-26-1916. Beverly National Cemetery, Edgewater Park, Burlington County.
HUNT*, JOSEPH Pvt, K, 124th NY Inf, 1926. Midvale Cemetery, Midvale, Passaic County.
HUNT, LEWIS L. Pvt, D, PA Emerg NJ Militia, 11-12-1905. Mount Hope Presbyterian Cemetery, Lambertville, Hunterdon County.
HUNT, LOUIS W. Pvt, A, 36th NY Inf, 1-16-1909. Fairmount Cemetery, Newark, Essex County.
HUNT, MICHAEL Pvt, E, 3rd NJ Militia, DoD Unknown. St. Mary's Cemetery, Hamilton, Mercer County.
HUNT, NELSON T. Pvt, L, 1st NJ Cav, 12-15-1865. Presbyterian Church Cemetery, Kingston, Somerset County.
HUNT, PETER Pvt, I, 21st PA Cav, 8-4-1923. Fairview Cemetery, Columbia, Warren County.
HUNT, ROBERT Pvt, K, 28th NJ Inf, DoD Unknown. Christ Church Cemetery, Morgan, Middlesex County.
HUNT, ROBERT GASTON Bvt Lt Col, U.S. Volunteers, 6-24-1872. Presbyterian Church Cemetery, Marksboro, Warren County.
HUNT, SAMUEL E. Pvt, F, 12th NY State Militia, 7-18-1890. Old North Church Cemetery, Dumont, Bergen County.
HUNT, SYLVESTER H. Asst Surg, 5th U.S. Vet Vol Inf 5-5-1891. Presbyterian Church Cemetery, Shrewsbury, Monmouth County.
HUNT, THEODORE Pvt, H, 8th NJ Inf, 3-23-1892. Presbyterian Church Cemetery, Hampton, Hunterdon County.
HUNT*, THEOPHILUS Pvt, C, 10th NJ Inf, 12-25-1916. Greenwood Cemetery, Hamilton, Mercer County.
HUNT*, THOMAS R. Pvt, G, 5th NJ Inf, 2-2-1915. Mount Hope Presbyterian Cemetery, Lambertville, Hunterdon County.
HUNT, WHITFIELD Pvt, D, 7th (Claiborne's) Confederate States Partisan Rangers (CSA), DoD Unknown. Newton Cemetery, Newton, Sussex County.
HUNT, WILLIAM 7-12-1896. Baptist Church Cemetery, Canton, Salem County.
HUNT*, WILLIAM C. Pvt, Btty D, 1st NJ Light Art, 7-1-1909. Mount Prospect Cemetery, Neptune, Monmouth County.
HUNT, WILLIAM G. Pvt, E, 13th MS Inf (CSA), 4-1-1864. Finn's Point National Cemetery, Pennsville, Salem County.
HUNT, WILLIAM H. Pvt, I, 70th NY Inf, [Wounded 8-27-1862 at Bristoe Station, VA.] 1918. Presbyterian Church Cemetery, Andover, Sussex County.
HUNT, WILLIAM SCHENCK Pvt, H, 21st NJ Inf, 4-18-1907. United Methodist Church Cemetery, Wayside, Monmouth County.
HUNT, WILLIAM T. DoD Unknown. Huntsville Cemetery, Huntsville, Sussex County.
HUNT, WILLIAM W. Pvt, B, 92nd IL Inf, 10-14-1908. Presbyterian Church Cemetery, Mount Pleasant, Hunterdon County.

Our Brothers Gone Before

HUNT, WILLIAM W. Pvt, C, 44th GA Inf (CSA), [Wounded 9-17-1862 at Sharpsburg, MD. Captured 5-10-1864 at Spotsylvania CH, VA. Died of smallpox.] 1-5-1865. Finn's Point National Cemetery, Pennsville, Salem County.
HUNTER, ALEXANDER Landsman, U.S. Navy, USS Montgomery, 5-25-1910. Arlington Cemetery, Kearny, Hudson County.
HUNTER, BENJAMIN T. Pvt, H, 20th GA Inf (CSA), 10-23-1863. Finn's Point National Cemetery, Pennsville, Salem County.
HUNTER, DAVID Bvt Maj Gen, U.S. Army, 2-2-1886. Princeton Cemetery, Princeton, Mercer County.
HUNTER, DAVID A. Pvt, A, 2nd PA Cav, 8-13-1923. Eglington Cemetery, Clarksboro, Gloucester County.
HUNTER, DAVID O. Pvt, I, 215th PA Inf, 10-20-1903. Evergreen Cemetery, Camden, Camden County.
HUNTER, EMANUEL Pvt, E, 15th NJ Inf, 5-23-1891. Fairmount Cemetery, Newark, Essex County.
HUNTER, FRANKLIN W. Pvt, Btty C, 1st PA Light Art, 1-26-1896. Bethel Cemetery, Pennsauken, Camden County.
HUNTER, ISAAC Pvt, G, 26th U.S. CT, 11-13-1914. Jordan Lawn Cemetery, Pennsauken, Camden County.
HUNTER, ISAAC Pvt, G, 24th NJ Inf, 11-19-1914. Evergreen Cemetery, Camden, Camden County.
HUNTER, JOHN H. Pvt, H, 71st NY Inf, 1-23-1905. Hackensack Cemetery, Hackensack, Bergen County.
HUNTER, JOHN P. Pvt, F, 16th NC Inf (CSA), [Captured 7-6-1863 at Gettysburg, PA. Died of diarrhea.] 9-6-1863. Finn's Point National Cemetery, Pennsville, Salem County.
HUNTER, JOSEPH M. Pvt, K, 2nd NJ Cav, 8-26-1922. Baptist Church Cemetery, Mullica Hill, Gloucester County.
HUNTER, LEWIS BOUDINOT Surg, U.S. Navy, 6-24-1887. Princeton Cemetery, Princeton, Mercer County.
HUNTER, ROBERT Sgt, D, 26th NJ Inf, 12-6-1908. Rosedale Cemetery, Orange, Essex County.
HUNTER*, SAMUEL L. (aka: Hunter, Sanford) Pvt, D, 2nd NH Inf, 4-8-1908. Arlington Cemetery, Kearny, Hudson County.
HUNTER, SANFORD (see: Hunter, Samuel L.) Arlington Cemetery, Kearny, Hudson County.
HUNTER, THOMAS S. Pvt, A, 1st PA Cav, 1915. Baptist Church Cemetery, Mullica Hill, Gloucester County.
HUNTER, WILLIAM Pvt, 8th NY Ind Btty 1-5-1920. Holy Name Cemetery, Jersey City, Hudson County.
HUNTER, WILLIAM V. Pvt, D, 31st NJ Inf, 7-3-1901. Arlington Cemetery, Kearny, Hudson County.
HUNTINGDON, FREEMAN F. 1st Lt, Btty A, 16th NY Heavy Art, 1919. St. Rose of Lima Cemetery, Millburn, Essex County.
HUNTINGTON, JAMES H. Pvt, A, 6th Bttn DC Inf, 3-1-1920. Hillside Cemetery, Scotch Plains, Union County.
HUNTLEY, EDWIN A. Sgt, H, 9th NY Cav, [Wounded 9-19-1864 at Winchester, VA.] 7-20-1930. Roadside Cemetery, Manchester Township, Ocean County.
HUNTLEY*, JESPER Pvt, K, 61st VA Inf (CSA), [Captured 7-6-1863 at Fayetteville, PA. Died of diarrhea.] 7-27-1863. Finn's Point National Cemetery, Pennsville, Salem County.
HUNTLEY, JOHN 8-30-1896. St. Paul's Methodist Church Cemetery, Port Republic, Atlantic County.

New Jersey Civil War Burials

HUNTLEY, THOMAS Pvt, C, 39th NJ Inf, 10-21-1921. Holy Sepulchre Cemetery, East Orange, Essex County.

HUNTLEY, THOMAS (see: Horner, Thomas) St. Peter's Cemetery, Perth Amboy, Middlesex County.

HUNTON, GEORGE Pvt, K, 8th NJ Inf, 4-13-1912. Arlington Cemetery, Kearny, Hudson County.

HUNTON, HENRY Pvt, A, 22nd NJ Inf, 1-4-1864. Old 1st Reformed Church Cemetery, Hackensack, Bergen County.

HUNTON*, ROBERT Pvt, F, 11th NJ Inf, 11-25-1901. Grove Church Cemetery, North Bergen, Hudson County.

HUNTSINGER, ROBERT F. Pvt, H, 24th NJ Inf, 1-27-1872. 7th Day Baptist Church Cemetery, Marlboro, Salem County.

HUNTSMAN, CHARLES H. Pvt, E, 10th NJ Inf, [Killed in action at Cedar Creek, VA.] 10-19-1864. Methodist-Episcopal Cemetery, Vincentown, Burlington County.

HUNTSMAN, GEORGE W. 2nd Lt, D, 19th IN Inf, [Wounded 8-28-1862 at 2nd Bull Run, VA. and 7-3-1863 at Gettysburg, PA.] 9-15-1906. Batsto/Pleasant Mills Methodist Church Cemetery, Pleasant Mills, Atlantic County.

HURD, ALFRED PAUL Pvt, A, 4th MA Inf, 4-18-1906. Brookside Cemetery, Englewood, Bergen County.

HURD, BYRAM P. Pvt, C, 2nd NJ Cav, [Missing in action at Egypt Station, MS. Declared dead.] 12-28-1864. Presbyterian Church Cemetery, Sparta, Sussex County.

HURD, BYRAM PITNEY Sgt, K, 27th NJ Inf, 2-23-1883. United Methodist Church Cemetery, Waterloo, Sussex County.

HURD, CHARLES W. Pvt, Btty D, 1st NY Light Art, 1905. United Methodist Cemetery, Gladstone, Somerset County.

HURD, FREEMAN A. Seaman, U.S. Navy, 5-6-1904. Fairview Cemetery, Fairview, Monmouth County.

HURD, HARLEN PAGE Corp, 17th NY Ind Btty 10-28-1901. Bloomfield Cemetery, Bloomfield, Essex County.

HURD, JOHN Pvt, K, 27th NJ Inf, 1915. United Methodist Church Cemetery, Waterloo, Sussex County.

HURD, LEROY C. Pvt, I, 11th NY Cav, 10-14-1897. Fairmount Cemetery, Newark, Essex County.

HURD, LEVI PARSON Pvt, 17th NY Ind Btty 10-28-1901. Evergreen Cemetery, Hillside, Union County.

HURD, STOCKTON Sgt, M, 1st NJ Cav, 5-10-1927. Arlington Cemetery, Kearny, Hudson County.

HURD, SUMNER FLORENTINE 1st Lt, E, 5th NH Inf, [Wounded in action three times.] 1-16-1924. Siloam Cemetery, Vineland, Cumberland County.

HURD, WILLIAM S. Corp, B, 37th NJ Inf, 8-18-1893. Cedar Lawn Cemetery, Paterson, Passaic County.

HURLBURT, JOHN M. Pvt, H, 17th VT Inf, 1928. Baptist Church Cemetery, Alloway, Salem County.

HURLBURT*, KELLOGG THOMAS Pvt, Btty H, 9th NY Heavy Art, 7-21-1896. Evergreen Cemetery, Lakewood, Ocean County.

HURLBURT, PIERRE PROAL Musc, B, 14th CT Inf, 3-25-1914. Rosedale Cemetery, Orange, Essex County.

HURLEY, CHARLES (see: Hurling, Charles) Hillside Cemetery, Madison, Morris County.

HURLEY, CLARK Pvt, K, 29th NJ Inf, 9-5-1916. Mount Prospect Cemetery, Neptune, Monmouth County.

HURLEY, DANIEL Pvt, A, 38th NJ Inf, 1899. Oak Grove Cemetery, Hammonton, Atlantic County.

Our Brothers Gone Before

HURLEY, DANIEL 1-21-1905. St. John's RC Church Cemetery, Lakehurst, Ocean County.
HURLEY, DAVID B. Pvt, K, 4th NJ Inf, 2-6-1906. Eastview Cemetery, Salem, Salem County.
HURLEY, FREEMAN Pvt, K, 34th NC Inf (CSA), [Wounded 6-27-1862 at Gaines' Mill, VA. Captured 7-3-1863 at Gettysburg, PA.] 10-5-1863. Finn's Point National Cemetery, Pennsville, Salem County.
HURLEY, JOHN H. Pvt, A, 14th NJ Inf, [Wounded in action.] 9-14-1901. Maplewood Cemetery, Freehold, Monmouth County.
HURLEY, JOSEPH B. Pvt, K, 29th NJ Inf, 3-10-1899. Methodist Cemetery, Hamilton, Monmouth County.
HURLEY, JOSEPH L. 1915. Fairview Cemetery, Fairview, Monmouth County.
HURLEY, MICHAEL DoD Unknown. Old St. Mary's Cemetery, Gloucester City, Camden County.
HURLEY, PATRICK Pvt, H, 6th NJ Inf, 11-8-1887. St. John's Cemetery, Lambertville, Hunterdon County.
HURLEY, SAMUEL M. Pvt, K, 29th NJ Inf, 7-15-1875. Methodist Church Cemetery, Point Pleasant, Ocean County.
HURLEY, THOMAS P. (aka: Henley, Thomas) Pvt, H, 29th NJ Inf, DoD Unknown. 1st Methodist Church Cemetery, Williamstown, Gloucester County.
HURLEY, WILLIAM H. Pvt, D, 9th NJ Inf, [Wounded in action.] 3-4-1893. Riverside Cemetery, Toms River, Ocean County.
HURLING, CHARLES (aka: Hurley, Charles) Pvt, B, 25th U.S. CT, DoD Unknown. Hillside Cemetery, Madison, Morris County.
HURLING, MARTIN (see: Herling, Martin) Hillside Cemetery, Scotch Plains, Union County.
HURLOCKE, WILLIAM J. Pvt, K, 8th MD Inf, 1-26-1890. Evergreen Cemetery, Camden, Camden County.
HURSCH, HUBERT Pvt, L, 1st NJ Cav, 12-19-1903. Fairmount Cemetery, Newark, Essex County.
HURSH, WARREN C. Pvt, G, 1st NJ Cav, [Wounded in action.] 3-24-1914. Bevans Church Cemetery, Peters Valley, Sussex County.
HURST, SEMPHOREAMUS (aka: Hurst, Symbinanus) Pvt, G, 9th NJ Inf, 5-15-1890. Fairmount Cemetery, Newark, Essex County.
HURST, SYMBINANUS (see: Hurst, Semphoreamus) Fairmount Cemetery, Newark, Essex County.
HURT, M.B. Pvt, E, 7th (Duckworth's) TN Cav (CSA), 7-23-1864. Finn's Point National Cemetery, Pennsville, Salem County.
HURTT, CHARLES M. Pvt, H, 37th NJ Inf, 10-21-1922. Arlington Cemetery, Kearny, Hudson County.
HURTT, LURAINE C. 1st Sgt, B, 1st NJ Cav, 10-3-1904. Hillside Cemetery, Scotch Plains, Union County.
HUSBAND, STONE M. 1895. Mount Olivet Cemetery, Newark, Essex County.
HUSCH, HEINRICH Corp, G, 54th NY Inf, 3-3-1906. Bayview-New York Bay Cemetery, Jersey City, Hudson County.
HUSE, JESSE H. Pvt, K, 57th VA Inf (CSA), [Wounded and captured 7-3-1863 at Gettysburg, PA. Died of wounds.] 10-13-1863. Finn's Point National Cemetery, Pennsville, Salem County.
HUSEBACK, ALFRED Pvt, A, MD Emerg NJ Militia, 2-10-1883. Methodist-Episcopal Cemetery, Mullica Hill, Gloucester County.
HUSEBACK, WILLIAM 1911. Bible Church Cemetery, Hardingville, Gloucester County.
HUSELTON, SIMEON R. Capt, I, 3rd NJ Militia, 7-30-1874. Mount Hope Presbyterian Cemetery, Lambertville, Hunterdon County.
HUSEMYER, LEWIS 1880. New Somerville Cemetery, Somerville, Somerset County.

New Jersey Civil War Burials

HUSH, AARON Pvt, H, 32nd U.S. CT, 1-20-1916. Sand Hills Cemetery, Sand Hills, Middlesex County.
HUSHEER, HENRY 8-30-1926. Palisade Cemetery, North Bergen, Hudson County.
HUSK, ALFRED W. Corp, C, 7th NJ Inf, [Wounded in action 7-2-1863 at Gettysburg, PA.] 11-4-1909. Prospect Hill Cemetery, Caldwell, Essex County.
HUSK, GEORGE W. Pvt, H, 1st MD Cav, 11-17-1864. Beverly National Cemetery, Edgewater Park, Burlington County.
HUSK, WILLIAM Pvt, G, 27th NJ Inf, 6-4-1920. Reformed Church Cemetery, Montville, Morris County.
HUSK, WILLIAM 8-29-1899. Reformed Church Cemetery, Fairfield, Essex County.
HUSS, JOHN G. Pvt, B, 3rd NJ Militia, DoD Unknown. Rahway Cemetery, Rahway, Union County.
HUSS, THOMAS (see: Henry, Thomas) Finn's Point National Cemetery, Pennsville, Salem County.
HUSSEY, SIMEON N. Pvt, Btty L, 4th MA Heavy Art, 9-3-1905. Harleigh Cemetery, Camden, Camden County.
HUSTED, CHARLES H. 11-23-1875. Cohansey Baptist Church Cemetery, Bowentown, Cumberland County.
HUSTED, DANIEL W. Pvt, D, 25th NJ Inf, 3-21-1914. Cedar Hill Cemetery, Cedarville, Cumberland County.
HUSTED*, DAVID B. Corp, F, 3rd NJ Inf, 5-11-1935. Cedar Hill Cemetery, Cedarville, Cumberland County.
HUSTED, DELANE S. Pvt, C, 2nd MD Inf (ES), 1-11-1865. Cohansey Baptist Church Cemetery, Bowentown, Cumberland County.
HUSTED, EDWARD R. Pvt, F, 24th NJ Inf, 7-19-1876. Cohansey Baptist Church Cemetery, Bowentown, Cumberland County.
HUSTED, JAMES R. Pvt, K, 6th NJ Inf, [Wounded in action.] 10-14-1903. Overlook Cemetery, Bridgeton, Cumberland County.
HUSTED, JAMES S. Pvt, D, 10th NJ Inf, [Died of lung inflammation at Washington, DC.] 1-15-1863. 1st United Methodist Church Cemetery, Bridgeton, Cumberland County.
HUSTED, JEREMIAH Pvt, K, 12th NJ Inf, 12-24-1925. New Hopewell Cemetery, Florence, Camden County.
HUSTED*, JONATHAN Pvt, F, 7th NJ Inf, 5-20-1915. Presbyterian Church Cemetery, Bridgeton, Cumberland County.
HUSTED, JOSEPH B. Corp, K, 12th NJ Inf, 6-14-1871. Baptist Church Cemetery, Bridgeton, Cumberland County.
HUSTED, JOSIAH 1913. New Presbyterian Church Cemetery, Daretown, Salem County.
HUSTED, WILLIAM C. Pvt, G, 24th NJ Inf, DoD Unknown. Overlook Cemetery, Bridgeton, Cumberland County.
HUSTER, HENRY Pvt, G, 24th NJ Inf, 1917. United Methodist Church Cemetery, Woodruff, Cumberland County.
HUSTER, JOSIAH Pvt, F, 3rd NJ Inf, 3-27-1893. Presbyterian Church Cemetery, Bridgeton, Cumberland County.
HUSTON, CHARLES 1-27-1899. Newton Cemetery, Newton, Sussex County.
HUSTON, CLARK Pvt, Btty D, 5th PA Heavy Art, 12-29-1879. Macphelah Cemetery, North Bergen, Hudson County.
HUSTON, GARRETT R. 1881. Newton Cemetery, Newton, Sussex County.
HUSTON, JESSE E. (aka: Houston, Jesse E.) Chaplain, 102nd IL Inf 2-12-1886. Evergreen Cemetery, Camden, Camden County.
HUSTON, JOSIAH S. Pvt, C, 34th NJ Inf, 12-9-1921. Baptist Cemetery, Vincentown, Burlington County.
HUSTON, ROBERT Pvt, F, 12th NJ Inf, DoD Unknown. Phillipsburg Cemetery, Phillipsburg, Warren County.

Our Brothers Gone Before

HUSTWAITE, JOHN Pvt, L, 1st NJ Cav, 12-4-1907. Harlingen Cemetery, Belle Mead, Somerset County.
HUSTWAITE*, THOMAS G. Sgt, K, 2nd NJ Inf, 1886. Highland Cemetery, Hopewell Boro, Mercer County.
HUTCHERSON, CYRUS A. Pvt, K, 5th NH Inf, [Died of disease at New York, NY.] 8-22-1862. Fairmount Cemetery, Newark, Essex County.
HUTCHESON, GEORGE W. Pvt, B, 22nd VA Inf (CSA), [Captured 11-6-1863 at Droop Mountain, WV.] 6-10-1865. Finn's Point National Cemetery, Pennsville, Salem County.
HUTCHESON, J.H. Pvt, 3rd Richmond VA Howitzers (CSA) 7-7-1864. Finn's Point National Cemetery, Pennsville, Salem County.
HUTCHINGS, EZRA (aka: Hutchins, Ezra) Pvt, I, 12th NJ Inf, 11-1-1896. Fairmount Cemetery, Newark, Essex County.
HUTCHINGS, EZRA J. Pvt, D, 1st NJ Inf, [Wounded in action.] 1-14-1906. Mansfield/Washington Cemetery, Washington, Warren County.
HUTCHINGS, JOHN Landsman, U.S. Navy, USS North Carolina, 1866. Mount Pleasant Cemetery, Newark, Essex County.
HUTCHINGS, PHILIP C. Pvt, B, 31st NJ Inf, [Died of typhoid at Belle Plain, VA.] 3-23-1863. Mansfield/Washington Cemetery, Washington, Warren County.
HUTCHINGS, SOLOMON W. Seaman, U.S. Navy, USS Brandywine, 5-9-1929. Oddfellows Cemetery, Burlington, Burlington County.
HUTCHINGS, WILLIAM H. Quartermaster, U.S. Navy, 1892. Greenmount Cemetery, Hammonton, Atlantic County.
HUTCHINS, ASHEL W. Pvt, K, 7th ME Inf, DoD Unknown. Finn's Point National Cemetery, Pennsville, Salem County.
HUTCHINS, EZRA (see: Hutchings, Ezra) Fairmount Cemetery, Newark, Essex County.
HUTCHINS, FRANK A. Pvt, F, 6th NJ Inf, 1910. Evergreen Cemetery, Lumberton, Burlington County.
HUTCHINS, JAMES Pvt, D, 7th NJ Inf, 4-23-1891. Riverview Cemetery, Trenton, Mercer County.
HUTCHINS, JAMES A. Pvt, E, 53rd MA Inf, 2-29-1894. Riverview Cemetery, Trenton, Mercer County.
HUTCHINS, JOHN F. Seaman, U.S. Navy, [U.S. receiving ship at New York, NY.] 1-6-1900. St. Mary's Cemetery, Hamilton, Mercer County.
HUTCHINS, THEODORE P. 2nd Lt, B, 72nd PA Inf, 11-22-1889. Berlin Cemetery, Berlin, Camden County.
HUTCHINSON, ALFRED B. 2nd Lt, I, 5th NJ Inf, 2-18-1921. Greenwood Cemetery, Hamilton, Mercer County.
HUTCHINSON, ANDREW B. 1st Sgt, G, 26th NJ Inf, 1890. Hollywood Cemetery, Union, Union County.
HUTCHINSON, ANDREW J. Pvt, A, 85th PA Inf, 1907. Ramseyburg Cemetery, Ramseyburg, Warren County.
HUTCHINSON, CLARK Sgt, C, 4th NJ Inf, 7-28-1905. Princeton Cemetery, Princeton, Mercer County.
HUTCHINSON, D. Pvt, B, 20th VA Inf (CSA), 3-29-1865. Finn's Point National Cemetery, Pennsville, Salem County.
HUTCHINSON, DANIEL C. Sgt, F, 35th NJ Inf, 6-8-1913. Alpine Cemetery, Perth Amboy, Middlesex County.
HUTCHINSON, DAVID Pvt, F, 22nd U.S. CT, 7-23-1865. Mount Zion AME Cemetery, Swedesboro, Gloucester County.
HUTCHINSON, EDWARD Pvt, G, 28th NJ Inf, 10-19-1918. Baptist Church Cemetery, Haddonfield, Camden County.
HUTCHINSON, EDWARD Pvt, K, 6th NJ Inf, 4-15-1874. Cedar Grove Cemetery, Gloucester City, Camden County.

New Jersey Civil War Burials

HUTCHINSON, GEORGE B. 1-9-1936. Bloomfield Cemetery, Bloomfield, Essex County.
HUTCHINSON, GEORGE F. Pvt, B, 10th U.S. Inf, 11-3-1921. Monument Cemetery, Edgewater Park, Burlington County.
HUTCHINSON*, GEORGE F. Pvt, K, 95th PA Inf, [Wounded 5-3-1863 at Salem Heights, VA.] 1-1-1908. New Camden Cemetery, Camden, Camden County.
HUTCHINSON*, GEORGE H. Pvt, E, PA Emerg NJ Militia, 7-21-1874. Mercer Cemetery, Trenton, Mercer County.
HUTCHINSON*, GIDEON H. Pvt, K, 35th NJ Inf, 12-1-1924. Greenwood Cemetery, Hamilton, Mercer County.
HUTCHINSON, HENRY B. Sgt, E, 21st NJ Inf, 12-8-1878. Baptist Church Cemetery, Hamilton Square, Mercer County.
HUTCHINSON, HENRY C. Pvt, C, 4th NJ Inf, 9-30-1906. Riverview Cemetery, Trenton, Mercer County.
HUTCHINSON, HENRY F. Pvt, F, 24th NJ Inf, 7-1-1898. Mount Pleasant Cemetery, Millville, Cumberland County.
HUTCHINSON, JACKSON 2nd Lt, I, 32nd PA Inf, 10-22-1877. Bordentown/Old St. Mary's Catholic Cemetery, Bordentown, Burlington County.
HUTCHINSON, JAMES Pvt, K, 24th NJ Inf, 3-3-1919. Methodist-Episcopal Church Cemetery, Penns Grove, Salem County.
HUTCHINSON, JAMES C. Pvt, A, PA Emerg NJ Militia, 12-17-1876. Riverview Cemetery, Trenton, Mercer County.
HUTCHINSON, JAMES H. Pvt, G, 28th NJ Inf, 5-11-1933. Wenonah Cemetery, Mantua, Gloucester County.
HUTCHINSON, JOHN Pvt, H, 104th PA Inf, DoD Unknown. Rosemont Cemetery, Rosemont, Hunterdon County.
HUTCHINSON, JOHN Sgt, H, 14th NJ Inf, [Wounded in action.] 1914. Brainerd Cemetery, Cranbury, Middlesex County.
HUTCHINSON, JOHN Pvt, B, 1st VT Cav, 12-5-1915. Evergreen Cemetery, Lakewood, Ocean County.
HUTCHINSON, JOHN H. Pvt, F, 1st NJ Inf, 4-25-1918. Fairmount Cemetery, Newark, Essex County.
HUTCHINSON, JOHN S. Maj, [New Jersey Home Guards.] 4-5-1911. Evergreen Cemetery, Hillside, Union County.
HUTCHINSON, JOHN W. DoD Unknown. Greenwood Cemetery, Hamilton, Mercer County.
HUTCHINSON, MARTIN V.B. Corp, K, 67th PA Inf, 8-4-1921. Evergreen Cemetery, Camden, Camden County.
HUTCHINSON*, MATTHIAS Teamster, Btty B, 11th U.S. CHA, 11-27-1912. Arlington Cemetery, Kearny, Hudson County.
HUTCHINSON, RICHARD Pvt, F, 5th NJ Inf, 1917. Methodist Church Cemetery, Sharptown, Salem County.
HUTCHINSON, SAMUEL S. Sgt, C, 11th NJ Inf, [Died at Trenton, NJ.] 9-15-1862. Riverview Cemetery, Trenton, Mercer County.
HUTCHINSON*, SAMUEL W. Pvt, C, 2nd NJ Cav, 4-12-1886. Methodist-Episcopal Cemetery, Burlington, Burlington County.
HUTCHINSON*, WILLIAM Pvt, A, 116th PA Inf, [Wounded 7-2-1863 at Gettysburg, PA.] 12-25-1869. Evergreen Cemetery, Camden, Camden County.
HUTCHINSON, WILLIAM DoD Unknown. Cedar Grove Cemetery, Gloucester City, Camden County.
HUTCHINSON, WILLIAM F. Leader, 7th NJ Inf Band [Died of typhoid at Annapolis, MD.] 7-23-1862. Princeton Cemetery, Princeton, Mercer County.
HUTCHINSON, WILLIAM H. Pvt, A, 3rd NJ Militia, 2-7-1917. Greenwood Cemetery, Hamilton, Mercer County.

Our Brothers Gone Before

HUTCHINSON, WILLIAM R. Pvt, H, 2nd PA Inf, 3-11-1929. Greenwood Cemetery, Pleasantville, Atlantic County.
HUTCHINSON, WILLIAM S. Corp, K, 24th NJ Inf, 2-2-1863. Methodist-Episcopal Church Cemetery, Penns Grove, Salem County.
HUTCHISON, JOHN G. 5-30-1896. Evergreen Cemetery, Camden, Camden County.
HUTMAN, JOHN Pvt, G, 39th NJ Inf, 6-9-1922. Evergreen Cemetery, Hillside, Union County.
HUTMAN, MAY Nurse, 9-21-1904. Evergreen Cemetery, Hillside, Union County.
HUTSON, WILEY E. Pvt, E, 53rd NC Inf (CSA), [Wounded 7-1-1863 and captured 7-5-1863 at Gettysburg, PA. Died of scurvy.] 10-24-1863. Finn's Point National Cemetery, Pennsville, Salem County.
HUTT, BENJAMIN (aka: Henft, Benjamin) Pvt, C, 8th U.S. CT, 10-3-1898. Johnson Cemetery, Camden, Camden County.
HUTT, JACOB L. Capt, C, 4th NJ Inf, 6-22-1915. Greenwood Cemetery, Boonton, Morris County.
HUTT, JOHN Pvt, F, 51st NY Inf, [Wounded in action.] 7-9-1892. Fairmount Cemetery, Newark, Essex County.
HUTTMAN, BELL G. Corp, A, 8th NJ Inf, 1-27-1915. Fairmount Cemetery, Newark, Essex County.
HUTTMAN, HENRY G. Corp, B, 8th NJ Inf, [Wounded in action.] 11-17-1900. Fairmount Cemetery, Newark, Essex County.
HUTTON, DAVID W.J. Pvt, B, PA Emerg NJ Militia, 12-12-1891. Harleigh Cemetery, Camden, Camden County.
HUTTON*, EMORY Musc, B, 148th PA Inf, 3-22-1916. Valleau Cemetery, Ridgewood, Bergen County.
HUTTON, EVAN N. QM Sgt, B, 19th PA Cav, 7-25-1867. Baptist Church Cemetery, Flemington, Hunterdon County.
HUTTON, LORENZO D. Pvt, G, 24th NJ Inf, 6-1-1888. Mount Pleasant Cemetery, Millville, Cumberland County.
HUTTON, SAMUEL (aka: Hooten, Samuel) Pvt, E, 4th NJ Inf, DoD Unknown. Cedar Grove Cemetery, Gloucester City, Camden County.
HUTTON, WILLIAM Pvt, B, 2nd NJ Inf, 4-30-1898. Fairmount Cemetery, Newark, Essex County.
HUYCK, JOSEPH G. Corp, H, 34th NJ Inf, [Died of typhoid at Union City, TN.] 12-29-1863. Evergreen Cemetery, Camden, Camden County.
HUYLER, ADAM (JR.) Pvt, B, 14th NJ Inf, [Wounded 7-9-1864 at Monocacy, MD.] 1911. Greengrove Cemetery, Keyport, Monmouth County.
HUYLER, CORNELIUS A. Sgt, C, 22nd NJ Inf, 1-12-1901. Maple Grove Cemetery, Hackensack, Bergen County.
HUYLER, DAVID J. Pvt, K, 39th NJ Inf, 3-23-1886. Midvale Cemetery, Midvale, Passaic County.
HUYLER, MARTIN BUNN Seaman, U.S. Navy, USS Britannia, [U.S. receiving ship at Washington, DC.] 12-17-1938. United Methodist Cemetery, Gladstone, Somerset County.
HUYLER, THOMAS J. Pvt, A, 8th NJ Inf, [Killed in action at Chancellorsville, VA.] 5-3-1863. Union Cemetery, Marcella, Morris County.
HUYLER, WILLIAM C. Pvt, K, 27th NJ Inf, DoD Unknown. Stanhope-Union Cemetery, Netcong, Morris County.
HUYZER, WILLIAM DoD Unknown. Preakness Reformed Church Cemetery, Wayne, Passaic County.
HYATT*, CHARLES E. 1st Lt, F, 20th NY Cav, 6-22-1901. Arlington Cemetery, Kearny, Hudson County.
HYATT, PETER S. Pvt, Btty A, 1st NJ Light Art, 1892. Balesville Cemetery, Balesville, Sussex County.

New Jersey Civil War Burials

HYATT, THOMAS J. Sgt, K, 118th PA Inf, [Wounded 9-20-1862 at Sheperdstown, WV.] 2-15-1905. Manalapan Cemetery, Manalapan, Monmouth County.
HYATT*, WILLIAM C. Pvt, E, 33rd NJ Inf, 7-29-1907. Fairmount Cemetery, Newark, Essex County.
HYATT, WILLIAM D. Pvt, G, 29th PA Inf, 7-12-1909. Harleigh Cemetery, Camden, Camden County.
HYDE, ALONZO G. Musc, I, 8th NY State Militia, 6-24-1909. Rosedale Cemetery, Orange, Essex County.
HYDE, AMOS Pvt, D, 30th NJ Inf, 10-25-1864. Unitarian Church Cemetery, Kingwood, Hunterdon County.
HYDE, EDWARD GOODRICH Sgt, F, 26th CT Inf, 1888. Clinton Cemetery, Irvington, Essex County.
HYDE, FRANCIS A. Pvt, N, 198th PA Inf, 11-15-1902. Newton Cemetery, Newton, Sussex County.
HYDE, HIRAM Corp, C, 11th NJ Inf, 4-13-1924. Greenwood Cemetery, Hamilton, Mercer County.
HYDE*, HOLCOMBE Corp, I, 2nd NJ Cav, 8-2-1869. Mount Salem Cemetery, Mount Salem, Hunterdon County.
HYDE, JAMES S. Corp, I, 33rd PA Inf, 6-25-1911. Soldier's Home Cemetery, Vineland, Cumberland County.
HYDE, MARTIN Pvt, D, 30th NJ Inf, 6-30-1921. Union Cemetery, Frenchtown, Hunterdon County.
HYDE, WILLIAM H. Pvt, E, 7th DE Inf, 3-29-1922. Arlington Cemetery, Kearny, Hudson County.
HYER, GEORGE H. Pvt, I, 29th NJ Inf, 11-20-1919. Wall Church Cemetery, Wall, Monmouth County.
HYER, JAMES L. Pvt, I, 29th NJ Inf, 2-2-1906. Old Mount Pleasant Cemetery, Matawan, Monmouth County.
HYER, WILLIAM H. HARRISON Corp, K, 29th NJ Inf, 2-15-1895. Methodist Cemetery, Hamilton, Monmouth County.
HYERS*, BARZILLA Pvt, D, 14th NJ Inf, 12-20-1930. Old 1st Methodist Church Cemetery, West Long Branch, Monmouth County.
HYERS, EDWIN B. Pvt, H, 10th NJ Inf, 6-10-1913. Oak Hill Cemetery, Vineland, Cumberland County.
HYERS, GARRETT VINCENT Pvt, D, 9th NJ Inf, [Wounded in action.] 7-21-1918. Riverside Cemetery, Toms River, Ocean County.
HYERS*, GEORGE H. Pvt, A, 38th NJ Inf, 11-13-1911. Maplewood Cemetery, Freehold, Monmouth County.
HYERS, GILBERT H. (aka: Heyers, Gilbert H.) Corp, D, 9th NJ Inf, 1920. Riverside Cemetery, Toms River, Ocean County.
HYERS, GILBERT S. Pvt, E, 28th NJ Inf, 5-13-1912. Greenlawn Cemetery, West Long Branch, Monmouth County.
HYERS, JOHN A. Pvt, G, 29th NJ Inf, 1913. Methodist Church Cemetery, Harmony, Ocean County.
HYLAND, JOHN Pvt, G, 39th NJ Inf, 1-19-1899. Flower Hill Cemetery, North Bergen, Hudson County.
HYLAND, JOHN (aka: Highland, John) Pvt, H, 35th NJ Inf, 11-9-1916. Mount Olivet Cemetery, Fairview, Monmouth County.
HYLAND, WILLIAM H. Corp, E, 27th NJ Inf, 2-7-1901. St. Vincent Martyr Cemetery, Madison, Morris County.
HYLER, RICHARD CORWIN Pvt, G, 27th NJ Inf, [Died of consumption at Stamford, KY.] 4-25-1863. Reformed Church Cemetery, Montville, Morris County.

Our Brothers Gone Before

HYLTON, JACOB S. Pvt, K, 22nd VA Inf (CSA), [Captured 11-6-1863 at Droop Mountain, WV.] 3-15-1864. Finn's Point National Cemetery, Pennsville, Salem County.

HYMER, JAMES Pvt, G, 3rd NJ Inf, 4-18-1918. Immaculate Conception Cemetery, Somerville, Somerset County.

HYMERS, ABNER D. Pvt, B, 24th NJ Inf, DoD Unknown. Presbyterian Church Cemetery, Bridgeton, Cumberland County.

HYSON, JOSEPH Pvt, B, 1st MD Cav (PHB), DoD Unknown. Mount Pleasant Cemetery, Millville, Cumberland County.

I'ANSON, ROBERT J. Pvt, E, 13th VA Cav (CSA), DoD Unknown. Mount Pleasant Cemetery, Newark, Essex County.

IBBS, CHARLES Pvt, L, 6th NY Cav, 4-6-1897. Riverview Cemetery, Trenton, Mercer County.

IBBS, GEORGE T. Sgt, G, 21st NJ Inf, 8-1-1888. Bayview-New York Bay Cemetery, Jersey City, Hudson County.

IBBS, JOHN M. Pvt, B, 5th NJ Inf, 1912. Christ Church Cemetery, Morgan, Middlesex County.

IBBS, STEPHEN Pvt, C, 6th NJ Inf, 3-22-1916. Bayview-New York Bay Cemetery, Jersey City, Hudson County.

IBEN, W.I. DoD Unknown. Greenlawn Cemetery, West Long Branch, Monmouth County.

ICKE, HEINRICH Corp, Btty I, 15th NY Heavy Art, 9-8-1906. Bayview-New York Bay Cemetery, Jersey City, Hudson County.

ICKE, JOHN Pvt, K, 13th NJ Inf, 9-21-1873. Cedar Lawn Cemetery, Paterson, Passaic County.

IDELL, FRANCIS A. Pvt, H, 22nd NJ Inf, 7-3-1863. Presbyterian Church Cemetery, Hamilton Square, Mercer County.

IDELL, JAMES O. Pvt, K, 22nd NJ Inf, 3-16-1896. Presbyterian Church Cemetery, Hamilton Square, Mercer County.

IDLEY, PETER (see: Aydlotte, Peter) Atlantic City Cemetery, Pleasantville, Atlantic County.

IHLE, CHARLES Corp, Btty A, 15th NY Heavy Art, 4-7-1911. Bayview-New York Bay Cemetery, Jersey City, Hudson County.

IHRIE, GEORGE PETER Bvt Brig Gen, U.S. Army, [Lt. Colonel, 3rd California Infantry.] 2-26-1903. Riverview Cemetery, Trenton, Mercer County.

IHRIE, WARREN Capt, C, 61st IL Inf, [Died of disease.] 9-9-1862. Riverview Cemetery, Trenton, Mercer County.

IKE, ALBERT F. Pvt, D, 27th NJ Inf, 7-12-1918. Stanhope-Union Cemetery, Netcong, Morris County.

ILER, JOSEPH D. Corp, K, 101st OH Inf, 1920. Newton Cemetery, Newton, Sussex County.

ILIFF, ALPHEUS Sgt, E, 11th NJ Inf, 4-5-1912. Methodist Church Cemetery, Fairmount, Hunterdon County.

IMLAY, ABIEL (aka: Emley, Abial) Pvt, H, 29th NJ Inf, 2-22-1890. Old Methodist Cemetery, Toms River, Ocean County.

IMLAY, CHARLES H. Pvt, D, 34th NJ Inf, 1926. Emleys Hill United Methodist Church Cemetery, Upper Freehold, Monmouth County.

IMLAY, JAMES Pvt, I, 93rd NY Inf, 1894. Presbyterian Cemetery, Cream Ridge, Monmouth County.

IMLAY, JOHN Pvt, D, 14th NJ Inf, 9-8-1881. Mount Prospect Cemetery, Neptune, Monmouth County.

IMLAY, NICHOLAS (aka: Emory, Nicholas) Pvt, G, 1st NJ Cav, [Died of typhoid pneumonia at Washington, DC.] 3-1-1862. Old 1st Methodist Church Cemetery, West Long Branch, Monmouth County.

New Jersey Civil War Burials

IMLAY, THEODORE E. Pvt, G, 14th NJ Inf, 8-13-1917. Greenlawn Cemetery, West Long Branch, Monmouth County.

IMLAY*, THOMAS (aka: Emley, Thomas) Pvt, L, 1st NJ Cav, 11-5-1901. Baptist Church Cemetery, Jacobstown, Burlington County.

IMLAY, WILLIAM B. Pvt, A, 28th NJ Inf, DoD Unknown. Old 1st Methodist Church Cemetery, West Long Branch, Monmouth County.

IMMER, WILLIAM (see: Emmer, William) Grove Church Cemetery, North Bergen, Hudson County.

IMSLEE, P.T. Seaman, U.S. Navy, 10-21-1900. Fairmount Cemetery, Newark, Essex County.

INGERSOLL, DANIEL WESLEY Pvt, B, 1st NJ Cav, 3-16-1917. Atlantic City Cemetery, Pleasantville, Atlantic County.

INGERSOLL, DAVID T. Pvt, G, 25th NJ Inf, DoD Unknown. Overlook Cemetery, Bridgeton, Cumberland County.

INGERSOLL, DENMAN BEVIS Medical Cadet, U.S. Army, [Assigned to Satterlee U.S. Hospital, Philadelphia, PA, 1863-65.] 8-30-1890. Presbyterian Church Cemetery, Mays Landing, Atlantic County.

INGERSOLL, ELISHA S. Sgt, B, 25th NJ Inf, 1-27-1903. Asbury United Methodist Church Cemetery, English Creek, Atlantic County.

INGERSOLL, RICHARD Pvt, G, 25th NJ Inf, 4-18-1896. Trinity Methodist-Episcopal Church Cemetery, Marmora, Cape May County.

INGERSOLL, THOMAS Seaman, U.S. Navy, 1-12-1889. Eglington Cemetery, Clarksboro, Gloucester County.

INGHAM*, GEORGE TRENCHARD Bvt Maj, 11th U.S. Inf 10-31-1899. St. John's Episcopal Church Cemetery, Salem, Salem County.

INGHAM, WILLIAM HENRY Pvt, A, 25th NJ Inf, 1-16-1903. St. John's Episcopal Church Cemetery, Salem, Salem County.

INGLE*, DAVID P. Sgt, D, 2nd NJ Inf, 6-22-1878. Fairmount Cemetery, Newark, Essex County.

INGLE, JAMES M. Pvt, F, 15th NJ Inf, 3-27-1906. Pleasant Hill Cemetery, Pleasant Hill, Morris County.

INGLE, WILLIAM (see: Inglis, William J) Finn's Point National Cemetery, Pennsville, Salem County.

INGLE, WILLIAM J Pvt, B, 5th KY Mtd Inf (CSA), 4-14-1864. Finn's Point National Cemetery, Pennsville, Salem County.

INGLIES, NEIL Pvt, K, 69th NY Inf, 10-5-1930. Oak Hill Cemetery, Vineland, Cumberland County.

INGLIN, ALFRED Sgt, A, 23rd NJ Inf, 7-10-1910. Methodist-Episcopal Cemetery, Burlington, Burlington County.

INGLIN, CORTLAND 1st Lt, G, 1st NJ Cav, 5-7-1923. Methodist Church Cemetery, Pemberton, Burlington County.

INGLIS, EDWARD (see: Engles, Edward) Bayview-New York Bay Cemetery, Jersey City, Hudson County.

INGLIS, JAMES (JR.) Capt, RQM, 25th NJ Inf 6-1-1914. Cedar Lawn Cemetery, Paterson, Passaic County.

INGOLD, HENRY Pvt, C, 26th U.S. CT, 3-1-1906. Greenwood Cemetery, Pleasantville, Atlantic County.

INGOLD, J.W. Pvt, C, 42nd MS Inf (CSA), 7-30-1863. Finn's Point National Cemetery, Pennsville, Salem County.

INGOLD, PETER Pvt, F, 26th NJ Inf, 1904. Prospect Hill Cemetery, Caldwell, Essex County.

INGOLD, WASHINGTON Pvt, K, 7th NC Inf (CSA), [Captured 7-3-1863 at Gettysburg, PA.] 7-30-1863. Finn's Point National Cemetery, Pennsville, Salem County.

Our Brothers Gone Before

INGRAHAM, JOSEPH A. Pvt, 27th NY Ind Btty 7-4-1910. Arlington Cemetery, Kearny, Hudson County.

INGRAHAM, NELSON (see: Ingram, Nelson) Atlantic City Cemetery, Pleasantville, Atlantic County.

INGRAHAM, WILLIAM J. (aka: Ingrahm, William) 1st Sgt, H, 14th NJ Inf, [Wounded 9-19-1864 at Winchester, VA.] 12-23-1916. Brainerd Cemetery, Cranbury, Middlesex County.

INGRAHM, WILLIAM (see: Ingraham, William J.) Brainerd Cemetery, Cranbury, Middlesex County.

INGRAM, BRYANT Pvt, G, 55th NC Inf (CSA), [Wounded 9-6-1862 at Washington, NC. Captured 7-1-1863 at Gettysburg, PA. Died of typhoid.] 8-30-1863. Finn's Point National Cemetery, Pennsville, Salem County.

INGRAM, GEORGE W. Pvt, Btty E, 2nd PA Heavy Art, 5-16-1910. Baptist/St. Andrew's Cemetery, Mount Holly, Burlington County.

INGRAM, J.L. Pvt, F, 8th AL Inf (CSA), 1-22-1864. Finn's Point National Cemetery, Pennsville, Salem County.

INGRAM, JOHN Pvt, K, 25th U.S. CT, 9-1-1904. Jordan Lawn Cemetery, Pennsauken, Camden County.

INGRAM, NATHAN Pvt, H, 22nd U.S. CT, 2-4-1923. Jordan Lawn Cemetery, Pennsauken, Camden County.

INGRAM, NELSON (aka: Ingraham, Nelson) Sgt, U.S. Marine Corps, USS Baltimore, 1911. Atlantic City Cemetery, Pleasantville, Atlantic County.

INGRAM, ROBERT B. Fireman, U.S. Navy, 3-22-1913. Bayview-New York Bay Cemetery, Jersey City, Hudson County.

INGRAM, WILLIAM Corp, H, 22nd U.S. CT, 8-19-1917. Jordan Lawn Cemetery, Pennsauken, Camden County.

INMAN*, ISAAC M. Pvt, D, 9th NJ Inf, 7-10-1894. Cedar Run/Greenwood Cemetery, Manahawkin, Ocean County.

INMAN, JACOB Pvt, H, 3rd NJ Inf, 3-24-1919. Methodist Church Cemetery, Pemberton, Burlington County.

INMAN*, JOSEPH H. Pvt, G, 12th NJ Inf, 1896. Atlantic City Cemetery, Pleasantville, Atlantic County.

INMAN, OLIVER P. Pvt, D, 9th NJ Inf, 8-5-1900. Old Baptist Church Cemetery, Manahawkin, Ocean County.

INMAN, STEPHEN C. Landsman, U.S. Navy, USS Princeton, 7-12-1914. Masonic Cemetery, Barnegat, Ocean County.

INMAN, WILLIAM Pvt, D, 4th NJ Inf, [Wounded 5-12-1864 at Spotsylvania CH, VA.] 5-15-1910. Oddfellows Cemetery, Pemberton, Burlington County.

INMAN, WILLIAM A. Pvt, B, 25th NC Inf (CSA), [Captured 7-3-1863 at Gettysburg, PA.] 10-2-1863. Finn's Point National Cemetery, Pennsville, Salem County.

INMAN, WILLIAM H. Musc, G, 34th NJ Inf, 1897. Greenwood Cemetery, Hamilton, Mercer County.

INNESS, GEORGE 2nd Lt, B, 13th NY Cav, 5-19-1887. Rosedale Cemetery, Orange, Essex County.

INSCHO, LEVI W. Pvt, B, 1st NJ Cav, 4-18-1895. Broadway Cemetery, Broadway, Warren County.

INSCHO, WILLIAM W. Pvt, C, 31st NJ Inf, 8-11-1870. Broadway Cemetery, Broadway, Warren County.

INSCO, ISAAC Pvt, F, 14th VA Inf (CSA), [Captured 7-3-1863 at Gettysburg, PA. Died of scurvy.] 11-25-1863. Finn's Point National Cemetery, Pennsville, Salem County.

INSCO, ROBERT O. Pvt, F, 14th VA Inf (CSA), [Captured 7-3-1863 at Gettysburg, PA. Died of pneumonia.] 8-28-1863. Finn's Point National Cemetery, Pennsville, Salem County.

New Jersey Civil War Burials

INSLEE, ISAAC (JR.) Capt, F, 28th NJ Inf, 8-19-1903. Alpine Cemetery, Perth Amboy, Middlesex County.

IREDELL, SAMUEL Corp, F, 12th NJ Inf, [Wounded in action.] 9-9-1915. Friends Cemetery, Mullica Hill, Gloucester County.

IREDELL, WHITTEN G. Pvt, H, 28th NJ Inf, [Died of fever at Washington, DC.] 3-9-1863. Methodist Cemetery, Mantua, Gloucester County.

IRELAN*, RICHMAN (aka: Ireland, Richmond) Pvt, I, 9th NJ Inf, 11-8-1909. Presbyterian Church Cemetery, Bridgeton, Cumberland County.

IRELAND, AMOS W. Corp, D, 6th NJ Inf, 10-27-1870. Evergreen Cemetery, Camden, Camden County.

IRELAND, CLEMENT H. Pvt, D, 10th NJ Inf, 5-13-1901. Oak Hill Cemetery, Vineland, Cumberland County.

IRELAND, DANIEL Pvt, H, 190th PA Inf, 9-30-1887. United Methodist Church Cemetery, Absecon, Atlantic County.

IRELAND, DANIEL Pvt, B, 25th NJ Inf, 5-23-1905. Greenwood Cemetery, Pleasantville, Atlantic County.

IRELAND, DANIEL 10-16-1907. United Methodist Church Cemetery, Tuckahoe, Cape May County.

IRELAND, DANIEL L. Pvt, H, 24th NJ Inf, DoD Unknown. Church of Christ Cemetery, Fairton, Cumberland County.

IRELAND, EDMOND S. Pvt, B, 25th NJ Inf, DoD Unknown. Zion Methodist Church Cemetery, Bargaintown, Atlantic County.

IRELAND, ENOCH Pvt, B, 25th NJ Inf, 9-9-1916. Atlantic City Cemetery, Pleasantville, Atlantic County.

IRELAND, JACOB Pvt, F, 23rd NJ Inf, 1906. Mount Pleasant Cemetery, Millville, Cumberland County.

IRELAND, JAMES Corp, __, __ __ __, DoD Unknown. Old Camden Cemetery, Camden, Camden County.

IRELAND, JAMES B. Pvt, Btty E, 1st NJ Light Art, 2-3-1917. Zion Methodist Church Cemetery, Bargaintown, Atlantic County.

IRELAND, JAMES S. 2-23-1908. Zion Methodist Church Cemetery, Bargaintown, Atlantic County.

IRELAND, JAPHET Pvt, B, 25th NJ Inf, 10-14-1902. Salem Cemetery, Pleasantville, Atlantic County.

IRELAND, JAPHET A. Pvt, A, 8th NJ Inf, 1925. Friends United Methodist-Episcopal Church Cemetery, Linwood, Atlantic County.

IRELAND*, JAPHET J. Pvt, I, 2nd NJ Inf, DoD Unknown. Mount Pleasant Methodist Cemetery, Pleasantville, Atlantic County.

IRELAND, JOHN Pvt, I, 4th NJ Inf, 1909. Atlantic City Cemetery, Pleasantville, Atlantic County.

IRELAND, JOHN H. Pvt, E, 24th NJ Inf, 10-12-1905. St. Paul's United Methodist Church Cemetery, Paulsboro, Gloucester County.

IRELAND, JOHN S. 10-1-1905. Atlantic City Cemetery, Pleasantville, Atlantic County.

IRELAND*, JOHN S. Pvt, I, 2nd NJ Inf, 4-5-1915. Atlantic City Cemetery, Pleasantville, Atlantic County.

IRELAND, JOSEPH Pvt, H, 34th NJ Inf, 11-2-1915. Union Cemetery, Clarkstown, Atlantic County.

IRELAND, JOSEPH W. Pvt, A, 7th NJ Inf, 2-11-1889. Presbyterian Church Cemetery, Cedarville, Cumberland County.

IRELAND, RICHMOND (see: Irelan, Richman) Presbyterian Church Cemetery, Bridgeton, Cumberland County.

IRELAND, THOMAS G. Pvt, D, 1st NJ Cav, 12-1-1908. Eglington Cemetery, Clarksboro, Gloucester County.

Our Brothers Gone Before

IRELAND, TOWNSEND Pvt, A, 7th NJ Inf, [Killed in action at Williamsburg, VA.] 5-5-1862. Presbyterian Church Cemetery, Cold Spring, Cape May County.
IRELAND, WILLIAM Pvt, H, 24th NJ Inf, 3- -1886. Church of Christ Cemetery, Fairton, Cumberland County.
IRELAND, WILLIAM B. Pvt, F, 38th NJ Inf, 2-22-1912. Old 1st Methodist Church Cemetery, West Long Branch, Monmouth County.
IREMAN, BASIL Pvt, Btty B, 1st NJ Light Art, 6-3-1906. Arlington Cemetery, Kearny, Hudson County.
IRETON, FRANKLIN Pvt, H, 6th U.S. Cav, 5-8-1901. Harleigh Cemetery, Camden, Camden County.
IRETON, GEORGE A. Fireman, U.S. Navy, [Killed.] 1-31-1863. Bordentown/Old St. Mary's Catholic Cemetery, Bordentown, Burlington County.
IRETON, WILLIAM G. Pvt, B, 23rd NJ Inf, 2-28-1913. Oddfellows Cemetery, Burlington, Burlington County.
IRETON, WILLIAM G. 4-27-1912. New Camden Cemetery, Camden, Camden County.
IRICK, JOHN STOCKTON Sgt, I, 11th MI Cav, 8-4-1894. Baptist/St. Andrew's Cemetery, Mount Holly, Burlington County.
IRICK, WILLIAM Pvt, C, 70th IN Inf, 8-17-1864. Baptist/St. Andrew's Cemetery, Mount Holly, Burlington County.
IRISH, HUGH C. Capt, K, 13th NJ Inf, [Killed in action at Antietam, MD.] 9-17-1862. Cedar Lawn Cemetery, Paterson, Passaic County.
IRON, MATTHIAS S. Pvt, G, 61st PA Inf, 3-16-1900. Evergreen Cemetery, Hillside, Union County.
IRONS, AARON Pvt, K, 38th NJ Inf, 3-10-1902. Ardena Baptist Church Cemetery, Adelphia, Monmouth County.
IRONS, AARON PITNEY 1st Lt, 1st NJ Cav [Regimental Commissary. Wounded in action.] 1906. Riverside Cemetery, Toms River, Ocean County.
IRONS, BARZILLA P. Pvt, F, 1st NJ Cav, 5-16-1926. Riverside Cemetery, Toms River, Ocean County.
IRONS, CHARLES Pvt, B, 12th NJ Inf, 3-24-1909. Roadside Cemetery, Manchester Township, Ocean County.
IRONS, CHARLES 1917. Baptist Church Cemetery, Jacobstown, Burlington County.
IRONS, CHARLES HENRY Pvt, L, 2nd NJ Cav, 2-5-1915. Riverside Cemetery, Toms River, Ocean County.
IRONS, EDWARD S. Pvt, M, 6th PA Cav, 2-28-1876. 1st United Methodist Church Cemetery, Bridgeton, Cumberland County.
IRONS, GEORGE GIBERSON 1st Lt, D, 9th NJ Inf, 5-1-1904. Riverside Cemetery, Toms River, Ocean County.
IRONS, GILBERT Pvt, A, 38th NJ Inf, 12-11-1912. Methodist Cemetery, Cassville, Ocean County.
IRONS, IVINS Pvt, F, 14th NJ Inf, 3-28-1868. Old Methodist Cemetery, Toms River, Ocean County.
IRONS, JAMES Pvt, B, 39th NJ Inf, 10-22-1884. Riverside Cemetery, Toms River, Ocean County.
IRONS, JAMES B. 3-21-1906. Riverside Cemetery, Toms River, Ocean County.
IRONS, JOHN B. Pvt, H, 29th NJ Inf, 1893. Riverside Cemetery, Toms River, Ocean County.
IRONS, JOSEPH 11-22-1866. Osbornville Protestant Church Cemetery, Breton Woods, Ocean County.
IRONS, WALLACE Pvt, D, 9th NJ Inf, 1884. Riverside Cemetery, Toms River, Ocean County.
IRONS, WILLIAM C. Pvt, C, 10th NJ Inf, 1919. Miller's Cemetery, New Gretna, Burlington County.

New Jersey Civil War Burials

IRONS, WILLIAM H. Pvt, H, 29th NJ Inf, 7-25-1873. Riverside Cemetery, Toms River, Ocean County.

IRVIN, GEORGE (see: Ervin, George) Old Scots Cemetery, Marlboro, Monmouth County.

IRVIN, HIRAM (see: Irvine, Hiram) Cedar Grove Cemetery, Gloucester City, Camden County.

IRVIN, JAMES Pvt, I, 2nd NJ Inf, DoD Unknown. Laurel Grove Cemetery, Totowa, Passaic County.

IRVIN, MARTIN Pvt, E, 25th NJ Inf, 1-5-1913. Laurel Grove Cemetery, Totowa, Passaic County.

IRVIN, P.C. (aka: Ervin, Christopher C.P.) Pvt, B, 59th (Cooke's) TN Mtd Inf (CSA), 7-6-1863. Finn's Point National Cemetery, Pennsville, Salem County.

IRVIN, PATRICK Pvt, B, 33rd NJ Inf, 6-11-1882. Holy Sepulchre Cemetery, East Orange, Essex County.

IRVIN, SOLOMON DYE Pvt, C, 3rd ___ ___, 1-19-1917. Presbyterian Church Cemetery, Pennington, Mercer County.

IRVIN, WILLIAM Pvt, K, 14th NJ Inf, 8-22-1885. Riverview Cemetery, Trenton, Mercer County.

IRVIN, WILLIAM (see: Erving, William) Old Scots Cemetery, Marlboro, Monmouth County.

IRVIN, WILLIAM H. Pvt, H, 72nd PA Inf, 11-25-1879. Baptist Church Cemetery, Haddonfield, Camden County.

IRVINE, CHARLES D. Pvt, H, 10th NJ Inf, 9-28-1883. Cedar Grove Cemetery, Gloucester City, Camden County.

IRVINE, HIRAM (aka: Irvin, Hiram) Pvt, D, 6th NJ Inf, 2-25-1881. Cedar Grove Cemetery, Gloucester City, Camden County.

IRVINE, ROBERT L. Pvt, A, 3rd PA Cav, 3-10-1903. Cedar Grove Cemetery, Gloucester City, Camden County.

IRVING, JAMES H. (aka: Irwin, James) Pvt, A, 28th NJ Inf, 2-2-1915. Tennent Church Cemetery, Tennent, Monmouth County.

IRVING, JOHN J. Pvt, G, 5th NJ Inf, 9-12-1895. Holy Name Cemetery, Jersey City, Hudson County.

IRVING, WILLIAM 1905. Presbyterian Church Cemetery, Liberty Corners, Somerset County.

IRVING, WILLIAM H. Landsman, U.S. Navy, USS Princeton, 1921. New Camden Cemetery, Camden, Camden County.

IRWIN, BARCLAY F. (aka: Barkley, Irwin) 1st Sgt, D, 96th OH Inf, 1919. Berlin Cemetery, Berlin, Camden County.

IRWIN, CHARLES L. Pvt, C, 29th NJ Inf, 3-20-1912. Cedar Hill Cemetery, Hightstown, Mercer County.

IRWIN, DANIEL W. Pvt, G, 29th NJ Inf, 9-21-1920. Holmdel Cemetery, Holmdel, Monmouth County.

IRWIN, GILBERT Pvt, A, 28th NJ Inf, DoD Unknown. Old Scots Cemetery, Marlboro, Monmouth County.

IRWIN, HARRISON Pvt, D, 29th NJ Inf, 2-19-1908. Glenwood Cemetery, West Long Branch, Monmouth County.

IRWIN, JAMES Pvt, B, 31st NJ Inf, 11-12-1889. Old Calvary Cemetery, Sayreville, Middlesex County.

IRWIN, JAMES (see: Irving, James H.) Tennent Church Cemetery, Tennent, Monmouth County.

IRWIN, JAMES S. 10-27-1913. Atlantic City Cemetery, Pleasantville, Atlantic County.

IRWIN, JOHN H. (aka: Erwin, John) Pvt, I, 2nd NJ Cav, DoD Unknown. Baptist Cemetery, Burlington, Burlington County.

IRWIN, MARION M. 1st Corp, D, 9th GA Inf (CSA), [Captured 7-2-1863 at Gettysburg, PA.] 10-11-1863. Finn's Point National Cemetery, Pennsville, Salem County.

Our Brothers Gone Before

IRWIN, SCHUREMAN (see: Ervin, Schureman) Old Scots Cemetery, Marlboro, Monmouth County.
IRWIN, WILLIAM A. Pvt, G, 29th NJ Inf, 5-29-1892. Greenlawn Cemetery, West Long Branch, Monmouth County.
IRWIN, WILLIAM C. 12-20-1902. Holmdel Cemetery, Holmdel, Monmouth County.
IRWIN, WILLIAM R. Pvt, B, 95th NY Inf, 1-4-1904. Elmwood Cemetery, New Brunswick, Middlesex County.
ISAAC, JULIUS (aka: Isack, Julius) Pvt, H, 41st NY Inf, 6-22-1895. Evergreen Cemetery, Hillside, Union County.
ISACK, JULIUS (see: Isaac, Julius) Evergreen Cemetery, Hillside, Union County.
ISARD, CHARLES T. 8-25-1906. Presbyterian Church Cemetery, Cold Spring, Cape May County.
ISARD, JOHN (see: Iszard, John) Cedar Green Cemetery, Clayton, Gloucester County.
ISBILLS, WILLIAM Pvt, K, 21st NJ Inf, 4-6-1918. Bayview-New York Bay Cemetery, Jersey City, Hudson County.
ISDELL, CHARLES C. Pvt, A, 21st NJ Inf, 1-18-1925. Bayview-New York Bay Cemetery, Jersey City, Hudson County.
ISELE, MORRITZ (aka: Isell, Maritz) Pvt, K, 12th NJ Inf, DoD Unknown. 7th Day Baptist Church Cemetery, Marlboro, Salem County.
ISELL, MARITZ (see: Isele, Morritz) 7th Day Baptist Church Cemetery, Marlboro, Salem County.
ISENHOUR, J. (see: Isonhour, John A.) Finn's Point National Cemetery, Pennsville, Salem County.
ISHAM, CHARLES Pvt, D, 5th AL Cav (CSA), 10-26-1863. Finn's Point National Cemetery, Pennsville, Salem County.
ISLEY, WILLIAM HENRY Pvt, B, 21st NJ Inf, 4-18-1892. Bayview-New York Bay Cemetery, Jersey City, Hudson County.
ISOM, JOHN W. Pvt, F, 1st (Gregg's) SC Inf (CSA), [Captured 5-13-1864 at Spotsylvania CH, VA. Died of lung inflammation.] 7-4-1864. Finn's Point National Cemetery, Pennsville, Salem County.
ISONHOUR, JOHN A. (aka: Isenhour, J.) Pvt, A, 7th NC Inf (CSA), [Captured 7-3-1863 at Gettysburg, PA. Died of dysentery.] 1-1-1864. Finn's Point National Cemetery, Pennsville, Salem County.
ISSELLE, FRANK Pvt, Btty A, 1st NJ Light Art, 4-11-1881. Hoboken Cemetery, North Bergen, Hudson County.
ISZARD, JOHN (aka: Isard, John) Pvt, G, 27th NC Inf (CSA), 1-22-1884. Cedar Green Cemetery, Clayton, Gloucester County.
ITEN, CHARLES Pvt, Btty A, 1st NJ Light Art, 7-18-1921. Flower Hill Cemetery, North Bergen, Hudson County.
ITZEL, PETER (aka: Jtzel, Peter) Pvt, H, 41st NY Inf, 8-13-1899. Rosedale Cemetery, Orange, Essex County.
IVENS, WILLIAM Pvt, E, 198th PA Inf, 1-28-1912. Oak Hill Cemetery, Vineland, Cumberland County.
IVERS, EDWARD M. Corp, E, 81st PA Inf, [Wounded 3-31-1865 at Petersburg, VA.] 12-15-1907. Evergreen Cemetery, Camden, Camden County.
IVES, EDWIN 1907. Mount Hebron Cemetery, Montclair, Essex County.
IVES, MILTON J. Pvt, A, 9th NJ Inf, 1-30-1924. Brainerd Cemetery, Cranbury, Middlesex County.
IVESTER, JACOB B. Pvt, E, 16th GA Inf (CSA), [Captured 7-5-1863 at Gettysburg, PA. Died of disease.] 11-23-1863. Finn's Point National Cemetery, Pennsville, Salem County.
IVEY, ROBERT A. Pvt, G, 3rd AL Cav (CSA), 10-14-1863. Finn's Point National Cemetery, Pennsville, Salem County.

New Jersey Civil War Burials

IVEY, TRAVIS J. Corp, H, 9th (Malone's) AL Cav (CSA), 8-19-1863. Finn's Point National Cemetery, Pennsville, Salem County.

IVINS, ALFRED Pvt, E, 6th NJ Inf, 4-16-1905. Evergreen Cemetery, Camden, Camden County.

IVINS, ALFRED 2-6-1869. Evergreen Cemetery, Hillside, Union County.

IVINS, BENJAMIN W. Pvt, E, 34th NJ Inf, 2-13-1906. Bethel Cemetery, Pennsauken, Camden County.

IVINS, JAMES G. Pvt, H, 48th NY Inf, 5-22-1895. Cedarwood Cemetery, Hazlet, Monmouth County.

IVINS, MAHLON F. Sgt, D, 6th NJ Inf, 3-6-1916. Evergreen Cemetery, Camden, Camden County.

IVINS, THOMAS Pvt, F, 37th NJ Inf, 12-19-1913. Cedar Green Cemetery, Clayton, Gloucester County.

IZLETON*, JEREMIAH Seaman, U.S. Navy, USS Fort Jackson, 1924. Cedarwood Cemetery, Hazlet, Monmouth County.

JACK, DAVID Pvt, G, 18th VA Cav (CSA), 12-4-1863. Finn's Point National Cemetery, Pennsville, Salem County.

JACK, JOHN (see: Jacques, Jean) Woodland Cemetery, Newark, Essex County.

JACK, MARTIN Pvt, F, 39th NJ Inf, 11-21-1911. Woodland Cemetery, Newark, Essex County.

JACKAWAY, AVERY S. 9-29-1861. Old Camden Cemetery, Camden, Camden County.

JACKAWAY, JOHN W. Pvt, A, 6th NJ Inf, 3-24-1916. Greenlawn Cemetery, West Long Branch, Monmouth County.

JACKES, AUGUST (aka: Jaques, August) Pvt, F, 39th NJ Inf, 11-1-1927. St. Mary's Cemetery, East Orange, Essex County.

JACKMAN, WALTER E. Pvt, H, 1st NJ Inf, 3-20-1891. Jersey City Cemetery, Jersey City, Hudson County.

JACKSON, ALONZO J. Pvt, C, 27th NJ Inf, [Died of laryngitis at Washington, DC.] 3-17-1863. Presbyterian Cemetery, Springfield, Union County.

JACKSON, ANDREW Pvt, K, 2nd U.S. CT, 4-26-1904. Mount Peace Cemetery, Lawnside, Camden County.

JACKSON, ANDREW Pvt, I, 22nd U.S. CT, 5-16-1907. Greens Cemetery, Janvier, Gloucester County.

JACKSON, ANDREW Colored Cook, F, 34th NJ Inf, 5-8-1866. Locust Hill Cemetery, Trenton, Mercer County.

JACKSON, ANDREW Pvt, E, 165th NY Inf, 2-16-1896. Fairmount Cemetery, Newark, Essex County.

JACKSON, ANDREW (see: Crosby, Andrew Jackson) Evergreen Cemetery, Morristown, Morris County.

JACKSON, ANDREW Pvt, K, 201st PA Inf, 9-4-1920. Cedar Grove Cemetery, Gloucester City, Camden County.

JACKSON, BENJAMIN P. Pvt, C, 27th NJ Inf, 2-15-1912. Presbyterian/Methodist-Episcopal Cemetery, Succasunna, Morris County.

JACKSON, CHARLES M. Pvt, B, 22nd U.S. CT, [Wounded 6-15-1864 at Petersburg, VA.] 11-17-1887. Bethel AME Cemetery, Freehold, Monmouth County.

JACKSON*, CHARLES R. Sgt, A, 15th NJ Inf, [Died of wounds received at Spotsylvania CH, VA.] 8-1-1864. United Methodist Church Cemetery, Richwood, Gloucester County.

JACKSON, CHARLES SMITH 1-9-1935. Eglington Cemetery, Clarksboro, Gloucester County.

JACKSON, DRAPER Pvt, A, 22nd U.S. CT, 9-18-1922. Spencer African Methodist Church Cemetery, Woodstown, Salem County.

JACKSON, EBENEZER B. Pvt, L, 1st NJ Cav, 7-29-1920. Hazelwood Cemetery, Rahway, Union County.

Our Brothers Gone Before

JACKSON, EDMUND G. Capt, A, 34th NJ Inf, 11-29-1891. Evergreen Cemetery, Camden, Camden County.

JACKSON, EDWARD Pvt, H, 29th CT Inf, 9-3-1885. 1st Baptist Cemetery, New Brunswick, Middlesex County.

JACKSON, EDWARD M. (aka: Jackson, John) Pvt, E, 23rd NY Inf, 4-15-1900. Prospect Hill Cemetery, Caldwell, Essex County.

JACKSON, ELLWOOD Pvt, B, 2nd NJ Inf, 1931. Memorial Park Cemetery, Gouldtown, Cumberland County.

JACKSON, FRANCIS Landsman, U.S. Navy, USS North Carolina, 1921. Westwood Cemetery, Westwood, Bergen County.

JACKSON, FRANCIS D. (aka: Jackson, Franklin) Pvt, C, 22nd U.S. CT, 9-12-1904. Arlington Cemetery, Kearny, Hudson County.

JACKSON, FRANCIS W. Seaman, U.S. Navy, [U.S. Naval Hospital at Norfolk, VA.] 2-28-1922. Rosedale Cemetery, Orange, Essex County.

JACKSON, FRANK Musc, G, 29th CT Inf, [Wounded in action 9-30-1864.] 4-3-1907. Arlington Cemetery, Kearny, Hudson County.

JACKSON, FRANKLIN (see: Jackson, Francis D.) Arlington Cemetery, Kearny, Hudson County.

JACKSON, GEORGE Pvt, A, 41st U.S. CT, 3-16-1889. Rahway Cemetery, Rahway, Union County.

JACKSON, GEORGE W. 1st Lt, H, 5th NJ Inf, 9-15-1905. Rahway Cemetery, Rahway, Union County.

JACKSON, GUSTAVUS A. Pvt, A, 2nd NJ Militia, DoD Unknown. Hackensack Cemetery, Hackensack, Bergen County.

JACKSON, HARRY S. DoD Unknown. Maple Grove Cemetery, Hackensack, Bergen County.

JACKSON, HENRY Pvt, K, 22nd U.S. CT, 12-24-1890. Fairmount Cemetery, Newark, Essex County.

JACKSON, HENRY L. Pvt, D, 20th U.S. CT, 2-18-1926. Evergreen Cemetery, Hillside, Union County.

JACKSON*, HILLIARD Pvt, Btty H, 11th U.S. CHA, DoD Unknown. Elmwood Cemetery, New Brunswick, Middlesex County.

JACKSON, HUNTINGTON WOLCOTT Bvt Lt Col, 4th NJ Inf [Aide-de-Camp to General John Newton.] 1-3-1901. Mount Pleasant Cemetery, Newark, Essex County.

JACKSON, J.H. Pvt, E, 60th (Crawford's) TN Mtd Inf (CSA), [Captured 5-17-1863 at Big Black River Bridge, MS.] 10-28-1863. Finn's Point National Cemetery, Pennsville, Salem County.

JACKSON, JAMES Pvt, D, 4th NJ Inf, DoD Unknown. Riverview Cemetery, Trenton, Mercer County.

JACKSON, JAMES Pvt, I, 40th NJ Inf, 4-23-1928. Baptist Cemetery, Pemberton, Burlington County.

JACKSON, JAMES Pvt, A, 43rd U.S. CT, 3-15-1916. Mount Zion Cemetery, Kresson, Camden County.

JACKSON*, JAMES Pvt, Btty C, 11th U.S. CHA, 6-19-1889. Greenwood Cemetery, Hamilton, Mercer County.

JACKSON*, JAMES H. Pvt, Btty I, 11th U.S. CHA, 10-24-1905. Beverly National Cemetery, Edgewater Park, Burlington County.

JACKSON, JAMES M. Pvt, I, 5th U.S. Cav, 12-27-1909. Fairmount Cemetery, Newark, Essex County.

JACKSON, JAMES M. Hosp Steward, U.S. Army, DoD Unknown. Presbyterian Cemetery, Springfield, Union County.

JACKSON, JOHN Pvt, B, 29th CT Inf, 11-7-1904. Brookside Cemetery, Englewood, Bergen County.

New Jersey Civil War Burials

JACKSON, JOHN Pvt, H, 127th U.S. CT, 12-23-1924. Arlington Cemetery, Kearny, Hudson County.
JACKSON, JOHN Pvt, C, 32nd U.S. CT, 1889. Reformed Church Cemetery, Montville, Morris County.
JACKSON, JOHN Pvt, A, 25th NJ Inf, DoD Unknown. Laurel Grove Cemetery, Totowa, Passaic County.
JACKSON, JOHN (see: Jackson, Edward M.) Prospect Hill Cemetery, Caldwell, Essex County.
JACKSON, JOHN Corp, D, 69th NY State Militia, 3-23-1922. Holy Sepulchre Cemetery, East Orange, Essex County.
JACKSON, JOHN C. Pvt, F, 12th NJ Inf, [Died of chronic diarrhea at Philadelphia, PA.] 2-1-1864. United Methodist Church Cemetery, Richwood, Gloucester County.
JACKSON*, JOHN E. Corp, M, 3rd NJ Cav, 4-25-1897. Riverview Cemetery, Trenton, Mercer County.
JACKSON, JOHN J. Pvt, F, 28th NJ Inf, 4- -1894. Presbyterian Church Cemetery, Woodbridge, Middlesex County.
JACKSON, JOHN L. Pvt, K, 31st U.S. CT, 11-22-1901. Jordan Lawn Cemetery, Pennsauken, Camden County.
JACKSON, JOHN M. Pvt, E, 4th KY Cav (CSA), 10-14-1863. Finn's Point National Cemetery, Pennsville, Salem County.
JACKSON, JOHN (SR.) Pvt, C, 11th NJ Inf, 7- -1864. Riverview Cemetery, Trenton, Mercer County.
JACKSON, JOSEPH Pvt, F, 32nd U.S. CT, 10-6-1913. Reformed Church Cemetery, Montville, Morris County.
JACKSON, LAMBERT WARDELL Pvt, E, 40th NJ Inf, [Wounded in action.] 12-1-1929. Old 1st Methodist Church Cemetery, West Long Branch, Monmouth County.
JACKSON, LEONARD L. Pvt, A, 124th NY Inf, [Wounded 5-5-1864 at Wilderness, VA.] 11-22-1900. Laurel Grove Cemetery, Totowa, Passaic County.
JACKSON, MOSES W. Pvt, L, 1st U.S. Colored Cav, 4-29-1894. Evergreen Cemetery, Morristown, Morris County.
JACKSON, NATHANIEL T. Pvt, I, 124th NY Inf, [Wounded 7-2-1863 at Gettysburg, PA.] 2-19-1918. Laurel Grove Cemetery, Totowa, Passaic County.
JACKSON, PETER Corp, F, 24th U.S. CT, 7-6-1904. Mount Peace Cemetery, Lawnside, Camden County.
JACKSON, PETER 7-6-1904. Johnson Cemetery, Camden, Camden County.
JACKSON, PETER Colored Cook, B, 1st NJ Inf, 4-24-1894. Fairmount Cemetery, Newark, Essex County.
JACKSON, PHILLIP 1st Sgt, H, 32nd U.S. CT, 7-11-1867. Reformed Church Cemetery, Montville, Morris County.
JACKSON, PRESTON Pvt, C, 6th LA Inf (CSA), [Captured 7-4-1863 at South Mountain, MD. Died of smallpox.] 10-24-1863. Finn's Point National Cemetery, Pennsville, Salem County.
JACKSON, PRINCE Pvt, D, 30th U.S. CT, 2-23-1888. Fairmount Cemetery, Newark, Essex County.
JACKSON, RICHARD Pvt, C, 45th U.S. CT, 6-6-1907. Memorial Park Cemetery, Gouldtown, Cumberland County.
JACKSON, ROBERT Pvt, K, 28th NJ Inf, 1-26-1901. Elmwood Cemetery, New Brunswick, Middlesex County.
JACKSON*, ROBERT Pvt, D, 112th NY Inf, [Wounded 10-27-1864 at Darbytown Road, VA.] 1893. Macphelah Cemetery, North Bergen, Hudson County.
JACKSON, RUTH Nurse, 8-10-1877. Friends Cemetery, Wall, Monmouth County.
JACKSON, SAMUEL Landsman, U.S. Navy, USS Princeton, 2-4-1917. Butler Cemetery, Camden, Camden County.

Our Brothers Gone Before

JACKSON, SAMUEL Pvt, H, 25th U.S. CT, 12-26-1887. Johnson Cemetery, Camden, Camden County.
JACKSON, SAMUEL Pvt, K, 27th NJ Inf, DoD Unknown. St. Peter's Church Cemetery, Belleville, Essex County.
JACKSON, SAMUEL 11-18-1899. Valleau Cemetery, Ridgewood, Bergen County.
JACKSON, SIMEON Pvt, A, 6th AL Inf (CSA), 10-1-1863. Finn's Point National Cemetery, Pennsville, Salem County.
JACKSON, THEODORE E. Pvt, F, 32nd U.S. CT, 9-28-1878. Evergreen Cemetery, Morristown, Morris County.
JACKSON, THOMAS Pvt, D, 26th U.S. CT, 8-22-1894. Evergreen Cemetery, Morristown, Morris County.
JACKSON, THOMAS Pvt, H, 3rd NJ Inf, 11-21-1866. Old Somerville Cemetery, Somerville, Somerset County.
JACKSON, THOMAS A. Pvt, A, 9th NJ Inf, 2-23-1903. Willow Grove Cemetery, New Brunswick, Middlesex County.
JACKSON, THOMAS H. Musc, I, 45th U.S. CT, 9-19-1910. Evergreen Cemetery, Hillside, Union County.
JACKSON, THOMAS L. Pvt, I, 8th NJ Inf, [Died of diarrhea at Petersburg, VA.] 1-13-1865. Riverside Cemetery, Toms River, Ocean County.
JACKSON, THOMAS R. Pvt, A, 41st U.S. CT, 7-3-1897. Rahway Cemetery, Rahway, Union County.
JACKSON, THOMAS W. Pvt, B, 13th NJ Inf, 5-15-1878. Bayview-New York Bay Cemetery, Jersey City, Hudson County.
JACKSON, TOBIAS Pvt, A, 127th U.S. CT, 9-11-1891. Valleau Cemetery, Ridgewood, Bergen County.
JACKSON, W.BARTLETT Pvt, E, 13th GA Inf (CSA), [Captured 5-12-1864 at Spotsylvania CH, VA. Died of lung congestion.] 11-27-1864. Finn's Point National Cemetery, Pennsville, Salem County.
JACKSON, W. SCOTT 1926. Riverside Cemetery, Toms River, Ocean County.
JACKSON, WALTER Pvt, G, 22nd U.S. CT, DoD Unknown. Grove Church Cemetery, North Bergen, Hudson County.
JACKSON, WATSON HENRY Pvt, A, 22nd U.S. CT, 5-14-1895. Fairmount Cemetery, Newark, Essex County.
JACKSON, WILLIAM Pvt, I, 26th PA Inf, [Wounded 6-30-1862 at Glendale, VA.] 4-12-1909. Union Cemetery, Gloucester City, Camden County.
JACKSON, WILLIAM Pvt, D, 22nd U.S. CT, 1-1-1887. Mount Zion Methodist Church Cemetery, Lawnside, Camden County.
JACKSON, WILLIAM Artificer, B, 15th NY Eng, 3-8-1877. Evergreen Cemetery, Hillside, Union County.
JACKSON, WILLIAM CLARK Musc, G, 10th U.S. Inf, 5-24-1902. Mount Pleasant Cemetery, Newark, Essex County.
JACKSON*, WILLIAM DECOURSEY 2nd Lt, C, 38th NJ Inf, 4-22-1885. United Methodist Church Cemetery, Ellisdale, Burlington County.
JACKSON, WILLIAM H. Pvt, G, 13th AL Inf (CSA), 3-6-1864. Finn's Point National Cemetery, Pennsville, Salem County.
JACKSON, WILLIAM H. Pvt, G, 29th CT Inf, 4-25-1916. Rahway Cemetery, Rahway, Union County.
JACKSON, WILLIAM H.H. Pvt, H, 1st NJ Cav, 1905. Cedar Hill Cemetery, East Millstone, Somerset County.
JACKSON, WILLIAM J. Pvt, B, 42nd GA Inf (CSA), 7-8-1863. Finn's Point National Cemetery, Pennsville, Salem County.
JACOBI, AUGUST (aka: Jakoby, August) Pvt, D, 2nd NJ Inf, 3-6-1915. Woodland Cemetery, Newark, Essex County.

New Jersey Civil War Burials

JACOBS, AUGUSTUS H. L. Corp, D, 11th NJ Inf, [Died of diarrhea at Newark, NJ.] 4-16-1863. Woodland Cemetery, Newark, Essex County.

JACOBS, BENJAMIN L. Pvt, MD QM Dept (CSA) 10-2-1863. Finn's Point National Cemetery, Pennsville, Salem County.

JACOBS, CHARLES Pvt, D, 4th NY Cav, 8-22-1895. Fairmount Cemetery, Newark, Essex County.

JACOBS*, HENRY D. Pvt, G, 39th NJ Inf, 10-20-1885. Woodland Cemetery, Newark, Essex County.

JACOBS, JOHN (see: Jacobus, John) St. Mary's Cemetery, East Orange, Essex County.

JACOBS, JOHN G. Pvt, C, 5th NY Inf, 7-11-1899. Palisade Cemetery, North Bergen, Hudson County.

JACOBS, JOSEPH S. Pvt, I, 12th NJ Inf, DoD Unknown. Baptist Church Cemetery, Alloway, Salem County.

JACOBUS, ABRAHAM Pvt, F, 15th NJ Inf, 1922. Boonton Cemetery, Boonton, Morris County.

JACOBUS, ABRAHAM J. Pvt, K, 26th NJ Inf, 1-18-1899. Rosedale Cemetery, Orange, Essex County.

JACOBUS, ABRAM RAPP Pvt, G, 27th NJ Inf, 1-12-1918. Whitehall Cemetery, Towaco, Morris County.

JACOBUS, CHARLES H. Pvt, H, 39th NJ Inf, 4-18-1918. Arlington Cemetery, Kearny, Hudson County.

JACOBUS, CHARLES H. DoD Unknown. Canfield Cemetery, Cedar Grove, Essex County.

JACOBUS, DAVID N. (aka: Dobbins, David N.) Pvt, D, 26th NJ Inf, 3-24-1894. Prospect Hill Cemetery, Caldwell, Essex County.

JACOBUS*, HENRY (aka: Gatfield, Henry) Pvt, F, 33rd NJ Inf, DoD Unknown. Boonton Cemetery, Boonton, Morris County.

JACOBUS, ISAAC M. Corp, I, 26th NJ Inf, 1-9-1918. Mount Pleasant Cemetery, Newark, Essex County.

JACOBUS, JACOB G. (aka: Jacobus, James C.) Pvt, H, 2nd DC Inf, 7-10-1873. Fairmount Cemetery, Newark, Essex County.

JACOBUS, JAMES Sgt, A, 47th NY Inf, 4-5-1922. Clinton Cemetery, Irvington, Essex County.

JACOBUS, JAMES C. (see: Jacobus, Jacob G.) Fairmount Cemetery, Newark, Essex County.

JACOBUS, JAMES H. Corp, E, 13th NJ Inf, 12-13-1902. Rosedale Cemetery, Orange, Essex County.

JACOBUS, JOHN (aka: Jacobs, John) Pvt, F, 33rd NJ Inf, 4-30-1890. St. Mary's Cemetery, East Orange, Essex County.

JACOBUS, JOHN A. Pvt, H, 40th NY Inf, [Wounded 7-2-1863 at Gettysburg, PA.] 9-25-1881. Fairmount Cemetery, Newark, Essex County.

JACOBUS, JOHN D. DoD Unknown. Hillside Cemetery, Fairfield, Essex County.

JACOBUS, JOHN H. Musc, K, 25th NJ Inf, DoD Unknown. East Ridgelawn Cemetery, Clifton, Passaic County.

JACOBUS, JOHN H.A. Corp, C, 9th NJ Inf, 10-16-1906. Cedar Lawn Cemetery, Paterson, Passaic County.

JACOBUS, JOHN J.H. Pvt, B, 7th NJ Inf, [Wounded 5-3-1863 at Chancellorsville, VA.] 7-29-1914. Mount Hebron Cemetery, Montclair, Essex County.

JACOBUS, JOHN U. Pvt, G, 27th NJ Inf, 2-22-1909. Whitehall Cemetery, Towaco, Morris County.

JACOBUS, NICHOLAS 5-24-1900. 1st Reformed Church Cemetery, Pompton Plains, Morris County.

JACOBUS, PETER Pvt, H, 25th NJ Inf, 10- -1915. Valleau Cemetery, Ridgewood, Bergen County.

Our Brothers Gone Before

JACOBUS, PETER Artificer, 2nd MA Light Art 7-19-1896. Fairmount Cemetery, Newark, Essex County.
JACOBUS*, PETER E. Corp, H, 39th NJ Inf, 4-24-1904. Prospect Hill Cemetery, Caldwell, Essex County.
JACOBUS, PETER E. 8-28-1866. Mount Pleasant Cemetery, Newark, Essex County.
JACOBUS, RICHARD DUDLEY Pvt, F, 26th NJ Inf, 8-28-1915. Bloomfield Cemetery, Bloomfield, Essex County.
JACOBUS, RODGER 2-15-1863. Whitehall Cemetery, Towaco, Morris County.
JACOBUS*, THEODORE Pvt, K, 7th NJ Inf, 7-26-1906. Arlington Cemetery, Kearny, Hudson County.
JACOBUS*, WILLIAM Musc, I, 40th NJ Inf, 11-30-1920. Rosedale Cemetery, Orange, Essex County.
JACOBUS, WILLIAM B. Pvt, E, 13th NJ Inf, 12-24-1903. Fairmount Cemetery, Newark, Essex County.
JACOBUS, WILLIAM D. Pvt, G, 26th NJ Inf, 11-27-1909. Rosedale Cemetery, Orange, Essex County.
JACOBUS, WILLIAM F. 10-29-1928. Fairmount Cemetery, Newark, Essex County.
JACOBUS, WILLIAM G. Pvt, D, 26th NJ Inf, 4-8-1880. Canfield Cemetery, Cedar Grove, Essex County.
JACOBUS, WILLIAM S. Pvt, I, 27th NJ Inf, 5-18-1884. Reformed Church Cemetery, Fairfield, Essex County.
JACQUES, ALBERT Pvt, A, 11th NJ Inf, 6-27-1873. Trinity Episcopal Church Cemetery, Woodbridge, Middlesex County.
JACQUES, AUGUSTUS Pvt, H, 5th NJ Inf, 12-21-1891. Fairmount Cemetery, Newark, Essex County.
JACQUES, CHARLES B. Asst Surg, 7th NJ Inf 11-2-1866. Old Somerville Cemetery, Somerville, Somerset County.
JACQUES, JEAN (aka: Jack, John) Pvt, D, 4th NJ Inf, 1-5-1905. Woodland Cemetery, Newark, Essex County.
JACQUES, JOHN (aka: Battish, John) Pvt, G, 7th NJ Inf, 6-23-1890. Cedar Lawn Cemetery, Paterson, Passaic County.
JACQUES, MORTIMER Pvt, F, 28th NJ Inf, 5-24-1903. Fairmount Cemetery, Newark, Essex County.
JACQUES, PETER L. Pvt, B, 23rd NJ Inf, [Died of disease at Washington, DC.] 12-3-1862. Methodist Church Cemetery, Groveville, Mercer County.
JACQUILARD, ANDREW (aka: Jaquillard, Andrew) Pvt, G, 1st OR Cav, 5-23-1872. Evergreen Cemetery, Hillside, Union County.
JAEGER, CHRISTIAN Pvt, B, 103rd NY Inf, 10-27-1880. Woodland Cemetery, Newark, Essex County.
JAEGER, JOHN Sgt, E, 5th NY National Guard, 4-24-1903. Weehawken Cemetery, North Bergen, Hudson County.
JAEGER, JULIUS (aka: Haeger, Judas J.) Pvt, B, 40th NJ Inf, 10-4-1905. Fairmount Cemetery, Newark, Essex County.
JAEGER, MARTIN Musc, 2nd NJ Inf Band 4-9-1876. Holy Sepulchre Cemetery, East Orange, Essex County.
JAEGER, MAX (see: Yeager, Max) Hoboken Cemetery, North Bergen, Hudson County.
JAEGER, ROBERT 1st Sgt, D, 71st NY Inf, 8- -1875. Holy Sepulchre Cemetery, East Orange, Essex County.
JAEGER, WILLIAM H. (aka: Jaggers, William) Pvt, B, 4th NJ Inf, 4-6-1891. Riverview Cemetery, Trenton, Mercer County.
JAEHING, WILLIAM E. __, E, 1st __ Inf, DoD Unknown. Clinton Cemetery, Irvington, Essex County.
JAGER, ANSON A. Pvt, A, 27th NJ Inf, 11-18-1892. Old Gumaer Cemetery, Sandyston, Sussex County.

New Jersey Civil War Burials

JAGERS, JOHN C. Pvt, C, 38th NJ Inf, 4-26-1912. Arlington Cemetery, Kearny, Hudson County.

JAGGARD*, CHARLES Pvt, E, 150th PA Inf, 1-1-1896. 1st Baptist Cemetery, Cape May Court House, Cape May County.

JAGGARD*, JOHN CLEMENT Pvt, G, 12th NJ Inf, 10-26-1924. Berlin Cemetery, Berlin, Camden County.

JAGGARD*, ROBERT W. Pvt, A, 3rd NJ Inf, 1-7-1923. St. John's United Methodist Cemetery, Turnersville, Gloucester County.

JAGGERS, ALBERT Pvt, D, 1st NJ Cav, 1880. Old Stone Church Cemetery, Fairton, Cumberland County.

JAGGERS, DANIEL Pvt, G, 24th NJ Inf, 1-9-1883. Presbyterian Church Cemetery, Bridgeton, Cumberland County.

JAGGERS, GEORGE M. Landsman, U.S. Navy, USS North Carolina, 10-17-1896. Fairmount Cemetery, Newark, Essex County.

JAGGERS, JOHN W. Pvt, I, 38th NJ Inf, 7-12-1886. Riverview Cemetery, Trenton, Mercer County.

JAGGERS, JOSEPH Pvt, G, 24th NJ Inf, 11-18-1907. Friendship United Methodist Church Cemetery, Upper Deerfield, Cumberland County.

JAGGERS, STEPHEN Pvt, E, 26th NJ Inf, [Died of disease at White Oak Church, VA.] 2-8-1863. Clinton Cemetery, Irvington, Essex County.

JAGGERS, WILLIAM (see: Jaeger, William H.) Riverview Cemetery, Trenton, Mercer County.

JAGGERS, WILLIAM FILER Pvt, I, 24th NJ Inf, 4-3-1927. Harmony Methodist-Episcopal Church Cemetery, Piney Hollow, Gloucester County.

JAGGERS, WILLIAM H. Pvt, D, 1st NJ Cav, 8-10-1919. Old Stone Church Cemetery, Fairton, Cumberland County.

JAHN, MARTIN (aka: John, Martin) Pvt, H, 46th NY Inf, 2-9-1914. Arlington Cemetery, Kearny, Hudson County.

JAIDE, FREDERICK (see: Jaide, Fritz) Rosedale Cemetery, Orange, Essex County.

JAIDE*, FRITZ (aka: Jaide, Frederick) Corp, I, 20th NY Inf, 8-3-1911. Rosedale Cemetery, Orange, Essex County.

JAKOBY, AUGUST (see: Jacobi, August) Woodland Cemetery, Newark, Essex County.

JAMES, ALBERT F. DoD Unknown. Presbyterian Church Cemetery, Upper Deerfield, Cumberland County.

JAMES, CALVIN T. Capt, I, 31st NJ Inf, 10-31-1895. Mount Pleasant Cemetery, Newark, Essex County.

JAMES*, CHARLES T. Pvt, G, 10th NJ Inf, 8-19-1918. Methodist Church Cemetery, Groveville, Mercer County.

JAMES*, DAVID Pvt, C, 8th NJ Inf, 4-8-1898. Fairmount Cemetery, Newark, Essex County.

JAMES, ELI Pvt, A, 24th U.S. CT, 1-3-1910. Greenwood Cemetery, Hamilton, Mercer County.

JAMES, ELI T. 10-12-1890. Riverside Cemetery, Riverside, Burlington County.

JAMES, FREDERICK T. Pvt, B, 4th __ Inf, 2-9-1907. Mount Pleasant Cemetery, Newark, Essex County.

JAMES*, HARRISON M. Corp, B, 93rd IL Inf, 11-1-1889. Arlington Cemetery, Kearny, Hudson County.

JAMES, HIRAM H. Actg Asst Surg, U.S. Navy, USS Kensington, 9-11-1885. Hazelwood Cemetery, Rahway, Union County.

JAMES, JACOB (aka: James, Shems) Pvt, K, 7th NJ Inf, 1-27-1913. Evergreen Cemetery, Camden, Camden County.

JAMES*, JAMES Pvt, C, 8th NJ Inf, 4-12-1909. Fairmount Cemetery, Newark, Essex County.

Our Brothers Gone Before

JAMES, JAMES H. Pvt, C, 24th NJ Inf, 1-21-1895. Presbyterian Cemetery, Salem, Salem County.
JAMES, JOEL R. (JR.) Pvt, A, 23rd NJ Inf, 3-21-1906. Bordentown/Old St. Mary's Catholic Cemetery, Bordentown, Burlington County.
JAMES, JOHN Pvt, C, 8th NJ Inf, 10-16-1864. Mount Pleasant Cemetery, Newark, Essex County.
JAMES, JOHN R. Pvt, H, 23rd NJ Inf, 11-16-1908. Bordentown/Old St. Mary's Catholic Cemetery, Bordentown, Burlington County.
JAMES*, JOHN W. Pvt, G, 7th NJ Inf, 3-31-1926. Cedar Lawn Cemetery, Paterson, Passaic County.
JAMES, JOSEPH Pvt, H, 7th NJ Inf, 3-8-1917. New Episcopal Church Cemetery, Swedesboro, Gloucester County.
JAMES, JOSEPH Sgt, A, 30th PA Inf, 12-2-1923. Monument Cemetery, Edgewater Park, Burlington County.
JAMES, LEVI 2nd Lt, E, 89th IN Inf, 3-19-1905. New Camden Cemetery, Camden, Camden County.
JAMES, SAMUEL C. Pvt, I, 28th NJ Inf, 10-26-1906. Christ Church Cemetery, Morgan, Middlesex County.
JAMES, SHEMS (see: James, Jacob) Evergreen Cemetery, Camden, Camden County.
JAMES, SILAS Pvt, G, 21st NJ Inf, 2-4-1896. Arlington Cemetery, Kearny, Hudson County.
JAMES, THEODORE 6-5-1933. Princeton Cemetery, Princeton, Mercer County.
JAMES, THOMAS (aka: Thomas, James) Pvt, K, 5th CT Inf, 7-19-1873. Rosehill Cemetery, Newfield, Gloucester County.
JAMES, THOMAS 1st Asst Eng, U.S. Navy, DoD Unknown. Arlington Cemetery, Kearny, Hudson County.
JAMES, WILLIAM Pvt, C, 41st U.S. CT, DoD Unknown. Mount Zion AME Cemetery, Swedesboro, Gloucester County.
JAMES*, WILLIAM B. Pvt, B, 34th NJ Inf, 8-3-1909. Methodist Church Cemetery, Hurffville, Gloucester County.
JAMES, WILLIAM D. Pvt, G, 2nd NJ Militia, 12-1-1896. Mount Pleasant Cemetery, Newark, Essex County.
JAMES, WILLIAM I. 11-14-1887. Riverside Cemetery, Toms River, Ocean County.
JAMESON, JOHN Capt, B, 36th PA Inf, [Wounded 9-17-1862 at Antietam, MD.] 4-12-1908. Union Cemetery, Milford, Hunterdon County.
JAMESON, SAMUEL Wagoner, I, 28th NJ Inf, 2-14-1885. Fernwood Cemetery, Jamesburg, Middlesex County.
JAMESON, WILLIAM Lt Col, 4th NY Inf 1896. Brookside Cemetery, Englewood, Bergen County.
JAMIESON, SAMUEL Sgt, K, 67th NY Inf, 1893. Bayview-New York Bay Cemetery, Jersey City, Hudson County.
JAMIESON, THOMPSON (aka: Jamison, Thomas) Pvt, B, 3rd PA Cav, 8-17-1905. Eastview Cemetery, Salem, Salem County.
JAMISON, ALBERT S. Pvt, H, 26th NJ Inf, 2-3-1880. Rosedale Cemetery, Orange, Essex County.
JAMISON*, ANDREW A. Pvt, E, 5th NJ Inf, 2-17-1893. Brainerd Cemetery, Cranbury, Middlesex County.
JAMISON, DAVID Sgt, 2nd Bttn U.S. VRC 4-15-1910. New Camden Cemetery, Camden, Camden County.
JAMISON, DAVID P. Pvt, H, 1st DE Inf, 11-15-1918. Methodist Cemetery, Haddonfield, Camden County.
JAMISON, ELLISON Pvt, F, 14th NJ Inf, [Wounded in action.] 1898. Methodist Cemetery, Cassville, Ocean County.

New Jersey Civil War Burials

JAMISON, JOHN ALLEN Pvt, C, 10th NJ Inf, 1918. Bloomfield Cemetery, Bloomfield, Essex County.
JAMISON, SHINN C. Pvt, A, 6th NJ Inf, [Wounded in action.] 7-17-1929. Riverside Cemetery, Toms River, Ocean County.
JAMISON, THOMAS (see: Jamieson, Thompson) Eastview Cemetery, Salem, Salem County.
JAMISON, WILLIAM A. Pvt, E, 25th U.S. CT, 1911. Johnson Cemetery, Matawan, Monmouth County.
JAMISON*, WILLIAM H. Pvt, E, 8th NJ Inf, 11-8-1864. Methodist Cemetery, Cassville, Ocean County.
JANCOVIOUS*, CHARLES FREDERICK ROBERT Pvt, 32nd NY Ind Btty 10-16-1904. Evergreen Cemetery, Hillside, Union County.
JANDRO*, WILLIAM (aka: Gandro, William) Pvt, G, 1st MA Cav, [Wounded in action 4--1864.] 12-4-1907. Laurel Grove Cemetery, Totowa, Passaic County.
JANES*, WILLIAM H. Pvt, G, 8th NJ Inf, 11-6-1905. United Methodist Church Cemetery, Alloway, Salem County.
JANEWAY, HUGH HARTSHORNE Col, 1st NJ Cav [Killed in action at Amelia CH, VA.] 4-5-1865. Elmwood Cemetery, New Brunswick, Middlesex County.
JANEWAY, JACOB JONES Bvt Col, 14th NJ Inf 1926. Elmwood Cemetery, New Brunswick, Middlesex County.
JANEWAY, JOHN HOWELL Asst Surg, U.S. Army, [Medical Staff. Brevet Lt Col.] 4-14-1911. Princeton Cemetery, Princeton, Mercer County.
JANEWAY, JOSHUA BLACKWELL HOWELL Chaplain, 199th PA Inf 1-17-1920. Elmwood Cemetery, New Brunswick, Middlesex County.
JANSON, HENRY D. Pvt, K, 2nd DC Inf, 4-7-1889. Chestnut Cemetery, Dover, Morris County.
JANTON, FRANK Pvt, B, 213th PA Inf, 1-23-1933. Harleigh Cemetery, Camden, Camden County.
JANTZEN, NICHOLAS Sgt, H, 5th NY State Militia, 9-13-1913. Bayview-New York Bay Cemetery, Jersey City, Hudson County.
JAQUES, AUGUST (see: Jackes, August) St. Mary's Cemetery, East Orange, Essex County.
JAQUES, DAVID H. Pvt, I, 39th NJ Inf, DoD Unknown. Arlington Cemetery, Kearny, Hudson County.
JAQUES, JOHN B. Musc, I, 40th NJ Inf, 6-13-1911. Fairmount Cemetery, Newark, Essex County.
JAQUES, SAMUEL 2-18-1936. Bordentown/Old St. Mary's Catholic Cemetery, Bordentown, Burlington County.
JAQUES, WILLIAM A. Pvt, B, 30th NJ Inf, [Died of typhoid at Division hospital.] 4-9-1863. Rahway Cemetery, Rahway, Union County.
JAQUES, WILLIAM H.H. Pvt, A, 38th NJ Inf, 4-21-1906. Cedarwood Cemetery, Hazlet, Monmouth County.
JAQUETT, FRANCIS F. Pvt, A, 24th NJ Inf, 12-29-1923. Baptist Church Cemetery, Canton, Salem County.
JAQUETT, JAMES J. Pvt, A, 24th NJ Inf, [Died of fever at Washington, DC.] 11-3-1862. Baptist Church Cemetery, Canton, Salem County.
JAQUETT, POWELL Pvt, A, 24th NJ Inf, [Died of fever at Washington, DC.] 10-9-1862. Baptist Church Cemetery, Canton, Salem County.
JAQUILLARD, ANDREW (see: Jacquilard, Andrew) Evergreen Cemetery, Hillside, Union County.
JAQUINS*, STEPHEN F. Pvt, B, 39th NJ Inf, 9-12-1902. Jersey City Cemetery, Jersey City, Hudson County.
JARDIN, MARTIN Sgt, H, 41st NY Inf, 4-19-1900. Fairmount Cemetery, Newark, Essex County.

Our Brothers Gone Before

JARDINE, ALBERT J. Hosp Steward, U.S. Navy, 2-23-1909. Bayview-New York Bay Cemetery, Jersey City, Hudson County.

JARDINE, ROBERT (see: Jardine, Thomas) Canfield Cemetery, Cedar Grove, Essex County.

JARDINE, THOMAS (aka: Jardine, Robert) 1st Sgt, Btty G, 3rd RI Heavy Art, 11-20-1888. Canfield Cemetery, Cedar Grove, Essex County.

JARMIN, RICHARD Pvt, G, 25th NJ Inf, [Wounded 12-13-1862 at Fredericksburg, VA.] 3-15-1890. Wesley United Methodist Church Cemetery, Petersburg, Cape May County.

JARQUIN, WILHELM (aka: Farquier, William) Pvt, Btty A, 7th NY Heavy Art, 11-27-1907. Fairmount Cemetery, Newark, Essex County.

JARRELL, J.E. (see: Jerrold, James E. (Jr.)) Finn's Point National Cemetery, Pennsville, Salem County.

JARRETT, JOSEPH Landsman, U.S. Navy, USS Home, 3-2-1900. Bordentown/Old St. Mary's Catholic Cemetery, Bordentown, Burlington County.

JARVIS, ALEXANDER Pvt, Btty A, 1st NJ Light Art, 5-15-1911. Fairmount Cemetery, Newark, Essex County.

JARVIS, ALFRED 1st Lt, G, 12th MS Inf (CSA), 1912. Old South Church Cemetery, Bergenfield, Bergen County.

JARVIS*, ALFRED E. Corp, Btty K, 11th U.S. CHA, 7-16-1916. Fairmount Cemetery, Newark, Essex County.

JARVIS, BENJAMIN Pvt, K, 10th NJ Inf, 8-15-1911. Elwood Rural Cemetery, Elwood, Atlantic County.

JARVIS, EBENEZER C. Pvt, C, 13th NJ Inf, 9-6-1938. Fairmount Cemetery, Newark, Essex County.

JARVIS, HARVEY 4-28-1891. Glenwood Cemetery, West Long Branch, Monmouth County.

JARVIS, ISAAC Pvt, K, 10th NJ Inf, 12-2-1876. Elwood Rural Cemetery, Elwood, Atlantic County.

JARVIS, JAMES M. Pvt, H, 33rd NJ Inf, 3-9-1910. Branchville Cemetery, Branchville, Sussex County.

JARVIS, JOHN E. Pvt, I, 127th NY Inf, 2-16-1903. Bayview-New York Bay Cemetery, Jersey City, Hudson County.

JARVIS, JOHN RICHARDSON 1st Lt, K, 104th NY Inf, 1-11-1921. Evergreen Cemetery, Hillside, Union County.

JARVIS, JOHN W. Pvt, C, 8th AL Inf (CSA), 2-21-1864. Finn's Point National Cemetery, Pennsville, Salem County.

JARVIS, STACY Pvt, B, 2nd NJ Inf, 8-1-1885. Elwood Rural Cemetery, Elwood, Atlantic County.

JARVIS, THOMAS 12-5-1897. St. John's Episcopal Church Cemetery, Chews Landing, Camden County.

JAUDEL, ALEXANDER Hosp Steward, U.S. Army, 2-7-1916. Arlington Cemetery, Kearny, Hudson County.

JAUSS, GOTTLIEB Pvt, F, 22nd NJ Inf, 1-3-1913. Weehawken Cemetery, North Bergen, Hudson County.

JAY, DAVID Pvt, A, 5th AL Inf (CSA), 9-9-1863. Finn's Point National Cemetery, Pennsville, Salem County.

JAYCOX*, JAMES C. Pvt, C, 40th NY Inf, [Wounded in action.] 12-30-1922. Mount Prospect Cemetery, Neptune, Monmouth County.

JAYNE, DAVID Pvt, B, 2nd NY Cav, 4-24-1917. Methodist Church Cemetery, Liberty, Warren County.

JAYNE, GEORGE F. Corp, H, 8th U.S. CT, 1-4-1901. Atlantic City Cemetery, Pleasantville, Atlantic County.

New Jersey Civil War Burials

JAYNE*, JOSEPH C. Wagoner, B, 61st NY Inf, 1924. Presbyterian Church Cemetery, Rockaway, Morris County.

JEANNE, LEON Pvt, B, 74th NY Inf, 9-17-1910. Fairview Cemetery, Fairview, Bergen County.

JEFFERIES, FRANK 1907. 1st Reformed Church Cemetery, Pompton Plains, Morris County.

JEFFERIES, WILLIAM N. Pvt, C, 37th NJ Inf, 3-31-1910. Mercer Cemetery, Trenton, Mercer County.

JEFFERS, CHARLES (see: Jeffery, Charles) Mansfield/Washington Cemetery, Washington, Warren County.

JEFFERS, ISAAC 1923. Bayview-New York Bay Cemetery, Jersey City, Hudson County.

JEFFERS, JAMES J. Pvt, B, 4th NJ Inf, DoD Unknown. Union Cemetery, Frenchtown, Hunterdon County.

JEFFERSON, F. Pvt, I, 10th VA Inf (CSA), 3-20-1864. Finn's Point National Cemetery, Pennsville, Salem County.

JEFFERSON, GEORGE Pvt, A, 41st U.S. CT, [Wounded in action.] DoD Unknown. Clinton Cemetery, Irvington, Essex County.

JEFFERSON, NOAH Pvt, I, 29th US CT, 12-13-1914. Arlington Cemetery, Kearny, Hudson County.

JEFFERSON, RALPH 1st Lt,RQM, 8th NJ Inf 9-25-1906. Woodland Cemetery, Newark, Essex County.

JEFFERSON, THOMAS Landsman, U.S. Navy, USS Seneca, 3-8-1905. Union Bethel Cemetery, Erma, Cape May County.

JEFFERSON, THOMAS Pvt, Unassigned, 10th NJ Inf, 1911. Methodist-Episcopal Cemetery, Whitehouse, Hunterdon County.

JEFFERSON, THOMAS (see: Morris, Thomas Jefferson) Evergreen Cemetery, Morristown, Morris County.

JEFFERY, CHARLES (aka: Jeffers, Charles) QM Sgt, C, 2nd NY Cav, 1924. Mansfield/Washington Cemetery, Washington, Warren County.

JEFFREY, BARTINE A. Pvt, F, 29th NJ Inf, 3-30-1895. Bayview-New York Bay Cemetery, Jersey City, Hudson County.

JEFFREY*, FRANCIS Corp, H, 35th NJ Inf, 5-2-1900. Old 1st Methodist Church Cemetery, West Long Branch, Monmouth County.

JEFFREY, NOAH E. Pvt, D, 9th NJ Inf, 4-1-1917. Good Luck Cemetery, Murray Grove, Ocean County.

JEFFREY, WILLIAM Sgt, F, 38th NJ Inf, 2-7-1914. Old 1st Methodist Church Cemetery, West Long Branch, Monmouth County.

JEFFREY, WILLIAM (see: Jeffreys, William J.) Rosedale Cemetery, Orange, Essex County.

JEFFREY*, WILLIAM W. Pvt, F, 38th NJ Inf, 1-28-1921. Old 1st Methodist Church Cemetery, West Long Branch, Monmouth County.

JEFFREYS, WILLIAM J. (aka: Jeffrey, William) Pvt, H, 71st NY State Militia, 3-18-1907. Rosedale Cemetery, Orange, Essex County.

JEFFRIES, JACOB Pvt, C, 13th NJ Inf, 4-15-1913. 1st Reformed Church Cemetery, Pompton Plains, Morris County.

JEFFRIES, JOHN T. Pvt, D, 3rd Bttn MO Cav (CSA), 6-20-1863. Finn's Point National Cemetery, Pennsville, Salem County.

JEFFRIES, JOSEPH Pvt, F, 24th NJ Inf, 7-3-1869. Baptist Church Cemetery, Greenwich, Cumberland County.

JEFFRIES, JOSEPH C. Pvt, D, 28th NJ Inf, 2-3-1900. St. Peter's Cemetery, New Brunswick, Middlesex County.

JEHN, MAX T. (aka: Yan, Max) Pvt, I, 117th NY Inf, 11-30-1918. Cedar Lawn Cemetery, Paterson, Passaic County.

Our Brothers Gone Before

JELICO, EDWARD B. __, B, 9th NY Inf, 12-21-1891. St. Peter's Cemetery, New Brunswick, Middlesex County.

JELLICO, THOMAS D. 1st Lt, F, 169th NY Inf, DoD Unknown. St. Peter's Cemetery, New Brunswick, Middlesex County.

JELLY, JOHN Pvt, H, 1st NJ Inf, DoD Unknown. Bayview-New York Bay Cemetery, Jersey City, Hudson County.

JELLY*, ROBERT Sgt, D, 21st NJ Inf, 8-16-1897. Bayview-New York Bay Cemetery, Jersey City, Hudson County.

JELLY, WILLIAM Pvt, A, 21st NJ Inf, 3-28-1885. Bayview-New York Bay Cemetery, Jersey City, Hudson County.

JEMISON, ELWOOD Pvt, I, 38th NJ Inf, 3-21-1914. Riverview Cemetery, Trenton, Mercer County.

JEMISON, HENRY Pvt, C, 1st NJ Cav, 10-26-1884. Riverview Cemetery, Trenton, Mercer County.

JEMISON*, ISAAC Pvt, D, 14th NJ Inf, 1899. Cedar Hill Cemetery, Hightstown, Mercer County.

JEMISON, JOSEPH J. Pvt, B, 28th NJ Inf, 3-25-1894. Cedar Hill Cemetery, Hightstown, Mercer County.

JENKINS, ALFRED A. Pvt, D, 38th NJ Inf, 6-30-1931. Eastview Cemetery, Salem, Salem County.

JENKINS, AZARIAH Pvt, B, 24th U.S. CT, 5-15-1919. Riverview Cemetery, Trenton, Mercer County.

JENKINS, DAVID Corp, B, 39th NJ Inf, 1-1-1929. Vincent Methodist-Episcopal Cemetery, Nutley, Essex County.

JENKINS, DAVID B. Capt, K, 86th U.S. CT, 3-10-1881. Evergreen Cemetery, Hillside, Union County.

JENKINS, DAVID LEFERRIS Pvt, A, 132nd IL Inf, 12-5-1906. Fairmount Cemetery, Newark, Essex County.

JENKINS, EDWARD 6-18-1901. Cedar Lawn Cemetery, Paterson, Passaic County.

JENKINS, ENOS Pvt, A, 124th NY Inf, 3-26-1941. Laurel Grove Cemetery, Totowa, Passaic County.

JENKINS, FAYETTE Pvt, E, 9th NJ Inf, DoD Unknown. Bateman Memorial Cemetery, Newport, Cumberland County.

JENKINS, FREDERICK Pvt, C, 26th NJ Inf, 1904. Vincent Methodist-Episcopal Cemetery, Nutley, Essex County.

JENKINS, HARVEY 1st Sgt, D, 29th NJ Inf, 8-4-1909. Fairview Cemetery, Fairview, Monmouth County.

JENKINS, HARVEY Pvt, L, 10th VA Inf (CSA), [Captured 5-12-1864 at Spotsylvania CH, VA. Died of diarrhea.] 9-15-1864. Finn's Point National Cemetery, Pennsville, Salem County.

JENKINS, HENRY Pvt, F, 12th NJ Inf, 1906. Methodist-Episcopal Church Cemetery, Aura, Gloucester County.

JENKINS, HENRY Pvt, H, 4th NC Cav (CSA), [Captured 7-4-1863 at South Mountain, MD. Died of diarrhea.] 7-11-1863. Finn's Point National Cemetery, Pennsville, Salem County.

JENKINS, ISRAEL 8-15-1866. Methodist-Episcopal Church Cemetery, Penns Grove, Salem County.

JENKINS, J. NEWTON Sgt, H, 30th NJ Inf, 1890. Baptist/Evergreen Methodist Cemetery, Plainfield, Union County.

JENKINS, JACOB K. Pvt, K, 25th NJ Inf, 11-26-1896. Cedar Lawn Cemetery, Paterson, Passaic County.

JENKINS, JOHN Pvt, Btty C, 16th NY Heavy Art, DoD Unknown. Midvale Cemetery, Midvale, Passaic County.

JENKINS, JOHN 12-26-1902. Bloomfield Cemetery, Bloomfield, Essex County.

New Jersey Civil War Burials

JENKINS, JOHN W. 7-31-1871. 1st Baptist Cemetery, Cape May Court House, Cape May County.

JENKINS, JOSEPH H. 1st Lt, C, 39th NJ Inf, 7-29-1887. Fairmount Cemetery, Newark, Essex County.

JENKINS*, LEANDER Pvt, D, 13th NJ Inf, [Wounded in action.] 4-7-1917. Fairmount Cemetery, Newark, Essex County.

JENKINS, MILLER Pvt, D, 7th U.S. Hancock Corps, 2-14-1918. Baptist Church Cemetery, Alloway, Salem County.

JENKINS, SAMUEL 7-6-1868. Macphelah Cemetery, North Bergen, Hudson County.

JENKINS, W. Pvt, A, 10th (Johnson's) KY Cav (CSA), 4-28-1864. Finn's Point National Cemetery, Pennsville, Salem County.

JENKINS, WILLIAM K. Pvt, F, 3rd SC Cav (CSA), [Captured 8-17-1864 at South Newport, GA.] 3-1-1865. Finn's Point National Cemetery, Pennsville, Salem County.

JENKINS, WILLIAM R. Pvt, H, 13th GA Inf (CSA), [Captured 7-3-1863 at Gettysburg, PA. Died of smallpox.] 11-7-1863. Finn's Point National Cemetery, Pennsville, Salem County.

JENKINSON*, ABRAHAM Pvt, B, 12th U.S. Inf, 6-2-1914. Fairmount Cemetery, Newark, Essex County.

JENKINSON, JOHN H. Pvt, K, 1st NJ Cav, 7-27-1887. Fairmount Cemetery, Newark, Essex County.

JENKS, JOHN G. Pvt, B, 22nd NJ Inf, DoD Unknown. Willow Grove Cemetery, New Brunswick, Middlesex County.

JENKS, RUSSELL DoD Unknown. Riverview Cemetery, Trenton, Mercer County.

JENNESS, CHARLES H. Pvt, K, 40th MA Inf, 10-5-1924. Evergreen Cemetery, Camden, Camden County.

JENNINGS*, CHARLES S. Pvt, Btty G, 11th U.S. CHA, 2-22-1928. AME Cemetery, Pennington, Mercer County.

JENNINGS, FRANKLIN F. Farrier, Btty B, 1st NJ Light Art, 9-12-1893. Cedarwood Cemetery, Hazlet, Monmouth County.

JENNINGS, GEORGE W. Corp, F, 12th NJ Inf, 2-2-1898. Eglington Cemetery, Clarksboro, Gloucester County.

JENNINGS, GEORGE W. 11-5-1881. Zion United Methodist Church Cemetery, Clarksboro, Gloucester County.

JENNINGS, H. Pvt, B, 1st Bttn (Colm's) TN Inf (CSA), 4-21-1864. Finn's Point National Cemetery, Pennsville, Salem County.

JENNINGS, JACOB M. Pvt, H, 30th NJ Inf, 12-18-1898. Hillside Cemetery, Scotch Plains, Union County.

JENNINGS, JESSE Sgt, K, 2nd DC Inf, 5-4-1915. Locust Hill Cemetery, Dover, Morris County.

JENNINGS, JOHN Pvt, K, 37th NY Inf, 11-24-1915. Holy Name Cemetery, Jersey City, Hudson County.

JENNINGS, JOHN 3-20-1887. Flower Hill Cemetery, North Bergen, Hudson County.

JENNINGS, JOHN Pvt, B, 40th NJ Inf, 11-17-1915. Holy Name Cemetery, Jersey City, Hudson County.

JENNINGS, JOHN Pvt, E, 25th NJ Inf, 3-23-1889. Canistear Cemetery, Vernon, Sussex County.

JENNINGS, JOHN D. Pvt, E, 9th NJ Inf, 1919. Chestnut Cemetery, Dover, Morris County.

JENNINGS, JOSEPH 4-6-1914. Evergreen Cemetery, Camden, Camden County.

JENNINGS, R.H. Pvt, F, 3rd (Howard's) Confederate States Cav (CSA), 8-8-1863. Finn's Point National Cemetery, Pennsville, Salem County.

Our Brothers Gone Before

JENNINGS, WILLIAM D. Pvt, F, 8th NJ Inf, [Died at Fort Monroe, VA. of wounds received 5-5-1862 at Williamsburg, VA.] 5-8-1862. Mount Pleasant Cemetery, Newark, Essex County.

JENNINGS, WILLIAM H. Pvt, D, 67th PA Inf, 1-3-1913. Belvidere/Catholic Cemetery, Belvidere, Warren County.

JENNINGS, WILLIAM P. Corp, I, 4th (Russell's) AL Cav (CSA), 7-14-1864. Finn's Point National Cemetery, Pennsville, Salem County.

JENNINGS*, WILTON T. Sgt, C, 94th NY Inf, 1887. Jersey City Cemetery, Jersey City, Hudson County.

JENSEN, J.H. (see: Jensen, Julius) Bloomfield Cemetery, Bloomfield, Essex County.

JENSEN, JULIUS (aka: Jensen, J.H.) Pvt, A, 4th LA Militia (CSA), [European Brigade.] DoD Unknown. Bloomfield Cemetery, Bloomfield, Essex County.

JERGES, ADAM (see: George, Adam) Arlington Cemetery, Kearny, Hudson County.

JERGUS, CHRISTOPHER (aka: Decker, Christopher) Pvt, C, 22nd NJ Inf, 3-22-1915. Old South Church Cemetery, Bergenfield, Bergen County.

JERNIGAN, H.M. Pvt, D, 5th NC Inf (CSA), [Wounded 7-1-1863 at Gettysburg, PA. Captured 5-12-1864 at Spotsylvania CH, VA. Died of diarrhea.] 3-23-1865. Finn's Point National Cemetery, Pennsville, Salem County.

JEROLAMON*, ABRAHAM Corp, B, 8th NJ Inf, 3-8-1897. Mount Pleasant Cemetery, Newark, Essex County.

JEROLAMON, CORNELIUS A. Pvt, C, 39th NJ Inf, 3-9-1887. Fairmount Cemetery, Newark, Essex County.

JEROLEMAN, WILLIAM H. Corp, D, 13th NJ Inf, 2-3-1916. Mount Pleasant Cemetery, Newark, Essex County.

JEROLOMAN, ABRAM Pvt, B, 30th NJ Inf, 9-9-1909. Greenlawn Cemetery, West Long Branch, Monmouth County.

JEROLOMAN, AMZI Pvt, A, 8th NJ Inf, 2-10-1912. Fairmount Cemetery, Newark, Essex County.

JERRELL, ISAAC F. Pvt, K, 12th NJ Inf, 4-2-1910. Calvary Baptist Church Cemetery, Ocean View, Cape May County.

JERRELL, JOHN P. Pvt, D, 25th NJ Inf, 5-11-1902. Old Stone Church Cemetery, Fairton, Cumberland County.

JERRELL, NATHAN P. (aka: Gerls, Nathan) Pvt, G, 24th NJ Inf, [Died of wounds received 12-13-1862 at Fredericksburg, VA.] 12-14-1862. Methodist Church Cemetery, Haleyville, Cumberland County.

JERRING, ALFRED Pvt, G, 26th NJ Inf, 12-26-1900. Rosedale Cemetery, Orange, Essex County.

JERROLD, JAMES E. (JR.) (aka: Jarrell, J.E.) Pvt, E, 7th VA Inf (CSA), [Captured 7-3-1863 at Gettysburg, PA. Died of diarrhea.] 9-21-1863. Finn's Point National Cemetery, Pennsville, Salem County.

JERSEY, JOHN J. Wagoner, D, 22nd NJ Inf, 8-17-1880. Pascack Reformed Cemetery, Park Ridge, Bergen County.

JERVIS, BETHUEL Pvt, D, 27th NJ Inf, 1-8-1911. Balesville Cemetery, Balesville, Sussex County.

JERVIS, JAMES N. Pvt, D, 15th NJ Inf, DoD Unknown. Balesville Cemetery, Balesville, Sussex County.

JERVIS, JOHN Artificer, A, 15th NY Eng, 1915. Batsto/Pleasant Mills Methodist Church Cemetery, Pleasant Mills, Atlantic County.

JESS, ADAM S. Pvt, K, 24th NJ Inf, 12-28-1907. Riverview Cemetery, Penns Grove, Salem County.

JESS, CHARLES Pvt, E, 10th NJ Inf, 4-12-1904. Baptist Church Cemetery, Blackwood, Camden County.

JESS, DAVID Pvt, K, 24th NJ Inf, DoD Unknown. Methodist-Episcopal Church Cemetery, Penns Grove, Salem County.

New Jersey Civil War Burials

JESS, HENRY Sgt, D, 25th NJ Inf, 2-19-1903. Cedar Green Cemetery, Clayton, Gloucester County.
JESS, LORENZO Corp, F, 4th NJ Inf, 12-5-1884. Baptist Church Cemetery, Haddonfield, Camden County.
JESS, MARY ANN Nurse, 4-6-1882. Baptist Cemetery, Salem, Salem County.
JESS, WESLEY Pvt, E, 10th NJ Inf, 7-30-1912. Baptist Church Cemetery, Blackwood, Camden County.
JESSUP, BENJAMIN Corp, C, 4th GA Inf (CSA), [Captured 7-5-1863 at Gettysburg, PA. Died of diarrhea.] 1-7-1864. Finn's Point National Cemetery, Pennsville, Salem County.
JESTER*, GEORGE W. Pvt, I, 12th NJ Inf, 11-11-1904. Baptist Cemetery, Salem, Salem County.
JETTER, JOHN Pvt, A, 11th NJ Inf, [Wounded in action.] 8-11-1910. Fairmount Cemetery, Newark, Essex County.
JEWELL, EDWARD Pvt, I, 8th NJ Inf, DoD Unknown. Fairmount Cemetery, Newark, Essex County.
JEWELL, ELIHU Pvt, K, 26th NJ Inf, 4-15-1890. Fairmount Cemetery, Newark, Essex County.
JEWELL, GEORGE W. 1886. Rahway Cemetery, Rahway, Union County.
JEWELL, THEODORE A. Pvt, A, 41st U.S. CT, DoD Unknown. New Somerville Cemetery, Somerville, Somerset County.
JEWELL, WILLIAM H. Pvt, H, 1st NJ Cav, 1890. Tennent Church Cemetery, Tennent, Monmouth County.
JINKINS, ROBERT __, __, __ PA __, 11-3-1898. Presbyterian Church Cemetery, Williamstown, Gloucester County.
JOBES, BENJAMIN Pvt, E, 23rd NJ Inf, 3-29-1895. Mount Holly Cemetery, Mount Holly, Burlington County.
JOBES, BENJAMIN F. Pvt, B, 23rd NJ Inf, 3-11-1917. Bordentown/Old St. Mary's Catholic Cemetery, Bordentown, Burlington County.
JOBES, CHARLES (see: Jobs, Charles) White Ridge Cemetery, Eatontown, Monmouth County.
JOBES, CHARLES S. Corp, D, 14th NJ Inf, 1907. Baptist Church Cemetery, Jacobstown, Burlington County.
JOBES, CHARLES W. Pvt, A, 37th NJ Inf, 12-7-1902. Bayview-New York Bay Cemetery, Jersey City, Hudson County.
JOBES*, GEORGE A. Pvt, E, 8th NJ Inf, 1-10-1916. Oddfellows Cemetery, Burlington, Burlington County.
JOBES*, GEORGE W. 1st Sgt, G, 8th NJ Inf, 2-16-1916. Old Camden Cemetery, Camden, Camden County.
JOBES, JAMES Pvt, A, 4th NJ Militia, 7-12-1914. Bordentown/Old St. Mary's Catholic Cemetery, Bordentown, Burlington County.
JOBES, JOSEPH Pvt, E, 23rd NJ Inf, 7-7-1903. Cedar Hill Cemetery, Florence, Burlington County.
JOBES, RICHARD Pvt, E, 6th NJ Inf, 12- -1862. Bordentown/Old St. Mary's Catholic Cemetery, Bordentown, Burlington County.
JOBES*, WILLIAM G. Wagoner, G, 7th NJ Inf, 11-9-1895. Oddfellows Cemetery, Burlington, Burlington County.
JOBLER, JOHN W.H. (see: Tabler, W.H.) Windsor Burial Grounds Cemetery, East Windsor, Mercer County.
JOBS, CHARLES (aka: Jobes, Charles) Pvt, H, 28th U.S. CT, 7-5-1863. White Ridge Cemetery, Eatontown, Monmouth County.
JOBS, ROBERT (JR.) 1-22-1866. White Ridge Cemetery, Eatontown, Monmouth County.

Our Brothers Gone Before

JOCELYN, GEORGE M. (aka: Joslin, George) Pvt, C, 10th NJ Inf, 5-27-1910. Arlington Cemetery, Kearny, Hudson County.

JOERGER*, OTTO (aka: Jorger, Otto) Pvt, A, 39th NJ Inf, 5-22-1906. Woodland Cemetery, Newark, Essex County.

JOHN, AUGUST Pvt, H, 29th NJ Inf, 1-19-1907. Woodlawn Cemetery, Lakewood, Ocean County.

JOHN, EDMUND Pvt, Btty I, 1st CT Heavy Art, 1-29-1913. Arlington Cemetery, Kearny, Hudson County.

JOHN, GOTTLIEB (aka: Gottlieb, John) Pvt, G, 20th NY Inf, 3-10-1878. Woodland Cemetery, Newark, Essex County.

JOHN, MARTIN (see: Jahn, Martin) Arlington Cemetery, Kearny, Hudson County.

JOHN, RICHARD Pvt, I, 33rd NJ Inf, 2-21-1917. Cedar Lawn Cemetery, Paterson, Passaic County.

JOHN II, EDMUND Pvt, Btty I, 1st CT Heavy Art, DoD Unknown. Arlington Cemetery, Kearny, Hudson County.

JOHNDREW, ABRAHAM Corp, C, 2nd NJ Inf, 9-1-1900. St. John's Evangelical Church Cemetery, Orange, Essex County.

JOHNES, ARTHUR Corp, E, 5th NY Inf, [Wounded 6-27-1862 at Gaines' Mill, VA.] 3-27-1880. Weehawken Cemetery, North Bergen, Hudson County.

JOHNS, MARION Pvt, E, 51st AL Cav (CSA), 10-18-1863. Finn's Point National Cemetery, Pennsville, Salem County.

JOHNS, WILLIAM H. Seaman, U.S. Navy, 1-2-1910. Jericho/Oddfellows Cemetery, Deptford, Gloucester County.

JOHNSEY, JAMES T. Pvt, K, 35th GA Inf (CSA), [Captured 7-3-1863 at Gettysburg, PA. Died of smallpox.] 7-11-1864. Finn's Point National Cemetery, Pennsville, Salem County.

JOHNSON, ABRAHAM J. Pvt, D, 9th NJ Inf, 4-23-1928. Kettle Creek Cemetery, Silverton, Ocean County.

JOHNSON, ABRAHAM L. Pvt, C, 32nd U.S. CT, 9-10-1905. Evergreen Cemetery, Morristown, Morris County.

JOHNSON, ABRAHAM W. Pvt, D, 15th NJ Inf, 6-26-1893. Mount Pleasant Cemetery, Newark, Essex County.

JOHNSON, ABRAM Pvt, A, 22nd U.S. CT, 1-21-1910. Mount Moriah Cemetery, Hainesport, Burlington County.

JOHNSON, ABRAM B. Pvt, D, 8th (Wade's) Confederate States Cav (CSA), 10-5-1863. Finn's Point National Cemetery, Pennsville, Salem County.

JOHNSON, ADOLPHUS JAMES (JR.) 1st Cl Boy, U.S. Navy, USS Adela, [Died aboard ship off the coast of Florida.] 11-9-1863. Evergreen Cemetery, Hillside, Union County.

JOHNSON*, ADOLPHUS JAMES (SR.) Col, 8th NJ Inf [Wounded 5-5-1862 at Williamsburg, VA.] 5-29-1893. Evergreen Cemetery, Hillside, Union County.

JOHNSON, ALBERT Pvt, K, 23rd NJ Inf, 2-25-1912. Community Church Cemetery, Leeds Point, Atlantic County.

JOHNSON, ALBERT DoD Unknown. Presbyterian/Methodist-Episcopal Cemetery, Succasunna, Morris County.

JOHNSON, ALBERT WILLIAM Pvt, A, 21st PA Cav, 1-24-1911. Elmwood Cemetery, New Brunswick, Middlesex County.

JOHNSON, ALEXANDER D. Pvt, D, 33rd NJ Inf, 11-24-1911. Fairmount Cemetery, Newark, Essex County.

JOHNSON, ALFRED Pvt, I, 33rd NJ Inf, 12-2-1912. 1st Reformed Church Cemetery, Pompton Plains, Morris County.

JOHNSON, ALFRED Pvt, F, 1st NJ Cav, 1-10-1882. Woodlawn Cemetery, Lakewood, Ocean County.

New Jersey Civil War Burials

JOHNSON, ALFRED Corp, G, 1st NY Eng, 9-17-1877. Methodist-Episcopal Cemetery, Harmony, Monmouth County.
JOHNSON, ALFRED H. Pvt, B, 8th U.S. CT, 3-4-1897. Johnson Cemetery, Camden, Camden County.
JOHNSON, ANDERSON R. 6-1-1876. Rosemont Cemetery, Rosemont, Hunterdon County.
JOHNSON, ANDREW Pvt, I, 35th NJ Inf, 11-24-1882. Fairmount Cemetery, Newark, Essex County.
JOHNSON, ANDREW __, __, __ NY Inf, 2-16-1896. Fairmount Cemetery, Newark, Essex County.
JOHNSON, ANDREW Pvt, I, 22nd U.S. CT, 5-20-1869. Bayview-New York Bay Cemetery, Jersey City, Hudson County.
JOHNSON, ANDREW (JR.) Pvt, F, 7th NJ Inf, 8-8-1883. Mount Pleasant Cemetery, Newark, Essex County.
JOHNSON, ANTHONY Pvt, F, 22nd NJ Inf, 4-27-1868. Cedar Hill Cemetery, Hightstown, Mercer County.
JOHNSON*, ANTHONY I. Pvt, I, 40th NJ Inf, 3-10-1916. Old 1st Methodist Church Cemetery, West Long Branch, Monmouth County.
JOHNSON, ANTHONY S. Pvt, F, 14th NJ Inf, 1887. Masonic Cemetery, Barnegat, Ocean County.
JOHNSON, ARCHARD C. Sgt, I, 1st NJ Cav, 9-16-1891. Riverview Cemetery, Trenton, Mercer County.
JOHNSON, ASHER Pvt, I, 22nd U.S. CT, 10-6-1899. Harlingen Cemetery, Belle Mead, Somerset County.
JOHNSON, BARZILLA Pvt, D, 9th NJ Inf, 1909. Old Baptist Church Cemetery, Manahawkin, Ocean County.
JOHNSON, BENAJAH O. Pvt, B, 12th NJ Inf, 6-4-1911. Silverton Cemetery, Silverton, Ocean County.
JOHNSON, BENJAMIN D. Musc, H, 48th NY Inf, 1930. Old 1st Methodist Church Cemetery, West Long Branch, Monmouth County.
JOHNSON, C.R. Pvt, A, 1st U.S. Inf, DoD Unknown. Fairmount Cemetery, Newark, Essex County.
JOHNSON, CHARLES Pvt, G, 10th NJ Inf, DoD Unknown. Johnson Cemetery, Lower Bank, Burlington County.
JOHNSON, CHARLES Pvt, F, 26th NJ Inf, 4-19-1916. Arlington Cemetery, Kearny, Hudson County.
JOHNSON, CHARLES Corp, I, 31st NJ Inf, DoD Unknown. Sandy Ridge Cemetery, Sandy Ridge, Hunterdon County.
JOHNSON, CHARLES Pvt, G, 14th NJ Inf, 3- -1872. Fairview Cemetery, Fairview, Monmouth County.
JOHNSON, CHARLES Sgt, C, 24th NJ Inf, 10-11-1925. Lutheran Church Cemetery, Friesburg, Salem County.
JOHNSON, CHARLES (see: Burnett, Charles) Arlington Cemetery, Kearny, Hudson County.
JOHNSON*, CHARLES A. Pvt, D, 9th NJ Inf, 1883. Whitelawn Cemetery, Point Pleasant, Ocean County.
JOHNSON, CHARLES F. Pvt, C, 13th NY State Militia, 1911. Atlantic City Cemetery, Pleasantville, Atlantic County.
JOHNSON, CHARLES H. Pvt, I, 29th CT Inf, 4-22-1902. Beverly National Cemetery, Edgewater Park, Burlington County.
JOHNSON, CHARLES H. Corp, E, 11th NJ Inf, 11-11-1919. Fairmount Cemetery, Newark, Essex County.
JOHNSON, CHARLES H. 10-12-1909. Jersey City Cemetery, Jersey City, Hudson County.

Our Brothers Gone Before

JOHNSON, CHARLES H. Pvt, K, 7th NJ Inf, 1916. United Methodist Church Cemetery, Rockaway Valley, Morris County.
JOHNSON, CHARLES L. Pvt, C, 2nd NJ Cav, 2-1-1875. Methodist-Episcopal Cemetery, Vincentown, Burlington County.
JOHNSON, CHARLES P. Pvt, H, 7th NJ Inf, 1905. United Methodist Church Cemetery, Absecon, Atlantic County.
JOHNSON, CHARLES P. Pvt, I, 12th PA Cav, 1-28-1895. Mount Pleasant Cemetery, Millville, Cumberland County.
JOHNSON, CHARLES P. Pvt, Btty F, 1st CT Heavy Art, DoD Unknown. Connecticut Farms Cemetery, Union, Union County.
JOHNSON, CHARLES W. Pvt, D, 13th PA Cav, 8-9-1896. United Methodist Church Cemetery, Almonessen, Gloucester County.
JOHNSON, CHARLES W. Capt, E, 13th NJ Inf, 11-11-1905. Evergreen Cemetery, Hillside, Union County.
JOHNSON, CORNELIUS (aka: Johnson, John) Pvt, K, 1st NY Eng, 1899. Macphelah Cemetery, North Bergen, Hudson County.
JOHNSON, DANIEL Pvt, C, 95th PA Inf, 3-31-1905. Riverview Cemetery, Trenton, Mercer County.
JOHNSON, DAVID A. Pvt, D, 9th NJ Inf, 7-21-1899. Old Baptist Church Cemetery, Manahawkin, Ocean County.
JOHNSON, DAVID C. Pvt, F, 14th NJ Inf, 4-6-1918. Greenville Cemetery, Lakewood, Ocean County.
JOHNSON, DAVID C. Pvt, K, 8th U.S. CT, 1918. Mount Hope United Methodist Church Cemetery, Salem, Salem County.
JOHNSON, DAVID E. Pvt, B, 2nd NJ Inf, 9-12-1923. Rosedale Cemetery, Orange, Essex County.
JOHNSON, DAVID G. Pvt, B, 10th NJ Inf, 1885. Mount Pleasant Cemetery, Millville, Cumberland County.
JOHNSON*, DAVID G. Pvt, A, 26th NJ Inf, 3-4-1900. Riverview Cemetery, Trenton, Mercer County.
JOHNSON, DAVID L. Pvt, A, 27th NJ Inf, 1907. Bevans Church Cemetery, Peters Valley, Sussex County.
JOHNSON, DAVID R. Landsman, U.S. Navy, USS Daiching, 2-21-1928. Atlantic City Cemetery, Pleasantville, Atlantic County.
JOHNSON, DAVID S. Pvt, H, 9th NJ Inf, 8-31-1903. Fairmount Cemetery, Newark, Essex County.
JOHNSON*, EDMUND Capt, E, 68th NY Inf, 8-5-1915. Siloam Cemetery, Vineland, Cumberland County.
JOHNSON*, EDWARD Pvt, F, 8th NJ Inf, 10-13-1867. Bordentown/Old St. Mary's Catholic Cemetery, Bordentown, Burlington County.
JOHNSON, EDWARD 3-20-1882. Riverview Cemetery, Trenton, Mercer County.
JOHNSON, EDWARD B. 1-21-1916. Fairmount Cemetery, Newark, Essex County.
JOHNSON, EDWARD H. Pvt, K, 6th NJ Inf, 5-22-1896. Preakness Reformed Church Cemetery, Wayne, Passaic County.
JOHNSON, EDWIN A.C. 12-6-1865. Berlin Cemetery, Berlin, Camden County.
JOHNSON, ELI M. Pvt, B, 1st NJ Cav, 6-25-1901. St. Paul's Methodist Church Cemetery, Port Republic, Atlantic County.
JOHNSON, ELI P. Pvt, G, 42nd MA Militia, DoD Unknown. Eglington Cemetery, Clarksboro, Gloucester County.
JOHNSON, ELWOOD Pvt, D, 95th PA Inf, 1930. Methodist-Episcopal Church Cemetery, Medford, Burlington County.
JOHNSON, ELWOOD E. Pvt, E, 23rd NJ Inf, 9-23-1922. Evergreen Cemetery, Lumberton, Burlington County.

New Jersey Civil War Burials

JOHNSON, F. Pvt, B, 3rd GA Res Inf (CSA), 4-23-1865. Finn's Point National Cemetery, Pennsville, Salem County.
JOHNSON, FESTUS Pvt, D, 9th U.S. CT, 8-25-1921. Mount Peace Cemetery, Lawnside, Camden County.
JOHNSON, FRANCIS 1892. Presbyterian Church Cemetery, Shrewsbury, Monmouth County.
JOHNSON, FRANK NEWTON Pvt, K, 179th NY Inf, 8-4-1916. Methodist Church Cemetery, Lebanon, Hunterdon County.
JOHNSON, FRANKLIN Landsman, U.S. Navy, USS Resolute, 3-7-1891. Mount Salem Church Cemetery, Fenwick, Salem County.
JOHNSON, FREDERICK Pvt, F, 39th IL Inf, [Died of wounds.] 8-24-1864. Beverly National Cemetery, Edgewater Park, Burlington County.
JOHNSON, FREDERICK T. Hosp Steward, U.S. Army, 10-8-1885. Mount Pleasant Cemetery, Newark, Essex County.
JOHNSON, GARRY Seaman, U.S. Navy, 1-13-1918. Fairmount Cemetery, Newark, Essex County.
JOHNSON, GEORGE Corp, H, 23rd U.S. CT, DoD Unknown. Mount Zion Cemetery, Kresson, Camden County.
JOHNSON, GEORGE Pvt, F, 24th U.S. CT, 7-1-1897. Johnson Cemetery, Camden, Camden County.
JOHNSON, GEORGE Pvt, I, 9th U.S. CT, 3-1-1903. Fairmount Cemetery, Newark, Essex County.
JOHNSON, GEORGE Pvt, D, 40th NJ Inf, 9-25-1915. Bayview-New York Bay Cemetery, Jersey City, Hudson County.
JOHNSON, GEORGE Pvt, H, 29th NJ Inf, 1899. Old Baptist Church Cemetery, Manahawkin, Ocean County.
JOHNSON, GEORGE DoD Unknown. Old 1st Methodist Meeting House Cemetery, Manahawkin, Ocean County.
JOHNSON, GEORGE A. Pvt, E, 37th NJ Inf, 8-23-1905. Fairmount Cemetery, Newark, Essex County.
JOHNSON, GEORGE A. Pvt, B, 26th NJ Inf, 9-10-1913. Mount Pleasant Cemetery, Newark, Essex County.
JOHNSON*, GEORGE F. Sgt, Btty C, 11th U.S. CHA, DoD Unknown. White Ridge Cemetery, Eatontown, Monmouth County.
JOHNSON, GEORGE F. DoD Unknown. Mount Prospect Cemetery, Neptune, Monmouth County.
JOHNSON*, GEORGE H. Landsman, U.S. Navy, USS Cayuga, 10-21-1900. Whitelawn Cemetery, Point Pleasant, Ocean County.
JOHNSON, GEORGE H. (see: Rhodes, George H.) Evergreen Cemetery, Hillside, Union County.
JOHNSON, GEORGE O. Musc, Btty C, 3rd RI Heavy Art, 5-12-1908. Bayview-New York Bay Cemetery, Jersey City, Hudson County.
JOHNSON, GEORGE S. Pvt, F, 6th U.S. CT, 11-4-1910. Riverview Cemetery, Trenton, Mercer County.
JOHNSON, GEORGE W. 4-7-1891. Evergreen Cemetery, Camden, Camden County.
JOHNSON, GEORGE W. Pvt, H, 3rd NJ Inf, [Killed in action at Salem Heights, VA.] 5-3-1863. Mount Pleasant Cemetery, Millville, Cumberland County.
JOHNSON, GEORGE W. 12-14-1917. White Ridge Cemetery, Eatontown, Monmouth County.
JOHNSON, GEORGE W. Pvt, I, 18th VA Inf (CSA), [Captured 7-3-1863 at Gettysburg, PA. Died of disease.] 10-28-1863. Finn's Point National Cemetery, Pennsville, Salem County.
JOHNSON, GILBERT J. Capt, L, 1st NJ Cav, 6-5-1926. Riverview Cemetery, Trenton, Mercer County.

Our Brothers Gone Before

JOHNSON, GILBERT J. 1882. Holy Sepulchre Cemetery, East Orange, Essex County.
JOHNSON, GILBERT S. Pvt, K, 15th NJ Inf, 12-25-1888. Rural Hill Cemetery, Whitehouse, Hunterdon County.
JOHNSON, HART 1915. Sandy Ridge Cemetery, Sandy Ridge, Hunterdon County.
JOHNSON, HENRY Pvt, G, 6th U.S. CT, 4-13-1901. Fairmount Cemetery, Newark, Essex County.
JOHNSON, HENRY Colored Cook, H, 3rd NJ Cav, 1-17-1924. Riverview Cemetery, Trenton, Mercer County.
JOHNSON, HENRY C. Pvt, A, 25th U.S. CT, 5-1-1903. Riverview Cemetery, Trenton, Mercer County.
JOHNSON, HENRY L. Pvt, D, 6th NJ Inf, 10-1-1894. Evergreen Cemetery, Camden, Camden County.
JOHNSON, HENRY P. Pvt, A, 15th NJ Inf, 11-11-1899. New Somerville Cemetery, Somerville, Somerset County.
JOHNSON, ISAAC C. Landsman, U.S. Navy, 5-12-1922. Tennent Church Cemetery, Tennent, Monmouth County.
JOHNSON, ISAAC N. 2nd Cl Boy, U.S. Navy, USS James Adger, 2-23-1923. Greengrove Cemetery, Keyport, Monmouth County.
JOHNSON, ISAAC P. Pvt, I, 24th NJ Inf, 1903. 1st Baptist Cemetery, Cape May Court House, Cape May County.
JOHNSON*, ISAIAH E. 2nd Lt, B, 2nd NJ Inf, 4-20-1889. Mount Pleasant Cemetery, Millville, Cumberland County.
JOHNSON, ISAIAH W. Pvt, K, 34th NJ Inf, 8-4-1865. Fairmount Cemetery, Newark, Essex County.
JOHNSON, IVINS L. 1-5-1907. Woodlawn Cemetery, Lakewood, Ocean County.
JOHNSON, J.D. Pvt, E, 7th GA Militia (CSA), 3-29-1865. Finn's Point National Cemetery, Pennsville, Salem County.
JOHNSON, J.G. DoD Unknown. Old Camden Cemetery, Camden, Camden County.
JOHNSON, J.P. 12-17-1913. Brainerd Cemetery, Cranbury, Middlesex County.
JOHNSON, JACOB Pvt, D, 10th NJ Inf, 5- -1918. Presbyterian Church Cemetery, Cold Spring, Cape May County.
JOHNSON, JACOB Pvt, C, 22nd U.S. CT, 1-24-1909. Arlington Cemetery, Kearny, Hudson County.
JOHNSON, JACOB Pvt, E, 38th NJ Inf, [Wounded in action.] 1935. Mount Hope Presbyterian Cemetery, Lambertville, Hunterdon County.
JOHNSON, JACOB B. Corp, I, 3rd U.S. CT, 3-12-1907. Presbyterian Church Cemetery, Bridgeton, Cumberland County.
JOHNSON, JAMES Pvt, B, 2nd NJ Inf, DoD Unknown. Cedar Hill Cemetery, Florence, Burlington County.
JOHNSON, JAMES Pvt, C, 8th NJ Inf, [Committed suicide at Newark, NJ.] 2-18-1865. Fairmount Cemetery, Newark, Essex County.
JOHNSON, JAMES Pvt, C, 62nd NY Inf, DoD Unknown. St. James Cemetery, Woodbridge, Middlesex County.
JOHNSON, JAMES DoD Unknown. Laurel Grove Cemetery, Totowa, Passaic County.
JOHNSON, JAMES Pvt, D, 15th NJ Inf, [Died of typhoid at Philadelphia, PA.] 7-6-1864. Tranquility Cemetery, Tranquility, Sussex County.
JOHNSON, JAMES (CSA) DoD Unknown. Cedar Grove Cemetery, Gloucester City, Camden County.
JOHNSON, JAMES 1927. Methodist Church Cemetery, Groveville, Mercer County.
JOHNSON, JAMES (aka: Johnson, Joseph) Musc, I, 5th MA Colored Cav, 5-13-1911. Fairmount Cemetery, Newark, Essex County.
JOHNSON, JAMES (see: Craft, William) Arlington Cemetery, Kearny, Hudson County.
JOHNSON, JAMES B. Pvt, D, 23rd NJ Inf, 6-16-1917. Silverton Cemetery, Silverton, Ocean County.

New Jersey Civil War Burials

JOHNSON*, JAMES B. Pvt, D, 9th NJ Inf, DoD Unknown. Old Baptist Church Cemetery, Manahawkin, Ocean County.

JOHNSON, JAMES D. Pvt, K, 11th VA Inf (CSA), [Wounded 12-20-1861 at Dranesville, VA. Wounded and captured 7-3-1863 at Gettysburg, PA. Died of dysentery.] 10-23-1863. Finn's Point National Cemetery, Pennsville, Salem County.

JOHNSON, JAMES H. Landsman, U.S. Navy, USS Juniata, 12-5-1864. Bloomfield Cemetery, Bloomfield, Essex County.

JOHNSON, JAMES H. Pvt, D, 4th U.S. Cav, 8-2-1865. Clinton Cemetery, Irvington, Essex County.

JOHNSON, JAMES H. Pvt, F, 28th NJ Inf, 1-19-1922. Evergreen Cemetery, New Brunswick, Middlesex County.

JOHNSON, JAMES H. Sgt, G, 1st NY Eng, 12-23-1914. Greengrove Cemetery, Keyport, Monmouth County.

JOHNSON, JAMES L. Pvt, Btty L, 13th NY Heavy Art, 6-11-1931. Riverside Cemetery, Toms River, Ocean County.

JOHNSON, JAMES L. Pvt, F, 1st NJ Cav, 2-13-1902. Greenville Cemetery, Lakewood, Ocean County.

JOHNSON, JAMES M. Sgt, I, 22nd U.S. CT, 12-18-1907. Jordan Lawn Cemetery, Pennsauken, Camden County.

JOHNSON, JAMES M. Landsman, U.S. Navy, USS Miami, 2-6-1904. Fairmount Cemetery, Newark, Essex County.

JOHNSON, JAMES M. Corp, B, 39th IL Inf, 1902. Stanhope-Union Cemetery, Netcong, Morris County.

JOHNSON, JAMES M. Pvt, L, 1st NJ Cav, 1924. Walpack Methodist Cemetery, Walpack, Sussex County.

JOHNSON, JAMES MORGAN Pvt, A, 3rd U.S. CT, 4-19-1909. Spencer African Methodist Church Cemetery, Woodstown, Salem County.

JOHNSON, JAMES P. Pvt, A, 47th OH Inf, 3-19-1938. New Camden Cemetery, Camden, Camden County.

JOHNSON, JAMES R. Pvt, C, 3rd NJ Inf, 1898. Berlin Cemetery, Berlin, Camden County.

JOHNSON, JAMES S. Actg Ensign, U.S. Navy, 6-11-1903. Bayview-New York Bay Cemetery, Jersey City, Hudson County.

JOHNSON, JASPER (aka: Johnson, Joseph) Pvt, C, 3rd (Forrest's) TN Cav (CSA), 9-24-1863. Finn's Point National Cemetery, Pennsville, Salem County.

JOHNSON, JASPER W. Corp, C, 43rd U.S. CT, 2-8-1880. Mount Moriah Cemetery, Hainesport, Burlington County.

JOHNSON, JEREMIAH Corp, A, 25th U.S. CT, 1-4-1887. Presbyterian Church Cemetery, Flemington, Hunterdon County.

JOHNSON*, JEREMIAH Pvt, Btty E, 11th U.S. CHA, 2-27-1886. Hamilton Cemetery, Allentown, Monmouth County.

JOHNSON*, JESSE L.B. Pvt, F, 3rd PA Prov Cav, 9-26-1892. Riverview Cemetery, Trenton, Mercer County.

JOHNSON, JOB J. Sgt, B, 2nd NJ Inf, 1923. Locust Hill Cemetery, Dover, Morris County.

JOHNSON, JOHN (CSA) DoD Unknown. Cedar Grove Cemetery, Gloucester City, Camden County.

JOHNSON, JOHN Pvt, G, 9th NJ Inf, 4-15-1902. Atlantic City Cemetery, Pleasantville, Atlantic County.

JOHNSON, JOHN Pvt, B, 6th U.S. CT, 4-10-1896. Timbuctoo Cemetery, Timbuctoo, Burlington County.

JOHNSON, JOHN Corp, A, 22nd U.S. CT, 5-1-1892. Fairmount Cemetery, Newark, Essex County.

Our Brothers Gone Before

JOHNSON, JOHN Pvt, L, 5th MA Colored Cav, 12-11-1911. Fairmount Cemetery, Newark, Essex County.
JOHNSON, JOHN Corp, B, 27th NJ Inf, 8-8-1903. Little Valley Cemetery, Middle Valley, Morris County.
JOHNSON, JOHN Pvt, F, 22nd U.S. CT, [Died at (New) Providence, NJ.] 2-7-1864. Presbyterian Church Cemetery, New Providence, Union County.
JOHNSON, JOHN (see: Johnson, Cornelius) Macphelah Cemetery, North Bergen, Hudson County.
JOHNSON, JOHN C. 1907. Cedar Ridge Cemetery, Blairstown, Warren County.
JOHNSON, JOHN C. Pvt, A, 1st NJ Cav, 11-17-1875. Mount Pleasant Cemetery, Newark, Essex County.
JOHNSON, JOHN D. Lt Col, 10th NJ Inf 12- -1875. Mount Holly Cemetery, Mount Holly, Burlington County.
JOHNSON, JOHN E. Landsman, U.S. Navy, USS St. Lawrence, 8-4-1883. Alpine Cemetery, Perth Amboy, Middlesex County.
JOHNSON*, JOHN H. Pvt, H, 2nd NJ Inf, 3-13-1907. St. Paul's Methodist Church Cemetery, Port Republic, Atlantic County.
JOHNSON, JOHN H. Pvt, G, 38th NJ Inf, 1-13-1918. Old Bethel Cemetery, Plainsboro, Middlesex County.
JOHNSON, JOHN H. Pvt, H, 5th NJ Inf, [Killed in action at Gettysburg, PA.] 7-3-1863. Rahway Cemetery, Rahway, Union County.
JOHNSON, JOHN H. Landsman, U.S. Navy, USS Dakota, 6-30-1897. Bloomfield Cemetery, Bloomfield, Essex County.
JOHNSON, JOHN J. Pvt, K, 15th NJ Inf, 4-30-1880. Deckertown-Union Cemetery, Papakating, Sussex County.
JOHNSON, JOHN P. Pvt, Btty A, 1st U.S. Art, 7-28-1889. Peter Young Farm Cemetery, Montgomery, Somerset County.
JOHNSON, JOHN QUINCY ADAMS Pvt, K, 42nd MS Inf (CSA), 10-3-1863. Finn's Point National Cemetery, Pennsville, Salem County.
JOHNSON, JOHN S. Pvt, D, 29th NJ Inf, 3-24-1911. Greengrove Cemetery, Keyport, Monmouth County.
JOHNSON, JOHN S. Musc, I, 39th IL Inf, 1-28-1917. Arlington Cemetery, Kearny, Hudson County.
JOHNSON, JOHN T. Pvt, D, 6th NJ Inf, 6-16-1914. Cedar Grove Cemetery, Gloucester City, Camden County.
JOHNSON, JOHN V. Corp, B, 27th NJ Inf, 12-22-1901. Rural Hill Cemetery, Whitehouse, Hunterdon County.
JOHNSON, JOHN W. Pvt, G, 10th NJ Inf, 4-26-1886. Cedar Hill Cemetery, Hightstown, Mercer County.
JOHNSON, JOHN W. Gunner, (CSA) [At Wilmington, NC.] 8-13-1929. Bayview-New York Bay Cemetery, Jersey City, Hudson County.
JOHNSON, JONATHAN E. Pvt, D, 9th NJ Inf, [Died of diarrhea at Fort Monroe, VA.] 8-29-1864. Kettle Creek Cemetery, Silverton, Ocean County.
JOHNSON, JOSEPH 1874. Mount Hope Presbyterian Cemetery, Lambertville, Hunterdon County.
JOHNSON, JOSEPH Pvt, K, 15th NJ Inf, [Died of typhoid at Baltimore, MD.] 12-8-1864. Reformed Church Cemetery, Readington, Hunterdon County.
JOHNSON, JOSEPH Pvt, G, 38th NJ Inf, 12-7-1915. Methodist Church Cemetery, Titusville, Mercer County.
JOHNSON, JOSEPH Pvt, M, 2nd NJ Cav, DoD Unknown. Greenwood Cemetery, Lakewood, Ocean County.
JOHNSON, JOSEPH (see: Johnson, James) Fairmount Cemetery, Newark, Essex County.

New Jersey Civil War Burials

JOHNSON, JOSEPH (see: Johnson, Jasper) Finn's Point National Cemetery, Pennsville, Salem County.

JOHNSON, JOSEPH B. Pvt, H, 29th NJ Inf, 1890. United Methodist Church Cemetery, Wayside, Monmouth County.

JOHNSON, JOSEPH C. Pvt, E, 11th NJ Inf, 1-26-1909. 1st United Methodist Church Cemetery, Bridgeton, Cumberland County.

JOHNSON, JOSEPH C. Pvt, E, 26th NJ Inf, 12-21-1872. Fairmount Cemetery, Newark, Essex County.

JOHNSON, JOSEPH E. 1916. Greenville Cemetery, Lakewood, Ocean County.

JOHNSON, JOSEPH H. Pvt, K, 2nd NJ Cav, 3-16-1886. Greenville Cemetery, Lakewood, Ocean County.

JOHNSON, JOSEPH H. Sgt, G, 14th NJ Inf, [Wounded 4-22-1864 at Fishers Hill, VA. and 5-12-1864 at Spotsylvania CH, VA.] 2-20-1903. Greengrove Cemetery, Keyport, Monmouth County.

JOHNSON, JOSEPH H. 2nd Lt, H, 7th NJ Inf, [Killed in action at Williamsburg, VA.] 5-5-1862. Union Cemetery, Mantua, Gloucester County.

JOHNSON, JOSEPH N. 5-22-1907. Friends Cemetery, Mansfield, Burlington County.

JOHNSON, JOSEPH S. 10-21-1923. Yellow Meeting House Cemetery, Imlaytown, Monmouth County.

JOHNSON, JOSHUA G. Mate, U.S. Navy, USS Augusta, 10-29-1896. Riverview Cemetery, Trenton, Mercer County.

JOHNSON, LARRY Landsman, U.S. Navy, 1-3-1918. Fairmount Cemetery, Newark, Essex County.

JOHNSON, LEMUEL P. Landsman, U.S. Navy, DoD Unknown. Presbyterian Church Cemetery, Bridgeton, Cumberland County.

JOHNSON, LEVI E. Pvt, A, 7th NJ Inf, 5-15-1912. Presbyterian Church Cemetery, Cold Spring, Cape May County.

JOHNSON, LEWIS Pvt, I, 2nd MA Inf, [Wounded 3-16-1865 at Averysboro, NC.] 6-30-1880. Bayview-New York Bay Cemetery, Jersey City, Hudson County.

JOHNSON, LEWIS DoD Unknown. Van Liew Cemetery, North Brunswick, Middlesex County.

JOHNSON, LOUIS Pvt, I, 27th NJ Inf, 3-25-1912. Mount Pleasant Cemetery, Newark, Essex County.

JOHNSON, LUTHER Pvt, C, 4th VT Inf, 8-11-1906. Fairmount Cemetery, Newark, Essex County.

JOHNSON, LUTHER H. Pvt, Btty D, 1st NJ Light Art, 7-24-1897. Mount Pleasant Cemetery, Newark, Essex County.

JOHNSON, MAHLON G. Pvt, E, 3rd NJ Cav, 2-20-1922. Branchville Cemetery, Branchville, Sussex County.

JOHNSON, MANUEL Corp, C, 15th NJ Inf, 12-29-1929. Evergreen Cemetery, Morristown, Morris County.

JOHNSON, MARSHALL H. Musc, 8th NJ Inf Band 1929. New Somerville Cemetery, Somerville, Somerset County.

JOHNSON*, MARTIN Pvt, H, 98th PA Inf, 5-9-1896. Riverview Cemetery, Trenton, Mercer County.

JOHNSON, MARTIN Pvt, H, 30th NJ Inf, 7-2-1904. Fairview Cemetery, Westfield, Union County.

JOHNSON, MATTHIAS Pvt, I, 28th NJ Inf, [Wounded 12-13-1862 at Fredericksburg, VA.] DoD Unknown. Alpine Cemetery, Perth Amboy, Middlesex County.

JOHNSON, MICHAEL Seaman, U.S. Navy, DoD Unknown. Mount Pleasant Cemetery, Millville, Cumberland County.

JOHNSON, MICHAEL H. 2nd Lt, I, 37th NJ Inf, 6-14-1918. Baptist/St. Andrew's Cemetery, Mount Holly, Burlington County.

Our Brothers Gone Before

JOHNSON, MOSES W. Pvt, Btty D, 1st NJ Light Art, 2-3-1879. Fairmount Cemetery, Newark, Essex County.

JOHNSON, NATHAN G. Pvt, H, 37th NJ Inf, 1923. Methodist Church Cemetery, Pemberton, Burlington County.

JOHNSON*, NICHOLAS Pvt, G, 15th NJ Inf, 8-3-1892. Union Methodist Church Cemetery, Center Square, Gloucester County.

JOHNSON, OLIVER H. Pvt, D, 31st NJ Inf, 1925. Amwell Ridge Cemetery, Larisons Corner, Hunterdon County.

JOHNSON, OLIVER SPENCER Capt, B, 8th NJ Inf, 11-8-1876. Mount Pleasant Cemetery, Newark, Essex County.

JOHNSON, OTTO B. Master-at-Arms, U.S. Navy, DoD Unknown. East Ridgelawn Cemetery, Clifton, Passaic County.

JOHNSON, PARENT Corp, E, 29th NJ Inf, 2-8-1898. Maplewood Cemetery, Freehold, Monmouth County.

JOHNSON, PATRICK 10-19-1909. Evergreen Cemetery, Morristown, Morris County.

JOHNSON, PETER Pvt, H, 29th NJ Inf, 2-11-1926. Riverside Cemetery, Toms River, Ocean County.

JOHNSON, PETER P. Pvt, K, 31st NJ Inf, 10-3-1879. Fountain Grove Cemetery, Glen Gardner, Hunterdon County.

JOHNSON*, PETER V. Pvt, Unassigned, 33rd NJ Inf, 3-12-1880. Fountain Grove Cemetery, Glen Gardner, Hunterdon County.

JOHNSON, PHILIP J. (see: Rice, Philip J.) Bayview-New York Bay Cemetery, Jersey City, Hudson County.

JOHNSON, PIERSON Pvt, B, 7th NJ Inf, 12-5-1904. Presbyterian/Methodist-Episcopal Cemetery, Succasunna, Morris County.

JOHNSON, PLEASANT M. Pvt, I, 3rd AR Inf (CSA), [Captured 7-2-1863 at Gettysburg, PA. Died of chronic bronchitis.] 8-14-1863. Finn's Point National Cemetery, Pennsville, Salem County.

JOHNSON, REUBEN Pvt, H, 29th NJ Inf, 1894. Old 1st Methodist Church Cemetery, West Long Branch, Monmouth County.

JOHNSON, RICHARD Pvt, A, 3rd U.S. CT, 8-14-1906. Atlantic City Cemetery, Pleasantville, Atlantic County.

JOHNSON, RICHARD Pvt, B, 12th NJ Inf, 5-2-1928. Greenwood Cemetery, Pleasantville, Atlantic County.

JOHNSON, RICHARD Pvt, K, 10th NJ Inf, 11-12-1915. Bordentown/Old St. Mary's Catholic Cemetery, Bordentown, Burlington County.

JOHNSON, RICHARD Pvt, A, 111th PA Inf, 7-10-1903. Woodland Cemetery, Newark, Essex County.

JOHNSON, RILEY Pvt, E, 28th NJ Inf, 5-5-1924. Whitelawn Cemetery, Point Pleasant, Ocean County.

JOHNSON, ROBERT Pvt, M, 2nd OH Cav, 3-6-1926. New Camden Cemetery, Camden, Camden County.

JOHNSON, ROBERT Pvt, G, 39th NJ Inf, 1-8-1919. Fairmount Cemetery, Newark, Essex County.

JOHNSON, ROBERT Pvt, D, 38th NJ Inf, 6-29-1904. Greenwood Cemetery, Hamilton, Mercer County.

JOHNSON, ROBERT DoD Unknown. Johnson Cemetery, Camden, Camden County.

JOHNSON*, ROBERT A. 2nd Lt, K, 47th NY Inf, 10-20-1914. Fairview Cemetery, Fairview, Monmouth County.

JOHNSON, ROBERT CARNEY Col, 12th NJ Inf 3-25-1881. St. John's Episcopal Church Cemetery, Salem, Salem County.

JOHNSON, ROLAND Pvt, D, 9th (Malone's) AL Cav (CSA), 8-24-1863. Finn's Point National Cemetery, Pennsville, Salem County.

New Jersey Civil War Burials

JOHNSON, RUSSELL C. Pvt, C, 14th NJ Inf, 1916. Mount Pleasant Cemetery, Newark, Essex County.
JOHNSON*, SAMUEL Sgt, K, 6th NC Cav (CSA), [Captured 8-6-1863.] 4-12-1865. Finn's Point National Cemetery, Pennsville, Salem County.
JOHNSON, SAMUEL Pvt, C, 23rd NJ Inf, [Died of consumption at Philadelphia, PA.] 11-11-1862. Baptist/St. Andrew's Cemetery, Mount Holly, Burlington County.
JOHNSON, SAMUEL 1870. Sandy Ridge Cemetery, Sandy Ridge, Hunterdon County.
JOHNSON, SAMUEL Pvt, F, 7th NJ Inf, 5-11-1870. Old Presbyterian Church Cemetery, Daretown, Salem County.
JOHNSON, SAMUEL T. 1916. Manahath Cemetery, Glassboro, Gloucester County.
JOHNSON*, SILAS D. Corp, Btty F, 11th U.S. CHA, 8-16-1915. Bayview-New York Bay Cemetery, Jersey City, Hudson County.
JOHNSON, SIMON Pvt, B, 41st U.S. CT, 10-14-1888. Bethel AME Cemetery, Freehold, Monmouth County.
JOHNSON, SPOTTSWOOD P. Pvt, F, 23rd VA Inf (CSA), [Captured 7-2-1863 at Gettysburg, PA.] 1-19-1864. Finn's Point National Cemetery, Pennsville, Salem County.
JOHNSON, STEPHEN 1st Sgt, G, 25th U.S. CT, DoD Unknown. Bethel AME Cemetery, Freehold, Monmouth County.
JOHNSON*, STEPHEN B. Corp, K, 3rd NY Inf, 7-21-1892. Pequest Union Cemetery, Great Meadows, Warren County.
JOHNSON, STEPHEN DESBRO Pvt, C, 11th NJ Inf, 4-13-1919. Overlook Cemetery, Bridgeton, Cumberland County.
JOHNSON, STEPHEN M. Pvt, A, 12th U.S. Inf, 10-7-1867. Fairmount Cemetery, Newark, Essex County.
JOHNSON, STEPHEN S. 8-18-1898. Palmer-Wood Cemetery, Keansburg, Monmouth County.
JOHNSON, THEODORE Pvt, I, 14th NJ Inf, 1879. Christ Church Cemetery, Morgan, Middlesex County.
JOHNSON, THOMAS Pvt, H, 29th NJ Inf, 10-31-1928. Riverside Cemetery, Toms River, Ocean County.
JOHNSON, THOMAS Pvt, H, 127th U.S. CT, 6-13-1895. Woodland Cemetery, Newark, Essex County.
JOHNSON, THOMAS CARR Pvt, C, 24th NJ Inf, 1901. Sandy Ridge Cemetery, Sandy Ridge, Hunterdon County.
JOHNSON, THOMAS P. Pvt, D, 9th NJ Inf, [Died of congestive fever at Fort Monroe, VA.] 4-7-1864. Kettle Creek Cemetery, Silverton, Ocean County.
JOHNSON, THOMAS SAMUEL Pvt, D, 1st DE Cav, 1910. Trinity Bible Church Cemetery, Glassboro, Gloucester County.
JOHNSON, TIMOTHY Pvt, F, 20th U.S. CT, 3-31-1919. Jacob's Chapel AME Church Cemetery, Colemantown, Burlington County.
JOHNSON, TUNIS D. 1st Sgt, E, 15th NJ Inf, [Died at Baltimore, MD. of wounds received 10-19-1864 at Cedar Creek, VA.] 11-19-1864. Rural Hill Cemetery, Whitehouse, Hunterdon County.
JOHNSON, W.H.H. Pvt, I, 31st MS Inf (CSA), 6-27-1863. Finn's Point National Cemetery, Pennsville, Salem County.
JOHNSON, W.T. Sgt, D, 51st AL Cav (CSA), 10-5-1863. Finn's Point National Cemetery, Pennsville, Salem County.
JOHNSON, WESLEY H. Landsman, U.S. Navy, USS Ohio, 5-24-1904. Riverview Cemetery, Trenton, Mercer County.
JOHNSON, WESLEY H. (SR.) Landsman, U.S. Navy, USS Ohio, 1-21-1890. Phillipsburg Cemetery, Phillipsburg, Warren County.
JOHNSON, WILLIAM Eng, U.S. Navy, USS Emma, 9-20-1912. Holy Name Cemetery, Jersey City, Hudson County.

Our Brothers Gone Before

JOHNSON, WILLIAM 1st Sgt, F, 47th NY Inf, 8-19-1912. Riverview Cemetery, Trenton, Mercer County.
JOHNSON, WILLIAM Pvt, I, 2nd NJ Inf, [Wounded in action.] 8-3-1911. Greenwood Cemetery, Boonton, Morris County.
JOHNSON, WILLIAM Pvt, A, 41st U.S. CT, 2-27-1866. Methodist Cemetery, Cassville, Ocean County.
JOHNSON, WILLIAM DoD Unknown. Finn's Point National Cemetery, Pennsville, Salem County.
JOHNSON, WILLIAM Landsman, U.S. Navy, USS Maryland, 10-22-1919. Holy Name Cemetery, Jersey City, Hudson County.
JOHNSON, WILLIAM (see: Jonsen, William) Hillside Cemetery, Lyndhurst, Bergen County.
JOHNSON, WILLIAM (see: Waldrip, William T.) Fairmount Cemetery, Newark, Essex County.
JOHNSON, WILLIAM (see: Johnston, William D.) Baptist Church Cemetery, Scotch Plains, Union County.
JOHNSON*, WILLIAM A. Pvt, I, 2nd NJ Cav, 1921. Emleys Hill United Methodist Church Cemetery, Upper Freehold, Monmouth County.
JOHNSON, WILLIAM ALFRED Pvt, H, 23rd NJ Inf, 1-5-1911. Elmwood Cemetery, New Brunswick, Middlesex County.
JOHNSON, WILLIAM C. Pvt, H, 40th NY Inf, 8-11-1901. Fairmount Cemetery, Newark, Essex County.
JOHNSON, WILLIAM D. 1st Sgt, E, 31st NJ Inf, 8-10-1863. Maple Grove Cemetery, Hackensack, Bergen County.
JOHNSON, WILLIAM H. 8-21-1908. Greenwood Cemetery, Pleasantville, Atlantic County.
JOHNSON, WILLIAM H. Pvt, K, 45th PA Inf, [Wounded in action.] 8-20-1925. Monument Cemetery, Edgewater Park, Burlington County.
JOHNSON, WILLIAM H. Pvt, I, 1st NJ Inf, 12-31-1912. Arlington Cemetery, Kearny, Hudson County.
JOHNSON, WILLIAM H. Pvt, B, 12th NJ Inf, 3-6-1868. Fairview Cemetery, Fairview, Monmouth County.
JOHNSON, WILLIAM H. Pvt, D, 25th U.S. CT, DoD Unknown. Mount Salem Church Cemetery, Fenwick, Salem County.
JOHNSON, WILLIAM H. Pvt, Carter's Btty, VA Light Art (CSA), 11-4-1864. Finn's Point National Cemetery, Pennsville, Salem County.
JOHNSON, WILLIAM H. Pvt, E, 34th NJ Inf, 1-9-1874. Locust Hill Cemetery, Trenton, Mercer County.
JOHNSON*, WILLIAM J. Sgt, D, 40th NJ Inf, 3-29-1922. Baptist/St. Andrew's Cemetery, Mount Holly, Burlington County.
JOHNSON, WILLIAM J. Pvt, F, 14th NJ Inf, 7-10-1893. Woodlawn Cemetery, Lakewood, Ocean County.
JOHNSON, WILLIAM J. Pvt, F, 1st NJ Cav, 8-22-1888. Greenville Cemetery, Lakewood, Ocean County.
JOHNSON*, WILLIAM J. Pvt, K, 22nd NJ Inf, 5-20-1910. Brookside Cemetery, Englewood, Bergen County.
JOHNSON, WILLIAM L. (aka: Johnston, William L.) Pvt, Btty A, 3rd PA Heavy Art, 1911. Presbyterian Church Cemetery, Kingston, Somerset County.
JOHNSON, WILLIAM M. Pvt, C, 9th NJ Inf, 1-27-1918. Harleigh Cemetery, Camden, Camden County.
JOHNSON, WILLIAM N. Musc, H, 12th NJ Inf, 7-20-1911. Presbyterian Church Cemetery, Upper Deerfield, Cumberland County.
JOHNSON*, WILLIAM O. Pvt, H, 4th NJ Inf, 1-25-1900. Mount Pleasant Cemetery, Millville, Cumberland County.

New Jersey Civil War Burials

JOHNSON, WILLIAM P. Pvt, E, 15th PA Cav, 11-21-1900. Riverview Cemetery, Trenton, Mercer County.
JOHNSON, WILLIAM T. Pvt, D, 9th NJ Inf, 3-25-1910. Greenville Cemetery, Lakewood, Ocean County.
JOHNSON, WILLIAM T.H. Pvt, A, 45th U.S. CT, 1916. Bordentown/Old St. Mary's Catholic Cemetery, Bordentown, Burlington County.
JOHNSON, WILLIAM Y. Pvt, A, 3rd NJ Cav, 5-13-1915. Baptist Cemetery, Hopewell Boro, Mercer County.
JOHNSTON, ABRAHAM V. 4-22-1887. Methodist-Episcopal Cemetery, Glendola, Monmouth County.
JOHNSTON, ANDREW Pvt, C, 2nd NJ Inf, 11-10-1875. St. John's Evangelical Church Cemetery, Orange, Essex County.
JOHNSTON, ANDREW Capt, A, 29th PA Inf, 1-25-1923. Mount Holly Cemetery, Mount Holly, Burlington County.
JOHNSTON, ARTHUR 2-14-1881. Rosedale Cemetery, Orange, Essex County.
JOHNSTON, BAYARD S. Pvt, F, 21st NJ Inf, 10-16-1925. Arlington Cemetery, Kearny, Hudson County.
JOHNSTON, BENJAMIN S. 1st Lt, H, 21st NJ Inf, 2-4-1882. Lawrenceville Cemetery, Lawrenceville, Mercer County.
JOHNSTON, CHARLES Pvt, D, 1st NJ Militia, 8-29-1900. Fairmount Cemetery, Newark, Essex County.
JOHNSTON, DAVID Seaman, U.S. Navy, 4-13-1901. Bayview-New York Bay Cemetery, Jersey City, Hudson County.
JOHNSTON, EDWARD Corp, G, 84th NY National Guard, 2-17-1921. Fairmount Cemetery, Newark, Essex County.
JOHNSTON, ELISHA Pvt, G, 4th NJ Inf, 6-4-1885. St. Paul's Methodist Church Cemetery, Port Republic, Atlantic County.
JOHNSTON, ENOCH L. Pvt, A, 3rd NJ Inf, DoD Unknown. Union Cemetery, Mantua, Gloucester County.
JOHNSTON, JAMES H. Pvt, B, 139th NY Inf, 12-25-1908. Arlington Cemetery, Kearny, Hudson County.
JOHNSTON, JESSE Pvt, A, 3rd (Forrest's) TN Cav (CSA), 7-3-1863. Finn's Point National Cemetery, Pennsville, Salem County.
JOHNSTON*, JOSEPH Pvt, A, 33rd NJ Inf, 1917. Lakewood-Hope Cemetery, Lakewood, Ocean County.
JOHNSTON, ROBERT H. Pvt, A, 33rd NJ Inf, DoD Unknown. Bayview-New York Bay Cemetery, Jersey City, Hudson County.
JOHNSTON, ROBERT S. Capt, B, 4th NJ Inf, 3-12-1909. Presbyterian Church Cemetery, Ewing, Mercer County.
JOHNSTON, ROBERT S. Pvt, H, 8th PA Cav, 9-28-1919. St. Peter's Cemetery, New Brunswick, Middlesex County.
JOHNSTON, W.W. Pvt, K, 44th NC Inf (CSA), [Captured 4-2-1865 at Petersburg, VA. Died of lung inflammation.] 6-5-1865. Finn's Point National Cemetery, Pennsville, Salem County.
JOHNSTON, WILLIAM Pvt, H, 32nd U.S. CT, 8-21-1907. Riverview Cemetery, Trenton, Mercer County.
JOHNSTON, WILLIAM Pvt, F, 2nd NJ Inf, 2-1-1927. Minisink Reformed Church Cemetery, Montague, Sussex County.
JOHNSTON, WILLIAM Landsman, U.S. Navy, 4-30-1915. Riverview Cemetery, Trenton, Mercer County.
JOHNSTON, WILLIAM 3-30-1891. AME Cemetery, Pennington, Mercer County.
JOHNSTON, WILLIAM D. (aka: Johnson, William) Pvt, Btty C, 6th NY Heavy Art, 5-22-1908. Baptist Church Cemetery, Scotch Plains, Union County.

Our Brothers Gone Before

JOHNSTON, WILLIAM L. (see: Johnson, William L.) Presbyterian Church Cemetery, Kingston, Somerset County.
JOHNSTON, ZACHARIAH A. Pvt, E, 11th NJ Inf, 10-31-1869. Osbornville Protestant Church Cemetery, Breton Woods, Ocean County.
JOINER, ANDREW E. 1-3-1919. Mount Hope Presbyterian Cemetery, Lambertville, Hunterdon County.
JOINER*, BENJAMIN H. Pvt, E, 11th NJ Inf, 12-19-1906. Mount Hope Presbyterian Cemetery, Lambertville, Hunterdon County.
JOINER, FRANK S. Pvt, B, 38th NJ Inf, 1932. Belvidere/Catholic Cemetery, Belvidere, Warren County.
JOINER, MOSES Pvt, I, 25th U.S. CT, 10-17-1923. Mount Peace Cemetery, Lawnside, Camden County.
JOLINE*, BORDEN G. Sgt, G, 1st NJ Cav, 1864. Old 1st Methodist Church Cemetery, West Long Branch, Monmouth County.
JOLINE, DANIEL 1890. Presbyterian Church Cemetery, Metuchen, Middlesex County.
JOLINE, JOHN WESLEY Corp, I, 11th NJ Inf, [Cenotaph. Died of wounds received 7-2-1863 at Gettysburg, PA.] 8-17-1863. Old 1st Methodist Church Cemetery, West Long Branch, Monmouth County.
JOLINE, THEODORE Pvt, F, 3rd NJ Militia, 7-23-1914. Glenwood Cemetery, West Long Branch, Monmouth County.
JOLINE, WILLIAM Pvt, A, 192nd PA Inf, 8-16-1916. Soldier's Home Cemetery, Vineland, Cumberland County.
JOLLEY, EDWARD S. Sgt, A, 7th NJ Inf, DoD Unknown. Evergreen Cemetery, Morristown, Morris County.
JOLLY, JOHN Pvt, K, 29th NJ Inf, DoD Unknown. Ardena Baptist Church Cemetery, Adelphia, Monmouth County.
JOLLY, ROBERT L. Pvt, K, 7th NJ Inf, [Died of wounds received 7-2-1863 at Gettysburg, PA.] 7-22-1863. Evergreen Cemetery, Morristown, Morris County.
JONES, A.G. Seaman, U.S. Navy, 9-16-1878. Rahway Cemetery, Rahway, Union County.
JONES, ABNER W. Pvt, D, 9th GA Inf (CSA), [Captured 7-2-1863 at Gettysburg, PA.] 12-5-1863. Finn's Point National Cemetery, Pennsville, Salem County.
JONES, ABRAM Pvt, D, 24th NJ Inf, 5-11-1897. United Methodist Church Cemetery, Cross Keys, Gloucester County.
JONES, ABRAM W. Pvt, E, 23rd NJ Inf, 3-15-1893. Fairmount Cemetery, Newark, Essex County.
JONES, ALBERT B. Corp, G, 24th NJ Inf, [Died of wounds received 12-13-1862 at Fredericksburg, VA.] 12-22-1862. Old Stone Church Cemetery, Fairton, Cumberland County.
JONES, ALFRED Corp, F, 12th NJ Inf, 9-7-1888. Methodist Episcopal/Methodist Protestant Cemetery, Bridgeport, Gloucester County.
JONES, ALFRED M. 2nd Lt, B, 78th U.S. CT, 5-12-1930. Fairmount Cemetery, Chatham, Morris County.
JONES, ALFRED P. DoD Unknown. Hackensack Cemetery, Hackensack, Bergen County.
JONES, ALGE Blacksmith, __, __ U.S. CT, DoD Unknown. Mount Prospect Cemetery, Neptune, Monmouth County.
JONES, ALPHONSO A. Pvt, F, 25th NJ Inf, 10-20-1911. Mount Pleasant Cemetery, Millville, Cumberland County.
JONES, BENEDICT Pvt, E, 21st NJ Inf, 1893. Windsor Burial Grounds Cemetery, East Windsor, Mercer County.
JONES, BENJAMIN Pvt, C, 10th NJ Inf, 1898. Methodist Church Cemetery, Pemberton, Burlington County.
JONES, BENJAMIN Pvt, G, 28th NJ Inf, 6-18-1899. Methodist Episcopal/Methodist Protestant Cemetery, Bridgeport, Gloucester County.

New Jersey Civil War Burials

JONES, BENJAMIN F. Sgt, E, 4th NJ Inf, 1-24-1901. Evergreen Cemetery, Camden, Camden County.

JONES, BERRYMAN E. Pvt, E, 43rd GA Inf (CSA), [Captured 5-16-1863 at Baker's Creek, MS.] 6-27-1863. Finn's Point National Cemetery, Pennsville, Salem County.

JONES, CASPER (JR.) Corp, D, 11th NJ Inf, 1-9-1918. Union Cemetery, Washington, Morris County.

JONES*, CATO Pvt, Btty B, 11th U.S. CHA, 2-18-1927. Jordan Lawn Cemetery, Pennsauken, Camden County.

JONES*, CHARLES Pvt, D, 40th NY Inf, [Wounded 12-13-1862 at Fredericksburg, VA.] 7-3-1917. Osage Cemetery, East Brunswick, Middlesex County.

JONES*, CHARLES D. Pvt, B, 40th NJ Inf, 5-20-1934. Greenwood Cemetery, Hamilton, Mercer County.

JONES, CHARLES F. 6-27-1925. Cedar Grove Cemetery, Waretown, Ocean County.

JONES, CHARLES H. Pvt, H, 100th PA Inf, 3-29-1922. Evergreen Cemetery, Camden, Camden County.

JONES, CHARLES H. Corp, E, 25th U.S. CT, 5-14-1895. Johnson Cemetery, Camden, Camden County.

JONES, CHARLES H. 1st Sgt, K, 132nd NY Inf, 2-13-1892. Bayview-New York Bay Cemetery, Jersey City, Hudson County.

JONES, CHARLES S. Pvt, A, 7th PA Cav, 2-6-1916. Eglington Cemetery, Clarksboro, Gloucester County.

JONES, CHARLES S. Pvt, G, 1st NJ Cav, 4-18-1865. Presbyterian Church Cemetery, Ewing, Mercer County.

JONES, CORNELIUS Pvt, A, 28th US CT, 6-20-1909. Oddfellows Cemetery, Burlington, Burlington County.

JONES, CORNELIUS C. Sgt, K, 132nd NY Inf, DoD Unknown. Alpine Cemetery, Perth Amboy, Middlesex County.

JONES, CORNELIUS S. Pvt, D, 10th NY Inf, 4-10-1903. Fairmount Cemetery, Newark, Essex County.

JONES, DANIEL A. Pvt, I, 38th NJ Inf, 4-28-1926. Methodist Church Cemetery, Titusville, Mercer County.

JONES, DAVID Pvt, C, 127th U.S. CT, 11-2-1911. White Ridge Cemetery, Eatontown, Monmouth County.

JONES, DAVID S. Pvt, F, 23rd NJ Inf, 3-13-1911. Brotherhood Cemetery, Hainesport, Burlington County.

JONES, DAVID S.K. 1-28-1927. Macphelah Cemetery, North Bergen, Hudson County.

JONES, DAVID W. Pvt, A, 31st NJ Inf, 1887. Presbyterian Church Cemetery, Califon, Hunterdon County.

JONES, DUNCAN Pvt, F, 2nd U.S. Colored Cav, 8-27-1915. Rosedale Cemetery, Orange, Essex County.

JONES, E. Pvt, G, 5th MO Cav (CSA), 5-13-1864. Finn's Point National Cemetery, Pennsville, Salem County.

JONES, E.M. Pvt, D, 71st PA Inf, DoD Unknown. St. Stephens Episcopal Church Cemetery, Mullica Hill, Gloucester County.

JONES, EDWARD D. Pvt, I, 21st NJ Inf, 8-7-1892. Bayview-New York Bay Cemetery, Jersey City, Hudson County.

JONES, EDWARD F. Seaman, U.S. Navy, 7-3-1901. Fairmount Cemetery, Newark, Essex County.

JONES, EDWARD J. Seaman, U.S. Navy, USS Brooklyn, 1891. Evergreen Cemetery, Hillside, Union County.

JONES, ELLIOTTE POPE Col, 109th VA Militia (CSA) 7-10-1864. Finn's Point National Cemetery, Pennsville, Salem County.

Our Brothers Gone Before

JONES, ENOCH Pvt, C, 5th PA Cav, 2-17-1915. Riverview Cemetery, Trenton, Mercer County.
JONES, ENOCH Pvt, F, 2nd NJ Cav, 1870. Cedar Grove Methodist Church Cemetery, Toms River, Ocean County.
JONES, EVAN C. Artificer, K, 1st NY Eng, 9-24-1910. Laurel Grove Cemetery, Totowa, Passaic County.
JONES, EZEKIEL C. Pvt, I, 3rd U.S. CT, 5-9-1901. Oak Hill Cemetery, Vineland, Cumberland County.
JONES, FRANCIS Pvt, A, 34th NJ Inf, DoD Unknown. Fairmount Cemetery, Newark, Essex County.
JONES, FRANK Pvt, D, 39th NJ Inf, 11-4-1890. Fairmount Cemetery, Newark, Essex County.
JONES, FRANK S. Pvt, H, 4th NJ Inf, 6-9-1903. Harleigh Cemetery, Camden, Camden County.
JONES*, FRANKLIN S. Corp, I, 5th NJ Inf, 9-29-1907. Methodist-Episcopal Cemetery, Vincentown, Burlington County.
JONES, GEORGE H. Pvt, C, 71st PA Inf, 12-13-1901. Presbyterian Church Cemetery, Basking Ridge, Somerset County.
JONES, GEORGE S. Pvt, H, 2nd NJ Militia, 4-25-1889. Evergreen Cemetery, Camden, Camden County.
JONES, GEORGE W. Corp, A, 21st NJ Inf, [Died of typhoid at White Oak Church, VA.] 3-17-1863. Bayview-New York Bay Cemetery, Jersey City, Hudson County.
JONES, GEORGE W. Pvt, K, 10th NJ Inf, 12-13-1908. Cedar Lawn Cemetery, Paterson, Passaic County.
JONES, GEORGE W. Coal Heaver, U.S. Navy, USS North Carolina, 1896. Greenwood Cemetery, Tuckerton, Ocean County.
JONES, GRIFFITH Corp, E, 1st NJ Cav, 4-2-1869. St. Stephen's Cemetery, Millburn, Essex County.
JONES, HARRISON Pvt, C, Cobb's Legion GA Inf (CSA), 3-27-1865. Finn's Point National Cemetery, Pennsville, Salem County.
JONES, HARRY 1st Lt, B, 1st NJ Cav, 9-11-1893. Baptist Cemetery, Salem, Salem County.
JONES, HENRY Pvt, B, 1st NJ Inf, 10-26-1870. Mount Pleasant Cemetery, Millville, Cumberland County.
JONES, HENRY Sgt, E, 103rd U.S. CT, 5-9-1887. Evergreen Cemetery, Hillside, Union County.
JONES, HENRY B. Pvt, E, 21st NJ Inf, 9-5-1877. Riverview Cemetery, Trenton, Mercer County.
JONES, HENRY F. Pvt, I, 2nd NJ Inf, 12-7-1908. Holy Sepulchre Cemetery, East Orange, Essex County.
JONES, HENRY H. Landsman, U.S. Navy, USS James L. Davis, 11-2-1900. Johnson Cemetery, Camden, Camden County.
JONES, HENRY M. Landsman, U.S. Navy, 2-10-1880. Mount Pleasant Cemetery, Newark, Essex County.
JONES, HENRY PHINEAS (aka: Cook, Henry) Musc, Btty F, 7th NY Heavy Art, 3-17-1923. Mount Pleasant Cemetery, Newark, Essex County.
JONES, HENRY W. Pvt, C, 8th U.S. CT, DoD Unknown. Johnson Cemetery, Camden, Camden County.
JONES, ISAAC Corp, I, 2nd NJ Cav, 3-7-1912. Maplewood Cemetery, Freehold, Monmouth County.
JONES, ISAIAH Pvt, C, 22nd U.S. CT, 4-3-1893. Spencer African Methodist Church Cemetery, Woodstown, Salem County.
JONES, J.E. Pvt, H, 3rd (Howard's) Confederate States Cav (CSA), 10-25-1863. Finn's Point National Cemetery, Pennsville, Salem County.

New Jersey Civil War Burials

JONES, J. WYNNE Sgt, G, 23rd WI Inf, 10-12-1918. Princeton Cemetery, Princeton, Mercer County.
JONES, JAMES Pvt, E, 33rd NY Inf, 1-1-1915. Oak Grove Cemetery, Hammonton, Atlantic County.
JONES*, JAMES Pvt, H, 7th NJ Inf, 8-8-1904. Cedar Green Cemetery, Clayton, Gloucester County.
JONES, JAMES (see: Lowe, James) St. John's AME Cemetery, Chesilhurst, Camden County.
JONES, JAMES C. Pvt, I, 24th NJ Inf, 1911. Methodist-Episcopal Cemetery, Lake, Gloucester County.
JONES, JAMES E. Pvt, B, 8th NJ Inf, 9-7-1903. Clinton Cemetery, Irvington, Essex County.
JONES, JAMES G. Sgt, U.S. Marine Corps, 5-18-1911. Fairmount Cemetery, Newark, Essex County.
JONES, JAMES J. Pvt, K, 7th (Gregg's) TX Inf (CSA), 7-31-1864. Finn's Point National Cemetery, Pennsville, Salem County.
JONES, JAMES M. Pvt, I, 12th NJ Inf, 3-5-1877. Baptist Church Cemetery, Canton, Salem County.
JONES, JAMES P. 4-3-1893. Old South Church Cemetery, Bergenfield, Bergen County.
JONES, JAMES P. Pvt, E, 22nd NJ Inf, 12-27-1901. Bloomfield Cemetery, Bloomfield, Essex County.
JONES, JAMES T. Pvt, B, 4th NJ Inf, 5-10-1874. Riverview Cemetery, Trenton, Mercer County.
JONES, JAMES T. Pvt, I, 44th VA Inf (CSA), [Wounded 5-3-1863 at Chancellorsville, VA. Captured 5-12-1864 at Spotsylvania CH, VA. Died of lung inflammation.] 1-10-1865. Finn's Point National Cemetery, Pennsville, Salem County.
JONES, JASPER M. Pvt, A, 40th MS Inf (CSA), 7-29-1863. Finn's Point National Cemetery, Pennsville, Salem County.
JONES, JESSE Pvt, K, 10th NJ Inf, DoD Unknown. Methodist Church Cemetery, Hurffville, Gloucester County.
JONES, JESSE (see: Jones, Josiah) Greenwood Cemetery, Hamilton, Mercer County.
JONES*, JOB Pvt, Btty E, 1st NJ Light Art, 8-6-1920. Baptist Cemetery, Vincentown, Burlington County.
JONES, JOEL Pvt, G, 26th NJ Inf, 3-9-1905. Rosedale Cemetery, Orange, Essex County.
JONES, JOHN Pvt, G, 118th NY Inf, 12-28-1895. 1st Methodist Church Cemetery, Williamstown, Gloucester County.
JONES, JOHN Pvt, B, 6th NY Cav, 7-23-1905. Jersey City Cemetery, Jersey City, Hudson County.
JONES, JOHN Pvt, G, 8th U.S. CT, 8-31-1903. Belvidere/Catholic Cemetery, Belvidere, Warren County.
JONES, JOHN DoD Unknown. Mansfield/Washington Cemetery, Washington, Warren County.
JONES, JOHN B. Pvt, A, 25th NJ Inf, 1-3-1874. Old Stone Church Cemetery, Fairton, Cumberland County.
JONES*, JOHN B. 2nd Lt, C, 44th WI Inf, 9-25-1921. Evergreen Cemetery, Hillside, Union County.
JONES, JOHN B. (JR.) Pvt, D, 25th NJ Inf, [Wounded in action at Fredericksburg, VA.] 1-3-1874. Old Stone Church Cemetery, Fairton, Cumberland County.
JONES, JOHN E. Pvt, B, 34th NJ Inf, 10-5-1899. St. Paul's Methodist-Episcopal Church Cemetery, Thorofare, Gloucester County.
JONES, JOHN E. Landsman, U.S. Navy, USS St. Marys, 12-23-1891. Cedar Grove Cemetery, Waretown, Ocean County.
JONES, JOHN E. Pvt, I, 22nd NJ Inf, 3-22-1904. Brookside Cemetery, Englewood, Bergen County.

Our Brothers Gone Before

JONES, JOHN J. Pvt, D, 28th NJ Inf, 12-31-1891. Fairmount Cemetery, Newark, Essex County.
JONES, JOHN P. Pvt, I, 23rd NJ Inf, 4-5-1917. Colestown Cemetery, Cherry Hill, Camden County.
JONES, JOHN R. Corp, I, 4th U.S. CT, 3-16-1888. Siloam Cemetery, Vineland, Cumberland County.
JONES, JOHN T. 1863. Baptist/Evergreen Methodist Cemetery, Plainfield, Union County.
JONES, JOHN W. Pvt, I, 26th NJ Inf, 2-1-1895. Fairmount Cemetery, Newark, Essex County.
JONES, JOHN W. Pvt, C, 42nd MS Inf (CSA), 7-30-1863. Finn's Point National Cemetery, Pennsville, Salem County.
JONES, JONATHAN E. Pvt, C, 14th NJ Inf, 1-2-1916. Evergreen Cemetery, Hillside, Union County.
JONES, JOSEPH W. Pvt, C, 27th NJ Inf, DoD Unknown. Presbyterian/Methodist-Episcopal Cemetery, Succasunna, Morris County.
JONES*, JOSHUA Pvt, C, 12th NJ Inf, 9-19-1905. Harleigh Cemetery, Camden, Camden County.
JONES, JOSHUA Pvt, C, 52nd NC Inf (CSA), [Captured 7-3-1863 at Gettysburg, PA. Died of disease.] 2-3-1864. Finn's Point National Cemetery, Pennsville, Salem County.
JONES*, JOSIAH (aka: Jones, Jesse) Pvt, H, 21st NJ Inf, 11-19-1921. Greenwood Cemetery, Hamilton, Mercer County.
JONES*, LEANDER Pvt, D, 6th NC Cav (CSA), [Died of chronic diarrhea.] 8-27-1864. Finn's Point National Cemetery, Pennsville, Salem County.
JONES, MICHAEL Pvt, D, 1st DE Cav, 1919. Harleigh Cemetery, Camden, Camden County.
JONES, OBADIAH F. Pvt, E, 14th NJ Inf, [Wounded in action.] 1-31-1917. Hazelwood Cemetery, Rahway, Union County.
JONES, PAUL J. Pvt, G, 12th NJ Inf, 6-17-1930. Baptist Church Cemetery, Blackwood, Camden County.
JONES, PAUL T. Capt, Btty L, 2nd PA Heavy Art, [Wounded in action.] 1883. Presbyterian Church Cemetery, Bridgeton, Cumberland County.
JONES, PETER Pvt, A, 9th NJ Inf, 1-14-1933. Evergreen Cemetery, New Brunswick, Middlesex County.
JONES, R. 5-7-1891. Mount Salem Church Cemetery, Fenwick, Salem County.
JONES, R.B. Pvt, K, 55th NC Inf (CSA), [Captured 5-5-1864 at Wilderness, VA. Died of diarrhea.] 2-9-1865. Finn's Point National Cemetery, Pennsville, Salem County.
JONES, RALPH Pvt, H, 21st NJ Inf, 5-31-1902. Greenwood Cemetery, Hamilton, Mercer County.
JONES*, RANDOLPH Musc, Btty L, 11th U.S. CHA, 1-15-1904. AME Cemetery, Pennington, Mercer County.
JONES, REUBEN Pvt, F, 8th ME Inf, 8-21-1864. Beverly National Cemetery, Edgewater Park, Burlington County.
JONES, RICHARD Pvt, E, 24th NJ Inf, [Killed in action at Fredericksburg, VA.] 12-13-1862. 7th Day Baptist Church Cemetery, Shiloh, Cumberland County.
JONES, ROBERT Pvt, I, 23rd NC Inf (CSA), [Captured 7-1-1863 at Gettysburg, PA. Died of smallpox.] 10-20-1863. Finn's Point National Cemetery, Pennsville, Salem County.
JONES, RUSH Corp, I, 26th NJ Inf, 10-19-1889. Fairmount Cemetery, Newark, Essex County.
JONES, SAMUEL Pvt, A, 26th AL Inf (CSA), [Captured 7-3-1863 at Gettysburg, PA. Died of influx of the lungs.] 12-23-1863. Finn's Point National Cemetery, Pennsville, Salem County.

New Jersey Civil War Burials

JONES, SAMUEL Pvt, D, 127th PA Inf, 3-20-1941. Hope Christian Church Cemetery, Marlton, Burlington County.
JONES, SAMUEL BRADFORD Bvt Brig Gen, U.S. Volunteers, [Colonel, 78th United States Colored Troops.] 11-3-1908. Fairmount Cemetery, Chatham, Morris County.
JONES, SAMUEL H. 2-8-1900. Arlington Cemetery, Kearny, Hudson County.
JONES, SAMUEL K. Corp, C, 11th NJ Inf, 11-6-1900. Riverview Cemetery, Trenton, Mercer County.
JONES, SAMUEL M. Pvt, F, 47th NY Inf, 11-26-1926. St. Mary's Cemetery, Hainesport, Burlington County.
JONES, SAMUEL MINOT 1st Lt, A, 59th IL Inf, 10-10-1912. Evergreen Cemetery, Morristown, Morris County.
JONES, THEODORE Pvt, D, 4th NJ Inf, [Wounded 9-14-1862 at Crampton's Pass, MD.] DoD Unknown. Old South Church Cemetery, Bergenfield, Bergen County.
JONES, THOMAS Pvt, F, 6th U.S. CT, 2-3-1898. Johnson Cemetery, Camden, Camden County.
JONES, THOMAS Pvt, A, 3rd NJ Inf, 1-17-1902. Baptist Cemetery, Rio Grande, Cape May County.
JONES, THOMAS Pvt, D, 150th NY Inf, 8-4-1915. Rosedale Cemetery, Orange, Essex County.
JONES, THOMAS Pvt, B, 5th NY Vet Inf, [Wounded 3-31-1865 at White Oak Road, VA.] 5-29-1891. Holy Name Cemetery, Jersey City, Hudson County.
JONES, THOMAS Pvt, E, 51st GA Inf (CSA), [Captured 7-2-1863 at Gettysburg, PA.] 10-23-1863. Finn's Point National Cemetery, Pennsville, Salem County.
JONES, THOMAS (see: Farlow, Thomas) Presbyterian Church Cemetery, Rockaway, Morris County.
JONES, THOMAS B. Pvt, B, 32nd U.S. CT, 6-28-1912. Mount Peace Cemetery, Lawnside, Camden County.
JONES, THOMAS J. Seaman, U.S. Navy, USS Donegal, 11-21-1876. Fairmount Cemetery, Chatham, Morris County.
JONES, THOMAS W. Sgt, D, 2nd NY Cav, 4-4-1929. St. John's Evangelical Church Cemetery, Orange, Essex County.
JONES, W.A. Pvt, B, 16th VA Cav (CSA), 5-22-1864. Finn's Point National Cemetery, Pennsville, Salem County.
JONES, W.B. Asst Surg, 2-23-1869. Fairmount Cemetery, Newark, Essex County.
JONES, W.J.W. Pvt, I, 3rd (Howard's) Confederate States Cav (CSA), 9-9-1863. Finn's Point National Cemetery, Pennsville, Salem County.
JONES*, WESLEY Pvt, A, 8th NJ Inf, 1-28-1879. Fairmount Cemetery, Newark, Essex County.
JONES, WESLEY W. 1887. New Somerville Cemetery, Somerville, Somerset County.
JONES, WILLIAM Pvt, A, 33rd NC Inf (CSA), [Captured 7-5-1863 at Gettysburg, PA.] 9-25-1863. Finn's Point National Cemetery, Pennsville, Salem County.
JONES*, WILLIAM Pvt, Btty I, 11th U.S. CHA, 1-15-1894. Greenmount Cemetery, Hammonton, Atlantic County.
JONES, WILLIAM Pvt, E, 187th PA Inf, 1932. Baptist Church Cemetery, Haddonfield, Camden County.
JONES, WILLIAM Seaman, U.S. Navy, USS Cimmarron, 1-6-1900. Mount Peace Cemetery, Lawnside, Camden County.
JONES, WILLIAM Seaman, U.S. Navy, USS North Carolina, 11-27-1920. Mount Olivet Cemetery, Newark, Essex County.
JONES, WILLIAM Pvt, G, 3rd NJ Cav, 1-6-1912. Arlington Cemetery, Kearny, Hudson County.
JONES, WILLIAM Corp, Btty M, 13th U.S. CHA, 1-1-1915. Bayview-New York Bay Cemetery, Jersey City, Hudson County.

Our Brothers Gone Before

JONES, WILLIAM Corp, G, 62nd NY Inf, [Wounded 6-1-1862 at Fair Oaks, VA.] 10-19-1930. Bayview-New York Bay Cemetery, Jersey City, Hudson County.

JONES, WILLIAM Seaman, U.S. Navy, USS Lancaster, 5-17-1894. Jersey City Cemetery, Jersey City, Hudson County.

JONES, WILLIAM Pvt, B, 6th AL Inf (CSA), 10-15-1863. Finn's Point National Cemetery, Pennsville, Salem County.

JONES, WILLIAM Pvt, Fry's Btty, VA Light Art (CSA), 1-23-1865. Finn's Point National Cemetery, Pennsville, Salem County.

JONES, WILLIAM DoD Unknown. Methodist Church Cemetery, Pemberton, Burlington County.

JONES, WILLIAM A. Ordinary Seaman, U.S. Navy, USS Princeton, 4-27-1922. Evergreen Cemetery, Camden, Camden County.

JONES, WILLIAM E. 10-13-1890. Baptist/Evergreen Methodist Cemetery, Plainfield, Union County.

JONES, WILLIAM H. Pvt, L, 6th NY Cav, 9-4-1896. Edgewater Cemetery, Edgewater, Bergen County.

JONES, WILLIAM H. Pay Steward, U.S. Navy, 8-12-1921. New Camden Cemetery, Camden, Camden County.

JONES, WILLIAM H. Corp, C, 12th TN Cav, 5-30-1889. Evergreen Cemetery, Camden, Camden County.

JONES, WILLIAM H. Pvt, F, 8th U.S. CT, 2-8-1891. Johnson Cemetery, Camden, Camden County.

JONES, WILLIAM H. Pvt, G, 6th NJ Inf, 11-10-1910. Overlook Cemetery, Bridgeton, Cumberland County.

JONES, WILLIAM H. Pvt, E, 179th PA Inf, DoD Unknown. 1st Methodist Church Cemetery, Williamstown, Gloucester County.

JONES, WILLIAM H. 5-26-1896. Holy Sepulchre Cemetery, Totowa, Passaic County.

JONES, WILLIAM H. DoD Unknown. Woodland Cemetery, Englewood Cliffs, Bergen County.

JONES*, WILLIAM H.H. Pvt, A, 110th NY Inf, 1-7-1908. Evergreen Cemetery, Lakewood, Ocean County.

JONES, WILLIAM HENRY Pvt, B, 150th NY Inf, 2-10-1917. Macphelah Cemetery, North Bergen, Hudson County.

JONES, WILLIAM J. Corp, K, 69th PA Inf, 5-3-1920. Evergreen Cemetery, Camden, Camden County.

JONES, WILLIAM J. Pvt, H, 21st NJ Inf, DoD Unknown. Lawrenceville Cemetery, Lawrenceville, Mercer County.

JONES, WILLIAM L. 1892. Evergreen/Bishop Jaynes Cemetery, Basking Ridge, Somerset County.

JONES, WILLIAM M. DoD Unknown. White Ridge Cemetery, Eatontown, Monmouth County.

JONSEN, WILLIAM (aka: Johnson, William) Pvt, H, 2nd NJ Cav, 4-19-1910. Hillside Cemetery, Lyndhurst, Bergen County.

JOPLIN, JAMES M. Pvt, K, 40th MS Inf (CSA), 11-10-1863. Finn's Point National Cemetery, Pennsville, Salem County.

JORALEMON, WALTER Pvt, F, 1st NJ Militia, 3-8-1897. Mount Pleasant Cemetery, Newark, Essex County.

JORDAN, ADAM Pvt, H, 5th NJ Inf, 4-1-1878. Trinity Episcopal Church Cemetery, Woodbridge, Middlesex County.

JORDAN, ADAM Pvt, G, 12th NJ Inf, DoD Unknown. Overlook Cemetery, Bridgeton, Cumberland County.

JORDAN, ALEXANDER Landsman, U.S. Navy, USS Maryland, 3-19-1916. Fairmount Cemetery, Newark, Essex County.

New Jersey Civil War Burials

JORDAN, CHARLES W. Pvt, L, 2nd MS Inf (CSA), [Wounded 7-1-1862 at Malvern Hill, VA. Captured 7-1-1863 at Gettysburg, PA. Died of disease.] 3-30-1865. Finn's Point National Cemetery, Pennsville, Salem County.
JORDAN, EDWARD J. 8-10-1904. Bayview-New York Bay Cemetery, Jersey City, Hudson County.
JORDAN*, ELEAZOR Pvt, A, 1st ME Cav, 1-20-1911. Siloam Cemetery, Vineland, Cumberland County.
JORDAN, GEORGE Pvt, L, 5th PA Cav, 2-14-1916. Green Cemetery, Woodbury, Gloucester County.
JORDAN, GEORGE H. Pvt, B, 24th U.S. CT, 12-19-1900. Princeton Cemetery, Princeton, Mercer County.
JORDAN, GEORGE W. Pvt, D, 37th NJ Inf, 3-24-1913. Coopertown Meeting House Cemetery, Edgewater Park, Burlington County.
JORDAN, ISAIAH Coal Heaver, U.S. Navy, USS Potomac, 9-11-1903. Mount Peace Cemetery, Lawnside, Camden County.
JORDAN, JACOB H. Pvt, M, 100th PA Inf, 3-3-1914. New Camden Cemetery, Camden, Camden County.
JORDAN, JAMES Pvt, B, 24th GA Inf (CSA), [Captured 7-3-1863 at Gettysburg, PA. Died of diarrhea.] 9-20-1863. Finn's Point National Cemetery, Pennsville, Salem County.
JORDAN, JAMES Pvt, I, 25th U.S. CT, 5-18-1907. Jordan Lawn Cemetery, Pennsauken, Camden County.
JORDAN, JAMES H. 2nd Lt, K, 10th NJ Inf, DoD Unknown. Methodist Episcopal/Methodist Protestant Cemetery, Bridgeport, Gloucester County.
JORDAN, JAMES T. Landsman, U.S. Navy, 2-1-1918. Holy Name Cemetery, Jersey City, Hudson County.
JORDAN, JOHN Actg 2nd Asst Eng, U.S. Navy, 2-5-1901. Holy Sepulchre Cemetery, Totowa, Passaic County.
JORDAN, JOHN (aka: McDonald, James) Pvt, D, 11th NJ Inf, DoD Unknown. Union Cemetery, Gloucester City, Camden County.
JORDAN, JOHN J. Pvt, H, 22nd NJ Inf, 5-29-1909. Laurel Grove Cemetery, Totowa, Passaic County.
JORDAN, JOHN L. Pvt, E, 24th NJ Inf, 3-23-1905. Green Cemetery, Woodbury, Gloucester County.
JORDAN, JOHN W. Pvt, C, 12th NJ Inf, 11-10-1888. Zion Methodist Church Cemetery, Porchtown, Gloucester County.
JORDAN, LOUIS Pvt, F, 8th NJ Inf, 6-1-1915. Woodland Cemetery, Newark, Essex County.
JORDAN, RICHARD K. Pvt, G, 23rd NJ Inf, 3-3-1895. Coopertown Meeting House Cemetery, Edgewater Park, Burlington County.
JORDAN, WILLIAM Pvt, K, 24th NJ Inf, 5-16-1898. Mount Hope Cemetery, Deerfield, Cumberland County.
JORDAN, WILLIAM Pvt, D, 24th U.S. CT, 1-6-1912. Mount Peace Cemetery, Lawnside, Camden County.
JORDAN, WILLIAM H. Pvt, E, 13th NJ Inf, 2-3-1916. Mount Pleasant Cemetery, Newark, Essex County.
JORDAN, WILLIAM P. Seaman, U.S. Navy, 4-20-1892. Methodist-Episcopal Church Cemetery, Penns Grove, Salem County.
JORDAN, WILLIAM T.C. Pvt, D, 25th NJ Inf, 2-26-1899. Methodist Church Cemetery, Centre Grove, Cumberland County.
JORDON, SAMUEL J. 1863. Laurel Grove Cemetery, Totowa, Passaic County.
JORELOMAN, HENRY C. Corp, B, 7th NJ Inf, 10-10-1917. Mount Pleasant Cemetery, Newark, Essex County.
JORGER, OTTO (see: Joerger, Otto) Woodland Cemetery, Newark, Essex County.

Our Brothers Gone Before

JOSEPH, CHARLES Sgt, B, 19th PA Cav, 3-7-1934. Beverly National Cemetery, Edgewater Park, Burlington County.
JOSEPH, THEODORE Corp, A, 5th U.S. Cav, 3-10-1900. Beverly National Cemetery, Edgewater Park, Burlington County.
JOSIAH, J.W. 1912. Mount Prospect Cemetery, Neptune, Monmouth County.
JOSLIN, DAVID Pvt, H, 40th NJ Inf, 7-17-1903. Baptist Cemetery, Pemberton, Burlington County.
JOSLIN, GEORGE (see: Jocelyn, George M.) Arlington Cemetery, Kearny, Hudson County.
JOSLIN, SAMUEL Pvt, G, 24th NJ Inf, 8-29-1916. Chestnut Grove Cemetery, Elmer, Salem County.
JOSLIN, URIAH B. Pvt, H, 12th NJ Inf, [Wounded in action at Chancellorsville, VA.] 3-23-1871. Methodist-Episcopal Cemetery, Olivet, Salem County.
JOSLYN, THOMAS C. Pvt, D, 9th NJ Inf, 1918. Union Cemetery, Clarkstown, Atlantic County.
JOULES, WILLIAM Pvt, B, 1st NJ Cav, 5-26-1899. Laurel Grove Cemetery, Totowa, Passaic County.
JOUNTRY, CHARLES C. Pvt, F, 14th NJ Inf, 7-12-1919. Harleigh Cemetery, Camden, Camden County.
JOWERS, THOMAS Pvt, H, 1st (Regulars) SC Inf (CSA), [Captured 12-21-1864 at Savannah, GA. Died of scurvy.] 7-30-1865. Finn's Point National Cemetery, Pennsville, Salem County.
JOY, ALEXANDER Pvt, K, 62nd OH Inf, [Died at Beverly, NJ.] 12-22-1864. Beverly National Cemetery, Edgewater Park, Burlington County.
JOY*, EDMUND LEWIS (aka: Joy, Edward) Maj, U.S. Volunteers, [Judge Advocate, 7th Corps. Captain, 36th Iowa Infantry.] 2-14-1892. Mount Pleasant Cemetery, Newark, Essex County.
JOY, EDWARD (see: Joy, Edmund Lewis) Mount Pleasant Cemetery, Newark, Essex County.
JOY, THOMAS W. Sgt, E, 118th PA Inf, [Wounded in action.] 2-27-1904. Bordentown/Old St. Mary's Catholic Cemetery, Bordentown, Burlington County.
JOYCE, ALLEN N. (JR.) Pvt, F, 23rd NJ Inf, 11-14-1920. Baptist Cemetery, Vincentown, Burlington County.
JOYCE*, EDWARD C. Pvt, C, 34th NJ Inf, 2-9-1897. Baptist Cemetery, Vincentown, Burlington County.
JOYCE*, JOHN Pvt, 2nd Btty, VT Light Art, 11-3-1866. Presbyterian Church Cemetery, Titusville, Mercer County.
JOYCE, JOSHUA Pvt, M, 21st NC Inf (CSA), [Wounded 5-4-1863 at Chancellorsville, VA. Captured 7-2-1863 at Gettysburg, PA.] 9-20-1863. Finn's Point National Cemetery, Pennsville, Salem County.
JOYCE, JOSHUA L. Pvt, F, 23rd NJ Inf, [Died of typhoid at White Oak Church, VA.] 2-19-1863. Baptist Cemetery, Vincentown, Burlington County.
JOYCE, MICHAEL 12-6-1910. Mount Olivet Cemetery, Newark, Essex County.
JOYCE, ROBERT Pvt, B, 21st NJ Inf, 1-1-1909. Holy Name Cemetery, Jersey City, Hudson County.
JOYCE, SAMUEL Pvt, G, 213th PA Inf, 12-8-1909. Methodist-Episcopal Cemetery, Pointville, Burlington County.
JOYCE, WILLIAM Landsman, U.S. Navy, USS Princeton, 3-8-1904. New Camden Cemetery, Camden, Camden County.
JOYNES, KING M. Corp, K, 62nd (Rowan's) TN Inf (CSA), 8-12-1863. Finn's Point National Cemetery, Pennsville, Salem County.
JTZEL, PETER (see: Itzel, Peter) Rosedale Cemetery, Orange, Essex County.
JUBILEE, SAMUEL C. Pvt, K, 1st U.S. Colored Cav, 8-14-1897. Johnson Cemetery, Camden, Camden County.

New Jersey Civil War Burials

JUDD, FRANK M. 1st Lt, Btty I, 8th U.S. CHA, DoD Unknown. Siloam Cemetery, Vineland, Cumberland County.
JUDSON, SILAS Corp, K, 8th OH Inf, [Died of wounds received 7-2-1863 at Gettysburg, PA.] 9-9-1863. Fairmount Cemetery, Newark, Essex County.
JUFFA, JULIUS (aka: Gaffa, Julius) Pvt, Btty B, 1st NJ Light Art, 11-21-1882. Woodland Cemetery, Newark, Essex County.
JULIAN, W.H.H. Pvt, A, 37th AR Inf (CSA), [Captured 7-4-1863 at Helena, AR. Died of lung inflammation.] 4-3-1864. Finn's Point National Cemetery, Pennsville, Salem County.
JULIUS, JOHN D. Sgt, C, 6th U.S. CT, 5-18-1916. Arlington Cemetery, Kearny, Hudson County.
JULREY, WILLIAM 8-30-1920. Hoboken Cemetery, North Bergen, Hudson County.
JUMP, HENRY Pvt, A, 23rd PA Inf, 1-3-1909. Atlantic City Cemetery, Pleasantville, Atlantic County.
JUMPER, AMOS Sgt, A, 47th PA Inf, 7-13-1910. Belvidere/Catholic Cemetery, Belvidere, Warren County.
JUNE, ADAM H. Pvt, G, 15th SC Inf (CSA), [Captured 7-5-1863 at Gettysburg, PA. Died of typhoid.] 6-11-1863. Finn's Point National Cemetery, Pennsville, Salem County.
JUNE, ISAAC Sgt, E, 9th NJ Inf, 1-2-1917. Methodist Church Cemetery, Liberty, Warren County.
JUNE, LEWIS S. Pvt, F, 1st NY Mounted Rifles, 5-25-1911. Siloam Cemetery, Vineland, Cumberland County.
JUNG*, FREDERICK Pvt, F, 45th NY Inf, 9-19-1895. Bayview-New York Bay Cemetery, Jersey City, Hudson County.
JUNG, GEORGE (aka: Young, George) Pvt, I, 66th NY Inf, 8-1-1911. Grove Church Cemetery, North Bergen, Hudson County.
JUNG, HEINRICH (see: Young, Henry) St. John's Evangelical Church Cemetery, Orange, Essex County.
JUNG, VALENTINE (see: Young, Valentine) Fairmount Cemetery, Newark, Essex County.
JUNGE, HERMAN Pvt, H, 1st CT Cav, 9-16-1915. Jersey City Cemetery, Jersey City, Hudson County.
JUNGK, JOHANN (see: Jungk, John) Beverly National Cemetery, Edgewater Park, Burlington County.
JUNGK, JOHN (aka: Jungk, Johann) Pvt, F, 46th NY Inf, [Died of wounds received 9-30-1864 at Poplar Springs Church, VA.] 10-12-1864. Beverly National Cemetery, Edgewater Park, Burlington County.
JUNKIN, WILLIAM M. Seaman, U.S. Navy, 9-29-1864. Presbyterian Church Cemetery, Bloomsbury, Hunterdon County.
JURGENS, JOHN R. Pvt, B, 9th NJ Inf, 3-31-1921. Bayview-New York Bay Cemetery, Jersey City, Hudson County.
JUSSEN, CARL 1st Lt, Adj, 23rd WI Inf 3-8-1919. English Neighborhood Reformed Church Cemetery, Ridgefield, Bergen County.
JUST, AUGUSTUS Pvt, E, 2nd NJ Inf, 12-6-1914. Bayview-New York Bay Cemetery, Jersey City, Hudson County.
JUSTICE, EDWARD Pvt, F, 140th NY Inf, [Died at Beverly, NJ.] 12-19-1864. Beverly National Cemetery, Edgewater Park, Burlington County.
JUSTICE, JOHN Pvt, F, 22nd NJ Inf, 1-5-1890. Mount Hope Presbyterian Cemetery, Lambertville, Hunterdon County.
JUSTICE, JOSEPH Musc, D, 134th PA Inf, DoD Unknown. Mercer Cemetery, Trenton, Mercer County.
JUSTICE, NATHAN S. Pvt, F, 79th IL Inf, 1917. Eglington Cemetery, Clarksboro, Gloucester County.

Our Brothers Gone Before

JUSTICE, TIMOTHY Pvt, K, 29th NJ Inf, 5-24-1890. Atlantic View Cemetery, Manasquan, Monmouth County.
JUSTIN, JACOB Pvt, E, 31st NY Inf, 7-22-1908. Arlington Cemetery, Kearny, Hudson County.
JUSTUS, GEORGE T. Sgt, Btty D, 2nd PA Heavy Art, DoD Unknown. Atlantic City Cemetery, Pleasantville, Atlantic County.
JUTZ, ANTONE (aka: Tutz, Henry) Pvt, Btty A, 1st NJ Light Art, 12-20-1876. Rosedale Cemetery, Orange, Essex County.
KABIS, JOHN Artificer, A, 1st Bttn U.S. Eng, DoD Unknown. Arlington Cemetery, Kearny, Hudson County.
KABRICK, GEORGE (aka: Kaebrieg, George) Pvt, Btty A, Schaffer's Ind PA Heavy Art, 1-9-1925. Evergreen Cemetery, Camden, Camden County.
KABUS, JACOB Pvt, I, 2nd DC Inf, 12-8-1907. Woodland Cemetery, Newark, Essex County.
KACHLINE, AARON P. Corp, G, 45th PA Militia, 4-6-1909. Union Cemetery, Frenchtown, Hunterdon County.
KADLE, JAMES M. Pvt, F, 7th SC Inf (CSA), [Captured 7-3-1863 at Gettysburg, PA. Died of scurvy.] 11-5-1863. Finn's Point National Cemetery, Pennsville, Salem County.
KAEBRIEG, GEORGE (see: Kabrick, George) Evergreen Cemetery, Camden, Camden County.
KAECHELE, DAVID (see: Kuchelle, Davis) Evergreen Cemetery, Camden, Camden County.
KAFER, CHARLES Pvt, C, 4th NJ Inf, 12-31-1865. Mercer Cemetery, Trenton, Mercer County.
KAFER*, JOHN C. 3rd Asst Eng, U.S. Navy, USS Kearsarge, 3-30-1906. Riverview Cemetery, Trenton, Mercer County.
KAFER, PETER M. Actg 3rd Asst Eng, U.S. Navy, USS Ft. Donalson, 1-6-1922. Lawrenceville Cemetery, Lawrenceville, Mercer County.
KAHLE, HENRY Pvt, A, 7th NJ Inf, 3-21-1884. Greenlawn Cemetery, West Long Branch, Monmouth County.
KAHLE, LOUIS Sgt, E, 68th NY Inf, 4-13-1907. Maplewood Cemetery, Freehold, Monmouth County.
KAHLERT*, GEORGE LEWIS 2nd Lt, 9th NY Ind Btty 11-17-1891. Flower Hill Cemetery, North Bergen, Hudson County.
KAHN, CARL (see: Kahn, Charles) Grove Church Cemetery, North Bergen, Hudson County.
KAHN, CHARLES (aka: Kahn, Carl) Pvt, A, 54th NY Inf, 3-8-1909. Grove Church Cemetery, North Bergen, Hudson County.
KAIGHN, WILLIAM C. Pvt, Ind, PA Emerg NJ Militia, 1-31-1883. Methodist-Episcopal Church Cemetery, Blackwood, Camden County.
KAIGHN*, WILLIAM H. Landsman, U.S. Navy, USS John Adams, 12-17-1899. Evergreen Cemetery, Camden, Camden County.
KAIN, DAVID (see: Kane, David) Fairmount Cemetery, Newark, Essex County.
KAIN, ISAAC Corp, D, 10th NJ Inf, 1909. 7th Day Baptist Church Cemetery, Shiloh, Cumberland County.
KAIN*, JAMES Pvt, E, 13th NJ Inf, 4-17-1923. Holy Sepulchre Cemetery, East Orange, Essex County.
KAIN, JAMES Pvt, G, 24th NJ Inf, 9-4-1897. Baptist Church Cemetery, Canton, Salem County.
KAIN, PETER M. Pvt, K, 7th NJ Inf, 7-31-1902. Holy Rood Cemetery, Morristown, Morris County.
KAIN, THEODORE W. Sgt, I, 23rd NJ Inf, 2-11-1873. Greenwood Cemetery, Hamilton, Mercer County.

New Jersey Civil War Burials

KAIN, THEODORE W. Sgt, I, 23rd NJ Inf, DoD Unknown. Colestown Cemetery, Cherry Hill, Camden County.

KAINE, DENNIS M. Pvt, G, 7th NJ Inf, 3-29-1896. Old St. Mary's Cemetery, Gloucester City, Camden County.

KAISER, FRIEDRICH (aka: Keizer, Frederick) Musc, F, 8th NY Cav, 9-22-1886. Weehawken Cemetery, North Bergen, Hudson County.

KAISER, GEORGE L. Pvt, Btty C, 15th NY Heavy Art, 2-26-1911. Fairmount Cemetery, Newark, Essex County.

KAISER, HARRIS Pvt, A, 9th NJ Inf, DoD Unknown. Grove Street Jewish Cemetery, Newark, Essex County.

KAISER*, JOHN Sgt, B, 3rd NJ Cav, 10-28-1908. Branchville Cemetery, Branchville, Sussex County.

KAISER, JOHN JACOB (aka: Keyser, John) Pvt, I, 14th NJ Inf, 2-10-1907. St. Francis Cemetery, Trenton, Mercer County.

KAISER, RUDOLPH (see: Kaiser, William) Fairmount Cemetery, Newark, Essex County.

KAISER, RUDOLPH (see: Kiser, Rudolph) Arlington Cemetery, Kearny, Hudson County.

KAISER, WILLIAM (aka: Kaiser, Rudolph) Pvt, B, 1st NJ Cav, 4-24-1894. Fairmount Cemetery, Newark, Essex County.

KAISER, WILLIAM Pvt, I, 20th NY Inf, 10-3-1886. Weehawken Cemetery, North Bergen, Hudson County.

KAISER, WILLIAM Capt, D, 52nd NY Inf, 12-19-1888. Mount Hope Presbyterian Cemetery, Lambertville, Hunterdon County.

KAISER, WILLIAM Pvt, A, 12th U.S. Inf, 6-21-1884. Holy Sepulchre Cemetery, East Orange, Essex County.

KALBER, JACOB Pvt, E, 2nd NJ Inf, 3-26-1895. Fairmount Cemetery, Newark, Essex County.

KALLING, GARRETT (see: Walling, Garrett A.) Dorsett Family Cemetery, Holmdel, Monmouth County.

KALT, CHARLES (aka: Kelt, Charles) Pvt, F, 44th PA Militia, 3-2-1907. Old Camden Cemetery, Camden, Camden County.

KALTHOFF, JOHN C. 1878. Weehawken Cemetery, North Bergen, Hudson County.

KALTON, NATHANIEL (see: Calton, Nathaniel F.) Jersey City Cemetery, Jersey City, Hudson County.

KALVIO, PETER 1918. Vincent Methodist-Episcopal Cemetery, Nutley, Essex County.

KAMMERMAN*, JOHN Pvt, A, 11th MO Inf, 5-1-1864. Baptist Church Cemetery, Alloway, Salem County.

KAMPF, ADAM Pvt, E, 2nd NJ Inf, 12-23-1897. Holy Sepulchre Cemetery, East Orange, Essex County.

KANDLE, JOHN M. Landsman, U.S. Navy, USS New Ironsides, 1911. Cedar Grove Cemetery, Gloucester City, Camden County.

KANDLE, SAMUEL (aka: Kendell, Samuel) Fireman, U.S. Navy, USS Newbern, 6-22-1883. St. John's Methodist Church Cemetery, Harrisonville, Gloucester County.

KANE, BENJAMIN Corp, F, 15th NJ Inf, 8-1-1903. Union Cemetery, Mount Olive, Morris County.

KANE, CHARLES W. Pvt, B, 9th DE Inf, 10-22-1900. Methodist Church Cemetery, Pemberton, Burlington County.

KANE, DANIEL Pvt, H, 84th NY National Guard, DoD Unknown. Holy Name Cemetery, Jersey City, Hudson County.

KANE, DAVID (aka: Kain, David) Pvt, G, 2nd NJ Inf, 12-2-1867. Fairmount Cemetery, Newark, Essex County.

KANE, DAVID (aka: Baldwin, David) Pvt, I, 35th NJ Inf, 3-25-1919. Fairmount Cemetery, Newark, Essex County.

Our Brothers Gone Before

KANE, HUGH Pvt, F, 100th NY Inf, 1-19-1907. St. Rose of Lima Cemetery, Freehold, Monmouth County.

KANE, JAMES Pvt, E, 48th NY Inf, [Wounded 1-15-1865 at Fort Fisher, NC.] 12-13-1901. St. James Cemetery, Woodbridge, Middlesex County.

KANE, JAMES (see: Cain, James) St. Joseph's Cemetery, Keyport, Monmouth County.

KANE, JAMES DoD Unknown. Cedar Grove Cemetery, Gloucester City, Camden County.

KANE, JOHN Sgt, C, 2nd NJ Inf, 1881. Holy Sepulchre Cemetery, East Orange, Essex County.

KANE, JOHN Pvt, E, 5th U.S. Inf, 4-13-1906. Holy Sepulchre Cemetery, Totowa, Passaic County.

KANE, JOHN Sgt, B, 1st NJ Cav, 12-26-1886. Holy Sepulchre Cemetery, East Orange, Essex County.

KANE, JOHN F. 1st Sgt, H, 64th NY Inf, DoD Unknown. Holy Name Cemetery, Jersey City, Hudson County.

KANE, JOHN H. Pvt, U.S. Marine Corps, 7-9-1907. Old Stone Church Cemetery, Fairton, Cumberland County.

KANE*, JOHN W. Pvt, U.S. Army, [Signal Corps.] 6-25-1907. Holy Name Cemetery, Jersey City, Hudson County.

KANE, MICHAEL CHARLES Pvt, A, 6th NY Inf, 6-4-1916. Holy Name Cemetery, Jersey City, Hudson County.

KANE, MICHAEL (SR.) (aka: Cain, Michael) Pvt, H, 66th NY Inf, 12-18-1879. Holy Name Cemetery, Jersey City, Hudson County.

KANE, PETER (see: Kline, Peter) Arlington Cemetery, Kearny, Hudson County.

KANE, PHILIP Corp, G, 2nd DC Inf, 9-20-1865. St. John's Evangelical Church Cemetery, Orange, Essex County.

KANE, THOMAS Sgt, D, 90th NY Inf, DoD Unknown. Holy Name Cemetery, Jersey City, Hudson County.

KANE, THOMAS Seaman, U.S. Navy, 8-5-1893. Greenwood Cemetery, Hamilton, Mercer County.

KANE, THOMAS DoD Unknown. Immaculate Conception Cemetery, Montclair, Essex County.

KANE, WILLIAM Landsman, U.S. Navy, USS Vandalia, 1-5-1909. St. Joseph's Church Cemetery, Perrineville, Monmouth County.

KANE, WILLIAM H. Corp, I, 115th NY Inf, [Died of wounds received 8-16-1864 at Deep Bottom, VA.] 9-26-1864. Beverly National Cemetery, Edgewater Park, Burlington County.

KANE*, WILLIAM W. Corp, C, 39th NJ Inf, 8-3-1885. Evergreen Cemetery, Camden, Camden County.

KANIPER, WILLIAM (aka: Kniper, William) Pvt, Btty B, 1st NJ Light Art, DoD Unknown. Presbyterian Church Cemetery, Harmony, Warren County.

KANOUSE, HENRY F. Pvt, L, 27th NJ Inf, [Died of pleurisy at Stamford, KY.] 5-19-1863. United Methodist Church Cemetery, Rockaway Valley, Morris County.

KANOUSE, JOHN F. Pvt, H, 26th NJ Inf, [Died of typhoid at White Oak Church, VA.] 3-14-1863. Rosedale Cemetery, Orange, Essex County.

KANOUSE, STEPHEN 1-8-1889. Ponds Church Cemetery, Oakland, Bergen County.

KANOUSE, THEODORE B. Pvt, H, 26th NJ Inf, 10-23-1922. Reformed Church Cemetery, Fairfield, Essex County.

KANS, JOHN (aka: Koons, John) Corp, G, 143rd PA Inf, DoD Unknown. Van Liew Cemetery, North Brunswick, Middlesex County.

KANT, ALEXANDER Pvt, I, 28th NJ Inf, 9-24-1900. Alpine Cemetery, Perth Amboy, Middlesex County.

KANUP, A. (see: Corry, Alexander) Finn's Point National Cemetery, Pennsville, Salem County.

New Jersey Civil War Burials

KARASCH, CARL (aka: Karsh, Carl) Pvt, E, 40th NY Inf, 1918. Flower Hill Cemetery, North Bergen, Hudson County.
KARCHER, JOHN 7-1-1884. Phillipsburg Cemetery, Phillipsburg, Warren County.
KARGE', JOSEPH Bvt Brig Gen, U.S. Volunteers, [Colonel, 2nd New Jersey Cavalry.] 12-27-1892. Princeton Cemetery, Princeton, Mercer County.
KARGE, PETER Sgt, A, 34th NJ Inf, 3-26-1909. Cedar Grove Cemetery, Gloucester City, Camden County.
KARGE, PHILIPP (see: Carr, Philip W.) Pvt, H, 3rd NJ Inf, 1-14-1916. Beverly National Cemetery, Edgewater Park, Burlington County.
KARL, NICHOLAS (see: Carl, Nicholas) Jersey City Cemetery, Jersey City, Hudson County.
KARN, CHARLES 11-30-1886. Fairmount Cemetery, Newark, Essex County.
KARR, FRANK D. Pvt, D, 7th NY State Militia, 12-18-1891. Evergreen Cemetery, Hillside, Union County.
KARR, JOHN 1930. Union Cemetery, Washington, Morris County.
KARR, SAMUEL Pvt, Btty D, 1st NJ Light Art, 5-8-1891. Baptist Church Cemetery, Port Murray, Warren County.
KARR, WILLIAM 5-21-1891. Baptist Church Cemetery, Port Murray, Warren County.
KARSEBOON*, WILLIAM P. Pvt, I, 14th NJ Inf, [Wounded 11-27-1863 at Locust Grove, VA.] 1-3-1910. Fairmount Cemetery, Newark, Essex County.
KARSH, CARL (see: Karasch, Carl) Flower Hill Cemetery, North Bergen, Hudson County.
KASE, JOHN F. Corp, G, 39th NJ Inf, 1881. Phillipsburg Old Catholic Cemetery, Phillipsburg, Warren County.
KASE, JOHN W. (JR.) Pvt, B, 7th NY State Militia, 4-15-1912. Arlington Cemetery, Kearny, Hudson County.
KASS, EARNEST (aka: Kassimer, Ebver) Pvt, B, 1st NY Cav, 4-28-1907. Arlington Cemetery, Kearny, Hudson County.
KASS, GEORGE Pvt, F, 8th NJ Inf, 7-11-1911. Fairmount Cemetery, Newark, Essex County.
KASSIMER, EBVER (see: Kass, Earnest) Arlington Cemetery, Kearny, Hudson County.
KASTNER*, ADAM (aka: Castler, Adam) Saddler, C, 4th NY Prov Cav, 12-3-1906. Laurel Grove Cemetery, Totowa, Passaic County.
KATAN, GEORGE R. Pvt, Btty L, 13th NY Heavy Art, 7-27-1899. New Camden Cemetery, Camden, Camden County.
KATES, CHARLES H. Sgt, H, 12th NJ Inf, [Killed in action at Dabneys Mills, VA.] 2-28-1865. New Presbyterian Church Cemetery, Daretown, Salem County.
KATES, CLARK W. Pvt, K, 24th NJ Inf, DoD Unknown. Methodist-Episcopal Church Cemetery, Penns Grove, Salem County.
KATES, FRANCIS Pvt, I, 25th NJ Inf, 11-20-1902. Overlook Cemetery, Bridgeton, Cumberland County.
KATES, JACOB B. Corp, B, 24th NJ Inf, 4-1-1895. Mount Pleasant Cemetery, Millville, Cumberland County.
KATES, JAMES Pvt, G, 28th NJ Inf, 10-14-1895. New Camden Cemetery, Camden, Camden County.
KATES, MICHAEL P. Pvt, A, 24th NJ Inf, 9-1-1904. Cedar Hill Cemetery, Cedarville, Cumberland County.
KATES, ROBERT R. 1st Lt, G, 12th NJ Inf, 1922. Harleigh Cemetery, Camden, Camden County.
KATHCART, WILLIAM (see: Kithcart, William H.) Presbyterian Church Cemetery, Mount Freedom, Morris County.
KATON, RICHARD Musc, C, 29th NJ Inf, 11-5-1894. Christ Church Cemetery, Morgan, Middlesex County.
KAUFFMAN, ANDREW Pvt, I, 9th NJ Inf, 11-4-1887. Eastview Cemetery, Salem, Salem County.

Our Brothers Gone Before

KAUFFMAN, CHRISTIAN Pvt, E, 40th NJ Inf, 5-19-1891. Phillipsburg Cemetery, Phillipsburg, Warren County.

KAUFMAN*, IGNATZ Pvt, E, 2nd NJ Inf, 8-15-1895. Holy Sepulchre Cemetery, East Orange, Essex County.

KAUFMAN, JOHN Pvt, H, 7th NJ Inf, [Died of wounds received 5-7-1862 at Williamsburg, VA.] 5-28-1862. Green Cemetery, Woodbury, Gloucester County.

KAUFMANN, JOHN K. Pvt, Btty B, 15th NY Heavy Art, DoD Unknown. Bayview-New York Bay Cemetery, Jersey City, Hudson County.

KAUNMILLER, JOHN (see: Cronmiller, John B.) German Valley Rural Cemetery, Naughright, Morris County.

KAUPP, GEORGE Pvt, A, 39th NJ Inf, 9-4-1898. Bloomfield Cemetery, Bloomfield, Essex County.

KAVANAGH, FRANCIS J. (aka: Cavanaugh, Francis) Corp, C, 2nd NJ Inf, DoD Unknown. Holy Sepulchre Cemetery, East Orange, Essex County.

KAVANAUGH, DANIEL (aka: Cavanaugh, Daniel) Pvt, E, 14th NJ Inf, 8-5-1906. Rosedale Cemetery, Linden, Union County.

KAVANAUGH, EDWARD Pvt, F, 10th NJ Inf, DoD Unknown. Holy Sepulchre Cemetery, Totowa, Passaic County.

KAVANAUGH, EDWARD (see: Cavanaugh, Edward) Holy Sepulchre Cemetery, Totowa, Passaic County.

KAY, ALFRED Pvt, A, 25th NJ Inf, 4-10-1889. Laurel Grove Cemetery, Totowa, Passaic County.

KAY, JAMES S. Pvt, C, 25th NJ Inf, 2-25-1895. Laurel Grove Cemetery, Totowa, Passaic County.

KAY, JOHN Pvt, E, 8th PA Cav, 3-27-1927. Baptist Church Cemetery, Haddonfield, Camden County.

KAY*, JOHN Pvt, K, 13th NJ Inf, 9- -1884. Cedar Lawn Cemetery, Paterson, Passaic County.

KAY, RICHARD H. Pvt, F, 55th VA Inf (CSA), [Captured 7-4-1863 at Gettysburg, PA. Died of diarrhea.] 9-21-1863. Finn's Point National Cemetery, Pennsville, Salem County.

KAY, SAMUEL D. 10-9-1923. Bayview-New York Bay Cemetery, Jersey City, Hudson County.

KAY, SETH H. Pvt, C, 25th NJ Inf, 6-3-1885. Cedar Lawn Cemetery, Paterson, Passaic County.

KAY, WILLIAM H. Pvt, E, 25th NJ Inf, 7-12-1884. Laurel Grove Cemetery, Totowa, Passaic County.

KAYHART*, CORNELIUS H. Corp, G, 13th NJ Inf, 11-22-1898. Pine Brook Cemetery, Pine Brook, Morris County.

KAYS, JAMES Pvt, A, 10th NJ Inf, 1-13-1933. Presbyterian Church Cemetery, Sparta, Sussex County.

KAYS, JOHN B. Pvt, D, 27th NJ Inf, 12-29-1895. Newton Cemetery, Newton, Sussex County.

KAYS, OSCAR HENRY Pvt, F, 9th NJ Inf, 7-11-1921. Fairmount Cemetery, Phillipsburg, Warren County.

KAYSER, WILLIAM J. Pvt, E, 1st NY Cav, 10-6-1908. Hoboken Cemetery, North Bergen, Hudson County.

KEACH*, ELISHA Pvt, G, 14th NJ Inf, 7-23-1925. Fairview Cemetery, Fairview, Monmouth County.

KEADEL, I.W. Pvt, C, 33rd VA Inf (CSA), 6-26-1865. Finn's Point National Cemetery, Pennsville, Salem County.

KEAFER, JEREMIAH (aka: Keifer, Jeremiah) Pvt, B, 31st NJ Inf, 1-27-1909. Mansfield/Washington Cemetery, Washington, Warren County.

KEAL, FREDERICK 1922. Hackensack Cemetery, Hackensack, Bergen County.

New Jersey Civil War Burials

KEALHOFER, EDWARD (see: Potts, Edward) 1st Baptist Cemetery, Cape May Court House, Cape May County.
KEAN, CHRISTOPHER C. Pvt, A, 18th VA Inf (CSA), [Wounded 6-1-1862 at Seven Pines, VA. Captured 7-3-1863 at Gettysburg, PA. Died of diarrhea.] 11-21-1863. Finn's Point National Cemetery, Pennsville, Salem County.
KEARNEY*, EDWARD Pvt, A, 59th NY Inf, [Wounded 9-17-1862 at Antietam, MD.] 2-20-1920. Holy Sepulchre Cemetery, East Orange, Essex County.
KEARNEY, JAMES Pvt, C, 4th NJ Inf, 10- -1879. Baptist/St. Andrew's Cemetery, Mount Holly, Burlington County.
KEARNEY, MATTHEW Pvt, B, 33rd NJ Inf, 1-15-1878. Holy Sepulchre Cemetery, East Orange, Essex County.
KEARNEY, TIMOTHY Seaman, U.S. Navy, USS Pontoosic, 3-21-1886. Holy Sepulchre Cemetery, East Orange, Essex County.
KEARNS, ANTHONY Pvt, C, 90th NY Inf, 8-31-1898. Holy Name Cemetery, Jersey City, Hudson County.
KEARNS, JAMES Pvt, I, 2nd NJ Inf, 9-8-1908. Holy Sepulchre Cemetery, Totowa, Passaic County.
KEARNS*, MICHAEL Pvt, Unassigned, 33rd NJ Inf, 10-18-1896. St. Joseph's Cemetery, Washington, Warren County.
KEARNS, THOMAS D. Corp, B, 11th PA Cav, 4-1-1925. Soldier's Home Cemetery, Vineland, Cumberland County.
KEARNY, ALFRED D. Pvt, K, 1st NJ Militia, 5-29-1898. Fairmount Cemetery, Newark, Essex County.
KEARNY*, THOMAS H. Pvt, C, 8th NJ Inf, 3-13-1900. Fairmount Cemetery, Newark, Essex County.
KEARS, JOHN H. Corp, B, 25th NJ Inf, DoD Unknown. Greenmount Cemetery, Hammonton, Atlantic County.
KEARS, SAMUEL (aka: Cears, Samuel) Pvt, B, 24th NJ Inf, DoD Unknown. Mount Pleasant Cemetery, Millville, Cumberland County.
KEARS, WILLIAM P. Pvt, G, 4th NJ Inf, 1918. Cedar Hill Cemetery, Hightstown, Mercer County.
KEARSING, AMBROSE W. Pvt, K, 84th NY Inf, 3-14-1921. Cedar Lawn Cemetery, Paterson, Passaic County.
KEARSING, WILLIAM H. Pvt, B, 56th NY National Guard, 9-2-1909. Cedar Lawn Cemetery, Paterson, Passaic County.
KEASBEY, JOHN B. Surg, 2nd DC Inf 8-25-1886. St. John's Episcopal Church Cemetery, Salem, Salem County.
KEATES, GEORGE (SR.) Coal Heaver, U.S. Navy, USS Vermont, 1894. Atlantic City Cemetery, Pleasantville, Atlantic County.
KEATING*, JAMES Pvt, Btty H, 6th NY Heavy Art, 8-11-1896. St. Peter's Cemetery, Jersey City, Hudson County.
KEATING*, MICHAEL Pvt, M, 3rd NJ Cav, 1878. St. John's Evangelical Church Cemetery, Orange, Essex County.
KEATING, MICHAEL Fireman, U.S. Navy, USS Vermont, 2-21-1903. St. Peter's Church Cemetery, Belleville, Essex County.
KEATING, THOMAS Pvt, H, 33rd NJ Inf, 3-6-1869. Holy Sepulchre Cemetery, East Orange, Essex County.
KEATING, WILLIAM E.J. Seaman, U.S. Navy, 1-4-1919. Cedar Lawn Cemetery, Paterson, Passaic County.
KEBLER, FRANK Sgt, E, 4th NJ Inf, 3-18-1923. St. Peter's Cemetery, Riverside, Burlington County.
KECKEISEN, PETER 4-8-1916. St. Francis Cemetery, Trenton, Mercer County.
KEDNEY, JOHN STEINFORT 3-8-1911. St. John's Episcopal Church Cemetery, Salem, Salem County.

Our Brothers Gone Before

KEEBLER, BENJAMIN Pvt, E, 2nd __ Inf, 5-11-1932. Riverside Cemetery, Riverside, Burlington County.
KEEFE, DANIEL E. Pvt, E, 9th NJ Inf, 7-18-1914. Cedar Lawn Cemetery, Paterson, Passaic County.
KEEFE, LAWRENCE J. Corp, C, 30th NJ Inf, 8-2-1889. Rahway Cemetery, Rahway, Union County.
KEEFE, MICHAEL Chief Bugler, 1st NJ Cav 3-11-1912. Laurel Grove Cemetery, Totowa, Passaic County.
KEEFE, MICHAEL Sgt, A, 1st NJ Cav, 11-10-1866. St. Mary's Cemetery, Elizabeth, Union County.
KEEFE, PATRICK (see: O'Keefe, Patrick) St. Mary's Cemetery, Clark, Union County.
KEEGAN, CONSTANTINE Corp, B, 21st NJ Inf, 12-22-1898. Palisade Cemetery, North Bergen, Hudson County.
KEEGAN, EDWARD G. 1st Lt, K, 4th NJ Militia, 11-16-1871. St. Mary's Episcopal Church Cemetery, Burlington, Burlington County.
KEEGAN, REUBEN Landsman, U.S. Navy, USS Princeton, DoD Unknown. Holy Sepulchre Cemetery, East Orange, Essex County.
KEEGAN*, THOMAS J. Pvt, G, 8th NJ Inf, 8-15-1865. Old St. Mary's Cemetery, Gloucester City, Camden County.
KEELE, JOSEPH Capt, B, 182nd NY Inf, [Awarded the Medal of Honor.] 10-16-1906. Bayview-New York Bay Cemetery, Jersey City, Hudson County.
KEELER, CHARLES C. Pvt, C, 3rd NJ Militia, 5-24-1916. Arlington Cemetery, Kearny, Hudson County.
KEELER, GEORGE W. Pvt, H, 3rd NJ Militia, 8-12-1930. Evergreen Cemetery, Morristown, Morris County.
KEELER, HENRY Farrier, B, 3rd PA Cav, 3-26-1875. Baptist Cemetery, Pemberton, Burlington County.
KEELER, SAMUEL BUDD 1st Sgt, A, 4th NJ Inf, 1925. Fairview Cemetery, Fairview, Monmouth County.
KEELER, SAMUEL J. Pvt, B, 3rd NJ Cav, 1-16-1908. Adelphia Cemetery, Adelphia, Monmouth County.
KEELER, SAMUEL T. Corp, H, 61st NY Inf, 6-2-1916. Fair Lawn Cemetery, Fair Lawn, Bergen County.
KEEN, CHARLES 3-23-1895. Eglington Cemetery, Clarksboro, Gloucester County.
KEEN, CHARLES PERDUE Sgt, I, 9th NJ Inf, [Wounded in action.] 1928. Methodist Church Cemetery, Sharptown, Salem County.
KEEN, DENNIS Pvt, B, 106th PA Inf, 11-5-1908. 1st Methodist Church Cemetery, Williamstown, Gloucester County.
KEEN, EDWARD H. Pvt, A, 24th NJ Inf, 1-3-1913. Methodist-Episcopal Church Cemetery, Penns Grove, Salem County.
KEEN, GEORGE M. Pvt, C, 38th NJ Inf, 1918. Mount Pleasant Cemetery, Millville, Cumberland County.
KEEN, HENRY Pvt, A, 39th NJ Inf, 11-1-1905. Newton Cemetery, Newton, Sussex County.
KEEN, JOHN Pvt, D, 48th NY Inf, 2-14-1912. 1st Baptist Church Cemetery, Woodstown, Salem County.
KEEN, JOHN L. Pvt, H, 12th NJ Inf, DoD Unknown. St. John's Methodist Church Cemetery, Harrisonville, Gloucester County.
KEEN, PETER C. Pvt, K, 4th NJ Inf, 7-13-1898. Harleigh Cemetery, Camden, Camden County.
KEEN, THOMAS B. Pvt, F, 3rd NJ Inf, [Killed in action at Crampton's Pass, MD.] 9-14-1862. 7th Day Baptist Church Cemetery, Shiloh, Cumberland County.
KEEN, WILEY Pvt, K, 38th NC Inf (CSA), [Captured 7-2-1863 at Gettysburg, PA.] 10-14-1863. Finn's Point National Cemetery, Pennsville, Salem County.

New Jersey Civil War Burials

KEEN, WILLIAM Pvt, D, 23rd NJ Inf, [Died of diarrhea at White Oak Church, VA.] 1-17-1863. Columbus Cemetery, Columbus, Burlington County.
KEEN, WILLIAM A. Pvt, F, 2nd NJ Cav, DoD Unknown. Frankford Plains Cemetery, Frankford, Sussex County.
KEENAN, FRANCIS Pvt, G, 47th NY Inf, 11-7-1894. Old Calvary Cemetery, Sayreville, Middlesex County.
KEENAN*, HENRY C. Corp, F, 5th NY Vet Inf, 4-15-1920. Old Bergen Church Cemetery, Jersey City, Hudson County.
KEENAN, JOHN Pvt, A, 1st NJ Cav, DoD Unknown. Speer Cemetery, Jersey City, Hudson County.
KEENAN, THOMAS Pvt, A, 7th NJ Inf, 1-2-1894. Presbyterian Church Cemetery, Cold Spring, Cape May County.
KEENAN*, THOMAS Pvt, A, 2nd NJ Inf, DoD Unknown. Evergreen Cemetery, Hillside, Union County.
KEENAN, WILLIAM W. Pvt, Btty E, 5th NY Heavy Art, 11-13-1913. Bayview-New York Bay Cemetery, Jersey City, Hudson County.
KEENE, CHARLES 2-5-1916. Hollywood Cemetery, Union, Union County.
KEENE, JESSE 1st Lt, G, 1st NJ Militia, 10-26-1870. Fairmount Cemetery, Newark, Essex County.
KEENEY, CHARLES L. Pvt, B, 20th CT Inf, 10-12-1898. Evergreen Cemetery, Hillside, Union County.
KEENY, HENRY (see: Kinney, Henry S.) Presbyterian Church Cemetery, Mount Pleasant, Hunterdon County.
KEEPER, JESSE S. Pvt, C, 24th NJ Inf, 5-2-1922. Presbyterian Church Cemetery, Bridgeton, Cumberland County.
KEER, JOHN Pvt, A, 25th NJ Inf, 10-5-1903. Fairmount Cemetery, Newark, Essex County.
KEER, WILLIAM H. Pvt, A, 28th NJ Inf, 12-17-1939. Maplewood Cemetery, Freehold, Monmouth County.
KEESLING, JULIUS P. (see: Kiesling, Julius P.) Fairmount Cemetery, Newark, Essex County.
KEETCH, STEPHEN T. Seaman, U.S. Navy, USS New Hampshire, 4-19-1920. Greenwood Cemetery, Tuckerton, Ocean County.
KEETH, ADAM (see: Beam, Adam) Prospect Hill Cemetery, Caldwell, Essex County.
KEHOE, EDWARD Pvt, C, 35th NJ Inf, [Died of diarrhea at Newark, NJ.] 5-2-1865. Fairmount Cemetery, Newark, Essex County.
KEHOE, JAMES Pvt, D, 1st DE Inf, 9-29-1923. Fairmount Cemetery, Newark, Essex County.
KEHOE*, JOHN Sgt, H, 39th NJ Inf, [Wounded in action.] 3-30-1914. Hillside Cemetery, Lyndhurst, Bergen County.
KEHR, HENRY D. (SR.) Pvt, K, 2nd NJ Militia, 2-24-1917. Riverview Cemetery, Trenton, Mercer County.
KEHRL, ALBERT (see: Kehrle, Albert) Finn's Point National Cemetery, Pennsville, Salem County.
KEHRLE, ALBERT (aka: Kehrl, Albert) Pvt, A, 68th NY Inf, [Wounded 7-2-1863 at Gettysburg, PA.] 12-7-1900. Finn's Point National Cemetery, Pennsville, Salem County.
KEIDERLING, HENRY Pvt, E, 30th NJ Inf, 7-9-1915. Old Somerville Cemetery, Somerville, Somerset County.
KEIDERLING, NICHOLAS 3-14-1865. Old Somerville Cemetery, Somerville, Somerset County.
KEIFER, JACOB Sgt, A, 59th NY Inf, 7-18-1876. Fairmount Cemetery, Newark, Essex County.

Our Brothers Gone Before

KEIFER, JEREMIAH (see: Keafer, Jeremiah) Mansfield/Washington Cemetery, Washington, Warren County.

KEIFER, THEODORE Musc, I, 132nd PA Inf, 1-7-1917. Grove Church Cemetery, North Bergen, Hudson County.

KEIFFER*, JOSEPH E. 2nd Lt, K, 63rd GA Inf (CSA), [Captured 12-19-1864 at Franklin, TN. Died of erysipelas.] 3-28-1865. Finn's Point National Cemetery, Pennsville, Salem County.

KEIL, HENRY AUGUST Pvt, I, 2nd DC Inf, 6-24-1888. Fairmount Cemetery, Newark, Essex County.

KEILER, VALENTINE Pvt, E, 9th NJ Inf, 1-28-1906. Rahway Cemetery, Rahway, Union County.

KEIM, CONRAD V. Pvt, A, 28th NY State Militia, 3-29-1908. Flower Hill Cemetery, North Bergen, Hudson County.

KEIM, FRANK Hosp Steward, 3rd MO Inf 8-6-1911. Palisade Cemetery, North Bergen, Hudson County.

KEIMIG, CHARLES B. Sgt, K, 3rd NJ Inf, 4-8-1911. Mount Olivet Cemetery, Newark, Essex County.

KEIPER, WILLIAM H. Musc, 7th NJ Inf Band 11-17-1888. Mount Hope Presbyterian Cemetery, Lambertville, Hunterdon County.

KEISER, WILLIAM Pvt, E, 20th NY Inf, 10-3-1886. Palisade Cemetery, North Bergen, Hudson County.

KEISLER, JACOB Pvt, E, 9th NJ Inf, 11-1-1889. Mount Hebron Cemetery, Montclair, Essex County.

KEISLER*, JACOB (aka: Kessler, Jacob) Pvt, C, 7th NY Vet Inf, DoD Unknown. Mount Hebron Cemetery, Montclair, Essex County.

KEISLER, RUFUS 2nd Lt, A, 8th NJ Inf, 3-27-1932. Fairmount Cemetery, Newark, Essex County.

KEISLER, SIMEON (aka: Keisler, Simpson) Pvt, E, 9th NJ Inf, 4-26-1918. Mount Hebron Cemetery, Montclair, Essex County.

KEISLER, SIMPSON (see: Keisler, Simeon) Mount Hebron Cemetery, Montclair, Essex County.

KEITH, ADAM 4-2-1887. Fairmount Cemetery, Newark, Essex County.

KEIZER, FREDERICK (see: Kaiser, Friedrich) Weehawken Cemetery, North Bergen, Hudson County.

KELBER, JOHN 9-9-1910. Mount Olivet Cemetery, Newark, Essex County.

KELL, NATHAN Pvt, I, 9th NJ Inf, DoD Unknown. Mount Pleasant Cemetery, Millville, Cumberland County.

KELL, SAMUEL Pvt, Btty I, 2nd PA Heavy Art, 10-22-1904. Presbyterian Church Cemetery, Bridgeton, Cumberland County.

KELLAM, FRANCIS (aka: Cartey, Francis) Pvt, K, 28th PA Inf, 2-25-1908. Bordentown/Old St. Mary's Catholic Cemetery, Bordentown, Burlington County.

KELLAR, HENRY Sgt, B, 7th NJ Inf, 1-25-1932. Overlook Cemetery, Bridgeton, Cumberland County.

KELLER, A. Pvt, A, 21st VA Inf (CSA), 1-27-1865. Finn's Point National Cemetery, Pennsville, Salem County.

KELLER, ALBERT A. Pvt, G, 11th U.S. Inf, DoD Unknown. Evergreen Cemetery, Hillside, Union County.

KELLER*, ANDREW Pvt, D, 7th NJ Inf, 11-14-1878. Berlin Cemetery, Berlin, Camden County.

KELLER, ANTHONY (see: Keller, Anton) Fairmount Cemetery, Newark, Essex County.

KELLER, ANTON (aka: Keller, Anthony) Pvt, B, 35th NJ Inf, 3-24-1893. Fairmount Cemetery, Newark, Essex County.

KELLER, CHARLES QM Sgt, C, 8th U.S. Inf, 11-6-1893. Holy Sepulchre Cemetery, East Orange, Essex County.

New Jersey Civil War Burials

KELLER, CHRISTOPHER Pvt, F, 28th NJ Inf, 6-12-1885. Evergreen Cemetery, New Brunswick, Middlesex County.
KELLER, FRANK Pvt, D, 129th PA Inf, 11-19-1904. Fairmount Cemetery, Phillipsburg, Warren County.
KELLER, FRANKLIN Pvt, B, 12th NJ Inf, 1-21-1903. Riverview Cemetery, Trenton, Mercer County.
KELLER, GEORGE (see: Kelly, George W.) Evergreen Cemetery, Camden, Camden County.
KELLER, HEINRICH Pvt, Btty A, Schaffer's Ind PA Heavy Art, [Died at Fort Delaware.] 7-18-1862. Finn's Point National Cemetery, Pennsville, Salem County.
KELLER, HENRY Pvt, A, 57th PA Inf, 11-5-1930. Fairview Cemetery, Westfield, Union County.
KELLER, JOHN Sgt, A, 73rd PA Inf, 1878. United Methodist Church Cemetery, Winslow, Camden County.
KELLER, JOHN Pvt, E, 24th NJ Inf, 7-11-1908. Eglington Cemetery, Clarksboro, Gloucester County.
KELLER, JOHN Pvt, D, 9th NJ Inf, 11-23-1899. Mercer Cemetery, Trenton, Mercer County.
KELLER*, JOHN JACOB Seaman, U.S. Navy, USS Tonawanda, 3-27-1914. Woodland Cemetery, Newark, Essex County.
KELLER, JOSEPH L. Pvt, 98, 2nd U.S. VRC, 4-21-1870. Methodist Church Cemetery, Buttzville, Warren County.
KELLER*, LEWIS Sgt, F, 8th NJ Inf, 6-3-1882. Bordentown/Old St. Mary's Catholic Cemetery, Bordentown, Burlington County.
KELLER, MACBALENA 1877. Old Camden Cemetery, Camden, Camden County.
KELLER, PHILIP 7-27-1916. Bloomfield Cemetery, Bloomfield, Essex County.
KELLER, PHILIP M. Pvt, I, 3rd NJ Cav, 4-26-1880. Evergreen Cemetery, Morristown, Morris County.
KELLER*, SMITH W. Pvt, A, 3rd NJ Cav, 7-13-1894. Riverview Cemetery, Trenton, Mercer County.
KELLETT*, JOHN Pvt, A, 71st NY Inf, DoD Unknown. Holy Sepulchre Cemetery, East Orange, Essex County.
KELLEY, DANIEL Pvt, C, 67th NY Inf, [Died at Washington, DC of wounds received 6-1-1864 at Cold Harbor, VA.] 6-19-1864. St. John's Evangelical Church Cemetery, Orange, Essex County.
KELLEY, DANIEL C. Pvt, C, 3rd DE Inf, DoD Unknown. 1st Methodist Church Cemetery, Williamstown, Gloucester County.
KELLEY, EDMOND P. DoD Unknown. St. Vincent Martyr Cemetery, Madison, Morris County.
KELLEY*, EDWARD B.P. (aka: Kelly, Edward B.P.) Surg, U.S. Volunteers, [6th Corps. Also: Surg, 95th PA Inf. Wounded in action.] 11-25-1891. Westminster Cemetery, Cranbury, Middlesex County.
KELLEY, EDWIN A. Corp, B, 119th PA Inf, 11-2-1906. Greenwood Cemetery, Hamilton, Mercer County.
KELLEY, GEORGE W.C. 5-28-1879. Bible Church Cemetery, Hardingville, Gloucester County.
KELLEY, HENRY CLAY Pvt, B, 127th NY Inf, 7-11-1909. Rosedale Cemetery, Orange, Essex County.
KELLEY, JAMES Seaman, U.S. Navy, USS Jamestown, 6-7-1899. New Camden Cemetery, Camden, Camden County.
KELLEY, JAMES Pvt, G, 2nd U.S. Inf, 2-16-1895. Mansfield/Washington Cemetery, Washington, Warren County.
KELLEY, JAMES P. Pvt, I, 15th NJ Inf, 1905. Locust Hill Cemetery, Dover, Morris County.

Our Brothers Gone Before

KELLEY, JOHN Pvt, K, 6th NY Inf, 4-7-1875. Fairmount Cemetery, Newark, Essex County.
KELLEY, JOHN L. 1873. Mount Pleasant Cemetery, Newark, Essex County.
KELLEY, JOHN R. Pvt, D, 3rd NJ Militia, 9-30-1900. Riverview Cemetery, Trenton, Mercer County.
KELLEY, JOHN W. Sgt, K, 10th NJ Inf, 8-11-1898. Masonic Cemetery, Barnegat, Ocean County.
KELLEY, M.J. Seaman, U.S. Navy, DoD Unknown. Holy Name Cemetery, Jersey City, Hudson County.
KELLEY, MUNSON P. Pvt, K, 1st NJ Militia, 4-1-1910. Fairmount Cemetery, Newark, Essex County.
KELLEY, PATRICK Pvt, A, 14th NJ Inf, 3-13-1924. Mount Olivet Cemetery, Newark, Essex County.
KELLEY, PATRICK Landsman, U.S. Navy, USS Sebago, 12-17-1919. St. John's Cemetery, Hamilton, Mercer County.
KELLEY, PATRICK Pvt, B, 6th NJ Inf, 11-12-1921. St. Rose of Lima Cemetery, Millburn, Essex County.
KELLEY, RICHARD D. Pvt, D, 15th NJ Inf, 5-30-1911. Clove Cemetery, Wantage, Sussex County.
KELLEY, STACY D. (aka: Thompson, Stacy) Pvt, E, 4th NJ Inf, [Wounded in action.] 5-1-1913. Riverview Cemetery, Trenton, Mercer County.
KELLEY, THOMAS H. Pvt, I, 44th GA Inf (CSA), [Captured 5-10-1864 at Spotsylvania CH, VA. Died of disease.] 2-25-1865. Finn's Point National Cemetery, Pennsville, Salem County.
KELLEY, WALTER E. Pvt, H, 1st NJ Cav, 10-15-1902. Fairmount Cemetery, Newark, Essex County.
KELLEY, WILLIAM Ordinary Seaman, U.S. Navy, USS New Ironsides, 9-14-1902. Fairmount Cemetery, Chatham, Morris County.
KELLEY, WILLIAM Pvt, C, 39th NJ Inf, 4-23-1908. Fairmount Cemetery, Newark, Essex County.
KELLINGER*, SAMUEL M. 2nd Lt, G, 65th NY Inf, 1892. Whitelawn Cemetery, Point Pleasant, Ocean County.
KELLITT, JAMES Pvt, G, 7th CT Inf, 4-13-1907. Arlington Cemetery, Pennsauken, Camden County.
KELLNER, BERNHARDT J. Corp, A, 20th NY Inf, 4-13-1895. Fairmount Cemetery, Newark, Essex County.
KELLNER, DANIEL Pvt, Btty A, 1st NJ Light Art, [Wounded in action.] 12-31-1901. Woodland Cemetery, Newark, Essex County.
KELLOGG, CHARLES BRYCE DoD Unknown. Canfield Cemetery, Cedar Grove, Essex County.
KELLOGG, ROBERT DoD Unknown. Fairmount Cemetery, Newark, Essex County.
KELLUM*, BENJAMIN L. Corp, B, 6th U.S. Cav, 3-31-1909. Arlington Cemetery, Pennsauken, Camden County.
KELLUM, EDWARD M. Wagoner, H, 28th NJ Inf, 9-12-1906. Berlin Cemetery, Berlin, Camden County.
KELLUM, JAMES Pvt, E, 8th IL Cav, 8-13-1890. Bordentown/Old St. Mary's Catholic Cemetery, Bordentown, Burlington County.
KELLUM, SAMUEL K. Corp, K, 36th U.S. CT, 11-2-1908. Rosehill Cemetery, Linden, Union County.
KELLY, ALEXANDER P. Pvt, G, 1st NJ Inf, 6-13-1874. Riverview Cemetery, Trenton, Mercer County.
KELLY, ANSON H. Pvt, D, 17th NY Inf, 2-21-1898. Calvary Cemetery, Cherry Hill, Camden County.

New Jersey Civil War Burials

KELLY, ARTHUR IRA DoD Unknown. Hackensack Cemetery, Hackensack, Bergen County.
KELLY, BERNARD __, __, __ U.S. __, DoD Unknown. Finn's Point National Cemetery, Pennsville, Salem County.
KELLY*, CHARLES H. Pvt, D, 2nd NJ Inf, 5-15-1874. Woodland Cemetery, Newark, Essex County.
KELLY, CORNELIUS Pvt, H, 29th NJ Inf, 6-29-1912. Baptist Cemetery, West Creek, Ocean County.
KELLY*, CURTIS Q. 1st Sgt, C, 11th NJ Inf, 9-7-1881. Greenwood Cemetery, Tuckerton, Ocean County.
KELLY, DANIEL Pvt, H, 13th NY Inf, 3-26-1917. Baptist Church Cemetery, Haddonfield, Camden County.
KELLY, DANIEL Pvt, B, 8th PA Cav, DoD Unknown. Old St. Mary's Cemetery, Gloucester City, Camden County.
KELLY*, DANIEL J. Sgt, Btty K, 13th NY Heavy Art, 1-14-1898. Holy Name Cemetery, Jersey City, Hudson County.
KELLY, DAVID Pvt, B, 25th U.S. CT, 12-27-1898. Johnson Cemetery, Camden, Camden County.
KELLY, EDWARD Pvt, G, 1st NJ Inf, 11-21-1922. Arlington Cemetery, Kearny, Hudson County.
KELLY, EDWARD B.P. (see: Kelley, Edward B.P.) Westminster Cemetery, Cranbury, Middlesex County.
KELLY, EDWARD F. Pvt, D, 69th NY Inf, 10-22-1911. St. Joseph's Cemetery, Hackensack, Bergen County.
KELLY*, EDWIN G. Pvt, E, 8th NJ Inf, 6-13-1885. Beverly National Cemetery, Edgewater Park, Burlington County.
KELLY, FRANCIS Pvt, C, 8th NJ Inf, 11-28-1899. Holy Name Cemetery, Jersey City, Hudson County.
KELLY, FRANCIS (see: Kennedy, Francis) Holy Sepulchre Cemetery, East Orange, Essex County.
KELLY, FRANK J. Pvt, H, 3rd NJ Militia, DoD Unknown. St. John's Evangelical Church Cemetery, Orange, Essex County.
KELLY, GEORGE Pvt, F, 37th VA Inf (CSA), [Wounded 3-23-1862 at Kernstown, VA. Captured 5-12-1864 at Spotsylvania CH, VA. Died of disease.] 5-17-1865. Finn's Point National Cemetery, Pennsville, Salem County.
KELLY*, GEORGE W. Pvt, H, 5th NJ Inf, 10-24-1906. Alpine Cemetery, Perth Amboy, Middlesex County.
KELLY, GEORGE W. (aka: Keller, George) Corp, B, 2nd MD Inf (PHB), 2-25-1890. Evergreen Cemetery, Camden, Camden County.
KELLY, J. Pvt, B, 4th (Russell's) AL Cav (CSA), 3-8-1864. Finn's Point National Cemetery, Pennsville, Salem County.
KELLY, JAMES Pvt, C, 7th NJ Inf, [Died at Annapolis, MD.] 1-3-1865. St. John's Evangelical Church Cemetery, Orange, Essex County.
KELLY*, JAMES Pvt, Unassigned, 33rd NJ Inf, 5-8-1897. Holy Sepulchre Cemetery, East Orange, Essex County.
KELLY, JAMES Wagoner, F, 8th NJ Inf, 11-6-1897. Mercer Cemetery, Trenton, Mercer County.
KELLY, JAMES Pvt, K, 3rd NJ Inf, [Wounded in action.] DoD Unknown. Holy Sepulchre Cemetery, East Orange, Essex County.
KELLY, JAMES 5-16-1907. St. John's Evangelical Church Cemetery, Orange, Essex County.
KELLY, JAMES E. Seaman, U.S. Navy, USS Princess Royal, 10-1-1874. St. John's Evangelical Church Cemetery, Orange, Essex County.

Our Brothers Gone Before

KELLY, JOEL F. Wagoner, K, 31st ME Inf, 10-14-1864. Beverly National Cemetery, Edgewater Park, Burlington County.
KELLY*, JOHN Pvt, I, 35th NJ Inf, 7-14-1905. Fairmount Cemetery, Newark, Essex County.
KELLY, JOHN Pvt, E, 5th U.S. Inf, 5-25-1914. Holy Sepulchre Cemetery, East Orange, Essex County.
KELLY, JOHN Pvt, C, 6th NJ Inf, 3-7-1919. Bayview-New York Bay Cemetery, Jersey City, Hudson County.
KELLY, JOHN Pvt, B, 41st NY Inf, 2-10-1872. Holy Name Cemetery, Jersey City, Hudson County.
KELLY, JOHN 1-30-1885. Flower Hill Cemetery, North Bergen, Hudson County.
KELLY, JOHN 6-14-1919. Holy Name Cemetery, Jersey City, Hudson County.
KELLY, JOHN Pvt, C, 29th NJ Inf, 2-13-1903. St. Rose of Lima Cemetery, Freehold, Monmouth County.
KELLY, JOHN Pvt, K, 1st NJ Inf, [Cenotaph. Died while prisoner at Andersonville, GA.] 10-17-1864. Old Somerville Cemetery, Somerville, Somerset County.
KELLY, JOHN 9-30-1900. Riverview Cemetery, Trenton, Mercer County.
KELLY, JOHN 1892. Mount Olivet Cemetery, Fairview, Monmouth County.
KELLY, JOHN H. Pvt, E, 1st NJ Inf, 2-9-1901. Holy Sepulchre Cemetery, East Orange, Essex County.
KELLY, JOHN J. Pvt, I, 176th NY Inf, 11-19-1891. Holy Rood Cemetery, Morristown, Morris County.
KELLY, JOHN R. Landsman, U.S. Navy, USS Seneca, 9-30-1911. St. John's Evangelical Church Cemetery, Orange, Essex County.
KELLY, JOHN R. 1903. Presbyterian Church Cemetery, Greenwich, Warren County.
KELLY, JOSEPH 9-3-1894. Hoboken Cemetery, North Bergen, Hudson County.
KELLY, JOSEPH T. Corp, K, 72nd PA Inf, [Wounded in action.] DoD Unknown. Bible Church Cemetery, Hardingville, Gloucester County.
KELLY, MARTIN Pvt, E, 2nd NJ Cav, 12-12-1898. Holy Name Cemetery, Jersey City, Hudson County.
KELLY, MICHAEL Pvt, A, 1st DE Inf, 9-3-1908. Arlington Cemetery, Kearny, Hudson County.
KELLY, MICHAEL Pvt, C, 1st NJ Cav, 1910. Holy Sepulchre Cemetery, Totowa, Passaic County.
KELLY*, PATRICK Pvt, I, 38th NY Inf, 12-2-1928. Mount Olivet Cemetery, Newark, Essex County.
KELLY, PATRICK Pvt, A, 38th NJ Inf, 7- -1865. Mount Olivet Cemetery, Fairview, Monmouth County.
KELLY, PATRICK (aka: Raley, Patrick) Pvt, L, 2nd NJ Cav, 5-7-1872. St. John's Evangelical Church Cemetery, Orange, Essex County.
KELLY, PETER B. Pvt, K, 7th NJ Inf, 2-21-1928. Cedar Lawn Cemetery, Paterson, Passaic County.
KELLY, RICHARD Pvt, H, 23rd NJ Inf, 10-10-1868. Bordentown/Old St. Mary's Catholic Cemetery, Bordentown, Burlington County.
KELLY, ROBERT Pvt, C, 25th NJ Inf, 3-14-1903. Laurel Grove Cemetery, Totowa, Passaic County.
KELLY, ROBERT N. Pvt, K, 38th NJ Inf, 10-8-1913. Baptist Church Cemetery, Flemington, Hunterdon County.
KELLY, THOMAS Landsman, U.S. Navy, 5-30-1875. St. John's Evangelical Church Cemetery, Orange, Essex County.
KELLY*, THOMAS Fireman, U.S. Navy, USS Shawmut, 1907. St. John's Cemetery, Hamilton, Mercer County.
KELLY, THOMAS Pvt, E, 26th NJ Inf, 5-8-1873. Holy Sepulchre Cemetery, East Orange, Essex County.

New Jersey Civil War Burials

KELLY, THOMAS Pvt, G, 13th NJ Inf, [Died of exposure at Fairfax, VA.] 12-21-1862. Holy Sepulchre Cemetery, East Orange, Essex County.

KELLY, THOMAS Landsman, U.S. Navy, USS Macedonia, 10-24-1871. St. John's Evangelical Church Cemetery, Orange, Essex County.

KELLY, THOMAS DoD Unknown. Evergreen Cemetery, Camden, Camden County.

KELLY, THOMAS B. Seaman, U.S. Navy, DoD Unknown. Arlington Cemetery, Kearny, Hudson County.

KELLY, WALTER Pvt, H, 1st NJ Cav, 10-18-1902. Fairmount Cemetery, Newark, Essex County.

KELLY, WARREN S. Pvt, E, 27th NJ Inf, 6-9-1884. Fairmount Cemetery, Newark, Essex County.

KELLY, WILLIAM Ordinary Seaman, U.S. Navy, USS New Ironsides, 7-9-1905. Brotherhood Cemetery, Hainesport, Burlington County.

KELLY, WILLIAM H. Pvt, I, 33rd NJ Inf, 8-21-1907. Fairmount Cemetery, Newark, Essex County.

KELSALL, JOSHUA Pvt, B, 14th NJ Inf, 7-10-1901. Fairmount Cemetery, Newark, Essex County.

KELSEY, EDWARD Pvt, A, 25th U.S. CT, 5-1-1924. Mansfield/Washington Cemetery, Washington, Warren County.

KELSEY, ISAAC Pvt, K, 13th NJ Inf, 10-15-1906. Hardyston Cemetery, North Church, Sussex County.

KELSEY, OSCAR A. Musc, G, 10th NY Inf, 4-10-1901. Holy Name Cemetery, Jersey City, Hudson County.

KELSEY, RUFUS B. Capt, F, 47th PA Militia, 6-11-1896. Baptist Church Cemetery, Slabtown, Salem County.

KELSEY, WILLIAM Pvt, H, 4th NJ Inf, [Wounded in action.] 1-2-1907. United Methodist Church Cemetery, Absecon, Atlantic County.

KELSOE, JOHN W. Sgt, I, 8th (Wade's) Confederate States Cav (CSA), 10-31-1863. Finn's Point National Cemetery, Pennsville, Salem County.

KELT, CHARLES (see: Kalt, Charles) Old Camden Cemetery, Camden, Camden County.

KELTER, JAMES E. Pvt, B, 72nd PA Inf, 9-10-1929. New Camden Cemetery, Camden, Camden County.

KELTEY, JESSE F. Pvt, F, 100th PA Inf, [Died at Beverly, NJ.] 12-4-1864. Beverly National Cemetery, Edgewater Park, Burlington County.

KEMBLE, ALBERT (aka: Kimble, Albert) Pvt, C, 24th PA Inf, DoD Unknown. Evergreen Cemetery, Camden, Camden County.

KEMBLE*, ISAAC J. Pvt, F, 7th NJ Inf, 11-14-1910. Greenwood Cemetery, Hamilton, Mercer County.

KEMBLE, JAMES D. (aka: Kimbel, James) Pvt, Btty C, 5th NY Heavy Art, 10-10-1914. Hillside Cemetery, Madison, Morris County.

KEMBLE*, JAMES H. Pvt, H, 1st U.S. Cav, 12-7-1866. Methodist Church Cemetery, New Albany, Burlington County.

KEMBLE, JOSEPH M. Pvt, C, 23rd NJ Inf, 3-9-1895. Baptist/St. Andrew's Cemetery, Mount Holly, Burlington County.

KEMBLE, WILLIAM C. Pvt, H, 10th NJ Inf, 3-14-1898. Monument Cemetery, Edgewater Park, Burlington County.

KEMBLE, WILLIAM G. Pvt, B, 23rd NJ Inf, 6-10-1922. Cedar Hill Cemetery, Florence, Burlington County.

KEMMER, HENRY Fireman, U.S. Navy, 4-8-1900. Palisade Cemetery, North Bergen, Hudson County.

KEMP, CHARLES (see: Kempe, Charles) Rose Hill Cemetery, Matawan, Monmouth County.

KEMP, JACOB Pvt, D, 33rd VA Inf (CSA), 8-10-1864. Finn's Point National Cemetery, Pennsville, Salem County.

Our Brothers Gone Before

KEMP, JESSE 2nd Lt, C, 22nd SC Inf (CSA), [Captured 7-30-1864 at the Crater, Petersburg, VA. Died of chronic diarrhea.] 3-12-1865. Finn's Point National Cemetery, Pennsville, Salem County.

KEMP, JOHN M. Pvt, F, 22nd CT Inf, 3-14-1910. Cedar Lawn Cemetery, Paterson, Passaic County.

KEMP, JOHN S. Pvt, B, 2nd FL Inf (CSA), [Captured 7-3-1863 at Gettysburg, PA. Died of bronchitis.] 9-14-1863. Finn's Point National Cemetery, Pennsville, Salem County.

KEMP, THOMAS Pvt, F, 1st NJ Inf, DoD Unknown. 1st Methodist-Episcopal Cemetery, New Brunswick, Middlesex County.

KEMPE, CHARLES (aka: Kemp, Charles) Pvt, Btty M, 6th NY Heavy Art, [Cenotaph. Killed in action at North Anna River, VA.] 5-23-1864. Rose Hill Cemetery, Matawan, Monmouth County.

KEMPF, HENRY Pvt, Btty C, 1st NJ Light Art, 3-15-1895. Flower Hill Cemetery, North Bergen, Hudson County.

KEMPF, O.AUGUST Pvt, Btty K, 15th NY Heavy Art, DoD Unknown. Macphelah Cemetery, North Bergen, Hudson County.

KEMPF, WILLIAM Pvt, E, 11th NY Inf, 9-17-1921. Berry Lawn Cemetery, Carlstadt, Bergen County.

KEMPPE, SELEG (see: Solnek, Penkus) Chew's United Methodist Church Cemetery, Glendora, Camden County.

KEMPTON, EMORY Pvt, Btty A, 1st MA Light Art, DoD Unknown. Good Luck Cemetery, Murray Grove, Ocean County.

KEMPTON, JOHN H. Musc, 3rd NJ Inf Band DoD Unknown. 1st Methodist-Episcopal Cemetery, New Brunswick, Middlesex County.

KENDALL, GEORGE H. Pvt, C, 25th NJ Inf, 3-15-1908. Prospect Hill Cemetery, Caldwell, Essex County.

KENDALL, JAMES Pvt, A, 118th NY Inf, 4-1-1915. Greenwood Cemetery, Pleasantville, Atlantic County.

KENDALL, JAMES D. Pvt, G, 3rd NJ Cav, 3-16-1920. Presbyterian Church Cemetery, Bridgeton, Cumberland County.

KENDELL, SAMUEL (see: Kandle, Samuel) St. John's Methodist Church Cemetery, Harrisonville, Gloucester County.

KENDRICK, JOHN H. Pvt, G, 33rd MA Inf, [Wounded 6-9-1863 at Beverlys Ford, VA.] 10-17-1902. Mount Carmel Cemetery, West Moorestown, Burlington County.

KENE, CHARLES (see: Cane, Charles) Holy Sepulchre Cemetery, East Orange, Essex County.

KENELLER, CHARLES (aka: Kneller, Charles) Pvt, A, 12th U.S. Inf, 11-3-1896. Fairmount Cemetery, Newark, Essex County.

KENLAN, CHARLES (aka: Kershaw, Charles A.) Sgt, G, 1st NJ Inf, 8-2-1918. Holy Sepulchre Cemetery, East Orange, Essex County.

KENNA, THOMAS Pvt, D, 28th NJ Inf, 8-26-1890. St. Peter's Cemetery, New Brunswick, Middlesex County.

KENNEDY, ANDREW J. Pvt, I, 3rd NJ Cav, 4-13-1886. Evergreen Cemetery, Camden, Camden County.

KENNEDY, CHARLES P. Pvt, B, 51st NY Inf, 10-10-1907. Evergreen Cemetery, Hillside, Union County.

KENNEDY, CHARLES W. 1st Lt, C, 8th NJ Inf, 10-15-1914. Fairmount Cemetery, Newark, Essex County.

KENNEDY, CORNELIUS Pvt, E, 26th NJ Inf, 1891. Immaculate Conception Cemetery, Montclair, Essex County.

KENNEDY, DANIEL Pvt, Btty E, 1st NJ Light Art, DoD Unknown. St. Peter's Cemetery, New Brunswick, Middlesex County.

New Jersey Civil War Burials

KENNEDY, DANIEL F. Pvt, H, 31st NJ Inf, 8-24-1912. Methodist-Episcopal Cemetery, Whitehouse, Hunterdon County.

KENNEDY, EDWARD Pvt, C, 9th NY Inf, 6-25-1881. Holy Name Cemetery, Jersey City, Hudson County.

KENNEDY, EDWARD Pvt, K, 3rd NJ Militia, DoD Unknown. St. Peter's Cemetery, New Brunswick, Middlesex County.

KENNEDY, FRANCIS Pvt, G, 42nd NY Inf, 4-3-1924. Rosedale Cemetery, Linden, Union County.

KENNEDY, FRANCIS (aka: Kelly, Francis) Corp, E, 37th NJ Inf, 2-11-1886. Holy Sepulchre Cemetery, East Orange, Essex County.

KENNEDY, GEORGE S. Sgt, G, 46th PA Inf, [Wounded in action.] 8-12-1898. Hillside Cemetery, Oxford, Warren County.

KENNEDY, JAMES Pvt, K, 27th NJ Inf, 11-26-1905. Immaculate Conception Cemetery, Montclair, Essex County.

KENNEDY, JARED Pvt, F, 2nd NJ Inf, [Killed in action at Gaines' Farm, VA.] 6-27-1862. Mount Pleasant Cemetery, Newark, Essex County.

KENNEDY, JOHN DoD Unknown. St. Peter's Cemetery, Jersey City, Hudson County.

KENNEDY, JOHN Pvt, 10th NY Ind Btty 12-8-1899. Holy Sepulchre Cemetery, Totowa, Passaic County.

KENNEDY, JOHN H. 10-24-1900. Mount Hope Presbyterian Cemetery, Lambertville, Hunterdon County.

KENNEDY, JOHN W. Sgt, C, 10th NY Inf, 10-22-1915. Fairmount Cemetery, Newark, Essex County.

KENNEDY, MICHAEL J. __, __, __ U.S. __, 1907. Soldier's Home Cemetery, Vineland, Cumberland County.

KENNEDY, PATRICK F. Pvt, K, 1st NJ Cav, 9-15-1913. Holy Sepulchre Cemetery, East Orange, Essex County.

KENNEDY*, PETER Pvt, A, 10th NJ Inf, 1-4-1924. Evergreen Cemetery, Hillside, Union County.

KENNEDY, Q.W. (aka: Kennedy, William D.) Pvt, A, 20th TN Cav (CSA), 3-21-1864. Finn's Point National Cemetery, Pennsville, Salem County.

KENNEDY, REDDING Pvt, F, 11th NJ Inf, 3-29-1908. Arlington Cemetery, Kearny, Hudson County.

KENNEDY*, RICHARD T. Pvt, D, 17th MA Inf, 6-22-1912. St. Mary's Cemetery, Hainesport, Burlington County.

KENNEDY, SAMUEL R. Pvt, D, 33rd PA Inf, 1924. Soldier's Home Cemetery, Vineland, Cumberland County.

KENNEDY, THEODORE Pvt, A, 25th U.S. CT, 2-9-1901. Riverview Cemetery, Trenton, Mercer County.

KENNEDY, THOMAS Pvt, Btty E, 16th NY Heavy Art, 12-5-1915. Holy Sepulchre Cemetery, East Orange, Essex County.

KENNEDY, THOMAS 8-19-1880. St. Peter's Church Cemetery, Belleville, Essex County.

KENNEDY, WILLIAM Coal Heaver, U.S. Navy, USS Wilderness, DoD Unknown. Holy Sepulchre Cemetery, East Orange, Essex County.

KENNEDY, WILLIAM 2-2-1882. St. Peter's Church Cemetery, Belleville, Essex County.

KENNEDY, WILLIAM (see: Harris, Ira) Holy Sepulchre Cemetery, East Orange, Essex County.

KENNEDY, WILLIAM D. (see: Kennedy, Q.W.) Finn's Point National Cemetery, Pennsville, Salem County.

KENNEDY, WILLIAM F. Pvt, D, 37th NJ Inf, 10-30-1895. Methodist-Episcopal Cemetery, Whitehouse, Hunterdon County.

KENNEDY, WILLIAM H. Pvt, K, 6th U.S. Cav, DoD Unknown. Arlington Cemetery, Kearny, Hudson County.

Our Brothers Gone Before

KENNEDY, WILLIAM HENRY Pvt, E, 3rd GA Inf (CSA), [Captured 7-2-1863 at Gettysburg, PA. Died of diarrhea.] 9-8-1863. Finn's Point National Cemetery, Pennsville, Salem County.
KENNELLY*, MAURICE V. Pvt, I, 176th NY Inf, 8-28-1924. Bayview-New York Bay Cemetery, Jersey City, Hudson County.
KENNEMER, FRANKLIN (aka: Cameron, Franklin) Pvt, A, 35th AL Inf (CSA), 7-5-1865. Finn's Point National Cemetery, Pennsville, Salem County.
KENNEY*, JAMES Pvt, E, 7th NJ Inf, 4-3-1881. Holy Sepulchre Cemetery, East Orange, Essex County.
KENNEY, JAMES Pvt, A, 9th NJ Inf, 6-2-1913. Holy Sepulchre Cemetery, East Orange, Essex County.
KENNEY, JAMES Pvt, F, 2nd NJ Militia, DoD Unknown. Holy Name Cemetery, Jersey City, Hudson County.
KENNEY, JOHN Pvt, D, 10th NJ Inf, 12-18-1900. Holy Name Cemetery, Jersey City, Hudson County.
KENNEY, JOHN Pvt, C, 91st NY Inf, 5-13-1867. Holy Name Cemetery, Jersey City, Hudson County.
KENNEY, JOHN Pvt, E, 8th NJ Inf, 3-2-1914. Greenwood Cemetery, Hamilton, Mercer County.
KENNEY, JOHN DoD Unknown. Old St. Mary's Cemetery, Gloucester City, Camden County.
KENNEY, JOHN T. Pvt, H, 7th NJ Inf, 12-12-1887. St. Joseph's Cemetery, Swedesboro, Gloucester County.
KENNEY, LEWIS Actg Ens, U.S. Navy, DoD Unknown. Evergreen Cemetery, Camden, Camden County.
KENNEY, PATRICK Pvt, K, 24th NJ Inf, 9-24-1922. Lake Park Cemetery, Swedesboro, Gloucester County.
KENNEY, THOMAS Pvt, Btty E, 1st NJ Light Art, 2-21-1908. Fairmount Cemetery, Newark, Essex County.
KENNEY, THOMAS Pvt, L, 8th NY Cav, 12-4-1916. Holy Name Cemetery, Jersey City, Hudson County.
KENNEY, THOMAS Pvt, L, 13th NY Cav, 6-20-1874. Holy Sepulchre Cemetery, East Orange, Essex County.
KENNEYBROOK*, CHARLES Pvt, G, 8th NJ Inf, DoD Unknown. Mansfield/Washington Cemetery, Washington, Warren County.
KENNY, ANDREW 6-22-1889. Holy Name Cemetery, Jersey City, Hudson County.
KENNY, D. Pvt, F, 10th VA Cav (CSA), 9-15-1864. Finn's Point National Cemetery, Pennsville, Salem County.
KENNY, FRANK 5-16-1905. Holy Name Cemetery, Jersey City, Hudson County.
KENNY, JAMES Seaman, U.S. Navy, USS Princeton, 3-5-1890. St. John's Evangelical Church Cemetery, Orange, Essex County.
KENNY, JOHN Corp, A, 10th NJ Inf, 1913. Holy Sepulchre Cemetery, East Orange, Essex County.
KENNY*, JOHN Musc, A, 16th U.S. Inf, 10-2-1922. Arlington Cemetery, Kearny, Hudson County.
KENNY, JOHN Pvt, Unassigned, 62nd NY Inf, DoD Unknown. Holy Name Cemetery, Jersey City, Hudson County.
KENNY, MARTIN (see: Kinney, Martin) St. John's Evangelical Church Cemetery, Orange, Essex County.
KENNY, W.D. Pvt, A, 4th GA Inf (CSA), 12-6-1863. Finn's Point National Cemetery, Pennsville, Salem County.
KENSELL, KASIMER Pvt, H, 14th NJ Inf, 9-14-1906. Evergreen Cemetery, Hillside, Union County.

New Jersey Civil War Burials

KENSTLER, FRANK 1st Sgt, K, 8th U.S. Inf, 12-18-1913. St. Mary's Cemetery, Wharton, Morris County.
KENT, ALEXANDER (aka: Kent, Sandy) Pvt, C, 102nd NY Inf, [Wounded in action 7-4-1864.] 2-11-1919. Old Hook Cemetery, Westwood, Bergen County.
KENT, CHARLES 3-17-1875. Rosedale Cemetery, Orange, Essex County.
KENT, CHARLES Wagoner, H, 2nd NJ Cav, 6-8-1869. Riverview Cemetery, Trenton, Mercer County.
KENT, CHARLES W. Pvt, D, 137th IL Inf, DoD Unknown. Old South Church Cemetery, Bergenfield, Bergen County.
KENT, CORNELIUS C. Pvt, B, 22nd NJ Inf, 1-24-1902. Pascack Reformed Cemetery, Park Ridge, Bergen County.
KENT, DAVID (aka: Kint, David) Pvt, E, 9th NJ Inf, 3-7-1928. Balesville Cemetery, Balesville, Sussex County.
KENT, EDWARD B. Pvt, E, 88th NY Inf, 6-30-1927. Fairmount Cemetery, Newark, Essex County.
KENT, FRANK Pvt, F, 2nd NJ Cav, 1904. New Somerville Cemetery, Somerville, Somerset County.
KENT, GEORGE W. Pvt, D, 6th CT Inf, 8-18-1898. Woodland Cemetery, Newark, Essex County.
KENT, HENRY C. Pvt, D, 11th NJ Inf, 2-19-1924. Fairmount Cemetery, Newark, Essex County.
KENT, JAMES (aka: Kent, John) Pvt, G, 1st AL Cav (CSA), 10-9-1863. Finn's Point National Cemetery, Pennsville, Salem County.
KENT, JAMES GILES Pvt, C, 21st NJ Inf, 10-2-1914. Brookside Cemetery, Englewood, Bergen County.
KENT, JOHN (see: Kent, James) Finn's Point National Cemetery, Pennsville, Salem County.
KENT*, JOHN T. Pvt, D, 33rd NJ Inf, 1-11-1866. Evergreen Cemetery, Morristown, Morris County.
KENT, LEVI Pvt, D, 26th NJ Inf, 2-5-1925. Prospect Hill Cemetery, Caldwell, Essex County.
KENT, LEWIS L. Pvt, K, 15th NJ Inf, [Killed in action at Spotsylvania CH, VA.] 5-12-1864. Hardyston Cemetery, North Church, Sussex County.
KENT, NAHUM Sgt, K, 14th NJ Inf, 3-7-1896. Van Liew Cemetery, North Brunswick, Middlesex County.
KENT, PERRY Pvt, E, 8th NJ Inf, 2-16-1919. Arlington Cemetery, Kearny, Hudson County.
KENT, PETER H. Pvt, E, 102nd NY Inf, 1-1-1918. Fairmount Cemetery, Newark, Essex County.
KENT, SANDY (see: Kent, Alexander) Old Hook Cemetery, Westwood, Bergen County.
KENT, WILLIAM Pvt, A, 10th NJ Inf, 9-6-1883. Willow Grove Cemetery, New Brunswick, Middlesex County.
KENT, WILLIAM A. Pvt, A, 1st NY Cav, 12-28-1894. Siloam Cemetery, Vineland, Cumberland County.
KENT, WILLIAM F. Sgt, K, 67th NY Inf, 8-5-1886. Old Hook Cemetery, Westwood, Bergen County.
KENTNER, CONRAD (see: Kintner, John L.) Baptist Cemetery, Hopewell Boro, Mercer County.
KENTY, GEORGE Pvt, D, 2nd NJ Cav, DoD Unknown. Mount Pleasant Cemetery, Millville, Cumberland County.
KENTZ, BALTHAZAR Pvt, F, 26th NJ Inf, 12-11-1898. Bloomfield Cemetery, Bloomfield, Essex County.
KENTZ, JOHN J. Sgt, G, 20th PA Cav, 2-3-1923. Riverview Cemetery, Trenton, Mercer County.

Our Brothers Gone Before

KENWORTHY, JAMES Pvt, D, 33rd NJ Inf, 1902. Midvale Cemetery, Midvale, Passaic County.
KENWORTHY, JOHN J. Pvt, D, 6th NJ Inf, 1-22-1907. Cedar Grove Cemetery, Gloucester City, Camden County.
KENYON, D. RANDOLPH 1901. New Somerville Cemetery, Somerville, Somerset County.
KEOGH, THOMAS Pvt, A, 88th NY Inf, 12-8-1908. Holy Name Cemetery, Jersey City, Hudson County.
KEOUGH, JOHN Pvt, B, 1st NJ Militia, 9-1-1896. Holy Sepulchre Cemetery, East Orange, Essex County.
KEOUGH, MICHAEL Pvt, G, 39th NJ Inf, 8-15-1921. Holy Sepulchre Cemetery, East Orange, Essex County.
KEOUGH, PATRICK Pvt, C, 35th NJ Inf, [Wounded 5-13-1864 at Resaca, GA.] 5-9-1883. Holy Sepulchre Cemetery, East Orange, Essex County.
KEOWN, SAMUEL Pvt, D, 3rd NJ Cav, 3-6-1895. Harleigh Cemetery, Camden, Camden County.
KEPHART, WILLIAM Pvt, F, 106th PA Inf, 8-13-1912. Greenwood Cemetery, Pleasantville, Atlantic County.
KER, ISAAC N. 12-21-1902. Fairmount Cemetery, Newark, Essex County.
KER, ISAAC N. Musc, A, 28th NJ Inf, 11-20-1920. Glenwood Cemetery, West Long Branch, Monmouth County.
KER*, LOUIS F. Pvt, F, 7th NJ Inf, 1911. 1st Reformed Church Cemetery, Pompton Plains, Morris County.
KERIN, JOSEPH Bvt Capt, E, 6th U.S. Cav, 9-24-1890. Siloam Cemetery, Vineland, Cumberland County.
KERKER, JOSEPH (see: Kircher, Joseph) Eglington Cemetery, Clarksboro, Gloucester County.
KERKHOFF, H. ANTON 3-20-1914. Cedar Green Cemetery, Clayton, Gloucester County.
KERLIN*, WILLIAM Pvt, F, 38th NJ Inf, 12-15-1898. Riverview Cemetery, Trenton, Mercer County.
KERN, ABRAM C. Seaman, U.S. Navy, DoD Unknown. Epworth Methodist Cemetery, Palmyra, Burlington County.
KERN, DAVID Coal Heaver, U.S. Navy, USS Althea, 12-12-1874. Methodist-Episcopal Cemetery, Wantage, Sussex County.
KERN, EFFINGER Pvt, B, 93rd PA Inf, 5-19-1891. New Presbyterian Church Cemetery, Daretown, Salem County.
KERN, GEORGE C. Pvt, D, 5th NY National Guard, 4-6-1893. Bayview-New York Bay Cemetery, Jersey City, Hudson County.
KERN, R. Pvt, I, 12th VA Cav (CSA), 8-30-1864. Finn's Point National Cemetery, Pennsville, Salem County.
KERN, WILLIAM H. Pvt, U.S. Marine Corps, DoD Unknown. Fairmount Cemetery, Newark, Essex County.
KERNAN, CHARLES Corp, I, 13th NJ Inf, 7-21-1865. Fairmount Cemetery, Newark, Essex County.
KERNAN, JOHN L. Pvt, A, 31st PA Inf, [Wounded 6-26-1862 at Mechanicsville, VA.] 8-30-1969. 1st Baptist Cemetery, Cape May Court House, Cape May County.
KERNS, JAMES H. DoD Unknown. Evergreen Cemetery, Camden, Camden County.
KERR, ABEL Pvt, H, 34th NJ Inf, 6-5-1923. Union Cemetery, Frenchtown, Hunterdon County.
KERR, ANDREW Pvt, G, 8th NJ Inf, 6-3-1908. Brotherhood Cemetery, Hainesport, Burlington County.
KERR, BARTLETT Pvt, H, 34th NJ Inf, 8-6-1917. Rosemont Cemetery, Rosemont, Hunterdon County.

New Jersey Civil War Burials

KERR, HUGH Pvt, G, 38th NJ Inf, 2-26-1910. Union Cemetery, Frenchtown, Hunterdon County.
KERR, HUGH 1901. Holy Sepulchre Cemetery, Totowa, Passaic County.
KERR, JAMES W. Pvt, H, 34th NJ Inf, 5-19-1891. Union Cemetery, Frenchtown, Hunterdon County.
KERR*, JOHN Pvt, B, 50th PA Inf, 5-22-1927. Rosemont Cemetery, Rosemont, Hunterdon County.
KERR, JOHN A. Pvt, A, 23rd NJ Inf, 7-24-1899. Oddfellows Cemetery, Burlington, Burlington County.
KERR, JOHN A. 10-8-1903. Fairmount Cemetery, Newark, Essex County.
KERR, JONATHAN Pvt, C, 18th PA Cav, [Died at Philadelphia, PA.] 1-17-1865. New Episcopal Church Cemetery, Swedesboro, Gloucester County.
KERR, LORENZO L.D. Pvt, H, 34th NJ Inf, 10-27-1916. Union Cemetery, Frenchtown, Hunterdon County.
KERR, SAMUEL Sgt, G, 11th NJ Inf, [Killed in action on picket line at Armstrong House ,Petersburg, VA.] 3-25-1865. Presbyterian Church Cemetery, Hamilton Square, Mercer County.
KERR, THOMAS (JR.) Pvt, B, 1st NJ Cav, [Died of typhoid at Washington, DC.] 10-26-1861. 1st Baptist Church Cemetery, Trenton, Mercer County.
KERR, WILLIAM J. Pvt, G, 2nd NJ Militia, 2-11-1906. Bayview-New York Bay Cemetery, Jersey City, Hudson County.
KERR, WILLIAM T. Pvt, E, 4th GA Inf (CSA), [Captured 5-10-1864 at Spotsylvania CH, VA. Died of disease.] 2-9-1865. Finn's Point National Cemetery, Pennsville, Salem County.
KERRICK, ADAM Pvt, G, 25th NJ Inf, 3-15-1863. Mount Pleasant Cemetery, Millville, Cumberland County.
KERRICK, ADAM (see: Merrick, Adam) Mount Pleasant Cemetery, Millville, Cumberland County.
KERRICK, PHILIP Corp, A, 58th PA Inf, 1925. Mount Pleasant Cemetery, Millville, Cumberland County.
KERSEY, JAMES Pvt, Tanner's Btty, VA Light Art (CSA), 7-29-1864. Finn's Point National Cemetery, Pennsville, Salem County.
KERSEY, WILLIAM H. Pvt, M, 3rd NJ Cav, 1-27-1874. Riverview Cemetery, Trenton, Mercer County.
KERSHAW, CHARLES A. (see: Kenlan, Charles) Holy Sepulchre Cemetery, East Orange, Essex County.
KERSHAW, JAMES Musc, A, 3rd NJ Inf, 7-21-1897. Mount Pleasant Cemetery, Millville, Cumberland County.
KERSHAW, THOMAS 6-18-1864. Methodist Church Cemetery, Sicklerville, Camden County.
KERWIN, EDWARD (aka: Kerwin, Edwin) Pvt, H, 182nd NY Inf, 6-17-1903. Holy Name Cemetery, Jersey City, Hudson County.
KERWIN, EDWIN (see: Kerwin, Edward) Holy Name Cemetery, Jersey City, Hudson County.
KERWIN, JOHN Pvt, F, 28th NJ Inf, 7-16-1894. Holy Sepulchre Cemetery, East Orange, Essex County.
KESIGLE, ADAM Pvt, C, 76th PA Inf, DoD Unknown. Beverly National Cemetery, Edgewater Park, Burlington County.
KESLAR, SEPLAR Pvt, A, 28th NJ Inf, 11-6-1882. Methodist Church Cemetery, Groveville, Mercer County.
KESSEL, FREDERICK C. Pvt, A, 5th PA Cav, 3-21-1925. Fairmount Cemetery, Newark, Essex County.
KESSLER, EDWIN J. Pvt, G, 14th U.S. Inf, 3-22-1917. Fairmount Cemetery, Newark, Essex County.

Our Brothers Gone Before

KESSLER, JACOB (see: Keisler, Jacob) Mount Hebron Cemetery, Montclair, Essex County.

KESSLER, JOHN Pvt, B, 91st NY Inf, 11-27-1895. Holy Sepulchre Cemetery, East Orange, Essex County.

KESTNER, JACOB J. Pvt, A, 8th NJ Inf, 2-3-1886. Fairmount Cemetery, Newark, Essex County.

KETCHAM, ELIPHALET S. Pvt, Btty D, 1st NJ Light Art, 10-26-1906. Rosedale Cemetery, Orange, Essex County.

KETCHAM, JACOB Pvt, A, 40th NY Inf, 5-24-1921. Evergreen Cemetery, Morristown, Morris County.

KETCHAM, JOHN D. Pvt, C, 8th NJ Inf, 1922. Baptist Church Cemetery, Port Murray, Warren County.

KETCHAM, JONAS 1-17-1917. Bayview-New York Bay Cemetery, Jersey City, Hudson County.

KETCHAM, SOLOMON (aka: Ketchum, Solomon) Pvt, K, 41st IL Inf, 9-25-1906. Fairview Cemetery, Fairview, Monmouth County.

KETCHAM, WILLIAM Pvt, A, 2nd NJ Militia, 9-9-1914. Evergreen Cemetery, Farmingdale, Monmouth County.

KETCHELL, THEODORE W. (see: Kitchell, Theodore Ward) New Presbyterian Cemetery, Hanover, Morris County.

KETCHUM, ERASTUS Artificer, A, 15th NY Eng, 7-31-1894. Atlantic View Cemetery, Manasquan, Monmouth County.

KETCHUM, SOLOMON (see: Ketcham, Solomon) Fairview Cemetery, Fairview, Monmouth County.

KETH, ADAM Pvt, K, 68th NY Inf, 4-5-1887. Fairmount Cemetery, Newark, Essex County.

KETTERER, GEORGE Pvt, Btty K, 15th NY Heavy Art, 10-18-1873. Fairmount Cemetery, Newark, Essex County.

KETTING, WILLIAM Pvt, G, 21st NJ Inf, DoD Unknown. Bayview-New York Bay Cemetery, Jersey City, Hudson County.

KETTLE, JAMES Pvt, B, 8th U.S. Inf, DoD Unknown. Arlington Cemetery, Kearny, Hudson County.

KEVE, DAVID C. Pvt, D, 11th NJ Inf, [Wounded in action.] 4-30-1886. Fairmount Cemetery, Newark, Essex County.

KEVE, ISAAC M. Pvt, H, 2nd DC Inf, 12-24-1902. Fairmount Cemetery, Newark, Essex County.

KEY, DAVID H. Sgt, G, 3rd NJ Cav, 1-3-1892. Mount Pleasant Cemetery, Millville, Cumberland County.

KEY, JOSEPH C. Pvt, B, 2nd NJ Inf, 4-6-1908. Harleigh Cemetery, Camden, Camden County.

KEY, THOMAS W. Pvt, D, 19th MS Inf (CSA), 9-15-1863. Finn's Point National Cemetery, Pennsville, Salem County.

KEY, WILLIAM Pvt, K, 22nd NJ Inf, 2-14-1907. Edgewater Cemetery, Edgewater, Bergen County.

KEYES, JOHN Pvt, Btty B, 1st MD Light Art, [Died of disease.] 8-22-1862. Fairmount Cemetery, Newark, Essex County.

KEYPORT, JACOB A. Pvt, K, 12th NJ Inf, 9-8-1890. Presbyterian Church Cemetery, Bridgeton, Cumberland County.

KEYS, NICHOLAS Pvt, C, 69th NY Inf, 1902. Soldier's Home Cemetery, Vineland, Cumberland County.

KEYSER, EDMUND (aka: Kiser, James) Pvt, B, 27th U.S. CT, 5-3-1909. Siloam Cemetery, Vineland, Cumberland County.

KEYSER, JOHN (see: Kaiser, John Jacob) St. Francis Cemetery, Trenton, Mercer County.

New Jersey Civil War Burials

KEYSER, WILLIAM R. Corp, F, 17th CT Inf, 11-1-1914. Fairmount Cemetery, Newark, Essex County.
KIBBE, OLIVER A. Capt, F, 30th NJ Inf, 7-27-1892. Evergreen Cemetery, New Brunswick, Middlesex County.
KIBBLE, ISAAC (see: Kittle, Isaac) Layton Cemetery, Layton, Sussex County.
KICK, HENRY Pvt, K, 1st NJ Inf, 6-2-1909. Palisade Cemetery, North Bergen, Hudson County.
KIDD, ALEXANDER Pvt, K, 13th NJ Inf, 2-16-1873. Cedar Lawn Cemetery, Paterson, Passaic County.
KIDD, B.F. Pvt, __, Nelson's Bttn VA Light Art (CSA), 3-21-1865. Finn's Point National Cemetery, Pennsville, Salem County.
KIDD, JAMES F. Pvt, H, 19th MS Inf (CSA), 9-14-1863. Finn's Point National Cemetery, Pennsville, Salem County.
KIDD*, JOHN W. Pvt, H, 12th NJ Inf, 2-4-1922. Presbyterian Church Cemetery, Bridgeton, Cumberland County.
KIDD, WILLIAM Pvt, A, 25th NJ Inf, 12-16-1884. Laurel Grove Cemetery, Totowa, Passaic County.
KIDD, WILLIAM Pvt, F, 35th NJ Inf, 5-20-1900. St. Peter's Cemetery, New Brunswick, Middlesex County.
KIDGER, GEORGE E. Sgt, C, 8th NJ Inf, [Killed in action at Hatchers Run, VA.] 2-5-1865. Fairmount Cemetery, Newark, Essex County.
KIDGER*, JAMES H. Pvt, F, 13th NJ Inf, 12-14-1905. Fairmount Cemetery, Newark, Essex County.
KIDGER, JOSEPH B. 3-6-1867. Fairmount Cemetery, Newark, Essex County.
KIDNEY*, JAMES M. Pvt, H, 33rd NJ Inf, DoD Unknown. Newton Cemetery, Newton, Sussex County.
KIEB, ANTON J. Pvt, LA Inf (CSA) 12-11-1902. Fairmount Cemetery, Newark, Essex County.
KIEFER, CONRAD Pvt, G, 24th NJ Inf, 1-5-1894. Cohansey Baptist Church Cemetery, Bowentown, Cumberland County.
KIELHOFFER, FRANCIS (see: Koellhoffer, Francis) St. Mary's Cemetery, East Orange, Essex County.
KIEM, JOHN Pvt, K, 35th NJ Inf, DoD Unknown. Stanhope-Union Cemetery, Netcong, Morris County.
KIENHAFER, CHARLES (aka: Kienhoefer, Charles) Pvt, E, 4th U.S. Inf, 4-6-1896. Fairmount Cemetery, Newark, Essex County.
KIENHOEFER, CHARLES (see: Kienhafer, Charles) Fairmount Cemetery, Newark, Essex County.
KIENZLE, GOTTLIEB (see: Kienzle, Gottlob) Berry Lawn Cemetery, Carlstadt, Bergen County.
KIENZLE, GOTTLOB (aka: Kienzle, Gottlieb) Corp, A, 45th NY Inf, 12-17-1909. Berry Lawn Cemetery, Carlstadt, Bergen County.
KIERNAN, FRANCIS Sgt, D, 93rd NY National Guard, 7-2-1891. Bayview-New York Bay Cemetery, Jersey City, Hudson County.
KIERNAN, JAMES H. Pvt, G, 21st NJ Inf, 1-15-1915. Holy Name Cemetery, Jersey City, Hudson County.
KIERNON, LOUIS J. Pvt, Btty D, 5th U.S. Art, DoD Unknown. Bayview-New York Bay Cemetery, Jersey City, Hudson County.
KIERSTED, JOHN S. Pvt, D, 26th NJ Inf, 10-6-1892. Fairmount Cemetery, Newark, Essex County.
KIESEWETHER, RUDOLPH Artificer, C, 15th NY Eng, 6-2-1900. Fairmount Cemetery, Newark, Essex County.
KIESLING, JULIUS P. (aka: Keesling, Julius P.) Pvt, K, 2nd NJ Inf, 2-27-1926. Fairmount Cemetery, Newark, Essex County.

Our Brothers Gone Before

KIESSEL, AUGUST (aka: Kissle, August) Pvt, G, 167th PA Inf, 3-26-1895. Greenwood Cemetery, Hamilton, Mercer County.
KIESSHIEGEL, JOHN A. Pvt, E, 37th NJ Inf, [Wounded in action.] 5-19-1895. Fairmount Cemetery, Newark, Essex County.
KIETH, JOHN C. Pvt, F, 44th Consolidated TN Inf (CSA), 5-3-1865. Finn's Point National Cemetery, Pennsville, Salem County.
KIGER, AMANDA Nurse, 1-24-1921. Chestnut Grove Cemetery, Elmer, Salem County.
KIGER, JAMES B. Pvt, H, 90th PA Inf, 1-15-1912. United Methodist Church Cemetery, Hainesneck, Salem County.
KIGER*, JAMES S. Sgt, A, 12th NJ Inf, 3-31-1925. Riverview Cemetery, Trenton, Mercer County.
KIGER*, JOSEPH M. Pvt, D, 5th NJ Inf, 1924. Eastview Cemetery, Salem, Salem County.
KIGER, THOMAS H. Pvt, I, 9th NJ Inf, 4-4-1900. Methodist Church Cemetery, Sharptown, Salem County.
KIGER, WILLIAM H. Pvt, C, 3rd PA Cav, [Cenotaph. Died while prisoner at Andersonville, GA.] 8-22-1864. Methodist Church Cemetery, Sharptown, Salem County.
KIGGINS, JOHN T. Pvt, B, 30th NJ Inf, [Died of fever at Aquia Creek, VA.] 12-27-1862. Evergreen Cemetery, Hillside, Union County.
KIHULE, JACOB F. Pvt, B, 4th NJ Inf, 9-8-1893. Greenwood Cemetery, Blue Anchor, Camden County.
KIKER, PETER Pvt, H, 197th PA Inf, 4-8-1932. Arlington Cemetery, Pennsauken, Camden County.
KILBORN, CHAUNCEY W. Capt, C, 94th NY Inf, [Wounded 8-30-1862 at 2nd Bull Run, VA.] 5-31-1915. Mount Pleasant Cemetery, Millville, Cumberland County.
KILBOURNE, DAVID G. Pvt, D, 207th PA Inf, 10-2-1892. Elmwood Cemetery, New Brunswick, Middlesex County.
KILBURN, DANIEL V. Pvt, E, 2nd NJ Militia, 1-30-1904. Arlington Cemetery, Kearny, Hudson County.
KILBURN, IRA G. Com Sgt, 26th NJ Inf 3-4-1907. Rosedale Cemetery, Orange, Essex County.
KILEY, DANIEL 3-9-1884. Old St. Mary's Cemetery, Clinton, Hunterdon County.
KILLE, DAVID 1st Lt, I, 9th NJ Inf, 4-15-1906. Union Methodist Church Cemetery, Center Square, Gloucester County.
KILLE, JOHN Corp, H, 12th NJ Inf, 1926. Cedar Green Cemetery, Clayton, Gloucester County.
KILLE, JOSEPH A. Pvt, H, 12th NJ Inf, [Killed in action at Wilderness, VA.] 5-6-1864. St. John's Episcopal Church Cemetery, Salem, Salem County.
KILLIAN, HENRY N. Pvt, Btty C, 1st PA Light Art, 10-23-1903. Riverside Cemetery, Riverside, Burlington County.
KILLIAN, JOHN D. Pvt, E, 10th PA Inf, 2-3-1916. Chestnut Hill Cemetery, East Brunswick, Middlesex County.
KILLIAN, WILLIAM Seaman, U.S. Navy, USS Juniata, 4-6-1889. New Camden Cemetery, Camden, Camden County.
KILLINGBECK, JOSHUA Pvt, F, 4th NJ Inf, 12-6-1894. Harleigh Cemetery, Camden, Camden County.
KILLINGSWORTH, WILLIAM J. Corp, G, 42nd MS Inf (CSA), [Captured 7-3-1863 at Gettysburg, PA.] 2-10-1864. Finn's Point National Cemetery, Pennsville, Salem County.
KILLIP, WILLIAM (see: McKillip, William F.) Methodist Cemetery, Woodstown, Salem County.
KILLMURRY, PATRICK Pvt, I, 28th NJ Inf, 10-17-1917. St. Mary's Cemetery, Perth Amboy, Middlesex County.

New Jersey Civil War Burials

KILLORAN, MICHAEL Corp, H, 170th NY Inf, [Wounded 5-24-1864 at North Anna River, VA.] 6-8-1877. Willow Grove Cemetery, New Brunswick, Middlesex County.
KILPATRICK*, ISAAC B. Pvt, C, 102nd NY Inf, 2-1-1890. Evergreen Cemetery, Hillside, Union County.
KIMBALL, EDWARD (see: Kimble, Edward) Mount Hebron Cemetery, Montclair, Essex County.
KIMBALL, GEORGE W. Pvt, B, 13th ME Inf, 12-7-1882. Baptist Church Cemetery, Hamilton Square, Mercer County.
KIMBALL, HENRY (see: Kimble, Henry) Cedar Lawn Cemetery, Paterson, Passaic County.
KIMBALL, JOSHUA Pvt, H, 23rd NJ Inf, 1-27-1893. Riverview Cemetery, Trenton, Mercer County.
KIMBALL, ORLANDO A. 8-9-1862. Presbyterian Church Cemetery, Shrewsbury, Monmouth County.
KIMBEL, JAMES (see: Kemble, James D.) Hillside Cemetery, Madison, Morris County.
KIMBLE, ALBERT (see: Kemble, Albert) Evergreen Cemetery, Camden, Camden County.
KIMBLE, CHARLES BENJAMIN Corp, Btty L, 6th NY Heavy Art, 3-31-1939. Woodland Cemetery, Englewood Cliffs, Bergen County.
KIMBLE, EDWARD (aka: Kimball, Edward) Pvt, K, 11th NJ Inf, 9-12-1923. Mount Hebron Cemetery, Montclair, Essex County.
KIMBLE*, GEORGE Pvt, Btty D, 1st NJ Light Art, DoD Unknown. Presbyterian Church Cemetery, Oak Ridge, Passaic County.
KIMBLE, HENRY (aka: Kimball, Henry) Pvt, C, 25th NJ Inf, 3-4-1908. Cedar Lawn Cemetery, Paterson, Passaic County.
KIMBLE, JAMES J. Pvt, K, 15th NJ Inf, 10-26-1903. Hardyston Cemetery, North Church, Sussex County.
KIMBLE*, JOHN Pvt, E, 2nd NJ Inf, DoD Unknown. Methodist Cemetery, Newfoundland, Morris County.
KIMBLE*, JOHN E. Landsman, U.S. Navy, USS Atlantic, [Naval station at Bay Point, SC.] 9-9-1917. Baptist Cemetery, Rio Grande, Cape May County.
KIMBLE, LEWIS Pvt, K, 1st NJ Cav, 11-26-1918. Methodist Cemetery, Newfoundland, Morris County.
KIMBLE, MARTIN D. Pvt, I, 39th NY Inf, 3-28-1901. Alpine Cemetery, Perth Amboy, Middlesex County.
KIMBLE, WARREN Pvt, M, 102nd PA Inf, 1-17-1916. Riverview Cemetery, Trenton, Mercer County.
KIMBLE, ZENAS Pvt, G, 43rd U.S. CT, 5-13-1891. Evergreen Cemetery, Morristown, Morris County.
KIMBROUGH, JOHN H. Pvt, B, 13th MS Inf (CSA), 11-9-1863. Finn's Point National Cemetery, Pennsville, Salem County.
KIMMICK, ANTON A. Pvt, A, 9th NJ Inf, 12-28-1905. St. Mary's Cemetery, Clark, Union County.
KIMSEY, WILLIAM H. (aka: Kinsey, William) Pvt, A, 7th NJ Inf, 1925. Tabernacle Baptist Church Cemetery, Erma, Cape May County.
KINCAID, JOSEPH L. Pvt, G, 24th NJ Inf, DoD Unknown. 1st United Methodist Church Cemetery, Bridgeton, Cumberland County.
KINCAID, T. Pvt, B, 20th VA Inf (CSA), 7-14-1864. Finn's Point National Cemetery, Pennsville, Salem County.
KINCAID, THOMAS Pvt, K, 124th NY Inf, [Wounded 7-30-1864 at Petersburg, VA.] 7-16-1919. United Methodist Church Cemetery, Rockaway Valley, Morris County.
KINCAID, W.W. Pvt, D, 11th (Bethel) NC Inf (CSA), [Captured 5-15-1864 at Spotsylvania CH, VA. Died of disease.] 4-26-1865. Finn's Point National Cemetery, Pennsville, Salem County.

Our Brothers Gone Before

KINCH, LEONIDAS TOWSEND 4-16-1867. Bordentown/Old St. Mary's Catholic Cemetery, Bordentown, Burlington County.

KINDLEN, CHARLES H. Pvt, G, 1st NY Inf, 8-2-1918. Holy Sepulchre Cemetery, East Orange, Essex County.

KINER, ADAM Seaman, U.S. Navy, 11-29-1911. Baptist/St. Andrew's Cemetery, Mount Holly, Burlington County.

KING, ABRAHAM L. 5-16-1885. Old 1st Methodist Church Cemetery, West Long Branch, Monmouth County.

KING, ABRAM B. Pvt, I, 14th NJ Inf, 6-24-1921. Hillside Cemetery, Scotch Plains, Union County.

KING, ADAM P. Ordinary Seaman, U.S. Navy, USS Princeton, 1907. New Camden Cemetery, Camden, Camden County.

KING, ALBERT W. 1933. Methodist Cemetery, Hamilton, Monmouth County.

KING, ALLEN Pvt, Btty D, 1st NJ Light Art, 11-1-1875. New Somerville Cemetery, Somerville, Somerset County.

KING, ANNA Nurse, 66th NY Inf DoD Unknown. Bayview-New York Bay Cemetery, Jersey City, Hudson County.

KING*, ASHER Sgt, A, 8th NJ Inf, 2-10-1868. Fairmount Cemetery, Newark, Essex County.

KING, AUGUSTUS Pvt, E, 5th NJ Inf, [Wounded in action.] 6-6-1912. Bordentown/Old St. Mary's Catholic Cemetery, Bordentown, Burlington County.

KING, AUGUSTUS DoD Unknown. White Ridge Cemetery, Eatontown, Monmouth County.

KING, BARNABUS B. Maj, 21st MO Inf [Cenotaph. Killed in action at Shiloh, TN.] 4-6-1862. Presbyterian Church Cemetery, Rockaway, Morris County.

KING, BENJAMIN F. Pvt, H, 30th TN Inf (CSA), 6-28-1864. Finn's Point National Cemetery, Pennsville, Salem County.

KING, CHARLES __, F, 1st __ Cav, DoD Unknown. Holy Name Cemetery, Jersey City, Hudson County.

KING, CHARLES 2-11-1896. Lower Springfield-Copany Meeting House Cemetery, Jacksonville, Burlington County.

KING*, CHARLES A. Pvt, E, 8th NJ Inf, 1-29-1872. Fairmount Cemetery, Newark, Essex County.

KING, CHARLES A. (aka: King, Christian) Corp, F, 54th NY Inf, 1-11-1931. Arlington Cemetery, Kearny, Hudson County.

KING*, CHARLES H. Pvt, F, 13th NJ Inf, 1872. Bloomfield Cemetery, Bloomfield, Essex County.

KING, CHARLES H. Pvt, B, 33rd NJ Inf, 7-19-1892. Fairmount Cemetery, Newark, Essex County.

KING*, CHARLES H. Pvt, C, 14th NJ Inf, DoD Unknown. Presbyterian Cemetery, North Plainfield, Somerset County.

KING, CHARLES H. Pvt, F, 13th NJ Inf, 10-20-1889. St. Mary's Cemetery, East Orange, Essex County.

KING*, CHARLES H. (JR.) Seaman, U.S. Navy, [Western Gunboat Service.] 1-3-1915. Greengrove Cemetery, Keyport, Monmouth County.

KING, CHRISTIAN (see: King, Charles A.) Arlington Cemetery, Kearny, Hudson County.

KING, CONSTANT V. Pvt, H, 11th NJ Inf, 11-26-1898. Carey Cemetery, Carey, Morris County.

KING, CORTLANDT Corp, C, 14th NJ Inf, 12-12-1874. Fairmount Cemetery, Newark, Essex County.

KING, DENCY HURD 11-20-1882. Oak Hill Cemetery, Vineland, Cumberland County.

KING, EDO M. Sgt, E, 9th NJ Inf, 12-28-1884. Laurel Grove Cemetery, Totowa, Passaic County.

New Jersey Civil War Burials

KING, EDWARD D. 1st Lt, H, 66th NY Inf, 5-8-1907. Bayview-New York Bay Cemetery, Jersey City, Hudson County.

KING, EDWARD J. 2nd Lt, A, 48th IN Inf, DoD Unknown. Greenwood Cemetery, Boonton, Morris County.

KING, EDWARD J.C. Pvt, B, 37th VA Inf (CSA), [Captured 5-12-1864 at Spotsylvania CH, VA. Died of measles.] 9-3-1864. Finn's Point National Cemetery, Pennsville, Salem County.

KING, F. 10-28-1897. Fairmount Cemetery, Newark, Essex County.

KING, FREDERICK C. Pvt, K, 13th NJ Inf, [Died of wounds received 9-17-1862 at Antietam, MD.] 9-30-1862. Laurel Grove Cemetery, Totowa, Passaic County.

KING, GEORGE C. Capt, F, 15th NJ Inf, 2-6-1866. Congregational Church Cemetery, Chester, Morris County.

KING, GEORGE H. Sgt, F, 33rd NJ Inf, 7-16-1892. Fairmount Cemetery, Newark, Essex County.

KING, GEORGE W. Pvt, E, Phillips' Legion GA Inf (CSA), 3-3-1865. Finn's Point National Cemetery, Pennsville, Salem County.

KING, GILBERT F. Sgt, D, 1st RI Cav, [Wounded in action.] 5-31-1881. Fairmount Cemetery, Newark, Essex County.

KING, H.F. Pvt, A, 7th (Duckworth's) TN Cav (CSA), 9-12-1864. Finn's Point National Cemetery, Pennsville, Salem County.

KING, H.L. Pvt, B, 1st (Carter's) TN Cav (CSA), 2-17-1865. Finn's Point National Cemetery, Pennsville, Salem County.

KING, HENRY Seaman, U.S. Navy, DoD Unknown. Bayview-New York Bay Cemetery, Jersey City, Hudson County.

KING, HOWARD Capt, C, 4th NJ Inf, 8-12-1870. Baptist Cemetery, Pemberton, Burlington County.

KING, HUBBARD D. 1931. Balesville Cemetery, Balesville, Sussex County.

KING, ISAAC B. Pvt, C, 14th NJ Inf, 9-21-1866. Evergreen Cemetery, Hillside, Union County.

KING, ISAIAH C. Seaman, U.S. Navy, 1-9-1903. Mount Holly Cemetery, Mount Holly, Burlington County.

KING, J.C. Pvt, H, 1st TX Inf (CSA), [Captured 7-2-1863 at Gettysburg, PA.] 4-14-1865. Finn's Point National Cemetery, Pennsville, Salem County.

KING, J. HARRY 10-28-1909. Batsto/Pleasant Mills Methodist Church Cemetery, Pleasant Mills, Atlantic County.

KING, J.W. Pvt, I, 9th (Malone's) AL Cav (CSA), 10-7-1863. Finn's Point National Cemetery, Pennsville, Salem County.

KING, JACOB Pvt, H, 34th NJ Inf, 6-28-1918. Baptist Cemetery, Pemberton, Burlington County.

KING, JAMES Pvt, K, 5th NJ Inf, 10-20-1899. Mount Olivet Cemetery, Fairview, Monmouth County.

KING, JAMES Pvt, B, 52nd NC Inf (CSA), [Captured 7-4-1863 at Gettysburg, PA. Died of disease.] 8-10-1863. Finn's Point National Cemetery, Pennsville, Salem County.

KING, JAMES Pvt, F, 72nd NY Inf, 8-5-1893. St. John's Evangelical Church Cemetery, Orange, Essex County.

KING, JAMES H. Ordinary Seaman, U.S. Navy, USS Macedonia, DoD Unknown. Holy Sepulchre Cemetery, East Orange, Essex County.

KING, JAMES H. Pvt, A, 38th NJ Inf, 10-21-1934. Old Brick Reformed Church Cemetery, Marlboro, Monmouth County.

KING, JAMES J. Pvt, I, 2nd NJ Inf, DoD Unknown. Cedar Lawn Cemetery, Paterson, Passaic County.

KING, JEREMIAH DoD Unknown. Methodist Church Cemetery, Mount Hermon, Warren County.

Our Brothers Gone Before

KING, JESSE Pvt, D, 24th NJ Inf, 1-24-1881. St. John's United Methodist Cemetery, Turnersville, Gloucester County.
KING, JOHN Pvt, E, 1st NJ Militia, 12-17-1902. Fairmount Cemetery, Newark, Essex County.
KING, JOHN 9-9-1909. Bayview-New York Bay Cemetery, Jersey City, Hudson County.
KING, JOHN A. Pvt, A, 29th NJ Inf, 6-12-1881. Old 1st Methodist Church Cemetery, West Long Branch, Monmouth County.
KING, JOHN E. 2nd Lt, E, 3rd NC Inf (CSA), [Captured 5-12-1864 at Spotsylvania CH, VA. Died of dysentery.] 6-15-1865. Finn's Point National Cemetery, Pennsville, Salem County.
KING, JOHN E. 2nd Lt, H, 9th NJ Inf, DoD Unknown. Reformed Church Cemetery, Belleville, Essex County.
KING, JOHN H. Pvt, D, 29th NJ Inf, 4-27-1912. Bloomfield Cemetery, Bloomfield, Essex County.
KING, JOHN H. 4-24-1873. Whitesville Cemetery, Whitesville, Ocean County.
KING, JOHN R. Pvt, K, 15th NJ Inf, 7-1-1881. Baptist Church Cemetery, Hamburg, Sussex County.
KING, JOHN W. Pvt, I, 4th NJ Inf, 7-23-1922. Oddfellows-Friends Cemetery, Medford, Burlington County.
KING, JOHN W. Pvt, F, 189th OH Inf, 1-1-1913. Cedar Lawn Cemetery, Paterson, Passaic County.
KING, JOSEPH Pvt, I, 4th NJ Inf, 5-16-1892. Baptist Cemetery, Pemberton, Burlington County.
KING, JOSEPH D. Pvt, C, 15th NJ Inf, 3-4-1876. Presbyterian Church Cemetery, Rockaway, Morris County.
KING, JULIUS (see: Koenig, Julius) Woodland Cemetery, Newark, Essex County.
KING, LEVI G. Pvt, A, 13th NJ Inf, 8-28-1900. Fairmount Cemetery, Newark, Essex County.
KING, LEWIS Pvt, C, 28th NJ Inf, 10-16-1888. St. James Episcopal Church Cemetery, Piscatawaytown, Middlesex County.
KING, LEWIS (aka: Koenig, Louis) Pvt, A, 10th NJ Inf, 1907. Mount Pleasant Cemetery, Millville, Cumberland County.
KING, METTLER (aka: Mettler, King) Corp, H, 3rd NJ Inf, [Wounded in action.] 8-26-1910. Baptist Church Cemetery, Cherryville, Hunterdon County.
KING, MICHAEL Pvt, F, 51st NY Inf, 12-30-1883. Holy Name Cemetery, Jersey City, Hudson County.
KING, MONROE H. 1st Sgt, G, 1st NJ Militia, 8-17-1882. Fairmount Cemetery, Newark, Essex County.
KING*, MOSES W. Pvt, G, 2nd DC Inf, 10-23-1897. Fairmount Cemetery, Newark, Essex County.
KING, PATRICK Pvt, H, 11th NJ Inf, [Wounded 7-2-1863 at Gettysburg, PA.] 4-29-1887. St. Mary's Cemetery, Wharton, Morris County.
KING, PETER R. Pvt, E, 8th PA Cav, 3-18-1915. Immaculate Conception Cemetery, Bridgeton, Cumberland County.
KING, RUFUS (JR.) Bvt Maj, 4th U.S. Art [Awarded the Medal of Honor.] 3-18-1900. Evergreen Cemetery, Hillside, Union County.
KING, SAMUEL H. 3-4-1876. Cedar Hill Cemetery, Hightstown, Mercer County.
KING, THOMAS Pvt, F, 72nd NY Inf, 3-14-1891. St. John's Evangelical Church Cemetery, Orange, Essex County.
KING, THOMAS Pvt, I, 34th NJ Inf, 1867. St. John's Evangelical Church Cemetery, Orange, Essex County.
KING, THOMAS BIRCH Pvt, I, 84th NY National Guard, 10-14-1908. Hillside Cemetery, Scotch Plains, Union County.

New Jersey Civil War Burials

KING, THOMAS L. Sgt, C, 27th NJ Inf, 3-5-1926. Presbyterian/Methodist-Episcopal Cemetery, Succasunna, Morris County.
KING, W.T.E. Pvt, C, 11th (Holman's) TN Cav (CSA), 8-18-1864. Finn's Point National Cemetery, Pennsville, Salem County.
KING, WILLIAM Pvt, U.S. Marine Corps, 9-4-1905. 1st Methodist Church Cemetery, Williamstown, Gloucester County.
KING, WILLIAM Pvt, B, 40th NJ Inf, 2-11-1915. Flower Hill Cemetery, North Bergen, Hudson County.
KING, WILLIAM Corp, G, 29th NJ Inf, 10-17-1883. Greenwood Cemetery, Hamilton, Mercer County.
KING, WILLIAM B. Pvt, F, 4th NJ Inf, DoD Unknown. Eglington Cemetery, Clarksboro, Gloucester County.
KING, WILLIAM H. Pvt, B, 1st NJ Inf, 3-3-1915. Baptist Cemetery, Pemberton, Burlington County.
KING, WILLIAM H. Landsman, U.S. Navy, 6-5-1908. Fairmount Cemetery, Newark, Essex County.
KING, WILLIAM H. Pvt, B, 8th NJ Inf, 5-25-1907. Clinton Cemetery, Irvington, Essex County.
KING, WILLIAM M. Sgt, H, 25th NJ Inf, 11-7-1889. Cedar Lawn Cemetery, Paterson, Passaic County.
KING, WILLIAM RAY (SR.) Saddler Sgt, 8th PA Cav 9-18-1924. Evergreen Cemetery, Hillside, Union County.
KING, WILSON C. Pvt, B, 26th NJ Inf, 1917. Mount Pleasant Cemetery, Newark, Essex County.
KINGLEY, EDWARD DoD Unknown. Holy Sepulchre Cemetery, Totowa, Passaic County.
KINGMAN, EUGENE Sgt, H, 12th ME Inf, DoD Unknown. Arlington Cemetery, Kearny, Hudson County.
KINGSBURY, JOHN Pvt, G, 21st NJ Inf, 11-4-1898. Bayview-New York Bay Cemetery, Jersey City, Hudson County.
KINGSLAND, ABRAHAM Pvt, K, 2nd DC Inf, 1925. Boonton Cemetery, Boonton, Morris County.
KINGSLAND, BENJAMIN Pvt, F, 35th NJ Inf, 3-31-1906. Arlington Cemetery, Kearny, Hudson County.
KINGSLAND, GEORGE 1st Lt, H, 22nd NJ Inf, DoD Unknown. Christ Church Cemetery, Belleville, Essex County.
KINGSLAND, GEORGE G. Corp, K, 7th NJ Inf, 3-24-1911. Arlington Cemetery, Kearny, Hudson County.
KINGSLAND, GEORGE O. Pvt, C, 26th NJ Inf, 10-10-1905. Bayview-New York Bay Cemetery, Jersey City, Hudson County.
KINGSLAND, JACOB Pvt, H, 25th NJ Inf, 4-27-1918. Cedar Lawn Cemetery, Paterson, Passaic County.
KINGSLAND, JEREMIAH Pvt, B, 8th NJ Inf, 5-31-1903. Mount Pleasant Cemetery, Newark, Essex County.
KINGSLAND, JOHN P. (aka: Paine, John) Pvt, B, 124th NY Inf, [Wounded 5-5-1864 at Wilderness, VA.] 6-22-1930. Lodi Cemetery, Lodi, Bergen County.
KINGSLEY, WILLETT W. Hosp Steward, D, 8th CT Inf, [Wounded 9-29-1864 at Fort Harrison, VA.] 11-12-1898. Fairmount Cemetery, Newark, Essex County.
KINGSLEY, WILLIAM HENRY Pvt, C, 49th NY Inf, [Wounded 8-21-1864 at Flowing Springs, Va.] 1-13-1899. Fairmount Cemetery, Newark, Essex County.
KINKLE, CHARLES F. Pvt, B, 9th NJ Inf, 10-5-1905. New Camden Cemetery, Camden, Camden County.
KINLEY, FREDERICK Pvt, Btty B, 3rd PA Heavy Art, 5-8-1908. Oddfellows Cemetery, Pemberton, Burlington County.

Our Brothers Gone Before

KINLEY, WILLIAM H. (aka: Kinly, William) 2nd Lt, D, 6th NJ Inf, 2-21-1900. Mount Calvary Cemetery, Mount Calvary, Atlantic County.
KINLY, WILLIAM (see: Kinley, William H.) Mount Calvary Cemetery, Mount Calvary, Atlantic County.
KINMOTH*, HUGH S. (aka: Kinmouth, Hugh) Pvt, I, 13th NY Cav, 1933. Mount Prospect Cemetery, Neptune, Monmouth County.
KINMOUTH, HUGH (see: Kinmoth, Hugh S.) Mount Prospect Cemetery, Neptune, Monmouth County.
KINN, JACOB Sgt, C, 30th NJ Inf, DoD Unknown. Holy Name Cemetery, Jersey City, Hudson County.
KINNE, THEODORE YOUNG Asst Surg, 184th NY Inf 3-4-1904. Cedar Lawn Cemetery, Paterson, Passaic County.
KINNER*, ASA C. Pvt, K, 15th NJ Inf, 2-20-1884. Newton Cemetery, Newton, Sussex County.
KINNEY, AMOS 1st Sgt, D, 27th NJ Inf, 12-9-1897. Fairmount Cemetery, Newark, Essex County.
KINNEY, CHARLES (see: Kinney, Chester T.) Cedar Lawn Cemetery, Paterson, Passaic County.
KINNEY*, CHARLES A. Pvt, E, 11th NJ Inf, [Wounded 7-2-1863 at Gettysburg, PA.] 9-9-1889. Fairmount Cemetery, Newark, Essex County.
KINNEY, CHARLES H. Pvt, D, 22nd U.S. CT, 3-29-1915. Riverview Cemetery, Trenton, Mercer County.
KINNEY, CHESTER T. (aka: Kinney, Charles) Pvt, E, 35th NJ Inf, 1-1-1903. Cedar Lawn Cemetery, Paterson, Passaic County.
KINNEY, DANIEL Pvt, D, 4th NJ Militia, 1-29-1883. Old St. Mary's Cemetery, Gloucester City, Camden County.
KINNEY, DANIEL W. Corp, F, 1st NJ Inf, 1-15-1912. Weller Cemetery, Willow Grove, Warren County.
KINNEY, EDWARD J. Sgt, E, 11th NJ Inf, 9-18-1893. Chestnut Cemetery, Dover, Morris County.
KINNEY, GEORGE C. Pvt, K, 27th NJ Inf, 2-28-1916. Laurel Grove Cemetery, Totowa, Passaic County.
KINNEY, GEORGE P. 3-21-1895. Reformed Church Cemetery, Three Bridges, Hunterdon County.
KINNEY*, GEORGE W. Pvt, I, 57th MA Inf, [Died of wounds received 8-9-1864 at Petersburg, VA.] 9-29-1864. Beverly National Cemetery, Edgewater Park, Burlington County.
KINNEY, GIDEON L. 3-24-1923. Fairview Cemetery, Wantage, Sussex County.
KINNEY, HENRY S. (aka: Keeny, Henry) Pvt, G, 207th PA Inf, 11-21-1920. Presbyterian Church Cemetery, Mount Pleasant, Hunterdon County.
KINNEY, ISAAC Com Sgt, 35th PA Inf 10-19-1915. Balesville Cemetery, Balesville, Sussex County.
KINNEY, JACOB M. Pvt, A, 8th NJ Inf, [Taken prisoner at the hospital in Fair Oaks, VA. Supposed to have died at Richmond, VA.] 8-5-1862. Presbyterian Church Cemetery, Rockaway, Morris County.
KINNEY, JOHN W. Pvt, E, 7th NJ Inf, [Killed in action at Williamsburg, VA.] 5-5-1862. Belvidere/Catholic Cemetery, Belvidere, Warren County.
KINNEY, JOSEPH D. Sgt, D, 31st NJ Inf, 3-20-1900. Holcomb-Riverview Cemetery, Lambertville, Hunterdon County.
KINNEY, MARTIN (aka: Kenny, Martin) Pvt, E, 71st NY Inf, 6-9-1864. St. John's Evangelical Church Cemetery, Orange, Essex County.
KINNEY, MICHAEL Pvt, E, 71st NY Inf, [Wounded 8-27-1862 at Bristoe Station, VA.] 8-30-1875. St. John's Evangelical Church Cemetery, Orange, Essex County.

New Jersey Civil War Burials

KINNEY, RENSSELAER WEST Sgt, D, 3rd NY Cav, 3-13-1910. Rosedale Cemetery, Orange, Essex County.
KINNEY*, SIMON H. Pvt, C, PA Emerg NJ Militia, 5-10-1880. Union Cemetery, Washington, Morris County.
KINNEY*, THOMAS T. Pvt, I, 7th NJ Inf, 12-2-1900. Mount Pleasant Cemetery, Newark, Essex County.
KINNEY, WILLIAM Pvt, A, 2nd NJ Cav, 10-2-1932. Fairmount Cemetery, Newark, Essex County.
KINSELL, ISAAC P. Pvt, F, 12th NJ Inf, 1920. Siloam Cemetery, Vineland, Cumberland County.
KINSELLA, THOMAS Pvt, A, 8th Bttn Confederate States Inf (CSA), 6-14-1889. Grove Church Cemetery, North Bergen, Hudson County.
KINSEY, CHARLES Sgt, H, 27th NJ Inf, 3-20-1897. Fairmount Cemetery, Newark, Essex County.
KINSEY, CHARLES V. Pvt, A, 26th NJ Inf, 6-7-1900. Bloomfield Cemetery, Bloomfield, Essex County.
KINSEY, DAVID T. Pvt, A, 7th NJ Inf, 4-13-1881. 1st Baptist Cemetery, Cape May Court House, Cape May County.
KINSEY, GEORGE Pvt, D, 13th NJ Inf, 10-25-1884. Fairmount Cemetery, Newark, Essex County.
KINSEY, GEORGE W. Corp, C, 30th NJ Inf, 1879. Hazelwood Cemetery, Rahway, Union County.
KINSEY*, HARRISON Pvt, Btty C, 1st NJ Light Art, 1-25-1909. Fairmount Cemetery, Newark, Essex County.
KINSEY, JAMES 1906. New Somerville Cemetery, Somerville, Somerset County.
KINSEY, JOHN WARNER QM, 37th NJ Inf 12-29-1906. Harleigh Cemetery, Camden, Camden County.
KINSEY, JOSEPH H.C. Sgt, E, 1st NJ Militia, 12-9-1913. Fairmount Cemetery, Newark, Essex County.
KINSEY*, PETER Pvt, A, 26th NJ Inf, 6-22-1883. Fairmount Cemetery, Newark, Essex County.
KINSEY, ROBERT B. Pvt, M, 1st NJ Cav, 1923. Union Cemetery, Washington, Morris County.
KINSEY, SMITH P. Pvt, E, 3rd NJ Militia, 4-1-1864. Sandy Ridge Cemetery, Sandy Ridge, Hunterdon County.
KINSEY, WILLIAM (see: Kimsey, William H.) Tabernacle Baptist Church Cemetery, Erma, Cape May County.
KINSILLA, CHARLES P. Pvt, I, 15th NJ Inf, 3-23-1932. Cedar Lawn Cemetery, Paterson, Passaic County.
KINSLER, FREDERICK Pvt, D, 33rd NJ Inf, 12-6-1895. Locust Hill Cemetery, Dover, Morris County.
KINSLER, GEORGE A. Principal Musc, 56th NY Inf 4-17-1921. Mount Carmel Cemetery, Tenafly, Bergen County.
KINSLEY, CALEB G. 1912. Columbus Cemetery, Columbus, Burlington County.
KINSLEY, DENNIS Pvt, Ahl's Btty, DE Heavy Art, DoD Unknown. Finn's Point National Cemetery, Pennsville, Salem County.
KINSLEY*, EDWARD T. Pvt, H, 2nd NJ Inf, 8-22-1909. Bordentown/Old St. Mary's Catholic Cemetery, Bordentown, Burlington County.
KINT, DAVID (see: Kent, David) Balesville Cemetery, Balesville, Sussex County.
KINTNER, JOHN L. (aka: Kentner, Conrad) QM Sgt, E, 2nd CO Cav, 12-25-1909. Baptist Cemetery, Hopewell Boro, Mercer County.
KINTNER, MARTIN Sgt, I, 15th NJ Inf, 1929. Newton Cemetery, Newton, Sussex County.

Our Brothers Gone Before

KIPLE, JACOB Pvt, B, 2nd NJ Inf, 1903. Mount Pleasant Cemetery, Millville, Cumberland County.

KIPLE, MOSES H. Pvt, G, 23rd NJ Inf, 2-16-1931. Monument Cemetery, Edgewater Park, Burlington County.

KIPP*, CHARLES JOHN Asst Surg, 15th NY Heavy Art [Also Surgeon, 5th NYNG.] 1-13-1911. Mount Pleasant Cemetery, Newark, Essex County.

KIPP, ISAAC Pvt, I, 22nd NJ Inf, 1892. Westwood Cemetery, Westwood, Bergen County.

KIPP, JAMES H. Pvt, G, 29th NJ Inf, [Died of typhoid at Washington, DC.] 1-23-1863. Holmdel Cemetery, Holmdel, Monmouth County.

KIPP, JOHN Pvt, H, 1st NJ Cav, 2-7-1898. Palisade Cemetery, North Bergen, Hudson County.

KIPP, JOHN G. Pvt, D, 29th NJ Inf, 3-15-1899. Greengrove Cemetery, Keyport, Monmouth County.

KIPP*, JOHN HENRY Corp, I, 2nd NJ Inf, 11-6-1917. Woodland Cemetery, Newark, Essex County.

KIRBY, ASA Corp, A, 2nd PA Cav, 6-15-1907. Evergreen Cemetery, Camden, Camden County.

KIRBY, J.W. Pvt, D, 15th SC Inf (CSA), [Captured 7-5-1863 at Gettysburg, PA. Died of smallpox.] 11-20-1863. Finn's Point National Cemetery, Pennsville, Salem County.

KIRBY*, JOHN Pvt, E, 1st NJ Cav, 3-4-1903. Fairmount Cemetery, Newark, Essex County.

KIRBY*, MICHAEL S. Pvt, G, 81st PA Inf, 1-21-1913. St. Peter's Cemetery, New Brunswick, Middlesex County.

KIRBY, RICHARD S. Pvt, H, 12th NJ Inf, [Died at Potomac Creek, VA. of wounds received at Chancellorsville, VA.] 5-17-1863. Friends Cemetery, Woodstown, Salem County.

KIRBY, SAMUEL S. Pvt, A, 29th NJ Inf, 11-1-1885. Old 1st Methodist Church Cemetery, West Long Branch, Monmouth County.

KIRBY*, WILLIAM H. Pvt, A, 7th NJ Inf, 11-11-1913. Evergreen Cemetery, Camden, Camden County.

KIRCHER, JOHN Pvt, A, 3rd NJ Cav, 2-17-1914. Hedding Methodist-Episcopal Church Cemetery, Bellmawr, Camden County.

KIRCHER, JOSEPH (aka: Kerker, Joseph) Blacksmith, D, 5th PA Cav, 10-10-1907. Eglington Cemetery, Clarksboro, Gloucester County.

KIRCHMAUER*, FERDINAND Pvt, F, 95th NY Inf, [Wounded 6-11-1864 on picket.] 2-16-1888. Fairmount Cemetery, Newark, Essex County.

KIRCHNER, AUGUST Pvt, C, 9th NJ Inf, 11-30-1923. Holy Sepulchre Cemetery, East Orange, Essex County.

KIRCHNER, JACOB Corp, F, 31st NY Inf, DoD Unknown. Weehawken Cemetery, North Bergen, Hudson County.

KIRCHNER, PETER Corp, F, 86th NY Inf, 6-12-1916. Bayview-New York Bay Cemetery, Jersey City, Hudson County.

KIREKER, CHARLES F. Lt Col, 116th U.S. CT 4-29-1910. Cedar Lawn Cemetery, Paterson, Passaic County.

KIRK, J.A. Pvt, K, 16th VA Cav (CSA), 9-1-1864. Finn's Point National Cemetery, Pennsville, Salem County.

KIRK, JOSIAH (see: Kirkpatrick, Josiah L.) Presbyterian Cemetery, North Plainfield, Somerset County.

KIRK, PAUL Coal Heaver, U.S. Navy, USS Iroquois, DoD Unknown. Grove Church Cemetery, North Bergen, Hudson County.

KIRKBRIDE, ELWOOD H. Capt, B, 23rd NJ Inf, 8-3-1908. Methodist-Episcopal Church Cemetery, Medford, Burlington County.

New Jersey Civil War Burials

KIRKBRIDE, JOSIAH R. Corp, G, PA Emerg NJ Militia, 7-26-1932. Harleigh Cemetery, Camden, Camden County.
KIRKENDALL, JACOB M. Pvt, E, 47th PA Inf, [Wounded 9-22-1864 at Fishers Hill, VA. and 3- -1865 at Charlestown, VA.] 5-20-1922. Phillipsburg Cemetery, Phillipsburg, Warren County.
KIRKENDALL*, JOSIAH Pvt, E, 41st PA Inf, 8-6-1883. Phillipsburg Cemetery, Phillipsburg, Warren County.
KIRKHUFF*, GEORGE B. Pvt, D, 35th NJ Inf, 5-1-1899. Cedar Ridge Cemetery, Blairstown, Warren County.
KIRKLAND, ABRAM Pvt, E, 8th AL Inf (CSA), 10-27-1863. Finn's Point National Cemetery, Pennsville, Salem County.
KIRKLAND, WILLIAM Pvt, H, 20th AR Inf (CSA), [Captured 5-16-1863 at Champion's Hill, MS.] 3-30-1864. Finn's Point National Cemetery, Pennsville, Salem County.
KIRKMAN, WILLIAM Pvt, B, 34th NJ Inf, 7-25-1885. Riverview Cemetery, Trenton, Mercer County.
KIRKMAN, WILLIAM W. Pvt, B, 45th NC Inf (CSA), [Wounded 7-3-1863 and captured 7-5-1863 at Gettysburg, PA. Died of diarrhea.] 10-25-1863. Finn's Point National Cemetery, Pennsville, Salem County.
KIRKPATRICK, HUGH J. Pvt, G, 8th NJ Inf, [Died at City Point, VA of wounds received 5-5-1864 at Wilderness, VA.] 5-15-1864. Mount Pleasant Cemetery, Newark, Essex County.
KIRKPATRICK, JAMES D. Pvt, I, 57th NC Inf (CSA), [Captured 7-5-1863 at Gettysburg, PA. Died of debility.] 8-24-1863. Finn's Point National Cemetery, Pennsville, Salem County.
KIRKPATRICK, JOHN Pvt, G, 1st NJ Inf, 1-7-1877. Bayview-New York Bay Cemetery, Jersey City, Hudson County.
KIRKPATRICK, JOSIAH L. (aka: Kirk, Josiah) Pvt, I, 21st NJ Inf, [Died of typhoid at Falmouth, VA.] 12-22-1862. Presbyterian Cemetery, North Plainfield, Somerset County.
KIRKPATRICK, RUFUS F. Pvt, E, 4th (Russell's) AL Cav (CSA), 9-20-1863. Finn's Point National Cemetery, Pennsville, Salem County.
KIRKPATRICK, SAMUEL Pvt, K, 2nd NJ Cav, DoD Unknown. Boonton Cemetery, Boonton, Morris County.
KIRKPATRICK, SAMUEL W. Pvt, H, 4th GA Inf (CSA), [Captured 5-10-1864 at Spotsylvania CH, VA. Died of smallpox.] 6-19-1864. Finn's Point National Cemetery, Pennsville, Salem County.
KIRKPATRICK, WILLIAM 1-29-1872. Presbyterian Cemetery, North Plainfield, Somerset County.
KIRKPATRICK, WILLIAM Pvt, K, 4th NJ Inf, DoD Unknown. Overlook Cemetery, Bridgeton, Cumberland County.
KIRKS, HENRY T. Pvt, A, 60th VA Inf (CSA), [Captured 5-20-1863 in Fayette County, WV. Died of diarrhea.] 11-29-1863. Finn's Point National Cemetery, Pennsville, Salem County.
KIRKWOOD, HENRY Pvt, A, 13th AL Inf (CSA), [Captured at Gettysburg, PA.] 9-13-1863. Finn's Point National Cemetery, Pennsville, Salem County.
KIRKWOOD, HUGH Pvt, Btty G, 4th NY Heavy Art, 1-3-1913. Arlington Cemetery, Kearny, Hudson County.
KIRKWOOD, THOMAS Pvt, C, 12th U.S. Inf, DoD Unknown. Cedar Lawn Cemetery, Paterson, Passaic County.
KIRLIN, MICHAEL (see: Kivlon, Michael) Holy Name Cemetery, Jersey City, Hudson County.
KIRLIN, PATRICK (see: Kivlon, Patrick) St. Peter's Cemetery, Jersey City, Hudson County.

Our Brothers Gone Before

KIRSCHGASNER, HENRY Pvt, C, 30th NJ Inf, 4-3-1900. Rahway Cemetery, Rahway, Union County.
KIRSCHLER, HENRY Pvt, H, 12th U.S. Inf, [Wounded in action.] 5-4-1884. Evergreen Cemetery, Hillside, Union County.
KIRST*, MATTHIAS Corp, E, 38th NJ Inf, 12-26-1906. Holcomb-Riverview Cemetery, Lambertville, Hunterdon County.
KIRTLAND, JOHN C. 2nd Lt, A, 89th NY Inf, 11-2-1926. Rosedale Cemetery, Orange, Essex County.
KIRWIN, JOHN Pvt, C, 26th NJ Inf, 2-28-1891. Holy Sepulchre Cemetery, East Orange, Essex County.
KISE*, JACOB Pvt, D, 35th NJ Inf, 2-16-1899. Cedar Ridge Cemetery, Blairstown, Warren County.
KISE, SOLOMON Pvt, A, 15th NJ Inf, 1-18-1894. Rosemont Cemetery, Rosemont, Hunterdon County.
KISER*, AMBROSE (aka: Ambrose, Kiser) Pvt, G, 8th NJ Inf, [Wounded in action.] 7-25-1906. Arlington Cemetery, Kearny, Hudson County.
KISER, JAMES Pvt, M, 16th NC Inf (CSA), [Wounded 5-31-1862 at Seven Pines, VA.] 8-23-1863. Finn's Point National Cemetery, Pennsville, Salem County.
KISER, JAMES (see: Keyser, Edmund) Siloam Cemetery, Vineland, Cumberland County.
KISER, JOHN H. Pvt, D, 53rd NC Inf (CSA), [Captured 7-5-1863 at Gettysburg, PA.] 10-10-1863. Finn's Point National Cemetery, Pennsville, Salem County.
KISER, NATHANIEL Pvt, I, 33rd NJ Inf, 1915. Presbyterian Church Cemetery, Mendham, Morris County.
KISER, RUDOLPH (aka: Kaiser, Rudolph) Pvt, G, 1st NJ Cav, 1-6-1926. Arlington Cemetery, Kearny, Hudson County.
KISHEGEL, FERDINAND (see: Kiskegel, Ferdinand F.) Woodland Cemetery, Newark, Essex County.
KISHNER, VALENTINE Pvt, I, 40th NJ Inf, 2-5-1914. Rahway Cemetery, Rahway, Union County.
KISKEGEL, FERDINAND F. (aka: Kishegel, Ferdinand) Pvt, D, 8th NJ Inf, 3-24-1904. Woodland Cemetery, Newark, Essex County.
KISSAM, AUGUST H. Corp, D, 37th NY National Guard, 10-25-1921. Rosedale Cemetery, Orange, Essex County.
KISSAM, EDGAR Capt, D, 9th NJ Inf, 6-6-1868. Jersey City Cemetery, Jersey City, Hudson County.
KISSAM, FRANKLIN Actg 3rd Asst Eng, U.S. Navy, 11-17-1922. Clinton Cemetery, Irvington, Essex County.
KISSAM, RUFUS A. Pvt, A, 37th NJ Inf, DoD Unknown. Jersey City Cemetery, Jersey City, Hudson County.
KISSAM, WILLIAM Corp, F, 27th NJ Inf, 11-28-1905. Fairview Cemetery, Westfield, Union County.
KISSELBACH, JOHN C. Pvt, E, 153rd PA Inf, 12-24-1916. Phillipsburg Cemetery, Phillipsburg, Warren County.
KISSICK, WILLIAM Pvt, D, 7th NJ Inf, 10-3-1905. Laurel Grove Cemetery, Totowa, Passaic County.
KISSLE, AUGUST (see: Kiessel, August) Greenwood Cemetery, Hamilton, Mercer County.
KISTNER, HENRY Pvt, F, 2nd NJ Inf, 9-29-1891. Fairmount Cemetery, Newark, Essex County.
KITCHELL, ALFRED FREEMAN Pvt, A, 59th NY Inf, [Killed in action at Antietam, MD.] 9-17-1862. New Presbyterian Cemetery, Hanover, Morris County.
KITCHELL, DAVID F. Pvt, F, 27th NJ Inf, 1913. Whitehall Cemetery, Towaco, Morris County.

New Jersey Civil War Burials

KITCHELL, EDWARD E. Pvt, H, 15th NJ Inf, 12-11-1913. Whitehall Cemetery, Towaco, Morris County.

KITCHELL, HORACE B. Pvt, B, 127th NY Inf, DoD Unknown. Presbyterian Church Cemetery, Rockaway, Morris County.

KITCHELL, HUDSON Capt, E, 27th NJ Inf, 10-27-1923. Evergreen Cemetery, Hillside, Union County.

KITCHELL, J. WARREN 1st Lt, I, 33rd NJ Inf, 7-29-1895. Evergreen Cemetery, Morristown, Morris County.

KITCHELL*, JARED LUDLOW Pvt, Btty E, 1st NJ Light Art, 8-29-1918. South Orange Cemetery, South Orange, Essex County.

KITCHELL, SAMUEL FARRAND Pvt, C, 7th NJ Inf, [Cenotaph. Died of diarrhea while prisoner at Andersonville, GA.] 9-12-1864. Presbyterian Church Cemetery, Rockaway, Morris County.

KITCHELL, SILAS M. Pvt, Btty B, 1st NJ Light Art, 8-21-1871. Fairmount Cemetery, Newark, Essex County.

KITCHELL, THEODORE WARD (aka: Ketchell, Theodore W.) Artificer, F, 1st NY Eng, 3-6-1898. New Presbyterian Cemetery, Hanover, Morris County.

KITCHEN, CHARLES Pvt, I, 28th PA Inf, 4-25-1893. 1st Methodist Church Cemetery, Williamstown, Gloucester County.

KITCHEN, CHARLES T. Sgt, I, 3rd NJ Militia, 11-23-1887. Mount Hope Presbyterian Cemetery, Lambertville, Hunterdon County.

KITCHEN, CHARLES W. 1st Lt, B, 38th NJ Inf, 12-2-1881. Mount Hope Presbyterian Cemetery, Lambertville, Hunterdon County.

KITCHEN, DAVID M. Pvt, G, 31st NJ Inf, 5-20-1881. Methodist-Episcopal Cemetery, Columbia, Warren County.

KITCHEN, ELWOOD Musc, B, 38th NJ Inf, 2-12-1920. Riverview Cemetery, Trenton, Mercer County.

KITCHEN, HENRY B. Pvt, I, 3rd NJ Militia, 11-11-1919. Holcomb-Riverview Cemetery, Lambertville, Hunterdon County.

KITCHEN, JOHN Musc, U.S. Navy, 5-30-1902. Elmwood Cemetery, New Brunswick, Middlesex County.

KITCHEN, JOHN Pvt, F, 9th NJ Inf, [Wounded in action at Cold Harbor, VA.] 8-18-1870. New Somerville Cemetery, Somerville, Somerset County.

KITCHEN*, MARCUS LAWRENCE WARD Lt Col, 2nd NJ Cav 8-28-1896. Mount Pleasant Cemetery, Newark, Essex County.

KITCHEN, PHILIP A. Pvt, E, 7th NJ Inf, 6-23-1916. Union Cemetery, Milford, Hunterdon County.

KITCHEN, ROBERT H. Pvt, F, 9th NJ Inf, 5-27-1900. New Somerville Cemetery, Somerville, Somerset County.

KITCHEN, WARREN THOMAS Pvt, C, 31st NJ Inf, 1913. Calvary Community Church Cemetery, Harmony, Warren County.

KITCHIN, JAMES E. Pvt, A, 50th PA Inf, 10-25-1919. Eglington Cemetery, Clarksboro, Gloucester County.

KITCHIN, SENECA B. Pvt, I, 31st NJ Inf, 1895. Belvidere/Catholic Cemetery, Belvidere, Warren County.

KITE, JOHN Corp, D, 12th NJ Inf, 5-10-1905. Oak Hill Cemetery, Vineland, Cumberland County.

KITE, JOHN H. Pvt, B, 1st NJ Inf, 12-28-1911. Riverview Cemetery, Trenton, Mercer County.

KITE, JOSEPH C. Pvt, D, 12th NJ Inf, 1920. Overlook Cemetery, Bridgeton, Cumberland County.

KITHCART, DANIEL D. Pvt, D, 27th NJ Inf, 6-10-1916. Deckertown-Union Cemetery, Papakating, Sussex County.

Our Brothers Gone Before

KITHCART*, DANIEL W. Sgt, D, 2nd NJ Inf, 1892. Balesville Cemetery, Balesville, Sussex County.
KITHCART, WILLIAM H. DoD Unknown. Deckertown-Union Cemetery, Papakating, Sussex County.
KITHCART, WILLIAM H. (aka: Kathcart, William) Pvt, H, 61st NY Inf, [Died of wounds received 7-1-1862 at Malvern Hill, VA.] 8-7-1863. Presbyterian Church Cemetery, Mount Freedom, Morris County.
KITTLE, ISAAC (aka: Kibble, Isaac) Corp, B, 2nd NY Cav, 10-12-1864. Layton Cemetery, Layton, Sussex County.
KITTLE, MANSON DoD Unknown. Layton Cemetery, Layton, Sussex County.
KIVLON, MICHAEL (aka: Kirlin, Michael) Pvt, I, 1st NJ Inf, 5-8-1910. Holy Name Cemetery, Jersey City, Hudson County.
KIVLON, PATRICK (aka: Kirlin, Patrick) Pvt, I, 1st NJ Inf, 3-6-1884. St. Peter's Cemetery, Jersey City, Hudson County.
KLAG, HENRY (SR.) Musc, 95th PA Inf Band 8-13-1912. Greenwood Cemetery, Hamilton, Mercer County.
KLAGG, FRANCIS C. Pvt, H, 27th PA Inf, 8-24-1896. Fairmount Cemetery, Newark, Essex County.
KLAPROUTH, HENRY Corp, C, 17th IL Cav, 5-6-1892. Bayview-New York Bay Cemetery, Jersey City, Hudson County.
KLASE, GEORGE W. Sgt, I, 48th PA Inf, 1908. Bayview-New York Bay Cemetery, Jersey City, Hudson County.
KLAUSER, FRANCIS (see: Klauser, Franz) Rosedale Cemetery, Orange, Essex County.
KLAUSER*, FRANZ (aka: Klauser, Francis) Corp, 30th NY Ind Btty 8-21-1886. Rosedale Cemetery, Orange, Essex County.
KLAUSER, WILLIAM Pvt, A, 33rd NJ Inf, 11-27-1928. Madonna Cemetery, Leonia, Bergen County.
KLEAVER, CHARLES H. Pvt, D, 118th PA Inf, 11-18-1874. Old Camden Cemetery, Camden, Camden County.
KLEIN, CHARLES T. 4-14-1904. Brookside Cemetery, Englewood, Bergen County.
KLEIN, JOHN Sgt, C, 28th NY Inf, 6-2-1861. Flower Hill Cemetery, North Bergen, Hudson County.
KLEIN, JOHN Pvt, F, 1st NJ Inf, 1-15-1906. St. Peter's Cemetery, New Brunswick, Middlesex County.
KLEIN, JOHN F.L. Pvt, B, 59th IL Inf, 11-6-1906. Bayview-New York Bay Cemetery, Jersey City, Hudson County.
KLEIN, PETER Pvt, Btty A, 15th NY Heavy Art, 1-18-1886. Flower Hill Cemetery, North Bergen, Hudson County.
KLEIN, THEODORE H. Pvt, Btty G, 3rd PA Heavy Art, 6-15-1903. Egg Harbor Cemetery, Egg Harbor, Atlantic County.
KLEINADAM, AUGUST Pvt, F, 37th __ Inf, DoD Unknown. St. Mary's Cemetery, East Orange, Essex County.
KLEINDIENST, FREDERICK Musc, __, 1st __ Cav, DoD Unknown. Flower Hill Cemetery, North Bergen, Hudson County.
KLEINE, CHRISTIAN Pvt, 13th NY Ind Btty 1-21-1919. Arlington Cemetery, Kearny, Hudson County.
KLEINE, WILLIAM (see: Klien, F. William) Laurel Grove Cemetery, Totowa, Passaic County.
KLEINGART, JOHN Pvt, B, 21st NJ Inf, 2-17-1904. Palisade Cemetery, North Bergen, Hudson County.
KLEINSCHMIDT, CHARLES (aka: Kleinsmith, Charles) Pvt, I, 35th NJ Inf, 10-19-1880. Fairmount Cemetery, Newark, Essex County.
KLEINSMITH, CHARLES (see: Kleinschmidt, Charles) Fairmount Cemetery, Newark, Essex County.

New Jersey Civil War Burials

KLEIS, MICHAEL Pvt, E, 48th NY Inf, DoD Unknown. Grove Church Cemetery, North Bergen, Hudson County.
KLEM, BALTHASAR Pvt, D, 2nd NJ Inf, 5-11-1914. Holy Sepulchre Cemetery, East Orange, Essex County.
KLEME, HENRY Pvt, F, 39th NJ Inf, 5-2-1917. Fairmount Cemetery, Newark, Essex County.
KLEMM, AUGUST (aka: Clemm, August) Pvt, C, 186th PA Inf, 9-12-1918. Oddfellows Cemetery, Burlington, Burlington County.
KLEMMER, JACOB Corp, B, 4th NJ Inf, 1-31-1897. Riverview Cemetery, Trenton, Mercer County.
KLEPP, HENRI (see: Klepp, Henry) Holy Sepulchre Cemetery, East Orange, Essex County.
KLEPP, HENRY (aka: Klepp, Henri) Sgt, A, 39th NJ Inf, 9-25-1891. Holy Sepulchre Cemetery, East Orange, Essex County.
KLIDELIN, GEORGE Pvt, I, 43rd MA Inf, 11-18-1900. Fairmount Cemetery, Newark, Essex County.
KLIEN, F. WILLIAM (aka: Kleine, William) Pvt, E, 2nd NJ Inf, [Wounded in action at Crampton's Pass, MD.] 1925. Laurel Grove Cemetery, Totowa, Passaic County.
KLINE, ANDREW Pvt, A, 41st U.S. CT, 8-1-1904. New Somerville Cemetery, Somerville, Somerset County.
KLINE, AUGUSTUS (aka: Kline, Jesse) Pvt, A, 3rd DE Inf, 1-3-1908. St. Francis Cemetery, Trenton, Mercer County.
KLINE, BENJAMIN F. Pvt, G, 38th NJ Inf, 11-7-1905. Rosemont Cemetery, Rosemont, Hunterdon County.
KLINE, CHARLES Pvt, I, 38th NJ Inf, 2-23-1886. Union Cemetery, Frenchtown, Hunterdon County.
KLINE, DAVID Pvt, Btty D, 1st NJ Light Art, 1-2-1897. Fairmount Cemetery, Newark, Essex County.
KLINE, EDWARD S. 1st Sgt, F, 116th PA Inf, [Wounded 8-25-1864 at Reams Station, VA.] 7-26-1904. Phillipsburg Cemetery, Phillipsburg, Warren County.
KLINE, ELISHA W. Pvt, G, 38th NJ Inf, 1921. Rosemont Cemetery, Rosemont, Hunterdon County.
KLINE, JESSE (see: Kline, Augustus) St. Francis Cemetery, Trenton, Mercer County.
KLINE, JOHN Corp, I, 5th PA Cav, 1-19-1911. Arlington Cemetery, Kearny, Hudson County.
KLINE, JOHN Pvt, F, 22nd U.S. CT, 2-16-1891. New Somerville Cemetery, Somerville, Somerset County.
KLINE, JOHN C. Corp, A, 31st NJ Inf, 12-17-1910. Old & New Lutheran Cemetery, Lebanon, Hunterdon County.
KLINE, MANUEL K. 2nd Lt, H, 15th NJ Inf, 7-8-1921. Riverview Cemetery, Trenton, Mercer County.
KLINE, MARTIN S. Pvt, B, 17th IL Inf, 1902. Rural Hill Cemetery, Whitehouse, Hunterdon County.
KLINE, PETER Pvt, C, 71st NY State Militia, 3-28-1907. Old & New Lutheran Cemetery, Lebanon, Hunterdon County.
KLINE*, PETER (aka: Kane, Peter) Pvt, Btty H, 6th NY Heavy Art, DoD Unknown. Arlington Cemetery, Kearny, Hudson County.
KLINE, PETER (see: Cline, Peter) Grove Church Cemetery, North Bergen, Hudson County.
KLINE*, PETER L. Pvt, I, 2nd NJ Inf, 2-18-1887. Reformed Church Cemetery, Readington, Hunterdon County.
KLINE, SAMUEL Pvt, C, 34th NJ Inf, DoD Unknown. Baptist Cemetery, Vincentown, Burlington County.

Our Brothers Gone Before

KLINE, WILLIAM Pvt, I, 4th NJ Inf, 6-1-1868. Presbyterian Church Cemetery, Harmony, Warren County.
KLINESMITH*, CHARLES Pvt, I, 35th NJ Inf, 1-7-1873. Palisade Cemetery, North Bergen, Hudson County.
KLING*, AUGUST Pvt, C, 7th NJ Inf, 10-18-1884. Fairmount Cemetery, Newark, Essex County.
KLING, JOSEPH A. Pvt, C, 30th NJ Inf, 3-14-1870. Rahway Cemetery, Rahway, Union County.
KLINGENSTEIN*, JACOB Pvt, H, 58th NY Inf, 5-2-1880. Bayview-New York Bay Cemetery, Jersey City, Hudson County.
KLINGENSTEIN, M. 12-21-1876. Bayview-New York Bay Cemetery, Jersey City, Hudson County.
KLOCK, EDMOND A. Pvt, Btty K, 5th NY Heavy Art, 1926. Union Cemetery, Washington, Morris County.
KLOEPPING, CHARLES (aka: Klopping, Carl) Pvt, Btty G, 15th NY Heavy Art, 8-6-1913. Hoboken Cemetery, North Bergen, Hudson County.
KLOEPPING, SIMON (aka: Klopping, Simon) Pvt, B, 58th NY Inf, 2-8-1923. Flower Hill Cemetery, North Bergen, Hudson County.
KLOPPING, CARL (see: Kloepping, Charles) Hoboken Cemetery, North Bergen, Hudson County.
KLOPPING*, PHILIP A. Pvt, K, 68th NY Inf, 9-8-1884. Flower Hill Cemetery, North Bergen, Hudson County.
KLOPPING, SIMON (see: Kloepping, Simon) Flower Hill Cemetery, North Bergen, Hudson County.
KLUG, GEORGE Corp, C, 54th NY Inf, 9-7-1909. Berry Lawn Cemetery, Carlstadt, Bergen County.
KLUGE, HERMAN Pvt, D, 119th NY Inf, [Wounded 5-2-1863 at Chancellorsville, VA.] 4-25-1882. Jersey City Cemetery, Jersey City, Hudson County.
KLUMP, JOHN Pvt, Btty B, 1st NJ Light Art, 6-20-1894. Woodland Cemetery, Newark, Essex County.
KLUTTS, EDMOND M. Pvt, K, 57th NC Inf (CSA), [Captured 7-5-1863 at Gettysburg, PA. Died of smallpox.] 12-25-1863. Finn's Point National Cemetery, Pennsville, Salem County.
KLUTZ, ADAM Pvt, C, 18th NC Inf (CSA), [Captured 7-12-1863 at Hagerstown, MD.] 9-10-1863. Finn's Point National Cemetery, Pennsville, Salem County.
KNACK, ALBERT F. Artificer, D, 1st NY Eng, 12-30-1907. Weehawken Cemetery, North Bergen, Hudson County.
KNAPP, ANDREW Pvt, A, 39th NJ Inf, 1-14-1914. Fairmount Cemetery, Newark, Essex County.
KNAPP, BENJAMIN FRANKLIN Pvt, L, 27th NJ Inf, 5-13-1926. Hillside Cemetery, Madison, Morris County.
KNAPP, BENJAMIN S. Pvt, H, 39th NJ Inf, 2-19-1924. Mount Pleasant Cemetery, Newark, Essex County.
KNAPP, CHARLES E. Pvt, B, 8th NJ Inf, 6-1-1896. Fairmount Cemetery, Newark, Essex County.
KNAPP, DAVID S. Pvt, C, 95th PA Inf, 7-27-1909. Methodist Church Cemetery, Groveville, Mercer County.
KNAPP, JOHN Pvt, I, 111th NY Inf, [Died at Beverly, NJ.] 10-5-1864. Beverly National Cemetery, Edgewater Park, Burlington County.
KNAPP, JOHN Pvt, G, 9th NJ Inf, 6-5-1914. Lady of Lourdes/Holy Sepulchre Cemetery, Hamilton, Mercer County.
KNAPP, JOHN G. Corp, H, 1st __ Inf, 1-23-1917. Fairmount Cemetery, Newark, Essex County.

New Jersey Civil War Burials

KNAPP, NEHEMIAH 2-4-1917. Bayview-New York Bay Cemetery, Jersey City, Hudson County.
KNAPP, W.HENRY Pvt, B, 12th NY Inf, 3-29-1912. Laurel Grove Cemetery, Totowa, Passaic County.
KNAPP, WILLIAM Pvt, B, 53rd NY Inf, 3-28-1909. Clinton Cemetery, Irvington, Essex County.
KNAPP, WILLIAM A. Pvt, K, 70th NY Inf, [Wounded 7-2-1863 at Gettysburg, PA.] 5-6-1915. Mount Pleasant Cemetery, Newark, Essex County.
KNAPP, WILLIAM J. Pvt, G, 1st NJ Militia, 12-22-1919. Fairmount Cemetery, Newark, Essex County.
KNAPP, WILLIAM R. Sgt, K, 9th NJ Inf, 9-29-1910. Fairmount Cemetery, Newark, Essex County.
KNAUSS, JOHN D. Musc, B, 51st PA Inf, 1-25-1922. Phillipsburg Cemetery, Phillipsburg, Warren County.
KNEASA, JOHN (see: Schmidt, John) Woodland Cemetery, Newark, Essex County.
KNEELAND, JOSEPH Landsman, U.S. Navy, DoD Unknown. St. John's Evangelical Church Cemetery, Orange, Essex County.
KNEER, GEORGE 3-18-1915. Jersey City Cemetery, Jersey City, Hudson County.
KNEFFNER, FREDERICK (see: Caspar, Frederick C.H.) Presbyterian Cemetery, North Plainfield, Somerset County.
KNELLER, CHARLES Pvt, A, 12th U.S. Inf, 11-6-1897. Fairmount Cemetery, Newark, Essex County.
KNELLER, CHARLES (see: Keneller, Charles) Fairmount Cemetery, Newark, Essex County.
KNELLER, FREDERICK Pvt, K, 9th NJ Inf, 5-26-1900. Woodland Cemetery, Newark, Essex County.
KNELLER, WILLIAM Pvt, K, 9th NJ Inf, 12-23-1906. Woodland Cemetery, Newark, Essex County.
KNERT, FRANCIS (see: Kurt, Francis) Brotherhood Cemetery, Hainesport, Burlington County.
KNESPEL, CHRISTIAN J. (see: Knispel, Christian J.) Woodland Cemetery, Newark, Essex County.
KNICKERBOCKER, EDWARD Pvt, E, 5th CT Inf, 11-21-1922. Greengrove Cemetery, Keyport, Monmouth County.
KNIEF, FREDERICK 6-11-1914. Palisade Cemetery, North Bergen, Hudson County.
KNIERIEN, FLORIAN 8-1-1890. Reformed Church Cemetery, North Branch, Somerset County.
KNIES, JOHN C. Pvt, A, 10th NY Inf, [Wounded 5-10-1864 at Spotsylvania CH, VA.] 6-9-1911. Palisade Cemetery, North Bergen, Hudson County.
KNIGHT, ALBERT H. Pvt, B, 21st IA Inf, 3-26-1927. Cedar Lawn Cemetery, Paterson, Passaic County.
KNIGHT, ALFRED Seaman, U.S. Navy, USS Cumberland, 5-1-1895. Evergreen Cemetery, Morristown, Morris County.
KNIGHT, EDWARD D. 1st Sgt, K, 121st PA Inf, 9-19-1899. Evergreen Cemetery, Camden, Camden County.
KNIGHT, ENGELBERT 6-10-1920. Evergreen Cemetery, Camden, Camden County.
KNIGHT*, FRANKLIN L. Lt Col, 24th NJ Inf 11-16-1895. Evergreen Cemetery, Camden, Camden County.
KNIGHT, JAMES C. Pvt, I, 2nd MS Inf (CSA), [Wounded 9-17-1862 at Sharpsburg, MD. Captured 7-3-1863 at Gettysburg, PA. Died of pneumonia.] 4-16-1865. Finn's Point National Cemetery, Pennsville, Salem County.
KNIGHT, JAMES D. Pvt, A, 197th PA Inf, 9-5-1892. Coopertown Meeting House Cemetery, Edgewater Park, Burlington County.

Our Brothers Gone Before

KNIGHT, JOHN B. Corp, C, 2nd NJ Inf, [Died of fever at Philadelphia, PA.] 9-2-1862. South Orange Cemetery, South Orange, Essex County.

KNIGHT, JOHN S. Pvt, F, 9th IA Inf, 7-11-1922. Cedar Lawn Cemetery, Paterson, Passaic County.

KNIGHT*, MONTVILLE SMITH (aka: Smith, Montreville) Pvt, B, 1st MD Inf, [Wounded in action.] 8-13-1924. Phillipsburg Cemetery, Phillipsburg, Warren County.

KNIGHT, PIERSON K. Pvt, A, 7th WV Inf, 1918. Riverview Cemetery, Penns Grove, Salem County.

KNIGHT, S.N. Pvt, B, 30th VA Inf (CSA), 10-29-1863. Finn's Point National Cemetery, Pennsville, Salem County.

KNIGHT, SEPTIMUS N. Corp, A, 15th PA Cav, 5-25-1917. Arlington Cemetery, Pennsauken, Camden County.

KNIGHT, STEPHEN R. Pvt, E, 39th NJ Inf, 2-5-1928. Clinton Cemetery, Irvington, Essex County.

KNIGHT, WILLIAM 10-8-1898. Friends Hicksite Cemetery, Woodbury, Gloucester County.

KNIGHTEN, JAMES W. Pvt, B, 4th NC Cav (CSA), [Captured 7-4-1863 at Monterey, PA. Died of tonsil inflammation.] 11-4-1863. Finn's Point National Cemetery, Pennsville, Salem County.

KNIPER, WILLIAM (see: Kaniper, William) Presbyterian Church Cemetery, Harmony, Warren County.

KNIPSCHILD, CLEMENS Capt, A, 41st NY Inf, 1901. Holy Sepulchre Cemetery, East Orange, Essex County.

KNISPEL, CHRISTIAN J. (aka: Knespel, Christian J.) Musc, C, 9th NJ Inf, 3-19-1902. Woodland Cemetery, Newark, Essex County.

KNOBLE, CHARLES E. Pvt, K, 13th NJ Inf, 12-23-1917. Cedar Lawn Cemetery, Paterson, Passaic County.

KNODLER, AUGUST Pvt, H, 2nd NJ Militia, 10-13-1887. Bayview-New York Bay Cemetery, Jersey City, Hudson County.

KNOELER, CHARLES P. (aka: Knowler, Charles) Pvt, B, 21st NJ Inf, 2-1-1906. Bayview-New York Bay Cemetery, Jersey City, Hudson County.

KNOLES, WILLIAM Pvt, Btty A, 1st NJ Light Art, 5-29-1903. St. John's Evangelical Church Cemetery, Orange, Essex County.

KNOLL, JOSEPH (aka: Knowles, Joseph) Pvt, F, 9th NJ Inf, DoD Unknown. Jersey City Cemetery, Jersey City, Hudson County.

KNOLLES, JAMES (see: Knolles, John) Harleigh Cemetery, Camden, Camden County.

KNOLLES, JOHN (aka: Knolles, James) Pvt, E, 1st MI Inf, 5-2-1896. Harleigh Cemetery, Camden, Camden County.

KNORR, LEONARD Pvt, D, 24th NJ Inf, 1907. Chickory Chapel Baptist Church Cemetery, Elk, Gloucester County.

KNOTT, DANIEL Pvt, K, 1st NJ Inf, 8-12-1887. Boonton Cemetery, Boonton, Morris County.

KNOTT, DANIEL Pvt, G, 39th PA Militia, 6-22-1898. Riverview Cemetery, Trenton, Mercer County.

KNOTT, JOHN F. Pvt, F, 14th NJ Inf, 1-15-1874. Methodist Cemetery, Hamilton, Monmouth County.

KNOTT, SAMUEL Pvt, D, 71st NY State Militia, 5-21-1919. Woodland Cemetery, Newark, Essex County.

KNOTT, THOMAS A. Pvt, A, 23rd (Martin's) TN Inf (CSA), 11-16-1863. Finn's Point National Cemetery, Pennsville, Salem County.

KNOTT, THOMAS G.F. DoD Unknown. Presbyterian Church Cemetery, Bridgeton, Cumberland County.

New Jersey Civil War Burials

KNOWLDEN, WILLIAM N. (aka: Nolan, William N.) Sgt, I, 39th NY Inf, [Wounded 5-10-1864 at Po River, VA.] 3-24-1871. Laurel Grove Cemetery, Totowa, Passaic County.

KNOWLER, CHARLES (see: Knoeler, Charles P.) Bayview-New York Bay Cemetery, Jersey City, Hudson County.

KNOWLES, ALVAH A. Pvt, C, 42nd MA Militia, 2-26-1930. Arlington Cemetery, Kearny, Hudson County.

KNOWLES*, ANTHONEY (aka: Nolles, Anthony) Ordinary Seaman, U.S. Navy, USS Kansas, 1-25-1885. Mount Hope United Methodist Church Cemetery, Salem, Salem County.

KNOWLES, CHARLES HOWARD Pvt, B, 21st NJ Inf, 1-23-1923. Greenwood Cemetery, Hamilton, Mercer County.

KNOWLES, CHARLES V. Pvt, F, 23rd OH Inf, 6-28-1873. Hainesburg Cemetery, Hainesburg, Warren County.

KNOWLES*, DAVID G. Farrier, E, 2nd NJ Cav, 3-13-1866. Baptist Church Cemetery, Penns Neck, Mercer County.

KNOWLES, GEORGE F. Corp, Btty F, 1st MA Heavy Art, 1-6-1899. Siloam Cemetery, Vineland, Cumberland County.

KNOWLES, HENDERSON W. Pvt, K, 30th NJ Inf, 9-13-1926. Presbyterian Church Cemetery, Kingston, Somerset County.

KNOWLES, JOHN P. Pvt, E, 21st NJ Inf, 12-18-1902. Riverview Cemetery, Trenton, Mercer County.

KNOWLES, JONATHAN C. Pvt, E, 11th NJ Inf, 6-12-1907. Riverview Cemetery, Trenton, Mercer County.

KNOWLES, JOSEPH (see: Knoll, Joseph) Jersey City Cemetery, Jersey City, Hudson County.

KNOWLES*, OLIVER H. Pvt, I, 38th NJ Inf, 8-26-1912. Mercer Cemetery, Trenton, Mercer County.

KNOWLES*, ROBERT J. Pvt, A, 5th NY Inf, 3-24-1875. Bayview-New York Bay Cemetery, Jersey City, Hudson County.

KNOWLES, WILLIAM Pvt, A, 17th NY Inf, 7-17-1880. Rosedale Cemetery, Orange, Essex County.

KNOWLTON, CHARLES H. Pvt, C, 25th MA Inf, [Wounded 5-9-1864 at Arrowfield Church, VA.] 1898. Harleigh Cemetery, Camden, Camden County.

KNOWLTON*, IRA Pvt, A, 12th NJ Inf, 10-15-1899. Mount Laurel/Eldridge Cemetery, Mount Laurel, Burlington County.

KNOWLTON, MINOR Capt, Btty B, 1st U.S. Art, 12-24-1870. St. Mary's Episcopal Church Cemetery, Burlington, Burlington County.

KNOX, ANDREW G. C. Pvt, D, 18th NY Inf, [Wounded in action.] 6-2-1903. Fairmount Cemetery, Newark, Essex County.

KNOX, BENJAMIN E. 2nd Lt, C, 2nd NY Cav, 1910. Branchville Cemetery, Branchville, Sussex County.

KNOX, EDWARD D. Pvt, K, 33rd NJ Inf, 7-18-1916. Arlington Cemetery, Kearny, Hudson County.

KNOX, GEORGE (see: Wentworth, George P.L.) Riverview Cemetery, Trenton, Mercer County.

KNOX*, JAMES SUYDAM Hosp Steward, U.S. Army, 6-28-1892. Old Somerville Cemetery, Somerville, Somerset County.

KNOX, JOHN POLK Sgt, D, 20th NY Inf, 2-26-1874. Presbyterian Church Cemetery, Newton, Sussex County.

KNOX, PATRICK DoD Unknown. Elmwood Cemetery, New Brunswick, Middlesex County.

KNOX, WILLIAM A. Corp, 5th NY Ind Btty 12-15-1922. Grove Church Cemetery, North Bergen, Hudson County.

Our Brothers Gone Before

KNOX, WILLIAM C. Bvt 2nd Lt, D, 4th TN Cav (CSA), 4-11-1865. Finn's Point National Cemetery, Pennsville, Salem County.

KNUBEL, JOHN F. Pvt, E, 9th NY Inf, [Wounded 9-17-1862 at Antietam, MD.] 12-16-1920. Bayview-New York Bay Cemetery, Jersey City, Hudson County.

KOBEL, GEORGE Pvt, Btty A, 1st NJ Light Art, 8-1-1900. Weehawken Cemetery, North Bergen, Hudson County.

KOCH, FREDERICK 2nd Lt, E, 7th NJ Inf, 10-27-1867. Lutheran Cemetery, East Stewartsville, Warren County.

KOCH, HEINRICH F. Pvt, B, 39th NY Inf, 1-5-1882. Palisade Cemetery, North Bergen, Hudson County.

KOCH*, HENRY Pvt, B, 39th NY Inf, [Wounded 7-2-1863 at Gettysburg, PA.] DoD Unknown. Berry Lawn Cemetery, Carlstadt, Bergen County.

KOCH, JACOB Pvt, F, 9th NJ Inf, 12-24-1902. Weehawken Cemetery, North Bergen, Hudson County.

KOCH, JACOB Pvt, K, 7th NJ Inf, 1881. Reformed Church Cemetery, Pluckemin, Somerset County.

KOCH, JOHN Pvt, G, 2nd NJ Cav, DoD Unknown. Berry Lawn Cemetery, Carlstadt, Bergen County.

KOCH, JOSEPH 7-29-1892. Palisade Cemetery, North Bergen, Hudson County.

KOCHER, JOHN Drum Major, 7th NJ Inf 5-19-1879. Fairmount Cemetery, Newark, Essex County.

KOCHLAND, NATHAN (see: Kowler, Nathan) Baptist Church Cemetery, Haddonfield, Camden County.

KOEBER*, JOHN G. (aka: Deachant, John) Pvt, M, 3rd NJ Cav, 2-18-1904. Bloomfield Cemetery, Bloomfield, Essex County.

KOEFFLER, MARTIN Pvt, L, 3rd NJ Cav, 2-8-1903. Riverview Cemetery, Trenton, Mercer County.

KOEHN, HENRY (aka: Kohn, Heinrich) Pvt, D, 20th NY Inf, 7-3-1913. Fairmount Cemetery, Newark, Essex County.

KOELBLE, AUGUST Pvt, Btty B, 2nd PA Heavy Art, 5-16-1914. Fairmount Cemetery, Newark, Essex County.

KOELLE, FRIEDRICH A. (SR.) (aka: Koello, Frederick) 1st Sgt, Btty B, 15th NY Heavy Art, 12-26-1929. Harleigh Cemetery, Camden, Camden County.

KOELLER, HERMAN A. Pvt, D, 3rd NY Cav, 1916. Rural Hill Cemetery, Whitehouse, Hunterdon County.

KOELLHOFFER, AUGUST Pvt, B, 25th NY Cav, 1-23-1910. St. Mary's Cemetery, East Orange, Essex County.

KOELLHOFFER, FRANCIS (aka: Kielhoffer, Francis) Pvt, B, 33rd NJ Inf, DoD Unknown. St. Mary's Cemetery, East Orange, Essex County.

KOELLO, FREDERICK (see: Koelle, Friedrich A. (Sr.)) Harleigh Cemetery, Camden, Camden County.

KOELSCH, WILLIAM (see: Kotsch, William) Woodland Cemetery, Newark, Essex County.

KOELTER, WILLIAM Pvt, H, 33rd NJ Inf, DoD Unknown. Weehawken Cemetery, North Bergen, Hudson County.

KOENIG*, ALBERT A. Pvt, L, 9th NJ Inf, [Wounded in action.] 3-19-1900. Fairmount Cemetery, Newark, Essex County.

KOENIG, BERTHOLD F. Pvt, E, 2nd NJ Inf, 11-8-1926. Fairmount Cemetery, Newark, Essex County.

KOENIG, CHARLES A. Corp, G, 11th NJ Inf, [Wounded 7-2-1863 at Gettysburg, PA.] 1912. United Methodist Church Cemetery, Ellisdale, Burlington County.

KOENIG, GUSTAVE (see: Koening, Gustave) Rosehill Cemetery, Linden, Union County.

KOENIG*, JOHN M. Pvt, Btty C, 1st NJ Light Art, 8-14-1908. Woodland Cemetery, Newark, Essex County.

New Jersey Civil War Burials

KOENIG, JOHN M. Pvt, K, 9th NJ Inf, 1-1-1936. Jacobstown Masonic Cemetery, Jacobstown, Burlington County.
KOENIG, JULIUS (aka: King, Julius) Pvt, H, 73rd NY Inf, 7-28-1922. Woodland Cemetery, Newark, Essex County.
KOENIG, LOUIS (see: King, Lewis) Mount Pleasant Cemetery, Millville, Cumberland County.
KOENIG, RICHARD Pvt, A, 47th PA Inf, 4-21-1870. Mercer Cemetery, Trenton, Mercer County.
KOENIG, WILLIAM (aka: Konig, William) Pvt, E, 119th NY Inf, 2-17-1929. Fairmount Cemetery, Newark, Essex County.
KOENIGSDOERFFER*, ADOLPH (aka: Konigsdoffer, Adolph) Pvt, E, 120th NY Inf, 2-11-1902. Fairmount Cemetery, Newark, Essex County.
KOENING*, GUSTAVE (aka: Koenig, Gustave) Pvt, H, 7th NJ Inf, 12-7-1914. Rosehill Cemetery, Linden, Union County.
KOEPKE, FRIEDRICH (aka: Kophe, Frederic) Pvt, K, 34th WI Inf, DoD Unknown. Berry Lawn Cemetery, Carlstadt, Bergen County.
KOERKLE, JOHN (see: Kurkel, John) Woodland Cemetery, Newark, Essex County.
KOERNER, CHARLES (aka: Horner, Charles) Pvt, K, 8th NJ Inf, 9-9-1911. Fairmount Cemetery, Newark, Essex County.
KOERNER, JOHN Pvt, Btty D, 15th NY Heavy Art, [Wounded in action 5-31-1864.] 11-21-1903. Edgewater Cemetery, Edgewater, Bergen County.
KOERT, CORNELIUS Pvt, E, 22nd NJ Inf, 5-5-1887. Fair Lawn Cemetery, Fair Lawn, Bergen County.
KOHL, JOSEPH Pvt, A, 104th PA Inf, 3-7-1922. Greenwood Cemetery, Hamilton, Mercer County.
KOHLBECKER, CORNELIUS (aka: Becker, Charles) Pvt, E, 3rd NJ Cav, 4-28-1917. St. Mary's Cemetery, East Orange, Essex County.
KOHLBERGER, PHILIP Pvt, D, 8th U.S. Inf, 6-5-1906. Lodi Cemetery, Lodi, Bergen County.
KOHLER, ANTHONY Pvt, B, 11th NJ Inf, 10-19-1881. Fairmount Cemetery, Newark, Essex County.
KOHLER, GEORGE W. (aka: Williamson, James) Pvt, I, 6th NH Inf, 7-1-1896. Hackensack Cemetery, Hackensack, Bergen County.
KOHLER, JACOB Pvt, F, 33rd NJ Inf, 2-21-1893. Rosedale Cemetery, Orange, Essex County.
KOHLER, JOHN Pvt, H, 1st NJ Cav, DoD Unknown. St. Peter's Cemetery, New Brunswick, Middlesex County.
KOHLHEPP, JOHN K. (aka: Calhepp, John) Pvt, H, 1st NJ Cav, DoD Unknown. Elmwood Cemetery, New Brunswick, Middlesex County.
KOHN, CHARLES H. Pvt, Unassigned, 93rd NY Inf, 2-2-1872. Fairmount Cemetery, Newark, Essex County.
KOHN, HEINRICH (see: Koehn, Henry) Fairmount Cemetery, Newark, Essex County.
KOLB, ADAM (JR.) Pvt, Btty M, 3rd PA Heavy Art, 4-7-1877. Old Camden Cemetery, Camden, Camden County.
KOLB, ADAM (SR.) Pvt, Btty M, 3rd PA Heavy Art, 3-1-1872. Old Camden Cemetery, Camden, Camden County.
KOLB, CHARLES Pvt, B, 54th NY Inf, 4-24-1884. Hoboken Cemetery, North Bergen, Hudson County.
KOLB, CHARLES M. Pvt, 9th NY Ind Btty 1-9-1903. Oddfellows Cemetery, Burlington, Burlington County.
KOLB, NICHOLAS Sgt, E, 2nd NJ Cav, 8-23-1893. Princeton Cemetery, Princeton, Mercer County.
KOLB, PETER Sgt, D, 45th NY Inf, 3-7-1871. Hoboken Cemetery, North Bergen, Hudson County.

Our Brothers Gone Before

KOLENBERG, GEORGE Pvt, K, 153rd NY Inf, 7-15-1911. Fairmount Cemetery, Newark, Essex County.
KOLSTER, ABRAHAM J. Musc, G, 2nd DC Inf, 1-8-1917. Presbyterian Cemetery, Springfield, Union County.
KOMST, LEOPOLD Musc, A, 9th NJ Inf, DoD Unknown. Mount Pleasant Cemetery, Newark, Essex County.
KOMST, LEOPOLD (aka: Krunpst, Leopold) Musc, C, 9th NY Inf, 10-21-1886. Woodland Cemetery, Newark, Essex County.
KONERT, FRANK Pvt, E, 39th NJ Inf, DoD Unknown. Holy Sepulchre Cemetery, East Orange, Essex County.
KONIETZKO, FREDERICK W. Landsman, U.S. Navy, 9-2-1924. Princeton Cemetery, Princeton, Mercer County.
KONIG, WILLIAM Pvt, E, 119th NY Inf, 2-16-1929. Fairmount Cemetery, Newark, Essex County.
KONIG, WILLIAM (see: Koenig, William) Fairmount Cemetery, Newark, Essex County.
KONIGSDOFFER, ADOLPH (see: Koenigsdoerffer, Adolph) Fairmount Cemetery, Newark, Essex County.
KOONS, CHARLES H. Pvt, F, 213th PA Inf, 2-10-1903. Rosedale Cemetery, Orange, Essex County.
KOONS, JOHN Pvt, A, 3rd NJ Cav, 2-1-1879. Mount Hope Presbyterian Cemetery, Lambertville, Hunterdon County.
KOONS, JOHN (see: Kans, John) Van Liew Cemetery, North Brunswick, Middlesex County.
KOOSE, WILLIAM Pvt, C, 31st NJ Inf, 1-13-1921. Phillipsburg Cemetery, Phillipsburg, Warren County.
KOPF, JOHN Pvt, A, 39th NJ Inf, 5-7-1874. Bloomfield Cemetery, Bloomfield, Essex County.
KOPHE, FREDERIC (see: Koepke, Friederich) Berry Lawn Cemetery, Carlstadt, Bergen County.
KOPP*, JOHN Corp, F, 39th NJ Inf, 9-10-1900. Fairmount Cemetery, Newark, Essex County.
KOPP, LORENZ Pvt, Btty A, 1st NJ Light Art, 6-10-1870. Woodland Cemetery, Newark, Essex County.
KORAN, CHARLES (see: Korn, Charles A.) Fairmount Cemetery, Newark, Essex County.
KORBEL, WILLIAM HENRY Pvt, E, 12th NJ Inf, 9-23-1897. Macphelah Cemetery, North Bergen, Hudson County.
KORN, CHARLES A. (aka: Koran, Charles) Pvt, E, 25th NY Cav, 12-2-1886. Fairmount Cemetery, Newark, Essex County.
KORN, EMIL CARL Pvt, Btty C, 1st NJ Light Art, 5-5-1891. Flower Hill Cemetery, North Bergen, Hudson County.
KORRIGAN, THOMAS (see: Corrigan, Thomas) Holy Name Cemetery, Jersey City, Hudson County.
KORSKE, JOHN F. Pvt, Btty L, 3rd __ Art, 1-3-1908. Fairmount Cemetery, Newark, Essex County.
KORTZENDORFER, NICHOLAS Pvt, G, 3rd NJ Inf, 5-10-1895. Fairmount Cemetery, Newark, Essex County.
KOSEROWSKI, JULIUS (aka: Kossakowski, Julius) Pvt, I, 28th OH Inf, 2-19-1888. Elmwood Cemetery, New Brunswick, Middlesex County.
KOSS, ERNST (see: Krons, Ernst) Evergreen Cemetery, Hillside, Union County.
KOSSAKOWSKI, JULIUS (see: Koserowski, Julius) Elmwood Cemetery, New Brunswick, Middlesex County.
KOST*, EMIL Corp, Btty A, 1st NJ Light Art, 1-20-1917. Grove Church Cemetery, North Bergen, Hudson County.

New Jersey Civil War Burials

KOSTER, ALBERT B. Pvt, L, 6th NY Cav, 2-12-1926. New York/New Jersey Mausoleum Cemetery, North Bergen, Hudson County.
KOSTER, OTTO Pvt, A, 11th NJ Inf, 1-23-1912. 1st Methodist-Episcopal Cemetery, New Brunswick, Middlesex County.
KOTHE, GEORGE Pvt, G, 6th CT Inf, 10-5-1932. Woodland Cemetery, Newark, Essex County.
KOTSCH, WILLIAM (aka: Koelsch, William) Pvt, A, 20th NY Inf, 2-28-1867. Woodland Cemetery, Newark, Essex County.
KOTTA, FREDERICK __, __, 3rd NY Cav, 1898. Bayview-New York Bay Cemetery, Jersey City, Hudson County.
KOUST, HENRY 8-7-1870. Baptist Cemetery, Burlington, Burlington County.
KOWLER, NATHAN (aka: Kochland, Nathan) Pvt, D, 34th NJ Inf, DoD Unknown. Baptist Church Cemetery, Haddonfield, Camden County.
KOYT, MARSHALL J. Pvt, G, 31st NJ Inf, 4-3-1889. Fairmount Cemetery, Newark, Essex County.
KOYT, SYLVESTER Sgt, H, 31st NJ Inf, 4-14-1900. Newton Cemetery, Newton, Sussex County.
KRACKE, JOHN 7-2-1916. Bayview-New York Bay Cemetery, Jersey City, Hudson County.
KRAEMER, CHARLES Pvt, A, 20th NY Inf, DoD Unknown. Fairmount Cemetery, Newark, Essex County.
KRAEMER, FRIEDRICH J. Pvt, E, 22nd CT Inf, 6-14-1901. Grove Church Cemetery, North Bergen, Hudson County.
KRAEMER, GOTTLIEB W. Pvt, K, 41st NY Inf, 10-28-1870. Woodland Cemetery, Newark, Essex County.
KRAFT, CHARLES Corp, B, 1st NJ Inf, 6-3-1918. Greenwood Cemetery, Hamilton, Mercer County.
KRAFT, CONRAD Corp, L, 9th NJ Inf, 3-17-1873. Woodland Cemetery, Newark, Essex County.
KRAFT, EDWARD DoD Unknown. Old Camden Cemetery, Camden, Camden County.
KRAFT*, FREDERICK Pvt, D, 11th NJ Inf, 10-23-1880. Woodland Cemetery, Newark, Essex County.
KRAFT, JACOB (aka: Craft, Jacob) Corp, E, 188th PA Inf, 1918. Arlington Cemetery, Pennsauken, Camden County.
KRAFT, JOHN Pvt, D, 7th NY Inf, 11-15-1864. Beverly National Cemetery, Edgewater Park, Burlington County.
KRAFT, PETER (see: Craft, Peter) Atlantic City Cemetery, Pleasantville, Atlantic County.
KRAFT, WILLIAM 1st Lt, D, 1st NC Inf (US), 3-18-1914. Evergreen Cemetery, Camden, Camden County.
KRAHL, CHRISTIAN (see: Kroehl, Christian) Holy Sepulchre Cemetery, East Orange, Essex County.
KRAIL*, CHARLES Pvt, I, 33rd PA Inf, 12-29-1902. Monument Cemetery, Edgewater Park, Burlington County.
KRALL, ISAAC Pvt, I, 200th PA Inf, 1928. Evergreen Cemetery, Clinton, Hunterdon County.
KRAMER, FREDERICK Sgt, I, 35th NJ Inf, 6-22-1875. Phillipsburg Cemetery, Phillipsburg, Warren County.
KRAMER, HENRY Pvt, C, 1st NJ Inf, 12-6-1889. Fairmount Cemetery, Newark, Essex County.
KRAUS, FREDERICK J. 2nd Lt, G, 37th NJ Inf, 1-23-1902. Fairmount Cemetery, Newark, Essex County.
KRAUS, HERMAN Pvt, A, 9th NJ Inf, 5-2-1895. Woodland Cemetery, Newark, Essex County.

Our Brothers Gone Before

KRAUSE, HENNING W. Pvt, Btty A, 1st NJ Light Art, 10-28-1906. Bayview-New York Bay Cemetery, Jersey City, Hudson County.
KRAUSE, RUDOLPH H. Corp, H, 8th NJ Inf, 2- -1907. Riverside Cemetery, Riverside, Burlington County.
KRAUSE*, WILLIAM Pvt, D, 2nd NJ Inf, 11-6-1896. Fairmount Cemetery, Newark, Essex County.
KRAUSS, FREDERICK Pvt, G, 1st NJ Cav, 11-5-1889. Greenlawn Cemetery, West Long Branch, Monmouth County.
KRAUSS, JOHN Pvt, K, 83rd PA Inf, [Wounded in action at Wilderness, VA. and Hatchers Run, VA.] 10-24-1892. Fairmount Cemetery, Newark, Essex County.
KREAMER, JOHN H. Corp, A, 72nd PA Inf, 5-25-1910. Greenwood Cemetery, Pleasantville, Atlantic County.
KREBS, GEORGE Pvt, H, 34th NJ Inf, 4-25-1915. Egg Harbor Cemetery, Egg Harbor, Atlantic County.
KREBS, JACOB 12-19-1865. Laurel Grove Cemetery, Totowa, Passaic County.
KREBS, JOHN (aka: Glibbs, John) Pvt, C, 4th NJ Inf, 10-3-1912. Mount Hope Cemetery, Deerfield, Cumberland County.
KREBS, MARTIN (see: Grapes, Martin) Laurel Grove Cemetery, Totowa, Passaic County.
KREIG, DAVID Pvt, 52, U.S. VRC, 11-2-1908. Evergreen Cemetery, Hillside, Union County.
KREIGER, DAVID (see: Criger, David) Pequest Union Cemetery, Great Meadows, Warren County.
KREIGER, JOHN FREDERICK Pvt, H, 25th NJ Inf, 2-1-1890. Laurel Grove Cemetery, Totowa, Passaic County.
KREILING, HENRY DIETRICH __, __, __ NY __, 9-3-1880. Berry Lawn Cemetery, Carlstadt, Bergen County.
KREIS, CHRISTIAN (aka: Christian, Creiss) Sgt, B, 39th NJ Inf, 12-11-1881. Woodland Cemetery, Newark, Essex County.
KREIS, PHILIP Pvt, I, 42nd NY Inf, 8-21-1896. Evergreen Cemetery, Hillside, Union County.
KREISS, BARTHOLOMAUS Pvt, A, 29th NY Inf, 11-20-1904. Bayview-New York Bay Cemetery, Jersey City, Hudson County.
KREMICK, ADAM (see: Kremrick, Adam) Bloomfield Cemetery, Bloomfield, Essex County.
KREMRICK, ADAM (aka: Kremick, Adam) Pvt, D, 15th NY Eng, 5-3-1888. Bloomfield Cemetery, Bloomfield, Essex County.
KRESS, JOHN Pvt, D, 29th NJ Inf, 4-18-1921. Woodland Cemetery, Newark, Essex County.
KRESSBACH, JOSEPH Pvt, Btty A, 1st NJ Light Art, 3-8-1904. Grove Church Cemetery, North Bergen, Hudson County.
KRESSLER, FRANKLIN Pvt, G, 23rd NJ Inf, 1-20-1912. Oddfellows Cemetery, Burlington, Burlington County.
KRETER, FREDERICK Pvt, A, 9th NJ Inf, 1880. Fairmount Cemetery, Newark, Essex County.
KRETZLER*, ARTHUR C. Corp, G, 5th NY Inf, [Wounded 6-27-1862 at Gaines' Mill, VA.] 11-20-1906. Grove Church Cemetery, North Bergen, Hudson County.
KREWSON*, AMOS A. Pvt, H, 6th NJ Inf, 2-11-1897. Mount Hope Presbyterian Cemetery, Lambertville, Hunterdon County.
KREWSON*, CHARLES Pvt, K, 99th PA Inf, [Wounded in action at Chancellorsville, VA.] DoD Unknown. Presbyterian Church Cemetery, Bridgeton, Cumberland County.
KRIEGSMANN, MICHAEL (see: Christmann, Michael) Laurel Grove Cemetery, Totowa, Passaic County.

New Jersey Civil War Burials

KRIGER, JOHN Pvt, I, 8th NJ Inf, 4-3-1913. Laurel Grove Cemetery, Totowa, Passaic County.
KRILL, AUGUST H. 6-21-1888. Fairmount Cemetery, Newark, Essex County.
KRIPPS, RICHARD Pvt, A, 34th NJ Inf, 8-6-1915. New Camden Cemetery, Camden, Camden County.
KRIPS, THOMAS W. Pvt, D, 12th NJ Inf, 3-6-1911. Evergreen Cemetery, Camden, Camden County.
KRISE*, DAVID Pvt, B, 31st NJ Inf, 11-15-1911. Mansfield/Washington Cemetery, Washington, Warren County.
KRITZMACHER, JACOB Pvt, E, 39th NJ Inf, 2-18-1891. Woodland Cemetery, Newark, Essex County.
KROCK, CHARLES F. (aka: Crock, Charles) Sgt, F, 33rd NJ Inf, 11-27-1865. Fairmount Cemetery, Newark, Essex County.
KROCK, HENRY E. (aka: Crock, Henry) Corp, K, 2nd NJ Cav, 7-2-1901. Fairmount Cemetery, Newark, Essex County.
KROECKLE, GEORGE Pvt, B, 39th NJ Inf, 1874. Fairmount Cemetery, Newark, Essex County.
KROEGER, MARTIN J. Pvt, H, 213th PA Inf, 12-26-1913. Old St. Mary's Cemetery, Gloucester City, Camden County.
KROEGER, WILLIAM (SR.) Pvt, F, 26th NJ Inf, 4-17-1915. Woodland Cemetery, Newark, Essex County.
KROEHL, CHRISTIAN (aka: Krahl, Christian) Pvt, G, 1st NJ Cav, 5-5-1880. Holy Sepulchre Cemetery, East Orange, Essex County.
KROEHL, JOHN Pvt, H, 68th NY Inf, [Wounded 7-1-1863 at Gettysburg, PA.] 10-25-1911. Holy Sepulchre Cemetery, East Orange, Essex County.
KROENLEIN, FRANCIS (see: Kroenlein, Franz) Holy Sepulchre Cemetery, East Orange, Essex County.
KROENLEIN*, FRANZ (aka: Kroenlein, Francis) Pvt, F, 68th NY Inf, 2-26-1891. Holy Sepulchre Cemetery, East Orange, Essex County.
KROENTHALER, ROBERT Pvt, K, 154th NY Inf, 8- -1905. Palisade Cemetery, North Bergen, Hudson County.
KROESEN*, HENRY S. (aka: Krosin, Harry) Pvt, H, 6th NJ Inf, 5-21-1920. Mount Hope Presbyterian Cemetery, Lambertville, Hunterdon County.
KROHN, WILHELM G. (aka: Cron, Wilhelm) Pvt, I, 39th NJ Inf, 1901. Grove Church Cemetery, North Bergen, Hudson County.
KRONMEYER, CHARLES J. Capt, C, 52nd NY Inf, [Wounded 5-10-1864 at Po River, VA.] 6-5-1897. Flower Hill Cemetery, North Bergen, Hudson County.
KRONS, ERNST (aka: Koss, Ernst) Pvt, B, 8th NY Inf, [Wounded 6-8-1862 at Cross Keys, VA.] 10-18-1900. Evergreen Cemetery, Hillside, Union County.
KROSIN, HARRY (see: Kroesen, Henry S.) Mount Hope Presbyterian Cemetery, Lambertville, Hunterdon County.
KROTTENTHALER, FREDERICK Pvt, H, 41st NY Inf, 3-28-1899. Weehawken Cemetery, North Bergen, Hudson County.
KROUSE, BERNARD (see: Krouse, Bernhart) St. James Cemetery, Woodbridge, Middlesex County.
KROUSE, BERNHART (aka: Krouse, Bernard) Pvt, K, 31st NJ Inf, 4-16-1915. St. James Cemetery, Woodbridge, Middlesex County.
KROUSE, JOHN W. Pvt, C, 73rd PA Inf, 10-15-1915. Woodlands Cemetery, Ocean View, Cape May County.
KROUSE, WILLIAM H. (see: Force, William H.) Mount Hebron Cemetery, Montclair, Essex County.
KROWN, WILLIAM MERCER (aka: Mercer, William) Pvt, C, 50th PA Inf, 11-3-1917. Evergreen Cemetery, Camden, Camden County.

Our Brothers Gone Before

KRUG*, FERDINAND W. Sgt, G, 11th NJ Inf, [Wounded in action.] DoD Unknown. Old 1st Methodist Church Cemetery, West Long Branch, Monmouth County.

KRUG, GEORGE HENRY (aka: Crook, Henry) Pvt, E, 22nd NJ Inf, 1-15-1899. Berry Lawn Cemetery, Carlstadt, Bergen County.

KRUG, PETER J. Pvt, A, 33rd NJ Inf, 1914. Cedar Lawn Cemetery, Paterson, Passaic County.

KRUG, PHILIP Pvt, D, 79th NY Inf, DoD Unknown. Holy Sepulchre Cemetery, East Orange, Essex County.

KRUGER, CHARLES Pvt, H, 17th MO Inf, 8-13-1917. Harleigh Cemetery, Camden, Camden County.

KRUGER, CHARLES Pvt, H, 2nd NJ Inf, 3-31-1887. Riverview Cemetery, Trenton, Mercer County.

KRUGER, PAUL (see: Ross, Paul) Palisade Cemetery, North Bergen, Hudson County.

KRUM, JOHN H. (aka: Crum, John) Pvt, A, 1st NY Mounted Rifles, 1906. Mount Prospect Cemetery, Neptune, Monmouth County.

KRUMRICH*, GEORGE Landsman, U.S. Navy, USS Miami, 1-6-1922. St. Mary's Cemetery, East Orange, Essex County.

KRUNPST, LEOPOLD (see: Komst, Leopold) Woodland Cemetery, Newark, Essex County.

KRUSE, HENRY (see: Crews, Henry T.) Finn's Point National Cemetery, Pennsville, Salem County.

KRUSE*, HENRY G.C. Actg Ensign, U.S. Navy, USS Shamrock, 11-20-1916. Macphelah Cemetery, North Bergen, Hudson County.

KRUSEN*, GEORGE Corp, C, 199th PA Inf, 7-16-1876. Baptist Cemetery, Medford, Burlington County.

KRUYSMAN*, NICHOLAS L. (aka: Crossman, Nicholas) Pvt, Btty B, 1st NJ Light Art, 12-2-1886. Fairmount Cemetery, Newark, Essex County.

KRYEZIEMER, __?__ __, Btty C, 5th U.S. Art, DoD Unknown. Bayview-New York Bay Cemetery, Jersey City, Hudson County.

KRYMER, JOHN P. Pvt, A, 30th NJ Inf, [Died of typhoid at Belle Plain, VA.] 2-18-1863. Reformed Church Cemetery, Bedminster, Somerset County.

KUCH, LOCUS (see: Kuch, Lukus) Beverly National Cemetery, Edgewater Park, Burlington County.

KUCH, LUKUS (aka: Kuch, Locus) Pvt, I, 74th PA Inf, 5-18-1879. Beverly National Cemetery, Edgewater Park, Burlington County.

KUCHELLE, DAVIS (aka: Kaechele, David) Pvt, I, 73rd PA Inf, 7-20-1877. Evergreen Cemetery, Camden, Camden County.

KUCK, MARTIN (aka: Cook, Martin) Corp, D, 7th NJ Inf, [Wounded in action.] 11-29-1907. Greenmount Cemetery, Hammonton, Atlantic County.

KUEBLER, PAUL H. Seaman, U.S. Navy, 7-10-1920. Fairmount Cemetery, Newark, Essex County.

KUGLER, ANDREW V. 10-12-1903. Union Cemetery, Frenchtown, Hunterdon County.

KUGLER, CHARLES Saddler, I, 3rd NJ Cav, 12- -1921. Mount Pleasant Cemetery, Millville, Cumberland County.

KUHL, HENRIQUES Pvt, A, 88th NY Inf, 2-3-1885. Fairmount Cemetery, Newark, Essex County.

KUHL, PAUL 1st Sgt, A, 15th NJ Inf, [Cenotaph. Killed in action at Spotsylvania CH, VA.] 5-12-1864. Presbyterian Church Cemetery, Flemington, Hunterdon County.

KUHL, WILHELM F. (aka: Kuhl, William F.) Pvt, K, 7th NY Inf, 9-25-1906. Hillside Cemetery, Scotch Plains, Union County.

KUHL, WILLIAM F. (see: Kuhl, Wilhelm F.) Hillside Cemetery, Scotch Plains, Union County.

KUHLENKAMP, DIETRICH Pvt, I, 3rd NJ Cav, 11-17-1886. Fairmount Cemetery, Newark, Essex County.

New Jersey Civil War Burials

KUHN*, ADAM (JR.) Pvt, G, 3rd NJ Inf, 1-17-1907. St. Mary's Cemetery, Boonton, Morris County.
KUHN, HEINRICH Pvt, C, 7th NY Inf, 9-21-1882. Cedar Lawn Cemetery, Paterson, Passaic County.
KUHN, JOHN Pvt, D, 68th NY Inf, 7-3-1918. Woodland Cemetery, Newark, Essex County.
KUHN, MICHAEL Corp, C, 37th NJ Inf, 5-23-1892. Riverview Cemetery, Trenton, Mercer County.
KUHN, MICHAEL G. 12-5-1932. Grove Church Cemetery, North Bergen, Hudson County.
KUHNE, CHARLES (aka: Coon, Charles) Pvt, E, 22nd NJ Inf, 11-14-1919. Arlington Cemetery, Kearny, Hudson County.
KUHNE, WILLIAM HENRY Sgt, F, 20th NY Inf, 8-30-1923. Weehawken Cemetery, North Bergen, Hudson County.
KULLER, PETER Pvt, K, 3rd NJ Inf, 2-21-1867. Evergreen Cemetery, Hillside, Union County.
KULTHAU, HENRY 1st Sgt, L, 1st NJ Cav, [Killed in action at Hawe's Shop, VA.] 5-28-1864. Van Liew Cemetery, North Brunswick, Middlesex County.
KUMANN, JOHN EDWARD (aka: Kunsmann, John) Pvt, F, 1st NJ Militia, 11-13-1877. Fairmount Cemetery, Newark, Essex County.
KUMMER, VALENTINE (aka: Spatz, Peter) Pvt, C, 2nd MA Cav, 5-30-1925. Woodland Cemetery, Newark, Essex County.
KUNKEL, MICHAEL Pvt, G, 9th NJ Inf, 2-23-1893. Fairmount Cemetery, Newark, Essex County.
KUNKLE, DAVID R. Pvt, G, 31st NJ Inf, DoD Unknown. Stillwater Cemetery, Stillwater, Sussex County.
KUNSMANN, JOHN (see: Kumann, John Edward) Fairmount Cemetery, Newark, Essex County.
KUNSTANT, WALTER 6-29-1890. Riverside Cemetery, Riverside, Burlington County.
KUNTZ, JOSEPH L. Pvt, A, 9th NJ Inf, 9-25-1899. Woodland Cemetery, Newark, Essex County.
KUNTZ, PETER (aka: Smith, George) Pvt, D, 17th NY Inf, 8-17-1905. Holy Name Cemetery, Jersey City, Hudson County.
KUNTZE*, FREDERICK Pvt, M, 14th NY Cav, 10-22-1918. Bayview-New York Bay Cemetery, Jersey City, Hudson County.
KUNZELMAN, JOHN Musc, A, 5th PA Cav, 1-23-1913. Riverview Cemetery, Trenton, Mercer County.
KUONY, JOSEPH Pvt, D, 11th NY State Militia, DoD Unknown. Jersey City Cemetery, Jersey City, Hudson County.
KUPPER, ADAM Pvt, B, 21st NJ Inf, 12-13-1888. Palisade Cemetery, North Bergen, Hudson County.
KUPPINGER, GOTTLIEB (aka: Cuppinger, Gottlieb) Corp, D, 68th NY Inf, 1-2-1907. Riverview Cemetery, Trenton, Mercer County.
KURKEL, JOHN (aka: Koerkle, John) Pvt, D, 2nd NJ Inf, 8-17-1872. Woodland Cemetery, Newark, Essex County.
KURT, FRANCIS (aka: Knert, Francis) Pvt, G, 118th PA Inf, 12-7-1913. Brotherhood Cemetery, Hainesport, Burlington County.
KURTZ, ANTON (aka: Kurz, Anton) Pvt, E, 103rd NY Inf, 4-13-1874. Woodland Cemetery, Newark, Essex County.
KURTZ, F. DoD Unknown. Methodist Cemetery, Mantua, Gloucester County.
KURTZ, HERMAN Corp, B, 91st PA Inf, 7- -1921. Mount Pleasant Cemetery, Millville, Cumberland County.
KURTZ, MILTON (SR.) Corp, B, 14th NJ Inf, 12-14-1914. Riverview Cemetery, Trenton, Mercer County.

Our Brothers Gone Before

KURTZ, WILHELM (see: Kurz, William) Harleigh Cemetery, Camden, Camden County.
KURZ, ANTON (see: Kurtz, Anton) Woodland Cemetery, Newark, Essex County.
KURZ, WILLIAM (aka: Kurtz, Wilhelm) Corp, K, 29th NY Inf, 10-2-1901. Harleigh Cemetery, Camden, Camden County.
KURZEL, GUSTAVE Pvt, 2nd NY Ind Btty 11-28-1915. Jersey City Cemetery, Jersey City, Hudson County.
KURZSCHEUKEL, JOHN Pvt, A, 13th NJ Inf, 7-12-1880. Fairmount Cemetery, Newark, Essex County.
KUSSMAUL, LEWIS F. Pvt, C, 7th NJ Inf, 4-28-1913. Reformed Church Cemetery, Fairfield, Essex County.
KUTCHER, GEORGE Corp, B, 123rd OH Inf, 10-21-1907. Rosedale Cemetery, Orange, Essex County.
KUTH*, ANTON Pvt, D, 2nd NJ Inf, 1-22-1873. St. Mary's Cemetery, Boonton, Morris County.
KUTTER, JOHN A. Corp, A, 15th NJ Inf, [Wounded 5-3-1863 at Salem Heights, VA.] 4-3-1877. Mount Hope Presbyterian Cemetery, Lambertville, Hunterdon County.
KUTTLER, CHARLES (aka: Cutler, Charles) Pvt, G, 9th NJ Inf, 4-26-1905. Holy Name Cemetery, Jersey City, Hudson County.
KYLE*, SAMUEL Pvt, K, 22nd NJ Inf, 10-3-1924. Woodland Cemetery, Englewood Cliffs, Bergen County.
KYNOR, ABIATHAR L. Pvt, K, 39th NJ Inf, 10-19-1931. Greenwood Cemetery, Boonton, Morris County.
KYRK, JOHN A. Capt, A, 35th IA Inf, DoD Unknown. Mount Salem Cemetery, Mount Salem, Sussex County.
KYRK, WILLIAM L. Sgt, M, 1st NJ Cav, 1-8-1866. Mount Salem Cemetery, Mount Salem, Sussex County.
KYSE, WILLIAM HENRY Pvt, K, 59th IL Inf, 2-5-1930. Arlington Cemetery, Kearny, Hudson County.
KYTE, GEORGE Pvt, 7th NY Ind Btty 5-5-1900. Baptist Church Cemetery, Scotch Plains, Union County.